TRAVELING WITH YOUR PET
THE AAA PETBOOK®

The AAA guide to more than 13,000
pet-friendly, AAA-RATED® lodgings
and 400 campgrounds
across the United States and Canada

9th Edition

AAA PUBLISHING

President & CEO	**Robert Darbelnet**
Executive Vice President, Publishing & Administration	**Rick Rinner**
Managing Director, Travel Information	**Bob Hopkins**
Director, Product Development & Sales	**Bill Wood**
Director, Publishing Marketing	**Patty Wight**
Director, Manufacturing & Quality	**Susan Sears**
Director, Tourism Information Development (TID)	**Michael Petrone**
Director, Publishing Operations/Travel Information	**Jeff Zimmerman**
Director, Publishing/GIS Systems & Development	**Ramin Kalhor**
Director, GIS/Cartography	**Jan Coyne**
Director, Purchasing & Corporate Services	**Rebecca A. Barrett**
Director, Business Development	**Gary Sisco**
Product Manager	**Marquita Dudley**
Manager, Public Relations	**Mike Pina**
Marketing Communications Manager	**Renuka Sastri**
Buyer	**Bob Bailes**
TID Regional Managers	**Lisa Brenneman, Todd Cronson, Michel Mousseau, Stacy Brunick, Patrick Schardin**
TID Field Operations Manager	**Laurie DiMinico**
Manager, Travel Information Operations	**Brenda Daniels**
Publishing Business Manager	**Linda Indolfi**
Manager, Electronic Media Design	**Mike McCrary**
Manager, Pre-Press/Photo Services & Product Support	**Tim Johnson**
Manager, Graphic Communication Services	**Yvonne Macklin**
Manager, Application Development	**Scott Chrisien**
Development Editor	**Alison Lockwood**
Art Director	**Barbra Natali**
Cover Design	**Kelly Smith**
Photo Research	**Denise Campbell**
Quality Services	**Terry Lane, Andrea Payne-Lecky**
Electronic Pagination Specialist	**Christine Carter**
Technical Specialist	**Roland Levett**
Planning Analyst	**Lorne Corbett**
System Analyst	**Samuel Allen**
Programmer	**James Cothrine**
Data Processors	**Kelly Giewont, Andrea Tlumacki, Paula Bourgeois, Lucy Quintana, Linda Barnard, Dawn Garrison, Jennifer Lopresti**
Proofreader	**Janet D'Amico**

AAA wishes to acknowledge the following for their assistance:
Dogpark.com®
Veterinary Emergency & Critical Care Society

Cover Photos

Cover: Puppy in front of hotel	**istockphoto**
Back Cover: Willow and owner kayaking on Anahim Lake, British Columbia	**Photo Contest winner Kim Meeker**
Spine: Linus riding in a vehicle	**Photo Contest winner Emily Fairchild**

Published by AAA Publishing
1000 AAA Drive, Heathrow, Florida 32746

Ninth Edition Copyright © 2007 AAA Publishing. All rights reserved.
ISBN 10: 1-59508-208-5 ISBN 13: 978-1-59508-208-4 Stock Number 552207
Printed in the USA by Rose Printing

Traveling with Your Pet
Photo Contest Entry Form

The next time you go on vacation with your pet, be sure to take along your camera.

The winning entry in AAA's PetBook Photo Contest will appear on the cover of the 10th edition of *Traveling With Your Pet: The AAA PetBook®*. The winner also will receive $100, five complimentary copies of the book as well as a year's supply of Milk-bone® dog snacks.

MILK-BONE

Please print

Name: _____

Address: _____

City: _____ **State:** ____ **Zip code:** _____

Daytime phone: _____ **Evening phone:** _____

Pet's name/gender: _____ **Animal breed:** _____

Photo taken: _____

Please answer the following questions:

   *1. Why do you travel with your pet? _____

   _____

   *2. What is your favorite place or city to take your pet, and why? _____

   _____

   3. Tell us about an adventure you had while traveling with your pet. _____

   _____

*Required answer

Traveling with Your Pet: The AAA PetBook® **Photo Contest Official Rules**

1. Email one digital photo to Petbookcontest@national.aaa.com. Please send the photo as a .jpeg file attachment no larger than 2 MB, and include the information requested on the entry form in the body of the email. The digital photo **must** have a minimum resolution of 1200 pixels by 1600 pixels. The entry form information (name, address, phone, pet's name/gender, animal breed and answers to questions) **must** be included in the email for contest consideration. Minor digital enhancement for cropping, red-eye removal, filters and correction functions are permitted, but images that are determined to be significantly altered will be disqualified. Photographers are not permitted to place borders or frames around their image or to place a watermark, signature, date or copyright notices on the image.

OR

2. Send printed color 8" x 10" unmounted photo that is in focus, along with the completed entry form to:

   PetBook Photo Contest
   AAA
   1000 AAA Drive, MS 64
   Heathrow, FL 32746

Official Rules *continued*

3. Photos must be postmarked by Nov. 26, 2007, and received by Nov. 30, 2007, to be eligible for the contest.

4. Photo must feature at least one pet and have a travel theme.

5. Only **one** photo may be entered per household.

6. The entrant must be the person who took the photo and who has full rights to the photo.

7. The entrant must obtain full consent from all models or persons appearing in the photo for full use of the photo, including use and publishing in this contest and the other uses stated herein.

8. All photos entered in the contest, including the prize-winning photo(s), along with all rights of every kind therein, become the sole and exclusive property of AAA and will not be returned.

9. A panel of judges will choose the winning photo based on the following qualities: impact, lighting, composition and effectively conveying the idea that *Traveling With Your Pet: The AAA PetBook* is about traveling on vacation with your pet. Posed or studio photographs will be disqualified.

10. The winner will be notified **by mail** early January 2008.

Disclaimer

By participating, entrants agree that: (i) these rules and the decisions of AAA shall be final in all respects, and (ii) AAA may put the winner's photo on the front or back cover or spine of the 10th edition of *Traveling With Your Pet: The AAA PetBook*. The winner grants AAA the right to use his or her name, likeness, portrait, picture, photo, answers on entry form and/or prize information for advertising, publicity and promotional purposes relating to the book, *Traveling With Your Pet: The AAA PetBook*, and the contest without compensation or permission (unless prohibited by law).Each entrant agrees to hold harmless and release AAA from any injuries, losses or damages of any kind that may result from taking a photo intended to be submitted. The pet travel accessories prize will be selected at the sole discretion of AAA. The winner agrees to hold harmless and release AAA from use of the pet travel accessories. AAA is not responsible for late, lost or misdirected entries or mail; for technical, hardware or software malfunctions, lost or unavailable network connections, or failed, incorrect, inaccurate, incomplete, garbled or delayed electronic communications, whether caused by the sender or by any of the equipment or programming associated with or utilized in this promotion, or by any human error that may occur in the processing of entries; or for loss of or damage to any entries. AAA retains the right to not award the prize should no acceptable photos be received. By participating in the contest, each entrant agrees that AAA becomes the owner of each photo submitted and AAA may use said photo in any manner and medium it chooses and entrant relinquishes all rights in and to said photo(s).

Eligibility

No purchase is necessary to enter the contest or claim the prize. Open to U.S. or Canadian residents 18 years or older except for employees of AAA, CAA and their clubs.

By submitting an entry I agree that I have read the Contest Rules, assent thereto, and submit the enclosed photo in accordance therewith; I attest that I own all rights to the photo and it has not been published or accepted for publication in any medium; and if the photo portrays any living person or persons, I have secured a model release or releases. I further agree that should my entry be chosen as the winning entry I will execute all necessary paperwork/releases as requested by AAA.

ABOUT THIS BOOK

Welcome to the 9th edition of *Traveling With Your Pet — The AAA PetBook*®. *Traveling With Your Pet* is a must for the traveler who's also an animal lover. This comprehensive book provides all the information you need to know about taking a four-legged friend on the road. Will Spot be a good car passenger? Is it safe to take Snowball on a plane? What are the important rules of pet etiquette? Is pet insurance a good idea? *Traveling With Your Pet* answers all of these questions and more. Here are just some of the features covered:

- Dog parks where you and your furry friends can play, exercise or just relax.

- An extensive listing of emergency animal clinics compiled by the Veterinary Emergency & Critical Care Society. Names, addresses and phone numbers provide valuable information for unexpected or emergency situations, both en route and at your destination.

- A roundup of pet-friendly attractions.

- National public lands in the United States and Canada that allow pets, along with recreation information.

- Border crossing procedures and tips for travelers — both entering Canada from the United States and vice versa.

- Policies pertaining to service animals.

Traveling With Your Pet lists more than 13,000 AAA-RATED® lodgings. And the listings show AAA's trustworthy diamond ratings, the traveler's assurance of quality. Other handy features include:

- Informative highway directions.

- Specific information about lodgings' pet policies: deposits and fees (rounded to the nearest dollar), housekeeping service, designated rooms and other stipulations relating to travelers with pets.

- Additional details about the lodgings themselves, including icons for amenities, recreation, dining and accessibility.

- Icons designating AAA's member discount programs.

- Listings for AAA's highest rated campgrounds, including rate and pet policy information and service/amenity icons.

All of this valuable information is packaged in a contemporary, easy-to-read format, making *Traveling With Your Pet — The AAA PetBook* as indispensable an on-the-road companion as Spot's water dish or Snowball's litter box. Don't leave home without it, and remember: It always pays to *Travel With Someone You Trust*®.

TABLE OF CONTENTS

Traveling With Pets

Pet-Friendly Places in the U.S. and Canada

Pet-Friendly Lodgings

U.S. Lodgings

Canadian Lodgings

Pet-Friendly Campgrounds

TRAVELING WITH PETS

Many people view their pets as full-fledged members of the family. Spot and Snowball often have their own beds, premium-quality foods, a basketful of toys and a special place in their humans' hearts.

Until it's time to go on vacation, that is. Then the family dog or cat is consigned to "watching the fort" at home while everyone else experiences the joy of traveling. Many animal lovers hesitate to take their pet with them because they don't think they'll be able to find accommodations that accept four-legged guests. Others aren't sure how — or if — their furry friends will adapt.

The truth is, including a pet in the family vacation is fairly easy, so long as you plan ahead. Most pets respond well to travel, a fact that isn't lost on the tourism industry. More than 13,000 AAA-RATED® hotels and motels from coast to coast are pet-friendly, and airline bookings for pet passengers are on the rise. Great companions at home, pets are earning their stripes on the road, too.

So if you've been longing to hit the trail with a canine or feline companion, read the tips on the following pages. You may find that a getaway can be far more enjoyable with than without your pet.

Should Your Pet Travel?

Before you make reservations, determine if your pet is able to travel. Most animals can and do make the most of the experience, but a small percentage simply are not cut out for traveling. Illness, physical condition and temperament are important factors, as is your pet's ability to adjust to such stresses as changes to his environment and routine. When in doubt, check with your veterinarian. If you feel your pet isn't up to the trip, it's better for everyone if he stays home.

❧ Rule 1: Pets who are very young, very old, pregnant, sick, injured, prone to biting or excessive vocalizing, or who cannot follow basic obedience commands should not travel.

Even if Spot and Snowball are seasoned travelers, take into account the type of vacation and activities you have planned. No pet is going to be happy (or safe) cooped up in a car or hotel room. Likewise, the family dog may love camping and hiking, but the family cat may not. Putting a little thought toward your animal's needs and safety will pay off in a more enjoyable vacation for everyone.

❧ Rule 2: If your pet can't actively participate in the trip, she should stay home.

Most of the information in this book pertains to cats and dogs. If you own a bird, hamster, pig, ferret, lizard or other exotic creature, remember that unusual animals are not always accepted as readily as more conventional pets. Always specify the type of pet you have when making arrangements.

Also check states' animal policies. **Hawaii** imposes 120-day or 5-days-or-less quarantines for all imported dogs, cats and other carnivores to prevent the importation of rabies. Guide dogs and other service animals are exempt from the quarantine provided they have: a standard health certificate; a current rabies vaccination with documentation of the product name, lot number and lot expiration date; and an electronic identification microchip implanted and operational. Upon arrival, guide dogs still must be examined for external parasites and undergo serum antibody testing and a microchip scan. For additional details, obtain the Hawaii Rabies Quarantine Information Brochure from the Hawaii Department of Agriculture, Animal Quarantine Station, 99-951 Halawa Valley St., Aiea, HI 96701-5602; phone (808) 483-7151 or (808) 837-8092, fax (808) 483-7161. The Web site address is www.hawaiiag.org/hdoa/ai_aqs_info.htm.

North Carolina has stringent restrictions regarding pets in lodgings. Make certain you understand an accommodation's specific policies before making reservations.

❧ Rule 3: Be specific when making travel plans that include your pet. Nobody wants unpleasant surprises on vacation.

If Spot and Snowball stay behind, leave them in good hands while you're gone. **Family, friends and neighbors** make good sitters (provided they're willing), especially if they know your pet and can care for him in your home. Provide detailed instructions for feeding, exercise and medication, as well as phone numbers for your destination, your veterinarian and your local animal emergency clinic.

Professional pet sitters offer a range of services, from feeding and walking your pet daily to full-time house sitting while you are gone. Interview several candidates, and always check credentials and references. For additional information, contact the National Association of Professional Pet Sitters or Pet Sitters International. *(See sidebars on p. 8 and p. 9.)*

Kennels board many animals simultaneously and generally are run by professionals who will provide food and exercise according to your instructions. Pets usually are kept in a run (dogs) or cage (cats and small dogs) and may not get the same level of human interaction as at home. **Veterinary clinics** also board pets and may be the best choice if yours is sick, injured or needs special medical care. For further information on how to select a kennel, contact the American Boarding Kennels Association.

Veterinarians, fellow pet owners and professional associations are a good source of referrals for sitters and kennels.

❧ Rule 4: Never leave your pet with someone you don't trust.

Travelers Who Have Disabilities

Individuals with disabilities who own service animals to assist them with everyday activities undoubtedly face challenges, but traveling should not be one of them. Service animals (the accepted term for animals trained to help people with disabilities) are not pets and thus are not subject to many of the laws or policies pertaining to pets.

The Americans With Disabilities Act (ADA) defines a service animal as "any guide dog, signal dog or other animal individually trained to provide assistance to an individual with a disability." ADA regulations stipulate that public accommodations are required to modify policies, practices and procedures to permit the use of a service animal by an individual with a disability.

The purpose of these regulations is to provide equal access opportunities for people with disabilities and to ensure that they are not separated from their service animals. A tow truck operator, for example, must allow a service animal to ride in the truck with her owner rather than in the towed vehicle.

Public accommodations may charge a fee or deposit to an individual who has a disability — provided that fee or deposit is required of all customers — but no fees or deposits may be charged for the service animal, even those normally charged for pets.

The handler/owner is responsible for the animal's care and behavior; if the dog creates an altercation or poses a direct threat, the handler may be required to remove it from the premises and pay for any resulting damages.

Choosing a Pet Sitter

Before hiring a pet sitter, ask:
- Is he or she insured (for commercial liability) and bonded?
- What is included in the fee?
- Does the sitter require that your pet have a current vaccination?
- What kind of animals does the sitter typically care for?
- How will a medical, weather or home emergency be handled?
- Does he or she fully understand your pet's medical or dietary needs?
- How much time will be spent with your pet?

The pet sitter should:
- Have a polished, professional attitude.
- Provide references.
- Have a standard contract outlining terms of service.
- Have experience in caring for animals.
- Insist on current vaccinations.
- Ask about your pet's health, temperament, schedule and needs.
- Visit and interact with your pet before you leave.
- Devote time and attention to your pet.
- Be affiliated with pet care organizations.

Be sure you:
- Explain your pet's personality — favorite toys, good and bad habits, hiding spots, general health, etc.
- Leave care instructions, keys, food and water dishes, extra supplies (food, medication, etc.), and phone numbers for your veterinarian and an emergency contact.
- Bring pets inside before leaving.

Choosing a Kennel

Before reserving a kennel, ask:
- What is included in the fee?
- Are current vaccinations required?
- What kind of animals do they board?
- How will a medical or weather emergency be handled?
- Will your pet be kept in a cage or run?
- Will your pet receive daily exercise?
- Does the kennel fully understand your pet's medical or dietary needs?
- How and how often will staff interact with your pet?

The kennel should:
- Require proof of current vaccinations.
- Be clean, well-ventilated and offer adequate protection from the elements.
- Have separate areas for dogs, cats and other animals, with secure fencing and caging.
- Clean and disinfect facilities daily.
- Give your pet his regular food on his regular schedule.
- Provide soft bedding in runs/cages.
- Understand your pet's medical needs.
- Provide or obtain veterinary care if necessary.
- Offer sufficient supervision.
- Have a friendly, animal-loving staff.

Be sure you:
- Notify staff of behavior quirks (dislike of other animals, children, etc.).
- Provide food and medication.
- Leave a familiar object with your pet.
- Leave phone numbers for your veterinarian and an emergency contact.
- Spend time with your pet before boarding him.

The **Delta Society,** an organization devoted to companion and service animals, has information about laws that affect people and service animals in public accommodations. Phone (425) 679-5500 for a catalog, or visit www.deltasociety.org.

Preparing Your Pet for Travel

Happily, many vacations can be planned to include fun activities for pets. Trips to parks, nature trails, the ocean or lakes offer exposure to the world beyond the window or fence at home, as well as the chance to explore new sights and sounds. Even the streets of an unfamiliar city can provide a smorgasbord of discoveries for your animal friend to enjoy.

Once you decide Spot and Snowball are ready to hit the road, plan accordingly:

❖ **Get a clean bill of health from the veterinarian.** Update your pet's vaccinations, check his general physical condition and obtain a health certificate showing proof of up-to-date inoculations, particularly rabies, distemper and kennel cough. Such documentation will be necessary if you cross state or country lines, and also may come in handy in the unlikely event your pet gets lost and must be retrieved from the local shelter. Don't forget to ask the doctor about potential health risks at your destination (Lyme disease, heartworm infection) and the necessary preventive measures.

If your pet is taking prescribed medicine, pack a sufficient supply plus a few days' extra. Also take the prescription in case you need a refill. Be prepared for emergencies by getting the names and numbers of clinics or doctors at your destination from your veterinarian or the American Animal Hospital Association. **Hint:** Obtain these references before you leave and keep them handy throughout the trip.

Make sure your pet is in good physical shape overall, especially if you are planning an active vacation. If your animal is primarily sedentary or overweight, he may not be up to lengthy hikes through the woods.

Note: Some owners believe a sedated animal will travel more easily than one that is fully aware, but this is rarely the case. In fact, tranquilizing an animal can make travel much more stressful. Always consult a veterinarian about what is best for your pet, and administer sedatives only under the doctor's direction. In addition, never give an animal medication that is specifically prescribed for humans. The dosage may be too high for an animal's much smaller body mass, or may cause dangerous side effects.

❖ **Acclimate your pet to car travel.** Even if you're flying, your pet will have to ride in the car to get to the airport or terminal, and you don't want any unpleasant surprises before departure.

CONTACT INFORMATION

The following organizations offer information, tips, brochures and other travel materials designed to help you and your pet enjoy a happy and safe vacation.

American Animal Hospital Association
12575 W. Bayaud Ave., Lakewood, CO 80228
(303) 986-2800 — www.healthypet.com

American Boarding Kennels Association
1702 East Pikes Peak Ave.
Colorado Springs, CO 80909
(719) 667-1600 — www.abka.com

American Society for the Prevention of Cruelty to Animals
424 E. 92nd St., New York, NY 10128-6804
(212) 876-7700 — www.aspca.org

American Veterinary Medical Association
1931 N. Meacham Rd., Suite 100
Schaumburg, IL 60173
(847) 925-8070 — www.avma.org

Dogpark.com ®
716 Fourth St., San Rafael, CA 94901
www.dogpark.com

Humane Society of the United States
2100 L St. NW, Washington, DC 20037
(202) 452-1100 — www.hsus.org

National Association of Professional Pet Sitters
15000 Commerce Pkwy., Suite C
Mt. Laurel, NJ 08054
(856) 439-0324 — www.petsitters.org

PetGroomer.com
P.O. Box 2489
Yelm, WA 98597
(360) 446-5348 — www.petgroomer.com

Pet Sitters International
201 E. King St., King, NC 27021
(336) 983-9222 — www.petsit.com

USDA-APHIS
USDA-APHIS-Animal Care
4700 River Rd., Unit 84
Riverdale, MD 20737-1234
(301) 734-7833 — www.aphis.usda.gov/ac

Some animals are used to riding in the car and even enjoy it. But most associate the inside of the carrier or the car with one thing only: the annual visit to the V-E-T. Considering that these visits usually end with a jab from a sharp needle, it's no wonder that some pets forget their training and act up in the car. If this is your situation, you will have to re-train your animal to view a drive as a reward, not a punishment.

Begin by allowing your pet to become used to the car without actually going anywhere. Then take short trips to places that are fun for animals, such as the park or the drive-through window at a fast-food restaurant. (Keep those indulgent snacks to a minimum!) Be sure to praise her for good behavior with words, petting and healthy treats. It shouldn't take long before you and your furry friend are enjoying leisurely drives without incident. *(See Traveling by Car, p. 12.)*

❧ **Brush up on behavior.** Will Snowball make a good travel companion? Or will he be an absolute terror on the road? Don't wait until the vacation is already under way to find out; review general behavioral guidelines with respect to your animal, keeping in mind that the unfamiliarity of travel situations may test the temperament of even the most well-behaved pet.

It's a good idea to socialize Spot by exposing her to other people and animals (especially if she normally stays inside). You're likely to encounter both on your trip, and it is important that she learns to behave properly in the company of strangers. Make her introduction to the outside world gradual, such as a walk in a new neighborhood or taking her along while you run errands. Exposure to new situations will help reduce fear of the unknown and result in more socially acceptable behavior.

Is your pet housebroken? How is he around children? Does he obey vocal commands? Be honest about your animal's ability to cope in unfamiliar surroundings. Depending on the length and nature of the trip and your pet's level of command response, an obedience refresher course might be a good idea.

❧ **Learn about your destination.** Check into quarantines or other restrictions well in advance, and make follow-up calls as your departure date approaches. Find out what types of documentation will be required — not just en route, but on the way home as well.

Be aware of potential safety or health risks where you're going, and plan accordingly. For example, the southeastern United States — particularly Florida — is home to alligators and heartworm-carrying mosquitoes, and many mountainous and wooded areas may harbor ticks that transmit Lyme disease.

Confirm all travel plans within a few days of your departure, especially with lodgings and airlines; their policies may have changed after you made the reservations. If you plan to visit state parks or attractions that accept pets on the premises, obtain their animal regulations in advance.

WHAT TO TAKE

- ❑ Carrier or crate. *(See Selecting a Carrier or Crate, p. 11, for specifications.)*
- ❑ Nylon or leather collar or harness, license tag, ID tag(s) and leash. All should be sturdy and should fit your pet properly.
- ❑ Food and water dishes.
- ❑ Can opener and spoon (for canned food).
- ❑ An ample supply of food, plus a few days' extra.
- ❑ Bottled water from home. (Many animals are finicky about their drinking water.)
- ❑ Cooler with ice.
- ❑ Healthy treats.
- ❑ Medications, if necessary.
- ❑ Health certificate and other required documents.
- ❑ A blanket or other bedding. (If your pet is used to sleeping on the furniture, bring an old blanket or sheet to place on top of the hotel's bedding.)
- ❑ Litter supplies (for cats or other small animals), a scooper and plastic bags (for dogs).
- ❑ Favorite toys.
- ❑ Carpet deodorizer.
- ❑ Chewing preventative.

- ❑ A recent photograph and a written description including name, breed, gender, height, weight, coloring and distinctive markings.
- ❑ Grooming supplies:
  comb/brush
  nail clippers
  shampoo
  cloth and paper towels
  cotton balls/tissues
- ❑ First-aid kit:
  gauze, bandages and adhesive tape
  hydrogen peroxide
  rubbing alcohol
  ointment
  muzzle
  scissors
  tweezers (for removing ticks, burrs, splinters, etc.)
  local emergency phone numbers
  first-aid guide (such as *Pet First Aid: Cats & Dogs*, published by The Humane Society of the United States and the American Red Cross)

❧ **Determine the best mode of transportation.** Most people traveling with pets drive. Many airlines do accept animals in the passenger cabin or cargo hold, and as more people choose to fly with their pet airlines are becoming more pet-conscious. Restrictions vary as to the type and number of pets an airline will carry, however, so inquire about animal shipping and welfare policies before making reservations. If your pet must travel in the cargo hold, heed the cautionary advice in the Traveling by Air section. *(See p. 13.)*

Flying is really the only major option to car travel. Amtrak, as well as Greyhound and other interstate bus lines, do not accept pets. **Note:** Seeing-eye dogs and other service animals are exempt from the regulations prohibiting pets on Amtrak and interstate bus lines. Local rail and bus companies may allow pets in small carriers, but this is an exception rather than a rule.

The only cruise ship that currently permits pets is the Cunard Line's *Queen Elizabeth 2* (on trans-Atlantic crossings); kennels are provided, but animals are accepted on a very limited basis. Some charter and sightseeing boat companies permit pets onboard, however.

A word of advice: Never try to sneak your pet onto any mode of public transportation where she is not permitted. You may face legal action or fines, and the animal may be confiscated if discovered.

❧ **Pack as carefully for your pet as you do for yourself.** *(See What To Take, p. 10.)* Make sure she has a collar with a license tag and ID tag(s) listing her name and yours, along with your address and phone number. As an added precaution, some owners outfit their dog with a second tag listing the name and number of a contact person at home. Popular backup identification methods are to have your animal tattooed with an ID number (usually a social security number) or to implant a microchip under her skin.

If your pet requires medication, make sure that is specified on his tag. This helps others understand your animal's needs and also may prevent people from keeping a found pet or from stealing one to sell.

Note: Choke chains, collars that tighten when they are pulled, may be useful during training sessions, but they do not make good full-time collars. If the chain catches on something, your pet could choke herself trying to pull free. For regular wear, use a harness or a conventional collar made of nylon or leather.

Selecting a Carrier or Crate

This is one of the most important steps in ensuring your pet's safety when traveling. A good-quality carrier not only contains your pet during transit, it also gives him a safe, reassuring place to stay when confinement is necessary at your destination. Acclimate the animal before the trip so he views the crate as a cozy den, not a place of exile.

If you plan to travel by car, a carrier will confine your pet en route, and also may come in handy if Spot or Snowball must stay in the room unsupervised. A secured crate will prevent your pet from escaping from the room when the cleaning staff arrives, or at night if camping in the open. *(See At Your Destination, p. 16.)*

Some airlines allow small pets to travel in the passenger cabin as carry-on luggage. There are no laws dictating the type of carrier to use, but remember that it must be small enough to fit under a standard airplane seat and should not exceed 45 linear inches (length + width + height), or roughly **23 by 13 by 9 inches.** If your pet will be flying in the cargo hold, you must use a carrier that meets U.S. Department of Agriculture Animal and Plant Health Inspection Service (USDA-APHIS) specifications. *(See Traveling by Air, p. 13.)*

Crates are available at pet supply stores; some airlines also sell carriers. Soft-sided travel bags are handy for flyers with small pets. Before you make the investment, make sure your carrier is airline-approved.

Even if you never take to the skies, these common-sense guidelines provide a good rule of thumb in selecting a crate for other uses. USDA-APHIS rules stipulate the following:

❧ The crate must be enclosed, but with ventilation openings occupying at least 14 percent of total wall space, at least one-third of which must be located on the top half of the kennel. A three-quarter-inch lip or rim must surround the exterior to prevent air holes from being blocked.

❧ The crate must open easily, but must be sufficiently strong to hold up during normal cargo transit procedures (loading, unloading, etc.).

❧ The floor must be solid and leakproof, and must be covered with an absorbent lining or material (such as an old towel or litter).

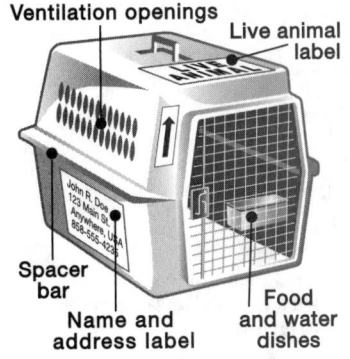

Ventilation openings · **Live animal label** · **Spacer bar** · **Name and address label** · **Food and water dishes**

Heatstroke

and

Hypothermia

The best way to treat heatstroke or hypothermia is to prevent it. Do not leave pets unattended in a car, even if only for a few minutes. Also heed airlines' restrictions on pet travel, and carefully investigate animal welfare policies to make certain the airline has safeguards to protect your pet from both conditions.

Other preventive measures are to avoid strenuous exercise — including such activities as hiking and "fetch" — when the sun is strongest (10 a.m.-2 p.m.), and to provide your pet access to clean, fresh drinking water at all times.

Following are the warning signs and basic first aid for heatstroke and hypothermia. Always be alert to your pet's physical condition and watch for symptoms — immediate attention to the situation may mean the difference between life and death. If your pet is struck with either disorder, take him to an animal hospital or veterinarian as fast as safely possible.

HEATSTROKE

Symptoms
- rapid, shallow breathing
- excessive salivation
- heavy panting
- hot to the touch
- glazed eyes
- unsteadiness, dizziness
- deep red or purple tongue or gums
- vomiting
- body temperature of 104 F or higher

First Aid
- place pet in the shade
- quickly dampen with cool water, especially on the head and neck
- give small amounts of water

HYPOTHERMIA

Symptoms
- shivering
- weakness
- lethargy
- cold to the touch
- body temperature of 95 F or lower

First Aid
- place in a warm area
- wrap in towels or a blanket
- quickly warm by gently massaging the head, chest and extremities

❧ The crate must be just large enough to allow the animal to turn freely while standing, and to have a full range of normal movement while standing or lying down.

❧ The crate must offer exterior grips or handles so that handlers do not have to place their hands or fingers inside.

❧ Food and water dishes must be securely attached and accessible without opening the kennel.

❧ If the carrier has wheels, they must be removed or immobilized prior to loading.

❧ One-inch lettering stating "Live Animal" or "Wild Animal" must be placed visibly on the exterior, and must be accompanied by directional arrows showing the crate's proper orientation. It also is a good idea to label the crate with your name, home address and home phone number, as well as an address and phone number where you can be reached during the trip. (Hint: Use an adhesive label or an indelible marker and write directly on the crate, as paper may be ripped off accidentally in transit.)

❧ Attach a list of care instructions (feeding, watering, etc.) for a 24-hour period to the exterior of the carrier. This will help airport workers care for your pet if he is sent to the wrong destination.

❧ If you are traveling with multiple pets, note that crates may contain only one animal whose weight exceeds 20 pounds. Smaller animals may travel together under the following guidelines: one species to a crate, except compatible dogs and cats of similar size; two puppies or kittens under 6 months of age; 15 guinea pigs or rabbits; 50 hamsters. **Note:** These are federal limits; airlines may impose more stringent regulations.

Traveling by Car

The first step in ensuring your pet's well-being during a vacation is to train her to ride in the car. For safety reasons, pets should be confined to the back seat, either in a carrier or a harness attached to the car's seat belt. This keeps the animal from interfering with or distracting the driver, and also may save her life in the event of an accident. And a restrained animal will not be able to break free and run away the second the car door is opened.

To help prevent car sickness, feed your pet a light meal four to six hours before departing. Do not give an animal food or water in a moving vehicle.

Never allow your pet to ride in the bed of a pickup truck. It's illegal in some states; he also can jump out or be thrown, endangering himself and others on the road. Harnessing or leashing him to the truck bed is not advisable either: If he tries to jump out, he could be dragged along the road or the restraint could become a noose. Avoid placing animals in campers or trailers as well. **If your pet cannot ride in the car with you, leave him at home.**

Don't let your dog stick her head out the window, no matter how enjoyable it seems. Road debris and other flying objects can injure delicate eyes and ears, and the animal is at greater risk for severe injury if the vehicle should stop suddenly or be struck. If it is hot outside, run the air conditioner instead of opening the windows, and be sure that the air flow is reaching your pet.

AAA recommends that drivers stop every two hours to stretch their legs and take a quick break from driving. Your pet will appreciate the same break. Plan to visit a rest stop every four hours or so to let him have a drink and a chance to answer the call of nature. (Cat owners should bring along a litter box; dog owners should clean up afterward.)

Be sure your pet is leashed before opening the car door. This is not merely a courtesy to fellow travelers; it will prevent her from unexpectedly breaking free and running away. Keep in mind that even the most obedient pet may become disoriented during travel or in strange places and set off for home. **Hint:** If your pet is not used to traveling, use a harness instead of a collar; it is more difficult for an animal to wriggle out of a harness.

NEVER leave an animal in a parked car, even if the windows are partially open. Even on pleasant days the temperature inside a car can soar to well over 100 degrees in less than 10 minutes, placing your pet at risk for heatstroke and possibly death. On very cold days, hypothermia is a risk. Also, animals left unattended in parked cars frequently are stolen.

Traveling by Air

(Service animals are normally exempt from most of the regulations and fees specified in this section. Check policies with the airline when making reservations.)

Opinion is divided as to whether air travel is truly safe for pets. Statistically, it is less dangerous than being a passenger in a car, but some experts warn of potentially deadly conditions for animals. The truth lies somewhere in between: Most pets arrive at their destination in fine condition, but death or injury is always a possibility. Before you decide to fly, know the risk factors and the necessary precautions to keep your pet safe.

✿ **Determine whether your pet is fit to fly.** The Animal Welfare Act (AWA), administered by USDA-APHIS, specifies that dogs and cats must be at least 8 weeks old and weaned at least 5 days before air travel. Animals that are very young, very old, pregnant, ill or injured should not fly at all. Cats, snub-nosed dogs (pugs, boxers, etc.) and long-nosed dogs (shelties, collies, etc.) are prone to severe respiratory difficulties in an airplane's poorly ventilated cargo hold and should travel only in the passenger cabin (if size allows) with their owner. Some airlines will not accept snub-nosed breeds if the temperature exceeds 70 degrees anywhere in the routing.

✿ **Decide where your pet will fly.** Most animals fly in the hold as checked baggage when traveling with their owners, or as cargo when they are unaccompanied. The AWA was enacted to ensure animals traveling in this manner are treated humanely and are not subjected to dangerous or life-threatening conditions. For specific requirements pertaining to your animal, check with the airline in advance, as policies vary. Some airlines will not ship dogs as checked baggage, and others will only accept dogs shipped as cargo from "known shippers"; i.e., commercial shippers or licensed pet breeders. Except for service animals, Southwest accepts no pets in the cabin or cargo department.

Items classified as "dangerous goods" (dry ice or toxic chemicals, for example) must be transported in a different part of the hold from where live animals are carried. Some planes are designed to have separate hold areas,

---

AIRLINE CONTACT INFORMATION

Following is a list of the major North American airlines and their toll-free reservation numbers.

Web site addresses include information about flying with animals. Hint: Look under links for baggage, cargo or special travel needs, or do a site search for "pets."

Air Canada . . . . (888) 247-2262
www.aircanada.ca (only service animals in cabin)

Alaska Airlines . . . . (800) 252-7522
www.alaskaair.com

American Airlines . . . . (800) 433-7300
www.aa.com

Continental Airlines . . . . (800) 523-3273
www.continental.com

Delta Airlines . . . . (800) 221-1212
www.delta.com

Northwest Airlines . . . . (800) 225-2525
www.nwa.com

Southwest Airlines . . . . (800) 435-9792
www.iflyswa.com (accepts service animals only)

United Airlines . . . . (800) 864-8331
www.ual.com

US Airways . . . . (800) 428-4322
www.usair.com

but so-called "people mover" airlines that are primarily interested in getting human passengers from one point to another as quickly as possible may not give priority to this feature. Check your airline's specific baggage policies so you know exactly where in the hold your pet will be traveling.

Small pets may be taken into the passenger cabin with you as carry-on luggage on most airlines. This places the animal's welfare squarely in your hands but is feasible only if he is very well-behaved and fits comfortably in a container that meets standard carry-on regulations. *(See Selecting a Carrier or Crate, p. 11.)* Keep in mind that the carrier — with the animal inside — must be kept under the seat in front of you throughout the flight. Some airlines charge a fee ($50-$95) for carry-on pets. **Note:** AWA regulations do not apply to animals traveling in the cabin.

❖ Do your homework. Investigate the airline's animal transport and welfare policies, especially if you are flying with a small or commuter airline. All airlines are subject to basic AWA regulations, but specific standards of care vary greatly from one company to another. Do your research well in advance and confirm the information 24-48 hours before departing.

The more information an airline provides, the better care your pet is likely to receive. Beware of companies that

---

Pet Insurance

Just like their owners, pets can experience major medical problems at some point in their lifetime — even those that live indoors. And if illness strikes while you're on the road, it may be necessary to obtain care quickly. As a result, more and more people who travel with their devoted companion are considering pet health insurance.

Insurance plans run the gamut from basic coverage and routine care for illness and injury to comprehensive health maintenance, vaccinations and exams. Annual premiums range from less than $100 to more than $350, depending on the type of pet and plan. When choosing your plan, consider the following:

- What are the enrollment guidelines (age, breed, specific restrictions, etc.)?
- Which expenses are covered and which are excluded?
- What is the plan's policy concerning existing health problems?
- Does the plan allow you to use your own veterinarian?
- How are veterinary fees paid?
- Is a multiple pet discount offered?

---

have vague animal welfare guidelines, or none at all. All major airlines provide information about pet transport on their Web sites. Also talk to fellow travelers and pet owners about their experiences. Finally, keep in mind that airlines are not required to transport live animals and can refuse to carry them for any reason.

❖ Protect your investment. Most people think of their pets as part of the family, but the legal system assigns them the same value as a piece of luggage. Inquire about insurance — an airline that won't insure animals in its care may not be the right one for your pet. (Always read the fine print before purchasing any insurance policy.) Also ask if the airline's workers are trained to handle animals. Few are, but it doesn't hurt to check. Remember, it's up to you to choose an airline that values pets and will treat yours with care.

❖ Understand the potential hazards. Because a plane's cargo hold is neither cooled nor heated until take-off, the most dangerous time for your pet is that spent on the ground in this unventilated compartment. In summer the space absorbs heat while the plane sits on the tarmac; the reverse is true in winter, when it is no warmer inside the hold than outside. Both instances expose pets to the possibility of serious injury or death from heatstroke or hypothermia. **Note:** The latter also may be a concern during flight if the hold's heater is disabled or turned off, allowing the temperature to drop to near-freezing levels.

To minimize these risks, USDA-APHIS rules prohibit animals from being kept in the hold or on the tarmac for more than 45 minutes when temperatures are above 85 F or below 45 F. Some airlines impose even tighter temperature restrictions and may not permit animals to fly on planes going to cities where the ground temperatures may exceed these limits. Delta, for example, does not carry animals in the cargo hold May 15 through Sept. 15. (Exceptions may be made for animals whose veterinarians certify they are acclimated to colder temperatures, but never warmer.)

❖ Make stress-free travel arrangements. Once you decide to fly, reserve space for Spot or Snowball when you arrange your own tickets, preferably well in advance of your travel date. Airlines accept only a limited number of animals per flight — usually two to four in the passenger cabin and one pet per passenger — on a first-come, first-served basis. More animals are generally allowed in the cargo hold.

Prepare to pay an additional fee, about $75-$100 each way; the cost is often greater for large animals traveling on a flight without their owner. (Unfortunately, pets are not eligible for frequent flyer miles.) Always reconfirm your reservations and flight information 24-48 hours before departure.

If your pet will be flying in the hold, travel on the same plane and reserve a nonstop flight. This not only reduces the danger of heatstroke or hypothermia during layovers, it also eliminates the possibility that she will be placed on the wrong connecting flight. In summer, fly during the early morning or late evening when temperatures are cooler. Because of large crowds and the chance of heavy air traffic causing delays, avoid holiday travel whenever possible.

Additional precautions may be necessary when traveling outside the United States and Canada. Other countries may impose lengthy quarantines, and airline workers outside North America may not be bound by animal welfare laws. *(See International Travel, p. 18.)*

❧ **Play an active role in your pet's well-being.** Flying safely with your pet requires careful planning and attention to his welfare. See the veterinarian within 10 days of departure for a health certificate (required by most airlines) and a pre-flight check-up.

Address any concerns you have about your pet traveling by air, especially if you are considering tranquilization. Sedation usually is not recommended for cats and dogs, regardless of whether they fly in the cabin or in the hold. Exposure to increased altitude pressure can create respiratory and cardiovascular problems; animals with short, wide heads are particularly susceptible to disorientation and possible injury. Sedation should never be administered without your veterinarian's approval.

Obtain an airline-approved carrier and acclimate your pet to its presence by leaving it open with a familiar object inside. A sturdy, well-ventilated crate adds an additional measure of protection.

Because animals are classified as luggage, they may be loaded on the plane via conveyor belt. If the crate falls off the belt, your pet could be injured or released. Ask that she be hand-carried on and off the plane, and that you be permitted to watch both procedures. Also ask about "counter-to-counter" shipping, in which the animal is loaded immediately before departure and unloaded immediately after arrival. There usually is an additional fee for this service.

Make sure you will have access to your pet if there is a lengthy layover or delay. Think twice about flying on an airline that won't allow you to check on your animal under such circumstances.

❧ **Prepare for the flight.** Keep in mind that traveling with an animal will require additional pre-flight time and preparation on your part. Exercise your pet before the flight, and arrive at least two but not more than four hours before departure. If he is traveling as carry-on luggage, check-in is normally at the passenger terminal; if he is traveling as checked baggage or as cargo in the cargo hold, proceed to the airline's cargo terminal, which is often in a different location. Find this out when making reservations and again when confirming flight information.

Make sure your animal's crate is properly labeled and secured, but do not lock it in case airline personnel have to provide emergency care. Include an ice pack for extra comfort on a hot day or a hot water bottle on a cold day. **Hint:** Wrap in a towel to prevent leaking.

Do not feed your pet less than four hours before departure, but provide water up until boarding. **Hint:** Freeze water in the bowl so that it melts throughout the trip, providing a constant drinking source.

Spot or Snowball should wear a sturdy collar (breakaway collars are recommended for cats) and two identification tags marked with your name, home address and phone number, and travel address and phone number. It's also a good idea to clip your pet's nails before departure so they won't accidentally get caught on any part of the carrier.

Note: You may be required to take your pet out of the carrier as you pass through security on your way to the gate. Make sure the animal is wearing a collar and leash or harness.

Attach food and water dishes inside the carrier so that airline workers can reach them without opening the door. If the trip will take longer than 12 hours, also attach a plastic bag with at least one meal's worth of dry food. Animals under 16 weeks of age must be fed every 12 hours, adult animals every 24 hours. Water must be provided at least every 12 hours, regardless of the animal's age.

Allow your pet to answer the call of nature before boarding, but do not take her out of the carrier while in the terminal. As a courtesy, wait until you are outside and away from fellow travelers. Keep her leash with you — do not leave it inside or attached to the kennel.

If your pet is traveling as carry-on luggage, let the passenger sitting next to you know. Someone with allergies may want to change seats.

Perhaps the most important precaution is to alert the flight crew and the captain that your pet is aboard. The pilot must activate the heater for the cargo hold; make sure this is done once you are in the air. If there are layovers or delays, ask the flight crew to be sure your pet has adequate shelter and/or ventilation; better yet, ask them to allow you to check in person.

If you have arranged to watch your pet being unloaded, ask a flight attendant to call the baggage handlers and let them know you are on the way. Above all, do not hesitate to voice any concerns you have for your pet's welfare — it is your responsibility to do so.

❧ **Be prepared for emergencies.** In the unlikely event your pet gets lost en route, contact the airline, local humane shelters, animal control agencies or USDA-APHIS. Many airlines can trace a pet that was transferred to the wrong flight. If your pet is injured in transit, proceed to the nearest animal hospital; register any complaints with USDA-APHIS. **Hint:** Carry a list of emergency contact numbers and a current photograph of your pet in your wallet or purse, just in case.

At Your Destination

How well you and your companion behave on the road directly affects the way future furry travelers will be treated. Always clean up after your pet and keep him under your control. This is not only a courtesy to fellow human travelers; it's the surest way to enjoy a safe and happy vacation.

Inquire about pet policies before making lodging reservations. Properties may impose restrictions on the type or size of pet allowed, or they may designate only certain rooms, such as smoking rooms, for travelers with animals. If you have a dog, get a room on the first floor with direct access outside, preferably near a walking area; keep her leashed on any excursion.

Lodgings may have supervision policies requiring that pets be crated when unattended or that they may not be left alone at all. Allow your pet only in designated exercise or animal-approved areas; never take him into such off-limits places as the lobby, pool area, patio or restaurant. Prepare to receive limited housekeeping service, or none at all.

Expect to pay some type of additional charge, which may be per room or per pet and may include any of the following: refundable deposit, non-refundable deposit, daily fee, weekly fee.

If staying with friends or relatives, make certain your pet is a welcome guest. Know and respect their "house rules," especially if they have small children or pets of their own.

Once in the room, check for such hazards as chemically treated toilet water, hiding spaces and electrical cords before freeing your pet. Give her time to adjust to her new surroundings under your supervision.

Above all, practice good "petiquette":

🐾 Try not to leave your pet alone, but if you must, crate or otherwise confine her.

🐾 Crate at night as well.

🐾 To keep your pet and the housekeeper from having an unexpected encounter, leave the "Do Not Disturb" sign on the door when you go out without him.

🐾 Barking dogs make poor hotel neighbors — keep your pet quiet.

🐾 Don't allow your pet on the furniture. If she insists on sleeping on the bed, bring a bedspread or sheet from home and place that on top of the hotel bedding.

🐾 Clean up after your pet immediately — inside the room and out — and leave no trace of him behind when checking out.

🐾 Dispose of litter and other "accidents" properly — check with housekeeping.

🐾 Notify the management immediately if something is damaged, and be ready to pay for repairs.

🐾 Add a little extra to the housekeeping tip.

🐾 When you take your pet out of the room, keep her leashed, especially in wilderness areas and around small children. No matter how obedient she is at home, new stimuli and distractions may cause her to forget or ignore vocal commands. Know and obey animal policies at parks, beaches and other public areas. Check before arriving to make certain animals still are welcome, even if you've been there before — the rules may have changed.

🐾 Look for outdoor cafes when selecting restaurants. For health reasons, pets are not permitted inside eating establishments, but many restaurants allow animals to sit quietly with their owners at outdoor tables. Drive-through restaurants are another alternative.

In Case of Emergency

Be prepared for any turn of events by knowing how to get to the nearest animal hospital. *(See Animal Clinics, p. 49.)* Also have the name and number of a local animal shelter and a local veterinarian handy — ask your veterinarian for a recommendation. Take first-aid supplies with you and know how to use them. An animal in pain may become aggressive, so exercise caution at all times.

Emergency evacuation shelters do not accept pets, and domesticated animals do not fare well if left to weather an emergency on their own, especially when far from home. Avert a potential tragedy by planning in advance where you will go with your pet in case of evacuation. Use the listings in this book to find other lodgings willing to take you and your pet. Above all, don't wait for disaster to strike. Leave as soon as the evacuation order is announced, and take your animal with you.

The Great Outdoors

Travelers planning an active or camping vacation should make some additional preparations. Check in advance to be sure your pet is permitted at campgrounds, parks, beaches, trails and anywhere else you will be visiting. If there are restrictions — and there usually are — follow them. Remember that pets other than service animals usually are not allowed in public buildings.

Note: It is not advisable to take animals other than dogs into wilderness areas. For example, bringing a pet is not recommended at some national parks in Alaska. Also keep in mind that rural areas often have few veterinarians and even fewer boarding kennels.

Use common sense. Clean up after your pet, do not allow excessive vocalizing and keep her under your control. If the property requires your pet to be leashed or crated at all times, do so. Few parks or natural areas will allow a pet to be unattended, even when chained — the risk of disagreeable encounters with other travelers or wildlife is too great. The National Park Service may confiscate pets that harm wildlife or other visitors.

If camping, crate your pet at night to protect him from the elements and predators. (Chaining confines the animal but won't keep him from becoming a midnight snack.)

When hiking, stick to the trail and keep your pet on a short leash. It is all too easy for an unleashed pet to wander off and get lost or fall prey to a larger animal. Keep an eye out for such wildlife as alligators, bears, big cats, porcupines and skunks, and avoid other dogs and small children. Be aware of indigenous poisonous plants, such as English ivy and oleander, or those causing physical injury, such as cactus, poison ivy or stinging nettle. Your veterinarian or local poison control center should be able to give you a full list of hazardous flora.

Before setting out on the trail, make sure both of you are in good physical shape. An animal that rarely exercises at home will not suddenly be ready for a 10-mile trek across uneven terrain. Plan a hike well within the limits of your pet's endurance, and don't push — remember, if Spot gets too tired to make it back on her own, you'll have to carry her.

Carry basic first-aid supplies, including a first-aid guide. *(See What to Take, p. 10.)* Also carry fresh drinking water for both of you — "found" water may contain harmful germs or toxins. Drink often, not just when thirst strikes, and have your pet do the same. Watch for signs of dehydration, leg or foot injuries, heat exhaustion or heatstroke. Stop immediately and return home or to camp if any of these occur.

Note: Dogs can carry their own backpacks (check your local pet store for specially designed packs), but should never carry more than one-third of their body weight. Train the dog to accept the pack beforehand, and only use it with a strong, healthy animal in excellent physical condition.

No matter where or how you spend your vacation, visit the veterinarian when you return home to check for injuries, parasites and general health.

Note: Most campgrounds accept pets. The AAA CampBook guides are an excellent source for obtaining detailed information regarding pet policies, restrictions and extra charges for campgrounds in the United States and Canada. AAA members may obtain complimentary copies of the CampBook guides at their local AAA club.

Traveling Between the United States and Canada

Traveling across the international border with your pet — either from the United States into Canada or from Canada into the United States — should prove largely hassle-free, although some basic regulations need to be kept in mind.

Effective Jan. 23, 2007, the Western Hemisphere Travel Initiative requires all passengers — including U.S. citizens — to have a passport for air travel to and from Canada. The requirement will be extended to land and sea border crossings as early as January 1, 2008, but no exact date has been set. AAA recommends that all travelers carry a passport for visits outside the United States to simplify the travel process. Visit the U.S. State Department's travel Web site at www.travel.state.gov, or phone (877) 4882-778 for more information.

U.S. Customs grants returning U.S. citizens who stay in Canada more than 48 hours an individual $800 duty-free exemption (if not used within the prior 30 days). Any amount over the $800 exemption is subject to duty.

The exemption is based on fair retail value and applies to goods acquired for personal or household use or as gifts but not intended for sale. All items for which the exemption is claimed must accompany you upon return.

A 7 percent Goods and Service Tax (GST) is levied on most items sold and most services rendered in Canada. In New Brunswick, Nova Scotia or Newfoundland and Labrador, a Harmonized Sales Tax (HST) of 15 percent (which includes the GST) is charged on goods and services. Rebates can be claimed on some items. Brochures that explain the GST and contain a rebate form are available at tourist information centers, customs offices and duty free shops at the border and in airports.

U.S. citizens taking pet cats and dogs three months of age and older into Canada must carry a health certificate signed by a licensed veterinarian that describes the animal and provides proof of rabies vaccination within the past 12 or 36 months, depending on the type of vaccine. Collar tags are not sufficient proof of immunization. The certificate also is needed to bring a pet back into the United States; make sure the vaccination doesn't expire while you're in Canada. **Note:** Pit bulls are not permitted into Ontario.

Service animals are exempt from import restrictions. Also exempt are up to two puppies or kittens under three months old; obtain a certificate of health from your veterinarian indicating that the animal is too young to vaccinate. **Note:** For details on pet imports, contact the Canadian Embassy; 501 Pennsylvania Ave. N.W., Washington, DC 20001; phone (202) 682-1740. The Web site address is www.canadianembassy.org.

The Canadian Food Inspection Agency (CFIA) provides additional pet information; phone (613) 225-2342 or visit the Web site at www.inspection.gc.ca. If you need assistance while in Canada, contact the U.S. Embassy, 490 Sussex Dr., Ottawa, ON, Canada K1N 1G8; phone (613) 238-5335.

Canadian Customs allows Canadian citizens to bring back from the United States, duty and tax free, goods valued up to $200 any number of times per year, provided the visit is 48 hours or more. A $50 exemption, excluding alcoholic beverages and tobacco products, may be claimed if the visit is 24 hours or more and no other exemption is being used. If returning from a visit of 7 days or more (not counting the day of departure from Canada), the exemption goes up to $750.

Canadian travelers may take pet cats and dogs into the United States with no restrictions, but U.S. Customs requires that dogs have proof of rabies vaccination no less than 30 days before arrival. For additional information on U.S. regulations, contact the Animal and Veterinary Services department of the USDA-APHIS National Center for Import and Export, (301) 734-3277.

International Travel

If you plan to travel abroad with Spot or Snowball, prepare for a lengthy flight and at least a short quarantine period. Be aware that airline and animal workers in other countries may not be bound by the same animal welfare laws that exist in the United States and Canada. Contact the embassy or consulate at your destination for information about documentation and quarantine requirements, animal control laws and animal welfare regulations.

As with any trip, have your pet checked by your regular veterinarian within 10 days of departure to obtain a health certificate showing proof of rabies and other inoculations. If you are traveling with an animal other than a domesticated dog or cat, check with USDA-APHIS for restrictions or additional documentation required.

The booklet "Pets and Wildlife: Licensing and Health Requirements" has general information about traveling abroad with animals; write U.S. Customs & Border Protection, 1300 Pennsylvania Ave. N.W., Washington, D.C. 20229; phone (202) 354-1000, or visit www.customs.gov.

Note: Island nations such as Australia and the United Kingdom, which are rabies-free, have adopted the Pet Travel Scheme (PETS) to allow entry for dogs and cats from the U.S. and Canada without the usual 6-month quarantine. Pets must be tested and vaccinated for rabies at least 6 months prior to travel, be implanted with microchip identification and receive a certificate of treatment from an official government veterinarian. For information, visit the U.K. Web site for the Department for Environment, Food and Rural Affairs (DEFRA) at www.defra.gov.uk. Hawaii, which has a standard 120-day quarantine for all imported animals except guide dogs, has adopted a similar expedited program of 5 days or less; a pet must have been vaccinated at least *twice* for rabies in its lifetime.

Loss Prevention Tips

Searching the woods or an unfamiliar town for a missing pet is easily prevented by following these helpful tips:

- Have your pet wear a sturdy nylon or leather collar with current ID and rabies tags firmly attached. Be sure the ID tag includes the phone number of an emergency contact. Consider having your pet implanted with microchip identification; it's a simple procedure similar to a vaccination.

- Keep your pet on a leash or harness. Even trained animals can become agitated or disoriented in unfamiliar surroundings and fail to obey vocal commands.

- Attach the leash or harness while your pet is still inside the closed car or crate.

- Do not leave your pet unattended at any time, anywhere. A stolen pet is extremely difficult to recover.

- Escape-proof your hotel room by crating your pet and asking hotel management to make certain no one enters your room while you are gone. (Inform the property that you're traveling with an animal when making reservations.)

- Take along a recent picture and a detailed written description of your pet.

If your pet gets lost these steps will improve your chances of recovery:

- If your pet is lost in transit, contact the airline immediately. Ask to trace the animal via the airline's automated baggage tracking system.

- Contact local police, animal control, animal shelters, humane organizations and veterinary clinics with a description and a recent photograph. Stay in contact until your pet is found, and provide your home and destination phone numbers.

- Post signs and place an ad in the local newspaper so that anyone who comes across your pet knows she is lost and how to reach you.

The Last Word

You are ultimately responsible for your pet's welfare and behavior while traveling. Since animals cannot speak for themselves, it is up to you to focus on your pet's well-being every step of the way. It also is important to make sure he conducts himself properly so that other pets will be welcome visitors in the future. Following the common-sense information in this book will help ensure that both you and your animal companion have a safe and happy trip.

PET-FRIENDLY
PLACES

IN THE U.S. AND CANADA

Dog Parks
Attractions
National Public Lands
Emergency Animal Clinics

DOG PARKS

A dog park is a place where people and their dogs can play together. These places offer dogs an area to play, exercise and socialize with other dogs while their owners enjoy the park-like setting. Dog park size and features vary greatly from location to location, from several hundred square feet in urban areas to several hundred acres in the suburbs and rural locations. Dog owners should remember to always keep their animal leashed until they reach the dog park entrance, to maintain voice control of their animal at all times, to bring their own supply of bags for picking up after their pet (and to be diligent in doing so), and to always have fresh water available for their dog. Please observe all dog park rules.

This list of dog parks in the United States and Canada is provided by Dogpark.com®. Dogpark.com is all about dogs — all breeds, all mixes of breeds, and all shapes, sizes and dispositions. It provides articles and information about dogs and their care, health and play. Online, visit www.dogpark.com.

The dog parks listed here welcome people who travel with their dogs; private parks or parks requiring local residency are not included. **Note:** Fence types and heights vary, and some areas have no fencing at all, requiring that the dog be under firm voice control.

United States

ARIZONA

Chaparral Park - Scottsdale
scottsdaleaz.gov/Parks/OffLeashAreas/default.asp
5401 N. Hayden Rd. (at the southeast corner of McDonald Drive and Hayden Road)
Daily dawn-9 p.m.
Fenced, 2.2 acres, benches, shade, restroom, water, separate areas for large and small dogs.

Horizon Park - Scottsdale
scottsdaleaz.gov/Parks/OffLeashAreas/default.asp
15444 N. 100th St. (Thompson Peak Parkway and 100th Street, east of SR 101 off Frank Lloyd Wright Boulevard)
Daily dawn-10:30 p.m.
Fenced, lighted, benches, little shade, tables, disposal bags, trash cans, parking, phones, restrooms; bring your own water.

Vista del Camino Park - Scottsdale
scottsdaleaz.gov/Parks/OffLeashAreas/default.asp
7700 East Pierce St. (take Pierce Street heading west from Hayden Road)
Daily dawn-10:30 p.m.
Fenced, lighted, 1 acre, grass turf, benches, restrooms nearby, dog and people water fountains, mutt mitt stations.

Creamery Park - Tempe
tempe.gov/pkrec/parkfacil/offleash.htm
8th Street and Una Avenue (just south of University near Rural)
Daily 6 a.m.-10 p.m.
Fenced, lighted, benches, disposal bags, trash cans, parking, water.

Jaycee Park - Tempe
tempe.gov/pkrec/parkfacil/offleash.htm
5th Street and Hardy Drive
Daily 6 a.m.-10 p.m.
Fenced, lighted, trees, benches, disposal bags, trash cans, parking, water. Access for the disabled.

Mitchell Park - Tempe
tempe.gov/pkrec/parkfacil/offleash.htm
Mitchell Drive and 9th Street
Daily 6 a.m.-10 p.m.
Fenced, lighted, trees, benches, disposal bags, trash cans, parking, water. Access for the disabled.

Papago Park - Tempe
tempe.gov/pkrec/parkfacil/offleash.htm
Curry Road and College Avenue
Daily 6 a.m.-10 p.m.
Fenced, lighted, trees, disposal bags, trash cans, parking, water.

Tempe Sports Complex - Tempe
tempe.gov/pkrec/parkfacil/offleash.htm
Warner Road and Hardy Drive
Daily 6 a.m.-midnight
Fenced, lighted, trees, disposal bags, trash cans, parking, water.

CALIFORNIA

Calabasas Bark Park - Calabasas
cityofcalabasas.com/recreation/barkpark.html
4232 Las Virgenes Rd., south of the Las Virgenes Municipal Water District (approximately 2 miles west of US 101 on the south side)
Daily 5 a.m.-9 p.m.
Fenced, lighted, trees, benches, scoops, trash cans, paved parking, dog water fountain, separate areas for large and small dogs.

Costa Mesa Bark Park - Costa Mesa
cmbarkpark.org
Arlington Drive and Newport Boulevard, across from the Orange County Fairgrounds Equestrian Center
Wed.-Mon. dawn-dusk; phone ahead in rainy conditions
Fenced, 2.1 acres, grass turf, trees, benches, tables, disposal bags, trash cans, parking, restrooms, water. Access for the disabled.

Ernie Smith Dog Park - El Verano
sonoma-county.org/parks/pk_smith.htm
18776 Gilman Dr.
Daily dawn-dusk. Parking free.
Fenced, double-gated entry, .5 acre, picnic tables, waste bags, garbage can, dog water fountain.

CALIFORNIA (CONT'D)

Elizabeth Anne Perrone Dog Park - Glen Ellen
sonoma-county.org/PARKS/foundation/
perrone_dog_park.htm
13630 Sonoma Hwy. in Sonoma Valley Regional Park (SR 12 between Arnold Drive and Madrone Road)
Daily dawn-dusk. Parking fee $5 or annual park pass.
Fenced, 1 acre, double-gated entry, covered gazebo, shade trees, dog water fountain.

Huntington Dog Beach - Huntington Beach
dogbeach.org
Pacific Coast Highway between 21st and Seapoint streets
Daily 5 a.m.-10 p.m.; parking lot closes at 10 p.m.
Unfenced, benches and tables on the bluffs above the beach, disposal bags, trash cans, metered parking, restrooms. Dogs may be off leash anywhere on the beach while under an owner's supervision. Access for the disabled to the sand.

Laguna Niguel Pooch Park - Laguna Niguel
ci.laguna-niguel.ca.us/index.asp?SID=481
31461 Golden Lantern near Chapparosa Park
Tues.-Thurs. and Sat. 7 a.m.-dusk, Sun. 8 a.m.-dusk, Mon. and Fri. noon-dusk
Fenced, 1 acre, Wood chip ground cover, picnic tables, shelters, disposal bag dispenser, parking, restroom, water faucet with hose.

Long Beach Recreation Dog Park - Long Beach
geocities.com/lbdogpark
5201 East 7th St. at Park
Daily dawn-10 p.m.
Fenced, lighted, trees, crushed-granite surface, benches, tables, disposal bags, trash cans, parking, water, separate fenced area for small dogs. Access for the disabled.

Palm Springs Dog Park - Palm Springs
ci.palm-springs.ca.us/dogpark.html
3200 E Tahquitz Canyon Way, behind City Hall
Daily dawn-10 p.m.
Fenced, lighted, double-gated entry, trees, benches, tables, shelter, disposal bags, trash cans, parking, phones, dual-level drinking fountains, separate areas for large and small dogs, antique fire hydrants. Unusual iron fence created by sculptor Phill Evans. Access for the disabled.

Redondo Beach Dog Park - Redondo Beach
rbdogpark.com
Southeast corner of 190th Street and Flagler Lane
Daily dawn-dusk; closed Wed. dawn-noon for maintenance
Fenced, trees, benches, disposal bags, trash cans, parking, phones, water, separate fenced area for small dogs. Access for the disabled.

Bannon Creek Park - Sacramento
cityofsacramento.org/parksandrecreation/parks/
dogpark1.htm
Bannon Creek Park, 2780 Azevedo Dr. off of Azevedo Dr., near West El Camino
Daily 5 a.m.-10 p.m.
Fenced, double-gated entry, .6 acres, benches, disposal bag dispensers, dog drinking fountain/faucet.

Granite Dog Park - Sacramento
cityofsacramento.org/parksandrecreation/parks/
dogpark1.htm
Ramona Avenue off Power Inn Road in Granite Regional Park
Daily dawn-10 p.m.
Fenced, double-gated entry, 2 acres, bench, disposal bags, trash cans, water spigot for dogs. Access for the disabled.

Partner Park - Sacramento
cityofsacramento.org/parksandrecreation/parks/
dogpark1.htm
5699 South Land Park Dr. at Fruitridge Road, behind Belle Cooledge Community Center
Daily dawn-10 p.m.
Fenced, lighted, double-gated entry, 2 acres landscaped with turf and mature trees, bench, disposal bags, trash cans, water spigot for dogs. Access for the disabled.

Balboa Park - San Diego
sandiego.gov/park-and-recreation/general-info/dogs.shtml
Two off-leash areas:
(1) Nate's Point at El Prado, on the southwest side of Cabrillo Bridge
(2) Morley Field, northwest of the tennis courts
Daily 24 hours
Unfenced, large field.

Cadman Community Park - San Diego
sandiego.gov/park-and-recreation/general-info/dogs.shtml
4280 Avati Dr.
Phone (858) 581-9929 for specific hours
Unfenced.

Capehart Park (Pacific Beach) - San Diego
sandiego.gov/park-and-recreation/general-info/dogs.shtml
Soledad Mountain Road and Feldspar Street
Daily 24 hours
Fenced, 1 acre, picnic tables, benches, parking, separate grass-turf areas for large and small dogs, areas to provide water for dogs, drinking fountain.

Dog Beach - San Diego
sandiego.gov/park-and-recreation/general-info/dogs.shtml
Voltaire Street in Ocean Beach; enter the parking lot at the west end of Voltaire
Daily 24 hours
Unfenced, disposal bags, trash cans, water, restrooms nearby. Access for the disabled.

Doyle Community Park - San Diego
sandiego.gov/park-and-recreation/general-info/dogs.shtml
8175 Regents Rd. behind Doyle Recreation Center
Daily 24 hours.
Fenced, no lights, separate grass-turf areas for large and small dogs.

Fiesta Island - San Diego
sandiego.gov/park-and-recreation/general-info/dogs.shtml
Mission Bay Park; this island allows dogs anywhere outside the fenced areas.
Daily 6 a.m.-10 p.m.

CALIFORNIA (CONT'D)

Grape Street Park - San Diego
sandiego.gov/park-and-recreation/general-info/dogs.shtml
Grape Street and Granada Avenue
Mon.-Fri. 7:30 a.m.-9 p.m.; Sat.-Sun. and holidays 9-9
Unfenced, 5 acres, lighted, trees, benches, tables, trash
cans, parking, restrooms, water.

Alamo Square Park - San Francisco
sfgov.org/site/recpark_index.asp?id=1448
Scott Street between Hayes and Fulton streets in the
western half of the park
Daily 6 a.m.-10 p.m.
Unfenced; dogs must be under firm voice control.

Alta Plaza Park - San Francisco
sfgov.org/site/recpark_index.asp?id=1448
Clay Street between Scott and Steiner streets, on the
second terrace of the park
Daily 6 a.m.-10 p.m.
Unfenced; dogs must be under firm voice control.

Bernal Heights - San Francisco
sfgov.org/site/recpark_index.asp?id=1448
Bernal Heights Boulevard at the top of the hill
Daily 6 a.m.-10 p.m.
Unfenced; dogs must be under firm voice control.

Brotherhood Mini Park - San Francisco
sfgov.org/site/recpark_index.asp?id=1448
Head Street and Brotherhood Way on Department of
Public Works property, improved by Recreation and Parks
Dept.
Daily 6 a.m.-10 p.m.
Unfenced; dogs must be under firm voice control.

Buena Vista Park - San Francisco
sfgov.org/site/recpark_index.asp?id=1448
Buena Vista West at Central Avenue
Daily 6 a.m.-10 p.m.
Unfenced; dogs must be under firm voice control.

Corona Heights - San Francisco
sfgov.org/site/recpark_index.asp?id=1448
Roosevelt Way and Museum Way in the field next to
Randall Museum
Daily 6 a.m.-10 p.m.
Fenced.

Crocker Amazon Playground - San Francisco
sfgov.org/site/recpark_index.asp?id=1448
Between LaGrande and Dublin streets in the northern
portion of park, adjacent to community garden
Daily 6 a.m.-10 p.m.
Unfenced; dogs must be under firm voice control.

Dolores Park - San Francisco
sfgov.org/site/recpark_index.asp?id=1448
Between Church and Dolores streets, south of tennis
courts and soccer field to central lawn
Daily 6 a.m.-10 p.m.
Unfenced; dogs must be under firm voice control.

Douglass Park - San Francisco
sfgov.org/site/recpark_index.asp?id=1448
27th and Douglass streets, upper field
Daily 6 a.m.-10 p.m.
Unfenced; dogs must be under firm voice control.

Eureka Valley Recreation Center - San Francisco
sfgov.org/site/recpark_index.asp?id=1448
Collingwood Street, adjacent to the tennis courts, east of
baseball diamond
Daily 6 a.m.-10 p.m.
Fenced.

Golden Gate Park - San Francisco
sfgov.org/site/recpark_index.asp?id=1448
Four off-leash areas:
(1) Southeast section bounded by Lincoln Way, King Drive
and 2nd and 7th avenues
(2) Northeast section at Fulton and Willard streets
(3) South-central area bounded by Martin Luther King Jr.
Drive, Middle Drive and 34th and 38th avenues
(4) Fenced dog-training area near 38th Avenue and Fulton
Street

Jefferson Park - San Francisco
sfgov.org/site/recpark_index.asp?id=1448
Eddy and Laguna Streets at the northwest end of the park
Daily 6 a.m.-10 p.m.
Unfenced; dogs must be under firm voice control.

Lafayette Park - San Francisco
sfgov.org/site/recpark_index.asp?id=1448
Near Sacramento Street between Octavia and Gough
streets
Daily 6 a.m.-10 p.m.
Unfenced; dogs must be under firm voice control.

Lake Merced - San Francisco
sfgov.org/site/recpark_index.asp?id=1448
Lake Merced Boulevard and Middlefield Drive, northern
lake area
Daily 6 a.m.-10 p.m.
Unfenced; dogs must be under firm voice control.

McKinley Square - San Francisco
sfgov.org/site/recpark_index.asp?id=1448
San Bruno Avenue and 20th Street, on the west slope
Daily 6 a.m.-10 p.m.
Unfenced; dogs must be under firm voice control.

McLaren Park - San Francisco
sfgov.org/site/recpark_index.asp?id=1448
Two off-leash areas:
(1) A 59-acre hilltop bounded by Shelly Drive with trails,
open areas, reservoir and fence at roadway. Includes
natural area, excludes group picnic facilities, children's play
area and custodian housing. Leash restrictions during
performances at amphitheater.
(2) South entrance at 1600 block of Geneva adjacent to
natural area with open area fenced on roadway
Daily 6 a.m.-10 p.m.

Mountain Lake Park - San Francisco
sfgov.org/site/recpark_index.asp?id=1448
North of Lake Street at 8th Avenue, east end of park
Daily 6 a.m.-10 p.m.
Unfenced; dogs must be under firm voice control.

Pine Lake Park - San Francisco
sfgov.org/site/recpark_index.asp?id=1448
Crestlake and Vale streets, west of and contiguous to
Stern Grove and adjacent to the parking lot
Daily 6 a.m.-10 p.m.
Unfenced; dogs must be under firm voice control.

CALIFORNIA (CONT'D)

Potrero Hill Mini Park - San Francisco
sfgov.org/site/recpark_index.asp?id=1448
22nd Street between Arkansas and Connecticut streets
Daily 6 a.m.-10 p.m.
Unfenced; dogs must be under firm voice control.

St. Mary's Recreation Center - San Francisco
sfgov.org/site/recpark_index.asp?id=1448
Justin and Benton Streets, lower terrace of the park
Daily 6 a.m.-10 p.m.
Fenced.

Stern Grove - San Francisco
sfgov.org/site/recpark_index.asp?id=1448
Wawona Street between 21st and 23rd avenues, north side
Daily 6 a.m.-10 p.m.
Unfenced; dogs must be under firm voice control.

Upper Noe Recreation Center - San Francisco
sfgov.org/site/recpark_index.asp?id=1448
30th Street between Church and Sanchez streets, behind and along the baseball field
Daily 6 a.m.-10 p.m.
Fenced.

Walter Haas Playground - San Francisco
sfgov.org/site/recpark_index.asp?id=1448
Diamond Heights Boulevard on upper terrace of the park
Daily 6 a.m.-10 p.m.
Unfenced; dogs must be under firm voice control.

Field of Dogs - San Rafael
fieldofdogs.org
3540 Civic Center Dr. near the intersection of US 101 and North San Pedro Road
Daily dawn-dusk
Fenced, double-gated entry, trees, benches, tables, shelter, disposal bags, trash cans, parking, water. Access for the disabled.

DeTurk Roundbarn Park - Santa Rosa
ci.santa-rosa.ca.us/rp/
819 Donahue St. between West 8th and 9th streets
Daily dawn-dusk
Fenced, water (small neighborhood park).

Doyle Park Dog Park - Santa Rosa
ci.santa-rosa.ca.us/rp/
700 Hoen Ave. within Doyle Park (go west on Sonoma Avenue, turn left on Hoen and then turn right into the parking lot; the fenced dog park is behind the stadium)
Daily dawn-dusk
Fenced, 3/4 acre, bench, disposal bags, water.

Galvin Dog Park - Santa Rosa
ci.santa-rosa.ca.us/rp/
3330 Yulupa Ave. in Don Galvin Park, next to Bennet Valley Golf Course
Daily dawn-dusk
Fenced, double-gated entry, trees, trash cans, parking, water. Access for the disabled.

Northwest Community Dog Park - Santa Rosa
ci.santa-rosa.ca.us/rp/
2620 W. Steele Lane in Northwest Community Park (go west on Gurneville Road, turn right on Marlow and then turn right at the first traffic light into the park's parking lot; walk east along the path to the dog park on the left)
Daily dawn-dusk
Fenced, 1 acre, benches, disposal bags, trash cans, restrooms nearby, water, separate area for small dogs.

Rincon Valley Dog Park - Santa Rosa
ci.santa-rosa.ca.us/rp/
5108 Badger Rd. in Rincon Valley Community Park
Daily dawn-dusk
Fenced, 1/2 acre, trees, benches, tables, disposal bags, trash cans, parking, phones, restrooms, water, separate fenced areas for large and small dogs (large-dog area closed during the winter), fenced pond area for dogs (open year-round). Monitors are present during peak hours to enforce rules. Access for the disabled.

Off-leash, unfenced, under voice control areas:

700 Doyle Park Drive - Santa Rosa
ci.santa-rosa.ca.us/rp/
700 Doyle Park Dr. (go west on Sonoma, turn left on Hoen and then turn right into the parking lot; the unfenced, off-leash area is to the right of the fenced dog park)
Daily 6-9 a.m., early Apr.-late Oct.

Doyle Park - Santa Rosa
ci.santa-rosa.ca.us/rp/
700 Hoen Ave. (the fenced dog park is behind the stadium)
Mon.-Fri. 6-9 a.m.
Dogs may be off leash within the park, but must be kept on leash from the parking lot to the park entrance.

Franklin Park - Santa Rosa
ci.santa-rosa.ca.us/rp/
2095 Franklin Ave.
Daily 6-8 a.m.

Southwest Community - Santa Rosa
ci.santa-rosa.ca.us/rp/
1698 Hearn Ave.
Daily 6-8 a.m.

Youth Community - Santa Rosa
ci.santa-rosa.ca.us/rp/
1725 Fulton Rd.
Daily 6-8 a.m.

Remington Dog Park - Sausalito
ci.sausalito.ca.us/business/park-rec/parks.htm
Ebbtide at Bridgeway
Mon.-Fri. 7-7, Sat.-Sun. 8-7
Fully fenced, lighted, safety-gated entry, picnic tables, benches, tents for shelter, scoops and scooper cleaning station, trash cans, parking, water, tennis balls and racquets provided.

Animal Care Center Dog Park - Sebastopol
sonoma-county.org/parks/pk_ragle_dog.htm
500 Ragle Rd.
Daily dawn-dusk. Parking fee $5 or annual park pass
Fenced, double-gated entry, .5 acre, waste bags & garbage can, dog water fountain.

CALIFORNIA (CONT'D)

Sierra Madre Dog Park - Sierra Madre
cityofsierramadre.com/index.php?mod=police_services
611 East Sierra Madre Blvd. in Sierra Vista Park, south of the tennis courts
Daily 6 a.m.-10 p.m. Permit required; daily permit $5. Daily and annual permits are available at City Hall; the Sierra Madre Police Department, 242 W. Sierra Madre Blvd.; or the Sierra Madre Community Recreation Center, 611 E. Sierra Madre Blvd.
Fenced, lighted, double-gated entry, trees, benches, disposal bags, trash cans, parking, phones, restrooms, water, separate fenced areas for large/active dogs and "special needs" dogs. Access for the disabled.

Baldy View Dog Park - Upland
baldyviewdogpark.com
Located on 11th street in the city of upland between Mountain Ave. and San Antonio Ave.
Daily dawn-dusk.
Fenced, double-gated entry and exit, 1.3 acres, grass turf, shade trees, benches, free parking, small and large dog sections, dog water stations.

COLORADO

Grandview Off-Leash Dog Park - Aurora
For additional information phone (303) 739-7160
17900 E. Quincy Ave., west of Quincy Reservoir and just east of Pitkin Street
Daily dawn-dusk
Fenced, trash cans, parking, water.

East Boulder Community - Boulder City
bouldercolorado.gov/
5660 Sioux Dr.
Daily dawn-dusk
Fenced, disposal bags, trash cans, parking, water, fenced-off swimming area. Access for the disabled.

Foothills Community Park - Boulder City
bouldercolorado.gov/
Locust Avenue and Lee Hill Road, west of Broadway
Daily dawn-dusk
Fenced, disposal bags, trash cans, parking, water. Access for the disabled.

Howard H. Hueston Park - Boulder City
bouldercolorado.gov/
34th Street near O'Neal Parkway
Daily dawn-dusk
Unfenced, trees, benches, tables, trash cans, parking. Dogs must be under voice and sight control. Access for the disabled.

Valmont Dog Park - Boulder City
bouldercolorado.gov/
Valmont and Airport roads
Daily dawn-dusk
Fenced, disposal bags, trash cans, parking, water. Access for the disabled.

Palmer Park - Colorado Springs
http://www.springsgov.com/Page.asp?NavID=5109
Maizeland Road and Academy Boulevard
Daily 5 a.m.-11 p.m., May-Oct.; 5 a.m.-9 p.m., rest of year
Fenced, benches, tables, disposal bags, trash cans, parking, restrooms, water. Access for the disabled.

Rampart Dog Park - Colorado Springs
http://www.springsgov.com/Page.asp?NavID=5109
8270 Lexington Dr. (from the intersection of Lexington Drive and N. Union Boulevard, go north on Lexington, then turn left into the park entrance)
Daily 5 a.m.-11 p.m., May-Oct.; 5 a.m.-9 p.m., rest of year
Fenced, trees, benches, disposal bags, trash cans, parking, water. Access for the disabled.

Barnum Park - Denver
www.denvergov.org/PRdogsoffleash/ or Dogs-off-leash hotline: (303) 964-1006
Hooker and West 5th
Daily 5:00 a.m.-11:00 p.m
Natural barriers (turf with split-rail fencing to delineate boundaries), 3 acres, trees, trash bags and cans, parking, restroom, bulletin board.

Berkeley Park - Denver
www.denvergov.org/PRdogsoffleash/ or Dogs-off-leash hotline: (303) 964-1006
Sheridan and West 46th
Daily 5:00 a.m.-11:00 p.m.
Fenced, 2 acres, turf, double-gate entry, trees, trash bags and cans, parking, bulletin board.

Denver Off-Leash Dog Park - Denver
denvergov.org
678 South Jason St. behind the Denver Municipal Animal Shelter
Daily dawn-dusk
Fenced, grass turf, parking, toys. Access for the disabled.

Fuller Park - Denver
www.denvergov.org/PRdogsoffleash/ or Dogs-off-leash hotline: (303) 964-1006
Franklin and East 29th
Daily 5:00 a.m.-11:00 p.m.
Fenced, 1 acre, turf, double-gate entry, trash bags and cans, bulletin board, on-street neighborhood parking only.

Green Valley Ranch East Park - Denver
www.denvergov.org/PRdogsoffleash/ or Dogs-off-leash hotline: (303) 964-1006
Jebel and East 45th
Daily 5:00 a.m.-11:00 p.m.
Natural barriers (native vegetation and split-rail fencing to delineate boundaries), 2 acres, trash bags and cans, parking.

Kennedy Park - Denver
www.denvergov.org/PRdogsoffleash/ or Dogs-off-leash hotline: (303) 964-1006
Hampden and South Dayton
Daily 5:00 a.m.-11:00 p.m.
Natural barriers (native vegetation and split-rail fencing to delineate boundaries), 3 acres, trash bags and cans, bulletin board, very limited parking.

FLORIDA

Happy Tails Canine Park - Bradenton
51st Street West at G.T. Bray Park, about halfway between Manatee Avenue and Cortez Road
Daily dawn-dusk
Eight-foot fence, 3 acres, trees, benches, tables, disposal bags, trash cans, parking (including handicapped spaces), restrooms nearby, water.

Dr. Paul's Pet Care Center Dog Park - Coral Springs
TopPetCare.com
Sportsplex Drive in the Sportsplex Regional Park Complex (park off Sportsplex Drive at the west pedestrian entrance)
Daily dawn-9:30 p.m.
Enclosed, lighted, trees, shaded area, paved running path, picnic table, gazebo, disposal bag dispensers, trash cans, indoor restroom, separate areas for large and small dogs, dog and people water fountains, dog shower, dog statues, weatherproof dog agility equipment.

The Dog Park in Lake Ida Park - Delray Beach
pbcgov.com/parks/dogparks/lakeida
2929 Lake Ida Rd. (take the Atlantic Avenue West exit off I-95, proceed west to Congress Avenue, go north on Congress for 1 mile, turn right onto Lake Ida Road and proceed east under I-95; park entrance is on the left)
Daily dawn-dusk; closed Thurs. noon-3 for maintenance
Fenced, 2.5 acres, partial paved pathway, eight shaded sitting areas, disposal bag dispensers and receptacles, restrooms and parking nearby, separate fenced areas for large and small dogs, two canine drinking stations, dog washing area, information kiosk.

Pooch Pines Dog Park at Okeeheelee Park - Delray Beach
pbcgov.com/parks/dogparks/lakeida
7715 Forest Hill Blvd. (off I-95 exit Forest Hill Boulevard, west to the main Okeeheelee Park entrance on the north side of the road; follow the park road to the Pooch Pines sign, turn right and continue to the top of the hill)
Daily dawn-dusk; closed Wed. noon-3 for maintenance
Fenced, 5 acres, paved pathways, shaded sitting areas, disposal bag dispensers and receptacles, trash cans, restrooms and parking nearby, separate areas for large and small dogs, canine drinking stations, dog washing area.

Bark Park at Snyder Park - Fort Lauderdale
ci.fort-lauderdale.fl.us/cityparks/snyder/barkpark
3299 S.W. 4th Ave.
Daily 7 a.m.-7:30 p.m., Apr.-Oct.; 7-6:30, rest of year.
Fee Mon.-Fri. $2; senior citizens and ages 6-12, $1.50.
Fee Sat.-Sun. and holidays $2.50; senior citizens and ages 6-12, $2.
Fenced, two open-air pavilions, benches, disposal bags, trash cans, parking, restrooms, water, separate area for small dogs, two hose stations, drinking fountains, agility equipment, small nature area with more than 20 labeled native trees. Freshwater dog swim Sat.-Sun. and holidays 10-5, first weekend in Mar.-first Sun. in Dec.; fee $1. Dogs must remain in the car until arrival at Bark Park and are not permitted in the remainder of Snyder Park. Access for the disabled.

Dog Wood Off-Leash Park - Gainesville
dogwoodpark.com
5505 S.W. Archer Rd. (1 mile west of I-75)
Sat.-Sun. noon-5; once in the park, visitors may stay until dusk
Fee $9 plus tax for the first dog, $1 plus tax for each additional dog per family (otherwise $2.50 plus tax for each additional dog in the group)
Six-foot fence, 15 acres, double-gated entry and exit, jogging trail, hammocks, gazebo, picnic tables, lounge chairs, swinging and regular benches, multiple clean-up stations with disposal bags, indoor restrooms, free bottled water, soft drinks for sale, two large swimming ponds for dogs, wading pools, dog shower, agility course, sunny and shady areas for small dogs, park-provided tennis balls. Park also offers a do-it-yourself dog wash, a doggie boutique, dog day care and agility and obedience training. All male dogs over 7 months must be neutered in order to enter the park. Children under 4 feet tall are not permitted. Phone (352) 335-1919 for details.

Paw Park of Historic Sanford - Sanford
pawparksanford.org
427 French Ave. (US 17/92) in Sanford's Historic District, 20 minutes north of downtown Orlando. From I-4, take the SR 46 exit (exit 101C, Sanford/Mount Dora), proceed east on SR 46 approximately 4 miles to French Avenue, turn right (southbound) and get into the left thru-lane; the Paw Park is on the left just past the Burger King
Daily 7:30 a.m.-8 p.m.
Fenced, double-gated entry, shaded with mature oak trees, historic lighting, paved walkway, benches, tables, disposal bag dispensers, parking, self-watering bowls, water misting station, dog showers, separate area for small dogs, community bulletin board. Access for the disabled.

17th Street Park & Paw Park - Sarasota
scgov.net/Content/Content.aspx?C7A6C692B2=A69A99
4570 17th St.
Daily dawn-dusk
Six-foot fence, 6 acres, lighted, double-gated entry, trees, benches, tables, disposal bags, trash cans, parking, restrooms, water, dog shower, separate area for small dogs, community bulletin board.

Lakeview Park - Sarasota
scgov.net/Content/Content.aspx?C7A6C692B2=A69A99
7150 Lago St.
Daily dawn-midnight
Six-foot fence, double-gated entry, many trees, benches, tables, disposal bags, trash cans, parking, restrooms, water, dog shower, separate area for small dogs, community bulletin board. Access for the disabled.

Brohard Beach & Paw Park - Venice
scgov.net/Content/Content.aspx?C7A6C692B2=A69A99
1600 Harbor Dr. South
Paw Park daily dawn-midnight. Dog Beach daily 7:30 a.m.-dusk
Six-foot fence, trees, benches, tables, shelter, disposal bags, trash cans, parking, water, dog shower, separate area for small dogs, community bulletin board. Dog Beach is accessed by boardwalk from Paw Park. Dogs are permitted in a restricted area along Brohard Beach as indicated by beach signs. Access for the disabled.

FLORIDA (CONT'D)

Woodmere Park & Woodmere Paw Park - Venice
scgov.net/Content/Content.aspx?C7A6C692B2=A69A99
3951 Woodmere Park Blvd. (two blocks north of U.S. 41
on Jacaranda Boulevard)
Daily dawn-dusk
Fenced, double-gated entry, trees, benches, tables,
disposal bags, trash cans, parking, restrooms, water,
double-gated section for small dogs near the front gate,
dog shower, community bulletin board.

GEORGIA

Royal Paws Dog Park - Alpharetta
royalpaws.com
13475 Providence Rd.
Mon.-Fri. 10-dusk, Sat.-Sun. 8-5
Off-leash area fee $16 per day for large dogs over 20
lbs., $5 per day for small dogs. Application and
vaccination proof required.
Two fenced off-leash areas on grassy hills, including a
10-acre area with lake swimming for large dogs and a
1-acre area for small dogs. Gated access, disposal bags,
well-water drinking bowls, dog bathing facilities, free
parking. Tennis balls, tosses and discs are provided. The
park is always staffed by experienced dog handlers; dog
day care is available.

ILLINOIS

Rover's Run Dog Park - Homewood
hfparks.com/parks/roversrun.htm
At 191st St. and Center Ave. in Apollo Park
Daily dawn-dusk.
Membership fee $15 per year for residents, $25 per year
for non-residents. A list of current vaccinations is required.
Phone (708)957-0300 for details.
Fenced, 3 acres, double-gated entry, separate training
area and entrance, benches, covered picnic tables, free
parking, walking path, owner/dog drinking fountain.

MICHIGAN

Orion Oaks Bark Park - Lake Orion
oakgov.com/parksrec/activities/dogpark.html
Joslyn Road, south of Clarkston Road (park at the north
Joslyn Road entrance and follow the signs)
Daily half-hour before dawn to half-hour after dusk
Resident park pass $7 per day, $30 annual pass.
Non-resident park pass $12 per vehicle per day, $46
annual pass. Over 62, park pass $4 per vehicle per day,
$28 annual pass. Park pass required; a daily pass is
available at the Lake Orion Township office (open
Mon.-Fri.) on Joslyn Road south of the park; or at
Independence Oaks County Park (open daily) on
Sashabaw Road 2.5 miles north of I-75.
Fenced, 7 acres, trees, benches, tables, disposal bags,
trash cans, parking, portable toilet, water. A portion of Lake
Sixteen is reserved for canine swimmers. Access for the
disabled.

Lyon Oaks Bark Park - Lyon Township
oakgov.com/parksrec/activities/dogpark.html
Pontiac Trail between Wixom and Old Plank roads
Daily half-hour before dawn to half-hour after dusk
Resident park pass $7 per day, $30 annual pass.
Non-resident park pass $12 per vehicle per day, $46
annual pass. Over 62, park pass $4 per vehicle per day,
$28 annual pass. Park pass required; daily and annual
passes are available at the park.
Fenced, 13 acres of open fields, benches, tables, disposal
bags, trash cans, parking, restrooms, water pump.

MINNESOTA

Note: In the greater Minneapolis area there are multiple
off-leash sites within a 15-minute drive of downtown
Minneapolis/St. Paul. There are additional sites in
rural/suburban areas of the seven-county metropolitan
area. Some parks require a permit for use; please read
descriptions carefully.

Alimagnet Dog Park - Burnsville (south metro suburb)
alimagnetdogpark.org
1200 Alimagnet Pkwy. (from central St. Paul, go south on
I-35E to the CR 42 exit, east to CR 11, then north on CR
11 to Alimagnet Parkway and turn right; the dog park is on
the right)
Daily 5 a.m.-10 p.m. Permit required; phone the
Recreation Department at (952) 895-4500.
Fenced, 7 acres, double-gated entry, wooded areas, open
fields, mowed prairie-grass trail, benches, tables, disposal
bags, trash cans, parking, phones, restrooms, water, pond.

Coates/Dakota County (south metro rural)
co.dakota.mn.us/Parks/faq.htm
Blaine Avenue south of CR 46 (160th Street E.) in the
center of Dakota County near Coates
Daily 5 a.m.-10 p.m. Permit required.
Fenced, 16 acres of wooded and open spaces with a
walking trail loop, tables, disposal bag dispensers and
receptacles, parking, portable toilets, no surface water;
bring drinking water for your dog.

Elm Creek Park Reserve - Dayton (northwest metro rural)
threeriversparkdistrict.org/trails/trails_pet.cfm
13080 Territorial Rd.
Daily 5 a.m.-dusk. Permit required; day permits are
available at the site. Annual special-use permits may be
obtained by phoning Park Guest Services at (763)
559-9000.
Fenced, 30 acres with a mowed trail, trees, tables, trash
cans, parking, restrooms.

Battle Creek Off-Leash Site - Maplewood (east central metro)
co.ramsey.mn.us/parks/parks/offleash.asp
Lower Afton and McKnight
Daily dawn-dusk. No permit required.
Partially fenced, 12 acres, tables, trash cans, parking.

MINNESOTA (CONT'D)

Franklin Terrace - Minneapolis
dogromp.org
Franklin Terrace and 30th Avenue S.
minneapolisparks.org/default.asp?PageID=851
Daily 6 a.m.-10 p.m. Permit required; phone (612)
348-4250 for information.
Fully fenced, 2.6 acres, double-gated entry at the east and
west ends of the site, bench, disposal bag dispensers,
on-street parking.

Lake of the Isles Park - Minneapolis
dogromp.org
Lake of the Isles Parkway and W. 28th Street
minneapolisparks.org/default.asp?PageID=851
Daily 6 a.m.-10 p.m. Permit required; phone (612)
348-4250 for information.
Fully fenced, 2.6 acres, double-gated entry at the northern
end of the site, lighted at the southern end, benches,
disposal bag dispensers.

Minnehaha Park - Minneapolis
minneapolisparks.org/default.asp?PageID=851
Minnehaha Avenue and E. 54th Street
Daily 6 a.m.-10 p.m. Permit required; phone (612)
348-4250 for information.
Partially fenced, 4.2 acres along the Mississippi River
(where dogs can swim), disposal bag dispensers, lighted
parking area (parking permit required), portable toilet in
parking area.

Saint Anthony Parkway - Minneapolis
minneapolisparks.org/default.asp?PageID=851
St. Anthony Pkwy. off Central Ave.
Daily 6 a.m.-10 p.m. Permit required; phone (612)
348-4250 for information.
Fully fenced, 2 acres, double-gated entry at the east and
west ends of the park, bench, disposal bag dispensers,
parking.

Egan Park's Off-Leash Area - Plymouth
http://www2.ci.plymouth.mn.us, Parks & Recreation Dept.
phone (763) 509-5200
CR 47 in northwest Plymouth, about two blocks west of
Dunkirk Lane on the south side of CR 47
Daily dawn-dusk. No permit required.
Unfenced, 10 acres, trash cans; bring your own drinking
water.

Cleary Lake Regional Park - Prior Lake (south metro rural)
threeriversparkdistrict.org/trails/trails_pet.cfm
18106 Texas Ave.
Daily 5 a.m.-dusk. Permit required; day permits are
available at the site. Annual special-use permits may be
obtained by phoning Park Guest Services at (763)
559-9000.
Fenced, 35 acres, tables, trash cans, parking, restrooms,
pond. Trails are mowed in summer, packed in winter.

Lake Sarah Regional Park - Rockford (west metro rural)
threeriversparkdistrict.org/trails/trails_pet.cfm
Lake Sarah Drive, 30 miles west of Minneapolis and east
of CR 92 (take US 55 west to CR 92, proceed south to
Lake Sarah Drive, turn left and then left again onto the
first gravel road; the parking lot for the off-leash area is on
the left side)
Daily 5 a.m.-dusk. Permit required; day permits are
available at the site. Annual special-use permits may be
obtained by phoning Park Guest Services at (763)
559-9000.
Unfenced, 30 acres, trees, mowed parking area, trash
cans, restrooms.

Crow-Hassan Park Reserve - Rogers (northwest metro rural)
threeriversparkdistrict.org/trails/trails_pet.fmc
Sylvan Lake Road west of Rogers (from I-94, take the
Rogers exit and go south through town to the T
intersection, turn right on CR 116 and proceed to CR 203,
turn left and follow CR 203 to the park entrance)
Daily 5 a.m.-dusk. Permit required; day permits are
available at the site. Annual special-use permits may be
obtained by phoning Park Guest Services at (763)
559-9000.
Fenced, 30 acres with a mowed trail, trees, tables, trash
cans, parking, restrooms.

Woodview Dog Park - Roseville (central)
co.ramsey.mn.us/parks/parks/offleash.asp
Larpenteur Avenue, just east of Dale Street (access gate
to main off-leash area is about 100 yards down the bike
trail)
Daily dawn-dusk. No permit required.
Partially fenced (along bike trail only), 3 acres, trees,
tables, disposal bags, trash cans, parking, water, separate
fenced area for small dogs. Access for the disabled.

Rice Creek Off-Leash Site - Shoreview (northeast metro)
co.ramsey.mn.us/parks/parks/offleash.asp
Lexington Avenue, just south of CR J
Daily dawn-dusk. No permit required.
Unfenced, 12 acres of flat prairie vegetation, tables, trash
cans, parking, small pond.

Bass Lake/Belt Line - St. Louis Park (west central)
stlouispark.org/experience/off_leash_dog_park.htm
West 36th Street and Belt Line Boulevard at Bass Lake
Preserve, east of the tennis courts
Daily 7:30 a.m. - 8:30 p.m. Permit required.
Fenced, 1.5 acres; bring drinking water for your dog.

Arlington-Arkwright (ArlArk) Dog Park - St. Paul
stpaul.gov/depts/parks/userguide/dogpark
Arkwright Street at Arlington Avenue (from I-35E, take the
Maryland Avenue exit east to Arkwright Street, then go
north; the park is on the right-hand side)
Daily dawn-9 p.m. No permit required.
Fenced, 4.5 acres with trails and woods, tables, disposal
bags, trash cans, parking. Park users sometimes leave
gates open; keep your dog under voice control to prevent
escapes.

MINNESOTA (CONT'D)

Otter Lake Dog Park - White Bear Township (northeast suburban)

co.ramsey.mn.us/parks/parks/offleash.htm
Otter Lake Road (take I-35E to the CR J exit, then CR J east to Otter Lake Road, following it south to the dog park; the entrance is next to the boat launch)
Daily dawn-dusk. No permit required.
Partially fenced, 10 acres of rolling hills with wooded and open prairie vegetation, separate 1-acre fenced area for small dogs. The park is fenced adjacent to Otter Lake Road and along most of the south boundary, bounded on the east by a large wetland and on the north by Otter Lake.

NEVADA

All Clark County/Las Vegas dog park areas include water, seating and waste receptacles.

Desert Breeze Park Dog Park - Clark County/Las Vegas (NW)

accessclarkcounty.com/parks/Dog_Parks.htm
8425 W. Spring Mountain Rd. at Durango
Daily 6 a.m.-11 p.m.

Desert Inn Dog Park - Clark County/Las Vegas (SE)

accessclarkcounty.com/parks/Dog_Parks.htm
3570 Vista del Monte, near Lamb and Boulder Highway
Daily 6 a.m.-11 p.m.

Dog Fancier's Park - Clark County/Las Vegas (SE)

accessclarkcounty.com/parks/Dog_Parks.htm
5800 E. Flamingo Rd., off E. Flamingo and Jimmy Durante
Daily 6 a.m.-11 p.m.
This 12-acre park is also used for dog shows and training.

Molasky Park Dog Park - Clark County/Las Vegas (SE)

accessclarkcounty.com/parks/Dog_Parks.htm
1065 E. Twain, west of Maryland Parkway; dog run is south of Twain
Daily 6 a.m.-11 p.m.

Shadow Rock Dog Park - Clark County/Las Vegas (NE)

accessclarkcounty.com/parks/Dog_Parks.htm
2650 Los Feliz (cross streets Lake Mead past Hollywood); dog run is east of the park area
Daily 6 a.m.-11 p.m.

Sunset Park - Clark County/Las Vegas (SE)

accessclarkcounty.com/parks/Dog_Parks.htm
2601 E. Sunset Rd.; closest parking is off Eastern between Sunset and Warm Springs roads
Daily 6 a.m.-11 p.m.

NEW HAMPSHIRE

Derry Dog Park - Derry

ci.derry.nh.us
45 Fordway St.
Daily dawn-dusk
Fenced, .5 acres, gazebo, picnic tables, water in summer only. Tunnel, seesaw, tire jump and other agility items are provided. Children under 9 are not permitted. Rules are posted on fence inside and out. Parking is free but somewhat limited after 25 vehicles.

NEW YORK

New York City (Manhattan and boroughs)

urbanhound.com
nycgovparks.org/sub_things_to_do/facilities/af_dog_runs.html

Canine Court, Van Cortlandt Park - Bronx

West 252nd Street and Broadway (enter on the path on 252nd and follow it about 100 feet to the left)
Daily dawn-dusk
Fenced with two large runs: a basic dog run and a canine agility playground with teeter-totter, hurdles, ladder, three chutes and a hanging tire.

Ewen Park ("John's Run") - Bronx (Riverdale)

Riverdale to Johnson avenues, south of West 232nd Street and down the steps in the clearing on the right
Daily dawn-dusk
Unfenced, plastic lawn furniture, scenic views.

Seton Park - Bronx (Riverdale)

West 235th Street and Independence Avenue (west of Independence on 235th Street, near the Spuyten Duyvil Library)
Daily dawn-dusk

Prospect Park - Brooklyn

fidobrooklyn.org, (888) 604-3422
Grand Army Plaza and Flatbush; off-leash areas may be accessed from all park entrances
Daily 9 p.m.-9 a.m., Apr.-Oct.; 5 p.m.-9 a.m., rest of year (in the 80-acre Long Meadow and 6-acre Peninsula Meadow). Dogs may be off-leash in the 15-acre Nethermead Mon.-Fri. 5 p.m-9 a.m. year-round (closed holidays). On holidays and weekends, the hours above apply to Nethermead as well. At all other times, dogs must be on a leash, minimum fine for non-compliance $100. Trees, restrooms (at Long Meadow only; may not be available early in the morning), water (some fountains equipped with troughs for dogs). No separate area for small dogs. Small swimming area in the Long Meadow near the 9th Street entrance. Note: Use of the park is at the owner's risk. Dogs may be off-leash with appropriate supervision in three large meadows at the hours specified above; please observe all off-leash rules. Rules are posted online and at park entrances. Dogs must be on a leash at all other places and times.

Owl's Head Park - Brooklyn (Bay Ridge)

68th Street and Shore Road
Tree, grass surface, disposal bags.

Hillside Park - Brooklyn Heights

Columbia Heights and Middagh Street
Daily 24 hours
Fenced.

Palmetto Playground - Brooklyn Heights

Columbia Place and State Street (in the corner by the Brooklyn-Queens Expressway)
Daily 24 hours
Benches, one park light, water.

Tompkins Square Park - Manhattan (East Village)

East 9th Street at Avenue B
Daily 6 a.m.-midnight
Benches, picnic tables, water, a canine memorial.

NEW YORK (CONT'D)

Madison Square Park - Manhattan (Gramercy/Flatiron/Union Square)
East 24th Street at Fifth Avenue
Daily 6 a.m.-midnight
Trees, benches, disposal bags, water.

Thomas Jefferson Park - Manhattan (Harlem)
East 112th Street at First Avenue
Daily 24 hours
Benches, wood chips surface.

J. Hood Wright Park - Manhattan (Inwood/Ft. George/Washington Heights)
West 173rd Street between Fort Washington Avenue and Haven Avenue

Fishbridge Park - Manhattan (Lower East Side)
Dover Street at Pearl Street, just south of the Brooklyn Bridge
Daily dawn-dusk
Benches, water hose, summer wading pool, lockbox for toys, lockbox with newspapers for picking up after your dog.

Peter Detmold Park — Manhattan (Midtown East)
East 49th Street at FDR Drive (behind Beeckman Place)
Daily dawn-9 p.m., June-Sept.; dawn-8 p.m., Mar.-May and Oct.-Nov.; dawn-7 p.m., rest of year
Trees, benches, historical lamps, disposal bags.

Carl Shurz Park - Manhattan (Upper East Side)
East 86th Street at East End Avenue
Daily dawn-1 a.m.
Benches, scoops, pea gravel surface. A second run for small dogs (past the main run, toward the East River) has a scenic view of the river and the 59th Street Bridge.

Riverside Park at 72nd Street - Manhattan (Upper West Side/Morningside Heights)
West 72nd Street
Daily 6 a.m.-1 a.m.
Bench, hanging flowerpots, disposal bags, scoopers.

Riverside Park at 87th Street - Manhattan (Upper West Side/Morningside Heights)
West 87th Street
Daily dawn-dusk
Separate areas for large and small dogs, fountain and hose.

Riverside Park at 105th Street - Manhattan (Upper West Side/Morningside Heights)
riversidedog.org
West 105th Street, Riverside Park Central Promenade
Daily dawn-dusk
Trees, crushed granite surface, benches, disposal bag dispensers, drinking fountain, dog water faucet, separate area for small dogs.

Theodore Roosevelt Park - Manhattan (Upper West Side/Morningside Heights)
West 81st Street at Columbus Avenue
Daily 8 a.m.-10 p.m.
Shade trees, benches, dog water faucet, separate run for small dogs.

Washington Square Park - Manhattan (West Village)
West 4th Street at Thompson Street
Daily 6 a.m.-midnight
Trees, pea gravel surface, benches, scoopers, water hose, water bowls.

Doughboy Plaza - Queens (Woodside)
Woodside Avenue from 54th to 56th streets (also south of Woodside at 56th Street) at Windmuller Park
Daily dawn-dusk
Fenced, trash can.

NORTH CAROLINA

Down East Dog Park - New Bern
newbern-nc.org/RP/parks.php
303 Glenburnie Dr. in Glenburnie Park
Daily dawn-dusk
Annual fee $35 for first dog, $20 each additional dog; weekly passes $5. Proof of current rabies vaccination is required. Contact 252-639-7588 for more information. Fenced; the main 1-acre area is for large dogs over 25 lbs., but dogs of any size may use it; a separate area is set aside for puppies and small dogs.

OHIO

Mt. Airy Dog Park - Cincinnati
cincinnati-oh.gov/cityparks/pages/-4327-/
Westwood Northern Boulevard within Mt. Airy Forest's Highpoint Picnic Area, between Montana Avenue and North Bend Road
Daily dawn-dusk
Fenced, trees, benches, tables, shelter, trash cans, parking, restrooms, water. Access for the disabled.

Big Walnut Dog Park - Columbus
bigwalnutdogpark.com
5000 E. Livingston Ave. in Big Walnut Park, across from Walnut Ridge High School
Daily 7 a.m.-11p.m.
Fenced, 2 double-gate entries, 3 acres, swimming pond, shade trees, picnic tables, paved parking; no restrictions on breeds or spay/neuter.

OREGON

Alton Baker Park - Eugene
www.eugene-or.gov/parks
South of Leo Harris Parkway; park in the lot south of Autzen Stadium and cross the pedestrian bridge to the dog park
Daily 6 a.m.-11 p.m.
Fenced, benches, tables, simple shelters for protection from sun and rain, disposal bag receptacles, water.

Amazon Park - Eugene
www.eugene-or.gov/parks
East of 29th Street and Amazon Parkway
Daily 6 a.m.-11 p.m.
Fenced, benches, tables, simple shelters for protection from sun and rain, disposal bag receptacles, water, parking nearby.

OREGON (CONT'D)

Morse Ranch - Eugene
www.eugene-or.gov/parks
Crest Drive and Lincoln Street (park in the main parking area at 595 Crest Dr. and take the trail east)
Daily 6 a.m.-11 p.m.
Fenced, benches, tables, simple shelters for protection from sun and rain, disposal bag receptacles, water.

Brentwood Park - Portland
http://www.portlandonline.com/parks/index.cfm?c=39523
SE 60th Avenue and Duke Street
Daily 5 a.m.-midnight
Fenced.

Chimney Park - Portland
http://www.portlandonline.com/parks/index.cfm?c=39523
9360 N. Columbia Blvd.
Daily 5 a.m.-midnight
Unfenced, 6 acres of off-leash meadow and trails. Dogs should be under excellent voice command.

East Delta Park - Portland
http://www.portlandonline.com/parks/index.cfm?c=39523
N. Denver and Martin Luther King Jr. Boulevard (off I-5 exit 307 across from the East Delta Sports Complex)
Daily 5 a.m.-midnight, May-Oct. (open during dry season only)
Fenced, 5 acres of off-leash field, trees, benches; bring drinking water for your dog. Dogs are not allowed on the sports fields.

Gabriel Park - Portland
http://www.portlandonline.com/parks/index.cfm?c=39523
S.W. 45th Street and Vermont
Daily 5 a.m.-midnight, May-Oct. (open during dry season only)
Fenced, 1 5 acres of off-leash area, trees, picnic tables, water. Dogs must remain leashed when not in the off-leash area.

Normandale Park - Portland
http://www.portlandonline.com/parks/index.cfm?c=39523
NE 57th Avenue and Halsey Street
Daily 5 a.m.-midnight
Fenced.

TEXAS

White Rock Lake Dog Park - Dallas
dallasdogparks.org
Mockingbird Point within White Rock Lake Park
Tues.-Sun. 5 a.m.-midnight (weather permitting)
Fenced, 2.5 acres, trees, benches, disposal bags, trash cans, parking, restrooms, water fountains, separate fenced areas for large and small dogs, fenced swimming area for dogs in White Rock Lake.

VIRGINIA

Note: Disposal bag receptacles are provided at Alexandria parks; patrons must provide their own bags.

Ben Brenman Park - Alexandria
ci.alexandria.va.us/recreation/parks/dogpark.html#fenced
Cameron Station along Backlick Creek
Daily 6 a.m.-10 p.m.
Fenced, disposal bag receptacles, trash cans, parking.

Dog Park - Alexandria
ci.alexandria.va.us/recreation/parks/dogpark.html#fenced
5000 block of Duke Street east of the Charles E. Beatley Jr. Library
Daily 6 a.m.-10 p.m.
Fenced, disposal bag receptacles, trash cans, parking.

Montgomery Park - Alexandria
ci.alexandria.va.us/recreation/parks/dogpark.html#fenced
Fairfax and 1st streets
Daily 6 a.m.-10 p.m.
Fenced, disposal bag receptacles, trash cans, parking.

Simpson Stadium Park - Alexandria
ci.alexandria.va.us/recreation/parks/dogpark.html#fenced
Monroe Avenue
Daily 6 a.m.-10 p.m.
Fenced, disposal bag receptacles, trash cans, parking, dog water fountains.

Off-leash, unfenced, under voice control areas:

Braddock Road - Alexandria
ci.alexandria.va.us/recreation/parks/dogpark.html#unfenced
Southeast corner of Braddock Road and Commonwealth Avenue
Daily 6 a.m.-10 p.m.
Unfenced.

Chambliss Street - Alexandria
ci.alexandria.va.us/recreation/parks/dogpark.html#unfenced
Chambliss Street at Grigsby Avenue, south of the tennis courts
Daily 6 a.m.-10 p.m.
Unfenced; area is marked by traffic barriers.

Chinquapin Park - Alexandria
ci.alexandria.va.us/recreation/parks/dogpark.html#unfenced
King Street at the east end of the loop road
Daily 6 a.m.-10 p.m.
Unfenced; area is marked by traffic barriers.

Edison Street - Alexandria
ci.alexandria.va.us/recreation/parks/dogpark.html#unfenced
Edison Street, west of the cul-de-sac between the bike trail and Berkey Photo Processing
Daily 6 a.m.-10 p.m.
Unfenced; area is marked by traffic barriers.

Ft. Williams - Alexandria
ci.alexandria.va.us/recreation/parks/dogpark.html#unfenced
Ft. Williams and New Ft. Williams Parkway
Daily 6 a.m.-10 p.m.
Unfenced; area is marked by traffic barriers.

Founders Park - Alexandria
ci.alexandria.va.us/recreation/parks/dogpark.html#unfenced
Oronoco Street and Union Street, northeast corner
Daily 6 a.m.-10 p.m.
Unfenced; 100-by-100-foot area is marked by traffic barriers.

VIRGINIA (CONT'D)

Off-leash, unfenced, under voice control areas:

Hooff's Run - Alexandria
ci.alexandria.va.us/recreation/parks/
dogpark.html#unfenced
East of Commonwealth Avenue between Oak and
Chapman streets
Daily 6 a.m.-10 p.m.
Unfenced; area is marked by traffic barriers.

Monticello Park - Alexandria
ci.alexandria.va.us/recreation/parks/
dogpark.html#unfenced
Beverly Drive, east of the entrance
Daily 6 a.m.-10 p.m.
Unfenced; 50-by-200-foot area is marked by traffic
barriers.

North Fort Ward Park - Alexandria
ci.alexandria.va.us/recreation/parks/
dogpark.html#unfenced
Braddock Road, east side of entrance
Daily 6 a.m.-10 p.m.
Unfenced; 100-by-100-foot area is marked by traffic
barriers.

Tarleton Park - Alexandria
ci.alexandria.va.us/recreation/parks/
dogpark.html#unfenced
Old Mill Run west of Gordon Street
Daily 6 a.m.-10 p.m.
Unfenced.

Timberbranch Parkway - Alexandria
ci.alexandria.va.us/recreation/parks/
dogpark.html#unfenced
Median to Timberbranch Parkway between Braddock
Road and Oakley Place
Daily 6 a.m.-10 p.m.
Unfenced; area is marked by traffic barriers.

Windmill Hill Park - Alexandria
ci.alexandria.va.us/recreation/parks/
dogpark.html#unfenced
Gibbon and Union streets
Daily 6 a.m.-10 p.m.
Unfenced.

W&OD Railroad - Alexandria
ci.alexandria.va.us/recreation/parks/
dogpark.html#unfenced
Raymond Avenue (200 feet of the W&OD Railroad
right-of-way south of Raymond)
Daily 6 a.m.-10 p.m.
Unfenced; area is marked by traffic barriers.

Benjamin Banneker Park - Arlington County
arlingtondogs.org
1600 block of North Sycamore Street (take I-66 west to
Sycamore Street/exit 69, turn left on Sycamore and
proceed past the East Falls Church Metro Station, turn
right onto North 16th Street and take the first right, which
dead-ends at the dog exercise area)
Daily dawn to half-hour after dusk
Fully fenced, picnic table and benches, water.

Fort Barnard Park - Arlington County
arlingtondogs.org
South Pollard Street and South Walter Reed Drive (from
Rte. 50, take Glebe Road south, turn right on South
Walter Reed Drive and proceed to Pollard Street; the park
is on the right side)
Daily dawn to half-hour after dusk
Fully fenced, picnic table and benches, water.

Glencarlyn Park - Arlington County
arlingtondogs.org
301 South Harrison St. (from Rte. 50, head west to Carlin
Springs Road, exit right and then turn left at the stop sign,
pass under Rte. 50 and follow Carlin Springs to 4th
Street, turn left on 4th Street and proceed five blocks until
the road ends at the Glencarlyn Park sign, following the
park road until it ends; park and walk over a small bridge
and stream to the exercise area)
Daily dawn to half-hour after dusk
Unfenced area near a creek and woods, picnic table,
benches.

Shirlington Park - Arlington County
arlingtondogs.org
2601 S. Arlington Mill Dr., bordering South Four Mile Run
between Shirlington Road and South Walter Reed Drive
along the bicycle path between a storage facility and the
water, near but not in Jennie Dean Park (from South Four
Mile Run, turn south onto Nelson and park behind the
storage facility; there are no signs indicating the dog park)
Daily dawn to half-hour after dusk
Partially fenced, picnic table, benches, water.

Towers Park - Arlington County
arlingtondogs.org
801 South Scott St. behind the tennis courts
Daily dawn to half-hour after dusk
Fully fenced, separate small dog area, parking.

Red Wing Park - Virginia Beach
vbgov.com/e-gov/vbcsg/faqinfo/0,1172,5353,00.html
1398 General Booth Blvd.
Daily 7:30 a.m.-dusk; closed Jan. 1, Martin Luther King
Day, Veterans Day, Thanksgiving and Dec. 25
Annual fee for first-time visitors $10; owners must register
at the park office, show proof of pet's rabies shot and
vaccines, and obtain a city dog license.
Fenced, benches, disposal bags, parking, restrooms,
water. Access for the disabled.

Woodstock Community Park - Virginia Beach
vbgov.com/e-gov/vbcsg/faqinfo/0,1172,5353,00.html
5709 Providence Rd.
Daily 7:30 a.m.-dusk; closed Jan. 1, Martin Luther King
Day, Veterans Day, Thanksgiving and Dec. 25
Annual fee for first-time visitors $10; owners must register
at the park office, show proof of pet's rabies shot and
vaccines, and obtain a city dog license.
Fenced, benches, disposal bags, restrooms, parking.
Access for the disabled.

WASHINGTON

I-5 Colonnade Park - Seattle
coladog.org
Lakeview Boulevard and Franklin Avenue East in the Eastlake neighborhood beneath I-5, south of East Howe Street
Daily 6 a.m.-11 p.m.
Fenced, 1.2 acres, double-gated entry, dog water fountain; the I-5 freeway deck provides shelter from the elements.

I-90 "Blue Dog Pond" - Seattle
coladog.org
Martin Luther King Jr. Way and South Massachusetts Street, on the northwest corner
Daily 6 a.m.-11 p.m.
Fenced, 1 acre, parking, dog water fountain, Blue Dog sculpture. No off-leash areas in I-90 Lid Park, just east of Blue Dog Pond.

Dr. Jose Rizal Park - Seattle
coladog.org
1008 12th Ave. S. on North Beacon Hill; off-leash area is in the lower portion of the park
Daily 6 a.m.-11 p.m.
Fenced, 4 acres, double-gated entry, parking, dog water fountain, scenic view of downtown.

Genesee Park - Seattle
coladog.org
46th Avenue South and South Genesee Street
Daily 6 a.m.-11 p.m.
Fenced, 3 acres, double-gated entry, parking, dog water fountain.

Golden Gardens Park - Seattle
coladog.org
8498 Seaview Pl. N.W. in Ballard
Daily 6 a.m.-11 p.m.
Fenced, lighted, 1 acre, parking, dog water fountain. The off-leash area is in the upper (eastern) portion of the park; dogs are not allowed on the lower beach area.

Magnuson Park - Seattle
coladog.org
6500 Sandpoint Way N.E. (enter the park at 74th Street and drive to the end of the road)
Daily 6 a.m.-11 p.m.
Fenced, 9 acres, double-gated entry, shelter, parking, separate area for small/shy dogs, dog water fountain, beach access.

Northacres Park - Seattle
coladog.org
N. 130th Street, west of I-5; off-leash area is in the northeast corner of the park at 12530 Third Ave. N.E., north of the ball field. Parking is available on the west side of the park along 1st Street N.E. and on the south side along North 125th Street
Daily 6 a.m.-11 p.m.
Fenced, double-gated entry, parking, dog water fountain.

Plymouth Pillars Park - Seattle
coladog.org
Boren Avenue and Pike Street on Capitol Hill above I-5
Daily 6 a.m.-11 p.m.
Fenced, 9,800 square feet, double-gated entry, dog water fountain, scenic view of downtown Seattle.

Regrade Park - Seattle
coladog.org
3rd Avenue and Bell Street, downtown
Fenced, 13,000 square feet, double-gated entry, dog water fountain.

Westcrest Park - Seattle
coladog.org
8806 8th Ave. S.W. in West Seattle
Daily 6 a.m.-11 p.m.
Fenced, 5 acres, parking, dog water fountain. The off-leash area is along the east side of the reservoir.

Woodland Park - Seattle
coladog.org
West Green Lake Way North, west of the tennis courts
Daily 6 a.m.-11 p.m.
Fenced, 1 acre, double-gated entry, parking, dog water fountain.

Canada

ALBERTA

91 Street Right of Way - Edmonton
gov.edmonton.ab.ca, (780) 496-1475
Berm east of 91 Street from 10 Avenue north to Whitemud Freeway and east to 76 Street
Unfenced.

Buena Vista Great Meadow - Edmonton
gov.edmonton.ab.ca, (780) 496-1475
North of Laurier Park and Buena Vista Drive and south of Melton Ravine in the vicinity of 88 Avenue
Unfenced; area does not include the pedestrian bridge access trail, Yorath property or the trail north to McKenzie Ravine. This is a hot-air balloon site, so please leash your dog during balloon launches.

Hermitage Park North - Edmonton
gov.edmonton.ab.ca, (780) 496-1475
129 Avenue to 137 Avenue; also 22 Street along the riverbank where signs designate an off-leash area.
Unfenced. This is a multi-use area in the valley north of the park's fishing pond and picnic area.

Jackie Parker Park - Edmonton
gov.edmonton.ab.ca, (780) 496-1475
Whitemud Freeway and 50th Street
Unfenced. Includes the area south of the 44 Avenue entrance; dogs are not allowed on the golf course.

Keehewin Blackmud - Edmonton
gov.edmonton.ab.ca, (780) 496-1475
Pipeline corridor, 104 Street and 20 Avenue to the south end of 109 Street (excludes Bearspaw Drive West and Blackmud Creek and Ravine)
Unfenced.

ALBERTA (CONT'D)

Kennedale - Edmonton
gov.edmonton.ab.ca, (780) 496-1475
Ravine west of the 40 Street loop, west to 47 Street and
the top of the bank
Unfenced.

Lauderdale - Edmonton
gov.edmonton.ab.ca, (780) 496-1475
South end of Grand Trunk Park, from 127 to 129 Avenue
and 113A to 109 Street
Unfenced.

Mill Creek Ravine - Edmonton
gov.edmonton.ab.ca, (780) 496-1475
68 Avenue and 93 Street; access is from the west or
north sides of Argyll Park
Unfenced. A granular trail along the bottom of the ravine
leads to the Whyte (82) Avenue overpass.

Terwillegar Park - Edmonton
gov.edmonton.ab.ca, (780) 496-1475
Rabbit Hill Road
Unfenced. This is a multi-use area.

MANITOBA

Bourkevale Park - Winnipeg
winnipeg.ca/publicworks/parks/fieldsforfido.asp
100 Ferry Rd., south of the dike along the riverbank
Daily 6 a.m.-10 p.m.
Unfenced, trash cans, parking; bring your own disposal
bags.

Juba Park & Pioneer Avenue - Winnipeg
winnipeg.ca/publicworks/parks/fieldsforfido.asp
Pioneer Avenue, all vacant land west of the walkway to
Juba Park
Daily 6 a.m.-10 p.m.
Unfenced, trash cans, parking; bring your own disposal
bags.

Kil-Cona Park - Winnipeg
winnipeg.ca/publicworks/parks/fieldsforfido.asp
Lagimodiere Boulevard in the area north of the west
parking lot
Daily 6 a.m.-10 p.m.
Unfenced, trash cans, parking; bring your own disposal
bags.

King's Park - Winnipeg
winnipeg.ca/publicworks/parks/fieldsforfido.asp
King's Drive, south end of park, south of the lake
Daily 6 a.m.-10 p.m.
Unfenced, trash cans, parking; bring your own disposal
bags.

Little Mountain Park - Winnipeg
winnipeg.ca/publicworks/parks/fieldsforfido.asp
West side of park adjacent to Klimpike Road entrance
Daily 6 a.m.-10 p.m.
Unfenced, trash cans, parking; bring your own disposal
bags.

Maple Grove Park - Winnipeg
winnipeg.ca/publicworks/parks/fieldsforfido.asp
Frobisher Road, north area of park
Daily 6 a.m.-10 p.m.
Unfenced, trash cans, parking; bring your own disposal
bags.

St. Boniface Industrial Park - Winnipeg
winnipeg.ca/publicworks/parks/fieldsforfido.asp
Area surrounding retention pond, bordered by Mazenod
Rd., Camiel Sys St. and Beghin St.
Daily 6 a.m.-10 p.m.
Unfenced, trash cans, parking; bring your own disposal
bags.

Westview Park - Winnipeg
winnipeg.ca/publicworks/parks/fieldsforfido.asp
Midland Street; entire park is an off-leash area
Daily 6 a.m.-10 p.m.
Unfenced, trash cans, parking; bring your own disposal
bags.

Wordsworth Park - Winnipeg
winnipeg.ca/publicworks/parks/fieldsforfido.asp
Northeast of King Edward Avenue and Park Lane
Daily 6 a.m.-10 p.m.
Unfenced, trash cans, parking; bring your own disposal
bags.

United States

CALIFORNIA

 Disneyland® Resort

(714) 781-4565, 1313 S. Harbor Blvd. via I-5 Disneyland Drive and Disney Way exits, Anaheim
Disneyland® Resort consists of two family-oriented theme parks — Disneyland Park and Disney's California Adventure Park — and the shops, restaurants and entertainment of Downtown Disney®. Indoor kennel facilities $15. Both theme parks are open daily with extended hours during the summer, on some holidays and on weekends. Admission to either park $63; over 60, $57; ages 3-9, $53. Parking fee. disneyland.disney.go.com

 SeaWorld

(619) 226-3901 or (800) 380-3203, 500 SeaWorld Dr., San Diego
SeaWorld offers four major animal shows, rides and playgrounds, a marina and exhibits featuring marine creatures from around the world. Pet facility provided for a nominal charge on a first-come, first-serve basis. Opens daily at 9, mid-June through Labor Day; at 10, rest of year. Closing times vary and may be extended during summer and holiday periods; phone ahead. Admission $56; ages 3-9, $46. Parking fee. www.seaworld.com/

 Universal Studios Hollywood

(800) 864-8377, is off Hollywood Frwy. (US 101) at 100 Universal City Plaza, Universal City
In addition to thrill rides and attractions, Universal Studios gives visitors a behind-the-scenes look at the workings of a major film and TV studio. Complimentary kennel service. Daily 9-8 in summer, 10-6 rest of year. Box office closes at 5 in summer, at 4 rest of year. Hours may vary; phone ahead to confirm. Closed Thanksgiving and Dec. 25. Admission $59; under 48 inches tall $49. Parking fee. universalstudioshollywood.com

DISTRICT OF COLUMBIA

Washington Monument

(202) 426-6841, 15th Street and Constitution Avenue N.W., Washington, D.C.
This instantly recognizable 555-foot marble obelisk commemorates our nation's first president and is surrounded by expansive grounds. Pets on leash. Daily 9-5; closed Dec. 25. Free. www.nps.gov/wamo

FLORIDA

Busch Gardens Tampa Bay

(866) 353-8622 or (888) 800-5447, 3000 E. Busch Blvd., Tampa
This African-themed family entertainment park and outstanding zoological facility features all kinds of thrill rides and numerous opportunities for animal observation. Indoor kennel facilities. Generally open daily at 9 a.m.; closing times vary. Phone ahead to confirm hours. Admission $61.95; ages 3-9, $51.95. Parking fee. www.buschgardens.com

 SeaWorld Orlando

(407) 351-3600 or (800) 327-2424, 7007 SeaWorld Dr. at I-4 and SR 528 (Beachline Expressway), Orlando
A research facility as well as a theme park, SeaWorld Orlando presents crowd-pleasing animal shows starring a family of performing killer whales. Air-conditioned kennels. Generally opens daily at 9; closing times vary. Phone ahead to confirm hours. Admission $64.95; ages 3-9, $53.95.
Parking fee. www.seaworld.com

 Universal Orlando Resort

(407) 363-8000, off I-4 exit 75A (eastbound) or 74B (westbound) following signs, Orlando
At Universal Orlando you can "ride the movies" at the Universal Studios theme park, cavort with superheroes and cartoon characters at Universal's Islands of Adventure theme park, or visit the specialty shops, celebrity-themed restaurants and entertainment venues at CityWalk. Air-conditioned kennels. Theme parks open daily at 9 a.m.; closing times vary by season. Phone ahead to confirm hours. CityWalk open daily 11 a.m.-2 a.m. One-day admission to either theme park $67; ages 3-9, $56. Individual CityWalk venue charges vary. Parking fee. www.universalorlando.com/

 Walt Disney World® Resort

(407) 824-4321, theme parks accessible from US 192, Osceola Parkway and several I-4 exits, Lake Buena Vista
Walt Disney World has — count 'em — four theme parks: Magic Kingdom® Park, Epcot®, Disney's Animal Kingdom® Theme Park and Disney-MGM Studios, plus shopping, dining and entertainment at the Downtown Disney® Area. Air-conditioned kennels. Theme parks generally open daily at 9 a.m., closing times vary. One-day, one-park admission $67; ages 3-9, $56. Parking fee. disneyworld.disney.go.com

GEORGIA

Six Flags Over Georgia

(770) 948-9290, 275 Riverside Pkwy. (off I-20), Austell
Six Flags offers more than 100 rides, attractions and shows, a 12,000-seat concert amphitheater, Broadway-style musical shows and a July 4 fireworks display. Kennels (water provided, but not food). Open daily at 10 a.m., late May to mid-Aug.; Sat.-Sun. at 10, mid-Mar. to late May and mid-Aug. to late Oct. Closing times vary. Admission $49.99, over 54 and under 49 inches tall $29.99, under 2 free. Parking fee. www.sixflags.com

ILLINOIS

 Six Flags Great America

(847) 249-4636 or (847) 249-1776, 542 N. Route 21, Gurnee
Batman the Ride, Iron Wolf and Raging Bull are among the thrill rides at this family theme park, which also has a section of rides and attractions for children under 54 inches tall. Kennel facilities. Open daily at 10 a.m., late Apr. to mid-Sept.; Sat.-Sun. at 10, mid-Sept. to late Oct. Closing times vary; phone ahead to confirm hours. Admission $54.99, over 60 and under 55 inches tall $34.99, under 4 free. Parking fee. www.sixflags.com

IOWA

 Pella Historical Village

(641) 628-2409 or 628-4311, 507 Franklin St., Pella
A country store, log cabin, grist mill, windmill, smithy and other buildings (including Wyatt Earp's boyhood home) are reminders of this town's Dutch Heritage. Pets on leash (grounds only). Mon.-Sat. 9-5, Mar.-Dec. Admission $8; ages 5-18, $2.

MASSACHUSETTS

 Bunker Hill Monument

(617) 242-5641, in Monument Square on Breed's Hill, Charlestown
Part of Boston National Historical Park, this 221-foot-tall granite obelisk commemorates the site of the Battle of Bunker Hill on June 17, 1775. Pets on leash (grounds only); must pick up after pet. Visitor lodge and exhibits daily 9-5. Free. www.nps.gov/bost/Bunker_Hill/htm

MISSISSIPPI

 Vicksburg National Military Park

(601) 636-0583, entered via I-20 exit 4B, then .2 mi. w. on Clay St. (US 80)
More than 1,260 memorials, monuments, statues and markers honor the Union and Confederate troops who engaged in the siege of Vicksburg in 1863. Pets on leash. Grounds open daily dawn-dusk; visitor center daily 8-5. Admission $8 per private vehicle. www.nps.gov/vick

MISSOURI

 The Gateway Arch

(877) 982-1410, Memorial Drive and Market Street, St. Louis
This curved, stainless steel monument soars 630 feet high and symbolizes the gateway to the West. A tram ride takes visitors to an observation deck. Pets on leash (grounds only). Tram ticket center open daily 8 a.m.-10 p.m., Memorial Day-Labor Day; 9-6, rest of year. Closed Jan. 1, Thanksgiving and Dec. 25. Tram ride $10; ages 13-15, $7; ages 3-15, $3. www.gatewayarch.com

NORTH CAROLINA

 Paramount's Carowinds Theme Park

(704) 588-2600 in N.C., (803) 548-5300 or (800) 888-4386, 10 miles south on I-77 to exit 90, Charlotte
Themed areas at this park depict the past and present of the Carolinas, and offer roller coasters and water rides, children's play areas and other family entertainment. Air-conditioned kennels. Open daily at 10, Jun. to mid-Aug.; open weekends Mar.-May and late Aug.-Oct. Hours vary seasonally; phone ahead. Admission $44.95; over 62 and ages 3-6 or under 48 inches tall, $19.95. Parking fee. www.carowinds.com

OHIO

 Paramount's Kings Island

(513) 754-5700 or (800) 288-0808, Kings Island Drive (off I-71 exits 24 and 25), Kings Mills
Kings Island is a family entertainment park featuring 14 hair-raising roller coasters; Boomerang Bay, a water recreation playground; costumed cartoon characters; and a variety of live shows. Kennel facilities (fee). Open daily at 10, late May-Aug.; Sat.-Sun. at 10, late Mar. to late May and Sept.-Oct. Phone ahead to confirm hours. Admission $49.99; over 59, ages 3-6 or under 48 inches tall, $26.99. Parking fee. www.pki.com

PENNSYLVANIA

 Hersheypark

(800) 437-7439, 100 W. Hersheypark Dr. (just off SR 743 and US 422), Hershey
The emphasis is on thrill rides at Hersheypark, plus live entertainment that includes a marine mammal show, song and dance reviews and big-name performers. Zooamerica North American Wildlife Park covers 11 acres. Kennel facilities. Open daily at 10 a.m., mid-May to late Sept.; Fri.-Sun. at 10, selected weekends in May. Closing times vary; phone ahead to confirm hours. Admission $45.95; ages 3-8 and 55-69, $26.95; over 70, $18.95. Parking fee. www.hersheypark.com

TEXAS

 SeaWorld San Antonio

(800) 700-7786, 10500 SeaWorld Dr. (off SR 151 at the junction of Westover Hills Boulevard), San Antonio
Killer and beluga whales, sea lions, otters, walruses and dolphins perform at this marine life park, which also has shark exhibits, a penguin habitat and a children's playground. Outdoor kennel facilities (owner must provide food and water containers). Open daily at 10 a.m., early Mar.-late Nov.; closing times vary. Admission $46.99; ages 3-9, $36.99 (phone to confirm times and admission). Parking fee. www.seaworld.com

 Six Flags Fiesta Texas

(817) 530-6000, 2201 Road to Six Flags (at the junction of I-30 and SR 360 exit 30), Arlington
Themed areas, each featuring thrill rides, food and entertainment, depict Texas under six different flags: Spain, France, Mexico, the Republic of Texas, the Confederate States of America and the United States. Air-conditioned kennels (fee). Open daily, June 1 to mid-Aug.; Sat.-Sun (also Labor Day), late Mar. through May 31, mid-Aug. through Oct. 31 and early to mid-Dec. Hours vary; phone ahead to confirm schedule. Admission $45; over 54 and under 48 inches tall, $35; under 3 free. Parking fee. www.sixflags.com

VIRGINIA

 Busch Gardens Europe

(800) 343-7946, 3 miles east on US 60 or off I-64 exit 242A, Williamsburg
This European-themed adventure park offers something for the entire family, from thrill rides to dance and music shows to villages representing England, Germany, France and other nations. Kennel facilities (England parking lot); fee $6 per pet per day. Open daily at 10 a.m., early May-Labor Day; closing times vary. Open at 10, late Mar.-early May and day after Labor Day-late Oct.; days and closing times vary. Admission $51.95; ages 3-6, $44.95. Parking fee. www.buschgardens.com

 Kings Dominion

(804) 876-5000, 16000 Theme Park Way (on SR 30 1/2 mile east off I-95 exit 98), Doswell
Eight themed areas make up Kings Dominion, a full-scale theme park with thrill rides, kiddie play areas, costumed characters, live shows and specialty shopping. Kennel facilities (fee); water provided, but not food. Park open daily, Memorial Day-Labor Day; Sat.-Sun., late Mar. to day before Memorial Day and first Sat. after Labor Day to late Oct. Hours vary seasonally; phone ahead. Admission $44.95; over 62, $24.95; under 3 free. Parking fee. www.kingsdominion.com

WASHINGTON

 Hovander Homestead

(360) 384-3444, 1 mile south via Hovander Road, Ferndale
This restored house, dating from 1903 and furnished with antiques, is within a large park encompassing gardens, picnic sites and a children's farm area. Pets on leash (grounds only). Grounds open daily 8 a.m.-dusk; house open Thurs.-Sun. noon-4:30, June 1-Labor Day. House $1; ages 5-12, 50 cents. www.co.whatcom.wa.us/parks/hovander/hovander.jsp

Canada

ONTARIO

 Upper Canada Village

(613) 543-4328 or (800) 437-2233, 7 miles (11 kilometers) east on CR 2 off Hwy. 401, Morrisburg
Upper Canada Village re-creates life during the 1860s through a working community of artisans and costumed interpreters who perform chores typical of the era. Pets on leash (grounds only). Daily 9:30-5, late May-early Oct. Village admission $16.95; over 65, $15.95; students with ID $10.50; ages 5-12, $7.50. www.uppercanadavillage.com

 Canada's Wonderland

(905) 832-7000 or 832-8131, off Hwy. 400 (Rutherford Road exit northbound or Major MacKenzie Drive E. exit southbound) at 9580 Jane St., Vaughan
Thrill rides at this theme park include the Top Gun coaster and Drop Zone, a free-fall plunge, while Scooby Doo's Haunted Mansion and Hanna-Barbera Land will entertain little ones. Air-conditioned kennels (fee). Open daily at 10 a.m., late May-Labour Day; some weekends early to late May and day after Labour Day-second Sun. in Oct. Closing times vary. Grounds admission $25.99. Grounds and rides passport $44.95; over 59 and ages 3-6, $19.95. Parking fee. www.canadas-wonderland.com

NATIONAL PUBLIC LANDS

The National Public Lands listed below permit pets on a leash. Keep in mind that animals may be prohibited from entering public buildings and even some areas outdoors, particularly those that are ecologically sensitive. Where swimming is permitted, there are usually no lifeguards on duty; people and pets swim at their own risk. Specific pet policies vary from park to park and are subject to change. Always check in advance regarding any applicable regulations and to confirm that pets are still permitted where you are going.

Be aware of dangers to your pet in natural areas, including snakes, ticks and fast-moving currents in rivers and streams. An unleashed dog may chase after a wild animal and become separated from its owner, increasing the risk of loss or injury. Never leave your pet unattended. Keep him leashed or crated at all times. Follow park guidelines faithfully, and monitor your pet's behavior; the National Park Service may confiscate pets that harm wildlife or other visitors. *For additional information on outdoor vacations, see The Great Outdoors, p. 16.*

United States

ALABAMA

Conecuh National Forest
On the Alabama-Florida border.
(334) 222-2555
🚲 🅰 🥾 🌲 🏊

Eufaula National Wildlife Refuge
On the Chattahoochee River.
(334) 687-4065
🚲 🥾 🏠

Horseshoe Bend National Military Park
12 mi. north of Dadeville on SR 49.
(256) 234-7111
🚲 🥾 🌲 🏠

Talladega National Forest
In central Alabama.
(256) 362-2909
🅰 🥾 🌲 🏠 🍴

Tuskegee National Forest
Northeast of Tuskegee.
(334) 727-2652
🅰 🥾 🌲 🏠

William B. Bankhead National Forest
In northwestern Alabama.
(205) 489-5111
🚲 🅰 🥾 🌲 🏊 🏠

Wheeler National Wildlife Refuge
Between Decatur and Huntsville.
(256) 350-6639
🚲 🥾 🌲 🏠

ALASKA

Chugach National Forest
Along the Gulf of Alaska from Cape Suckling to Seward.
(907) 743-9500
🚲 🅰 🥾 🌲 🏠

Denali National Park and Preserve
In south-central Alaska.
(907) 683-2294
🚲 🅰 🥾 🌲 🏠 🍴

Glacier Bay National Park and Preserve
North of Cross Sound to the Canadian border.
(907) 697-2230
🚲 🅰 🥾 🏠

Kenai Fjords National Park
Southeastern side of the Kenai Peninsula.
(907) 224-7500 or (907) 224-2132
🅰 🥾 🌲 🏠

Lake Clark National Park and Preserve
In southern Alaska.
(907) 781-2218 or (907) 644-3626
🅰 🥾 🏠

Tongass National Forest
In southeastern Alaska.
(907) 586-8800 or (907) 228-6220
🚲 🅰 🥾 🌲 🏊 🏠

Wrangell-St. Elias National Park and Preserve
In southeastern Alaska, northwest of Tongass National Forest.
(907) 822-5234
🚲 🅰 🥾 🏠 🍴

ARIZONA

Apache-Sitgreaves National Forests
In east-central Arizona.
(928) 333-4301
🚲 🅰 🥾 🌲 🏠 🍴

Bill Williams River National Wildlife Refuge
Off SR 95 near Parker.
(928) 667-4144
🥾 🌲 🏠

Buenos Aires National Wildlife Refuge
North of Sasabe on SR 286.
(520) 823-4251
🚲 🅰 🥾 🌲 🏠

🚲 Bicycling Trails   🅰 Camping   🥾 Hiking Trails   🌲 Picnic Facilities
🏊 Swimming   🏠 Visitor Center   🍴 Food Service

Coconino National Forest
In north-central Arizona.
(928) 527-3600
🚲 🏕 🥾 🍽 🚶 🏛 🍴

Coronado National Forest
In southeastern Arizona and southwestern New Mexico.
(520) 388-8300
🚲 🏕 🥾 🍽 🚶

Glen Canyon National Recreation Area
In north-central Arizona.
(928) 608-6200
🏕 🥾 🍽 🏛 🚶 🍴

Grand Canyon National Park
In northwestern Arizona.
(928) 638-7888
🏕 🥾 🍽 🚶 🍴

Kaibab National Forest
In north-central Arizona.
(928) 635-4061 or (800) 863-0546
🚲 🏕 🥾 🍽 🚶 🍴

Lake Mead National Recreation Area
In northwestern Arizona and southeastern Nevada.
(702) 293-8990
🚲 🏕 🥾 🍽 🏛 🚶 🍴

Petrified Forest National Park
In east-central Arizona, east of Holbrook.
(928) 524-6228
🥾 🍽 🚶 🍴

Prescott National Forest
In central Arizona.
(928) 443-8000
🚲 🏕 🥾 🍽 🍴

Saguaro National Park
Two districts, 15 mi. east and west of Tucson.
(520) 733-5153
🚲 🥾 🍽 🚶

Tonto National Forest
In central Arizona.
(602) 225-5200
🚲 🏕 🥾 🍽 🏛 🚶 🍴

ARKANSAS

Buffalo National River
In northwestern Arkansas.
(870) 741-5443 or (870) 439-2502
🏕 🥾 🍽 🏛 🚶 🍴

Felsenthal National Wildlife Refuge
7 mi. west of Crossett on US 82.
(870) 364-3167
🏕 🥾 🚶

Hot Springs National Park
In western Arkansas.
(501) 624-2701, (501) 620-6701 or TDD (501) 624-2308
🏕 🥾 🍽 🚶 🍴

Ouachita National Forest
In west-central Arkansas and southeastern Oklahoma.
(501) 321-5202
🚲 🏕 🥾 🍽 🏛 🚶 🍴

Ozark-St. Francis National Forests
In northwestern and east-central Arkansas.
(479) 964-7200
🚲 🏕 🥾 🍽 🏛 🚶 🍴

Pea Ridge National Military Park
East of Rogers in northwest Arkansas.
(479) 451-8122
🚲 🥾 🍽 🚶

CALIFORNIA

Angeles National Forest
In southern California.
(626) 574-5200
🚲 🏕 🥾 🍽 🏛 🚶 🍴

Cleveland National Forest
In southwestern California.
(858) 673-6180
🚲 🏕 🥾 🍽 🚶 🍴

Death Valley National Park
Along the Nevada border in east-central California.
(760) 786-2331
🚲 🏕 🥾 🍽 🚶 🍴

Eldorado National Forest
In central California.
(530) 644-6048
🚲 🏕 🥾 🍽 🏛 🚶 🍴

Golden Gate National Recreation Area
North of the Golden Gate Bridge and in northern and western San Francisco.
(415) 561-4730
🚲 🏕 🥾 🍽 🏛 🚶 🍴

Inyo National Forest
In east-central California.
(760) 873-2400
🚲 🏕 🥾 🍽 🏛 🚶 🍴

Joshua Tree National Park
East of Desert Hot Springs.
(760) 367-5500
🚲 🏕 🥾 🍽 🚶

Klamath National Forest
In northern California.
(530) 842-6131
🚲 🏕 🥾 🍽 🏛 🍴

🚲 Bicycling Trails   🏕 Camping   🥾 Hiking Trails   🍽 Picnic Facilities
🏛 Swimming   🚶 Visitor Center   🍴 Food Service

Lassen National Forest
In northeastern California.
(530) 257-2151
🚴 ⛺ 🥾 🏕 🚤 🧍 📷

Lassen Volcanic National Park
In northeastern California.
(530) 595-4444
🚴 ⛺ 🥾 🏕 🚤 🧍 📷

Los Padres National Forest
In southern California.
(805) 968-6640
🚴 ⛺ 🥾 🏕 🚤 🧍

Mendocino National Forest
In northwestern California.
(530) 934-2350 or (530) 934-3316, or TDD (530) 934-7724
🚴 ⛺ 🥾 🏕 🚤 🧍

Modoc National Forest
In northeastern California.
(530) 233-5811
🚴 ⛺ 🥾 🏕 🚤 🧍

Mojave National Preserve
Between I-15 and I-40 in southeastern California.
(760) 252-6100
🚴 ⛺ 🥾 🏕 🧍

Plumas National Forest
In northern California.
(530) 283-2050
🚴 ⛺ 🥾 🏕 🚤 📷

Point Reyes National Seashore
Along the California coast just north of San Francisco.
(415) 464-5100
🚴 ⛺ 🥾 🏕 🧍

Redwood National and State Parks
On the northern California coast.
(707) 465-7306
🚴 ⛺ 🥾 🏕 🚤 🧍

San Bernardino National Forest
In southern California.
(909) 382-2600
🚴 ⛺ 🥾 🏕 🚤 🧍 📷

Santa Monica Mountains National Recreation Area
West from Griffith Park in Los Angeles to the Ventura County line.
(805) 370-2301
🚴 ⛺ 🥾 🏕 🧍 📷

Sequoia and Kings Canyon National Parks
In east-central California.
(559) 565-3341
⛺ 🥾 🏕 🧍 📷

Sequoia National Forest
In south-central California.
(559) 784-1500
🚴 ⛺ 🥾 🏕 🚤 📷

Shasta-Trinity National Forests
In northern California.
(530) 226-2500
🚴 ⛺ 🥾 🏕 🚤 🧍 📷

Sierra National Forest
In central California.
(559) 297-0706
🚴 ⛺ 🥾 🏕 🚤 📷

Six Rivers National Forest
In northwestern California.
(707) 442-1721
🚴 ⛺ 🥾 🏕 🚤 🧍 📷

Smith River National Recreation Area
Within Six Rivers National Forest in northwestern California.
(707) 457-3131
🚴 ⛺ 🥾 🏕 🚤 🧍

Stanislaus National Forest
In central California.
(209) 532-3671
🚴 ⛺ 🥾 🏕 🚤 📷

Tahoe National Forest
In north-central California.
(530) 265-4531
🚴 ⛺ 🥾 🏕 🚤 🧍 📷

Whiskeytown-Shasta-Trinity National Recreation Area
North and west of Redding.
(530) 242-3400, (530) 275-1589 in Shasta or (530) 623-2121 in Trinity
🚴 ⛺ 🥾 🏕 🚤 🧍

Yosemite National Park
In central California.
(209) 372-0200
🚴 ⛺ 🥾 🏕 🚤 🧍 📷

COLORADO

Arapaho and Roosevelt National Forests and Pawnee National Grassland
In north-central Colorado.
(970) 295-6700
🚴 ⛺ 🥾 🏕 🧍 📷

Arapaho National Recreation Area
In north-central Colorado.
(970) 887-4100
🚴 ⛺ 🥾 🏕 🚤 🧍

Black Canyon of the Gunnison National Park
In western Colorado.
(970) 641-2337
🚴 ⛺ 🥾 🏕 🧍

Curecanti National Recreation Area
In south-central Colorado between Gunnison and Montrose, paralleling US 50.
(970) 641-2337
🚴 ⛺ 🥾 🏕 🚤 🧍 📷

Grand Mesa-Uncompahgre-Gunnison National Forests
In west-central Colorado.
(970) 874-6600
🚲 ⛺ 🥾 🏕 👥

Great Sand Dunes National Park and Preserve
Northeast of Alamosa.
(719) 378-6300
⛺ 🥾 🏕 🏊 👥

Mesa Verde National Park
In southwestern Colorado.
(970) 529-4465
⛺ 🥾 🏕 👥 🍽

Pike and San Isabel National Forest
In south-central Colorado.
(719) 553-1400
🚲 ⛺ 🥾 🏕 👥

Rio Grande National Forest
In south-central Colorado.
(719) 852-5941
🚲 ⛺ 🥾 🏕 👥

Rocky Mountain National Park
In north-central Colorado.
(970) 586-1206 or (970) 586-1333
⛺ 🥾 🏕 👥

Routt National Forest
In northwestern Colorado.
(970) 879-1870
🚲 ⛺ 🥾 🏕 👥

San Juan National Forest
In southwestern Colorado.
(970) 247-4874
🚲 ⛺ 🥾 🏕 🏊 👥

White River National Forest
In west-central Colorado.
(970) 945-2521
🚲 ⛺ 🥾 🏕 🏊 👥

DELAWARE

Bombay Hook National Wildlife Refuge
South of Smyrna.
(302) 653-9345
🚲 🥾 🏕 👥

Prime Hook National Wildlife Refuge
North of Milton via SR 1.
(302) 684-8419
🚲 🥾 🏕 👥

FLORIDA

Apalachicola National Forest
In northwestern Florida.
(850) 926-3561
🚲 ⛺ 🥾 🏕 🏊

Biscayne National Park
In southeast Florida.
(305) 230-7275
⛺ 🏕 🏊 👥

J.N. "Ding" Darling National Wildlife Refuge
1 Wildlife Dr. in Sanibel.
(239) 472-1100
🚲 🥾

Ocala National Forest
In north-central Florida.
(352) 236-0288
🚲 ⛺ 🥾 🏕 🏊 👥 🍽

Osceola National Forest
Near the Georgia border.
(386) 752-2577
🚲 ⛺ 🥾 🏕 🏊 👥

GEORGIA

Chattahoochee and Oconee National Forests
In central and northern Georgia.
(770) 297-3000
🚲 ⛺ 🥾 🏕 🏊 👥 🍽

Chattahoochee River National Recreation Area
North of Atlanta.
(678) 538-1200
🚲 🥾 🏕 🏊 👥

Chickamauga and Chattanooga National Military Park
On the Georgia-Tennessee border.
(706) 866-9241 or (423) 752-5213, ext 123
🚲 🥾 🏕 👥

Kennesaw Mountain National Battlefield Park
Northwest of Marietta.
(770) 427-4686
🥾 🏕 👥

IDAHO

Boise National Forest
In southwestern Idaho.
(208) 373-4007
🚲 ⛺ 🥾 🏕 🏊 👥 🍽

Caribou-Targhee National Forest
In southeastern Idaho.
(208) 524-7500 or (208) 624-3151
🚲 ⛺ 🥾 🏕 🏊 👥 🍽

Clearwater National Forest
In northeastern Idaho.
(208) 476-4541
🚲 ⛺ 🥾 🏕 🏊 👥 🍽

Hells Canyon National Recreation Area
In western Idaho and northeastern Oregon.
(509) 758-0616
🚲 ⛺ 🥾 🏕 🏊 👥

🚲 Bicycling Trails   ⛺ Camping   🥾 Hiking Trails   🏕 Picnic Facilities
🏊 Swimming   👥 Visitor Center   🍽 Food Service

Idaho Panhandle National Forests
In northern and northwestern Idaho.
(208) 765-7223

Nez Perce National Forest
In northwestern Idaho.
(208) 983-1950

Payette National Forest
In west-central Idaho.
(208) 634-0700

Salmon-Challis National Forest
In east-central Idaho.
(208) 756-5100

Sawtooth National Forest
In south-central Idaho.
(208) 737-3200 or (800) 260-5970

Sawtooth National Recreation Area
In south-central Idaho.
(208) 727-5013 or (800) 260-5970

ILLINOIS
Chautauqua National Wildlife Refuge
Near Havana.
(309) 535-2290

Shawnee National Forest
In southern Illinois.
(618) 253-7114 or (800) 699-6637

INDIANA
George Rogers Clark National Historical Park
Off US 50 and US 41 near Vincennes.
(812) 882-1776, ext. 110

Hoosier National Forest
In southern Indiana.
(812) 275-5987

Indiana Dunes National Lakeshore
On the southern shore of Lake Michigan.
(219) 926-7561, ext. 225

Muscatatuck National Wildlife Refuge
East of jct. I-65 and US 50 near Seymour.
(812)522-4352

KANSAS
Kirwin National Wildlife Refuge
702 E. Xavier Rd.
(785) 543-6673

KENTUCKY
Big South Fork National River and Recreation Area
In southeastern Kentucky and northeastern Tennessee.
(423) 286-7275 or (606) 376-5073

Cumberland Gap National Historical Park
At the borders of Kentucky, Tennessee and Virginia.
(606) 248-2817

Daniel Boone National Forest
Five districts in eastern and southeastern Kentucky.
(859) 745-3100

Land Between the Lakes National Recreation Area
In western Kentucky and Tennessee.
(270) 924-2000 or (800) 525-7077

Mammoth Cave National Park
In south-central Kentucky 10 mi. west of Cave City.
(270) 758-2180

LOUISIANA
Bayou Sauvage National Wildlife Refuge
Within the New Orleans city limits.
(985) 882-2000

Kisatchie National Forest
In central and northern Louisiana.
(318) 473-7160

MAINE
Acadia National Park
Along the Atlantic coast southeast of Bangor.
(207) 288-3338

Moosehorn National Wildlife Refuge
Near Baring and Dennysville.
(207) 454-7161

MARYLAND
Assateague Island National Seashore
In southeastern Maryland south of Ocean City.
(410) 641-1441 or (410) 641-3030

Chesapeake and Ohio Canal National Historical Park
From Georgetown to Cumberland.
(301) 739-4200

MASSACHUSETTS

Cape Cod National Seashore
Occupies 40 miles along the shoreline.
(508)349-3785, ext. 200
⛷ 𝄞 ⛱ ⚓ ♿

MICHIGAN

Hiawatha National Forest
In Michigan's Upper Peninsula.
(906) 786-4062
⛷ ⛺ 𝄞 ⛱ ⚓ ♿ 🍴

Huron-Manistee National Forests
In the northern part of the Lower Peninsula.
(231) 775-2421 or (800) 821-6263
⛷ ⛺ 𝄞 ⛱ ⚓ ♿ 🍴

Ottawa National Forest
In Michigan's Upper Peninsula.
(906) 932-1330 or (800) 562-1201
⛷ ⛺ 𝄞 ⛱ ⚓ ♿ 🍴

Pictured Rocks National Lakeshore
Along Lake Superior in Michigan's Upper Peninsula.
906-387-3700 or (906) 387-2607
⛺ 𝄞 ⛱ ⚓ ♿

Sleeping Bear Dunes National Lakeshore
Along Lake Michigan in the northwestern part of the Lower Peninsula.
(231) 326-5134
⛺ 𝄞 ⛱ ⚓ ♿ 🍴

MINNESOTA

Chippewa National Forest
In north-central Minnesota.
(218) 335-8600
⛷ ⛺ 𝄞 ⛱ ⚓ ♿ 🍴

Minnesota Valley National Wildlife Refuge
3815 E. American Blvd, Bloomington
(952) 854-5900
⛷ 𝄞 ♿

Superior National Forest
In northeastern Minnesota.
(218) 626-4300
⛷ ⛺ 𝄞 ⛱ ⚓ ♿ 🍴

MISSISSIPPI

Bienville National Forest
In central Mississippi.
(601) 469-3811
⛺ 𝄞 ⛱ ⚓ ♿ 🍴

Gulf Islands National Seashore
Along the Gulf of Mexico in southern Mississippi.
(228) 875-9057
⛷ 𝄞 ⛱ ⚓ ♿

MISSOURI

Mark Twain National Forest (Big Bay)
1 mi. southeast of Shell Knob on SR 39, then 3 mi. southeast on CR YY.
(573) 364-4621
⛷ ⛱ ⚓

Mark Twain National Forest (Council Bluff)
13 mi. s. of Potosi on CR P, 4 mi. w. on CR C , then 8 mi. s. on CR DD.
(573) 364-4621
⛷ ⛺ 𝄞 ⛱ ⚓

Mark Twain National Forest (Crane Lake)
12 mi. south of Ironton off SR 49 and CR E.
(573) 364-4621
⛷ 𝄞 ⛱ ⚓

Mark Twain National Forest (Fourche Lake)
18 mi. west of Doniphan on SR 160.
(573) 364-4621
𝄞 ⛱ ⚓

Mark Twain National Forest (Noblett Lake)
8 mi. west of Willow Springs on SR 76, then 1.5 mi. south on SR 181, 3 mi. southeast on CR AP and 1 mi. southwest on FR 857.
(573) 364-4621
⛷ 𝄞 ⛱

Mark Twain National Forest (Pinewoods Lake)
2 mi. west of Ellsinore on SR 60.
(573) 364-4621
⛷ 𝄞 ⛱ ⚓

Mark Twain National Forest (Red Bluff)
1 mi. east of Davisville on CR V, then 1 mi. north on FR 2011.
(573) 364-4621
⛺ 𝄞 ⛱ ⚓

Ozark National Scenic Riverways
In southeastern Missouri.
(573) 323-4236
⛺ 𝄞 ⛱ ⚓ ♿ 🍴

MONTANA

Beaverhead-Deerlodge National Forest
In southwestern Montana.
(406) 683-3900
⛷ ⛺ 𝄞 ⛱ ⚓ 🍴

Bighorn Canyon National Recreation Area
In southern Montana and northern Wyoming.
(406) 666-2412
⛺ 𝄞 ⛱ ⚓ ♿ 🍴

⛷ Bicycling Trails   ⛺ Camping   𝄞 Hiking Trails   ⛱ Picnic Facilities
⚓ Swimming   ♿ Visitor Center   🍴 Food Service

Bitterroot National Forest
In western Montana.
(406) 363-7100
▲ 𝖒 ⛱ ⛵ 🏠

Custer National Forest
In southeastern Montana.
(406) 657-6200
🚲 ▲ 𝖒 ⛱ ⛵

Flathead National Forest
In northwestern Montana.
(406) 758-5204
🚲 ▲ 𝖒 ⛱ ⛵ 🏠

Gallatin National Forest
In south-central Montana.
(406) 522-2520
🚲 ▲ 𝖒 ⛱ ⛵ 🏠

Glacier National Park
In northwestern Montana.
(406) 888-7800
🚲 ▲ 𝖒 ⛱ ⛵ 🏠 🍴

Helena National Forest
In west-central Montana.
(406) 449-5201
🚲 ▲ 𝖒 ⛱ ⛵ 🏠

Kootenai National Forest
In northwestern Montana.
(406) 293-6211
🚲 ▲ 𝖒 ⛱ ⛵ 🏠 🍴

Lewis and Clark National Forest
In central Montana.
(406) 791-7700
🚲 ▲ 𝖒 ⛱ 🏠

NEBRASKA

Fort Niobrara National Wildlife Refuge
East of Valentine on SR 12.
(402) 376-3789
𝖒 ⛱

Nebraska National Forest
In central and northwestern Nebraska.
(308) 432-0300 or TDD (308) 432-0304
🚲 ▲ 𝖒 ⛱ ⛵

Oglala National Grassland
In northwestern Nebraska, 6 mi. north of Crawford via SR 2.
(308) 432-4475 or (308) 665-3900
▲ 𝖒 ⛱ 🏠

NEVADA

Great Basin National Park
In central Nevada, 5 mi. west of Baker near the Nevada-Utah border.
(775) 234-7331
▲ 𝖒 ⛱ 🏠 🍴

Humboldt-Toiyabe National Forest
In central, western, northern and southern Nevada and eastern California.
(775) 331-6444
🚲 ▲ 𝖒 ⛱ 🍴

Lake Mead National Recreation Area
In southeastern Nevada and northwestern Arizona.
(702) 293-8990
🚲 ▲ 𝖒 ⛱ ⛵ 🏠 🍴

NEW HAMPSHIRE

White Mountain National Forest
In northern New Hampshire.
(603) 528-8721 or TDD (603) 528-8722
🚲 ▲ 𝖒 ⛱ ⛵ 🏠

NEW JERSEY

Edwin B. Forsythe National Wildlife Refuge
US 9 and Great Creek Road near Oceanville
(609) 652-1665
🚲 𝖒 ⛱ 🏠

Gateway National Recreation Area (Sandy Hook Unit)
In northeastern New Jersey.
(732) 872-5970
🚲 𝖒 ⛱ ⛵ 🏠 🍴

Morristown National Historical Park
Four units in Morristown and southwest.
(973) 539-2016
𝖒 🏠

NEW MEXICO

Carson National Forest
In north-central New Mexico.
(505) 758-6200
🚲 ▲ 𝖒 ⛱ 🏠 🍴

Chaco Culture National Historical Park
In northwestern New Mexico.
(505) 786-7014
🚲 ▲ 𝖒 ⛱ 🏠

Cibola National Forest
In central New Mexico.
(505) 346-3900
🚲 ▲ 𝖒 ⛱ ⛵ 🏠 🍴

Gila National Forest
In southwestern New Mexico.
(505) 388-8201
🚲 ▲ 𝖒 ⛱ 🏠 🍴

Lincoln National Forest
In south-central New Mexico.
(505) 434-7200
🚲 ▲ 𝖒 ⛱ 🍴

Santa Fe National Forest
In north-central New Mexico between the San Pedro Mountains and the Sangre de Cristo Mountains.
(505) 438-7840
🚲 ▲ 𝖒 ⛱ 🏠 🍴

NEW YORK
Finger Lakes National Forest
In south-central New York on a ridge between Seneca and Cayuga lakes, via I-90, I-81 and SR 17.
(607) 546-4470

Fire Island National Seashore
In southeastern New York on Fire Island, off the south shore of Long Island.
(631) 687-4750

Gateway National Recreation Area (Jamaica Bay Unit)
In Brooklyn and Queens boroughs in New York City.
(718) 338-3799

Gateway National Recreation Area (Staten Island Unit)
On Staten Island borough in New York City.
(718) 354-4500

Saratoga National Historical Park
8 miles south of Schuylerville on US 4.
(518) 664-9821, ext. 224

NORTH CAROLINA
Cape Hatteras National Seashore
In eastern North Carolina along the Outer Banks.
(252) 473-2111 or (252) 441-5711

Croatan National Forest
In southeastern North Carolina.
(252) 638-5628

Great Smoky Mountains National Park
In western North Carolina and eastern Tennessee.
(865) 436-1200

Nantahala National Forest
At North Carolina's southwestern tip.
(828) 257-4200 or (828) 526-3765

Pisgah National Forest
In western North Carolina.
(828) 257-4200

Pisgah National Forest (Lake Powhatan)
7 mi. southwest of Asheville on SR 191 and FR 3807.
(828) 257-4200

Pisgah National Forest (Rocky Bluff)
3 mi. south of Hot Springs on SR 209.
(828) 257-4200

Uwharrie National Forest
In central North Carolina.
(910) 576-6391

NORTH DAKOTA
Little Missouri National Grassland
Between the Missouri River and South Dakota.
(701) 227-7800

Sheyenne National Grassland
Along the Sheyenne River south of Fargo.
(701) 683-4342

Theodore Roosevelt National Park (North Unit)
In western North Dakota.
(701) 842-2333

Theodore Roosevelt National Park (South Unit)
In western North Dakota.
(701) 623-4466

OHIO
Cuyahoga Valley National Park
In northeastern Ohio.
(216) 524-1497

Hopewell Culture National Historical Park
About 3 mi. north of Chillicothe on SR 104.
(740) 774-1126

Wayne National Forest
In southeast Ohio.
(740) 753-0101

OKLAHOMA
Chickasaw National Recreation Area
In south-central Oklahoma.
(580) 622-3165 or (580) 622-3161

Ouachita National Forest
In southeastern Oklahoma and west-central Arkansas.
(501) 321-5202

🚲 Bicycling Trails   🔺 Camping   🥾 Hiking Trails   ⛱ Picnic Facilities
🏊 Swimming   👥 Visitor Center   🍴 Food Service

Salt Plains National Wildlife Refuge
Off SR 38, 2 mi. south of jct. SRs 11 and 38 at Cherokee.
(580) 626-4794
🚴 🏕 💁

OREGON

Crater Lake National Park
On the crest of the Cascade Range off SR 62.
(541) 594-3100
🚴 🏕 🥾 🏕 💁 🍽

Deschutes National Forest
In central Oregon 6 mi. south of Bend via US 97.
(541) 383-5300
🚴 🏕 🥾 🏕 🛶 💁 🍽

Fremont-Winema National Forests
In south-central Oregon.
(541) 947-2151
🚴 🏕 🥾 🏕 🛶 💁

Hells Canyon National Recreation Area
In northeastern Oregon and western Idaho.
(541) 426-5546
🚴 🏕 🥾 🏕 💁

Malheur National Forest
In eastern Oregon.
(541) 575-3000
🚴 🏕 🥾 🏕 🛶 🍽

Mount Hood National Forest
In northwestern Oregon.
(888) 622-4822
🚴 🏕 🥾 🏕 🛶 💁 🍽

Ochoco National Forest
In central Oregon off US 26.
(541) 416-6500
🚴 🏕 🥾 🏕 🛶

Oregon Dunes National Recreation Area
Between North Bend and Florence.
(541) 271-6000
🚴 🏕 🥾 🏕 🛶 💁

Rogue River-Siskiyou National Forest
In southwestern Oregon off I-5 from Medford.
(541) 858-2200
🚴 🏕 🥾 🏕 🛶 💁 🍽

Siuslaw National Forest
In western Oregon.
(541) 750-7000
🚴 🏕 🥾 🏕 🛶 💁 🍽

Umatilla National Forest
In northeastern Oregon.
(541) 278-3716
🚴 🏕 🥾 🏕 🛶 💁

Umpqua National Forest
In southwestern Oregon 33 mi. east of Roseburg on SR 138.
(541) 672-6601
🚴 🏕 🥾 🏕 🛶 💁 🍽

Wallowa-Whitman National Forest
In northeastern Oregon.
(541) 523-6391
🚴 🏕 🥾 🏕 🛶 💁 🍽

Willamette National Forest
In western Oregon.
(541) 225-6300
🚴 🏕 🥾 🏕 🛶 💁 🍽

PENNSYLVANIA

Allegheny National Forest
In northwestern Pennsylvania.
(814) 723-5150 or TDD (814) 726-2710
🚴 🏕 🥾 🏕 🛶 💁 🍽

Delaware Water Gap National Recreation Area
In eastern Pennsylvania and northwestern New Jersey.
(570) 426-2457
🚴 🏕 🥾 🏕 🛶 💁

Gettysburg National Military Park
Surrounding the town of Gettysburg at SR 134.
(717) 334-1124
🚴 🏕 🏕 💁

John Heinz National Wildlife Refuge at Tinicum
I-95S exit 14 near Philadelphia
(215) 365-3118
🚴 🏕 💁

Valley Forge National Historical Park
Extending east of Valley Forge along SR 23.
(610) 783-1077
🚴 🏕 🏕 💁 🍽

SOUTH CAROLINA

Congaree National Park
Southeast of Hopkins.
(803) 776-4396
🏕 🏕 🏕 💁

Francis Marion National Forest
On the Coastal Plain north of Charleston.
(803) 561-4000
🚴 🏕 🥾 🏕 🛶 💁 🍽

Kings Mountain National Military Park
South of Kings Mountain, N.C., off I-85.
(864) 936-7921
🏕 🥾

Sumter National Forest
In western South Carolina.
(803) 561-4000
🚴 🏕 🥾 🏕 🛶 🍽

SOUTH DAKOTA

Badlands National Park
In southwestern South Dakota.
(605) 433-5361, ext. 100
🏕 🥾 🏕 💁 🍽

Black Hills National Forest
In southwestern South Dakota.
(605) 673-9200 or TDD (605) 673-4954
🚲 🅰 🥾 🏕 🏊 🏠 🍽

Custer National Forest
In northwestern South Dakota and southeastern Montana.
(605) 797-4432
🚲 🅰 🥾 🏕

Wind Cave National Park
In southwestern South Dakota.
(605) 745-4600
🅰 🥾 🏕 🏠

TENNESSEE

Big South Fork National River and Recreation Area
In northeastern Tennessee and southeastern Kentucky.
(423) 286-7275
🚲 🅰 🥾 🏕 🏊 🏠

Cherokee National Forest
In eastern Tennessee.
(423) 476-9700
🚲 🅰 🥾 🏕 🏊 🏠

Chickamauga and Chattanooga National Military Park
On the Georgia-Tennessee border.
(706) 866-9241
🚲 🥾 🏕 🏠

Great Smoky Mountains National Park
In eastern Tennessee and western North Carolina.
(865) 436-1200
🚲 🅰 🥾 🏕 🏠

Land Between the Lakes National Recreation Area
In western Kentucky and Tennessee.
(270) 924-2000 or (800) 525-7077
🚲 🅰 🥾 🏕 🏊 🏠

TEXAS

Amistad National Recreation Area
Northwest of Del Rio via US 90.
(830) 775-7491
🅰 🥾 🏕 🏊 🏠

Angelina National Forest
In east Texas.
(936) 897-1068
🅰 🥾 🏕 🏊

Big Bend National Park
Southeast of Alpine on SR 118 and US 385.
(432) 477-2251 or (432) 477-1187
🚲 🅰 🥾 🏕 🏠 🍽

Davy Crockett National Forest
In east Texas.
(936) 655-2299
🅰 🥾 🏕 🏊 🍽

Guadalupe Mountains National Park
110 mi. east of El Paso on US 62/180.
(915) 828-3251
🅰 🥾 🏕 🏠

Lake Meredith National Recreation Area
45 mi. northeast of Amarillo and 9 mi. west of Borger via SR 136.
(806) 857-3151
🅰 🏕 🏊 🍽

Padre Island National Seashore
On Padre Island near Corpus Christi.
(361) 949-8068
🚲 🅰 🥾 🏕 🏊 🏠 🍽

Sabine National Forest
In east Texas.
(409) 787-3870
🅰 🥾 🏕 🏊

Sam Houston National Forest
40 mi. north of Houston in east Texas.
(936) 344-6205 or (888) 361-6908
🚲 🅰 🥾 🏕 🏊 🍽

UTAH

Ashley National Forest
In northeastern Utah.
(435) 789-1181
🚲 🅰 🥾 🏕 🏊 🏠

Canyonlands National Park
In southeastern Utah.
(435) 719-2100 or TTY (435) 259-5279
🅰 🥾 🏕 🏠

Capitol Reef National Park
10 mi. east of Torrey on SR 24.
(435) 425-3791, ext. 111
🚲 🅰 🥾 🏕 🏠

Dixie National Forest
In southwestern Utah.
(435) 865-3700
🚲 🅰 🥾 🏕 🏊 🏠 🍽

Fishlake National Forest
In south-central Utah.
(435) 896-9233
🚲 🅰 🥾 🏕 🏊 🏠 🍽

Flaming Gorge National Recreation Area
In northeastern Utah.
(435) 784-3445
🚲 🅰 🥾 🏕 🏊 🏠 🍽

Glen Canyon National Recreation Area
In south-central Utah.
(928) 608-6200
🅰 🥾 🏕 🏊 🏠 🍽

🚲 Bicycling Trails   🅰 Camping   🥾 Hiking Trails   🏕 Picnic Facilities
🏊 Swimming   🏠 Visitor Center   🍽 Food Service

Manti-La Sal National Forest
In southeastern Utah.
(435) 637-2817
⬛⬛⬛⬛⬛⬛

Uinta National Forest
In central Utah.
(801) 342-5100
⬛⬛⬛⬛

Wasatch-Cache National Forest
In north-central and northeastern Utah.
(801) 236-3400 or (801) 466-6411
⬛⬛⬛⬛⬛⬛⬛

Zion National Park
In southwestern Utah.
(435) 772-3256
⬛⬛⬛⬛⬛⬛

VERMONT
Green Mountain National Forest
In south-central Vermont.
(802) 747-6700
⬛⬛⬛⬛⬛

Marsh-Billings-Rockefeller National Historical Park
Off SR 12 near Woodstock.
(802) 457-3368, ext. 22
⬛

VIRGINIA
George Washington and Jefferson National Forests
In western Virginia and the eastern edge of West Virginia.
(540) 265-5100 or (888) 265-0019
⬛⬛⬛⬛⬛⬛

Mount Rogers National Recreation Area
In southwestern Virginia.
(276) 783-5196 or (800) 628-7202
⬛⬛⬛⬛⬛⬛⬛

Shenandoah National Park
In northwestern Virginia.
(540) 999-3500
⬛⬛⬛⬛⬛⬛

WASHINGTON
Colville National Forest
In northeastern Washington.
(509) 684-7000
⬛⬛⬛⬛⬛⬛

Gifford Pinchot National Forest
In southwestern Washington.
(360) 891-5000
⬛⬛⬛⬛⬛⬛

Lake Chelan National Recreation Area
In north-central Washington.
(509) 682-2549
⬛⬛⬛⬛⬛⬛

Lake Roosevelt National Recreation Area
In northeastern Washington.
(509) 633-9441
⬛⬛⬛⬛⬛⬛⬛

Mount Baker-Snoqualmie National Forest
2 mi. east of Glacier on SR 542.
(425) 775-9702, (800) 627-0062, ext. 0, or TTY (425) 744-3577
⬛⬛⬛⬛⬛⬛

Okanogan National Forest
In north-central Washington.
(509) 996-4000
⬛⬛⬛⬛⬛⬛

Olympic National Forest
In northwestern Washington.
(360) 956-2400
⬛⬛⬛⬛⬛⬛⬛

Ross Lake National Recreation Area
Between the north and south sections of North Cascades National Park.
(360) 856-5700, ext. 515, or (360) 206-386-4495, ext. 11
⬛⬛⬛⬛⬛

WEST VIRGINIA
Monongahela National Forest
In eastern West Virginia.
(304) 636-1800
⬛⬛⬛⬛⬛⬛⬛

New River Gorge National River
Between Fayetteville and Hinton.
(304) 465-0508
⬛⬛⬛⬛⬛

Spruce Knob-Seneca Rocks National Recreation Area
In east-central West Virginia.
(304) 257-4488
⬛⬛⬛⬛⬛

WISCONSIN
Apostle Islands National Lakeshore
Off northern Wisconsin's Bayfield Peninsula in Lake Superior.
(715) 779-3397
⬛⬛⬛⬛⬛

Chequamegon-Nicolet National Forest
In north-central and northeastern Wisconsin.
(715) 762-2461 (Chequamegon) or (715) 362-1300 (Nicolet)
⬛⬛⬛⬛⬛

St. Croix National Scenic Riverway
Running 252 mi. from Cable to Prescott.
(715) 483-3284
⬛⬛⬛⬛⬛⬛

WYOMING

Bighorn Canyon National Recreation Area
In Montana and northern Wyoming.
(307) 548-2251
🚴 ⛺ 🥾 ⛱ 🏊 🏠

Bighorn National Forest
In north-central Wyoming.
(307) 674-2600
🚴 ⛺ 🥾 ⛱ 🏠 🍽

Devils Tower National Monument
Between Sundance and Hulett.
(307) 467-5283
⛺ 🥾 ⛱ 🏠

Flaming Gorge National Recreation Area
On the Wyoming-Utah border.
(435) 784-3445
🚴 ⛺ 🥾 ⛱ 🏊 🏠 🍽

Fossil Butte National Monument
14 mi. west of Kemmerer on US 30.
(307) 877-4455
🥾 ⛱ 🏠

Grand Teton National Park
In northwestern Wyoming.
(307) 739-3300
🚴 ⛺ 🥾 ⛱ 🏊 🏠 🍽

Medicine Bow National Forest
In southeastern Wyoming.
(307) 745-2300
🚴 ⛺ 🥾 ⛱ 🏠

Shoshone National Forest
In northwestern Wyoming.
(307) 527-6241
🚴 ⛺ 🥾 ⛱ 🏠 🍽

Yellowstone National Park
In northwestern Wyoming.
(307) 344-7311
⛺ 🥾 ⛱ 🏊 🏠 🍽

Canada

ALBERTA

Banff National Park of Canada
In southwestern Alberta, west of Calgary.
(403) 762-1550
🚴 ⛺ 🥾 ⛱ 🏠 🍽

Elk Island National Park of Canada
In central Alberta, east of Edmonton.
(780) 992-2950
🚴 ⛺ 🥾 ⛱ 🏠 🍽

Jasper National Park of Canada
In west-central Alberta along the British Columbia border.
(780) 852-6176
🚴 ⛺ 🥾 ⛱ 🏊 🏠 🍽

Waterton Lakes National Park of Canada
In Alberta's southwestern corner.
(403) 859-5133, or (403) 859-2224 during the winter
🚴 ⛺ 🥾 ⛱ 🏊 🏠 🍽

BRITISH COLUMBIA

Gulf Islands National Park Reserve of Canada
Off the southeast coast of Vancouver Island.
(250) 654-4000
⛺ 🥾 ⛱ 🏊

Glacier National Park of Canada
In southeastern British Columbia.
(250) 837-7500
⛺ 🥾 ⛱ 🏠 🍽

Kootenay National Park of Canada
In southeastern British Columbia.
(250) 347-9505 or (888) 773-8888
🚴 ⛺ 🥾 ⛱ 🏊 🏠 🍽

Mount Revelstoke National Park of Canada
In southeastern British Columbia.
(250) 837-7500
🚴 ⛺ 🥾 ⛱

Pacific Rim National Park Reserve of Canada
On the southwestern coast of Vancouver Island.
(250) 726-7721 or (250) 726-4212, Jun. 1 to mid-Sept.
⛺ 🥾 ⛱ 🏊 🏠 🍽

Yoho National Park of Canada
On the British Columbia-Alberta border.
(250) 343-6783
🚴 ⛺ 🥾 ⛱ 🏠 🍽

MANITOBA

Riding Mountain National Park of Canada
In southwestern Manitoba.
(204) 848-7275
🚴 ⛺ 🥾 ⛱ 🏊 🏠 🍽

🚴 Bicycling Trails   ⛺ Camping   🥾 Hiking Trails   ⛱ Picnic Facilities
🏊 Swimming   🏠 Visitor Center   🍽 Food Service

NEW BRUNSWICK

Fundy National Park of Canada
On Hwy. 114, 130 km. southwest of Moncton.
(506) 887-6000

Kouchibouguac National Park of Canada
On Hwy. 134, north of Moncton.
(506) 876-2443 or TDD (506) 876-4205

NEWFOUNDLAND

Gros Morne National Park of Canada
On Newfoundland's western coast.
(709) 458-2417 or TDD (709) 772-4564

Terra Nova National Park of Canada
In eastern Newfoundland.
(709) 533-2801

NORTHWEST TERRITORIES

Nahanni National Park Reserve of Canada
145 km. west of Fort Simpson in southwestern Northwest Territories.
(867) 695-3151

Wood Buffalo National Park of Canada
On the Northwest Territories-Alberta border.
(867) 872-7960

NOVA SCOTIA

Cape Breton Highlands National Park of Canada
5 km. northeast of Chéticamp on Cabot Tr.
(902) 224-2306 or (888) 773-8888

Kejimkujik National Park and National Historic Site of Canada
In southwestern Nova Scotia off Hwy. 8 at Maitland Bridge.
(902) 682-2772

ONTARIO

Bruce Peninsula National Park of Canada
In southwestern Ontario.
(519) 596-2233

Georgian Bay Islands National Park
Along the southeastern portion of Georgian Bay.
(705) 526-9804

Point Pelee National Park of Canada
South of Leamington.
(519) 322-2365 or (888) 773-8888

Pukaskwa National Park of Canada
On the north shore of Lake Superior.
(807) 229-0801, ext. 242

St. Lawrence Islands National Park of Canada
In the St. Lawrence River between Kingston and Brockville.
(613) 923-5261

PRINCE EDWARD ISLAND

Port La Joye-Fort Amherst National Historic Site of Canada
West of Charlottetown on Hwy. 1.
(902) 566-7626

Prince Edward Island National Park of Canada
Along the island's northern shore.
(902) 566-7050

QUEBEC

Forillon National Park of Canada
20 km. northeast of Gaspé via Hwy. 132.
(418) 368-5505 or (888) 773-8888

La Mauricie National Park of Canada
North of Trois-Rivières via Hwy. 55.
(819) 538-3232 or (888) 773-8888

SASKATCHEWAN

Grasslands National Park of Canada
Between Val Marie and Killdeer in southern Saskatchewan.
(306) 298-2257

Prince Albert National Park of Canada
In central Saskatchewan.
(306) 663-4522

YUKON TERRITORY

Kluane National Park of Canada
West of Haines Junction.
(867) 634-7250

This list of emergency animal clinics in the United States and Canada is provided by the Veterinary Emergency & Critical Care Society (VECCS) as a service to the community for information purposes only. This is not to be construed as a certification or an endorsement of any clinic listed. For further information, contact the society at (210) 698-5575 or online at www.veccs.org. Note: Hours frequently change, and not all clinics are open 24 hours or in the evening. In addition, not all facilities listed here are emergency clinics. In non-emergency situations, it's best to call first.

If you are traveling to an area not covered in this list, be prepared for an emergency by asking your regular veterinarian to recommend a clinic or veterinarian at your destination. The American Animal Hospital Association also provides a veterinary locator service to clinics that meet the association's high standards for veterinary care. Contact the association at (303) 986-2800 or online at www.healthypet.com.

United States

ALABAMA

Auburn University Small Animal Teaching Hospital
Hoerlein Hall, Wire Rd., Auburn
(334) 844-4690

Animal Medical Center
2864 Acton Rd., Birmingham
(205) 967-7389

Emergency Pet Care
4524 Southlake Pkwy., Suite 28, Birmingham
(205) 988-5998

Animal Emergency Clinic of North Alabama
2112 Memorial Pkwy South, Huntsville
(256) 533-7600

ALASKA

Pet Emergency Treatment, Inc.
2320 E Dowling Rd., Anchorage
(907) 274-5636

After Hours Veterinary Emergency Clinic
8 Bonnie Ave., Fairbanks
(907) 479-2700

ARIZONA

First Regional Animal Hospital
1233 W. Warner Rd., Chandler
(480) 732-0335

Emergency Animal Clinic, PLC
86 W. Juniper, Gilbert
(480) 497-0222

1st Emergency Pet Care
1423 S. Highley Rd. #102, Mesa
(480) 924-1123

Mesa Veterinary Hospital
858 N. Country Club, Mesa
(480) 833-7330

Emergency Animal Clinic
9875 W. Peoria Ave., Peoria
(623) 974-1520

Emergency Animal Clinic, PLC
2260 W. Glendale Ave., Phoenix
(602) 995-3757

North Valley Animal Emergency Center
3134 W. Carefree Hwy., Suite A-2, Phoenix
(623) 516-8571

Sonora Veterinary Specialists
4015 E. Cactus Rd., Phoenix
(602) 765-3700

Emergency Animal Clinic
14202 N. Scottsdale Rd., Suite 163, Scottsdale
(480) 949-8001

Paradise Valley Emergency Animal Clinic
6969 E. Shea Blvd. #225, Scottsdale
(480) 991-1848

Ina Road Animal Hospital
7320 N. La Cholla, Suite 114, Tucson
(520) 544-7700

Pima Pet Clinic - Animal Emergency Service
4832 E Speedway Blvd., Tucson
(520) 327-5624

Southern Arizona Veterinary
Specialty and Emergency Center
141 E. Fort Lowell, Tucson
(520) 888-3177

Veterinary Specialty Center of Tucson
4909 N. La Canada Dr., Tucson
(520) 795-9955

ARKANSAS

Ft. Smith Animal Emergency Clinic
4301 Regions Park Dr., Suite 3, Fort Smith
(479) 649-3100

Pulaski County Veterinary Emergency Clinic
801 John Barrow #6, Little Rock
(501) 224-3784

After Hours Animal Hospital
290 Smokey Lane, North Little Rock
(501) 955-0911

Animal Emergency & Specialty Clinic
8735 Sheltie Dr., Suite G, North Little Rock
(501) 224-3784

Animal Emergency Clinic of Northwest Arkansas
1110 Mathias Dr., Suite E, Springdale
(501) 927-0007

CALIFORNIA

Pet Emergency Treatment Service
1048 University Ave., Anoyo Grande
(510) 548-6684

East Bay Veterinary Emergency
1312 Sunset Dr., Antioch
(925) 754-5001

Central Coast Pet Emergency Clinic
1558 W. Branch St., Arroyo Grande
(805) 489-6573

Atascadero Pet Hospital and Emergency Center
9575 El Camino Real, Atascadero
(805) 466-3880

Animal Emergency & Urgent Care
4300 Easton Dr., Suite 1, Bakersfield
(661) 322-6019

East of the River Veterinary Emergency Clinic
222 Boston Turnpike, Bolton
(860) 647-0264

United Emergency Animal Clinic
1657 South Bascom Ave., Campbell
(408) 371-6282

Pacific Veterinary Specialists and Emergency Critical Care Center
1980 41st Ave., Capitola
(831) 476-2584

Sacramento Animal Medical Group
4990 Manzanita Ave., Carmichael
(916) 331-7430

Contra Costa Veterinary Emergency Center
1410 Monument Blvd., Suite 108, Concord
(925) 798-2900

Advanced Critical Care and Internal Medicine Los Angeles
9599 Jefferson Blvd., Culver City
(310) 558 6100

UC Davis Veterinary Medical Teaching Hospital Small Animal Clinic
One Shields Ave., Davis
(530) 752-0186

Vetcare Emergency & Specialty Care Center
7660 Amador Valley Blvd., Dublin
(925) 556-1234

Emergency Pet Clinic of San Gabriel Valley
3254 Santa Anita Ave., El Monte
(626) 579-4550

North Coast Veterinary and Emergency
414 Encinitas Blvd., Encinitas
(760) 632-1072

Animal Urgent Care
2430 A.S. Escondido Blvd., Escondido
(760) 738-9600

Escondido Animal Urgent Care
2525 S. Center City Pkwy., Escondido
(760) 738-9600

Animal Emergency Center
3954 A Jacobs Ave., Eureka
(707) 443-2776

Solano-Napa Pet Emergency Clinic
4437 Central Pl., Fairfield
(707) 864-1444

VCA All-Care Animal Referral Center
18440 Amistad St., Suite E, Fountain Valley
(714) 963-0909

Ohlone Veterinary Emergency Clinic
1618 Washington Blvd., Fremont
(510) 657-6620

Central California Veterinary Specialty Center
6606 N. Blackstone Ave., Fresno
(559) 451-0800

Veterinary Emergency Service, Inc.
1639 N. Fresno St., Fresno
(559) 486-0520

Orange County Emergency Pet Clinic
12750 Garden Grove Blvd., Garden Grove
(714) 537-3032

EMASH - Emergency & Mobile Animal Services Hospital
10825 Watsonville Rd., Gilroy
(408) 847-1122

Animal Emergency Clinic
12022 La Crosse Ave., Grand Terrace
(909) 825-9350

North Orange County Emergency Pet Clinic
1474 S. Harbor Blvd., La Habra
(714) 441-2925

Pet Emergency and Specialty Center
5232 Jackson Dr. #105, La Mesa
(619) 462-4800

Animal Emergency Clinic
1055 W. Avenue M, Suite 101, Lancaster
(661) 723-3959

Animal Specialty group
4641 Colorado Blvd., Los Angeles
(818) 244-7977

Animal Surgical and Emergency Center (ASEC)
1535 S. Sepulveda Blvd., Los Angeles
(310) 473-5906

Eagle Rock Emergency Pet Clinic
4254 Eagle Rock Blvd., Los Angeles
(323) 254-7382

VCA West Los Angeles Animal Hospital
1818 S. Sepulveda Blvd., Los Angeles
(310) 473-2951

Animal Urgent Care
2805 Hillcrest, Mission Viejo
(949) 364 6228

Modesto Veterinary Emergency Clinic
1800 Prescott Rd., Modesto
(209) 527-8844

Monterey Peninsula-Salinas Vet Emergency Clinic
#2 Harris Ct., Suite A-1, Monterey
(831) 373-7374

Central Orange County Emergency Animal Clinic
3720 Campus Dr., Suite D, Newport Beach
(949) 261-7979

Crossroads Animal Emergency and Referral Clinic
11057 E. Rosecrans, Norwalk
(562) 863-2522

Orange Veterinary Hospital
1100 W. Chapman Ave., Orange
(714) 997-8200

Extraordinary Veterinary Services
5714 Los Coyotes Dr., Palm Springs
(760) 202-8710

South Peninsula Veterinary Emergency Clinic
3045 Middlefield Rd., Palo Alto
(650) 494-1461

Animal Emergency Clinic of Pasadena
2121 E. Foothill Blvd., Pasadena
(626) 564-0704

Animal Emergency Clinic of San Diego
12775 Poway Rd., Poway
(858) 748-7387

Veterinary Specialty Hospital
6525 Calle Del Nido, Rancho Santa Fe
(858) 759-1777

Animal Care Center
6470 Redwood Dr., Rohnert Park
(707) 584-4343

Atlantic St. Veterinary Hospital and Pet Emergency Center
1100 Atlantic St., Roseville
(916) 783-4655

Mueller Animal Hospital
6420 Freeport Blvd., Sacramento
(916) 428-9202

Sacramento Emergency Vet Clinic
2201 El Camino, Sacramento
(916) 922-3425

Sacramento Veterinary Surgical Services
9700 Business Park Dr., Suite 404, Sacramento
(916) 362-3111

Animal E.R. of San Diego
5610 Kearny Mesa Rd., Suite A, San Diego
(858) 569-0600

VCA Emergency Animal Hospital and Referral Center
2317 Hotel Circle South, San Diego
(619) 299-2400

All Animals Emergency Hospital
1333 Ninth Ave., San Fransisco
(415) 566-0531

Pets Unlimited
2343 Fillmore St., San Fransisco
(415) 563-6700

San Francisco Veterinary Specialists
600 Alabama St., San Fransisco
(415) 401-9200

Emergency Animal Clinic of Suth San Jose
5440 Thornwood Dr., Suite E, San Jose
(408) 578-5623

Bay Area Veterinary Emergency Clinic
14790 Washington Ave., San Leandro
(510) 352-6080

California Veterinary Specialists
100 N. Rancho Santa Fe Rd., San Marcos
(760) 734-4433

North Peninsula Veterinary Emergency Clinic, Inc.
227 N. Amphlett Blvd., San Mateo
(650) 348-2576

The Pet Emergency and Specialty Center
901 E. Francisco Blvd., Suite C, San Rafael
(415) 456-7372

California Animal Referral & Emergency Hospital
301 E. Haley St., Santa Barbara
(805) 899-2273

Pacific Emergency Pet Hospital, Inc.
2963 State St., Santa Barbara
(805) 682-5120

Santa Cruz Veterinary Hospital
2585 Soquel Dr., Santa Cruz
(831) 475-5400

North Bay Animal Emergency Hospital
1304 Wilshire Blvd., Santa Monica
(310) 451-8962

Emergency Animal Hospital of Santa Rosa
1946 Santa Rosa Ave., Santa Rosa
(707) 544-1647

PetCare Veterinary Hospital
1370 Fulton Rd., Santa Rosa
(707) 579-5900

TLC Pet Medical Centers-South Pasadena
1412 Huntington Dr., South Pasadena
(626) 441-8555

Associated Veterinary Emergency Services
3008 E. Hammer Ln. #115, Stockton
(209) 952-8387

Animal Emergency Centre
11740 Ventura Blvd., Studio City
(818) 760-3882

Emergency Pet Clinic of Temecala
27443 Jefferson Ave., Temecala
(909) 695-5044

Pet Emergency Clinic, Inc.
2967 N. Moorepark Rd., Thousand Oaks
(805) 492-2436

Animal Emergency Medical Center
3511 Pacific Coast Hwy., Torrance
(310) 325-3000

Emergency Pet Clinic of South Bay
2325 Torrance Blvd., Torrance
(310) 320-8300

Monte Vista Small Animal Hospital
901 E. Monte Vista Ave., Turlock
(209) 634-0023

Advanced Critical Care & Internal Medicine
2965 Edinger Ave., Tustin
(949) 654-8950

Inland Valley Emergency Pet Clinic
10 West 7th St., Upland
(909) 931-7871

Pet Emergency Clinic, Inc.
2301 S. Victoria Ave., Ventura
(805) 642-8562

Veterinary Medical and Surgical Group
2199 Sperry Ave., Ventura
(805) 339-2290

Animal Emergency Clinic
15532 Bear Valley Rd., Victorville
(760) 962-1122

Pinnacle Veterinary Service, Inc.
2300 S. Divisadero ST, Visalia
(559) 732-8000

Tulare-Kings Veterinary Emergency Service
4946 W. Mineral King Ave., Visalia
(559) 739-7054

Coastal Emergency Animal Hospital
1900 Hacienda Dr., Vista
(760) 630-6343

TLC Pet Medical Centers-West Hollywood
8725 Santa Monica Blvd., West Hollywood
(310) 859-4852

COLORADO

Valley Emergency Pet Care
180 Fiou Lane, Suite 101, Basalt
(970) 927-5066

Animal Emergency & Referral Center
1480 W. Midway Blvd., Boulder
(303) 464-7744

Boulder Emergency Pet Clinic
1658 30th St., Boulder
(303) 440-7722

VCA Douglas County Animal Hospital
531 Jerry St., Castle Rock
(303) 688-2480

Animal Emergency Care Centers, Inc.
3775 Airport Rd., Colorado Springs
(719) 578-9300

Animal Emergency Care, Inc.
5752 N. Academy Blvd., Colorado Springs
(719) 260-7141

Alameda East Veterinary Hospital
9770 E. Alameda Ave., Denver
(303) 366-2639

Central Veterinary Emergency Services
3550 S. Jason St., Englewood
(303) 874-7387

Pet Emergency Treatment Services of N. Colorado
3629 23rd Ave., Evans
(970) 339-8700

Fort Collins Veterinary Emergency Hospital
816 S. Lemay, Fort Collins
(970) 484-8080

James L. Voss Veterinary Teaching Hospital Colorado State University
300 W. Drake, Fort Collins
(970) 221-4535

Grand Valley Veterinary Emergency Center
1660 North Ave., Grand Junction
(970) 255-1911

Animal Hospital Center
5640 County Line Place, Suite 1, Highland Ranch
(303) 740-9595

Animal Critical Care & Emergency Services, Inc.
1597 Wadsworth Blvd., Lakewood
(303) 239-1200

Animal E.R.
221 W. County Line Rd., Littleton
(720) 283-9348

Columbine Animal Hospital & Emergency Clinic
5546 W. Canyon Tr., Littleton
(303) 929-4040

Animal Emergency Center of Longmont
230 S. Main St., Longmont
(303) 678-8844

Animal Emergency Services of Northern Colorado
201 W. 67th Ct., Loveland
(970) 663-5760

Animal Emergency & Urgent Care
17701 Cottonwood Dr., Parker
(720) 842-5050

Emergency Animal Hospital of Pueblo
472 S. Joe Martinez Blvd., Pueblo
(719) 229-7030

Northside Emergency Pet Clinic
945 W 124th Ave., Westminster
(303) 252-7722

Wheat Ridge Animal Hospital / Wheat Ridge Veterinary Specialists
3695 Kipling St., Wheat Ridge
(303) 424-3325

CONNECTICUT

Farmington Valley Veterinary Emergency Hospital
9 Avonwood Rd., Avon
(860) 674-1886

Cheshire Veterinary Hospital
1572 S. Main St., Chesire
(203) 271-1577

New Haven Hospital for Veterinary Medicine, Inc.
843 State St., New Haven
(203) 865-0878

Veterinary Referral & Emergency Center
123 W. Cedar St., Norwalk
(203) 854-9960

V-E-T-S (Veterinary Emergency Treatment Services)
8 Enterprise Ln., Oakdale
(860) 444-8870

Shoreline Animal Emergency Clinic
7365 Main St., Stratford
(203) 375-6500

Connecticut Veterinary Center
470 Oakwood Ave., West Hartford
(860) 233-8564

DELAWARE

VCA Newark Animal Hospital
1360 Marrows Rd., Newark
(302) 737-8100

Veterinary Emergency Center of Delaware
1212 E. Newport Pike, Wilmington
(302) 691-3647

Wincrest Animal Emergency Hospital
3705 Lancaster Pike, Wilmington
(302) 998-2995

DISTRICT OF COLUMBIA

Friendship Hospital for Animals
4105 Brandywire St., Washington
(202) 363-7300

FLORIDA

Boca Veterinary Emergency Center
5030 Champion Blvd., Boca Raton
(861) 443-3699

Animal Emergency Clinic of Brandon
693 W. Lumsden Rd., Brandon
(813) 684-3013

Veterinary Emergency Clinic of Central Florida, Inc.
195 Concord Dr., Casselberry
(407) 740-5500

Animal Emergency and Critical Care Services of S. Florida
9410 Stirling Rd., Cooper City
(954) 432-5611

Coral Springs Animal Hospital
1730 University Dr., Coral Gables
(954) 753-1800

Florida Veterinary Referral Center & 24 Hour Emergency & Critical Care
9220 Estero Park Commons Blvd., Suite 7, Estero
(239) 992 8878

Animal Emergency Trauma Center
2200 W. Oakland Park Blvd., Fort Lauderdale
(954) 731-4228

Pet Emergency Center
921 E. Cypress, Fort Lauderdale
(954) 772-0420

Emergency Veterinary Clinic, Inc.
2045 Collier Ave., Fort Myers
(239) 939-5542

Animal Emergency and Referral Center
3984 S. US 1, Fort Pierce
(772) 466-3441

Affiliated Pet Emergency Services
7520 West University Ave., Gainesville
(352) 373-4444

Hollywood Animal Hospital
2864 Hollywood Blvd., Hollywood
(954) 920-3556

Animal ER
3444 Southside Blvd., Suite 101, Jacksonville
(904) 642-4357

Emergency Pet Care, LLC
14185-7 Beach Blvd., Jacksonville
(904) 223-8000

Emergency Pet Care of Jupiter
300 Central Blvd., Jupiter
(561) 746-0555

Tampa Bay Veterinary Emergency Service
1501-A Belcher Rd., Suite 1A, Largo
(727) 531-5752

Animal Emergency and Critical Care Center of Brevard
2281 W. Eau Gallie Blvd., Melbourne
(321) 725-5365

AEC-Animal Emergency Clinic South
8429 SW 132 St., Miami
(305) 251-2096

Miami Central Veterinary Emergency Hospital
2009 SW 67 Ave., Miami
(305) 261-2374

Miami Pet Emergency
298 Granello Ave., Miami
(305) 666-3224

Snapper Creek Emergency Clinic (Knowles Animal Clinics)
9933 Sunset Dr., Miami
(305) 279-2323

Emergency Pet Hospital of Collier County
1217 Airport Rd. South, Naples
(941) 263-8010

Animal ER Of SW Florida
15201 N. Cleveland Ave. #1400, North Fort Meyers
(941) 995-7775

Clay-Duval Pet Emergency Clinic
275 Corporate Way, Suite 200, Orange Park
(904) 264-8281

Veterinary Emergency Clinic of Central Florida, South Facility
2080 Principal Row, Orlando
(407) 438-4449

Pet Emergency and Critical Care Clinic
3816 Northlake Blvd., Palm Beach Gardens
(561) 691-9999

A.A. Animal ER Center, LLC
36401 US 19N, Palm Harbor
(727) 787-5402

Animal Emergency of Countryside, Inc.
30606 US 19N, Palm Harbor
(727) 786-5755

After Hours Emergency Animal Clinic of Hollywood, Inc.
6602 Pines Blvd., Pembroke Pines
(954) 962-0300

Pensacola Animal Emergency Clinic
3998 N. Palafox St., Pensacola
(850) 434-2924

The Veterinary Emergency Clinic
17829 Murdock Circle, Port Charlotte
(941) 255-5222

Emergency Veterinary Clinic of Sarasota
7517 South Tamiami Tr., Sarasota
(941) 923-7260

Animal Emergency Clinic of St. Petersburg
3165 22 Ave. N., St. Petersburg
(727) 321-1311

Noahs Animal Hospital and 24 Hour Emergency
2050 62nd Ave. N, St. Petersburg
(727) 522-6640

Pet Emergency & Critical Care Clinic, Inc.
2239 S. Kanner Hwy., Stuart
(772) 781-3302

FVS (Florida Veterinary Specialists)
3000 Busch Lake Blvd., Tampa
(813) 933-8944

Tampa Bay Veterinary Emergency Service
14925 N. Florida Ave., Tampa
(813) 265-4043

Animal E.R.
8239 Cooper Creek Blvd., University Park
(941) 355-2884

Animal Emergency Clinic
3425 Forest Hill Blvd., West Palm Beach
(561) 433-2244

Palm Beach Veterinary Referral and Critical Care Center
3092 Forest Hill Blvd., West Palm Beach
(561) 434-5700

GEORGIA

All Pets Emergency and Referral Center, P.C.
6460 Hwy. 9N, Alpharetta
(678) 366-2125

University of Georgia - Vet Teaching Hospital
College of Veterinary Medicine, Athens
(706) 542-3221

Animal Emergency Center of Sandy Springs
228 Sandy Springs Place NE, Atlanta
(404) 252-7881

Georgia Veterinary Specialists and Emergency Care
455 Abernathy Rd. NE, Atlanta
(404) 459-0963

Southern Crescent Animal Emergency
1270 Hwy. 54 E, Fayetteville
(770) 460-8166

An-Emerg Animal Emergency Center
275 #3 Pearl Nix Pkwy., Gainesville
(770) 534-2911

Animal Emergency Center of Gwinnett
1956 Lawrenceville-Suwanee Rd., Lawrenceville
(770) 277 3220

Cobb Emergency Veterinary Clinic
630 Cobb Pkwy. N, Suite C, Marietta
(770) 424-9157

Animal Emergency Center of North Fulton
900 Mansell Rd., Suite 19, Roswell
(770) 594-2266

DeKalb-Gwinnet Animal Emergency Clinic
6430 Lawrenceville Hwy., Tucker
(770) 491-0661

Cherokee Emergency Veterinary Clinic
719 Bascomb Commercial Pkwy., Woodstock
(770) 924-3720

IDAHO

Animal Emergency & Referral Center of Idaho
5019 N. Sawyer, Boise
(208) 376-4510

Mountain View Animal Hospital/Pet ER
3435 N Cole Rd., Boise
(208) 375-0251

North Idaho Pet Emergency
2700 E. Seltice Way #12, Post Falls
(208) 777-2707

ILLINOIS

Animal E.R. of Arlington Heights
1201 E. Palatine Rd., Arlington Heights
(847) 394-6049

VCA Franklin Park Animal Hospital
9846 W. Grand Ave., Arlington Heights
(847) 455-4922

VCA Animal Animal Hospital
2600 W. Galena Blvd., Aurora
(630) 896-8541

Animal Emergency Clinic of McLean County
2505 E. Oakland Ave., Bloomington
(309) 665-5020

Veterinary Specialty Center Emergency & Critical Care
1515 Busch Pkwy., Buffalo Grove
(847) 459-7535

Animal Emergency Cinic of Champaign County
1713 S. State St. #4, Champaign
(217) 359-1977

Chicago Veterinary Emergency Service
3123 N. Clybourne Ave., Chicago
(773) 281-7110

Animal Emergency Center
2005 Mall St., Collinsville
(618) 346-1898

Emergency Veterinary Care South Assoc.
13715 S. Cicero Ave., Crestwood
(708) 388-3771

Animal Emergency Of Mchenry County
1095 Pingree Rd., Suite 120, Crystal Lake
(815) 479-9119

Arboretum View Animal Hospital
2551 Warrenville Rd., Downers Grove
(630) 963-0424

Dundee Animal Hospital
199 Penny Ave., Dundee
(847) 428-6114

Animal Emergency & Treatment Center
1810 E. Belvidere Rd., Grayslake
(847) 548-5300

Emergency Veterinary Services
820 Ogden Ave., Lisle
(630) 960-2900

Animal Emergency of Mokena
19110 S. 88th Ave., Mokena
(708) 326-4800

Animal Emergency Clinic of McLeon County
704B S. Main St., Normal
(309) 454-8802

Animal Emergency and Critical Care Center
1810 Frontage Rd., Northbrook
(847) 564-5775

Animal Emergency Clinic of Rockford
4236 Maray Dr., Rockford
(815) 229-7791

Animal 911
3735 W. Dempster St., Skokie
(847) 673-9110

Animal Emergency Clinic of Springfield
1333 W. Wabash Ave., Springfield
(617) 698-0870

Emergency Veterinary Services of St. Charles
530 Dunham Rd., St. Charles
(630) 584-7447

University of Illinois College of Veterinary Medicine
1008 W. Hazelwood Dr., Urbana
(217) 333-5300

INDIANA

Northwood Veterinary Emergency Practice
3255 N. SR 9, Anderson
(765) 649-5218

St. Francis Family Pet Health Care
822 W. Plymouth St., Breman
(574) 546-9005

Emergency and Critical Animal Care
5818 Maplecrest Rd., Fort Wayne
(219) 426-1062

Airport Animal Emergi-Center
5235 W. Washington St., Indianapolis
(317) 248-0832

Animal Emergency Center of Indianapolis
8250 Bash St., Indianapolis
(317) 849-4925

Indianapolis Veterinary Emergency Center
5245 Victory Dr., Indianapolis
(317) 782-4484

Noahs Animal Hospital, P.C.
5510 Millersville Rd., Indianapolis
(317) 253-1327

Animal Emergency Clinic of Tippecanoe County
1343 Sagamore Pkwy. N, Lafayette
(765) 449-2001

Calumet Emergency Veterinary Clinic
216 W. Lincoln Hwy., Schererville
(219) 865-0970

Animal Emergency Clinic
17903 SR 23, South Bend
(574) 272-9611

North Central Veterinary Emergency Center
1645 S. US 421, Westville
(219) 785-7300

IOWA

Iowa State University Veterinary Clinical Sciences Teaching Hospital
S. 16th St., Ames
(515) 294-4900

Animal Emergency Center of the Quad Cities
1510 State St., Bettendorf
(563) 344-9599

Eastern Iowa Veterinary Specialty Center
755 Capitan Dr., SW, Cedar Rapids
(319) 841-5161

Animal Emergency & Referral Center of Central Iowa
6110 Cresden Ave., Des Moines
(515) 280-3051

KANSAS

Kansas State University Vet. Med. Teaching Hospital
1800 Denison Ave., Manhattan
(785) 532-4100

Mission MedVet
5914 Johnson Dr., Mission
(913) 722-5566

Veterinary Specialty & Emergency Center
11950 W. 110th St., Overland Park
(913) 642-9563

Central Kansas Veterinary Center
515 W. Blanchard Ave., South Hutchinson
(620) 663 8387

Emergency Animal Clinic of Topeka
839 S.W. Fairlawn Rd., Topeka
(785) 272-2926

Veterinary Emergency and Specialty Hospital Of Wichita
727 S. Washington, Wichita
(316) 262-5321

KENTUCKY

AA Small Animal Emergency Service
200 Southland Dr., Lexington
(859) 276-2505

Jefferson Animal Hospital and Regional Emergency Center
4504 Outer Loop, Louisville
(502) 966-4104

Louisville Veterinary Specialty and Emergency Services
12905 Shelbyville Rd., Suite 3, Louisville
(502) 244-3036

Greater Cincinnati Veterinary Specialists & Emergency Services
11 Beacon Dr., Wilder
(859) 572-0560

LOUISIANA

Animal Emergency Clinic of Baton Rouge
7353 Jefferson Hwy., Baton Rouge
(225) 927-8800

Baton Rouge Pet Emergency Hospital
1514 Cottondale Dr., Baton Rouge
(225) 925-5566

Veterinary Emergency and Critical Care, LLC
2611 Florida St., Mandeville
(985) 626-4862

Southeast Veterinary Emergency and Critical Care
400 N. Causeway Blvd., Metairie
(504) 219-0444

MAINE

Eastern Maine Emergency Veterinary Clinic
Twin City Plaza, 268 State St., Brewer
(207) 989-6267

Animal Emergency Clinic of Mid-Maine
37 Strawberry Ave., Lewiston
(207) 777-1110

Animal Emergency Clinic
352 Warren Ave., Portland
(207) 878-3121

MARYLAND

Anne Arundel Veterinary Emergency Clinic
808 Bestgate Rd., Annapolis
(410) 224-0331

Harford Emergency Veterinary Services
526 Underwood Lane, Bel Air
(410) 420-8000

Emergency Veterinary Clinic, Inc.
32 Mellor Ave., Catonsville
(410) 788-7042

Emergency Animal Hospital of Elliott City
10270 Baltimore National Pike (SR 40W), Elliott City
(410) 750-1177

Frederick Emergency Animal Hospital
434 Prospect Blvd., Frederick
(301) 662-6622

VCA Veterinary Referral Association
15021 Dufief Mill Rd., Gaithersburg
(301) 340-3224

Emergency Animal Center
1896 Urbana Pike, Suite 23, Hyattstown
(301) 831-1088

Metropolitan Emergency Animal Clinic
12106 Nebel St., Rockville
(301) 770-5226

Pets ER
Gateway Crossing, 329 Tilghman Rd., Suite 100, Salisbury
(410) 543-8400

PET ER
1209 Cromwell Bridge Rd., Towson
(410) 252-8387

Southern Maryland Veterinary Referral Center
3485 Rockefeller Ct., Waldorf
(301) 638-0988

Westminister Veterinary Hospital and Emergency /Trauma Center
269 W. Main St., Westminister
(410) 848-3363

MASSACHUSETTS

Animal Emergency Care
164 Great Rd., Acton
(978) 263-1742

Angell Memorial Animal Hospital
350 South Huntington Ave., Boston
(617) 522-7282

Cape Cod Veterinary Specialists Emergency Service
230 Main St., Buzzards Bay
(508) 759-5125

Wignall Animal Hospital
1837 Bridge St., Dracut
(978) 454-8272

Fall River Animal Hospital, Inc.
33 18th St., Fall River
(508) 675-6374

Essex County Veterinary Emergency Hospital
247 Chickering Rd., North Andover
(978) 725-5544

Tufts University School of Veterinary Medicine
200 Westboro Rd., North Grafton
(508) 839-7826

VCA South Shore Animal Hospital
595 Columbian St., South Weymouth
(781) 337-6622

Boston Road Animal Hospital
1235 Boston Rd., Springfield
(413) 783-1203

Rowley Memorial Animal Hospital/MSPCA
171 Union St., Springfield
(413) 785-1221

TUFTS Veterinary Emergency Treatment and Specialties
920 Main St., Walpole
(508) 668-5454

Veterinary Emergency & Specialty Center of New England
180 Bear Hill Rd., Waltham
(781) 684-8387

New England Animal Medical Center
595 West Center St., West Bridgewater
(508) 580-2515

Massachusetts Veterinary Referral Hospital
21 Cabot Rd., Woburn
(781) 932-5802

Woburn Animal Hospital
373 Russell St., Woburn
(781) 933-0170

MICHIGAN

Animal Emergency Clinic
4126 Packard Rd., Ann Arbor
(734) 971-8774

Ann Arbor Animal Hospital Emergency Service
2150 W. Liberty, Ann Arbor
(734) 662-4474

Michigan Veterinary Specialists
3412 E. Walton Blvd., Auburn Hills
(248) 371-3713

Oakland Veterinary Emergency & Critical Care
1400 Telegraph Rd., Bloomfield Hills
(248) 334-6877

Oakland Veterinary Emergency Group
1948 Telegraph Rd., Bloomfield Hills
(248) 334-1555

Veterinary Emergency Service-West
24400 Ford Rd., Dearborn Heights
(313) 274-3300

Michigan State University Veterinary Teaching Hospital
Michigan State University, East Lansing
(517) 353-5420

Animal Emergency Hospital-Genesee
1007 S. Ballenger Hwy., Flint
(810) 238 7557

Animal Emergency Hospital
3260 Planfield Ave. NE, Grand Rapids
(616) 361-9911

Southwest Michigan Animal Emergency Hospital
3301 S. Burdick, Kalamazoo
(616) 381-5228

Lansing Veterinary Urgent Care
3276 E. Jolly Rd., Lansing
(517) 393-9200

Veterinary Emergency Service East
28223 John Rd., Madison Heights
(248) 547-4677

Veterinary Care Specialists
205 Rowe Rd., Milford
(248) 684-0468

Animal Emergency Center
24255 Novi Rd., Novi
(248) 348-1788

Veterinary Emergency Service West
40850 Ann Arbor Rd., Plymouth
(734) 207-8500

Great Lakes Pet Emergencies
1221 Tittabawasse Rd., Saginaw
(989) 752-1960

Michigan Veterinary Specialists
21600 W. Eleven Mile Rd., Southfield
(248) 354-6660

Affiliated Veterinary Emergency Service, P.C.
14085 Northline Rd., Southgate
(734) 284-1700

MINNESOTA

South Metro Animal Emergency Care
14960 Pennock Ave., Apple Valley
(952) 953-3737

Midwest Veterinary Specialty Group
11850 Aberdeen St., NE, Blaine
(763) 754-5000

Affiliated Emergency Veterinary Hospital
1615 Coon Rapids Blvd., Coon Rapids
(763) 754-9434

Affiliated Emergency Veterinary Service
7717 Flying Cloud Dr., Eden Prairie
(952) 942-8272

Affiliated Emergency Veterinary Service
4708 Hwy. 55, Golden Valley
(763) 529-6560

Animal Emergency Clinic
7166 10th St. N, Oakdale
(651) 501-3766

Animal Emergency Clinic
301 University Ave., St. Paul
(651) 293-1800

University of Minnesota, College of Veterinary Medicine
1365 Gortner Ave., St. Paul
(612) 625-9711

Alliliated Emergency Veterinary Service
4180 Thielman Lane, St. Cloud
(320) 258-3481

MISSOURI

DBA Animal Emergency Clinic
7095 Metropolitan, Suite 6, Barnhart
(636) 464-2846

DBA: Animal Emergency Clinic
12501 Natural Bridge, Bridgeton
(314) 739-1500

University of Missouri-Columbia Veterinary Med. Teaching Hospital
379 E. Campus Dr., Columbia
(573) 882-7821

Animal Emergency Center
409 N.E. 42nd St., Kansas City
(816) 455-5430

Animal Emergency & Referral Hospital
3495 N.E. Ralph Powell Rd., Lees Summit
(816) 554-4990

Animal Emergency Clinic
334 Fort Zumwalt Sq., O Fallon
(636) 240-5496

Emergency Veterinary Clinic of Southwest Missouri
2130 Glenstone Ave., Springfield
(417) 890-1600

DBA: Animal Emergency Clinic
9937 Big Bend, St. Louis
(314) 822-7600

Mid-Rivers Equine Centre
404 Stable Ln., Wentzville
(636) 332-5373

MONTANA
Western Montana Small Animal Emergency Clinic
1914 S. Reserve St., Missoula
(406) 829-9300

NEBRASKA
United Vet Emergency Treatment Services
2540 S. 48th St., Lincoln
(402) 489-6800

Animal Emergency Clinic
9664 Mockingbird Dr., Omaha
(402) 339-6232

NEVADA
Animal Emergency Center of Las Vegas
3340 E. Patrick Ln., Las Vegas
(702) 207-1024

Las Vegas Animal Emergency Hospital
5231 W. Charleston Blvd., Las Vegas
(702) 822-1045

Animal Emergency Center of Reno
6425 S. Virginia St., Reno
(775) 851-3600

Charles River Laboratories, Proclinical Service, NV
587 Dunn Ct., Sparks
(775) 331-2201

NEW HAMPSHIRE
Capital Area Veterinary Emergency Service
22 Bridge St., Concord
(603) 227-1199

Animal Emergency Clinic of Southern NH
2626 Brown Ave., Pine Island Plaza, Manchester
(603) 666-6677

Animal Medical Center of New England
168 Main Dunstable Rd., Nashua
(603) 821-7222

Emergency Veterinary Clinic of the Seacoast Region
300 Gosling Rd., Portsmouth
(603) 431-3600

NEW JERSEY
Veterinary Surgical & Diagnostic Specialists
34 Trenton-Lakewood Rd., Clarksburg
(609) 259-8300

Animal Emergency Referral Associates
1237 Broomfield Ave., Fairfield
(973) 226-3282

Central Jersey Veterinary Emergency Service
643 Rt. 27, Iselin
(732) 283-3535

Jersey Shore Veterinary Emergency Service
1000 Rt. 70, Lakewood
(732) 363-3200

South Jersey Veterinary Emergency Services
535 Maple Ave., Linwood
(609) 926-5300

Animal Emergency Service of South Jersey
220 Moorestown-Mount Laurel Rd., Mount Laurel
(856) 727-1332

Oradell Animal Hospital
580 Winters Ave., Paramus
(201) 262-0010

Alliance Emergency Veterinary Clinic
540 Rt. 10W, Randolph
(973) 328-2844

Animerge
21 Rt. 206N, Raritan
(908) 707-9077

Garden State Veterinary Specialists
One Pine St., Tinton Falls
(732) 922-0011

Red Bank Veterinary Hospital
197 Hance Ave., Tinton Falls
(732) 747-3636

Animal Emergency and Referral Center
647 Bloomfield Ave., West Caldwell
(973) 226-3282

NEW MEXICO
Staleys Veterinary Medical Clinic
1407 Indian Walls Rd., Alamogordo
(505) 437-3063

Albuquerque Animal Emergency Clinic
4000 Montgomery Blvd. NE, Albuquerque
(505) 884-3433

Urgent Care Veterinary Hospital
9032 Montgomery Blvd. NE, Albuquerque
(505) 275-2273

Emergency Veterinary Clinic of Santa Fe
1311 Calle Mava, Santa Fe
(505) 984-0625

NEW YORK

Greater Buffalo Veterinary Emergency Services
4949 Main St., Amherst
(716) 839-4044

Veterinary Emergency & Critical Care Center
2115 Downer Street Rd., Baldwinsville
(315) 638-3500

Katonah Bedford Veterinary Center
546 N. Bedford Rd., Bedford Hills
(914) 241-7700

Atlantic Coast Veterinary Specialists
3250 Veterans Hwy., Bohemia
(631) 285-7780

Brooklyn Veterinary Emergency Service
453 Bay Ridge Ave., Brooklyn
(718) 748-5180

Capital District Animal Emergency Clinic
1086 New Loudon Rd., Cohoec
(578) 785-1094

Animal Emergency Service
6230-C Jericho Turnpike, Commack
(631) 462-6044

Animal Emergency Service
2233 Broadhollow Rd., Farmingdale
(631) 249-2899

Animal Emergency Center of Queens, P.C.
187-11 Hillside Ave., Jamaica
(718) 454-4141

Capital District Animal Emergency Clinic
222 Troy-Schenectady Rd., Latham
(518) 785-1094

Orange County Animal Emergency Service
517 Rt 211E, Middletown
(845) 692-0260

The Veterinary Referral Center of Ultravet Diagnostics
220 E. Jericho Turnpike, Mineola
(516) 294-6680

Manhattan Veterinary Group
240 E. 80th St., New York
(212) 988-1000

NYC Veterinary Specialists and Cancer Treatment Center
410 West 55th St., New York
(212) 767 0099

Orchard Park Veterinary Medical Center
3507 Orchard Park Rd., Orchard Park
(716) 662-6660

Long Island Veterinary Specialists / Animal Emergency & Critical Care Center
163 South Service Rd., Plainview
(516) 501-1700

Animal Emergency Clinic of Hudson Valley
84 Patrick Lane, Poughkeepsie
(845) 471-8242

East End Veterinary Emergency Center
67 Commerce Dr., Riverhead
(631) 369-4513

Animal Hospital of Pittsford (Monroe Emergency Service)
2816 Monroe Ave., Rochester
(716) 271-7700

Veterinary Specialists of Rochester/Animal Emergency Service
825 White Spruce Blvd., Rochester
(585) 424-1277

Animal Emergency Service
280-L Middle Country Rd., Selden
(631) 698-2225

Veterinary Medical Center of Central New York
2612 Erie Blvd. E, Syracuse
(315) 446-7933

Valley Cottage Animal Hospital
202 Rt. 303, Valley Cottage
(845) 268-9263

Nassau Animal Emergency Clinic
740 Old Country Rd., Westbury
(516) 333-6262

The Center for Specialized Veterinary Care
609-5 Cantiague Rock Rd., Westbury
(516) 420-0000

NORTH CAROLINA

REACH Hospital
677 Brevard Rd., Asheville
(828) 665-4399

Animal Emergency Clinic Of High Country
1126 Blowing Roack Rd., Suite A, Boone
(828) 268-2833

Animal Emergency Clinic of Cary
220 High House Rd., Cary
(919) 462-8989

Veterinary Specialty Hospital of the Carolinas
6405 Tryon Rd., Cary
(919) 233-4911

Animal Medical Hospital
3832 Monroe Rd., Charlotte
(704) 334-4684

Carolina Veterinary Specialists-Animal Emergency and Trauma Center
2225 Township Rd., Charlotte
(704) 504-9608

Triangle Pet Emergency Treatment Service
3319 Chapel Hill Blvd., Durham
(919) 489-0615

After Hours Veterinary Emergency Clinic
5505 W. Friendly Ave., Greensboro
(336) 851-1990

Carolina Veterinary Spec., Animal Emergency
501 Nicholas Rd., Greensboro
(336) 632-0605

After Hours Emergency Veterinary Clinic
126 Hwy 321 SW, Hickory
(828) 328-2660

Animal Emergency Center
12117 Statesville Rd., Huntersville
(704) 949-1100

Cabarrus Emergency Veterinary Clinic
1317 S. Cannon Blvd., Kannapolis
(704) 932-1182

Emergency Veterinary Clinic, PA
2440 Plantation Center Dr., Mathews
(704) 844-6834

After Hours Small Animal Emergency Clinic
409 Vick Ave., Raleigh
(919) 781-5145

Quail Corners Animal Hospital & 24 Hour Emergency Care
1613 E. Millbrook Rd., Raleigh
(919) 876-0739

Eastern Carolina Veterinary Emergency Treatment Service
4909-D Expressway Dr., Wilson
(252) 265-9920

Forsyth Veterinary Emergency Clinic
7781 North Point Blvd., Winston-Salem
(336) 896-0902

OHIO

Akron Veterinary Referral & Emergency Center
1321 Centerview Circle, Akron
(330) 665-4996

Animal Emergency Clinic West
2101 N. Cleveland-Massillon Rd., Akron
(216) 362-6001

Metropolitan Veterinary Hospital
1053 S. Cleveland-Massillon Rd., Akron
(330) 666-2976

Veterinary Referral Clinic & Emergency Center
5035 Richmond Rd., Bedford Heights
(216) 831-6789

Stark County Veterinary Emergency Clinic, LLC
2705 Fulton Dr. NW, Canton
(330) 452-5117

Cincinnati Animal Referral and Emergency Care Center
6995 E. Kemper Rd., Cincinnati
(513) 530-0911

Capital Veterinary Referral & Emergency Clinic
5230 Renner Rd., Columbus
(614) 870-0480

Ohio State University Veterinary Hospital
601 Vernon Tharp, Columbus
(614) 293-3551

Dayton Emergency Veterinary Clinic
2714 Springboro West, Dayton
(937) 293-2714

After Hours Animal Emergency Clinic, Inc.
2680 W. Liberty St., Girard
(330) 530-8387

Animal Emergency Center, Inc.
1909 North Ridge Rd., Lorain
(440) 240-1400

Ohio State University
2634 CR 15, Marengo
(614) 292-3551

Aaron Animal Clinic and Emergency Hospital
7640 Broadview Rd., Parma
(216) 901-9980

Animal Emergency & Critical Care Center of Toledo, Inc.
2785 W. Central Ave., Toledo
(419) 473-0328

Green Animal Medical Center
1620 Corporate Woods Cir., Uniontown
(330) 896-4040

MedVet Associates, Ltd.
300 E. Wilson Bridge Rd., Worthington
(800) 890-9010

OKLAHOMA

Animal Emergency Center
931 SW 74th, Oklahoma City
(405) 631-7828

Neel Veterinary Hospital
2700 N. McArthur, Oklahoma City
(405) 947-8387

Veterinary Emergency and Critical Care Hospital
1800 W. Memorial Rd., Oklahoma City
(405) 749-6989

Animal Emergency Center, Inc.
7220 E. 41st St., Tulsa
(918) 665-0508

OREGON

Animal Emergency Center Of Central Oregon
1245 SE 3rd St., Suite C3, Bend
(541) 385-9110

Cascade Animal Emergency Clinic
425 NE Windy Knolls, Suite 4, Bend
(541) 318-5829

Northwest Veterinary Specialists Emergency Service
16756 SE 82nd Dr., Clackamas
(503) 656-3999

Animal Emergency and Critical Care Center
650 SW 3rd St., Corvallis
(541) 753-5750

Dove Lewis Emergency Animal Hospital
1984 NW Pettygroove, Portland
(503) 228-7282

VCA SE Portland Animal Hospital
13830 SE Stark St., Portland
(503) 255-8139

Salem Veterinary Emergency Clinic
3215 Market St. NE, Salem
(503) 588-8082

Springfield-Eugene Emergency Veterinary Hospital
103 W. Q St., Springfield
(541) 746-0112

Emergency Veterinary Clinic of Tualatin
19314 SW Mohave Ct., Tualatin
(503) 691-7922

PENNSYLVANIA

Center for Animal Referral and Emergency Services
2010 Cabot Blvd. W, Suite D, Langhorne
(215) 750-2774

Veterinary Specialty & Emergency Center
1900 W. Old Lincoln Hwy., Langhorne
(215) 750-7884

Guynell Veterinary Hospital
1615 West Poin Pine, Lansdale
(215) 699-9294

Allegheny Veterinary Emergency Trauma & Specialty
4224 Northern Pike, Monroeville
(412) 373-4200

Emergency Service, Veterinary Hospital of the University of PA
3900 Delancey St., Philadelphia
(215) 898-4685

VCA Castle Shannon Animal Hospital Service
3610 Library Rd., Pittsburgh
(412) 885-2500

Veterinary Emergency Clinic
882 Butler St., Pittsburgh
(412) 492-9855

Hickory Veterinary Hospital
2303 Hickory Rd., Plymouth Meeting
(610) 828-3054

Metropolitan Emergency Service
915 Trooper Rd., Valley Forge
(610) 666-0914

Bucks County Veterinary Emergency Trauma Service
978 Easton Rd., Warrington
(215) 918-2200

Animal Emergency Center
395 Susquehanna Trail, Watsontown
(570) 742-7400

Valley Central Emergency Veterinary Hospital
210 Fullerton Ave., Whitehall
(610) 435-5588

RHODE ISLAND

Ocean State Veterinary Specialists
1480 S. County Trail, East Greenwich
(401) 886-6787

SOUTH CAROLINA

Greater Charleston Emergency Veterinary Clinic
3163 W. Montague Ave., Charleston
(843) 744-3372

South Carolina Veterinary Emergency Care
132 Stonemark Ln., Columbia
(803) 798-3837

Palmetto Regional Emergency Hospital for Animals
921 Spears Creek Ct., Elgin
(803) 865-1418

Mt. Pleasant Emergency Veterinary Hospital
930B Pine Hollow Rd., Mt. Pleasant
(843) 216-7554

Animal Emergency Hospital of the Strand
303-1 Hwy. 15, Myrtle Beach
(843) 445-9797

Spartanburg Veterinary Emergency Clinic
1291 Asheville Hwy., Spartanburg
(864) 591-1923

SOUTH DAKOTA

Veterinary Emergency Hospital
3508 S. Minnesota Ave., Suite 104, Sioux Falls
(605) 977-6200

TENNESSEE

Midland Pet Emergency Center, Inc.
235 Calderwood St., Alcoa
(865) 982-1007

Airport Pet Emergency Clinic
2436 Hwy. 75, Blountville
(423) 279-0574

Pet Emergency Treatment Service
1668 Mallory Ln., Brentwood
(615) 333-1212, ext. 1

River Region Institute For Veterinary Emergencies Referrals
2223 E. 23rd St., Chattanooga
(423) 698-4612

Animal Emergency Clinic of Maury County, LLC
1900B Shady Brook St., Columbia
(931) 380-1929

PetMed Emergency Center, LLC
830 N. Germantown Pkwy., Suite 105, Cordova
(901) 624-9002

Knoxville Pet Emergency Clinic
1819 Ailor Ave., Knoxville
(865) 637-0114

University of Tennessee
C247 Veterinary Teaching Hospital, Knoxville
(865) 974-8387

TEXAS

I-20 Animal Medical Center
5820 W. I-20, Arlington
(817) 478-9238

Animal Emergency Hospital of Austin
4106 N. Lamar, Austin
(512) 459-4336

Emergency Animal Hospital of NWA
12034 Research Blvd., Suite 8, Austin
(512) 331-6121

Emergency Animal Hospital of NWA - South Branch
4434 Frontier Tr., Austin
(512) 899-0955

Animal Emergency Clinic of Southeast Texas, Inc.
3420 W. Cardinal Dr., Beaumont
(409) 842-3239

North Texas Emergency Pet Clinic
1712 W. Frankford Rd. 3108, Carrolton
(972) 323-1310

Heritage Veterinary Hospital
3930 Glade Rd., Suite 120, Colleyville
(817) 358-0404

Emergency Animal Clinic
12101 Greenville Ave., Suite 118, Dallas
(972) 994-9110

The E-Clinic, Inc.
3337 Fitzhugh Ave., Dallas
(214) 520-8388

Denton County Animal Emergency Room
4145 S. I-35E, Suite 100, Denton
(940) 271-1200

El Paso Animal Emergency Center
2101 Texas Ave., El Paso
(915) 545-1148

Airport Frwy. Animal Emergency Clinic
411 N. Main St., Euless
(817) 571-2088

Metro West Emergency Veterinary Center
3201 Hulen St., Fort Worth
(817) 731-3734

Animal Emergency & Urgent Care Center of The Woodlands
27870 I-45N, Houston
(281) 367-5444

Animal Emergency Center of West Houston
4823 Hwy. 6N, Houston
(832) 593-8387

Animal Emergency Clinic SH 249
18707 SH 249, Houston
(281) 890-8875

Animal Emergency Clinic Southeast
10331 Gulf Frwy., Houston
(713) 941-8460

Houston Veterinary Services, Inc.
111 West Loop S. #200, Houston
(713) 693-1100

Veterinary Emergency Referral Group, Inc.
8921 Katy Frwy., Houston
(713) 932-9589

Metroplex Veterinary Centre
700 W. Airport Frwy., Irving
(972) 438-7113

After Hours Veterinary Services
2501 S. W.S. Young, Suite 413, Killeen
(254) 628-5017

Animal Emercency Clinic Southeast-Calder Rd.
1100 Gulf Frwy. S, Suite 104, League City
(800) 356-3692

Lake Ray Hubbard Emergency Pet Care Center
4651 N. Beltline Rd., Mesquite
(972) 226-3377

LRH Emergency Pet Care Center
9501 Lakeview Pkwy, Rowlett
(972) 475-5349

Angel of Mercy Animal Critical Care, Inc.
8734 Grissom Rd., San Antonio
(210) 684-2105

Animal Emergency Room
4315 Fredericksburg Rd., Suite 2, San Antonio
(210) 737-7380

Emergency Pet Clinic, Inc.
8503 Broadway #105, San Antonio
(210) 822-2873

Northeast Emergency Animal Clinic
8365 Perrin Beitel, San Antonio
(210) 650-3141

Animal Emergency Hospital of North Texas
2340 W. Southlake Blvd., Southlake
(817) 410-2273

Animal Emergency Clinic 59 Southwest
9920 Hwy. 90A, Suite 100C, Sugar Land
(281) 340-8387

Southwest Frwy. Animal Hospital & Emergency Center
15575 Southwest Frwy., Sugarland
(281) 491-8387

Texas Animal Medical Center
4900 Steinbeck Bend, Waco
(254) 753-0901

UTAH

Central Emergency Animal Hospital
55 E. Miller Ave., Salt Lake City
(801) 487-1325

Pet E.R. - The Pet Emergency Room
6360 S. Highland Dr., Salt Lake City
(801) 278-3367

Animal Emergency Center
2465 N. Main St., Sunset
(801) 776-8118

VERMONT

Veterinary Emergency Service, LLP
8 Calkins Court, S. Burlington
(802) 865-1205

VIRGINIA

Alexandria Veterinary Emergency Service
2660 Duke St., Alexandria
(703) 823-3601

Veterinary Emergency Treatment Services, Inc.
370 Greenbriar Dr., Suite A-2, Charlottesville
(434) 973-3519

Greenbrier Veterinary Emergency Center
1100 Eden Way N, Suite 101B, Chesapeake
(757) 366-9000

SouthPaws Veterinary Referral Center
8500 Arlington Blvd., Fairfax
(703) 752-9100

Animal Emergency Hospital and Referral Center
2 Cardinal Park Dr. 101B, Leesburg
(703) 777-5755

Animal Emergency & Critical Care of Lynchburg
3432 Odd Fellows Rd., Lynchburg
(434) 846-1504

Veterinary Referral & Critical Care (VRCC)
1596 Hockett Rd., Manakin Sabot
(804) 784-8722

Prince William Emergency Veterinary Clinic
8610 Centerville Rd., Manassas
(703) 361-8287

Animal Emergency Care
12501 Hull St. Rd., Midlothian
(804) 744-9800

Veterinary Emergency Center, Inc.
3312 W. Cary St., Richmond
(804) 353-9000

Emergency Veterinary Services of Roanoke
4902 Frontage Rd., Roanoke
(540) 563-8575

Regional Veterinary Referral Center
6651 Backlick Rd., Springfield
(703) 451-8900

Emergency Veterinary Clinic of North Virginia
416 Maple Ave. W., Vienna
(703) 281-5614

Beach Veterinary Emergency Clinic
1124 Lynnhaven Pkwy., Viriginia Beach
(757) 468-4900

Tidewater Veterinary Emergency and Critical Care Center
5425 Virginia Beach Blvd., Viriginia Beach
(757) 499-5463

Woodbridge Animal Hospital
2703 Caton Hill Rd., Woodbridge
(703) 897-5665

Emergency Veterinary Clinic
1120 George Washington Memorial Hwy., Yorktown
(757) 874-8115

WASHINGTON

After Hours Animal Emergency Clinic
718 Auburn Way N., Auburn
(253) 939-6272

Animal Emergency Care
317 Telegraph Rd., Bellingham
(360) 758-2200

Animal Emergency Clinic of Everett
3625 Rucker Ave., Everett
(425) 258-4466

Alpine Animal Hospital
888 N.W. Sammamish Rd., Issaquah
(425) 392-8888

Mid-Columbia Pet Emergency Service
8802 W. Gage Blvd., Kennewick
(509) 783-7391

Animal Emergency Service, East
636 7th Ave., Kirkland
(425) 827-8727

Agape Pet Emergency Center
16418 7th Place W., Lynnwood
(425) 741-2688

Veterinary Specialty Center of Seattle
20115 44th Ave. W., Lynnwood
(425) 697-6106

Pet Emergency Center
14434 Avon Allen Rd., Mount Vernon
(360) 848-5911

Animal Emergency & Trauma Center
320 Lindwig Way, Poulsbo
(360) 697-7771

Washington State University
Veterinary Teaching Hospital, Pullman
(509) 335-0711

Animal Critical Care & Emergency Services (ACCES)
11536 Lake City Way, NE, Seattle
(206) 364-1660

Emerald City Emergency Clinic
4102 Stone Way N., Seattle
(206) 634-9000

Five Corners Veterinary Hospital
15707 1st Ave. S., Seattle
(206) 243-2982

PSCVM Small Animal Emergency and Critical Care Center
11308 92nd St. SE, Snohomish
(360) 563-5300

Pet Emergency Clinic
E. 21 Mission, Spokane
(509) 326-6670

Puget Sound Pet Pavilion
2505 S. 80th St., Tacoma
(253) 983-1000

The Animal Emergency Clinic
5608 S. Durango St., Tacoma
(253) 474-0791

Emergency Veterinary Service, Inc.
6818 E. 4th Plain Blvd., Suite C, Vancouver
(360) 694-3007

St. Francis 24 Hr. Animal Hospital
12010 NE 65th St., Vancouver
(360) 253-5446

WEST VIRGINIA

Kanawha Valley Animal Emergency Clinic
5304 Mac Corkle Ave., Charleston
(304) 768-2911

Animal Urgent Care, Inc.
4201 Wood St., Wheeling
(304) 233-0002

WISCONSIN
Fox Valley Animal Referral Center
4706 New Horizons Blvd., Appleton
(920) 993-9193

Animal Emergency Center
2100 W. Silver Spring Dr., Glendale
(414) 540-6710

Green Bay Animal Emergency Center
933 Anderson Dr., Suite F, Green Bay
(920) 494-9400

Crawford Animal Hospital
4607 S. 108th St., Greenfield
(414) 543-3499

Emergency Clinic for Animals
229 W. Beltline Hwy, Madison
(608) 274-7772

Emergency Vets Of Central Wisconsin, Llc
1420 Kronenwetter Dr., Mosinee
(715) 693-6934

The Animal Er Of Kenasha & Racine
4333 S. Green Bay Rd., Racine
(262) 553-9223

Wisconsin Veterinary Referred Center
360 Bluemound Rd., Woukesha
(262) 542-3241

Canada

ALBERTA
Calgary North Veterinary Hospital and Emergency Service
4204 4 St. NW, Calgary
(403) 277-0135

Animal Emergency Hospital South Ltd.
3823 99 St., Edmonton
(780) 436-5880

Edmonton Veterinarians Emergency Clinic
11104 102 Ave., Edmonton
(780) 433-9505

BRITISH COLUMBIA
Animal Critical Care Group
1410 Boundary Rd., Burnabay
(604) 473-4882

Central Animal Emergency Clinic
812 Roderick Ave., Coquitlam
(604) 931-1911

Animal Emergency Clinic of the Fraser Valley
#306-6325 204th St., Langley
(604) 514-1711

Vancouver Animal Emergency Clinic, Ltd.
1590 W. 4th St., Vancouver
(604) 734-5104

Central Victoria Veterinary Hospital
760 Roderick St., Victoria
(250) 475-2495

MANITOBA
Winnipeg Animal Emergency Clinic
400 Pembina Hwy., Winnipeg
(204) 452-9427

NOVA SCOTIA
Metro Animal Emergency Clinic
201 Brownlow Ave., Unit 9, Dartmouth
(902) 468-0674

ONTARIO
Veterinary Emergency Clinic of York Region
14879 Yonge St., Aurora
(905) 713-2323

Huronia Veterinary Emergency Clinic
4-130 Bell Farm Rd., Barrie
(705) 722-3077

Emergency Veterinary Clinic
#1 Wexford Rd., Brampton
(905) 495-9907

North Town Veterinary Hospital
496 Main St. N., Brampton
(905) 451-2000

London Veterinary Emergency Clinic
41 Adelaide St. N., #43, London
(519) 432-7341

Mississauga-Oakville Veterinary Emergency Hospital
2285 Bristol Cir., Oakville
(905) 829 9444

Alta Vista Animal Hospital
2616 Bank St., Ottawa
(613) 731-9911

Niagara Veterinary Emergency Clinic
2F Tremont Dr., Unit 1, St. Catharines
(905) 641-3185

Veterinary Emergency Clinic
920 Yonge St. #117, Toronto
(416) 920-2002

Animal Emergency Clinic
1910 Dundas St. East, Unit 122, Whitby
(905) 576-3031

QUEBEC
Centre Veterinaire DMV
2300 54 IEME Ave., Montreal
(514) 633-8888

University of Montreal
3200 Sicotte St., Saint Hyacinthe
(450) 778-8111

PET-FRIENDLY LODGINGS

How to Use the Listings
U.S. Lodgings
Canadian Lodgings
Campground Listings

How to Use the Listings

Some 13,000 AAA-RATED® properties across North America accept traveling pets. This guide provides listings for those lodgings in the United States and Canada that roll out the welcome mat for pets as well as the people who love them.

For the purpose of this book, "pets" are domestic cats or dogs. If you are planning to travel with any other kind of animal — particularly such exotic pets as birds or reptiles — check with the property before making definite plans. Expect to keep nontraditional pets crated at all times.

Note: Always inform the management that you are traveling with an animal; you may be fined if you do not declare your pet. Many properties require guests with pets to sign a waiver or release form and to pay for the room with a credit card. Of course, whether you pay in cash or by credit card, you will be held liable for any damages caused by your pet, even if the property does not charge a deposit or pet fee. It is not a good idea to leave your pet unattended in the room, but if you must, crate him and notify the management. When in public areas, keep your pet leashed and do not allow him to disturb other guests.

About the Listings

Geographic listings are used for accuracy and consistency; lodgings are listed under the city or town in which they physically are located — or in some cases under the nearest recognized city or town. For a complete list of all cities within a state or province, see the comprehensive City Index at the beginning of the corresponding section.

U.S. properties are shown first, followed by Canadian properties. Most listings are alphabetically organized by state or province, city and establishment name. Reflecting contemporary travel patterns, properties in some cities or towns may instead be listed within destination cities or areas. Such "vicinity cities" and their listings will be shown alphabetically in the destination city or area, and the vicinity city also will appear in alphabetical order in the City Index, along with the page number on which the listings begin.

Each listing provides the following information (see sample listing, next page):

❶ Symbol denoting Official Appointment (OA) properties. The OA program permits properties to display and advertise the 🅰🅰🅰 or 🅲🅰🅰 logo. OAs have a special interest in serving AAA/CAA members. Ask if they offer special member amenities such as free breakfast, early check-in/late check-out, free room upgrade, free local phone calls, etc.

❷ Diamond rating. See next page.

❸ Property name.

❹ Lodging classification. See p. 69.

❺ Special amenities offered. These properties provide an additional benefit to pets, such as treats, toys or gifts, pet sitting and/or walking, a pet menu, food/water dishes, pet sheets or pillows, pet beds or other extras.

❻ Telephone number.

❼ Two-person (2P) rate year-round, and cancellation notice validity period (if more than 48 hours). Rates listed are usually daily, but weekly rates also may be listed. Note: Most properties accept any or all of the major credit cards, including American Express, MasterCard and VISA. If a property accepts only cash, the phrase "(no credit cards)" follows the rates.

❽ Physical address and highway location, if available.

❾ Exterior or interior corridors.

❿ Pet policies. If the phrase "pets accepted" appears, the property does accept pets but specific information was unavailable at press time. Otherwise, pet-specific policies are denoted as follows:

Size. "Very small" denotes pets weighing up to 10 pounds; "small," up to 25 pounds; "medium," up to 50 pounds; and "large," up to 100 pounds. If no size is specified, the property accepts pets of all sizes.

Species. "Other" indicates the property accepts animals other than dogs and cats. Always call ahead and specify the type of pet you plan to bring.

Deposits and fees. Includes the dollar amount, the type of charge (refundable deposit or nonrefundable fee), the frequency of the charge and whether the charge is per pet or per room.

Designated rooms. Guests with pets are placed in certain rooms, often smoking rooms or those on the ground floor.

Housekeeping service. The phrase "service with restrictions" denotes properties that require the pet to be crated, removed or attended by the owner during housekeeping service.

Supervision. The pet is required to be supervised at all times.

Crate. The pet must be crated when the owner is not present.

⓫ Property discounts and amenities:

- 🆂🅰🆅🅴 Minimum 10% discount.
- 🅰🆂🅺 May offer discount.
- 🆂 Senior discount.
- ⊠ Non-smoking rooms.
- ♿ Semi-accessible or ♿ fully accessible.
- ⑦ Hearing impaired.
- 🛁 Roll-in showers.
- 🅱 Refrigerator.
- ☕ Coffee maker.

Ⓣ Restaurant on premises.

Ⓟ Pool.

Ⓧ Recreational activities.

Ⓚ No air conditioning.

Ⓣ No TV.

Ⓣ No telephones.

Please note: Some in-room amenities represented by the icons in the listings may be available only in selected rooms, and may incur an extra fee. Please inquire when making your reservations.

It is important to remember that animal policies do change; always confirm policies, restrictions and fees with the lodging when making reservations and again 1-2 days before departure.

Listing information is subject to change. All listing information was accurate at press time. However, lodging rates and policies change and the publisher cannot be held liable for changes occurring after publication. AAA cannot guarantee the safety of guests or their pets at any facility.

AAA Diamond Ratings

Before a property is listed by AAA, it must satisfy a set of minimum standards regarding basic lodging needs as identified by AAA members. If a property meets those requirements, it is assigned a diamond rating reflecting the overall quality of the establishment.

AAA ratings range from one to five diamonds and indicate the property's physical and service standards as measured against the standards of each diamond level. The rating process takes into account the property's classification; i.e., its physical structure and style of operation.

◈ These establishments typically appeal to the budget-minded traveler. They provide essential, no-frills accommodations. They meet the basic requirements pertaining to comfort, cleanliness, and hospitality.

◈◈ These establishments appeal to the traveler seeking more than the basic accommodations. There are modest enhancements to the overall physical attributes, design elements, and amenities of the facility typically at a modest price.

◈◈◈ These establishments appeal to the traveler with comprehensive needs. Properties are multifaceted with a distinguished style, including marked upgrades in the quality of physical attributes, amenities and level of comfort provided.

◈◈◈◈ These establishments are upscale in all areas. Accommodations are progressively more refined and stylish. The physical attributes reflect an obvious enhanced level of quality throughout. The fundamental hallmarks at this level include an extensive array of amenities combined with a high degree of hospitality, service, and attention to detail.

◈◈◈◈◈ These establishments reflect the characteristics of the ultimate in luxury and sophistication. Accommodations are first-class. The physical attributes are extraordinary in every manner. The fundamental hallmarks at this level are to meticulously serve and exceed all guest expectations while maintaining an impeccable standard of excellence. Many personalized services and amenities enhance an unmatched level of comfort.

Lodging Classifications

Ⓑⓑ **Bed & Breakfast:** Usually smaller establishments emphasizing a more personal relationship between operators and guests, leading to an "at home" feeling. Guest units tend to be individually decorated. Rooms may not include some modern amenities such as televisions and telephones, and may have a shared bathroom. Usually owner-operated, with a common room or parlor separate from the innkeeper's living quarters, where guests and operators can interact during evening and breakfast hours. Evening office closures are normal. A continental or full, hot breakfast is served and is included in the room rate.

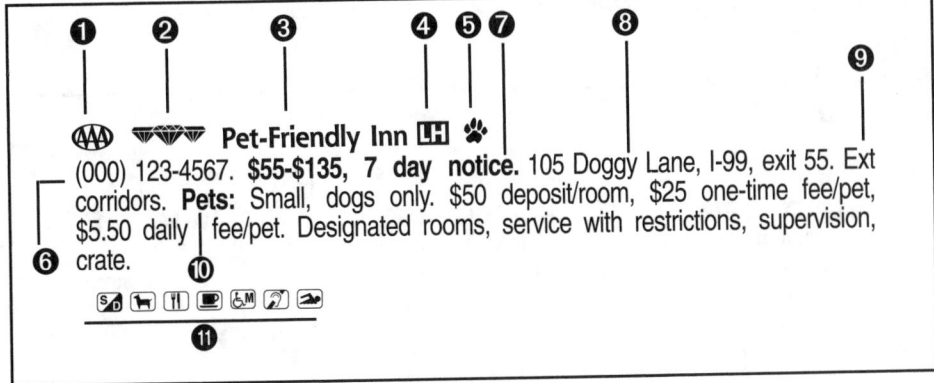

❶ ❷ ❸ ❹❺❼ ❽ ❾

Ⓐ ◈◈◈◈ Pet-Friendly Inn 🄻🄷 🐾
(000) 123-4567. **$55-$135, 7 day notice.** 105 Doggy Lane, I-99, exit 55. Ext corridors. **Pets:** Small, dogs only. $50 deposit/room, $25 one-time fee/pet, $5.50 daily fee/pet. Designated rooms, service with restrictions, supervision,
❻ crate. ❿

🔟 🛏 Ⓣ 🖥 ♿ 📶 🏊

⓫

Cabin/Cottage: Vacation-oriented, small-scale, free-standing houses or cabins. Units vary in design and decor and often contain one or more bedrooms, living room, kitchen, dining area and bathroom. Studio-type models combine the sleeping and living areas into one room. Typically, basic cleaning supplies, kitchen utensils, and complete bed and bath linens are supplied. The guest registration area may be located off-site.

Country Inn: Although similar in definition to a bed and breakfast, country inns are usually larger in size, provide more spacious public areas and offer a dining facility that serves at least breakfast and dinner. May be located in a rural setting or downtown area.

Condominium: Establishments that primarily offer guest accommodations that are privately owned by individuals and available for rent. These can include apartment-style units or homes. A variety of room styles and decor treatments are offered, and limited housekeeping service is typical. May have off-site registration.

Large-scale Hotel: A multistory establishment with interior room entrances. A variety of guest unit styles are offered. Public areas are spacious and include a variety of facilities such as a restaurant, shops, fitness center, spa, business center or meeting rooms.

Motel: Low-rise or multistory establishment offering limited public and recreational facilities.

Ranch: Often offers rustic decor treatments and food and beverage facilities. Entertainment and recreational activities are geared to a Western-style adventure vacation. May provide some meeting facilities.

Small-scale Hotel: A multistory establishment typically with interior room entrances. A variety of guest unit styles are offered. Public areas are limited in size and/or the variety of facilities available.

Vacation Home: Vacation-oriented or extended-stay, large-scale, freestanding houses that are routinely available for rent through a management company. Houses vary in design and décor and often contain two or more bedrooms, living room, full kitchen, dining room and multiple bathrooms. Typically, basic cleaning supplies, kitchen utensils, and complete bed and bath linens are supplied. The guest registration area may be located off-site.

Campground Listings

Geographic listings are used for accuracy and consistency. Campgrounds are listed under the city or town in which they physically are located — or in some cases under the nearest recognized city or town. Not all listings include physical addresses. U.S. campgrounds are given first, followed by Canadian campgrounds. Listings are alphabetically organized by state or province, city and campground name.

Note: Call first before taking your pet on a camping trip, as campground policies regarding pets may change.

Each listing provides the following information (see sample listing):

❶ Location.

❷ Campground name.

❸ Symbol denoting Official Appointment (OA) campgrounds. The OA program permits privately operated campgrounds to display and advertise the AAA or CAA logo. OAs have a special interest in serving AAA/CAA members.

❹ Telephone number.

❺ Fee range for a specified number of persons, including the fee for an extra person (XP) staying at the campground.

❻ Most campgrounds accept any or all of the major credit cards, including American Express, MasterCard and Visa. If a campground accepts only cash, the sentence "(no credit cards)." appears.

❼ Physical address (if available), highway location and mailing address (if available).

❽ Pet policies (as applicable). When pets up to 25 pounds are permitted, the phrase "small pets allowed" will appear. If no size is specified, the campground accepts pets of all sizes.

❾ Campground discounts and amenities:

　🏷 10% senior discount for members over 59
　🚫 No Tents.
　🏊 Pool.
　🎯 Recreational activities.

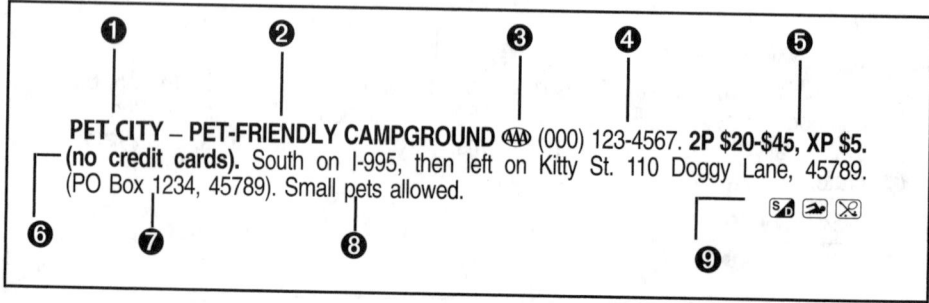

United States

ALABAMA

ABBEVILLE

◆◆ **Best Western-Abbeville Inn** M
(334) 585-5060. **$59-$79.** 1237 US Hwy 431. Jct SR 27. Ext corridors.
Pets: Small, other species. $10 daily fee/pet. Service with restrictions, crate.
⊠ 📶 🛏 🏊

ALBERTVILLE

◆◆ **Jameson Inn** SH
(256) 891-2600. **$54-$120.** 315 Martling Rd. On US 431, just e of SR
75. Ext corridors. **Pets:** Small. $10 daily fee/pet. Service with restrictions,
crate.
A$K ⊠ 🖥 🛏 💻 🏊

ALEXANDER CITY

◆◆ **Jameson Inn** SH
(256) 234-7099. **$54-$120.** 4335 US Hwy 280. US 280, just s of jct SR
22; just w of jct SR 63. Ext corridors. **Pets:** Small. $10 daily fee/pet.
Service with restrictions, crate.
A$K ⊠ 🖥 🛏 💻 🏊

ANDALUSIA

◆◆ **Days Inn** M
(334) 427-0050. **$59.** 1604 Dr. MLK Jr Expwy. On US 84 Bypass. Ext
corridors. **Pets:** Accepted.
A$K 🛏 ⊠ 🛏 💻 🏊

◆◆◆ **Scottish Inn** M
(334) 222-7511. **$45-$60.** 1421 Dr. MLK Jr Expwy. On US 84 Bypass.
Ext corridors. **Pets:** Small. $10 daily fee/pet. Service with restrictions,
supervision.
SAVE 🛏 ⊠ 🛏 💻 🏊

ANNISTON

◆◆ **Long Leaf Lodge at McClellan** M
(256) 820-9494. **$60-$75.** 74 Exchange Ave. I-20, exit 185, 10 mi n on
SR 21, then 1.5 mi e into McClellan-Ballzell Gate. **Pets:** Designated
rooms.
A$K 🛏 ⊠ 🛏 💻

◆◆◆ **The Victoria, A Country Inn** CI 🐾
(256) 236-0503. **$99.** 1600 Quintard Ave. I-20, exit 185, 4 mi n on SR
21/US 431. Ext/int corridors. **Pets:** Small. $25 one-time fee/room. Desig-
nated rooms, service with restrictions, crate.
A$K 🛏 ⊠ 🛏 💻 🍴 🏊

ARAB

◆◆ **Jameson Inn** SH
(256) 586-5777. **$54-$120.** 706 N Brindlee Mountain Pkwy. On US 231,
0.5 mi n of jct SR 69. Ext corridors. **Pets:** Small. $10 daily fee/pet.
Service with restrictions, crate.
A$K ⊠ 🖥 🛏 💻 🏊

ATHENS

◆◆◆ ◆◆ **Best Western Athens Inn** SH
(256) 233-4030. **$69-$109, 7 day notice.** 1329 Hwy 72. I-65, exit 351,
just w. Ext corridors. **Pets:** Accepted.
SAVE 🛏 ⊠ 🛏 💻 🏊

◆◆◆ ◆◆ **Country Hearth Inn** SH
(256) 232-1520. **$53-$79.** 1500 Hwy 72 E. I-65, exit 351, just e on US
72. Ext corridors. **Pets:** Small, other species. $10 daily fee/room. Service
with restrictions, crate.
SAVE 🛏 ⊠ 🛏 💻 🏊

ATTALLA

◆◆ **Americas Best Value Inn & Suites** SH
(256) 570-0117. **$50-$180.** 915 E 5th Ave. I-59, exit 183 southbound,
just e; exit northbound, through first set of lights, then just e. Ext
corridors. **Pets:** Accepted.
⊠ 🛏

◆◆ **Days Inn Attalla** SH
(256) 538-7861. **$60-$65.** 801 Cleveland Ave. I-59, exit 183 northbound, just e; exit southbound, through first set of lights, then just e.
Ext corridors. **Pets:** Dogs only. $15 daily fee/room. Service with restric-
tions, supervision.
A$K 🛏 ⊠ 🖥 🛏 💻 🏊

◆◆ **Econo Lodge** SH
(256) 538-9925. **$59-$150.** 507 Cherry St. I-59, exit 183, just w. Int
corridors. **Pets:** Accepted.
A$K 🛏 ⊠ 🛏 💻 🍴 🏊

AUBURN

◆◆◆ ◆◆ **Best Western University Convention
Center** SH
(334) 821-7001. **$81-$225.** 1577 S College St. I-85, exit 51, 1.4 mi n on
US 29/SR 147. Ext corridors. **Pets:** Accepted.
SAVE 🛏 ⊠ 🛏 💻 🏊

◆◆◆ ◆◆◆ **The Hotel at Auburn University & Dixon
Conference Center** LH
(334) 821-8200. **$89-$119.** 241 S College St. I-85, exit 51, 3.5 mi n on
US 29/SR 147. Int corridors. **Pets:** Accepted.
SAVE ⊠ 🛏M 🗐 🛏 💻 🍴 🏊 ⊠

◆◆ **Jameson Inn** M
(334) 502-5020. **$54-$120.** 1212 Mall Pkwy. I-85, exit 58, 1.5 mi n on
US 280 W, then 2.1 mi s on US 29/SR 14. Ext corridors. **Pets:** Small.
$10 daily fee/pet. Service with restrictions, crate.
A$K ⊠ 🛏 💻 🏊

◆◆◆ ◆◆ **Microtel Inn & Suites** SH
(334) 826-1444. **$55-$200, 14 day notice.** 2174 S College St. I-85, exit
51, just n. Int corridors. **Pets:** Small. $10 daily fee/pet. Service with
restrictions, supervision.
SAVE 🛏 ⊠ 🖥 🛏 💻

BIRMINGHAM METROPOLITAN AREA

BESSEMER

AAA ♦♦♦♦ Best Western Hotel & Suites SH
(205) 481-1950. **$89-$250.** 5041 Academy Ln. I-20/59, exit 108, just sw. Int corridors. **Pets:** Accepted.
SAVE S X 🐾 🔥 ♿ 🏊 ⚊

♦♦ Jameson Inn SH
(205) 428-3194. **$54-$120.** 5021 Academy Ln. I-20/59, exit 108, just sw. Ext corridors. **Pets:** Small. $10 daily fee/pet. Service with restrictions, crate.
ASK X 🔥 ♿ 🏊 ⚊

♦ Motel 6 #426 M
(205) 426-9646. **$45-$58.** 1000 Shiloh Ln. I-20/59, exit 108, 1 mi ne on US 11. Ext corridors. **Pets:** Medium, other species. Service with restrictions, supervision.
S X 🔥 ⚊

♦♦ Sleep Inn SH 🐾
(205) 424-0000. **$59-$139.** 1259 Greenmor Dr. I-459, exit 6, just e, then just s. Int corridors. **Pets:** Small, other species. $10 daily fee/pet. Designated rooms, no service, supervision.
ASK S X 🔥 ♿ 🏊 ⚊

BIRMINGHAM

AAA ♦♦♦♦ Best Western Carlton Suites SH
(205) 940-9990. **$109-$198.** 140 State Farm Pkwy. I-65, exit 255, just w to Wildwood Pkwy, then just n. Int corridors. **Pets:** Small, dogs only. $10 daily fee/pet. Designated rooms, no service, supervision.
SAVE S X 🐾 🔥 ♿ 🏊 ⚊

AAA ♦♦♦♦ Best Western Mountain Brook M
(205) 991-9977. **$80-$200.** 4627 Hwy 280 E. I-459, exit 19 (US 280), 1.4 mi e. Ext corridors. **Pets:** Small. $20 one-time fee/pet. Service with restrictions, supervision.
SAVE S X ♿ 🏊 ⚊ ✕

♦♦♦♦ Drury Inn & Suites-Birmingham Southeast SH
(205) 967-2450. **$95-$140.** 3510 Grandview Pkwy. I-459, exit 19, just e on US 280; in Grandview. Int corridors. **Pets:** Large, other species. Service with restrictions, supervision.
ASK X 🔥 ♿ 🏊 ⚊

AAA ♦♦♦ Embassy Suites Birmingham LH
(205) 879-7400. **$139-$359.** 2300 Woodcrest Pl. Just n of jct US 31 and 280, exit 21st Ave southbound, then 0.3 mi s. Int corridors. **Pets:** Accepted.
SAVE X 🐾 ♿ 🏊 🍴 ⚊ ✕

♦♦ Extended Stay Studio Plus SH
(205) 408-0107. **$49-$69.** 101 Cahaba Park Cir. I-459, exit 19 (US 200), 1.9 mi se, then just n. Int corridors. **Pets:** Accepted.
X ♿ 🏊 ⚊

♦♦ Homestead Studio Suites Hotel-Birmingham Perimeter Park South SH
(205) 967-3800. **$65-$95.** 12 Perimeter Park S. I-459, exit 19 (US 280), 0.5 mi e, then just s. Ext corridors. **Pets:** Accepted.
ASK S X 🐾 🔥 ♿ 🏊

♦♦♦♦ Homewood Suites by Hilton SH 🐾
(205) 995-9823. **$129-$169.** 215 Inverness Center Dr. I-459, exit 19 (US 280), 1.8 mi e, then just s. Int corridors. **Pets:** Other species. $75 one-time fee/room.
ASK S X 🔥 ♿ 🏊 ⚊ ✕

♦♦♦ La Quinta Inn & Suites Birmingham SH
(205) 995-9990. **$74-$94.** 513 Cahaba Park Cir. I-459, exit 19 (US 280), 1.2 mi e. Int corridors. **Pets:** Medium. Service with restrictions.
ASK X ♿ 🏊

♦♦♦♦ Pickwick Hotel & Conference Center SH
(205) 933-9555. **$88.** 1023 20th St S. 1.5 mi s of downtown (Five Points area). Int corridors. **Pets:** Accepted.
ASK S X 🔥 ♿ 🏊

AAA ♦♦♦♦ Residence Inn By Marriott SH 🐾
(205) 991-8686. **$164-$209.** 3 Greenhill Pkwy. I-459, exit 19 (US 280), 2 mi e. Ext corridors. **Pets:** Medium, other species. $75 one-time fee/room. Service with restrictions.
SAVE X 🔥 ♿ 🏊 ✕

AAA ♦♦♦♦ Sheraton Birmingham Hotel LH
(205) 324-5000. **$89-$249.** 2101 Richard Arrington Blvd N. I-20/59, exit 22nd St. Int corridors. **Pets:** Accepted.
SAVE X 🐾 🔥 ♿ 🍴 🏊 ✕

AAA ♦♦♦♦ The Tutwiler-A Wyndham Historic Hotel LH
(205) 322-2100. **$152.** 2021 Park Pl N. Between Richard Arrington Jr Blvd and 20th St; just s of Woodrow Wilson Park. Int corridors. **Pets:** Accepted.
SAVE S X 🐾 🔥 ♿ 🍴

CALERA

♦♦ Holiday Inn Express SH
(205) 668-3641. **$85.** 357 Hwy 304. I-65, exit 231, just se. Ext corridors. **Pets:** Accepted.
ASK S X 🔥 ♿ 🏊 ⚊

HOMEWOOD

♦♦♦♦ Drury Inn & Suites-Birmingham Southwest SH
(205) 940-9500. **$90-$140.** 160 State Farm Pkwy. I-65, exit 255, 0.5 mi on northwest frontage road. Int corridors. **Pets:** Large, other species. Service with restrictions, supervision.
ASK X 🔥 ♿ 🏊 ⚊

♦♦♦♦ La Quinta Inn & Suites Birmingham (Homewood) SH
(205) 290-0150. **$109-$125.** 60 State Farm Pkwy. I-65, exit 255, 0.9 mi on northwest frontage road. Int corridors. **Pets:** Medium. Service with restrictions.
ASK X 🔥 ♿ 🏊 ⚊

AAA ♦♦♦♦ Ramada Inn SH
(205) 916-0464. **$59-$199.** 226 Summit Pkwy. I-65, exit 256 northbound; exit 256A southbound, just w. Int corridors. **Pets:** Small, other species. $25 daily fee/pet. Designated rooms, service with restrictions, supervision.
SAVE S X 🔥 ♿ 🏊

♦♦ Red Roof Inn M
(205) 942-9414. **$43-$58.** 151 Vulcan Rd. I-65, exit 256 northbound; exit 256A southbound, just nw. Ext corridors. **Pets:** Medium, other species. Service with restrictions, supervision.
X 🔥

AAA ♦♦♦♦ Residence Inn by Marriott SH
(205) 943-0044. **$108-$189.** 50 State Farm Pkwy. I-65, exit 255, 1 mi on northwest frontage road. Int corridors. **Pets:** Accepted.
SAVE X 🔥 ♿ 🏊 ⚊ ✕

♦♦ StudioPLUS M
(205) 290-0102. **$59-$69.** 40 Statefarm Pkwy. I-65, exit 256, just w. Int corridors. **Pets:** Accepted.
X ♿ 🏊 ⚊

♦♦ Super 8 Motel SH
(205) 945-9888. **$44-$63.** 140 Vulcan Rd. I-65, exit 256 northbound; exit 256A southbound, just nw. Int corridors. **Pets:** Small, dogs only. $5 daily fee/pet. Service with restrictions.
ASK S X 🔥 ♿

△△△ ▽▽▽▽ **TownePlace Suites by Marriott** SH ❀
(205) 943-0114. **$149-$159.** 500 Wildwood Cir. I-65, exit 255, 0.6 mi w, then just n. Int corridors. **Pets:** Medium, other species. $75 one-time fee/room. Service with restrictions, supervision.

SAVE S♦ ✕ ⌖M ⌐ ⎕ ▣ ⇌

HOOVER

▽▽◆ **La Quinta Inn & Suites Birmingham (Hoover/Riverchase)** SH
(205) 403-0096. **$109-$125.** 120 Riverchase Pkwy E. I-65, exit 247 (Valleydale Rd), just w. Int corridors. **Pets:** Accepted.

A$K ✕ ⌐ ⎕ ▣ ⇌

△△△ ▽▽ ▽▽ **The Wynfrey Hotel** LH
(205) 987-1600. **$169-$239.** 1000 Riverchase Galleria. I-459, exit 13 (US 31), adjacent to the Riverchase Galleria. Int corridors. **Pets:** $150 deposit/pet. Service with restrictions, supervision.

SAVE S♦ ✕ ⌖ ⌐ ⎕ ▣ ⍦ ⇌ ⌧

LEEDS

△△△ ▽▽ **Days Inn of Leeds** M
(205) 699-9833. **$59-$200.** 1838 Ashville Rd. I-20, exit 144A eastbound; exit 144B westbound, just s. Ext corridors. **Pets:** Medium, other species. $7 daily fee/pet. Service with restrictions, supervision.

SAVE S♦ ✕ ⌐ ⇌

MOODY

▽▽ ▽ **Super 8 Motel** M
(205) 640-7091. **$67-$78.** 2451 Moody Pkwy. I-20, exit 144, 1 mi n on US 411. Ext corridors. **Pets:** Accepted.

A$K S♦ ✕ ⌐

END METROPOLITAN AREA

CHILDERSBURG

▽▽ ◆ **Days Inn** SH
(256) 378-6007. **$55-$100.** 33669 US Hwy 280. 0.8 mi s of jct SR 76. Ext corridors. **Pets:** Other species. $10 one-time fee/pet. Service with restrictions, supervision.

A$K S♦ ✕ ⌐ ⎕ ⇌

CLANTON

△△△ ▽▽▽ **Best Western Inn** SH
(205) 280-1006. **$75-$85, 5 day notice.** 801 Bradberry Ln. I-65, exit 205, 0.5 mi e. Ext corridors. **Pets:** Very small. $10 daily fee/pet. Service with restrictions, supervision.

SAVE ✕ ⌖ ⌐ ⎕ ⇌

△△△ ▽▽▽ **GuestHouse International Inn** SH
(205) 280-0306. **$61-$71.** 946 Lake Mitchell Rd. I-65, exit 208, just w. Ext corridors. **Pets:** Accepted.

SAVE S♦ ✕ ⌐ ⎕ ⇌

CULLMAN

△△△ ▽▽▽▽ **Best Western Fairwinds Inn** SH
(256) 737-5009. **$55-$125.** 1917 Commerce Ave NW. I-65, exit 310, just e. Ext corridors. **Pets:** Other species. $9 daily fee/room. Service with restrictions, crate.

SAVE S♦ ✕ ⌐ ⎕ ⇌

▽▽ ▽ **Comfort Inn** SH
(256) 734-1240. **$80-$120.** 5917 Alabama Hwy 157 NW. I-65, exit 310, just e. Ext corridors. **Pets:** Accepted.

A$K S♦ ✕ ⌐ ⎕ ⇌

ONEONTA

△△△ ▽▽▽ **Best Western Colonial Inn** SH
(205) 274-2200. **$85-$150, 7 day notice.** 293 Valley Rd. On SR 75, 0.5 mi n of jct US 231. Ext corridors. **Pets:** Accepted.

SAVE S♦ ✕ ⌖ ⌐ ⎕ ⇌

PELHAM

△△△ ▽▽▽▽ **Best Western at Oak Mountain** SH
(205) 982-1113. **$109-$199.** 100 Bishop Cir. I-65, exit 246, just sw, then just s on State Park Rd. Int corridors. **Pets:** Accepted.

SAVE S♦ ✕ ⌖ ⌐ ⎕ ⇌

△△△ ▽▽ ▽ **Quality Inn** SH
(205) 444-9200. **$89-$160, 14 day notice.** 110 Cahaba Valley Pkwy. I-65, exit 246, just nw. Ext corridors. **Pets:** Very small, dogs only. $25 daily fee/room. No service, supervision.

SAVE ✕ ⌐ ⎕ ⇌

TRUSSVILLE

▽▽ ▽ **Jameson Inn** SH
(205) 661-9323. **$54-$120.** 4730 Norrell Dr. I-59, exit 141, just e on Chalkville Rd, then just n. Ext corridors. **Pets:** Small. $10 daily fee/pet. Service with restrictions, crate.

A$K ✕ ⌖ ⌐ ⎕ ⇌

▽▽ ▽ **Days Inn** M
(256) 739-3800. **$61-$80.** 1841 4th St SW. I-65, exit 308, just e. Ext corridors. **Pets:** Medium, other species. $5 one-time fee/room. Service with restrictions, crate.

A$K S♦ ✕ ⌐ ⎕ ⍦ ⇌

△△△ ▽▽ **Econo Lodge** M ❀
(256) 734-2691. **$60-$75, 7 day notice.** 1655 CR 437. I-65, exit 304, just e. Ext corridors. **Pets:** Very small, dogs only. $10 daily fee/pet. Designated rooms, service with restrictions, crate.

SAVE S♦ ✕ ⌐ ⎕

DECATUR

△△△ ▽▽▽ **Best Western River City Hotel** SH
(256) 301-1388. **$79-$89.** 1305 Front Ave. I-65, exit 334, 8 mi n. Int corridors. **Pets:** Other species. $15 one-time fee/pet. Service with restrictions, supervision.

A$K S♦ ✕ ⌖M ⌖ ⌐ ⎕ ⇌

△△△ ▽▽▽ **Comfort Inn & Suites** SH ❀
(256) 355-1999. **$71-$91.** 2212 Danville Rd SW. SR 67, jct Beltline Rd SW. Int corridors. **Pets:** Large. $35 deposit/pet, $10 daily fee/pet. Service with restrictions, supervision.

SAVE S♦ ✕ ⌖ ⌐ ⎕ ⇌

▽▽▽▽ **Holiday Inn Hotel & Suites** SH
(256) 355-3150. **$70-$119.** 1101 6th Ave NE. Just w of jct US 31, 72A and SR 20. Ext/int corridors. **Pets:** Small. $15 one-time fee/room. Designated rooms, service with restrictions.

A$K S♦ ✕ ⌐ ⎕ ⍦ ⇌ ⌧

▼▼ ▼▼ Jameson Inn SH
(256) 355-2229. **$54-$120.** 2120 Jameson Pl SW. SR 67, 1.6 mi s of jct US 72A; 3.9 mi n of jct US 31. Ext corridors. **Pets:** Small. $10 daily fee/pet. Service with restrictions, crate.

[ASK] [X] [icons]

▼▼ Microtel Inn & Suites SH 🐾
(256) 301-9995. **$49-$89.** 2226 Beltline Rd SW. On SR 67, 4 mi w of jct US 31. Int corridors. **Pets:** Medium. $2500.00 one-time fee/pet. Service with restrictions, crate.

[ASK] [icons]

DOTHAN

▲▲▲ ▼▼ Americas Best Value Inn & Suites M
(334) 793-5200. **$47-$99.** 2901 Ross Clark Cir. 0.8 mi s of jct US 84; west end of town. Ext corridors. **Pets:** Small, dogs only. $10 daily fee/pet. Service with restrictions, supervision.

[SAVE] [icons]

▲▲▲ ▼▼▼ Comfort Inn SH
(334) 793-9090. **$85-$106.** 3593 Ross Clark Cir. Just w of jct US 231; northwest part of town. Int corridors. **Pets:** Small, other species. $10 daily fee/pet. Supervision.

[SAVE] [icons]

▼▼ ▼▼ Days Inn M
(334) 793-2550. **$46-$51.** 2841 Ross Clark Cir. 0.9 mi s of jct US 84; west end of town. Ext corridors. **Pets:** Accepted.

[ASK] [icons]

▲▲▲ ▼▼ ▼▼ Holiday Inn Express M
(334) 671-3700. **$80-$90.** 3071 Ross Clark Cir. Just s of jct US 84; west end of town. Ext corridors. **Pets:** Accepted.

[SAVE] [icons]

▼▼ ▼▼ ▼▼ Holiday Inn-South SH
(334) 794-8711. **$60-$125.** 2195 Ross Clark Cir. Just e of US 231; in south part of town. Ext corridors. **Pets:** Accepted.

[ASK] [icons]

▼▼ ▼▼ Howard Johnson Express Inn M
(334) 792-3339. **$62-$75.** 2244 Ross Clark Cir. 1.4 mi s of jct SR 52; west end of town. Ext corridors. **Pets:** Accepted.

[ASK] [icons]

▼▼ Motel 6 #1233 M
(334) 793-6013. **$39-$51.** 2907 Ross Clark Cir. 0.8 mi s of jct US 84; west end of town. Ext corridors. **Pets:** Medium, other species. Service with restrictions, supervision.

[icons]

▲▲▲ ▼▼ ▼▼ Quality Inn M
(334) 794-6601. **$65-$85.** 3053 Ross Clark Cir. Just s of jct US 84, west end of town. Ext corridors. **Pets:** Accepted.

[SAVE] [icons]

ENTERPRISE

▲▲▲ ▼▼ ▼▼ Comfort Inn M
(334) 393-2304. **$70.** 615 Boll Weevil Cir. On US 84 Bypass. Ext corridors. **Pets:** Accepted.

[SAVE] [icons]

EUFAULA

▼▼ ▼▼ ▼▼ Eufaula Comfort Suites SH
(334) 616-0114. **$69-$129, 30 day notice.** 12 Paul Lee Pkwy. 1.7 mi s on US 431 from jct US 82 E, then just e. Int corridors. **Pets:** Other species. $25 one-time fee/room. Service with restrictions, crate.

[ASK] [icons]

▼▼ ▼▼ Jameson Inn M
(334) 687-7747. **$54-$120.** 136 Towne Center Blvd. On US 431, 1 mi s of US 82 E. Ext corridors. **Pets:** Small. $10 daily fee/pet. Service with restrictions, crate.

[ASK] [icons]

EVERGREEN

▲▲▲ ▼▼ ▼▼ Comfort Inn M
(251) 578-4701. **$60-$110.** I-65 Hwy 83 Bates Rd. I-65, exit 96, just w. Ext corridors. **Pets:** Accepted.

[SAVE] [icons]

▼▼ ▼▼ Days Inn of Evergreen M 🐾
(251) 578-2100. **$70.** Rt 2. I-65, exit 96, just w. Ext corridors. **Pets:** Very small. $10 one-time fee/pet. Service with restrictions, supervision.

[ASK] [icons]

FAIRHOPE

▼▼ ▼▼ Key West Inn M
(251) 990-7373. **$69-$99.** 231 S Greeno Rd. On US 98, 1.9 mi s of jct SR 104. Ext corridors. **Pets:** Small. $10 daily fee/pet. Designated rooms, service with restrictions, supervision.

[ASK] [icons]

FLORENCE

▼▼ Jameson Inn SH
(256) 764-5326. **$54-$120.** 115 Ana Dr. On US 43/72, just nw of jct SR 133 (Cox Creek Pkwy). Ext corridors. **Pets:** Small. $10 daily fee/pet. Service with restrictions, crate.

[ASK] [icons]

▼▼ Knights Inn Florence M
(256) 766-2620. **$43-$66.** 1915 Florence Blvd (US 72). 2 mi w; jct Cox Creek Pkwy (SR 133) and US 72. Ext corridors. **Pets:** Medium. $10 daily fee/room. Service with restrictions, crate.

[ASK] [icons]

▼▼ ▼▼ ▼▼ Marriott Shoals Hotel and Spa LH
(256) 246-3600. **Call for rates.** 800 Cox Creek Pkwy S. From jct US 13/72 and SR 133 (Cox Creek Pkwy), 1.5 mi s; at Wilson Dam. Int corridors. **Pets:** Accepted.

[icons]

▲▲▲ ▼▼ Super 8 Motel M 🐾
(256) 757-2167. **$51-$110.** 101 Hwy 72 & 43 E. 3.8 mi e on US 43/72 from jct SR 133 (Cox Creek Pkwy). Ext corridors. **Pets:** Small. $25 deposit/pet, $10 daily fee/pet. Designated rooms, service with restrictions, supervision.

[SAVE] [icons]

FOLEY

▲▲▲ ▼▼ ▼▼ Holiday Inn Express SH
(251) 943-9100. **$95-$187.** 2682 S McKenzie St. On SR 59, 1.9 mi s of jct US 98. Ext corridors. **Pets:** Accepted.

[SAVE] [icons]

▼▼ ▼▼ Key West Inn M
(251) 943-1241. **$60-$120.** 2520 S McKenzie St. On SR 59, 1.8 mi s of jct US 98. Ext corridors. **Pets:** Small, dogs only. $20 daily fee/pet. Designated rooms, service with restrictions, supervision.

[ASK] [icons]

GADSDEN

▼▼ ▼▼ Motel 6 #1495 SH
(256) 543-1105. **$41-$53.** 1600 Rainbow Dr. I-759, exit 4A, 0.8 mi s on US 411. Ext corridors. **Pets:** Medium, other species. Service with restrictions, supervision.

[icons]

GREENVILLE

◆◆◆ ▼▼ Days Inn M
(334) 382-3118. **$60-$80.** 946 Fort Dale Rd. I-65, exit 130, just s on SR 185. Ext corridors. **Pets:** Medium. $15 daily fee/pet. Service with restrictions, supervision.

[SAVE] [S&] [✕] [🛏] [💻] [🏊]

▼▼◆ Jameson Inn M
(334) 382-6300. **$54-$120.** 71 Jameson Ln. I-65, exit 130, just n on SR 185, then just w on Cahaba Rd. Ext corridors. **Pets:** Small. $10 daily fee/pet. Service with restrictions, crate.

[ASK] [✕] [🛏] [💻] [🏊]

GULF SHORES

◆▼ La Quinta Inn SH
(251) 967-3500. **$60-$309.** 213 W Fort Morgan Rd. On SR 180, just w of jct SR 59. Int corridors. **Pets:** Small, other species. Designated rooms, service with restrictions, supervision.

[ASK] [S&] [✕] [♿] [🐾] [✎] [🛏] [💻] [🏊] [✕]

HAMILTON

◆◆◆ ▼◆ Days Inn SH
(205) 921-1790. **$65.** 1849 Military St S. US 78, exit 14, 1 mi n, then 1 mi w on US 43. Ext corridors. **Pets:** $10 daily fee/pet. Service with restrictions, supervision.

[SAVE] [✕] [✎] [🛏] [💻] [🏊]

▼▼ Econo Lodge Inn & Suites SH
(205) 921-7831. **$59-$64.** 2031 Military St S. US 78, exit 14, 1 mi n, then 1 mi w on US 43. Ext corridors. **Pets:** Accepted.

[ASK] [S&] [✕] [🛏] [💻] [🍴] [🏊]

HUNTSVILLE

◆◆◆ ▼▼ America's Best Inns M
(256) 539-9671. **$59-$79.** 1304 N Memorial Pkwy. I-565, exit 19B, 0.5 mi n on US 231/431, Cook Ave exit. Ext corridors. **Pets:** Very small. $15 one-time fee/room. Designated rooms, service with restrictions, supervision.

[SAVE] [S&] [✕] [🛏] [🏊]

▼ Extended StayAmerica Huntsville-U.S. Space and Rocket Center M
(256) 830-9110. **$64-$79.** 4751 Govenors House Dr. I-565, exit 17A, just s, then 0.5 mi w. Ext corridors. **Pets:** Accepted.

[ASK] [S&] [✕] [♿] [🐾] [✎] [🛏] [💻]

◆◆◆ ▼▼◆ Holiday Inn Hunstville Downtown LH 🐾
(256) 533-1400. **$88-$100.** 401 Williams Ave SW. Just w of Church St; downtown. Int corridors. **Pets:** Small, other species. $25 one-time fee/pet. Service with restrictions, supervision.

[SAVE] [S&] [✕] [🛏] [💻] [🍴] [🏊]

▼▼▼ La Quinta Inn & Suites Huntsville SH
(256) 830-8999. **$74-$94.** 4890 University Dr SE. I-565, exit 14B, 2.6 mi n on Research Park Blvd, then 1 mi e on US 72. Int corridors. **Pets:** Medium. Service with restrictions.

[ASK] [✕] [🛏] [💻] [🏊]

▼▼▼▼ La Quinta Inn Huntsville (Research Park) SH
(256) 830-2070. **$86-$96.** 4870 University Dr NW. I-565, exit 14B, 2.6 mi n on Research Park Blvd, then 1 mi e on US 72. Ext corridors. **Pets:** Medium. Service with restrictions.

[ASK] [✕] [✎] [🛏] [💻] [🏊]

▼▼▼ La Quinta Inn Huntsville (Space Center) SH
(256) 533-0756. **$76-$86.** 3141 University Dr (Hwy 72). I-565, exit 17A, 1.1 mi n on SR 53 (Jordan Ln), then 0.6 mi e on US 72. Ext corridors. **Pets:** Medium. Service with restrictions.

[ASK] [✕] [🛏] [💻] [🏊]

JACKSON

◆◆◆ ▼▼◆ Econo Lodge M
(251) 246-4111. **$58-$68.** 3680 N College Ave. I-I-65, exit 19, On US 43. Ext corridors. **Pets:** Accepted.

[SAVE] [S&] [✕] [🛏] [💻]

JASPER

▼▼ Jameson Inn SH
(205) 387-7710. **$54-$120.** 1100 Hwy 118. SR 118, 1.8 mi w of jct SR 69. Ext corridors. **Pets:** Small. $10 daily fee/pet. Service with restrictions, crate.

[ASK] [✕] [♿] [✎] [🛏] [💻] [🏊]

MADISON

▼ Motel 6–1087 M
(256) 772-7479. **$43-$55.** 8995 Madison Blvd. I-565, exit 8, just n on Wall Triana Hwy, then just w. Ext corridors. **Pets:** Medium, other species. Service with restrictions, supervision.

[S&] [✕] [✎] [🛏] [🏊]

▼▼▼ Ramada Inn & Conference Center LH
(256) 772-0701. **$90.** 8716 Madison Blvd. I-565, exit 8, just n on Wall Triana Hwy, then 0.4 mi e. Int corridors. **Pets:** Accepted.

[ASK] [S&] [✕] [♿] [🛏] [💻] [🍴] [🏊]

MOBILE

▼▼▼ Americas Best Value Inn & Suites M
(251) 344-2121. **$60-$100.** 162 W I-65 Service Rd. I-65, exit 4, just w on Dauphin St, then 0.5 mi s. Ext corridors. **Pets:** Accepted.

[ASK] [S&] [✕] [♿] [🛏] [💻] [🏊]

▼▼▼ Drury Inn-Mobile SH
(251) 344-7700. **$80-$130.** 824 W I-65 Service Rd S. I-65, exit 3 (Airport Blvd), just w, then just s on service road. Int corridors. **Pets:** Large, other species. Service with restrictions, supervision.

[ASK] [✕] [🛏] [💻] [🏊]

▼▼◆ Holiday Inn-Bellingrath Gardens SH 🐾
(251) 666-5600. **$84-$111.** 5465 Hwy 90 W. I-10, exit 15B, just e on US 90, then just s on Coca Cola Rd. Int corridors. **Pets:** Medium, other species. $25 daily fee/room. Service with restrictions, supervision.

[ASK] [✕] [🐾] [✎] [🛏] [💻] [🍴] [🏊]

▼▼▼ La Quinta Inn Mobile M
(251) 343-4051. **$95-$105.** 816 W I-65 Service Rd S. I-65, exit 3 (Airport Blvd), just w, then just s. Ext/int corridors. **Pets:** Medium. Service with restrictions.

[ASK] [✕] [🛏] [💻] [🏊]

▼ Motel 6 #608 M
(251) 660-1483. **$55-$68.** 5488 Inn Rd. I-10, exit 15B, just e on US 90, then just n. Ext corridors. **Pets:** Medium, other species. Service with restrictions, supervision.

[S&] [✕] [✎] [🛏] [🏊]

◆◆◆ ▼ Olsson Motel M
(251) 661-5331. **$65-$80, 15 day notice.** 4137 Government Blvd. I-65, exit 1, 2 mi w on US 90. Ext corridors. **Pets:** Small, dogs only. $7 daily fee/pet. Service with restrictions, supervision.

[SAVE] [✕] [🛏]

▼▼ Red Roof Inn North M
(251) 476-2004. **$54-$70.** 33 I-65 Service Rd E. I-65, exit 4, just e on Dauphin St, just s on Springdale Blvd, then just w. Ext corridors. **Pets:** Medium, other species. Service with restrictions, supervision.

[✕]

▼▼▼ Residence Inn by Marriott Mobile SH
(251) 304-0570. **$119-$159.** 950 W I-65 Service Rd S. I-65, exit 3 (Airport Blvd), just w, then 0.4 mi s. Int corridors. **Pets:** Accepted.

[ASK] [✕] [♿] [✎] [🛏] [💻] [🏊] [✕]

▼▼▼ **TownePlace Suites by Marriott** SH
(251) 345-9588. **$98-$149.** 1075 Montlimar Dr. I-65, exit 3 (Airport Blvd), 0.5 mi w, then 0.5 mi s. Int corridors. **Pets:** $75 one-time fee/room. Service with restrictions.
ASK S✗ X ✖ 🖥 🏊

MONROEVILLE

🔺🔺🔺 ▼▼ **Americas Best Value Inn** M
(251) 743-3154. **$50-$95.** 50 Hwy 21. On SR 21, just s of jct US 84. Ext corridors. **Pets:** Accepted.
SAVE S✗ X ✖

▼▼ **Best Western of Monroeville** M
(251) 575-9999. **$52-$99.** 4419 S Alabama Ave. On SR 21, 0.5 mi n of jct US 84. Ext corridors. **Pets:** Accepted.
ASK S✗ X ✖ 🖥 🏊

▼▼ **Days Inn of Monroeville** M
(251) 743-3297. **$60-$90.** 4389 S Alabama Ave. On SR 21, 0.5 mi n of jct US 84. Ext corridors. **Pets:** Accepted.
ASK S✗ X ✖ 🖥 🏊

🔺🔺🔺 ▼▼▼ **Holiday Inn Express** SH
(251) 743-3333. **$75-$185.** 120 Hwy 21 S. On SR 21, just s of jct US 84. Int corridors. **Pets:** Accepted.
SAVE S✗ X ✖ 🖥 🏊

MONTGOMERY

▼▼ **America's Best Inns** SH
(334) 270-9199. **$66-$99, 3 day notice.** 5135 Carmichael Rd. I-85, exit 6, just s on Eastern Blvd, then just w. Int corridors. **Pets:** Small, other species. Service with restrictions, supervision.
ASK X 🏊 🖥 🏊

▼▼ **Best Western Monticello Inn** M
(334) 277-4442. **$62.** 5837 Monticello Dr. I-85, exit 6, just n on Eastern Blvd, then just e. Ext corridors. **Pets:** Accepted.
ASK S✗ X ✖ 🖥 🏊

🔺🔺🔺 ▼▼▼ **Days Inn Midtown** M
(334) 269-9611. **$59-$64.** 2625 Zelda Rd. I-85, exit 3, just s on Ann St. Ext corridors. **Pets:** $5 daily fee/pet. Service with restrictions, supervision.
SAVE S✗ X ✖ 🖥 🏊

▼▼▼ **Drury Inn & Suites-Montgomery** SH
(334) 273-1101. **$80-$170.** 1124 Eastern Blvd. I-85, exit 6, just n. Int corridors. **Pets:** Large, other species. Service with restrictions, supervision.
ASK X 🏊 🖥 🏊

▼▼ **Econo Lodge** M
(334) 284-3400. **$60-$70.** 4135 Troy Hwy. On US 82/231, 0.7 mi e of jct South and East blvds. Ext corridors. **Pets:** Very small, dogs only. $10 daily fee/pet. Designated rooms, no service, supervision.
ASK S✗ X ✖ 🖥 🏊

🔺🔺🔺 ▼▼▼ **Embassy Suites Montgomery Conference Center** LH
(334) 269-5055. **$99-$229.** 300 Tallapoosa St. Between Motton and Commerce sts; in historic downtown. Int corridors. **Pets:** Accepted.
SAVE X 🏊 🖥 🍴 🏊 ✖

▼▼ **Extended StayAmerica Montgomery-Eastern Blvd** M
(334) 279-1204. **$54-$69.** 2491 Eastern Blvd. I-85, exit 6, 1.3 mi s on US 231. Ext corridors. **Pets:** Accepted.
ASK S✗ X ✖ 🖥

▼▼ **Holiday Inn-East** SH
(334) 272-0370. **$65-$79.** 1185 Eastern Bypass. I-85, exit 6, just n. Ext/int corridors. **Pets:** Accepted.
ASK S✗ X 🏊 🖥 🍴 🏊 ✖

▼▼▼ **La Quinta Inn & Suites Montgomery** SH
(334) 277-6000. **$74-$94.** 5225 Carmichael Rd. I-85, exit 6, just s on Eastern Blvd, then just w. Int corridors. **Pets:** Medium. Service with restrictions.
ASK X 🖥 🏊

▼▼▼ **La Quinta Inn Montgomery** M
(334) 271-1620. **$85-$95.** 1280 East Blvd. I-85, exit 6, just s. Ext corridors. **Pets:** Medium. Service with restrictions.
ASK X 🖥 🏊

▼ **Motel 6 #149** M
(334) 277-6748. **$45-$61.** 1051 Eastern Blvd. I-85, exit 6, just n. Ext corridors. **Pets:** Medium, other species. Service with restrictions, supervision.
S✗ X 🏊

🔺🔺🔺 ▼▼▼ **Residence Inn by Marriott** SH
(334) 270-3300. **$169-$179.** 1200 Hilmar Ct. I-85, exit 6, just s on Eastern Blvd, then just e. Ext/int corridors. **Pets:** Accepted.
SAVE S✗ X 🖥 🖥 🏊 ✖

▼▼ **StudioPLUS** SH
(334) 273-0075. **Call for rates.** 5115 Carmichael Rd. I-85, exit 6, 0.5 mi s on US 231. Int corridors. **Pets:** Accepted.
X 🖥 🏊

▼▼ **TownePlace Suites by Marriott** SH
(334) 396-5505. **$119.** 5047 Towneplace Dr. I-85, exit 6, just s on Eastern Blvd, then just w on Carmichael Rd. Int corridors. **Pets:** Accepted.
ASK S✗ X 🏊 🖥 🏊

OPELIKA

▼▼ **Days Inn Opelika** M
(334) 749-5080. **$68-$70, 14 day notice.** 1014 Anand Ave. I-85, exit 62, just e on US 280. Ext corridors. **Pets:** Small. $20 daily fee/pet. Designated rooms, service with restrictions, supervision.
ASK S✗ X 🖥 🏊

OXFORD

🔺🔺🔺 ▼▼ **Econo Lodge Oxford** M
(256) 831-9480. **$48-$180.** 25 Elm St. I-20, exit 185, just s. Ext corridors. **Pets:** Other species. $10 daily fee/pet. Service with restrictions, crate.
SAVE S✗ X 🖥 🖥 🏊

▼▼ **Jameson Inn Oxford** M
(256) 835-2170. **$54-$120.** 161 Colonial Dr. I-20, exit 188, just n, then w. Ext corridors. **Pets:** Small. $10 daily fee/pet. Service with restrictions, crate.
ASK X 🏊 🖥 🏊

▼ **Motel 6 #542** M
(256) 831-5463. **$40-$53.** 202 Grace St. I-20, exit 185, just s. Ext corridors. **Pets:** Medium, other species. Service with restrictions, supervision.
S✗ X 🏊 🖥 🏊

▼▼ **Quality Inn** SH
(256) 831-3410. **$49-$199.** US 78 & SR 21. I-20, exit 185, just n. Ext corridors. **Pets:** Accepted.
X 🖥 🍴 🏊

OZARK

🔺🔺🔺 ▼▼ **All American Ozark Inn** M
(334) 774-5166. **$55-$65.** 2064 Hwy 231 S. 1 mi s of jct SR 249. Ext corridors. **Pets:** Accepted.
SAVE S✗ X 🖥 🖥 🏊

▼▼ **Jameson Inn** M
(334) 774-0233. **$54-$120.** 1360 S US Hwy 231. 0.3 mi s of jct SR 249. Ext corridors. **Pets:** Small. $10 daily fee/pet. Service with restrictions, crate.
ASK X 🏊 🖥 🖥 🏊

(AAA) ▼▼▼▼ Quality Inn & Suites-Ozark/Ft Rucker SH
(334) 774-7300. **$70.** 858 US 231 S. Just n of jct SR 249. Ext corridors.
Pets: Large, other species. $25 one-time fee/pet. Service with restrictions,
supervision.
[SAVE] [Sₒ] [✕] [🖥] [💻] [🍴] [≈]

PRATTVILLE

▼▼ Jameson Inn SH
(334) 361-6463. **$54-$120.** 104 Jameson Ct. I-65, exit 179, 1 mi w. Ext
corridors. **Pets:** Small. $10 daily fee/pet. Service with restrictions, crate.
[ASK] [✕] [🗁] [🖥] [💻] [≈]

PRICEVILLE

(AAA) ▼▼▼ Comfort Inn SH
(256) 355-1037. **$59-$150.** 3239 Point Mallard Pkwy. I-65, exit 334, just
w. Int corridors. **Pets:** Accepted.
[SAVE] [Sₒ] [✕] [🗁] [🖥] [💻] [≈]

▼▼ Days Inn SH
(256) 355-3297. **$49-$99.** 63 Marco Dr. I-65, exit 334, just e. Ext
corridors. **Pets:** Accepted.
[ASK] [Sₒ] [✕] [🖥] [💻] [≈]

SCOTTSBORO

▼▼ Americas Best Value Inn & Suites SH
(256) 259-4300. **$49-$59.** 46 Micah Way. On US 72, just s of jct SR 35.
Ext corridors. **Pets:** Accepted.
[ASK] [Sₒ] [✕] [🖥] [💻] [≈]

▼▼ Jameson Inn SH
(256) 574-6666. **$54-$120.** 208 Micah Way. On US 72, just s of jct SR
35. Ext corridors. **Pets:** Small. $10 daily fee/pet. Service with restrictions,
crate.
[ASK] [✕] [🖥] [💻] [≈]

SELMA

▼▼ Comfort Inn SH
(334) 875-5700. **$60-$75.** 1812 Hwy 14 E. Jct SR 14 and US 80
Bypass. Int corridors. **Pets:** Accepted.
[ASK] [Sₒ] [✕] [🖥] [💻] [≈]

▼▼ Jameson Inn M
(334) 874-8600. **$54-$120.** 2420 Broad St. On SR 22, just n of jct US
80. Ext corridors. **Pets:** Small. $10 daily fee/pet. Service with restrictions,
crate.
[ASK] [✕] [🖥] [💻] [≈]

STEVENSON

▼ Budget Host Inn M
(256) 437-2215. **$50-$55, 3 day notice.** 42973 US Hwy 72. On US 72,
just s of CR 85. Ext corridors. **Pets:** Accepted.
[ASK] [Sₒ] [✕] [🖥] [💻]

SYLACAUGA

▼▼ Jameson Inn SH
(256) 245-4141. **$54-$120.** 89 Gene Stewart Blvd. Off US 280, just s.
Ext corridors. **Pets:** Small. $10 daily fee/pet. Service with restrictions,
crate.
[ASK] [✕] [🖥] [💻] [≈]

TROY

▼▼ Holiday Inn Express M
(334) 670-0012. **$74.** Hwy 231 at US 29. On US 231, just n of jct US
29. Ext corridors. **Pets:** $10 daily fee/room. Service with restrictions,
supervision.
[ASK] [✕] [🖥] [💻]

(AAA) ▼▼▼▼ Holiday Inn of Troy SH
(334) 566-1150. **$74-$99.** Hwy 231 at US 29. On US 231, just n of jct
US 29. Ext corridors. **Pets:** Accepted.
[SAVE] [Sₒ] [✕] [🖥] [💻] [🍴] [≈]

TUSCALOOSA

(AAA) ▼▼ Americas Best Value Inn SH
(205) 556-7950. **$45-$100.** 3501 McFarland Blvd. I-59/20, exit 73, just
ne on US 82. Ext corridors. **Pets:** Medium, other species. Designated
rooms, service with restrictions, supervision.
[SAVE] [✕] [🖥] [💻] [≈]

▼▼ Jameson Inn SH
(205) 345-5018. **$54-$120.** 5021 Oscar Baxter Rd. I-59/20, exit 71A,
just s. Ext corridors. **Pets:** Small. $10 daily fee/pet. Service with restric-
tions, crate.
[ASK] [✕] [🖥] [💻] [≈]

▼▼ La Quinta Inn Tuscaloosa M
(205) 349-3270. **$80-$90.** 4122 McFarland Blvd E. I-59/20, exit 73, just
sw on US 82. Ext corridors. **Pets:** Medium. Service with restrictions.
[ASK] [✕] [🖥] [💻] [≈]

(AAA) ▼ Masters Inn M
(205) 556-2010. **$35-$39.** 3600 McFarland Blvd. I-59/20, exit 73, just
nw on US 82. Ext corridors. **Pets:** Small. $20 one-time fee/pet. Service
with restrictions, crate.
[SAVE] [Sₒ] [✕] [🖥] [≈]

▼ Motel 6 #432 M
(205) 759-4942. **$45-$58.** 4700 McFarland Blvd E. I-59/20, exit 73, just
se on US 82. Ext corridors. **Pets:** Medium, other species. Service with
restrictions, supervision.
[Sₒ] [✕] [🗁] [🖥] [≈]

VANCE

▼▼▼ Baymont Inn & Suites SH
(205) 556-3606. **$72-$100, 14 day notice.** 11170 Will Walker
Rd/Daimler Benz Blvd. I-59/20, exit 89 southbound, just s; exit north-
bound, 0.8 mi n on Mercedes Dr, 0.3 mi w, then just s. Int corridors.
Pets: Accepted.
[ASK] [Sₒ] [✕] [🅼] [🗁] [🖥] [💻]

ALASKA

ANCHORAGE

Best Western Barratt Inn SH
(907) 243-3131. **$85-$189.** 4616 Spenard Rd. International Airport Rd; just ne of jct Jewel Lake and Spenard rds. Ext/int corridors. **Pets:** Medium. $10 daily fee/pet. Designated rooms, service with restrictions, supervision.

Comfort Inn Ship Creek SH
(907) 277-6887. **$79-$249.** 111 W Ship Creek Ave. At 3rd and E sts, 0.3 mi n on E St, across the railway, just e on Ship Creek Ave; downtown. Int corridors. **Pets:** $100 deposit/pet. Designated rooms, service with restrictions, supervision.

Days Inn Downtown SH
(907) 276-7226. **$62-$250.** 321 E 5th Ave. At Cordova and E 5th Ave; downtown. Ext/int corridors. **Pets:** Accepted.

Hilton Anchorage LH
(907) 272-7411. **$109-$419, 3 day notice.** 500 W 3rd Ave. At E St; downtown. Int corridors. **Pets:** Dogs only. $25 daily fee/room. Service with restrictions, supervision.

Long House Alaskan Hotel SH
(907) 243-2133. **$69-$189.** 4335 Wisconsin St. International Airport Rd, 1.5 mi ne on Spenard Rd, nw on Wisconsin St at 43rd Ave, then just e. Int corridors. **Pets:** Other species. $150 deposit/pet. Designated rooms, service with restrictions, supervision.

Merrill Field Inn M
(907) 276-4547. **$55-$145.** 420 Sitka St. 1 mi e via US 1 (Glenn Hwy). Ext corridors. **Pets:** $7 one-time fee/pet. Service with restrictions, supervision.

Microtel Inn & Suites SH
(907) 245-5002. **$63-$135.** 5205 Northwood Dr. 1.7 mi e of airport. Int corridors. **Pets:** Accepted.

Millennium Alaskan Hotel Anchorage LH
(907) 243-2300. **$140-$269.** 4800 Spenard Rd. International Airport Rd; just ne from jct Jewel Lake and Spenard rds. Int corridors. **Pets:** Accepted.

Parkwood Inn M
(907) 563-3590. **$69-$179.** 4455 Juneau St. Jct International Airport Rd and Old Seward Hwy, 0.4 mi n on Old Seward Hwy, just e on 45th St. Ext corridors. **Pets:** Other species. $50 deposit/pet, $5 daily fee/pet. Designated rooms, service with restrictions.

Ramada Anchorage Downtown SH
(907) 272-7561. **$79-$209.** 115 E 3rd Ave. Jct Barrow St; downtown. Ext/int corridors. **Pets:** Medium, dogs only. $100 deposit/pet, $10 daily fee/pet. Designated rooms, service with restrictions, supervision.

Red Roof Inn M
(907) 274-1650. **$59-$149.** 1104 E 5th Ave. At Karluk St. Ext/int corridors. **Pets:** Medium. Service with restrictions, supervision.

Sheraton Anchorage Hotel LH
(907) 276-8700. **$199-$359.** 401 E 6th Ave. 6th Ave and Denali St. Int corridors. **Pets:** Medium, dogs only. Service with restrictions, supervision.

Westmark Anchorage LH
(907) 276-7676. **$80-$179.** 720 W 5th Ave. At G St and W 5th Ave; downtown. Int corridors. **Pets:** Accepted.

CANTWELL

Backwoods Lodge M
(907) 768-2232. **$90-$160, 10 day notice.** Denali Hwy MM 133.8. Parks Hwy, (Milepost 210), just e on Denali Hwy. Ext corridors. **Pets:** Medium. Service with restrictions, supervision.

DENALI NATIONAL PARK AND PRESERVE

McKinley Chalet Resort LH
(907) 683-8200. **$199-$269, 7 day notice.** Milepost 238 (Parks Hwy). Milepost 238.5 on SR 3 (Parks Hwy). Ext/int corridors. **Pets:** Accepted.

EAGLE RIVER

Eagle River Microtel Inn & Suites SH
(907) 622-6000. **$69-$159.** 13049 Old Glenn Hwy. Jct Glenn Hwy (SR 1), exit Eagle River, just e, then just s. Int corridors. **Pets:** Other species. $15 daily fee/pet. Designated rooms, service with restrictions, crate.

Eagle River Motel M
(907) 694-5000. **$54-$109, 3 day notice.** 11111 Old Eagle River Rd. Glenn Hwy, exit Eagle River, just e; center. Ext corridors. **Pets:** Other species. $10 daily fee/pet. Designated rooms, service with restrictions, supervision.

FAIRBANKS

Best Western Fairbanks Inn SH
(907) 456-6602. **$89-$179.** 1521 S Cushman St. Just s of Airport Way. Int corridors. **Pets:** Large. $10 daily fee/pet. Designated rooms, service with restrictions, supervision.

Comfort Inn-Chena River SH
(907) 479-8080. **$79-$180.** 1908 Chena Landings Loop. Airport Way, just n on Peger Rd, then just e on Phillips Field Rd, follow signs in wooded area south of road. Int corridors. **Pets:** Accepted.

Pike's Waterfront Lodge SH
(907) 456-4500. **$99-$285.** 1850 Hoselton Rd. Jct Airport and Hoselton rds. Ext/int corridors. **Pets:** Accepted.

▼ Regency Fairbanks Hotel SH
(907) 452-3200. **$99-$250.** 95 10th Ave. Just w of SR 2 (Steese Expwy). Int corridors. **Pets:** Accepted.

▼ Super 8 Motel M
(907) 451-8888. **$75-$161.** 1909 Airport Way. Airport Way at Wilbur St. Int corridors. **Pets:** Other species. $10 one-time fee/pet. Service with restrictions, crate.

GUSTAVUS

▼▼▼ Glacier Bay's Bear Track Inn SH
(907) 697-3017. **$924-$1024.** 255 Rink Creek Rd. 7 mi e of airport; at end of Rink Creek Rd. Int corridors. **Pets:** Accepted.

HAINES

▲▲▲ ▼ Captain's Choice Inc Motel M
(907) 766-3111. **$86-$120.** 108 2nd Ave N. Jct 2nd Ave and Dalton St. Ext corridors. **Pets:** Other species. $15 one-time fee/room. Service with restrictions, supervision.

HOMER

▲▲▲ ▼▼ Best Western Bidarka Inn M
(907) 235-8148. **$70-$134.** 575 Sterling Hwy. 0.3 mi n on (SR 1) Sterling Hwy. Ext/int corridors. **Pets:** Other species. $10 daily fee/pet. Designated rooms, service with restrictions, supervision.

JUNEAU

▲▲▲ ▼▼ Westmark Baranof SH
(907) 586-2660. **$139-$179.** 127 N Franklin St. At 2nd and Franklin sts; downtown. Int corridors. **Pets:** Accepted.

KETCHIKAN

▲▲▲ ▼▼▼ Best Western Landing SH
(907) 225-5166. **$109-$210.** 3434 Tongass Ave. Across from the Alaska Marine Hwy ferry terminal. Ext/int corridors. **Pets:** Other species. $10 daily fee/pet. Designated rooms, service with restrictions, supervision.

▲▲▲ ▼▼▼ Cape Fox Lodge LH
(907) 225-8001. **$100-$200.** 800 Venetia Way. Above Creek St (Tramway from Creek St). Ext/int corridors. **Pets:** No service.

KODIAK

▲▲▲ ▼▼▼ Best Western Kodiak Inn SH
(907) 486-5712. **$99-$179.** 236 W Rezanof Dr. 0.3 mi w of ferry terminal; center. Ext/int corridors. **Pets:** Medium. $50 deposit/room, $25 one-time fee/pet. Designated rooms.

▼▼ Comfort Inn Kodiak SH
(907) 487-2700. **$117-$235.** 1395 Airport Way. Adjacent to airport. Int corridors. **Pets:** Accepted.

PALMER

▲▲▲ ▼ Peak Inn Motel M
(907) 746-5757. **$50-$99.** 775 W Evergreen Ave. Just w of Glenn Hwy (SR 1). Ext corridors. **Pets:** $10 daily fee/room. Service with restrictions, supervision.

SITKA

▲▲▲ ▼▼▼ Shee Atika Totem Square Inn SH ❀
(907) 747-3693. **$89-$199.** 201 Katlian St. Center; in Totem Square Complex, near Municipal Office. Int corridors. **Pets:** Small, other species. $50 deposit/room, $10 daily fee/pet. Service with restrictions, crate.

SKAGWAY

▲▲▲ ▼ Westmark Inn Skagway SH
(907) 983-6000. **$99-$129.** 3rd & Spring St. Downtown. Ext/int corridors. **Pets:** Accepted.

SOLDOTNA

▲▲▲ ▼▼▼ Alaskan Serenity Bed and Breakfast BB
(907) 262-6648. **$59-$180, 30 day notice.** 41598 Aksala Ln. Sterling Hwy (SR 1), 1.5 mi e, 1.6 mi n on Mackey Lake Rd, then 0.5 mi e on Denise Lake Rd. Ext/int corridors. **Pets:** Other species. $25 one-time fee/pet. Designated rooms, supervision.

TOK

▲▲▲ ▼▼▼ Cleft of the Rock Bed & Breakfast CA
(907) 883-4219. **$65-$150, 3 day notice.** 122 Sundog Tr. Jct SR 1 and 2 (Alaskan Hwy), 3 mi w on SR 2 (Alaskan Hwy) to Sundog Trail, then 0.5 mi n. Ext/int corridors. **Pets:** Other species. $10 daily fee/pet. Service with restrictions, supervision.

▲▲▲ ▼▼▼ Westmark Inn Tok M
(907) 883-5174. **$129.** Jct Alaska Hwy & Glenn Hwy. On SR 1; jct SR 2 (Alaskan Hwy). Ext corridors. **Pets:** Accepted.

TRAPPER CREEK

▼▼ Gate Creek Cabins CA
(907) 733-1393. **$98-$130, 10 day notice.** Mile 10.5 Petersville Rd. From MM 114 (Parks Hwy), 10.5 mi w at Petersville Rd. Ext corridors. **Pets:** Accepted.

VALDEZ

▲▲▲ ▼▼▼ Best Western Valdez Harbor Inn SH
(907) 835-3434. **$99-$179.** 100 N Harbor Dr. Just s at Meals Dr. Int corridors. **Pets:** Small. $50 deposit/pet, $10 daily fee/pet. Designated rooms, service with restrictions, supervision.

WASILLA

▲▲▲ ▼▼▼ Best Western Lake Lucille Inn SH
(907) 373-1776. **$99-$219.** 1300 W Lake Lucille Dr. George Parks Hwy (SR 3), just w on Hallea Ln; center. Int corridors. **Pets:** Accepted.

▲▲▲ ▼▼▼ Grandview Inn & Suites SH
(907) 357-7666. **$79-$199.** 2900 E Parks Hwy. 1 mi n of jct Parks Hwy and Fairview Loop exit. Int corridors. **Pets:** Other species. $10 daily fee/pet. Designated rooms, service with restrictions, supervision.

ARIZONA

AJO

◇ La Siesta Motel Ⓜ
(520) 387-6569. **$50.** 2561 N Ajo-Gila Bend Hwy. On SR 85, 1.8 mi n of town plaza. Ext corridors. **Pets:** Service with restrictions, supervision.

BELLEMONT

◆◆◆ Bellemont Microtel Inn 🆂🅷
(928) 556-9599. **$49-$99.** 12380 W Interstate Hwy 40. I-40, exit 185, just n. Int corridors. **Pets:** Very small, dogs only. $20 daily fee/pet. Designated rooms, service with restrictions, supervision.

BENSON

◆◆ Baymont Inn & Suites Ⓜ
(520) 586-3646. **$69-$99.** 699 N Ocotillo Rd. I-10, exit 304, just s. Ext corridors. **Pets:** Accepted.

BISBEE

◆◆◆ Audrey's Inn 🅲🅾
(520) 227-6120. **$95.** 20 Brewery Ave. Just ne of Main St; in historic district. Int corridors. **Pets:** Accepted.

◆◆◆ San Jose Lodge Ⓜ
(520) 432-5761. **$75-$145, 3 day notice.** 1002 Naco Hwy. Off of SR 92 W, 1.5 mi s on Naco Hwy. Ext corridors. **Pets:** Medium, dogs only. $10 daily fee/pet. Designated rooms, service with restrictions, supervision.

BULLHEAD CITY

◆◆◆◆ Best Western Bullhead City Inn 🆂🅷
(928) 754-3000. **$59-$89.** 1126 Hwy 95. 1.8 mi s of Laughlin Bridge. Ext corridors. **Pets:** Medium. $20 one-time fee/room. Service with restrictions, supervision.

◆◆◆ Budget Host Inn Ⓜ
(928) 763-1002. **$65-$75.** 1616 Hwy 95. Jct SR 68, 3.2 mi s. Int corridors. **Pets:** Very small. $5 daily fee/pet. Service with restrictions, supervision.

◆◆◆ Lake Mohave Resort Motel Ⓜ 🐾
(928) 754-3245. **$60-$120, 3 day notice.** 2690 E Katherine Spur Rd. Jct SR 95, 1.5 mi e on SR 68, 1 mi n, then 5.4 mi e; at Katherine Landing; in Lake Mead National Recreation area. Ext corridors. **Pets:** Large, other species. $10 daily fee/pet. Service with restrictions, supervision.

AJO *(continued)*

◆◆ Lodge on The River Ⓜ 🐾
(928) 758-8080. **$40-$99, 3 day notice.** 1717 Hwy 95. 3.8 mi s of Laughlin Bridge. Ext corridors. **Pets:** Large. $10 daily fee/pet. Designated rooms, service with restrictions, supervision.

CAMERON

◆◆◆ Cameron Trading Post Motel, Restaurant & Gift Shop 🆂🅷
(928) 679-2231. **$59-$99.** US 89. 1 mi from the east gate turn off. Ext corridors. **Pets:** Accepted.

CAMP VERDE

◆◆◆ Comfort Inn-Camp Verde 🆂🅷
(928) 567-9000. **$59-$139.** 340 N Goswick Way. I-17, exit 287, just e, then just s. Int corridors. **Pets:** Medium, other species. $15 one-time fee/pet. Designated rooms, service with restrictions, supervision.

◆◆◆ Days Inn & Suites of Camp Verde 🆂🅷
(928) 567-3700. **$50-$99.** 1640 W Hwy 260. I-17, exit 287, just e, then just n. Int corridors. **Pets:** Other species. $10 daily fee/pet. Designated rooms, service with restrictions, supervision.

◆◆◆ The Lodge At Cliff Castle Casino 🆂🅷
(928) 567-6611. **$70-$110.** 333 Middle Verde Rd. I-17, exit 289, 0.4 mi se. Ext corridors. **Pets:** Medium. $20 one-time fee/pet. Designated rooms, service with restrictions, supervision.

◆◆ Super 8 Motel-Camp Verde Ⓜ
(928) 567-2622. **$59-$139.** 1550 W Hwy 260. I-17, exit 287, just e. Int corridors. **Pets:** Small. $10 daily fee/pet. Designated rooms, service with restrictions, supervision.

CASA GRANDE

◆◆◆◆ Best Western Casa Grande 🆂🅷
(520) 836-1600. **$79-$169.** 665 N Via Del Cielo Rd. I-10, exit 194 (SR 287), 1 mi w. Ext corridors. **Pets:** Very small, dogs only. $10 daily fee/pet. Designated rooms, service with restrictions, supervision.

◆◆ Holiday Inn Casa Grande 🆂🅷
(520) 426-3500. **$70-$199.** 777 N Pinal Ave. I-10, exit 194 (SR 287), 3.9 mi w. Int corridors. **Pets:** Accepted.

◆ **Motel 6-1263** [M]
(520) 836-3323. **$45-$65.** 4965 N Sunland Gin Rd. I-10, exit 200, just w. Ext corridors. **Pets:** Medium, other species. Service with restrictions, supervision.
[SD] 🚭 ♿ ▣ 🏊

[AAA] ◆◆ **Super 8 Motel** [SH]
(520) 836-8800. **$99-$150.** 2066 E Florence Blvd. I-10, exit 194 (SR 287), 0.6 mi w. Int corridors. **Pets:** Dogs only. $10 daily fee/pet. Service with restrictions, supervision.
[SAVE] [SD] 🚭 ♿ ▣ 🏊

CHAMBERS

[AAA] ◆◆ **Chieftain Inn** [M]
(928) 688-2754. **$75-$150.** I-40 & 191 Interchange. I-40, exit 333, just s at jct US 191 N. Ext corridors. **Pets:** Accepted.
[SAVE] [SD] 🚭 🦻 ☕ 🍴

COTTONWOOD

[AAA] ◆◆◆ **Best Western Cottonwood Inn** [M]
(928) 634-5575. **$79-$129.** 993 S Main St. On SR 89A, at SR 260. Ext corridors. **Pets:** Small, dogs only. $10 daily fee/pet. Designated rooms, service with restrictions, supervision.
[SAVE] [SD] 🚭 ♿ ▣ ☕ 🏊

[AAA] ◆ **Little Daisy Motel** [M]
(928) 634-7865. **$50-$55.** 34 S Main St. On SR 89A, just n. Ext corridors. **Pets:** Other species. $20 deposit/room, $5 daily fee/pet. Service with restrictions, crate.
[SAVE] [SD] 🚭 ▣

[AAA] ◆◆ **Pines Motel** [M]
(928) 634-9975. **$54-$89.** 920 S Camino Real. Jct SR 260, just nw on SR 89A, then just s. Ext corridors. **Pets:** $10 one-time fee/room. Service with restrictions.
[SAVE] [SD] 🚭 ▣ ☕ 🏊

[AAA] ◆◆ **Quality Inn** [M]
(928) 634-4207. **$89-$99.** 301 W SR 89A. On SR 89A, 1.8 mi s of jct SR 260. Ext corridors. **Pets:** Medium. $20 one-time fee/room. Designated rooms, service with restrictions, supervision.
[SAVE] [SD] 🚭 ▣ ☕ 🍴 🏊

[AAA] ◆ **The View Motel** [M]
(928) 634-7581. **$58-$70.** 818 S Main St. On SR 89A, 0.4 mi nw of jct SR 260. Ext corridors. **Pets:** Dogs only. $10 daily fee/pet. Service with restrictions, supervision.
[SAVE] [SD] 🚭 ▣ 🏊

DOUGLAS

◆ **Motel 6 #305** [M]
(520) 364-2457. **$45-$55.** 111 16th St (SR 80). 1.2 mi e of jct SR 191. Ext corridors. **Pets:** Medium, other species. Service with restrictions, supervision.
[SD] 🚭 ▣ 🏊

EAGAR

◆◆ **Best Western Sunrise Inn** [M]
(928) 333-2540. **$75-$95.** 128 N Main St. From jct SR 260, just n; from jct US 60, 1.5 mi s. Ext corridors. **Pets:** Accepted.
🚭 🦻 ▣ ☕

EHRENBERG

[AAA] ◆◆ **Best Western Flying J Motel** [SH]
(928) 923-9711. **$79-$169, 5 day notice.** S Frontage Rd. I-10, exit 1, just s; 0.5 mi e of the Colorado River. Int corridors. **Pets:** Accepted.
[SAVE] [SD] 🚭 ▣ ☕ 🏊

FLAGSTAFF

[AAA] ◆◆ **Best Western Kings House** [M]
(928) 774-7186. **$45-$129.** 1560 E Route 66. I-40, exit 198 (Butler Ave), just w, just n on Enterprise, then just w. Ext corridors. **Pets:** Medium. $15 daily fee/pet. Service with restrictions, supervision.
[SAVE] [SD] 🚭 ▣ ☕ 🏊

[AAA] ◆◆◆ **Best Western Pony Soldier Inn and Suites** [SH] 🐾
(928) 526-2388. **$59-$119.** 3030 E Route 66. I-40, exit 201, just n, then 1 mi w. Int corridors. **Pets:** $15 one-time fee/room. Designated rooms, service with restrictions, supervision.
[SAVE] [SD] 🚭 🦻 ▣ ☕ 🏊

[AAA] ◆◆ **Comfort Inn I-17/I-40** [SH]
(928) 774-2225. **$59-$159.** 2355 S Beulah Blvd. I-40, exit 195, just n to Forest Meadows St, then 1 blk w. Int corridors. **Pets:** Accepted.
[SAVE] [SD] 🚭 🦻 ▣ ☕ 🏊

[AAA] ◆◆ **Days Inn East** [SH]
(928) 527-1477. **$49-$159.** 3601 E Lockett Rd. I-40, exit 201, just n, 0.5 mi w on I-40 business loop, then just n. Int corridors. **Pets:** Accepted.
[SAVE] [SD] 🚭 ▣ ☕ 🏊

[AAA] ◆◆ **Days Inn Route 66** [M] 🐾
(928) 774-5221. **$45-$115.** 1000 W Route 66. I-40, exit 195, 1.5 mi n on Milton Rd, then just w. Ext corridors. **Pets:** Other species. $10 daily fee/pet. Service with restrictions.
[SAVE] [SD] 🚭 🦻 ▣ ☕ 🏊

[AAA] ◆◆ **Econo Lodge-University** [M]
(928) 774-7326. **$49-$119.** 914 S Milton Rd. I-40, exit 195, 1.2 mi n. Ext corridors. **Pets:** Large, other species. $10 daily fee/pet. Supervision.
[SAVE] [SD] 🚭 ▣ ☕ 🏊

[AAA] ◆◆ **Howard Johnson Inn-Lucky Lane** [M]
(928) 779-5121. **$50-$150.** 2520 E Lucky Ln. I-40, exit 198 (Butler Ave), just n, then just e. Ext corridors. **Pets:** Small. $15 daily fee/pet. Designated rooms, service with restrictions, supervision.
[SAVE] [SD] 🚭 🦻 ▣ ☕ 🏊

◆◆◆ **La Quinta Inn & Suites** [SH]
(928) 556-8666. **$85-$164.** 2015 S Beulah Blvd. I-40, exit 195, just n to Forest Meadow St, then just w. Int corridors. **Pets:** No service, supervision.
[A$K] 🚭 🦻 ♿ ▣ ☕ 🏊

◆ **Motel 6-Flagstaff West #1000** [M]
(928) 779-3757. **$42-$59.** 2745 S Woodlands Village. I-40, exit 195, just n to Forest Meadows St, w to Beulah Blvd, just s, then just w. Ext corridors. **Pets:** Medium, other species. Service with restrictions, supervision.
[SD] 🚭 ♿M ♿ ▣ 🏊

[AAA] ◆◆ **Quality Inn I-40/I-17** [SH]
(928) 774-8771. **$47-$109.** 2000 S Milton Rd. I-40, exit 195, just n to Forest Meadows, then right. Int corridors. **Pets:** Other species. $10 daily fee/pet. Service with restrictions, supervision.
[SAVE] [SD] 🚭 🦻 ♿ ☕ 🏊

[AAA] ◆◆ **Quality Inn-Lucky Lane** [M]
(928) 226-7111. **$51-$65, 7 day notice.** 2500 E Lucky Ln. I-40, exit 198 (Butler Ave), just n, then just e. Ext corridors. **Pets:** Accepted.
[SAVE] [SD] 🚭 🦻 ▣ ☕ 🏊

[AAA] ◆◆ **Ramada Limited-Lucky Lane** [M]
(928) 779-3614. **$49-$119.** 2350 E Lucky Ln. I-40, exit 198 (Butler Ave), just n, then just e. Ext corridors. **Pets:** Accepted.
[SAVE] [SD] 🚭 🦻 ▣ ☕ 🏊

▼▼▼▼ **Residence Inn by Marriott Flagstaff** Ⓜ ❀
(928) 526-5555. **$60-$199.** 3440 N Country Club Dr. I-40, exit 201, 0.5 mi s. Ext/int corridors. **Pets:** Other species. $25 daily fee/room. Designated rooms, service with restrictions, supervision.

(ASK) (X) (🖊) (🖼) 🞐 🖵 🏊 (X)

ⒶⒶⒶ ▼▼▼ **Rodeway Inn East** 🅂🄷
(928) 526-2200. **$35-$89.** 2650 E Route 66. I-40, exit 201, 0.5 mi n, then 1.6 mi w. Ext corridors. **Pets:** Small, other species. $10 daily fee/pet. Designated rooms, crate.

(SAVE) (S🗗) (X) 🞐 🖵

ⒶⒶⒶ ▼▼▼ **Sleep Inn** Ⓜ
(928) 556-3000. **$60-$140.** 2765 S Woodlands Village Blvd. I-40, exit 195, just n to Forest Meadows St, w to Beulah Rd, just s, then just w. Int corridors. **Pets:** $50 deposit/room, $10 daily fee/pet. Service with restrictions, supervision.

(SAVE) (S🗗) (X) (🛏M) (🖊) (🖼) 🞐 🖵 🏊

ⒶⒶⒶ ▼▼▼ **Super 8-Lucky Lane** Ⓜ
(928) 773-4888. **$55-$239.** 2540 E Lucky Ln. I-40, exit 198 (Butler Ave), just n, then just e. Ext corridors. **Pets:** Small. $15 daily fee/pet. Designated rooms, service with restrictions, supervision.

(SAVE) (S🗗) (🖊) 🞐 🖵 🏊

ⒶⒶⒶ ▼▼▼ **Super 8 Motel** Ⓜ
(928) 774-4581. **$39-$125.** 602 W Route 66. I-40, exit 195, 1.5 mi n on SR 89A (Milton Rd), then just w. Ext corridors. **Pets:** Accepted.

(SAVE) (S🗗) (X) 🞐 🏊

ⒶⒶⒶ ▼▼▼ **Super 8 Motel East Flagstaff** Ⓜ
(928) 526-0818. **$39-$149.** 3725 Kasper Ave. I-40, exit 201, just n, 0.5 mi w on I-40 business loop, then just n. Int corridors. **Pets:** Accepted.

(SAVE) (S🗗) (X) (🖼) 🞐

ⒶⒶⒶ ▼▼ **Travel Inn** Ⓜ
(928) 774-3381. **$39-$109.** 801 W Route 66. I-40, exit 195, 1.2 mi n on Milton Rd, then just w. Ext corridors. **Pets:** Accepted.

(SAVE) (S🗗) (X) (🖊) 🞐

FLORENCE

▼▼▼ **Rancho Sonora Inn** Ⓜ
(520) 868-8000. **$79-$99, 7 day notice.** 9198 N Hwy 79. On SR 79, 5 mi s of SR 287. Ext corridors. **Pets:** Accepted.

(X) 🞐 🖵

FOREST LAKES

ⒶⒶⒶ ▼▼▼ **Forest Lakes Lodge** Ⓜ
(928) 535-4727. **$54-$79.** 876 AZ Hwy 260. On SR 260. Ext corridors. **Pets:** Small, dogs only. $10 one-time fee/pet. Service with restrictions, supervision.

(SAVE) (S🗗) (X) 🞐 (🗚)

GILA BEND

▼▼▼ **America's Choice Inn & Suites** Ⓜ ❀
(928) 683-6311. **$75.** 2888 Butterfield Tr. I-8, exit 119, just nw. Int corridors. **Pets:** Medium, other species. $5 one-time fee/room. Service with restrictions, supervision.

(ASK) (S🗗) (X) 🞐 🖵 🏊

ⒶⒶⒶ ▼▼▼ **Best Western Space Age Lodge** Ⓜ
(928) 683-2273. **$69-$149.** 401 E Pima St. Business Loop I-8; center. Ext corridors. **Pets:** Other species. Service with restrictions, supervision.

(SAVE) (S🗗) (X) 🞐 🖵 (¶¶) 🏊

GLOBE

▼▼▼ **Comfort Inn at Round Mountain Park** 🅂🄷
(928) 425-7575. **$69-$209.** 1515 South St. On US 60, 1 mi e of town. Ext corridors. **Pets:** Accepted.

(ASK) (S🗗) (X) 🞐 🖵 🏊

ⒶⒶⒶ ▼▼▼ **Motel 6 #4223** 🅂🄷
(928) 425-5741. **$50-$63.** 1699 E Ash St. On US 60, 1.3 mi e of town. Ext/int corridors. **Pets:** Medium, other species. Service with restrictions, supervision.

(SAVE) (S🗗) (X) (🖼) 🞐 🖵 🏊

GOLD CANYON

▼▼▼▼ **Gold Canyon Golf Resort** 🅻🄷
(480) 982-9090. **$135-$310, 3 day notice.** 6100 S Kings Ranch Rd. US 60, exit Kings Ranch Rd, 1 mi n. Ext corridors. **Pets:** Medium, other species. $75 one-time fee/room. Service with restrictions, supervision.

(ASK) (S🗗) (X) 🖵 (¶¶) 🏊 (X)

Grand Canyon National Park

GRAND CANYON NATIONAL PARK - SOUTH RIM

▼▼▼▼ **The Grand Hotel** 🅂🄷 ❀
(928) 638-3333. **$99-$199.** Hwy 64. On SR 64; 2 mi s of South Rim entrance. Int corridors. **Pets:** Medium. $50 deposit/pet, $25 daily fee/pet. Designated rooms, service with restrictions, supervision.

(ASK) (S🗗) (X) (🖼) 🞐 🖵 (¶¶) 🏊

ⒶⒶⒶ ▼▼▼ **Red Feather Lodge** 🅂🄷
(928) 638-2414. **$69-$159.** Hwy 64. On SR 64; 2 mi s of South Rim entrance. Ext/int corridors. **Pets:** Other species. $75 deposit/pet, $25 one-time fee/room. Designated rooms, service with restrictions, supervision.

(SAVE) (S🗗) (X) (🖊) (🖼) 🞐 🖵 (¶¶) 🏊

End Area

HEBER

ⒶⒶⒶ ▼▼▼ **Best Western Sawmill Inn** 🅂🄷
(928) 535-5053. **$72-$77.** 1877 Hwy 260. 0.5 mi e of center. Ext corridors. **Pets:** Accepted.

(SAVE) (X) (🖊) (🖼) 🞐 🖵

HOLBROOK

ⒶⒶⒶ ▼▼▼ **American Best Inn** Ⓜ
(928) 524-2654. **$40-$55.** 2211 E Navajo Blvd. I-40, exit 289, 1 mi w. Ext corridors. **Pets:** Other species. $5 one-time fee/pet. Designated rooms, supervision.

(SAVE) (S🗗) (X) 🞐 🖵

Best Western Adobe Inn M
(928) 524-3948. **$49-$99.** 615 W Hopi Dr. I-40, exit 285, 1 mi e on US 180 (Hopi Dr). Ext corridors. **Pets:** $10 daily fee/pet. Service with restrictions, supervision.

Best Western Arizonian Inn SH
(928) 524-2611. **$77-$90.** 2508 Navajo Blvd. I-40, exit 289, 0.5 mi w. Ext corridors. **Pets:** Medium, other species. $50 deposit/pet. Designated rooms, service with restrictions, supervision.

Comfort Inn SH
(928) 524-6131. **$55-$89.** 2602 E Navajo Blvd. I-40, exit 289, just w. Ext corridors. **Pets:** Accepted.

Econo Lodge SH
(928) 524-1448. **$39-$54.** 2596 E Navajo Blvd. I-40, exit 289, just w. Ext corridors. **Pets:** Accepted.

Holbrook Holiday Inn Express M
(928) 524-1466. **$99-$119.** 1308 E Navajo Blvd. I-40, exit 286, just e. Int corridors. **Pets:** Accepted.

JEROME

Connor Hotel of Jerome SH
(928) 634-5006. **$95-$155, 3 day notice.** 164 Main St. Center. Int corridors. **Pets:** Accepted.

KAYENTA

Hampton Inn of Kayenta SH
(928) 697-3170. **$59-$139, 3 day notice.** Hwy 160. On US 160, just w. Int corridors. **Pets:** Accepted.

KINGMAN

Best Western A Wayfarer's Inn SH
(928) 753-6271. **$80-$115.** 2815 E Andy Devine Ave. I-40, exit 53, 0.5 mi w on Route 66. Ext corridors. **Pets:** Medium. $8 one-time fee/pet. Service with restrictions, supervision.

Best Western King's Inn & Suites SH
(928) 753-6101. **$87-$102.** 2930 E Route 66. I-40, exit 53, just w on Route 66. Ext corridors. **Pets:** Accepted.

Days Inn West M
(928) 753-7500. **$39-$89, 3 day notice.** 3023 E Andy Devine Ave. I-40, exit 53, just w on Route 66. **Pets:** Accepted.

Hill Top Motel M
(928) 753-2198. **$40-$92, 3 day notice.** 1901 E Andy Devine Ave. I-40, exit 53, 2 mi w on Route 66. **Pets:** Dogs only. $5 daily fee/pet. Service with restrictions, supervision.

Motel 6-1114 M
(928) 753-9222. **$48-$61.** 424 W Beale St. I-40, exit 48, just se on Business Loop I-40/US 93. Ext corridors. **Pets:** Medium, other species. Service with restrictions, supervision.

Motel 6-1366 M
(928) 757-7151. **$45-$57.** 3351 E Andy Devine Ave. I-40, exit 53, just e on Route 66. Ext corridors. **Pets:** Medium, other species. Service with restrictions, supervision.

Quality Inn M
(928) 753-4747. **$55-$130.** 1400 E Andy Devine Ave. I-40, exit 53, 2.5 mi sw on Route 66. Ext corridors. **Pets:** Medium. $10 one-time fee/room. Designated rooms, service with restrictions, supervision.

Super 8 Motel SH
(928) 757-4808. **$44-$99.** 3401 E Andy Devine Ave. I-40, exit 53, just e on Route 66. Int corridors. **Pets:** Other species. $15 daily fee/pet. Designated rooms, no service, supervision.

KOHLS RANCH

Kohl's Ranch Lodge CO
(928) 478-4211. **Call for rates (no credit cards).** 202 S Kohl's Ranch Lodge Rd. Jct SR 87 and 260 E, 16.6 mi e, just s. Ext/int corridors. **Pets:** Other species. $250 deposit/pet. Service with restrictions, supervision.

LAKE HAVASU CITY

Best Western Lake Place Inn SH
(928) 855-2146. **$69-$300, 3 day notice.** 31 Wing's Loop. 1 mi e of SR 95 via Swanson Ave; downtown. Ext corridors. **Pets:** Medium, dogs only. $10 daily fee/pet. Service with restrictions, supervision.

Hampton Inn Lake Havasu SH
(928) 855-4071. **$59-$159.** 245 London Bridge Rd. 0.5 mi n of London Bridge. Ext/int corridors. **Pets:** Accepted.

The Havasu Inn M
(928) 855-7841. **$50-$139.** 1700 N McCulloch Blvd. Just ne of Lake Havasu Ave; center. Ext corridors. **Pets:** Accepted.

Island Inn Hotel SH
(928) 680-0606. **$69-$300.** 1300 W McCulloch Blvd. 0.7 mi w of London Bridge/SR 95. Int corridors. **Pets:** Medium, dogs only. $10 daily fee/pet. Service with restrictions, supervision.

Island Suites SH
(928) 855-7333. **$50-$199, 3 day notice.** 236 S Lake Havasu Ave. Just s of jct McCulloch Blvd. Int corridors. **Pets:** Accepted.

Lake Havasu City Super 8 M
(928) 855-8844. **$55-$169.** 305 London Bridge Rd. Just w of SR 95, exit Palo Verde; 0.5 mi n of London Bridge. Int corridors. **Pets:** Accepted.

Motel 6 Lake Havasu M
(928) 855-3200. **$55-$103, 3 day notice.** 111 London Bridge Rd. 0.3 mi n of London Bridge. Int corridors. **Pets:** Medium, other species. Service with restrictions, supervision.

Ramada Inn Havasu M
(928) 855-1111. **$69-$139.** 271 S Lake Havasu Ave. SR 95, just e on Swanson Ave, just s. Ext corridors. **Pets:** $20 daily fee/room. Designated rooms, service with restrictions, supervision.

◆◆◆ ▼▼▼ **Travelodge-Lake Havasu City** 🅂🄷
(928) 680-9202. **$59-$89, 7 day notice.** 480 London Bridge Rd. 1 mi n of London Bridge. Int corridors. **Pets:** Medium, dogs only. $50 deposit/room, $10 daily fee/pet. Designated rooms, service with restrictions, supervision.

SAVE S🄳 ✕ 🖥 🖵

NOGALES

◆◆◆ ▼▼▼ **Best Western Siesta Motel** 🄼
(520) 287-4671. **$76-$85, 7 day notice.** 673 N Grand Ave. On Business Loop I-19, 1 mi n of International border. Ext corridors. **Pets:** Very small, dogs only. $10 daily fee/pet. Designated rooms, service with restrictions, supervision.

SAVE S🄳 ✕ 🖥 🖵 ≋

▼▼▼ **Motel 6 Nogales #71** 🄼
(520) 281-2951. **$45-$63.** 141 W Mariposa Rd. I-19, exit 4, 0.9 mi e. Ext corridors. **Pets:** Medium, other species. Service with restrictions, supervision.

S🄳 ✕ 🎖 🖥 ≋

PAGE

◆◆◆ ▼▼ **Americas Best Value Inn** 🄼
(928) 645-2858. **$54-$79, 3 day notice.** 75 S 7th Ave. 1 mi e of US 89 via SR 89L, just n of Lake Powell Blvd. Ext corridors. **Pets:** Accepted.

SAVE S🄳 ✕ 🎖

◆◆◆ ▼▼▼ **Best Western Arizona Inn** 🅂🄷
(928) 645-2466. **$54-$112.** 716 Rimview Dr. 0.7 mi e of US 89 via SR 89L. Int corridors. **Pets:** Small. $10 daily fee/pet, $10 one-time fee/pet. Designated rooms, service with restrictions, supervision.

SAVE S🄳 ✕ 🎖 🖥 🖵 ≋

◆◆◆ ▼▼▼ **Best Western at Lake Powell** 🅂🄷
(928) 645-5988. **$59-$139.** 208 N Lake Powell Blvd. 0.8 mi e of US 89 via SR 89L. Int corridors. **Pets:** Small. $20 one-time fee/pet. Designated rooms, service with restrictions, supervision.

SAVE S🄳 ✕ 🎖 🖥 🖵 ≋

◆◆◆ ▼▼▼ **Lake Powell Days Inn & Suites** 🅂🄷
(928) 645-2800. **$69-$189.** 961 N Hwy 89. On US 89, just s. Int corridors. **Pets:** $10 daily fee/pet. Service with restrictions, supervision.

SAVE S🄳 ✕ 🎖 🎖 🖥 🖵 ≋

◆◆◆ ▼▼▼ **Lake Powell Resort and Marina** 🄻🄷
(928) 645-2433. **$94-$198.** 100 Lakeshore Dr. 4 mi n of Glen Canyon Dam via US 89. Int corridors. **Pets:** $20 daily fee/pet. Designated rooms, service with restrictions, crate.

SAVE S🄳 ✕ 🎖 🖥 🖵 🍴 ≋ ✕

▼▼ **Linda's Lake Powell Condos** 🄲🄾
(928) 353-4591. **$88-$114, 3 day notice.** 1019 Tower Butte. 6 mi n on US 89. Ext corridors. **Pets:** Accepted.

A$K ✕ 🖥 🖵

◆◆◆ ▼ **Motel 6-Page/Lake Powell #4013** 🅂🄷
(928) 645-5888. **$55-$81.** 637 S Lake Powell Blvd. On Business Loop SR 89L, just e of US 89. Int corridors. **Pets:** Medium, other species. Service with restrictions, supervision.

SAVE S🄳 ✕ 🎖 ≋

◆◆◆ ▼▼▼ **Quality Inn, At Lake Powell** 🅂🄷
(928) 645-8851. **$54-$104.** 287 N Lake Powell Blvd. 0.8 mi e of US 89/SR 89L. Int corridors. **Pets:** Large, other species. Designated rooms, service with restrictions, supervision.

SAVE S🄳 ✕ 🎖 🖥 🖵 🍴 ≋

◆◆◆ ▼▼ **Super 8 Gateway to Lake Powell** 🅂🄷
(928) 645-5858. **$44-$84, 3 day notice.** 649 S Lake Powell Blvd. On SR 89L, just e of US 89. Int corridors. **Pets:** Small. $50 deposit/pet. Designated rooms, service with restrictions, supervision.

SAVE S🄳 ✕ 🎖 🖥 ≋

PARKER

◆◆◆ ▼▼ **Best Western Parker Inn** 🅂🄷
(928) 669-6060. **$69-$167, 7 day notice.** 1012 Geronimo Ave. SR 95, just e. Int corridors. **Pets:** Small. Designated rooms, service with restrictions, supervision.

SAVE S🄳 ✕ 🎖 🖥 🖵 ≋

PAYSON

◆◆◆ ▼ **Americas Best Value Inn** 🄼
(928) 474-2283. **$55-$100.** 811 S Beeline Hwy. On SR 87, 0.7 mi s of SR 260. Ext/int corridors. **Pets:** Small, dogs only. $15 daily fee/pet. Designated rooms, service with restrictions, supervision.

SAVE S🄳 ✕ 🖥 🖵

◆◆◆ ▼▼▼▼ **Best Western Payson Inn** 🅂🄷
(928) 474-3241. **$69-$149.** 801 N Beeline Hwy. On SR 87, 0.6 mi n of SR 260. Ext corridors. **Pets:** Dogs only. $10 daily fee/room. Service with restrictions, supervision.

SAVE S🄳 ✕ 🎖 🎖 🖥 🖵 ≋

◆◆◆ ▼▼ **Days Inn & Suites** 🅂🄷
(928) 474-9800. **$59-$149.** 301-A S Beeline Hwy. On SR 87, just s of SR 260. Int corridors. **Pets:** Small, other species. $10 daily fee/pet. Designated rooms, service with restrictions, supervision.

SAVE S🄳 ✕ 🎖 🖥 🖵 ≋

▼▼ **Majestic Mountain Inn** 🅂🄷
(928) 474-0185. **$69-$150.** 602 E Hwy 260. On SR 260, 0.5 mi e of SR 87. Ext corridors. **Pets:** Accepted.

A$K S🄳 ✕ 🎖 🖥 🖵 ≋

◆◆◆ ▼▼ **Paysonglo Lodge** 🅂🄷
(928) 474-2382. **$55-$92.** 1005 S Beeline Hwy. On SR 87, 0.9 mi s of SR 260. Ext corridors. **Pets:** Accepted.

SAVE S🄳 ✕ 🖥 🖵 ≋

◆◆◆ ▼▼ **Super 8 Inn & Suites of Payson** 🄼
(928) 474-5241. **$69-$99, 3 day notice.** 809 E Hwy 260. On SR 260, 0.8 mi e of SR 87. Ext corridors. **Pets:** Accepted.

SAVE S🄳 ✕ 🖥 🖵 ≋

PHOENIX METROPOLITAN AREA

APACHE JUNCTION

Apache Junction Motel
(480) 982-7702. **$45-$71, 3 day notice.** 1680 W Apache Tr. US 60, exit 195, 2 mi n, then just w. Ext corridors. **Pets:** Very small, dogs only. $20 one-time fee/pet. Designated rooms, service with restrictions, supervision.

Apache Junction Super 8
(480) 288-8888. **$54-$103.** 251 E 29th Ave. US 60, exit 196 (Idaho Rd/SR 88 E), just n. Ext/int corridors. **Pets:** Accepted.

BUCKEYE

Days Inn-Buckeye
(623) 386-5400. **$70-$200.** 25205 W Yuma Rd. I-10, exit 114 (Miller Rd), just sw. Ext corridors. **Pets:** Accepted.

CAREFREE

The Boulders Resort & Golden Door Spa
(480) 488-9009. **$119-$749, 21 day notice.** 34631 N Tom Darlington Dr. Scottsdale Rd, 11 mi n of Bell Rd. Ext corridors. **Pets:** Medium, dogs only. $100 one-time fee/room.

Carefree Resort & Villas
(480) 488-5300. **$120-$750, 3 day notice.** 37220 Mule Train Rd. SR 101, exit 36 (Pima Rd), 12.2 mi n to Cave Creek Rd, 1 mi w, then 0.4 mi n. Ext/int corridors. **Pets:** Accepted.

CHANDLER

Chandler Super 8
(480) 961-3888. **$85-$105.** 7171 W Chandler Blvd. I-10, exit 160 (Chandler Blvd), just e. Int corridors. **Pets:** Small, other species. $5 daily fee/pet. Designated rooms, service with restrictions.

Comfort Inn
(480) 705-8882. **$79-$149.** 255 N Kyrene Rd. I-10, exit 160 (Chandler Blvd), 1.5 mi e, then just n. Int corridors. **Pets:** Small. $10 daily fee/pet. Designated rooms, service with restrictions, supervision.

Crowne Plaza San Marcos Golf Resort
(480) 812-0900. **$129-$229.** 1 San Marcos Pl. Jct Chandler Blvd, just s on Arizona Ave, then just w on Buffalo St; in historic downtown. Ext corridors. **Pets:** Accepted.

Hawthorn Suites Chandler
(480) 705-8881. **$89-$169.** 5858 W Chandler Blvd. I-10, exit 160 (Chandler Blvd), 1.5 mi e. Int corridors. **Pets:** Accepted.

Homewood Suites by Hilton
(480) 753-6200. **$79-$239.** 7373 W Detroit St. I-10, exit 160 (Chandler Blvd), 0.4 mi e, n on 54th St, then just w. Int corridors. **Pets:** Accepted.

Park Plaza Phoenix/Chandler
(480) 961-4444. **$79-$147.** 7475 W Chandler Blvd. I-10, exit 160 (Chandler Blvd), just e, then just s on Southgate Dr. Int corridors. **Pets:** Accepted.

Red Roof Inn-Chandler
(480) 857-4969. **$49-$79.** 7400 W Boston St. I-10, exit 160 (Chandler Blvd), just e, then s on Southgate Dr. Int corridors. **Pets:** Medium, other species. Service with restrictions, supervision.

Residence Inn-Chandler Fashion Center
(480) 782-1551. **$135-$195.** 200 N Federal St. I-10, exit 160 (Chandler Blvd), 4.2 mi e, just n on N Metro Blvd, then just e. Int corridors. **Pets:** Accepted.

Southgate Motel
(480) 940-0308. **$45-$80.** 7445 W Chandler Blvd. I-10, exit 160 (Chandler Blvd), just e, then just s on Southgate Dr. Ext corridors. **Pets:** Accepted.

Windmill Suites of Chandler
(480) 812-9600. **$89-$179.** 3535 W Chandler Blvd. I-10, exit 160 (Chandler Blvd), 4 mi e. Int corridors. **Pets:** Other species. Service with restrictions, supervision.

FOUNTAIN HILLS

Holiday Inn Hotel & Suites-Fountain Hills/Mayo Clinic
(480) 837-6565. **$79-$219.** 12800 N Saguaro Blvd. Jct Shea Blvd, 2.2 mi n; across from the Fountain; center. Int corridors. **Pets:** Medium, other species. $25 one-time fee/pet. Service with restrictions, supervision.

GLENDALE

Quality Inn
(623) 939-9431. **$59-$159.** 7116 N 59th Ave. I-17, exit 205 (Glendale Ave), 4.3 mi w, then just n. Ext corridors. **Pets:** Accepted.

Ramada
(623) 412-2000. **$72-$143.** 7885 W Arrowhead Towne Center Dr. Loop 101, exit 14 (Bell Rd), 0.3 mi n, then just n on 79th Ave. Ext corridors. **Pets:** Small, other species. $10 daily fee/pet. Designated rooms, service with restrictions, crate.

GOODYEAR

Best Western Phoenix Goodyear Inn
(623) 932-3210. **$69-$159.** 55 N Litchfield Rd. I-10, exit 128, 0.8 mi s. Ext/int corridors. **Pets:** Large, other species. $10 daily fee/room.

Hampton Inn & Suites
(623) 536-1313. **$99-$199.** 2000 N Litchfield Rd. I-10, exit 128, 0.5 mi n. Int corridors. **Pets:** Accepted.

Holiday Inn Express
(623) 535-1313. **$99-$179.** 1313 N Litchfield Rd. I-10, exit 128, just n. Int corridors. **Pets:** Accepted.

Residence Inn by Marriott
(623) 866-1313. **$109-$199.** 2020 N Litchfield Rd. I-10, exit 128, 0.6 mi n. Int corridors. **Pets:** Other species. $100 one-time fee/room.

▼▼▼ **Wingate Inn & Suites** SH ❀
(623) 547-1313. **$99-$299.** 1188 N Dysart Rd. I-10, exit 129 (Dysart Rd), just n. Int corridors. **Pets:** $35 one-time fee/pet. Service with restrictions, crate.
ASK S❍ ✕ ❤ ❸ ▦ ➣

LITCHFIELD PARK

❹❹❹ ▼▼▼▼ **The Wigwam Resort** LH
(623) 935-3811. **$275-$925, 7 day notice.** 300 Wigwam Blvd. I-10, exit 128 (Litchfield Rd), 2.4 mi n, then 0.4 mi e. Ext corridors. **Pets:** Medium, dogs only. Service with restrictions, supervision.
SAVE S❍ ✕ ❤ ❸ ▦ ¶¶ ➣ ✕

MESA

❹❹❹ ▼▼▼▼ **Arizona Golf Resort & Conference Center** LH
(480) 832-3202. **$149-$219.** 425 S Power Rd. 1.3 mi n of US 60 (Superstition Frwy), exit 188 (Power Rd); southeast corner of Broadway and Power rds; entrance on Broadway Rd. Ext corridors. **Pets:** Other species. Service with restrictions.
SAVE ✕ ❤ ❸ ▦ ¶¶ ➣ ✕

❹❹❹ ▼▼▼ **Best Western Dobson Ranch Inn** LH
(480) 831-7000. **$75-$165.** 1666 S Dobson Rd. Just s of US 60 (Superstition Frwy), exit 177 (Dobson Rd). Ext/int corridors. **Pets:** Accepted.
SAVE S❍ ✕ ❸ ▦ ¶¶ ➣

❹❹❹ ▼▼▼ **Best Western Mesa Inn** SH ❀
(480) 964-8000. **$59-$131.** 1625 E Main St. 2 mi n of US 60 (Superstition Frwy), exit Stapley Dr, 0.5 mi e. Ext corridors. **Pets:** Other species. $20 one-time fee/room. Service with restrictions, supervision.
SAVE S❍ ✕ ❸ ▦ ➣

❹❹❹ ▼▼▼ **Best Western Mezona Inn** SH
(480) 834-9233. **$69-$169.** 250 W Main St. Just e of Country Club Dr; downtown. Ext corridors. **Pets:** Medium. $10 daily fee/room. Designated rooms, service with restrictions, supervision.
SAVE S❍ ✕ ❤ ❸ ▦ ➣

❹❹❹ ▼▼▼ **Best Western Superstition Springs Inn** SH
(480) 641-1164. **$74-$129.** 1342 S Power Rd. Just n of US 60 (Superstition Frwy), exit 188 (Power Rd); northwest corner of Power Rd and Hampton Ave. Ext corridors. **Pets:** Small, other species. $10 daily fee/pet. Designated rooms, service with restrictions, supervision.
SAVE S❍ ✕ ❤ ❸ ▦ ➣

❹❹❹ ▼▼▼ **Days Inn** SH
(480) 844-8900. **$59-$149.** 333 W Juanita. US 60 (Superstition Frwy), exit 179 (Country Club Dr), just s, then just e. Int corridors. **Pets:** Accepted.
SAVE S❍ ✕ ❤ ❸ ▦ ➣ ✕

▼▼ **Days Inn-East Mesa** M
(480) 981-8111. **$54-$119.** 5531 E Main St. 0.4 mi e of Higley Rd. Ext corridors. **Pets:** Accepted.
ASK S❍ ✕ ⎘ ❸ ▦ ➣

▼▼ **Extended StayAmerica-Phoenix/Mesa** SH
(480) 632-0201. **$59-$99.** 455 W Baseline Rd. US 60 (Superstition Frwy), exit 179 (Country Club Dr), 0.4 mi s on SR 87, then just w. Int corridors. **Pets:** Accepted.
ASK S❍ ✕ ❤ ❸

❹❹❹ ▼▼▼▼ **Holiday Inn Hotel & Suites** LH
(480) 964-7000. **$79-$139.** 1600 S Country Club Dr. US 60 (Superstition Frwy), exit 179 (Country Club Dr), just s. Ext/int corridors. **Pets:** Small. $20 one-time fee/room. Service with restrictions, supervision.
SAVE S❍ ✕ ❤ ❸ ▦ ¶¶ ➣

▼▼ **Homestead Studio Suites Hotel Phoenix-Mesa** SH
(480) 752-2266. **$64-$90.** 1920 W Isabella. Just s of US 60 (Superstition Frwy), exit 177 (Dobson Rd). Ext corridors. **Pets:** Accepted.
ASK S❍ ✕ ❤ ❸ ▦

▼▼▼ **La Quinta Inn & Suites Phoenix (Mesa East)** SH
(480) 654-1970. **$116-$169.** 6530 E Superstition Springs Blvd. US 60 (Superstition Frwy), exit 187 (Superstition Springs Blvd) eastbound, just se; exit 188 (Power Rd) westbound, just sw. Int corridors. **Pets:** Medium. Service with restrictions.
ASK ✕ ⚹M ⎘ ❤ ❸ ▦ ➣ ✕

❹❹❹ ▼▼▼ **La Quinta Inn & Suites Phoenix (Mesa West)** SH
(480) 844-8747. **$106-$169.** 902 W Grove Ave. US 60 (Superstition Frwy), exit 178 (Alma School Rd), just n, then just e. Int corridors. **Pets:** Medium. Service with restrictions.
SAVE S❍ ⎘ ❸ ▦ ➣

▼ **Motel 6-Mesa South #1030** M
(480) 834-0066. **$45-$65.** 1511 S Country Club Dr. US 60 (Superstition Frwy), exit 179 (Country Club Dr), northeast corner. Ext corridors. **Pets:** Medium, other species. Service with restrictions, supervision.
S❍ ✕ ❤ ❸ ➣

▼▼▼ **Residence Inn by Marriott Mesa** SH ❀
(480) 610-0100. **$109-$279.** 941 W Grove Ave. US 60 (Superstition Frwy), exit 178 (Alma School Rd), just n, then just e. Int corridors. **Pets:** Large, other species. $75 one-time fee/room. Service with restrictions, supervision.
ASK ✕ ⚹M ⎘ ❤ ❸ ▦ ➣ ✕

▼▼ **Sleep Inn of Mesa** SH
(480) 807-7760. **$59-$109.** 6347 E Southern Ave. US 60 (Superstition Frwy), exit 188 (Power Rd), 0.8 mi n, then 0.4 mi w to mall entrance. Int corridors. **Pets:** Accepted.
ASK S❍ ✕ ❤ ❸ ▦

❹❹❹ ▼ **Super 8 Motel-Mesa/Gilbert Rd** SH
(480) 545-0888. **$66-$129.** 1550 S Gilbert Rd. US 60 (Superstition Frwy), exit 182 (Gilbert Rd), 1 blk n. Int corridors. **Pets:** Very small. $5 daily fee/pet. Designated rooms, service with restrictions, supervision.
SAVE S❍ ✕ ❤ ❸ ➣

▼ **Travelodge Suites Mesa** SH
(480) 832-5961. **$49-$109.** 4244 E Main St. US 60 (Superstition Frwy), exit 185 (Greenfield Rd), 2 mi n, then just w. Ext corridors. **Pets:** Accepted.
ASK S❍ ✕ ❤ ❸ ▦ ➣

❹❹❹ ▼▼▼ **Windemere Hotel and Conference Center** SH
(480) 985-3600. **$59-$139.** 5750 E Main St. 0.6 mi e of Higley Rd. Ext corridors. **Pets:** Accepted.
SAVE S❍ ✕ ❸ ▦ ¶¶ ➣

PARADISE VALLEY

▼▼▼ **Hermosa Inn** SH ❀
(602) 955-8614. **$169-$729, 7 day notice.** 5532 N Palo Cristi Rd. 1 mi s of Lincoln Dr; corner of Stanford Dr. Ext corridors. **Pets:** Other species. $50 one-time fee/room. Supervision.
ASK S❍ ✕ ❤ ▦ ¶¶ ➣ ✕

PEORIA

▼▼◆ **Comfort Suites by Choice Hotels/Sports Complex** SH
(623) 334-3993. **$75-$95.** 8473 W Paradise Ln. Loop 101, exit 14 (Bell Rd), just e to 83rd Ave, just s, then just w. Int corridors. **Pets:** Accepted.
ASK S❍ ✕ ⎘ ❤ ❸ ▦ ➣

▼▼ **Extended StayAmerica Phoenix-Peoria** SH
(623) 487-0020. **$79-$114.** 7345 W Bell Rd. Loop 101, exit 14 (Bell Rd), 1.2 mi e. Int corridors. **Pets:** Accepted.
ASK S❍ ✕ ❤ ❸ ▦

▼▼◆ **Holiday Inn Express Hotel & Suites** SH
(623) 853-1313. **$99-$199.** 16771 N 84th Ave. Loop 101, exit 14 (Bell Rd), just w, then just s. Int corridors. **Pets:** Accepted.
ASK S❍ ✕ ⚹M ❤ ❸ ▦ ➣

▼▼▼▼ **La Quinta Inn & Suites Phoenix (West/Peoria)** **SH**
(623) 487-1900. **$138-$207.** 16321 N 83 Ave. Loop 101, exit 14 (Bell Rd), just e, then just s. Int corridors. **Pets:** Medium. Service with restrictions.
(ASK) ⊠ 🖉 🖋 🖥 💻 ⊃

▼▼▼ **Residence Inn by Marriott** **SH**
(623) 979-2074. **$125-$265.** 8435 W Paradise Ln. Loop 101, exit 14 (Bell Rd), just e, just s on 83rd Ave, then just w. Int corridors. **Pets:** Accepted.
(ASK) 🏊 ⊠ 🖋 🖥 💻 ⊃ ⊠

PHOENIX

🔷🔷🔷 ▼▼ ▼▼ **Arizona Biltmore Resort & Spa** **T** ☙
(602) 955-6600. **$205-$1955, 7 day notice.** 2400 E Missouri Ave. Jct Camelback Rd, 0.5 mi n on 24th St, then 0.4 mi e. Ext/int corridors. **Pets:** Medium. $50 deposit/room, $50 one-time fee/room. Designated rooms, supervision.
(SAVE) ⊠ 🖋 💻 🍴 ⊃ ⊠

🔷🔷🔷 ▼▼ **Best Western Airport Inn** **SH**
(602) 273-7251. **$75-$159.** 2425 S 24th St. I-10, exit 150B westbound, just s; exit 151 (University Dr) eastbound, just n to I-10 westbound, 1 mi w to exit 150B (24th St), then just s. Ext/int corridors. **Pets:** Accepted.
(SAVE) 🏊 ⊠ 🖉 🖥 💻 🍴 🏊

🔷🔷🔷 ▼▼ **Best Western Bell Hotel** **SH** ☙
(602) 993-8300. **$60-$150.** 17211 N Black Canyon Hwy. I-17, exit 212, just e, then just n. Ext corridors. **Pets:** Other species. $10 daily fee/pet. Designated rooms, service with restrictions, supervision.
(SAVE) 🏊 ⊠ 🖉 🖥 💻 🏊

🔷🔷🔷 ▼▼▼ **Best Western InnSuites Hotel & Suites Phoenix Northern** **SH** ☙
(602) 997-6285. **$69-$149.** 1615 E Northern Ave. SR 51, exit 7, 0.6 mi w. Ext corridors. **Pets:** Medium, other species. $25 one-time fee/pet. Designated rooms, service with restrictions, crate.
(SAVE) 🏊 ⊠ 🖉 🖋 🖥 💻 🏊

🔷🔷🔷 ▼▼▼ **Best Western Phoenix/I-17 Metrocenter Inn** **SH**
(602) 864-6233. **$69-$139.** 8101 N Black Canyon Hwy. I-17, exit 206 (Northern Ave), just e, then just n; on east side of freeway. Ext corridors. **Pets:** Accepted.
(SAVE) 🏊 ⊠ 🖉 🖥 💻 🏊

▼▼▼ **Candlewood Suites** **SH**
(602) 861-4900. **$79-$169.** 11411 N Black Canyon Hwy. I-17, exit 208 (Peoria Ave), just e, then 0.4 mi n. Int corridors. **Pets:** Accepted.
(ASK) ⊠ 🖋 🖥 💻 🏊

🔷🔷🔷 ▼▼🔷▼ **Clarion Hotel @ Phoenix Tech Center** **SH** ☙
(480) 893-3900. **$69-$169.** 5121 E La Puenta Ave. I-10, exit 157 (Elliot Rd), just w, just n on 51st St, then just e. Ext corridors. **Pets:** Other species. $25 one-time fee/pet.
(SAVE) 🏊 ⊠ 🖉 🖥 💻 🏊

🔷🔷🔷 ▼▼▼ **Comfort Inn Black Canyon** **SH**
(602) 242-8011. **$70-$350, 14 day notice.** 5050 N Black Canyon Hwy. I-17, exit 203 (Camelback Rd), just w, then just n on west side of freeway. Ext corridors. **Pets:** Accepted.
(SAVE) 🏊 ⊠ 🖋 🖥 💻 🏊

🔷🔷🔷 ▼▼▼ **Comfort Inn I-10 West/Central** **SH**
(602) 415-1623. **$60-$140.** 1344 N 27th Ave. I-10, exit 27th Ave eastbound, just n; exit 141 (35th Ave) westbound, just n, 1 mi e on McDowell Rd, then s. Int corridors. **Pets:** Accepted.
(SAVE) 🏊 ⊠ 🖋 🖥 💻 🏊

▼▼▼ **Comfort Suites by Choice Hotels** **SH**
(602) 861-3900. **$95-$100.** 10210 N 26th Dr. I-17, exit 208 (Peoria Ave), just e, just s on 25th Ave, then 0.3 mi w on W Beryl Ave. Int corridors. **Pets:** Accepted.
(ASK) 🏊 ⊠ 🖋 🖥 💻 🏊

▼▼▼ **Comfort Suites Conference Center** **SH**
(602) 279-3211. **$62-$143.** 3210 NW Grand Ave. I-17, exit 201 (Thomas Rd), just w to 27th Ave, just n, then 0.7 mi nw. Ext corridors. **Pets:** Accepted.
(ASK) 🏊 ⊠ 🖋 🖥 💻 🏊

▼ **Crossland Economy Studios-Phoenix West** **SH**
(602) 272-8571. **Call for rates.** 4861 W McDowell Rd. I-10, exit 139, just n, then just e. Ext corridors. **Pets:** Accepted.
⊠ 🖋 🖥 💻 🏊

🔷🔷🔷 ▼▼🔷▼ **Crowne Plaza Phoenix** **SH**
(602) 943-2341. **$62-$209.** 2532 W Peoria Ave. I-17, exit 208 (Peoria Ave), just e, then just n on 25th Ave. Int corridors. **Pets:** Accepted.
(SAVE) 🏊 ⊠ 🖋🅼 🖉 🖋 🖥 💻 🍴 🏊 ⊠

🔷🔷🔷 ▼▼🔷▼ **Crowne Plaza Phoenix Airport** **SH**
(602) 273-7778. **$71-$152.** 4300 E Washington St. Loop 202, exit 2 (44th St), 0.7 mi s. Int corridors. **Pets:** Other species. $50 one-time fee/pet. Service with restrictions.
(SAVE) ⊠ 🖉 🖋 🖥 💻 🍴 🏊

🔷🔷🔷 ▼▼🔷▼ **Days Inn-Airport** **M**
(602) 244-8244. **$69-$309.** 3333 E Van Buren St. Loop 202, exit 1C (32nd St), 0.6 mi s, then just e. Ext/int corridors. **Pets:** Other species. $20 one-time fee/pet. Service with restrictions, supervision.
(SAVE) 🏊 🔷 🖉 🖥 💻 🍴 🏊

🔷🔷🔷 ▼▼🔷▼ **Embassy Suites Phoenix Airport at 24th St** **SH**
(602) 957-1910. **$89-$199.** 2333 E Thomas Rd. SR 51, exit 2, just e. Ext corridors. **Pets:** Accepted.
(SAVE) 🏊 ⊠ 🖋 🖥 🖥 💻 🍴 🏊 ⊠

▼▼🔷▼ **Embassy Suites Phoenix-Biltmore** **SH**
(602) 955-3992. **$129-$429.** 2630 E Camelback Rd. Just n of Camelback Rd, on 26th St. Int corridors. **Pets:** Accepted.
⊠ 🖉 🖥 💻 🍴 🏊

🔷🔷🔷 ▼▼🔷▼ **Embassy Suites Phoenix North** **LH**
(602) 375-1777. **$129-$239.** 2577 W Greenway Rd. I-17, exit 211, just e. Ext corridors. **Pets:** Accepted.
(SAVE) 🏊 ⊠ 🖉 🖋 🖥 💻 🍴 🏊 ⊠

▼▼ **Extended StayAmerica-Chandler** **SH**
(480) 785-0464. **$64-$114.** 14245 S 50th St. I-10, exit 159, just w on Ray Rd, just s, then just e. Int corridors. **Pets:** Accepted.
(ASK) 🏊 ⊠ 🖋🅼 🖋 🖥 💻

▼▼ **Extended StayAmerica Pheonix-Chandler-E Chandler Blvd** **SH**
(480) 753-6700. **$69-$90.** 5035 E Chandler Blvd. I-10, exit 160 (Chandler Blvd), just w. Ext corridors. **Pets:** Accepted.
(ASK) 🏊 ⊠ 🖋 🖥 💻 🏊

▼▼ **Extended StayAmerica-Phoenix Airport** **SH**
(602) 438-2900. **$64-$94.** 3421 E Elwood St. I-10, exit 151 (University Dr), just n, then just e. Int corridors. **Pets:** Accepted.
(ASK) 🏊 ⊠ 🖋 🖥 💻 🏊

▼▼ **Extended StayAmerica Phoenix/Airport/E Oak St** **SH**
(602) 225-2998. **$74-$104.** 4357 E Oak St. Loop 202, exit 2 (44th St), 1 mi n. Ext corridors. **Pets:** Accepted.
(ASK) 🏊 ⊠ 🖋🅼 🖥 💻 🏊

▼▼ Extended StayAmerica Phoenix-Deer Valley **SH**
(623) 879-6609. **$65-$109.** 20827 N 27th Ave. I-10, exit 217A, just w. Int corridors. **Pets:** Accepted.
[A$K] [S/D] [✕] [🐾] [🛏] [💻]

▼▼ Extended StayAmerica Phoenix-Metro Center **SH**
(602) 870-2999. **$64-$94.** 11211 N Black Canyon Hwy. I-17, exit 208 (Peoria Ave), just e, then 0.3 mi n; on east side of freeway. Ext corridors. **Pets:** Accepted.
[A$K] [S/D] [✕] [🐾] [🛏] [💻]

▼▼▼ Extended Stay Deluxe Phoenix-Biltmore **SH**
(602) 265-6800. **$84-$134.** 5235 N 16th St. Jct SR 51, just w on Camelback Rd, then just n. Int corridors. **Pets:** Accepted.
[A$K] [S/D] [✕] [🐾] [🛏] [💻] [≈]

▼▼▼ Extended Stay Deluxe (Phoenix/Midtown) **SH**
(602) 279-9000. **$94-$119.** 217 W Osborn Rd. Just w of Central Ave; between Indian School and Thomas rds. Int corridors. **Pets:** Accepted.
[A$K] [S/D] [✕] [&M] [🐾] [🛏] [💻] [≈]

(AAA) ▼▼ Hilton Suites-Phoenix **LH**
(602) 222-1111. **$99-$309.** 10 E Thomas Rd. Just e of Central Ave; in Phoenix Plaza. Int corridors. **Pets:** Large, dogs only. $50 deposit/pet. Service with restrictions, supervision.
[SAVE] [✕] [&M] [🐾] [🛏] [💻] [🍴] [≈] [✕]

(AAA) ▼▼▼ Holiday Inn Express Hotel & Suites **SH**
(480) 785-8500. **$199-$225.** 15221 S 50th St. I-10, exit 160 (Chandler Blvd), just w, then just n. Int corridors. **Pets:** Medium. $25 one-time fee/room. Designated rooms, supervision.
[SAVE] [S/D] [✕] [🐾] [🛏] [💻] [≈]

▼▼▼ Holiday Inn Express Hotel & Suites **SH**
(602) 453-9900. **$69-$119.** 3401 E University Dr. I-10, exit 151 (University Dr), just n. Int corridors. **Pets:** Accepted.
[A$K] [S/D] [✕] [🐾] [🛏] [💻] [≈]

(AAA) ▼▼▼ Holiday Inn West **SH**
(602) 484-9009. **$99-$141.** 1500 N 51st Ave. I-10, exit 139 (51st Ave), just n. Int corridors. **Pets:** Accepted.
[SAVE] [S/D] [✕] [&M] [🐾] [🐾] [🛏] [💻] [🍴] [≈]

▼▼ Homestead Studio Suites Hotel-Phoenix North/Metro Center **M**
(602) 944-7828. **$59-$84.** 2102 W Dunlap Ave. I-17, exit 207, 0.7 mi e. Ext corridors. **Pets:** Accepted.
[A$K] [S/D] [✕] [🐾] [🛏] [💻]

▼▼ Homewood Suites by Hilton **SH**
(602) 508-0937. **$89-$219.** 2001 E Highland Ave. Just e of 20th St. Int corridors. **Pets:** Accepted.
[A$K] [✕] [🐾] [🛏] [💻] [≈] [✕]

(AAA) ▼▼▼ Homewood Suites Hotel **SH** ❀
(602) 674-8900. **$99-$259.** 2536 W Beryl Ave. I-17, exit 208 (Peoria Ave), just e, just s on 25th Ave, then just w. Int corridors. **Pets:** Medium. $25 one-time fee/room. Designated rooms, service with restrictions, crate.
[SAVE] [✕] [&M] [🐾] [🛏] [💻] [≈]

(AAA) ▼▼▼ La Quinta Inn & Suites Phoenix (Chandler) **SH**
(480) 961-7700. **$111-$169.** 15241 S 50th St. I-10, exit 160 (Chandler Blvd), just w, then just n. Int corridors. **Pets:** Medium. Service with restrictions.
[SAVE] [✕] [&M] [🐾] [🐾] [🛏] [💻] [≈]

(AAA) ▼▼ La Quinta Inn Phoenix Airport North **SH**
(602) 956-6500. **$70-$144.** 4727 E Thomas Rd. Just w of 48th St. Ext/int corridors. **Pets:** Small, dogs only. $60 deposit/room. Service with restrictions, supervision.
[SAVE] [S/D] [✕] [🛏] [💻] [≈]

▼▼▼ La Quinta Inn Phoenix (North) **SH**
(602) 993-0800. **$106-$154.** 2510 W Greenway Rd. I-17, exit 211, just e. Ext corridors. **Pets:** Medium. Service with restrictions.
[A$K] [✕] [🐾] [🛏] [💻] [≈] [✕]

▼▼ La Quinta Inn Phoenix (Thomas Road) **M**
(602) 258-6271. **$95-$126.** 2725 N Black Canyon Hwy. I-17, exit 201 (Thomas Rd), just e, then just s on east side of freeway. Ext corridors. **Pets:** Medium. Service with restrictions.
[A$K] [✕] [🐾] [🛏] [💻] [≈]

▼▼ MainStay Suites **SH**
(602) 395-0900. **$69-$149.** 9455 N Black Canyon Hwy. I-17, exit 207, just e, then 0.4 mi n. Int corridors. **Pets:** Small. $100 one-time fee/pet. Service with restrictions, crate.
[A$K] [S/D] [✕] [🐾] [🛏] [≈]

▼ Motel 6 Phoenix-Black Canyon #1304 **M**
(602) 277-5501. **$45-$65.** 4130 N Black Canyon Hwy. I-17, exit 202 (Indian School Rd), just w. Ext corridors. **Pets:** Medium, other species. Service with restrictions, supervision.
[S/D] [✕] [≈]

▼ Motel 6 Phoenix East #18 **M**
(602) 267-8555. **$45-$65.** 5315 E Van Buren St. Loop 202 eastbound, exit 4 (52nd St/Van Buren St) just s, then just e. Ext corridors. **Pets:** Medium, other species. Service with restrictions, supervision.
[S/D] [✕] [🐾] [🛏] [≈]

▼ Motel 6 Phoenix-North #344 **M**
(602) 993-2353. **$45-$67.** 2330 W Bell Rd. I-17, exit 212, just e. Ext corridors. **Pets:** Medium, other species. Service with restrictions, supervision.
[S/D] [🐾] [≈]

▼ Motel 6 Phoenix-Northern Ave #1185 **M**
(602) 995-7592. **$43-$63.** 8152 N Black Canyon Hwy. I-17, exit 206, just w, then just n. Ext corridors. **Pets:** Medium, other species. Service with restrictions, supervision.
[S/D] [✕] [🐾] [≈]

▼ Motel 6 Phoenix West #696 **M**
(602) 272-0220. **$45-$69.** 1530 N 52nd Dr. I-10, exit 139, just n to McDowell, just w, then just s. Ext corridors. **Pets:** Medium, other species. Service with restrictions, supervision.
[S/D] [✕] [🐾] [≈]

(AAA) ▼▼▼ Park Plaza Hotel Phoenix North **SH**
(602) 978-2222. **$89-$219.** 2641 W Union Hills Dr. I-17, exit 214A (Union Hills Dr), just w. Int corridors. **Pets:** Accepted.
[SAVE] [S/D] [✕] [🐾] [🛏] [💻] [🍴] [≈]

(AAA) ▼▼▼▼ Pointe Hilton Squaw Peak Resort **LH**
(602) 997-2626. **$89-$379, 3 day notice.** 7677 N 16th St. Loop 51, exit Glendale Ave, 0.4 mi w, then 0.6 mi n. Ext corridors. **Pets:** Accepted.
[SAVE] [✕] [🐾] [🐾] [🛏] [💻] [🍴] [≈] [✕]

(AAA) ▼▼▼▼ Pointe Hilton Tapatio Cliffs Resort **LH**
(602) 866-7500. **$89-$379, 3 day notice.** 11111 N 7th St. I-17, exit 207 (Dunlap Ave), 3 mi e, then 2 mi n. Ext corridors. **Pets:** Accepted.
[SAVE] [✕] [&M] [🐾] [🐾] [💻] [🍴] [≈] [✕]

(AAA) ▼ Premier Inns **M**
(602) 943-2371. **$39-$109.** 10402 Black Canyon Frwy. I-17, exit 208 (Peoria Ave), 0.3 mi w to 28th Dr, just s, just e on Metro Pkwy E, then just n on 27th Ave. Ext corridors. **Pets:** Accepted.
[SAVE] [S/D] [✕] [🛏] [💻] [≈]

(AAA) ▼▼▼ Radisson Hotel Phoenix Airport North **SH**
(602) 220-4400. **$139-$249.** 427 N 44th St. Loop 202, exit 2 (44th St), 0.5 mi s. Int corridors. **Pets:** Accepted.
[SAVE] [S/D] [✕] [&M] [🐾] [🛏] [💻] [🍴] [≈]

ΑΑΑ ▼▼ Ramada Plaza Hotel and Suites SH
(602) 866-7000. **$145-$300.** 12027 N 28th Dr. I-17, exit 209 (Cactus Rd), just w, then just s. Int corridors. **Pets:** Medium. $25 daily fee/room. Designated rooms, service with restrictions.
SAVE 🆂 ⊠ 🎨 🔋 🖵 🍴 🏊

▼▼ Red Roof Inn SH
(602) 233-8004. **$66-$84.** 5215 W Willetta. I-10, exit 139 (51st Ave), just n, just e on McDowell Rd, then just s. Int corridors. **Pets:** Medium, other species. Service with restrictions, supervision.
⊠ ♿ 🐾 🏊

▼▼ Red Roof Inn-Camelback SH
(602) 264-9290. **$49-$79.** 502 W Camelback Rd. I-17, exit 203 (Camelback Rd), 1.8 mi e. Int corridors. **Pets:** Medium, other species. $25 deposit/room. Service with restrictions, supervision.
ASK ⊠ 🔋 🏊

ΑΑΑ ▼▼▼ Residence Inn by Marriott SH ❀
(602) 864-1900. **$119-$209.** 8242 N Black Canyon Hwy. I-17, exit 207 (Dunlap Ave), just w, then 0.8 mi s. Ext/int corridors. **Pets:** Medium. $100 one-time fee/room. Service with restrictions.
SAVE 🆂 ⊠ ♿ 🐾 🔋 🖵 🏊 ⊠

▼▼▼ Residence Inn by Marriott Phoenix Airport SH ❀
(602) 273-9220. **$79-$219.** 801 N 44th St. Loop 202, exit 2 (44th St), just s. Int corridors. **Pets:** $11 daily fee/pet, $100 one-time fee/room. Designated rooms, service with restrictions.
ASK 🆂 ⊠ ♿ 🐾 🔋 🖵 🏊 ⊠

ΑΑΑ ▼▼▼▼ The Ritz-Carlton, Phoenix LH
(602) 468-0700. **$349-$429.** 2401 E Camelback Rd. Southeast corner of Camelback Rd and 24th St. Int corridors. **Pets:** Accepted.
⊠ ♿ 🎨 🔋 🖵 🍴 🏊 ⊠

ΑΑΑ ▼▼▼▼ Royal Palms Resort and Spa LH
(602) 840-3610. **$179-$1600, 7 day notice.** 5200 E Camelback Rd. Just e of 52nd St. Ext/int corridors. **Pets:** Accepted.
SAVE ⊠ 🐾 🔋 🖵 🍴 🏊 ⊠

ΑΑΑ ▼▼▼▼ Sheraton Crescent Hotel LH
(602) 943-8200. **$79-$295, 3 day notice.** 2620 W Dunlap Ave. I-17, exit 207 (Dunlap Ave), just e. Int corridors. **Pets:** Accepted.
SAVE 🆂 ⊠ ♿ 🎨 🐾 🔋 🖵 🍴 🏊 ⊠

ΑΑΑ ▼▼▼▼ Sheraton Wild Horse Pass Resort & Spa LH ❀
(602) 225-0100. **$169-$850, 7 day notice.** 5594 W Wild Horse Pass Blvd. I-10, exit 162, 2.4 mi w. Int corridors. **Pets:** Medium, dogs only. Designated rooms, service with restrictions, supervision.
SAVE 🆂 ⊠ 🐾 🖵 🍴 🏊 ⊠

ΑΑΑ ▼▼▼ Sleep Inn Phoenix North SH
(602) 504-1200. **$69-$409.** 18235 N 27th Ave. I-17, exit 214A, just w, then just s. Int corridors. **Pets:** Small. $15 daily fee/pet. Designated rooms, service with restrictions, supervision.
SAVE 🆂 ⊠ ♿ 🐾 🔋 🖵 🏊

ΑΑΑ ▼▼▼ Sleep Inn Sky Harbor Airport SH
(480) 967-7100. **$55-$139.** 2621 S 47th Pl. I-10, exit 151 (University Dr), 2 mi n, then just w. Int corridors. **Pets:** Accepted.
SAVE 🆂 ⊠ 🐾 🔋 🖵 🏊

▼▼ Studio 6 Phoenix-Deer Valley #6030 SH
(602) 843-1151. **$57-$73.** 18405 N 27th Ave. I-17, exit 214A (Union Hills Dr), just w, then just s. Ext corridors. **Pets:** Accepted.
🆂 ⊠ 🐾 🔋 🖵

ΑΑΑ ▼▼▼ Super 8-Airport M
(602) 244-1627. **$59-$299.** 3401 E Van Buren St. Loop 202, exit 1C (32nd St), 0.6 mi s, then just e. Ext/int corridors. **Pets:** Accepted.
SAVE 🆂 ⊠ 🎨 🔋 🖵

▼▼ Super 8 Motel-Phoenix SH
(602) 415-0888. **$69-$199.** 1242 N 53rd Ave. I-10, exit 139 (51st Ave), just s to Latham Rd, then just w. Int corridors. **Pets:** Accepted.
ASK 🆂 ⊠ 🔋 🐾

▼▼ TownePlace Suites by Marriott SH
(602) 943-9510. **$95-$125.** 9425 N Black Canyon Hwy. I-17, exit 207, just e, then 0.3 mi n. Int corridors. **Pets:** Accepted.
ASK 🆂 ⊠ 🐾 🔋 🖵 🐾

ΑΑΑ ▼▼▼ Wingate Inn Phoenix SH
(602) 716-9900. **$79-$175.** 2520 N Central Ave. I-10, exit 145 (7th St), just n to McDowell Rd, 0.4 mi w, then 0.7 mi n. Int corridors. **Pets:** Other species. $25 deposit/room. Service with restrictions, supervision.
SAVE ⊠ 🐾 🔋 🖵 🏊

SCOTTSDALE

ΑΑΑ ▼▼▼ Best Western Papago Inn & Resort SH
(480) 947-7335. **$59-$169, 3 day notice.** 7017 E McDowell Rd. From Scottsdale Rd, just w. Ext corridors. **Pets:** Accepted.
SAVE 🆂 ⊠ 🐾 🔋 🖵 🏊

▼▼▼ Best Western Scottsdale Airpark Suites SH
(480) 951-4000. **$69-$189.** 7515 E Butherus Dr. 0.8 mi n of Thunderbird Rd; 0.5 mi e of Scottsdale Rd. Ext corridors. **Pets:** Accepted.
ASK 🆂 ⊠ 🎨 🔋 🖵 🍴 🏊

ΑΑΑ ▼▼▼▼ Camelback Inn, A JW Marriott Resort & Spa LH ❀
(480) 948-1700. **$129-$549, 7 day notice.** 5402 E Lincoln Dr. 0.5 mi e of Tatum Blvd; on north side of Lincoln Dr. Ext corridors. **Pets:** Small, dogs only. $250 deposit/room. Service with restrictions, supervision.
SAVE 🆂 ⊠ ♿ 🎨 🐾 🔋 🖵 🏊 ⊠

ΑΑΑ ▼▼▼ Chaparral Suites Resort SH
(480) 949-1414. **$159-$229.** 5001 N Scottsdale Rd. At Chaparral Rd. Ext corridors. **Pets:** Medium, dogs only. $25 one-time fee/pet. Service with restrictions, supervision.
SAVE ⊠ 🐾 🎨 🐾 🔋 🖵 🍴 🏊

▼▼▼ Comfort Suites by Choice Hotels-Old Town SH
(480) 946-1111. **$65-$85.** 3275 N Drinkwater Blvd. N of Thomas Rd; just e of Scottsdale Rd. Int corridors. **Pets:** Accepted.
ASK 🆂 ⊠ ♿ 🐾 🔋 🖵 🐾

▼▼▼ Country Inn & Suites By Carlson SH
(480) 314-1200. **$85-$135.** 10801 N 89th Pl. Loop 101, exit 41, just e on Shea Blvd, then just n. Int corridors. **Pets:** Medium. $50 one-time fee/room. Designated rooms, service with restrictions, supervision.
ASK 🆂 ⊠ 🐾 🔋 🖵 🐾

ΑΑΑ ▼▼▼ DoubleTree Paradise Valley Resort-Scottsdale LH
(480) 947-5400. **$89-$299.** 5401 N Scottsdale Rd. Just n of Chaparral Rd; on east side of Scottsdale Rd. Ext corridors. **Pets:** Accepted.
SAVE 🆂 ⊠ 🎨 🔋 🖵 🍴 🏊 ⊠

▼▼ Extended StayAmerica-Phoenix-Scottsdale SH
(480) 607-3767. **$75-$114.** 15501 N Scottsdale Rd. Loop 101, exit Frank Lloyd Wright, 2 mi w, 0.5 s on Scottsdale Rd, then just e on Tierra Buena Ln. Ext corridors. **Pets:** Accepted.
ASK 🆂 ⊠ 🎨 🐾 🔋 🖵

▼▼▼ Extended Stay Deluxe Phoenix-Scottsdale SH
(480) 483-1333. **$94-$134.** 10660 N 69th St. From jct Scottsdale Rd, just w on Shea Blvd, then just n. Int corridors. **Pets:** Accepted.
ASK 🆂 ⊠ 🐾 🔋 🖵 🐾 ⊠

△△△ ▽▽▽▽▽ The Fairmont Scottsdale Princess [LH]
(480) 585-4848. **$129-$819.** 7575 E Princess Dr. 0.6 mi n of Bell Rd, 0.5 mi e of Scottsdale Rd; on south side of Princess Dr. Ext/int corridors. **Pets:** Accepted.

△△△ ▽▽▽▽▽ Four Seasons Resort Scottsdale at Troon North [LH] ☙
(480) 515-5700. **$225-$5500, 7 day notice.** 10600 E Crescent Moon Dr. SR 101, exit 36 (Pima Rd), 4.7 mi n, 2 mi e on Happy Valley, then 1.5 mi n on Alma School Rd. Ext corridors. **Pets:** Small, other species. Service with restrictions.

▽▽▽▽ Hampton Inn-Oldtown/Fashion Square Scottsdale [SH]
(480) 941-9400. **$69-$179.** 4415 N Civic Center Plaza. Scottsdale Rd, just e on Camelback Rd, just s on 75th St. Ext/int corridors. **Pets:** Accepted.

△△△ ▽▽▽ ▽▽▽ Hilton Scottsdale Resort & Villas [LH]
(480) 948-7750. **$79-$389, 3 day notice.** 6333 N Scottsdale Rd. Loop 101, exit 45, 2.1 mi w on McDonald Dr, then 0.3 mi n. Int corridors. **Pets:** Accepted.

△△△ ▽▽▽ Holiday Inn Express Hotel & Suites-Scottsdale [SH]
(480) 675-7665. **$89-$209.** 3131 N Scottsdale Rd. Northeast corner of Scottsdale Rd and Earll Dr. Int corridors. **Pets:** Other species. $25 deposit/room. Service with restrictions, supervision.

▽▽ Homestead Studio Suites Hotel-Phoenix-Scottsdale [SH]
(480) 994-0297. **$64-$104.** 3560 N Marshall Way. Just w of Scottsdale Rd on Goldwater, just s. Ext corridors. **Pets:** Accepted.

△△△ ▽▽▽ The Inn at Pima, A Condominium Suite Hotel [CO]
(480) 948-3800. **$79-$338.** 7330 N Pima Rd. 0.4 mi n of Indian Bend Rd; on west side of Pima Rd. Ext/int corridors. **Pets:** Accepted.

△△△ ▽▽▽▽ La Quinta Inn & Suites Phoenix (Scottsdale) [SH]
(480) 614-5300. **$116-$190.** 8888 E Shea Blvd. Loop 101, exit Shea Blvd, northeast corner. Int corridors. **Pets:** Medium. Service with restrictions.

△△△ ▽▽▽▽ Millennium Resort Scottsdale, McCormick Ranch [LH]
(480) 948-5050. **$69-$319, 3 day notice.** 7401 N Scottsdale Rd. 0.8 mi n of Indian Bend Rd. Int corridors. **Pets:** Accepted.

▽▽ Motel 6 Scottsdale #29 [M]
(480) 946-2280. **$48-$85.** 6848 E Camelback Rd. Just w of Scottsdale Rd. Ext corridors. **Pets:** Medium, other species. Service with restrictions, supervision.

△△△ ▽▽▽▽▽ The Phoenician [LH]
(480) 941-8200. **$199-$775, 7 day notice.** 6000 E Camelback Rd. 0.5 mi w of 64th St. Ext/int corridors. **Pets:** Small, dogs only. $100 one-time fee/pet. Designated rooms.

△△△ ▽▽▽▽ Radisson Fort McDowell Resort & Casino [LH] ☙
(480) 789-5300. **$99-$259.** 10438 N Fort McDowell Rd. Jct Shea Blvd, 1.6 mi ne on SR 87. Int corridors. **Pets:** Dogs only. $50 deposit/room, $10 daily fee/room. Service with restrictions, supervision.

▽▽ ▽▽ Ramada Limited Scottsdale [M]
(480) 994-9461. **$50-$150.** 6935 5th Ave. Just w of Scottsdale Rd; just n of Indian School Rd; on south side of 5th Ave. Ext corridors. **Pets:** Accepted.

△△△ ▽▽▽▽ Renaissance Scottsdale Resort [LH]
(480) 991-1414. **$129-$399.** 6160 N Scottsdale Rd. Just n of McDonald Dr. Ext corridors. **Pets:** Accepted.

△△△ ▽▽▽▽ Residence Inn by Marriott, Scottsdale/Paradise Valley [SH]
(480) 948-8666. **$89-$249.** 6040 N Scottsdale Rd. Just n of McDonald Dr. Ext/int corridors. **Pets:** Other species. $100 one-time fee/room. Service with restrictions, crate.

▽▽▽▽ Residence Inn Scottsdale North [SH] ☙
(480) 563-4120. **$129-$389.** 17011 N Scottsdale Rd. SR 101, exit 34 (Scottsdale Rd), 1.1 mi s, then just e on 17050 N. Int corridors. **Pets:** Small. $100 one-time fee/room. Service with restrictions, crate.

△△△ ▽▽▽▽ Scottsdale Marriott at McDowell Mountains [SH]
(480) 502-3836. **$99-$339.** 16770 N Perimeter Dr. Loop 101, exit 36 (Princess Dr), just w to N Perimeter Dr, then 0.6 mi s. Int corridors. **Pets:** Accepted.

△△△ ▽▽ ▽▽ Sleep Inn [SH]
(480) 998-9211. **$59-$149.** 16630 N Scottsdale Rd. Just s of Bell Rd. Int corridors. **Pets:** Accepted.

▽▽▽▽ Summerfield Suites-Scottsdale [SH] ☙
(480) 946-7700. **$99-$399.** 4245 N Drinkwater Blvd. 0.3 mi e of Scottsdale Rd. Ext corridors. **Pets:** Medium. $200 one-time fee/room. Service with restrictions, crate.

▽▽ ▽▽ TownePlace Suites by Marriott [SH]
(480) 551-1100. **$59-$139.** 10740 N 90th St. Loop 101, exit Shea Blvd, just e to 90th St, then just n. Int corridors. **Pets:** Other species. $100 one-time fee/room. Service with restrictions.

△△△ ▽▽▽▽ The Westin Kierland Resort & Spa [LH]
(480) 624-1000. **$149-$619, 7 day notice.** 6902 E Greenway Pkwy. 0.5 mi w of Scottsdale Rd. Int corridors. **Pets:** Accepted.

SURPRISE

▽▽ Days Inn & Suites [SH]
(623) 933-4000. **$90-$160.** 12477 W Bell Rd. US 60 (Grand Ave), 1.1 mi e, then just s on Greasewood St. Int corridors. **Pets:** Accepted.

AAA ▼▼▼ Windmill Suites at Sun City West SH
(623) 583-0133. **$78-$169.** 12545 W Bell Rd. US 60 (Grand Ave), 1 mi e. Int corridors. **Pets:** Accepted.
SAVE S6 X 🛎 🔌 🖥 🏊 ⊠

TEMPE

AAA ▼▼ Best Western Inn of Tempe SH
(480) 784-2233. **$49-$149.** 670 N Scottsdale Rd. SR 202 Loop (Red Mountain Frwy), exit 7, just s. Int corridors. **Pets:** Small. $25 deposit/room. Designated rooms, service with restrictions.
SAVE S6 X 🔌 🛎 🖥 🏊

AAA ▼▼▼ Best Western Tempe by the Mall SH
(480) 820-7500. **$59-$109.** 5300 S Priest Dr. I-10, exit 155 (Baseline Rd), 0.4 mi e, then just s. Int corridors. **Pets:** Small. $25 one-time fee/pet. Designated rooms, service with restrictions, supervision.
SAVE S6 X 🛎 🖥 🏊

AAA ▼▼▼ The Buttes, A Marriott Resort SH
(602) 225-9000. **$159-$309.** 2000 Westcourt Way. I-10, exit 153 (Broadway Rd) westbound, 0.8 mi w to 48th St, then 0.3 mi s; exit 48th St eastbound, 0.5 mi s. Int corridors. **Pets:** Accepted.
SAVE X 🔌 🖥 🍴 🏊 ⊠

▼▼ Candlewood Suites SH
(480) 777-0440. **$85-$160.** 1335 W Baseline Rd. I-10, exit 155 (Baseline Rd), 0.5 mi e; just e of Priest Dr. Int corridors. **Pets:** Accepted.
ASK S6 X 🔌 🛎 🖥 🏊

AAA ▼▼▼ Comfort Inn & Suites Tempe/ASU SH
(480) 966-7202. **$59-$139.** 1031 E Apache Blvd. SR 202 Loop (Red Mountain Frwy), exit 7 (Rural Rd S), 1.5 mi s, then just e. Int corridors. **Pets:** Other species. $50 deposit/pet. Service with restrictions, supervision.
SAVE S6 X 🔌 🛎 🖥 🏊 ⊠

▼▼▼ Country Inn & Suites By Carlson SH
(480) 345-8585. **$90-$160.** 1660 W Elliot Rd. I-10, exit 157, just e. Ext corridors. **Pets:** Small, other species. $25 one-time fee/room. Service with restrictions.
ASK S6 X 🔌 🛎 🖥 🏊

AAA ▼▼ Econo Lodge/Tempe ASU M
(480) 966-5832. **$42-$72.** 2101 E Apache Blvd. Loop 101, exit University Blvd, just w to Price Rd; exit southbound 0.9 mi s, then 0.5 mi w. Ext corridors. **Pets:** Accepted.
SAVE X 🛎 🏊

AAA ▼▼▼ Hampton Inn & Suites SH
(480) 675-9799. **$109-$169.** 1429 N Scottsdale Rd. SR 202 Loop (Red Mountain Frwy), exit 7, 0.5 mi n. Ext corridors. **Pets:** Accepted.
SAVE S6 X 🔌 🛎 🖥 🏊 ⊠

▼▼▼ Hawthorn Suites SH
(480) 633-2744. **$69-$159.** 2301 E Southern Ave. Loop 101, exit 54 (Southern Ave/Baseline Rd); at southeast corner. Int corridors. **Pets:** Accepted.
ASK S6 X 👤 🔌 🛎 🖥 🏊

AAA ▼▼ Holiday Inn SH
(480) 968-3451. **$59-$139.** 915 E Apache Blvd. US 60 (Superstition Frwy), exit 174 (Rural Rd), 2 mi n. Int corridors. **Pets:** Accepted.
SAVE S6 X 🔌 🛎 🖥 🍴 🏊 ⊠

▼▼ Homestead Studio Suites Hotel-Phoenix/Airport/Tempe SH
(480) 557-8880. **$79-$104.** 2165 W 15th St. I-10, exit 153 (Broadway Rd), 0.3 mi ne, just nw on S 52nd St, then just w. Int corridors. **Pets:** Accepted.
ASK S6 X 🔌 🛎 🖥 🏊

AAA ▼▼▼ InnSuites Hotels & Suites Tempe/Phoenix Airport SH ❀
(480) 897-7900. **$69-$139.** 1651 W Baseline Rd. I-10, exit 155 (Baseline Rd), just e. Ext corridors. **Pets:** Medium, other species. $25 one-time fee/pet. Designated rooms, service with restrictions, supervision.
SAVE S6 X 🛎 🖥 🍴 🏊 ⊠

▼▼▼ La Quinta Inn Phoenix (Sky Harbor South) SH
(480) 967-4465. **$91-$169.** 911 S 48th St. I-10, exit 153 (Broadway Rd) eastbound; exit 153A (University Dr) westbound, 0.8 mi n; on south side of University Dr; east side of SR 143 (Hohokam Expwy). Ext corridors. **Pets:** Medium. Service with restrictions.
ASK X 🔌 👤 🛎 🖥 🏊

▼ Motel 6 #1315 M
(480) 945-9506. **$49-$75.** 1612 N Scottsdale Rd. Loop 202 (Red Mountain Frwy), exit 7, 0.6 mi n. Ext corridors. **Pets:** Medium, other species. Service with restrictions, supervision.
S6 X 🏊

AAA ▼▼ Quality Inn-Phoenix Airport-Tempe M
(480) 967-3000. **$89-$129.** 1550 S 52nd St. I-10, exit 153B (Broadway Rd) westbound; exit 153A (48th St) eastbound, 0.3 mi ne. Ext corridors. **Pets:** Accepted.
SAVE S6 X 🔌 🛎 🖥 🏊

AAA ▼▼ Ramada Limited SH
(480) 413-1188. **$60-$90.** 1701 W Baseline Rd. I-10, exit 155 (Baseline Rd), just e. Ext corridors. **Pets:** Other species. $10 daily fee/room. Service with restrictions, supervision.
SAVE S6 X 🔌 👤 🛎 🖥 🏊

AAA ▼▼ Ramada Limited Tempe-University M
(480) 736-1700. **$64-$129, 3 day notice.** 1915 E Apache Blvd. US 60 (Superstition Frwy), exit 175, 1.9 mi n on McClintock Dr, then 0.3 mi e. Ext corridors. **Pets:** Medium, dogs only. $50 deposit/pet. Service with restrictions, crate.
SAVE S6 X 🛎 🖥 🏊

▼▼ Red Roof Inn Phoenix Airport SH
(480) 449-3205. **$70-$85.** 2135 W 15th St. I-10, exit 153 (Broadway Rd), just nw on S 52nd St, then just w. Int corridors. **Pets:** Medium, other species. Service with restrictions, supervision.
X 👤 🛎 🏊

▼▼▼ Residence Inn by Marriott SH
(480) 756-2122. **$79-$219.** 5075 S Priest Dr. I-10, exit 155 (Baseline Rd), 0.4 mi e, then just n. Ext/int corridors. **Pets:** Other species. $100 one-time fee/room. Service with restrictions.
ASK S6 X 🔌 👤 🛎 🖥 🏊 ⊠

AAA ▼▼▼ Sheraton Phoenix Airport Hotel-Tempe LH ❀
(480) 967-6600. **$189-$319.** 1600 S 52nd St. I-10, exit 153B Broadway Rd westbound; exit 153A 48th St eastbound, 0.3 mi ne. Int corridors. **Pets:** Small, dogs only. $75 deposit/pet. Designated rooms, service with restrictions, supervision.
SAVE S6 X 🔌 👤 🛎 🖥 🍴 🏊 ⊠

▼▼ Studio 6 Extended Stay #6031 SH
(602) 414-4470. **$53-$77.** 4909 S Wendler Dr. I-10, exit 155 (Baseline Rd), just w, then 0.4 mi n. Ext corridors. **Pets:** Accepted.
S6 X 🛎 🖥 🏊

AAA ▼▼▼ Tempe Mission Palms Hotel SH
(480) 894-1400. **$129-$259, 3 day notice.** 60 E 5th St. Jct University Dr, just n on Mill Ave, then just e; downtown. Int corridors. **Pets:** Accepted.
SAVE S6 X 🔌 👤 🛎 🖥 🍴 🏊 ⊠

▼▼ Tempe Super 8 **M**
(480) 967-8891. **$49-$129.** 1020 E Apache Blvd. Just e of Rural Rd. Ext corridors. **Pets:** Accepted.

🆎 🔊 ⊠ 🔋 ➴

YOUNGTOWN

🔺 ▼▼ Best Western Inn & Suites of Sun City **SH** 🐾
(623) 933-8211. **$80-$140.** 11201 Grand Ave. On US 60, just se of 113th Ave. Ext/int corridors. **Pets:** Medium. Designated rooms, service with restrictions, supervision.

SAVE 🔊 ⊠ 🗐 🗐 🔋 🖵 ➴

END METROPOLITAN AREA

PINETOP-LAKESIDE

🔺 ▼▼ Bear Mountain Inn & Suites **SH**
(928) 368-6600. **$55-$109.** 1637 W White Mountain Blvd. On SR 260. Int corridors. **Pets:** Accepted.

SAVE 🔊 ⊠ 🔋

🔺 ▼▼ Best Western Inn of Pinetop **M** 🐾
(928) 367-6667. **$74-$99.** 404 E White Mountain Blvd. On SR 260. Ext corridors. **Pets:** Other species. $10 daily fee/pet. Service with restrictions, supervision.

SAVE 🔊 ⊠ 🔋 🖵

🔺 ▼▼▼ Holiday Inn Express **SH**
(928) 367-6077. **$79-$169.** 431 E White Mountain Blvd. On SR 260. Int corridors. **Pets:** Very small. $25 daily fee/room. Service with restrictions, supervision.

SAVE 🔊 ⊠ 🔋 🖵 ⊠

▼▼ Lazy Oaks Resort **CA**
(928) 368-6203. **$71-$90 (no credit cards), 21 day notice.** 1075 Larson Rd. Jct SR 260, 0.8 mi s on Rainbow Lake Dr, then 0.6 mi w. Ext corridors. **Pets:** Medium. Designated rooms, supervision.

🔋 🖵 ⊠ ⊠ ⊠

▼▼ Mountain Hacienda Lodge **M**
(928) 367-4146. **$45-$59.** 1023 E White Mountain Blvd. On SR 260. Ext corridors. **Pets:** Accepted.

⊠ 🔋 🖵 ⊠

▼▼▼ Northwoods Resort **CA**
(928) 367-2966. **$79-$149, 14 day notice.** 165 E White Mountain Blvd. On SR 260. Ext corridors. **Pets:** Other species. $12 daily fee/pet. Designated rooms, no service, supervision.

⊠ 🔋 🖵 ⊠ ⊠ ⊠

🔺 ▼▼ Super 8 Motel **SH**
(928) 367-3161. **$75-$150.** 1202 E White Mountain Blvd. On SR 260, east end of town. Int corridors. **Pets:** Accepted.

SAVE 🔊 ⊠ 🔋 ➴

▼▼ Timber Lodge **M** 🐾
(928) 367-4463. **$49-$89.** 1078 E White Mountain Blvd. On SR 260. Ext corridors. **Pets:** Other species. $10 daily fee/pet. Service with restrictions, crate.

🆎 🔊 ⊠ 🔋 🖵 ⊠

🔺 ▼▼ Woodland Inn & Suites **M**
(928) 367-3636. **$69-$159, 3 day notice.** 458 E White Mountain Blvd. On SR 260. Ext corridors. **Pets:** Medium, other species. $10 daily fee/pet. Service with restrictions, supervision.

SAVE 🔊 ⊠ 🔋 🖵

PRESCOTT

🔺 ▼ America's Best Value Inn **M** 🐾
(928) 776-1282. **$64-$84.** 1105 E Sheldon St. 0.4 mi e of jct SR 89. Int corridors. **Pets:** Dogs only. $10 one-time fee/room. Designated rooms, service with restrictions, supervision.

SAVE 🔊 ⊠ 🗐 🔋 🖵 ➴

▼▼ Best Western Prescottonian Motel **M**
(928) 445-3096. **$79-$139, 3 day notice.** 1317 E Gurley St. On SR 89, just s of jct SR 69. Ext corridors. **Pets:** Accepted.

🆎 🔊 ⊠ 🗐 🔋 🖵 🍴 ➴

🔺 ▼▼ Comfort Inn of Prescott **M**
(928) 778-5770. **$65-$169.** 1290 White Spar Rd. On SR 89, 1.5 mi s of town center. Ext corridors. **Pets:** Accepted.

SAVE 🔊 ⊠ 🗐 🔋 🖵

▼ Motel 6 #0166 **M**
(928) 776-0160. **$55-$65.** 1111 E Sheldon St. 0.4 mi e of jct SR 89; center. Ext corridors. **Pets:** Medium, other species. Service with restrictions, supervision.

🔊 ⊠ 🗐 🔋 ➴

▼▼ Prescott Cabin Rentals **M**
(928) 778-9573. **$80-$351.** 5555 Onyx Dr. Jct SR 89, 5 mi e on SR 69, 0.4 mi s on dirt/gravel road. Ext corridors. **Pets:** Other species. $20 daily fee/pet. No service, crate.

⊠ 🔋 🖵 ⊠

🔺 ▼▼▼ Quality Inn & Suites and Conference Center **SH** 🐾
(928) 777-0770. **$89-$209.** 4499 Hwy 69. On SR 69, 3.6 mi e of jct SR 89. Int corridors. **Pets:** Medium, other species. $40 one-time fee/pet. Designated rooms, service with restrictions, supervision.

SAVE 🔊 ⊠ 🗐 🔋 🖵 🍴 ➴ ⊠

PRESCOTT VALLEY

🔺 ▼▼ Days Inn/Prescott Valley **M**
(928) 772-8600. **$7-$100.** 7875 E Hwy 69. On SR 69; corner of Windsong Rd. Ext corridors. **Pets:** Other species. $50 deposit/room. Service with restrictions.

SAVE 🔊 ⊠ 🗐 🔋 🖵 ➴

QUARTZSITE

▼ Super 8 Motel-Quartzsite **M** 🐾
(928) 927-8080. **$75-$135.** 2050 W Dome Rock Rd. I-10, exit 17, just s to Frontage Rd, then 0.6 mi w. Int corridors. **Pets:** Other species. $10 daily fee/pet. Service with restrictions, supervision.

🆎 ⊠ 🗐 🔋

RIO RICO

▼▼▼ Esplendor Resort at Rio Rico **LH**
(520) 281-1901. **$109-$159.** 1069 Camino Caralampi. I-19, exit 17 (Rio Rico Dr), just w to Camino Caralampi, then just s to resort entrance. Ext corridors. **Pets:** Accepted.

🆎 🔊 ⊠ 🗐 🗐 🔋 🖵 🍴 ➴ ⊠

SAFFORD

🔺 ▼▼ Best Western Desert Inn **M**
(928) 428-0521. **$80-$95.** 1391 W Thatcher Blvd. US 191, 1 mi w on US 70. Ext corridors. **Pets:** Accepted.

SAVE 🔊 ⊠ 🔋 🖵 ➴

ⓐⓐⓐ ▽▽◈ Days Inn M
(928) 428-5000. **$85-$160, 10 day notice.** 520 E Hwy 70. US 191, 0.5 mi e. Ext corridors. **Pets:** Medium. $10 daily fee/room. Service with restrictions, supervision.
[SAVE] [S🔊] [✕] [&M] [🍴] [⛱] [🛏] [🖭] [🏊]

ST. JOHNS

▽ Days Inn M
(928) 337-4422. **$65-$85.** 125 E Commercial St. On SR 191/61; center. Ext corridors. **Pets:** Accepted.
[ASK] [S🔊] [✕] [🛏]

ST. MICHAELS

ⓐⓐⓐ ▽▽◈ Navajoland Days Inn SH
(928) 871-5690. **$70-$95.** 392 W Hwy 264. From jct SR 12, 1.5 mi w. Ext corridors. **Pets:** Accepted.
[SAVE] [S🔊] [✕] [🍴] [🛏] [🖭] [🍴] [⛱] [🏊]

SEDONA

ⓐⓐⓐ ▽▽◈▽ Best Western Inn of Sedona SH
(928) 282-3072. **$174-$229.** 1200 W Hwy 89A. Jct SR 179, 1.2 mi w. Ext corridors. **Pets:** Large. $20 daily fee/room. Service with restrictions, crate.
[SAVE] [S🔊] [✕] [🍴] [🛏] [🖭] [🏊]

ⓐⓐⓐ ▽▽▽ Desert Quail Inn M
(928) 284-1433. **$74-$149.** 6626 Hwy 179. Jct Bell Rock Blvd, 0.9 mi s. Ext corridors. **Pets:** Small, dogs only. $15 daily fee/pet. Designated rooms, service with restrictions, supervision.
[SAVE] [S🔊] [✕] [🍴] [🍴] [🛏] [🖭] [🏊]

ⓐⓐⓐ ▽▽◈▽ El Portal Sedona SH ✿
(928) 203-9405. **$250-$495, 15 day notice.** 95 Portal Ln. Jct SR 89A, just s on SR 179, then just w. Ext/int corridors. **Pets:** Other species. Designated rooms, service with restrictions, supervision.
[SAVE] [✕] [🍴] [🛏]

ⓐⓐⓐ ▽▽▽▽ Hilton Sedona Resort & Spa LH
(928) 284-4040. **$149-$339, 3 day notice.** 90 Ridge Trail Dr. Jct SR 89A, 7.3 mi s on SR 179. Int corridors. **Pets:** Medium. $50 one-time fee/pet. Designated rooms, service with restrictions, supervision.
[SAVE] [✕] [🍴] [🛏] [🖭] [🍴] [🏊] [🏊]

ⓐⓐⓐ ▽▽◈ King's Ransom Inn SH
(928) 282-7151. **$69-$189.** 771 Hwy 179. 0.7 mi s of jct SR 89A. Ext/int corridors. **Pets:** Accepted.
[SAVE] [S🔊] [✕] [🛏] [🖭] [🏊] [🏊]

ⓐⓐⓐ ▽▽◈▽ La Quinta Inn Sedona SH
(928) 284-0711. **$85-$169.** 6176 Hwy 179. Jct Bell Rock Blvd, just s. Int corridors. **Pets:** Other species. Designated rooms, service with restrictions.
[SAVE] [S🔊] [✕] [&M] [🍴] [🛏] [🏊]

ⓐⓐⓐ ▽▽◈▽ L'Auberge de Sedona Resort SH ✿
(928) 282-1661. **$189-$325, 14 day notice.** 301 L'Auberge Ln. Jct SR 179, just n on SR 89A, then ne; down the hill. Ext/int corridors. **Pets:** Dogs only. $35 daily fee/pet. Designated rooms, service with restrictions.
[SAVE] [S🔊] [✕] [🍴] [🛏] [🖭] [🍴] [🏊] [🏊]

▽▽◈▽ The Lodge at Sedona BB ✿
(928) 204-1942. **$160-$325, 14 day notice.** 125 Kallof Pl. Jct SR 179, 1.8 mi w on SR 89A, then just s. Ext/int corridors. **Pets:** Large, dogs only. $35 one-time fee/room. Designated rooms, no service, supervision.
[✕] [🍴] [🏊] [🍴]

ⓐⓐⓐ ▽▽◈▽ Matterhorn Inn M ✿
(928) 282-7176. **$79-$159.** 230 Apple Ave. Jct SR 179, just ne on SR 89A; uptown. Ext corridors. **Pets:** Other species. $10 daily fee/room. Designated rooms, service with restrictions, crate.
[SAVE] [S🔊] [✕] [🛏] [🖭] [🏊]

ⓐⓐⓐ ▽▽◈ Sedona Real Inn & Suites SH
(928) 282-1414. **$89-$349.** 95 Arroyo Pinon. Jct SR 179, 3.4 mi w on SR 89A, just sw. Ext corridors. **Pets:** Medium, other species. $20 one-time fee/pet. Designated rooms, supervision.
[SAVE] [✕] [🛏] [🏊]

ⓐⓐⓐ ▽▽◈▽◈ Sedona Rouge Hotel & Spa SH ✿
(928) 203-4111. **$249-$279, 3 day notice.** 2250 W Hwy 89A. Jct SR 179, 2 mi w. Ext/int corridors. **Pets:** Medium, dogs only. $100 deposit/room, $50 one-time fee/room. Designated rooms, supervision.
[SAVE] [✕] [🍴] [🛏] [🖭] [🍴] [🏊] [🍴]

▽▽◈▽ Sedona Super 8 SH
(928) 282-1533. **$69-$119.** 2545 W Hwy 89A. Jct SR 179, 2.4 mi w. Int corridors. **Pets:** Small. $25 one-time fee/pet. Service with restrictions, supervision.
[ASK] [S🔊] [✕] [🍴] [🛏] [🏊]

ⓐⓐⓐ ▽▽▽ Sky Ranch Lodge M
(928) 282-6400. **$75-$189.** Airport Rd. Jct SR 179, 1 mi w on SR 89A, then 1 mi s. Ext corridors. **Pets:** Medium, other species. $10 daily fee/pet. Service with restrictions, supervision.
[SAVE] [✕] [🛏] [🖭] [🏊]

ⓐⓐⓐ ▽▽◈ The Views Inn Sedona M
(928) 284-2487. **$65-$150.** 65 E Cortez Dr. Jct Bell Rock Blvd, 0.9 mi s on SR 179, just e. Ext corridors. **Pets:** Accepted.
[SAVE] [S🔊] [✕] [🛏] [🖭] [🏊]

ⓐⓐⓐ ▽◈ Village Lodge M
(928) 284-3626. **$49-$69, 3 day notice.** 78 Bell Rock Blvd. Jct SR 179, just w. Ext/int corridors. **Pets:** Dogs only. Supervision.
[SAVE] [✕] [🛏] [🖭]

SELIGMAN

ⓐⓐⓐ ▽◈ Deluxe Inn Motel M
(928) 422-3244. **$47-$52.** 203 E Chino. I-40, exit 121 eastbound, 1 mi n, then 0.7 mi e on Route 66; exit 123 westbound, just ne on I-40 business loop, then 2.4 mi w. Ext corridors. **Pets:** Other species. $10 one-time fee/room. Service with restrictions, supervision.
[SAVE] [S🔊] [✕] [🛏]

SHOW LOW

ⓐⓐⓐ ▽▽▽ Best Western Paint Pony Lodge M
(928) 537-5773. **$79-$120.** 581 W Deuce of Clubs Ave. On US 60 and SR 260. Ext corridors. **Pets:** Accepted.
[SAVE] [S🔊] [✕] [🛏] [🖭]

ⓐⓐⓐ ▽▽ Days Inn M
(928) 537-4356. **$65-$77.** 480 W Deuce of Clubs. On US 60 and SR 260. Ext/int corridors. **Pets:** Small. $10 one-time fee/pet. Supervision.
[SAVE] [S🔊] [✕] [🍴] [🛏] [🍴] [🏊]

▽ Motel 6 #4102 M
(928) 537-7694. **$50-$74.** 1941 E Deuce of Clubs Ave. Just e of jct SR 260. Ext corridors. **Pets:** Medium, other species. Service with restrictions, supervision.
[ASK] [S🔊] [✕] [🛏]

ⓐⓐⓐ ▽▽◈ Sleep Inn SH
(928) 532-7323. **$69-$120.** 1751 W Deuce of Clubs Ave. Jct SR 260 and US 60, just w. Int corridors. **Pets:** Large. $50 deposit/room, $15 daily fee/pet. Service with restrictions, supervision.
[SAVE] [S🔊] [✕] [&M] [🍴] [🍴] [🛏] [🖭] [🏊]

SIERRA VISTA

ⓐⓐⓐ ▽◈ America's Best Value Inn M ✿
(520) 459-5380. **$65-$85.** 100 Fab Ave. Jct Business SR 90 and Fry Blvd, then just e of main gate to Fort Huachuca. Ext corridors. **Pets:** Dogs only. $10 one-time fee/room. Designated rooms, service with restrictions, supervision.
[SAVE] [S🔊] [✕] [🍴] [🛏] [🖭] [🏊]

AAA ▼▼▼ Best Western Mission Inn M
(520) 458-8500. **$79-$99.** 3460 E Fry Blvd. Just w of jct SR 90/92. Ext corridors. **Pets:** Medium, other species. $10 daily fee/pet. Service with restrictions, supervision.
(SAVE) (S🐾) (✕) (🛏M) (🍴) (🖥) (➪)

AAA ▼▼▼ Quality Inn SH
(520) 458-7900. **$79-$89.** 1631 S Hwy 92. On SR 92, 1 mi s of jct SR 90. Int corridors. **Pets:** $15 daily fee/pet. Designated rooms, service with restrictions, crate.
(SAVE) (S🐾) (✕) (🍴) (🖥) (➪)

▼▼▼ Windemere Hotel & Conference Center SH
(520) 459-5900. **$89-$159.** 2047 S Hwy 92. 1.5 mi s of jct SR 90. Int corridors. **Pets:** $25 daily fee/room. Designated rooms, service with restrictions, supervision.
(ASK) (S🐾) (✕) (🍴) (🖥) (🍴) (➪)

SNOWFLAKE

AAA ▼▼▼ Comfort Inn SH
(928) 536-3888. **$59-$119.** 2055 S Main. SR 77, just s of town. Int corridors. **Pets:** Accepted.
(SAVE) (S🐾) (✕) (🖋) (🍴) (🖥) (➪)

TAYLOR

AAA ▼▼▼ Silver Creek Inn-Rodeway Inn M
(928) 536-2600. **$59-$79.** 825 N Main St. On SR 77. Ext corridors. **Pets:** Other species. $15 daily fee/room. Service with restrictions, supervision.
(SAVE) (S🐾) (✕) (🍴) (🖥)

TOMBSTONE

AAA ▼▼▼ Best Western Lookout Lodge SH 🐾
(520) 457-2223. **$75-$95.** 801 US Hwy 80 W. On SR 80, 1 mi n. Ext corridors. **Pets:** $20 daily fee/pet. Designated rooms, service with restrictions, crate.
(SAVE) (S🐾) (✕) (🖥) (🍴) (➪)

TUBAC

AAA ▼▼▼▼ Tubac Golf Resort SH 🐾
(520) 398-2211. **$110-$415, 7 day notice.** 1 Otero Rd. I-19, exit 40 (Chavez Siding Rd), on east side, then 2 mi s. Ext corridors. **Pets:** $25 deposit/pet. Designated rooms, service with restrictions.
(SAVE) (✕) (🖋) (🍴) (🖥) (🍴) (➪) (✕)

TUBA CITY

AAA ▼▼▼ Quality Inn SH
(928) 283-4545. **$88-$113.** Main St & Moenave Rd. 1 mi n of US 160. Int corridors. **Pets:** Medium. $10 daily fee/pet. Service with restrictions, supervision.
(SAVE) (S🐾) (✕) (🍴) (🖥) (🍴)

CATALINA

▼▼ Super 8 Motel-Tucson/Catalina M
(520) 818-9500. **$64-$90.** 15691 N Oracle Rd. 4.6 mi n of Tangerine Rd. Ext/int corridors. **Pets:** Dogs only. $5 daily fee/pet. Service with restrictions, crate.
(ASK) (S🐾) (✕) (🖋) (🍴) (🖥) (➪)

GREEN VALLEY

AAA ▼▼▼▼ Baymont Inn & Suites SH
(520) 399-3736. **$75-$144.** 90 W Esperanza Blvd. I-19, exit 65, just w. Int corridors. **Pets:** Accepted.
(SAVE) (S🐾) (✕) (🌀) (🖋) (🍴) (🖥) (➪)

AAA ▼▼▼▼ Best Western Green Valley SH
(520) 625-2250. **$64-$124.** 111 S La Canada Dr. I-19, exit 65, just w, then just s. Int corridors. **Pets:** Very small, dogs only. $10 daily fee/pet. Designated rooms, service with restrictions, supervision.
(SAVE) (S🐾) (✕) (🍴) (🖥) (🍴) (➪)

▼▼ Holiday Inn Express SH
(520) 625-0900. **$70-$135.** 19200 S I-19 Frontage Rd. I-19, exit 69 (Duval Mine Rd), west side of interstate, then just s. Int corridors. **Pets:** Small, dogs only. $20 daily fee/pet. Designated rooms, service with restrictions, supervision.
(ASK) (S🐾) (✕) (🌀) (🖋) (🍴) (🖥) (➪)

MARANA

AAA ▼▼▼ La Quinta Inn & Suites SH
(520) 572-4235. **$60-$280.** 6020 W Hospitality Rd. I-10, exit 246 (Cortaro Rd), just w, then just n. Int corridors. **Pets:** Medium. Designated rooms, service with restrictions, supervision.
(SAVE) (S🐾) (✕) (🛏M) (🖋) (🍴) (🖥) (➪)

▼▼ Red Roof Inn Tucson North SH
(520) 744-8199. **$60-$82.** 4940 W Ina Rd. I-10, exit 248 (Ina Rd), just w. Int corridors. **Pets:** Medium, other species. Service with restrictions, supervision.
(✕) (🖋) (🍴) (➪)

▼▼ Super 8 Motel SH
(520) 572-0300. **$89-$199.** 8351 N Cracker Barrel Rd. I-10, exit 246 (Cortaro Rd), just w. Int corridors. **Pets:** Accepted.
(ASK) (S🐾) (✕) (🖋) (🍴) (➪)

ORO VALLEY

AAA ▼▼▼ ▼▼▼ Hilton Tucson El Conquistador Golf & Tennis Resort LH
(520) 544-5000. **$89-$279, 3 day notice.** 10000 N Oracle Rd. I-10, exit 248 (Ina Rd), jct Ina Rd, 4.4 mi n. Ext/int corridors. **Pets:** Accepted.
(SAVE) (✕) (🛏M) (🖋) (🍴) (🖥) (🍴) (➪) (✕)

TUCSON

AAA ▼▼▼ Americas Best Value Inn-Tucson M
(520) 884-5800. **$50-$259.** 810 E Benson Hwy. I-10, exit 262, just s. Ext corridors. **Pets:** Other species. $25 deposit/room. Service with restrictions, supervision.
(SAVE) (S🐾) (✕) (🍴) (➪)

AAA ▼▼▼ Best Western Executive Inn SH
(520) 791-7551. **$89-$179, 30 day notice.** 333 W Drachman St. I-10, exit 257 (Speedway Blvd), 0.4 mi e to Main St, then 0.3 mi n. Int corridors. **Pets:** $25 one-time fee/pet. Designated rooms, supervision.
(SAVE) (S🐾) (✕) (🌀) (🍴) (🖥) (➪)

Best Western InnSuites Hotel & Suites Tucson-Catalina Foothills SH ❖
(520) 297-8111. **$69-$159.** 6201 N Oracle Rd. I-10, exit 250 (Orange Grove Rd), 4 mi e, then just s. Ext corridors. **Pets:** Medium, other species. $25 one-time fee/pet. Designated rooms, service with restrictions, supervision.
[icons]

Clarion Hotel-Randolph Park SH
(520) 795-0330. **$74-$164, 3 day notice.** 102 N Alvernon Way. Jct Campbell Ave, 2.2 mi e on Broadway, then just n. Ext/int corridors. **Pets:** Medium. $25 one-time fee/pet. Designated rooms, service with restrictions, supervision.
[icons]

Comfort Suites SH
(520) 295-4400. **$59-$159.** 6935 S Tucson Blvd. Just n of Tucson International Airport. Int corridors. **Pets:** Accepted.
[icons]

Comfort Suites at Tucson Mall SH ❖
(520) 888-6676. **$89-$169.** 515 W Auto Mall Dr. I-10, exit 254 (Prince Rd), 1.9 mi e, then 1.2 mi n. Int corridors. **Pets:** Other species. $10 one-time fee/pet. Service with restrictions, crate.
[icons]

Comfort Suites Tanque Verde/Sabino Canyon SH
(520) 298-2300. **$59-$159.** 7007 E Tanque Verde Rd. Jct Grand Rd, 0.4 mi ne. Ext corridors. **Pets:** Medium, other species. $15 daily fee/pet. Service with restrictions, supervision.
[icons]

Country Inn & Suites By Carlson SH
(520) 575-9255. **$79-$139.** 7411 N Oracle Rd. SR 77 (Oracle Rd), just n of Ina Rd. Ext corridors. **Pets:** Accepted.
[icons]

Crossland Economy Studios-Tucson-Butterfield Dr SH
(520) 745-3612. **Call for rates.** 4800 S Butterfield Dr. I-10, exit 264B eastbound, just n to Irvington, just e to Hotel Dr, just n; exit 264 westbound, just n. Ext corridors. **Pets:** Accepted.
[icons]

DoubleTree Hotel at Reid Park LH ❖
(520) 881-4200. **$79-$289.** 445 S Alvernon Way. I-10, exit 259 (22nd St), 4 mi e, then just n. Ext/int corridors. **Pets:** Medium. $25 one-time fee/room. Designated rooms, service with restrictions.
[icons]

Econo Lodge M
(520) 622-6714. **$39-$149.** 1136 N Stone Ave. I-10, eastbound, just e, then just n. Ext corridors. **Pets:** Medium, dogs only. $10 deposit/room, $10 one-time fee/room. Designated rooms, service with restrictions, supervision.
[icons]

Econo Lodge M
(520) 623-5881. **$39-$99.** 3020 S 6th Ave. I-10, exit 261 (4th-6th Ave), just n. Ext corridors. **Pets:** Accepted.
[icons]

Extended StayAmerica-Tucson-Grant Rd SH
(520) 795-9510. **$64-$104.** 5050 E Grant Rd. 0.5 mi e of Swan Rd. Ext corridors. **Pets:** Accepted.
[icons]

Hampton Inn North SH
(520) 206-0602. **$79-$149.** 1375 W Grant Rd. I-10, exit 256 (Grant Rd), just w. Int corridors. **Pets:** Accepted.
[icons]

Holiday Inn Express Hotel & Suites Tucson Airport SH
(520) 889-6600. **$72-$189.** 2548 E Medina Rd. 0.5 mi n of entrance to Tucson International Airport. Int corridors. **Pets:** Accepted.
[icons]

The Hotel Arizona LH
(520) 624-8711. **$89-$139.** 181 W Broadway. I-10, exit 258 (Broadway Blvd/Congress St), just e. Int corridors. **Pets:** $50 one-time fee/room. Service with restrictions.
[icons]

La Posada Lodge & Casitas SH
(520) 887-4800. **$79-$189.** 5900 N Oracle Rd. 0.5 mi s of Orange Grove Rd. Ext corridors. **Pets:** Medium, other species. $50 one-time fee/room. Service with restrictions, supervision.
[icons]

La Quinta Inn & Suites Tucson Airport SH
(520) 573-3333. **$95-$169.** 7001 S Tucson Blvd. Just n of Tucson International Airport. Int corridors. **Pets:** Medium. Service with restrictions.
[icons]

La Quinta Inn Downtown SH
(520) 624-4455. **$59-$129.** 750 Starr Pass Blvd. I-10, exit 259 (Starr Pass Blvd), just w. Int corridors. **Pets:** Other species. Service with restrictions.
[icons]

La Quinta Inn Tucson (East) SH
(520) 747-1414. **$98-$147.** 6404 E Broadway. Just e of Wilmot Rd. Ext corridors. **Pets:** Medium. Service with restrictions.
[icons]

The Lodge At Ventana Canyon LH
(520) 577-1400. **$93-$297, 21 day notice.** 6200 N Clubhouse Ln. I-10, exit 256 (Grant Rd), 8.6 mi e to Tanque Verde Rd, 0.6 mi e to Sabino Canyon Rd, 2 mi n, then 3.2 mi n on Kolb Rd. Ext/int corridors. **Pets:** Accepted.
[icons]

Lodge on the Desert SH ❖
(520) 325-3366. **$94-$309.** 306 N Alvernon Way. I-10, exit 258 (Broadway Blvd/Congress St), 4 mi e, then just n. Ext corridors. **Pets:** Large. $20 daily fee/pet. Service with restrictions, supervision.
[icons]

Loews Ventana Canyon Resort LH ❖
(520) 299-2020. **$165-$495, 7 day notice.** 7000 N Resort Dr. I-10, exit 256 (Grant Rd), 8.6 mi e, 0.6 mi ne on Tanque Verde Rd, 2 mi n on Sabino Canyon Rd, then 3.5 mi n on Kolb Rd. Ext/int corridors. **Pets:** Other species.
[icons]

Motel 6 Tucson-22nd Street #1196 M
(520) 624-2516. **$45-$87.** 1222 S Freeway Rd. I-10, exit 259 (Starr Pass Blvd), just w, then just s on frontage road. Ext corridors. **Pets:** Medium, other species. Service with restrictions, supervision.
[icons]

Motel 6 Tucson-Congress Street #50 M
(520) 628-1339. **$43-$59.** 960 S Freeway. I-10, exit 258 (Broadway Blvd/Congress St), 0.7 mi s on west side of interstate. Ext corridors. **Pets:** Medium, other species. Service with restrictions, supervision.
[icons]

Motel 6 Tucson North #1127 M
(520) 744-9300. **$45-$58.** 4630 W Ina Rd. I-10, exit 248 (Ina Rd), just e to Camino de Oeste, then just n. Int corridors. **Pets:** Medium, other species. Service with restrictions, supervision.
[icons]

Quality Inn at Tucson Airport SH
(520) 294-2500. **$65-$220.** 2803 E Valencia Rd. 1 mi ne of Tucson International Airport; just e of Tucson Blvd. Ext/int corridors. **Pets:** Large. $10 daily fee/pet. Service with restrictions, supervision.

Quality Inn Tucson SH
(520) 623-7792. **$59-$149.** 1025 E Benson Hwy. I-10, exit 262, just s. Int corridors. **Pets:** Other species. $15 one-time fee/pet. Designated rooms, service with restrictions.

Radisson Suites Tucson LH
(520) 721-7100. **$79-$229.** 6555 E Speedway Blvd. Just e of Wilmot Rd. Ext corridors. **Pets:** $50 one-time fee/pet. Service with restrictions, crate.

Ramada Inn & Suites Foothills Resort SH
(520) 886-9595. **$49-$199.** 6944 E Tanque Verde Rd. Jct Campbell Ave, 5.5 mi e on Grant Rd, then just ne. Ext corridors. **Pets:** Accepted.

Red Roof Inn-Tucson South M
(520) 571-1400. **$50-$76.** 3704 E Irvington Rd. I-10, exit 264 westbound; exit 264B eastbound. Ext corridors. **Pets:** Medium, other species. Service with restrictions, supervision.

Residence Inn by Marriott Williams Centre SH 🐾
(520) 790-6100. **$99-$399.** 5400 E Williams Cir. Jct Campbell Ave, 3.8 mi e on Broadway Blvd, then just s and just e on Williams Centre. Int corridors. **Pets:** Other species. $100 one-time fee/room. Service with restrictions, supervision.

Riverpark Inn SH
(520) 239-2300. **$79-$149.** 350 S Freeway. I-10, exit 258 (Broadway Blvd/Congress St), just w, then 0.4 mi s. Ext/int corridors. **Pets:** Accepted.

Rodeway Inn I-10 & Grant Rd M
(520) 622-7791. **$70-$136.** 1365 W Grant Rd. I-10, exit 256 (Grant Rd), just w. Ext corridors. **Pets:** Accepted.

Sheraton Tucson Hotel & Suites SH
(520) 323-6262. **$169-$279.** 5151 E Grant Rd. Jct Campbell Ave, 3.6 mi e. Ext/int corridors. **Pets:** Small. Designated rooms, no service, supervision.

Studio 6 Extended Stay #6002 M
(520) 746-0030. **$53-$79.** 4950 S Outlet Center Dr. I-10, exit 264A eastbound; exit 264B westbound, just s, then just nw on Julian Dr. Ext corridors. **Pets:** Accepted.

TownePlace Suites by Marriott SH
(520) 292-9697. **$89-$169.** 405 W Rudasill Rd. Jct Orange Grove Rd, 0.5 mi s on Oracle Rd, then just e. Int corridors. **Pets:** Other species. $75 one-time fee/room. Designated rooms, service with restrictions.

The Westin La Paloma Resort & Spa LH 🐾
(520) 742-6000. **$129-$489, 7 day notice.** 3800 E Sunrise Dr. From SR 77 (Oracle Rd), 4.6 mi e on Ina Rd via Skyline and Sunrise drs, just s on Via Palomita. Ext corridors. **Pets:** Medium, dogs only. Service with restrictions, supervision.

Westward Look Resort LH
(520) 297-1151. **$79-$339, 7 day notice.** 245 E Ina Rd. I-10, exit 248 (Ina Rd), 6 mi e, then just n on Westward Look Dr. Ext corridors. **Pets:** Small, other species. $75 one-time fee/room. Designated rooms, service with restrictions, crate.

Windmill Suites at St. Philip's Plaza SH
(520) 577-0007. **$79-$189.** 4250 N Campbell Ave. I-10, exit 254 (Prince Rd), 4 mi e, then 1 mi n. Int corridors. **Pets:** Accepted.

END METROPOLITAN AREA

WICKENBURG

AmericInn SH
(928) 684-5461. **$69-$87, 10 day notice.** 850 E Wickenburg Way. 1.3 mi se on US 60. Int corridors. **Pets:** Small. $6 daily fee/pet. Service with restrictions, supervision.

Best Western Rancho Grande SH
(928) 684-5445. **$64-$116.** 293 E Wickenburg Way. On US 60; center. Ext corridors. **Pets:** Accepted.

Super 8 Motel M
(928) 684-0808. **$70-$80.** 975 N Tegner St. 1 mi n of US 60 and 93. Ext/int corridors. **Pets:** Other species. $10 daily fee/pet. Designated rooms, service with restrictions, supervision.

WILLCOX

Best Western Plaza Inn SH
(520) 384-3556. **$64-$89.** 1100 W Rex Allen Dr. I-10, exit 340, just s. Ext corridors. **Pets:** Other species. $15 daily fee/pet. Service with restrictions, supervision.

Days Inn M
(520) 384-4222. **$60-$65.** 724 N Bisbee Ave. I-10, exit 340, just s. Ext corridors. **Pets:** Medium. $7 daily fee/pet. Service with restrictions, supervision.

Motel 6 Willcox #410 M
(520) 384-2201. **$39-$50.** 921 N Bisbee Ave. I-10, exit 340, just s. Ext corridors. **Pets:** Medium, other species. Service with restrictions, supervision.

WILLIAMS

Days Inn M
(928) 635-4051. **$56-$96.** 2488 W Route 66. I-40, exit 161, just e. Int corridors. **Pets:** Medium, other species. $20 deposit/pet. Designated rooms, service with restrictions, supervision.

El Rancho Motel M
(928) 635-2552. **$35-$73.** 617 E Route 66. I-40, exit 163, 0.6 mi s, then just e. Ext corridors. **Pets:** Dogs only. $5 daily fee/pet. Designated rooms, service with restrictions, supervision.

Grand Canyon Railway Hotel SH
(928) 635-4010. **$99-$179.** 235 N Grand Canyon Blvd. I-40, exit 163, 0.5 mi s. Int corridors. **Pets:** Accepted.

Holiday Inn Williams SH
(928) 635-4114. **$69-$169.** 950 N Grand Canyon Blvd. I-40, exit 163, just s. Int corridors. **Pets:** Large, other species. No service.

Motel 6-4010 M
(928) 635-9000. **$45-$83.** 831 W Route 66. I-40, exit 161, 1 mi e. Int corridors. **Pets:** Medium, other species. Service with restrictions, supervision.

Quality Inn Mountain Ranch Resort SH
(928) 635-2693. **$59-$149.** 6701 E Mountain Ranch Rd. I-40, exit 171 (Deer Farm Rd), just s. Ext corridors. **Pets:** Medium. $35 one-time fee/room. Service with restrictions, supervision.

Rodeway Inn M
(928) 635-2619. **$40-$105.** 334 E Route 66. I-40, exit 163, 0.5 mi s, then just e. Ext corridors. **Pets:** Accepted.

Travelodge Williams M
(928) 635-2651. **$39-$99.** 430 E Route 66. I-40, exit 163, 0.5 mi s, then just e. Ext corridors. **Pets:** Dogs only. $10 one-time fee/pet. No service, supervision.

WINDOW ROCK

Quality Inn Navajo Nation Capital SH
(928) 871-4108. **$64-$83.** 48 W Hwy 264. Center. Ext corridors. **Pets:** Small. $50 deposit/room. Service with restrictions, crate.

WINSLOW

Comfort Inn-Winslow SH
(928) 289-4638. **$80-$219, 7 day notice.** 1701 N Park Dr. I-40, exit 253. Int corridors. **Pets:** Accepted.

Days Inn SH
(928) 289-1010. **$55-$105.** 2035 W Hwy 66. I-40, exit 252, just s. Int corridors. **Pets:** Accepted.

Econo Lodge SH
(928) 289-4687. **$69-$109.** 1706 N Park Dr. I-40, exit 253, just s. Ext corridors. **Pets:** Small. $5 one-time fee/room. Service with restrictions, crate.

La Posada Hotel SH
(928) 289-4366. **$99-$149, 3 day notice.** 303 E 2nd St. I-40, exit 253, 1 mi s to Route 66 (2nd St), then just e; in historic downtown. Int corridors. **Pets:** Other species. $10 one-time fee/room. Designated rooms, service with restrictions, supervision.

Motel 6 Winslow #4012 M
(928) 289-9581. **$47-$59.** 520 W Desmond St. I-40, exit 253, just s on N Park Dr, then just w. Int corridors. **Pets:** Medium, other species. Service with restrictions, supervision.

Super 8 Motel M
(928) 289-4606. **$51-$79.** 1916 W Third St. I-40, exit 252, just s, then just e on Route 66. Int corridors. **Pets:** Accepted.

YUMA

Best Western Coronado Motor Hotel M
(928) 783-4453. **$79-$129.** 233 4th Ave. I-8, exit 4th Ave eastbound, 0.5 mi s; exit 1 (Giss Pkwy) westbound, 1 mi w. Ext corridors. **Pets:** Small. $50 deposit/pet. Designated rooms, service with restrictions, crate.

Best Western InnSuites Hotel & Suites Yuma SH
(928) 783-8341. **$79-$169.** 1450 Castle Dome Ave. I-8, exit 2 (16th St/US 95), just ne. Ext corridors. **Pets:** Medium, other species. $25 one-time/pet. Designated rooms, service with restrictions, supervision.

Clarion Suites SH
(928) 726-4830. **$147-$400.** 2600 S 4th Ave. I-8, exit 2 (16 St/US 95) eastbound, 1 mi w, then 1.3 mi s; exit 3 (SR 280) westbound, 0.5 mi s, then 2 mi w. Ext corridors. **Pets:** Accepted.

Comfort Inn SH
(928) 782-1200. **$109-$199, 7 day notice.** 1691 S Riley Ave. I-8, exit 2 (16th St/US 95), just w. Int corridors. **Pets:** Medium. $10 daily fee/room. Service with restrictions, supervision.

Holiday Inn SH
(928) 782-9300. **Call for rates (no credit cards).** 1901 E 18th St. I-8, exit 2 (16th St/US 95), 0.4 mi e on 16th St, just s on Pacific Ave, then just w. Int corridors. **Pets:** Medium. $10 deposit/pet, $5 daily fee/pet. Designated rooms, service with restrictions, supervision.

Howard Johnson Inn SH
(928) 344-1420. **$49-$120.** 3181 S 4th Ave. I-8, exit 3E (SR 280 S), 1 mi s to 32nd St, then 2 mi w. Ext corridors. **Pets:** Other species. $10 daily fee/room. Service with restrictions, crate.

Microtel Inn & Suites SH
(928) 345-1777. **$54-$108.** 11274 S Fortuna Rd, Suite H. I-8, exit 12 (Fortuna Rd), just s, then w on frontage road. Int corridors. **Pets:** Very small, other species. Service with restrictions, supervision.

Motel 6 Yuma East #1031 M
(928) 782-9521. **$45-$68.** 1445 E 16th St. I-8, exit 2 (16th St/US 95), just e. Ext corridors. **Pets:** Medium, other species. Service with restrictions, supervision.

▼▼ **Oak Tree Inn** SH
(928) 539-9000. **$85-$109, 7 day notice.** 1731 Sunridge Dr. I-8, exit 2 (16th St/US 95), just e, then just s. Int corridors. **Pets:** Medium. $10 daily fee/pet. Service with restrictions, supervision.

(ASK) (SD) (✕) (🗎) (🖵) (∿)

AAA ▼▼ **Quality Inn Airport** SH
(928) 726-4721. **$80-$109.** 711 E 32nd St. I-8, exit 3E (SR 280), 1.2 mi s, then 1.9 mi w. Ext corridors. **Pets:** $25 one-time fee/room. Service with restrictions, supervision.

(SAVE) (SD) (✕) (👤) (🗎) (🖵) (¶) (∿)

AAA ▼▼ **Shilo Inn Hotel-Yuma** SH 🐾
(928) 782-9511. **$122-$200.** 1550 S Castle Dome Rd. I-8, exit 2 (16th St/US 95), just e to Yuma Palms Pkwy, just n, then just w. Int corridors. **Pets:** Other species. $25 one-time fee/room. Supervision.

(SAVE) (SD) (✕) (👤) (🗎) (🖵) (¶) (∿) (✕)

AAA ▼▼ **Yuma Cabana Motel** M
(928) 783-8311. **$44-$83.** 2151 S 4th Ave. I-8, exit 2 (16th St/US 95), 1 mi w, then 0.5 mi s. Int corridors. **Pets:** Small. $6 daily fee/pet. Service with restrictions, supervision.

(SAVE) (SD) (✕) (🗎) (∿)

▼▼ **Yuma Super 8 Motel** SH
(928) 782-2000. **$89-$189, 7 day notice.** 1688 S Riley Ave. I-8, exit 2 (16th St/US 95), just w. Int corridors. **Pets:** Medium. $10 daily fee/room. Service with restrictions, supervision.

(ASK) (SD) (✕) (👤M) (👤) (🗎) (🖵) (∿)

ARKANSAS

ARKADELPHIA

Best Western-Continental Inn SH
(870) 246-5592. **$69-$99.** 136 Valley St. I-30, exit 78, just e. Ext corridors. **Pets:** Large. $9 daily fee/pet. Service with restrictions, supervision.

Super 8 Motel SH
(870) 246-8585. **$48-$78.** 118 Valley St. I-30, exit 78, just e. Ext corridors. **Pets:** Accepted.

BATESVILLE

Ramada Inn of Batesville SH
(870) 698-1800. **$70-$149.** 1325 N St Louis St. 1 mi n on US 167. Ext corridors. **Pets:** Small, dogs only. $20 daily fee/pet. Service with restrictions, supervision.

Super 8 Motel-Batesville M ❖
(870) 793-5888. **$59-$62.** 1287 N St. Louis St. 1 mi n on US 167. Ext corridors. **Pets:** Dogs only. $25 one-time fee/room. Service with restrictions, supervision.

BEEBE

Days Inn SH
(501) 882-2008. **$60-$120.** 100 Tammy Ln. US 67/167, exit 28, just e. Ext corridors. **Pets:** Small, dogs only. $10 one-time fee/pet. Designated rooms, service with restrictions, supervision.

BENTONVILLE

La Quinta Inn & Suites SH
(479) 271-7555. **$134-$164.** 1001 SE Walton Blvd. I-540, exit 85, 0.7 mi w. Int corridors. **Pets:** $75 deposit/pet. Service with restrictions, supervision.

TownePlace Suites by Marriott Bentonville/Rogers SH
(479) 621-0202. **$134-$189.** 3100 SE 14th St. I-540, exit 86, just e. Int corridors. **Pets:** $100 one-time fee/room. Service with restrictions, crate.

BLYTHEVILLE

Comfort Inn of Blytheville SH
(870) 763-7081. **$59-$69, 7 day notice.** 1520 E Main. I-55, exit 67, just w. Ext corridors. **Pets:** Accepted.

Hampton Inn SH
(870) 763-5220. **$79-$109.** 301 N Access Rd. I-55, exit 67, just nw. Ext corridors. **Pets:** Accepted.

Holiday Inn SH
(870) 763-5800. **$109-$139.** 1121 E Main. I-55, exit 67, just w. Ext/int corridors. **Pets:** Accepted.

Super 8 Motel-Blytheveille SH
(870) 763-2300. **$62-$69.** 239 N Service Rd. I-55, exit 67, just nw. Int corridors. **Pets:** Accepted.

BRYANT

Americas Best Value Inn & Suites M
(501) 653-7800. **$48-$78.** 407 W Commerce St. I-30, exit 123, just sw. Ext corridors. **Pets:** Medium, dogs only. $10 daily fee/pet. Service with restrictions, supervision.

Comfort Inn & Suites SH
(501) 653-4000. **$90-$130.** 209 W Commerce St. I-30, exit 123, just w. Int corridors. **Pets:** Accepted.

Super 8 Motel M
(501) 847-7888. **$53-$56.** 201 Dell Dr. I-30, exit 123, just e. Ext corridors. **Pets:** Medium, dogs only. $10 one-time fee/pet. Service with restrictions, supervision.

CABOT

Super 8 of Cabot M
(501) 941-3748. **$59-$64.** 15 Ryeland Dr. US 67/167, exit 19 (SR 89), just e. Ext corridors. **Pets:** Accepted.

CAMDEN

Holiday Inn Express SH ❖
(870) 836-8100. **$90-$110.** 1450 US Hwy 278 W. 1 mi w of jct US 79 and 278. Int corridors. **Pets:** Medium. Designated rooms, service with restrictions, supervision.

CLARKSVILLE

Best Western Sherwood Inn SH
(479) 754-7900. **$42-$74, 10 day notice.** 1203 S Rogers Ave. I-40, exit 58, just n. Ext corridors. **Pets:** Other species. Service with restrictions, supervision.

CONWAY

Days Inn SH
(501) 450-7575. **$59-$119.** 1002 E Oak St. I-40, exit 127, just n. Ext corridors. **Pets:** Accepted.

◆◆◆ ▼▼▼ Quality Inn SH
(501) 329-0300. **$69-$149.** 150 Hwy 65 N. I-40, exit 125, just n. Ext corridors. **Pets:** Accepted.
SAVE S6 ⊗ ⌀ 目 ▣ ≋

EL DORADO

▼▼▼▼ La Quinta Inn El Dorado SH
(870) 863-6677. **$65-$75.** 2303 Junction City Rd. Just e of jct US 167 and 82B. Ext/int corridors. **Pets:** Accepted.
ASK S6 ⊗ ⌀ 目 ▣ ≋

EUREKA SPRINGS

◆◆◆ ▼▼▼▼ 1886 Crescent Hotel & Spa SH
(479) 253-9766. **$93-$164, 3 day notice.** 75 Prospect Ave. 1.3 mi n of jct SR 23 on US 62B Historic Loop. Int corridors. **Pets:** Small, other species. $10 daily fee/pet. Service with restrictions, crate.
SAVE S6 ⊗ 目 ▣ ¶¶ ≋ ⊗

▼▼ 1905 Basin Park Hotel SH
(479) 253-7837. **$93-$139, 3 day notice.** 12 Spring St. 0.7 mi n of jct US 62 via SR 23 N; downtown. Int corridors. **Pets:** Small, other species. $10 daily fee/pet. Designated rooms, service with restrictions, crate.
ASK S6 ⊗ 目 ▣ ¶¶ ≋

▼▼▼ Arsenic & Old Lace B&B BB ❀
(479) 253-5454. **$139-$249, 15 day notice.** 60 Hillside Ave. 1.2 mi n on SR 23, just sw; downtown. Ext/int corridors. **Pets:** Dogs only. $30 one-time fee/room. Designated rooms, service with restrictions, crate.
ASK ⊗

▼▼ Bavarian Inn SH
(479) 253-8128. **$68-$128, 3 day notice.** 325 W Van Buren St. 1 mi w of jct US 62 and SR 23. Ext corridors. **Pets:** Accepted.
⊗ 目 ▣ ≋

◆◆◆ ▼▼▼ Best Western-Eureka Inn SH
(479) 253-9551. **$49-$139.** 101 E Van Buren St. Just w of jct US 62 and SR 23 N. Ext/int corridors. **Pets:** Accepted.
SAVE S6 ⊗ 目 ▣ ¶¶ ≋ ⊗

◆◆◆ ▼▼▼ Best Western Inn of the Ozarks SH ❀
(479) 253-9768. **$49-$129, 3 day notice.** 207 W Van Buren St. On US 62, 0.5 mi w of jct SR 23. Ext corridors. **Pets:** Medium, dogs only. $7 daily fee/pet. Service with restrictions, supervision.
SAVE S6 ⊗ ⌀ 🖳 目 ▣ ¶¶ ≋ ⊗

▼▼ Brackenridge Lodge M
(479) 253-6803. **$39-$149, 7 day notice.** 352 W Van Buren St. 1 mi w of jct US 62 and SR 23. Ext corridors. **Pets:** Small, dogs only. $50 deposit/room. Designated rooms, service with restrictions, crate.
ASK S6 ⊗ 目 ▣ ≋ ℤ

◆◆◆ ▼▼▼ Budget Host Inn SH ❀
(479) 253-7300. **$48-$88.** 154 Huntsville Rd. Just s of jct US 62 and SR 23. Ext/int corridors. **Pets:** Very small. $4 daily fee/room. Designated rooms, supervision.
SAVE S6 ⊗ 目 ▣ ≋

▼▼ Comfort Inn SH
(479) 253-5241. **$49-$179.** 196 E Van Buren St. Just w of jct US 62 and SR 23 S. Ext/int corridors. **Pets:** Designated rooms, service with restrictions, crate.
ASK S6 ⊗ ⌀ 目 ▣ ≋

▼▼ Days Inn M ❀
(479) 253-8863. **$49-$169, 3 day notice.** 120 W Van Buren St. On US 62, just w of jct SR 23 N. Ext corridors. **Pets:** Medium, dogs only. $15 daily fee/room. Service with restrictions, supervision.
ASK S6 ⊗ 目 ▣ ≋

◆◆◆ ▼▼▼ Howard Johnson Express SH
(479) 253-6665. **$45-$150.** 4042 E Van Buren St. 1.8 mi e of jct US 62 and SR 23. Ext corridors. **Pets:** Accepted.
SAVE S6 ⊗ 目 ▣ ≋

▼▼ Road Runner Inn M
(479) 253-8166. **$59-$89, 14 day notice.** 3034 Mundell Rd. On US 62, 4.3 mi w, 3.9 mi s on SR 187, then 3 mi se. Ext corridors. **Pets:** Other species. $10 daily fee/pet. Designated rooms, service with restrictions, supervision.
ASK ⊗ 目 ▣ ℤ

▼ Travelers Inn M
(479) 253-8386. **$38-$58, 3 day notice.** 2044 E Van Buren St. On US 62, just e of jct US 62 and SR 23. Ext corridors. **Pets:** Accepted.
ASK S6 ⊗ 目 ≋

◆◆◆ ▼▼▼ Travelodge SH
(479) 253-8992. **$45-$150.** 110 Huntsville Dr. Jct US 62 and SR 23. Ext corridors. **Pets:** Accepted.
SAVE S6 ⊗ 目 ▣ ≋

FAYETTEVILLE

◆◆◆ ▼▼▼ Best Western Windsor Suites SH
(479) 587-1400. **$89-$109.** 1122 S Futrall Dr. I-540, exit 62, just se. Ext corridors. **Pets:** Accepted.
SAVE S6 ⊗ 目 ▣ ≋

◆◆◆ ▼▼▼ Quality Inn SH
(479) 444-9800. **$62-$110.** 523 S Shiloh Dr. I-540, exit 62, just w. Ext corridors. **Pets:** Accepted.
SAVE S6 ⊗ 目 ▣ ≋

▼▼▼ Sleep Inn by Choice Hotels SH
(479) 587-8700. **$75-$95.** 728 Millsap Rd. I-540, exit 67, 1.6 mi e, then just s on US 71B. Int corridors. **Pets:** Accepted.
ASK S6 ⊗ 🖳 目 ▣

FORDYCE

▼▼ Days Inn SH
(870) 352-2400. **$69-$89.** 2500 W 4th St. On US 79/167; 1 mi w of center. Ext/int corridors. **Pets:** Small. $10 daily fee/pet. Service with restrictions, supervision.
ASK S6 ⊗ 目 ▣ ≋

FORREST CITY

▼▼ Days Inn SH
(870) 633-0777. **$70-$120, 7 day notice.** 350 Barrow Hill Rd. I-40, exit 241B, just n. Ext corridors. **Pets:** Small. $5 one-time fee/pet. No service, supervision.
ASK S6 ⊗ 🖳 目 ▣ ≋

▼▼▼ Holiday Inn SH
(870) 633-6300. **$81-$90.** 200 Holiday Dr. I-40, exit 241B, just n. Ext corridors. **Pets:** Accepted.
ASK S6 ⊗ 目 ▣ ¶¶ ≋

FORT SMITH

▼▼▼ Aspen Hotel & Suites SH
(479) 452-9000. **$99-$202.** 2900 S 68th St. I-540, exit 8B (Rogers Ave), just e. Int corridors. **Pets:** Other species. Service with restrictions, supervision.
ASK S6 ⊗ 目 ▣ ≋

◆◆◆ ▼▼▼ Baymont Inn & Suites Fort Smith SH
(479) 484-5770. **$74-$114.** 2123 Burnham Rd. I-540, exit 8A (Rogers Ave), just w. Int corridors. **Pets:** Medium. Service with restrictions.
SAVE ⊗ ⌀ 目 ▣ ≋

▼▼▼ ◆ Comfort Inn SH
(479) 484-0227. **$99.** 2120 Burnham Rd. I-540, exit 8A (Rogers Ave), just w. Int corridors. **Pets:** Accepted.
ASK ✕ 🎲 🔌 💻 ➢ ✕

▼▼▼▼ Holiday Inn City Center Fort Smith LH
(479) 783-1000. **$79-$109.** 700 Rogers Ave. Just s of US 64 (Garrison Ave); downtown. Int corridors. **Pets:** Medium. $25 one-time fee/room. Designated rooms, service with restrictions, supervision.
SAVE 🎲 ✕ ♿ 🎲 🐾 🔌 💻 🍴 ➢ ✕

▼▼▼▼ Residence Inn by Marriott SH
(479) 478-8300. **$109-$149.** 3005 S 74th. I-540, exit 8A (Rogers Ave), 0.8 mi e. Int corridors. **Pets:** Other species. $150 one-time fee/room.
ASK 🎲 ✕ 🎲 🐾 🔌 💻 ➢ ✕

GENTRY

▼▼▼▼ Apple Crest Inn Bed & Breakfast BB
(479) 736-8201. **$100-$185, 14 day notice.** 12758 S Hwy 59. On SR 59, 1 mi s. Int corridors. **Pets:** Other species. $25 one-time fee/room. Designated rooms, service with restrictions, crate.
ASK 🎲 ✕

HARRISON

▼▼ ◆ Comfort Inn SH
(870) 741-7676. **$85-$105.** 1210 Hwy 62/65 N. 1 mi n on US 62/65/412. Ext/int corridors. **Pets:** Small. $25 daily fee/pet, $25 one-time fee/pet. Service with restrictions, supervision.
ASK ✕ 🎲 🔌 💻 ➢

▼ Family Budget Inn M 🐾
(870) 743-1000. **$39-$43.** 401 S Main (Hwy 65B S). 0.7 mi s of jct SR 7. Ext corridors. **Pets:** Small. $5 daily fee/room. Designated rooms, no service, supervision.
SAVE 🎲 ✕ 🔌 💻 ➢

▼▼ ◆ Holiday Inn Express Hotel & Suites SH
(870) 741-3636. **$105-$125.** 117 Hwy 43 E. Just e from jct US 62/65/412 and SR 43. Int corridors. **Pets:** Small. $25 one-time fee/pet. Service with restrictions, supervision.
ASK 🎲 ✕ 🐾 🔌 💻 ➢ ✕

HAZEN

▼▼ ◆ Super 8 Motel SH
(870) 255-2888. **$64-$79.** 4167 Hwy 63. I-40, exit 193, just s. Ext corridors. **Pets:** Small. $10 daily fee/pet. Service with restrictions, supervision.
SAVE 🎲 ✕ 🔌 💻 ➢

HOPE

▼▼▼ Best Western of Hope SH
(870) 777-9222. **$63-$65.** 1800 Holiday Dr. I-30, exit 30, just nw. Ext corridors. **Pets:** Other species. Service with restrictions, crate.
SAVE 🎲 ✕ 🔌 💻 ➢

HOT SPRINGS

▼▼▼▼ Clarion Resort SH
(501) 525-1391. **$89-$249.** 4813 Central Ave. 5.5 mi s of jct US 270 and SR 7. Int corridors. **Pets:** Medium. $35 daily fee/room. Designated rooms, service with restrictions, supervision.
SAVE 🎲 ✕ 🐾 🔌 💻 🍴 ➢ ✕

▼▼▼▼ Embassy Suites Hot Springs LH 🐾
(501) 624-9200. **$129-$179.** 400 Convention Blvd. Just w of jct US 70. Int corridors. **Pets:** Small, other species. $25 daily fee/pet. Designated rooms, service with restrictions, supervision.
SAVE ✕ ♿ 🎲 🐾 🔌 💻 🍴 ➢ ✕

▼▼▼ Travelier Inn M
(501) 624-4681. **$50-$65.** 1045 E Grand Ave. 1 mi e of jct US 270B and 70. Ext corridors. **Pets:** Accepted.
SAVE 🎲 ✕ 🔌 ➢

▼▼▼ Velda Rose Resort Hotel & Spa LH
(501) 623-3311. **$79-$95.** 217 Park Ave. On US 70B and SR 7; center. Int corridors. **Pets:** Medium. $10 one-time fee/pet. Designated rooms, service with restrictions, supervision.
SAVE 🎲 ✕ 🔌 💻 🍴 ➢

JONESBORO

▼▼▼ ◆ Comfort Inn & Suites SH
(870) 972-9000. **$70-$85.** 2911 Gilmore Dr. US 63, exit Stadium Blvd/Caraway Rd, just n. Int corridors. **Pets:** Small, other species. $10 daily fee/room. Service with restrictions.
SAVE 🎲 ✕ 🎲 🔌 💻 ➢

▼▼▼▼ Holiday Inn Express SH
(870) 932-5554. **$85.** 2407 Phillips Dr. US 63, exit Stadium Blvd/Caraway Rd, just n. Int corridors. **Pets:** Medium. Service with restrictions, supervision.
ASK 🎲 ✕ 🔌 💻 ➢

LITTLE ROCK

▼▼▼▼ Comfort Inn & Suites, Downtown Little Rock @ The Clinton Library SH
(501) 687-7700. **$81-$99.** 707 I-30. I-30, exit 140A, just e. Int corridors. **Pets:** Medium. $25 one-time fee/room. Service with restrictions, supervision.
SAVE 🎲 ✕ ♿ 🔌 💻 ➢

▼▼▼▼ Embassy Suites Hotel Little Rock LH
(501) 312-9000. **$119-$219.** 11301 Financial Center Pkwy. Jct I-430 and 630, just w. Int corridors. **Pets:** Accepted.
SAVE ✕ ♿ 🎲 🐾 🔌 💻 🍴 ➢ ✕

▼▼▼ La Quinta Inn SH
(501) 225-7007. **$71-$107.** 1010 Breckenridge Rd. I-430, exit 8, just e to Breckenridge Rd, then just s. Int corridors. **Pets:** Medium. Service with restrictions.
SAVE ✕ 🎲 🔌 💻

▼▼▼ ◆ La Quinta Inn Little Rock (Medical Center Area) SH
(501) 664-7000. **$65-$99.** 901 Fair Park Blvd. I-630, exit 4, just s. Ext corridors. **Pets:** Medium. Service with restrictions.
ASK ✕ ♿ 🎲 🔌 💻 ➢

▼▼▼ La Quinta Inn Little Rock (Otter Creek Area) SH
(501) 455-2300. **$76-$106.** 11701 I-30. I-30, exit 128, just e. Ext corridors. **Pets:** Medium. Service with restrictions.
SAVE ✕ 💻 ➢

▼▼▼ La Quinta Inn Little Rock (West) SH
(501) 224-0900. **$78-$168.** 200 S Shackleford Rd. I-430, exit 6; I-630, exit Shackleford Rd N; jct I-430 and 630. Ext corridors. **Pets:** Medium. Service with restrictions.
SAVE ✕ 💻 ➢

LONOKE

▼▼▼ Days Inn SH
(501) 676-5138. **$65-$90.** 105 Dee Dee Ln. I-40, exit 175, just n. Ext corridors. **Pets:** Medium, other species. $10 daily fee/pet. Designated rooms, service with restrictions, supervision.
SAVE 🎲 ✕ 🐾 🔌 💻 ➢

▲▲▲ ◆◆◆ Holiday Inn Express Hotel & Suites SH
(501) 676-7800. **$99-$119.** 104 Dee Dee Ln. I-40, exit 175, just n. Int corridors. **Pets:** Small. $25 daily fee/pet. Designated rooms, service with restrictions, supervision.
SAVE S☐ ☒ ☒ ⬚ ⬚ ⬚ ⬚ ⬚

▲▲▲ ◆◆ Super 8 Motel SH
(501) 676-8880. **$65-$80.** 102 Dee Dee Ln. I-40, exit 175, just n. Int corridors. **Pets:** Small. $10 daily fee/pet. Service with restrictions, supervision.
SAVE S☐ ☒ ⬚ ⬚ ⬚

MARION

◆◆ Best Western-Regency Motor Inn SH
(870) 739-3278. **$65-$75.** 3635 I-55. I-55, exit 10, just nw. Ext corridors. **Pets:** Medium. Service with restrictions, supervision.
ASK S☐ ☒ ☒ ⬚ ⬚ ⬚

MAUMELLE

▲▲▲ ◆◆◆ Comfort Suites SH
(501) 851-8444. **$79-$139.** 14322 Frontier Dr. I-40, exit 142, just sw. Int corridors. **Pets:** Accepted.
SAVE S☐ ☒ ☒ ⬚ ⬚ ⬚

◆◆ Quality Inn-Maumelle SH
(501) 851-3500. **$75.** 14325 Frontier Dr. I-40, exit 142, just sw. Ext corridors. **Pets:** Medium. $10 one-time fee/room. Designated rooms, service with restrictions, supervision.
ASK S☐ ☒ ⬚ ⬚ ⬚

MOUNTAIN HOME

◆◆ Days Inn SH
(870) 425-1010. **$65-$70.** 1746 E Hwy 62B. On US 62B, 2.3 mi e. Int corridors. **Pets:** Small, other species. $8 daily fee/pet. Service with restrictions, supervision.
ASK S☐ ☒ ☒ ⬚ ⬚ ⬚

◆◆ Holiday Inn Express SH
(870) 425-6200. **$80-$119.** 1005 Coley Dr. 1.4 mi e on US 62B. Int corridors. **Pets:** Accepted.
ASK S☐ ☒ ☒ ⬚ ⬚ ⬚ ⬚

▲▲▲ ◆◆◆ Teal Point Resort CA
(870) 492-5145. **$69-$379, 45 day notice.** 715 Teal Point Rd. 7 mi e on US 62, 0.6 mi n on CR 406, follow signs. Ext corridors. **Pets:** $7 daily fee/pet. Designated rooms, service with restrictions, supervision.
SAVE ⬚ ⬚ ⬚ ⬚

MOUNTAIN VIEW

◆◆ Best Western Fiddlers Inn M
(870) 269-2828. **$58-$95.** 601 Sylomore. 1 mi n on SR 5, 9 and 14. Ext corridors. **Pets:** Accepted.
ASK S☐ ☒ ⬚ ⬚ ⬚

NORTH LITTLE ROCK

▲▲▲ ◆◆◆ Baymont Inn & Suites SH
(501) 758-8888. **$69-$104.** 4100 E McCain Blvd. Jct US 67/167, exit 1A northbound; exit 1 southbound. Ext corridors. **Pets:** Medium. Service with restrictions.
SAVE ☒ ☒ ⬚ ⬚

◆◆◆ Hampton Inn SH
(501) 771-2090. **$99-$119.** 500 W 29th St. I-40, exit 152. Int corridors. **Pets:** Accepted.
ASK S☐ ☒ ☒ ⬚ ⬚

▲▲▲ ◆◆◆ Holiday Inn-North SH
(501) 758-1851. **$89-$99, 30 day notice.** 120 W Pershing Blvd. I-40, exit 152 westbound; exit 153A eastbound. Int corridors. **Pets:** Large, other species. Service with restrictions, supervision.
SAVE S☐ ☒ ⬚ ⬚ ⬚

▲▲▲ ◆◆◆ La Quinta Inn & Suites SH
(501) 945-0808. **$81-$117.** 4311 Warden Rd. US 67/167, exit 1B northbound; exit 1 southbound. Int corridors. **Pets:** Medium. Service with restrictions.
SAVE ☒ ☒ ⬚ ⬚ ⬚ ⬚

▲▲▲ ◆◆◆ Red Roof Inn SH
(501) 945-0080. **$60-$70.** 5711 Pritchard Dr. I-40, exit 157, just s. Int corridors. **Pets:** Medium, other species. Service with restrictions, supervision.
SAVE S☐ ☒ ⬚ ⬚

◆◆◆◆ Residence Inn by Marriott-North SH
(501) 945-7777. **$145-$185.** 4110 Healthcare Dr. I-40, exit 156. Int corridors. **Pets:** Accepted.
ASK S☐ ☒ ☒ ⬚ ⬚ ⬚ ⬚ ☒

OZARK

◆ Oxford Inn M
(479) 667-1131. **$50.** 305 N 18th St. I-40, exit 35, 3 mi s on SR 23. Ext corridors. **Pets:** Accepted.
ASK ☒ ⬚ ⬚

PINE BLUFF

◆◆ Days Inn & Suites SH
(870) 534-1800. **$64-$85.** 406 N Blake St. Just n of jct US 65B and 79B. Ext corridors. **Pets:** Accepted.
ASK S☐ ☒ ☒ ⬚ ⬚ ⬚

◆◆◆ Holiday Inn Express Hotel & Suites SH
(870) 879-3800. **$85-$150.** 3620 Camden Rd. I-530, exit 39, just sw. Int corridors. **Pets:** Small, other species. $25 one-time fee/room. Service with restrictions, supervision.
ASK S☐ ☒ ☒ ⬚ ⬚ ⬚ ⬚

POCAHONTAS

◆◆ Days Inn & Suites SH
(870) 892-9500. **$77.** 2805 Hwy 67 S. 1.7 mi s. Int corridors. **Pets:** Medium. $25 deposit/pet, $10 daily fee/pet. Designated rooms, service with restrictions, supervision.
ASK S☐ ☒ ⬚ ⬚ ⬚ ⬚ ☒

ROGERS

▲▲▲ ◆◆◆◆ Embassy Suites Northwest Arkansas LH 🐾
(479) 254-8400. **$139-$239.** 3303 Pinnacle Hills Pkwy. I-540, exit 83, just w, then 0.6 mi s. Int corridors. **Pets:** Small. $75 one-time fee/room. Service with restrictions, crate.
SAVE ☒ ⬚ ☒ ⬚ ⬚ ⬚ ⬚ ⬚ ☒

◆◆◆◆ Residence Inn by Marriott SH
(479) 636-5900. **$69-$179.** 4611 W Locust St. I-540, exit 85, 0.4 mi n on 46th St. Int corridors. **Pets:** Other species. $75 one-time fee/pet. Service with restrictions, crate.
ASK S☐ ☒ ☒ ⬚ ⬚ ⬚ ⬚ ☒

RUSSELLVILLE

◆◆ Comfort Inn M
(479) 967-7500. **$69.** 3019 E Parkway Dr. I-40, exit 84, just s. Ext corridors. **Pets:** Accepted.
ASK S☐ ☒ ⬚ ⬚ ⬚

▲▲▲ ◆◆ Holiday Inn SH
(479) 968-4300. **$74-$89.** 2407 N Arkansas Ave. I-40, exit 81, just s. Ext corridors. **Pets:** Medium, other species. $10 one-time fee/room. Designated rooms, service with restrictions, supervision.
SAVE S☐ ☒ ⬚ ⬚ ⬚ ⬚

▼ **Motel 6 Russellville #265** Ⓜ
(479) 968-3666. **$40-$53.** 215 W Birch St. I-40, exit 81, just n. Ext corridors. **Pets:** Medium, other species. Service with restrictions, supervision.
🔊 ⊠ ⟨☕⟩ 🛄 ⚼

🔷 ▼ **Super 8 Motel-Russellville** 🆂🅷
(479) 968-8898. **$60-$70.** 2404 N Arkansas Ave. I-40, exit 81, just s. Int corridors. **Pets:** Medium. $10 one-time fee/pet. Designated rooms, service with restrictions, supervision.
🆂🅰🆅🅴 🔊 ⊠ ⟨✎⟩ 🛄 ⚼

SEARCY

▼▼▼ **Hampton Inn** 🆂🅷
(501) 268-0654. **$99-$109.** 3204 E Race Ave. US 67, exit 46, just w. Ext/int corridors. **Pets:** Accepted.
🅰🆂🅺 🔊 ⊠ ⟨✎⟩ 🛄 ⚼ 🌊 ⊠

🔷 ▼ **Royal Inn** Ⓜ
(501) 268-3511. **$55-$70.** 2203 E Race Ave. US 67, exit 46, 1.1 mi w. Ext corridors. **Pets:** Small, dogs only. $5 daily fee/pet. Designated rooms, service with restrictions, supervision.
🆂🅰🆅🅴 🔊 ⊠ 🛄 ⚼

SILOAM SPRINGS

▼▼ **Super 8 Motel** Ⓜ
(479) 524-8898. **$52-$60.** 1800 Hwy 412 W. Center. Ext corridors. **Pets:** Accepted.
🅰🆂🅺 🔊 ⊠ ⟨☕⟩ 🛄 ⚼ 🌊

SPRINGDALE

🔷 ▼▼▼ **Comfort Suites** 🆂🅷
(479) 725-1777. **$90-$179.** 1099 Rieff St. I-540, exit 72, just w. Int corridors. **Pets:** Accepted.
🆂🅰🆅🅴 🔊 ⊠ ⟨☕⟩ 🛄 ⚼ 🌊 ⊠

🔷 ▼▼▼ **Hampton Inn & Suites** 🆂🅷
(479) 756-3500. **$109-$169.** 1700 S 48th St. I-540, exit 72, just e. Int corridors. **Pets:** $50 one-time fee/room. Service with restrictions, supervision.
🆂🅰🆅🅴 ⊠ ♿ ⟨✎⟩ ⟨☕⟩ 🛄 ⚼ 🌊

🔷 ▼▼▼ **Holiday Inn Northwest AR Hotel & Convention Center** 🅻🅷
(479) 751-8300. **$89-$129.** 1500 S 48th St. I-540, exit 72, just e on US 412. Int corridors. **Pets:** Other species. $10 one-time fee/room. Service with restrictions, supervision.
🆂🅰🆅🅴 🔊 ⊠ ⟨✎⟩ ⟨☕⟩ 🛄 ⚼ 🍴 🌊 ⊠

🔷 ▼▼ **La Qunita Inn-Springdale** 🆂🅷
(479) 751-2626. **$82-$129.** 1300 S 48th St. I-540, exit 72, just e on US 412. Int corridors. **Pets:** Medium. Service with restrictions.
🆂🅰🆅🅴 ⊠ ♿ ⟨✎⟩ ⟨☕⟩ 🛄 ⚼ 🌊 ⊠

STAR CITY

▼▼ **Super 8 Motel-Star City** 🆂🅷
(870) 628-6883. **$57-$70.** 1308 N Lincoln St. Just n on US 425. Int corridors. **Pets:** Accepted.
🅰🆂🅺 🔊 ⊠ 🛄 ⚼ 🌊

STUTTGART

🔷 ▼▼◆ **Days Inn & Suites** 🆂🅷
(870) 673-3616. **$62-$125.** 708 W Michigan. Just w on US 63/79. Ext corridors. **Pets:** Accepted.
🆂🅰🆅🅴 ⊠ 🛄 ⚼ 🌊

TEXARKANA

🔷 ▼▼▼ **Holiday Inn Texarkana** 🆂🅷
(870) 774-3521. **$72-$77.** 5100 N State Line Ave. I-30, exit 223B, just n. Int corridors. **Pets:** Other species. $50 one-time fee/room. Service with restrictions, crate.
🆂🅰🆅🅴 ⊠ ⟨☕⟩ 🛄 ⚼ 🍴 🌊 ⊠

🔷 ▼▼◆ **La Quinta Inn & Suites** 🆂🅷
(870) 773-1000. **$80-$111.** 5102 N State Line Ave. I-30, exit 223B, just n. Int corridors. **Pets:** Medium. Service with restrictions.
🆂🅰🆅🅴 ⊠ ⟨✎⟩ 🛄 ⚼ 🌊

TRUMANN

🔷 ▼▼◆ **Days Inn & Suites** 🆂🅷
(870) 483-8383. **$59-$65.** 400 Commerce Dr. US 63, exit 29, just e. Ext/int corridors. **Pets:** Medium, other species. $10 daily fee/pet. Service with restrictions, crate.
🆂🅰🆅🅴 🔊 ⊠ ⟨✎⟩ ⟨☕⟩ 🛄 ⚼ 🌊

VAN BUREN

▼▼ **Comfort Inn** 🆂🅷
(479) 474-2223. **$55-$95.** 3131 Cloverleaf. I-540, exit 2A, just s. Int corridors. **Pets:** Accepted.
🅰🆂🅺 🔊 ⊠ 🛄 ⚼ 🌊

WEST HELENA

🔷 ▼▼◆ **Best Western Inn** 🆂🅷
(870) 572-2592. **$64-$125.** 1053 Hwy 49 W. US 49, 3 mi w. Ext corridors. **Pets:** Small. $20 deposit/pet. Designated rooms, service with restrictions, supervision.
🆂🅰🆅🅴 🔊 ⊠ 🛄 ⚼ 🌊

CALIFORNIA

CITY INDEX

ALTURAS

Best Western Trailside Inn Ⓜ
(530) 233-4111. **$73-$80.** 343 N Main St. On US 395. Ext corridors.
Pets: Small, dogs only. $20 daily fee/pet. Designated rooms, service with restrictions, supervision.

Super 8 Motel Ⓜ
(530) 233-3545. **$65-$99.** 511 N Main St. On US 395. Ext corridors.
Pets: Accepted.

ANAHEIM

(AAA) ▼▼▼▼ Anabella Hotel SH
(714) 905-1050. **$129-$159, 3 day notice.** 1030 W Katella Ave. I-5, exit Katella Ave, exit 109 (Katella Ave/Disney Way) northbound; exit 109A (Katella Ave/Orangewood Ave) southbound, 1.2 mi w. Ext corridors. **Pets:** Medium, dogs only. $100 one-time fee/pet. Designated rooms, service with restrictions, supervision.
[SAVE] [S○] [✕] [🛏] [💻] [¶¶] [≈]

▼▼▼ Anaheim Candlewood Suites SH
(714) 808-9000. **$149-$229.** 1733 S Anaheim Blvd. I-5, exit 109 (Katella Ave/Disney Way) northbound; 109A (Katella Ave/Orangewood Ave) southbound, just w, then just n. Int corridors. **Pets:** Accepted.
[✕] [🛏] [💻] [≈]

▼▼▼ Anaheim Marriott Hotel LH
(714) 750-8000. **$159-$299.** 700 W Convention Way. I-5, exit Katella Ave, exit 109 (Katella Ave/Disney Way) northbound; exit 109A (Katella Ave/Orangewood Ave) southbound, 0.8 mi w on Katella Ave, just s on Harbor Blvd, then just w. Int corridors. **Pets:** Large, other species. $50 one-time fee/room. Designated rooms, service with restrictions.
[A$K] [✕] [S·M] [🐾] [🖊] [🛏] [💻] [¶¶] [≈] [✕]

(AAA) ▼▼ Anaheim Plaza Hotel & Suites SH
(714) 772-5900. **$99-$159.** 1700 S Harbor Blvd. I-5, exit Katella Ave, exit 110 (Harbor Blvd/Ball Rd) northbound; exit 110A (Harbor Blvd) southbound, 0.6 mi s. Ext corridors. **Pets:** Accepted.
[SAVE] [S○] [✕] [🛏] [💻] [¶¶] [≈]

(AAA) ▼▼ Anaheim Quality Inn Maingate M
(714) 750-5211. **$59-$129.** 2200 S Harbor Blvd. I-5, exit Chapman Ave, exit 109 (Katella Ave/Disney Way) northbound; exit 109A (Katella Ave/Orangewood Ave) southbound, 0.8 mi w, then 0.6 mi s. Ext corridors. **Pets:** Accepted.
[SAVE] [S○] [✕] [🛏] [💻] [≈]

(AAA) ▼▼ Anaheim TownePlace Suites By Marriott M
(714) 939-9700. **$99-$159.** 1730 S State College Blvd. I-5, exit 109 (Katella Ave/Disney Way) northbound; exit 109A (Katella Ave/Orangewood Ave) southbound, 0.7 mi e, then just n. Int corridors. **Pets:** Other species. $100 one-time fee/room. Service with restrictions, supervision.
[SAVE] [✕] [🛏] [💻] [≈] [✕]

(AAA) ▼▼ Clarion Hotel Anaheim Resort LH
(714) 750-3131. **$69-$169, 3 day notice.** 616 Convention Way. I-5, exit 109 (Katella Ave/Disney Way) northbound; exit 109A (Katella Ave/Orangewood Ave) southbound, 0.8 mi w to Harbor Blvd, just s, then just w. Int corridors. **Pets:** Accepted.
[SAVE] [S○] [✕] [🛏] [💻] [¶¶] [≈]

(AAA) ▼▼▼▼ Embassy Suites Hotel Anaheim-North Near Disneyland Resort LH
(714) 632-1221. **$129-$319.** 3100 E Frontera St. SR 91, exit 31 (Kraemer Blvd/Glassell St) eastbound; exit 32 westbound just s, then just e. Int corridors. **Pets:** Large, other species. $50 one-time fee/pet. Service with restrictions.
[SAVE] [✕] [🛏] [💻] [¶¶] [≈] [✕]

▼▼ Extended StayAmerica-Orange County-Anaheim Convention Center SH
(714) 502-9988. **$74-$114.** 1742 S Clementine St. I-5, exit 109 (Katella Ave/Disney Way) northbound; exit 109A (Katella Ave/Orangewood Ave) southbound, just w, then just n. Int corridors. **Pets:** Accepted.
[A$K] [S○] [✕] [🛏] [💻] [≈]

▼▼ Extended StayAmerica-Orange County-Anaheim Hills SH
(714) 630-4006. **$79-$119.** 1031 N Pacificenter Dr. SR 91, exit 33 (Tustin Ave), just n, then just w. Int corridors. **Pets:** Accepted.
[A$K] [S○] [✕] [🛏] [💻]

(AAA) ▼▼▼ La Quinta Inn and Suites SH
(714) 635-5000. **$129-$209.** 1752 S Clementine St. I-5, exit 109 (Katella Ave/Disney Way)northbound; exit 109A (Katella Ave/Orangewood Ave) southbound, just w, then just n. Int corridors. **Pets:** Medium. Service with restrictions.
[SAVE] [✕] [🛏] [💻] [≈] [✕]

(AAA) ▼▼ Lemon Tree Hotel M
(714) 772-0200. **$59-$139.** 1600 E Lincoln Ave. I-5, exit 111 (Lincoln Ave), 2 mi e. Ext/int corridors. **Pets:** Accepted.
[SAVE] [S○] [✕] [🛏] [💻] [≈]

▼▼ Red Roof Inn Anaheim-Maingate M
(714) 520-9696. **$75-$105.** 100 Disney Way. I-5, exit Disney Way. Ext corridors. **Pets:** Medium, other species. Service with restrictions, supervision.
[✕] [🛏] [≈]

(AAA) ▼▼▼▼ Residence Inn by Marriott Anaheim Maingate SH ❖
(714) 533-3555. **$179.** 1700 S Clementine St. I-5, exit Katella Ave, exit 109 (Katella Ave/Disney Way) northbound; exit 109A (Katella Ave/Orangewood Ave) southbound, just w on Katella Ave, then just n. Ext corridors. **Pets:** Medium, other species. $75 one-time fee/room. Service with restrictions, crate.
[SAVE] [S○] [✕] [S·M] [🖊] [🐾] [🛏] [💻] [≈] [✕]

(AAA) ▼▼▼▼ Sheraton Anaheim Hotel LH ❖
(714) 778-1700. **$125.** 900 S Disneyland Dr. I-5, exit 110 (Harbor Blvd/Ball Rd) northbound; exit 110A (Harbor Blvd) southbound, just n on Harbor Blvd, just w on Ball Rd, then just n. Int corridors. **Pets:** Other species. $25 daily fee/room. Service with restrictions, supervision.
[SAVE] [✕] [🐾] [🛏] [💻] [¶¶] [≈] [✕]

(AAA) ▼▼▼▼ Sheraton Park Hotel at the Anaheim Resort LH ❖
(714) 750-1811. **$119-$262, 3 day notice.** 1855 S Harbor Blvd. I-5, exit Katella Ave, exit 109 (Katella Ave/Disney Way) northbound; exit 109A (Katella Ave/Orangewood Ave) southbound, 0.8 mi w, then just s. Int corridors. **Pets:** Medium, dogs only. Designated rooms, service with restrictions, supervision.
[SAVE] [S○] [✕] [🛏] [💻] [¶¶] [≈] [✕]

(AAA) ▼▼▼ Staybridge Suites by Holiday Inn-Anaheim Resort SH
(714) 748-7700. **$119-$279.** 1855 S Manchester Ave. I-5, exit 109 (Katella Ave/Disney Way) northbound; exit 109A (Katella Ave/Orangewood Ave) southbound, just w on Katella Ave, then 0.3 mi s; adjacent to west side of freeway. Int corridors. **Pets:** Accepted.
[SAVE] [S○] [✕] [🛏] [💻] [≈] [✕]

ANAHEIM HILLS

▼▼▼ Best Western Anaheim Hills M
(714) 779-0252. **$79-$99.** 5710 E La Palma Ave. SR 91, exit 36 (Imperial Hwy), 0.3 mi n. Ext/int corridors. **Pets:** Small. $15 daily fee/pet. Designated rooms, service with restrictions, supervision.
[A$K] [S○] [✕] [🛏] [≈] [✕]

ANDERSON

(AAA) ▼▼▼ AmeriHost Inn-Anderson SH
(530) 365-6100. **$74.** 2040 Factory Outlet Dr. I-5, exit Factory Outlet Dr, just w. Int corridors. **Pets:** Accepted.
[SAVE] [S○] [✕] [S·M] [🖊] [🛏] [💻] [≈] [✕]

(AAA) ▼▼ Best Western Knights Inn SH
(530) 365-2753. **$70-$85.** 2688 Gateway Dr. I-5, exit 668 (Central Anderson) eastbound; exit Lassen Park westbound, just e. Ext corridors. **Pets:** Accepted.
[SAVE] [S○] [✕] [🛏] [💻] [≈]

ANGELS CAMP

Angels Inn Motel M
(209) 736-4242. **$85-$145.** 600 N Main St. SR 49, north end of town. Ext corridors. **Pets:** Dogs only. $50 deposit/room, $10 daily fee/pet. Designated rooms, service with restrictions, supervision.

Best Western Cedar Inn & Suites SH
(209) 736-4000. **$89-$189.** 444 S Main St. On SR 49; center. Ext/int corridors. **Pets:** Dogs only. $15 daily fee/room. Designated rooms, service with restrictions, supervision.

Gold Country Inn M
(209) 736-4611. **$49-$135.** 720 S Main St. 1 mi s of jct SR 49 and 4. Ext corridors. **Pets:** Medium, other species. $5 daily fee/pet. Service with restrictions, supervision.

Jumping Frog Motel M
(209) 736-2191. **$60-$150.** 330 Murphys Grade Rd. SR 49, n of Angels Camp Center, just left. Ext corridors. **Pets:** Small, dogs only. $10 daily fee/pet. Service with restrictions, supervision.

ANTIOCH

Best Western Heritage Inn M
(925) 778-2000. **$74-$104.** 3210 Delta Fair Blvd. SR 4, exit Somersville Rd. Ext corridors. **Pets:** Large. $15 one-time fee/room. Service with restrictions, supervision.

APTOS

Bayview Hotel CI
(831) 688-8654. **$109-$269, 10 day notice.** 8041 Soquel Dr. SR 1, exit State Park Dr E, 0.8 mi s. Int corridors. **Pets:** Accepted.

ARCATA

Arcata Super 8 SH
(707) 822-8888. **$70-$100.** 4887 Valley West Blvd. US 101, exit Giuntoli Ln/Janes Rd, just e, then just s. Int corridors. **Pets:** Accepted.

Best Western Arcata Inn M
(707) 826-0313. **$79-$189.** 4827 Valley West Blvd. US 101, exit Giuntoli Ln/Janes Rd, just e, then just s. Ext corridors. **Pets:** Dogs only. $20 one-time fee/room. Designated rooms, service with restrictions, supervision.

Comfort Inn M
(707) 826-2827. **$65-$185.** 4701 Valley West Blvd. US 101, exit Giuntoli Ln/Janes Rd, just e, then 0.3 mi s. Ext corridors. **Pets:** Medium, dogs only. $50 deposit/pet, $10 daily fee/pet. Service with restrictions, supervision.

Hotel Arcata SH
(707) 826-0217. **$84-$185.** 708 9th St. Corner of G St; downtown. Int corridors. **Pets:** Other species. $50 deposit/pet, $5 daily fee/pet. Service with restrictions, supervision.

North Coast Inn SH
(707) 822-4861. **$55-$115.** 4975 Valley West Blvd. US 101, exit Giuntoli Ln/Janes Rd, just e, then s. Int corridors. **Pets:** Medium. Designated rooms, supervision.

Quality Inn Arcata SH
(707) 822-0409. **$84-$224.** 3535 Janes Rd. US 101, exit Giuntoli Ln/Janes Rd, just w. Int corridors. **Pets:** Other species. $100 deposit/room, $10 daily fee/pet. Designated rooms, service with restrictions, supervision.

ARROYO GRANDE

Premier Inns M
(805) 481-4774. **$49-$119.** 555 Camino Mercado. US 101, exit 188 (Oak Park Rd), then 0.3 mi s. Ext corridors. **Pets:** Medium, dogs only. $20 deposit/room. No service, supervision.

AUBURN

Best Western Golden Key SH
(530) 885-8611. **$86-$120.** 13450 Lincoln Way. I-80, exit Foresthill Rd. Ext corridors. **Pets:** $15 one-time fee/pet. Designated rooms, service with restrictions, supervision.

Foothills Motel M
(530) 885-8444. **$68-$98.** 13431 Bowman Rd. I-80, exit Foresthill Rd. Ext corridors. **Pets:** Dogs only. $50 deposit/room, $10 daily fee/pet. Designated rooms, service with restrictions, supervision.

Holiday Inn-Auburn SH
(530) 887-8787. **$124-$159.** 120 Grass Valley Hwy. I-80, exit SR 49. Int corridors. **Pets:** Small, dogs only. $20 daily fee/pet. Designated rooms, service with restrictions, supervision.

Motel 6 #4152 M
(530) 888-7829. **$65-$89.** 1819 Auburn Ravine Rd. I-80, exit Foresthill and Auburn Ravine rds. Int corridors. **Pets:** Medium, other species. Service with restrictions, supervision.

Travelodge M
(530) 885-7025. **$110-$150.** 13490 Lincoln Way. I-80, exit Foresthill Rd. Ext/int corridors. **Pets:** Small. $15 daily fee/pet. Designated rooms, service with restrictions, supervision.

BAKERSFIELD

America's Best Inn M
(661) 764-5221. **$69-$79.** 200 Trask St. I-5, exit 253 (Stockdale Hwy), just e. Ext corridors. **Pets:** Medium. $5 daily fee/pet. Designated rooms, service with restrictions, supervision.

Bakersfield Red Lion Hotel SH
(661) 327-0681. **$69-$169.** 2400 Camino Del Rio Ct. SR 99, exit 26 (SR 58 W/Rosedale Hwy), just w, then just s. Ext/int corridors. **Pets:** Accepted.

Best Western Crystal Palace Inn & Suites SH
(661) 327-9651. **$79-$140.** 2620 Buck Owens Blvd. SR 99, exit 26B (Buck Owens Blvd) northbound, just s; exit 26 (SR 58 W/SR 178 E) southbound, just e, then just n. Int corridors. **Pets:** Accepted.

Best Western Heritage Inn M
(661) 764-6268. **$95-$100.** 253 Trask St. I-5, exit 253 (Stockdale Hwy), just e. Ext corridors. **Pets:** Small. $10 daily fee/pet. Service with restrictions, supervision.

Best Western Hill House SH ❀
(661) 327-4064. **$69-$119.** 700 Truxtun Ave. SR 99, exit 25 (California Ave), 1.2 mi e, 0.4 mi n on Chester Ave, then 0.4 mi e. Int corridors. **Pets:** Medium. $15 daily fee/pet. Designated rooms, service with restrictions, supervision.

DoubleTree Hotel Bakersfield LH
(661) 323-7111. **$105-$210.** 3100 Camino Del Rio Ct. SR 99, exit 26 (SR 58 W/Rosedale Hwy), just w, then just s. Int corridors. **Pets:** Medium. $30 one-time fee/room. Designated rooms, service with restrictions, supervision.

Holiday Inn Select Convention Center LH
(661) 323-1900. **$98-$116.** 801 Truxtun Ave. SR 99, exit 25 (California Ave), 1.2 mi e, 0.4 mi n on Chester Ave, then 0.3 mi e. Int corridors. **Pets:** Accepted.

Howard Johnson Express Inn M
(661) 396-1425. **$55-$60.** 2700 White Ln. SR 99, exit 21 (White Ln), just e. Ext corridors. **Pets:** Accepted.

La Quinta Inn & Suites SH
(661) 393-7775. **$99-$129.** 8858 Spectrum Pkwy. SR 99, exit 30 (SR 65) northbound, just n to 7th Standard Rd, just w, then just s; exit 31 (7th Standard Rd) southbound, just e, then just s. Int corridors. **Pets:** Accepted.

La Quinta Inn Bakersfield M
(661) 325-7400. **$90-$129.** 3232 Riverside Dr. SR 99, exit 26 (SR 58 W/Rosedale Hwy) southbound, just e, then just n; exit 26B (Buck Owens Blvd) northbound, just s. Ext corridors. **Pets:** Medium. Service with restrictions.

Quality Inn M
(661) 325-0772. **$76-$130.** 1011 Oak St. SR 99, exit 25 (California Ave), just e, then just s. Ext/int corridors. **Pets:** Accepted.

Ramada Limited-Central M
(661) 831-1922. **$70-$120, 7 day notice.** 830 Wible Rd. SR 99, exit 23 (Ming Ave), just e, then 0.8 mi n. Ext corridors. **Pets:** Accepted.

Residence Inn by Marriott SH
(661) 321-9800. **$184-$249.** 4241 Chester Ln. SR 99, exit 25 (California Ave), 0.5 mi w, then just n. Ext corridors. **Pets:** Other species. $75 one-time fee/room. Service with restrictions.

Super 8 Motel Bakersfield M
(661) 322-1012. **$65-$85.** 901 Real Rd. SR 99, exit 25 (California Ave), just w, then just s. Ext corridors. **Pets:** Small. $10 daily fee/pet. Service with restrictions, supervision.

Vagabond Inn North M
(661) 392-1800. **$45-$65.** 6100 Knudsen Dr. SR 99, exit 28 (Olive Dr), just w, then just n. Int corridors. **Pets:** Accepted.

Vagabond Inn South M
(661) 831-9200. **$45-$65.** 6501 Colony St. SR 99, exit 20 (Panama Ln), just e, then just s. Ext corridors. **Pets:** Accepted.

BANNING

Banning Travelodge M
(951) 849-1000. **$59-$199.** 1700 W Ramsey St. I-10, exit 99 (22nd St), 0.5 mi e, then just n. Ext corridors. **Pets:** Accepted.

Days Inn M
(951) 849-0092. **$79-$199.** 2320 W Ramsey St. I-10, exit 99 (22nd St), just n, then just w. Ext corridors. **Pets:** Accepted.

Super 8 Motel M
(951) 849-8888. **$75-$499.** 1690 W Ramsey St. I-10, exit 99 (22nd St), just n, then 0.4 mi e. Int corridors. **Pets:** Accepted.

BARSTOW

Barstow-Super 8 Motel M
(760) 256-8443. **$72-$77.** 170 Coolwater Ln. I-15, exit E Main St, exit 184B (E Main St) northbound; exit 184 (E Main St/I-40 E/Needles) southbound, 0.3 mi w, then just s; I-40 westbound, exit 1 (E Main St), 0.7 mi w, then just s. Ext corridors. **Pets:** Other species. $5 daily fee/pet. Service with restrictions, supervision.

Best Western Desert Villa Inn M
(760) 256-1781. **$64-$129.** 1984 E Main St. I-15, exit 184B (E Main St) northbound; exit 184 (E Main St/I-40/Needles) southbound, 0.5 mi e; I-40 westbound, exit 1 (E Main St), just w. Ext corridors. **Pets:** Accepted.

Days Inn M
(760) 256-1737. **$59-$65.** 1590 Coolwater Ln. I-15, exit 184B (E Main St) northbound; exit 184 (E Main St/I-40 E/Needles) southbound, just w, then just s; I-40, exit 1 (E Main St) westbound, 0.7 mi w, then just s. Ext corridors. **Pets:** Small. $10 daily fee/pet. Service with restrictions, supervision.

Holiday Inn Express, Barstow-Historic Route 66 SH
(760) 256-1300. **$99-$109.** 1861 W Main St. I-15, exit 181 (L St), 0.5 mi n, then just e. Int corridors. **Pets:** Other species. $20 deposit/room. Service with restrictions, supervision.

Holiday Inn Express Hotel & Suites SH
(760) 253-9200. **$99-$219.** 2700 Lenwood Rd. I-15, exit 178 (Lenwood Rd), just e, then 0.5 mi s. Int corridors. **Pets:** Other species. $25 deposit/room. Service with restrictions, supervision.

Motel 6 Barstow #1355 M
(760) 256-1752. **$45-$55.** 150 N Yucca Ave. I-15, 184B (E Main St) northbound; exit 184 (E Main St/I-40 E/Needles) southbound, 0.5 mi w, then just n; I-40, exit 1 (E Main St) westbound, 1 mi w, then just n. Ext corridors. **Pets:** Medium, other species. Service with restrictions, supervision.

Ramada Inn SH
(760) 256-5673. **$85-$129.** 1511 E Main St. I-15, exit 184B (E Main St) northbound; exit 184 (E Main St/I-40 E/Needles) southbound, 0.3 mi w; I-40, exit 1 (E Main St) westbound, 0.8 mi w. Int corridors. **Pets:** Medium. $20 one-time fee/room. Service with restrictions, crate.

Red Roof Inn M
(760) 253-2121. **$57-$109.** 2551 Commerce Pkwy. I-15, exit 178 (Lenwood Rd), just w; 8 mi s of town. Ext corridors. **Pets:** Medium, other species. Service with restrictions, supervision.

AAA ▼ **Rodeway Inn** M
(760) 256-7581. **$40-$60.** 1261 E Main St. I-15, exit E Main St, exit 184B (E Main St) northbound; exit 184 (E Main St/I-40 E/Needles) southbound, 0.8 mi w; I-40, exit 1 (E Main St) westbound, 1.3 mi w. Ext corridors. **Pets:** Accepted.
[SAVE] [X] [fridge] [pool]

AAA ▼ **Stardust Inn** M
(760) 256-7116. **$35-$60.** 901 E Main St. I-15, exit 183 (Barstow Rd), 0.8 mi n, then 0.4 mi e. Ext corridors. **Pets:** Small. $5 daily fee/pet. Designated rooms, service with restrictions, supervision.
[SAVE] [S] [X] [fridge] [pool]

AAA ▼ **Travelodge** M
(760) 256-8931. **$69-$99.** 1630 E Main St. I-15, exit 184B (E Main St) northbound; exit 184 (E Main St/I-40 E/Needles) southbound, just e; I-40 westbound, exit 1 (E Main St), just w. Ext corridors. **Pets:** Accepted.
[SAVE] [S] [X] [fridge] [pool]

BEAUMONT

AAA ▼ **Americas Best Value Inn** M
(951) 845-2185. **$70-$200.** 625 E 5th St. I-10, exit 94 (SR 79/Beaumont Ave), just n. Ext corridors. **Pets:** Medium. $5 daily fee/pet. Service with restrictions, supervision.
[SAVE] [S] [X] [fridge] [pool]

AAA ▼▼▼ **Best Western El Rancho Motor Inn** M
(951) 845-2176. **$95-$195, 3 day notice.** 480 E 5th St. I-10, exit 94 (SR 79/Beaumont Ave), just n, then just e. Ext corridors. **Pets:** Very small. $15 daily fee/pet. Designated rooms, service with restrictions, crate.
[SAVE] [S] [X] [fridge] [screen] [food] [pool]

BENICIA

AAA ▼▼▼ **Best Western Heritage Inn** SH
(707) 746-0401. **$101-$149.** 1955 E 2nd St. I-780, exit Central Benicia/E 2nd St, just e. Int corridors. **Pets:** Small. $25 one-time fee/pet. Service with restrictions, supervision.
[SAVE] [S] [X] [fridge] [screen] [pool]

BEN LOMOND

AAA ▼▼▼ **Econo Lodge** M
(831) 336-2292. **$70-$230, 7 day notice.** 9733 Hwy 9. SR 9, 0.3 mi n; on San Lorenzo River. Ext corridors. **Pets:** Accepted.
[SAVE] [S] [X] [fridge] [screen] [pool]

BERKELEY

AAA ▼▼▼ **Best Value Golden Bear Inn** M
(510) 525-6770. **$79-$119.** 1620 San Pablo Ave. I-80, exit Gilman E, 2 mi s. Ext corridors. **Pets:** Other species. $10 daily fee/room. Designated rooms, supervision.
[SAVE] [S] [X] [fridge] [screen]

AAA ▼▼▼▼ **Claremont Resort and Spa** LH
(510) 843-3000. **$199-$399.** 41 Tunnel Rd. SR 13 and 24, exit SR 24 (Claremont Ave), 1 mi n; in Berkeley Hills. Int corridors. **Pets:** Accepted.
[SAVE] [S] [X] [screen] [food] [pool] [X]

AAA ▼▼▼▼ **DoubleTree Hotel and Executive Meeting Center Berkeley Marina** SH
(510) 548-7920. **$119-$485.** 200 Marina Blvd. I-80, exit University Ave, 0.5 mi w; on Berkeley Marina. Int corridors. **Pets:** Accepted.
[SAVE] [S] [X] [key] [fridge] [screen] [food] [pool] [X]

BERRY CREEK

▼▼▼ **Lake Oroville Bed & Breakfast** BB ❀
(530) 589-0700. **$125-$175, 5 day notice.** 240 Sunday Dr. SR 162, 15 mi e to Bell Ranch Rd, 0.5 mi w. Int corridors. **Pets:** Other species. $10 daily fee/pet. Supervision.
[ASK] [S] [X] [access] [key] [fridge]

BIG BEAR LAKE

▼▼ **Alpine Village Inn** M
(909) 866-5460. **$119-$219, 5 day notice.** 546 Pine Knot Ave. SR 18 business route; in the village. Ext/int corridors. **Pets:** $100 deposit/pet, $10 daily fee/pet. Designated rooms, no service, supervision.
[ASK] [S] [X] [fridge] [screen] [AC]

▼▼ **Bear Manor Cabins** CA
(909) 866-6800. **$119-$399, 30 day notice.** 40393 Big Bear Blvd. SR 18, 0.8 mi w of village. Ext corridors. **Pets:** Small, dogs only. $100 deposit/room. Designated rooms, no service, supervision.
[ASK] [S] [X] [fridge] [screen] [AC]

AAA ▼▼▼ **Best Western Big Bear Chateau** SH
(909) 866-6666. **$99-$259.** 42200 Moonridge Rd. SR 18, 1.5 mi e of Pine Knot Ave, then 0.5 mi s. Int corridors. **Pets:** Medium, dogs only. $30 daily fee/room. Designated rooms, service with restrictions, supervision.
[SAVE] [X] [fridge] [screen] [food] [pool] [X]

AAA ▼ **Big Bear Lakefront Lodge** M ❀
(909) 866-8271. **$65-$220, 3 day notice.** 40360 Lakeview Dr. SR 18, 0.5 mi w of Pine Knot Ave, 0.5 mi nw. Ext/int corridors. **Pets:** Small, other species. $50 deposit/room, $10 daily fee/pet. Designated rooms, service with restrictions, supervision.
[SAVE] [S] [X] [fridge] [screen] [X] [AC] [Z]

AAA ▼▼▼ **Cozy Hollow Lodge** CA
(909) 866-9694. **$49-$279, 15 day notice.** 40409 Big Bear Blvd. SR 18, 0.8 mi w. Ext corridors. **Pets:** Medium, dogs only. $100 deposit/room, $10 daily fee/pet, $25 one-time fee/room. Designated rooms, service with restrictions, supervision.
[SAVE] [X] [fridge] [screen] [AC]

▼▼ **Eagle's Nest Bed & Breakfast** BB ❀
(909) 866-6465. **$110-$170, 5 day notice.** 41675 Big Bear Blvd. SR 18, 1 mi e of Pine Knot Ave. Ext/int corridors. **Pets:** Other species. $10 daily fee/pet. Designated rooms, service with restrictions, supervision.
[ASK] [S] [X] [fridge] [screen]

AAA ▼▼ **Golden Bear Cottages** CA
(909) 866-2010. **$89-$129, 60 day notice.** 39367 Big Bear Blvd. SR 18, 2 mi w of village. Ext corridors. **Pets:** Accepted.
[SAVE] [S] [X] [fridge] [screen] [X] [AC]

AAA ▼▼ **Grey Squirrel Resort** CA ❀
(909) 866-4335. **$85-$127, 14 day notice.** 39372 Big Bear Blvd. SR 18, 2.5 mi w of village. Ext corridors. **Pets:** $10 one-time fee/pet. Designated rooms, no service, supervision.
[SAVE] [S] [X] [fridge] [screen] [pool] [X] [AC]

▼▼ **Pine Knot Guest Ranch** CA ❀
(909) 866-6500. **$89-$189.** 908 Pine Knot Ave. Just s of SR 18 and downtown area. Ext corridors. **Pets:** Other species. $10 one-time fee/pet. Designated rooms, service with restrictions.
[ASK] [S] [X] [fridge] [screen]

AAA ▼▼▼ **Timber Haven Lodge** CA ❀
(909) 866-7207. **$69-$259, 14 day notice.** 877 Tulip Ln. SR 18, 1.8 mi w of Pine Knot Ave, 0.4 mi s. Ext corridors. **Pets:** Dogs only. $15 daily fee/pet. Designated rooms, service with restrictions, supervision.
[SAVE] [S] [X] [fridge] [screen] [X] [AC]

BIG PINE

▼▼ **Big Pine Motel** M
(760) 938-2282. **$55-$64.** 370 S Main St. On US 395. Ext corridors. **Pets:** Accepted.
[ASK] [S] [X] [fridge] [screen]

AAA ▼▼▼ **Bristlecone Motel** M
(760) 938-2067. **$48-$75.** 101 N Main St. On US 395. Ext corridors. **Pets:** Other species. Service with restrictions, supervision.
[SAVE] [S] [X] [fridge] [screen]

BISHOP

Best Western Bishop Holiday Spa Lodge M
(760) 873-3543. **$80-$110.** 1025 N Main St. On US 395. Ext corridors. **Pets:** Medium. Designated rooms, service with restrictions, supervision.

Comfort Inn M
(760) 873-4284. **$79-$229.** 805 N Main St. On US 395. Ext corridors. **Pets:** Other species. $5 daily fee/pet. Supervision.

Holiday Inn Express Hotel & Suites SH
(760) 872-2423. **$109-$179.** 636 N Main St. On US 395. Int corridors. **Pets:** Medium, dogs only. $50 one-time fee/pet. Designated rooms, service with restrictions, supervision.

Motel 6-4094 M
(760) 873-8426. **$59.** 1005 N Main St. On US 395. Ext corridors. **Pets:** Medium, other species. Service with restrictions, supervision.

Ramada Limited M ✿
(760) 872-1771. **$80-$110.** 155 E Elm St. On US 395, just e. Ext corridors. **Pets:** $10 daily fee/pet. Designated rooms, service with restrictions, supervision.

Rodeway Inn M
(760) 873-3564. **$80-$150.** 150 E Elm St. On US 395, just e. Ext/int corridors. **Pets:** Small. $5 daily fee/pet. Designated rooms, service with restrictions, supervision.

Thunderbird Motel M
(760) 873-4215. **$60-$109.** 190 W Pine St. Just w of US 395. Ext corridors. **Pets:** Accepted.

Vagabond Inn M ✿
(760) 873-6351. **$74-$185.** 1030 N Main St. On US 395. Ext corridors. **Pets:** $10 daily fee/pet. Designated rooms, service with restrictions, supervision.

BLYTHE

Best Western Sahara Motel M
(760) 922-7105. **$79-$159.** 825 W Hobsonway. I-10, exit 239 (Lovekin Blvd), just n, then just w. Ext corridors. **Pets:** Accepted.

Comfort Suites M
(760) 922-9209. **$89-$159.** 545 E Hobsonway. I-10, exit 240 (7th St), just n, then just w. Ext corridors. **Pets:** Other species. $10 daily fee/pet. Service with restrictions, supervision.

Super 8 Motel M
(760) 922-8881. **$70-$130.** 550 W Donlon St. I-10, exit 239 (Lovekin Blvd), just e. Int corridors. **Pets:** Accepted.

Travelers Inn Express M
(760) 922-3334. **$69-$139.** 1781 E Hobsonway. I-10, exit 241 (Intake Blvd), just n, then just w. Ext corridors. **Pets:** Medium, other species. Designated rooms, service with restrictions, supervision.

BORREGO SPRINGS

Borrego Springs Resort Hotel SH
(760) 767-5700. **$75-$160.** 1112 Tilting T Dr. SR 22, 1.5 mi s on Borrego Valley Rd, just w. Int corridors. **Pets:** Small. $50 deposit/pet. Service with restrictions, supervision.

La Casa del Zorro Desert Resort LH
(760) 767-5323. **$295-$1660, 3 day notice.** 3845 Yaqui Pass Rd. 5.5 mi se on CR S-3; jct Yaqui Pass and Borrego Springs rds. Ext corridors. **Pets:** Medium, other species. $100 deposit/room, $50 daily fee/pet. Service with restrictions.

BRAWLEY

Brawley Inn M
(760) 344-1199. **$79-$150.** 575 W Main St. On SR 86 and 78. Ext/int corridors. **Pets:** Accepted.

BREA

Homestead Studio Suites Hotel-Orange County-Brea M
(714) 528-2500. **$80-$110.** 3050 E Imperial Hwy. SR 57, exit 9 (SR 90), 1.4 mi e on Imperial Hwy (SR 90). Ext corridors. **Pets:** Accepted.

Woodfin Suite Hotel M
(714) 579-3200. **$129-$194.** 3100 E Imperial Hwy. SR 57, exit 9 (SR 90), 1.5 mi e on Imperial Hwy (SR 90). Ext corridors. **Pets:** Large, other species. $150 deposit/pet, $10 daily fee/pet. Designated rooms, service with restrictions.

BRIDGEPORT

Best Western Ruby Inn M ✿
(760) 932-7241. **$125-$180.** 333 Main St. On US 395; center. Ext corridors. **Pets:** Medium. Designated rooms, service with restrictions, supervision.

Redwood Motel M ✿
(760) 932-7060. **$55-$199, 5 day notice.** 425 Main St. On US 395; on north side of town. Ext corridors. **Pets:** Large. $5 daily fee/pet. Service with restrictions, supervision.

Silver Maple Inn M ✿
(760) 932-7383. **$60-$120.** 310 Main St. On US 395; center. Ext corridors. **Pets:** Other species. Service with restrictions, supervision.

Walker River Lodge M
(760) 932-7021. **$55-$225.** 100 Main St. On US 395; at south end of town. Ext corridors. **Pets:** $10 daily fee/pet. Service with restrictions, supervision.

BUELLTON

Quality Inn Solvang/Buellton M
(805) 688-0022. **$59-$169.** 630 Ave of the Flags. US 101, exit 140B (Ave of the Flags) southbound, just s; exit 140A (SR 246) northbound, just w, then just n. Ext/int corridors. **Pets:** Medium. $25 one-time fee/room. Designated rooms, service with restrictions, supervision.

Santa Ynez Valley Marriott SH
(805) 688-1000. **$149-$399.** 555 McMurray Rd. US 101, exit 140A (SR 246), just e, then just n. Int corridors. **Pets:** Accepted.

BURNEY

(AAA) ▽▽ Charm Motel M ❀
(530) 335-2254. **$55-$95, 3 day notice.** 37363 Main St. 0.8 mi e on SR 299. Ext corridors. **Pets:** Other species. $10 daily fee/pet. Designated rooms, service with restrictions, supervision.
[SAVE] [S🐾] [✕] [🛏] [▣]

(AAA) ▽▽◇ Green Gables Motel M ❀
(530) 335-2264. **$55-$95, 3 day notice.** 37385 Main St. 0.8 mi e on SR 299. Ext corridors. **Pets:** Other species. $10 daily fee/pet. Service with restrictions, supervision.
[SAVE] [S🐾] [✕] [🛏] [▣] [🏊]

BUTTONWILLOW

(AAA) ▽▽ Super 8 Motel M
(661) 764-5117. **$70-$75.** 20681 Tracy Ave. I-5, exit 257 (SR 58), just e, then just n. Ext corridors. **Pets:** Accepted.
[SAVE] [S🐾] [✕] [♿] [🏋] [🛏] [▣] [🏊]

(AAA) ▽ Willow Inn & Suites M
(661) 764-5121. **$50.** 20645 Tracy Ave. I-5, exit 257 (SR 58), just e, then just n. Ext corridors. **Pets:** Accepted.
[SAVE] [✕] [🛏] [▣] [🏊]

CALEXICO

(AAA) ▽▽◇ Best Western John Jay Inn M
(760) 768-0442. **$84-$119.** 2421 Scaroni Rd. I-8, exit 118A (SR 111 S), 5.5 mi s, just w on West Cole Rd, then just n. Int corridors. **Pets:** Dogs only. $100 deposit/room, $10 daily fee/pet. Designated rooms, service with restrictions, supervision.
[SAVE] [S🐾] [✕] [♿] [🛏] [▣] [🏊]

CALIMESA

(AAA) ▽▽◇ Calimesa Inn Motel M
(909) 795-2536. **$70-$150.** 1205 Calimesa Blvd. I-10, exit 88 (Calimesa Blvd), just ne. Ext corridors. **Pets:** Small. $10 daily fee/pet. Designated rooms, service with restrictions, supervision.
[SAVE] [✕] [🛏] [🏊]

CALIPATRIA

(AAA) ▽▽◇ Calipatria Inn & Suites M
(760) 348-7348. **$85-$300.** 700 N Sorenson Ave. On SR 111. Ext corridors. **Pets:** Accepted.
[SAVE] [S🐾] [✕] [🛏] [▣] [🍴] [🏊]

CAMBRIA

▽▽◇▽ Blue Dolphin Inn SH
(805) 927-3300. **$159-$239, 3 day notice.** 6470 Moonstone Beach Dr. SR 1, exit Moonstone Beach Dr, 0.7 mi n. Int corridors. **Pets:** $25 daily fee/pet. Designated rooms, service with restrictions, supervision.
[ASK] [✕] [🛏] [▣] [📶]

▽▽◇ Cambria Shores Inn M
(805) 927-8644. **$135-$250, 7 day notice.** 6276 Moonstone Beach Dr. SR 1, exit Moonstone Beach Dr, just w, then 0.8 mi s. Ext corridors. **Pets:** Accepted.
[✕] [🛏] [▣] [📶]

▽▽◇▽ Fog Catcher Inn M ❀
(805) 927-1400. **$119-$379.** 6400 Moonstone Beach Dr. SR 1, exit Moonstone Beach Dr, just w, then 0.7 mi s. Ext corridors. **Pets:** Large, other species. $25 one-time fee/room. Designated rooms, service with restrictions, supervision.
[ASK] [S🐾] [✕] [🛏] [▣] [🏊] [📶]

(AAA) ▽▽ Mariners Inn by the Sea M
(805) 927-4624. **$89-$275, 5 day notice.** 6180 Moonstone Beach Dr. SR 1, exit Moonstone Beach Dr, just w, then 1 mi s. Ext corridors. **Pets:** Dogs only. $15 one-time fee/pet. Designated rooms, service with restrictions, supervision.
[SAVE] [✕] [🛏] [📶]

▽▽◇▽ Pelican Cove Inn SH
(805) 927-1500. **$149-$389, 3 day notice.** 6316 Moonstone Beach Dr. SR 1, exit Moonstone Beach Dr, just w, then 0.8 mi s. Ext/int corridors. **Pets:** $25 daily fee/pet. Designated rooms, service with restrictions, supervision.
[ASK] [✕] [🛏] [▣] [🏊] [📶]

▽▽◇▽ Sand Pebbles Inn SH
(805) 927-5600. **$99-$279, 3 day notice.** 6252 Moonstone Beach Dr. SR 1, exit Moonstone Beach Dr, just w, then 0.9 mi s. Int corridors. **Pets:** $25 daily fee/pet. Designated rooms, service with restrictions, supervision.
[ASK] [✕] [🛏] [▣] [📶]

▽▽◇▽ Sea Otter Inn M
(805) 927-5888. **$179-$239.** 6656 Moonstone Beach Dr. SR 1, exit Moonstone Beach Dr, just w, then 0.5 mi s. Ext corridors. **Pets:** $25 daily fee/pet. Designated rooms, service with restrictions, supervision.
[ASK] [✕] [🛏] [▣] [🏊] [📶]

CAMERON PARK

▽▽◇▽ Cameron Park Inn & Suites SH
(530) 677-2203. **$99-$149.** 3361 Coach Ln. 12 mi w of Placerville on US 50, exit Cameron Park Dr. Ext corridors. **Pets:** Accepted.
[ASK] [S🐾] [✕] [🏋] [🛏] [▣] [🏊]

▽ Motel 6 Cameron Park #4289 SH
(530) 677-7177. **$66-$75.** 3444 Coach Ln. 12 mi w of Placerville on US 50, exit Cameron Park Dr. Int corridors. **Pets:** Medium, other species. Service with restrictions, supervision.
[ASK] [S🐾] [✕] [🏋] [🏊]

CAMINO

(AAA) ▽▽ Camino Hotel-Seven Mile House BB
(530) 644-7740. **$88-$118, 14 day notice.** 4103 Carson Rd. US 50, exit 54 (Camino), just n. Int corridors. **Pets:** Accepted.
[SAVE] [S🐾] [✕] [🏋] [📶] [Ⓦ] [Ⓩ]

CAMPBELL

(AAA) ▽▽◇ Campbell Inn SH
(408) 374-4300. **$99-$250.** 675 E Campbell Ave. SR 17, exit Hamilton Ave E, 0.3 mi to Bascom Ave, 0.3 mi s, then 0.3 mi w. Ext corridors. **Pets:** Accepted.
[SAVE] [S🐾] [✕] [🛏] [▣] [🏊] [🐕]

▽▽◇ Residence Inn by Marriott-San Jose SH
(408) 559-1551. **$135-$179.** 2761 S Bascom Ave. SR 17, exit Camden Ave E, just n. Ext corridors. **Pets:** Accepted.
[ASK] [S🐾] [✕] [▣] [🏊]

▽▽◇ TownePlace Suites by Marriott-San Jose/Campbell SH
(408) 370-4510. **$89-$159.** 700 E Campbell Ave. SR 17, exit Hamilton Ave E, 0.3 mi to Bascom Ave, 0.3 mi s, then 0.3 mi w. Int corridors. **Pets:** Other species. $75 one-time fee/room. Service with restrictions.
[ASK] [S🐾] [✕] [▣]

CAPITOLA

(AAA) ▽▽◇ Best Western Capitola By-the-Sea Inn & Suites SH ❀
(831) 477-0607. **$99-$269.** 1435 41st Ave. SR 1, exit 41st Ave, 0.8 mi w. Int corridors. **Pets:** Dogs only. $20 daily fee/room. Designated rooms, service with restrictions, supervision.
[SAVE] [S🐾] [✕] [🏋] [♿] [🛏] [▣] [🏊]

Capitola Inn M
(831) 462-3004. **$55-$135.** 822 Bay Ave. SR 1, exit Bay Ave, just w. Ext/int corridors. **Pets:** Accepted.
SAVE S X █ ➛

CARLSBAD

Four Seasons Resort Aviara LH ❀
(760) 603-6800. **$415-$650, 3 day notice.** 7100 Four Seasons Point. I-5, exit 45 (Poinsettia Ln/Aviara Pkwy), 1 mi e on Poinsettia Ln, then 1 mi s on Aviara Pkwy. Int corridors. **Pets:** Small. Service with restrictions.
SAVE X █ ▐ ➛ X

Quality Inn & Suites SH
(760) 931-1185. **$89-$149.** 751 Raintree Dr. I-5, exit 45 (Poinsetta Ln), just w to Ave Encinas, then just n. Ext corridors. **Pets:** Accepted.
SAVE S X █ █ ▐ ➛

West Inn & Suites SH
(760) 448-4500. **$179-$369, 3 day notice.** 4970 Avenida Encinas. I-5, exit 48 (Cannon Rd), just w, then just n. Int corridors. **Pets:** Accepted.
SAVE S X ⬆M ⬚ ⬚ █ █ ▐ ➛

CARPINTERIA

Holiday Inn Express Hotel & Suites SH
(805) 566-9499. **$99-$299.** 5606 Carpinteria Ave. US 101, exit 86A (Casitas Pass Rd), just s, then just e. Int corridors. **Pets:** Accepted.
SAVE S X ⬆M ⬚ ⬚ █ █ ➛

CASSEL

Burney Mountain Guest Ranch RA
(530) 335-4087. **$175-$300, 61 day notice.** 22800 Hat Creek Powerhouse #2. I-5, exit 299 E, 2.7 mi; jct SR 89/299 e. Ext corridors. **Pets:** Accepted.
ASK S X █ █ ➛ X

CASTAIC

Comfort Inn M
(661) 295-1100. **$59-$99.** 31558 Castaic Rd. I-5, exit 175A (Parker Rd) northbound, just e on Ridge Route Rd, then just n; exit 176 (Lake Hughes/Castaic) southbound, just s on The Old Rd, just e on Sloan Canyon Rd, then 0.4 mi s; in Castaic. Ext corridors. **Pets:** Other species. $10 one-time fee/pet. Designated rooms, service with restrictions, supervision.
SAVE S X ⬚ █ █ ➛

CASTRO VALLEY

Holiday Inn Express SH
(510) 538-9501. **$90-$120.** 2532 Castro Valley Blvd. I-580, exit Castro Valley Blvd, 0.3 mi n. Int corridors. **Pets:** Small, other species. $20 daily fee/pet. Service with restrictions, supervision.
ASK S X ⬆M ⬚ █ █ ➛

CATHEDRAL CITY

Comfort Suites M
(760) 324-5939. **$79-$209.** 69-151 E Palm Canyon Dr. I-10, exit 126 (Date Palm Dr), 5 mi s, then just e. Ext corridors. **Pets:** Accepted.
ASK S X █ █ ➛

Doral Desert Princess Resort, Palm Springs LH
(760) 322-7000. **$159-$299, 3 day notice.** 67-967 Vista Chino. I-10, exit 126 (Date Palm Dr), 0.5 mi s, then 1 mi w. Int corridors. **Pets:** Accepted.
SAVE X █ █ ▐ ➛ X

CAYUCOS

Beachwalker Inn M
(805) 995-2133. **$65-$169, 3 day notice.** 501 S Ocean Ave. On SR 1 business route. Ext corridors. **Pets:** Accepted.
ASK S X █ █ ▐ ⬚

Cayucos Beach Inn M ❀
(805) 995-2828. **$95-$215, 3 day notice.** 333 S Ocean Ave. On SR 1 business route. Ext corridors. **Pets:** Other species. $5 daily fee/room, $10 one-time fee/room. Service with restrictions.
X █ █

Cypress Tree Motel M ❀
(805) 995-3917. **$49-$119.** 125 S Ocean Ave. On SR 1 business route. Ext corridors. **Pets:** Other species. $10 one-time fee/room. Service with restrictions.
SAVE S X █ █ ▐ ⬚

Estero Bay Motel M
(805) 995-3614. **$55-$169, 7 day notice.** 25 S Ocean Ave. On SR 1 business route. Ext corridors. **Pets:** Medium, dogs only. $10 one-time fee/pet. Service with restrictions, supervision.
SAVE S X █ █ ▐ ⬚

Shoreline Inn M
(805) 995-3681. **$85-$180.** 1 N Ocean Ave. On SR 1 business route. Ext corridors. **Pets:** Accepted.
SAVE S X ⬆M █ █ ▐ ⬚

CEDARVILLE

Sunrise Motel M
(530) 279-2161. **$62-$66, 7 day notice.** 54889 Hwy 299. On SR 299, 0.5 mi w. Ext corridors. **Pets:** Medium. $10 one-time fee/pet. Designated rooms, service with restrictions, supervision.
SAVE X █ █

CHESTER

Almanor Lakeside Resort M
(530) 596-4530. **$95-$175, 30 day notice.** 325 Peninsula Dr. SR 36, right on CR A-13, left on Peninsula Dr, then 0.5 mi. Ext corridors. **Pets:** Accepted.
SAVE X █ X

Best Western Rose Quartz Inn SH
(530) 258-2002. **$106-$146.** 306 Main St. On SR 36; center. Int corridors. **Pets:** $15 daily fee/pet. Designated rooms, service with restrictions, supervision.
SAVE S X ⬚ █ █

CHICO

Budget Inn of Chico SH
(530) 342-9472. **$45-$150.** 1717 Park Ave. SR 99, exit 20th St E, then right. Ext corridors. **Pets:** Small, dogs only. $15 daily fee/pet. Designated rooms, service with restrictions, supervision.
SAVE S X █ X

Deluxe Inn M
(530) 342-8386. **$45-$79, 7 day notice.** 2507 Esplanade. 2 mi n on SR 99 business route. Ext corridors. **Pets:** Medium, dogs only. $10 daily fee/pet. Designated rooms, service with restrictions, supervision.
SAVE S X ➛

Heritage Inn Express M
(530) 343-4527. **$89-$109.** 725 Broadway. SR 32, exit SR 99, 1 mi w. Ext corridors. **Pets:** Medium. $20 one-time fee/room. Designated rooms, service with restrictions, supervision.
SAVE S X █ █ ➛

△△△ ▼▼▼▼ Holiday Inn of Chico SH
(530) 345-2491. **$89-$169.** 685 Manzanita Ct. Just w of SR 99, via Cohasset Rd. Int corridors. **Pets:** Medium. $35 daily fee/pet. Designated rooms, service with restrictions, supervision.
SAVE S⊘ ⊠ ⌧M ⌂ ⬛ ▭ ⍀ ⌁

▼▼▼▼ Music Express Inn BB
(530) 345-8376. **$76-$125.** 1145 El Monte Ave. SR 99, exit SR 32, 1 mi e to El Monte Ave, then just n. Ext/int corridors. **Pets:** Medium, other species. $15 daily fee/pet. Designated rooms, service with restrictions, supervision.
⊠ ⌧M ⌂ ⬛

▼▼▼▼ Oxford Suites SH ❀
(530) 899-9090. **$99-$109.** 2035 Business Ln. SR 99, exit 20th St E. Int corridors. **Pets:** Medium. $38 one-time fee/room. Designated rooms, service with restrictions, supervision.
ASK S⊘ ⊠ ⌧M ⌂ ⬛ ▭ ⍀ ⊠

▼▼▼▼ Residence Inn SH
(530) 894-5500. **Call for rates (no credit cards).** 2485 Carmichael Dr. SR 99, exit Park Ave, 0.5 mi nw. Int corridors. **Pets:** Accepted.
⊠ ⬛ ▭ ⍀ ⊠

△△△ ▼ Safari Garden Motel M
(530) 343-3201. **$45-$55.** 2352 Esplanade. 2 mi n on SR 99 business route. Ext corridors. **Pets:** Accepted.
SAVE S⊘ ⊠ ⬛ ▭ ⍀

△△△ ▼▼▼▼ Super 8 Motel M
(530) 345-2533. **$70-$170.** 655 Manzanita Ct. Just w of SR 99, via Cohasset Rd. Int corridors. **Pets:** Medium. $6 daily fee/pet. Service with restrictions, supervision.
SAVE S⊘ ⊠ ⬛ ⍀

CHOWCHILLA

△△△ ▼▼▼ Days Inn M
(559) 665-4821. **$65-$85.** 220 E Robertson Blvd. SR 99, exit Robertson Blvd W. Ext corridors. **Pets:** Other species. $10 daily fee/pet. Service with restrictions, crate.
SAVE S⊘ ⊠ ⬛ ▭ ⍀

CLIO

▼▼▼▼ Molly's Bed & Breakfast BB ❀
(530) 836-4436. **$90-$110, 7 day notice.** 276 Lower Main St. Just e of SR 89. Int corridors. **Pets:** Dogs only. $10 daily fee/pet. Designated rooms, service with restrictions, supervision.
ASK S⊘ ⊠ W ⌁

COALINGA

△△△ ▼▼▼▼ Best Western Big Country Inn M
(559) 935-0866. **$89-$149.** 25020 W Dorris Ave. I-5, exit SR 198/Hanford-Lemoore, just w. Ext corridors. **Pets:** Medium. $10 daily fee/pet. Designated rooms, service with restrictions, supervision.
SAVE S⊘ ⊠ ⬛ ▭ ⍀

△△△ ▼▼▼▼ The Inn at Harris Ranch LH
(559) 935-0717. **$125-$139.** 24505 W Dorris Ave. I-5, exit SR 198/Hanford-Lemoore, just e. Ext/int corridors. **Pets:** Accepted.
SAVE S⊘ ⊠ ⌧M ⬛ ▭ ⍀

COLTON

△△△ ▼▼▼▼ Hampton Inn & Suites SH
(909) 370-2424. **$89-$199.** 250 N 9th St. I-10, exit 70B (9th St), just n. Int corridors. **Pets:** Accepted.
SAVE S⊘ ⊠ ⬛ ▭ ⍀

COLUMBIA

▼ Columbia Gem Motel M
(209) 532-4508. **$79-$139.** 22131 Parrotts Ferry Rd. 3 mi n of Sonora; 1 mi from Columbia State Historic Park. Ext corridors. **Pets:** Dogs only. Service with restrictions, supervision.
⊠ ⬛ ▭ ⌁

CONCORD

△△△ ▼▼▼ Best Western Heritage Inn SH
(925) 686-4466. **$69-$119.** 4600 Clayton Rd. 3 mi e at Wharton Way. Ext corridors. **Pets:** Medium. $100 deposit/pet. Service with restrictions, supervision.
SAVE S⊘ ⊠ ⬛ ▭ ⍀

△△△ ▼▼▼▼ Holiday Inn Concord LH
(925) 687-5500. **$80-$160.** 1050 Burnett Ave. I-680, exit E Concord Ave, just e. Ext/int corridors. **Pets:** $10 daily fee/pet. Designated rooms, service with restrictions, supervision.
SAVE S⊘ ⊠ ⬛ ▭ ⍀ ⍀

△△△ ▼▼▼ Premier Inns M
(925) 674-0888. **$61-$81.** 1581 Concord Ave. SR 242, exit Clayton Rd northbound; exit Concord Ave southbound, just e. Ext corridors. **Pets:** Accepted.
SAVE S⊘ ⊠ ⌂ ⬛ ⍀

CORNING

△△△ ▼▼▼▼ Best Western Inn Corning M
(530) 824-2468. **$79-$120.** 2165 Solano St. I-5, exit 631 (Central Corning), just e. Ext corridors. **Pets:** $10 daily fee/pet. Designated rooms, service with restrictions, supervision.
SAVE S⊘ ⊠ ⌧M ⬛ ▭ ⍀

△△△ ▼▼▼▼ Comfort Inn SH
(530) 824-5200. **$100-$189.** 910 Hwy 99 W. I-5, exit 631 (Central Corning), just e. Int corridors. **Pets:** Medium. $10 daily fee/room. Designated rooms, no service, supervision.
SAVE S⊘ ⊠ ⌧M ⌂ ⬛ ▭ ⍀

△△△ ▼▼▼▼ Days Inn SH ❀
(530) 824-2000. **$50-$139.** 3475 Hwy 99 W. I-5, exit 630 (South Ave), 0.3 mi s. Int corridors. **Pets:** Other species. $50 deposit/pet. Service with restrictions, supervision.
SAVE S⊘ ⊠ ⌧M ⬛ ⍀

▼▼▼▼ Holiday Inn Express Hotel & Suites SH ❀
(530) 824-6400. **$79-$129.** 3350 Sunrise Way. I-5, exit 630 (South Ave), just s. Int corridors. **Pets:** Other species. $10 daily fee/room. Designated rooms, service with restrictions.
ASK S⊘ ⊠ ⌂ ⬛ ▭ ⍀ ⊠

CORONA

▼▼ Hotel Paseo "Dynasty Suites" M
(951) 371-7185. **$82-$99.** 1805 W 6th St. SR 91, exit 48 (Maple St/W 6th St) eastbound; exit 48 (Maple St) westbound, just s. Ext corridors. **Pets:** Small. $20 daily fee/pet. Service with restrictions, crate.
ASK ⊠ ⬛ ▭ ⍀

▼▼▼▼ Residence Inn by Marriott Corona SH
(951) 371-0107. **$165-$205.** 1015 Montecito Dr. I-15, exit 95 (Magnolia Ave), just e, just n on El Camino, just w on Carly Way, then just n. Int corridors. **Pets:** Accepted.
ASK S⊘ ⊠ ⬛ ▭ ⍀ ⊠

COSTA MESA

▼▼▼▼ Hilton Orange County/Costa Mesa LH
(714) 540-7000. **$109-$329, 3 day notice.** 3050 Bristol St. I-405, exit 9B (Bristol St), just s. Int corridors. **Pets:** Medium. $100 one-time fee/room. Service with restrictions, crate.
⊠ ⬛ ▭ ⍀ ⍀ ⊠

▼▼▼ **Holiday Inn-Costa Mesa/Orange County Airport** 🅛🅗
(714) 557-3000. **$89-$199.** 3131 Bristol St. I-405, exit 9B (Bristol St), just s. Int corridors. **Pets:** Small. $50 one-time fee/room. Designated rooms, service with restrictions, supervision.
ⒶⓈⓀ Ⓢ◐ ✕ 🛢 💻 🍽 ➿

ⒶⒶⒶ ▼▼▼▼ **La Quinta Inn Costa Mesa (John Wayne/Orange Co. Airport)** 🅜
(714) 957-5841. **$85-$139.** 1515 S Coast Dr. I-405, exit 11B (Harbor Blvd), just n, then just w. Ext corridors. **Pets:** Medium. Service with restrictions.
Ⓢ🅐🅥🅔 ✕ 🛢 💻 ➿

ⒶⒶⒶ ▼▼▼▼ **Ramada Limited & Suites** 🅢🅗 🐾
(949) 645-2221. **$79-$184.** 1680 Superior Ave. Just w of SR 55 (Newport Blvd) at 17th St. Ext corridors. **Pets:** Medium. $150 deposit/room, $5 daily fee/room. Designated rooms, service with restrictions, supervision.
Ⓢ🅐🅥🅔 Ⓢ◐ ✕ 🅛🅜 🎣 🅕 🛢 💻 ➿

▼▼▼▼ **Residence Inn by Marriott** 🅢🅗 🐾
(714) 241-8800. **$209-$259.** 881 W Baker St. SR 73, exit 17B (Bear St); SR 55, exit 5B (Baker St). Ext corridors. **Pets:** Other species. $100 one-time fee/room.
ⒶⓈⓀ Ⓢ◐ ✕ 🛢 💻 ➿ ✕

ⒶⒶⒶ ▼ **Travelodge-Orange County Airport** 🅜
(714) 557-8700. **$87-$97.** 1400 SE Bristol St. Adjacent to SR 73, just w of Red Hill Ave. Ext corridors. **Pets:** Small, dogs only. $100 deposit/pet. Designated rooms, service with restrictions, crate.
Ⓢ🅐🅥🅔 Ⓢ◐ ✕ 🛢 💻 ➿

ⒶⒶⒶ ▼ **Vagabond Inn** 🅜 🐾
(714) 557-8360. **$74-$84.** 3205 Harbor Blvd. I-405, exit 11 (Harbor Blvd), just s; entrance from Gisler Ave, just w of Harbor. Ext corridors. **Pets:** Small. $10 daily fee/pet. Service with restrictions, supervision.
Ⓢ🅐🅥🅔 ✕ 🛢 💻 ➿

▼▼▼ **The Westin South Coast Plaza Hotel** 🅛🅗
(714) 540-2500. **$149-$289.** 686 Anton Blvd. I-405, exit 9B (Bristol St), just n, then just e. Int corridors. **Pets:** Accepted.
ⒶⓈⓀ Ⓢ◐ ✕ 🅛🅜 🎣 🅕 🛢 🍽 ➿ ✕

ⒶⒶⒶ ▼▼▼▼ **Wyndham Orange County Airport** 🅛🅗
(714) 751-5100. **$109-$209.** 3350 Ave of the Arts. I-405, exit 9B (Bristol St), n to Anton Blvd, just e, then just n. Int corridors. **Pets:** Accepted.
Ⓢ🅐🅥🅔 ✕ 🎣 🛢 💻 🍽 ➿

CRESCENT CITY

ⒶⒶⒶ ▼ **Americas Best Value Inn** 🅜
(707) 464-4141. **$49-$110.** 440 Hwy 101 N. Center. Ext corridors. **Pets:** Medium, dogs only. $10 daily fee/pet. Designated rooms, service with restrictions, supervision.
Ⓢ🅐🅥🅔 Ⓢ◐ ✕ 🛢 💻

ⒶⒶⒶ ▼▼▼ **Anchor Beach Inn** 🅜
(707) 464-2600. **$59-$140.** 880 Hwy US 101 S. On US 101. Ext corridors. **Pets:** Accepted.
Ⓢ🅐🅥🅔 Ⓢ◐ ✕ 🛢 💻

ⒶⒶⒶ ▼▼▼▼ **Comfort Inn & Suites** 🅢🅗
(707) 464-3885. **$84-$254.** 100 Walton St. Just w of US 101. Ext corridors. **Pets:** Accepted.
Ⓢ🅐🅥🅔 Ⓢ◐ ✕ 🅕 🛢 💻

▼ **Hiouchi Motel** 🅜
(707) 458-3041. **$60-$65.** 2097 Hwy 199. On US 199, 5.5 mi e of jct US 101. Ext corridors. **Pets:** Dogs only. Service with restrictions, supervision.
ⒶⓈⓀ ✕ 🅕 🛢 🅚 🅩

▼▼▼ **Super 8** 🅜 🐾
(707) 464-4111. **$50-$110.** 685 Hwy 101 S. On US 101. Ext corridors. **Pets:** Medium, dogs only. $10 daily fee/pet. Designated rooms, service with restrictions, supervision.
Ⓢ🅐🅥🅔 Ⓢ◐ ✕ 🛢 💻 🅚

CUPERTINO

ⒶⒶⒶ ▼▼▼▼ **Cypress Hotel** 🅛🅗
(408) 253-8900. **$109-$249.** 10050 S De Anza Blvd. I-280, exit De Anza Blvd, just s. Int corridors. **Pets:** Accepted.
Ⓢ🅐🅥🅔 Ⓢ◐ ✕ 🛢 💻 🍽 ➿

CYPRESS

▼▼ **Homestead Studio Suites Hotel-Orange County-Cypress** 🅢🅗
(714) 761-2766. **$104-$124.** 5990 Corporate Ave. I-605, exit 1D (Katella Ave) southbound; exit 1B (Katella Ave/Willow St) northbound, 3 mi e, 0.4 mi n on Valley View Ave, then just w. Int corridors. **Pets:** Accepted.
ⒶⓈⓀ Ⓢ◐ ✕ 🛢 💻 ➿

ⒶⒶⒶ ▼▼▼ **Woodfin Suite Hotel-Cypress** 🅢🅗
(714) 828-4000. **$154-$184.** 5905 Corporate Ave. I-605, exit 1D (Katella Ave) southbound; exit 1B (Katella Ave/Willow St) northbound, 3 mi e, 0.4 mi n on Valley View Ave, then just w. Int corridors. **Pets:** Accepted.
Ⓢ🅐🅥🅔 Ⓢ◐ ✕ 🛢 💻 ➿

DANA POINT

ⒶⒶⒶ ▼▼▼▼ **St. Regis Resort, Monarch Beach** 🅛🅗 🐾
(949) 234-3200. **$575-$1925, 7 day notice.** One Monarch Beach Resort. I-5, exit 79 (Pacific Coast Hwy) northbound, 3 mi n; exit 86 (Crown Valley Pkwy) southbound, 3 mi w, 1 mi s on Pacific Coast Hwy, then 0.5 mi e on Niguel Rd. Int corridors. **Pets:** Medium. $100 one-time fee/room. Designated rooms, supervision.
Ⓢ🅐🅥🅔 Ⓢ◐ ✕ 🅛🅜 🎣 🅕 🍽 ➿ ✕

DAVIS

ⒶⒶⒶ ▼▼▼ **Best Western University Lodge** 🅢🅗
(530) 756-7890. **$79-$99.** 123 B St. Just e of University of California Davis campus. Ext corridors. **Pets:** Other species. $20 daily fee/pet. Service with restrictions, supervision.
Ⓢ🅐🅥🅔 Ⓢ◐ ✕ 🅛🅜 🛢 💻 ✕

ⒶⒶⒶ ▼▼▼ **Howard Johnson Hotel** 🅜
(530) 792-0800. **$99-$199.** 4100 Chiles Rd. I-80, exit Mace Blvd, just s, then 0.3 mi w. Int corridors. **Pets:** Accepted.
Ⓢ🅐🅥🅔 Ⓢ◐ ✕ 🅛🅜 🅕 🛢 💻 🍽 ➿

ⒶⒶⒶ ▼▼▼ **University Park Inn & Suites** 🅢🅗
(530) 756-0910. **$80-$129.** 1111 Richards Blvd. I-80, exit Richards Blvd, just n. Ext corridors. **Pets:** Other species. $250 deposit/room, $10 daily fee/pet. Designated rooms, service with restrictions, crate.
Ⓢ🅐🅥🅔 Ⓢ◐ ✕ 🅛🅜 🛢 💻 ➿

DEATH VALLEY NATIONAL PARK

▼ **Stovepipe Wells Village** 🅜
(303) 297-2757. **$87-$112.** SR 190. On SR 190; 24 mi nw of visitor center. Ext corridors. **Pets:** Accepted.
✕ 🅛🅜 🅕 🛢 🍽 ➿ 🅩

DELANO

ⒶⒶⒶ ▼▼▼ **Rodeway Inn** 🅜
(661) 725-1022. **$59-$89.** 2211 Girard St. SR 99, exit 58 (County Line Rd), just e, then just s. Ext corridors. **Pets:** Small. $10 daily fee/pet. Service with restrictions, supervision.
Ⓢ🅐🅥🅔 Ⓢ◐ ✕ 🛢 💻 ➿

DINUBA

◆◆◆ Reedley Country Inn [BB]
(559) 638-2585. **$85-$115, 3 day notice.** SR 99, exit 121 (Manning Ave), 10 mi e, then 1 mi s on Rd 52 (Reed Ave). Ext/int corridors. **Pets:** Accepted.
[ASK] [S☐] [X]

DIXON

△△△ ◆◆◆◆ Best Western Inn Dixon [SH]
(707) 678-1400. **$95-$135, 3 day notice.** 1345 Commercial Way. I-80, exit Pitt School Rd; 8 mi w of University of California Davis campus. Ext/int corridors. **Pets:** $15 one-time fee/room. Service with restrictions, supervision.
[SAVE] [S☐] [X] [&M] [&] [B] [◻] [≈] [X]

◆◆◆ Super 8 [SH]
(707) 678-3399. **$65-$105.** 2500 Plaza Ct. I-80, exit West A St, just s. Int corridors. **Pets:** Accepted.
[ASK] [S☐] [X] [B] [≈]

DORRIS

◆ Golden Eagle Motel [SH]
(530) 397-3114. **$45-$96.** 100 N Main St. US 97; center. **Pets:** Medium. $5 daily fee/pet. Designated rooms, service with restrictions, supervision.
[ASK] [S☐] [X] [&] [B]

DOWNIEVILLE

◆◆ Riverside Inn [M]
(530) 289-1000. **$75-$165, 3 day notice.** 206 Commercial St. SR 49; center. Ext corridors. **Pets:** Medium, other species. $10 one-time fee/pet. Service with restrictions, supervision.
[ASK] [S☐] [X] [B] [◻] [X] [X]

DUNNIGAN

△△△ ◆◆◆ Americas Best Value Inn [SH]
(530) 724-3333. **$65-$89.** 3930 Rd 89. I-5, exit Dunnigan. Int corridors. **Pets:** Medium, other species. $10 one-time fee/pet. Service with restrictions, supervision.
[SAVE] [S☐] [X] [&M] [B] [≈]

△△△ ◆◆◆ Best Western Country [M]
(530) 724-3471. **$69-$119.** 3930 Rd 89. I-5, exit Dunnigan. Ext corridors. **Pets:** Medium, other species. $10 one-time fee/pet. Service with restrictions, supervision.
[SAVE] [S☐] [X] [&M] [B] [◻] [≈]

DUNSMUIR

△△△ ◆◆◆ Caboose Motel-Railroad Park Resort [M]
(530) 235-4440. **$90-$100, 3 day notice.** 100 Railroad Park Rd. I-5, exit 728 (Railroad Park Rd), 1 mi s. **Pets:** Dogs only. $10 daily fee/pet. Designated rooms, service with restrictions, supervision.
[SAVE] [X] [B] [◻] [¶] [≈]

△△△ ◆ Cedar Lodge Motel [M]
(530) 235-4331. **$59-$74.** 4201 Dunsmuir Ave. I-5, exit 732, 0.5 mi w. Ext corridors. **Pets:** Accepted.
[SAVE] [X] [B] [◻]

EL CENTRO

◆◆ Barbara Worth Golf Resort and Convention Center [SH]
(760) 356-2806. **$78-$112.** 2050 Country Club Dr. I-8, exit 120 (Bowker Rd), 2 mi n, then 3 mi e on CR S-80; 9 mi e of SR 86. Ext/int corridors. **Pets:** Accepted.
[ASK] [S☐] [X] [B] [◻] [¶] [≈] [X]

◆◆ Brunner's Inns & Suites [M]
(760) 337-5550. **$79-$149, 3 day notice.** 215 N Imperial Ave. I-8, exit 114 (Imperial Ave), 1 mi n. Ext corridors. **Pets:** Accepted.
[ASK] [S☐] [X] [B] [◻] [¶] [≈]

△△△ ◆◆◆ Ramada Inn El Centro [M]
(760) 352-5152. **$101-$160.** 1455 Ocotillo Dr. I-8, exit 114 (Imperial Ave), just n, then just e. Ext corridors. **Pets:** Accepted.
[SAVE] [S☐] [X] [B] [◻] [¶] [≈]

◆◆ Super Star Inn-El Centro [M]
(760) 352-0715. **$59-$64.** 611 N Imperial Ave. I-8, exit 114 (Imperial Ave), 1.5 mi n. Ext corridors. **Pets:** Accepted.
[ASK] [S☐] [X] [B]

◆◆ Vacation Inn [M]
(760) 352-9700. **$69-$99.** 2015 Cottonwood Cir. I-8, exit 114 (Imperial Ave), just n, then just w. Ext corridors. **Pets:** Accepted.
[ASK] [S☐] [X] [B] [◻] [¶] [≈]

△△△ ◆◆ Value Inn & Suites [M]
(760) 352-6620. **$46-$65.** 455 W Wake Ave. I-8, exit 115 (4th St/SR 86), just s, then just w. Ext corridors. **Pets:** Small. $5 daily fee/pet. Service with restrictions, supervision.
[SAVE] [S☐] [X] [B] [≈]

ELK GROVE

◆◆ Extended StayAmerica-Sacramento-Elk Grove [SH]
(916) 683-3753. **$109-$119.** 2201 Long Port Ct. I-5, exit Laguna Blvd, 0.5 mi e, just s on Harbour Point Dr, then just w. Int corridors. **Pets:** Accepted.
[ASK] [S☐] [X] [&] [B]

EL PORTAL

△△△ ◆◆◆ Yosemite View Lodge [SH]
(209) 379-2681. **$95-$709, 7 day notice.** 11136 Hwy 140. Just w of Yosemite National Park West Gate. Ext corridors. **Pets:** Medium. $10 daily fee/pet. Designated rooms, service with restrictions, supervision.
[SAVE] [X] [&M] [◻] [&] [B] [◻] [≈] [X]

EMERYVILLE

△△△ ◆◆◆◆ Woodfin Suite Hotel San Francisco Bay Bridge [LH]
(510) 601-5880. **$159-$229.** 5800 Shellmound St. I-80, exit Powell St. Int corridors. **Pets:** Other species. $150 deposit/pet, $5 daily fee/pet. Designated rooms, service with restrictions, supervision.
[SAVE] [S☐] [X] [B] [◻] [≈]

ENCINITAS

△△△ ◆◆◆◆ Best Western Encinitas Inn & Suites at Moonlight Beach [M]
(760) 942-7455. **$109-$184.** 85 Encinitas Blvd. I-5, exit 41B (Encinitas Blvd), just w. Ext corridors. **Pets:** Medium. $50 one-time fee/room. Designated rooms, service with restrictions, supervision.
[SAVE] [X] [B] [◻] [¶] [≈]

△△△ ◆◆◆◆ Howard Johnson-Encinitas [M]
(760) 944-3800. **$69-$169.** 607 Leucadia Blvd. I-5, exit 43 (Leucadia Blvd), east side. Ext corridors. **Pets:** Accepted.
[SAVE] [S☐] [X] [B] [◻] [≈]

◆◆ Portofino Beach Inn [M]
(760) 944-0301. **$79-$169.** 186 N Coast Hwy. I-5, exit 41B (Encinitas Blvd), 0.6 mi w, then just n. Ext corridors. **Pets:** Accepted.
[ASK] [S☐] [X] [B] [◻]

ESCONDIDO

△△△ ◆◆◆◆ Best Western Escondido [SH]
(760) 740-1700. **$109-$139, 14 day notice.** 1700 Seven Oaks Rd. I-15, exit 33 (El Norte Pkwy), just e. Int corridors. **Pets:** Small, other species. $25 one-time fee/pet. Service with restrictions, supervision.
[SAVE] [S☐] [X] [B] [◻] [≈]

Rodeway Inn M
(760) 746-0441. **$54-$159.** 250 W El Norte Pkwy. I-15, exit 33 (El Norte Pkwy), 1 mi e. Ext corridors. **Pets:** Accepted.
SAVE S⊙ ✕ 🖥 💻

ETNA

Motel Etna M
(530) 467-5330. **$47.** 317 Collier Way. Just w of SR 3. Ext corridors. **Pets:** Accepted.
✕ 🖥

EUREKA

Bayview Motel M ❖
(707) 442-1673. **$80-$150.** 2844 Fairfield St. E of US 101, at Henderson St, top of hill. Ext corridors. **Pets:** Small. $10 daily fee/room. Designated rooms, supervision.
ASK S⊙ ✕ 🖉 🖥 💻

Best Western Bayshore Inn M
(707) 268-8005. **$89-$179.** 3500 Broadway. US 101; south end of town. Ext corridors. **Pets:** Medium, dogs only. $40 one-time fee/pet. Designated rooms, service with restrictions, supervision.
SAVE S⊙ ✕ 🖉 🖥 💻 🍴 ➹ ✕

Carter House Inns CI
(707) 444-8062. **$155-$595, 3 day notice.** 301 L St. Just w of US 101 S. Int corridors. **Pets:** Medium. $50 one-time fee/pet. Designated rooms, service with restrictions.
SAVE S⊙ ✕ 🖥 🍴 ✗

Eureka Town House Motel M
(707) 443-4536. **$55-$125.** 933 4th St. On US 101 southbound; corner of K St. Ext corridors. **Pets:** Small, dogs only. $10 daily fee/pet. Designated rooms, service with restrictions, supervision.
SAVE S⊙ ✕ 🖥 💻 ✗

Eureka Travelodge M
(707) 443-6345. **$54-$126.** 4 4th St. On US 101; corner of 4th and B sts. Ext corridors. **Pets:** Accepted.
ASK S⊙ ✕ 🖥 💻 ➹ ✗

Quality Inn Eureka M
(707) 443-1601. **$78-$150.** 1209 4th St. On US 101 southbound; between M and N sts. Ext corridors. **Pets:** Accepted.
SAVE ✕ 🖥 💻 ➹ ✗

Ramada Eurekan SH
(707) 443-2206. **$63-$92.** 270 5th St. On US 101 northbound; corner of D St. Int corridors. **Pets:** Accepted.
SAVE S⊙ ✕ 🖥 💻

Red Lion Hotel Eureka SH ❖
(707) 445-0844. **$109-$195.** 1929 4th St. On US 101 southbound; between T and V sts. Int corridors. **Pets:** Small, dogs only. $20 daily fee/pet. Service with restrictions, crate.
SAVE ✕ 🖉 🖥 💻 🍴 ➹

Sunrise Inn & Suites M
(707) 443-9751. **$50-$110.** 129 4th St. On US 101 southbound; corner of C St. Ext corridors. **Pets:** Small, dogs only. $8 daily fee/pet. Service with restrictions, supervision.
SAVE S⊙ ✕ 🖥 💻 ✗

FAIRFIELD

Days Inn M
(707) 864-1728. **$60-$110.** 4376 Central Pl. I-80, exit Suisun Valley Rd, just e. Ext corridors. **Pets:** Medium. $15 daily fee/pet. Service with restrictions, supervision.
SAVE S⊙ ✕ 🖥 ➹

Econo Lodge Inn & Suites M
(707) 864-2426. **$59-$109.** 4625 Central Way. I-80, exit Suisun Valley Rd, just e. Ext corridors. **Pets:** Accepted.
SAVE S⊙ ✕ &M 🖥 💻

FALLBROOK

Pala Mesa Resort LH ❖
(760) 728-5881. **$145-$315.** 2001 Old Hwy 395. I-15, exit 46 (SR 76/Pala/Oceanside), just w, then 2 mi n. Ext corridors. **Pets:** Medium. $75 one-time fee/pet. Service with restrictions, supervision.
ASK S⊙ ✕ 🖥 💻 🍴 ➹ ✗

FALL RIVER MILLS

Hi-Mont Motel M ❖
(530) 336-5541. **$86-$94, 3 day notice.** 43021 Bridge St. 1 mi w on SR 299. Ext corridors. **Pets:** Other species. $10 daily fee/pet. Service with restrictions, supervision.
SAVE S⊙ ✕ 🖥 💻

FERNDALE

Collingwood Inn Bed & Breakfast BB ❖
(707) 786-9219. **$125-$300, 14 day notice.** 831 Main St. Center. Int corridors. **Pets:** Other species. $25 daily fee/pet.
ASK S⊙ ✕ 🖥 ✗

Shaw House Inn Bed & Breakfast BB
(707) 786-9958. **$100-$275, 15 day notice.** 703 Main St. Center. Ext/int corridors. **Pets:** Medium, other species. $30 daily fee/pet. Designated rooms, service with restrictions, crate.
SAVE ✕ 🖥 🖉 ✗

FILLMORE

Best Western La Posada Motel M
(805) 524-0440. **$85-$99.** 827 Ventura Ave. On SR 126. Ext corridors. **Pets:** Small, dogs only. $15 one-time fee/pet. No service, supervision.
SAVE S⊙ ✕ 🖥 💻 ➹

FIREBAUGH

Best Western Apricot Inn M
(559) 659-1444. **$79-$109.** 46290 W Panoche Rd. I-5, exit W Panoche Rd, just w. Ext corridors. **Pets:** Medium, other species. $10 daily fee/pet. Service with restrictions, supervision.
SAVE S⊙ ✕ 🖥 💻 ➹

FISH CAMP

Apple Tree Inn SH ❖
(559) 683-5111. **$99-$219.** 1110 Hwy 41. 2 mi from South Gate to Yosemite National Park. Ext corridors. **Pets:** Other species. $50 one-time fee/pet. Designated rooms, service with restrictions, supervision.
SAVE S⊙ ✕ &M ☺ 🖥 💻 ➹ ✗ ✗

The Narrow Gauge Inn SH ❖
(559) 683-7720. **$79-$245, 4 day notice.** 48571 Hwy 41. 4 mi from South Gate to Yosemite National Park. Ext corridors. **Pets:** Medium, other species. $25 one-time fee/pet. Designated rooms, service with restrictions, supervision.
✕ 🖥 💻 🍴 ➹

Tenaya Lodge at Yosemite LH
(559) 683-6555. **$129-$369, 7 day notice.** 1122 Hwy 41. 2 mi from South Gate to Yosemite National Park. Int corridors. **Pets:** Accepted.
SAVE ✕ &M ☺ 🖉 🖥 💻 🍴 ➹ ✗

FOLSOM

Lake Natoma Inn SH
(916) 351-1500. **$106-$159.** 702 Gold Lake Dr. US 50, exit Folsom Blvd, 3 mi n; behind The Lakes Specialty Shopping Center. Int corridors. **Pets:** Accepted.
SAVE S⊙ ✕ &M 🖥 💻 🍴 ➹ ✗

Larkspur Landing Home Suite Hotel Folsom SH
(916) 355-1616. **$139-$179.** 121 Iron Point Rd. US 50, exit Folsom Blvd, 0.5 mi n to Iron Point Rd, then 0.3 mi e. Int corridors. **Pets:** Medium. $75 one-time fee/pet. Designated rooms, service with restrictions, supervision.

Residence Inn by Marriott SH
(916) 983-7289. **$170-$200.** 2555 Iron Point Rd. US 50, exit Bidwell St, just n. Int corridors. **Pets:** Accepted.

FORTUNA

Best Western Country Inn M
(707) 725-6822. **$89-$145.** 2025 Riverwalk Dr. US 101, exit 687 (Kenmar Rd), just w. Ext corridors. **Pets:** Dogs only. $10 one-time fee/pet. Designated rooms, service with restrictions, supervision.

Fortuna Super 8 M
(707) 725-2888. **$66-$126.** 1805 Alamar Way. US 101, exit 687 (Kenmar Rd), 0.3 mi w on Riverwalk Dr to Alamar Way. Ext corridors. **Pets:** Medium, dogs only. $10 daily fee/pet. Designated rooms, service with restrictions, supervision.

Holiday Inn Express M ❀
(707) 725-5500. **$99-$199.** 1859 Alamar Way. US 101, exit 687 (Kenmar Rd), 0.3 mi w on Riverwalk Dr to Alamar Way. Ext corridors. **Pets:** Small. $10 daily fee/pet. Designated rooms, service with restrictions, supervision.

Travel Inn M
(707) 725-6993. **$79, 3 day notice.** 275 12th St. US 101, exit 12th St, 0.5 mi w. Ext corridors. **Pets:** Very small. $10 daily fee/pet. Service with restrictions, supervision.

FOUNTAIN VALLEY

Residence Inn by Marriott SH ❀
(714) 965-8000. **$209-$259.** 9930 Slater Ave. I-405, exit 14 (Brookhurst St), just n, then just w. Ext corridors. **Pets:** Small, other species. $100 one-time fee/room. Service with restrictions, supervision.

FREMONT

Best Western Garden Court Inn SH
(510) 792-4300. **$59-$139.** 5400 Mowry Ave. I-880, exit Mowry Ave, just e. Int corridors. **Pets:** Accepted.

Extended StayAmerica-Fremont-Newark SH
(510) 794-8040. **$84-$94.** 5355 Farwell Pl. I-880, exit Mowry Ave, just e. Int corridors. **Pets:** Accepted.

Extended Stay Deluxe-Fremont-Newark SH
(510) 794-9693. **$94-$99.** 5375 Farwell Pl. I-880, exit Mowry Ave, just e. Int corridors. **Pets:** Accepted.

Fremont Marriott LH
(510) 413-3700. **$149-$199.** 46100 Landing Pkwy. I-880, exit Fremont Blvd/Cushing Pkwy, then w. Int corridors. **Pets:** Accepted.

Homestead Studio Suites Hotel-Fremont Blvd. South SH
(510) 353-1664. **$85-$95.** 46080 Fremont Blvd. I-880, exit Fremont Blvd/Cushing Pkwy, just w. Int corridors. **Pets:** Accepted.

La Quinta Inn & Suites Fremont SH
(510) 445-0808. **$105-$139.** 46200 Landing Pkwy. I-880, exit Fremont Blvd/Cushing Pkwy, just w. Int corridors. **Pets:** Medium. Service with restrictions.

FRESNO

Days Inn-Parkway M
(559) 268-6211. **$79-$84.** 1101 N Parkway Dr. SR 99, exit Olive Ave, just w. Ext corridors. **Pets:** Accepted.

Holiday Inn Express Hotel & Suites-Barcus SH
(559) 277-5700. **$95-$125.** 5046 N Barcus. SR 99, exit Shaw Ave, just e. Int corridors. **Pets:** Medium, other species. $20 one-time fee/room. Service with restrictions, supervision.

La Quinta Inn Fresno/Yosemite SH
(559) 442-1110. **$86-$122.** 2926 Tulare St. SR 99, exit Fresno St, 1 mi e to R St, then s, then just e. Ext corridors. **Pets:** Medium. Service with restrictions.

Quality Inn M
(559) 275-2727. **$99-$119.** 4278 W Ashlan Ave. SR 99, exit Ashlan Ave, just w. Ext corridors. **Pets:** Accepted.

Red Roof Inn SH
(559) 431-3557. **$59-$99.** 6730 N Blackstone Ave. SR 41, exit Herndon Ave, then w. Ext corridors. **Pets:** Medium, other species. Service with restrictions, supervision.

Red Roof Inn M
(559) 276-1910. **$55-$91.** 5021 N Barcus Ave. SR 99, exit Shaw Ave, just e. Ext corridors. **Pets:** Medium, other species. Service with restrictions, supervision.

Residence Inn by Marriott SH ❀
(559) 222-8900. **$169-$208.** 5322 N Diana Ave. SR 41, exit Shaw Ave, 0.3 mi w, n on Blackstone Ave, then e on Barstow Ave. Int corridors. **Pets:** Other species. $75 one-time fee/room. Service with restrictions, supervision.

Super 8-Parkway M
(559) 268-0741. **$67-$89.** 1087 N Parkway Dr. SR 99, exit Olive Ave, just w. Ext corridors. **Pets:** Accepted.

TownePlace Suites by Marriott SH
(559) 435-4600. **$99-$132.** 7127 N Fresno St. SR 41, exit Herndon Ave E. Int corridors. **Pets:** Other species. $100 one-time fee/room. Service with restrictions, supervision.

University Inn SH
(559) 294-0224. **$44-$90.** 2655 E Shaw Ave. SR 168, exit Shaw Ave, just w. Ext corridors. **Pets:** Other species. $25 deposit/room. Service with restrictions, supervision.

AAA WW Valley Inn **M**
(559) 233-3913. **$40-$50.** 933 N Parkway Dr. SR 99, exit Olive Ave, then w. Ext corridors. **Pets:** Small, dogs only. $10 daily fee/pet. Designated rooms, service with restrictions, supervision.
SAVE X 🔵

FULLERTON

WWWW Fullerton Marriott Hotel at California State Univ **SH**
(714) 738-7800. **$114-$179.** 2701 E Nutwood Ave. SR 57, exit 7 (Nutwood Ave) northbound; exit 7 (Nutwood Ave/Chapman Ave) southbound, just w. Int corridors. **Pets:** $100 deposit/room, $35 one-time fee/room.
ASK S X &M 🔒 🔵 🔵 ⛟ 🍴 🚫

WWWW Wyndham Anaheim Park Hotel **SH**
(714) 992-1700. **$109-$149.** 222 W Houston Ave. SR 91, exit 28 (Harbor Blvd), just n, then just w. Int corridors. **Pets:** Accepted.
ASK S X 🍴 ⛟

GARBERVILLE

AAA WWW Best Western Humboldt House Inn **M**
(707) 923-2771. **$99-$135.** 701 Redwood Dr. US 101, exit Garberville, just e. Ext corridors. **Pets:** Medium, dogs only. $5 one-time fee/pet. Designated rooms, service with restrictions, supervision.
SAVE S X 🔒 🔵 ⛟

GARDEN GROVE

AAA WWWW Anaheim Marriott Suites **SH**
(714) 750-1000. **$119-$199.** 12015 Harbor Blvd. I-5, exit 107B (Champman Ave) northbound, 1.5 mi w on Chapman Ave, then just s; exit 107C (State College/The City Dr) southbound, just s on State College Blvd, 1.5 mi w on Chapman Ave, then just s. Int corridors. **Pets:** Accepted.
SAVE S X 🔒 🔵 🔵 🍴 ⛟ 🚫

WWWW Candlewood Suites Anaheim-South **SH**
(714) 539-4200. **$89-$129.** 12901 Garden Grove Blvd. SR 22, exit 13 (Haster St) westbound; exit 13 (Fairview St) eastbound, just n, then just w. Int corridors. **Pets:** Accepted.
ASK S X 🔒 🔵

AAA WWWW Residence Inn Anaheim Resort Area **SH**
(714) 591-4000. **$139-$369, 3 day notice.** 11931 Harbor Blvd. I-5, exit 107B (Chapman Ave) northbound, 1.5 mi w, then just n; exit 107C (State College/The City Dr) southbound, just s on State College Blvd, 1.5 mi w on Chapman Ave, then just n. Int corridors. **Pets:** Accepted.
SAVE S X 🔒 🔵 🔵 ⛟ 🚫

GLENNVILLE

WW The Bunkhouse Motel **M**
(661) 536-9100. **$65-$85.** 12044 Hwy 155 S. On SR 155 at Granite Rd. Ext corridors. **Pets:** Accepted.
ASK S X 🔒 🔵 🍴

GRAEAGLE

WWWW Chalet View Lodge **SH**
(530) 832-5528. **$90-$166.** 72056 Hwy 70. 5 mi e on SR 70 (Feather River Hwy) from jct SR 89. Ext corridors. **Pets:** $15 daily fee/room. Designated rooms, service with restrictions, supervision.
X 🔒 🔵 🍴 ⛟ 🚫

GRASS VALLEY

AAA WWW Alta Sierra Village Inn **M** 🐾
(530) 273-9102. **$59-$175, 7 day notice.** 11858 Tammy Way. 6 mi s, 1.1 mi e on Alta Sierra Dr, 0.8 mi w on Norlene, then 0.5 mi e; follow signs to Alta Sierra Country Club. Ext corridors. **Pets:** Large. $10 one-time fee/room. Service with restrictions, supervision.
SAVE S X &M 🔒 🔵 🚫

AAA WW Best Western Gold Country Inn **M**
(530) 273-1393. **$89-$140.** 11972 Sutton Way. SR 20 and 49, exit Brunswick Rd, just e; midway between Grass Valley and Nevada City. Ext corridors. **Pets:** Small. $20 one-time fee/pet. Designated rooms, service with restrictions, supervision.
SAVE S X &M 🔒 🔵 ⛟

AAA WW Coach N' Four Motel **M**
(530) 273-8009. **$60-$122, 7 day notice.** 628 S Auburn St. SR 49, exit E Empire St, 0.3 mi e, then just s. Ext corridors. **Pets:** Medium, other species. $10 deposit/pet. Designated rooms, service with restrictions, supervision.
SAVE S X &M 🔒

AAA WW Golden Chain Resort Motel **M**
(530) 273-7279. **$65-$109, 3 day notice.** 13413 State Hwy 49. On SR 49, 2.5 mi s. Ext corridors. **Pets:** Small. $10 one-time fee/pet. Service with restrictions, supervision.
SAVE S X &M 🔒 ⛟

AAA WWW Grass Valley Courtyard Suites **SH** 🐾
(530) 272-7696. **$150-$265, 3 day notice.** 210 N Auburn St. SR 49, exit Central Grass Valley. Ext corridors. **Pets:** Dogs only. $50 one-time fee/pet. Supervision.
SAVE S X & 🔒 🔵 ⛟ 🚫

AAA WW Stagecoach Motel **M**
(530) 272-3701. **$55-$90.** 405 S Auburn St. SR 49, exit Colfax Ave, 0.4 mi s. Ext corridors. **Pets:** Medium. $15 one-time fee/pet. Designated rooms, service with restrictions, supervision.
SAVE S X &M 🔒 🔵

GRIDLEY

AAA WW Gridley Inn **M** 🐾
(530) 846-4520. **$60-$80.** 1490 Hwy 99, Suite A. On SR 99, 1 mi s. Ext corridors. **Pets:** $10 daily fee/pet. Service with restrictions, supervision.
SAVE X 🔒 🔵 ⛟

AAA WW Pacific Motel **M**
(530) 846-4580. **$58-$68, 3 day notice.** 1308 Hwy 99. On SR 99, 1 mi s. Ext corridors. **Pets:** Accepted.
SAVE S X 🔒 ⛟

GROVELAND

AAA WWW Americas Best Value Inn -Yosemite Westgate Lodge **SH**
(209) 962-5281. **$79-$250, 3 day notice.** 7633 Hwy 120. On SR 120, 12 mi e. Ext corridors. **Pets:** $25 daily fee/pet. Designated rooms, no service, supervision.
SAVE X 🔒 🔵 ⛟

AAA WWWW Groveland Hotel at Yosemite National Park **CI**
(209) 962-4000. **$145-$185.** 18767 Main St. Center. Int corridors. **Pets:** Accepted.
SAVE X 🔵 🍴

HANFORD

AAA WW Sequoia Inn **SH**
(559) 582-0338. **$74-$85, 3 day notice.** 1655 Mall Dr. SR 198, exit 12th Ave, then n. Int corridors. **Pets:** Accepted.
SAVE S X 🔒 🔵 ⛟

HAYWARD

AAA WWWW Comfort Inn **SH**
(510) 538-4466. **$89-$170.** 24997 Mission Blvd. 1.8 mi e of I-880, exit SR 92 (Jackson St), 0.5 mi s on SR 238 (Mission Blvd). Ext corridors. **Pets:** Small. $150 deposit/room, $15 daily fee/room. Designated rooms, service with restrictions, supervision.
SAVE S X 🔒 🔵

▼▼▼ **La Quinta Inn & Suites Hayward/Oakland Airport** SH
(510) 732-6300. **$119.** 20777 Hesperian Blvd. I-880, exit A St, 0.5 mi w. Int corridors. **Pets:** Medium. Supervision.

ASK S⃝ X⃝ 🐾 📶 💻 🏊

⊕⊕⊕ ▼▼▼ **MainStay Suites** SH
(510) 731-3571. **$79-$99.** 835 West A St. I-880, exit A St, just w. Int corridors. **Pets:** Small, other species. $15 daily fee/pet. Service with restrictions, supervision.

SAVE X⃝ 🐾 🏊 💻 🏊

HEMET

⊕⊕⊕ ▼▼▼ **Best Western Inn of Hemet** M
(951) 925-6605. **$99-$156.** 2625 W Florida Ave. 2.4 mi w of SR 79 N (San Jacino St) on SR 74/79. Ext corridors. **Pets:** Accepted.

SAVE S⃝ X⃝ 📶 💻 🏊

⊕⊕⊕ ▼ **Coach Light Motel** M
(951) 658-3237. **$65-$70.** 1640 W Florida Ave. 1.7 mi w of SR 74 N (San Jacino St) on SR 74/79. Ext corridors. **Pets:** Dogs only. $10 daily fee/pet. No service, supervision.

SAVE S⃝ X⃝ 📶 🏊

⊕⊕⊕ ▼▼▼ **Quality Inn** M
(951) 766-1902. **$80-$90.** 1201 W Florida Ave. 1.5 mi w of SR 79 N (San Jacino St) on SR 74/79. Ext corridors. **Pets:** Small, dogs only. $20 daily fee/pet. Service with restrictions, supervision.

SAVE X⃝ 📶 💻

HESPERIA

⊕⊕⊕ ▼▼▼ **Days Inn Suites-Hesperia/Victorville** M
(760) 948-0600. **$62-$185.** 14865 Bear Valley Rd. I-15, exit 147 (Bear Valley Rd), 0.5 mi e of Victor Valley Mall. Ext corridors. **Pets:** Accepted.

SAVE S⃝ X⃝ 📶 💻

⊕⊕⊕ ▼▼▼ **Holiday Inn Express Hotel & Suites** SH
(760) 244-7674. **$79-$180.** 9750 Key Pointe Dr. I-15, exit 143 (Hesperia/Main St), just w on Main St, then just n. Int corridors. **Pets:** Small. $25 daily fee/room. Designated rooms, service with restrictions, supervision.

SAVE S⃝ X⃝ 🏊 📶 🐾 📶 💻 🏊

▼▼▼ **La Quinta Inn & Suites Victorville** SH
(760) 949-9900. **$105-$145.** 12000 Mariposa Rd. I-15, exit 147 (Bear Valley Rd), just e, then just s. Int corridors. **Pets:** Medium. $50 deposit/room. Designated rooms, service with restrictions, supervision.

ASK S⃝ X⃝ 📶 💻 🏊 🐾

⊕⊕⊕ ▼▼▼ **Super 8 Motel** M
(760) 949-3231. **$59-$82.** 12033 Oakwood Ave. I-15, exit 147 (Bear Valley Rd), just se. Ext corridors. **Pets:** Accepted.

SAVE S⃝ X⃝ 📶 💻 🏊

HUNTINGTON BEACH

▼▼▼ **Extended StayAmerica-Orange County/Huntington Beach** SH
(714) 799-4887. **$99-$119.** 5050 Skylab W Cir. I-405, exit 21 (SR 22 Valley View Blvd) northbound, 1.8 mi s; exit 18 (Bolsa Ave) southbound, 2 mi s. Int corridors. **Pets:** Accepted.

ASK S⃝ X⃝ 🏊 📶 🐾 📶 💻

⊕⊕⊕ ▼▼▼▼ **Hilton Waterfront Beach Resort** LH
(714) 845-8000. **$199-$599, 3 day notice.** 21100 Pacific Coast Hwy. I-405, exit 16 (Beach Blvd), 6 mi s, then just w. Int corridors. **Pets:** Medium, dogs only. $50 daily fee/pet. Service with restrictions, supervision.

SAVE X⃝ 📶 💻 🍴 🏊 🐾

IDYLLWILD

▼▼▼ **Cedar Street Inn** CA
(951) 659-4789. **$70-$150, 10 day notice.** 25880 Cedar St. From SR 243 and town center, 0.3 mi ne on N Circle Dr. Ext corridors. **Pets:** Accepted.

ASK X⃝ 📶 💻 🐾 📞

⊕⊕⊕ ▼▼▼ **Fireside Inn** CA
(951) 659-2966. **$65-$130, 10 day notice.** 54540 N Circle Dr. From SR 243 and town center, 0.3 mi ne. Ext corridors. **Pets:** Medium, dogs only. $20 one-time fee/room. Designated rooms, no service, supervision.

SAVE S⃝ X⃝ 📶 💻

▼▼ **Woodland Park Manor** M
(951) 659-2657. **$95-$195, 10 day notice.** 55350 S Circle Dr. From SR 243 and town center, 1 mi ne. Ext corridors. **Pets:** Designated rooms, no service, supervision.

ASK X⃝ 📶 💻 🏊 📞

INDEPENDENCE

⊕⊕⊕ ▼ **Independence Courthouse Motel** M
(760) 878-2732. **$38-$78.** 157 N Edwards. On US 395. Ext corridors. **Pets:** $5 one-time fee/pet. Service with restrictions, supervision.

SAVE S⃝ X⃝ 📶 💻

⊕⊕⊕ ▼▼▼ **Ray's Den Motel** M
(760) 878-2122. **$78.** 405 N Edwards. On US 395. Ext corridors. **Pets:** Accepted.

SAVE X⃝ 📶 💻

INDIO

⊕⊕⊕ ▼▼▼ **Best Western Date Tree Hotel** M 🐾
(760) 347-3421. **$69-$249.** 81-909 Indio Blvd. I-10, exit 139 (Jefferson St/Indio Blvd) westbound, 2 mi se; eastbound, south across freeway, then 2.8 mi e. Int corridors. **Pets:** Other species. $10 daily fee/pet. Service with restrictions, crate.

SAVE S⃝ X⃝ 📶 💻 🏊

⊕⊕⊕ ▼▼▼ **Indian Palms Country Club & Resort** SH
(760) 775-4444. **$84-$199.** 48-630 Monroe St. I-10, exit 142 (Monroe St), 2 mi s. Ext corridors. **Pets:** Accepted.

SAVE S⃝ X⃝ 📶 💻 🍴 🏊 🐾

▼▼ **Palm Shadow Inn** M
(760) 347-3476. **$59-$144.** 80-761 Hwy 111. I-10, exit 139 (Jefferson St/Indio Blvd), 2.5 mi s, then 0.7 mi e. Ext corridors. **Pets:** Small. Service with restrictions, supervision.

ASK S⃝ X⃝ 📶 💻 🏊 🐾

⊕⊕⊕ ▼▼▼ **Quality Inn** M
(760) 347-4044. **$75-$255.** 43505 Monroe St. I-10, exit 142 (Monroe St), 0.5 mi s. Int corridors. **Pets:** Accepted.

SAVE S⃝ X⃝ 📶 💻 🏊

⊕⊕⊕ ▼▼▼ **Super 8 Motel** M
(760) 342-0264. **$59-$199.** 81753 Hwy 111. I-10, exit 142 (Monroe St), 1.5 mi s, then 0.5 mi w. Ext corridors. **Pets:** Accepted.

SAVE S⃝ X⃝ 📶 💻 🏊

IRVINE

⊕⊕⊕ ▼▼▼▼ **Hilton Irvine/Orange County Airport** LH 🐾
(949) 833-9999. **$119-$299.** 18800 MacArthur Blvd. I-405, exit MacArthur Blvd, exit 8 (MacArthur Blvd/John Wayne Airport), 0.5 mi s. Int corridors. **Pets:** Large. $50 one-time fee/room. Designated rooms, service with restrictions.

SAVE S⃝ X⃝ 📶 💻 🍴 🏊 🐾

▼▼▼ **La Quinta Inn Irvine Spectrum (Old Historic Site)** **M**
(949) 551-0909. **$97-$127.** 14972 Sand Canyon Ave. I-5, exit 96 (Sand Canyon Ave) northbound; exit 96A (Sand Canyon Ave) southbound, just w. Ext/int corridors. **Pets:** Medium. Service with restrictions.
ASK ✕ 🛏 💻 🏊

▼▼▼ **Residence Inn by Marriott Irvine John Wayne Airport** **SH** 🐾
(949) 261-2020. **$249-$299.** 2855 Main St. I-405, exit 7 (Jamboree Blvd), just n, then just e. Int corridors. **Pets:** Large, other species. $100 one-time fee/room. Service with restrictions, crate.
ASK S🛏 ✕ 🛏 💻 🏊 ✕

▼▼▼ **Residence Inn by Marriott-Irvine Spectrum** **SH** 🐾
(949) 380-3000. **$209-$259.** 10 Morgan. I-5, exit 94B (Alton Pkwy) northbound; exit 94 (Alton Pkwy) southbound, 2 mi e. Ext corridors. **Pets:** Other species. $100 one-time fee/room. Service with restrictions, crate.
ASK S🛏 ✕ 🛏 💻 🏊 ✕

JACKSON

🔺 ▼ **Amador Motel** **M**
(209) 223-0970. **$54-$66, 5 day notice.** 12408 Kennedy Flat Rd. 1.5 mi n at jct SR 49 and 88 on Frontage Rd. Ext corridors. **Pets:** Dogs only. $10 one-time fee/pet. Designated rooms, service with restrictions, supervision.
SAVE S🛏 ✕ 🛏 💻 🏊

▼▼ **Best Western Amador Inn** **SH**
(209) 223-0211. **$79-$99.** 200 S Hwy 49. On SR 49. Int corridors. **Pets:** Medium. $10 daily fee/room. Designated rooms, service with restrictions, supervision.
ASK S🛏 ✕ 🛏 💻 🏊

🔺 ▼▼ **The Jackson Lodge** **M**
(209) 223-0486. **$59-$159.** 850 N Hwy 49/88. On SR 88/49, 0.5 mi w. Ext corridors. **Pets:** Medium, dogs only. $100 deposit/pet, $10 daily fee/ pet. Designated rooms, service with restrictions, supervision.
SAVE ✕ 🛏 💻 🏊

JAMESTOWN

🔺 ▼▼▼ **1859 Historic National Hotel, A Country Inn** **CI** 🐾
(209) 984-3446. **$140-$160, 3 day notice.** 18183 Main St. Downtown. Int corridors. **Pets:** Medium, dogs only. $15 daily fee/pet. Service with restrictions, supervision.
SAVE S🛏 ✕ 🍴 🎦 🕹

▼▼▼ **Country Inn Sonora** **M**
(209) 984-0315. **$69-$289.** 18730 Hwy 108. On SR 108 and 49, 1 mi e of town. Ext corridors. **Pets:** Medium. $10 daily fee/pet. Designated rooms, service with restrictions, supervision.
ASK S🛏 ✕ 🛏 💻 🏊

🔺 ▼▼▼ **Jamestown Hotel** **BB**
(209) 984-3902. **$81-$175, 7 day notice.** 18153 Main St. 0.5 mi n of jct SR 49 and 108; downtown. Int corridors. **Pets:** Accepted.
SAVE S🛏 ✕ 🍴 🕹

🔺 ▼ **Jamestown Railtown Motel** **M**
(209) 984-3332. **$59-$80, 3 day notice.** 10301 Willow St. Center. Ext corridors. **Pets:** Small, dogs only. $10 daily fee/pet. Supervision.
SAVE S🛏 ✕ 🏊

🔺 ▼▼ **Royal Carriage Inn** **SH**
(209) 984-5271. **$65-$109, 3 day notice.** 18239 Main St. SR 108 and 49, exit Central Business District. Int corridors. **Pets:** Accepted.
SAVE S🛏 ✕ 🛏 💻 🕹

JUNE LAKE

🔺 ▼▼▼ **Double Eagle Resort/Spa** **CA**
(760) 648-7004. **$229-$349, 30 day notice.** 5587 Hwy 158. On SR 158; 3 mi w of village. Ext corridors. **Pets:** Large. $15 daily fee/room. Designated rooms, service with restrictions, supervision.
SAVE ✕ 🛏 🎦 🛏 💻 🍴 🏊 ✕ 🅰️

▼▼ **Gull Lake Lodge** **M**
(760) 648-7516. **$75-$180, 7 day notice.** 132 Leonard Ave. Just n of SR 158; via Knoll and Bruce sts; in village. Ext corridors. **Pets:** Other species. Designated rooms, service with restrictions, supervision.
ASK ✕ 🛏 💻 🅰️ 🕹

▼▼ **June Lake Villager** **M** 🐾
(760) 648-7712. **$65-$95, 30 day notice.** 85 Boulder Dr. On SR 158; center of village. Ext corridors. **Pets:** Other species. Service with restrictions, supervision.
✕ 🛏 💻 🅰️

KERNVILLE

◆ ▼ **Barewood Motel** **M**
(760) 376-1910. **$79-$99, 3 day notice.** 7013 Wofford Blvd. In Wofford Heights. Ext corridors. **Pets:** Accepted.
ASK S🛏 ✕ 🛏 💻

▼▼ **River View Lodge** **M** 🐾
(760) 376-6019. **$79-$129, 3 day notice.** 2 Sirretta St. On Kernville Rd; at the bridge; center. Ext corridors. **Pets:** $20 daily fee/pet. Service with restrictions, supervision.
ASK S🛏 ✕ 🛏

KETTLEMAN CITY

🔺 ▼▼▼ **Best Western Kettleman Inn and Suites** **M**
(559) 386-0804. **$79-$169.** 33410 Powers Dr. E of and adjacent to I-5, exit SR 41 N, 0.3 mi to Bernard, then 0.3 mi n. Ext corridors. **Pets:** Accepted.
SAVE S🛏 ✕ 🛏 💻 🏊

🔺 ▼ **Super 8** **M**
(559) 386-9530. **$49-$79.** 33415 Powers Dr. E of and adjacent to I-5, exit SR 41 N, 0.3 mi to Bernard, then 0.3 mi n. Ext corridors. **Pets:** Small. $10 daily fee/pet. Designated rooms, service with restrictions, supervision.
SAVE S🛏 ✕ 🎦 🛏 🏊

KING CITY

▼▼ **Courtesy Inn** **M**
(831) 385-4646. **$49-$89.** 4 Broadway Cir. US 101, exit Broadway St, just w. Ext corridors. **Pets:** Small. $25 daily fee/pet. Designated rooms, service with restrictions, supervision.
ASK S🛏 ✕ 🦽 🎦 🦽 🛏 💻 🏊

KINGSBURG

🔺 ▼▼ **Swedish Inn** **M**
(559) 897-1022. **$68, 4 day notice.** 401 Conejo St. SR 99, exit Conejo St, just w. Ext corridors. **Pets:** Accepted.
SAVE S🛏 ✕ 🛏 💻 🏊

KLAMATH

🔺 ▼ **Motel Trees** **M**
(707) 482-3152. **$60-$70.** 15495 Hwy 101 N. On US 101, 4.5 mi n. Ext corridors. **Pets:** $25 daily fee/pet. Designated rooms, service with restrictions, supervision.
SAVE S🛏 ✕ 🛏 💻 🍴 🅰️

KYBURZ

AAA ◆◆◆ **Kyburz Resort Motel** **M**
(530) 293-3382. **$59-$99.** 13666 Hwy 50. On US 50; halfway between Placerville and South Lake Tahoe. Ext corridors. **Pets:** Other species. $10 one-time fee/room. Service with restrictions, crate.

[SAVE] [S🐾] [✕] [🛁M] [🔔] [🛏] [🦮]

LAGUNA BEACH

AAA ◆◆◆ **Best Western Laguna Brisas Spa Hotel** **M**
(949) 497-7272. **$119-$449, 3 day notice.** 1600 S Coast Hwy. SR 133, 1 mi s on SR 1. Ext/int corridors. **Pets:** Accepted.

[SAVE] [S🐾] [✕] [🛏] [🦮]

◆◆◆ **The Carriage House-Bed & Breakfast** **BB**
(949) 494-8945. **$140-$200, 3 day notice.** 1322 Catalina St. SR 133, 1 mi s on S Coast Hwy to Cress St, then just e. Ext corridors. **Pets:** Other species. $15 daily fee/pet. Supervision.

[✕] [🛏] [🦮] [🔔]

AAA ◆◆◆ **Casa Laguna Inn** **BB** 🐾
(949) 494-2996. **$175-$400, 5 day notice.** 2510 S Coast Hwy. SR 133, 1.3 mi s on SR 1. Ext corridors. **Pets:** Dogs only. $25 daily fee/pet. Service with restrictions, supervision.

[SAVE] [S🐾] [✕] [🛏] [🦮] [🏊]

AAA ◆◆◆ **The Tides Inn** **M**
(949) 494-2494. **$104-$280.** 460 N Coast Hwy. SR 133, 0.5 mi n on SR 1. Ext corridors. **Pets:** Medium. $25 daily fee/pet. Designated rooms, service with restrictions, supervision.

[SAVE] [S🐾] [✕] [🛏] [🦮]

LAGUNA HILLS

◆◆◆ **Holiday Inn Laguna Hills** **SH** 🐾
(949) 586-5000. **$169-$199.** 25205 La Paz Rd. I-5, exit 89 (La Paz Rd), just w. Int corridors. **Pets:** Medium, other species. $100 one-time fee/room. Designated rooms.

[ASK] [S🐾] [✕] [🛁M] [🔔] [🦮] [🛏] [🍴] [🏊]

LAKE ARROWHEAD

AAA ◆◆◆ **Arrowhead Saddleback Inn** **CI**
(909) 336-3571. **$117-$179, 7 day notice.** On SR 173, jct SR 189; across from entrance to Lake Arrowhead Village. Ext/int corridors. **Pets:** Other species. $8 daily fee/pet. Designated rooms, service with restrictions, crate.

[SAVE] [✕] [🛏] [🦮] [🍴]

◆◆◆ **Arrowhead Tree Top Lodge** **M**
(909) 337-2311. **$129-$176, 7 day notice.** 27992 Rainbow Dr. 0.3 mi s of Lake Arrowhead Village on SR 173. Ext corridors. **Pets:** Accepted.

[ASK] [S🐾] [✕] [🛏] [🦮] [🏊] [🔔] [🛁]

◆◆◆ **Storybook Inn** **BB**
(909) 337-0011. **$99-$299.** 28717 SR 18. SR 18, 1.1 mi e of jct SR 173. Ext/int corridors. **Pets:** Other species. Designated rooms, service with restrictions.

[ASK] [S🐾] [✕] [🛏] [🦮] [🍴]

LAKE TAHOE AREA

SOUTH LAKE TAHOE

AAA ◆◆◆ **Alpenrose Inn** **M**
(530) 544-2985. **$50-$135, 7 day notice.** 4074 Pine Blvd. 0.3 mi n of US 50 via Park Ave, 3 blks from casino area. Ext corridors. **Pets:** Accepted.

[SAVE] [S🐾] [✕] [🛏] [🦮] [✕]

AAA ◆◆◆ **Ambassador Motor Lodge** **M**
(530) 544-6461. **$55-$150, 3 day notice.** 4130 Manzanita Ave. Just s of US 50 on Stateline Ave. Ext corridors. **Pets:** Accepted.

[SAVE] [S🐾] [✕] [🛏] [🦮] [🏊] [🔔]

AAA ◆◆◆ **Best Western Timber Cove Lodge** **SH**
(530) 541-6722. **$74-$299.** 3411 Lake Tahoe Blvd. 1.5 mi w of casino center; 0.5 mi w of Ski Run Blvd. Ext corridors. **Pets:** Medium. $100 deposit/room, $25 daily fee/pet. Designated rooms, service with restrictions, supervision.

[SAVE] [S🐾] [✕] [🛁M] [🔔] [🦮] [🛏] [🍴] [🏊] [✕]

AAA ◆◆◆ **Capri Motel** **M**
(530) 544-3665. **$55-$150, 72 day notice.** 932 Stateline Ave. Just s of US 50; in casino area. Ext corridors. **Pets:** Accepted.

[SAVE] [S🐾] [✕] [🛏] [🦮] [🏊] [🔔]

AAA ◆◆◆ **Cedar Lodge** **M**
(530) 544-6453. **$60-$230, 3 day notice.** 4069 Cedar Ave. N off US 50 toward lake; at Cedar and Friday aves; 3 blks from the casino center. Ext corridors. **Pets:** Dogs only. $10 daily fee/pet. Designated rooms, service with restrictions, supervision.

[SAVE] [S🐾] [✕] [🛏] [🦮] [🏊]

AAA ◆◆◆ **Days Inn-Casino Area/Lake Resort** **M**
(530) 541-4800. **$49-$289, 3 day notice.** 968 Park Ave. 3 blks w of casino area; 1 blk n off US 50 toward lake, at Park and Cedar aves. Int corridors. **Pets:** Accepted.

[SAVE] [S🐾] [✕] [🛏] [🏊]

AAA ◆◆◆ **Fireside Lodge B&B** **BB** 🐾
(530) 544-5515. **$69-$165, 30 day notice.** 515 Emerald Bay Rd. SR 89, 1 mi n of US 50. Ext corridors. **Pets:** Dogs only. $100 deposit/room, $20 daily fee/pet. Service with restrictions, crate.

[SAVE] [S🐾] [✕] [🛏] [🦮] [🔔]

AAA ◆◆◆ **High Country Lodge LLC** **M**
(530) 541-0508. **$45-$175, 3 day notice.** 1227 Emerald Bay Rd. US 50, 0.5 mi n of airport. Ext corridors. **Pets:** Accepted.

[SAVE] [✕] [🛏] [🦮]

AAA ◆◆◆ **Pistantes Coyote Den** **M**
(530) 541-2282. **$55-$250, 4 day notice.** 1211 Emerald Bay Rd. US 50, 0.5 mi n of airport. Ext corridors. **Pets:** Medium, dogs only. $10 one-time fee/room. Designated rooms, service with restrictions, supervision.

[SAVE] [✕] [🛏] [🔔]

◆◆◆ **Tahoe Hacienda Inn** **M**
(530) 541-3805. **$38-$198, 3 day notice.** 3820 Lake Tahoe Blvd. US 50, 0.7 mi w of casino area. Ext corridors. **Pets:** Small. $10 daily fee/pet. Designated rooms, no service, supervision.

[ASK] [S🐾] [✕] [🛁M] [🔔] [🛏] [🦮] [🏊]

AAA ◆◆◆ **Tahoe Keys Resort** **CO** 🐾
(530) 544-5397. **$100-$1800.** 599 Tahoe Keys Blvd. US 50, exit Tahoe Keys Blvd, 1 mi w. Ext corridors. **Pets:** Dogs only. $100 deposit/pet, $25 one-time fee/pet. Designated rooms, service with restrictions, supervision.

[SAVE] [S🐾] [✕] [🛏] [🦮] [🏊] [✕] [🔔]

AAA ◆◆◆ **Tahoe Valley Lodge** **M**
(530) 541-0353. **$95-$495, 7 day notice.** 2241 Lake Tahoe Blvd. 0.5 mi e of jct US 50 and SR 89. Ext corridors. **Pets:** Small, dogs only. $10 daily fee/pet. Designated rooms, service with restrictions, supervision.

[SAVE] [S🐾] [✕] [🛏] [🦮] [🏊]

TAHOE CITY

▲▲▲ ▼▼▼ ◆ **Mother Nature's Inn** Ⓜ
(530) 581-4278. **$55-$115, 3 day notice.** 551 N Lake Blvd. SR 28, 0.5 mi e of jct SR 89; behind Mother Nature's Store. Int corridors. **Pets:** Accepted.
[SAVE] ⊗ 🖥 🖵

TAHOE VISTA

▼▼ ▼ **Holiday House** Ⓜ ❀
(530) 546-2369. **$125-$225.** 7276 N Lake Blvd. SR 28, 1 mi w of SR 267. Ext corridors. **Pets:** Other species. $10 daily fee/pet, $30 one-time fee/pet. Supervision.
⊗ ⓜ 🖥 🖵 Ⓚ

END AREA

LANCASTER

▲▲▲ ▼▼▼ ◆ **Best Western Antelope Valley Inn** Ⓜ
(661) 948-4651. **$109-$119, 3 day notice.** 44055 N Sierra Hwy. SR 14, exit 42 (Ave K), 2.3 mi e. Ext/int corridors. **Pets:** $50 one-time fee/pet. Designated rooms, no service, supervision.
[SAVE] ⓢ ⊗ ⓜ 🖥 ¶ 🏊

▼▼▼▼ **Oxford Inn & Suites** Ⓜ ❀
(661) 949-3423. **$99-$129.** 1651 W Ave K. SR 14, exit 42 (Ave K), just w. Int corridors. **Pets:** Dogs only. $50 one-time fee/pet. Service with restrictions, supervision.
[ASK] ⓢ ⊗ ⓜ ⓓ ⓔ 🖥 🖵 🏊

LA PALMA

▼▼▼ **La Quinta Inn & Suites Orange County (Buena Park)** [SH]
(714) 670-1400. **$119-$165.** 3 Center Pointe Dr. SR 91, exit 21 (Orangethorpe Ave/Valley View St) eastbound; exit 22 (Orangethorpe Ave/Valley View St) westbound, just n. Int corridors. **Pets:** Medium. Service with restrictions.
[ASK] ⊗ ⓓ 🖥 🖵 🏊

LATHROP

▼▼ **Days Inn** [SH]
(209) 982-1959. **$80-$86.** 14750 S Harlan Rd. I-5, exit Lathrop Rd, just e. Int corridors. **Pets:** Other species. $10 daily fee/pet. Service with restrictions, supervision.
[ASK] ⓢ ⊗ ⓜ 🖥 🏊

LEBEC

▼▼▼ **Best Rest Inn** Ⓜ
(661) 248-2700. **$79-$119.** 51541 N Peace Valley Rd. I-5, exit 205 (Frazier Park), just w. Int corridors. **Pets:** Other species. $10 daily fee/pet. Designated rooms, service with restrictions, supervision.
[ASK] ⓢ ⊗ ⓜ 🖥 🖵 ¶ 🏊

▲▲▲ ▼▼▼▼ **Ramada Limited Grapevine** Ⓜ
(661) 248-1530. **$69-$99.** 9000 Country Side Ct. I-5, exit 215 (Grapevine Rd), just w. Ext corridors. **Pets:** Accepted.
[SAVE] ⓢ ⊗ ⓜ ⓔ 🖥 🖵 🏊

LEE VINING

▲▲▲ ▼▼▼ **Murphey's Motel** Ⓜ
(760) 647-6316. **$53-$113.** 51493 Hwy 395. US 395; in town. Ext corridors. **Pets:** Medium. $5 one-time fee/pet. Designated rooms, service with restrictions, supervision.
[SAVE] ⊗ 🖥 🖵

TRUCKEE

▼▼▼ **The Cedar House Sport Hotel** [SH] ❀
(530) 582-5655. **$150-$325.** 10918 Brockway Rd. I-80, exit SR 267, 1.5 mi s. Int corridors. **Pets:** Large, dogs only. $25 daily fee/room. Designated rooms, service with restrictions, supervision.
[ASK] ⓢ ⊗ ⓓ 🖥 🖵

LEMOORE

▼▼ ▼ **Days Inn/Lemoore** Ⓜ
(559) 924-1261. **$85.** 877 E "D" St. SR 198, exit Houston St, 0.8 mi nw. Ext corridors. **Pets:** Other species. $25 daily fee/pet. Designated rooms, service with restrictions, supervision.
[ASK] ⓢ ⊗ ⓜ 🖥 🖵 🏊

LINDSAY

▲▲▲ ▼▼▼ **Super 8 Motel** Ⓜ
(559) 562-5188. **$69-$89.** 390 N Hwy 65. SR 65. Ext corridors. **Pets:** Very small, dogs only. $10 daily fee/pet. Designated rooms, no service, supervision.
[SAVE] ⓢ ⊗ 🖥 🏊

LIVERMORE

▼▼▼ **Hampton Inn** [SH]
(925) 606-6400. **$69-$149.** 2850 Constitution Dr. I-580, exit Airway Blvd/Collier Canyon Rd. Int corridors. **Pets:** Small, dogs only. $35 one-time fee/pet. Designated rooms, service with restrictions, supervision.
[ASK] ⓢ ⊗ ⓜ ⓓ 🖥 🖵 🏊

◆ ▼▼ **La Quinta Inn** [SH]
(925) 373-9600. **$79-$139.** 7700 Southfront Rd. I-580, exit Greenville Rd, just s. Int corridors. **Pets:** Medium. $10 daily fee/pet. Service with restrictions, crate.
[ASK] ⓢ ⊗ 🖥 🖵 🏊 ⊗

▼▼▼▼ **Residence Inn by Marriott** Ⓜ
(925) 373-1800. **$149-$174.** 1000 Airway Blvd. I-580, exit Airway Blvd/Collier Canyon Rd, just n. Ext corridors. **Pets:** Accepted.
[ASK] ⊗ 🖵 🏊 ⊗

LODI

▲▲▲ ▼ **El Rancho Motel** Ⓜ ❀
(209) 368-0651. **$60-$75.** 603 N Cherokee Ln. SR 99, exit Turner Rd, just s. Ext corridors. **Pets:** Small. $10 one-time fee/pet. Service with restrictions, supervision.
[SAVE] ⓢ ⊗ ⓜ 🖥 🏊

▼▼ **Microtel Inn & Suites** [SH] ❀
(209) 367-9700. **$69-$99.** 6428 W Banner St. I-5, exit SR 12, just e. Int corridors. **Pets:** $10 daily fee/pet. Designated rooms, service with restrictions, supervision.
[ASK] ⓢ ⊗ ⓜ ⓓ 🖥 🖵 🏊

▼▼▼ **Wine & Roses Hotel and Restaurant** [CI]
(209) 334-6988. **$159-$239, 7 day notice.** 2505 W Turner Rd. I-5, exit Turner Rd, 5 mi e; SR 99, exit Turner Rd, 2 mi w. Int corridors. **Pets:** Small, other species. $45 daily fee/pet. Designated rooms, service with restrictions, supervision.
[ASK] ⓢ ⊗ ⓜ 🖥 🖵 ¶

LOMA LINDA

(AAA) ◆ Loma Linda Inn M
(909) 583-2500. **$75-$80.** 24532 University Pl. I-10, exit 74 (Anderson St/Tippecanoe Ave) eastbound; westbound, 1 mi s, just w on Stewart, just s on Campus, then just w. Ext corridors. **Pets:** Accepted.
[SAVE] [X] [⊟] [▦]

LOMPOC

(AAA) ◆◆ Americas Best Value Inn M
(805) 735-3737. **$79-$169.** 1200 N H St. SR 1, 1.3 mi n of Ocean Ave. Ext corridors. **Pets:** Accepted.
[SAVE] [S✓] [X] [&M] [✆] [⊟] [AC]

(AAA) ◆◆ Days Inn M
(805) 735-7744. **$89-$179.** 1122 N H St. SR 1, 1.2 mi n of Ocean Ave. Ext/int corridors. **Pets:** Accepted.
[SAVE] [S✓] [X] [⊟] [▦] [➤]

(AAA) ◆◆ Quality Inn & Executive Suites SH
(805) 735-8555. **$99-$209, 7 day notice.** 1621 N H St. SR 1, 1.8 mi n of Ocean Ave. Int corridors. **Pets:** Accepted.
[SAVE] [S✓] [X] [⊟] [▦] [➤] [✗]

(AAA) ◆◆ Super 8 Motel M
(805) 735-6444. **$55-$120.** 1020 E Ocean Ave. SR 1, 1.5 mi w of H St. Ext corridors. **Pets:** Medium. $15 daily fee/room. Designated rooms, service with restrictions, supervision.
[SAVE] [S✓] [X] [&M] [✆] [⊟] [☕]

(AAA) ◆◆ White Oaks Hotel M ❀
(805) 733-5000. **$79-$169.** 3955 Apollo Way. SR 1, exit 211 (Constellation Blvd), just e; 3.5 mi n of Ocean Ave. Ext/int corridors. **Pets:** Dogs only. $50 deposit/room, $10 daily fee/pet. Designated rooms, service with restrictions, supervision.
[SAVE] [S✓] [X] [⊟] [▦] [🍽] [➤] [✗]

LONE PINE

(AAA) ◆◆◆ Best Western Frontier Motel M
(760) 876-5571. **$66-$114.** 1008 S Main St. US 395; at south end of town. Ext corridors. **Pets:** Service with restrictions, supervision.
[SAVE] [S✓] [X] [&M] [✆] [&] [⊟] [▦] [➤]

(AAA) ◆◆◆ Comfort Inn SH
(760) 876-8700. **$59-$199.** 1920 S Main St. US 395, 1.5 mi s of town. Int corridors. **Pets:** $20 daily fee/pet. Service with restrictions, supervision.
[SAVE] [S✓] [X] [&M] [⊟] [▦] [➤]

(AAA) ◆◆◆ Dow Villa Motel M
(760) 876-5521. **$66-$140.** 310 S Main St. US 395. Ext corridors. **Pets:** Medium, other species. $50 deposit/room. Designated rooms, service with restrictions, supervision.
[SAVE] [S✓] [X] [&M] [✆] [&] [⊟] [▦] [➤]

(AAA) ◆◆ Lone Pine Budget Inn Motel M
(760) 876-5655. **$45-$99, 3 day notice.** 138 W Willow St. US 395, just w. Ext corridors. **Pets:** Very small, dogs only. $10 daily fee/pet. Designated rooms, no service, supervision.
[SAVE] [X] [⊟] [▦]

LOS ALAMITOS

◆◆◆ Residence Inn by Marriott-Cypress/Orange County SH
(714) 484-5700. **$189-$239.** 4931 Katella Ave. I-605, exit 1D (Katella Ave) southbound; exit 1B (Katella Ave/Willow St) northbound, 1.5 mi e. Int corridors. **Pets:** Small, other species. $100 one-time fee/room. Service with restrictions, supervision.
[ASK] [X] [⊟] [▦] [➤] [✗]

LOS ALTOS

◆◆◆ Marriott Residence Inn-Palo Alto/Los Altos SH ❀
(650) 559-7890. **$129-$279.** 4460 El Camino Real. US 101, exit San Antonio Rd, 2 mi w to SR 82, then just n. Int corridors. **Pets:** Medium, other species. $100 one-time fee/pet. Designated rooms, service with restrictions, crate.
[ASK] [X] [&M] [&] [▦] [➤] [✗]

LOS ANGELES METROPOLITAN AREA

ALHAMBRA

(AAA) ◆◆◆ Super 8 Motel M
(323) 225-2310. **$60-$70.** 5350 Huntington Dr S. I-10, exit 22 (Fremont Ave), 2.5 mi n, then 0.5 mi w. Ext corridors. **Pets:** Medium. $10 daily fee/pet. Designated rooms, service with restrictions, supervision.
[SAVE] [S✓] [X] [⊟]

ARCADIA

◆◆ Extended StayAmerica-Los Angeles-Arcadia SH
(626) 446-6422. **$89-$109.** 401 E Santa Clara St. I-210, exit 33 (Huntington Dr), just w to 5th, just n, then just w. Int corridors. **Pets:** Accepted.
[ASK] [S✓] [X] [&M] [✆] [&] [⊟] [▦]

(AAA) ◆◆◆ Residence Inn by Marriott SH ❀
(626) 446-6500. **$209-$259.** 321 E Huntington Dr. I-210, exit 33 (Huntington Dr), 0.5 mi w, then just n on Gateway Dr. Ext corridors. **Pets:** Other species. $100 one-time fee/room.
[SAVE] [S✓] [X] [&M] [✆] [&] [⊟] [▦] [➤] [✗]

BELL GARDENS

(AAA) ◆◆◆ Vagabond Inn M
(323) 560-8221. **$65-$99.** 6344 S Eastern Ave. I-710, exit 15 (Florence Ave), just e, then 0.5 mi n. Ext corridors. **Pets:** Accepted.
[SAVE] [S✓] [X] [⊟] [▦]

BEVERLY HILLS

◆◆◆◆ Avalon Hotel SH
(310) 277-5221. **$269-$529.** 9400 W Olympic Blvd. I-10, exit 6 (Robertson Blvd), 1.7 mi n, then 0.8 mi w. Ext/int corridors. **Pets:** Accepted.
[X] [▦] [🍽] [➤]

(AAA) ◆◆◆◆ The Beverly Hills Hotel and Bungalows LH
(310) 276-2251. **$485-$630.** 9641 Sunset Blvd. I-405, exit 57 (Sunset Blvd), 3.7 mi e. Int corridors. **Pets:** Accepted.
[SAVE] [X] [&M] [✆] [&] [🍽] [➤] [✗]

◆◆◆◆ Beverly Hilton LH
(310) 274-7777. **$215-$1500.** 9876 Wilshire Blvd. I-405, exit 55 (Wilshire Blvd), 2.2 mi e. Int corridors. **Pets:** Accepted.
[ASK] [X] [&M] [✆] [&] [▦] [🍽] [➤] [✗]

AAA ◈◈◈ Luxe Hotel Rodeo Drive SH
(310) 273-0300. **$425-$575.** 360 N Rodeo Dr. I-405, exit 55 (Wilshire Blvd), 4.4 mi e, then just n. Int corridors. **Pets:** Accepted.
[SAVE] [S▣] [✕] [🔒] [💻] [≈]

◈◈◈ The Mosaic Hotel SH ❧
(310) 278-0303. **$315-$350.** 125 S Spalding Dr. I-405, exit 55 (Wilshire Blvd), 2.2 mi e, then just s. Ext/int corridors. **Pets:** Other species. Service with restrictions.
[ASK] [S▣] [✕] [💻] [🍴] [≈]

AAA ◈◈◈◈ The Peninsula Beverly Hills SH ❧
(310) 551-2888. **$495-$3500.** 9882 S Santa Monica Blvd. I-405, exit 55A (Santa Monica Blvd), 2.2 mi e at Wilshire Blvd. Int corridors. **Pets:** Other species. $35 daily fee/pet. Supervision.
[SAVE] [✕] [&M] [🔒] [💻] [🍴] [≈] [✕]

AAA ◈◈◈◈ Raffles L'Ermitage Beverly Hills SH ❧
(310) 278-3344. **$468-$548, 7 day notice.** 9291 Burton Way. I-10, exit 6 (Robertson Blvd), 3.1 mi n, then just w. Int corridors. **Pets:** Medium. $50 one-time fee/pet.
[SAVE] [✕] [&M] [🔒] [✦] [💻] [🍴] [≈] [✕]

◈◈◈◈ Regent Beverly Wilshire LH ❧
(310) 275-5200. **$400-$515.** 9500 Wilshire Blvd. I-405, exit 55 (Wilshire Blvd), 4.5 mi e. Int corridors. **Pets:** Small, other species. Supervision.
[✕] [&M] [🔒] [✦] [🍴] [≈] [✕]

BURBANK

◈◈◈ Burbank Airport Hilton & Convention Center LH
(818) 843-6000. **$99-$350.** 2500 Hollywood Way. I-5, exit 149 (Hollywood Way), 1 mi s. Int corridors. **Pets:** Accepted.
[ASK] [S▣] [✕] [&M] [🔒] [✦] [🔒] [💻] [🍴] [≈]

◈◈◈ Extended StayAmerica-Los angeles-Burbank Airport SH
(818) 567-0952. **$124-$144.** 2200 Empire Ave. I-5, exit 146B (Burbank Blvd), just w, then 0.7 mi n on Victory Pl. Int corridors. **Pets:** Accepted.
[ASK] [S▣] [✕] [🔒] [💻]

◈◈◈ The Graciela Burbank SH ❧
(818) 842-8887. **$235-$2000.** 322 N Pass Ave. SR 134, exit 2 (Hollywood Way) westbound, just w on Alameda Ave, then 0.5 mi n; exit 2 (Pass Ave) eastbound, 0.5 mi n. Ext corridors. **Pets:** Large. $75 one-time fee/room. Designated rooms, service with restrictions, supervision.
[ASK] [S▣] [✕] [&M] [🔒] [✦] [🔒] [💻] [🍴] [✕]

AAA ◈◈◈ Safari Inn, A Coast Hotel M
(818) 845-8586. **$109-$299.** 1911 W Olive Ave. I-5, exit 146A (Olive Ave), 1.3 mi sw. Ext corridors. **Pets:** Other species. $200 deposit/pet, $25 one-time fee/room. Supervision.
[SAVE] [S▣] [✕] [🔒] [🔒] [💻] [🍴] [≈]

CARSON

◈◈ Extended StayAmerica-Los Angeles/Carson SH
(310) 323-2080. **$89-$109.** 401 E Albertoni St. SR 91, exit 7B (Avalon Blvd) just s, then just w. Int corridors. **Pets:** Accepted.
[ASK] [S▣] [✕] [&M] [🔒] [✦] [🔒] [💻]

CERRITOS

◈◈◈ Sheraton Cerritos Hotel at Towne Center SH
(562) 809-1500. **$109-$159.** 12725 Center Court Dr. SR 91, exit 19B (Artesia/Bloomfield Dr), just s to Town Center Dr, just e, then just s. Int corridors. **Pets:** Accepted.
[ASK] [S▣] [✕] [&M] [🔒] [✦] [💻] [🍴] [≈]

CHATSWORTH

◈◈ Ramada Inn SH
(818) 998-5289. **$89-$110.** 21340 Devonshire St. SR 118, exit 35 (De Soto Ave), 1.5 mi s, then 0.5 mi w. Int corridors. **Pets:** Small. $50 deposit/pet, $10 daily fee/pet. Designated rooms, service with restrictions, supervision.
[ASK] [S▣] [✕] [&M] [🔒] [🔒] [💻] [≈]

CHINO

◈◈ Extended StayAmerica SH
(909) 597-8675. **Call for rates.** 4325 Corporate Center Ave. SR 71, exit Chino Hills Pkwy, just e to Ramona Ave, just n, then just w. Int corridors. **Pets:** Accepted.
[✕] [🔒] [💻]

CLAREMONT

◈◈ Hotel Claremont & Tennis Club M ❧
(909) 621-4831. **$89-$99.** 840 S Indian Hill Blvd. I-10, exit 47 (Indian Hill Blvd), just s; enter on Auto Center Dr. Ext corridors. **Pets:** Supervision.
[ASK] [S▣] [✕] [🔒] [💻] [≈] [✕]

CULVER CITY

AAA ◈◈◈ Four Points by Sheraton Culver City LH
(310) 641-7740. **$125-$250.** 5990 Green Valley Cir. I-405, exit 49 (Howard Hughes Pkwy), just n, then just e. Int corridors. **Pets:** Accepted.
[SAVE] [S▣] [✕] [🔒] [💻] [🍴] [≈]

AAA ◈◈◈ Radisson Hotel-LA Westside LH
(310) 649-1776. **$169-$199.** 6161 W Centinela Ave. I-405, exit 50 (Jefferson Blvd), just s, then just nw. Int corridors. **Pets:** Large, other species. $50 one-time fee/room. Designated rooms, service with restrictions, crate.
[SAVE] [S▣] [✕] [🔒] [💻] [🍴] [≈]

DOWNEY

AAA ◈◈◈ Embassy Suites Hotel LH
(562) 861-1900. **$139-$202.** 8425 Firestone Blvd. I-605, exit 10 (Firestone Blvd), 2 mi w. Int corridors. **Pets:** Accepted.
[SAVE] [✕] [&M] [🔒] [✦] [🔒] [💻] [🍴] [≈] [✕]

EL SEGUNDO

◈◈◈ Embassy Suites-LAX South LH
(310) 640-3600. **$154-$219.** 1440 E Imperial Ave. I-405, exit 45B (Imperial Hwy), 1.6 mi w. Int corridors. **Pets:** Small, other species. $25 daily fee/pet. Service with restrictions, supervision.
[✕] [🔒] [🍴] [≈]

◈◈ Homestead Studio Suites Hotel-Los Angeles-LAX Airport-El Segundo M
(310) 607-4000. **$84-$124.** 1910 E Mariposa Ave. I-105, exit 1B (Sepulveda Blvd), 1 mi s. Ext corridors. **Pets:** Accepted.
[ASK] [S▣] [✕] [&M] [🔒] [✦] [🔒] [💻]

◈◈◈ Residence Inn by Marriott-LAX/El Segundo SH
(310) 333-0888. **$199-$249.** 2135 E El Segundo Blvd. I-405, exit 44 (El Segundo Blvd), 1.4 mi w. Int corridors. **Pets:** Small. $150 one-time fee/pet. Service with restrictions, supervision.
[ASK] [S▣] [✕] [&M] [🔒] [✦] [🔒] [💻] [≈] [✕]

◈◈◈ Summerfield Suites by Wyndham-El Segundo M ❧
(310) 725-0100. **$169-$189.** 810 S Douglas St. I-405, exit 43 (Rosecrans Ave), 0.5 mi e, then just n. Ext/int corridors. **Pets:** Other species. $200 one-time fee/room. Service with restrictions, crate.
[ASK] [✕] [&M] [🔒] [✦] [🔒] [💻] [≈] [✕]

GLENDALE

▼▼▼ Homestead Studio Suites Hotel-Los Angeles-Glendale SH
(818) 956-6665. **$104.** 1377 W Glenoaks Blvd. I-5, exit 145A (Western Ave), 0.4 mi e, then 0.6 mi s. Int corridors. **Pets:** Accepted.
[ASK] [S♦] [X] [♿M] [🐾] [🛗] [📶] [📺]

▼▼ Los Angeles Days Inn-Glendale SH
(818) 956-0202. **$114, 3 day notice.** 450 W Pioneer Dr. SR 134, exit 7A (Pacific Ave), just s, then just e. Int corridors. **Pets:** Small, other species. $50 deposit/room. Designated rooms, service with restrictions, supervision.
[ASK] [S♦] [X] [🛗] [📶] [🍴] [🏊]

▲ ▼▼ ◆ Vagabond Inn Glendale M
(818) 240-1700. **$89-$140.** 120 W Colorado St. SR 134, exit 7B (Brand Blvd), 1 mi s, then just w. Ext corridors. **Pets:** Large. $5 daily fee/pet. Designated rooms, service with restrictions, supervision.
[SAVE] [S♦] [X] [♿M] [🐾] [📺] [🛗] [📶] [🏊]

HAWTHORNE

▼▼ TownePlace Suites by Marriott M
(310) 725-9696. **$119-$249.** 14400 Aviation Blvd. I-405, exit 43 (Rosecrans Ave), 0.4 mi w. Int corridors. **Pets:** Accepted.
[ASK] [S♦] [X] [🛗] [📶] [🏊]

HOLLYWOOD

▲ ▼▼◆ Best Western Hollywood Hills Hotel M
(323) 464-5181. **$109-$209.** 6141 Franklin Ave. US 101, exit Gower St, just n, then just e. Ext/int corridors. **Pets:** Medium, other species. $25 daily fee/pet. Service with restrictions.
[SAVE] [S♦] [X] [🛗] [📶] [🏊]

▲ ▼▼◆ Hollywood Hotel Near Universal Studios-A Ramada Hotel SH
(323) 315-1800. **$90-$150.** 1160 N Vermont Ave. US 101, exit 6A (Vermont Ave), 0.5 mi n. Int corridors. **Pets:** Small. $50 daily fee/pet. Designated rooms, service with restrictions, supervision.
[SAVE] [S♦] [X] [♿M] [🐾] [📺] [🛗] [📶] [🍴] [🏊] [X]

INDUSTRY

▼▼▼ Pacific Palms Conference Resort LH
(626) 810-4455. **$169-$249.** One Industry Hills Pkwy. SR 60, exit 18 (Azusa Ave), 1.3 mi n, 0.5 mi w. Int corridors. **Pets:** Other species. $25 one-time fee/room. Supervision.
[ASK] [X] [♿M] [🐾] [📺] [📶] [🍴] [🏊] [X]

LA MIRADA

▼▼▼ Residence Inn by Marriott SH
(714) 523-2800. **$164.** 14419 Firestone Blvd. I-5, exit 118 (Valley View), just n, then 0.5 mi e. Ext corridors. **Pets:** Medium, other species. $100 one-time fee/room. Service with restrictions, crate.
[ASK] [X] [♿M] [🐾] [📺] [📶] [🏊] [X]

LONG BEACH

▲ ▼▼◆ The Coast Long Beach Hotel SH
(562) 435-7676. **$145-$225.** 700 Queensway Dr. I-710, exit 14 (Harbor Scenic Dr/Queen Mary), 1 mi s. Ext corridors. **Pets:** Other species. $55 one-time fee/room. Service with restrictions, supervision.
[SAVE] [S♦] [X] [🛗] [📶] [🍴] [🏊] [X]

▼▼ Extended StayAmerica-Los Angeles-Long Beach SH
(562) 989-4601. **$114-$134.** 4105 E Willow St. I-405, exit 27 (Lakewood Blvd), 0.3 mi sw. Int corridors. **Pets:** Accepted.
[ASK] [S♦] [X] [♿M] [🐾] [📺] [🛗] [📶]

▲▲▲ ▼▼▼ GuestHouse Hotel Long Beach M
(562) 597-1341. **$85-$139.** 5325 E Pacific Coast Hwy. I-405, exit 23 (SR 22/Long Beach) northbound, 2 mi nw; exit 27 (Lakewood Blvd) southbound, 2 mi se on SR 1. Ext corridors. **Pets:** Medium. $10 one-time fee/room. Designated rooms, service with restrictions, crate.
[SAVE] [S♦] [X] [🐾] [📺] [🛗] [📶] [🍴] [🏊]

▼▼▼▼ Hilton Long Beach LH
(562) 983-3400. **$169-$329, 3 day notice.** Two World Trade Center. I-710, exit Downtown/Broadway, just e to Daisy Ave, just s to Ocean Blvd, then just w. Int corridors. **Pets:** Small. $150 deposit/room. Service with restrictions, crate.
[ASK] [X] [📶] [X]

▲▲▲ ▼▼▼▼ Holiday Inn-Long Beach Airport LH
(562) 597-4401. **$199-$219.** 2640 Lakewood Blvd. I-405, exit 27 (Lakewood Blvd), just s. Ext/int corridors. **Pets:** Accepted.
[SAVE] [X] [🛗] [📶] [🍴] [🏊]

▼▼▼ Residence Inn by Marriott Long Beach SH
(562) 595-0909. **Call for rates.** 4111 E Willow St. I-405, exit 27 (Lakewood Blvd), just s, then just w. Ext corridors. **Pets:** Accepted.
[X] [♿M] [🐾] [📺] [🛗] [📶] [🏊] [X]

▲▲▲ ▼▼▼ The Westin Long Beach LH
(562) 436-3000. **$369-$480.** 333 E Ocean Blvd. I-710, exit Downtown/Broadway, 0.8 mi e to Long Beach Blvd, then just s. **Pets:** Accepted.
[SAVE] [S♦] [X] [📶] [🍴] [🏊] [X]

LOS ANGELES

▲▲▲ ▼▼ Beverly Laurel Motor Hotel M
(323) 651-2441. **$103-$118.** 8018 Beverly Blvd. I-10, exit 7B (Fairfax Ave), 2.8 mi n, then just w. Ext corridors. **Pets:** Medium. $25 daily fee/pet. Service with restrictions, supervision.
[SAVE] [S♦] [X] [🛗] [🍴] [📶]

▼▼ Extended StayAmerica-Los Angeles/LAX Airport SH
(310) 568-9337. **$114-$134.** 6531 S Sepulveda Blvd. I-405, exit 49 (Howard Hughes Pkwy), 0.9 mi w, then just n. Int corridors. **Pets:** Accepted.
[ASK] [S♦] [X] [♿M] [🐾] [📺] [🛗] [📶]

▲▲▲ ▼▼▼▼ Four Points by Sheraton LAX LH 🌸
(310) 645-4600. **$109-$129.** 9750 Airport Blvd. I-405, exit 46 (Century Blvd), 1.5 mi w, then just n. Ext/int corridors. **Pets:** Medium, other species. $25 one-time fee/room. Designated rooms, service with restrictions, supervision.
[SAVE] [S♦] [X] [🛗] [📶] [🍴] [🏊]

▲▲▲ ▼▼▼▼ Four Seasons Hotel Los Angeles at Beverly Hills LH 🌸
(310) 273-2222. **$425-$5400.** 300 S Doheny Dr. I-10, exit 6 (Robertson Blvd), 3 mi n to Burton Way, then just w. Int corridors. **Pets:** Very small. Service with restrictions, supervision.
[SAVE] [X] [♿M] [🐾] [📺] [📶] [🍴] [🏊] [X]

▼▼ ▼▼ Hotel Bel-Air SH
(310) 472-1211. **$395-$600, 3 day notice.** 701 Stone Canyon Rd. I-405, exit 57 (Sunset Blvd), 2 mi e, then 0.8 mi n. Ext corridors. **Pets:** Accepted.
[X] [🛗] [🍴] [🏊]

▲▲▲ ▼▼ ▼▼ Hyatt Regency Century Plaza LH
(310) 277-2000. **$209-$405.** 2025 Avenue of the Stars. I-10, exit 6 (Robertson Blvd), 2.7 mi n to Olympic Blvd, 1.9 mi w, then just n. Int corridors. **Pets:** Small. $30 daily fee/pet. Service with restrictions, supervision.
[SAVE] [X] [♿M] [🐾] [📺] [📶] [🍴] [🏊] [X]

▲▲▲ ▼▼▼ La Quinta Inn & Suites-LAX LH
(310) 645-2200. **$117-$160.** 5249 W Century Blvd. I-405, exit 46 (Century Blvd), just w. Int corridors. **Pets:** Medium. Service with restrictions.
[SAVE] [X] [🛗] [📶] [🍴] [🏊]

▼▼▼▼ Los Angeles Airport Hilton & Towers LH
(310) 410-4000. **$169-$269.** 5711 W Century Blvd. I-405, exit 46 (Century Blvd), 0.8 mi w. Int corridors. **Pets:** Small, dogs only. $50 deposit/pet. Designated rooms, service with restrictions, supervision.

⊠ 🖥 💻 🍴 ➰ ⊠

▼▼▼▼ Los Angeles Airport Marriott Hotel LH
(310) 641-5700. **$139-$299.** 5855 W Century Blvd. I-405, exit 46 (Century Blvd), 1 mi w. Int corridors. **Pets:** Accepted.

⊠ 🔊 🖥 💻 ➰ ⊠

▲▲▲ ▼▼▼ ▼▼▼ Omni Los Angeles Hotel LH 🐾
(213) 617-3300. **$299.** 251 S Olive St. SR 110, exit 4th St southbound; exit 6th St northbound, just e, then just n. Int corridors. **Pets:** Medium, dogs only. $50 one-time fee/pet. Designated rooms, service with restrictions, crate.

SAVE 🔊 ⊠ 🔊M 🖥 💻 🍴 ➰

▼▼▼▼ Radisson Hotel at Los Angeles Airport LH
(310) 670-9000. **$109-$199.** 6225 W Century Blvd at Sepulveda Blvd. I-405, exit 46 (Century Blvd), 1.6 mi w. Int corridors. **Pets:** Accepted.

ASK 🔊 ⊠ 💻 🍴 ➰ ⊠

▼▼▼▼ Residence Inn by Marriott-Beverly Hills SH 🐾
(310) 277-4427. **$199-$299.** 1177 S Beverly Dr. I-10, exit 6 (Robertson Blvd), 1.6 mi n to Pico Blvd, then 0.6 mi w. Int corridors. **Pets:** Medium. $10 daily fee/pet, $100 one-time fee/room. Service with restrictions, supervision.

ASK 🔊 ⊠ 🖥 💻

▼▼▼▼ Sheraton Gateway Hotel, Los Angeles Airport LH
(310) 642-1111. **$109-$249.** 6101 W Century Blvd. I-405, exit 46 (Century Blvd), 1.3 mi w. Int corridors. **Pets:** Accepted.

ASK 🔊 ⊠ 🔊M 🖥 💻 🍴 ➰

▲▲▲ ▼▼▼▼ Sheraton Los Angeles Downtown LH
(213) 488-3500. **$129-$329.** 711 S Hope St. SR 110, exit 6th St southbound, just e, then just s. Int corridors. **Pets:** Accepted.

SAVE 🔊 ⊠ 🔊M 🖥 💻 🍴

▲▲▲ ▼▼▼▼ The Tower–Beverly Hills LH
(310) 277-2800. **$229-$329.** 1224 S Benverwil Dr. I-10, exit 6 (Robertson Blvd), 1.8 mi n, then 0.7 mi e. Int corridors. **Pets:** Accepted.

SAVE 🔊 ⊠ 💻 🍴 ➰

▲▲▲ ▼▼▼ Travelodge Hotel at Lax SH
(310) 649-4000. **$65-$120.** 5547 W Century Blvd. I-405, exit 46 (Century Blvd), 0.5 mi w. Ext/int corridors. **Pets:** Medium. $10 daily fee/pet. Designated rooms, service with restrictions, crate.

SAVE 🔊 ⊠ 🖥 💻 🍴 ➰

▲▲▲ ▼▼ Vagabond Inn Los Angeles-USC M
(213) 746-1531. **$74-$109.** 3101 S Figueroa St. SR 110, exit Adams Blvd, 0.5 mi s. Ext corridors. **Pets:** Small. $10 daily fee/pet. Designated rooms, service with restrictions, supervision.

SAVE 🔊 ⊠ 🖥 💻 ➰

▼▼▼▼ The Westin Bonaventure Hotel & Suites LH
(213) 624-1000. **$149-$189.** 404 S Figueroa St. I-SR 110, exit 23A (6th St), just n on Figueroa, e on 4th St, then s on Flower. Int corridors. **Pets:** Accepted.

ASK 🔊 ⊠ 🔊M 🖥 💻 🍴 ➰

▼▼▼▼ The Westin Hotel-Los Angeles Airport LH
(310) 216-5858. **$109-$309.** 5400 W Century Blvd. I-405, exit 46 (Century Blvd), just w. Int corridors. **Pets:** Accepted.

ASK 🔊 ⊠ 🔊M 🖥 💻 🍴 ➰ ⊠

MANHATTAN BEACH

▼▼▼▼ Residence Inn by Marriott SH
(310) 421-3100. **$119-$239, 3 day notice.** 1700 N Sepulveda Blvd. I-405, exit 43B (Rosecrans Ave), 1.5 mi w, then 1 mi s on SR 1. Ext corridors. **Pets:** Large. $100 one-time fee/room. Service with restrictions, supervision.

ASK 🔊 ⊠ 🔊M 🖥 💻 ➰ ⊠

MARINA DEL REY

▲▲▲ ▼▼▼▼ The Ritz-Carlton, Marina del Rey LH
(310) 823-1700. **$369-$469.** 4375 Admiralty Way. SR 90 (Marina Frwy), just s on Lincoln Blvd (SR 1), just w on Bali Way. Int corridors. **Pets:** Accepted.

SAVE ⊠ 🔊M 🖥 💻 🍴 ➰ ⊠

MONROVIA

▼▼▼▼ Homestead Studio Suites Hotel-Los Angeles-Monrovia SH
(626) 256-6999. **$94-$115.** 930 S Fifth Ave. I-210, exit 33 (Huntington Dr), just w, then just n. Int corridors. **Pets:** Accepted.

ASK 🔊 ⊠ 🔊M 🖥 💻

NORTHRIDGE

▼▼▼ Extended StayAmerica-Los Angeles/Northridge SH
(818) 734-1787. **$104-$124.** 19325 Londelius St. SR 118, exit 37 (Tampa Ave), 3 mi s. Int corridors. **Pets:** Accepted.

ASK 🔊 ⊠ 🔊M 🖥 💻

PASADENA

▲▲▲ ▼▼▼ Quality Inn Pasadena M
(626) 796-9291. **$81-$99.** 3321 E Colorado Blvd. I-210, exit 29B (Madre St), just s, then 0.3 mi e. Ext corridors. **Pets:** Other species. $20 daily fee/pet. Designated rooms, service with restrictions, supervision.

SAVE 🔊 ⊠ 🖥 💻 ➰

▲▲▲ ▼▼▼▼ The Ritz-Carlton, Huntington Hotel & Spa LH
(626) 568-3900. **$335-$585.** 1401 S Oak Knoll Ave. I-210, exit 26B (Lake Ave), 2 mi s. Ext/int corridors. **Pets:** Accepted.

SAVE ⊠ 🔊M 🖥 💻 🍴 ➰ ⊠

▼▼▼▼ Sheraton Pasadena Hotel LH 🐾
(626) 449-4000. **$169-$245.** 303 E Cordova St. I-210, exit 26B (Lake Ave), 0.7 mi s, then just w. Int corridors. **Pets:** Large, dogs only. Service with restrictions, supervision.

ASK 🔊 ⊠ 🔊M 🖥 💻 🍴 ➰ ⊠

▲▲▲ ▼▼ Super 8 M
(626) 449-3020. **$63-$250.** 2863 E Colorado Blvd. I-210, exit 29A (San Gabriel Blvd), 0.3 mi s, then just e. Ext corridors. **Pets:** Very small. $20 daily fee/pet. Designated rooms, service with restrictions, supervision.

SAVE 🔊 ⊠ 🖥 💻

▲▲▲ ▼▼ Vagabond Inn M
(626) 449-3170. **$78-$98.** 1203 E Colorado Blvd. I-210, exit 27A (Hill Ave), just s, then just w. Ext/int corridors. **Pets:** Accepted.

SAVE 🔊 ⊠ 🖥 💻

▲▲▲ ▼▼▼ The Westin-Pasadena LH 🐾
(626) 792-2727. **$149-$375.** 191 N Los Robles Ave. I-210, exit Los Robles Ave, just s; in Plaza Las Fuentes. Int corridors. **Pets:** Small, dogs only. Service with restrictions, supervision.

SAVE 🔊 ⊠ 🔊M 🖥 💻 🍴 ➰ ⊠

▲▲▲ ▼▼ ▼▼ Westway Inn M
(626) 304-9678. **$75-$350, 30 day notice.** 1599 E Colorado Blvd. I-210, exit 27B (Allen Ave) westbound; exit 27 (Hill Ave) eastbound, 0.8 mi s. Ext corridors. **Pets:** Small. $10 daily fee/pet. Designated rooms, service with restrictions, crate.

SAVE ⊠ 🖥 💻 ➰

POMONA

▼▼▼▼ Sheraton Suites Fairplex 🄻🄷 ❀
(909) 622-2220. **$239-$259.** 601 W McKinley Ave. I-10, exit 45A (White Ave) eastbound, 0.5 mi n, then just w; exit 43 (Fairplex Dr) westbound, 1 mi n, then 0.7 mi e. Int corridors. **Pets:** Medium, other species. $150 deposit/pet. Designated rooms, service with restrictions, supervision.
(ASK) (S🄳) (✕) (🄶🄼) (🖉) (🖧) (🖥) (🖳) (🍽) (🏊) (✕)

▼▼▼ Shilo Inn Pomona Hotel 🅂🄷 ❀
(909) 598-0073. **$92-$152.** 3200 Temple Ave. SR 57, exit 20 (Temple Ave), just w. Int corridors. **Pets:** Other species. $25 one-time fee/room. Supervision.
(ASK) (S🄳) (✕) (🄶🄼) (🖉) (🖧) (🖥) (🖳) (🍽) (🏊) (✕)

SAN DIMAS

▼▼ Extended StayAmerica-Los Angeles-San Dimas 🅂🄷
(909) 394-1022. **$84-$104.** 601 W Bonita Ave. SR 57, exit 45 (Arrow Hwy), just e, then just ne. Int corridors. **Pets:** Accepted.
(ASK) (S🄳) (✕) (🄶🄼) (🖉) (🖧) (🖥) (🖳)

▼▼ Red Roof Inn 🄼
(909) 599-2362. **$64-$99.** 204 N Village Ct. SR 57, exit 45 (Arrow Hwy), just e, then just n. Ext corridors. **Pets:** Medium, other species. Service with restrictions, supervision.
(ASK) (S🄳) (✕) (🄶🄼) (🖧) (🖥) (🏊)

SAN PEDRO

▲▲▲ ▼ Vagabond Inn 🄼
(310) 831-8911. **$65-$75.** 215 S Gaffey St. I-110, exit Gaffey St, just s of terminus. Ext corridors. **Pets:** Small. $25 one-time fee/pet. Designated rooms, service with restrictions, supervision.
(SAVE) (S🄳) (✕) (🖥) (🖳) (🖳)

SANTA CLARITA

▲▲▲ ▼▼▼ Best Western Valencia Inn 🄼 ❀
(661) 255-0555. **$99-$139, 14 day notice.** 27413 Wayne Mills Pl. I-5, exit 170 (Magic Mountain Pkwy), just e. Ext corridors. **Pets:** Medium. $10 daily fee/pet. Designated rooms, service with restrictions, crate.
(SAVE) (S🄳) (✕) (🖥) (🖳) (🏊)

▼▼ Extended StayAmerica 🅂🄷
(661) 255-1044. **$99-$119.** 24940 W Pico Canyon Rd. I-5, exit 167 (Lyons Ave), just w. Int corridors. **Pets:** Accepted.
(ASK) (S🄳) (✕) (🖥)

▼▼▼ Residence Inn by Marriott 🅂🄷 ❀
(661) 290-2800. **$159-$229.** 25320 The Old Rd. I-5, exit 167 (Lyons Ave), just w. Int corridors. **Pets:** Large. $10 daily fee/pet, $75 one-time fee/room. Service with restrictions, crate.
(ASK) (S🄳) (✕) (🄶🄼) (🖉) (🖧) (🖥) (🖳) (🏊) (✕)

SANTA MONICA

▲▲▲ ▼▼▼▼ The Fairmont Miramar Hotel Santa Monica 🄻🄷 ❀
(310) 576-7777. **$339-$399.** 101 Wilshire Blvd. I-10, exit 1B (Lincoln Blvd), 0.6 mi n, then 0.6 mi w. Ext/int corridors. **Pets:** Small, dogs only. $125 deposit/room. Service with restrictions, supervision.
(SAVE) (✕) (🖳) (🍽) (🏊) (✕)

▼▼▼ The Georgian 🅂🄷
(310) 395-9945. **$235-$355.** 1415 Ocean Ave. I-10, exit 1B (Lincoln Blvd), just n, then 0.5 mi w on Broadway. Int corridors. **Pets:** Accepted.
(ASK) (✕) (🖳)

▲▲▲ ▼▼▼▼ Le Merigot–A JW Marriott Beach Hotel & Spa 🄻🄷 ❀
(310) 395-9700. **$350-$400.** 1740 Ocean Ave. I-10, exit 1B (Lincoln Blvd), 0.3 mi s, 0.6 mi w on Pico Blvd, then just n. Int corridors. **Pets:** $100 one-time fee/room. Service with restrictions.
(SAVE) (S🄳) (✕) (🍽) (🏊) (✕)

▲▲▲ ▼▼▼ ▼▼ Loews Santa Monica Beach Hotel 🄻🄷 ❀
(310) 458-6700. **$309-$489.** 1700 Ocean Ave. I-10, exit 1B (Lincoln Blvd), 0.3 mi s, 0.6 mi w on Pico Blvd, then just n. Int corridors. **Pets:** Medium. Service with restrictions.
(SAVE) (✕) (🄶🄼) (🖉) (🖧) (🖥) (🍽) (🏊) (✕)

▼▼▼ Sheraton Delfina Santa Monica 🄻🄷 ❀
(310) 399-9344. **$209-$359.** 530 Pico Blvd. I-10, exit 1B (Lincoln Blvd), just s. Int corridors. **Pets:** Medium, dogs only. $50 one-time fee/room. Designated rooms, service with restrictions, supervision.
(ASK) (S🄳) (✕) (🖥) (🖳) (🍽) (🏊)

▲▲▲ ▼▼▼ Travelodge-Santa Monica/Pico Blvd 🄼
(310) 450-5766. **$89-$199.** 3102 W Pico Blvd. I-10, exit 2 (Centinela Ave), just n, then just w. Ext corridors. **Pets:** Small. Designated rooms, service with restrictions, supervision.
(SAVE) (S🄳) (✕) (🖥) (🖳)

SHERMAN OAKS

▲▲▲ ▼▼▼ Best Western Carriage Inn 🄼
(818) 787-2300. **$99-$189.** 5525 Sepulveda Blvd. I-405, exit 64 (Burbank Blvd), just e, then just s. Ext/int corridors. **Pets:** Accepted.
(SAVE) (S🄳) (✕) (🄶🄼) (🖉) (🖧) (🖥) (🖳) (🍽) (🏊)

SOUTH EL MONTE

▼▼ Rodeway Inn South El Monte 🄼
(626) 579-4490. **$74-$99.** 1228 N Durfee Rd. SR 60, exit 11 (Peck Rd), just s, then just e. Ext corridors. **Pets:** Accepted.
(ASK) (S🄳) (✕) (🖥) (🖳) (🏊)

TARZANA

▲▲▲ ▼▼▼ St. George Inn & Suites 🄼 ❀
(818) 345-6911. **$77-$89.** 19454 Ventura Blvd. US 101, exit 24 (Tampa Ave), just s, then just w. Ext corridors. **Pets:** Medium, other species. $150 deposit/room. Designated rooms, service with restrictions.
(SAVE) (S🄳) (✕) (🖥) (🖳) (🏊)

TORRANCE

▼▼ Extended StayAmerica-Los Angeles-Torrance 🅂🄷
(310) 540-5442. **$99-$119.** 3525 Torrance Blvd. I-405, exit 42A (Hawthorne Blvd), 3.5 mi s, then 0.4 mi e. Int corridors. **Pets:** Accepted.
(ASK) (S🄳) (✕) (🄶🄼) (🖉) (🖧) (🖥) (🖳)

▼▼ Extended StayAmerica-Los Angeles/Torrance Harbor Gateway 🅂🄷
(310) 328-6000. **$99-$119.** 19200 Harborgate Way. I-405, exit 38A (Normandie Ave), just s, then just w via 190th St. Int corridors. **Pets:** Accepted.
(ASK) (S🄳) (✕) (🄶🄼) (🖉) (🖧) (🖥) (🖳)

▼▼▼ Holiday Inn Torrance 🄻🄷
(310) 781-9100. **$129-$229.** 19800 S Vermont Ave. I-110, exit 9 (190th St), just e, then 0.4 mi n. Int corridors. **Pets:** Large, other species. $50 deposit/room. Service with restrictions, crate.
(ASK) (S🄳) (✕) (🖥) (🖳) (🍽) (🏊) (✕)

▼▼ Homestead Studio Suites Hotel-Los Angeles-Torrance 🅂🄷
(310) 543-0048. **$84-$120.** 3995 Carson St. I-405, exit 42A (Hawthorne Blvd), 3.6 mi s; I-110, exit 7B (Carson St), 4.5 mi w. Int corridors. **Pets:** Accepted.
(ASK) (S🄳) (✕) (🄶🄼) (🖉) (🖧) (🖥) (🖳)

▼▼▼ Residence Inn by Marriott 🅂🄷
(310) 543-4566. **$99-$179.** 3701 Torrance Blvd. I-405, exit 42A (Hawthorne Blvd), 3.2 mi s, then just e. Ext corridors. **Pets:** Accepted.
(ASK) (S🄳) (✕) (🖥) (🖳) (🏊) (✕)

▼▼▼ **Staybridge Suites** **M**
(310) 371-8525. **$149-$209.** 19901 Prairie Ave. I-405, exit 39 (Crenshaw Blvd), just s to 190th St, 1 mi w, then just s. Ext/int corridors. **Pets:** Accepted.

ASK S6 X 🔒 🖥 🏊 ✕

UNIVERSAL CITY

AAA ▼▼▼ **Sheraton Universal Hotel, at Universal Studios** **LH** ❀
(818) 980-1212. **$199-$339.** 333 Universal Hollywood Dr. US 101, exit 12A (Lankershim Blvd), just n, then just e. Int corridors. **Pets:** Designated rooms, service with restrictions, supervision.

SAVE X 🔒 🖥 🍴 🏊 ✕

WEST HOLLYWOOD

▼▼▼ **The Grafton on Sunset** **SH**
(323) 654-4600. **$175-$315.** 8462 Sunset Blvd. I-10, exit 7A (La Cienega Blvd), 4.4 mi n, then just e. Int corridors. **Pets:** Accepted.

ASK X 🖥M 🐾 🔒 🏊

▼▼▼ **Le Montrose Suite Hotel** **SH**
(310) 855-1115. **$395-$549.** 900 Hammond St at Cynthia St. I-10, exit 7A (La Cienega Blvd), 2.6 mi n to San Vicente Blvd, 1.3 mi nw, then just w on Cynthia St. Int corridors. **Pets:** Accepted.

ASK X 🔒 🖥 🍴 🏊 ✕

▼▼▼ **Le Parc Suite Hotel** **LH**
(310) 855-8888. **$259-$549.** 733 N West Knoll Dr. I-10, exit 7A (La Cienega Blvd), 3.5 mi n, just w on Melrose Ave, then just n. Int corridors. **Pets:** Medium. $75 one-time fee/room. Service with restrictions.

ASK S6 X 🔒 🖥 🍴 🏊 ✕

AAA ▼▼▼ **Ramada Plaza Hotel** **LH**
(310) 652-6400. **$129-$199.** 8585 Santa Monica Blvd. I-10, exit 7A (La Cienega Blvd), 4 mi n, then just w. Int corridors. **Pets:** Accepted.

SAVE S6 X 🔒 🖥 🍴 🏊

WHITTIER

AAA ▼▼▼ **Radisson Hotel Whittier** **LH**
(562) 945-8511. **$159-$189.** 7320 Greenleaf Ave. I-605, exit 15 (Whittier Blvd), 2.5 mi e, then 0.6 mi n. Int corridors. **Pets:** Accepted.

SAVE S6 X 🖥M 🖥 🍴 🏊

AAA ▼ **Vagabond Inn** **M**
(562) 698-9701. **$60-$73.** 14125 E Whittier Blvd. I-605, exit 15 (Whittier Blvd), 3.5 mi e. Ext corridors. **Pets:** Other species. $10 daily fee/pet. Designated rooms, service with restrictions, supervision.

SAVE S6 X 🔒 🖥 🏊

WOODLAND HILLS

▼▼◆ **Extended StayAmerica-Los Angeles-Woodland Hills** **SH**
(818) 710-1170. **$94-$114.** 20205 Ventura Blvd. US 101, exit 25 (Winnetka Ave), just s, then just w. Int corridors. **Pets:** Accepted.

ASK S6 X 🔒 🖥

AAA ▼▼◆ **Warner Center Marriott Hotel** **LH** 🐾
(818) 887-4800. **$139-$269.** 21850 Oxnard St. US 101, exit 270 (Topanga Canyon Blvd), 0.6 mi n, then just e. Int corridors. **Pets:** Other species. $50 one-time fee/room. Service with restrictions, crate.

SAVE S6 X 🖥M 🐾 🐾 🔒 🖥 🍴 🏊 ✕

END METROPOLITAN AREA

LOS BANOS

AAA ▼▼◆ **Best Western Executive Inn** **SH**
(209) 827-0954. **$69-$99.** 301 W Pacheco Blvd. On SR 152. Int corridors. **Pets:** Small, dogs only. $20 one-time fee/pet. Service with restrictions, supervision.

SAVE S6 X 🖥M 🐾 🔒 🖥 🏊 ✕

LOS GATOS

AAA ▼▼▼ **Los Gatos Lodge** **SH**
(408) 354-3300. **$149-$199.** 50 Los Gatos/Saratoga Rd. SR 17, exit E Los Gatos, just e. Ext/int corridors. **Pets:** Accepted.

SAVE S6 X 🖥M 🐾 🔒 🖥 🍴 🏊 ✕

AAA ▼▼▼ **Toll House Hotel** **SH**
(408) 395-7070. **$179-$229.** 140 S Santa Cruz Ave. I-880/SR 17, exit SR 9, 0.3 mi w. Int corridors. **Pets:** Accepted.

SAVE S6 X 🐾 🔒 🖥 🍴 ✕

LOS OLIVOS

AAA ▼▼▼◆ **Fess Parker's Wine Country Inn & Spa** **CI**
(805) 688-7788. **$280-$380, 7 day notice.** 2860 Grand Ave. SR 154, 0.5 mi s. Ext/int corridors. **Pets:** Accepted.

SAVE S6 X 🔒 🍴 🏊 ✕

MADERA

AAA ▼▼▼▼ **Madera Valley Inn** **SH**
(559) 664-0100. **$79-$129.** 317 North G St. SR 99, exit Central Madera, just e. Int corridors. **Pets:** Other species. $15 one-time fee/pet. Service with restrictions, supervision.

SAVE S6 X 🔒 🖥 🍴 🏊

▼▼ **Motel 6 #4247** **SH**
(559) 675-8697. **$54-$85, 3 day notice.** 22683 Ave 18 1/2. SR 99, exit Ave 18 1/2, just w. Int corridors. **Pets:** Medium, other species. Service with restrictions, supervision.

ASK S6 X 🐾 🔒 🏊

▼▼ **Super 8** **M**
(559) 661-1131. **$60-$70.** 1855 W Cleveland Ave. SR 99, exit Cleveland Ave, just w. Ext corridors. **Pets:** Dogs only. $5 daily fee/pet. Service with restrictions, supervision.

ASK S6 X 🔒 🖥 🏊

MAMMOTH LAKES

AAA ▼▼▼ **Econo Lodge Wildwood Inn** **M**
(760) 934-6855. **$79-$199, 7 day notice.** 3626 Main St. On SR 203, 0.7 mi w of Old Mammoth Rd. Ext corridors. **Pets:** Medium. $10 daily fee/pet. Service with restrictions, supervision.

SAVE S6 X 🔒 🖥 🏊 🐾

▼▼▼ **Mammoth Ski & Racquet Club** **CO**
(760) 934-7368. **$110-$330, 30 day notice.** 248 Mammoth Slopes Dr. From Old Mammoth Rd, 1 mi w on SR 203, just n; Canyon Blvd, 0.8 mi w, then just s. Int corridors. **Pets:** Accepted.

ASK S6 X 🔒 🖥 🏊 ✕ 🐾

▼▼▼ **Shilo Inn** **SH** ❀
(760) 934-4500. **$130-$210.** 2963 Main St. On SR 203, just e of Old Mammoth Rd. Int corridors. **Pets:** Other species. $25 one-time fee/room. Supervision.

ASK S6 X 🖥M 🐾 🔒 🖥 🏊 ✕

AAA ▼▼◆ **Sierra Lodge** **SH**
(760) 934-8881. **$59-$199.** 3540 Main St. On SR 203, 0.6 mi w of Old Mammoth Rd. Int corridors. **Pets:** Other species. No service.

SAVE S6 X 🔒 🐾

△△△ ▼▼ Sierra Nevada Rodeway Inn 🆂🅷
(760) 934-2515. **$109-$757, 7 day notice.** 164 Old Mammoth Rd. Just s of SR 203. Ext/int corridors. **Pets:** Accepted.

[SAVE] [S🅓] [✕] [🛏] [📺] [🏊]

◆◆ Swiss Chalet Motel 🅼
(760) 934-2403. **$70-$130, 7 day notice.** 3776 Viewpoint Rd. 0.7 mi w of Old Mammoth Rd; adjacent to SR 203. Ext corridors. **Pets:** Accepted.

[ASK] [S🅓] [✕] [🛏] [🄰🄲]

MANTECA

△△△ ▼▼▼ Best Western Executive Inn & Suites 🆂🅷
(209) 825-1415. **$88-$96.** 1415 E Yosemite Ave. Jct SR 99 and 120, exit E Yosemite Ave. Ext corridors. **Pets:** Accepted.

[SAVE] [S🅓] [✕] [🅶🅼] [🛏] [📺] [🏊]

MARIPOSA

△△△ ▼▼ Americas Best Value Inn–Mariposa Lodge 🆂🅷
(209) 966-3607. **$59-$129, 3 day notice.** 5052 Hwy 140. Center. Ext corridors. **Pets:** Medium. $10 daily fee/pet. Service with restrictions, supervision.

[SAVE] [S🅓] [✕] [🛏] [📺] [🏊]

△△△ ▼▼◆ Best Western Yosemite Way Station Motel 🆂🅷
(209) 966-7545. **$59-$119, 7 day notice.** 4999 Hwy 140. SR 140 at SR 49 S. Ext corridors. **Pets:** $10 daily fee/pet. Designated rooms, service with restrictions, supervision.

[SAVE] [✕] [🅶🅼] [🄲] [📺] [🏊]

△△△ ▼▼◆ Comfort Inn-Mariposa 🆂🅷
(209) 966-4344. **$49-$99.** 4994 Bullion St. Jct SR 140 and 49 S, just e. Ext corridors. **Pets:** Small. $15 daily fee/pet. Service with restrictions, supervision.

[SAVE] [S🅓] [✕] [🅶🅼] [🄲] [📺] [🏊]

△△△ ▼▼◆ Miners Inn 🆂🅷
(209) 742-7777. **$59-$169.** 5181 Hwy 49 N. On SR 49, n at SR 140. Ext/int corridors. **Pets:** Other species. $10 daily fee/pet. Designated rooms, service with restrictions, supervision.

[SAVE] [✕] [📺] [🍴] [🏊]

MERCED

△△△ ▼▼▼ Merced-Yosemite Travelodge 🅼
(209) 722-6224. **$55-$75.** 1260 Yosemite Pkwy. SR 99, exit SR 140, just e. Ext corridors. **Pets:** Medium. $25 deposit/pet, $10 daily fee/pet. No service, supervision.

[SAVE] [S🅓] [✕] [🅶🅼] [🄲] [🛏] [📺] [🏊]

MILPITAS

△△△ ▼▼▼ Americas Best Value Inn & Suites 🅼
(408) 946-8383. **$49-$89.** 485 S Main St. I-880, exit Calaveras Blvd (SR 237), 0.5 mi e, then just s. Ext corridors. **Pets:** Small, dogs only. $10 daily fee/pet. Service with restrictions, supervision.

[SAVE] [S🅓] [✕] [🛏]

△△△ ▼▼▼ Best Western Brookside Inn 🆂🅷
(408) 263-5566. **$89-$129.** 400 Valley Way. I-880, exit Calaveras Blvd (SR 237), just e. Ext/int corridors. **Pets:** Accepted.

[SAVE] [S🅓] [✕] [🄲] [🛏] [📺] [🏊]

△△△ ▼▼▼ Beverly Heritage Hotel 🅻🅷
(408) 943-9080. **$59-$179.** 1820 Barber Ln. Northwest quadrant of I-880 and Montague Expwy. Int corridors. **Pets:** Accepted.

[SAVE] [S🅓] [✕] [🄲] [🛏] [📺] [🍴] [🏊] [✕]

△△△ ▼▼▼ Days Inn Milpitas 🆂🅷
(408) 946-8889. **$49-$189.** 270 S Abbott Ave. I-880, exit Calaveras Blvd (SR 237), just e. Ext corridors. **Pets:** Accepted.

[SAVE] [✕] [🛏] [📺] [🏊]

▼▼▼▼ Embassy Suites Milpitas/Silicon Valley 🅻🅷
(408) 942-0400. **$109-$229.** 901 E Calaveras Blvd. I-680, exit Calaveras Blvd (SR 237), just w. Int corridors. **Pets:** $50 one-time fee/pet. Service with restrictions, crate.

[ASK] [S🅓] [✕] [🛏] [📺] [🍴] [🏊] [✕]

◆ Extended StayAmerica-San Jose/Milpitas 🆂🅷
(408) 941-9977. **$94-$104.** 1000 Hillview Ct. I-680, exit Calaveras Blvd (SR 237) W, just n. Int corridors. **Pets:** Accepted.

[ASK] [S🅓] [✕] [📺]

◆◆ Homestead Studio Suites Hotel-San
    Jose-Milpitas 🅼
(408) 433-9700. **$125-$135.** 330 Cypress Dr. SR 237, exit McCarthy S. Ext/int corridors. **Pets:** Accepted.

[ASK] [S🅓] [✕] [♿] [🄲] [📺]

△△△ ▼▼◆ Sheraton San Jose at Silicon Valley 🅻🅷 ❀
(408) 943-0600. **$79-$259.** 1801 Barber Ln. 4 mi n of San Jose International Airport; 0.3 mi nw of I-880 and Montague Expwy. Ext/int corridors. **Pets:** Other species. $50 deposit/room. Service with restrictions, supervision.

[SAVE] [S🅓] [✕] [🛏] [📺] [🍴] [🏊] [✕]

▼▼▼ TownePlace Suites by Marriott 🆂🅷
(408) 719-1959. **$79-$179.** 1428 Falcon Dr. I-680, exit Montague Expwy, just w, then just n. Int corridors. **Pets:** Accepted.

[ASK] [S🅓] [✕] [🅶🅼] [🄲] [📺] [🏊]

MIRANDA

△△△ ▼▼◆ Miranda Gardens Resort 🄲🄰
(707) 943-3011. **$105-$265, 7 day notice.** 6766 Ave of the Giants. US 101, exit 650 (Miranda), just e on French Rd, 0.3 mi s on Maple Hills Rd, then 1.5 mi e. Ext corridors. **Pets:** Medium. $150 deposit/room, $15 daily fee/pet. Designated rooms, supervision.

[SAVE] [S🅓] [✕] [🛏] [📺] [🄰🄲] [✕]

MI-WUK VILLAGE

△△△ ▼▼ Christmas Tree Inn 🅼
(209) 586-1005. **$89-$109, 3 day notice.** 24685 Hwy 108. On SR 108, 15 mi e of Sonora. Ext corridors. **Pets:** Small, dogs only. $15 daily fee/room. Designated rooms, service with restrictions, supervision.

[SAVE] [S🅓] [✕] [🛏] [📺] [🏊]

△△△ ▼▼◆ Mi-Wuk Village Inn, Resort & Conference
    Center 🆂🅷 ❀
(209) 586-3031. **$125-$350, 21 day notice.** 24680 SR 108. On SR 108, 15 mi e of Sonora. Ext corridors. **Pets:** Dogs only. $150 deposit/room, $20 daily fee/pet. Designated rooms, service with restrictions, supervision.

[SAVE] [S🅓] [✕] [🛏] [📺] [🏊]

MODESTO

△△△ ▼▼ Best Western Town House Lodge 🅼
(209) 524-7261. **$90-$115.** 909 16th St. SR 99, exit Central Modesto, 1 mi e, at I St. Ext corridors. **Pets:** Accepted.

[SAVE] [S🅓] [✕] [🅶🅼] [🛏] [📺] [🏊]

△△△ ▼▼▼ Days Inn 🆂🅷
(209) 527-1010. **$79-$149.** 1312 McHenry Ave. SR 99, exit Briggsmore Ave, 2.3 mi e, then 0.5 mi s. Ext/int corridors. **Pets:** Accepted.

[SAVE] [S🅓] [✕] [🄲] [🛏] [📺] [🏊]

△△△ ▼▼▼ Howard Johnson Express Inn 🅼
(209) 537-4821. **$79-$99.** 1672 Herndon Rd. SR 99, exit Hatch Rd E, then s. Ext corridors. **Pets:** Small, other species. $100 deposit/pet. Designated rooms, service with restrictions, supervision.

[SAVE] [S🅓] [✕] [🅶🅼] [🛏] [📺] [🏊]

(AAA) ▼▼▼ Microtel Inn & Suites SH
(209) 538-6466. **$82-$110.** 1760 Herndon Rd. SR 99, exit Hatch Rd E, just s. Int corridors. **Pets:** Small, other species. $100 deposit/pet. Designated rooms, service with restrictions, supervision.
[SAVE] [S☆] [✕] [&M] [🐾] [🛏] [📺] [🏊]

(AAA) ▼ Travelodge M
(209) 524-3251. **$45-$70.** 722 Kansas Ave. SR 99, exit Kansas Ave, then w. Ext corridors. **Pets:** $10 daily fee/pet. No service, supervision.
[SAVE] [S☆] [✕] [&M] [🛏] [📺] [🏊]

MOJAVE

(AAA) ▼▼▼ Americas Best Value Inn M
(661) 824-9317. **$60-$80.** 16352 Sierra Hwy. On SR 14 and 58. Ext corridors. **Pets:** Accepted.
[SAVE] [S☆] [✕] [🛏] [📺] [🏊]

(AAA) ▼▼▼ Best Western Desert Winds M
(661) 824-3601. **$84.** 16200 Sierra Hwy. On SR 14 and 58. Ext corridors. **Pets:** Medium, other species. $10 daily fee/pet. Designated rooms, service with restrictions, supervision.
[SAVE] [S☆] [✕] [🛏] [📺] [🏊]

(AAA) ▼▼ Desert Inn M
(661) 824-2518. **$49-$59.** 1954 Hwy 58. Just e of SR 14. Ext corridors. **Pets:** Medium. Service with restrictions, crate.
[SAVE] [S☆] [✕] [🛏] [📺]

(AAA) ▼▼ Econo Lodge M
(661) 824-2463. **$59-$99.** 2145 Hwy 58. Just e of SR 14. Ext corridors. **Pets:** Accepted.
[SAVE] [S☆] [✕] [🛏] [📺] [🏊]

(AAA) ▼▼▼▼ Mariah Country Inn & Suites SH
(661) 824-4980. **$95-$120.** 1385 Hwy 58. 1.5 mi e of SR 14. Int corridors. **Pets:** Medium, other species. $10 daily fee/room. Designated rooms, service with restrictions, supervision.
[SAVE] [S☆] [✕] [&M] [🐾] [🔧] [🛏] [📺] [🍽] [🏊]

MONTEREY PENINSULA AREA

CARMEL-BY-THE-SEA

(AAA) ▼▼▼▼ Best Western Carmel Mission Inn SH
(831) 624-1841. **$79-$599.** 3665 Rio Rd. 1 mi s on SR 1. Ext/int corridors. **Pets:** Medium. $35 one-time fee/room. Designated rooms, service with restrictions, crate.
[SAVE] [S☆] [✕] [🛏] [📺] [🍽] [🏊]

(AAA) ▼▼▼ Briarwood Inn BB
(831) 624-2277. **$85-$265, 7 day notice.** San Carlos St. 3 blks n off Ocean Ave; at San Carlos St and 4th Ave. Ext corridors. **Pets:** Medium, dogs only. $25 daily fee/pet. Designated rooms, service with restrictions, supervision.
[SAVE] [✕] [🛏] [📺] [AC]

▼▼▼▼ Carmel Country Inn BB 🐾
(831) 625-3263. **$175-$375, 7 day notice.** 4 blks n of Ocean Ave; at Dolores St and 3rd Ave. Ext corridors. **Pets:** Other species. $20 daily fee/pet. Designated rooms, supervision.
[✕] [🛏] [📺] [AC]

(AAA) ▼▼▼▼ Carmel Fireplace Inn Bed & Breakfast BB
(831) 624-2277. **$99-$275, 7 day notice.** 3 blks n off Ocean Ave; at San Carlos St and 4th Ave. Ext corridors. **Pets:** Medium, dogs only. $25 daily fee/pet. Designated rooms, service with restrictions, supervision.
[SAVE] [✕] [🛏] [📺] [AC]

(AAA) ▼▼▼▼ Carmel Garden Court BB 🐾
(831) 624-6926. **$160-$225, 7 day notice.** 4th & Torres. 3 blks n off Ocean Ave; at 4th Ave and Torres St. Ext corridors. **Pets:** Medium. $50 one-time fee/pet. Service with restrictions, supervision.
[SAVE] [✕] [🛏] [📺] [AC]

▼▼ Carmel River Inn M
(831) 624-1575. **$69-$169, 3 day notice.** 1 mi s on SR 1; n of Carmel River Bridge at Oliver Rd. Ext corridors. **Pets:** Accepted.
[ASK] [S☆] [✕] [🛏] [📺] [🏊] [AC]

(AAA) ▼▼▼ Coachman's Inn M 🐾
(831) 624-6421. **$135-$425, 3 day notice.** San Carlos at Seventh. Just s of Ocean Ave on San Carlos St; between 7th and 8th aves. Ext corridors. **Pets:** Dogs only. $20 daily fee/pet. Designated rooms, service with restrictions, supervision.
[SAVE] [S☆] [✕] [&M] [🛏] [📺] [AC]

▼▼▼ Cypress Inn SH 🐾
(831) 624-3871. **$125-$595, 3 day notice.** Just s off Ocean Ave; at Lincoln St and 7th Ave. Ext/int corridors. **Pets:** $30 daily fee/pet. Supervision.
[✕] [🍽] [AC]

(AAA) ▼▼ Hofsas House M 🐾
(831) 624-2745. **$85-$250, 3 day notice.** Between 3rd & 4th on San Carlos. 3 blks n off Ocean Ave; between 3rd and 4th aves on San Carlos St. Ext corridors. **Pets:** Dogs only. $20 daily fee/pet. Designated rooms, service with restrictions, supervision.
[SAVE] [S☆] [✕] [🛏] [📺] [🏊] [AC]

(AAA) ▼▼▼ Horizon Inn & Ocean View Lodge M
(831) 624-5327. **$99-$350, 3 day notice.** 3rd Ave & Junipero SWC. 4 blks n off Ocean Ave. Ext corridors. **Pets:** Large, dogs only. $20 daily fee/pet. Designated rooms, service with restrictions, supervision.
[SAVE] [S☆] [✕] [🛏] [📺] [AC]

(AAA) ▼▼▼ Quail Lodge SH 🐾
(831) 624-2888. **$205-$405, 3 day notice.** 8205 Valley Greens Dr. 3.5 mi e of SR 1, via Carmel Valley Rd. Ext corridors. **Pets:** $25 one-time fee/pet. Service with restrictions, crate.
[SAVE] [✕] [🔧] [&M] [🍽] [🏊] [✕]

▼▼▼ Tradewinds Carmel SH 🐾
(831) 624-2776. **$225-$575, 3 day notice.** 4 blks n off Ocean Ave; at Mission St and 3rd Ave. Ext corridors. **Pets:** Medium. $25 daily fee/pet. Designated rooms, service with restrictions, supervision.
[ASK] [S☆] [✕] [🛏] [📺] [AC]

(AAA) ▼▼▼ Wayside Inn SH
(831) 624-5336. **$132-$414, 7 day notice.** 1 blk s off Ocean Ave; at Mission St and 7th Ave. Ext corridors. **Pets:** Accepted.
[SAVE] [S☆] [✕] [🛏] [📺] [AC]

CARMEL VALLEY

▼▼▼ Los Laureles Lodge SH
(831) 659-2233. **$89-$695, 3 day notice.** 313 W Carmel Valley Rd. 10.5 mi e of SR 1. Ext corridors. **Pets:** Medium, dogs only. $20 daily fee/pet. Service with restrictions, supervision.
[ASK] [S☆] [✕] [🛏] [📺] [🍽] [🏊] [AC]

MONTEREY

Bay Park Hotel ⚫ ⚫
(831) 649-1020. **$89-$299.** 1425 Munras Ave. SR 1, exit Soledad Dr/Munras Ave, just w. Int corridors. **Pets:** Medium, other species. $20 daily fee/pet. Designated rooms, service with restrictions, supervision.

Best Western Beach Resort Monterey ⚫ ⚫
(831) 394-3321. **$99-$469.** 2600 Sand Dunes Dr. SR 1, exit Del Rey Oaks, just w. Ext corridors. **Pets:** Large, other species. $25 daily fee/pet. Designated rooms, service with restrictions, supervision.

Best Western Victorian Inn ⚫ ⚫
(831) 373-8000. **$99-$319, 3 day notice.** 487 Foam St. SR 1, exit Monterey, 3.4 mi w. Ext/int corridors. **Pets:** $150 deposit/room, $30 daily fee/pet. Designated rooms, service with restrictions, crate.

Casa Munras, a Larkspur Hotel ⚫
(831) 375-2411. **$109-$329, 3 day notice.** 700 Munras Ave. SR 1, exit Soledad Dr/Munras Ave, 0.8 mi w. Ext/int corridors. **Pets:** Accepted.

El Adobe Inn ⚫ ⚫
(831) 372-5409. **$49-$199, 3 day notice.** 936 Munras Ave. SR 1, exit Soledad Dr/Munras Ave, 0.6 mi w. Ext corridors. **Pets:** Medium, dogs only. $15 daily fee/pet. Designated rooms, service with restrictions, supervision.

Hyatt Regency-Monterey Resort & Conference Center ⚫ ⚫
(831) 372-1234. **$105-$349.** 1 Old Golf Course Rd. SR 1, exit Aguajito Rd northbound; exit Monterey southbound, just e. Int corridors. **Pets:** Large, other species. $50 one-time fee/room. Designated rooms, service with restrictions, crate.

Monterey Bay Lodge ⚫ ⚫
(831) 372-8057. **$89-$319.** 55 Camino Aguajito. SR 1, exit Aguajito Rd, just w. Ext corridors. **Pets:** Dogs only. $15 daily fee/pet. Designated rooms, service with restrictions, supervision.

Monterey Bay Travelodge ⚫
(831) 373-3381. **$59-$159.** 2030 N Fremont St. Jct SR 1 and Fremont St, at SR 68. Ext/int corridors. **Pets:** Other species. $20 daily fee/room. Designated rooms, service with restrictions, supervision.

Monterey Fireside Lodge ⚫
(831) 373-4172. **$69-$249, 3 day notice.** 1131 10th St. SR 1, exit Aguajito Rd or Monterey, just w. Ext corridors. **Pets:** Other species. $20 daily fee/pet. Designated rooms, no service, supervision.

PACIFIC GROVE

Bide-A-Wee Inn & Cottages ⚫ ⚫
(831) 372-2330. **$69-$169, 3 day notice.** 221 Asilomar Blvd. 1 mi n of SR 68. Ext corridors. **Pets:** Medium. $14 daily fee/pet. Service with restrictions, supervision.

Olympia Lodge ⚫
(831) 373-2777. **$80-$180, 3 day notice.** 1140 Lighthouse Ave. 1 mi w. Ext corridors. **Pets:** Accepted.

Sea Breeze Inn and Cottages ⚫ ⚫
(831) 372-7771. **$69-$259.** 1100 Lighthouse Ave. Just w of Seventeen Mile Dr; jct Lighthouse Ave and Grove Acre. Ext/int corridors. **Pets:** $25 one-time fee/pet. Designated rooms, service with restrictions, supervision.

Sea Breeze Lodge ⚫ ⚫
(831) 372-3431. **$69-$259.** 1101 Lighthouse Ave. Just w of Seventeen Mile Dr. Ext corridors. **Pets:** $25 one-time fee/pet. Designated rooms, service with restrictions, supervision.

PEBBLE BEACH

The Lodge at Pebble Beach ⚫ ⚫
(831) 624-3811. **$610-$995, 3 day notice.** 1700 Seventeen Mile Dr. Off SR 1. Ext/int corridors. **Pets:** Medium, dogs only.

SEASIDE

Econo Lodge Bay Breeze ⚫
(831) 899-7111. **$49-$199.** 2049 Fremont Blvd. SR 1, exit Sand City/Seaside, just e. Ext/int corridors. **Pets:** Very small. Service with restrictions, supervision.

END AREA

MORENO VALLEY

Best Western Image Inn & Suites ⚫
(951) 924-4546. **$84.** 24840 Elder Ave. SR 60, exit 62 (Perris Blvd) westbound, just n, then just w; eastbound, just e on Sunnymead Blvd, just n on Perris Blvd, then just w. Ext corridors. **Pets:** $10 daily fee/pet, $10 one-time fee/pet. Service with restrictions, supervision.

Comfort Inn ⚫
(951) 242-0699. **$69-$149.** 23330 Sunnymead Blvd. SR 60, exit 62 (Perris Blvd) westbound, just s, then 1.3 mi w; eastbound, 1 mi w. Ext/int corridors. **Pets:** Small, other species. $50 deposit/pet, $10 daily fee/pet. Designated rooms, service with restrictions, supervision.

MORGAN HILL

Extended StayAmerica-Morgan Hill ⚫
(408) 779-9660. **$84-$94.** 605 Jarvis Dr. US 101, exit Cochrane W, s on Sutter Blvd, then just e. Int corridors. **Pets:** Accepted.

Quality Inn ⚫
(408) 779-0447. **$66-$100.** 16525 Condit Rd. US 101, exit Tennant Ave or E Dunne Ave, just e. Int corridors. **Pets:** Medium. $15 daily fee/pet. Service with restrictions, supervision.

Residence Inn by Marriott ⚫
(408) 782-8311. **$145-$225.** 18620 Madrone Pkwy. US 101, exit Cochrane W, just n. Int corridors. **Pets:** Accepted.

MORRO BAY

AAA ▼▼▼ Best Western El Rancho M ❀
(805) 772-2212. **$95-$160, 3 day notice.** 2460 Main St. SR 1, exit SR 41, 0.5 mi n. Ext corridors. **Pets:** Other species. $15 one-time fee/pet. Service with restrictions, supervision.
[SAVE] [S6] [✕] [🛏] [💻] [🏊] [📷]

▼▼▼ Days Inn M
(805) 772-2711. **$55-$159, 3 day notice.** 1095 Main St. SR 1, exit Morro Bay Blvd, 0.7 mi w, then just n. Ext corridors. **Pets:** Accepted.
[S6] [✕] [🛏] [💻] [📷]

AAA ▼▼ Econo Lodge South M ❀
(805) 772-7503. **$49-$185, 3 day notice.** 540 Main St. SR 1, exit Morro Bay Blvd, 0.7 mi w, then 0.4 mi s. Ext corridors. **Pets:** Small. $15 one-time fee/room. Designated rooms, service with restrictions, supervision.
[SAVE] [✕] [S/M] [🌀] [♿] [🛏] [💻] [📷]

AAA ▼▼▼ Sea Pines Golf Resort M ❀
(805) 528-5252. **$119-$179.** 1945 Solano St. SR 1, exit Los Osos/Baywood Park, 4 mi s on S Bay Blvd, 1.6 mi w on Los Osos Valley Rd, 0.3 mi n on Pecho Rd, then just w on Skyline Dr; in Los Osos. Ext corridors. **Pets:** Small, dogs only. $25 daily fee/pet. Designated rooms, service with restrictions, supervision.
[SAVE] [S6] [✕] [S/M] [♿] [🛏] [💻] [🍴] [✕]

AAA ▼▼▼ Sundown Inn M
(805) 772-7381. **$38-$159.** 640 Main St. SR 1, exit Morro Bay Blvd, 0.7 mi w, then just s. Ext corridors. **Pets:** Small, dogs only. $8 daily fee/pet. Designated rooms, service with restrictions, supervision.
[SAVE] [S6] [✕] [S/M] [♿] [🛏] [💻] [📷]

MOUNTAIN VIEW

▼▼ Homestead Studio Suites Hotel-San Jose, Mountain View M
(650) 962-1500. **$120-$130.** 190 E El Camino Real. On SR 82, just w of SR 85. Ext corridors. **Pets:** Accepted.
[ASK] [S6] [✕] [S/M] [♿] [🛏] [💻]

AAA ▼▼ Tropicana Lodge M
(650) 961-0220. **$75-$95.** 1720 El Camino Real W. US 101, exit Shoreline Blvd, 2 mi to SR 82, then just n. Ext/int corridors. **Pets:** Designated rooms, service with restrictions, crate.
[SAVE] [S6] [✕] [S/M] [🛏] [💻] [🏊]

MOUNT SHASTA

AAA ▼▼ A-1 Choice Inn M
(530) 926-4811. **$69-$119, 3 day notice.** 1340 S Mount Shasta Blvd. I-5, exit McCloud/SR 89, just n at 1st left, then 1 mi. Ext corridors. **Pets:** Very small, dogs only. $10 daily fee/pet. Designated rooms, service with restrictions, supervision.
[SAVE] [S6] [✕] [🛏] [💻] [🏊]

AAA ▼▼▼ Best Western Tree House Motor Inn SH
(530) 926-3101. **$107-$199.** 111 Morgan Way. I-5, just e. Ext/int corridors. **Pets:** Medium. $10 daily fee/pet. Service with restrictions, supervision.
[SAVE] [S6] [✕] [🌀] [🛏] [💻] [🍴] [🏊]

▼▼ Cold Creek Inn M ❀
(530) 926-9851. **$55-$89, 3 day notice.** 724 N Mt Shasta Blvd. I-5, exit 738. Ext corridors. **Pets:** Other species. $10 daily fee/pet. Designated rooms, service with restrictions, supervision.
[ASK] [S6] [✕] [🛏] [💻]

▼▼ Mt Shasta Ranch Bed & Breakfast BB
(530) 926-3870. **$70-$125, 3 day notice.** 1008 W A Barr Rd. I-5, exit 738 (Central Mount Shasta), 1.5 mi w. Ext/int corridors. **Pets:** Other species. $10 one-time fee/pet. Supervision.
[ASK] [S6] [✕] [🛏] [✕]

AAA ▼▼▼ Swiss Holiday Lodge M ❀
(530) 926-3446. **$60-$80.** 2400 S Mount Shasta Blvd. I-5, exit McCloud/SR 89, just n at 1st left. Ext corridors. **Pets:** Small. $10 daily fee/pet. Service with restrictions, supervision.
[SAVE] [S6] [✕] [🛏] [🏊]

NEEDLES

▼▼▼ Americas Best Value Inn M ❀
(760) 326-4501. **$45-$75.** 1102 E Broadway. I-40, exit 144 (US 95/E Broadway), just sw. Ext corridors. **Pets:** Other species. $10 daily fee/room.
[ASK] [S6] [✕] [🛏] [🏊]

AAA ▼▼▼ Best Western Royal Inn M
(760) 326-5660. **$60-$80, 30 day notice.** 1111 Pashard St. I-40, exit 141 (W Broadway/River Rd). Ext corridors. **Pets:** Accepted.
[SAVE] [S6] [✕] [🛏] [💻]

AAA ▼▼▼ Days Inn & Suites M
(760) 326-5836. **$89-$135.** 1215 Hospitality Ln. I-40, exit 142 (J St), just se. Ext corridors. **Pets:** Other species. $10 daily fee/pet. Supervision.
[SAVE] [S6] [✕] [♿] [🛏] [🏊]

AAA ▼▼ Travelers Inn M
(760) 326-4900. **$60-$120.** 1195 3rd St Hill. I-40, exit 142 (J St), just e, then just s. Ext corridors. **Pets:** Medium, other species. $10 one-time fee/room. Designated rooms, service with restrictions, supervision.
[SAVE] [S6] [✕] [🌀] [🛏] [🏊]

NEVADA CITY

AAA ▼▼▼ Nevada City Inn M
(530) 265-2253. **$65-$109.** 760 Zion St. SR 20 and 49, exit Gold Flat/Ridge Rd, 0.3 mi w, then 0.3 mi n. Ext corridors. **Pets:** Medium, other species. $10 daily fee/pet. Service with restrictions, supervision.
[SAVE] [S6] [✕] [S/M] [🛏] [💻]

NEWARK

AAA ▼▼▼▼ Hilton Newark/Fremont LH
(510) 490-8390. **$79-$199.** 39900 Balentine Dr. I-880, exit Stevenson Blvd, just w. Int corridors. **Pets:** Accepted.
[SAVE] [S6] [✕] [🛏] [💻] [🍴] [🏊] [✕]

▼▼▼▼ Homewood Suites by Hilton SH
(510) 791-7700. **$149-$169.** 39270 Cedar Blvd. I-880, exit Mowry Ave, w to Cedar Blvd, then 0.3 mi s. Int corridors. **Pets:** Accepted.
[ASK] [✕] [♿] [🛏] [💻] [🏊] [✕]

▼▼▼ Residence Inn by Marriott Newark/Silicon Valley SH ❀
(510) 739-6000. **$65-$139.** 34566 Dumbarton Ct. SR 84, exit Newark Blvd, just s. Int corridors. **Pets:** Medium. $100 one-time fee/pet. Service with restrictions.
[ASK] [✕] [S/M] [♿] [💻] [🏊] [✕]

AAA ▼▼▼ Woodfin Suites SH
(510) 795-1200. **$129-$169.** 39150 Cedar Blvd. I-880, exit Mowry Ave, just w, then 0.3 mi s. Ext corridors. **Pets:** Accepted.
[SAVE] [S6] [✕] [♿] [💻] [🏊]

NEWPORT BEACH

▼▼▼ Extended StayAmerica-Orange County/John Wayne Airport SH
(949) 851-2711. **$104-$124.** 4881 Birch St. I-408, exit 8 (MacArthur Blvd), 0.8 mi s, then just e. Int corridors. **Pets:** Accepted.
[ASK] [S6] [✕] [S/M] [🌀] [♿] [🛏] [💻]

The Island Hotel Newport Beach LH 🐾
(949) 759-0808. **$345-$480.** 690 Newport Center Dr. SR 73, exit 14 (MacArthur Blvd) northbound, 3 mi s to San Joaquin Hills Rd, then 0.5 mi w; exit 15 (Jamboree Rd) southbound, 2.5 mi s to San Joaquin Hills Rd, then 0.5 mi e. Int corridors. **Pets:** Small, other species. $100 one-time fee/room. Designated rooms, service with restrictions.

NIPOMO

Kaleidoscope Inn & Gardens B&B BB
(805) 929-5444. **$125-$160, 7 day notice.** 130 E Dana St. US 101, exit 179 (Tefft St), 0.7 mi e, just s on Thompson Rd, then just e. Ext/int corridors. **Pets:** Other species. $50 deposit/pet. Designated rooms, service with restrictions, supervision.

NOVATO

Inn Marin SH 🐾
(415) 883-5952. **$109-$149.** 250 Entrada Dr. US 101, exit Ignacio Blvd, just w, then just n on Enfrente Rd. Ext corridors. **Pets:** Other species. $20 one-time fee/pet. Service with restrictions.

Novato Days Inn SH
(415) 897-7111. **$69-$124.** 8141 Redwood Blvd. US 101, exit San Marin Dr, 1 mi n. Ext corridors. **Pets:** Small, dogs only. $10 daily fee/pet. Designated rooms, no service, supervision.

OAKHURST

Americas Best Value Inn SH
(559) 658-5500. **$49-$259.** 48800 Royal Oaks Dr. SR 41, just s of SR 49. Int corridors. **Pets:** Small. $10 one-time fee/pet. Designated rooms, no service, supervision.

Best Western Yosemite Gateway Inn SH
(559) 683-2378. **$56-$114.** 40530 Hwy 41. SR 49, 0.8 mi n. Ext corridors. **Pets:** Accepted.

Chateau du Sureau CI
(559) 683-6860. **$435-$575, 15 day notice.** 48688 Victoria Ln. Just w of jct SR 41 and 49. Int corridors. **Pets:** Accepted.

Comfort Inn Yosemite Area SH
(559) 683-8282. **$49-$149.** 40489 Hwy 41. SR 49, 0.5 mi n. Ext corridors. **Pets:** Large, other species. $10 daily fee/pet. Service with restrictions, supervision.

Days Inn M
(559) 642-2525. **$50-$150.** 40662 Hwy 41. SR 49, 0.8 mi n. Ext corridors. **Pets:** Accepted.

OAKLAND

Best Western Inn at the Square SH
(510) 452-4565. **$89-$169.** 233 Broadway. I-880, exit Broadway, 0.3 mi w. Int corridors. **Pets:** Small. $100 deposit/room. Service with restrictions, supervision.

Hilton Oakland Airport LH
(510) 635-5000. **$89-$249.** 1 Hegenberger Rd. I-880, exit Hegenberger Rd, 1 mi w; 1.3 mi e of Metropolitan Oakland International Airport. Int corridors. **Pets:** Accepted.

Homewood Suites SH
(510) 663-2700. **$169-$279.** 1103 Embarcadero. I-880, exit 16th Ave/Embarcadero southbound; exit 5th Ave/Embarcadero northbound, just w. Int corridors. **Pets:** Medium, other species. $50 one-time fee/room. Designated rooms, service with restrictions.

Quality Inn SH
(510) 562-4888. **$79-$109.** 8471 Enterprise Way. I-880, exit Hegenberger Rd, just e. Ext corridors. **Pets:** Medium. $100 deposit/room, $10 daily fee/pet.

OCEANO

Oceano Inn M
(805) 473-0032. **$69-$219, 3 day notice.** 1252 Pacific Blvd. On SR 1. Ext corridors. **Pets:** Accepted.

OCEANSIDE

Best Western Marty's Valley Inn M
(760) 757-7700. **$69-$129.** 3240 E Mission Ave. I-5, exit 53 (Misson Ave), 2 mi e. Ext/int corridors. **Pets:** Other species. $10 daily fee/room. Designated rooms, service with restrictions, crate.

Best Western Oceanside Inn Hotel & Suites M
(760) 722-1821. **$69.** 1680 Oceanside Blvd. I-5, exit 52 (Oceanside Blvd), just w. Ext/int corridors. **Pets:** Medium. $50 one-time fee/pet. Service with restrictions, supervision.

Extended StayAmerica-San Diego/Oceanside SH
(760) 439-1499. **$94-$144.** 3190 Vista Way. I-5, exit 51B (SR 78 E) 1.5 mi e to El Camino Real, just n, then just e. Int corridors. **Pets:** Accepted.

La Quinta Inn SH
(760) 450-0730. **$99-$129, 3 day notice.** 937 N Coast Hwy. I-5, exit 54 (Coast Hwy), just w. Int corridors. **Pets:** Accepted.

Motel 6 #4208 M
(760) 721-1543. **$65-$85.** 909 N Coast Hwy. I-5, exit 54B (Coast Hwy), just w. Int corridors. **Pets:** Medium, other species. Service with restrictions, supervision.

OJAI

Best Western Casa Ojai M 🐾
(805) 646-8175. **$104-$195.** 1302 E Ojai Ave. 0.8 mi e on SR 150. Ext corridors. **Pets:** Medium, dogs only. $25 daily fee/pet. Designated rooms, service with restrictions, supervision.

Blue Iguana Inn M
(805) 646-5277. **$99-$169, 7 day notice.** 11794 N Ventura Ave. 2.5 mi w of town on SR 33. Ext corridors. **Pets:** Dogs only. $20 daily fee/pet. Service with restrictions, supervision.

Oakridge Inn M
(805) 649-4018. **$85-$145.** 780 N Ventura Ave. 4 mi s on SR 33; 2 mi e of Lake Casitas; in Oak View. Ext corridors. **Pets:** Medium. $15 one-time fee/pet. Designated rooms, service with restrictions, supervision.

AAA ▼▼▼▼ Ojai Valley Inn & Spa LH ✿
(805) 646-1111. **$400-$3000, 3 day notice.** 905 Country Club Rd. 1 mi
w on SR 150, 0.3 mi s. Ext/int corridors. **Pets:** Medium, dogs only. $50
daily fee/pet. Designated rooms, service with restrictions.
[SAVE] ⊠ [⛟] [📷] [🅿] 🔒 🖥 🍴 ⌦ ⊠

ONTARIO

**AAA ▼▼▼▼ Ayres Inn & Suites Ontario at the Mills
Mall SH**
(909) 987-5940. **$119-$149.** 4395 E Ontario Mills Pkwy. I-10, exit 57
(Milliken Ave), just n, then just e. Int corridors. **Pets:** Accepted.
[SAVE] [⛟] ⊠ 🖥 ⌦

AAA ▼▼▼▼ Best Western InnSuites Ontario SH ✿
(909) 466-9600. **$89-$129.** 3400 Shelby St. I-10, exit 56 (Haven Ave),
just n to Inland Empire Blvd, then just se. Ext corridors. **Pets:** Medium,
other species. $25 one-time fee/pet. Designated rooms, service with restric-
tions, supervision.
[SAVE] [⛟] ⊠ 🔒 🖥 🍴 ⌦ ⊠

AAA ▼▼▼▼ Country Inn & Suites by Carlson M
(909) 937-6000. **$95-$199.** 231 N Vineyard Ave. I-10, exit 54 (Vineyard
Ave), just s. Ext corridors. **Pets:** $50 one-time fee/room. Service with
restrictions.
[SAVE] [⛟] ⊠ [⛟] 🔒 🖥 ⌦

AAA ▼▼▼▼ DoubleTree Hotel Ontario LH
(909) 937-0900. **$99-$219.** 222 N Vineyard Ave. I-10, exit 54 (Vineyard
Ave), 0.4 mi s. Int corridors. **Pets:** Accepted.
[SAVE] ⊠ [⛟] [⛟] 🔒 🖥 🍴 ⌦

**▼▼ Extended StayAmerica-Los Angeles-Ontario
Airport SH**
(909) 944-8900. **$99-$119.** 3990 E Inland Empire Blvd. I-10, exit 56
(Haven Ave), just n, then 0.5 mi e. Int corridors. **Pets:** Accepted.
[ASK] [⛟] ⊠ 🖥

▼▼▼ Hilton Ontario Airport LH
(909) 980-0400. **$69-$179.** 700 N Haven Ave. I-10, exit 56 (Haven
Ave), just n. Int corridors. **Pets:** Small. $75 deposit/pet. Service with
restrictions, supervision.
[ASK] [⛟] ⊠ [⛟] 🔒 🖥 🍴 ⌦

▼▼▼▼ La Quinta Inn & Suites Ontario (Airport) SH
(909) 476-1112. **$119-$169.** 3555 Inland Empire Blvd. I-10, exit 56
(Haven Ave), just n, then just e. Int corridors. **Pets:** Medium. Service
with restrictions.
[ASK] ⊠ [⛟] [⛟] 🔒 🖥 ⌦

▼▼▼▼ Residence Inn by Marriott SH ✿
(909) 937-6788. **$159-$189.** 2025 Convention Center Way. I-10, exit 54
(Vineyard Ave), just s, then 1 blk e. Ext corridors. **Pets:** $75 one-time
fee/room. Service with restrictions, crate.
[ASK] [⛟] ⊠ 🔒 🖥 ⌦ ⊠

AAA ▼▼▼▼ Sheraton Ontario Airport Hotel LH ✿
(909) 937-8000. **$229.** 429 N Vineyard Ave. I-10, exit 54 (Vineyard
Ave), just s. Int corridors. **Pets:** Small, other species. Service with restrictions, crate.
[SAVE] [⛟] ⊠ 🖥 🍴 ⌦

ORLAND

AAA ▼▼▼ Amber Light Inn Motel M ✿
(530) 865-7655. **$54-$62.** 828 Newville Rd. I-5, exit Chico (SR 32), 0.3
mi e. Ext corridors. **Pets:** Small. $10 one-time fee/pet. Service with restric-
tions, supervision.
[SAVE] [⛟] ⊠ 🔒 ⌦

AAA ▼▼▼ Orland Inn M
(530) 865-7632. **$59-$67.** 1052 South St. I-5, exit South St northbound;
exit CR 16 southbound, just e; in Stony Creek Shopping Center. Ext
corridors. **Pets:** Medium, other species. $5 daily fee/pet. Service with
restrictions, supervision.
[SAVE] [⛟] ⊠ [⛟] 🔒 🖥

OROVILLE

AAA ▼▼▼ Americas Best Value Inn M
(530) 533-7070. **$65-$110.** 580 Oro Dam Blvd. SR 70, exit Oroville
Dam Blvd, 0.3 mi e. Ext corridors. **Pets:** Other species. $20 deposit/pet,
$6 daily fee/pet. Designated rooms, service with restrictions, supervision.
[SAVE] [⛟] ⊠ [📷] 🔒 🖥

AAA ▼▼▼ Comfort Inn M
(530) 533-9673. **$80-$161.** 1470 Feather River Blvd. SR 70, exit E
Montgomery St. Int corridors. **Pets:** Dogs only. $100 deposit/room, $10
daily fee/pet. Designated rooms, service with restrictions, supervision.
[SAVE] [⛟] ⊠ [⛟] 🔒 🖥 ⌦ ⊠

AAA ▼▼▼ Days Inn-Oroville M
(530) 533-3297. **$60-$75.** 1745 Feather River Blvd. SR 70, exit E
Montgomery St, just e to Feather River Blvd, then 0.5 mi s. Ext
corridors. **Pets:** Medium. $10 daily fee/pet. Service with restrictions, super-
vision.
[SAVE] [⛟] ⊠ 🔒 🖥 ⌦

AAA ▼▼ Sunset Inn M
(530) 533-8201. **$60-$150.** 1835 Feather River Blvd. SR 70, exit E
Montgomery St, 0.5 mi s. Ext corridors. **Pets:** Accepted.
[SAVE] [⛟] ⊠ 🔒 🖥 ⌦

OXNARD

AAA ▼▼▼▼ Best Western Oxnard Inn M
(805) 483-9581. **$89-$129.** 1156 S Oxnard Blvd. US 101, exit 61 (Rose
Ave) northbound, 3 mi s, then 1 mi se; exit 62B (Oxnard Blvd) southbound, 3.5 mi s. Ext corridors. **Pets:** Accepted.
[SAVE] [⛟] ⊠ [⛟] [📷] [⛟] 🔒 🖥 ⌦

▼▼▼▼ Residence Inn At River Ridge SH
(805) 278-2200. **$129-$149.** 2101 W Vineyard Ave. US 101, exit 62A
(Vineyard Ave), 1.8 mi w. Ext corridors. **Pets:** Accepted.
[ASK] [⛟] ⊠ [⛟] [📷] [⛟] 🔒 🖥 ⌦ ⊠

AAA ▼▼▼ Vagabond Inn Oxnard M ✿
(805) 983-0251. **$79-$299.** 1245 N Oxnard Blvd. US 101, exit 62A
(Vineyard Ave) northbound; exit 62B (Oxnard Blvd) southbound, 1.5
mi s. Ext corridors. **Pets:** Other species. $5 daily fee/pet. Service with
restrictions, supervision.
[SAVE] [⛟] ⊠ [⛟] [📷] [⛟] 🔒 🖥 ⌦

PALMDALE

▼▼▼▼ Residence Inn by Marriott SH
(661) 947-4204. **$180-$225.** 514 W Ave P. SR 14, exit Ave P, just w. Int
corridors. **Pets:** Accepted.
[ASK] [⛟] ⊠ [⛟] [📷] [⛟] 🔒 🖥 ⌦ ⊠

PALM DESERT

AAA ▼▼▼▼ Best Western Palm Desert Resort M
(760) 340-4441. **$79-$199.** 74-695 Hwy 111. I-10, exit 134 (Cook St),
4.4 mi s, then 0.3 mi w. Ext corridors. **Pets:** Other species. $10 daily
fee/room. No service, supervision.
[SAVE] [⛟] ⊠ 🔒 🖥 ⌦ ⊠

AAA ▼▼▼▼ Comfort Suites M
(760) 360-3337. **$99-$249.** 39-585 Washington St. I-10, exit 137
(Washington St), just n. Int corridors. **Pets:** Accepted.
[SAVE] [⛟] ⊠ 🔒 🖥 ⌦ ⊠

Fairfield Inn M
(760) 341-9100. **$69-$189.** 72-322 Hwy 111. I-10, exit 131 (Monterey Ave), 5.7 mi s, then 0.6 mi w. Int corridors. **Pets:** Other species. $75 one-time fee/room. Service with restrictions, supervision.

The Inn at Deep Canyon M
(760) 346-8061. **$47-$127, 3 day notice.** 74470 Abronia Tr. I-10, exit 134 (Cook St), 4.4 mi s to SR 111, 0.5 mi w, then just s on Deep Canyon Rd. Ext corridors. **Pets:** Large, other species. $10 daily fee/pet. Designated rooms, service with restrictions.

International Lodge CO
(760) 346-6161. **$84-$178, 3 day notice.** 74-380 El Camino. I-10, exit 136 (Cook St), 4.4 mi s to SR 111, 0.6 mi w to Panorama Dr, just s, then just e. Ext corridors. **Pets:** Medium, other species. $10 daily fee/pet. Designated rooms, service with restrictions, supervision.

Residence Inn by Marriott SH
(760) 776-0050. **$109-$349.** 38-305 Cook St. I-10, exit 134 (Cook St), 0.8 mi s. Ext corridors. **Pets:** Small, other species. $75 one-time fee/pet. Service with restrictions, supervision.

PALM SPRINGS

Americas Best Value Inn M
(760) 322-3757. **$65-$100.** 1900 N Palm Canyon Dr. 1.4 mi n of Tahquitz Canyon Way. Ext corridors. **Pets:** Dogs only. $10 one-time fee/room. Designated rooms, service with restrictions, supervision.

A Place In The Sun M
(760) 325-0254. **$79-$319, 7 day notice.** 754 San Lorenzo Rd. Just e of Palm Canyon Dr via Mesquite Ave and Random Rd. Ext corridors. **Pets:** Other species. $15 daily fee/pet. Service with restrictions, crate.

Best Western Las Brisas Hotel M
(760) 325-4372. **$59-$229.** 222 S Indian Canyon Dr. 0.3 mi s of Tahquitz Canyon Way. Ext corridors. **Pets:** Dogs only. $10 daily fee/pet, $35 one-time fee/pet. Service with restrictions, supervision.

Casa Cody Country Inn M
(760) 320-9346. **$99-$209, 7 day notice.** 175 S Cahuilla Rd. SR 111, just w on Tahquitz Canyon Way, then just s. Ext corridors. **Pets:** Other species. $15 daily fee/pet. Service with restrictions, supervision.

Hilton Palm Springs Resort LH
(760) 320-6868. **$170-$295, 3 day notice.** 400 E Tahquitz Canyon Way. Just e of Indian Canyon Dr. Int corridors. **Pets:** Accepted.

Hotel California M
(760) 322-8855. **$89-$250, 3 day notice.** 424 E Palm Canyon Dr. 1.5 mi s of Tahquitz Canyon Way. Ext corridors. **Pets:** Small, dogs only. $15 one-time fee/pet. Designated rooms, service with restrictions, supervision.

Hotel Zoso LH
(760) 325-9676. **$139-$339.** 150 S Indian Canyon Dr. Just s of Tahquitz Canyon Way. Int corridors. **Pets:** Medium. $100 one-time fee/room. Supervision.

Quality Inn Resort M
(760) 323-2775. **$59-$259.** 1269 E Palm Canyon Dr. 2.3 mi se of Tahquitz Canyon Way. Ext corridors. **Pets:** Other species. Designated rooms, service with restrictions, supervision.

Ramada Palm Springs M
(760) 320-0555. **$49-$299.** 2000 N Palm Canyon Dr. 1.5 mi n of Tahquitz Canyon Way. Ext/int corridors. **Pets:** Small, dogs only. $10 daily fee/pet. Service with restrictions, supervision.

Shilo Inn Suites M
(760) 320-7676. **$99-$183.** 1875 N Palm Canyon Dr. 1.5 mi n of Tahquitz Canyon Way. Ext corridors. **Pets:** Small, other species. $25 one-time fee/room. Designated rooms, supervision.

Vagabond Inn Palm Springs M
(760) 325-7211. **$60-$99.** 1699 S Palm Canyon Dr. 1.5 mi s of Tahquitz Canyon Way. Ext corridors. **Pets:** Small. $10 daily fee/room. Service with restrictions, supervision.

Wyndham Palm Springs LH
(760) 322-6000. **$99-$119.** 888 Tahquitz Canyon Way. 0.4 mi e of Indian Canyon Dr. Int corridors. **Pets:** Accepted.

PALO ALTO

Crowne Plaza Cabana Hotel SH
(650) 857-0787. **$184.** 4290 El Camino Real. US 101, exit San Antonio Rd, 0.4 mi n. Ext/int corridors. **Pets:** Medium, other species. $50 one-time fee/room. Designated rooms, service with restrictions.

The Westin Palo Alto LH
(650) 321-4422. **Call for rates.** 675 El Camino Real. US 101, exit Embarcadero, 1.8 mi w, then just n on SR 82. Int corridors. **Pets:** Large, dogs only. Service with restrictions, supervision.

PARADISE

Comfort Inn SH
(530) 876-0191. **$75-$115.** 5475 Clark Rd. SR 191, 0.5 mi s of Pearson Rd. Int corridors. **Pets:** Dogs only. $100 deposit/room, $10 daily fee/pet. Designated rooms, service with restrictions, supervision.

Lantern Inn M
(530) 877-5553. **$65-$98.** 5799 Wildwood Ln. 1 blk w off Skyway. Ext corridors. **Pets:** Accepted.

Paradise Inn M
(530) 877-2127. **$59-$99.** 5423 Skyway. 1.5 mi w. Ext corridors. **Pets:** Small, dogs only. $10 daily fee/pet. Designated rooms, no service, supervision.

Ponderosa Gardens Motel M
(530) 872-9094. **$75-$95.** 7010 Skyway. 2 blks e; center. Ext corridors. **Pets:** Other species. $10 daily fee/pet. Designated rooms, service with restrictions, supervision.

PASO ROBLES

Hampton Inn & Suites SH
(805) 226-9988. **$125-$209.** 212 Alexa Ct. US 101, exit 231B (SR 46/Fresno/Bakersfield), just sw. Int corridors. **Pets:** Small. $50 deposit/room. Service with restrictions, supervision.

PATTERSON

AAA ▼▼▼▼ Best Western Villa Del Lago Inn **SH**
(209) 892-5300. **$79-$139.** 2959 Speno Dr. I-5, exit Sperry Rd, just e. Int corridors. **Pets:** Medium. Service with restrictions, supervision.

[SAVE] [S‑D] [X] [■] [▣] [Y1] [≈] [X]

PHELAN

AAA ▼▼▼ Best Western Cajon Pass **M**
(760) 249-6777. **$69-$129.** 8317 Hwy 138. I-15, exit 131 (SR 138/Palmdale), just w. Ext corridors. **Pets:** Accepted.

[SAVE] [X] [■] [▣] [≈]

PIRU

▼▼▼▼ Heritage Valley Inn **CI**
(805) 521-0700. **$135-$195, 3 day notice.** 691 N Main St. SR 126, 0.7 mi n. Int corridors. **Pets:** Other species. $100 deposit/pet. Service with restrictions, supervision.

[ASK] [S‑D] [X] [Y1]

PISMO BEACH

▼▼▼▼ Cliffs Resort **SH**
(805) 773-5000. **$134-$259, 3 day notice.** 2757 Shell Beach Rd. US 101, exit 193 (Spyglass Dr) northbound; exit 193 (Shell Beach Rd) southbound, just w, then just n. Int corridors. **Pets:** Accepted.

[ASK] [S‑D] [X] [≈M] [⊘] [≈] [■] [▣] [Y1] [≈] [X]

▼▼▼▼ Cottage Inn by the Sea **M** ☙
(805) 773-4617. **$109-$399.** 2351 Price St. US 101, exit 191B (Shell Beach Rd) northbound, just w, 0.5 mi s; exit 191B (Price St) southbound, just w, then just s. Ext corridors. **Pets:** Large, other species. $10 daily fee/room. Service with restrictions, supervision.

[ASK] [S‑D] [X] [≈M] [⊘] [≈] [■] [▣] [≈] [K]

AAA ▼▼▼▼ Oxford Suites **SH** ☙
(805) 773-3773. **$109-$249.** 651 Five Cities Dr. US 101, exit 189 (4th St), just w, then just n. Ext corridors. **Pets:** Medium. $10 daily fee/pet. Designated rooms, service with restrictions, supervision.

[SAVE] [S‑D] [X] [≈M] [⊘] [■] [▣] [≈] [X]

▼▼▼▼ Sandcastle Inn **M**
(805) 773-2422. **$139-$459.** 100 Stimson Ave. US 101, exit 190 (Price St) northbound, 0.3 mi s, then just w; exit 190B (Hinds Ave) southbound, just w, then just s. Ext/int corridors. **Pets:** $10 daily fee/pet. Designated rooms, service with restrictions, supervision.

[ASK] [S‑D] [X] [≈M] [⊘] [≈] [■] [▣]

▼▼ Sea Gypsy Motel **CO**
(805) 773-1801. **$55-$175.** 1020 Cypress St. US 101, exit 191A (Wadsworth Ave) northbound, 0.3 mi w to Cypress St, then just s; exit 191A (SR 1) southbound, just w on Wadsworth Ave, then just s. Ext/int corridors. **Pets:** Other species. $15 daily fee/pet. Service with restrictions, supervision.

[X] [■] [▣] [≈] [K]

AAA ▼▼▼ Shell Beach Inn **M**
(805) 773-4373. **$83-$165.** 653 Shell Beach Rd. US 101, exit 191B (Shell Beach Rd) northbound, just w, then 1.2 mi s; exit 191B (Price St) southbound, just w, then 1 mi n. Ext corridors. **Pets:** Accepted.

[SAVE] [S‑D] [X] [■] [▣] [≈] [K]

▼▼▼▼ Spyglass Inn **SH**
(805) 773-4855. **$99-$399.** 2705 Spyglass Dr. US 101, exit 193 (Spyglass Dr) northbound; exit 193 (Shell Beach Rd) southbound, just w, then just n. Ext corridors. **Pets:** Dogs only. $15 daily fee/pet. Designated rooms, service with restrictions, supervision.

[ASK] [S‑D] [X] [≈M] [⊘] [≈] [■] [▣] [Y1] [≈] [K]

PLACENTIA

▼▼▼▼ Residence Inn by Marriott **SH**
(714) 996-0555. **$119-$249.** 700 W Kimberly Ave. SR 57, exit 6 (Orangethorpe Ave) southbound; exit 6A (Orangethorpe Ave) northbound, just w, just n on Placentia Ave, then just e. Ext corridors. **Pets:** Medium, other species. $100 one-time fee/room. Service with restrictions.

[S‑D] [X] [■] [▣] [≈] [X]

PLACERVILLE

AAA ▼▼▼▼ Best Western Placerville Inn **SH**
(530) 622-9100. **$89-$399.** 6850 Green Leaf Dr. US 50, exit Missouri Flat Rd S, 0.5 mi w. Int corridors. **Pets:** Accepted.

[SAVE] [S‑D] [X] [≈M] [■] [▣] [≈]

AAA ▼ Mother Lode Motel **M**
(530) 622-0895. **$52-$78, 3 day notice.** 1940 Broadway. 2 mi e; adjacent to US 50, exit Point View Dr. Ext corridors. **Pets:** Dogs only. $10 daily fee/pet. Designated rooms, service with restrictions, supervision.

[SAVE] [X] [≈M] [⊘] [■] [▣] [≈]

PLEASANT HILL

▼▼▼▼ Residence Inn by Marriott-Pleasant Hill **SH** ☙
(925) 689-1010. **$179-$259.** 700 Ellinwood Way. I-680, exit Willow Pass Rd W to S Contra Costa Blvd, e on Ellinwood Dr, then n. Ext/int corridors. **Pets:** Large, other species. $100 one-time fee/room. Service with restrictions, supervision.

[ASK] [S‑D] [X] [▣] [≈] [X]

▼▼▼▼ Summerfield Suites by Wyndham-Pleasant Hill **SH** ☙
(925) 934-3343. **$99-$299.** 2611 Contra Costa Blvd. I-680, exit Contra Costa Blvd, then w. Int corridors. **Pets:** Medium. $150 one-time fee/room. Service with restrictions, crate.

[ASK] [X] [≈M] [⊘] [■] [≈] [X]

PLEASANTON

▼▼▼▼ Best Western Pleasanton Inn **M**
(925) 463-1300. **$69-$109, 7 day notice.** 5375 Owens Ct. I-580, exit Hopyard Rd, just s. Ext corridors. **Pets:** Medium, dogs only. $100 deposit/room, $20 daily fee/pet. Designated rooms, service with restrictions, supervision.

[ASK] [S‑D] [X] [■] [▣] [≈] [X]

▼▼▼▼ Extended Stay Deluxe **SH**
(925) 730-0000. **$100-$110.** 4555 Chabot Dr. I-580, exit Hopyard Rd, 1 mi s, e on Stoneridge Dr, then s. Int corridors. **Pets:** Accepted.

[ASK] [S‑D] [X] [▣] [≈]

AAA ▼▼▼▼ Larkspur Landing Home Suite Hotel Pleasanton **SH**
(925) 463-1212. **$164-$180.** 5535 Johnson Dr. I-580, exit Hopyard Rd S, w on Owen. Int corridors. **Pets:** Medium. $75 one-time fee/pet. Designated rooms, service with restrictions, crate.

[SAVE] [S‑D] [X] [▣]

AAA ▼▼▼▼ Residence Inn by Marriott **SH**
(925) 227-0500. **$83-$149.** 11920 Dublin Canyon Rd. I-580, exit Foothill Blvd S, then w. Int corridors. **Pets:** Accepted.

[SAVE] [S‑D] [X] [≈M] [⊘] [■] [▣] [≈] [X]

▼▼▼▼ Summerfield Suites-Pleasanton **SH**
(925) 730-0070. **$89-$299.** 4545 Chabot Dr. I-580, exit Hopyard Rd, 1 mi s, e on Stoneridge Dr, then s. Ext corridors. **Pets:** Medium. $150 one-time fee/room. Service with restrictions, crate.

[ASK] [X] [≈M] [⊘] [▣] [≈] [X]

AAA ▼▼▼▼ Wyndham Garden Hotel-Pleasanton **SH**
(925) 463-3330. **$153-$180.** 5990 Stoneridge Mall Rd. Jct I-580 and 680, 0.5 mi sw; I-580, exit Foothill Rd, 0.3 mi s, then 0.3 mi e on Canyon Way. Int corridors. **Pets:** Accepted.

[SAVE] [S‑D] [X] [■] [▣] [Y1] [≈] [X]

POLLOCK PINES

Best Western Stagecoach Inn M
(530) 644-2029. **$118-$138.** 5940 Pony Express Tr. US 50, exit Pollock Pines eastbound, 1 mi e; exit Sly Park westbound. Ext corridors. **Pets:** Accepted.

Westhaven Inn M
(530) 644-7800. **$79-$89.** 5658 Pony Express Tr. US 50, exit Pollock Pines, just n. Ext corridors. **Pets:** Small. $11 one-time fee/pet. Designated rooms, service with restrictions, supervision.

PORTERVILLE

Best Western Porterville Inn SH
(559) 781-7411. **$99-$129.** 350 W Montgomery Ave. SR 65, 0.8 mi e, just s on Jaye St, then just e; adjacent to SR 190. Int corridors. **Pets:** Accepted.

PORTOLA

Sleepy Pines Motel M
(530) 832-4291. **$64-$99.** 74631 Hwy 70. On SR 70. Ext corridors. **Pets:** Dogs only. Service with restrictions, supervision.

QUINCY

Pine Hill Motel M
(530) 283-1670. **$75-$85, 3 day notice.** 42075 Hwy 70. 1 mi n. Ext corridors. **Pets:** Medium. $5 daily fee/pet. Service with restrictions, supervision.

RAMONA

Ramona Valley Inn M
(760) 789-6433. **$68-$88.** 416 Main St. On SR 78, 0.5 mi e of jct SR 67. Ext corridors. **Pets:** Very small, dogs only. $100 one-time fee/pet. Designated rooms, service with restrictions, supervision.

RANCHO CORDOVA

Best Western, The Venetian Court SH
(916) 635-4040. **$69-$119.** 11269 Point East Dr. US 50, exit Sunrise Blvd S; 12 mi e of Sacramento. Int corridors. **Pets:** Accepted.

Crossland Studios-Sacramento-Point East Dr SH
(916) 859-0280. **$60.** 11299 Point East Dr. US 50, exit Sunrise Blvd, just s, then 9 mi e of Sacramento. Ext corridors. **Pets:** Accepted.

Days Inn M
(916) 351-1213. **$69-$99.** 12249 Folsom Blvd. US 50, exit Hazel Ave, just s. Ext corridors. **Pets:** Accepted.

Extended StayAmerica-Sacramento-White Rock Rd SH
(916) 635-2363. **$79-$89.** 10721 White Rock Rd. US 50, exit Zinfandel Dr, just s. Ext corridors. **Pets:** Accepted.

Hawthorn Suites SH
(916) 351-9192. **$129-$139.** 12180 Tributary Point Dr. US 50, exit Hazel Ave, just n. Int corridors. **Pets:** Medium, other species. $50 one-time fee/room. Service with restrictions, supervision.

Residence Inn by Marriott SH
(916) 851-1550. **$205-$225.** 2779 Prospect Park Dr. US 50, exit Zinfandel Dr. Int corridors. **Pets:** Accepted.

Wingate Inn SH
(916) 858-8680. **$79-$109.** 10745 Gold Center Dr. US 50, exit Zinfandel Dr, just s. Int corridors. **Pets:** Other species. $25 deposit/room. Service with restrictions, supervision.

RANCHO CUCAMONGA

Homewood Suites SH
(909) 481-6480. **Call for rates.** 11433 Mission Vista Dr. I-15, exit 110 (4th St), just w to Richmond Pl, just n, then just w. Int corridors. **Pets:** Medium. $75 one-time fee/room. Service with restrictions, crate.

Marriott TownePlace Suites SH
(909) 466-1100. **$99-$169.** 9625 Milliken Ave. I-10, exit 57 (Milliken Ave), 0.6 mi n. Int corridors. **Pets:** Other species. $100 one-time fee/room. Service with restrictions, supervision.

RANCHO MIRAGE

The Westin Mission Hills Resort LH
(760) 328-5955. **$129-$450, 7 day notice.** 71-333 Dinah Shore Dr. I-10, exit 130 (Ramon Rd), 0.3 mi w on Ramon Rd, 1 mi s on Bob Hope Dr, then 0.6 mi w. Ext corridors. **Pets:** Accepted.

RED BLUFF

Best Western Antelope Inn M
(530) 527-8882. **$80-$165.** 203 Antelope Blvd. I-5, exit SR 36 W (Central District). Int corridors. **Pets:** Large, other species. $7 daily fee/pet. Service with restrictions, supervision.

Days Inn & Suites M
(530) 527-6130. **$60-$66.** 5 John Sutter St. I-5, exit 647 northbound, just e; exit 647A southbound, 0.4 mi e. Ext corridors. **Pets:** Accepted.

Lamplighter Lodge M
(530) 527-1150. **$85-$95.** 210 S Main St. I-5, exit business loop. Ext corridors. **Pets:** Medium, dogs only. $10 daily fee/pet. Service with restrictions, supervision.

Sportsman Lodge M
(530) 527-2888. **$85-$170, 3 day notice.** 768 Antelope Blvd. I-5, exit SR 36 W (Central District), 1.5 mi e. Ext corridors. **Pets:** $7 daily fee/pet. No service, supervision.

Super 8–Red Bluff M
(530) 529-2028. **$60-$110, 7 day notice.** 30 Gilmore Rd. I-5, exit 649 (Central Red Bluff), just sw on SR 36. Ext corridors. **Pets:** Medium, other species. $7 daily fee/pet. Service with restrictions, supervision.

Travelodge Red Bluff M
(530) 527-6020. **$60-$110.** 38 Antelope Blvd. I-5, exit 649 (Central Red Bluff), just w. Ext corridors. **Pets:** Medium. $7 daily fee/pet. Service with restrictions, supervision.

REDCREST

Redcrest Resort 🅲🅰
(707) 722-4208. **$60-$140, 14 day notice.** 26459 Ave of the Giants. US 101, exit Redcrest southbound; exit Redcrest/Holmes northbound, just e, then just n. Ext corridors. **Pets:** $6 daily fee/pet. Designated rooms, no service, supervision.

REDDING

AmeriHost Inn & Suites-Redding SH
(530) 722-9100. **$99-$160.** 2600 Larkspur Ln. I-5, exit Cypress Ave, just e, then right at Larkspur Ln. Int corridors. **Pets:** Accepted.

Best Western Hospitality House SH
(530) 241-6464. **$59-$119.** 532 N Market St. I-5, exit Lake Blvd northbound, just w, 0.5 mi to Market St, then 0.5 mi s; exit Market St southbound, 2 mi s. Ext corridors. **Pets:** Medium, dogs only. $10 daily fee/pet. Designated rooms, service with restrictions, supervision.

Grand Manor Inn & Suites SH
(530) 221-4472. **$87-$110.** 850 Mistletoe Ln. I-5, exit Cypress Ave E, 0.8 mi n on Hilltop Dr. Int corridors. **Pets:** Medium. $10 daily fee/pet. Designated rooms, service with restrictions, supervision.

Holiday Inn SH
(530) 221-7500. **$119-$145.** 1900 Hilltop Dr. I-5, exit Hilltop Dr, just s. Int corridors. **Pets:** Dogs only. $100 deposit/room, $10 daily fee/pet. Designated rooms, service with restrictions, supervision.

Holiday Inn Express SH
(530) 241-5500. **$94-$199.** 1080 Twin View Blvd. I-5, exit Twin View Blvd, just w. Int corridors. **Pets:** Accepted.

La Quinta Inn Redding SH
(530) 221-8200. **$86-$123.** 2180 Hilltop Dr. I-5, exit Cypress Ave E, 0.5 mi n. Int corridors. **Pets:** Medium. Service with restrictions.

Oxford Suites SH ❧
(530) 221-0100. **$99-$129.** 1967 Hilltop Dr. I-5, exit Cypress Ave E, 0.5 mi n. Ext/int corridors. **Pets:** Medium. $25 one-time fee/room. Designated rooms, service with restrictions, supervision.

Quality Inn M
(530) 221-6530. **$85-$179.** 2059 Hilltop Dr. I-5, exit Cypress Ave E, 0.3 mi n. Ext corridors. **Pets:** Medium. $15 one-time fee/pet. Service with restrictions, supervision.

Ramada Limited SH ❧
(530) 246-2222. **$110-$200.** 1286 Twin View Blvd. I-5, exit Twin View Blvd E, just n. Int corridors. **Pets:** Medium. $20 daily fee/pet. Designated rooms, service with restrictions.

Redding Travelodge SH ❧
(530) 243-5291. **$72-$120.** 540 N Market St. I-5, exit Lake Blvd northbound, just w, 0.5 mi to Market St, then 0.5 mi s; exit Market St southbound, 2 mi s. Ext corridors. **Pets:** Other species. $8 daily fee/pet. Designated rooms, service with restrictions, supervision.

Red Lion Hotel Redding SH
(530) 221-8700. **$90-$135.** 1830 Hilltop Dr. I-5, exit SR 44/ Hilltop Dr. Int corridors. **Pets:** Medium. $50 deposit/pet. Designated rooms, service with restrictions, supervision.

REDLANDS

Best Western Sandman Motel M
(909) 793-2001. **$59-$129.** 1120 W Colton Ave. I-10, exit 77C (Tennessee St) eastbound; exit 77B (Tennessee St) westbound, just s, then just e. Ext corridors. **Pets:** Accepted.

Dynasty Suites-Redlands M
(909) 793-6648. **$86-$119.** 1235 W Colton Ave. I-10, exit 77C (Tennessee St) eastbound; 77B (Tennessee St) westbound, just s, then just w. Ext corridors. **Pets:** Accepted.

REDWAY

Dean Creek Resort M
(707) 923-2555. **$65-$135.** 4112 Redwood Dr. US 101, exit Redwood Dr northbound; exit Redway/Shelter Cove southbound, just w. Ext corridors. **Pets:** Dogs only. $6 one-time fee/pet. Service with restrictions, supervision.

REDWOOD CITY

Sofitel San Francisco Bay LH
(650) 598-9000. **$125-$599.** 223 Twin Dolphin Dr. US 101, exit Marine Pkwy E, 0.5 mi s. Int corridors. **Pets:** Accepted.

REEDLEY

Edgewater Inn M
(559) 637-7777. **$70-$75.** 1977 W Manning Ave. 12 mi e of SR 99 via Manning Ave. Ext corridors. **Pets:** Dogs only. $8 daily fee/pet. Service with restrictions, supervision.

RIALTO

Best Western Empire Inn M
(909) 877-0690. **$90-$120, 3 day notice.** 475 W Valley Blvd. I-10, exit 68 (Riverside Ave), just n, then 0.5 mi w. Ext corridors. **Pets:** Medium. $30 deposit/pet, $20 daily fee/pet. Service with restrictions, supervision.

RIDGECREST

Best Western China Lake Inn M
(760) 371-2300. **$90-$120.** 400 S China Lake Blvd. On US 395 business route. Ext corridors. **Pets:** Small, dogs only. $10 one-time fee/pet. Designated rooms, service with restrictions, crate.

Carriage Inn M
(760) 446-7910. **$89.** 901 N China Lake Blvd. On SR 178 and US 395 business route. Ext corridors. **Pets:** Small, dogs only. $25 daily fee/room. Designated rooms, service with restrictions, crate.

Comfort Inn M
(760) 375-9731. **$90-$100.** 507 S China Lake Blvd. On US 395 business route. Ext corridors. **Pets:** Small, dogs only. $10 one-time fee/pet. Designated rooms, service with restrictions, supervision.

Econo Lodge M
(760) 446-2551. **$70-$88.** 201 Inyokern Rd. On SR 178 and US 395 business route, just w of China Lake Blvd. Ext corridors. **Pets:** Small, dogs only. Service with restrictions, supervision.

🔺 ▼▼▼▼ **Heritage Inn & Suites** 🆂🅷
(760) 446-7951. **$75-$91.** 1050 N Norma. On US 395 business route, just w. Int corridors. **Pets:** Other species. $100 deposit/room. Service with restrictions, supervision.
⟦SAVE⟧ ⟦S⟧ ⟦✕⟧ ⟦🌙⟧ ⟦🖥⟧ ⟦🍴⟧ ⟦≋⟧

▼▼ **Rodeway Inn** 🅼
(760) 384-3575. **$50-$80.** 131 W Upjohn Ave. On US 395 business route, just w. Ext corridors. **Pets:** Accepted.
⟦ASK⟧ ⟦S⟧ ⟦✕⟧ ⟦🖥⟧ ⟦≋⟧

🔺 ▼▼▼ **Vagabond Inn** 🅼
(760) 375-2220. **$65-$70.** 426 China Lake Blvd. On US 395 business route. Ext corridors. **Pets:** Accepted.
⟦SAVE⟧ ⟦S⟧ ⟦✕⟧ ⟦🌙⟧ ⟦🖥⟧ ⟦≋⟧

RIO DELL

🔺 ▼ **Humboldt Gables Motel** 🅼
(707) 764-5609. **$50-$85.** 40 W Davis St. US 101, exit Wildwood Ave, 0.5 mi w. Ext corridors. **Pets:** Small, dogs only. $10 daily fee/pet. Service with restrictions, supervision.
⟦SAVE⟧ ⟦S⟧ ⟦✕⟧ ⟦🌙⟧ ⟦🖥⟧ ⟦🐾⟧

RIPON

▼▼▼▼ **La Quinta Inn & Suites** 🆂🅷
(209) 599-8999. **$70-$100, 7 day notice.** 1524 Colony Rd. SR 99, exit Jack Tone Rd, just e. Int corridors. **Pets:** Other species. No service, supervision.
⟦ASK⟧ ⟦S⟧ ⟦✕⟧ ⟦🖥⟧ ⟦≋⟧

RIVERSIDE

🔺 ▼▼▼ **Best Western of Riverside** 🅼
(951) 359-0770. **$79-$199.** 10518 Magnolia Ave. SR 91, exit 56 (Tyler St), 0.5 mi nw, then 0.3 mi sw. Ext corridors. **Pets:** Accepted.
⟦SAVE⟧ ⟦S⟧ ⟦✕⟧ ⟦🖥⟧ ⟦≋⟧

ROCKLIN

🔺 ▼▼▼ **Heritage Inn Express, Rocklin** 🆂🅷
(916) 632-3366. **$79-$89.** 4480 Rocklin Rd. I-80, exit Rocklin Rd. Int corridors. **Pets:** $25 one-time fee/room. Service with restrictions, supervision.
⟦SAVE⟧ ⟦S⟧ ⟦✕⟧ ⟦🖥⟧ ⟦≋⟧

🔺 ▼▼▼ **Howard Johnson Hotel** 🆂🅷 🐾
(916) 624-4500. **$89-$149.** 4420 Rocklin Rd. I-80 E, exit Rocklin Rd. Int corridors. **Pets:** Small. $100 deposit/room, $25 one-time fee/room. Service with restrictions, supervision.
⟦SAVE⟧ ⟦S⟧ ⟦✕⟧ ⟦🌙⟧ ⟦🖥⟧ ⟦≋⟧

🔺 ▼▼▼ **Rocklin Park Hotel** 🆂🅷
(916) 630-9400. **$139-$159.** 5450 China Garden Rd. I-80, exit Rocklin Rd, just e, s on Aguilar Rd, then e. Int corridors. **Pets:** Other species. $75 one-time fee/room. Designated rooms, service with restrictions, supervision.
⟦SAVE⟧ ⟦S⟧ ⟦✕⟧ ⟦🌙⟧ ⟦🖥⟧ ⟦🍴⟧ ⟦≋⟧

ROSEVILLE

🔺 ▼▼▼ **Best Western Roseville Inn** 🅼
(916) 782-4434. **$80-$85, 7 day notice.** 220 Harding Blvd. I-80, exit Douglas Blvd, just w, then just n. Ext corridors. **Pets:** $10 daily fee/pet. Service with restrictions, supervision.
⟦SAVE⟧ ⟦S⟧ ⟦✕⟧ ⟦🖥⟧ ⟦≋⟧

▼▼▼ **Extended StayAmerica-Sacramento-Roseville** 🆂🅷
(916) 781-9001. **$104-$114.** 1000 Lead Hill Blvd. I-80, exit Douglas Blvd W, just n. Int corridors. **Pets:** Accepted.
⟦ASK⟧ ⟦S⟧ ⟦✕⟧ ⟦🖥⟧ ⟦≋⟧

🔺 ▼▼▼ **Heritage Inn Express** 🅼
(916) 782-4466. **$75-$80.** 204 Harding Blvd. I-80, exit Douglas Blvd, just w, then just n. Ext corridors. **Pets:** Accepted.
⟦SAVE⟧ ⟦S⟧ ⟦✕⟧ ⟦🌙⟧ ⟦🖥⟧ ⟦≋⟧

▼▼▼▼ **Homewood Suites by Hilton** 🆂🅷
(916) 783-7455. **$164-$184.** 401 Creekside Ridge Ct. I-80, exit SR 65, 1 mi w to Galleria Blvd, 0.5 mi s to Antelope Creek Rd, then just e to Creekside Ridge Ct. Int corridors. **Pets:** Accepted.
⟦ASK⟧ ⟦S⟧ ⟦✕⟧ ⟦🌙⟧ ⟦🖥⟧ ⟦≋⟧

🔺 ▼▼▼ **Orchid Suites** 🆂🅷
(916) 784-2222. **$89-$169.** 130 N Sunrise Ave. I-80, exit Douglas Blvd, just e, then 0.3 mi n. Ext/int corridors. **Pets:** Accepted.
⟦SAVE⟧ ⟦S⟧ ⟦✕⟧ ⟦🌙⟧ ⟦🖥⟧ ⟦≋⟧

▼▼▼▼ **Residence Inn by Marriott** 🆂🅷
(916) 772-5500. **$175-$205.** 1930 Taylor Rd. I-80, exit Eureka-Taylor Rd, just s. Int corridors. **Pets:** Accepted.
⟦ASK⟧ ⟦S⟧ ⟦✕⟧ ⟦🌙⟧ ⟦🖥⟧ ⟦≋⟧ ⟦✕⟧

SACRAMENTO

🔺 ▼▼▼ **Best Western Expo Inn** 🆂🅷
(916) 922-9833. **$95.** 1413 Howe Ave. Jct SR 16 and US 50, exit Howe Ave, 2.5 mi n. Int corridors. **Pets:** Medium. $50 one-time fee/room. Designated rooms, service with restrictions, crate.
⟦SAVE⟧ ⟦S⟧ ⟦✕⟧ ⟦🌙⟧ ⟦🖥⟧ ⟦≋⟧

🔺 ▼▼▼▼ **Best Western Harbor Inn & Suites** 🆂🅷
(916) 371-2100. **$69-$159.** 1250 Halyard Dr. 4 mi w; exit Business Rt I-80 via Harbor Blvd. Ext/int corridors. **Pets:** Accepted.
⟦SAVE⟧ ⟦S⟧ ⟦✕⟧ ⟦🌙⟧ ⟦🖥⟧ ⟦≋⟧

▼▼▼ **Canterbury Inn** 🅼
(916) 927-0927. **$59-$89.** 1900 Canterbury Rd. Business Rt I-80, exit Exposition Blvd, 0.4 mi w to Leisure Ln; just n of SR 160. Ext corridors. **Pets:** Accepted.
⟦ASK⟧ ⟦S⟧ ⟦✕⟧ ⟦🌙⟧ ⟦🖥⟧ ⟦≋⟧

▼▼▼ **Clarion Hotel Mansion Inn** 🆂🅷
(916) 444-8000. **$89-$129.** 700 16th St. On SR 160, 1.3 mi n of Business Rt I-80, exit 16th St. Int corridors. **Pets:** Medium. $50 one-time fee/pet. Service with restrictions, supervision.
⟦ASK⟧ ⟦S⟧ ⟦✕⟧ ⟦🌙⟧ ⟦🌙⟧ ⟦🖥⟧ ⟦🍴⟧ ⟦≋⟧

🔺 ▼▼▼ **Clarion Hotel Near Calexpo** 🆂🅷
(916) 487-7600. **$79.** 2600 Auburn Blvd. Business Rt I-80, exit Fulton Ave. Int corridors. **Pets:** Accepted.
⟦SAVE⟧ ⟦S⟧ ⟦✕⟧ ⟦🌙⟧ ⟦🖥⟧ ⟦🍴⟧ ⟦≋⟧

▼▼▼ **DoubleTree Hotel** 🅻🅷
(916) 929-8855. **$95-$250.** 2001 Point West Way. 1 blk off Business Rt I-80, exit via Arden Way. Int corridors. **Pets:** Accepted.
⟦ASK⟧ ⟦S⟧ ⟦✕⟧ ⟦🌙⟧ ⟦🖥⟧ ⟦🍴⟧ ⟦≋⟧

🔺 ▼▼ **Econo Lodge** 🅼
(916) 443-6631. **$60-$129.** 711 16th St. Business Rt I-80, exit 15th St eastbound; exit 16th St westbound; I-5, exit J St (Old Sacramento). Ext corridors. **Pets:** $6 daily fee/pet. Designated rooms, service with restrictions.
⟦SAVE⟧ ⟦S⟧ ⟦✕⟧ ⟦🌙⟧ ⟦🖥⟧

▼▼ **Extended StayAmerica-Sacramento-Arden Way** 🆂🅷
(916) 921-9942. **$89-$99.** 2100 Harvard St. I-80 business route, exit Arden Way, just w. Ext corridors. **Pets:** Accepted.
⟦ASK⟧ ⟦S⟧ ⟦🖥⟧

🔺 ▼▼▼ **Holiday Inn Express Sacramento** 🆂🅷
(916) 444-4436. **$109-$159.** 728 16th St. On SR 160. Int corridors. **Pets:** Medium. $50 one-time fee/pet. Service with restrictions, supervision.
⟦SAVE⟧ ⟦S⟧ ⟦✕⟧ ⟦🌙⟧ ⟦🖥⟧ ⟦≋⟧

▼▼▼ Homestead Studio Suites Hotel-Sacramento-S. Natomas M
(916) 564-7500. **$100-$110.** 2810 Gateway Oaks Dr. I-5, exit W El Camino Ave, just w, then 0.4 mi n. Ext corridors. **Pets:** Accepted.

(ASK) (S🐾) (✕) (🚾) (🖥️) (💻)

▼▼ Host Airport Hotel SH
(916) 922-8071. **$90-$180.** 6945 Airport Blvd. 11 mi nw of state capitol; 6 mi nw of I-80; off I-5. Ext corridors. **Pets:** Accepted.

(ASK) (S🐾) (✕) (🚾) (💻)

▼▼▼ La Quinta Inn Sacramento (Downtown) M
(916) 448-8100. **$95-$138.** 200 Jibboom St. I-5, exit Richards Blvd W, 2.3 mi nw of Business Loop I-80. Ext corridors. **Pets:** Medium. Service with restrictions.

(ASK) (✕) (🚾) (🖥️) (💻) (🏊)

▼▼▼ La Quinta Inn Sacramento (North) M
(916) 348-0900. **$102-$132.** 4604 Madison Ave. I-80, exit Madison Ave, 0.3 mi e. Ext corridors. **Pets:** Medium. Service with restrictions.

(ASK) (✕) (🚾) (💻) (🏊)

▲▲▲ ▼▼▼ Larkspur Landing Home Suite Hotel Sacramento SH
(916) 646-1212. **$99-$179.** 555 Howe Ave. US 50, exit Howe Ave, 1.5 mi n. Int corridors. **Pets:** Medium. $75 one-time fee/pet. Designated rooms, service with restrictions, crate.

(SAVE) (S🐾) (✕) (🚾) (🖥️) (🖥️) (💻)

▼▼▼ Marriott Residence Inn SH
(916) 920-9111. **$159.** 1530 Howe Ave. 2.5 mi n of jct SR 16 and US 50, exit Howe Ave. Ext corridors. **Pets:** Accepted.

(ASK) (S🐾) (✕) (🚾) (🐾) (🖥️) (💻) (🏊)

▲▲▲ ▼▼▼ Quality Inn Notomas SH
(916) 927-7117. **$65-$135.** 3796 Northgate Blvd. I-80, exit Northgate Blvd, just s. Ext corridors. **Pets:** Medium. $25 daily fee/pet. Designated rooms, service with restrictions, supervision.

(SAVE) (S🐾) (✕) (🚾) (🖥️) (💻) (🏊)

▲▲▲ ▼▼▼ Radisson Hotel SH
(916) 922-2020. **$109-$189.** 500 Leisure Ln. Business Rt I-80, exit Exposition Blvd, 0.4 mi w. Ext corridors. **Pets:** Accepted.

(SAVE) (S🐾) (✕) (🚾) (🐾) (🖥️) (💻) (🍴) (🏊) (✕)

▲▲▲ ▼▼▼ Ramada Limited-Discovery Park SH
(916) 442-6971. **$75-$110.** 350 Bercut Dr. I-5, exit E Richards Blvd, 2.3 mi nw of Business Loop I-80. Ext corridors. **Pets:** Medium. $20 daily fee/room. Designated rooms, service with restrictions, supervision.

(SAVE) (S🐾) (✕) (🚾) (🖥️) (💻) (🏊)

▼▼▼ Red Lion Hotel Sacramento SH
(916) 922-8041. **$149-$169.** 1401 Arden Way. I-80, exit Arden Way; in Arden Fair Shopping Plaza. Ext/int corridors. **Pets:** Small, other species. $25 one-time fee/pet. Designated rooms, service with restrictions, supervision.

(ASK) (S🐾) (✕) (🚾) (🖥️) (💻) (🍴) (🏊)

▼▼▼ Residence Inn by Marriott M
(916) 649-1300. **$115-$189.** 2410 W El Camino Ave. I-5, exit W El Camino Ave. Ext corridors. **Pets:** Other species. $100 one-time fee/room. Service with restrictions.

(ASK) (S🐾) (✕) (🚾) (🖥️) (🖥️) (💻) (🏊) (✕)

▲▲▲ ▼▼▼ Vagabond Executive Inn Old Town SH
(916) 446-1481. **$99-$149.** 909 3rd St. I-5, exit J St (Old Sacramento); 8 blks w of state capitol. Ext corridors. **Pets:** Small. $10 daily fee/pet. Designated rooms, service with restrictions, supervision.

(SAVE) (S🐾) (✕) (🚾) (🐾) (🖥️) (💻) (🏊)

SALINAS

▲▲▲ ▼▼▼ Ramada Limited M
(831) 424-4801. **$59-$299, 7 day notice.** 109 John St. US 101, exit John St, 0.7 mi w. Ext corridors. **Pets:** Accepted.

(SAVE) (S🐾) (✕) (🖥️) (🖥️) (💻)

▼▼▼ Residence Inn by Marriott-Salinas SH
(831) 775-0410. **$215-$315.** 17215 El Rancho Way. US 101, exit Laurel Dr, just w. Int corridors. **Pets:** Accepted.

(ASK) (S🐾) (✕) (🚾) (🖥️) (💻) (🏊) (✕)

▲▲▲ ▼▼▼ Vagabond Inn M
(831) 758-4693. **$59-$199.** 131 Kern St. US 101, exit Market St, just e. Ext corridors. **Pets:** Accepted.

(SAVE) (S🐾) (✕) (🚾) (🖥️) (💻) (🏊)

SAN ANDREAS

▼▼▼ The Robins Nest BB 🐾
(209) 754-1076. **$95-$175, 7 day notice.** 247 W St. Charles St. SR 49; north end of town. Int corridors. **Pets:** Large, other species. Designated rooms, service with restrictions, supervision.

(ASK) (S🐾) (✕) (🖥️) (💻)

SAN BERNARDINO

▲▲▲ ▼▼▼ Best Western Hospitality Lane M
(909) 381-1681. **$104-$159.** 294 E Hospitality Ln. I-10, exit 73 (Waterman Ave) westbound; exit 73B (Waterman Ave) eastbound, just nw. Ext corridors. **Pets:** Medium, dogs only. $50 deposit/room, $10 daily fee/pet. Service with restrictions, supervision.

(SAVE) (S🐾) (✕) (🖥️) (💻) (🏊)

▲▲▲ ▼▼▼ Econo Lodge M
(909) 383-1188. **$65-$70.** 606 N "H" St. I-215, exit 44 (SR 66 W/5th St) southbound; exit 44A (SR 66 W/5th St) northbound, just e, then just n. Ext corridors. **Pets:** Accepted.

(SAVE) (S🐾) (✕) (🖥️) (💻) (🏊)

▼▼▼ Hilton-San Bernardino LH
(909) 889-0133. **$139-$279.** 285 E Hospitality Ln. I-10, exit 73 (Waterman Ave) westbound; exit 73B (Waterman Ave) eastbound, just n, then just w. Int corridors. **Pets:** Accepted.

(✕) (🖥️) (💻) (🍴) (🏊) (✕)

▼▼▼ La Quinta Inn San Bernardino M
(909) 888-7571. **$109-$139.** 205 E Hospitality Ln. I-10, exit 73 (Waterman Ave) westbound; 73B (Waterman Ave N) eastbound, just n, then 0.3 mi w. Ext corridors. **Pets:** Medium. Service with restrictions.

(ASK) (✕) (🚾) (🐾) (🖥️) (💻)

▼▼ Quality Inn M
(909) 888-4827. **$69-$249.** 1750 S Waterman Ave. I-10, exit 73 (Waterman Ave), 0.5 mi n. Ext corridors. **Pets:** Accepted.

(ASK) (S🐾) (✕) (🖥️) (🖥️) (🏊)

▼▼▼ Residence Inn San Bernardino SH
(909) 382-4564. **$159-$199.** 1040 E Harriman Pl. I-10, exit 74 (Tippecanoe Ave) eastbound; exit 74 (Anderson St/Tippecanoe Ave) westbound, just n, then just w. Int corridors. **Pets:** Accepted.

(ASK) (S🐾) (✕) (🖥️) (💻) (🏊) (✕)

SAN CLEMENTE

AAA ▼▼▼▼ Country Plaza Inn SH ❄
(949) 498-8800. **$79-$149.** 35 Via Pico Plaza. I-5, exit 76 (Avenida Pico), just w, then just s. Int corridors. **Pets:** Small, dogs only. $100 deposit/pet, $20 daily fee/pet. Designated rooms, service with restrictions, supervision.
SAVE ⓢ ✕ ♿ ✍ 🐾 ♿ 🖥 ➪

▼▼▼▼ Holiday Inn-San Clemente Resort SH
(949) 361-3000. **$139-$159.** 111 S Avenida de la Estrella. I-5, exit 75 (Avenida Palizada) southbound; exit 75 (Avenida Presidio) northbound, just s, then just w. Int corridors. **Pets:** Accepted.
✕ ♿ 🖥 🍴 ➪

SAN DIEGO METROPOLITAN AREA

CHULA VISTA

▼▼▼▼ La Quinta Inn San Diego (Chula Vista) M
(619) 691-1211. **$119-$159.** 150 Bonita Rd. I-805, exit 7C (E St/Bonita Rd), just w. Ext corridors. **Pets:** Medium. Service with restrictions.
ASK ✕ ♿ 🖥 ➪

CORONADO

▼▼▼▼ Coronado Island Marriott Resort LH ❄
(619) 435-3000. **$233-$340.** 2000 2nd St. I-5, exit 14A (Coronado Bridge), 1.5 mi w to Glorietta Blvd, then just ne. Ext corridors. **Pets:** Other species. $75 one-time fee/room. Service with restrictions, crate.
ASK ⓢ ✕ 🐾 ♿ 🖥 🍴 ➪ ✕

▼▼ Crown City Inn M ❄
(619) 435-3116. **$99-$249.** 520 Orange Ave. I-5, exit 14A (Coronado Bridge), 1.5 mi w, then just s. Ext corridors. **Pets:** Other species. $8 daily fee/pet. Designated rooms, service with restrictions, supervision.
ASK ⓢ ✕ 🐾 ♿ 🖥 🍴 ➪

AAA ▼▼▼▼ Loews Coronado Bay Resort LH ❄
(619) 424-4000. **$265-$425.** 4000 Coronado Bay Rd. I-5, exit 14A (Coronado Bridge), 1.7 mi w to Orange Ave, 1 mi sw to Silver Strand Blvd, then 4.5 mi s to Coronado Cays. Ext/int corridors. **Pets:** Other species. $25 one-time fee/pet.
SAVE ✕ ♿ 🖥 🍴 ➪ ✕

DEL MAR

AAA ▼▼▼▼ Best Western Stratford Inn M
(858) 755-1501. **$99-$179, 3 day notice.** 710 Camino Del Mar. I-5, exit 34 (Del Mar Heights Rd), 1 mi w, then 0.3 mi n. Int corridors. **Pets:** Medium, other species. $50 one-time fee/room. Designated rooms, service with restrictions, supervision.
SAVE ⓢ ✕ 🐾 ✍ 🐾 ♿ 🖥 ➪

AAA ▼▼▼▼ Del Mar Inn, A Clarion Carriage House SH
(858) 755-9765. **$99-$259, 3 day notice.** 720 Camino Del Mar. I-5, exit 34 (Del Mar Heights Rd), 1 mi w, then 0.3 mi n. Int corridors. **Pets:** Accepted.
SAVE ⓢ ✕ ♿ 🖥 ➪

▼▼▼▼ Hilton San Diego Del Mar LH
(858) 792-5200. **$159-$599.** 15575 Jimmy Durante Blvd. I-5, exit 36 (Via de la Valle), just w. Int corridors. **Pets:** Accepted.
ASK ⓢ ✕ ♿ 🖥 🍴 ➪

EL CAJON

AAA ▼▼▼ Best Western Courtesy Inn M
(619) 440-7378. **$79-$130.** 1355 E Main St. I-8, exit 19 (2nd St), 0.5 mi s, then just e. Ext corridors. **Pets:** Other species. $6 daily fee/pet. Designated rooms, service with restrictions, supervision.
SAVE ⓢ ✕ ♿ 🖥 ➪

AAA ▼▼▼ Quality Inn & Suites Grossmont SH ❄
(619) 588-8808. **$75-$115.** 1250 El Cajon Blvd. I-8, exit 14C (Severin Dr) westbound, 1 mi e on Murray Rd; exit 15 (El Cajon Blvd) eastbound, 0.5 mi w. Ext corridors. **Pets:** Medium. $25 one-time fee/room. Designated rooms, service with restrictions, supervision.
SAVE ⓢ ✕ ♿ 🖥 ➪

LA JOLLA

AAA ▼▼▼ La Jolla Cove Suites SH ❄
(858) 459-2621. **$134-$549, 3 day notice.** 1155 Coast Blvd. I-5, exit 28 (La Jolla Village Dr), 1 mi w to Torrey Pines Rd, 2.5 mi to Prospect St, 0.5 mi s to Girard Ave, then just w. Ext corridors. **Pets:** Small. $25 daily fee/pet. Designated rooms, service with restrictions, supervision.
SAVE ⓢ ✕ ♿ 🖥 ➪ ✕

▼▼▼▼ La Valencia Hotel LH ❄
(858) 454-0771. **$275-$795.** 1132 Prospect St. I-5, exit 26A (La Jolla Pkwy) northbound, 1.5 mi w to Torrey Pines Rd, 1 mi w, then 0.6 mi sw; exit 28 (La Jolla Village Dr) southbound, 1 mi w to Torrey Pines Rd, 2.7 mi sw, then 0.6 mi sw. Ext/int corridors. **Pets:** Medium. $75 daily fee/pet. Service with restrictions.
✕ ♿ 🖥 🍴 ➪ ✕

▼▼▼ Residence Inn by Marriott La Jolla SH
(858) 587-1770. **$169-$269.** 8901 Gilman Dr. I-5, exit 27 (Gilman Dr), 1.5 mi nw. Ext corridors. **Pets:** Other species. $100 one-time fee/room. Service with restrictions.
ASK ⓢ ✕ ♿ 🖥 ➪ ✕

▼▼▼ San Diego Marriott La Jolla LH
(858) 587-1414. **$149-$299.** 4240 La Jolla Village Dr. I-5, exit 28 (La Jolla Village Dr), 0.5 mi e. Int corridors. **Pets:** Small. $75 one-time fee/room. Service with restrictions, supervision.
ASK ✕ 🐾 ✍ 🐾 ♿ 🖥 🍴 ➪ ✕

LA MESA

▼ Motel 6 San Diego-La Mesa #1319 M
(619) 464-7151. **$55-$71.** 7621 Alvarado Rd. I-8, exit 12 (Fletcher Pkwy), just s, then just w. Ext corridors. **Pets:** Medium, other species. Service with restrictions, supervision.
ⓢ ✕

NATIONAL CITY

AAA ▼▼▼ Howard Johnson Express Inn-San Diego South M
(619) 474-6517. **$59-$190.** 521 Roosevelt Ave. I-5, exit 11B (8th St) southbound; exit 11B (Plaza Blvd) northbound, just e, then just n. Ext corridors. **Pets:** Accepted.
SAVE ⓢ ✕ ♿ 🖥 ➪

POWAY

AAA ▼▼▼▼ Best Western Country Inn M
(858) 748-6320. **$99-$149.** 13845 Poway Rd. I-15, exit 18 (Poway Rd), 4 mi e. Ext corridors. **Pets:** Accepted.
SAVE ⓢ ✕ 🐾 ✍ 🐾 ♿ 🖥 ➪

RANCHO BERNARDO

AAA ▼▼▼▼ La Quinta Inn San Diego (Rancho Penasquitos) SH
(858) 484-8800. **$105-$142.** 10185 Paseo Montril. I-15, exit 18 (Rancho Penasquitos Blvd), just w. Ext corridors. **Pets:** Medium. Service with restrictions.
SAVE ✕ 🐾 ♿ 🖥 ➪

Staybridge Suites Carmel Mountain SH
(858) 487-0900. **$159-$699.** 11855 Ave of Industry. I-15, exit 21 (Carmel Mountain Rd), 1 mi ne to second Rancho Carmel Dr, just w to Innovation Dr, just n, then just e. Int corridors. **Pets:** Accepted.

RANCHO SANTA FE

The Inn at Rancho Santa Fe SH
(858) 756-1131. **$245-$850, 3 day notice.** 5951 Linea del Cielo. I-5, exit 37 (Lomas Sante Fe Dr), 4 mi e on CR S-8. Ext/int corridors. **Pets:** Medium, dogs only. Supervision.

SAN DIEGO

Best Western Lamplighter Inn & Suites M
(619) 582-3088. **$80-$135.** 6474 El Cajon Blvd. I-8, exit 11 (70th St), 0.5 mi s, then 1 mi w. Ext corridors. **Pets:** Medium, other species. $10 daily fee/pet. Service with restrictions, supervision.

Best Western Mission Bay Inn M
(619) 275-5700. **$79-$179.** 2575 Clairemont Dr. I-5, exit 22 (Clairemont Dr/Mission Bay Dr), just e. Ext corridors. **Pets:** Small, dogs only. $20 daily fee/pet. Designated rooms, service with restrictions, supervision.

The Bristol LH
(619) 232-6141. **$119-$199.** 1055 First Ave. I-5, exit 17 (Front St), 0.5 mi s at C St. Int corridors. **Pets:** Accepted.

Doubletree Club Hotel San Diego Zoo/SeaWorld Area LH
(619) 881-6900. **$119-$199, 3 day notice.** 1515 Hotel Cir S. I-8, exit 4A (Hotel Cir), south side. Int corridors. **Pets:** Medium. $75 one-time fee/room.

DoubleTree Hotel San Diego-Mission Valley LH
(619) 297-5466. **$149-$339.** 7450 Hazard Center Dr. SR 163, exit 4 (Friars Rd), 0.3 mi e to Frazee Rd, then just s. Int corridors. **Pets:** Medium. $50 one-time fee/pet. Service with restrictions.

Extended StayAmerica-San Diego/Hotel Circle SH
(619) 296-5570. **$104-$144.** 2087 Hotel Cir S. I-8, exit 4A (Hotel Cir), south side. Int corridors. **Pets:** Accepted.

Extended StayAmerica–San Diego/Mission Valley Stadium SH
(858) 292-8927. **Call for rates.** 3860 Murphy Canyon Dr. I-15, exit 8 (Aero Dr), just w, then 1 mi n. Int corridors. **Pets:** Accepted.

Four Points by Sheraton San Diego SH
(858) 277-8888. **$125-$275.** 8110 Aero Dr. SR 163, exit 7B (Balboa Ave E) southbound, 1 mi se via Kearny Villa Rd; exit 10 (Kearny Villa Rd) northbound, 0.8 mi ne. Int corridors. **Pets:** Accepted.

Hampton Inn SeaWorld/Airport SH
(619) 299-6633. **$129-$209.** 3888 Greenwood St. I-8, exit Sports Arena Blvd, 0.5 mi s, 0.3 mi e on Hancock St, then 0.4 mi s on Kurtz St. Int corridors. **Pets:** Accepted.

Holiday Inn on the Bay LH
(619) 232-3861. **$129-$189.** 1355 N Harbor Dr at Ash St. I-5, exit 17 (Hawthorn St) northbound, 0.4 mi w, then 0.4 mi s; exit 17 (Front Ave) southbound, 0.5 mi s to Ash St, then just w. Int corridors. **Pets:** Accepted.

Homestead Studio Suites Hotel-San Diego/Mission Valley M
(619) 299-2292. **$99-$129.** 7444 Mission Valley Rd. SR 163, exit 4 (Friars Rd), 1 mi ne via Mission Center Dr. Ext corridors. **Pets:** Accepted.

Homestead Studio Suites Hotel-San Diego/Sorrento Mesa M
(858) 623-0100. **$114-$144.** 9880 Pacific Heights Blvd. I-805, exit 27 (Mira Mesa Blvd), 1 mi e. Ext corridors. **Pets:** Accepted.

Hotel Solamar LH
(619) 531-8740. **$279-$409.** 435 6th Ave. I-5, exit 17 (Front St/Civic Center), 0.3 mi s, 0.3 mi e on A St, then 0.4 mi s. Int corridors. **Pets:** Accepted.

Kona Kai Resort SH
(619) 221-8000. **$149-$249.** 1551 Shelter Island Dr. I-5, exit 20 (Rosecrans St) southbound; 3 mi sw; exit 17 (Hawthorn St) northbound, 3 mi nw on Harbor Dr to Scott Rd, then 0.5 mi w. Ext/int corridors. **Pets:** Accepted.

Mission Valley Resort SH
(619) 298-8281. **$79-$129.** 875 Hotel Cir S. I-8, exit 4A (Hotel Cir), south side. Ext corridors. **Pets:** Small, other species. $35 one-time fee/pet. Service with restrictions, supervision.

Ocean Villa Inn M
(619) 224-3481. **$89-$289.** 5142 W Point Loma Blvd. I-8, exit Sunset Cliff Blvd, 1.5 mi sw. Ext corridors. **Pets:** Other species. Designated rooms.

Old Town Inn M
(619) 260-8024. **$65-$155.** 4444 Pacific Hwy. I-5, exit 21 (SeaWorld Dr), just w, then 1 mi s. Ext corridors. **Pets:** Medium, other species. $10 daily fee/pet. Service with restrictions, supervision.

Omni San Diego Hotel LH
(619) 231-6664. **$349-$379.** 675 L St. I-5, exit 17 (Front St/Civic Center), 0.3 mi s, 0.3 mi e on A St, 0.6 mi s on Sixth Ave, then just e; connected via skybridge to Petco Park. Int corridors. **Pets:** Medium, dogs only. $50 one-time fee/room. Designated rooms, service with restrictions, supervision.

Premier Inns Mission Valley/Hotel Circle M
(619) 291-8252. **$60-$139.** 2484 Hotel Circle Pl. I-8, exit 3 (Taylor St), just n. Int corridors. **Pets:** Accepted.

Premier Inn-Sports Arena/Mission Bay M
(619) 223-9500. **$60-$139, 3 day notice.** 3333 Channel Way. I-5/8, exit 20 (Rosecrans St), 0.5 mi s, 1 mi nw on Sports Arena Blvd, then just e. Ext corridors. **Pets:** Accepted.

◆◆◆ **Residence Inn by Marriott-San Diego Central** [SH]
(858) 278-2100. **$169-$219.** 5400 Kearny Mesa Rd. SR 163, exit 8 (Clairemont Mesa Blvd). Ext corridors. **Pets:** Medium, other species. $75 one-time fee/room. Service with restrictions.
[A$K] [SD] ✕ ▣ 📺 🏊 🏋

◆◆◆ **Residence Inn by Marriott San Diego Downtown** [SH] 🐾
(619) 338-8200. **$249.** 1747 Pacific Hwy. I-5, exit 17 (Front St) southbound, just s to Grape St, 0.3 mi w, then just n; exit 17 (Hawthorn St) northbound, 0.4 mi w, then just s. Int corridors. **Pets:** Medium. $75 one-time fee/room. Service with restrictions, supervision.
[A$K] [SD] ✕ ▣ 📺 🏊

[AAA] ◆◆◆ **Residence Inn San Diego/Mission Valley/ SeaWorld Area** [SH]
(619) 881-3600. **$159-$359, 3 day notice.** 1865 Hotel Cir S. I-8, exit 4A (Hotel Cir), south side. Int corridors. **Pets:** Accepted.
[SAVE] [SD] ✕ ♿M 👂 ♿ ▣ 📺 🏊 🏋

◆◆◆ **Residence Inn San Diego Ranch Bernardo/Scripps Poway** [SH]
(858) 635-5724. **$129-$209.** 12011 Scripps Highland Dr. I-805, exit 17 (Mercy Rd/Scripps Poway Pkwy), just e, then just n. Int corridors. **Pets:** Other species. $75 one-time fee/room. Service with restrictions, crate.
[A$K] [SD] ✕ ♿M 👂 ♿ ▣ 📺 🏊 🏋

◆◆◆ **Residence Inn San Diego-Sorrento Mesa** [SH] 🐾
(858) 552-9100. **$189-$229.** 5995 Pacific Mesa Ct. I-805, exit 27 (Mira Mesa Blvd), 1.5 mi e. Int corridors. **Pets:** Other species. $150 one-time fee/room.
[A$K] ✕ ▣ 📺 🏊 🏋

[AAA] ◆◆◆ **Sheraton San Diego Hotel, Mission Valley** [LH]
(619) 260-0111. **$139-$299.** 1433 Camino del Rio S. I-8, exit 5 (Mission Center Rd), south side. Int corridors. **Pets:** Accepted.
[SAVE] [SD] ✕ 📺 🍴 🏊

◆◆◆◆ **San Diego Marriott Hotel & Marina** [LH] 🐾
(619) 234-1500. **$195-$460.** 333 W Harbor Dr. I-5, exit 17 (Front St), 1.3 mi s, then just w. Int corridors. **Pets:** Other species. $75 daily fee/room. Service with restrictions.
[A$K] [SD] ✕ ▣ 📺 🍴 🏊 🏋

[AAA] ◆◆◆ **Sheraton Suites San Diego** [LH] 🐾
(619) 696-9800. **$199-$369.** 701 A St/7th Ave. I-5, exit 17 (Front St), 0.5 mi s. Int corridors. **Pets:** Medium, other species. $50 deposit/pet. No service, supervision.
[SAVE] ✕ ♿M 👂 ♿ 📺 🍴 🏊

◆◆◆ **Sommerset Suites Hotel** [SH]
(619) 692-5200. **$129-$299.** 606 Washington St. SR 163, exit 2B (Washington St), just w. Ext/int corridors. **Pets:** Small. $35 one-time fee/room. Service with restrictions, crate.
[A$K] [SD] ✕ ▣ 📺 🏊

◆◆◆ **Staybridge Suites by Holiday Inn-Sorrento Mesa** [SH]
(858) 453-5343. **$149-$359.** 6639 Mira Mesa Blvd. I-805, exit 27 (Mira Mesa Blvd), 2.3 mi e. Int corridors. **Pets:** Accepted.
[A$K] ✕ ♿M 👂 ♿ ▣ 📺 🏊

[AAA] ◆◆ **Vagabond Inn-Point Loma** [M]
(619) 224-3371. **$104-$239.** 1325 Scott St. I-8, exit Nimintz Blvd, 2 mi s to Rosecrans St, just w to Jarvis St, then just s; in Point Loma area. Ext corridors. **Pets:** Medium. $10 daily fee/pet. Designated rooms, service with restrictions, supervision.
[SAVE] [SD] ✕ ▣ 📺 🏊

◆◆◆ **The Westin Horton Plaza** [LH]
(619) 239-2200. **$199-$369.** 910 Broadway Cir. I-5, exit 17 (Front St) southbound, 0.9 mi s to Broadway, just e, then just s; exit 16B (6th Ave) northbound, 0.6 mi s, just w, then just s. Int corridors. **Pets:** Accepted.
[A$K] [SD] ✕ ♿M 👂 ♿ ▣ 📺 🍴 🏊 🏋

[AAA] ◆◆◆ **Woodfin Suite Hotel** [SH] 🐾
(858) 597-0500. **$299-$349.** 10044 Pacific Mesa Blvd. I-805, exit 27 (Mira Mesa Blvd), 1.1 mi e, then just n. Int corridors. **Pets:** $250 deposit/room, $10 daily fee/pet. Designated rooms, service with restrictions, crate.
[SAVE] [SD] ✕ ♿M 👂 ♿ ▣ 📺 🍴 🏊

SAN FRANCISCO METROPOLITAN AREA

BELMONT

◆◆◆ **Hyatt Summerfield Suites** [SH]
(650) 591-8600. **$199-$259.** 400 Concourse Dr. US 101, exit Marine World Pkwy, just e, then just n on Oracle Pkwy. Ext corridors. **Pets:** Small. $250 one-time fee/room. Service with restrictions.
[A$K] ✕ ♿M ♿ 📺 🏊

BRISBANE

◆◆◆ **Homewood Suites By Hilton** [SH]
(650) 589-1600. **$169-$279.** 2000 Shoreline Ct. US 101, exit Sierra Point Pkwy, just e. Int corridors. **Pets:** Medium. $75 one-time fee/room. Designated rooms, service with restrictions, supervision.
[A$K] [SD] ✕ ♿M 👂 ♿ ▣ 📺 🏊

BURLINGAME

◆◆◆ **Crowne Plaza** [LH] 🐾
(650) 342-9200. **$149-$169.** 1177 Airport Blvd. US 101, exit Broadway-Burlingame or Old Bayshore Hwy, just e. Int corridors. **Pets:** Large. $100 deposit/room. Designated rooms, service with restrictions, supervision.
[A$K] [SD] ✕ ♿M 👂 ♿ ▣ 📺 🍴 🏊

[AAA] ◆◆◆ **DoubleTree Hotel-San Francisco Airport** [LH]
(650) 344-5500. **$99-$229.** 835 Airport Blvd. US 101, exit Broadway-Burlingame or Anza Blvd, just e. Int corridors. **Pets:** Accepted.
[SAVE] ✕ ♿M 👂 ♿ ▣ 📺 🍴

◆◆ **Red Roof Inn** [M]
(650) 342-7772. **$80-$140.** 777 Airport Blvd. US 101, exit Broadway-Burlingame or E Anza Blvd; just s of airport. Ext corridors. **Pets:** Medium, other species. Service with restrictions, supervision.
✕ ♿M 👂 ♿ 🏊

◆◆◆◆ **San Francisco Airport Marriott** [LH]
(650) 692-9100. **$129-$249.** 1800 Old Bayshore Hwy. US 101, exit Millbrae Ave, just e. Int corridors. **Pets:** $75 one-time fee/room. Designated rooms, service with restrictions, supervision.
[A$K] [SD] ✕ ♿M 👂 ♿ ▣ 📺 🍴 🏊 🏋

[AAA] ◆◆◆ **Sheraton Gateway Hotel-San Francisco International Airport** [LH]
(650) 340-8500. **$280.** 600 Airport Blvd. US 101, exit Broadway-Burlingame or Anza Blvd, 0.3 mi e. Int corridors. **Pets:** Accepted.
[SAVE] [SD] ✕ ♿M 👂 ▣ 📺 🍴 🏊

AAA ▼▼ Vagabond Inn-SFO M
(650) 692-4040. **$79-$139.** 1640 Bayshore Hwy. US 101, exit Millbrae Ave, just e. Ext corridors. **Pets:** Other species. $10 daily fee/pet. Designated rooms, service with restrictions, supervision.
[SAVE] [S☼] [✕] [♿] [🖥] [▭]

CORTE MADERA

AAA ▼▼ Marin Suites Hotel SH
(415) 924-3608. **$154-$204.** 45 Tamal Vista Blvd. US 101, exit Tamalpais Rd/Paradise Dr. Ext corridors. **Pets:** Other species. $10 daily fee/pet. Service with restrictions, supervision.
[SAVE] [S☼] [✕] [♿] [🖥] [▭] [≈] [✕] [K]

HALF MOON BAY

AAA ▼▼▼ Comfort Inn Half Moon Bay SH ❀
(650) 712-1999. **$80-$180.** 2930 N Cabrillo Hwy. On SR 1. Ext corridors. **Pets:** $20 daily fee/room. Service with restrictions, supervision.
[SAVE] [S☼] [✕] [♿] [🖥] [▭]

▼▼ Days Inn M
(650) 726-9700. **$69-$350.** 3020 N Cabrillo Hwy. 2 mi n of jct SR 92 and 1; w of SR 1. Ext corridors. **Pets:** Dogs only. $15 daily fee/pet. Designated rooms, service with restrictions, supervision.
[ASK] [S☼] [✕] [♿] [🖥] [▭]

AAA ▼▼▼ Harbor View Inn M
(650) 726-2329. **$90-$200.** 51 Ave Alhambra. 4 mi n of jct SR 92 and 1; e of SR 1. Ext corridors. **Pets:** Accepted.
[SAVE] [S☼] [✕] [♿] [🖥] [K]

AAA ▼▼▼ Holiday Inn Express M
(650) 726-3400. **$95-$169.** 230 S Cabrillo Hwy. On SR 1, just s of SR 92. Ext corridors. **Pets:** $10 daily fee/pet. Designated rooms, service with restrictions, supervision.
[SAVE] [S☼] [✕] [♿] [🖥] [▭]

▼▼▼▼▼ The Ritz-Carlton, Half Moon Bay LH
(650) 712-7000. **$295-$395, 7 day notice.** 1 Miramontes Point Rd. 3 mi s of jct SR 92 and 1; w of SR 1 at Miramontes Point Rd. Ext/int corridors. **Pets:** Accepted.
[ASK] [✕] [♿] [▭] [🍴] [≈] [✕]

MILLBRAE

AAA ▼▼▼ Clarion Hotel-San Francisco Airport LH
(650) 692-6363. **$109-$149.** 401 E Millbrae Ave. US 101, exit Millbrae Ave, just e. Int corridors. **Pets:** Accepted.
[SAVE] [S☼] [✕] [♿] [♿] [🖥] [▭] [🍴] [≈]

▼▼▼ The Westin Hotel-San Francisco Airport LH
(650) 692-3500. **$329.** 1 Old Bayshore Hwy. Just e of US 101, exit Millbrae Ave. Int corridors. **Pets:** Accepted.
[ASK] [✕] [♿] [🗐] [♿] [▭] [🍴] [≈] [✕]

SAN BRUNO

AAA ▼▼▼ Regency Inn M
(650) 589-7535. **$89-$109.** 411 E San Bruno Ave. US 101, exit San Bruno Ave, 0.4 mi w. Ext corridors. **Pets:** Large. $15 daily fee/pet. Service with restrictions, supervision.
[SAVE] [S☼] [✕] [♿] [🖥] [▭]

AAA ▼▼▼ Staybridge Suites SH
(650) 588-0770. **$109-$159.** 1350 Huntington Ave. I-380, exit El Camino Real N, e on Sneath Ln. Ext corridors. **Pets:** Other species. $150 one-time fee/pet.
[SAVE] [S☼] [✕] [♿] [🖥] [▭] [≈] [✕]

SAN CARLOS

▼▼ Homestead Studio Suites Hotel-San Francisco San Carlos SH
(650) 368-2600. **$105-$115.** 3 Circle Star Way. US 101, exit Whipple Ave, w to Industrial, then just n. Int corridors. **Pets:** Accepted.
[ASK] [S☼] [✕] [♿] [♿] [🖥] [▭]

SAN FRANCISCO

AAA ▼▼▼ ▼▼▼ Argonaut Hotel LH ❀
(415) 563-0800. **$149-$379.** 495 Jefferson St. Fisherman's Wharf; adjacent to The Cannery. Int corridors. **Pets:** Other species. Designated rooms, service with restrictions, supervision.
[SAVE] [S☼] [✕] [♿] [♿] [▭] [K]

▼▼▼ Beresford Arms SH
(415) 673-2600. **$99-$119.** 701 Post St. 3 blks w of Union Square. Int corridors. **Pets:** Accepted.
[ASK] [S☼] [✕] [♿] [♿] [🖥] [▭] [K]

▼▼▼ Best Western Tuscan Inn at Fisherman's Wharf SH
(415) 561-1100. **$129-$329.** 425 Northpoint St. Just s of Fisherman's Wharf at Mason St. Int corridors. **Pets:** Accepted.
[SAVE] [✕] [🗐] [🍴]

▼▼▼▼ Campton Place Hotel SH ❀
(415) 781-5555. **$235-$455.** 340 Stockton St. Just n of Union Square. Int corridors. **Pets:** Medium. $100 one-time fee/room. Service with restrictions, supervision.
[ASK] [S☼] [✕] [♿] [♿] [🍴]

AAA ▼▼▼ Cartwright Hotel SH
(415) 421-2865. **$119-$179, 3 day notice.** 524 Sutter St. Union Square at Powell St. Int corridors. **Pets:** Small. $75 one-time fee/pet. Designated rooms, service with restrictions, crate.
[SAVE] [✕] [♿]

AAA ▼▼▼ Crowne Plaza Union Square LH
(415) 398-8900. **$139-$299.** 480 Sutter St. Just n off Union Square; corner of Powell St. Int corridors. **Pets:** Accepted.
[SAVE] [✕] [♿] [🗐] [♿] [🖥] [▭] [🍴]

AAA ▼▼▼ Diva Hotel SH ❀
(415) 885-0200. **$119-$269.** 440 Geary St. Just w of Union Square. Int corridors. **Pets:** Medium, dogs only. $75 one-time fee/room. Service with restrictions, crate.
[SAVE] [S☼] [✕] [🍴]

AAA ▼▼▼ Executive Hotel Vintage Court SH
(415) 392-4666. **$199-$329.** 650 Bush St. 2 blks n of Union Square. Int corridors. **Pets:** Accepted.
[SAVE] [S☼] [✕] [♿]

▼▼▼▼ The Fairmont San Francisco LH
(415) 772-5000. **$289-$409.** 950 Mason St. Atop Nob Hill at California St. Int corridors. **Pets:** Small. $35 one-time fee/pet. Supervision.
[ASK] [S☼] [✕] [♿] [🗐] [♿] [🍴]

▽▽▽▽ Four Seasons San Francisco 🄻🄷
(415) 633-3000. **$460-$560.** 757 Market St. Between 3rd and 4th sts. Int corridors. **Pets:** Accepted.

[icons]

▲▲▲ ▽▽▽ Galleria Park Hotel 🅂🄷
(415) 781-3060. **$269-$319.** 191 Sutter St. 2 blks ne of Union Square. Int corridors. **Pets:** Accepted.

[icons]

▲▲▲ ▽▽▽ Harbor Court Hotel 🅂🄷
(415) 882-1300. **$309.** 165 Steuart St. On Embarcadero; between Howard and Mission sts. Int corridors. **Pets:** Accepted.

[icons]

▲▲▲ ▽▽▽ Holiday Inn Civic Center 🄻🄷
(415) 626-6103. **$85-$189.** 50 8th St. 2 blks from civic auditorium; just s of Market St and BART Station. Int corridors. **Pets:** Accepted.

[icons]

▲▲▲ ▽▽▽ Holiday Inn Fisherman's Wharf 🄻🄷
(415) 771-9000. **$119-$259.** 1300 Columbus Ave. Jct North Point St. Int corridors. **Pets:** $50 deposit/room. Designated rooms, service with restrictions, crate.

[icons]

▽▽ Hotel Beresford 🅂🄷
(415) 673-9900. **$89-$119.** 635 Sutter St. 1 blk nw of Union Square at Mason St. Int corridors. **Pets:** Accepted.

[icons]

▲▲▲ ▽▽ Hotel Metropolis 🅂🄷 🐾
(415) 775-4600. **$109-$189.** 25 Mason St. Jct Market St. Int corridors. **Pets:** Medium, dogs only. $75 one-time fee/room. Designated rooms, service with restrictions, crate.

[icons]

▲▲▲ ▽▽▽ ▽▽ Hotel Monaco 🄻🄷
(415) 292-0100. **$199-$399.** 501 Geary St. Just w of Union Square at Taylor St. Int corridors. **Pets:** Accepted.

[icons]

▲▲▲ ▽▽▽ ▽▽ Hotel Nikko San Francisco 🄻🄷
(415) 394-1111. **$139-$495.** 222 Mason St. Just w of Union Square. Int corridors. **Pets:** Small, dogs only. $70 one-time fee/room. Service with restrictions, supervision.

[icons]

▲▲▲ ▽▽▽ ▽▽ Hotel Palomar 🅂🄷 🐾
(415) 348-1111. **$189-$489.** 12 Fourth St. At Market St; downtown. Int corridors. **Pets:** Other species. Designated rooms, service with restrictions, supervision.

[icons]

▲▲▲ ▽▽▽ Hotel Triton 🅂🄷
(415) 394-0500. **$149-$249.** 342 Grant Ave. Near Union Square at Bush St. Int corridors. **Pets:** Accepted.

[icons]

▲▲▲ ▽▽▽ Hotel Union Square 🅂🄷
(415) 397-3000. **$119-$199.** 114 Powell St. US 101 (Van Ness Ave), exit Market St E to Powell St; just n of cable car turnaround. Int corridors. **Pets:** Accepted.

[icons]

▽▽▽ ▽▽▽ Hotel Vitale 🅂🄷
(415) 278-3700. **$199-$699.** 8 Mission St. At Embarcadero. Int corridors. **Pets:** Accepted.

[icons]

▽▽▽ ▽▽▽ J.W. Marriott Hotel San Francisco 🄻🄷
(415) 771-8600. **$219-$450.** 500 Post St. Just w of Union Square at Mason St. Int corridors. **Pets:** Accepted.

[icons]

▲▲▲ ▽▽▽ Kensington Park Hotel 🅂🄷 🐾
(415) 788-6400. **$129-$189.** 450 Post St. Just w of Union Square. Int corridors. **Pets:** Medium, dogs only. $75 one-time fee/room. Service with restrictions, crate.

[icons]

▽▽▽▽ La Quinta Inn & Suites 🅂🄷
(415) 673-4711. **$79-$159.** 1050 Van Ness Ave. On US 101 (Van Ness Ave). Int corridors. **Pets:** Accepted.

[icons]

▲▲▲ ▽▽▽▽ The Laurel Inn 🅂🄷 🐾
(415) 567-8467. **$189-$219.** 444 Presidio Ave. 1 mi w of US 101 (Van Ness Ave); 1 mi e of Park Presidio Blvd (SR 1) at California St. Int corridors. **Pets:** Service with restrictions, supervision.

[icons]

▽▽▽▽ ▽▽▽▽ Mandarin Oriental, San Francisco 🄻🄷 🐾
(415) 276-9888. **$530-$760.** 222 Sansome St. US 101, 1.2 mi e on Bush St, then just n. Int corridors. **Pets:** Small, dogs only. $25 daily fee/pet. Service with restrictions, supervision.

[icons]

▲▲▲ ▽▽▽▽ Monticello Inn 🅂🄷
(415) 392-8800. **$119-$209.** 127 Ellis St. Just w of Union Square at Mason St. Int corridors. **Pets:** Accepted.

[icons]

▽▽▽▽ ▽▽▽▽ Omni San Francisco Hotel 🄻🄷 🐾
(415) 677-9494. **$199-$599.** 500 California St. At Montgomery St; downtown; in financial district. Int corridors. **Pets:** Small. $50 one-time fee/pet. Service with restrictions, crate.

[icons]

▲▲▲ ▽▽ Pacific Heights Inn 🄼 🐾
(415) 776-3310. **$79-$155.** 1555 Union St. Just w of US 101 (Van Ness Ave). Ext corridors. **Pets:** $15 daily fee/room. Service with restrictions, supervision.

[icons]

▽▽▽▽ ▽▽▽▽ Palace Hotel 🄻🄷
(415) 512-1111. **$229-$629.** 2 New Montgomery St. Just e of Union Square at Market St. Int corridors. **Pets:** Accepted.

[icons]

▲▲▲ ▽▽▽▽ The Prescott Hotel 🅂🄷
(415) 563-0303. **$199-$439.** 545 Post St. Just w of Union Square. Int corridors. **Pets:** Accepted.

[icons]

▲▲▲ ▽▽▽▽▽ The Ritz-Carlton, San Francisco 🄻🄷 🐾
(415) 296-7465. **$545-$745.** 600 Stockton St. Just n of Union Square at California St. Int corridors. **Pets:** Very small, dogs only. $125 one-time fee/room. Service with restrictions.

[icons]

▲▲▲ ▽▽▽▽ San Francisco Marriott Fisherman's Wharf 🄻🄷 🐾
(415) 775-7555. **$189-$299.** 1250 Columbus Ave. Just s of Fisherman's Wharf at Bay St. Int corridors. **Pets:** Medium, other species. $100 one-time fee/room. Service with restrictions, supervision.

[icons]

▲▲▲ ▽▽▽ Serrano Hotel 🅂🄷 🐾
(415) 885-2500. **$319-$339.** 405 Taylor St. Just w of Union Square at O'Farrell St. Int corridors. **Pets:** Medium. Service with restrictions, supervision.

[icons]

▲▲▲ ▽▽▽ Sheraton Fisherman's Wharf 🄻🄷 🐾
(415) 362-5500. **$139-$349.** 2500 Mason St. Just se of Fisherman's Wharf at Beach St. Int corridors. **Pets:** Medium, dogs only. Service with restrictions, supervision.

[icons]

AAA ◆◆◆ Sir Francis Drake Hotel LH
(415) 392-7755. **$149-$259.** 450 Powell St. Just n of Union Square at Sutter St. Int corridors. **Pets:** Accepted.

(SAVE) (S) (X) (&M) (.e) (Y)

AAA ◆◆◆◆ The Stanford Court, A Renaissance Hotel LH
(415) 989-3500. **$199-$449.** 905 California St. Atop Nob Hill; corner of California and Powell sts. Int corridors. **Pets:** Small, dogs only. $75 one-time fee/room.

(SAVE) (X) (&M) (a) (.e) (B) (Y)

AAA ◆◆◆ Travelodge By The Bay M ❀
(415) 673-0691. **$79-$139.** 1450 Lombard St. On US 101 (Lombard St). Ext/int corridors. **Pets:** Large, dogs only. $23 daily fee/pet. Designated rooms, service with restrictions, crate.

(SAVE) (X) (&M) (.e) (B)

AAA ◆◆◆ Villa Florence Hotel SH
(415) 397-7700. **$119-$259.** 225 Powell St. Just s of Union Square; between O'Farrell and Geary sts. Int corridors. **Pets:** Accepted.

(SAVE) (S) (X) (&M) (a) (B) (Y)

AAA ◆◆◆◆ The Westin St. Francis LH ❀
(415) 397-7000. **$149-$489.** 335 Powell St. On Union Square. **Pets:** Medium, dogs only. $75 one-time fee/room. Service with restrictions, supervision.

(SAVE) (S) (X) (&M) (.e) (B) (Y) (X)

◆◆◆ W Hotel LH ❀
(415) 777-5300. **Call for rates.** 181 3rd St. At Howard St. Int corridors. **Pets:** Medium. $25 daily fee/room, $100 one-time fee/room.

(X) (a) (.e) (B) (B) (Y) (X)

SAN MATEO

◆◆ Homestead Studio Suites Hotel-San Francisco-SFO SH
(650) 574-1744. **$105-$115.** 1830 Gateway Dr. SR 92, exit Edgewater Blvd; se of jct US 101 and SR 92. Ext corridors. **Pets:** Accepted.

(ASK) (S) (X) (&M) (.e) (B)

END METROPOLITAN AREA

SAN JOSE

AAA ◆◆◆ Best Western Gateway Inn SH
(408) 435-8800. **$89-$119.** 2585 Seaboard Ave. US 101, exit Trimble Rd E; 1 mi ne of San Jose International Airport. Int corridors. **Pets:** Accepted.

(SAVE) (S) (X) (B) (B) (B)

AAA ◆◆◆◆ Crowne Plaza Hotel and Resort San Jose LH
(408) 998-0400. **$99-$269.** 282 Almaden Blvd. I-280, exit Almaden-Vine, 6 blks n. Int corridors. **Pets:** Accepted.

(SAVE) (S) (X) (&M) (.e) (B) (B) (Y)

AAA ◆◆◆ ◆◆ DoubleTree Hotel San Jose LH
(408) 453-4000. **$89-$289.** 2050 Gateway Pl. 0.3 mi e of San Jose International Airport via Airport Blvd; w of US 101, exit N 1st St; US 101 northbound, exit Brokaw Rd. Int corridors. **Pets:** Other species. $50 deposit/room. Service with restrictions.

(SAVE) (S) (X) (B) (B) (Y) (B)

◆◆◆◆ Extended Stay Deluxe-San Jose-Downtown SH
(408) 453-3000. **$135-$145.** 55 E Brokaw Rd. US 101, exit 1st St/Brokaw Rd, just e. Int corridors. **Pets:** Accepted.

(X) (.e) (B) (B)

◆◆◆ Residence Inn by Marriott SH
(650) 574-4700. **$159-$189.** 2000 Winward Way. 0.8 mi se from jct US 101 and SR 92; exit SR 92 via Edgewater Blvd. Ext corridors. **Pets:** Large. $100 one-time fee/room. Service with restrictions.

(ASK) (S) (X) (&M) (.e) (B) (B) (B) (X)

SAN RAFAEL

◆◆ Villa Inn M
(415) 456-4975. **$69-$120.** 1600 Lincoln Ave. Off US 101 at Lincoln Ave off-ramp; exit Central San Rafael northbound, 0.3 mi w on 4th St, then 0.5 mi n. Ext corridors. **Pets:** Medium, dogs only. $20 deposit/room. Designated rooms, service with restrictions, supervision.

(ASK) (X) (&M) (.e) (B) (B)

SOUTH SAN FRANCISCO

◆◆◆ Embassy Suites San Francisco Airport-South San Francisco LH
(650) 589-3400. **$139-$239.** 250 Gateway Blvd. US 101, exit Grand Ave, just e. Int corridors. **Pets:** Accepted.

(ASK) (X) (&M) (a) (B) (B) (Y) (B) (X)

AAA ◆◆◆ La Quinta Inn San Francisco (Airport) SH
(650) 583-2223. **$102-$142.** 20 S Airport Blvd. US 101, exit S Airport Blvd, just w. Int corridors. **Pets:** Medium. Service with restrictions.

(SAVE) (X) (&M) (.e) (B) (B) (B)

◆◆ ◆◆ The Fairmont San Jose LH ❀
(408) 998-1900. **$152-$259.** 170 S Market St. At Fairmont Plaza. Int corridors. **Pets:** Medium. $75 one-time fee/room. Service with restrictions, supervision.

(ASK) (S) (X) (B) (Y) (B) (X)

AAA ◆◆◆◆ Hilton San Jose LH
(408) 287-2100. **$129-$329.** 300 Almaden Blvd. Downtown. Int corridors. **Pets:** Accepted.

(SAVE) (S) (X) (&M) (B) (B) (Y) (B)

◆◆◆ Homestead Studio Suites Hotel-San Jose-Downtown SH
(408) 573-0648. **$115-$125.** 1560 N 1st St. 1 mi e of Norman Y. Mineta San Jose International Airport; US 101, exit N 1st St, then s. Int corridors. **Pets:** Accepted.

(ASK) (S) (X) (B)

◆◆◆◆ Homewood Suites by Hilton SH
(408) 428-9900. **$149-$225.** 10 W Trimble Rd. 2 mi ne of San Jose International Airport; US 101, exit Trimble Rd, 1.3 mi e. Ext/int corridors. **Pets:** Accepted.

(ASK) (X) (&M) (a) (B) (B) (X)

AAA ◆◆◆◆ Hotel De Anza LH
(408) 286-1000. **$99-$399.** 233 W Santa Clara St. Downtown. Int corridors. **Pets:** Small. $30 one-time fee/room. Service with restrictions.

(SAVE) (S) (X) (B) (Y)

AAA ▼▼▼ Howard Johnson Express Inn M
(408) 280-5300. **$99-$159.** 1215 S 1st St. Jct I-280 and SR 82, 0.8 mi s. Ext corridors. **Pets:** Large. $5 daily fee/room. Service with restrictions, supervision.
SAVE ⎃ ⊠ ⊞ ⊡ ⇌

▼▼▼ Residence Inn by Marriott SH
(408) 226-7676. **$163-$189.** 6111 San Ignacio Ave. US 101, exit Bernal Rd, then e. Int corridors. **Pets:** Accepted.
ASK ⎃ ⊠ ⊞ ⊡ ⊞ ⊡ ⇌ ⊠

AAA ▼▼▼ Staybridge Suites San Jose SH
(408) 436-1600. **$140-$190.** 1602 Crane Ct. US 101, exit 1st St/Brokaw Rd, 0.4 mi e to Bering S, then 0.5 mi. Ext corridors. **Pets:** Accepted.
SAVE ⎃ ⊠ ⊞ ⊡ ⇌

▼▼ TownePlace Suites by Marriott San Jose/Cupertino SH
(408) 984-5903. **$89-$149.** 440 Saratoga Ave. I-280, exit Saratoga Ave, just n. Int corridors. **Pets:** Accepted.
ASK ⎃ ⊠ ⊡ ⇌

AAA ▼ Vagabond Inn San Jose M
(408) 453-8822. **$79.** 1488 N 1st St. I-880, exit N 1st St, then w. Ext corridors. **Pets:** Accepted.
SAVE ⎃ ⊠ ⊞ ⊡ ⇌

SAN JUAN BAUTISTA

AAA ▼▼▼ San Juan Inn M
(831) 623-4380. **$69-$99.** 410 The Alameda. Jct SR 156. Ext corridors. **Pets:** Other species. $15 daily fee/pet.
SAVE ⎃ ⊠ ⊞ ⊡ ⇌

SAN JUAN CAPISTRANO

AAA ▼▼▼▼ Best Western Capistrano Inn M
(949) 493-5661. **$80-$180.** 27174 Ortega Hwy. I-5, exit 82 (SR 74/Ortega Hwy), just e. Ext corridors. **Pets:** Large, other species. $25 one-time fee/room. Supervision.
SAVE ⎃ ⊠ ⊞ ⊡ ⇌

SAN LUIS OBISPO

AAA ▼▼▼ Best Western Royal Oak Hotel M ❀
(805) 544-4410. **$79-$189.** 214 Madonna Rd. US 101, exit 201 (Madonna Rd), just s. Ext/int corridors. **Pets:** $15 one-time fee/pet. Service with restrictions, supervision.
SAVE ⎃ ⊠ ⊞ ⊡ ⊡ ⊞ ⊡ ⇌

AAA ▼▼▼▼ Days Inn M ❀
(805) 549-9911. **$69-$199.** 2050 Garfield St. US 101, exit 204 (Monterey St), just sw. Ext corridors. **Pets:** Medium, dogs only. $10 daily fee/pet. Designated rooms, service with restrictions, supervision.
SAVE ⎃ ⊠ ⊞ ⊡ ⊡ ⊡ ⊞ ⊡ ⇌ ⊠

▼▼ Heritage Inn Bed & Breakfast BB
(805) 544-7440. **$85-$175, 7 day notice.** 978 Olive St. US 101, exit 203B (SR 1/Morro Bay) northbound, just w on Santa Rosa St, then just s; exit 203A (Santa Rosa St) southbound, just ne. Int corridors. **Pets:** Medium, other species. $100 deposit/pet, $15 one-time fee/room. Designated rooms, service with restrictions, supervision.
ASK ⊠ ⊡ ⊡ ⊡

▼▼▼ Holiday Inn Express SH
(805) 544-8600. **$89-$149.** 1800 Monterey St. US 101, exit 204 (Monterey St), just w. Int corridors. **Pets:** Large. $25 one-time fee/room. Service with restrictions, supervision.
ASK ⎃ ⊠ ⊞ ⊡ ⊞ ⊡ ⇌

AAA ▼▼▼ Ramada Inn Olive Tree M
(805) 544-2800. **$79-$219.** 1000 Olive St. US 101, exit 203B (Morro Bay) northbound, just w on Santa Rosa St, then just s; exit 203A (Santa Rosa St) southbound, just ne. Ext corridors. **Pets:** Accepted.
SAVE ⎃ ⊠ ⊞ ⊡ ⊡ ⊡ ⊞ ⊡ ⇌

AAA ▼▼▼ Sands Suites & Motel M
(805) 544-0500. **$59-$219.** 1930 Monterey St. US 101, exit 204 (Monterey St), just sw. Ext corridors. **Pets:** Other species. $10 one-time fee/pet. Service with restrictions, supervision.
SAVE ⎃ ⊠ ⊞ ⊡ ⊞ ⊡ ⇌ ⊠

AAA ▼▼▼ Super 8 Motel M
(805) 544-6888. **$49-$139.** 1951 Monterey St. US 101, exit 204 (Monterey St), just e. Ext corridors. **Pets:** Medium, dogs only. $10 daily fee/pet. Designated rooms, service with restrictions, supervision.
SAVE ⎃ ⊠ ⊡ ⊡ ⊞ ⇌

SAN MARCOS

AAA ▼▼▼▼ Lake San Marcos Resort SH ❀
(760) 744-0120. **$189-$219.** 1025 La Bonita Dr. SR 78, exit Rancho Santa Fe Rd, 2 mi s, then 0.5 mi e via Lake San Marcos Dr and San Marino Dr; at Lake San Marcos. Ext/int corridors. **Pets:** Other species. $50 one-time fee/room. Designated rooms, service with restrictions, supervision.
SAVE ⎃ ⊠ ⊞ ⊡ ⊞ ⇌ ⊠

SAN RAMON

▼▼ Homestead Studio Suites Hotel-San Ramon-Bishop Ranch M
(925) 277-0833. **$110-$120.** 18000 San Ramon Valley Blvd. I-680, exit Bollinger Canyon Rd E, just n. Ext corridors. **Pets:** Accepted.
ASK ⎃ ⊠ ⊡ ⊞ ⊡

▼▼▼ Residence Inn by Marriott SH
(925) 277-9292. **$114-$249.** 1071 Market Pl. I-680, exit Bollinger Canyon Rd E, 0.5 mi e. Ext corridors. **Pets:** Medium, other species. $100 one-time fee/room. Service with restrictions, crate.
ASK ⎃ ⊠ ⊡ ⊡ ⇌

▼▼▼ San Ramon Marriott at Bishop Ranch LH
(925) 867-9200. **$79-$229.** 2600 Bishop Dr. I-680, exit Bollinger Canyon Rd E, n on Sunset, then just w. Int corridors. **Pets:** Accepted.
ASK ⊠ ⊞ ⊡ ⊞ ⇌ ⊠

▼▼▼ Sierra Suites Hotel San Ramon SH
(925) 743-1882. **$99-$249.** 2323 San Ramon Valley Blvd. I-680, exit Crow Canyon Rd W, just n. Int corridors. **Pets:** Accepted.
ASK ⎃ ⊠ ⊡ ⊡ ⇌

SAN SIMEON

AAA ▼▼▼ Courtesy Inn M
(805) 927-4691. **$70-$180.** 9450 Castillo Dr. East side of SR 1. Ext corridors. **Pets:** Accepted.
SAVE ⎃ ⊠ ⊞ ⊡ ⇌

▼▼▼ Motel 6 Premiere–1212 SH
(805) 927-8691. **$45-$105.** 9070 Castillo Dr. Just e of SR 1. Int corridors. **Pets:** Medium, other species. Service with restrictions, supervision.
⎃ ⊠ ⊡ ⊡ ⊡ ⊞ ⊞ ⇌

▼▼ San Simeon Lodge SH
(805) 927-4601. **$50-$215, 3 day notice.** 9520 Castillo Dr. On SR 1. Ext corridors. **Pets:** $10 daily fee/pet. Designated rooms, service with restrictions, supervision.
ASK ⎃ ⊠ ⊞ ⊡ ⊞ ⇌ ⊠

AAA ▼▼▼ Silver Surf Motel M ❀
(805) 927-4661. **$49-$189.** 9390 Castillo Dr. Just e of SR 1. Ext corridors. **Pets:** $10 daily fee/pet. Designated rooms, service with restrictions, supervision.
SAVE ⎃ ⊠ ⊞ ⊡ ⇌ ⊠

SANTA ANA

La Quinta Inn Santa Ana M
(714) 540-1111. **$89-$129.** 2721 Hotel Terrace Rd. SR 55, exit 8 (Dyer Rd) northbound; exit 8B (Dyer Rd W) southbound, just w, then just s. Ext corridors. **Pets:** Medium. Service with restrictions.

Motel 6 #738 M
(714) 558-0500. **$51-$65.** 1623 E 1st St. I-5, 103C (1st St/4th St) northbound; exit 104A (1st St/4th St) southbound, just w. Ext corridors. **Pets:** Medium, other species. Service with restrictions, supervision.

Red Roof Inn M
(714) 542-0311. **$75-$90.** 2600 N Main St. I-5, exit 105B (Main St), 0.3 mi n. Ext/int corridors. **Pets:** Medium, other species. Service with restrictions, supervision.

SANTA BARBARA

Best Western Beachside Inn M
(805) 965-6556. **$119-$329.** 336 W Cabrillo Blvd. US 101, exit 97 (Bath St) northbound, just w on Haley St to Castillo St, then 0.4 mi s; exit 97 (Castillo St) southbound, 0.3 mi s. Ext corridors. **Pets:** Large, other species. $20 daily fee/pet. Designated rooms, service with restrictions, supervision.

Blue Sands Motel M
(805) 965-1624. **$95-$225, 3 day notice.** 421 S Milpas St. US 101, exit 96A (Milpas St), 0.3 mi s. Ext corridors. **Pets:** Medium, dogs only. $10 daily fee/pet. Designated rooms, service with restrictions.

Fess Parker's DoubleTree Resort LH ❖
(805) 564-4333. **$235-$610, 3 day notice.** 633 E Cabrillo Blvd. US 101, exit 96A (Milpas St), just s, then just w. Ext/int corridors. **Pets:** Other species. $40 one-time fee/room. Designated rooms, service with restrictions, supervision.

Four Seasons Biltmore Santa Barbara LH ❖
(805) 969-2261. **$550-$4000, 3 day notice.** 1260 Channel Dr. US 101, exit 94A (Olive Mill Rd), 0.3 mi s. Ext/int corridors. **Pets:** Medium. Designated rooms, supervision.

Harbor House Inn M
(805) 962-9745. **$99-$325.** 104 Bath St. US 101, exit 94B (Cabrillo Blvd) (left hand exit), 3 mi n, then just e; exit 97 (Castillo St) southbound, 0.4 mi w, just s on Cabrillo Blvd, then just e. Ext corridors. **Pets:** Medium. $15 daily fee/pet. Designated rooms, service with restrictions, supervision.

Hotel MarMonte LH
(805) 963-0744. **$130-$329, 3 day notice.** 1111 E Cabrillo Blvd. US 101, exit 96A (Milpas St), 0.3 mi s, then just e. Int corridors. **Pets:** Accepted.

Marina Beach Motel M
(805) 963-9311. **$99-$289.** 21 Bath St. US 101, exit 96B (Garden St), 0.3 mi w to Cabrillo Blvd, 0.4 mi n to Bath St, then just e. Ext corridors. **Pets:** Small. $15 daily fee/pet. Designated rooms, supervision.

Pacifica Suites SH
(805) 683-6722. **$179-$329.** 5490 Hollister Ave. US 101, exit 104A (Patterson Ave), 0.5 mi w, then 0.5 mi n. Ext/int corridors. **Pets:** Small. $100 deposit/pet. Designated rooms, service with restrictions.

The Parkside Inn M
(805) 963-0744. **$109-$179, 3 day notice.** 424 Por La Mar. US 101, exit 96A (Milpas St), 0.3 mi s, just e on Cabrillo Blvd, then just n. Int corridors. **Pets:** Accepted.

SANTA CATALINA ISLAND

Best Western Catalina Canyon Hotel & Spa M ❖
(310) 510-0325. **$99-$279, 3 day notice.** 888 Country Club Dr. 0.5 mi from the harbor via Sumner Ave. Ext corridors. **Pets:** Medium. Service with restrictions, supervision.

SANTA CLARA

GuestHouse Inn & Suites M
(408) 241-3010. **$85-$95.** 2930 El Camino Real. SR 82, 0.5 mi w of San Tomas Expwy; US 101, exit S Bowers Ave. Ext corridors. **Pets:** Medium. $10 daily fee/pet. Service with restrictions, supervision.

Ramada Limited SH
(408) 244-8313. **$69-$109.** 1655 El Camino Real. I-880, exit The Alameda, 2 mi w. Ext corridors. **Pets:** Accepted.

Santa Clara Marriott Hotel LH
(408) 988-1500. **$109-$269.** 2700 Mission College Blvd. 0.5 mi e off US 101, exit Great America Pkwy; 0.8 mi s of Great America Theme Park. Int corridors. **Pets:** Accepted.

Sierra Suites Hotel-Santa Clara SH
(408) 486-0800. **$89-$269.** 3915 Rivermark Plaza. US 101, exit Montague Expwy E. Int corridors. **Pets:** Accepted.

The Vagabond Inn M
(408) 241-0771. **$49-$119.** 3580 El Camino Real. On SR 82, southeast corner of Lawrence Expwy Cloverleaf. Ext corridors. **Pets:** Accepted.

SANTA CRUZ

Bay Front Inn M
(831) 423-8564. **$58-$260.** 325 Pacific Ave. 6 blks se of SR 1. Ext corridors. **Pets:** Medium. $15 daily fee/pet. Service with restrictions, supervision.

Continental Inn M
(831) 429-1221. **$75-$260.** 60 Oak Knoll Dr. 5 blks from beach; between Broadway and Soquel aves. Ext corridors. **Pets:** Dogs only. $15 daily fee/room. Service with restrictions, supervision.

GuestHouse International Pacific Inn SH ❖
(831) 425-3722. **$59-$199.** 330 Ocean St. 1 mi from jct SR 1 and 17. Int corridors. **Pets:** Dogs only. $10 daily fee/pet. Supervision.

Hilton Santa Cruz/Scotts Valley SH
(831) 440-1000. **$189-$279.** 6001 La Madrona Dr. SR 17, exit Mt. Hermon Rd. Int corridors. **Pets:** Accepted.

The Inn at Pasatiempo SH ❖
(831) 423-5000. **$145-$209.** 555 Hwy 17. 0.8 mi n of jct SR 1 and 17; exit SR 17, exit Pasatiempo Dr. Ext corridors. **Pets:** Medium, dogs only. $25 daily fee/pet. Designated rooms, service with restrictions, supervision.

Santa Cruz Beach Inn M
(831) 458-9660. **$70-$269.** 600 Riverside Ave. 4 blks from beach. Ext corridors. **Pets:** Medium, dogs only. $25 daily fee/pet. Designated rooms, service with restrictions, supervision.
SAVE 🐾 ✕ 🍴 💻 🏊 🛄

SANTA MARIA

Best Western Big America M
(805) 922-5200. **$95-$169.** 1725 N Broadway. US 101, exit 173 (SR 135/S Broadway), 0.5 mi s. Ext corridors. **Pets:** Medium, other species. Service with restrictions, supervision.
SAVE 🐾 ✕ 🍴 💻 🏊

Historic Santa Maria Inn LH 🐾
(805) 928-7777. **$134-$174.** 801 S Broadway. US 101, exit 171 (Main St), 1 mi w, then 0.5 mi s. Int corridors. **Pets:** Small. $50 one-time fee/room. Designated rooms, service with restrictions, supervision.
ASK 🐾 ✕ 🔧 💻 🍴 🏊 🛄

Holiday Inn Hotel & Suites LH
(805) 928-6000. **$159-$239.** 2100 N Broadway. US 101, exit 173 (SR 135/S Broadway), just s. Int corridors. **Pets:** Medium. $25 daily fee/pet. Designated rooms, service with restrictions, supervision.
SAVE 🐾 ✕ 🔧 📷 🍴 💻 🏊 🛄

SANTA NELLA

Holiday Inn Express SH
(209) 826-8282. **$75-$97.** 28976 W Plaza Dr. I-5, exit 407 (SR 33), just e. Ext corridors. **Pets:** Medium. $8 daily fee/room. Designated rooms, service with restrictions, supervision.
SAVE 🐾 ✕ 🍴 💻 🏊

Ramada Mission de Oro M
(209) 826-4444. **$79-$104, 3 day notice.** 13070 S Hwy 33. I-5, exit 407 (SR 33), just w. Ext/int corridors. **Pets:** Other species. $10 daily fee/room. Designated rooms.
SAVE 🐾 ✕ 🍴 💻 🍴 🏊

Super 8 M
(209) 827-8700. **$60.** 28821 W Gonzaga Rd. 2.5 mi w of I-5; SR 152, exit Gonzaga Rd, just s. Ext corridors. **Pets:** Accepted.
SAVE 🐾 ✕ 🍴 💻 🏊

SCOTTS VALLEY

Best Western Inn Scotts Valley SH
(831) 438-6666. **$89-$225.** 6020 Scotts Valley Dr. SR 17, exit Granite Creek, just w. Ext corridors. **Pets:** Accepted.
SAVE 🐾 ✕ 🔧 📷 🍴 💻 🏊

SELMA

Super 8 Motel SH
(559) 896-2800. **$95-$135.** 3142 S Highland Ave. SR 99, exit Floral Ave. Int corridors. **Pets:** Accepted.
SAVE 🐾 ✕ 🍴 🏊

SHASTA LAKE

Bridge Bay Resort SH 🐾
(530) 275-3021. **$85-$108, 3 day notice.** 10300 Bridge Bay Rd. I-5, exit 690, e of I-5, exit Bridge Bay Rd; 12 mi n of Redding. Ext corridors. **Pets:** $50 deposit/room, $15 daily fee/pet. Service with restrictions, supervision.
SAVE 🐾 ✕ 🍴 💻 🍴 🏊 🛄

Fawndale Lodge & RV Resort M
(530) 275-8000. **$59-$83.** I-5, exit 689, 1 mi s of Shasta Lake; e of I-5, exit Fawndale Rd; 10 mi n of Redding. Ext corridors. **Pets:** Other species. Service with restrictions.
SAVE 🐾 ✕ 🍴 💻 🏊 🛄

SHELTER COVE

Inn of the Lost Coast M 🐾
(707) 986-7521. **$145.** 205 Wave Dr. US 101, exit Shelter Cove, 1.7 mi s on Redwood Dr, 21.1 mi w on Briceland Rd/Shelter Cove Rd, 0.4 mi n on Upper Pacific Rd, then just w on Lower Pacific Rd. Ext corridors. **Pets:** Other species. $10 one-time fee/pet. Designated rooms, service with restrictions, supervision.
SAVE ✕ 🍴 💻 🍴 🛄 🛄

SIERRA CITY

Herrington's Sierra Pines M
(530) 862-1151. **$79-$110, 7 day notice.** 104 Main St. 0.5 mi w on SR 49; 12 mi n of Downieville Center. Ext corridors. **Pets:** Other species. Supervision.
SAVE 🐾 ✕ 🍴 💻 🍴 🛄 🛄 🛄

SIMI VALLEY

Extended StayAmerica-Los Angeles-Simi Valley SH
(805) 584-8880. **Call for rates.** 2498 Stearns St. SR 118, exit Stearns St, just s. Int corridors. **Pets:** Accepted.
✕ 🍴 💻

SMITH RIVER

Ship Ashore Motel M
(707) 487-3141. **$60-$140.** 12370 Hwy 101. On US 101, 3.7 mi s of Oregon border. Ext corridors. **Pets:** Very small, other species. Supervision.
ASK 🐾 ✕ 🍴 💻 🍴 🛄

SOLEDAD

Best Western Valley Harvest Inn SH
(831) 678-3833. **$79-$180.** 1155 Front St. US 101, exit Soledad, just e. Ext/int corridors. **Pets:** Small, dogs only. $10 daily fee/pet. Designated rooms, service with restrictions, supervision.
SAVE 🐾 ✕ 🍴 💻 🍴 🏊

SOLVANG

Meadowlark Inn M 🐾
(805) 688-4631. **$120-$275, 14 day notice.** 2644 Mission Dr. On SR 246, 1.6 mi e. Ext corridors. **Pets:** Dogs only. $100 deposit/room, $25 daily fee/room. Designated rooms, supervision.
ASK 🐾 ✕ 🍴 💻 🏊

Royal Copenhagen Inn M 🐾
(805) 688-5561. **$85-$219, 3 day notice.** 1579 Mission Dr. On SR 246. Ext/int corridors. **Pets:** $100 deposit/room. Designated rooms, service with restrictions, supervision.
SAVE 🐾 ✕ 🍴 💻 🏊

Wine Valley Inn & Cottages SH
(805) 688-2111. **$89-$319.** 1564 Copenhagen Dr. SR 246, just s on 5th St. Ext/int corridors. **Pets:** $100 deposit/pet, $25 daily fee/pet. Designated rooms, no service, supervision.
SAVE ✕ 🍴 💻 🛄

SONORA

Aladdin Motor Inn SH 🐾
(209) 533-4971. **$68-$89.** 14260 Mono Way (Hwy 108). On SR 108, 3.5 mi e. Ext/int corridors. **Pets:** Medium. $15 one-time fee/room. Designated rooms, service with restrictions, supervision.
SAVE ✕ 🍴 💻 🏊

Best Western Sonora Oaks SH 🐾
(209) 533-4400. **$109-$143.** 19551 Hess Ave. 3.5 mi e on SR 108. Ext/int corridors. **Pets:** Medium. $25 daily fee/room. Designated rooms, service with restrictions, supervision.
SAVE 🐾 ✕ 📷 🍴 💻 🏊

Miners Motel M
(209) 532-7850. **$59-$75, 3 day notice.** 18740 SR 108. On SR 108 and 49, 1 mi e of Jamestown. Ext corridors. Pets: Medium, dogs only. $10 daily fee/pet. Service with restrictions.

Sonora Days Inn SH
(209) 532-2400. **$69-$114.** 160 S Washington St. Downtown. Ext/int corridors. Pets: Medium, other species. $10 daily fee/room. Designated rooms, service with restrictions, supervision.

Union Hill Inn BB
(209) 533-1494. **$150-$195, 3 day notice.** 21645 Parrotts Ferry Rd. Jct SR 49 and Parrotts Ferry Rd; 3 mi n of downtown. Ext corridors. Pets: Accepted.

STANTON

Best Western Cypress Inn & Suites M
(714) 527-6680. **$109-$139, 3 day notice.** 7161 W Katella Ave. SR 22, exit 7 (Knott Ave/Golden West St.), 2 mi n, then just w. Ext/int corridors. Pets: Accepted.

STOCKTON

Comfort Inn M
(209) 478-4300. **$49-$120.** 2654 W March Ln. I-5, exit March Ln, just e. Ext corridors. Pets: Other species. $25 deposit/room. Service with restrictions, supervision.

Econo Lodge of Stockton M
(209) 466-5741. **$59-$69.** 2210 S Manthey Rd. I-5, exit 8th St W, 0.3 mi s of jct SR 4. Int corridors. Pets: Very small, dogs only. $20 one-time fee/pet. Designated rooms, service with restrictions, supervision.

Holiday Inn SH
(209) 474-3301. **$89-$139.** 111 E March Ln. I-5, exit March Ln, 2.5 mi e; corner of El Dorado St. Int corridors. Pets: Accepted.

Howard Johnson Express Inn-Marina SH
(209) 948-6151. **$70-$85.** 33 N Center St. 1 blk n; w off El Dorado St via Weber; SR 99, exit Wilson Way southbound; exit northbound, w via Mariposa Rd to Charter Way; I-5, exit downtown. Ext corridors. Pets: Medium. $10 daily fee/pet. Designated rooms, service with restrictions, supervision.

La Quinta Inn Stockton SH
(209) 952-7800. **$88-$118.** 2710 W March Ln. I-5, exit March Ln, just w. Ext corridors. Pets: Medium. Service with restrictions.

Residence Inn by Marriott SH
(209) 472-9800. **$139-$250.** 3240 W March Ln. I-5, exit March Ln, 0.5 mi w. Int corridors. Pets: Accepted.

SUNNYVALE

Homestead Studio Suites Hotel-San Jose-Sunnyvale M
(408) 734-3431. **$110-$120.** 1255 Orleans Dr. N of SR 237, exit Mathilda Ave, e on Moffett Park Dr. Ext corridors. Pets: Accepted.

Maple Tree Inn SH ❀
(408) 720-9700. **$69-$129.** 711 E El Camino Real. On SR 82; between Fair Oaks and Wolfe Rd; 2.5 mi w of US 101. Int corridors. Pets: Medium, other species. $10 daily fee/pet. Designated rooms, service with restrictions, supervision.

Quality Inn-Sunnyvale SH ❀
(408) 744-1100. **$69-$279.** 1280 Persian Dr. US 101, exit Lawrence Expwy N, 1 mi n to Persian Dr, then 0.3 mi w. Int corridors. Pets: Small. $100 deposit/room, $10 daily fee/pet. Designated rooms, service with restrictions, supervision.

Residence Inn by Marriott SH
(408) 720-8893. **$89-$109.** 1080 Stewart Dr. US 101, exit Lawrence Expwy S, w on Duane Ave W. Ext corridors. Pets: Accepted.

Residence Inn by Marriott SH
(408) 720-1000. **Call for rates.** 750 Lakeway Dr. US 101, exit Lawrence Expwy S, e on Oakmead. Ext corridors. Pets: Accepted.

Staybridge Suites SH
(408) 745-1515. **$70-$299.** 900 Hamlin Ct. SR 237, exit Mathilda Ave S, w on Ross Dr. Ext corridors. Pets: Accepted.

TownePlace Suites by Marriott Sunnyvale/Mountain View SH
(408) 733-4200. **$89-$199.** 606 S Bernardo Ave. SR 85, exit SR 82, 0.5 mi s. Int corridors. Pets: Accepted.

Vagabond Inn M
(408) 734-4607. **$59-$219.** 816 Ahwanee Ave. US 101, exit Mathilda Ave S, then s. Ext corridors. Pets: Other species. $10 daily fee/pet. Designated rooms, service with restrictions, supervision.

SUSANVILLE

Americas Best Inns M
(530) 257-4522. **$60-$159.** 2705 Main St. 1.5 mi e on SR 36. Ext corridors. Pets: Medium, other species. $10 daily fee/pet. Service with restrictions, supervision.

River Inn M
(530) 257-6051. **$52-$62.** 1710 Main St. 0.8 mi e on SR 36. Ext corridors. Pets: Accepted.

Super 8 Motel M
(530) 257-2782. **$72.** 2975 Johnstonville Rd. SR 36, 1.8 mi e. Ext corridors. Pets: Accepted.

TEHACHAPI

Best Western Mountain Inn M
(661) 822-5591. **$89-$99.** 418 W Tehachapi Blvd. SR 58, exit 148 (SR 202), 1 mi e. Ext corridors. Pets: Other species. Designated rooms.

Tehachapi Summit Travelodge M
(661) 823-8000. **$72-$85.** 500 Steuber Rd. SR 58, exit 151 (Monolith), just s. Int corridors. Pets: Accepted.

TEMECULA

▼▼▼ **Extended StayAmerica-Temecula-Wine Country** 🅜
(951) 587-8881. **$94-$159.** 27622 Jefferson Ave. I-15, exit 61 (SR 79 N), just w on Winchester Rd, then 0.4 mi s. Int corridors. **Pets:** Accepted.
🅐🅢🅚 🔊 ✖ 🔒 🖵

THOUSAND OAKS

▼▼▼ **Best Western Thousand Oaks Inn** 🆂🅷 ❖
(805) 497-3701. **$120-$200.** 75 W Thousand Oaks Blvd. US 101, exit 44 (Moorpark Rd), just n, then just w. Ext corridors. **Pets:** Medium. $45 one-time fee/pet. Designated rooms, service with restrictions, supervision.
🅐🅢🅚 🔊 ✖ 🕭 🔊 🔒 🖵 ➰

▼▼▼ **Holiday Inn** 🅜
(805) 499-5910. **$89-$200.** 1320 Newbury Rd. US 101, exit 46 (Ventu Park Rd), just se. Ext corridors. **Pets:** Service with restrictions, supervision.
🅐🅢🅚 ✖ 🕭 🔊 🔊 🔒 🖵 🍴 ➰

▼ **Motel 6 #1360 Thousand Oaks** 🅜
(805) 499-0711. **$53-$65.** 1516 Newbury Rd. US 101, exit 46 (Ventu Park Rd), just w, then just n. Ext corridors. **Pets:** Medium, other species. Service with restrictions, supervision.
🔊 ✖ ➰

▲▲▲ ▼▼▼ **Premier Inns** 🅜
(805) 499-0755. **$59-$79.** 2434 W Hillcrest Dr. US 101, exit 47A (Borchard Rd), just e, then just n. Ext corridors. **Pets:** Medium, dogs only. Designated rooms, service with restrictions, supervision.
🆂🅰🆅🅴 🔊 ✖ 🕭 🔒 ➰

THOUSAND PALMS

▲▲▲ ▼▼▼ **Red Roof Inn** 🅜
(760) 343-1381. **$61-$189.** 72-215 Varner Rd. I-10, exit 130 (Ramon Rd), just n, then just w. Ext corridors. **Pets:** Medium, other species. Service with restrictions, supervision.
🆂🅰🆅🅴 ✖ 🔒 🖵 ➰

THREE RIVERS

▲▲▲ ▼▼▼ **Americas Best Value Inn–Lazy J Ranch** 🅜
(559) 561-4449. **$90-$115, 3 day notice.** 39625 Sierra Dr. SR 198, 3 mi sw of town center. Ext corridors. **Pets:** Other species. $5 one-time fee/pet. Service with restrictions, supervision.
🆂🅰🆅🅴 🔊 ✖ 🔒 🖵 ➰ ⊠

▲▲▲ ▼▼▼ **Buckeye Tree Lodge** 🅜 🐾
(559) 561-5900. **$69-$132, 7 day notice.** 46000 Sierra Dr. SR 198, 6 mi ne of town center; 0.5 mi sw of entrance to Sequoia National Park. Ext corridors. **Pets:** Other species. Supervision.
🆂🅰🆅🅴 🔊 ✖ 🔒 🖵 ➰

▲▲▲ ▼▼▼ **Gateway Lodge** 🅜
(559) 561-4133. **$79-$149, 3 day notice.** 45978 Sierra Dr. SR 198, 6 mi ne of town center; 0.5 mi sw of entrance to Sequoia National Park. Ext corridors. **Pets:** Accepted.
🆂🅰🆅🅴 🔊 ✖ 🔒 🖵 🍴 ➰

▼▼▼ **Sequoia River Dance Bed & Breakfast** 🅱🅱 ❖
(559) 561-4411. **Call for rates.** 40534 Cherokee Oaks Dr. SR 198, 2 mi sw of town center, then 0.3 mi e. **Pets:** $10 daily fee/pet. Supervision.
🅦 ➰

▲▲▲ ▼▼▼ **Sequoia Village Inn** 🅒🅐 ❖
(559) 561-3652. **$69-$269, 7 day notice.** 45971 Sierra Dr. SR 198, 6 mi ne of town center; 0.5 mi sw of entrance to Sequoia National Park. Ext corridors. **Pets:** Other species. Supervision.
🆂🅰🆅🅴 🔊 ✖ 🔒 🖵 ➰ 🅩

TRINIDAD

▲▲▲ ▼ **Bishop Pine Lodge** 🅒🅐
(707) 677-3314. **$100-$145, 7 day notice.** 1481 Patrick's Point Dr. US 101, exit Seawood Dr, just w, then 0.8 mi s. Ext corridors. **Pets:** Accepted.
🆂🅰🆅🅴 🔊 ✖ 🔒 🖵 🅺

▼▼◆ **Lost Whale Bed & Breakfast Inn** 🅱🅱
(707) 677-3425. **$170-$250, 7 day notice.** 3452 Patrick's Point Dr. US 101, exit Patrick's Point Dr, 1.1 mi w. Int corridors. **Pets:** Accepted.
✖ 🅺

▲▲▲ ▼▼▼ **Trinidad Inn** 🆂🅷
(707) 677-3349. **$95-$175.** 1170 Patrick's Point Dr. US 101, exit Trinidad, just w on Main St, then 1.3 mi n. Ext corridors. **Pets:** Accepted.
🆂🅰🆅🅴 ✖ 🔒 🖵 🅺

TULARE

▲▲▲ ▼▼▼ **Best Western Town & Country Lodge** 🅜
(559) 688-7537. **$79-$150.** 1051 N Blackstone St. SR 99, exit 88 (Prosperity Ave/Blackstone St), just w. Int corridors. **Pets:** Medium. $20 one-time fee/room. Service with restrictions, supervision.
🆂🅰🆅🅴 🔊 ✖ 🔊 🔒 🖵 ➰

▲▲▲ ▼▼▼ **Charter Inn** 🆂🅷
(559) 685-9500. **$94-$134.** 1016 E Prosperity Ave. SR 99, exit 88 (Prosperity Ave/Blackstone St), just e. Int corridors. **Pets:** Accepted.
🆂🅰🆅🅴 🔊 ✖ 🕭 🔊 🔊 🔒 🖵 ➰

▲▲▲ ▼▼▼ **Quality Inn** 🅜
(559) 686-3432. **$73-$85.** 1010 E Prosperity Ave. SR 99, exit 88 (Prosperity Ave/Blackstone St), just e. Int corridors. **Pets:** Small, dogs only. $10 daily fee/pet. Service with restrictions, supervision.
🆂🅰🆅🅴 🔊 ✖ 🔊 🔒 🖵 ➰ ⊠

TURLOCK

▲▲▲ ▼▼▼ **Best Western Orchard Inn** 🅜
(209) 667-2827. **$87-$97.** 5025 N Golden State Blvd. SR 99, exit Taylor Rd, just e. Ext corridors. **Pets:** Accepted.
🆂🅰🆅🅴 🔊 ✖ 🕭 🔒 🖵 ➰

▲▲▲ ▼▼▼ **Travelodge** 🅜
(209) 668-3400. **$66-$80.** 201 W Glenwood Ave. SR 99, exit Lander W. Ext corridors. **Pets:** Accepted.
🆂🅰🆅🅴 🔊 ✖ 🕭 🔊 🔒 🖵 ➰

TWAIN HARTE

▲▲▲ ▼▼▼▼ **McCaffrey House B & B Inn** 🅱🅱
(209) 586-0757. **$135-$175, 8 day notice.** 23251 Hwy 108. 0.5 mi on SR 108; just beyond 4000' elevation marker. Int corridors. **Pets:** Other species. $25 daily fee/pet. Designated rooms, service with restrictions, supervision.
🆂🅰🆅🅴 ✖

TWENTYNINE PALMS

▼▼ **Circle C Lodge** 🅜
(760) 367-7615. **$84-$103, 3 day notice.** 6340 El Rey Ave. On SR 62, just n; 1.5 mi w of Adobe Rd. Ext corridors. **Pets:** Accepted.
🅐🅢🅚 🔊 ✖ 🔒 🖵

▲▲▲ ▼▼▼ **Roughley Manor** 🅱🅱
(760) 367-3238. **$135-$160, 3 day notice.** 74744 Joe Davis Rd. SR 62, 0.5 mi n on Utal Trail, 0.5 mi e on Joe Davis Rd, then just n. Ext/int corridors. **Pets:** Dogs only. Designated rooms, service with restrictions, supervision.
🆂🅰🆅🅴 ✖ 🔒 🖵 ➰ 🅩

▼▼ **Sunnyvale Garden Suites Hotel** ⬛ ❀
(760) 361-3939. **$89-$175.** 73843 Sunnyvale Dr. SR 62, 0.7 mi n on Adobe Rd, just e on S Slope, just n on Ocotillo, then just e. Ext corridors. **Pets:** Medium. $35 one-time fee/pet. Designated rooms, service with restrictions, crate.

(ASK) (S⬛) (✕) (🔒) (💻) (✖)

UNION CITY

⬤⬤⬤ ▼▼▼▼ **Crowne Plaza Oakland South/Union City** 🄻🄷
(510) 489-2200. **$99-$149.** 32083 Alvarado-Niles Rd. I-880, exit Alvarado-Niles Rd, just e. Int corridors. **Pets:** Small. $100 deposit/room, $35 daily fee/pet. Supervision.

(SAVE) (S⬛) (✕) (🔒) (💻) (🍴) (⇌) (✖)

VACAVILLE

⬤⬤⬤ ▼▼ **Best Western Heritage Inn** Ⓜ
(707) 448-8453. **$98-$103.** 1420 E Monte Vista Ave. I-80, exit Monte Vista Ave, just n. Ext corridors. **Pets:** Medium, other species. $20 one-time fee/room. Service with restrictions, supervision.

(SAVE) (S⬛) (✕) (🔒) (💻) (⇌)

▼▼▼ **Extended StayAmerica-Sacramento-Vacaville** 🅂🄷
(707) 469-1371. **$104-$114.** 799 Orange Dr. I-80, exit Leisure Town Rd. Int corridors. **Pets:** Accepted.

(ASK) (S⬛) (✕) (💻) (⇌)

▼▼▼ **Residence Inn by Marriott** 🅂🄷
(707) 469-0300. **$185-$205.** 360 Orange Dr. I-80, exit Orange Dr eastbound, 0.5 mi; exit Monte Vista westbound, freeway overpass to E Nut Tree Pkwy. Int corridors. **Pets:** Accepted.

(ASK) (S⬛) (✕) (🔒) (🔓) (💻) (⇌) (✖)

⬤⬤⬤ ▼▼▼ **Vacaville Super 8** Ⓜ
(707) 449-8884. **$59-$69.** 101 Allison Ct. I-80, exit Monte Vista Ave, just n. Int corridors. **Pets:** Medium. $10 daily fee/pet. Designated rooms, service with restrictions, supervision.

(SAVE) (S⬛) (✕) (🔒) (💻) (⇌)

VALLEJO

⬤⬤⬤ ▼▼▼▼ **Best Western Inn & Suites at Marine World** 🅂🄷
(707) 554-9655. **$69-$169.** 1596 Fairgrounds Dr. I-80, exit SR 37 (Marine World Pkwy) N, 0.3 mi w. Int corridors. **Pets:** $35 one-time fee/pet. Designated rooms, service with restrictions, supervision.

(SAVE) (S⬛) (✕) (🔒) (🔓) (🔒) (💻) (⇌)

▼▼▼ **Courtyard by Marriott** 🅂🄷
(707) 644-1200. **$149-$229.** 1000 Fairgrounds Dr. I-80, exit SR 37 (Marine World Pkwy), 0.3 mi n. Int corridors. **Pets:** Accepted.

(ASK) (✕) (🔒) (🔓) (💻) (🍴) (⇌)

▼▼ **Ramada Inn** 🅂🄷
(707) 643-2700. **$65-$169.** 1000 Admiral Callaghan Ln. I-80, exit Columbus Pkwy, 0.5 mi w. Ext corridors. **Pets:** Large, other species. $25 one-time fee/room. Service with restrictions, supervision.

(ASK) (S⬛) (✕) (🔒) (💻) (⇌)

VENTURA

⬤⬤⬤ ▼▼▼▼ **Crowne Plaza Ventura Beach Resort** 🄻🄷
(805) 648-7731. **$95-$229.** 450 E Harbor Blvd. US 101, exit 70A (California St) northbound, just s; exit 71 (Main St) southbound, 0.5 mi e to California St, then just s. Int corridors. **Pets:** Dogs only. $50 one-time fee/room. Designated rooms, service with restrictions, supervision.

(SAVE) (S⬛) (✕) (🔒) (🔓) (🔒) (💻) (🍴) (⇌)

▼▼▼ **Four Points by Sheraton Ventura Harbortown** 🅂🄷
(805) 658-1212. **$99-$249.** 1050 Schooner Dr. US 101, exit 68 (Seaward Ave), just w, then 1.5 mi s; at Ventura Harbor. Ext corridors. **Pets:** $75 one-time fee/pet. Designated rooms, service with restrictions, supervision.

(ASK) (✕) (🔓) (🔒) (🔒) (🔒) (💻) (🍴) (⇌) (✖)

⬤⬤⬤ ▼▼▼▼ **La Quinta Inn Ventura** Ⓜ
(805) 658-6200. **$93-$142.** 5818 Valentine Rd. US 101, exit 64 (Victoria Ave), just s, then just n. Ext/int corridors. **Pets:** Medium. Service with restrictions.

(SAVE) (✕) (🔒) (🔓) (💻) (💻) (⇌)

▼▼▼ **Marriott Ventura Beach Hotel** 🄻🄷
(805) 643-6000. **$149-$399.** 2055 Harbor Blvd. US 101, exit 68 (Seaward Ave), just w, then 0.5 mi n. Int corridors. **Pets:** Large, other species. $75 one-time fee/room. Service with restrictions, supervision.

(ASK) (✕) (🔒) (🔓) (🔒) (🔒) (💻) (🍴) (⇌)

⬤⬤⬤ ▼▼▼ **Vagabond Inn Ventura** Ⓜ
(805) 648-5371. **$79-$299.** 756 E Thompson Blvd. US 101, exit 70A (California St) northbound, just n, then just e; exit 70A (Ventura Ave) southbound, 0.6 mi s. Ext corridors. **Pets:** $10 daily fee/pet. Service with restrictions, supervision.

(SAVE) (S⬛) (✕) (✕) (💻) (🍴) (⇌)

VICTORVILLE

⬤⬤⬤ ▼▼▼▼ **Comfort Suites Hotel** 🅂🄷
(760) 245-6777. **$110-$140.** 12281 Mariposa Rd. I-15, exit 147 (Bear Valley Rd), just e, then just n. Int corridors. **Pets:** Accepted.

(SAVE) (S⬛) (✕) (🔒) (🔓) (🔒) (💻) (⇌)

▼▼▼ **Hawthorn Suites by Hyatt** 🅂🄷
(760) 949-4700. **$97-$156.** 11750 Dunia Rd. I-15, exit 147 (Bear Valley Rd), just w, just s on Amargosa Rd, then just w. Int corridors. **Pets:** Accepted.

(ASK) (S⬛) (✕) (🔒) (🔓) (🔒) (🔒) (💻) (⇌) (✖)

▼▼ **Red Roof Inn** Ⓜ 🐾
(760) 241-1577. **$69-$78.** 13409 Mariposa Rd. I-15, exit 147 (Bear Valley Rd) northbound, just e, then 1.5 mi n; exit 150 (SR 18 W/Palmdale Rd) southbound, just e, then 1.5 mi s. Ext corridors. **Pets:** Large. Service with restrictions, supervision.

(ASK) (S⬛) (✕) (🔒) (💻) (⇌)

⬤⬤⬤ ▼▼▼ **Travelodge Victorville** Ⓜ
(760) 241-7200. **$65-$95.** 12175 Mariposa Rd. I-15, exit 147 (Bear Valley Rd), just e, then just n. Ext corridors. **Pets:** Medium, dogs only. $8 one-time fee/pet. Service with restrictions, supervision.

(SAVE) (S⬛) (✕) (🔒) (⇌)

VISALIA

◆◇ **Best Western Visalia Inn** Ⓜ
(559) 732-4561. **$88-$94.** 623 W Main St. SR 198, exit 105B (SR 63 S/Mooney Blvd), just n, then 0.9 mi e. Ext corridors. **Pets:** Small, other species. $10 one-time fee/pet. Designated rooms, service with restrictions, crate.

(ASK) (S⬛) (✕) (🔒) (💻) (⇌)

⬤⬤⬤ ◆◇◇ **Holiday Inn Hotel & Conference Center** 🄻🄷 ❀
(559) 651-5000. **$125-$175.** 9000 W Airport Dr. SR 99, exit 102 (Plaza Dr), then just s. Int corridors. **Pets:** Medium. $25 daily fee/pet. Designated rooms, service with restrictions, supervision.

(SAVE) (S⬛) (✕) (🔒) (🔓) (🔒) (🔒) (💻) (🍴) (⇌) (✖)

⬤⬤⬤ ◆◇ **Lamp Liter Inn** Ⓜ
(559) 732-4511. **$79-$129.** 3300 W Mineral King Ave. SR 198, exit 105B (SR 63/S Mooney Blvd), 0.5 mi w. Ext corridors. **Pets:** Accepted.

(SAVE) (S⬛) (✕) (🔒) (💻) (🍴) (⇌)

⬤⬤⬤ ◆ **Super 8** Ⓜ
(559) 627-2885. **$60-$85.** 4801 W Noble Ave. SR 198, exit 104 (Akers St), just s, then 0.5 mi e. Ext corridors. **Pets:** Other species. $20 daily fee/pet. Service with restrictions, crate.

(SAVE) (✕) (🔒) (⇌)

VISTA

▼▼▼▼ La Quinta Inn San Diego (Vista) M
(760) 727-8180. **$98-$134.** 630 Sycamore Ave. SR 78, exit Sycamore Ave, just sw. Ext/int corridors. **Pets:** Medium. Service with restrictions.

(ASK) (X) (🛏) (💻) (🏊)

WALNUT CREEK

▼▼▼▼ Embassy Suites Hotel LH
(925) 934-2500. **$139-$239.** 1345 Treat Blvd. I-680, exit Geary Rd/Treat Blvd northbound; exit Oak Park Blvd southbound, then e; at Pleasant Hill BART Station. Int corridors. **Pets:** Large. $15 daily fee/pet, $75 one-time fee/pet. Service with restrictions, supervision.

(ASK) (X) (🐾) (🛏) (💻) (🍴) (🏊) (✕)

▲▲▲ ▼▼▼▼ Holiday Inn Walnut Creek SH
(925) 932-3332. **$79-$169.** 2730 N Main St. I-680, exit N Main St, just n. Int corridors. **Pets:** Accepted.

(SAVE) (S🐾) (X) (🛏) (💻) (🍴) (🏊)

WATSONVILLE

▲▲▲ ▼▼▼ Best Western Rose Garden Inn M ✿
(831) 724-3367. **$69-$199.** 740 Freedom Blvd. On SR 152. Ext corridors. **Pets:** Dogs only. $15 daily fee/room. Service with restrictions, supervision.

(SAVE) (S🐾) (X) (🛏) (💻) (🏊)

▲▲▲ ▼▼▼ Comfort Inn Watsonville SH
(831) 728-2300. **$89-$120.** 112 Airport Blvd. SR 1, exit Airport Blvd, 1 mi e. Int corridors. **Pets:** Accepted.

(SAVE) (S🐾) (X) (🛏) (💻)

▲▲▲ ▼▼▼ Red Roof Inn SH ✿
(831) 740-4520. **$56-$92.** 1620 W Beach St. SR 1, exit Riverside Dr (SR 129), just w. Int corridors. **Pets:** Other species. Service with restrictions, supervision.

(SAVE) (S🐾) (X) (🛏) (💻) (🏊)

WEAVERVILLE

▲▲▲ ▼▼ ▼ 49er Gold Country Inn M
(530) 623-4937. **$60-$110.** 880 Main St. On SR 299. Ext corridors. **Pets:** Medium, dogs only. Service with restrictions, supervision.

(SAVE) (S🐾) (X) (🛏) (💻) (🏊) (✕)

▲▲▲ ▼▼▼▼ Best Western Weaverville Victorian Inn SH
(530) 623-4432. **$85-$169.** 1709 Main St. On SR 299. Ext corridors. **Pets:** Accepted.

(SAVE) (S🐾) (X) (🌀) (🛏) (💻) (🍴) (🏊)

▲▲▲ ▼ Motel Trinity M
(530) 623-2129. **$50-$80, 3 day notice.** 1270 Main St. Just s on SR 3. Ext corridors. **Pets:** Dogs only. $5 daily fee/pet. Service with restrictions, supervision.

(SAVE) (S🐾) (X) (🛏) (💻) (🏊)

▼▼ Red Hill Motel M
(530) 623-4331. **$37-$84.** Red Hill Rd. SR 299, just w of SR 3. Ext corridors. **Pets:** Medium. $5 one-time fee/pet. Service with restrictions, supervision.

(🛏) (💻)

WEED

▲▲▲ ▼▼▼▼ Comfort Inn SH
(530) 938-1982. **$79-$129.** 1844 Shastina Dr. I-5, exit S Weed, just e. Int corridors. **Pets:** Dogs only. $50 deposit/room, $10 daily fee/pet. Designated rooms, service with restrictions, supervision.

(SAVE) (S🐾) (X) (🐾) (🛏) (💻) (🏊)

▲▲▲ ▼▼▼▼ Holiday Inn Express SH
(530) 938-1308. **$69-$99.** 1830 Black Butte Dr. just e. Int corridors. **Pets:** Accepted.

(SAVE) (S🐾) (X) (🛏) (💻)

▲▲▲ ▼▼▼ Sis-Q-Inn Motel M
(530) 938-4194. **$60-$125.** 1825 Shastina Dr. I-5, exit S Weed. Int corridors. **Pets:** Small. $10 daily fee/pet. Service with restrictions, supervision.

(SAVE) (S🐾) (X) (🛏)

WESTLEY

▲▲▲ ▼▼▼ Econo Lodge M
(209) 894-3900. **$70-$95, 3 day notice.** 7100 McCracken Rd. I-5, exit Westley, just e. Ext corridors. **Pets:** Medium. $10 daily fee/pet. No service, supervision.

(SAVE) (S🐾) (X) (🛏) (💻) (🏊)

▲▲▲ ▼▼▼▼ Holiday Inn Express SH ✿
(209) 894-8940. **$99-$109.** 4525 Howard Rd. I-5, exit Westley, just e. Int corridors. **Pets:** Small. $25 one-time fee/pet. Service with restrictions, supervision.

(SAVE) (S🐾) (X) (🛏) (💻) (🏊)

WESTMORLAND

▲▲▲ ▼▼▼ Super 8 Motel M
(760) 351-7100. **$75-$120.** 351 W Main St. On SR 86. Int corridors. **Pets:** Accepted.

(SAVE) (S🐾) (X) (🛏) (🏊)

WEST SACRAMENTO

▼▼▼ Extended StayAmerica-Sacramento-West Sacramento SH
(916) 371-1270. **$99-$109.** 795 Stillwater Ave. I-80, exit Reed Ave, just w. Int corridors. **Pets:** Accepted.

(ASK) (S🐾) (X) (🐾) (🛏) (💻)

WILLIAMS

▲▲▲ ▼▼▼ Comfort Inn M
(530) 473-2381. **$69-$89.** 400 C St. I-5, exit Williams, just w on E St, then just n on 4th St. Ext corridors. **Pets:** $10 daily fee/pet. Service with restrictions, supervision.

(SAVE) (S🐾) (X) (🐾M) (🛏) (💻) (🏊)

▲▲▲ ▼▼▼▼ Granzella's Inn M
(530) 473-3310. **$80-$105.** 391 6th St. I-5, exit Williams, 0.5 mi w. Int corridors. **Pets:** Other species. $10 one-time fee/room. Designated rooms, no service, supervision.

(SAVE) (S🐾) (X) (🐾M) (🐾) (🛏) (💻) (🍴) (🏊)

▲▲▲ ▼▼▼▼ Holiday Inn Express Hotel & Suites M
(530) 473-5120. **$89-$109.** 374 Ruggieri Way. I-5, exit Williams, just e. Int corridors. **Pets:** Accepted.

(SAVE) (S🐾) (X) (🐾M) (🐾) (🛏) (💻)

▲▲▲ ▼▼ Stage Stop Inn M
(530) 473-2281. **$45-$50.** 300 N 7th St. I-5, exit SR 20 business route, 3 blks w. Ext corridors. **Pets:** Accepted.

(SAVE) (S🐾) (X) (🛏) (💻) (🏊)

WILLOW CREEK

▲▲▲ ▼ Bigfoot Motel M
(530) 629-2142. **$69-$160, 7 day notice.** 39039 Hwy 299. On SR 299; just e of SR 96; center. Ext corridors. **Pets:** Accepted.

(SAVE) (X) (🐾) (🛏) (🏊)

WILLOWS

▲▲▲ ▼▼▼ Days Inn M
(530) 934-4444. **$49-$89.** 475 N Humboldt Ave. I-5, exit 162 (Willows-Elk Creek-Glenn Rd), just e. Ext corridors. **Pets:** $10 daily fee/pet. Designated rooms, service with restrictions, supervision.

(SAVE) (S🐾) (X) (🐾M) (🛏) (💻) (🏊)

△△△ ▼ Economy Inn M
(530) 934-4224. **$55-$75.** 435 N Tehama St. I-5, exit SR 162 (Willows-Elk Creek-Glenn Rd), 1 mi e. Ext corridors. **Pets:** Small. $5 one-time fee/pet. Designated rooms, service with restrictions, supervision.
[SAVE] [S☼] [✕] [⊟]

△△△ ▼▼ Motel 6 #4273 M
(530) 934-7026. **$46-$86.** 452 N Humboldt Ave. I-5, exit 162 (Willows-Elk Creek-Glenn Rd), just e. Ext corridors. **Pets:** Medium, other species. Service with restrictions, supervision.
[SAVE] [S☼] [✕] [⊟] [⊃]

△△△ ▼▼▼ Super 8 Motel of Willows SH
(530) 934-2871. **$59-$64.** 457 Humboldt Ave. I-5, exit 162 (Willows-Elk Creek-Glenn Rd). Int corridors. **Pets:** Accepted.
[SAVE] [S☼] [✕] [⊟] [≋]

WINE COUNTRY AREA

ALBION

▼▼▼ Fensalden Inn BB
(707) 937-4042. **$119-$239, 7 day notice.** 33810 Navarro Ridge Rd. 0.5 mi e of jct SR 1. Ext/int corridors. **Pets:** Medium, dogs only. $100 deposit/room. Designated rooms, service with restrictions, supervision.
[ASK] [S☼] [✕] [⊟] [⊡] [K] [W] [✇]

CALISTOGA

△△△ ▼▼▼ Brannan Cottage Inn BB 🐾
(707) 942-4200. **$145-$210.** 109 Wapoo Ave. At Lincoln Ave. Ext corridors. **Pets:** Other species. $100 deposit/pet, $25 daily fee/pet. Designated rooms, service with restrictions, crate.
[SAVE] [✕]

▼▼▼ Washington Street Lodging CA
(707) 942-6968. **$95-$140 (no credit cards), 3 day notice.** 1605 Washington St. On SR 29. Ext corridors. **Pets:** Other species. $15 one-time fee/pet. Service with restrictions.
[✕] [&M] [⊟] [⊡] [✇]

CLOVERDALE

△△△ ▼ Cloverdale Oaks Inn M
(707) 894-2404. **$69-$169, 3 day notice.** 123 S Cloverdale Blvd. US 101, exit Citrus Fair Dr, 0.4 mi w to S Cloverdale Blvd, then just n. Ext corridors. **Pets:** Accepted.
[SAVE] [S☼] [✕] [&M] [⊟] [⊡]

FORT BRAGG

△△△ ▼▼▼ Americas Best Value Inn Seabird Lodge M
(707) 964-4731. **$72-$130, 3 day notice.** 191 South St. 0.8 mi n of Noyo River Bridge; 1 blk e off SR 1. Ext corridors. **Pets:** Medium, other species. $8 daily fee/room. Designated rooms, service with restrictions, supervision.
[SAVE] [S☼] [✕] [⊟] [⊡] [⊃] [K]

△△△ ▼▼▼ Beachcomber Motel M
(707) 964-2402. **$69-$260.** 1111 N Main St. 1 mi n on SR 1. Ext corridors. **Pets:** Accepted.
[SAVE] [✕] [⊟] [⊡] [K]

△△△ ▼▼▼ Beach House Inn M
(707) 961-1700. **$59-$158.** 100 Pudding Creek Rd. 0.7 mi n on SR 1. Int corridors. **Pets:** $10 daily fee/pet. Service with restrictions, supervision.
[SAVE] [S☼] [✕] [⊟] [⊡] [K]

▼▼▼ Emerald Dolphin Inn & Mini Golf M 🐾
(707) 964-6699. **$60-$200, 7 day notice.** 1211 S Main St. On SR 1. Ext corridors. **Pets:** Dogs only. $10 daily fee/room. Designated rooms, service with restrictions, supervision.
[ASK] [S☼] [✕] [⊟] [⊡] [⊠] [K]

△△△ ▼▼▼ Mariah Country Inn & Suites M
(707) 964-4787. **$60-$79, 3 day notice.** 763 N Main St. SR 1, 0.5 mi n. Ext corridors. **Pets:** Accepted.
[SAVE] [S☼] [✕] [⊟] [⊡] [K]

△△△ ▼▼▼ Pine Beach Inn & Suites M
(707) 964-5603. **$79-$159, 3 day notice.** 16801 N Hwy 1. On SR 1, 4 mi s. Ext corridors. **Pets:** Accepted.
[SAVE] [✕] [⊟] [⊡] [⊤] [⊠] [K]

△△△ ▼▼▼ Quality Inn & Suites M
(707) 964-4761. **$69-$229.** 400 S Main St. 6 blks s on SR 1. Ext corridors. **Pets:** Other species. $10 daily fee/room. Designated rooms, service with restrictions, supervision.
[SAVE] [S☼] [✕] [⊟] [⊡] [⊤] [⊃] [⊠] [K]

▼▼ Super 8 M
(707) 964-4003. **$49-$135.** 888 S Main St. 0.5 mi s on SR 1; north end of Noyo Bridge. Ext corridors. **Pets:** Accepted.
[ASK] [S☼] [✕] [⊡] [⊟]

△△△ ▼▼▼ Surf Motel M
(707) 964-5361. **$51-$110, 3 day notice.** 1220 S Main St. 1 mi s on SR 1; s of Noyo River Bridge; 0.3 mi n of jct SR 20. Ext corridors. **Pets:** Accepted.
[SAVE] [S☼] [✕] [⊟] [⊡] [K]

GUALALA

▼▼ Gualala Country Inn M
(707) 884-4343. **$95-$175, 3 day notice.** 47955 Center St. East side of SR 1. Ext/int corridors. **Pets:** Other species. $10 one-time fee/pet. Service with restrictions, supervision.
[✕] [⊟] [⊡] [K]

△△△ ▼▼▼ North Coast Country Inn BB 🐾
(707) 884-4537. **$156-$235, 5 day notice.** 34591 S Hwy 1. On SR 1, 4.5 mi n. Ext corridors. **Pets:** Dogs only. $25 one-time fee/pet. Designated rooms, service with restrictions, supervision.
[SAVE] [S☼] [✕] [⊟] [⊡] [K] [W] [✇]

▼▼ Surf Motel M
(707) 884-3571. **$105-$190.** 39170 S Hwy 1. Center. Ext/int corridors. **Pets:** Other species. $10 one-time fee/pet. Service with restrictions, supervision.
[✕] [⊟] [⊡] [K]

GUERNEVILLE

△△△ ▼▼▼ Ferngrove Cottages CA 🐾
(707) 869-8105. **$89-$239, 3 day notice.** 16650 Hwy 116. On SR 116, just sw. Ext corridors. **Pets:** Large, other species. $15 daily fee/pet. Designated rooms, service with restrictions, supervision.
[SAVE] [S☼] [✕] [&M] [⊟] [⊡] [⊃] [⊠] [K] [✇]

HEALDSBURG

△△△ ▼▼▼ Americas Best Value Inn & Suites M
(707) 433-5548. **$99-$129.** 74 Healdsburg Ave. US 101, exit Central Healdsburg, just e. Ext corridors. **Pets:** Small. $100 deposit/room, $10 daily fee/room. Service with restrictions, supervision.
[SAVE] [S☼] [✕] [&M] [⊟] [⊡] [⊃]

(AAA) ▼▼▼▼ Best Western Dry Creek Inn **M**
(707) 433-0300. **$99-$325.** 198 Dry Creek Rd. US 101, exit Dry Creek Rd, just e. Ext corridors. **Pets:** $20 daily fee/pet. Service with restrictions, supervision.

[SAVE] [S❄] [✕] [&M] [⊘] [⊟] [▣] [⇌]

JENNER

(AAA) ▼▼▼▼ Jenner Inn & Cottages **CI** ✿
(707) 865-2377. **$108-$298, 10 day notice.** 10400 Hwy 1. On SR 1 at SR 116. Ext corridors. **Pets:** Dogs only. $35 one-time fee/pet. Designated rooms, supervision.

[SAVE] [S❄] [✕] [&M] [⊟] [▣] [⊓] [Ⓐ] [⊠]

LEGGETT

(AAA) ▼▼ Redwoods River Resort **CA** ✿
(707) 925-6249. **$59-$145, 7 day notice.** 75000 Hwy 101. 6.5 mi n of jct SR 1. Ext corridors. **Pets:** $10 daily fee/pet. Designated rooms, no service, supervision.

[SAVE] [✕] [⊟] [▣] [⇌] [✕] [Ⓐ] [Ⓩ]

LITTLE RIVER

(AAA) ▼▼▼▼ Auberge Mendocino-Rachel's Inn **BB** ✿
(707) 937-0088. **$179-$225, 14 day notice.** 8200 N Hwy 1. On SR 1, 2 mi s of Mendocino. Ext/int corridors. **Pets:** Medium, dogs only. $100 deposit/room, $35 one-time fee/pet. Designated rooms, service with restrictions, crate.

[SAVE] [S❄] [✕] [&] [⊟] [▣] [Ⓐ] [Ⓩ]

▼▼▼▼ The Inn at Schoolhouse Creek **BB** ✿
(707) 937-5525. **$120-$350, 14 day notice.** 7001 N Hwy 1. On SR 1, 0.8 mi s of Van Damme State Park entrance. Ext corridors. **Pets:** Other species. $50 one-time fee/room. Service with restrictions.

[ASK] [S❄] [✕] [▼] [⊟] [▣] [Ⓐ]

(AAA) ▼▼▼▼ Stevenswood Spa Resort **CI** ✿
(707) 937-2810. **$149-$625, 99 day notice.** 8211 SR 1. 2 mi s of Mendocino. Int corridors. **Pets:** Other species. $50 one-time fee/pet.

[SAVE] [S❄] [✕] [&] [⊟] [▣] [⊓] [✕] [Ⓐ]

MENDOCINO

▼▼▼▼ Abigail's Bed & Breakfast **BB**
(707) 937-0934. **$99-$179, 14 day notice.** 951 Ukiah St. Just e of Lansing St; center. Ext/int corridors. **Pets:** Accepted.

[ASK] [S❄] [✕] [⊟] [▣] [Ⓐ] [Ⓩ]

▼▼▼▼ Agate Cove Inn **CA**
(707) 937-0551. **$149-$325, 14 day notice.** 11201 N Lansing St. Just w on Little Lake Rd from jct SR 1, 0.6 mi n. Ext corridors. **Pets:** Small, dogs only. $20 one-time fee/room. Designated rooms, supervision.

[✕] [▣] [Ⓐ] [Ⓩ]

(AAA) ▼▼▼▼ Blackberry Inn **M** ✿
(707) 937-5281. **$115-$260, 5 day notice.** 44951 Larkin Rd. Just e of jct SR 1. Ext corridors. **Pets:** $10 daily fee/pet. Designated rooms, supervision.

[SAVE] [S❄] [✕] [⊟] [▣] [Ⓐ]

▼▼▼▼ Hill House Inn **CI** ✿
(707) 937-0554. **$121-$295, 3 day notice.** 10701 Pallette Dr. Just w on Little Lake St from jct SR 1, just n on Lansing St. Ext corridors. **Pets:** Medium, dogs only. $25 one-time fee/pet. Designated rooms, service with restrictions, supervision.

[ASK] [S❄] [✕] [⊟] [▣] [⊓] [Ⓐ]

(AAA) ▼▼▼▼ MacCallum House Inn **CI**
(707) 937-0289. **$150-$395, 7 day notice.** 45020 Albion St. Just w of Lansing St; center. Ext/int corridors. **Pets:** Accepted.

[SAVE] [✕] [⊟] [▣] [⊓] [✕] [Ⓐ]

(AAA) ▼▼▼▼ Mendocino Seaside Cottage **BB**
(707) 485-0239. **$155-$301, 14 day notice.** 10940 Lansing St. Just w on Little Lake Rd from jct SR 1, then 0.3 mi n. Ext/int corridors. **Pets:** Accepted.

[SAVE] [S❄] [✕] [⊟] [▣] [✕] [Ⓐ]

(AAA) ▼▼▼▼ ▼▼▼▼ Stanford Inn by the Sea & Spa **CI** ✿
(707) 937-5615. **$202-$475, 7 day notice.** 44850 Comptche-Ukiah Rd. SR 1, exit Comptche-Ukiah Rd, 0.5 mi s of town, then 0.5 mi e. Ext corridors. **Pets:** Other species. $25 one-time fee/pet.

[SAVE] [S❄] [✕] [&M] [⊘] [⊟] [▣] [⊓] [⇌] [✕] [Ⓐ]

NAPA

▼▼▼▼ The Chablis Inn **M** ✿
(707) 257-1944. **$79-$185, 3 day notice.** 3360 Solano Ave. Just w off SR 29 via Redwood Rd, then just s. Ext corridors. **Pets:** Dogs only. $10 daily fee/pet. Designated rooms, supervision.

[ASK] [S❄] [✕] [&M] [⊘] [⊟] [▣] [⇌]

(AAA) ▼▼▼▼ The Napa Inn **BB**
(707) 257-1444. **$125-$295, 10 day notice.** 1137 Warren St. SR 29, exit 1st St, 0.5 mi e, then 0.3 mi n. Int corridors. **Pets:** Accepted.

[SAVE] [S❄] [✕] [&M] [⊟] [▣]

▼▼▼▼ Napa River Inn **SH** ✿
(707) 251-8500. **$179-$499.** 500 Main St. Downtown. Int corridors. **Pets:** Medium. $25 daily fee/room. Service with restrictions, supervision.

[ASK] [S❄] [✕] [&M] [⊘] [⊟] [▣]

(AAA) ▼▼ Napa Valley Redwood Inn **M** ✿
(707) 257-6111. **$75-$135.** 3380 Solano Ave. Just w off SR 29 via Redwood Rd, just s. Ext corridors. **Pets:** Other species. Supervision.

[SAVE] [S❄] [✕] [⊘] [⊟] [▣] [⇌]

OCCIDENTAL

(AAA) ▼▼▼ Occidental Lodge **M**
(707) 874-3623. **$74-$129.** 3610 Bohemian Hwy. In the village. Ext corridors. **Pets:** Medium. $8 daily fee/pet. Service with restrictions, supervision.

[SAVE] [S❄] [✕] [&M] [⊟] [▣] [⇌]

PETALUMA

(AAA) ▼▼▼▼ Best Western Petaluma Inn **SH**
(707) 763-0994. **$89-$149.** 200 S McDowell Blvd. US 101, exit Washington St, 1 blk e. Ext corridors. **Pets:** Medium. $10 one-time fee/room. Service with restrictions, supervision.

[SAVE] [S❄] [✕] [&M] [⊘] [⊟] [▣] [⇌]

(AAA) ▼▼▼▼ Quality Inn-Petaluma **SH**
(707) 664-1155. **$103-$200.** 5100 Montero Way. US 101, exit Old Redwood Hwy-Penngrove northbound; exit Petaluma Blvd N-Penngrove southbound (east side). Ext/int corridors. **Pets:** Accepted.

[SAVE] [✕] [&M] [⊘] [⊟] [▣] [⇌] [✕]

(AAA) ▼▼▼▼ Sheraton Sonoma County-Petaluma **SH** ✿
(707) 283-2888. **$149-$249.** 745 Baywood Dr. US 101, exit SR 116 (Lakeville Hwy), just se. Int corridors. **Pets:** Medium, dogs only. Designated rooms, service with restrictions, supervision.

[SAVE] [S❄] [✕] [&M] [⊘] [⊟] [▣] [⊓] [⇌]

POINT ARENA

(AAA) ▼▼▼ Wharf Master's Inn **M**
(707) 882-3171. **$79-$250, 3 day notice.** 785 Port Rd. 1 mi w on Iversen Ave from jct SR 1; at wharf. Ext corridors. **Pets:** Accepted.

[SAVE] [✕] [&M] [⊘] [▣] [Ⓐ]

ROHNERT PARK

△△△ ▽▽▽ Best Western Inn **SH**
(707) 584-7435. **$89-$130, 3 day notice.** 6500 Redwood Dr. US 101, exit Rohnert Park Expwy, just w. Ext corridors. **Pets:** $10 one-time fee/room. Service with restrictions, supervision.

[SAVE] [S🐾] [✕] [&M] [🛏] [💻] [≈]

ST. HELENA

△△△ ▽▽▽▽ El Bonita Motel **SH**
(707) 963-3216. **$89-$279, 3 day notice.** 195 Main St. 0.8 mi s on SR 29. Ext corridors. **Pets:** Large, other species. $15 daily fee/pet. Service with restrictions.

[SAVE] [✕] [&M] [✎] [🛏] [💻] [≈]

△△△ ▽▽▽▽ Harvest Inn **SH**
(707) 963-9463. **$299-$599, 7 day notice.** One Main St. 1.5 mi s on SR 29. Ext corridors. **Pets:** Accepted.

[SAVE] [✕] [&M] [✎] [🛏] [💻] [≈] [✕]

SANTA ROSA

△△△ ▽▽▽ Americas Best Value Inn **M**
(707) 523-3480. **$60-$149.** 1800 Santa Rosa Ave. US 101, exit Baker Ave northbound; exit Corby Ave southbound. Ext corridors. **Pets:** Other species. $10 daily fee/pet. Service with restrictions, crate.

[SAVE] [✕] [&M] [🛏]

△△△ ▽▽▽▽ Best Western Garden Inn **SH** ❖
(707) 546-4031. **$79-$139, 3 day notice.** 1500 Santa Rosa Ave. US 101, exit Baker Ave northbound; exit Corby Ave southbound. Ext corridors. **Pets:** Medium, dogs only. $15 daily fee/pet. Designated rooms, no service, supervision.

[SAVE] [S🐾] [✕] [&M] [🛏] [💻] [🍴] [≈]

△△△ ▽▽▽▽ Fountaingrove Inn, Hotel & Conference
                Center **SH** ❖
(707) 578-6101. **$119-$189.** 101 Fountaingrove Pkwy. 2.5 mi n on US 101, exit Mendocino Ave/Old Redwood Hwy, just e. Int corridors. **Pets:** $25 daily fee/pet. Designated rooms, service with restrictions, supervision.

[SAVE] [S🐾] [✕] [&M] [🏊] [✎] [🛏] [💻] [🍴] [≈]

△△△ ▽▽▽▽ Holiday Inn Express **M**
(707) 545-9000. **$89-$190.** 870 Hopper Ave. US 101, exit Mendocino Ave/Old Redwood Hwy northbound, just w; exit Hopper Ave southbound. Ext corridors. **Pets:** Medium, dogs only. $20 one-time fee/room. Designated rooms, service with restrictions, supervision.

[SAVE] [S🐾] [✕] [&M] [🛏] [💻] [≈]

△△△ ▽▽▽▽ Sandman Motel **SH** ❖
(707) 544-8570. **$89-$125, 3 day notice.** 3421 Cleveland Ave. US 101, exit W Mendocino Ave/Old Redwood Hwy. Ext corridors. **Pets:** Dogs only. $25 one-time fee/pet. Service with restrictions, supervision.

[SAVE] [S🐾] [✕] [&M] [✎] [🛏] [💻] [≈]

△△△ ▽▽ Travelodge **M**
(707) 542-3472. **$59-$119.** 1815 Santa Rosa Ave. 1.5 mi s on US 101 business route; US 101, exit Baker Ave northbound; exit Corby Ave southbound. Ext corridors. **Pets:** $20 daily fee/pet. Service with restrictions, supervision.

[SAVE] [S🐾] [✕] [&M] [🛏] [💻] [≈]

THE SEA RANCH

△△△ ▽▽▽▽ Sea Ranch Lodge **SH** ❖
(707) 785-2371. **$230-$495, 7 day notice.** 60 Sea Walk Dr. Just w of SR 1. Ext corridors. **Pets:** Medium, dogs only. $50 one-time fee/room. Designated rooms, service with restrictions, supervision.

[SAVE] [S🐾] [✕] [&M] [✎] [💻] [🍴] [✕] [🐾]

SONOMA

△△△ ▽▽▽▽ Best Western Sonoma Valley Inn **SH**
(707) 938-9200. **$116-$329, 3 day notice.** 550 2nd St W. 1 blk w of town plaza. Ext corridors. **Pets:** Accepted.

[SAVE] [S🐾] [✕] [&M] [✎] [🛏] [💻] [≈]

UKIAH

△△△ ▽▽▽ Americas Best Value Inn **M**
(707) 462-6657. **$49-$99, 7 day notice.** 1070 S State St. US 101, exit Talmage Rd, 1 mi w. Ext corridors. **Pets:** $10 daily fee/pet. Service with restrictions, supervision.

[SAVE] [S🐾] [✕] [🛏] [≈]

△△△ ▽▽▽ Days Inn **M**
(707) 462-7584. **$60-$129.** 950 N State St. US 101, exit N State St, 0.5 mi s. Ext corridors. **Pets:** Other species. $10 daily fee/pet. Designated rooms, service with restrictions, supervision.

[SAVE] [S🐾] [✕] [🛏] [💻] [≈]

△△△ ▽▽▽▽ Discovery Inn **SH** ❖
(707) 462-8873. **$69-$129, 3 day notice.** 1340 N State St. 1.5 mi n on US 101 business route; US 101, exit N State St. Ext corridors. **Pets:** Other species. $25 one-time fee/room. Designated rooms, service with restrictions, supervision.

[SAVE] [S🐾] [✕] [✎] [🛏] [💻] [≈]

△△△ ▽▽ Rodeway Inn **M**
(707) 462-2906. **$69-$89.** 1050 S State St. US 101, exit Talmage Rd, 0.5 mi w. Ext corridors. **Pets:** Medium, dogs only. $10 daily fee/pet. Designated rooms, service with restrictions, supervision.

[SAVE] [S🐾] [✕] [🛏] [💻] [≈]

△△△ ▽ Super 8 **M** ❖
(707) 468-8181. **$49-$99.** 693 S Orchard Ave. US 101, exit Gobbi St W. Ext corridors. **Pets:** $10 daily fee/pet. Designated rooms, service with restrictions, supervision.

[SAVE] [S🐾] [✕] [🛏] [💻] [≈]

WILLITS

△△△ ▽▽▽ Baechtel Creek Inn & Spa **M** ❖
(707) 459-9063. **$69-$175.** 101 Gregory Ln. US 101, just w. Ext corridors. **Pets:** Medium, dogs only. $20 one-time fee/room. Designated rooms, service with restrictions, supervision.

[SAVE] [S🐾] [✕] [🛏] [💻] [≈]

YOUNTVILLE

△△△ ▽▽▽▽ Vintage Inn **SH**
(707) 944-1112. **$230-$610, 7 day notice.** 6541 Washington St. SR 29, exit Yountville; center. Ext corridors. **Pets:** Accepted.

[SAVE] [S🐾] [✕] [&M] [✎] [🛏] [💻] [≈] [✕]

END AREA

WOODLAND

▲▲▲ ▼▼ Days Inn SH
(530) 666-3800. **$75-$115.** 1524 E Main St. I-5, exit Main St (Woodland) northbound; exit SR 113 (Davis) southbound. Int corridors. **Pets:** Dogs only. $10 daily fee/pet. Designated rooms, service with restrictions, supervision.
🆂🅰🅴 🆂🔟 ✖ 🅼 🖥 🐾

YERMO

▲▲▲ ▼▼ Oak Tree Inn SH
(760) 254-1148. **$65-$75.** 35450 Yermo Rd. I-15, exit 191 (Ghost Town Rd), just e, then just s. Int corridors. **Pets:** Accepted.
🆂🅰🅴 🆂🔟 ✖ 🅴 🖥 🖥 🍴 🐾

YREKA

▲▲▲ ▼▼▼ AmeriHost Inn-Yreka SH
(530) 841-1300. **$70-$90.** 148 Moonlit Oaks Ave. I-5, exit SR 3 (Fort Jones Rd). Int corridors. **Pets:** Small. $10 one-time fee/pet. Designated rooms, service with restrictions, supervision.
🆂🅰🅴 🆂🔟 ✖ 🅴 🖥 🖥 🐾 ✖

▲▲▲ ▼▼▼▼ Best Western Miner's Inn M ❀
(530) 842-4355. **$79-$120.** 122 E Miner St. I-5, exit Central Yreka, just w. Ext corridors. **Pets:** Medium. $10 daily fee/pet. Designated rooms, service with restrictions, supervision.
🆂🅰🅴 🆂🔟 ✖ 🅴 🖥 🖥 🐾 ✖

▲▲▲ ▼▼▼▼ Comfort Inn SH
(530) 842-1612. **$65-$95.** 1804-B Fort Jones Rd. I-5, exit SR 3 (Fort Jones Rd). Int corridors. **Pets:** Medium, other species. $20 deposit/pet. Designated rooms, service with restrictions, supervision.
🆂🅰🅴 🆂🔟 ✖ 🅼 🖥 🖥 🐾

▲▲▲ ▼▼▼ Econo Lodge Inn & Suites M
(530) 842-4404. **$51-$95.** 526 S Main St. I-5, exit Central Yreka, 0.3 mi s. Ext corridors. **Pets:** Medium. $20 deposit/pet. Designated rooms, service with restrictions, supervision.
🆂🅰🅴 🆂🔟 ✖ 🅼 🖥 🖥 🐾

▲▲▲ ▼▼▼ Mountain View Inn/Motel M
(530) 842-1940. **$43-$89.** 801 N Main St. I-5, exit Montague Rd, 0.5 mi w. Ext corridors. **Pets:** Small. $5 daily fee/pet. Designated rooms, service with restrictions, supervision.
🆂🅰🅴 🆂🔟 ✖ 🖥 🖥 🐾

▲▲▲ ▼▼▼▼ Super 8-Yreka M
(530) 842-5781. **$60-$80.** 136 Montague Rd. I-5, exit Montague Rd, just w. Ext corridors. **Pets:** $5 daily fee/pet. Service with restrictions, supervision.
🆂🅰🅴 🆂🔟 ✖ 🖥 🖥 🐾

YUBA CITY

▲▲▲ ▼ Days Inn-Downtown-Yuba City M
(530) 674-1711. **$45-$80.** 700 N Palora Ave. SR 99, exit Bridge St, 0.5 mi s of SR 20. Ext corridors. **Pets:** Accepted.
🆂🅰🅴 🆂🔟 ✖ 🅼 🅴 🖥 🖥 🏊

▼▼ Fireside Inn SH
(530) 674-0201. **$99.** 4228 S Hwy 99. On SR 99, 4.5 mi s of SR 20. Ext corridors. **Pets:** Accepted.
🅰🆂🅺 🆂🔟 ✖ 🅼 🅴 🖥 🖥 🍴 🐾

YUCCA VALLEY

▲▲▲ ▼▼▼ Americas Best Value Inn & Suites-Oasis of Eden M
(760) 365-6321. **$59-$139.** 56377 Twentynine Palms Hwy. 1 mi w of jct SR 62 and 247. Ext corridors. **Pets:** Small, dogs only. $15 daily fee/pet. Service with restrictions, supervision.
🆂🅰🅴 🆂🔟 ✖ 🖥 🖥 🐾

▲▲▲ ▼ Super 8 Motel M
(760) 228-1773. **$59-$79.** 57096 Twentynine Palms Hwy. On SR 62, 0.3 mi w of jct SR 247. Int corridors. **Pets:** Other species. $20 deposit/pet, $10 daily fee/room. Service with restrictions.
🆂🅰🅴 🆂🔟 ✖ 🖥 🐾

COLORADO

ALAMOSA

🔺🔺 ▼▼▼▼ Best Western Alamosa Inn SH
(719) 589-2567. $59-$84. 2005 W Main St. 1 mi w on US 160 and 285. Ext corridors. Pets: Accepted.

▼▼▼ Holiday Inn Express Hotel & Suites SH
(719) 589-4026. $69-$110. 3418 Mariposa St. 1.8 mi w on US 160; in shopping complex. Int corridors. Pets: Small. $10 daily fee/pet. Service with restrictions, supervision.

🔺🔺 ▼▼▼▼ Inn of the Rio Grande SH
(719) 589-5833. $79-$89. 333 Santa Fe Ave. Just e of jct SR 17 on US 160. Int corridors. Pets: Other species. $25 deposit/pet. Service with restrictions, supervision.

ASPEN

▼▼▼ Aspen Meadows Resort A Dolce Conference Destination LH
(970) 925-4240. $143-$450, 14 day notice. 845 Meadows Rd. 3 blks e of SR 82 via 7th Ave. Ext/int corridors. Pets: Accepted.

▼▼▼ Aspen Mountain Lodge SH
(970) 925-7650. $109-$395, 7 day notice. 311 W Main St. Just w on SR 82; between 2nd and 3rd sts. Int corridors. Pets: $20 daily fee/pet. Supervision.

🔺🔺 ▼▼▼ Hotel Aspen SH
(970) 925-3441. $109-$245, 30 day notice. 110 W Main St. On SR 82, just w. Ext/int corridors. Pets: Dogs only. $20 daily fee/pet. Supervision.

▼▼▼ Hotel Lenado BB ❀
(970) 925-6246. $115-$525, 30 day notice. 200 S Aspen St. Just s of SR 82 via Aspen St at jct Hopkins St. Ext/int corridors. Pets: Dogs only. Designated rooms, service with restrictions.

🔺🔺 ▼▼▼▼▼ The Little Nell LH ❀
(970) 920-4600. $470-$4800, 30 day notice. 675 E Durant Ave. Beside the gondola at base of Aspen Mountain. Int corridors. Pets: Other species.

▼▼▼▼ St. Regis Resort, Aspen LH
(970) 920-3300. $145-$800, 30 day notice. 315 E Dean St. SR 82, s on Monarch St, then just e. Int corridors. Pets: Accepted.

🔺🔺 ▼▼▼▼ Sky Hotel LH
(970) 925-6760. $179-$589, 30 day notice. 709 E Durant Ave. At base of Aspen Mountain. Ext/int corridors. Pets: Accepted.

AVON

▼▼ Comfort Inn-Vail/Beaver Creek SH
(970) 949-5511. $69-$209. 161 W Beaver Creek Blvd. I-70, exit 167, just s on Avon Rd, then just w. Int corridors. Pets: Accepted.

BEAVER CREEK

🔺🔺 ▼▼▼▼▼ The Ritz-Carlton, Bachelor Gulch LH ❀
(970) 748-6200. $195-$8000, 60 day notice. 130 Daybreak Ridge. I-70, exit 167, s on Avon and Village rds (beyond gatehouse), w on Prater Rd, follow signs to Bachelor Gulch Village. Int corridors. Pets: Dogs only. $125 one-time fee/room. Service with restrictions, crate.

BOULDER

🔺🔺 ▼▼▼▼ Best Western Boulder Inn SH
(303) 449-3800. $89-$334. 770 28th St. US 36 (28th St) at Baseline Rd. Int corridors. Pets: Medium, dogs only. $100 deposit/room. Designated rooms, supervision.

▼▼▼▼ Boulder Broker Inn SH
(303) 444-3330. $99-$249. 555 30th St. US 36 (28th St), exit Baseline Rd, 0.3 mi e to 30th St, then just s. Int corridors. Pets: Accepted.

🔺🔺 ▼▼▼▼ Boulder Outlook Hotel & Suites SH ❀
(303) 443-3322. $69-$139. 800 28th St. US 36 (28th St), exit Baseline Rd via Frontage Rd. Ext/int corridors. Pets: $10 daily fee/room. Designated rooms, service with restrictions, supervision.

🔺🔺 ▼▼▼ Boulder University Inn M ❀
(303) 417-1700. $50-$119. 1632 Broadway. US 36 (28th St), exit Baseline (SR 93) Rd, 0.3 mi s, then 3 mi nw. Ext corridors. Pets: Other species. $100 deposit/room, $15 daily fee/pet. Service with restrictions, supervision.

Foot of The Mountain Motel M
(303) 442-5688. **$70-$85.** 200 Arapahoe Ave. 1.8 mi w of US 36 (28th St). Ext corridors. **Pets:** Other species. $50 deposit/room, $5 daily fee/pet. Designated rooms, supervision.
SAVE ⊠ 📶 (AC)

Holiday Inn Express SH
(303) 442-6600. **$89-$169.** 4777 N Broadway. 4 mi n of Pearl St Pedestrian Mall, then 0.3 mi s of jct US 36 (28th St). Int corridors. **Pets:** Other species. $20 daily fee/room. Service with restrictions, crate.
ASK ⊠ 📶 📶 💻 ➥

Homewood Suites by Hilton SH
(303) 499-9922. **$139-$189.** 4950 Baseline Rd. 0.3 mi e of US 36 (28th St); SR 157 (Foothills Pkwy), exit Baseline Rd, just w; entry off Baseline Rd. Ext/int corridors. **Pets:** Other species. $50 one-time fee/room. Service with restrictions, crate.
ASK S⊠ ⊠ 📶 📶 💻 ➥ ⊠

Millennium Harvest House Boulder LH
(303) 443-3850. **$124-$299.** 1345 28th St. Just s of jct Arapahoe Rd and US 36 (28th St). Int corridors. **Pets:** Medium. $100 deposit/room. Designated rooms, supervision.
SAVE ⊠ 📶 💻 ⍾ ➥ ⊠

Quality Inn & Suites Boulder Creek SH ❀
(303) 449-7550. **$79-$149.** 2020 Arapahoe Ave. US 36 (28th St), 0.5 mi w. Ext/int corridors. **Pets:** Large, other species. $100 deposit/pet, $15 daily fee/pet. Service with restrictions, supervision.
SAVE S⊠ ⊠ 📶 💻 ➥ ⊠

Residence Inn by Marriott SH
(303) 449-5545. **$159-$229.** 3030 Center Green Dr. 0.5 mi e of US 36 (28th St), e on Valmont Rd; corner of Foothills Pkwy. Ext corridors. **Pets:** Accepted.
ASK S⊠ ⊠ 📶 📶 📶 💻 ➥ ⊠

BRECKENRIDGE

Great Divide Lodge LH ❀
(970) 547-5758. **$110-$275, 21 day notice.** 550 Village Rd. I-70, exit 203, 10.7 mi s on SR 9, just w on S Park Ave, then just s. Int corridors. **Pets:** Dogs only. Designated rooms.
ASK ⊠ 📶 📶 📶 💻 ⍾ ➥ ⊠ (AC)

The Hunt Placer Inn BB
(970) 453-7573. **$149-$218, 14 day notice.** 275 Ski Hill Rd. SR 9, just w toward Peak 8. Int corridors. **Pets:** Accepted.
ASK S⊠ ⊠ (AC) (W)

The Lodge and Spa at Breckenridge SH ❀
(970) 453-9300. **$75-$475, 45 day notice.** 112 Overlook Dr. I-70, exit 203, jct SR 9, 2.1 mi e on Boreas Pass Rd, then just sw. Ext/int corridors. **Pets:** Dogs only. $20 daily fee/pet. Designated rooms, service with restrictions, crate.
ASK S⊠ ⊠ 📶 💻 ⍾ ➥ ⊠

The Village at Breckenridge Hotel SH
(970) 453-2000. **$99-$265, 21 day notice.** 535 S Park Ave. 0.3 mi w of SR 9. Int corridors. **Pets:** Accepted.
ASK ⊠ 📶 📶 💻 ⊠

BROOMFIELD

Omni Interlocken Resort LH
(303) 438-6600. **$229-$399.** 500 Interlocken Blvd. US 36 (Boulder Tpke), exit Interlocken Loop, then w, just s via signs. Int corridors. **Pets:** Accepted.
SAVE S⊠ ⊠ 📶 📶 📶 📶 💻 ⍾ ➥ ⊠

TownePlace Suites by Marriott Boulder/Broomfield SH ❀
(303) 466-2200. **$79-$139.** 480 Flatiron Blvd. US 36 (Boulder Tpke), exit Interlocken Loop, to first traffic light, w on Interlocken Blvd, then s. Int corridors. **Pets:** Other species. $100 one-time fee/room. Service with restrictions, supervision.
⊠ 📶 📶 📶 📶 💻 ➥

BRUSH

Americas Best Value Inn Brush SH
(970) 842-5146. **$55-$75.** 1208 N Colorado Ave. I-76, exit 90B, just n. Ext/int corridors. **Pets:** Accepted.
SAVE S⊠ ⊠ 📶 💻 ➥

Microtel Inn SH
(970) 842-4241. **$56-$74.** 975 N Colorado Ave. I-76, exit 90A, just s. Int corridors. **Pets:** Large, dogs only. $20 deposit/room, $15 daily fee/pet. Designated rooms, service with restrictions, supervision.
ASK S⊠ ⊠ 📶 📶 💻 ➥

BUENA VISTA

Alpine Lodge M
(719) 395-2415. **$60-$100, 15 day notice.** 12845 Hwy 24 & 285. 2 mi s on US 24, 0.5 mi e on US 24 and 285. Ext corridors. **Pets:** Accepted.
SAVE S⊠ ⊠ 📶

Best Western Vista Inn M ❀
(719) 395-8009. **$77-$147.** 733 US Hwy 24 N. 0.5 mi n. Int corridors. **Pets:** Medium, dogs only. $10 daily fee/pet. Designated rooms, service with restrictions, supervision.
SAVE S⊠ ⊠ 📶 📶 💻 ➥

BURLINGTON

Burlington Comfort Inn SH
(719) 346-7676. **$69-$109, 5 day notice.** 282 S Lincoln St. I-70, exit 437, just n on US 385. Int corridors. **Pets:** Accepted.
ASK S⊠ ⊠ 📶 📶 💻 ➥

Chaparral Motor Inn M
(719) 346-5361. **$45-$59.** 405 S Lincoln St. I-70, exit 437, just n on jct US 385. Ext corridors. **Pets:** Medium, other species. $7 daily fee/pet.
SAVE S⊠ ⊠ 📶 💻 ➥

CANON CITY

Budget Host Royal Gorge Inn M
(719) 269-1100. **$45-$95.** 217 N Raynolds Ave. 1 mi e on US 50, just n. Int corridors. **Pets:** Accepted.
SAVE S⊠ ⊠ 📶 ➥

Comfort Inn SH
(719) 276-6900. **$64-$190.** 311 Royal Gorge Blvd. On US 50, just w of downtown. Int corridors. **Pets:** Accepted.
ASK S⊠ ⊠ 📶 📶 📶 💻 ➥

Holiday Inn Express SH
(719) 275-2400. **$79-$99.** 110 Latigo Ln. 2.5 mi e of SR 115 on US 50. Int corridors. **Pets:** Small. $15 daily fee/pet. Designated rooms, service with restrictions, supervision.
ASK S⊠ ⊠ 📶 📶 📶 💻 ➥

Quality Inn & Suites M
(719) 275-8676. **$59-$179.** 3075 E Hwy 50. 12 mi w of jct SR 115; center. Int corridors. **Pets:** Other species. Designated rooms, service with restrictions, supervision.
⊠ 📶 💻 ⍾ ➥

CARBONDALE

Comfort Inn & Suites SH
(970) 963-8880. **$99-$149.** 920 Cowen Dr. Jct of SR 82 and 133, just s via signs. Int corridors. **Pets:** Accepted.
SAVE S⊠ ⊠ 📶 📶 💻 ➥ ⊠

AAA ▼▼▼ **Days Inn-Carbondale** SH
(970) 963-9111. **$59-$159.** 950 Cowen Dr. Jct SR 82 and 133. Int corridors. **Pets:** $10 daily fee/pet. Service with restrictions, supervision.

SAVE S X X & ♦ ➤ X

CASTLE ROCK

AAA ▼▼▼ **Best Western Inn & Suites of Castle**
Rock SH ❀
(303) 814-8800. **$79-$159.** 595 Genoa Way. I-25, exit 184 (Meadows Pkwy), just w to Castleton Way, just s, then e. Int corridors. **Pets:** Medium. $15 daily fee/pet. Designated rooms, service with restrictions, supervision.

SAVE S X Ð & ♦ ➤ ➤

▼▼ **Castle Rock Days Inn and Suites** SH
(303) 814-5825. **$50-$99.** 4961 Castleton Way. I-25, exit 184 (Meadows Pkwy), 0.5 mi e, just s on Castleton Way, then just se. Int corridors. **Pets:** Medium. $10 daily fee/room. Service with restrictions, supervision.

ASK S X & ♦ ➤ ➤

▼▼▼ **Comfort Suites** SH
(303) 814-9999. **$79-$99.** 4755 Castleton Way. I-25, exit 184 (Meadows Pkwy), w to Castleton Way; entry on east side. Int corridors. **Pets:** Medium. $10 daily fee/room. Service with restrictions, supervision.

ASK S X &M Ð & ♦ ➤ ➤ X

▼▼▼ **Hampton Inn** SH
(303) 660-9800. **$89-$149.** 4830 Castleton Way. I-25, exit 184 (Meadows Pkwy), sw to N Castleton Rd, just s, then e. Int corridors. **Pets:** $5 daily fee/room, $25 one-time fee/room. Designated rooms, service with restrictions.

ASK S X &M Ð & ♦ ➤ ➤

▼▼▼ **Holiday Inn Express** SH
(303) 660-9733. **$70-$120.** 884 Park St. I-25, exit 182, just w. Int corridors. **Pets:** Large, other species. $10 daily fee/pet. Service with restrictions, supervision.

ASK S X & ♦ ➤ ➤

CEDAREDGE

AAA ▼▼▼ **Howard Johnson Express Inn** M
(970) 856-7824. **$69-$99.** 530 S Grand Mesa Dr. Just s on SR 65. Int corridors. **Pets:** $10 daily fee/pet. Designated rooms, service with restrictions, supervision.

SAVE S X & ♦ ➤ ➤

CIMARRON

AAA ▼▼▼ **The Inn at Arrowhead** BB
(970) 862-8206. **$120-$165, 14 day notice.** 21401 Alpine Plateau Rd. 11 mi e; from US 50, 5.3 mi s on Dirt Rd; look for signs. Int corridors. **Pets:** Accepted.

SAVE S X Ð ¶ X Ä ₩ ✑

COLORADO SPRINGS METROPOLITAN AREA

CHIPITA PARK

▼▼▼ **Chipita Lodge B&B** BB ❀
(719) 684-8454. **$80-$135, 7 day notice.** 9090 Chipita Park Rd. Jct US 24, just s on Fountain Blvd (Pine Peak Hwy), then 1.5 mi w; go right at fork. Ext/int corridors. **Pets:** Other species. $50 deposit/room. Designated rooms, no service, supervision.

ASK S X ♦ ➤ Ä

COLORADO SPRINGS

AAA ▼▼ **Airport Value Inn & Suites** SH
(719) 596-5588. **$59-$89.** 6875 Space Village Ave. I-25, exit 141, 1 mi e on Cimarron Ave, 0.7 mi n on Wahsatch Ave, 6.3 mi e on Platte Ave, then exit Space Village Ave. Ext/int corridors. **Pets:** Medium. $35 one-time fee/room. Designated rooms, service with restrictions, supervision.

SAVE S X &M ♦ ➤

AAA ▼▼ **Apollo Park Executive Suites** CO ❀
(719) 634-0286. **$55-$75, 3 day notice.** 805 S Circle Dr, 2-B. I-25, exit 138, 2.5 mi e. Int corridors. **Pets:** Other species. $5 daily fee/room. Designated rooms, service with restrictions.

SAVE S X ♦ ➤ ➤

AAA ▼▼▼ **Best Western Airport Inn** SH
(719) 574-7707. **$79-$109.** 1780 Aeroplaza Dr. I-25, exit 139, 4 mi e on US 24 Bypass. Int corridors. **Pets:** Small. $10 daily fee/pet. Designated rooms, service with restrictions, supervision.

SAVE S X &M ♦ ➤ ➤

AAA ▼▼▼ **Best Western Executive Inn & Suites** SH
(719) 576-2371. **$59-$109.** 1440 Harrison Rd. I-25, exit 138, just w; on northwest corner of interchange; entry through restaurant. Int corridors. **Pets:** Small, dogs only. $10 daily fee/pet. Designated rooms, service with restrictions, supervision.

SAVE S X &M Ð & ♦ ➤ ➤

AAA ▼▼▼ **Best Western The Academy Hotel** LH
(719) 598-5770. **$69-$149.** 8110 N Academy Blvd. I-25, exit 150, just s. Int corridors. **Pets:** Accepted.

SAVE X &M Ð & ♦ ➤ ¶ ➤ X

AAA ▼▼▼▼ **The Broadmoor** LH ❀
(719) 634-7711. **$280-$560, 7 day notice.** 1 Lake Ave. I-25, exit 138, 3 mi w on Circle Dr (which becomes Lake Ave). Int corridors. **Pets:** Other species. $35 daily fee/pet. Service with restrictions, supervision.

SAVE X &M Ð & ♦ ➤ ¶ ➤ X

AAA ▼ **Chief Motel** M
(719) 473-5228. **$35-$65.** 1624 S Nevada Ave. I-25, exit 140, just s. Ext corridors. **Pets:** Accepted.

SAVE S X ♦

▼▼▼▼ **Clarion Hotel Downtown** SH
(719) 471-8680. **$69-$139.** 314 W Bijou St. I-25, exit 142, just w. Int corridors. **Pets:** Medium, other species. $10 daily fee/pet. Designated rooms, service with restrictions, crate.

ASK S X Ð ♦ ➤ ¶ ➤

AAA ▼▼▼ **Colorado Springs Marriott** LH
(719) 260-1800. **$129-$179.** 5580 Tech Center Dr. I-25, exit 147 (Rockrimmon Blvd), 0.5 mi w. Int corridors. **Pets:** Accepted.

SAVE S X Ð ♦ ➤ ¶ ➤ X

AAA ▼▼▼ **Comfort Inn North** SH
(719) 262-9000. **$79-$119.** 6450 Corporate Dr. I-25, exit 149 (Woodmen Rd), just w, then 0.3 mi s. Int corridors. **Pets:** Accepted.

SAVE S X &M Ð & ♦ ➤ ➤

AAA ▼▼▼ **Comfort Inn South** SH
(719) 579-6900. **$69-$124.** 1410 Harrison Rd. I-25, exit 138, just w to Rand Rd, then ne. Int corridors. **Pets:** Other species. $25 deposit/pet. Designated rooms, service with restrictions, supervision.

SAVE S X Ð & ♦ ➤ ➤

▼▼▼▼ Comfort Suites SH
(719) 536-0731. **$79-$124.** 1055 Kelly Johnson Blvd. I-25, exit 150, just s on Academy Blvd to Kelly Johnson Blvd, then w. Int corridors. **Pets:** Small, other species. $20 one-time fee/pet. Service with restrictions, supervision.
ASK SD ✕ ⬛M ⬛' ⬛ ⬛ ⬛ ➣ ✕

▼▼ Days Inn-Air Force Academy SH
(719) 266-1317. **$49-$94.** 8350 Razorback Rd. I-25, exit 150, just s, then e. Int corridors. **Pets:** Accepted.
ASK SD ✕ ⬛' ⬛ ⬛ ➣

▼▼▼▼ DoubleTree Hotel Colorado Springs, World Arena SH
(719) 576-8900. **$119-$209.** 1775 E Cheyenne Mountain Blvd. I-25, exit 138, just w. Int corridors. **Pets:** Medium. $10 daily fee/pet. Supervision.
ASK ✕ ⬛M ⬛ ⬛' ⬛ ⬛ ⬛ ➣ ✕

▼▼▼▼ Drury Inn-Pikes Peak SH
(719) 598-2500. **$72-$152.** 8155 N Academy Blvd. I-25, exit 150, just s, then e. Int corridors. **Pets:** Large, other species. Service with restrictions, supervision.
ASK ✕ ⬛ ⬛ ⬛ ➣

AAA ▼▼▼ Econo Lodge Inn & Suites SH ❀
(719) 632-6651. **$45-$75.** 1623 S Nevada Ave. I-25, exit 140, just s. Ext corridors. **Pets:** Other species. $10 deposit/pet, $10 one-time fee/pet. Service with restrictions, supervision.
SAVE SD ✕ ⬛' ⬛ ⬛ ➣

▼▼▼▼ Homewood Suites by Hilton SH
(719) 265-6600. **$119-$199.** 9130 Explorer Dr. I-25, exit 151, 0.8 mi e; across from Focus on the Family. Int corridors. **Pets:** Medium, other species. $25 one-time fee/pet. Service with restrictions, crate.
ASK SD ✕ ⬛M ⬛ ⬛' ⬛ ⬛ ➣ ✕

▼▼▼▼ Homewood Suites by Hilton Colorado Springs Airport SH
(719) 574-2701. **$105-$127.** 2875 Zeppelin Rd. I-25, exit 139, 4 mi e on US 24 Bypass, 1.1 mi s on Powers Blvd, then just e. Int corridors. **Pets:** Small. $50 one-time fee/pet. Service with restrictions, crate.
ASK SD ✕ ⬛ ⬛' ⬛ ⬛ ➣ ✕

AAA ▼▼▼▼ La Quinta Inn & Suites Colorado Springs (South/Airport) SH
(719) 527-4788. **$88-$151.** 2750 Geyser Dr. I-25, exit 138 (Circle Dr), just w to Cheyenne Mountain Blvd, then just s. Int corridors. **Pets:** Medium. Service with restrictions.
SAVE ✕ ⬛M ⬛ ⬛' ⬛ ⬛ ➣

AAA ▼▼▼▼ La Quinta Inn Colorado Springs (Garden of the Gods) SH
(719) 528-5060. **$80-$147.** 4385 Sinton Rd. I-25, exit 146, just e. Ext/int corridors. **Pets:** Medium. Service with restrictions.
SAVE ✕ ⬛ ⬛ ⬛ ➣

AAA ▼▼▼ Microtel Inn & Suites SH
(719) 598-7500. **$59-$120.** 7265 Commerce Center Dr. I-25, exit 149, just w, then n. Int corridors. **Pets:** Other species. $20 one-time fee/room. Designated rooms, service with restrictions.
SAVE SD ✕ ⬛M ⬛ ⬛' ⬛ ⬛ ➣

AAA ▼▼▼ Radisson Hotel Colorado Springs Airport LH
(719) 597-7000. **$99-$119.** 1645 N Newport Rd. I-25, exit 139, 4 mi e on US 24 Bypass. Int corridors. **Pets:** Medium. $100 deposit/room, $25 one-time fee/pet. Service with restrictions, crate.
SAVE ✕ ⬛M ⬛ ⬛' ⬛ ⬛ ⬛ ➣ ✕

AAA ▼▼▼ Rainbow Lodge and Inn M
(719) 632-4551. **$52-$95, 7 day notice.** 3709 W Colorado Ave. I-25, exit 141, 2.5 mi w on US 24, just n on 31st St, then 0.7 mi w. Ext corridors. **Pets:** Accepted.
SAVE SD ✕ ⬛ ➣

▼▼ ▼▼ Ramada Limited East-Airport SH
(719) 596-7660. **$63-$83.** 520 N Murray Blvd. I-25, exit 141, 1 mi e on Cimarron Ave, 0.7 mi n on Wahsatch Ave, 3.7 mi e on Platte Ave, just n. Ext/int corridors. **Pets:** Other species. $25 deposit/room. Designated rooms, crate.
ASK SD ✕ ⬛' ⬛ ⬛ ➣

▼▼▼▼ Residence Inn by Marriott-Central SH
(719) 574-0370. **$69-$139.** 3880 N Academy Blvd. I-25, exit 146, 4.5 mi e on Garden of the Gods/Austin Bluffs Pkwy, then 0.3 mi s. Ext corridors. **Pets:** Other species. $75 one-time fee/room. Service with restrictions.
ASK SD ✕ ⬛ ⬛' ⬛ ⬛ ➣ ✕

▼▼▼▼ Residence Inn by Marriott Colorado Springs North at Interquest Pkwy SH ❀
(719) 388-9300. **$99-$299.** 9805 Federal Dr. I-25, exit 153, just e, then s. Int corridors. **Pets:** Medium. $75 one-time fee/pet. Service with restrictions, supervision.
ASK SD ✕ ⬛M ⬛' ⬛ ⬛ ➣ ✕

▼▼▼▼ Residence Inn by Marriott-Colorado Springs South SH
(719) 576-0101. **$79-$229.** 2765 Geyser Dr. I-25, exit 138, just w to E Cheyenne Mountain Blvd, then just s. Int corridors. **Pets:** Accepted.
ASK SD ✕ ⬛M ⬛' ⬛ ⬛ ➣ ✕

▼▼▼▼ Sheraton Colorado Springs Hotel LH
(719) 576-5900. **$99-$159.** 2886 S Circle Dr. I-25, exit 138, just e. Int corridors. **Pets:** Accepted.
✕ ⬛ ⬛' ⬛ ⬛ ⬛ ➣ ✕

AAA ▼▼▼▼ Silverwood Hotel & Conference Center LH ❀
(719) 598-7656. **$79-$139.** 505 Popes Bluff Tr. I-25, exit 146, just w, then n on Hilton Pkwy. Int corridors. **Pets:** Other species. $50 deposit/room. Designated rooms, service with restrictions, crate.
SAVE SD ✕ ⬛M ⬛ ⬛ ⬛ ⬛ ⬛ ➣ ✕

▼▼▼ Sleep Inn SH
(719) 260-6969. **$59-$94.** 1075 Kelly Johnson Blvd. I-25, exit 150, just s on Academy Blvd to Kelly Johnson Blvd, then w. Int corridors. **Pets:** Small, other species. $20 one-time fee/pet. Service with restrictions, supervision.
ASK SD ✕ ⬛M ⬛' ⬛

AAA ▼ Stagecoach Motel M
(719) 633-3894. **$49-$69.** 1647 S Nevada Ave. I-25, exit 140, just s. Ext corridors. **Pets:** Small. $5 daily fee/pet. Service with restrictions, crate.
SAVE SD ✕ ⬛

AAA ▼▼▼ Staybridge Suites-Air Force Academy SH ❀
(719) 590-7829. **$99-$199.** 7130 Commerce Center Dr. I-25, exit 149, just w, then n. Int corridors. **Pets:** Other species. $150 one-time fee/pet. Designated rooms, no service, supervision.
SAVE SD ✕ ⬛M ⬛ ⬛' ⬛ ⬛ ⬛ ➣ ✕

▼▼▼▼ TownePlace Suites by Marriott-Colorado Springs SH
(719) 594-4447. **$79-$109.** 4760 Centennial Blvd. I-25, exit 146, 1 mi w on Garden of the Gods Rd, just n on Centennial Blvd, then first left. Int corridors. **Pets:** Accepted.
ASK SD ✕ ⬛M ⬛' ⬛ ⬛ ➣

AAA ▼▼▼ Travel Inn M
(719) 636-3986. **$39-$89.** 512 S Nevada Ave. I-25, exit 141, 0.7 mi e to Nevada Ave, then just s. Ext/int corridors. **Pets:** Other species. $20 deposit/room, $5 one-time fee/pet. Service with restrictions, supervision.
SAVE SD ✕ ⬛

Travelodge SH
(719) 632-4600. **$50-$95.** 2625 Ore Mill Rd. I-25, exit 141, 2.3 mi nw on US 24; entry via 26th St. Int corridors. **Pets:** Other species. $20 one-time fee/room. Service with restrictions, supervision.

[SAVE] [S] [X] [H] [P] [≈]

Travelodge South Colorado Springs SH
(719) 632-7077. **$45-$69.** 1703 S Nevada Ave. I-25, exit 140, 0.4 mi sw. Ext corridors. **Pets:** Accepted.

[ASK] [S] [X] [H] [P] [≈]

MANITOU SPRINGS

El Colorado Lodge CA
(719) 685-5485. **$76-$170, 7 day notice.** 23 Manitou Ave. I-25, exit 141, 4 mi w on US 24, then just ne on US 24 business route. Ext corridors. **Pets:** Medium. $75 deposit/room. Designated rooms, service with restrictions, crate.

[SAVE] [X] [H] [P] [≈] [X]

Park Row Lodge M ❀
(719) 685-5216. **$45-$69.** 54 Manitou Ave. I-25, exit 141, 4 mi w on US 24, then just ne on US 24 business route. Ext corridors. **Pets:** Small. $5 one-time fee/pet. Designated rooms, service with restrictions, supervision.

[SAVE] [S] [X] [H]

END METROPOLITAN AREA

CORTEZ

Best Western Turquoise Inn & Suites SH ❀
(970) 565-3778. **$79-$152.** 535 E Main St. On US 160. Ext corridors. **Pets:** Other species. $15 one-time fee/room. Service with restrictions, supervision.

[SAVE] [S] [X] [&] [H] [P] [≈]

Budget Host Inn M
(970) 565-3738. **$44-$98.** 2040 E Main St. 1.3 mi e on US 160, w of jct SR 145. Ext corridors. **Pets:** $5 daily fee/pet. Designated rooms, service with restrictions, supervision.

[SAVE] [S] [X] [H] [P] [≈]

Comfort Inn SH
(970) 565-3400. **$70-$140.** 2321 E Main St. 1.3 mi e on US 160. Ext/int corridors. **Pets:** Large, other species. $10 one-time fee/room. Designated rooms, service with restrictions.

[SAVE] [S] [X] [H] [P] [≈]

Days Inn SH
(970) 565-8577. **$49-$119.** US Hwy 160 at State 145. 1.5 mi e on US 160, at SR 145. Ext/int corridors. **Pets:** $10 daily fee/pet. Service with restrictions, supervision.

[SAVE] [S] [X] [H] [P] [¶] [≈]

Econo Lodge M
(970) 565-3474. **$56-$79.** 2020 E Main St. 1.3 mi e on US 160. Ext corridors. **Pets:** Accepted.

[ASK] [S] [X] [&] [H] [P] [≈]

Holiday Inn Express SH
(970) 565-6000. **$90-$169.** 2121 E Main St. 1.3 mi e on US 160. Int corridors. **Pets:** Medium, other species. Designated rooms, service with restrictions, supervision.

[SAVE] [S] [X] [2] [&] [H] [P] [¶] [≈] [X]

Mesa Verde Inn M
(970) 565-3773. **$65-$80.** 640 S Broadway. 0.5 mi sw on US 160 and 491. Ext corridors. **Pets:** Medium, other species. $50 deposit/room. Designated rooms, service with restrictions, crate.

[SAVE] [S] [X] [&] [H] [¶] [≈] [X]

Red Wing Motel M ❀
(719) 685-5656. **$45-$129.** 56 El Paso Blvd. I-25, exit 141, 4 mi w on US 24, just ne on US 24 business route/Manitou Ave., then just w on Beckers Ln. Ext corridors. **Pets:** Large, other species. $5 daily fee/pet. Service with restrictions.

[SAVE] [S] [X] [H] [P] [≈]

Silver Saddle Motel M
(719) 685-5611. **$70-$100.** 215 Manitou Ave. I-25, exit 141, 4 mi w on US 24, then just sw on US 24 business route. Ext corridors. **Pets:** Other species. Service with restrictions, supervision.

[SAVE] [S] [X] [H] [P] [≈]

Rodeway Inn M
(970) 565-3761. **$49-$98.** 1120 E Main St. 0.3 mi e on US 160. Ext/int corridors. **Pets:** Accepted.

[SAVE] [S] [X] [H] [P] [≈]

Tomahawk Lodge M
(970) 565-8521. **$49-$99.** 728 S Broadway. 1 mi sw on US 160 and 491. Ext corridors. **Pets:** Dogs only. $25 deposit/pet. Designated rooms, service with restrictions, supervision.

[SAVE] [S] [X] [P] [≈]

CRAIG

Best Western Deer Park Inn and Suites SH
(970) 824-9282. **$89-$129.** 262 Commerce St (Hwy 13). Jct US 40, just 0.3 mi s on SR 13. Int corridors. **Pets:** Medium. $50 deposit/room, $10 daily fee/room. Service with restrictions, supervision.

[SAVE] [S] [X] [&M] [2] [H] [P] [≈]

Black Nugget Motel M
(970) 824-8161. **$69-$79, 7 day notice.** 2855 W Victory Way. 1.5 mi w on US 40, 0.3 mi w of jct SR 13. Ext corridors. **Pets:** Accepted.

[SAVE] [S] [X] [H]

Craig Holiday Inn SH
(970) 824-4000. **$89-$169.** 300 S Hwy 13. 0.3 mi s on SR 13, from jct US 40. Int corridors. **Pets:** Accepted.

[ASK] [S] [X] [2] [&] [H] [P] [¶] [≈] [X]

CRESTED BUTTE

Grand Lodge Crested Butte LH
(970) 349-8000. **$79-$359, 3 day notice.** 6 Emmons Loop. 2.5 mi n on SR 135. Int corridors. **Pets:** Accepted.

[ASK] [S] [X] [&] [H] [P] [¶] [≈] [X]

Old Town Inn SH
(970) 349-6184. **$78-$129, 14 day notice.** 708 6th St. Se on SR 135. Int corridors. **Pets:** Accepted.

[ASK] [S] [X] [H]

DELTA

⚑⚑⚑ ▼▼▼ Best Western Sundance M
(970) 874-9781. **$105, 7 day notice.** 903 Main St. 0.5 mi s on US 50. Ext corridors. **Pets:** Other species. $10 daily fee/pet. Designated rooms, service with restrictions, supervision.

[SAVE] [S🐾] [✖] [🛏] [🖥] [🍴] [≈] [✖]

▼▼ Comfort Inn M
(970) 874-1000. **$90.** 180 Gunnison River Dr. Just n, w of jct US 50 and 92. Int corridors. **Pets:** Accepted.

[ASK] [S🐾] [✖] [🛏] [🖥]

⚑⚑⚑ ▼▼ Riverwood Inn M
(970) 874-5787. **$45-$65.** 677 US 50. 0.5 mi n. Int corridors. **Pets:** Other species. Service with restrictions, supervision.

[SAVE] [S🐾] [✖] [🛏] [🖥]

⚑⚑⚑ ▼▼ Southgate Inns M
(970) 874-9726. **$46-$90.** 2124 S Main St. 1.5 mi s on US 50. Ext corridors. **Pets:** Dogs only. $10 daily fee/room. No service, supervision.

[SAVE] [✖] [🛏] [🖥] [≈]

DENVER METROPOLITAN AREA

AURORA

⚑⚑⚑ ▼▼▼▼ Best Western Gateway Inn & Suites SH
(720) 748-4800. **$49-$169.** 800 S Abilene St. I-225, exit 7 (Mississippi Ave), just e, then 3 blks n. Int corridors. **Pets:** Small. $15 daily fee/pet. Service with restrictions, crate.

[SAVE] [S🐾] [✖] [🕭M] [🖍] [🖍] [🛏] [🖥] [≈] [✖]

▼▼ Comfort Inn Denver Southeast SH
(303) 755-8000. **$64-$89.** 14071 E Iliff Ave. I-225, exit 5, just e. Int corridors. **Pets:** Accepted.

[ASK] [S🐾] [✖] [🕭M] [🖍] [🖍] [🛏] [🖥]

⚑⚑⚑ ▼▼▼ Comfort Inn DIA Airport SH
(303) 367-5000. **$69-$210.** 16921 E 32nd Ave. I-70, exit 285, just s on Airport Blvd; on southeast corner. Int corridors. **Pets:** Medium, other species. $10 one-time fee/pet. Designated rooms, service with restrictions, crate.

[SAVE] [S🐾] [✖] [🕭M] [🖍] [🛏] [🖥] [≈]

▼▼ Crestwood Suites Extended Stay Hotels SH
(303) 481-0379. **$60-$90.** 14090 E Evans Ave. I-225, exit 5 (E Iliff Ave), e to Blackhawk St, then 0.4 mi nw. Int corridors. **Pets:** Small. $50 one-time fee/pet. Designated rooms, service with restrictions, supervision.

[ASK] [✖] [🖍] [🛏] [🖥]

⚑⚑⚑ ▼▼▼ Crystal Inn DIA SH
(303) 340-3800. **$129-$149.** 3300 N Ouray St. I-70, exit 285, just s on Airport Blvd, then w on 32nd Ave. Int corridors. **Pets:** Small. $20 daily fee/room.

[SAVE] [S🐾] [✖] [🕭M] [🖍] [🖍] [🛏] [🖥] [≈]

▼▼ Extended Stay Deluxe SH
(303) 337-7000. **$67-$84.** 14095 E Evans Ave. I-225, exit 5 (E Iliff Ave), just e to Blackhawk St, then 0.4 mi nw. Int corridors. **Pets:** Accepted.

[ASK] [S🐾] [✖] [🕭M] [🖍] [🖍] [🛏] [🖥]

▼▼ Homestead Studio Suites Hotel-Denver/Aurora M
(303) 750-9116. **$54-$69.** 13941 E Harvard Ave. I-225, exit 5 (Iliff Ave), just e to Blackhawk St, then just s. Ext corridors. **Pets:** Accepted.

[ASK] [S🐾] [✖] [🕭M] [🖍] [🖍] [🛏] [🖥]

▼▼▼▼ La Quinta Inn Denver (Aurora) M
(303) 337-0206. **$77-$124.** 1011 S Abilene St. I-225, exit 7, just e, then n. Ext corridors. **Pets:** Medium. Service with restrictions.

[ASK] [✖] [🕭M] [🖍] [🖥] [≈]

⚑⚑⚑ ▼▼▼ Sleep Inn Denver International Airport SH
(303) 373-1616. **$65-$125.** 15900 E 40th Ave. I-70, exit 283; from airport, Pena Blvd S to 40th Ave W. Int corridors. **Pets:** Other species. $10 daily fee/room.

[SAVE] [S🐾] [✖] [🕭M] [🖍] [🖍] [🛏] [🖥] [≈]

⚑⚑⚑ ▼▼▼ Super 8 Motel M
(303) 366-7333. **$51-$64, 7 day notice.** 14200 E 6th Ave. I-225, exit 9, just e. Ext corridors. **Pets:** Small. $20 one-time fee/room. Service with restrictions, supervision.

[SAVE] [S🐾] [✖] [🛏] [≈]

CENTENNIAL

▼▼▼▼ Bradford HomeSuites Denver Tech Center SH
(303) 858-9990. **$59-$149.** 7150 S Clinton St. I-25, exit 197, just e to S Clinton St, then just s. Int corridors. **Pets:** Accepted.

[ASK] [✖] [🕭M] [🖍] [🛏] [🖥] [≈]

▼▼ Days Inn Denver Tech Center SH
(303) 768-9400. **$50-$100.** 9719 E Geddes Ave. I-25, exit 196 (Dry Creek Rd), just e to S Clinton St, just n, then just e. Int corridors. **Pets:** Accepted.

[ASK] [S🐾] [✖] [🕭M] [🖍] [🛏] [🖥]

⚑⚑⚑ ▼▼▼▼ Embassy Suites Denver Tech Center SH
(303) 792-0433. **$69-$700.** 10250 E Costilla Ave. I-25, exit 197, 1 mi e on Arapahoe Rd, 0.3 mi s on Havana St, then w. Int corridors. **Pets:** Accepted.

[SAVE] [S🐾] [✖] [🕭M] [🖍] [🖍] [🛏] [🖥] [🍴] [≈]

DENVER

⚑⚑⚑ ▼▼▼ Best Western Central Denver SH
(303) 296-4000. **$59-$129.** 200 W 48th Ave. I-25, exit 215 northbound; exit 214B southbound, just w to Broadway, then 1.2 mi s. Int corridors. **Pets:** Medium. $10 daily fee/pet. Designated rooms, service with restrictions, crate.

[SAVE] [S🐾] [✖] [🛏] [🖥] [🍴] [≈]

⚑⚑⚑ ▼▼▼ ▼▼▼ Brown Palace Hotel & Spa LH ✿
(303) 297-3111. **$159-$229.** 321 17th St, Tremont Pl & Broadway. I-25, exit 210 (E Colfax Ave) to Lincoln St, just n on Lincoln St, just w on 18th St, then s. Int corridors. **Pets:** Medium, dogs only. $75 one-time fee/room. Designated rooms, service with restrictions, supervision.

[SAVE] [S🐾] [✖] [🖍] [🖍] [🛏] [🖥] [🍴]

⚑⚑⚑ ▼▼ Cameron Motel M
(303) 757-2100. **$55-$58, 7 day notice.** 4500 E Evans Ave. I-25, exit 203, then w. Ext corridors. **Pets:** Medium, other species. $5 daily fee/pet. Designated rooms, service with restrictions, supervision.

[SAVE] [S🐾] [✖] [🛏]

⚑⚑⚑ ▼▼▼ Comfort Inn Central SH ✿
(303) 297-1717. **$89-$114.** 401 E 58th Ave. I-25, exit 215, just e, then left on Logan St. Int corridors. **Pets:** Medium, dogs only. $10 daily fee/pet. Designated rooms, service with restrictions, crate.

[SAVE] [S🐾] [✖] [🕭M] [🛏] [🖥] [🍴] [≈]

⚑⚑⚑ ▼▼▼ Comfort Inn Downtown Denver SH
(303) 296-0400. **$89-$159.** 401 17th St. I-25, exit 210 (E Colfax Ave) to Lincoln St, n to 18th St, then just w; opposite Brown Palace Hotel & Spa. Int corridors. **Pets:** Accepted.

[SAVE] [S🐾] [✖] [🖍] [🖥] [🍴]

▼▼▼ DoubleTree Hotel Denver LH
(303) 321-3333. **$79-$199.** 3203 Quebec St. I-70, exit 278, 0.5 mi s; I-270, exit 4. Int corridors. **Pets:** Dogs only. $25 one-time fee/room. Service with restrictions, supervision.

[ASK] [✖] [🖍] [🖍] [🛏] [🖥] [🍴] [≈] [✖]

▼▼▼ Drury Inn-Denver East SH
(303) 373-1983. $77-$127. 4380 E Peoria St. I-70, exit 281, just n. Int corridors. **Pets:** Large, other species. Service with restrictions, supervision.

A$K ⊠ ◉ 📺 🏊

△△△ ▼▼▼ Embassy Suites Denver-Aurora LH ❀
(303) 375-0400. $86-$158. 4444 N Havana St. I-70, exit 280, just n. Int corridors. **Pets:** Dogs only. Service with restrictions, supervision.

SAVE ⊠ &M ◉ 🖥 📺 ▮▮ 🏊 ⊠

▼▼▼ The Four Points by Sheraton Denver Southeast LH
(303) 758-7000. $89-$199. 6363 E Hampden Ave. I-25, exit 201, just e. Ext/int corridors. **Pets:** Accepted.

A$K S🔊 &M ◉ 🖥 🖥 📺 ▮▮ 🏊 ⊠

△△△ ▼▼▼ Guesthouse Hotel Denver Stapleton SH
(303) 388-6161. $59-$105. 3737 Quebec St. I-70, exit 278, just s. Int corridors. **Pets:** Accepted.

SAVE S🔊 ⊠ 🖥 📺 ▮▮ 🏊

▼▼▼ Hampton Inn & Suites Denver Tech Center SH ❀
(303) 804-9900. $69-$149. 5001 S Ulster St. I-25, exit 199, e to Ulster St, then just n. Int corridors. **Pets:** Medium. $50 deposit/room. Designated rooms, service with restrictions, supervision.

A$K S🔊 ⊠ &M ◉ 🖥 🖥 📺 🏊

△△△ ▼▼▼▼ Hampton Inn DIA SH
(303) 371-0200. $120-$125. 6290 Tower Rd. I-70, exit 286 (Tower Rd), 3.5 mi n. Int corridors. **Pets:** Small. $50 one-time fee/room. Designated rooms, service with restrictions, crate.

SAVE S🔊 ⊠ &M ◉ 🖥 📺 🏊

△△△ ▼▼▼ Holiday Chalet A Victorian Bed & Breakfast BB ❀
(303) 437-8245. $94-$145. 1820 E Colfax Ave. I-25, exit 210 (Colfax Ave), 2.3 mi e on US 40. Int corridors. **Pets:** Other species. $5 daily fee/room. Supervision.

SAVE S🔊 ⊠ 🖥 📺

▼▼▼ Holiday Inn-Denver Central LH
(303) 292-9500. $106-$110. 4849 Bannock St. I-25, exit 215 northbound; exit 214B southbound, just w to Broadway, then 1.2 mi s. Ext/int corridors. **Pets:** Accepted.

A$K S🔊 ⊠ &M ◉ 🖥 🖥 📺 ▮▮

△△△ ▼▼▼ Holiday Inn DIA LH
(303) 371-9494. $129-$164, 21 day notice. 15500 E 40th Ave. I-70, exit 283 (Chambers Rd), just n, then just e. Int corridors. **Pets:** Large, other species. $100 deposit/pet, $50 one-time fee/room. Service with restrictions, crate.

SAVE ⊠ &M ◉ 🖥 🖥 📺 ▮▮ 🏊 ⊠

△△△ ▼▼▼ Hotel Monaco Denver SH ❀
(303) 296-1717. $175-$339. 1717 Champa St. I-25, exit 212A (Speer Blvd S), s to Curtis St, w to 19th St, 1 blk s to Champa St, then 2 blks w. Int corridors. **Pets:** Large, other species.

SAVE S🔊 ⊠ &M ◉ 🖥 📺 ▮▮ ⊠

△△△ ▼▼▼ Hotel Teatro SH ❀
(303) 228-1100. $185-$380. 1100 14th St. I-25, exit 212 (Speer Blvd), just ne on Lawrence St, then e to 14th St; exit Auraria Pkwy northbound. Int corridors. **Pets:** Dogs only.

SAVE S🔊 ⊠ ◉ 🖥 🖥 📺 ▮▮ ⊠

△△△ ▼▼▼ The Inn at Cherry Creek SH ❀
(303) 350-4440. $161-$188. 233 Clayton St. Entrance on Clayton St; between 2nd and 3rd aves; in Cherry Creek Village. Int corridors. **Pets:** Dogs only. Designated rooms, service with restrictions, supervision.

SAVE S🔊 ⊠ 🖥 📺 ▮▮

△△△ ▼▼▼ ▼▼▼ JW Marriott Denver At Cherry Creek SH ❀
(303) 316-2700. $269-$399. 150 Clayton Ln. I-25, exit 5 (University Blvd), 2.4 mi n to 1st Ave, just e, then just n. Int corridors. **Pets:** Dogs only. Service with restrictions, supervision.

SAVE S🔊 ⊠ &M 🖥 📺 ⊠

▼▼▼▼ La Quinta Inn & Suites Denver (Airport/DIA) SH
(303) 371-0888. $106-$149. 6801 Tower Rd. I-70, exit 286, 4.2 mi n; 0.8 mi s of Pena Blvd. Int corridors. **Pets:** Medium. Service with restrictions.

A$K ⊠ &M ◉ 🖥 🖥 📺 🏊

▼▼▼ La Quinta Inn Denver (Central) SH
(303) 458-1222. $74-$139. 3500 Park Ave W. I-25, exit 213, take 38th Ave, just s, left at Fox St, left on Park Ave to 2nd light, then U-turn. Ext/int corridors. **Pets:** Medium. Service with restrictions.

A$K ⊠ &M ◉ 🖥 📺 🏊

△△△ ▼▼▼ La Quinta Inn Denver (Cherry Creek) SH
(303) 758-8886. $85-$122. 1975 S Colorado Blvd. I-25, exit 204, just s. Ext corridors. **Pets:** Medium. Service with restrictions.

SAVE ⊠ ◉ 🖥 📺 🏊

▼▼▼ Magnolia Hotel-Downtown SH
(303) 607-9000. $125-$265. 818 17th St. I-25, exit 212A (Speer Blvd S) to Market St, e to 17th St, then s to jct 17th and Stout sts. Int corridors. **Pets:** Medium, dogs only. $20 one-time fee/pet. Designated rooms, service with restrictions, supervision.

A$K ⊠ &M ◉ 🖥 📺

▼▼▼ Marriott Courtyard Denver Cherry Creek SH
(303) 757-8797. $89-$179. 1475 S Colorado Blvd. I-25, exit 204, 0.5 mi n; entry on Arkansas St. Int corridors. **Pets:** Accepted.

A$K S🔊 ⊠ &M ◉ 🖥 🖥 📺 🏊

△△△ ▼▼▼ Microtel Inn D.I.A SH
(303) 371-8300. $71. 18600 E 63rd Ave. I-70, exit 286 (Tower Rd), 3.6 mi n. Int corridors. **Pets:** Small. $10 daily fee/pet. Supervision.

SAVE ⊠ &M 🖥

▼▼▼ The Oxford Hotel SH
(303) 628-5400. $189-$229. 1600 17th St. Corner of 17th and Wazee sts. Int corridors. **Pets:** Accepted.

A$K S🔊 ⊠ ▮▮

△△△ ▼▼▼ Quality Inn Denver East SH
(303) 371-5640. $59-$89. 3975 Peoria Way. I-70, exit 281 eastbound; exit 282 westbound, just s. Ext corridors. **Pets:** Medium, other species. $15 daily fee/room. Service with restrictions, supervision.

SAVE S🔊 ⊠ 🖥 📺 🏊

△△△ ▼▼▼ Radisson Hotel Denver Stapleton Plaza LH
(303) 321-3500. $79-$109. 3333 Quebec St. I-70, exit 278, 0.3 mi s; I-270, exit 4. Int corridors. **Pets:** Accepted.

SAVE S🔊 ⊠ &M ◉ 🖥 📺 ▮▮ 🏊 ⊠

▼▼▼▼ Ramada Continental Hotel SH
(303) 433-6677. $60-$80. 2601 Zuni St. I-25, exit 212B, just w on Speer Blvd, then just e. Ext/int corridors. **Pets:** Accepted.

A$K ⊠ 🖥 🖥 📺 ▮▮ 🏊

△△△ ▼▼▼ Ramada Inn Denver Downtown LH
(303) 831-7700. $74-$119. 1150 E Colfax Ave. I-25, exit 210 (E Colfax Ave), 1 mi e on US 40; 0.5 mi e of State Capitol. Int corridors. **Pets:** Other species. $100 one-time fee/room. Service with restrictions.

SAVE S🔊 ⊠ &M 🖥 📺 ▮▮ 🏊

△△△ ▼▼▼ Ramada Suites at Denver International Airport SH
(303) 373-1600. $90-$129. 7020 Tower Rd. I-70, exit 286 (Tower Rd), 4.5 mi n. Int corridors. **Pets:** Accepted.

SAVE S🔊 ⊠ &M 🖥 📺 🏊

▼▼▼▼ Red Lion Denver Central SH
(303) 321-6666. **$59-$109.** 4040 Quebec St. I-70, exit 278, s on Quebec St, exit Smith Rd, then e to Frontage Rd; I-270, exit 4. Ext/int corridors. **Pets:** Small. $20 one-time fee/room. Service with restrictions, crate.
ASK S✿ ✕ 🐾 🖧 🛏 🖳 🍴 🏊

▲▲▲ ▼▼▼▼ Red Lion Hotel Denver Downtown at Invesco Field SH
(303) 433-8331. **$79-$149.** 1975 Bryant St. I-25, exit 210B, just w. Int corridors. **Pets:** Accepted.
SAVE S✿ ✕ 🛏 🖳 🍴 🏊

▲▲▲ ▼▼▼▼ Red Roof Inn & Suites SH
(303) 371-5300. **$52-$100.** 6890 Tower Rd. I-70, exit 286, 4.2 mi n; 0.8 mi s of Pena Blvd. Int corridors. **Pets:** Medium, other species. Service with restrictions, supervision.
SAVE ✕ 🐾 🗐 🖧 🛏 🖳 🏊

▼▼▼▼ Residence Inn by Marriott Denver City Center SH 🐾
(303) 296-3444. **$209-$259.** 1725 Champa St. I-70, exit I-25 via Speer Blvd S, left on Stout St via 18th St, left on 18th St via Champa St. Int corridors. **Pets:** Other species. $100 one-time fee/room. No service.
ASK S✿ ✕ 🖧 🛏 🖳

▼▼▼▼ Residence Inn by Marriott Denver Downtown SH
(303) 458-5318. **$149.** 2777 Zuni St. I-25, exit 212B, just w. Ext corridors. **Pets:** Accepted.
ASK S✿ ✕ 🗐 🛏 🖳 🏊

▼▼ Diamond TownePlace Suites by Marriott Downtown Denver SH
(303) 722-2322. **$149-$189.** 685 Speer Blvd. I-25, exit Speer Blvd S, 2.2 mi s, stay in right lane, just past second Bannock St, exit towards Broadway, then right on Acoma St. Int corridors. **Pets:** Accepted.
ASK S✿ ✕ 🐾 🖧 🛏 🖳

▲▲▲ ▼▼▼▼ The Warwick Hotel-Denver SH 🐾
(303) 861-2000. **$119-$650.** 1776 Grant St at 18th St. I-25, exit 210 (E Colfax Ave) to Logan St, n to 18th St, then just w. Int corridors. **Pets:** Small, dogs only. $25 one-time fee/pet. Designated rooms, service with restrictions, supervision.
SAVE S✿ ✕ 🗐 🖧 🛏 🖳 🍴 🏊

▲▲▲ ▼▼▼▼ The Westin Tabor Center Denver LH 🐾
(303) 572-9100. **$319.** 1672 Lawrence St. I-25, exit 212A (Speer Blvd S), 1 mi s to Lawrence St, then e. Int corridors. **Pets:** Small, dogs only. Designated rooms, service with restrictions, supervision.
SAVE ✕ 🐾 🗐 🖧 🛏 🖳 🏊 ✕

ENGLEWOOD

▼▼▼▼ Drury Inn & Suites-Denver Near the Tech Center SH
(303) 694-3400. **$70-$117.** 9445 E Dry Creek Rd. I-25, exit 196 (Dry Creek Rd), just w, on northwest corner. Int corridors. **Pets:** Large, other species. Service with restrictions, supervision.
ASK ✕ 🖧 🛏 🖳 🏊

▼▼▼▼ Holiday Inn Express Hotel & Suites SH
(303) 662-0777. **$81-$100.** 7380 S Clinton St. I-25, exit 196 (Dry Creek Rd), e to S Clinton St, then just n. Int corridors. **Pets:** Accepted.
ASK S✿ ✕ 🗐 🖧 🛏 🖳 🏊

▼▼ Diamond Homestead Studio Suites Hotel-Denver/Tech CenterSouth-Inverness M
(303) 708-8888. **$59-$74.** 9650 E Geddes Ave. I-25, exit 196 (Dry Creek Rd), just e, then n on S Clinton St. Ext corridors. **Pets:** Accepted.
ASK S✿ ✕ 🖧 🛏 🖳

▼▼▼▼ Quality Suites Denver Tech SH
(303) 858-0700. **$105-$125.** 7374 S Clinton St. I-25, exit 196 (Dry Creek Rd), just e, then n. Int corridors. **Pets:** Accepted.
ASK S✿ ✕ 🐾 🗐 🖧 🛏 🖳 🏊

▼▼▼▼ Residence Inn by Marriott-Denver Tech Center SH
(303) 740-7177. **$89-$169.** 6565 S Yosemite St. I-25, exit 197, just w on Arapahoe Rd, then n. Ext corridors. **Pets:** Accepted.
ASK S✿ ✕ 🛏 🖳 🏊 ✕

▼▼▼▼ Residence Inn Park Meadows SH
(720) 895-0200. **$149-$189.** 8322 S Valley Hwy. I-25, exit 195 (County Line Rd), just e to S Valley Hwy, then just s. Int corridors. **Pets:** Accepted.
ASK ✕ 🐾 🖧 🛏 🖳 🏊 ✕

▼▼ Diamond StudioPLUS-Denver-Tech Center South SH
(303) 858-0292. **Call for rates.** 9604 E Easter Ave. I-25, exit 197. Int corridors. **Pets:** Accepted.
✕ 🖧 🛏 🖳 🏊

▼▼▼▼ TownePlace Suites Denver Tech Center SH
(720) 875-1113. **$119-$129.** 7877 S Chester St. I-25, exit 196 (Dry Creek Rd), just w to Chester St, then 0.3 mi s. Int corridors. **Pets:** Large, other species. $75 one-time fee/room. Service with restrictions, crate.
ASK S✿ ✕ 🐾 🖧 🛏 🖳 🏊

GLENDALE

▼▼ Diamond Crossland Studios-Denver/Cherry Creek M
(303) 333-2545. **$65-$75.** 4850 Leetsdale Dr. I-25, exit 201, just e, 3.3 mi n on Monaco Pkwy, then 1.4 mi e. Ext corridors. **Pets:** Accepted.
ASK S✿ ✕ 🛏 🖳

▲▲▲ ▼▼▼ ▼▼▼ Loews Denver Hotel LH 🐾
(303) 782-9300. **$139-$299.** 4150 E Mississippi Ave. I-25, exit 204, 1 mi n on Colorado Blvd, then just e. Int corridors. **Pets:** Other species.
SAVE S✿ ✕ 🐾 🗐 🖧 🛏 🍴

▼▼▼▼ Staybridge Suites Denver/Cherry Creek SH
(303) 321-5757. **$109-$149.** 4220 E Virginia Ave. I-25, exit 204, 1.5 mi n on Colorado Blvd to Virginia Ave, then just e. Int corridors. **Pets:** Accepted.
ASK S✿ ✕ 🐾 🗐 🖧 🛏 🖳 ✕

GOLDEN

▼▼▼▼ Clarion Collection The Golden Hotel SH 🐾
(303) 279-0100. **$149-$289.** 800 11th St. At 11th St and Washington Ave; downtown. Int corridors. **Pets:** Medium. $100 deposit/room, $15 daily fee/room. Service with restrictions, supervision.
ASK S✿ ✕ 🗐 🛏 🖳 🍴

▼▼ ▼▼ Days Inn Denver West SH
(303) 277-0200. **$69-$119.** 15059 W Colfax Ave. I-70, exit 262 (Colfax Ave), just e. Int corridors. **Pets:** Other species. $6 daily fee/pet. Service with restrictions, supervision.
ASK S✿ ✕ 🗐 🖧 🛏 🖳 🍴 🏊 ✕

▼▼▼▼ Denver Marriott West LH
(303) 279-9100. **$99-$189.** 1717 Denver W Blvd. I-70, exit 263, just n, then w. Int corridors. **Pets:** Large. $75 one-time fee/pet. Designated rooms, service with restrictions, crate.
ASK S✿ ✕ 🐾 🗐 🖧 🛏 🖳 🍴 🏊 ✕

▲▲▲ ▼▼▼▼ La Quinta Inn Denver (Golden) SH
(303) 279-5565. **$86-$126.** 3301 Youngfield Service Rd. I-70, exit 264 (32nd Ave), just w, then n. Ext corridors. **Pets:** Medium. Service with restrictions.
SAVE ✕ 🛏 🖳 🏊

▼▼▼▼ Quality Suites at Evergreen Parkway SH 🐾
(303) 526-2000. **$99-$139.** 29300 US Hwy 40. I-70, exit 252 (Evergreen Pkwy), on west side of El Rancho Restaurant; exit 251 eastbound. Int corridors. **Pets:** Large, other species. $50 deposit/pet, $10 daily fee/room. Designated rooms, service with restrictions, crate.
ASK S✿ ✕ 🖧 🛏 🖳 🏊 ✕

▼▼▼ **Residence Inn by Marriott Denver West/Golden** 🆂🅷 ❀
(303) 271-0909. **$99-$189.** 14600 W 6th Ave Frontage Rd. US 6, exit Indiana Ave to frontage road, just e. Int corridors. **Pets:** Medium, other species. $100 one-time fee/room. Designated rooms, service with restrictions.

🄰🄴🅺 🆂🅱 ⊠ 🅫 🅲 🛢 🖥 ➠ ⊠

▲▲▲ ▼▼▼ **Table Mountain Inn** 🆂🅷 ❀
(303) 277-9898. **$116-$148.** 1310 Washington Ave. US 6, exit 19th St, 0.5 mi n to Washington Ave, 0.5 mi w; downtown, just s of arch. Int corridors. **Pets:** $10 daily fee/pet. Designated rooms, service with restrictions.

🆂🄰🅅🄴 🆂🅱 ⊠ 🅫 🅲 🛢 🖥 🍴

GREENWOOD VILLAGE

▼▼▼▼ **Hampton Inn Denver Southeast** 🆂🅷 ❀
(303) 792-9999. **$119-$179.** 9231 E Arapahoe Rd. I-25, exit 197, just e. Int corridors. **Pets:** Other species. $25 daily fee/pet. Designated rooms, service with restrictions.

⊠ 🅫 🕖 🛢 🖥 ➰

▼▼ **Homestead Studio Suites Hotel-Denver/Tech Center South-Greenwood Village** 🆂🅷
(303) 858-1669. **$64-$79.** 9253 E Costilla Ave. I-25, exit 197, just e on Arapahoe Rd, se on Clinton St to Costilla St, then w. Int corridors. **Pets:** Accepted.

🄰🅂🅺 🆂🅱 ⊠ 🅫 🕖 🅲 🛢 🖥

▲▲▲ ▼▼▼▼ **Hyatt Summerfield Suites Hotel** 🆂🅷
(303) 706-1945. **$59-$289.** 9280 E Costilla Ave. I-25, exit 197, e to Clinton St, then just s. Int corridors. **Pets:** Medium, other species. $200 one-time fee/room. Service with restrictions, crate.

🆂🄰🅅🄴 🆂🅱 ⊠ 🅫 🕖 🅲 🛢 🖥 ➠ ⊠

▲▲▲ ▼▼▼▼ **La Quinta Inn & Suites** 🆂🅷
(303) 799-4555. **$103-$143.** 9009 E Arapahoe Rd. I-25, exit 197, just e to Boston, n to Southtech, then just w. Int corridors. **Pets:** Medium. Service with restrictions.

🆂🄰🅅🄴 ⊠ 🅫 🕖 🅲 🛢 🖥 ➠ ⊠

▼▼▼▼ **La Quinta Inn & Suites Denver Tech Center** 🆂🅷
(303) 649-9969. **$109-$159.** 7077 S Clinton St. I-25, exit 197, e to Clinton St, then s. Int corridors. **Pets:** Medium. Service with restrictions.

🄰🅂🅺 ⊠ 🅫 🕖 🅲 🛢 🖥 ➠

▼▼▼▼ **Sheraton Denver Tech Center Hotel** 🆂🅷 ❀
(303) 799-6200. **$59-$189.** 7007 S Clinton St. I-25, exit 197, e on Arapahoe Rd, then s. Int corridors. **Pets:** Medium, dogs only. Service with restrictions, supervision.

🄰🅂🅺 🆂🅱 ⊠ 🅫 🕖 🅲 🖥 🍴 ➠

HIGHLANDS RANCH

▼▼▼ **Residence Inn Denver South Highlands Ranch** 🆂🅷
(303) 683-5500. **$179.** 93 Centennial Blvd. SR 470, exit Broadway, just s, then w. Int corridors. **Pets:** Accepted.

🆂🅱 ⊠ 🅫 🕖 🅲 🛢 🖥 ➠ ⊠

LAKEWOOD

▲▲▲ ▼▼▼▼ **Best Western-Denver Southwest** 🆂🅷
(303) 989-5500. **$55-$75, 14 day notice.** 3440 S Vance St. Just ne of jct US 285 (Hampden Ave) and S Wadsworth Blvd, e on Girton Dr, then just s. Int corridors. **Pets:** Accepted.

🆂🄰🅅🄴 🆂🅱 ⊠ 🕖 🅲 🛢 🖥 ➠

▼▼▼▼ **Comfort Suites** 🆂🅷
(303) 231-9929. **$69-$149, 3 day notice.** 11909 W 6th Ave. US 6, exit Simms/Union, westbound travelers must turn right at stop light, but do not use right turn lane, follow signs to frontage road. Int corridors. **Pets:** Accepted.

🄰🅂🅺 🆂🅱 ⊠ 🅫 🕖 🅲 🛢 🖥 ➠ ⊠

▲▲▲ ▼▼▼▼ **La Quinta Inn & Suites Denver (Southwest/Lakewood)** 🄼
(303) 969-9700. **$74-$115.** 7190 W Hampden Ave. Just se of jct US 285 (W Hampden Ave) and Wadsworth Blvd, e on Jefferson Ave, just n, then e on frontage road. Int corridors. **Pets:** Medium. Service with restrictions.

🆂🄰🅅🄴 ⊠ 🅫 🕖 🅲 🛢 🖥 ➰

▼▼▼ **Quality Suites Lakewood** 🆂🅷
(303) 988-8600. **$79-$129.** 7260 W Jefferson Ave. Just se of US 285 (W Hampden Ave) and Wadsworth Blvd, then e. Int corridors. **Pets:** Accepted.

🄰🅂🅺 🆂🅱 ⊠ 🅫 🕖 🅲 🛢 🖥 ➠

▼▼▼ **Residence Inn by Marriott Denver SW/Lakewood** 🆂🅷
(303) 985-7676. **$169.** 7050 W Hampden Ave. Just se of jct US 285 (W Hampden Ave) and Wadsworth Blvd, e on Jefferson Ave, then n to frontage road. Int corridors. **Pets:** Medium, other species. $75 one-time fee/room.

🄰🅂🅺 🆂🅱 ⊠ 🅫 🕖 🅲 🛢 🖥 ➠ ⊠

▲▲▲ ▼▼▼▼ **Sheraton-Denver West Hotel** 🅻🅷 ❀
(303) 987-2000. **$109-$119.** 360 Union Blvd. US 6, exit Simms/Union, s on Union Blvd; 3 mi e of jct I-70, exit 261. Int corridors. **Pets:** Large, dogs only. $50 deposit/room. Designated rooms, service with restrictions, supervision.

🆂🄰🅅🄴 🆂🅱 ⊠ 🛢 🖥 🍴 ➠ ⊠

▼▼▼ **Super 8 Motel-SW Denver** 🄼
(303) 989-4600. **$49-$89.** 7240 W Jefferson Ave. Just se of US 285 (W Hampden Ave) and Wadsworth Blvd, then e. Int corridors. **Pets:** Accepted.

🄰🅂🅺 🆂🅱 ⊠ 🅲 🛢 🖥

▼▼▼ **TownePlace Suites by Marriott-Denver West/Federal Center** 🆂🅷
(303) 232-7790. **$89-$109.** 800 Tabor St. US 6, exit Simms/Union, just n to 8th, then w. Int corridors. **Pets:** Accepted.

🄰🅂🅺 🆂🅱 ⊠ 🅫 🕖 🅲 🛢 🖥 ➠ ⊠

LITTLETON

▲▲▲ ▼▼▼▼ **Holiday Inn Express** 🆂🅷
(720) 981-1000. **$99-$119.** 12683 W Indore Pl. I-70 to SR 470 and Ken Caryl Ave; I-25 to SR 470 and Ken Caryl Ave, to Shaffer Ave, just n, then w. Int corridors. **Pets:** Accepted.

🆂🄰🅅🄴 ⊠ 🅫 🅲 🛢 🖥 ➰

LONE TREE

▼▼▼▼ **Staybridge Suites Denver South-Lone Tree** 🆂🅷
(303) 649-1010. **$99-$162.** 7820 Park Meadows Dr. I-25, exit 195 (County Line Rd), w on County Line Rd to Acres Green, s to E Park Meadows Dr, then just w; SR 470, exit Quebec St, just se. Int corridors. **Pets:** Accepted.

🄰🅂🅺 🆂🅱 ⊠ 🅫 🕖 🅲 🛢 🖥 ➠ ⊠

NORTHGLENN

▲▲▲ ▼▼▼▼ **Ramada Plaza & Conference Center** 🅻🅷
(303) 452-4100. **$99-$129.** 10 E 120th Ave. I-25, exit 223, just e. Int corridors. **Pets:** Accepted.

🆂🄰🅅🄴 🆂🅱 ⊠ 🅫 🕖 🅲 🛢 🖥 🍴 ➠ ⊠

THORNTON

▼▼ **Crossland Studios-Denver-Thornton** 🆂🅷
(303) 430-4474. **Call for rates.** 8750 Grant St. I-25, exit 219, e to Grant St, then 0.5 mi n. Ext corridors. **Pets:** Accepted.

⊠ 🅲 🛢 🖥

ⒶⒶⒶ ▼▼▼ Sleep Inn North Denver 🆂🅷
(303) 280-9818. **$54-$109.** 12101 Grant St. I-25, exit 223, e to Grant St, then n. Int corridors. **Pets:** Accepted.

🆂🅰🆅🅴 🆂🅵 ⊠ 🔥M 🗐 🖋 🎁 💻 🌊

WESTMINSTER

ⒶⒶⒶ ▼▼▼ Comfort Inn Northwest 🆂🅷
(303) 428-3333. **$70-$200.** 8500 Turnpike Dr. US 36 (Boulder Tpke), exit Sheridan Ave, just s, left on Turnpike Dr at 87th Ave, then 0.4 mi. Int corridors. **Pets:** Medium. $10 daily fee/pet. Service with restrictions, supervision.

🆂🅰🆅🅴 🆂🅵 ⊠ 🔥M 🗐 🖋 🎁 💻 🌊

ⒶⒶⒶ ▼▼▼▼ DoubleTree Hotel Denver North 🆂🅷 🐾
(303) 427-4000. **$89-$199.** 8773 Yates Dr. US 36 (Boulder Tpke), exit Sheridan Ave, n to 92nd Ave, e to Yates Dr, then 0.5 mi s. Int corridors. **Pets:** Other species. Service with restrictions, supervision.

🆂🅰🆅🅴 ⊠ 🗐 🖋 💻 🍴 🌊 ⊠

**ⒶⒶⒶ ▼▼▼▼ La Quinta Inn & Suites Westminster
(Promenade)** 🆂🅷 🐾
(303) 438-5800. **$77-$80, 3 day notice.** 10179 Church Ranch Way. US 36 (Boulder Tpke), exit Church Ranch Blvd, just s to 103rd Pl, then e. Int corridors. **Pets:** Medium. Service with restrictions, crate.

🆂🅰🆅🅴 🆂🅵 ⊠ 🔥M 🖋 🎁 💻 🌊

▼▼ La Quinta Inn Denver (Northglenn) 🆂🅷
(303) 252-9800. **$80-$122.** 345 W 120th Ave. I-25, exit 223, just w. Ext/int corridors. **Pets:** Medium. Service with restrictions.

🅰🆂🅺 ⊠ 🗐 🎁 💻 🌊

ⒶⒶⒶ ▼▼▼▼ La Quinta Inn Denver (Westminster Mall) 🆂🅷
(303) 425-9099. **$72-$125.** 8701 Turnpike Dr. US 36 (Boulder Tpke), exit Sheridan Ave, just s, then left on Turnpike Dr at 87th Ave. Ext/int corridors. **Pets:** Medium. Service with restrictions.

🆂🅰🆅🅴 ⊠ 🔥M 🗐 🎁 💻 🌊

▼▼▼▼ Residence Inn by Marriott 🆂🅷
(303) 427-9500. **$190-$210.** 5010 W 88th Pl. US 36 (Boulder Tpke), exit Sheridan Ave, n to 92nd Ave, e to Yates Dr, then s. Int corridors. **Pets:** Accepted.

🅰🆂🅺 🆂🅵 ⊠ 🔥M 🗐 🖋 🎁 💻 🌊 ⊠

▼▼▼▼ The Westin Westminster 🅻🅷 🐾
(303) 410-5000. **$189-$289.** 10600 Westminster Blvd. US 36 (Boulder Tpke), exit 104th Ave, just n. Int corridors. **Pets:** Other species. Service with restrictions, crate.

🅰🆂🅺 🆂🅵 ⊠ 🔥M 🗐 🖋 🎁 💻 🍴 🌊 ⊠

▼▼ Westminster-Super 8 🆂🅷
(303) 451-7200. **$69.** 12055 Melody Dr. I-25, exit 223, just w. Int corridors. **Pets:** $5 daily fee/pet. Service with restrictions, supervision.

🅰🆂🅺 🆂🅵 ⊠ 🗐 🖋 🎁 💻 ⊠

DILLON

ⒶⒶⒶ ▼▼▼▼ Best Western Ptarmigan Lodge 🆂🅷
(970) 468-2341. **$62-$159, 7 day notice.** 652 Lake Dillon Dr. I-70, exit 205, 1.3 mi se on US 6, then 0.3 mi s. Ext/int corridors. **Pets:** Other species. $15 one-time fee/pet. Designated rooms, service with restrictions, supervision.

🆂🅰🆅🅴 🆂🅵 ⊠ 🎁 💻 ⊠ 🄰

ⒶⒶⒶ ▼▼▼ Dillon Super 8 Motel 🆂🅷
(970) 468-8888. **$60-$135.** 808 Little Beaver Tr. I-70, exit 205, just s, then e. Int corridors. **Pets:** Medium. $15 one-time fee/pet. Designated rooms, service with restrictions, supervision.

🆂🅰🆅🅴 🆂🅵 ⊠ 🎁 💻

DURANGO

ⒶⒶⒶ ▼▼▼ Alpine Inn 🅼
(970) 247-4042. **$48-$102.** 3515 N Main Ave. 2.7 mi n of jct US 160 W and 550, on US 550. Ext corridors. **Pets:** Other species. $5 daily fee/room. Supervision.

🆂🅰🆅🅴 🆂🅵 ⊠ 🎁

ⒶⒶⒶ ▼▼ Caboose Motel 🅼
(970) 247-1191. **$42-$130.** 3363 Main Ave. 2.5 mi n of jct US 550 and 160. Ext corridors. **Pets:** Small, dogs only. $7 daily fee/pet. Designated rooms, service with restrictions, supervision.

🆂🅰🆅🅴 🆂🅵 ⊠ 🎁

ⒶⒶⒶ ▼▼▼ Comfort Inn 🆂🅷
(970) 259-5373. **$59-$159.** 2930 N Main Ave. 2.1 mi n of jct US 160 and 550, on US 550. Ext corridors. **Pets:** Medium, other species. $10 daily fee/pet. Designated rooms, service with restrictions, supervision.

🆂🅰🆅🅴 🆂🅵 ⊠ 💻 🌊

▼▼▼ DoubleTree Hotel Durango 🆂🅷
(970) 259-6580. **$69-$234.** 501 Camino Del Rio. Jct US 160 and 550. Int corridors. **Pets:** Accepted.

🅰🆂🅺 🆂🅵 ⊠ 🔥M 🗐 🖋 🎁 💻 🍴 🌊 ⊠

ⒶⒶⒶ ▼▼▼▼ Holiday Inn 🆂🅷
(970) 247-5393. **$89-$159.** 800 Camino Del Rio. On US 550, just n of jct US 160. Ext corridors. **Pets:** Other species. $10 daily fee/pet. Service with restrictions, supervision.

🆂🅰🆅🅴 ⊠ 🗐 🖋 💻 🍴 🌊 ⊠

ⒶⒶⒶ ▼▼▼▼ Quality Inn & Suites 🆂🅷
(970) 259-7900. **$79-$300.** 455 S Camino Del Rio. On US 160 (Frontage Rd), 1.5 mi e of jct US 550. Int corridors. **Pets:** Other species. $50 deposit/room, $10 daily fee/room. Designated rooms, service with restrictions, supervision.

🆂🅰🆅🅴 🆂🅵 ⊠ 🔥M 🖋 🎁 💻 🌊 ⊠

ⒶⒶⒶ ▼▼▼▼ Residence Inn by Marriott 🆂🅷
(970) 259-6200. **$119-$299, 3 day notice.** 21691 Hwy 160 W. On US 160, just w. Int corridors. **Pets:** Medium, other species. $75 one-time fee/room. Service with restrictions, crate.

🆂🅰🆅🅴 ⊠ 🖋 🎁 💻 🌊 ⊠

▼▼▼▼ The Rochester Hotel 🅱🅱 🐾
(970) 385-1920. **$109-$249, 14 day notice.** 726 E 2nd Ave. Just e of Main Ave via 7th St, then just n. Int corridors. **Pets:** Dogs only. $20 daily fee/pet. Designated rooms, service with restrictions, crate.

🅰🆂🅺 🆂🅵 ⊠ 🎁 💻

ⒶⒶⒶ ▼▼ Siesta Motel 🅼
(970) 247-0741. **$36-$78.** 3475 N Main Ave. 2.6 mi n of jct US 160 W and 550, on US 550. Ext corridors. **Pets:** Medium, dogs only. $10 daily fee/pet. Designated rooms, service with restrictions, supervision.

🆂🅰🆅🅴 🆂🅵 ⊠ 🎁 💻

[AAA] ♦♦ **Travelodge** [M]
(970) 247-1741. **$59-$119.** 2970 Main Ave. 2.2 mi n of jct US 160 and 550, on US 550. Ext corridors. **Pets:** Medium. $8 daily fee/pet. Designated rooms, service with restrictions, supervision.
[SAVE] [SD] 🚭 ▣ 📺

EAGLE

[AAA] ♦♦♦ **Best Western Eagle Lodge & Suites** [SH]
(970) 328-6316. **$90-$140.** 200 Loren Ln. I-70, exit 147, just s. Int corridors. **Pets:** Accepted.
[SAVE] [SD] 🚭 ♿ ▣ 📺 🏊 🏋

EDWARDS

[AAA] ♦♦♦ **Inn and Suites at Riverwalk** [SH]
(970) 926-0606. **$120-$810, 14 day notice.** 27 Main St. I-70, exit 163, 0.3 mi s. Int corridors. **Pets:** Large, other species. $5 daily fee/pet, $25 one-time fee/pet. No service, crate.
[SAVE] [SD] 🚭 👂 ▣ 📺 🍴 🏊

ESTES PARK

[AAA] ♦♦ **Budget Host Four Winds Motor Lodge** [M]
(970) 586-3313. **$52-$109, 5 day notice.** 1120 Big Thompson Ave. 1 mi e on US 34. Ext corridors. **Pets:** Medium. $15 daily fee/pet. Designated rooms, supervision.
[SAVE] [SD] 🚭 ▣ 📺 🏊 🏋

[AAA] ♦♦ **Castle Mountain Lodge** [CA]
(970) 586-3664. **$85-$235, 30 day notice.** 1520 Fall River Rd. 1 mi w on US 34. Ext corridors. **Pets:** Dogs only. $15 daily fee/pet. Designated rooms, supervision.
[SAVE] [SD] 🚭 ▣ 📺 🏋 [AC] ☎

[AAA] ♦♦♦ **Holiday Inn** [SH]
(970) 586-2332. **$89-$299, 3 day notice.** 101 S St Vrain Ave. 0.5 mi se; on SR 7 at US 36. Int corridors. **Pets:** Dogs only. $30 one-time fee/room. Designated rooms, service with restrictions.
[SAVE] [SD] 🚭 [♿M] 👂 ♿ ▣ 📺 🍴 🏊

[AAA] ♦♦ **Lake Estes Inn & Suites** [M]
(970) 586-3386. **$59-$149, 7 day notice.** 1650 Big Thompson Ave. 1.7 mi e on US 34. Ext corridors. **Pets:** Other species. $100 deposit/room, $25 daily fee/pet. Designated rooms, service with restrictions.
[SAVE] [SD] 🚭 ♿ ▣ 📺 🏊 🏋 [AC]

[AAA] ♦♦ **McGregor Mountain Lodge** [CA]
(970) 586-3457. **$65-$309, 30 day notice.** 2815 Fall River Rd. 3.5 mi w on US 34. Ext corridors. **Pets:** Dogs only. $20 daily fee/pet. Designated rooms, supervision.
[SAVE] 🚭 ▣ 📺 🏋 [AC] ☎

[AAA] ♦♦ **Mountain Sage Inn** [M]
(970) 586-2833. **$40-$110, 7 day notice.** 553 W Elkhorn Ave. 0.5 mi w on US 34. Ext/int corridors. **Pets:** Dogs only. $20 daily fee/room. Designated rooms, service with restrictions, supervision.
[SAVE] 🚭 ▣ 📺

[AAA] ♦♦♦ **Silver Moon Inn** [M]
(970) 586-6006. **$70-$180.** 175 Spruce Dr. Just w on US 34, then just ne. Ext corridors. **Pets:** Accepted.
[SAVE] 🚭 ▣ 📺 🏊

EVANS

[AAA] ♦ **Americas Best Value Inn** [SH]
(970) 339-2492. **$36-$79.** 800 31st St. Jct US 85 and 31st St. Ext corridors. **Pets:** Other species. $10 daily fee/pet. Designated rooms, service with restrictions, crate.
[SAVE] [SD] 🚭 ▣ 🏊

[AAA] ♦♦ **Sleep Inn Greeley/Evans** [SH]
(970) 356-2180. **$59-$99.** 3025 8th Ave. Just sw of jct US 34 and 85 Bypass. Int corridors. **Pets:** Other species. $15 one-time fee/room. Service with restrictions, crate.
[SAVE] [SD] 🚭 [♿M] 👂 ♿ ▣ 📺 🏊

FORT COLLINS

[AAA] ♦♦ **AmericInn Lodge & Suites** [SH]
(970) 226-1232. **$99-$169.** 7645 Westgate Dr. I-25, exit 262, just se off SR 392. Int corridors. **Pets:** Accepted.
[SAVE] 🚭 [♿M] 👂 ♿ ▣ 📺 🏊 🏋

[AAA] ♦♦♦ **Best Western Kiva Inn** [SH]
(970) 484-2444. **$69-$119.** 1638 E Mulberry St (Hwy 14). I-25, exit 269B, 1.5 mi w on SR 14. Ext/int corridors. **Pets:** Dogs only. $10 daily fee/pet. Designated rooms, service with restrictions, supervision.
[SAVE] [SD] 🚭 ♿ ▣ 📺 🏊 🏋

[AAA] ♦♦ **Best Western University Inn** [M] 🐾
(970) 484-1984. **$69-$129.** 914 S College Ave. I-25, exit 268, 4 mi w to College Ave, then just n on US 287. Ext/int corridors. **Pets:** Other species. $10 daily fee/pet. Designated rooms, service with restrictions, supervision.
[SAVE] [SD] 🚭 ▣ 📺 🏊

♦♦♦ **Comfort Suites by Choice Hotels** [SH]
(970) 206-4597. **$115-$135.** 1415 Oakridge Dr. I-25, exit 265, 3.3 mi w to McMurray Ave, just s, then w. Int corridors. **Pets:** Accepted.
[A$K] [SD] 🚭 👂 ♿ ▣ 📺 🏊

♦♦♦ **Courtyard by Marriott** [SH]
(970) 282-1700. **$85-$119.** 1200 Oakridge Dr. I-25, exit 265, 3.3 mi w; entry via Lemay Ave. Int corridors. **Pets:** $75 one-time fee/pet. Designated rooms, service with restrictions, supervision.
[A$K] 🚭 [♿M] 👂 ♿ ▣ 📺 🍴 🏊

♦♦♦ **Fort Collins Marriott** [LH]
(970) 226-5200. **$99-$179, 5 day notice.** 350 E Horsetooth Rd. I-25, exit 265, 4 mi w to John F Kennedy, then n; just beyond Horsetooth Rd. Int corridors. **Pets:** Accepted.
[A$K] 🚭 [♿M] 👂 ♿ ▣ 📺 🍴 🏊

♦♦♦ **Hampton Inn** [SH]
(970) 229-5927. **$89-$159.** 1620 Oakridge Dr. I-25, exit 265, 3.3 mi w, s on McMurray Ave to Oakridge Dr, then just e. Int corridors. **Pets:** Accepted.
[A$K] [SD] 🚭 [♿M] ♿ ▣ 📺 🏊

[AAA] ♦♦♦ **Hilton Ft Collins** [SH]
(970) 482-2626. **$109-$229.** 425 W Prospect Rd. I-25, exit 268, 4.3 mi w. Int corridors. **Pets:** Accepted.
[SAVE] [SD] 🚭 👂 ♿ ▣ 📺 🍴 🏊 🏋

[AAA] ♦♦♦ **Quality Inn & Suites** [SH]
(970) 282-9047. **$79-$149.** 4001 S Mason St. I-25, exit 265, 4.6 mi w to Mason St, then 0.5 mi n. Int corridors. **Pets:** Accepted.
[SAVE] [SD] 🚭 [♿M] 👂 ♿ ▣ 📺 🏊

♦♦♦ **Residence Inn Fort Collins** [SH] 🐾
(970) 223-5700. **$149-$189.** 1127 Oakridge Dr. I-25, exit 265, 3.3 mi w on Harmony Rd to Lemay Ave, then s to Oakridge Dr. Int corridors. **Pets:** Other species. $75 one-time fee/room.
[A$K] 🚭 ♿ ▣ 📺 🏊 🏋

♦♦ **Sleep Inn** [SH]
(970) 484-5515. **$69-$129.** 3808 E Mulberry St. I-25, exit 269B, just nw. Int corridors. **Pets:** Large, other species. $5 one-time fee/pet. Designated rooms, service with restrictions, crate.
[A$K] [SD] 🚭 ♿ ▣ 📺

▼▼ **Super 8 Motel** 🆂🅷
(970) 493-7701. **$55-$100.** 409 Centro Way. I-25, exit 269B, just w. Int corridors. **Pets:** Medium. $5 daily fee/pet. Service with restrictions, supervision.
🅰🆂🅺 🆂🗙 🗙 🖥 🗙

FORT MORGAN

▼▼ **Best Western Park Terrace Inn** 🆂🅷 🐾
(970) 867-8256. **$69-$89.** 725 Main St. I-76, exit 80, 0.5 mi s. Ext corridors. **Pets:** $10 one-time fee/pet. Designated rooms, service with restrictions, crate.
🅰🆂🅺 🆂🗙 🗙 🖥 🖥 🍴 🏊

🅰🅰🅰 ▼▼▼ **Central Motel** 🅼
(970) 867-2401. **$49-$62.** 201 W Platte Ave. I-76, exit 80, 0.6 mi s, then w on US 34. Ext corridors. **Pets:** Other species. $10 one-time fee/room. Service with restrictions, supervision.
🆂🗙 🆂🗙 🗙 🖥 🖥

▼▼ **Rodeway Inn** 🅼 🐾
(970) 867-9481. **$69-$119.** 1409 Barlow Rd. I-76, exit 82, just n. Ext/int corridors. **Pets:** $10 daily fee/room. Designated rooms, service with restrictions, supervision.
🗙 🖥 🍴

FRISCO

🅰🅰🅰 ▼▼▼▼ **Best Western Lake Dillon Lodge** 🆂🅷
(970) 668-5094. **$79-$229, 7 day notice.** 1202 Summit Blvd. I-70, exit 203, just s. Int corridors. **Pets:** Accepted.
🆂🗙 🆂🗙 🗙 🖥 🖥 🍴 🏊 🗙

🅰🅰🅰 ▼▼▼ **Holiday Inn-Frisco** 🆂🅷
(970) 668-5000. **$79-$199.** 1129 N Summit Blvd. I-70, exit 203, just s. Ext/int corridors. **Pets:** Accepted.
🆂🗙 🆂🗙 🗙 🅼 🗙 🗙 🖥 🖥 🍴 🏊 🗙

▼▼ **Hotel Frisco** 🆂🅷 🐾
(970) 668-5009. **$59-$199, 14 day notice.** 308 Main. I-70, exit 201, 0.7 mi s; center. Ext/int corridors. **Pets:** Other species. $10 daily fee/pet. Service with restrictions.
🅰🆂🅺 🗙 🖥 🖥 🗙

🅰🅰🅰 ▼▼▼ **New Summit Inn** 🆂🅷
(970) 668-3220. **$49-$159, 3 day notice.** 1205 N Summit Blvd. I-70, exit 203, just s, then just e. Int corridors. **Pets:** Dogs only. $10 daily fee/pet. Supervision.
🆂🗙 🆂🗙 🗙 🖥 🖥

🅰🅰🅰 ▼▼▼ **Ramada Limited Frisco** 🆂🅷
(970) 668-8783. **$49-$169.** 990 Lakepoint Dr. I-70, exit 203, just s. Int corridors. **Pets:** Other species. $10 daily fee/room. Designated rooms, no service, supervision.
🆂🗙 🆂🗙 🗙 🅼 🗙 🖥 🖥

🅰🅰🅰 ▼▼▼ **Snowshoe Motel** 🅼
(970) 668-3444. **$49-$140.** 521 Main St. I-70, exit 203 westbound, 1 mi s to Main St, then just w; exit 201 eastbound. Ext corridors. **Pets:** $10 deposit/pet, $10 one-time fee/pet. Designated rooms, supervision.
🆂🗙 🗙 🖥 🖥 🗙

FRUITA

🅰🅰🅰 ▼▼ **Balanced Rock Motel** 🅼
(970) 858-7333. **$40-$60.** 126 S Coulson. I-70, exit 19, just n to Aspen Ave, then just w. Ext corridors. **Pets:** Dogs only. $5 daily fee/pet. No service, supervision.
🆂🗙 🗙 🖥

🅰🅰🅰 ▼▼▼ **Comfort Inn** 🆂🅷 🐾
(970) 858-1333. **$70-$135.** 400 Jurassic Ave. I-70, exit 19, 0.3 mi s; just e of Dinosaur Journey Museum. Int corridors. **Pets:** Medium. Designated rooms, service with restrictions, supervision.
🆂🗙 🆂🗙 🗙 🅼 🗙 🗙 🖥 🖥 🏊

🅰🅰🅰 ▼ **H-Motel** 🅼
(970) 858-7198. **$35-$55, 3 day notice.** 333 Hwy 6 & 50. I-70, exit 19, just n to Aspen St, e to Plum St, just s, then just e. Ext corridors. **Pets:** Accepted.
🆂🗙 🗙 🖥

▼▼▼ **La Quinta Inn & Suites** 🆂🅷
(970) 858-8850. **$62-$102.** 570 Raptor Rd. I-70, exit 19, 0.3 mi s; next to Dinosaur Journey Museum. Int corridors. **Pets:** Accepted.
🅰🆂🅺 🆂🗙 🗙 🗙 🖥 🖥 🏊

🅰🅰🅰 ▼▼▼ **Super 8** 🆂🅷 🐾
(970) 858-0808. **$50-$86.** 399 Jurassic Ave. I-70, exit 19, 0.3 mi s; just e of Dinosaur Journey Museum. Int corridors. **Pets:** Medium. $5 one-time fee/pet. Designated rooms, service with restrictions, supervision.
🆂🗙 🆂🗙 🗙 🅼 🗙 🗙 🖥 🏊

GEORGETOWN

🅰🅰🅰 ▼▼▼ **Georgetown Mountain Inn** 🅼
(303) 569-3201. **$57-$79.** 1100 Rose St. I-70, exit 228, just s, then 0.3 mi w. Ext corridors. **Pets:** Other species. $10 one-time fee/room. Designated rooms, service with restrictions, crate.
🆂🗙 🆂🗙 🗙 🖥 🖥 🏊 🗙

GLENWOOD SPRINGS

🅰🅰🅰 ▼▼▼▼ **Hotel Colorado** 🆂🅷
(970) 945-6511. **$175-$197.** 526 Pine St. I-70, exit 116, just ne. Int corridors. **Pets:** Accepted.
🆂🗙 🗙 🗙 🖥 🖥 🍴 🗙 🗙

▼▼▼▼ **Quality Inn & Suites** 🆂🅷
(970) 945-5995. **$89-$189.** 2650 Gilstrap. I-70, exit 114, just s, then w. Int corridors. **Pets:** Accepted.
🅰🆂🅺 🆂🗙 🗙 🅼 🗙 🗙 🖥 🖥 🏊

▼▼▼▼ **Ramada Inn & Suites** 🆂🅷
(970) 945-2500. **$90-$150.** 124 W 6th St. I-70, exit 116, just w. Ext/int corridors. **Pets:** Medium. $15 daily fee/room. Designated rooms, service with restrictions, supervision.
🅰🆂🅺 🆂🗙 🗙 🖥 🖥 🍴 🏊

🅰🅰🅰 ▼▼▼ **Silver Spruce Motel** 🅼
(970) 945-5458. **$50-$120.** 162 W 6th St. I-70, exit 116, just w on frontage road. Ext corridors. **Pets:** Dogs only. $10 daily fee/pet. Designated rooms, service with restrictions, supervision.
🆂🗙 🆂🗙 🗙 🖥 🖥

GRANBY

🅰🅰🅰 ▼▼▼▼ **The Inn at Silver Creek** 🅻🅷 🐾
(970) 887-2131. **$59-$249, 15 day notice.** 62927 Hwy 40. 2 mi se on US 40. Int corridors. **Pets:** $25 one-time fee/room. Designated rooms, service with restrictions.
🆂🗙 🆂🗙 🗙 🖥 🖥 🍴 🏊 🗙 🗙

GRAND JUNCTION

🅰🅰🅰 ▼▼▼ **Americas Best Value Inn** 🆂🅷
(970) 245-1410. **$55-$89.** 754 Horizon Dr. I-70, exit 31, 0.3 mi n. Ext corridors. **Pets:** Service with restrictions, supervision.
🆂🗙 🆂🗙 🗙 🅼 🗙 🖥 🖥 🏊

🅰🅰🅰 ▼▼▼ **Best Western Sandman Motel** 🆂🅷 🐾
(970) 243-4150. **$69-$110, 3 day notice.** 708 Horizon Dr. I-70, exit 31, 0.3 mi s. Ext/int corridors. **Pets:** Medium. $25 one-time fee/room. Designated rooms, service with restrictions, supervision.
🆂🗙 🆂🗙 🗙 🖥 🖥 🏊

🅰🅰🅰 ▼▼▼ **Grand Junction Super 8** 🆂🅷
(970) 248-8080. **$50-$86.** 728 Horizon Dr. I-70, exit 31, just s. Int corridors. **Pets:** Accepted.
🆂🗙 🆂🗙 🗙 🖥 🏊

Grand Vista Hotel SH
(970) 241-8411. **$79-$89.** 2790 Crossroads Blvd. I-70, exit 31, 0.3 mi n. Int corridors. **Pets:** Small. $10 daily fee/room. Designated rooms, service with restrictions, supervision.

Hampton Inn SH
(970) 243-3222. **$100-$124.** 205 Main St. At 2nd and Main sts; downtown. Int corridors. **Pets:** Large, other species. $25 daily fee/room. Service with restrictions, supervision.

Hawthorn Suites SH
(970) 242-2525. **$99-$239.** 225 Main St. At 2nd and Main sts; downtown. Int corridors. **Pets:** Large, other species. $25 daily fee/room. Service with restrictions, supervision.

Holiday Inn SH
(970) 243-6790. **$79-$99.** 755 Horizon Dr. I-70, exit 31; northwest corner. Ext/int corridors. **Pets:** Other species. Service with restrictions, supervision.

La Quinta Inn & Suites Grand Junction SH
(970) 241-2929. **$92-$139.** 2761 Crossroads Blvd. I-70, exit 31, n to Crossroads Blvd, then just w. Int corridors. **Pets:** Medium. Service with restrictions.

Mesa Inn M
(970) 245-3080. **$45-$80.** 704 Horizon Dr. I-70, exit 31, 0.5 mi s. Ext corridors. **Pets:** Service with restrictions, supervision.

Quality Inn of Grand Junction SH
(970) 245-7200. **$70-$100.** 733 Horizon Dr. I-70, exit 31, just s. Int corridors. **Pets:** Designated rooms, service with restrictions, supervision.

Ramada Inn SH
(970) 243-5150. **$79-$159.** 752 Horizon Dr. I-70, exit 31, just n. Int corridors. **Pets:** Accepted.

West Gate Inn M
(970) 241-3020. **$63-$89.** 2210 Hwy 6 & 50. I-70, exit 26, just se. Ext corridors. **Pets:** Other species. $50 deposit/room. Designated rooms, service with restrictions, crate.

GRAND LAKE

Spirit Lake Lodge M
(970) 627-3344. **$55-$180, 7 day notice.** 829 Grand Ave. Just e of US 34; downtown. Ext corridors. **Pets:** Accepted.

GREAT SAND DUNES NATIONAL PARK AND PRESERVE

Great Sand Dunes Lodge M
(719) 378-2900. **$89-$95.** 7900 Hwy 150 N. From Alamosa, 16 mi e on US 160, 16 mi n on SR 150; at entrance to Great Sand Dunes National Monument. Ext corridors. **Pets:** Large. $10 daily fee/room. Designated rooms.

GREELEY

Best Western Regency Hotel SH
(970) 353-8444. **$59-$139.** 701 8th St. On US 85 business route; downtown. Int corridors. **Pets:** $25 one-time fee/room. Service with restrictions, crate.

Comfort Inn-Greeley SH
(970) 330-6380. **$70-$100, 30 day notice.** 2467 W 29th St. US 34 Bypass, exit 23rd Ave, just sw. Int corridors. **Pets:** Accepted.

Country Inn & Suites By Carlson SH
(970) 330-3404. **$85-$115.** 2501 W 29th St. US 34 Bypass, exit 23rd Ave, just s, then w. Int corridors. **Pets:** Small. $15 daily fee/room. Designated rooms, service with restrictions, supervision.

Days Inn SH
(970) 392-1530. **$62-$110.** 5630 W 10th St. 5 mi w on US 34 business route; entry via 54th Ave off 10th St. Int corridors. **Pets:** Large, other species. $15 daily fee/pet. Service with restrictions, crate.

GUNNISON

ABC Motel M
(970) 641-2400. **$48-$89.** 212 E Tomichi Ave. On US 50; near Western State College. Ext corridors. **Pets:** $5 daily fee/pet. Designated rooms, service with restrictions, supervision.

Alpine Inn M
(970) 641-2804. **$45-$129.** 1011 W Rio Grande. Jct US 50 and SR 135, 1.1 mi w. Int corridors. **Pets:** Accepted.

Gunnison Inn M
(970) 641-0700. **$45-$85.** 412 E Tomichi Ave. On US 50; near Western State College. Ext corridors. **Pets:** Dogs only. $5 daily fee/pet. Service with restrictions, supervision.

Rodeway Inn SH
(970) 641-0500. **Call for rates.** 37760 W Hwy 50. US 50, 2.3 mi w. Ext corridors. **Pets:** Medium. $5 daily fee/pet. Designated rooms, service with restrictions, supervision.

Water Wheel Inn SH
(970) 641-1650. **$49-$99.** 37478 W Hwy 50. Jct SR 135, 2.5 mi w. Ext/int corridors. **Pets:** Other species. $5 daily fee/pet. Designated rooms, supervision.

HOT SULPHUR SPRINGS

Canyon Motel M
(970) 725-3395. **$54-$99.** 221 Byers Ave. On US 40. Ext corridors. **Pets:** $10 one-time fee/room. Supervision.

IDAHO SPRINGS

H & H Motor Lodge M
(303) 567-2838. **$59-$69.** 2445 Colorado Blvd. I-25, exit 241, just w. Ext corridors. **Pets:** Other species. $5 daily fee/pet. Designated rooms, service with restrictions, supervision.

JULESBURG

Budget Host Platte Valley Inn SH
(970) 474-3336. **$44-$65.** 15225 Hwy 385 & I-76. I-76, exit 180, just n. Ext corridors. **Pets:** Dogs only. $7 daily fee/pet. Designated rooms, service with restrictions, supervision.

KEYSTONE

The Inn at Keystone SH ❖
(970) 496-4825. **$99-$262, 21 day notice.** 23044 Hwy 6. I-70, exit 205, 6.5 mi e on US 6; at Keystone Ski area. Int corridors. **Pets:** $25 daily fee/room. Designated rooms, service with restrictions.

LA JUNTA

Holiday Inn Express M
(719) 384-2900. **$89.** 27994 US Hwy 50 Frontage Rd. On US 50, 0.8 mi w. Int corridors. **Pets:** Accepted.

LAKE CITY

Matterhorn Mountain Motel M
(970) 944-2210. **$85-$95.** 409 Bluff St. SR 149, just w via 4th St. Ext corridors. **Pets:** Other species. $10 one-time fee/pet. No service, supervision.

LAMAR

Best Western Cow Palace Inn M
(719) 336-7753. **$80-$100.** 1301 N Main St. 0.8 mi n on US 50 and 287. Ext/int corridors. **Pets:** Accepted.

Blue Spruce Motel M ❖
(719) 336-7454. **$45-$55.** 1801 S Main St. 1.3 mi s on US 287 and 385. Ext corridors. **Pets:** Medium, other species. $5 daily fee/pet. Designated rooms, supervision.

El Mar Motel M ❖
(719) 336-4331. **$43-$55.** 1210 S Main St. 1 mi s on US 287 and 385. Ext corridors. **Pets:** Medium, other species. $5 daily fee/pet. Designated rooms, supervision.

LAS ANIMAS

Best Western Bent's Fort Inn M
(719) 456-0011. **$71-$79.** 10950 E US 50. On US 50, 1.5 mi e on frontage road. Int corridors. **Pets:** Other species. $7 one-time fee/pet. Service with restrictions.

LEADVILLE

Alps Motel M
(719) 486-1223. **$59-$115, 5 day notice.** S Hwy 24. Just s on US 24. Int corridors. **Pets:** Large, dogs only. $15 daily fee/pet. Designated rooms, service with restrictions, supervision.

Silver King Inn SH
(719) 486-2610. **$119-$150.** 2020 N Poplar. US 24, just s of jct SR 91. Ext/int corridors. **Pets:** Medium, other species. $35 daily fee/pet. Designated rooms, no service, supervision.

LIMON

Best Western Limon Inn SH
(719) 775-0277. **$55-$100.** 925 T Ave. I-70, exit 359. Int corridors. **Pets:** Accepted.

Safari Motel M
(719) 775-2363. **$44-$92.** 637 Main St. I-70, exit 361, 0.8 mi w. Ext corridors. **Pets:** Medium, other species. $5 daily fee/pet. Designated rooms, service with restrictions, supervision.

Super 8 Motel SH
(719) 775-2889. **$55-$99.** 937 Hwy 24. I-70, exit 359, just s. Int corridors. **Pets:** Accepted.

Tyme Square Inn SH
(719) 775-0700. **$65-$105.** 2505 6th St. I-70, exit 359, then s. Int corridors. **Pets:** Large, other species. $15 daily fee/pet. Designated rooms, service with restrictions, supervision.

LONGMONT

Hawthorn Suites SH
(303) 774-7100. **$69-$179.** 2000 Sunset Way. 1 mi s on US 287, 1.3 mi sw on SR 119, just n on Sunset St, then just w on Korte Pkwy. Int corridors. **Pets:** Other species. $50 one-time fee/room. Service with restrictions, supervision.

Radisson Hotel & Conference Center Longmont-Boulder SH ❖
(303) 776-2000. **$89-$155.** 1900 Ken Pratt Blvd. 1 mi s on US 287, 1.3 mi sw on SR 119. Int corridors. **Pets:** Other species. $50 deposit/pet. Designated rooms, service with restrictions, crate.

Residence Inn by Marriott Boulder/Longmont SH
(303) 702-9933. **$99-$199.** 1450 Dry Creek Dr. I-25, exit 235, jct Hover Rd and SR 119. Int corridors. **Pets:** Other species. $100 one-time fee/room. Service with restrictions, crate.

Super 8 Motel M
(303) 772-0888. **$56-$81.** 10805 Turner Blvd. I-25, exit 240, jct SR 119; 7 mi e of town. Int corridors. **Pets:** Accepted.

LOUISVILLE

Comfort Inn of Boulder County SH ❖
(303) 604-0181. **$69-$129.** 1196 Dillon Rd. US 36 (Boulder Tpke), exit Superior (SR 170), just n on McCaslin Blvd, then just w. Int corridors. **Pets:** Other species. $10 daily fee/room. No service, supervision.

La Quinta Inn & Suites Denver (Louisville/Boulder) SH
(303) 664-0100. **$85-$139.** 902 Dillon Rd. US 36 (Boulder Tpke), exit Superior (SR 170), just n on McCaslin Blvd, then e. Int corridors. **Pets:** Medium. Service with restrictions.

Quality Inn and Suites SH ❖
(303) 327-1215. **$59-$149.** 960 W Dillon Rd. US 36 (Boulder Tpke), exit Superior (SR 170), n on McCaslin Blvd to Dillon Rd, then e. Int corridors. **Pets:** $15 daily fee/pet. Service with restrictions, crate.

Residence Inn by Marriott-Boulder/Louisville SH
(303) 665-2661. **$139-$149.** 845 Coal Creek Cir. US 36 (Boulder Tpke), exit Superior (SR 170), n on McCaslin Blvd to Dillon Rd, then 0.6 mi e. Int corridors. **Pets:** Medium. $100 one-time fee/room. Service with restrictions.

LOVELAND

Budget Host Exit 254 Inn M ❖
(970) 667-5202. **$50-$79.** 2716 SE Frontage Rd. I-25, exit 254, just e. Ext corridors. **Pets:** Other species. $5 daily fee/pet. Supervision.

MARBLE

▼▼◊◊ Ute Meadows Inn Bed & Breakfast 🅱🅱 ❧
(970) 963-7088. **$119-$159, 14 day notice.** 2880 CR 3. From jct SR 133, 3 mi e. Int corridors. **Pets:** Large, dogs only. $15 daily fee/pet. Service with restrictions, supervision.
Ⓐ$Ⓚ Ⓢ⑥ ☒ 🍴 ⊠ 🎟 ☎

MESA VERDE NATIONAL PARK

◊◊◊ ▼▼◊◊ Far View Lodge in Mesa Verde Ⓜ
(970) 529-4421. **$120-$148, 3 day notice.** 1 Navajo Hill, MM 15. 15 mi from park gate; near park visitors center. Ext corridors. **Pets:** Accepted.
ⓈⒶⓋⒺ Ⓢ⑥ ☒ ⓚ 🚪 💻 🍴 🌀

MONTE VISTA

◊◊◊ ▼▼▼▼ Best Western Movie Manor Motel 🆂🅷
(719) 852-5921. **$55-$110, 10 day notice.** 2830 W Hwy 160. On US 160, 2 mi w. Ext corridors. **Pets:** Accepted.
Ⓢ🅐🅥🅔 ☒ 💻 🍴

◊◊◊ ▼▼◊◊ Pecosa Inn Ⓜ
(719) 852-0612. **$105.** 1519 Grande Ave. 0.3 mi e on US 160. Int corridors. **Pets:** Other species. Service with restrictions, supervision.
Ⓢ🅐🅥🅔 Ⓢ⑥ ☒ 💻 ➰

MONTROSE

▼▼◊◊▼ Best Western Red Arrow 🆂🅷
(970) 249-9641. **$69-$109.** 1702 E Main St. 1 mi e on US 50. Ext/int corridors. **Pets:** $8 daily fee/pet. Service with restrictions, crate.
Ⓐ$Ⓚ Ⓢ⑥ ☒ 🚪 💻 ➰ ☒

◊◊◊ ▼▼◊◊ Black Canyon Motel Ⓜ
(970) 249-3495. **$45-$95.** 1605 E Main St. 1 mi e on US 50. Ext corridors. **Pets:** Accepted.
Ⓢ🅐🅥🅔 Ⓢ⑥ ☒ ⓚ 🚪 💻 ➰

◊◊◊ ▼ Canyon Trails Inn Ⓜ
(970) 249-3426. **$50-$80.** 1225 E Main St. 0.8 mi e on US 50. Ext corridors. **Pets:** Other species. Designated rooms, service with restrictions.
Ⓢ🅐🅥🅔 Ⓢ⑥ ☒ 💻 ➰

▼▼◊◊▼ Hampton Inn Montrose 🆂🅷 ❧
(970) 252-3300. **$99-$129.** 1980 N Townsend Ave. On US 550, just n of jct US 50. Int corridors. **Pets:** Large, other species. Designated rooms, service with restrictions, supervision.
Ⓐ$Ⓚ ☒ ⓛM 🖋 ⓚ 💻 ➰ ☒

◊◊◊ ▼▼◊◊◊ Holiday Inn Express Hotel & Suites 🆂🅷
(970) 240-1800. **$89-$159.** 1391 S Townsend Ave. 1 mi s on US 550, e on Niagara Ave. Int corridors. **Pets:** Designated rooms, service with restrictions, supervision.
Ⓢ🅐🅥🅔 ☒ ⓛM 🖋 ⓚ 🚪 💻 ➰

▼▼◊◊▼ Quality Inn & Suites-Montrose 🆂🅷
(970) 249-1011. **$63-$119.** 2751 Commercial Way. 2 mi s on US 550, w on O'Delle. Int corridors. **Pets:** Medium. $10 daily fee/pet. Service with restrictions, supervision.
☒ 🖋 ⓚ 🚪 💻 ➰

▼▼ Uncompahgre Bed & Breakfast 🅱🅱
(970) 240-4000. **$70-$115.** 21049 Uncompahgre Rd. 8 mi s on US 550. Int corridors. **Pets:** Dogs only. Service with restrictions, supervision.
Ⓐ$Ⓚ Ⓢ⑥ ☒ 🚪

▼ Western Motel Ⓜ
(970) 249-3481. **$45-$105.** 1200 E Main St. 0.8 mi e on US 50. Ext corridors. **Pets:** Accepted.
Ⓐ$Ⓚ Ⓢ⑥ ☒ 🚪 💻 ➰

NEDERLAND

◊◊◊ ▼▼◊◊ Best Western Lodge at Nederland 🆂🅷
(303) 258-9463. **$115, 3 day notice.** 55 Lakeview Dr. SR 119; across street from Visitor's Center. Int corridors. **Pets:** Accepted.
Ⓢ🅐🅥🅔 Ⓢ⑥ ☒ 🚪 💻 ☒

NEW CASTLE

▼▼◊◊ New Castle Rodeway Inn 🆂🅷
(970) 984-2363. **$69-$119.** 781 Burning Mountain Ave. I-70, exit 105, just n, then w. Int corridors. **Pets:** Accepted.
Ⓐ$Ⓚ Ⓢ⑥ ☒ ⓚ 🚪 💻 ➰

OURAY

◊◊◊ ▼▼◊◊ Best Western Twin Peaks Hot Springs Ⓜ ❧
(970) 325-4427. **$85-$250.** 125 3rd Ave. Just w of US 550. Ext corridors. **Pets:** Large, dogs only. $10 one-time fee/room. Designated rooms, service with restrictions, supervision.
Ⓢ🅐🅥🅔 Ⓢ⑥ ☒ 🚪 💻 🌀

▼ Comfort Inn Ⓜ
(970) 325-7203. **$59-$159.** 191 5th Ave. Just w of US 550. Ext corridors. **Pets:** Dogs only. $10 daily fee/pet. Service with restrictions.
Ⓐ$Ⓚ Ⓢ⑥ ☒ ⓛM 🚪 💻

◊◊◊ ▼▼◊◊ Matterhorn Motel Ⓜ
(970) 325-4938. **$79-$139.** 201 6th Ave. Just w of US 550. Ext corridors. **Pets:** Accepted.
Ⓢ🅐🅥🅔 Ⓢ⑥ ☒ 🚪 💻 ➰ 🎟

◊◊◊ ▼▼◊◊ Ouray Riverside Inn & Cabins Ⓜ ❧
(970) 325-4061. **$38-$160.** 1805 N Main St. Just n on US 550. Ext corridors. **Pets:** Large. Designated rooms, service with restrictions, supervision.
Ⓢ🅐🅥🅔 ☒ 🚪 💻

◊◊◊ ▼▼◊◊ Ouray Victorian Inn Ⓜ
(970) 325-7222. **$65-$100.** 50 3rd Ave. Just w of US 550. Ext corridors. **Pets:** Accepted.
Ⓢ🅐🅥🅔 Ⓢ⑥ ☒ 🚪 💻 🎟

◊◊◊ ▼▼◊◊ Rivers Edge Motel Ⓜ ❧
(970) 325-4621. **$80-$250.** 110 7th Ave. Just w of US 550 via 7th Ave. Ext corridors. **Pets:** Large, dogs only. $10 one-time fee/pet. Service with restrictions, supervision.
Ⓢ🅐🅥🅔 Ⓢ⑥ ☒ 🚪 💻 🎟

PAGOSA SPRINGS

◊◊◊ ▼▼◊◊ Americas Best Value High Country Lodge Ⓜ ❧
(970) 264-4181. **$65-$96.** 3821 E Hwy 160. On US 160, 3 mi e. Ext corridors. **Pets:** Other species. $25 one-time fee/room. Service with restrictions, crate.
Ⓢ🅐🅥🅔 Ⓢ⑥ ☒ 🚪 💻 ☒

◊◊◊ ▼▼◊◊ Best Western Oak Ridge Lodge Ⓜ
(970) 264-4173. **$109-$159.** 158 Hot Springs Blvd. Just s of US 160. Int corridors. **Pets:** $100 deposit/pet, $15 one-time fee/pet. Service with restrictions, supervision.
Ⓢ🅐🅥🅔 Ⓢ⑥ ☒ 🚪 💻 🍴 ➰ ☒

▼▼ Econo Lodge Ⓜ
(970) 731-2701. **$69-$129.** 315 Navajo Trail Dr. 4 mi w on US 160. Int corridors. **Pets:** Accepted.
Ⓐ$Ⓚ Ⓢ⑥ ☒ ⓚ 🚪 ➰

▼▼ Fireside Inn Cabins 🅲🅰 ❧
(970) 264-9204. **$105-$184.** 1600 E Hwy 160. On US 160, 1.3 mi e. Ext corridors. **Pets:** Dogs only. $8 daily fee/pet. No service.
Ⓐ$Ⓚ Ⓢ⑥ ☒ 🚪 💻 ☒ 🎟

A A A ▼▼▼▼ Pagosa Lodge SH
(970) 731-4141. **$114-$128.** 3505 W Hwy 160. On US 160, 3.5 mi w.
Int corridors. **Pets:** Accepted.
[SAVE] [S🌙] [✕] [👤] [🛏] [💻] [♉] [≋] [⊠]

▼▼ The Pagosa Springs Inn & Suites SH
(970) 731-3400. **$65-$159.** 519 Village Dr. 3.8 mi w on US 160. Int
corridors. **Pets:** Medium. $10 daily fee/pet. Service with restrictions, super-
vision.
[A$K] [S🌙] [✕] [🛏] [💻] [≋]

A A A ▼ Super 8 Motel M
(970) 731-4005. **$42-$105.** 8 Solomon Dr. 2.5 mi w on US 160. Ext/int
corridors. **Pets:** Accepted.
[SAVE] [S🌙] [✕] [🛏] [💻]

PARKER

▼▼ Microtel Inn & Suites SH
(720) 851-2644. **$79-$109.** 6230 E Pine Ln. E-470 toll road, exit 5
(Parker Rd/SR 83), 0.4 mi se, then just e. Int corridors. **Pets:** Accepted.
[✕] [👤] [🛏] [💻]

PLACERVILLE

A A A ▼▼▼▼ The Blue Jay Lodge & Cafe SH
(970) 728-0830. **$105-$135.** 22332 Hwy 145. Just n. Int corridors.
Pets: Other species. $25 one-time fee/pet. Designated rooms, no service,
supervision.
[SAVE] [S🌙] [✕] [🛏] [💻] [♉] [⊠]

PUEBLO

▼▼▼ Best Western Eagle Ridge Inn & Suites SH
(719) 543-4644. **$65-$130.** 4727 N Elizabeth St. I-25, exit 102, just w,
then just n. Int corridors. **Pets:** $15 daily fee/pet. Service with restrictions,
supervision.
[A$K] [S🌙] [✕] [🛏] [💻] [≋] [⊠]

A A A ▼▼▼ GuestHouse International Inn & Suites M
(719) 543-6530. **$43-$65.** 730 N Santa Fe Ave. I-25, exit 99B, just w,
then just s. Ext corridors. **Pets:** Other species. $10 one-time fee/room.
Service with restrictions, supervision.
[SAVE] [S🌙] [✕] [👤] [🛏] [💻] [♉] [≋]

▼▼▼▼ Hampton Inn SH
(719) 544-4700. **$79-$109.** 4703 N Freeway. I-25, exit 102, just w. Ext
corridors. **Pets:** Accepted.
[A$K] [S🌙] [✕] [🛏] [💻] [≋]

▼▼▼ La Quinta Inn & Suites Pueblo SH
(719) 542-3500. **$91-$129.** 4801 N Elizabeth St. I-25, exit 102, just nw.
Int corridors. **Pets:** Medium. Service with restrictions.
[A$K] [✕] [🖉] [👤] [🛏] [💻]

▼▼▼ Microtel Inn & Suites SH
(719) 242-2020. **$60-$98.** 3343 Gateway Dr. I-25, exit 94. Int corridors.
Pets: Accepted.
[A$K] [S🌙] [✕] [🔊M] [👤] [🛏] [💻]

▼ Motel 6–1186 M
(719) 543-8900. **$40-$57.** 960 Hwy 50 W. I-25, exit 101, 0.3 mi w. Ext
corridors. **Pets:** Medium, other species. Service with restrictions, supervision.
[✕] [👤] [🛏]

▼▼ Sleep Inn SH
(719) 583-4000. **$55-$106.** 3626 N Freeway. I-25, exit 101, just ne on
frontage road. Int corridors. **Pets:** Medium, dogs only. $15 daily fee/pet.
Service with restrictions, supervision.
[A$K] [S🌙] [✕] [🔊M] [👤] [🛏] [💻] [≋]

RIDGWAY

A A A ▼▼▼▼ Chipeta Sun Lodge and Spa SH
(970) 626-3737. **$95-$255.** 304 S Lena St. Jct US 550, just w on SR
62, then just s. Ext/int corridors. **Pets:** Medium, dogs only. $35 one-time
fee/pet. Designated rooms, service with restrictions, supervision.
[SAVE] [S🌙] [✕] [👤] [🛏] [💻] [♉] [⊠]

A A A ▼▼▼ Ridgway-Ouray Lodge & Suites M
(970) 626-5444. **$70-$93.** 373 Palomino Tr. From US 550, just ne on
SR 62, then just e. Int corridors. **Pets:** Large. $10 daily fee/pet. Service
with restrictions, supervision.
[SAVE] [S🌙] [✕] [🛏] [💻] [≋] [⊠]

RIFLE

A A A ▼▼▼ Rusty Cannon Motel M
(970) 625-4004. **$76-$84, 7 day notice.** 701 Taughenbaugh Blvd. I-70,
exit 90, just s. Ext corridors. **Pets:** Medium, dogs only. $25 one-time
fee/pet. Designated rooms, service with restrictions, supervision.
[SAVE] [S🌙] [✕] [🛏] [💻] [≋]

SALIDA

A A A ▼▼ Aspen Leaf Lodge M 🐾
(719) 539-6733. **$45-$99.** 7350 W Hwy 50. Just w of Hot Springs Pool.
Ext corridors. **Pets:** Other species. $5 daily fee/pet. Service with restric-
tions, supervision.
[SAVE] [✕] [🛏]

A A A ▼ Circle R Motel M
(719) 539-6296. **$49-$94.** 304 E US Hwy 50. On US 50. Ext corridors.
Pets: Medium. $5 one-time fee/pet. No service, crate.
[SAVE] [✕] [🛏] [💻]

A A A ▼ Econo Lodge SH
(719) 539-2895. **$49-$199.** 1310 E Hwy 50. Just e on US 50; between
Blake and Palmer sts. Ext corridors. **Pets:** Accepted.
[SAVE] [S🌙] [✕] [🛏] [💻]

A A A ▼▼▼ Great Western Colorado Lodge M
(719) 539-2514. **$43-$80.** 352 W Rainbow Blvd. On US 50. Ext corridors. **Pets:** Medium. $10 daily fee/pet. Service with restrictions, supervi-
sion.
[SAVE] [S🌙] [✕] [🛏] [💻] [≋]

A A A ▼▼▼ Silver Ridge Lodge M 🐾
(719) 539-2553. **$45-$100, 3 day notice.** 545 W Rainbow Blvd. US 50,
just w of Chamber of Commerce. Ext corridors. **Pets:** Small, dogs only.
$10 daily fee/pet. Designated rooms, service with restrictions, supervision.
[SAVE] [S🌙] [✕] [🛏] [💻] [≋]

▼▼ Super 8 Motel M
(719) 539-6689. **$69-$119.** 525 W Rainbow Blvd. On US 50. Ext corridors. **Pets:** Accepted.
[A$K] [S🌙] [✕] [🛏] [💻] [≋]

A A A ▼ Travelodge M
(719) 539-2528. **$59-$109.** 7310 Hwy 50. On US 50 W, just w of Hot
Springs Pool. Ext corridors. **Pets:** Other species. $10 one-time fee/pet.
Service with restrictions, supervision.
[SAVE] [S🌙] [✕] [🛏] [💻] [≋]

▼▼▼▼ The Tudor Rose Bed & Breakfast BB
(719) 539-2002. **$72-$175, 7 day notice.** 6720 CR 104. Just e on US
50, s on CR 104, 0.5 mi up the hill, follow signs. Int corridors.
Pets: Accepted.
[✕] [🛏] [⊠] [AC]

A A A ▼▼ Woodland Motel M 🐾
(719) 539-4980. **$47-$124.** 903 W 1st St. From center of historic downtown, 0.5 mi w on 1st St (SR 291). Ext corridors. **Pets:** Other species.
[SAVE] [✕] [🛏] [💻]

SILVERTHORNE

AAA **WWW** Days Inn Summit County **SH**
(970) 468-8661. **$59-$139, 14 day notice.** 580 Silverthorne Ln. I-70, exit 205, just n on SR 9, just e on Rainbow Dr, then just e on Tanglewood Ln. Int corridors. **Pets:** $10 daily fee/pet. Service with restrictions, supervision.

WWW Quality Inn & Suites **SH**
(970) 513-1222. **$79-$219.** 530 Silverthorne Ln. I-70, exit 205, just n on SR 9, just e on Rainbow Rd, then just e on Tanglewood Ln. Int corridors. **Pets:** Accepted.

SILVERTON

AAA **WWW** Silverton's Inn of the Rockies at the Historic Alma House **BB**
(970) 387-5336. **$85-$110, 7 day notice.** 220 E 10th St. From SR 110 (Greene St), just se. Int corridors. **Pets:** Accepted.

WW Villa Dallavalle B & B **BB**
(970) 387-5555. **$99-$125.** 1257 Blair St. SR 110, off US 550, se on 12th St, then just ne. Int corridors. **Pets:** Accepted.

AAA **WWWW** The Wyman Hotel & Inn **BB**
(970) 387-5372. **$120-$170, 14 day notice.** 1371 Greene St. Northeast corner of Greene (Main St) and 14th sts. Int corridors. **Pets:** Small, dogs only. $25 one-time fee/pet. Designated rooms, supervision.

SNOWMASS VILLAGE

AAA **WWW** Snowmass Mountain Chalet **SH**
(970) 923-3900. **$89-$350, 45 day notice.** 115 Daly Ln. 4 mi sw of SR 82 via Brush Creek and Lower Village rds, Lot 5. Ext/int corridors. **Pets:** Accepted.

SOUTH FORK

AAA **WWW** Americas Best Value Inn Wolf Creek Lodge **M**
(719) 873-5547. **$64-$89, 3 day notice.** 31042 Hwy 160 W. On US 160. Ext corridors. **Pets:** Accepted.

W Ute Bluff Lodge and RV Park **M**
(719) 873-5595. **$59-$69, 14 day notice.** 27680 W Hwy 160. 2.5 mi e of jct US 160 and SR 149. Ext corridors. **Pets:** Medium, dogs only. $10 daily fee/pet. Designated rooms, service with restrictions, supervision.

STEAMBOAT SPRINGS

AAA **WWWW** The Alpiner Lodge **M**
(970) 879-1430. **$65-$109, 3 day notice.** 424 Lincoln Ave. US 40, just w of Hot Springs Pool. Ext/int corridors. **Pets:** Large. $15 one-time fee/pet. Designated rooms, service with restrictions, crate.

AAA **WWWW** Best Western Ptarmigan Inn **SH** ❀
(970) 879-1730. **$84-$274.** 2304 Apres Ski Way. 2.3 mi e on US 40, 0.8 mi n on Mt Werner Rd, then take Apres Ski Way. Int corridors. **Pets:** Other species. $25 one-time fee/room. Designated rooms, service with restrictions, supervision.

WW Comfort Inn **SH** ❀
(970) 879-6669. **$74-$499.** 1055 Walton Creek Rd. 2.8 mi e on US 40. Int corridors. **Pets:** Dogs only. $20 daily fee/pet. Designated rooms, service with restrictions, supervision.

AAA **WWWW** Holiday Inn Steamboat **SH** ❀
(970) 879-2250. **$119-$279, 3 day notice.** 3190 S Lincoln Ave. 3 mi e on US 40. Int corridors. **Pets:** Other species. $25 deposit/room, $10 daily fee/room. Designated rooms, service with restrictions, supervision.

AAA **WWW** Iron Horse Inn-Steamboat Springs **SH**
(970) 879-6505. **$59-$299.** 333 S Lincoln Ave. 1 mi e on US 40. Ext/int corridors. **Pets:** Accepted.

AAA **WWW** Nordic Lodge **M**
(970) 879-0531. **$59-$199, 14 day notice.** 1036 Lincoln Ave. Between 10th and 11th sts; downtown. Ext corridors. **Pets:** Other species. $10 daily fee/room. Service with restrictions, supervision.

AAA **WWW** Rabbit Ears Motel **M** ❀
(970) 879-1150. **$79-$149, 3 day notice.** 201 Lincoln Ave. Just e on US 40. Ext corridors. **Pets:** Other species. $12 one-time fee/room. Service with restrictions, supervision.

WWWW Sheraton Steamboat Resort **LH**
(970) 879-2220. **$129-$399, 30 day notice.** 2200 Village Inn Ct. 2.3 mi e on US 40, 1 mi n on Mt Werner Rd; at ski area. Int corridors. **Pets:** Accepted.

WW Super 8 Motel **SH**
(970) 879-5230. **$63-$118.** 3195 S Lincoln Ave. 3 mi e on US 40. Int corridors. **Pets:** Medium, dogs only. Designated rooms, crate.

STERLING

AAA **WWW** Best Western Sundowner **M** ❀
(970) 522-6265. **$77-$119.** 125 Overland Trail St. I-76, exit 125, just w. Ext/int corridors. **Pets:** Other species. $10 daily fee/pet. No service, supervision.

AAA **WW** Colonial Motel **M**
(970) 522-3382. **$46-$65.** 915 S Division. I-76, exit 125, 1.8 mi w on US 6 to 3rd traffic light (4th St), then 1.7 mi s. Ext corridors. **Pets:** Accepted.

AAA **WWW** Ramada Inn **SH**
(970) 522-2625. **$69-$109.** 22140 E Hwy 6. I-76, exit 125, 0.5 mi e on US 6. Ext/int corridors. **Pets:** Other species. $25 deposit/room. Designated rooms, service with restrictions, supervision.

STRATTON

AAA **WWW** Best Western Golden Prairie Inn **SH**
(719) 348-5311. **$69-$109.** 700 Colorado Ave. I-70, exit 419, just n. Ext corridors. **Pets:** Accepted.

TELLURIDE

AAA **WWWW** Hotel Columbia **SH** ❀
(970) 728-0660. **$125-$475, 30 day notice.** 300 W San Juan Ave. Just s of SR 145 Spur, at Aspen St and San Juan Ave; opposite gondola. Int corridors. **Pets:** Dogs only. $20 daily fee/room. Designated rooms, service with restrictions.

AAA **WWWW** The Hotel Telluride **SH**
(970) 369-1188. **$149-$519.** 199 N Cornet St. Just n of jct SR 145 (Colorado Ave). Ext/int corridors. **Pets:** Accepted.

TRINIDAD

Best Western Trinidad Inn **M**
(719) 846-2215. **$99-$119.** 900 W Adams St. I-25, exit 13A northbound; exit Cross Bridge southbound, just ne. Ext corridors. **Pets:** Accepted.

Budget Host Derrick Motel **M**
(719) 846-3307. **$59-$69.** 10301 Santa Fe Trail Dr. I-25, exit 11, 0.5 mi ne. Ext corridors. **Pets:** Accepted.

Budget Summit Inn **M**
(719) 846-2251. **$45-$70.** 9800 Santa Fe Trail Dr. I-25, exit 11, just se. Ext/int corridors. **Pets:** Accepted.

Quality Inn Trinidad **SH** ❖
(719) 846-4491. **$85-$139.** 3125 Toupal Dr. I-25, exit 11, just w. Int corridors. **Pets:** Small, dogs only. $15 one-time fee/pet. Designated rooms, service with restrictions, supervision.

Super 8 Motel **M**
(719) 846-8280. **$50-$96.** 1924 Freedom Rd. I-25, exit 15, just ne. Int corridors. **Pets:** Accepted.

VAIL

Antlers at Vail **CO** ❖
(970) 476-2471. **$175-$485, 14 day notice.** 680 W Lionshead Pl. I-70, exit 176, 0.5 mi w, then just s on Lionshead Cir. Ext corridors. **Pets:** Other species. $15 daily fee/pet. Designated rooms, service with restrictions, crate.

Holiday Inn Apex Vail **SH**
(970) 476-2739. **$119-$299.** 2211 N Frontage Rd. I-70, exit 173, just e. Int corridors. **Pets:** Medium, dogs only. $25 daily fee/pet. Designated rooms, supervision.

The Lodge at Vail, A Rock Resort **SH** ❖
(970) 476-5011. **$139-$3599, 30 day notice.** 174 E Gore Creek Dr. I-70, exit 176, s on Vail Rd to center of village. Ext/int corridors. **Pets:** Dogs only. $25 daily fee/pet. Designated rooms, service with restrictions.

Sonnenalp Resort of Vail **SH**
(970) 476-5656. **$170-$3000, 14 day notice.** 20 Vail Rd. I-70, exit 176, just s. Int corridors. **Pets:** Accepted.

WALSENBURG

Anchor Motel **M**
(719) 738-2800. **$40-$75.** 1001 Main St. I-25, exit 49, 0.5 mi nw. Ext corridors. **Pets:** Very small, other species. $10 one-time fee/pet. Designated rooms, service with restrictions, supervision.

Best Western Rambler **SH** ❖
(719) 738-1121. **$67-$125.** 457 US Hwy 85-87. I-25, exit 52, just w. Ext corridors. **Pets:** Medium. $10 daily fee/room. Designated rooms, service with restrictions, supervision.

WELLINGTON

Comfort Inn Wellington **SH**
(970) 568-0444. **$69-$139.** 7860 6th St. I-25, exit 278, just w, then just s. Int corridors. **Pets:** $25 one-time fee/room. Designated rooms, service with restrictions, supervision.

WINDSOR

Super 8 Motel **SH**
(970) 686-5996. **$59-$124.** 1265 Main St. I-25, exit 262, 3.8 mi e; in shopping/restaurant complex. Int corridors. **Pets:** Other species. $15 daily fee/pet. Service with restrictions, crate.

WINTER PARK

Best Western Alpenglo Lodge **SH** ❖
(970) 726-8088. **$69-$159, 30 day notice.** 78665 US Hwy 40. On US 40; center. Int corridors. **Pets:** Large. $10 daily fee/room. Designated rooms, crate.

Winter Park Mountain Lodge **SH**
(970) 726-4211. **$60-$529.** 81699 US Hwy 40. 2.3 mi se on US 40; near Winter Park ski area. Int corridors. **Pets:** Accepted.

YAMPA

Oak Tree Inn **SH**
(970) 638-1000. **$80-$100.** 98 Moffat Ave. Just off SR 131. Int corridors. **Pets:** Other species. $10 one-time fee/room. Service with restrictions, supervision.

CONNECTICUT

BETHEL

Microtel Inn & Suites SH
(203) 748-8318. **$79-$99.** 80 Benedict Rd. I-84, exit 8, 1 mi e on US 6. Int corridors. **Pets:** $100 deposit/room, $10 daily fee/pet. Service with restrictions, crate.

BRIDGEPORT

Bridgeport Holiday Inn & Convention Center SH
(203) 334-1234. **$119-$159.** 1070 Main St. SR 8, exit 2 northbound, 0.7 mi se; exit southbound, just s, then just e. Int corridors. **Pets:** Accepted.

BROOKFIELD

Twin Tree Inn M
(203) 775-0220. **$85-$95.** 1030 Federal Rd (Rt 7 & 202). Jct SR 25, 0.9 mi nw on US 7 and 202. Ext/int corridors. **Pets:** Other species. $10 one-time fee/room. Designated rooms, service with restrictions, supervision.

DANBURY

Ethan Allen Hotel SH
(203) 744-1776. **$145.** 21 Lake Ave Extension. I-84, exit 4, 0.3 mi w on US 6 and 202. Int corridors. **Pets:** Accepted.

Holiday Inn SH ☘
(203) 792-4000. **$129-$159.** 80 Newtown Rd. I-84, exit 8 (Newtown Rd), 0.5 mi s on US 6 W. Int corridors. **Pets:** Large, other species. $15 daily fee/pet. Designated rooms, service with restrictions, supervision.

Maron Hotel & Suites SH
(203) 791-2200. **$119-$179.** 42 Lake Ave Extension. I-84, exit 4, 0.5 mi w on US 6 and 202. Int corridors. **Pets:** Accepted.

Residence Inn by Marriott SH ☘
(203) 797-1256. **$109-$229.** 22 Segar St. I-84, exit 4 eastbound, just n; exit westbound, just e on Lake Ave Extension, then just s. Int corridors. **Pets:** Other species. $75 one-time fee/room. Service with restrictions.

Sheraton Danbury LH
(203) 794-0600. **$169-$209.** 18 Old Ridgebury Rd. I-84, exit 2 eastbound; exit 2A westbound. Int corridors. **Pets:** Accepted.

DAYVILLE

Holiday Inn Express SH
(860) 779-3200. **$120-$140.** 16 Tracy Rd. I-395, exit 94, just w. Int corridors. **Pets:** $10 daily fee/pet. Service with restrictions, supervision.

FAIRFIELD

Best Western Black Rock Inn SH
(203) 659-2200. **$109-$189.** 100 Kings Hwy Cutoff. I-95, exit 24, just sw. Int corridors. **Pets:** Accepted.

GRISWOLD

AmericInn Lodge & Suites SH
(860) 376-3200. **$69-$179.** 375 Voluntown Rd. I-395, exit 85, w on SR 138. Int corridors. **Pets:** Small, dogs only. $100 deposit/pet, $25 daily fee/pet. Designated rooms, service with restrictions, supervision.

HARTFORD METROPOLITAN AREA

AVON

Residence Inn by Marriott Hartford-Avon SH ☘
(860) 678-1666. **$169.** 55 Simsbury Rd (SR 202). Jct US 44, just n. Int corridors. **Pets:** $75 one-time fee/room. Service with restrictions, supervision.

BERLIN

Hawthorne Inn SH ☘
(860) 828-4181. **$69-$200.** 2387 Berlin Tpke. I-91, exit 17 northbound, 4.7 mi n on SR 15 (Berlin Tpke); exit 22N southbound, 2.5 mi n on SR 9 to exit 22, follow signs onto US 5 and SR 15 (Berlin Tpke), then 3 mi s. Int corridors. **Pets:** Large, other species. $20 one-time fee/pet. Designated rooms, service with restrictions, crate.

CROMWELL

Comfort Inn SH
(860) 635-4100. **$94-$139.** 111 Berlin Rd. I-91, exit 21, just e on SR 372. Int corridors. **Pets:** Accepted.

EAST HARTFORD

Sheraton Hartford Hotel SH
(860) 528-9703. **$99-$179.** 100 E River Dr. I-84, exit 53 eastbound, just s; exit 54 westbound to exit 3 (Darlin St), just n. Int corridors. **Pets:** Accepted.

EAST WINDSOR

▲▲▲ ▼▼▼ Holiday Inn Express Hartford Airport Area M
(860) 627-6585. **$79-$129.** 260 Main St (US 5). I-91, exit 44, just s. Int corridors. **Pets:** Medium. $35 one-time fee/pet. Service with restrictions, supervision.
[SAVE] [S₆] [✕] [&M] [⌂] [&] [🖬] [💻]

ENFIELD

▼▼ Red Roof Inn # 7105 M
(860) 741-2571. **$61-$87.** 5 Hazard Ave. I-91, exit 47E. Ext corridors. **Pets:** Medium, other species. Service with restrictions, supervision.
[✕] [&M] [⌂] [&] [🖬]

FARMINGTON

▲▲▲ ▼▼▼▼ Centennial Inn Suites CO
(860) 677-4647. **$81-$239.** 5 Spring Ln. US 6, 0.3 mi e of jct SR 177. Ext/int corridors. **Pets:** Other species. $15 daily fee/pet. Designated rooms, service with restrictions.
[SAVE] [S₆] [✕] [&M] [&] [🖬] [💻] [≈]

▼▼ Extended StayAmerica Deluxe Hartford-Farmington SH
(860) 676-2790. **$114-$129.** 1 Batterson Park Rd. I-84, exit 37, just ne. Int corridors. **Pets:** Accepted.
[ASK] [S₆] [✕] [⌂] [&] [🖬] [💻]

▼▼▼ Homewood Suites by Hilton SH ❀
(860) 321-0000. **$179.** 2 Farm Glen Blvd. I-84, exit 39, 0.6 mi e on SR 4. Int corridors. **Pets:** Other species. $200 one-time fee/room. Service with restrictions.
[ASK] [S₆] [✕] [&M] [&] [🖬] [💻] [≈]

GLASTONBURY

▼▼▼ Homewood Suites by Hilton Hartford South-Glastonbury SH
(860) 652-8111. **$129-$289.** 65 Glastonbury Blvd. SR 3, exit Main St, just se. Int corridors. **Pets:** Large. $150 one-time fee/room. Service with restrictions, crate.
[ASK] [S₆] [✕] [&M] [⌂] [&] [🖬] [💻] [≈] [✕]

HARTFORD

▼▼▼ Crowne Plaza Hartford Downtown LH
(860) 549-2400. **$179-$199.** 50 Morgan St. I-91, exit 32B; I-84, exit 50 eastbound; exit 52 westbound. Int corridors. **Pets:** Accepted.
[ASK] [S₆] [✕] [&M] [&] [🖬] [💻] [▯▯] [≈]

▼▼▼ Goodwin Hotel SH
(860) 246-7500. **$99-$1050.** 1 Haynes St. Downtown; entrance on Asylum St. Int corridors. **Pets:** Accepted.
[ASK] [S₆] [✕] [&M] [&] [🖬] [💻] [▯▯]

▼▼▼ Residence Inn by Marriott Downtown Hartford SH
(860) 524-5550. **$144-$359.** 942 Main St. I-91, exit 29A northbound; exit 31 southbound. Int corridors. **Pets:** Accepted.
[S₆] [✕] [&] [🖬] [💻]

MANCHESTER

▼▼ Extended StayAmerica SH
(860) 643-5140. **$99-$119.** 340 Tolland Tpke. I-84, exit 63, 0.3 mi se on SR 30, then just sw. Int corridors. **Pets:** Accepted.
[ASK] [S₆] [✕] [&M] [&] [🖬] [💻]

▲▲▲ ▼▼▼ Residence Inn Manchester SH
(860) 432-4242. **$154-$199.** 201 Hale Rd. I-84, exit 63, 0.5 mi nw, then 0.6 mi sw. Int corridors. **Pets:** Other species. $75 one-time fee/room. Service with restrictions.
[SAVE] [S₆] [✕] [&M] [⌂] [&] [🖬] [💻] [≈] [✕]

MIDDLETOWN

▼▼▼ Inn at Middletown SH
(860) 854-6300. **$159-$179.** 70 Main St. SR 9, exit 15, just sw on Dr. Martin Luther King Jr Way, then 0.4 mi se. Int corridors. **Pets:** Medium. $75 one-time fee/room. Designated rooms.
[ASK] [S₆] [✕] [&M] [⌂] [&] [🖬] [💻] [▯▯] [≈]

ROCKY HILL

▼▼▼ Residence Inn by Marriott Hartford-Rocky Hill SH
(860) 257-7500. **$99-$189.** 680 Cromwell Ave. I-91, exit 23, 0.4 mi w on West St, then just n. Int corridors. **Pets:** Other species. $75 one-time fee/room. Supervision.
[ASK] [S₆] [✕] [&M] [⌂] [&] [🖬] [💻] [≈] [✕]

SOUTHINGTON

◆ Motel 6-1018 M
(860) 621-7351. **$48-$61.** 625 Queen St. I-84, exit 32, just ne. Ext corridors. **Pets:** Medium, other species. Service with restrictions, supervision.
[S₆] [✕] [&]

▲▲▲ ▼▼▼ Residence Inn by Marriott SH
(860) 621-4440. **$139-$255.** 778 West St. I-84, exit 31, just s. Int corridors. **Pets:** Accepted.
[SAVE] [✕] [&M] [&] [🖬] [💻] [≈] [✕]

WETHERSFIELD

◆ Motel 6-1028 M
(860) 563-5900. **$45-$61.** 1341 Silas Deane Hwy. I-91, exit 24, just n on SR 99. Ext corridors. **Pets:** Medium, other species. Service with restrictions, supervision.
[S₆] [✕] [&]

WINDSOR

▼▼▼ The Residence Inn by Marriott Hartford-Windsor SH ❀
(860) 688-7474. **$129-$169.** 100 Dunfey Ln. I-91, exit 37, just w on SR 305 to Dunfey Ln, then 0.3 mi n. Ext corridors. **Pets:** Other species. $75 one-time fee/room. Service with restrictions.
[ASK] [S₆] [✕] [&M] [⌂] [&] [🖬] [💻] [≈] [✕]

WINDSOR LOCKS

▼▼▼ Homewood Suites by Hilton SH
(860) 627-8463. **$159.** 65 Ella T Grasso Tpke. I-91, exit 40, 2.5 mi w on SR 20, then just n on SR 75. Ext/int corridors. **Pets:** Accepted.
[ASK] [S₆] [✕] [&M] [⌂] [&] [🖬] [💻] [≈] [✕]

▲▲▲ ▼▼▼ La Quinta Inn Hartford-Airport SH
(860) 623-3336. **$84-$149.** 64 Ella T Grasso Tpke. I-91, exit 40, 2.5 mi w on SR 20, then just n on SR 75. Int corridors. **Pets:** Medium. Service with restrictions.
[SAVE] [✕] [&M] [⌂] [🖬] [💻]

▼▼ Ramada Inn Bradley International Airport SH ❀
(860) 623-9494. **$109-$159.** 5 Ella T Grasso Tpke. I-91, exit 40, 2.5 mi w on SR 20, then just n on SR 75. Int corridors. **Pets:** $49 one-time fee/pet. Service with restrictions, supervision.
[ASK] [✕] [🖬] [💻] [▯▯] [≈]

▲▲▲ ▼▼▼▼ Sheraton Hotel At Bradley International Airport LH
(860) 627-5311. **$239-$259.** 1 Bradley International Airport. At Bradley International Airport terminal. Int corridors. **Pets:** Medium. Service with restrictions, supervision.
[SAVE] [S₆] [✕] [&M] [⌂] [&] [🖬] [💻] [▯▯] [≈]

IVORYTON

The Copper Beech Inn CI
(860) 767-0330. **$175-$425, 14 day notice.** 46 Main St. SR 9, exit 3, 1.7 mi w. Int corridors. Pets: Accepted.
SAVE S X T

LAKEVILLE

Inn at Iron Masters M
(860) 435-9844. **$95-$195.** 229 Main St (Rt 44 & 41). 0.5 mi ne. Ext corridors. Pets: Dogs only. Designated rooms, supervision.
SAVE X

Interlaken Inn Resort and Conference Center SH
(860) 435-9878. **$139-$259, 7 day notice.** 74 Interlaken Rd. On SR 112, 0.5 mi w of jct SR 41. Ext/int corridors. Pets: Dogs only. $15 daily fee/room. Designated rooms, service with restrictions, supervision.
SAVE X

LEDYARD

Almost In Mystic/Mares Inn BB
(860) 572-7556. **$100-$200, 14 day notice.** 333 Colonel Ledyard Hwy. I-95, exit 89, 1 mi ne to Gold Star Hwy, 0.6 mi w, then 0.7 mi n. Int corridors. Pets: Accepted.
ASK X

LITCHFIELD

Litchfield Inn CI
(860) 567-4503. **$160-$300, 3 day notice.** 432 Bantam Rd. 1.5 mi w on US 202. Int corridors. Pets: Medium, dogs only. $25 daily fee/pet. Designated rooms, service with restrictions, supervision.
SAVE S X

MERIDEN

Extended StayAmerica Hartford-Meriden SH
(203) 630-1927. **$84-$104.** 366 Bee St. I-91, exit 17 northbound, just e on E Main St, then 0.7 mi n; exit 19 southbound, 0.5 mi w on Baldwin Ave, then 0.6 mi s. Int corridors. Pets: Accepted.
ASK S X

Four Points by Sheraton Meriden SH
(203) 238-2380. **$105-$205.** 275 Research Pkwy. I-91, exit 17 southbound; exit 16 northbound, 0.5 mi e, then 0.5 mi s. Int corridors. Pets: Accepted.
ASK S X

Residence Inn by Marriott SH
(203) 634-7770. **$89-$139.** 390 Bee St. I-91, exit 16 northbound, just e on E Main St, then 0.7 mi n; exit 19 southbound, 0.5 mi w on Baldwin Ave, then 0.5 mi s. Ext/int corridors. Pets: Accepted.
ASK X

MILFORD

Residence Inn by Marriott SH
(203) 283-2100. **$99-$199.** 62 Rowe Ave. I-95, exit 35, just nw. Int corridors. Pets: Accepted.
ASK S X

MYSTIC

Days Inn of Mystic SH
(860) 572-0574. **$49-$179.** 55 Whitehall Ave. I-95, exit 90, just n. Int corridors. Pets: Accepted.
SAVE S X

Inn at Mystic M
(860) 536-9604. **$95-$295.** 3 Williams Ave. On US 1 at SR 27. Ext/int corridors. Pets: Large. $15 daily fee/pet. Designated rooms, service with restrictions, supervision.
SAVE S X

Residence Inn by Marriott SH
(860) 536-5150. **$149-$399.** 40 Whitehall Ave. I-95, exit 90, just n on SR 27. Int corridors. Pets: Other species. $100 one-time fee/room. Service with restrictions, crate.
SAVE S X

NEW HAVEN

Omni New Haven Hotel at Yale LH
(203) 772-6664. **$169-$449.** 155 Temple St. Center of downtown. Int corridors. Pets: Small. $50 one-time fee/pet. Service with restrictions, supervision.
SAVE S X

NEW LONDON

Red Roof Inn #7145 M
(860) 444-0001. **$61-$108.** 707 Colman St. I-95, exit 82A northbound, 0.8 mi n, just w, then 0.6 mi on Bayonet St; exit 83 southbound, 0.6 mi s. Ext corridors. Pets: Medium, other species. Service with restrictions, supervision.
X

NEW MILFORD

The Homestead Inn BB
(860) 354-4080. **$100-$160.** 5 Elm St. Just e of village green off Main St; center. Ext/int corridors. Pets: Other species. $10 daily fee/pet. Designated rooms, service with restrictions, supervision.
ASK S X

NIANTIC

Motel 6-1063 M
(860) 739-6991. **$47-$71.** 269 Flanders Rd. I-95, exit 74, just s. Ext corridors. Pets: Medium, other species. Service with restrictions, supervision.
S X

NORTH STONINGTON

The Inn at Lower Farm BB
(860) 535-9075. **$100-$170, 10 day notice.** 119 Mystic Rd. I-95, exit 90, 1.5 mi n on SR 27, 1.4 mi e on SR 184, then 3.4 mi n on SR 201. Int corridors. Pets: Medium, dogs only. Designated rooms, service with restrictions, supervision.
ASK S X

NORWALK

Four Points by Sheraton Norwalk SH
(203) 849-9828. **$135-$145.** 426 Main Ave. I-95, exit 15, 3.5 mi n via US 7, just e, then 0.7 mi s. Int corridors. Pets: Accepted.
SAVE S X

Homestead Studio Suites Hotel-Norwalk SH
(203) 847-6888. **$134-$154.** 400 Main Ave. I-95, exit 15, 3.5 mi n via US 7, just e, then 1 mi s. Int corridors. Pets: Accepted.
ASK S X

The Silvermine Tavern CI
(203) 847-4558. **$130-$210, 3 day notice.** 194 Perry Ave. Merritt Pkwy, exit 40A, 0.5 mi s on Main Ave, then 1.7 mi ne. Int corridors. Pets: Medium. Designated rooms, service with restrictions.
SAVE X

OLD LYME

Old Lyme Inn 🔲
(860) 434-2600. **$135-$185, 10 day notice.** 85 Lyme St. I-95, exit 70 northbound, just n on SR 156, then 0.5 mi e on US 1; exit southbound, just n. Int corridors. **Pets:** Other species. $50 deposit/pet. Designated rooms, service with restrictions, supervision.

OLD SAYBROOK

Saybrook Point Inn & Spa 🔲 🐾
(860) 395-2000. **$179-$799, 3 day notice.** 2 Bridge St. On SR 154, 2.2 mi s of jct US 1; at Saybrook Point. Int corridors. **Pets:** Medium, dogs only. $25 one-time fee/pet. Designated rooms, service with restrictions, supervision.

PUTNAM

King's Inn 🔲
(860) 928-7961. **$62-$98.** 5 Heritage Rd. I-395, exit 96, just sw. Int corridors. **Pets:** $5 one-time fee/room. Service with restrictions, supervision.

RIVERTON

Old Riverton Inn 🔲
(860) 379-8678. **$85-$200, 10 day notice.** 436 E River Rd (SR 20). Center. Int corridors. **Pets:** Medium, dogs only. $20 one-time fee/room. Designated rooms, service with restrictions, supervision.

SHELTON

Homestead Studio Suites Hotel-Shelton-Fairfield County 🔲
(203) 926-6868. **$124-$144.** 945 Bridgeport Ave. SR 8, exit 11, 0.5 mi w. Int corridors. **Pets:** Accepted.

Residence Inn by Marriott 🔲
(203) 926-9000. **$107-$152.** 1001 Bridgeport Ave. SR 8, exit 11, 0.3 mi w. Ext corridors. **Pets:** Accepted.

SOUTHBURY

Cornucopia at Oldfield Bed and Breakfast 🔲
(203) 267-6772. **$120-$275, 14 day notice.** 782 Main St N. I-84, exit 15, 1.5 mi n. Int corridors. **Pets:** Accepted.

Crowne Plaza Southbury 🔲
(203) 598-7600. **$99-$169.** 1284 Strongtown Rd. I-84, exit 16, just n on SR 188. Int corridors. **Pets:** Medium. $25 one-time fee/pet. Designated rooms, service with restrictions, supervision.

The Heritage Resort & Conference Center 🔲
(203) 264-8200. **$135.** 522 Heritage Rd. I-84, exit 15, 0.4 mi n on SR 67, then 1 mi w. Int corridors. **Pets:** Accepted.

STAMFORD

Amsterdam Hotel–Greenwich/Stamford 🔲
(203) 327-4300. **$80-$100.** 19 Clark Ave. I-95, exit 8 northbound, just n on Atlantic St, 0.6 mi ne on Tresser Blvd, exit southbound, just nw on Elm St, ne on Main St, then just s. Int corridors. **Pets:** $20 daily fee/pet. Designated rooms, service with restrictions, supervision.

Holiday Inn Select 🔲
(203) 358-8400. **$120-$260.** 700 Main St. I-95, exit 8 southbound, just n on Elm; exit northbound, n on Atlantic St, 0.3 mi e on Tresser Blvd, then just n on Elm; downtown. Int corridors. **Pets:** Accepted.

Marriott Stamford Hotel & Spa 🔲 🐾
(203) 357-9555. **$289-$319.** Two Stamford Forum. I-95, exit 8, just n under viaduct, then n on Tresser Blvd. Int corridors. **Pets:** Other species. $35 one-time fee/room. Designated rooms, service with restrictions, supervision.

Sheraton Stamford Hotel 🔲
(203) 359-1300. **$309.** 2701 Summer St. I-95, exit 8 northbound, 1.7 mi w on Atlantic and Bedford sts; exit 7 southbound, n on Atlantic and Bedford sts. Int corridors. **Pets:** Accepted.

Super 8 Motel 🔲
(203) 324-8887. **$90-$159.** 32 Grenhart Rd. I-95, exit 6, just n. Int corridors. **Pets:** Accepted.

The Westin Stamford 🔲
(203) 967-2222. **$109-$199.** 1 First Stamford Pl. I-95, exit 7 northbound, just s on Greenwich Ave, then just w; exit 6 southbound, just s on West Ave, 0.3 mi w on Baxter Ave, just n on Fairfield Ave, then just e. Int corridors. **Pets:** Medium. $25 one-time fee/room.

STONINGTON

Another Second Penny Inn 🔲 🐾
(860) 535-1710. **$99-$225, 7 day notice.** 870 Pequot Tr. I-95, exit 91, 0.8 mi s on SR 234. Int corridors. **Pets:** Medium, other species. $25 one-time fee/pet. Designated rooms, service with restrictions, supervision.

STRATFORD

Homewood Suites by Hilton 🔲 🐾
(203) 377-3322. **$179-$259.** 6905 Main St. SR 15, exit 53, just n. Int corridors. **Pets:** Medium. $20 daily fee/room, $350 one-time fee/room. Service with restrictions, supervision.

WATERBURY

House on the Hill Bed & Breakfast 🔲
(203) 757-9901. **$175-$250, 14 day notice.** 92 Woodlawn Terr. I-84, exit 21, 0.6 mi n on Meadow St, then 0.4 mi ne on Pine St. Int corridors. **Pets:** Accepted.

WATERFORD

Oakdell Motel 🔲
(860) 442-9446. **$60-$145.** 983 Hartford Tpke. I-95, exit 82, 2 mi n on SR 85. Ext/int corridors. **Pets:** Dogs only. Service with restrictions, supervision.

WESTPORT

The Westport Inn 🔲 🐾
(203) 259-5236. **$169-$229.** 1595 Post Rd E. I-95, exit 18 northbound, n to US 1, then 1.5 mi e; exit 19 southbound, 1 mi w. Ext/int corridors. **Pets:** Small, other species. $49 one-time fee/room. Designated rooms, service with restrictions.

DELAWARE

CLAYMONT

 **Holiday Inn Select Wilmington** 🔲
(302) 792-2700. **$155-$175.** 630 Naamans Rd. I-95, exit 11, just w on
SR 92; I-495, exit 6 (Naamans Rd). Int corridors. **Pets:** Small, other
species. $50 one-time fee/pet. Service with restrictions, supervision.
(ASK) (S$) (✕) (&M) (🔊) (🖋) (🔲) (🍴) (🏊)

DEWEY BEACH

🔺🔻🔻 **Atlantic Oceanside Motel** Ⓜ ☙
(302) 227-8811. **$45-$229, 7 day notice.** 1700 Hwy 1. Jct SR 1 and
McKinley St. Ext corridors. **Pets:** Dogs only. $10 daily fee/pet. Service
with restrictions, crate.
(SAVE) (✕) (🔲) (🏊)

🔻🔻 **Bellbuoy Motel** Ⓜ ☙
(302) 227-6000. **$65-$195, 3 day notice.** 21 Van Dyke St. SR 1, on
oceanside block of Van Dyke St. Ext corridors. **Pets:** Dogs only. $10
daily fee/pet. Designated rooms, service with restrictions.
(✕) (🔲) (🏊)

🔺🔻🔻 **Best Western Gold Leaf** 🔲
(302) 226-1100. **$59-$289, 3 day notice.** 1400 Hwy 1. On SR 1;
center. Int corridors. **Pets:** Other species. $20 daily fee/pet. Designated
rooms, service with restrictions, supervision.
(SAVE) (S$) (✕) (🔊) (🔲) (🖳) (🏊)

🔺🔻 **Sea-Esta Motel I** Ⓜ
(302) 227-7666. **$49-$189.** 2306 Hwy 1. SR 1 at Houston St. Ext
corridors. **Pets:** Accepted.
(SAVE) (✕) (🔲)

🔺🔻🔻 **Sea-Esta Motel III** Ⓜ
(302) 227-4343. **$59-$209.** 1409 Hwy 1. Jct SR 1 and Rodney St. Ext
corridors. **Pets:** Accepted.
(SAVE) (✕) (🔲) (🖳)

DOVER

🔺🔻🔻 **Comfort Inn-Dover** Ⓜ
(302) 674-3300. **$85-$129.** 222 S DuPont Hwy. SR 1, exit 95, 2 mi n on
US 113, then 0.3 mi n on US 13. Ext corridors. **Pets:** Small, other
species. $35 one-time fee/room. Designated rooms, service with restric-
tions, crate.
(SAVE) (S$) (✕) (🔊) (🔲) (🖳) (🏊)

🔻🔻🔻 **Little Creek Inn** 🅱🅱
(302) 730-1300. **$150-$195.** 2623 N Little Creek Rd. SR 1, exit 98, 1 mi
e on SR 8; 2.2 mi e of jct US 13. Int corridors. **Pets:** Accepted.
(ASK) (✕) (🏊)

🔺🔻🔻🔻 **Sheraton Dover Hotel** 🔲
(302) 678-8500. **$109-$325.** 1570 N DuPont Hwy. SR 1, exit 104, 1 mi
s on US 13. Int corridors. **Pets:** Accepted.
(SAVE) (S$) (✕) (🔊) (🖳) (🍴) (🏊)

GEORGETOWN

🔺🔻🔻🔻 **Comfort Inn & Suites-Georgetown** 🔲
(302) 854-9400. **$69-$249, 3 day notice.** 20530 DuPont Blvd. On US
113, 0.5 mi n of jct SR 404. Int corridors. **Pets:** Other species. $15 daily
fee/room. Designated rooms, service with restrictions, supervision.
(SAVE) (S$) (✕) (🔊) (🔲) (🖳) (🏊)

HARRINGTON

🔻🔻🔻 **AmericInn Lodge & Suites of Harrington** 🔲 ☙
(302) 398-3900. **$99-$139, 30 day notice.** 1259 Corn Crib Rd. On US
13, 0.6 mi s of jct SR 14. Int corridors. **Pets:** Medium, dogs only. $20
daily fee/pet. Designated rooms, service with restrictions, crate.
(ASK) (S$) (✕) (&M) (🔊) (🖋) (🔲) (🖳) (🏊)

LEWES

🔺🔻🔻 **The Inn at Canal Square** 🔲 ☙
(302) 644-3377. **$105-$300, 7 day notice.** 122 Market St. On the
canal. Int corridors. **Pets:** Medium. $100 deposit/room. Designated rooms,
service with restrictions.
(SAVE) (S$) (✕) (🔲) (🖳) (✕)

🔺🔻🔻 **Sleep Inn & Suites** 🔲 ☙
(302) 645-6464. **$79-$249.** 1595 Hwy 1. On SR 1, 1.5 mi s. Int corridors. **Pets:** Medium, other species. $25 daily fee/pet. Designated rooms,
service with restrictions, supervision.
(SAVE) (S$) (✕) (🔊) (🖋) (🔲) (🖳) (🏊)

LONG NECK

🔺🔻🔻 **Sea Esta II** Ⓜ
(302) 945-5900. **$49-$149.** A19 Long Neck Rd. On SR 23, 1.1 mi s of
jct SR 24, 5 and 23. Ext corridors. **Pets:** Accepted.
(SAVE) (✕) (🔲) (🖳) (🏊)

MILLSBORO

🔻🔻 **Atlantic Inn-Millsboro** Ⓜ
(302) 934-6711. **$69-$189.** 210 E DuPont Hwy. US 113, just s of SR
24. Ext corridors. **Pets:** Accepted.
(ASK) (✕) (🔲) (🏊)

NEWARK

🔺🔻🔻🔻 **Best Western Delaware Inn and Conference**
Center-Wilmington/Newark 🔲
(302) 738-3400. **$89-$179.** 260 Chapman Rd. I-95, exit 3 southbound;
exit 3A northbound, 0.3 mi e on SR 273 E, then just n. Int corridors.
Pets: Other species. $15 daily fee/pet. Designated rooms, service with
restrictions, supervision.
(SAVE) (S$) (✕) (🔊) (🔲) (🖳) (🍴) (🏊)

🔺🔻🔻 **Days Inn Wilmington/Newark** Ⓜ
(302) 368-2400. **$50-$170.** 900 Churchmans Rd. I-95, exit 4B, 0.3 mi n
on SR 7, exit 166, then 0.3 mi w on SR 58 (Churchmans Rd). Ext
corridors. **Pets:** Accepted.
(SAVE) (S$) (✕) (🔲) (🖳) (🏊)

🔺🔻🔻🔻 **Hilton Wilmington/Christiana** 🔲 ☙
(302) 454-1500. **$109-$299.** 100 Continental Dr. I-95, exit 4B, 0.3 mi n
on SR 7, exit 166, then 0.4 mi w on SR 58 (Churchmans Rd). Int
corridors. **Pets:** Medium. $49 one-time fee/room. Designated rooms, serv-
ice with restrictions, crate.
(SAVE) (S$) (✕) (🔊) (🔲) (🖳) (🍴) (🏊) (✕)

🔻🔻 **Homestead Studio Suites**
Hotel-Newark/Christiana 🔲
(302) 283-0800. **$89-$109.** 333 Continental Dr. I-95, exit 4B, 0.3 mi n
on SR 7, exit 166, then 0.4 mi w on SR 58 (Churchmans Rd). Int
corridors. **Pets:** Accepted.
(ASK) (S$) (✕) (&M) (🔊) (🖋) (🔲) (🖳)

▼▼▼▼ Homewood Suites by Hilton Newark/Wilmington South SH
(302) 453-9700. **$99-$269.** 640 S College Ave. I-95, exit 1B south-bound; exit 1 northbound, 0.8 mi n on SR 896. Int corridors. **Pets:** Accepted.

AAA ▼▼▼ Howard Johnson Inn & Suites-Wilmington/Newark SH
(302) 368-8521. **$55-$99.** 1119 S College Ave. I-95, exit 1B south-bound; exit 1 northbound, 0.3 mi n on SR 896. Int corridors. **Pets:** Accepted.

▼▼▼ Red Roof Inn-Wilmington M
(302) 292-2870. **$66-$77.** 415 Stanton Christiana Rd. I-95, exit 4B, 0.5 mi n on SR 7. Ext corridors. **Pets:** Medium, other species. Service with restrictions, supervision.

▼▼▼▼ Residence Inn by Marriott SH
(302) 453-9200. **$99-$169.** 240 Chapman Rd. I-95, exit 3 southbound; exit 3A northbound, 0.3 mi e on SR 273 E, then 0.5 mi s. Ext corridors. **Pets:** Accepted.

NEW CASTLE

AAA ▼▼▼ Quality Inn Skyways M ❖
(302) 328-6666. **$115-$170.** 147 N DuPont Hwy. I-95, exit 5A, 0.8 mi s on SR 141, exit 1B, 0.5 mi s on US 13, 40 and 301; I-295, exit New Castle Airport/US 13 S, 1.8 mi s on US 13, 40 and 301. Ext/int corridors. **Pets:** Other species. $10 daily fee/room. Designated rooms, service with restrictions, supervision.

REHOBOTH BEACH

▼▼ AmericInn Lodge & Suites of Rehoboth Beach SH ❖
(302) 226-0700. **$50-$249.** 329Z Airport Rd. Just w of SR 1; 1.3 mi n of jct SR 1A. Int corridors. **Pets:** Dogs only. $20 daily fee/pet. Designated rooms, service with restrictions, supervision.

▼▼ The Atlantis Inn M
(302) 227-9446. **$85-$275, 7 day notice.** 154 Rehoboth Ave. At Reho-both Ave and 2nd St; downtown. Ext corridors. **Pets:** Accepted.

AAA ▼▼▼ Sea-Esta IV M
(302) 227-5882. **$49-$189.** 3101 Hwy 1. 1 mi s. Ext corridors. **Pets:** Accepted.

WILMINGTON

AAA ▼▼▼▼ Best Western Brandywine Valley Inn SH
(302) 656-9436. **$104-$175.** 1807 Concord Pike. I-95, exit 8, 1 mi n on US 202. Ext corridors. **Pets:** Other species. $25 one-time fee/pet. Service with restrictions, crate.

AAA ▼▼▼ Days Inn Wilmington M
(302) 478-0300. **$65-$70.** 5209 Concord Pike. I-95, exit 8, 4 mi n on US 202; jct SR 92 (Naamans Rd). Ext corridors. **Pets:** Large. $10 daily fee/pet. Designated rooms, service with restrictions, crate.

AAA ▼▼▼▼ Sheraton Suites Wilmington LH
(302) 654-8300. **$105-$179.** 422 Delaware Ave. I-95, exit 7, 0.3 mi e; downtown. Int corridors. **Pets:** Accepted.

DISTRICT OF COLUMBIA

WASHINGTON

▼▼▼▼ Doubletree Guest Suites, Washington DC SH
(202) 785-2000. $159-$600. 801 New Hampshire Ave NW. Just sw at Washington Circle. Int corridors. **Pets:** Other species. $20 daily fee/pet. Designated rooms, service with restrictions.
[X] [&M] [🐾] [&] [🛏] [💻] [🍴] [≈]

AAA ▼▼▼▼ The Fairmont Washington, D.C. LH ❀
(202) 429-2400. $189-$619. 2401 M St NW. 24th and M sts NW. Int corridors. **Pets:** Other species. Service with restrictions, supervision.
[SAVE] [S&] [X] [&M] [🐾] [&] [🛏] [💻] [🍴] [≈] [X]

AAA ▼▼▼▼ Four Seasons Hotel Washington D.C. LH ❀
(202) 342-0444. $395-$7155. 2800 Pennsylvania Ave NW. In Georgetown. Int corridors. **Pets:** Small, other species. Service with restrictions, supervision.
[SAVE] [X] [&M] [🐾] [&] [🛏] [💻] [🍴] [≈] [X]

▼▼▼▼ Hamilton Crowne Plaza Hotel Washington DC LH
(202) 682-0111. $109-$399. 1001 14th St NW. 14th and K sts NW. Int corridors. **Pets:** Accepted.
[ASK] [S&] [X] [&M] [🐾] [&] [🛏] [💻] [🍴]

▼▼▼▼ The Hay-Adams SH
(202) 638-6600. $600-$1000. 800 16th St NW. 16th and H sts NW; just n of the White House. Int corridors. **Pets:** Accepted.
[X] [🐾] [&] [🛏] [🍴]

AAA ▼▼▼ The Hotel George SH ❀
(202) 347-4200. $174-$454. 15 E St NW. On Capitol Hill, just n of Capitol grounds. Int corridors. **Pets:** Other species. Service with restrictions, crate.
[SAVE] [S&] [X] [&M] [🐾] [&] [🛏] [🍴]

AAA ▼▼▼ Hotel Helix SH
(202) 462-9001. $129-$329. 1430 Rhode Island Ave NW. Just e of Scott Circle. Int corridors. **Pets:** Accepted.
[SAVE] [S&] [X] [🐾] [&] [🛏] [💻] [🍴]

AAA ▼▼▼ Hotel Madera SH
(202) 296-7600. $139-$389. 1310 New Hampshire Ave NW. Between 20th and N sts NW. Int corridors. **Pets:** Accepted.
[SAVE] [S&] [X] [🐾] [&] [🛏] [💻] [🍴]

AAA ▼▼▼▼ Hotel Monaco Washington DC SH
(202) 628-7177. $229-$429. 700 F St NW. Between 7th and 8th sts NW. Int corridors. **Pets:** Accepted.
[SAVE] [S&] [X] [🐾] [&] [💻] [🍴]

AAA ▼▼▼ Hotel Rouge SH ❀
(202) 232-8000. $129-$339. 1315 16th St NW. Just n of Scott Circle. Int corridors. **Pets:** Other species. Service with restrictions, crate.
[SAVE] [S&] [X] [🐾] [&] [🛏] [💻] [🍴]

AAA ▼▼▼ Hotel Washington LH
(202) 638-5900. $129-$400. 515 15th St NW. 1 blk e of the White House at Pennsylvania Ave and 15th St NW; 2 blks from Metro Center. Int corridors. **Pets:** Accepted.
[SAVE] [X] [🐾] [&] [💻] [🍴]

AAA ▼▼▼ The Jefferson SH
(202) 347-2200. $473-$625. 1200 16th St NW. 16th and M sts NW. Int corridors. **Pets:** Accepted.
[SAVE] [X] [&M] [&] [🛏] [💻] [🍴]

▼▼▼▼ L'Enfant Plaza Hotel LH
(202) 484-1000. $109-$409. 480 L SW. I-395, exit L. Int corridors. **Pets:** Accepted.
[ASK] [S&] [X] [🐾] [🛏] [💻] [🍴] [≈]

AAA ▼▼▼▼ The Madison, a Loews Hotel LH ❀
(202) 862-1600. $180-$999. 1177 15th St NW. 15th and M sts NW. Int corridors. **Pets:** Designated rooms.
[SAVE] [S&] [X] [🐾] [&] [🛏] [🍴] [X]

▼▼▼▼ Mandarin Oriental, Washington D.C. LH ❀
(202) 554-8588. $495-$8000. 1330 Maryland Ave SW. Jct Independence Ave SW; just s on 12th St SW. Int corridors. **Pets:** Small. $100 one-time fee/room. Crate.
[X] [&M] [🐾] [&] [🍴] [≈]

▼▼▼▼ Marriott Wardman Park Hotel LH
(202) 328-2000. $299-$409. 2660 Woodley Rd NW. Just w of Connecticut Ave; at Woodley Park/Zoo Metro Station. Int corridors. **Pets:** Accepted.
[ASK] [X] [&M] [🐾] [&] [🛏] [💻] [🍴] [≈] [X]

AAA ▼▼▼ The Melrose Hotel, Washington DC SH
(202) 955-6400. $269-$409. 2430 Pennsylvania Ave NW. Between 24th and 25th sts NW. Int corridors. **Pets:** Accepted.
[SAVE] [X] [🐾] [&] [💻] [🍴]

AAA ▼▼▼▼ Omni Shoreham Hotel LH
(202) 234-0700. $489, 3 day notice. 2500 Calvert St NW. Just w of Connecticut Ave. Int corridors. **Pets:** $50 one-time fee/room. Service with restrictions, supervision.
[SAVE] [S&] [X] [🐾] [&] [🛏] [💻] [🍴] [≈] [X]

AAA ▼▼▼ The Quincy SH
(202) 223-4320. $119-$379. 1823 L St NW. Between 18th and 19th sts NW. Int corridors. **Pets:** Small, other species. $150 one-time fee/pet. Service with restrictions, supervision.
[SAVE] [S&] [X] [🐾] [&] [🛏] [💻] [🍴]

▼▼▼▼ Red Roof Inn Downtown Washington, D.C. SH
(202) 289-5959. $155-$205. 500 H St NW. At 5th and H sts NW; in Chinatown. Int corridors. **Pets:** Medium, other species. Service with restrictions, supervision.
[X] [🐾] [&] [🛏] [💻]

AAA ▼▼▼▼ Renaissance Mayflower Hotel LH ❀
(202) 347-3000. $379-$436. 1127 Connecticut Ave NW. Just n of K St NW; in business district. Int corridors. **Pets:** Medium, dogs only. $100 one-time fee/pet. Designated rooms, service with restrictions, supervision.
[SAVE] [X] [&M] [🐾] [&] [🍴]

▼▼▼▼ Residence Inn by Marriott Capitol SH
(202) 484-8280. $229. 333 E St SW. Between 3rd and 4th sts SW. Int corridors. **Pets:** Medium. $10 daily fee/pet, $200 one-time fee/pet. Service with restrictions, crate.
[ASK] [S&] [X] [&M] [&] [🛏] [💻] [≈]

▼▼▼▼ Residence Inn by Marriott-Dupont Circle SH
(202) 466-6800. $269-$379. 2120 P St NW. Between 21st and 22nd sts NW; just w of Dupont Circle. Int corridors. **Pets:** Accepted.
[X] [&M] [🐾] [&] [🛏] [💻]

▼▼▼▼ Residence Inn by Marriott-Washington DC-Vermont Ave SH
(202) 898-1100. $259. 1199 Vermont Ave NW. Jct 14th St and Vermont Ave NW, at Thomas Circle. Int corridors. **Pets:** Accepted.
[ASK] [S&] [X] [&M] [🐾] [&] [🛏] [💻]

▼▼▼▼ The Ritz-Carlton, Georgetown SH
(202) 912-4100. $260-$550. 3100 South St NW. Just s of jct M St and Wisconsin Ave; off Wisconsin Ave, just e; in Georgetown. Int corridors. **Pets:** Accepted.
[X] [🐾] [&] [🛏] [🍴] [X]

▼▼▼▼ The Ritz-Carlton, Washington, DC 🄻🄷
(202) 835-0500. **$259-$645.** 1150 22nd St NW. At 22nd and M sts NW. Int corridors. **Pets:** Accepted.
⊠ 🅖🄼 🗝 🖾 🖬 🖵 🍴 🏊 ⊠

▼▼▼ The River Inn 🅂🄷
(202) 337-7600. **$99-$269.** 924 25th St NW. Between K and I sts NW. Int corridors. **Pets:** Accepted.
🄰🅂🄺 🅂🅃 ⊠ 🗝 🖬 🖵 🍴

🄰🄰🄰 ▼▼▼▼ St. Regis, Washington, D.C. 🄻🄷
(202) 638-2626. **$325-$750.** 923 16th St NW. 16th and K sts; just n of the White House. Int corridors. **Pets:** Accepted.
🅂🄰🅅🄴 ⊠ 🗝 🍴

🄰🄰🄰 ▼▼▼▼ Sofitel Lafayette Square Washington
DC 🅂🄷 🐾
(202) 730-8800. **$700-$1000.** 806 15th St NW. Jct 15th and H sts NW. Int corridors. **Pets:** Large. Service with restrictions, supervision.
🅂🄰🅅🄴 ⊠ 🅖🄼 🗝 🖾 🍴

🄰🄰🄰 ▼▼▼▼ Topaz Hotel 🅂🄷
(202) 393-3000. **$139-$359.** 1733 N St NW. Just e of Connecticut Ave. Int corridors. **Pets:** Accepted.
🅂🄰🅅🄴 🅂🅃 ⊠ 🗝 🖾 🖵 🍴

▼▼ ▼ Travelodge Gateway 🅂🄷
(202) 832-8600. **$69-$139.** 1917 Bladensburg Rd NE. US 50 (New York Ave) and Alternate Rt 1; just w of entrance to Baltimore-Washington Pkwy. Ext/int corridors. **Pets:** Accepted.
🄰🅂🄺 🅂🅃 ⊠ 🗝 🖾 🖬 🖵 🍴 🏊

🄰🄰🄰 ▼▼▼▼ Washington Suites Georgetown 🅂🄷
(202) 333-8060. **$148-$288.** 2500 Pennsylvania Ave NW. Jct 25th St NW and Pennsylvania Ave; 2 blks from Foggy Bottom metro station. Int corridors. **Pets:** Accepted.
🅂🄰🅅🄴 🅂🅃 ⊠ 🅖🄼 🗝 🖾 🖬 🖵

🄰🄰🄰 ▼▼▼▼ The Westin Embassy Row 🅂🄷
(202) 293-2100. **$159-$419.** 2100 Massachusetts Ave NW. Just w of Dupont Circle; at 21st St. Int corridors. **Pets:** Medium. Service with restrictions.
🅂🄰🅅🄴 🅂🅃 ⊠ 🗝 🖾 🖬 🖵 🍴 ⊠

▼▼▼▼ The Westin Grand 🄻🄷
(202) 429-0100. **$209-$289.** 2350 M St NW. 24th and M sts NW. Int corridors. **Pets:** Accepted.
🄰🅂🄺 🅂🅃 ⊠ 🗝 🖾 🖵 🍴 🏊

▼▼▼ The Willard InterContinental 🄻🄷 🐾
(202) 628-9100. **$610-$4200.** 1401 Pennsylvania Ave NW. Just e of the White House. Int corridors. **Pets:** Medium, dogs only. $100 one-time fee/room. Service with restrictions, supervision.
🅂🅃 ⊠ 🅖🄼 🗝 🖾 🖵 🍴 ⊠

FLORIDA

CITY INDEX

APALACHICOLA

♦♦♦ ▼▼▼▼ Coombs House Inn BB
(850) 653-9199. **$79-$225, 7 day notice.** 80 6th St. Corner of US 98 and 6th St; center. Int corridors. **Pets:** Accepted.
SAVE S■ ✕ ■ ▣

♦♦♦ ▼▼▼▼ Gibson Inn CI
(850) 653-2191. **$85-$200, 14 day notice.** Market St & Ave C. On US 98 at west end of bridge. Int corridors. **Pets:** Other species. $25 daily fee/pet. Designated rooms, service with restrictions, supervision.
SAVE S■ ✕ ▮▮

ARCADIA

♦♦♦ ▼▼▼ Best Western Arcadia Inn M
(863) 494-4884. **$79-$149.** 504 S Brevard Ave. 0.6 mi s of SR 70; on US 17. Ext corridors. **Pets:** Small. $15 daily fee/room. Service with restrictions, supervision.
SAVE S■ ✕ ■ ▣ ⇌

AVON PARK

♦♦♦ ▼▼▼ Econo Lodge M
(863) 453-2000. **$69-$109.** 2511 US Hwy 27. On US 27; 2.5 mi s of jct SR 17 and 64. Ext corridors. **Pets:** Other species. $10 daily fee/room. Service with restrictions, crate.
SAVE S■ ✕ ▨ ⇌

BOCA RATON

▼▼ Homestead Studio Suites Hotel-Boca Raton/Commerce M
(561) 994-2599. **$84-$164.** 501 NW 77th St. I-95, exit 50, just s on Congress Ave to NW 6th Ave. Ext corridors. **Pets:** Accepted.
A$K S■ ✕ ▥ ■ ▣

♦♦♦ ▼▼▼▼ Residence Inn-By Marriott-Boca Raton SH
(561) 994-3222. **$143-$233.** 525 NW 77th St. I-95, exit 50, W on Congress Ave to NW 6th Ave, then to NW 77th St. Ext corridors. **Pets:** Other species. $75 one-time fee/room. Service with restrictions.
SAVE ✕ ▨ ▥ ■ ▣ ⇌ ✕

♦♦♦ ▼▼▼▼ TownePlace Suites by Marriott SH 🐾
(561) 994-7232. **$129-$289.** 5110 NW 8th Ave. I-95, exit 48B (Yamato Rd), just w; in Arvida Corporate Park. Int corridors. **Pets:** Other species. $100 one-time fee/room. Service with restrictions, crate.
SAVE ✕ ▥M ▨ ▥ ■ ▣ ⇌

BONITA SPRINGS

▼▼▼▼ AmericInn Hotel & Suites SH
(239) 495-9255. **$79-$200.** 28600 Trails Edge Blvd. I-75, exit 116, 3.5 mi w on CR 865 (Bonita Beach Rd SE), 0.7 mi s on US 41 (Tamiami Trail), then just w; in Woods Edge. Int corridors. **Pets:** Accepted.
S■ ✕ ▥M ▨ ▥ ■ ▣ ⇌

♦♦♦ ▼▼▼▼ Inn at The Springs CO
(239) 949-5913. **$109-$249, 3 day notice.** 8900 Brighton Ln. I-75, exit 116, 3.5 mi w on CR 865 (Bonita Beach Rd SE), 1.4 mi n on US 41 (Tamiami Trail), then e. Int corridors. **Pets:** Accepted.
SAVE S■ ✕ ▥M ▨ ▥ ■ ▣ ⇌

BOYNTON BEACH

▼▼▼ Holiday Inn-Boynton Beach SH
(561) 737-4600. **$119-$199.** 1601 N Congress Ave. I-95, exit 59 (SR 806/Gateway Blvd), 1.2 mi w to SR 807 (Congress Ave); 0.3 mi s of jct SR 806 (Gateway Blvd); adjacent to Catalina Shopping Center. Ext/int corridors. **Pets:** Accepted.
A$K S■ ✕ ▨ ■ ▣ ▮▮ ⇌ ✕

BRADENTON

(AAA) ▼▼▼ Econo Lodge Airport M
(941) 758-7199. **$59-$139.** 6727 14th St W. On US 41, 2 mi s of jct SR 70. Ext corridors. **Pets:** Small, dogs only. $10 daily fee/pet. Designated rooms, service with restrictions, supervision.
[SAVE] [S☼] [✕] [📶] [💻] [↝]

(AAA) ▼▼ Howard Johnson Express Inn M
(941) 756-8399. **$65-$149.** 6511 14th St W. On US 41, 1.5 mi s of jct SR 70. Ext corridors. **Pets:** Small, dogs only. $10 daily fee/pet. Service with restrictions, supervision.
[SAVE] [S☼] [✕] [📶] [💻] [↝]

BRADENTON BEACH

(AAA) ▼▼▼ Tortuga Inn Beach Resort CO
(941) 778-6611. **$125-$400, 14 day notice.** 1325 Gulf Dr N. On SR 789, 0.3 mi n of jct SR 684. Ext corridors. **Pets:** Small. $25 one-time fee/pet. Designated rooms, service with restrictions.
[SAVE] [✕] [📶] [💻] [↝]

(AAA) ▼▼▼ Tradewinds Resort CA
(941) 779-0010. **$145-$300, 14 day notice.** 1603 Gulf Dr N. On SR 789, 0.5 mi n of jct SR 684. Ext corridors. **Pets:** Other species. $50 one-time fee/room.
[SAVE] [✕] [📶] [💻] [↝]

BROOKSVILLE

▼▼ Best Western Brooksville I-75 M
(352) 796-9481. **$79-$109.** 30307 Cortez Blvd. I-75, exit 301, just w on US 98/SR 50. Ext corridors. **Pets:** Large, other species. $25 one-time fee/room. Designated rooms, service with restrictions, supervision.
[ASK] [S☼] [✕] [&M] [&] [💻] [🍴] [↝]

(AAA) ▼▼ Days Inn Heritage Inn M
(352) 796-9486. **$79-$99.** 6320 Windmere Rd. I-75, exit 301, just e on US 98/SR 50. Ext corridors. **Pets:** $25 one-time fee/pet. Service with restrictions.
[SAVE] [S☼] [✕] [&M] [🔇] [📶] [💻] [↝]

BUSHNELL

▼▼ Guest House Inn M
(352) 793-5010. **$49-$99.** 2224 W Hwy 48. I-75, exit 314, just e. Ext corridors. **Pets:** Accepted.
[ASK] [S☼] [✕] [📶] [💻] [↝]

CAPE CANAVERAL

(AAA) ▼▼▼ Residence Inn by Marriott Cape Canaveral/ Cocoa Beach SH ❀
(321) 323-1100. **$139-$229.** 8959 Astronaut Blvd. On SR A1A, 0.3 mi s of jct SR 528. Int corridors. **Pets:** Medium, other species. $15 one-time fee/room. Service with restrictions.
[SAVE] [✕] [🔇] [&] [📶] [💻] [↝] [✕]

CAPE CORAL

(AAA) ▼ Dockside Inn M
(239) 542-0061. **$89-$159, 7 day notice.** 3817 Del Prado Blvd. 1.2 mi n of jct Cape Coral Pkwy. Ext corridors. **Pets:** Accepted.
[SAVE] [S☼] [✕] [📶] [↝] [✕]

▼▼▼ Quality Hotel SH
(239) 542-2121. **$89-$189.** 1538 Cape Coral Pkwy. Jct Del Prado Blvd. Int corridors. **Pets:** Accepted.
[ASK] [S☼] [✕] [🔇] [&] [📶] [💻] [↝]

CARRABELLE

▼▼ The Moorings At Carrabelle SH
(850) 697-2800. **$100-$175.** 1000 Hwy 98. On US 98, just e of bridge. Ext corridors. **Pets:** Other species. $50 deposit/room, $10 daily fee/pet. Designated rooms.
[ASK] [S☼] [✕] [📶] [💻] [↝] [✕]

CEDAR KEY

(AAA) ▼▼▼ Park Place Motel & Condominiums M
(352) 543-5737. **$65-$110.** 211 2nd St. At A St. Ext corridors. **Pets:** Small, other species. $7 daily fee/pet. Designated rooms, service with restrictions, supervision.
[SAVE] [✕] [📶] [💻]

(AAA) ▼▼▼ Seahorse Landing Condominiums CO
(352) 543-5860. **$150-$190, 3 day notice.** 4050 G St. Just w on 6th St. Ext corridors. **Pets:** Medium, dogs only. $15 daily fee/pet. Designated rooms, no service, supervision.
[✕] [📶] [💻] [↝] [✕]

CHARLOTTE HARBOR

▼ Banana Bay Waterfront Motel M
(941) 743-4441. **$450-$850 (weekly).** 23285 Bayshore Rd. Jct US 41. Ext corridors. **Pets:** Accepted.
[✕] [📶] [💻]

CHIEFLAND

(AAA) ▼▼ Best Western Suwannee Valley Inn SH
(352) 493-0663. **$87-$97.** 1125 N Young Blvd. On US 19/98, just n of jct US 129. Ext corridors. **Pets:** Very small. $30 deposit/room, $20 daily fee/pet. Designated rooms, service with restrictions, supervision.
[SAVE] [S☼] [✕] [📶] [💻] [↝]

CHIPLEY

▼▼ Super 8 Motel M
(850) 638-8530. **$59-$74.** 1150 Motel Dr. I-10, exit 120, just n. Ext corridors. **Pets:** Accepted.
[ASK] [S☼] [✕] [📶]

COCOA

▼▼ Best Western Cocoa Inn SH
(321) 632-1065. **$65-$139.** 4225 W King St. I-95, exit 201 (SR 520), 0.3 mi e. Ext corridors. **Pets:** Accepted.
[ASK] [S☼] [✕] [🔇] [&] [📶] [💻] [↝]

(AAA) ▼▼▼ Econo Lodge-Space Center SH
(321) 632-4561. **$71-$199.** 3220 N Cocoa Blvd. US 1, just n of jct SR 528. Ext corridors. **Pets:** Accepted.
[SAVE] [✕] [🔇] [📶] [💻] [🍴] [↝]

COCOA BEACH

▼▼▼ Four Points by Sheraton Cocoa Beach SH
(321) 783-8717. **$125-$225.** 4001 N Atlantic Ave. SR A1A, just s of SR 520. Int corridors. **Pets:** Accepted.
[ASK] [S☼] [✕] [&M] [&] [📶] [💻] [🍴] [↝]

(AAA) ▼▼▼ Holiday Inn Cocoa Beach Oceanfront Resort SH
(321) 783-2271. **$89-$199.** 1300 N Atlantic Ave. SR A1A, 1.8 mi s of jct SR 520. Ext corridors. **Pets:** Accepted.
[SAVE] [S☼] [✕] [&M] [🔇] [&] [📶] [💻] [🍴] [↝] [✕]

(AAA) ▼▼▼ La Quinta Inn Cocoa Beach SH
(321) 783-2252. **$79-$159.** 1275 N Atlantic Ave. On SR A1A, 1.7 mi s. Ext corridors. **Pets:** Small, other species. Designated rooms, service with restrictions, crate.
[SAVE] [S☼] [✕] [🔇] [📶] [💻] [🍴] [↝]

▼▼▼▼ **Quality Suites Cocoa Beach** SH
(321) 783-6868. **$89-$199.** 3655 N Atlantic Ave. SR A1A, 0.3 mi s of jct SR 520. Int corridors. **Pets:** Accepted.

ASK S✗ ✗ &M ☕ ⌨ 🛏

▼▼ **Surf Studio Beach Resort** M
(321) 783-7100. **$85-$205.** 1801 S Atlantic Ave. SR A1A northbound, 5 mi s of jct SR 520 at Francis St; 1.3 mi n of Partrick AFB. Ext corridors. **Pets:** Medium. $20 daily fee/pet. No service, supervision.

🏊 🛏 ⌨ 🛏

CRESCENT BEACH

▲▲▲ ▼▼▼ **Beacher's Lodge** SH
(904) 471-8849. **$79-$250.** 6970 A1A S. Just s of jct SR 206. Ext corridors. **Pets:** Small. $50 one-time fee/pet. Designated rooms, service with restrictions, supervision.

SAVE S✗ ✗ 🛏 ⌨ 🛏

CRESCENT CITY

▼▼ **Lake View Motel** M
(386) 698-1090. **$55-$85.** 1004 N Summit St. 1 mi n on US 17. Ext corridors. **Pets:** Small. $5 daily fee/pet. Designated rooms, service with restrictions, supervision.

ASK ✗ 🛏 ⌨ 🛏

CRESTVIEW

▼▼▼▼ **Jameson Inn** SH
(850) 683-1778. **$54-$120.** 151 Cracker Barrel Dr. I-10, exit 56, just s. Int corridors. **Pets:** Small. $10 daily fee/pet. Service with restrictions, crate.

ASK ✗ 🛏 ⌨ 🛏

▲▲▲ ▼▼▼ **Regency Inn** SH
(850) 682-6111. **$90.** 4050 S Ferdon Blvd. I-10, exit 56, 0.5 mi s. Ext corridors. **Pets:** Accepted.

ASK S✗ ✗ & 🛏 ⌨ 🍴 🛏

▲▲▲ ▼▼▼ **Super 8 Motel** M
(850) 682-9649. **$54-$74.** 3925 S Ferdon Blvd. I-10, exit 56, 0.3 mi s. Ext corridors. **Pets:** Other species. $5 daily fee/pet. Designated rooms, service with restrictions.

SAVE S✗ ✗ 🛏

CRYSTAL RIVER

▲▲▲ ▼▼▼ **Best Western Crystal River Resort** SH
(352) 795-3171. **$101-$150.** 614 NW Hwy 19. On US 19/98, 0.8 mi n of jct SR 44. Ext corridors. **Pets:** Medium, other species. $3 daily fee/pet. Service with restrictions, supervision.

SAVE S✗ ✗ 🏊 & 🛏 ⌨ 🛏 ✗

▲▲▲ ▼▼▼ **Days Inn** SH
(352) 795-2111. **$55-$130.** 2380 NW Hwy 19. US 19, 2.2 mi n of jct SR 44. Ext corridors. **Pets:** Other species. $10 daily fee/pet. Service with restrictions, supervision.

SAVE S✗ ✗ & 🛏 🍴

DAYTONA BEACH

▲▲▲ ▼▼ **Days Inn Speedway** M
(386) 255-0541. **$59-$298, 30 day notice.** 2900 W International Speedway Blvd. I-95, exit 261B southbound; exit 261 northbound, just w on US 92. Ext corridors. **Pets:** Medium, other species. $15 daily fee/pet. Service with restrictions, supervision.

SAVE S✗ ✗ 🛏 🍴 🛏

▼▼ **Extended Stay Deluxe Daytona Beach-International Speedway** SH
(386) 257-4311. **$90-$105.** 255 Bill France Blvd. I-95, exit 261, 2.5 mi e, then just n. Int corridors. **Pets:** Accepted.

ASK S✗ ✗ & 🛏 ⌨ 🛏

▼▼ ▼▼ **Homewood Suites by Hilton Daytona Speedway/Airport** SH
(386) 258-2828. **Call for rates.** 165 Bill France Blvd. I-95, exit 261, 2.5 mi e, then just n. Int corridors. **Pets:** Accepted.

✗ &M ⌨ 🛏 ⌨ 🛏 ✗

▲▲▲ ▼▼▼ **LaPlaya Resort & Suites** SH
(386) 672-0990. **$79-$459, 7 day notice.** 2500 N Atlantic Ave. On SR A1A, 3.3 mi n of jct US 92. Ext corridors. **Pets:** Accepted.

SAVE S✗ ✗ 🏊 🛏 ⌨ 🍴 🛏 ✗

▲▲▲ ▼▼▼ **La Quinta Inn & Suites** SH
(386) 944-0060. **$79-$279, 3 day notice.** 816 N Atlantic Ave. On SR A1A, 1.4 mi n of US 92. Ext corridors. **Pets:** Small. $50 deposit/room, crate.

SAVE S✗ ✗ & 🛏 ⌨ 🛏

▲▲▲ ▼▼▼ **Plaza Ocean Club** SH
(386) 239-9800. **$69-$399, 7 day notice.** 640 N Atlantic Ave. On SR A1A, 1 mi n of jct SR 90. Int corridors. **Pets:** Small, other species. $15 daily fee/pet. Designated rooms, service with restrictions.

SAVE S✗ ✗ &M 🏊 & 🛏 ⌨ 🍴 🛏

▼▼▼ **Ramada Inn Speedway** SH 🐾
(386) 255-2422. **$89-$99, 30 day notice.** 1798 W International Speedway Blvd. I-95, exit 261A southbound; exit 261 northbound, 2 mi e on US 92. Ext corridors. **Pets:** Medium. $25 one-time fee/room. Designated rooms, service with restrictions.

ASK S✗ ✗ 🏊 🛏 ⌨ 🍴 🛏

▼▼▼ **Residence Inn by Marriott** SH
(386) 252-3949. **$109-$199.** 1725 Richard Petty Blvd. I-95, exit 261, 2.6 mi e, then just s. Int corridors. **Pets:** Accepted.

ASK S✗ ✗ &M 🏊 & 🛏 ⌨ 🛏 ✗

▲▲▲ ▼▼▼ **Super 8-Oceanfront** M
(386) 253-0666. **$59-$136, 7 day notice.** 133 S Ocean Ave. Jct US 92 and SR A1A N, just e, then n. Ext corridors. **Pets:** Other species. $10 daily fee/pet. Service with restrictions, crate.

SAVE S✗ ✗ & 🛏

DAYTONA BEACH SHORES

▲▲▲ ▼▼▼ **Atlantic Ocean Palm Inn** M
(386) 761-8450. **$69-$159, 30 day notice.** 3247 S Atlantic Ave. On SR A1A, 5 mi s of jct US 92. Ext corridors. **Pets:** Accepted.

SAVE S✗ ✗ 🛏 🛏

▲▲▲ ▼▼▼ ▼▼▼ **The Shores Resort & Spa** LH
(386) 767-7350. **$159-$369, 3 day notice.** 2637 S Atlantic Ave. On SR A1A, 3.2 mi s of jct US 92. Int corridors. **Pets:** Small, dogs only. $200 deposit/room, $25 one-time fee/room. Service with restrictions, supervision.

SAVE S✗ ✗ &M 🏊 & 🛏 ⌨ 🍴 🛏 ✗

DE FUNIAK SPRINGS

▼▼ ▼▼ **Best Western Crossroads Inn** SH
(850) 892-5111. **$69-$99.** 2343 Freeport Rd. I-10, exit 85, just s. Ext/int corridors. **Pets:** Small. $10 one-time fee/room. Designated rooms, service with restrictions, supervision.

ASK S✗ ✗ 🛏 ⌨ 🍴 🛏

DELAND

▲▲▲ ▼▼▼ **Holiday Inn** SH 🐾
(386) 738-5200. **$74-$229.** 350 E International Speedway Blvd. 0.3 mi ne on US 92 from jct US 17. Int corridors. **Pets:** Medium. $25 one-time fee/room. Designated rooms, service with restrictions, supervision.

SAVE S✗ ✗ 🏊 🛏 ⌨ 🍴 🛏

▲▲▲ ▼▼▼ **University Inn** M
(386) 734-5711. **$79-$189.** 644 N Woodland Blvd. US 17, 0.9 mi n of jct SR 44. Ext corridors. **Pets:** Medium. $10 daily fee/pet. Designated rooms, service with restrictions, supervision.

SAVE S✗ ✗ & 🛏 ⌨ 🛏

DELRAY BEACH

⬤⬤⬤ ▼◆▼◆ Colony Hotel & Cabana Club SH ❀
(561) 276-4123. **$129-$319, 3 day notice.** 525 E Atlantic Ave. On SR 806 (Atlantic Ave) at US 1 northbound; center. Int corridors. **Pets:** Other species. $25 daily fee/pet.

SAVE ⬤ ⤫ ⬤ ⬤

▼◆▼◆ Residence Inn Delray Beach SH ❀
(561) 276-7441. **$199-$659.** 1111 E Atlantic Ave. I-95, exit 52 (SR 806/Atlantic Ave), 1.7 mi e. Int corridors. **Pets:** $100 one-time fee/pet. Service with restrictions.

ASK ⬤ ⤫ ⬤M ⬤ ⬤ ⬤ ⬤ ⬤

DELTONA

⬤⬤⬤ ▼◆▼◆ Best Western Deltona Inn SH
(386) 860-3000. **$75-$240, 3 day notice.** 481 Deltona Blvd. I-4, exit 108, just ne. Ext corridors. **Pets:** Medium. $10 daily fee/pet. Service with restrictions, supervision.

SAVE ⬤ ⤫ ⬤ ⬤ ⬤ ⬤ ⬤ ⬤

DESTIN

▼◆▼◆ Beachside Inn SH ❀
(850) 337-8000. **Call for rates.** 2931 Scenic Hwy 98. 1 mi s of US 98. Ext corridors. **Pets:** Other species. $25 one-time fee/room. Designated rooms.

ASK ⤫ ⬤ ⬤ ⬤ ⬤ ⬤

DUNDEE

⬤⬤⬤ ▼◆▼◆▼◆ Quality Inn-Dundee SH ❀
(863) 438-9800. **$59-$149.** 28610 US Hwy 27. On US 27; center. Ext corridors. **Pets:** Medium. $20 one-time fee/room. Designated rooms, service with restrictions.

SAVE ⬤ ⤫ ⬤ ⬤ ⬤ ⬤

ELKTON

⬤⬤⬤ ▼◆▼◆ Comfort Inn St. Augustine SH
(904) 829-3435. **$74-$179.** 2625 SR 207. I-95, exit 311, just w. Ext corridors. **Pets:** Accepted.

SAVE ⬤ ⤫ ⬤ ⬤ ⬤

ELLENTON

▼◆▼◆ GuestHouse International Inn M
(941) 729-0600. **$70-$120.** 4915 17th St E. I-75, exit 224, 0.3 mi s on US 301, just w on 51st Ave E, then just n. Ext corridors. **Pets:** Other species. $10 one-time fee/room. Service with restrictions, supervision.

ASK ⬤ ⤫ ⬤M ⬤ ⬤ ⬤ ⬤ ⬤

▼◆▼◆ Sleep Inn & Suites Riverfront M ❀
(941) 721-4933. **$90-$154.** 5605 18th St E. I-75, exit 224, just n on US 301, just e on 19th St E, then 0.3 mi sw. Int corridors. **Pets:** $20 daily fee/pet. Designated rooms, service with restrictions, supervision.

ASK ⬤ ⤫ ⬤M ⬤ ⬤ ⬤ ⬤

FLAGLER BEACH

▼◆▼◆ Beach Front Motel M
(386) 439-0089. **$64-$89.** 1544 S A1A. On SR A1A, 1 mi s of SR 100. Ext corridors. **Pets:** Medium, dogs only. $15 one-time fee/room. Service with restrictions, crate.

ASK ⬤ ⤫ ⬤ ⬤

⬤⬤⬤ ▼◆▼◆ Topaz Motel SH
(386) 439-3301. **$70-$180, 14 day notice.** 1224 S Oceanshore Blvd. On SR A1A, 0.5 mi s of SR 100. Ext/int corridors. **Pets:** Accepted.

SAVE ⤫ ⬤ ⬤ ⬤ ⬤ ⬤

FLORAL CITY

▼◆▼◆ Moonrise Resort CA
(352) 726-2553. **$75-$110 (no credit cards).** 8801 E Moonrise Ln, Lot 18. Just e on CR 48, then 1.5 mi n on Old Floral City Rd. Ext corridors. **Pets:** Dogs only. $20 daily fee/pet. No service.

⬤ ⬤ ⤫ ⬤

THE FLORIDA KEYS AREA

ISLAMORADA

⬤⬤⬤ ▼◆▼◆ Sands of Islamorada M
(305) 664-2791. **$105-$320, 3 day notice.** 80051 Overseas Hwy. US 1 at MM 80. Ext corridors. **Pets:** Other species. $20 daily fee/pet. Service with restrictions.

SAVE ⬤ ⬤ ⬤ ⬤ ⤫

KEY LARGO

⬤⬤⬤ ▼◆▼◆ Key Largo Grande Resort & Beach Club LH
(305) 852-5553. **$94-$189.** 97000 S Overseas Hwy. US 1 at MM 97. Ext corridors. **Pets:** Medium, dogs only. $50 one-time fee/room. Service with restrictions, supervision.

SAVE ⤫ ⬤ ⬤ ⬤ ⬤ ⬤ ⬤ ⤫

▼◆▼◆▼◆ Marina Del Mar Resort & Marina SH
(305) 451-4107. **$79-$239.** 527 Caribbean Dr. US 1 at MM 100. Ext corridors. **Pets:** Accepted.

ASK ⤫ ⬤ ⬤ ⬤ ⬤ ⬤ ⤫

KEY WEST

▼◆▼◆▼◆ Ambrosia Too At Fleming St BB
(305) 296-9838. **$125-$535, 30 day notice.** 622 Fleming St. Just n of Simonton St; in Old Town. Ext corridors. **Pets:** Accepted.

⤫ ⬤ ⬤ ⬤

▼◆▼◆▼◆ Center Court Historic Inn & Cottages BB ❀
(305) 296-9292. **$98-$608, 30 day notice.** 1075 Duval, C-19 St. Just e of Truman Ave; in Duval Square. Ext/int corridors. **Pets:** Other species. $10 daily fee/pet. Designated rooms, service with restrictions.

⤫ ⬤ ⬤ ⤫

⬤⬤⬤ ▼◆▼◆▼◆ Chelsea House Pool & Gardens BB
(305) 296-2211. **$109-$369, 7 day notice.** 709 Truman Ave. Corner of Elizabeth St and Truman Ave. Ext/int corridors. **Pets:** Medium, dogs only. $20 daily fee/pet. Designated rooms, service with restrictions, supervision.

SAVE ⤫ ⬤ ⬤ ⬤

⬤⬤⬤ ▼◆▼◆ Courtney's Place Historic Cottages & Inn CA ❀
(305) 294-3480. **$89-$389, 21 day notice.** 720 Whitmarsh Ln. Just e of jct Petronia and Simonton sts; in Old Town. Ext corridors. **Pets:** Large, other species. $25 one-time fee/pet. Designated rooms, service with restrictions.

SAVE ⬤ ⬤ ⬤ ⬤ ⬤

▼◆▼◆▼◆ The Cuban Club Suites M
(305) 294-5269. **$159-$599, 14 day notice.** 1108 Duval St. Corner of Duval and Amelia sts; in Old Town. Int corridors. **Pets:** Accepted.

⤫ ⬤ ⬤

(AAA) ▼▼▼▼ Curry Mansion Inn BB
(305) 294-5349. **$165-$335, 15 day notice.** 511 Caroline St. Just n of jct Duval St; in Old Town. Ext/int corridors. **Pets:** Small. Service with restrictions, supervision.
[SAVE] [X] [▬] [≈]

▼▼▼▼ Frances Street Bottle Inn BB
(305) 294-8530. **$99-$229, 14 day notice.** 535 Frances St. US 1/Roosevelt Blvd, w on White St, then just s on Southard St; corner of Frances and Southard sts; in Old Town. Int corridors. **Pets:** Other species. $35 one-time fee/pet. Designated rooms, service with restrictions.
[ASK] [X] [▬] [≈]

(AAA) ▼▼▼▼ Hyatt Key West Resort & Marina LH
(305) 809-1234. **$236-$599, 14 day notice.** 601 Front St. Simonton and Front sts; just n of Mallory Square; in Old Town. Ext corridors. **Pets:** Large, dogs only. $250 one-time fee/room. Service with restrictions, crate.
[SAVE] [X] [≈] [≈] [▬] [¶] [≈] [≈]

(AAA) ▼▼▼ The Palms Hotel BB ❀
(305) 294-3146. **$120-$325, 7 day notice.** 820 White St. Just w of Truman Ave. Ext corridors. **Pets:** Small. Designated rooms, service with restrictions, crate.
[SAVE] [S6] [≈]

(AAA) ▼▼▼▼ Sheraton Suites-Key West LH ❀
(305) 292-9800. **$159-$489, 3 day notice.** 2001 S Roosevelt Blvd. Jct US 1 and SR A1A, 3 mi s. Ext/int corridors. **Pets:** Medium. Service with restrictions, supervision.
[SAVE] [S6] [X] [≈M] [≈] [▬] [¶] [≈] [≈]

FORT LAUDERDALE METROPOLITAN AREA

CORAL SPRINGS

▼▼ La Quinta Inn & Suites Coral Springs South SH
(954) 344-2200. **$89-$219.** 3100 N University Dr. SR 817, just s of jct SR 834 (Sample Rd). Int corridors. **Pets:** Medium. Service with restrictions.
[ASK] [X] [≈] [≈] [▬] [▬] [≈]

▼▼▼▼ La Quinta Inn Ft. Lauderdale (Coral Springs) SH
(954) 753-9000. **$119-$209.** 3701 University Dr. SR 817, just n of jct SR 834 (Sample Rd). Int corridors. **Pets:** Medium. Service with restrictions.
[ASK] [X] [≈M] [≈] [≈] [▬] [▬] [≈]

▼▼ Studio 6 #6027 M
(954) 796-0011. **$78-$88.** 5645 University Dr. SR 869 (Sawgrass Expwy), exit 12 (University Dr), just s. Ext corridors. **Pets:** Accepted.
[S6] [X] [≈] [≈] [▬] [▬]

DANIA BEACH

▼▼ Motel 6 E. Dania Beach Blvd #376 M
(954) 921-5505. **$75-$91.** 825 E Dania Beach Blvd. I-95, exit 22, 1.1 mi e on Stirling Rd, just n on US 1 (Federal Hwy), then 0.8 mi e. Ext corridors. **Pets:** Medium, other species. Service with restrictions, supervision.
[S6] [X] [≈] [≈]

▼▼▼▼ Sheraton Fort Lauderdale Airport Hotel LH
(954) 920-3500. **$110-$309.** 1825 Griffin Rd. I-95, exit 23. Int corridors. **Pets:** Accepted.
[ASK] [S6] [X] [≈M] [≈] [≈] [▬] [▬] [¶] [≈] [≈]

DAVIE

▼▼ Homestead Studio Suites Hotel-Fort Lauderdale-Plantation M
(954) 476-1211. **$84-$124.** 7550 SR 84 E. I-595, exit 5, 0.3 mi. Ext corridors. **Pets:** Accepted.
[ASK] [S6] [X] [≈M] [≈] [≈] [▬] [▬]

DEERFIELD BEACH

(AAA) ▼▼▼▼ Comfort Inn-Oceanside M ❀
(954) 428-0650. **$124-$325.** 50 S Ocean Dr Ave. SR A1A, jct SR 810 (Hillsboro Blvd). Int corridors. **Pets:** Medium, other species. $25 daily fee/pet. Service with restrictions, supervision.
[SAVE] [S6] [X] [≈] [≈] [▬] [▬] [≈]

(AAA) ▼▼▼▼ Comfort Suites SH
(954) 570-8887. **$95-$399.** 1040 E Newport Center Dr. I-95, exit 41, jct SW 10th St to SW 12th Ave, then s; in Newport Center Complex. Ext corridors. **Pets:** Accepted.
[SAVE] [S6] [X] [≈] [≈] [▬] [▬] [≈]

(AAA) ▼▼▼▼ Embassy Suites-Deerfield Beach Resort LH
(954) 426-0478. **$149-$1000, 3 day notice.** 950 Ocean Dr (SR A1A). SR A1A, 0.5 mi s of jct SR 810 (Hillsboro Blvd). Int corridors. **Pets:** Small, dogs only. $20 daily fee/pet. Designated rooms, service with restrictions, crate.
[SAVE] [X] [≈] [≈] [▬] [▬] [¶] [≈] [≈]

▼▼ Extended StayAmerica-Deerfield Beach SH
(954) 428-5997. **$84-$134.** 1200 FAU Research Park Blvd. I-95, exit 41, just e to Fall Research Park Rd, then just s. Int corridors. **Pets:** Accepted.
[ASK] [S6] [X] [≈M] [≈] [▬] [▬]

▼▼ Holiday Park Hotel & Suites M
(954) 427-2200. **$59-$220.** 1250 W Hillsboro Blvd. I-95, exit 42B, just w on SR 810 (Hillsboro Blvd), then just s on 12th Ave SW. Ext corridors. **Pets:** Accepted.
[ASK] [S6] [X] [≈] [≈] [▬] [▬] [¶] [≈]

▼▼ La Quinta Inn & Suites Deerfield Beach SH
(954) 428-0661. **$129-$229.** 100 12th Ave SW. I-95, exit 42B, just w on SR 810 (Hillsboro Blvd), then just s. Int corridors. **Pets:** Medium. Service with restrictions.
[ASK] [X] [≈M] [≈] [≈] [▬] [▬] [≈]

▼▼▼▼ La Quinta Inn Ft. Lauderdale (Deerfield Beach) M
(954) 421-1004. **$112-$206.** 351 W Hillsboro Blvd. I-95, exit 42A, 0.3 mi e on SR 810. Ext corridors. **Pets:** Medium. Service with restrictions.
[ASK] [X] [≈M] [≈] [▬] [▬] [≈]

FORT LAUDERDALE

▼▼ Angela's Beach Inn M
(954) 563-7926. **$59-$230, 21 day notice.** 3016 Windamar St. On SR A1A, 6 blks s of SR 838 (Sunrise Blvd); west corner of Breakers Ave and Windamar St. Ext corridors. **Pets:** Accepted.
[ASK] [X] [▬] [▬] [≈]

▼▼ Crossland Studios-Fort Lauderdale/Commercial Blvd M
(954) 484-5115. **$64-$99.** 3031 W Commercial Blvd. I-95, exit 32 (SR 870/Commercial Blvd), 2 mi w; Florida Tpke, exit 62, 1.5 mi e. Ext corridors. **Pets:** Accepted.
[ASK] [S6] [X] [≈] [▬]

▼▼▼▼ **Embassy Suites-Fort Lauderdale** 🅛🄷
(954) 527-2700. **$129-$289.** 1100 SE 17th St Cswy. On SR A1A, just e of jct US 1 (Federal Hwy). Int corridors. **Pets:** Accepted.
[icons]

▼▼ **Extended StayAmerica-Cypress Creek/Andrews Ave** 🄼
(954) 776-9447. **$74-$109.** 5851 N Andrews Ave. I-95, exit 33 (Cypress Creek), just w, 0.3 mi s on N Andrews Ave, then left. Ext corridors. **Pets:** Accepted.
[icons]

▼▼ **Extended StayAmerica-Marina/Convention Center** 🄼
(954) 761-9055. **$74-$109.** 1450 SE 17th Street Cswy. SR A1A, 1 mi e of US 1 (Federal Hwy). Int corridors. **Pets:** Accepted.
[icons]

▼▼▼▼ **Hampton Inn Fort Lauderdale Airport North** 🅂🄷
(954) 524-9900. **$139-$219.** 2301 SW 12th Ave. I-95, exit 25 (SR 84), 0.7 mi e to SW 12th Ave, then just n. Int corridors. **Pets:** Small. $75 one-time fee/pet. Designated rooms, service with restrictions.
[icons]

▼▼▼▼ **La Quinta Inn** 🅂🄷
(954) 491-2500. **$69-$159, 3 day notice.** 5727 N Federal Hwy. 0.5 mi n on US 1 (Federal Hwy) from SR 870 (Commercial Blvd). Ext corridors. **Pets:** Medium. Service with restrictions.
[icons]

▼▼▼▼ **La Quinta Inn Ft. Lauderdale (Cypress Creek/I-95)** 🅂🄷
(954) 491-7666. **$106-$156.** 999 W Cypress Creek Rd. I-95, exit 33 southbound, 0.8 mi; exit 33B northbound, at Powerline Rd. Int corridors. **Pets:** Medium. Service with restrictions.
[icons]

▼ **Motel 6-Ft. Lauderdale #55** 🅂🄷
(954) 760-7999. **$75-$87.** 1801 SR 84. I-95, exit 25 (SR 84 E), just e, then U-turn at light. Int corridors. **Pets:** Medium, other species. Service with restrictions, supervision.
[icons]

▼▼ **Red Roof Inn** 🅂🄷
(954) 776-6333. **$85-$130.** 4800 Powerline Rd. I-95, exit 32, just w of jct Commercial Blvd, then n. Int corridors. **Pets:** Medium, other species. Service with restrictions, supervision.
[icons]

🄰🄰🄰 ▼▼▼ **Royal Saxon Apartments** 🄼
(954) 566-7424. **$75-$250, 30 day notice.** 551 Breakers Ave. Just w of SR A1A, 0.5 mi s of SR 838 (Sunrise Blvd); corner of Breakers Ave and Terramar St. Ext corridors. **Pets:** Accepted.
[icons]

🄰🄰🄰 ▼▼▼▼ **Sheraton Suites Cypress Creek** 🅛🄷
(954) 772-5400. **$229-$359.** 555 NW 62nd St. I-95, exit 33B northbound, then w; exit 33 southbound, then w SR 811 (Cypress Creek Rd). Int corridors. **Pets:** Accepted.
[icons]

🄰🄰🄰 ▼▼▼▼ **TownePlace Suites by Marriott** 🅂🄷 🐾
(954) 484-2214. **$124-$309.** 3100 Prospect Rd. I-95, exit 33, 2.7 mi w, then 0.5 mi s on NW 31st St. Int corridors. **Pets:** Other species. $100 one-time fee/room. Service with restrictions, crate.
[icons]

HOLLYWOOD

▼▼▼▼ **Days Inn Fort Lauderdale/Hollywood Airport South** 🅂🄷
(954) 923-7300. **$79-$299.** 2601 N 29th Ave. I-95, exit 21, just nw on SR 822 (Sheridan St). Int corridors. **Pets:** Dogs only. $10 daily fee/pet. Designated rooms, service with restrictions.
[icons]

🄰🄰🄰 ▼▼▼▼ **Econo Lodge Inn & Suites Hollywood Blvd** 🄼
(954) 981-1800. **$69-$199.** 4900 Hollywood Blvd. I-95, exit 20, 1.6 mi w; Florida Tpke, exit 49, 1.3 mi e. Ext corridors. **Pets:** Accepted.
[icons]

▼▼▼▼ **La Quinta Inn & Suites Ft. Lauderdale (Airport)** 🅂🄷
(954) 922-2295. **$125-$225.** 2620 N 26th Ave. I-95, exit 21, just e to Oakwood, then just left. Int corridors. **Pets:** Medium. Service with restrictions.
[icons]

🄰🄰🄰 ▼▼ **Sandy Shores Motel & Family Lodging** 🄼
(954) 923-3750. **$85-$135, 7 day notice.** 342 Van Buren St. From SR 820 (Hollywood Blvd), just s on SR A1A (S Ocean Dr), then e. Ext corridors. **Pets:** Accepted.
[icons]

🄰🄰🄰 ▼▼▼▼ **Seminole Hard Rock Hotel & Casino Hollywood** 🅛🄷
(954) 327-7625. **$139-$579.** 1 Seminole Way. I-95, exit 22, 2.9 mi w, then just n on SR 7/US 441; Florida Tpke, exit 53, 0.5 mi n, then 0.8 mi s. Int corridors. **Pets:** Accepted.
[icons]

PLANTATION

▼▼▼▼ **Best Western Plantation-Sawgrass** 🅂🄷 🐾
(954) 556-8200. **$79-$329.** 1711 N University Dr. On SR 817 (University Blvd), just s of Sunrise Blvd (SR 838). Ext/int corridors. **Pets:** Large. $25 one-time fee/room. Service with restrictions, supervision.
[icons]

▼▼▼ **Extended StayAmerica-Fort Lauderdale/Plantation** 🅂🄷
(954) 382-8888. **Call for rates.** 7755 SW 6th St. Just w of University Blvd (SR 817); next to Broward Mall. Int corridors. **Pets:** Accepted.
[icons]

▼▼▼▼ **Holiday Inn Express Plantation** 🅂🄷 🐾
(954) 472-5600. **$129-$239.** 1701 N University Dr. SR 817 (University Dr), just s of jct SR 838 (Sunrise Blvd). Int corridors. **Pets:** Large. $25 one-time fee/pet. Designated rooms, service with restrictions, crate.
[icons]

▼▼▼▼ **La Quinta Inn & Suites Ft. Lauderdale (Plantation)** 🅂🄷
(954) 476-6047. **$125-$195.** 8101 Peters Rd. I-595, exit 5 (SR 817 N/University Dr), just n, then just w; in Crossroad Office Park. Int corridors. **Pets:** Medium. Service with restrictions.
[icons]

▼▼▼ **La Quinta Inn Plantation** 🅂🄷
(954) 473-8257. **$129-$209.** 7901 SW 6th St. 0.3 mi w of SR 817 (University Dr); 0.5 mi sw of jct SR 842 (Broward Blvd). Int corridors. **Pets:** Medium. Service with restrictions.
[icons]

🄰🄰🄰 ▼▼▼▼ **Sheraton Suites-Plantation** 🅛🄷
(954) 424-3300. **$179-$259.** 311 N University Dr. I-595, exit 5 (SR 817/University Dr), 0.7 mi n; 0.3 mi n of jct Broward Blvd (SR 842); at Fashion Mall. Int corridors. **Pets:** Accepted.
[icons]

🄰🄰🄰 ▼▼▼▼ **Staybridge Suites Ft Lauderdale-Plantation** 🅂🄷
(954) 577-9696. **$166-$320, 7 day notice.** 410 N Pine Island Rd. I-595, exit 4 (Pine Island Rd), 1.7 mi n. Int corridors. **Pets:** Medium. $75 deposit/pet, $25 one-time fee/pet. Service with restrictions.
[icons]

POMPANO BEACH

▼▼▼ Extended Stay Deluxe–Cypress Creek Park North SH
(954) 783-1050. $84-$134. 1401 SW 15th St. I-95, exit 33B (Cypress Creek Rd) to Andrews Ave, just s, then left on McNab St. Int corridors. Pets: Accepted.

ASK Sᴅ ⊠ 🐾 🖉 🖬 🖵 🐾

▼ Motel 6–Pompano Beach #371 M
(954) 977-8011. $55-$79. 1201 NW 31st Ave. Florida Tpke, exit 67 (Coconut Creek Pkwy/Martin Luther King Blvd), just s. Pets: Medium, other species. Service with restrictions, supervision.

Sᴅ ⊠ 🖬 🐾

SUNRISE

▼ ▼ La Quinta Inn & Suites Sunrise SH
(954) 845-9929. $119-$219. 13600 NW 2nd St. SW 136th Ave, 0.3 mi n of jct I-595, exit 1A and SR 84; 0.5 mi e of jct I-75 and Sawgrass Expwy. Int corridors. Pets: Medium. Service with restrictions.

ASK ⊠ 🖉 🖫 🖬 🖵 🐾

▼▼▼ La Quinta Inn & Suites Sunrise at Sawgrass SH
(954) 846-1200. $129-$179. 13651 NW 2nd St. SW 136th Ave, 0.3 mi n of jct I-595, exit 1A and SR 84; 0.5 mi e of jct I-75 and Sawgrass Expwy. Int corridors. Pets: Medium. Service with restrictions.

ASK ⊠ 🖉 🖫 🖬 🖵 🐾

TAMARAC

▼ ▼ Homestead Studio Suites Hotel-Ft Lauderdale-Tamarac M
(954) 733-6644. $74-$99. 3873 W Commercial Blvd. SR 870 (Commercial Blvd), 0.7 mi e of Florida Tpke, exit 62; just e of jct US 441 and SR 7. Ext corridors. Pets: Accepted.

ASK Sᴅ ⊠ 🖉 🖫 🖬

▼▼▼ La Quinta Inn & Suites Ft. Lauderdale SH
(954) 485-7900. $85-$145. 3800 W Commercial Blvd. On SR 870 (Commercial Blvd), 0.8 mi e of Florida Tpke, exit 62; just e of jct SR 7 and US 441. Int corridors. Pets: Medium. Service with restrictions.

ASK ⊠ 🖉 🖫 🖬 🖵 🐾

WESTON

🔷 ▼▼▼ Bonaventure Resort & Conference Center LH 🐾
(954) 389-3300. $189-$589. 250 Racquet Club Rd. I-75, exit 21 (Indian Trace) southbound, 1.6 mi e on SR 84 to E Mall Dr, then just s; exit northbound, U-turn to SR 84, 1.6 mi to E Mall Dr, then just s. Ext corridors. Pets: Small. $150 one-time fee/room. Service with restrictions, supervision.

SAVE Sᴅ ⊠ 🖉 🖫 🖬 🖵 🍴 🐾 ⊠

▼▼▼ Residence Inn by Marriott Weston SH
(954) 659-8585. $179-$279. 2605 Weston Rd. I-75, exit 15 to Weston Rd, just s. Int corridors. Pets: Other species. $100 one-time fee/room. Service with restrictions, supervision.

ASK Sᴅ ⊠ ᴹ 🖫 🖬 🖵 🐾 ⊠

▼▼▼ TownePlace Suites by Marriott Weston SH
(954) 659-2234. $119-$209. 1545 Three Village Rd. I-75, exit 15, 1 mi e on Arvida Pkwy to Bonaventure Blvd, n to Three Village Rd, then w. Int corridors. Pets: Accepted.

ASK Sᴅ ⊠ 🖬 🖵 🐾

END METROPOLITAN AREA

FORT MYERS

🔷 ▼▼▼ Best Western Airport Inn SH
(239) 561-7000. $99-$199. 8955 Daniels Pkwy. I-75, exit 131, 0.6 mi w. Int corridors. Pets: Small. $10 daily fee/pet. Designated rooms, no service, supervision.

ASK Sᴅ ⊠ 🖫 🖬 🖵 🐾 ⊠

🔷 ▼▼▼ Best Western Fort Myers Island Gateway SH
(239) 466-1200. $109-$239, 14 day notice. 20091 Summerlin Rd SW. Jct John Morris Rd. Ext corridors. Pets: Accepted.

SAVE ⊠ 🖉 🖫 🖬 🖵 🍴 🐾

🔷 ▼▼▼ Best Western Springs Resort M
(239) 267-7900. $94-$159. 18051 S Tamiami Tr. On US 41 at Constitution Blvd. Ext corridors. Pets: Accepted.

SAVE Sᴅ ⊠ 🖬 🖵 🍴 🐾

▼ ▼ Comfort Suites Airport/University M
(239) 768-0005. $79-$159. 13651 Indian Paint Ln. I-75, exit 131, just w. Int corridors. Pets: Accepted.

ASK Sᴅ ⊠ 🖉 🖬 🖵

🔷 ▼▼▼ Country Inn & Suites By Carlson Sanibel-Gateway SH
(239) 454-9292. $115-$229. 13901 Shell Point Plaza. Jct McGregor Blvd; in Shell Point. Int corridors. Pets: Accepted.

SAVE Sᴅ ⊠ ᴹ 🖉 🖫 🖬 🖵 🐾

🔷 ▼▼▼ Crowne Plaza LH
(239) 482-2900. $129-$329, 3 day notice. 13051 Bell Tower Dr. Jct Daniels Pkwy; in Bell Tower Shops. Int corridors. Pets: Accepted.

SAVE Sᴅ ⊠ ᴹ 🖉 🖫 🖬 🖵 🍴 🐾 ⊠

🔷 ▼▼▼ Holiday Inn Downtown Historic District SH
(239) 332-3232. $129-$219, 3 day notice. 2431 Cleveland Ave. On US 41, just s of jct Edison Ave. Int corridors. Pets: Small. $50 one-time fee/room. Designated rooms, service with restrictions.

SAVE Sᴅ ⊠ 🖫 🖬 🖵 🍴 🐾

▼▼▼ Homewood Suites by Hilton-Ft. Myers SH
(239) 275-6000. $109-$329. 5255 Big Pine Way. Just e of jct US 41; in Bell Tower Shops. Int corridors. Pets: Medium. $75 one-time fee/room. Service with restrictions, supervision.

ASK ⊠ ᴹ 🖉 🖫 🖬 🖵 🐾

▼▼▼ La Quinta Inn Fort Myers M
(239) 275-3300. $99-$189. 4850 S Cleveland Ave. On US 41, just s of jct N Airport Rd. Ext corridors. Pets: Medium. Service with restrictions.

ASK ⊠ ᴹ 🖉 🖫 🖬 🖵 🐾

▼▼▼ Residence Inn by Marriott SH
(239) 936-0110. $124-$329. 2960 Colonial Blvd. I-75, exit 136, 3.5 mi w on SR 884 (Colonial Blvd). Int corridors. Pets: Accepted.

ASK Sᴅ ⊠ ᴹ 🖉 🖫 🖬 🖵 🐾 ⊠

▼ ▼ Suburban Extended Stay Hotel SH
(239) 938-0100. $68-$170. 10150 Metro Pkwy. I-75, exit 136, 3.4 mi w on SR 884 (Colonial Blvd); just s on SR 739. Int corridors. Pets: Medium. $15 daily fee/pet, $110 one-time fee/pet. Designated rooms, service with restrictions, supervision.

ASK Sᴅ ⊠ ᴹ 🖉 🖫 🖬 🖵 🐾

▼▼▼ Wynstar Inn & Suites SH
(239) 791-5000. $59-$269. 10150 Daniels Pkwy. I-75, exit 131, just e. Int corridors. Pets: Small. $100 deposit/room, $25 daily fee/pet. Designated rooms, service with restrictions, supervision.

ASK Sᴅ ⊠ ᴹ 🖉 🖫 🖬 🖵 🐾

FORT MYERS BEACH

Best Western Beach Resort SH
(239) 463-6000. **$109-$269, 7 day notice.** 684 Estero Blvd. 0.4 mi n of Matanzas Pass Bridge (SR 865). Ext corridors. **Pets:** Small. $10 daily fee/pet. Designated rooms, service with restrictions, supervision.
[SAVE] [S6] [X] [🐾] [🛏] [🍴] [🖥] [🏊] [X]

Lighthouse Resort Inn & Suites SH
(239) 463-9392. **$79-$325, 3 day notice.** 1051 5th St. Jct Matanzas Pass Bridge (SR 865). Ext corridors. **Pets:** Accepted.
[SAVE] [S6] [X] [🛏] [🖥] [🍴] [🏊]

FORT PIERCE

Dockside Inn & Resort SH
(772) 468-3555. **$79-$250, 3 day notice.** 1160 Seaway Dr. SR A1A southbound, 2 mi e of jct US 1. Ext corridors. **Pets:** Small. $50 one-time fee/pet. Designated rooms, service with restrictions.
[SAVE] [S6] [X] [🛏] [🖥] [🏊] [X]

Fountain Resort M
(772) 466-7041. **$89-$119, 3 day notice.** 4889 N US 1. I-95, exit 138 (Indrio Rd), 5.5 mi e, then just n. Ext corridors. **Pets:** Medium. $50 one-time fee/pet. Service with restrictions, crate.
[SAVE] [S6] [X] [🛏] [🖥] [🏊] [X]

Holiday Inn Express SH
(772) 464-5000. **$99-$165.** 7151 Okeechobee Rd. I-95, exit 129, 0.7 mi w on SR 70; Florida Tpke, exit 152. Ext corridors. **Pets:** Accepted.
[ASK] [S6] [X] [🛏] [🐾] [🖥] [🏊]

Motel 6-Fort Pierce #1207 M
(772) 461-9937. **$75-$91.** 2500 Peters Rd. I-95, exit 129, just w, then n. Ext corridors. **Pets:** Medium, other species. Service with restrictions, supervision.
[S6] [X] [🏊]

FORT WALTON BEACH

Marina Motel & Marina M
(850) 244-1129. **$50-$100.** 1345 Miracle Strip Pkwy SE. On US 98, 1 mi e. Ext/int corridors. **Pets:** Accepted.
[ASK] [S6] [X] [🛏] [🖥]

GAINESVILLE

A Newberry Inn & Conference Center SH
(352) 332-8001. **$89-$169.** 7413 W Newberry Rd. I-75, exit 387, just w. Ext corridors. **Pets:** Accepted.
[SAVE] [S6] [X] [🛏] [🖥] [🍴] [🏊]

Best Western Gateway Grand SH
(352) 331-3336. **$99-$139.** 4200 NW 97th Blvd. I-75, exit 390, just n of SR 222, then just w. Int corridors. **Pets:** Accepted.
[SAVE] [S6] [X] [🆖] [🐾] [🛏] [🖥] [🍴] [🏊] [X]

Comfort Inn West SH
(352) 264-1771. **$99-$169.** 3440 SW 40th Blvd. I-75, exit 384, just e, then just n. Int corridors. **Pets:** $10 daily fee/pet. Designated rooms, service with restrictions, crate.
[ASK] [S6] [X] [🆖] [🐾] [🛏] [🖥] [🏊]

Econo Lodge University M
(352) 373-7816. **$52-$135.** 2649 SW 13th St. I-75, exit 382, 2 mi e on SR 331, then 0.5 mi n on US 441. Ext corridors. **Pets:** Small, other species. $10 daily fee/pet. Service with restrictions, supervision.
[SAVE] [S6] [X] [🛏] [🖥] [🏊]

Extended StayAmerica SH
(352) 375-0073. **$73-$88.** 3600 SW 42nd St. I-75, exit 384, just e. Ext corridors. **Pets:** Accepted.
[ASK] [S6] [X] [🐾] [🛏] [🖥]

Holiday Inn Express SH
(352) 376-0004. **$85-$209.** 3905 SW 43rd St. I-75, exit 384, just w; behind Cracker Barrel Restaurant. Int corridors. **Pets:** Other species. $10 daily fee/pet. Designated rooms, service with restrictions, supervision.
[SAVE] [S6] [X] [🆖] [🐾] [🛏] [🖥] [🏊]

Holiday Inn-West SH
(352) 332-7500. **$89-$169, 14 day notice.** 7417 Newberry Rd. I-75, exit 387, just w. Ext corridors. **Pets:** Accepted.
[SAVE] [X] [🛏] [🖥] [🍴] [🏊]

Homewood Suites SH 🐾
(352) 335-3133. **Call for rates.** 3333 SW 42nd St. I-75, exit 384, just e. Int corridors. **Pets:** Other species. Service with restrictions, crate.
[X] [🛏] [🖥] [🏊] [X]

La Quinta Inn Gainesville SH
(352) 332-6466. **$92-$136.** 920 NW 69th Terrace. I-75, exit 387, just e, then just n. Ext corridors. **Pets:** Accepted.
[ASK] [X] [🐾] [🛏] [🖥] [🏊]

Motel 6 #414 SH
(352) 373-1604. **$47-$65.** 4000 SW 40th Blvd. I-75, exit 384, just e. Ext corridors. **Pets:** Medium, other species. Service with restrictions, supervision.
[S6] [X] [🛏] [🏊]

Quality Inn SH
(352) 378-2405. **$71-$129.** 3455 SW Williston Rd. I-75, exit 382, just w. Ext/int corridors. **Pets:** Accepted.
[SAVE] [S6] [X] [🛏] [🖥] [🏊]

Red Roof Inn-Gainesville SH
(352) 336-3311. **$60-$74.** 3500 SW 42nd St. I-75, exit 384, just e. Int corridors. **Pets:** Medium, other species. Service with restrictions, supervision.
[X] [🆖] [🐾] [🆖] [🛏] [🏊]

HAINES CITY

Best Western Lake Hamilton M
(863) 421-6929. **$66-$100.** 605 B Moore Rd. On US 27, just s of jct SR 544; 2 mi s of jct US 17-92. Ext corridors. **Pets:** Small, other species. $20 daily fee/pet. Designated rooms, service with restrictions, crate.
[SAVE] [S6] [X] [🆖] [🛏] [🖥] [🏊] [X]

HERNANDO

Best Western Citrus Hills Lodge SH
(352) 527-0015. **$83-$105.** 350 E Norvell Bryant Hwy. CR 486 at Citrus Hills Blvd, 3.3 mi w of US 41. Ext corridors. **Pets:** Accepted.
[ASK] [S6] [X] [🆖] [🐾] [🛏] [🖥] [🍴] [🏊]

HOLMES BEACH

Haley's Motel M 🐾
(941) 778-5405. **$99-$199, 30 day notice.** 8102 Gulf Dr N. On CR 789, 1.2 mi n of jct SR 64, jct Palm Dr; on Anna Maria Island. Ext corridors. **Pets:** Other species. $30 one-time fee/room. Service with restrictions.
[SAVE] [X] [🛏] [🏊]

HOMOSASSA SPRINGS

Bella Oasis Hotel & Spa SH
(352) 628-4311. **$66-$85.** 4076 S Suncoast Blvd. Just s of jct CR 490 and US 19. Ext corridors. **Pets:** Large, other species. $15 daily fee/pet. Designated rooms, service with restrictions, crate.
[SAVE] [S6] [X] [🛏] [🏊] [X]

INDIALANTIC

Oceanfront Cottages CA
(321) 725-8474. **$790 (weekly), 60 day notice.** 612 Wavecrest Ave. Just s of east end of US 192. Ext corridors. **Pets:** Small. $50 one-time fee/room. Service with restrictions, supervision.
[X] [🛏] [🖥] [🏊]

INDIAN HARBOUR BEACH

(AAA) ▼▼▼ Lexington Hotel on the Island SH
(321) 773-0325. **$75-$120.** 1894 S Patrick Dr. I-95, exit 183, 8 mi e, then 1 mi n on SR 513. Ext/int corridors. **Pets:** Medium, other species. $75 one-time fee/pet. Service with restrictions.

SAVE Sₒ ✕ ⌕ ⊙ 🖪 🖵 ⇌

INGLIS

(AAA) ▼▼▼ Pine Lodge Bed & Breakfast BB
(352) 447-7463. **$149-$179, 7 day notice.** 649 Hwy 40 W. 1.5 mi w of US 19. Ext/int corridors. **Pets:** $25 one-time fee/pet. Designated rooms, service with restrictions, supervision.

SAVE Sₒ ✕ 🖪 🖵 ⇌ 🖾

JACKSONVILLE METROPOLITAN AREA

BALDWIN

(AAA) ▼▼▼ Best Western Baldwin Inn M
(904) 266-9759. **$65-$199.** 1088 US 301 S. I-10, exit 343, just s. Ext corridors. **Pets:** Accepted.

SAVE Sₒ ✕ 🖵 ⇌

FERNANDINA BEACH

(AAA) ▼▼▼▼ Amelia Island Plantation-Amelia Inn & Beach Club LH
(904) 261-6161. **$251-$366, 14 day notice.** 6800 First Coast Hwy. In Fernandina Beach; SR A1A, 6.5 mi s of the bridge. Ext corridors. **Pets:** Accepted.

SAVE ✕ ⌕ ⊙ 🖵 ⑪ ⇌ ✕

▼▼▼ Hoyt House BB
(904) 277-4300. **$129-$239, 7 day notice.** 804 Atlantic Ave. In Fernandina Beach; on Atlantic Ave/SR 200 at Centre and S 8th sts; in historic district. Int corridors. **Pets:** Small. $35 one-time fee/room. Designated rooms, service with restrictions, crate.

✕ ⇌

JACKSONVILLE

(AAA) ▼▼▼ Best Western Hotel JTB/Southpoint LH ❖
(904) 281-0900. **$65-$169, 3 day notice.** 4660 Salisbury Rd. I-95, exit 344 (SR 202), just ne, then just s. Int corridors. **Pets:** Small. $10 daily fee/pet. Designated rooms, service with restrictions.

SAVE Sₒ ✕ ⌕ 🖪 🖵 ⇌ ✕

(AAA) ▼▼▼ Best Western Jacksonville Airport SH
(904) 741-4980. **$69-$149.** 1170 Airport Entrance Rd. I-95, exit 363B, just w, then just s on Duval Rd. Ext corridors. **Pets:** Medium. $10 daily fee/pet. Designated rooms, service with restrictions, supervision.

SAVE Sₒ ✕ ⌕ᴹ ⌕ ⊙ 🖪 🖵 ⇌

▼▼▼ Candlewood Suites SH
(904) 296-7785. **$79-$89.** 4990 Belfort Rd. I-95, exit 344 (SR 202), ne to Belfort Rd, then just s. Int corridors. **Pets:** Accepted.

ASK Sₒ ✕ ⌕ᴹ ⌕ ⊙ 🖪 🖵

(AAA) ▼▼▼ Days Inn South SH
(904) 733-3890. **$65, 3 day notice.** 5649 Cagle Rd. I-95, exit 346B southbound; exit 345 northbound, just w, then 0.5 mi n. Ext corridors. **Pets:** Accepted.

SAVE Sₒ ✕ ⌕ ⊙ ⇌

▼▼▼ Extended StayAmerica-Jacksonville-Butler Blvd SH
(904) 296-0181. **$65-$75.** 6961 Lenoir Ave. I-95, exit 344 (SR 202), just sw, then 0.3 mi n. Int corridors. **Pets:** Accepted.

ASK Sₒ ✕ 🖪 🖵

▼▼▼ Extended StayAmerica-Riverwalk SH
(904) 396-1777. **$85-$90.** 1413 Prudential Dr. South side of Main St Bridge. Int corridors. **Pets:** Accepted.

ASK Sₒ ✕ 🖪 🖵

▼▼ Extended Stay Deluxe-Butler Blvd-Jacksonville SH
(904) 332-6512. **$85-$95.** 4699 Lenoir Ave S. I-95, exit 344 (SR 202), just sw, then just n. Int corridors. **Pets:** Accepted.

ASK Sₒ ✕ 🖪 🖵 ⇌

▼▼▼ Extended Stay Deluxe (Jacksonville/Deerwood Park) SH
(904) 620-9008. **$90-$100.** 8801 Perimeter Park Blvd. I-95, exit 344 (SR 202), 2.5 mi e on J Turner Butler Blvd to Southside Blvd, then just n on west side of road. Int corridors. **Pets:** Accepted.

ASK Sₒ ✕ ⌕ᴹ ⌕ ⊙ 🖪 🖵 ⇌

▼▼▼ Holiday Inn Baymeadows SH
(904) 737-1700. **$89-$189.** 9150 Baymeadows Rd. I-95, exit 341, 0.3 mi e. Ext/int corridors. **Pets:** Accepted.

ASK Sₒ ✕ ⌕ 🖪 🖵 ⑪ ⇌

▼▼▼ Holiday Inn Express & Suites Jacksonville SH
(904) 696-3333. **$97-$189.** 10148 New Berlin Rd. I-95, exit 362A southbound, 4.9 mi s on SR 9A to Heckscher Dr, then just w; exit 358A northbound, 5.8 mi ne on Heckscher Dr; 0.6 mi from Jaxport Cruise Terminal. Int corridors. **Pets:** Accepted.

ASK Sₒ ✕ ⌕ 🖪 🖵 ⇌ ✕

▼▼▼ Homestead Studio Suites Hotel-Jacksonville/Baymeadows SH
(904) 739-1881. **$60-$85.** 8300 Western Way. I-95, exit 341, just e to Western Way, then just s. Int corridors. **Pets:** Accepted.

ASK Sₒ ✕ ⌕ ⊙ 🖪 🖵

▼▼▼ Homestead Studio Suites Hotel-Jacksonville/Southeast SH
(904) 296-0661. **$90-$105.** 4693 Jacksonville-Salisbury Rd S. I-95, exit 344 (SR 202), e on J Turner Butler Blvd, then just s. Int corridors. **Pets:** Accepted.

ASK Sₒ ✕ ⌕ᴹ ⌕ ⊙ 🖪 🖵 ⇌

▼▼ Homestead Studio Suites Hotel-Jacksonville/Southside M
(904) 642-9911. **$70-$80.** 10020 Skinner Lake Rd. I-95, exit 344 (SR 202), 3.5 mi e on J Turner Butler Blvd to Gate Pkwy, just n, then just w. Ext corridors. **Pets:** Accepted.

ASK Sₒ ✕ ⌕ᴹ ⌕ 🖪 🖵

▼▼▼ Homewood Suites by Hilton SH ❖
(904) 733-9299. **$95-$209.** 8737 Baymeadows Rd. I-95, exit 341, 0.3 mi w. Ext/int corridors. **Pets:** Medium, other species. $125 one-time fee/room. Service with restrictions, supervision.

ASK Sₒ ✕ 🖪 🖵 ⇌ ✕

▼▼▼ Homewood Suites by Hilton Jacksonville South/Town Center SH
(904) 641-7988. **Call for rates.** 10434 Midtown Pkwy. I-95, exit 344 (SR 202), 3.5 mi e on J Turner Butler Blvd to Gate Blvd, 0.3 mi n to Town Center Pkwy, 0.5 mi e to Midtown Pkwy, then 0.3 mi s. Int corridors. **Pets:** Small. $125 one-time fee/room. Service with restrictions, supervision.

✕ 🖪 🖵 ⇌ ✕

▼▼▼ Jameson Inn SH
(904) 296-0968. **$54-$120.** 7030 Bonneval Rd. I-95, exit 344 (SR 202), just w. Int corridors. **Pets:** Small. $10 daily fee/pet. Service with restrictions, crate.

ASK ✕ 🖪 🖵 ⇌

▼▼ ▼▼ **La Quinta Inn & Suites Jacksonville** SH
(904) 268-9999. **$81-$115.** 3199 Hartley Rd. I-295, exit 5A northbound; exit 5 southbound at SR 13. Int corridors. **Pets:** Medium. Service with restrictions.

ASK ✕ 🐾 🛏 💻 ➰

▼▼ ▼▼ **La Quinta Inn & Suites Jacksonville (Butler Blvd)** SH
(904) 296-0703. **$96-$166.** 4686 Lenoir Ave S. I-95, exit 344 (SR 202), just sw, then just nw. Int corridors. **Pets:** Medium. Service with restrictions.

ASK ✕ &M 🐾 🐾 🛏 💻 ➰

▼▼ ▼▼ **La Quinta Inn Jacksonville (Airport/North)** SH
(904) 751-6960. **$91-$126.** 812 Dunn Ave. I-95, exit 360, southwest corner. Ext corridors. **Pets:** Medium. Service with restrictions.

ASK ✕ 🐾 🛏 💻 ➰

▼▼ ▼▼ **La Quinta Inn Jacksonville (Baymeadows)** M
(904) 731-9940. **$92-$139.** 8255 Dix Ellis Tr. I-95, exit 341, southwest corner. Ext corridors. **Pets:** Medium. Service with restrictions.

ASK ✕ 🛏 💻 ➰

▼▼ ▼▼ **La Quinta Inn Jacksonville (Orange Park)** SH
(904) 778-9539. **$91-$116.** 8555 Blanding Blvd. I-295, exit 12, just s on SR 21. Ext corridors. **Pets:** Medium. Service with restrictions.

ASK ✕ 🐾 🛏 💻 ➰

🐾🐾🐾 ▼▼ ▼▼ **Microtel Inn & Suites–Jacksonville** SH
(904) 281-2244. **$54-$64.** 4940 Mustang Rd. I-95, exit 344 (SR 202), just sw, then just nw. Int corridors. **Pets:** Accepted.

SAVE S🐾 ✕ &M 🐾 🛏

▼▼ **Motel 6 Jacksonville SW (Orange Park) #415** M
(904) 777-6100. **$45-$57.** 6107 Youngerman Cir. I-295, exit 12, just sw. Ext corridors. **Pets:** Medium, other species. Service with restrictions, supervision.

S🐾 ✕ ➰

🐾🐾🐾 ▼▼ ▼▼ **Omni Jacksonville Hotel** LH
(904) 355-6664. **$107-$350, 3 day notice.** 245 Water St. Corner of Pearl and Water sts; on northside of St. Johns River; downtown; adjacent to The Landing. Int corridors. **Pets:** Accepted.

SAVE S🐾 ✕ 🐾 🛏 💻 🍴 ➰

🐾🐾🐾 ▼▼ ▼▼ **Ramada Inn Conference Center** SH
(904) 268-8080. **$99.** 3130 Hartley Rd. I-295, exit 5A northbound; exit 5 southbound, just n on SR 13. Ext corridors. **Pets:** Medium, other species. $50 deposit/room, $20 one-time fee/room. Service with restrictions, supervision.

SAVE S🐾 ✕ 🐾 🛏 💻 🍴 ➰

▼▼ ▼▼ **Residence Inn by Marriott** SH
(904) 996-8900. **$125-$170.** 10551 Deerwood Park Blvd. I-95, exit 344 (SR 202), 3.5 mi e on J Turner Butler Blvd to Gate Blvd, just s, then just w. Int corridors. **Pets:** Other species. $75 one-time fee/room.

ASK S🐾 ✕ &M 🐾 🐾 🛏 💻 ➰ ✕

🐾🐾🐾 ▼▼ ▼▼ **Residence Inn by Marriott** SH
(904) 733-8088. **$79-$500.** 8365 Dix Ellis Tr. I-95, exit 341 (SR 152), just w to Freedom Commerce Pkwy, then just s. Ext corridors. **Pets:** Medium, other species. $75 one-time fee/room. Service with restrictions.

SAVE ✕ 🐾 🐾 🛏 💻 ➰ ✕

JACKSONVILLE BEACH

🐾🐾🐾 ▼▼ ▼▼ **Hampton Inn Ponte Vedra at Jacksonville Beach** SH 🐾
(904) 280-9101. **$99-$169.** 1220 Marsh Landing Pkwy. Just s of J Turner Butler Blvd; east of Intracoastal Bridge. Int corridors. **Pets:** Medium. $75 one-time fee/pet. Service with restrictions, supervision.

SAVE ✕ &M 🐾 🐾 🛏 💻 ➰

🐾🐾🐾 ▼▼ ▼▼ **Quality Suites Oceanfront** SH 🐾
(904) 435-3535. **$179-$279.** 11 1st St N. Just n of Beach Blvd (US 90). Int corridors. **Pets:** Medium. $35 daily fee/pet. Service with restrictions, crate.

SAVE S🐾 ✕ 🛏 💻 ➰

ORANGE PARK

▼▼ ▼▼ **Comfort Inn** SH
(904) 644-4444. **$65-$95.** 341 Park Ave. I-295, exit 10 (US 17), just s. Ext corridors. **Pets:** Other species. $30 one-time fee/pet. Service with restrictions, supervision.

ASK S🐾 ✕ 🛏 💻 ➰

PONTE VEDRA BEACH

🐾🐾🐾 ▼▼ ▼▼ **The Sawgrass Marriott Resort & Beach Club** LH
(904) 285-7777. **$149-$299.** 1000 PGA Tour Blvd. 2.5 mi s of J Turner Butler Blvd. Ext/int corridors. **Pets:** $25 daily fee/room. Designated rooms, service with restrictions.

SAVE S🐾 ✕ 🛏 💻 🍴 ➰ ✕

YULEE

▼▼ ▼▼ **Comfort Inn** SH
(904) 225-2600. **$85-$99.** 76043 Sidney Pl. I-95, exit 373, just e on SR 200/A1A. Int corridors. **Pets:** Small. $20 daily fee/pet. Designated rooms, no service, supervision.

ASK S🐾 ✕ 🐾 🛏 💻 ➰

END METROPOLITAN AREA

JUNO BEACH

▼▼ ▼▼ **Holiday Inn Express-North Palm Beach** SH
(561) 622-4366. **$99-$159.** 13950 US Hwy 1. Jct Donald Ross Rd. Ext/int corridors. **Pets:** Other species. $10 daily fee/pet. Designated rooms, no service, supervision.

ASK S🐾 ✕ 🐾 🐾 🛏 💻 ➰

JUPITER

▼▼ ▼▼ ▼▼ **Fairfield Inn & Suites by Marriott** SH
(561) 748-5252. **$89-$199.** 6748 W Indiantown Rd. I-95, exit 87A, 0.8 mi e on SR 706 (Indiantown Rd). Int corridors. **Pets:** Medium. $50 one-time fee/pet. Service with restrictions, crate.

ASK S🐾 ✕ 🐾 🛏 💻 ➰

LAKE CITY

Best Western Lake City Inn SH
(386) 752-3801. **$65-$110.** 3598 W Hwy 90. I-75, exit 427, just w. Ext corridors. **Pets:** Medium, other species. $10 daily fee/pet. Designated rooms, service with restrictions, supervision.

Days Inn I-10 SH
(386) 758-4224. **$65-$120.** 3430 N Hwy 441. I-10, exit 303, just s. Ext corridors. **Pets:** $10 daily fee/pet. Service with restrictions, supervision.

Driftwood Inn M
(386) 755-3545. **$40-$70.** 2764 W Hwy 90. I-75, exit 427, 0.7 mi e. Ext corridors. **Pets:** Small, dogs only. $10 daily fee/pet. Designated rooms, no service, supervision.

Jameson Inn SH
(386) 758-8440. **$54-$120.** 285 SW Commerce Blvd. I-75, exit 427, just e, then just s. Int corridors. **Pets:** Small. $10 daily fee/pet. Service with restrictions, crate.

Rodeway Inn M
(386) 755-5203. **$50-$66.** 205 SW Commerce Dr. I-75, exit 427, just e. Ext corridors. **Pets:** Accepted.

LAKELAND

Comfort Inn & Suites SH
(863) 859-0100. **$80-$160.** 3520 Hwy US 98. I-4, exit 32, just nw; at Lakeland Square Mall. Int corridors. **Pets:** Accepted.

Holiday Inn Lakeland Hotel & Conference Center SH
(863) 688-8080. **$80-$100.** 3260 US Hwy 98 N. I-4, exit 32, just e. Int corridors. **Pets:** $25 one-time fee/pet. Designated rooms.

Jameson Inn SH
(863) 858-9070. **$54-$104.** 4375 Lakeland Park Dr. I-4, exit 33, just nw. Int corridors. **Pets:** Small. $10 daily fee/pet. Service with restrictions, crate.

Lakeland Residence Inn by Marriott SH ❖
(863) 680-2323. **$139-$199.** 3701 Harden Blvd. I-4, exit 27 (Polk Pkwy), se on SR 570 (toll road) to exit 5, then just n. Int corridors. **Pets:** Medium. $75 one-time fee/room. Service with restrictions, crate.

La Quinta Inn & Suites Lakeland SH
(863) 859-2866. **$110-$165.** 1024 Crevasse St. I-4, exit 32, just n on US 98. Int corridors. **Pets:** Medium. Service with restrictions.

La Quinta Inn & Suites Lakeland SH
(863) 815-0606. **$89-$159.** 4315 Lakeland Park Dr. I-4, exit 33; jct SR 33, just nw. Int corridors. **Pets:** Medium. Service with restrictions.

LAKE WORTH

Lago Motor Inn M
(561) 585-5246. **$80-$195, 14 day notice.** 714 S Dixie Hwy. I-95, exit 63, 0.7 mi e, then just s on US 1; US 1, just s of jct 6th Ave S. Ext corridors. **Pets:** Other species. $10 daily fee/pet. Designated rooms, service with restrictions, supervision.

LANTANA

Motel 6 Lantana #688 M
(561) 585-5833. **$55-$81.** 1310 W Lantana Rd. I-95, exit 61 (SR 812), just e, then s. Ext corridors. **Pets:** Medium, other species. Service with restrictions, supervision.

LIVE OAK

Econo Lodge SH
(386) 362-7459. **$62-$85.** 6811 N US 129 & I-10. I-10, exit 283, just s. Ext corridors. **Pets:** Large, other species. $10 one-time fee/pet. Service with restrictions, supervision.

Suwannee River Best Western Inn SH
(386) 362-6000. **$45-$150, 7 day notice.** 6819 US 129 N. I-10, exit 283, 0.3 mi s. Ext corridors. **Pets:** Very small, other species. $10 daily fee/pet. Service with restrictions, supervision.

LONGBOAT KEY

Cedars Tennis Resort CO
(941) 383-4621. **$800-$2075 (weekly), 90 day notice.** 645 Cedars Ct. Just e of jct SR 789 (Gulf of Mexico Dr), on Campanion Way. Ext corridors. **Pets:** Accepted.

Riviera Beach Resort M
(941) 383-2552. **$139-$249, 30 day notice.** 5451 Gulf of Mexico Dr. On SR 789, 5 mi se of jct SR 684 (Cortez Rd). Ext corridors. **Pets:** Small, dogs only. $100 deposit/pet, $10 daily fee/pet. No service.

LYNN HAVEN

Wingate Inn SH ❖
(850) 248-8080. **$125-$150.** 2610 Lynn Haven Pkwy. Jct 23rd St, 2.3 mi n on SR 77. Int corridors. **Pets:** Small. $50 one-time fee/pet. Designated rooms, service with restrictions, supervision.

MACCLENNY

Econo Lodge M
(904) 259-3000. **$52-$85.** 151 Woodlawn Rd. I-10, exit 335, just s of jct SR 121. Ext corridors. **Pets:** Large, other species. $10 one-time fee/pet. Service with restrictions.

MARIANNA

Best Western Marianna Inn SH ❖
(850) 526-5666. **$50-$100.** 2086 Hwy 71 S. I-10, exit 142, 0.3 mi s. Ext corridors. **Pets:** Other species. $10 deposit/pet. Service with restrictions, supervision.

Quality Inn SH
(850) 526-5600. **$59-$99.** 2175 Hwy 71 S. I-10, exit 142, just n. Ext corridors. **Pets:** Accepted.

MELBOURNE

Crane Creek Inn Waterfront Bed & Breakfast BB ❖
(321) 768-6416. **$139-$199, 14 day notice.** 907 E Melbourne Ave. Jct US 192, just s on Babcock, then 0.9 mi e. Ext/int corridors. **Pets:** Dogs only. $10 daily fee/pet. Supervision.

▼▼ ▼▼ **Extended Stay Deluxe Melbourne-Airport** 🆂🅷
(321) 733-6050. **$95-$120.** 1701 Evans Rd. I-95, exit 180 (US 192), 3 mi e, then 0.3 mi n. Int corridors. **Pets:** Accepted.
🅰🆂🅺 🆂🅱 ✕ 🖉 🔋 🖥 🏊

▼▼ ▼▼ **Hilton Melbourne Rialto Place** 🆂🅷
(321) 768-0200. **$119-$269.** 200 Rialto Pl. 1 mi w of US 1, 0.8 mi n of US 192 via Airport Blvd. Int corridors. **Pets:** $50 deposit/pet. Service with restrictions, supervision.
🆂🅱 ✕ 🕭M 🖉 🖉 🔋 🖥 🍴 🏊 ✕

▼▼ ▼▼ **La Quinta Inn & Suites Melbourne** 🆂🅷
(321) 242-9400. **$125-$195.** 7200 George T Edwards Dr. I-95, exit 191 (CR 509), just w. Int corridors. **Pets:** Medium. Service with restrictions.
🅰🆂🅺 ✕ 🖉 🖉 🔋 🖥 🏊

▼▼ ▼▼ **Wisteria Inn Bed & Breakfast** 🅱🅱
(321) 727-0717. **$109-$149, 14 day notice.** 1924 Catterton Dr. I-95, exit 180 (US 192), 4.5 mi e on US 192, then just n. Int corridors. **Pets:** Accepted.
✕ 🔋 🖥

MIAMI-MIAMI BEACH METROPOLITAN AREA

AVENTURA

🅰🅰🅰 ▼▼▼ ▼▼▼ **The Fairmont Turnberry Isle Resort & Club** 🅻🅷 ❀
(305) 932-6200. **$169-$709, 3 day notice.** 19999 W Country Club Dr. 0.5 mi w of SR A1A via SR 856; from US 1 at NE 199th St and Biscayne Blvd. Ext/int corridors. **Pets:** Small. $25 daily fee/pet. Service with restrictions, crate.
🆂🅰🆅🅴 🆂🅱 ✕ 🖉 🖉 🔋 🖥 🍴 🏊 ✕

🅰🅰🅰 ▼▼▼▼ **Residence Inn by Marriott-Aventura Mall** 🆂🅷 ❀
(786) 528-1001. **$199-$899.** 19900 W Country Club Dr. 0.5 mi w of SR A1A via SR 856; from US 1 at NE 199th St and Biscayne Blvd. Int corridors. **Pets:** Large, other species. $75 one-time fee/pet. Service with restrictions, supervision.
🆂🅰🆅🅴 🆂🅱 ✕ 🕭M 🖉 🖉 🔋 🖥 🏊

COCONUT GROVE

🅰🅰🅰 ▼▼▼ ▼▼▼ **Grand Bay-Miami** 🆂🅷 ❀
(305) 858-9600. **$129-$1500.** 2669 S Bayshore Dr. On Water Front Dr. Int corridors. **Pets:** Other species. $50 one-time fee/pet. Designated rooms, service with restrictions, crate.
🆂🅰🆅🅴 🆂🅱 ✕ 🕭M 🖉 🔋 🖥 🍴 🏊 ✕

▼▼▼ ▼▼▼ **Mayfair Hotel & Spa** 🆂🅷
(305) 441-0000. **$159-$399.** 3000 Florida Ave. At Florida Ave and Virginia St; center. Ext/int corridors. **Pets:** Accepted.
🅰🆂🅺 🆂🅱 ✕ 🖉 🖉 🔋 🖥 🍴 🏊 ✕

▼▼▼ ▼▼▼ **Residence Inn by Marriott** 🆂🅷
(305) 285-9303. **$123-$229.** 2835 Tigertail Ave. S Bayshore Dr, w on SW 27th Ave/Cornelia Dr, then s; in CocoWalk and May Fair Shops. Ext corridors. **Pets:** Accepted.
🅰🆂🅺 🆂🅱 ✕ 🖉 🔋 🖥 🏊

CORAL GABLES

▼▼▼ ▼▼▼ **The Biltmore Hotel Coral Gables** 🅻🅷
(305) 445-1926. **$234-$369.** 1200 Anastasia Ave. 1 mi w of Le Jeune Rd. Int corridors. **Pets:** Accepted.
✕ 🖉 🔋 🍴 🏊 ✕

▼▼ ▼▼ **Extended StayAmerica-Miami-Coral Gables** 🆂🅷
(305) 443-7444. **$89-$134.** 3640 Coral Way/SW 22nd St. Just e of Douglas Rd. Int corridors. **Pets:** Accepted.
🅰🆂🅺 🆂🅱 ✕ 🕭M 🔋 🖥

CUTLER RIDGE

🅰🅰🅰 ▼▼▼▼ **Best Western Floridian Hotel** 🆂🅷
(305) 253-9960. **$79-$139.** 10775 Caribbean Blvd. Florida Tpke, exit 12 (US 1), then w. Ext corridors. **Pets:** Accepted.
🆂🅰🆅🅴 🆂🅱 ✕ 🔋 🖥 🍴 🏊

▼▼▼ ▼▼▼ **La Quinta Inn & Suites Miami-Cutler Ridge** 🆂🅷
(305) 278-0001. **$85-$155.** 10821 Caribbean Blvd. Florida Tpke, exit 12 (US 1), northwest corner. Int corridors. **Pets:** Medium. Service with restrictions.
🅰🆂🅺 ✕ 🕭M 🖉 🖉 🔋 🖥 🏊

FLORIDA CITY

🅰🅰🅰 ▼▼ ▼▼ **Coral Roc Motel** 🅼
(305) 246-2888. **$42-$139, 3 day notice.** 1100 N Krome Ave. On SR 997; just w of US 1; 0.5 mi s of Homestead. Ext corridors. **Pets:** Medium, dogs only. $50 deposit/pet. Service with restrictions, supervision.
🆂🅰🆅🅴 🆂🅱 ✕ 🔋 🏊

▼▼ ▼▼ **Hampton Inn** 🅼
(305) 247-8833. **$120-$145.** 124 E Palm Dr. On US 1, 0.3 mi s of Florida Tpke terminus. Ext corridors. **Pets:** Accepted.
🅰🆂🅺 🆂🅱 ✕ 🖉 🔋 🖥 🏊

🅰🅰🅰 ▼▼ ▼▼ **Travelodge** 🅼
(305) 248-9777. **$69-$199, 30 day notice.** 409 SE 1st Ave. On US 1, just s of Florida Tpke terminus. Ext corridors. **Pets:** $10 daily fee/pet. Designated rooms, service with restrictions, supervision.
🆂🅰🆅🅴 🆂🅱 ✕ 🕭M 🖉 🖉 🔋 🖥 🏊

HIALEAH GARDENS

🅰🅰🅰 ▼▼▼ ▼▼▼ **Howard Johnson Plaza Hotel & Conference Center-Miami Airport** 🅻🅷
(305) 825-1000. **$89-$349.** 7707 NW 103rd St. SR 826 (Palmetto Expwy), exit NW 103rd St, just w. Int corridors. **Pets:** Accepted.
🆂🅰🆅🅴 🆂🅱 ✕ 🔋 🖥 🍴 🏊 ✕

HOMESTEAD

🅰🅰🅰 ▼▼ **Everglades Motel** 🅼
. **$32-$129.** 605 S Krome Ave. Just w of US 1; between Lucy and 6th sts; on SR 997, 0.5 mi s of center of town. Ext corridors. **Pets:** Accepted.
🆂🅰🆅🅴 🆂🅱 ✕ 🔋 🏊

KENDALL

🅰🅰🅰 ▼▼ ▼▼ **Country Inn & Suites Miami/Kendall** 🆂🅷
(305) 270-0359. **$110-$400.** 11750 Mills Dr. Florida Tpke, exit 20 (SW 88th/Kendall Dr), 0.3 mi e on SR 94, then 0.3 mi n on SW 117th Ave. Int corridors. **Pets:** Accepted.
🆂🅰🆅🅴 🆂🅱 ✕ 🕭M 🖉 🖉 🔋 🖥 🏊

KEY BISCAYNE

🅰🅰🅰 ▼▼▼ ▼▼▼ **The Ritz-Carlton, Key Biscayne** 🅻🅷
(305) 365-4500. **$309-$4000.** 455 Grand Bay Dr. Crandon Blvd, just e. Int corridors. **Pets:** Accepted.
🆂🅰🆅🅴 ✕ 🔋 🍴 🏊 ✕

MIAMI

▼▼ America's Best Inn-Miami Airport M
(305) 592-5440. **$69-$99.** 7330 NW 36th St. Just e of jct SR 826 (Palmetto Expwy). Int corridors. **Pets:** Accepted.

◆◆◆◆ Candlewood Suites Miami Airport West SH
(305) 591-9099. **$105-$246.** 8855 NW 27th St. SR 826 (Palmetto Expwy), 0.8 mi w on nw 36th St, 0.4 mi s. Int corridors. **Pets:** Large. $75 one-time fee/room. Service with restrictions, crate.

▼▼ Clarion Collection Las Palmas Hotel & Suites SH
(305) 592-4799. **$79-$269.** 8436 NW 36th St. 0.8 mi w of jct SR 826 (Palmetto Expwy). Int corridors. **Pets:** Accepted.

▼▼ Extended StayAmerica-Airport at Doral SH
(786) 331-7717. **$84-$124.** 8655 NW 21 Terrace. SR 836 (Dolphin Expwy), exit 87th Ave NW, then just n. Int corridors. **Pets:** Accepted.

▼▼ Extended StayAmerica-Miami-Brickell-Port of Miami SH
(305) 856-3700. **$74-$144.** 298 SW 15th Rd/Broadway Rd. I-95, exit 1B (SW 7th St) to SW 8th St, then e, s on SW 2nd Ave, then w. Int corridors. **Pets:** Accepted.

▼▼ Extended Stay Deluxe-Miami Airport SH
(305) 716-9005. **$94-$124.** 7750 NW 25th St. From SR 836, exit NW 25th St, then w; turn into The Shoppes at MICC Center. Int corridors. **Pets:** Accepted.

◆◆◆ ▼▼▼▼▼ Four Seasons Hotel Miami LH ❀
(305) 358-3535. **$350-$3500.** 1435 Brickell Ave. On US 1 (Brickell Ave) and 14th St. Int corridors. **Pets:** Small. Service with restrictions, supervision.

▼▼ Homestead Studio Suites Hotel-Miami/Airport at Doral M
(305) 436-1811. **$84-$124.** 8720 NW 33rd St. SR 826 (Palmetto Expwy), 0.8 mi w on NW 36th St, just s. Ext corridors. **Pets:** Accepted.

▼▼ Homestead Studio Suites Hotel–Miami Airport–Blue Lagoon M
(305) 260-0085. **$79-$124.** 6605 NW 7th St. SR 836 (Dolphin Expwy), exit Milam Dairy Rd S, 0.3 mi e; in Blue Lagoon Office Park. Ext corridors. **Pets:** Accepted.

◆◆◆◆ Homewood Suites by Hilton-Miami Airport/Blue Lagoon SH
(305) 261-3335. **$119-$199.** 5500 Blue Lagoon Dr. Se of jct SR 836 (Dolphin Expwy), exit Red Rd. Int corridors. **Pets:** Accepted.

▼▼▼▼ La Quinta Inn & Suites Miami (Airport West) SH
(305) 436-0830. **$125-$195.** 8730 NW 27th St. SR 836 (Dolphin Expwy), just n on 87th NW Ave. Int corridors. **Pets:** Medium. Service with restrictions.

▼▼▼▼ La Quinta Inn Miami (Airport North) M
(305) 599-9902. **$95-$165.** 7401 NW 36th St. Just e of jct SR 826 (Palmetto Expwy). Ext corridors. **Pets:** Medium. Service with restrictions.

◆◆◆ ▼▼▼▼ Mandarin Oriental, Miami LH ❀
(305) 913-8288. **$415-$860.** 500 Brickell Key Dr. US 1 (Brickell Ave), just e on SE 8th St (Brickell Key Dr). Int corridors. **Pets:** Small. $100 deposit/room, $100 one-time fee/room. Supervision.

◆◆◆◆ Miami River Inn BB ❀
(305) 325-0045. **$69-$199, 3 day notice.** 118 SW South River Dr. I-95, exit 1B (SW 7th St), just w to SW 5th Ave, just n to SW 2nd St, then e. Ext/int corridors. **Pets:** $25 daily fee/room.

◆◆◆ ▼▼▼▼ Quality Inn-South at The Falls M
(305) 251-2000. **$98-$140.** 14501 S Dixie Hwy (US 1). US 1 at SW 145th St. Ext corridors. **Pets:** Medium, other species. $10 daily fee/room. Service with restrictions.

▼▼▼▼ Residence Inn by Marriott SH
(305) 591-2211. **$149-$299.** 1212 NW 82nd Ave. SR 836 (Dolphin Expwy), exit 87th Ave NW, just n to NW 82nd Ave, then e. Ext corridors. **Pets:** Accepted.

◆◆◆ ▼▼▼▼ Sofitel Miami LH
(305) 264-4888. **$339-$379.** 5800 Blue Lagoon Dr. Just sw of jct SR 836 (Dolphin Expwy), exit Red Rd. Int corridors. **Pets:** Accepted.

▼▼▼▼ Staybridge Suites Miami/Doral Area SH
(305) 500-9100. **$102-$159, 3 day notice.** 3265 NW 87th Ave. 0.4 mi s of jct NW 36th St. Int corridors. **Pets:** Small. $125 one-time fee/pet. Service with restrictions, supervision.

◆◆◆ ▼▼▼▼ Summerfield Suites-Miami Airport SH
(305) 269-1922. **$159-$259.** 5710 Blue Lagoon Dr. Se of jct SR 836 (Dolphin Expwy), exit Red Rd, just w. Int corridors. **Pets:** Accepted.

◆◆◆ ▼▼▼▼ TownePlace Suites by Marriott SH
(305) 718-4144. **$79-$249.** 10505 NW 36th St. Florida Tpke, exit 29, 1.2 mi e to 107th Ave, just s. Int corridors. **Pets:** Accepted.

MIAMI BEACH

▼▼▼▼ Cadet Hotel SH
(305) 672-6688. **$99-$225, 3 day notice.** 1701 James Ave. Just w of SR A1A (Collins Ave) on 17th St; corner of James Ave and 17th St. Int corridors. **Pets:** Accepted.

▼▼▼▼ Casa Grande Suite Hotel SH
(305) 672-7003. **$215-$1500, 3 day notice.** 834 Ocean Dr. E of SR A1A (Collins Ave) and 8th St. Int corridors. **Pets:** Accepted.

▼▼▼▼ Century Hotel SH
(305) 674-8855. **$100-$250, 7 day notice.** 140 Ocean Dr. Just e of SR A1A (Collins Ave), just s of 2nd St. Int corridors. **Pets:** Accepted.

◆◆◆ ▼▼▼▼ Eden Roc Renaissance Resort & Spa LH
(305) 531-0000. **$179-$450, 3 day notice.** 4525 Collins Ave. SR A1A (Collins Ave), just n of 41st St. Int corridors. **Pets:** Accepted.

◆◆◆ ▼▼▼▼ Fontainebleau Resort LH
(305) 538-2000. **$199-$629, 3 day notice.** 4441 Collins Ave. On SR A1A. Int corridors. **Pets:** Accepted.

◆ **Greenview Hotel** [SH]
(305) 531-6588. **Call for rates.** 1671 Washington Ave. From Collins Ave (SR A1A), just e on Lincoln Rd, then just n. Int corridors. **Pets:** Accepted.

[AAA] ◆◆◆ **Hotel Ocean** [SH]
(305) 672-2579. **$230-$575, 3 day notice.** 1230 Ocean Dr. E of jct SR A1A (Collins Ave) and 12th St. Int corridors. **Pets:** Accepted.
[SAVE] [SD] ⊠ ▣

◆◆◆ **The Kent Hotel** [SH]
(305) 604-5068. **$140-$175, 3 day notice.** 1131 Collins Ave. On SR A1A, at Collins Ave and 11th St. Int corridors. **Pets:** Accepted.
[A$K] [SD] ⊠ 👂 ♿ ▣

[AAA] ◆◆◆◆ **Loews Miami Beach Hotel** [LH] 🐾
(305) 604-1601. **$189-$4000, 3 day notice.** 1601 Collins Ave. On SR A1A, at Collins and 16th aves. Int corridors. **Pets:** Large, other species. Service with restrictions.
[SAVE] ⊠ ♿M 👂 ♿ ▣ 🖥 🍴 🏊 🏋

◆◆◆ **The Marlin** [SH]
(305) 604-3595. **$135-$895, 14 day notice.** 1200 Collins Ave. On SR A1A, at Collins Ave and 12th St. Int corridors. **Pets:** Accepted.
[A$K] [SD] 👂 ▣ 🖥 🍴

[AAA] ◆◆◆ **Marriott South Beach** [LH]
(305) 536-7700. **$219-$519, 3 day notice.** 161 Ocean Dr. Just e of SR A1A (Collins Ave); just s of 2nd St. Int corridors. **Pets:** Accepted.
[SAVE] ⊠ 👂 ♿ ▣ 🖥 🍴 🏊 🏋

◆◆◆◆ **The Ritz-Carlton, South Beach** [LH]
(786) 276-4000. **$649-$5500, 3 day notice.** 1 Lincoln Rd. Jct SR A1A (Collins Ave) and Lincoln Rd. Int corridors. **Pets:** Accepted.
⊠ ♿M 👂 ♿ ▣ 🖥 🍴 🏊 🏋

◆◆◆◆ **The Setai** [SH]
(305) 520-6000. **Call for rates.** 2001 Collins Ave. On SR A1A (Collins Ave); at 20th St. Int corridors. **Pets:** Accepted.
⊠ ♿M 👂 ▣ 🖥 🍴 🏊 🏋

[AAA] ◆◆◆◆ **The Tides Hotel** [SH]
(305) 604-5070. **$350-$1100, 3 day notice.** 1220 Ocean Dr. E of jct SR A1A (Collins Ave) and 12th St. Int corridors. **Pets:** Accepted.
[SAVE] ⊠ ♿M 👂 ♿ ▣ 🍴 🏊

◆◆◆ **Villa Capri All Suites Hotel** [SH]
(305) 531-7742. **$170-$415, 3 day notice.** 3010 Collins Ave. On SR A1A (Collins Ave); at 30th St. Int corridors. **Pets:** Accepted.
[A$K] [SD] ⊠ ▣ 🖥 🍴 🏊

[AAA] ◆◆◆ **The Waldorf Towers Hotel** [SH]
(305) 531-7684. **$219.** 860 Ocean Dr. Corner of 8th St and Ocean Dr; just e of A1A (Collins Ave). Int corridors. **Pets:** Medium, dogs only. $20 daily fee/pet. Designated rooms, service with restrictions, crate.
[SAVE] ⊠ ▣ 🍴

MIAMI LAKES

◆◆ **La Quinta Inn & Suites** [SH]
(305) 821-8274. **$89-$219.** 7925 NW 154th St. Jct SR 826 (Palmetto Expwy), just w. Int corridors. **Pets:** Medium. Service with restrictions.
[A$K] ⊠ 👂 ♿ ▣ 🖥 🏊

[AAA] ◆◆◆ **TownePlace Suites by Marriott** [SH]
(305) 512-9191. **$109-$159.** 8079 NW 154th St. SR 826 (Palmetto Expwy), exit 154th St, 0.4 mi w. Int corridors. **Pets:** Small. $75 one-time fee/room. Service with restrictions, supervision.
[SAVE] [SD] ⊠ ▣ 🖥 🏊

MIAMI SPRINGS

[AAA] ◆◆◆ **Comfort Inn & Suites-Miami International Airport** [SH]
(305) 871-6000. **$149-$599.** 5301 NW 36th St. Between Le Jeune Rd and SR 826 (Palmetto Expwy). Int corridors. **Pets:** Accepted.
[SAVE] [SD] ⊠ 👂 ▣ 🖥 🍴 🏊 🏋

◆◆◆ **Homestead Studio Suites Hotel-Miami/Airport/Miami Springs** [SH]
(305) 870-0448. **$104-$144.** 101 Fairway Dr. I-95 to SR 112 W, exit NW 36th St, then w, right on Palmetto Dr, then w; between Le Jeune Rd and SR 826 (Palmetto Expwy); behind Clarion Hotel. Int corridors. **Pets:** Accepted.
[A$K] [SD] ⊠ 👂 ▣ 🖥 🏊

◆◆◆ **La Quinta Inn & Suites Miami-Airport** [SH]
(305) 871-1777. **$99-$179.** 3501 NW Le Jeune Rd. SR 953 (Le Jeune Rd) at jct SR 112. Int corridors. **Pets:** Medium. Service with restrictions.
[A$K] ⊠ 👂 ▣ 🖥 🏊

◆◆◆ **Red Roof Inn Miami Airport** [SH]
(305) 871-4221. **$80-$116.** 3401 NW Le Jeune Rd. On SR 953 at SR 112; 0.5 mi n of airport entrance. Int corridors. **Pets:** Medium, other species. Service with restrictions, supervision.
⊠ 👂 🏊

SUNNY ISLES BEACH

[AAA] ◆◆◆◆ **Le Meridien Sunny Isles Beach Miami** [CO] 🐾
(305) 503-6000. **$299-$679, 5 day notice.** 18683 Collins Ave. From north, just s from William Lehman Cswy, U-turn at 186th St, then just n; from south, SR 826, 1.3 mi n. Int corridors. **Pets:** Small, dogs only. $200 deposit/pet, $50 one-time fee/pet. Service with restrictions, supervision.
[SAVE] ⊠ 👂 ▣ 🖥 🍴 🏊 🏋

[AAA] ◆◆◆ **Newport Beachside Hotel & Resort** [LH]
(305) 949-1300. **$79-$439.** 16701 Collins Ave. SR A1A, jct SR 826 and Sunny Isles Blvd. Int corridors. **Pets:** Accepted.
[SAVE] [SD] 👂 ▣ 🖥 🍴 🏊 🏋

[AAA] ◆◆◆◆ **Trump International Sonesta Beach Resort** [LH]
(305) 692-5600. **$159-$409, 3 day notice.** 18001 Collins Ave. On SR A1A, just s of The William Lehman Cswy. Int corridors. **Pets:** Small, dogs only. $100 one-time fee/pet. Service with restrictions, supervision.
[SAVE] [SD] ⊠ ▣ 🖥 🍴 🏊 🏋

END METROPOLITAN AREA

MILTON

◆◆ **Comfort Inn** [SH]
(850) 623-1511. **$89-$149.** 8936 S Hwy 87. I-10, exit 31, just s. Int corridors. **Pets:** Accepted.
[A$K] [SD] ⊠ ▣ 🖥 🏊

◆◆ **Red Roof Inn & Suites** [SH]
(850) 995-6100. **$89-$110, 3 day notice.** 2672 Avalon Blvd. I-10, exit 22, just s. Int corridors. **Pets:** Medium, other species. Service with restrictions, supervision.
[A$K] [SD] ⊠ ♿M ♿ ▣ 🖥 🏊

MOSSY HEAD

▼▼ ▼▼ **Rodeway Inn** Ⓜ
(850) 951-9780. **$54-$70.** 326 Green Acres Dr. I-10, exit 70, just s. Ext corridors. **Pets:** $25 daily fee/pet. Service with restrictions, supervision.
⊠ 🖻 🍴

NAPLES

ⒶⒶⒶ ▼▼ ▼▼ **The Fairways Resort** Ⓜ
(239) 597-8181. **$75-$220, 3 day notice.** 103 Palm River Blvd. I-75, exit 111, 2.2 mi w on CR 846 (Immokalee Rd). Ext corridors. **Pets:** Small. $50 one-time fee/pet. Designated rooms, no service, supervision.
[SAVE] Ⓢⓓ ⊠ 🖻 🖳 ⊃

ⒶⒶⒶ ▼▼▼▼ **Hawthorn Suites of Naples** SH
(239) 593-1300. **$104-$339.** 3557 Pine Ridge Rd. I-75, exit 107, 0.5 mi w on CR 896. Int corridors. **Pets:** Accepted.
[SAVE] ⊠ Ⓜ 🐾 🦮 🖻 🖳 ⊃ ⊠

ⒶⒶⒶ ▼▼▼▼ **Holiday Inn** Ⓜ
(239) 263-3434. **$79-$179.** 1100 Tamiami Tr N. I-75, exit 107, 3.8 mi w on CR 896 (Pine Ridge Rd); 3.8 mi s on US 41. Ext corridors. **Pets:** Medium, other species. $20 daily fee/room. Designated rooms, service with restrictions, supervision.
[SAVE] Ⓢⓓ ⊠ 🖻 🖳 🍴 ⊃

▼▼▼▼ **Inn at Park Shore** SH
(239) 649-5500. **$79-$249, 3 day notice.** 4055 Tamiami Tr N. I-75, exit 107, 3.8 mi w on CR 896 (Pine Ridge Rd), then 1.1 3 s on US 41. Int corridors. **Pets:** Accepted.
[ASK] Ⓢⓓ ⊠ Ⓜ 🦮 🖻 🖳 ⊃

▼▼▼▼ **LaPlaya Beach & Golf Resort** LH
(239) 597-3123. **$279-$1450, 14 day notice.** 9891 Gulf Shore Dr. I-75, exit 111, 3.6 mi w on CR 846 (Immokalee Rd), 1.5 mi s on US 41 (Tamiami Trail), 1.3 mi w on Vanderbilt Beach Rd (CR 862), then 0.5 mi n. Ext/int corridors. **Pets:** Accepted.
[ASK] ⊠ 🦮 🖻 🖳 🍴 ⊃ ⊠

▼▼▼▼ **La Quinta Inn & Suties** SH
(239) 352-8400. **$105-$185.** 185 Bedzel Cir. I-75, exit 101, just w on SR 84 (Davis Blvd). Int corridors. **Pets:** Medium. Service with restrictions.
[ASK] ⊠ Ⓜ 🐾 🦮 🖻 🖳 ⊃

▼▼ ▼▼ **La Quinta Inns & Suites** SH
(239) 793-4646. **$109-$239.** 1555 5th Ave S. I-75, exit 101, 6.8 mi w on SR 84. Int corridors. **Pets:** Medium. Service with restrictions.
[ASK] ⊠ 🐾 🦮 🖻 🖳 ⊃

▼▼▼ **Red Roof Inn** SH
(239) 774-3117. **$50-$130.** 1925 Davis Blvd. I-75, exit 101, 6.4 mi w on SR 84; just e of jct US 41 (Tamiami Trail). Ext corridors. **Pets:** Medium, other species. Service with restrictions, supervision.
⊠ 🦮 🖻 🖳 ⊃

▼▼▼▼ **Residence Inn by Marriott, Naples** SH 🐾
(239) 659-1300. **$109-$399.** 4075 Tamiami Tr N. I-75, exit 107, 3.8 mi w on CR 896 (Pine Ridge Rd), then 1 mi s on US 41. Int corridors. **Pets:** Other species. $75 one-time fee/room. Service with restrictions.
[ASK] Ⓢⓓ ⊠ Ⓜ 🐾 🦮 🖻 🖳 ⊃ ⊠

ⒶⒶⒶ ▼▼▼▼▼ **The Ritz-Carlton Golf Resort** LH 🐾
(239) 593-2000. **$139-$2000, 14 day notice.** 2600 Tiburon Dr. I-75, exit 111, 1.6 mi w on CR 846 (Immokalee Rd), 1.3 mi s on CR 31 (Airport-Pulling Rd), then just e. Int corridors. **Pets:** Small. $150 one-time fee/room. Designated rooms, service with restrictions, supervision.
[SAVE] ⊠ Ⓜ 🐾 🦮 🖻 🖳 🍴 ⊃ ⊠

ⒶⒶⒶ ▼▼▼▼ **Staybridge Suites by Holiday Inn** SH
(239) 643-8002. **$90-$320, 3 day notice.** 4805 Tamiami Tr N. I-75, exit 107, 3.8 mi w on CR 896 (Pine Ridge Rd), then 0.9 mi s on US 41. Int corridors. **Pets:** Other species. $100 deposit/room, $150 one-time fee/room. Service with restrictions.
[SAVE] Ⓢⓓ ⊠ Ⓜ 🐾 🦮 🖻 🖳 ⊃

NEW SMYRNA BEACH

▼▼▼ **Buena Vista Inn** Ⓜ
(386) 428-5565. **$75-$95, 14 day notice.** 500 N Causeway. 2 mi e on SR Business Rt 44, at west end of North Causeway Bridge. Ext corridors. **Pets:** Accepted.
[ASK] Ⓢⓓ ⊠ 🖻 🖳 ⊠

ⒶⒶⒶ ▼▼▼▼ **Holiday Inn Hotel & Suites** SH
(386) 426-0020. **$140-$375.** 1401 S Atlantic Ave. SR A1A, s of SR 44. Int corridors. **Pets:** Accepted.
[SAVE] Ⓢⓓ ⊠ 🖻 🖳 🍴 ⊃

ⒶⒶⒶ ▼▼▼▼ **Longboard Inn** BB
(386) 428-3499. **$105-$130, 14 day notice.** 312 Washington St. 0.25 mi w of jct N Riverside Dr. Ext corridors. **Pets:** Accepted.
[SAVE] Ⓢⓓ ⊠ 🖻

ⒶⒶⒶ ▼▼▼▼ **Night Swan Intracoastal Bed & Breakfast** BB
(386) 423-4940. **$100-$225, 3 day notice.** 512 S Riverside Dr. Just s of SR 44 Intracoastal Waterway bridge; west side of Intracoastal Waterway. Ext/int corridors. **Pets:** Accepted.
[SAVE] Ⓢⓓ ⊠ 🦮 🖻 🖳 ⊠

NORTH FORT MYERS

ⒶⒶⒶ ▼▼ ▼▼ **Best Western Fort Myers Waterfront** SH
(239) 997-5511. **$89-$210.** 13021 N Cleveland Ave. On US 41, 0.6 mi s of SR 78A (Pondella Rd), jct N Bay Dr and Caloosahatchee Bridge. Ext corridors. **Pets:** Medium, dogs only. $35 one-time fee/pet. Designated rooms, service with restrictions, supervision.
[SAVE] ⊠ 🐾 🦮 🖻 🖳 🍴 ⊃ ⊠

ⒶⒶⒶ ▼▼ ▼▼ **Econo Lodge** Ⓜ
(239) 995-0571. **$49-$149.** 13301 N Cleveland Ave. On US 41, 1.1 mi n of Caloosahatchee Bridge. Ext corridors. **Pets:** $6 daily fee/pet. Service with restrictions.
[SAVE] ⊠ 🖻 🖳 ⊃

OCALA

ⒶⒶⒶ ▼▼ ▼▼ **Budget Host Inn** Ⓜ
(352) 732-6940. **$45-$92.** 4013 NW Bonnie Heath Blvd. I-75, exit 354, 0.3 mi n on US 27. Ext corridors. **Pets:** Medium, other species. $10 daily fee/pet. Service with restrictions, supervision.
[SAVE] Ⓢⓓ ⊠ 🖻

ⒶⒶⒶ ▼▼ ▼▼ **Comfort Inn** SH
(352) 629-8850. **$68-$150.** 4040 W Silver Springs Blvd. I-75, exit 352, just w on SR 40. Ext corridors. **Pets:** Accepted.
[SAVE] Ⓢⓓ ⊠ 🖻 🖳 ⊃

ⒶⒶⒶ ▼▼ **Days Inn** SH
(352) 629-7041. **$56-$110.** 3811 NW Bonnie Heath Blvd. I-75, exit 354, just n on US 27. Ext/int corridors. **Pets:** $5 daily fee/pet. Service with restrictions, supervision.
[SAVE] Ⓢⓓ ⊠ 🖻 🖳 ⊃

▼▼ ▼▼ **Days Inn** SH
(352) 629-0091. **$59-$129.** 3620 W Silver Springs Blvd. I-75, exit 352, just e. Ext/int corridors. **Pets:** $10 daily fee/pet. Service with restrictions.
[ASK] Ⓢⓓ ⊠ 🖳 ⊃

▼▼▼▼ **Hilton Ocala** LH
(352) 854-1400. **$99-$229.** 3600 SW 36th Ave. I-75, exit 350, 0.3 mi n on SR 200. Int corridors. **Pets:** Accepted.
[ASK] Ⓢⓓ ⊠ 🐾 🖻 🖳 🍴 ⊃

ⒶⒶⒶ ▼▼▼▼ **Howard Johnson Inn & Restaurant** Ⓜ
(352) 629-7021. **$50-$200.** 3951 NW Bonnie Heath Blvd. I-75, exit 354, just w. Ext corridors. **Pets:** Other species. $20 daily fee/pet. Service with restrictions, supervision.
[SAVE] Ⓢⓓ ⊠ 🖻 🖳 🍴 ⊃ ⊠

▼▼▼▼ La Quinta Inn & Suites Ocala SH
(352) 861-1137. **$105-$185.** 3530 SW 36th Ave. I-75, exit 350, just e on SR 200. Int corridors. **Pets:** Medium. Service with restrictions.

(ASK) ⊠ 🔊 ② 🛏 🛋 ➿

△△△ ▼▼▼ Quality Inn Ocala Hotel and Conference Center SH ❀
(352) 629-0381. **$60-$145.** 3621 W Silver Springs Blvd. I-75, exit 352, just e on SR 40. Ext corridors. **Pets:** Small. $10 daily fee/pet. Service with restrictions, supervision.

(SAVE) 🔊 ⊠ 🛏 🛋 ¶¶ ➿

△△△ ▼▼▼▼ Red Roof Inn & Suites SH
(352) 732-4590. **$70-$130.** 120 NW 40th Ave. I-75, exit 352, just w. Int corridors. **Pets:** Medium, other species. Service with restrictions, supervision.

(SAVE) 🔊 ⊠ 🛏 🛋 ➿

▼▼▼▼ Seven Sisters Inn BB ❀
(352) 867-1170. **$119-$279.** 820 SE Fort King St. Just s of jct SR 40 on SE Winona Ave; in downtown historic district. Int corridors. **Pets:** Medium. $35 one-time fee/pet. Designated rooms, service with restrictions, supervision.

⊠ 🛋 🛋

△△△ ▼▼▼ Steinbrenner's Ramada Inn & Conference Center SH
(352) 732-3131. **$79-$139.** 3810 NW Bonnie Heath Blvd. I-75, exit 354, just w. Ext corridors. **Pets:** Medium. $25 one-time fee/room. Designated rooms, service with restrictions, supervision.

(SAVE) 🔊 ⊠ 🛏 🛋 ¶¶ ➿ ⊠

OKEECHOBEE

△△△ ▼▼ Budget Inn M
(863) 763-3185. **$89-$185.** 201 S Parrott Ave (US 441). US 98 and 441, just s of jct SR 70. Ext corridors. **Pets:** Accepted.

(SAVE) 🔊 ⊠ 🛏 ➿

△△△ ▼▼ Economy Inn M
(863) 763-1148. **$59-$129, 3 day notice.** 507 N Parrott Ave. US 441, 0.3 mi n of jct SR 70. Ext corridors. **Pets:** Very small. $10 daily fee/pet. Service with restrictions, supervision.

(SAVE) 🔊 ⊠ 🛏

OLD TOWN

△△△ ▼▼▼ Suwanee Gables Motel M ❀
(352) 542-7752. **$85-$99, 7 day notice.** 27659 SE Hwy 19, Alt 27. US 19, 98 and 27A; 2 mi s of jct SR 349. Ext corridors. **Pets:** Medium, other species. $12 daily fee/pet. Service with restrictions, supervision.

(SAVE) 🔊 ⊠ 🛏 ➿

ORANGE CITY

△△△ ▼▼▼ Comfort Inn M
(386) 775-7444. **$79-$225, 30 day notice.** 445 S Volusia Ave. I-4, exit 114, 2.8 mi w on SR 472, then 2 mi s on US 17-92. Ext corridors. **Pets:** Medium. $25 deposit/room, $15 daily fee/pet. Service with restrictions, crate.

(SAVE) 🔊 ⊠ 🛏 🛋 ➿

△△△ ▼▼▼ Days Inn M
(386) 775-4522. **$60-$250, 7 day notice.** 2501 N Volusia Ave. I-4, exit 114, 2.8 mi w on SR 472, then 0.3 mi s on US 17-92. Ext corridors. **Pets:** Small. $25 one-time fee/pet. Designated rooms, no service, supervision.

(SAVE) 🔊 ⊠ 🛏 🛋 ➿

ORLANDO METROPOLITAN AREA

ALTAMONTE SPRINGS

▼▼▼▼ Candlewood Suites SH
(407) 767-5757. **$79-$99.** 644 Raymond Ave. I-4, exit 92, just w to Douglas Ave, 0.8 mi n to Central Pkwy, then just e. Int corridors. **Pets:** Accepted.

(ASK) 🔊 ⊠ 🗚 ② 🛏 🛋 ➿

△△△ ▼▼▼ Days Inn Altamonte Springs SH
(407) 788-1411. **$50-$150, 3 day notice.** 150 S Westmonte Dr. I-4, exit 92, 0.3 mi w on SR 436, then just s. Ext corridors. **Pets:** Other species. $10 daily fee/pet. Designated rooms, no service, crate.

(SAVE) 🔊 ⊠ ② 🛏 🛋 ➿

△△△ ▼▼▼▼ Embassy Suites Orlando North SH ❀
(407) 834-2400. **$115-$229.** 225 Shorecrest Dr. I-4, exit 92, 0.3 mi e on SR 436, then just n on North Lake Blvd. Int corridors. **Pets:** Large, other species. $20 daily fee/pet. Designated rooms, service with restrictions, crate.

(SAVE) ⊠ 🗚 ② 🛏 🛋 ¶¶ ➿ ⊠

△△△ ▼▼▼▼ Holiday Inn Orlando North/Altamonte Springs SH
(407) 862-4455. **$79-$129.** 230 W SR 436. I-4, exit 92, just sw. Ext/int corridors. **Pets:** Accepted.

(SAVE) 🔊 ⊠ 🗚 ② 🛏 🛋 ¶¶ ➿

▼▼▼▼ Homestead Studio Suites Hotel-Orlando/Altamonte Springs SH
(407) 332-9300. **$74-$84.** 302 S North Lake Blvd. I-4, exit 92, just e, then 0.3 mi s. Int corridors. **Pets:** Accepted.

(ASK) 🔊 ⊠ 🗚 ② 🛏 🛋

▼▼▼▼ Residence Inn by Marriott SH
(407) 788-7991. **$99-$299.** 270 Douglas Ave. I-4, exit 92, just w on SR 436, then just n. Ext corridors. **Pets:** Medium. $75 one-time fee/room. Service with restrictions, supervision.

(ASK) 🔊 ⊠ 🗚 ② 🛏 🛋 ➿ ⊠

DAVENPORT

△△△ ▼▼▼▼ Best Western Main Gate South SH
(863) 424-2596. **$59-$129.** 2425 Frontage Rd. I-4, exit 55, just s on US 27. Ext corridors. **Pets:** Accepted.

(ASK) 🔊 ⊠ 🗚 ② 🛏 🛋 ➿

▼▼▼▼ Calabay Parc-The Florida Store VH
(407) 846-1722. **$89-$399, 30 day notice.** 215 Orista Dr. I-4, exit 68, 3.5 mi s on SR 535, then 3.8 mi e on US 192. Ext corridors. **Pets:** Medium. $150 one-time fee/pet. No service, crate.

(ASK) 🔊 ⊠ 🛏 🛋 ➿

▼▼▼▼ Hampton Inn Orlando-S of Walt Disney World Resorts SH
(863) 420-9898. **$89-$189.** 44117 Hwy 27. I-4, exit 55, just nw. Int corridors. **Pets:** Accepted.

(ASK) 🔊 ⊠ 🗚 ② 🛏 🛋 ➿

▼▼▼▼ Highlands Reserve-Superior Resorts VH
(863) 424-6141. **$149-$239, 3 day notice.** 2700 Sand Mine Rd. 0.5 mi s of jct US 27 and 192. Ext corridors. **Pets:** Accepted.

(ASK) 🔊 🛏 🛋 ➿ ⊠

Omni Orlando Resort at ChampionsGate LH 🐾
(407) 390-6664. **$179-$309, 3 day notice.** 1500 Masters Blvd. I-4, exit 58, 0.3 mi w. Int corridors. **Pets:** Small, other species. $50 one-time fee/room. Designated rooms, service with restrictions, crate.

Southern Dunes-The Florida Store VH
(407) 846-1722. **$89-$399, 30 day notice.** 3479 Hemingway Dr. I-4, exit 68, 3.5 mi s on SR 535, then 3.8 mi e on US 192. Ext corridors. **Pets:** Medium. $150 one-time fee/pet. No service, crate.

Super 8 Motel Maingate South SH
(863) 420-8888. **$39-$149.** 44199 Hwy 27. I-4, exit 55, 0.5 mi n. Ext corridors. **Pets:** Accepted.

KISSIMMEE

Best Western Maingate East Hotel & Suites SH
(407) 870-2000. **$79-$129, 3 day notice.** 4018 W Vine St. I-4, exit 64A, 7 mi e on US 192. Ext corridors. **Pets:** Medium. $50 one-time fee/room. Designated rooms, service with restrictions, supervision.

Country Inn & Suites at Calypso Cay SH
(407) 997-1400. **$99-$179.** 5001 Calypso Cay Way. I-4, exit 68, 3 mi s on SR 535; just s of Osceola Pkwy; just n of US 192. Int corridors. **Pets:** Small. $10 daily fee/pet. Service with restrictions, supervision.

Days Inn Maingate East SH
(407) 396-7969. **$59-$129.** 5840 W Irlo Bronson Memorial Hwy. I-4, exit 64A, 1 mi e on US 192. Ext corridors. **Pets:** Accepted.

Fantasy World Club Villas CO
(407) 396-8530. **$99-$195.** 5005 Kyngs Heath Rd. I-4, exit 64A, 3.5 mi e on US 192 and just n; at MM 11. Ext corridors. **Pets:** Accepted.

Flamingo Inn M
(407) 846-1935. **$28-$38, 3 day notice.** 801 E Vine St. 0.3 mi e of jct US 441 and 192 on US 192. Ext corridors. **Pets:** Small, dogs only. $8 daily fee/pet. Service with restrictions.

Hampton Lakes-The Florida Store VH
(407) 846-1722. **$89-$399, 30 day notice.** 740 Bloomingdale Dr. I-4, exit 68, 3.5 mi s on SR 535, then 3.8 mi e on US 192. Ext corridors. **Pets:** Medium. $150 one-time fee/pet. No service, crate.

Howard Johnson Enchantedland Hotel SH
(407) 396-4343. **$39-$99.** 4985 W Irlo Bronson Memorial Hwy. I-4, exit 64A, 3.2 mi e on US 192. Ext corridors. **Pets:** Small. $10 daily fee/pet. Designated rooms, service with restrictions, crate.

Howard Johnson Maingate Resort West LH 🐾
(407) 396-4500. **$59-$129.** 8660 W Irlo Bronson Memorial Hwy. I-4, exit 64B, 5.6 mi w on US 192. Ext corridors. **Pets:** Medium, other species. $35 one-time fee/room. Designated rooms, service with restrictions, supervision.

Indian Creek-The Florida Store VH
(407) 846-1722. **$89-$399, 30 day notice.** 8092 Santee Dr. I-4, exit 68, 3.5 mi s on SR 535, then 3.8 mi e on US 192. Ext corridors. **Pets:** Medium. $150 one-time fee/pet. No service, crate.

Lake Suites Hotel SH
(407) 997-2700. **$60-$127.** 4786 W Irlo Bronson Memorial Hwy. I-4, exit 64A, 4 mi e on US 192; 4.8 mi w of jct US 17-92 and 441. Ext corridors. **Pets:** Medium, other species. $100 one-time fee/room. Service with restrictions, supervision.

La Quinta Inn & Suites Kissimmee (Orlando Maingate) SH
(407) 997-1700. **$99-$179.** 3484 Polynesian Isle Blvd. I-4, exit 68, s on SR 535, then just e. Int corridors. **Pets:** Accepted.

Masters Inn-Kissimmee SH
(407) 396-4020. **$49-$59, 3 day notice.** 5367 W Irlo Bronson Memorial Hwy. I-4, exit 25, 2.5 mi e on US 192. Ext corridors. **Pets:** Small. $20 one-time fee/pet. Service with restrictions, crate.

Masters Inn-Main Gate SH
(407) 396-7743. **$31-$150, 3 day notice.** 2945 Entry Point Blvd. I-4, exit 25, 2.5 mi w on US 192; 1 mi w of Disney World main gate. Ext corridors. **Pets:** Small. $20 one-time fee/pet. Service with restrictions, crate.

Motel 6-#0436 SH
(407) 396-6422. **$41-$65.** 7455 W Irlo Bronson Memorial Hwy. I-4, exit 64B, 1.3 mi w on US 192. Ext corridors. **Pets:** Medium, other species. Service with restrictions, supervision.

Motel 6-#0464 M
(407) 396-6333. **$41-$65.** 5731 W Hwy 192. I-4, exit 64A, 2 mi e. Ext corridors. **Pets:** Medium, other species. Service with restrictions, supervision.

The Palms Hotel and Villas CO
(407) 396-2229. **$89-$129.** 3100 Parkway Blvd. I-4, exit 64A, 0.3 mi e on US 192, then 0.5 mi n. Ext/int corridors. **Pets:** Accepted.

Quality Suites Maingate East SH 🐾
(407) 396-8040. **$89-$299, 3 day notice.** 5876 W Irlo Bronson Memorial Hwy. I-4, exit 64A, 1 mi e on US 192. Ext corridors. **Pets:** Small, dogs only. $10 daily fee/pet. Designated rooms, service with restrictions, crate.

Radisson Resort WorldGate LH
(407) 396-1400. **$69-$99, 3 day notice.** 3011 Maingate Ln. US 192, 2.8 mi w of I-4, 1 mi w of Disney World main gate access road. Int corridors. **Pets:** Medium, other species. $50 one-time fee/room. Service with restrictions, crate.

Red Roof Inn SH
(407) 396-0065. **$39-$129.** 4970 Kyngs Heath Rd. I-4, exit 64A, 3.6 mi e on US 192; jct SR 535. Ext corridors. **Pets:** Designated rooms, supervision.

Rodeway Inn Eastgate M 🐾
(407) 396-1212. **$49-$109.** 4559 W Hwy 192. I-4, exit 68, 4 mi s on SR 535, then 3 mi e. Ext corridors. **Pets:** Small. $50 deposit/pet. Designated rooms, service with restrictions, supervision.

Rodeway Inn Maingate SH
(407) 396-4300. **$39-$94, 7 day notice.** 5995 W Irlo Bronson Memorial Hwy. I-4, exit 64A, 1 mi e. Ext corridors. **Pets:** Accepted.

△△△ ▽▽▽▽ Seralago Hotel & Suites Main Gate East 🅂🄷
(407) 396-4488. **$59-$119.** 5678 W Irlo Bronson Memorial Hwy. I-4, exit 64A; between MM 9 and 10. Ext corridors. **Pets:** Medium, other species. $40 one-time fee/room. Service with restrictions, crate.

🆂🄰🆅🄴 🆂🄳 ☒ ⊗ 🗎 🖥 ▤ 🖥 🍴 ➳ ☒

▽▽▽▽ Ventura Resort Rentals 🅅🄷
(407) 273-8770. **$96-$291.** 4008 San Gallo Dr. 0.6 mi e of SR 436. Ext corridors. **Pets:** Accepted.

🄰🆂🄺 🆂🄳 ⊗ 🗎 🖥 ➳

△△△ ▽▽▽ Westgate Inn 🅂🄷
(863) 424-2621. **$59-$99.** 9200 W US Hwy 192. I-4, exit 64B, 6 mi w. Ext corridors. **Pets:** Accepted.

🆂🄰🆅🄴 🆂🄳 ☒ 🗎 🖥 ➳

▽▽▽▽ Wonderland Inn 🄼 🐾
(407) 847-2477. **$79-$159.** 3601 S Orange Blossom Tr. US 192, 3 mi s on US 17-92 (John Young Pkwy/Bermuda Ave). Ext corridors. **Pets:** Designated rooms.

🄰🆂🄺 🆂🄳 ☒ 🗎 🖥

LADY LAKE

△△△ ▽▽▽▽ Comfort Suites in the Villages 🅂🄷
(352) 259-6578. **$99-$159.** 1202 Avenida Central N. Just n on US 441. Int corridors. **Pets:** Medium, dogs only. $35 one-time fee/room. Service with restrictions, supervision.

🆂🄰🆅🄴 🆂🄳 🗎 🖥 ➳

△△△ ▽▽▽▽ Holiday Inn Express Hotel & Suites 🅂🄷
(352) 750-3888. **$99-$135.** 1205 Avenida Central N. Just n on US 441. Int corridors. **Pets:** Small, dogs only. $35 one-time fee/room. Service with restrictions, supervision.

🆂🄰🆅🄴 🆂🄳 ☒ 🗎 🖥 ➳

▽▽ ▽▽ Microtel Inn & Suites 🅂🄷
(352) 259-0184. **$59-$89.** 850 US 27/441. 1 mi s. Int corridors. **Pets:** Medium. $25 one-time fee/pet. Designated rooms, service with restrictions, supervision.

🄰🆂🄺 ☒ 🗎 🖥 ➳

LAKE BUENA VISTA

△△△ ▽▽▽▽ Blue Tree Resort at Lake Buena Vista-Westgate Resorts 🄲🄾
(407) 597-2200. **$89-$259, 7 day notice.** 12007 Cypress Run Rd. I-4, exit 68, 0.5 mi n on SR 535, just n on Apopka Vineland Rd, then just e on Vinings Way Blvd. Ext corridors. **Pets:** Accepted.

🆂🄰🆅🄴 ☒ 🗎 ⊗ 🖥 🖥 ➳ ☒

△△△ ▽▽▽▽ Buena Vista Suites 🅂🄷
(407) 239-8588. **$109-$159.** 8203 World Center Dr. I-4, exit 67, 1.3 mi e; jct SR 535 and 536. Int corridors. **Pets:** Accepted.

🆂🄰🆅🄴 🆂🄳 ☒ ⊗ ⊙ 🗎 🖥 🍴 ➳ ☒

△△△ ▽▽▽ Comfort Inn Lake Buena Vista 🄻🄷 🐾
(407) 996-7300. **$59-$89.** 8442 Palm Pkwy. I-4, exit 68, 0.6 mi n on SR 535, then 0.5 mi e. Ext corridors. **Pets:** Medium. $50 deposit/pet, $10 daily fee/pet. Designated rooms, service with restrictions, crate.

🆂🄰🆅🄴 🆂🄳 ☒ 🗎 ⊗ 🗎 🖥 🍴 ➳

▽▽▽▽ Holiday Inn Express Lake Buena Vista 🅂🄷
(407) 239-8400. **$89-$179.** 8686 Palm Pkwy. I-4, exit 68, 0.5 mi n on CR 535, then 0.3 mi e. Int corridors. **Pets:** Medium, other species. $50 one-time fee/room. Service with restrictions, supervision.

🄰🆂🄺 🆂🄳 ☒ ⊗ 🖥 🖥 ☒

△△△ ▽▽▽▽ Holiday Inn-SunSpree Resort-Lake Buena Vista 🅂🄷
(407) 239-4500. **$89-$129.** 13351 SR 535. I-4, exit 68, 0.3 mi se. Ext corridors. **Pets:** Medium. $40 one-time fee/pet. Service with restrictions, crate.

🆂🄰🆅🄴 🆂🄳 ☒ 🗎 ⊗ ⊙ 🗎 🖥 🍴 ➳ ☒

△△△ ▽▽▽▽ Residence Inn Orlando Lake Buena Vista 🅂🄷
(407) 465-0075. **$89-$299.** 11450 Marbella Palms Ct. I-4, exit 68, 0.4 mi n on SR 535, then 0.5 mi e on Palm Pkwy. Int corridors. **Pets:** Accepted.

🆂🄰🆅🄴 🆂🄳 ☒ 🗎 ➳ ☒

△△△ ▽▽▽▽ Sheraton Safari Hotel 🅂🄷 🐾
(407) 239-0444. **$119-$259, 3 day notice.** 12205 Apopka-Vineland Rd. I-4, exit 68, 0.5 mi n on SR 535. Ext/int corridors. **Pets:** Medium, dogs only. Designated rooms, service with restrictions, supervision.

🆂🄰🆅🄴 🆂🄳 ☒ 🗎 ⊗ 🗎 🖥 🍴 ➳ ☒

△△△ ▽▽▽▽ SpringHill Suites at The Marriott Village 🅂🄷
(407) 938-9001. **$85-$135.** 8623 Vineland Ave. I-4, exit 68, just e, then n on SR 535. Int corridors. **Pets:** Accepted.

🆂🄰🆅🄴 🆂🄳 ☒ 🗎 🖥 ➳

LAKE MARY

▽▽▽▽ Candlewood Suites Lake Mary-Heathrow 🅂🄷
(407) 585-3000. **$59-$139.** 1130 Greenwood Blvd. I-4, exit 98, just e to Lake Emma Rd, 0.5 mi s to Greenwood Blvd, then 0.6 mi w. Int corridors. **Pets:** Accepted.

🄰🆂🄺 🆂🄳 ☒ 🗎 ⊗ 🗎 🖥 ➳

▽▽ ▽▽ Extended StayAmerica-Orlando-Lake Mary 🅂🄷
(407) 833-0011. **$79-$89.** 1036 Greenwood Blvd. I-4, exit 98, just e to Lake Emma Rd, then 1 mi. Int corridors. **Pets:** Accepted.

🄰🆂🄺 ☒ 🗎 🖥

▽▽▽▽ Homestead Studio Suites-Orlando/Lake Mary 🅂🄷
(407) 829-2332. **$79-$89.** 1040 Greenwood Blvd. I-4, exit 98, 0.5 mi s on Lake Emma Rd; in Commerce Park. Int corridors. **Pets:** Accepted.

🄰🆂🄺 🆂🄳 ☒ ⊗ 🗎 ⊗ 🗎 🖥 ➳

△△△ ▽▽▽ Homewood Suites by Hilton 🅂🄷 🐾
(407) 805-9111. **$129-$199.** 755 Currency Cir. I-4, exit 98, just ne via Lake Mary Blvd and Primera. Int corridors. **Pets:** Medium. $55 one-time fee/pet. Service with restrictions, crate.

🆂🄰🆅🄴 🆂🄳 ☒ ⊗ 🗎 ⊗ 🗎 🖥 ➳

▽▽▽▽ La Quinta Inn & Suites Orlando (Lake Mary) 🅂🄷
(407) 805-9901. **$105-$145.** 1060 Greenwood Blvd. I-4, exit 98, just se via Lake Mary Blvd. Int corridors. **Pets:** Medium. Service with restrictions.

🄰🆂🄺 ☒ ⊗ 🗎 ⊗ 🗎 🖥 ➳

LEESBURG

△△△ ▽▽▽ Super 8 Motel 🅂🄷
(352) 787-6363. **$45-$100, 7 day notice.** 1392 North Blvd. Jct US 27 and 441. Int corridors. **Pets:** Large. $15 daily fee/pet. Service with restrictions, supervision.

🆂🄰🆅🄴 🆂🄳 ☒ ⊗ 🗎 🖥 ➳

MAITLAND

▽▽ ▽▽ Extended StayAmerica-Orlando -Maitland Pembrook Dr 🅂🄷
(407) 667-0474. **$54-$74.** 1760 Pembrook Dr. I-4, exit 90B, 0.5 mi w. Int corridors. **Pets:** Accepted.

🄰🆂🄺 🆂🄳 ☒ 🗎 🖥 ➳

▽▽ ▽▽ Extended Stay Deluxe-Orlando-Maitland-Pembrook Dr 🅂🄷
(407) 475-1675. **$64-$84.** 1776 Pembrook Dr. I-4, exit 90B, 0.5 mi w. Int corridors. **Pets:** Accepted.

🄰🆂🄺 🆂🄳 ⊗ 🗎 🖥 ➳

△△△ ▽▽▽▽ Homewood Suites by Hilton Orlando North 🅂🄷
(407) 875-8777. **$169-$279.** 290 Southhall Ln. I-4, exit 90, just w, then just s on Lake Destiny. Int corridors. **Pets:** Accepted.

🆂🄰🆅🄴 🆂🄳 ☒ ⊗ 🗎 ⊗ 🗎 🖥 ➳

MOUNT DORA

▼▼ ▼▼ Heron Cay Lakeview Bed & Breakfast BB
(352) 383-4050. $155-$285, 15 day notice. 495 Old Hwy 441. On CR 441 (Old US 441), 0.3 mi w. Int corridors. Pets: Other species. $25 daily fee/room. Service with restrictions.

(ASK) (X) (&) (B) (Z)

OCOEE

▼▼ Best Western Turnpike West-Orlando SH
(407) 656-5050. $69-$94. 10945 W Colonial Dr. I-4, exit 84, 10 mi w on SR 50; 0.5 mi e of Florida Tpke, exit 267B. Ext corridors. Pets: Accepted.

(ASK) (&) (X) (&) (B) (I) (I) (=)

▼▼ Red Roof Inn Orlando West SH
(407) 347-0140. $79-$99. 11241 W Colonial Dr. I-4, exit 84, 10 mi w on SR 50; 0.6 mi e of Florida Tpke, exit 267. Int corridors. Pets: Small. Designated rooms, service with restrictions, supervision.

(ASK) (&) (X) (&) (B) (=)

ORLANDO

▼▼ Best Western Orlando West SH ❀
(407) 841-8600. $59-$150. 2014 W Colonial Dr. I-4, exit 84, 1.5 mi w on SR 50; 0.4 mi e of SR 423. Int corridors. Pets: Small. $5 daily fee/pet. Service with restrictions, supervision.

(ASK) (&) (X) (&) (B) (I) (I) (=)

▲▲▲ ▼▼▼ Comfort Inn-North SH
(407) 629-4000. $60-$65. 830 Lee Rd. I-4, exit 88, 0.4 mi w on SR 423. Int corridors. Pets: Accepted.

(SAVE) (X) (&) (B) (I) (=) (X)

▲▲▲ ▼▼▼ Comfort Inn Universal Studios SH
(407) 363-7886. $69-$149. 6101 Sand Lake Rd. I-4, exit 74A, 0.3 mi e on SR 482 (Sand Lake Rd), at Universal Blvd. Ext corridors. Pets: Accepted.

(SAVE) (&) (X) (&M) (&) (B) (I) (=)

▲▲▲ ▼▼▼ Comfort Suites Orlando SH ❀
(407) 351-5050. $65-$75. 9350 Turkey Lake Rd. I-4, exit 74A, just w on SR 482 (Sand Lake Rd), then 1.5 mi s. Ext corridors. Pets: $25 one-time fee/pet. Designated rooms, service with restrictions, crate.

(SAVE) (&) (X) (&M) (I) (&) (B) (=)

▼▼▼▼ Country Inn & Suites by Carlson-Orlando International Airport SH
(407) 856-8896. $110-$130. 5440 Forbes Pl. SR 528 (Beachline Expwy), exit 11, 0.6 mi n on SR 436, then just w. Int corridors. Pets: Accepted.

(ASK) (&) (X) (I) (B) (=) (=)

▲▲▲ ▼▼▼ Days Inn North of Universal SH
(407) 841-3731. $59-$99. 2500 W 33rd St. I-4, exit 79, just e. Ext corridors. Pets: Medium. $10 daily fee/pet. Designated rooms, service with restrictions, supervision.

(SAVE) (&) (X) (I) (&) (B) (I) (=)

▼▼ ▼▼ Extended StayAmerica-Orlando-Convention Center-Westwood Blvd SH
(407) 352-3454. $74-$84. 6451 Westwood Blvd. I-4, exit 72, just e on SR 528 (Beachline Expwy) to exit 1 (International Dr), just s, then just w. Int corridors. Pets: Accepted.

(ASK) (&) (X) (B) (=)

▼▼▼ Extended Stay Deluxe Orlando Convention Center/ Pointe Orlando SH
(407) 903-1500. $84-$114. 8750 Universal Blvd. I-4, exit 74A, 0.5 mi e on SR 482 (Sand Lake Rd), then 0.7 mi s. Int corridors. Pets: Accepted.

(ASK) (&) (X) (&M) (I) (&) (B) (=) (X)

▼▼ ▼▼ Extended Stay Deluxe/Orlando Convention Center/ Westwood Blvd. SH
(407) 351-1982. $70-$115. 6443 Westwood Blvd. I-4, exit 72, just e on SR 528 (Beachline Expwy) to exit 1 (International Dr), just s, then just w. Int corridors. Pets: Accepted.

(X) (I) (B) (=) (=)

▼▼▼ Extended Stay Deluxe Orlando-John Young Parkway SH
(407) 248-8010. $84-$94. 8687 Commodity Cir. Just sw of jct SR 423 (John Young Pkwy) and 482 (Sand Lake Rd). Int corridors. Pets: Accepted.

(ASK) (&) (X) (I) (&) (B) (=) (=)

▼▼▼ Extended Stay Deluxe-Orlando-Universal Studios SH
(407) 370-4428. $69-$79. 5610 Vineland Rd. I-4, exit 75B, just n, then e. Int corridors. Pets: Accepted.

(ASK) (&) (X) (&M) (&) (B) (=) (=)

▲▲▲ ▼▼▼ ▼▼▼ Hard Rock Hotel, at Universal Orlando, a Loews Hotel LH
(407) 503-2000. $229-$429, 5 day notice. 5800 Universal Blvd. I-4, exit 75A, 1 mi n, follow signs. Int corridors. Pets: Accepted.

(SAVE) (X) (&M) (I) (&) (B) (=) (I) (=) (X)

▲▲▲ ▼▼▼▼ Hawthorn Suites Orlando Airport SH
(407) 438-2121. $89-$299. 7450 Augusta National Dr. SR 528 (Beachline Expwy), exit 11, 0.5 mi n on SR 436, just e, then just s. Int corridors. Pets: Accepted.

(SAVE) (&) (X) (&M) (I) (&) (B) (=) (=) (X)

▲▲▲ ▼▼▼▼ Holiday Inn & Suites At Universal Orlando SH ❀
(407) 351-3333. $89-$169, 3 day notice. 5905 S Kirkman Rd. I-4, exit 75B, 0.5 mi n on SR 435 (Kirkman Rd). Int corridors. Pets: Medium, other species. $50 one-time fee/room. Service with restrictions, supervision.

(SAVE) (&) (X) (&M) (I) (&) (B) (=) (=)

▼▼▼ Holiday Inn-International Drive Resort SH
(407) 351-3500. $89-$169. 6515 International Dr. I-4, exit 74A, just e on SR 482 (Sand Lake Rd), then 0.5 mi n. Ext/int corridors. Pets: Large. $500 deposit/room, $15 daily fee/room, $35 one-time fee/room. Service with restrictions, crate.

(ASK) (X) (&M) (I) (&) (B) (=) (I) (=) (X)

▼▼▼ Homestead Studio Suites Hotel-Orlando/John Young Parkway SH
(407) 352-5577. $79-$89. 4101 Equity Row. Just sw of jct SR 423 (John Young Pkwy) and 482 (Sand Lake Rd). Int corridors. Pets: Accepted.

(ASK) (&) (X) (&M) (I) (&) (B) (=) (=)

▼▼▼ Howard Johnson Inn-International Drive SH ❀
(407) 351-2900. $89-$125. 6603 International Dr. I-4, exit 74A, just e on SR 482 (Sand Lake Rd), then 0.4 mi n. Ext corridors. Pets: Small, dogs only. $25 daily fee/room. Designated rooms, no service, supervision.

(ASK) (X) (I) (B) (=) (=)

▲▲▲ ▼▼ ▼▼ La Quinta Inn SH
(407) 351-4100. $69-$149, 7 day notice. 5825 International Dr. I-4, exit 75A, just w. Ext corridors. Pets: Accepted.

(SAVE) (&) (X) (I) (B) (=) (=)

▼▼▼ La Quinta Inn & Suites Orlando (Airport North) SH
(407) 240-5000. $115-$155. 7160 N Frontage Rd. SR 528 (Beachline Expwy), exit 11, 0.5 mi n on SR 436, then just w. Int corridors. Pets: Medium. Service with restrictions.

(ASK) (X) (&M) (I) (&) (B) (=) (=)

▼▼▼▼ La Quinta Inn & Suites Orlando (Convention Center) SH
(407) 345-1365. **$95-$165.** 8504 Universal Blvd. I-4, exit 74A, 0.5 mi e on SR 482 (Sand Lake Rd), then 0.5 mi s. Int corridors. **Pets:** Medium. Service with restrictions.
A$K ⊠ ⅃M 🐾 ⌂ ⊟ ⊡ ⇌

▼◆▼ La Quinta Inn & Suites Orlando South SH
(407) 240-0500. **$89-$139.** 2051 Consulate Dr. US 17-92 and 441, just s of SR 528 (Beachline Expwy); off Florida Tpke, exit 254. Int corridors. **Pets:** Medium. Service with restrictions.
A$K ⊠ 🐾 ⌂ ⊟ ⊡ ⇌

▼◆▼ La Quinta Inn & Suites Orlando (U.C.F.) SH
(407) 737-6075. **$105-$155.** 11805 Research Pkwy. Just se of jct University Blvd and SR 434 (Alafaya Trail). Int corridors. **Pets:** Medium. Service with restrictions.
A$K ⊠ ⅃M 🐾 ⌂ ⊟ ⊡ ⇌

▼▼▼ La Quinta Inn Orlando (Airport West) SH
(407) 857-9215. **$95-$155.** 7931 Daetwyler Dr. SR 528 (Beachline Expwy), exit 9 (Tradeport), via McCoy Rd. Ext corridors. **Pets:** Medium. Service with restrictions.
A$K 🐾 ⊡ ⇌

▼◆▼ La Quinta Inn Orlando (International Drive) SH
(407) 351-1660. **$85-$155.** 8300 Jamaican Ct. I-4, exit 74A, just e on SR 482 (Sand Lake Rd), then just s on International Dr. Ext corridors. **Pets:** Medium. Service with restrictions.
A$K ⊠ ⅃M 🐾 ⌂ ⊟ ⊡ ⇌ ⊠

▲▲▲ ▼◆▼ La Quinta Inn Orlando-Winter Park SH
(407) 645-5600. **$79-$125.** 626 Lee Rd. I-4, exit 88 (Lee Rd), just w on SR 438. Int corridors. **Pets:** Small. Service with restrictions, crate.
SAVE S🐾 ⊠ 🐾 ⌂ ⊟ ⊡ ⅋ ⇌

▲▲▲ ▼◆▼ Masters Inn International Drive SH
(407) 345-1172. **$50-$120.** 8222 Jamaican Ct. I-4, exit 74A, e on SR 482 (Sand Lake Rd), then just s on International Dr. Ext corridors. **Pets:** Small. $20 one-time fee/pet. Service with restrictions, crate.
SAVE S🐾 ⊠ 🐾 ⊟ ⇌

▲▲▲ ▼◆▼ Microtel Inn & Suites SH
(407) 226-9887. **$90, 3 day notice.** 7531 Canada Ave. I-4, exit 74A, just e on SR 482 (Sand Lake Rd), then n. Int corridors. **Pets:** Accepted.
SAVE S🐾 ⊠ 🐾 ⊟ ⊡ ⇌

▼◆▼ Motel 6 Orlando-International Drive #1079 SH
(407) 351-6500. **$53-$71.** 5909 American Way. I-4, exit 75A, just w of SR 435, then just n. Int corridors. **Pets:** Medium, other species. Service with restrictions, supervision.
S🐾 ⊠ 🐾 ⌂ ⇌

▲▲▲ ▼◆▼▼ Portofino Bay Hotel, at Universal Orlando, a Loews Hotel LH
(407) 503-1000. **$259-$429, 5 day notice.** 5601 Universal Blvd. I-4, exit 74B westbound; exit 75A eastbound, 1 mi n, follow signs. Int corridors. **Pets:** Accepted.
SAVE ⊠ ⅃M 🐾 ⌂ ⊟ ⊡ ⅋ ⇌ ⊠

▼◆▼ Quality Inn International LH 🐾
(407) 996-1600. **$59-$99.** 7600 International Dr. I-4, exit 74A, just e on SR 482 (Sand Lake Rd), then just n. Ext corridors. **Pets:** Medium. $10 daily fee/pet. Service with restrictions, supervision.
A$K S🐾 ⊠ ⅃M 🐾 ⌂ ⊟ ⊡ ⅋ ⇌

▼◆▼ Quality Inn Plaza LH 🐾
(407) 996-8585. **$49-$129.** 9000 International Dr. I-4, exit 74A, just e on SR 482 (Sand Lake Rd), then 1 mi s. Ext corridors. **Pets:** Medium, other species. $50 deposit/pet. Service with restrictions.
A$K S🐾 ⊠ ⅃M 🐾 ⌂ ⊟ ⊡ ⅋ ⇌ ⊠

▼◆▼ Red Roof Inn Convention Center SH
(407) 352-1507. **$48-$100.** 9922 Hawaiian Ct. I-4, exit 72, 0.9 mi e on SR 528 (Beachline Expwy) to exit 1, then just n. Ext corridors. **Pets:** Medium, other species. Service with restrictions, supervision.
⊠ ⅃M 🐾 ⌂ ⊟ ⇌

▲▲▲ ▼◆▼ Residence Inn by Marriott Orlando Convention Center SH
(407) 226-0288. **$139-$239, 3 day notice.** 8800 Universal Blvd. I-4, exit 74A, 0.5 mi e on SR 482 (Sand Lake Rd), then 0.8 mi s. Int corridors. **Pets:** Accepted.
SAVE S🐾 ⊠ ⅃M 🐾 ⌂ ⊟ ⊡ ⇌ ⊠

▼◆▼ Residence Inn by Marriott/Orlando East SH
(407) 513-9000. **$169-$199.** 11651 University Blvd. 2.2 mi e of SR 417 on University Blvd; just w of SR 434 (Alafaya Trail). Int corridors. **Pets:** Accepted.
A$K S🐾 ⊠ 🐾 ⌂ ⊟ ⊡ ⇌ ⊠

▲▲▲ ▼◆▼ Residence Inn by Marriott-Orlando International Dr SH
(407) 345-0117. **$99-$199.** 7975 Canada Ave. I-4, exit 74A, just e on SR 482 (Sand Lake Rd). Ext corridors. **Pets:** Medium, other species. $75 one-time fee/pet. Service with restrictions, crate.
SAVE S🐾 ⊠ 🐾 ⌂ ⊟ ⊡ ⇌ ⊠

▲▲▲ ▼◆▼ Residence Inn by Marriott SeaWorld International Center SH
(407) 313-3600. **$115-$140.** 11000 Westwood Blvd. I-4, exit 72. Int corridors. **Pets:** Medium, other species. $75 one-time fee/pet. Service with restrictions, supervision.
SAVE S🐾 ⊠ ⅃M 🐾 ⌂ ⊟ ⊡ ⅋ ⇌ ⊠

▼◆▼ Rodeway Inn International SH
(407) 996-4444. **$46-$80.** 6327 International Dr. I-4, exit 74A, just e on SR 482 (Sand Lake Rd), then 0.7 mi n. Ext/int corridors. **Pets:** Medium. $50 deposit/pet, $10 daily fee/pet. Service with restrictions, supervision.
A$K S🐾 ⊠ 🐾 ⌂ ⊟ ⊡ ⅋ ⇌

▲▲▲ ▼◆▼▼ Royal Pacific Resort, at Universal Orlando, a Loews Hotel LH 🐾
(407) 503-3000. **$199-$369, 5 day notice.** 6300 Hollywood Way. I-4, exit 74B, just n. Int corridors. **Pets:** $25 one-time fee/room. Designated rooms, service with restrictions, supervision.
SAVE ⊠ 🐾 ⌂ ⊟ ⊡ ⅋ ⇌ ⊠

▲▲▲ ▼◆▼▼ Sheraton Suites Orlando Airport SH
(407) 240-5555. **$99-$179.** 7550 Augusta National Dr. 2 mi n of airport terminal via SR 436 and TG Lee Blvd. Int corridors. **Pets:** Accepted.
SAVE S🐾 ⊠ ⅃M 🐾 ⌂ ⊟ ⊡ ⅋ ⇌

▼◆▼ Sheraton World Resort LH
(407) 352-1100. **$109-$149, 3 day notice.** 10100 International Dr. I-4, exit 72, just s on International Dr; SR 528 (Beachline Expwy), exit 1, just e. Ext/int corridors. **Pets:** Small. $100 deposit/room. Service with restrictions, crate.
A$K S🐾 ⊠ ⅃M 🐾 ⌂ ⊟ ⊡ ⅋ ⇌ ⊠

▼◆▼ Ventura Country Club-Ventura Resort Rentals CO
(407) 273-8770. **$79-$199.** 5946 Curry Ford Rd. 0.6 mi e of SR 436. Ext corridors. **Pets:** Accepted.
A$K S🐾 🐾 ⊟ ⊡ ⇌ ⊠

▲▲▲ ▼◆▼▼ Westin Grand Bohemian LH
(407) 313-9000. **$199-$499.** 325 S Orange Ave. Corner of Jackson St. Int corridors. **Pets:** Accepted.
SAVE ⊠ ⅃M 🐾 ⌂ ⊡ ⅋ ⇌ ⊠

▲▲▲ ▼◆▼▼ Wyndham Orlando Resort LH 🐾
(407) 351-2420. **$79, 3 day notice.** 8001 International Dr. I-4, exit 74A, just e at SR 482 (Sand Lake Rd). Ext/int corridors. **Pets:** Large, other species. $50 one-time fee/room. Service with restrictions, crate.
SAVE S🐾 ⊠ ⅃M 🐾 ⌂ ⊟ ⊡ ⅋ ⇌ ⊠

ST. CLOUD

AAA **WWW** Budget Inn of St Cloud **M**
(407) 892-2858. **$45-$90, 3 day notice.** 602 13th St. On US 192, 0.5 mi e of The Water Tower, 2 mi w of jct CR 15. Ext corridors. **Pets:** Very small, dogs only. $10 daily fee/pet. Service with restrictions, supervision.
SAVE S X @ H

TAVARES

W Budget Inn **M**
(352) 343-4666. **$59-$99, 7 day notice.** 101 W Burleigh Blvd. On US 441, 0.3 mi e of jct SR 19 S. Ext corridors. **Pets:** Accepted.
ASK S X H

END METROPOLITAN AREA

ORMOND BEACH

AAA **WWW** Comfort Inn Interstate **SH**
(386) 672-8621. **$69-$300, 3 day notice.** 1567 N US 1. I-95, exit 273, just e. Ext corridors. **Pets:** Accepted.
SAVE S X @ H P

WW Comfort Inn On The Beach **M**
(386) 677-8550. **$95-$265, 10 day notice.** 507 S Atlantic Ave. On SR A1A, 1 mi s of jct SR 40. Ext corridors. **Pets:** Very small. $20 daily fee/pet. Service with restrictions, supervision.
ASK S X H P

WWW Jameson Inn **SH**
(386) 672-3675. **$54-$120.** 175 Interchange Blvd. I-95, exit 268, just w, then just s. Int corridors. **Pets:** Small. $10 daily fee/pet. Service with restrictions, crate.
ASK X &M @ & H P

OSPREY

WW Ramada Inn-Sarasota South **M**
(941) 966-2121. **$79-$129.** 1660 S Tamiami Tr. On US 41, 1.8 mi n of jct SR 681. Ext/int corridors. **Pets:** Small. $75 one-time fee/room. Designated rooms, service with restrictions, supervision.
ASK S X H P Y

PALM BAY

WW Jameson Inn **SH**
(321) 725-2952. **$54-$120.** 890 Palm Bay Rd. I-95, exit 176. Int corridors. **Pets:** Small. $10 daily fee/pet. Service with restrictions, crate.
ASK X &M @ & H P

PALM BEACH

WWWW Brazilian Court Hotel **SH**
(561) 655-7740. **$250-$700, 4 day notice.** 301 Australian Ave. From Royal Palm Way (SR 704), s on Cocoanut Row, 2 blks to Australian Ave, then just e; corner of Hibiscus and Australian aves. Int corridors. **Pets:** Accepted.
ASK S X & Y

AAA **WWWW** The Chesterfield Hotel **SH**
(561) 659-5800. **$160-$1700, 3 day notice.** 363 Cocoanut Row. Just w of SR A1A; at Australian Ave and Cocoanut Row. Int corridors. **Pets:** Accepted.
SAVE S X @ H Y

AAA **WWWW** The Four Seasons Resort, Palm Beach **LH**
(561) 582-2800. **$305-$931, 14 day notice.** 2800 S Ocean Blvd. SR A1A, 0.3 mi n of jct SR 802. Int corridors. **Pets:** Accepted.
SAVE X &M @ H P Y

WWW Heart of Palm Beach Hotel **SH**
(561) 655-5600. **$99-$1000, 3 day notice.** 160 Royal Palm Way. Just e of SR A1A; center. Int corridors. **Pets:** Accepted.
ASK X @ H P Y

AAA **WWWW** The OC Beach Resort **SH** 🐾
(561) 586-6542. **$89-$499, 3 day notice.** 2842 S Ocean Blvd. On SR A1A; just n of jct SR 802. Int corridors. **Pets:** Small, other species. $100 one-time fee/room. Designated rooms, service with restrictions, supervision.
SAVE S X @ H Y P Y

PALM BEACH SHORES

AAA **WWW** Best Western Seaspray Inn **SH**
(561) 844-0233. **$110-$240, 14 day notice.** 123 S Ocean Ave. On Singer Island; 0.5 mi s of SR A1A. Int corridors. **Pets:** Accepted.
SAVE S X H P Y

PALM COAST

WW Microtel Inn & Suites **SH**
(386) 445-8976. **$57-$189.** 16 Kingswood Dr. I-95, exit 289, 0.5 mi se via Old Kings Rd. Int corridors. **Pets:** Small, dogs only. $25 one-time fee/pet. Designated rooms, service with restrictions, supervision.
ASK S X &M & H P Y

AAA **WWWW** Palm Coast Villas **M** 🐾
(386) 445-3525. **$59-$79, 7 day notice.** 5454 N Oceanshore Blvd. I-95, exit 289, 2.8 mi e to SR A1A, then 1.8 mi n. Ext corridors. **Pets:** $500 daily fee/pet. Designated rooms, service with restrictions, supervision.
SAVE S X H P Y

PANAMA CITY

WWWW Howard Johnson Inn **SH**
(850) 785-0222. **$54-$129, 3 day notice.** 4601 W Hwy 98. US 98, 0.8 mi e of Hathaway Bridge. Ext/int corridors. **Pets:** Medium, other species. $25 one-time fee/room. Designated rooms, service with restrictions, crate.
ASK S X H P Y

WWWW La Quinta Inn & Suites Panama City **SH**
(850) 914-0022. **$109-$149.** 1030 E 23rd St. Jct US 231 and CR 390A. Int corridors. **Pets:** Medium. Service with restrictions.
ASK X &M & H P Y

WWW Super 8 Motel **M**
(850) 784-1988. **$60-$120.** 207 Hwy 231 N. Just n of jct US 98. Ext/int corridors. **Pets:** Small, dogs only. $15 daily fee/pet. Designated rooms, service with restrictions, crate.
ASK S X H Y

PENSACOLA

AAA **WWW** Americas Best Value Inn & Suites **SH**
(850) 479-1099. **$59-$89.** 8240 N Davis Hwy. I-10, exit 13, 0.8 mi n. Ext/int corridors. **Pets:** Medium. $10 one-time fee/pet. Service with restrictions, supervision.
SAVE S X & H P Y

WWW Ashton Inn & Suites **SH**
(850) 454-0280. **$75-$99.** 4 New Warrington Rd. Just n of jct US 98 and SR 295. Int corridors. **Pets:** Accepted.
ASK S X H P Y

WWW Extended StayAmerica-Pensacola-University Mall **SH**
(850) 473-9323. **$59-$79.** 809 Bloodworth Ln. I-10, exit 13, just s on Davis Hwy, then e. Int corridors. **Pets:** Accepted.
ASK S X H P

▼▼▼ **La Quinta Inn Pensacola** SH
(850) 474-0411. **$106-$150.** 7750 N Davis Hwy. I-10, exit 13, just n. Ext corridors. **Pets:** Medium. Service with restrictions.
[ASK] [⊠] [⌐] [🖶] [🖵] [⇌]

▼ **Motel 6 #1105** M
(850) 474-1060. **$50-$65.** 7226 Plantation Rd. I-10, exit 13, sw on Mall Rd. Ext corridors. **Pets:** Medium, other species. Service with restrictions, supervision.
[🖎] [⊠] [⌐] [⇌]

▼ **Motel 6 #1183** M
(850) 476-5386. **$47-$63.** 7827 N Davis Hwy. I-10, exit 13, 0.3 mi n. Ext corridors. **Pets:** Medium, other species. Service with restrictions, supervision.
[🖎] [⊠] [⌐] [⇌]

◈◈◈ ▼▼▼ **Quality Inn** SH
(850) 477-0711. **$89.** 6550 N Pensacola Blvd. I-10, exit 10A, 1.2 mi s on US 29. Ext/int corridors. **Pets:** Small. $50 one-time fee/pet. Designated rooms, service with restrictions, supervision.
[SAVE] [🖎] [⊠] [🗗] [🖶] [🖵] [⇌]

◈◈◈ ▼▼▼ **Quality Inn Pensacola West** SH
(850) 944-0333. **$70-$100.** 8060 Lavalle Way. I-10, exit 7, just s. Ext corridors. **Pets:** Accepted.
[SAVE] [🖎] [⊠] [🗗] [🖶] [🖵] [⇌]

▼▼ **Red Roof Inn** M
(850) 476-7960. **$57-$73.** 7340 Plantation Rd. I-10, exit 13, just s. Ext corridors. **Pets:** Medium, other species. Service with restrictions, supervision.
[⊠] [🖶]

◈◈◈ ▼▼▼ **Residence Inn By Marriott** SH
(850) 479-1000. **$159.** 7230 Plantation Rd. I-10, exit 13, just s. Ext corridors. **Pets:** Small. $100 one-time fee/room. Service with restrictions, supervision.
[SAVE] [⊠] [⌐M] [🗗] [🖶] [🖵] [⇌] [⊠]

PENSACOLA BEACH

◈◈◈ ▼▼▼ **Best Western Resort Pensacola Beach** M
(850) 934-3300. **$79-$299, 3 day notice.** 16 Via De Luna. 0.5 mi e on SR 399. Ext corridors. **Pets:** Other species. Service with restrictions, crate.
[SAVE] [🖎] [⊠] [🖶] [🖵] [⇌]

PERRY

◈◈◈ ▼ **Best Budget Inn** M
(850) 584-6231. **$50-$55.** 2220 US 19 S. US 19 and 98, 0.4 mi s of jct US 221. Ext corridors. **Pets:** Accepted.
[SAVE] [🖎] [⊠] [🖶] [⇌]

PORT ST. LUCIE

▼▼▼▼ **Holiday Inn-Port St Lucie** SH
(772) 337-2200. **$139-$209.** 10120 S Federal Hwy, Rt 1. US 1, 0.5 mi n of jct SR 716, Port St Lucie Blvd. Int corridors. **Pets:** Accepted.
[ASK] [🖎] [⊠] [🗗] [🖶] [🖵] [🍽] [⇌]

QUINCY

▼▼▼▼ **Allison House Inn** BB 🐾
(850) 875-2511. **$105-$140, 14 day notice.** 215 N Madison St. Just e of town center; in historic district. Int corridors. **Pets:** Small, dogs only. Designated rooms, service with restrictions, supervision.
[ASK] [🖎] [⊠]

ST. AUGUSTINE

◈◈◈ ▼▼ ◈ **Avenida Inn Saint Augustine** SH 🐾
(904) 829-6581. **$61-$139.** 2800 N Ponce de Leon Blvd. US 1 at SR 16; in historic district. Ext corridors. **Pets:** Medium, dogs only. $10 daily fee/pet. Designated rooms, service with restrictions, supervision.
[SAVE] [🖎] [⊠] [🗗] [🖶] [🖵] [🍽] [⇌]

▼▼▼▼ **Bayfront Westcott House** BB
(904) 824-4301. **$119-$279, 7 day notice.** 146 Avenida Menendez. 1 blk s of Bridge of Lions. Ext/int corridors. **Pets:** Accepted.
[ASK] [🖎] [⊠]

◈◈◈ ▼▼ ◈ **Casablanca Inn on the Bay** BB
(904) 829-0928. **$99-$369, 7 day notice.** 24 Avenida Menendez. US 1 business route and SR A1A, then just n. Int corridors. **Pets:** Large. $15 daily fee/pet. Designated rooms, service with restrictions, supervision.
[SAVE] [⊠] [🖶] [🖵]

▼▼▼▼ **Cedar House Inn Victorian B & B** BB
(904) 829-0079. **$149-$299, 14 day notice.** 79 Cedar St. Jct King St, just s on Granda St, then just w. Ext/int corridors. **Pets:** Accepted.
[ASK] [⊠] [🖶]

◈◈◈ ▼▼ ◈ **The Cozy Inn** M
(904) 824-2449. **$49-$99.** 202 San Marco Ave. 0.3 mi s of jct SR 16. Ext corridors. **Pets:** Accepted.
[SAVE] [🖎] [⊠] [🖶] [🖵]

◈◈◈ ▼▼▼ **Days Inn-West** SH
(904) 824-4341. **$69-$199, 14 day notice.** 2560 SR 16. I-95, exit 318, just w. Ext corridors. **Pets:** Accepted.
[SAVE] [🖎] [⊠] [🖶] [🖵] [🍽] [⇌]

▼▼▼ **The Inn At Camachee Harbor** SH 🐾
(904) 825-0003. **$99-$189, 3 day notice.** 201 Yacht Club Dr. On Intracoastal Waterway at west side of Usine Bridge; 1 mi e of jct N SR A1A and San Marco Blvd. Ext/int corridors. **Pets:** Other species. $15 daily fee/room. Designated rooms, service with restrictions.
[ASK] [🖎] [⊠] [🖶] [🖵] [⊠]

◈◈◈ ▼▼▼▼ **St. Francis Inn** BB
(904) 824-6068. **$99-$269, 7 day notice.** 279 St George St. Just s; in historic district. Ext/int corridors. **Pets:** Medium, other species. $15 daily fee/pet. Designated rooms.
[SAVE] [⊠] [🖶] [🖵] [⇌] [⊠]

◈◈◈ ▼▼▼ **Scottish Inns** M
(904) 824-2871. **$50-$99.** 110 San Marco Ave. Old Mission and San Marco aves; center. Ext corridors. **Pets:** Small, dogs only. $10 daily fee/pet. No service, crate.
[SAVE] [🖎] [⊠] [⇌]

ST. AUGUSTINE BEACH

◈◈◈ ▼▼▼ **Comfort Inn at St. Augustine Beach** SH
(904) 471-1474. **$79-$105, 10 day notice.** 901 A1A Beach Blvd. On Business Rt SR A1A, 1.6 mi s of jct SR 312 and A1A. Ext corridors. **Pets:** Designated rooms, supervision.
[SAVE] [🖎] [⊠] [🖶] [🖵] [⇌]

◈◈◈ ▼▼▼ **Holiday Inn-St Augustine Beach** SH
(904) 471-2555. **$114-$199.** 860 A1A Beach Blvd. On Business Rt SR A1A, 1.8 mi s of jct SR 312 and A1A. Ext/int corridors. **Pets:** Medium. $20 daily fee/pet. Designated rooms, no service, supervision.
[SAVE] [🖎] [⊠] [⌐] [🖶] [🖵] [🍽] [⇌]

◈◈◈ ▼▼▼ **Super 8 By The Beach** SH
(904) 471-2330. **$59-$129.** 311 A1A Beach Blvd. On Business Rt SR A1A, 1 mi s of jct SR 312 and A1A. Ext corridors. **Pets:** $15 one-time fee/room. Service with restrictions, supervision.
[SAVE] [🖎] [⊠] [🗗] [🖶] [🖵] [⇌]

SARASOTA

◇◇◇ Comfort Inn Sarasota Airport SH
(941) 351-7734. **$80-$140.** 5000 N Tamiami Tr. On US 41, just s of jct University Pkwy. Ext corridors. **Pets:** Small, other species. $10 daily fee/pet. Service with restrictions, supervision.
ASK S✗ ✗ ᴳᴹ ⬚ ⬚ 🖥 ➥

◇◇ Comfort Inn, Sarasota I-75 SH
(941) 921-7750. **$79-$189.** 5778 Clark Rd. I-75, exit 205, just w on SR 72. Int corridors. **Pets:** Accepted.
ASK S✗ ✗ ᴳᴹ ⬚ ⬚ ⬚ 🖥 ➥

◇◇◇ Coquina on the Beach Resort M
(941) 388-2141. **$99-$369.** 1008 Benjamin Franklin Dr. On St. Armands Key of Lido Beach; 0.9 mi s of St. Armands Circle. Ext corridors. **Pets:** Accepted.
SAVE S✗ ⬚ 🖥 ➥

◇◇◇ Hibiscus Suites Inn M
(941) 921-5797. **$109-$379, 3 day notice.** 1735 Stickney Point Rd. On SR 72, 0.3 mi sw of jct US 41. Ext corridors. **Pets:** Dogs only. $25 daily fee/room. Service with restrictions, supervision.
SAVE S✗ ✗ ᴳᴹ ⬚ 🖥 ➥

◇◇◇◇ Homewood Suites by Hilton SH
(941) 365-7300. **$117-$225.** 3470 Fruitville Rd. I-75, exit 210, 3.2 mi w on SR 780 (Fruitville Rd). Int corridors. **Pets:** Accepted.
SAVE S✗ ✗ ᴳᴹ ⬚ ⬚ ⬚ 🖥 ➥ ✗

◇◇◇◇ Hyatt Sarasota LH
(941) 953-1234. **$135-$265.** 1000 Blvd of the Arts. Just w of jct US 41. Int corridors. **Pets:** Small. $150 one-time fee/room. Designated rooms, service with restrictions, supervision.
SAVE ✗ ᴳᴹ ⬚ ⬚ ⬚ 🖥 ⑪ ➥ ✗

◇◇◇◇ La Quinta Inn & Suites Sarasota Airport SH
(941) 366-5128. **Call for rates.** 1803 N Tamiami Tr. On US 41, 1 mi n of jct SR 780 (Fruitville Rd). Int corridors. **Pets:** Medium. Service with restrictions.
ASK ✗ ᴳᴹ ⬚ ⬚ ⬚ 🖥 ➥

◇◇◇◇ The Ritz-Carlton, Sarasota LH ❀
(941) 309-2000. **$349-$539.** 1111 Ritz-Carlton Dr. On US 41, jct John Ringling Blvd. Int corridors. **Pets:** Small. $125 one-time fee/pet. Designated rooms, service with restrictions, supervision.
ASK ✗ ᴳᴹ ⬚ ⬚ ⬚ 🖥 ⑪ ➥ ✗

◇◇◇ Sarasota Cay Club Resort & Marina M
(941) 355-2781. **$79-$169, 10 day notice.** 7150 N Tamiami Tr. On US 41, 2.4 mi n of jct University Pkwy. Ext/int corridors. **Pets:** Accepted.
SAVE S✗ ✗ ᴳᴹ ⬚ ⬚ ⬚ 🖥 ➥ ✗

◇◇ Sleep Inn SH
(941) 359-8558. **$80-$110.** 900 University Pkwy. Just e of jct US 41; in Airport Business Park. Int corridors. **Pets:** Accepted.
SAVE S✗ ✗ ⬚ 🖥 ➥

SEBRING

◇◇◇ Four Points by Sheraton Sebring Chateau Elan SH
(863) 655-6252. **$90-$130.** 150 Midway Dr. From US 27, 2.2 mi e on US 98; at entrance to Sebring International Raceway. Int corridors. **Pets:** Accepted.
ASK S✗ ✗ ⬚ ⬚ ⬚ 🖥 ⑪ ➥ ✗

◇◇◇ Inn On The Lakes SH ❀
(863) 471-9400. **$84-$120.** 3100 Golfview Rd. On US 27, 1.5 mi n of jct SR 17. Ext/int corridors. **Pets:** Other species. $40 one-time fee/room. Designated rooms, service with restrictions, supervision.
SAVE S✗ ✗ ⬚ 🖥 ⑪ ➥

◇◇◇ Kenilworth Lodge SH
(863) 385-0111. **$70-$100, 3 day notice.** 1610 Lakeview Dr. US 27, 1 mi e on SR 17. Ext/int corridors. **Pets:** Other species. $15 daily fee/pet. Designated rooms, service with restrictions, crate.
SAVE S✗ ✗ ⬚ ⬚ 🖥 ➥ ✗

◇◇◇ Quality Inn & Suites Conference Center SH
(863) 385-4500. **$79-$99.** 6525 US 27 N. On US 27, 7 mi n of jct SR 17. Ext corridors. **Pets:** Accepted.
SAVE S✗ ✗ ᴳᴹ ⬚ ⬚ 🖥 ⑪ ➥

SIESTA KEY

◇◇◇ Tropical Breeze Resort & Spa of Siesta Key M
(941) 349-1125. **$108-$418.** 5150 Ocean Blvd. Jct Avenida Messina; in Siesta Village. Ext corridors. **Pets:** $75 one-time fee/pet. No service, crate.
SAVE S✗ ✗ ⬚ 🖥 ➥ ✗

SILVER SPRINGS

◇◇ Days Inn M
(352) 236-2891. **$55-$95.** 5001 E Silver Springs Blvd. SR 40, 0.5 mi w of jct CR 35. Ext corridors. **Pets:** Accepted.
SAVE S✗ ✗ ⬚ ➥

STARKE

◇◇◇ Best Western Motor Inn SH
(904) 964-6744. **$69-$79.** 1290 N Temple Ave. 1 mi n on US 301 from jct SR 100. Ext corridors. **Pets:** Medium. $10 daily fee/pet. Service with restrictions, supervision.
SAVE S✗ ✗ ⬚ 🖥 ➥

◇◇◇ Days Inn SH
(904) 964-7600. **$65-$179.** 1101 N Temple Ave. 0.5 mi n of jct SR 16 and US 301. Ext corridors. **Pets:** Accepted.
SAVE S✗ ✗ ⬚ ⬚ ⑪ ➥

STEINHATCHEE

◇◇◇◇ Steinhatchee Landing Resort CA
(352) 498-3513. **$132-$525, 14 day notice.** SR 51. SR 51, 8 mi w of jct US 19/98. Ext corridors. **Pets:** Small, dogs only. $100 deposit/room. Designated rooms, supervision.
ASK ✗ ⬚ 🖥 ➥ ✗

◇◇ Steinhatchee River Inn M ❀
(352) 498-4049. **$69-$139, 14 day notice.** 1111 Riverside Dr. Center. Ext corridors. **Pets:** Small, dogs only. $10 daily fee/pet. Designated rooms, service with restrictions, supervision.
ASK S✗ ✗ ⬚ 🖥 ➥

STUART

◇◇◇ Pirates Cove Resort & Marina SH
(772) 287-2500. **$130-$175.** 4307 SE Bayview St. 0.3 mi e of SR A1A. Ext corridors. **Pets:** Large, other species. $20 one-time fee/pet. Designated rooms, service with restrictions, supervision.
SAVE S✗ ⬚ ⬚ 🖥 ⑪ ➥ ✗

TALLAHASSEE

◇◇◇ Best Western Seminole Inn M
(850) 656-2938. **$55-$150, 3 day notice.** 6737 Mahan Dr. I-10, exit 209A, just w on US 90. Ext corridors. **Pets:** Accepted.
SAVE ✗ ⬚ 🖥 ➥

◇◇◇ Days Inn SH
(850) 222-3219. **$59-$189, 30 day notice.** 1350 W Tennessee St. 1.6 mi w of US 27. Int corridors. **Pets:** Accepted.
SAVE S✗ ✗ ⬚ ➥

[AAA] ♦♦ **Econo Lodge** [M]
(850) 385-6155. **$54-$109.** 2681 N Monroe St. I-10, exit 199, 0.5 mi s. Ext corridors. **Pets:** Large, other species. $10 one-time fee/pet. Service with restrictions.
[SAVE] [SD] ⊠ ■ 🖥

♦♦♦ **Homewood Suites by Hilton** [SH]
(850) 402-9400. **$89-$299.** 2987 Apalachee Pkwy. US 27, 3.5 mi s. Int corridors. **Pets:** Accepted.
[A$K] [SD] ⊠ ■ 🖥 🏊 🏋

♦♦♦ **La Quinta Inn Tallahassee (North)** [SH]
(850) 385-7172. **$98-$125.** 2905 N Monroe St. I-10, exit 199, just s on US 27. Ext corridors. **Pets:** Medium. Service with restrictions.
[A$K] ⊠ ■ 🖥 🏊

♦♦♦ **La Quinta Inn Tallahassee (South)** [SH]
(850) 878-5099. **$95-$119.** 2850 Apalachee Pkwy. 3 mi se on US 27. Ext corridors. **Pets:** Medium. Service with restrictions.
[A$K] ⊠ [♿M] 🦻 ♿ ■ 🖥 🏊

♦ **Motel 6 #1073** [SH]
(850) 877-6171. **$50-$85.** 1027 Apalachee Pkwy. 1 mi se on US 27. Ext corridors. **Pets:** Medium, other species. Service with restrictions, supervision.
[SD] ⊠ ■ 🖥 🏊

♦♦ **Motel 6 #1191** [SH]
(850) 386-7878. **$45-$85.** 2738 N Monroe St. I-10, exit 199, just s on US 27. Ext corridors. **Pets:** Medium, other species. Service with restrictions, supervision.
[SD] ⊠ ■ 🖥 🏊

♦ **Motel 6–420** [M]
(850) 668-2600. **$45-$85.** 1481 Timberlane Rd. I-10, exit 203, just n, then w. Ext corridors. **Pets:** Medium, other species. Service with restrictions, supervision.
[SD] ⊠ 🏊

♦♦ **Ramada Conference Center** [LH]
(850) 386-1027. **$60-$90.** 2900 N Monroe St. I-10, exit 199, just s. Ext/int corridors. **Pets:** Medium. $15 daily fee/room. Designated rooms, service with restrictions, supervision.
[A$K] [SD] ⊠ ■ 🖥 🍴 🏊

♦♦ **StudioPLUS-Tallahassee-Killearn** [SH]
(850) 383-1700. **$75-$100.** 1950 Raymond Diehl Rd. I-10, exit 203, 0.8 mi e. Int corridors. **Pets:** Accepted.
[A$K] [SD] ⊠ [♿M] ♿ ■ 🖥 🏊

Tampa Bay Metropolitan Area

BRANDON

♦♦ **Homestead Studio Suites Hotel-Tampa/Brandon** [M]
(813) 643-5900. **$74-$104.** 330 Grand Regency Blvd. I-75, exit 257, just e on SR 60, then 0.4 mi n; in Regency Office Park. Ext corridors. **Pets:** Accepted.
[A$K] [SD] ⊠ [♿M] 🦻 ♿ ■ 🖥

♦♦♦ **La Quinta Inn & Suites Tampa Bay (Brandon)** [SH]
(813) 643-0574. **$99-$169.** 310 Grand Regency Blvd. I-75, exit 257, just e on SR 60, then 0.5 mi n; in Regency Office Park. Int corridors. **Pets:** Medium. Service with restrictions.
[A$K] ⊠ [♿M] 🦻 ♿ ■ 🖥 🏊

CLEARWATER

[AAA] ♦♦♦ **Belleview Biltmore Resort & Spa** [SH] 🐾
(727) 373-3000. **$219-$269.** 25 Belleview Blvd. 2 mi s on US Alternate 19 (Ft Harrison Ave); from jct SR 60, 0.5 mi w. Int corridors. **Pets:** Small. $25 one-time fee/room. Designated rooms, service with restrictions, crate.
[SAVE] [SD] ⊠ 🦻 ♿ ■ 🍴 🏊 🏋

[AAA] ♦♦ **Days Inn-St. Pete/Clearwater Airport** [SH]
(727) 573-3334. **$59-$129.** 3910 Ulmerton Rd. I-275, exit 31 southbound; exit 30 northbound, 2 mi w on SR 688. Int corridors. **Pets:** Small, other species. $20 one-time fee/room. Designated rooms, service with restrictions.
[SAVE] [SD] ⊠ [♿M] 🦻 ♿ ■ 🖥 🏊

♦♦ **Extended StayAmerica-St. Petersburg-Clearwater** [SH]
(727) 561-9032. **$74-$99.** 3089 Executive Dr. I-275, exit 31 southbound; exit 30 northbound, 1.8 mi w on SR 699, just n on 34th St N, then 0.3 mi ne. Int corridors. **Pets:** Accepted.
[A$K] [SD] ⊠ [♿M] 🦻 ♿ ■ 🖥

♦♦♦ **Hampton Inn-Clearwater/St. Petersburg Airport** [M]
(727) 577-9200. **$79-$109.** 3655 Hospitality at Ulmerton Rd. I-275, exit 31 southbound; exit 30 northbound, 1.8 mi w on SR 688. Ext corridors. **Pets:** Accepted.
[A$K] [SD] ⊠ 🦻 🖥 🏊 🏋

♦♦♦ **Holiday Inn Express** [SH] 🐾
(727) 536-7275. **$79-$159.** 13625 Icot Blvd. 0.5 mi e of jct US 19; just n of Ulmerton Rd (SR 688); in Icot Center Business Park. Int corridors. **Pets:** Medium. $50 one-time fee/pet. Designated rooms, service with restrictions, crate.
[A$K] [SD] ⊠ [♿M] 🦻 ♿ ■ 🖥 🏊

♦♦ **Homestead Studio Suites Hotel-St Petersburg-Clearwater** [M]
(727) 572-4800. **$74-$104.** 2311 Ulmerton Rd. I-275, exit 31 southbound; exit 30 northbound, 1.3 mi w on SR 688. Ext corridors. **Pets:** Accepted.
[A$K] [SD] ⊠ [♿M] 🦻 ♿ ■ 🖥 🏊

♦♦♦ **Homewood Suites by Hilton** [SH]
(727) 573-1500. **$119-$249.** 2233 Ulmerton Rd. I-275, exit 31 southbound; exit 30 northbound, 1.3 mi w on SR 688 (Ulmerton Rd). Int corridors. **Pets:** Accepted.
[A$K] ⊠ [♿M] 🦻 ♿ ■ 🖥 🏊

♦♦ **Howard Johnson Inn & Suites** [M]
(727) 796-0135. **$60-$96.** 27988 US Hwy 19 N. On US 19, 0.6 mi n of jct SR 580. Ext corridors. **Pets:** Small. $10 daily fee/pet. Designated rooms, service with restrictions, supervision.
[A$K] [SD] ⊠ ♿ ■ 🖥 🏊

♦♦♦ **La Quinta Inn Tampa Bay (Clearwater-Airport)** [SH]
(727) 572-7222. **$101-$145.** 3301 Ulmerton Rd. I-275, exit 31 southbound; exit 30 northbound, 1.7 mi w on SR 688; in The Centres Office Park. Int corridors. **Pets:** Medium. Service with restrictions.
[A$K] ⊠ 🦻 ♿ ■ 🖥 🏊 🏋

♦♦♦ **Radisson Hotel Clearwater Central** [SH]
(727) 799-1181. **$75-$89.** 20967 US 19 N. On US 19, just n of jct SR 60. Ext/int corridors. **Pets:** Accepted.
[A$K] [SD] ⊠ [♿M] 🦻 ♿ ■ 🖥 🍴 🏊 🏋

[AAA] ♦♦♦ **Residence Inn by Marriott** [SH]
(727) 573-4444. **$169-$299.** 5050 Ulmerton Rd. On SR 688, 1 mi e of jct US 19. Ext corridors. **Pets:** Accepted.
[SAVE] ⊠ 🦻 ♿ ■ 🖥 🏊 🏋

AAA ▼▼ Super 8 Clearwater/St. Petersburg Airport 🆂🅷
(727) 572-8881. **$60-$120.** 13260 34th St N. I-275, exit 31 southbound;
exit 30 northbound, 1.8 mi w on SR 688 (Ulmerton Rd), then just s. Int
corridors. **Pets:** Large. $10 daily fee/pet. Designated rooms, service with
restrictions, supervision.
[SAVE] [S🐾] [✕] [🛏] [💻] [🏊]

▼▼▼ TownePlace Suites by Marriott St.
Petersburg/Clearwater 🆂🅷
(727) 299-9229. **$79-$169.** 13200 49th St N. I-275, exit 31 southbound;
exit 30 northbound, 3 mi w on SR 688, then just s; in Turtle Creek. Int
corridors. **Pets:** Accepted.
[ASK] [S🐾] [✕] [🔥M] [🍳] [♿] [🛏] [💻] [🏊]

INDIAN ROCKS BEACH

▼▼ Sea Star Motel & Apartments 🅼 ❀
(727) 596-2525. **$65-$115, 30 day notice.** 1805 Gulf Blvd. On SR 699,
1.2 mi n of jct SR 688 (Walsingham Rd). Ext corridors. **Pets:** Other
species. $10 daily fee/pet. No service, crate.
[✕] [🛏] [💻] [🏊] [🔒]

LARGO

AAA ▼▼▼ Hampton Inn & Suites 🆂🅷
(727) 585-3333. **$109-$189.** 100 E Bay Dr. On SR 686, 3.4 mi w of jct
US 19. Int corridors. **Pets:** Accepted.
[SAVE] [S🐾] [✕] [🔥M] [🍳] [🛏] [💻] [🏊]

MADEIRA BEACH

AAA ▼▼ Snug Harbor Inn Waterfront Bed &
Breakfast 🅼 ❀
(727) 395-9256. **$72-$128, 21 day notice.** 13655 Gulf Blvd. On SR
699, 0.9 mi s of jct Tom Stuart Cswy. Ext corridors. **Pets:** Other species.
Service with restrictions.
[SAVE] [✕] [🛏] [💻] [🏊] [🔒]

NEW PORT RICHEY

AAA ▼▼ Riverside Inn 🅼
(727) 845-4990. **$50-$120.** 7631 US 19. On US 19, 0.8 mi n of jct Main
St. Ext corridors. **Pets:** Small. $6 daily fee/room. Designated rooms, no
service, supervision.
[SAVE] [S🐾] [✕] [🛏] [💻] [🏊]

OLDSMAR

AAA ▼▼▼ Residence Inn Tampa/Oldsmar 🆂🅷
(813) 818-9400. **$139-$219.** 4012 Tampa Rd. Just s on St. Pete Dr. Int
corridors. **Pets:** Medium, other species. $100 one-time fee/pet. Service
with restrictions, crate.
[SAVE] [S🐾] [✕] [🔥M] [🍳] [♿] [🛏] [💻] [🏊] [🔒]

PALM HARBOR

AAA ▼▼▼ Best Western Palm Harbor Hotel 🅲🅾
(727) 942-0358. **$80-$125.** 37611 US 19 N. On US 19, 3 mi s of jct SR
582. Ext corridors. **Pets:** Medium, other species. $10 daily fee/pet. Service
with restrictions, crate.
[SAVE] [S🐾] [✕] [♿] [🛏] [💻] [🍴] [🏊] [🔒]

▼ Knights Inn-Clearwater/Palm Harbor 🅼
(727) 789-2002. **$56-$89.** 34106 US 19 N. On US 19, 1.8 mi n of CR
752 (Tampa Rd). Ext corridors. **Pets:** Medium, other species. $10 daily
fee/room. Service with restrictions, crate.
[ASK] [S🐾] [✕] [🔥M] [♿] [🛏] [💻] [🏊]

AAA ▼▼ Red Roof Inn 🅼
(727) 786-2529. **$45-$150.** 32000 US 19 N. On US 19, 0.4 mi s of jct
CR 752 (Tampa Rd). Ext corridors. **Pets:** $15 daily fee/pet. Designated
rooms, service with restrictions, supervision.
[SAVE] [S🐾] [✕] [🍳] [♿] [🛏] [💻] [🏊]

AAA ▼▼▼ The Westin Innisbrook Golf Resort 🅲🅾 ❀
(727) 942-2000. **$109-$189.** 36750 US Hwy 19. On US 19, 2.8 mi s of
jct SR 582. Int corridors. **Pets:** Medium. $50 one-time fee/pet. Service
with restrictions.
[SAVE] [✕] [🛏] [💻] [🍴] [🏊] [🔒]

PINELLAS PARK

▼▼▼ La Quinta Inn Tampa (Pinellas Park/Clearwater) 🆂🅷
(727) 545-5611. **$90-$145.** 7500 US Hwy 19 N. I-275, exit 28, 1.4 mi s
on Gandy Blvd (SR 694), then just n. Ext/int corridors. **Pets:** Medium.
Service with restrictions.
[ASK] [✕] [🔥M] [🍳] [🛏] [💻] [🏊]

PLANT CITY

AAA ▼▼▼ Ramada Plantation House 🅼
(813) 752-3141. **$89-$189.** 2011 N Wheeler St. I-4, exit 21, 0.4 mi ne;
at jct SR 39. Ext corridors. **Pets:** Accepted.
[SAVE] [S🐾] [✕] [🔥M] [🍳] [♿] [🛏] [💻] [🍴] [🏊]

PORT RICHEY

▼▼ Comfort Inn 🅼
(727) 863-3336. **$59-$99.** 11810 US 19. On US 19, just s of jct SR 52.
Ext corridors. **Pets:** Accepted.
[ASK] [S🐾] [✕] [🍳] [🛏] [💻] [🏊]

SAFETY HARBOR

AAA ▼▼▼ Safety Harbor Resort and Spa on Tampa
Bay 🆂🅷
(727) 726-1161. **$169-$469, 3 day notice.** 105 N Bayshore Dr. Jct SR
590 (Main St); downtown. Int corridors. **Pets:** Accepted.
[SAVE] [S🐾] [✕] [🔥M] [🍳] [♿] [🛏] [💻] [🍴] [🏊] [🔒]

ST. PETE BEACH

AAA ▼▼ Bayview Plaza Waterfront Resort 🅼
(727) 367-1387. **$49-$149, 14 day notice.** 4321 Gulf Blvd. On SR 699;
0.8 mi n of Pinellas Bayway. Ext/int corridors. **Pets:** Accepted.
[SAVE] [S🐾] [✕] [🛏]

AAA ▼▼▼▼ Beach House Suites By The Don Cesar 🆂🅷
(727) 363-0001. **$179-$489, 5 day notice.** 3860 Gulf Blvd. On SR 699,
0.4 mi n of jct Pinellas Bayway. Ext corridors. **Pets:** Accepted.
[SAVE] [S🐾] [✕] [🍳] [🛏] [💻] [🏊] [🔒]

AAA ▼▼▼▼ Don CeSar Beach Resort, A Loews
Hotel 🅻🅷 ❀
(727) 360-1881. **$234-$559, 5 day notice.** 3400 Gulf Blvd. On SR 699,
jct Pinellas Bayway. Int corridors. **Pets:** Small, other species. $25 one-
time fee/pet. Service with restrictions.
[SAVE] [S🐾] [✕] [🔥M] [🍳] [♿] [🛏] [💻] [🍴] [🏊] [🔒]

ST. PETERSBURG

▼▼▼ Days Inn Tropicana Field North 🅼 ❀
(727) 522-3191. **$50-$80.** 2595 54th Ave N. I-275, exit 26 southbound;
exit 26B northbound, just w. Ext corridors. **Pets:** Medium, other species.
$25 daily fee/pet. Designated rooms, service with restrictions, supervision.
[ASK] [S🐾] [✕] [🍳] [🛏] [💻] [🏊]

▼▼▼ La Quinta Inn Tampa Bay Area (St.
Petersburg) 🅼
(727) 527-8421. **$95-$135.** 4999 34th St N. I-275, exit 26 southbound;
exit 26B northbound, just w on 54th Ave N, then just s on US 19. Ext
corridors. **Pets:** Medium. Service with restrictions.
[ASK] [✕] [🔥M] [🍳] [♿] [🛏] [💻] [🏊]

▼▼▼ Mansion House B & B 🅱🅱
(727) 821-9391. **$139-$250, 14 day notice.** 105 5th Ave NE. 0.5 mi n
at 1st St N; downtown. Ext/int corridors. **Pets:** Accepted.
[ASK] [✕] [🛏] [🏊]

Ramada Inn Mirage M
(727) 525-1181. $60-$105. 5005 34th St N. I-275, exit 26 southbound; exit 26B northbound,0.8 mi w on 54th Ave N, then 0.3 mi s on US 19. Ext corridors. Pets: Accepted.

SEFFNER

Hampton Inn & Suites Tampa-East SH
(813) 630-4321. $115-$125. 11740 Tampa Gateway Blvd. I-4, exit 10, just n of CR 579. Int corridors. Pets: Small. Service with restrictions, crate.

TAMPA

Best Western All Suites Hotel Near USF Behind Busch Gardens SH
(813) 971-8930. $95-$139, 3 day notice. 3001 University Center Dr. I-275, exit 51, 1.8 mi e on SR 582 (Fowler Ave), then 0.5 mi s on N 30th St. Ext corridors. Pets: Large. $25 daily fee/pet. Designated rooms, service with restrictions, supervision.

Best Western Brandon Hotel & Conference Center M
(813) 621-5555. $52-$102. 9331 Adamo Dr. I-75, exit 257, 1.2 mi w on SR 60. Ext corridors. Pets: Large, other species. $30 one-time fee/room. Designated rooms, service with restrictions, crate.

Chase Suite Hotel by Woodfin M
(813) 281-5677. $109-$239. 3075 N Rocky Point Dr. I-275, exit 39 southbound; exit 39B northbound, 3 mi w on SR 60, then just n; in Rocky Point Harbor. Ext corridors. Pets: Accepted.

Clarion Hotel and Conference Center near Busch Gardens SH
(813) 971-4710. $69-$179. 2701 E Fowler Ave. I-275, exit 51, 1.5 mi e on SR 582. Ext/int corridors. Pets: Accepted.

Comfort Inn and Conference Center Near Busch Gardens SH
(813) 933-4011. $79-$109. 820 E Busch Blvd. I-275, exit 50, just e on SR 580. Ext/int corridors. Pets: Accepted.

Comfort Inn Hotel & Suites Tampa Stadium/Airport M
(813) 877-6061. $70-$269. 4732 N Dale Mabry Hwy. I-275, exit 41B, 2 mi n. Ext corridors. Pets: Accepted.

Extended StayAmerica-Tampa Airport-West Shore SH
(813) 873-2850. $89-$124. 4312 W Spruce St. I-275, exit 40B, 0.6 mi n on Lois Ave, then just w. Int corridors. Pets: Accepted.

Extended Stay Deluxe Tampa–Airport SH
(813) 886-5253. $89-$114. 4811 Memorial Hwy. Veteran's Expwy, exit 3, just sw on CR 576. Int corridors. Pets: Accepted.

Extended Stay Deluxe-Tampa-Airport-N West Shore Blvd SH
(813) 637-8990. $89-$124. 1805 N Westshore Blvd. I-275, exit 40A southbound, 0.5 mi n; exit 39A northbound, 1 mi e on Kennedy Blvd, then 1.3 mi n. Int corridors. Pets: Accepted.

Grand Hyatt Tampa Bay LH
(813) 874-1234. $135-$410. 2900 Bayport Plaza. SR 60, east end of Courtney Campbell Cswy. Ext/int corridors. Pets: Other species. $75 one-time fee/room. Designated rooms, service with restrictions, supervision.

Hampton Inn Veterans Expressway SH
(813) 901-5900. $109-$179. 5628 W Waters Ave. SR 589 (Veteran's Expwy), exit 6A, just e on CR 584. Int corridors. Pets: Accepted.

Holiday Inn Express & Suites SH
(813) 910-7171. $99-$179. 8310 Galbraith Rd. I-75, exit 270, 0.3 mi n on CR 581 (Bruce B Downs Blvd), just w on Highwoods Preserve Pkwy, then just n; in Highwoods Preserve. Int corridors. Pets: Accepted.

Holiday Inn Express Hotel & Suites SH
(813) 885-3700. $99-$149. 9402 Corporate Lake Dr. SR 589 (Veteran's Expwy), exit 6B, just ne; in Westlake Corporate Center. Int corridors. Pets: $35 one-time fee/pet. Designated rooms, no service.

Homestead Studio Suites Hotel-Tampa/North Airport M
(813) 243-1913. $64-$94. 5401 Beaumont Ctr Blvd. SR 589 (Veterans Expwy), exit 4, just w on SR 580. Ext/int corridors. Pets: Accepted.

La Quinta Inn & Suites M
(813) 626-0885. $81-$145. 4811 US 301 N. I-4, exit 6 westbound; exit 6A eastbound, just se. Int corridors. Pets: Medium. Service with restrictions.

La Quinta Inn & Suites Tampa Bay (U.S.F./Near Busch Gardens) SH
(813) 910-7500. $105-$155. 3701 E Fowler. I-275, exit 51, 2.2 mi e on SR 582. Int corridors. Pets: Medium. Service with restrictions.

La Quinta Inn & Suites Tampa-Brandon SH
(813) 684-4007. $89-$149. 602 S Falkenburg Rd. I-75, exit 257, just w on SR 60, then just n. Int corridors. Pets: Medium. Service with restrictions.

La Quinta Inn & Suites Tampa/near Busch Gardens SH
(813) 930-6900. $75-$149. 9202 N 30th St. I-275, exit 50, 2 mi e on SR 580, then just n. Ext corridors. Pets: Medium. Service with restrictions.

La Quinta Inn Tampa Bay (Airport) M
(813) 287-0440. $101-$155. 4730 Spruce St. I-275, exit 40A, 0.7 mi w on Westshore Blvd; exit 39A, 1 mi e on Kennedy Blvd, 1.2 mi n on Westshore Blvd, then just w. Ext corridors. Pets: Pets: Medium. Service with restrictions.

La Quinta Inn Tampa South SH
(813) 835-6262. $119-$199. 4620 W Gandy Blvd. Just e of jct S West Shore Blvd. Int corridors. Pets: Small. Designated rooms, service with restrictions, supervision.

Motel 6 #1192 M
(813) 628-0888. $53-$65. 6510 US 301 N. I-4, exit 7 westbound; exit 7B eastbound, 0.7 mi n. Ext corridors. Pets: Medium, other species. Service with restrictions, supervision.

Red Roof Inn
(813) 932-0073. **$49-$79.** 2307 E Busch Blvd. I-275, exit 50, 1.4 mi e on SR 580. Ext corridors. **Pets:** Medium, other species. Service with restrictions, supervision.

Red Roof Inn-Fairgrounds M
(813) 623-5245. **$60-$90.** 5001 N US 301. I-4, exit 7 westbound; exit 7A eastbound, just se. Ext corridors. **Pets:** Medium, other species. Service with restrictions, supervision.

Residence Inn by Marriott Sabal Park SH
(813) 627-8855. **$84-$209.** 9719 Princess Palm Ave. I-75, exit 260 southbound; exit 260B northbound, just w on SR 574 (Dr. Martin Luther King Jr Blvd), just s on Falkenburg Rd, then 0.4 mi w; in Sabal Corporate Center. Int corridors. **Pets:** Accepted.

Seminole Hard Rock Hotel and Casino Tampa LH ❀
(813) 627-7625. **$209-$329.** 5223 N Orient Rd. I-4, exit 6, just w. Int corridors. **Pets:** Medium, other species. $50 one-time fee/pet. Designated rooms, service with restrictions, crate.

Sheraton Suites Tampa Airport LH ❀
(813) 873-8675. **$139-$209.** 4400 W Cypress St. I-275, exit 40B, n to Cypress St, then 0.3 mi w. Int corridors. **Pets:** Medium. Service with restrictions, supervision.

Tahitian Inn SH
(813) 877-6721. **$119-$259.** 601 S Dale Mabry Hwy. I-275, exit 41A, 1.1 mi s. Ext/int corridors. **Pets:** Accepted.

Westin Harbour Island LH
(813) 229-5000. **$149-$289.** 725 S Harbour Island Blvd. I-275, exit 44, just e, then 2 mi s on Tampa St, follow signs to Convention Center and Harbour Island. Int corridors. **Pets:** Accepted.

TEMPLE TERRACE

Extended StayAmerica–Temple Terrace SH
(813) 989-2264. **$69-$94.** 12242 Morris Bridge Rd. I-75, exit 266, just w on Fletcher Ave (CR 582A). Int corridors. **Pets:** Accepted.

END METROPOLITAN AREA

TITUSVILLE

Best Western Space Shuttle Inn Kennedy Space Center SH
(321) 269-9100. **$69-$169.** 3455 Cheney Hwy. I-95, exit 215 (SR 50), just e. Ext corridors. **Pets:** Accepted.

Comfort Inn Titusville SH
(321) 269-7110. **$79-$250.** 3655 Cheney Hwy. I-95, exit 215 (SR 50), just w. Ext corridors. **Pets:** Small. $10 daily fee/pet. Designated rooms, service with restrictions, supervision.

Days Inn-Kennedy Space Center SH
(321) 269-4480. **$69-$169, 14 day notice.** 3755 Cheney Hwy. I-95, exit 215 (SR 50). Ext corridors. **Pets:** Accepted.

Hampton Inn Titusville/Kennedy Space Center SH
(321) 383-9191. **$119-$199.** 4760 Helen Hauser Blvd. I-95, exit 215 (SR 50), just w. Int corridors. **Pets:** Medium, other species. $25 one-time fee/pet. Designated rooms, service with restrictions.

Ramada Inn & Suites-Kennedy Space Center SH
(321) 269-5510. **$99-$119.** 3500 Cheney Hwy. I-95, exit 215 (SR 50), just e. Int corridors. **Pets:** Other species. $10 daily fee/pet. Service with restrictions, supervision.

VENICE

Holiday Inn Venice M ❀
(941) 485-5411. **$69-$179.** 455 US 41 Bypass N. 0.5 mi s of jct US 41. Ext/int corridors. **Pets:** Other species. $30 one-time fee/pet.

Horse and Chaise Inn A Bed & Breakfast BB
(941) 488-2702. **$125-$169, 7 day notice.** 317 Ponce de Leon. Just s of jct Venice Ave on Nassau St, just sw; downtown. Ext/int corridors. **Pets:** Small. $10 one-time fee/room. Designated rooms, service with restrictions.

Motel 6-364 M
(941) 485-8255. **$55-$95.** 281 US 41 Bypass N. Just n of jct Venice Ave. Ext corridors. **Pets:** Medium, other species. Service with restrictions, supervision.

WEEKI WACHEE

Best Western Weeki Wachee Resort M
(352) 596-2007. **$79-$129.** 6172 Commercial Way. On US 19, jct SR 50 (Cortez Blvd). Ext corridors. **Pets:** Other species. Service with restrictions.

WEST MELBOURNE

Howard Johnson SH
(321) 768-8439. **$70-$110.** 4431 W New Haven Ave. I-95, exit 180, just e on US 192. Ext corridors. **Pets:** Medium. $20 one-time fee/pet. Service with restrictions, supervision.

WEST PALM BEACH

Comfort Inn & Conference Center M
(561) 689-6100. **$109-$199.** 1901 Palm Beach Lakes Blvd. I-95, exit 71, just w. Int corridors. **Pets:** Accepted.

Hibiscus House Bed & Breakfast BB
(561) 863-5633. **$100-$210, 14 day notice.** 501 30th St. 1.2 mi n on Flagler Dr from jct Palm Beach Lakes Blvd, 0.3 mi w. Int corridors. **Pets:** Other species.

▼▼ La Quinta Inn M

(561) 697-3388. **$119-$329.** 5981 Okeechobee Blvd. SR 704, at east side of Florida Tpke, exit 99. Ext corridors. **Pets:** Accepted.

ASK SD X 🐾 🛏 🖥 🏊

▼▼ La Quinta Inn & Suites SH

(561) 689-8540. **$99-$279.** 1910 Palm Beach Lakes Blvd. I-95, exit 71, just w. Int corridors. **Pets:** Medium. Service with restrictions.

ASK X 🐾 🛏 🖥 🏊

▼▼ Red Roof Inn-West Palm Beach M

(561) 697-7710. **$85-$145.** 2421 Metrocenter Blvd E. I-95, exit 74 (45th St), just w on CR 702; in Metrocenter Corporate Park. Ext/int corridors. **Pets:** Medium, other species. Service with restrictions, supervision.

X 🐾 🛏 🖥 🏊

▼▼▼ Residence Inn by Marriott West Palm Beach SH 🐾

(561) 687-4747. **$119-$359.** 2461 Metrocenter Blvd. I-95, exit 74, just w on 45th St; in Metrocenter Corporate Park. Int corridors. **Pets:** Medium. $75 one-time fee/room. Service with restrictions.

ASK X 🐾 🛏 🖥 🏊 X

WINTER HAVEN

ⒶⒶⒶ ▼▼▼ Best Western Admiral's Inn and Conference Center SH 🐾

(863) 324-5950. **$98-$299.** 5665 Cypress Gardens Blvd. SR 540, 3 mi e of jct US 17; 3.9 mi w of jct US 27. Ext/int corridors. **Pets:** Small, other species. $15 daily fee/pet. Designated rooms, service with restrictions, crate.

SAVE SD X 🐾 🛏 🖥 🍴 🏊 X

ⒶⒶⒶ ▼▼▼ Holiday Inn Winter Haven-Cypress Gardens SH

(863) 294-4451. **$79-$139.** 1150 Third St SW. 0.8 mi s on US 17. Ext corridors. **Pets:** Medium, other species. $25 one-time fee/room. Designated rooms, service with restrictions, supervision.

SAVE SD X 🐾 🛏 🖥 🍴 🏊

GEORGIA

ADAIRSVILLE

◆◆◆ ▼▼▼ Comfort Inn SH
(770) 773-2886. **$50-$90.** 107 Princeton Blvd. I-75, exit 306, just w. Ext corridors. **Pets:** Small. $10 daily fee/pet. Service with restrictions, supervision.

▼▼▼ Ramada Limited SH ❀
(770) 769-9726. **$50-$110.** 500 Georgia North Cir. I-75, exit 306, 0.3 mi w. Ext corridors. **Pets:** Medium. $8 daily fee/pet. Designated rooms, service with restrictions, supervision.

ADEL

▼▼▼ Hampton Inn SH
(229) 896-3099. **$99.** 1500 W 4th St. I-75, exit 39, just w. Int corridors. **Pets:** Other species. $10 daily fee/pet. Designated rooms, service with restrictions, supervision.

▼▼ Super 8 Motel I-75 M
(229) 896-2244. **$45-$65.** 1103 W 4th St. I-75, exit 39, just e. Ext corridors. **Pets:** Accepted.

ALBANY

▼▼ ▼ Jameson Inn SH
(229) 435-3737. **$54-$120.** 2720 Dawson Rd. 0.5 mi s of jct US 82 and SR 520. Ext corridors. **Pets:** Small. $10 daily fee/pet. Service with restrictions, crate.

▼ Motel 6 #172 M
(229) 439-0078. **$35-$45.** 201 S Thornton Dr. Just e of US 19/82. Ext corridors. **Pets:** Medium, other species. Service with restrictions, supervision.

▼▼ Quality Inn-Merry Acres M
(229) 435-7721. **$65-$85.** 1500 Dawson Rd. 3.3 mi w. Ext corridors. **Pets:** Small. $10 daily fee/pet. Designated rooms, service with restrictions, crate.

▼▼▼ Wingate Inn SH
(229) 883-9800. **$101-$125.** 2735 Dawson Rd. Jct US 82 and SR 520, 0.4 mi s. Int corridors. **Pets:** Other species. $25 one-time fee/room. Service with restrictions, crate.

AMERICUS

◆◆◆ ▼▼▼▼ 1906 Pathway Inn Bed & Breakfast BB
(229) 928-2078. **$89-$145, 3 day notice.** 501 S Lee St. 0.5 mi s of US 280 on SR 377. Int corridors. **Pets:** Small, other species. $50 deposit/pet, $20 daily fee/pet. Designated rooms, service with restrictions, crate.

▼▼▼ Holiday Inn Express SH
(229) 928-5400. **$55-$85.** 1611 E Lomar St. On US 280, just w of jct US 27. Ext corridors. **Pets:** Accepted.

▼▼ Ramada Inn SH
(229) 924-4431. **$77.** 1205 Martin Luther King Jr Blvd. On US 19 S, 1 mi w of downtown. Ext corridors. **Pets:** Small, other species. $10 daily fee/pet. Designated rooms, service with restrictions, crate.

ASHBURN

◆◆◆ ▼▼▼▼ Best Western Ashburn Inn SH
(229) 567-0080. **$55-$65.** 820 Shoney's Dr. I-75, exit 82, just w. Ext corridors. **Pets:** Small. $10 daily fee/pet. Designated rooms, service with restrictions, supervision.

◆◆◆ ▼▼▼ Days Inn SH
(229) 567-3346. **$52-$62.** 823 E Washington Ave. I-75, exit 82, just w on SR 112. Ext corridors. **Pets:** Small. $10 daily fee/pet. Designated rooms, service with restrictions, supervision.

◆◆◆ ▼▼▼ Ramada Limited SH
(229) 567-3295. **$52-$60.** 156 Whittle Cir. I-75, exit 82, just w. Ext corridors. **Pets:** Medium. $5 daily fee/pet. Service with restrictions, supervision.

▼▼ ▼▼ Super 8 Motel 🆂🅷
(229) 567-4688. **$45.** 749 E Washington Ave. I-75, exit 82, just w. Ext corridors. **Pets:** Very small. $5 one-time fee/pet. Service with restrictions, supervision.

🅰🅂🄺 🆂🄳 ⊠ 🅱

ATHENS

🄰🄰🄰 ▼▼ ▼▼ Best Western-Colonial Inn Ⓜ
(706) 546-7311. **$53-$200, 3 day notice.** 170 N Milledge Ave. Jct US 78 business route (Broad St), 0.5 mi w on SR 15. Ext corridors. **Pets:** Accepted.

🆂🄰🆅🄴 ⊠ 🅱 🖵 ⇆

▼▼ ▼▼ Comfort Suites Athens 🆂🅷 ❀
(706) 995-4000. **$79-$199, 30 day notice.** 255 North Ave. SR 10 Loop, exit 11B (Dougherty St/North Ave); 1 mi n of downtown. Int corridors. **Pets:** $20 daily fee/pet. Service with restrictions, supervision.

🅰🅂🄺 🆂🄳 ⊠ 🖏 🅱 🖵 ⇆

ATLANTA METROPOLITAN AREA

ACWORTH

🄰🄰🄰 ▼▼ ▼▼ Acworth Comfort Suites 🆂🅷
(678) 574-4222. **$70-$99.** 200 N Point Way. I-75, exit 277, just e. Int corridors. **Pets:** Accepted.

🆂🄰🆅🄴 🆂🄳 ⊠ 🄼 🕭 🖏 🅱 🖵 ⇆

🄰🄰🄰 ▼▼ ▼▼ America's Best Inn Ⓜ
(770) 974-5400. **$45-$56, 7 day notice.** 5320 Cherokee St. I-75, exit 278, just w. Ext corridors. **Pets:** $5 one-time fee/pet. Service with restrictions, supervision.

🆂🄰🆅🄴 🆂🄳 ⊠ 🕭 🅱 ⇆

🄰🄰🄰 ▼▼ ▼▼ Best Western Acworth Inn Ⓜ
(770) 974-0116. **$55-$75.** 5155 Cowan Rd. I-75, exit 277, just w. Ext corridors. **Pets:** Other species. $10 daily fee/pet. Service with restrictions, supervision.

🆂🄰🆅🄴 🆂🄳 ⊠ 🅱 🖵 ⇆

🄰🄰🄰 ▼▼ ▼▼ Days Inn Ⓜ
(770) 974-1700. **$50-$80.** 5035 Cowan Rd. I-75, exit 277, just w. Ext corridors. **Pets:** Accepted.

🆂🄰🆅🄴 🆂🄳 ⊠ 🅱 🖵 ⇆

🄰🄰🄰 ▼▼ ▼▼ Econo Lodge Ⓜ
(770) 974-1922. **$50-$80.** 4980 Cowan Rd. I-75, exit 277, just w. Ext corridors. **Pets:** Accepted.

🆂🄰🆅🄴 🆂🄳 ⊠ 🅱 🖵 ⇆

🄰🄰🄰 ▼▼ ▼▼ Super 8 Motel Ⓜ
(770) 966-9700. **$50-$99.** 4970 Cowan Rd. I-75, exit 277, just w. Ext corridors. **Pets:** Medium. $10 daily fee/pet. Service with restrictions, supervision.

🆂🄰🆅🄴 🆂🄳 ⊠ 🕭 🅱 ⇆

ALPHARETTA

▼▼ ▼▼ Extended StayAmerica 🆂🅷
(770) 475-2676. **$64-$74.** 1950 Rock Mill Rd. SR 400, exit 9, just e. Int corridors. **Pets:** Accepted.

🄼 🕭 🖏 🅱 🖵

**▼▼ ▼▼ ▼▼ Extended Stay Deluxe
Atlanta-Alpharetta-Northpoint** 🆂🅷
(770) 569-1730. **$80-$90.** 3329 Old Milton Pkwy. SR 400, exit 10, just e. Int corridors. **Pets:** Accepted.

🅰🅂🄺 🆂🄳 ⊠ 🄼 🕭 🖏 🅱 🖵 ⇆

🄰🄰🄰 ▼▼ ▼▼ Homewood Suites 🆂🅷
(770) 998-1622. **$89-$169.** 10775 Davis Dr. SR 400, exit 8, northwest corner. Int corridors. **Pets:** Accepted.

🆂🄰🆅🄴 🆂🄳 ⊠ 🄼 🕭 🖏 🅱 🖵 ⇆

▼▼ ▼▼ ▼▼ La Quinta Inn & Suites Atlanta (Alpharetta) 🆂🅷
(770) 754-7800. **$84-$114.** 1350 North Point Dr. SR 400, exit 9, 0.5 mi e. Int corridors. **Pets:** Medium. Service with restrictions.

🅰🅂🄺 ⊠ 🄼 🕭 🖏 🅱 🖵 ⇆

🄰🄰🄰 ▼▼ ▼▼ ▼▼ Residence Inn by Marriott 🆂🅷
(770) 664-0664. **$84-$159.** 5465 Windward Pkwy W. SR 400, exit 11, 0.4 mi w. Ext/int corridors. **Pets:** Accepted.

🆂🄰🆅🄴 🆂🄳 ⊠ 🄼 🕭 🖏 🅱 🖵 ⇆ ⊠

▼▼ ▼▼ ▼▼ Sierra Suites Alpharetta 🆂🅷
(678) 339-0505. **$69-$199.** 12505 Cingular Way. SR 400, exit 11, 0.5 mi w. Int corridors. **Pets:** Accepted.

🅰🅂🄺 🆂🄳 ⊠ 🄼 🕭 🖏 🅱 🖵 ⇆

▼▼ ▼▼ ▼▼ Staybridge Suites 🆂🅷 ❀
(770) 569-7200. **$130-$165.** 3980 North Point Pkwy. SR 400, exit 10, 0.5 mi e. Int corridors. **Pets:** Medium, other species. $150 one-time fee/room. Service with restrictions.

🅰🅂🄺 🆂🄳 ⊠ 🄼 🕭 🖏 🅱 🖵 ⇆

▼▼ ▼▼ StudioPLUS 🆂🅷
(770) 475-7871. **$70-$85.** 3331 Old Milton Pkwy. SR 400, exit 10, just e. Int corridors. **Pets:** Accepted.

🅰🅂🄺 🆂🄳 ⊠ 🖏 🅱 🖵 ⇆

▼▼ ▼▼ ▼▼ TownePlace Suites by Marriott 🆂🅷
(770) 664-1300. **$51-$179.** 7925 S Westside Pkwy. SR 400, exit 9, 0.3 mi w. Int corridors. **Pets:** Medium. $75 one-time fee/room. Service with restrictions.

🅰🅂🄺 🆂🄳 ⊠ 🄼 🕭 🖏 🅱 🖵 ⇆

▼▼ ▼▼ Wingate Inn 🆂🅷
(770) 649-0955. **$80-$115.** 1005 Kingswood Pl. SR 400, exit 8, 0.7 mi w. Int corridors. **Pets:** Accepted.

🅰🅂🄺 🆂🄳 ⊠ 🄼 🕭 🖏 🅱 🖵

ATLANTA

🄰🄰🄰 ▼▼ ▼▼ Best Western Granada Suite Hotel 🆂🅷
(404) 876-6100. **$89-$149.** 1302 W Peachtree St. I-75/85, exit 250 (14th St), just e, then just n on W Peachtree St to 16th St. Int corridors. **Pets:** Large, other species. $50 one-time fee/pet. Service with restrictions.

🆂🄰🆅🄴 🆂🄳 ⊠ 🕭 🅱 🖵

▼▼ ▼▼ Holiday Inn 🅻🅷
(706) 549-4433. **$80.** 197 E Broad St. On US 78 business route (Broad St); jct N Hull St; center. Ext/int corridors. **Pets:** Accepted.

⊠ 🕭 🖏 🅱 🖵 🍴 ⇆

▼▼ ▼▼ ▼▼ Microtel Inn 🆂🅷
(706) 548-5676. **$55-$130.** 1050 Ultimate Dr. Jct US 78 business route (Broad St) and SR 10 Loop, 1.4 mi e. Int corridors. **Pets:** Medium, dogs only. $25 one-time fee/room. Designated rooms, service with restrictions, crate.

🅰🅂🄺 🆂🄳 ⊠ 🄼 🕭 🅱 🖵

Best Western Inn at the Peachtrees SH
(404) 577-6970. **$89-$259, 3 day notice.** 330 W Peachtree St. I-75/85, exit 248C northbound, 0.4 mi w to Peachtree St, then 0.3 mi n; exit 249C southbound, just s to Peachtree Pl, then just e. Ext/int corridors. **Pets:** Medium. $50 one-time fee/room. Service with restrictions, crate.

SAVE 🚭 🕉 🔒 🖵

Beverly Hills Inn BB
(404) 233-8520. **$110-$249, 3 day notice.** 65 Sheridan Dr NE. Jct Piedmont and Peachtree rds, 1.1 mi s on Peachtree Rd to Sheridan Dr, then just e. Int corridors. **Pets:** Accepted.

ASK 🚭 🔒 🖵

Crowne Plaza Atlanta Perimeter NW LH
(770) 955-1700. **$69-$269.** 6345 Powers Ferry Rd NW. I-285, exit 22, southeast corner. Int corridors. **Pets:** Small, other species. $75 one-time fee/room. Service with restrictions, supervision.

ASK 🚭 🚫 ♿ 🕉 📶 🔒 🖵 ⑪ ⌇

Extended StayAmerica SH
(770) 396-5600. **Call for rates (no credit cards).** 905 S Crestline Pkwy. I-285, exit 28 westbound, 0.7 mi n; exit 26 eastbound, 0.5 mi n to Hammond Dr, 0.5 mi e, then 0.3 mi n. Int corridors. **Pets:** Accepted.

🚫 ♿ 🕉 🔒 🖵

Extended StayAmerica SH
(404) 679-4333. **Call for rates (no credit cards).** 3115 Clairmont Rd. I-85, exit 91, 0.6 mi w. Int corridors. **Pets:** Accepted.

🚫 ♿ 📶 🔒 🖵

Extended Stay Deluxe Atlanta-Lenox SH
(404) 237-9100. **$80-$100.** 3967 Peachtree Rd. I-85, exit 89, 2.8 mi w. Int corridors. **Pets:** Accepted.

ASK 🚭 🚫 ♿ 📶 🔒 🖵 ⌇

Extended Stay Deluxe (Atlanta/Marietta/Powers Ferry Rd) SH
(770) 933-8010. **$75-$95.** 2010 Powers Ferry Rd. I-75, exit 260 (Windy Hill Rd), 0.5 mi e, then just s. Int corridors. **Pets:** Accepted.

ASK 🚭 🚫 ♿ 📶 🔒 🖵 ⌇

Extended Stay Deluxe (Atlanta/Marietta/Windy Hill/Int N Pkwy) SH
(770) 226-0242. **$65-$85.** 2225 Interstate North Pkwy. I-75, exit 260 (Windy Hill Rd), just e to Interstate North Pkwy, then just s. Int corridors. **Pets:** Accepted.

ASK 🚭 🚫 ♿ 🕉 📶 🔒 🖵 ⌇

Extended Stay Deluxe Atlanta-Perimeter SH
(770) 379-0111. **$80-$90.** 6330 Peachtree-Dunwoody Rd NE. I-285, exit 28 westbound, 0.7 mi n; exit 26 eastbound, 0.5 mi n to Hammond Dr, 0.5 mi e, then 0.3 mi n. Int corridors. **Pets:** Accepted.

ASK 🚭 🚫 ♿ 🕉 📶 🔒 🖵 ⌇

Four Seasons Hotel Atlanta SH ❀
(404) 881-9898. **$230-$505.** 75 14th St. I-75/85, exit 250 (14th St), 0.3 mi e. Int corridors. **Pets:** Very small. Service with restrictions, crate.

🚫 ♿ 🕉 ⑪ ⌇ 🚫

Grand Hyatt Atlanta LH
(404) 365-8100. **$179-$409.** 3300 Peachtree Rd. Corner of Peachtree and Piedmont rds NE. Int corridors. **Pets:** Accepted.

SAVE 🚫 ♿ 🕉 📶 🔒 🖵 ⑪ ⌇ 🚫

Hampton Inn-Perimeter Center SH ❀
(404) 303-0014. **$109-$139, 7 day notice.** 769 Hammond Dr. I-285, exit 26 eastbound, 0.5 mi n to Hammond Dr, then 0.5 mi e; exit 28 westbound, 0.5 mi n to Hammond Dr, then 0.5 mi w. Int corridors. **Pets:** Medium, dogs only. $50 one-time fee/pet. Designated rooms, service with restrictions, crate.

SAVE 🚭 🚫 ♿ 🕉 📶 🔒 🖵 ⌇

Hawthorn Suites-Atlanta NW SH
(770) 952-9595. **$69.** 1500 Parkwood Cir. I-75, exit 260 (Windy Hill Rd), 0.5 mi e, then 0.3 mi s on Powers Ferry Rd. Ext corridors. **Pets:** Medium. $125 one-time fee/room. Service with restrictions, crate.

SAVE 🚭 🚫 ♿ 🔒 🖵 ⌇ 🚫

Holiday Inn Express Hotel & Suites-Atlanta Buckhead SH
(404) 262-7880. **$109-$159.** 505 Pharr Rd. Jct Pharr Rd and Maple Dr; just w of Piedmont Rd. Ext/int corridors. **Pets:** Accepted.

ASK 🚫 🕉 🔒 🖵 ⌇

Holiday Inn Select Atlanta Perimeter SH
(770) 457-6363. **$84-$124.** 4386 Chamblee-Dunwoody Rd. I-285, exit 30 eastbound, southwest corner; exit westbound, follow access road 1.3 mi to Chamblee-Dunwoody Rd, then just s. Int corridors. **Pets:** $100 deposit/pet, $25 one-time fee/pet. Service with restrictions, supervision.

ASK 🚫 ♿ 🕉 📶 🔒 🖵 ⑪ ⌇

Homestead Studio Suites Hotel-Atlanta/North Druid Hills SH
(404) 325-1223. **$70-$80.** 1339 Executive Park Dr NE. I-85, exit 89, just e to Executive Park Dr, then just s. Ext corridors. **Pets:** Accepted.

ASK 🚭 🚫 ♿ 🕉 📶 🔒 🖵

Homestead Studio Suites Hotel-Atlanta/Perimeter SH
(770) 522-0025. **$65-$75.** 1050 Hammond Dr. I-285, exit 26 eastbound, 0.5 mi n to Hammond Dr, then 0.5 mi e; exit 28 westbound, just n to Hammond Dr, then just w. Ext corridors. **Pets:** Accepted.

ASK 🚭 🚫 ♿ 🕉 📶 🔒 🖵

Homewood Suites-Cumberland SH
(770) 988-9449. **$145.** 3200 Cobb Pkwy SW. I-285, exit 19 eastbound; exit 20 westbound, 0.7 mi se on US 41 (Cobb Pkwy). Ext/int corridors. **Pets:** Accepted.

ASK 🚭 🚫 ♿ 🕉 🔒 🖵 ⌇ 🚫

Hotel Indigo SH ❀
(404) 874-9200. **$99-$299.** 683 Peachtree St NE. I-75/85, exit 249D, 0.5 mi e to Peachtree St, then just n. Int corridors. **Pets:** Other species.

ASK 🚫 🕉 🖵 ⑪

Intercontinental Buckhead Atlanta LH 🐾
(404) 946-9000. **$219-$489.** 3315 Peachtree Rd NE. Jct Piedmont and Peachtree rds NE, just e. Int corridors. **Pets:** Designated rooms, supervision.

SAVE 🚭 🚫 ♿ 🕉 📶 🖵 ⑪ ⌇ 🚫

La Quinta Inn & Suites Atlanta-Buckhead/Lenox SH
(404) 321-0999. **$106-$126.** 2535 Chantilly Dr NE. I-85, exit 88 southbound; exit 86 northbound, 2 mi on Buford Hwy to Lenox Rd, then just e under highway. Int corridors. **Pets:** Medium. Service with restrictions.

ASK 🚫 🕉 🔒 🖵

La Quinta Inn & Suites Atlanta (Paces Ferry/Vinings) SH
(770) 801-9002. **$99-$119.** 2415 Paces Ferry Rd SE. I-285, exit 18, just w. Int corridors. **Pets:** Medium. Service with restrictions.

ASK 🚫 🕉 📶 🔒 🖵 ⌇

La Quinta Inn & Suites Atlanta (Perimeter/Medical Center) SH
(770) 350-6177. **$95-$143.** 6260 Peachtree-Dunwoody. I-285, exit 28 westbound, 0.7 mi n; exit 26 eastbound, 0.5 mi n to Hammond Dr, 0.7 mi e, then 0.5 mi n. Int corridors. **Pets:** Medium. Service with restrictions.

ASK 🚫 ♿ 🕉 📶 🔒 🖵 ⌇

(AAA) ▼▼▼ Omni Hotel at CNN Center LH
(404) 659-0000. **$139-$379, 3 day notice.** 100 CNN Center. I-75/85, exit 248C northbound, 0.8 mi w; exit 249C southbound to International Blvd, then 0.5 mi w. Int corridors. **Pets:** Small, dogs only. $50 one-time fee/pet. Service with restrictions, supervision.

▼▼▼ Red Roof Inn-Druid Hills M
(404) 321-1653. **$60-$84.** 1960 N Druid Hills Rd. I-85, exit 89, just w. Ext corridors. **Pets:** Medium, other species. Service with restrictions, supervision.

▼▼▼ Residence Inn Atlanta Midtown at 17th Street SH
(404) 745-1000. **$119-$290.** 1365 Peachtree St. I-75/85, exit 250 (14th St), 0.5 mi e to Peachtree St, then 0.3 mi n. Int corridors. **Pets:** Medium. $100 one-time fee/room. Service with restrictions.

▼▼▼ Residence Inn-Buckhead/Lenox SH
(404) 467-1660. **$174-$194.** 2220 Lake Blvd. I-85, exit 89, 1.6 mi w on N Druid Hills (becomes E Roxboro), then just n on Lenox Park Blvd. Int corridors. **Pets:** Large. $75 one-time fee/room. Service with restrictions, supervision.

(AAA) ▼▼ Residence Inn by Marriott-Atlanta/Buckhead SH
(404) 239-0677. **$179-$209.** 2960 Piedmont Rd NE. Jct Piedmont and Pharr rds, just s. Ext corridors. **Pets:** Accepted.

(AAA) ▼▼▼ Residence Inn by Marriott-Atlanta Downtown SH
(404) 522-0950. **$169-$199.** 134 Peachtree St NW. I-75/85, exit 248C northbound, 0.4 mi w, then just s; exit 249A southbound to International Blvd, just w, then just s. Int corridors. **Pets:** Accepted.

(AAA) ▼▼▼ Residence Inn by Marriott Atlanta Dunwoody SH
(770) 455-4446. **$129-$169.** 1901 Savoy Dr. I-285, exit 30, just e. Ext corridors. **Pets:** Accepted.

▼▼▼ Residence Inn by Marriott Midtown SH
(404) 872-8885. **$74-$234.** 1041 W Peachtree St. I-75/85, exit 250 (10th St), just e to W Peachtree St, then just n; corner of 11th St. Int corridors. **Pets:** Accepted.

(AAA) ▼▼▼ Residence Inn by Marriott-Perimeter Center SH
(404) 252-5066. **$89-$249.** 6096 Barfield Rd. I-285, exit 26 eastbound, 0.5 mi n on Glenridge to Hammond Dr, then 0.3 mi e to Barfield Rd; exit 28 westbound (Peachtree-Dunwoody Rd), 0.5 mi n to Hammond Dr, then just w. Ext corridors. **Pets:** Other species. $75 one-time fee/ room. Service with restrictions, crate.

(AAA) ▼▼▼▼ The Ritz-Carlton, Atlanta LH ❀
(404) 659-0400. **$395.** 181 Peachtree St NE. I-75/85, exit 248C northbound, 0.4 mi w, then just s; exit 249A southbound, just s to International Blvd, just w, then just s. Int corridors. **Pets:** Small. $300 deposit/ pet. Service with restrictions, supervision.

(AAA) ▼▼▼▼ The Ritz-Carlton, Buckhead LH
(404) 237-2700. **$479.** 3434 Peachtree Rd NE. I-85, exit 86, 1.8 mi n on Cheshire Bridge-Lenox Rd. Int corridors. **Pets:** Accepted.

(AAA) ▼▼▼ Sheraton Atlanta Hotel LH ❀
(404) 659-6500. **$79-$349.** 165 Courtland St. I-75/85, exit 249A southbound; exit 248C northbound, just w. Int corridors. **Pets:** Medium, dogs only. $150 deposit/room. Designated rooms, service with restrictions, supervision.

(AAA) ▼▼▼▼ Sheraton Buckhead Hotel Atlanta LH
(404) 261-9250. **$289.** 3405 Lenox Rd NE. I-85, exit 88 southbound; exit 86 northbound, 1.8 mi n. Int corridors. **Pets:** Accepted.

(AAA) ▼▼▼▼ Sheraton Midtown Atlanta Hotel at Colony Square LH
(404) 892-6000. **$89-$289.** 188 14th St NE. I-75/85, exit 250 (14th St), 0.5 mi e. Int corridors. **Pets:** Accepted.

▼▼▼ Sheraton Suites Galleria LH
(770) 955-3900. **$89-$189.** 2844 Cobb Pkwy SE. I-285, exit 20 westbound; exit 19 eastbound, just s on US 41 (Cobb Pkwy). Int corridors. **Pets:** Accepted.

▼▼▼ Staybridge Suites SH
(404) 842-0800. **$149-$169.** 540 Pharr Rd. Jct Pharr and Piedmont rds, just w. Int corridors. **Pets:** Accepted.

▼▼▼ Staybridge Suites-Atlanta-Mt. Vernon SH
(404) 250-0110. **$160.** 760 Mt Vernon Hwy NE. I-285, exit 25, 0.8 mi n on Roswell Rd, then 1 mi e. Ext/int corridors. **Pets:** Accepted.

▼▼▼ Staybridge Suites Atlanta Perimeter SH
(678) 320-0111. **$90-$170.** 4601 Ridgeview Rd. I-285, exit 29 (Ashford-Dunwoody Rd), 0.5 mi n, 0.5 mi w on Perimeter Center W to Crowne Pointe Dr, then just n. Int corridors. **Pets:** Medium, other species. $150 one-time fee/room. Service with restrictions.

▼▼▼ StudioPLUS-Atlanta-Vinings SH
(770) 436-1511. **Call for rates.** 2474 Cumberland Pkwy SE. I-285, exit 18, just e. Int corridors. **Pets:** Accepted.

▼▼▼ TownePlace Suites Atlanta Buckhead SH
(404) 949-4820. **$99-$249.** 820 Sidney Marcus Blvd. I-85, exit 86 northbound, 1.9 mi n to Sidney Marcus Blvd, then just w; exit 88 southbound, just w to Sidney Marcus Blvd, then just w. Int corridors. **Pets:** Accepted.

(AAA) ▼▼▼ University Inn at Emory SH
(404) 634-7327. **$79-$175.** 1767 N Decatur Rd. I-85, exit 91, 3.8 mi s on Clairmont Rd to N Decatur Rd, then 0.8 mi w. Ext corridors. **Pets:** Accepted.

▼▼▼ The Westin Atlanta North LH
(770) 395-3900. **$169-$300.** 7 Concourse Pkwy. I-285, exit 28 westbound; exit 26 eastbound, 0.5 mi n to Hammond Dr, then 0.4 mi e. Int corridors. **Pets:** Accepted.

▼▼▼ The Westin Buckhead Atlanta LH
(404) 365-0065. **$159-$389.** 3391 Peachtree Rd NE. Adjacent to Lenox Mall. Int corridors. **Pets:** Accepted.

▼▼▼ The Westin Peachtree Plaza LH
(404) 659-1400. **$109-$385, 3 day notice.** 210 Peachtree St. I-75/85, exit 248C northbound, 0.4 mi w; exit 249C southbound, 0.5 mi s. Int corridors. **Pets:** Accepted.

AUSTELL

▼▼▼▼ La Quinta Inn Atlanta (West/Near Six Flags) 🆂🅷
(770) 944-2110. **$69-$105.** 7377 Six Flags Dr. I-20, exit 46 eastbound; exit 46B westbound, just n. Ext/int corridors. **Pets:** Accepted.

(ASK) ⊠ 🗐 🖬 🖳 🛋

COLLEGE PARK

▼▼ Econo Lodge Ⓜ
(404) 768-1241. **Call for rates.** 4874 Old National Hwy. I-285, exit 62, just n. Ext corridors. **Pets:** Accepted.

(ASK) ⊠ 🛋

▼▼ Howard Johnson Express Inn 🆂🅷
(404) 766-0000. **$55-$75, 3 day notice.** 2480 Old National Pkwy. I-285, exit 62, just s. Int corridors. **Pets:** Accepted.

(ASK) 🆂🅾 ⊠ 🖬 🖳

▼▼ Ramada Hotel Atlanta Airport South 🆂🅷
(770) 996-4321. **$59-$99.** 1551 Phoenix Blvd. I-285, exit 60 (Riverdale Rd N), just sw. Ext/int corridors. **Pets:** Other species. Designated rooms, service with restrictions.

(ASK) 🆂🅾 ⊠ 🗐 🖬 🖬 🖳 🍴 🛋

ⒶⒶⒶ ▼▼▼▼ Sheraton Gateway Hotel, Atlanta Airport 🅻🅷
(770) 997-1100. **$209-$309.** 1900 Sullivan Rd. I-85, exit 71, just e to Sullivan Rd, then just s. Int corridors. **Pets:** Accepted.

(SAVE) 🆂🅾 ⊠ 🗐 🖬 🖳 🍴 🛋

ⒶⒶⒶ ▼▼▼▼ The Westin Hotel-Atlanta Airport 🅻🅷 ❀
(404) 762-7676. **$99-$294.** 4736 Best Rd. I-85, exit 71, just w, se on access road to Best Rd, then just s. Int corridors. **Pets:** $100 deposit/room. Service with restrictions, crate.

(SAVE) ⊠ 🛦🅼 🗐 🖬 🖬 🖳 🍴 🛋 ⊠

DECATUR

▼▼▼▼ America's Best Inn & Suites Ⓜ
(404) 286-2500. **$65.** 4095 Covington Hwy. I-285, exit 43, just w. Ext corridors. **Pets:** $10 daily fee/pet. Service with restrictions, supervision.

(ASK) 🆂🅾 ⊠ 🛦🅼 🗐 🖬 🛋

▼▼▼▼ Holiday Inn Select 🆂🅷
(404) 371-0204. **$99-$169.** 130 Clairmont Ave. Downtown. Int corridors. **Pets:** Accepted.

(ASK) 🆂🅾 ⊠ 🗐 🖬 🖳 🍴 🛋

DORAVILLE

ⒶⒶⒶ ▼▼▼ Super 8 Motel Ⓜ
(770) 458-2671. **$43-$50.** 2822 Chamblee Tucker Rd. I-85, exit 94, just w. Ext corridors. **Pets:** Accepted.

(SAVE) 🆂🅾 ⊠ 🖬

DOUGLASVILLE

▼▼ Days Inn Ⓜ
(770) 949-1499. **$60-$75.** 5489 Westmoreland Plaza. I-20, exit 37, just n. Ext corridors. **Pets:** Small. $25 daily fee/pet. Service with restrictions, supervision.

(ASK) 🆂🅾 ⊠ 🖬 🛋

DULUTH

▼▼▼▼ Candlewood Suites-Atlanta 🆂🅷
(678) 380-0414. **$72-$95.** 3665 Shackleford Rd. I-85, exit 104, just e, then just s. Int corridors. **Pets:** Medium. $150 one-time fee/room. Service with restrictions, crate.

(ASK) 🆂🅾 ⊠ 🗐 🖬 🖬 🖳

▼▼ Extended StayAmerica 🆂🅷
(770) 622-0270. **Call for rates (no credit cards).** 3430 Venture Pkwy. I-85, exit 104, just w to Venture Pkwy, then just n. Int corridors. **Pets:** Accepted.

⊠ 🛦🅼 🗐 🖬 🖬 🖳

ⒶⒶⒶ ▼▼▼▼ Hampton Inn & Suites-Gwinnett 🆂🅷 ❀
(770) 931-9800. **$81-$135.** 1725 Pineland Rd. I-85, exit 104, 0.3 mi e to Crestwood, then just s. Int corridors. **Pets:** Medium. $75 one-time fee/room. Designated rooms, service with restrictions, supervision.

(SAVE) 🆂🅾 ⊠ 🛦🅼 🗐 🖬 🖬 🖳 🛋

ⒶⒶⒶ ▼▼▼▼ Holiday Inn-Gwinnett Center 🆂🅷
(770) 476-2022. **$79-$149.** 6310 Sugarloaf Pkwy. I-85, exit 108, just w. Int corridors. **Pets:** Accepted.

(SAVE) 🆂🅾 ⊠ 🛦🅼 🗐 🖬 🖬 🖳 🍴 🛋

▼▼▼▼ La Quinta Inn Duluth 🆂🅷
(678) 957-0500. **$79-$89.** 2370 Stephen Center Dr. I-85, exit 107, just w. Int corridors. **Pets:** Service with restrictions, crate.

(ASK) 🆂🅾 ⊠ 🛦🅼 🗐 🖬 🖬 🖳 🛋

ⒶⒶⒶ ▼▼▼ Quality Inn–Gwinnett Mall 🆂🅷
(770) 623-9300. **$65-$125.** 3500 Venture Pkwy. I-85, exit 104, just w to Venture Pkwy, then just n. Ext/int corridors. **Pets:** Other species. $10 daily fee/pet. Service with restrictions, supervision.

(SAVE) 🆂🅾 ⊠ 🛦🅼 🗐 🖬 🖳

▼▼▼▼ Residence Inn-Atlanta Gwinnett 🆂🅷 🐾
(770) 921-2202. **$149-$199.** 1760 Pineland Rd. I-85, exit 104, just e to Shackleford Rd, just s to Pineland Rd, then just e. Int corridors. **Pets:** Small, other species. $75 one-time fee/room. Service with restrictions.

(ASK) ⊠ 🛦🅼 🗐 🖬 🖬 🖳 🛋 ⊠

▼▼ Studio 6 #6023 🆂🅷
(770) 931-3113. **$49-$59.** 3525 Breckinridge Blvd. I-85, exit 104, just e to Breckinridge Blvd, then just n. Ext corridors. **Pets:** Accepted.

🆂🅾 ⊠ 🛦🅼 🗐 🖬 🖳

▼▼▼▼ Wellesley Inn & Suites (Atlanta/Gwinnett Mall) 🆂🅷
(770) 623-6800. **$89-$99, 3 day notice.** 3390 Venture Pkwy NW. I-85, exit 104, just w to Venture Pkwy, then just n. Int corridors. **Pets:** Accepted.

(ASK) 🆂🅾 ⊠ 🛦🅼 🗐 🖬 🖳 🛋

EAST POINT

ⒶⒶⒶ ▼▼▼ Comfort Inn & Suites Atlanta Airport Camp Creek 🆂🅷
(404) 762-5566. **$109.** 3601 N Desert Dr. I-285, exit 2, just e. Int corridors. **Pets:** Accepted.

(SAVE) 🆂🅾 ⊠ 🛦🅼 🗐 🖬 🖳 🛋

▼▼▼▼ Crowne Plaza Hotel and Resort Atlanta Airport 🅻🅷
(404) 768-6660. **$79-$209.** 1325 Virginia Ave. I-85, exit 73 southbound; exit 73B northbound, just w. Int corridors. **Pets:** Accepted.

(ASK) ⊠ 🛦🅼 🗐 🖬 🖬 🖳 🍴 🛋

▼▼▼▼ Drury Inn & Suites-Atlanta Airport 🆂🅷
(404) 761-4900. **$90-$140.** 1270 Virginia Ave. I-85, exit 73 southbound; exit 73A northbound, just e. Int corridors. **Pets:** Large, other species. Service with restrictions, supervision.

(ASK) ⊠ 🛦🅼 🗐 🖬 🖬 🖳 🛋

ⒶⒶⒶ ▼▼▼▼ Holiday Inn Atlanta Airport North 🅻🅷
(404) 762-8411. **$79-$169.** 1380 Virginia Ave. I-85, exit 73 southbound; exit 73B northbound, just w. Ext/int corridors. **Pets:** Small, other species. $100 deposit/room, $50 one-time fee/room. Service with restrictions, supervision.

(SAVE) ⊠ 🛦🅼 🗐 🖬 🖬 🖳 🍴 🛋

▼▼▼▼ Red Roof Inn-Atlanta Airport North 🆂🅷
(404) 209-1800. **$71-$86.** 1200 Virginia Ave. I-85, exit 73 southbound; exit 73A northbound, just e. Int corridors. **Pets:** Medium, other species. Service with restrictions, supervision.

(ASK) 🆂🅾 ⊠ 🛦🅼 🗐 🖬 🖬 🖳

 **Wellesley Inn (Atlanta/Hartsfield Int'l Airport)** SH
(404) 762-5111. **$69-$89.** 1377 Virginia Ave. I-85, exit 73 southbound; exit 73B northbound, just w. Int corridors. **Pets:** Accepted.
SAVE SD X ... ...

FOREST PARK

 **Days Inn-Airport East** M
(404) 768-6400. **$55-$130.** 5116 Hwy 85. I-75, exit 237A southbound; exit 237 northbound, 0.5 mi w. **Pets:** Medium, other species. $25 daily fee/room. Designated rooms, service with restrictions, supervision.
ASK SD X ... ...

▼▼ **Super 8 Motel** SH
(404) 363-8811. **$59-$99.** 410 Old Dixie Way. I-75, exit 235, just e. Ext corridors. **Pets:** Accepted.
ASK SD X ... ...

HAPEVILLE

 **Hilton Atlanta Airport** LH
(404) 767-9000. **$99-$299.** 1031 Virginia Ave. I-85, exit 73 southbound; exit 73A northbound, just e. Int corridors. **Pets:** $50 deposit/pet. Designated rooms, service with restrictions.
SAVE X ... ...

▲▲▲ ▼▼▼▼ **Residence Inn Atlanta Airport** SH
(404) 761-0511. **$119-$259.** 3401 International Blvd. I-85, exit 73 southbound; exit 73A northbound, 0.5 mi e to International Blvd, then just n. Ext/int corridors. **Pets:** Other species. $75 one-time fee/pet. Service with restrictions.
SAVE SD X ... ...

JONESBORO

 **Holiday Inn Atlanta South Jonesboro** SH
(770) 968-4300. **$90-$160.** 6288 Old Dixie Hwy. I-75, exit 235, just w. Int corridors. **Pets:** $15 one-time fee/room.
ASK SD X ... ...

KENNESAW

▲▲▲ ▼▼ **Best Western Kennesaw Inn** SH
(770) 424-7666. **$79-$99.** 3375 Busbee Dr. I-75, exit 271, just e. Ext corridors. **Pets:** Medium, other species. $10 daily fee/pet. Designated rooms, service with restrictions, supervision.
SAVE SD X ... ...

▼▼ **Extended StayAmerica** SH
(770) 422-1403. **Call for rates (no credit cards).** 3000 George Busbee Pkwy. I-75, exit 269, just e to George Busbee Pkwy, then 0.8 mi n. Int corridors. **Pets:** Accepted.
X ... ...

▼▼▼ **La Quinta Inn** SH
(770) 426-0045. **$69-$89.** 2625 George Busbee Pkwy. I-75, exit 269, just e to George Busbee Pkwy, then just n. Int corridors. **Pets:** Accepted.
ASK SD X ... ...

▼▼ **Red Roof Inn-Town Center Mall** M
(770) 429-0323. **$45-$57.** 520 Roberts Ct NW. I-75, exit 269, just e. Ext corridors. **Pets:** Medium, other species. Service with restrictions, supervision.
X ... ...

▲▲▲ ▼▼▼ **Residence Inn by Marriott Town Center** SH
(770) 218-1018. **$169-$199.** 3443 Busbee Dr. I-75, exit 271, just e. Int corridors. **Pets:** Medium, other species. $100 one-time fee/room. Service with restrictions.
SAVE SD X ... ...

▼▼▼ **StudioPlus Atlanta-Kennesaw** SH
(770) 425-6101. **$60-$70.** 3316 Busbee Dr. I-75, exit 271, just e to Busbee Dr, then just s. Int corridors. **Pets:** Accepted.
ASK SD X ... ...

▼▼▼▼ **TownePlace Suites by Marriott** SH
(770) 794-8282. **$75-$169.** 1074 Cobb Place Blvd NW. I-75, exit 269, 1.1 mi w to Second Cobb Place Blvd entrance. Int corridors. **Pets:** Accepted.
ASK SD X ... ...

▼▼▼ **Travelodge** M
(770) 590-0519. **$45-$70.** 1460 George Busbee Pkwy. I-75, exit 273, just e. Ext corridors. **Pets:** Accepted.
ASK SD X ... ...

LAWRENCEVILLE

 **Days Inn** M
(770) 995-7782. **$55-$70.** 731 Duluth Hwy. Jct SR 316, just e on SR 120. Ext corridors. **Pets:** $20 one-time fee/pet. Service with restrictions, supervision.
SAVE SD X ...

▼▼▼ **Extended StayAmerica Atlanta-Lawrenceville** SH
(770) 962-5660. **Call for rates.** 474 W Pike St. SR 316, exit SR 120, 0.8 mi s. Ext corridors. **Pets:** Accepted.
X ... ...

▼▼▼▼ **Hampton Inn** SH
(770) 338-9600. **$99-$119.** 1135 Lakes Pkwy. I-85, exit 106 northbound, 4 mi e to Riverside Pkwy, then just n; exit 115 southbound, 4.4 mi s on SR 20 to SR 316, then 1.1 mi w. Int corridors. **Pets:** Accepted.
ASK SD X ... ...

LITHIA SPRINGS

▼▼▼ **SuiteOne Hotel of Douglas County** SH
(770) 948-8331. **$69-$99.** 637 W Market Cir. I-20, exit 44, 1 mi n. Ext corridors. **Pets:** Accepted.
ASK SD X ... ...

MARIETTA

▼▼▼ **Comfort Inn-Marietta** SH
(770) 952-3000. **$79-$99.** 2100 Northwest Pkwy. I-75, exit 261, 0.3 mi w to Franklin Rd, then just s. Ext corridors. **Pets:** Small. $25 one-time fee/pet. Designated rooms, service with restrictions, crate.
ASK SD X ... ...

▼▼▼ **Drury Inn & Suites-Atlanta Northwest** SH
(770) 612-0900. **$80-$130.** 1170 Powers Ferry Pl. I-75, exit 261, just e. Int corridors. **Pets:** Large, other species. Service with restrictions, supervision.
ASK X ... ...

▲▲▲ ▼▼▼ **Econo Lodge Northwest** SH
(770) 952-0052. **$49-$99.** 1940 Leland Dr. I-75, exit 260, just e, then 0.3 mi n. Ext/int corridors. **Pets:** Small. $5 daily fee/pet. Service with restrictions.
SAVE SD X ...

▼▼▼ **Extended StayAmerica Atlanta-Marietta Windy Hill** SH
(770) 690-9477. **$55-$65.** 1967 Leland Dr. I-75, exit 260, just e to Leland Dr, then just n. Int corridors. **Pets:** Accepted.
ASK SD X ... ...

 **Homestead Studio Suites Hotel-Atlanta-Marrietta-Powers Ferry Rd** SH
(770) 303-0043. **$70-$90.** 2239 Powers Ferry Rd. I-285, exit 22, just n. Int corridors. **Pets:** Accepted.
ASK SD X ... ...

Hyatt Regency Suites Perimeter Northwest LH
(770) 956-1234. **$99-$259.** 2999 Windy Hill Rd. I-75, exit 260, 0.5 mi e at Powers Ferry Rd. Int corridors. **Pets:** Small. $50 one-time fee/room. Supervision.

La Quinta Inn SH
(770) 951-0026. **$89-$104.** 2170 Delk Rd. I-75, exit 261, 0.3 mi w. Ext/int corridors. **Pets:** Medium. Service with restrictions.

Masters Inn Marietta M
(770) 951-2005. **$50-$54, 21 day notice.** 2682 Windy Hill Rd. I-75, exit 260, just w to Circle 75 Pkwy, then just s. Ext corridors. **Pets:** Small. $20 one-time fee/pet. Service with restrictions, crate.

Ramada Limited Suites SH
(770) 919-7878. **$49-$59.** 630 Franklin Rd. I-75, exit 263, 0.3 mi w to Franklin Rd, then 0.3 mi s. Ext corridors. **Pets:** Accepted.

Super 8 Motel SH
(770) 919-2340. **$49-$59.** 610 Franklin Rd. I-75, exit 263, 0.3 mi w to Franklin Rd, then 0.3 mi s. Ext corridors. **Pets:** Accepted.

MORROW

Best Western Southlake Inn SH
(770) 961-6300. **$44-$69, 3 day notice.** 6437 Jonesboro Rd. I-75, exit 233, just e. Ext corridors. **Pets:** Small. $10 daily fee/room. Designated rooms, service with restrictions, supervision.

Days Inn SH
(770) 961-6044. **$45-$100.** 1599 Adamson Pkwy. I-75, exit 233, just e. Ext/int corridors. **Pets:** Accepted.

Drury Inn & Suites-Atlanta South SH
(770) 960-0500. **$80-$130.** 6520 S Lee St. I-75, exit 233, just e. Int corridors. **Pets:** Large, other species. Service with restrictions, supervision.

Extended StayAmerica-Atlanta-Morrow SH
(770) 472-0727. **$65-$80.** 2265 Mt. Zion Pkwy. I-75, exit 231, just w, then 1.3 mi s. Int corridors. **Pets:** Accepted.

Quality Inn & Suites SH
(770) 960-1957. **$49-$79.** 6597 Jonesboro Rd. I-75, exit 233, just w. Ext corridors. **Pets:** Medium. $10 daily fee/pet. Service with restrictions, crate.

Red Roof Inn-South M
(770) 968-1483. **$49-$70.** 1348 Southlake Plaza Dr. I-75, exit 233, just e to Southlake Plaza Dr, then just n. Ext corridors. **Pets:** Medium, other species. Service with restrictions, supervision.

Sleep Inn SH
(770) 472-9800. **$54-$169.** 2185 Mt Zion Pkwy. I-75, exit 231, just w to Mt Zion Pkwy, then just s. Int corridors. **Pets:** Medium. $100 deposit/pet, $10 daily fee/pet. Designated rooms, service with restrictions, supervision.

NORCROSS

Amberley Suite Hotel SH
(770) 263-0515. **$69-$79.** 5885 Oakbrook Pkwy. I-85, exit 99, 0.5 mi e to Live Oak Pkwy, 0.8 mi n, then w. Int corridors. **Pets:** Accepted.

Baymont Inn & Suites SH
(770) 449-5144. **$63-$74.** 5375 Peachtree Industrial Blvd. I-285, exit 31B, 5.5 mi n; I-85, exit 99, 4 mi w to Peachtree Industrial Blvd, then 1.5 mi n. Ext/int corridors. **Pets:** Accepted.

Best Western Diplomat Inn SH
(770) 448-8686. **$49-$79.** 6187 Dawson Blvd. I-85, exit 99, just e to McDonough Dr, then just s. Ext corridors. **Pets:** Small. $20 one-time fee/room. Service with restrictions, supervision.

Comfort Inn & Suites SH
(770) 263-8883. **$64-$99, 7 day notice.** 5200 Peachtree Industrial Blvd. I-285, exit 31B, 5.5 mi n; I-85, exit 99, 4 mi w to Peachtree Industrial Blvd, then 1.5 mi n. Int corridors. **Pets:** Small, other species. $25 one-time fee/pet. Service with restrictions, supervision.

Comfort Inn & Suites SH
(770) 662-8175. **$59-$129.** 5985 Oakbrook Pkwy. I-85, exit 99, 0.5 mi e to Live Oak Pkwy, 0.8 mi n, then w. Int corridors. **Pets:** Small, other species. $10 one-time fee/room. Designated rooms, service with restrictions, supervision.

Days Inn Atlanta NE M
(770) 368-0218. **$59-$109.** 5990 Western Hills Dr. I-85, exit 99, 0.8 mi w to Norcross Tucker Rd to Western Hills Dr, then just n. Ext corridors. **Pets:** Accepted.

Drury Inn & Suites-Atlanta Northeast SH
(770) 729-0060. **$70-$125.** 5655 Jimmy Carter Blvd. I-85, exit 99, just w. Int corridors. **Pets:** Large, other species. Service with restrictions, supervision.

Extended StayAmerica Atlanta-Jimmy Carter Blvd. SH
(770) 446-9245. **Call for rates.** 6295 Jimmy Carter Blvd. I-85, exit 99, 2.5 mi w. Ext corridors. **Pets:** Accepted.

Extended StayAmerica Atlanta-Norcross SH
(770) 729-8100. **Call for rates.** 200 Lawrenceville St. Downtown; behind post office. Ext corridors. **Pets:** Accepted.

GuestHouse Inn SH
(770) 564-0492. **$49-$99, 7 day notice.** 2050 Willowtrail Pkwy. I-85, exit 101, just e. Ext corridors. **Pets:** Accepted.

Hilton Atlanta Northeast LH ❀
(770) 447-4747. **$69-$169.** 5993 Peachtree Industrial Blvd. I-285, exit 31B, 4.5 mi ne. Int corridors. **Pets:** Medium, other species. $25 one-time fee/room. Service with restrictions.

Homestead Studio Suites Hotel-Atlanta/Peachtree Corners SH
(770) 449-9966. **$50-$60.** 7049 Jimmy Carter Blvd. I-85, exit 99, 4 mi n; I-285, exit 31B, 4 mi n. Ext corridors. **Pets:** Accepted.

Homewood Suites by Hilton SH
(770) 448-4663. **$114.** 450 Technology Pkwy. I-85, exit 99, 4 mi w to Peachtree Industrial Blvd, 0.4 mi n, w on Holcomb Bridge Rd, then 2 blks n on Peachtree Pkwy; I-285, exit 31B, 5 mi n on SR 141. Ext/int corridors. **Pets:** Accepted.

 La Quinta Inn SH
(770) 368-9400. **$63-$69.** 5945 Oakbrook Pkwy. I-85, exit 99, 0.5 mi e to Live Oak Pkwy, then 0.8 mi w. Int corridors. **Pets:** Small, other species. $20 deposit/room. Service with restrictions, supervision.

Ramada Limited SH
(770) 449-7322. **$59-$99.** 6045 Oakbrook Pkwy. I-85, exit 99, just e to Live Oak Pkwy, 1 mi n, then w. Ext/int corridors. **Pets:** Accepted.

Red Roof Inn & Suites SH
(770) 446-2882. **$52-$67.** 5395 Peachtree Industrial Blvd. I-285, exit 31B, 5.5 mi n; I-85, exit 99, 4 mi w to Peachtree Industrial Blvd, then 1.5 mi n. Int corridors. **Pets:** Small, other species. Service with restrictions, supervision.

Red Roof Inn-Indian Trail M
(770) 448-8944. **$43-$60.** 5171 Brook Hollow Pkwy. I-85, exit 101, just w to Brook Hollow Pkwy, then just s. Ext corridors. **Pets:** Medium, other species. Service with restrictions, supervision.

StudioPlus SH
(770) 582-9984. **$60-$70.** 7065 Jimmy Carter Blvd. I-85, exit 99, 4 mi n; I-285, exit 31B, 4 mi n. Int corridors. **Pets:** Accepted.

ROSWELL

Days Inn- Perimeter SH
(770) 587-5161. **$55-$60.** 9995 Old Dogwood Rd. SR 400, exit 7B, just w to Old Dogwood Rd, then just n. Ext corridors. **Pets:** Accepted.

La Quinta Inn & Suites Atlanta-Roswell SH
(770) 552-0200. **$80-$100.** 575 Old Holcomb Bridge Rd. SR 400, exit 7B, just w. Int corridors. **Pets:** Medium. Service with restrictions.

Studio 6 #6025 SH
(770) 992-9449. **$53-$63.** 9955 Old Dogwood Rd. SR 400, exit 7B, just w. Ext corridors. **Pets:** Accepted.

SMYRNA

AmeriHost Inn SH
(404) 794-1600. **$70-$100, 3 day notice.** 5130 S Cobb Dr. I-285, exit 15, 0.3 mi w. Int corridors. **Pets:** Very small. $15 one-time fee/room. Designated rooms, service with restrictions, supervision.

Comfort Inn & Suites SH
(678) 309-1200. **$80-$100.** 2800 Highlands Pkwy. I-285, exit 15, just w to Highlands Pkwy, then just s. Int corridors. **Pets:** Accepted.

Holiday Inn Express Cobb Galleria SH
(770) 435-4990. **$75.** 2855 Springhill Pkwy. I-285, exit 20 westbound; exit 19 eastbound, just n on US 41 (Cobb Pkwy), then just w on Spring Rd. Int corridors. **Pets:** $50 one-time fee/pet. Service with restrictions, crate.

Homestead Studio Suites Hotel-Atlanta/Cumberland Mall SH
(770) 432-4000. **$60-$75.** 3103 Sports Ave. I-285, exit 20 westbound; exit 19 eastbound, just n to Spring Rd, then 0.3 mi w. Ext corridors. **Pets:** Accepted.

Red Roof Inn-North M
(770) 952-6966. **$47-$55.** 2200 Corporate Plaza. I-75, exit 260, just w to Corporate Plaza, then just s. Ext corridors. **Pets:** Medium, other species. Service with restrictions, supervision.

Residence Inn-Atlanta Cumberland SH
(770) 433-8877. **$89-$179.** 2771 Cumberland Blvd. I-285, exit 20 westbound; exit 19 eastbound, just n to Spring Rd, 0.3 mi w to Cumberland Blvd, then just n. Ext corridors. **Pets:** $75 one-time fee/room. Service with restrictions.

SNELLVILLE

Super 8 Motel SH
(770) 736-4723. **$79-$99.** 2971 W Main St. Jct US 78 and SR 124, 0.6 mi w. Int corridors. **Pets:** Accepted.

STONE MOUNTAIN

Best Western Stone Mountain SH
(770) 465-1022. **$79-$120.** 1595 E Park Place Blvd. US 78, exit E Park Place Blvd, just n. Ext corridors. **Pets:** Medium. $25 daily fee/pet. Designated rooms, service with restrictions, supervision.

SUWANEE

Comfort Inn SH
(770) 945-1608. **$69-$119.** 2945 Hwy 317. I-85, exit 111, just e. Ext corridors. **Pets:** Other species. $25 one-time fee/room. Service with restrictions, crate.

TUCKER

Atlanta Northlake TownePlace Suites SH
(770) 938-0408. **$111-$144.** 3300 Northlake Pkwy. I-285, exit 36 southbound, just w; exit 37 northbound, just w to Parklake Dr, 0.5 mi n, then just w. Int corridors. **Pets:** Other species. $75 one-time fee/room.

Econo Lodge M
(770) 939-8440. **$55-$80.** 1820 Mountain Industrial Blvd. US 78, exit 4, just n. Int corridors. **Pets:** Medium, dogs only. $10 daily fee/pet. Designated rooms, service with restrictions, supervision.

Masters Inn Tucker M
(770) 938-3552. **$46-$56.** 1435 Montreal Rd. I-285, exit 38, just w. Ext corridors. **Pets:** Small. $10 daily fee/pet. Service with restrictions, crate.

Quality Inn Atlanta/Northlake SH
(770) 491-7444. **$64.** 2155 Ranchwood Dr. I-285, exit 37, 0.4 mi w, then just n. Ext/int corridors. **Pets:** Small. $25 deposit/room, $10 daily fee/pet. Designated rooms, service with restrictions, crate.

Red Roof Inn-Atlanta Tucker NE M
(770) 496-1311. **$43-$53.** 2810 Lawrenceville Hwy. I-285, exit 38, just w. Ext corridors. **Pets:** Medium, other species. Service with restrictions, supervision.

UNION CITY

▼▼◆ Holiday Inn Express Hotel & Suites SH
(770) 969-4567. $59-$129. 6743 Shannon Pkwy. I-85, exit 64, 0.3 mi w, then just n. Int corridors. Pets: Accepted.
A$K S🔒 ⊗ &M 🕐 🐾 🔋 💻 ≈

◆◆ ▼▼ Microtel Inn & Suites SH ❀
(770) 306-3800. $49-$59. 6690 Shannon Pkwy. I-85, exit 64, 0.3 mi w to Shannon Pkwy, then just n. Int corridors. Pets: Small. $10 daily fee/pet. Service with restrictions, supervision.
SAVE S🔒 ⊗ &M 🕐 🐾 🔋 💻

END METROPOLITAN AREA

AUGUSTA

▼▼ Comfort Inn SH
(706) 855-6060. $63-$99. 629 Frontage Rd NW. I-20, exit 196B, 0.3 mi n to Scott Nixon Memorial, just w, then just s. Int corridors. Pets: Accepted.
A$K S🔒 ⊗ 🔋 💻 ≈

◆◆ ▼▼◆ Comfort Inn Medical Center SH
(706) 722-2224. $76, 10 day notice. 1455 Walton Way. I-20, exit 199 (Washington Rd), 4.5 mi e on SR 28, then just sw on 15th St. Ext corridors. Pets: Medium, other species. $50 deposit/pet. Service with restrictions, supervision.
SAVE S🔒 ⊗ 🐾 🔋 💻 ≈

▼▼◆ DoubleTree Augusta SH
(706) 855-8100. $109-$139. 2651 Perimeter Pkwy. I-520, exit 1C (Wheeler Rd), just w to Perimeter Pkwy, then just n. Int corridors. Pets: Accepted.
A$K S🔒 ⊗ &M 🔋 💻 🍴 ≈ ⊗

▼▼◆ Holiday Inn Gordon Highway at Bobby Jones SH
(706) 737-2300. $82-$92. 2155 Gordon Hwy. I-520, exit 3A (US 78), just w. Ext corridors. Pets: Large. $35 one-time fee/room. Service with restrictions, crate.
A$K S🔒 ⊗ 🔋 💻 🍴 ≈

▼▼◆ Howard Johnson Inn M
(706) 863-2882. $45-$89. 601 Frontage Rd NW. I-20, exit 196B (Bobby Jones Expwy), just nw. Ext corridors. Pets: Accepted.
A$K S🔒 ⊗ 🔋 💻 ≈

▼▼◆ La Quinta Inn Augusta SH
(706) 733-2660. $77-$97. 3020 Washington Rd. I-20, exit 199 (Washington Rd), just w. Ext/int corridors. Pets: Medium. Service with restrictions.
A$K ⊗ &M 🕐 🔋 💻 ≈

◆◆ ▼▼◆ Marriott Augusta Hotel & Suites LH
(706) 722-8900. $129-$189. 2 10th St. I-20, exit 200 (River Watch Pkwy), 5.4 mi se, then just n; downtown. Int corridors. Pets: Accepted.
SAVE S🔒 ⊗ &M 🕐 🔋 💻 🍴 ≈ ⊗

◆◆ ▼▼◆ The Partridge Inn SH
(706) 737-8888. $139-$219, 7 day notice. 2110 Walton Way. 1.3 mi w off 15th St. Int corridors. Pets: Accepted.
SAVE S🔒 ⊗ 🐾 🔋 💻 🍴 ≈

BAINBRIDGE

▼▼ Jameson Inn SH
(229) 243-7000. $54-$120. 1403 Tallahassee Hwy. Just s of US 84 Bypass on US 27. Ext corridors. Pets: Small. $10 daily fee/pet. Service with restrictions, crate.
A$K ⊗ 🐾 🔋 💻 ≈

BARNESVILLE

◆◆ ▼▼◆ Country Hearth Inn SH
(770) 358-0967. $55. 648 Hwy 341 S. Jct US 341 and 41, 2.3 mi s. Int corridors. Pets: Accepted.
SAVE S🔒 ⊗ 🔋 💻

BLUE RIDGE

▼▼◆ Douglas Inn & Suites M
(706) 258-3600. $59-$89. 1192 Windy Ridge Rd. Just off SR 515 and US 76. Ext corridors. Pets: Accepted.
A$K S🔒 ⊗ 🔋 💻 ≈

BRASELTON

◆◆ ▼▼◆ Chateau Elan Lodge by Holiday Inn Express SH
(770) 867-8100. $89-$129. 2069 Hwy 211. I-85, exit 126, just w. Int corridors. Pets: Other species. $25 one-time fee/room. Service with restrictions, supervision.
SAVE S🔒 💻 ≈

BREMEN

◆◆ ▼▼◆ Days Inn SH ❀
(770) 537-4646. $49-$149. 35 Price Creek Rd. I-75, exit 11, just n. Ext corridors. Pets: Medium, dogs only. $10 one-time fee/pet. Service with restrictions, crate.
SAVE S🔒 ⊗ 🔋 ≈

▼▼◆ Holiday Inn Express Hotel & Suites SH
(770) 537-3770. $94-$104. 125 US Hwy 27 Bypass. I-20, exit 11, just n. Int corridors. Pets: Accepted.
A$K S🔒 ⊗ &M 🕐 🐾 🔋 💻 ≈

BRUNSWICK

◆◆ ▼▼◆ Best Western Brunswick Inn SH ❀
(912) 264-0144. $68-$88. 5323 New Jesup Hwy. I-95, exit 36B (New Jesup Hwy/US 25), just nw. Ext corridors. Pets: Small, other species. Service with restrictions, supervision.
SAVE S🔒 ⊗ 🔋 💻 🍴 ≈

▼▼◆ Embassy Suites Hotel SH ❀
(912) 264-6100. $109-$209. 500 Mall Blvd. I-95, exit 38 (Golden Isles Pkwy), 2 mi se, then just e. Int corridors. Pets: $15 daily fee/room. Service with restrictions, supervision.
⊗ 🕐 🔋 💻 ≈

◆◆ ▼▼◆ Hampton Inn SH ❀
(912) 261-0002. $99-$119. 230 Warren Mason Blvd. I-95, exit 36A (New Jesup Hwy/US 25), just se, then just sw on Tourist Dr. Ext/int corridors. Pets: Other species. $25 one-time fee/room. Service with restrictions, crate.
SAVE S🔒 ⊗ 🕐 🔋 💻 ≈

▼▼◆ Jameson Inn Brunswick SH
(912) 267-0800. $54-$120. 661 Scranton Rd. I-95, exit 38 (Golden Isles Pkwy), 1.6 mi se, then just sw. Ext corridors. Pets: Small. $10 daily fee/pet. Service with restrictions, crate.
A$K ⊗ 🔋 💻 ≈

▼▼ La Quinta Inn & Suites Brunswick SH
(912) 265-7725. $72-$82. 165 Warren Mason Blvd. I-95, exit 36A (New Jesup Hwy/US 25), just se, then sw on Tourist Dr. Int corridors. Pets: Medium. Service with restrictions.
A$K ⊗ 🕐 🔋 💻 ≈

AAA ▼▼▼▼ Park Inn SH ❀
(912) 264-4033. **$69-$109.** 5252 New Jesup Hwy. I-95, exit 36B (New Jesup Hwy/US 25), just nw. Ext corridors. **Pets:** Other species. $25 one-time fee/room. Service with restrictions.

SAVE S X & 🛏 💻 ¶ ⊇

▼▼ Red Roof Inn & Suites I-95 SH
(912) 264-4720. **$59-$104.** 25 Tourist Dr. I-95, exit 36A (New Jesup Hwy/US 25), just se. Int corridors. **Pets:** Other species. Service with restrictions, supervision.

ASK S X ⟋ 🛏 💻 ⊇

AAA ▼ Super 8 Motel M
(912) 264-8800. **$56-$151.** 5280 New Jesup Hwy. I-95, exit 36B (New Jesup Hwy/US 25), just nw. Int corridors. **Pets:** Small. $10 daily fee/pet. Service with restrictions, supervision.

SAVE S X 🛏

BYRON

AAA ▼▼▼ Best Western Inn and Suites SH
(478) 956-3056. **$59.** 101 Dunbar Rd. I-75, exit 149 (SR 49), just ne. Ext corridors. **Pets:** Other species. $10 daily fee/pet. Service with restrictions, supervision.

SAVE S X & 🛏 💻 ⊇

AAA ▼▼▼ Comfort Inn SH
(478) 956-1600. **$54-$99.** 115 Chapman Rd. I-75, exit 149 (SR 49), just sw, then n. Ext corridors. **Pets:** Accepted.

SAVE S X & 🛏 💻 ⊇

CALHOUN

AAA ▼▼▼ Americas Best Inn M
(706) 625-1511. **$40-$65.** 1438 US Hwy 41 N. I-75, exit 318, just w. Ext corridors. **Pets:** Medium. $8 daily fee/pet. Service with restrictions, supervision.

SAVE S X 🛏 💻 ⊇

▼▼ Budget Host Shepherd Motel M
(706) 629-8644. **$40-$48.** 1007 Fairmount Hwy 53. I-75, exit 312, just e. Ext corridors. **Pets:** Accepted.

ASK S X & 🛏 💻

▼▼ Comfort Inn SH
(706) 629-8271. **$60-$70.** 742 Hwy 53 SE. I-75, exit 312, just w. Ext corridors. **Pets:** Large. $10 daily fee/pet. Service with restrictions, crate.

ASK S X 🛏 💻 ¶ ⊇

▼▼ Jameson Inn SH
(706) 629-8133. **$54-$120.** 189 Jameson St. I-75, exit 312, just w. Ext corridors. **Pets:** Small. $10 daily fee/pet. Service with restrictions, crate.

ASK X ⟋ & 🛏 💻 ⊇

AAA ▼▼▼ Quality Inn Calhoun SH 🐾
(706) 629-9501. **$65-$75.** 915 Hwy 53 E SE. I-75, exit 312, just e. Ext corridors. **Pets:** Small. $6 daily fee/pet. Service with restrictions, crate.

SAVE S X 🛏 💻 ¶ ⊇

▼▼ Ramada Limited M
(706) 629-9207. **$54-$99.** 1204 Red Bud Rd NE. I-75, exit 315, just w. Ext corridors. **Pets:** Accepted.

ASK S X ⟋ 🛏 💻 ⊇

AAA ▼▼▼ Smith Motel M
(706) 629-8427. **$28-$35.** 1437 US Hwy 41 N. I-75, exit 318, just w. Ext corridors. **Pets:** Accepted.

SAVE S X 🛏 ⊇

CARROLLTON

▼▼▼ Jameson Inn SH
(770) 834-2600. **$54-$120.** 700 S Park St. On US 27, just s of downtown. Ext corridors. **Pets:** Small. $10 daily fee/pet. Service with restrictions, crate.

ASK &M ⟋ 🛏 💻 ⊇

CARTERSVILLE

AAA ▼▼▼▼ Best Western Garden Inn & Suites SH
(770) 386-1569. **$52-$90.** 5663 Hwy 20 NE. I-75, exit 290, 0.3 mi e. Ext corridors. **Pets:** Very small. $10 daily fee/pet. Designated rooms, service with restrictions, supervision.

SAVE S X &M ⟋ & 🛏 💻 ⊇

▼▼ Budget Host Inn M
(770) 386-0350. **$38-$51.** 851 Cass-White Rd. I-75, exit 296, just w. Ext corridors. **Pets:** $4 daily fee/pet. Service with restrictions, supervision.

ASK S X 🛏 ⊇

AAA ▼▼▼ Comfort Inn M
(770) 387-1800. **$50-$72.** 28 SR 20 Spur. I-75, exit 290, 0.3 mi se. Ext corridors. **Pets:** $5 daily fee/pet. Service with restrictions, supervision.

SAVE S X 🛏 💻 ⊇

▼▼▼ Country Inn & Suites by Carlson SH
(770) 386-5888. **$71-$152.** 43 SR 20 Spur. I-75, exit 290, 0.3 mi se. Int corridors. **Pets:** Small. Service with restrictions, supervision.

ASK S X &M ⟋ 🛏 💻 ⊇

AAA ▼▼▼ Days Inn SH
(770) 382-1824. **$55-$70.** 5618 Hwy 20 SE. I-75, exit 290, just w. Ext corridors. **Pets:** Other species. $10 daily fee/pet.

SAVE S X 🛏 ⊇

▼▼▼ Holiday Inn SH
(770) 386-0830. **$76-$86.** 2336 Hwy 411. I-75, exit 293, southwest corner. Int corridors. **Pets:** Accepted.

ASK S X &M ⟋ 🛏 💻 ¶ ⊇

AAA ▼▼▼ Howard Johnson Express M
(770) 386-0700. **$40.** 25 Carson Loop NW. I-75, exit 296, just w. Ext corridors. **Pets:** Accepted.

SAVE X 🛏 💻 ¶ ⊇

AAA ▼▼▼ Knights Inn M
(770) 386-7263. **$55-$70, 14 day notice.** 420 E Church St. I-75, exit 288, 1.5 mi w. Ext corridors. **Pets:** Medium. $10 one-time fee/pet. Service with restrictions, crate.

SAVE S X 🛏 ⊇

▼▼▼ Motel 6-4046 M
(770) 386-1449. **$42-$46.** 5657 Hwy 20 NE. I-75, exit 290, 0.3 mi e. Ext corridors. **Pets:** Medium, other species. Service with restrictions, supervision.

S X ⟋ ⊇

AAA ▼▼▼ Quality Inn SH
(770) 386-0510. **$59-$87.** 235 Dixie Ave. I-75, exit 288, 2.5 mi w. Ext corridors. **Pets:** Small, dogs only. $5 daily fee/pet. Designated rooms, service with restrictions, supervision.

SAVE S X 🛏 💻 ¶ ⊇

AAA ▼▼▼ Super 8 Motel M
(770) 382-8881. **$40-$70.** 41 SR 20 Spur SE. I-75, exit 290, 0.3 mi e. Int corridors. **Pets:** $5 daily fee/pet. Service with restrictions, supervision.

SAVE S X ⟋ 🛏

CEDARTOWN

▼▼ ▼▼ Country Hearth Inn SH
(770) 749-9951. **$45-$85.** 925 N Main St. 1.5 mi n on US 27. Int corridors. **Pets:** Accepted.

ASK S X &M ⟋ & 🛏 💻

CHATSWORTH

▼▼ **Key West Inn** M
(706) 517-1155. **$49-$55.** 501 GI Maddox Pkwy. Jct SR 76 and US 411. Ext corridors. **Pets:** Accepted.
ASK S�❍ ✕ ▤

CLAYTON

AAA ▼▼ **Quality Inn & Suites** SH
(706) 782-2214. **$70-$80.** 834 Hwy 441 S. 0.8 mi s. Ext corridors. **Pets:** Accepted.
SAVE S☐ ✕ ▤ ▣ ≈

AAA ▼ **Regal Inn** M
(706) 782-4269. **$37-$95, 3 day notice.** 707 Hwy 441 S. 0.8 mi s. Ext corridors. **Pets:** Small, dogs only. $5 daily fee/pet. Designated rooms, service with restrictions, supervision.
SAVE S☐ ✕ ▤

AAA ▼▼ **Stonebrook Inn** SH
(706) 782-4702. **$39-$99.** 698 Hwy 441 S. 0.8 mi s. Int corridors. **Pets:** Accepted.
SAVE S☐ ✕ ▤ ▣

COLUMBUS

▼▼ **Extended StayAmerica-Columbus-Airport** SH
(706) 653-0131. **$65-$75.** 5020 Armour Rd. I-185, exit 8, 1.5 mi e, then just 0.5 mi n. Ext corridors. **Pets:** Accepted.
ASK S☐ ✕ ▤

▼▼ **Extended StayAmerica-Columbus-Bradley Park** SH
(706) 653-9938. **$70-$80.** 1721 Rollins Way. US 80 and SR 22, exit 3A, just s to Whittlesey Rd, 0.3 mi e to Rollins Way, then just n. Int corridors. **Pets:** Accepted.
ASK S☐ ✕ ▤

▼▼ **Howard Johnson Express Inn** SH
(706) 322-6641. **$65-$100.** 1011 Veterans Pkwy. I-185, exit 7 southbound; exit 7A northbound, 1.2 mi w to Veterans Pkwy, then 3.2 mi s. Ext corridors. **Pets:** Other species. $25 one-time fee/room. Service with restrictions, supervision.
ASK S☐ ✕ ▤ ▣ ▯ ≈

▼▼ **La Quinta Inn & Suites Columbus** SH
(706) 323-4344. **$91-$111.** 2919 Warm Springs Rd. I-185, exit 7 southbound; exit 7A northbound, just e. Int corridors. **Pets:** Medium. Service with restrictions.
ASK ✕ ▤ ▣ ≈

▼ **La Quinta Inn Columbus** SH
(706) 568-1740. **$91-$111.** 3201 Macon Rd. I-185, exit 6, just w. Ext corridors. **Pets:** Medium. Service with restrictions.
ASK ✕ ▤ ▣

▼ **Motel 6 #58** M
(706) 687-7214. **$45-$57.** 3050 Victory Dr. I-185, exit 1B, 3 mi w. Ext corridors. **Pets:** Medium, other species. Service with restrictions, supervision.
S☐ ✕ ≈

▼▼ **Super 8 Motel of Columbus** M
(706) 322-6580. **$52-$68.** 2935 Warm Springs Rd. I-185, exit 7 southbound; exit 7A northbound, just e. Int corridors. **Pets:** Accepted.
ASK S☐ ✕ ▤

COMMERCE

AAA ▼▼ **Comfort Inn** M
(706) 335-9001. **$55-$90, 3 day notice.** 165 Eisenhower Dr. I-85, exit 149, just ne. Ext corridors. **Pets:** Small. $10 daily fee/pet. Service with restrictions, supervision.
SAVE S☐ ✕ ▣ ▤ ▣ ≈

▼▼ **Howard Johnson Inn & Suites** M
(706) 335-5581. **$43-$140.** 148 Eisenhower Dr. I-85, exit 149, just ne. Ext corridors. **Pets:** Medium. $10 one-time fee/pet. Service with restrictions, supervision.
ASK S☐ ✕ ▤ ▣ ≈

▼▼ **Jameson Inn** M
(706) 335-3738. **$59-$95.** 267 Steven B Tanger Blvd. I-85, exit 149, just nw. Ext corridors. **Pets:** Small. $10 daily fee/pet. Service with restrictions, crate.
ASK S☐ ✕ ▤ ▣ ≈

AAA ▼ **Scottish Inn** M
(706) 335-5147. **$34-$129.** 30934 US 441 S. I-85, exit 149, 0.3 mi e. Ext corridors. **Pets:** Other species. $10 daily fee/pet. Service with restrictions, supervision.
SAVE S☐ ✕ ▤ ≈

▼ **Super 8 Motel** M
(706) 336-8008. **$39-$139.** 152 Eisenhower Dr. I-85, exit 149, just ne. Ext corridors. **Pets:** Medium. $10 one-time fee/pet. Service with restrictions, supervision.
ASK S☐ ✕

CONYERS

▼▼ **Comfort Inn** SH
(770) 760-0300. **$79-$129, 14 day notice.** 1363 Klondike Rd. I-20, exit 80, just s. Int corridors. **Pets:** Medium, other species. $25 one-time fee/pet. Designated rooms, service with restrictions, supervision.
ASK S☐ ✕ ▤M ▤ ▣ ≈

▼▼▼ **Hampton Inn** SH
(770) 483-8838. **$109.** 1340 Dogwood Dr. I-20, exit 82, just n, then just e. Int corridors. **Pets:** Accepted.
ASK S☐ ✕ ▤M ▱ ▣ ▤ ▣ ≈

▼▼ **Holiday Inn** SH
(770) 483-3220. **$68-$75.** 1351 Dogwood Dr. I-20, exit 80, just n, then 0.4 mi w. Ext corridors. **Pets:** Accepted.
ASK S☐ ✕ ▤M ▱ ▤ ▣ ▯ ≈

▼▼ **Jameson Inn** SH
(770) 760-1230. **$54-$120.** 1164 Dogwood Dr. I-20, exit 82, just n, then just w. Ext corridors. **Pets:** Small. $10 daily fee/pet. Service with restrictions, crate.
ASK ✕ ▤ ▣ ≈

▼▼ **La Quinta Inn & Suites Atlanta (Conyers)** SH
(770) 918-0092. **$109-$135.** 1184 Dogwood Dr. I-20, exit 82, just n, then just w. Int corridors. **Pets:** Medium. Service with restrictions.
ASK ✕ ▤M ▱ ▤ ▣ ≈

CORDELE

AAA ▼▼▼ **Best Western Colonial Inn** SH ❀
(229) 273-5420. **$65-$69.** 1706 E 16th Ave (US 280). I-75, exit 101 (US 280), just w. Ext/int corridors. **Pets:** Medium, other species. $10 daily fee/pet. Service with restrictions, supervision.
SAVE S☐ ✕ ▣ ≈

AAA ▼▼▼ **Lake Blackshear Resort & Golf Club** SH
(229) 276-1004. **$99-$179, 7 day notice.** 2459-H US 280 W. I-75, exit 101 (US 280), 10 mi w. Ext/int corridors. **Pets:** Other species. $50 one-time fee/room. Designated rooms, service with restrictions, crate.
SAVE S☐ ✕ ▤ ▣ ▯ ≈ ⊠

AAA ▼▼ **Ramada Inn** SH
(229) 273-5000. **$79.** 2016 E 16th Ave (US 280). I-75, exit 101 (US 280), just e. Ext corridors. **Pets:** Other species. $10 daily fee/pet. Service with restrictions, supervision.
SAVE S☐ ✕ ▤ ▣ ≈

AAA **Super 8** **M**
(229) 273-2456. **$55, 7 day notice.** 1618 16th Ave E (US 280). I-75, exit 101 (US 280), just w. Ext corridors. **Pets:** Designated rooms, supervision.
SAVE S6 X B

CORNELIA

Comfort Inn **SH**
(706) 778-9573. **$55-$99.** 2965 J Warren Rd. Jct SR 365 and US 441 business route, just w. Int corridors. **Pets:** Medium. $35 one-time fee/pet. Designated rooms, service with restrictions, supervision.
ASK S6 X 6M B

Holiday Inn Express **SH**
(706) 778-3600. **$73-$140.** 1105 Business 441. Jct SR 365 and US 441, just e. Int corridors. **Pets:** Medium. $35 one-time fee/pet. Designated rooms, service with restrictions, supervision.
ASK S6 X 6M B

COVINGTON

AAA **Best Western Executive Inn** **M**
(770) 787-4900. **$68-$82.** 10111 Alcovy Rd. I-20, exit 92, just n. Ext corridors. **Pets:** Accepted.
SAVE S6 X 6M B

AAA **Super 8 Motel-Covington** **SH**
(770) 786-5800. **$85, 3 day notice.** 10130 Alcovy Rd. I-20, exit 92, just n. Ext corridors. **Pets:** Accepted.
SAVE S6 X B

DAHLONEGA

Super 8 Motel **M**
(706) 864-4343. **$45-$99, 7 day notice.** 20 Mountain Dr. 0.5 mi s on US 19 and SR 60. Ext corridors. **Pets:** Accepted.
ASK S6 X B

DALLAS

Days Inn **M**
(770) 505-4567. **$56-$62.** 1007 Old Harris Rd. Jct Business Rt SR 6 (Atlanta Hwy). Ext corridors. **Pets:** Medium. $15 daily fee/pet. Supervision.
X 6M B

DALTON

AAA **Americas Best Inn** **M**
(706) 226-1100. **$42-$88, 15 day notice.** 1529 W Walnut Ave. I-75, exit 333, just e. Ext corridors. **Pets:** Other species. $10 daily fee/pet. Service with restrictions, supervision.
SAVE S6 X B

AAA **Best Western Inn of Dalton** **SH**
(706) 226-5022. **$54-$60.** 2106 Chattanooga Rd. I-75, exit 336, just w. Ext corridors. **Pets:** Small, dogs only. $5 one-time fee/pet. Service with restrictions, supervision.
SAVE S6 X B

AAA **Comfort Inn & Suites** **SH**
(706) 259-2583. **$74-$82.** 905 Westbridge Rd. I-75, exit 333, just w to Westbridge Rd, then just s. Int corridors. **Pets:** Small. $15 daily fee/pet. Designated rooms, service with restrictions, supervision.
SAVE S6 X 6M B

AAA **Econo Lodge** **M**
(706) 278-4300. **$50.** 2007 Tampico Way. I-75, exit 336, just e. Int corridors. **Pets:** Accepted.
SAVE S6 X B

Jameson Inn **SH**
(706) 281-1880. **$54-$120.** 422 Holiday Dr. I-75, exit 333, just w, then 0.3 mi n. Ext corridors. **Pets:** Small. $10 daily fee/pet. Service with restrictions, crate.
ASK X B

Motel 6 #761 **M**
(706) 278-5522. **$37-$49.** 2200 Chattanooga Rd. I-75, exit 336, 0.3 mi w. Ext corridors. **Pets:** Medium, other species. Service with restrictions, supervision.
S6 X 6M

Wingate Inn **SH**
(706) 272-9099. **$72-$76.** 715 College Dr. I-75, exit 333, just w to Holiday Dr, then 0.5 mi n. Int corridors. **Pets:** Accepted.
ASK S6 X 6M B

DARIEN

AAA **Comfort Inn** **SH**
(912) 437-4200. **$89-$129.** 703 Frontage Rd. I-95, exit 49 (SR 251), just nw. Int corridors. **Pets:** Accepted.
SAVE S6 X B

Quality Inn **SH**
(912) 437-5373. **$55-$149.** GA Hwy 251 & I-95 exit 49. I-95, exit 49 (SR 251), just w. Int corridors. **Pets:** Other species. $10 daily fee/pet. Service with restrictions, supervision.
ASK S6 X B

DAWSONVILLE

AAA **Best Western (Dawson Village Inn)** **SH**
(706) 216-4410. **$65-$149.** 76 N Georgia Ave. Jct SR 400/53, 0.5 mi s. Int corridors. **Pets:** Small, dogs only. $10 daily fee/pet. Designated rooms, service with restrictions, supervision.
SAVE S6 X 6M B

Comfort Inn **SH**
(706) 216-1900. **$59-$135, 30 day notice.** 127 Beartooth Pkwy. Jct SR 400/53, 0.5 mi s. Int corridors. **Pets:** Other species. $10 daily fee/pet. No service, crate.
ASK S6 X 6M B

Super 8 Motel **SH**
(706) 216-6801. **$50-$175.** 205 N 400 Center Ln. Jct SR 400/53, just n. Int corridors. **Pets:** Small, other species. $10 daily fee/pet. Service with restrictions, supervision.
ASK S6 X 6M B

DILLARD

AAA **Dillard House** **SH**
(706) 746-5348. **$59-$219.** 768 Franklin St. US 441, just e via Old Dillard Rd. Ext corridors. **Pets:** Medium, dogs only. $10 daily fee/pet. Designated rooms.
SAVE X B

AAA **Mountain Valley Inn** **M**
(706) 746-5373. **$40-$100.** 13 Royalty Ln. Just n of town center. Ext corridors. **Pets:** Medium. $10 daily fee/pet. Designated rooms, service with restrictions, supervision.
SAVE S6 X B

Ramada Limited **M**
(706) 746-5321. **$49-$119.** 3 Best Inn Way. Center. Ext corridors. **Pets:** Very small, dogs only. $10 daily fee/pet. Service with restrictions, supervision.
ASK S6 X B

DOUGLAS

Jameson Inn **M**
(912) 384-9432. **$54-$104.** 1628 S Peterson Ave. Jct US 221/441/SR 31 and SR 206/353, just s. Ext corridors. **Pets:** Small. $10 daily fee/pet. Service with restrictions, crate.
ASK X B

DUBLIN

(AAA) ▼▼◆ Best Western Executive Inn & Suites SH
(478) 275-2650. **$62.** 2121 Hwy 441 S. I-16, exit 51 (US 441), 0.5 mi n. Ext corridors. **Pets:** Other species. $15 one-time fee/room. Designated rooms, service with restrictions, crate.
SAVE S⬚ ⊠ ⟲ ⯐ ▣ ⇴

▼▼◆ Comfort Inn SH
(478) 274-8000. **$55-$80.** 2110 Hwy 441 S. I-16, exit 51 (US 441), 0.6 mi n. Ext corridors. **Pets:** Accepted.
ASK S⬚ ⊠ ⯪M ⟲ ⯐ ▣ ⇴

▼ Econo Lodge M
(478) 296-1223. **$49-$120 (no credit cards).** 2184 Hwy 441 S. I-16, exit 51 (US 441), just n. Ext corridors. **Pets:** Accepted.
ASK S⬚ ⊠ ⯐

▼▼ Jameson Inn M
(478) 275-3008. **$54-$120.** 100 PM Watson Dr. I-16, exit 51 (US 441), just n. Ext corridors. **Pets:** Small. $10 daily fee/pet. Service with restrictions, crate.
ASK ⊠ ⯐ ▣ ⇴

EAST ELLIJAY

(AAA) ▼▼◆ Stratford Motor Inn SH
(706) 276-1080. **$50-$120.** 79 Maddox Cir. Jct Maddox Dr and SR 515; behind KFC. Ext corridors. **Pets:** Medium, other species. $10 daily fee/pet. Designated rooms, service with restrictions, supervision.
SAVE S⬚ ⊠ ⯐ ⇴

FITZGERALD

▼▼ Country Hearth Inn SH
(229) 409-9911. **$50-$85.** 125 Stuart Way. Just n of US 319/107, just e. Int corridors. **Pets:** Medium, other species. Service with restrictions, supervision.
ASK S⬚ ⊠ ⯐ ▣

▼▼◆ Western Motel SH
(229) 424-9500. **$54-$104.** 111 Bull Run Rd. Just n of US 319/107, on US 129. Ext corridors. **Pets:** Small, dogs only. $10 one-time fee/pet. Service with restrictions, supervision.
ASK ⊠ ⯐ ▣ ⇴

FORSYTH

(AAA) ▼▼◆ Best Western Hilltop Inn SH
(478) 994-9260. **$50-$99.** 951 Hwy 42 N. I-75, exit 188 (SR 42), just ne via Frontage Rd. Ext corridors. **Pets:** Medium. $15 daily fee/pet. Designated rooms, service with restrictions, supervision.
SAVE S⬚ ⊠ ▣ ⇴

(AAA) ▼▼◆ Econo Lodge SH ❀
(478) 994-5603. **$48-$80.** 320 Cabiness Rd. I-75, exit 187 (SR 83), just ne. Int corridors. **Pets:** Medium. $6 daily fee/pet. Service with restrictions, supervision.
SAVE S⬚ ▣ ⇴

▼▼▼ Hampton Inn SH
(478) 994-9697. **$89-$119.** 520 Holiday Cir. I-75, exit 186 (Juliette Rd), just w, then just s on Aaron St. Int corridors. **Pets:** Accepted.
ASK S⬚ ⊠ ⯪M ⟲ ⯐ ▣

▼▼▼ Holiday Inn Forsyth SH ❀
(478) 994-5691. **$81-$85.** 480 Holiday Cir. I-75, exit 186 (Juliette Rd), just w, then just s on Aaron St. Ext corridors. **Pets:** Other species. $25 one-time fee/room. Service with restrictions, supervision.
ASK S⬚ ⊠ ⟲ ⯪ ⯐ ▣ ¶↑ ⇴

(AAA) ▼▼▼ Super 8 Motel SH
(478) 994-5101. **$42-$150.** 436 Tift College Dr. I-75, exit 186 (Juliette Rd), just w. Ext/int corridors. **Pets:** Accepted.
SAVE S⬚ ⊠ ⯐ ⇴

GAINESVILLE

(AAA) ▼▼◆ Days Inn SH
(770) 535-8100. **$55-$95.** 520 Queen City Pkwy SW. I-985, exit 20, 1.8 mi nw on SR 60/Queen City Pkwy. Ext corridors. **Pets:** Other species. $15 daily fee/pet. Service with restrictions, supervision.
SAVE S⬚ ⊠ ⯐ ▣ ⇴

▼▼ Ramada Limited M
(770) 287-3205. **$45-$89.** 766 Jesse Jewell Pkwy. I-985, exit 20, 1.9 mi w to Jesse Jewell Pkwy, then just s. Ext corridors. **Pets:** Other species. $10 one-time fee/pet. Supervision.
ASK S⬚ ⊠ ⯐ ▣

GARDEN CITY

(AAA) ▼▼◆ Masters Inn Garden City SH
(912) 964-4344. **$47-$52.** 4200 Hwy 21 N (Augusta Rd). I-95, exit 109 (SR 21), 6.7 mi s. Ext/int corridors. **Pets:** Small. $20 one-time fee/pet. Service with restrictions, crate.
SAVE S⬚ ⊠ ⟲ ⯐ ⇴

GLENNVILLE

(AAA) ▼ Cheeri-O Inn M
(912) 654-2176. **$40-$42.** 820 Musgrove St. 0.8 mi s on US 25 and 301. Ext corridors. **Pets:** Medium. $5 daily fee/pet. Service with restrictions, supervision.
SAVE S⬚ ⊠ ⯐ ▣

GOLDEN ISLES AREA

JEKYLL ISLAND

(AAA) ▼▼▼ Quality Inn & Suites SH
(912) 635-2202. **$84-$124, 7 day notice.** 700 N Beachview Dr. Jct Ben Fortson Pkwy (SR 520)/Beachview Dr, 1.5 mi n. Ext corridors. **Pets:** Medium. $10 daily fee/pet. Service with restrictions, supervision.
SAVE S⬚ ⊠ ⯪ ⯐ ▣ ⇴ ⊠

END AREA

GRAY

▼▼ Days Inn M
(478) 986-4200. **$58.** 288 W Clinton St. Jct SR 44/US 129, 0.9 mi w on US 129. Ext/int corridors. **Pets:** Accepted.
ASK S⬚ ⊠ ⯪ ⯐ ⇴

GREENSBORO

▼▼ Microtel Inn M
(706) 453-7300. **$45-$49.** 2470 Old Eatonton Rd. I-20, exit 130, just n on SR 44 E. Int corridors. **Pets:** $10 daily fee/pet. Service with restrictions.
ASK S⬚ ⊠ ⯪M ⟲ ⯪ ⯐

▼▼▼▼▼ The Ritz-Carlton Lodge, Reynolds
Plantation 🄻🄷
(706) 467-0600. **$225-$5000.** One Lk Oconee Tr. I-20, exit 130, 7.2 mi
sw on SR 44 (Old Eatonton Rd), 1.5 mi e on Linger Longer Rd, then
2 mi ne. Ext/int corridors. **Pets:** Accepted.

ASK S☉ ✕ ✗M ⚷ 🛆 ▣ 🍽 ⚓ ✗

GROVETOWN

⬩⬩⬩ ▼▼ Motel 6 of Augusta 🅂🄷
(706) 651-8300. **$49-$225.** 459 Parkwest Dr. I-20, exit 194 (SR 383),
just s, then w. Int corridors. **Pets:** Medium, other species. Service with
restrictions, supervision.

SAVE S☉ ✕ ⚷ 🛆 ⚓

▼▼ Quality Inn 🅂🄷
(706) 855-2088. **$60.** 4073 Jimmie Dyess Pkwy. I-20, exit 194 (SR
383), just s. Ext corridors. **Pets:** Small. $35 one-time fee/pet. Designated
rooms, no service, supervision.

ASK S☉ ✕ ✗M ⚷ 🛆 ▣ ⚓

HAHIRA

▼▼ Super 8 Motel I-75 🄼
(229) 794-8000. **$42-$62.** 1300 Georgia Hwy 122 W. I-75, exit 29, just
w. Ext corridors. **Pets:** Accepted.

ASK S☉ ✕ 🛆

HARTWELL

▼▼▼ Best Western Lake Hartwell Inn & Suites 🅂🄷
(706) 376-4700. **$69-$89.** 1357 E Franklin St. I-85, exit 177, 2 mi on
US 29 E. Int corridors. **Pets:** Medium. $20 one-time fee/room. Service
with restrictions.

ASK S☉ ✕ 🛆 ▣ ⚓

HELEN

▼▼ The Helendorf River Inn & Conference Center 🅂🄷
(706) 878-2271. **$54-$109, 10 day notice.** 33 Munichstrasse. SR 17
and 75; center. Ext corridors. **Pets:** Other species. $10 daily fee/pet.
Designated rooms, service with restrictions, supervision.

✕ 🛆 ▣ ⚓

▼▼ Kountry Peddler Tanglewood Resort Cabins 🄲🄰
(706) 878-3286. **$87-$535, 14 day notice.** 3387 Hwy 356. 1 mi n on
SR 75, then 3 mi ne. Ext corridors. **Pets:** Small, dogs only. $25 one-time
fee/pet. Designated rooms, supervision.

ASK S☉ ✕ 🛆 ▣ ⚓ ✗

⬩⬩⬩ ▼▼▼▼ Premier Vacation Rentals Inc 🅅🄷
(706) 348-8323. **$105-$395, 14 day notice.** 5156 Helen Hwy. 3.5 mi s
on SR 75. Ext corridors. **Pets:** Small, dogs only. $15 daily fee/pet. Des-
ignated rooms, no service, supervision.

SAVE S☉ 🛆 ▣

HIAWASSEE

▼▼▼ Enota B & B, Cabins & Conference Lodge 🄲🄰 ✿
(706) 896-9966. **$100-$165, 10 day notice.** 1000 Hwy 180. E on US
76 to SR 75/17, 6 mi s to SR 180, then 3 mi w. Ext corridors.
Pets: Other species. $15 daily fee/pet. No service.

✕ 🛆 ▣ ✗ ✍

▼▼▼▼ Holiday Inn Express Hotel & Suites 🅂🄷
(706) 896-8884. **$59-$79.** 300 Big Sky Dr. On US 76; center. Int corridors. **Pets:** Accepted.

ASK S☉ ✕ ✗M 🝙 ⚷ 🛆 ▣ ⚓ ✗

HINESVILLE

▼▼ Quality Inn at Fort Stewart 🅂🄷 ✿
(912) 876-4466. **$69-$89.** 706 E Oglethrope Hwy. Just sw of jct US 84
and SR 38C. Ext corridors. **Pets:** $15 one-time fee/room. Designated
rooms, service with restrictions, crate.

ASK S☉ ✕ 🝙 ⚷ 🛆 ▣ ⚓

HIRAM

▼▼▼ Country Inn & Suites by Carlson 🅂🄷
(770) 222-0456. **$79-$129.** 70 Enterprise Path. Jct SR 92/6 and US
278, 0.3 mi w. Int corridors. **Pets:** Very small, other species. $10 daily
fee/pet, $20 one-time fee/pet. Designated rooms, service with restrictions,
supervision.

ASK S☉ ✕ ⚷ 🛆 ▣ ⚓

HOGANSVILLE

⬩⬩⬩ ▼▼▼ Econo Lodge 🅂🄷
(706) 637-9395. **$65-$105.** 1888 E Main St. I-85, exit 28, just w. Ext
corridors. **Pets:** Accepted.

SAVE S☉ ✕ 🛆 ▣ ⚓

JASPER

▼▼▼ Super 8 Motel 🄼
(706) 253-3297. **$76-$86.** 100 Whitfield Dr. Jct SR 515/53; in Lawsons
Crossing. Ext corridors. **Pets:** Small. $10 daily fee/pet. Service with
restrictions, supervision.

ASK S☉ ✕ ✗M ⚷ 🛆 ▣ ⚓

JESUP

▼▼ Jameson Inn of Jesup 🄼
(912) 427-6800. **$54-$120.** 205 N Hwy 301. Jct US 341, just n. Ext
corridors. **Pets:** Small. $10 daily fee/pet. Service with restrictions, crate.

ASK ✕ ✍ 🛆 ▣ ⚓

KINGSLAND

⬩⬩⬩ ▼▼▼ Best Western/Kings Bay Inn 🅂🄷
(912) 729-7666. **$60-$80.** 1353 Hwy 40 E. I-95, exit 3 (SR 40), just se.
Ext corridors. **Pets:** Accepted.

SAVE S☉ ✕ 🛆 ▣ ⚓

▼▼ Econo Lodge 🄼
(912) 673-7336. **$52-$60.** 1135 E King Ave. I-95, exit 3 (SR 40), just
nw. Ext corridors. **Pets:** Small. $5 daily fee/pet. Service with restrictions,
supervision.

ASK S☉ ✕ ✗M ✍ ⚷ 🛆 ▣ ⚓

▼▼ Jameson Inn 🄼
(912) 729-9600. **$54-$120.** 105 May Creek Dr. I-95, exit 3 (SR 40), just
w, then s at Boone Ave. Ext corridors. **Pets:** Small. $10 daily fee/pet.
Service with restrictions, crate.

ASK ✕ ✗M 🛆 ▣ ⚓

⬩⬩⬩ ▼▼▼ Ramada Inn & Suites 🅂🄷
(912) 729-3000. **$55-$80.** 1215 E King Ave. I-95, exit 3 (SR 40), just
nw. Ext corridors. **Pets:** Accepted.

SAVE S☉ ✕ ⚷ 🛆 ▣ 🍽 ⚓

⬩⬩⬩ ▼▼ Super 8 Motel 🄼
(912) 729-6888. **$40-$150.** 120 Edenfield Dr. I-95, exit 3 (SR 40), just
se. Int corridors. **Pets:** Other species. $10 daily fee/pet. Service with
restrictions.

SAVE S☉ ✕ 🛆

LA FAYETTE

⬩⬩⬩ ▼▼▼ Days Inn 🄼
(706) 639-9362. **$50-$60.** 2209 N Main St. 2.5 mi n on US 27. Ext
corridors. **Pets:** Other species. $10 daily fee/pet. Service with restrictions,
crate.

SAVE S☉ ✕ 🛆 ⚓

▼▼ Key West Inn 🄼
(706) 638-8200. **$60-$75, 14 day notice.** 2221 N Main St. 2.5 mi n on
US 27. Ext corridors. **Pets:** Accepted.

ASK S☉ ✕ ✗M 🛆 ⚓

LAGRANGE

AAA ▼▼◆ AmeriHost Inn-LaGrange SH ❀
(706) 885-9002. **$62-$82.** 107 Hoffman Dr. I-85, exit 18 (Lafayette Pkwy), just w. Int corridors. **Pets:** Small, dogs only. $10 one-time fee/pet. Service with restrictions, supervision.
SAVE 🐾 ✕ 🐕 📶 🖥 🏊

AAA ▼▼◆ Days Inn-LaGrange/Callaway Gardens SH
(706) 882-8881. **$60.** 2606 Whitesville Rd. I-85, exit 13, just e. Ext corridors. **Pets:** $10 daily fee/pet. Service with restrictions, supervision.
SAVE 🐾 ✕ 🐕 📶 🖥 🏊

▼▼ Jameson Inn SH
(706) 882-8700. **$54-$120.** 110 Jameson Dr. I-85, exit 18 (Lafayette Pkwy), 0.3 mi w. Ext corridors. **Pets:** Small. $10 daily fee/pet. Service with restrictions, crate.
ASK ✕ 🐾M 🐕 📶 🖥 🏊

LAKE PARK

▼▼ Days Inn SH
(229) 559-0229. **$59-$79.** 4913 Timber Dr. I-75, exit 5, just w, then n. Ext corridors. **Pets:** Accepted.
ASK 🐾 ✕ 🖥 🏊

▼▼ Holiday Inn Express SH
(229) 559-5181. **$75.** 1198 Lakes Blvd. I-75, exit 5, just e. Ext corridors. **Pets:** Other species. $10 daily fee/pet. Service with restrictions.
✕ 📶 🖥 🏊

AAA ▼▼ Super 8 Motel SH
(229) 559-8111. **$50-$80.** 4907 Timber Dr. I-75, exit 5, just w, then n. Ext corridors. **Pets:** Accepted.
SAVE 🐾 ✕ 📶

LOCUST GROVE

AAA ▼▼ Econo Lodge M
(770) 957-2601. **$50-$125, 3 day notice.** 4829 Bill Gardner Pkwy. I-75, exit 212, just e. Ext corridors. **Pets:** Small. $7 daily fee/pet. Designated rooms, service with restrictions, supervision.
SAVE 🐾 ✕ 📶 🖥

AAA ▼▼◆ Red Roof Inn & Suites SH
(678) 583-0004. **$60-$99.** 4832 Bill Gardner Pkwy. I-75, exit 212, just e. Int corridors. **Pets:** Medium. Service with restrictions, supervision.
SAVE 🐾 ✕ 🐾M 🐕 📶 🖥 🏊

MACON

▼▼ Baymont Inn & Suites M
(478) 474-8004. **$54-$104.** 150 Plantation Inn Dr. I-475, exit 9 (Zebulon Rd), just e to Peake Rd, then just s. Ext corridors. **Pets:** Accepted.
ASK ✕ 📶 🖥 🏊

AAA ▼▼ Best Western Inn & Suites of Macon M
(478) 781-5300. **$59.** 4681 Chambers Rd. I-475, exit 3 (Eisenhower Pkwy/US 80), just ne, then just se. Ext corridors. **Pets:** Accepted.
SAVE 🐾 ✕ 🐕 📶 🖥 🏊

AAA ▼▼ Best Western Riverside Inn SH ❀
(478) 743-6311. **$60-$65.** 2400 Riverside Dr. I-75, exit 167 (Riverside Dr), just w, then 0.4 mi se. Int corridors. **Pets:** Medium. $10 daily fee/pet. Service with restrictions, crate.
SAVE 🐾 ✕ 📶 🖥 🏊

AAA ▼▼◆ Crowne Plaza Hotel LH
(478) 746-1461. **$59-$139, 7 day notice.** 108 First St. Between Walnut St and Riverside Dr; downtown. Int corridors. **Pets:** Large, other species. $50 one-time fee/room. Service with restrictions, crate.
SAVE 🐾 ✕ 📶 🖥 🍴 🏊 ✕

▼▼ Days Inn-Macon West M
(478) 784-1000. **$50-$75.** 6000 Harrison Rd. I-475, exit 3 (Eisenhower Pkwy/US 80), just w. Ext corridors. **Pets:** Accepted.
ASK 🐾 ✕ 🎿 📶 🏊

AAA ▼▼◆ Econo Lodge M ❀
(478) 474-1661. **$42-$60, 3 day notice.** 4951 Romeiser Dr. I-475, exit 3 (Eisenhower Pkwy/US 80), just sw, then s. Ext corridors. **Pets:** Other species. $10 daily fee/pet. Designated rooms, no service, supervision.
SAVE 🐾 ✕ 📶 🖥 🏊

AAA ▼▼◆ Holiday Inn West SH
(478) 788-0120. **$72.** 4755 Chambers Rd. I-475, exit 3 (Eisenhower Pkwy/US 80), just nw, then se. Ext corridors. **Pets:** Large. $20 one-time fee/room. Service with restrictions, supervision.
SAVE 🐾 ✕ 📶 🖥 🍴 🏊

▼ La Quinta Inn & Suites Macon SH
(478) 475-0206. **$101-$139.** 3944 River Place Dr. I-75, exit 169 (Arkwright Rd), just n, then e. Int corridors. **Pets:** Medium. Service with restrictions.
ASK ✕ 🐾M 🐕 📶 🖥 🏊

▼ Motel 6 #4246 M
(478) 474-2870. **$39-$42.** 4991 Harrison Rd. I-475, exit 3 (Eisenhower Pkwy/US 80), just ne, then n. Ext corridors. **Pets:** Medium, other species. Service with restrictions, supervision.
🐾 ✕ 📶 🏊

AAA ▼▼ Rodeway Inn M ❀
(478) 781-4343. **$49.** 4999 Eisenhower Pkwy. I-475, exit 3 (Eisenhower Pkwy/US 80), just ne. Ext corridors. **Pets:** Medium. $5 daily fee/pet. Service with restrictions, crate.
SAVE 🐾 ✕ 📶 🖥 🏊

AAA ▼▼◆ Sleep Inn I-475 SH
(478) 476-8111. **$62-$63.** 140 Plantation Inn Dr. I-475, exit 9 (Zebulon Rd), just e to Peake Rd, then just s. Int corridors. **Pets:** Very small, other species. $10 daily fee/pet. Designated rooms, no service, supervision.
SAVE 🐾 ✕ 🐾M 🎿 🐕 📶 🖥 🏊

MADISON

AAA ▼▼ Days Inn SH
(706) 342-1839. **$45-$90.** 2001 Eatonton Hwy. I-20, exit 114, just n. Ext corridors. **Pets:** Accepted.
SAVE 🐾 ✕ 📶 🖥 🏊

▼▼ Red Roof Inn SH
(706) 342-3433. **$44-$59.** 2080 Eatonton Rd. I-20, exit 114, 0.3 mi s. Ext corridors. **Pets:** Medium, other species. Service with restrictions, supervision.
ASK 🐾 ✕ 📶 🖥 🏊

MCDONOUGH

AAA ▼▼◆ Comfort Inn SH ❀
(770) 954-9110. **$85-$95.** 80 Hwy 81 W. I-75, exit 218, just nw. Ext corridors. **Pets:** Medium. $10 daily fee/pet. Service with restrictions, crate.
SAVE 🐾 ✕ 🎿 📶 🖥 🏊

AAA ▼▼◆ Country Hearth Inn & Suites M
(770) 957-2458. **$60.** 1170 Hampton Rd. I-75, exit 218, just e. Ext/int corridors. **Pets:** $7 daily fee/pet. No service, supervision.
SAVE 🐾 ✕ 📶

AAA ▼▼ Days Inn SH
(770) 957-5261. **$55-$77.** 744 Hwy 155 S. I-75, exit 216, just e. Ext corridors. **Pets:** Medium. $7 daily fee/pet. No service, supervision.
SAVE 🐾 ✕ 🎿 📶 🖥 🏊

AAA ▼ Econo Lodge M
(770) 957-2651. **$49-$150.** 1279 Hampton Rd. I-75, exit 218, just w. Ext corridors. **Pets:** Accepted.
SAVE 🐾 ✕ 📶 🖥 🏊

△△△ ▽▼▽▼▽ Quality Inn & Suites Conference Center 🆂🅷 ❀
(770) 957-5291. **$79-$170.** 930 Hwy 155 S. I-75, exit 216, just w. Ext corridors. **Pets:** Large, other species. $10 daily fee/room. Service with restrictions.
🆂🅰🆅🅴 🆂🅳 ⨉ 🕭 ⚟ 🕮 ⎙ 🍴 ⇌

△△△ ▽▼▽ Super 8 🅼
(770) 957-5818. **$45.** 1311 Hampton Rd. I-75, exit 218, just w. Ext corridors. **Pets:** Accepted.
🆂🅰🆅🅴 🆂🅳 ⨉ 🕭 ⇌

MILLEDGEVILLE

▽▼▽▼ Holiday Inn Express 🆂🅷
(478) 454-9000. **$65-$69.** 1839 N Columbia St. US 441, 2 mi n of downtown. Int corridors. **Pets:** Small. $25 one-time fee/room. Designated rooms, service with restrictions, supervision.
🅰🆂🅺 🆂🅳 ⨉ ♿ 🕭 ⚟ 🕮 ⎙ ⇌

MONROE

▽▼▽▼ Country Hearth Inn 🆂🅷
(770) 207-1977. **$65-$70.** 1222 W Spring St. 1 mi w of downtown on Business Rt SR 10. Int corridors. **Pets:** Very small, dogs only. $10 daily fee/pet. No service, supervision.
⨉ ♿ 🕮 ⎙

NEWNAN

△△△ ▽▼▽ Best Western-Shenandoah Inn 🆂🅷
(770) 304-9700. **$55-$85.** 620 Hwy 34 E. I-85, exit 47, just w. Ext corridors. **Pets:** Medium, other species. $10 daily fee/pet. Designated rooms, service with restrictions, supervision.
🆂🅰🆅🅴 🆂🅳 ⨉ ♿ 🕭 🕮 ⎙ ⇌

▽▼▽ Howard Johnson Inn 🆂🅷
(770) 683-1499. **$55-$85.** 1310 Hwy 29 S. I-85, exit 41, just w. Ext corridors. **Pets:** Medium. $15 daily fee/room. Service with restrictions, supervision.
🅰🆂🅺 🆂🅳 ⨉ ⚟ 🕮 ⎙ ⇌

▽▼▽▼ Jameson Inn 🆂🅷
(770) 252-1236. **$54-$120.** 40 Lakeside Way. I-85, exit 47, 0.6 mi e. Int corridors. **Pets:** Small. $10 daily fee/pet. Service with restrictions, crate.
🅰🆂🅺 ⨉ ♿ ⚟ 🕭 🕮 ⎙ ⇌

OAKWOOD

▽▼▽▼ Country Inn & Suites by Carlson 🆂🅷
(770) 535-8080. **$85-$185.** 4535 Oakwood Rd. I-985, exit 16, just sw. Int corridors. **Pets:** Accepted.
🅰🆂🅺 🆂🅳 ⨉ ⚟ 🕭 🕮 ⎙ ⇌

▽▼▽ Jameson Inn of Oakwood/Gainesville 🆂🅷
(770) 533-9400. **$54-$104.** 3780 Merchants Way. I-985, exit 16, 0.4 mi w. Ext corridors. **Pets:** Small. $10 daily fee/pet. Service with restrictions, crate.
🅰🆂🅺 ⨉ ♿ 🕭 🕮 ⇌

PERRY

▽▼▽ America's Best Inns 🆂🅷 ❀
(478) 987-4454. **$39-$69.** 110 Perimeter Rd. I-75, exit 136 (Sam Nunn Blvd), just se. Ext corridors. **Pets:** Other species. $10 daily fee/room. Service with restrictions, crate.
🅰🆂🅺 🆂🅳 ⨉ 🕭 ⇌

△△△ ▽▼▽▼ Best Western Bradbury Inn & Suites 🆂🅷
(478) 218-5200. **$59-$119.** 205 Lect Dr. I-75, exit 135 (US 41), just e, then just n. Int corridors. **Pets:** Accepted.
🆂🅰🆅🅴 🆂🅳 ⨉ ⚟ 🕭 🕮 ⇌

△△△ ▽▼▽▼ Henderson Village 🅲🅸
(478) 988-8696. **$175-$350, 3 day notice.** 125 S Langston Cir. I-75, exit 127 (SR 26), 1.3 mi w. Ext/int corridors. **Pets:** $250 deposit/room. Designated rooms, service with restrictions, crate.
🆂🅰🆅🅴 🆂🅳 ⨉ 🕭 ⚟ 🕮 🍴 ⇌ ⨉

▽▼▽ Jameson Inn-Perry 🅼
(478) 987-5060. **$54-$104.** 200 Market Place Dr. I-75, exit 136 (Sam Nunn Blvd), just se, then sw. Ext corridors. **Pets:** Small. $10 daily fee/pet. Service with restrictions, crate.
🅰🆂🅺 ⨉ 🕭 ⚟ ⇌

▽▼▽ New Perry Hotel 🆂🅷
(478) 987-1000. **$69-$99.** 800 Main St. I-75, exit 136 (Sam Nunn Blvd) southbound, 1.2 mi se on US 341, then just w; exit 135 (US 41) northbound, 1.5 mi ne, then just s. Ext/int corridors. **Pets:** Accepted.
🅰🆂🅺 🆂🅳 ⨉ 🕭 ⚟ 🍴 ⇌

△△△ ▽▼▽ Quality Inn 🅼
(478) 987-1345. **$57-$65.** 1504 Sam Nunn Blvd. I-75, exit 136 (Sam Nunn Blvd), just nw. Ext corridors. **Pets:** Medium. $10 daily fee/room. Designated rooms, service with restrictions, supervision.
🆂🅰🆅🅴 🆂🅳 ⨉ 🕭 ⚟ 🍴 ⇌

△△△ ▽▼▽ Super 8 Motel 🆂🅷 ❀
(478) 987-0999. **$50-$80, 3 day notice.** 102 Plaza Dr. I-75, exit 136 (Sam Nunn Blvd), just se. Ext corridors. **Pets:** Medium, other species. $10 daily fee/pet. Service with restrictions, crate.
🆂🅰🆅🅴 🆂🅳 ⨉ ♿ 🕭 ⇌

PINE MOUNTAIN

△△△ ▽▼▽▼ Callaway Gardens' Mountain Creek Inn 🅻🅷
(706) 663-2281. **$109-$149, 7 day notice.** Hwy 27. On US 27, 2.8 mi s. Ext corridors. **Pets:** Accepted.
🆂🅰🆅🅴 🆂🅳 ⨉ ♿ ⚟ ♿ 🕭 🕮 ⎙ 🍴 ⇌ ⨉

△△△ ▽▼▽ Days Inn 🆂🅷
(706) 663-2121. **$70-$80.** 368 S Main Ave. Just s on US 27 and SR 18. Ext corridors. **Pets:** Small. $10 daily fee/pet. Designated rooms, no service, supervision.
🆂🅰🆅🅴 🆂🅳 ⨉ ⚟ ♿ 🕭 🕮 ⇌

▽▼ White Columns Motel 🅼 ❀
(706) 663-2312. **$59-$79, 3 day notice.** 524 S Main Ave. 1 mi s on US 27. Ext corridors. **Pets:** Medium. $10 daily fee/pet. Designated rooms, service with restrictions, supervision.
🅰🆂🅺 ⨉ 🕭

POOLER

△△△ ▽▼▽▼ Best Western Bradbury Suites 🆂🅷 ❀
(912) 330-0330. **$94-$159.** 155 Bourne Ave. I-95, exit 102 (US 80), just e. Int corridors. **Pets:** Very small, other species. Service with restrictions.
🆂🅰🆅🅴 🆂🅳 ⨉ ♿ ⚟ ♿ 🕭 🕮 ⎙ ⇌ ⨉

△△△ ▽▼ Econo Lodge-Savannah Pooler 🅼 ❀
(912) 748-4124. **$60-$100.** 500 E Hwy 80. I-95, exit 102 (US 80), just nw. Ext corridors. **Pets:** Large, other species. $10 daily fee/pet. Designated rooms, service with restrictions.
🆂🅰🆅🅴 🆂🅳 ⨉ ⚟ ♿ 🕭 🕮 ⎙ ⇌

▽▼▽ Jameson Inn 🆂🅷
(912) 748-0017. **$54-$120.** 125 Bourne Ave. I-95, exit 102 (US 80), just e. Int corridors. **Pets:** Small. $10 daily fee/pet. Service with restrictions, crate.
🅰🆂🅺 ⨉ ⚟ ♿ 🕭 🕮 ⇌

▽▼▽▼ Quality Inn & Suites Conference Center 🆂🅷
(912) 748-6464. **$69-$199.** 301 Governor Treutlen Dr. I-95, exit 102 (US 80), just nw, then just se. Int corridors. **Pets:** Accepted.
🅰🆂🅺 ⨉ 🕭 🕮 ⎙ ⇌

▼▼▼ Red Roof Inn & Suites SH
(912) 748-4050. **$74-$89.** 20 Mill Creek Cir. I-95, exit 104 (Pooler Pkwy), just w. Int corridors. **Pets:** Small. No service, supervision.
ASK S₆ ✕ ⌐ ☒ 🛏 🖵 ≈

🔺🔺🔺 Travelodge Suites SH
(912) 748-6363. **$69-$109.** 130 Continental Blvd. I-95, exit 102 (US 80), just e. Int corridors. **Pets:** Accepted.
SAVE S₆ ✕ ⌐ 🛏 🖵 ≈

PORT WENTWORTH

▼▼▼▼ Wingate Inn SH
(912) 964-0840. **$94-$154.** 115 O'Leary Rd. I-95, exit 109 (SR 21), just e, then just n. Int corridors. **Pets:** Medium, dogs only. $20 daily fee/pet. Designated rooms, service with restrictions, supervision.
✕ &M ⌐ ☒ 🛏 🖵

RICHMOND HILL

🔺🔺 ▼▼▼▼ Best Western Richmond Hill Inn SH
(912) 756-7070. **$69-$90.** 4564 Hwy. I-95, exit 87 (Ocean Hwy/US 17), just w. Int corridors. **Pets:** Accepted.
SAVE S₆ ✕ 🛏 🖵 ≈

🔺🔺🔺 ▼▼▼▼ Comfort Suites SH
(912) 756-6668. **$89-$189.** 4601 Hwy 17. I-95, exit 87 (Ocean Hwy/US 17), 0.4 mi sw. Int corridors. **Pets:** Small. $20 daily fee/room. Designated rooms, service with restrictions, supervision.
SAVE S₆ ✕ 🛏 🖵 ≈ ✕

RINGGOLD

🔺🔺🔺 ▼▼▼▼ Comfort Inn SH
(706) 935-4000. **$69-$89.** 177 Industrial Blvd. I-75, exit 348, just w. Int corridors. **Pets:** Small. $10 daily fee/pet. Designated rooms, service with restrictions, supervision.
SAVE S₆ ✕ ⌐ 🛏 🖵 ≈

▼▼ Super 8 Motel M
(706) 965-7080. **$47-$100.** 5400 Alabama Hwy. I-75, exit 348, just e. Ext corridors. **Pets:** Medium. $8 daily fee/pet. Designated rooms, service with restrictions, supervision.
ASK S₆ ✕ &M 🛏 ≈

ROCKMART

▼▼ Days Inn M
(770) 684-9955. **$50-$60.** 105 GTM Pkwy. Jct US 278 and SR 101, just n. Ext corridors. **Pets:** Accepted.
ASK S₆ ✕ &M ⌐ 🛏

ROME

▼▼▼ ▼ Holiday Inn-Sky Top Center SH
(706) 295-1100. **$79.** 20 US 411 E. 2 mi e. Ext corridors. **Pets:** Accepted.
✕ &M ⌐ 🛏 🖵 ❚❘ ≈

▼▼ Jameson Inn SH
(706) 291-7797. **$54-$120.** 40 Grace Dr. On US 411, 2.2 mi e. Int corridors. **Pets:** Small. $10 daily fee/pet. Service with restrictions, crate.
ASK ✕ &M ⌐ ☒ 🛏 🖵 ≈

SAVANNAH

🔺🔺 ▼ Americas Best Value Inn M
(912) 927-2999. **$45-$65, 5 day notice.** 390 Canebrake Rd. I-95, exit 94 (SR 204), just e, then just s. Ext corridors. **Pets:** Accepted.
SAVE S₆ ✕ ⌐ 🛏 🖵 ≈

▼▼▼ Catherine Ward House Inn BB
(912) 234-8564. **$149-$339, 3 day notice.** 118 E Waldburg St. Between Drayton and Abercorn sts. Ext/int corridors. **Pets:** Accepted.
ASK ✕ 🛏

🔺🔺 ▼▼▼ ClubHouse Inn & Suites SH
(912) 356-1234. **$92-$125.** 6800 Abercorn St. 1 mi s of jct SR 21/204 (Abercorn St). Int corridors. **Pets:** Accepted.
SAVE S₆ ✕ 🛏 🖵 ≈

🔺🔺 ▼▼▼ East Bay Inn CI
(912) 238-1225. **$149-$269, 7 day notice.** 225 E Bay St. I-16, exit 167 (Montgomery St), 0.8 mi ne, then 0.4 mi se; in historic district. Int corridors. **Pets:** Small. $35 one-time fee/pet. Designated rooms, service with restrictions, crate.
SAVE S₆ ✕ 🖵 ❚❘

▼▼ Extended StayAmerica-Midtown SH
(912) 692-0076. **Call for rates.** 5511 Abercorn St. Jct SR 21 and 204, just s. Int corridors. **Pets:** Accepted.
✕ 🛏 🖵

▼▼▼▼ The Forsyth Park Inn BB 🐾
(912) 233-6800. **$150-$275, 7 day notice.** 102 W Hall St. Between Whitaker and Howard sts; on Forsyth Park. Int corridors. **Pets:** Medium. $40 one-time fee/room. Designated rooms, service with restrictions.
ASK ✕ 🛏

▼▼▼ Homewood Suites by Hilton SH
(912) 353-8500. **$129-$229.** 5820 White Bluff Rd. Jct SR 21/204, 0.5 mi s. Ext/int corridors. **Pets:** Other species. $50 one-time fee/room. Service with restrictions, crate.
ASK S₆ ✕ 🛏 🖵 ≈ ✕

▼▼ Joan's on Jones B & B BB 🐾
(912) 234-3863. **$160-$185 (no credit cards), 7 day notice.** 17 W Jones St. Between Whitaker and Bull sts. Ext corridors. **Pets:** Dogs only. $50 one-time fee/room. Crate.
✕ 🛏 🖵

▼▼ La Quinta Inn & Suites Savannah SH
(912) 927-7660. **$85-$115.** 8484 Abercorn St. 2.4 mi s of jct SR 21/204 (Abercorn St). Int corridors. **Pets:** Accepted.
ASK ✕ ⌐ 🛏 🖵 ≈

▼▼ La Quinta Inn Savannah (I-95) SH
(912) 925-9505. **$84-$105.** 6 Gateway Blvd S. I-95, exit 94 (SR 204), just e, then s. Ext corridors. **Pets:** Medium. Service with restrictions.
ASK ✕ &M ⌐ ☒ 🖵 ≈

▼▼ La Quinta Inn Savannah (Midtown) SH
(912) 355-3004. **$95-$115.** 6805 Abercorn St. 1 mi s of jct SR 21/204 (Abercorn St). Ext/int corridors. **Pets:** Medium. Service with restrictions.
ASK ✕ ⌐ ☒ 🖵 ≈

🔺🔺🔺 ▼▼▼▼ The Mansion on Forsyth Park LH
(912) 238-5158. **$249-$899, 3 day notice.** 700 Drayton St. Between E Hall and E Gwinnett sts; on Forsyth Park. Int corridors. **Pets:** Dogs only. Designated rooms.
SAVE S₆ ✕ 🛏 🖵 ❚❘ ≈

🔺🔺🔺 ▼▼▼ Olde Harbour Inn BB
(912) 234-4100. **$159-$269, 7 day notice.** 508 E Factors Walk. Lincoln St ramp off E Bay St; in historic riverfront district. Ext corridors. **Pets:** Small. $35 one-time fee/pet. Designated rooms, service with restrictions, crate.
SAVE S₆ ✕ 🛏 🖵

▼▼ ▼ Quality Inn Savannah South SH 🐾
(912) 925-2770. **$70-$129.** 3 Gateway Blvd S. I-95, exit 94 (SR 204), just e, then just s. Ext corridors. **Pets:** Medium, other species. $10 daily fee/pet. Service with restrictions, supervision.
ASK S₆ ✕ ⌐ 🛏 🖵 ❚❘ ≈

🔺🔺 ▼▼ Red Roof Inn SH
(912) 920-3535. **$50-$90.** 405 Al Henderson Blvd. I-95, exit 94 (SR 204), just e. Int corridors. **Pets:** Medium, other species. Service with restrictions, supervision.
SAVE S₆ ✕ &M ☒ 🛏 🖵 ≈

▼▼▼▼ Savannah Residence Inn by Marriott SH
(912) 356-3266. **$119-$179.** 5710 White Bluff Rd. Jct SR 21, 0.5 mi s. Int corridors. **Pets:** Small. $100 one-time fee/room. Service with restrictions, supervision.
[X] [🐾] [🛏] [💻] [🏊] [X]

▲▲▲ ▼▼▼ Suites on Lafayette CO
(912) 233-7815. **$169-$299, 14 day notice.** 201-205 E Charlton St. Off Abercorn St at Lafayette Square. Int corridors. **Pets:** Dogs only. $45 one-time fee/pet. No service.
[SAVE] [X] [🛏] [💻]

▲▲▲ ▼▼ Travelodge M
(912) 925-2640. **$40-$259.** 1 Ft Argyle Rd. I-95, exit 94 (SR 204), just w. Ext corridors. **Pets:** $10 daily fee/pet. Supervision.
[SAVE] [S🐾] [X] [🐾] [🛏] [💻] [🏊]

▲▲▲ ▼▼▼▼ Westin Savannah Harbor Golf Resort and Spa LH
(912) 201-2000. **$149-$329, 3 day notice.** 1 Resort Dr. On Hutchinson Island; 1 mi se of first exit after Eugene Talmadge Memorial Bridge and US 17. Int corridors. **Pets:** Accepted.
[SAVE] [X] [🐾] [🗐] [🐾] [🛏] [💻] [🍴] [🏊] [X]

STATESBORO

▼▼◆ Best Western University Inn M
(912) 681-7900. **$62-$68.** 1 Jameson Ave. Jct US 25/301 and SR 67, 0.9 mi s on US 25/301. Ext corridors. **Pets:** Accepted.
[ASK] [S🐾] [X] [🛏] [💻] [🏊]

▼▼ Hometown Inn M
(912) 681-4663. **Call for rates.** 126 Rushing Ln. Jct US 301 Bypass and SR 67, just n, then w. Ext corridors. **Pets:** Accepted.
[ASK] [X] [🐾] [🛏]

▼▼◆ La Quinta Inn Statesboro SH
(912) 871-2525. **$69-$119.** 225 Lanier Dr. Jct US 301 Bypass and SR 67, 1.2 mi w on US 301, just n of Georgia Southern University. Int corridors. **Pets:** Accepted.
[ASK] [S🐾] [X] [🐾M] [🗐] [🐾] [🛏] [💻] [🏊]

▼▼▼▼ Statesboro Inn & Restaurant CI 🐾
(912) 489-8628. **$95-$115.** 106 S Main St (US 301/25). US 301/25, just s of town center; downtown. Int corridors. **Pets:** Small. $25 daily fee/pet. Designated rooms, service with restrictions, supervision.
[ASK] [S🐾] [X] [🛏] [💻] [🍴]

STOCKBRIDGE

▼▼▼ Best Western Atlanta South SH
(770) 474-8771. **$60-$100.** 619 Hwy 138. I-75, exit 228, just e; I-675, exit 1, 0.5 mi w. Ext corridors. **Pets:** Accepted.
[ASK] [S🐾] [X] [🛏] [💻] [🍴] [🏊]

▲▲▲ ▼▼▼ Super 8 Motel Atlanta South SH
(770) 474-5758. **$65-$110.** 1451 Hudson Bridge Rd. I-75, exit 224, just w. Ext corridors. **Pets:** Accepted.
[SAVE] [S🐾] [X] [🛏] [💻] [🏊]

SWAINSBORO

▲▲▲ ▼▼▼ Best Western Bradford Inn M
(478) 237-2400. **$50-$100.** 688 S Main St. I-16, exit 90 (US 1), 12.4 mi n. Ext corridors. **Pets:** Small, dogs only. $10 daily fee/pet. No service, supervision.
[SAVE] [S🐾] [X] [🛏] [💻] [🏊]

THOMASTON

▼▼ Jameson Inn SH
(706) 648-2232. **$54-$120.** 1010 Hwy 19 N. Jct SR 74, 2.3 mi n. Ext corridors. **Pets:** Small. $10 daily fee/pet. Service with restrictions, crate.
[ASK] [X] [🛏] [💻] [🏊]

THOMASVILLE

▼▼ Comfort Inn M
(229) 228-5555. **$65-$76.** 14866 US 19 S. Jct SR 300/US 19 and 84/SR 122. Ext corridors. **Pets:** Medium. $35 deposit/pet. Service with restrictions, crate.
[ASK] [S🐾] [🛏] [💻] [🏊]

▼▼ Jameson Inn M
(229) 227-9500. **$54-$120.** 1470 Remington Ave. US 19, just w on CR 122. Ext corridors. **Pets:** Small. $10 daily fee/pet. Service with restrictions, crate.
[ASK] [X] [🐾M] [🗐] [🐾] [🛏] [💻] [🏊]

▼◆◆ Quality Inn & Suites Conference Center M
(229) 225-2134. **$72.** 15138 Hwy 19 S. 0.3 mi s of US 319. Ext corridors. **Pets:** Large. $30 deposit/pet. Service with restrictions, crate.
[ASK] [S🐾] [X] [🐾M] [🗐] [🛏] [💻] [🍴] [🏊]

THOMSON

▲▲▲ ▼▼▼▼ Best Western White Columns Inn SH 🐾
(706) 595-8000. **$59-$139, 30 day notice.** 1890 Washington Rd. I-20, exit 172 (US 78), just s. Ext corridors. **Pets:** Small, other species. $10 daily fee/pet. Service with restrictions.
[SAVE] [S🐾] [X] [🛏] [💻] [🍴] [🏊] [X]

▲▲▲ ▼▼ Days Inn M
(706) 595-2262. **$59-$89.** 2658 Cobbham Rd. I-20, exit 175 (SR 150), just n. Ext corridors. **Pets:** Accepted.
[SAVE] [S🐾] [X] [🛏]

TIFTON

▼▼ Days Inn & Suites SH
(229) 382-8505. **$57-$77.** 1199 Hwy 82 W. I-75, exit 62, just w. Int corridors. **Pets:** Accepted.
[ASK] [S🐾] [X] [🛏] [💻] [🏊]

▲▲▲ ▼▼▼▼ Hampton Inn SH
(229) 382-8800. **$94-$102.** 720 Hwy 319 S. I-75, exit 62, just e. Ext corridors. **Pets:** Medium, other species. Service with restrictions.
[SAVE] [S🐾] [X] [🛏] [💻] [🏊]

▲▲▲ ▼▼▼ Holiday Inn SH 🐾
(229) 382-6687. **$80-$109.** 1208 Hwy 82 W. I-75, exit 62, at jct US 82 and 319. Ext corridors. **Pets:** Medium. Service with restrictions, supervision.
[SAVE] [S🐾] [X] [🗐] [🛏] [💻] [🍴] [🏊]

▲▲▲ ▼▼ Microtel Inns & Suites SH
(229) 387-0112. **$49-$75.** 196 S Virginia Ave. I-75, exit 62, just n. Int corridors. **Pets:** Accepted.
[ASK] [S🐾] [X] [🐾M] [🐾] [🛏] [💻] [🏊]

◆ Motel 6 #4074 SH
(229) 388-8777. **$38, 7 day notice.** 579 Old Omega Rd. I-75, exit 61, just w. Int corridors. **Pets:** Medium, other species. Service with restrictions, supervision.
[ASK] [S🐾] [X] [🏊]

▼▼ Ramada Limited and Conference Center SH
(229) 382-8500. **$55-$75.** 1211 Hwy 82 W. I-75, exit 62, just w. Ext corridors. **Pets:** Medium, other species. $10 daily fee/pet. Service with restrictions, crate.
[ASK] [S🐾] [X] [🛏] [💻] [🏊]

TOWNSEND

▼ Days Inn M
(912) 832-4411. **$60-$65.** Hwy 57. I-95, exit 58 (SR 57), just nw. Ext corridors. **Pets:** Medium. $10 daily fee/pet. Service with restrictions, supervision.
[ASK] [S🐾] [X] [🛏] [🏊]

TRENTON

▼▼ Days Inn SH
(706) 657-2550. **$53-$55.** 95 Killian Ave. I-59, exit 11, just e. Ext corridors. **Pets:** Accepted.

ASK S⬛ ✕ ⬛M ⬛ ⬛ ⬛

VALDOSTA

▼▼ Best Western King of the Road SH
(229) 244-7600. **$69-$89.** 1403 N St Augustine Rd. I-75, exit 18, just w off of SR 94. Ext corridors. **Pets:** Accepted.

ASK S⬛ ✕ ⬛ ⬛ ⬛ ⬛ ⬛ ⬛

▲▲▲ ▼▼ Comfort Inn Conference Center SH
(229) 242-1212. **$84-$157.** 2101 W Hill Ave. I-75, exit 16, just w. Ext/int corridors. **Pets:** Medium. Designated rooms, service with restrictions, crate.

SAVE S⬛ ✕ ⬛ ⬛ ⬛ ⬛ ⬛

▼▼ Days Inn Conference Center SH
(229) 249-8800. **$52-$72.** 1827 W Hill Ave. I-75, exit 16, just e. Ext corridors. **Pets:** Accepted.

ASK S⬛ ✕ ⬛M ⬛ ⬛ ⬛ ⬛

▼▼ Days Inn I-75 North SH
(229) 244-4460. **$49-$69.** 4598 N Valdosta Rd. I-75, exit 22, just w. Ext corridors. **Pets:** Medium, other species. $10 daily fee/pet. Service with restrictions, crate.

ASK S⬛ ✕ ⬛ ⬛ ⬛

▲▲▲ ▼▼ Econo Lodge SH
(229) 671-1511. **$60-$100.** 3022 James Rd. I-75, exit 18, just w. Int corridors. **Pets:** Accepted.

SAVE S⬛ ✕ ⬛ ⬛ ⬛

▲▲▲ ▼▼ Holiday Inn SH
(229) 242-3881. **$78-$89.** 1309 St Augustine Rd. I-75, exit 18, just e on SR 94. Ext corridors. **Pets:** Accepted.

SAVE S⬛ ✕ ⬛ ⬛ ⬛ ⬛

◆ ▼ Jameson Inn SH
(229) 253-0009. **$54-$120.** 1725 Gornto Rd. I-75, exit 18, 0.3 mi e on north side of SR 94. Ext corridors. **Pets:** Small. $10 daily fee/pet. Service with restrictions, crate.

ASK ✕ ⬛ ⬛ ⬛ ⬛

▼◆▼ La Quinta Inn & Suites Valdosta SH ❀
(229) 247-7755. **$79-$114.** 1800 Clubhouse Dr. I-75, exit 18, 0.3 mi e, then just s off SR 94. Int corridors. **Pets:** Large, other species. Service with restrictions, supervision.

ASK S⬛ ✕ ⬛ ⬛ ⬛ ⬛

▲▲▲ ▼▼ Quality Inn North SH ❀
(229) 244-8510. **$69-$75.** 1209 St Augustine Rd. I-75, exit 18, 0.3 mi e on SR 94. Ext corridors. **Pets:** Small, dogs only. $5 daily fee/pet. Service with restrictions, supervision.

SAVE S⬛ ✕ ⬛ ⬛ ⬛ ⬛

▼▼ Quality Inn South SH
(229) 244-4520. **$49-$89.** 1902 W Hill Ave. I-75, exit 16, just e on US 84. Ext corridors. **Pets:** Medium. $5 daily fee/pet. Service with restrictions, crate.

ASK S⬛ ✕ ⬛ ⬛ ⬛

◆ ▼ Ramada Limited M
(229) 242-1225. **$79.** 2008 W Hill Ave. I-75, exit 16, just e on US 84. Ext corridors. **Pets:** Accepted.

ASK S⬛ ✕ ⬛ ⬛ ⬛

VIDALIA

▲▲▲ ▼▼ Days Inn SH
(912) 537-9251. **$80.** 1503 Lyons E. 1 mi e on US 280. Ext corridors. **Pets:** Medium. $5 daily fee/pet. Service with restrictions, supervision.

SAVE S⬛ ✕ ⬛ ⬛ ⬛

▼▼ Holiday Inn Express SH
(912) 537-9000. **$70-$100.** 2619 E First St. 2.5 mi e on US 280. Ext corridors. **Pets:** Accepted.

ASK S⬛ ✕ ⬛ ⬛ ⬛ ⬛

VILLA RICA

▼▼ Days Inn SH
(770) 459-8888. **$54-$89.** 195 Hwy 61 Connector. I-20, exit 24, just n. Int corridors. **Pets:** Accepted.

ASK S⬛ ✕ ⬛M ⬛ ⬛

WARM SPRINGS

▼▼▼ Best Western White House Inn SH
(706) 655-2750. **$55-$90.** 2526 White House Pkwy. Jct US 41/27, 1.4 mi s. Ext/int corridors. **Pets:** Accepted.

ASK S⬛ ✕ ⬛M ⬛ ⬛ ⬛

WARNER ROBINS

▲▲▲ ▼▼ Best Western Peach Inn SH
(478) 953-3800. **$47-$65.** 2739 Watson Blvd. I-75, exit 146 (SR 247C), 4.1 mi e. Ext corridors. **Pets:** Small. $8 daily fee/pet. Designated rooms, no service, crate.

SAVE S⬛ ✕ ⬛ ⬛ ⬛ ⬛

▲▲▲ ▼▼ Comfort Inn & Suites SH
(478) 922-7555. **$70-$150.** 95 S Hwy 247. Jct SR 247C and US 129/SR 247, 1.6 mi s on US 129/SR 247. Ext/int corridors. **Pets:** Small, other species. $25 one-time fee/room. Designated rooms, service with restrictions, crate.

SAVE S⬛ ✕ ⬛ ⬛ ⬛ ⬛ ⬛

▼▼ Jameson Inn-Warner Robins SH
(478) 953-5522. **$54-$120.** 2731 Watson Blvd. I-75, exit 146 (SR 247C), 4.1 mi e. Ext corridors. **Pets:** Small. $10 daily fee/pet. Service with restrictions, crate.

ASK ✕ ⬛ ⬛ ⬛ ⬛

WAYCROSS

▼▼ Holiday Inn Waycross SH
(912) 283-4490. **$73-$100, 14 day notice.** 1725 Memorial Dr. Jct US 1 and 82. Ext corridors. **Pets:** Medium. $15 one-time fee/room. No service, crate.

ASK S⬛ ✕ ⬛ ⬛ ⬛ ⬛ ⬛ ⬛ ⬛

▼▼ Jameson Inn SH
(912) 283-3800. **$54-$120.** 950 City Blvd. Between US 1 and 82, east of city. Ext corridors. **Pets:** Small. $10 daily fee/pet. Service with restrictions, crate.

ASK ✕ ⬛M ⬛ ⬛ ⬛ ⬛

WAYNESBORO

▼▼ Jameson Inn M
(706) 437-0500. **$54-$120.** 1436 N Liberty St. 0.9 mi n of downtown center on US 25. Ext corridors. **Pets:** Small. $10 daily fee/pet. Service with restrictions, crate.

ASK ✕ ⬛ ⬛ ⬛ ⬛

WINDER

◈◈ Jameson Inn [M]
(770) 867-1880. **$54-$120.** 9 Stafford St. Jct SR 81, 11, 53 and 8; center. Ext corridors. **Pets:** Small. $10 daily fee/pet. Service with restrictions, crate.

[ASK] [✕] [🐾] [📇] [💻] [🏊]

WOODSTOCK

◈◈ SuiteOne of Woodstock [SH]
(770) 592-7848. **$54-$79.** 470 Parkway 575. I-575, exit 7, just e to Parkway 575, then just n. Ext corridors. **Pets:** Accepted.

[ASK] [S🐾] [✕] [♿M] [🐾] [📇] [💻]

YOUNG HARRIS

◈◈◈ Brasstown Valley Resort [LH]
(706) 379-9900. **$89-$259, 3 day notice.** 6321 US Hwy 76. US 76 and US 76/SR 515. Int corridors. **Pets:** Medium. $75 daily fee/room. Designated rooms, service with restrictions.

[ASK] [✕] [🐾] [♿] [📇] [💻] [🍴] [🏊] [✕]

HAWAII

HONOLULU

▼▼▼ ▼▼▼ The Kahala 🄻🄷
(808) 739-8888. **$475-$940, 3 day notice.** 5000 Kahala Ave. E of
Diamond Head at end of Kahala Ave. Int corridors. **Pets:** Accepted.
🗙 ⓜ 🕗 🔧 🍴 🏊 🗙

KAUPULEHU

▼▼▼ ▼▼▼ Four Seasons Resort Hualalai at Historic
Ka'upulehu 🄻🄷 🐾
(808) 325-8000. **$625-$1000, 30 day notice.** 100 Ka'upulehu Dr. Off
SR 19, 6 mi n of Kona International Airport. Ext corridors. **Pets:** Very
small, dogs only. Service with restrictions, supervision.
🗙 ⓜ 🕗 🔧 🖥 🍴 🏊 🗙

WAILEA

🅐🅐🅐 ▼▼▼ ▼▼▼ Four Seasons Resort, Maui at
Wailea 🄻🄷 🐾
(808) 874-8000. **$395-$11500, 21 day notice.** 3900 Wailea Alanui Dr.
From end of SR 31, 0.5 mi s. Int corridors. **Pets:** Small. Service with
restrictions, supervision.
SAVE 🗙 ⓜ 🕗 🔧 🖥 🖥 🍴 🏊 🗙

IDAHO

AHSAHKA

The High Country Inn 🅱🅱
(208) 476-7570. **$85-$125, 5 day notice.** 4231 Old Ahsahka Grade. 0.5 mi w to Dworshak Visitors Center Rd, 2 mi n, just w. Ext/int corridors. **Pets:** Accepted.

BLACKFOOT

Best Western Blackfoot Inn 🆂🅷
(208) 785-4144. **$65-$109.** 750 Jensen Grove Dr. I-15, exit 93, just e on Bergener, then 0.4 mi n on Parkway. Int corridors. **Pets:** Designated rooms, service with restrictions, supervision.

Super 8 🆂🅷
(208) 785-9333. **$66-$80.** 1279 Parkway Dr. I-15, exit 93, just e; shared driveway with McDonald's. Int corridors. **Pets:** Other species. $10 one-time fee/room. Service with restrictions, crate.

BLISS

Amber Inn Motel 🆂🅷
(208) 352-4441. **$41.** 17286 US Hwy 30. I-84, exit 141, just s. Int corridors. **Pets:** Other species. $5 one-time fee/pet. Designated rooms, service with restrictions, supervision.

BOISE

Boise Super 8 Motel 🆂🅷 🐾
(208) 344-8871. **$52-$75.** 2773 Elder St. I-84, exit 53 (Vista Ave), just n. Int corridors. **Pets:** $25 deposit/room, $25 one-time fee/room. Designated rooms, service with restrictions, supervision.

Budget Host Inn 🅼
(208) 322-4404. **$75-$85, 3 day notice.** 8002 Overland Rd. I-84, exit 50A westbound, just s, just w, then just n; exit 50B eastbound, just w, then just n. Ext corridors. **Pets:** Other species. $10 one-time fee/room. Service with restrictions, crate.

DoubleTree Club Hotel 🆂🅷
(208) 345-2002. **$67-$169.** 475 W Parkcenter Blvd. I-84, exit 54 (Broadway Ave), 2 mi n, then 0.3 mi e on Beacon and Parkcenter Blvd. Int corridors. **Pets:** Accepted.

DoubleTree Hotel Riverside 🆂🅷
(208) 343-1871. **$89-$169.** 2900 Chinden Blvd. I-84, exit 3 (Fairview Ave), just n, then just w on Garden. Int corridors. **Pets:** Medium. $25 one-time fee/room. Designated rooms, service with restrictions, crate.

Fairfield Inn by Marriott 🆂🅷 🐾
(208) 331-5656. **$73-$199.** 3300 S Shoshone St. I-84, exit 53 (Vista Ave), just n to Elder St, then just w. Int corridors. **Pets:** Large, other species. $10 daily fee/room. Crate.

Hampton Inn 🆂🅷 🐾
(208) 331-5600. **$99-$129.** 3270 S Shoshone St. I-84, exit 53 (Vista Ave), just n to Elder St, then just w. Int corridors. **Pets:** Small. $10 daily fee/pet. Service with restrictions, supervision.

Holiday Inn Boise Airport 🆂🅷
(208) 343-4900. **$89-$119.** 3300 Vista Ave. I-84, exit 53 (Vista Ave), just n. Int corridors. **Pets:** Accepted.

Holiday Inn Express 🆂🅷
(208) 388-0800. **$69-$114.** 2613 S Vista Ave. I-84, exit 53 (Vista Ave), 0.5 mi n. Int corridors. **Pets:** Accepted.

Oxford Suites 🆂🅷
(208) 322-8000. **$119-$169.** 1426 S Entertainment Ave. I-84, exit 50A westbound; exit 50B eastbound, just s to Spectrum St, just w, then n. Int corridors. **Pets:** Medium. $25 deposit/pet, $25 one-time fee/pet. Supervision.

Red Lion Hotel Boise Downtowner 🅻🅷
(208) 344-7691. **$79-$225.** 1800 Fairview Ave. I-84, exit 3 (Fairview Ave), 1 mi n. Int corridors. **Pets:** Accepted.

Residence Inn by Marriott-Boise Central 🆂🅷 🐾
(208) 344-1200. **$159-$189.** 1401 Lusk Ave. I-84, exit 53 (Vista Ave), 2.4 mi n. Ext corridors. **Pets:** Other species. $75 one-time fee/room.

Residence Inn by Marriott-Boise West 🆂🅷 🐾
(208) 385-9000. **$159-$189.** 7303 W Denton. I-84, exit 50A westbound; exit 50B eastbound, 2 mi n on Cole Rd, just w, then just n. Int corridors. **Pets:** Other species. $100 one-time fee/room. Designated rooms, service with restrictions, supervision.

Rodeway Inn of Boise 🆂🅷
(208) 376-2700. **$60-$100.** 1115 N Curtis Rd. I-84, exit 2, just se. Ext/int corridors. **Pets:** Accepted.

Safari Inn Downtown 🆂🅷 🐾
(208) 344-6556. **$75-$85.** 1070 Grove St. At 11th and Grove sts; center. Int corridors. **Pets:** $10 one-time fee/room. Designated rooms, service with restrictions, supervision.

Shilo Inn Suites-Boise Airport 🆂🅷 🐾
(208) 343-7662. **$57-$110.** 4111 Broadway Ave. I-84, exit 54 (Broadway Ave), just sw. Int corridors. **Pets:** Other species. $25 one-time fee/room. Supervision.

▼▼▼▼ **SpringHill Suites by Marriott-Boise ParkCenter** SH
(208) 342-1044. **$79-$116.** 424 E ParkCenter Blvd. I-84, exit 54 (Broadway Ave), 2.3 mi n, then just e on Beacon and Parkcenter Blvd. Int corridors. **Pets:** Accepted.

[ASK] [S5] [X] [&M] [🐾] [&] [🔲] [💻] [🏊] [🐾]

BONNERS FERRY

🔺🔺🔺 ▼▼▼▼ **Best Western Kootenai River Inn Casino &**
Spa SH
(208) 267-8511. **$89-$134.** 7169 Plaza St. On US 95; city center. Int corridors. **Pets:** Medium. $15 daily fee/pet. Service with restrictions, supervision.

[SAVE] [S5] [X] [🐾] [&] [🔲] [💻] [🍴] [🏊] [🐾]

BURLEY

🔺🔺🔺 ▼▼▼▼ **Best Western Burley Inn & Convention**
Center SH
(208) 678-3501. **$69-$84.** 800 N Overland Ave. I-84, exit 208, just s. Ext/int corridors. **Pets:** Medium. $25 one-time fee/pet. Designated rooms, service with restrictions, supervision.

[SAVE] [S5] [X] [🐾] [&] [🔲] [💻] [🍴] [🏊] [🐾]

🔺🔺🔺 ▼▼ **Budget Motel** M
(208) 678-2200. **$54-$69.** 900 N Overland Ave. I-84, exit 208, just s. Ext corridors. **Pets:** Medium. $25 one-time fee/pet. Designated rooms, service with restrictions, supervision.

[SAVE] [S5] [X] [&M] [🐾] [&] [🔲] [🏊]

CALDWELL

🔺🔺🔺 ▼▼▼ **Best Western Caldwell Inn & Suites** M 🐾
(208) 454-7225. **$81-$94.** 908 Specht Ave. I-84, exit 29, just s. Int corridors. **Pets:** Large. $5 daily fee/pet. Designated rooms, service with restrictions, supervision.

[SAVE] [S5] [X] [🐾] [&] [🔲] [💻] [🏊]

▼▼▼▼ **La Quinta Inn Caldwell** SH 🐾
(208) 454-2222. **$69-$109.** 901 Specht Ave. I-84, exit 29, just s. Int corridors. **Pets:** Other species. Service with restrictions, supervision.

[ASK] [S5] [X] [🔲] [💻] [🏊]

COEUR D'ALENE

🔺🔺🔺 ▼▼▼▼ **Best Western Coeur d'Alene Inn & Conference**
Center SH 🐾
(208) 765-3200. **$89-$185.** W 506 Appleway Ave. I-90, exit 12, just nw. Int corridors. **Pets:** Large, dogs only. $25 daily fee/room. Service with restrictions, supervision.

[SAVE] [S5] [X] [&M] [🐾] [&] [🔲] [💻] [🍴] [🏊]

🔺🔺🔺 ▼▼▼ ▼▼▼ **The Coeur d'Alene Resort** LH 🐾
(208) 765-4000. **$99-$459, 7 day notice.** 115 S 2nd St. I-90, exit 11, 2 mi s. Ext/int corridors. **Pets:** Small. $75 one-time fee/room. Designated rooms, service with restrictions, supervision.

[SAVE] [S5] [X] [💻] [🍴] [🏊] [🐾]

▼▼▼ **Days Inn-Coeur d'Alene** SH 🐾
(208) 667-8668. **$57.** 2200 Northwest Blvd. I-90, exit 11, just se. Int corridors. **Pets:** Medium. $1000.00 daily fee/pet. Service with restrictions, supervision.

[ASK] [S5] [X] [&M] [🐾] [&] [🔲] [💻] [🐾]

▼▼▼ **Guest House Inn & Suites** SH
(208) 765-3011. **$39-$99.** 330 W Appleway. I-90, exit 12, just n, then just e. Int corridors. **Pets:** Large, other species. $10 one-time fee/room. Designated rooms, service with restrictions, supervision.

[ASK] [S5] [X] [🔲] [💻]

▼▼▼ **Holiday Inn Express Hotel & Suites**
Coeurd'Alene SH 🐾
(208) 667-3100. **Call for rates.** 2300 W Seltice Way. I-90, exit 11, just s. Int corridors. **Pets:** Medium, dogs only. $50 one-time fee/pet. Designated rooms, no service, supervision.

[X] [&] [🔲] [💻] [🏊]

🔺🔺🔺 ▼▼▼▼ **La Quinta Inn & Suites Coeur D'Alene**
(East) SH
(208) 667-6777. **$59-$199.** 2209 E Sherman Ave. I-90, exit 15 (Sherman Ave), just s. Int corridors. **Pets:** Other species. Service with restrictions, supervision.

[SAVE] [X] [&M] [🐾] [🔲] [💻] [🏊]

🔺🔺🔺 ▼▼▼▼ **La Quinta Inn Coeur D'Alene**
(Appleway) SH 🐾
(208) 765-5500. **$69-$199.** 280 W Appleway Ave. I-90, exit 12, just ne. Int corridors. **Pets:** Large, other species. Service with restrictions, supervision.

[SAVE] [S5] [X] [&M] [🐾] [🔲] [💻] [🏊] [🐾]

🔺🔺🔺 ▼▼▼▼ **The Roosevelt Inn** BB
(208) 765-5200. **$89-$319, 14 day notice.** 105 Wallace Ave. I-90, exit 13, 2 mi s, then just w; downtown. Int corridors. **Pets:** Accepted.

[SAVE] [X] [&] [🐾] [W] [🅩]

🔺🔺🔺 ▼▼▼▼ **Shilo Inn Suites Coeur d'Alene** SH 🐾
(208) 664-2300. **$87-$158.** 702 W Appleway Ave. I-90, exit 12, just n, then just w. Int corridors. **Pets:** Other species. $25 one-time fee/room. Supervision.

[SAVE] [S5] [X] [&M] [&] [🔲] [💻] [🏊] [🐾]

DRIGGS

🔺🔺🔺 ▼▼ **Teton Valley Cabins** CA
(208) 354-8153. **$69-$109, 7 day notice.** 34 Ski Hill Rd. 0.8 mi e on Little Ave from SR 33 E. Ext corridors. **Pets:** Dogs only. $50 deposit/ room, $10 daily fee/room. Supervision.

[SAVE] [X] [🔲] [🐾] [🅚]

HAGERMAN

🔺🔺🔺 ▼▼▼ **Hagerman Valley Inn** M
(208) 837-6196. **$59-$89.** 661 Frog's Landing. South end of town on US 30. Ext/int corridors. **Pets:** $7 daily fee/pet. Designated rooms, service with restrictions, supervision.

[SAVE] [S5] [X] [🔲]

HAILEY

▼▼ **Airport Inn** M 🐾
(208) 788-2477. **$85-$135.** 820 4th Ave S. Just n of SR 75 at 4th Ave; near airport. Ext corridors. **Pets:** Medium. $10 daily fee/pet. Designated rooms, service with restrictions, supervision.

[X] [🔲] [💻]

▼▼▼ **Wood River Inn** SH
(208) 578-0600. **$89-$147.** 603 N Main. Just n of downtown on SR 75. Int corridors. **Pets:** $25 one-time fee/room. Service with restrictions, supervision.

[ASK] [S5] [X] [&M] [&] [🔲] [💻] [🏊]

HAYDEN

▼▼▼▼ **Holiday Inn Express Hotel & Suites** SH 🐾
(208) 772-7900. **$62-$350.** 151 W Orchard Ave. I-90, exit 12, 3.5 mi n. Int corridors. **Pets:** Other species. $10 daily fee/pet. Supervision.

[ASK] [S5] [X] [&M] [🐾] [&] [🔲] [💻] [🏊] [🐾]

HEYBURN

AAA ◆◆◆ **Super 8–Burley** SH
(208) 678-7000. **$59-$80.** 336 S 600 W. I-84, exit 208, just n. Int corridors. **Pets:** Small. $10 daily fee/pet. Designated rooms, service with restrictions, supervision.
SAVE ⬛ ✕ ⬛ ⬛ ⬛ ⬛ ⬛ ⬛

IDAHO FALLS

AAA ◆◆◆ **Best Western Driftwood Inn** SH
(208) 523-2242. **$65-$139.** 575 River Pkwy. I-15, exit 118 (Broadway), 0.5 mi e, then 0.3 mi n. Ext corridors. **Pets:** Other species. $10 one-time fee/room. Service with restrictions, supervision.
SAVE ⬛ ✕ ⬛ ⬛ ⬛ ⬛

◆◆ **Comfort Inn** SH
(208) 528-2804. **$73-$110.** 195 S Colorado Ave. I-15, exit 118 (Broadway), just w to Colorado Ave, then just s. Int corridors. **Pets:** Accepted.
ASK ⬛ ✕ ⬛ ⬛ ⬛ ⬛

◆◆ **GuestHouse Inn & Suites** SH 🐾
(208) 523-6260. **$55-$95.** 850 Lindsay Blvd. I-15, exit 119, just e. Ext/int corridors. **Pets:** $10 daily fee/pet. Designated rooms, service with restrictions, supervision.
ASK ⬛ ✕ ⬛ ⬛ ⬛ ⬛

AAA ◆◆◆ **Le Ritz Hotel & Suites** SH 🐾
(208) 528-0880. **$79-$99.** 720 Lindsay Blvd. I-15, exit 118 (Broadway), 0.5 mi e, then just n. Int corridors. **Pets:** Other species. $10 daily fee/room. Designated rooms, service with restrictions, crate.
SAVE ⬛ ✕ ⬛ ⬛ ⬛ ⬛

◆◆ **Red Lion Hotel on the Falls** SH
(208) 523-8000. **$67-$108.** 475 River Pkwy. I-15, exit 118 (Broadway), 0.5 mi n, then just n. Ext/int corridors. **Pets:** Accepted.
ASK ⬛ ✕ ⬛ ⬛ ⬛ ⬛ ⬛ ⬛

AAA ◆◆ **Shilo Inn Suites Conference Hotel** SH 🐾
(208) 523-0088. **$84-$190.** 780 Lindsay Blvd. I-15, exit 119, just se. Int corridors. **Pets:** Other species. $25 one-time fee/room. Supervision.
SAVE ⬛ ✕ ⬛ ⬛ ⬛ ⬛ ⬛ ⬛

JEROME

AAA ◆◆◆ **Best Western Sawtooth Inn and Suites** SH
(208) 324-9200. **$79-$119.** 2653 S Lincoln. I-84, exit 168, just n on SR 79. Int corridors. **Pets:** Other species. $50 deposit/room. Designated rooms, service with restrictions, supervision.
SAVE ⬛ ✕ ⬛ ⬛ ⬛

KELLOGG

AAA ◆◆◆ **Baymont Inn & Suites** SH
(208) 783-1234. **$54-$94.** 601 Bunker Ave. I-90, exit 49, 0.5 mi s. Int corridors. **Pets:** Accepted.
SAVE ⬛ ✕ ⬛ ⬛ ⬛ ⬛

◆◆◆ **Morning Star Lodge** SH
(208) 783-0202. **$115-$285.** 602 Bunker Ave. I-90, exit 49, 0.5 mi se. Int corridors. **Pets:** Large. $30 one-time fee/room. Designated rooms, service with restrictions, supervision.
ASK ⬛ ✕ ⬛ ⬛ ⬛ ⬛

◆ **Silverhorn Motor Inn** SH 🐾
(208) 783-1151. **$53-$75.** 699 W Cameron Ave. I-90, exit 49, just ne. Int corridors. **Pets:** Other species. Supervision.
ASK ✕ ⬛ ⬛

KETCHUM

AAA ◆◆◆ **Best Western Tyrolean Lodge** SH
(208) 726-5336. **$85-$149, 3 day notice.** 260 Cottonwood. South end of town; just w of SR 75 (Main St) on Rivers St, just s on 3rd Ave. Int corridors. **Pets:** Accepted.
SAVE ⬛ ✕ ⬛ ⬛ ⬛ ⬛

◆◆ **Tamarack Lodge** M
(208) 726-3344. **$104-$174, 14 day notice.** 291 Walnut Ave N. Just ne on Sun Valley Rd from jct SR 75 (Main St); downtown. Ext/int corridors. **Pets:** Other species. $25 one-time fee/room. No service, supervision.
ASK ⬛ ✕ ⬛ ⬛ ⬛

LEWISTON

◆◆ **Comfort Inn** SH
(208) 798-8090. **$60-$156.** 2128 8th Ave. 1.2 mi s on US 12 from jct US 95, just s on 21st St. Int corridors. **Pets:** Accepted.
ASK ⬛ ✕ ⬛ ⬛ ⬛ ⬛ ⬛

◆◆ **GuestHouse Inn & Suites** SH 🐾
(208) 746-3311. **$45-$89.** 1325 Main St. Downtown. Int corridors. **Pets:** Large, other species. $10 one-time fee/pet. Designated rooms, service with restrictions, supervision.
ASK ⬛ ✕ ⬛ ⬛ ⬛

AAA ◆◆◆ **Holiday Inn Express** SH
(208) 750-1600. **$79-$149.** 2425 Nez Perce Dr. 1.2 mi s on US 12 from jct US 95, 1.2 mi s on 21st St, then just e. Int corridors. **Pets:** Other species. $20 one-time fee/room. Service with restrictions, supervision.
SAVE ⬛ ✕ ⬛ ⬛ ⬛ ⬛ ⬛

◆ **Super 8 Motel** SH
(208) 743-8808. **$49-$51.** 3120 North & South Hwy. Just e on US 12 from jct US 95. Int corridors. **Pets:** Other species. $10 daily fee/pet. Service with restrictions, supervision.
ASK ⬛ ✕ ⬛

LOWER STANLEY

AAA ◆ **Salmon River Cabins & Motel** CA
(208) 774-3566. **$65-$100, 30 day notice.** 55 Lower Stanley (Hwy US 75). 1 mi n on US 75 from jct SR 21. Ext corridors. **Pets:** Small. $10 daily fee/pet. Service with restrictions, supervision.
SAVE ✕ ⬛ ⬛ ⬛

MCCALL

AAA ◆◆◆ **Best Western McCall** SH
(208) 634-6300. **$89-$169.** 415 3rd St. SR 55, just s of jct with Lake St. Ext/int corridors. **Pets:** Accepted.
SAVE ✕ ⬛ ⬛ ⬛ ⬛ ⬛

AAA ◆◆◆ **McCall Super 8 Lodge** M
(208) 634-4637. **$74-$99.** 303 S 3rd St. South end of town on SR 55. Int corridors. **Pets:** Accepted.
SAVE ⬛ ✕ ⬛ ⬛ ⬛

MONTPELIER

AAA ◆◆◆ **Best Western Clover Creek Inn** SH
(208) 847-1782. **$69-$99.** 243 N 4th St. Just n on US 30 from jct US 89 S. Ext corridors. **Pets:** Accepted.
SAVE ⬛ ✕ ⬛ ⬛

MOSCOW

AAA ◆◆◆ **Best Western University Inn** SH
(208) 882-0550. **$94-$135.** 1516 Pullman Rd. Jct US 95, 1 mi w on SR 8. Int corridors. **Pets:** Small, other species. $25 daily fee/room. Designated rooms, service with restrictions, crate.
SAVE ⬛ ✕ ⬛ ⬛ ⬛ ⬛ ⬛ ⬛ ⬛

◆◆◆ **La Quinta Inn** SH
(208) 882-5365. **$89-$179.** 185 Warbonnet Dr. 1.6 mi w on SR 8 from jct US 93, just n. Int corridors. **Pets:** Other species. Service with restrictions, supervision.
ASK ⬛ ✕ ⬛ ⬛ ⬛ ⬛

◆◆ **Super 8 Motel** SH
(208) 883-1503. **$49-$109.** 175 Peterson Dr. Jct US 95, 0.8 mi w on SR 8, just n. Int corridors. **Pets:** Accepted.
⬛ ✕ ⬛

MOUNTAIN HOME

▼▼▼▼ Best Western Foothills Motor Inn SH
(208) 587-8477. **$72-$107.** 1080 Hwy 20. I-84, exit 95, just n. Ext corridors. **Pets:** Accepted.

ASK SD ⊠ ⅁M 🐾 ⌨ 🛌 🖥 ⋙

▼▼▼ Sleep Inn SH
(208) 587-9743. **$67-$82.** 1180 Hwy 20. I-84, exit 95, just n. Int corridors. **Pets:** Accepted.

ASK SD ⊠ 🛌 🖥

NAMPA

▼▼▼▼ Hampton Inn & Suites at the Idaho Center SH
(208) 442-0036. **$89-$109.** 5750 E Franklin Rd. I-84, exit 38, 0.4 mi n on Garrity Blvd to Franklin Rd, then just e; in front of Idaho Center. Int corridors. **Pets:** Accepted.

ASK SD ⊠ ⅁M 🐾 ⌨ 🛌 🖥 ⋙

▼▼▼▼ Shilo Inn Nampa Suites SH 🐾
(208) 465-3250. **$82-$115.** 1401 Shilo Dr. I-84, exit 36, just nw. Int corridors. **Pets:** Other species. $25 one-time fee/room. Supervision.

ASK SD ⊠ 🐾 🛌 🖥 ⅂⅂ ⋙ ⊠

OROFINO

▼▼▼▼ Best Western Lodge at River's Edge SH
(208) 476-9999. **$76-$110.** 615 Main St. Downtown. Int corridors. **Pets:** Small. $20 daily fee/pet. Designated rooms, service with restrictions, supervision.

ASK SD ⊠ 🛌 🖥 ⅂⅂ ⋙ ⊠

⊕⊕ ▼▼▼ Konkolville Motel M
(208) 476-5584. **$44-$75.** 2000 Konkolville Rd. 2.7 mi e on Michigan Ave. Ext corridors. **Pets:** $10 daily fee/pet. Designated rooms, service with restrictions, supervision.

SAVE SD ⊠ 🛌 🖥 ⋙

POCATELLO

⊕⊕ ▼▼▼▼ Best Western CottonTree Inn SH 🐾
(208) 237-7650. **$85-$179.** 1415 Bench Rd. I-15, exit 71, just e. Int corridors. **Pets:** $25 deposit/room. Designated rooms, service with restrictions, crate.

SAVE SD ⊠ 🛌 🖥 ⋙

▼▼▼ Holiday Inn-Pocatello SH
(208) 237-1400. **$68-$95.** 1399 Bench Rd. I-15, exit 71, just e. Ext/int corridors. **Pets:** Medium, other species. $10 daily fee/room. Designated rooms, service with restrictions, supervision.

ASK SD ⊠ 🐾 ⌨ 🛌 🖥 ⅂⅂ ⋙ ⊠

⊕⊕ ▼▼▼ Pocatello Super 8 Motel SH
(208) 234-0888. **$57-$99.** 1330 Bench Rd. I-15, exit 71, just e. Int corridors. **Pets:** Other species. $10 one-time fee/room. Designated rooms, supervision.

SAVE SD ⊠ ⌨ 🛌

▼▼▼ Ramada Inn & Convention Center SH
(208) 237-0020. **$73-$141.** 133 W Burnside. I-86, exit 61, just n. Int corridors. **Pets:** Medium. $10 daily fee/pet. Service with restrictions, supervision.

ASK SD ⊠ 🛌 🖥 ⅂⅂ ⋙ ⊠

⊕⊕ ▼▼▼ Red Lion Hotel Pocatello SH
(208) 233-2200. **$89-$119.** 1555 Pocatello Creek Rd. I-15, exit 71, just e. Int corridors. **Pets:** Medium, other species. $10 one-time fee/pet. Service with restrictions, crate.

SAVE SD ⊠ 🛌 🖥 ⅂⅂ ⋙ ⊠

▼ Thunderbird Motel M
(208) 232-6330. **$49-$59.** 1415 S 5th Ave. I-15, exit 67, 1.3 mi n; just s of Idaho State University. Ext corridors. **Pets:** Other species. $5 daily fee/pet. Service with restrictions, supervision.

ASK SD ⊠ 🛌 ⋙

PONDERAY

⊕⊕ ▼▼▼ Sandpoint Motel 6–4163 SH
(208) 263-5383. **$64-$85.** 477255 Hwy 95 N. 1.2 mi n on US 95 from jct SR 200. Int corridors. **Pets:** Medium, other species. Service with restrictions, supervision.

SAVE ⊠ ⅁M ⌨ 🛌

▼▼ Super 8 Motel SH 🐾
(208) 263-2210. **$49-$99.** 476841 Hwy 95 N. 0.7 mi n on US 95 from jct SR 200. Int corridors. **Pets:** Other species. $10 one-time fee/room. Designated rooms, service with restrictions, supervision.

ASK SD ⊠ ⅁M 🛌

POST FALLS

⊕⊕ ▼▼▼ Howard Johnson Express SH
(208) 773-4541. **$64-$159.** 3647 W 5th Ave. I-90, exit 2, just ne. Int corridors. **Pets:** Dogs only. $15 daily fee/pet. Designated rooms, service with restrictions, supervision.

SAVE SD ⊠ ⅁M 🐾 ⌨ 🛌 🖥 ⋙

⊕⊕ ▼▼▼▼ Post Falls Comfort Inn SH 🐾
(208) 773-8900. **$89-$139.** 3175 E Seltice Way. I-90, exit 7, just sw. Int corridors. **Pets:** $20 one-time fee/room. Service with restrictions, supervision.

SAVE SD ⊠ ⅁M 🐾 🛌 🖥

⊕⊕ ▼▼▼▼ Red Lion Templin's Hotel on the River–Post Falls SH
(208) 773-1611. **$89-$169, 3 day notice.** 414 E First Ave. I-90, exit 5 eastbound, just s to First Ave; exit 6 westbound, 0.7 mi w on Seltice Way to Spokane St, 0.5 mi s, then just e. Int corridors. **Pets:** Other species. $10 daily fee/pet. Service with restrictions, supervision.

SAVE SD ⊠ ⅁M 🐾 ⌨ 🛌 🖥 ⅂⅂ ⋙ ⊠

⊕⊕ ▼▼▼ Sleep Inn SH
(208) 777-9394. **$49-$179.** 157 S Pleasant View Rd. I-90, exit 2, just s. Int corridors. **Pets:** Accepted.

SAVE SD ⊠ 🐾 ⌨ 🖥 ⋙

PRIEST RIVER

▼▼ Eagle's Nest Motel M
(208) 448-2000. **$45-$89.** 1007 Albeni Hwy (US 2). US 2, 0.5 mi w. Ext corridors. **Pets:** $100 deposit/room. Designated rooms, service with restrictions, supervision.

ASK ⊠ ⅁M 🐾 ⌨ 🛌 🖥

REXBURG

▼▼▼ AmericInn Lodge & Suites SH
(208) 356-5333. **$69-$89.** 1098 Golden Beauty Dr. US 20, exit 332 (S Rexburg). Int corridors. **Pets:** $20 one-time fee/room. Designated rooms, service with restrictions, supervision.

ASK SD ⊠ 🛌 🖥 ⋙ ⊠

⊕⊕ ▼▼▼ Best Western CottonTree Inn SH
(208) 356-4646. **$67-$76.** 450 W 4th St S. US 20, exit 332 (S Rexburg), 1 mi e. Int corridors. **Pets:** Medium, other species. $15 one-time fee/room. Designated rooms, service with restrictions, supervision.

SAVE SD ⊠ 🛌 🖥 ⅂⅂ ⋙

⊕⊕ ▼▼▼ Comfort Inn SH
(208) 359-1311. **$65-$109.** 885 W Main St. US 20, exit 333 (Salmon), just e. Int corridors. **Pets:** Other species. Designated rooms, service with restrictions, supervision.

SAVE SD ⊠ 🛌 🖥 ⋙

RIGGINS

▼ Pinehurst Resort Cottages CA
(208) 628-3323. **$50-$70.** MM 182 on US 95. On US 95, 13 mi s. Ext corridors. **Pets:** Accepted.

ASK ⊠ 🛌 🖥 〽 ⊠

SAGLE

▽▽ Bottle Bay Resort & Marina CA
(208) 263-5916. **$99-$159, 90 day notice.** 115 Resort Rd. 8.3 mi e on Bottle Bay Rd from US 95. Ext corridors. **Pets:** Medium, dogs only. $10 daily fee/pet. No service, supervision.

ST. ANTHONY

▽▽ GuestHouse Int'l Inn Henry's Fork SH
(208) 624-3711. **$49-$89.** 115 S Bridge St. US 20, exit St. Anthony, just w. Ext corridors. **Pets:** Other species. $10 one-time fee/room. Service with restrictions, supervision.

SALMON

▽ Motel DeLuxe M
(208) 756-2231. **$45-$52.** 112 S Church St. Just s of Main St; downtown. Ext corridors. **Pets:** Other species. Supervision.

SANDPOINT

▽▽ Best Western Edgewater Resort SH
(208) 263-3194. **$89-$199.** 56 Bridge St. Just e of US 95 N; downtown. Int corridors. **Pets:** Accepted.

▽▽▽ Coit House Bed & Breakfast BB
(208) 265-4035. **$79-$150, 3 day notice.** 502 N Fourth Ave. Just ne of US 95 at Fourth Ave and Alder St. Int corridors. **Pets:** Accepted.

▽ The K2 Inn M
(208) 263-3441. **$39-$139, 3 day notice.** 501 N Fourth Ave. US 95, just e. Ext corridors. **Pets:** Service with restrictions, supervision.

◆◆◆ ▽▽▽ La Quinta Inn Sandpoint SH ❀
(208) 263-9581. **$99-$229.** 415 Cedar St. Jct US 2 and 95; downtown. Ext/int corridors. **Pets:** Service with restrictions, supervision.

▽▽ Quality Inn Sandpoint SH
(208) 263-2111. **$79-$149.** 807 N 5th. US 2 and 95, just s of jct SR 200. Int corridors. **Pets:** Other species. $10 daily fee/pet. Service with restrictions, supervision.

TWIN FALLS

◆◆◆ ▽▽ Apollo Motor Inn M
(208) 733-2010. **$55-$75.** 296 Addison Ave W. I-84, exit 173, 5.7 mi s on US 93, then 1.2 mi w. Ext corridors. **Pets:** Other species. $10 daily fee/room. Designated rooms, service with restrictions, supervision.

▽▽ Comfort Inn M
(208) 734-7494. **$62-$200.** 1893 Canyon Springs Rd. I-84, exit 173, 3.5 mi s on US 93. Int corridors. **Pets:** Medium. $10 daily fee/pet. Service with restrictions, supervision.

◆◆◆ ▽▽ Days Inn M ❀
(208) 324-6400. **$59-$109.** 1200 Centennial Spur. I-84, exit 173, just n on US 93. Int corridors. **Pets:** Other species. $50 deposit/room, $10 daily fee/pet. Designated rooms, service with restrictions, supervision.

◆◆◆ ▽▽▽ Red Lion Hotel Canyon Springs SH
(208) 734-5000. **$93-$159.** 1357 Blue Lakes Blvd N. I-84, exit 173, 4 mi s on US 93. Int corridors. **Pets:** Accepted.

▽▽◆ Shilo Inn Suites Twin Falls SH ❀
(208) 733-7545. **$99-$170.** 1586 Blue Lakes Blvd N. I-84, exit 173, 3.7 mi s on US 93. Int corridors. **Pets:** Other species. $25 one-time fee/room. Designated rooms, supervision.

▽▽ Twin Falls Super 8 Motel M
(208) 734-5801. **$59-$80.** 1260 Blue Lakes Blvd N. I-84, exit 173, 4.1 mi s on US 93. Int corridors. **Pets:** Other species. $10 one-time fee/room. Service with restrictions, supervision.

WALLACE

◆◆ Stardust Motel M
(208) 752-1213. **$52-$72.** 410 Pine St. I-90, exit 61 (Business Rt 90), 0.7 mi e; downtown. Ext corridors. **Pets:** Other species. $15 daily fee/pet. Service with restrictions, supervision.

◆◆◆ ▽▽▽ The Wallace Inn SH
(208) 752-1252. **$80-$94.** 100 Front St. I-90, exit 61 (Business Rt 90), just se. Int corridors. **Pets:** Other species. $15 one-time fee/pet. Supervision.

WHITE BIRD

▽ Hells Canyon Jet Boat Trips & Lodging M ❀
(208) 839-2255. **Call for rates.** HC01 Box 160. 1 mi s of White Bird on Old Hwy 95. Ext corridors. **Pets:** Dogs only. $20 daily fee/pet. Service with restrictions, supervision.

WORLEY

◆◆◆ ▽▽▽ Coeur d'Alene Casino Resort Hotel SH
(208) 686-0248. **$70-$400.** 27068 S Hwy 95. On US 95, 3 mi n. Int corridors. **Pets:** Accepted.

ILLINOIS

ALTON

🔺🔺 🔻🔻🔻 Comfort Inn SH
(618) 465-9999. $85-$99. 11 Crossroads Ct. Off SR 3, jct SR 140. Int corridors. Pets: Accepted.

SAVE 🔲 🔲 🔲 🔲 🔲 🔲 🔲 🔲

🔻🔻🔻 Super 8 Motel SH
(618) 465-8885. $54-$80. 1800 Homer Adams Pkwy. On SR 111, 1.8 mi e of jct US 67. Int corridors. Pets: Medium. $50 deposit/room. Service with restrictions, supervision.

ASK 🔲 🔲 🔲 🔲 🔲

ARCOLA

🔻🔻 Comfort Inn SH
(217) 268-4000. $49-$120. 610 E Springfield Rd. I-57, exit 203 (SR 133), just w. Int corridors. Pets: Medium. $7 one-time fee/pet. Service with restrictions, supervision.

ASK 🔲 🔲 🔲 🔲 🔲 🔲 🔲

BELLEVILLE

🔺🔺 🔻 The Shrine Hotel SH
(618) 397-1162. $75. 451 S Demazenod Dr. I-255, exit 17A, 1 mi e on SR 15; in Shrine of Our Lady of the Snows Complex. Int corridors. Pets: Other species. Service with restrictions, crate.

SAVE 🔲 🔲 🔲 🔲 🔲 🔲

BLOOMINGTON

🔻🔻 Baymont Inn & Suites SH
(309) 662-2800. $79-$99. 604 1/2 IAA Dr. I-55, exit 167 southbound, follow I-55 business route (Veterans Pkwy), 2.8 mi s to jct SR 9, just e, then just n via service road; exit 157B (Veterans Pkwy) northbound, 4 mi n to SR 9. Int corridors. Pets: Small. $25 deposit/room, $15 one-time fee/room. Service with restrictions, supervision.

ASK 🔲 🔲 🔲 🔲 🔲 🔲

🔻🔻🔻 Country Inn & Suites By Carlson Bloomington/Normal-Airport SH
(309) 662-3100. $114-$129. 2403 E Empire St. Jct I-55 business route (Veterans Pkwy) and SR 9, 0.8 mi e. Int corridors. Pets: Medium, dogs only. $10 daily fee/room. Designated rooms, service with restrictions, supervision.

ASK 🔲 🔲 🔲 🔲 🔲 🔲 🔲 🔲

🔻🔻🔻 Country Inn & Suites By Carlson Bloomington/Normal-West SH
(309) 828-7177. $76. 923 Maple Hill Rd. I-55/74, exit 160 (SR 9), 0.3 mi w to Wylie Dr, just n, then just e. Int corridors. Pets: Accepted.

ASK 🔲 🔲 🔲 🔲 🔲 🔲

🔻🔻 DoubleTree Bloomington Hotel & Conference Center LH
(309) 664-6446. $135. 10 Brickyard Dr. I-55 business route (Veterans Pkwy), just n of US 150. Int corridors. Pets: Accepted.

ASK 🔲 🔲 🔲 🔲 🔲 🔲 🔲 🔲 🔲 🔲

🔻🔻 Eastland Suites Hotel & Conference Center SH
(309) 662-0000. $79-$94. 1801 Eastland Dr. Jct I-55 business route (Veterans Pkwy) and SR 9, just s to Eastland Dr, then just e. Ext/int corridors. Pets: Accepted.

ASK 🔲 🔲 🔲 🔲 🔲 🔲

🔻🔻 Econo Lodge by Choice Hotels M
(309) 829-3100. $45-$100. 403 Brock Dr. I-55/74, exit 160 (SR 9), just e. Ext corridors. Pets: Accepted.

ASK 🔲 🔲 🔲 🔲

🔻🔻 Ramada Limited & Suites Bloomington/Normal-West SH
(309) 828-0900. $64. 919 Maple Hill Rd. I-55/74, exit 160 (SR 9), 0.3 mi w to Wylie Rd, just n, then just e. Int corridors. Pets: Other species. $10 daily fee/pet. Service with restrictions, crate.

ASK 🔲 🔲 🔲 🔲 🔲

🔻🔻🔻 Wingate Inn SH
(309) 820-9990. $84-$149, 3 day notice. 1031 Wylie Dr. I-55/74, exit 160 (SR 9), just w, then just n. Int corridors. Pets: Accepted.

ASK 🔲 🔲 🔲 🔲 🔲 🔲 🔲

BOURBONNAIS

🔻🔻 Hampton Inn Bradley/Kankakee SH
(815) 932-8369. $88-$98. 60 Ken Hayes Dr. I-57, exit 315 (SR 50). Int corridors. Pets: Small. Service with restrictions, crate.

ASK 🔲 🔲 🔲 🔲 🔲 🔲

CARBONDALE

🔻 Super 8 Motel SH
(618) 457-8822. $56-$95. 1180 E Main St. I-57, exit 54B, 13.9 mi w on SR 13. Int corridors. Pets: Accepted.

ASK 🔲 🔲 🔲 🔲 🔲

CARLINVILLE

▼▼ **Best Western Carlinville Inn** SH
(217) 324-2100. **$85-$92.** 19067 W Frontage Rd. I-55, exit 60 (SR 108), just w. Int corridors. **Pets:** Accepted.

A$K ✕ 🖥 💻 ¶¶ ➦

CASEY

ⒶⒶⒶ ▼▼▼ **Comfort Inn** SH
(217) 932-2212. **$70-$87, 5 day notice.** 933 SR 49. I-70, exit 129, 0.3 mi se. Int corridors. **Pets:** Other species. $5 daily fee/pet. Designated rooms, service with restrictions, supervision.

SAVE S🖊 ✕ 🖥 💻 ➦

CHAMPAIGN

▼▼ **Baymont Inn & Suites** SH
(217) 356-8900. **$60-$135.** 302 W Anthony Dr. I-74, exit 182 (Neil St), just nw. Int corridors. **Pets:** Designated rooms, service with restrictions, supervision.

A$K S🖊 ✕ 🖥 💺 🖥 💻

ⒶⒶⒶ ▼▼▼▼ **Country Inn & Suites By Carlson** SH
(217) 355-6666. **$89.** 602 W Marketview Dr. I-74, exit 181 (Prospect Rd), just n, then just e. Int corridors. **Pets:** Accepted.

SAVE S🖊 ✕ 🖥M 🖥 💺 🖥 💻 ➦

▼▼▼▼ **Drury Inn & Suites-Champaign** SH
(217) 398-0030. **$97-$147.** 905 W Anthony Dr. I-74, exit 181 (Prospect Blvd), just n. Int corridors. **Pets:** Large, other species. Service with restrictions, supervision.

A$K ✕ 🖥M 🖥 💺 🖥 💻 ➦

▼▼ **Extended Stay America-Champaign-Urbana** SH
(217) 351-8899. **$65-$165.** 610 W Marketview Dr. I-74, exit 181 (Prospect Rd), just n, then just e. Int corridors. **Pets:** Accepted.

A$K S🖊 ✕ 🖥 💺 🖥 💻 📦

ⒶⒶⒶ ▼▼▼▼ **La Quinta Inn Champaign** SH
(217) 356-4000. **$85-$99.** 1900 Center Dr. I-74, exit 182B (Neil St), just n. Int corridors. **Pets:** Medium. Service with restrictions.

SAVE ✕ 🖥M 🖥 🖥 💻 ➦

ⒶⒶⒶ ▼▼▼ **Microtel Inn** SH
(217) 398-4136. **$48-$89, 7 day notice.** 1615 Rion Dr. I-57, exit 238, just w. Int corridors. **Pets:** Accepted.

SAVE S🖊 ✕ 🖥

▼▼▼▼ **Red Roof Inn #170** SH
(217) 352-0101. **$45-$69.** 212 W Anthony Dr. I-74, exit 182B (Neil St), just n to Anthony Dr, then just w. Ext corridors. **Pets:** Medium, other species. Service with restrictions, supervision.

✕ 🖥 💺 🖥

CHESTER

ⒶⒶⒶ ▼▼▼▼ **Best Western Reids' Inn** SH
(618) 826-3034. **$64-$119.** 2150 State St. SR 150, 1 mi e of SR 3. Int corridors. **Pets:** Accepted.

SAVE S🖊 ✕ 🖥M 🖥 💻 ➦

CHICAGO METROPOLITAN AREA

ALGONQUIN

ⒶⒶⒶ ▼▼▼▼ **Holiday Inn Express Hotel & Suites** SH
(847) 458-6000. **$84-$114, 7 day notice.** 2595 Bunker Hill Rd. I-90, exit Randall Rd N, 6.1 mi n to Bunker Hill Rd, then just w. Int corridors. **Pets:** Small. $50 one-time fee/room. Designated rooms, service with restrictions, supervision.

SAVE S🖊 ✕ 🖥M 🖥 💺 🖥 💻 ➦ ✕

ALSIP

▼▼ **Baymont Inn-Midway South** SH
(708) 597-3900. **$68-$79.** 12801 S Cicero Ave. I-294, exit SR 50 (Cicero Ave S). Int corridors. **Pets:** Accepted.

A$K S🖊 ✕ 🖥 💺 🖥 💻

ⒶⒶⒶ ▼▼▼▼ **DoubleTree Hotel Chicago/Alsip** LH
(708) 371-7300. **$129-$189.** 5000 W 127th St. I-294, exit SR 50 (Cicero Ave S), just w. Int corridors. **Pets:** Accepted.

SAVE S🖊 ✕ 🖥M 🖥 🖥 💻 ¶¶ ➦

ANTIOCH

ⒶⒶⒶ ▼▼▼ **Best Western Regency Inn** SH
(847) 395-3606. **$89-$127, 3 day notice.** 350 Rt 173. SR 173, 0.5 mi w of jct SR 83. Int corridors. **Pets:** Accepted.

SAVE S🖊 ✕ 🖥 💻 ➦

ARLINGTON HEIGHTS

▼▼▼▼ **DoubleTree Hotel Chicago-Arlington Heights** LH
(847) 364-7600. **$89-$199.** 75 W Algonquin Rd. I-90, exit Arlington Heights Rd, just n to Algonquin Rd, then just w. Int corridors. **Pets:** $250 deposit/room. Designated rooms, service with restrictions, crate.

✕ 🖥M 🖥 💺 🖥 💻 ¶¶ ➦

▼▼▼▼ **La Quinta Inn Chicago (Arlington Heights)** SH
(847) 253-8777. **$99-$129.** 1415 W Dundee Rd. SR 53, exit Dundee Rd, just e. Int corridors. **Pets:** Medium. Service with restrictions.

A$K ✕ 🖥 🖥 💻 ➦

▼ **Motel 6-1048** SH
(847) 806-1230. **$51-$65.** 441 W Algonquin Rd. I-90, exit Arlington Heights Rd, 0.5 mi n, then 0.5 mi w. Int corridors. **Pets:** Medium, other species. Service with restrictions, supervision.

S🖊 ✕ 🖥M

▼ **Red Roof Inn #7102** M
(847) 228-6650. **$57-$82.** 22 W Algonquin Rd. I-90, exit Arlington Heights Rd, 0.5 mi n, then just w. Ext corridors. **Pets:** Medium, other species. Service with restrictions, supervision.

✕ 💺

ⒶⒶⒶ ▼▼▼▼ **Sheraton Chicago Northwest** LH
(847) 394-2000. **$99-$289.** 3400 W Euclid Ave. SR 53, exit Euclid Ave, just e. Int corridors. **Pets:** Accepted.

SAVE S🖊 ✕ 🖥 🖥 💻 ¶¶ ➦ ✕

AURORA

▼▼▼▼ **Staybridge Suites by Holiday Inn Aurora/Naperville** SH
(630) 978-2222. **$159-$264.** 4320 Meridian Pkwy. I-88, exit SR 59, 2 mi s to Meridian Pkwy, then just w. Int corridors. **Pets:** $75 one-time fee/room. Service with restrictions, crate.

A$K S🖊 ✕ 🖥M 💺 🖥 💻 ➦ ✕

BANNOCKBURN

(AAA) ▼▼▼▼ La Quinta Inn & Suites
Bannockburn-Deerfield SH
(847) 317-7300. **$139-$169.** 2000 S Lakeside Dr. I-94, exit Half Day Rd
(SR 22), just e to Lakeside Dr, then just s. Int corridors. **Pets:** Medium.
Designated rooms, service with restrictions, supervision.

BEDFORD PARK

▼▼▼▼ Extended StayAmerica Chicago-Midway SH
(708) 496-8211. **Call for rates.** 7524 State Rd. Jct SR 50, just w. Int
corridors. **Pets:** Accepted.

BLOOMINGDALE

▼▼▼▼ Residence Inn by Marriott SH
(630) 893-9200. **$170-$200.** 295 Knollwood Dr. I-355, exit Army Trail
Rd, 4 mi w, then just n. Int corridors. **Pets:** Accepted.

BOLINGBROOK

(AAA) ▼▼▼ AmericInn Lodge & Suites SH 🐾
(630) 378-5300. **$79-$114.** 175 W Remington Blvd. I-55, exit 267, just n
on SR 53. Int corridors. **Pets:** Medium, dogs only. Designated rooms,
service with restrictions.

▼▼▼▼ Holiday Inn Hotel & Suites Bolingbrook LH
(630) 679-1600. **$129.** 205 Remington Blvd. I-55, exit 267, just n, then
0.4 mi sw. Int corridors. **Pets:** Accepted.

▼▼▼▼ La Quinta Inn Bolingbrook SH
(630) 226-0000. **$114-$144.** 225 W South Frontage Rd. I-55, exit 267,
0.5 mi sw. Int corridors. **Pets:** Accepted.

BRIDGEVIEW

(AAA) ▼▼ Exel Inn of Bridgeview SH
(708) 430-1818. **$69-$99.** 9625 S 76th Ave. I-294, exit 95th St, just s.
Int corridors. **Pets:** Small, other species. Designated rooms, service with
restrictions, supervision.

BURR RIDGE

▼▼▼ Extended StayAmerica Chicago-Burr Ridge SH
(630) 323-6630. **Call for rates.** 15 W 122nd S Frontage Rd. I-55, exit
276A (County Line Rd), just sw. Int corridors. **Pets:** Accepted.

(AAA) ▼▼▼▼ The Oaks Hotel & Conference Center SH
(630) 325-2900. **$95-$209.** 300 S Frontage Rd. I-55, exit 276A (County
Line Rd), just sw. Int corridors. **Pets:** Accepted.

CHICAGO

(AAA) ▼▼▼▼ Affinia Chicago SH
(312) 787-6000. **$325-$462.** 166 E Superior St. Just e of Michigan Ave.
Int corridors. **Pets:** Other species. $200 deposit/pet. Service with restric-
tions, crate.

(AAA) ▼▼▼▼ Allegro Chicago, A Kimpton Hotel SH
(312) 236-0123. **$135-$315.** 171 W Randolph St. Jct La Salle St; in
theater district. Int corridors. **Pets:** Accepted.

(AAA) ▼▼▼▼ Allerton Crowne Plaza LH
(312) 440-1500. **$109-$489.** 701 N Michigan Ave. Jct Huron St. Int
corridors. **Pets:** Accepted.

(AAA) ▼▼▼▼ Amalfi Hotel Chicago SH 🐾
(312) 395-9000. **$189-$499.** 20 W Kinzie St. Between State and Dearborn sts. Int corridors. **Pets:** Small.

(AAA) ▼▼▼▼ Best Western Hawthorne Terrace SH
(773) 244-3434. **$159-$219.** 3434 N Broadway St. Between Belmont
Ave and Addison St. Int corridors. **Pets:** Accepted.

(AAA) ▼▼▼ Carlton Inn Midway M
(773) 582-0900. **$99-$149.** 4944 S Archer Ave. I-55, exit 287 (Pulaski),
1.8 mi s to Archer Ave, then just e. Ext corridors. **Pets:** Medium. $50
deposit/pet. Service with restrictions, supervision.

(AAA) ▼▼▼▼ Conrad Chicago LH 🐾
(312) 645-1500. **$225-$625.** 521 N Rush St at Michigan Ave. Jct Grand
Ave. Int corridors. **Pets:** Small, other species. Service with restrictions,
crate.

▼▼▼▼ Crowne Plaza Chicago Metro SH 🐾
(312) 829-5000. **$189-$499.** 733 W Madison St. I-90/94, exit 51D
(Madison St), at Monroe St. Int corridors. **Pets:** Small. $50 one-time
fee/pet. Service with restrictions, crate.

▼▼▼▼ The Drake Hotel, Chicago LH
(312) 787-2200. **$185-$435.** 140 E Walton Pl. N Michigan Ave at Lake
Shore Dr and Walton Pl. Int corridors. **Pets:** Accepted.

▼▼▼▼ The Fairmont Chicago LH 🐾
(312) 565-8000. **$149-$509.** 200 N Columbus Dr. Jct Michigan Ave and
Wacker Dr, just e. Int corridors. **Pets:** Small. $25 daily fee/room. Service
with restrictions, supervision.

(AAA) ▼▼▼▼ Four Seasons Hotel Chicago LH 🐾
(312) 280-8800. **$305-$3500.** 120 E Delaware Pl. Jct Michigan Ave; just
nw of John Hancock building. Int corridors. **Pets:** Very small. Designated
rooms, service with restrictions, crate.

(AAA) ▼▼▼▼ Hard Rock Hotel Chicago LH
(312) 345-1000. **$119-$499.** 230 N Michigan Ave. Between Lake St and
Wacker Dr. Int corridors. **Pets:** Accepted.

(AAA) ▼▼▼▼ Hilton Chicago LH
(312) 922-4400. **$159-$399.** 720 S Michigan Ave. I-290 (Congress
Pkwy), just s. Int corridors. **Pets:** Accepted.

(AAA) ▼▼▼▼ Hilton Chicago O'Hare Airport LH
(773) 686-8000. **$119-$379.** OHare Intl Airport. Opposite and connected
to terminal buildings at O'Hare International Airport, accessed via
I-190. Int corridors. **Pets:** Small. Designated rooms, service with restrictions, crate.

(AAA) ▼▼▼▼ Holiday Inn Chicago Mart Plaza LH 🐾
(312) 836-5000. **$129-$369, 3 day notice.** 350 N Orleans. Atop the
Mart Center along the Chicago River. Int corridors. **Pets:** Medium.
Designated rooms, service with restrictions, crate.

▲▲▲ ▼▼▼▼ Holiday Inn Chicago-O'Hare Kennedy 🅂🅷
(773) 693-2323. **$120-$170.** 8201 W Higgins Rd. I-90, exit 79B (Cumberland Ave N), just n to Higgins Rd (SR 72), then just e. Int corridors. **Pets:** Accepted.

[SAVE] ⓧ 🖉 🖥 🖳 ❙❙ ⇌

▲▲▲ ▼▼▼▼ Hotel Burnham Chicago 🅂🅷 🐾
(312) 782-1111. **$152-$399.** One W Washington St. Jct State St. Int corridors. **Pets:** Other species. Designated rooms, service with restrictions, crate.

[SAVE] ⓧ 🖉 🖳 🖥 ❙❙ ⊠

▲▲▲ ▼▼▼▼ Hotel Monaco Chicago 🅂🅷 🐾
(312) 960-8500. **$149-$499, 3 day notice.** 225 N Wabash Ave. Jct Wacker Dr. Int corridors. **Pets:** Other species. Service with restrictions.

[SAVE] 🆂🄳 ⓧ 🖉 🖳 🖥 ❙❙ ⊠

▲▲▲ ▼▼▼▼ Hotel Sax Chicago 🅻🅷
(312) 245-0333. **$199-$495.** 333 N Dearborn St. Between Dearborn and State sts. Int corridors. **Pets:** Accepted.

[SAVE] 🆂🄳 ⓧ 🖉 🖳 🖥 ❙❙

▲▲▲ ▼▼▼▼ InterContinental Chicago 🅻🅷
(312) 944-4100. **$229-$499.** 505 N Michigan Ave. Just n of Chicago River. Int corridors. **Pets:** Accepted.

[SAVE] ⓧ 🖉 🖳 🖥 ❙❙ ⇌ ⊠

▼▼▼▼ The James 🅻🅷 🐾
(312) 337-1000. **$289-$519.** 55 E Ontario. At Ontario St, just w of N Michigan Ave. Int corridors. **Pets:** $75 one-time fee/room. Service with restrictions.

[ASK] 🆂🄳 ⓧ 🖦 🖉 🖳 🖥 ❙❙

▲▲▲ ▼▼▼▼ Omni Chicago Hotel 🅻🅷
(312) 944-6664. **$369-$899.** 676 N Michigan Ave. Jct Huron St. Int corridors. **Pets:** Small. $50 one-time fee/room. Service with restrictions, supervision.

[SAVE] 🆂🄳 ⓧ 🖦 🖉 🖥 🖳 ⇌ ⊠

▲▲▲ ▼▼▼▼ The Palmer House Hilton 🅻🅷
(312) 726-7500. **$129-$454.** 17 E Monroe St. Between State St and Wabash Ave. Int corridors. **Pets:** Accepted.

[SAVE] ⓧ 🖉 🖳 🖥 ❙❙ ⊠

▲▲▲ ▼▼▼▼ Park Hyatt Chicago 🅻🅷
(312) 335-1234. **$279-$495.** 800 N Michigan Ave. Jct Chicago and Michigan aves at Water Tower Square. Int corridors. **Pets:** Accepted.

[SAVE] ⓧ 🖉 🖳 ❙❙ ⇌ ⊠

▲▲▲ ▼▼▼▼ The Peninsula Chicago 🅻🅷
(312) 337-2888. **$490-$7020.** 108 E Superior St. Jct Michigan Ave. Int corridors. **Pets:** Accepted.

[SAVE] ⓧ 🖉 🖳 🖥 ❙❙ ⇌ ⊠

▲▲▲ ▼▼▼▼ Radisson Hotel & Suites Chicago 🅻🅷
(312) 787-2900. **$199-$419.** 160 E Huron St. Just e of N Michigan Ave. Int corridors. **Pets:** Small. $100 deposit/room. Service with restrictions, supervision.

[SAVE] 🆂🄳 ⓧ 🖉 🖳 🖥 🖦 ❙❙ ⇌

▲▲▲ ▼▼▼▼ Renaissance Chicago Hotel 🅻🅷
(312) 372-7200. **$199-$529.** One W Wacker Dr. Jct State St. Int corridors. **Pets:** Accepted.

[SAVE] 🆂🄳 ⓧ 🖦 🖉 🖳 🖥 ❙❙ ⇌ ⊠

▲▲▲ ▼▼▼▼ Residence Inn by Marriott Chicago Downtown 🅂🅷
(312) 943-9800. **$129-$579.** 201 E Walton St. Just e of Michigan Ave at Mies van der Rohe. Int corridors. **Pets:** Other species. $75 one-time fee/pet. Designated rooms, service with restrictions.

[SAVE] ⓧ 🖦 🖉 🖳 🖥 🖦

▲▲▲ ▼▼▼▼ The Ritz-Carlton, Chicago (A Four Seasons Hotel) 🅻🅷
(312) 266-1000. **$500-$5000.** 160 E Pearson St. Jct N Michigan Ave. Int corridors. **Pets:** Accepted.

[SAVE] 🆂🄳 ⓧ 🖦 🖉 🖳 🖥 ❙❙ ⇌ ⊠

▲▲▲ ▼▼▼▼ Sheraton Chicago Hotel & Towers 🅻🅷 🐾
(312) 464-1000. **$139-$699.** 301 E North Water St. Columbus Dr at Chicago River; just e of Michigan Ave. Int corridors. **Pets:** Medium, dogs only. Service with restrictions, crate.

[SAVE] 🆂🄳 ⓧ 🖉 🖳 🖥 ❙❙ ⇌ ⊠

▲▲▲ ▼▼▼▼ Sofitel Chicago Water Tower 🅻🅷 🐾
(312) 324-4000. **$525-$2000.** 20 E Chestnut St. Jct Wabash Ave and Chestnut St, 1/2 blk w of Rush St. Int corridors. **Pets:** Small, dogs only. Service with restrictions, supervision.

[SAVE] 🆂🄳 ⓧ 🖉 🖳 🖥 ❙❙ ⊠

▲▲▲ ▼▼▼▼ The Sutton Place Hotel 🅻🅷
(312) 266-2100. **$177-$386.** 21 E Bellevue Pl. Jct Rush St. Int corridors. **Pets:** Accepted.

[SAVE] 🆂🄳 ⓧ 🖉 🖳 ❙❙

▼▼▼▼ The Talbott Hotel 🅂🅷
(312) 944-4970. **$371-$431.** 20 E Delaware Pl. Jct Rush St, just w. Int corridors. **Pets:** Accepted.

[ASK] ⓧ 🖳 🖥 ❙❙

▼▼▼▼ W Chicago-City Center 🅻🅷
(312) 332-1200. **$179-$499.** 172 W Adams St. Between La Salle and Wells sts. Int corridors. **Pets:** Accepted.

[ASK] 🆂🄳 ⓧ 🖉 🖳 🖥 ❙❙

▼▼▼▼ W Chicago Lakeshore 🅻🅷 🐾
(312) 943-9200. **$250-$275.** 644 N Lake Shore Dr. Jct Ontario St. Int corridors. **Pets:** Medium. $25 daily fee/room, $100 one-time fee/room. Designated rooms, service with restrictions, supervision.

[ASK] ⓧ 🖉 🖳 🖥 ❙❙ ⇌

▲▲▲ ▼▼▼▼ The Westin Chicago River North 🅻🅷
(312) 744-1900. **$209-$529.** 320 N Dearborn St. Just n of Chicago River; between Dearborn and Clark sts; in River North area. Int corridors. **Pets:** Accepted.

[SAVE] 🆂🄳 ⓧ 🖉 🖳 🖥 ❙❙ ⊠

▲▲▲ ▼▼▼▼ The Westin Michigan Avenue Chicago 🅻🅷 🐾
(312) 943-7200. **$499.** 909 N Michigan Ave. Across from John Hancock Center. Int corridors. **Pets:** Accepted.

[SAVE] 🆂🄳 ⓧ 🖦 🖉 🖳 🖥 ❙❙

CRESTWOOD

▼▼▼ Hampton Inn-Chicago/Crestwood 🅂🅷
(708) 597-3330. **Call for rates.** 13330 S Cicero Ave. On SR 50 and 83, 0.8 mi s of jct I-294. Int corridors. **Pets:** Accepted.

ⓧ 🖳 🖥 ⇌

DARIEN

▼▼▼ Extended StayAmerica Chicago-Darien 🅂🅷
(630) 985-4708. **Call for rates.** 2345 Sokol Ct. I-55, exit 271A, 0.5 mi s to Westgate Rd, then 0.5 mi ne via frontage road. Int corridors. **Pets:** Accepted.

ⓧ 🖉 🖳 🖳 🖥

DES PLAINES

▼▼▼ Des Plaines Inn & Suites Chicago/O'Hare Airport 🅂🅷
(847) 635-1300. **$90-$175.** 2175 E Touhy Ave. I-294, exit Touhy Ave westbound, just w; exit Golf Rd (SR 58) eastbound, 0.3 mi w to River Rd, then 5.5 mi s. Int corridors. **Pets:** Accepted.

[ASK] 🆂🄳 ⓧ 🖉 🖳 🖳 🖥 ❙❙

▼▼ **Extended StayAmerica-Chicago-O'Hare** SH
(847) 294-9693. **Call for rates.** 1201 E Touhy Ave. At SR 72 (Higgins Rd), 0.6 mi, w of US 12/45 (Mannheim Rd). Int corridors. **Pets:** Accepted.

🅧 🖳 🗐 🖉 🔲 🖵

▼▼ **Extended Stay Deluxe Chicago-O'Hare** SH
(847) 768-0395. **Call for rates.** 1207 E Touhy Ave. At SR 72 (Higgins Rd), 0.6 mi w of US 12/45 (Mannheim Rd). Int corridors. **Pets:** Accepted.

🅧 🖳 🗐 🖉 🔲 🖵

DOWNERS GROVE

▼ **Red Roof Inn #7087** M
(630) 963-4205. **$53-$88.** 1113 Butterfield Rd. I-355, exit Butterfield Rd (SR 56), on frontage road; I-88, exit Highland Ave N, just w. Ext corridors. **Pets:** Medium, other species. Service with restrictions, supervision.

🅧 🗐 🔲

ELGIN

🄰🄰🄰 ▼▼ **Quality Inn-Elgin** SH
(847) 608-7300. **$75.** 500 Tollgate Rd. I-90, exit SR 31 N, just n. Int corridors. **Pets:** Accepted.

SAVE 🆂 🅧 🖳 🗐 🖉 🔲 🖵

ELK GROVE VILLAGE

🄰🄰🄰 ▼▼ **Best Western Chicago West** SH
(847) 981-0010. **$74-$129.** 1600 Oakton St. Jct SR 72 (Higgins Rd) and 83 (Busse Rd). Int corridors. **Pets:** Accepted.

SAVE 🆂 🅧 🗐 🔲 🖵 🍴 🏊 🅧

🄰🄰🄰 ▼ **Exel Inn of Elk Grove Village** SH
(847) 895-2085. **$60-$90.** 1000 W Devon Ave. I-290, exit Thorndale Ave, 0.5 mi w to Rohlwing Rd, 0.3 mi n to Devon Ave, then 0.3 mi e. Int corridors. **Pets:** Small, other species. Designated rooms, service with restrictions, supervision.

SAVE 🆂 🅧 🗐 🔲 🖵

🄰🄰🄰 ▼ **Exel Inn of O'Hare** SH
(847) 803-9400. **$67-$97.** 2881 Touhy Ave. Jct SR 72 (Higgins Rd) and 83 (Busse Rd), 1.5 mi e on SR 72 (Higgins Rd). Int corridors. **Pets:** Small, other species. Designated rooms, service with restrictions, supervision.

SAVE 🆂 🅧 🗐 🔲 🖵

▼▼▼ **La Quinta Inn Chicago (O'Hare Airport)** SH
(847) 439-6767. **$64-$159.** 1900 E Oakton St. Jct SR 72 (Higgins Rd) and 83 (Busse Rd). Int corridors. **Pets:** Medium, other species. Service with restrictions, crate.

ASK 🆂 🅧 🗐 🔲 🖵 🏊

🄰🄰🄰 ▼▼ **Super 8 Motel O'Hare** SH
(847) 827-3133. **$69-$99.** 2951 Touhy Ave. Jct SR 72 (Higgins Rd) and 83 (Busse Rd), 1.5 mi e on SR 72 (Higgins Rd). Int corridors. **Pets:** Small. $10 daily fee/pet. Designated rooms, service with restrictions, supervision.

SAVE 🆂 🅧 🖳 🗐 🖉 🔲 🖵 🏊

ELMHURST

▼▼ **Extended StayAmerica Chicago-Elmhurst** SH
(630) 530-4353. **$77.** 550 W Grand Ave. Jct US 20 (Lake St), 0.4 mi ne; adjacent to I-290 overpass. Int corridors. **Pets:** Accepted.

ASK 🆂 🅧 🖳 🖉 🔲 🖵

EVANSTON

🄰🄰🄰 ▼▼▼ ▼▼▼ **Hotel Orrington** LH 🐾
(847) 866-8700. **$149-$239.** 1710 Orrington Ave. Jct Church St. Int corridors. **Pets:** Medium, other species. $50 one-time fee/pet. Designated rooms, service with restrictions, supervision.

SAVE 🆂 🅧 🖳 🗐 🖉 🔲 🖵 🍴

FRANKLIN PARK

🄰🄰🄰 ▼▼ ▼ **Comfort Inn by Choice Hotels** SH
(847) 233-9292. **$109.** 3001 N Mannheim Rd. Jct US 12/45 (Mannheim Rd) and Grand Ave, just n. Int corridors. **Pets:** Accepted.

SAVE 🆂 🅧 🖉 🔲 🖵 🏊

🄰🄰🄰 ▼▼ ▼ **Super 8 O'Hare South** SH
(847) 288-0600. **$69-$99.** 3010 N Mannheim Rd. Jct US 12/45 (Mannheim Rd) and Grand Ave, just n. Int corridors. **Pets:** Accepted.

SAVE 🆂 🅧 🔲

GLEN ELLYN

▼▼ ▼ **Holiday Inn-Glen Ellyn** SH
(630) 629-6000. **$79-$109.** 1250 Roosevelt Rd. I-355, exit Roosevelt Rd, 0.8 mi e on SR 38. Int corridors. **Pets:** Accepted.

ASK 🆂 🅧 🖳 🗐 🖉 🔲 🖵 🍴 🏊

GLENVIEW

▼▼ ▼ **Baymont Inn & Suites Chicago-Glenview** SH
(847) 635-8300. **$69-$129.** 1625 Milwaukee Ave. I-294, exit Willow Rd, 0.4 mi e to Landwehr Rd, 1.3 mi s to Lake Ave, then 0.5 mi w. Int corridors. **Pets:** Accepted.

ASK 🆂 🅧 🗐 🔲 🖵

🄰🄰🄰 ▼▼▼ ▼ **Staybridge Suites** SH
(847) 657-0002. **$99-$155.** 2600 Lehigh Ave. I-294, exit Willow Rd, 2.4 mi e. Int corridors. **Pets:** Accepted.

SAVE 🆂 🅧 🖳 🗐 🖉 🔲 🖵 🏊

GURNEE

▼▼ ▼ **Comfort Suites by Choice Hotels** SH
(847) 782-0890. **$69-$299.** 5430 Grand Ave. I-94, exit Grand Ave (SR 132 E), 0.5 mi e. Int corridors. **Pets:** Medium, dogs only. $50 one-time fee/room. Service with restrictions, supervision.

ASK 🆂 🅧 🖳 🗐 🖉 🔲 🖵 🏊

▼▼▼ ▼ **Country Inn & Suites By Carlson** SH
(847) 625-9700. **$69-$299.** 5420 Grand Ave. I-94, exit Grand Ave (SR 132), 0.5 mi e. Int corridors. **Pets:** Medium, dogs only. $50 one-time fee/room. Service with restrictions, supervision.

ASK 🆂 🅧 🖳 🗐 🖉 🔲 🖵 🏊

▼▼ ▼ **Extended StayAmerica-Chicago-Gurnee** SH
(847) 662-3060. **Call for rates.** 5724 Northridge Dr. I-94, exit Grand Ave (SR 132 E), just e via service road. Int corridors. **Pets:** Accepted.

🅧 🖳 🖉 🔲 🖵

🄰🄰🄰 ▼▼ ▼ **La Quinta Chicago-Gurnee** SH
(847) 662-7600. **$76-$131.** 5688 Northridge Dr. I-94, exit Grand Ave (SR 132), just e via service road. Int corridors. **Pets:** Medium. Service with restrictions.

SAVE 🅧 🖳 🗐 🖉 🔲 🖵 🏊

HARVEY

▼▼ ▼ **Sleep Inn by Choice Hotels** SH 🐾
(708) 331-3400. **$55-$95.** 16940 Halsted St. I-80/294, exit Halsted St, just n. Int corridors. **Pets:** Medium, other species. $15 daily fee/pet. Service with restrictions, supervision.

ASK 🆂 🅧 🗐 🖉 🔲

HOFFMAN ESTATES

▼▼ **Baymont Inn & Suites Chicago-Hoffman Estates** 🆂🅷
(847) 882-8848. **$75-$150.** 2075 Barrington Rd. I-90, exit Barrington Rd westbound, 0.3 mi s; exit SR 59 eastbound, 0.5 mi n to SR 72 (Higgins Rd), 2 mi e to Barrington Rd, then just n. Int corridors. **Pets:** Accepted.
A$K S🔒 ✕ 🕭 🔒 💻

▼▼▼ **La Quinta Inn Chicago (Hoffman Estates)** 🆂🅷
(847) 882-3312. **$99-$115.** 2280 Barrington Rd. I-90, exit Barrington Rd westbound, 0.3 mi s; exit SR 59 eastbound, 0.5 mi n to SR 72 (Higgins Rd), 2 mi e to Barrington Rd, then just n. Int corridors. **Pets:** Medium. Service with restrictions.
A$K ✕ 🕭 🔒 🔒 💻 ⇌

▼ **Red Roof Inn #7199** Ⓜ
(847) 885-7877. **$56-$88.** 2500 Hassell Rd. I-90, exit Barrington Rd westbound, 0.3 mi s; exit SR 59 eastbound, 0.5 mi n to SR 72 (Higgins Rd), 2 mi e to Barrington Rd, then just n. Ext corridors. **Pets:** Medium, other species. Service with restrictions, supervision.
✕ 🕭 🔒

ITASCA

▼▼ **Extended StayAmerica-Chicago-Itasca** 🆂🅷
(630) 250-1111. **$75-$95.** 1181 Rohlwing Rd. I-290, exit Thorndale Ave, 0.5 mi w. Int corridors. **Pets:** Accepted.
A$K S🔒 ✕ 🕭M 🕭 🔒 🔒 💻

JOLIET

▼▼ **Comfort Inn by Choice Hotels North** 🆂🅷
(815) 436-5141. **$85-$105.** 3235 Norman Ave. I-55, exit 257, just e. Int corridors. **Pets:** Accepted.
A$K S🔒 ✕ 🕭 🔒 💻 ⇌

▼▼ **Comfort Inn by Choice Hotels-South** 🆂🅷
(815) 744-1770. **$80-$100.** 135 S Larkin Ave. I-80, exit 130B, 0.5 mi n. Int corridors. **Pets:** Accepted.
A$K S🔒 ✕ 🕭 🔒 💻 ⇌

▼▼▼ **Holiday Inn Convention Center-Joliet** 🆂🅷
(815) 729-2000. **$69-$129.** 411 S Larkin Ave. I-80, exit 130B, just nw. Int corridors. **Pets:** Accepted.
A$K S🔒 ✕ 🕭M 🕭 🔒 💻 🍴 ⇌

▼ **Red Roof Inn #7071** Ⓜ
(815) 741-2304. **$52-$80.** 1750 McDonough St. I-80, exit 130B, just off Larkin Ave. Ext corridors. **Pets:** Medium, other species. Service with restrictions, supervision.
✕ 🕭 🔒

🅐🅐🅐 ▼▼▼ **Super 8 Motel I-55 North** 🆂🅷
(815) 439-3838. **$61-$70.** 3401 Mall Loop Dr. I-55, exit 257, 0.4 mi e on US 30, then just s. Int corridors. **Pets:** Medium, dogs only. $8 daily fee/room. Service with restrictions, supervision.
SAVE S🔒 ✕ 🕭 🔒 🔒 ⇌

LANSING

▼▼ **Extended StayAmerica-Chicago-Lansing** 🆂🅷
(708) 895-6402. **$77-$87.** 2520 173rd St. I-80, exit 161 (Torrence Ave), just n. Int corridors. **Pets:** Accepted.
A$K ✕ 🕭M 🕭 🔒 🔒 💻

▼ **Red Roof Inn #7078** Ⓜ
(708) 895-9570. **$57-$90.** 2450 E 173rd St. I-80/94, exit 161 (Torrence Ave), just n. Ext corridors. **Pets:** Medium, other species. Service with restrictions, supervision.
✕ 🕭 🔒

LIBERTYVILLE

▼▼▼ **Holiday Inn Express Hotel & Suites** 🆂🅷
(847) 549-7878. **$89-$129.** 77 Buckley Rd. I-94, exit SR 137 (Buckley Rd), 2.3 mi w. Int corridors. **Pets:** Small, dogs only. $50 one-time fee/pet. Service with restrictions, supervision.
A$K S🔒 ✕ 🕭 🔒 💻 ⇌

LINCOLNSHIRE

▼▼▼ **Homewood Suites by Hilton Chicago-Lincolnshire** 🆂🅷
(847) 945-9300. **$79-$179.** 10 Westminister Way. I-94, exit Half Day Rd, just w. Int corridors. **Pets:** Accepted.
A$K S🔒 ✕ 🕭 🔒 💻 ⇌ ✕

LISLE

▼▼ **Extended StayAmerica-Chicago-Lisle** 🆂🅷
(630) 434-7710. **Call for rates.** 445 Warrenville Rd. I-355, exit Ogden Ave E. Int corridors. **Pets:** Accepted.
✕ 🔒 🔒 💻

LOMBARD

▼▼▼ **Homestead Studio Suites Hotel-Chicago/Lombard-Oak Brook** 🆂🅷
(630) 928-0202. **$91-$104.** 2701 Technology Dr. I-88, exit Highland Ave, just n, 0.6 mi e on Butterfield Rd (SR 56), then just s. Int corridors. **Pets:** Accepted.
A$K S🔒 ✕ 🕭M 🕭 🔒 🔒 💻

MATTESON

🅐🅐🅐 ▼▼▼ **La Quinta Inn & Suites Chicago-Matteson** 🆂🅷
(708) 503-0999. **$79-$129.** 5210 W Southwick Dr. I-57, exit 340A, 0.3 mi e on US 30, then 0.3 mi s on Cicero Ave (SR 50). Int corridors. **Pets:** Medium. Service with restrictions, crate.
SAVE ✕ 🕭 🔒 💻

MUNDELEIN

▼▼▼ **Crowne Plaza Chicago North Shore** 🆂🅷 🐾
(847) 949-5100. **$100-$300.** 510 SR 83 E. Jct US 45 and SR 83. Int corridors. **Pets:** Designated rooms, service with restrictions, crate.
A$K S🔒 ✕ 🕭 🔒 💻 🍴 ⇌

NAPERVILLE

🅐🅐🅐 ▼ **Exel Inn of Naperville** 🆂🅷
(630) 357-0022. **$56-$86.** 1585 N Naperville/Wheaton Rd. I-88, exit Naperville Rd, 0.5 mi s. Int corridors. **Pets:** Small, other species. Designated rooms, service with restrictions, supervision.
SAVE S🔒 ✕ 🔒 ⇌

▼▼ **Extended StayAmerica-Chicago-Naperville** 🆂🅷
(630) 983-0000. **Call for rates.** 1575 Bond St. I-88, exit SR 59, just s. Int corridors. **Pets:** Accepted.
✕ 🔒 💻

▼▼▼ **Fairfield Inn & Suites by Marriott Naperville/Aurora** 🆂🅷
(630) 548-0966. **$100-$120.** 1847 W Diehl Rd. I-88, exit SR 59, just s. Int corridors. **Pets:** Accepted.
A$K S🔒 ✕ 🕭 🕭 🔒 🔒 💻 ⇌

🅐🅐🅐 ▼▼▼ **Holiday Inn Select Hotel & Conference Center** 🅛🅗
(630) 505-4900. **$69-$189.** 1801 N Naper Blvd. I-88, exit Naperville Rd, just s. Int corridors. **Pets:** Accepted.
SAVE S🔒 ✕ 🕭 🔒 💻 🍴 ⇌

▼▼ Homestead Studio Suites
Hotel-Chicago-Naperville SH
(630) 577-0200. **$86-$100.** 1827 Centre Point Cir. I-88, exit Naperville Rd, just s to Diehl Rd, 0.8 mi w, then just n. Int corridors. **Pets:** Accepted.

ASK Sᴅ ✕ ᕫ ⊞ ⊟ ▭

▼ Red Roof Inn #7195 M
(630) 369-2500. **$58-$84.** 1698 W Diehl Rd. I-88, exit SR 59, just s. Ext corridors. **Pets:** Medium, other species. Service with restrictions, supervision.

✕ ᕫ ⊟

▼▼▼ TownePlace Suites by Marriott Naperville SH
(630) 548-0881. **$185-$205.** 1843 W Diehl Rd. I-88, exit SR 59, just s to Diehl Rd, then just w. Int corridors. **Pets:** Accepted.

ASK Sᴅ ✕ ᕫ ᕫ ⊞ ⊟ ▭ ➤ ✕

NORTHBROOK

▲▲▲ ▼▼▼ Radisson Hotel Northbrook LH
(847) 298-2525. **$125-$179.** 2875 N Milwaukee Ave. I-294, exit Willow Rd, 1 mi w to SR 21 and US 45, then 0.6 mi s. Int corridors. **Pets:** Accepted.

SAVE Sᴅ ✕ ᕫ ᕫ ⊞ ⊟ ▭ ⑪ ➤

▼ Red Roof Inn #7188 M
(847) 205-1755. **$62-$82.** 340 Waukegan Rd. I-94, exit SR 43 (Waukegan Rd). Ext corridors. **Pets:** Medium, other species. Service with restrictions, supervision.

✕ ⊟

OAK BROOK

▲▲▲ ▼▼▼ Renaissance Oak Brook Hotel SH
(630) 573-2800. **$89-$269.** 2100 Spring Rd. Just e of SR 83 and just n of 22nd St (Cermak Rd). Int corridors. **Pets:** Accepted.

SAVE Sᴅ ✕ ᕫ ᕫ ⊞ ⊟ ▭ ⑪ ➤

▼▼▼ Residence Inn by Marriott Chicago/Oak Brook SH
(630) 571-1200. **$99-$189.** 790 Jorie Blvd. I-88, exit Midwest Rd eastbound, just n to 22nd St (Cermak Rd), 1.7 mi e to Jorie Blvd, then just sw; exit 22nd St (Cermak Rd) westbound, 0.4 mi e to Jorie Blvd. Int corridors. **Pets:** Medium, other species. $100 one-time fee/room. Service with restrictions.

ASK Sᴅ ✕ ᕫ ᕫ ⊞ ⊟ ▭ ➤

OAKBROOK TERRACE

▲▲▲ ▼▼▼ La Quinta Inn Chicago (Oak Brook) SH
(630) 495-4600. **$99-$125.** 1 S 666 Midwest Rd. I-88, exit Midwest Rd eastbound, 0.4 mi n, then just n of 22nd St (Cermak Rd); exit 22nd St (Cermak Rd) westbound, 1.1 mi w to Midwest Rd, then just n. Int corridors. **Pets:** Medium. Service with restrictions.

SAVE ✕ ᕫ ⊞ ⊟ ▭ ➤

▼▼▼ Staybridge Suites Chicago-Oakbrook Terrace SH
(630) 953-9393. **$81-$198.** 200 Royce Blvd. I-88, exit Midwest Rd eastbound to 22nd St (Cermak Rd), 0.4 mi w to SR 56, just n, then just n on Renaissance Blvd; exit 22nd St (Cermak) westbound, 2.5 mi w on 22nd St to SR 56, just n, then just n on Renaissance Blvd. Int corridors. **Pets:** Large, other species. $75 one-time fee/room. Service with restrictions.

ASK Sᴅ ✕ ᕫ ᕫ ⊞ ⊟ ▭ ✕

PALATINE

▼▼▼ Holiday Inn Express Palatine/Arlington Heights SH
(847) 934-4900. **$80-$143.** 1550 E Dundee Rd. SR 53, exit Dundee Rd (SR 68), just w. Int corridors. **Pets:** Medium, other species. Designated rooms, service with restrictions, supervision.

ASK Sᴅ ✕ ᕫ ᕫ ⊞ ⊟ ▭ ➤ ✕

▲▲▲ ▼▼ Hotel Indigo SH ❀
(847) 359-6900. **$119-$299.** 920 E Northwest Hwy (US 14). SR 53, exit Northwest Hwy (US 14), just w. Int corridors. **Pets:** Small, other species. $25 daily fee/pet. Service with restrictions, supervision.

SAVE Sᴅ ✕ ᕫ ᕫ ⊞ ⊟ ⑪ ➤

PROSPECT HEIGHTS

▲▲▲ ▼▼ Exel Inn of Prospect Heights SH
(847) 459-0545. **$53-$83.** 540 Milwaukee Ave. Jct SR 21 and US 45. Int corridors. **Pets:** Small, other species. Designated rooms, no service, supervision.

SAVE Sᴅ ✕ ᕫ ⊟ ▭

RICHMOND

◆◆ Save Inn Richmond/Geneva Lakes SH
(815) 678-4711. **$69-$120.** 11200 N Rt 12. 0.5 mi n of jct SR 173. Int corridors. **Pets:** Large, other species. $10 daily fee/pet. Designated rooms, service with restrictions, supervision.

ASK Sᴅ ✕ ▭ ➤

ROMEOVILLE

▼▼ Comfort Inn by Choice Hotels
Bolingbrook/Romeoville SH
(630) 226-1900. **$72-$84.** 1235 Lake View Dr. I-55, exit 263, just n. Int corridors. **Pets:** Accepted.

ASK Sᴅ ✕ ⊟ ▭ ➤

▼▼ Extended StayAmerica Chicago-Romeoville SH
(630) 226-8966. **$95-$108.** 1225 Lakeview Dr. I-55, exit 263, just n. Int corridors. **Pets:** Accepted.

ASK Sᴅ ✕ ᕫ ⊟ ▭

ROSEMONT

▲▲▲ ▼▼▼ Crowne Plaza Chicago O'Hare LH
(847) 671-6350. **$109-$319.** 5440 N River Rd. I-190, exit 1B, just s. Int corridors. **Pets:** Medium, dogs only. $50 one-time fee/room. Service with restrictions, crate.

SAVE Sᴅ ✕ ᕫ ᕫ ᕫ ⊞ ⊟ ▭ ⑪ ➤ ✕

▼▼▼ DoubleTree Hotel Chicago O'Hare
Airport-Rosemont LH
(847) 292-9100. **$79-$369.** 5460 N River Rd. I-190, exit 1B, just s. Int corridors. **Pets:** Accepted.

ASK ✕ ᕫ ᕫ ᕫ ⊟ ▭ ⑪ ➤

▲▲▲ ▼▼▼ Embassy Suites Hotel O'Hare Rosemont LH
(847) 678-4000. **$109-$379.** 5500 N River Rd. I-190, exit 1B, just s. Int corridors. **Pets:** Medium. $75 deposit/room, $25 one-time fee/room. Service with restrictions, crate.

SAVE ✕ ᕫ ᕫ ⊞ ⊟ ▭ ⑪ ➤ ✕

▼▼▼ Residence Inn by Marriott Chicago-O'Hare SH
(847) 375-9000. **$189-$209.** 7101 Chestnut St. Jct US 12 and 45 and Touhy Ave. Int corridors. **Pets:** Other species. $100 one-time fee/room. Service with restrictions.

ASK Sᴅ ✕ ᕫ ᕫ ⊞ ⊟ ▭ ➤ ✕

▼▼▼ Sheraton Gateway Suites O'Hare LH
(847) 699-6300. **$89-$289.** 6501 N Mannheim Rd. On US 12 and 45, at SR 72 (Higgins Rd). Int corridors. **Pets:** Accepted.

✕ ᕫ ⊞ ⊟ ▭ ⑪ ➤ ✕

▲▲▲ ▼▼▼▼ The Westin O'Hare LH
(847) 698-6000. **$199-$259.** 6100 N River Rd. I-190, exit 1B, just n. Int corridors. **Pets:** Accepted.

SAVE ✕ ᕫ ᕫ ᕫ ⊟ ▭ ⑪ ➤ ✕

▲▲▲ ▼▼▼▼ Wyndham O'Hare LH
(847) 297-1234. **$114-$140.** 6810 N Mannheim Rd. On US 12 and 45, 0.3 mi n of SR 72 (Higgins Rd). Int corridors. **Pets:** Accepted.

SAVE ✕ ᕫ ᕫ ⊞ ⊟ ▭ ⑪ ➤ ✕

ST. CHARLES

Best Western Inn of St. Charles SH
(630) 584-4550. **$89-$109, 3 day notice.** 1635 E Main St. On SR 64, 0.5 mi e of SR 25. Ext/int corridors. **Pets:** Dogs only. $10 daily fee/pet. Designated rooms, service with restrictions, supervision.

Courtyard by Marriott Chicago-St Charles SH
(630) 377-6370. **$109-$139.** 700 Courtyard Dr. Jct SR 59 and 64, 3.4 mi w on SR 64, just n on Kirk Rd, then just w on Foxfield. Int corridors. **Pets:** $100 one-time fee/room. Service with restrictions, supervision.

Holiday Inn Express SH
(630) 584-5300. **$109.** 1600 E Main St. On SR 64, 0.5 mi e of SR 25. Int corridors. **Pets:** Accepted.

Super 8 Motel-St. Charles SH
(630) 377-8388. **$69-$109, 4 day notice.** 1520 E Main St. On SR 64, 1 mi e. Int corridors. **Pets:** Very small. $15 daily fee/pet. Designated rooms, service with restrictions, supervision.

SCHAUMBURG

Drury Inn-Schaumburg SH
(847) 517-7737. **$87-$137.** 600 N Martingale Rd. I-290, exit SR 72 (Higgins Rd), just w, then just n. Int corridors. **Pets:** Large, other species. Service with restrictions, supervision.

Extended StayAmerica-Chicago-Schaumburg SH
(847) 882-7011. **$95-$113.** 2000 N Roselle Rd. I-90, exit Roselle Rd, just sw. Int corridors. **Pets:** Accepted.

Hawthorn Suites Schaumburg SH
(847) 706-9007. **$79-$149.** 1251 E American Ln. I-290, exit SR 72 (Higgins Rd), 0.5 mi w to Meacham Rd, 0.5 mi n to American Ln, then just w. Int corridors. **Pets:** Accepted.

Holiday Inn Schaumburg SH
(847) 310-0500. **$89-$109.** 1550 N Roselle Rd. I-90, exit Roselle Rd, 0.8 mi s. Int corridors. **Pets:** Medium, other species. $50 deposit/pet. Service with restrictions, crate.

Homestead Studio Suites Hotel-Chicago-Schaumburg SH
(847) 882-6900. **$100-$109.** 51 E State Pkwy. I-90, exit Roselle Rd, 0.8 mi s, then just e. Int corridors. **Pets:** Accepted.

Homewood Suites by Hilton-Schaumburg SH
(847) 605-0400. **$89-$299.** 815 E American Ln. I-290, exit SR 72 (Higgins Rd), 1.5 mi w, 0.4 mi n on Plum Grove Rd. Ext/int corridors. **Pets:** Medium. $50 one-time fee/room. Service with restrictions, crate.

La Quinta Inn (Schaumburg) SH
(847) 517-8484. **$99-$129.** 1730 E Higgins Rd. I-290, exit SR 72 (Higgins Rd), just w. Int corridors. **Pets:** Medium. Service with restrictions.

Residence Inn by Marriott-Chicago/Schaumburg SH
(847) 517-9200. **$169-$289.** 1610 McConnor Pkwy. I-290, exit 1A (Woodfield/Golf rds) northbound, follow signs just n to Golf Rd, just w to McConnor Pkwy, then just n; exit 1B (Woodfield/Golf rds) southbound. Int corridors. **Pets:** Accepted.

Staybridge Suites Chicago/Schaumburg SH
(847) 619-6677. **$134-$154.** 901 E Woodfield Office Ct. I-290, exit SR 72 (Higgins Rd), 1.5 mi w, then 0.3 mi n on Plum Grove Rd. Ext/int corridors. **Pets:** Accepted.

SCHILLER PARK

Comfort Suites O'Hare SH
(847) 233-9000. **$79-$129.** 4200 N River Rd. Jct SR 19 (Irving Park Rd) and Des Plaines St/River Rd, just n. Int corridors. **Pets:** Accepted.

Four Points by Sheraton Chicago O'Hare Airport LH
(847) 671-6000. **$95-$140.** 10249 W Irving Park Rd. Jct US 12 and 45 and SR 19 (Irving Park Rd). Int corridors. **Pets:** Very small. $50 deposit/pet. Designated rooms, service with restrictions.

SKOKIE

Comfort Inn Northshore-Skokie SH
(847) 679-4200. **$119-$159.** 9333 Skokie Blvd. I-94, exit Old Orchard Rd, 0.4 mi e to Skokie Blvd (US 41), then 0.3 mi s. Int corridors. **Pets:** Accepted.

Holiday Inn Chicago-Skokie SH
(847) 679-8900. **$159-$199.** 5300 W Touhy Ave. I-94, exit 39A, 0.5 mi w. Ext/int corridors. **Pets:** Accepted.

TINLEY PARK

La Quinta Inn & Suites Chicago-Tinley Park SH
(708) 633-1200. **$89-$129.** 7255 W 183rd St. I-80, exit 148B, 0.5 mi n to 183rd St, then just w to North Creek Business Center. Int corridors. **Pets:** Medium. Service with restrictions.

VERNON HILLS

Homestead Studio Suites Hotel-Chicago/Vernon Hills-Lincolnshire SH
(847) 955-1111. **$100-$109.** 675 Woodlands Pkwy. I-94, exit SR 60 (Townline Rd), 2.1 mi w to SR 21 (Milwaukee Ave), 1.9 mi s to Woodlands Pkwy, then just w. Int corridors. **Pets:** Accepted.

WARRENVILLE

Residence Inn by Marriott Chicago Naperville/Warrenville SH
(630) 393-3444. **$149-$249.** 28500 Bella Vista Pkwy. I-88, exit Winfield Rd, just n to Ferry Rd, then just e. Int corridors. **Pets:** Other species. $100 one-time fee/room. Service with restrictions, supervision.

WAUKEGAN

Candlewood Suites Chicago/Waukegan SH
(847) 578-5250. **$79-$119.** 1151 S Waukegan Rd. I-94, exit SR 137 (Buckley Rd), 0.5 mi e to SR 43 (Waukegan Rd), then 1.9 mi n. Int corridors. **Pets:** Accepted.

Crossland Studios-Chicago-Waukegan SH
(847) 688-0402. **$72-$81.** 1177 S Northpoint Blvd. At US 41; between US 41 and SR 43. Ext corridors. **Pets:** Accepted.

▼▼▼ Residence Inn by
      Marriott-Waukegan/Gurnee 🅢🅗 🌸
(847) 689-9240. **$99-$169.** 1440 S White Oak Dr. I-94, exit SR 137
(Buckley Rd), 0.5 mi e to SR 43 (Waukegan Rd), 1.5 mi n to Lakeside
Dr, then just e. Int corridors. **Pets:** $100 one-time fee/room.

🅐🅢🅚 ⊠ 🖼 🎷 🎙 📶 🖥 🛎 ⊠

WEST DUNDEE

▼▼ TownePlace Suites by Marriott-Chicago/Elgin 🅢🅗
(847) 608-6320. **$119-$134.** 2185 Marriott Dr. I-90, exit SR 31, 0.4 mi n
to Marriott Dr, then just e. Int corridors. **Pets:** Accepted.

🅐🅢🅚 ⊠ 🎷 🎙 🖥 🛎

WESTMONT

🅐🅐🅐 ▼▼▼ ClubHouse Inn & Suites 🅢🅗
(630) 920-2200. **$97-$117.** 630 Pasquinelli Dr. Just off US 34 (Ogden
Ave), 0.3 mi nw of jct SR 83. Int corridors. **Pets:** Accepted.

🆂🅰🆅🅴 🆂 ⊠ 🖥 🛎 🔄 ⊠

▼▼ Homestead Studio Suites Hotel-Chicago/Westmont-Oak
      Brook 🅢🅗
(630) 323-9292. **$91-$104.** 855 Pasquinelli Dr. SR 83, exit US 34
(Ogden Ave), just w to Pasquinelli Dr, then 0.5 mi n. Int corridors.
Pets: Accepted.

🅐🅢🅚 🆂 ⊠ 🎙 🎷 🎙 🖥 🛎

WILLOWBROOK

🅐🅐🅐 ▼▼▼ La Quinta Inn & Suites
                Chicago-Willowbrook 🅢🅗
(630) 654-0077. **$85-$109.** 855 79th St. I-55, exit 274, just n. Int corridors. **Pets:** Pets: Medium. Service with restrictions.

🆂🅰🆅🅴 ⊠ 🎷 🖥 🛎

▼ Red Roof Inn #7167 🅜
(630) 323-8811. **$57-$87.** 7535 Kingery Hwy. I-55, exit 274, 0.5 mi n on
SR 83. Ext corridors. **Pets:** Medium, other species. Service with restrictions, supervision.

⊠ 🎷 🖥

▼▼ Super 8 Motel-Willowbrook 🅢🅗
(630) 789-6300. **$64-$99.** 820 W 79th St. I-55, exit 274, 0.3 mi n to
Midway Dr, then e on frontage road. Ext/int corridors. **Pets:** $20 one-
time fee/room. Service with restrictions, supervision.

🅐🅢🅚 🆂 ⊠ 🎷 🖥 🛎 🔄

WOODSTOCK

▼ Super 8 Motel 🅢🅗
(815) 337-8808. **$55-$106, 3 day notice.** 1220 Davis Rd. On SR 47, s
of jct US 14. Int corridors. **Pets:** Accepted.

🅐🅢🅚 🆂 ⊠ 🖥

END METROPOLITAN AREA

CHILLICOTHE

▼▼🔷 Super 8 Motel 🅢🅗
(309) 274-2568. **$57-$63.** 615 S Fourth St. 1.1 mi s on SR 29. Int
corridors. **Pets:** Accepted.

🅐🅢🅚 🆂 ⊠ 🖥

COLLINSVILLE

▼▼ Drury Inn-St. Louis/Collinsville 🅢🅗
(618) 345-7700. **$80-$149.** 602 N Bluff Rd. I-55/70, exit 11 (SR 157),
just n. Int corridors. **Pets:** Large, other species. Service with restrictions,
supervision.

🅐🅢🅚 ⊠ 🎙 🎷 🖥 🛎 🔄

DANVILLE

🅐🅐🅐 ▼▼▼ Best Western Regency Inn 🅢🅗
(217) 446-2111. **$57-$110.** 360 Eastgate Dr. I-74, exit 220 (Lynch Dr),
just n. Ext/int corridors. **Pets:** Small, dogs only. $10 daily fee/pet. Desig-
nated rooms, service with restrictions, supervision.

🆂🅰🆅🅴 🆂 ⊠ 🖥 🛎 🔄

🅐🅐🅐 ▼▼▼ Best Western Riverside Inn 🅢🅗
(217) 431-0020. **$57-$115.** 57 S Gilbert St. I-74, exit 215B, 0.8 mi n on
US 150 and SR 1. Ext/int corridors. **Pets:** Small, dogs only. $10 daily
fee/pet. Designated rooms, service with restrictions, supervision.

🆂🅰🆅🅴 🆂 ⊠ 🖥 🛎 🔄

▼▼ Comfort Inn by Choice Hotels 🅢🅗
(217) 443-8004. **$70-$90.** 383 Lynch Dr. I-74, exit 220 (Lynch Dr), just
n. Int corridors. **Pets:** Accepted.

🅐🅢🅚 🆂 ⊠ 🎷 🖥 🛎 🔄

▼▼ Sleep Inn & Suites 🅢🅗
(217) 442-6600. **$75-$99.** 361 Lynch Dr. I-74, exit 220 (Lynch Dr), just
n. Int corridors. **Pets:** Small, dogs only. $10 daily fee/pet. Designated
rooms, service with restrictions, supervision.

🅐🅢🅚 🆂 ⊠ 🖥 🛎 🔄

▼▼ Super 8 🅢🅗
(217) 443-4499. **$65-$85.** 377 Lynch Dr. I-74, exit 220 (Lynch Dr), just
n. Int corridors. **Pets:** Accepted.

🅐🅢🅚 🆂 ⊠ 🖥 🛎

DECATUR

▼▼🔷▼ Country Inn & Suites By Carlson 🅢🅗
(217) 872-2402. **$79.** 5150 Hickory Point Frontage Rd. I-72, exit 141B
(US 51 N), s on frontage road. Int corridors. **Pets:** Accepted.

🅐🅢🅚 🆂 ⊠ 🎙 🎷 🎙 🖥 🛎 🔄 ⊠

▼▼▼▼ Decatur Conference Center & Hotel 🅛🅗
(217) 422-8800. **$79-$109.** 4191 W Hwy 36. I-72, exit 133A (US 36), 1
mi e. Int corridors. **Pets:** Accepted.

🅐🅢🅚 🆂 ⊠ 🎙 🎷 🎙 🖥 🛎 🍴 🔄 ⊠

▼▼ Ramada Limited Decatur 🅢🅗
(217) 876-8011. **$69-$175.** 355 E Hickory Point Rd. I-72, exit 141B (US
51 N), just n, then s via frontage road. Int corridors. **Pets:** Other
species. Service with restrictions, supervision.

🅐🅢🅚 🆂 ⊠ 🎷 🎙 🖥 🛎 🔄

🅐🅐🅐 ▼▼▼ Sleep Inn of Decatur 🅢🅗
(217) 872-7700. **$69-$84.** 3920 E Hospitality Ln. I-72, exit 144 (SR 48),
just s to Brush College Rd, then just e. Int corridors. **Pets:** Medium.
Service with restrictions, supervision.

🆂🅰🆅🅴 🆂 ⊠ 🎷 🎙 🖥 🛎 🔄 ⊠

▼▼▼▼ Wingate Inn 🅢🅗
(217) 875-5500. **$89, 6 day notice.** 5170 Wingate Dr. I-72, exit 141, 0.5
mi n on US 51, then just e. Int corridors. **Pets:** Accepted.

🅐🅢🅚 🆂 ⊠ 🎙 🎷 🎙 🖥 🛎 🔄 ⊠

DEKALB

▼▼▼ Baymont Inn & Suites Dekalb/Sycamore 🅢🅗
(815) 748-4800. **$69-$110.** 1314 W Lincoln Hwy. I-88, exit Annie Glid-
den Rd, 2 mi n to W Lincoln Hwy (SR 38), then 0.4 mi w. Int corridors.
Pets: Accepted.

🅐🅢🅚 🆂 ⊠ 🎙 🎷 🎙 🖥 🛎 🔄

🅐🅐🅐 ▼▼▼ Best Western DeKalb Inn & Suites 🅢🅗
(815) 758-8661. **$79-$149.** 1212 W Lincoln Hwy. I-88, exit Annie Glid-
den Rd, 2 mi n to W Lincoln Hwy (SR 38), then just w. Ext/int
corridors. **Pets:** $10 daily fee/room. Service with restrictions, supervision.

🆂🅰🆅🅴 ⊠ 🎷 🖥 🛎 🔄

DIXON

Comfort Inn by Choice Hotels SH
(815) 284-0500. **$69-$94.** 136 Plaza Dr. I-88, exit SR 26, just n, then just e. Int corridors. **Pets:** Medium, other species. $100 deposit/room. Service with restrictions, supervision.

Quality Inn & Suites by Choice Hotels SH
(815) 288-2001. **$79-$115.** 154 Plaza Dr. I-88, exit SR 26, just n, then just e. Int corridors. **Pets:** Large, other species. $100 deposit/room, $15 daily fee/room. Service with restrictions, supervision.

EAST MOLINE

Ramada-East Moline SH
(309) 792-4660. **$75-$119.** 2209 John Deere Expwy. I-74, exit 4B (John Deere Rd), 5 mi e; I-80, exit 4A, 6 mi w. Int corridors. **Pets:** Small. $25 daily fee/pet. Service with restrictions, supervision.

Super 8 Motel-East Moline SH
(309) 796-1999. **$59-$99, 4 day notice.** 2201 John Deere Rd. I-74, exit 4B (John Deere Rd), 5.5 mi e on SR 5. Int corridors. **Pets:** Medium. $10 daily fee/pet. Designated rooms, service with restrictions, supervision.

EAST PEORIA

Super 8 Motel SH
(309) 698-8889. **$57-$97.** 725 Taylor St. I-74, exit 96, just e. Int corridors. **Pets:** Accepted.

EFFINGHAM

Best Western Raintree Inn SH
(217) 342-4121. **$47-$67.** 1811 W Fayette Ave. I-57/70, exit 159, just n. Ext/int corridors. **Pets:** Medium. Designated rooms, service with restrictions, supervision.

Comfort Inn SH
(217) 347-5050. **$59-$75.** 1304 W Evergreen Dr. I-57/70, exit 160 (SR 32/33), just e, then just n. Int corridors. **Pets:** Accepted.

Comfort Suites SH
(217) 342-3151. **$59-$89.** 1310 W Fayette Ave. I-57/70, exit 159, 0.4 mi e. Int corridors. **Pets:** Accepted.

Holiday Inn Express SH ❄
(217) 540-1111. **$85.** 1103 Ave of Mid-America. I-57/70, exit 160 (SR 32/33), just n. Int corridors. **Pets:** $20 one-time fee/room. Designated rooms, service with restrictions, supervision.

Paradise Inn M
(217) 342-2165. **$42-$48.** 1000 W Fayette Ave. I-57/70, exit 159, 1 mi e. Ext corridors. **Pets:** Small. $7 one-time fee/pet. Designated rooms, service with restrictions, supervision.

Rodeway Inn M ❄
(217) 342-9271. **$39-$79.** 1412 W Fayette Ave. I-57/70, exit 159, just e. Ext corridors. **Pets:** $5 daily fee/pet. Service with restrictions, supervision.

Super 8 Motel-Effingham M
(217) 342-6888. **$59-$88.** 1400 Thelma Keller Ave. I-57/70, exit 160 (SR 32/33), 0.5 mi n. Int corridors. **Pets:** Service with restrictions, supervision.

FAIRVIEW HEIGHTS

Drury Inn & Suites-Fairview Heights SH
(618) 398-8530. **$90-$140.** 12 Ludwig Dr. I-64, exit 12 (SR 159). Int corridors. **Pets:** Large, other species. Service with restrictions, supervision.

FLORA

Best Western Lorson Inn SH
(618) 662-3054. **$70.** 201 Gary Hagen Dr. Jct US 45 and 50. Int corridors. **Pets:** Accepted.

FORSYTH

Comfort Inn by Choice Hotels SH
(217) 875-1166. **$65-$85.** 134 Barnett Ave. I-72, exit 141B (US 51), 0.5 mi n. Int corridors. **Pets:** Accepted.

FREEPORT

AmeriHost Inn & Suites-Freeport SH
(815) 599-8510. **$60-$90.** 1060 Riverside Dr. Jct US 20 Bypass and SR 26, just s. Int corridors. **Pets:** Small. $25 daily fee/room. Supervision.

GALENA

Best Western Quiet House & Suites SH
(815) 777-2577. **$90-$205.** 9923 US Rt 20 W. 1 mi e. Ext/int corridors. **Pets:** Small, dogs only. $15 daily fee/pet. Designated rooms, supervision.

Eagle Ridge Resort & Spa LH
(815) 777-5000. **$159-$279, 7 day notice.** 444 Eagle Ridge Dr. 6 mi e on US 20, 4.5 mi n. Ext/int corridors. **Pets:** Accepted.

GALESBURG

Best Western Prairie Inn SH ❖
(309) 343-7151. **$96.** 300 S Soangetaha Rd. I-74, exit 48 (Main St), just e, then just s. Int corridors. **Pets:** Medium, other species. Designated rooms, service with restrictions, crate.

Comfort Inn by Choice Hotels SH
(309) 344-5445. **$80-$100.** 907 W Carl Sandburg Dr. US 34, exit US 150 E. Int corridors. **Pets:** Accepted.

Holiday Inn Express SH
(309) 343-7100. **$74.** 2285 Washington St. I-74, exit 48A (US 150), just w to Michigan Ave, just s to Washington St, then just e. Int corridors. **Pets:** $25 one-time fee/room. No service, supervision.

GILMAN

Super 8 Motel SH
(815) 265-7000. **$68-$81.** 1301 S Crescent St. I-57, exit 283, 0.3 mi e. Int corridors. **Pets:** Small, other species. $20 deposit/pet, $5 daily fee/pet. Service with restrictions, supervision.

Travel Inn M
(815) 265-7283. **$60-$70.** 834 US 24 W. I-57, exit 283, just e. Ext/int corridors. **Pets:** Accepted.

GRAYVILLE

▼▼ Best Western Windsor Oaks Inn SH
(618) 375-7930. **$73-$88.** 2200 S Court St. I-64, exit 130 (SR 1), just n. Int corridors. **Pets:** $5 daily fee/room. Designated rooms, service with restrictions, crate.

(ASK) (S) (X) (⏄) (☎) (➡) (¶¶) (≋)

▼▼ Super 8 Motel SH
(618) 375-7288. **$55-$68.** 2060 CR 2450 North. I-64, exit 130 (SR 1), just n. Int corridors. **Pets:** Large, other species. $10 one-time fee/room. Designated rooms, service with restrictions, supervision.

(ASK) (S) (X) (&M) (⏄) (☎) (➡)

JACKSONVILLE

▼▼ AmeriHost Inn-Jacksonville SH
(217) 245-4500. **$59-$84.** 1709 W Morton Ave. I-72, exit 64, 2.3 mi n on SR 267 (Main St) to SR 104 (Morton Ave), then 1.5 mi w. Int corridors. **Pets:** Accepted.

(ASK) (S) (X) (⏄) (☎) (➡) (≋) (✕)

▲▲ ▼ Starlite Motel M ✿
(217) 245-7184. **$45-$55, 7 day notice.** 1910 W Morton Ave. I-72, exit 64, 2.3 mi n on SR 267 (Main St) to SR 104 (Morton Ave), then 1.8 mi w. Ext corridors. **Pets:** Small. $5 daily fee/pet. Service with restrictions, supervision.

(SAVE) (S) (X) (☎)

▼ Super 8 Motel SH ✿
(217) 479-0303. **$40-$70.** 1003 W Morton Ave. I-72, exit 64, 2.3 mi n on SR 267 (Main St) to SR 104 (Morton Ave), then 0.8 mi w. Int corridors. **Pets:** Other species. $10 daily fee/room. Service with restrictions.

(ASK) (S) (X) (☎) (➡)

LINCOLN

▼▼ Holiday Inn Express SH
(217) 735-5800. **$89-$140, 14 day notice.** 130 Olson Dr. I-55, exit 126 (US 121), just e to Heitman Dr, just w to Olson Dr, then just n. Int corridors. **Pets:** Large, other species. Designated rooms, service with restrictions, supervision.

(ASK) (S) (X) (⏄) (&M) (☎) (➡) (≋)

LITCHFIELD

▼▼▼ Hampton Inn SH
(217) 324-4441. **$74-$119.** 11 Thunderbird Cir. I-55, exit 52 (SR 16), on Corvette Dr, then just e. Int corridors. **Pets:** $100 deposit/room. Service with restrictions, supervision.

(ASK) (S) (X) (&M) (⏄) (☎) (➡) (≋)

▼▼ Holiday Inn Express SH
(217) 324-4556. **$79-$89.** 1405 W Hudson Dr. I-55, exit 52 (SR 16), just e to Ohren Ln, just s to W Hudson Dr, then just w. Int corridors. **Pets:** Small. Service with restrictions, supervision.

(ASK) (S) (X) (☎) (➡) (≋)

LOVES PARK

▼▼ Days Inn & Suites Rockford/Loves Park SH
(815) 282-9300. **$89-$94.** 4313 Bell School Rd. I-39/90, exit E Riverside Blvd, just nw. Int corridors. **Pets:** Small, other species. $10 daily fee/pet. Service with restrictions, supervision.

(ASK) (S) (X) (&M) (⏄) (☎) (➡) (≋)

MACOMB

▼ Super 8 Motel SH ✿
(309) 836-8888. **$45-$125.** 313 University Dr. 1.1 mi n on US 67 to University Dr, 0.5 mi w. Int corridors. **Pets:** Other species. $10 one-time fee/pet. Service with restrictions, supervision.

(ASK) (S) (X) (⏄) (☎)

MANTENO

▲▲▲ ▼▼▼ Country Inn & Suites by Carlson SH
(815) 468-2600. **$109.** 380 S Cypress St. I-57, exit 322, just se via frontage road. Int corridors. **Pets:** Medium. $100 deposit/room, $25 daily fee/room. Service with restrictions, supervision.

(SAVE) (S) (X) (&M) (⏄) (☎) (➡)

MARION

▼▼▼ Comfort Inn SH
(618) 993-6221. **$65-$80.** 2600 W Main St. I-57, exit 53 (Main St), just w. Int corridors. **Pets:** Accepted.

(ASK) (S) (X) (⏄) (☎) (➡) (≋)

▼▼ Drury Inn-Marion SH
(618) 997-9600. **$83-$142.** 2706 W DeYoung St. I-57, exit 54B (SR 13), 0.5 mi w. Int corridors. **Pets:** Large, other species. Service with restrictions, supervision.

(ASK) (X) (&M) (⏄) (☎) (➡) (≋)

▼ Super 8 Motel SH
(618) 993-5577. **$50-$90.** 2601 W DeYoung St. I-57, exit 54B (SR 13), just w. Int corridors. **Pets:** Accepted.

(ASK) (S) (X) (⏄) (☎)

MATTOON

▼▼▼ Super 8 Motel M
(217) 235-8888. **$51-$79.** 205 McFall Rd. I-57, exit 190B, just w. Int corridors. **Pets:** Small, other species. $10 one-time fee/pet. Designated rooms, service with restrictions, supervision.

(ASK) (S) (X) (☎) (➡)

METROPOLIS

▼▼▼ Isle of View Bed & Breakfast BB
(618) 524-5838. **$95-$165, 7 day notice.** 205 Metropolis St. I-24, exit 37 (US 45), 3.4 mi w, then just s on Metropolis St. Int corridors. **Pets:** Accepted.

MONTICELLO

▲▲▲ ▼▼▼▼ Best Western Monticello Gateway Inn SH
(217) 762-9436. **$55-$80.** 805 Iron Horse Pl. I-72, exit 166, just s. Ext/int corridors. **Pets:** Other species. $10 daily fee/pet. Service with restrictions, supervision.

(SAVE) (S) (X) (☎) (➡)

MORRIS

▼▼▼ Holiday Inn SH
(815) 942-6600. **$71.** 200 Gore Rd. I-80, exit 112, 0.3 mi nw. Int corridors. **Pets:** Accepted.

(ASK) (S) (X) (⏄) (☎) (➡) (¶¶) (≋) (✕)

MORTON

▲▲▲ ▼▼▼▼ Best Western Ashland House Inn & Conference Center SH
(309) 263-5116. **$99-$109, 30 day notice.** 201 E Ashland St. I-74, exit 102, 0.3 mi ne. Int corridors. **Pets:** Accepted.

(SAVE) (S) (X) (☎) (➡) (¶¶) (≋)

MOUNT VERNON

▲▲▲ ▼▼▼ Holiday Inn LH
(618) 244-7100. **$50-$150.** 222 Potomac Blvd. I-57/64, exit 95 (SR 15), just w to Potomac Blvd, then just n. Int corridors. **Pets:** Medium, other species. $10 one-time fee/pet. Designated rooms, service with restrictions, crate.

(SAVE) (S) (X) (&M) (⏄) (☎) (➡) (¶¶) (≋) (✕)

NASHVILLE

AAA ◈◈ Best Western U.S. Inn SH
(618) 478-5341. **$65-$79.** 11640 SR 127. I-64, exit 50 (SR 127), 0.3 mi s. Int corridors. **Pets:** Small. $10 daily fee/pet. Designated rooms, service with restrictions, supervision.
SAVE 🄂 ✕ 🄼 ♿ 🖥 💳 ≋

NORMAL

AAA ◈◈ Best Western University Inn SH
(309) 454-4070. **$75.** 6 Traders Cir. I-55, exit 165A (US 51), just s, then return on frontage road. Int corridors. **Pets:** Other species. $10 one-time fee/room. Service with restrictions.
SAVE 🄂 ✕ 🄐 🖥 💳 ≋

**◈◈ Comfort Suites by Choice Hotels
Bloomington/Normal** SH
(309) 452-8588. **$115-$135.** 310 B Greenbriar Dr. I-55, exit 167, follow I-55 business route (Veterans Pkwy), 1.3 mi s; jct Fort Jesse Rd. Int corridors. **Pets:** Accepted.
ASK 🄂 ✕ 🄼 ♿ 🖥 💳 ≋

**◈◈◈ Holiday Inn Express Hotel & Suites
Bloomington/Normal** SH
(309) 862-1600. **$79-$159.** 1715 Parkway Plaza Dr. I-55, exit 167, follow I-55 business route (Veterans Pkwy), 1.7 mi s to Parkway Plaza Dr, then just e. Int corridors. **Pets:** Accepted.
ASK 🄂 ✕ 🄐 ♿ 🖥 💳 ≋ 🚫

◈◈ Signature Inn-Bloomington/Normal SH
(309) 454-4044. **$87.** 101 S Veterans Pkwy. I-55, exit 167, follow I-55 business route (Veterans Pkwy), 1.5 mi s. Int corridors. **Pets:** Small. $10 daily fee/pet. Service with restrictions, crate.
ASK 🄂 ✕ 🄐 🖥 💳 ≋

O'FALLON

AAA ◈◈ Comfort Inn SH
(618) 624-6060. **$79-$149.** 1100 Eastgate Dr. I-64, exit 19B (SR 158), 0.5 mi n, then just sw. Int corridors. **Pets:** Other species. $50 deposit/pet.
SAVE 🄂 ✕ 🖥 💳 ≋

◈◈ Extended Stay America-O'Fallon Illinois SH
(618) 624-1757. **Call for rates.** 154 Regency Park Dr. I-64, exit 14, just w to Regency Park Dr, then 0.4 mi s. Int corridors. **Pets:** Accepted.
✕ 🄼 🄐

OGLESBY

AAA ◈◈ Holiday Inn Express
(815) 883-3535. **$89-$199.** 900 Holiday St. I-39, exit 54, just e. Int corridors. **Pets:** Accepted.
SAVE 🄂 ✕ 🖥 💳 ≋

OTTAWA

◈◈◈ Hampton Inn SH
(815) 434-6040. **$94-$104.** 4115 Holiday Ln. I-80, exit 90 (SR 23), just n. Int corridors. **Pets:** Small, other species. Designated rooms, service with restrictions, supervision.
ASK 🄂 ✕ 🄼 🄐 ♿ 🖥 💳 ≋

◈◈ Holiday Inn Express SH
(815) 433-0029. **$94-$179.** 120 W Stevenson Rd. I-80, exit 90 (SR 23), just n. Int corridors. **Pets:** Accepted.
ASK 🄂 ✕ 🖥 💳 ≋

PEKIN

AAA ◈◈◈ Econo Lodge Inn & Suites SH
(309) 353-4047. **$55-$90.** 3240 Vandever Ave. Just n of SR 9; 3 mi e of jct SR 29. Int corridors. **Pets:** Dogs only. $5 daily fee/pet. No service, supervision.
SAVE 🄂 ✕ 🖥 💳 ≋

PEORIA

◈◈ AmericInn Lodge & Suites SH
(309) 692-9200. **$96-$180.** 9106 N Lindbergh Dr. SR 6, exit 6, 0.5 mi s. Int corridors. **Pets:** Small, dogs only. $15 daily fee/room. Service with restrictions, supervision.
ASK 🄂 ✕ 🄐 🄐 🖥 💳 ≋ 🚫

◈◈ Baymont Inn & Suites SH
(309) 686-7600. **$79.** 2002 W War Memorial Dr. I-74, exit 89 (US 150/War Memorial Dr), just n; entrance through Northwoods Mall. Ext/int corridors. **Pets:** Accepted.
ASK 🄂 ✕ 🄐 🖥 💳 ≋

◈◈ Best Western Signature Inn SH
(309) 685-2556. **$74-$99.** 4112 N Brandywine Dr. I-74, exit 89 (US 150/War Memorial Dr), just e, then just n. Int corridors. **Pets:** Small. $10 daily fee/pet. Service with restrictions, crate.
ASK ✕ 🄐 🖥 💳 ≋

◈◈ Comfort Suites by Choice Hotels SH
(309) 688-3800. **$115-$135.** 1812 W War Memorial Dr. I-74, exit 89 (US 150/War Memorial Dr), just e, then just s. Int corridors. **Pets:** Accepted.
ASK 🄂 ✕ 🄐 🖥 💳 ≋

◈◈ Extended StayAmerica-Peoria-North SH
(309) 688-3110. **Call for rates.** 4306 N Brandywine Dr. I-74, exit 89 (US 150/War Memorial Dr), just w to Brandywine Dr, then just ne. Int corridors. **Pets:** Accepted.
✕ 🄐 ♿ 🖥 💳

◈ Red Roof Inn #7057 M
(309) 685-3911. **$56-$74.** 1822 W War Memorial Dr. I-74, exit 89 (US 150/War Memorial Dr), just e. Ext corridors. **Pets:** Medium, other species. Service with restrictions, supervision.
✕ 🄐 ♿ 🖥 💳

◈◈◈ Residence Inn by Marriott SH
(309) 681-9000. **$110-$130.** 2000 W War Memorial Dr. I-74, exit 89 (US 150/War Memorial Dr), just w; entrance through Northwoods Mall. Int corridors. **Pets:** Accepted.
ASK 🄂 ✕ 🄐 ♿ 🖥 💳 ≋ 🚫

◈ Super 8 Motel SH
(309) 688-8074. **$61-$86.** 1816 W War Memorial Dr. I-74, exit 89 (US 150/War Memorial Dr), just e. Int corridors. **Pets:** Medium. $50 deposit/pet. Service with restrictions, supervision.
ASK 🄂 ✕ 🄐 🖥 💳

PERU

◈◈ La Quinta Inn Peru SH
(815) 224-9000. **$72-$120.** 4389 Venture Dr. I-80, exit 75 (SR 251), 0.4 mi s to 38th St, just w to Venture Dr, then 0.4 mi nw. Int corridors. **Pets:** Medium, other species. Service with restrictions, supervision.
ASK 🄂 ✕ 🖥 💳 ≋

PONTIAC

◈◈ Comfort Inn by Choice Hotels SH
(815) 842-2777. **$69-$125, 14 day notice.** 1821 W Reynolds St. I-55, exit 197 (SR 116), just e. Int corridors. **Pets:** Accepted.
ASK 🄂 ✕ 🖥 💳 ≋

QUAD CITIES AREA

MOLINE

▼▼ Comfort Inn by Choice Hotels SH
(309) 762-7000. **$80-$100.** 2600 52nd Ave. I-280/74, exit 18A eastbound; exit 5B westbound, just s on US 6 and 150, then 0.5 mi nw on 27th St. Int corridors. **Pets:** Accepted.
[ASK] [S6] [X] [🔌] [💻] [🏊]

▲▲▲ ▼▼▼ Econo Lodge SH
(309) 762-1548. **$39-$69.** 6920 27th St. I-280/74, exit 18A eastbound; exit 5B westbound, just s on US 6 and 150, then just nw. Int corridors. **Pets:** Accepted.
[SAVE] [S6] [X] [🔌] [💻] [🏊]

▲▲▲ ▼ Exel Inn of Moline SH
(309) 797-5580. **$46-$76.** 2501 52nd Ave. I-280/74, exit 18A eastbound; exit 5B westbound, just s on US 6 and 150, then 1 mi nw on 27th St. Int corridors. **Pets:** Small, other species. Designated rooms, service with restrictions, supervision.
[SAVE] [S6] [X] [🔊] [🔌] [💻]

▲▲▲ ▼▼▼ Holiday Inn Express-Moline Airport SH
(309) 762-8300. **$89-$159.** 6910 27th St. I-280/74, exit 18A eastbound; exit 5B westbound, just s on US 6 and 150, then just nw. Int corridors. **Pets:** Large, other species. $10 one-time fee/room. Service with restrictions, crate.
[SAVE] [S6] [X] [🔊] [🔌] [💻]

▲▲▲ ▼▼▼ Holiday Inn-Moline Convention Center at the Airport SH
(309) 762-8811. **$79-$139.** 6902 27th St. I-280/74, exit 18A eastbound; exit 5B westbound, just s on US 6 and 150, then just nw. Int corridors. **Pets:** Accepted.
[SAVE] [S6] [X] [🔊] [🔌] [🔌] [💻] [🍴] [🏊] [X]

▲▲▲ ▼▼▼▼ La Quinta Inn Moline SH
(309) 762-9008. **$85-$109.** 5450 27th St. I-280/74, exit 18A eastbound; exit 5B westbound, just s on US 6 and 150 to traffic light, then just nw. Int corridors. **Pets:** Medium. Service with restrictions.
[SAVE] [X] [🔊] [🔌] [🔌] [💻] [🏊]

▲▲▲ ▼▼▼ Quality Inn & Suites by Choice Hotels SH
(309) 762-1711. **$50-$80.** 6920 27th St. I-280/74, exit 18A eastbound; exit 5B westbound, just s on US 6 and 150, then just nw. Int corridors. **Pets:** Accepted.
[SAVE] [S6] [X] [🔌] [💻] [🏊]

ROCK ISLAND

▲▲▲ ▼▼▼▼ Four Points by Sheraton LH
(309) 794-1212. **$89-$129.** 226 17th St. Just e of Centennial Bridge; at 3rd Ave and 17th St; downtown. Int corridors. **Pets:** Accepted.
[SAVE] [S6] [X] [🔊] [🔌] [💻] [🍴] [🏊] [X]

END AREA

QUINCY

▼▼ Comfort Inn by Choice Hotels SH
(217) 228-2700. **$80-$100.** 4122 Broadway. I-172, exit 14 (SR 104), 1.3 mi w. Int corridors. **Pets:** Accepted.
[ASK] [S6] [X] [🔌] [💻] [🏊]

▲▲▲ ▼ Super 8 Motel SH
(217) 228-8808. **$65-$79.** 224 N 36th St. I-172, exit 14 (SR 104), 1.8 mi w, then just s. Int corridors. **Pets:** Accepted.
[SAVE] [S6] [X] [♿M] [🔌]

RANTOUL

▲▲▲ ▼▼◆ Best Western Heritage Inn SH
(217) 892-9292. **$60.** 420 S Murray Rd. I-57, exit 250 (US 136), 0.5 mi e, then just s. Ext corridors. **Pets:** Small, other species. $5 daily fee/pet. Service with restrictions, crate.
[SAVE] [S6] [X] [🔌] [💻] [🏊]

▼▼ Super 8 Motel SH
(217) 893-8888. **$54-$94.** 207 S Murray Rd. I-57, exit 250 (US 136), just e. Int corridors. **Pets:** Accepted.
[ASK] [S6] [X] [🔌] [💻]

ROBINSON

▼▼ Best Western Robinson Inn SH
(618) 544-8448. **$73-$83.** 1500 W Main St. 1 mi w on SR 33. Int corridors. **Pets:** Other species. $5 daily fee/room. Service with restrictions.
[ASK] [S6] [X] [🔊] [🔌] [🔌] [💻]

ROCHELLE

▲▲▲ ▼▼▼ AmeriHost Inn-Rochelle SH
(815) 562-9530. **$69-$169.** 567 E Hwy 38. I-39, exit 99 (SR 38), 1 mi w. Int corridors. **Pets:** Accepted.
[SAVE] [S6] [X] [🔌] [💻] [🏊]

▲▲▲ ▼▼▼ Comfort Inn & Suites by Choice Hotels SH
(815) 562-5551. **$74-$194.** 1131 N 7th St. I-39, exit 99 (SR 38), 2.5 mi w; jct SR 38 and 251; downtown. Int corridors. **Pets:** Accepted.
[SAVE] [S6] [X] [🔌] [💻] [🍴] [🏊] [X]

▼▼▼ U. S. Express Hotel SH
(815) 562-9994. **$99.** 1240 Dement Rd. I-39, exit 99 (SR 38), just nw. Int corridors. **Pets:** Accepted.
[ASK] [S6] [X] [♿M] [🔊] [🔌] [🔌] [💻] [🏊]

ROCKFORD

▲▲▲ ▼▼▼ Baymont Inn & Suites Rockford SH
(815) 229-8200. **$69-$150.** 662 N Lyford Rd. I-90, exit US 20 business route, just e, then just n. Int corridors. **Pets:** Small. No service, supervision.
[SAVE] [S6] [X] [🔊] [🔌] [💻] [🏊] [X]

▼▼▼ Candlewood Suites SH
(815) 229-9300. **$119-$139.** 7555 Walton St. I-90, exit US 20 business route, 0.3 mi e to Bell School Rd, just s to Walton St, then just e. Int corridors. **Pets:** Large, other species. $75 one-time fee/pet. Designated rooms, service with restrictions, supervision.
[ASK] [X] [🔌] [🔌]

▼▼▼ Comfort Inn by Choice Hotels SH
(815) 398-7061. **$95-$115.** 7392 Argus Dr. I-90, exit US 20 business route, just w to Bell School Rd, then just n. Int corridors. **Pets:** Accepted.
[ASK] [S6] [X] [🔌] [💻] [🏊]

▲▲▲ ▼ Exel Inn of Rockford SH
(815) 332-4915. **$51-$81.** 220 S Lyford Rd. I-90, exit US 20 business route, just e, then just s. Int corridors. **Pets:** Small, other species. Designated rooms, service with restrictions, supervision.
[SAVE] [S6] [X] [🔌] [💻]

◆ ▼▼▼ Quality Suites SH
(815) 227-1300. **$99-$199.** 7401 Walton St. I-90, exit US 20 business route, just w to Bell School Rd, then just s. Int corridors. **Pets:** Accepted.

[SAVE] [S❄] [X] [🐾] [🛏] [🖥] [📺] [≈] [X]

▼ Red Roof Inn #7035 M
(815) 398-9750. **$57-$81.** 7434 E State St. I-90, exit US 20 business route, just w. Ext corridors. **Pets:** Medium, other species. Service with restrictions, supervision.

[X] [🐾] [🛏]

▼▼▼ Residence Inn by Marriott SH
(815) 227-0013. **$170-$210.** 7542 Colosseum Dr. I-90, exit US 20 business route, just w. Int corridors. **Pets:** Accepted.

[ASK] [S❄] [X] [🐾] [🛏] [🖥] [📺] [≈] [X]

◆ ▼▼▼ Sleep Inn-Rockford SH
(815) 398-8900. **$69-$179.** 725 Clark Dr. I-90, exit US 20 business route, just w to Bell School Rd, just n to Clark Dr, then 0.4 mi ne. Int corridors. **Pets:** Medium. $15 one-time fee/room. Designated rooms, service with restrictions, supervision.

[SAVE] [S❄] [X] [🛏] [🖥] [📺]

◆ ▼▼▼ Sweden House Lodge SH
(815) 398-4130. **$60-$90.** 4605 E State St. I-90, exit US 20 business route, 4 mi w. Ext/int corridors. **Pets:** Accepted.

[SAVE] [S❄] [X] [🛏] [🖥] [📺] [≈]

SALEM

▼ Super 8 Motel of Salem SH
(618) 548-5882. **$60-$87.** 118 Woods Ln. I-57, exit 116 (US 50), just w. Ext/int corridors. **Pets:** Accepted.

[ASK] [S❄] [X] [🖥] [🐾] [🛏] [🖥] [📺]

SAVOY

▼▼ Best Western Paradise Inn SH
(217) 356-1824. **$70-$99, 7 day notice.** 709 N Dunlap. I-57, exit 229, 1 mi e to US 45, then 2.5 mi n. Ext corridors. **Pets:** Small. $5 daily fee/pet. Service with restrictions, crate.

[ASK] [S❄] [X] [🛏] [🖥] [📺] [≈]

SOUTH JACKSONVILLE

◆ ▼▼▼ Comfort Inn-South Jacksonville SH ❀
(217) 245-8372. **$69-$99.** 200 Comfort Dr. I-72, exit 64, just n. Int corridors. **Pets:** Other species. $15 daily fee/room. Service with restrictions, supervision.

[SAVE] [S❄] [X] [🛏] [🖥] [📺] [≈]

◆ ▼▼▼ Econo Lodge Inn & Suites by Choice Hotels SH
(217) 245-9575. **$54-$63.** 1914 Southbrooke Rd. I-72, exit 64, just n. Int corridors. **Pets:** Medium. $20 one-time fee/room. Service with restrictions, supervision.

[SAVE] [S❄] [X] [🖥] [🐾] [🛏] [🖥] [📺]

SPRINGFIELD

▼▼ Baymont Inn & Suites Springfield SH
(217) 529-6655. **$80.** 5871 S 6th St. I-55, exit 90 (Toronto Rd), just e to 6th St, then just n. Int corridors. **Pets:** Accepted.

[ASK] [S❄] [X] [🖥] [🐾] [🛏] [🖥] [📺] [≈]

▼▼▼ Drury Inn & Suites-Springfield SH
(217) 529-3900. **$82-$130.** 3180 S Dirksen Pkwy. I-55, exit 94 (Stevenson Dr), just w to Dirksen Pkwy, then just n. Int corridors. **Pets:** Large, other species. Service with restrictions, supervision.

[ASK] [X] [🖥] [🐾] [🐾] [🛏] [🖥] [📺] [≈]

◆ ▼▼▼ Holiday Inn Express Hotel & Suites SH
(217) 529-7771. **$89-$115.** 3050 S Dirksen Pkwy. I-55, exit 94 (Stevenson Dr), just w to S Dirksen Pkwy, then 0.4 mi n. Int corridors. **Pets:** Accepted.

[SAVE] [S❄] [X] [🖥] [🐾] [🐾] [🛏] [🖥]

▼▼ Microtel Inn & Suites SH
(217) 753-2636. **$79-$99, 3 day notice.** 2636 Sunrise Dr. I-55, exit 94 (Stevenson Dr), just w to Dirksen Pkwy, then 0.4 mi n. Int corridors. **Pets:** Small. $5 daily fee/pet. Service with restrictions, crate.

[ASK] [X] [🖥] [🐾] [🐾] [🛏] [🖥] [📺] [≈]

▼▼ Pear Tree Inn by Drury-Springfield SH
(217) 529-9100. **$55-$110.** 3190 S Dirksen Pkwy. I-55, exit 94 (Stevenson Dr), just w. Int corridors. **Pets:** Large, other species. Service with restrictions, supervision.

[ASK] [X] [🐾] [📺]

▼▼ Red Roof Inn #7040 M
(217) 753-4302. **$47-$68.** 3200 Singer Ave. I-55, exit 96B, just w. Ext corridors. **Pets:** Medium, other species. Service with restrictions, supervision.

[X] [🐾] [🐾]

▼▼▼ Sleep Inn by Choice Hotels SH
(217) 787-6200. **$95-$115.** 3470 Freedom Dr. I-72, exit 93 (Veterans Pkwy), 0.7 mi n to Lindbergh Blvd, just w to Freedom Dr, then just s. Int corridors. **Pets:** Accepted.

[ASK] [S❄] [X] [🐾] [🛏] [🖥]

◆ ▼▼▼ The State House Inn-A Clarion Collection Hotel SH
(217) 528-5100. **$92-$106.** 101 E Adams St. Jct 1st and Adams sts; just n of State House. Int corridors. **Pets:** Accepted.

[SAVE] [S❄] [X] [🖥] [🐾] [🐾] [🛏] [🖥]

▼▼▼ Staybridge Suites Springfield South SH
(217) 793-6700. **$115-$159.** 4231 Schooner Dr. I-72, exit 93, 0.4 mi se. Int corridors. **Pets:** Medium. $75 one-time fee/room. Service with restrictions, supervision.

[ASK] [S❄] [X] [🖥] [🐾] [🐾] [🛏] [🖥] [📺] [X]

STAUNTON

▼ Staunton Super 8 SH
(618) 635-5353. **$53-$63.** 1527 Herman Rd. I-55, exit 41, 0.5 mi w. Int corridors. **Pets:** Medium. $10 one-time fee/room. Service with restrictions, supervision.

[ASK] [S❄] [X] [🐾] [🛏] [🖥]

STOCKTON

▼▼▼ Country Inn & Suites By Carlson SH
(815) 947-6060. **$84-$134.** 200 Dillon Ave. On US 20, just e of SR 78. Int corridors. **Pets:** Large. $15 daily fee/pet. Designated rooms, service with restrictions, supervision.

[ASK] [S❄] [X] [🖥] [🐾] [🛏] [🖥] [≈]

SYCAMORE

◆ ▼▼▼ Americas Best Value Inn & Suites SH
(815) 899-6500. **$69-$99.** 1860 Dekalb Ave. On SR 23, 0.9 mi s of Peace Rd. Int corridors. **Pets:** Accepted.

[SAVE] [S❄] [X] [🖥] [🐾] [🛏] [🖥]

◆ ▼▼▼ Comfort Inn-Sycamore SH
(815) 895-4979. **$80-$100.** 1475 S Peace Rd. I-88, exit Peace Rd, 5.5 mi n to jct SR 23. Int corridors. **Pets:** Small, dogs only. $10 daily fee/pet. Designated rooms, no service, supervision.

[SAVE] [S❄] [X] [🐾] [🐾] [🛏] [🖥] [≈]

TUSCOLA

◆◆ AmeriHost Inn-Tuscola SH
(217) 253-3500. **$60-$100.** 1006 Southline Rd. I-57, exit 212 (US 36), 0.3 mi w. Int corridors. **Pets:** Accepted.
ASK SØ ⊠ ᏕM Ꮥ᷂ 🖬 💻 ⇶

◆◆ Holiday Inn Express SH
(217) 253-6363. **$79-$89.** 1201 Tuscola Blvd. I-57, exit 212 (US 36), 0.3 mi w to Progress Blvd, just s to Tuscola Blvd, then 0.4 mi se. Int corridors. **Pets:** Medium. Service with restrictions, supervision.
ASK SØ ⊠ ᏕM Ꮥ᷂ 🖬 💻 ⇶

◆◆ Super 8 Motel-Tuscola SH
(217) 253-5488. **$69, 10 day notice.** 1007 E Southline Dr. I-57, exit 212 (US 36), 0.4 mi w. Int corridors. **Pets:** Other species. $10 daily fee/pet. Designated rooms, no service, supervision.
ASK SØ ⊠ 🖬 💻

URBANA

◍ ◆◆ Ramada Limited-Urbana/Champaign SH ❖
(217) 328-4400. **$99-$150.** 902 W Killarney St. I-74, exit 183 (Lincoln Ave), just s to Killarney St, then just w. Int corridors. **Pets:** $50 deposit/room. Service with restrictions, supervision.
SAVE SØ ⊠ 🖬 💻 ⇶

◍ ◆◆ Sleep Inn SH ❖
(217) 367-6000. **$76-$105.** 1908 N Lincoln Ave. I-74, exit 183 (Lincoln Ave), 0.5 mi s. Int corridors. **Pets:** Other species. $7 one-time fee/room. Service with restrictions, supervision.
SAVE SØ ⊠ Ꮥᴹ 🖬 💻 ⇶

VANDALIA

◍ ◆◆ Days Inn M
(618) 283-4400. **$74-$84.** 1920 Kennedy Blvd. I-70, exit 63 (US 51), 0.6 mi n. Ext corridors. **Pets:** Other species. $10 deposit/room. Service with restrictions.
SAVE SØ ⊠ 🖬 💻 ⇶

◍ ◆◆ Jay's Inn M
(618) 283-1200. **$52-$63.** 720 Gochenour St. I-70, exit 63 (US 51), just s. Ext corridors. **Pets:** Other species. Service with restrictions.
SAVE ⊠ 🖬 💻

◍ ◆◆ Ramada Vandalia SH
(618) 283-1400. **$57-$100.** 2707 Veterans Ave. I-70, exit 61, just s. Int corridors. **Pets:** Other species. $10 one-time fee/room. Designated rooms, no service, crate.
SAVE ⊠ 🖬 💻 ⇶

WASHINGTON

◆ Super 8 Motel-Peoria Area SH
(309) 444-8881. **$60-$80.** 1884 Washington Rd. On Business Rt SR 24, 1.5 mi w. Int corridors. **Pets:** Medium. $8 daily fee/pet. Service with restrictions, supervision.
ASK SØ ⊠ 🖬

WATSEKA

◍ ◆◆ Super 8 Motel SH ❖
(815) 432-6000. **$68-$81.** 710 W Walnut. On US 24; center of downtown. Int corridors. **Pets:** Small. $25 deposit/pet, $5 daily fee/pet. Service with restrictions, supervision.
SAVE SØ ⊠ 🖬

WENONA

◆ Super 8 Motel SH
(815) 853-4371. **$55-$110.** 5 Cavalry Dr. I-39, exit 35. Int corridors. **Pets:** $5 daily fee/pet. Designated rooms, service with restrictions, supervision.
ASK SØ ⊠ 🖬

INDIANA

ANGOLA

Ramada Inn SH
(260) 665-9471. **$70-$150.** 3855 N SR 127. I-69, exit 154, just e, then 0.4 mi s. Int corridors. **Pets:** $20 daily fee/room. Service with restrictions, supervision.

AUBURN

Holiday Inn Express SH
(260) 925-1900. **$85-$95.** 404 Touring Dr. I-69, exit 129, just e off SR 8. Int corridors. **Pets:** Accepted.

La Quinta Inn Auburn SH
(260) 920-1900. **$81-$88.** 306 Touring Dr. I-69, exit 129, 0.5 mi e on SR 8. Int corridors. **Pets:** Service with restrictions.

Super 8 Motel-Auburn SH
(260) 927-8800. **$68-$78.** 503 Ley Dr. I-69, exit 129, just e. Int corridors. **Pets:** Accepted.

BEDFORD

Bedford Super 8 SH
(812) 275-8881. **$65-$125.** 501 Bell Back Rd. Jct SR 37 and 58, just e on SR 58. Int corridors. **Pets:** $10 daily fee/pet. Service with restrictions, crate.

BERNE

Black Bear Inn & Suites SH
(260) 589-8955. **$69.** 1335 US 27 N. On US 27, 1 mi n. Int corridors. **Pets:** Accepted.

BLOOMINGTON

Fairfield Inn by Marriott SH
(812) 331-1122. **$99-$229.** 120 Fairfield Dr. Just e from SR 37 at 3rd St. Int corridors. **Pets:** Accepted.

Hampton Inn SH
(812) 334-2100. **$109-$219, 7 day notice.** 2100 N Walnut St. 1 mi e of jct SR 37 on SR 45/46 Bypass, then just s on College Ave/Walnut St. Int corridors. **Pets:** Accepted.

TownePlace Suites By Marriott SH
(812) 334-1234. **$89-$169.** 105 S Franklin Rd. Just e from SR 37 at 3rd St, then 0.3 mi n. Int corridors. **Pets:** Other species. $75 one-time fee/room. Service with restrictions.

CHESTERTON

Gray Goose Inn BB
(219) 926-5781. **$100-$190, 10 day notice.** 350 Indian Boundary Rd. I-94, exit 26A, 0.6 mi s to Indian Boundary Rd, then just w. Int corridors. **Pets:** Large. Service with restrictions, crate.

NEARBY OHIO
CINCINNATI METROPOLITAN AREA

LAWRENCEBURG

Comfort Inn & Suites SH
(812) 539-3600. **Call for rates.** 1610 Flossie Dr. I-275, exit 16, 0.3 mi e. Int corridors. **Pets:** Accepted.

END METROPOLITAN AREA

CLARKSVILLE

Best Western Green Tree Inn M
(812) 288-9281. **$75.** 1425 Broadway St. I-65, exit 4, just w. Ext corridors. **Pets:** Medium, dogs only. Service with restrictions, supervision.

CLOVERDALE

Super 8 Motel Cloverdale/Greencastle SH
(765) 795-7373. **$52-$135.** 1020 N Main St. I-70, exit 41, just s. Int corridors. **Pets:** Dogs only. $10 one-time fee/room. Service with restrictions, supervision.

COLUMBIA CITY

AmeriHost Inn & Suites SH
(260) 248-4551. **$75.** 701 W Connexion Way. 1 mi w, just off US 30. Int corridors. **Pets:** Accepted.

COLUMBUS

Columbus Holiday Inn and Conference Center SH
(812) 372-1541. **$101-$143.** 2480 Jonathan Moore Pike. I-65, exit 68, just e on SR 46. Ext/int corridors. **Pets:** $25 one-time fee/pet. Designated rooms, service with restrictions, supervision.

Days Inn Columbus SH
(812) 376-9951. **$59-$64.** 3445 Jonathan Moore Pike. I-65, exit 68, just w. Int corridors. **Pets:** Accepted.

Ramada Inn SH
(812) 376-3051. **$99-$139.** 2485 Jonathan Moore Pike. I-65, exit 68, just e on SR 46. Int corridors. **Pets:** $25 one-time fee/pet. Service with restrictions, crate.

CORYDON

Holiday Inn Express SH
(812) 738-1623. **$74-$199.** 249 Federal Dr. I-64, exit 105, 0.6 mi s, then just w. Int corridors. **Pets:** Accepted.

CRAWFORDSVILLE

Comfort Inn SH
(765) 361-0665. **$89-$199, 7 day notice.** 2991 N Gandhi Dr. I-74, exit 34, just s on US 231. Int corridors. **Pets:** $15 daily fee/room. Service with restrictions, supervision.

Holiday Inn-Crawfordsville SH
(765) 362-8700. **$72-$90.** 2500 N Lafayette Rd. I-74, exit 34, 0.3 mi s on US 231. Ext corridors. **Pets:** Small. $15 daily fee/pet. Designated rooms, service with restrictions, supervision.

DALE

Baymont Inn & Suites Dale SH
(812) 937-7000. **$60-$235.** 1339 N Washington St. I-64, exit 57 (US 231), just s. Int corridors. **Pets:** Other species. $50 deposit/room. Designated rooms, service with restrictions, supervision.

DALEVILLE

Value 8 Motel SH
(765) 378-0888. **$49-$57.** 15701 W Commerce Rd. I-69, exit 34, just w. Ext/int corridors. **Pets:** Accepted.

DECATUR

AmeriHost Inn Decatur SH
(260) 728-4600. **$69-$189.** 1201 S 13th St. On US 27 and 33, 1 mi s of jct US 224. Int corridors. **Pets:** Accepted.

Comfort Inn of Decatur SH
(260) 724-8888. **$79-$89.** 1302 S 13th St. 1 mi s on US 27 and 33. Int corridors. **Pets:** Accepted.

Days Inn SH
(260) 728-2196. **$45-$69.** 1033 N 13th St. On US 27 and 33, 0.5 mi n of jct US 224. Ext/int corridors. **Pets:** Accepted.

ELKHART

Candlewood Suites SH
(574) 262-8600. **Call for rates.** 300 Northpointe Blvd. I-80/90, exit 92, just n on SR 19, then just w. Int corridors. **Pets:** Medium, other species. $75 one-time fee/pet. Service with restrictions, supervision.

Jameson Inn Elkhart SH
(574) 264-7222. **$82.** 3010 Brittany Ct. I-80/90, exit 92, 0.3 mi s on SR 19. Int corridors. **Pets:** Small. $10 daily fee/pet. Service with restrictions, crate.

Ramada SH
(574) 262-1581. **$79-$149, 21 day notice.** 3011 Belvedere Rd. I-80/90, exit 92, 0.3 mi s on SR 19. Int corridors. **Pets:** Small. $10 daily fee/pet. Designated rooms, service with restrictions, crate.

Red Roof Inn-Elkhart #018 M
(574) 262-3691. **$53-$78.** 2902 Cassopolis St. I-80/90, exit 92, 0.5 mi s. Ext corridors. **Pets:** Medium, other species. Service with restrictions, supervision.

EVANSVILLE

Baymont Inn & Suites Evansville East SH
(812) 477-2677. **$79-$139.** 8005 E Division St. I-164, exit 7B (SR 66/Lloyd Expwy), 0.5 mi w to Cross Pointe Blvd, just n to Division St, then 0.5 mi e. Int corridors. **Pets:** Small, other species. $10 one-time fee/room. Designated rooms, service with restrictions, crate.

Baymont Inn & Suites Evansville West SH
(812) 421-9773. **$89-$109.** 5737 Pearl Dr. Jct US 41 and SR 62, 5.7 mi w on SR 62, then just s on Boehne Camp Rd. Int corridors. **Pets:** Other species. $15 one-time fee/room. Service with restrictions, supervision.

Best Western Gateway Inn & Suites SH
(812) 868-8000. **$85-$95, 7 day notice.** 324 Rusher Creek Rd. I-64, exit 25A (US 41), 0.5 mi s, then just w. Int corridors. **Pets:** Other species. $15 one-time fee/pet. Service with restrictions, crate.

Casino Aztar Hotel LH
(812) 433-4000. **$79-$129.** 421 NW Riverside Dr. SR 62 (Lloyd Expwy), just s on Fulton. Int corridors. **Pets:** Accepted.

▼▼▼ **Comfort Inn East** SH
(812) 476-3600. **$79.** 8331 E Walnut St. I-164, exit 7B (SR 66/Lloyd Expwy), 0.5 mi w to Eagle Crest Blvd, 0.3 mi se to Fuquay St, just s to Walnut St, then 0.4 mi e. Int corridors. **Pets:** Medium. $10 daily fee/room. Service with restrictions, supervision.
ASK Sᴅ ✕ ᴍ ⌨ ⟨ ⊟ ⊡ ⤳

▼▼▼ **Drury Inn & Suites-Evansville East** SH
(812) 471-3400. **$80-$127.** 100 Cross Pointe Blvd. I-164, exit 7B (SR 66/Lloyd Expwy), 0.5 mi w. Int corridors. **Pets:** Large, other species. Service with restrictions, supervision.
ASK ✕ ᴍ ⌨ ⟨ ⊟ ⊡ ⤳ ✕

▼▼▼ **Drury Inn & Suites-Evansville North** SH
(812) 423-5818. **$75-$127.** 3901 US 41 N. On US 41, 2.5 mi n of jct SR 62 and 66 (Lloyd Expwy), 3.3 mi sw of Regional Airport entrance. Int corridors. **Pets:** Large, other species. Service with restrictions, supervision.
ASK ✕ ⊟ ⊡ ⤳ ✕

▼▼▼ **Jameson Inn Evansville** SH
(812) 476-9626. **$71.** 1101 N Green River Rd. I-164, exit 9 (SR 62 E/Morgan Ave), 1.5 mi w on SR 62, then just s. Int corridors. **Pets:** Small. $10 daily fee/pet. Service with restrictions, crate.
ASK Sᴅ ✕ ᴍ ⌨ ⟨ ⊟ ⊡ ⤳ ✕

▼▼▼ **Residence Inn Hotel** SH
(812) 471-7191. **$114-$149.** 8283 E Walnut St. I-164, exit 7B (SR 66/Lloyd Expwy), 0.5 mi w to Eagle Crest Blvd, 0.3 mi se to Fuquay St, then 0.3 mi e. Int corridors. **Pets:** $100 one-time fee/room. Service with restrictions, crate.
ASK Sᴅ ✕ ᴍ ⌨ ⟨ ⊟ ⊡ ⤳ ✕

FORT WAYNE

▼▼ **Baymont Inn Fort Wayne** SH
(260) 489-2220. **$52-$91.** 1005 W Washington Center Rd. I-69, exit 111B, just w on SR 3, then just n. Int corridors. **Pets:** Accepted.
ASK Sᴅ ✕ ᴍ ⌨ ⊟ ⊡

▲▲▲ ▼▼ **Best Western Luxbury Inn Fort Wayne** SH
(260) 436-0242. **$83-$96.** 5501 Coventry Ln. I-69, exit 102. Int corridors. **Pets:** Accepted.
SAVE ✕ ⊟ ⊡ ⤳

▼▼▼ **Candlewood Suites** SH
(260) 484-1400. **Call for rates.** 5250 Distribution Dr. I-69, exit 111A, just e. Int corridors. **Pets:** Large. $75 one-time fee/room. Service with restrictions.
✕ ᴍ ⟨ ⊟ ⊡ ⤳

▲▲▲ ▼▼▼ **Don Hall's Guesthouse** SH
(260) 489-2524. **$89-$150.** 1313 W Washington Center Rd. I-69, exit 111B, just n on SR 3, then 0.3 mi e. Ext/int corridors. **Pets:** Accepted.
SAVE Sᴅ ✕ ⊟ ⊡ 🍴 ⤳ ✕

▼▼▼ **Fort Wayne Marriott** LH
(260) 484-0411. **$189.** 305 E Washington Center Rd. I-69, exit 112A. Int corridors. **Pets:** Accepted.
ASK ✕ ⌨ ⊟ ⊡ 🍴 ⤳ ✕

▲▲▲ ▼▼▼ **Hilton Fort Wayne at Grand Wayne Center** SH
(260) 420-1100. **$99-$134, 3 day notice.** 1020 S Calhoun St. Jct Jefferson Blvd; center. Int corridors. **Pets:** Accepted.
SAVE ✕ ᴍ ⌨ ⟨ ⊟ ⊡ 🍴 ⤳ ✕

▼▼▼ **Residence Inn by Marriott Fort Wayne** SH
(260) 484-4700. **$89-$149.** 4919 Lima Rd. I-69, exit 111A, 0.4 mi s on US 27. Ext corridors. **Pets:** Accepted.
ASK Sᴅ ✕ ⟨ ⊟ ⊡ ⤳ ✕

▼▼▼ **Residence Inn Southwest** SH
(260) 432-8000. **$99-$119.** 7811 W Jefferson Blvd. I-69, exit 102, 0.5 mi e. Int corridors. **Pets:** Accepted.
ASK Sᴅ ✕ ⟨ ⊟ ⊡ ⤳ ✕

GEORGETOWN

▼ **Motel 6-4097** SH
(812) 923-0441. **$49-$56.** 1079 N Luther Rd. I-64, exit 118, just w on SR 64. Int corridors. **Pets:** Medium, other species. Service with restrictions, supervision.
ASK Sᴅ ✕ ⟨ ⊟ ⤳

GOSHEN

▲▲▲ ▼▼ **Best Western Inn** M
(574) 533-0408. **$89.** 900 Lincolnway E. 1 mi se on US 33. Ext corridors. **Pets:** Service with restrictions, crate.
SAVE Sᴅ ✕ ⊟ ⊡

GREENCASTLE

▲▲▲ ▼ **College Inn** M
(765) 653-4167. **$65-$75.** 315 Bloomington St. I-70, exit 41, 8 mi n on US 231. Ext corridors. **Pets:** Accepted.
SAVE Sᴅ ✕ ⊟

GREENSBURG

▼▼▼ **Holiday Inn Express** SH
(812) 663-5500. **$84-$135.** 915 Ann Blvd. I-74, exit 134A, 1.4 mi s on SR 3. Int corridors. **Pets:** Other species. $20 deposit/room. Designated rooms, service with restrictions, supervision.
ASK Sᴅ ✕ ᴍ ⌨ ⟨ ⊟ ⊡ ⤳

HAMMOND

▼▼ **Best Western Northwest Indiana Inn** SH
(219) 844-2140. **$79-$99, 7 day notice.** 3830 179th St. I-80/94, exit 5 (Cline Ave), 0.6 mi s to frontage road, then 0.6 mi n. Int corridors. **Pets:** Medium, other species. $30 deposit/room, $5 daily fee/pet. Designated rooms, service with restrictions, supervision.
ASK Sᴅ ✕ ⌨ ⊟ ⊡ 🍴 ⤳

▼▼▼ **Residence Inn by Marriott Chicago Southeast** SH
(219) 844-8440. **$199-$229.** 7740 Corinne Dr. I-80/94, exit 3 (Kennedy Ave S), just s. Int corridors. **Pets:** Medium, other species. $100 one-time fee/room. Service with restrictions, crate.
ASK Sᴅ ✕ ᴍ ⌨ ⟨ ⊟ ⊡ ⤳ ✕

HOWE

▲▲▲ ▼▼ **Super 8 Motel** SH 🐾
(260) 562-2828. **$65-$120.** 7333 N SR 9. I-80/90, exit 121 (US 66), 0.5 mi s. Int corridors. **Pets:** Small, dogs only. $15 one-time fee/pet. Service with restrictions, supervision.
SAVE Sᴅ ✕ ᴍ ⌨ ⟨ ⊟

HUNTINGTON

▼▼▼ **AmeriHost Inn & Suites Huntington** SH
(260) 359-9000. **$69-$159.** 2820 Hotel Ave. 0.6 mi nw of jct US 24/224 and SR 5. Int corridors. **Pets:** Medium. $50 deposit/room, $10 daily fee/pet. Service with restrictions, supervision.
ASK Sᴅ ✕ ⌨ ⟨ ⊟ ⊡ ⤳

INDIANAPOLIS METROPOLITAN AREA

CARMEL

▼▼▼ Jameson Inn Carmel SH
(317) 816-1616. **$114.** 10201 N Meridian St. I-465, exit 31, 0.3 mi n on US 31. Int corridors. **Pets:** Small. $10 daily fee/pet. Service with restrictions, crate.

ASK 🔊 ✕ 🎿 🔋 💻 🏊 ✕

◆◆◆◆ Residence Inn by Marriott Indianapolis/Carmel SH
(317) 846-2000. **$149-$359.** 11895 N Meridian St. I-465, exit 31, 2 mi n on US 31, just e on 116th St, then just n on Pennsylvania Rd. Int corridors. **Pets:** Accepted.

ASK ✕ 🔊M 🎿 🔋 💻 🏊 ✕

▼▼▼ SpringHill Suites by Marriott Indianapolis/Carmel SH
(317) 846-1800. **$99-$399.** 11855 N Meridian St. I-465, exit 31, 2 mi n on US 31, just e on 116th St, then just n on Pennsylvania Rd. Int corridors. **Pets:** Accepted.

ASK 🔊 ✕ 🔊M 🎿 🔋 💻 🏊 ✕

EDINBURGH

◆◆◆ ▼▼ Best Western Horizon Inn SH
(812) 526-9883. **$65-$139.** 11780 N US 31. I-65, exit 76B, just n. Int corridors. **Pets:** Other species. $10 one-time fee/room. Designated rooms, service with restrictions, supervision.

SAVE 🔊 ✕ 🔋 💻 🏊

FISHERS

◆◆◆ ▼▼▼ Comfort Suites SH
(317) 578-1200. **$99-$200.** 9760 Crosspoint Blvd. I-69, exit 3, just w on 96th St, then just n. Int corridors. **Pets:** Accepted.

SAVE 🔊 ✕ 🎿 🔋 💻 🏊

▼▼▼ Frederick-Talbott Inn BB
(317) 578-3600. **$75-$175, 7 day notice.** 13805 Allisonville Rd. I-465, exit 35 (Allisonville Rd), 6.2 mi n; I-69, exit 5, 1.8 mi w on 116th St to Allisonville Rd, then 2.2 mi n. Int corridors. **Pets:** Accepted.

ASK 🔊 ✕

◆◆ ▼ Ramada Inn Indianapolis Northeast SH
(317) 558-4100. **$99-$185.** 9791 North by Northeast Blvd. I-69, exit 3, just ne. Int corridors. **Pets:** Accepted.

ASK 🔊 ✕ 🎿 🔋 💻 🏊

▼▼▼ Residence Inn by Marriott Indianapolis/Fishers SH 🐾
(317) 842-1111. **$139-$279.** 9765 Crosspoint Blvd. I-69, exit 3, just nw. Int corridors. **Pets:** Other species. $100 one-time fee/room. Service with restrictions, crate.

✕ 🔊M 🎿 🎿 🔋 💻 🏊 ✕

▼▼▼ Staybridge Suites Indianapolis-Fishers SH
(317) 577-9500. **$119.** 9780 Crosspoint Blvd. I-69, exit 3, just nw. Int corridors. **Pets:** Large. $125 one-time fee/room. Service with restrictions, crate.

ASK 🔊 ✕ 🔊M 🎿 🎿 🔋 💻 🏊 ✕

GREENWOOD

▼▼ Red Roof Inn M
(317) 887-1515. **$54-$174.** 110 Sheek Rd. I-65, exit 99, just w. Ext corridors. **Pets:** Medium, other species. Service with restrictions, supervision.

ASK 🔊 ✕ 🔋 💻 🏊

INDIANAPOLIS

◆◆◆ ▼▼▼ Best Western Airport Suites SH
(317) 246-1505. **$79-$250.** 55 S High School Rd. I-465, exit 13B, just w. Int corridors. **Pets:** Accepted.

SAVE 🔊 ✕ 🔋 💻

▼▼ Candlewood Suites SH
(317) 595-9292. **$89-$109.** 8111 Bash St. I-69, exit 1, just w. Int corridors. **Pets:** Other species. $75 one-time fee/room. Service with restrictions.

ASK 🔊 ✕ 🔋 💻 🏊 ✕

▼▼ Drury Inn-Indianapolis SH
(317) 876-9777. **$87-$132.** 9320 N Michigan Rd. I-465, exit 27, just s. Int corridors. **Pets:** Large, other species. Service with restrictions, supervision.

ASK ✕ 🎿 🔋 💻 🏊

▼▼ Extended StayAmerica-Indianapolis North SH
(317) 843-1181. **$45-$145.** 9750 Lakeshore Dr. I-465, exit 33, 0.3 mi n on Keystone Dr, 0.4 mi e on 96th St, then just n on Bauer Dr. Int corridors. **Pets:** Accepted.

ASK 🔊 ✕ 🔋 💻 🏊

▼▼ Extended Stay America-Indianapolis-Northwest-College Park SH
(317) 872-3090. **$40-$160.** 9030 Wesleyan Rd. I-465, exit 27, just s to Depauw Blvd, just e, then just s. Int corridors. **Pets:** Accepted.

ASK 🔊 ✕ 🔋 💻

▼▼▼ Hawthorn Suites East SH
(317) 322-0011. **$89-$119.** 7035 Western Select Dr. I-70, exit 89, 0.5 mi w of jct I-465. Int corridors. **Pets:** Small. $50 one-time fee/room. Service with restrictions, supervision.

ASK 🔊 ✕ 🔊M 🎿 🔋 💻 🏊

▼▼▼ Holiday Inn City Express City Center Hotel & Suites SH
(317) 822-6400. **$139-$179.** 410 S Missouri St. Jct Missouri and South sts. Int corridors. **Pets:** Other species. $25 one-time fee/pet. Service with restrictions, crate.

ASK 🔊 ✕ 🔊M 🎿 🔋 💻 🏊

◆◆◆ ▼▼▼ Holiday Inn East SH
(317) 359-5341. **$69-$210, 60 day notice.** 6990 E 21st St. I-70, exit 89, 0.5 mi w of jct I-465. Int corridors. **Pets:** $25 daily fee/pet. Service with restrictions, supervision.

SAVE 🔊 ✕ 🎿 🔋 💻 🍽 🏊 ✕

▼▼ Homestead Studio Suites Hotel-Indianapolis/Northwest SH
(317) 334-7829. **$55-$105.** 8520 Northwest Blvd. I-465, exit 23, just e. Int corridors. **Pets:** Accepted.

ASK 🔊 ✕ 🔊M 🎿 🎿 🔋 💻 🏊

▼▼▼ Indianapolis Marriott East LH
(317) 352-1231. **$99-$169.** 7202 E 21st St. I-70, exit 89, 0.3 mi se; 0.5 mi w of jct I-465. Int corridors. **Pets:** $75 one-time fee/room. Service with restrictions, crate.

ASK 🔊 ✕ 🎿 🔋 💻 🍽 🏊 ✕

▼▼▼ Jameson Inn Indianapolis Castleton SH
(317) 849-8555. **$74-$99.** 8380 Kelly Ln. I-465, exit 35 (Allisonville Rd), just s. Int corridors. **Pets:** Small. $10 daily fee/pet. Service with restrictions, crate.

ASK ✕ 🔊M 🎿 🔋 💻 🏊

▼▼▼ Jameson Inn of Indianapolis South SH
(317) 784-7006. **$74-$99.** 4402 E Creekview Dr. I-65, exit 103, just w. Int corridors. **Pets:** Small. $10 daily fee/pet. Service with restrictions, crate.

ASK ✕ 🎿 🔋 💻 🏊

(AAA) ▼▼▼ **La Quinta Inn & Suites Indianapolis-Airport** SH
(317) 244-8100. **$85-$105.** 2650 Executive Dr. I-465, exit 11A southbound; exit 11B northbound, 0.3 mi e. Int corridors. **Pets:** Medium.
Service with restrictions.
[SAVE] [X] [&M] [] [] [] []

(AAA) ▼▼▼ **La Quinta Inn Indianapolis Airport** SH
(317) 247-4281. **$104-$129.** 5316 W Southern Ave. I-465, exit 11A, 0.5
mi e on Airport Expwy to Lynhurst Dr. Int corridors. **Pets:** Medium.
Service with restrictions.
[SAVE] [X] [] [] [] []

▼▼ **La Quinta Inn Indianapolis (East)** SH
(317) 359-1021. **$49-$99.** 7304 E 21st St. I-70, exit 89, just s, then just
e; 0.5 mi w of jct I-465. Int corridors. **Pets:** Medium. Service with
restrictions, supervision.
[ASK] [SB] [X] [] [] [] []

▼▼ **Microtel Inn & Suites** SH
(317) 870-7765. **$40-$60.** 9140 N Michigan Rd. I-465, exit 27, just s. Int
corridors. **Pets:** Medium. $15 one-time fee/room. Service with restrictions,
supervision.
[ASK] [SB] [X] [] []

(AAA) ▼▼▼▼ **Omni Severin Hotel** LH
(317) 634-6664. **$119-$299.** 40 W Jackson Pl. Opposite Union Station.
Int corridors. **Pets:** Small, dogs only. $50 one-time fee/room. Service with
restrictions, crate.
[SAVE] [SB] [X] [] [] [] [] [] []

▼▼ **Quality Inn & Suites Airport** SH
(317) 381-1000. **$89-$229.** 2631 S Lynhurst Dr. I-465, exit 11A, 0.5 mi
e on Airport Expwy to Lynhurst Dr. Int corridors. **Pets:** Accepted.
[ASK] [SB] [X] [] [] [] []

▼▼ **Ramada Limited** SH
(317) 297-1848. **$69-$175, 15 day notice.** 3851 Shore Dr. I-465, exit
17, just w on 38th St, then just n. Ext corridors. **Pets:** Medium. $15 daily
fee/pet. No service, supervision.
[ASK] [SB] [X] [] [] []

▼▼▼ **Residence Inn by Marriott Indianapolis Airport** SH
(317) 244-1500. **$149-$199.** 5224 W Southern Ave. I-465, exit 11A, 0.5
mi e on Airport Expwy to Lynhurst Dr. Int corridors. **Pets:** Accepted.
[ASK] [SB] [X] [] [] [] [] [] []

▼▼▼ **Residence Inn by Marriott Indianapolis Downtown on
the Canal** SH
(317) 822-0840. **$179.** 350 W New York St. At New York St and Senate
Ave. Int corridors. **Pets:** Medium, other species. $100 one-time fee/room.
Service with restrictions.
[ASK] [SB] [X] [&M] [] [] [] [] []

▼▼▼ **Residence Inn by Marriott
Northwest-Indianapolis** SH
(317) 275-6000. **$84-$199.** 6220 Digital Way. I-465, exit 21, just w. Int
corridors. **Pets:** Medium. $75 one-time fee/room. Service with restrictions,
crate.
[ASK] [SB] [X] [&M] [] [] [] [] []

▼▼▼ **Sheraton Indianapolis Hotel & Suites** LH
(317) 846-2700. **$229.** 8787 Keystone Crossing. I-465, exit 33, 0.5 mi s
on SR 431, just e on 86th St, then just n. Int corridors. **Pets:** Accepted.
[ASK] [SB] [X] [&M] [] [] [] [] [] []

▼▼▼ **TownePlace Suites by Marriott Keystone** SH
(317) 255-3700. **Call for rates (no credit cards).** 8468 Union Chapel
Rd. I-465, exit 33, 0.5 mi s on SR 431, just e on 86th st, then just s.
Int corridors. **Pets:** Accepted.
[X] [] [] []

▼▼▼ **TownePlace Suites by Marriott Park 100** SH
(317) 290-8900. **Call for rates (no credit cards).** 5802 W 71st St.
I-465, exit 21, 0.3 mi e. Int corridors. **Pets:** Accepted.
[X] [] []

(AAA) ▼▼▼▼ **The Westin Indianapolis** LH ✿
(317) 262-8100. **$359-$389.** 50 S Capitol Ave. At Washington and
Maryland sts and Capitol Ave. Int corridors. **Pets:** Medium, dogs only.
Service with restrictions, crate.
[SAVE] [SB] [X] [] [] [] [] [] []

LEBANON

(AAA) ▼▼▼ **Comfort Inn** SH
(765) 482-4800. **$70-$120.** 210 N Sam Ralston Rd. I-65, exit 140. Int
corridors. **Pets:** $10 daily fee/pet. Service with restrictions, supervision.
[SAVE] [SB] [X] [] [] []

▼▼▼ **Holiday Inn Express** SH
(765) 483-4100. **$89-$169.** 335 N Mt. Zion Rd. I-65, exit 140, just w. Int
corridors. **Pets:** Small. $10 one-time fee/room. Service with restrictions,
supervision.
[ASK] [SB] [X] [&M] [] [] [] []

▼▼ **Super 8 Motel** SH
(765) 482-9999. **$57.** 405 N Mount Zion Rd. I-65, exit 140, just w. Int
corridors. **Pets:** Accepted.
[ASK] [SB] [X] []

SHELBYVILLE

(AAA) ▼▼ **Best Western Shelbyville Inn** SH
(317) 398-0472. **$59-$99.** 68 E Rampart St. I-74, exit 113, just w. Int
corridors. **Pets:** Accepted.
[SAVE] [SB] [X] [&M] [] [] []

END METROPOLITAN AREA

JASPER

▼▼ **Days Inn Jasper** SH
(812) 482-6000. **$64-$90.** 272 Brucke Strasse. Jct SR 164, just w.
Ext/int corridors. **Pets:** $10 daily fee/pet. Designated rooms, service with
restrictions, crate.
[ASK] [SB] [X] [] [] [] [] [] []

JEFFERSONVILLE

▼▼ **TownePlace Suites by Marriott** SH
(812) 280-8200. **$75-$95.** 703 N Shore Dr. I-65, exit 0, just w. Int
corridors. **Pets:** Accepted.
[ASK] [SB] [X] [] [] [] []

KENDALLVILLE

(AAA) ▼▼▼ **Best Western Kendallville Inn** SH
(260) 347-5263. **$69-$129.** 621 Professional Way. 1 mi e on US 6. Int
corridors. **Pets:** Medium, dogs only. $25 one-time fee/room. Service with
restrictions, supervision.
[SAVE] [SB] [X] [] [] [] []

KOKOMO

▼▼ **Comfort Inn by Choice Hotels** SH
(765) 452-5050. **$70-$90.** 522 Essex Dr. Jct US 35, 0.3 mi n on US 31.
Int corridors. **Pets:** Accepted.
[ASK] [SB] [X] [] [] [] []

Days Inn & Suites M
(765) 453-7100. **$56-$86.** 264 S 00 EW. US 31, 2.8 mi s of jct US 35.
Ext corridors. **Pets:** $10 one-time fee/room. Service with restrictions,
supervision.
ASK S□ X 🖥 🖵 ¶ ⇔

Hampton Inn & Suites SH
(765) 455-2900. **$99-$179.** 2920 S Reed Rd (US Hwy 31). US 31, 2 mi
s of jct US 35. Int corridors. **Pets:** Medium. Designated rooms, service
with restrictions, crate.
ASK S□ X ⅙M 🖉 ⅙ 🖥 🖵 ⇔ ⊠

LAFAYETTE

Best Western Lafayette Executive Plaza &
Conference Center SH
(765) 447-0575. **$84-$199, 30 day notice.** 4343 SR 26 E. I-65, exit
172, just w. Int corridors. **Pets:** Very small. $15 daily fee/room. Desig-
nated rooms, service with restrictions, supervision.
SAVE S□ X 🖉 ⅙ 🖥 🖵 ¶ ⇔ ⊠

Comfort Suites-Lafayette SH
(765) 447-0016. **$95-$126.** 31 Frontage Rd. I-65, exit 172, just e. Int
corridors. **Pets:** Other species. $10 one-time fee/pet. Service with restric-
tions, supervision.
SAVE S□ X ⅙M 🖉 ⅙ 🖥 🖵 ⇔ ⊠

Days Inn & Suites SH 🐾
(765) 446-8558. **$80, 3 day notice.** 151 Frontage Rd. I-65, exit 172,
just e. Int corridors. **Pets:** $75 deposit/pet. Service with restrictions, crate.
ASK S□ X 🖥 🖵

Holiday Inn Express SH
(765) 449-4808. **$100-$200, 15 day notice.** 201 Frontage Rd. I-65, exit
172, just e on SR 26, then just n. Int corridors. **Pets:** Other species. No
service.
SAVE S□ X ⅙ 🖥 🖵

Homewood Suites by Hilton SH
(765) 448-9700. **$124-$189.** 3939 SR 26 E. I-65, exit 172, 0.8 mi w.
Ext/int corridors. **Pets:** $10 daily fee/pet, $50 one-time fee/pet. Crate.
ASK S□ X 🖉 🖥 🖵 ⇔ ⊠

Loeb House Inn BB
(765) 420-7737. **$95-$175, 14 day notice.** 708 Cincinnati St. SR 38,
0.4 mi n on 9th St, then just w. Int corridors. **Pets:** Accepted.
ASK S□ X

Motel 6 M
(765) 447-7566. **$44-$73.** 139 Frontage Rd. I-65, exit 172. Ext corridors. **Pets:** Medium, other species. Service with restrictions, supervision.
SAVE S□ X 🖥

Red Roof Inn-Lafayette #7062 M
(765) 448-4671. **$52-$63.** 4201 SR 26 E. I-65, exit 172, 0.3 mi w. Ext
corridors. **Pets:** Medium, other species. Service with restrictions, supervision.
X ⅙ 🖥

TownePlace Suites by Marriott SH
(765) 446-8668. **$119-$299.** 163 Frontage Rd. I-65, exit 172, just e. Int
corridors. **Pets:** $75 one-time fee/room. Service with restrictions, crate.
ASK S□ X 🖥 🖵 ⇔

LOGANSPORT

Ramada SH
(574) 753-6351. **$65-$100.** 3550 E Market St. 2.5 mi e on Business Rt
US 24. Int corridors. **Pets:** Medium. Service with restrictions, supervision.
ASK S□ X ⅙M ⅙ 🖥 🖵 ¶ ⇔

MADISON

Country Hearth Inn SH
(812) 273-0757. **$45-$150.** 308 Demaree Dr. Jct SR 7 and 62, 2 mi e
on SR 62. Int corridors. **Pets:** Other species. $10 daily fee/pet, $10
one-time fee/pet. Service with restrictions, crate.
SAVE S□ X 🖥 🖵

Super 8 Motel SH
(812) 273-4443. **$50-$145.** 3767 Clifty Dr. Jct SR 56/62/256. Int corridors. **Pets:** Accepted.
SAVE S□ X ⅙ 🖥 🖵 ⇔

MARION

Comfort Suites-Marion SH
(765) 651-1006. **$85-$131.** 1345 N Baldwin Ave. 1.5 mi n of jct SR 9
and 18. Int corridors. **Pets:** Other species. $10 one-time fee/room. Desig-
nated rooms, service with restrictions, supervision.
SAVE S□ X 🖉 ⅙ 🖥 🖵 ⇔ ⊠

MARKLE

Super 8 Motel Fort Wayne South/Markle SH
(260) 758-8888. **$63-$95.** 610 Annette Dr. I-69, exit 86, just e. Int
corridors. **Pets:** Accepted.
ASK S□ X 🖥 🖵

MERRILLVILLE

Extended StayAmerica-Merrillville-US Rte 30 SH
(219) 769-4740. **$87-$103.** 1355 E 83rd Ave. I-65, exit 253 (US 30), 0.3
mi e, just s on Mississippi St, then 0.4 mi w. Int corridors.
Pets: Accepted.
ASK S□ X 🖉 ⅙ 🖥 🖵

Residence Inn by Marriott Merrillville SH
(219) 791-9000. **$139-$179.** 8018 Delaware Pl. I-65, exit 253B (US 30),
0.3 mi nw. Int corridors. **Pets:** $100 one-time fee/room. Service with
restrictions.
ASK S□ X ⅙M 🖉 ⅙ 🖥 🖵 ⇔ ⊠

Super 8 Motel SH
(219) 736-8383. **$50-$70, 7 day notice.** 8300 Louisiana St. I-65, exit
253 (US 30), 0.3 mi e, just s on Mississippi St, then just w on 83rd
Ave. Int corridors. **Pets:** Medium. $20 deposit/pet. Designated rooms,
service with restrictions, supervision.
SAVE S□ X ⅙M 🖉 🖥

MONTGOMERY

Gasthof Amish Village Inn SH
(812) 486-2600. **$60-$100.** 6747 E Garth of Village Rd E. US 50, 0.8
mi n on First St. Int corridors. **Pets:** Accepted.
ASK S□ X 🖉 ⅙ 🖥 🖵 ¶ ⇔ ⊠

MONTICELLO

Best Western Brandywine Inn & Suites SH
(574) 583-6333. **$80-$190.** 304 S 6th St. SR 24, just s. Int corridors.
Pets: Accepted.
SAVE S□ X ⅙M ⅙ 🖥 🖵 ⇔ ⊠

MOUNT VERNON

Four Seasons Motel M
(812) 838-4821. **$59-$100.** 70 Hwy 62 W. 1.8 mi w. Ext corridors.
Pets: Accepted.
ASK S□ X 🖥 🖵 ⇔

MUNCIE

▼▼ Days Inn Muncie SH
(765) 288-2311. **$48-$64.** 3509 N Everbrook Ln. I-69, exit 41, 6.3 mi e on SR 332, then just n. Int corridors. **Pets:** Dogs only. $10 one-time fee/room. Service with restrictions, supervision.
ASK SO ⊠ ⊟ 💻

▼▼▼▼ The Roberts Hotel LH
(765) 741-7777. **$72-$139.** 420 S High St. Downtown; opposite Horizon Convention Center. Int corridors. **Pets:** Accepted.
ASK SO ⊠ ⊟ 💻 🍴 🏊

▼▼▼ Signature Inn-Muncie SH
(765) 284-4200. **$71.** 3400 N Chadam Ln. I-69, exit 41, 6.3 mi e on SR 332. Int corridors. **Pets:** Small. $10 daily fee/pet. Service with restrictions, crate.
ASK SO ⊠ ⊘ ⊟ 💻 🏊

▼▼ Super 8 Motel SH
(765) 286-4333. **$42-$75.** 3601 W Fox Ridge Ln. I-69, exit 41, 6.3 mi e on SR 332. Int corridors. **Pets:** Medium, dogs only. $10 daily fee/pet. Service with restrictions, supervision.
ASK SO ⊠ ⊟

NEW ALBANY

◉◉◉ ▼▼▼ Holiday Inn Express SH
(812) 945-2771. **$79-$199.** 411 W Spring St. I-64, exit 123. Int corridors. **Pets:** Small, dogs only. $25 one-time fee/pet. Service with restrictions, supervision.
SAVE SO ⊠ ♿ ⊟ 💻 🏊

NEW CASTLE

◉◉◉ ▼▼ Best Western Raintree Inn SH
(765) 521-0100. **$70-$136.** 2836 S SR 3. I-70, exit 123, 2.5 mi n. Ext/int corridors. **Pets:** Medium, other species. $20 one-time fee/pet. Service with restrictions.
SAVE SO ⊠ ♿ ⊟ 💻 🍴 🏊

NORTH VERNON

▼▼ Comfort Inn SH
(812) 352-9999. **$79-$119.** 150 FDR Dr. Jct US 50, 0.6 mi n on SR 7. Int corridors. **Pets:** Small. $25 one-time fee/room. Service with restrictions, supervision.
ASK SO ⊠ ♿ ⊟ 💻 🏊

PERU

▼▼▼ Best Western Circus City Inn SH
(765) 473-8800. **$86-$96.** 2642 Business 31 S. Just e of jct US 31. Int corridors. **Pets:** Other species. $5 daily fee/pet. Supervision.
ASK SO ⊠ ⊘ ♿ ⊟ 💻 🏊

PLYMOUTH

▼▼▼ Swan Lake Resort SH
(574) 935-5680. **$98-$258, 3 day notice.** 5203 Plymouth-LaPorte Tr. 2.5 mi w on US 30, 4 mi nw on Queen Rd/Plymouth-LaPorte Trail. Int corridors. **Pets:** Small. $200 deposit/room. Service with restrictions, crate.
ASK SO ⊠ ⊟ 💻 🍴 🏊 ⊠

PORTAGE

▼▼ Super 8 Motel Portage SH
(219) 762-8857. **$49-$109.** 6118 Melton Rd. I-94, exit 19, just s on SR 249, then just w on US 20. Int corridors. **Pets:** Accepted.
ASK SO ⊠ ⊟ 💻

PORTLAND

▼▼ Hoosier Inn M
(260) 726-7113. **$42-$85.** 1620 Meridian St. 1.4 mi n on US 27. Ext corridors. **Pets:** $5 daily fee/pet. Service with restrictions, supervision.
ASK ⊠ ⊟ 💻

PRINCETON

▼▼ Fairfield Inn by Marriott SH
(812) 385-4300. **$60-$99.** 2828 Dixon St. Jct US 41 and SR 64, 0.3 mi w. Int corridors. **Pets:** Other species. $50 one-time fee/room. Service with restrictions, supervision.
ASK SO ⊠ ♿ ⊘ ♿ ⊟ 💻 🏊

RENSSELAER

◉◉◉ ▼▼▼ Holiday Inn Express SH
(219) 866-7111. **$85-$105.** 4788 Nesbitt Dr. I-65, exit 215, just e. Int corridors. **Pets:** Medium. $25 daily fee/pet. Designated rooms, service with restrictions, supervision.
SAVE ⊠ ♿ ♿ ⊟ 💻

RICHMOND

▼▼▼ Holiday Inn-Richmond SH
(765) 966-7511. **$85-$325.** 5501 National Rd E. I-70, exit 156A, 0.3 mi w. Int corridors. **Pets:** Accepted.
ASK SO ⊠ ♿ ⊘ ♿ ⊟ 💻 🍴 🏊 ⊠

◉◉◉ ▼▼▼ Knights Inn SH
(765) 966-1505. **$49-$84.** 3020 E Main St. I-70, exit 156A, 2 mi w. Ext corridors. **Pets:** Small. $8 daily fee/pet. Service with restrictions, supervision.
SAVE SO ⊠ ⊟ 💻 🏊

▼▼▼ Lees Inn & Suites SH
(765) 966-6559. **$79-$89.** 6030 National Rd E. I-70, exit 156A, jct US 40. Int corridors. **Pets:** Designated rooms, service with restrictions, supervision.
ASK SO ⊠ ⊟ 💻 🏊

▼▼ Motel 6 Richmond #4170 M
(765) 966-6682. **$40-$89.** 419 Commerce Dr. I-70, exit 156A, just s on US 40. Ext corridors. **Pets:** Medium, other species. Service with restrictions, supervision.
ASK SO ⊠ 🏊

ROSELAND

◉◉◉ ▼▼▼ Comfort Suites South Bend SH
(574) 272-1500. **$100-$165.** 52939 SR 933 N. I-80/90, exit 77, just e to Business Rt US 31/33, then 1 mi n. Int corridors. **Pets:** Large, other species. $20 one-time fee/room. Service with restrictions, crate.
SAVE SO ⊠ ♿ ⊟ 💻 🏊 ⊠

▼▼ Quality Inn-University Area SH
(574) 272-6600. **$70-$100.** 515 N Dixie Way. I-80/90, exit 77, on US 31 and SR 933, 0.8 mi n. Ext/int corridors. **Pets:** Accepted.
ASK SO ⊠ ♿ ⊟ 💻 🍴 🏊

SCOTTSBURG

◉◉◉ ▼▼▼ Mariann Travel Inn M
(812) 752-3396. **$58-$61.** I-65 and SR 56. I-65, exit 29A, just e. Ext corridors. **Pets:** Accepted.
SAVE SO ⊠ ⊟ 🍴 🏊 ⊠

SELLERSBURG

▼▼ Home Lodge SH
(812) 246-6332. **$319 (weekly), 14 day notice.** 363 Triangle Dr. I-65, exit 9, just e. Int corridors. **Pets:** Accepted.
⊠ ⊘ ⊟ 💻

▼▼▼ Ramada Limited & Suites SH
(812) 246-3131. **$79, 14 day notice.** 360 Triangle Dr. I-65, exit 9, just e. Int corridors. **Pets:** Accepted.
ASK SO ⊠ ♿ ⊟ 💻 🏊

SEYMOUR

▼▼▼ Holiday Inn SH
(812) 522-6767. **$79-$99.** 2025 E Tipton St. I-65, exit 50B, 0.5 mi w on US 50. Ext corridors. **Pets:** Service with restrictions, supervision.
(ASK) (So) (X) (♿) (f) (TI) (≈)

▼ Motel 6 Seymour #4153 SH
(812) 524-7443. **$36-$99.** 365 Tanger Blvd. I-65, exit 50A. Int corridors. **Pets:** Medium, other species. Service with restrictions, supervision.
(ASK) (So) (X) (&M) (♿) (f) (➡) (≈)

SHIPSHEWANA

▲▲▲ ▼▼▼ Super 8 Motel SH
(260) 768-4004. **$55-$125.** 740 S Van Buren St. US 20, 0.8 mi n on SR 5. Int corridors. **Pets:** Medium, other species. $10 daily fee/pet. Service with restrictions, supervision.
(SAVE) (So) (X) (♿) (f) (➡)

SOUTH BEND

▼▼▼ Oliver Inn Bed & Breakfast BB 🐾
(574) 232-4545. **$95-$329, 14 day notice.** 630 W Washington St. 0.3 mi w of jct US 933 and 31 S. Int corridors. **Pets:** $10 daily fee/room. Designated rooms, supervision.
(ASK) (So) (X) (f) (➡)

▲▲▲ ▼▼▼▼ Quality Inn & Suites SH
(574) 288-3800. **$64-$119, 30 day notice.** 4124 Lincolnway W. I-80/90, exit 72 (US 31), 1.5 mi s to South Bend Airport exit, then 2 mi e. Int corridors. **Pets:** Medium, other species. $10 daily fee/pet. Service with restrictions, supervision.
(SAVE) (So) (X) (&M) (♿) (f) (➡) (≈)

▲▲▲ ▼▼▼ Super 8 Motel SH
(574) 243-0200. **$59-$84.** 4124 Ameritech Dr. I-80/90, exit 72 (US 31), 0.7 mi n, just e on Cleveland Rd, then just s. Int corridors. **Pets:** Medium, other species. $10 daily fee/pet. Designated rooms, service with restrictions, supervision.
(SAVE) (So) (X) (♿) (f) (➡) (≈)

TAYLORSVILLE

▼▼ Red Roof Inn M
(812) 526-9747. **$59-$110.** 10330 US 31. I-65, exit 76A, just s. Ext corridors. **Pets:** Medium, other species. Service with restrictions, supervision.
(ASK) (So) (X) (♿) (f) (➡) (≈)

TELL CITY

▼▼ Ramada Limited SH
(812) 547-3234. **$56-$99.** 235 Orchard Hill Dr. Just off SR 66, 1.7 mi se of jct SR 37. Int corridors. **Pets:** Medium, other species. $50 deposit/pet. Service with restrictions, crate.
(ASK) (So) (X) (♿) (f) (➡) (≈)

TERRE HAUTE

▼▼ Comfort Suites by Choice Hotels SH
(812) 235-1770. **$95-$115.** 501 E Margaret Ave. I-70, exit 7 (US 41/150), just ne. Int corridors. **Pets:** Accepted.
(ASK) (So) (X) (&M) (♿) (f) (➡)

▼▼ Drury Inn-Terre Haute SH
(812) 238-1206. **$102-$152.** 3040 Hwy 41 S. I-70, exit 7 (US 41/150), just n. Int corridors. **Pets:** Large, other species. Service with restrictions, supervision.
(ASK) (X) (&M) (♿) (f) (➡) (🐾)

◆ Econo Lodge M
(812) 234-9931. **$59-$124.** 401 E Margaret Ave. I-70, exit 7 (US 41/150), just n, then e. Ext corridors. **Pets:** Large, other species. $10 one-time fee/room. Service with restrictions.
(ASK) (So) (X) (f) (➡) (≈)

▼▼▼ Holiday Inn LH
(812) 232-6081. **$104-$149.** 3300 US 41 S. I-70, exit 7 (US 41/150), just s. Int corridors. **Pets:** Medium, other species. $25 one-time fee/room. Service with restrictions, supervision.
(ASK) (So) (X) (♿) (f) (➡) (TI) (≈) (🐾)

▼▼ Pear Tree Inn by Drury-Terre Haute SH
(812) 234-4268. **$70-$117.** 3050 US 41 S. I-70, exit 7 (US 41/150), just n. Int corridors. **Pets:** Large, other species. Service with restrictions, supervision.
(ASK) (X) (♿) (➡)

◆ Super 8 Motel-Terre Haute SH
(812) 232-4890. **$50-$65.** 3089 S 1st St. I-70, exit 7 (US 41/150), just nw. Int corridors. **Pets:** Service with restrictions, supervision.
(ASK) (So) (X) (f)

VALPARAISO

◆◆ Courtyard by Marriott Valparaiso SH
(219) 465-1700. **$89-$129.** 2301 E Morthland Dr. US 30, w of jct SR 49 Bypass. Int corridors. **Pets:** Accepted.
(X) (♿) (f) (➡) (TI) (≈)

WARREN

▼▼ Comfort Inn Warren SH
(260) 375-4800. **$59-$85, 7 day notice.** 7275 S 75 E. I-69, exit 78, just n on SR 5. Int corridors. **Pets:** Accepted.
(So) (X) (&M) (♿) (f) (➡) (≈)

WARSAW

▲▲▲ ▼▼▼▼ Comfort Inn & Suites-Warsaw SH
(574) 269-6655. **$90-$125.** 3328 E Center St. 3.2 mi e of SR 15 on US 30. Int corridors. **Pets:** Accepted.
(SAVE) (So) (X) (♿) (f) (➡) (🐾)

▼▼▼▼ Ramada Plaza Hotel of Warsaw SH 🐾
(574) 269-2323. **$104-$120.** 2519 E Center St. 2.8 mi e of SR 15 on US 30, just s. Int corridors. **Pets:** Medium. Service with restrictions, crate.
(ASK) (So) (X) (f) (➡) (TI) (➡) (🐾)

WASHINGTON

▼▼▼ Baymont Inn & Suites Washington SH
(812) 254-7000. **$70-$88.** 7 Cumberland Dr. Just ne of jct US 50 and SR 257. Int corridors. **Pets:** Small, dogs only. $50 deposit/pet. Service with restrictions, supervision.
(ASK) (So) (X) (♿) (f) (➡) (≈) (🐾)

IOWA

ADAIR

Adair Budget Inn M
(641) 742-5553. **$39-$49.** 100 S 5th St. I-80, exit 76. Ext corridors.
Pets: Accepted.

Adair Super 8 SH
(641) 742-5251. **$54-$79.** 111 S 5th St. I-80, exit 76. Int corridors.
Pets: Accepted.

ALBIA

Indian Hills Inn SH
(641) 932-7181. **$65-$90.** 100 Hwy 34 E. Just e of jct US 34 and SR 5.
Ext/int corridors. **Pets:** Medium. $6 daily fee/room. Designated rooms,
service with restrictions, crate.

ALGONA

AmericInn Motel SH
(515) 295-3333. **$78-$131.** 600 Hwy 18 W. Just w of jct US 169/18. Int
corridors. **Pets:** Accepted.

ALTOONA

Motel 6 Des Moines East #1420 SH
(515) 967-5252. **$43-$89.** 3225 Adventureland Dr. I-80, exit 142A. Int
corridors. **Pets:** Medium, other species. Service with restrictions, supervision.

Settle Inn & Suites-Altoona SH
(515) 967-7888. **$60-$95.** 2101 Adventureland Dr. I-80, exit 142A, just
se. Int corridors. **Pets:** Accepted.

AMES

AmericInn & Suites SH
(515) 233-1005. **$69-$109.** 2507 SE 16th St. I-35, exit 111B, just w on
US 30, then exit 150. Int corridors. **Pets:** Accepted.

Baymont Inn & Suites SH
(515) 296-2500. **$80-$100.** 2500 Elwood Dr. I-35, exit 111B, 3.5 mi w
on US 30, exit 146 (Elwood Dr), then just s. Int corridors.
Pets: Accepted.

Comfort Inn-Ames SH
(515) 232-0689. **$65-$129.** 1605 S Dayton Ave. I-35, exit 111B, just w
on US 30, then exit 150. Int corridors. **Pets:** Medium, other species. $5
daily fee/pet. Service with restrictions.

Gateway Hotel & Conference Center LH
(515) 292-8600. **$89-$179.** 2100 Green Hills Dr. I-35, exit 111B, 3.5 mi
w on US 30, exit 146 (Elwood Dr). Int corridors. **Pets:** Other species.
Designated rooms, service with restrictions, crate.

GrandStay Residential Suites SH
(515) 232-8363. **$75-$100.** 1606 S Kellogg Ave. I-35, exit 111, 1 mi w,
then just nw on Duff Ave to Kellogg Ave. Int corridors. **Pets:** Accepted.

Holiday Inn SH
(515) 268-8808. **$109-$250.** 2609 Elwood Dr. I-35, exit 111B, 3.5 mi w
on US 30, exit 146 (Elwood Dr), then just s. Int corridors.
Pets: Accepted.

**Quality Inn & Suites Starlite Village Conference
Center** SH 🐾
(515) 232-9260. **$90-$150.** 2601 E 13th St. I-35, exit 113 (13th St), 0.5
mi w. Int corridors. **Pets:** Small. $10 one-time fee/pet.

ANAMOSA

Super 8 Motel-Anamosa SH
(319) 462-3888. **$58-$68.** 100 Grant Wood Dr. Just e on US 64 from
US 151. Int corridors. **Pets:** Medium. $10 one-time fee/pet. Service with
restrictions, supervision.

ARNOLDS PARK

Fillenwarth Beach SH
(712) 332-5646. **$68-$880 (no credit cards), 21 day notice.** 87 Lake
Shore Dr. Just w of US 71; on West Lake Okoboji. Ext corridors.
Pets: Other species.

ATLANTIC

Days Inn SH
(712) 243-4067. **$49-$60.** 64968 Boston Rd. I-80, exit 60 (US 71), 0.5
mi s. Int corridors. **Pets:** Large, other species. $5 one-time fee/room.
Designated rooms, service with restrictions, supervision.

▼▼▼ **Super 8 Motel** SH
(712) 243-4723. **$59-$89.** 1902 E 7th St. I-80, exit 60 (US 71), 6 mi s, then 2 mi w; east side of town. Int corridors. **Pets:** Accepted.
ASK S▢ ✕ ⟨⟩ ▤ ▣ ⇌

BOONE

AAA ▼▼▼ **AmeriHost Inn & Suites** SH
(515) 432-8168. **$59-$109.** 1745 SE Marshall. Jct US 30 and Story St, just e on US 30. Int corridors. **Pets:** Accepted.
SAVE S▢ ✕ ⟨M ⟨⟩ ▤ ▣ ⇌

BURLINGTON

AAA ▼▼▼ **Best Western Pzazz Fun City** SH
(319) 753-2223. **$79-$149, 30 day notice.** 3001 Winegard Dr. Jct US 61 and 34, just n. Int corridors. **Pets:** Other species. Designated rooms, service with restrictions, crate.
SAVE S▢ ✕ ⟨M ⟨⟩ ⟨⟩ ▤ ▣ ▥ ⇌ ✕⟩

▼▼▼ **Comfort Suites Hotel & Conference Center** SH
(319) 753-1300. **$79-$109.** 1780 Stonegate Center Dr. On US 61, 2 mi s of US 34. Int corridors. **Pets:** Accepted.
ASK S▢ ✕ ⟨M ⟨⟩ ▤ ▣ ▥ ⇌ ✕⟩

AAA ▼▼▼ **Quality Inn** SH
(319) 753-0000. **$65-$85.** 3051 Kirkwood Ave. Jct US 61 and 34, just n. Int corridors. **Pets:** Accepted.
SAVE S▢ ✕ ▤ ▣ ⇌

▼▼▼ **Super 8 Motel-Burlington** SH
(319) 752-9806. **$48-$79.** 3001 Kirkwood Ave. Jct US 61 and 34, just n. Int corridors. **Pets:** Small. $25 daily fee/pet. Service with restrictions, supervision.
ASK S▢ ✕ ▤

CARROLL

▼▼▼ **Super 8 Motel** SH
(712) 792-4753. **$60-$90.** 1757 US 71 N. Just n of jct US 30 and 71. Int corridors. **Pets:** $10 daily fee/pet. Designated rooms, service with restrictions, supervision.
ASK S▢ ✕

CARTER LAKE

AAA ▼▼▼▼ **Holiday Inn Express Hotel & Suites** SH
(402) 505-4900. **$80-$160.** 2510 Abbott Plaza. I-480 W, exit 4 to 10th St, 2 mi n, follow Eppley Airfield signs. Int corridors. **Pets:** Accepted.
SAVE S▢ ✕ ⟨M ⟨⟩ ⟨⟩ ▤ ▣ ⇌

AAA ▼▼▼▼ **La Quinta Inn & Suites** SH
(712) 347-6595. **$89-$139.** 1201 Ave H. I-480 W, exit 4 to 10th St, 2 mi n, follow Eppley Airfield signs. Int corridors. **Pets:** Medium.
SAVE S▢ ✕ ⟨M ⟨⟩ ⟨⟩ ▤ ▣ ⇌

AAA ▼▼▼ **Super 8 Motel** SH
(712) 347-5588. **$75-$90.** 3000 Airport Dr. I-480 W, exit 4 to 10th St, 2.3 mi n, follow Eppley Airfield signs. Int corridors. **Pets:** Accepted.
SAVE S▢ ✕ ⟨M ⟨⟩ ▤ ⇌

CEDAR FALLS

AAA ▼▼▼ **Days Inn** M
(319) 266-1222. **$59-$84.** 5826 University Ave, Suite 2. 0.7 mi e of jct SR 58. Int corridors. **Pets:** Accepted.
SAVE S▢ ✕ ▤ ▣

AAA ▼▼▼ **University Inn** SH
(319) 277-1412. **$45-$69.** 4711 University Ave. 1.6 mi e of jct SR 58. Ext/int corridors. **Pets:** $30 deposit/pet. Designated rooms, service with restrictions, crate.
SAVE S▢ ✕ ▤ ▣

CEDAR RAPIDS

▼▼ **Best Western Cooper's Mill Hotel & Restaurant** SH
(319) 366-5323. **$69-$89.** 100 F Ave NW. I-380, exit 19C northbound, take right at end of exit, make immediate U-turn and go under I-380; exit 20A southbound, cross river, right on 1st St NW. Int corridors. **Pets:** Medium, other species. $5 daily fee/pet. Service with restrictions, supervision.
ASK S▢ ✕ ▤ ▣ ▥ ⇌ ✕⟩

AAA ▼▼▼▼ **Best Western Longbranch Hotel & Convention Center** SH
(319) 377-6386. **$79-$99.** 90 Twixt Town Rd NE. I-380, exit 24A (SR 100/Collins Rd), 2.5 mi e, then just n. Int corridors. **Pets:** Medium, other species. $5 daily fee/pet. Designated rooms, service with restrictions, supervision.
SAVE S▢ ✕ ▤ ▣ ▥ ⇌ ✕⟩

AAA ▼▼▼ **Clarion Hotel & Convention Center** LH 🐾
(319) 366-8671. **$90-$97.** 525 33rd Ave SW. I-380, exit 17 (33rd Ave SW), just w. Int corridors. **Pets:** $15 one-time fee/room. Designated rooms, service with restrictions.
SAVE S▢ ✕ ⟨⟩ ▤ ▣ ▥ ⇌ ✕⟩

▼▼ ▼ **Comfort Inn by Choice Hotels North** SH
(319) 393-8247. **$75-$95.** 5055 Rockwell Dr NE. I-380, exit 24A (SR 100/Collins Rd), 1 mi e. Int corridors. **Pets:** Accepted.
ASK S▢ ✕ ⟨⟩ ▤ ▣

▼▼ ▼ **Comfort Inn by Choice Hotels-South** SH
(319) 363-7934. **$75-$95.** 390 33rd Ave SW. I-380, exit 17 (33rd Ave SW), just w. Int corridors. **Pets:** Accepted.
ASK S▢ ✕ ▤ ▣

AAA ▼▼▼ **Country Inn & Suites Cedar Rapids Airport** SH 🐾
(319) 363-3789. **$99-$129.** 9100 Atlantic Dr SW. I-380, exit 13, just w. Int corridors. **Pets:** Other species. $10 daily fee/pet. Service with restrictions, supervision.
SAVE S▢ ✕ ⟨M ⟨⟩ ▤ ▣ ⇌

AAA ▼▼▼ **Crowne Plaza Five Seasons** LH
(319) 363-8161. **$99-$179.** 350 1st Ave NE. I-380, exit 20B, just e; downtown. Int corridors. **Pets:** $25 one-time fee/room. Designated rooms, service with restrictions, supervision.
SAVE S▢ ✕ ⟨⟩ ▤ ▣ ▥ ⇌ ✕⟩

▼▼ **Economy Inn & Suites** SH
(319) 365-4339. **$49-$79.** 3245 Southgate Pl SW. I-380, exit 17 (33rd Ave SW), just w. Int corridors. **Pets:** Accepted.
ASK S▢ ✕ ⟨⟩ ▤ ▣ ⇌

AAA ▼▼▼ **Exel Inn of Cedar Rapids** M
(319) 366-2475. **$48-$78.** 616 33rd Ave SW. I-380, exit 17 (33rd Ave SW), 0.3 mi w. Int corridors. **Pets:** Small, other species. Designated rooms, service with restrictions, supervision.
SAVE S▢ ✕ ▤

▼▼▼ **Hawthorn Suites Ltd** SH
(319) 294-8700. **$95-$101.** 4444 Czech Ln NE. I-380, exit 24A (SR 100/Collins Rd), just s. Int corridors. **Pets:** Other species. Service with restrictions, crate.
ASK S▢ ✕ ⟨M ⟨⟩ ⟨⟩ ▤ ▣ ⇌

▼▼▼ **Mainstay Suites** SH
(319) 363-7829. **$75-$120.** 5145 Rockwell Dr NE. I-380, exit 24A (SR 100/Collins Rd), 1 mi e, then just n. Int corridors. **Pets:** Accepted.
ASK S▢ ✕ ⟨⟩ ▤ ▣ ⇌

AAA ▼▼▼▼ **Marriott Cedar Rapids** LH
(319) 393-6600. **$129-$199.** 1200 Collins Rd NE. I-380, exit 24A (SR 100/Collins Rd), 1 mi e. Int corridors. **Pets:** Accepted.
SAVE S▢ ✕ ⟨M ⟨⟩ ⟨⟩ ▤ ▣ ▥ ⇌

▼▼ Motel 6 #1485 M
(319) 366-7523. **$37-$57.** 3325 Southgate Ct SW. I-380, exit 17 (33rd Ave SW), just sw. Ext corridors. **Pets:** Medium, other species. Service with restrictions, supervision.
[S₀] [✕] [&M] [⌂] [🐾]

▲▲▲ ▼▼ Quality Inn of Cedar Rapids SH
(319) 393-8800. **$64-$110.** 4747 1st Ave SE. I-380, exit 24A (SR 100/Collins Rd), 2.5 mi e, then 1st Ave SE. Int corridors. **Pets:** Accepted.
[SAVE] [S₀] [✕] [&M] [⌂] [🐾] [🍴] [💻] [🏊]

▼▼ Ramada Limited SH
(319) 396-5000. **$75-$125.** 4011 16th Ave SW. I-380, exit 16 (US 30), 2.4 mi w, 1.4 mi n (exit 250) on Edgewood Rd to 16th Ave, then just w. Int corridors. **Pets:** Small. $10 daily fee/room. Service with restrictions, crate.
[A$K] [S₀] [✕] [&M] [🍴] [💻] [🏊]

▼▼ Ramada Limited Suites SH
(319) 378-8888. **$75-$135.** 2025 Werner Ave NE. I-380, exit 24A (SR 100/Collins Rd), just se. Int corridors. **Pets:** Small. Service with restrictions, supervision.
[A$K] [S₀] [✕] [🐾] [🍴] [💻] [🏊]

▼▼▼ Residence Inn by Marriott SH
(319) 395-0111. **$145-$165.** 1900 Dodge Rd NE. I-380, exit 24A (SR 100/Collins Rd), just e. Int corridors. **Pets:** Accepted.
[A$K] [S₀] [✕] [&M] [⌂] [🐾] [🍴] [💻] [🏊] [✕]

▼▼◆ Super 8 Motel SH
(319) 363-1755. **$65-$70.** 400 33rd Ave SW. I-380, exit 17 (33rd Ave SW), just w. Int corridors. **Pets:** Small, other species. $10 one-time fee/room. Designated rooms, service with restrictions, supervision.
[A$K] [S₀] [✕] [&M] [⌂] [🍴]

▼▼◆ Super 8 Motel SH
(319) 362-6002. **$65-$70.** 720 33rd Ave SW. I-380, exit 17 (33rd Ave SW), 0.4 mi w. Int corridors. **Pets:** Small, other species. $10 one-time fee/room. Designated rooms, service with restrictions, supervision.
[A$K] [S₀] [✕] [&M] [⌂] [🍴]

CHARLES CITY

▲▲▲ ▼▼◆ Hartwood Inn M
(641) 228-4352. **$40.** 1312 Gilbert St. Jct US 18 and CR B35, exit 212, 2.2 mi e. Ext corridors. **Pets:** Accepted.
[SAVE] [S₀] [✕] [&M] [🍴] [💻]

▼▼▼▼ Sleep Inn & Suites SH ❀
(641) 257-6700. **$60-$99.** 1416 S Grand Ave. Jct US 18 and 218 (exit 218), 0.7 mi n on US 218 business route; south side of town. Int corridors. **Pets:** Other species. $10 daily fee/pet. Designated rooms, service with restrictions, supervision.
[A$K] [S₀] [✕] [&M] [⌂] [🍴] [💻] [🏊] [✕]

▼▼ Super 8 Motel-Charles City SH ❀
(641) 228-2888. **$68-$74.** 1411 S Grand Ave. Jct US 18 and 218 (exit 118), 0.8 mi n on US 218 business route; south side of town. Int corridors. **Pets:** Medium. $10 one-time fee/pet. Service with restrictions, crate.
[A$K] [S₀] [✕] [&M] [🍴]

CHEROKEE

▲▲▲ ▼▼ Best Western La Grande Hacienda SH
(712) 225-5701. **$79-$89, 3 day notice.** 1401 N 2nd St. Jct US 59 and SR 3, 0.4 mi s. Int corridors. **Pets:** Medium, other species. $50 deposit/room. Service with restrictions, supervision.
[SAVE] [S₀] [✕] [&M] [⌂] [💻] [🍴] [🏊]

CLARINDA

▼▼ Clarinda Super 8 Motel SH
(712) 542-6333. **$55-$60.** 1203 S 12th St. Jct US 71 and SR 2, just e. Int corridors. **Pets:** Medium. Service with restrictions, supervision.
[A$K] [S₀] [✕] [&M] [⌂] [🍴] [💻] [🏊]

CLEAR LAKE

▼▼ AmericInn Lodge & Suites of Clear Lake SH
(641) 357-8954. **$69-$89.** 1406 25th St. I-35, exit 194 (SR 122). Int corridors. **Pets:** Other species. Service with restrictions, supervision.
[A$K] [✕] [⌂] [🍴] [💻] [🏊] [✕]

▲▲▲ ▼▼ Best Western Holiday Lodge SH
(641) 357-5253. **$64-$99.** 2023 7th Ave N. I-35, exit 194 (SR 122), 0.3 mi w. Ext/int corridors. **Pets:** Other species. $10 daily fee/room. Designated rooms, service with restrictions, crate.
[SAVE] [S₀] [✕] [&M] [⌂] [🍴] [💻] [🍴] [🏊]

▲▲▲ ▼▼▼ Budget Inn M
(641) 357-8700. **$45-$65.** 1306 N 25th St. I-35, exit 194 (US 18), just nw. Int corridors. **Pets:** Medium. $3 one-time fee/pet. Service with restrictions, supervision.
[SAVE] [S₀] [✕] [🍴] [🏊]

▼▼ Lake Country Inn M
(641) 357-2184. **$39-$64.** 518 Hwy 18. I-35, exit 194 (US 18), 2 mi w. Ext corridors. **Pets:** Accepted.
[A$K] [S₀] [✕] [🍴] [💻]

▼▼ Microtel Inn SH
(641) 357-0966. **$56-$91.** 1305 N 25th St. I-35, exit 194 (SR 122), just nw. Int corridors. **Pets:** Service with restrictions, supervision.
[A$K] [S₀] [✕] [&M] [⌂] [🍴] [💻]

▼▼ Super 8 Motel SH
(641) 357-7521. **$50-$80.** 2809 4th Ave S. I-35, exit 193, just e. Int corridors. **Pets:** Accepted.
[A$K] [S₀] [✕] [&M]

CLINTON

▲▲▲ ▼▼▼ Best Western-Frontier Motor Inn SH ❀
(563) 242-7112. **$69-$109.** 2300 Lincoln Way. On US 30, just e of jct US 30 and 67. Int corridors. **Pets:** Very small, other species. $10 daily fee/room. Service with restrictions.
[SAVE] [S₀] [✕] [&M] [⌂] [🍴] [💻] [🍴] [🏊] [✕]

▲▲▲ ▼▼▼▼ Country Inn & Suites By Carlson SH ❀
(563) 244-9922. **$69-$109.** 2224 Lincoln Way. On US 30, just e of jct US 30 and 67. Int corridors. **Pets:** Medium, other species. $10 daily fee/pet. Service with restrictions.
[SAVE] [S₀] [✕] [&M] [⌂] [🍴] [💻] [🏊]

▲▲▲ ▼▼◆ Oak Tree Inn SH
(563) 243-1000. **$65-$77.** 2300 Valley West Ct. Just n of jct US 30 and 67, west side of town. Int corridors. **Pets:** Accepted.
[SAVE] [S₀] [✕] [&M] [⌂] [🍴] [💻]

▼◆ Super 8 Motel-Clinton SH ❀
(563) 242-8870. **$52-$70.** 1711 Lincoln Way. On US 30, 0.7 mi e of jct US 67. Int corridors. **Pets:** Other species. $10 daily fee/pet, $10 one-time fee/pet. Service with restrictions, crate.
[A$K] [S₀] [✕] [&M] [⌂] [🍴]

CLIVE

▲▲▲ ▼▼▼▼ Best Western Clive Inn & Suites SH
(515) 221-2345. **$72-$95.** 1450 NW 118th St. I-80/35, exit 124 (University Ave), just nw. Int corridors. **Pets:** Accepted.
[SAVE] [S₀] [✕] [&M] [⌂] [🍴] [💻]

▲▲▲ ▼▼▼▼ Chase Suite Hotel by Woodfin SH
(515) 223-7700. **$119-$219.** 11428 Forest Ave. I-80/35, exit 124 (University Ave), just ne. Ext corridors. **Pets:** Other species. $10 deposit/pet. Service with restrictions, crate.
[SAVE] [S₀] [✕] [&M] [⌂] [🐾] [🍴] [💻] [🏊] [✕]

AAA ♦♦ La Quinta Inn & Suites West Des Moines-Clive **SH**
(515) 221-9200. **$85-$109.** 1390 NW 118th St. I-80/35, exit 124 (University Ave). Int corridors. **Pets:** Medium. Service with restrictions.
[SAVE] [X] [&M] [⊘] [🛏] [🖥] [🍴] [≋] [🛎]

COLFAX

AAA ♦♦ Comfort Inn **SH**
(515) 674-4455. **$59-$170.** 1402 N Walnut. I-80, exit 155, just ne. Int corridors. **Pets:** Accepted.
[SAVE] [S🐾] [X] [&M] [⊘] [🛏] [🖥] [≋] [🛎]

CORALVILLE

♦♦ Days Inn **M**
(319) 354-4400. **$59-$129.** 205 2nd St. I-80, exit 242, 1 mi s to 2nd St, then just w. Ext corridors. **Pets:** Accepted.
[ASK] [S🐾] [X] [🛏]

AAA ♦♦ Super 8 Motel-Iowa City **SH** 🐾
(319) 337-8388. **$67-$70.** 611 1st Ave. I-80, exit 242, 0.4 mi s. Int corridors. **Pets:** $10 daily fee/pet. Designated rooms, service with restrictions, supervision.
[SAVE] [S🐾] [X] [&M] [⊘] [🛏]

COUNCIL BLUFFS

AAA ♦♦ Best Western Crossroads of the Bluffs **SH**
(712) 322-3150. **$79-$140.** 2216 27th Ave. I-29/80, exit 1B (24th St), just ne. Int corridors. **Pets:** Accepted.
[SAVE] [S🐾] [X] [⊘] [&M] [🛏] [🖥] [≋]

♦♦ Days Inn **SH**
(712) 366-9699. **$45-$70, 14 day notice.** 3208 S 7th St. I-29/80, exit 3 (US 92), just sw. Int corridors. **Pets:** Accepted.
[ASK] [S🐾] [X] [⊘] [🛏] [🖥] [🍴]

AAA ♦♦ Days Inn **SH**
(712) 323-2200. **$55-$100.** 3619 9th Ave. I-29, exit 53A (9th Ave). Int corridors. **Pets:** Accepted.
[SAVE] [S🐾] [X] [⊘] [🛏] [🖥]

♦ Motel 6 Council Bluffs, IA #1153 **SH**
(712) 366-2405. **$51-$71.** 3032 S Expressway St. I-29/80, exit 3 (US 92). Int corridors. **Pets:** Medium, other species. Service with restrictions, supervision.
[S🐾] [X] [⊘] [&M] [🛏] [🖥] [≋]

AAA ♦♦ Quality Inn & Suites **SH**
(712) 328-3171. **$70-$80.** 3537 W Broadway. I-29, exit 53A (9th Ave), just e, 0.5 mi n on S 35th St, then just w. Ext/int corridors. **Pets:** Other species. $10 daily fee/room. Service with restrictions.
[SAVE] [S🐾] [X] [⊘] [&M] [🛏] [🖥] [≋]

♦ Super 8 Motel **SH**
(712) 322-2888. **$60-$66.** 2712 S 24th St. I-29/80, exit 1B (24th St), just nw. Int corridors. **Pets:** No service, supervision.
[ASK] [S🐾] [X] [🛏]

AAA ♦♦ Western Inn **SH**
(712) 322-4499. **$65-$86.** 1842 Madison Ave. I-80, exit 5 (Madison Ave), just s. Int corridors. **Pets:** Small. $10 one-time fee/room. Service with restrictions, supervision.
[SAVE] [S🐾] [X] [&M] [🛏] [≋]

CRESCO

AAA ♦ Cresco Motel **M**
(563) 547-2240. **$50-$83.** 620 2nd Ave SE. On SR 9; on east side of town. Ext corridors. **Pets:** Other species. Service with restrictions, supervision.
[SAVE] [S🐾] [X] [&M] [⊘] [🛏]

CRESTON

♦♦ Super 8 Motel-Creston **SH**
(641) 782-6541. **$60-$78, 7 day notice.** 804 W Taylor. Jct US 34 and SR 25, on US 34. Int corridors. **Pets:** $20 one-time fee/pet. Service with restrictions, supervision.
[ASK] [X] [&M] [⊘] [🛏]

DENISON

♦♦ Denison Super 8 **SH**
(712) 263-5081. **$54-$64.** 502 Boyer Valley Rd. Jct US 30/59 and SR 141, 0.3 mi sw. Int corridors. **Pets:** Accepted.
[ASK] [S🐾] [X] [🛏]

DES MOINES

AAA ♦♦ Baymont Inn & Suites **SH**
(515) 265-4777. **$69-$112.** 4685 NE 14th St. I-80, exit 136 (US 69), just s. Int corridors. **Pets:** Accepted.
[SAVE] [X] [🛏] [🖥] [🍴] [≋] [🛎]

AAA ♦♦♦ Best Western Des Moines Airport **SH**
(515) 287-6464. **$115.** 1810 Army Post Rd. Across from airport. Int corridors. **Pets:** Accepted.
[SAVE] [S🐾] [X] [&M] [⊘] [🛏] [🖥] [🍴] [≋]

♦♦ Comfort Inn by Choice Hotels **SH**
(515) 287-3434. **$80-$100.** 5231 Fleur Dr. Opposite the airport. Int corridors. **Pets:** Accepted.
[ASK] [S🐾] [X] [&M] [⊘] [🛏] [🖥] [≋]

♦♦ Motel 6–30 **M**
(515) 287-6364. **$43-$58.** 4817 Fleur Dr. Opposite the airport. Ext corridors. **Pets:** Medium, other species. Service with restrictions, supervision.
[S🐾] [X] [⊘] [🛏]

AAA ♦♦♦ Quality Inn & Suites Event Center **LH**
(515) 282-5251. **$69-$179.** 929 3rd St. I-235, exit 3rd St; downtown. Int corridors. **Pets:** Accepted.
[SAVE] [S🐾] [X] [⊘] [&M] [🛏] [🖥] [🍴] [≋]

AAA ♦♦ Red Roof Inn & Suites **SH**
(515) 266-6800. **$66-$82.** 4950 NE 14th St. I-80, exit 136 (US 69). Int corridors. **Pets:** Medium, other species. Service with restrictions, supervision.
[SAVE] [S🐾] [X] [&M] [⊘] [🛏] [🖥] [≋]

♦♦ Super 8 Motel **SH**
(515) 278-8858. **$45-$80.** 4755 Merle Hay Rd. I-80/35, exit 131 (Merle Hay Rd), just s. Int corridors. **Pets:** Accepted.
[ASK] [S🐾] [X] [🛏]

DE SOTO

♦ Edgetowner Motel **M**
(515) 834-2641. **$48-$50.** 804 Guthrie. I-80, exit 110, just s. Ext corridors. **Pets:** Dogs only. $5 daily fee/room. Service with restrictions, crate.
[S🐾] [X] [🛏]

DUBUQUE

AAA ♦♦♦ Best Western Midway Hotel **LH**
(563) 557-8000. **$79-$129.** 3100 Dodge St. US 20, 2.3 mi w of jct US 52/61/151 and Mississippi Bridge. Int corridors. **Pets:** Medium. Designated rooms, service with restrictions, supervision.
[SAVE] [S🐾] [X] [⊘] [🛏] [🖥] [🍴] [≋] [🛎]

♦♦ Comfort Inn by Choice Hotels **SH**
(563) 556-3006. **$70-$90.** 4055 McDonald Dr. US 20, 3.8 mi w of jct US 52/61/151 and Mississippi Bridge. Int corridors. **Pets:** Accepted.
[ASK] [S🐾] [X] [⊘] [🛏] [🖥] [≋]

AAA ▼▼▼ Holiday Inn Dubuque/Galena LH
(563) 556-2000. **$90-$120.** 450 Main St. At Main and 4th sts; downtown. Int corridors. **Pets:** Accepted.
[SAVE] [S♦] [✕] [♿] [♦] [▯] [▭] [¶] [≈] [✕]

▼▼▼ MainStay Suites SH
(563) 557-7829. **$89-$114.** 1275 Associates Dr. Just n of jct US 20 and NW Arterial Rd; west side of town. Int corridors. **Pets:** Small, other species. $100 deposit/room. Service with restrictions, crate.
[ASK] [S♦] [✕] [♿] [♦] [▯] [▭]

DYERSVILLE

▼▼ Comfort Inn-Dyersville SH
(563) 875-7700. **$75-$159.** 527 16th Ave SE. US 20, exit 294 (SR 136), just nw. Int corridors. **Pets:** Medium. $13 daily fee/room. Service with restrictions, supervision.
[ASK] [S♦] [✕] [♿] [▯] [▭] [≈] [✕]

◆ ▼ Super 8 Motel-Dyersville SH
(563) 875-8885. **$49-$110.** 925 15th Ave SE. US 20, exit 294 (SR 136), just n. Int corridors. **Pets:** Supervision.
[ASK] [S♦] [✕] [♿] [▯] [▭]

ELDRIDGE

AAA ▼▼▼ Quality Inn & Suites SH ❀
(563) 285-4600. **$69-$139.** 1000 E Iowa St. I-80, exit 295B (US 61), 4 mi n to exit 127 (CR F45). Int corridors. **Pets:** Small, dogs only. $13 daily fee/room. Designated rooms, service with restrictions, crate.
[SAVE] [S♦] [✕] [♿] [▯] [▭] [≈] [✕]

ELK HORN

▼▼ AmericInn Motel & Suites SH
(712) 764-4000. **$76-$80.** 4037 Main St. I-80, exit 54 (SR 173), 6.4 mi n. Int corridors. **Pets:** Other species. $15 daily fee/room. Designated rooms, service with restrictions, supervision.
[ASK] [S♦] [✕] [♿] [♦] [▯] [▭] [≈]

ESTHERVILLE

AAA ▼▼▼ Sleep Inn & Suites SH
(712) 362-5522. **$89-$109.** 2008 Central Ave. Jct SR 4 and 9, 1 mi e. Int corridors. **Pets:** $15 one-time fee/room. Service with restrictions, supervision.
[SAVE] [S♦] [✕] [♿] [▯] [▭] [≈]

▼▼ Super 8 Motel SH
(712) 362-2400. **$50-$60.** 1919 Central Ave. Jct SR 4 and 9, 1 mi e. Int corridors. **Pets:** Medium. $4 daily fee/pet. Supervision.
[ASK] [S♦] [✕] [♿] [▯] [▭]

EVANSDALE

▼▼ Days Inn SH
(319) 235-1111. **$89.** 450 Evansdale Dr. I-380/20, exit 68, just n. Int corridors. **Pets:** Small. $10 daily fee/pet. Service with restrictions.
[ASK] [S♦] [✕] [♿] [▯] [▭] [≈]

FAIRFIELD

AAA ▼▼▼ Best Western Fairfield Inn SH
(641) 472-2200. **$89-$109.** 2200 W Burlington Ave. On US 34, 1 mi w of jct SR 1. Int corridors. **Pets:** Accepted.
[SAVE] [S♦] [✕] [♿] [▯] [▭] [¶] [≈]

AAA ▼▼▼ Super 8 Motel SH
(641) 469-2000. **$57-$68.** 3001 W Burlington Ave. On US 34, 1.5 mi w of jct SR 1. Int corridors. **Pets:** Medium. $50 deposit/room, $5 daily fee/pet. Designated rooms, service with restrictions, supervision.
[SAVE] [S♦] [✕] [♿] [▯] [▭] [≈]

FORT DODGE

AAA ▼▼▼ Comfort Inn SH
(515) 573-5000. **$80-$150.** 2938 5th Ave S. US 20, exit 124 (Coalville), 3.5 mi n on CR P59, then 1.3 mi w on 5th Ave and Business Rt US 20. Int corridors. **Pets:** Accepted.
[SAVE] [S♦] [✕] [♿] [▯] [▭] [≈]

▼▼ Days Inn SH
(515) 576-8000. **$50-$70.** 3040 5th Ave S. US 20, exit 124 (Coalville), 3.5 mi n on CR P59, then 1.2 mi w on Business Rt US 20. Int corridors. **Pets:** $25 daily fee/room. Designated rooms, service with restrictions, supervision.
[ASK] [S♦] [✕] [♿] [▭]

FORT MADISON

AAA ▼▼▼ Comfort Inn & Suites SH
(319) 372-6800. **$90, 3 day notice.** 6169 Reve Ct S 61. Just e of jct US 61 and SR 2, on US 61. Int corridors. **Pets:** Other species. $25 daily fee/room. Designated rooms, service with restrictions, crate.
[SAVE] [S♦] [✕] [♿] [▯] [▭] [≈] [✕]

AAA ▼▼▼ Knights Inn M
(319) 372-7740. **$45-$120, 7 day notice.** 3440 Ave L. 2.1 mi e of jct US 61 and SR 2. Ext corridors. **Pets:** Medium. $10 daily fee/pet. Designated rooms, no service, crate.
[SAVE] [S♦] [✕] [▯] [▭]

▼▼ Super 8 Motel-Ft Madison SH
(319) 372-8500. **$53-$69.** US 61 W, 5107 Ave O. 1 mi e of jct US 61 and SR 2. Ext/int corridors. **Pets:** $10 daily fee/room. Service with restrictions, supervision.
[ASK] [S♦] [✕] [♦] [▯]

GRIMES

▼▼ AmericInn Lodge & Suites SH ❀
(515) 986-9900. **$69-$164.** 251 Gateway. Just sw of jct US 44 and SR 141. Int corridors. **Pets:** Medium, dogs only. $50 deposit/room, $10 daily fee/room. Designated rooms, service with restrictions, supervision.
[ASK] [✕] [♿] [♦] [▯] [▭] [≈] [✕]

HAMPTON

▼▼ AmericInn Lodge & Suites SH ❀
(641) 456-5559. **$76-$130.** 702 Central Ave W. On SR 3 (Central Ave W), 0.7 mi w of jct US 65 and SR 3. Int corridors. **Pets:** Medium. $50 deposit/pet, $10 one-time fee/pet. Designated rooms, service with restrictions, supervision.
[ASK] [✕] [♦] [♦] [▯] [▭] [≈] [✕]

▼▼ Country Heritage Bed & Breakfast BB
(641) 456-4036. **$65-$100, 15 day notice.** 1034 Hwy 3. I-35, exit 165, 4 mi e. Int corridors. **Pets:** Accepted.
[✕] [▭] [☎]

IDA GROVE

▼ Delux Motel M
(712) 364-3317. **$45-$60.** 5981 US Hwy 175. Jct US 59 S and 175. Ext corridors. **Pets:** $10 daily fee/pet. Designated rooms, service with restrictions, supervision.
[✕] [▯]

INDEPENDENCE

▼▼ Super 8 Motel SH
(319) 334-7041. **$65-$135.** 2000 1st St W. US 20, exit 252, 1.4 mi n. Int corridors. **Pets:** Small. $10 daily fee/pet. Service with restrictions, crate.
[ASK] [S♦] [✕] [♿] [▯]

IOWA CITY

▼▼▼▼ hotelVetro conference center **SH**
(319) 337-4961. **$139-$349.** 201 S Linn St. I-80, exit 244, s on Dubuque St, e on Washington St, then s. Int corridors. **Pets:** Accepted.
⊠ 🗐 📺 🏊

ⒶⒶⒶ ▼▼▼ Quality Inn & Suites **LH** ❀
(319) 354-2000. **$69-$139.** 2525 N Dodge. I-80, exit 246, just ne. Int corridors. **Pets:** Medium, other species. $10 one-time fee/room. Service with restrictions, supervision.
SAVE 🗐 ⊠ 👌 📺 🗐 📺 🍴 🏊 ⊠

ⒶⒶⒶ ▼▼▼▼ Sheraton Iowa City Hotel **LH** ❀
(319) 337-4058. **$99-$299.** 210 S Dubuque St. Dubuque and Burlington sts (SR 1); downtown. Int corridors. **Pets:** Medium, dogs only. Service with restrictions, supervision.
SAVE ⊠ 👌 🗂 🗐 🗐 📺 🍴 🏊 ⊠

JOHNSTON

ⒶⒶⒶ ▼▼▼ America's Best Inn **SH**
(515) 270-1111. **$50-$89.** 5050 Merle Hay Rd. I-80/35, exit 131 (Merle Hay Rd), just n. Int corridors. **Pets:** Accepted.
SAVE 🗐 ⊠ 👌 🗂 🗐 📺 🏊

ⒶⒶⒶ ▼▼▼ Best Western-Des Moines North **SH**
(515) 276-5411. **$67-$78.** 5055 Merle Hay Rd. I-35/80, exit 131 (Merle Hay Rd), just n. Int corridors. **Pets:** Accepted.
SAVE 🗐 ⊠ 🗂 🗐 📺 🍴 🏊

KEOKUK

▼▼▼▼ Hampton Inn **SH**
(319) 524-6700. **$89-$129.** 3201 Main St. 1.8 mi n of jct US 136. Int corridors. **Pets:** Accepted.
ASK 🗐 ⊠ 👌 🗐 📺 🏊

▼▼▼ Super 8 Motel-Keokuk **SH**
(319) 524-3888. **$53-$79.** 3511 Main St. On Business US 61/US 218, 2 mi n of jct US 136. Int corridors. **Pets:** $10 daily fee/room. Service with restrictions, supervision.
ASK 🗐 ⊠ 👌 🗐 📺

LE CLAIRE

ⒶⒶⒶ ▼▼▼ Comfort Inn & Suites-Riverview **SH**
(563) 289-4747. **$70-$160.** 902 Mississippi View Ct. I-80, exit 306 (US 67), 0.5 mi n to Eagle Ridge Rd, then just sw. Int corridors. **Pets:** Large. $25 deposit/room. Service with restrictions, crate.
SAVE 🗐 ⊠ 👌 🗐 🗐 📺 🏊

ⒶⒶⒶ ▼▼▼▼ Holiday Inn Express **SH**
(563) 289-9978. **$89-$149.** 1201 Canal Shore Dr. I-80, exit 306, just n. Int corridors. **Pets:** $12 daily fee/pet. Service with restrictions, supervision.
SAVE 🗐 ⊠ 🗐 🗐 📺 🏊

ⒶⒶⒶ ▼▼▼ Super 8 of LeClaire **SH**
(563) 289-5888. **$62-$110.** 1552 Welcome Center Dr. I-80, exit 306 (US 67), 0.5 mi n to Eagle Ridge Rd, then just sw to Mississippi View Ct. Int corridors. **Pets:** Large. $25 deposit/room. Service with restrictions.
SAVE 🗐 ⊠ 👌 🗐 🗐

LE MARS

▼▼▼ Super 8 Motel **SH**
(712) 546-8800. **$50-$75.** 1201 Hawkeye Ave SW. 1.2 mi s of jct US 75/SR 3, on US 75; south end of town. Int corridors. **Pets:** Medium, dogs only. $10 daily fee/pet. Designated rooms, service with restrictions, supervision.
ASK 🗐 ⊠ 👌 🗐 📺 🏊

MANCHESTER

▼▼▼ ▼▼ Super 8 of Manchester **SH**
(563) 927-2533. **$62-$100.** 1020 W Main. Jct US 20 and SR 13, exit 275, 1.3 mi n, then 0.3 mi e. Int corridors. **Pets:** $10 one-time fee/room. Designated rooms, service with restrictions, supervision.
ASK ⊠ 🗐 📺

MARION

▼▼ ▼▼ Microtel Inn & Suites **SH**
(319) 373-7400. **$55-$80.** 5500 Dyer Ave. Jct US 151 and SR 13. Int corridors. **Pets:** Small. $50 deposit/pet. Service with restrictions, supervision.
ASK 🗐 ⊠ 👌 🗐 📺

MARQUETTE

▼▼ The Frontier Motel **M**
(563) 873-3497. **$50-$110.** 101 S 1st St. Just s of jct US 18 and SR 76; between Mississippi River Bridge and casino. Ext corridors. **Pets:** Accepted.
⊠ 🗐 📺 🏊

MARSHALLTOWN

▼▼▼ ▼ Best Western Regency Inn **SH**
(641) 752-6321. **$80-$95.** 3303 S Center St. Jct US 30 and SR 14. Int corridors. **Pets:** Other species. $10 one-time fee/room. Service with restrictions, supervision.
ASK 🗐 ⊠ 👌 🗂 🗐 🗐 📺 🍴 🏊

▼▼ ▼▼ Comfort Inn **SH**
(641) 752-6000. **$70-$85.** 2613 S Center St. 0.5 mi n of jct US 30 and SR 14. Int corridors. **Pets:** $10 one-time fee/room.
ASK 🗐 ⊠ 👌 🗂 🗐 🗐 📺

▼▼ ▼▼ Super 8 Motel **SH**
(641) 753-3333. **$57-$70.** 3315 S Center St. Just n of jct US 30 and SR 14. Int corridors. **Pets:** $10 one-time fee/room.
ASK 🗐 ⊠ 🗂 🗐 📺

MASON CITY

ⒶⒶⒶ ▼▼▼ Americas Best Value Inn **M**
(641) 424-2910. **$40-$69.** 24 5th St SW. Just w of jct US 65 and SR 122; just s of downtown. Ext/int corridors. **Pets:** Other species. Crate.
SAVE 🗐 ⊠ 🗐 🏊

▼▼ ▼▼ Days Inn Mason City **SH**
(641) 424-0210. **$54-$66.** 2301 4th St SW. I-35, exit 194 (SR 122), 6 mi e. Int corridors. **Pets:** $10 one-time fee/room. Service with restrictions.
ASK 🗐 ⊠ 🗐 🗐

ⒶⒶⒶ ▼▼▼▼ Holiday Inn **SH** ❀
(641) 423-1640. **$74-$92.** 2101 4th St SW (Hwy 122). I-35, exit 194 (SR 122), 6 mi e. Ext/int corridors. **Pets:** $15 one-time fee/room. Service with restrictions, crate.
SAVE 🗐 ⊠ 👌 🗐 🗐 📺 🍴 🏊 ⊠

MISSOURI VALLEY

ⒶⒶⒶ ▼▼▼ Oak Tree Inn **SH**
(712) 642-3000. **$89-$109.** 128 S Willow Rd. I-29, exit 75, just ne. Int corridors. **Pets:** Small. $5 one-time fee/room. Service with restrictions, supervision.
SAVE 🗐 ⊠ 👌 🗐 🗐 📺 🍴

MONTICELLO

▼▼ ▼▼ The Blue Inn **SH**
(319) 465-6116. **$56-$105.** 250 N Main St. North end of town on Business Rt US 151. Int corridors. **Pets:** Other species. $20 deposit/room, $6 daily fee/pet. Designated rooms, service with restrictions, supervision.
ASK 🗐 ⊠ 📺 🍴 🏊

MOUNT PLEASANT

▼▼▼ **Brazelton Hotel** 🆂🅷
(319) 385-8803. **$71-$127.** 1200 E Baker. US 218/27, exit 45, 0.6 mi s on Grand Ave. Int corridors. **Pets:** Medium. $8 daily fee/room. Designated rooms, service with restrictions, supervision.
🅰🆂🅺 🆂🔌 ⊠ 🖉 🖵 🖥 💻 ⊇ ⊠

▼▼ **Super 8 Motel-Mt Pleasant** 🆂🅷
(319) 385-8888. **$55-$60.** 1000 N Grand Ave. US 218/27, exit 45, 0.6 mi s. Int corridors. **Pets:** Small. $10 daily fee/pet. Service with restrictions, supervision.
🅰🆂🅺 🆂🔌 ⊠ 🖥 💻

MOUNT VERNON

🔷🔷🔷 **Sleep Inn & Suites** 🆂🅷
(319) 895-0055. **$74-$120.** 310 Virgil Ave. Jct US 30 and SR 1, just se. Int corridors. **Pets:** $13 one-time fee/room. Service with restrictions, supervision.
🆂🄰🅅🄴 🆂🔌 ⊠ 🖵 💻 ⊇

MUSCATINE

▼▼ **Super 8 Motel-Muscatine** 🆂🅷
(563) 263-9100. **$53-$64.** 2900 N Hwy 61. Jct US 61 and SR 38. Int corridors. **Pets:** Other species. $5 daily fee/room. Service with restrictions, supervision.
🅰🆂🅺 🆂🔌 ⊠ 🖉 🖥

NEWTON

▼▼ **Days Inn of Newton** 🆂🅷
(641) 792-2330. **$75-$140.** 1605 W 19th St S. I-80, exit 164 (SR 14), just n. Int corridors. **Pets:** Medium, other species. $10 daily fee/room. Service with restrictions, supervision.
🅰🆂🅺 🆂🔌 ⊠ 🖵 🖥 💻

🔷🔷🔷 **Quality Inn of Newton Iowa** 🆂🅷
(641) 792-7722. **$90.** 1700 W 19th St S. I-80, exit 164 (SR 14), just nw. Int corridors. **Pets:** Medium. $15 daily fee/room. Designated rooms, service with restrictions, supervision.
🆂🄰🅅🄴 🆂🔌 ⊠ 🖵 🖥 💻 ⊇

🔷🔷🔷🔷 **HomeRidge Inn & Suites** 🆂🅷
(641) 792-3333. **$105-$115.** 208 W 4th St N. Downtown. Int corridors. **Pets:** Accepted.
🆂🄰🅅🄴 🆂🔌 ⊠ 🔌 🖵 🖥 💻 ⊇

🔷🔷🔷 **Ramada Limited** 🆂🅷
(641) 792-8100. **$49-$140.** 1405 W 19th St S. I-80, exit 164 (SR 14), just n. Int corridors. **Pets:** Accepted.
🆂🄰🅅🄴 🆂🔌 ⊠ 🖥 💻

OELWEIN

▼▼ **Super 8 Motel-Oelwein** 🅼
(319) 283-2888. **$65-$135.** 210 10th St SE. Jct SR 3 and 150, 1 mi s. Int corridors. **Pets:** $10 daily fee/pet. Service with restrictions, crate.
🅰🆂🅺 🆂🔌 ⊠ 🖥 💻

OKOBOJI

▼▼ **AmericInn Lodge & Suites** 🆂🅷
(712) 332-9000. **$75-$195, 7 day notice.** 1005 Brooks Park Dr. Jct US 71 and SR 9, 2.5 mi s on US 71. Int corridors. **Pets:** Dogs only. $50 deposit/room, $10 one-time fee/room. Service with restrictions, supervision.
⊠ 🔌 🖵 🖥 💻 ⊇

▼▼▼ **Arrowwood Resort & Conference Center** 🆂🅷
(712) 332-2161. **$89-$189, 7 day notice.** 1405 US 71 S. Jct US 71 and SR 9, 3 mi s. Ext/int corridors. **Pets:** Accepted.
🅰🆂🅺 🆂🔌 ⊠ 🖵 🖉 🖵 🖥 💻 🍽 ⊇ ⊠

OSCEOLA

▼▼ **AmericInn Lodge & Suites** 🆂🅷
(641) 342-9400. **$79-$164.** 111 Ariel Cir. I-35, exit 33. Int corridors. **Pets:** Medium. $50 deposit/pet, $10 one-time fee/pet. Designated rooms, service with restrictions, supervision.
🅰🆂🅺 🆂🔌 ⊠ 🖵 🖵 🖥 💻 ⊇

▼▼ **Days Inn** 🆂🅷
(641) 342-6666. **$90.** 710 Warren Ave. I-35, exit 33, just e. Int corridors. **Pets:** $10 daily fee/pet. Designated rooms, no service, supervision.
🅰🆂🅺 🆂🔌 ⊠ 🖵 🖥 💻 ⊇

OSKALOOSA

🔷🔷 ▼▼ **Americas Best Value Inn** 🅼
(641) 673-8351. **$59-$69.** 1315 A Ave E. On SR 92, just w of jct SR 23. Ext/int corridors. **Pets:** Medium, dogs only. $5 daily fee/pet. Designated rooms, service with restrictions, supervision.
🆂🄰🅅🄴 🆂🔌 ⊠ 🖥 💻

▼▼ **Comfort Inn** 🆂🅷
(641) 676-6000. **$84-$260.** 2401 A Ave W. SR 163, exit 57 (SR 92), just e. Int corridors. **Pets:** Medium. $10 daily fee/pet. Designated rooms, service with restrictions, supervision.
🅰🆂🅺 🆂🔌 ⊠ 🖵 🖥 💻 ⊇

▼▼ **Super 8 Motel-Oskaloosa** 🆂🅷
(641) 673-8481. **$60-$80.** 306 S 17th St. Just s of SR 92 and 23. Int corridors. **Pets:** Small. $10 daily fee/pet. Designated rooms, service with restrictions, supervision.
🅰🆂🅺 🆂🔌 ⊠ 🖵 🖥 💻

OTTUMWA

▼▼ **Days Inn** 🆂🅷
(641) 683-3000. **$65-$75.** 2824 N Court St. On US 63; north side of town. Int corridors. **Pets:** Small. $10 daily fee/pet. Designated rooms, service with restrictions, supervision.
🅰🆂🅺 🆂🔌 ⊠ 🖵 🖥 💻 ⊇

▼▼ **Super 8 Motel** 🆂🅷
(641) 684-5055. **$65-$79.** 2823 N Court Rd. Jct US 63 and 34, 1.8 mi n. Int corridors. **Pets:** Small. $10 daily fee/pet. Service with restrictions, supervision.
🅰🆂🅺 🆂🔌 ⊠ 🖥 💻 ⊇ ⊠

PELLA

▼▼▼ **Comfort Inn & Suites** 🆂🅷
(641) 621-1421. **$80-$95.** 910 W 16th St. SR 163, exit 40, just s. Int corridors. **Pets:** Accepted.
🅰🆂🅺 🆂🔌 ⊠ 🖵 🖵 🖥 💻 ⊇

▼▼ **Super 8 Motel-Pella** 🆂🅷
(641) 628-8181. **$45-$90.** 105 E Oskaloosa St. SR 163, exit 42, 1 mi n, then 0.5 mi e. Int corridors. **Pets:** Other species. $5 one-time fee/room. Designated rooms, service with restrictions, crate.
🅰🆂🅺 🆂🔌 ⊠ 🖵 🖉 🖥 💻

PERCIVAL

AAA ▼▼▼ Americas Best Value Inn & Suites SH
(712) 382-2100. **$65-$120.** 2113 Sapp Brothers Dr. I-29, exit 10 (SR 2), just w. Int corridors. **Pets:** Small, dogs only. $10 daily fee/pet. Service with restrictions, supervision.
SAVE S🐾 ✕ 🐾 🎁 💻 🏊

AAA ▼▼ Nebraska City Super 8 Motel SH
(712) 382-2828. **$50-$75.** 2103 249th St. I-29, exit 10, just w. Int corridors. **Pets:** $10 one-time fee/room. Supervision.
SAVE S🐾 ✕ 🐾M 🐾 🎁 💻

PLEASANT HILL

AAA ▼▼▼▼ Sleep Inn & Suites SH
(515) 299-9922. **$79-$189.** 5850 Morning Star Ct. US 65, exit 79 (SR 163/E University Ave), just e. Int corridors. **Pets:** Large, other species. $13 daily fee/room. Service with restrictions, supervision.
SAVE S🐾 ✕ 🐾 🎁 💻 🏊

QUAD CITIES AREA

BETTENDORF

▼▼▼ The Lodge-Hotel & Conference Center LH
(563) 359-7141. **$90-$176.** 900 Spruce Hills Dr. I-74, exit 2, just e. Int corridors. **Pets:** Accepted.
ASK S🐾 ✕ 🐾 🎁 💻 🍽 🏊 ✕

▼▼▼ Ramada Inn SH
(563) 355-7575. **$79-$109.** 3020 Utica Ridge Rd. I-74, exit 2, just e. Int corridors. **Pets:** Medium. $10 one-time fee/pet. Designated rooms, service with restrictions, crate.
ASK S🐾 ✕ 🐾M 🎁 💻 🏊 ✕

DAVENPORT

▼▼ Baymont Inn & Suites Davenport SH
(563) 386-1600. **$75-$89.** 400 Jason Way Ct. I-80, exit 295A (US 61), just s to 65th St, then 0.5 mi ne on frontage road. Int corridors. **Pets:** Medium. Service with restrictions.
ASK ✕ 🐾 🐾 🎁 💻 🏊

AAA ▼▼▼ Best Western SteepleGate Inn SH
(563) 386-6900. **$89-$119.** 100 W 76th St. I-80, exit 295A (US 61), 0.5 mi s to 65th St and West frontage road entrance, then just nw. Int corridors. **Pets:** Accepted.
SAVE S🐾 ✕ 🐾 🎁 💻 🍽 🏊 ✕

AAA ▼▼▼▼ Clarion Hotel & Conference Center SH
(563) 391-1230. **$69-$109.** 5202 Brady St. I-80, exit 295A (US 61), 1.6 mi s. Int corridors. **Pets:** Medium, other species. $10 one-time fee/room. Service with restrictions, supervision.
SAVE S🐾 ✕ 🐾M 🐾 🎁 💻 🍽 🏊 ✕

▼▼▼ Country Inn & Suites by Carlson SH
(563) 388-6444. **$115-$135.** 140 E 55th St. I-80, exit 295A (US 61), 1.4 mi s. Int corridors. **Pets:** Accepted.
ASK S🐾 ✕ 🐾M 🐾 🎁 💻 🏊

AAA ▼▼▼ Davenport Super 8 Motel SH
(563) 388-9810. **$57-$70, 7 day notice.** 410 E 65th St. I-80, exit 295A (US 61), 0.5 mi s, then just e. Int corridors. **Pets:** Other species. $5 daily fee/pet. Service with restrictions.
SAVE ✕ 🐾M 🎁 💻

▼▼▼ Econolodge Inn & Suites SH 🐾
(563) 391-8222. **$55-$75.** 7222 Northwest Blvd. I-80, exit 292 (North-west Blvd), 0.3 mi s. Ext corridors. **Pets:** Large, other species. $5 daily fee/pet. Service with restrictions, supervision.
ASK S🐾 ✕ 🐾 🎁 💻

AAA ▼▼▼ Exel Inn of Davenport SH
(563) 386-6350. **$46-$76.** 6310 N Brady St. I-80, exit 295A (US 61), 0.5 mi s; use frontage road on west side. Int corridors. **Pets:** Small, other species. Designated rooms, service with restrictions, supervision.
SAVE S🐾 ✕ 🐾 🎁 💻

▼▼▼ Fairfield Inn by Marriott SH
(563) 355-2264. **$95-$115.** 3206 E Kimberly Rd. I-74, exit 2, just w. Int corridors. **Pets:** Accepted.
ASK S🐾 ✕ 🐾 🎁 💻 🏊

▼▼▼ Howard Johnson Plaza Hotel LH
(563) 326-1786. **$49-$99.** 227 LeClare St. Downtown. Int corridors. **Pets:** Other species. $20 one-time fee/room. Designated rooms, no service, supervision.
ASK S🐾 ✕ 🐾 🎁 💻 🍽 🏊 ✕

AAA ▼▼▼ La Quinta Inn SH
(563) 359-3921. **$79.** 3330 E Kimberly Rd. I-74, exit 2, just w, then just s. Int corridors. **Pets:** Other species. Service with restrictions, crate.
SAVE S🐾 ✕ 🎁 💻 🏊

▼▼▼▼ Residence Inn by Marriott SH
(563) 391-8877. **$150-$170.** 120 E 55th St. I-80, exit 295 (US 61), 1.4 mi s. Int corridors. **Pets:** Accepted.
ASK S🐾 ✕ 🐾M 🐾 🎁 💻 🏊 ✕

END AREA

RED OAK

AAA ▼▼▼ Super 8-Red Oak SH
(712) 623-6919. **$71-$84.** 800 Senate Ave. Just e of jct US 34 and SR 48 on US 34. Int corridors. **Pets:** Other species. $5 daily fee/pet. Service with restrictions, supervision.
SAVE S🐾 ✕ 🎁 🏊

SIBLEY

▼▼ Super 8 Motel SH
(712) 754-3603. **$54-$63.** 1108 2nd Ave. On SR 60. Int corridors. **Pets:** Accepted.
ASK S🐾 ✕ 🐾M 🎁

SIOUX CITY

▼▼▼ AmericInn Lodge & Suites SH
(712) 255-1800. **$79-$156.** 4230 S Lewis Blvd. I-29, exit 143, just e. Int corridors. **Pets:** Other species. $50 deposit/room, $10 daily fee/room. Designated rooms, service with restrictions, supervision.
ASK S🐾 ✕ 🐾M 🐾 🎁 💻 🏊 ✕

AAA ▼▼▼ Clarion Hotel and Conference Center LH
(712) 277-4101. **$89-$119.** 707 4th St. Downtown. Int corridors. **Pets:** Accepted.
SAVE S🐾 ✕ 🐾 🎁 💻 🍽 🏊 ✕

▼▼ Comfort Inn by Choice Hotels SH
(712) 274-1300. **$90-$110.** 4202 S Lakeport St. I-29, exit 144A, 1 mi e on US 20, then just s; do not use Business Rt US 20. Int corridors. **Pets:** Accepted.
ASK SD X ✈ 🖥 📺 ➰

▲▲ ▼▼ Quality Inn Hotel & Conference Center M
(712) 277-3211. **$59-$89.** 1401 Zenith Dr. I-29, exit 149 (Hamilton Blvd). Int corridors. **Pets:** Other species. Service with restrictions, supervision.
SAVE SD X ✈ 🖥 📺 ⫧ ➰ ⊠

▼▼ Super 8 Motel SH
(712) 274-1520. **$54-$69.** 4307 Stone Ave. I-29, exit 144A northbound, US 75 to exit 4B, 1 mi n on Gordon Dr; exit 147B southbound to Gordon Dr, 3 mi s. Int corridors. **Pets:** Small. $10 daily fee/pet. Designated rooms, service with restrictions, supervision.
ASK SD X ♿ 🖥 📺

SLOAN

▼▼ Winna Vegas Inn SH
(712) 428-4280. **$58-$68.** 1862 Hwy 141. I-29, exit 127, just e. Int corridors. **Pets:** Accepted.
ASK SD X ♿ 🖥 📺

SPIRIT LAKE

▼▼ Ramada Limited SH
(712) 336-3984. **$69-$159, 3 day notice.** 2704 17th St. Jct US 71 and SR 9, just w. Int corridors. **Pets:** $10 one-time fee/room. Service with restrictions, supervision.
X 🖥 📺 ➰

▼ Shamrock Inn SH
(712) 336-2668. **$49-$119, 3 day notice.** 1905 18th St. 0.6 mi e on SR 9 from jct US 71. Ext/int corridors. **Pets:** $10 daily fee/room. Designated rooms, service with restrictions, supervision.
ASK SD X 🖥 📺 ➰

▼▼ Spirit Lake Super 8 SH
(712) 336-4901. **$55-$110, 3 day notice.** 2203 Circle Dr W. Jct US 71 and SR 9. Int corridors. **Pets:** $10 one-time fee/room. Service with restrictions, supervision.
X ♿ 🖥 📺

SPRINGDALE

▼ Econo Lodge M
(319) 627-2171. **$50-$80.** 1943 Garfield Ave. I-80, exit 259, just sw. Ext corridors. **Pets:** Medium. $5 daily fee/pet. Service with restrictions, crate.
ASK SD X 📺

STORY CITY

▲▲ ▼▼▼ Comfort Inn SH
(515) 733-6363. **$75-$115.** 425 Timberland Dr. I-35, exit 124, just sw. Int corridors. **Pets:** Other species. $12 daily fee/room. Service with restrictions, supervision.
SAVE SD X ♿ 🖥 📺 ➰ ⊠

▼▼ Super 8 Motel SH
(515) 733-5281. **$55-$75.** 515 Factory Outlet Dr. I-35, exit 124, just sw. Int corridors. **Pets:** Small. $10 one-time fee/pet. Service with restrictions, supervision.
ASK SD X ♿ 🖥

▼ Viking Hotel M 🐾
(515) 733-4306. **$54-$62.** 1520 Broad St. I-35, exit 124, just w. Int corridors. **Pets:** Other species. $5 daily fee/room. Service with restrictions, supervision.
ASK SD X 🖥

STUART

▼▼ AmericInn Motel & Suites SH
(515) 523-9000. **$70-$160.** 420 SW 8th St. I-80, exit 93, just w. Int corridors. **Pets:** Medium, other species. $50 deposit/room, $10 daily fee/pet. Designated rooms, service with restrictions, supervision.
ASK X ♿ ✈ ⬡ 🖥 📺 ➰ ⊠

TOLEDO

▲▲ ▼▼ Designer Inn & Suites SH 🐾
(641) 484-5678. **$45-$69.** 403 US 30 W. On US 30, just w of jct US 63 and 30. Int corridors. **Pets:** $7 daily fee/pet. Service with restrictions, supervision.
SAVE SD X 🖥 📺

▲▲ ▼▼▼ Super 8 Motel-Toledo SH 🐾
(641) 484-5888. **$89-$169.** 207 Hwy 30 W. On US 30, just w of jct US 63 and 30. Ext/int corridors. **Pets:** Other species. $5 daily fee/room. Service with restrictions.
SAVE SD X ♿ 🖥 📺

URBANA

▼▼ Super 8 Urbana Iowa SH 🐾
(319) 443-8888. **$60-$96.** 5369 Hutton Dr. I-380, exit 43, just s on east access road. Int corridors. **Pets:** $15 one-time fee/pet. Service with restrictions, supervision.
ASK SD X 🖥 📺 ➰ ⊠

URBANDALE

▲▲ ▼▼▼ Comfort Inn-Merle Hay SH
(515) 270-1037. **$69-$89.** 5900 Sutton Dr. I-80, exit 131 (Merle Hay Rd), just s, then w. Int corridors. **Pets:** Other species. $5 daily fee/pet. Service with restrictions, supervision.
SAVE SD X ✈ 🖥 📺 ➰

▼▼ Extended StayAmerica SH
(515) 276-1929. **Call for rates.** 3940 114th St. I-35/80, exit 126 (Douglas Ave), just e to 114th St, then 0.4 mi nw. Int corridors. **Pets:** Accepted.
X ♿ ⬡ 🖥 📺

▼▼ Microtel Inn and Suites SH
(515) 727-5424. **$56-$66.** 8711 Plum Dr. I-35/80, exit 129. Int corridors. **Pets:** Accepted.
ASK SD X ♿ ⬡ 🖥 📺

▼▼▼ Ramada Inn Northwest SH
(515) 278-0271. **$59-$89.** 5000 Merle Hay Rd. I-35/80, exit 131 (Merle Hay Rd), just s. Ext/int corridors. **Pets:** Medium, other species. $10 one-time fee/room. Service with restrictions, crate.
ASK SD X ♿ 🖥 📺 ⫧ ➰ ⊠

▼▼ Sleep Inn SH 🐾
(515) 270-2424. **$90-$100.** 11211 Hickman Rd. I-35/80, exit 125 (Hickman Rd), just ne. Int corridors. **Pets:** Other species. $15 daily fee/room. Designated rooms.
ASK SD X ♿ ✈ ⬡ 🖥 📺 ➰ ⊠

WALNUT

▼▼ Super 8 Motel SH
(712) 784-2221. **$50-$60.** 2109 Antique City Dr. I-80, exit 46, just n. Int corridors. **Pets:** Other species. $5 one-time fee/room. Designated rooms, service with restrictions, supervision.
ASK SD X ♿ ⬡ 🖥 📺 ➰

WATERLOO

▼▼ Comfort Inn by Choice Hotels SH
(319) 234-7411. **$80-$100.** 1945 La Porte Rd. I-380, exit 72 (E San Marnan). Int corridors. **Pets:** Accepted.
ASK SD X ✈ 🖥 📺 ➰

▼▼▼ **Holiday Inn Express** SH
(319) 233-9191. **$81.** 2141 La Porte Rd. I-380, exit 72 (E San Marnan). Int corridors. **Pets:** Accepted.
[ASK] [S6] [X] [6M] [🌡] [🛏] [💻] [🏊]

▼▼▼ **Ramada Hotel & Convention Center** LH
(319) 233-7560. **$77-$99.** 205 W 4th St. 4th and Commercial sts; downtown. Int corridors. **Pets:** Other species. Designated rooms, service with restrictions, supervision.
[ASK] [S6] [X] [6M] [🌡] [🛏] [💻] [🍴] [🏊] [✕]

WAVERLY

▼▼▼ **Americas Best Value Inn & Suites** SH
(319) 352-5330. **$60-$99.** 1900 Heritage Way. On SR 3, 2 mi e of jct US 218 and SR 3 (exit 203). Ext/int corridors. **Pets:** Accepted.
[ASK] [X] [🌡] [🛏] [🍴] [🏊] [✕]

▼▼▼ **AmeriHost Inn-Waverly** SH
(319) 352-0399. **$73-$149.** 404 29th Ave SW. Business Rt US 218, exit 198, 0.5 mi n. Int corridors. **Pets:** Medium, dogs only. $10 daily fee/pet. Designated rooms, service with restrictions, supervision.
[ASK] [S6] [X] [6M] [🌡] [🛏] [🏊] [✕]

▼▼▼ **Super 8 Waverly** SH
(319) 352-0888. **$65-$110.** 301 13th Ave SW. Business Rt US 218 S, exit 198, 1.2 mi n. Int corridors. **Pets:** Accepted.
[ASK] [S6] [X] [6M] [🛏]

WEBSTER CITY

▼▼▼ **AmericInn Motel & Suites of Webster City** SH
(515) 832-3999. **$75-$125.** 411 Closz Dr. Just s of jct US 20 and SR 17. Int corridors. **Pets:** Accepted.
[ASK] [S6] [X] [6M] [🌡] [🛏] [💻]

▼▼▼ **The Executive Inn** SH
(515) 832-3631. **$54-$89.** 1700 Superior St. Jct US 20 and SR 17, exit 140, 0.5 mi n. Int corridors. **Pets:** Accepted.
[ASK] [X] [🛏] [💻] [🏊]

▼▼▼ **Super 8 Motel** SH
(515) 832-2000. **$57-$72.** 305 Closz Dr. Just s of jct US 20 and SR 17. Int corridors. **Pets:** $6 daily fee/pet. Service with restrictions, supervision.
[ASK] [S6] [X] [🛏] [🏊]

WEST BEND

AAA ▼▼▼ **Park View Inn & Suites and Conference Center** SH
(515) 887-3611. **$58-$75.** 13 4th St NE. Jct CR B63, 1 mi n on SR 15, then just w. Int corridors. **Pets:** Small, other species. $10 daily fee/room. Supervision.
[SAVE] [X] [🌡] [🛏] [🏊]

WEST BURLINGTON

▼▼ **AmericInn** SH
(319) 758-9000. **$70-$129.** 628 S Gear Ave. US 34, exit 260 (Gear Ave), just ne. Int corridors. **Pets:** $10 daily fee/room. Designated rooms, service with restrictions, supervision.
[ASK] [S6] [X] [6M] [🌡] [🌡] [🛏] [💻] [🏊] [✕]

WEST DES MOINES

▼▼▼ **Candlewood Suites-West Des Moines** SH
(515) 221-0001. **$69-$119.** 7625 Office Plaza Dr N. I-80, exit 121 (Jordan Creek Pkwy), just sw. Int corridors. **Pets:** Medium, other species. $75 one-time fee/pet. Service with restrictions, supervision.
[ASK] [S6] [X] [6M] [🌡] [🛏] [💻]

▼▼▼ **Hawthorn Suites Ltd** SH
(515) 223-0000. **$105-$116.** 6905 Lake Dr. I-80, exit 121 (Jordan Creek Pkwy), just ne. Int corridors. **Pets:** Service with restrictions, crate.
[ASK] [S6] [X] [6M] [🌡] [🛏] [💻] [🏊] [✕]

▼▼▼ **Motel 6–1408** SH
(515) 267-8885. **$45-$59.** 7655 Office Plaza Dr N. I-80, exit 121 (Jordan Creek Pkwy), just sw. Int corridors. **Pets:** Medium, other species. Service with restrictions, supervision.
[S6] [X] [6M] [🌡] [🏊]

▼▼▼ **Residence Inn-Des Moines West** SH
(515) 267-0338. **$155-$175.** 160 S Jordan Creek Pkwy. I-35, exit 70 (Mills Civic Pkwy), 1.2 mi w to 68th, then just nw. Int corridors. **Pets:** Accepted.
[ASK] [S6] [X] [🌡] [🛏] [💻] [🏊] [✕]

AAA ▼▼▼ **Sheraton West Des Moines** LH
(515) 223-1800. **$109-$145.** 1800 50th St. I-80/35, exit 124 (University Ave), just e. Int corridors. **Pets:** Accepted.
[SAVE] [S6] [X] [6M] [🌡] [🌡] [🛏] [💻] [🍴] [🏊] [✕]

▼▼▼ **StudioPLUS** SH
(515) 327-9100. **Call for rates.** 2701 Westown Pkwy. I-235, exit 2 (22nd St), just n to Westown Pkwy, then just w. Int corridors. **Pets:** Accepted.
[X] [6M] [🌡] [🛏] [💻] [🏊]

▼▼▼ **Valley West Inn** SH
(515) 225-2524. **$89-$109.** 3535 Westown Pkwy. I-235, exit 1 (Valley West Dr), just nw. Int corridors. **Pets:** $10 daily fee/room. Designated rooms, service with restrictions, crate.
[ASK] [S6] [X] [🌡] [🛏] [💻] [🍴] [🏊] [✕]

▼▼▼ **West Des Moines Marriott** LH 🐾
(515) 267-1500. **$179-$209.** 1250 Jordan Creek Pkwy. I-80, exit 121 (Jordan Creek Pkwy), just sw. Int corridors. **Pets:** Large. $75 one-time fee/room. Service with restrictions.
[ASK] [S6] [X] [6M] [🌡] [🛏] [💻] [🍴] [🏊] [✕]

▼▼▼ **West Des Moines SpringHill Suites by Marriott** SH
(515) 223-9005. **$89-$149.** 1236 Jordan Creek Pkwy. I-80, exit 121 (Jordon Creek Pkwy), just s. Int corridors. **Pets:** Accepted.
[ASK] [S6] [X] [6M] [🌡] [🌡] [🛏] [💻] [🏊] [✕]

WILLIAMS

▼▼▼ **Best Western Norseman Inn** M
(515) 854-2281. **$60-$64.** 3086 220th St. I-35, exit 144, just e. Int corridors. **Pets:** Medium, dogs only. Service with restrictions, supervision.
[ASK] [S6] [X] [🛏] [💻]

WILLIAMSBURG

▼▼▼▼ **Amana Holiday Inn** SH
(319) 668-1175. **$189.** 2211 U Ave. I-80, exit 225 (US 151). Int corridors. **Pets:** Other species. Service with restrictions, supervision.
[ASK] [S6] [X] [6M] [🌡] [🌡] [🛏] [💻] [🍴] [🏊] [✕]

AAA ▼▼▼ **Best Western Quiet House Suites** SH
(319) 668-9777. **$90-$160.** 1708 N Highland St. I-80, exit 220, 0.8 mi n. Int corridors. **Pets:** Accepted.
[SAVE] [S6] [X] [🌡] [🌡] [🛏] [💻] [🏊]

AAA ▼▼▼ **Crest Country Inn** M
(319) 668-1522. **$50-$85.** 340 W Evans St. I-80, exit 220, just nw. Ext corridors. **Pets:** Accepted.
[SAVE] [S6] [X] [🌡]

▼▼▼ **Heritage Inn Hotel & Suites Amana Colonies** SH 🐾
(319) 668-2700. **$58-$145.** 2185 U Ave. I-80, exit 225 (US 151), just n. Int corridors. **Pets:** Other species. $10 daily fee/pet. Service with restrictions, supervision.
[ASK] [S6] [X] [6M] [🌡] [🛏] [💻] [🏊]

AAA ▼▼▼ **Super 8 Motel** SH
(319) 668-9718. **$70-$100.** 1708 N Highland St. I-80, exit 220, 0.8 mi n. Ext/int corridors. **Pets:** Accepted.
[SAVE] [S6] [X] [🌡]

KANSAS

ABILENE

⚫⚫⚫ ▼▼▼ Best Western President's Inn SH
(785) 263-2050. **$46-$58.** 2210 N Buckeye. I-70, exit 275, just s. Ext corridors. **Pets:** Accepted.
[SAVE] [S₀] [✕] [&M] [🖊] [🛏] [💻] [🍴] [🏊]

▼▼▼▼ Holiday Inn Express Hotel & Suites SH
(785) 263-4049. **$81.** 110 E Lafayette Ave. I-70, exit 275, just n. Int corridors. **Pets:** Accepted.
[ASK] [✕] [&M] [🖊] [🖊] [🛏] [💻] [🏊] [✕]

▼▼▼ Super 8 Motel SH 🐾
(785) 263-4545. **$55-$75.** 2207 N Buckeye. I-70, exit 275, just s. Int corridors. **Pets:** $10 daily fee/pet. Service with restrictions, supervision.
[ASK] [S₀] [✕] [&M] [🛏] [💻]

ATCHISON

▼▼▼ AmericInn Lodge & Suites SH
(913) 367-4000. **$70-$80.** 500 US 73. Just s at US 59 and 73. Int corridors. **Pets:** Small. $50 deposit/room, $10 daily fee/room. Designated rooms, service with restrictions, supervision.
[ASK] [S₀] [✕] [&M] [🖊] [🛏] [💻] [🏊]

BAXTER SPRINGS

▼▼▼ Baxter Inn-4-Less SH
(620) 856-2106. **$45-$50.** 2451 Military Ave. On US 69 alternate route, 1 mi s of jct US 166. Int corridors. **Pets:** Other species. Service with restrictions, supervision.
[ASK] [S₀] [✕] [🛏]

BELLEVILLE

▼▼▼ Americas Best Value Inn M
(785) 527-2231. **$53-$63.** 215 Hwy 36. Jct US 81 and 36; northwest corner; just up hill. Ext corridors. **Pets:** Dogs only. Designated rooms, service with restrictions, supervision.
[ASK] [S₀] [✕] [🛏] [💻] [🏊]

▼▼▼ Super 8 Motel SH
(785) 527-2112. **$52-$100.** 1410 28th St. On US 36, 0.5 mi e of jct US 81. Int corridors. **Pets:** Accepted.
[ASK] [S₀] [✕] [🛏]

BELOIT

▼▼▼ Super 8 Motel-Beloit SH
(785) 738-4300. **$58-$68.** 3018 US 24 Hwy. Just e of jct SR 14. Ext/int corridors. **Pets:** Accepted.
[ASK] [✕] [&M] [🖊] [🛏] [💻]

BURLINGTON

▼▼ Country Haven Inn SH
(620) 364-8260. **$60-$65.** 207 Cross St. Just e of US 75; 1 mi n of center. Int corridors. **Pets:** Accepted.
[ASK] [S₀] [✕] [🛏] [💻]

CHANUTE

▼▼ Chanute Safari Inn M
(620) 431-9460. **$35.** 3428 S Santa Fe. US 169, exit 35th St, 1.5 mi e. Ext corridors. **Pets:** Small. $5 one-time fee/pet. Service with restrictions, crate.
[ASK] [✕] [🛏] [🏊]

⚫⚫⚫ ▼ Guest House Motor Inn M
(620) 431-0600. **$40.** 1814 S Santa Fe. US 169, exit 35th St, 2.5 mi ne. Ext corridors. **Pets:** Small. $5 one-time fee/pet. Service with restrictions, crate.
[SAVE] [✕] [🛏] [🏊]

CLAY CENTER

▼▼ Cedar Court Motel SH
(785) 632-2148. **$49-$79.** 905 Crawford. On US 24, just e of jct SR 15. Ext corridors. **Pets:** Accepted.
[ASK] [S₀] [✕] [&M] [🖊] [🛏] [💻] [🍴] [🏊]

COFFEYVILLE

⚫⚫⚫ ▼▼▼ Appletree Inn M
(620) 251-0002. **$69-$80.** 820 E 11th St. 0.8 mi e of center. Int corridors. **Pets:** Accepted.
[SAVE] [S₀] [✕] [🛏] [💻] [🏊] [✕]

⚫⚫⚫ ▼▼▼ Super 8 Motel M
(620) 251-2250. **$57-$64.** 104 W 11th St. On US 169 and 166; center. Ext corridors. **Pets:** Medium, dogs only. $10 one-time fee/pet. Designated rooms, service with restrictions, supervision.
[SAVE] [S₀] [✕] [🛏] [🏊]

COLBY

⚫⚫⚫ ▼▼▼ Comfort Inn SH
(785) 462-3833. **$79-$119.** 2225 S Range. I-70, exit 53 (SR 25), just s. Int corridors. **Pets:** Small. $10 one-time fee/room. Designated rooms, service with restrictions, supervision.
[SAVE] [S₀] [✕] [🖊] [🖊] [🛏] [💻] [🍴] [🏊]

⚫⚫⚫ ▼▼▼ Days Inn SH
(785) 462-8691. **$59-$85.** 1925 S Range. I-70, exit 53 (SR 25), 0.3 mi n. Int corridors. **Pets:** Accepted.
[SAVE] [S₀] [✕] [🛏] [💻] [🏊]

⚫⚫⚫ ▼▼▼ Holiday Inn Express Hotel & Suites SH
(785) 462-8787. **$85-$130.** 645 W Willow. I-70, exit 53 (SR 25), just ne. Int corridors. **Pets:** Large, other species. $10 daily fee/room. Service with restrictions, crate.
[SAVE] [S₀] [✕] [🖊] [🖊] [🛏] [💻] [🏊] [✕]

▼▼ Motel 6 #4245 SH
(785) 462-8201. **$41-$51.** 1985 S Range. I-70, exit 53 (SR 25), just n. Ext/int corridors. **Pets:** Medium, other species. Service with restrictions, supervision.
[ASK] [S₀] [✕]

Quality Inn SH
(785) 462-3933. **$55-$85, 7 day notice.** 1950 S Range. I-70, exit 53 (SR 25), just n. Ext/int corridors. **Pets:** Accepted.

CONCORDIA

Super 8 Motel-Concordia SH
(785) 243-4200. **$54-$64.** 1320 Lincoln. On US 81, 1 mi s of center. Ext/int corridors. **Pets:** Accepted.

COTTONWOOD FALLS

Grand Central Hotel CI
(620) 273-6763. **$160-$190.** 215 Broadway. Just w of US 177; center of downtown. Int corridors. **Pets:** Service with restrictions, supervision.

COUNCIL GROVE

The Cottage House Hotel & Motel SH
(620) 767-6828. **$55-$175, 7 day notice.** 25 N Neosho. Just n of Main St; downtown. Ext/int corridors. **Pets:** Accepted.

DODGE CITY

Holiday Inn Express SH
(620) 227-5000. **$93-$103.** 2320 W Wyatt Earp Blvd. 1.4 mi w on US 50 business route. Int corridors. **Pets:** Other species. Service with restrictions, crate.

Super 8 Motel SH
(620) 225-3924. **$93-$103.** 1708 W Wyatt Earp Blvd. 1.2 mi w on US 50 business route. Int corridors. **Pets:** Other species. Service with restrictions, crate.

EL DORADO

Best Western Red Coach Inn SH
(316) 321-6900. **$55.** 2525 W Central Ave. I-35, exit 71, 0.5 mi e. Ext corridors. **Pets:** Small, dogs only. $15 daily fee/pet. Designated rooms, service with restrictions, supervision.

Super 8 Motel-El Dorado M
(316) 321-4888. **$45-$95.** 2530 W Central Ave. I-35, exit 71, 0.5 mi e. Int corridors. **Pets:** Small, dogs only. $15 daily fee/pet. Designated rooms, service with restrictions, supervision.

ELLSWORTH

Best Western Garden Prairie Inn SH
(785) 472-3116. **$79-$89.** Jct SR 140 & 156. Jct SR 140 and 156. Ext/int corridors. **Pets:** Accepted.

EMPORIA

Americas Best Value Inn M
(620) 342-7567. **$56-$67.** 2913 W Hwy 50. I-35, exit 127, 0.8 mi e. Int corridors. **Pets:** Dogs only. $10 one-time fee/room. Designated rooms, service with restrictions, supervision.

Best Western Hospitality House SH
(620) 342-7587. **$58-$99.** 3021 W Hwy 50. I-35, exit 127, just e. Ext/int corridors. **Pets:** Accepted.

Candlewood Suites SH
(620) 343-7756. **$79-$99.** 2602 Candlewood Dr. I-35, exit 128 (Industrial St), just n, then e. Int corridors. **Pets:** Accepted.

Comfort Inn SH
(620) 342-9700. **Call for rates.** 2836 W 18th Ave. I-35, exit 128, just nw. Int corridors. **Pets:** Accepted.

FORT SCOTT

Fort Scott Inn SH
(620) 223-0100. **$56-$65.** 101 State St. On US 69 Bypass, exit US 54 southbound; exit 3rd St northbound. Ext/int corridors. **Pets:** Medium, other species. $25 daily fee/pet. Service with restrictions, supervision.

GARDEN CITY

AmericInn Lodge & Suites SH
(620) 272-9860. **$160.** 3020 E Kansas Ave. Jct US 50, 83 and SR 156. Int corridors. **Pets:** Medium. $50 deposit/room, $10 daily fee/pet. Service with restrictions, crate.

Best Western Red Baron Hotel SH
(620) 275-4164. **$69-$75.** 2205 E Hwy 50. 2.3 mi e on US 50 business route, at US 83 Bypass. Ext corridors. **Pets:** Accepted.

Best Western Wheat Lands Hotel & Conference Center SH
(620) 276-2387. **$67-$92.** 1311 E Fulton. 1 mi e on US 50 business route. Ext corridors. **Pets:** Other species. Service with restrictions, crate.

Comfort Inn SH
(620) 275-5800. **$60-$149, 14 day notice.** 2608 E Kansas Ave. Jct US 50, 83 and SR 156. Int corridors. **Pets:** Medium, other species. $10 deposit/pet. Service with restrictions, supervision.

Holiday Inn Express Hotel & Suites SH
(620) 275-5900. **$95-$105.** 2502 E Kansas Ave. Jct US 50, 83 and SR 156. Int corridors. **Pets:** Other species. Service with restrictions, crate.

GODDARD

Express Inn M
(316) 794-3366. **$46-$52.** 19941 W Kellogg Dr. Just se of jct US 54/400 and 199th St. Ext corridors. **Pets:** Accepted.

GOODLAND

Best Western Buffalo Inn SH
(785) 899-3621. **$72-$74, 5 day notice.** 830 W Hwy 24. I-70, exit 17 or 19, n to jct US 24 and SR 27. Ext corridors. **Pets:** Accepted.

Comfort Inn SH
(785) 899-7181. **$85-$105.** 2519 Enterprise Rd. I-70, exit 17, just n. Int corridors. **Pets:** Medium, dogs only. $15 daily fee/pet. Designated rooms, service with restrictions, supervision.

Super 8 Motel-Goodland SH
(785) 890-7566. **$56-$100, 14 day notice.** 2520 Commerce Rd. I-70, exit 17 (SR 27), just n. Ext corridors. **Pets:** Accepted.

GREAT BEND

🛆🛆🛆 ▼▼▼ Best Western Angus Inn 🖼
(620) 792-3541. **$75.** 2920 10th St. 0.8 mi w on US 56 and SR 96/156. Ext/int corridors. **Pets:** Crate.
SAVE ⬛ ⊠ 🖉 🗄 🖵 🍴 ⋈ 🐾

🛆🛆🛆 ▼▼▼ Highland Hotel & Convention Center 🖼
(620) 792-2431. **$71-$85.** 3017 10th St. 1 mi w on US 56 and SR 96/156. Ext/int corridors. **Pets:** $10 daily fee/room. Designated rooms, service with restrictions, supervision.
SAVE ⬛ ⊠ ♿ 🗄 🖵 🍴 ⋈ 🐾

GREENSBURG

▼▼ Best Western J-Hawk Motel 🖼
(620) 723-2121. **$72-$75.** 515 W Kansas Ave. Just w on US 54. Ext corridors. **Pets:** Service with restrictions, supervision.
⊠ 🗄 🖵 ⋈

HAYS

▼▼ Best Western Vagabond Motel 🅼
(785) 625-2511. **$57-$76.** 2524 Vine St. I-70, exit 159 (US 183), 1 mi s. Ext corridors. **Pets:** Designated rooms, service with restrictions, supervision.
ASK ⬛ ⊠ ♿ 🗄 🖵 🍴 ⋈

🛆🛆🛆 ▼▼▼ Hampton Inn-Hays 🖼
(785) 625-8103. **$64-$89.** 3801 Vine St. I-70, exit 159 (US 183), just sw. Ext/int corridors. **Pets:** Other species. No service, supervision.
SAVE ⬛ ⊠ 🖉 ♿ 🖵

▼▼◆ Holiday Inn-Hays 🖼
(785) 625-7371. **$89-$109, 3 day notice.** 3603 Vine St. I-70, exit 159 (US 183), just s. Ext/int corridors. **Pets:** Accepted.
ASK ⬛ ⊠ ♿ 🖉 ♿ 🗄 🖵 🍴 ⋈ 🐾

HESSTON

▼▼ AmericInn Lodge & Suites-Hesston 🖼
(620) 327-2053. **$64-$99.** 2 Leonard Ct. I-135, exit 40, just e. Int corridors. **Pets:** Medium. $50 deposit/room. Designated rooms, no service, supervision.
ASK ⬛ ⊠ 🗄 🖵 ⋈

HILLSBORO

▼▼ Country Haven Inn 🖼
(620) 947-2929. **$60-$65.** 804 Western Heights. On US 56; center. Int corridors. **Pets:** Small, other species. $35 deposit/room, $15 one-time fee/room. Service with restrictions, crate.
ASK ⬛ ⊠ 🗄

HUTCHINSON

🛆🛆🛆 ▼ Americas Best Value Inn 🅼 🐾
(620) 662-6394. **$61-$81.** 1315 E 11th Ave. Just se of jct SR 61. Int corridors. **Pets:** Dogs only. $10 one-time fee/room. Designated rooms, service with restrictions, supervision.
SAVE ⬛ ⊠ 🖉 🖵

▼▼ Comfort Inn 🖼
(620) 663-7822. **$55-$129.** 1621 Super Plaza. Just w of jct SR 61 and N 17th Ave. Int corridors. **Pets:** Small, other species. $10 daily fee/room. Designated rooms, service with restrictions, supervision.
ASK ⬛ ⊠ 🖉 ♿ 🗄 🖵 ⋈

🛆🛆🛆 ▼▼▼ Grand Prairie Hotel & Convention Center 🕮🖼
(620) 669-9311. **$99-$129, 30 day notice.** 1400 N Lorraine St. Just nw of jct SR 61 and N 11th Ave. Ext/int corridors. **Pets:** Medium, dogs only. $35 one-time fee/room. Service with restrictions, crate.
SAVE ⬛ ⊠ ♿ 🗄 🖵 🍴 ⋈ 🐾

▼▼▼ Holiday Inn Express Hotel & Suites 🖼
(620) 669-5200. **$93-$103.** 1601 Super Plaza. Just w of jct SR 61 and N 17th Ave. Int corridors. **Pets:** Other species. Service with restrictions, crate.
ASK ⬛ ⊠ ♿ 🖉 ♿ 🗄 🖵 ⋈

▼▼ Microtel Inn & Suites 🖼
(620) 665-3700. **$64-$135.** 1420 N Lorraine. Just nw of jct SR 61 and N 11th Ave. Int corridors. **Pets:** Small. $10 one-time fee/pet. Service with restrictions, supervision.
ASK ⬛ ⊠ ♿ 🗄 🖵

INDEPENDENCE

▼▼ Appletree Inn 🖼
(620) 331-5500. **$85.** 201 N 8th St. At 8th and Laurel sts. Ext/int corridors. **Pets:** Accepted.
⊠ 🗄 ⋈

🛆🛆🛆 ▼▼▼ Knights Inn 🖼
(620) 331-7300. **$49-$59.** 3222 W Main St. 1.4 mi e of jct US 75 and 160. Ext corridors. **Pets:** Small. $10 daily fee/pet. Designated rooms, service with restrictions, supervision.
SAVE ⬛ ⊠ 🗄 🖵 ⋈

▼▼ Microtel Inn & Suites 🖼
(620) 331-0088. **$66-$83.** 2917 W Main St. 1.2 mi e of jct US 75 and 160. Int corridors. **Pets:** Accepted.
ASK ⬛ ⊠ ♿ 🖉 ♿ 🗄 🖵

IOLA

🛆🛆🛆 ▼▼▼ Best Western Inn 🅼
(620) 365-5161. **$54-$59.** 1315 N State St. Jct US 54 and 169, 1.5 mi w on US 54, then 0.8 mi n. Ext corridors. **Pets:** Accepted.
SAVE ⬛ ⊠ ♿ 🖉 ♿ 🗄 🖵 🍴 ⋈

▼▼ Super 8 Iola 🖼
(620) 365-3030. **$69-$79.** 200 Bills Way. Jct US 54 and 169. Int corridors. **Pets:** Accepted.
ASK ⬛ ⊠ ♿ 🗄 🖵 ⋈

JUNCTION CITY

🛆🛆🛆 ▼▼▼▼ Courtyard by Marriott Junction City 🖼
(785) 210-1500. **$94.** 310 Hammons Dr. I-70, exit 298, just w. Int corridors. **Pets:** Medium. $75 one-time fee/room. Service with restrictions, supervision.
SAVE ⊠ ♿ ♿ 🗄 🖵 ⋈

▼▼▼ Days Inn 🖼
(785) 762-2727. **$55-$75.** 1024 S Washington St. I-70, exit 296, just n. Ext/int corridors. **Pets:** Other species. Designated rooms, crate.
ASK ⬛ ⊠ 🖉 🗄 🖵 ⋈ 🐾

▼▼▼ Holiday Inn Express 🖼
(785) 762-4200. **$84-$95.** 120 N East St. I-70, exit 298, just nw. Int corridors. **Pets:** Small. $50 deposit/room, $5 daily fee/pet. Service with restrictions, supervision.
ASK ⬛ ⊠ ♿ 🖉 🗄 🖵 ⋈ 🐾

KANSAS CITY METROPOLITAN AREA

GARDNER

◆◆ ▼▼ **Super 8 Motel** SH
(913) 856-8887. **$65-$120, 3 day notice.** 2001 E Santa Fe. I-35, exit 210. Int corridors. **Pets:** Medium, other species. $10 daily fee/pet. Service with restrictions, supervision.

ASK S✆ ⊗ &M ⊟

KANSAS CITY

◆◆◆ ▼▼ **Best Western Inn and Conference Center** SH ❧
(913) 677-3060. **$79-$89.** 501 Southwest Blvd. I-35, exit 234 (7th St), just s. Int corridors. **Pets:** Service with restrictions, supervision.

SAVE S✆ ⊗ ⊟ ⊑ ⇒

▼▼ **Microtel Inn & Suites at the Speedway** SH
(913) 334-3028. **$59-$69.** 7721 Elizabeth St. I-70, exit 414 (78th St N), just ne. Int corridors. **Pets:** Accepted.

ASK S✆ ⊗ &M ⊙ ⊟ ⊑ ⇒

LENEXA

▼▼▼ **Extended StayAmerica -Kansas City-Lenexa-87th St** SH
(913) 894-5550. **$70-$130.** 8015 Lenexa Dr. I-35, exit 227 (75th St), 1 mi s on east frontage road. Ext corridors. **Pets:** Accepted.

ASK S✆ ⊗ &M ⊙ ⊙ ⊟ ⊑ ⇒

▼▼ **La Quinta Inn Kansas City (Lenexa)** SH
(913) 492-5500. **$78-$108.** 9461 Lenexa Dr. I-35, exit 224 (95th St), just ne; entrance left on Monrovia Rd, off 95th St. Int corridors. **Pets:** Medium. Service with restrictions.

ASK ⊗ ⊙ ⊟ ⊑ ⇒

MERRIAM

▼▼ **Comfort Inn-Merriam** SH
(913) 262-2622. **$46-$190.** 6401 E Frontage Rd. I-35, exit 228B (Shawnee Mission Pkwy), just se. Int corridors. **Pets:** Accepted.

ASK S✆ ⊗ ⊙ ⊟ ⊑ ⇒

▼▼▼ **Drury Inn-Merriam/Shawnee Mission Parkway** SH
(913) 236-9200. **$80-$120.** 9009 W Shawnee Mission Pkwy. I-35, exit 228B (Shawnee Mission Pkwy). Int corridors. **Pets:** Large, other species. Service with restrictions, supervision.

ASK ⊗ &M ⊙ ⊟ ⊑ ⇒

▼▼▼ **Hampton Inn & Suites** SH
(913) 722-0800. **$103-$114.** 7400 W Frontage Rd. I-35, exit 227, just nw. Int corridors. **Pets:** Small, other species. Service with restrictions, crate.

ASK S✆ ⊗ &M ⊙ ⊟ ⊑ ⇒

▼▼ **Homestead Studio Suites Hotel-Kansas City-Shawnee Mission** M
(913) 236-6006. **$60-$120.** 6451 E Frontage Rd. I-35, exit 228B (Shawnee Mission Pkwy), just se. Ext corridors. **Pets:** Accepted.

ASK S✆ ⊗ &M ⊙ ⊙ ⊟ ⊑

◆◆◆ ▼▼ **Quality Inn** SH
(913) 262-4448. **$39-$199.** 6601 E Frontage Rd. I-35, exit 228A, just ne. Ext/int corridors. **Pets:** Accepted.

SAVE S✆ ⊗ &M ⊙ ⊙ ⊟ ⊑ ⇒

OLATHE

▼▼▼ **Holiday Inn** SH
(913) 829-4000. **$83-$105.** 101 W 151st St. I-35, exit 215 (151st St). Int corridors. **Pets:** Other species. Service with restrictions, crate.

ASK S✆ ⊗ ⊙ ⊟ ⊑ ⊞ ⇒

◆◆◆ ▼▼ **Sleep Inn** SH
(913) 390-9500. **$74-$85.** 20662 W 151st St. I-35, exit 215 (151st St), 0.4 mi sw, follow signs. Int corridors. **Pets:** Small. $10 one-time fee/pet. Service with restrictions, crate.

SAVE S✆ ⊗ &M ⊙ ⊙ ⊟ ⊑ ⇒

OVERLAND PARK

▼▼▼ **Candlewood Suites** SH
(913) 469-5557. **$75-$92.** 11001 Oakmont. I-435, exit 82 (Quivira Rd), 0.5 mi s, 0.3 mi w on College Ave, then just n. Int corridors. **Pets:** Small. $75 one-time fee/pet. Service with restrictions, supervision.

ASK S✆ ⊗ &M ⊙ ⊙ ⊟ ⊑

◆◆◆ ▼▼▼ **Chase Suites by Woodfin** SH
(913) 491-3333. **$89-$152.** 6300 W 110th. I-435, exit 79 (Metcalf Ave/US 169), 0.3 mi s on US 169, 0.5 mi e on College Blvd to Lamar Ave, then just n. Ext corridors. **Pets:** Accepted.

SAVE S✆ ⊗ &M ⊙ ⊙ ⊟ ⊑ ⇒ ⊗

▼▼▼ **Comfort Inn & Suites** SH
(913) 648-7858. **$79-$110.** 7200 W 107th St. I-435, exit 79 (Metcalf Ave/US 169), just nw. Int corridors. **Pets:** Medium. $10 daily fee/room. Designated rooms, service with restrictions, supervision.

ASK S✆ ⊗ &M ⊙ ⊟ ⊑ ⇒

▼▼▼ **Drury Inn & Suites-Overland Park** SH
(913) 345-1500. **$85-$140.** 10963 Metcalf Ave. I-435, exit 79 (Metcalf Ave/US 169), just se. Int corridors. **Pets:** Large, other species. Service with restrictions, supervision.

ASK ⊗ &M ⊙ ⊟ ⊑ ⇒ ⊗

▼▼ **Extended StayAmerica-Kansas City-Overland Park** SH
(913) 661-9299. **$75-$155.** 10750 Quivira Rd. I-435, exit 82 (Quivira Rd), just sw. Int corridors. **Pets:** Accepted.

⊗ &M ⊙ ⊟ ⊑

▼▼▼ **Extended Stay Deluxe Kansas City-Overland Park-Metcalf** SH
(913) 642-2299. **$75-$165.** 7201 W 106th St. I-435, exit 79 (Metcalf Ave/US 169), just nw. Int corridors. **Pets:** Accepted.

ASK S✆ ⊗ &M ⊙ ⊟ ⊑

▼▼▼ **Holiday Inn of Mission-Overland Park** LH
(913) 262-3010. **$99-$139.** 7240 Shawnee Mission Pkwy. I-35, exit 228B (Shawnee Mission Pkwy), 1 mi e. Ext/int corridors. **Pets:** Accepted.

ASK S✆ ⊗ &M ⊙ ⊙ ⊟ ⊑ ⊞ ⇒ ⊗

◆◆◆ ▼▼▼ **Holtze Executive Village** SH
(913) 344-8100. **$62-$269.** 11400 College Blvd. I-435, exit 82 (Quivira Rd), 0.5 mi s, then just e. Ext/int corridors. **Pets:** Medium, other species. $250 deposit/pet. Service with restrictions, supervision.

SAVE S✆ ⊗ &M ⊙ ⊙ ⊟ ⊑ ⇒ ⊗

▼▼▼ **Homestead Studio Suites Hotel-Kansas City-Overland Park** SH
(913) 661-7111. **$75-$155.** 5401 W 110th St. I-435, exit 77B (Nall Ave), just s. Int corridors. **Pets:** Accepted.

ASK S✆ ⊗ &M ⊙ ⊟ ⊑ ⇒

▼▼▼ **La Quinta Inn & Suites** SH
(913) 648-5555. **$89-$139.** 10610 Marty Ave. I-435, exit 79 (Metcalf Ave/US 169), just nw. Int corridors. **Pets:** Accepted.

ASK S✆ ⊗ ⊙ ⊟ ⊑ ⇒ ⊗

▼▼▼ **Pear Tree Inn by Drury-Overland Park** SH
(913) 451-0200. **$60-$115.** 10951 Metcalf Ave. I-435, exit 79 (Metcalf Ave/US 169), just se. Int corridors. **Pets:** Large, other species. Service with restrictions, supervision.

ASK ⊗ &M ⊙ ⊟ ⊑ ⇒

▼▼ Red Roof Inn-Overland Park Ⓜ
(913) 341-0100. **$48-$73.** 6800 W 108th St. I-435, exit 79 (Metcalf Ave/US 169), just ne. Ext corridors. **Pets:** Medium, other species. Service with restrictions, supervision.

▼▼▼ Residence Inn by Marriott 🆂🅷
(913) 491-4444. **$179-$299.** 12010 Blue Valley Pkwy. I-435, exit 79 (Metcalf Ave/US 169), 1.3 mi s. Int corridors. **Pets:** Accepted.

🅐🅐🅐 ▼▼ Settle Inn 🆂🅷
(913) 381-5700. **$54-$129.** 4401 W 107th St. I-435, exit 77A (Roe Ave), just ne. Ext/int corridors. **Pets:** Small, dogs only. $15 daily fee/pet. Designated rooms, service with restrictions, supervision.

▼▼▼ Sheraton Overland Park Hotel at the Convention Center 🅻🅷 🐾
(913) 234-2100. **$99-$299.** 6100 College Blvd. I-435, exit 79 (Metcalf Ave/US 169), just s to College Blvd, then 0.6 mi e. Int corridors. **Pets:** Medium, dogs only. Service with restrictions, supervision.

▼▼ Super 8 Motel 🆂🅷
(913) 341-4440. **$50-$109.** 10750 Barkley St. I-435, exit 79 (Metcalf Ave/US 169), just n to 107th St, then just e. Int corridors. **Pets:** Medium, other species. $10 one-time fee/pet. Service with restrictions, supervision.

▼▼ White Haven Motor Lodge Ⓜ
(913) 649-8200. **$58-$60.** 8039 Metcalf Ave. I-435, exit 79 (Metcalf Ave/US 169), 3.5 mi n. Ext corridors. **Pets:** Medium. Service with restrictions, crate.

END METROPOLITAN AREA

LANSING

🅐🅐🅐 ▼▼ Econo Lodge 🆂🅷
(913) 727-2777. **$55-$100.** 504 N Main. I-70, exit 224 (Leavenworth), 10 mi n on US 73 and SR 7. Int corridors. **Pets:** Accepted.

▼▼▼ Holiday Inn Express Hotel & Suites 🆂🅷
(913) 250-1000. **$75-$86.** 120 Express Dr. I-70, exit 224 (Leavenworth), 10 mi n on US 73 and SR 7. Int corridors. **Pets:** Accepted.

LARNED

🅐🅐🅐 ▼▼ Best Western Townsman Inn 🆂🅷
(620) 285-3114. **$59-$69.** 123 E 14th St. Jct US 56 and SR 156. Ext corridors. **Pets:** Small. $10 daily fee/pet. Service with restrictions, supervision.

LAWRENCE

🅐🅐🅐 ▼▼▼ Best Western Lawrence 🆂🅷
(785) 843-9100. **$79-$129.** 2309 Iowa St. On US 59; jct SR 10. Ext/int corridors. **Pets:** Small, dogs only. $8 daily fee/pet. Designated rooms, no service, supervision.

▼▼ Econo Lodge 🆂🅷
(785) 842-7030. **$63-$110.** 2222 W 6th St. I-70, exit 202, 1 mi s. Int corridors. **Pets:** $10 one-time fee/room. Service with restrictions, crate.

🅐🅐🅐 ▼▼▼ Golden Rule Motel 🆂🅷 🐾
(785) 842-5721. **$63-$83.** 515 McDonald Dr. I-70, exit 202, 0.8 mi s, then just w. Int corridors. **Pets:** Dogs only. $10 one-time fee/room. Designated rooms, service with restrictions, supervision.

🅐🅐🅐 ▼▼▼ Holiday Inn 🅻🅷
(785) 841-7077. **$79-$119.** 200 McDonald Dr. I-70, exit 202, 0.5 mi s on US 59. Ext/int corridors. **Pets:** Other species. $25 daily fee/pet. Service with restrictions, supervision.

▼▼ Quality Inn 🆂🅷 🐾
(785) 842-5100. **$64-$124.** 801 N Iowa St. I-70, exit 202, 1 mi s on US 59. Ext/int corridors. **Pets:** $10 one-time fee/pet. Service with restrictions, crate.

LIBERAL

🅐🅐🅐 ▼▼ Americas Best Value Inn Ⓜ
(620) 624-6203. **$48.** 564 E Pancake Blvd. 0.8 w of jct US 54 and 83. Ext corridors. **Pets:** $5 daily fee/pet. Service with restrictions, supervision.

🅐🅐🅐 ▼▼ Liberal Inn 🆂🅷
(620) 624-7254. **$60-$75.** 603 E Pancake Blvd. 0.5 mi w of jct US 54 and 83. Int corridors. **Pets:** Medium. Designated rooms, service with restrictions, crate.

LINDSBORG

▼▼ Viking Motel Ⓜ
(785) 227-3336. **$49-$64.** 446 Harrison. I-135, exit 78, 4 mi sw. Ext corridors. **Pets:** Small. $500 daily fee/pet. Service with restrictions, supervision.

MANHATTAN

▼▼▼ Best Western Manhattan Inn 🆂🅷
(785) 537-8300. **Call for rates.** 601 E Poyntz Ave. SR 177, 0.4 mi e on US 24 (Frontage Rd). Int corridors. **Pets:** Accepted.

🅐🅐🅐 ▼▼▼ Clarion Hotel 🅻🅷
(785) 539-5311. **$65-$160.** 530 Richards Dr. On SR 18 (Ft. Riley Blvd), 0.3 mi e of jct SR 113. Ext/int corridors. **Pets:** Other species. $10 daily fee/pet. Designated rooms, service with restrictions, crate.

▼▼▼ Holiday Inn at the Campus 🆂🅷 🐾
(785) 539-7531. **$89-$169.** 1641 Anderson. 1 mi n of SR 18 (Ft. Riley Blvd). Int corridors. **Pets:** Other species. $10 daily fee/room. Service with restrictions, supervision.

◆ **Motel 6–152** **M**
(785) 537-1022. **$43-$55.** 510 Tuttle Creek Blvd. 0.3 mi ne on US 24 (Frontage Rd) and SR 177. Ext corridors. **Pets:** Medium, other species. Service with restrictions, supervision.

🛏️ ✖️ 🔧 📶 🏊

◆◆ **Super 8 Motel-Manhattan** **SH**
(785) 537-8468. **$65-$125.** 200 Tuttle Creek Blvd. Jct US 24 (Frontage Rd) and SR 177. Int corridors. **Pets:** Medium, other species. $50 one-time fee/room. Service with restrictions, supervision.

ASK 🛏️ ✖️ 📶 🔧 📺

MARYSVILLE

◆◆ **Best Western Surf Motel** **SH**
(785) 562-2354. **$45-$65.** 2105 Center St. 1 mi e on US 36 (Pony Express Hwy). Ext/int corridors. **Pets:** Accepted.

ASK 🛏️ ✖️ 🔧 🔧 📺 ✖️

◆◆◆ ◆◆ **Oak Tree Inn-Marysville** **SH**
(785) 562-1234. **$65.** 1127 Pony Express Hwy. 1.6 mi e on US 36 (Pony Express Hwy). Int corridors. **Pets:** Accepted.

SAVE 🛏️ ✖️ 📶 🔧 🔧 📺 🍴

◆◆ **Super 8 Motel** **SH**
(785) 562-5588. **$45-$88.** 1155 Pony Express Hwy. 2 mi e on US 36 (Pony Express Hwy). Int corridors. **Pets:** Other species. $10 one-time fee/room. Designated rooms, supervision.

ASK 🛏️ ✖️ 📶 🔧

MCPHERSON

◆◆◆ ◆◆ **Americas Best Value Inn** **M** 🐾
(620) 241-8881. **$54-$74.** 2110 E Kansas Ave. I-135, exit 60, just w. Int corridors. **Pets:** Dogs only. $10 one-time fee/room. Designated rooms, service with restrictions, supervision.

SAVE 🛏️ ✖️ 📶 🔧

◆◆ **Best Western Holiday Manor Motel** **SH** 🐾
(620) 241-5343. **$57-$85.** 2211 E Kansas Ave. I-135, exit 60, just w. Ext/int corridors. **Pets:** Medium, other species. $10 daily fee/pet. Service with restrictions, supervision.

ASK 🛏️ ✖️ 📶 🔧 🔧 📺 🍴 🏊 ✖️

◆◆◆ ◆ **Red Coach Inn** **SH**
(620) 241-6960. **$54-$150, 30 day notice.** 2111 E Kansas Ave. I-135, exit 60, just w. Ext/int corridors. **Pets:** $15 one-time fee/room. Designated rooms, service with restrictions, supervision.

SAVE 🛏️ ✖️ 🍴 🏊 ✖️

NEWTON

◆◆ **Days Inn Newton** **SH**
(316) 283-3330. **$66-$68.** 105 Manchester St. I-135, exit 31, just e. Int corridors. **Pets:** Large, other species. $10 one-time fee/pet. Service with restrictions, supervision.

ASK 🛏️ ✖️ 🔧 📺 🏊

OBERLIN

◆◆◆ ◆ **Frontier Motel** **M**
(785) 475-2203. **$49-$79.** 207 E Frontier Pkwy. On US 36, 0.5 mi e of jct US 83. Ext corridors. **Pets:** Accepted.

SAVE ✖️ 🔧 🍴 🏊

OTTAWA

◆◆ **Best Western Ottawa Inn** **SH**
(785) 242-2224. **$80-$100.** 606 E 23rd St. I-35, exit 183 (US 59). Ext/int corridors. **Pets:** Accepted.

ASK 🛏️ ✖️ 📶 🔧 📺 🏊

◆◆ **Days Inn** **M**
(785) 242-4842. **$54-$90.** 1641 S Main. I-35, exit 183 (US 59), 1 mi n. Ext corridors. **Pets:** Accepted.

ASK 🛏️ ✖️ 📶 🔧 📺 🏊

◆◆◆ ◆◆ **Econo Lodge** **SH**
(785) 242-3400. **$55-$100.** 2331 S Cedar Rd. I-35, exit 183 (US 59). Int corridors. **Pets:** $10 daily fee/pet. Service with restrictions, supervision.

SAVE 🛏️ ✖️ 🔧 📺 🏊

◆◆ **Travelodge** **M**
(785) 242-7000. **Call for rates.** 2209 S Princeton Rd. I-35, exit 183 (US 59), just n. Ext corridors. **Pets:** Accepted.

ASK ✖️ 🔧 📺 🏊

PARK CITY

◆ **Super 8 Motel-Wichita North/Park City** **SH**
(316) 744-2071. **$45-$85.** 6075 Air Cap Dr. I-135, exit 14, just sw. Int corridors. **Pets:** $10 daily fee/pet. Service with restrictions, supervision.

ASK 🛏️ ✖️ 📶 🔧

PARSONS

◆ **Super 8 Motel-Parsons** **SH**
(620) 421-8000. **$59-$79.** 229 E Main. 1.3 mi e of jct US 59 and 400. Int corridors. **Pets:** Small. $10 daily fee/pet. Designated rooms, service with restrictions, supervision.

ASK 🛏️ ✖️ 🔧 📺 🏊

PHILLIPSBURG

◆◆◆ ◆◆ **Cottonwood Inn** **M**
(785) 543-2125. **$69-$99, 7 day notice.** 1200 State St. 1 mi e on US 36/183. Ext corridors. **Pets:** Accepted.

SAVE 🛏️ ✖️ 🔧 🏊

PITTSBURG

◆◆◆ ◆◆ **Econo Lodge** **SH** 🐾
(620) 231-8300. **$49-$89.** 2408 S Broadway. Jct US 69 and Broadway; south side of town. Ext corridors. **Pets:** Small. $10 daily fee/pet. Designated rooms, service with restrictions, supervision.

SAVE 🛏️ ✖️ 🔧 🏊

◆◆ **Super 8 Motel-Pittsburg** **SH**
(620) 232-1881. **$53-$69.** 3108 N Broadway St. 2.1 mi n on US 69 from jct SR 126. Int corridors. **Pets:** Small. $25 one-time fee/room. Service with restrictions, supervision.

ASK 🛏️ ✖️ 📶 🔧 📺

PRATT

◆◆ **Days Inn** **SH** 🐾
(620) 672-9465. **$58-$92.** 1901 E 1st St. 1.7 mi e on US 54. Ext corridors. **Pets:** Medium. $10 daily fee/pet. Service with restrictions, supervision.

ASK 🛏️ ✖️ 🔧 📺 🏊

◆◆ **Econo Lodge** **SH**
(620) 672-6407. **$46-$74.** 1336 E 1st St. 1 mi e on US 54. Ext corridors. **Pets:** Accepted.

ASK 🛏️ ✖️ 🔧 📺 🏊

◆◆◆ ◆ **Economy Inn** **M**
(620) 672-5588. **$45-$65, 4 day notice.** 1401 E 1st St. 1 mi e on US 54. Ext corridors. **Pets:** Medium. $5 daily fee/pet. Designated rooms, service with restrictions, supervision.

SAVE 🛏️ ✖️ 🔧 🏊

◆ **Evergreen Inn** **M**
(620) 672-6431. **$50-$65.** 20001 W US Hwy 54. On US 54, 3 mi w. Ext corridors. **Pets:** Accepted.

✖️ 🔧 🏊

◆◆◆ **Leisure Hotel** **SH**
(620) 672-9433. **$80-$92.** 1401 W Hwy 54. On US 54, 2 mi w. Int corridors. **Pets:** Other species. Service with restrictions, supervision.

ASK 🛏️ ✖️ 📶 🔧 🔧 📺 🏊

▼▼ ▼▼ Super 8 Motel of Pratt SH
(620) 672-5945. **$50-$59.** 1906 E 1st St. 1.7 mi e on US 54. Int corridors. **Pets:** Accepted.

⊠ 🖪

RUSSELL

▼▼▼ AmericInn Lodge & Suites SH 🐾
(785) 483-4200. **$75-$95.** 1430 S Fossil St. I-70, exit 184 (US 281), just n. Int corridors. **Pets:** Large, other species. $50 deposit/pet, $10 daily fee/pet. Service with restrictions, crate.

ASK S🐾 ⊠ &M 🝏 &👁 🖪 💻 🗪 ⊠

▼▼ Days Inn M
(785) 483-6660. **$55-$74.** 1225 S Fossil St. I-70, exit 184 (US 281), just n. Ext corridors. **Pets:** Accepted.

ASK S🐾 ⊠ 🖪 🗪

SALINA

▼▼▼ Americas Best Inn SH
(785) 825-2500. **$56-$66.** 429 W Diamond Dr. I-70, exit 252, just n. Int corridors. **Pets:** Other species. $10 daily fee/pet. Designated rooms, supervision.

ASK S🐾 ⊠ &M 🖪

▼▼▼ Baymont Inn & Suites SH
(785) 493-9800. **$70-$90.** 745 W Schilling Rd. I-135, exit 89 (Schilling Rd), just w. Int corridors. **Pets:** Accepted.

ASK S🐾 ⊠ &M &👁 🖪 💻 🗪 ⊠

▲▲▲ ▼▼▼ Best Western Mid-America Inn SH
(785) 827-0356. **$60-$85.** 1846 N 9th St. I-70, exit 252, just s. Ext corridors. **Pets:** $50 deposit/pet. Designated rooms, service with restrictions, crate.

SAVE S🐾 ⊠ &M &👁 💻 🍴 🗪

▼▼▼ Candlewood Suites SH
(785) 823-6939. **$49-$129.** 2650 Planet Ave. I-135, exit 89 (Schilling Rd), just e to S 9th St, 0.5 mi n to Belmont, then just w. Int corridors. **Pets:** Medium. $20 one-time fee/pet. Service with restrictions, crate.

ASK ⊠ &M &👁 💻 🗪

▼▼▼ Comfort Inn SH
(785) 826-1711. **$60-$120.** 1820 W Crawford St. I-135, exit 92, just e. Int corridors. **Pets:** Small, dogs only. $20 one-time fee/pet. Service with restrictions, supervision.

ASK S🐾 ⊠ &M 🝏 🖪 💻 🗪

▲▲▲ ▼▼▼ EconoLodge SH
(785) 825-8211. **$60-$70.** 1949 N 9th St. I-70, exit 252, just s. Ext corridors. **Pets:** Medium. $10 daily fee/pet. Designated rooms, service with restrictions, supervision.

SAVE S🐾 ⊠ 🖪 💻 🗪

▼▼▼ Holiday Inn Express Hotel & Suites-Salina SH
(785) 827-9000. **$79-$109.** 201 E Diamond Dr. I-70, exit 252, just ne. Int corridors. **Pets:** Accepted.

ASK ⊠ &M 🝏 &👁 🖪 💻 🗪

▼▼▼ Holiday Inn of Salina SH
(785) 823-1739. **$75-$95.** 1616 W Crawford St. I-135, exit 92, 0.5 mi e. Int corridors. **Pets:** Accepted.

ASK S🐾 ⊠ &M 🝏 &👁 🖪 💻 🍴 🗪 ⊠

▲▲▲ ▼▼▼ Red Coach Inn SH 🐾
(785) 825-2111. **$59-$109.** 2110 W Crawford St. I-135, exit 92, just w. Int corridors. **Pets:** $15 one-time fee/pet. Designated rooms, service with restrictions, supervision.

SAVE S🐾 ⊠ &M 🝏 &👁 🖪 💻 🍴 🗪 ⊠

▲▲▲ ▼▼ Super 8 I-70 SH
(785) 823-8808. **$61-$82.** 120 E Diamond Dr. I-70, exit 252, just ne. Int corridors. **Pets:** Medium. $50 deposit/room, $5 one-time fee/pet. Service with restrictions, supervision.

SAVE S🐾 ⊠ &M &👁 🖪 💻 🗪

SHARON SPRINGS

▼▼ Oak Tree Inn SH
(785) 852-4664. **$73-$79.** 801 N Hwy 27. Jct US 40 and SR 27. Ext/int corridors. **Pets:** Other species. $10 deposit/pet. Service with restrictions, supervision.

ASK S🐾 ⊠ 🝏 &👁 🖪 💻 🍴

SMITH CENTER

▲▲▲ ▼ U.S. Center Motel M
(785) 282-6611. **$36-$42.** 116 E Hwy 36. Jct US 36 and 281. Ext corridors. **Pets:** Accepted.

SAVE S🐾 ⊠ 🖪 🗪

TOPEKA

▼▼▼ Best Western Candlelight Inn M
(785) 272-9550. **$55-$139.** 2831 SW Fairlawn Rd. I-470, exit 3. Ext corridors. **Pets:** Accepted.

ASK ⊠ &👁 🖪 💻 🗪 ⊠

▲▲▲ ▼▼▼▼ Capitol Plaza Hotel LH
(785) 431-7200. **$99-$114.** 1717 SW Topeka Blvd. I-70, exit SE 8th Ave, 1.6 mi s; I-470, exit Topeka Blvd, 2.9 mi n. Int corridors. **Pets:** Other species. Service with restrictions, supervision.

SAVE ⊠ &M 🝏 &👁 🖪 💻 🍴 🗪 ⊠

▲▲▲ ▼▼▼▼ ClubHouse Inn & Suites SH
(785) 273-8888. **$109-$125.** 924 SW Henderson. I-70, exit 356 (Wanamaker Rd). Int corridors. **Pets:** Accepted.

SAVE S🐾 ⊠ 🝏 &👁 🖪 💻 🗪

▼▼ Comfort Inn by Choice Hotels SH
(785) 273-5365. **$70-$90.** 1518 SW Wanamaker Rd. I-470, exit 1 (Wanamaker Rd). Int corridors. **Pets:** Accepted.

ASK S🐾 ⊠ 🖪 💻 🗪

▼▼▼▼ Country Inn & Suites By Carlson-Topeka-West SH
(785) 478-9800. **$79-$150.** 6020 SW 10th St. I-70, exit 356 (Wanamaker Rd). Int corridors. **Pets:** Accepted.

ASK S🐾 ⊠ &M &👁 🖪 💻 🗪

▲▲▲ ▼▼▼ Quality Inn SH
(785) 273-6969. **$54-$129, 5 day notice.** 1240 SW Wanamaker Rd. I-470, exit 1 (Wanamaker Rd), just ne; I-70, exit 356A (Wanamaker Rd), 1 mi s. Int corridors. **Pets:** Other species. $10 one-time fee/pet. Supervision.

SAVE S🐾 ⊠ 🝏 🖪 💻 🗪

▼▼▼ Ramada Downtown Hotel & Convention Center LH
(785) 234-5400. **$59-$109.** 420 SE Sixth St. I-70, exit 362B, just e. Int corridors. **Pets:** Accepted.

ASK S🐾 ⊠ &M &👁 🖪 💻 🍴 🗪 ⊠

▼▼▼ Residence Inn by Marriott SH
(785) 271-8903. **$145-$185.** 1620 SW Westport Dr. I-470, exit 1 (Wanamaker Rd), just se. Int corridors. **Pets:** Accepted.

ASK S🐾 ⊠ &M 🝏 &👁 🖪 💻 🗪 ⊠

▼▼▼ The Senate Luxury Suites SH
(785) 233-5050. **$85-$120.** 900 SW Tyler. Just w of state capitol; downtown. Int corridors. **Pets:** Accepted.

ASK ⊠ 🖪 💻

Sleep Inn & Suites SH
(785) 228-2500. **$49-$89.** 1024 SW Wanamaker Rd. I-70, exit 356 (Wanamaker Rd), just s. Int corridors. **Pets:** Medium, other species. $10 daily fee/pet. Service with restrictions, supervision.
SAVE S X &M 🛎 🖥 💻 ≈

Super 8 at Forbes Landing SH ❀
(785) 862-2222. **$70-$140.** 5922 S Topeka Blvd. I-470, exit 6, 2.2 mi s. Int corridors. **Pets:** Dogs only. $20 one-time fee/room. Service with restrictions, supervision.
SAVE S X &M 🛎 🖥 💻 ≈

ULYSSES

Single Tree Inn SH
(620) 356-1500. **$73-$84.** 2033 W Oklahoma St. 1.5 mi w on US 160. Int corridors. **Pets:** Other species. $25 deposit/room. Service with restrictions, crate.
ASK S X 🛎 🖥 💻

UNIONTOWN

Wyatt Earp Inn & B&B SH ❀
(620) 756-4990. **$60-$150, 30 day notice.** 100 5th St. On SR 3; on west side of town. Int corridors. **Pets:** Other species. $25 deposit/pet, $10 one-time fee/pet. Supervision.
ASK S X

WAMEGO

Simmer Motel M
(785) 456-2304. **$44-$90.** 1215 Hwy 24 W. Jct SR 99, 0.5 mi w. Ext corridors. **Pets:** Large. $5 one-time fee/pet. Designated rooms, service with restrictions, supervision.
SAVE X 🛎 💻 ≈

WICHITA

Best Western Airport Inn & Conference Center SH
(316) 942-5600. **$89-$175.** 6815 W Kellogg. I-235, exit 7, 0.6 mi w on US 54 (S Frontage Rd). Int corridors. **Pets:** Small. Service with restrictions, supervision.
SAVE X 🛎 🖥 💻 ¶ ≈ ⊠

Best Western Governors Inn & Suites SH
(316) 522-0775. **$69-$79.** 4742 S Emporia. I-135, exit 1B, just sw. Int corridors. **Pets:** Accepted.
SAVE S X 🛎 💻 ≈

Best Western Hotel & Suites SH
(316) 832-9387. **$75-$99.** 915 E 53rd St N. I-135, exit 13, just w. Ext/int corridors. **Pets:** $20 one-time fee/pet. Service with restrictions, supervision.
SAVE S X 🛎 🖥 💻 ¶ ≈ ⊠

Candlewood Suites SH
(316) 942-0400. **$79-$139.** 570 S Julia. I-235, exit 7, 0.4 mi nw on Dugan Rd. Int corridors. **Pets:** Medium, other species. $150 one-time fee/room. Service with restrictions, crate.
ASK S X 🛎 🖥

Comfort Inn SH ❀
(316) 522-1800. **$69.** 4849 S Laura. I-135, exit 1A/B (47th St S), just e. Int corridors. **Pets:** Other species. $10 one-time fee/room. Service with restrictions, supervision.
SAVE S X 🛎 🖥 💻 ≈

Comfort Inn by Choice Hotels SH
(316) 686-2844. **$74-$104.** 9525 E Corporate Hills Dr. I-35, exit 50, just ne. Int corridors. **Pets:** Accepted.
ASK S X 🛎 🖥 💻

Comfort Suites Airport SH
(316) 945-2600. **$85-$95, 10 day notice.** 658 Westdale. Jct I-235 and US 54. Int corridors. **Pets:** Accepted.
SAVE S X 🛎 🖥 💻 ≈

Cresthill Suites Hotel SH
(316) 689-8000. **$129.** 12111 E Central Ave. 1.7 mi e of jct Rock Rd. Int corridors. **Pets:** Accepted.
ASK S X 🛎 🖥 💻

Econo Lodge Inn & Suites SH
(316) 722-8730. **$49-$54, 3 day notice.** 600 S Holland. I-235, exit 7, 1.1 mi w on US 54. Int corridors. **Pets:** Accepted.
SAVE S X 🛎 🖥 💻 ≈

Four Points by Sheraton Wichita Airport SH
(316) 942-7911. **$69-$129.** 5805 W Kellogg. I-235, exit 7A, just w. Int corridors. **Pets:** Accepted.
SAVE X 🛎 🖥 💻 ¶ ≈

Hampton Inn by Hilton SH
(316) 686-3576. **$89-$129.** 9449 E Corporate Hills Dr. I-35, exit 50, just ne. Int corridors. **Pets:** Other species. Service with restrictions.
ASK S X &M 🛎 🖥 💻 ≈

Hawthorn Suites at Reflection Ridge SH
(316) 729-5700. **$104-$122.** 2405 N Ridge Rd. I-235, exit 10, 1.7 mi w on Zoo Blvd/21st St N, then just n. Int corridors. **Pets:** $20 one-time fee/room. Service with restrictions, crate.
ASK S X 🛎 🖥 💻

Holiday Inn Express SH
(316) 529-4848. **$85-$120.** 4848 S Laura. I-35, exit 1B, just ne. Int corridors. **Pets:** Other species. $25 one-time fee/room. Crate.
SAVE X 🛎 🖥 💻 ≈

Holiday Inn Hotel & Suites Convention Center SH
(316) 269-2090. **$89-$149.** 221 E Kellogg. Just sw of jct US 54/400 and Broadway. Int corridors. **Pets:** Medium, other species. Service with restrictions, crate.
ASK S X &M 🛎 🖥 💻 ¶ ≈ ⊠

Holiday Inn Select SH
(316) 686-7131. **$79-$99.** 549 S Rock Rd. I-35, exit 50, 0.5 mi w. Ext/int corridors. **Pets:** Small. $25 one-time fee/room. Designated rooms, service with restrictions, supervision.
SAVE X 🛎 🖥 💻 ¶ ≈ ⊠

La Quinta Inn & Suites SH
(316) 943-2181. **$72-$81.** 5500 W Kellogg. I-235, exit 7, just w. Int corridors. **Pets:** Accepted.
SAVE S X 🛎 🖥 💻 ¶ ≈ ⊠

Residence Inn by Marriott SH
(316) 686-7331. **$154.** 411 S Webb Rd. I-35, exit 50, just ne. Ext corridors. **Pets:** Accepted.
ASK S X 🛎 💻 ≈ ⊠

Residence Inn by Marriott at Plazzio SH
(316) 682-7300. **$134-$199, 3 day notice.** 1212 N Greenwich. SR 96, exit 13th St, 0.5 mi sw. Int corridors. **Pets:** Accepted.
ASK S X &M 🛎 🖥 💻 ≈ ⊠

Super 8 Motel-Wichita/East M
(316) 686-3888. **$50-$55.** 527 S Webb Rd. I-35, exit 50, just e. Int corridors. **Pets:** $25 daily fee/room.
SAVE S X 🛎 🖥 💻

TownePlace Suites by Marriott SH
(316) 631-3773. **$109.** 9444 E 29th St N. SR 96, exit Webb Rd, just sw. Int corridors. **Pets:** Accepted.
ASK S X &M 🛎 🖥 💻 ⊠

▼▼ Wesley Inn SH
(316) 858-3343. **$55-$65.** 3343 E Central Ave. Just e of jct Hillside. Int corridors. **Pets:** Accepted.
(ASK) (SD) (X) (&) (📶) (💻)

WINFIELD

▼▼▼ Comfort Inn SH
(620) 221-7529. **$91-$179.** Hwy 77 at Quail Ridge Dr. On US 77, 1 mi s. Ext/int corridors. **Pets:** Accepted.
(ASK) (SD) (X) (🐾) (📶) (💻) (🏊)

▼▼ Econo Lodge M
(620) 221-9050. **$56-$71.** 1710 Main St. 0.5 mi s of jct US 77 and 160. Ext corridors. **Pets:** Medium. $10 daily fee/pet. Designated rooms, service with restrictions, supervision.
(ASK) (SD) (X) (📶) (💻)

CITY INDEX

BARDSTOWN

◈ ▽▽ Bardstown-Parkview Motel M
(502) 348-5983. **$60-$85.** 418 E Stephen Foster Ave. 0.5 mi e on US 150; e of jct US 62. Ext corridors. **Pets:** Small. Service with restrictions, supervision.

▽▽ Best Western General Nelson Motel SH
(502) 348-3977. **$62-$79, 7 day notice.** 411 W Stephen Foster Ave. 0.5 mi w on US 62. Ext corridors. **Pets:** Small. $10 one-time fee/pet. Service with restrictions, crate.

◈ ▽▽▽ Hampton Inn SH
(502) 349-0100. **$89-$99.** 985 Chambers Blvd. Just s of US 245. Int corridors. **Pets:** Medium. $50 one-time fee/room. Supervision.

▽▽ Old Bardstown Inn SH
(502) 349-0776. **$55-$99, 3 day notice.** 510 E Stephen Foster Ave. 0.5 mi e on US 150; e of jct US 62. Ext corridors. **Pets:** Medium. $15 deposit/room, $5 daily fee/pet. Service with restrictions, crate.

BEAVER DAM

▽▽▽ Days Inn Beaver Dam SH
(270) 274-0851. **$64-$90.** 1750 US Hwy 231. Kentucky Pkwy, exit 75, just n. Int corridors. **Pets:** Accepted.

BENTON

▽▽▽ Holiday Inn Express Hotel & Suites SH
(270) 527-5300. **$71-$89.** 173 Carroll Rd. Purchase Pkwy, exit 47. Int corridors. **Pets:** Accepted.

BEREA

◈ ▽▽▽ Boone Tavern Hotel-Berea College SH
(859) 985-3700. **$92-$125.** 100 Main St. I-75, exit 76, 1.5 mi ne on SR 21. Int corridors. **Pets:** Accepted.

◈ ▽▽▽ Comfort Inn & Suites SH
(859) 985-5500. **$59-$89.** 1003 Paint Lick Rd. I-75, exit 76, just w. Int corridors. **Pets:** Small. $10 one-time fee/pet. Service with restrictions, supervision.

◈ ▽▽▽ Knights Inn Berea M
(859) 986-2384. **$40-$60.** 715 Chestnut St. I-75, exit 76, 0.3 mi e. Ext corridors. **Pets:** Other species. $6 daily fee/pet. Supervision.

BOWLING GREEN

◈ ▽▽ Continental Inn SH
(270) 781-5200. **$58-$65, 3 day notice.** 700 Interstate Dr. I-65, exit 28, 0.3 mi w. Ext corridors. **Pets:** Small. $10 daily fee/room. Designated rooms, no service, supervision.

◈ ▽▽▽ Country Hearth Inn SH
(270) 783-4443. **$49-$54.** 395 Corvette Dr. I-65, exit 28, just w. Int corridors. **Pets:** Very small. $20 deposit/room. Service with restrictions, supervision.

▽▽▽ Drury Inn-Bowling Green SH
(270) 842-7100. **$90-$140.** 3250 Scottsville Rd. I-65, exit 22 (Scottsville Rd), just w. Int corridors. **Pets:** Large, other species. Service with restrictions, supervision.

◈ ▽▽▽ Holiday Inn University Plaza LH ❀
(270) 745-0088. **$109-$149.** 1021 Wilkinson Trace. I-65, exit 22 (Scottsville Rd), 2.5 mi w, then just n. Int corridors. **Pets:** Small, other species. $25 one-time fee/room. Service with restrictions, supervision.

◈ ▽▽▽ News Inn of Bowling Green M
(270) 781-3460. **$49-$69.** 3160 Scottsville Rd. I-65, exit 22 (Scottsville Rd). Ext corridors. **Pets:** Large. $5 daily fee/pet. Service with restrictions, supervision.

◈ ▽▽▽ Red Roof Inn SH
(270) 781-6550. **$59-$99.** 3140 Scottsville Rd. I-65, exit 22 (Scottsville Rd), 0.3 mi w. Ext corridors. **Pets:** Large. Service with restrictions, supervision.

CADIZ

▽▽▽▽ Holiday Inn Express SH
(270) 522-3700. **$72-$80.** 153 Broad Bent Blvd. I-24, exit 65, just s. Int corridors. **Pets:** Small, other species. $20 one-time fee/room. Designated rooms, service with restrictions, supervision.

▽▽ Super 8 Motel SH
(270) 522-7007. **$59-$65.** 154 Hospitality Ln. I-24, exit 65. Ext corridors. **Pets:** Accepted.

CAMPBELLSVILLE

Best Western Campbellsville Lodge SH
(270) 465-7001. **$60.** 1400 E Broadway. 2 mi e on US 68 and SR 55.
Int corridors. **Pets:** Very small. $10 daily fee/pet. Designated rooms, service with restrictions, supervision.

Holiday Inn Express SH
(270) 465-2727. **$68.** 102 Plantation Dr. Jct US 68 and SR 55, 0.5 mi
n. Int corridors. **Pets:** Other species. $10 daily fee/pet. Service with restrictions, crate.

Lakeview Motel SH
(270) 465-8139. **$45-$48.** 1291 Old Lebanon Rd. 1 mi n on SR 289.
Ext corridors. **Pets:** Accepted.

CARROLLTON

Best Western Executive Inn SH
(502) 732-8444. **$65-$119.** 10 Slumber Ln. I-71, exit 44, just nw. Int
corridors. **Pets:** Accepted.

Days Inn Carrollton SH
(502) 732-9301. **$49-$99.** 61 Inn Rd. I-71, exit 44, just nw. Int corridors.
Pets: Accepted.

Super 8 Carrollton SH
(502) 732-0252. **$55-$99.** 130 Slumber Ln. I-71, exit 44, just nw. Int
corridors. **Pets:** Accepted.

CATLETTSBURG

Ramada Limited Hotel SH
(606) 739-5700. **$82-$92.** 6000 Crider Dr. I-64, exit 191, 0.5 mi n on US
23. Int corridors. **Pets:** $10 daily fee/pet. Designated rooms, service with
restrictions, supervision.

CAVE CITY

Comfort Inn SH
(270) 773-2030. **$45-$110, 3 day notice.** 801 Mammoth Cave St. I-65,
exit 53, just ne. Ext corridors. **Pets:** Very small. $10 daily fee/pet. Designated rooms, service with restrictions, supervision.

Super 8 Motel SH
(270) 773-2500. **$49-$85.** 799 Mammoth Cave St. I-65, exit 53, just ne.
Ext corridors. **Pets:** Accepted.

CENTRAL CITY

Days Inn SH
(270) 754-1222. **$60-$85.** 640 S 2nd St. Western Kentucky Pkwy, exit
58, just n. Int corridors. **Pets:** Accepted.

CORBIN

Baymont Inn & Suites-Corbin SH
(606) 523-9040. **$65-$165.** 174 Adams Rd. I-75, exit 29. Int corridors.
Pets: Accepted.

Best Western-Corbin Inn SH
(606) 528-2100. **$59-$99.** 2630 Cumberland Falls Hwy. I-75, exit 25.
Ext corridors. **Pets:** Small. $10 daily fee/pet. Designated rooms, service
with restrictions, supervision.

Comfort Suites SH
(606) 526-6646. **$74-$100.** 47 Adams Rd. I-75, exit 29. Int corridors.
Pets: Accepted.

COVINGTON

Embassy Suites Cincinnati RiverCenter LH
(859) 261-8400. **$139-$229.** 10 E RiverCenter Blvd. I-71/75, exit 192,
0.8 mi e on 5th St, then 0.3 mi n on Madison Ave. Int corridors.
Pets: Medium. $25 daily fee/room. Designated rooms, service with restrictions, supervision.

Extended StayAmerica SH
(859) 581-3000. **Call for rates.** 650 W 3rd St. I-71/75, exit 192, 0.5 mi
ne on SR 8. Int corridors. **Pets:** Accepted.

DANVILLE

Holiday Inn Express-Danville SH
(859) 236-8600. **$69-$109.** 96 Daniel Dr. Just e of US 127 on US 150
Bypass. Int corridors. **Pets:** Other species. $50 deposit/room. Service with
restrictions, supervision.

DRY RIDGE

Holiday Inn Express SH
(859) 824-7121. **$67-$89.** 1050 Fashion Ridge Rd. I-75, exit 159, just
nw. Int corridors. **Pets:** Medium. $10 one-time fee/pet. Designated rooms,
service with restrictions, supervision.

Microtel Inn and Suites SH
(859) 824-2000. **$39-$59.** 79 Blackburn Ln. I-75, exit 159, just ne. Int
corridors. **Pets:** Other species. $7 one-time fee/pet. Service with restrictions, supervision.

EDDYVILLE

Eddy Creek Resort & Marina CA
(270) 388-2271. **$74, 45 day notice.** 7612 SR 93 S. I-24, exit 45, 4 mi
s. Ext corridors. **Pets:** Medium. $100 deposit/room. Service with restrictions, supervision.

ELIZABETHTOWN

Best Western Atrium Gardens SH
(270) 769-3030. **$89-$130.** 1043 Executive Dr. I-65, exit 94, just nw. Int
corridors. **Pets:** Other species. $15 one-time fee/pet. Service with restrictions, crate.

Country Hearth Inn & Suites SH
(270) 769-2344. **$69-$75, 5 day notice.** 1058 N Mulberry St. I-65, exit
94, just nw. Ext corridors. **Pets:** Accepted.

Holiday Inn Express SH
(270) 769-1334. **$99-$120.** 107 Buffalo Creek Dr. I-65, exit 94, just w.
Int corridors. **Pets:** Small. $25 daily fee/room. Designated rooms, service
with restrictions, supervision.

Kentucky Cardinal Inn SH
(270) 765-6139. **$76-$136.** 642 E Dixie Ave. I-65, exit 91 (US 31 W),
0.3 mi nw. Ext/int corridors. **Pets:** Accepted.

La Quinta Inn Elizabethtown SH
(270) 765-4747. **$70-$100.** 210 Commerce Dr. I-65, exit 94, just nw. Int corridors. **Pets:** Accepted.

Quality Inn & Suites SH
(270) 765-4166. **$69-$129.** 2009 N Mulberry St. I-65, exit 94, just sw. Int corridors. **Pets:** Accepted.

ERLANGER

Comfort Inn-Cincinnati Airport SH
(859) 727-3400. **$70-$90.** 630 Donaldson Rd. I-71/75, exit 184, off SR 236 southbound; exit 184B northbound. Int corridors. **Pets:** Medium. $10 daily fee/room. Service with restrictions, supervision.

Days Inn SH
(859) 342-7111. **$59-$69.** 599 Donaldson Ave. I-75, exit 184. Ext corridors. **Pets:** Small, dogs only. $15 daily fee/room. Service with restrictions, supervision.

Residence Inn by Marriott, Cincinnati Airport SH
(859) 282-7400. **$134-$199.** 2811 Circleport Dr. I-275, exit 2. Int corridors. **Pets:** Other species. $100 one-time fee/room. Service with restrictions.

FLORENCE

Ashley Quarters SH
(859) 525-9997. **$84-$114.** 4880 Houston Rd. I-71/75, exit 182, 0.6 mi w on Turfway and Houston rds. Int corridors. **Pets:** Accepted.

Best Western Inn Florence SH
(859) 525-0090. **$54-$125.** 7821 Commerce Dr. I-71/75, exit 181, just ne. Int corridors. **Pets:** Small, dogs only. $15 daily fee/pet. Designated rooms, service with restrictions, supervision.

Extended StayAmerica SH
(859) 282-7829. **Call for rates.** 7350 Turfway Rd. I-71/75, exit 182, just w. Int corridors. **Pets:** Accepted.

Florence Super 8 SH
(859) 283-1221. **$70-$90.** 7928 Dream St. I-71/75, exit 180, just e on US 42, then just n. Int corridors. **Pets:** Accepted.

La Quinta Inn & Suites SH
(859) 282-8212. **$89-$119.** 350 Meijer Dr. I-71/85, exit 182, 0.4 mi sw. Int corridors. **Pets:** Service with restrictions, supervision.

Red Roof Inn M
(859) 647-2700. **$58-$76.** 7454 Turfway Rd. I-71/75, exit 182, 0.8 mi sw. Int corridors. **Pets:** Medium. Service with restrictions, supervision.

StudioPLUS-Cincinnati-Florence SH
(859) 746-0172. **$65-$125.** 200 Meijer Dr. I-71/75, exit 182, 0.3 mi w, then 0.4 mi s. Int corridors. **Pets:** Accepted.

FORT MITCHELL

Best Western Fort Mitchell SH
(859) 331-1500. **$79-$149.** 2100 Dixie Hwy. I-71/75, exit 188, just w. Ext/int corridors. **Pets:** Accepted.

FRANKFORT

Americas Best Value Inn SH 🐾
(502) 875-3220. **$61-$81.** 1225 US Hwy 127 S. I-64, exit 53B, 1.2 mi n. Int corridors. **Pets:** Dogs only. $10 one-time fee/room. Designated rooms, service with restrictions, supervision.

Bluegrass Inn M
(502) 695-1800. **$48-$64.** 635 Versailles Rd. I-64, exit 58, 1 mi n on US 60. Ext corridors. **Pets:** Medium. $10 daily fee/pet. Designated rooms, service with restrictions, supervision.

Capital Plaza Hotel LH
(502) 227-5100. **$81-$125.** 405 Wilkinson Blvd. Adjacent to Frankfort Convention Center. Int corridors. **Pets:** Medium. $25 deposit/room. Designated rooms, service with restrictions, supervision.

FRANKLIN

Comfort Inn SH
(270) 586-6100. **$69-$99.** 3794 Nashville Rd. I-65, exit 2. Ext corridors. **Pets:** Medium. $10 daily fee/room. Service with restrictions, supervision.

Super 8 Motel SH
(270) 586-5090. **$55-$70.** 3811 Nashville Rd. I-65, exit 2, just w. Ext corridors. **Pets:** Small, dogs only. $10 daily fee/pet. Designated rooms, no service, supervision.

GEORGETOWN

Days Inn of Georgetown M
(502) 863-5000. **$37-$80.** 385 Cherry Blossom Way. I-75, exit 129, just se. Ext corridors. **Pets:** $5 daily fee/pet. Service with restrictions, supervision.

GLASGOW

Comfort Inn SH
(270) 651-9099. **$70-$90.** 210 Calvary Dr. Cumberland Pkwy, exit 11, just n. Ext corridors. **Pets:** Small. $10 daily fee/room. Service with restrictions, supervision.

GRAND RIVERS

Best Western Kentucky-Barkley Lakes Inn SH
(270) 928-2700. **$56.** 720 Complex Dr. I-24, exit 31 (SR 453), just s. Ext/int corridors. **Pets:** Accepted.

Microtel Inn & Suites SH
(270) 928-2740. **$51-$74.** 1017 Dover Rd. I-24, exit 31 (SR 453), just n. Int corridors. **Pets:** Accepted.

GRAYSON

Super 8 Motel SH
(606) 474-8811. **$39-$89.** 125 Super 8 Ln. I-64, exit 172, just s. Int corridors. **Pets:** Small. $10 daily fee/pet. Designated rooms, service with restrictions, supervision.

HARLAN

Holiday Inn Express Harlan SH
(606) 573-3385. **$74-$79.** 2608 S Hwy 421. On US 421, 2.8 mi s. Int corridors. **Pets:** Small. $7 daily fee/room. Designated rooms, service with restrictions, supervision.

HARRODSBURG

▼▼ ▼▼ Country Hearth Inn SH
(859) 734-2400. **$59-$75.** 105 Commercial Dr. 0.6 mi n on College St. Int corridors. **Pets:** Small. $20 one-time fee/pet. Service with restrictions, supervision.
ASK S✆ ⊠ 🛏 💻

▼▼ ▼▼ Days Inn Danville and Harrodsburg SH
(859) 734-9431. **$60-$80.** 1680 Danville Rd. 3 mi s on US 127. Ext/int corridors. **Pets:** Accepted.
ASK S✆ ⊠ 🛏 💻 ⇌

HENDERSON

▼▼▼▼ Ramada Inn SH
(270) 826-6600. **$70.** 2044 US 41 N. 1 mi n on US 41. Int corridors. **Pets:** Accepted.
ASK S✆ ⊠ 🐾 🛏 💻 🍴 ⇌

HOPKINSVILLE

▼▼▼▼ Holiday Inn SH
(270) 886-4413. **$89-$109.** 2910 Ft Campbell Blvd. Pennyrile Pkwy, exit 7A, 0.6 mi n on US 41A. Int corridors. **Pets:** Medium. $25 deposit/room. Designated rooms, service with restrictions, supervision.
ASK S✆ ⊠ 🛏 💻 🍴 ⇌ ⊠

▲▲▲ ▼▼▼ Hopkinsville Best Western SH
(270) 886-9000. **$69-$79.** 4101 Ft Campbell Blvd. Pennyrile Pkwy, exit 7A, just s on US 41A. Int corridors. **Pets:** Accepted.
SAVE ⊠ 🛏 💻 ⇌

HORSE CAVE

▼▼▼▼ Hampton Inn SH
(270) 786-5000. **$59-$79.** 750 Flint Ridge Rd. I-65, exit 58, just nw. Int corridors. **Pets:** Accepted.
ASK S✆ ⊠ 🛏 💻 ⇌ ⊠

KUTTAWA

▼▼ ▼▼ Days Inn SH 🐾
(270) 388-4060. **$56-$105.** 139 Days Inn Dr. I-24, exit 40 (US 62), just s. Ext corridors. **Pets:** Large, other species. $10 one-time fee/room. No service, supervision.
ASK ⊠ 🕹M 🗝 🛏 💻 ⇌

LEBANON

▼▼▼▼ Hampton Inn Lebanon SH
(270) 699-4000. **$77-$87.** 1125 Loretto Rd. Jct SR 49 and 84. Int corridors. **Pets:** Medium, other species. $25 one-time fee/room. Service with restrictions, crate.
ASK S✆ ⊠ 🕹M 🐾 🗝 🛏 💻 ⇌

LEITCHFIELD

▼▼ ▼▼ Hatfield Inn SH
(270) 259-0464. **$63-$80.** 769 White St. Western Kentucky Pkwy, exit 107, just nw. Int corridors. **Pets:** $10 daily fee/pet. Service with restrictions, supervision.
ASK S✆ ⊠ 🛏

LEWISPORT

▼▼▼▼ Best Western Hancock Inn M
(270) 295-3234. **$59-$99.** 9040 US Hwy 60 W. On US 60. Int corridors. **Pets:** Other species. $50 deposit/pet. Service with restrictions, supervision.
ASK S✆ ⊠ 🛏 💻 ⇌

LEXINGTON

▲▲▲ ▼▼ ▼▼ Days Inn-South SH
(859) 263-3100. **$54-$65.** 5575 Athens-Boonesboro Rd. I-75, exit 104, just e. Ext corridors. **Pets:** Other species. $10 daily fee/pet. Service with restrictions.
SAVE S✆ ⊠ 🕹M 🛏 💻

▼▼ ▼▼ Econo Lodge SH
(859) 263-5101. **$40-$59.** 5527 Athens Boonesboro Rd. I-75, exit 104. Ext corridors. **Pets:** Accepted.
ASK S✆ ⊠ 🛏

▼▼ ▼▼ Extended StayAmerica-Nicholasville Rd SH
(859) 278-9600. **Call for rates.** 2650 Wilhite Dr. Jct US 27 and SR 4. Ext corridors. **Pets:** Accepted.
⊠ 🕹M 🐾 🗝 🛏 💻

▼▼ ▼▼ Extended StayAmerica-Tates Creek SH
(859) 271-6160. **Call for rates.** 3575 Tates Creek Rd. New Circle Rd (SR 4), exit 18, 0.4 mi s. Int corridors. **Pets:** Accepted.
⊠ 🛏 💻

▼▼ ▼▼ ▼▼ Griffin Gate Marriott Resort LH
(859) 231-5100. **$109-$329.** 1800 Newtown Pike. I-75/64, exit 115, 0.5 mi sw. Int corridors. **Pets:** Other species. $75 one-time fee/room. Designated rooms, service with restrictions, crate.
ASK S✆ ⊠ 🕹M 🐾 🗝 🛏 💻 🍴 ⇌ ⊠

▲▲▲ ▼▼▼▼ Hampton Inn I-75 SH
(859) 299-2613. **$89-$129.** 2251 Elkhorn Rd. I-75, exit 110, 0.4 mi nw. Int corridors. **Pets:** Large. Service with restrictions, supervision.
SAVE S✆ ⊠ 🕹M 🛏 💻 ⇌

▼▼▼▼ Holiday Inn Express Hotel & Suites-Lexington SH
(859) 389-6800. **$79-$139.** 1000 Export St. I-75, exit 113, 4.5 mi s, then just e. Int corridors. **Pets:** Medium. $25 one-time fee/room. Designated rooms, service with restrictions, supervision.
ASK S✆ ⊠ 🕹M 🗝 🛏 💻 ⇌

▲▲▲ ▼▼▼▼ Holiday Inn-Lexington North LH 🐾
(859) 233-0512. **$109-$209.** 1950 Newtown Pike. I-75/64, exit 115, just s. Ext/int corridors. **Pets:** Small. $50 one-time fee/room. Service with restrictions, supervision.
SAVE S✆ ⊠ 🕹M 🐾 🛏 💻 🍴 ⇌ ⊠

▲▲▲ ▼▼▼▼ Holiday Inn Lexington South SH
(859) 263-5241. **$74-$99.** 5532 Athens-Boonesboro Rd. I-75, exit 104, just e. Int corridors. **Pets:** Small. $15 daily fee/pet. Service with restrictions, supervision.
SAVE S✆ ⊠ 🐾 🛏 💻 🍴 ⇌ ⊠

▲▲▲ ▼▼▼▼ Hyatt Regency Lexington LH
(859) 253-1234. **$99-$235.** 401 W High St. Center. Int corridors. **Pets:** Accepted.
SAVE ⊠ 🕹M 🐾 🛏 💻 🍴 ⇌

▼▼▼▼ La Quinta Inn Lexington SH
(859) 231-7551. **$80-$101.** 1919 Stanton Way. I-75/64, exit 115, just se off SR 922. Int corridors. **Pets:** Accepted.
ASK ⊠ 🛏 💻 ⇌

▼▼ ▼▼ Microtel Inn SH
(859) 299-9600. **$45-$125, 14 day notice.** 2240 Buena Vista Rd. I-75, exit 110, just w. Int corridors. **Pets:** Other species. $20 one-time fee/room. Service with restrictions.
⊠

▲▲▲ ▼▼▼▼ Radisson Plaza Hotel Lexington LH
(859) 231-9000. **$99-$179.** 369 W Vine St. Corner of Vine St and Broadway. Int corridors. **Pets:** Accepted.
SAVE S✆ ⊠ 🕹M 🐾 🗝 🛏 💻 🍴 ⇌ ⊠

▼▼ **Ramada Conference Center** SH
(859) 299-1261. **$79-$89.** 2143 N Broadway. I-75/64, exit 113, just e. Int corridors. **Pets:** $10 daily fee/pet. Service with restrictions, supervision.
[ASK] [S] [X] [&M] [🐾] [🐾] [🖥] [💻] [📺] [🍴] [🏊] [🐾]

▼ **Red Roof Inn-North** SH
(859) 293-2626. **$52-$69.** 1980 Haggard Ct. I-75/64, exit 113, 0.3 mi nw. Ext corridors. **Pets:** Medium, other species. Service with restrictions, supervision.
[X]

▼▼ **Red Roof Inn South** SH
(859) 277-9400. **$57-$72.** 2651 Wilhite Dr. Jct US 27 and SR 4. Ext corridors. **Pets:** Medium, other species. Service with restrictions, supervision.
[X] [&M] [🖥]

▼▼ **Red Roof Inn Southeast** SH
(859) 543-1877. **$45-$85, 14 day notice.** 100 Canebrake Dr. I-75, exit 104, just e. Int corridors. **Pets:** Medium, other species. Supervision.
[ASK] [S] [X] [🖥] [💻] [🏊]

▼▼▼ **Residence Inn by Marriott** SH
(859) 231-6191. **$129-$189.** 1080 Newtown Pike. I-75/64, exit 115, 1 mi s on SR 922. Ext corridors. **Pets:** Accepted.
[ASK] [S] [X] [🐾] [🖥] [💻] [🏊] [X]

▼▼▼ **Residence Inn South @ Hamburg** SH 🐾
(859) 263-9979. **$99-$189, 14 day notice.** 2688 Pink Pigeon Pkwy. I-75, exit 108, just se. Int corridors. **Pets:** Other species.
[ASK] [S] [X] [&M] [🐾] [🐾] [🖥] [💻] [🍴] [🏊] [X]

▼▼▼ **Sheraton Suites Lexington** LH 🐾
(859) 268-0060. **$109-$350.** 2601 Richmond Rd. I-75, exit 104, 5.5 mi w. Int corridors. **Pets:** Service with restrictions, crate.
[ASK] [S] [X] [&M] [🐾] [🖥] [💻] [🍴] [🏊]

▼▼ **Sleep Inn Lexington** SH
(859) 543-8400. **$69-$129.** 1920 Plaudit Pl. I-75, exit 108, just sw. Int corridors. **Pets:** Accepted.
[ASK] [S] [X] [🐾] [🖥] [💻] [🏊]

LIBERTY

🆔 ▼ **Royal Inn Express** SH
(606) 787-6224. **$42-$44.** 579 N Wallace Wilkinson Blvd. 1 mi n on US 127; 0.5 mi n of jct SR 70. Ext corridors. **Pets:** Medium. $5 daily fee/pet. No service, supervision.
[SAVE] [X] [🖥]

LONDON

▼ **Budget Host Westgate Inn** SH 🐾
(606) 878-7330. **$45-$54, 3 day notice.** 254 Russell Dyche Memorial Hwy. I-75, exit 41, just w on SR 80. Ext/int corridors. **Pets:** Small. Designated rooms, service with restrictions, supervision.
[S] [X] [&M] [🐾] [🖥] [🏊]

▼▼▼▼ **Holiday Inn Express** SH
(608) 862-0077. **$80-$150.** 506 Minton Dr. I-75, exit 38, just e. Int corridors. **Pets:** Accepted.
[ASK] [S] [X] [&M] [🐾] [🐾] [🖥] [💻] [🏊]

▼▼ **Red Roof Inn** SH
(606) 862-8844. **$50-$80.** 110 Melcon Ln. I-75, exit 41, southwest corner. Int corridors. **Pets:** Medium, other species. Service with restrictions, supervision.
[ASK] [X] [&M] [🖥] [💻] [🏊]

LOUISVILLE METROPOLITAN AREA

BROOKS

▼▼▼ **Comfort Inn** SH 🐾
(502) 957-6900. **$69-$250.** 149 Willabrook Dr. I-65, exit 121, just nw. Int corridors. **Pets:** Other species. $10 daily fee/room. Service with restrictions.
[ASK] [S] [X] [🖥] [💻] [🏊] [X]

HURSTBOURNE

▼▼▼▼ **Drury Inn & Suites-Louisville** SH
(502) 326-4170. **$80-$140.** 9501 Blairwood Rd. I-64, exit 15. Int corridors. **Pets:** Large, other species. Service with restrictions, supervision.
[ASK] [X] [&M] [🐾] [🐾] [🖥] [💻] [🏊]

▼▼ **Red Roof Inn Louisville–East #034** SH
(502) 426-7621. **$53-$72.** 9330 Blairwood Rd. I-64, exit 15, 0.3 mi nw of Hurstbourne Pkwy. Ext corridors. **Pets:** Medium, other species. Service with restrictions, supervision.
[X] [&M] [🐾] [🖥]

JEFFERSONTOWN

🆔 ▼▼▼▼ **Clarion Hotel and Conference Center** LH
(502) 491-4830. **$60-$299.** 9700 Bluegrass Pkwy. I-64, exit 15, 0.5 mi se of Hurstbourne Pkwy. Int corridors. **Pets:** Very small, dogs only. $35 one-time fee/pet. Designated rooms, service with restrictions, crate.
[SAVE] [X] [🐾] [🖥] [💻] [🍴] [🏊] [X]

▼▼▼ **Comfort Suites** SH
(502) 266-6509. **$74-$400.** 1850 Resource Way. I-64, exit 17, 0.5 mi s of Blankenbaker Rd. Int corridors. **Pets:** Accepted.
[S] [X] [&M] [🖥] [💻] [🏊]

▼▼ **Extended StayAmerica** SH
(502) 499-6215. **Call for rates.** 9801 Bunsen Way. I-64, exit 15A, 0.5 mi e on Hurstbourne Pkwy. Int corridors. **Pets:** Accepted.
[X] [🐾] [🖥] [💻] [🏊]

🆔 ▼▼▼▼ **Holiday Inn-Hurstbourne** LH
(502) 426-2600. **$79-$179.** 1325 S Hurstbourne Pkwy. I-64, exit 15. Ext/int corridors. **Pets:** Large, other species. $39 one-time fee/room. Service with restrictions.
[SAVE] [S] [X] [🐾] [🖥] [💻] [🍴] [🏊] [X]

▼▼▼▼ **Homestead Studio Suites Louisville–Alliant Drive** SH
(502) 267-4454. **$60-$135.** 1650 Alliant Ave. I-64, exit 17, just s. Int corridors. **Pets:** Accepted.
[ASK] [S] [X] [&M] [🐾] [🖥] [💻] [🏊]

▼▼▼ **Jameson Inn Louisville East** SH
(502) 267-8100. **$54-$120.** 1301 Kentucky Mills Dr. I-64, exit 17. Ext/int corridors. **Pets:** Small. $10 daily fee/pet. Service with restrictions, crate.
[ASK] [X] [&M] [🐾] [🖥] [💻] [🏊] [X]

▼▼ **Microtel Inn** SH
(502) 266-6590. **$65-$225.** 1221 Kentucky Mills Dr. I-64, exit 17. Int corridors. **Pets:** Small. $20 one-time fee/pet. Service with restrictions, supervision.
[ASK] [S] [X] [&M] [🐾] [🐾]

▼▼ **Sleep Inn** SH
(502) 266-6776. **$59-$250.** 1850 Priority Way. I-64, exit 17, 0.5 mi s of Blankenbaker Rd. Int corridors. **Pets:** Accepted.
[ASK] [S] [X] [🖥] [💻]

▼▼ **Super 8 Motel & Suites** SH
(502) 267-8889. **$50-$350.** 1501 Alliant Ave. I-64, exit 17, just e. Int corridors. **Pets:** Medium, other species. $20 daily fee/pet. Designated rooms, no service, supervision.

ASK S✿ ⊠ &M (≀ 🖥 💻 ⇋

LA GRANGE

▼▼▼ **Comfort Suites** SH ❋
(502) 225-4125. **$72-$180.** 1500 Crystal Dr. I-71, exit 22, just e. Int corridors. **Pets:** Large. $50 deposit/pet, $10 one-time fee/pet. Service with restrictions, supervision.

ASK S✿ ⊠ &M (≀ 🖥 💻 ⇋ ⊠

▼▼▼▼ **Holiday Inn Express** SH
(502) 222-5678. **$90-$200.** 1001 Paige Pl. I-71, exit 22, just se. Int corridors. **Pets:** Accepted.

ASK S✿ ⊠ (≀ 🖥 💻 ⇋

LOUISVILLE

▼▼▼ **Aleksander House Bed and Breakfast** BB
(502) 585-9167. **$95-$169, 3 day notice.** 1213 S 1st St. I-65, exit 135 (St Catherine St), just s. Int corridors. **Pets:** Accepted.

ASK ⊠ 🖥 💻

▼▼▼ **Breckinridge Inn** LH
(502) 456-5050. **$69-$89.** 2800 Breckinridge Ln. I-264, exit 18A, just s. Int corridors. **Pets:** Accepted.

ASK S✿ ⊠ 🖥 💻 ¶¶ ⇋ ⊠

AAA ▼▼▼ **Executive West** LH
(502) 367-2251. **$79-$169.** 830 Phillips Ln. I-264, exit 11 (Fairgrounds/Expo Center Main Gate). Int corridors. **Pets:** Other species. $100 daily fee/pet. Service with restrictions.

SAVE S✿ ⊠ ⟲ (≀ 🖥 💻 ¶¶ ⇋ ⊠

AAA ▼▼▼ **Holiday Inn Airport East** SH
(502) 452-6361. **$115.** 4004 Gardiner Point Dr. I-264, exit 15B westbound; exit 15 eastbound. Int corridors. **Pets:** Accepted.

SAVE ⊠ (≀ 🖥 💻 ¶¶ ⇋

▼▼▼ **Holiday Inn South-Airport** LH
(502) 964-3311. **$95-$145.** 2715 Fern Valley Rd. I-65, exit 128 (Fern Valley Rd), northeast corner. Int corridors. **Pets:** Other species. $35 one-time fee/room. Service with restrictions, crate.

ASK S✿ ⊠ &M ⟲ (≀ 🖥 💻 ¶¶ ⇋

▼▼▼ **Jameson Inn Airport South** SH
(502) 968-4100. **$54-$120.** 6515 Signature Dr. I-65, exit 128 (Fern Valley Rd), southeast corner. Int corridors. **Pets:** Small. $10 daily fee/pet. Service with restrictions, crate.

ASK ⊠ 🖥 💻 ⇋

AAA ▼▼▼ **La Quinta Inn & Suites Airport & Expo-Louisville** SH ❋
(502) 368-0007. **$79-$335.** 4125 Preston Hwy. I-65, exit 130, 1 mi w. Int corridors. **Pets:** Other species. Service with restrictions, supervision.

SAVE S✿ ⊠ &M ⟲ (≀ 🖥 💻 ⇋

▼▼ **Red Roof Inn-Airport-Fairgrounds** SH
(502) 968-0151. **$55-$70.** 4704 Preston Hwy. I-65, exit 130, northeast corner. Ext corridors. **Pets:** Medium, other species. Service with restrictions, supervision.

⊠

▼▼ **Red Roof Inn-Southeast-Fairgrounds** SH
(502) 456-2993. **$53-$71.** 3322 Red Roof Inn Pl. I-264, 15B westbound, 0.3 mi s; exit 15 eastbound. Ext corridors. **Pets:** Medium, other species. Service with restrictions, supervision.

⊠ 🖥

▼▼▼ **Residence Inn by Marriott-Louisville Airport** SH
(502) 363-8800. **$116-$129.** 700 Phillips Ln. I-264, exit 11 (Fairgrounds/Expo Center Main Gate), 0.4 mi w. Int corridors. **Pets:** Accepted.

ASK ⊠ ⟲ (≀ 🖥 💻 ⇋

▼▼▼ **Residence Inn by Marriott Louisville Downtown** SH
(502) 589-8998. **Call for rates.** 333 E Market St. Corner of Preston and E Market. Int corridors. **Pets:** Accepted.

⊠ &M ⟲ (≀ 🖥 💻 ⇋

▼▼▼ **Residence Inn by Marriott-Louisville NE** SH
(502) 412-1311. **$139-$189.** 3500 Springhurst Commons Dr. I-265, exit 32, 0.5 mi w on Westport Rd, then just n. Int corridors. **Pets:** Accepted.

ASK S✿ ⊠ &M (≀ 🖥 💻 ⇋ ⊠

▼▼▼ **Residence Inn Louisville East** SH
(502) 425-1821. **$79-$99.** 120 N Hurstbourne Pkwy. I-64, exit 15, 1.8 mi n. Ext corridors. **Pets:** Accepted.

⊠ 🖥 💻 ⇋ ⊠

AAA ▼▼▼ ▼▼▼ **The Seelbach Hilton Louisville** LH
(502) 585-3200. **$119-$239.** 500 4th St. I-65, exit 136C (Muhammad Ali), 0.3 mi w, then just s. Int corridors. **Pets:** Other species. $50 deposit/pet. Service with restrictions, supervision.

SAVE ⊠ &M ⟲ (≀ 🖥 💻 ¶¶ ⊠

▼▼▼ **Sleep Inn Fairgrounds** SH ❋
(502) 368-9597. **$69-$189.** 3330 Preston Hwy. I-264, exit 11 (Fairgrounds/Expo Center Main Gate), 0.5 mi e on Phillips Ln, then just n. Int corridors. **Pets:** Other species. $10 daily fee/room. Service with restrictions, supervision.

ASK S✿ ⊠ (≀ 🖥 💻

▼▼▼ **Staybridge Suites by Holiday Inn** SH
(502) 244-9511. **$110-$160.** 11711 Gateworth Way. I-64, exit 17, just n. Int corridors. **Pets:** Small, dogs only. $200 one-time fee/room. Designated rooms, service with restrictions.

ASK S✿ ⊠ &M ⟲ (≀ 🖥 💻 ⇋

ST. MATTHEWS

▼▼ **Extended StayAmerica** SH
(502) 897-2559. **Call for rates.** 1401 Browns Ln. I-264, exit 18B, just e, 1 mi e on Dutchmans Ln, then just s. Int corridors. **Pets:** Accepted.

⊠ ⟲ 🖥 💻 ⇋

SHEPHERDSVILLE

AAA ▼▼▼ **Best Western South** SH
(502) 543-7097. **$69-$79, 30 day notice.** 211 S Lakeview Dr. I-65, exit 117 (SR 44 W), just se. Int corridors. **Pets:** Accepted.

SAVE S✿ ⊠ 🖥 💻 ⇋

▼▼ **Super 8** SH
(502) 543-8870. **$46-$150.** 275 Keystone Crossroads. I-65, exit 117, just w. Int corridors. **Pets:** Accepted.

ASK S✿ ⊠ (≀ 🖥

SHIVELY

AAA ▼▼▼ **Holiday Inn-Southwest** LH
(502) 448-2020. **$95-$145.** 4110 Dixie Hwy. I-264, exit 8B, just n on US 31 W and 60. Int corridors. **Pets:** Small, other species. $25 deposit/room. Service with restrictions, crate.

SAVE S✿ ⊠ ⟲ 🖥 💻 ¶¶ ⇋

END METROPOLITAN AREA

MAYFIELD

Super 8 Motel SH
(270) 247-8899. **$42-$94.** 1100 Links Ln. Purchase Pkwy, exit 24, just s on SR 121. Int corridors. **Pets:** Small. $10 daily fee/pet. Service with restrictions, supervision.

MAYSVILLE

Super 8 Motel, Maysville KY SH
(606) 759-8888. **$57-$63.** 550 Tucker Dr. Just e of US 68. Int corridors. **Pets:** Accepted.

MOREHEAD

Comfort Inn & Suites SH
(606) 780-7378. **$59-$109.** 2650 Kentucky 801 N. I-64, exit 133, just s. Int corridors. **Pets:** Other species. $10 daily fee/room. Service with restrictions, crate.

Holiday Inn Express of Morehead SH
(606) 784-5796. **$76-$90.** 110 Toms Dr. I-64, exit 137 (SR 32), just sw. Int corridors. **Pets:** Medium, other species. $10 daily fee/pet. Service with restrictions, supervision.

MORTONS GAP

Best Western Pennyrile Inn SH
(270) 258-5201. **$56-$64, 4 day notice.** White City Rd. Pennyrile Pkwy, exit 37 (US 41). Ext corridors. **Pets:** $7 daily fee/pet. Supervision.

MOUNT VERNON

Kastle Inn Motel M
(606) 256-5156. **$52-$70.** Hwy 25 S. I-75, exit 59. Ext corridors. **Pets:** Accepted.

MUNFORDVILLE

Super 8 SH
(270) 524-4888. **$51-$99.** 88 Bull Run Rd. I-65, exit 65, 0.5 mi s. Int corridors. **Pets:** Other species. $10 one-time fee/room. Supervision.

MURRAY

Days Inn-Murray, KY SH
(270) 753-6706. **$50-$75.** 517 S 12th St. 1 mi s on US 641. Ext corridors. **Pets:** Accepted.

NEWPORT

Comfort Suites Riverfront SH
(859) 291-6700. **$99-$135.** 420 Riverboat Row. I-471, exit 5, just e on SR 8. Int corridors. **Pets:** Medium, other species. $25 one-time fee/room. Service with restrictions, supervision.

OAK GROVE

Comfort Inn-Oak Grove SH
(270) 439-3311. **$68-$78.** 201 Auburn St. I-24, exit 86, just s. Ext corridors. **Pets:** Small. $20 daily fee/pet. Designated rooms, service with restrictions, supervision.

Holiday Inn Express SH
(270) 439-0022. **$76.** 12759 Ft Campbell Blvd. I-24, exit 86. Int corridors. **Pets:** Small. $10 daily fee/pet. Designated rooms, service with restrictions, supervision.

OLIVE HILL

Spanish Manor Inn M
(606) 286-4141. **$45-$49.** 10095 US Rt 60. I-64, exit 161, 0.4 mi n. Ext corridors. **Pets:** Supervision.

OWENSBORO

Motel 6 #205 SH
(270) 686-8606. **$42-$54.** 4585 Frederica St. US 60 Bypass, exit 4 at US 431, just n. Ext corridors. **Pets:** Medium, other species. Service with restrictions, supervision.

Super 8 Motel-Owensboro SH
(270) 685-3388. **$50-$90.** 1027 Goetz Dr. US 60 Bypass, exit 4 at US 431. Int corridors. **Pets:** Accepted.

OWINGSVILLE

Super 8 Owingsville SH
(606) 674-2200. **$54-$60.** 201 Williams Ave. I-64, exit 121, just n. Int corridors. **Pets:** Accepted.

PADUCAH

Baymont Inn-Paducah SH
(270) 443-4343. **$65-$95.** 5300 Old Cairo Rd. I-24, exit 3 (SR 305), just w. Int corridors. **Pets:** Accepted.

Days Inn SH
(270) 442-7500. **$55-$100.** 3901 Hinkleville Rd. I-24, exit 4 (US 60), just e. Ext corridors. **Pets:** Small, dogs only. $10 one-time fee/room. No service, supervision.

Drury Inn-Paducah SH
(270) 443-3313. **$85-$135.** 3975 Hinkleville Rd. I-24, exit 4 (US 60), just e. Int corridors. **Pets:** Large, other species. Service with restrictions, supervision.

Drury Suites-Paducah SH
(270) 441-0024. **$100-$145.** 2930 James-Sanders Blvd. I-24, exit 4 (US 60), just w. Int corridors. **Pets:** Large, other species. Service with restrictions, supervision.

Hampton Inn-Paducah SH
(270) 442-4500. **$114-$144.** 5006 Hinkleville Rd. I-24, exit 4 (US 60), just w. Int corridors. **Pets:** Small. Service with restrictions, crate.

Thrifty Inn SH
(270) 444-7200. **$70-$105.** 5002 Hinkleville Rd. I-24, exit 4 (US 60), just w. Ext corridors. **Pets:** Small. Service with restrictions, crate.

PRESTONSBURG

Holiday Inn-Prestonsburg SH
(606) 886-0001. **$80, 10 day notice.** 1887 N US 23. 2 mi s. Ext corridors. **Pets:** Accepted.

RICHMOND

▼▼▼▼ **Holiday Inn Express Hotel & Suites** SH
(859) 624-4005. **$84-$159.** 1990 Colby Taylor Dr. I-75, exit 87, just w.
Int corridors. **Pets:** Other species. $15 daily fee/pet. Service with restrictions, supervision.
ASK S☉ ✕ &M ⟨? ⟨✓ 🖥 ▣ ⇌

▼▼▼ **Jameson Inn** SH
(859) 623-0063. **$54-$120.** 1007 Colby Taylor Dr. I-75, exit 87, just w.
Int corridors. **Pets:** Small. $10 daily fee/pet. Service with restrictions, crate.
ASK ✕ &M ⟨? ⟨✓ 🖥 ▣ ⇌

▼▼▼ **Red Roof Inn** M
(859) 625-0084. **$52-$72.** 111 Bahama Ct. I-75, exit 90 northbound; exit 90A southbound. Int corridors. **Pets:** Medium. Service with restrictions, supervision.
ASK S☉ ✕ ⟨✓ 🖥 ▣ ⇌

AAA ▼▼ **Super 8 Motel** SH
(859) 624-1550. **$57-$62, 7 day notice.** 107 N Keeneland Dr. I-75, exit 90. Int corridors. **Pets:** Very small. $6 daily fee/pet. Designated rooms, service with restrictions, supervision.
SAVE S☉ ✕ &M 🖥 ▣

SCOTTSVILLE

AAA ▼▼▼ **Executive Inn** SH
(270) 622-7770. **$52-$56.** 57 Burnley Rd. US 31 E, jct SR 231. Ext corridors. **Pets:** Small. $6 daily fee/room. Service with restrictions.
SAVE S☉ ✕ 🖥 ⇌

SHELBYVILLE

▼▼▼▼ **Best Western Shelbyville Lodge** SH
(502) 633-4400. **$72-$82.** 115 Isaac Shelby Dr. I-64, exit 32, 0.5 mi n on SR 55. Int corridors. **Pets:** Accepted.
ASK S☉ ✕ 🖥 ▣ ⇌

▼▼▼▼ **Holiday Inn Express** SH
(502) 647-0109. **$75-$125.** 110 Club House Dr. I-64, exit 35, just s. Int corridors. **Pets:** Other species. Service with restrictions, supervision.
ASK S☉ ✕ &M ⟨? ⟨✓ 🖥 ▣ ⇌

▼▼▼ **Ramada** SH
(502) 633-9933. **Call for rates.** 251 Breighton Cir. I-64, exit 32, just s. Int corridors. **Pets:** Other species. $25 one-time fee/room.
✕ &M ⟨? ⟨✓ 🖥 ▣ ⇌

SMITHS GROVE

AAA ▼▼▼ **Bryce Inn** SH
(270) 563-5141. **$53-$65.** 592 S Main St. I-65, exit 38, 0.3 mi w. Ext corridors. **Pets:** Small, dogs only. $6 one-time fee/pet. Designated rooms, service with restrictions, supervision.
SAVE S☉ ✕ 🖥 ▣ ⇌

SOMERSET

▼▼▼▼ **Comfort Inn** SH
(606) 677-1500. **$65-$139, 3 day notice.** 82 Jolin Dr. Cumberland Pkwy, 4.3 mi s on US 27. Int corridors. **Pets:** Accepted.
ASK S☉ ✕ &M ⟨✓ 🖥 ▣ ⇌

SPARTA

▼▼▼▼ **Ramada at the Kentucky Speedway** SH
(859) 567-7223. **$69-$129, 3 day notice.** 525 Dale Dr. I-71, exit 57, just w. Int corridors. **Pets:** Medium, other species. $25 one-time fee/room. Designated rooms, service with restrictions.
ASK S☉ ✕ &M ⟨✓ 🖥 ▣ ⇌

VERSAILLES

▼▼▼▼ **1823 Historic Rose Hill Inn** BB
(859) 873-5957. **$109-$179, 7 day notice.** 233 Rose Hill. Just s on SR 33 (S Main St), then just w. Ext/int corridors. **Pets:** Accepted.
✕ 🖥 ⇌

WEST LIBERTY

▼▼ **Days Inn** SH
(606) 743-4206. **$53-$69.** 1613 W Main St. Jct SR 519 and 460, just w. Int corridors. **Pets:** Accepted.
ASK S☉ ✕ &M ⟨✓

WILLIAMSBURG

▼▼▼▼ **Cumberland Inn** SH
(606) 539-4100. **$74-$79.** 649 S 10th St. I-75, exit 11. Int corridors. **Pets:** Accepted.
ASK S☉ ✕ &M 🖥 ▣ ⟨¶⟩ ⇌

WILLIAMSTOWN

AAA ▼▼▼ **Americas Best Value Inn & Suites** SH
(859) 824-7177. **$40-$69, 5 day notice.** 10 Skyway Dr. I-75, exit 154, just w. Ext corridors. **Pets:** Small. $5 daily fee/pet. Designated rooms, service with restrictions, supervision.
SAVE S☉ ✕ 🖥 ⇌

AAA ▼▼▼ **Days Inn** SH
(859) 824-5025. **$47-$59.** 211 SR 36 W. I-75, exit 154, just n. Ext corridors. **Pets:** Accepted.
SAVE S☉ ✕ 🖥 ▣ ⇌

WINCHESTER

AAA ▼▼▼ **Best Western-Country Squire** SH
(859) 744-7210. **$59-$109.** 1307 W Lexington Rd. I-64, exit 94 (US 60), 0.9 mi se. Ext corridors. **Pets:** Small. $5 one-time fee/pet. Service with restrictions, supervision.
SAVE S☉ ✕ 🖥 ▣ ⇌

LOUISIANA

ALEXANDRIA

Best Western Inn & Suites & Conference Center of Alexandria SH
(318) 445-5530. **$75-$95, 3 day notice.** 2720 W MacArthur Dr. I-49, exit 86 (MacArthur Dr), 1.3 mi sw. Ext/int corridors. **Pets:** Small. $10 daily fee/pet. Designated rooms, service with restrictions, crate.

La Quinta Inn & Suites Alexandria SH
(318) 442-3700. **$116-$126.** 6116 W Calhoun Dr. I-49, exit 90 (Air Base Rd), just w. Int corridors. **Pets:** Medium. Service with restrictions.

Ramada Limited SH
(318) 448-1611. **$55-$99.** 742 MacArthur Dr. 0.4 mi s of jct SR 28 and US 71/165 (MacArthur Dr). Ext corridors. **Pets:** Medium. $10 daily fee/ pet. Designated rooms, service with restrictions, supervision.

Super 8 Motel M
(318) 445-6541. **$51-$70.** 700 MacArthur Dr. I-49, exit 86 (MacArthur Dr), 2.4 mi sw. Ext/int corridors. **Pets:** Accepted.

BATON ROUGE

Chase Suites by Woodfin SH
(225) 927-5630. **$169-$199.** 5522 Corporate Blvd. I-10, exit 158, just n on College Dr, then just e. Ext corridors. **Pets:** Accepted.

Crestwood Suites Hotel SH
(225) 291-5200. **$70-$130.** 5222 S Sherwood Forest Blvd. I-12, exit 4, 1.7 mi s. Int corridors. **Pets:** Accepted.

Holiday Inn Select Executive Center Baton Rouge LH
(225) 925-2244. **$99-$129.** 4728 Constitution Ave. I-10, exit 158, just se on frontage road. Int corridors. **Pets:** Large. $25 one-time fee/room. Designated rooms, service with restrictions, supervision.

La Quinta Inn & Suites Baton Rouge SH
(225) 291-6600. **$84-$94.** 10555 Rieger Rd. I-10, exit 163 (Siegen Ln), just n, then just e. Int corridors. **Pets:** Medium. Service with restrictions.

La Quinta Inn Baton Rouge SH
(225) 924-9600. **$95-$105.** 2333 S Acadian Thruway. I-10, exit 157B. Ext corridors. **Pets:** Medium. Service with restrictions.

Ramada I-12/Airline Highway SH
(225) 706-5500. **$80-$100.** 10045 Gwenadele Ave. I-12, exit 2B, just n on US 61. Ext corridors. **Pets:** Accepted.

Residence Inn by Marriott-Baton Rouge SH
(225) 293-8700. **$139-$179.** 10333 N Mall Dr. I-10, exit 163 westbound, just s on Siegen Ln, then just e; exit eastbound, 0.5 mi to S Mall Dr, just e to Andrea (at Lowe's), then just n. Int corridors. **Pets:** Small. $75 one-time fee/room. Service with restrictions, crate.

Sheraton Baton Rouge Convention Center Hotel LH
(225) 242-2600. **$169-$199.** 102 France St. I-110, exit 1A (Government St), 0.8 mi w to St. James, then just s. Int corridors. **Pets:** Accepted.

TownePlace Suites by Marriott SH
(225) 819-2112. **$129-$199.** 8735 Summa Ave. I-10, exit 162 (Bluebonnet Blvd), just s to Picardy, just w to Summa Ave, then 0.5 mi nw. Int corridors. **Pets:** Other species. $75 one-time fee/room. Service with restrictions, crate.

BOSSIER CITY

Best Western-Airline Motor Inn SH
(318) 742-6000. **$75-$125.** 1984 Airline Dr. I-20, exit 22 (Airline Dr), just n. Ext corridors. **Pets:** Accepted.

Crossland Studios Shreveport-Bossier City SH
(318) 747-5800. **Call for rates.** 3070 E Texas St. I-20, exit 22, just s. Ext corridors. **Pets:** Accepted.

Hampton Inn SH
(318) 752-1112. **$84-$144.** 1005 Gould Dr. I-20, exit 21, 0.5 mi ne on service road. Int corridors. **Pets:** Accepted.

La Quinta Inn Bossier City SH
(318) 747-4400. **$82-$109.** 309 Preston Blvd. I-20, exit 21, just n. Ext corridors. **Pets:** Medium. Service with restrictions.

Microtel Inn & Suites SH
(318) 742-7882. **$59-$79.** 2713 Village Ln. I-20, exit 22 (Airline Dr), just s, then just w. Int corridors. **Pets:** Medium, other species. $25 one-time fee/room. Service with restrictions, supervision.

Quality Inn & Suites SH
(318) 742-7890. **$79-$89.** 2717 Village Ln. I-20, exit 22 (Airline Dr), just s, then just w. Int corridors. **Pets:** Small, other species. $25 one-time fee/pet. No service, supervision.

Residence Inn by Marriott-Shreveport/Bossier City SH
(318) 747-6220. **$129-$230.** 1001 Gould Dr. I-20, exit 21, just ne. Ext corridors. **Pets:** Other species. $100 one-time fee/room. Service with restrictions.

BREAUX BRIDGE

▼▼ Holiday Inn Express of Breaux Bridge SH
(337) 667-8913. **$73.** 2942 H Grand Point Hwy. I-10, exit 115, just n. Int corridors. **Pets:** Accepted.

CONVENT

▼▼▼ Poche Plantation Bed & Breakfast and RV Resort BB
(225) 562-7728. **$59-$149, 30 day notice.** 6554 Louisiana Hwy 44. Jct SR 44 and 641; 10.1 mi s of Sunshine Bridge (SR 70), then 10.2 mi n. Ext/int corridors. **Pets:** $15 one-time fee/room. Service with restrictions, supervision.

CROWLEY

▼▼ Days Inn SH
(337) 783-2378. **$46-$79.** 9571 Egan Hwy. I-10, exit 80. Ext corridors. **Pets:** Accepted.

DERIDDER

▲▲▲ ▼▼ Stagecoach Inn SH
(337) 462-0022. **$79.** 505 E 1st St. 2 mi on east side; between US 171. Ext corridors. **Pets:** Accepted.

HAMMOND

▲▲▲ ▼▼ Best Western Hammond Inn & Suites SH
(985) 419-2001. **$80-$100.** 107 Duo Dr. I-12, exit 40 (US 51), just ne. Ext corridors. **Pets:** Other species. $10 daily fee/pet. Service with restrictions, supervision.

▲▲▲ ▼▼▼ Michabelle-A Little Inn CI
(985) 419-0550. **$75-$100, 5 day notice.** 1106 S Holly St. I-12, exit 40 (US 51), 0.8 mi n, just e on Old Covington Hwy, then n, follow signs. Ext/int corridors. **Pets:** Accepted.

KINDER

▲▲▲ ▼▼▼ Best Western Inn At Coushatta SH
(337) 738-4800. **$89-$119, 7 day notice.** 12102 US Hwy 165 N. 5 mi n of jct US 190/165. Int corridors. **Pets:** Small, other species. Service with restrictions, supervision.

▼▼ Holiday Inn Express Hotel & Suites SH
(337) 738-3381. **$79-$150.** 11750 US Hwy 165. 5.2 mi n of jct US 190/165, 5.1 mi on US 165. Ext/int corridors. **Pets:** Accepted.

LAFAYETTE

▼▼ America's Best Suites of Lafayette SH
(337) 235-1367. **$99-$149.** 125 E Kaliste Saloom Rd. I-10, exit 103A, 1 mi w of jct E Kaliste Saloom Rd and US 90 (SW Evangeline Thruway). Int corridors. **Pets:** Small, other species. Service with restrictions, supervision.

▼▼▼ Best Western Hotel Acadiana SH
(337) 233-8120. **$79-$109.** 1801 W Pinhook Rd. SR 182, 1.5 mi s of US 90 (Evangeline Thruway). Int corridors. **Pets:** Accepted.

▼▼ Best Western-Lafayette SH
(337) 289-9907. **$75-$125.** 126 Alcide Dominique. I-10, exit 101, just s. Int corridors. **Pets:** Other species. Service with restrictions, supervision.

▼▼ Comfort Inn Lafayette SH
(337) 232-9000. **$84-$101.** 1421 SE Evangeline Thruway. 3 mi s of I-10 at jct US 90 (Evangeline Thruway). Int corridors. **Pets:** Designated rooms, service with restrictions, crate.

▼▼ Days Inn-Lafayette M
(337) 237-8880. **$65.** 1620 N University. I-10, exit 101. Ext corridors. **Pets:** Other species. $10 daily fee/pet. Service with restrictions, supervision.

▼▼▼ Drury Inn & Suites-Lafayette SH
(337) 262-0202. **$85-$130.** 120 Alcide Dominique. I-10, exit 101 (SR 182), just s on University Ave, then just w. Int corridors. **Pets:** Large, other species. Service with restrictions, supervision.

▲▲▲ ▼▼▼ Holiday Inn Lafayette-Holidome SH ✿
(800) 465-4329. **$70-$189.** 2032 NE Evangeline Thruway. I-10, exit 103A, just s. Ext/int corridors. **Pets:** Small, dogs only. $50 one-time fee/room. Crate.

▼▼ Jameson Inn of Lafayette SH
(337) 291-2916. **$54-$120.** 2200 NE Evangeline Thruway. I-10, exit 103A, just s. Int corridors. **Pets:** Small. $10 daily fee/pet. Service with restrictions, crate.

▼▼▼ La Quinta Inn & Suites Lafayette Oil Center SH
(337) 291-1088. **$109-$139.** 1015 W Pinhook Rd. I-10, exit 101 (University Ave), 3.5 mi to SR 182 (Pinhook Rd), then 0.5 mi w. Int corridors. **Pets:** Accepted.

▼▼ La Quinta Inn Lafayette (North) SH
(337) 233-5610. **$79-$95.** 2100 NE Evangeline Thruway. I-10, exit 103A, 0.3 mi s on US 167. Ext corridors. **Pets:** Medium. Service with restrictions.

▼ Motel 6 #461 M
(337) 233-2055. **$41-$55.** 2724 NE Evangeline Thruway. I-49, exit 1B (Pont des Mouton Rd), just e, then just s on frontage road. Ext corridors. **Pets:** Medium, other species. Service with restrictions, supervision.

▼▼ Ramada Inn SH
(337) 235-0858. **$64.** 120 E Kaliste Saloom Rd. I-10, exit 103A, 4.4 mi e on US 90 (Evangeline Thruway), then 1 mi s. Ext corridors. **Pets:** Medium, other species. $10 one-time fee/room. Service with restrictions, crate.

LAKE CHARLES

▼▼ Baymont Inn & Suites SH
(337) 310-7666. **Call for rates.** 1004 MLK Hwy (171 N). I-10, exit 33, just n. Ext corridors. **Pets:** Accepted.

▼▼▼ Best Suites of America SH
(337) 439-2444. **$94-$150.** 401 Lakeshore Dr. I-10, exit 29 (business district/tourist bureau); exit 30B (Ryan St business district) westbound, just s to Pine, then just w. Int corridors. **Pets:** Accepted.

▲▲▲ ▼▼▼ Best Western Richmond Suites Hotel SH
(337) 433-5213. **$89-$99.** 2600 Moeling St. I-10, exit 33, just n. Ext/int corridors. **Pets:** Accepted.

(AAA) WWW La Quinta Inn Lake Charles SH
(337) 436-5998. **$70-$140.** 1320 MLK Hwy 171 N. I-10, exit 33, 0.8 mi n. Int corridors. **Pets:** Accepted.
SAVE S X X 8 B B S

LIVONIA

WW Oak Tree Inn SH
(225) 637-2590. **$53.** 7875 Airline Hwy. Jct SR 77 and US 190, 0.3 mi w. Ext corridors. **Pets:** Accepted.
ASK S X X 8 B B

MINDEN

(AAA) WWW Best Western Minden Inn SH
(318) 377-1001. **$70-$80.** 1411 Sibley Rd. I-20, exit 47, just n. Ext corridors. **Pets:** Medium. $10 daily fee/pet. Service with restrictions, supervision.
SAVE S X X 8 8 B B S

MONROE

WWW Holiday Inn Hotel & Suites Conference Center SH
(318) 387-5100. **$69-$129.** 1051 Hwy 165 Bypass. I-20, exit 118B, just ne on US 165 service road. Ext/int corridors. **Pets:** Medium, other species. $20 one-time fee/pet. Service with restrictions, supervision.
X X X 8 8 B B S

WW La Quinta Inn Monroe SH
(318) 322-3900. **$78-$94.** 1035 Hwy 165 Bypass. I-20, exit 118B, just ne on US 165 service road. Ext corridors. **Pets:** Medium. Service with restrictions.
ASK X X B S

WWW Residence Inn by Marriott SH 🐾
(318) 387-0210. **$107-$123.** 4960 Millhaven Rd. I-20, exit 120, just n of Pecanland Mall. Int corridors. **Pets:** Medium, other species. $100 one-time fee/pet. Service with restrictions, supervision.
X X X X 8 8 B B X

MORGAN CITY

WWW Holiday Inn-Morgan City SH
(985) 385-2200. **$109-$209.** 520 Roderick St. 1.5 mi s of jct US 90 and SR 70. Ext corridors. **Pets:** Small. $50 one-time fee/room. Service with restrictions, supervision.
ASK S X X X X 8 B B S

NEW IBERIA

(AAA) WWW Best Western Inn & Suites SH
(337) 364-3030. **$70-$84, 3 day notice.** 2714 Hwy 14. 0.3 mi e of jct US 90. Ext/int corridors. **Pets:** Small. $25 one-time fee/pet. Designated rooms, service with restrictions, supervision.
SAVE S X 8 B B T S

WW Holiday Inn New Iberia-Avery Island SH
(337) 367-1201. **$89-$99.** 2915 Hwy 14. SR 14, just e of jct US 90. Ext corridors. **Pets:** Accepted.
ASK X 8 B B T S

NEW ORLEANS METROPOLITAN AREA

COVINGTON

WWW Holiday Inn & Suites Covington Northshore SH
(985) 893-3580. **$109-$199, 5 day notice.** 501 N Hwy 190. I-12, exit 63B, just n. Ext/int corridors. **Pets:** Accepted.
ASK X X X 8 B B T S X

GRETNA

WW La Quinta Inn New Orleans (West Bank) SH
(504) 368-5600. **$109-$149.** 50 Terry Pkwy. S US 90 business route, exit 9A (Terry Pkwy); N US 90 (Westbank Expwy), exit 9 (Terry Pkwy/General DeGaulle). Ext corridors. **Pets:** Medium. Service with restrictions.
ASK X X 8 B B S

KENNER

WWW La Quinta Inn New Orleans (Airport) SH
(504) 466-1401. **$109-$149.** 2610 Williams Blvd. I-10, exit 223A (Williams Blvd), 0.3 mi s. Int corridors. **Pets:** Medium. Service with restrictions.
ASK X 8 B B S

LA PLACE

(AAA) WWW Best Western La Place Inn SH
(985) 651-4000. **$69-$109.** 4289 Main St. I-10, exit 209, just s. Ext corridors. **Pets:** Very small. $25 daily fee/room. Service with restrictions.
SAVE X X 8 B B S

WWW Quality Inn-La Place SH
(985) 652-5544. **$77-$99.** 3900 Hwy 51. I-10, exit 209, 0.5 mi s. Ext corridors. **Pets:** Small, dogs only. $75 one-time fee/room. Service with restrictions, supervision.
ASK S X X X X 8 B B T S

METAIRIE

WW La Quinta Inn New Orleans (Causeway) SH
(504) 835-8511. **$109-$149.** 3100 I-10 Service Rd. I-10, exit 228 (Causeway Blvd), just s. Ext corridors. **Pets:** Medium. Service with restrictions.
ASK X X X 8 B B S

WW La Quinta Inn New Orleans (Veterans) SH
(504) 456-0003. **$109-$149.** 5900 Veterans Memorial Blvd. I-10, exit 225, just n. Ext corridors. **Pets:** Medium. Service with restrictions.
ASK X X X 8 B B S

(AAA) WWW Residence Inn by Marriott-Metairie SH
(504) 832-0888. **$149-$299, 3 day notice.** 3 Galleria Blvd. I-10, exit 228 (Causeway Blvd), just se to 36th St, then just e. Int corridors. **Pets:** Other species. $100 one-time fee/room. Service with restrictions, crate.
SAVE S X X 8 B B S X

NEW ORLEANS

(AAA) WWWW Best Western St. Christopher Hotel SH
(504) 648-0444. **$79-$269, 3 day notice.** 114 Magazine St. Between Canal and Common sts. Int corridors. **Pets:** Accepted.
SAVE X X B S

(AAA) WWWW Chateau Sonesta Hotel LH
(504) 586-0800. **$99-$249, 3 day notice.** 800 Iberville St. Between Dauphine and Bourbon sts. Int corridors. **Pets:** Accepted.
SAVE X X X X B T S

WWW Drury Inn & Suites-New Orleans SH
(504) 529-7800. **$105-$195.** 820 Poydras St. Between Baronne and Carondelet sts. Int corridors. **Pets:** Large, other species. Service with restrictions, supervision.
ASK X X X X 8 B B S

AAA ▼▼ ▼▼ Elysian Fields Inn BB
(504) 948-9420. **$99-$250, 15 day notice.** 930 Elysian Fields Ave. I-610, exit 3 (Elysian Fields), 1.2 mi s. Int corridors. **Pets:** $25 one-time fee/room. Service with restrictions, crate.
[SAVE] [X]

AAA ▼▼ ▼▼ The Fairmont New Orleans LH
(504) 529-7111. **$139-$319.** 123 Baronne St. Between Canal and University sts; entrance on University St; downtown. Int corridors. **Pets:** Accepted.
[SAVE] [X] [🐾] [&] [🛏] [🍴] [≈] [X]

▼▼ ▼▼ French Quarter Suites Hotel SH ❀
(504) 524-7725. **$59-$299, 7 day notice.** 1119 N Rampart St. Between Ursuline and Governor Nicholls. Ext corridors. **Pets:** Other species. $15 daily fee/pet. Service with restrictions.
[ASK] [S🐾] [X] [🛏] [🖥] [≈]

▼▼ ▼▼ Holiday Inn Express-New Orleans French Quarter Downtown SH
(504) 962-0800. **$189-$249, 3 day notice.** 221 Carondelet St. Between Common and Gravier sts. Int corridors. **Pets:** Accepted.
[ASK] [S🐾] [X] [&] [🛏] [🖥] [≈]

AAA ▼▼ ▼▼ Holiday Inn French Quarter SH
(504) 529-7211. **$89-$299.** 124 Royal St. Between Iberville and Canal sts. Int corridors. **Pets:** Accepted.
[SAVE] [S🐾] [X] [&M] [🐾] [&] [🛏] [🖥] [🍴] [≈]

AAA ▼▼ ▼▼ The Iberville Suites SH
(504) 523-2400. **$99-$268, 3 day notice.** 910 Iberville St. Between Burgundy and Dauphine sts. Int corridors. **Pets:** Accepted.
[SAVE] [S🐾] [X] [&] [🛏] [🖥]

▼▼ ▼▼ La Quinta Inn & Suites New Orleans–Downtown Flagship SH
(504) 598-9977. **$109-$189.** 301 W Camp St. Corner of Gravier and Camp sts; downtown. Int corridors. **Pets:** Medium. Service with restrictions.
[ASK] [X] [&M] [🐾] [&] [🛏] [🖥] [≈]

▼▼ ▼▼ Loews New Orleans Hotel LH ❀
(504) 595-3300. **$149-$319, 3 day notice.** 300 Poydras St. Corner of S Peters St; downtown. Int corridors. **Pets:** Other species. Service with restrictions, crate.
[ASK] [S🐾] [X] [&] [🛏] [🖥] [🍴] [≈] [X]

AAA ▼▼ ▼▼ The Maison Orleans-Ritz Carlton SH
(504) 670-2900. **$209-$419.** 904 Iberville St. Between Burgundy and Dauphine sts. Int corridors. **Pets:** Accepted.
[SAVE] [S🐾] [X] [&M] [&] [🍴] [≈] [X]

AAA ▼▼ ▼▼ Maison St. Charles Quality Inn & Suites SH ❀
(504) 522-0187. **$79-$268.** 1319 St. Charles Ave. I-90 business, exit St. Charles Ave, just w; between Thalia and Erato sts. Ext corridors. **Pets:** Small, other species. $10 daily fee/pet. Designated rooms, service with restrictions, crate.
[SAVE] [S🐾] [X] [🐾] [&] [🛏] [🖥] [🍴] [≈]

▼▼ ▼▼ Omni Royal Crescent Hotel SH
(504) 527-0006. **$89-$169.** 535 Gravier St. 0.3 mi w of Canal St; downtown. Int corridors. **Pets:** Accepted.
[ASK] [S🐾] [X] [🐾] [&] [🛏] [🖥] [🍴] [X]

AAA ▼▼ ▼▼ Omni Royal Orleans Hotel LH
(504) 529-5333. **$129-$320, 3 day notice.** 621 St. Louis St. At Royal and St. Louis sts. Int corridors. **Pets:** Small. $50 one-time fee/room. Service with restrictions, crate.
[SAVE] [S🐾] [X] [&] [🛏] [🖥] [🍴] [≈]

AAA ▼▼ ▼▼ Residence Inn by Marriott SH
(504) 522-1300. **$239.** 345 St. Joseph's St. Jct Tchoupitoulas St. Int corridors. **Pets:** Accepted.
[SAVE] [S🐾] [X] [&M] [&] [🛏] [🖥] [≈] [X]

AAA ▼▼ ▼▼ The Ritz-Carlton New Orleans LH ❀
(504) 524-1331. **$419-$459, 3 day notice.** 921 Canal St. Between Dauphine and Burgundy sts. Int corridors. **Pets:** Medium, other species. $150 one-time fee/pet.
[SAVE] [X] [&M] [🐾] [&] [🍴] [≈]

AAA ▼▼ ▼▼ Royal Sonesta Hotel New Orleans LH
(504) 586-0300. **$109-$329, 3 day notice.** 300 Bourbon St. Garage entrance on Conti or Bienville sts. Int corridors. **Pets:** Small, other species. $50 one-time fee/room. Service with restrictions, supervision.
[SAVE] [S🐾] [X] [&M] [🐾] [&] [🛏] [🍴] [≈]

▼▼ ▼▼ St. James Hotel SH
(504) 304-4000. **$99-$249, 3 day notice.** 330 Magazine St. Jct Magazine and Natchez sts; downtown. Int corridors. **Pets:** Accepted.
[ASK] [S🐾] [X] [&] [🛏] [🖥] [≈]

AAA ▼▼ ▼▼ The Sheraton New Orleans Hotel LH
(504) 525-2500. **$109-$249, 3 day notice.** 500 Canal St. Between Camp and Magazine sts. Int corridors. **Pets:** Accepted.
[SAVE] [S🐾] [X] [&M] [🐾] [&] [🖥] [🍴] [≈] [X]

AAA ▼▼ ▼▼ W French Quarter SH
(504) 581-1200. **$139-$369, 3 day notice.** 316 rue Chartres St. Between Conti and Bienville sts. Int corridors. **Pets:** Accepted.
[SAVE] [S🐾] [X] [&] [🖥] [🍴] [≈]

AAA ▼▼ ▼▼ Windsor Court Hotel LH
(504) 523-6000. **$200-$455.** 300 Gravier St. Between Magazine and Tchoupitoulas sts. Int corridors. **Pets:** Accepted.
[SAVE] [X] [🐾] [🛏] [🍴] [≈] [X]

AAA ▼▼ ▼▼ W New Orleans LH
(504) 525-9444. **$139-$369, 3 day notice.** 333 Poydras St. Close to Riverfront area/convention center; jct Poydras and S Peters sts; downtown. Int corridors. **Pets:** Accepted.
[SAVE] [S🐾] [X] [&M] [🐾] [&] [🖥] [🍴] [≈]

SLIDELL

▼▼ ▼▼ La Quinta Inn New Orleans/Slidell SH
(985) 643-9770. **$77-$87.** 794 E I-10 Service Rd. I-10, exit 266 (Gause Blvd), just se. Ext corridors. **Pets:** Medium. Service with restrictions.
[ASK] [X] [&] [🛏] [🖥] [≈]

END METROPOLITAN AREA

OPELOUSAS

▼▼ Days Inn & Suites SH
(337) 407-0004. $70-$150. 5761 I-49 S Service Rd. I-49, exit 18 (Creswell Ln). Ext corridors. Pets: Accepted.
ASK S✆ ✕ &' 🛏 🖵 ≈

PORT ALLEN

▼ Motel 6 Baton Rouge-Port Allen #406 M
(225) 343-5945. $51-$61. 2800 I-10 Frontage Rd. I-10, exit 151, just s. Ext corridors. Pets: Medium, other species. Service with restrictions, supervision.
S✆ ✕ 🛏 🖵 ≈

RAYVILLE

▼▼ Days Inn M
(318) 728-4500. $60-$70. 125 Maxwell Dr. I-20, exit 138, just n. Ext corridors. Pets: Accepted.
ASK S✆ ✕ 🛏 🖵 ≈

RUSTON

▼▼ Budget Lodge SH
(318) 255-0354. $55-$75, 3 day notice. 1301 Goodwin Rd. I-20, exit 85, just n on US 167, then just e on N Service Rd. Ext corridors. Pets: Accepted.
ASK S✆ ✕ 🐾 🛏 🖵

▼▼ Ramada Inn SH
(318) 255-5901. $76-$85. 401 N Service Rd. I-20, exit 85, just ne. Ext corridors. Pets: Accepted.
✕ 🛏 🖵 🍴 ≈

ST. FRANCISVILLE

▼▼ Lake Rosemound Inn Bed & Breakfast BB
(225) 635-3176. $80-$135, 3 day notice. 10473 Lindsey Ln. 13 mi n on SR 61, then 3 mi w using Rosemound Loop, Sligo Rd, Lake Rosemound Rd and Lindsey Ln, follow signs. Ext/int corridors. Pets: Other species. No service, crate.
✕ 🐾

SCOTT

▼▼ Howard Johnson SH
(337) 593-0849. $60-$70. 103 Harold Gauthe Dr. I-10, exit 97. Int corridors. Pets: Small, other species. $20 deposit/pet. Service with restrictions, supervision.
ASK S✆ ✕ 🛏 🖵 ≈

SHREVEPORT

AAA ▼▼▼ Best Western Richmond Suites Hotel SH
(318) 635-6431. $89-$99, 21 day notice. 5101 Monkhouse Dr. I-20, exit 13 (Monkhouse Rd), just s. Int corridors. Pets: Accepted.
SAVE S✆ ✕ &' 🛏 🖵 ≈ 🐾

AAA ▼▼▼▼ Clarion Hotel Shreveport LH
(318) 797-9900. $139. 1419 E 70th St. I-20, exit 19A (SR 1 S), 6 mi s to E 70th St, then 0.4 mi w. Int corridors. Pets: Accepted.
SAVE S✆ ✕ 🐾 🛏 🖵 🍴 ≈

▼▼▼ Holiday Inn Downtown LH
(318) 222-7717. $77-$89. 102 Lake St. I-20, exit 19A (Spring St), just n. Int corridors. Pets: Medium, other species. $25 one-time fee/room. Service with restrictions, supervision.
S✆ ✕ &M 🐾 🛏 🖵 🍴 ≈

▼▼▼ Holiday Inn Financial Plaza LH
(318) 688-3000. $90-$105. 5555 Financial Plaza. I-20, exit 10 (Pines Rd), 1 mi e on frontage road. Int corridors. Pets: Medium, other species. $25 one-time fee/pet. Service with restrictions, supervision.
ASK S✆ ✕ 🛏 🖵 🍴 ≈ ✕

▼▼▼▼ La Quinta Inn & Suites Shreveport SH
(318) 671-1100. $105-$125. 6700 Financial Cir. I-20, exit 10 (Pines Rd), 0.5 mi e on frontage road. Int corridors. Pets: Medium. Service with restrictions.
ASK ✕ &M &' 🛏 🖵 ≈

SPRINGFIELD

▼▼▼▼ The Villas at Carter Plantation SH
(225) 294-7555. $99-$220. 23475 Carter Trace. I-12, exit 32, 2.7 mi s on SR 43, 1.1 mi e on SR 42, 1.5 mi s on Carter Cemetery Rd. Ext corridors. Pets: Small. $125 one-time fee/room. Service with restrictions, supervision.
ASK S✆ ✕ &' 🛏 🖵 🍴 ≈

SULPHUR

▼▼▼ Wingate Inn SH
(337) 527-5151. $69-$79. 300 Arena Rd. I-10, exit 20 (SR 27), just s, then just w. Int corridors. Pets: Accepted.
ASK S✆ ✕ &' 🛏 🖵 ≈

WEST MONROE

▼▼ Jameson Inn SH
(318) 361-0750. $54-$120. 213 Constitution Dr. I-20, exit 114 (Thomas Rd), just s to Constitution Dr, then just w. Int corridors. Pets: Small. $10 daily fee/pet. Service with restrictions, crate.
ASK ✕ &' 🛏 🖵 ≈

▼▼▼ Quality Inn & Suites-West Monroe SH
(318) 387-2711. $72-$104. 503 Constitution Dr. I-20, exit 114 (Thomas Rd), just s to Constitution Dr, then 0.6 mi w. Int corridors. Pets: Medium. $20 one-time fee/room. Designated rooms, service with restrictions, supervision.
ASK S✆ ✕ &M 🐾 &' 🛏 🖵 ≈

▼▼ Red Roof Inn M
(318) 388-2420. $50-$59. 102 Constitution Dr. I-20, exit 114 (Thomas Rd), just s. Ext corridors. Pets: Medium, other species. Service with restrictions, supervision.
&'

ZACHARY

AAA ▼▼▼ Best Western Zachary Inn SH
(225) 658-2550. $68. 4030 Hwy 19. Just s of jct SR 64. Int corridors. Pets: Other species. $50 one-time fee/room. Service with restrictions, supervision.
SAVE S✆ ✕ 🛏 🖵 ≈

MAINE

AUBURN

▼▼▼ A Fireside Inn & Suites SH
(207) 777-1777. $80-$180. 1777 Washington St. I-95 (Maine Tpke), exit 75, 5 mi s on US 202, SR 4 and 100. Ext/int corridors. Pets: Other species. $10 daily fee/room. Service with restrictions, supervision.
ASK S⊘ ✕ 🖥 💻 🍴 ➳

⚠ ▼▼ Econo Lodge SH
(207) 784-1331. $69-$250. 170 Center St. North side on SR 4. Ext/int corridors. Pets: Medium. $10 daily fee/pet. Designated rooms, service with restrictions, supervision.
SAVE S⊘ ✕ 🖥

⚠ ▼ Sleepy Time Motel M
(207) 783-1435. $65-$85. 46 Danville Corner Rd. I-95 (Maine Tpke), exit 75, 0.5 mi ne on US 202, just e. Ext corridors. Pets: Accepted.
SAVE S⊘ ✕ 🖥

AUGUSTA

⚠ ▼▼▼ Best Western Senator Inn & Spa SH �
(207) 622-5804. $119-$269. 284 Western Ave. I-95, exit 109 (Augusta-Winthrop) northbound; exit 109A southbound, on US 202, SR 11 and 100. Ext/int corridors. Pets: $50 deposit/room, $9 one-time fee/pet. Designated rooms, service with restrictions, supervision.
SAVE S⊘ ✕ 🖥 💻 🍴 ➳ ✕

▼▼▼ Comfort Inn SH
(207) 623-1000. $99-$209, 3 day notice. 281 Civic Center Dr. I-95, exit 112B northbound; exit 112 southbound. Int corridors. Pets: Accepted.
ASK S⊘ ✕ 🖉 🖥 💻 🍴 ➳

⚠ ▼▼ Econo Lodge Inn & Suites SH �
(207) 622-6371. $59-$249. 390 Western Ave. I-95, exit 109 northbound, exit 109B southbound on US 202, SR 11 and 100. Ext corridors. Pets: Large. Service with restrictions, supervision.
SAVE S⊘ ✕ 🖥 💻 🍴 ➳

▼▼▼ Holiday Inn SH
(207) 622-4751. $99-$199, 3 day notice. 110 Community Dr. I-95, exit 112A northbound; exit 112 southbound, just s on SR 8, 11 and 27. Int corridors. Pets: Service with restrictions, supervision.
ASK S⊘ ✕ 🖉 🖉 🖥 💻 🍴 ➳

BANGOR

▼▼ America's Best Inn SH
(207) 942-1234. $80-$120, 7 day notice. 570 Main St. I-395, exit 3B. Int corridors. Pets: Other species. Service with restrictions, supervision.
ASK S⊘ ✕ 🖥 💻 🍴

▼▼▼ Best Western White House SH �
(207) 862-3737. $72-$133. 155 Littlefield Ave. I-95, exit 180 (Coldbrook Rd), 5.5 mi s of downtown. Ext/int corridors. Pets: $100 deposit/room. Designated rooms, service with restrictions, supervision.
ASK S⊘ ✕ 🖥 💻 ➳

▼▼ Comfort Inn SH
(207) 942-7899. $84-$134. 750 Hogan Rd. I-95, exit 187 (Hogan Rd), 0.5 mi w. Int corridors. Pets: $6 one-time fee/room. Service with restrictions, supervision.
S⊘ ✕ 💻 ➳

▼▼ Days Inn SH
(207) 942-8272. $79-$109. 250 Odlin Rd. I-95, exit 182B, 0.3 mi e on US 2 and SR 100. Int corridors. Pets: Dogs only. $10 one-time fee/room. Service with restrictions, supervision.
ASK S⊘ ✕ 🖥 🖥 💻 ➳

▼▼ Econo Lodge M
(207) 945-0111. $49-$129. 327 Odlin Rd. I-95, exit 182B, just e on US 2 and SR 100. Int corridors. Pets: Large, other species. $10 one-time fee/pet. Service with restrictions, supervision.
ASK ✕ 🖥 🖥 💻 ➳

▼▼▼ Four Points by Sheraton Bangor SH
(207) 947-6721. $135-$195. 308 Godfrey Blvd. At Bangor International Airport. Int corridors. Pets: Accepted.
ASK S⊘ ✕ 🖥 🖥 💻 🍴

▼▼▼ Holiday Inn-Bangor SH
(207) 947-0101. $160-$170. 404 Odlin Rd. I-95, exit 182B at jct Odlin Rd and I-395. Int corridors. Pets: Accepted.
ASK S⊘ ✕ 🖥 🖥 💻 🍴 ➳

▼▼ Holiday Inn Bangor-Civic Center SH
(207) 947-8651. $81-$99. 500 Main St. I-395, exit 3B, just n. Int corridors. Pets: Accepted.
ASK S⊘ ✕ 🖥 💻 🍴 ➳

⚠ ▼▼ Howard Johnson Inn SH
(207) 942-5251. $45-$100. 336 Odlin Rd. I-95, exit 182B; Odlin Rd and I-395. Int corridors. Pets: Other species. $10 daily fee/pet. Supervision.
SAVE S⊘ ✕ 🖥 💻 🍴 ➳

▼▼ Ramada Inn SH
(207) 947-6961. $89-$119. 357 Odlin Rd. I-95, exit 182B, at Odlin Rd and I-395. Int corridors. Pets: Accepted.
ASK S⊘ ✕ 🖥 💻 🍴 ➳

▼▼ Riverside Inn SH
(207) 973-4100. $69-$129, 7 day notice. 495 State St. Adjacent to Eastern Maine Medical Center. Int corridors. Pets: Accepted.
✕ 🖥 💻

▼▼ Travelodge M
(207) 942-6301. $60-$90. 482 Odlin Rd. I-95, exit 182B, just left. Ext corridors. Pets: Accepted.
ASK S⊘ ✕ 🖥 💻

BAR HARBOR

△△△ ▽▽▽ Anchorage Motel M
(207) 288-3959. **$54-$129, 3 day notice.** 51 Mt Desert St. In town on SR 3. Ext corridors. **Pets:** $15 daily fee/room. Service with restrictions, supervision.
[SAVE] [X] [🛏]

▽▽ A Wonder View Inn & Suites SH
(207) 288-3358. **$50-$230, 3 day notice.** 50 Eden St. 0.5 mi w on SR 3. Ext corridors. **Pets:** Other species. $10 daily fee/room. Service with restrictions, crate.
[X] [🛏] [💻] [🍽] [≈]

△△△ ▽▽▽▽ Balance Rock Inn 1903 BB
(207) 288-2610. **$125-$595, 14 day notice.** 21 Albert Meadow. S on Main St, just e; center. Ext/int corridors. **Pets:** Other species. $30 daily fee/pet. Service with restrictions, supervision.
[SAVE] [X] [≈]

△△△ ▽▽▽ Best Western Inn SH ❀
(207) 288-5823. **$80-$150.** 452 State Hwy 3. 4.8 mi w. Ext corridors. **Pets:** Service with restrictions, supervision.
[SAVE] [S🐾] [X] [🛏] [💻] [≈]

△△△ ▽▽▽ Days Inn M
(207) 288-3321. **$89-$165.** 120 Eden St. 1 mi w on SR 3. Ext corridors. **Pets:** Accepted.
[SAVE] [X] [🛏]

▽▽ Hutchins Mountain View Cottages CA
(207) 288-4833. **$58-$98, 14 day notice.** 286 State Rt 3. 4 mi w. Ext corridors. **Pets:** Other species. Service with restrictions.
[X] [🛏] [💻] [≈] [🐾] [✆]

BATH

△△△ ▽▽▽▽ Holiday Inn Bath/Brunswick SH
(207) 443-9741. **$80-$199.** 139 Richardson St. 0.3 mi s on US 1. Int corridors. **Pets:** Designated rooms, service with restrictions, supervision.
[SAVE] [S🐾] [X] [♿M] [🐾] [🐾] [🛏] [💻] [🍽] [≈] [✕]

BELFAST

▽▽▽ Belfast Harbor Inn SH
(207) 338-2740. **$54-$149.** 91 Searsport Ave (Rt 1). On US 1, 1.2 mi n from jct SR 3. Ext/int corridors. **Pets:** Accepted.
[ASK] [S🐾] [X] [≈]

▽▽▽▽ Comfort Inn Ocean's Edge SH ❀
(207) 338-2090. **$85-$369.** 159 Searsport Ave. On US 1, 2 mi n from jct SR 3. Int corridors. **Pets:** $10 daily fee/pet. Designated rooms, service with restrictions, supervision.
[ASK] [S🐾] [X] [♿M] [🐾] [🐾] [🛏] [💻] [🍽] [≈] [✕]

▽▽ Gull Motel M
(207) 338-4030. **$39-$89, 3 day notice.** 196 Searsport Ave. On US 1, 3 mi n from jct SR 3. Ext corridors. **Pets:** $10 daily fee/pet. Designated rooms, service with restrictions, supervision.
[ASK] [X] [🛏]

▽▽ Seascape Motel & Cottages M ❀
(207) 338-2130. **$52-$139, 3 day notice.** 202 Searsport Ave. On US 1, 3 mi n from jct SR 3. Ext corridors. **Pets:** Small. $10 one-time fee/pet. Designated rooms, service with restrictions, supervision.
[X] [🛏] [💻] [≈]

BETHEL

▽▽▽▽ Briar Lea Inn & The Jolly Drayman English Pub CI
(207) 824-4717. **$89-$159, 14 day notice.** 150 Mayville Rd (US 2). 1 mi n of jct US 2, SR 5 and 26. Int corridors. **Pets:** Dogs only. $10 daily fee/pet. Service with restrictions, crate.
[ASK] [X] [🍽]

▽▽▽ The Inn At the Rostay M
(207) 824-3111. **$60-$130, 14 day notice.** 186 Mayville Rd (US 2). On US 2, 2 mi e. Ext corridors. **Pets:** Accepted.
[ASK] [S🐾] [X] [🛏] [🍽] [≈]

BOOTHBAY

▽▽▽ The 1828 Vintage House and Cottages M ❀
(207) 633-3411. **$65-$149, 14 day notice.** 301 Adams Pond Rd. US 1, 9 mi s on SR 27, then just w. Ext/int corridors. **Pets:** $18 daily fee/pet. Designated rooms, service with restrictions, supervision.
[X] [🛏] [💻] [≈] [🐾] [✆]

▽▽▽ Kenniston Hill Inn BB
(207) 633-2159. **$85-$135, 14 day notice.** 988 Wiscasset Rd. US 1 to SR 27, 10 mi s. Ext/int corridors. **Pets:** Medium. Designated rooms, service with restrictions, supervision.
[ASK] [X] [✆]

△△△ ▽▽ White Anchor Inn M
(207) 633-3788. **$45-$80.** 609 Wiscasset Rd. US 1 to SR 27, 7.5 mi s. Ext/int corridors. **Pets:** Other species. $10 one-time fee/room. Designated rooms, service with restrictions, supervision.
[SAVE] [X] [🛏]

BOOTHBAY HARBOR

△△△ ▽▽▽▽ Welch House Inn BB
(207) 633-3431. **$85-$205, 14 day notice.** 56 McKown St. Center. Ext/int corridors. **Pets:** Small, dogs only. $25 one-time fee/pet. Designated rooms, service with restrictions, supervision.
[SAVE] [X]

BRIDGTON

▽▽ Pleasant Mountain Inn M ❀
(207) 647-4505. **$80-$205, 7 day notice.** 656 N High St. On US 302, 3 mi w of center. Ext corridors. **Pets:** Dogs only. $10 daily fee/pet. Service with restrictions, supervision.
[ASK] [S🐾] [X] [🛏] [💻] [🍽]

BRUNSWICK

△△△ ▽▽▽ Viking Motor Inn M
(207) 729-6661. **$59-$159.** 287 Bath Rd. US 1, exit Cooks Corner, left on Bath Rd, then 1 mi w. Ext/int corridors. **Pets:** Medium, other species. $10 daily fee/pet. Service with restrictions, supervision.
[SAVE] [X] [🛏]

BRYANT POND

▽▽ Mollyockett Motel & Swim Spa M
(207) 674-2345. **$70-$95.** 1132 S Main St. 1.3 mi n on SR 26 from jct SR 219. Ext/int corridors. **Pets:** Accepted.
[ASK] [S🐾] [X] [🛏] [💻] [≈] [✕]

BUCKSPORT

▽▽ Bucksport Motor Inn M
(207) 469-3111. **$59-$99.** 70 Main St. On US 1; center. Ext corridors. **Pets:** $10 one-time fee/room. Designated rooms, service with restrictions, supervision.
[ASK] [S🐾] [X] [🛏] [💻]

CAMDEN

▽▽▽▽ The Camden Riverhouse Hotel & Inns SH ❀
(207) 236-0500. **$99-$250, 14 day notice.** 11 Tannery Ln. Center. Int corridors. **Pets:** Dogs only. $10 daily fee/room. Designated rooms, service with restrictions, supervision.
[ASK] [S🐾] [X] [🛏] [💻] [≈]

AAA ▽▽▽ Lord Camden Inn **BB** ❀
(207) 236-4325. **$89-$289, 4 day notice.** 24 Main St. Center. Int corridors. **Pets:** Dogs only. $20 daily fee/pet. Service with restrictions, supervision.
SAVE 🛇 ✕ 🖃 📟

CARIBOU

AAA ▽▽▽ Caribou Inn & Convention Center **SH**
(207) 498-3733. **$106.** 19 Main St. 3 mi s on US 1. Int corridors. **Pets:** Other species. Service with restrictions.
SAVE 🛇 ✕ 🖃 📟 ⫙ ➥ 🗙

CASTINE

▽▽▽ Pentagoet Inn **CI**
(207) 326-8616. **$95-$205, 14 day notice.** 26 Main St. Center. Int corridors. **Pets:** Accepted.
🗙 ⫙ 🗙 🗙 🗙

EAGLE LAKE

▽▽ Overlook Motel & Lakeside Cabins **M** ❀
(207) 444-4535. **$58-$150.** 3232 Aroostook Rd. On SR 11; center. Ext/int corridors. **Pets:** Other species. $5 daily fee/pet. Service with restrictions, supervision.
🖃 📟 🗙

ELLSWORTH

▽ The Colonial Inn **SH** ❀
(207) 667-5548. **$78-$159.** 321 High St. 1.3 mi e on SR 3. Ext/int corridors. **Pets:** Large, other species. Service with restrictions, supervision.
ASK 🛇 ✕ 🗙 🖃 📟 ⫙ ➥

▽▽▽ Holiday Inn **SH**
(207) 667-9341. **$90-$160.** 215 High St. Jct US 1, 1A and SR 3. Int corridors. **Pets:** Accepted.
ASK ✕ 🗙M 🖃 📟 ⫙ ➥ 🗙

AAA ▽ Jasper's Motel **SH**
(207) 667-5318. **$48-$87, 3 day notice.** 200 High St. 1 mi e on US 1 and SR 3. Ext corridors. **Pets:** Accepted.
SAVE 🛇 ✕ 🖃 ⫙

AAA ▽▽▽ Twilite Motel **M**
(207) 667-8165. **$66-$119, 3 day notice.** 147 Bucksport Rd. Jct US 1A, 1.5 mi w on US 1/SR 3. Ext corridors. **Pets:** Small, dogs only. $15 daily fee/pet. Designated rooms, service with restrictions, supervision.
SAVE ✕ 🖃 📟

FARMINGTON

AAA ▽ Mount Blue Motel **M**
(207) 778-6004. **$45-$60.** 454 Wilton Rd. 2 mi w on US 2 and SR 4. Ext corridors. **Pets:** $10 one-time fee/room. Supervision.
SAVE 🛇 ✕ 🖃

FREEPORT

AAA ▽▽▽ Best Western Freeport Inn **SH** ❀
(207) 865-3106. **$85-$175.** 31 US 1 S. I-295, exit 17, 1 mi n. Ext/int corridors. **Pets:** Other species. Designated rooms, service with restrictions.
SAVE 🛇 ✕ 🖃 📟 ⫙ ➥

▽▽ Econo Lodge **M**
(207) 865-3777. **$59-$149.** 537 US Rt 1. I-295, exit 20, 0.3 mi s. Ext corridors. **Pets:** Accepted.
ASK 🛇 ✕ 🖃 📟

AAA ▽▽▽ Harraseeket Inn **CI**
(207) 865-9377. **$123-$304, 3 day notice.** 162 Main St. I-295, exit 22, 0.5 mi e. Int corridors. **Pets:** Accepted.
SAVE 🛇 ✕ 🗙M 🗙 🗙 🖃 📟 ⫙ ➥

GREENVILLE

▽▽ Chalet Moosehead Lakefront Motel **M**
(207) 695-2950. **$70-$136, 3 day notice.** 12 N Birch St. 1.5 mi w on SR 15. Ext corridors. **Pets:** Dogs only. $10 daily fee/pet. Designated rooms, service with restrictions, supervision.
✕ 🖃 📟 🗙

AAA ▽▽▽ Kineo View Motor Lodge **M**
(207) 695-4470. **$69-$105, 7 day notice.** Overlook Dr. 2.5 mi s on SR 15; gravel access road from highway. Ext corridors. **Pets:** Other species. $10 daily fee/room. Designated rooms, service with restrictions, supervision.
SAVE 🛇 ✕ 🖃 📟

HOULTON

AAA ▽▽ Shiretown Motor Inn **SH**
(207) 532-9421. **$79-$99.** 282 North St. I-95, exit 302, 0.3 mi n on US 1. Ext/int corridors. **Pets:** Designated rooms.
SAVE 🛇 ✕ 🖃 📟 ⫙ ➥

KENNEBUNK

AAA ▽▽▽ Turnpike Motel **M**
(207) 985-4404. **$49-$119, 3 day notice.** 77 Old Alewive Rd. I-95 (Maine Tpke), exit 25 (Kennebunk) northbound; exit 25 (Kennebunk) southbound, just e on SR 35. Ext/int corridors. **Pets:** Very small, other species. $10 daily fee/pet. Service with restrictions, supervision.
SAVE 🛇 ✕ 🖃 📟

KENNEBUNKPORT

AAA ▽▽▽ The Captain Jefferds Inn **BB** ❀
(207) 967-2311. **$115-$350, 14 day notice.** 5 Pearl St. From Dock Square, 0.3 mi e on Maine St, just s; corner of Pearl and Pleasant sts. Ext/int corridors. **Pets:** Dogs only. $30 daily fee/pet. Designated rooms, supervision.
SAVE ✕ 🖃

AAA ▽▽▽ The Colony Hotel **SH** ❀
(207) 967-3331. **$225-$1150, 3 day notice.** 140 Ocean Ave. From Dock Square, 1 mi s. Int corridors. **Pets:** Other species. $25 daily fee/pet.
SAVE ✕ 🗙 🖃 ⫙ ➥ 🗙

AAA ▽▽▽ Lodge At Turbat's Creek **M**
(207) 967-8700. **$79-$169, 14 day notice.** 7 Turbat Rd. From Dock Square, 0.5 mi e on Maine St, 0.6 mi ne on Wildes, then just se. Ext corridors. **Pets:** Accepted.
SAVE 🛇 ✕ 🗙M 🖃 ➥

AAA ▽▽▽▽ The Yachtsman Lodge & Marina **SH**
(207) 967-2511. **$179-$379, 30 day notice.** 57 Ocean Ave. From Dock Square, 0.3 mi se. Ext corridors. **Pets:** Accepted.
SAVE ✕ 🖃 📟 🗙

LEWISTON

AAA ▽▽▽ Chalet Motel **SH**
(207) 784-0600. **$60-$70.** 1243 Lisbon St. I-95 (Maine Tpke), exit 80. Ext/int corridors. **Pets:** Accepted.
SAVE 🛇 ✕ 🖃 ⫙ ➥ 🗙

LINCOLNVILLE

▽ Abbingtons Seaview Motel & Cottages **M** ❀
(207) 236-3471. **$49-$139, 5 day notice.** 6 Seaview Dr. On US 1, 1.2 mi s of jct SR 173. Ext corridors. **Pets:** Other species. $15 daily fee/pet. Designated rooms, service with restrictions, supervision.
ASK 🛇 ✕ 🖃 📟 ➥

▼▼▼ Pine Grove Cottages CA
(207) 236-2929. **$85-$175, 7 day notice.** 2076 Atlantic Hwy. On US 1, 2 mi s of jct SR 173. Ext corridors. **Pets:** Service with restrictions, supervision.

⊗ 🛏 ▣

LUBEC

🆎 ▼▼ The Eastland Motel M
(207) 733-5501. **$58-$74.** 395 County Rd. Jct US 1 and SR 189, 8.4 mi e on SR 189. Ext/int corridors. **Pets:** Accepted.

(SAVE) ⊗ 🛏

LUCERNE IN MAINE

🆎 ▼▼▼ The Lucerne Inn CI
(207) 843-5123. **$59-$199.** 2517 Main Rd. On US 1A. Int corridors. **Pets:** Accepted.

(SAVE) (S🐾) ⊗ 🛏 ▣ 🍴 ≈

MACHIAS

🆎 ▼▼ The Bluebird Motel M
(207) 255-3332. **$65-$75.** Dublin St. On US 1, 1 mi s. Ext corridors. **Pets:** Accepted.

(SAVE) (S🐾) ⊗ (🐾M) 🛏

🆎 ▼▼ Machias Motor Inn M
(207) 255-4861. **$70-$115.** 26 E Main St. 0.5 mi e on US 1. Ext corridors. **Pets:** Dogs only. $5 daily fee/pet. Service with restrictions, supervision.

(SAVE) ⊗ 🛏 ▣

MEDWAY

▼ Katahdin Shadows Motel M
(207) 746-5162. **$54-$59, 7 day notice.** 2166 Medway Rd. I-95, exit 244, 1.5 mi w on SR 157. Ext corridors. **Pets:** Service with restrictions, supervision.

⊗ 🛏 ≈ ⊗

MILFORD

▼▼ Milford Motel On The River M
(207) 827-3200. **$60-$84.** 174 Main Rd. 0.5 mi n on US 2. Ext/int corridors. **Pets:** Medium, dogs only. Service with restrictions, supervision.

(ASK) ⊗ 🛏

MILLINOCKET

▼▼▼ Americas Best Value Heritage Inn SH
(207) 723-9777. **$79-$89.** 935 Central St. 0.8 mi e on SR 11 and 157. Int corridors. **Pets:** Other species. $10 daily fee/pet. Service with restrictions, supervision.

(ASK) (S🐾) ⊗ 🛏 ▣ 🍴 ≈

🆎 ▼▼ Econo Lodge Inn & Suites SH
(207) 723-4555. **$59-$135, 3 day notice.** 740 Central St. On SR 157; center. Int corridors. **Pets:** $10 daily fee/pet. Designated rooms, no service, supervision.

(SAVE) (S🐾) ⊗ 🛏 ▣ ≈ ⊗

OGUNQUIT

▼▼ Studio East Motor Inn M
(207) 646-7297. **$49-$189, 7 day notice.** 267 Main St. On US 1; center. Ext corridors. **Pets:** Accepted.

⊗ 🛏

OLD ORCHARD BEACH

🆎 ▼▼▼ Alouette Beach Resort M 🐾
(207) 934-4151. **$49-$275, 14 day notice.** 91 E Grand Ave. 0.9 mi e on SR 9 (E Grand Ave). Ext/int corridors. **Pets:** Dogs only. $50 deposit/room, $8 daily fee/pet. Designated rooms, supervision.

(SAVE) ⊗ 🛏 ▣ 🍴 ≈

🆎 ▼▼▼ Grand Beach Inn SH
(207) 934-4621. **$69-$179, 3 day notice.** 198 E Grand Ave. On SR 9 (E Grand Ave); center. Ext corridors. **Pets:** Medium, dogs only. $10 daily fee/pet. Designated rooms.

(SAVE) (S🐾) ⊗ 🛏 ▣ 🍴 ≈

🆎 ▼▼▼ Old Colonial Motel M 🐾
(207) 934-9862. **$70-$230, 14 day notice.** 61 W Grand Ave. On SR 9 (W Grand Ave), 0.5 mi w. Ext corridors. **Pets:** Small, other species. $50 deposit/room, $10 daily fee/pet. Designated rooms, service with restrictions, crate.

(SAVE) (S🐾) ⊗ 🛏 ▣ ≈ ⊗

🆎 ▼▼▼ Sea View Motel SH
(207) 934-4180. **$52-$280, 14 day notice.** 65 W Grand Ave. 0.5 mi w on SR 9 (W Grand Ave). Ext corridors. **Pets:** Medium, dogs only. $100 deposit/pet, $10 daily fee/pet. Designated rooms, supervision.

(SAVE) (S🐾) ⊗ 🛏 ≈

ORONO

▼▼▼ Best Western Black Bear Inn & Conference
        Center SH
(207) 866-7120. **$94-$139.** 4 Godfrey Dr. I-95, exit 193 (Stillwater Ave). Int corridors. **Pets:** $3 daily fee/pet. Designated rooms, service with restrictions, supervision.

(ASK) (S🐾) ⊗ (🐾M) 🛏 ▣

▼▼ University Inn Academic Suites SH
(207) 866-4921. **$69-$95.** 5 College Ave. I-95, exit 191, 1.6 mi n on US 2; 8 mi n of Bangor. Int corridors. **Pets:** Designated rooms, service with restrictions, supervision.

(ASK) ⊗ 🛏 ▣ ≈

PORTLAND

▼▼▼ Doubletree Hotel LH
(207) 774-5611. **$89-$269.** 1230 Congress St. I-295, exit 5 southbound, w on SR 22; exit 5B northbound. Int corridors. **Pets:** Accepted.

(ASK) ⊗ (🐾M) 🐾 🛏 ▣ 🍴 ≈

🆎 ▼▼▼ Eastland Park Hotel LH
(207) 775-5411. **$79-$249, 3 day notice.** 157 High St. At Congress Square; center. Int corridors. **Pets:** Accepted.

(SAVE) ⊗ 🛏 ▣ 🍴 ⊗

🆎 ▼▼▼ Embassy Suites Hotel LH 🐾
(207) 775-2200. **$109-$329.** 1050 Westbrook St. At Portland International Jetport. Int corridors. **Pets:** Designated rooms, service with restrictions.

(SAVE) ⊗ (🐾M) 🐾 🛏 ▣ 🍴 ≈ ⊗

🆎 ▼▼▼ Holiday Inn-West SH
(207) 774-5601. **$109-$199.** 81 Riverside St. I-95 (Maine Tpke), exit 48. Int corridors. **Pets:** Medium. $50 one-time fee/room. Designated rooms, service with restrictions, supervision.

(SAVE) (S🐾) ⊗ (🐾M) 🐾 🐾 🛏 ▣ 🍴 ≈ ⊗

🆎 ▼▼▼ Howard Johnson Plaza Hotel SH
(207) 774-5861. **$85-$205.** 155 Riverside St. I-95 (Maine Tpke), exit 48, jct SR 25. Int corridors. **Pets:** $50 deposit/room. Service with restrictions, supervision.

(SAVE) ⊗ 🛏 ▣ 🍴 ≈

🆎 ▼▼▼ ▼▼ Portland Harbor Hotel SH
(207) 775-9090. **$149-$259.** 468 Fore St. In the Old Port. Int corridors. **Pets:** $25 daily fee/pet. Service with restrictions, supervision.

(SAVE) (S🐾) ⊗ (🐾M) 🐾 🐾 🛏 🍴

PRESQUE ISLE

🆎 ▼▼ Northern Lights Motel M
(207) 764-4441. **$57-$90.** 72 Houlton Rd. 2 mi s on US 1. Ext corridors. **Pets:** Accepted.

(SAVE) ⊗ 🛏

(AAA) ♦♦ Presque Isle Inn & Convention Center SH
(207) 764-3321. **$78-$124.** 116 Main St. 1 mi s on US 1. Int corridors.
Pets: Other species. Service with restrictions.
SAVE S⊘ ✕ 🖶 🖵 🍴 ⌘

RANGELEY

♦♦ Country Club Inn CI
(207) 864-3831. **$99-$125, 7 day notice.** 56 Country Club Rd. 2.5 mi w
on SR 4 and 16, 0.8 mi s, follow signs. Ext/int corridors. **Pets:** $10 daily
fee/pet. Service with restrictions, supervision.
ASK ✕ 🍴 ⌘ 🐾 📺 ☎

(AAA) ♦♦♦ Rangeley Inn & Motor Lodge CI ❀
(207) 864-3341. **$84-$139, 15 day notice.** 2443 Main St. Center. Ext/
int corridors. **Pets:** Other species. $15 daily fee/room. Designated rooms,
service with restrictions, supervision.
SAVE ✕ 🖶 🖵 🍴

ROCKLAND

(AAA) ♦♦ Navigator Motor Inn SH
(207) 594-2131. **$65-$165.** 520 Main St. On US 1. Ext/int corridors.
Pets: Dogs only. Designated rooms, service with restrictions, supervision.
SAVE S⊘ ✕ 🖶 🍴

(AAA) ♦♦♦ Trade Winds Motor Inn SH
(207) 596-6661. **$59-$179.** 2 Park Dr. On US 1; center. Ext/int corridors. **Pets:** Dogs only. Designated rooms, service with restrictions, crate.
SAVE S⊘ ✕ 🖶 🍴 ⌘ ✕

ROCKPORT

**(AAA) ♦♦♦♦ The Country Inn At
Camden-Rockport SH ❀**
(207) 236-2725. **$94-$209, 3 day notice.** 8 Country Inn Way. Jct SR
90, 0.9 mi n on US 1. Ext/int corridors. **Pets:** Other species. $10 daily
fee/pet. Designated rooms, service with restrictions, supervision.
SAVE S⊘ ✕ 🖶 🖵 ⌘ ✕

RUMFORD

(AAA) ♦♦♦ Linnell Motel & RestInn Conference Center SH
(207) 364-4511. **$60-$75.** 986 Prospect Ave. 2 mi w, just off US 2.
Ext/int corridors. **Pets:** Accepted.
SAVE S⊘ ✕ 🖶 🖵

SACO

(AAA) ♦♦♦ Hampton Inn SH
(207) 282-7222. **$79-$149.** 48 Industrial Park Rd. I-95 (Maine Tpke),
exit 36; I-195, exit 1. Int corridors. **Pets:** Other species. Designated
rooms, service with restrictions, supervision.
SAVE S⊘ ✕ ♿M 🖶 🖵 ⌘

(AAA) ♦ Saco Motel M
(207) 284-6952. **$55-$90, 3 day notice.** 473 Main St. I-95 (Maine
Tpke), exit 36, 0.5 mi s on US 1. Ext corridors. **Pets:** Accepted.
SAVE S⊘ ✕ 🖶 ⌘

♦♦ Wagon Wheel Motel M
(207) 284-6387. **$55-$125, 3 day notice.** 726 Portland Rd. 1.8 mi n on
US 1; 0.8 mi n of jct I-95 (Maine Tpke), exit 36. Ext corridors.
Pets: Accepted.
✕ 🖶 🖵 ⌘

SANFORD

♦♦ Super 8 Motel SH
(207) 324-8823. **$57-$95.** 1892 Main St (Rt 109). I-95 (Maine Tpke),
exit 19, 7 mi w. Int corridors. **Pets:** Accepted.
✕ 🔲 🖶

SCARBOROUGH

♦ Pride Motel & Cottages CA ❀
(207) 883-4816. **$45-$160.** 677 US 1. I-95 (Maine Tpke), exit 36, 0.5 mi
e to US 1, then 4.5 mi n. Ext corridors. **Pets:** Other species. $15 daily
fee/room. Service with restrictions, supervision.
✕ 🖶 ⌘ ✕

♦♦ Residence Inn by Marriott SH
(207) 883-0400. **$125-$216.** 800 Roundwood Dr. I-95 (Maine Tpke),
exit 42, 1.5 mi n on Payne Rd. Int corridors. **Pets:** Other species. $75
one-time fee/room. Service with restrictions.
ASK S⊘ ✕ ♿M 🐾 🔲 🖶 🖵 ⌘ ✕

♦♦ TownePlace Suites by Marriott SH ❀
(207) 883-6800. **$89-$179.** 700 Roundwood Dr. I-95 (Maine Tpke), exit
42, 1.5 mi n on Payne Rd. Int corridors. **Pets:** Other species. $75
one-time fee/room. Service with restrictions, crate.
ASK S⊘ ✕ ♿M 🔲 🖶 🖵 ⌘

SKOWHEGAN

(AAA) ♦ Breezy Acres Motel M
(207) 474-2703. **$58-$79, 7 day notice.** 315 Waterville Rd. 1.5 mi s on
US 201. Ext corridors. **Pets:** Accepted.
SAVE S⊘ ✕ 🖶 🖵 ⌘ ✕

SOUTHPORT

(AAA) ♦♦♦ The Lawnmere Inn CI ❀
(207) 633-2544. **$99-$189, 14 day notice.** 65 Hendricks Hill Rd. 2 mi s
of Boothbay Harbor on SR 27, just s of bridge to Southport Island.
Ext/int corridors. **Pets:** Other species. $20 daily fee/pet. Designated
rooms, service with restrictions.
SAVE ✕ 🖶 🍴

(AAA) ♦♦♦ Ocean Gate Inn SH
(207) 633-3321. **$53-$179, 8 day notice.** 70 Ocean Gate Rd. SR 27,
2.5 mi s of Boothbay Harbor, 0.5 mi s of bridge to Southport Island.
Ext corridors. **Pets:** Accepted.
SAVE S⊘ ✕ 🖶 🖵 ⌘ ✕

SOUTH PORTLAND

♦♦♦ Best Western Merry Manor Inn SH
(207) 774-6151. **$99-$169.** 700 Main St. I-95 (Maine Tpke), exit 45, 1.3
mi e to US 1. Ext/int corridors. **Pets:** Other species. Designated rooms,
service with restrictions, supervision.
ASK S⊘ ✕ ♿M 🔲 🖶 🖵 🍴 ⌘ ✕

(AAA) ♦♦♦ Comfort Inn SH ❀
(207) 775-0409. **$89-$199.** 90 Maine Mall Rd. I-95, exit 45, 1 mi n. Int
corridors. **Pets:** Other species. $25 one-time fee/room. Service with restric-
tions, supervision.
SAVE S⊘ ✕ ♿M 🔲 🖶 🖵

♦♦ Hampton Inn Hotel SH
(207) 773-4400. **$109-$229.** 171 Philbrook Ave. I-95 (Maine Tpke), exit
45. Int corridors. **Pets:** Other species. $50 one-time fee/room. Designated
rooms, service with restrictions, supervision.
ASK S⊘ ✕ ♿M 🐾 🖶 🖵

(AAA) ♦♦♦ Holiday Inn Express SH
(207) 775-3900. **$99-$239.** 303 Sable Oaks Dr. I-95 (Maine Tpke), exit
45, just n on Maine Mall Rd, then just w on Running Hill Rd. Int
corridors. **Pets:** Other species. $20 one-time fee/room. Service with restric-
tions.
SAVE S⊘ ✕ ♿ 🖶 🖵 ⌘

(AAA) ♦♦♦ Howard Johnson Hotel SH
(207) 775-5343. **$72-$179.** 675 Main St. I-95 (Maine Tpke), exit 45, 1.3
mi e to US 1. Int corridors. **Pets:** Other species. Designated rooms,
service with restrictions, supervision.
SAVE ✕ 🖶 🖵 ⌘

▼▼▼ **Portland Marriott Hotel & Golf Resort** 🇱🇭
(207) 871-8000. **$169-$329.** 200 Sable Oaks Dr. I-95 (Maine Tpke), exit 45, just n on Maine Mall Rd, then just w on Running Hill Rd. Int corridors. **Pets:** $35 one-time fee/room. Designated rooms, service with restrictions, supervision.

SPRUCE HEAD

🔺🔺 ▼▼▼ **Craignair Inn** 🇨🇮 🐾
(207) 594-7644. **$75-$154, 14 day notice.** 5 Third St. 2.5 mi w on SR 73, 1.5 mi s on Clark Island Rd; 10 mi s of Rockland. Ext/int corridors. **Pets:** $10 daily fee/room. Designated rooms, service with restrictions, supervision.

WATERVILLE

🔺🔺 ▼▼▼ **Budget Host Airport Inn** 🇸🇭
(207) 873-3366. **$40-$110.** 400 Kennedy Memorial Dr. I-95, exit 127, 0.3 mi e on SR 11 (Kennedy Memorial Dr). Ext/int corridors. **Pets:** $10 one-time fee/pet. Designated rooms, service with restrictions, supervision.

🔺🔺 ▼▼▼ **Econo Lodge** 🇸🇭
(207) 872-5577. **$40-$110.** 455 Kennedy Memorial Dr. I-95, exit 127 on SR 11 (Kennedy Memorial Dr) at Waterville-Oakland. Ext/int corridors. **Pets:** Accepted.

▼▼▼ **Holiday Inn** 🇸🇭
(207) 873-0111. **$105-$139, 7 day notice.** 375 Main St. I-95, exit 130 (Main St) on SR 104. Int corridors. **Pets:** Other species. Service with restrictions.

WELLS

🔺🔺 ▼▼▼ **Ne'r Beach Motel** 🇲
(207) 646-2636. **$44-$149, 14 day notice.** 395 Post Rd (Rt 1). I-95 (Maine Tpke), exit 19, on US 1; 1 mi e on SR 109, then 2.5 mi s. Ext corridors. **Pets:** Accepted.

WEST FORKS

🔺🔺 ▼▼▼ **Inn by the River** 🇨🇮
(207) 663-2181. **$75-$200, 30 day notice.** 2777 US Rt 201. Center. Int corridors. **Pets:** Other species. Designated rooms, service with restrictions.

WESTPORT

▼▼▼ **The Squire Tarbox Inn** 🇨🇮 🐾
(207) 882-7693. **$99-$195, 14 day notice.** 1181 Main Rd. Jct US 1 and SR 144; in Wiscasset; 8.5 mi s on SR 144, follow signs. Ext/int corridors. **Pets:** Supervision.

WILTON

🔺🔺 ▼▼▼ **Whispering Pines Motel** 🇲
(207) 645-3721. **$60-$109, 3 day notice.** 183 Lake Rd. SR 2, 1 mi w of jct SR 4. Ext corridors. **Pets:** Accepted.

YARMOUTH

🔺🔺 ▼▼▼ **Down-East Village Motel** 🇲
(207) 846-5161. **$65-$118.** 705 US Rt 1. I-295, exit 15 northbound; exit 17 southbound. Ext corridors. **Pets:** Other species. $8 daily fee/pet. Service with restrictions, supervision.

MARYLAND

BALTIMORE METROPOLITAN AREA

ABERDEEN

Clarion Aberdeen SH
(410) 273-6300. **$99-$110.** 980 Hospitality Way. I-95, exit 85, just e on SR 22. Int corridors. **Pets:** Medium, other species. Service with restrictions, supervision.

Holiday Inn Chesapeake House SH
(410) 272-8100. **$112-$121.** 1007 Beards Hill Rd. I-95, exit 85, just e on SR 22. Int corridors. **Pets:** Accepted.

Red Roof Inn M
(410) 273-7800. **$55-$70.** 988 Hospitality Way. I-95, exit 85, just e on SR 22. Ext corridors. **Pets:** Medium, other species. Service with restrictions, supervision.

Super 8 Motel SH
(410) 272-5420. **$50-$65.** 1008 Beards Hill Rd. I-95, exit 85, just e on SR 22. Int corridors. **Pets:** Dogs only. Supervision.

ANNAPOLIS

DoubleTree Hotel Annapolis SH
(410) 224-3150. **$119-$269.** 210 Holiday Ct. 2.3 mi sw on US 50 and 301, exit 22 to Riva Rd, 0.3 mi n. Int corridors. **Pets:** Small. Designated rooms, service with restrictions, supervision.

Extended StayAmerica-Annapolis/Naval Academy SH
(410) 571-9988. **Call for rates.** 1 Womack Dr. 2.3 mi sw on US 50 and 301, exit 22, just s on Admiral Cochrane Dr, then just n on Spruill Rd. Int corridors. **Pets:** Accepted.

Historic Inns of Annapolis SH
(410) 263-2641. **$119-$269.** 58 State Circle. Facing the State Capitol; in historic district. Int corridors. **Pets:** Accepted.

Homestead Studio Suites Hotel-Annapolis SH
(410) 571-6600. **$95-$139.** 120 Admiral Cochrane Dr. 2.3 mi sw on US 50 and 301, exit 22, just s, then just e. Int corridors. **Pets:** Accepted.

Loews Annapolis Hotel LH ❖
(410) 263-7777. **$129-$409.** 126 West St. US 50 and 301, exit 24 eastbound; exit 24A westbound, 1.4 mi s on SR 70, just sw on Calvert St, then just w. Int corridors. **Pets:** Service with restrictions, supervision.

Residence Inn by Marriott-Annapolis SH
(410) 573-0300. **$199-$299.** 170 Admiral Cochrane Dr. 2.3 mi sw on US 50 and 301, exit 22 to Riva Rd, just s on Riva Rd, then just e. Ext corridors. **Pets:** Accepted.

Sheraton Annapolis Hotel LH ❖
(410) 266-3131. **$99-$299.** 173 Jennifer Rd. North side of US 50 and 301, exit 23B westbound; exit 23 eastbound. Int corridors. **Pets:** Medium, dogs only. Service with restrictions, supervision.

ANNAPOLIS JUNCTION

TownePlace Suites by Marriott-Baltimore/Ft. Meade SH
(301) 498-7477. **$59-$139.** 120 National Business Pkwy. I-95, exit 38A, 2.5 mi e on SR 32 to exit 11 (Dorsey Run Rd), then 1.3 mi e. Int corridors. **Pets:** Accepted.

BALTIMORE

Admiral Fell Inn SH
(410) 522-7377. **$179-$299.** 888 S Broadway St. Corner of Broadway and Thames sts; facing the waterfront. Int corridors. **Pets:** Accepted.

Baltimore's Tremont Park Hotel SH
(410) 576-1200. **$89-$289.** 8 E Pleasant St. Just s of US 40 E, off Charles St. Int corridors. **Pets:** Accepted.

Brookshire Suites SH
(410) 625-1300. **$119-$206.** 120 E Lombard St. Corner of Calvert and Lombard sts. Int corridors. **Pets:** Accepted.

Hampton Inn & Suites Baltimore Inner Harbor SH ❖
(410) 539-7888. **$179-$249, 30 day notice.** 131 E Redwood St. Between Lombard and Baltimore sts; corner of Calvert and E Redwood sts. Int corridors. **Pets:** Medium. $100 one-time fee/pet. Service with restrictions, crate.

Peabody Court-A Clarion Hotel SH
(410) 727-7101. **$179-$309.** 612 Cathedral St. Cathedral St and Mt Vernon Square. Int corridors. **Pets:** Small. $15 daily fee/pet, $45 one-time fee/room. Service with restrictions, supervision.

Pier 5 Hotel SH
(410) 539-2000. **$199-$349.** 711 Eastern Ave. On the Inner Harbor, at Pier 5. Int corridors. **Pets:** Accepted.

▼▼▼ **Residence Inn by Marriott-Baltimore Downtown/Inner Harbor** SH
(410) 962-1220. **$169-$229.** 17 Light St. Between Mercer and E Redwood sts. Int corridors. **Pets:** Medium. $100 one-time fee/pet. Service with restrictions.

▼▼▼ **Sheraton Inner Harbor Hotel** LH
(410) 962-8300. **$339-$369.** 300 S Charles St. At Conway St. Int corridors. **Pets:** Accepted.

BELCAMP

▼▼▼ **Extended StayAmerica-Bel Air** SH
(410) 273-0194. **Call for rates.** 1361 James Way. I-95, exit 80 (SR 543), just ne. Int corridors. **Pets:** Accepted.

COLUMBIA

▼▼▼ **Extended StayAmerica-Columbia 100 Parkway** SH
(410) 772-8800. **$104-$119.** 8870 Columbia 100 Pkwy. I-95, exit 43B, 4 mi w on SR 100, exit 1B, then just e. Int corridors. **Pets:** Accepted.

▼▼▼ **Extended Stay Deluxe Columbia Corporate Park** SH
(410) 872-2994. **$124-$144.** 8890 Stanford Blvd. I-95, exit 41B, 1.3 mi w on SR 175 (Little Patuxent Pkwy), 0.5 mi s on Snowden River Pkwy, just w on McGaw Rd, then 0.3 mi nw. Int corridors. **Pets:** Accepted.

▼▼▼ **Homewood Suites by Hilton** SH
(410) 872-9200. **$89-$269.** 8320 Benson Dr. I-95, exit 41B, 0.5 mi w on SR 175 (Little Patuxent Pkwy), just nw on SR 108, then just w on Lark Brown Rd. Int corridors. **Pets:** $75 one-time fee/room. Service with restrictions, supervision.

▼▼▼ **Sheraton Columbia Hotel** LH
(410) 730-3900. **$149-$269.** 10207 Wincopin Cir. 1.2 mi w on SR 175 (Little Patuxent Pkwy) from jct US 29, then just s; center. Int corridors. **Pets:** Medium, dogs only. Designated rooms, service with restrictions, supervision.

▼▼▼ **Staybridge Suites Baltimore-Columbia** SH
(410) 964-9494. **$99-$239.** 8844 Columbia 100 Pkwy. I-95, exit 43B, 4 mi w on SR 100, exit 1B, then just e. Int corridors. **Pets:** Accepted.

EDGEWOOD

AAA ▼▼▼ **Best Western Invitation Inn** M ❀
(410) 679-9700. **$69-$99.** 1709 Edgewood Rd. I-95, exit 77A, just e on SR 24. Ext corridors. **Pets:** Other species. $15 daily fee/room. Service with restrictions, supervision.

ELLICOTT CITY

▼▼▼ **Residence Inn by Marriott Columbia** SH
(410) 997-7200. **$119-$299.** 4950 Beaver Run Way. I-95, exit 43B, 4 mi w on SR 100, exit 1B (Executive Park Dr). Int corridors. **Pets:** Accepted.

GLEN BURNIE

AAA ▼▼▼ **Days Inn-Glen Burnie** SH
(410) 761-8300. **$79-$149.** 6600 Ritchie Hwy. I-695, exit 3B eastbound; exit 2 westbound, 0.5 mi s on SR 2. Ext corridors. **Pets:** Accepted.

▼▼▼ **Extended StayAmerica Baltimore-Glen Burnie** SH
(410) 761-2708. **$114-$134.** 104 Chesapeake Centre Ct. I-695, exit 3B, 0.9 mi s on SR 2, just e on E Ordance Rd, then just s. Int corridors. **Pets:** Accepted.

HANOVER

▼▼▼ **Red Roof Inn-BWI Parkway** M
(410) 712-4070. **$66-$96.** 7306 Parkway Dr S. I-95, exit 43A, 2 mi e on SR 100, exit 8 (Coca-Cola Dr), then 0.5 mi se. Ext corridors. **Pets:** Medium, other species. Service with restrictions, supervision.

▼▼▼ **Residence Inn by Marriott-Arundel Mills/BWI** SH ❀
(410) 799-7332. **$139-$249.** 7035 Arundel Mills Cir. I-95, exit 43A, 3.6 mi e on SR 100, exit 10A (Arundel Mills Blvd). Int corridors. **Pets:** Medium, other species. $100 one-time fee/room. Designated rooms.

JESSUP

▼▼ **Extended StayAmerica-Jessup** SH
(301) 725-3877. **Call for rates.** 8550 Washington Blvd. I-95, exit 38A, 1.4 mi e on SR 32, 0.5 mi n on US 1. Int corridors. **Pets:** Accepted.

▼▼ **Red Roof Inn-Columbia/Jessup** M
(410) 796-0380. **$74-$101.** 8000 Washington Blvd. I-95, exit 41A; 0.3 mi s of jct US 1 and SR 175. Ext corridors. **Pets:** Medium, other species. Service with restrictions, supervision.

LINTHICUM HEIGHTS

▼▼ **Candlewood Suites-BWI** SH ❀
(410) 850-9214. **$117-$129.** 1247 Winterson Rd. I-695, exit 7A, 1 mi s on SR 295, 1.3 mi e on W Nursery Rd, then 0.3 mi w. Int corridors. **Pets:** Other species. $75 one-time fee/room. Designated rooms, service with restrictions, crate.

AAA ▼▼▼ **Comfort Inn Airport** SH
(410) 789-9100. **$89-$179.** 6921 Baltimore Annapolis Blvd. I-695, exit 6A eastbound; exit 5 westbound, at SR 170 and 648. Int corridors. **Pets:** Accepted.

AAA ▼▼▼ **Comfort Suites-BWI Airport** SH
(410) 691-1000. **$89-$159.** 815 Elkridge Landing Rd. I-695, exit 7A, 1 mi s on SR 295, then 1.3 mi e on W Nursery Rd. Int corridors. **Pets:** Accepted.

▼▼ **Extended StayAmerica BWI Airport** SH
(410) 850-0400. **$95-$115.** 1500 Aero Dr. I-695, exit 7A, 1 mi s on SR 295, 0.6 mi e on W Nursery Rd, then just n. Int corridors. **Pets:** Accepted.

AAA ▼▼▼ **Four Points by Sheraton BWI Airport** SH
(410) 859-3300. **$90-$240.** 7032 Elm Rd. I-195, exit 1A, 0.5 mi n on SR 170, then just e. Int corridors. **Pets:** Accepted.

▼▼▼ **Hampton Inn BWI Airport** SH
(410) 850-0600. **$89-$179.** 829 Elkridge Landing Rd. I-695, exit 7A, 1 mi s on SR 295, 1.3 mi e on W Nursery Rd, then just w. Int corridors. **Pets:** Accepted.

△△△ ▽▼▽▼ Holiday Inn-BWI Airport Conference Center LH
(410) 859-8400. **$89-$219.** 890 Elkridge Landing Rd. I-695, exit 7A, 1 mi s on SR 295, 1.3 mi e on W Nursery Rd, then 0.5 mi w. Int corridors. **Pets:** Accepted.
[SAVE] [S✺] [✕] [⚹M] [✎] [⚷] [🛏] [🖵] [¶] [➾]

▽▼ Homestead Studio Suites Hotel-Baltimore-BWI Airport M
(410) 691-2500. **$95-$115.** 939 International Dr. I-695, exit 7A, 1 mi s on SR 295, then 0.6 mi e on W Nursery Rd. Ext corridors. **Pets:** Accepted.
[ASK] [S✺] [✕] [⚹M] [✎] [⚷] [🛏] [🖵]

▽▼▽▼ Homewood Suites by Hilton-BWI Airport SH
(410) 684-6100. **$129-$189.** 1181 Winterson Rd. I-695, exit 7A, 1 mi s on SR 295, 0.7 mi e on W Nursery Rd, then just n. Int corridors. **Pets:** Accepted.
[ASK] [✕] [⚹M] [✎] [⚷] [🛏] [🖵] [➾] [✕]

▽▼ Microtel Inn & Suites-BWI Airport SH
(410) 865-7500. **$115-$125.** 1170 Winterson Rd. I-695, exit 7A, 1 mi s on SR 295, 0.7 mi e on W Nursery Rd, then just n. Int corridors. **Pets:** Accepted.
[ASK] [S✺] [✕] [⚹M] [✎] [⚷] [🛏] [🖵]

▽ Motel 6 Baltimore-Linthicum Heights #1201 M
(410) 636-9070. **$39-$65.** 5179 Raynor Ave. I-695, exit 8, just e on SR 168. Ext corridors. **Pets:** Medium, other species. Service with restrictions, supervision.
[S✺] [✕] [➾]

▽▼ Red Roof Inn-BWI Airport M
(410) 850-7600. **$76-$106.** 827 Elkridge Landing Rd. I-695, exit 7A, 1 mi s on SR 295, 1.3 mi e on W Nursery Rd, then just w. Ext corridors. **Pets:** Medium, other species. Service with restrictions, supervision.
[✕] [✎] [🛏]

▽▼▽▼ Residence Inn by Marriott-BWI Airport SH
(410) 691-0255. **$119-$199.** 1160 Winterson Rd. I-695, exit 7A, 1 mi s on SR 295, 0.7 mi e on W Nursery Rd, then just n. Int corridors. **Pets:** Accepted.
[ASK] [S✺] [✕] [⚹M] [⚷] [🛏] [🖵] [➾] [✕]

△△△ ▽▼▽▼ Sleep Inn & Suites Airport SH
(410) 789-7223. **$89-$159.** 6055 Belle Grove Rd. I-695, exit 6A eastbound; exit 5 westbound, 0.3 mi n to jct SR 170/648. Int corridors. **Pets:** Accepted.
[SAVE] [S✺] [✕] [⚹M] [✎] [⚷] [🛏] [🖵]

SYKESVILLE

▽▼▽▼ Inn at Norwood BB
(410) 549-7868. **$130-$220, 7 day notice.** 7514 Norwood Ave. I-70, exit 80 (SR 32), 8 mi n, just w on Main St, then just w on Church St. Int corridors. **Pets:** Medium, dogs only. $20 daily fee/pet. Designated rooms.
[ASK] [✕] [🛏] [🖵] [🗘]

TIMONIUM

▽▼▽▼ Extended StayAmerica-Baltimore-Timonium SH
(410) 628-1088. **$95-$115.** 9704 Beaver Dam Rd. I-83, exit 17, just e, follow signs to Beaver Dam Rd. Int corridors. **Pets:** Accepted.
[ASK] [S✺] [✕] [⚹M] [✎] [🛏] [🖵]

▽▼▽▼ Red Roof Inn-Timonium M
(410) 666-0380. **$63-$98.** 111 W Timonium Rd. I-83, exit 16A northbound; exit 16 southbound, just e. Ext corridors. **Pets:** Medium, other species. Service with restrictions, supervision.
[✕] [🛏]

TOWSON

△△△ ▽▼▽▼ Holiday Inn Baltimore-Towson SH
(410) 823-4410. **$89-$159.** 1100 Cromwell Bridge Rd. I-695, exit 29A, just s. Int corridors. **Pets:** Medium. $40 one-time fee/room. Crate.
[SAVE] [S✺] [✕] [✎] [🛏] [🖵] [¶] [➾]

△△△ ▽▼▽▼ Sheraton Baltimore North Hotel LH
(410) 321-7400. **$109-$179.** 903 Dulaney Valley Rd. I-695, exit 27A, 0.3 mi s. Int corridors. **Pets:** Accepted.
[SAVE] [S✺] [✕] [✎] [🛏] [🖵] [¶] [➾] [✕]

WESTMINSTER

▽ The Boston Inn M
(410) 848-9095. **$46-$77.** 533 Baltimore Blvd. 0.9 mi se on SR 97/140 from jct SR 27. Ext corridors. **Pets:** Dogs only. $50 deposit/pet. Service with restrictions, crate.
[ASK] [✕] [🛏] [➾]

WHITE MARSH

▽▼▽▼ Residence Inn by Marriott Baltimore/White Marsh SH
(410) 933-9554. **$109-$299.** 4980 Mercantile Rd. I-95, exit 67B, 0.5 mi w on SR 43 (White Marsh Blvd), just s to Mercantile Rd, then just e. Int corridors. **Pets:** Other species. $75 one-time fee/room. Service with restrictions.
[ASK] [✕] [⚹M] [⚷] [🛏] [🖵] [➾] [✕]

END METROPOLITAN AREA

CAMBRIDGE

△△△ ▽▼▽▼▽▼ Hyatt Regency Chesapeake Bay Golf Resort, Spa and Marina LH ❖
(410) 901-1234. **$159-$399, 3 day notice.** 100 Heron Blvd. US 50 E, 1.2 mi e of Frederick C Malkus Jr Bridge. Int corridors. **Pets:** Large. $25 daily fee/pet. Designated rooms, service with restrictions.
[SAVE] [✕] [⚹M] [✎] [⚷] [🛏] [🖵] [¶] [➾] [✕]

CHESTERTOWN

▽▼▽▼ Brampton Bed & Breakfast Inn BB ❖
(410) 778-1860. **$155-$265, 10 day notice.** 25227 Chestertown Rd. SR 213 to 291, 0.5 mi w to SR 20, 1 mi s. Ext/int corridors. **Pets:** Dogs only. $35 one-time fee/pet. Designated rooms, service with restrictions, crate.
[✕] [🖵] [🗘]

CUMBERLAND

Holiday Inn SH
(301) 724-8800. **$89-$129, 3 day notice.** 100 S George St. I-68, exit 43C, just n; downtown. Int corridors. **Pets:** Accepted.

(ASK) (S6) (X) (&) (B) (D) (I) (2)

Rocky Gap Lodge & Golf Resort LH
(301) 784-8400. **$79-$199, 3 day notice.** 16701 Lakeview Rd NE. I-68, exit 50, just n. Int corridors. **Pets:** Accepted.

(SAVE) (S6) (X) (&M) (B) (B) (D) (I) (2) (X)

DISTRICT OF COLUMBIA METROPOLITAN AREA

BELTSVILLE

Sheraton College Park Hotel SH ❀
(301) 937-4422. **$95-$129.** 4095 Powder Mill Rd. I-95, exit 29B, just w on SR 212; 2 mi n of I-495 (Capital Beltway). Int corridors. **Pets:** Medium. Service with restrictions, supervision.

(ASK) (X) (&M) (D) (&) (B) (D) (I) (2)

BETHESDA

Residence Inn by Marriott-Bethesda Downtown SH
(301) 718-0200. **$239-$279.** 7335 Wisconsin Ave. I-495, exit 34, 2.5 mi s on SR 355; entrance on Waverly St. Int corridors. **Pets:** Large. $10 daily fee/pet, $200 one-time fee/room. Service with restrictions, crate.

(X) (D) (&) (B) (D) (2)

BOWIE

Comfort Inn Hotel & Conference Center-Bowie SH
(301) 464-0089. **$121-$153.** 4500 NW Crain Hwy. US 50, exit 13A, jct US 50/301 and SR 3. Int corridors. **Pets:** Medium, other species. $15 daily fee/pet. Designated rooms, service with restrictions, supervision.

(ASK) (S6) (X) (&M) (D) (&) (B) (D) (I) (2)

Hampton Inn-Bowie SH
(301) 809-1800. **$109-$159.** 15202 Major Lansdale Blvd. US 50, exit 11, 0.4 mi s on SR 197. Int corridors. **Pets:** Accepted.

(SAVE) (S6) (X) (&M) (&) (B) (D) (2)

CAMP SPRINGS

Days Inn-Camp Springs/Andrews AFB SH
(301) 423-2323. **$76-$106.** 5001 Mercedes Blvd. I-95/495, exit 7B, 0.3 mi n on Auth Rd. Int corridors. **Pets:** Other species. $10 daily fee/pet. Service with restrictions, crate.

(SAVE) (S6) (X) (B) (D) (2)

GAITHERSBURG

Comfort Inn Shady Grove SH ❀
(301) 330-0023. **$79-$149.** 16216 Frederick Rd. I-270, exit 8, 1 mi e on Shady Grove Rd at SR 355. Int corridors. **Pets:** Medium. $15 daily fee/pet. Service with restrictions, crate.

(SAVE) (S6) (X) (D) (B) (D) (2)

Extended StayAmerica-Washington, DC-Gaithersburg SH
(301) 869-9814. **Call for rates.** 205 Professional Dr. I-270, exit 11, 0.4 mi e, then 0.9 mi n on SR 355. Int corridors. **Pets:** Accepted.

(X) (&M) (D) (&) (B) (D)

Extended Stay Deluxe-Washington, DC-Gaithersburg SH
(301) 963-3539. **Call for rates.** 201 Professional Dr. I-270, exit 11, 0.4 mi e, then 0.9 mi n on SR 355. Int corridors. **Pets:** Accepted.

(X) (D) (&) (B) (D)

Holiday Inn-Gaithersburg LH
(301) 948-8900. **$169-$189.** 2 Montgomery Village Ave. I-270, exit 11, 0.3 mi e. Int corridors. **Pets:** Small, other species. Service with restrictions, crate.

(SAVE) (S6) (X) (&M) (D) (&) (B) (D) (I) (2) (X)

Homestead Studio Suites Hotel-Gaithersburg/Rockville SH
(301) 987-9100. **$130-$140.** 2621 Research Blvd. I-270, exit 8, just w, then just n. Int corridors. **Pets:** Accepted.

(ASK) (S6) (X) (&M) (D) (&) (B) (D)

Residence Inn by Marriott-Gaithersburg SH
(301) 590-3003. **$99-$179.** 9721 Washingtonian Blvd. I-270, exit 9B (I-370/Sam Eig Hwy), just w to Fields Rd, 0.8 mi se, then just ne. Int corridors. **Pets:** Accepted.

(ASK) (S6) (X) (&M) (D) (&) (B) (D) (2) (X)

Summerfield Suites-Gaithersburg SH
(301) 527-6000. **$99-$299.** 200 Skidmore Blvd. I-370, exit SR 355, just n to Westland Rd. Ext corridors. **Pets:** Accepted.

(ASK) (X) (&M) (D) (&) (B) (D) (2) (X)

TownePlace Suites by Marriott-Gaithersburg SH ❀
(301) 590-2300. **$89-$209.** 212 Perry Pkwy. I-270, exit 10 northbound, just e; exit 11 southbound, just e on SR 124 to SR 355, 0.3 mi s, then 0.5 mi sw. Int corridors. **Pets:** $100 one-time fee/room. Service with restrictions.

(ASK) (S6) (X) (&M) (D) (&) (B) (D) (2)

GERMANTOWN

Extended StayAmerica-Washington, DC-Germantown SH
(301) 540-9369. **Call for rates.** 12450 Milestone Center Dr. I-270, exit 16, 0.6 mi e on SR 27 (Father Hurley Blvd), 0.7 mi n on Observation Dr, then just w. Int corridors. **Pets:** Accepted.

(X) (&M) (D) (&) (B) (D)

Homestead Studio Suites Hotel-Germantown M
(301) 515-4500. **$100-$110.** 20141 Century Blvd. I-270, exit 15B (SR 118 S/Germantown Rd), just w to Aircraft Dr, then just n. Ext corridors. **Pets:** Accepted.

(ASK) (S6) (X) (&M) (D) (&) (B) (D)

GREENBELT

Residence Inn by Marriott-Greenbelt SH
(301) 982-1600. **$249-$499.** 6320 Golden Triangle Dr. I-95/495, exit 23, 0.5 mi sw of jct SR 201; off SR 193, just n on Walker Dr. Int corridors. **Pets:** Accepted.

(ASK) (S6) (X) (&M) (D) (&) (B) (D) (2) (X)

LANHAM

Red Roof Inn-Lanham M
(301) 731-8830. **$69-$91.** 9050 Lanham Severn Rd. I-95/495, exit 20A, 0.3 mi e on SR 450. Ext corridors. **Pets:** Medium, other species. Service with restrictions, supervision.

(X) (B)

LARGO

Extended StayAmerica-Landover SH
(301) 333-9139. **Call for rates.** 9401 Largo Dr W. I-95/495, exit 17A, just e to Lottsford Rd, 1.3 mi s, then just e; I-95/545, exit 15A, just e. Int corridors. **Pets:** Accepted.

(X) (&) (B) (D)

LAUREL

AAA ▼▼▼ Comfort Suites Laurel Lakes SH
(301) 206-2600. **$79-$179.** 14402 Laurel Pl. On US 1, 0.9 mi s of jct SR 198. Int corridors. **Pets:** Accepted.
SAVE SD ⊠ ⚷ ☎ 🖥 ⇌

AAA ▼▼▼ Quality Inn & Suites Laurel SH
(301) 725-8800. **$89-$199.** One Second St. On US 1, 0.5 mi n of jct SR 198. Ext/int corridors. **Pets:** Small. $15 daily fee/room. Designated rooms, service with restrictions, crate.
SAVE SD ⊠ ⚷ ☎ 🖥 ⇌

▼▼ Red Roof Inn-Laurel M
(301) 498-8811. **$65-$90.** 12525 Laurel Bowie Rd. On SR 197, 0.3 mi w of Baltimore-Washington Pkwy. Ext corridors. **Pets:** Medium, other species. Service with restrictions, supervision.
⊠ ⚷ ⚷ ☎

ROCKVILLE

AAA ▼◆◆▼ The Atrium Court Hotel, a Clarion Collection SH
(301) 840-0200. **$149-$309.** 3 Research Ct. I-270, exit 8 (Shady Grove Rd), just sw. Int corridors. **Pets:** Accepted.
SAVE SD ⊠ ⚷ ⚷ ☎ 🖥 ⇌

AAA ▼▼ Best Western Washington Gateway Hotel LH
(301) 424-4940. **$79-$199.** 1251 W Montgomery Ave. I-270, exit 6B, just w on SR 28. Int corridors. **Pets:** Medium, dogs only. $10 daily fee/room. Service with restrictions, supervision.
SAVE SD ⊠ ⚷ ⚷ ☎ 🖥 🍴 ⇌

▼▼ Red Roof Inn-Rockville SH
(301) 987-0965. **$74-$107.** 16001 Shady Grove Rd. I-270, exit 8 (Shady Grove Rd), 0.5 mi e. Ext corridors. **Pets:** Medium, other species. Service with restrictions, supervision.
⊠ 🔥M ⚷ ⚷ ☎

AAA ▼▼▼ Woodfin Suites Hotel SH
(301) 590-9880. **$239-$289.** 1380 Piccard Dr. I-270, exit 8 (Shady Grove Rd), 0.3 mi s; 1 mi w of SR 355 via Redland Rd. Ext corridors. **Pets:** Accepted.
SAVE SD ⊠ ⚷ ⚷ ☎ 🖥 ⇌ ⊠

SILVER SPRING

▼◆◆▼ Residence Inn by Marriott Silver Spring SH
(301) 572-2322. **Call for rates.** 12000 Plum Orchard Dr. I-95, exit 29B, 1.2 mi w on SR 212, then 1 mi n on Cherry Hill Rd. Int corridors. **Pets:** Accepted.
⊠ 🔥M ⚷ ⚷ ☎ 🖥 ⇌ ⊠

END METROPOLITAN AREA

EMMITSBURG

AAA ▼▼ Sleep Inn & Suites in Emmitsburg SH 🐾
(301) 447-0044. **$65-$199.** 501 Silo Hill Pkwy. US 15, exit SR 140, just w, then just n on Silo Hill Pkwy. Int corridors. **Pets:** Other species. $25 daily fee/room. Service with restrictions, supervision.
SAVE SD ⊠ ⚷ ☎ 🖥 ⇌

FREDERICK

AAA ▼▼▼ Comfort Inn SH
(301) 668-7272. **$99-$139.** 7300 Executive Way. I-270, exit 31B, 0.9 mi sw on SR 85. Int corridors. **Pets:** Other species. $10 daily fee/pet. Service with restrictions, crate.
SAVE SD ⊠ 🔥M ⚷ ☎ 🖥

▼▼▼ Frederick Residence Inn by Marriott SH 🐾
(301) 360-0010. **$179-$219.** 5230 Westview Dr. I-270, exit 31B, 0.5 mi sw on SR 85, then 0.3 mi n on Crestwood Blvd. Int corridors. **Pets:** Medium, other species. $100 one-time fee/room. Service with restrictions.
ASK SD ⊠ ⚷ ☎ 🖥 ⇌ ⊠

AAA ▼▼▼ Hampton Inn SH
(301) 698-2500. **$109-$179.** 5311 Buckeystown Pike (SR 85). I-270, exit 31B, 0.6 mi w. Int corridors. **Pets:** Accepted.
SAVE SD ⊠ ⚷ ⚷ ☎ 🖥 🍴 ⇌

AAA ▼▼▼ Holiday Inn Express-FSK Mall SH
(301) 695-2881. **$119-$169.** 5579 Spectrum Dr. I-270, exit 31A, just e on SR 85. Int corridors. **Pets:** Accepted.
SAVE ⊠ ⚷ ⚷ ☎ 🖥

AAA ▼▼▼ Holiday Inn-Frederick/Ft Detrick SH 🐾
(301) 662-5141. **$79-$139.** 999 W Patrick St. Just w on US 40 from jct US 15. Ext corridors. **Pets:** $50 one-time fee/room. Service with restrictions, supervision.
SAVE SD ⊠ ⚷ ⚷ ☎ 🖥 🍴 ⇌ ⊠

AAA ▼▼▼ Holiday Inn-Holidome & Conference Center SH
(301) 694-7500. **$139-$189.** 5400 Holiday Dr. I-270, exit 31A, just se of SR 85. Int corridors. **Pets:** Large. $10 daily fee/room. Service with restrictions, supervision.
SAVE ⊠ ⚷ ☎ 🖥 🍴 ⇌ ⊠

AAA ▼▼▼ MainStay Suites SH
(301) 668-4600. **$119-$149.** 7310 Executive Way. I-270, exit 31B. Int corridors. **Pets:** Accepted.
SAVE SD ⊠ ⚷ ☎ 🖥 ⇌

GRANTSVILLE

▼▼▼ Comfort Inn SH
(301) 895-5993. **$69-$79.** 2541 Chestnut Ridge Rd. I-68, exit 22, just s on US 219. Int corridors. **Pets:** Accepted.
ASK SD ⊠ ☎ 🖥 ⇌

GRASONVILLE

AAA ▼▼ Best Western Kent Narrows Inn M 🐾
(410) 827-6767. **$82-$199.** 3101 Main St. US 50 and 301, exit 42; at Kent Narrows Bridge. Ext corridors. **Pets:** Medium, other species. $10 daily fee/pet. Service with restrictions, crate.
SAVE SD ⊠ ⚷ ☎ 🖥 ⇌ ⊠

HAGERSTOWN

▼▼▼ Halfway Hagerstown Super 8 SH
(301) 582-1992. **$64-$69.** 16805 Blake Rd. I-81, exit 5B, just w. Int corridors. **Pets:** Medium, dogs only. $15 deposit/pet, $11 one-time fee/pet. Designated rooms, service with restrictions, supervision.
ASK SD ⊠ ⚷ ☎ 🖥

AAA ▼▼ Quality Inn Antietam Creek SH
(301) 733-2700. **$59.** 1101 Dual Hwy. I-70, exit 32B, 2.2 mi w on US 40. Int corridors. **Pets:** Accepted.
SAVE SD ⊠ ☎ 🖥

△△△ ▽▽▽ **Sleep Inn & Suites** SH
(301) 766-9449. **$84-$169.** 18216 Col Henry K Douglas Dr. I-70, exit 29, just s. Int corridors. **Pets:** Other species. $10 daily fee/pet. Service with restrictions, supervision.
SAVE S₀ ✕ 🖥 🕭 🍴 ☎

HANCOCK

△△△ ▽▽▽ **Super 8 Motel** SH
(301) 678-6101. **$49-$109.** 118 Limestone Rd. I-70, exit 1B, just s. Ext/int corridors. **Pets:** $10 one-time fee/pet. Service with restrictions, supervision.
SAVE S₀ ✕ 🖥

INDIAN HEAD

△△△ ▽▽▽ **Super 8 Motel** SH
(301) 753-8100. **$65-$75.** 4694 Indian Head Hwy. SR 210, 0.6 mi s of jct SR 225. Int corridors. **Pets:** Medium, dogs only. $10 daily fee/pet. Designated rooms, service with restrictions, supervision.
SAVE S₀ ✕ 🕭M 🖥

LA VALE

△△△ ▽▽▽ **Red Roof Inn** SH
(301) 729-6700. **$50-$80.** 12310 Winchester Rd SW. I-68, exit 40, 0.6 mi s. Ext/int corridors. **Pets:** Other species. Service with restrictions, supervision.
SAVE S₀ ✕ 🕭 🕭 🖥 🍴

▽▽ **Super 8 Motel** M
(301) 729-6265. **$54.** 1301 National Hwy. I-68, exit 40, 0.4 mi n. Int corridors. **Pets:** Small. $10 daily fee/room. Service with restrictions, supervision.
ASK S₀ ✕ 🖥

LEXINGTON PARK

△△△ ▽▽▽ **Best Western Lexington Park** SH
(301) 862-4100. **$100.** Rt 235. On SR 235, 3.2 mi n of jct SR 246. Int corridors. **Pets:** Accepted.
SAVE S₀ ✕ 🖥 🍴 ☎ ✕

▽▽ **Extended StayAmerica Lexington Park-Pax River** SH
(240) 725-0100. **$89-$104.** 46565 Expedition Park Dr. SR 235, just s to Lexington Park. Int corridors. **Pets:** Accepted.
ASK S₀ ✕ 🕭M 🕭 🕭 🍴 🖥 🍴

MCHENRY

▽▽▽ **Wisp Mountain Resort/Hotel & Conference Center** SH
(301) 387-5581. **$59-$279, 14 day notice.** 290 Marsh Hill Rd. 1 mi s on US 219 from jct SR 42, just w on Sang Run Rd, then 0.3 mi s. Int corridors. **Pets:** Medium, dogs only. $50 one-time fee/room. Designated rooms, service with restrictions, supervision.
ASK S₀ ✕ 🕭 🕭 🖥 🍴 🍴 ☎ ✕

NORTH EAST

▽▽ **Crystal Inn** SH
(410) 287-7100. **$129-$149.** 1 Center Dr. I-95, exit 100 southbound; exit 100A northbound, just e on SR 272. Int corridors. **Pets:** Accepted.
ASK S₀ ✕ 🕭 🕭 🖥 ☎

OCEAN CITY

△△△ ▽▽▽▽ **Clarion Resort Fontainebleau Hotel** LH
(410) 524-3535. **$99-$399, 3 day notice.** 10100 Coastal Hwy. 101st St and the ocean. Int corridors. **Pets:** Accepted.
SAVE S₀ ✕ 🕭 🖥 🍴 🍴 ☎ ✕

△△△ ▽▽▽ **Fenwick Inn** SH
(410) 250-1100. **$79-$209, 3 day notice.** 13801 Coastal Hwy. 138th St and Coastal Hwy. Int corridors. **Pets:** Small. $10 daily fee/pet. Designated rooms, service with restrictions, supervision.
SAVE ✕ 🖥 🍴 ☎

PERRYVILLE

△△△ ▽▽▽ **Ramada Perryville** M ✿
(410) 642-2866. **$69-$104.** 61 Heather Ln. I-95, exit 93, just e. Ext corridors. **Pets:** Other species. $15 daily fee/room. Designated rooms, service with restrictions, crate.
SAVE S₀ ✕ 🕭 🖥 🍴

ROCK HALL

▽▽▽▽ **Inn at Huntingfield Creek** BB ✿
(410) 639-7779. **$135-$185, 14 day notice.** 4928 Eastern Neck Rd. 1.8 mi s on SR 445 from jct SR 20. Ext/int corridors. **Pets:** Designated rooms, supervision.
ASK S₀ ✕ 🖥 🍴 🖥 ☎ ✕ ✕

▽▽ **Mariners Motel** M ✿
(410) 639-2291. **$75-$85.** 5681 S Hawthorne Ave. 0.3 mi e of SR 20. Ext corridors. **Pets:** Other species. $10 one-time fee/room. Service with restrictions, supervision.
✕ 🖥 🍴 ☎

ST. MICHAELS

△△△ ▽▽▽ **The Parsonage Inn** BB
(410) 745-5519. **$100-$195, 10 day notice.** 210 N Talbot St. 0.3 mi w on SR 33. Ext/int corridors. **Pets:** Medium, dogs only. $25 one-time fee/pet. Designated rooms, service with restrictions, crate.
SAVE S₀ ✕ ✕

SALISBURY

△△△ ▽▽▽ **Best Western Salisbury Plaza** M
(410) 546-1300. **$59-$145.** 1735 N Salisbury Blvd. US 13 business route, 0.5 mi s of US 50 Bypass. Ext corridors. **Pets:** $10 daily fee/pet. Service with restrictions, crate.
SAVE S₀ ✕ 🖥 🍴 ☎

△△△ ▽▽▽ **Comfort Inn Salisbury** SH
(410) 543-4666. **$64-$139.** 2701 N Salisbury Blvd. US 13, 0.5 mi n of jct US 13 business route and Bypass. Int corridors. **Pets:** Medium. Service with restrictions, supervision.
SAVE S₀ ✕ 🕭 🖥

▽▽ ▽▽ **Ramada Inn and Conference Center** LH
(410) 546-4400. **$69-$125.** 300 S Salisbury Blvd. US 13 business route, 0.4 mi s of jct Business US 50; downtown. Int corridors. **Pets:** Accepted.
ASK S₀ ✕ 🖥 🍴 🖥 🍴 ☎

SNOW HILL

△△△ ▽▽▽▽ **River House Inn** BB
(410) 632-2722. **$125-$300, 7 day notice.** 201 E Market St. 1 mi w on SR 394 from jct SR 113. Ext/int corridors. **Pets:** Accepted.
SAVE ✕ 🖥 🍴 ☎ ✕

WILLIAMSPORT

△△△ ▽▽▽ **Red Roof Inn** SH
(301) 582-3500. **$54-$79.** 310 E Potomac St. I-81, exit 2, 0.3 mi sw on US 11. Ext corridors. **Pets:** Small. $5 daily fee/pet. Service with restrictions, supervision.
SAVE S₀ ✕ 🕭 🖥

MASSACHUSETTS

AMHERST

(AAA) ▼▼▼▼ The Lord Jeffery Inn SH
(413) 253-2576. **$89-$209.** 30 Boltwood Ave. I-91, exit 19, 6 mi e on SR 9 to Commons. Int corridors. **Pets:** Other species. $15 daily fee/room. Designated rooms, service with restrictions, crate.

[SAVE] [⊗] [🛏] [🍴]

▼▼ University Lodge M
(413) 256-8111. **$63-$135.** 345 N Pleasant St. 0.6 mi n. Ext corridors. **Pets:** Accepted.

[ASK] [S𝄐] [⊗] [🛏] [💻]

AUBURN

▼▼▼▼ Comfort Inn SH
(508) 832-8300. **$85-$139.** 426 Southbridge St. I-90, exit 10, 1 mi n on SR 12; I-290, exit 9 to SR 12. Int corridors. **Pets:** Accepted.

[ASK] [S𝄐] [⊗] [♿] [🐾] [🛏] [💻]

(AAA) ▼▼▼ La Quinta Inn & Suites Worcester-Auburn SH
(508) 832-7000. **$94-$145.** 446 Southbridge St. I-90, exit 10, 1.2 mi n on SR 12. Int corridors. **Pets:** Medium. Service with restrictions.

[SAVE] [⊗] [🛏] [💻]

BARRE

(AAA) ▼▼▼▼ Jenkins Inn CI 🌸
(978) 355-6444. **$170-$195, 7 day notice.** 7 West St. On SR 122 and 32. Int corridors. **Pets:** Dogs only. $5 daily fee/pet. Service with restrictions, supervision.

[SAVE] [S𝄐] [⊗] [💻] [🍴]

BOSTON METROPOLITAN AREA

ANDOVER

(AAA) ▼▼▼▼ Comfort Suites SH
(978) 475-6000. **$89-$109.** 4 Riverside Dr. I-93, exit 45, 0.5 mi e. Int corridors. **Pets:** Small. $75 one-time fee/pet. Designated rooms, service with restrictions, supervision.

[SAVE] [S𝄐] [⊗] [♿] [🐾] [💺] [🛏] [💻] [🏊] [⊗]

▼▼▼▼ La Quinta Inn & Suites SH
(978) 685-6200. **$99-$159.** 131 River Rd. I-93, exit 45, just w; I-495, exit 40B, 2 mi n. Int corridors. **Pets:** Medium. Service with restrictions.

[ASK] [⊗] [🛏] [🏊]

▼▼▼▼ Residence Inn by Marriott Boston-Andover SH
(978) 683-0382. **$89-$199.** 500 Minuteman Rd. I-93, exit 45, 0.3 mi w, then 0.5 mi n. Int corridors. **Pets:** Accepted.

[ASK] [S𝄐] [⊗] [♿] [🐾] [💺] [🛏] [💻] [🏊] [⊗]

(AAA) ▼▼▼▼ Staybridge Suites Boston/Andover SH
(978) 686-2000. **$139-$179.** 4 Tech Dr. I-93, exit 45, just sw via Shattuck Rd. Int corridors. **Pets:** Accepted.

[SAVE] [⊗] [♿] [💺] [🛏] [💻] [🏊]

(AAA) ▼▼▼▼ Wyndham Andover Hotel LH
(978) 975-3600. **$189-$239.** 123 Old River Rd. I-93, exit 45, just e on River Rd. Int corridors. **Pets:** Small. $50 one-time fee/pet. Designated rooms, service with restrictions.

[SAVE] [⊗] [🐾] [💺] [🛏] [💻] [🍴] [🏊] [⊗]

ARLINGTON

▼▼▼▼ Hawthorn Suites Ltd SH
(781) 643-7258. **$129-$399.** 1 Massachusetts Ave. On SR 2A, just n of SR 16. Int corridors. **Pets:** Accepted.

[ASK] [S𝄐] [⊗] [♿] [🐾] [💺] [🛏] [💻]

BILLERICA

▼▼▼▼ Homewood Suites by Hilton SH
(978) 670-7111. **$119-$159.** 35 Middlesex Tpke. I-95, exit 32B, 2.5 mi n. Int corridors. **Pets:** Accepted.

[ASK] [S𝄐] [⊗] [♿] [🐾] [💺] [🛏] [💻] [🏊]

BOSTON

(AAA) ▼▼▼▼▼ Boston Harbor Hotel LH 🌸
(617) 439-7000. **$250-$695.** 70 Rowes Wharf. At Rowes Wharf. Int corridors. **Pets:** Service with restrictions, crate.

[SAVE] [⊗] [🐾] [🍴] [🏊] [⊗]

(AAA) ▼▼▼▼ Boston Omni Parker House Hotel LH
(617) 227-8600. **$119-$419.** 60 School St. Corner of Tremont and School sts; northeast corner of Boston Common. Int corridors. **Pets:** Small, other species. $50 one-time fee/pet. Service with restrictions, crate.

[SAVE] [S𝄐] [⊗] [💻] [🍴]

AAA ▼▼▼ ▼▼▼ Bulfinch Hotel A Clarion Collection Hotel SH
(617) 624-0202. **$159-$369.** 107 Merrimac St. At Lancaster St. Int corridors. **Pets:** Accepted.
[SAVE] [X] [&] [▣] [¶]

The Colonnade Boston LH ❖
(617) 424-7000. **Call for rates.** 120 Huntington Ave. Just s of Copley Square. Int corridors. **Pets:** Medium. Service with restrictions.
[X] [¶] [≈]

AAA ▼▼▼ ▼▼▼ Comfort Inn Boston SH
(617) 287-9200. **$109-$199.** 900 William T Morrissey Blvd. I-93, exit 13 northbound, 0.5 mi sw; exit 12 southbound, follow signs. Int corridors. **Pets:** Service with restrictions, crate.
[SAVE] [SD] [X] [🗗] [&] [🖥] [🖥] [▣]

▼▼▼ ▼▼▼ Courtyard by Marriott Boston, Copley Square SH
(617) 437-9300. **$149-$349.** 88 Exeter St. I-90, exit 22, just n; between Huntington Ave and Boylston St. Int corridors. **Pets:** Accepted.
[ASK] [SD] [X] [&M] [🗗] [&] [▣] [🖥]

▼▼▼ ▼▼▼ DoubleTree Guest Suites-Boston/Cambridge SH
(617) 783-0090. **$99-$309.** 400 Soldiers Field Rd. I-90, exit 20 westbound; exit 18 eastbound. Int corridors. **Pets:** $250 deposit/room. Designated rooms, service with restrictions, crate.
[X] [🗗] [▣] [🖥] [¶] [≈] [🐾]

AAA ▼▼▼ ▼▼▼ The Eliot Hotel SH ❖
(617) 267-1607. **$225-$455.** 370 Commonwealth Ave. Corner of Commonwealth and Massachusetts aves. Int corridors. **Pets:** Other species. Service with restrictions, crate.
[SAVE] [X] [🗗] [&] [¶]

AAA ▼▼▼ ▼▼▼ The Fairmont Copley Plaza Boston LH ❖
(617) 267-5300. **$179-$499.** 138 St. James Ave. At Copley Square. Int corridors. **Pets:** $25 daily fee/pet. Service with restrictions, supervision.
[SAVE] [SD] [X] [&M] [🗗] [&] [▣] [🖥] [¶]

AAA ▼▼▼ ▼▼▼ Fifteen Beacon SH
(617) 670-1500. **$395-$1900.** 15 Beacon St. Just e of State House; just ne of Boston Common; center. Int corridors. **Pets:** Accepted.
[SAVE] [X] [🗗] [&] [¶] [🐾]

AAA ▼▼▼ ▼▼▼ Four Seasons Hotel Boston LH
(617) 338-4400. **$475-$875.** 200 Boylston St. Between Arlington and Charles sts. Int corridors. **Pets:** Accepted.
[SAVE] [X] [&M] [🗗] [&] [¶] [≈] [🐾]

AAA ▼▼▼ ▼▼▼ Hilton Boston Logan Airport LH
(617) 568-6700. **$109-$459.** One Hotel Dr. At General Edward Lawrence Logan International Airport. Int corridors. **Pets:** Medium. Service with restrictions, crate.
[SAVE] [X] [&M] [🗗] [&] [🖥] [▣] [¶] [≈] [🐾]

AAA ▼▼▼ ▼▼▼ Hotel Commonwealth LH ❖
(617) 933-5000. **$175-$485.** 500 Commonwealth Ave. On SR 2 at Beacon St and Brookline Ave. Int corridors. **Pets:** Small, dogs only. $25 one-time fee/pet. Service with restrictions, supervision.
[SAVE] [SD] [X] [&M] [🗗] [¶]

▼▼▼ Howard Johnson Hotel Fenway SH
(617) 267-8300. **$109-$199.** 1271 Boylston St. I-90, exit Brookline Ave S, backing onto Fenway Park. Int corridors. **Pets:** Accepted.
[ASK] [SD] [X] [🗗] [▣] [¶] [≈]

AAA ▼▼▼ ▼▼▼ Hyatt Regency Boston LH
(617) 912-1234. **$159-$399.** One Ave de Lafayette. Just e of Boston Common at Lafayette Pl. Int corridors. **Pets:** Accepted.
[SAVE] [X] [&M] [🗗] [&] [▣] [¶] [≈] [🐾]

AAA ▼▼▼ ▼▼▼ Langham Hotel Boston LH ❖
(617) 451-1900. **$405-$495.** 250 Franklin St. Center; on Post Office Square. Int corridors. **Pets:** Medium. $50 one-time fee/pet. Service with restrictions, crate.
[SAVE] [SD] [X] [🗗] [&] [▣] [¶] [≈] [🐾]

AAA ▼▼▼ ▼▼ The Midtown Hotel SH
(617) 262-1000. **$119-$279, 3 day notice.** 220 Huntington Ave. 3 blks sw of Copley Pl; just n of Symphony Hall and Massachusetts Ave; downtown. Int corridors. **Pets:** Accepted.
[SAVE] [X] [&] [🗗] [▣] [¶] [≈]

AAA ▼▼▼ ▼▼▼ Nine Zero Hotel SH
(617) 772-5800. **$189-$459.** 90 Tremont St. Just ne of Boston Common; motor entrance on Bosworth, just s of property; center. Int corridors. **Pets:** Accepted.
[SAVE] [X] [&M] [&] [¶]

AAA ▼▼▼ ▼▼▼ Onyx Hotel SH 🐾
(617) 557-9955. **$179-$409.** 155 Portland St. Just n of corner of Merrimac and Traverse sts; 3 blks s of Fleet Center. Int corridors. **Pets:** Other species.
[SAVE] [X] [🗗] [&] [▣] [¶]

AAA ▼▼▼ ▼▼▼ Ramada Boston SH
(617) 287-9100. **$109-$199.** 800 William T Morrissey Blvd. I-93, exit 13 northbound, 0.5 mi sw; exit 12 southbound, follow signs. Int corridors. **Pets:** Service with restrictions, crate.
[SAVE] [SD] [X] [🗗] [▣] [≈]

AAA ▼▼▼ ▼▼▼ Residence Inn by Marriott Boston Harbor on Tudor Wharf SH ❖
(617) 242-9000. **$179-$399.** 34-44 Charles River Ave. Just se of SR 99 at Charlestown Bridge. Int corridors. **Pets:** Large. $75 one-time fee/room. Service with restrictions.
[SAVE] [SD] [X] [&M] [🗗] [&] [🖥] [▣] [¶] [≈]

AAA ▼▼▼ ▼▼▼ The Ritz-Carlton, Boston LH
(617) 536-5700. **$335-$575.** 15 Arlington St. At Arlington and Newbury sts; overlooks the Public Gardens. Int corridors. **Pets:** Accepted.
[SAVE] [X] [🗗] [&] [¶] [🐾]

AAA ▼▼▼ ▼▼▼ The Ritz-Carlton, Boston Common SH
(617) 574-7100. **$295-$725.** 10 Avery St. At Washington and Avery sts; 1 blk e of Boston Common. Int corridors. **Pets:** Accepted.
[SAVE] [X] [&M] [🗗] [&] [¶] [≈]

AAA ▼▼▼ ▼▼▼ Seaport Hotel LH
(617) 385-4000. **$179-$339.** 1 Seaport Ln. At Seaport World Trade Center; MBTA-Silverline, World Trade Center Shop. Int corridors. **Pets:** Medium, other species. Supervision.
[SAVE] [SD] [X] [&M] [🗗] [&] [▣] [¶] [≈] [🐾]

AAA ▼▼▼ ▼▼▼ Sheraton Boston LH ❖
(617) 236-2000. **$349-$1800.** 39 Dalton St. I-90, exit 22. Int corridors. **Pets:** Medium. Designated rooms, service with restrictions, supervision.
[SAVE] [SD] [X] [&M] [🗗] [&] [🖥] [▣] [¶] [≈] [🐾]

▼▼▼ ▼▼▼ Westin Boston Waterfront LH ❖
(617) 532-4600. **$429-$499.** 425 Summer St. I-93, exit 23, se via Purchase St to Summer St. Int corridors. **Pets:** Medium, dogs only. Service with restrictions, supervision.
[ASK] [SD] [X] [&] [▣] [¶] [≈]

AAA ▼▼▼ ▼▼▼ The Westin Copley Place Boston LH
(617) 262-9600. **$199-$529.** 10 Huntington Ave. I-90, exit 22, at Copley Square. Int corridors. **Pets:** Accepted.
[SAVE] [X] [🗗] [&] [▣] [¶] [≈] [🐾]

BRAINTREE

▼▼ **Candlewood Suites Boston–Braintree** SH ❖
(781) 849-7450. **$80-$220.** 235 Wood Rd. I-93, exit 6, just n on SR 37, then 0.5 mi w. Int corridors. **Pets:** Large, other species. $150 one-time fee/room. Service with restrictions.
ASK S⊘ ⊠ 🛢 🖵

▼▼ **Extended StayAmerica Boston-Braintree** SH
(781) 356-8333. **$85-$130.** 20 Rockdale St. I-93, exit 6, just se. Int corridors. **Pets:** Accepted.
ASK S⊘ ⊠ ⟨M 🕾 🛢 🖵

◆◆◆ ▼▼▼ **Hampton Inn Braintree** SH
(781) 380-3300. **$119-$159.** 215 Wood Rd. I-93, exit 6, just n on SR 37, then 0.5 mi w. Int corridors. **Pets:** Accepted.
SAVE ⊠ ⟨M 🕾 🛢 🖵 ☇

◆◆◆ ▼▼▼ **Holiday Inn Express-Braintree** SH ❖
(781) 848-1260. **$89-$159.** 190 Wood Rd. I-93, exit 6, just n on SR 37, then 0.4 mi w. Int corridors. **Pets:** $10 daily fee/pet. Designated rooms, service with restrictions, supervision.
SAVE S⊘ ⊠ 🕾 🛢 🖵

▼▼▼ **Sheraton Braintree Hotel** LH
(781) 848-0600. **$109-$299.** 37 Forbes Rd. I-93, exit 6, just s on SR 37, then just w. Int corridors. **Pets:** Accepted.
ASK ⊠ 🕾 🕾 🛢 🖵 🍽 ☇ ⊠

BROOKLINE

◆◆◆ ▼▼▼ **Holiday Inn Brookline** SH
(617) 277-1200. **$136-$259.** 1200 Beacon St. 1 mi sw of Kenmore Square; at Beacon and St. Paul sts. Int corridors. **Pets:** Accepted.
SAVE S⊘ ⊠ ⟨M 🕾 🕾 🛢 🖵 🍽 ☇

BURLINGTON

▼▼▼ **Candlewood Suites Boston-Burlington** SH
(781) 229-4300. **$109-$119.** 130 Middlesex Tpke. I-95, exit 32B, just n. Int corridors. **Pets:** Accepted.
ASK S⊘ ⊠ ⟨M 🕾 🛢 🖵

▼▼▼ **Hilton Garden Inn Boston/Burlington** SH
(781) 272-8800. **$89-$209.** 5 Wheeler Rd. I-95, exit 32B, just s on Middlesex Tpke. Int corridors. **Pets:** Accepted.
ASK S⊘ ⊠ ⟨M 🕾 🛢 🖵 🍽 ☇

▼▼ **Homestead Studio Suites Hotel-Boston/Burlington** SH
(781) 359-9099. **$105.** 40 South Ave. I-95, exit 32B, just n. Int corridors. **Pets:** Accepted.
ASK S⊘ ⊠ 🕾 🕾 🛢 🖵

▼▼ **Staybridge Suites Boston-Burlington** SH
(781) 221-2233. **$149-$195, 3 day notice.** 11 Old Concord Rd. I-95, exit 32B, just s on Middlesex Tpke. Int corridors. **Pets:** Accepted.
ASK S⊘ ⊠ ⟨M 🕾 🕾 🛢 🖵 ☇

▼▼ **Summerfield Suites Burlington** SH
(781) 270-0800. **$99-$399.** 2 Van de Graaff Dr. I-95, exit 33A, just s on US 3, then 0.5 mi w on Wayside Rd. Int corridors. **Pets:** Accepted.
ASK ⊠ ⟨M 🕾 🕾 🛢 🖵 ☇ ⊠

CAMBRIDGE

▼▼▼ **Best Western Hotel Tria** SH ❖
(617) 491-8000. **$179-$299.** 220 Alewife Brook Pkwy. Jct SR 2, 16 and US 3; in N Cambridge; I-90 (Massachusetts Tpke), exit Cambridge/Allston to SR 2 W (Fresh Pond Pkwy). Int corridors. **Pets:** $25 daily fee/room. Service with restrictions.
ASK S⊘ ⊠ 🕾 🛢 🖵 🍽 ☇

◆◆◆ ▼▼▼ ▼▼ **The Charles Hotel, Harvard Square** LH
(617) 864-1200. **$250-$650.** One Bennett St. Just s of Harvard Square, at Eliot St. Int corridors. **Pets:** Accepted.
SAVE ⊠ ⟨M 🕾 🕾 🛢 🖵 🍽 ☇ ⊠

◆◆◆ ▼▼▼ ▼▼ **Hotel @ MIT** SH
(617) 577-0200. **$119-$439.** 20 Sidney St. On SR 2A, 1 mi n of the river. Int corridors. **Pets:** Accepted.
SAVE ⊠ ⟨M 🕾 🕾 🛢 🖵 🍽

◆◆◆ ▼▼▼ ▼▼ **Hotel Marlowe** SH ❖
(617) 868-8000. **$169-$349.** 25 Edwin H Land Blvd. Just sw of jct SR 28. Int corridors. **Pets:** Other species.
SAVE S⊘ ⊠ ⟨M 🕾 🕾 🍽 ⊠

◆◆◆ ▼▼▼ ▼▼ **Hyatt Regency Cambridge** LH
(617) 492-1234. **$169-$380.** 575 Memorial Dr. On US 3 and SR 2. Int corridors. **Pets:** Small. $50 one-time fee/pet. Service with restrictions, supervision.
SAVE ⊠ ⟨M 🕾 🕾 🛢 🖵 🍽 ☇ ⊠

▼▼▼ **Residence Inn by Marriott Cambridge** LH ❖
(617) 349-0700. **$209-$399.** 6 Cambridge Center. Corner of Ames St and Broadway. Int corridors. **Pets:** Large. $150 one-time fee/room. Service with restrictions, supervision.
ASK ⊠ ⟨M 🕾 🕾 🛢 🖵 ☇

▼▼▼ **Sheraton Commander Hotel** SH
(617) 547-4800. **$105-$375.** 16 Garden St. Just n of Harvard Square. Int corridors. **Pets:** Accepted.
ASK ⊠ 🕾 🕾 🛢 🖵 🍽

CHELMSFORD

◆◆◆ ▼▼▼ **Radisson Hotel & Suites** SH
(978) 256-0800. **$89-$169.** 10 Independence Dr. I-495, exit 34, 0.3 mi s on SR 110. Int corridors. **Pets:** Accepted.
SAVE ⊠ 🛢 🖵 🍽 ☇

CONCORD

▼▼▼ **Best Western at Historic Concord** SH
(978) 369-6100. **$99-$159.** 740 Elm St. 1.8 mi w, just off SR 2 and 2A. Int corridors. **Pets:** Other species. $10 daily fee/pet. Designated rooms, service with restrictions, supervision.
ASK S⊘ ⊠ 🛢 🖵 ☇

DANVERS

▼▼ **Extended StayAmerica Boston-Danvers** SH
(978) 762-7414. **$55-$95.** 102 Newbury St. On US 1 southbound. Int corridors. **Pets:** Accepted.
ASK S⊘ ⊠ ⟨M 🕾 🛢 🖵

▼ **Motel 6 Boston-Danvers #1078** M
(978) 774-8045. **$55-$75.** 65 Newbury St. On US 1 northbound, just n of SR 114. Int corridors. **Pets:** Medium, other species. Service with restrictions, supervision.
S⊘ ⊠ ☇

▼▼▼ **Residence Inn by Marriott** SH
(978) 777-7171. **$139-$199.** 51 Newbury St (Rt 1). US 1 N, just s of jct SR 114. Ext corridors. **Pets:** Accepted.
ASK S⊘ ⊠ 🕾 🛢 🖵 ☇ ⊠

◆◆◆ ▼▼▼ **Sheraton Ferncroft Resort** LH
(978) 777-2500. **$99-$219.** 50 Ferncroft Rd. I-95, exit 50, follow signs for US 1 S to Ferncroft Village. Int corridors. **Pets:** Accepted.
SAVE ⊠ ⟨M 🕾 🕾 🛢 🖵 🍽 ☇ ⊠

TownePlace Suites by Marriott SH
(978) 777-6222. **$109-$159.** 238 Andover St. Southwest corner of jct US 1 and SR 114; SR 114 eastbound, enter just w of US 1 (no westbound entrance); US 1 southbound, enter through shopping center. Int corridors. **Pets:** Accepted.

DEDHAM

Holiday Inn Boston/Dedham Hotel & Conference Center SH
(781) 329-1000. **$109-$189.** 55 Ariadne Rd. I-95, exit 15A, on US 1. Int corridors. **Pets:** Accepted.

Residence Inn by Marriott SH
(781) 407-0999. **$209-$269.** 259 Elm St. I-95, exit 15A, just n, then 0.4 mi e. Int corridors. **Pets:** Medium. $75 one-time fee/room.

FOXBORO

Foxborough Residence Inn by Marriott SH
(508) 698-2800. **$109-$209.** 250 Foxborough Blvd. I-95, exit 7A, 0.6 mi s on SR 140, 0.7 mi e, then just n. Int corridors. **Pets:** Accepted.

FRAMINGHAM

Best Western Framingham SH
(508) 872-8811. **$79-$109.** 130 Worcester Rd. I-90, exit 13, 0.5 mi s to SR 9; 1 mi w of Speen St; just w of Shopper's World Mall. Int corridors. **Pets:** Other species. Designated rooms, service with restrictions, supervision.

Red Roof Inn #7068 M
(508) 872-4499. **$70-$102.** 650 Cochituate Rd. I-90, exit 13, follow SR 30 E. Ext corridors. **Pets:** Medium, other species. Service with restrictions, supervision.

Residence Inn by Marriott SH
(508) 370-0001. **$109-$229.** 400 Staples Dr. SR 9 W to Crossing Blvd, then s. Int corridors. **Pets:** Other species. $75 one-time fee/room. Service with restrictions.

Sheraton Hotel Framingham LH
(508) 879-7200. **$99-$289.** 1657 Worcester Rd. I-90, exit 12, follow signs to SR 9 W. Int corridors. **Pets:** Accepted.

FRANKLIN

Franklin Residence Inn by Marriott SH
(508) 541-8188. **$119-$199.** 4 Forge Pkwy. I-495, exit 17, 0.7 mi nw off SR 140 N. Int corridors. **Pets:** $100 one-time fee/room. Service with restrictions, supervision.

Hawthorn Suites Ltd SH
(508) 553-3500. **$109-$129.** 835 UpperUnion St. I-495, exit 16, just s, then 0.3 mi e. Int corridors. **Pets:** Small. $100 one-time fee/room. Designated rooms, service with restrictions, crate.

GLOUCESTER

Cape Ann Motor Inn M
(978) 281-2900. **$75-$160, 7 day notice.** 33 Rockport Rd. 2 mi n of terminus of SR 128 via SR 127A. Ext corridors. **Pets:** Large, other species. Service with restrictions, supervision.

HAVERHILL

Best Western Merrimack Valley SH
(978) 373-1511. **$69-$179.** 401 Lowell Ave. I-495, exit 49 (SR 110). Int corridors. **Pets:** Medium. $20 daily fee/pet. Designated rooms, service with restrictions, supervision.

LAWRENCE

Hampton Inn Boston/North Andover SH
(978) 975-4050. **$79-$129.** 224 Winthrop Ave. I-495, exit 42A, just s on SR 114. Int corridors. **Pets:** Accepted.

LEXINGTON

Quality Inn & Suites SH
(781) 861-0850. **$89-$129.** 440 Bedford St. I-95, exit 31B, just n on SR 4 and 225, continue n and use jug handle to reverse direction. Ext corridors. **Pets:** Other species. $25 one-time fee/pet. Service with restrictions, supervision.

MARLBOROUGH

Embassy Suites Hotel-Boston Marlborough LH
(508) 485-5900. **$129-$189.** 123 Boston Post Rd W. I-495, exit 24B, 0.5 mi w; just off US 20. Int corridors. **Pets:** Accepted.

Homestead Studio Suites Hotel-Boston/Marlborough SH
(508) 490-9911. **$105.** 19 Northborough Rd E. I-495, exit 24B, just w on US 20. Int corridors. **Pets:** Accepted.

NATICK

Crowne Plaza Boston-Natick LH
(508) 653-8800. **$109-$299.** 1360 Worcester St. SR 9, 4 mi e of Framingham Center; I-90 (Massachusetts Tpke), exit 12, 5 mi e. Int corridors. **Pets:** Accepted.

NEEDHAM

Sheraton Needham Hotel LH
(781) 444-1110. **$159-$209.** 100 Cabot St. I-95, exit 19A, just e. Int corridors. **Pets:** Accepted.

NEWTON

Holiday Inn Newton SH
(617) 969-5300. **$99-$219, 3 day notice.** 399 Grove St. I-95, exit 22, just e; 0.3 mi s of I-90. Int corridors. **Pets:** Accepted.

Sheraton Newton Hotel LH
(617) 969-3010. **$129-$159.** 320 Washington St. I-90 (Massachusetts Tpke), exit 17 (SR 16). Int corridors. **Pets:** Accepted.

NORTH CHELMSFORD

Hawthorn Suites SH
(978) 256-5151. **$99-$129.** 25 Research Pl. US 3, exit 32, 0.3 mi ne on SR 4. Int corridors. **Pets:** Medium. $10 daily fee/room, $50 one-time fee/room. Designated rooms, service with restrictions, supervision.

NORWOOD

▼▼◆▼ Hampton Inn SH
(781) 769-7000. **$75-$119.** 434 Boston Providence Hwy. I-95, exit 15B, 2.3 mi s. Int corridors. **Pets:** Accepted.
ASK S⊘ ✕ &M 🐾 🦽 💻 🏊

▼▼◆▼ Residence Inn Boston-Norwood SH
(781) 278-9595. **$109-$199.** 275 Norwood Park S. I-95, exit 9, on US 1 southbound. Int corridors. **Pets:** Medium. $75 one-time fee/pet. Service with restrictions, crate.
ASK S⊘ ✕ &M 🦽 🛗 💻 🏊 ✕

PEABODY

◆◆◆ ▼▼▼ Holiday Inn Hotel & Suites SH
(978) 535-4600. **$89-$169.** 1 Newbury St. I-95 and SR 128, exit 44A northbound, U-turn before lights to US 1 N; exit 44 southbound, just s on US 1, then U-turn to US 1 N. Int corridors. **Pets:** Dogs only. $50 one-time fee/pet. Designated rooms, service with restrictions, supervision.
SAVE S⊘ ✕ 🛗 💻 🍽 🏊

▼▼◆▼ Homestead Studio Suites Hotel-Boston/Peabody SH
(978) 531-6632. **$85.** 200 Jubilee Dr. SR 128, exit 28, just s to Centennial Dr, w to the end, n to Jubilee Dr, then 1.1 mi e. Int corridors. **Pets:** Accepted.
ASK S⊘ ✕ 🐾 🦽 🛗 💻 🏊

▼▼◆▼ Homewood Suites by Hilton SH
(978) 536-5050. **$99-$174.** 57 Newbury St. On US 1, northbound; I-95 and SR 128, exit 44B, just n, then left on Dearborn Rd. Int corridors. **Pets:** Accepted.
ASK S⊘ ✕ &M 🐾 🦽 🛗 💻 🏊

REVERE

▼▼◆▼ Comfort Inn & Suites Boston Airport SH
(781) 485-3600. **$89-$209.** 85 American Legion Hwy. Jct SR 1A and 60, 3 mi n of General Edward Lawrence Logan International Airport. Int corridors. **Pets:** Medium, other species. $10 daily fee/room. Service with restrictions.
ASK S⊘ ✕ 🦽 🛗 💻 🍽 🏊

▼▼◆▼ Hampton Inn Boston Logan Airport SH
(781) 286-5665. **$109-$210.** 230 Lee Burbank Hwy. On SR 1A, 1.9 mi n of General Edward Lawrence Logan International Airport; 0.6 mi s of terminus SR 60. Int corridors. **Pets:** Accepted.
ASK S⊘ ✕ &M 🐾 🦽 🛗 💻 🍽 🏊

SALEM

▼▼◆▼ Hawthorne Hotel SH 🐾
(978) 744-4080. **$127-$212, 3 day notice.** 18 Washington Square W. On SR 1A. Int corridors. **Pets:** Other species. $100 deposit/room, $10 daily fee/pet. Designated rooms, service with restrictions, supervision.
ASK S⊘ ✕ 🛗 🍽

▼▼◆▼ The Salem Inn BB
(978) 741-0680. **$119-$250, 7 day notice.** 7 Summer St. On SR 114 at Essex St; SR 128, exit 25A, 3 mi e. Int corridors. **Pets:** Other species. $15 daily fee/pet. Designated rooms, service with restrictions, supervision.
✕ 🛗 💻

SAUGUS

▼▼ Red Roof Inn #7305 SH
(781) 941-1400. **$75-$105.** 920 Broadway (US 1). I-95, exit 44 northbound, 3.2 mi s on US 1; exit Main St/Saugus southbound to U-turn. Int corridors. **Pets:** Medium, other species. Service with restrictions, supervision.
✕ &M 🐾 🦽 🛗

SOMERVILLE

▼▼◆▼ La Quinta Inn & Suites Boston/ Somerville SH
(617) 625-5300. **$125-$229.** 23 Cummings St. I-93, exit 29 northbound, just ne on SR 28, then just s on Middlesex Ave; exit 31 southbound, 1 mi e on SR 16, then 0.5 mi s on SR 28 to Middlesex Ave. Int corridors. **Pets:** Accepted.
ASK ✕ &M 🦽 🛗 💻 🏊

SUDBURY

▼▼◆▼ Clarion Carriage House Inn SH
(978) 443-2223. **$129-$219.** 738 Boston Post Rd. I-495, exit 24A, 7.5 mi e on US 20; 4.7 mi w of jct SR 27 on US 20. Int corridors. **Pets:** Accepted.
ASK S⊘ ✕ 🛗 💻

TEWKSBURY

▼▼ Extended StayAmerica Boston-Tewksbury SH
(978) 863-9888. **$55-$95.** 1910 Andover St. I-93, exit 43B, just w; I-495, exit 39, just e. Int corridors. **Pets:** Accepted.
ASK S⊘ ✕ 🐾 🛗 💻

◆◆◆ ▼▼◆▼ Holiday Inn Tewksbury/Andover SH
(978) 640-9000. **$77-$150.** 4 Highwood Dr. I-495, exit 39, just w on SR 133. Int corridors. **Pets:** Accepted.
SAVE S⊘ ✕ 🐾 🛗 💻 🍽 🏊 ✕

▼▼ Motel 6 Boston-Tewksbury #1403 M
(978) 851-8677. **$65-$75.** 95 Main St. I-495, exit 38, just s on SR 38. Ext corridors. **Pets:** Medium, other species. Service with restrictions, supervision.
S⊘ ✕ 🦽 🏊

▼▼◆▼ Residence Inn by Marriott-Boston/Tewksbury SH
(978) 640-1003. **$89-$144.** 1775 Andover St. I-495, exit 39, 0.3 mi w on SR 133. Ext corridors. **Pets:** Other species. $75 one-time fee/room. Service with restrictions.
ASK S⊘ ✕ &M 🐾 🦽 🛗 💻 🏊 ✕

▼▼◆▼ TownePlace Suites by Marriott SH
(978) 863-9800. **$80-$139.** 20 International Pl. I-495, exit 39, 0.3 mi nw. Int corridors. **Pets:** Accepted.
ASK S⊘ ✕ &M 🐾 🦽 🛗 💻 🏊

WAKEFIELD

▼▼◆▼ Sheraton Colonial Hotel & Golf Club Boston North LH
(781) 245-9300. **$109-$249.** 1 Audubon Rd. I-95, exit 42, just n. Int corridors. **Pets:** Accepted.
ASK S⊘ ✕ 🐾 🦽 🛗 💻 🍽 🏊 ✕

WALTHAM

▼▼◆▼ Courtyard by Marriott Boston-Waltham SH
(781) 419-0900. **$89-$189.** 387 Winter St. I-95, exit 27A, on northeast corner. Int corridors. **Pets:** Accepted.
ASK S⊘ ✕ &M 🐾 🛗 💻 🍽 🏊

▼▼◆▼ Extended Stay Deluxe Boston-Waltham SH
(781) 622-1900. **$80-$155.** 32 Fourth Ave. I-95, exit 27A, just se. Int corridors. **Pets:** Accepted.
ASK S⊘ ✕ &M 🦽 🛗 💻 🏊

▼▼◆▼ Holiday Inn Express Boston/Waltham SH
(781) 890-2800. **$84-$152.** 385 Winter St. I-95, exit 27A, just ne. Ext/int corridors. **Pets:** Accepted.
ASK S⊘ ✕ &M 🐾 🦽 🛗 💻

▼▼ Homestead Studio Suites Hotel-Boston/Waltham SH
(781) 890-1333. **$90.** 52 Fourth Ave. I-95, exit 27A, just se; behind The Westin, Waltham-Boston. Int corridors. **Pets:** Accepted.
ASK S⊘ ✕ 🐾 🦽 🛗 💻

▼▼▼▼ Home Suites Inn of Boston-Waltham **SH**
(781) 890-3000. **$84-$150.** 455 Totten Pond Rd. I-95, exit 27A, just s. Int corridors. **Pets:** Accepted.

(ASK) (S6) (X) (⚖) (🛏) (💻) (†↑) (🐾)

▼▼▼▼ The Westin Waltham-Boston **LH**
(781) 290-5600. **$109-$309.** 70 Third Ave. I-95, exit 27A, just se. Int corridors. **Pets:** Accepted.

(ASK) (S6) (X) (&M) (⚖) (🛏) (💻) (†↑) (🐾) (X)

WESTFORD

▼▼▼▼ Residence Inn by Marriott **SH**
(978) 392-1407. **$149-$199.** 7 Lan Dr. I-495, exit 32, just s, then 0.5 w on SR 110. Int corridors. **Pets:** Accepted.

(ASK) (S6) (X) (&M) (⚖) (🛏) (💻) (🐾) (X)

WOBURN

(AAA) ▼▼▼▼ Best Western New Englander **SH**
(781) 935-8160. **$99-$159.** 1 Rainin Rd. I-93, exit 36, just e. Int corridors. **Pets:** Medium, other species. $10 daily fee/pet. Service with restrictions, supervision.

(SAVE) (S6) (X) (&M) (⚖) (🛏) (💻) (†↑) (🐾)

▼▼▼▼ Extended Stay Deluxe Boston-Woburn **SH**
(781) 938-3737. **$75-$110.** 831 Main St. I-95, exit 35, just n on SR 38. Int corridors. **Pets:** Accepted.

(ASK) (S6) (X) (&M) (⚖) (🛏) (💻) (🐾)

▼▼▼▼ Hilton **LH**
(781) 932-0999. **$116-$144, 30 day notice.** 2 Forbes Rd. I-95, exit 36, 0.5 mi s via Washington St, then just e at Lukoil; jct Cedar St. Int corridors. **Pets:** Accepted.

(ASK) (S6) (X) (⚖) (🛏) (💻) (†↑) (🐾)

▼▼▼▼ Holiday Inn Select **SH** 🐾
(781) 935-8760. **$89-$159.** 15 Middlesex Canal Park Rd. I-95, exit 35, s via SR 38. Int corridors. **Pets:** Other species. $50 one-time fee/room. Designated rooms, service with restrictions.

(ASK) (S6) (X) (&M) (⚖) (🛏) (💻) (†↑) (🐾)

▼▼ Red Roof Inn Woburn #7238 **SH**
(781) 935-7110. **$90-$126.** 19 Commerce Way. I-95, exit 36, just n, then just w on Mishawum Rd. Int corridors. **Pets:** Medium, other species. Service with restrictions, supervision.

(X) (&M) (⚖) (🛏) (🐾)

(AAA) ▼▼▼▼ Residence Inn by
Marriott-Boston/Woburn **SH**
(781) 376-4000. **$89-$249.** 300 Presidential Way. I-93, exit 37C, just nw. Int corridors. **Pets:** Other species. $75 one-time fee/room.

(SAVE) (S6) (X) (&M) (⚖) (🛏) (💻) (🐾) (X)

END METROPOLITAN AREA

BOXBOROUGH

▼◆▼◆ Holiday Inn Boxborough Woods **SH**
(978) 263-8701. **$99-$199.** 242 Adams Pl. I-495, exit 28, just e on SR 111. Int corridors. **Pets:** Medium, other species. $100 deposit/room, $35 one-time fee/room. Service with restrictions, crate.

(ASK) (S6) (X) (⚖) (🛏) (💻) (†↑) (🐾)

BROCKTON

▼▼▼▼ Residence Inn by Marriott **SH**
(508) 583-3600. **$109-$189.** 124 Liberty St. SR 24, exit 17B, just w, just s on Pearl St, then 0.3 mi se via Mill St connector. Int corridors. **Pets:** Other species. $100 one-time fee/room. Service with restrictions, supervision.

(ASK) (S6) (X) (&M) (⚖) (🛏) (💻) (†↑) (🐾) (X)

CAPE COD AREA

BUZZARDS BAY

(AAA) ▼▼▼ Bay Motor Inn **CA**
(508) 759-3989. **$51-$129, 10 day notice.** 223 Main St. SR 25, 0.5 mi w of Bourne rotary, exit 2. Ext corridors. **Pets:** $10 daily fee/pet. Service with restrictions, supervision.

(SAVE) (S6) (X) (🛏) (🐾)

CENTERVILLE

(AAA) ▼▼▼ Centerville Corners Inn **M**
(508) 775-7223. **$50-$190.** 369 S Main St. 1 mi s of SR 28, jct Craigville Beach Rd. Ext corridors. **Pets:** Large. Service with restrictions.

(SAVE) (S6) (X) (🛏) (🐾)

EAST FALMOUTH

▼▼▼ Capewind Waterfront Resort **M**
(508) 548-3400. **$100-$225, 30 day notice.** 34 Maravista Extension. 2.2 mi e via SR 28, then just s, follow signs. Ext corridors. **Pets:** Accepted.

(ASK) (S6) (X) (🛏) (💻) (🐾) (X)

FALMOUTH

▼▼▼ Capeside Cottage Bed & Breakfast **BB**
(508) 548-6218. **$100-$160, 14 day notice.** 320 Woods Hole Rd. 2.2 mi s on SR 28. Int corridors. **Pets:** Accepted.

(X) (🛏) (🐾) (W) (⚖)

(AAA) ▼▼▼ Mariner Motel **M**
(508) 548-1331. **$69-$169.** 555 Main St. 0.5 mi e on SR 28. Ext corridors. **Pets:** Accepted.

(SAVE) (X) (🛏) (🐾)

(AAA) ▼▼▼▼ The Palmer House Inn **BB**
(508) 548-1230. **$109-$295, 14 day notice.** 81 Palmer Ave. 0.5 mi nw on SR 28. Ext/int corridors. **Pets:** Small, dogs only. $35 one-time fee/room. Designated rooms, service with restrictions, supervision.

(SAVE) (X) (&M) (🛏) (💻)

HYANNIS

▼▼▼▼ Comfort Inn **SH** 🐾
(508) 771-4804. **$110-$180.** 1470 Iyanough Rd. On SR 132, US 6, exit 6, 1.3 mi se. Ext/int corridors. **Pets:** Large, other species. $20 daily fee/room. Designated rooms, service with restrictions, supervision.

(ASK) (S6) (X) (⚖) (🛏) (💻) (🐾) (X)

ORLEANS

▼▼ Orleans Inn **CI**
(508) 255-2222. **$175-$300.** 21 SR 6A. On SR 28 and 6A, exit rotary, just w. Int corridors. **Pets:** Other species.

(ASK) (X) (🛏) (†↑)

(AAA) ▼▼▼ Skaket Beach Motel **M** ❀
(508) 255-1020. **$58-$169, 10 day notice.** 203 Cranberry Hwy (Rt 6A). US 6, exit 12, just e. Ext corridors. **Pets:** Large. $10 daily fee/pet. Service with restrictions, supervision.
[SAVE] [X] [🛏] [📺] [🐾]

PROVINCETOWN

▼▼▼ Anchor Inn Beach House **SH**
(508) 487-0432. **$125-$385, 21 day notice.** 175 Commercial St. 2 blks se of SR 6A, just sw of the post office; center. Ext/int corridors. **Pets:** Accepted.
[X] [🐕] [🛏]

▼▼▼ Bayshore & Chandler **CO**
(508) 487-9133. **$100-$295, 30 day notice.** 493 Commercial St. 0.8 mi e of Town Hall. Ext corridors. **Pets:** $15 daily fee/pet. Service with restrictions.
[X] [🛏] [📺]

(AAA) ▼▼▼ Cape Inn **SH**
(508) 487-1711. **$99-$189.** 698 Commercial St. 1.5 mi se on SR 6A. Ext corridors. **Pets:** Accepted.
[SAVE] [S🐾] [X] [🐕] [🛏] [📺] [🍴] [🐾]

(AAA) ▼▼▼ Surfside Hotel & Suites **SH** ❀
(508) 487-1726. **$99-$309, 21 day notice.** 542-543 Commercial St. 1 mi e of Town Hall. Ext/int corridors. **Pets:** Medium, dogs only. $20 daily fee/pet. Service with restrictions, supervision.
[SAVE] [S🐾] [X] [🛏] [📺] [🐾]

END AREA

CHICOPEE

(AAA) ▼▼▼ Quality Inn-Chicopee **SH**
(413) 592-6171. **$79-$109.** 463 Memorial Dr. I-90 (Massachusetts Tpke), exit 5, just ne; upon exiting, use jug handle overpass to SR 33 N. Int corridors. **Pets:** Accepted.
[SAVE] [S🐾] [X] [🛏] [📺] [🐾]

DARTMOUTH

▼▼ Comfort Inn **SH**
(508) 996-0800. **$79-$139.** 171 Faunce Corner Rd. I-195, exit 12A westbound; exit 12 eastbound, then s. Int corridors. **Pets:** Accepted.
[ASK] [S🐾] [X] [🛏] [📺] [🐾]

▼▼▼ Residence Inn by Marriott **SH** ❀
(508) 984-5858. **$140-$190.** 181 Faunce Corner Rd. I-195, exit 12A westbound; exit 12 eastbound, just s. Int corridors. **Pets:** Other species. $75 one-time fee/room. Service with restrictions.
[ASK] [S🐾] [X] [🔥] [🐕] [🐕] [🛏] [📺] [🐾] [X]

DEERFIELD

▼▼▼ Deerfield Inn **CI** ❀
(413) 774-5587. **$169-$260, 7 day notice.** 81 Old Main St. Center. Int corridors. **Pets:** Small, dogs only. $25 daily fee/room. Designated rooms, service with restrictions, crate.
[ASK] [S🐾] [X] [🍴]

EAST WAREHAM

(AAA) ▼▼▼ Atlantic Motel **M**
(508) 295-0210. **$79-$189, 10 day notice.** 7 Depot St. Between eastbound and westbound lanes of US 6/SR 28; jct SR 25, exit 1. Ext corridors. **Pets:** Medium, dogs only. $20 daily fee/pet. Designated rooms, service with restrictions, supervision.
[SAVE] [S🐾] [X] [🛏] [🐾]

▼▼▼ White Wind Inn **BB**
(508) 487-1526. **$80-$275, 14 day notice.** 174 Commercial St. Just w of Town Hall. Int corridors. **Pets:** Dogs only. $15 daily fee/pet. Designated rooms.
[ASK] [X] [🛏]

SANDWICH

▼▼ The Earl of Sandwich Motel **M**
(508) 888-1415. **$55-$119, 7 day notice.** 378 SR 6A. At MM 5.1. Ext corridors. **Pets:** Accepted.
[X] [🛏] [🐾]

SOUTH YARMOUTH

(AAA) ▼▼▼ Best Western Blue Water on The Ocean **SH** ❀
(508) 398-2288. **$110-$440, 10 day notice.** 291 S Shore Dr. 1 mi s off SR 28. Ext/int corridors. **Pets:** Dogs only. $25 daily fee/room. Designated rooms, service with restrictions.
[SAVE] [S🐾] [X] [🔥] [🛏] [📺] [🍴] [🐾] [X]

FAIRHAVEN

(AAA) ▼▼▼▼ Holiday Inn Express Harborfront **SH**
(508) 997-1281. **$89-$149.** 110 Middle St. I-195, exit 15, 1 mi s, then just off US 6. Int corridors. **Pets:** Other species. $10 one-time fee/room. Service with restrictions, crate.
[SAVE] [S🐾] [X] [🛏] [📺]

FITCHBURG

(AAA) ▼▼▼▼ Best Western Royal Plaza Hotel & Trade Center **LH**
(978) 342-7100. **$84-$105.** 150 Royal Plaza Dr. Just s on SR 31; SR 2, exit 28. Int corridors. **Pets:** Other species. $10 daily fee/pet. Service with restrictions, supervision.
[SAVE] [X] [🔥] [🐕] [🛏] [📺] [🍴] [🐾] [X]

GARDNER

▼▼▼ Colonial Hotel **SH**
(978) 630-2500. **$85-$120.** 625 Betty Spring Rd. 0.9 mi n on SR 140, 0.5 mi w; SR 2, exit 24 eastbound; exit 24B westbound. Int corridors. **Pets:** Small, other species. $25 one-time fee/room. Designated rooms.
[ASK] [S🐾] [X] [🛏] [📺] [🍴] [🐾]

▼▼ Super 8 Motel **M**
(978) 630-2888. **$78-$93, 14 day notice.** 22 Pearson Blvd. SR 2, exit 23, just n. Int corridors. **Pets:** Medium. $10 daily fee/pet. Service with restrictions, supervision.
[ASK] [S🐾] [X] [🛏]

GREAT BARRINGTON

(AAA) ▼▼ Monument Mountain Motel **M**
(413) 528-3272. **$55-$199, 14 day notice.** 247 Stockbridge Rd. On US 7, 1.2 mi s of jct SR 183. Ext corridors. **Pets:** Dogs only. $20 daily fee/pet. No service, supervision.
[SAVE] [S🐾] [X] [🛏] [🐾]

AAA ▼▼▼ Travelodge M
(413) 528-2340. **$65-$295, 14 day notice.** 400 Stockbridge Rd. On US 7, 1.2 mi s of jct SR 183. Ext corridors. **Pets:** Accepted.
[SAVE] [X] [■] [■] [≈]

GREENFIELD

AAA ▼▼▼▼ The Brandt House B&B BB
(413) 774-3329. **$95-$295, 30 day notice.** 29 Highland Ave. I-91, exit 26, 1.8 mi e on SR 2A, then se via Crescent St. Int corridors. **Pets:** Accepted.
[SAVE] [S🔅] [X] [■]

HADLEY

AAA ▼▼▼ Howard Johnson SH
(413) 586-0114. **$77-$230.** 401 Russell Rd. I-91, exit 19 northbound, 4.3 mi e on SR 9; exit 24 southbound, 10 mi s on SR 116, then just w on SR 9. Int corridors. **Pets:** Other species. $20 daily fee/room. Designated rooms, service with restrictions, supervision.
[SAVE] [S🔅] [X] [✍M] [🐾] [■] [■] [≈]

AAA ▼▼▼ Quality Inn SH
(413) 584-9816. **$75-$185.** 237 Russell St (SR 9). I-91, exit 19 northbound; exit 20 southbound, 3 mi e on SR 9. Int corridors. **Pets:** Medium, dogs only. $25 one-time fee/pet. Designated rooms, service with restrictions, supervision.
[SAVE] [S🔅] [X] [✍] [■] [■] [≈]

HOLLAND

▼▼▼▼ Restful Paws Bed & Breakfast BB ❀
(413) 245-7792. **$145, 14 day notice.** 70 Allen Hill Rd. SR 20. 2.1 mi s on E. Brimfield Rd, 0.4 mi on Alexander Rd, then 0.7 mi n. Int corridors. **Pets:** Service with restrictions, supervision.
[ASK] [S🔅] [X] [■] [W] [☎]

KINGSTON

AAA ▼▼▼ Plymouth Bay Inn & Suites M ❀
(781) 585-3831. **$79-$159.** 149 Main St. SR 3, exit 9, just w. Int corridors. **Pets:** $100 deposit/room. Designated rooms, service with restrictions.
[SAVE] [S🔅] [X] [✍M] [✍] [■] [≈]

LANESBOROUGH

▼▼▼ Mt View Motel M
(413) 442-1009. **$85-$325, 7 day notice.** 499 S Main St. 1 mi s on US 7. Ext corridors. **Pets:** Accepted.
[ASK] [S🔅] [X] [■] [■]

AAA ▼▼ The Weathervane Motel M
(413) 443-3230. **$35-$110, 15 day notice.** 475 S Main St. 1.3 mi s on US 7. Ext corridors. **Pets:** Medium. $10 one-time fee/pet. Designated rooms, no service, supervision.
[SAVE] [X] [■] [■]

LENOX

▼▼▼ ▼▼▼ Blantyre CI ❀
(413) 637-3556. **$500-$1680, 30 day notice.** 16 Blantyre Rd. On US 20, 1 mi s from jct SR 183. Int corridors. **Pets:** Small, dogs only. $75 daily fee/pet. Designated rooms, service with restrictions, supervision.
[X] [■] [■] [¶] [≈] [X]

▼▼ Seven Hills Country Inn & Restaurant SH
(413) 637-0060. **$85-$340, 15 day notice.** 40 Plunkett St. Jct US 7/20, 0.6 mi se on US 20, 0.8 mi w. Ext/int corridors. **Pets:** Accepted.
[ASK] [X] [🖥] [■] [■] [¶] [≈] [X]

LEOMINSTER

AAA ▼▼▼ Super 8 Motel M
(978) 537-2800. **$59-$99, 14 day notice.** 482 N Main St. SR 2, exit 31B, just n on SR 12. Int corridors. **Pets:** Accepted.
[SAVE] [S🔅] [X] [✍M] [■]

MANSFIELD

AAA ▼▼▼▼ Holiday Inn Mansfield SH
(508) 339-2200. **$160-$180.** 31 Hampshire St. I-95, exit 7A, 0.5 mi s on SR 140, then 1 mi w on Forbes Rd; I-495, exit 12, 2 mi n on SR 140, then w on Forbes Rd. Int corridors. **Pets:** $10 daily fee/pet. Designated rooms, service with restrictions, supervision.
[SAVE] [S🔅] [X] [🖥] [■] [■] [¶] [≈] [X]

MARTHA'S VINEYARD AREA

EDGARTOWN

AAA ▼▼▼▼ Colonial Inn of Martha's Vineyard CI
(508) 627-4711. **$90-$425, 14 day notice.** 38 N Water St. Just n from Main St. Int corridors. **Pets:** Dogs only. $25 daily fee/room. Designated rooms, crate.
[SAVE] [S🔅] [X] [■] [¶]

VINEYARD HAVEN

AAA ▼▼▼▼ The Doctor's House BB
(508) 696-0859. **$125-$300, 21 day notice.** 60 Mt. Aldworth Rd. 0.4 mi sw to road to Edgartown, 1 blk e. Int corridors. **Pets:** Medium, dogs only. $10 daily fee/room. Service with restrictions, supervision.
[SAVE] [X] [☎]

END AREA

MIDDLEBORO

AAA ▼▼▼ Days Inn-Plymouth/Middleboro SH
(508) 946-4400. **$69-$119.** 30 E Clark St. I-495, exit 4, at SR 105. Int corridors. **Pets:** Medium. $10 daily fee/pet. Designated rooms, service with restrictions, crate.
[SAVE] [S🔅] [X] [✍] [■] [■] [≈]

MILFORD

AAA ▼▼▼▼ Holiday Inn Express SH
(508) 634-1054. **$79-$129.** 50 Fortune Blvd. I-495, exit 20, just sw on SR 85, then just se. Int corridors. **Pets:** Accepted.
[SAVE] [X] [✍M] [🐾] [✍] [■] [■] [≈]

▼▼▼ La Quinta Inn & Suites SH
(508) 478-8243. **$85-$149.** 24 Beaver St. I-495, exit 19, just w on SR 109. Int corridors. **Pets:** Medium. Service with restrictions.
[ASK] [X] [■] [■]

NEW BEDFORD

AAA ▼▼▼ Days Inn SH
(508) 997-1231. **$69-$149, 3 day notice.** 500 Hathaway Rd. SR 140, exit 3, just w. Ext/int corridors. **Pets:** Accepted.
[SAVE] [S🔅] [X] [■]

NORTH ADAMS

AAA ▼▼▼▼ **Jae's Inn** CI ❀
(413) 664-0100. **$95-$150, 3 day notice.** 1111 S State St. 2 mi s on SR 8; center. Int corridors. **Pets:** Large, other species. $20 daily fee/room. Designated rooms, service with restrictions, supervision.
SAVE ✕ ⊟ ¶¶ ⊸ ✕

NORTHAMPTON

▼▼▼▼ **Clarion Hotel & Conference Center** SH
(413) 586-1211. **$99-$189.** One Atwood Dr. I-91, exit 18, just s on US 5. Int corridors. **Pets:** $20 daily fee/room. Service with restrictions, crate.
ASK SD ✕ ⊙M ⌖ ⌖ ⊟ ⊑ ¶¶ ⊸ ✕

NORTHBOROUGH

AAA ▼▼▼ **Econo Lodge Inn & Suites** SH
(508) 842-8941. **$75-$95.** 380 SW Cutoff. Jct of US 20 and SR 9. Ext corridors. **Pets:** Medium. $10 daily fee/pet. Service with restrictions, supervision.
SAVE SD ✕ ⊟ ⊑

NORTON

▼▼▼ ◆ **Extended StayAmerica-Boston-Norton** SH
(508) 285-7800. **$60-$95.** 271 S Washington St. I-495, exit 9, 0.3 mi se on Bay St, then 0.5 mi nw via Industrial Park Rd. Int corridors. **Pets:** Accepted.
ASK SD ✕ ⊙M ⌖ ⌖ ⊟ ⊑

ORANGE

AAA ◆ **Executive Inn** M ❀
(978) 544-8864. **$55-$85.** 110 Daniel Shay Hwy. US 202, exit 16, just n of jct SR 2. Ext/int corridors. **Pets:** $7 daily fee/pet. Service with restrictions, supervision.
SAVE ✕ ⊟

PITTSFIELD

AAA ▼▼▼ **Comfort Inn** SH
(413) 443-4714. **$79-$309, 3 day notice.** 1055 South St. On US 7 and 20, 3 mi s. Int corridors. **Pets:** Accepted.
SAVE SD ✕ ⊙M ⌖ ⌖ ⊟ ⊑ ⊸

▼▼▼◆ **Crowne Plaza Hotel and Resort Pittsfield Berkshires** LH
(413) 499-2000. **$129-$349, 3 day notice.** 1 West St, Berkshire Common. Center. Int corridors. **Pets:** $25 one-time fee/room. Designated rooms, service with restrictions, supervision.
ASK SD ✕ ⊙M ⌖ ⊟ ⊑ ¶¶ ⊸ ✕

PLYMOUTH

AAA ▼▼▼▼ **Best Western Cold Spring** M
(508) 746-2222. **$89-$179, 3 day notice.** 188 Court St. Jct US 44, 0.5 mi n on SR 3A. Ext corridors. **Pets:** Medium. $10 daily fee/pet. Designated rooms, no service, supervision.
SAVE SD ✕ ⊟ ⊑ ⊸

RAYNHAM

AAA ▼▼▼ **Days Inn Taunton** M
(508) 824-8647. **$59-$99.** 164 New State Hwy. SR 24, exit 13B, 0.8 mi w on US 44. Ext/int corridors. **Pets:** $10 daily fee/pet. Designated rooms, service with restrictions, supervision.
SAVE SD ✕ ⌖ ⊟ ⊸

REHOBOTH

▼▼▼ **Five Bridge Inn Bed & Breakfast** BB ❀
(508) 252-3190. **$98-$135, 7 day notice.** 154 Pine St. 1.6 mi n of US 44; 3.3 mi w of jct SR 118; US 44, n on Blanding, e on Broad, n on Salisbury, then w. Int corridors. **Pets:** Medium. $15 one-time fee/room. Designated rooms, service with restrictions.
✕ ⊟ ⊑ ⊸ ✕

RICHMOND

▼▼▼ **The Inn at Richmond** BB
(413) 698-2566. **$135-$215, 15 day notice.** 802 State Rd (SR 41). 2.5 mi s of jct US 20. Ext/int corridors. **Pets:** Accepted.
✕ ⊟ ⊑

ROCKLAND

AAA ▼▼▼ **Best Western Rockland** SH
(781) 871-5660. **$109-$159, 3 day notice.** 909 Hingham St. SR 3, exit 14, 0.3 mi sw on SR 228. Int corridors. **Pets:** $20 daily fee/pet. Designated rooms, service with restrictions, supervision.
SAVE SD ✕ ⊟ ⊑

SCITUATE

▼▼ **The Inn at Scituate Harbor** M
(781) 545-5550. **$109-$209, 3 day notice.** 7 Beaver Dam Rd. Jct Front St; at Scituate Harbor. Int corridors. **Pets:** Other species. $20 daily fee/room. Designated rooms, supervision.
ASK SD ✕ ⊟ ⊸

SEEKONK

▼▼ **Motel 6-1289** M
(508) 336-7800. **$61-$75.** 821 Fall River Ave. I-195, exit 1, just n on SR 114A. Int corridors. **Pets:** Medium, other species. Service with restrictions, supervision.
SD ✕ ⌖ ⌖

SOMERSET

AAA ▼▼▼▼ **Quality Inn-Fall River/Somerset** SH
(508) 678-4545. **$89-$179.** 1878 Wilbur Ave. Jct SR 103 and I-195, exit 4 eastbound; exit 4A westbound. Int corridors. **Pets:** $50 deposit/room. Designated rooms, service with restrictions, supervision.
SAVE SD ✕ ⊟ ⊑ ⊸ ✕

SOUTHBOROUGH

▼▼▼◆ **Red Roof Inn # 7075** M
(508) 481-3904. **$68-$100.** 367 Turnpike Rd. I-495, exit 23A, just e on SR 9. Ext corridors. **Pets:** Medium, other species. Service with restrictions, supervision.
✕ ⌖ ⊟

SPRINGFIELD

AAA ▼▼▼◆ **Holiday Inn** LH
(413) 781-0900. **$109-$159.** 711 Dwight St. I-291, exit 2A, just e. Int corridors. **Pets:** Large, other species. $35 one-time fee/pet. Service with restrictions, supervision.
SAVE SD ✕ ⊙M ⌖ ⊟ ⊑ ¶¶ ⊸ ✕

▼▼▼▼ **Sheraton Springfield Monarch Place** LH
(413) 781-1010. **$109-$500.** 1 Monarch Pl. I-91, exit 6 northbound; exit 7 southbound, just n; downtown. Int corridors. **Pets:** Accepted.
ASK SD ✕ ⊙M ⌖ ⊟ ⊑ ¶¶ ⊸ ✕

STURBRIDGE

AAA ▼▼▼ **American Motor Lodge** M
(508) 347-9121. **$65-$109.** 350 Main St. Jct US 20 and SR 131. Int corridors. **Pets:** Accepted.
SAVE SD ✕ ¶¶ ⊸

▼▼▼ **Americas Best Value Inn** M
(508) 347-7327. **$49-$149, 7 day notice.** 408 Main St. I-90 (Massachusetts Tpke), exit 9, 0.8 mi w on US 20; I-84, exit 3B. Ext corridors. **Pets:** $10 daily fee/pet. Service with restrictions, supervision.
ASK SD ✕ ⊑ ⊸

AAA ▼▼▼ **Comfort Inn & Suites Colonial** SH
(508) 347-3306. **$89-$259.** 215 Charlton Rd. I-90 (Massachusetts Tpke), exit 9, 0.5 mi e; I-84, exit 3A. Ext/int corridors. **Pets:** Accepted.
SAVE SD ✕ ⊙M ⌖ ⌖ ⊟ ⊑ ⊸

▼▼▼ Days Inn M
(508) 347-3391. **$59-$149.** 66-68 Haynes St (SR 15). I-84, exit 2, 0.5 mi n, follow signs to SR 131, on I-84 service road. Ext/int corridors. **Pets:** Accepted.
ASK SÒ ⊠ 🛢 ▣ 🏊

AAA ▼▼▼ Publick House Historic Inn & Country Lodge SH 🐾
(508) 347-3313. **$69-$175.** 295 Main St. I-90 (Massachusetts Tpke), exit 9; I-84, exit 3B, 0.5 mi s of jct US 20. Ext/int corridors. **Pets:** Other species. $10 daily fee/pet. Designated rooms, service with restrictions, crate.
SAVE SÒ ⊠ 🛢 ▣ 🍴 🏊

AAA ▼▼▼ Quality Inn SH
(508) 347-1978. **$67-$120.** 400 (SR 15). I-84, exit 1, 0.5 mi w. Int corridors. **Pets:** Accepted.
SAVE SÒ ⊠ 🕸 🕹 🛢 ▣ 🏊

AAA ▼ Rodeway Inn M
(508) 347-9673. **$65-$120.** 172 Main St. On SR 131, 1.4 mi s of jct US 20. Ext corridors. **Pets:** Accepted.
SAVE SÒ ⊠ 🛢 ▣

AAA ▼ Scottish Inns M
(508) 347-9514. **$55-$100.** 142 Main St. On SR 131, 1.5 mi s of jct US 20. Ext corridors. **Pets:** Accepted.
SAVE SÒ ⊠ 🛢

AAA ▼ Sturbridge Heritage Motel M
(508) 347-3943. **$45-$65.** 499 Main St. I-84, exit 3B, 1.5 mi w on US 20. Ext corridors. **Pets:** Accepted.
SAVE SÒ ⊠ 🛢

AAA ▼▼▼ Sturbridge Host Hotel and Conference Center on Cedar Lake LH
(508) 347-7393. **$89-$149.** 366 Main St. I-90 (Massachusetts Tpke), exit 9, just w on US 20; I-84, exit 3B. Int corridors. **Pets:** Accepted.
SAVE ⊠ 🕸 🛢 ▣ 🍴 🏊 🕹

AAA ▼▼▼ Super 8 M
(508) 347-9000. **$53-$169.** 358 Main St. I-90 (Massachusetts Tpke), exit 9; I-84, exit 3B on US 20. Ext corridors. **Pets:** Small, other species. $10 daily fee/pet. Designated rooms, service with restrictions, crate.
SAVE SÒ ⊠ 🛢 ▣ 🏊

WESTBOROUGH

AAA ▼▼▼▼ Doubletree Hotel Boston/Westborough LH
(508) 366-5511. **$99-$219, 3 day notice.** 5400 Computer Dr. I-495, exit 23B, just w on SR 9, exit Computer/Research Dr. Int corridors. **Pets:** Accepted.
SAVE ⊠ 🕹M 🕸 🕹 🛢 ▣ 🍴 🏊 🕹

▼▼ Extended Stay Deluxe-Boston-Westborough SH
(508) 616-9213. **$70-$150.** 180 E Main St. I-495, exit 23B, 1.4 mi w, then just sw on SR 30. Int corridors. **Pets:** Accepted.
ASK SÒ ⊠ 🕹M 🕸 🛢 ▣

▼ Extended Stay Deluxe Boston-Westborough-Computer Dr SH
(508) 366-6100. **$70-$105.** 1800 Computer Dr. I-495, exit 23B, just w; north side of SR 9. Int corridors. **Pets:** Accepted.
ASK SÒ ⊠ 🕹M 🕸 🕹 🛢 ▣ 🏊

AAA ▼▼▼▼ Residence Inn by Marriott Boston/Westborough SH 🐾
(508) 366-7700. **$99-$249.** 25 Connector Rd. I-495, exit 23B, just w on SR 9, exit Computer/Research Dr, then 0.3 mi s. Ext/int corridors. **Pets:** Large, other species. $100 one-time fee/room. Designated rooms, service with restrictions, supervision.
SAVE SÒ ⊠ 🕹M 🕸 🕹 🛢 ▣ 🏊 🕹

WEST BOYLSTON

AAA ▼▼▼ Classic Suites & Inns SH
(508) 835-4456. **$90-$100.** 181 W Boylston St (SR 12). I-190, exit 4, 0.8 mi ne. Int corridors. **Pets:** Other species. $25 one-time fee/room. Service with restrictions, supervision.
SAVE ⊠ 🛢 ▣ 🏊

WESTFIELD

AAA ▼▼▼ Econo Lodge & Suites SH
(413) 568-2821. **$60-$160.** 2 Southampton Rd. I-90, exit 3, at US 202 and SR 10. Ext/int corridors. **Pets:** Medium. $25 one-time fee/pet. Service with restrictions, supervision.
SAVE SÒ ⊠ 🛢 ▣ 🏊

WESTMINSTER

AAA ▼▼▼▼ Wachusett Village Inn & Conference Center SH
(978) 874-2000. **$99-$189.** 9 Village Inn Rd. 0.7 mi w on Village Inn Rd; SR 2, exit 27 westbound, 0.3 mi e; exit 26 eastbound. Ext/int corridors. **Pets:** Small, other species. $250 deposit/pet, $25 daily fee/pet. Designated rooms, service with restrictions, crate.
SAVE SÒ ⊠ 🕹 🛢 ▣ 🍴 🏊 🕹

WEST SPRINGFIELD

AAA ▼▼▼ Hampton Inn SH
(413) 732-1300. **$99-$109.** 1011 Riverdale St (US 5). I-91, exit 13B, 0.3 mi s. Int corridors. **Pets:** Accepted.
SAVE ⊠ 🕹M 🕸 🕹 ▣ 🏊

AAA ▼▼▼ Quality Inn SH
(413) 739-7261. **$49-$159.** 1150 Riverdale St. I-91, exit 13B, jct US 5. Int corridors. **Pets:** Medium. $35 one-time fee/pet. Service with restrictions, crate.
SAVE SÒ ⊠ 🛢 ▣ 🍴 🏊

▼▼ Red Roof Inn #7193 M
(413) 731-1010. **$65-$99.** 1254 Riverdale St. I-91, exit 13A. Ext corridors. **Pets:** Medium, other species. Service with restrictions, supervision.
⊠ 🕹M 🕸

▼▼ Residence Inn by Marriott SH
(413) 732-9543. **$145-$165.** 64 Border Way. I-91, exit 13A, on US 5. Int corridors. **Pets:** Accepted.
ASK SÒ ⊠ 🕹M 🕸 🕹 🛢 ▣ 🏊 🕹

WEST STOCKBRIDGE

AAA ▼▼ Pleasant Valley Motel M 🐾
(413) 232-8511. **$45-$195, 10 day notice.** 42 Stockbridge Rd. I-90 (Massachusetts Tpke), exit B3 eastbound, 0.5 mi s on SR 22, then 3.5 mi e on SR 102; exit 1 westbound, 0.4 mi e. Ext corridors. **Pets:** $15 daily fee/pet. Service with restrictions.
SAVE SÒ ⊠ 🛢 🏊

WILLIAMSTOWN

▼▼ Cozy Corner Motel M
(413) 458-8006. **$55-$125, 7 day notice.** 284 Sand Springs Rd (US 7). On US 7, 1.5 mi n of jct SR 2. Ext corridors. **Pets:** Other species. $10 one-time fee/pet. Service with restrictions, supervision.
⊠ 🛢

AAA ▼▼ The Villager Motel M
(413) 458-4046. **$55-$125, 14 day notice.** 953 Simonds Rd. On US 7, 1.7 n of jct SR 2. Ext corridors. **Pets:** Medium. $10 daily fee. Service with restrictions, supervision.
SAVE SÒ ⊠ 🛢

WORCESTER

AAA ◆◆◆ **Crowne Plaza Hotel** LH
(508) 791-1600. **$109-$199.** 10 Lincoln Square. I-290, exit 17 eastbound; exit 18 westbound, 0.3 mi s. Int corridors. **Pets:** Medium. $20 daily fee/pet. Designated rooms, service with restrictions, crate.
[SAVE] 🆂🅳 ✕ 🖱 🈁 💺 🛄 💻 🍽 🏊 ✕

◆◆◆ **Residence Inn by Marriott Worcester** SH 🐾
(508) 753-6300. **$109-$209.** 503 Plantation St. I-290, exit 21, 0.5 mi sw. Int corridors. **Pets:** Medium, other species. $75 one-time fee/room. Designated rooms, service with restrictions, supervision.
[ASK] 🆂🅳 ✕ 🛄 💻 🏊

AAA ◆◆◆◆ **Worcester Hotel & Conference Center** SH
(508) 852-4000. **$139-$149.** 500 Lincoln St. I-290, exit 20, 0.5 mi n on SR 70. Int corridors. **Pets:** Accepted.
[SAVE] 🆂🅳 ✕ 🈁 💺 🛄 💻 🍽 🏊

ALBION

Days Inn SH
(517) 629-9411. **Call for rates.** 27644 C Dr N. I-94, exit 121 (28 Mile Rd), just nw. Int corridors. **Pets:** Accepted.

ALGONAC

Linda's Lighthouse Inn BB
(810) 794-2992. **$95-$135, 14 day notice.** 5965 Pointe Tremble Rd (SR 29). I-94, exit 243 (23 Mile Rd), 14.3 mi e. Int corridors. **Pets:** Other species. $15 daily fee/pet. Crate.

ALLEGAN

Castle In The Country B & B Inn BB
(269) 673-8054. **$125-$225, 14 day notice.** 340 SR 40 S. SR 40 S, 6 mi s. Int corridors. **Pets:** Accepted.

ALLENDALE

Sleep Inn & Suites SH
(616) 892-8000. **$70-$105.** 4869 Becker Dr. I-96, exit 16, 6 mi s, then 2.5 mi e on SR 45. Int corridors. **Pets:** Accepted.

ALPENA

Days Inn SH
(989) 356-6118. **$89-$120.** 1496 Hwy 32 W. 2.5 mi w of jct US 23. Int corridors. **Pets:** Dogs only. $10 daily fee/room. Service with restrictions, supervision.

Holiday Inn SH
(989) 356-2151. **$109-$129.** 1000 Hwy 23 N. On US 23, 1 mi n. Int corridors. **Pets:** Service with restrictions, supervision.

ANN ARBOR

Americas Best Value Inn & Suites M
(734) 665-3500. **$59-$69, 3 day notice.** 3505 S State St. I-94, exit 177 (State St), just ne. Ext corridors. **Pets:** Large. $25 one-time fee/room. Service with restrictions, supervision.

Best Western Executive Plaza SH
(734) 665-4444. **$79-$159.** 2900 Jackson Rd. I-94, exit 172 (Jackson Rd), just e. Ext/int corridors. **Pets:** Accepted.

Extended StayAmerica SH
(734) 332-1980. **$69.** 1501 Briarwood Circle Dr. I-94, exit 177 (State St), just ne. Int corridors. **Pets:** Accepted.

Fairfield Inn by Marriott SH
(734) 995-5200. **$74-$126.** 3285 Boardwalk St. I-94, exit 177 (State St), just n, then e on Victors Way. Int corridors. **Pets:** Medium, dogs only. $100 one-time fee/room. Designated rooms, service with restrictions, supervision.

Hampton Inn-North SH
(734) 996-4444. **$89-$119, 7 day notice.** 2300 Green Rd. US 23, exit 41 (Plymouth Rd), just nw. Int corridors. **Pets:** Medium. $25 one-time fee/room. Service with restrictions, supervision.

Hawthorn Suites SH
(734) 327-0011. **$130-$275.** 3535 Green Ct. US 23, exit 41 (Plymouth Rd), just sw. Int corridors. **Pets:** Other species. $100 one-time fee/room. Service with restrictions.

Red Roof Inn #7045 M
(734) 996-5800. **$66-$86.** 3621 Plymouth Rd. US 23, exit 41 (Plymouth Rd), just nw. Ext corridors. **Pets:** Medium, other species. Service with restrictions, supervision.

Residence Inn by Marriott SH
(734) 996-5666. **$149-$169.** 800 Victor Way. I-94, exit 177 (State St), just ne. Ext/int corridors. **Pets:** Accepted.

Studio Plus SH
(734) 997-7623. **Call for rates.** 3265 Boardwalk Dr. I-94, exit 177 (State St), just n, then e on Victors Way. Int corridors. **Pets:** Accepted.

AU GRES

▼▼▼ Best Western Pinewood Lodge SH
(989) 876-4060. **$56-$89.** 510 W US 23. On US 23, just w. Int corridors. **Pets:** Accepted.
S✪ ✕ ⊟ ▣ ⇌

BAD AXE

▲▲▲ ▼▼▼ Econo Lodge Inns & Suites SH
(989) 269-3200. **$49-$180.** 898 N Van Dyke Rd. Just s of jct SR 142 and 53 (Van Dyke Rd). Int corridors. **Pets:** Small. $10 one-time fee/room. Service with restrictions, supervision.
SAVE S✪ ✕ ▥ ⇌

BATTLE CREEK

▲▲▲ ▼▼▼ Baymont Inn & Suites-Battle Creek SH
(269) 979-5400. **$129.** 4725 Beckley Rd. I-94, exit 97 (Capital Ave), just sw. Int corridors. **Pets:** Accepted.
SAVE S✪ ✕ 🐾 ⌨ ⊟ ▣ ⇌

▼ Motel 6–4250 M
(269) 979-1141. **$42-$50.** 4775 Beckley Rd. I-94, exit 97 (Capital Ave), just sw. Ext corridors. **Pets:** Medium, other species. Service with restrictions, supervision.
S✪ ✕ ⚹ ⌨ ⇌

◆▼▼ Ramada Inn & Suites M
(269) 979-1100. **$69-$109, 14 day notice.** 5050 Beckley Rd. I-94, exit 97 (Capital Ave), just s. Ext corridors. **Pets:** Accepted.
ASK S✪ ✕ ⊟ ▣ ▥ ⇌

BAY VIEW

▲▲▲ ▼▼▼ Comfort Inn SH ❀
(231) 347-3220. **$60-$200.** 1314 US 31 N. Jct US 31 and SR 119. Int corridors. **Pets:** Other species. Service with restrictions, supervision.
SAVE S✪ ✕ ⊟ ▣

BEAR LAKE

▲▲▲ ▼▼ Bella Vista Inn M
(231) 864-3000. **$60-$109, 7 day notice.** 12273 US 31. On US 31; center. Ext corridors. **Pets:** Dogs only. $10 daily fee/room. Service with restrictions, supervision.
SAVE S✪ ✕ ⊟ ⇌

BEULAH

▲▲▲ ▼▼▼ Best Western Scenic Hill Resort SH
(231) 882-7754. **$105-$248.** 1400 US 31 Hwy. 0.8 mi e on US 31. Int corridors. **Pets:** Medium. $50 deposit/room, $20 daily fee/pet. Designated rooms, crate.
SAVE S✪ ✕ ⌨ ⊟ ▣ ⇌ ✕

BIG RAPIDS

▼▼ Holiday Inn Hotel & Conference Center SH ❀
(231) 796-4400. **$89-$179.** 1005 Perry St. US 131, exit 139, 1.3 mi e on SR 20. Int corridors. **Pets:** Other species. $15 daily fee/room. Service with restrictions, supervision.
ASK S✪ ✕ ⚹ ⌨ ⊟ ▣ ▥ ⇌ ✕

▲▲▲ ▼▼▼ Quality Inn & Suites M
(231) 592-5150. **$69-$129.** 1705 S State St. US 131, exit 139, 2.1 mi e on SR 20, then 1 mi s. Ext/int corridors. **Pets:** Medium, other species. $6 daily fee/pet. No service, supervision.
SAVE S✪ ✕ ⊟ ▣ ⇌

BIRCH RUN

▲▲▲ ▼▼▼ Super 8 Motel SH
(989) 624-4440. **$50-$88.** 9235 E Birch Run Rd. I-75, exit 136 (Birch Run Rd), just e. Int corridors. **Pets:** Medium. Service with restrictions, supervision.
SAVE S✪ ✕ ⊟ ✕

BRIDGEPORT

▲▲▲ ▼▼▼ Baymont Inn &
Suites-Frankenmuth/Bridgeport SH
(989) 777-3000. **$56-$129.** 6460 Dixie Hwy. I-75, exit 144A. Int corridors. **Pets:** Accepted.
SAVE S✪ ✕ ⌨ ⊟ ▣ ⇌

BROOKLYN

▼▼ Super 8 Motel SH
(517) 592-0888. **$58-$130.** 155 Wamplers Rd. Jct Main St (SR 50) and SR 124; downtown. Int corridors. **Pets:** Other species. $10 daily fee/pet. Service with restrictions, supervision.
ASK S✪ ✕ ⚹ ⌨ ⊟

BYRON CENTER

▼▼ Baymont Inn & Suites Grand Rapids Southwest/Byron Center SH
(616) 583-9535. **$79-$99.** 8282 Pfeiffer Farms Dr SW. US 131, exit 74, just w. Int corridors. **Pets:** Accepted.
ASK S✪ ✕ ⚹ 🐾 ⌨ ⊟ ▣ ▥ ⇌ ✕

CADILLAC

▲▲▲ ▼ Econo Lodge SH
(231) 775-6700. **$50-$115.** 2501 Sunnyside Dr. Jct SR 55 and 115. Ext/int corridors. **Pets:** Other species. $10 one-time fee/room. Designated rooms, service with restrictions, supervision.
SAVE S✪ ✕ ⊟ ▣

▲▲▲ ▼▼▼ McGuires Resort SH ❀
(231) 775-9947. **$89-$219, 7 day notice.** 7880 Mackinaw Trail. US 131, exit 177, 0.7 mi n, then 0.5 mi w. Int corridors. **Pets:** $15 daily fee/room. Designated rooms, service with restrictions, supervision.
SAVE S✪ ✕ ⌨ ⊟ ▣ ▥ ⇌ ✕

CALUMET

▼▼ AmericInn of Calumet SH
(906) 337-6463. **$95-$170.** 56925 S 6th St. On US 41, just w of Visitors Center. Int corridors. **Pets:** Accepted.
ASK ✕ ⌨ ⊟ ▣ ⇌ ✕

CASCADE

▲▲▲ ▼▼▼ Baymont Inn-Grand Rapids Airport SH
(616) 956-3300. **$69-$89.** 2873 Kraft Ave SE. I-96, exit 43B, just e. Int corridors. **Pets:** Accepted.
SAVE S✪ ✕ ⊟ ▣

▼▼ Country Inn & Suites by Carlson of Grand Rapids SH
(616) 977-0909. **$71-$79.** 5399 28th St. I-96, exit 43B, just e on SR 11. Int corridors. **Pets:** Accepted.
ASK S✪ ✕ 🐾 ⌨ ⌨ ⊟ ▣ ⇌

▼▼▼ Crowne Plaza Grand Rapids LH
(616) 957-1770. **$89-$149.** 5700 28th St SE. I-96, exit 43B, 0.3 mi e on SR 11. Int corridors. **Pets:** Accepted.
ASK S✪ ✕ ⌨ ⌨ ⊟ ▣ ▥ ⇌ ✕

▲▲▲ ▼ Exel Inn of Grand Rapids SH
(616) 957-3000. **$50-$80.** 4855 28th St SE. I-96, exit 43A, 0.5 mi w on SR 11. Int corridors. **Pets:** Small, other species. Designated rooms, service with restrictions, supervision.
SAVE S✪ ✕ ⊟ ▣

▼▼ Hampton Inn SH
(616) 956-9304. **$82-$92.** 4981 28th St SE. I-96, exit 43A, 0.5 mi w on SR 11. Int corridors. **Pets:** Small. Service with restrictions, supervision.
ASK S✪ ✕ ⌨ ⊟ ▣ ⇌

CHARLEVOIX

◆◆◆ AmericInn Lodge & Suites SH
(231) 237-0988. $75-$170. 11800 US 31 N. On US 31, 2.4 mi n. Int corridors. Pets: $50 deposit/room, $10 daily fee/room.
A$K S◇ ⊠ &M 🐾 🔒 💻 🏊

CHARLOTTE

◆◆◆ ▽▽▽ Super 8 Motel SH 🐾
(517) 543-8288. $75-$99, 7 day notice. 828 E Shepherd St. I-69, exit 60 (SR 50), just w. Int corridors. Pets: Other species. $15 one-time fee/room. Service with restrictions, supervision.
SAVE S◇ ⊠ 🔒

CHEBOYGAN

◆◆◆ ▽▽▽ Best Western River Terrace Motel M
(231) 627-5688. $49-$189. 847 S Main St. 1 mi s on SR 27. Ext/int corridors. Pets: Accepted.
SAVE S◇ ⊠ 🔒 💻 🏊 ⊠

◆◆◆ ▽ Birch Haus Motel M
(231) 627-5862. $40-$75. 1301 Mackinaw Ave. On US 23, 0.8 mi nw. Ext corridors. Pets: Medium. $5 daily fee/pet. Service with restrictions, supervision.
SAVE ⊠ 🔒

▽ Continental Inn M
(231) 627-7164. $49-$120. 613 N Main St. Jct US 23 and SR 27. Ext corridors. Pets: Other species. $6 daily fee/room. Service with restrictions, crate.
A$K S◇ ⊠ 🔒 🏊

◆◆◆ ▽ Pine River Motel M 🐾
(231) 627-5119. $30-$90. 102 Lafayette. On US 23, 0.5 mi e. Ext corridors. Pets: $10 one-time fee/pet. Service with restrictions, supervision.
SAVE ⊠ 🔒

CHELSEA

▽▽▽ Chelsea Comfort Inn & Conference Center SH
(734) 433-8000. $95-$230. 1645 Commerce Park Dr. I-94, exit 159 (SR 52/Main St), just n. Int corridors. Pets: Medium. $20 one-time fee/pet. Service with restrictions, supervision.
A$K S◇ ⊠ &M 🔒 💻 🏊

CHRISTMAS

◆◆◆ ▽▽▽ Pair-A-Dice Inn SH
(906) 387-3500. $85-$108. E7889 W Hwy M-28. On SR 28; center. Int corridors. Pets: Dogs only. $25 one-time fee/room. Service with restrictions, supervision.
SAVE S◇ ⊠ 🔒 💻

COLDWATER

◆◆◆ ▽▽▽ Red Roof Inn SH
(517) 279-1199. $60-$90. 348 S Willowbrook Rd. I-69, exit 13 (US 12), just e. Int corridors. Pets: Small. $10 daily fee/pet. Service with restrictions, supervision.
SAVE S◇ ⊠ &M 🔒 💻

◆◆◆ ▽▽▽ Super 8 Motel SH
(517) 278-8833. $59-$75. 600 Orleans Blvd. I-69, exit 13 (US 12), 0.3 mi w on E Chicago St, just n on N Michigan Ave, then just e. Int corridors. Pets: Accepted.
SAVE S◇ ⊠ &M 🔒

COMSTOCK PARK

▽ Swan Inn M
(616) 784-1224. $48-$80. 5182 Alpine Ave. Jct I-96 and Alpine Ave, 3 mi n on SR 37. Ext corridors. Pets: Other species. Service with restrictions, crate.
⊠ 🔒 💻 🍴 🏊

COPPER HARBOR

▽ Lake Fanny Hooe Resort M
(906) 289-4451. $75-$105, 7 day notice. 505 2nd St. Just s on Manganese Rd. Ext corridors. Pets: Other species. $7 daily fee/pet. Service with restrictions, supervision.
⊠ 🔒 💻 ⊠ 🐾 ⊠

DETROIT METROPOLITAN AREA

ALLEN PARK

◆◆◆ ▽▽▽ Best Western Greenfield Inn SH
(313) 271-1600. $84-$99. 3000 Enterprise Dr. I-94, exit 206 (Oakwood Blvd), just s, then just w. Int corridors. Pets: Small, dogs only. $100 deposit/room. Designated rooms, service with restrictions, supervision.
SAVE S◇ ⊠ 🐾 🔒 💻 🍴 🏊 ⊠

◆◆◆ ▽▽▽ Holiday Inn Express & Suites SH
(313) 323-3500. $109-$129. 3600 Enterprise Dr. I-94, exit 206 (Oakwood Blvd), just s, then just w. Int corridors. Pets: Accepted.
SAVE S◇ ⊠ &M 🔒 💻 🏊

AUBURN HILLS

▽▽▽ Candlewood Suites SH
(248) 373-3342. $92. 1650 N Opdyke Rd. I-75, exit 79 (University Dr), just w, then 0.4 mi n. Int corridors. Pets: Accepted.
A$K S◇ ⊠ 🔒 💻

▽▽▽ Homestead Studio Suites Hotel-Detroit/Auburn
       Hills SH
(248) 340-8888. $69-$79. 3315 University Dr. I-75, exit 79 (University Dr), 0.9 mi e. Int corridors. Pets: Accepted.
A$K S◇ ⊠ 🔒 💻

▽▽▽▽ Staybridge Suites SH
(248) 322-4600. $89-$155. 2050 Featherstone Rd. I-75, exit 79 (University Dr), just w, 0.5 mi s on Opdyke Rd, then just e. Int corridors. Pets: Other species. $75 one-time fee/room. Service with restrictions.
A$K S◇ ⊠ &M 🔒 💻 🏊

BELLEVILLE

▽▽▽ Red Roof Inn Metro Airport #7183 M
(734) 697-2244. $62-$83. 45501 N I-94 Service Dr. I-94, exit 190 (Belleville Rd), just n. Ext corridors. Pets: Medium, other species. Service with restrictions, supervision.
⊠ 🐾 &M 🔒

▽▽ Super 8 Motel SH
(734) 699-1888. $50-$99. 45707 S I-94 Service Dr. I-94, exit 190 (Belleville Rd), just s. Int corridors. Pets: Other species. $5 daily fee/pet. Service with restrictions, supervision.
A$K ⊠ 🔒

BIRMINGHAM

▼▼▼▼ Barclay Inn Birmingham SH
(248) 646-7300. **$79-$250.** 34952 Woodward Ave. On SR 1, jct Woodward Ave and Maple Rd; center. Ext/int corridors. **Pets:** Medium, other species. $25 one-time fee/room. Designated rooms, service with restrictions.

ASK S♂ ✕ ᰦM 〳 █ 💻

▲▲▲ ▼▼▼▼ Holiday Inn Express–Birmingham SH
(248) 642-6200. **$119-$179.** 35270 Woodward Ave. Jct Woodward Ave and Maple Rd; center. Int corridors. **Pets:** Small. $50 daily fee/room. Service with restrictions, crate.

SAVE S♂ ✕ █ 💻

CANTON

▲▲▲ ▼▼ La Quinta Inn & Suites Detroit-Canton SH
(734) 981-1808. **$85-$99.** 41211 Ford Rd. I-275, exit 25 (Ford Rd), just w to jct Haggerty Rd. Int corridors. **Pets:** Medium. Service with restrictions.

SAVE ✕ 〵 █ 💻

DEARBORN

▼▼ Extended StayAmerica SH
(313) 336-0021. **$89-$99.** 260 Towne Center Dr. SR 39 (Southfield Frwy); between Ford Rd and Michigan Ave exits; just w of jct Service and Hubbard drs. Int corridors. **Pets:** Accepted.

ASK S♂ ✕ ᰦM 〳 █ 💻

▼▼ Red Roof Inn-Dearborn #7182 M
(313) 278-9732. **$68-$93.** 24130 Michigan Ave. Jct US 24 (Telegraph Rd) and 12 (Michigan Ave). Ext corridors. **Pets:** Medium, other species. Service with restrictions, supervision.

✕ ᰦM 〵 〳 █

▲▲▲ ▼▼▼ ▼▼ The Ritz-Carlton, Dearborn LH 🐾
(313) 441-2000. **$309.** 300 Town Center Dr. SR 39 (Southfield Frwy); between Ford Rd and Michigan Ave exits, on Service Dr. Int corridors. **Pets:** Medium, dogs only. $75 one-time fee/room. Service with restrictions.

SAVE ✕ ᰦM 〵 〳 █ 💻 ⌚ ✕

▼▼ TownePlace Suites SH
(313) 271-0200. **$119-$300.** 6141 Mercury Dr. SR 39 (Southfield Frwy), exit 7 (Ford Rd), just e, then 0.8 mi n. Int corridors. **Pets:** Accepted.

ASK S♂ ✕ ᰦM 〳 █ 💻 ⌚

DETROIT

▲▲▲ ▼▼▼▼ Holiday Inn Express LH
(313) 887-7000. **$75-$399.** 1020 Washington Blvd. Corner of Washington Blvd and Michigan Ave. Int corridors. **Pets:** $25 one-time fee/room. Service with restrictions, supervision.

SAVE S♂ ✕ 〳 █ 💻 ⌚

▼▼▼▼ Residence Inn By Marriott-Dearborn SH
(313) 441-1700. **$59-$199.** 5777 Southfield Service Dr. SR 39 (Southfield Frwy), exit Ford Rd, just w. Ext corridors. **Pets:** Accepted.

ASK S♂ ✕ █ 💻 ⌚ ✕

▼▼ Woodbridge Star Bed & Breakfast BB 🐾
(313) 831-9668. **$60-$155, 10 day notice.** 3985 Trumbull St. Jct Alexandrine St. Int corridors. **Pets:** Medium. Supervision.

ASK ✕ ☏

FARMINGTON HILLS

▼▼ Candlewood Suites SH
(248) 324-0540. **$95-$120.** 37555 Hills Tech Dr. I-696, exit I-96 E/I-275 S/SR 5, just s to SR 5 N, 2 mi n to 12 Mile Rd, 1.3 mi e, then 0.3 mi s on Halsted Rd. Int corridors. **Pets:** Large. $75 one-time fee/room.

ASK S♂ ✕ ᰦM 〳 █ 💻

▼▼ ▼▼ Extended StayAmerica-Detroit-Farmington Hills SH
(248) 473-4000. **$65-$75.** 27775 Stansbury Blvd. I-696, exit 5 (Orchard Lake Rd), just n, just e on 12 Mile Rd, then just s. Int corridors. **Pets:** Accepted.

ASK S♂ ✕ ᰦM 〵 〳 █ 💻

▼▼ ▼▼ Red Roof Inn-Farmington Hills #7038 M
(248) 478-8640. **$60-$76.** 24300 Sinacola Ct. I-96/275 and SR 5, exit 165 (Grand River Ave), just w. Ext corridors. **Pets:** Medium, other species. Service with restrictions, supervision.

✕ ᰦM 〳 █

LAKE ORION

▲▲▲ ▼▼ Best Western Palace Inn SH
(248) 391-2755. **$100-$130.** 2755 N Lapeer Rd. I-75, exit 81 (Lapeer Rd), 3.3 mi n. Ext/int corridors. **Pets:** Accepted.

SAVE S♂ ✕ ᰦM 〵 █ 💻 ⌚

LIVONIA

▲▲▲ ▼▼▼▼ Residence Inn Detroit-Livonia SH
(734) 462-4201. **$159-$399.** 17250 Fox Dr. I-275, exit 170 (6 Mile Rd), just w. Int corridors. **Pets:** Accepted.

SAVE S♂ ✕ ᰦM 〵 〳 █ 💻 ⌚ ✕

▼▼▼▼ TownePlace Suites by Marriott SH
(734) 542-7400. **$79-$129.** 17450 Fox Dr. I-275, exit 170 (6 Mile Rd), just nw. Int corridors. **Pets:** Accepted.

ASK S♂ ✕ ᰦM 〳 █ 💻 ⌚

MADISON HEIGHTS

▼▼ Motel 6 Madison Heights #1109 M
(248) 583-0500. **$48-$58.** 32700 Barrington Rd. I-75, exit 65A (14 Mile Rd), just e. Ext corridors. **Pets:** Medium, other species. Service with restrictions, supervision.

S♂ ✕ ᰦM 〵 〳

▼▼ ▼▼ Red Roof Inn #7084 M
(248) 583-4700. **$61-$80.** 32511 Concord Dr. I-75, exit 65A (14 Mile Rd), just e, then just s. Ext corridors. **Pets:** Medium, other species. Service with restrictions, supervision.

✕ 〵 █

▼▼ ▼▼ Residence Inn by Marriott-Detroit Troy/Madison Heights SH
(248) 583-4322. **$159.** 32650 Stephenson Hwy. I-75, exit 65B (14 Mile Rd), just w, then just s. Ext corridors. **Pets:** Accepted.

✕ 〵 █ 💻 ⌚ ✕

NOVI

▼▼▼▼ Extended StayAmerica-Detroit-Novi SH
(248) 305-9955. **$75-$85.** 21555 Haggerty Rd. I-275, exit 167 (8 Mile Rd), just w, then 0.5 mi n. Int corridors. **Pets:** Accepted.

ASK S♂ ✕ 〵 〳 █ 💻

▼▼▼▼ Residence Inn by Marriott-Detroit/Novi SH
(248) 735-7400. **$169-$209.** 27477 Caberet Dr. I-96, exit 162 (Novi Rd), just n to 12 Mile Rd, then just w. Int corridors. **Pets:** Other species. $100 one-time fee/room. Service with restrictions, crate.

ASK S♂ ✕ ᰦM 〵 █ 💻 ⌚

▼▼▼▼ Sheraton-Detroit-Novi LH 🐾
(248) 349-4000. **$99-$249.** 21111 Haggerty Rd. I-275, exit 167 (8 Mile Rd), just w to Haggerty Rd, then just n. Int corridors. **Pets:** Medium, dogs only. Service with restrictions, supervision.

✕ ᰦM 〵 〳 █ 💻 ⑪ ⌚ ✕

▼▼▼ TownePlace Suites SH ❀
(248) 305-5533. $139-$149. 42600 11 Mile Rd. I-96, exit 162 (Novi Rd), just s, 0.5 mi e on Crescent Dr, then just s on Town Center Dr. Int corridors. Pets: Small. $75 one-time fee/room. Service with restrictions, crate.

ASK S☐ ✕ ☐ ☐ ☐ ☐ ~

PLYMOUTH

▼▼ Red Roof Inn-Plymouth #7016 M
(734) 459-3300. $62-$83. 39700 Ann Arbor Rd. I-275, exit 28 (Ann Arbor Rd), just e. Ext corridors. Pets: Medium, other species. Service with restrictions, supervision.

✕ ☐ ☐ ☐

PONTIAC

▼▼▼▼ Residence Inn by Marriott Detroit Pontiac/Auburn Hills SH
(248) 858-8664. $99-$199. 3333 Centerpoint Pkwy. I-75, exit 75 (Square Lake Rd), w via Opdyke Rd. Int corridors. Pets: $100 one-time fee/room. Service with restrictions.

ASK S☐ ✕ ☐ ☐ ☐ ☐ ~ ✕

ROCHESTER HILLS

▼▼ Red Roof Inn #7191 M
(248) 853-6400. $62-$87. 2580 Crooks Rd. Jct Hall (SR 59) and Crooks rds. Ext corridors. Pets: Medium, other species. Service with restrictions, supervision.

✕ ☐ ☐ ☐

ROMULUS

▼ Americas Best Value Inn & Suites SH
(734) 595-7400. $50-$90. 9095 Wickham Rd. I-94, exit 198 (Merriman Rd), just n, then just w. Int corridors. Pets: Accepted.

ASK S☐ ✕ ☐ ☐ ☐

▼▼ Baymont Inn & Suites Detroit-Airport SH
(734) 722-6000. $95-$99. 9000 Wickham Rd. I-94, exit 198 (Merriman Rd), just n, then just w. Int corridors. Pets: Medium. Service with restrictions.

ASK ✕ ☐ ☐ ☐

🅰🅰🅰 ▼▼▼ Clarion Hotel Detroit Metro Airport SH
(734) 728-7900. $90-$249, 3 day notice. 8600 Merriman Rd. I-94, exit 198 (Merriman Rd), just n. Int corridors. Pets: Large, other species. $10 daily fee/pet. Service with restrictions, supervision.

SAVE S☐ ✕ ☐ ☐ ☐ ~

▼▼▼ Detroit Metro Airport Marriott SH
(734) 729-7555. $89-$209. 30559 Flynn Dr. I-94, exit 198 (Merriman Rd), just n, then 0.3 mi e. Int corridors. Pets: Accepted.

ASK S☐ ✕ ☐M ☐ ☐ ☐ ☐ ~

▼▼▼ Four Points by Sheraton Detroit Metro Airport SH
(734) 729-9000. $170. 8800 Wickham Rd. I-94, exit 198 (Merriman Rd), just n, then just e. Int corridors. Pets: Accepted.

ASK S☐ ✕ ☐ ☐ ☐ ☐ ☐ ~

🅰🅰🅰 ▼▼▼ Ramada Detroit Airport SH
(734) 728-2322. $74-$94. 31119 Flynn Dr. I-94, exit 198 (Merriman Rd). Ext/int corridors. Pets: Accepted.

SAVE S☐ ✕ ☐M ☐ ☐ ☐ ~

🅰🅰🅰 ▼▼▼ Romulus Quality Inn & Suites SH
(734) 946-1400. $69-$89. 9555 Middlebelt Rd. I-94, exit 199 (Middlebelt Rd), 0.4 mi s. Int corridors. Pets: Accepted.

SAVE S☐ ✕ ☐ ☐ ☐

▼▼ Super 8 Motel-Romulus SH
(734) 946-8808. $59-$89. 9863 Middlebelt Rd. I-94, exit 199 (Middlebelt Rd), 0.8 mi s. Int corridors. Pets: Accepted.

ASK S☐ ✕ ☐M ☐

🅰🅰🅰 ▼▼▼ ▼ The Westin Detroit Metropolitan Airport LH ❀
(734) 942-6500. $99-$289. 2501 Worldgateway Pl. I-94, exit 198 (Merriman Rd); at McNamara Terminal. Int corridors. Pets: Medium, dogs only. Service with restrictions, supervision.

SAVE S☐ ✕ ☐M ☐ ☐ ☐ ☐ ~

ROSEVILLE

▼▼▼ Best Western Georgian Inn M
(586) 294-0400. $69-$189. 31327 Gratiot Ave. I-94, exit 232 (Little Mack Ave), just s, 0.5 mi n on 13 Mile Rd, then just n. Ext corridors. Pets: Medium, dogs only. $8 daily fee/pet. Service with restrictions, crate.

ASK S☐ ✕ ☐ ☐ ☐ ~

▼▼ Microtel Inn & Suites SH
(586) 415-1000. $49-$89. 20313 13 Mile Rd. I-94, exit 232 (Little Mack Ave), just s, then 0.4 mi w. Int corridors. Pets: Other species. Designated rooms, service with restrictions, supervision.

ASK S☐ ✕ ☐M ☐ ☐ ☐ ☐ ~

▼▼ Red Roof Inn #7012 M
(586) 296-0310. $55-$78. 31800 Little Mack Ave. I-94, exit 232 (Little Mack Ave), just n. Ext corridors. Pets: Medium, other species. Service with restrictions, supervision.

✕ ☐ ☐

SOUTHFIELD

▼▼ Candlewood Suites SH
(248) 945-0010. $100-$110. 1 Corporate Dr. SR 10 (Northwestern Hwy), exit Lasher Rd, just e. Int corridors. Pets: Accepted.

ASK S☐ ✕ ☐M ☐ ☐ ☐

▼▼▼ Hawthorn Suites Ltd SH
(248) 350-2400. $96-$104. 25100 Northwestern Hwy. SR 10 (Northwestern Hwy), exit 10 Mile Rd. Int corridors. Pets: Accepted.

ASK S☐ ✕ ☐M ☐ ☐ ☐ ~

▼▼ Holiday Inn-Southfield LH
(248) 353-7700. $109-$119. 26555 Telegraph Rd. I-696, exit 9 (Telegraph Rd), just s on US 24 (Telegraph Rd). Int corridors. Pets: Accepted.

ASK S☐ ✕ ☐M ☐ ☐ ☐ ☐ ☐ ~ ✕

▼▼ Homestead Studio Suites Hotel-Detroit/Southfield SH
(248) 213-4500. $84-$94. 28500 Northwestern Hwy. I-696, exit 9 (Telegraph Rd), just nw of jct US 24. Int corridors. Pets: Accepted.

ASK S☐ ✕ ☐M ☐ ☐ ☐ ☐

🅰🅰🅰 ▼▼ Marvin's Garden Inn M
(248) 353-6777. $60-$200, 3 day notice. 27650 Northwestern Hwy. I-696, exit 9 (Telegraph Rd), just nw. Ext/int corridors. Pets: Small, other species. $9 daily fee/room. Designated rooms, service with restrictions, supervision.

SAVE S☐ ✕ ☐ ☐

▼▼ Red Roof Inn-Southfield #7133 M
(248) 353-7200. $68-$86. 27660 Northwestern Hwy. I-696, exit 9 (Telegraph Rd), just nw. Ext corridors. Pets: Medium, other species. Service with restrictions, supervision.

✕ ☐M ☐ ☐

▼▼ Residence Inn by Marriott SH ❀
(248) 352-8900. $169-$199. 26700 Central Park Blvd. I-696, exit 11 (Evergreen Rd), just sw of jct 11 Mile and Evergreen rds. Ext corridors. Pets: Large, other species. $75 one-time fee/room. Service with restrictions, supervision.

ASK S☐ ✕ ☐M ☐ ☐ ☐ ~

🔷 🔷🔷 🔷🔷 Westin Hotel Southfield-Detroit [LH]
(248) 827-4000. $99-$309. 1500 Town Center. SR 10 (Northwestern Hwy), exit 10 (Mile/Evergreen rds), 0.3 mi n. Int corridors. Pets: Accepted.
[SAVE] 🔲 ⊠ 🔲 🔲 🔲 🔲 🔲 🔲 🔲

SOUTHGATE

🔷 🔷🔷 Americas Best Value Inn & Suites [M]
(734) 287-8340. $53. 18777 Northline Rd. I-75, exit 37 (Northline Rd), just w. Ext corridors. Pets: $5 one-time fee/pet. Service with restrictions, crate.
[SAVE] 🔲 ⊠ 🔲 🔲 🔲 🔲

🔷 🔷🔷🔷 La Quinta Inn & Suites Detroit-Southgate [SH]
(734) 374-3000. $79-$105. 12888 Reeck Rd. I-75, exit 37 (Northline Rd), just w. Int corridors. Pets: Medium. Service with restrictions.
[SAVE] ⊠ 🔲 🔲 🔲

STERLING HEIGHTS

🔷🔷 TownePlace Suites [SH]
(586) 566-0900. $89-$119. 14800 Lakeside Cir. 1 mi e of jct SR 53 (Van Dyke Ave) and 59 (Hall Rd). Int corridors. Pets: Accepted.
[ASK] 🔲 ⊠ 🔲 🔲 🔲 🔲 🔲

TAYLOR

🔷🔷 Red Roof Inn-Taylor #7189 [M]
(734) 374-1150. $63-$85. 21230 Eureka Rd. I-75, exit 36 (Eureka Rd), just w. Ext corridors. Pets: Medium, other species. Service with restrictions, supervision.
⊠ 🔲

TROY

🔷🔷🔷 Drury Inn & Suites-Troy [SH]
(248) 528-3330. $110-$166. 575 W Big Beaver Rd. I-75, exit 69 (Big Beaver Rd), just e. Int corridors. Pets: Large, other species. Service with restrictions, supervision.
[ASK] ⊠ 🔲 🔲 🔲 🔲 🔲 🔲

🔷🔷 Holiday Inn-Troy [SH]
(248) 689-7500. $79-$129. 2537 Rochester Ct. I-75, exit 67 (Rochester Rd), 0.3 mi sw, then just w. Int corridors. Pets: $30 one-time fee/room. Service with restrictions.
[ASK] 🔲 ⊠ 🔲 🔲 🔲 🔲

🔷🔷 Red Roof Inn-Troy #7021 [M]
(248) 689-4391. $63-$88. 2350 Rochester Ct. I-75, exit 67 (Rochester Rd), 0.3 mi sw. Ext corridors. Pets: Medium, other species. Service with restrictions, supervision.
⊠ 🔲 🔲 🔲 🔲

🔷🔷🔷 Residence Inn by Marriott [SH]
(248) 689-6856. $89-$169. 2600 Livernois Rd. I-75, exit 69 (Big Beaver Rd), 0.5 mi e to Livernois Rd, then 0.5 mi s. Ext corridors. Pets: Accepted.
[ASK] 🔲 ⊠ 🔲 🔲 🔲 🔲 🔲 ⊠

UTICA

🔷 🔷🔷🔷 La Quinta Inn & Suites Detroit-Utica [SH]
(586) 731-4700. $99-$129. 45311 Park Ave. Jct Van Dyke Ave (SR 53) and Hall Rd (SR 59), just n. Int corridors. Pets: Medium. Service with restrictions.
[SAVE] ⊠ 🔲 🔲 🔲 🔲 🔲

🔷 🔷🔷🔷 Staybridge Suites-Utica [SH]
(586) 323-0101. $134-$154. 46155 Utica Park Blvd. Jct Van Dyke Ave (SR 53) and Hall Rd (SR 59), just n. Int corridors. Pets: Accepted.
[SAVE] 🔲 ⊠ 🔲 🔲 🔲 🔲 🔲 🔲

WARREN

🔷🔷 Comfort Inn [SH]
(586) 268-9020. $85-$160. 7001 Convention Blvd. I-696, exit 23 (Van Dyke Ave), 2.8 mi n. Int corridors. Pets: Accepted.
[ASK] 🔲 ⊠ 🔲 🔲 🔲

🔷🔷 Extended Stay Deluxe [SH]
(586) 558-5554. Call for rates. 30125 N Civic Center Blvd. I-696, exit 23 (Van Dyke Ave), 1.5 mi n, then just e. Int corridors. Pets: Accepted.
⊠ 🔲 🔲 🔲

🔷 🔷🔷🔷 Hawthorn Suites Ltd [SH]
(586) 264-8800. $89-$94. 7601 Chicago Rd. I-696, exit 23 (Van Dyke Ave), 1.8 mi n. Int corridors. Pets: Accepted.
[SAVE] 🔲 ⊠ 🔲 🔲 🔲 🔲 🔲

🔷 🔷🔷 🔷🔷 La Quinta Inn & Suites Detroit-Warren Tech Center [SH]
(586) 574-0550. $79-$99. 30900 Van Dyke Ave. I-696, exit 23 (Van Dyke Ave), 2 mi n on SR 53. Int corridors. Pets: Medium. Service with restrictions.
[SAVE] ⊠ 🔲 🔲 🔲

🔷🔷 🔷🔷 Red Roof Inn-Warren #7070 [M]
(586) 573-4300. $61-$83. 26300 Dequindre Rd. I-696, exit 20 (Dequindre Rd), just ne. Ext corridors. Pets: Medium, other species. Service with restrictions, supervision.
⊠ 🔲 🔲 🔲

END METROPOLITAN AREA

DE WITT

🔷 🔷🔷 Sleep Inn [SH]
(517) 669-8823. $85-$109. 1101 Commerce Park Dr. I-69, exit 87 (Business Rt US 127), 0.8 mi n. Int corridors. Pets: Accepted.
[SAVE] 🔲 ⊠ 🔲 🔲 🔲 🔲

DOUGLAS

🔷🔷 🔷🔷 AmericInn of Saugatuck/Douglas [SH] 🐾
(269) 857-8581. $63-$254. 2905 Blue Star Hwy. I-196, exit 36, 0.3 mi n. Int corridors. Pets: Dogs only. $20 daily fee/room. Designated rooms, service with restrictions, supervision.
[ASK] ⊠ 🔲 🔲 🔲 🔲 🔲

DOWAGIAC

🔷 🔷🔷 AmeriHost Inn & Suites-Dowagiac [SH]
(269) 782-4270. $69-$79. 29291 Amerihost Dr. 0.4 mi s of jct SR 51 and 62. Int corridors. Pets: Medium. $25 deposit/room. Designated rooms, service with restrictions, crate.
[SAVE] 🔲 ⊠ 🔲 🔲 🔲 🔲

EAST LANSING

🔷 🔷🔷🔷 Candlewood Suites [SH] 🐾
(517) 351-8181. $85-$149. 3545 Forest Rd. I-496, exit 11 (Jolly Rd), just e to Collins Rd, 0.3 mi n, then just e. Int corridors. Pets: Medium. $75 one-time fee/room. Service with restrictions, supervision.
[SAVE] 🔲 ⊠ 🔲 🔲 🔲 🔲 🔲

Residence Inn by Marriott SH
(517) 332-7711. **$89-$159.** 1600 E Grand River Ave. US 127, exit Grand River Ave, 2.6 mi se on SR 43. Ext corridors. **Pets:** Accepted.

TownePlace Suites SH ✿
(517) 203-1000. **$89-$189.** 2855 Hannah Blvd. I-96, exit 110 (Okemos Rd), just n, 0.5 mi w on Jolly Rd, then 0.4 mi n on Hagedorn Rd. Int corridors. **Pets:** $75 one-time fee/room.

ESCANABA

Hiawatha Motel M
(906) 786-1341. **$50-$60.** 2400 Ludington St. 0.5 mi w on US 2/41. Ext corridors. **Pets:** Accepted.

FENTON

Holiday Inn Express Hotel & Suites SH
(810) 714-7171. **$89-$159.** 17800 Silver Pkwy. US 23, exit 78 (Owen Rd), just w, then 0.4 mi n. Int corridors. **Pets:** Medium. Service with restrictions, supervision.

FLINT

Baymont Inn & Suites-Flint SH
(810) 732-2300. **$60-$99.** 4160 Pier North Blvd. I-75, exit 122 (Pierson Rd), just w. Int corridors. **Pets:** Accepted.

Holiday Inn Express SH
(810) 238-7744. **$80-$169.** 1150 Robert T Longway Blvd. I-475, exit 8A (Robert T Longway Blvd), just w. Int corridors. **Pets:** Accepted.

Red Roof Inn-Flint #7004 M
(810) 733-1660. **$48-$71.** G-3219 Miller Rd. I-75, exit 117B (Miller Rd), just w. Ext corridors. **Pets:** Medium, other species. Service with restrictions, supervision.

Residence Inn by Marriott SH
(810) 424-7000. **$145-$165.** 2202 W Hill Rd. US 23, exit 90 (Hill Rd), just e. Int corridors. **Pets:** Accepted.

FRANKENMUTH

Drury Inn & Suites-Frankenmuth SH
(989) 652-2800. **$92-$147.** 260 S Main St. On SR 83; downtown. Int corridors. **Pets:** Large, other species. Service with restrictions, supervision.

GAYLORD

Best Western Alpine Lodge SH ✿
(989) 732-2431. **$69-$109.** 833 W Main St. I-75, exit 282, 0.3 mi e on SR 32. Ext/int corridors. **Pets:** Medium, dogs only. Service with restrictions, supervision.

Quality Inn SH ✿
(989) 732-7541. **$60-$110.** 137 West St. I-75, exit 282, 0.3 mi e on SR 32. Int corridors. **Pets:** Other species. $10 daily fee/room. Designated rooms, service with restrictions, supervision.

Royal Crest Lodge of Gaylord SH
(989) 732-6451. **$44-$89.** 803 S Otsego Ave. I-75, exit 279, 2.3 mi ne on I-75 business loop. Int corridors. **Pets:** Accepted.

Timberly Motel M
(989) 732-5166. **$48-$84, 5 day notice.** 881 S Otsego Ave. I-75, exit 279, 2.5 mi n on I-75 business loop (Old US 27). Ext corridors. **Pets:** Other species. $6 one-time fee/pet. Service with restrictions, supervision.

GRAND MARAIS

Voyageur's Motel M
(906) 494-2389. **$75.** 21914 E Wilson St. 0.5 mi e of SR 77. Ext corridors. **Pets:** Dogs only. $20 daily fee/pet. Designated rooms, service with restrictions, supervision.

GRAND RAPIDS

Homewood Suites by Hilton SH
(616) 285-7100. **$130-$150.** 3920 Stahl Dr SE. I-96, exit 43A (28th St SW), 1.5 mi w to E Paris Ave, then just n. Int corridors. **Pets:** Accepted.

Radisson Hotel Grand Rapids Riverfront LH
(616) 363-9001. **$99-$109.** 270 Ann St NW. US 131, exit 88, 1.8 mi n. Int corridors. **Pets:** Medium. $20 one-time fee/room. Service with restrictions, crate.

GRANDVILLE

Residence Inn by Marriott Grand Rapids West SH
(616) 538-1100. **$99-$139.** 3451 Rivertown Point Ct SW. I-196, exit 67, 1.7 mi e. Int corridors. **Pets:** Small. $75 one-time fee/room. Service with restrictions.

GRAYLING

Holiday Inn SH
(989) 348-7611. **$79-$129.** 2650 S Business Loop. I-75 business loop, 0.8 mi s. Ext/int corridors. **Pets:** Accepted.

North Country Lodge M
(989) 348-8471. **$58-$170.** 617 N I-75 Business Loop. 1 mi n. Ext corridors. **Pets:** Accepted.

Super 8 Motel SH
(989) 348-8888. **$57-$99.** 5828 Nelson A Miles Pkwy. I-75, exit 251, just w. Int corridors. **Pets:** Accepted.

HANCOCK

Best Western Copper Crown Motel SH
(906) 482-6111. **$65-$100.** 235 Hancock Ave. On US 41 S; downtown. Ext/int corridors. **Pets:** Medium. $11 one-time fee/room. Designated rooms, service with restrictions, supervision.

HARRISON

Lakeside Motel & Cottages M ✿
(989) 539-3796. **$58-$99.** 515 E Park St, Business US 127, M-61. US 127, exit US 127 business route/SR 61, 2.2 mi w. Ext corridors. **Pets:** Other species. Service with restrictions, crate.

HART

Budget Host Motel SH
(231) 873-1855. **$49-$119.** 4143 Polk Rd. US 31, exit Mears/Hart, just e on US 31 business route. Int corridors. **Pets:** Small. $25 one-time fee/pet. Designated rooms, service with restrictions, supervision.

HOLLAND

▼▼ /▼▼ Microtel Inn & Suites Ⓜ
(616) 392-3235. **$49-$89.** 643 Hastings Ave. Just w of US 31 and 32nd
St. Int corridors. **Pets:** Accepted.
🅰🆂🅺 🆂🅳 ⊠ 🔥ᴹ 🄴 🔒 🖵

▼▼/▼▼ Residence Inn by Marriott 🆂🅷
(616) 393-6900. **$113-$149.** 631 Southpoint Ridge Rd. I-196, exit 49,
0.7 mi n on SR 40. Int corridors. **Pets:** Other species. $100 one-time
fee/room. Service with restrictions, crate.
🅰🆂🅺 ⊠ 🔥ᴹ 🄴 🔒 🖵 ⚓ ⊠

HOUGHTON

⒜⒜⒜ ▼▼/▼▼ Best Western-Franklin Square Inn 🆂🅷
(906) 487-1700. **$91-$119.** 820 Shelden Ave. On US 41; downtown. Int
corridors. **Pets:** $10 daily fee/room. Designated rooms, supervision.
🆂🄰🆅🄴 🆂🅳 ⊠ 🔒 🖵 🍴 ⚓ ⊠

▼▼/▼▼ Country Inn & Suites 🆂🅷
(906) 487-6700. **$89-$169.** 919 Razorback Dr. 1.3 mi w on SR 26. Int
corridors. **Pets:** Accepted.
🅰🆂🅺 🆂🅳 ⊠ 🔥ᴹ 🄴 🔒 🖵 ⚓ ⊠

HOUGHTON LAKE

▼▼/▼▼ Holiday Inn Express 🆂🅷
(989) 422-7829. **$49-$149.** 200 Cloverleaf Ln. Jct US 127 and SR 55,
just e. Int corridors. **Pets:** Accepted.
🅰🆂🅺 🆂🅳 ⊠ 🄴 🔒 ⚓

▼▼ /▼▼ Super 8 Motel 🆂🅷
(989) 422-3119. **$59-$109.** 9580 W Lake City Rd. Jct US 127 and SR
55. Int corridors. **Pets:** $10 daily fee/pet. No service, supervision.
🅰🆂🅺 🆂🅳 ⊠ 🔒 ⚓ ⊠

HOWELL

▼▼ /▼▼ Best Western Howell Ⓜ
(517) 548-2900. **$85-$145.** 1500 Pinckney Rd. I-96, exit 137 (Pickney
Rd), just s on CR D19. Ext corridors. **Pets:** Small, dogs only. $15 daily
fee/pet. Designated rooms, service with restrictions, supervision.
🅰🆂🅺 🆂🅳 ⊠ 🔒 🖵 ⊠

HUDSONVILLE

⒜⒜⒜ ▼▼ Super 8 Motel 🆂🅷
(616) 896-6710. **$59-$79.** 3005 Corporate Grove Dr. I-196, exit 62
(32nd Ave), just se. Int corridors. **Pets:** Medium, other species. $10
one-time fee/pet. Service with restrictions, supervision.
🆂🄰🆅🄴 🆂🅳 ⊠ 🄴 🔒 🖵 ⚓

IMLAY CITY

⒜⒜⒜ ▼▼/▼▼ Days Inn 🆂🅷
(810) 724-8005. **$69-$89.** 6692 Newark Rd. I-69, exit 168 (SR 53/Van
Dyke Rd), just n, then just w. Int corridors. **Pets:** Accepted.
🆂🄰🆅🄴 🆂🅳 ⊠ 🗎 🔒 🖵 ⚓

▼▼ /▼▼ Super 8 Motel-Imlay City 🆂🅷
(810) 724-8700. **$52-$99, 7 day notice.** 6951 Newark Rd. I-69, exit
168 (SR 53/Van Dyke Rd), just n, then just e. Int corridors. **Pets:** $10
one-time fee/room. Service with restrictions, supervision.
🅰🆂🅺 🆂🅳 ⊠ 🔒

INDIAN RIVER

⒜⒜⒜ ▼▼ Nor Gate Motel Ⓜ
(231) 238-7788. **$44-$50, 3 day notice.** 4846 S Straits Hwy. I-75, exit
310, 0.3 mi w, then 2 mi s on Old US 27. Ext corridors. **Pets:** Small,
dogs only. $500 one-time fee/pet. Designated rooms, service with restric-
tions, crate.
🆂🄰🆅🄴 🆂🅳 ⊠ 🔒 🖵 ⊠

IONIA

⒜⒜⒜ ▼▼/▼▼ Super 8 Motel 🆂🅷
(616) 527-2828. **$62-$110.** 7245 S State Rd. I-96, exit 67 (SR 66). Int
corridors. **Pets:** Accepted.
🆂🄰🆅🄴 🆂🅳 ⊠ 🔥ᴹ 🗎 🄴 🔒 🖵

IRON MOUNTAIN

⒜⒜⒜ ▼▼ Budget Host Inn Ⓜ ✿
(906) 774-6797. **$53-$58.** 1663 N Stephenson Ave. 1.5 mi nw on US 2
and 141. Ext corridors. **Pets:** Medium. $5 one-time fee/pet. Designated
rooms, service with restrictions, supervision.
🆂🄰🆅🄴 🆂🅳 ⊠ 🔒

IRONWOOD

⒜⒜⒜ ▼▼/▼▼ AmericInn of Ironwood 🆂🅷
(906) 932-7200. **$69-$129, 3 day notice.** 1117 E Cloverland Dr. 0.8 mi
e on US 2. Int corridors. **Pets:** Accepted.
🆂🄰🆅🄴 🆂🅳 ⊠ 🔥ᴹ 🄴 🔒 🖵 ⚓ ⊠

⒜⒜⒜ ▼▼ Crestview Motel Ⓜ
(906) 932-4845. **$55-$75.** 424 W Cloverland Dr. 0.4 mi w on US 2. Ext
corridors. **Pets:** Medium. $10 one-time fee/room. No service, supervision.
🆂🄰🆅🄴 🆂🅳 ⊠ 🔒 🖵

▼▼ Super 8 Motel 🆂🅷
(906) 932-3395. **$65-$95.** 160 E Cloverland Dr. Jct US 2 and 2 business route. Int corridors. **Pets:** Other species. $10 one-time fee/room.
Service with restrictions, supervision.
🅰🆂🅺 🆂🅳 ⊠ 🔒 🖵 ⊠

ISHPEMING

⒜⒜⒜ ▼▼/▼▼ Best Western Country Inn 🆂🅷
(906) 485-6345. **$83-$123.** 850 US 41 W. On US 41, just n of town. Int
corridors. **Pets:** Designated rooms, service with restrictions, supervision.
🆂🄰🆅🄴 🆂🅳 ⊠ 🖵 🍴 ⚓ ⊠

JACKSON

⒜⒜⒜ ▼▼/▼▼ Baymont Inn-Jackson 🆂🅷
(517) 789-6000. **$55-$129, 7 day notice.** 2035 Service Dr. I-94, exit
138 (US 127), just nw. Int corridors. **Pets:** Accepted.
🆂🄰🆅🄴 🆂🅳 ⊠ 🗎 🔒 🖵

▼▼/▼▼ Holiday Inn 🆂🅷
(517) 783-2681. **$79-$300.** 2000 Holiday Inn Dr. I-94, exit 138 (US
127), just n to Springport Rd, then just w. Ext/int corridors.
Pets: Accepted.
🅰🆂🅺 🆂🅳 ⊠ 🗎 🄴 🔒 🖵 🍴 ⚓ ⊠

▼▼ Motel 6-1088 Ⓜ
(517) 789-7186. **$42-$55.** 830 Royal Dr. I-94, exit 138 (US 127), just
se. Ext corridors. **Pets:** Medium, other species. Service with restrictions,
supervision.
🆂🅳 ⊠ 🗎 🄴 ⚓

KALAMAZOO

⒜⒜⒜ ▼▼/▼▼ Baymont Inn & Suites-Kalamazoo 🆂🅷
(269) 372-7999. **$59-$149.** 2203 S 11th St. US 131, exit 36B (Stadium
Dr), just w. Int corridors. **Pets:** Accepted.
🆂🄰🆅🄴 🆂🅳 ⊠ 🔒 🖵

⒜⒜⒜ ▼▼/▼▼/▼▼ Best Western Hospitality Inn 🆂🅷
(269) 381-1900. **$79-$149.** 3640 E Cork St. I-94, exit 80 (Sprinkle Rd),
just nw. Int corridors. **Pets:** $15 daily fee/pet. Designated rooms, service
with restrictions, crate.
🆂🄰🆅🄴 ⊠ 🖵 ⚓ ⊠

AAA ▼▼▼ Comfort Inn SH
(269) 381-7000. **$72-$100.** 3820 Sprinkle Rd. I-94, exit 80 (Sprinkle Rd), 0.3 mi s. Int corridors. **Pets:** $50 one-time fee/room. Service with restrictions, crate.

AAA ▼▼▼ Holiday Inn-West SH ❀
(269) 375-6000. **$99-$109.** 2747 S 11th St. US 131, exit 36B (Stadium Dr), just w. Int corridors. **Pets:** Medium. $25 one-time fee/room. Service with restrictions, supervision.

AAA ▼ Knights Inn M
(269) 381-5000. **$56-$100, 7 day notice.** 1211 S Westnedge Ave. I-94, exit 76B, 3 mi n, w on Park Pl, then just s. Ext/int corridors. **Pets:** Medium, other species. $25 daily fee/room. Designated rooms, no service, supervision.

▼▼ Red Roof Inn-East #7003 M
(269) 382-6350. **$55-$88.** 3701 E Cork St. I-94, exit 80 (Sprinkle Rd), just n, then just w. Ext corridors. **Pets:** Medium, other species. Service with restrictions, supervision.

▼▼ Red Roof Inn-West #7025 SH
(269) 375-7400. **$53-$74.** 5425 W Michigan Ave. US 131, exit 36B (Stadium Dr), just nw. Ext corridors. **Pets:** Medium, other species. Service with restrictions, supervision.

KENTWOOD

▼▼ Comfort Inn SH
(616) 957-2080. **$59-$139.** 4155 28th St SE. I-96, exit 43A, 1.5 mi w on SR 11. Int corridors. **Pets:** Large, other species. Service with restrictions, supervision.

▼▼ Residence Inn by Marriott East SH
(616) 957-8111. **$79-$169.** 2701 E Beltline Ave. Jct SR 11 and E Beltline Ave (SR 37). Ext corridors. **Pets:** Other species. $75 one-time fee/room. Service with restrictions.

▼▼▼ Staybridge Suites by Holiday Inn SH
(616) 464-3200. **$112-$269.** 3000 Lake Eastbrook Blvd SE. I-96, exit 43A, 2 mi w on SR 11, then just s. Int corridors. **Pets:** Accepted.

LAKE CITY

AAA ▼ Northcrest Motel M
(231) 839-2075. **$59-$79, 15 day notice.** 1341 S Lakeshore. 1 mi s on SR 55 and 66. Ext corridors. **Pets:** Small. $10 daily fee/pet. Designated rooms, service with restrictions, supervision.

LAKESIDE

▼▼▼ White Rabbit Inn BB
(269) 469-4620. **$95-$200, 7 day notice.** 14634 Red Arrow Hwy. I-94, exit 6 (Union Pier Rd), 1 mi w, then 2 mi n. Ext corridors. **Pets:** Designated rooms.

LANSING

AAA ▼▼▼ Best Western Midway Hotel SH
(517) 627-8471. **$69-$129.** 7711 W Saginaw Hwy. I-96, exit 93B (SR 43/Saginaw Hwy), just e. Int corridors. **Pets:** Accepted.

AAA ▼▼▼ Hampton Inn of Lansing SH ❀
(517) 627-8381. **$71-$99.** 525 N Canal Rd. I-96, exit 93B (SR 43/Saginaw Hwy), just e. Int corridors. **Pets:** Medium, other species. $100 deposit/room. Service with restrictions, crate.

AAA ▼▼▼ Lansing's Quality Suites Hotel SH
(517) 886-0600. **$79-$99.** 901 Delta Commerce Dr. I-96, exit 93B (SR 43/Saginaw Hwy), 0.3 mi e to Bennigan's Restaurant, then just n. Int corridors. **Pets:** Other species. $25 one-time fee/room. Service with restrictions, crate.

▼ Motel 6 Lansing West #1089 M
(517) 321-1444. **$45-$57.** 7326 W Saginaw Hwy. I-96, exit 93B (SR 43/Saginaw Hwy), just e. Ext corridors. **Pets:** Medium, other species. Service with restrictions, supervision.

▼▼ Red Roof Inn-East #7029 M
(517) 332-2575. **$61-$77.** 3615 Dunckel Rd. Just e of I-496 and US 127, exit 11 (Jolly Rd). Ext corridors. **Pets:** Medium, other species. Service with restrictions, supervision.

▼▼ Red Roof Inn-West #7020 SH
(517) 321-7246. **$53-$74.** 7412 W Saginaw Hwy. I-96, exit 93B (SR 43/Saginaw Hwy), just e. Ext corridors. **Pets:** Medium, other species. Service with restrictions, supervision.

▼▼▼ Residence Inn by Marriott West SH
(517) 886-5030. **$120-$140.** 922 Delta Commerce Dr. I-96, exit 93B (SR 43/Saginaw Hwy), 0.4 mi e; behind Bennigans. Int corridors. **Pets:** Accepted.

▼▼▼ Sheraton Lansing Hotel SH ❀
(517) 323-7100. **$99-$275.** 925 S Creyts Rd. I-496, exit 1 (Creyts Rd), just n. Int corridors. **Pets:** Medium. $30 one-time fee/pet. Service with restrictions, supervision.

LUDINGTON

AAA ▼▼▼ Holiday Inn Express SH ❀
(231) 845-7004. **$81-$180.** 5323 W US 10. Jct US 31, 1.3 mi w on US 10. Int corridors. **Pets:** Other species. $10 daily fee/pet. Designated rooms, service with restrictions, supervision.

▼▼ Super 8 Motel SH
(231) 843-2140. **$59-$380.** 5005 W US 10. Jct US 31, 1 mi w. Int corridors. **Pets:** Large, other species. $10 one-time fee/pet. Designated rooms, service with restrictions, supervision.

MACKINAW CITY

AAA ▼ Anchor Budget Inns M
(231) 436-5553. **$29-$109, 3 day notice.** 138 US 31. I-75, exit 338 southbound, 0.3 mi e; exit 337 northbound, just ne. Ext/int corridors. **Pets:** Accepted.

AAA ▼▼▼ Baymont Inn & Suites-Mackinaw City SH
(231) 436-7737. **$69-$149.** 109 S Nicolet St. I-75, exit 338 southbound, just n. Int corridors. **Pets:** Accepted.

AAA ▼ Beachcomber Motel on the Water M ❀
(231) 436-8451. **$29-$109, 3 day notice.** 1011 S Huron Ave. 1 mi s on US 23. Ext corridors. **Pets:** Small, dogs only. $5 daily fee/pet. Designated rooms, service with restrictions, supervision.

The Beach House 🄲🄰
(231) 436-5353. **$44-$170, 14 day notice.** 11490 W US 23. 1.3 mi s. Ext corridors. **Pets:** Dogs only. $15 one-time fee/pet. Designated rooms, service with restrictions.
〔SAVE〕🛇 ⊗ 🖨

Budget Inns-Starlite 🄼 ❀
(231) 436-5959. **$29-$135, 3 day notice.** 116 Old US 31. I-75, exit 338 southbound, 0.3 mi e; exit 337 northbound, just ne. Ext corridors. **Pets:** Medium, dogs only. $15 daily fee/pet. Designated rooms, service with restrictions, supervision.
〔SAVE〕🛇 ⊗ 🖨 ⊗ ⊗

Capri Motel 🄼
(231) 436-5498. **$39-$89.** 801 S Nicolet St. I-75, exit 338 southbound, just s. Ext corridors. **Pets:** Large. $5 daily fee/room. Designated rooms, service with restrictions, supervision.
〔SAVE〕🛇 ⊗ 🖨 🖨 ⊗ ⊗

Days Inn & Suites "Bridgeview Lodge" 🄼
(231) 436-8961. **$39-$269.** 206 N Nicolet St. I-75, exit 339; at bridge. Ext/int corridors. **Pets:** Dogs only. Designated rooms, service with restrictions, supervision.
〔SAVE〕🛇 ⊗ 🖨 🖨 ⊗

Days Inn Lakeview 🄼
(231) 436-5557. **$49-$199.** 825 S Huron Ave. I-75, exit 337 northbound, 0.5 mi n to US 23, then 0.3 mi e; exit 338 southbound, 0.8 mi se on US 23. Ext corridors. **Pets:** Medium, dogs only. $50 deposit/pet. Designated rooms, service with restrictions, supervision.
〔SAVE〕🛇 ⊗ 🖨 🖨 ⊗ ⊗

Holiday Inn Express at the Bridge 🆂🅷
(231) 436-7100. **$49-$270.** 364 Louvingny. I-75, exit 339. Int corridors. **Pets:** Medium, dogs only. $50 deposit/room. Designated rooms, service with restrictions, supervision.
〔SAVE〕🛇 ⊗ 🖨 🖨 🖨 ⊗ ⊗

Super 8 Motel Bridgeview 🆂🅷
(231) 436-5252. **$38-$198.** 601 N Huron Ave. I-75, exit 339 northbound, just n, then just e. Ext/int corridors. **Pets:** Accepted.
〔SAVE〕🛇 ⊗ ⊗ 🖨 🖨 ⊗ ⊗

MANISTIQUE

Beachcomber Motel 🄼 ❀
(906) 341-2567. **$55-$85.** 751 E Lakeshore Dr. 1 mi e on US 2. Ext corridors. **Pets:** Other species. $10 deposit/room. Designated rooms, service with restrictions, supervision.
〔SAVE〕🛇 ⊗ 🖨

Comfort Inn 🆂🅷
(906) 341-6981. **$70-$179.** 617 E Lakeshore Dr. 0.5 mi e on US 2. Int corridors. **Pets:** Other species. $10 daily fee/pet. Service with restrictions, supervision.
〔ASK〕🛇 ⊗ 🖨 🖨 ⊗

Econo Lodge Lakeshore 🄼
(906) 341-6014. **$60-$120.** 1101 E Lakeshore Dr. 1.5 mi e on US 2. Ext/int corridors. **Pets:** Accepted.
〔ASK〕🛇 ⊗ ⊗ 🖨 🖨 ⊗

MARQUETTE

Birchmont Motel 🄼
(906) 228-7538. **$46-$78, 10 day notice.** 2090 US 41 S. On US 41 and SR 28, 4.3 mi s. Ext corridors. **Pets:** Other species. $8 daily fee/pet. Service with restrictions, supervision.
〔SAVE〕⊗ 🖨 ⊗

Holiday Inn 🆂🅷
(906) 225-1351. **$99-$125.** 1951 US 41 W. On US 41 and SR 28, 1.8 mi w. Int corridors. **Pets:** Dogs only. $25 daily fee/room. Designated rooms, service with restrictions, crate.
〔ASK〕🛇 ⊗ 🖨M ⊗ 🖨 🖨 ⊗ ⊗ ⊗

MARSHALL

Arbor Inn of Historic Marshall 🄼 ❀
(269) 781-7772. **$45-$60.** 15435 W Michigan Ave. I-69, exit 36 (Michigan Ave), just w. Ext corridors. **Pets:** $5 daily fee/pet. Service with restrictions.
〔SAVE〕🛇 ⊗ 🖨 ⊗

MENOMINEE

Econo Lodge On The Bay 🆂🅷 ❀
(906) 863-4431. **$65-$105.** 2516 10th St. 1 mi n on US 41. Int corridors. **Pets:** Medium, other species. $25 daily fee/pet. Designated rooms, crate.
〔SAVE〕🛇 ⊗ 🖨 🖨

MIDLAND

Best Western Valley Plaza Resort 🆂🅷
(989) 496-2700. **$81-$90.** 5221 Bay City Rd. US 10, exit Midland/Bay City Rd. Int corridors. **Pets:** Small. Designated rooms, service with restrictions, supervision.
〔SAVE〕🛇 ⊗ 🖨 🖨 ⓘⓘ ⊗ ⊗

Fairview Inn & Suites 🆂🅷
(989) 631-0070. **$79-$99.** 2200 W Wackerly St. Jct US 10 and Eastman Rd. Int corridors. **Pets:** Accepted.
〔ASK〕🛇 ⊗ 🖨 🖨 ⊗

Holiday Inn 🆂🅷
(989) 631-4220. **$90-$194.** 1500 W Wackerly St. Jct US 10 and Eastman Rd. Ext/int corridors. **Pets:** Accepted.
〔ASK〕🛇 ⊗ 🖨 🖨 ⓘⓘ ⊗ ⊗

MIO

Mio Motel 🄼
(989) 826-3248. **$50-$70, 3 day notice.** 415 N Morenci St. Just n on SR 33 and 72. Ext corridors. **Pets:** Accepted.
⊗ 🖨

MONROE

Americas Best Value Inn & Suites 🄼 ❀
(734) 289-1080. **$40-$90.** 1885 Welcome Way. I-75, exit 15 (SR 50), just e. Ext corridors. **Pets:** Other species. $25 one-time fee/pet. Service with restrictions, supervision.
〔SAVE〕🛇 ⊗ 🖨

Best Western Prestige Inn 🄼
(734) 289-2330. **$60-$80.** 1900 Welcome Way. I-75, exit 15 (SR 50), just e. Ext corridors. **Pets:** $10 daily fee/pet. Service with restrictions, supervision.
〔SAVE〕🛇 ⊗ ⊗ ⊗ 🖨 🖨 ⊗

MOUNT PLEASANT

Holiday Inn 🆂🅷
(989) 772-2905. **$89-$199.** 5665 E Pickard Ave. Jct US 127 and SR 20 E. Ext/int corridors. **Pets:** Accepted.
〔ASK〕🛇 ⊗ 🖨M ⊗ 🖨 🖨 ⓘⓘ ⊗ ⊗

MUNISING

Alger Falls Motel 🄼
(906) 387-3536. **$40-$68.** E9427 E Hwy M-28. 2 mi e on SR 28 and 94. Ext corridors. **Pets:** Small, dogs only. Designated rooms, supervision.
〔SAVE〕🛇 ⊗ 🖨

AmericInn of Munising 🆂🅷
(906) 387-2000. **$81-$180.** E 9926 Hwy M-28 E. On SR 28, 2.7 mi e. Int corridors. **Pets:** Dogs only. $20 one-time fee/room. Designated rooms, service with restrictions, supervision.
〔ASK〕🛇 ⊗ 🖨M ⊗ 🖨 🖨 ⊗ ⊗

AAA ◈ Sunset Motel on the Bay M
(906) 387-4574. **$50-$85.** 1315 Bay St. 1 mi e on E Munising Ave (CR H58). Ext corridors. **Pets:** Dogs only. $10 one-time fee/room. Designated rooms, service with restrictions, supervision.
(SAVE) ⊠ 🗋 ▣ 🅇

AAA ◈ Terrace Motel M ☙
(906) 387-2735. **$40-$55.** 420 Prospect. 0.5 mi e, just off SR 28. Ext corridors. **Pets:** Medium, other species. $3 daily fee/pet. Designated rooms, service with restrictions, supervision.
(SAVE) ⊠ 🅇 🅐 🅩

NEW BUFFALO

AAA ◈◈◈ Best Western Plaza Hotel SH
(269) 469-4193. **$80-$200, 30 day notice.** 18800 La Porte Rd. I-94, exit 1 (La Porte Rd), just w. Int corridors. **Pets:** Accepted.
(SAVE) ⊠ 🅖🅜 🅒 🗋 ▣ 🏊

◈◈◈ Holiday Inn Express Hotel & Suites SH
(269) 469-1400. **$79-$189.** 11500 Holiday Dr. I-94, exit 1 (La Porte Rd), just w. Int corridors. **Pets:** Accepted.
(ASK) 🅢 ⊠ 🅖🅜 🅒 🗋 ▣ 🏊 🅇

NORWAY

◈◈◈ AmericInn of Norway SH ☙
(906) 563-7500. **$82-$84.** W 6002 US Hwy 2. 0.7 mi w. Int corridors. **Pets:** Medium. $10 one-time fee/room. Designated rooms, service with restrictions, supervision.
(ASK) ⊠ 🗋 ▣ 🏊 🅇

OKEMOS

◈◈◈ Holiday Inn Express & Suites-E Lansing/Okemos SH
(517) 349-8700. **$94-$199.** 2209 University Park. I-96, exit 110 (Okemos Rd), 0.3 mi n, then just e. Int corridors. **Pets:** Large, dogs only. $10 daily fee/pet. Designated rooms, service with restrictions, supervision.
(ASK) 🅢 ⊠ 🗋 ▣ 🏊 🅇

PAW PAW

◈◈ Comfort Inn & Suites SH
(269) 655-0303. **$59-$139.** 153 Ampey Rd. I-94, exit 60 (SR 40), just nw. Int corridors. **Pets:** Service with restrictions, crate.
(ASK) 🅢 ⊠ 🅖🅜 🅐 🅒 🗋 ▣ 🏊

AAA ◈◈ Super 8 Motel SH
(269) 657-1111. **$55-$169.** 111 Ampey Rd. I-94, exit 60 (SR 40). Int corridors. **Pets:** Other species. $15 one-time fee/room. Service with restrictions, supervision.
(SAVE) 🅢 ⊠ 🅖🅜 🅒 🗋 ▣ 🏊

PELLSTON

AAA ◈◈ Holiday Inn Express Pellston SH
(231) 539-7000. **$59-$199.** 1600 US 31 N. 1.2 mi n. Int corridors. **Pets:** $20 one-time fee/pet. Service with restrictions, supervision.
(SAVE) 🅢 ⊠ 🅒 🗋 ▣ 🏊 🅇

PETOSKEY

AAA ◈ Days Inn Petoskey M
(231) 348-3900. **$49-$135.** 1420 US 131 S. 1.3 mi s. Ext corridors. **Pets:** Other species. $10 daily fee/pet. Designated rooms, service with restrictions.
(SAVE) 🅢 ⊠ 🗋 ▣ 🍴

PLAINWELL

AAA ◈◈◈◈ Comfort Inn SH
(269) 685-9891. **$85-$200.** 622 Allegan St. US 131, exit 49A, just e. Int corridors. **Pets:** $10 daily fee/pet. Service with restrictions, supervision.
(SAVE) 🅢 ⊠ 🗋 ▣ 🏊

PORT HURON

AAA ◈ AmeriHost Inn-Port Huron SH
(810) 364-8000. **$69-$99.** 1611 Range Rd. I-94, exit 269 (Range Rd), just w. Int corridors. **Pets:** Accepted.
(SAVE) 🅢 ⊠ 🅒 🗋 ▣ 🏊 🅇

◈◈◈ Hampton Inn SH
(810) 966-9000. **$79-$149.** 1655 Yeager St. I-94, exit 274 (Water St), just s, then just w. Int corridors. **Pets:** Accepted.
(ASK) 🅢 ⊠ 🅒 🗋 ▣ 🏊

PORTLAND

AAA ◈◈◈ Best Western American Heritage Inn SH
(517) 647-2200. **$74-$84.** 1681 Grand River Ave. I-96, exit 77, just n. Int corridors. **Pets:** Accepted.
(SAVE) 🅢 ⊠ 🅖🅜 🅒 🗋 ▣ 🏊

SAGINAW

◈◈ Best Western–Saginaw SH
(989) 755-0461. **$59-$99.** 1408 S Outer Dr. I-75, exit 149B (SR 46). Int corridors. **Pets:** Large, other species. $25 one-time fee/room. Service with restrictions, supervision.
(ASK) 🅢 ⊠ 🗋 ▣ 🍴 🏊 🅇

◈◈ Four Points by Sheraton Saginaw SH
(989) 790-5050. **$89-$109.** 4960 Towne Centre Rd. I-675, exit 6, just w on Tittabawassee Rd. Int corridors. **Pets:** Accepted.
(ASK) 🅢 ⊠ 🗋 ▣ 🍴 🏊 🅇

◈ Motel 6 Saginaw #1496 M
(989) 754-8414. **$42-$55.** 966 S Outer Dr. I-75, exit 149B (SR 46). Ext corridors. **Pets:** Medium, other species. Service with restrictions, supervision.
🅢 ⊠ 🗋

AAA ◈◈ Ramada Inn & Suites SH
(989) 793-7900. **$59-$139.** 3325 Davenport Ave. I-675, exit 3, 2 mi w on SR 58. Int corridors. **Pets:** Medium, other species. Designated rooms, service with restrictions.
(SAVE) 🅢 ⊠ 🅒 🗋 ▣ 🍴

◈ Super 8 Motel SH
(989) 791-3003. **$59-$70.** 4848 Towne Centre Rd. I-675, exit 6, 0.3 mi w, then just s. Int corridors. **Pets:** Accepted.
(ASK) 🅢 ⊠ 🗋

ST. IGNACE

AAA ◈◈ Budget Host Inn SH
(906) 643-9666. **$61-$149.** 700 N State St. 1.8 mi n of bridge tollgate on I-75 business route. Ext/int corridors. **Pets:** Other species. $40 deposit/room. Service with restrictions, supervision.
(SAVE) 🅢 ⊠ 🗋 🏊 🅇

SAULT STE. MARIE

AAA ◈◈ Best Western Sault Ste Marie SH
(906) 632-2170. **$60-$110.** 4335 I-75 business loop. I-75, exit 392, 0.3 mi ne. Int corridors. **Pets:** Accepted.
(SAVE) 🅢 ⊠ 🅒 🗋 ▣ 🏊 🅇

AAA ◈ Budget Host Crestview Inn M
(906) 635-5213. **$59-$89.** 1200 Ashmun St. I-75, exit 392, 2.8 mi ne on I-75 business loop. Ext corridors. **Pets:** Other species. Designated rooms, service with restrictions, supervision.
(SAVE) 🅢 ⊠ 🗋

AAA ◈◈ Comfort Inn SH
(906) 635-1118. **$59-$199.** 4404 I-75 Business Spur. I-75, exit 392, at business loop. Int corridors. **Pets:** Accepted.
(SAVE) 🅢 ⊠ 🅒 🗋 ▣ 🏊 🅇

AAA WW Days Inn SH
(906) 635-5200. **$89-$189.** 3651 I-75 Business Spur. I-75, exit 392, 0.8 mi ne on I-75 business loop. Int corridors. **Pets:** Large. Designated rooms, service with restrictions, supervision.
[SAVE] [SD] [X] [H] [IP] [🏊] [X]

W Econo Lodge SH
(906) 632-6000. **$49-$99.** 3525 I-75 business spur. I-75, exit 392, 0.7 mi ne. Int corridors. **Pets:** Accepted.
[ASK] [SD] [X] [&M] [🐾] [H] [IP]

AAA WW Holiday Inn Express SH
(906) 632-3999. **$70-$150.** 1171 Riverview Way. I-75, exit 394. Int corridors. **Pets:** Medium, other species. $15 daily fee/room. Designated rooms, service with restrictions, crate.
[SAVE] [SD] [X] [&M] [🐾] [H] [IP] [🏊] [X]

AAA W La France Terrace Motel M
(906) 632-7823. **$42-$75.** 1608 Ashmun St. I-75, exit 392, 2.3 mi ne on I-75 business loop. Ext corridors. **Pets:** Dogs only. Designated rooms, service with restrictions, supervision.
[SAVE] [SD] [X] [H] [🏊]

AAA W Mid-City Motel M
(906) 632-6832. **$44-$60, 5 day notice.** 304 E Portage Ave. Just e of town, on I-75 business loop. Ext corridors. **Pets:** Accepted.
[SAVE] [SD] [X]

W Royal Motel M
(906) 632-6323. **$42-$52.** 1707 Ashmun St. I-75, exit 392, 2 mi ne on I-75 business loop. Ext corridors. **Pets:** Accepted.
[ASK] [SD] [X] [H] [IP]

AAA W Super 8 Motel SH 🐾
(906) 632-8882. **$49-$89.** 3826 I-75 Business Loop. I-75, exit 392, 0.5 mi ne. Int corridors. **Pets:** Other species. Designated rooms, service with restrictions, supervision.
[SAVE] [SD] [X] [🐾] [H]

AAA W TraveLodge Sault Ste Marie M 🐾
(906) 632-4366. **$50-$100.** 4281 I-75 Business Loop. I-75, exit 392, 0.3 mi ne. Ext corridors. **Pets:** $20 one-time fee/room. Designated rooms, service with restrictions, supervision.
[SAVE] [SD] [X] [H] [IP]

SILVER CITY

WW AmericInn Lodge & Suites SH
(906) 885-5311. **$79-$197.** 120 Lincoln Ave. On SR 107, 0.3 mi w of SR 64. Int corridors. **Pets:** Dogs only. $10 daily fee/room. Designated rooms, service with restrictions, supervision.
[ASK] [SD] [X] [🐾] [H] [IP] [TI] [🏊] [X]

W Mountain View Lodges CA
(906) 885-5256. **$119-$180, 30 day notice.** 34042 M-107. Jct SR 107 and 64, 0.8 mi w. Ext corridors. **Pets:** Accepted.
[X] [H] [IP] [🐾]

W Rainbow Lodging M
(906) 885-5348. **$50-$81, 3 day notice.** 32739 W State Hwy M 64. SR 64, just e of jct SR 107. Ext corridors. **Pets:** Accepted.
[X] [H] [IP] [TI] [X]

SOUTH HAVEN

AAA WWW Comfort Suites SH
(269) 639-2014. **$79-$249.** 1755 Phoenix St. I-196, exit 20, 0.5 mi e. Int corridors. **Pets:** Accepted.
[SAVE] [SD] [X] [&M] [🐾] [H] [IP] [🏊]

SPRING LAKE

WW Grand Haven Waterfront Holiday Inn SH 🐾
(616) 846-1000. **$89-$179.** 940 W Savidge St. On SR 104, just e of US 31. Int corridors. **Pets:** Dogs only. $25 daily fee/pet. Designated rooms, service with restrictions, supervision.
[ASK] [SD] [X] [&] [H] [IP] [TI] [🏊] [X]

STEVENSVILLE

AAA WW Candlewood Suites SH
(269) 428-4400. **$100-$200.** 2567 W Marquette Woods Rd. I-94, exit 23 (Red Arrow Hwy), just w. Int corridors. **Pets:** Medium. $75 one-time fee/pet. Designated rooms, service with restrictions, supervision.
[SAVE] [X] [&M] [🐾] [H]

WW Hampton Inn SH
(269) 429-2700. **$76-$129.** 5050 Red Arrow Hwy. I-94, exit 23 (Red Arrow Hwy), just se. Int corridors. **Pets:** Medium. Service with restrictions, supervision.
[ASK] [SD] [X] [&M] [🏊] [&] [H] [IP] [🏊]

AAA WW Park Inn International SH 🐾
(269) 429-3218. **$75-$110.** 4290 Red Arrow Hwy. I-94, exit 23 (Red Arrow Hwy), 0.5 mi n. Ext/int corridors. **Pets:** Other species. Designated rooms, service with restrictions, supervision.
[SAVE] [SD] [X] [&] [H] [IP] [TI] [🏊] [X]

STURGIS

AAA W Americas Best Value Inn M
(269) 651-2361. **$40-$55.** 71381 S Centerville Rd. I-80/90, exit 121 (SR 66), 0.4 mi n. Ext corridors. **Pets:** Very small, dogs only. $5 one-time fee/pet. Service with restrictions, supervision.
[SAVE] [SD] [X] [H] [🏊]

SUTTONS BAY

W Red Lion Motor Lodge M
(231) 271-6694. **$69-$125.** 4290 S West Bay Shore Rd. 5 mi s on SR 22. Ext corridors. **Pets:** Medium. $10 daily fee/pet. Designated rooms, service with restrictions, supervision.
[X] [&] [H] [IP] [🐾]

TAWAS CITY

AAA W Tawas Motel-Resort M
(989) 362-3822. **$50-$149.** 1124 US 23 S. On US 23, 1.8 mi s. Ext corridors. **Pets:** Accepted.
[SAVE] [SD] [X] [H] [IP] [🏊] [X]

TECUMSEH

W Tecumseh Inn Motel M
(517) 423-7401. **$56-$160.** 1445 W Chicago Blvd. On SR 50, 1.5 mi w of city center. Ext corridors. **Pets:** Accepted.
[SD] [X] [H] [IP] [TI]

THREE RIVERS

WW Super 8 Motel SH
(269) 279-8888. **$72-$79.** 711 US 131. Jct US 131 and SR 60 (W Broadway St). Int corridors. **Pets:** Accepted.
[ASK] [SD] [X] [&M] [&] [H] [🐾]

TRAVERSE CITY

WW Baymont Inn & Suites-Traverse City SH
(231) 933-4454. **$55-$200.** 2326 N US 31 S. 3.5 mi s on SR 37. Int corridors. **Pets:** Accepted.
[ASK] [SD] [X] [&] [H] [IP] [🏊] [X]

AAA WW Best Western Four Seasons M
(231) 946-8424. **$49-$249.** 305 Munson Ave. 2 mi e on US 31. Ext/int corridors. **Pets:** $10 daily fee/room. Service with restrictions, supervision.
[SAVE] [SD] [X] [H] [IP] [🏊]

AAA ▼▼▼ Days Inn & Suites SH ✿
(231) 941-0208. **$49-$179.** 420 Munson Ave. 2 mi e on US 31. Int corridors. **Pets:** Large, other species. $100 deposit/room, $10 daily fee/pet. Service with restrictions, supervision.
SAVE S✗ ✗ 🖥 💻 ⟿ ✗

AAA ▼▼▼ Holiday Inn SH ✿
(231) 947-3700. **$89-$280, 3 day notice.** 615 E Front St. 0.5 mi e on US 31. Int corridors. **Pets:** Other species. $10 daily fee/room. Designated rooms, service with restrictions, supervision.
SAVE S✗ ✗ M ✍ ✗ 🖥 💻 ⫙ ⟿ ✗

▼▼ Park Place Hotel SH
(231) 946-5000. **$99-$269, 3 day notice.** 300 E State St. Corner of E State and Park sts; downtown. Int corridors. **Pets:** Accepted.
ASK S✗ ✗ ✍ 🖥 💻 ⫙ ⟿ ✗

AAA ▼▼ Quality Inn SH
(231) 929-4423. **$40-$189.** 1492 US 31 N. On US 31, 3.3 mi e. Ext/int corridors. **Pets:** Accepted.
SAVE S✗ ✗ ✗ 🖥 💻 ⟿

▼▼ Traverse Victorian Inn SH
(231) 947-5525. **$69-$179.** 461 Munson Ave. 2.4 mi e on US 31. Int corridors. **Pets:** Small. $25 one-time fee/room. Designated rooms, service with restrictions, supervision.
ASK S✗ ✗ ✗ 🖥 💻 ⟿

WALKER

AAA ▼▼▼ Baymont Inn & Suites-Grand Rapids North SH
(616) 735-9595. **$79-$99.** 2151 Holton Ct NW. I-96, exit 28 (Walker Ave), just s. Int corridors. **Pets:** Accepted.
SAVE S✗ ✗ ✗ 🖥 💻 ⟿

AAA ▼▼▼ Quality Inn Grand Rapids North SH
(616) 791-8500. **$75-$115, 30 day notice.** 2171 Holton Ct. I-96, exit 28 (Walker Ave), just s. Int corridors. **Pets:** Medium. $10 daily fee/pet. No service, supervision.
SAVE S✗ ✗ ✗ 🖥 💻 ⟿

WATERSMEET

▼▼▼ Dancing Eagles Resort Lac Vieux Desert Casino SH
(906) 358-4949. **$70-$80.** N5384 US Hwy 45. 1.8 mi n of US 2. Int corridors. **Pets:** Other species. $100 deposit/room, $10 one-time fee/room. Designated rooms, service with restrictions, supervision.
ASK S✗ ✗ ✗ 🖥 💻 ⟿ ✗

WHITMORE LAKE

AAA ▼▼▼ Best Western Whitmore Lake M
(734) 449-2058. **$75-$125.** 9897 Main St. US 23, exit 53, just e. Ext corridors. **Pets:** Other species. $25 daily fee/pet. Service with restrictions, crate.
SAVE S✗ ✗ 🖥 💻 ⟿

WYOMING

AAA ▼▼▼ Howard Johnson Plaza Hotel SH
(616) 241-6444. **$63-$83.** 255 28th St SW. On SR 11, 0.3 mi e of jct US 131, exit 28th St. Int corridors. **Pets:** Other species. $25 one-time fee/pet.
SAVE S✗ ✗ 🖥 💻 ⫙ ⟿ ✗

▼ Super 8 Motel SH
(616) 530-8588. **$58-$80.** 727 44th St SW. US 131, exit 79. Int corridors. **Pets:** Other species. $10 daily fee/pet. Service with restrictions, supervision.
ASK S✗ ✗ 🖥

CITY INDEX

AITKIN

▼ Ripple River Motel & RV Park M
(218) 927-3734. $60-$80. 701 Minnesota Ave S. US 169, 0.8 mi s of jct SR 210. Ext corridors. Pets: $10 daily fee/pet. Designated rooms, service with restrictions, supervision.
(ASK) (×) (📶)

ALBERT LEA

▲▲▲ ▼▼▼ Albert Lea Countryside Inn Motel M
(507) 373-2446. $45-$75, 3 day notice. 2102 E Main St. I-35, exit 11, 1.3 mi w on CR 46. Ext/int corridors. Pets: Medium. $5 daily fee/pet. Designated rooms, service with restrictions, supervision.
(SAVE) (S/D) (×) (📶)

▲▲▲ ▼▼▼ Comfort Inn SH
(507) 377-1100. $69-$129. 810 Happy Trails Ln. I-35, exit 11, just se. Int corridors. Pets: Other species. $10 one-time fee/pet. Designated rooms, supervision.
(SAVE) (S/D) (×) (♿M) (🍳) (📺) (📶) (📼) (⊃) (×)

▲▲▲ ▼▼▼ Country Inn & Suites By Carlson SH
(507) 373-5513. $89. 2214 E Main St. I-35, exit 12 southbound; exit 11 northbound, 1 mi w. Int corridors. Pets: Small. $20 one-time fee/pet. Designated rooms, service with restrictions, crate.
(SAVE) (S/D) (×) (♿M) (🍳) (📶) (📼) (⊃)

▲▲▲ ▼▼▼ Days Inn SH
(507) 373-8291. $75-$90. 2301 E Main St. I-35, exit 11, 1 mi w on CR 46. Int corridors. Pets: Medium, other species. $8 daily fee/pet. Designated rooms, service with restrictions, supervision.
(SAVE) (×) (🍳) (📶) (🍴) (⊃) (×)

ALEXANDRIA

▲▲▲ ▼▼▼▼ Country Inn & Suites By Carlson SH
(320) 763-9900. $80-$115. 5304 Hwy 29 S. I-94, exit 103, just sw. Int corridors. Pets: Large, other species. $10 daily fee/pet. Designated rooms, service with restrictions, supervision.
(SAVE) (S/D) (×) (♿M) (🍳) (📶) (📼) (⊃)

▼▼▼ Holiday Inn Alexandria SH
(320) 763-6577. $90-$153. 5637 State Hwy 29 S. I-94, exit 103, just s. Int corridors. Pets: Other species. Service with restrictions, crate.
(ASK) (×) (📶) (📼) (🍴) (⊃) (×)

▲▲▲ ▼▼▼ Super 8 Motel SH
(320) 763-6552. $61-$83, 14 day notice. 4620 Hwy 29 S. I-94, exit 103, 0.3 mi n. Int corridors. Pets: Accepted.
(SAVE) (S/D) (×) (📶)

AUSTIN

▲▲▲ ▼▼▼ Country Side Inn SH
(507) 437-7774. $39-$79. 3303 Oakland Ave W. I-90, exit 175 (Oakland Ave), just nw. Int corridors. Pets: Accepted.
(SAVE) (S/D) (×) (📶) (📼)

▼▼ Days Inn SH
(507) 433-8600. $55-$80. 700 16th Ave NW. I-90, exit 178A (4th St NW), just nw. Int corridors. Pets: Other species. $25 one-time fee/room. Designated rooms, service with restrictions, crate.
(ASK) (S/D) (×) (🍳) (📶) (📼)

▼▼▼ Holiday Inn & Austin Conference Center SH
(507) 433-1000. $80-$130. 1701 4th St NW. I-90, exit 178A (4th St NW), just nw. Int corridors. Pets: Other species. $25 one-time fee/room. Designated rooms, service with restrictions, crate.
(ASK) (S/D) (×) (♿M) (🍳) (📺) (📶) (📼) (🍴) (⊃) (×)

BABBITT

▼▼▼▼ Timber Bay Lodge & Houseboats CA
(218) 827-3682. $730-$3500 (weekly), 60 day notice. 8347 Timber Bay Rd. 2.8 mi e of jct CR 21 via CR 70 and 623. Ext corridors. Pets: Other species. $14 daily fee/pet. Service with restrictions, supervision.
(📶) (📼) (×) (📠)

BAUDETTE

▼▼▼ AmericInn Lodge & Suites Lake of the Woods SH
(218) 634-3200. $74-$145. 1179 Main St W. 0.5 mi w on SR 11. Int corridors. Pets: Accepted.
(ASK) (S/D) (×) (♿M) (🍳) (📺) (📶) (📼) (⊃) (×)

BAXTER

▼▼▼▼ Hawthorn Inn & Suites SH
(218) 822-1133. $79-$369. 7208 Fairview Rd. Just nw of jct SR 371 on SR 210. Int corridors. Pets: Accepted.
(ASK) (S/D) (×) (♿M) (🍳) (📺) (📶) (📼) (⊃) (×)

▼▼▼ Holiday Inn Express, Three Bear Lodge Water & Theme Park SH 🐾
(218) 824-3232. $129-$189. 15739 Audubon Way. Just se of jct SR 371 and CR 77. Int corridors. Pets: Small, dogs only. $75 deposit/pet, $15 daily fee/pet. Designated rooms, service with restrictions, supervision.
(ASK) (S/D) (×) (♿M) (🍳) (📺) (📶) (📼)

BEMIDJI

△△△ ▽▽▽ AmericInn Lodge & Suites SH
(218) 751-3000. **$72-$128.** 1200 Paul Bunyan Dr NW. 0.5 mi e of northwest jct US 2, 71 and SR 197. Int corridors. **Pets:** Medium, dogs only. $30 one-time fee/pet. No service, supervision.
[SAVE] [S❍] [✕] [🐾] [🛏] [🖥] [🏊] [✕]

△△△ ▽▽▽ Best Western Bemidji SH
(218) 751-0390. **$45-$99.** 2420 Paul Bunyan Dr. Jct US 71 N and SR 197. Int corridors. **Pets:** Accepted.
[SAVE] [S❍] [✕] [🐾] [🛏] [🖥] [🏊] [✕]

△△△ ▽▽▽▽ Ruttger's Birchmont Lodge CA
(218) 444-3463. **$59-$370, 30 day notice.** 7598 Bemidji Rd NE. Jct SR 197, 3.6 mi n on CR 21 (Bemidji Ave N). Ext/int corridors. **Pets:** Large, other species. $10 daily fee/pet. Designated rooms, service with restrictions, crate.
[SAVE] [S❍] [✕] [🐾] [🛏] [🖥] [🍴] [🏊] [✕]

BLUE EARTH

△△ ▽▽ Super 8 Motel SH
(507) 526-7376. **$63-$72.** 1420 Giant Dr. I-90, exit 119 (US 169), just s. Int corridors. **Pets:** $10 one-time fee/pet. Service with restrictions, supervision.
[ASK] [S❍] [✕] [🛏] [🖥]

BRAINERD

△△△ ▽▽▽▽ Ramada Inn Brainerd SH
(218) 829-1441. **$64-$99.** 2115 S 6th St. On SR 371 business route, 1.8 mi s of jct SR 210. Ext/int corridors. **Pets:** Accepted.
[SAVE] [✕] [🐾] [🛏] [🖥] [🍴] [🏊] [✕]

BRECKENRIDGE

△△△ ▽▽▽ Select Inn of Breckenridge/Wahpeton SH
(218) 643-9201. **$54-$67.** 821 Hwy 75 N. Just sw of jct US 75 N and 210. Int corridors. **Pets:** $10 one-time fee/pet. Designated rooms, service with restrictions, crate.
[SAVE] [S❍] [✕] [🐾] [🛏] [🖥] [🏊]

CALEDONIA

▽▽▽ AmericInn Lodge & Suites SH
(507) 725-8000. **$70-$80.** 508 N Kruckow Ave. Just n of Main St on SR 44, just w on Esch Dr. Int corridors. **Pets:** $50 deposit/room. Supervision.
[ASK] [✕] [🐾] [🛏] [🖥] [🏊] [✕]

▽ Crest Red Carpet Inn M ❀
(507) 724-3311. **$65-$70.** 15944 State 76. Jct SR 44 and 76; on north end of town, 1.9 mi s. Ext/int corridors. **Pets:** $20 one-time fee/room. Designated rooms, service with restrictions, supervision.
[ASK] [S❍] [✕] [🛏]

CANNON FALLS

△△△ ▽▽▽ Best Western Saratoga Inn SH
(507) 263-7272. **$69-$145.** 31591 64th Ave. 1 mi s on US 52. Int corridors. **Pets:** Small. $15 daily fee/pet. Designated rooms, service with restrictions, supervision.
[SAVE] [S❍] [✕] [🛏] [🖥] [🏊]

CLOQUET

▽▽▽ Super 8 Motel SH ❀
(218) 879-1250. **$56-$138.** 121 Big Lake Rd. I-35, exit 237 (SR 33), 2 mi nw. Int corridors. **Pets:** Dogs only. $50 deposit/pet. Designated rooms, service with restrictions, supervision.
[ASK] [✕] [♿M] [🐾] [🛏] [🖥]

CROOKSTON

▽▽▽ Northland Inn of Crookston SH
(218) 281-5210. **$69-$89.** 2200 University Ave. On US 2 W and 75 N, 1.5 mi n. Int corridors. **Pets:** Other species. $10 daily fee/room. Designated rooms, service with restrictions, supervision.
[ASK] [S❍] [✕] [🐾] [🍴] [🏊]

DEER RIVER

△△△ ▽▽▽ White Oak Inn & Suites SH
(218) 246-9400. **$47-$160.** 201 4th Ave NW. On US 2. Int corridors. **Pets:** $100 deposit/room. Designated rooms, service with restrictions, supervision.
[SAVE] [S❍] [✕] [🛏] [🖥] [🏊] [✕]

DETROIT LAKES

△△△ ▽▽▽ AmericInn Lodge & Suites SH
(218) 847-8795. **$75-$160.** 777 Hwy 10 E. 1.4 mi se. Int corridors. **Pets:** Other species. $10 daily fee/room. Service with restrictions, supervision.
[SAVE] [S❍] [✕] [♿M] [🐾] [🛏] [🖥] [🏊] [✕]

△△△ ▽▽▽ Best Western Holland House & Suites SH ❀
(218) 847-4483. **$79-$219, 3 day notice.** 615 Hwy 10 E. 1.3 mi se. Ext/int corridors. **Pets:** Medium. $10 daily fee/pet. Designated rooms, service with restrictions, supervision.
[SAVE] [✕] [🐾] [🛏] [🖥] [🏊] [✕]

△△△ ▽▽▽ Budget Host Inn M ❀
(218) 847-4454. **$51-$115.** 895 Hwy 10 E. 1.5 mi se. Ext corridors. **Pets:** Medium. $10 daily fee/pet. Service with restrictions, supervision.
[SAVE] [S❍] [✕] [🛏] [🖥]

△△△ ▽▽▽▽ Country Inn & Suites By Carlson SH
(218) 847-2000. **$72-$125.** 1330 Hwy 10 E. Just e of jct US 10 and CR 54 E. Int corridors. **Pets:** Other species. $20 one-time fee/room. Designated rooms, service with restrictions, supervision.
[SAVE] [S❍] [✕] [♿M] [🛏] [🖥] [🏊]

DULUTH

△△△ ▽▽▽▽ AmericInn Hotel & Suites of Duluth/Proctor
(218) 624-1026. **$70-$210.** 185 US 2. Jct I-35 and US 2, 0.8 mi n. Int corridors. **Pets:** Accepted.
[SAVE] [S❍] [✕] [🐾] [🛏] [🖥] [🍴] [🏊]

△△△ ▽▽▽ Best Western Downtown Motel M
(218) 727-6851. **$44-$129.** 131 W 2nd St. 2nd St at 2nd Ave W; center. Ext/int corridors. **Pets:** Accepted.
[SAVE] [S❍] [✕] [🛏] [🖥]

△△△ ▽▽▽▽ Country Inn & Suites By Carlson SH
(218) 628-0668. **$73-$170.** 9330 W Skyline Pkwy. I-35, exit 249 (Boundary Ave), just se. Int corridors. **Pets:** Other species. $8 daily fee/room. Designated rooms, no service, supervision.
[SAVE] [S❍] [✕] [🐾] [🛏] [🖥] [🏊] [✕]

△△△ ▽▽▽▽ Country Inn & Suites-Duluth North SH ❀
(218) 740-4500. **$89-$199.** 4257 Haines Rd. Just n of US 53 at jct Haines Rd. **Pets:** Medium, other species. $10 daily fee/pet. Designated rooms, service with restrictions, supervision.
[SAVE] [S❍] [✕] [🛏] [🖥] [🏊] [✕]

▽▽▽ Days Inn-Duluth SH
(218) 727-3110. **$55-$159.** 909 Cottonwood Ave. SR 194, just n of jct US 53. Int corridors. **Pets:** Service with restrictions, supervision.
[ASK] [S❍] [✕] [🐾] [🛏]

AAA ▼▼▼ Econo Lodge Airport SH ☀
(218) 722-5522. **$51-$140.** 4197 Haines Rd. West side on US 53 and SR 194. Int corridors. **Pets:** $50 deposit/room, $10 one-time fee/room. Designated rooms, service with restrictions, supervision.
SAVE S⃝ ⊠ ◈ ➦ ⊠

AAA ▼▼▼ Edgewater Resort & Waterpark M
(218) 728-3601. **$89-$359.** 2400 London Rd. I-35, exit 258 (21st Ave E), just nw. Ext/int corridors. **Pets:** Accepted.
SAVE S⃝ ⊠ ⊘ ◈ ⊟ ◈ ➦ ⊠

AAA ▼◈▼ Hawthorn Suites at Waterfront Plaza SH
(218) 727-4663. **$89-$299.** 325 Lake Ave S. In Canal Park area. Int corridors. **Pets:** Accepted.
SAVE S⃝ ⊠ ♿ ⊘ ◈ ⊟ ◈ ⊺ ➦ ⊠

AAA ▼◈▼ The Inn on Lake Superior SH
(218) 726-1111. **$125-$369.** 350 Canal Park Dr. In Canal Park area. Int corridors. **Pets:** Accepted.
SAVE ⊠ ♿ ⊘ ◈ ⊟ ◈ ➦ ⊠

▼◈▼ Radisson Hotel Duluth-Harborview LH
(218) 727-8981. **$109-$199.** 505 W Superior St. At 5th Ave W; center. Int corridors. **Pets:** Other species. $10 daily fee/room. Designated rooms, service with restrictions, supervision.
ASK S⃝ ⊠ ⊟ ◈ ⊺ ➦ ⊠

▼◈▼ Voyageur Lakewalk Inn M
(218) 722-3911. **$35-$74.** 333 E Superior St. I-35, exit 256 (Superior St), just n at jct 4th Ave E and Superior St. Ext corridors. **Pets:** Other species. $15 one-time fee/room. Supervision.
⊠ ⊟ ◈

ELY

AAA ▼◈▼ Grand Ely Lodge Resort and Conference Center SH ☀
(218) 365-6565. **$100-$196, 14 day notice.** 400 N Pioneer Rd. SR 169 to Central Ave, just n to Pioneer Rd, then 1 mi n. Ext/int corridors. **Pets:** Other species. $15 daily fee/pet. Designated rooms, service with restrictions.
SAVE S⃝ ⊠ ⊘ ◈ ⊟ ◈ ⊺ ➦ ⊠

AAA ▼ Motel Ely-Budget Host M
(218) 365-3237. **$60-$100.** 1047 E Sheridan St. SR 1 and 169. Ext corridors. **Pets:** Accepted.
SAVE ⊠ ◈

EVELETH

▼▼ Super 8 Motel SH
(218) 744-1661. **$69-$123.** 1080 Industrial Park Dr. On US 53, 0.5 mi n of jct SR 37. Int corridors. **Pets:** Accepted.
ASK S⃝ ⊠ ♿ ◈ ⊟ ◈ ➦ ⊠

FAIRMONT

▼◈▼ Comfort Inn SH
(507) 238-5444. **$80-$90.** 2225 N State St. I-90, exit 102 (SR 15), just sw. Int corridors. **Pets:** Other species. Designated rooms, service with restrictions, supervision.
ASK S⃝ ⊠ ♿ ⊟ ◈ ➦

▼◈▼ Holiday Inn SH
(507) 238-4771. **$90-$115.** 1201 Torgerson Dr. I-90, exit 102 (SR 15), just se. Int corridors. **Pets:** Other species. Service with restrictions, supervision.
ASK S⃝ ⊠ ⊟ ◈ ⊺ ➦ ⊠

▼▼ Super 8 Motel SH
(507) 238-9444. **$55-$63.** 1200 Torgerson Dr. I-90, exit 102 (SR 15), just se. Int corridors. **Pets:** Other species. $10 daily fee/pet. Designated rooms, service with restrictions, supervision.
ASK ⊠ ◈

FARIBAULT

AAA ▼◈▼ AmericInn Motel SH
(507) 334-9464. **$80-$90.** 1801 Lavender Dr. I-35, exit 59 (SR 21), 0.3 mi e. Int corridors. **Pets:** $15 one-time fee/room. Designated rooms, service with restrictions, supervision.
SAVE S⃝ ⊠ ⊘ ◈ ⊟ ◈ ➦ ⊠

▼◈▼ Days Inn & Suites SH
(507) 334-6835. **$60-$85.** 1920 Cardinal Ln. I-35, exit 59 (SR 21), just ne. Int corridors. **Pets:** Medium. $10 daily fee/room. Service with restrictions, crate.
ASK ⊠ ♿ ⊘ ◈ ⊟ ◈ ➦

AAA ▼◈▼ Select Inn M
(507) 334-2051. **$50-$100.** 4040 SR 60 W. I-35, exit 56, just w. Int corridors. **Pets:** $7 daily fee/pet. Service with restrictions, crate.
SAVE S⃝ ⊠ ◈ ⊟ ◈ ➦

FERGUS FALLS

AAA ▼◈▼ AmericInn Lodge & Suites SH ☀
(218) 739-3900. **$76-$150.** 526 Western Ave N. I-94, exit 54 (SR 210), just se. Int corridors. **Pets:** Large, other species. $50 deposit/room, $10 one-time fee/room. Designated rooms, service with restrictions, crate.
SAVE ⊠ ♿ ⊘ ◈ ⊟ ◈ ➦ ⊠

▼◈ Motel 7 M
(218) 736-2554. **$42-$65.** 616 Frontier Dr. I-94, exit 54 (SR 210), just ne. Int corridors. **Pets:** Accepted.
⊠ ◈

FINLAYSON

▼◈▼ Banning Junction-North Country Inn SH
(320) 245-5284. **$59-$99.** 60671 State Hwy 23. I-35, exit 195 (SR 23), just ne. Int corridors. **Pets:** Accepted.
ASK S⃝ ⊠ ◈

FOSSTON

▼◈▼ Super 8 Motel SH
(218) 435-1088. **$65-$125.** 108 S Amber. US 2, 0.5 mi e. Int corridors. **Pets:** Dogs only. $5 one-time fee/room. Service with restrictions, supervision.
ASK S⃝ ⊠ ◈ ⊟ ◈

GARRISON

▼◈▼ Garrison Inn & Suites by Ruttger's SH
(320) 692-4050. **$65-$149.** 9243 Hwy 169. SR 169, just s of jct SR 18. Int corridors. **Pets:** Dogs only. $50 deposit/room, $10 daily fee/pet. Designated rooms, service with restrictions, supervision.
ASK S⃝ ⊠ ◈ ⊟ ◈ ➦

GAYLORD

▼◈▼ Gold Leaf Inn & Suites M
(507) 237-5860. **$57-$130.** 330 Main Ave E. 1.5 mi e. Int corridors. **Pets:** Small. Designated rooms, service with restrictions, supervision.
⊠ ◈ ◈

GRAND MARAIS

AAA ▼◈▼ Best Western Superior Inn & Suites SH ☀
(218) 387-2240. **$79-$289, 3 day notice.** 104 1st Ave E. SR 61, just ne of center. Int corridors. **Pets:** Medium, other species. $10 one-time fee/room. Designated rooms, service with restrictions, supervision.
SAVE ⊠ ⊘ ◈ ⊟ ◈

AAA ▼◈▼ Gunflint Lodge VH
(218) 388-2294. **$99-$699, 31 day notice.** 143 S Gunflint Lake. 43 mi n of town; 0.8 mi e of jct CR 12 (Gunflint Trail) and 50. Ext corridors. **Pets:** Accepted.
SAVE ♿ ◈ ⊟ ◈ ⊺ ⊠ ✗ ◈

▼▼ Nor'Wester Lodge and Outfitter CA
(218) 388-2252. **$99-$289, 60 day notice.** 7778 Gunflint Trail. 30 mi nw on CR 12 (Gunflint Trail) from jct SR 61. Ext corridors. **Pets:** Accepted.
🛏️ 📺 ⊠ 🐾 🐾 ⚟

▼ Outpost Motel M
(218) 387-1833. **$45-$95.** 2935 SR 61 E. 9 mi ne. Ext corridors. **Pets:** Other species. $10 daily fee/pet. Service with restrictions, supervision.
⊠ 🛏️ 📺 ⊠ 🐾

▲▲▲ ▼ Wedgewood Motel M
(218) 387-2944. **$49-$69, 3 day notice.** 1663 E Hwy 61. On SR 61, 2.5 mi ne. Ext corridors. **Pets:** Dogs only. $5 daily fee/pet. Designated rooms, service with restrictions, supervision.
SAVE S📶 ⊠ 🛏️ 🐾 ⚟

GRAND RAPIDS

▲▲▲ ▼▼ Budget Host Inn M ❀
(218) 326-3457. **$60-$80.** 311 E Hwy 2. Jct US 2 E and 169 N. Ext/int corridors. **Pets:** Designated rooms, service with restrictions, crate.
SAVE S📶 ⊠

▲▲▲ ▼▼▼ Country Inn By Carlson SH ❀
(218) 327-4960. **$92-$133.** 2601 S Hwy 169. US 2, 2 mi s. Int corridors. **Pets:** Medium, dogs only. Supervision.
SAVE ⊠ 🅼 🐾 🐾 🛏️ 📺 ➜

▲▲▲ ▼▼▼ Sawmill Inn SH ❀
(218) 326-8501. **$79-$109.** 2301 S Hwy 169. US 2, 2 mi s on US 169. Ext/int corridors. **Pets:** Other species. Service with restrictions, supervision.
SAVE S📶 ⊠ 🐾 🛏️ 📺 🍴 ➜ ⊠

GRANITE FALLS

▼▼ Super 8 Motel SH
(320) 564-4075. **$50-$92.** 845 W SR 212. Jct SR 23 and 212, 0.5 mi w. Int corridors. **Pets:** Accepted.
ASK S📶 ⊠ 🅼 🐾 🛏️ ➜

HIBBING

▼▼ Super 8 Motel SH
(218) 263-8982. **$72-$82, 7 day notice.** 1411 E 40th St. Just e of US 169 and SR 37. Int corridors. **Pets:** Accepted.
ASK S📶 ⊠ 🛏️

HINCKLEY

▼▼ Days Inn SH
(320) 384-7751. **$59-$129.** 104 Grindstone Ct. I-35, exit 183 (SR 48), just e. Int corridors. **Pets:** Accepted.
ASK S📶 ⊠ 🐾 🛏️ 📺 ➜

HUTCHINSON

▲▲▲ ▼▼▼ Best Western Victorian Inn SH
(320) 587-6030. **$73-$96.** 1000 Hwy 7 W. SR 15, 1 mi w. Int corridors. **Pets:** Accepted.
SAVE S📶 ⊠ 🛏️ 📺 ➜

INTERNATIONAL FALLS

▲▲▲ ▼▼▼ Hilltop Motel M
(218) 283-2505. **$46-$84.** 2002 2nd Ave W. US 53, 1 mi s of jct US 53 and SR 11. Ext corridors. **Pets:** Small, dogs only. $10 one-time fee/pet. Designated rooms, service with restrictions, supervision.
SAVE S📶 ⊠

▼▼▼ Holiday Inn SH
(218) 283-8000. **$99-$119.** 1500 US 71 W. 1.5 mi w on US 71 and SR 11 W. Int corridors. **Pets:** Accepted.
ASK S📶 ⊠ 🐾 🛏️ 📺 🍴 ➜ ⊠

JACKSON

▲▲▲ ▼▼◈ AmericInn Lodge & Suites SH
(507) 847-2444. **$85-$140.** 110 Belmont Ln. I-90, exit 73 (US 71), just sw. Int corridors. **Pets:** Medium, dogs only. $10 daily fee/pet. Designated rooms, service with restrictions, supervision.
SAVE ⊠ 🅼 🐾 🛏️ 📺 ➜

▼▼ Econo Lodge SH
(507) 847-3110. **$50-$75.** 2007 Hwy 71 N. I-90, exit 73 (US 71), just n. Ext/int corridors. **Pets:** Other species. $10 daily fee/pet. Service with restrictions, supervision.
ASK S📶 ⊠ 🛏️ 📺 🍴 ➜ ⊠

LAMBERTON

▼ Lamberton Motel M
(507) 752-7242. **$45-$55.** 601 1st Ave W. Just s of jct US 14 and Ilex St. Ext corridors. **Pets:** Accepted.
ASK S📶 ⊠ 🛏️ 📺

LITCHFIELD

▼▼ ScotWood Motel M
(320) 693-2496. **$50-$80.** 1017 E Frontage Rd. On US 12. Int corridors. **Pets:** Accepted.
ASK S📶 ⊠ 🛏️ ➜

LONG PRAIRIE

▲▲▲ ▼▼ Budget Host Inn M
(320) 732-6118. **$57-$75, 3 day notice.** 417 Lake St. On US 71 and SR 27, just s of jct SR 287. Ext corridors. **Pets:** $5 daily fee/room. Designated rooms, service with restrictions, supervision.
SAVE S📶 ⊠ 🛏️ 📺

LUTSEN

▲▲▲ ▼▼▼ Cascade Lodge CI
(218) 387-1112. **$45-$99, 14 day notice.** 3719 W SR 61. On SR 61, 7 mi ne of jct CR 4 (Caribou Trail). Ext/int corridors. **Pets:** Dogs only. $10 daily fee/pet. Designated rooms, no service, supervision.
SAVE S📶 ⊠ 🛏️ 📺 🍴 ⊠

▲▲▲ ▼▼▼ Solbakken Resort M
(218) 663-7566. **$51-$95, 14 day notice.** 4874 W SR 61. On SR 61, 1.3 mi n of jct CR 4 (Caribou Trail). Ext corridors. **Pets:** Other species. $10 daily fee/pet. Designated rooms, no service, supervision.
SAVE S📶 ⊠ 🐾 🛏️ 📺 ⊠ 🐾

MANKATO

▼▼▼ AmericInn of Mankato at MSU SH ❀
(507) 345-8011. **$55-$199.** 240 Stadium Rd. From jct US 14, 1.6 mi s on SR 22, 0.4 mi w on SR 83, just s on Victory Dr, then 1.5 mi w. Int corridors. **Pets:** Medium, dogs only. $20 one-time fee/room. Designated rooms, service with restrictions.
ASK ⊠ 🅼 🐾 🛏️ 📺 ➜ ⊠

▲▲▲ ▼▼▼◈ Best Western Hotel, Restaurant & Conference Center SH
(507) 625-9333. **$75-$138.** 1111 Range St. 1.3 mi n on US 169. Int corridors. **Pets:** Designated rooms, service with restrictions, crate.
SAVE S📶 ⊠ 🛏️ 📺 🍴 ➜ ⊠

▼▼ Comfort Inn by Choice Hotels SH
(507) 388-5107. **$95-$115.** 131 Apache Pl. Just s of jct US 14 and SR 22 S. Int corridors. **Pets:** Accepted.
ASK S📶 ⊠ 🐾 🛏️ 📺 ➜

▲▲▲ ▼▼ Days Inn SH ❀
(507) 387-3332. **$55-$90, 14 day notice.** 1285 Range St. US 169, 0.3 mi s of jct US 14. Int corridors. **Pets:** Other species. $5 daily fee/pet. Designated rooms, service with restrictions, supervision.
SAVE S📶 ⊠ 🛏️ 📺 ➜

▼▼▼▼ Grandstay Residential Suites 🆂🅷
(507) 388-8688. **$110-$150.** 1000 Raintree Rd. 1.3 mi s of jct US 14 and SR 22 on CR 3. Int corridors. **Pets:** Accepted.
🅰🆂🅺 ⊠ 🐾 ⟨⟩ 🛉 🖵 ⇝

▼▼▼▼ Holiday Inn 🆂🅷
(507) 345-1234. **$65-$129.** 101 E Main St. Main St at Riverfront Dr; downtown. Int corridors. **Pets:** Accepted.
🅰🆂🅺 🆂🏠 ⊠ 🔥ᴹ ⟨⟩ ⟨⟩ 🛉 🖵 ⫟⫠ ⇝ ⊠

▼▼ Microtel Inn & Suites 🆂🅷
(507) 388-2818. **$50-$74.** 200 St. Andrews Dr. US 14, exit CR 3, 0.4 mi n. Int corridors. **Pets:** Large, other species. $15 one-time fee/room. Service with restrictions, crate.
🅰🆂🅺 🆂🏠 ⊠ 🛉 🖵

▼▼ Super 8 Motel 🆂🅷 🐾
(507) 387-4041. **$64-$98.** 51578 US Hwy 169 N. Jct US 169 and 14, just n. Int corridors. **Pets:** Dogs only. $100 deposit/room. Service with restrictions, supervision.
🅰🆂🅺 🆂🏠 ⊠ 🛉 🖵 ⊠

MARSHALL

🆂🅾🅾 ▼▼▼▼ Best Western Marshall Inn 🆂🅷
(507) 532-3221. **$79-$99.** 1500 E College Dr. SR 19, just w of jct SR 23. Int corridors. **Pets:** Other species. $10 daily fee/room. Service with restrictions, supervision.
🆂🅰🆅🅴 🆂🏠 ⊠ 🛉 🖵 ⫟⫠ ⇝ ⊠

▼▼▼▼ Comfort Inn 🆂🅷
(507) 532-3070. **$75-$100, 7 day notice.** 1511 E College Dr. SR 19, w of jct SR 23. Int corridors. **Pets:** $10 daily fee/pet. Service with restrictions, crate.
🅰🆂🅺 🆂🏠 ⊠ 🔥ᴹ ⟨⟩ ⟨⟩ 🛉 🖵 ⇝

▼▼ Super 8 Motel 🆂🅷
(507) 537-1461. **$50-$69.** 1106 E Main St. 0.3 mi se on US 59 from jct SR 23. Int corridors. **Pets:** Large, other species. $10 one-time fee/room. Service with restrictions, supervision.
🅰🆂🅺 🆂🏠 ⊠ ⟨⟩ 🛉

MCGREGOR

▼▼ Country Meadows Inn 🆂🅷
(218) 768-7378. **$65-$114.** 403 Meadows Dr. Jct SR 65 and 210. Int corridors. **Pets:** Accepted.
🅰🆂🅺 🆂🏠 ⊠ ⟨⟩ 🛉 🖵 ⇝

MILACA

▼▼ Super 8 Motel 🆂🅷
(320) 983-2660. **Call for rates.** 215 10th Ave SE. Jct SR 23 and 169. Int corridors. **Pets:** Accepted.
🅰🆂🅺 ⊠ 🔥ᴹ ⟨⟩ 🛉

MINNEAPOLIS-ST. PAUL METROPOLITAN AREA

ANNANDALE

▼▼ AmericInn Lodge & Suites 🆂🅷
(320) 274-3006. **$75-$130.** 620 Elm St E. On SR 55. Int corridors. **Pets:** Other species. $50 deposit/room. Designated rooms, service with restrictions, crate.
🅰🆂🅺 🆂🏠 ⊠ 🔥ᴹ ⟨⟩ ⟨⟩ 🛉 🖵 ⇝

BECKER

🆂🅾🅾 ▼▼▼▼ Sleep Inn & Suites 🆂🅷
(763) 262-7700. **$64-$94.** 14435 Bank St. Just e on US 10. Int corridors. **Pets:** Medium, dogs only. $100 deposit/pet, $15 one-time fee/pet. Designated rooms, no service, supervision.
🆂🅰🆅🅴 🆂🏠 ⊠ 🛉 🖵 ⇝ ⊠

BLOOMINGTON

🆂🅾🅾 ▼▼▼▼ Hilton Minneapolis/St. Paul Airport Mall of America 🅻🅷
(952) 854-2100. **$89-$219.** 3800 American Blvd E. I-494, exit 1B (34th Ave), just se. Int corridors. **Pets:** Accepted.
🆂🅰🆅🅴 🆂🏠 ⊠ 🔥ᴹ ⟨⟩ ⟨⟩ 🛉 🖵 ⫟⫠ ⇝

🆂🅾🅾 ▼▼▼▼ Homewood Suites by Hilton 🆂🅷
(952) 854-0900. **$149-$219.** 2261 Killebrew Dr. I-494, exit 2A (24th Ave), 1 mi s, then just w. Int corridors. **Pets:** Medium, other species. $100 one-time fee/room. Service with restrictions, crate.
🆂🅰🆅🅴 🆂🏠 ⊠ ⟨⟩ 🛉 🖵 ⇝

🆂🅾🅾 ▼▼▼ La Quinta Inn Minneapolis-Airport (Bloomington) 🆂🅷
(952) 881-7311. **$95-$129.** 7815 Nicollet Ave S. I-494, exit 4A (Nicollet Ave), just s. Int corridors. **Pets:** Medium. Service with restrictions.
🆂🅰🆅🅴 ⊠ ⟨⟩ 🛉 🖵

🆂🅾🅾 ▼▼▼▼ Le Bourget Aero Suites 🆂🅷
(952) 893-9999. **$109-$169.** 7770 Johnson Ave. I-494, exit 6B (France Ave), 0.5 mi nw on frontage road (78th St). Int corridors. **Pets:** $150 deposit/room. Service with restrictions, crate.
🆂🅰🆅🅴 🆂🏠 ⊠ 🔥ᴹ ⟨⟩ 🛉 🖵 ⫟⫠ ⇝ ⊠

🆂🅾🅾 ▼▼▼ Ramada Inn Mall of America 🆂🅷
(952) 854-3411. **$99-$199, 30 day notice.** 2201 E 78th St. I-494, exit 2A (24th Ave), just s. Int corridors. **Pets:** Medium, dogs only. $25 one-time fee/room. Supervision.
🆂🅰🆅🅴 🆂🏠 ⊠ 🔥ᴹ ⟨⟩ 🛉 🖵 ⫟⫠ ⇝ ⊠

▼▼▼▼ Residence Inn by Marriott 🆂🅷
(952) 876-0900. **$89-$199, 30 day notice.** 7850 Bloomington Ave S. I-494, exit 3, on south frontage road. Int corridors. **Pets:** Other species. $75 one-time fee/room. Service with restrictions.
🅰🆂🅺 🆂🏠 ⊠ ⟨⟩ ⟨⟩ 🛉 🖵 ⇝

▼▼▼▼ Sheraton Bloomington Hotel Minneapolis South 🅻🅷 🐾
(952) 835-7800. **$89-$269.** 7800 Normandale Blvd. I-494, exit 7A (SR 100). Int corridors. **Pets:** Medium. $50 deposit/room. Designated rooms, service with restrictions, supervision.
🅰🆂🅺 🆂🏠 ⊠ ⟨⟩ 🛉 🖵 ⫟⫠ ⇝ ⊠

🆂🅾🅾 ▼▼▼▼ Sofitel Minneapolis 🅻🅷
(952) 835-1900. **$79-$439.** 5601 W 78th St. Just nw of jct I-494 and SR 100, access via SR 100 and Industrial Blvd. Int corridors. **Pets:** Medium. Designated rooms, service with restrictions, crate.
🆂🅰🆅🅴 ⊠ 🔥ᴹ ⟨⟩ ⟨⟩ 🛉 ⫟⫠ ⊠

▼▼▼▼ Staybridge Suites 🆂🅷
(952) 831-7900. **$169-$249.** 5150 American Blvd. I-494, exit 6B (France Ave), just se of SR 100, then 1 mi w on frontage road. Int corridors. **Pets:** Small. $150 one-time fee/room. Service with restrictions, supervision.
🅰🆂🅺 ⊠ 🔥ᴹ ⟨⟩ ⟨⟩ 🛉 🖵 ⇝ ⊠

BROOKLYN CENTER

🆂🅾🅾 ▼▼▼ Baymont Inn & Suites Minneapolis-Brooklyn Center 🆂🅷
(763) 561-8400. **$66-$116.** 6415 James Cir N. I-94/694, exit 34 (Shingle Creek Pkwy), just ne. Int corridors. **Pets:** Medium. $50 deposit/pet, $11 daily fee/pet. Service with restrictions, supervision.
🆂🅰🆅🅴 ⊠ ⟨⟩ 🛉 🖵

Comfort Inn by Choice Hotels SH
(763) 560-7464. **$85-$105.** 1600 James Cir N. I-694, exit 34 (Shingle Creek Pkwy), just ne. Int corridors. **Pets:** Accepted.

BROOKLYN PARK

La Quinta Inn & Suites SH
(763) 971-8000. **$69-$89.** 7011 Northland Cir. I-94/694, exit 30 (Boone Ave), just ne. Int corridors. **Pets:** Accepted.

BURNSVILLE

Americas Best Value Inn M ❀
(952) 894-3400. **$63-$83.** 1101 Burnsville Pkwy. I-35W, exit 2 (Burnsville Pkwy), just sw. Int corridors. **Pets:** Dogs only. $10 one-time fee/room. Designated rooms, service with restrictions, supervision.

Red Roof Inn M
(952) 890-1420. **$45-$83.** 12920 Aldrich Ave S. I-35W, exit 2 (Burnsville Pkwy), just sw. Ext corridors. **Pets:** Medium, other species. Service with restrictions, supervision.

CHANHASSEN

AmericInn Hotel & Suites SH
(952) 934-3888. **$99-$104.** 570 Pond Promenade. Just se of jct SR 5 and 101 S. Int corridors. **Pets:** $35 one-time fee/room. Designated rooms, service with restrictions, crate.

CHASKA

Best Western Chaska River Inn & Suites SH
(952) 448-7877. **$135.** One Riverbend. Jct US 212, 0.3 mi s on SR 41. Int corridors. **Pets:** Dogs only. $10 daily fee/room. Designated rooms, service with restrictions, supervision.

COON RAPIDS

Comfort Inn-Northtown SH
(763) 785-4746. **$69-$129.** 9052 University Ave NE. Just ne of jct US 10, exit University Ave. Int corridors. **Pets:** Accepted.

Country Suites By Carlson SH
(763) 780-3797. **$90-$130.** 155 Coon Rapids Blvd. 0.5 mi e of SR 610. Int corridors. **Pets:** Medium. $10 daily fee/pet. Designated rooms, service with restrictions, crate.

EAGAN

Days Inn SH
(651) 681-1770. **$79-$109.** 4510 Erin Dr. Just ne of jct SR 77 and Cliff Rd. Int corridors. **Pets:** Medium. $100 deposit/room, $10 daily fee/pet. Designated rooms, service with restrictions, supervision.

Homestead Studio Suites Hotel-Minneapolis-Airport-Eagan SH
(651) 905-1778. **$91-$100.** 3015 Denmark Ave. I-35E, exit 98 (Lone Oak Rd), just se. Int corridors. **Pets:** Accepted.

Microtel Inn & Suites SH
(651) 405-0988. **$56-$81.** 3000 Denmark Ave. I-35E, exit 98 (Lone Oak Rd), just se. Int corridors. **Pets:** Accepted.

Residence Inn by Marriott-Mpls/St. Paul Airport SH
(651) 688-0363. **$89-$199.** 3040 Eagandale Pl. I-35E, exit 98 (Lone Oak Rd), just sw. Ext corridors. **Pets:** Large, other species. $75 one-time fee/room. Service with restrictions, crate.

Staybridge Suites SH ❀
(651) 994-7810. **$109-$209.** 4675 Rahncliff Rd. I-35E, exit 93 (Cliff Rd), just w, then just s. Int corridors. **Pets:** Other species. $150 one-time fee/room. Service with restrictions, supervision.

TownePlace Suites SH
(651) 994-4600. **$79-$149.** 3615 Crestridge Dr. I-35E, exit 71 (Pilot Knob Rd), just se. Int corridors. **Pets:** Accepted.

EDEN PRAIRIE

Best Western Eden Prairie Inn SH
(952) 829-0888. **$65-$195.** 11500 W 78th St. I-494, exit 11A, just sw. Int corridors. **Pets:** Small, dogs only. $10 daily fee/pet. Designated rooms, service with restrictions, supervision.

Homestead Studio Suites Hotel-Minneapolis-Eden Prairie SH
(952) 942-6818. **$86-$109.** 11905 Technology Dr. Just sw of jct I-494 and US 212 (Flying Cloud Dr). Int corridors. **Pets:** Accepted.

EDINA

Residence Inn Minneapolis-Edina SH
(952) 893-9300. **$119-$289.** 3400 Edinborough Way. I-494, exit 6B (France Ave), 0.3 mi n to Minnesota Dr, then just e. Int corridors. **Pets:** Small, dogs only. $75 one-time fee/room. Designated rooms, service with restrictions, crate.

ELK RIVER

AmericInn Lodge & Suites of Elk River M ❀
(763) 441-8554. **$79-$199.** 17432 Hwy 10. 1.5 mi se on US 10/169. Int corridors. **Pets:** Medium. $10 daily fee/pet. Designated rooms, service with restrictions, supervision.

FOREST LAKE

AmericInn Motel SH
(651) 464-1930. **$69-$105.** 1291 W Broadway. I-35, exit 131 (CR 2), just ne. Int corridors. **Pets:** Accepted.

HASTINGS

Country Inn & Suites By Carlson SH
(651) 437-8870. **$79-$149.** 300 33rd St. Just e of US 61. Int corridors. **Pets:** Accepted.

LAKE ELMO

Wildwood Lodge SH
(651) 714-8068. **$179-$259.** 8511 Hudson Blvd. I-94, exit 250 (Inwood/Radio), just ne. Int corridors. **Pets:** Accepted.

MAPLE GROVE

AAA ▼▼▼ Select Inn SH
(763) 493-2277. **$63-$75.** 7285 Forest View Ln N. I-94, exit 28 (CR 61/Hemlock Ln), just se. Int corridors. **Pets:** Accepted.
SAVE SD X H H P

▼▼▼ Staybridge Suites Minneapolis-Maple Grove SH
(763) 494-8856. **$139-$399.** 7821 Elm Creek Blvd. Just ne of jct I-94/494/694. Int corridors. **Pets:** Medium. $150 one-time fee/pet. Service with restrictions, crate.
ASK SD X &M H H H P 2 X

MINNEAPOLIS

AAA ▼▼▼ Days Inn-University SH
(612) 623-3999. **$79-$169.** 2407 University Ave SE. I-35W, exit University Ave, 1 mi se. Int corridors. **Pets:** $20 one-time fee/room. Designated rooms, service with restrictions, supervision.
SAVE SD X H H H P

AAA ▼▼▼ ▼▼▼ Graves 601 Hotel LH
(612) 677-1100. **$209-$269.** 601 1st Ave N. Between 6th and 7th sts. Int corridors. **Pets:** Small, dogs only. $150 one-time fee/room. Designated rooms, service with restrictions, supervision.
SAVE SD X H H H P X

▼▼▼ Hilton Minneapolis LH
(612) 376-1000. **$109-$369.** 1001 Marquette Ave. Between S 10th and S 11th sts. Int corridors. **Pets:** Small. $100 deposit/pet. Service with restrictions, crate.
ASK X H H H P H 2 X

▼▼▼ Holiday Inn Minneapolis Metrodome LH
(612) 333-4646. **$139-$199.** 1500 Washington Ave S. Jct Washington and S 15th aves. Int corridors. **Pets:** Accepted.
ASK SD X H H H H P H 2 X

AAA ▼▼▼ The Marquette Hotel LH
(612) 333-4545. **$109-$375.** 7th St & Marquette Ave. Jct Marquette Ave and S 7th St. Int corridors. **Pets:** Accepted.
SAVE X H H H P H

AAA ▼▼▼ Millenium Hotel Minneapolis LH ❀
(612) 332-6000. **$109-$141.** 1313 Nicollet Mall. Jct Nicollet Ave and Grant St. Int corridors. **Pets:** $10 daily fee/pet. Service with restrictions.
SAVE X &M H H H P H 2 X

AAA ▼▼▼ Minneapolis Marriott City Center LH
(612) 349-4000. **$199-$259.** 30 S 7th St. Between Hennepin and Nicollet aves; in City Center Shopping Complex. Int corridors. **Pets:** Accepted.
SAVE X &M H H H P H X

AAA ▼▼▼ ▼▼▼ Radisson Plaza Hotel Minneapolis LH
(612) 339-4900. **$99-$399, 3 day notice.** 35 S 7th St. Between Nicollet and Hennepin aves. Int corridors. **Pets:** Accepted.
SAVE SD X &M H H H P H X

▼▼▼ Residence Inn by Marriott Minneapolis Downtown City Center SH
(612) 677-1000. **$109-$369.** 45 S 8th St. At 8th St and LaSalle Ave. Int corridors. **Pets:** Other species. $75 one-time fee/room. Service with restrictions, supervision.
ASK SD X H H H P

AAA ▼▼▼ Residence Inn Milwaukee Road Depot SH
(612) 340-1300. **$95-$299.** 425 S 2nd St. Jct S 2nd St and 5th Ave S. Int corridors. **Pets:** Accepted.
SAVE SD X H H H P

▼▼▼ Sheraton Minneapolis Midtown Hotel SH
(612) 821-7600. **Call for rates.** 2901 Chicago Ave S. At Lake St. Int corridors. **Pets:** Accepted.
X H H H P H 2

MINNETONKA

▼▼▼ Minneapolis Marriott-Southwest LH
(952) 935-5500. **$169-$189.** 5801 Opus Pkwy. Just nw of jct US 169 and Cross Town SR 62, exit Bren Rd off US 169. Int corridors. **Pets:** Accepted.
X H H H P H 2 X

AAA ▼▼▼ Sheraton Minneapolis West Hotel SH
(952) 593-0000. **$89-$169.** 12201 Ridgedale Dr. I-394, exit 1C (Plymouth Rd), 0.3 mi s. Int corridors. **Pets:** Accepted.
SAVE SD X H H H P H 2 X

MONTICELLO

AAA ▼▼▼ Best Western Chelsea Inn & Suites SH
(763) 271-8880. **$89-$139.** 89 Chelsea Rd. I-94, exit 193, just se. Int corridors. **Pets:** Medium. $10 daily fee/pet. Service with restrictions, supervision.
SAVE SD X H H H P 2

AAA ▼▼▼ Days Inn SH
(763) 295-1111. **$59-$79.** 200 E Oakwood Dr. I-94, exit 193, 0.3 mi se. Int corridors. **Pets:** Accepted.
SAVE SD X H H P

▼▼▼ Select Inn of Monticello SH
(763) 295-4000. **$66-$86.** 1114 Cedar St. I-94, exit 193, 0.3 mi se. Int corridors. **Pets:** Large. $10 daily fee/pet. Designated rooms, service with restrictions, crate.
ASK SD X H H P 2 X

NORTH BRANCH

AAA ▼▼▼ AmericInn Lodge & Suites SH ❀
(651) 674-8627. **$75-$181.** 38675 14th Ave. I-35, exit 147 (SR 95), just e, then s on Oakview, then w on Oak St. Int corridors. **Pets:** $30 one-time fee/room. Service with restrictions, supervision.
SAVE X H H P 2 X

AAA ▼▼▼ Budget Host Inn & Suites SH
(651) 277-8000. **$65-$110.** 6010 Main St. I-35, exit 147 (SR 95), just e. Int corridors. **Pets:** Small, dogs only. $20 one-time fee/pet. Designated rooms, service with restrictions, supervision.
SAVE SD X H H P 2

OAKDALE

▼▼▼ Wingate Inn SH ❀
(651) 578-8466. **$125-$135.** 970 Helena Ave N. I-694, exit 57, just e, then just s. Int corridors. **Pets:** Small, other species. $50 one-time fee/room. Designated rooms, service with restrictions, crate.
ASK X &M H H H P

OAK PARK HEIGHTS

AAA ▼▼▼ AmericInn Lodge & Suites SH
(651) 275-0980. **$76-$140.** 13025 60th St N. SR 36 at Stillwater Blvd. Int corridors. **Pets:** Accepted.
SAVE SD X H H P 2 X

PLYMOUTH

AAA ▼▼▼ Best Western Kelly Inn SH
(763) 553-1600. **$89-$129.** 2705 N Annapolis Ln. I-494, exit 22 (SR 55), just e. Int corridors. **Pets:** Large. Designated rooms, service with restrictions, supervision.
SAVE SD X H H P H 2 X

AAA ▼▼▼ Radisson Hotel & Conference Center Minneapolis LH
(763) 559-6600. **$110-$179.** 3131 Campus Dr. I-494, exit 22 (SR 55), just e to CR 61 (Northwest Blvd), then 0.8 mi nw. Int corridors. **Pets:** Accepted.
SAVE SD X H H H P H 2 X

▼▼/▼▼ Red Roof Inn **M**
(763) 553-1751. **$50-$74.** 2600 Annapolis Ln N. I-494, exit 22 (SR 55), just se. Ext corridors. **Pets:** Medium, other species. Service with restrictions, supervision.
⊠

RICHFIELD

▲▲▲ ▼▼/▼▼ Candlewood Suites **SH**
(612) 869-7704. **$95-$115.** 351 W 77th St. I-494, exit 4B (Lyndale Ave), just ne. Int corridors. **Pets:** Accepted.
[SAVE] [Ŝ₆] [⊠] [♿] [🐾] [♨] [📶] [🍴] [📺]

ROGERS

▼▼/▼▼ AmericInn Lodge & Suites **SH** 🐾
(763) 428-4346. **$75-$105.** 21800 Industrial Blvd. I-94, exit 207 (SR 101), just sw. Int corridors. **Pets:** $100 deposit/pet, $10 daily fee/pet. Designated rooms, service with restrictions, supervision.
[ASK] [Ŝ₆] [⊠] [♿] [🍴] [📺] [♨]

ROSEVILLE

▼▼/▼▼/▼▼ Residence Inn **SH**
(651) 636-0680. **$89-$159.** 2985 Centre Pointe Dr. I-35W, exit 25A (CR D), just se. Int corridors. **Pets:** Accepted.
[ASK] [Ŝ₆] [⊠] [♿] [🐾] [♨] [🍴] [📺] [♨] [⊠]

ST. LOUIS PARK

▲▲▲ ▼▼ Lakeland Inn **SH**
(952) 926-6575. **$65-$80.** 4025 Hwy 7. SR 7, 0.5 mi e of SR 100. Int corridors. **Pets:** $10 daily fee/pet. Designated rooms, service with restrictions, supervision.
[SAVE] [Ŝ₆] [⊠] [🍴]

▼▼/▼▼/▼▼ TownePlace Suites-Minneapolis West **SH**
(952) 847-6900. **$80-$159.** 1400 Zarthan Ave S. I-394, exit 5 (Park Place Blvd), 0.3 mi w on 16th, then just n. Int corridors. **Pets:** Medium. $75 one-time fee/room. Service with restrictions, supervision.
[ASK] [Ŝ₆] [⊠] [♿] [🍴] [📺] [♨]

ST. PAUL

▲▲▲ ▼▼/▼▼ Best Western Bandana Square **SH**
(651) 647-1637. **$79-$199.** 1010 Bandana Blvd W. I-94, exit 239B (Lexington Pkwy), 1.3 mi n, then 0.3 mi w on Energy Park Dr. Int corridors. **Pets:** Medium, other species. $10 one-time fee/pet. Service with restrictions, crate.
[SAVE] [Ŝ₆] [⊠] [♿] [🐾] [♨] [🍴] [📺] [♨] [⊠]

▲▲▲ ▼▼/▼▼ Best Western Kelly Inn **SH**
(651) 227-8711. **$89-$129.** 161 St. Anthony Ave. Jct I-35E and 94. Int corridors. **Pets:** Other species. Service with restrictions, crate.
[SAVE] [Ŝ₆] [⊠] [♿] [🍴] [📺] [🍴] [♨]

▲▲▲ ▼▼/▼▼ Exel Inn of St. Paul **SH**
(651) 771-5566. **$58-$88.** 1739 Old Hudson Rd. I-94, exit 245 (White Bear Ave), just nw. Int corridors. **Pets:** Small, other species. Designated rooms, service with restrictions, supervision.
[SAVE] [Ŝ₆] [⊠] [🐾] [🍴] [📺]

SHAKOPEE

▲▲▲ ▼▼/▼▼ AmericInn Lodge & Suites **SH**
(952) 445-6775. **$70-$170.** 4100 12th Ave E. Just ne of US 169. Int corridors. **Pets:** Small, dogs only. $100 deposit/room, $30 one-time fee/room. Service with restrictions, crate.
[SAVE] [⊠] [🐾] [♿] [🍴] [📺] [♨] [⊠]

▲▲▲ ▼▼/▼▼ Country Inn & Suites By Carlson **SH**
(952) 445-0200. **$79-$142.** 1204 Ramsey St. Just ne of US 169. Int corridors. **Pets:** Small. $100 deposit/pet, $30 one-time fee/pet. Service with restrictions.
[SAVE] [Ŝ₆] [⊠] [♿] [🐾] [🍴] [📺] [♨]

▲▲▲ ▼▼/▼▼/▼▼ Sandalwood Studios & Suites **SH**
(952) 277-0100. **$49-$129.** 3910 12th Ave E. Just nw of US 169. Int corridors. **Pets:** Very small, cats only. $10 daily fee/room, $10 one-time fee/room. Designated rooms, no service, supervision.
[SAVE] [Ŝ₆] [⊠] [🍴]

STILLWATER

▼▼/▼▼ Days Inn-Stillwater **SH**
(651) 430-1300. **$59-$99.** 1750 W Frontage Rd. SR 36 at Washington Ave, just ne. Int corridors. **Pets:** Accepted.
[ASK] [Ŝ₆] [⊠] [♿] [🐾] [🍴] [📺] [♨]

▼▼/▼▼ Super 8 Motel **M**
(651) 430-3990. **$66-$99.** 2190 W Frontage Rd. SR 36 at Washington Ave, 3.3 mi sw. Int corridors. **Pets:** $10 one-time fee/pet. Service with restrictions, supervision.
[ASK] [Ŝ₆] [⊠] [🐾] [🍴]

TAYLORS FALLS

▲▲▲ ▼▼/▼▼ The Springs Country Inn **M**
(651) 465-6565. **$70-$110.** 361 Government St. US 8 and SR 95, just w. Ext corridors. **Pets:** Accepted.
[SAVE] [Ŝ₆] [⊠] [🍴]

WACONIA

▼▼/▼▼ Super 8 Motel **M**
(952) 442-5147. **Call for rates.** 301 E Frontage Rd. On SR 5 at jct CR 10. Int corridors. **Pets:** Accepted.
[ASK] [⊠] [🐾] [♿] [🍴] [📺]

WHITE BEAR LAKE

▲▲▲ ▼▼/▼▼/▼▼ Best Western White Bear Country Inn **SH**
(651) 429-5393. **$99-$209.** 4940 N Hwy 61. Jct SR 96, 1 mi n. Int corridors. **Pets:** $10 daily fee/pet. Service with restrictions, supervision.
[SAVE] [Ŝ₆] [⊠] [🍴] [📺] [🍴] [♨] [⊠]

WOODBURY

▲▲▲ ▼▼/▼▼/▼▼ Holiday Inn Express Hotels & Suites **SH**
(651) 702-0200. **$119-$129.** 9840 Norma Ln. I-94, exit 251, just sw. Int corridors. **Pets:** Small. $10 daily fee/pet. Designated rooms, service with restrictions, supervision.
[SAVE] [Ŝ₆] [⊠] [♿] [🍴] [📺] [♨] [⊠]

▼▼/▼▼ Red Roof Inn #7063 **M**
(651) 738-7160. **$51-$72.** 1806 Wooddale Dr. I-494, exit 59 (Valley Creek Rd), just se. Ext corridors. **Pets:** Medium, other species. Service with restrictions, supervision.
[⊠] [🐾]

END METROPOLITAN AREA

A FAMILY VACATION SHOULD INCLUDE THE WHOLE FAMILY.

Best Western Advantages:

Exclusive AAA/CAA Preferred Gold Crown Club® International frequent-guest program

Continental or hot breakfast*

Fresh in-room coffee

Free high-speed internet access

Free local calls

And much more

AT OVER 1,900 BEST WESTERNS PETS ARE MORE THAN ALLOWED, THEY'RE WELCOMED.

Best Western® invites you to bring your pet on your next family trip. Your best friend will love being part of the fun, while the rest of you enjoy the 17 standard services and amenities that have made Best Western your choice for vacation travel.

Visit our website and click on "Trip Planner" to find one of our pet-friendly hotels. And plan your getaway today.

THE WORLD'S LARGEST HOTEL CHAIN

bestwestern.com/aaa
bestwestern.com/caa
1.866.430.9022

DISCOUNTS.
FREE NIGHTS.
REWARD POINTS.

ONE CARD DOES IT ALL.

MONTEVIDEO

▼▼▼▼ Country Inn & Suites By Carlson 🆂🅷
(320) 269-8000. **$79-$99.** 1805 E Hwy 7. On SR 7. Int corridors. **Pets:** Other species. $200 deposit/room. Designated rooms, service with restrictions, supervision.
A$K 🆂🏠 ✕ 🎯 🖵 ➿

MOORHEAD

◈◈◈ ▼ Grand Inn Of Moorhead 🆂🅷
(218) 233-7501. **$40-$45.** 810 Belsly Blvd. I-94, exit 1A (US 75), 0.5 mi s. Int corridors. **Pets:** Medium. $25 deposit/room. Designated rooms, service with restrictions, supervision.
SAVE 🆂🏠 ✕

▼▼ Super 8 Motel 🆂🅷
(218) 233-8880. **$39-$89.** 3621 S 8th St. I-94, exit 1A (US 75), 0.5 mi s. Int corridors. **Pets:** Medium. Designated rooms, service with restrictions, supervision.
A$K 🆂🏠 ✕ 🎯 🖵

◈◈◈ ▼▼▼ Travelodge & Suites 🆂🅷
(218) 233-5333. **$49-$149.** 3027 S Frontage Rd. Just s of US 10 E; east of downtown. Int corridors. **Pets:** Medium. Designated rooms, service with restrictions, supervision.
SAVE 🆂🏠 ✕ ♿ 🎯 🎯 🖵 ➿

MOOSE LAKE

▼▼▼▼ AmericInn Lodge & Suites 🆂🅷
(218) 485-8885. **$75-$180.** 400 Park Place Dr. I-35, exit 214 (SR 73), just sw. Int corridors. **Pets:** Other species. $50 deposit/room, $10 daily fee/room. Designated rooms, service with restrictions, supervision.
A$K ✕ 🎯 🖵 ➿

MORRIS

◈◈◈ ▼▼▼ Best Northland Prairie Inn 🆂🅷
(320) 589-3030. **$60-$92.** 200 SR 28 E. Jct US 59 and SR 28, just sw. Int corridors. **Pets:** Other species. Designated rooms, service with restrictions.
SAVE 🆂🏠 ✕ 🎯 🖵 🍽 ➿

NEW ULM

▼▼▼ Holiday Inn 🆂🅷
(507) 359-2941. **$85-$179.** 2101 S Broadway. SR 15/68, 1.8 mi se. Int corridors. **Pets:** Accepted.
A$K ✕ 🎯 🖵 🍽 ➿ 🎯

◈◈◈ ▼▼▼ Microtel Inn & Suites 🆂🅷
(507) 354-9800. **$57-$105.** 424 20th St S. Just e of jct SR 15/68 and CR 37. Int corridors. **Pets:** Other species. $10 daily fee/room. Service with restrictions.
SAVE ✕ ♿ 🎯 🎯 🎯 🖵 ➿

NISSWA

◈◈◈ ▼▼▼ Nisswa Motel Ⓜ
(218) 963-7611. **$59-$83, 5 day notice.** 5370 Merrill Ave. Just sw of Main St; center. Ext corridors. **Pets:** Dogs only. $5 daily fee/pet. Designated rooms, service with restrictions, crate.
SAVE ✕ 🎯 🖵

ONAMIA

▼▼ Econo Lodge 🆂🅷
(320) 532-3838. **$55-$100.** 40847 US 169. On US 169; 6 mi n. Int corridors. **Pets:** Accepted.
A$K 🆂🏠 ✕ 🎯 🎯 🖵

ORR

▼▼▼▼ AmericInn Lodge & Suites 🆂🅷
(218) 757-3613. **$80-$210.** 4675 Hwy 53. Just n. Int corridors. **Pets:** $20 one-time fee/room. Designated rooms, service with restrictions, supervision.
A$K 🆂🏠 ✕ 🎯 🎯 🎯 🖵 🍽 ➿ 🎯

▼▼ North Country Inn 🆂🅷
(218) 757-3778. **$64-$90.** 4483 Hwy 53. 0.3 mi s. Int corridors. **Pets:** $10 one-time fee/pet. Service with restrictions, supervision.
✕ ♿ 🎯

OWATONNA

▼▼▼ Comfort Inn 🆂🅷
(507) 444-0818. **$80-$140.** 2345 43rd St NW. I-35, exit 45 (Clinton Falls), just sw. Int corridors. **Pets:** $50 deposit/room, $5 one-time fee/pet. Designated rooms, service with restrictions, supervision.
A$K 🆂🏠 ✕ ♿ 🎯 🎯 🖵 ➿

◈◈◈ ▼▼▼ Microtel Inn & Suites 🆂🅷
(507) 446-0228. **$49-$89.** 150 St. John Dr NW. I-35, exit 41 (Bridge St), just nw. Int corridors. **Pets:** Accepted.
SAVE 🆂🏠 ✕ ♿ 🎯 🎯 🖵

◈◈◈ ▼▼▼ Owatonna Grand Hotel 🆂🅷
(507) 455-0606. **$59-$129.** 1212 N I-35. I-35, exit 42B, 0.3 mi nw. Int corridors. **Pets:** Accepted.
SAVE 🆂🏠 ✕ 🎯 🎯 🎯 🖵 ➿ 🎯

PEQUOT LAKES

◈◈◈ ▼▼▼ AmericInn Lodge & Suites 🆂🅷
(218) 568-8400. **$79-$149, 7 day notice.** 32912 Paul Bunyan Trail Dr (SR 371/CR 16). SR 371, n of downtown. Int corridors. **Pets:** Very small, dogs only. $10 daily fee/pet. Designated rooms, service with restrictions, supervision.
SAVE ✕ 🎯 🎯 🖵 ➿ 🎯

PERHAM

▼▼ Super 8 Motel 🆂🅷
(218) 346-7888. **$62-$95.** 106 Jake St SE. SR 78, just nw of jct US 10. Int corridors. **Pets:** Other species. $10 daily fee/pet. Service with restrictions, supervision.
A$K 🆂🏠 ✕ 🎯

PINE RIVER

▼▼ Econo Lodge Ⓜ
(218) 587-4499. **$50-$125, 10 day notice.** 2684 SR 371 SW. 1 mi s. Ext corridors. **Pets:** Accepted.
A$K 🆂🏠 ✕ 🎯 🖵 🎯

RED WING

◈◈◈ ▼▼◈▼ Best Western Quiet House & Suites 🆂🅷
(651) 388-1577. **$60-$180.** 752 Withers Harbor Dr. 1.5 mi n on US 61, at Withers Harbor Dr; opposite side of US 61 from Pottery Mall. Ext/int corridors. **Pets:** $15 daily fee/pet. Designated rooms, service with restrictions, supervision.
SAVE 🆂🏠 ✕ ♿ 🎯 🎯 🖵 ➿

▼▼ Days Inn Ⓜ
(651) 388-3568. **$65-$93.** 955 E 7th St. US 61/63, 1.7 mi se. Ext corridors. **Pets:** Other species. $7 daily fee/pet. Service with restrictions, supervision.
A$K 🆂🏠 ✕ 🎯 🖵 ➿

ROCHESTER

▼▼ Econo Lodge-South 🆂🅷
(507) 282-9905. **$50-$80.** 1850 S Broadway. Jct US 52 and 63 (Broadway), 1 mi s. Int corridors. **Pets:** $8 daily fee/pet. Designated rooms, service with restrictions, crate.
A$K 🆂🏠 ✕ 🎯 🎯 🎯

⦿⦿⦿ ▼▼▼▼ Heritage Suites 🆂🅷
(507) 281-1200. **$89-$169.** 2829 NW 43rd St. US 52, exit 41st St NW, just w, just n on W Frontage Rd, then just w. Int corridors. **Pets:** Accepted.
🆂🅰🆅🅴 🆂🅳 ⊠ 🅗🅜 🅐 🅒 🅗 🅛🅔 ⊠ ⊠

▼▼▼▼ Holiday Inn South 🆂🅷
(507) 288-1844. **$74-$109.** 1630 S Broadway. On US 63 (Broadway), 0.5 mi s of jct US 14. Ext/int corridors. **Pets:** $15 daily fee/pet. Service with restrictions, supervision.
🅰🆂🅺 🆂🅳 ⊠ 🅐 🅗 🅛🅔 🅗 🅛🅔 ⊠ ⊠

⦿⦿⦿ ▼▼▼▼ The Kahler Grand Hotel 🅻🅷
(507) 282-2581. **$159.** 20 2nd Ave SW. Opposite Mayo Clinic and Methodist Hospital. Int corridors. **Pets:** Accepted.
🆂🅰🆅🅴 ⊠ 🅐 🅗 🅗 🅛🅔 🅗 🅛🅔 ⊠ ⊠

⦿⦿⦿ ▼▼▼ Kahler Inn & Suites 🆂🅷
(507) 289-8646. **$85-$95.** 9 NW 3rd Ave. Just n of Mayo Clinic. Int corridors. **Pets:** Medium. $60 one-time fee/room. Service with restrictions, supervision.
🆂🅰🆅🅴 🆂🅳 ⊠ 🅐 🅗 🅗 🅛🅔 🅗 🅛🅔 ⊠

▼▼▼ Marriott Hotel 🅻🅷
(507) 280-6000. **$219.** 101 1st Ave SW. Just e of Mayo Clinic. Int corridors. **Pets:** Accepted.
⊠ 🅐 🅗 🅗 🅛🅔 🅗 🅛🅔 ⊠ ⊠

▼▼▼ Microtel Inn & Suites 🆂🅷
(507) 286-8780. **$58-$99.** 4210 Hwy 52 N. US 52, exit 41st St NW, just w. Int corridors. **Pets:** $5 daily fee/room. Service with restrictions, crate.
🅰🆂🅺 🆂🅳 ⊠ 🅗🅜 🅐 🅗 🅗 🅛🅔

⦿⦿⦿ ▼▼▼▼ Quality Inn & Suites 🆂🅷
(507) 282-8091. **$78-$199.** 1620 1st Ave SE. On US 63 (Broadway) from jct US 14, 0.5 mi s, just e on 16th St, then just s. Ext/int corridors. **Pets:** Other species. $5 daily fee/pet. Crate.
🆂🅰🆅🅴 🆂🅳 ⊠ 🅐 🅗 🅗 🅛🅔

⦿⦿⦿ ▼▼▼▼ Radisson Plaza Hotel 🅻🅷
(507) 281-8000. **$149-$219.** 150 S Broadway. On US 63 (Broadway); downtown. Int corridors. **Pets:** Accepted.
🆂🅰🆅🅴 🆂🅳 ⊠ 🅗 🅗 🅗 🅛🅔 🅗 🅛🅔 ⊠ ⊠

▼▼▼▼ Staybridge Suites 🆂🅷
(507) 289-6600. **$134-$229.** 1211 2nd St SW. SR 52, exit 2nd St SW, just e. Int corridors. **Pets:** Small. $75 one-time fee/pet. Service with restrictions, supervision.
🅰🆂🅺 🆂🅳 ⊠ 🅗🅜 🅐 🅗 🅗 🅗 🅛🅔 ⊠

ROSEAU

▼▼ AmericInn Lodge & Suites 🆂🅷
(218) 463-1045. **$70-$80.** 1090 3rd St NW. 1 mi w on SR 11. Int corridors. **Pets:** Other species. $25 one-time fee/room. Designated rooms, supervision.
🅰🆂🅺 ⊠ 🅗🅜 🅐 🅗 🅗 🅛🅔 ⊠

▼▼ North Country Inn 🆂🅷
(218) 463-9444. **$70-$130.** 902 3rd St NW. 0.8 mi w on SR 11. Int corridors. **Pets:** Accepted.
🅰🆂🅺 🆂🅳 ⊠ 🅗 🅗 🅛🅔

ST. CLOUD

⦿⦿⦿ ▼▼▼ AmericInn Lodge & Suites 🆂🅷
(320) 253-6337. **$69-$125.** 4385 Clearwater Rd. I-94, exit 171 (CR 75), just ne. Int corridors. **Pets:** Medium. $10 daily fee/pet. Service with restrictions, supervision.
🆂🅰🆅🅴 🆂🅳 ⊠ 🅗🅜 🅐 🅗 🅗 🅛🅔

⦿⦿⦿ ▼▼▼▼ Best Western Americanna Inn & Conference Center 🆂🅷
(320) 252-8700. **$60-$86.** 520 S US Hwy 10. Jct SR 23, 0.3 mi s. Ext/int corridors. **Pets:** Other species. $10 one-time fee/room. Service with restrictions, supervision.
🆂🅰🆅🅴 🆂🅳 ⊠ 🅐 🅗 🅗 🅛🅔 🅗 🅛🅔 ⊠

⦿⦿⦿ ▼▼▼▼ Best Western Kelly Inn 🆂🅷
(320) 253-0606. **$89-$149.** 100 4th Ave S. SR 23 at 4th Ave S; center. Int corridors. **Pets:** Other species. Service with restrictions, supervision.
🆂🅰🆅🅴 🆂🅳 ⊠ 🅗🅜 🅐 🅗 🅗 🅛🅔 🅗 🅛🅔 ⊠

▼▼▼ Comfort Inn 🆂🅷
(320) 251-1500. **$64-$134.** 4040 2nd St S. Jct SR 15 and 23 W, just w. Int corridors. **Pets:** Small, dogs only. $10 one-time fee/pet. Designated rooms, service with restrictions, crate.
🅰🆂🅺 🆂🅳 ⊠ 🅗🅜 🅐 🅗 🅗 🅛🅔 🅗 🅛🅔 ⊠

▼▼▼ Country Inn & Suites By Carlson 🆂🅷
(320) 259-8999. **$82-$102.** 235 S Park Ave. Jct SR 15 and 23 W, just w. Int corridors. **Pets:** Small. $15 daily fee/room. Designated rooms, service with restrictions, supervision.
🅰🆂🅺 🆂🅳 ⊠ 🅗🅜 🅗 🅗 🅛🅔

⦿⦿⦿ ▼▼▼ Days Inn Hotel and Waterslide 🆂🅷
(320) 253-4444. **$50-$100.** 70 37th Ave S. Jct SR 15 and 23, just e. Int corridors. **Pets:** Medium, other species. $10 daily fee/pet. Designated rooms, service with restrictions, supervision.
🆂🅰🆅🅴 🆂🅳 ⊠ 🅗🅜 🅐 🅗 🅗 🅗 🅛🅔

▼▼▼▼ Holiday Inn Express 🆂🅷 🐾
(320) 240-8000. **$79-$99.** 4322 Clearwater Rd. I-94, exit 171 (CR 75), just ne. Int corridors. **Pets:** Service with restrictions, supervision.
🅰🆂🅺 🆂🅳 ⊠ 🅗🅜 🅐 🅗 🅗 🅗 🅛🅔 ⊠

▼▼▼▼ Holiday Inn Hotel & Suites 🆂🅷
(320) 253-9000. **$80-$105.** 75 S 37th Ave. Jct SR 15 and 23. Int corridors. **Pets:** Large. Service with restrictions, supervision.
🅰🆂🅺 ⊠ 🅐 🅗 🅗 🅛🅔 🅗 🅛🅔 ⊠ ⊠

⦿⦿⦿ ▼▼▼▼ Ramada Limited & Suites 🆂🅷
(320) 253-3200. **$65-$115.** 121 Park Ave S. Jct SR 15 and 23, just w. Int corridors. **Pets:** Accepted.
🆂🅰🆅🅴 🆂🅳 ⊠ 🅗🅜 🅐 🅗 🅗 🅛🅔 ⊠

▼▼ Thrifty Motel 🅼
(320) 253-6320. **$38-$46.** 130 14th Ave NE. Jct US 10 and SR 23, 0.3 mi e. Int corridors. **Pets:** Small, other species. $5 daily fee/pet. Service with restrictions, supervision.
⊠ 🅐 🅗

SAUK CENTRE

⦿⦿⦿ ▼▼▼ AmericInn Lodge & Suites 🆂🅷 🐾
(320) 352-2800. **$75-$139.** 1230 Timberlane Dr. I-94, exit 127, just ne. Int corridors. **Pets:** Medium, dogs only. $10 one-time fee/pet. Designated rooms, service with restrictions, supervision.
🆂🅰🆅🅴 ⊠ 🅐 🅗 🅗 🅛🅔 🅗 🅛🅔 ⊠

SILVER BAY

⦿⦿⦿ ▼▼▼ AmericInn Lodge & Suites 🆂🅷
(218) 226-4300. **$79-$169.** 150 Mensing Dr. On SR 61, 0.5 mi ne of jct SR 61 and Outer Dr. Int corridors. **Pets:** $10 daily fee/pet. Designated rooms, service with restrictions.
🆂🅰🆅🅴 🆂🅳 ⊠ 🅗🅜 🅐 🅗 🅗 🅛🅔 🅗 🅛🅔 ⊠

⦿⦿⦿ ▼▼▼ Mariner Motel 🅼 🐾
(218) 226-4488. **$50-$70, 3 day notice.** 46 Outer Dr. Just w off SR 61; at traffic signal. Ext corridors. **Pets:** Dogs only. $5 daily fee/pet. Service with restrictions, supervision.
🆂🅰🆅🅴 ⊠ 🅗 🅗 🅗

SLEEPY EYE

△△△ ▽▽▼ Inn of Seven Gables 🄷
(507) 794-5390. **$65-$89.** 1100 E Main St. US 14, 0.8 mi e of jct CR 4 and US 14. Int corridors. **Pets:** Accepted.
【SAVE】❌ 🔲 💻 🏊

SPICER

▽▽ Northern Inn Hotel & Suites 🄷
(320) 796-2091. **$89-$119.** 154 Lake Ave S. On SR 23; center. Int corridors. **Pets:** Other species. $10 daily fee/pet. Designated rooms, service with restrictions, crate.
【ASK】❌ 🔲 💻 🏊

SPRING VALLEY

△△△ ▽▽▼ Spring Valley Inn & Suites 🄷
(507) 346-7788. **$75-$125.** 745 N Broadway. Just w on US 63. Int corridors. **Pets:** Accepted.
【SAVE】【S🐾】❌ 【&M】【&】🔲 💻

STEWARTVILLE

△△△ ▽▽▼ AmericInn Motel 🄼
(507) 533-4747. **$70-$85.** 1700 NW 2nd Ave. I-90, exit 209A, 1 mi s on US 63. Int corridors. **Pets:** Small, dogs only. $15 daily fee/pet. Designated rooms, service with restrictions, supervision.
【SAVE】【S🐾】❌ 【&M】🌀 【&】🔲 💻

TOFTE

△△△ ▽▽▼ AmericInn Lodge & Suites 🄷 🐾
(218) 663-7899. **$60-$249.** 7261 W SR 61. On SR 61. Int corridors. **Pets:** Dogs only. $10 daily fee/room. Designated rooms, service with restrictions, supervision.
【SAVE】❌ 【&】🔲 💻 🏊 ❌

▽▽▽▼ Bluefin Bay on Lake Superior 🄲🄾 🐾
(218) 663-7296. **$59-$549, 5 day notice.** 7198 W Hwy 61. On SR 61. Ext corridors. **Pets:** Other species. $20 daily fee/room. Designated rooms, crate.
❌ 🔲 💻 🍴 🏊 ❌ 🄺

TWO HARBORS

△△△ ▽▽▼ AmericInn Lodge & Suites 🄷 🐾
(218) 834-3000. **$66-$220.** 1088 SR 61. On SR 61, 0.7 mi s. Int corridors. **Pets:** Medium, dogs only. $20 daily fee/pet. Designated rooms, service with restrictions, supervision.
【SAVE】【S🐾】❌ 【&M】🔲 💻 🏊 ❌

△△△ ▽▽▽▼ Superior Shores Resort 🄲🄾
(218) 834-5671. **$49-$479, 14 day notice.** 1521 Superior Shores Dr. On SR 61, 1.5 mi n of center. Ext/int corridors. **Pets:** Accepted.
【SAVE】❌ 🔲 💻 🍴 🏊 ❌

VERGAS

▽▽▽▼ The Log House & Homestead on Spirit Lake 🄱🄱
(218) 342-2318. **$120-$215.** 44854 Fredholm Rd. 5 mi sw on CR 4. Ext/int corridors. **Pets:** Accepted.
❌ 🔲 💻 ❌ 🅆 🅩

VIRGINIA

▽▽ AmericInn Lodge & Suites 🄷 🐾
(218) 741-7839. **$89-$179.** 5480 Mountain Iron Dr. US 53, just s of jct US 169. Int corridors. **Pets:** Dogs only. $10 one-time fee/pet. Designated rooms, supervision.
❌ 【&M】【&】🔲 💻 🏊 ❌

▽ Lakeshor Motor Inn Downtown 🄼 🐾
(218) 741-3360. **$58.** 404 6th Ave N. Just n of Chestnut St; center. Ext corridors. **Pets:** Dogs only. Service with restrictions, supervision.
【ASK】【S🐾】❌ 🔲 💻

△△△ ▽▽▼ Pine View Inn 🄼
(218) 741-8918. **$46-$80.** 903 N 17th St. Jct US 53 and 169, 0.5 mi n on US 53, 0.7 mi e on 9th St N, then 0.5 mi n on 9th Ave W. Ext/int corridors. **Pets:** Medium, dogs only. $50 deposit/pet, $10 daily fee/pet. Service with restrictions, supervision.
【SAVE】❌ 💻

WABASHA

▽▽▽▼ AmericInn Lodge & Suites 🄷
(651) 565-5366. **$80-$170.** 150 Commerce Dr. Just ne of jct US 61 and SR 60. Int corridors. **Pets:** Accepted.
【ASK】❌ 【&M】【&】🔲 💻 🏊 ❌

WALKER

△△△ ▽▽▽▼ Country Inn & Suites By Carlson 🄷
(218) 547-1400. **$69-$101.** 442 Walker Bay Blvd. 1 mi s on SR 371. Int corridors. **Pets:** Other species. $50 deposit/pet. Designated rooms, service with restrictions, crate.
【SAVE】【S🐾】❌ 【&M】🔲 💻 🏊

WARROAD

▽▽▽▼ Can-Am Motel 🄷
(218) 386-3807. **$53-$64.** 406 Main Ave NE. 0.5 mi w on SR 11. Int corridors. **Pets:** No service, supervision.
【ASK】【S🐾】❌ 【&M】【&】

▽▽ The Patch Motel 🄷
(218) 386-2723. **$54-$65.** 801 N State Ave W. 0.6 mi w on SR 11. Int corridors. **Pets:** Accepted.
【ASK】【S🐾】❌ 【&M】【&】🔲 🍴

WILLMAR

▽▽▽▼ Comfort Inn 🄷
(320) 231-2601. **$90-$130.** 2200 E US 12. 1.8 mi e. Int corridors. **Pets:** Small. Designated rooms, service with restrictions, supervision.
【ASK】【S🐾】❌ 【&】🔲 💻 🏊 ❌

▽▽▽ Days Inn-Willmar 🄷
(320) 231-1275. **$66-$73.** 225 28th St SE. 2.3 mi e on US 12. Int corridors. **Pets:** Small. Designated rooms, service with restrictions, supervision.
【ASK】【S🐾】❌ 🌀 🔲 💻

▽▽▽▼ Holiday Inn & Willmar Conference Center 🄷
(320) 235-6060. **$100-$110.** 2100 US 12 E. 1.8 mi e. Int corridors. **Pets:** Small. Designated rooms, service with restrictions, supervision.
【ASK】【S🐾】❌ 🌀 🔲 💻 🍴 🏊 ❌

WINONA

△△△ ▽▽▽▼ Best Western Riverport Inn & Suites 🄷
(507) 452-0606. **$69-$109.** 900 Bruski Dr. Jct US 14/61 and SR 43. Int corridors. **Pets:** Accepted.
【SAVE】【S🐾】❌ 🔲 💻 🍴 🏊

▽▽▽▼ Holiday Inn Hotel and Suites 🄷
(507) 453-0303. **$90-$119.** 1025 Hwy 61 E. Jct SR 43, just sw. Int corridors. **Pets:** Accepted.
【ASK】❌ 【&M】🌀 【&】🔲 💻 🍴 🏊 ❌

▽▽▽ Quality Inn 🄷
(507) 454-4390. **$70-$150.** 956 Mankato Ave. Jct US 14/61 and SR 43. Ext/int corridors. **Pets:** Accepted.
【ASK】【S🐾】❌ 🔲 💻 🍴 🏊 ❌

WORTHINGTON

△△△ ▽▽▽▼ AmericInn Motel 🄷
(507) 376-4500. **$70-$130, 7 day notice.** 1475 Darling Dr. I-90, exit 43 (US 59), just se. Int corridors. **Pets:** Other species. $10 one-time fee/room. Supervision.
【SAVE】❌ 【&M】🌀 【&】🔲 💻 🏊 ❌

▽▽ ▽▽ **Days Inn** SH
(507) 376-6155. **$60-$75.** 207 Oxford St. I-90, exit 42, 0.7 mi s on SR 266, then just e. Ext/int corridors. **Pets:** Other species. $6 daily fee/pet. Service with restrictions, supervision.

ASK S⊘ ✕ &° 🖬 🖵 ⇝

▽▽ ▽▽ **Super 8 Motel** SH
(507) 372-7755. **$54-$125.** 850 Lucy Dr. I-90, exit 42, just sw. Int corridors. **Pets:** Other species. $10 one-time fee/room. Service with restrictions, supervision.

ASK S⊘ ✕ 🖬 🖵

ABERDEEN

🆎 ♦♦ Best Western Aberdeen Inn Ⓜ
(662) 369-4343. **$72-$80.** 801 E Commerce St. On US 45, just n of jct SR 25 and Tenn-Tom Bridge. Ext corridors. **Pets:** Accepted.
[SAVE] [S] [✕] [🔶] [💻] [🍴] [≈]

BATESVILLE

♦♦ Comfort Inn 🆂🅷
(662) 563-1188. **$58-$120.** 290 Power Dr. I-55, exit 243B, just ne on frontage road. Ext corridors. **Pets:** Accepted.
[ASK] [S] [✕] [🔶] [💻] [≈]

BAY ST. LOUIS

♦♦ Casino Magic Inn 🅻🅷
(228) 467-9257. **$59-$129.** 711 Casino Magic Dr. US 90, 0.6 mi n on Meadow Rd, then e, follow signs. Int corridors. **Pets:** Accepted.
[ASK] [✕] [⚙] [🔶] [💻] [🍴] [≈] [✕]

BOONEVILLE

♦♦ Super 8 Motel 🆂🅷
(662) 720-1688. **$55-$65.** 110 Hospitality Ave. Jct US 45 and SR 4/30, 1.7 mi e to SR 145, then 0.5 mi s. Int corridors. **Pets:** Medium. $5 daily fee/room. Service with restrictions, supervision.
[ASK] [S] [✕] [⚙] [🔶] [≈]

CANTON

🆎 ♦♦♦ Best Western-Canton Inn 🆂🅷
(601) 859-8600. **$60-$70, 7 day notice.** 137 Soldiers Colony Rd. I-55, exit 119, just se. Int corridors. **Pets:** Accepted.
[SAVE] [S] [✕] [🔶] [💻] [≈]

🆎 ♦♦♦ Comfort Inn 🆂🅷
(601) 859-7575. **$69-$85.** 145 Soldier Colony Rd. I-55, exit 119, just se. Int corridors. **Pets:** Medium, other species. $50 deposit/room. Service with restrictions, supervision.
[SAVE] [S] [✕] [⚙] [🔶] [💻] [≈]

CLARKSDALE

🆎 ♦♦♦ Best Western Executive Inn 🆂🅷
(662) 627-9292. **$69-$72, 7 day notice.** 710 S State St. 1 mi s of jct US 49 and SR 161. Ext/int corridors. **Pets:** Accepted.
[SAVE] [S] [✕] [🔶] [💻] [≈]

🆎 ♦♦ Econo Lodge Ⓜ
(662) 621-1110. **$55-$76.** 350 S State St. 0.5 mi s of jct US 49 amd SR 161. Ext corridors. **Pets:** Very small, dogs only. $10 daily fee/pet. Service with restrictions, supervision.
[SAVE] [S] [✕] [🔶] [💻]

CLEVELAND

♦♦ Comfort Inn of Cleveland Ⓜ
(662) 843-4060. **$49-$89.** 721 N Davis Ave. On US 61, 1 mi n of jct US 61 and SR 8. Ext corridors. **Pets:** Accepted.
[ASK] [S] [✕] [⚙] [🔶] [💻] [≈]

COLUMBIA

♦♦♦ Comfort Inn 🆂🅷
(601) 731-9955. **$89-$119.** 820 Hwy 98 Bypass. Just e of jct US 98 Bypass and SR 13. Int corridors. **Pets:** Medium. $20 one-time fee/room. Service with restrictions, supervision.
[ASK] [S] [✕] [⚙] [🔶] [💻] [≈]

COLUMBUS

♦♦ Master Hosts Inns & Suites 🆂🅷
(662) 328-5202. **$50-$65.** 506 Hwy 45 N. US 82, exit US 45 N, just s. Ext corridors. **Pets:** Medium. $5 daily fee/pet. Service with restrictions, crate.
[ASK] [S] [✕] [🔶] [💻] [🍴] [≈]

CORINTH

♦♦ Comfort Inn 🆂🅷 🐾
(662) 287-4421. **$41-$50.** 2101 Hwy 72 W. Jct US 72 and 45, just e. Ext corridors. **Pets:** Other species. $25 deposit/room.
[ASK] [S] [✕] [🔶] [💻] [≈]

FOREST

🆎 ♦♦♦ Comfort Inn 🆂🅷
(601) 469-2100. **$65-$75.** 1250 Hwy 35 S. I-20, exit 88, just n. Ext corridors. **Pets:** Accepted.
[SAVE] [S] [✕] [🔶] [💻] [≈]

GREENVILLE

♦♦♦ Comfort Inn of Greenville 🆂🅷
(662) 378-4976. **$59-$129.** 3080 US 82 E. 3 mi e of center. Ext corridors. **Pets:** $50 deposit/room. Service with restrictions, supervision.
[ASK] [S] [✕] [⚙] [🔶] [💻] [≈]

GREENWOOD

♦♦ Econo Lodge Inn & Suites 🆂🅷
(662) 453-5974. **$49-$79.** 401 Hwy 82 W. 0.4 mi w of Main St. Ext corridors. **Pets:** Accepted.
[ASK] [S] [✕] [🔶] [💻] [≈]

GRENADA

♦♦ Americas Best Value Inn 🆂🅷
(662) 226-7816. **$42-$59.** 1750 Sunset Dr. I-55, exit 206, just ne on frontage road. Ext corridors. **Pets:** Accepted.
[ASK] [S] [✕] [🔶] [💻] [🍴] [≈]

♦♦♦ Country Inn & Suites by Carlson 🆂🅷
(662) 227-8444. **$73-$100.** 255 SW Frontage Rd. I-55, exit 206, just sw. Int corridors. **Pets:** Medium. $25 one-time fee/room. Designated rooms, service with restrictions, supervision.
[ASK] [S] [✕] [🔶] [💻] [≈]

GULFPORT

🆎 ♦♦♦ Best Western Seaway Inn 🆂🅷
(228) 864-0050. **$50-$200.** 9475 Hwy 49. I-10, exit 34A, just sw. Ext corridors. **Pets:** Accepted.
[SAVE] [✕] [🎵] [⚙] [🔶] [💻] [≈]

▼▼▼▼ Holiday Inn Airport SH
(228) 868-8200. **$150.** 9415 Hwy 49. I-10, exit 34A, 0.6 mi s. Ext corridors. **Pets:** Medium, other species. $100 deposit/room, $35 one-time fee/room. Designated rooms, service with restrictions, supervision.
[icons]

▼▼▼ Holiday Inn Express SH
(228) 864-7222. **$89-$139.** 9435 Hwy 49. I-10, exit 34A, 0.6 mi s. Ext corridors. **Pets:** $35 one-time fee/room. Service with restrictions, crate.
[icons]

▼ Motel 6 #416 M
(228) 863-1890. **$65-$95.** 9355 US Hwy 49. I-10, exit 34A, just s. Ext corridors. **Pets:** Medium, other species. Service with restrictions, supervision.
[icons]

HATTIESBURG

▼▼▼▼ Comfort Inn University-The Lodge SH
(601) 264-1881. **$99-$139.** 6541 US Hwy 49. I-59, exit 67A, just s. Ext/int corridors. **Pets:** $25 one-time fee/room. Service with restrictions, supervision.
[icons]

▼▼▼▼ Hampton Inn of Hattiesburg SH
(601) 264-8080. **$81-$139.** 4301 Hardy St. I-59, exit 65, just nw. Ext/int corridors. **Pets:** Accepted.
[icons]

▲▲▲ ▼▼▼▼ Inn on the Hill at Convention Center SH
(601) 599-2001. **$81-$90.** 6595 Hwy 49 N. I-59, exit 67A, just se. Ext corridors. **Pets:** Medium, other species. $75 one-time fee/room. Service with restrictions, supervision.
[icons]

▼ Motel 6 #0235 M
(601) 544-6096. **$45-$62.** 6508 US Hwy 49 N. I-59, exit 67A, 0.5 mi e. Ext corridors. **Pets:** Medium, other species. Service with restrictions, supervision.
[icons]

▼▼▼ University Inn SH
(601) 268-2850. **$89.** 6563 Hwy 49 N. I-59, exit 67A, just se. Int corridors. **Pets:** Supervision.
[icons]

HOLLY SPRINGS

▼▼▼▼ Hampton Inn SH
(662) 252-5444. **$79-$129.** 100 Brooks Rd. US 78, exit 30, just sw. Int corridors. **Pets:** Accepted.
[icons]

HORN LAKE

▲▲▲ ▼▼▼ Days Inn SH
(662) 349-3493. **$72-$89.** 801 Desoto Cove. I-55, exit 289, just nw. Int corridors. **Pets:** Accepted.
[icons]

▼▼▼▼ Drury Inn & Suites-Memphis South SH
(662) 349-6622. **$95-$130.** 735 Goodman Rd W. I-55, exit 289, just sw. Int corridors. **Pets:** Large, other species. Service with restrictions, supervision.
[icons]

▼ Motel 6 SH
(662) 349-4439. **$55-$65.** 701 Southwest Dr. I-55, exit 289, just se. Int corridors. **Pets:** Medium, other species. Service with restrictions, supervision.
[icons]

JACKSON

▲▲▲ ▼▼▼▼ Cabot Lodge Millsaps SH
(601) 948-8650. **$79-$129.** 2375 N State St. I-55, exit 98A northbound, 1 mi w on Woodrow Wilson Blvd, then just s. Int corridors. **Pets:** Accepted.
[icons]

▼▼▼▼ The Edison Walthall Hotel LH
(601) 948-6161. **$99.** 225 E Capitol St. I-55, exit 96A (Pearl St), 0.8 mi w; between West and Lamar sts; downtown. Ext/int corridors. **Pets:** Accepted.
[icons]

▼▼▼ Extended StayAmerica Jackson-North M
(601) 956-4312. **$59-$69.** 5354 I-55 N. I-55, exit 100, just n. Ext corridors. **Pets:** Accepted.
[icons]

▲▲▲ ▼▼▼ Jackson Inn & Suites SH
(601) 899-9000. **$84-$100.** 5411 I-55 N. I-55, exit 102A northbound; exit 102 southbound, s on west service road. Int corridors. **Pets:** Accepted.
[icons]

▼▼▼ Jameson Inn SH
(601) 206-8923. **$54-$120.** 585 Beasley Rd. I-55, exit 102, just w. Int corridors. **Pets:** Small. $10 daily fee/pet. Service with restrictions, crate.
[icons]

▼▼▼ La Quinta Inn Jackson (North) SH
(601) 957-1741. **$70-$80.** 616 Briarwood Dr. I-55, exit 102A northbound, just ne on Frontage Rd. Ext corridors. **Pets:** Medium. Service with restrictions.
[icons]

▼▼ Red Roof Inn Fairgrounds M
(601) 969-5006. **$48-$63.** 700 Larson St. I-55, exit 96B (High St), e to Greymont, then just ne. Ext corridors. **Pets:** Medium, other species. Service with restrictions, supervision.
[icons]

▲▲▲ ▼▼▼▼ Regency Hotel & Conference Center SH
(601) 969-2141. **$89-$129.** 400 Greymont Ave. I-55, exit 96B, just w, then just s. Ext/int corridors. **Pets:** Small. $25 daily fee/pet. Service with restrictions, supervision.
[icons]

▼▼▼ Residence Inn by Marriott SH
(601) 355-3599. **$109-$160, 7 day notice.** 881 E River Pl. I-55, exit 96C, just e. Ext corridors. **Pets:** Accepted.
[icons]

KOSCIUSKO

▲▲▲ ▼▼▼ Americas Best Value Inn M
(662) 289-6252. **$55-$59.** 1052 Veterans Memorial Dr/Hwy 35 Bypass. Just sw of jct SR 35 and Natchez Trace Pkwy. Ext corridors. **Pets:** Accepted.
[icons]

MCCOMB

▲▲▲ ▼▼▼▼ Hawthorn Inn & Suites SH
(601) 684-8655. **$90.** 2001 Veteran's Blvd. I-55, exit 18, just off interstate. Int corridors. **Pets:** Medium, other species. $125 one-time fee/room. Service with restrictions, supervision.
[icons]

MERIDIAN

▲▲▲ ▼▼▼▼ Best Western of Meridian SH
(601) 693-3210. **$56-$70.** 2219 S Frontage Rd. I-20/59, exit 153, just sw. Ext/int corridors. **Pets:** Small, dogs only. $10 daily fee/pet. Designated rooms, service with restrictions, supervision.
[icons]

Days Inn M
(601) 483-3812. **$59-$69.** 145 Hwy 11 & 80 E. I-20/59, exit 154 westbound; exit 154B eastbound, just n to Frontage Rd, then just e. Ext corridors. **Pets:** Other species. $6 daily fee/pet. Service with restrictions, supervision.

Econo Lodge M
(601) 693-9393. **$45-$60.** 2405 S Frontage Rd. I-20/59, exit 153, 0.5 mi sw. Ext corridors. **Pets:** Accepted.

Holiday Inn Northeast SH
(601) 485-5101. **$89-$105.** 111 US 11 & 80. I-20/59, exit 154 westbound, just n to frontage road, then just e; exit 154B eastbound. Ext corridors. **Pets:** Accepted.

Jameson Inn SH
(601) 483-3315. **$54-$120.** 524 Bonita Lakes Dr. I-20/59, exit 154 southbound; exit 154A northbound, just s. Ext corridors. **Pets:** Small. $10 daily fee/pet. Service with restrictions, crate.

Motel 6 M
(601) 482-1182. **$35-$38.** 2309 S Frontage Rd. I-20/59, exit 153, 0.5 mi sw. Ext corridors. **Pets:** Medium, other species. Service with restrictions, supervision.

MOSS POINT

Best Western Flagship Inn SH
(228) 475-5000. **$70-$110.** 4830 Amoco Dr. I-10, exit 69, just s. Ext corridors. **Pets:** Accepted.

NATCHEZ

Days Inn of Natchez SH
(601) 445-8291. **$64-$90.** 109 US Hwy 61 S. Just se of jct US 61, 84 and 98. Ext corridors. **Pets:** Other species. Supervision.

OCEAN SPRINGS

Quality Inn Ocean Springs SH
(228) 875-7555. **$80-$110.** 7304 Washington Ave. I-10, exit 50, 0.4 mi s on SR 609. Ext corridors. **Pets:** Accepted.

Ramada Limited SH
(228) 872-2323. **$99-$159.** 8011 Tucker Rd. I-10, exit 50, just n. Ext corridors. **Pets:** Medium, other species. $15 daily fee/pet. Designated rooms, service with restrictions.

OLIVE BRANCH

Comfort Inn SH
(662) 895-0456. **$79-$84.** 7049 Enterprise. US 78, exit 2, SR 302, just w. Int corridors. **Pets:** Other species. $12 daily fee/room. Designated rooms, service with restrictions.

Holiday Inn Express Hotel & Suites SH
(662) 893-8700. **$89-$119.** 8900 Expressway Dr. US 78, exit 4, just e. Int corridors. **Pets:** Accepted.

Whispering Woods Hotel and Conference Center LH
(662) 895-2941. **$109-$149, 3 day notice.** 11200 E Goodman Rd. US 78, exit 2 (SR 302), 3.6 mi e. Int corridors. **Pets:** Accepted.

PASCAGOULA

LaFont Inn SH
(228) 762-7111. **$79-$99.** 2703 Denny Ave. I-10, exit 69, 3.5 mi s on SR 63, then 2 mi w on US 90. Ext corridors. **Pets:** Small. $30 one-time fee/pet. Service with restrictions, supervision.

Super 8 Motel M
(228) 762-9414. **$120-$170.** 4919 Denny Ave. I-10, exit 69, 3.5 mi s on SR 63, then just w on US 90. Int corridors. **Pets:** Accepted.

PEARL

Jameson Inn of Pearl SH
(601) 932-6030. **$54-$120.** 434 Riverwind Dr. I-20, exit 48, just nw. Int corridors. **Pets:** Small. $10 daily fee/pet. Service with restrictions, crate.

La Quinta Inn & Suites Jackson Airport (Pearl) SH
(601) 664-0065. **$65-$85.** 501 S Pearson Rd. I-20, exit 48, just s. Int corridors. **Pets:** Accepted.

PHILADELPHIA

Deluxe Inn & Suites SH
(601) 656-0052. **$44-$149.** 1004 Central Dr. Jct SR 15 and 16. Ext corridors. **Pets:** Medium. $10 daily fee/pet. No service, crate.

PICAYUNE

Days Inn SH
(601) 799-1339. **$59-$149.** 450 S Lofton Ave. I-59, exit 4, just nw. Ext corridors. **Pets:** Medium. $10 daily fee/pet. Designated rooms, service with restrictions, supervision.

PONTOTOC

Days Inn M
(662) 489-5200. **$50-$55.** 217 Hwy 15 N. Just n of jct SR 336 and 15. Ext corridors. **Pets:** Medium. $10 daily fee/pet. Designated rooms, service with restrictions, supervision.

RICHLAND

Executive Inn & Suites SH
(601) 664-3456. **$49-$59.** 390 Hwy 49 S. I-20, exit 47, just s. Ext corridors. **Pets:** Dogs only. $20 deposit/pet, $5 one-time fee/pet. Designated rooms, service with restrictions, supervision.

RIDGELAND

Drury Inn & Suites-Jackson, MS SH
(601) 956-6100. **$85-$135.** 610 E County Line Rd. I-55, exit 103 (County Line Rd), just w. Int corridors. **Pets:** Large, other species. Service with restrictions, supervision.

Econo Lodge M
(601) 956-7740. **$50-$60.** 839 Ridgewood Rd. I-55, exit 103 (County Line Rd), just e, then just n. Ext corridors. **Pets:** Accepted.

Homewood Suites by Hilton SH
(601) 899-8611. **$149.** 853 Centre St. I-55, exit 103 (County Line Rd), just e to Ridgewood Rd, 0.4 mi ne, then just e. Int corridors. **Pets:** Accepted.

♦♦ **Quality Inn North** [SH]
(601) 956-6203. **$70-$80.** 839 Ridgewood Rd. I-55, exit 103 (County Line Rd), just ne. Ext corridors. **Pets:** Accepted.
[ASK] [SD] ⊠ ▣ ☕ 🏊

♦♦ **Red Roof Inn Ridgeland** [M]
(601) 956-7707. **$51-$58.** 810 Adcock St. I-55, exit 103 (County Line Rd), just ne on Frontage Rd. Ext corridors. **Pets:** Medium, other species. Service with restrictions, supervision.
⊠ ♿ ▣

SENATOBIA

♦♦ **Days Inn & Suites** [SH]
(662) 562-5647. **$55-$61.** 513 E Main St. I-55, exit 265, just se. Ext corridors. **Pets:** Accepted.
[ASK] [SD] ⊠ ♿ ▣ ☕ 🏊

STARKVILLE

[AAA] ♦♦ **Days Inn & Suites** [SH]
(662) 324-5555. **$105-$125.** 119 Hwy 12 W. SR 12, 1.5 mi w of jct US 82. Ext corridors. **Pets:** Accepted.
[ASK] ⊠ ▣ ☕ 🏊

TUNICA

[AAA] ♦♦ **Cottage Inn** [CA]
(662) 363-2900. **$50-$150.** 4325 Casino Center Dr. Off US 61. Ext corridors. **Pets:** Other species. Service with restrictions.
[SAVE] ⊠ ▣ ☕

♦ **Key West Inn Tunica** [M] 🐾
(662) 363-0021. **$45-$149.** 11635 Hwy 61 N. US 61, 0.3 mi n of SR 304. Ext corridors. **Pets:** Other species. $10 daily fee/pet. Service with restrictions.
[ASK] [SD] ⊠ ▣ ☕

TUPELO

[AAA] ♦♦ **AmeriHost Inn-Tupelo** [SH]
(662) 844-7660. **$69.** 625 Spicer Dr. On SR 145, 0.4 mi n of McCullough Blvd. Int corridors. **Pets:** Medium. $25 one-time fee/pet. Designated rooms, service with restrictions, supervision.
[SAVE] [SD] ⊠ [♿M] ♿ ▣ ☕ 🏊 ✂

♦♦ **Comfort Inn** [SH]
(662) 842-5100. **$77-$95.** 1190 N Gloster St. Jct McCullough Blvd and SR 145, 1.3 mi s to McCullough Blvd, w to N Gloster St, then 0.3 mi n. Ext corridors. **Pets:** Small. $25 deposit/pet. Service with restrictions, supervision.
[ASK] [SD] ⊠ ▣ ☕

♦♦ **Jameson Inn** [SH]
(662) 840-2380. **$54-$120.** 879 Mississippi Dr. US 45, exit Barnes Crossing, 1 mi sw. Ext corridors. **Pets:** Small. $10 daily fee/pet. Service with restrictions, crate.
[ASK] ⊠ ♿ ▣ ☕ 🏊

[AAA] ♦♦ **Super 8 Motel** [M]
(662) 842-0448. **$51-$63.** 3898 McCullough Blvd. US 78, exit 81, just sw. Ext corridors. **Pets:** Small, dogs only. $10 one-time fee/pet. Designated rooms, service with restrictions, supervision.
[SAVE] [SD] ⊠ ▣ 🏊

VICKSBURG

[AAA] ♦♦♦ **Annabelle Bed & Breakfast** [BB]
(601) 638-2000. **$99, 7 day notice.** 501 Speed St. I-20, exit 1A, 2.3 mi n on Washington St, just w. Ext/int corridors. **Pets:** $50 one-time fee/pet. Designated rooms, service with restrictions, supervision.
[SAVE] ⊠ ▣ ☕ 🏊

[AAA] ♦♦ **Battlefield Inn** [SH]
(601) 638-5811. **$79.** 4137 I-20 N Frontage Rd. I-20, exit 4B, 1 mi ne. Ext/int corridors. **Pets:** Other species. $10 daily fee/pet. Service with restrictions.
[SAVE] [SD] ⊠ ▣ 🍴 🏊 ✂

[AAA] ♦♦♦ **Cedar Grove Mansion** [CI]
(601) 636-1000. **$100-$260, 3 day notice.** 2200 Oak St. I-20, exit 1A, 2.3 mi n on Washington St, then w on Klein; to gated entrance. Ext/int corridors. **Pets:** Other species. $50 one-time fee/room. Designated rooms, service with restrictions, supervision.
[SAVE] [SD] ⊠ ▣ ☕ 🍴 🏊 ✂

♦♦♦ **The Corners Bed & Breakfast** [BB]
(601) 636-7421. **$90-$130, 3 day notice.** 601 Klein St. I-20, exit 1A, 2.3 mi n on Washington St, just w. Ext/int corridors. **Pets:** Other species. $100 deposit/room. Designated rooms, service with restrictions, supervision.
[ASK] ⊠ ▣ ☕

♦ **Econo Lodge of Vicksburg** [M]
(601) 634-8766. **$50-$70.** 3330-A Clay St. I-20, exit 4B (Clay St), just n. Ext corridors. **Pets:** Accepted.
[ASK] [SD] ⊠ ▣ ☕

♦♦ **Jameson Inn** [SH]
(601) 619-7799. **$54-$120.** 3975 S Frontage Rd. I-20, exit 4A, on southeast frontage road. Ext corridors. **Pets:** Small. $10 daily fee/pet. Service with restrictions, crate.
[ASK] ⊠ [♿M] 👂 ♿ ▣ ☕ 🏊

♦♦ **Motel 6 #4189** [SH]
(601) 638-5077. **$55-$115, 7 day notice.** 4127 N Frontage Rd. I-20, exit 4B (Clay St), just ne. Int corridors. **Pets:** Medium, other species. Service with restrictions, supervision.
⊠ 🏊

♦♦♦ **Quality Inn and Suites** [M]
(601) 636-0804. **$65-$140.** 3332 Clay St. I-20, exit 4B (Clay St), just n. Ext corridors. **Pets:** $10 one-time fee/room.
[ASK] [SD] ⊠ ▣ ☕ 🏊

MISSOURI

AVA

▼▼▼ Ava Super 8 SH

(417) 683-1343. **$65-$80.** 1711 S Jefferson St. Jct SR 5 S and 76. Int corridors. **Pets:** Other species. $10 one-time fee/room. Designated rooms, service with restrictions, supervision.

BETHANY

◆◆◆ ▼▼▼ Best Western Bethany Inn SH

(660) 425-8006. **$60-$65, 3 day notice.** 496 S 39th St. I-35, exit 92, just nw. Int corridors. **Pets:** Medium. $10 daily fee/pet. Service with restrictions, supervision.

◆◆◆ ▼▼▼ Family Budget Inn M

(660) 425-7915. **$49-$59.** 4014 Miller St. I-35, exit 92. Int corridors. **Pets:** Other species. $20 deposit/pet, $5 daily fee/pet. Designated rooms, supervision.

BOONVILLE

◆◆◆ ▼▼ Boonville Comfort Inn SH ❀

(660) 882-5317. **$59-$109.** 2427 Mid America Industrial Dr. I-70, exit 101, just sw. Int corridors. **Pets:** Small, dogs only. $10 daily fee/pet. Designated rooms, service with restrictions, supervision.

BRANSON METROPOLITAN AREA

BRANSON

◆◆◆ ▼▼▼▼ Best Western Landing View Inn & Suites SH

(417) 334-6464. **$69-$129.** 403 W Main (Hwy 76). 0.3 mi e from SR 76 and US 65. Ext corridors. **Pets:** Medium. $10 daily fee/pet. Designated rooms, service with restrictions, crate.

◆◆◆ ▼▼▼ ▼▼ Chateau on the Lake Resort Spa & Convention Center LH

(417) 334-1161. **$109-$269, 3 day notice.** 415 N State Hwy 265. Just n of jct SR 165 and 265. Int corridors. **Pets:** Small. $25 one-time fee/room. Designated rooms, service with restrictions, crate.

◆◆◆ ▼▼ Eagles Inn a Rodeway Inn SH

(417) 336-2666. **$45-$85.** 3221 Shepherd of the Hills Expwy. 0.3 mi e of jct SR 76. Ext corridors. **Pets:** Accepted.

▼▼ Fall Creek Inn & Suites SH

(417) 348-1683. **$44-$79.** 995 Hwy 165. Jct SR 76 (Country Music Blvd), 1.5 mi s on SR 165. Ext corridors. **Pets:** Accepted.

▼▼▼ Grand Crowne Resorts CO

(417) 332-8330. **$109-$250.** 300 Golfview Dr. just sw of jct Wildwood Dr. Ext corridors. **Pets:** Medium, other species. Designated rooms, service with restrictions, supervision.

▼▼▼▼ Holiday Inn Express Hotel & Suites SH

(417) 336-1100. **$85-$97.** 1970 W Hwy 76 (Country Music Blvd). 1.8 mi w of jct SR 76 (Country Music Blvd) and US 65. Int corridors. **Pets:** Other species. $25 one-time fee/room. Designated rooms, service with restrictions, supervision.

◆◆◆ ▼▼▼ Howard Johnson SH

(417) 336-5151. **$59-$79.** 3027-A W Hwy 76. On SR 76 (Country Music Blvd), 3.5 mi w of jct US 65. Ext corridors. **Pets:** Medium, other species. $10 daily fee/pet. Service with restrictions.

▼▼▼▼ La Quinta Inn Branson (Music City Centre) SH

(417) 336-1600. **$50-$89.** 1835 W Hwy 76. 1.6 mi w of jct US 65. Ext/int corridors. **Pets:** Other species. No service.

◆◆◆ ▼▼ Ozark Valley Inn M

(417) 336-4666. **$45-$115.** 2693 Shepherd of the Hills Expwy. Jct SR 76 (Country Music Blvd), 0.9 mi e. Ext corridors. **Pets:** $10 one-time fee/room. Designated rooms, service with restrictions.

▼▼ ▼▼ Quality Inn SH

(417) 335-6776. **$45-$95.** 3269 Shepherd of the Hills Expwy. 0.3 mi e of jct SR 76 (Country Music Blvd). Ext/int corridors. **Pets:** Accepted.

▼▼ ▼▼ Ramada Inn & Conference Center SH

(417) 334-1000. **$40-$90.** 1700 Hwy 76 W. Jct SR 76 (Country Music Blvd) and US 65, 1.5 mi w. Ext corridors. **Pets:** Accepted.

▼▼ **Residence Inn by Marriott** SH
(417) 336-4077. **$89-$229.** 280 Wildwood Dr S. 2 mi w on SR 76 (Country Music Blvd), just s. Int corridors. **Pets:** Accepted.
ⒶⓈⓀ 🆂🅾 ✕ 🅼 🌀 🅲 🅸 📭 🔁 ✕

▼ **Rock View Resort** M
(417) 334-4678. **$53-$87, 21 day notice.** 1049 Park View Dr. Jct US 65, 4.4 mi w on SR 165, 0.3 mi s via Dale Dr, then 0.7 mi w. Ext corridors. **Pets:** Accepted.
✕ 🅸 📭 🔁 ✕ ☎

ⒶⒶ ▼▼ **Scenic Hills Inn** SH
(417) 336-8855. **$43-$70.** 2422 Shepherd of the Hills Expwy. Jct SR 76 (Country Music Blvd), 1.1 mi e. Int corridors. **Pets:** Small, other species. $7 daily fee/room. Designated rooms, service with restrictions.
🆂🅰🆅🅴 🆂🅾 ✕ 🅲 🅸 📭 🔁

ⒶⒶ ▼▼ **Settle Inn Resort & Conference Center** SH
(417) 335-4700. **$59-$119.** 3050 Green Mountain Dr. Jct SR 76 (Country Music Blvd) and US 65, 3 mi w on SR 76, 0.8 mi s. Int corridors. **Pets:** $10 daily fee/pet. Designated rooms, service with restrictions, supervision.
🆂🅰🆅🅴 🆂🅾 ✕ 🌀 🅲 🅸 📭 🍴 🔁 ✕

ⒶⒶ ▼▼▼ **The Village At Indian Point** CO
(417) 338-8800. **$95-$225, 14 day notice.** 24 Village Tr. 2.5 mi s of jct SR 76 on Indian Point Rd. Ext corridors. **Pets:** $10 daily fee/room. Designated rooms, crate.
🆂🅰🆅🅴 🆂🅾 ✕ 🅸 🔁 ✕

ⒶⒶⒶ ▼▼▼ **Westgate Branson Woods Resort** CO
(417) 334-2324. **$59-$139, 7 day notice.** 2201 Roark Valley Rd. US 65, exit SR 248 (Shepherd of the Hills Expwy), 3.7 mi w, just n. Ext corridors. **Pets:** Accepted.
🆂🅰🆅🅴 🆂🅾 ✕ 🅸 📭 🔁 ✕

BRANSON WEST

ⒶⒶⒶ ▼▼▼ **Best Western Branson Inn & Conference Center** SH
(417) 338-2141. **$49-$85.** 8514 State Hwy 76. Jct SR 265, 1.1 mi w on SR 76. Int corridors. **Pets:** Small. $10 daily fee/pet. Designated rooms, service with restrictions, supervision.
🆂🅰🆅🅴 🆂🅾 ✕ 🅸 📭 🔁 ✕

▼▼ **Shady Acre Motel** M
(417) 338-2316. **$42.** 8722 Hwy 76. Jct SR 265, 1.3 mi w. Ext corridors. **Pets:** Small, dogs only. $10 one-time fee/room. Service with restrictions, crate.
✕ 🅸 📭 🔁

BUTLER

▼ **Super 8 Motel–Butler** M
(660) 679-6183. **$40-$85.** 1114 W Fort Scott St. Just e of jct US 71 and SR 52. Ext corridors. **Pets:** Small, other species. $7 daily fee/pet. Designated rooms, service with restrictions, supervision.
ⒶⓈⓀ 🆂🅾 ✕ 🅸

CAMERON

ⒶⒶⒶ ▼▼ **Best Western Acorn Inn** M
(816) 632-2187. **$75-$85.** 2210 E US 36. I-35, exit 54, 0.3 mi e. Ext corridors. **Pets:** Accepted.
🆂🅰🆅🅴 🆂🅾 ✕ 🌀 🅲 🅸 📭 🔁

ⒶⒶⒶ ▼▼ **Comfort Inn** SH
(816) 632-5655. **$79-$164.** 1803 Comfort Ln. I-35, exit 54, just e. Int corridors. **Pets:** $10 daily fee/room. Designated rooms, service with restrictions, crate.
🆂🅰🆅🅴 🆂🅾 ✕ 🅼 🅸 📭 🔁

ⒶⒶⒶ ▼▼ **Econo Lodge** M
(816) 632-6571. **$49-$69.** 220 E Grand. I-35, exit 54, 0.5 mi w on US 36, then just s on US 69. Ext corridors. **Pets:** Other species. $5 daily fee/pet. Service with restrictions, supervision.
🆂🅰🆅🅴 🆂🅾 ✕ 🅸 🔁

▼▼ **Super 8 Motel** SH
(816) 632-8888. **$60-$78.** 1710 N Walnut St. I-35, exit 54, 0.5 mi w on US 36. Int corridors. **Pets:** Small. $10 one-time fee/room. Designated rooms, service with restrictions, supervision.
ⒶⓈⓀ 🆂🅾 ✕ 🅲 🅸 🔁

CANTON

▼▼ **Comfort Inn Canton** SH
(573) 288-8800. **$65-$105.** 1701 Oak St. US 61, exit CR P, just e. Int corridors. **Pets:** Accepted.
ⒶⓈⓀ 🆂🅾 ✕ 🅸 📭 🔁

CAPE GIRARDEAU

▼▼▼ **Drury Lodge-Cape Girardeau** SH
(573) 334-7151. **$85-$130.** 104 S Vantage Dr. I-55, exit 96 (William St), just e. Ext/int corridors. **Pets:** Large, other species. Service with restrictions, supervision.
ⒶⓈⓀ ✕ 🌀 🅸 📭 🍴 🔁

▼▼▼ **Drury Suites-Cape Girardeau** SH
(573) 339-9500. **$96-$136.** 3303 Campster Dr. I-55, exit 96 (William St), just w. Int corridors. **Pets:** Large, other species. Service with restrictions, supervision.
ⒶⓈⓀ ✕ 🅼 🌀 🅲 🅸 📭 🔁

▼▼ **Hampton Inn-Cape Girardeau** SH
(573) 651-3000. **$114-$144.** 103 Cape W Pkwy. I-55, exit 96 (William St), 0.3 mi sw. Int corridors. **Pets:** Accepted.
ⒶⓈⓀ ✕ 🌀 🅲 🅸 📭

▼▼▼ **Pear Tree Inn by Drury-Cape Girardeau** SH
(573) 334-3000. **$70-$110.** 3248 William St. I-55, exit 96 (William St), just e. Int corridors. **Pets:** Large, other species. Service with restrictions, supervision.
ⒶⓈⓀ ✕ 📭 🔁

▼▼▼ **Victorian Inn & Suites** SH
(573) 651-4486. **$69-$109.** 3265 William St. I-55, exit 96 (William St), just e. Ext/int corridors. **Pets:** Accepted.
ⒶⓈⓀ 🆂🅾 ✕ 🅼 🌀 🅲 🅸 📭 🔁 ✕

CARTHAGE

ⒶⒶⒶ ▼▼▼ **Best Western Precious Moments Hotel** SH 🐾
(417) 359-5900. **$69-$130.** 2701 Hazel St. Just e of jct US 71 and SR HH. Int corridors. **Pets:** Medium, dogs only. $10 daily fee/room. Designated rooms, service with restrictions, crate.
🆂🅰🆅🅴 🆂🅾 ✕ 🌀 🅲 🅸 📭 🔁

Econo Lodge SH
(417) 358-3900. **$58-$139.** 1441 W Central. On SR 96; jct US 71. Ext/int corridors. **Pets:** Accepted.

Super 8 Motel SH
(417) 359-9000. **$57.** 416 W Fir Rd. Just e of jct US 71 and SR HH. Int corridors. **Pets:** Medium. $5 daily fee/pet. Service with restrictions, supervision.

CASSVILLE

Super 8 Motel SH
(417) 847-4888. **$59-$69.** 101 S Hwy 37. Just s of jct SR 76, 86 and 37 business route. Int corridors. **Pets:** Small, dogs only. $5 daily fee/pet. Designated rooms, service with restrictions, supervision.

CHARLESTON

Comfort Inn M
(573) 683-4200. **$64-$100, 7 day notice.** 102 Drake St. I-57, exit 10, just nw. Ext corridors. **Pets:** Medium. $15 one-time fee/pet. No service, supervision.

CHILLICOTHE

Best Western Inn SH
(660) 646-0572. **$45-$65.** 1020 S Washington St. Jct US 36 and 65 (Washington St). Ext/int corridors. **Pets:** Other species. $25 one-time fee/room. Designated rooms, service with restrictions, supervision.

Chillicothe Super 8 Motel SH
(660) 646-7888. **$70-$77.** 580 Old Hwy 36 E. Jct US 36 and 65 (Washington St), 0.8 mi e. Int corridors. **Pets:** Accepted.

CLINTON

Best Western Colonial Motel M
(660) 885-2206. **$55-$65.** 106 S Baird St. Jct SR 7 and 13. Ext corridors. **Pets:** Medium, dogs only. $10 daily fee/pet. Designated rooms, service with restrictions.

Motel USA Inn M
(660) 885-2267. **$39-$69.** 1508 N 2nd St. Jct SR 7 and 13. Ext corridors. **Pets:** Very small, dogs only. $10 daily fee/pet. Designated rooms, service with restrictions, supervision.

COLUMBIA

Candlewood Suites SH
(573) 817-0525. **$79-$179.** 3100 Wingate Ct. I-70, exit 128A, just s to I-70 Dr SE, 0.3 mi e to Keene St, then 0.3 mi s to Wingate Ct. Int corridors. **Pets:** Accepted.

Drury Inn-Columbia SH
(573) 445-1800. **$90-$160.** 1000 Knipp St. I-70, exit 124 (Stadium Blvd), just s. Int corridors. **Pets:** Large, other species. Service with restrictions, supervision.

Extended StayAmerica-Columbia-Stadium Blvd SH
(573) 445-6800. **$60-$145.** 2000 W Business Loop 70. I-70, exit 124 (Stadium Blvd), just ne. Int corridors. **Pets:** Accepted.

Holiday Inn Select Executive Center LH
(573) 445-8531. **$85-$300.** 2200 I-70 Dr SW. I-70, exit 124 (Stadium Blvd), just w. Int corridors. **Pets:** Accepted.

Red Roof Inn-Columbia M
(573) 442-0145. **$50-$73.** 201 E Texas Ave. I-70, exit 126 (Providence Rd), just n. Ext corridors. **Pets:** Accepted.

Super 8 Motel-Clarke Lane in Columbia M
(573) 474-8488. **$57-$96.** 3216 Clark Ln. I-70, exit 128A, northeast corner. Int corridors. **Pets:** Other species. $15 daily fee/pet. Designated rooms, service with restrictions, supervision.

CUBA

Super 8 Motel M
(573) 885-2087. **$55-$63.** 28 Hwy P. I-44, exit 208 (SR 19), just nw. Ext/int corridors. **Pets:** Accepted.

FESTUS

Baymont Inn & Suites SH
(636) 937-2888. **$69-$79.** 1303 Veterans Blvd. I-55, exit 175, just w. Int corridors. **Pets:** Accepted.

Drury Inn-Festus SH
(636) 933-2400. **$75-$113.** 1001 Veterans Blvd. I-55, exit 175, just e. Int corridors. **Pets:** Large, other species. Service with restrictions, supervision.

FULTON

Loganberry Inn Bed & Breakfast BB
(573) 642-9229. **$99-$189, 14 day notice.** 310 W 7th St. 1 mi e of jct US 54 and CR F, n on Westminster, then just e. Int corridors. **Pets:** Dogs only. $10 one-time fee/pet. Designated rooms, service with restrictions, crate.

HANNIBAL

Quality Inn & Suites SH
(573) 221-4001. **$69-$89.** 120 Lindsey Dr. 2 mi w on US 36, exit Shinn Ln to south service road. Int corridors. **Pets:** Medium. $10 daily fee/room. Designated rooms, service with restrictions, crate.

Super 8 Motel M
(573) 221-5863. **$56-$90.** 120 Huckleberry Heights. Jct US 36, 1.5 mi s on US 61. Int corridors. **Pets:** Accepted.

HARRISONVILLE

Best Western Harrisonville M
(816) 884-3200. **$59-$99, 7 day notice.** 2201 Rockhaven Rd. Just n of jct US 71 and SR 291. Ext corridors. **Pets:** Very small. $10 daily fee/pet. Designated rooms, service with restrictions, supervision.

Slumber Inn Motel M
(816) 884-3100. **$40-$60, 3 day notice.** 21400 E 275th St. Jct US 71 and SR 7 S (Clinton exit), just w. Ext corridors. **Pets:** Small. $10 daily fee/pet. Designated rooms, service with restrictions, supervision.

HAYTI

▼▼ Drury Inn & Suites-Hayti Caruthersville SH
(573) 359-2702. **$79-$146.** 1317 Hwy 84. I-55, exit 19 (US 412/SR 84), just w. Int corridors. **Pets:** Large, other species. Service with restrictions, supervision.

A$K ✕ ⟲ 🛏 💻 ➿

HIGGINSVILLE

▼▼ Super 8 Motel-Higginsville SH
(660) 584-7781. **$61-$77.** 6471 Oakview Ln. I-70, exit 49 (SR 13), just se. Int corridors. **Pets:** Other species. $5 daily fee/pet. Service with restrictions, supervision.

A$K S⟲ ✕ ⟲

JACKSON

▼▼▼ Drury Inn & Suites-Jackson,MO SH
(573) 243-9200. **$77-$122.** 225 Drury Ln. I-55, exit 105 (SR 61), 0.3 mi w. Int corridors. **Pets:** Large, other species. Service with restrictions, supervision.

A$K ✕ &M ⟲ 🛏 💻 ➿

JANE

▼▼ Booneslick Lodge SH
(417) 226-1888. **$64-$79.** 21140 US Hwy 71. just s on US 71. Int corridors. **Pets:** Accepted.

A$K ✕ 🛏 ➿

JEFFERSON CITY

▲▲▲ ▼▼▼ Truman Hotel & Conference Center SH
(573) 635-7171. **$62-$80.** 1510 Jefferson St. US 54, exit Ellis Blvd, 0.5 mi nw. Ext/int corridors. **Pets:** $10 daily fee/pet. Service with restrictions, supervision.

SAVE S⟲ ✕ ⟲ 🛏 💻 🍴 ➿

JOPLIN

▲▲▲ ▼▼▼ Baymont Inn & Suites SH
(417) 623-0000. **$66-$96.** 3510 S Range Line Rd. I-44, exit 8B, just n. Ext/int corridors. **Pets:** Accepted.

SAVE S⟲ ✕ ⟲ 🛏 💻 ➿

▲▲▲ ▼▼▼ Best Western Oasis Inn & Suites SH ❀
(417) 781-6776. **$66-$86.** 3508 S Range Line Rd. I-44, exit 8B, just nw. Ext corridors. **Pets:** Medium. $10 daily fee/pet. Service with restrictions, supervision.

SAVE S⟲ ✕ 🛏 💻 ➿

▼▼▼▼ Drury Inn & Suites-Joplin SH
(417) 781-8000. **$80-$120.** 3601 Range Line Rd. I-44, exit 8B, just ne. Int corridors. **Pets:** Large, other species. Service with restrictions, supervision.

A$K ✕ &M ⟲ 🛏 💻 ➿ ✕

▲▲▲ ▼▼▼▼ Holiday Inn SH ❀
(417) 782-1000. **$99-$159.** 3615 Range Line Rd. I-44, exit 8B, just ne. Int corridors. **Pets:** $25 deposit/room. Designated rooms, service with restrictions.

SAVE S⟲ ✕ ⟲ 🛏 💻 🍴 ➿ ✕

▼ Microtel Inn & Suites Joplin SH
(417) 626-8282. **$47-$53.** 4101 Richard Joseph Blvd. I-44, exit 8A, just s. Int corridors. **Pets:** Accepted.

A$K S⟲ ✕ ⟲ ⟲ 🛏 💻 ➿

▼▼▼ Residence Inn by Marriott-Joplin SH ❀
(417) 782-0908. **$119-$159.** 3128 E Hammons Blvd. I-44, exit 8B, just ne. Int corridors. **Pets:** Large, other species. $75 one-time fee/room. Service with restrictions, crate.

A$K S⟲ ✕ &M ⟲ ⟲ 🛏 💻 ➿ ✕

▲▲▲ ▼▼▼ Sleep Inn SH
(417) 782-1212. **$69.** I-44 & State Hwy 43 S. I-44, exit 4, just s. Int corridors. **Pets:** Accepted.

SAVE S⟲ ✕ ⟲ 💻

KANSAS CITY METROPOLITAN AREA

BLUE SPRINGS

▼▼▼ Hampton Inn Blue Springs SH
(816) 220-3844. **$89-$140.** 900 NW South Outer Rd. I-70, exit 20, just s to South Outer Rd, then just w. Int corridors. **Pets:** Other species. Service with restrictions.

A$K ✕ ⟲ 🛏 💻 ➿

INDEPENDENCE

▲▲▲ ▼▼▼ Best Western Truman Inn M
(816) 254-0100. **$54-$69.** 4048 S Lynn Court Dr. I-70, exit 12, just n on Noland Rd, then just w. Ext corridors. **Pets:** Medium, other species. $8 one-time fee/pet. Service with restrictions, crate.

SAVE S⟲ ✕ 🛏 💻 ➿

▲▲▲ ▼▼▼ Super 8 Motel SH
(816) 833-1888. **$44-$59.** 4032 S Lynn Court Dr. I-70, exit 12, just nw. Int corridors. **Pets:** Medium. $30 deposit/room, $8 daily fee/pet. Service with restrictions, crate.

SAVE S⟲ ✕ 🛏 ➿

KANSAS CITY

▲▲▲ ▼▼▼ Baymont Inn & Suites Kansas City South SH
(816) 822-7000. **$71-$105.** 8601 Hillcrest Rd. I-435, exit 69 (87th St). Int corridors. **Pets:** Accepted.

SAVE ✕ &M ⟲ ⟲ 🛏 💻

▲▲▲ ▼▼▼ Best Western Country Inn-North M
(816) 459-7222. **$49-$139.** 2633 NE 43rd St. I-35, exit 8C (Antioch Rd), just s on SR 1, then just e. Ext corridors. **Pets:** Very small, other species. $10 daily fee/pet. Designated rooms, service with restrictions, supervision.

SAVE S⟲ ✕ ⟲ 🛏 💻 ➿

▲▲▲ ▼▼▼▼ Best Western Seville Plaza Hotel SH
(816) 561-9600. **$95-$189.** 4309 Main St. 43rd and Main sts, just se. Int corridors. **Pets:** Medium, dogs only. $40 one-time fee/pet. Designated rooms, service with restrictions.

SAVE S⟲ ✕ &M 🛏 💻

▲▲▲ ▼▼▼▼ Chase Suites by Woodfin SH ❀
(816) 891-9009. **$79-$159.** 9900 NW Prairie View Rd. I-29, exit 10. Ext corridors. **Pets:** $150 deposit/room, $10 daily fee/pet. Designated rooms, service with restrictions, crate.

SAVE S⟲ ✕ ⟲ ⟲ 🛏 💻 ➿ ✕

▼▼▼ Courtyard by Marriott-Country Club Plaza SH ❀
(816) 285-9755. **Call for rates.** 4600 J C Nichols Pkwy. Center of downtown. Int corridors. **Pets:** Medium. $75 one-time fee/pet. Service with restrictions.

✕ ⟲ 🛏 💻 🍴 ➿

▼ **Crossland Economy Studios Kansas City-Worlds of Fun** Ⓜ
(816) 413-0060. **Call for rates.** 4301 N Corrington Ave. I-435, exit 5A, just w. Ext corridors. **Pets:** Accepted.

[icons]

▼▼ **Drury Inn & Suites-Kansas City Airport** 🆂🅷
(816) 880-9700. **$80-$140.** 7900 NW Tiffany Springs Pkwy. I-29, exit 10, just w. Int corridors. **Pets:** Large, other species. Service with restrictions, supervision.

[icons]

▼▼▼ **Drury Inn & Suites-Kansas City Stadium** 🆂🅷
(816) 923-3000. **$80-$130.** 3830 Blue Ridge Cutoff. I-70, exit 9 (Blue Ridge Cutoff), just nw. Int corridors. **Pets:** Large, other species. Service with restrictions, supervision.

[icons]

🔺 ▼▼▼ **Embassy Suites Hotel KCI Airport** 🆂🅷
(816) 891-7788. **$99-$239.** 7640 NW Tiffany Springs Pkwy. I-29, exit 10, just e. Int corridors. **Pets:** Small. $10 daily fee/pet. Service with restrictions, supervision.

[icons]

▼ **Extended StayAmerica-Kansas City Airport** 🆂🅷
(816) 270-7829. **$50-$140.** 11712 NW Plaza Cir. I-29, exit 13, just se. Int corridors. **Pets:** Accepted.

[icons]

▼ **Extended StayAmerica-Kansas City South** 🆂🅷
(816) 943-1315. **$55-$145.** 550 E 105th St. I-435, exit 74, just s. Int corridors. **Pets:** Accepted.

[icons]

🔺 ▼▼ **Fairfield Inn Kansas City-Liberty** 🆂🅷
(816) 792-4000. **$80-$160.** 8101 N Church Rd. I-35, exit 16 (SR 152), just w, then s. Int corridors. **Pets:** Medium, other species. $75 one-time fee/room. Designated rooms, service with restrictions, supervision.

[icons]

🔺 ▼▼▼ **Holiday Inn At The Plaza, Kansas City** 🆂🅷
(816) 753-7400. **$139-$189.** One E 45th St. In Country Club Plaza. Int corridors. **Pets:** Accepted.

[icons]

▼▼▼ **Holiday Inn-Sports Complex** 🆂🅷
(816) 353-5300. **$59-$199.** 4011 Blue Ridge Cutoff. I-70, exit 9 (Blue Ridge Cutoff), just se. Int corridors. **Pets:** Accepted.

[icons]

▼▼ **Homestead Studio Suites Hotel-Kansas City/Country Club Plaza** 🆂🅷
(816) 531-2212. **$85-$150.** 4535 Main St. Just ne of Country Club Plaza. Int corridors. **Pets:** Accepted.

[icons]

🔺 ▼▼▼ **Homewood Suites by Hilton** 🆂🅷
(816) 880-9880. **$89-$239.** 7312 NW Polo Dr. I-29, exit 10, just e. Int corridors. **Pets:** Small, other species. $50 one-time fee/room. Service with restrictions, crate.

[icons]

🔺 ▼▼▼ **The InterContinental Kansas City at the Plaza** 🅻🅷 ✿
(816) 303-2900. **$119-$359.** 401 Ward Pkwy. Corner of Wornall Rd and Ward Pkwy; in Country Club Plaza. Int corridors. **Pets:** Medium. $25 daily fee/pet. Service with restrictions.

[icons]

▼▼▼ **Kansas City Marriott Downtown** 🅻🅷
(816) 421-6800. **$154-$220.** 200 W 12th St. Just s of I-70, US 24 and 40. Int corridors. **Pets:** Accepted.

[icons]

🔺 ▼▼▼ **La Quinta Inn** 🆂🅷
(816) 483-7900. **$87-$104.** 1051 N Cambridge Ave. I-435, exit 57, just w to Cambridge Ave, then just s. Int corridors. **Pets:** Service with restrictions, crate.

[icons]

🔺 ▼▼▼ **Quality Inn & Suites Airport** 🆂🅷
(816) 587-6262. **$80-$149.** 6901 NW 83rd St. I-29, exit 8. Int corridors. **Pets:** Large. $25 one-time fee/room. Service with restrictions, crate.

[icons]

🔺 ▼▼▼ **Radisson Hotel & Suites Kansas City, City Center** 🆂🅷
(816) 474-6664. **$89-$269.** 1301 Wyandotte St. Just s of I-70, US 24 and 40. Int corridors. **Pets:** Accepted.

[icons]

▼▼▼ **Radisson Hotel Kansas City Airport** 🆂🅷
(816) 464-2423. **$89-$119.** 11828 NW Plaza Cir. I-29, exit 13, just se. Int corridors. **Pets:** Accepted.

[icons]

▼▼ **Red Roof Inn-North** Ⓜ
(816) 452-8585. **$48-$73.** 3636 NE Randolph Rd. I-435, exit 55B northbound; exit 55 southbound, just e on SR 210, then just n. Ext corridors. **Pets:** Medium, other species. Service with restrictions, supervision.

[icons]

▼▼▼ **Residence Inn by Marriott Downtown/Union Hill** 🆂🅷
(816) 561-3000. **$123-$209.** 2975 Main St. Just n of 31st St. Ext corridors. **Pets:** Medium, other species. $75 one-time fee/room. Service with restrictions.

[icons]

▼▼▼ **Residence Inn Kansas City Country Club Plaza** 🆂🅷
(816) 753-0033. **$139-$259.** 4601 Broadway Blvd. In Country Club Plaza. Int corridors. **Pets:** Medium. $100 one-time fee/room. Service with restrictions, supervision.

[icons]

🔺 ▼▼▼ ✿ **Sheraton Suites Country Club Plaza** 🅻🅷 ✿
(816) 931-4400. **$299-$309.** 770 W 47th St. Corner of Summit and 47th St; in Country Club Plaza. Int corridors. **Pets:** Dogs only. Service with restrictions, supervision.

[icons]

🔺 ▼▼▼ ▼▼▼ **The Westin Crown Center** 🅻🅷
(816) 474-4400. **$129-$309.** 1 E Pershing Rd. 0.5 mi s. Int corridors. **Pets:** Accepted.

[icons]

KEARNEY

▼▼ **Kearney Super 8 Motel** 🆂🅷 🐾
(816) 628-6800. **$60-$110, 5 day notice.** 210 Platte Clay Way. I-35, exit 26, just e on SR 92, then just n. Int corridors. **Pets:** Medium, dogs only. $10 daily fee/room. Designated rooms, service with restrictions, supervision.

[icons]

LEE'S SUMMIT

▼▼ ▼▼ **Comfort Inn by Choice Hotels** 🆂🅷
(816) 524-8181. **$85-$105.** 607 SE Oldham Pkwy. Jct US 50 and SR 291 N. Int corridors. **Pets:** Accepted.

[icons]

▼▼ ▼▼ **Lee's Summit Holiday Inn Express** 🆂🅷
(816) 795-6400. **$90.** 4825 NE Lakewood Way. I-470, exit 14, just e on Bowlin Rd, then 0.4 mi s. Int corridors. **Pets:** Other species. Supervision.

[icons]

NORTH KANSAS CITY

▼▼ La Quinta Inn & Suites Kansas City North 🆂🅷
(816) 221-1200. **$88-$120.** 2214 Taney Rd. I-29/35, exit 6A, just e on SR 210, then just n. Int corridors. **Pets:** Medium. Service with restrictions.
Ⓐ🆂🅺 ☒ ⏎ 🛏 🖵

OAK GROVE (JACKSON COUNTY)

ⒶⒶⒶ ▼ Econo Lodge 🅼
(816) 690-3681. **$50-$89.** 410 SE 1st St. I-70, exit 28, just s on Broadway St, just e on SE 4th St, then just n. Ext corridors. **Pets:** Medium. $10 daily fee/pet. Service with restrictions, supervision.
🆂🅰🆅🅴 🆂🔟 ☒ 🛏

END METROPOLITAN AREA

KIRKSVILLE

▼ Super 8 Motel-Kirksville 🅼
(660) 665-8826. **$56-$73.** 1101 Country Club Dr. On US 63 and SR 6. Int corridors. **Pets:** Other species. $10 daily fee/pet. Designated rooms, service with restrictions, supervision.
Ⓐ🆂🅺 🆂🔟 ☒ 🛏

LEBANON

ⒶⒶⒶ ▼▼◈ Best Western Wyota Inn Lebanon 🆂🅷
(417) 532-6171. **$49-$99.** 1225 Mill Creek Rd. I-44, exit 130, just nw. Ext corridors. **Pets:** Medium, other species. $15 daily fee/pet. No service, crate.
🆂🅰🆅🅴 🆂🔟 ☒ 🛏 🖵 🍽 🏊

▼▼ Holiday Inn Express 🆂🅷
(417) 532-1111. **$89-$109.** 1955 W Elm St. I-44, exit 127, just n. Int corridors. **Pets:** Other species. $25 one-time fee/room. Service with restrictions, supervision.
Ⓐ🆂🅺 🆂🔟 ☒ 🛏 🖵 🏊

LICKING

▼ Scenic Rivers Inn 🅼
(573) 674-4809. **$50-$55.** 209 S Hwy 63. On US 63. Ext corridors. **Pets:** Small. $5 daily fee/pet. Service with restrictions, supervision.
Ⓐ🆂🅺 🆂🔟 ☒ 🐾 🛏 🖵 🏊

LOUISIANA

ⒶⒶⒶ ▼ River's Edge Motel 🅼
(573) 754-4522. **$60-$70.** 201 Mansion St. On US 54; at Champ Clark Bridge. Ext corridors. **Pets:** Dogs only. $8 one-time fee/pet. Service with restrictions, supervision.
🆂🅰🆅🅴 ☒ 🛏 🖵

MACON

▼▼ Best Western Inn 🅼
(660) 385-2125. **$59-$69.** 28933 Sunset Dr. On Outer Rd S; at US 36 and Long Branch Lake exit. Ext/int corridors. **Pets:** Accepted.
Ⓐ🆂🅺 🆂🔟 ☒ 🛏 🖵 🏊

▼ Super 8 Motel 🆂🅷
(660) 385-5788. **$56-$80.** 203 E Briggs Dr. Jct US 36 and 63. Int corridors. **Pets:** Accepted.
Ⓐ🆂🅺 ☒ 🛏 🖵

MARSHFIELD

▼▼ Holiday Inn Express 🆂🅷
(417) 859-6000. **$86-$110.** 1301 Banning St. I-44, exit 100 (SR 38), on southeast corner. Int corridors. **Pets:** Medium. $25 one-time fee/room. Service with restrictions, supervision.
Ⓐ🆂🅺 🆂🔟 ☒ ⚿🅼 🛏 🖵 🏊

MARYVILLE

▼▼ Super 8 Motel-Maryville 🆂🅷
(660) 582-8088. **$50-$55.** 222 Summit Dr. On Business Rt US 71; just n of US 71 Bypass. Int corridors. **Pets:** Other species. $25 deposit/pet. Service with restrictions, supervision.
Ⓐ🆂🅺 🆂🔟 ☒ 🛏 🖵

MINER

▼▼ Drury Inn-Sikeston 🆂🅷
(573) 471-4100. **$86-$130.** 2602 E Malone. I-55, exit 67, just sw. Int corridors. **Pets:** Large, other species. Service with restrictions, supervision.
Ⓐ🆂🅺 ☒ ⚿🅼 ⏎ 🐾 🛏 🖵 🏊

▼▼ Pear Tree Inn by Drury-Sikeston 🆂🅷
(573) 471-8660. **$60-$110.** 2602 E Malone. I-55, exit 67, just sw. Ext corridors. **Pets:** Large, other species. Service with restrictions, supervision.
Ⓐ🆂🅺 ☒ ⚿🅼 ⏎ 🖵 🏊

MOBERLY

▼▼ Best Western Moberly Inn 🆂🅷
(660) 263-6540. **$69-$127, 10 day notice.** 1200 Hwy 24 E. Jct US 24 and 63 business route. Ext/int corridors. **Pets:** Small, dogs only. $30 one-time fee/room. Designated rooms, service with restrictions, supervision.
Ⓐ🆂🅺 🆂🔟 ☒ ⚿🅼 🛏 🖵 🍽 🏊

MOUNTAIN GROVE

ⒶⒶⒶ ▼ Days Inn of Mountain Grove 🆂🅷
(417) 926-5555. **$54-$65.** 300 E 19th St. Jct US 60 and 95, just se. Ext corridors. **Pets:** Accepted.
🆂🅰🆅🅴 🆂🔟 ☒ 🏊

▼ TraveLodge 🅼
(417) 926-3152. **$49-$68.** 111 E 17th St. Jct US 60 and 95, just s. Ext corridors. **Pets:** Accepted.
Ⓐ🆂🅺 🆂🔟 ☒ 🖵 🏊

NEOSHO

▼ Super 8 Motel-Neosho 🆂🅷
(417) 455-1888. **$60.** 3085 Gardner/Edgewood Dr. Just s of jct US 60B and 71B. Int corridors. **Pets:** Medium. $10 daily fee/pet. Service with restrictions, supervision.
Ⓐ🆂🅺 🆂🔟 ☒ ⏎ 🛏

NEVADA

▼▼ Days Inn of Nevada 🆂🅷
(417) 667-6777. **$53-$69.** 2345 Marvel Rd. US 71, exit Camp Clark, just w. Ext/int corridors. **Pets:** Accepted.
🆂🔟 ☒ 🛏 🖵 🏊

AAA ❤❤❤ Super 8 Motel SH
(417) 667-8888. **$54-$57.** 2301 E Austin Blvd. US 71, exit Camp Clark, just w. Int corridors. **Pets:** Accepted.
SAVE S✗ ❌ 🖥 🏊

NEW FLORENCE

❤❤ Days Inn Booneslick Lodge SH
(573) 835-7777. **$54-$85.** 403 Booneslick Rd. I-70, exit 175, just w. Int corridors. **Pets:** Other species. $10 daily fee/pet. Service with restrictions, supervision.
ASK S✗ ❌ 🖥 🏊

OSAGE BEACH

AAA ❤❤❤ Best Western Dogwood Hills Resort Inn SH
(573) 348-1735. **$52-$116, 14 day notice.** 1252 State Hwy KK. 0.5 mi n, off US 54. Ext corridors. **Pets:** Other species. $25 one-time fee/pet. Service with restrictions, supervision.
SAVE S✗ ❌ 🖥 🍽 🏊

AAA ❤ Lake Chateau Resort M
(573) 348-2791. **$49-$139.** 5066 Hwy 54. Just s of Grand Glaize Bridge. Ext corridors. **Pets:** Accepted.
SAVE S✗ ❌ 🖥 🍽 🏊 ✗

AAA ❤ Scottish Inns M
(573) 348-3123. **$50-$95.** 5404 Hwy 54. 1 mi w of Grand Glaize Bridge. Ext/int corridors. **Pets:** Small. $10 daily fee/pet. Designated rooms, service with restrictions, crate.
SAVE S✗ ❌ 🏊

PACIFIC

AAA ❤ Quality Inn Near Six Flags M
(636) 257-8400. **$59-$99.** 1400 W Osage St. I-44, exit 257, just se. Ext/int corridors. **Pets:** Medium. $15 daily fee/pet. Designated rooms, service with restrictions, crate.
SAVE S✗ ❌ 🖥 🏊

POPLAR BLUFF

❤❤ Comfort Inn SH
(573) 686-5200. **$63.** 2582 N Westwood Blvd. 1.3 mi s from jct US 60 E. Int corridors. **Pets:** Accepted.
ASK S✗ ❌ 🖥 🏊

❤❤ Drury Inn-Poplar Bluff SH
(573) 686-2451. **$76-$120.** 2220 N Westwood Blvd. On US 67, 1.4 mi s from jct US 60 E. Int corridors. **Pets:** Large, other species. Service with restrictions, supervision.
ASK ❌ 🖥 🏊

❤ Pear Tree Inn by Drury-Poplar Bluff M
(573) 785-7100. **$55-$90.** 2218 N Westwood Blvd. On US 67, 1.4 mi s from jct US 60 E. Ext corridors. **Pets:** Large, other species. Service with restrictions, supervision.
ASK ❌ 🖥 🏊

❤ Super 8 SH
(573) 785-0176. **$51-$56, 15 day notice.** 2831 N Westwood Blvd. On US 67, 0.8 mi s from jct US 60 E. Int corridors. **Pets:** Other species. Supervision.
ASK S✗ ❌ 🖥

POTOSI

❤ Potosi Super 8 SH
(573) 438-8888. **$56-$65.** 820 E High St. Jct SR 8 and 21. Ext/int corridors. **Pets:** Other species. $10 daily fee/pet. Service with restrictions.
ASK S✗ ❌ 🖥

REPUBLIC

❤❤ AmericInn Lodge & Suites of Republic SH
(417) 732-5335. **$73-$159.** 950 Austin Ln. I-44, exit 67, 4.4 mi s to SR 174 (flashing red light/4-way stop), then 0.7 mi e to Highland Park Town Center; just nw of jct US 60, SR 413 and 174. Int corridors. **Pets:** Small. $10 daily fee/room. Designated rooms, service with restrictions, supervision.
ASK ❌ 🖥 🏊

RICH HILL

AAA ❤ Apache Motel M
(417) 395-2161. **$38-$42, 3 day notice.** Hwy 71 and B. Just e of jct US 71 and CR B. Ext corridors. **Pets:** Accepted.
SAVE S✗ ❌

ROLLA

AAA ❤❤❤ Best Western Coachlight M
(573) 341-2511. **$65-$99.** 1403 Martin Springs Dr. Jct I-44 and Business Rt 44 S, exit 184. Ext corridors. **Pets:** Other species. $10 one-time fee/pet. Designated rooms, service with restrictions, supervision.
SAVE S✗ ❌ 🖥 🏊

❤ Days Inn M
(573) 341-3700. **$59-$79.** 1207 Kingshighway. I-44, exit 184, just s. Ext corridors. **Pets:** $10 daily fee/pet. No service, supervision.
ASK S✗ ❌ 🖥 🏊

❤❤ Drury Inn-Rolla SH
(573) 364-4000. **$70-$115.** 2006 N Bishop Ave. I-44, exit 186 (US 63), just ne. Int corridors. **Pets:** Large, other species. Service with restrictions, supervision.
ASK ❌ 🖥 🏊

ST. CLAIR

AAA ❤❤ Budget Lodging M
(636) 629-1000. **$69-$79.** 866 S Outer Rd W. I-44, exit 240, just w. Ext/int corridors. **Pets:** Large, dogs only. $10 daily fee/room. Designated rooms, service with restrictions, crate.
SAVE S✗ ❌ 🖥 🏊

ST. JOSEPH

❤❤❤ Drury Inn & Suites-St. Joseph SH
(816) 364-4700. **$65-$110.** 4213 Frederick Blvd. I-29, exit 47. Int corridors. **Pets:** Large, other species. Service with restrictions, supervision.
ASK ❌ 🖥 🏊 ✗

AAA ❤❤❤ Ramada Inn LH
(816) 233-6192. **$57-$81.** 4016 Frederick Blvd. I-29, exit 47. Int corridors. **Pets:** Small. $25 one-time fee/pet. Service with restrictions, supervision.
SAVE S✗ ❌ 🖥 🍽 🏊 ✗

AAA ❤❤❤ St. Joseph Holiday Inn-Riverfront LH
(816) 279-8000. **$94-$114.** 102 S Third St. I-229, exit Edmond St northbound; exit Felix St southbound; downtown. Int corridors. **Pets:** Medium. $15 one-time fee/pet. Service with restrictions, supervision.
SAVE S✗ ❌ 🖥 🍽 🏊 ✗

ST. LOUIS METROPOLITAN AREA

CHESTERFIELD

▼▼▼▼▼ Drury Plaza Hotel-Chesterfield SH
(636) 532-3300. **$100-$160.** 355 Chesterfield Center E. I-64/US 40, exit 19B (Clarkson Rd/Olive Blvd); jct I-64/US 40 and Clarkson Rd; southwest corner. Int corridors. **Pets:** Large, other species. Service with restrictions, supervision.
(ASK) ⊠ ⓖ ⓜ 🔌 🛏 💻 ¶ 🏊

▼▼▼▼ Homewood Suites by Hilton SH
(636) 530-0305. **$89-$139.** 840 Chesterfield Pkwy W. I-64, exit 20, 1 mi n. Int corridors. **Pets:** Medium. $25 one-time fee/pet. Service with restrictions, supervision.
(ASK) S🔥 ⊠ 🔌 🛏 💻 🏊

CLAYTON

▲▲▲ ▼▼▼▼ Crowne Plaza St Louis-Clayton SH
(314) 726-5400. **$139-$209.** 7750 Carondelet Ave. I-64/US 40, exit 31 (Brentwood Blvd), 1.3 mi n, then 0.7 mi e. Int corridors. **Pets:** Dogs only. Designated rooms, service with restrictions, crate.
(SAVE) ⊠ 🔌 🔥 💻 ¶ 🏊 ⊠

▲▲▲ ▼▼▼▼▼ The Ritz-Carlton, St. Louis LH
(314) 863-6300. **$179-$251.** 100 Carondelet Plaza. I-64, exit 32B, 1.2 mi n on Hanley Rd, then just e. Int corridors. **Pets:** Accepted.
(SAVE) ⊠ 🔌 🔥 ¶ 🏊 ⊠

▲▲▲ ▼▼▼▼ Sheraton Clayton Plaza Hotel SH ❀
(314) 863-0400. **$239.** 7730 Bonhomme Ave. I-64/US 40, exit 31 (Brentwood Blvd), 1.3 mi n, then 0.7 mi e. Int corridors. **Pets:** Small. Service with restrictions, crate.
(SAVE) S🔥 ⊠ 🔌 🔥 🛏 💻 ¶ 🏊 ⊠

CREVE COEUR

▼▼▼▼ Drury Inn & Suites-Creve Coeur SH
(314) 989-1100. **$90-$150.** 11980 Olive Blvd. I-270, exit 14 (Olive Blvd). Int corridors. **Pets:** Large, other species. Service with restrictions, supervision.
(ASK) ⊠ ⓜ 🔌 🔥 🛏 💻 🏊

EARTH CITY

▼▼▼▼ Residence Inn St. Louis Airport/Earth City SH
(314) 209-0995. **$99-$189.** 3290 Rider Tr S. I-70, exit 231B (Earth City Expwy N), just e. Int corridors. **Pets:** Accepted.
(ASK) S🔥 ⊠ ⓜ 🔌 🔥 🛏 💻 🏊 ⊠

EDMUNDSON

▼▼▼ Drury Inn-St. Louis Airport SH
(314) 423-7700. **$93-$150.** 10490 Natural Bridge Rd. I-70, exit 236 (Lambert Airport), just se. Int corridors. **Pets:** Large, other species. Service with restrictions, supervision.
(ASK) ⊠ ⓜ 🔌 🛏 💻 🏊

EUREKA

▲▲▲ ▼▼▼▼ Holiday Inn at Six Flags SH ❀
(636) 938-6661. **$99-$239, 3 day notice.** 4901 Six Flags Rd. I-44, exit 261 (Allenton Rd). Ext/int corridors. **Pets:** Large, other species. $25 daily fee/room. Designated rooms, service with restrictions, crate.
(SAVE) S🔥 ⊠ 💻 ¶ 🏊 ⊠

FENTON

▼▼▼ Drury Inn & Suites-Fenton SH
(636) 343-7822. **$75-$125.** 1088 S Highway Dr. I-44, exit 274 (Bowles Ave), just se. Int corridors. **Pets:** Large, other species. Service with restrictions, supervision.
(ASK) ⊠ 🔌 🛏 💻 🏊 ⊠

▼▼ Pear Tree Inn by Drury-Fenton SH
(636) 343-8820. **$60-$110.** 1100 S Highway Dr. I-44, exit 274 (Bowles Ave), just s. Int corridors. **Pets:** Large, other species. Service with restrictions, supervision.
(ASK) ⊠ 🔌 🛏 💻 🏊

FORISTELL

▲▲▲ ▼▼▼▼ Best Western West 70 Inn SH
(636) 673-2900. **$62-$95.** 12 Hwy W. I-70, exit 203 (CR W), just n. Int corridors. **Pets:** Accepted.
(SAVE) S🔥 ⊠ 🛏 💻 🏊

HAZELWOOD

▼▼▼ La Quinta Inn St. Louis (Airport) SH
(314) 731-3881. **$85-$118.** 5781 Campus Ct. I-270, exit 23 (McDonnell Blvd), just s. Int corridors. **Pets:** Medium. Service with restrictions.
(ASK) ⊠ 🔌 🛏 💻 🏊

KIRKWOOD

▼▼▼ Best Western Kirkwood Inn SH ❀
(314) 821-3950. **$69-$129, 7 day notice.** 1200 S Kirkwood Rd. I-44, exit 277B (Lindbergh Blvd), just n. Int corridors. **Pets:** Large, other species. $10 daily fee/pet. Designated rooms, service with restrictions, supervision.
(ASK) S🔥 ⊠ 🔌 🛏 💻 ¶ 🏊

MARYLAND HEIGHTS

▼▼▼▼ DoubleTree Hotel St. Louis at Westport SH
(314) 434-0100. **Call for rates.** 1973 Craigshire Rd. I-270, exit 16A (Page Ave), just e to Lackland Rd, then 0.4 mi sw on Lackland and Craigshire rds. Int corridors. **Pets:** Accepted.
(ASK) ⊠ ⓜ 🔌 🔥 🛏 💻 ¶ 🏊 ⊠

▼▼▼ Drury Inn & Suites-St. Louis-Westport SH
(314) 576-9966. **$76-$130.** 12220 Dorsett Rd. I-270, exit 17 (Dorsett Rd), just se. Int corridors. **Pets:** Large, other species. Service with restrictions, supervision.
(ASK) ⊠ 🔌 🛏 💻 🏊

▲▲▲ ▼▼▼▼ Sheraton (West Port) Hotel-Lakeside Chalet LH
(314) 878-1500. **$89-$229.** 191 Westport Plaza Dr. I-270, exit 16A (Page Ave), 0.8 mi e to Lackland Rd exit, just w to Craig Rd, then 0.4 mi n. Int corridors. **Pets:** Accepted.
(SAVE) ⊠ ⓜ 🔌 🔥 🛏 💻 ¶ 🏊

▲▲▲ ▼▼▼▼ The Sheraton (West Port) Plaza Tower LH
(314) 878-1500. **$89-$219.** 900 Westport Plaza Dr. I-270, exit 16A (Page Ave), 0.8 mi e, exit Lackland Rd, just w to Craig Rd, then 0.4 mi n. Int corridors. **Pets:** Accepted.
(SAVE) S🔥 ⊠ ⓜ 🔌 🔥 🛏 💻 ¶ 🏊 ⊠

▲▲▲ ▼▼▼▼ Staybridge Suites SH ❀
(314) 878-1555. **$142-$163.** 1855 Craigshire Rd. I-270, exit 16A (Page Ave), 0.8 mi e, exit Lackland Rd, 1 mi w, then s via Lackland and Craigshire rds. Ext/int corridors. **Pets:** Medium. $10 one-time fee/pet. Service with restrictions, crate.
(SAVE) ⊠ 🔌 🛏 💻 🏊 ⊠

MEHLVILLE

▼▼▼ Holiday Inn St. Louis-South I-55 SH
(314) 894-0700. **$89-$175.** 4234 Butler Hill Rd. I-55, exit 195 (Butler Hill Rd), just se. Ext/int corridors. **Pets:** Accepted.
(ASK) S🔥 ⊠ 🔌 🔥 🛏 💻 ¶ 🏊 ⊠

O'FALLON

Country Inn & Suites SH
(636) 300-4844. **$86-$96.** 1175 Technology Dr. I 64/US 40, exit 9 (CR K), just nw. Int corridors. **Pets:** Accepted.

Hilton Garden Inn St. Louis/O'Fallon SH
(636) 625-2700. **$79-$149.** 2310 Technology Dr. I-70, exit 216 (Bryan Rd), 4.2 mi s. Int corridors. **Pets:** Accepted.

Staybridge Suites O'Fallon SH
(636) 300-0999. **$109-$259.** 1155 Technology Dr. I 64/US 40, exit 9 (CR K), just nw. Int corridors. **Pets:** Medium, other species. $100 one-time fee/room. Service with restrictions, crate.

RICHMOND HEIGHTS

Residence Inn By Marriott-St. Louis Galleria SH
(314) 862-1900. **$99-$169.** 1100 McMorrow Ave. I-170, exit 1C (Brentwood Ave) northbound; exit southbound, 0.5 mi e of Galleria via Galleria Pkwy. Ext corridors. **Pets:** Other species. $100 one-time fee/room. Designated rooms, service with restrictions.

ST. ANN

Hampton Inn-St. Louis Airport SH
(314) 429-2000. **$109-$165.** 10820 Pear Tree Ln. I-70, exit 236 (Airport Dr), just sw. Int corridors. **Pets:** Service with restrictions, supervision.

Pear Tree Inn by Drury-St. Louis Airport SH
(314) 427-3400. **$76-$134.** 10810 Pear Tree Ln. I-70, exit 236 (Airport Dr), just sw. Int corridors. **Pets:** Large, other species. Service with restrictions, supervision.

ST. CHARLES

Comfort Suites-St. Charles SH
(636) 949-0694. **$100-$130.** 1400 S 5th St. I-70, exit 229 (5th St), just ne. Int corridors. **Pets:** Other species. Service with restrictions, supervision.

Country Inn & Suites St. Charles SH
(636) 724-5555. **$92-$99, 3 day notice.** 1190 S Main St. I-70, exit 229A (5th St S), to S Main St, then 0.7 mi ne. Int corridors. **Pets:** Dogs only. Designated rooms, supervision.

ST. LOUIS

Drury Inn & Suites-St. Louis-Convention Center LH
(314) 231-8100. **$96-$165.** 711 N Broadway. I-70, exit 250B (Stadium/Memorial Dr), at convention center. Int corridors. **Pets:** Large, other species. Service with restrictions, supervision.

Drury Inn-St. Louis/Union Station SH
(314) 231-3900. **$100-$180.** 201 S 20th St. Just e of Jefferson Ave; between Market St and Clark Ave. Int corridors. **Pets:** Large, other species. Service with restrictions, supervision.

Drury Plaza Hotel-St. Louis At the Arch SH
(314) 231-3003. **$100-$170.** 4th & Market sts. I-70, 250B (Stadium/Memorial Dr), just w on Pine St to Broadway, just s to Walnut St, just e to 4th St, then just n. Int corridors. **Pets:** Large, other species. Service with restrictions, supervision.

Hampton Inn-St. Louis/Union Station SH
(314) 241-3200. **$159-$220.** 2211 Market St. I-64/US 40, exit 39, just n on Jefferson Ave, then just e. Int corridors. **Pets:** Large, other species. Service with restrictions, supervision.

Renaissance St. Louis Grand & Suites Hotel LH
(314) 621-9600. **$229.** 800 Washington Ave. Across from America's Center Convention Center. Int corridors. **Pets:** Other species. $45 one-time fee/pet. Service with restrictions, crate.

Sheraton St. Louis City Center Hotel & Suites LH
(314) 231-5007. **$399-$529.** 400 S 14th St. I-40, exit 39B (14th St), just ne. Int corridors. **Pets:** Accepted.

The Westin St. Louis LH
(314) 621-2000. **$359.** 811 Spruce St. Just w of Busch Stadium. Int corridors. **Pets:** Small, other species. Service with restrictions, supervision.

ST. PETERS

Drury Inn-St. Charles/St. Peters SH
(636) 397-9700. **$75-$155.** 170 Westfield Dr. I-70, exit 222 (Mid Rivers Mall Dr), just se. Int corridors. **Pets:** Large, other species. Service with restrictions, supervision.

SUNSET HILLS

Holiday Inn-Southwest & Viking Conference Center SH
(314) 821-6600. **$104-$159.** 10709 Watson Rd. I-44, exit 277B, just s. Int corridors. **Pets:** Medium. $25 one-time fee/pet. Service with restrictions, supervision.

TOWN AND COUNTRY

St. Louis Marriott West LH
(314) 878-2747. **$89-$189.** 660 Maryville Centre Dr. I-64/US40, exit 23 (Maryville Centre Dr), just n. Int corridors. **Pets:** Other species. $75 one-time fee/room. Service with restrictions, crate.

VALLEY PARK

Drury Inn & Suites-St. Louis Southwest SH
(636) 861-8300. **$70-$140.** 5 Lambert Drury Pl. I-44, exit 272 (SR 141), just sw. Int corridors. **Pets:** Large, other species. Service with restrictions, supervision.

Hampton Inn-St. Louis Southwest SH
(636) 529-9020. **$96-$126.** 9 Lambert Drury Pl. I-44, exit 272 (SR 141), just sw. Int corridors. **Pets:** Small. Service with restrictions, supervision.

END METROPOLITAN AREA

ST. ROBERT

◆◆◆ **MainStay Suites** [SH]
(573) 451-2700. **$90-$100.** 227 St. Robert Blvd. I-44, exit 159, 0.8 mi nw. Ext/int corridors. **Pets:** Medium, other species. $75 one-time fee/room. Service with restrictions, crate.
[A$K] [SD] ⊠ ■ ☕ 🏊

[AAA] ◆ **Motel 6 #4211** [SH]
(573) 336-3610. **$45-$55.** 545 Hwy Z. I-44, exit 161, just s, then 0.3 mi e on frontage road. Int corridors. **Pets:** Medium, other species. Service with restrictions, supervision.
[SAVE] [SD] ⊠ ♿M ■ ☕

SEDALIA

[AAA] ◆◆◆ **Hotel Bothwell, A Clarion Collection** [SH]
(660) 826-5588. **$70-$234.** 103 E 4th St. Corner of 4th and S Ohio sts; downtown. Int corridors. **Pets:** Other species. $25 one-time fee/pet. Service with restrictions, supervision.
[SAVE] [SD] ⊠ ☕ 🍴

SPRINGFIELD

[AAA] ◆◆ **Baymont Inn & Suites** [SH]
(417) 889-8188. **$76-$106.** 3776 S Glenstone Ave. On US 60. Int corridors. **Pets:** Accepted.
[SAVE] [SD] ⊠ ♿M 👂 ♿ ■ ☕ 🏊

[AAA] ◆◆ **Best Western Route 66 Rail Haven** [M]
(417) 866-1963. **$64-$84.** 203 S Glenstone Ave. I-44, exit 80A, 3 mi s. Ext corridors. **Pets:** Other species. $10 daily fee/room. Designated rooms, service with restrictions, supervision.
[SAVE] [SD] ⊠ ♿M ■ ☕ 🏊

◆◆◆ **Drury Inn & Suites-Springfield** [SH]
(417) 863-8400. **$90-$132.** 2715 N Glenstone Ave. I-44, exit 80A (Glenstone Ave), just s. Int corridors. **Pets:** Large, other species. Service with restrictions, supervision.
[A$K] ⊠ ♿M 👂 ♿ ■ ☕ 🏊

[AAA] ◆◆◆ **Holiday Inn Express Hotel & Suites** [SH]
(417) 862-0070. **$109-$169.** 1117 E St. Louis St. Just w of National Ave. Int corridors. **Pets:** Small, dogs only. $25 one-time fee/room. Service with restrictions, supervision.
[SAVE] ⊠ ♿ ■ ☕

[AAA] ◆◆ **Krystal Aire-A Non-Smoking Hotel** [SH]
(417) 869-0001. **$65-$99.** 2745 N Glenstone Ave. I-44, exit 80A, just sw. Ext/int corridors. **Pets:** Designated rooms, service with restrictions, crate.
[SAVE] [SD] ⊠ ■ ☕ 🏊

◆◆ **La Quinta Inn Springfield** [SH]
(417) 520-8800. **$62-$92.** 1610 E Evergreen. I-44, exit 80A. Int corridors. **Pets:** Small, other species. $100 deposit/room. Service with restrictions, supervision.
[A$K] [SD] ⊠ ♿M 👂 ■ ☕ 🏊

◆◆◆ **Quality Inn & Suites** [SH]
(417) 888-0898. **$69-$129.** 3930 S Overland Ave. US 60 (James River Expwy), exit Kansas Expwy, just n to Chesterfield Blvd, then just w. Int corridors. **Pets:** Accepted.
[A$K] [SD] ⊠ ♿M 👂 ♿ ■ ☕ 🏊

[AAA] ◆◆◆ **Residence Inn-Springfield** [SH] 🐾
(417) 890-0020. **$134-$229.** 1303 E Kingsley St. US 60 (James River Expwy), exit National St, just s, then just e. Int corridors. **Pets:** Other species. $100 one-time fee/room. Service with restrictions, supervision.
[SAVE] [SD] ⊠ ♿M 👂 ♿ ■ ☕ 🏊 🏋

◆◆ **Sleep Inn of Springfield** [SH]
(417) 886-2464. **$50-$85.** 233 El Camino Alto. US 60 (James River Expwy), exit Campbell Ave, just se. Int corridors. **Pets:** Accepted.
[A$K] [SD] ⊠ 👂 ♿ ■ ☕ 🏊

[AAA] ◆◆◆ **University Plaza Hotel and Convention Center** [LH]
(417) 864-7333. **$109-$159.** 333 John Q Hammons Pkwy. 0.5 mi e on St. Louis St. Int corridors. **Pets:** Accepted.
[SAVE] [SD] ⊠ ♿M 👂 ♿ ■ ☕ 🍴 🏊

SWEET SPRINGS

[AAA] ◆ **People's Choice Motel** [M]
(660) 335-6315. **$37-$41.** 1001 N Locust St. I-70, exit 66, just se. Ext corridors. **Pets:** $20 deposit/room. Service with restrictions, supervision.
[SAVE] [SD] ⊠

◆◆ **Super 8 Motel** [SH]
(660) 335-4888. **$55-$68.** 208 W 40 Hwy. I-70, exit 66, just se. Int corridors. **Pets:** Accepted.
[A$K] [SD] ⊠ ■ ☕

TRENTON

◆ **Super 8 Motel** [SH]
(660) 359-2988. **$60.** 1845A E 28th St. US 65, 1 mi n of jct SR 6 and US 65. Int corridors. **Pets:** Accepted.
[A$K] [SD] ⊠ ■

UNION

◆◆ **Super 8 Motel** [SH]
(636) 583-8808. **$65-$85.** 1015 E Main St. I-44, exit 247 (US 50), 4.7 mi w; just w of jct SR 47. Int corridors. **Pets:** Accepted.
[A$K] [SD] ⊠ ♿M 👂 ☕ 🏊

WARSAW

◆ **Super 8 Motel-Warsaw** [SH]
(660) 438-2882. **$85.** 1603 Commercial St. US 65 and SR 7, exit Clinton. Ext corridors. **Pets:** Accepted.
[A$K] [SD] ⊠ ■ ☕ 🏊

WASHINGTON

[AAA] ◆◆ **Sleep Inn & Suites** [SH]
(636) 390-8877. **$89-$149.** 4104 S Point Rd. I-44, exit 251, 8.5 mi w on SR 100 to S Point Rd. Int corridors. **Pets:** Medium, dogs only. $25 one-time fee/pet. Service with restrictions, supervision.
[SAVE] [SD] ⊠ ■ ☕ 🏊 🏋

◆ **Super 8 Washington** [SH]
(636) 390-0088. **$72-$102, 7 day notice.** 2081 Eckelkamp Ct. I-44, exit 251, 10 mi, w on SR 100; just s of SR 100 and 47. Int corridors. **Pets:** Small, dogs only. $10 one-time fee/pet. Service with restrictions, supervision.
[A$K] [SD] ⊠ ■ ☕

WEST PLAINS

◆ **Super 8 Motel-West Plains** [SH]
(417) 256-8088. **$55.** 1210 Porter Wagoner Blvd. On US 63B, 0.8 mi s of jct US 63. Int corridors. **Pets:** Small. $25 one-time fee/pet. Service with restrictions, supervision.
⊠ ☕

MONTANA

ALBERTON

The Ghost Rails Inn B & B BB
(406) 722-4990. **$49-$89, 3 day notice.** 702 Railroad Ave. Downtown. Int corridors. **Pets:** Medium, dogs only. Designated rooms, service with restrictions, supervision.

BELGRADE

Gallatin River Lodge CI
(406) 388-0148. **$155-$270, 7 day notice.** 9105 Thorpe Rd. I-90, exit 298, 2.7 mi s on SR 85, 1 mi w on Valley Center Rd (gravel), then 0.5 mi s, follow sign. Int corridors. **Pets:** Dogs only. $20 daily fee/room. Designated rooms, service with restrictions, supervision.

Holiday Inn Express SH
(406) 388-0800. **$69-$149.** 6261 Jackrabbit Ln. I-90, exit 298, just s on SR 85. Int corridors. **Pets:** Accepted.

La Quinta Inn & Suites Belgrade (Bozeman/Belgrade) SH
(406) 388-2222. **$69-$139.** 6445 Jackrabbit Ln. I-90, exit 298, just s on SR 85. Int corridors. **Pets:** Medium. Designated rooms, service with restrictions, supervision.

Super 8 Motel-Belgrade/Bozeman Airport SH
(406) 388-1493. **$89-$120.** 6450 Jackrabbit Ln. I-90, exit 298, just s. Int corridors. **Pets:** Accepted.

BIGFORK

Mountain Lake Lodge SH
(406) 837-3800. **$89-$285, 7 day notice.** 14735 Sylvan Dr. On US 35, 5 mi s. Ext corridors. **Pets:** Medium. $15 daily fee/pet. Designated rooms.

Timbers Motel M
(406) 837-6200. **$52-$118, 7 day notice.** 8540 Hwy 35. Just n on US 35 from jct SR 209. Ext corridors. **Pets:** $10 one-time fee/pet. Service with restrictions, supervision.

BIG SKY

Best Western Buck's T-4 Lodge SH
(406) 995-4111. **$89-$169, 7 day notice.** 46625 Gallatin Rd. US 191, 1 mi s of Big Sky entrance. Ext/int corridors. **Pets:** Large, other species. $10 daily fee/pet. Service with restrictions, supervision.

Rainbow Ranch Lodge RA
(406) 995-4132. **$185-$360.** 42950 Gallatin Rd. 5 mi s on US 191. Ext corridors. **Pets:** $40 daily fee/room. Service with restrictions, supervision.

BIG TIMBER

Big Timber Super 8 Motel SH
(406) 932-8888. **$54-$99.** 20A Big Timber Loop Rd. I-90, exit 367. Int corridors. **Pets:** Medium, dogs only. $5 daily fee/pet. Service with restrictions, supervision.

River Valley Inn M
(406) 932-4943. **$58-$88.** 600 W 2nd St. I-90, exit 367, just n, then 0.6 mi e. Int corridors. **Pets:** Small. $10 one-time fee/pet. Service with restrictions, supervision.

BILLINGS

Best Western Clocktower Inn SH
(406) 259-5511. **$94-$120, 3 day notice.** 2511 1st Ave N. On I-90 business loop; downtown. Ext/int corridors. **Pets:** Accepted.

Billings Hotel and Convention Center SH
(406) 248-7151. **$69-$99.** 1223 Mullowney Ln. I-90, exit 446, just s. Int corridors. **Pets:** Small. $10 daily fee/room. Service with restrictions, supervision.

Billings Super 8 Motel SH
(406) 248-8842. **$50-$95.** 5400 Southgate Dr. I-90, exit 447, just n on S Billings Blvd, 0.8 mi w on King Ave, then just s on Parkway Ln. Int corridors. **Pets:** Medium. $10 one-time fee/pet. Designated rooms, service with restrictions, supervision.

Cherry Tree Inn SH
(406) 252-5603. **$58-$63.** 823 N Broadway. I-90, exit 450, 2 mi n on 27th St, then just w on 9th Ave. Int corridors. **Pets:** Other species. Service with restrictions, crate.

Clubhouse Inn & Suites SH
(406) 248-9800. **$79-$129.** 5610 S Frontage Rd. I-90, exit 446, just s. Ext/int corridors. **Pets:** Other species. Designated rooms, supervision.

Comfort Inn by Choice Hotels SH
(406) 652-5200. **$90-$110.** 2030 Overland Ave. I-90, exit 446, 0.5 mi n, then just s. Int corridors. **Pets:** Accepted.

◆◆◆ **Days Inn** SH
(406) 252-4007. **$63-$103.** 843 Parkway Ln. I-90, exit 447, just n on S Billings Blvd, 0.8 mi w on King Ave, then just s. Int corridors. **Pets:** Other species. $5 daily fee/pet. Service with restrictions, supervision.
A$K S⬤ ✕ 🐾 ⬛ 💻

◆ **Dude Rancher Lodge** M
(406) 259-5561. **$55-$90.** 415 N 29th St. Just w of the 400 block of N 27th st; downtown. Ext/int corridors. **Pets:** Large, other species. $5 daily fee/room. Designated rooms, service with restrictions, supervision.
A$K S⬤ ✕ 🐾 ⬛ 💻 ❚❙

◆◆ **Extended StayAmerica-Billings-West End** SH
(406) 245-3980. **$80-$95.** 4950 Southgate Dr. I-90, exit 447, just w. Int corridors. **Pets:** Accepted.
A$K S⬤ ✕ ⬛M 🗐 🐾 ⬛ 💻

◆◆◆ ◆◆ **Hilltop Inn** SH ❀
(406) 245-5000. **$70-$80.** 1116 N 28th St. I-90, exit 450, 2 mi n on 27th St, just w on 11th Ave, then just n. Int corridors. **Pets:** $7 daily fee/pet. Service with restrictions, supervision.
SAVE S⬤ ✕ ⬛M ⬛ 💻

◆◆◆ ◆◆◆ **Holiday Inn Grand Montana Billings** LH
(406) 248-7701. **$124-$149.** 5500 Midland Rd. I-90, exit 446. Int corridors. **Pets:** Accepted.
SAVE S⬤ ✕ ⬛M 🗐 🐾 ⬛ 💻 ❚❙ 🏊 ✕

◆◆ ◆◆ **Kelly Inn** SH ❀
(406) 252-2700. **$69-$109.** 5425 Midland Rd. I-90, exit 446, just se. Ext/int corridors. **Pets:** Medium, other species. Service with restrictions, supervision.
A$K S⬤ ✕ 🐾 ⬛ 💻 🏊

◆ **Motel 6 #178** M
(406) 252-0093. **$41-$65.** 5400 Midland Rd. I-90, exit 446, just se. Ext corridors. **Pets:** Medium, other species. Service with restrictions, supervision.
S⬤ ✕ ⬛M 🗐 🐾

◆◆◆◆ **Quality Inn Homestead** SH
(406) 652-1320. **$61-$99.** 2036 Overland Ave. I-90, exit 446, n on King Ave W, then just s, first stoplight. Int corridors. **Pets:** Other species. $25 deposit/room. Supervision.
A$K S⬤ ✕ ⬛ 💻 🏊 ✕

◆ **Red Roof Inn #269** SH
(406) 248-7551. **$48-$68.** 5353 Midland Rd. I-90, exit 446, just se. Int corridors. **Pets:** Medium, other species. Service with restrictions, supervision.
✕ ⬛M 🗐 🐾 ⬛ 💻 🏊

◆◆◆ ◆ **Rimview Inn** M
(406) 248-2622. **$60-$70.** 1025 N 27th St. I-90, exit 450, 2 mi n. Ext/int corridors. **Pets:** Dogs only. $10 one-time fee/pet. Supervision.
SAVE S⬤ ✕ ⬛

◆◆◆ ◆◆ **Riverstone Billings Inn** SH ❀
(406) 252-6800. **$62-$67.** 880 N 29th St. I-90, exit 450, 2 mi n on 27th St, then just w on 9th Ave. Int corridors. **Pets:** Other species. $7 daily fee/pet. Designated rooms, service with restrictions, crate.
SAVE S⬤ ✕ ⬛ 💻

◆◆◆ ◆◆ **Western Executive Inn** SH
(406) 294-8888. **$56-$100.** 3141 King Ave W. I-90, exit 446, 2.5 mi w. Int corridors. **Pets:** Small. $20 daily fee/pet. Service with restrictions, supervision.
SAVE S⬤ ✕ ⬛M 🐾 ⬛ 💻

BOZEMAN

◆◆◆ ◆◆ **Americas Best Value Inn** SH
(406) 585-7888. **$56-$89.** 817 Wheat Dr. I-90, exit 306, just n. Int corridors. **Pets:** Accepted.
A$K S⬤ ✕ ⬛M 🐾 ⬛ 🏊

◆◆◆ ◆◆◆ **AmericInn Lodge & Suites** SH
(406) 522-8686. **$89-$169.** 1121 Reeves Rd W. I-90, exit 305, just n. Int corridors. **Pets:** $20 daily fee/pet. Designated rooms, service with restrictions, supervision.
SAVE ✕ ⬛M 🐾 ⬛ 💻 🏊 ✕

◆◆◆ ◆◆◆ ◆◆ **Best Western GranTree Inn** SH
(406) 587-5261. **$89-$159.** 1325 N 7th Ave. I-90, exit 306, just s. Int corridors. **Pets:** Service with restrictions, supervision.
SAVE S⬤ ✕ 🐾 ⬛ 💻 ❚❙ 🏊

◆◆ ◆◆ **Bozeman Days Inn & Suites** SH ❀
(406) 587-5251. **$65-$169.** 1321 N 7th Ave. I-90, exit 306, just s. Int corridors. **Pets:** Large, other species. $10 daily fee/pet. Service with restrictions, crate.
A$K S⬤ ✕ 🐾 ⬛ 💻 🏊 ✕

◆◆◆ ◆◆ **Bozeman Inn** M
(406) 587-3176. **$42-$85.** 1235 N 7th Ave. I-90, exit 306, just s. Ext corridors. **Pets:** Other species. $5 one-time fee/room. Service with restrictions, crate.
SAVE S⬤ ✕ ⬛ 🏊

◆ **Bozeman Super 8** SH ❀
(406) 586-1521. **$63-$100.** 800 Wheat Dr. I-90, exit 306, just n, then just w. Int corridors. **Pets:** Other species. $5 one-time fee/room. Designated rooms, service with restrictions, supervision.
A$K S⬤ ✕

◆◆◆ ◆◆ ◆◆ **Bozeman's Western Heritage Inn** SH ❀
(406) 586-8534. **$68-$108, 5 day notice.** 1200 E Main St. I-90 business loop, exit 309, 0.5 mi w. Int corridors. **Pets:** Dogs only. $8 daily fee/pet. Service with restrictions, supervision.
SAVE S⬤ ✕ ⬛ 💻 ✕

◆◆◆ ◆◆ ◆◆◆ **Holiday Inn Bozeman** SH ❀
(406) 587-4561. **$79-$179.** 5 Baxter Ln. I-90, exit 306, just s of jct I-90. Int corridors. **Pets:** Other species. Service with restrictions, supervision.
SAVE ✕ 🐾 ⬛ 💻 ❚❙ 🏊 ✕

◆◆◆ ◆◆ **Microtel Inn & Suites** SH
(406) 586-3797. **$74-$104.** 612 Nikles Dr. I-90, exit 306, just ne. Int corridors. **Pets:** Accepted.
SAVE S⬤ ✕ 🐾 ⬛ 💻 🏊

◆◆◆ ◆ **Rainbow Motel** M
(406) 587-4201. **$48-$70.** 510 N 7th Ave. I-90, exit 306, 0.8 mi s. Ext corridors. **Pets:** Small, dogs only. $5 daily fee/pet. Designated rooms, service with restrictions, supervision.
SAVE ✕ ⬛ 💻 🏊

◆◆ ◆ **Ramada Limited** M
(406) 585-2626. **$75-$120.** 2020 Wheat Dr. I-90, exit 306, just n, then just w. Ext/int corridors. **Pets:** Accepted.
A$K S⬤ ✕ 💻 🏊

◆◆◆ ◆◆ ◆◆ **Royal "7" Budget Inn** M ❀
(406) 587-3103. **$48-$67.** 310 N 7th Ave. I-90, exit 306, 0.8 mi s. Ext corridors. **Pets:** $2 daily fee/pet. Designated rooms, supervision.
SAVE S⬤ ✕ ⬛

BROWNING

◆◆◆ ◆ **Western Motel LLC** M
(406) 338-7572. **$45-$98.** 121 Central Ave E. On US 2; center. Ext corridors. **Pets:** Other species. $10 daily fee/pet. Supervision.
SAVE S⬤ ✕ ⬛

BUTTE

Best Western Butte Plaza Inn SH
(406) 494-3500. **$85-$120.** 2900 Harrison Ave. I-90/15, exit 127 (Harrison Ave). Int corridors. **Pets:** Medium. $50 deposit/room. Designated rooms, service with restrictions, supervision.

Comfort Inn of Butte SH
(406) 494-8850. **$94-$104.** 2777 Harrison Ave. I-90/15, exit 127 (Harrison Ave), just s. Int corridors. **Pets:** Accepted.

Copper King Hotel & Convention Center SH
(406) 494-6666. **$75-$115.** 4655 Harrison Ave S. I-90/15, exit 127A (Harrison Ave), 2 mi s on SR 2. Int corridors. **Pets:** Accepted.

Days Inn SH
(406) 494-7000. **$79-$250.** 2700 Harrison Ave. I-90/15, exit 127 (Harrison Ave), just n. Int corridors. **Pets:** Medium. Designated rooms, service with restrictions, supervision.

Red Lion Hotel SH
(406) 494-7800. **$75-$114.** 2100 Cornell Ave. I-90/15, exit 127B (Harrison Ave), just n, then just e. Int corridors. **Pets:** Medium. $10 deposit/room. Service with restrictions, supervision.

Rocker Inn M
(406) 723-5464. **$45-$57.** 122001 W Brown's Gulch Rd. I-90/15, exit 122 (Rocker). Int corridors. **Pets:** Medium. $5 daily fee/room. Designated rooms, service with restrictions, supervision.

Super 8 Motel of Butte SH
(406) 494-6000. **$65-$97.** 2929 Harrison Ave. I-90/15, exit 127 (Harrison Ave), just s. Int corridors. **Pets:** Large. $50 deposit/room, $5 daily fee/pet. Service with restrictions, supervision.

CHINOOK

Chinook Motor Inn SH
(406) 357-2248. **$65-$75.** 100 Indiana St. On US 2. Int corridors. **Pets:** Accepted.

CHOTEAU

Big Sky Motel M
(406) 466-5318. **$49.** 209 S Main Ave. Just s of town center on US 89. Ext corridors. **Pets:** Other species. Service with restrictions, supervision.

COLUMBIA FALLS

Meadow Lake Resort CO
(406) 892-8700. **$135-$180, 30 day notice.** 100 St Andrews Dr. Jct US 2 and SR 40, 1.4 mi e on US 2, 1.1 mi n on Meadow Lake Blvd. Ext/int corridors. **Pets:** Accepted.

COLUMBUS

Super 8 of Columbus SH
(406) 322-4101. **$75-$85.** 602 8th Ave N. I-90, exit 408, just s on SR 78. Int corridors. **Pets:** Accepted.

CONRAD

Super 8 Motel SH
(406) 278-7676. **$62-$80.** 215 N Main. I-15, exit 339, just w. Int corridors. **Pets:** Accepted.

COOKE CITY

Elk Horn Lodge M
(406) 838-2332. **$78, 7 day notice.** 103 Main St. Center. Ext corridors. **Pets:** Dogs only. $5 one-time fee/pet. No service, supervision.

CUT BANK

Glacier Gateway Inn SH
(406) 873-5544. **$55-$79, 7 day notice.** 1121 E Railroad St. US 2, just e from town center. Int corridors. **Pets:** $6 daily fee/pet. Supervision.

DEER LODGE

Super 8 Motel M
(406) 846-2370. **$50-$100.** 1150 N Main St. I-90, exit 184, 0.3 mi s. Int corridors. **Pets:** Accepted.

Western Big Sky Inn M
(406) 846-2590. **$52-$64.** 210 N Main St. I-90, exit 184, 1 mi w. Ext corridors. **Pets:** Designated rooms, service with restrictions, supervision.

DILLON

Best Western Paradise Inn M
(406) 683-4214. **$59-$79.** 650 N Montana St. I-15, exit 63, 0.3 mi s on SR 41. Ext corridors. **Pets:** Other species. Service with restrictions, supervision.

Comfort Inn of Dillon M
(406) 683-6831. **$84-$94.** 450 N Interchange. I-15, exit 63. Int corridors. **Pets:** Accepted.

GuestHouse International Inns & Suites SH
(406) 683-3636. **$74-$109.** 580 Sinclair St. I-15, exit 63. Int corridors. **Pets:** Accepted.

Sundowner Motel M
(406) 683-2375. **$40-$45.** 500 N Montana St. I-15, exit 63, just s. Ext corridors. **Pets:** Other species. Designated rooms, service with restrictions, supervision.

Super 8 Motel M
(406) 683-4288. **$54-$75.** 550 N Montana St. I-15, exit 63, just n on US 91. Int corridors. **Pets:** Dogs only. $10 daily fee/pet. Service with restrictions, supervision.

EAST GLACIER PARK

Dancing Bears Inn LLC M
(406) 226-4402. **$45-$146.** 40 Montana Ave. Just off US 2, follow signs; center. Ext/int corridors. **Pets:** Other species. $10 daily fee/pet. Supervision.

ENNIS

△△△ ▽▽▽ Fan Mountain Inn M
(406) 682-5200. **$50-$75, 14 day notice.** 204 N Main. US 287, just nw of city center. Ext corridors. **Pets:** Medium. $10 daily fee/pet. Designated rooms, service with restrictions, supervision.
SAVE ⊠ ᴹ ⌖ ▣

△△△ ▽▽ Riverside Motel & Outfitters M
(406) 682-4240. **$50-$145, 14 day notice.** 346 Main St. US 287, east of town. Ext corridors. **Pets:** Medium, dogs only. $10 one-time fee/pet. Designated rooms, service with restrictions, supervision.
SAVE ⊠ ⌖ ▣ ☐

FORSYTH

△△△ ▽▽▽ Best Western Sundowner Inn M ❖
(406) 346-2115. **$77-$87.** 1018 Front St. I-94, exit 95, 0.5 mi nw on north frontage road. Ext corridors. **Pets:** $10 one-time fee/pet. Service with restrictions, supervision.
SAVE Sᴏ̷ ⊠ ⌖ ▣

△△△ ▽▽▽ Rails Inn Motel SH
(406) 346-2242. **$69-$74, 4 day notice.** 3rd & Front sts. I-94, exit 93, just n, then 0.5 mi e on frontage road. Int corridors. **Pets:** $5 daily fee/pet. Service with restrictions, supervision.
SAVE Sᴏ̷ ⊠ ⌖ ⑪

△△△ ▽▽ Restwel Motel M
(406) 346-2771. **$50-$67.** 810 Front St. I-94, exit 95, 0.8 mi nw on north frontage road. Ext corridors. **Pets:** Medium. $5 daily fee/pet. Designated rooms, service with restrictions, supervision.
SAVE Sᴏ̷ ⊠ ⌖ ⌖

△△△ ▽▽ Westwind Motor Inn M
(406) 346-2038. **$60-$65, 3 day notice.** 225 Westwind Ln. I-94, exit 93, 0.3 mi n. Int corridors. **Pets:** $5 daily fee/pet. Service with restrictions, supervision.
SAVE ⊠ ⌖

GARDINER

△△△ ▽▽▽ Best Western by Mammoth Hot Springs SH
(406) 848-7311. **$69-$149, 3 day notice.** S Hwy 89. 0.5 mi n. Ext/int corridors. **Pets:** Accepted.
SAVE Sᴏ̷ ⊠ ⌖ ⌖ ▣ ⑪ ☞ ⊠

▽▽ Travelodge Yellowstone Park North M
(406) 848-7520. **$45-$115, 3 day notice.** PO Box 48. North entrance, just s on US 89; 0.5 mi n of Yellowstone north gate. Ext corridors. **Pets:** Small, dogs only. $10 one-time fee/pet. Service with restrictions, supervision.
ASK Sᴏ̷ ⊠ ⌖ ▣

△△△ ▽▽ Yellowstone River Motel M
(406) 848-7303. **$50-$88.** 14 E Park St. Just e of US 89. Ext corridors. **Pets:** Accepted.
SAVE Sᴏ̷ ⊠ ᴹ ⌖ ▣

▽▽ Yellowstone Super 8-Gardiner SH
(406) 848-7401. **$49-$109.** Hwy 89 S. On US 89. Int corridors. **Pets:** Other species. $10 daily fee/pet. Designated rooms, supervision.
ASK Sᴏ̷ ⊠ ⌖ ▣ ☞

GLASGOW

▽▽ Cottonwood Inn SH
(406) 228-8213. **$67-$87.** 45 1st Ave NE. 0.5 mi e on US 2. Int corridors. **Pets:** Designated rooms, service with restrictions, supervision.
ASK Sᴏ̷ ⊠ ⌖ ⌖ ▣ ⑪ ☞

GLENDIVE

△△△ ▽▽▽ Best Western Glendive Inn SH
(406) 377-5555. **$60-$90.** 223 N Merrill Ave. I-94, exit 215, on I-94 business loop; downtown. Ext/int corridors. **Pets:** Accepted.
SAVE Sᴏ̷ ⊠ ⌖ ▣ ☞

▽▽ Super 8 Glendive M
(406) 365-5671. **$59-$77.** 1904 Merrill Ave. I-94, exit 215, just n. Int corridors. **Pets:** Other species. $5 one-time fee/room. Service with restrictions, supervision.
ASK Sᴏ̷ ⊠

GREAT FALLS

△△△ ▽▽▽▽ Best Western Heritage Inn SH
(406) 761-1900. **$90-$110.** 1700 Fox Farm Rd. I-15, exit 278, 0.8 mi e on 10th Ave S and US 87/89 and SR 3/200. Int corridors. **Pets:** Accepted.
SAVE Sᴏ̷ ⊠ ⌖ ⌖ ▣ ⑪ ☞ ⊠

◇◇ Comfort Inn by Choice Hotels SH
(406) 454-2727. **$90-$110.** 1120 9th St S. I-15, exit 278, 3 mi e on 10th Ave S and US 87/89 and SR 3/200, then just s. Int corridors. **Pets:** Accepted.
ASK Sᴏ̷ ⊠ ᴹ ⌖ ⌖ ▣ ☞

△△△ ▽▽▽▽ Crystal Inn SH
(406) 727-7788. **$109-$129.** 3701 31st St SW. I-15, exit 277, just e. Int corridors. **Pets:** Accepted.
SAVE Sᴏ̷ ⊠ ⌖ ⌖ ▣ ☞

▽▽ Days Inn of Great Falls M
(406) 727-6565. **$65-$90.** 101 14th Ave NW. I-15, exit 280 (Central Ave), 1.3 mi e on Central Ave/Business Rt I-15, 0.8 mi n on 3rd St NW, then just w. Int corridors. **Pets:** Dogs only. $5 one-time fee/room. Designated rooms, service with restrictions, supervision.
ASK Sᴏ̷ ⊠ ⌖ ⌖ ▣

◇▽ Extended StayAmerica-Great Falls-Missouri River SH
(406) 761-7524. **$75-$90.** 800 River Dr S. I-15, exit 278, 1.7 mi e on 10th Ave S, then 0.7 mi n. Int corridors. **Pets:** Accepted.
ASK Sᴏ̷ ⊠ ᴹ ⌖ ⌖ ⌖ ▣

△△△ ▽▽▽ The Great Falls Inn SH ❖
(406) 453-6000. **$68-$74.** 1400 28th St S. I-15, exit 278, 5.3 mi e on 10th Ave S, 0.3 mi s on 26th St S, then just e on 15th Ave S. Int corridors. **Pets:** $7 daily fee/pet. Designated rooms, supervision.
SAVE Sᴏ̷ ⊠ ᴹ ⌖ ⌖ ▣

▽▽▽ Hampton Inn SH
(406) 453-2675. **$79-$129.** 2301 14th St SW. I-15, exit 278, just sw. Int corridors. **Pets:** Medium, dogs only. $20 one-time fee/pet. Designated rooms, service with restrictions, supervision.
ASK ⊠ ᴹ ⌖ ⌖ ▣ ☞

△△△ ▽▽▽▽ La Quinta Inn & Suites Great Falls SH ❖
(406) 761-2600. **$84-$209.** 600 River Dr S. I-15, exit 278, 1.7 mi e on 10th Ave S, then 0.8 mi n. Int corridors. **Pets:** Medium. Service with restrictions, supervision.
SAVE Sᴏ̷ ⊠ ⌖ ⌖ ⌖ ▣ ▣ ☞ ⊠

△△△ ▽▽ Motel 6 #4238 M
(406) 453-1602. **$55-$90.** 2 Treasure State Dr. I-15, exit 278, 0.8 mi e on 10th Ave S and US 87/89 and SR 3/200; next to Best Western. Int corridors. **Pets:** Accepted.
SAVE Sᴏ̷ ⊠ ⌖

△△△ ▽▽▽ Quality Inn SH
(406) 761-3410. **$74-$104.** 220 Central Ave. Downtown. Ext/int corridors. **Pets:** Small. $10 deposit/room. Service with restrictions, supervision.
SAVE Sᴏ̷ ⊠ ⌖ ▣ ☞

HAMILTON

AAA ▼▼▼ **Town House Inns** 🅂🄷 ❀
(406) 363-6600. **$66-$68.** 1113 N 1st St. North of city center on US 93. Int corridors. **Pets:** Other species. $10 daily fee/pet. Service with restrictions, supervision.

SAVE S♂ ✕ 🅔M 🄐 🄷 🖵

HARDIN

AAA ▼▼▼ **American Inn of Hardin** 🅂🄷
(406) 665-1870. **$60-$90.** 1324 N Crawford Ave. I-90, exit 495, just s on SR 47. Ext corridors. **Pets:** Accepted.

SAVE S♂ ✕ 🄐 🄷 🖵 🍴 ⇌

▼ **Western Motel** Ⓜ
(406) 665-2296. **$40-$80.** 830 W 3rd St. I-90, exit 495 eastbound, 1.3 mi s on SR 47 and CR 313, then just e; exit 497 westbound, 0.3 mi w on I-90 business loop, continue straight on 3rd St for 0.7 mi. Ext corridors. **Pets:** Accepted.

✕ 🄷

HARLOWTON

▼ **Corral Motel** Ⓜ
(406) 632-4331. **$40-$65.** Hwy 12 @ junction12 and 191. 0.5 mi e at jct US 12 and 191. Ext corridors. **Pets:** Dogs only. $5 one-time fee/pet. Service with restrictions, supervision.

A$K S♂ ✕ 🄷

▼ **Countryside Inn** Ⓜ
(406) 632-4119. **$56-$60.** 309 3rd St NE. US 12 E. Ext corridors. **Pets:** Other species. $5 daily fee/pet. Service with restrictions, supervision.

S♂ ✕ 🄷 ✕

HAVRE

▼▼ **AmericInn of Havre** 🅂🄷
(406) 395-5000. **Call for rates.** 2520 Hwy 2 W. On US 2, west side of town. Int corridors. **Pets:** Other species. $20 one-time fee/room. Designated rooms, service with restrictions, supervision.

✕ 🄷 🖵 ⇌

HELENA

▼▼▼ **Barrister Bed & Breakfast** 🄱🄱 ❀
(406) 443-7330. **$102-$117, 4 day notice.** 416 N Ewing St. I-15, exit 192 (Prospect Ave), 1.5 mi sw via Prospect and Montana aves to 9th Ave, 0.8 mi w, then just s. Int corridors. **Pets:** Dogs only.

A$K ✕ 🄩

AAA ▼▼▼▼ **Best Western Helena Great Northern Hotel** 🅂🄷
(406) 457-5500. **$110-$165.** 835 Great Northern Blvd. I-15, exit 193 (Cedar St), 2 mi w, just w on Lyndale Ave, then just s on Getchell; downtown. Int corridors. **Pets:** Accepted.

SAVE S♂ ✕ 🅔M 🄐 🄔 🄷 🖵 🍴 ⇌ ✕

▼▼ **Days Inn Helena** 🅂🄷
(406) 442-3280. **$75-$109.** 2001 Prospect Ave. I-15, exit 192 (Prospect Ave), just w. Int corridors. **Pets:** Accepted.

A$K S♂ ✕ 🅔M 🄐 🄔 🄷 🖵 ✕

AAA ▼▼▼ **Elkhorn Mountain Inn** 🅂🄷 ❀
(406) 442-6625. **$74-$86.** 1 Jackson Creek Rd. I-15, exit 187 (Montana City), just w. Int corridors. **Pets:** Other species. $5 daily fee/pet. Supervision.

SAVE S♂ ✕ 🅔M 🄔 🄷 🖵

AAA ▼▼▼ **Mountain Valley Inn & Suites** 🅂🄷
(406) 443-2300. **$69-$79.** 2101 E 11th Ave. I-15, exit 192B (capitol area), just sw. Ext/int corridors. **Pets:** Accepted.

SAVE S♂ ✕ 🄷 🖵 ⇌

AAA ▼▼▼▼ **Red Lion Colonial Hotel** 🅂🄷
(406) 443-2100. **$100-$120.** 2301 Colonial Dr. I-15, exit 192 southbound; exit 192B northbound. Int corridors. **Pets:** $20 one-time fee/pet. Service with restrictions, supervision.

SAVE S♂ ✕ 🄷 🖵 🍴 ⇌

AAA ▼▼▼ **Super 8 Motel** 🅂🄷 ❀
(406) 443-2450. **$53-$77.** 2200 11th Ave. I-15, exit 192B (capitol area) southbound; exit west business district northbound on US 12. Int corridors. **Pets:** Other species. $10 one-time fee/pet. Designated rooms, service with restrictions, supervision.

SAVE S♂ ✕ 🄐 🄔 🄷 🖵

▼▼▼ **Wingate Inn** 🅂🄷
(406) 449-3000. **$105-$130.** 2007 Oakes. I-15, exit 193 (Cedar St), just sw. Int corridors. **Pets:** Accepted.

A$K S♂ ✕ 🅔M 🄐 🄔 🄷 🖵 ⇌

HUNGRY HORSE

AAA ▼▼▼ **Mini Golden Inns Motel** Ⓜ
(406) 387-4313. **$85-$176, 90 day notice.** 8955 US 2 E. East end of town. Ext corridors. **Pets:** Accepted.

SAVE S♂ ✕ 🅔M 🄔 🄷 🖵

KALISPELL

AAA ▼ **Aero Inn** 🅂🄷
(406) 755-3798. **$44-$89.** 1830 US 93 S. 1.3 mi s on US 93 from jct US 2. Int corridors. **Pets:** $20 deposit/room. Designated rooms, service with restrictions, supervision.

SAVE S♂ ✕ 🄐 🄔 🄷 ⇌

AAA ▼▼ **Comfort Inn** 🅂🄷
(406) 755-6700. **$79-$149.** 1330 Hwy 2 W. 1 mi w on US 2 from jct US 93. Int corridors. **Pets:** Accepted.

SAVE S♂ ✕ 🄷 🖵 🍴 ⇌

▼▼ **Days Inn Kalispell** 🅂🄷
(406) 756-3222. **$65-$107.** 1550 Hwy 93 N. 1.3 mi n on US 93 from jct US 2. Int corridors. **Pets:** Small, other species. $10 deposit/pet. Designated rooms, service with restrictions, supervision.

A$K S♂ ✕ 🄷

AAA ▼▼▼ **Four Seasons Motor Inn** 🅂🄷
(406) 755-6123. **$60-$120.** 350 N Main St. US 93, just n of jct US 2. Ext/int corridors. **Pets:** $10 daily fee/room. Designated rooms, service with restrictions, supervision.

SAVE S♂ ✕ 🄷 🖵 🍴

▼▼ **Kalispell/Glacier Int'l Airport area Super 8 Motel** 🅂🄷
(406) 755-1888. **$67-$122.** 1341 1st Ave E. 1.2 mi s on US 93 from jct US 2. Int corridors. **Pets:** Other species. $10 daily fee/room. Designated rooms, service with restrictions, supervision.

A$K S♂ ✕ 🅔M 🄐 🄷 🖵

▼▼ **Kalispell Grand Hotel** 🅂🄷
(406) 755-8100. **$63-$155.** 100 Main St. On US 93; downtown. Int corridors. **Pets:** Large. Designated rooms, service with restrictions, supervision.

A$K S♂ ✕ 🍴

AAA ▼▼▼▼ **La Quinta Inn & Suites Kalispell** 🅂🄷
(406) 257-5255. **$79-$179.** 255 Montclair Dr. Jct US 93 and 2, 1 mi e. Int corridors. **Pets:** Accepted.

SAVE S♂ ✕ 🅔M 🄐 🄔 🄷 🖵 ⇌ ✕

AAA ▼▼▼▼ **Red Lion Hotel Kalispell** 🅂🄷
(406) 751-5050. **$109-$209, 15 day notice.** 20 N Main St. Just s on US 93 from jct of US 2; connected to Kalispell Center Mall. Int corridors. **Pets:** $20 one-time fee/pet. Designated rooms, service with restrictions, supervision.

SAVE S♂ ✕ 🅔M 🄷 🖵 🍴 ⇌ ✕

▼▼▼ WestCoast Outlaw Hotel-Kalispell SH
(406) 755-6100. **$69-$149.** 1701 Hwy 93 S. 1.4 mi s on US 93 from jct US 2. Int corridors. **Pets:** Accepted.
[ASK] [S♦] [✕] [🛏] [🖥] [🍴] [⊷] [✕]

LAKESIDE

▼▼ Bayshore Resort Motel Inc M
(406) 844-3131. **$55-$115.** 616 Lakeside Blvd. On US 93; center. Ext corridors. **Pets:** Other species. $10 daily fee/pet. Designated rooms, service with restrictions, crate.
[ASK] [✕] [🛏] [🖥] [✕] [AC]

LAUREL

▼▼ Best Western Yellowstone Crossing SH
(406) 628-6888. **$79-$89.** 205 SE 4th St. I-90, exit 434, just n, then just e. Int corridors. **Pets:** Medium. $10 daily fee/pet. Designated rooms, service with restrictions, supervision.
[ASK] [S♦] [✕] [&M] [🗂] [🖥] [🛏] [🖥] [⊷]

LEWISTOWN

AAA ▼ B & B Motel M ☙
(406) 535-5496. **$48-$70.** 520 E Main St. Downtown. Ext corridors. **Pets:** Dogs only. $10 daily fee/pet. Designated rooms, service with restrictions, supervision.
[SAVE] [✕] [🛏]

LIBBY

▼▼▼ Caboose Motel and Sportsman Information Center M ☙
(406) 293-6201. **$52-$66.** 714 W 9th St. Just w on US 2 from jct SR 37. Ext corridors. **Pets:** $5 one-time fee/room. Service with restrictions, crate.
[ASK] [✕] [🛏] [🖥]

▼▼ Sandman Motel M ☙
(406) 293-8831. **$39-$74.** 688 US Hwy 2 W. Just w on US 2 from jct SR 37. Ext corridors. **Pets:** Other species. $20 deposit/room, $5 daily fee/pet. Designated rooms, service with restrictions, supervision.
[ASK] [S♦] [✕] [🛏]

AAA ▼▼ Super 8 Motel SH
(406) 293-2771. **$60-$95.** 448 US 2 W. Just w on US 2 from jct SR 37. Int corridors. **Pets:** Accepted.
[SAVE] [S♦] [✕] [🗂] [🛏] [⊷]

LINCOLN

AAA ▼ Leeper's Ponderosa Motel M ☙
(406) 362-4333. **$53-$69.** Hwy 200 & 1st Ave. On SR 200, just w. Ext corridors. **Pets:** Other species. $5 daily fee/pet. Service with restrictions, supervision.
[SAVE] [S♦] [✕] [🛏] [🖥] [AC]

LIVINGSTON

AAA ▼▼ Best Western Yellowstone Inn & Conference Center SH
(406) 222-6110. **$79-$145.** 1515 W Park St. I-90, exit 333, just n. Int corridors. **Pets:** Medium. $10 daily fee/pet. Service with restrictions, supervision.
[SAVE] [✕] [🛏] [🖥] [⊷]

▼▼ Econo Lodge SH
(406) 222-0555. **$55-$115.** 111 Rogers Ln. I-90, exit 333, just n on US 89, then just w. Int corridors. **Pets:** Large, other species. $10 daily fee/pet. Designated rooms, service with restrictions, supervision.
[ASK] [S♦] [✕] [&M] [🗂] [🖥] [🛏] [🖥] [⊷]

AAA ▼▼ Travelodge Livingston M
(406) 222-6320. **$74-$120.** 102 Rogers Ln. I-90, exit 333, just n on US 89, then just w. Ext/int corridors. **Pets:** Large, other species. $10 daily fee/pet. Designated rooms, service with restrictions, supervision.
[SAVE] [✕] [🛏] [🖥] [🍴] [⊷]

MALTA

AAA ▼▼ Maltana Motel M
(406) 654-2610. **$52-$59.** 138 S 1st Ave W. Just s of US 2 via US 191, just w; downtown. Ext corridors. **Pets:** Dogs only. $8 one-time fee/pet. Service with restrictions, supervision.
[SAVE] [✕] [🛏] [🖥]

MILES CITY

AAA ▼▼ Best Western War Bonnet Inn SH ☙
(406) 234-4560. **$72-$97, 7 day notice.** 1015 S Haynes Ave. I-94, exit 138 (Broadus), 0.3 mi n. Ext corridors. **Pets:** Large, other species. $5 daily fee/pet. Service with restrictions, supervision.
[SAVE] [S♦] [✕] [🛏] [🖥] [⊷] [✕]

▼▼▼ GuestHouse International Inn & Suites SH
(406) 232-3661. **$75-$150.** 3111 Steel St. I-94, exit 138 (Broadus), just s. Int corridors. **Pets:** Large, other species. $15 daily fee/room. Designated rooms, service with restrictions, supervision.
[ASK] [S♦] [✕] [&M] [🗂] [🛏] [🖥] [⊷]

MISSOULA

▼▼ America's Best Inn SH
(406) 542-7550. **$74-$100.** 4953 N Reserve St. I-90 W, exit 101 (Reserve St), just s. Int corridors. **Pets:** Large, other species. $10 daily fee/pet. Designated rooms.
[ASK] [S♦] [✕] [🗂] [🖥] [🛏] [🖥]

AAA ▼▼▼ Best Western Grant Creek Inn SH
(406) 543-0700. **$95-$159.** 5280 Grant Creek Rd. I-90, exit 101 (Reserve St), just n. Int corridors. **Pets:** Small. $10 daily fee/room. Designated rooms, service with restrictions, supervision.
[SAVE] [S♦] [✕] [&M] [🗂] [🗂] [🛏] [🖥] [⊷] [✕]

AAA ▼▼ Broadway Inn Conference Center SH ☙
(406) 532-3300. **$69-$109.** 1609 W Broadway. I-90, exit 104 (Orange St), 0.5 mi s, then 1 mi w. Int corridors. **Pets:** Dogs only. $10 one-time fee/pet. Designated rooms, service with restrictions, supervision.
[SAVE] [S♦] [✕] [🛏] [🖥] [🍴] [⊷]

▼▼ Campus Inn M
(406) 549-5134. **$50-$100.** 744 E Broadway. I-90, exit 105 (Van Buren St), just s to Broadway, then just w. Ext/int corridors. **Pets:** Other species. $6 daily fee/pet. Supervision.
[ASK] [✕] [🗂] [🗂] [🛏] [🖥] [⊷]

▼▼▼ Comfort Inn SH
(406) 542-0888. **$89-$159, 3 day notice.** 4545 N Reserve St. I-90, exit 101 (Reserve St), 0.5 mi s. Int corridors. **Pets:** Small, other species. $10 daily fee/room. Service with restrictions, supervision.
[ASK] [S♦] [✕] [&M] [🗂] [🗂] [🛏] [🖥] [⊷]

AAA ▼▼▼ Days Inn/Missoula Airport SH ☙
(406) 721-9776. **$60-$105.** 8600 Truck Stop Rd. I-90, exit 96, just n. Int corridors. **Pets:** Other species. $5 daily fee/pet. Designated rooms, service with restrictions, supervision.
[SAVE] [✕] [🛏] [🖥]

AAA ▼▼▼ Days Inn University SH
(406) 543-7221. **$64-$84.** 201 E Main St. I-90, exit 104 (Orange St), 0.5 mi s to Broadway, 0.5 mi e to Washington, just s to Main St, then just w. Ext corridors. **Pets:** Small, dogs only. $15 daily fee/pet. Service with restrictions, supervision.
[SAVE] [S♦] [✕] [🛏] [🖥] [⊷]

AAA ▼▼▼▼ Doubletree Hotel Missoula/Edgewater SH
(406) 728-3100. **$134-$209.** 100 Madison. I-90, exit 105 (Van Buren St), just s, then w on Front St. Int corridors. **Pets:** Large. $20 one-time fee/room. Designated rooms, service with restrictions, supervision.
SAVE ✕ &M 🐾 & 🛢 🖳 🍴 ⊅

AAA ▼ Downtown Motel M
(406) 370-3830. **$41-$52.** 502 E Broadway. I-90, exit 105 (Van Buren St), just w. Ext corridors. **Pets:** Accepted.
SAVE ✕ 🛢 🖳

AAA ▼ Family Inn M
(406) 543-7371. **$62-$70.** 1031 E Broadway. I-90, exit 105 (Van Buren St), just s, then just e. Ext corridors. **Pets:** Medium. $50 deposit/room, $10 daily fee/pet. Designated rooms, service with restrictions.
SAVE S✄ ✕ 🛢 ⊅

AAA ▼▼▼▼ Holiday Inn Missoula-Parkside SH
(406) 721-8550. **$89-$169.** 200 S Pattee St. I-90, exit 104 (Orange St), 0.5 mi s to Broadway, just e to Pattee St, then just s. Int corridors.
Pets: Accepted.
SAVE S✄ ✕ 🐾 🛢 🖳 🍴 ⊅ ✕

▼▼ Microtel Inn & Suites SH
(406) 543-0959. **$60-$100.** 5059 N Reserve St. I-90, exit 101 (Reserve St), just s. Int corridors. **Pets:** Accepted.
ASK ✕ &M 🐾 & 🛢 🖳

AAA ▼▼ Orange Street Inn SH
(406) 721-3610. **$79-$89.** 801 N Orange St. I-90, exit 104 (Orange St), just s. Int corridors. **Pets:** Accepted.
SAVE S✄ ✕ 🛢 🖳

AAA ▼ Ponderosa Lodge M
(406) 543-3102. **$45-$80.** 800 E Broadway. I-90, exit 105 (Van Buren St), just s to Broadway, then w. Ext/int corridors. **Pets:** Other species. $10 daily fee/pet. Designated rooms, service with restrictions, supervision.
SAVE S✄ ✕ 🛢

AAA ▼▼▼ Quality Inn & Conference Center SH
(406) 251-2665. **$75-$140.** 3803 Brooks St. I-90, exit 101 (Reserve St), 5 mi s to Brooks St, then just w. Int corridors. **Pets:** Large, other species. $10 daily fee/pet. Designated rooms.
SAVE S✄ ✕ &M 🐾 & 🛢 🖳

AAA ▼▼▼ Red Lion Inn SH
(406) 728-3300. **$79-$149.** 700 W Broadway. I-90, exit 104 (Orange St), just s, then just w. Ext corridors. **Pets:** Accepted.
SAVE S✄ ✕ 🐾 🛢 🖳 ⊅

AAA ▼▼▼ Redwood Lodge M
(406) 721-2110. **$60-$65.** 8060 Hwy 93 N. I-90, exit 96, just s. Ext corridors. **Pets:** Other species. $5 daily fee/pet. Service with restrictions, supervision.
SAVE S✄ ✕ 🛢

AAA ▼ Royal Motel M
(406) 542-2184. **$40-$56.** 338 Washington St. I-90, exit 105 (Van Buren St), just s, then 0.5 mi w on Broadway. Ext corridors. **Pets:** $4 daily fee/pet. No service, supervision.
SAVE ✕ 🛢

AAA ▼▼▼ Ruby's Inn & Convention Center SH
(406) 721-0990. **$79-$99.** 4825 N Reserve St. I-90, exit 101 (Reserve St), just s. Ext/int corridors. **Pets:** Accepted.
SAVE S✄ ✕ &M 🐾 & 🛢 🖳 ⊅ ✕

▼▼ Sleep Inn by Choice Hotels SH
(406) 543-5883. **$90-$110.** 3425 Dore Ln. I-90, exit 101 (Reserve St), 5 mi s, then just e on Brooks St. Int corridors. **Pets:** Accepted.
ASK S✄ ✕ &M 🐾 & 🛢 🖳 ⊅

AAA ▼▼ Southgate Inn SH
(406) 251-2250. **$60-$120.** 3530 Brooks St. I-90, exit 101 (Reserve St), 5 mi s to Brooks St, then just e. Ext corridors. **Pets:** Accepted.
SAVE S✄ ✕ 🛢 🖳 ⊅ ✕

▼▼ Super 8-Brooks St SH
(406) 251-2255. **$54-$76.** 3901 Brooks St. I-90, exit 101 (Reserve St), 5 mi s to Brooks St, then just w. Int corridors. **Pets:** Accepted.
ASK S✄ ✕ 🛢

AAA ▼ Travelers Inn Motel Inc M
(406) 728-8330. **$55-$75.** 4850 N Reserve St. I-90, exit 101 (Reserve St), just s. Ext corridors. **Pets:** Small, dogs only. $5 daily fee/pet. Designated rooms, service with restrictions, supervision.
SAVE S✄ ✕ 🛢

OVANDO

▼▼▼ Lake Upsata Guest Ranch RA
(406) 793-5890. **$1260-$3360 (weekly).** 201 Lower Lakeside Ln. 7.5 mi w on SR 200 to MM 38, 3.4 mi n on Woodworth Rd, then 1 mi e. Ext corridors. **Pets:** Accepted.
✕ 🛢 🖳 ✕ ⚿ 🐾 ⊅

POLSON

AAA ▼▼▼▼ Best Western KwaTaqNuk Resort SH ☙
(406) 883-3636. **$89-$155, 3 day notice.** 303 US Hwy 93 E. Just s of downtown. Int corridors. **Pets:** $25 one-time fee/room. Designated rooms, service with restrictions.
SAVE S✄ ✕ &M 🛢 🖳 🍴 ⊅ ✕

RED LODGE

▼▼ Best Western Lu Pine Inn SH
(406) 446-1321. **$79-$139.** 702 S Hauser. 0.4 mi s, just w of US 212. Int corridors. **Pets:** Supervision.
ASK S✄ ✕ 🛢 🖳 ⊅ ✕

▼▼ Comfort Inn of Red Lodge SH
(406) 446-4469. **$60-$160.** 612 N Broadway. Jct US 212 and SR 78, north entrance. Int corridors. **Pets:** Designated rooms, service with restrictions, supervision.
ASK S✄ ✕ &M & 🛢 🖳 ⊅

AAA ▼▼ Super 8 of Red Lodge M
(406) 446-2288. **$69-$109.** 1223 S Broadway Ave. Just s on US 212. Ext/int corridors. **Pets:** Accepted.
SAVE S✄ ✕ 🛢 🖳 ⊅

AAA ▼ Yodeler Motel M
(406) 446-1435. **$55-$105.** 601 S Broadway. Just s on US 212. Ext corridors. **Pets:** $5 daily fee/pet. Designated rooms, service with restrictions, supervision.
SAVE S✄ ✕ 🛢 🖳

RONAN

▼ Starlite Motel M ☙
(406) 676-7000. **$52-$74.** 18 Main St SW. Just w of jct US 93 and Main St. Ext corridors. **Pets:** Medium. $20 deposit/room, $10 daily fee/pet. Designated rooms, service with restrictions, supervision.
ASK ✕ 🛢 🖳

ST. IGNATIUS

▼ Sunset Motel M
(406) 745-3900. **$39-$59.** 333 Mountain View. Just s of downtown, exit on US 93. Ext corridors. **Pets:** Dogs only. $5 daily fee/pet. Supervision.
ASK S✄ ✕ 🛢

ST. REGIS

▲▲▲ ▼ Little River Motel M
(406) 649-2713. **$40-$70.** 50 Old US Hwy 10 W. I-90, exit 33, just n to flashing light, just w, then just sw. Ext corridors. **Pets:** Small. $5 daily fee/pet. Service with restrictions, supervision.
〔SAVE〕〔S⌀〕✕ 🛄 🐾 🄺 ☎

▲▲▲ ▼ Super 8 Motel-St. Regis SH
(406) 649-2422. **$51-$73.** 9 Old Hwy 10 E. I-90, exit 33, just n. Ext/int corridors. **Pets:** $20 deposit/pet. Service with restrictions, supervision.
〔SAVE〕〔S⌀〕✕ 🄺 🛄 ▣

SEELEY LAKE

▲▲▲ ▼▼ Wilderness Gateway Inn M
(406) 677-2095. **$45-$60.** 2996 Hwy 83 N. South end of town on SR 83. Ext corridors. **Pets:** Accepted.
〔SAVE〕〔S⌀〕✕

SHELBY

▼▼◆ Comfort Inn of Shelby SH
(406) 434-2212. **$99-$109.** 455 McKinley Ave. I-15, exit 363, just e, then just s. Int corridors. **Pets:** Other species. $5 daily fee/pet. Designated rooms, service with restrictions, supervision.
〔ASK〕〔S⌀〕✕ 🄺 🄺 🛄 ▣ 🗶

▲▲▲ ▼ Crossroads Inn M
(406) 434-5134. **$47-$66.** 1200 Roosevelt Hwy. I-15, exit 363, just e. Int corridors. **Pets:** $10 daily fee/pet. Service with restrictions, supervision.
〔SAVE〕〔S⌀〕✕ 🄺 🛄 🏊

▲▲▲ ▼ O'Haire Manor Motel M
(406) 434-5555. **$60-$80.** 204 2nd St S. Just s of Main St via Maple Dr. Ext/int corridors. **Pets:** $5 daily fee/room. Designated rooms, service with restrictions, supervision.
〔SAVE〕〔S⌀〕✕ 🛄 ▣

SHERIDAN

▼ Moriah Motel M
(406) 842-5491. **$60-$68.** 220 S Main St. On SR 287; center. Ext corridors. **Pets:** Other species. $10 one-time fee/room. Service with restrictions, supervision.
〔ASK〕✕ 🛄

SIDNEY

▲▲▲ ▼▼ Richland Motor Inn M
(406) 433-6400. **$75-$90.** 1200 S Central Ave. 1.5 mi n of jct SR 200 and 16. Int corridors. **Pets:** Medium, other species. $5 one-time fee/pet. Service with restrictions, supervision.
〔SAVE〕〔S⌀〕✕ 🛄 ▣

SUPERIOR

▲▲▲ ▼▼◆ Budget Host Big Sky Motel M
(406) 822-4831. **$56-$65.** 103 4th Ave E. I-90, exit 47, just n. Ext corridors. **Pets:** Small. $10 one-time fee/room. Designated rooms, service with restrictions, supervision.
〔SAVE〕〔S⌀〕✕ 🛄

THOMPSON FALLS

▲▲▲ ▼▼ The Riverfront M
(406) 827-3460. **$55-$110.** 4907 Hwy 200 W. 1 mi w of city center. Ext corridors. **Pets:** Small. $7 daily fee/pet. Service with restrictions, supervision.
〔SAVE〕✕ 🛄 ▣ 🗶

THREE FORKS

▲▲▲ ▼ Broken Spur Motel M
(406) 285-3237. **$55-$79.** 124 W Elm (Hwy 2). I-90, exit 278 westbound, 1.3 mi sw; exit 274 eastbound, 1 mi s on SR 287 to jct SR 2, then 3 mi se. Ext corridors. **Pets:** Other species. $5 one-time fee/pet. Designated rooms, service with restrictions, supervision.
〔SAVE〕〔S⌀〕✕ 🛄

▲▲▲ ▼ Fort Three Forks Motel & RV Park M
(406) 285-3233. **$48-$75.** 10776 Hwy 287. I-90, exit 274. Ext corridors. **Pets:** Accepted.
〔SAVE〕〔S⌀〕✕ 🛄 ▣

VICTOR

▲▲▲ ▼▼▼ Wildlife Adventures Guest Ranch RA 🐾
(406) 642-3262. **$105-$170, 14 day notice.** 1765 Pleasant View Dr. Jct US 93 and Fifth St, 0.9 mi w, 3.2 mi s. Int corridors. **Pets:** Other species. $10 daily fee/pet. Designated rooms, service with restrictions, supervision.
〔SAVE〕〔S⌀〕✕ 🗶 🄺 🄿 ☎

WEST YELLOWSTONE

▲▲▲ ▼▼▼ Best Western Cross Winds Motor Inn SH
(406) 646-9557. **$55-$155, 3 day notice.** 201 Firehole Ave. Just w of US 191 and 287, on US 20 at Dunraven St and Firehole Ave. Ext corridors. **Pets:** Designated rooms, service with restrictions, supervision.
〔SAVE〕〔S⌀〕✕ 🛄 ▣ 🏊

▲▲▲ ▼▼▼ Best Western Desert Inn SH
(406) 646-7376. **$55-$185, 3 day notice.** 133 Canyon Ave. US 191 at US 20; corner of Canyon and Firehole aves. Int corridors. **Pets:** Designated rooms, service with restrictions, supervision.
〔SAVE〕〔S⌀〕✕ 〔⌀M〕🄺 🄺 🛄 ▣ 🏊

▲▲▲ ▼▼▼ Brandin' Iron Inn SH 🐾
(406) 646-9411. **$61-$119, 3 day notice.** 201 Canyon Ave. Just w and n of park entrance. Ext corridors. **Pets:** Other species. $15 one-time fee/room. Designated rooms, service with restrictions, crate.
〔SAVE〕〔S⌀〕✕ 〔⌀M〕🄺 🛄 ▣

▲▲▲ ▼ City Center Motel M
(406) 646-7337. **$49-$89, 3 day notice.** 214 Madison Ave. W off US 191 at Madison Ave and Dunraven St; just nw of park entrance. Ext corridors. **Pets:** Other species. $15 one-time fee/room. Designated rooms, service with restrictions, crate.
〔SAVE〕✕ ▣ ☎

▼▼▼ ClubHouse Inn SH 🐾
(406) 646-4892. **$79-$169.** 105 S Electric St. Just sw of jct US 191, 187 and 20; just w of park entrance. Int corridors. **Pets:** Other species. Designated rooms, service with restrictions, supervision.
〔ASK〕〔S⌀〕✕ 〔⌀M〕🄺 🄺 🛄 ▣ 🏊

▲▲▲ ▼▼ Days Inn West Yellowstone SH
(406) 646-7656. **$55-$165, 14 day notice.** 301 Madison Ave. W off US 191; just nw of park entrance. Ext/int corridors. **Pets:** Accepted.
〔SAVE〕〔S⌀〕✕ 〔⌀M〕🄺 🛄 ▣ 🍴 🏊 🗶

▲▲▲ ▼▼◆ Gray Wolf Inn & Suites SH
(406) 646-0000. **$69-$149.** 250 S Canyon Ave. Just w of Yellowstone National Park entrance. Int corridors. **Pets:** Other species. $50 deposit/room. Designated rooms, service with restrictions, supervision.
〔SAVE〕〔S⌀〕✕ 〔⌀M〕🄺 🄺 🛄 ▣ 🏊

▲▲▲ ▼▼▼▼ Holiday Inn SunSpree Resort West Yellowstone Conference Hotel SH
(406) 646-7365. **$69-$159.** 315 Yellowstone Ave. Just w of park entrance. Int corridors. **Pets:** Accepted.
〔SAVE〕〔S⌀〕✕ 〔⌀M〕🄺 🄺 🛄 ▣ 🍴 🏊 🗶

▼▼ **Kelly Inn** 🆂🅷
(406) 646-4544. **$59-$169.** 104 S Canyon Ave. S of jct US 191, 287 and 20; just w of park entrance. Ext/int corridors. **Pets:** Service with restrictions, supervision.
🅰🆂🄺 ☒ 🄲 🄷 ▣ ⇌

🅰🅰🅰 ▼▼ **Stage Coach Inn** 🆂🅷
(406) 646-7381. **$59-$139, 14 day notice.** 209 Madison Ave. Corner of Dunraven St and Madison Ave, just w of park entrance. Ext/int corridors. **Pets:** Other species. $50 deposit/room. Designated rooms, service with restrictions, supervision.
🆂🄰🅅🄴 🆂🅟 ☒ 🄷 🄲 🄷 ▣ 🍴 ☒

🅰🅰🅰 ▼▼▼ **The Three Bear Lodge** 🅼
(406) 646-7353. **$59-$115, 14 day notice.** 217 Yellowstone Ave. Just w of park entrance. Ext/int corridors. **Pets:** $10 daily fee/pet. Service with restrictions, crate.
🆂🄰🅅🄴 ☒ 🄷 ▣ 🍴 ⇌ ☒

🅰🅰🅰 ▼▼▼ **Yellowstone Lodge** 🆂🅷
(406) 646-0020. **$59-$159.** 251 S Electric St. Just w of park entrance. Int corridors. **Pets:** $10 daily fee/room. Designated rooms, service with restrictions, crate.
🆂🄰🅅🄴 🆂🅟 ☒ 🄲 🄷 ▣ ⇌

WHITEFISH

🅰🅰🅰 ▼▼▼ **Best Western Rocky Mountain Lodge** 🆂🅷 🐾
(406) 862-2569. **$83-$185.** 6510 Hwy 93 S. 1.3 mi s on US 93 from jct SR 487. Ext/int corridors. **Pets:** $20 one-time fee/room. Designated rooms, service with restrictions, supervision.
🆂🄰🅅🄴 🆂🅟 ☒ 🄻🄼 🄷 🄲 🄷 ▣ ⇌

🅰🅰🅰 ▼▼ **Kristianna Mountain Homes** 🄲🄾
(406) 862-2860. **$135-$1100.** 3842 Winter Ln. Jct US 93 and SR 487, 2.4 mi n on SR 487, at flashing light go 5.2 mi on Big Mountain Rd, just n on Gelande, then just w on Kristanna Close. Ext/int corridors. **Pets:** Accepted.
🆂🄰🅅🄴 ☒ 🄷 ▣ ☒ 🄴

▼▼ **North Forty Resort** 🄲🄰 🐾
(406) 862-7740. **$79-$249, 14 day notice.** 3765 Hwy 40 W. 2.5 mi e on SR 40 from jct of US 93. Ext corridors. **Pets:** Other species. $10 daily fee/pet. Designated rooms, service with restrictions, supervision.
☒ 🄷 ▣ ☒ 🄴

🅰🅰🅰 ▼▼▼ **Pine Lodge** 🆂🅷
(406) 862-7600. **$79-$149.** 920 Spokane Ave. 1 mi s on US 93. Int corridors. **Pets:** Large. Service with restrictions, supervision.
🆂🄰🅅🄴 🆂🅟 ☒ 🄻🄼 🄷 🄲 🄷 ▣ ⇌

▼ **Super 8 Motel** 🆂🅷
(406) 862-8255. **$50-$92.** 800 Spokane Ave. 1 mi s on US 93 from jct SR 487. Int corridors. **Pets:** $5 daily fee/pet. Service with restrictions, supervision.
🅰🆂🄺 🆂🅟 ☒ 🄷

WHITE SULPHUR SPRINGS

🅰🅰🅰 ▼▼ **All Seasons Inn & Suites** 🅼
(406) 547-8888. **$75-$120.** 808 3rd Ave SW. On US 89, south end of town. Int corridors. **Pets:** Other species. $6 daily fee/pet. Service with restrictions, supervision.
🆂🄰🅅🄴 🆂🅟 ☒ 🄻🄼 🄷 🄷

WIBAUX

🅰🅰🅰 ▼ **Beaver Creek Inn & Suites** 🅼
(406) 796-2666. **$58-$69.** 400 W 2nd Ave N. I-94, exit 241 westbound; exit 242 eastbound. Int corridors. **Pets:** Medium, other species. $8 daily fee/pet. Designated rooms, service with restrictions, supervision.
🆂🄰🅅🄴 🆂🅟 ☒ 🄷 ▣

NEBRASKA

AINSWORTH

Comfort Inn SH
(402) 387-1050. **$75.** 1124 E 4th St. 0.5 mi e on US 20. Int corridors. **Pets:** $10 daily fee/pet. Designated rooms, service with restrictions, supervision.

Super 8 Motel SH
(402) 387-0700. **$50.** 1025 E 4th St. 0.5 mi e on US 20. Int corridors. **Pets:** Other species. $50 deposit/room. Service with restrictions, crate.

ALLIANCE

Alliance Days Inn SH
(308) 762-8000. **$59-$96.** 117 Cody Ave. Jct US 385 and SR 2, 0.4 mi e, just s. Int corridors. **Pets:** Accepted.

BEATRICE

Holiday Inn Express Hotel & Suites SH
(402) 228-7100. **$79-$139.** 4005 N 6th St. 1 mi n on US 77. Int corridors. **Pets:** Accepted.

BELLEVUE

Settle Inn and Suites SH
(402) 292-1155. **$59-$175.** 2105 Pratt Ave. US 75, exit Cornhusker, just w. Int corridors. **Pets:** Small, dogs only. $15 daily fee/room. Designated rooms, service with restrictions, supervision.

CENTRAL CITY

Super 8 Motel SH
(308) 946-5055. **$55.** 1701 31st St. SR 14, 1 mi s of jct US 30. Ext/int corridors. **Pets:** Medium, other species. $5 daily fee/room. Service with restrictions, supervision.

CHADRON

Best Western West Hills Inn SH
(308) 432-3305. **$61-$127.** 1100 W 10th St. Just s of jct US 385 and 20. Ext/int corridors. **Pets:** $10 one-time fee/room. Service with restrictions, crate.

Grand Westerner Motel M
(308) 432-5595. **$46-$59.** 1050 W Hwy 20. 0.8 mi w on US 20; just e of jct US 385. Ext corridors. **Pets:** Dogs only. No service, supervision.

Motel 6 of Chadron #4259 SH
(308) 432-3000. **$45-$85.** 755 Microtel Dr. Just s of jct US 385 and 20. Int corridors. **Pets:** Medium, other species. Service with restrictions, supervision.

Westerner Motel M
(308) 432-5577. **$46-$59.** 300 Oak St. On US 20, 0.5 mi e of jct US 385 and SR 87. Ext corridors. **Pets:** Dogs only. $500 one-time fee/pet. No service, supervision.

COLUMBUS

Sleep Inn & Suites Hotel SH
(402) 562-5200. **$77-$130.** 303 23rd St. On US 30, 2 mi e of jct US 30 and 81; east side of town. Int corridors. **Pets:** Medium. $10 daily fee/pet. Designated rooms, service with restrictions, crate.

Super 8 Motel-Columbus SH
(402) 563-3456. **$50-$56.** 3324 20th St. On US 30 and 81, just s. Int corridors. **Pets:** Small. $10 one-time fee/pet. Service with restrictions, supervision.

COZAD

Motel 6-Cozad–4091 SH
(308) 784-4900. **$42-$56.** 809 S Meridian. I-80, exit 222, just n. Int corridors. **Pets:** Medium, other species. Service with restrictions, supervision.

CRETE

Super 8 Motel SH
(402) 826-3106. **$52-$65.** 1880 W 12th St. 1.3 mi sw at jct SR 33/103; west end of town. Int corridors. **Pets:** Small, dogs only. $5 daily fee/pet. Service with restrictions, supervision.

FREMONT

Comfort Inn SH
(402) 721-1109. **$49-$149.** 1649 E 23rd Ave. 2 mi e on US 30, just e of Business Rt US 275. Int corridors. **Pets:** Large. $10 daily fee/room. Designated rooms, service with restrictions, supervision.

Wilderness Lodge & Conference Center SH
(402) 727-1110. **$59-$80, 3 day notice.** 1220 E 23rd St. US 30, jct Business Rt US 275 and 30. Ext/int corridors. **Pets:** Dogs only. $25 deposit/room. Designated rooms, no service, supervision.

FULLERTON

Fullerton Inn M
(308) 536-2699. **$60.** S Hwy 14. Just s of center. Int corridors. **Pets:** Accepted.

GERING

▼▼▼ Microtel Inn & Suites SH
(308) 436-1950. **$65-$70.** 1130 M St. On SR 92, 1 mi e of SR 71. Int corridors. **Pets:** Other species. $10 one-time fee/room. Service with restrictions, supervision.
ASK S⌀ ✕ ⌖M ⌖ 🛏 🖵

GOTHENBURG

▲▲▲ ▼▼▼ Gothenburg Super 8 SH
(308) 537-2684. **$58-$72.** 401 Platte River Dr. I-80, exit 211 (SR 47), just n. Int corridors. **Pets:** Accepted.
SAVE S⌀ ✕ 🛏 🖵 ⊃

GRAND ISLAND

▼▼▼▼ Holiday Inn-Interstate 80 SH ❀
(308) 384-7770. **$59-$99.** 7838 S US Hwy 281. I-80, exit 312 (US 281), just s. Int corridors. **Pets:** $15 daily fee/room. Service with restrictions, supervision.
✕ ⌖M 🗗 ⌖ 🛏 🖵 ⊤⊤ ⊃ ⊠

▼▼ Super 8 Motel SH
(308) 384-4380. **$52-$60.** 2603 S Locust St. I-80, exit 314, 4.7 mi n. Int corridors. **Pets:** Accepted.
ASK ✕ 🛏 🖵 ⊃

▼▼ Travelodge SH
(308) 382-5003. **$53-$59.** 1311 S Locust St. I-80, exit 314 (US 281), 5.2 mi n. Int corridors. **Pets:** Accepted.
ASK S⌀ ✕ ⌖ 🛏 🖵

▲▲▲ ▼▼▼ USA Inns of America M
(308) 381-0111. **$52-$70.** 7501 S Hwy 281. I-80, exit 312 (US 281), just n. Ext/int corridors. **Pets:** Accepted.
SAVE S⌀ ✕ 🛏 🖵

HASTINGS

▲▲▲ ▼▼▼▼ Holiday Inn-Hastings SH ❀
(402) 463-6721. **$68-$90.** 2205 Osborne Dr E. Jct US 34 and 281, 2 mi n. Ext/int corridors. **Pets:** Other species. $30 deposit/room. Service with restrictions, crate.
SAVE S⌀ ✕ ⌖M 🗗 ⌖ 🛏 🖵 ⊤⊤ ⊃ ⊠

▲▲▲ ▼ Midlands Lodge M
(402) 463-2428. **$48-$59.** 910 W J St. Jct US 6, 34 and 281. Ext corridors. **Pets:** Accepted.
SAVE S⌀ ✕ 🛏 ⊃

▼▼ Super 8 SH
(402) 463-8888. **$54-$79.** 2200 N Kansas Ave. Jct US 34 and 281, 2 mi n. Int corridors. **Pets:** Accepted.
ASK S⌀ ✕ 🗗 ⌖ 🛏 🖵

HOLDREGE

▼▼▼ Super 8 SH
(308) 995-2793. **$64-$69.** 420 Broadway. US 183, 0.5 mi w on US 6/34. Int corridors. **Pets:** $10 daily fee/pet. Service with restrictions, supervision.
ASK S⌀ ✕ 🛏 ⊃

KEARNEY

▲▲▲ ▼▼▼ AmericInn Lodge & Suites of Kearney SH
(308) 234-7800. **$79-$99.** 215 W Talmadge Rd. I-80, exit 272 (SR 44), just n. Int corridors. **Pets:** Accepted.
SAVE ✕ ⌖M ⌖ 🛏 🖵 ⊃ ⊠

▲▲▲ ▼▼▼ Best Western Inn of Kearney SH ❀
(308) 237-5185. **$60-$95.** 1010 3rd Ave. I-80, exit 272 (SR 44), 1 mi n, then just w. Ext/int corridors. **Pets:** Large, other species. $10 one-time fee/room. Service with restrictions, crate.
SAVE S⌀ ✕ 🗗 ⌖ 🛏 🖵 ⊤⊤ ⊃ ⊠

▲▲▲ ▼▼▼ Days Inn of Kearney SH
(308) 234-5699. **$48-$65.** 619 2nd Ave. I-80, exit 272 (SR 44), 0.8 mi n. Int corridors. **Pets:** Accepted.
SAVE S⌀ ✕ 🛏 ⊃

▼▼ Fairfield Inn-Kearney SH ❀
(308) 237-0838. **$79.** 121 3rd Ave. I-80, exit 272 (SR 44), 0.3 mi n. Int corridors. **Pets:** Medium, other species. $25 one-time fee/room. Designated rooms, service with restrictions, supervision.
ASK S⌀ ✕ 🗗 ⌖ 🛏 🖵 ⊃

▲▲▲ ▼▼▼ Ramada Inn-Kearney SH
(308) 237-3141. **$59-$99.** 301 2nd Ave. I-80, exit 272 (SR 44), 0.7 mi n. Int corridors. **Pets:** Accepted.
SAVE S⌀ ✕ 🛏 🖵 ⊤⊤ ⊃ ⊠

▼▼ Super 8 Motel M ❀
(308) 234-5513. **$55-$75.** 15 W 8th St. I-80, exit 272 (SR44), 1 mi n, then just e. Int corridors. **Pets:** Dogs only. $10 one-time fee/room. Designated rooms, service with restrictions, supervision.
ASK S⌀ ✕

KIMBALL

▼▼ Days Inn-Kimball M
(308) 235-4671. **$70-$120.** 611 E 3rd St. I-80, exit 20, 1.5 ne on SR 71, then 0.5 mi e on US 30. Ext corridors. **Pets:** Large, other species. $10 daily fee/pet. Service with restrictions, supervision.
ASK S⌀ ✕ 🛏

LEXINGTON

▼▼ Days Inn SH
(308) 324-6440. **$55-$99.** 2506 Plum Creek Pkwy. I-80, exit 237 (US 283), 0.6 mi n. Int corridors. **Pets:** Dogs only. $6 daily fee/pet. Designated rooms, service with restrictions, supervision.
ASK S⌀ ✕ 🛏

▲▲▲ ▼▼▼▼ Holiday Inn Express Hotel & Suites SH
(308) 324-9900. **$90-$111.** 2605 Plum Creek Pkwy. I-80, exit 237 (US 283), 0.5 mi n. Int corridors. **Pets:** Other species. $10 one-time fee/room. Designated rooms, service with restrictions, supervision.
SAVE S⌀ ✕ ⌖M 🗗 ⌖ 🛏 🖵 ⊃

LINCOLN

▼▼▼▼ Candlewood Suites SH ❀
(402) 420-0330. **$85-$132.** 4100 Pioneer Woods Dr. 4.6 mi e on SR 2, 2.2 mi n via 70th St, e on Pioneers Blvd, then just n. Int corridors. **Pets:** Medium. $75 one-time fee/pet. Service with restrictions, crate.
ASK S⌀ ✕ ⌖M 🗗 ⌖ 🛏 🖵

▲▲▲ ▼▼▼▼ Chase Suites Hotel SH ❀
(402) 483-4900. **$79-$180.** 200 S 68th St Pl. On US 34, 4.3 mi e, just s of jct 68th St. Ext corridors. **Pets:** $150 deposit/pet, $5 daily fee/pet. Designated rooms, service with restrictions, crate.
SAVE S⌀ ✕ ⌖M 🗗 ⌖ 🛏 🖵 ⊃ ⊠

▲▲▲ ▼▼ Cobbler Inn SH
(402) 475-4800. **$53-$74.** 4808 West O St. I-80, exit 395. Int corridors. **Pets:** Medium. $6 daily fee/pet. Designated rooms, service with restrictions, supervision.
SAVE ✕ 🖵

▲▲▲ ▼▼▼▼ Country Inns & Suites By Carlson SH ❀
(402) 476-5353. **$95-$115.** 5353 N 27th St. I-80, exit 403 (27th St), 1.5 mi s. Int corridors. **Pets:** Medium. $10 daily fee/pet. Service with restrictions, supervision.
SAVE S⌀ ✕ ⌖M ⌖ 🛏 🖵 ⊤⊤ ⊃

▲▲▲ ▼▼▼ Days Inn South SH
(402) 423-7111. **$53-$99.** 1140 Calvert St. 2.5 mi s on SR 2. Ext/int corridors. **Pets:** Medium, dogs only. $5 daily fee/pet. Designated rooms, service with restrictions, crate.
SAVE S⌀ ✕ 🛏 🖵

(AAA) ▼▼▼ Econo Lodge M
(402) 475-4511. **$49-$69.** 1140 W Cornhusker Hwy. I-80, exit 399 (Airport), just w. Ext/int corridors. **Pets:** Dogs only. $10 daily fee/pet. Service with restrictions, supervision.
[SAVE] ⊗ 🛏 🖥 ▤

(AAA) ▼▼▼ Holiday Inn Express SH
(402) 435-0200. **$90-$140.** 1133 Belmont Ave. I-80, exit 401; exit 401A; 2 mi s on I-180, exit 2 (Cornhusker Hwy e), then just n on 11th St. Int corridors. **Pets:** Other species. $5 one-time fee/room. Designated rooms, service with restrictions, supervision.
[SAVE] 🛏 ⊗ 🛏 🖥 ▤ 🛏 🖥 ▤ ⊗

(AAA) ▼▼ Quality Suites SH
(402) 464-4400. **$76-$129.** 216 N 48th St. 2.5 mi e on US 6 and 34; just ne of jct O St; entrance off of 48th St. Int corridors. **Pets:** Other species. $10 daily fee/room. Designated rooms, service with restrictions, supervision.
[ASK] 🛏 ⊗ 🛏 🖥 ▤ 🖥 ▤

◆◆ Settle Inn & Suites SH
(402) 435-8100. **$59-$89.** 2800 Husker Cir. I-80, exit 403 (27th St), just s to Wildcat Dr, just e, then just n. Int corridors. **Pets:** Small, dogs only. $15 daily fee/pet. Designated rooms, service with restrictions, supervision.
[ASK] ⊗ 🛏 🖥 ▤ 🖥 ▤

▼▼▼ Staybridge Suites Lincoln-I-80 SH
(402) 438-7829. **$86-$200.** 2701 Fletcher Ave. I-80, exit 403 (27th St), 0.4 mi s. Int corridors. **Pets:** Other species. $75 one-time fee/room. Service with restrictions, crate.
[ASK] ⊗ 🛏 🖥 ▤ 🖥 ▤ ⊗

◆◆ Super 8 Motel-Lincoln/Cornhusker SH 🐾
(402) 467-4488. **$53-$80.** 2545 Cornhusker Hwy. I-80, exit 403 (27th St), 2.5 mi s. Int corridors. **Pets:** Medium, dogs only. $10 one-time fee/room. Service with restrictions, supervision.
[ASK] 🛏 ⊗ 🛏 🖥 ▤

(AAA) ▼▼▼ Super 8 Motel-Lincoln/West "O" Street SH
(402) 476-8887. **$56-$67.** 2635 West O St. I-80, exit 396 eastbound, 0.5 mi e; exit 397 westbound, 0.5 mi w. Int corridors. **Pets:** Other species. $10 daily fee/room. No service, supervision.
[SAVE] 🛏 ⊗ 🛏 🖥 🖥 ▤

(AAA) ▼▼▼ Town House Suites SH
(402) 475-3000. **$60-$85.** 1744 M St. Jct 18th and M St; downtown. Int corridors. **Pets:** Other species. Supervision.
[SAVE] 🛏 ⊗ 🖥 🖥 ▤

MCCOOK

▼▼▼▼ Holiday Inn Express SH
(308) 345-4505. **$70-$88.** 1 Holiday Bison Dr. On US 83, just n of jct US 6 and 34. Int corridors. **Pets:** Accepted.
[ASK] 🛏 ⊗ 🛏 🖥 🖥

MORRILL

(AAA) ▼▼▼ Oak Tree Inn SH
(308) 247-2111. **$55-$69.** 707 E Webster. 0.5 mi e on US 26. Ext/int corridors. **Pets:** $5 one-time fee/room. Service with restrictions.
[SAVE] 🛏 ⊗ 🛏 🖥 🖥 ▤ 🍴

NEBRASKA CITY

(AAA) ▼▼▼ Apple Inn SH
(402) 873-5959. **$58-$65.** 502 S 11th St. Jct 11th St and 4th Corso; center. Ext/int corridors. **Pets:** Small, dogs only. $8 daily fee/pet. Designated rooms, service with restrictions, supervision.
[SAVE] 🛏 ⊗ 🖥 🖥 ▤ 🖥

NORFOLK

(AAA) ▼▼▼▼ Norfolk Lodge & Suites- A Clarion Collection Hotel SH
(402) 379-3833. **$89-$169.** 4200 W Norfolk Ave. On US 275 Bypass, 3 mi w of jct US 81. Ext/int corridors. **Pets:** Accepted.
[SAVE] 🛏 ⊗ 🛏 🖥 🖥 🖥 🖥 ▤ 🍴 🖥 ⊗

▼ Super 8 Motel-Norfolk SH
(402) 379-2220. **$46-$60.** 1223 Omaha Ave. Jct US 275 Bypass and 81. Int corridors. **Pets:** Other species. $10 one-time fee/room. Service with restrictions, crate.
[ASK] 🛏 ⊗ 🖥 🖥

◆◆ White House Inn SH
(402) 371-3133. **$55-$60.** 2206 Market Ln. On US 275 Bypass, 1 mi w of jct US 81. Int corridors. **Pets:** Accepted.
[ASK] 🛏 ⊗ 🛏 🖥 🖥 ▤

NORTH PLATTE

(AAA) ▼▼ Americas Best Value Travelers Inn M
(308) 534-4020. **$40-$60.** 602 E 4th St. I-80, exit 177 (US 83), 1.5 mi n, then 0.3 mi e. Ext corridors. **Pets:** Medium, other species. Service with restrictions, supervision.
[SAVE] 🛏 ⊗ 🖥 ▤

(AAA) ▼▼ Best Western Chalet Lodge M
(308) 532-2313. **$55-$92.** 920 N Jeffers St. I-80, exit 177 (US 83), 2 mi n on US 30 and 83. Ext corridors. **Pets:** Other species. $7 daily fee/pet. Service with restrictions, supervision.
[SAVE] 🛏 ⊗ 🖥 ▤

(AAA) ▼▼▼▼ Holiday Inn Express Hotel & Suites SH
(308) 532-9500. **$89-$159.** 300 Holiday Frontage Rd. I-80, exit 177 (US 83), just s. Int corridors. **Pets:** Accepted.
[SAVE] 🛏 ⊗ 🛏 🖥 🖥 🖥 🖥 ▤ ⊗

▼▼▼▼ La Quinta Inn & Suites SH
(308) 534-0700. **$79-$149.** 2600 Eagles Wings Pl. I-80, exit 179, just n, then just w. Int corridors. **Pets:** Service with restrictions, supervision.
[ASK] 🛏 ⊗ 🛏 🖥 🖥 🖥 ▤

◆◆ Oak Tree Inn SH
(308) 535-9900. **$70-$95.** 451 Halligan Dr. I-80, exit 177 (US 83), 0.3 mi n, then 0.3 mi e on service road. Int corridors. **Pets:** Accepted.
[ASK] 🛏 ⊗ 🛏 🖥 🖥 🍴

(AAA) ▼▼▼▼ Quality Inn & Suites SH
(308) 532-9090. **$84-$159.** 2102 S Jeffers St. I-80, exit 177 (US 83), just n. Ext/int corridors. **Pets:** $10 daily fee/pet. Designated rooms, no service, supervision.
[SAVE] 🛏 ⊗ 🛏 🖥 🖥 🖥 🖥 ▤ 🍴 ▤ ⊗

(AAA) ▼▼▼ Ramada Inn SH
(308) 534-3120. **$59-$80.** 3201 S Jeffers St. I-80, exit 177 (US 83), 0.3 mi s. Int corridors. **Pets:** Other species. $10 one-time fee/room. Service with restrictions, supervision.
[SAVE] 🛏 ⊗ 🖥 🖥 ▤ 🍴 ▤

OGALLALA

(AAA) ▼▼▼ Best Western Stagecoach Inn SH 🐾
(308) 284-3656. **$60-$129.** 201 Stagecoach Tr. I-80, exit 126 (US 26/SR 61), just n, then e on Frontage Rd. Ext corridors. **Pets:** Other species. $7 deposit/pet. Designated rooms, no service, supervision.
[SAVE] 🛏 ⊗ 🛏 🖥 🍴 ▤ ⊗

(AAA) ▼▼▼ Days Inn M 🐾
(308) 284-6365. **$49-$79.** 601 Stagecoach Trail. I-80, exit 126 (US 26/SR 61), just n, then e on Frontage Rd. Int corridors. **Pets:** Dogs only. $6 daily fee/room. Service with restrictions, supervision.
[SAVE] 🛏 ⊗ 🖥

▼▼ ▼▼ **Holiday Inn Express** 🆂🅷 ❀
(308) 284-2266. **$85-$105, 10 day notice.** 501 Stagecoach Trail. I-80, exit 126 (US 26/SR 61), just n, then e on Frontage Rd. Ext/int corridors. **Pets:** Large. $7 daily fee/pet. Service with restrictions, supervision.
A$K 🆂🅳 ⊠ 🕸 🗝 🔔 💻

OMAHA

◆◆◆ ▼▼ ▼▼ **Best Western Kelly Inn Omaha** 🆂🅷 ❀
(402) 339-7400. **$89-$119.** 4706 S 108th St. I-80, exit 445 (L St E), 0.3 mi e, then just s. Int corridors. **Pets:** Service with restrictions, supervision.
SAVE 🆂🅳 ⊠ 🕸 🔔 💻 🍴 ⟿ ⊠

▼▼ ▼▼ **Best Western Settle Inn** 🆂🅷
(402) 431-1246. **$69-$109.** 650 N 109th Ct. I-680, exit 3 (Dodge St W), 0.8 mi w to 108th St and N Old Mill Rd, then just w on Mill Valley Rd. Int corridors. **Pets:** Accepted.
A$K 🆂🅳 ⊠ 🕸 🗝 🔔 💻 ⟿ ⊠

◆◆◆ ▼▼ ▼▼ **Best Western Seville Plaza** 🆂🅷
(402) 345-2222. **$79-$119.** 3001 Chicago. I-480, exit 2B westbound; exit 2A northbound, just w on Dodge St, then just n on 30th St. Int corridors. **Pets:** Small. $40 one-time fee/pet. Designated rooms, service with restrictions, crate.
SAVE 🆂🅳 ⊠ 🅼 🕸 🗝 🔔 💻

▼▼ ▼▼ ▼▼ **Candlewood Suites** 🆂🅷
(402) 758-2848. **$99-$129.** 360 S 108th Ave. I-680, exit 3 (Dodge St W), 0.7 mi to 108th St, then 0.8 mi s. Int corridors. **Pets:** Medium. $75 one-time fee/room. Service with restrictions.
⊠ 🅼 🕸 🗝 🔔 💻

▼▼ ▼▼ ▼▼ **Clarion Hotel-West** 🆂🅷 ❀
(402) 895-1000. **$49-$249.** 4888 S 118th St. I-80, exit 445 (L St W), 0.3 mi w on US 275/SR 92, then just s on 120th St. Int corridors. **Pets:** Large. $10 daily fee/room. Designated rooms, service with restrictions, crate.
A$K 🆂🅳 ⊠ 🅼 🕸 🗝 🔔 💻 🍴 ⟿

◆◆◆ ▼▼ ▼▼ **Comfort Inn** 🆂🅷
(402) 343-1000. **$75-$114.** 8736 W Dodge Rd. I-680, exit 3 (Dodge St E), 1.5 mi e. Int corridors. **Pets:** Accepted.
SAVE 🆂🅳 ⊠ 🅼 🕸 🔔 💻 ⟿

◆◆◆ ▼▼ ▼▼ ▼▼ **Comfort Inn-Southwest** 🆂🅷
(402) 593-2380. **$59-$150, 14 day notice.** 10728 L St. I-80, exit 445 (L St E), just n on 108th St, then e. Int corridors. **Pets:** Other species. $10 daily fee/room. Service with restrictions, supervision.
SAVE 🆂🅳 ⊠ 🔔 💻 ⟿

◆◆◆ ▼▼ ▼▼ **Countryside Suites** 🅼
(402) 884-2644. **$60-$80.** 9477 S 142nd St. I-80, exit 440, just ne. Ext corridors. **Pets:** Very small, dogs only. $20 deposit/pet, $10 daily fee/pet. Service with restrictions, supervision.
SAVE 🆂🅳 ⊠ 🅼 🔔 💻

▼▼ ▼▼ ▼▼ **Crowne Plaza Hotel** 🅻🅷
(402) 496-0850. **$79-$159.** 655 N 108th Ave. I-680, exit 3 (Dodge St W), 0.7 mi to 108th St to 108th Ave and N Old Mill Rd exits, then just n. Int corridors. **Pets:** Accepted.
⊠ 🕸 🗝 🔔 💻 🍴 ⟿ ⊠

▼▼ ▼▼ ▼▼ **DoubleTree Guest Suites Omaha** 🅻🅷
(402) 397-5141. **$69-$189.** 7270 Cedar St. I-80, exit 449 (72nd St), 1.3 mi n. Int corridors. **Pets:** Dogs only. $50 one-time fee/room. Service with restrictions, supervision.
⊠ 🕸 🗝 🔔 💻 🍴 ⟿ ⊠

◆◆◆ ▼▼ ▼▼ ▼▼ **Hawthorn Suites** 🆂🅷
(402) 331-0101. **$99-$189.** 11025 M St. I-80, exit 445 (L St E), 0.3 mi e, just s on 108th St, then just w. Ext corridors. **Pets:** Medium. $6 daily fee/room. Service with restrictions, crate.
SAVE 🆂🅳 ⊠ 🕸 🔔 💻 ⟿ ⊠

▼▼ ▼▼ **Homewood Suites** 🆂🅷
(402) 397-7500. **$129-$259, 30 day notice.** 7010 Hascall St. I-80, exit 449 (72nd St), just n, then just e. Ext/int corridors. **Pets:** Small. $50 one-time fee/pet. Service with restrictions, crate.
A$K ⊠ 🕸 🗝 🔔 💻

◆◆◆ ▼▼ ▼▼ **La Quinta Inn** 🆂🅷
(402) 592-5200. **$67-$107.** 10760 M St. I-80, exit 445 (L St E), 0.3 mi e, s on 108th St, then just e. Int corridors. **Pets:** Medium. Service with restrictions.
SAVE ⊠ 🕸 🔔 💻

◆◆◆ ▼▼ ▼▼ ▼▼ **La Quinta Inn Omaha** 🆂🅷
(402) 493-1900. **$69-$109.** 3330 N 104th Ave. I-680, exit 4 (Maple St), just w to 108th St, just n to Bedford, then just e. Int corridors. **Pets:** Medium. Service with restrictions.
SAVE ⊠ 🕸 🔔 💻 ⟿

▼▼ ▼▼ **Quality Inn & Suites** 🆂🅷
(402) 896-9500. **$72-$78.** 9505 S 142nd St. I-80, exit 440, just ne. Int corridors. **Pets:** Medium, dogs only. $10 daily fee/pet. Service with restrictions, supervision.
A$K ⊠ 🗝 🔔 💻 ⟿

◆◆◆ ▼▼ ▼▼ **Relax Inn Motel & Suites** 🅼
(402) 731-7300. **$50-$65.** 4578 S 60th St. I-80, exit 450 (60th St), 0.8 mi s. Ext corridors. **Pets:** Very small, dogs only. $20 deposit/pet, $10 daily fee/pet. Service with restrictions, supervision.
SAVE 🆂🅳 ⊠ 🔔 💻

◆◆◆ ▼▼ ▼▼ ▼▼ **Residence Inn by Marriott** 🆂🅷
(402) 553-8898. **$119-$219.** 6990 Dodge St. I-680, exit 3 (Dodge St E), 3 mi e. Ext corridors. **Pets:** Accepted.
SAVE 🆂🅳 ⊠ 🔔 💻 ⟿ ⊠

◆◆◆ ▼▼ **Satellite Motel** 🅼
(402) 733-7373. **$45-$55.** 6006 L St. I-80, exit 450 (60th St), 0.8 mi s; just n of US 275 and SR 92. Ext/int corridors. **Pets:** Accepted.
SAVE 🆂🅳 ⊠ 🔔 💻

◆◆◆ ▼▼ ▼▼ ▼▼ **Sheraton Omaha Hotel** 🅻🅷
(402) 342-2222. **$219-$229.** 1615 Howard St. Downtown. Int corridors. **Pets:** Accepted.
SAVE 🆂🅳 ⊠ 🕸 🗝 🔔 💻 🍴 ⊠

▼▼ ▼▼ **StudioPLUS-Omaha-West** 🆂🅷
(402) 343-9000. **$86-$109.** 9006 Burt St. I-680, exit 3 (Dodge St E), 1.1 mi e, then just n. Int corridors. **Pets:** Accepted.
A$K 🆂🅳 ⊠ 🗝 🔔 💻

▼▼ **Super 8 Motel-Omaha/Aksarben** 🆂🅷
(402) 390-0700. **$49-$85.** 7111 Spring St. I-80, exit 449 (72nd St), 0.3 mi n. Int corridors. **Pets:** $11 daily fee/room. Designated rooms, service with restrictions, supervision.
A$K 🆂🅳 ⊠ 🕸 🔔

▼▼ ▼▼ **Super 8 Motel-Omaha/West L** 🆂🅷
(402) 339-2250. **$69-$72.** 10829 M St. I-80, exit 445 (L St E), 0.3 mi e, just s on 108th St, then just w. Int corridors. **Pets:** Small. $10 daily fee/pet. Service with restrictions, supervision.
A$K 🆂🅳 ⊠ 🕸 🔔

O'NEILL

◆◆◆ ▼▼ **Elms Motel** 🅼 ❀
(402) 336-3800. **$48-$62.** 414 E Hwy 20. 1 mi se on US 20/275. Ext corridors. **Pets:** $7 one-time fee/room. Service with restrictions, supervision.
SAVE 🆂🅳 ⊠ 🔔 💻

▼▼ ▼▼ ▼▼ **Holiday Inn Express Hotel & Suites** 🆂🅷
(402) 336-4500. **$75-$79.** 1020 E Douglas St. 0.4 mi e on US 20/275. Int corridors. **Pets:** Accepted.
A$K ⊠ 🅼 🗝 🔔 💻 ⟿

▼▼ Super 8 Motel-O'Neill SH
(402) 336-3100. **$50.** 106 E Hwy 20. 0.5 mi e on US 20/275. Int corridors. **Pets:** $10 daily fee/pet. Designated rooms, service with restrictions, supervision.

PAXTON

◆◆◆ ▼▼ Paxton Days Inn M
(308) 239-4510. **$59-$95.** 851 Paxton Rd. I-80, exit 145, just n. Ext corridors. **Pets:** Other species. $10 one-time fee/room. Service with restrictions, supervision.

ST. PAUL

◆◆◆ ▼ Bel-Air Motel & RV Park M
(308) 754-4466. **$45-$49.** 1158 Highway 281. On US 281, 1 mi s. Ext corridors. **Pets:** Supervision.

SCOTTSBLUFF

▼▼▼ Barn Anew Bed & Breakfast BB
(308) 632-8647. **$85-$90.** 170549 CR L. 3.5 mi w of town, via 20th St, then 0.5 mi s on SR 92. Int corridors. **Pets:** Accepted.

▼▼ Comfort Inn SH
(308) 632-7510. **$60-$70.** 1902 21st Ave. 1.8 mi e on US 26, just n. Ext/int corridors. **Pets:** Other species. Service with restrictions, supervision.

◆▼ Lamplighter American Inn SH
(308) 632-7108. **$52-$64.** 606 E 27th St. US 26 business route, 0.5 mi e of jct SR 71, just s. Int corridors. **Pets:** Accepted.

SIDNEY

◆◆◆ ▼ Americas Best Value Inn & Suites M
(308) 254-2081. **$59-$73.** 2115 W Illinois. On US 30, west side of town. Int corridors. **Pets:** Medium. $10 daily fee/pet. Designated rooms, service with restrictions, supervision.

◆◆◆ ▼▼▼ AmericInn Lodge & Suites of Sidney SH 🐾
(308) 254-0100. **$86-$150.** 645 Cabela Dr. I-80, exit 59, just nw. Int corridors. **Pets:** Other species. $10 one-time fee/pet. Service with restrictions, supervision.

◆◆◆ ▼▼ Days Inn SH
(308) 254-2121. **$76-$125.** 3042 Silverberg Dr. I-80, exit 59, just n. Int corridors. **Pets:** Medium. $10 daily fee/pet. Designated rooms, service with restrictions, supervision.

◆▼▼ Holiday Inn & Conference Center SH
(308) 254-2000. **$79-$119.** 664 Chase Blvd. I-80, exit 59, just s. Int corridors. **Pets:** Dogs only. $20 one-time fee/pet. Designated rooms, service with restrictions, supervision.

SOUTH SIOUX CITY

▼▼▼ Marina Inn Conference Center SH
(402) 494-4000. **$109-$149, 3 day notice.** 4th & B sts. I-29, exit 148, on banks of Missouri River; e at stop light by Nebraska side of bridge. Int corridors. **Pets:** Accepted.

SYRACUSE

◆◆◆ ▼▼ Sleep Inn & Suites SH
(402) 269-2700. **$70.** 130 N 30th Rd. Jct SR 2, 1 mi n on SR 50. Int corridors. **Pets:** Accepted.

THEDFORD

◆◆◆ ▼▼ Roadside Inn SH
(308) 645-2284. **$56-$86.** HC 58 Box 1D. 1 mi e on SR 2, just w of US 83. Int corridors. **Pets:** Other species. $25 deposit/room, $7 daily fee/room. Service with restrictions, supervision.

VALENTINE

▼▼ Dunes Lodge & Suites M
(402) 376-3131. **$44-$89.** 340 E Hwys 20 & 83. Jct US 20/83, 0.3 mi e. Ext corridors. **Pets:** Accepted.

◆◆◆ ▼▼▼ Trade Winds Motel M
(402) 376-1600. **$40-$74.** E Hwys 20 & 83. Jct US 20/83, 1 mi se. Ext corridors. **Pets:** $4 daily fee/pet. Service with restrictions, supervision.

WAHOO

▼▼ Wahoo Heritage Inn SH
(402) 443-1288. **$57-$74.** 950 N Chestnut. On US 77 and SR 92, just nw of downtown. Ext/int corridors. **Pets:** Accepted.

YORK

◆◆◆ ▼▼▼ Best Western Palmer Inn M
(402) 362-5585. **$50-$71.** 2426 S Lincoln Ave. I-80, exit 353 (US 81), 1 mi n. Ext corridors. **Pets:** Accepted.

◆◆◆ ▼▼▼ Holiday Inn SH
(402) 362-6661. **$72-$79.** 4619 S Lincoln Ave. I-80, exit 353 (US 81), just s. Int corridors. **Pets:** Accepted.

◆▼ Yorkshire Inn Motel M
(402) 362-6633. **$42-$59.** 3402 S Lincoln Ave. I-80, exit 353 (US 81), 0.5 mi n. Ext/int corridors. **Pets:** Accepted.

NEVADA

BATTLE MOUNTAIN

Comfort Inn SH
(775) 635-5880. **$56-$78.** 521 E Front St. I-80, exit 229 or 233, just n. Int corridors. **Pets:** Other species. $10 one-time fee/room. Service with restrictions.

BEATTY

Exchange Club Motel M
(775) 553-2333. **$48-$68.** 119 Main St. SR 95 at SR 374; downtown. Ext corridors. **Pets:** Other species. $25 deposit/room, $5 daily fee/room. Service with restrictions, supervision.

Stagecoach Hotel Casino M
(775) 553-2419. **$47-$57.** Hwy 95 N. North end of town; west side of US 95. Ext/int corridors. **Pets:** Medium. $10 deposit/pet. Designated rooms, service with restrictions, supervision.

CARLIN

Comfort Inn SH
(775) 754-6110. **$67-$96.** 1018 Fir St. I-80, exit 280, just s. Int corridors. **Pets:** Dogs only. $100 deposit/room, $10 daily fee/pet. Designated rooms, service with restrictions, supervision.

CARSON CITY

Carson City Super 8 M
(775) 883-7800. **$43-$124.** 2829 S Carson St. South end of town. Int corridors. **Pets:** Small, other species. $25 deposit/pet. Designated rooms, no service, supervision.

Days Inn M
(775) 883-3343. **$49-$120.** 3103 N Carson St. US 395 N, north end of town. Ext corridors. **Pets:** Large. $10 daily fee/pet. Service with restrictions, crate.

Holiday Inn Express & Suites M
(775) 283-4055. **$89-$199.** 4055 N Carson St. US 395; north end of town. Int corridors. **Pets:** Accepted.

The Plaza Hotel M
(775) 883-9500. **$59-$109.** 801 S Carson St. South end of town. Ext/int corridors. **Pets:** Accepted.

Quality Inn M
(775) 883-7300. **$55-$189.** 1300 N Carson St. 0.5 mi n on US 395. Ext corridors. **Pets:** Accepted.

ELKO

Best Western Gold Country Motor Inn SH
(775) 738-8421. **$99-$159.** 2050 Idaho St. I-80, exit 303, just s. Ext corridors. **Pets:** Accepted.

Comfort Inn SH
(775) 777-8762. **$73-$130.** 2970 Idaho St. I-80, exit 303, just s, then just e. Int corridors. **Pets:** Very small, dogs only. $15 daily fee/pet. Service with restrictions, supervision.

Econo Lodge Inn & Suites SH
(775) 777-8000. **$55-$85.** 3320 E Idaho St. I-80, exit 303, just s. Int corridors. **Pets:** Medium, other species. $15 daily fee/pet. Service with restrictions, supervision.

High Desert Inn SH
(775) 738-8425. **$69-$99.** 3015 Idaho St. I-80, exit 303, just n. Ext/int corridors. **Pets:** Accepted.

Oak Tree Inn SH
(775) 777-2222. **$69-$99.** 95 Spruce Rd. I-80, exit 301, just n. Int corridors. **Pets:** $10 daily fee/pet. Service with restrictions, supervision.

Red Lion Inn & Casino Elko SH
(775) 738-2111. **$99-$259.** 2065 Idaho St. I-80, exit 303, just s. Int corridors. **Pets:** $15 one-time fee/room. Designated rooms, service with restrictions, crate.

Rodeway Inn M
(775) 738-7152. **$42-$99, 3 day notice.** 736 Idaho St. I-80, exit 301 or 303, 1 mi s. Ext corridors. **Pets:** Medium, dogs only. $15 daily fee/pet. Designated rooms, service with restrictions, supervision.

Shilo Inn SH
(775) 738-5522. **$85-$135.** 2401 Mountain City Hwy. I-80, exit 301, just n. Int corridors. **Pets:** Other species. $25 one-time fee/room. Supervision.

Thunderbird Motel M
(775) 738-7115. **$69-$89.** 345 Idaho St. I-80, exit 301 or 303, 1 mi s. Ext corridors. **Pets:** Other species. $15 one-time fee/room. Designated rooms, service with restrictions, crate.

ELY

4 Sevens Motel M
(775) 289-4747. **$30-$50.** 500 High St. Just n of 5th St; downtown. Ext corridors. **Pets:** Other species. Designated rooms, service with restrictions, supervision.

▲▲▲ ▼▼ Fireside Inn M
(775) 289-3765. **$40-$50.** McGill Hwy. 2 mi n on US 93. Ext corridors.
Pets: Other species. Service with restrictions, supervision.
[SAVE] [S🐾] [✕] [📶] [💻]

▲▲▲ ▼▼◆ Historic Hotel Nevada & Gambling Hall SH
(775) 289-6665. **$30-$50.** 501 Aultman St. Downtown. Int corridors.
Pets: Other species. Designated rooms, service with restrictions, supervision.
[SAVE] [S🐾] [✕] [📶] [💻] [🍴]

▲▲▲ ▼▼▼▼ Ramada Inn-Copper Queen Casino SH
(775) 289-4884. **$87-$199.** 805 Great Basin Blvd. 0.3 mi s of jct US 6,
50 and 93. Ext/int corridors. **Pets:** Service with restrictions, supervision.
[SAVE] [S🐾] [✕] [&M] [📶] [💻] [🍴] [🏊]

EUREKA

▲▲▲ ▼▼▼▼ Best Western Eureka Inn SH
(775) 237-5247. **$76.** 251 N Main St. On east side of Main St; center.
Int corridors. **Pets:** Accepted.
[SAVE] [S🐾] [✕] [&M] [📶] [📶] [📶] [💻]

FALLON

▲▲▲ ▼▼▼ Comfort Inn M
(775) 423-5554. **$59-$110.** 1830 W Williams Ave. US 50, 1 mi w of US
95. Int corridors. **Pets:** Medium. $10 daily fee/pet. Designated rooms,
service with restrictions, supervision.
[SAVE] [S🐾] [✕] [&M] [📶] [📶] [💻] [🏊]

▲▲▲ ▼▼ Motel 6 #4140 M
(775) 423-2277. **$49-$90.** 1705 S Taylor St. 0.5 mi s of US 50. Ext
corridors. **Pets:** Medium, other species. Service with restrictions, supervision.
[SAVE] [S🐾] [✕] [📶] [🏊]

▲▲▲ ▼▼▼ Super 8 Motel M
(775) 423-6031. **$45-$90.** 855 W Williams Ave. US 50, 0.5 mi w of US
95. Ext/int corridors. **Pets:** Other species. $5 daily fee/pet. Designated
rooms, service with restrictions.
[SAVE] [✕] [🍴]

FERNLEY

▲▲▲ ▼▼▼ Best Western Fernley Inn M
(775) 575-6776. **$75-$108.** 1405 E Newlands Dr. I-80, exit 48, just s.
Ext corridors. **Pets:** Small. $7 daily fee/room. Designated rooms, service
with restrictions.
[SAVE] [S🐾] [✕] [&M] [📶] [📶] [💻] [🏊]

GARDNERVILLE

▲▲▲ ▼▼▼ Best Western Topaz Lake Inn M
(775) 266-4661. **$59-$139.** 3410 Sandy Bowers Ave. US 395 at Topaz
Lake, 20 mi s. Ext/int corridors. **Pets:** Medium, dogs only. $12 daily
fee/pet. Designated rooms, service with restrictions, supervision.
[SAVE] [S🐾] [✕] [&M] [📶] [📶] [💻] [🏊]

▲▲▲ ▼▼▼ Topaz Lodge SH
(775) 266-3338. **$39-$105.** 1979 US 395 S. US 395 S at Topaz Lake,
22 mi s. Ext corridors. **Pets:** Accepted.
[SAVE] [✕] [🍴] [🏊]

▲▲▲ ▼▼▼ Westerner Motel M
(775) 782-3602. **$52-$73.** 1353 US 395. On US 395, south end of
town. Ext corridors. **Pets:** Other species. Designated rooms, service with
restrictions, supervision.
[SAVE] [S🐾] [✕] [📶] [💻] [🏊]

HAWTHORNE

▲▲▲ ▼▼▼ El Capitan Resort Casino M
(775) 945-3321. **$41-$45.** 540 F St. Just n of US 95. Ext corridors.
Pets: Accepted.
[SAVE] [✕] [📶] [💻] [🍴] [🏊]

JACKPOT

▲▲▲ ▼▼▼▼ Horseshu Hotel & Casino SH
(775) 755-7777. **$37-$160.** 1385 Hwy 93. On US 93. Int corridors.
Pets: Other species. Designated rooms, service with restrictions.
[SAVE] [✕] [💻] [🍴] [🏊] [✕]

LAKE TAHOE AREA

STATELINE

▲▲▲ ▼▼▼ ▼▼▼ Harrah's Lake Tahoe LH
(775) 588-6611. **$89-$699, 3 day notice.** US 50. In casino center. Int
corridors. **Pets:** Accepted.
[SAVE] [✕] [&M] [📶] [🍴] [🏊] [✕]

▲▲▲ ▼▼▼▼▼ Harveys Hotel, Casino & Resort LH
(775) 588-2411. **$79-$459, 3 day notice.** US 50. On US 50; in casino
center. Int corridors. **Pets:** Accepted.
[SAVE] [✕] [&M] [📶] [🍴] [🏊] [✕]

▲▲▲ ◆▼▼▼ Lake Village Resort CO
(775) 589-6065. **$139-$595.** 301 Hwy 50. 1 mi e of casino center. Ext
corridors. **Pets:** Accepted.
[SAVE] [S🐾] [✕] [📶] [💻] [🏊] [✕] [🐾]

ZEPHYR COVE

▼▼ ▼▼ Zephyr Cove Resort CA
(775) 589-4907. **$529, 14 day notice.** 760 Hwy 50. US 50. Ext corridors. **Pets:** Accepted.
[ASK] [S🐾] [✕] [📶] [💻] [🍴] [✕]

END AREA

LAS VEGAS METROPOLITAN AREA

BOULDER CITY

▼▼ Boulder Dam Hotel SH
(702) 293-3510. **$69-$119.** 1305 Arizona St. Center. Int corridors.
Pets: Accepted.
ASK ⊠ 🐾 🛏 💻 🍴

▼▼ Boulder Inn & Suites M
(702) 369-1000. **$69-$299.** 704 Nevada Way. On US 93. Ext corridors.
Pets: Dogs only. $10 daily fee/pet. Designated rooms, service with restrictions, supervision.
ASK 🔊 ⊠ 🐾 🛏 💻 ➰

▲▲▲ ▼▼▼ El Rancho Boulder Motel M
(702) 293-1085. **$65-$95, 3 day notice.** 725 Nevada Way. On US 93.
Ext corridors. **Pets:** Dogs only. $10 daily fee/pet. Service with restrictions, supervision.
SAVE ⊠ 🛏 💻 ➰

ECHO BAY

▲▲▲ ▼▼▼ Echo Bay Resort M
(702) 394-4000. **$85-$170, 3 day notice.** North Shore Rd. 4 mi e of SR 167; on Lake Mead. Int corridors. **Pets:** Accepted.
SAVE 🔊 ⊠ 🐾 🐾 🍴 ⊠

HENDERSON

▲▲▲ ▼▼▼▼ Green Valley Ranch LH 🐾
(702) 617-7777. **$129-$500.** 2300 S Paseo Verde Dr. I-215, exit Green Valley Pkwy, just s. **Pets:** Small, dogs only. $100 daily fee/pet. Designated rooms, service with restrictions.
SAVE 🔊 ⊠ 🐾 🐾 💻 🍴 ➰ ⊠

▲▲▲ ▼▼▼▼ Hawthorn Inn & Suites M
(702) 568-7800. **$79-$149, 3 day notice.** 910 S Boulder Hwy. S of Lake Mead Pkwy. Int corridors. **Pets:** Accepted.
SAVE 🔊 ⊠ 🐾 🛏 💻 ➰

▼▼▼ Residence Inn-Green Valley M
(702) 434-2700. **$169-$209.** 2190 Olympic Ave. I-215, exit Green Valley Pkwy N, 3 mi n at Sunset Rd. Int corridors. **Pets:** Accepted.
ASK ⊠ 🐾 🐾 🛏 💻 ➰ ⊠

▲▲▲ ▼▼▼▼▼ The Ritz-Carlton, Lake Las Vegas LH
(702) 567-4700. **$199-$379.** 1610 Lake Las Vegas Pkwy. I-215, e to end, n on Lake Las Vegas Pkwy, then 0.5 mi. Int corridors.
Pets: Accepted.
SAVE 🔊 ⊠ 🐾 🍴 🐾 🛏 🍴 ➰ ⊠

INDIAN SPRINGS

▲▲▲ ▼▼ Indian Springs Motor Hotel M
(702) 879-3700. **$49-$53.** 300 Tonopah Hwy. On US 95. Int corridors.
Pets: Medium, other species. $50 deposit/pet, $5 daily fee/pet. Designated rooms, service with restrictions, crate.
SAVE 🔊 ⊠ 🛏 🍴

LAS VEGAS

▲▲▲ ▼▼▼ Best Western Main Street Inn M
(702) 382-3455. **$54-$179.** 1000 N Main St. I-15, exit 43E northbound; exit 44E southbound. Ext corridors. **Pets:** Other species. $15 daily fee/pet. Service with restrictions.
SAVE 🔊 ⊠ 🛏 💻 🍴 ➰

▲▲▲ ▼▼▼ Best Western Nellis Motor Inn M
(702) 643-6111. **$55-$200.** 5330 E Craig Rd. I-15, exit 48, 2.8 mi e; 0.3 mi from Nellis AFB. Ext corridors. **Pets:** Small. $10 daily fee/pet. Service with restrictions, supervision.
SAVE 🔊 ⊠ 🛏 💻 ➰

▲▲▲ ▼▼▼ Best Western Parkview Inn M
(702) 385-1213. **$55-$199.** 921 Las Vegas Blvd N. I-15, exit US 93/95, 0.3 mi n at Washington. Ext corridors. **Pets:** Accepted.
SAVE 🔊 ⊠ 💻 ➰

▼▼▼▼ Candlewood Suites SH 🐾
(702) 836-3660. **$109-$249.** 4034 S Paradise Rd. I-15, exit E Flamingo Rd to Paradise Rd, just ne. Int corridors. **Pets:** Medium, other species. $75 one-time fee/pet. Designated rooms, service with restrictions, supervision.
ASK 🔊 ⊠ 🐾 🐾 🛏 💻 ➰

▲▲▲ ▼▼▼ Comfort Inn M
(702) 399-1500. **$90-$399.** 910 E Cheyenne Ave. I-15, exit Cheyenne Ave W, just w. Int corridors. **Pets:** Large, other species. $10 daily fee/pet. Service with restrictions, crate.
SAVE 🔊 ⊠ 🐾 🛏 💻 ➰

▼▼▼ Desert Rose Resort M
(702) 739-7000. **$79-$259.** 5051 Duke Ellington Way. I-15, exit E Tropicana Ave, 0.8 mi e to Duke Ellington Way, then just s. Ext corridors.
Pets: Accepted.
ASK 🔊 ⊠ 🐾 🍴 🐾 🛏 💻 ➰

▼▼▼ Extended StayAmerica-Valley View SH
(702) 221-7600. **$110-$120.** 4270 S Valley View Blvd. I-15, exit W Flamingo St, just sw. Ext corridors. **Pets:** Accepted.
ASK 🔊 ⊠ 🐾 🛏 💻 ➰

▼▼▼ Extended Stay Deluxe-Las Vegas-East Flamingo M
(702) 731-3111. **$100-$110.** 1550 E Flamingo Rd. I-15, exit E Flamingo Rd, 2 mi. Int corridors. **Pets:** Accepted.
ASK 🔊 ⊠ 🐾 🍴 🐾 🛏 💻 ➰

▲▲▲ ▼▼▼▼▼ Four Seasons Hotel Las Vegas LH
(702) 632-5000. **$255-$545.** 3960 Las Vegas Blvd S. I-15, exit E Tropicana Ave, just s on the Strip. Int corridors. **Pets:** Accepted.
SAVE ⊠ 🐾 🐾 💻 🍴 ➰ ⊠

▲▲▲ ▼▼ Highland Inn Motel M
(702) 896-4333. **$45-$200.** 8025 Dean Martin Dr. I-15, exit W Blue Diamond Rd, just nw. Ext corridors. **Pets:** Very small. $10 daily fee/pet. Service with restrictions, supervision.
SAVE 🔊 ⊠ 🛏

▼▼▼ Homestead Studio Suites Hotel-Las Vegas/Midtown M
(702) 369-1414. **$100-$110.** 3045 S Maryland Pkwy. I-15, exit Sahara Ave E, just s. Int corridors. **Pets:** Accepted.
ASK 🔊 ⊠ 🐾 🐾 🛏 💻

▲▲▲ ▼▼▼ Howard Johnson Las Vegas Strip M
(702) 388-0301. **$40-$300.** 1401 Las Vegas Blvd S. I-15, exit Las Vegas Blvd, just n. Ext/int corridors. **Pets:** Accepted.
SAVE 🔊 ⊠ 🛏 💻 🍴 ➰

▲▲▲ ▼▼▼▼ La Quinta Inn & Suites Las Vegas (Lakes/West) M
(702) 243-0356. **$99-$249.** 9570 W Sahara Ave. Just w of Fort Apache Rd. Int corridors. **Pets:** Designated rooms, service with restrictions, supervision.
SAVE 🔊 ⊠ 🐾 🐾 🛏 💻 ➰

▼▼▼▼ La Quinta Inn & Suites Las Vegas (Summerlin Tech Center) M
(702) 360-1200. **$112-$170.** 7101 Cascade Valley Ct. US 95, exit W Cheyenne Ave. Int corridors. **Pets:** Medium. Service with restrictions.
ASK ⊠ 🐾 🐾 🛏 💻 ➰

▼▼▼▼ La Quinta Inn Las Vegas (Convention Center) 🅼
(702) 796-9000. **$138-$169.** 3970 Paradise Rd. I-15, exit E Flamingo Rd, 0.8 mi s of convention center; 0.5 mi e of the Strip. Int corridors. **Pets:** Medium. Service with restrictions.

ⓐⓢⓚ ⌧ 🖥 🖥 🍽 🏊

ⒶⒶⒶ ▼▼▼▼ La Quinta Inn Las Vegas (Nellis) 🅼
(702) 632-0229. **$89-$169.** 4288 N Nellis Blvd. I-15, exit Craig Rd, e to N Las Vegas Blvd. Int corridors. **Pets:** Accepted.

ⓢⓐⓥⓔ ⓢ ⌧ 🅼 🕹 🖥 🖥 🏊

▼▼▼▼ La Quinta Inn Las Vegas (Tropicana) 🅼
(702) 798-7736. **$79-$159.** 4975 S Valley View Blvd. I-15, exit Tropicana Ave W, just w. Int corridors. **Pets:** Medium, other species. Designated rooms, service with restrictions.

ⓐⓢⓚ ⓢ ⌧ 🅼 🖥 🖥 🏊

▼ Motel 6 Boulder Highway #1337 🅼
(702) 457-8051. **$51-$85.** 4125 Boulder Hwy. Just s of Sahara Ave. Ext corridors. **Pets:** Medium, other species. Service with restrictions, supervision.

ⓢ ⌧ 🏊

▼ Mt. Charleston Hotel 🆂🅷
(702) 872-5500. **Call for rates.** 2 Kyle Canyon Rd. US 95, exit Mt Charleston, 17 mi w. Int corridors. **Pets:** Accepted.

⌧ 🍽 🔏

▼▼ Ramada Inn-Speedway Casino 🅼
(702) 399-3297. **$49-$99.** 3227 Civic Center Dr. I-15, exit Cheyenne Ave E, Just e. Int corridors. **Pets:** Other species. $25 daily fee/pet. Designated rooms, service with restrictions, supervision.

ⓐⓢⓚ ⓢ ⌧ 🅼 🖥 🖥 🍽 🏊

▼▼▼ Residence Inn by Marriott Las Vegas South 🆂🅷
(702) 795-7378. **$135-$185.** 5875 Dean Martin Rd. I-15, exit Russell Rd, just sw. Int corridors. **Pets:** Accepted.

ⓐⓢⓚ ⓢ ⌧ 🅼 🖥 🖥 🏊 🔏

▼▼▼ Residence Inn-Hughes Center 🆂🅷 🐾
(702) 650-0040. **$99-$499.** 370 Hughes Center Dr. I-15, exit Paradise Rd. Int corridors. **Pets:** Medium, other species. $100 one-time fee/room. Service with restrictions.

ⓐⓢⓚ ⓢ ⌧ 🅼 🖥 🖥 🏊

▼▼▼▼ Residence Inn Las Vegas Convention Center 🅼
(702) 796-9300. **$174-$409.** 3225 Paradise Rd. Opposite the convention center. Ext corridors. **Pets:** Medium. $100 one-time fee/room. Service with restrictions.

ⓐⓢⓚ ⓢ ⌧ 🅼 🖥 🖥 🏊 🔏

▼▼▼▼ St. Tropez All Suite Hotel 🆂🅷
(702) 369-5400. **$69-$199.** 455 E Harmon Ave. 2 mi s of convention center, at Paradise Rd. Ext/int corridors. **Pets:** Accepted.

ⓐⓢⓚ ⓢ ⌧ 🅼 🖥 🖥 🏊

▼ Super 8 Motel Las Vegas Strip 🅼 🐾
(702) 794-0888. **$72-$130.** 4250 Koval Ln. I-15, exit S Koval Ln. Int corridors. **Pets:** Other species. $15 daily fee/pet. Designated rooms, service with restrictions, supervision.

ⓐⓢⓚ ⓢ ⌧ 🏊

ⒶⒶⒶ ▼▼▼ Vagabond Inn , Las Vegas 🅼
(702) 733-0001. **$59-$69.** 2601 Westwood Dr. I-15, exit Sahara Ave E, just se. Int corridors. **Pets:** Medium. $30 daily fee/pet. Designated rooms, service with restrictions, supervision.

ⓢⓐⓥⓔ ⓢ ⌧ 🖥 🏊

ⒶⒶⒶ ▼▼▼▼ The Westin Casuarina Las Vegas Hotel & Spa 🅻🅷 🐾
(702) 836-5900. **$135-$499.** 160 E Flamingo Rd. I-15, exit Flamingo Rd E, 1.1 mi. Int corridors. **Pets:** $129 deposit/room, $35 one-time fee/room. Service with restrictions, supervision.

ⓢⓐⓥⓔ ⓢ ⌧ 🅼 🕹 🖥 🖥 🍽 🏊 🔏

LAUGHLIN

ⒶⒶⒶ ▼▼▼ Don Laughlin's Riverside Resort Hotel & Casino 🅻🅷
(702) 298-2535. **$42-$699.** 1650 S Casino Dr. 2 mi s of Davis Dam. Int corridors. **Pets:** Accepted.

ⓢⓐⓥⓔ ⌧ 🕹 🖥 🖥 🍽 🏊 🔏

MESQUITE

ⒶⒶⒶ ▼▼▼ Best Western Mesquite Inn 🅼
(702) 346-7444. **$79-$150.** 390 N Sandhill Blvd. I-15, exit 122. Ext corridors. **Pets:** Medium. $15 daily fee/pet. Designated rooms, service with restrictions, supervision.

ⓢⓐⓥⓔ ⓢ ⌧ 🕹 🖥 🖥 🏊

▼▼▼▼ Falcon Ridge Hotel 🆂🅷
(702) 346-2200. **$69-$179.** 1030 W Pioneer Blvd. I-15, exit 120, just w. Int corridors. **Pets:** Accepted.

ⓐⓢⓚ ⓢ ⌧ 🕹 🖥 🖥 🏊 🔏

▼▼ Virgin River Hotel Casino Bingo 🅼
(702) 346-7777. **$30-$90.** 100 Pioneer Blvd. I-15, exit 122, just w. Ext corridors. **Pets:** Medium, other species. $150 deposit/room. Designated rooms, no service, supervision.

⌧ 🅼 🕹 🍽 🏊

OVERTON

▼▼▼ Best Western North Shore Inn at Lake Mead 🅼
(702) 397-6000. **$67-$120.** 520 N Moapa Valley Blvd. I-15, exit 93, 10 mi ne on SR 169. Int corridors. **Pets:** Small, dogs only. $10 one-time fee/room. Designated rooms, supervision.

ⓐⓢⓚ ⓢ ⌧ 🖥 🖥 🏊

PAHRUMP

ⒶⒶⒶ ▼▼ Best Western Pahrump Station 🅼
(775) 727-5100. **$69-$110.** 1101 S Hwy 160. Downtown. Ext/int corridors. **Pets:** Accepted.

ⓢⓐⓥⓔ ⓢ ⌧ 🅼 🕹 🖥 🖥 🍽 🏊

ⒶⒶⒶ ▼▼▼ Saddle West Hotel & Casino 🅼
(775) 727-1111. **$48-$150.** 1220 S Hwy 160. Downtown. Ext corridors. **Pets:** Medium, dogs only. $10 daily fee/room. Designated rooms, service with restrictions, supervision.

ⓢⓐⓥⓔ ⓢ ⌧ 🅼 🕹 🖥 🖥 🍽 🏊

END METROPOLITAN AREA

LOVELOCK

▼▼▼ Sturgeon's Inn & Casino 🆂🅷
(775) 273-2971. **$54-$75.** 1420 Cornell Ave. I-80, exit 105 or 107, just n. Ext corridors. **Pets:** Other species. $50 deposit/room. Designated rooms, service with restrictions, supervision.

ⓐⓢⓚ ⓢ ⌧ 🕹 🖥 🖥 🍽 🏊

MINDEN

ⒶⒶⒶ ▼▼▼ Best Western Minden Inn 🅼
(775) 782-7766. **$65-$109.** 1795 Ironwood Dr. US 395, exit Ironwood Dr W, 0.5 mi n of jct US 395 and SR 88. Ext corridors. **Pets:** Dogs only. $18 daily fee/pet. Service with restrictions, supervision.

ⓢⓐⓥⓔ ⓢ ⌧ 🅼 🖥 🖥 🏊

▼▼ Holiday Lodge Ⓜ
(775) 782-2288. **$44-$56.** 1591 US 395 N. Center. Ext corridors. **Pets:** Small, dogs only. $30 deposit/pet. Designated rooms, service with restrictions, supervision.
ⒶⓈⓀ ⊠ 🛏 ≈

RENO

⬥⬥⬥ ▼▼▼ Atlantis Casino Resort-Reno 🅻🅷 🐾
(775) 825-4700. **$49-$299.** 3800 S Virginia St. 3 mi s on US 395. Ext/int corridors. **Pets:** $25 one-time fee/room. Designated rooms, service with restrictions.
SAVE ⓈⓄ ⊠ 🛏ᴹ 🐾 🦮 🖳 🍽 ≈ ⊠

⬥⬥⬥ ▼▼▼ Best Western Airport Plaza Hotel 🆂🅷 🐾
(775) 348-6370. **$90-$129.** 1981 Terminal Way. US 395, exit E Plumb Villanova. Int corridors. **Pets:** Medium. $50 deposit/room, $10 one-time fee/room. Designated rooms, service with restrictions, supervision.
SAVE ⓈⓄ ⊠ 🛏ᴹ 🦮 🛏 🖳 🍽 ≈ ⊠

⬥⬥⬥ ▼ Days Inn Ⓜ 🐾
(775) 786-4070. **$39-$199.** 701 E 7th St. I-80, exit Wells Ave, just s. Ext corridors. **Pets:** Other species. $10 daily fee/pet. Designated rooms, service with restrictions, crate.
SAVE ⓈⓄ ⊠ 🛏 ≈

▼▼ Extended StayAmerica-Reno-South Meadows 🆂🅷
(775) 852-5611. **$114-$124.** 9795 Gateway Dr. US 395, exit 60, just e. Int corridors. **Pets:** Accepted.
ⒶⓈⓀ ⓈⓄ ⊠ 🛏 🖳

⬥⬥⬥ ▼ GateKeeper Inn Ⓜ
(775) 786-3500. **$45-$225.** 221 W 5th St. Corner of West and 5th sts. Ext corridors. **Pets:** $10 one-time fee/room. Service with restrictions, supervision.
SAVE ⓈⓄ ⊠

⬥⬥⬥ ▼▼▼ Holiday Inn-Downtown 🆂🅷 🐾
(775) 786-5151. **$59-$89.** 1000 E 6th St. I-80, exit Wells Ave, 2 blks e. Int corridors. **Pets:** Other species. $20 daily fee/room. Service with restrictions, supervision.
SAVE ⓈⓄ ⊠ 🛏ᴹ 🐾 🦮 🛏 🖳 🍽 ≈

▼▼▼▼ La Quinta Inn Reno (Airport) Ⓜ
(775) 348-6100. **$88-$136.** 4001 Market St. US 395, exit airport northbound; exit Villanova Dr southbound. Ext corridors. **Pets:** Medium. Service with restrictions.
⊠ 🛏ᴹ 🐾 🛏 🖳 ≈

⬥⬥⬥ ▼▼▼ Reno Downtown Travelodge Ⓜ
(775) 329-3451. **$39-$69.** 655 W 4th St. I-80, exit Keystone, just e. Ext corridors. **Pets:** Accepted.
SAVE ⓈⓄ ⊠ 🛏 🖳 ≈

⬥⬥⬥ ▼▼▼▼ Residence Inn by Marriott 🆂🅷 🐾
(775) 853-8800. **$119-$269.** 9845 Gateway Dr. US 395, exit S Meadows Pkwy, then e. Int corridors. **Pets:** Large. $100 one-time fee/room. Supervision.
SAVE ⓈⓄ ⊠ 🛏ᴹ 🦮 🛏 🖳 ≈ ⊠

⬥⬥⬥ ▼▼▼▼ Super 8 Motel at Meadow Wood Courtyard 🆂🅷
(775) 829-4600. **$49-$129.** 5851 S Virginia St. Jct US 395 and S McCarran Blvd, 0.3 mi s. Ext corridors. **Pets:** Small. $50 deposit/room, $10 daily fee/pet. Designated rooms, service with restrictions, supervision.
SAVE ⓈⓄ ⊠ 🛏ᴹ 🐾 🛏 🖳 🍽 ≈

SPARKS

⬥⬥⬥ ▼▼▼ Quality Inn 🆂🅷
(775) 358-6900. **$75-$110.** 55 E Nugget Ave. I-80, exit E McCarran Blvd, just s. Int corridors. **Pets:** Medium, other species. $15 daily fee/pet. Designated rooms, service with restrictions, supervision.
SAVE ⓈⓄ ⊠ 🦮 🛏 🖳 🍽 ≈

▼▼ Sparks Super 8 🆂🅷
(775) 358-8884. **$54-$205.** 1900 E Greg St. I-80, exit 21, 3 mi sw. Int corridors. **Pets:** Other species. $10 daily fee/pet. Service with restrictions, supervision.
ⒶⓈⓀ ⓈⓄ ⊠ 🛏 🖳 ≈

TONOPAH

⬥⬥⬥ ▼▼▼ Best Western Hi-Desert Inn Ⓜ
(775) 482-3511. **$79-$105.** 320 Main St. On US 6 and 95. Int corridors. **Pets:** Dogs only. Designated rooms, service with restrictions, supervision.
SAVE ⓈⓄ ⊠ 🛏ᴹ 🐾 🦮 🛏 🖳 ≈

⬥⬥⬥ ▼▼▼ Jim Butler Inn and Suites Ⓜ
(775) 482-3577. **$55-$61.** 100 S Main St. On US 6 and 95; downtown. Ext corridors. **Pets:** Accepted.
SAVE ⓈⓄ ⊠ 🛏

⬥⬥⬥ ▼▼▼ Ramada Inn-Tonopah Station Ⓜ
(775) 482-9777. **$65-$75.** 1100 Main St. On US 6 and 95. Int corridors. **Pets:** Accepted.
SAVE ⓈⓄ ⊠ 🦮 🖳 🍽

UNIONVILLE

⬥⬥⬥ ▼▼▼ Old Pioneer Garden 🅱🅱
(775) 538-7585. **$85-$95 (no credit cards).** 2805 Unionville Rd. I-80, exit 149, 16 mi s, then 2.5 mi w. Int corridors. **Pets:** Accepted.
SAVE ⓈⓄ ⊠ Ⓦ 🐾

VIRGINIA CITY

▼▼ Gold Hill Hotel 🅱🅱
(775) 847-0111. **$45-$250.** 1540 Main St. 1 mi s on SR 342. Ext/int corridors. **Pets:** Accepted.
ⒶⓈⓀ 🛏 🖳 🍽

WELLS

⬥⬥⬥ ▼▼▼ Super 8 Motel Ⓜ 🐾
(775) 752-3384. **$40-$85.** 930 6th St. I-80, exit 351 eastbound, 1 mi n, then 0.8 mi e; exit 352A westbound, 0.3 mi n, then 0.5 mi w. Ext corridors. **Pets:** Other species. $5 daily fee/pet. Designated rooms, service with restrictions, supervision.
SAVE ⊠ 🛏 ≈

WEST WENDOVER

▼▼▼ Wendover Super 8 Ⓜ
(775) 664-2888. **$29-$129, 3 day notice.** 1325 Wendover Blvd. I-80, exit 410, 0.5 mi w. Int corridors. **Pets:** Accepted.
ⒶⓈⓀ ⓈⓄ ⊠ 🛏

WINNEMUCCA

⬥⬥⬥ ▼▼▼▼ Best Western Gold Country Inn 🆂🅷 🐾
(775) 623-6999. **$89-$119.** 921 W Winnemucca Blvd. I-80, exit 176 or 178, just s. Int corridors. **Pets:** Other species. $10 one-time fee/room. Designated rooms, service with restrictions, supervision.
SAVE ⓈⓄ ⊠ 🛏 🖳 ≈

⬥⬥⬥ ▼▼▼▼ Best Western Holiday Motel Ⓜ
(775) 623-3684. **$59-$89.** 670 W Winnemucca Blvd. I-80, exit 176 or 178, just s. Ext corridors. **Pets:** Other species. $10 deposit/room. Designated rooms, service with restrictions, supervision.
SAVE ⓈⓄ ⊠ 🛏 🖳 ≈

⬥⬥⬥ ▼▼▼▼ Days Inn Ⓜ
(775) 623-3661. **$69-$99.** 511 W Winnemucca Blvd. I-80, exit 176, just s. Ext corridors. **Pets:** Accepted.
SAVE ⊠ 🛏 🖳 ≈

▼▼▼ Holiday Inn Express M
(775) 625-3100. **$80-$149.** 1987 W Winnemucca Blvd. I-80, exit 178, just s. Int corridors. **Pets:** Medium. $50 deposit/pet, $20 daily fee/pet, $20 one-time fee/pet. Designated rooms, service with restrictions, supervision.

▲▲▲ ▼▼▼ Red Lion Hotel & Casino SH
(775) 623-2565. **$89-$119.** 741 W Winnemucca Blvd. I-80, exit 176 or 178, just s. Int corridors. **Pets:** Accepted.

▲▲▲ ▼ Scott Shady Court Motel M
(775) 623-3646. **$40-$55.** 400 1st St. I-80, exit 176 or 178, 0.3 mi n on Pavilion. Ext corridors. **Pets:** Accepted.

▼▼ Super 8 Motel M
(775) 625-1818. **$59.** 1157 W Winnemucca Blvd. I-80, exit 176, 0.5 mi e. Int corridors. **Pets:** Accepted.

▲▲▲ ▼▼▼ Town House Motel M
(775) 623-3620. **$53-$70.** 375 Monroe St. I-80, exit 176 or 178, just s. Ext corridors. **Pets:** Small, dogs only. Service with restrictions, supervision.

ANDOVER

Highland Lake Inn Bed & Breakfast BB
(603) 735-6426. **$160-$195.** 32 Maple St. I-93, exit 17, 15.5 mi nw on US 4, 3.5 mi e on SR 11, then just w. Int corridors. **Pets:** Accepted.

BARTLETT

The Bartlett Inn BB
(603) 374-2353. **$79-$255, 14 day notice.** White Mountain Hwy (US 302). On US 302, 7 mi w of jct SR 16. Ext/int corridors. **Pets:** Dogs only. $15 one-time fee/pet. Designated rooms, supervision.

The Villager Motel M
(603) 374-2742. **$49-$259, 10 day notice.** US 302. 1 mi e on US 302; 1.3 mi w of Attitash Mountain. Ext corridors. **Pets:** Dogs only. $10 daily fee/pet, $10 one-time fee/pet. Designated rooms, service with restrictions, supervision.

BRETTON WOODS

The Bretton Arms Country Inn CI
(603) 278-1000. **$149-$299, 15 day notice.** US 302. Center. Int corridors. **Pets:** Accepted.

The Townhomes at Bretton Woods CO
(603) 278-2000. **$199-$1099, 60 day notice.** Rt 302. Center. Ext corridors. **Pets:** Accepted.

CAMPTON

Days Inn Campton/Plymouth SH
(603) 536-3520. **$45-$150.** 1513 Rt 3. I-93, exit 27, just e, then just n. Int corridors. **Pets:** $20 daily fee/pet. Designated rooms, service with restrictions.

CHESTERFIELD

Chesterfield Inn CI
(603) 256-3211. **$150-$320, 5 day notice.** 20 Cross Rd. I-91, exit 3, 2 mi e on SR 9. Ext/int corridors. **Pets:** Medium, other species. Service with restrictions, supervision.

CLAREMONT

Best Budget Inn M
(603) 542-9567. **$49-$99.** 24 Sullivan St. Just n of jct SR 11/12/103/120; center. Ext corridors. **Pets:** Medium. $20 daily fee/room. Service with restrictions, supervision.

COLEBROOK

Northern Comfort Motel M
(603) 237-4440. **$66-$86, 3 day notice.** 1 Trooper Scott Phillips Hwy. 1.5 mi s on US 3. Ext corridors. **Pets:** Accepted.

CONCORD

Best Western Concord Inn & Suites SH
(603) 228-4300. **$69-$299.** 97 Hall St. I-93, exit 13, just n on Main St, then 0.5 mi w. Int corridors. **Pets:** Medium, other species. $20 daily fee/pet. Service with restrictions, supervision.

Concord Comfort Inn SH
(603) 226-4100. **$130-$210.** 71 Hall St. I-93, exit 13, just n on Main St, then 0.3 mi w. Int corridors. **Pets:** Dogs only. $15 daily fee/room. Designated rooms, service with restrictions, supervision.

CONWAY

White Deer Motel M
(603) 447-5366. **$49-$239, 14 day notice.** 379 White Mountain Hwy. 2.1 mi s of jct US 302; 0.5 mi n of village center on SR 16. Ext/int corridors. **Pets:** Accepted.

DOVER

Days Inn M
(603) 742-0400. **$99-$199.** 481 Central Ave. Spaulding Tpke, exit 7, 2 mi n on SR 108; downtown. Ext/int corridors. **Pets:** Other species. $50 deposit/room. Service with restrictions, supervision.

DURHAM

Hickory Pond Inn CI
(603) 659-2227. **$89-$146, 3 day notice.** 1 Stagecoach Rd. 2.8 mi s on SR 108. Int corridors. **Pets:** Accepted.

EATON CENTER

Inn at Crystal Lake & Restaurant CI
(603) 447-2120. **$89-$239, 14 day notice.** 2356 Eaton Rd. On SR 153; center. Ext/int corridors. **Pets:** Accepted.

FRANCONIA

Best Western White Mountain Resort SH
(603) 823-7422. **$89-$149.** 87 Wallace Hill Rd. I-93, exit 38, just e. Int corridors. **Pets:** $10 daily fee/pet. Designated rooms, service with restrictions, supervision.

▼▼◆ **Gale River Motel** Ⓜ ❀
(603) 823-5655. **$70-$140, 7 day notice.** 1 Main St. I-93, exit 38, 0.8 mi n on SR 18. Ext corridors. **Pets:** Other species. $10 daily fee/pet. Service with restrictions, supervision.
🆂🄰🅅🄴 Ⓢ❻ ☒ 🖪 💻 ⋙ ☒

GORHAM

▼ **Moose Brook Motel** Ⓜ
(603) 466-5400. **$39-$89, 7 day notice.** 65 Lancaster Rd. Jct SR 16, 0.5 mi w on US 2. Ext corridors. **Pets:** $5 one-time fee/pet. Designated rooms, service with restrictions, crate.
☒ 🖪 ⋙

▼▼ **Royalty Inn** 🆂🄷
(603) 466-3312. **$54-$114.** 130 Main St. On US 2 and SR 16; center. Ext/int corridors. **Pets:** Other species. $5 daily fee/pet. Designated rooms, service with restrictions.
☒ 🅶🄼 🖪 💻 🍴 ⋙ ☒

▲▲▲ ▼▼▼ **Top Notch Inn** Ⓜ ❀
(603) 466-5496. **$39-$142.** 265 Main St. On US 2 and SR 16; center. Ext/int corridors. **Pets:** Medium, dogs only. Designated rooms, service with restrictions, supervision.
🆂🄰🅅🄴 Ⓢ❻ ☒ 🚭 🖪 💻 ⋙

▼▼ **Town & Country Motor Inn** 🆂🄷
(603) 466-3315. **$60-$110.** 20 SR 2. 0.5 mi e of jct SR 16. Ext/int corridors. **Pets:** $6 daily fee/pet. Designated rooms, service with restrictions, crate.
☒ 🖪 🍴 ⋙ ☒

HAMPTON

▲▲▲ ▼▼◆ **Best Western The Inn at Hampton** 🆂🄷
(603) 926-6771. **$109-$189.** 815 Lafayette Rd. 0.5 mi n on US 1. Int corridors. **Pets:** Medium, other species. Designated rooms, supervision.
🆂🄰🅅🄴 Ⓢ❻ ☒ 🅶🄼 🚭 🖪 💻 🍴 ⋙ ☒

▲▲▲ ▼▼◆ **Lamie's Inn and The Old Salt** 🄲🄸 ❀
(603) 926-0330. **$105-$155, 3 day notice.** 490 Lafayette Rd. Jct SR 27 on US 1. Int corridors. **Pets:** Medium. $10 daily fee/pet. Designated rooms, service with restrictions, supervision.
🆂🄰🅅🄴 Ⓢ❻ ☒ 🚭 🖪 🍴

HAMPTON FALLS

▲▲▲ ▼▼◆ **Hampton Falls Inn** Ⓜ
(603) 926-9545. **$79-$179.** 11 Lafayette Rd. I-95, exit 1, 0.5 mi e on SR 107, then 1 mi n on US 1. Int corridors. **Pets:** Medium, dogs only. $50 deposit/pet. Service with restrictions, supervision.
🆂🄰🅅🄴 Ⓢ❻ ☒ 🖪 🍴 ⋙

HANCOCK

▼▼▼ **The Hancock Inn** 🄲🄸
(603) 525-3318. **$125-$295, 15 day notice.** 33 Main St. Jct of SR 123 and 137; center. Int corridors. **Pets:** Accepted.
☒ 🍴

HARTS LOCATION

▼▼▼ **Notchland Inn** 🄲🄸 ❀
(603) 374-6131. **$205-$350, 14 day notice.** US 302. On US 302, 6.4 mi w of town. Ext/int corridors. **Pets:** Other species. $10 daily fee/pet. Designated rooms, service with restrictions, crate.
☒ 🖪 💻 🍴 ☒

KEENE

◆▼ ▼ **Best Western Sovereign Hotel** 🆂🄷
(603) 357-3038. **$125-$250.** 401 Winchester St. SR 10, just s of jct SR 12 and 101. Int corridors. **Pets:** Accepted.
🄰🆂🄺 Ⓢ❻ ☒ 🚭 🖪 💻 🍴 ⋙

▼▼◆ **Holiday Inn Express** 🆂🄷 ❀
(603) 352-7616. **$119-$299.** 175 Key Rd. SR 101, just n, via Winchester St, 0.3 mi w. Int corridors. **Pets:** Medium, dogs only. $25 daily fee/pet. Designated rooms, service with restrictions, supervision.
🄰🆂🄺 Ⓢ❻ ☒ 🅶🄼 🚭 🖪 💻 🍴

▲▲▲ ▼▼◆ **Super 8 Keene** 🆂🄷
(603) 352-9780. **$72-$199.** 3 Ashbrook Rd. Jct SR 9 and 12, just w. Int corridors. **Pets:** $20 one-time fee/room. Service with restrictions, supervision.
🆂🄰🅅🄴 Ⓢ❻ ☒ 🅶🄼 🖪

LANCASTER

▲▲▲ ▼▼◆ **Coos Motor Inn** 🆂🄷
(603) 788-3079. **$39-$90.** 209 Main St. On US 2 and 3; center. Int corridors. **Pets:** Dogs only. $10 daily fee/pet. Service with restrictions, supervision.
🆂🄰🅅🄴 ☒ 🚭 🖪 💻

▲▲▲ ▼▼◆ **Lancaster Motor Inn** 🆂🄷
(603) 788-4921. **$39-$79.** 112 Main St. 0.5 mi w of jct US 2 and 3. Ext corridors. **Pets:** Accepted.
🆂🄰🅅🄴 Ⓢ❻ ☒ 🖪 🍴

LEBANON

▲▲▲ ▼▼◆ **Days Inn** Ⓜ
(603) 448-5070. **$89-$139.** 135 SR 120. I-89, exit 18, 0.8 mi n. Ext/int corridors. **Pets:** Accepted.
🆂🄰🅅🄴 Ⓢ❻ ☒ 🖪

▼▼▼ **Residence Inn by Marriott-Lebanon** 🆂🄷
(603) 643-4511. **$179-$399.** 32 Centerra Pkwy. I-89, exit 18, 2.5 mi n on SR 120. Int corridors. **Pets:** Other species. $75 one-time fee/room. Service with restrictions, supervision.
🄰🆂🄺 Ⓢ❻ ☒ 🅶🄼 🚭 🖪 💻 ⋙ ☒

LINCOLN

▲▲▲ ▼▼▼▼ **Comfort Inn & Suites** 🆂🄷 ❀
(603) 745-6700. **$99-$209, 3 day notice.** 21 Railroad St. I-93, exit 32, just e on SR 112; at Hobo Railroad. Int corridors. **Pets:** $15 daily fee/pet. Designated rooms, service with restrictions, supervision.
🆂🄰🅅🄴 Ⓢ❻ ☒ 🅶🄼 🚭 🖪 💻 ⋙ ☒

▲▲▲ ▼▼ ▼ **Econo Lodge Inn & Suites** Ⓜ
(603) 745-3661. **$59-$299, 3 day notice.** 381 US Rt 3. I-93, exit 33 (US 3), 0.3 mi ne. Ext/int corridors. **Pets:** Small. $10 daily fee/pet. Designated rooms, service with restrictions, crate.
🆂🄰🅅🄴 Ⓢ❻ ☒ 🚭 🖪 ⋙ ☒

▲▲▲ ▼ **Parker's Motel** Ⓜ ❀
(603) 745-8341. **$44-$109, 3 day notice.** 750 US Rt 3. I-93, exit 33 (US 3), 2 mi ne. Ext corridors. **Pets:** Medium. $5 daily fee/pet. Designated rooms, service with restrictions, supervision.
🆂🄰🅅🄴 Ⓢ❻ ☒ 🖪 💻 ⋙ ☒

LITTLETON

▼▼▼ **Beal House Inn and Restaurant** 🄲🄸
(603) 444-2661. **$125-$245, 7 day notice.** 2 W Main St. I-93, exit 42, 0.8 mi e on US 302 and SR 10. Int corridors. **Pets:** Accepted.
🄰🆂🄺 ☒ 🖪 💻 🍴

▲▲▲ ▼▼▼ **Eastgate Motor Inn** Ⓜ
(603) 444-3971. **$59-$119.** 335 Cottage St. I-93, exit 41, just e. Ext/int corridors. **Pets:** Other species. $25 one-time fee/room. Designated rooms, supervision.
🆂🄰🅅🄴 ☒ 💻 🍴 ⋙ ☒

▲▲▲ ▼▼ ▼ **Thayers Inn** 🆂🄷
(603) 444-6469. **$69-$119, 7 day notice.** 111 Main St. I-93, exit 42, 1.3 mi e on US 302 and SR 10; center. Int corridors. **Pets:** Accepted.
🆂🄰🅅🄴 Ⓢ❻ ☒ 🖪 💻 🍴

LOUDON

Red Roof Inn SH
(603) 225-8399. **$50-$90.** 2 Staniels Rd. I-393, exit 3, 1.5 mi n. Int corridors. **Pets:** Medium, other species. Service with restrictions, supervision.

SAVE ✕ 🔥M 🍴 📶 🔋 ⊒

MANCHESTER

Comfort Inn SH
(603) 668-2600. **$110-$300.** 298 Queen City Ave. I-293, exit 4, just w. Int corridors. **Pets:** Accepted.

ASK 🔥 ✕ 🔋 🖥 ⊒

Holiday Inn Express Hotel & Suites–Manchester Airport SH
(603) 669-6800. **$129-$139.** 1298 S Porter St. I-293, exit 1. Int corridors. **Pets:** $50 deposit/room. Service with restrictions, supervision.

SAVE 🔥 ✕ 🔥M 📶 🍴 🔋 🖥 ⊒

Homewood Suites by Hilton SH
(603) 668-2200. **$99-$249.** 1000 N Perimeter Rd. I-293, exit 2, follow signs to Manchester Airport. Int corridors. **Pets:** Accepted.

ASK 🔥 ✕ 🔥M 🍴 🔋 🖥 ⊒ ✕

Radisson Hotel Manchester LH
(603) 625-1000. **$109-$209.** 700 Elm St. Jct Granite St; downtown. Int corridors. **Pets:** Medium, other species. $25 one-time fee/room. Service with restrictions, supervision.

SAVE 🔥 ✕ 🔥M 📶 🍴 🔋 🖥 🍴 ⊒ ✕

TownePlace Suites by Marriott SH
(603) 641-2288. **$69-$189.** 686 Huse Rd. I-293, exit 1, 0.5 mi se on SR 28. Int corridors. **Pets:** Accepted.

ASK 🔥 ✕ 🔥M 🍴 🔋 🖥 ⊒

MERRIMACK

Residence Inn by Marriott SH ❀
(603) 424-8100. **$89-$279.** 246 Daniel Webster Hwy. Everett Tpke, exit 11, just e, then 0.6 mi s on US 3. Ext/int corridors. **Pets:** Other species. $75 one-time fee/room. Designated rooms.

ASK 🔥 ✕ 🔥M 📶 🍴 🔋 🖥 ⊒ ✕

NASHUA

Extended StayAmerica-Nashua SH
(603) 577-9900. **$70-$85.** 2000 Southwood Dr. US 3 (Everett Tpke), exit 8, just w. Int corridors. **Pets:** Accepted.

ASK 🔥 ✕ 🔥M 📶 🍴 🔋 🖥

Holiday Inn Nashua SH
(603) 888-1551. **$89-$139.** 9 Northeastern Blvd. US 3 (Everett Tpke), exit 4, just w, then 0.3 mi n. Int corridors. **Pets:** Accepted.

ASK 🔥 ✕ 🔥M 📶 🔋 🖥 🍴 ⊒

Red Roof Inn #7122 M
(603) 888-1893. **$64-$86.** 77 Spitbrook Rd. US 3 (Everett Tpke), exit 1, just e. Ext corridors. **Pets:** Medium, other species. Service with restrictions, supervision.

✕ 🔥M 📶 🍴 🔋

Sheraton Nashua Hotel LH ❀
(603) 888-9970. **$79-$169.** 11 Tara Blvd. US 3 (Everett Tpke), exit 1, just w. Int corridors. **Pets:** Large, dogs only. Designated rooms, supervision.

SAVE 🔥 ✕ 🔥M 📶 🍴 🔋 🖥 🍴 ⊒ ✕

NEWBURY

Best Western Sunapee Lake Lodge SH
(603) 763-2010. **$109-$349, 14 day notice.** 1403 SR 103. Jct SR 103B, just e. Int corridors. **Pets:** Accepted.

SAVE 🔥 ✕ 🔥M 📶 🍴 🔋 🖥 ⊒ ✕

NEW CASTLE

Wentworth By The Sea Marriott Hotel & Spa LH
(603) 422-7322. **$229-$459, 3 day notice.** 588 Wentworth Rd. On SR 1B, 2 mi e of SR 1A. Ext/int corridors. **Pets:** Small, dogs only. $50 deposit/room. Designated rooms, service with restrictions, supervision.

SAVE 🔥 ✕ 🍴 🔋 🖥 🍴 ⊒ ✕

NEW LONDON

New London Inn CI
(603) 526-2791. **$135-$225, 7 day notice.** 353 Main St. Center. Int corridors. **Pets:** Accepted.

SAVE ✕ 🍴

NORTH CONWAY

Mt Washington Valley Inn SH
(603) 356-5486. **$69-$159.** 1567 White Mountain Hwy. 2.5 mi s on US 302/SR 16; village center. Int corridors. **Pets:** Medium, dogs only. $10 daily fee/pet. Designated rooms, service with restrictions, supervision.

SAVE ✕ 🔋 🖥 ⊒

North Conway Mountain Inn M
(603) 356-2803. **$79-$169, 3 day notice.** 2114 White Mountain Hwy. 1 mi s on US 302/SR 16. Ext corridors. **Pets:** Accepted.

SAVE ✕

PITTSBURG

The Glen CA
(603) 538-6500. **$200-$260 (no credit cards), 7 day notice.** 118 Glen Rd. 9 mi n on US 3, from jct SR 145 to Varney Rd, then 0.3 mi s to Glen Rd, follow signs. Ext/int corridors. **Pets:** Other species. Designated rooms, service with restrictions, supervision.

✕ 🔋 🖥 🍴 ✕ 🔥 📶 ⊒

PORTSMOUTH

Hampton Inn-Portsmouth SH
(603) 431-6111. **$129-$219.** 99 Durgin Ln. I-95, exit 7, 1 mi w via Market St and Woodbury Ave to Durgin Ln, then 0.3 mi s. Int corridors. **Pets:** Medium. $50 one-time fee/room. Service with restrictions.

ASK 🔥 ✕ 🔥M 📶 🍴 🔋 🖥 ⊒ ✕

Hilton Garden Inn Portsmouth Downtown SH
(603) 431-1499. **$99-$329.** 100 High St. Downtown. Int corridors. **Pets:** Medium. $75 one-time fee/room. Designated rooms, service with restrictions, crate.

ASK ✕ 🔥M 📶 🍴 🔋 🖥 🍴 ⊒

Meadowbrook Inn M
(603) 436-2700. **$69-$139.** 549 US Hwy 1 Bypass. I-95, exit 5; jct US 1 Bypass and Portsmouth Traffic Circle. Ext/int corridors. **Pets:** Accepted.

ASK 🔥 ✕ 🔋 ⊒

Motel 6 Portsmouth #1424 M
(603) 334-6606. **$55-$85.** 3 Gosling Rd. I-95, exit 4 to Spaulding Tpke (US 4 and SR 16), exit 1, just e. Int corridors. **Pets:** Medium, other species. Service with restrictions, supervision.

🔥 ✕ 🔥M 🔋 ⊒

Residence Inn by Marriott SH
(603) 436-8880. **$129-$279.** 1 International Dr. SR 4/16, exit 1, just s. Int corridors. **Pets:** Medium. $75 one-time fee/room. Designated rooms, service with restrictions.

ASK 🔥 ✕ 🔥M 📶 🍴 🔋 🖥 ⊒ ✕

Sheraton Harborside Portsmouth Hotel & Conference Center LH ❀
(603) 431-2300. **$129-$309.** 250 Market St. Downtown. Int corridors. **Pets:** Large, dogs only. Service with restrictions, supervision.

🔥 ✕ 🔥M 📶 🍴 🔋 🖥 🍴 ⊒

ROCHESTER

Anchorage Inn M ❖
(603) 332-3350. **$69-$139.** 13 Wadleigh Rd. Jct Spaulding Tpke and SR 125, exit 12. Ext corridors. **Pets:** Medium. $15 deposit/pet. Designated rooms, service with restrictions, supervision.
SAVE 🛏 ✕ 🖥 ➦

The Governor's Inn CI
(603) 332-0107. **$88-$158.** 78 Wakefield St. On SR 125 and 108, just n of monument; center. Int corridors. **Pets:** Accepted.
ASK 🛏 ✕ 🖥 🖥 ❙❙

SALEM

Holiday Inn-Salem New Hampshire SH ❖
(603) 893-5511. **$99-$149.** 1 Keewaydin Dr. I-93, exit 2, just sw. Int corridors. **Pets:** $25 one-time fee/room. Service with restrictions, supervision.
SAVE 🛏 ✕ 🖥 🖥 🖥 ❙❙ ➦ ✕

Red Roof Inn #7151 M
(603) 898-6422. **$61-$105.** 15 Red Roof Ln. I-93, exit 2, just se. Ext corridors. **Pets:** Medium, other species. Service with restrictions, supervision.
✕ 🖥 🖥 🖥

SNOWVILLE

Snowvillage Inn CI ❖
(603) 447-2818. **$129-$269, 14 day notice.** 136 Stewart Rd. Jct SR 16, 5 mi s on SR 153, turn at Crystal Lake, then 1.5 mi s, follow signs. Ext/int corridors. **Pets:** Dogs only. $25 one-time fee/pet. Designated rooms, crate.
SAVE ✕ ❙❙ 🖥

SUGAR HILL

The Hilltop Inn BB
(603) 823-5695. **$100-$195, 8 day notice.** 9 Norton Ln. I-93, exit 38, 0.5 mi n on SR 18, then 2.8 mi w on SR 117. Int corridors. **Pets:** Accepted.
✕ 🖥 🖥 🖥

SUNAPEE

Dexter's Inn CI ❖
(603) 763-5571. **$110-$185, 14 day notice.** 258 Stagecoach Rd. Jct SR 103B and 11, 0.4 mi w on SR 11, 1.8 mi s (Winn Hill Rd). Ext/int corridors. **Pets:** Other species. $10 daily fee/pet. Designated rooms, service with restrictions.
ASK 🛏 ✕ 🖥 🖥 ❙❙ ➦ ✕

THORNTON

Shamrock Motel M
(603) 726-3534. **$50-$65, 7 day notice.** 2913 US 3. I-93, exit 29, 2.3 mi n. Ext corridors. **Pets:** Accepted.
ASK 🛏 ✕ 🖥 🖥 ➦ ❙❙ ✕

TROY

The Inn at East Hill Farm CI
(603) 242-6495. **$152-$256, 21 day notice.** 460 Monadnock St. Jct SR 12 and Monadock St, then 2 mi e. Ext/int corridors. **Pets:** $10 daily fee/pet. Designated rooms, service with restrictions.
✕ 🖥 ❙❙ ➦ ✕ ✕

WEST LEBANON

Airport Economy Inn M
(603) 298-8888. **$70-$120.** 45 Airport Rd. I-89, exit 20 (SR 12A), just s, then just e. Int corridors. **Pets:** Accepted.
SAVE 🛏 ✕ 🖥 🖥 ➦

Fireside Inn and Suites SH
(603) 298-5900. **$119-$200.** 25 Airport Rd. I-89, exit 20 (SR 12A), just s. Int corridors. **Pets:** Dogs only. $10 daily fee/pet. Designated rooms, service with restrictions, supervision.
ASK 🛏 ✕ 🖥 🖥 🖥 ❙❙ ➦ ✕

WOLFEBORO

The Lake Motel M ❖
(603) 569-1100. **$79-$139, 14 day notice.** 280 S Main St. 0.5 mi se on SR 28. Ext/int corridors. **Pets:** Other species. Supervision.
✕ 🖥 🖥 ✕

WOODSVILLE

All Seasons Motel M
(603) 747-2157. **$65-$95.** 36 Smith St. I-91, exit 17, 4.1 mi e on US 302, then just s. Ext corridors. **Pets:** Accepted.
SAVE 🛏 ✕ 🖥 ➦

Nootka Lodge M
(603) 747-2418. **$70-$150.** Jct 10 & 302. I-91, exit 17, 4.5 mi e on US 302. Ext corridors. **Pets:** Accepted.
SAVE 🛏 ✕ 🖥 ➦ ✕

NEW JERSEY

ALLAMUCHY

AAA WWWW The Inn at Panther Valley-A Clarion Collection Hotel SH
(908) 852-6000. **$114-$119.** CR 517. I-80, exit 19, 0.8 mi s. Ext/int corridors. **Pets:** Medium. $10 daily fee/pet. Designated rooms, service with restrictions, crate.
SAVE S▲ X ⌘ 🖥 🖨 ▯❮

ATLANTIC CITY METROPOLITAN AREA

ABSECON

WW WW Knights Inn-Atlantic City/ Absecon M
(609) 407-1919. **$39-$499.** 531 Absecon Blvd. Garden State Pkwy, exit 40, 6 mi e on US 30 (White Horse Pike). Ext corridors. **Pets:** Accepted.
ASK S▲ X 🖥

ATLANTIC CITY

AAA WWWW Sheraton Atlantic City Convention Center Hotel LH
(609) 344-3535. **$99-$459.** 2 Miss America Way. Garden State Expwy, exit 38 to Atlantic City Expwy to Artic Ave, just e to Michigan Ave, then just n. Int corridors. **Pets:** Accepted.
SAVE S▲ X ⌘ 🔧 🖥 🖨 ▯❮ ▰

SOMERS POINT

WWWW Residence Inn by Marriott SH
(609) 927-6400. **$269-$329.** 900 Mays Landing Rd. Garden State Pkwy, exit 30 southbound; exit 29 northbound, 1 mi e. Ext corridors. **Pets:** Other species. $100 one-time fee/room. Service with restrictions.
ASK S▲ X ⌘ 🔧 🖥 🖨 ▰ ❮

WEST ATLANTIC CITY

AAA WWW Quality Hotel Bayside Resort SH
(609) 641-3546. **$49-$299.** 8029 Black Horse Pike. Garden State Pkwy, exit 38 (Atlantic City Expwy), 2 mi e to exit 5, 0.5 mi s on US 9 to US 40/322, then 1.8 mi e. Int corridors. **Pets:** Accepted.
SAVE S▲ X 🖥 🖨 ▯❮ ▰ ❮

AAA WWW Ramada Limited-West Atlantic City SH
(609) 646-5220. **$49-$299.** 8037 Black Horse Pike. Garden State Pkwy, exit 38 (Atlantic City Expwy), 2 mi e to exit 5, 0.5 mi s on US 9 to US 40/322, then 1.8 mi e. Ext/int corridors. **Pets:** Medium. $100 deposit/room, $15 daily fee/pet. Service with restrictions, supervision.
SAVE S▲ X ⌘ 🖥 🖨 ▰

END METROPOLITAN AREA

BASKING RIDGE

WWWW The Inn at Somerset Hills SH
(908) 580-1300. **$116-$169.** 80 Allen Rd. I-78, exit 33, 0.3 mi n on CR 525, then 0.3 mi w. Int corridors. **Pets:** Medium. $25 daily fee/room. Designated rooms, service with restrictions, crate.
ASK S▲ X 🔧 🖥 🖨 ▯❮

BEACH HAVEN

AAA WWW Engleside Inn SH 🐾
(609) 492-1251. **$95-$439, 30 day notice.** 30 Engleside Ave. 6.9 mi s of SR 72 Cswy to Engleside Ave, then just e. Ext corridors. **Pets:** Other species. $10 daily fee/pet. Service with restrictions, supervision.
SAVE X 🔧 🖥 🖨 ▯❮ ▰

BRIDGEWATER

WWWW Summerfield Suites SH
(908) 725-0800. **$99-$419.** 530 Rt 22 E. I-287, exit 14B northbound; exit 17 southbound to US 22 W, then 0.8 mi. Ext corridors. **Pets:** Accepted.
ASK X ⌘M 🔧 🖥 🖨 ▰ ❮

BUDD LAKE

WW WW Extended StayAmerica Mt. Olive-Budd Lake SH
(973) 347-5522. **$89-$99.** 71 International Dr S. I-80, exit 25, just n, follow signs for International Trade Center; just e of jct US 46. Int corridors. **Pets:** Accepted.
ASK S▲ X 🔧 🖥 🖨

CAPE MAY

⬥⬥⬥ Marquis de Lafayette Hotel 🆂🅗
(609) 884-3500. **$109-$489.** 501 Beach Ave. Between Decatur and Ocean sts. Ext/int corridors. **Pets:** Other species. $100 deposit/room, $20 daily fee/pet. Designated rooms, service with restrictions, supervision.
🆂🅰🆅🅴 ⊠ 🛏 🖵 🍽 〰

⬥⬥⬥ Palace Hotel of Cape May 🆂🅗
(609) 898-8100. **$129-$289, 14 day notice.** 1101 Beach Ave. Jct Beach and Philadelphia aves. Int corridors. **Pets:** Other species. $25 daily fee/pet. Designated rooms, service with restrictions.
🆂🅰🆅🅴 🆂🅰 ⊠ 🛏 🖵

CAPE MAY COURT HOUSE

⬥⬥⬥ The Doctors Inn 🅱🅱
(609) 463-9330. **$135-$195, 21 day notice.** 2 N Main St. At Main (US 9) and Mechanic sts; just s of Garden State Pkwy. Int corridors. **Pets:** Small. $25 daily fee/pet. Crate.
🆂🅰🆅🅴 ⊠ 🛏 🍽

CLINTON

⬥⬥⬥ Hampton Inn 🆂🅗 🐾
(908) 713-4800. **$124-$134.** 16 Frontage Dr. I-78, exit 15, 0.3 mi s on CR 513, then left at next light. Int corridors. **Pets:** Small. $49 daily fee/pet. Service with restrictions, supervision.
🅰🆂🅺 🆂🅰 ⊠ 🕭 🕗 🕗 🛏 🖵 〰

⬥⬥⬥ Holiday Inn Select-Clinton 🆂🅗 🐾
(908) 735-5111. **$139-$149.** 111 Rt 173. I-78, exit 15, just nw. Int corridors. **Pets:** Small. $49 daily fee/pet. Service with restrictions, supervision.
🅰🆂🅺 🆂🅰 ⊠ 🕗 🛏 🖵 🍽 〰

CRANBURY

⬥⬥⬥ Residence Inn by Marriott/Cranbury-South Brunswick 🆂🅗
(609) 395-9447. **$99-$279.** 2662 Rt 130. New Jersey Tpke, exit 8A to SR 32 W toward town, 2 mi w on S River Rd. Int corridors. **Pets:** Large. $100 one-time fee/room. Service with restrictions.
🅰🆂🅺 🆂🅰 ⊠ 🕭 🕗 🕗 🛏 🖵 〰 ⊠

⬥⬥⬥ Staybridge Suites/Cranbury 🆂🅗
(609) 409-7181. **$139-$179.** 1272 S River Rd. New Jersey Tpke, exit 8A to SR 32 toward Cranbury, 2 mi w. Int corridors. **Pets:** Accepted.
🆂🅰🆅🅴 🆂🅰 ⊠ 🛏 🖵 〰

DENVILLE

⬥⬥⬥ Hampton Inn-The Inn At Denville 🆂🅗
(973) 664-1050. **$149.** 350 Morris Ave. I-80, exit 37 westbound, just s on Green Pond Rd, then just e; exit eastbound, just n on Hibernia Ave, then just e. Int corridors. **Pets:** Accepted.
🅰🆂🅺 🆂🅰 ⊠ 🕭 🕗 🕗 🛏 🖵 〰 ⊠

EAST BRUNSWICK

⬥ Motel 6, East Brunswick #1083 🆂🅗
(732) 390-4545. **$61-$75.** 244 SR 18 N. New Jersey Tpke, exit 9 (SR 18) to SR 18 S, 1 mi, exit Edgeboro Rd, w at U-turn, then just e. Ext/int corridors. **Pets:** Medium, other species. Service with restrictions, supervision.
🆂🅰 ⊠ 🕭 🕗 🕗

⬥ Studio 6 East Brunswick #6020 🆂🅗
(732) 238-3330. **$69-$79.** 246 Rt 18 @ Edgeboro Rd. New Jersey Tpke, exit 9 (SR 18) to SR 18 S, 1 mi, exit Edgeboro Rd, w at U-turn, then just e. Int corridors. **Pets:** Accepted.
🆂🅰 ⊠ 🕭 🕗 🕗 🛏 🖵

EAST HANOVER

⬥⬥⬥ Ramada Inn & Conference Center 🆂🅗
(973) 386-5622. **$89-$149.** 130 Rt 10 W. I-287, exit 39, 3 mi e. Int corridors. **Pets:** Accepted.
🅰🆂🅺 🆂🅰 ⊠ 🕭 🕗 🕗 🛏 🖵 🍽

EAST RUTHERFORD

⬥⬥ Homestead Studio Suites Hotel-Meadowlands/East Rutherford 🆂🅗
(201) 939-8866. **$104-$120.** 300 SR 3 E. New Jersey Tpke, exit 16W (from western spur), sports complex right after toll. Int corridors. **Pets:** Accepted.
🅰🆂🅺 🆂🅰 ⊠ 🕭 🕗 🕗 🛏 🖵

⬥⬥⬥ Sheraton Meadowlands Hotel & Conference Center 🅛🅗 🐾
(201) 896-0500. **$119-$409, 7 day notice.** 2 Meadowlands Plaza. New Jersey Tpke, exit 16W (from western spur), sports complex right after toll to Sheraton Plaza Dr. Int corridors. **Pets:** Medium, dogs only. $50 deposit/room. Service with restrictions, crate.
🆂🅰🆅🅴 ⊠ 🕭 🕗 🛏 🖵 🍽 〰 ⊠

EAST WINDSOR

⬥⬥⬥ Hampton Inn East Windsor 🆂🅗
(609) 426-1600. **$119-$159.** 384 Monmouth St. New Jersey Tpke, exit 8, just e, just n via Woodside Ave, then just w. Int corridors. **Pets:** Accepted.
🆂🅰🆅🅴 🆂🅰 ⊠ 🕭 🕗 🕗 🛏 🖵 〰

EATONTOWN

⬥⬥⬥ Staybridge Suites Hotel Eatontown-Tinton Falls 🆂🅗 🐾
(732) 380-9300. **$159-$249.** 4 Industrial Way E. Garden State Pkwy, exit 105, 0.7 mi e on SR 36, then 0.7 mi s on SR 35. Int corridors. **Pets:** Medium. $45 one-time fee/pet. Service with restrictions, supervision.
🅰🆂🅺 🆂🅰 ⊠ 🕭 🕗 🕗 🛏 🖵 〰

EDISON

⬥⬥⬥ Courtyard by Marriott Edison/Woodbridge 🆂🅗 🐾
(732) 738-1991. **$159-$164.** 3105 Woodbridge Ave. New Jersey Tpke, exit 10, 0.5 mi se on CR 514, then just e. Int corridors. **Pets:** Other species. $75 one-time fee/pet. Designated rooms, service with restrictions, crate.
🅰🆂🅺 ⊠ 🕭 🕗 🕗 🛏 🖵 〰

⬥ Red Roof Inn #7194 🅜
(732) 248-9300. **$78-$94.** 860 New Durham Rd. I-287, exit 2A northbound, 0.3 mi w via Bridge St, then left; exit 3 southbound, just w. Ext corridors. **Pets:** Medium, other species. Service with restrictions, supervision.
⊠ 🕭 🕗 🕗 🛏

⬥⬥⬥ Sheraton Edison 🅛🅗 🐾
(732) 225-8300. **$269.** 125 Raritan Center Pkwy. New Jersey Tpke, exit 10, 0.5 mi se on CR 514, keep right after tolls. Int corridors. **Pets:** Medium, other species. $50 deposit/room. Service with restrictions, supervision.
🅰🆂🅺 🆂🅰 ⊠ 🕭 🕗 🕗 🛏 🖵 🍽 〰 ⊠

ELIZABETH

⬥⬥ Extended StayAmerica 🆂🅗
(908) 355-4300. **Call for rates.** 45 Glimcher Realty Way. New Jersey Tpke, exit 13A, after toll follow signs to Jersey Garden Blvd; 1 mi, left on Kapkowski Rd, then just e. Int corridors. **Pets:** Accepted.
⊠ 🕭 🕗 🕗 🛏 🖵

⬥⬥⬥ Hilton Newark Airport 🅛🅗
(908) 351-3900. **$89-$269.** 1170 Spring St. New Jersey Tpke, exit 13A, on US 1 and 9 N, U-turn on McClellan St. Int corridors. **Pets:** Accepted.
🆂🅰🆅🅴 🆂🅰 ⊠ 🕭 🕗 🕗 🛏 🖵 🍽 〰

▼▼▼▼ Residence Inn by Marriott 🆂🅷 ❀
(908) 352-4300. **$199-$250.** 83 Glimcher Realty Way. New Jersey Tpke, exit 13A, after toll follow signs to Jersey Garden Blvd, 1 mi, left on Kapkowski Rd, then just e. Int corridors. **Pets:** Large, other species. $100 one-time fee/room. Designated rooms, service with restrictions.
🅰🆂🅺 ⊠ ♿ 🖉 🖥 🖵 🖵 🏊

FAIRFIELD

🅰🅰🅰 ▼▼▼▼ Fairfield Wellesley Inns 🆂🅷
(973) 575-1742. **$89-$149.** 38 Two Bridges Rd. I-80, exit 52 westbound; exit 47B (Caldwells) eastbound, 7 mi e on US 46, exit Passaic Ave. Int corridors. **Pets:** Accepted.
🆂🅰🆅🅴 🆂 ⊠ ♿ 🖉 🖫 🖥 🖵 🖵 🏊

FLEMINGTON

🅰🅰🅰 ▼▼▼ Ramada 🅼
(908) 782-7472. **$92-$120.** 250 Hwy 202 & SR 31. 0.5 mi s of the circle. Ext corridors. **Pets:** Small. $10 daily fee/pet. Designated rooms, service with restrictions, supervision.
🆂🅰🆅🅴 🆂 ⊠ 🖉 🖥 🖵 🖵 🖵 🏊

HILLSBOROUGH

▼▼ Days Inn Hillsborough Executive Inn 🆂🅷
(908) 685-9000. **$77-$199.** 118 Rt 206 S. 2.6 mi s of jct SR 28, US 202 and 206, at circle. Int corridors. **Pets:** Accepted.
🅰🆂🅺 🆂 ⊠ 🖉 🖥 🖵 🖵 🏊

ISELIN

▼▼▼▼ Sheraton at Woodbridge Place 🅻🅷
(732) 634-3600. **$109-$339.** 515 Rt 1 S. Garden State Pkwy, exit 131A northbound, 0.7 mi e, s on Middlesex Essex Tpke, 0.4 mi to Gill Ln, then 1.5 mi w; exit 130 southbound, 0.7 mi on US 1 N to Gill Ln, then U-turn; diagonal to Woodbridge Center. Int corridors. **Pets:** Accepted.
🅰🆂🅺 ⊠ 🖉 🖥 🖵 🖵 🖵 🏊

LAWRENCEVILLE

🅰🅰🅰 ▼▼▼ Howard Johnson Inn 🅼
(609) 896-1100. **$95-$129, 3 day notice.** 2995 Rt 1 S. On US 1 southbound, 0.5 mi s of I-295. Ext/int corridors. **Pets:** Medium. $10 daily fee/pet. Service with restrictions, supervision.
🆂🅰🆅🅴 🆂 ⊠ 🖉 🖥 🖵 🖵

▼ Red Roof Inn-Princeton #7111 🅼
(609) 896-3388. **$69-$94.** 3203 Brunswick Pike (US 1). I-295, exit 67A, just n. Ext corridors. **Pets:** Medium, other species. Service with restrictions, supervision.
⊠ 🖉 🖾 🖥

LEDGEWOOD

🅰🅰🅰 ▼▼▼ Days Inn 🆂🅷
(973) 347-5100. **$89-$99.** 1691 US 46 W. I-80, exit 27, 2 mi e via US 206 N and 183 N. Int corridors. **Pets:** Accepted.
🆂🅰🆅🅴 🆂 ⊠ 🖉 🖾 🖥 🖵 🏊

LONG BRANCH

▼ Ocean Place Resort & Spa 🅻🅷
(732) 571-4000. **$169-$599, 7 day notice.** 1 Ocean Blvd. 2.5 mi e from jct SR 71, 0.5 mi s. Int corridors. **Pets:** Medium, other species. $150 one-time fee/room. Designated rooms, service with restrictions, supervision.
🅰🆂🅺 🆂 ⊠ 🖥 🖵 🖵 🏊 🖾

MAHWAH

▼▼▼▼ Homewood Suites by Hilton 🆂🅷
(201) 760-9994. **$179-$239.** 375 Corporate Dr. I-287, exit 66, 1.7 mi on SR 17 S to MacArthur Blvd, then 0.4 mi w. Int corridors. **Pets:** Other species. $150 one-time fee/room.
🅰🆂🅺 🆂 ⊠ 🖉 🖥 🖵 🏊

🅰🅰🅰 ▼▼▼▼ Sheraton Mahwah Hotel 🅻🅷 ❀
(201) 529-1660. **$130-$198.** 1 International Blvd (Rt 17). I-287, exit 66, at SR 17 N. Int corridors. **Pets:** Dogs only. Service with restrictions.
🆂🅰🆅🅴 🆂 ⊠ 🖉 🖥 🖵 🖵 🖾

MIDDLETOWN

🅰🅰🅰 ▼▼▼ Comfort Inn Middletown 🅼 ❀
(732) 671-3400. **$105-$189.** 750 Hwy 35 S. Garden State Pkwy, exit 114, 2 mi on Red Hill Rd, 1 mi s on King's Hwy to SR 35, then 0.3 mi s. Int corridors. **Pets:** Other species. $25 daily fee/room. Service with restrictions, supervision.
🆂🅰🆅🅴 🆂 ⊠ 🖉 🖥 🖵 🖵

MONMOUTH JUNCTION

▼ Red Roof Inn/North Princeton #7198 🅼
(732) 821-8800. **$63-$85.** 208 New Rd. On US 1 S. Ext corridors. **Pets:** Medium, other species. Service with restrictions, supervision.
⊠ 🖉 🖥

▼▼▼ Residence Inn by Marriott 🆂🅷
(732) 329-9600. **$119-$179.** 4225 Rt 1 S. 0.5 mi s of Raymond Rd. Int corridors. **Pets:** Accepted.
🅰🆂🅺 🆂 ⊠ ♿ 🖉 🖾 🖥 🖵 🖵 🏊 🖾

MORRISTOWN

🅰🅰🅰 ▼▼▼ Best Western Morristown Inn 🆂🅷
(973) 540-1700. **$160-$170.** 270 South St. I-287, exit 35, just w on SR 124 (Madison Ave), then just s. Int corridors. **Pets:** Medium, dogs only. $10 daily fee/pet, $75 one-time fee/room. Designated rooms, service with restrictions, crate.
🆂🅰🆅🅴 🆂 ⊠ 🖉 🖥 🖵 🖵 🖾

🅰🅰🅰 ▼▼▼▼ Summerfield Suites Morristown 🆂🅷
(973) 971-0008. **$89-$270.** 194 Park Ave. SR 24, exit 2A (Morristown), stay in far left lane. Int corridors. **Pets:** Medium. $200 one-time fee/room. Designated rooms, service with restrictions, crate.
🆂🅰🆅🅴 ⊠ ♿ 🖉 🖾 🖥 🖵 🖵 🏊 🖾

🅰🅰🅰 ▼▼▼▼ The Westin Governor Morris 🅻🅷 ❀
(973) 539-7300. **$149-$409.** 2 Whippany Rd. I-287, exit 36 southbound, left lane to light, left to stop, then left 1 mi; exit 36A northbound thru Morris Ave, 0.8 mi, follow signs. Int corridors. **Pets:** Medium, other species. $50 one-time fee/room. Service with restrictions, supervision.
🆂🅰🆅🅴 ⊠ 🖉 🖾 🖥 🖵 🖵 🏊

MOUNT OLIVE

▼▼▼ Residence Inn Mt Olive at the International Trade Center 🆂🅷
(973) 691-1720. **$179-$189.** 271 Continental Dr. I-80, exit 25, just n, follow signs for International Trade Center. Int corridors. **Pets:** Accepted.
🅰🆂🅺 🆂 ⊠ 🖾 🖥 🖵 🏊 🖾

NEWARK

▼▼▼▼ Sheraton Newark Airport Hotel 🅻🅷
(973) 690-5500. **$109-$269, 4 day notice.** 128 Frontage Rd. New Jersey Tpke, exit 14 via Frontage Rd, 2nd right after toll booth. Int corridors. **Pets:** Accepted.
🅰🆂🅺 🆂 ⊠ ♿ 🖉 🖾 🖥 🖵 🖵 🏊 🖾

NEW PROVIDENCE

🅰🅰🅰 ▼▼▼▼ Best Western Murray Hill Inn 🆂🅷
(908) 665-9200. **$180-$235.** 535 Central Ave. I-78, exit 43 westbound to Diamond Hill Rd, 0.6 mi e on Mountain Ave, 0.8 mi to South Ave, then 0.8 mi n. Int corridors. **Pets:** Accepted.
🆂🅰🆅🅴 🆂 ⊠ 🖉 🖥 🖵 🖵 🖾

NORTH BERGEN

▼▼ Days Inn 🆂🅷
(201) 348-3600. **$15-$180.** 2750 Tonnelle Ave (US 1 & 9). Jct SR 3, 0.4 mi s. Int corridors. **Pets:** $100 deposit/room. Designated rooms, service with restrictions, supervision.

🄰$🄺 ⊠ 🕙 🖬 🖃 🍴

PARAMUS

▼▼ La Quinta Inn 🆂🅷
(201) 265-4200. **$109-$125.** 393 Rt 17 S. Garden State Pkwy, exit 163 northbound to SR 17 N, 0.6 mi to Midland Ave, then U-turn to SR 17 S; exit 165 southbound to Richwood Ave, 1 mi. Int corridors. **Pets:** Small. Service with restrictions, supervision.

🄰$🄺 🆂🄳 ⊠ 🖬 🖃

PARSIPPANY

▼▼▼ Embassy Suites 🅻🅷 ❀
(973) 334-1440. **$124-$259.** 909 Parsippany Blvd. I-80, exit 42 to US 202 N; just ne of jct US 202 and 46 W. Int corridors. **Pets:** Other species. $20 daily fee/room. Designated rooms, service with restrictions, crate.

🄰$🄺 ⊠ 🕙 🖬 🖃 🍴 🏊 ⊠

▼▼ Red Roof Inn #7072 🅼
(973) 334-3737. **$75-$82.** 855 US 46 E. I-80, exit 47 westbound; exit 45 eastbound, 0.5 mi e. Ext corridors. **Pets:** Medium, other species. Service with restrictions, supervision.

⊠ 🕙 🕙 🖬

🄰🄰🄰 ▼◆▼▼ Sheraton Parsippany Hotel 🅻🅷 ❀
(973) 515-2000. **$309-$379.** 199 Smith Rd. I-287, exit 41A northbound; exit 42 to US 46 E, 0.4 mi s. Int corridors. **Pets:** Large, dogs only. Designated rooms, service with restrictions, supervision.

🆂🄰🅅🄴 🆂🄳 ⊠ 🕙 🕙 🖬 🖃 🍴 🏊 ⊠

▼▼◆▼ Sierra Suites Hotel-Parsippany 🆂🅷
(973) 428-8875. **$99-$239.** 299 Smith Rd. I-287, exit 41A northbound; exit 42 southbound to US 46 E, 0.5 mi s. Int corridors. **Pets:** Accepted.

🄰$🄺 🆂🄳 ⊠ 🕙 🖬 🖃 🏊 ⊠

NEARBY PENNSYLVANIA
PHILADELPHIA METROPOLITAN AREA

BORDENTOWN

🄰🄰🄰 ▼ Imperial Inn 🅼
(609) 298-3355. **$50-$100.** 3312 US 206 S. New Jersey Tpke, exit 7, 0.8 mi s. Ext corridors. **Pets:** Medium, dogs only. $20 deposit/pet, $5 daily fee/pet. Service with restrictions, crate.

🆂🄰🅅🄴 🆂🄳 ⊠ 🖬

CARNEYS POINT

🄰🄰🄰 ▼◆▼▼ Holiday Inn Express Hotel & Suites 🆂🅷
(856) 351-9222. **$99-$153.** 506 Pennsville-Auburn Rd. I-295, exit 2B, just e. Int corridors. **Pets:** Large, other species. Supervision.

🆂🄰🅅🄴 🆂🄳 ⊠ 🕙 🖬 🖃

CHERRY HILL

▼◆▼▼ Clarion Hotel & Conference Center 🅻🅷
(856) 428-2300. **$99-$159.** 1450 SR 70 E. I-295, exit 34B, just w. Int corridors. **Pets:** Accepted.

🄰$🄺 🆂🄳 ⊠ 🕙🄼 🕙 🕙 🖬 🖃 🍴 🏊 ⊠

▼▼ Extended StayAmerica-Philadelphia-Cherry Hill 🆂🅷
(856) 616-1200. **$84-$99.** 1653 SR 70 (Marlton Pike). I-295, exit 34A, just e. Int corridors. **Pets:** Accepted.

🄰$🄺 🆂🄳 ⊠ 🕙 🖬 🖃

🄰🄰🄰 ▼▼ Holiday Inn Philadelphia-Cherry Hill 🆂🅷
(856) 663-5300. **$99-$159.** 2175 Marlton Pike. I-295, exit 34B, 2.5 mi w. Int corridors. **Pets:** Other species. $50 deposit/room. Service with restrictions, supervision.

🆂🄰🅅🄴 🆂🄳 ⊠ 🕙 🕙 🖬 🖃 🍴 🏊

▼▼◆▼ Residence Inn by Marriott 🆂🅷
(856) 429-6111. **$129-$229.** 1821 Old Cuthbert Rd. I-295, exit 34A, just e to Marlkress Rd jughandle, back to Old Cuthbert Rd, then just n. Ext corridors. **Pets:** Accepted.

🄰$🄺 🆂🄳 ⊠ 🕙 🖬 🖃 🏊 ⊠

DEPTFORD

▼▼◆▼ Residence Inn by Marriott 🆂🅷
(856) 686-9188. **$165-$185.** 1154 Hurffville Rd. SR 42, exit Deptford, Woodbury, Runnemede to CR 544, just e to CR 415. Int corridors. **Pets:** Accepted.

🄰$🄺 🆂🄳 ⊠ 🕙 🕙 🖬 🖃 🏊 ⊠

HADDONFIELD

▼▼◆▼ Haddonfield Inn 🅱🅱 ❀
(856) 428-2195. **$159-$229, 7 day notice.** 44 W End Ave. I-295, exit 28, 0.7 mi n on SR 168, 2.6 mi e on Kings Hwy, then just n. Int corridors. **Pets:** Dogs only. $30 daily fee/pet. Designated rooms.

🄰$🄺 ⊠ 🕙 🖬

MOUNT HOLLY

🄰🄰🄰 ▼▼ Best Western Burlington Inn 🆂🅷
(609) 261-3800. **$109-$144, 3 day notice.** 2020 Rt 541, Rd 1. New Jersey Tpke, exit 5, just n. Int corridors. **Pets:** Accepted.

🆂🄰🅅🄴 🆂🄳 ⊠ 🕙 🖬 🖃 🏊

MOUNT LAUREL

🄰🄰🄰 ▼▼ Candlewood Suites 🆂🅷
(856) 642-7567. **$104-$127.** 4000 Crawford Pl. New Jersey Tpke, exit 4, 1 mi s on SR 73 S. Int corridors. **Pets:** Accepted.

🆂🄰🅅🄴 🆂🄳 ⊠ 🕙 🖬 🖃

▼▼◆▼ Doubletree Guest Suites Hotel 🅻🅷
(856) 778-8999. **$124-$214.** 515 Fellowship Rd N. New Jersey Tpke, exit 4, just nw to Fellowship Rd, then just n; I-295, exit 36A, just se on SR 73 to Fellowship Rd, then just n. Int corridors. **Pets:** Accepted.

🄰$🄺 🆂🄳 ⊠ 🕙🄼 🕙 🖬 🖃 🍴 🏊

▼▼ Extended StayAmerica Philadelphia-Mt. Laurel 🆂🅷
(856) 778-4100. **$84-$94.** 101 Diemer Dr. New Jersey Tpke, exit 4, 1 mi se on SR 73, just n on Crawford Pl, then just e. Int corridors. **Pets:** Accepted.

🄰$🄺 🆂🄳 ⊠ 🕙 🕙 🖬 🖃

▼▼ **Extended Stay Deluxe-Mt. Laurel** 🆂🅷
(856) 608-9820. **$84-$104.** 500 Diemer Dr. New Jeresy Tpke, exit 4, 1 mi se on SR 73, just n on Crawford Pl, then just e. Int corridors. **Pets:** Accepted.

🄰🄼 🅂🄳 ⊠ 🗋 🄼 ❙ 🖵

▼ **Red Roof Inn #7066** Ⓜ
(856) 234-5589. **$60-$82.** 603 Fellowship Rd. New Jersey Tpke, exit 4, just nw on SR 73 to Fellowship Rd, then just s; I-295, exit 36A, just se on SR 73 to Fellowship Rd, then just s. Ext corridors. **Pets:** Medium, other species. Service with restrictions, supervision.

⊠ 🗋 🄼 ❙

🄰🄰🄰 ▼▼▼ **Staybridge Suites** 🆂🅷 ❀
(856) 722-1900. **$147-$189.** 4115 Church Rd. New Jersey Tpke, exit 4, 0.5 mi s on SR 73, then 0.5 mi w. Int corridors. **Pets:** Medium. $75 one-time fee/pet. Designated rooms, service with restrictions, supervision.

🆂🄰🅅🄴 🅂🄳 ⊠ ❙ 🖵 🌊 ⊠

▼▼ **Summerfield Suites-Mount Laurel** 🆂🅷
(856) 222-1313. **$139-$169.** 3000 Crawford Pl. New Jersey Tpke, exit 4, 1 mi s on SR 73; I-295, exit 36A, 1.5 mi s on SR 73. Ext corridors. **Pets:** Accepted.

🄰🄼 ⊠ 🄼 🗋 🄼 ❙ 🖵 🌊 ⊠

🄰🄰🄰 ▼▼▼▼ **Wyndham Mount Laurel** 🅻🅷
(856) 234-7000. **$169.** 1111 Rt 73. New Jersey Tpke, exit 4; I-295, exit 36A, 0.5 mi se. Int corridors. **Pets:** Other species. $100 deposit/room. Designated rooms, service with restrictions, crate.

🆂🄰🅅🄴 🅂🄳 ⊠ 🗋 🄼 ❙ 🖵 🍴 🌊 ⊠

END METROPOLITAN AREA

PISCATAWAY

▼▼▼ **Embassy Suites Hotel** 🅻🅷 ❀
(732) 980-0500. **$149-$229.** 121 Centennial Ave. I-287, exit 9 (Highland Park), just s to Centennial Ave. Int corridors. **Pets:** Medium. $20 daily fee/room. Designated rooms, service with restrictions, crate.

⊠ 🗋 🄼 ❙ 🖵 🍴 🌊 ⊠

▼ **Motel 6 Piscataway #1084** 🆂🅷
(732) 981-9200. **$61-$75.** 1012 Stelton Rd. I-287, exit 5, just e. Ext/int corridors. **Pets:** Medium, other species. Service with restrictions, supervision.

🅂🄳 🄼

▼▼▼ **Radisson Hotel Piscataway** 🅻🅷
(732) 980-0400. **$109-$149.** 21 Kingsbridge Rd. I-287, exit 9 (Highland Park) to Centennial Ave via River Rd S, then 0.4 mi s. Int corridors. **Pets:** Accepted.

🄰🄼 🅂🄳 ⊠ 🗋 🄼 ❙ 🖵 🍴 🌊

PLAINSBORO

▼▼▼ **Courtyard by Marriott Princeton** 🆂🅷
(609) 716-9100. **$194-$214.** 3815 US Rt 1. 0.4 mi s of Scudders Mill Rd at Mapleton Rd. Int corridors. **Pets:** Accepted.

🄰🄼 ⊠ 🄼 🄼 ❙ 🖵 🌊

PRINCETON

🄰🄰🄰 ▼▼▼▼ **Holiday Inn Princeton** 🆂🅷
(609) 520-1200. **$139-$179.** 100 Independence Way. I-295, exit 67A (SR 1) northbound; exit 67 (SR 1) southbound, 7 mi n. Int corridors. **Pets:** Accepted.

🆂🄰🅅🄴 🅂🄳 ⊠ 🗋 🄼 ❙ 🖵 🍴 🌊 ⊠

🄰🄰🄰 ▼▼▼ **Nassau Inn** 🆂🅷 ❀
(609) 921-7500. **$207-$275.** 10 Palmer Square. Center. Int corridors. **Pets:** $75 one-time fee/room. Designated rooms, service with restrictions, crate.

🆂🄰🅅🄴 🅂🄳 ⊠ 🗋 🄼 ❙ 🖵 🍴

▼▼▼ **Residence Inn by Marriott-Princeton at Carnegie Center** 🆂🅷
(609) 799-0550. **$119-$239.** 3563 US 1 S. 1.5 mi s of jct CR 527 and 571. Int corridors. **Pets:** Accepted.

🄰🄼 🅂🄳 ⊠ 🄼 🗋 🄼 ❙ 🖵 🌊 ⊠

▼▼▼ **Staybridge Suites** 🆂🅷 ❀
(609) 951-0009. **$199-$229.** 4375 US 1 S. Just past Ridge Rd. Ext corridors. **Pets:** Medium, other species. $10 daily fee/pet. Service with restrictions, crate.

🄰🄼 🅂🄳 ⊠ 🄼 🗋 🄼 🖵 🌊 ⊠

🄰🄰🄰 ▼▼▼ **Westin Princeton at Forrestal Village** 🅻🅷
(609) 452-7900. **$329-$349.** 201 Village Blvd. On US 1 southbound, 1.5 mi n of CR 571. Int corridors. **Pets:** Accepted.

🆂🄰🅅🄴 ⊠ 🄼 🗋 🄼 ❙ 🖵 🍴 🌊 ⊠

RAMSEY

🄰🄰🄰 ▼▼▼ **Best Western-The Inn at Ramsey** 🆂🅷
(201) 327-6700. **$89-$199, 7 day notice.** 1315 Rt 17 S. Jct I-287 and SR 17 S, 3 mi s. Int corridors. **Pets:** Accepted.

🆂🄰🅅🄴 🅂🄳 ⊠ 🗋 🄼 🍴

▼▼ **Extended StayAmerica Ramsey** 🆂🅷
(201) 236-9996. **Call for rates.** 112 SR 17 N. Just s of Lake St exit. Int corridors. **Pets:** Accepted.

⊠ 🄼 🗋 🄼 ❙ 🖵

RED BANK

▼▼ **Extended StayAmerica Red Bank-Middletown** 🆂🅷
(732) 450-8688. **Call for rates (no credit cards).** 329 Newman Springs Rd. Garden State Pkwy, exit 109, just e. Int corridors. **Pets:** Accepted.

⊠ 🄼 🗋 🄼 ❙ 🖵

ROCKAWAY

🄰🄰🄰 ▼▼▼ **Best Western-Rockaway Hotel** 🆂🅷
(973) 625-1200. **$99-$135.** 14 Green Pond Rd. I-80, exit 37, just n. Int corridors. **Pets:** Small. $25 daily fee/pet. Designated rooms, service with restrictions, supervision.

🆂🄰🅅🄴 🅂🄳 ⊠ 🗋 🄼 ❙ 🖵 🌊

RUTHERFORD

▼▼▼ **Extended StayAmerica-Meadowlands** 🆂🅷
(201) 635-0266. **Call for rates.** 750 Edwin L Ward Sr Memorial Hwy. I-95, exit 16W, 1.5 mi w on SR 3 to SR 17 N service road exit, then 0.5 mi e. Int corridors. **Pets:** Accepted.

⊠ 🗋 🄼 ❙ 🖵

SECAUCUS

▼▼▼ **Extended StayAmerica-Secaucus-Meadowlands** 🆂🅷
(201) 617-1711. **Call for rates.** 1 Meadowlands Pkwy. Between eastern and western spurs of New Jersey Tpke; exits 16E, 17, or 16W to SR 3, exit Meadowlands Pkwy, just n. Int corridors. **Pets:** Accepted.

⊠ 🄼 🗋 🄼 ❙ 🖵

▲▲▲ ▼▼▼▼ The Holiday Inn Harmon Meadow 🏠 ❀
(201) 348-2000. **$140-$260.** 300 Plaza Dr. New Jersey Tpke, exits 16E, 17, or 16W via SR 3 to Harmon Meadow Blvd. Int corridors. **Pets:** Dogs only. $25 one-time fee/room. Service with restrictions, crate.

▼▼▼ Homestead Studio Suites
Hotel-Secaucus/Meadowlands 🆂🅷
(201) 553-9700. **$124-$140.** 1 Plaza Dr. New Jersey Tpke, exit 16E northbound; exit 17E southbound, 0.3 mi e. Int corridors. **Pets:** Accepted.

▼▼ Red Roof Inn-Meadowlands #7150 Ⓜ
(201) 319-1000. **$81-$123.** 15 Meadowlands Pkwy. Between eastern and western spurs of New Jersey Tpke, exits 16E, 17 or 16W to SR 3, exit Meadowlands Pkwy. Ext corridors. **Pets:** Medium, other species. Service with restrictions, supervision.

▲▲▲ ▼▼▼▼ Wyndham Meadowlands Suites 🏠
(201) 863-8700. **$109-$289.** 350 Rt 3 W, at Mill Creek Dr. Between eastern and western spurs of New Jersey Tpke, exits 16E, 17 or 16W via SR 3 W and Harmon Meadow Blvd; in Mill Creek Mall. Int corridors. **Pets:** Accepted.

SOMERSET

▼▼ Candlewood Suites 🆂🅷
(732) 748-1400. **Call for rates.** 41 Worlds Fair Dr. I-287, exit 10 (CR 527), left on Ramp (CR 527 S/Easton Ave), 0.3 mi, then 0.5 mi w. Int corridors. **Pets:** Accepted.

▼▼▼ Doubletree Hotel & Executive Meeting Center
Somerset 🏠
(732) 469-2600. **$99-$210.** 200 Atrium Dr. I-287, exit 10 (CR 527), just n (direction Bound Brook) to Davidson Ave, 0.5 mi sw; in Atrium Corp Park. Int corridors. **Pets:** Accepted.

▼▼ Extended StayAmerica-Franklin 🆂🅷
(732) 469-8080. **Call for rates.** 30 World Fair Dr. I-287, exit 10 (CR 527), left on ramp (CR 527 S/Easton Ave), 0.3 mi, then 0.5 mi w. Int corridors. **Pets:** Accepted.

▲▲▲ ▼▼▼▼ Holiday Inn-Somerset 🆂🅷
(732) 356-1700. **$115-$145.** 195 Davidson Ave. I-287, exit 10 (CR 527), just n (direction Bound Brook), then 0.5 mi sw. Int corridors. **Pets:** $15 daily fee/room. Designated rooms, service with restrictions, supervision.

▼▼▼ Homewood Suites by Hilton-Somerset 🆂🅷
(732) 868-9155. **$179-$219.** 101 Pierce St. I-287, exit 10 (CR 527), left on ramp (CR 527 S/Easton Ave), 0.3 mi, 0.7 mi w on World Fair Dr, then just s. Int corridors. **Pets:** Medium. $20 daily fee/room. Designated rooms, service with restrictions, crate.

▼▼▼ Residence Inn by Marriott-Somerset 🆂🅷
(732) 627-0881. **$90-$153.** 37 World Fair Dr. I-287, exit 10 (CR 527), left on ramp (CR 527 S/Easton Ave) 0.3 mi, then 0.5 mi w. Int corridors. **Pets:** Accepted.

▼▼▼ Somerset Marriott Hotel 🏠
(732) 560-0500. **$79-$159, 3 day notice.** 110 Davidson Ave. I-287, exit 10 (CR 527), just n (direction Bound Brook) to Davidson Ave, then just sw. Int corridors. **Pets:** Accepted.

▼▼▼ Staybridge Suites Somerset 🆂🅷
(732) 356-8000. **$135-$171.** 260 Davidson Ave. I-287, exit 10 (CR 527), just n (direction Bound Brook) to Davidson Ave, then 0.8 mi sw. Ext corridors. **Pets:** Large. $150 one-time fee/room. No service.

SPRINGFIELD

▼▼▼ Holiday Inn Springfield 🆂🅷
(973) 376-9400. **$139-$159.** 304 Rt 22 W. Garden State Pkwy, exit 140 northbound, 4 mi w; exit 140A southbound. Int corridors. **Pets:** Service with restrictions, supervision.

TINTON FALLS

▲▲▲ ▼▼▼▼ Holiday Inn at Tinton Falls 🆂🅷 ❀
(732) 544-9300. **$160-$180.** 700 Hope Rd. Garden State Pkwy, exit 105. Int corridors. **Pets:** Medium, other species. $100 one-time fee/pet. Service with restrictions, crate.

▼▼ Red Roof Inn #7211 Ⓜ
(732) 389-4646. **$76-$114.** 11 Centre Plaza. Garden State Pkwy, exit 105, just right at 1st light after toll. Ext corridors. **Pets:** Medium, other species. Service with restrictions, supervision.

▼▼▼ Residence Inn by Marriott 🆂🅷
(732) 389-8100. **$119-$199, 30 day notice.** 90 Park Rd. Garden State Pkwy, exit 105, 1st jughandle after toll, immediate left before Courtyard by Marriott, just n, then e. Ext corridors. **Pets:** Accepted.

▼▼▼ Sunrise Suites Hotel 🆂🅷 ❀
(732) 389-4800. **$89-$209.** 3 Centre Plaza. Garden State Pkwy, exit 105, 1st right at Hope Rd after toll. Ext/int corridors. **Pets:** Small. $75 one-time fee/room. Service with restrictions, crate.

TOMS RIVER

▲▲▲ ▼▼▼ Howard Johnson Hotel-Toms River 🆂🅷
(732) 244-1000. **$85-$199.** 955 Hooper Ave. Garden State Pkwy, exit 82, 1 mi e on SR 37. Int corridors. **Pets:** Accepted.

WANTAGE

▼▼ High Point Country Inn Ⓜ ❀
(973) 702-1860. **$79-$300.** 1328 SR 23 N. 1 mi n of Colesville Village Center. Ext corridors. **Pets:** Other species. $10 daily fee/pet. Designated rooms, service with restrictions.

WARREN

▼▼▼▼ Somerset Hills Hotel 🆂🅷
(908) 647-6700. **$125-$179.** 200 Liberty Corner Rd. I-78, exit 33, just n on CR 525. Int corridors. **Pets:** Medium. $25 daily fee/room. Designated rooms, service with restrictions, crate.

WAYNE

▲▲▲ ▼▼▼ La Quinta Inn 🆂🅷
(973) 696-8050. **$74-$119.** 1850 Rt 23 & Ratzer Rd. I-80, exit 53 (Butler-Verona) westbound to SR 23 N, 3 mi to Ratzer Rd (service road); exit 54 eastbound to Minisink Rd to U-turn for I-80 W to exit 53. Int corridors. **Pets:** Accepted.

▼▼▼▼ Residence Inn by Marriott Wayne 🆂🅷
(973) 872-7100. **Call for rates (no credit cards).** 30 Nevins Rd. From jct CR 640 (Riverview Dr) and 681 (Valley Rd), 3.5 mi n, just w on Barbour Pond Dr, then just n. Int corridors. **Pets:** Small, other species. $100 one-time fee/room. Service with restrictions, crate.

⊠ 🅲 🖪 🖵 🏊 ⊠

WEEHAWKEN

🆔 ▼▼▼▼ Sheraton Suites On The Hudson 🅻🅷
(201) 617-5600. **$474-$524.** 500 Harbor Blvd. I-495 E toward Lincoln Tunnel, exit Weekawken/Hoboken, bear right at bottom of hill, then 0.4 mi e to Lincoln Harbor Complex; on 19th St. Int corridors. **Pets:** Accepted.

[SAVE] ⊠ 🎧 🅲 🖪 🖵 🍴 🏊

WEST ORANGE

▼▼▼▼ Residence Inn by Marriott-West Orange 🆂🅷
(973) 669-4700. **$199-$299.** 107 Prospect Ave. I-280, exit 8B, 1 mi n on CR 527 (Prospect Ave). Int corridors. **Pets:** Accepted.

[ASK] ⊠ 🅲 🖪 🖵 🏊

WHIPPANY

▼▼ Homestead Studio Suites
   Hotel-Hanover/Parsippany 🆂🅷
(973) 463-1999. **$110-$125.** 125 Rt 10 E. I-287, exit 39, 3.6 mi e. Int corridors. **Pets:** Accepted.

[ASK] [S.D.] ⊠ 🅼 🎧 🅲 🖪 🖵

▼▼▼ Summerfield Suites Parsippany/Whippany 🆂🅷
(973) 605-1001. **$67-$188.** 1 Ridgedale Ave. I-287, exit 39, just nw. Int corridors. **Pets:** Accepted.

[SAVE] ⊠ 🅼 🎧 🅲 🖪 🖵 🏊 ⊠

🆔 ▼▼▼ Wellesley Inn (Whippany) 🆂🅷
(973) 539-8350. **$65-$109.** 1255 Rt 10 E. I-287, exit 39B southbound; exit 39 northbound, just w. Int corridors. **Pets:** Accepted.

[SAVE] ⊠ 🎧 🅲 🖪 🖵 🏊

WOODBRIDGE

▼▼ Homestead Studio Suites
   Hotel-Woodbridge-Newark 🆂🅷
(732) 442-8333. **$95-$110.** 1 Hoover Way. New Jersey Tpke, exit 11, 1.4 mi to US 9 N, then just w on King George Post Rd. Int corridors. **Pets:** Accepted.

[ASK] [S.D.] ⊠ 🅼 🎧 🅲 🖪 🖵

ALAMOGORDO

▼▼ Quality Inn 🅂🄷 🐾
(505) 437-7100. **$105.** 1401 S White Sands Blvd. 1.6 mi s of jct US 54/70 and 82. Int corridors. **Pets:** Other species. $50 deposit/pet, $10 daily fee/pet. Service with restrictions, supervision.
🄰🄢🄺 🆂🄳 ⊠ ᴸᴹ 🔌 🖥 💻 🏊

▼▼ Super 8 Motel-Alamogordo 🅂🄷
(505) 434-4205. **$63-$79.** 3204 N White Sands Blvd. Just s of jct US 54/70 and 82. Int corridors. **Pets:** Small, other species. Service with restrictions, supervision.
🆂🄳 ⊠ 🖥

ALBUQUERQUE

🄰🄰🄰 ▼▼ Airport University Inn 🅂🄷
(505) 247-0512. **$59-$139.** 1901 University Blvd SE. I-25, exit 228A southbound; exit 222 northbound, just e. Int corridors. **Pets:** Accepted.
🆂🄰🆅🄴 🆂🄳 ⊠ 🔌 🖥 🍴 🏊

🄰🄰🄰 ▼▼ Best Western American Motor Inn 🅂🄷 🐾
(505) 298-7426. **$49-$119.** 12999 Central Ave NE. I-40, exit 167 westbound, 0.3 mi w on Central Ave; exit 166 eastbound, right on Juan Tabo, left on Central Ave, then 0.5 mi e. Ext corridors. **Pets:** Other species. $10 daily fee/pet. Service with restrictions, supervision.
🆂🄰🆅🄴 ⊠ 🖥 💻 🍴 🏊

🄰🄰🄰 ▼▼▼ Best Western InnSuites Hotel & Suites-Airport Albuquerque 🅂🄷 🐾
(505) 242-7022. **$69-$129.** 2400 Yale Blvd SE. I-25, exit 222 northbound; exit 222A southbound, 1 mi e, then just s. Int corridors. **Pets:** Medium, other species. $25 one-time fee/pet. Designated rooms, service with restrictions, supervision.
🆂🄰🆅🄴 🆂🄳 ⊠ 🔌 🖥 💻 🏊

🄰🄰🄰 ▼▼▼ Best Western Rio Grande Inn 🅂🄷 🐾
(505) 843-9500. **$98-$128.** 1015 Rio Grande Blvd NW. I-40, exit 157A, just s. Int corridors. **Pets:** Medium. $25 one-time fee/room. Designated rooms, service with restrictions, supervision.
🆂🄰🆅🄴 🆂🄳 ⊠ 🔌 🖥 💻 🍴 🏊

🄰🄰🄰 ▼▼▼ Brittania & W E Mauger Estate Bed & Breakfast 🄱🄱
(505) 242-8755. **$89-$229, 10 day notice.** 701 Roma Ave NW. I-25, exit 225, 1 mi w, then just s on 7th Ave. Int corridors. **Pets:** Dogs only. $30 one-time fee/pet. Designated rooms, service with restrictions, crate.
🆂🄰🆅🄴 🆂🄳 ⊠ 🖥 💻

▼▼▼ Candlewood Suites 🅂🄷
(505) 888-3424. **$79-$115.** 3025 Menaul Blvd NE. I-40, exit 160, just n to Menaul Blvd, then 0.5 mi w. Int corridors. **Pets:** Accepted.
🄰🄢🄺 🆂🄳 ⊠ ᴸᴹ 🌙 🖥 💻

🄰🄰🄰 ▼▼▼ ClubHouse Inn & Suites 🅂🄷
(505) 345-0010. **$79-$119.** 1315 Menaul Blvd NE. I-25, exit 227A, just e to University Blvd, 0.5 mi s to Menaul Blvd, then 0.5 mi w. Int corridors. **Pets:** Accepted.
🆂🄰🆅🄴 🆂🄳 ⊠ ᴸᴹ 🔌 🌙 🖥 💻 🏊

▼▼▼ Comfort Inn & Suites by Choice Hotels 🅂🄷
(505) 822-1090. **$68-$88.** 5811 Signal Ave NE. I-25, exit 233, just e via Alameda. Int corridors. **Pets:** Accepted.
🄰🄢🄺 🆂🄳 ⊠ ᴸᴹ 🔌 🌙 🖥 💻 🏊

🄰🄰🄰 ▼▼ Comfort Inn East 🅂🄷
(505) 294-1800. **$49-$99.** 13031 Central Ave NE. I-40, exit 167, just w. Ext corridors. **Pets:** Accepted.
🆂🄰🆅🄴 🆂🄳 ⊠ ᴸᴹ 🔌 🌙 🖥 💻 🍴 🏊

🄰🄰🄰 ▼▼ Comfort Inn-Midtown 🅂🄷
(505) 881-3210. **$54-$110.** 2015 Menaul Blvd NE. I-25, exit 225 northbound, 1.6 mi n of Frontage Rd to Menaul Blvd, then just e; exit 227 (Commanche Rd) southbound, s on Frontage Rd, 0.8 mi n to Menaul Blvd, then just e. Ext corridors. **Pets:** Accepted.
🆂🄰🆅🄴 ⊠ 🖥 💻 🏊

▼▼▼ Country Inn & Suites 🅂🄷 🐾
(505) 246-9600. **$89-$129.** 2601 Mulberry SE. I-25, exit 222 (Gibson Blvd), just e. Int corridors. **Pets:** Medium, other species. $25 one-time fee/room. Service with restrictions, supervision.
🄰🄢🄺 🆂🄳 ⊠ 🖥 💻 🏊

▼ Crossland Studios-Albuquerque-Northeast #413 🅂🄷
(505) 343-1100. **$50.** 5020 Ellison St NE. I-25, exit 231 (San Antonio Blvd), just w. Ext corridors. **Pets:** Accepted.
🄰🄢🄺 🆂🄳 ⊠ 🌙 🖥 💻

🄰🄰🄰 ▼▼▼ Days Inn-Hotel Circle 🅂🄷 🐾
(505) 275-3297. **$50-$80.** 10321 Hotel Ave NE. I-40, exit 165 (Eubank Blvd), just n. Ext corridors. **Pets:** $10 daily fee/pet. Service with restrictions.
🆂🄰🆅🄴 🆂🄳 ⊠ 🏊

▼▼ Days Inn Midtown 🅂🄷
(505) 884-0250. **$44-$84, 7 day notice.** 2120 Menaul Blvd NE. I-40, exit 160, just n to Menaul Blvd, then 0.8 mi w. Ext corridors. **Pets:** Small. $10 daily fee/pet. Service with restrictions, supervision.
🄰🄢🄺 🆂🄳 ⊠ ᴸᴹ 🔌 🖥 💻 🏊

▼▼ Days Inn West 🄼
(505) 836-3297. **$53-$85.** 6031 Iliff Rd NW. I-40, exit 155, just s on Coors Rd, then just w. Ext corridors. **Pets:** Accepted.
🄰🄢🄺 🆂🄳 ⊠ ᴸᴹ 🔌 🌙 🏊

▼▼▼ Drury Inn & Suites-Albuquerque 🅂🄷
(505) 341-3600. **$90-$135.** 4310 The 25 Way NE. I-25, exit Jefferson St NE, northwest quadrant of exchange. Int corridors. **Pets:** Large, other species. Service with restrictions, supervision.
🄰🄢🄺 ⊠ ᴸᴹ 🌙 🖥 💻 🏊

🄰🄰🄰 ▼▼ Econo Lodge Downtown/University 🅂🄷 🐾
(505) 243-1321. **$49-$89.** 817 Central Ave NE. I-25, exit 224A northbound; exit 224B southbound, just e. Ext corridors. **Pets:** Medium. $25 deposit/pet, $7 daily fee/pet. Designated rooms, service with restrictions, supervision.
🆂🄰🆅🄴 🆂🄳 ⊠ 🖥 💻 🏊

Econo Lodge East M
(505) 292-7600. **$45-$99.** 13211 Central Ave NE. I-40, exit 167 (Central Ave), just w. Ext corridors. **Pets:** Accepted.

Econo Lodge Midtown SH
(505) 880-0080. **$45-$85.** 2412 Carlisle Blvd NE. I-40, exit 160, just n. Ext corridors. **Pets:** Accepted.

Econo Lodge Old Town SH
(505) 243-8475. **$45-$95.** 2321 Central Ave NW. I-40, exit 157A, 0.6 mi s on Rio Grande Blvd, then 0.4 mi w. Ext corridors. **Pets:** Medium, dogs only. $10 daily fee/pet. Designated rooms, service with restrictions, supervision.

Fairfield Inn Airport SH
(505) 247-1621. **$64-$94.** 2300 Centre Ave SE. I-25, exit 222 northbound; exit 222A southbound, 1 mi e to Yale Blvd; northeast jct of Gibson and Yale blvds. Int corridors. **Pets:** Other species. $75 one-time fee/room. Service with restrictions, supervision.

GuestHouse Inn & Suites SH ❈
(505) 271-8500. **$39-$95.** 10331 Hotel Ave NE. I-40, exit 165, 2 blks n. Int corridors. **Pets:** Very small. $10 daily fee/pet. Service with restrictions, supervision.

Hacienda Antigua Inn BB ❈
(505) 345-5399. **$134-$189, 10 day notice.** 6708 Tierra Dr NW. I-25, exit 230 (Osuna Dr), 2 mi w, then just n. Ext/int corridors. **Pets:** Other species. $30 one-time fee/pet. Crate.

Hampton Inn-North SH
(505) 344-1555. **$89-$172.** 5101 Ellison NE. I-25, exit 231, just w. Ext corridors. **Pets:** Service with restrictions, supervision.

Hawthorn Inn & Suites SH
(505) 242-1555. **$72, 3 day notice.** 1511 Gibson Blvd SE. I-25, exit 222 northbound; exit 222A southbound, just e. Int corridors. **Pets:** Accepted.

Holiday Inn Express SH
(505) 275-8900. **$75.** 10330 Hotel Ave NE. I-40, exit 165 (Eubank Blvd), 2 blks n. Ext corridors. **Pets:** $5 daily fee/pet. Service with restrictions, supervision.

Holiday Inn Express-West SH
(505) 836-8600. **$99.** 6100 Iliff Rd NW. I-40, exit 155, just sw. Ext/int corridors. **Pets:** Accepted.

The Hotel Blue SH
(505) 924-2400. **$79-$109.** 717 Central Ave NW. 8th and Central Ave; downtown. Ext corridors. **Pets:** Accepted.

Howard Johnson Express Inn SH
(505) 828-1600. **$60-$75.** 7630 Pan American Frwy NE. I-25, exit 231, 0.8 mi n on frontage road. Int corridors. **Pets:** Large, other species. $10 daily fee/pet. Designated rooms, service with restrictions, supervision.

La Quinta Inn Albuquerque (Airport) SH
(505) 243-5500. **$84-$118.** 2116 Yale Blvd SE. I-25, exit 222 northbound; exit 222A southbound, 1 mi e. Ext/int corridors. **Pets:** Medium. Service with restrictions.

La Quinta Inn Albuquerque (I-40 East) SH
(505) 884-3591. **$67-$107.** 2424 San Mateo Blvd NE. I-40, exit 161 westbound; exit 161B eastbound, just n. Ext corridors. **Pets:** Medium. Service with restrictions.

La Quinta Inn Albuquerque (North) SH
(505) 821-9000. **$79-$114.** 5241 San Antonio Dr NE. I-25, exit 231, just e. Ext corridors. **Pets:** Medium. Service with restrictions.

La Quinta Inn & Suites Albuquerque (West) SH
(505) 839-1744. **$112-$154.** 6101 Iliff Rd NW. I-40, exit 155, just sw. Int corridors. **Pets:** Medium. Service with restrictions.

La Quinta Inn & Suites Northwest SH
(505) 345-7500. **$74-$139.** 7439 Pan American Frwy NE. I-25, exit 231, just w. Int corridors. **Pets:** Medium. Service with restrictions.

La Quinta Suites Midtown/University SH ❈
(505) 761-5600. **$89-$219.** 2011 Menaul Blvd. Jct University Blvd NE and Menaul Blvd, just e. Int corridors. **Pets:** Service with restrictions, supervision.

Microtel Inn & Suites SH
(505) 836-1686. **$65.** 9910 Avalon NW. I-40, exit 153 (98th St), just s; on western edge of city. Int corridors. **Pets:** Accepted.

Motel 6 #1349 M
(505) 243-8017. **$45-$57.** 1000 Avenida Cesar Chavez. I-25, exit 223, just w. Ext corridors. **Pets:** Medium, other species. Service with restrictions, supervision.

Motel 6 Albuquerque North #1290 SH
(505) 821-1472. **$45-$57.** 8510 Pan American Frwy NE. I-25, exit 232 (Paseo del Norte), just n on Frontage Rd. Int corridors. **Pets:** Medium, other species. Service with restrictions, supervision.

Motel 76 SH
(505) 836-3881. **$38-$55, 7 day notice.** 1521 Coors Blvd NW. I-40, exit 155 (Coors Blvd), just s. Ext corridors. **Pets:** Small. $25 deposit/room. Designated rooms, service with restrictions, supervision.

Nativo Lodge SH
(505) 798-4300. **$89-$109.** 6000 Pan American Frwy NE. I-25, exit 230, just e. Int corridors. **Pets:** Accepted.

Park Plaza Hotel and Conference Center Albuquerque LH
(505) 888-3311. **$62-$80.** 2500 Carlisle Blvd NE. I-40, exit 160, just n. Ext/int corridors. **Pets:** Accepted.

Plaza Inn Albuquerque SH
(505) 243-5693. **$89.** 900 Medical Arts NE. I-25, exit 225, just e. Int corridors. **Pets:** Accepted.

Quality Inn & Suites Albuquerque Downtown SH ❈
(505) 242-5228. **$55-$105.** 411 McKnight Ave NW. I-40, exit 159A, just s via 4th St N. Int corridors. **Pets:** Medium. $10 one-time fee/pet. Designated rooms, service with restrictions, supervision.

Quality Suites SH
(505) 797-0850. **$70-$95, 3 day notice.** 5251 San Antonio Dr NE. I-25, exit 231, just e. Int corridors. **Pets:** Medium, other species. $12 daily fee/pet. Designated rooms, service with restrictions, supervision.

Ramada Limited SH
(505) 858-3297. **$69-$79.** 5601 Alameda Blvd NE. I-25, exit 233, just w. Int corridors. **Pets:** Accepted.

Red Roof Inn SH
(505) 831-3400. **$45-$59.** 6015 Iliff Rd NW. I-40, exit 155 (Coors Blvd), just s, then just w. Ext corridors. **Pets:** Medium, other species. Service with restrictions, supervision.

Residence Inn North by Marriott SH
(505) 761-0200. **$109-$149.** 4331 The Lane at 25 NE. I-25, exit 229 (Jefferson St), just w, just n to The Lane at 25 NE, then just e. Int corridors. **Pets:** Small. $100 one-time fee/room. Designated rooms, service with restrictions, supervision.

Sandia Peak Inn SH
(505) 831-5036. **$60-$136, 7 day notice.** 4614 Central Ave SW. I-40, exit 159A (Rio Grande Blvd), just s, then 2 mi w. Ext corridors. **Pets:** Accepted.

Sheraton Albuquerque Uptown LH
(505) 881-0000. **$99-$139.** 2600 Louisiana Blvd NE. I-40, exit 162, 0.8 mi n. Int corridors. **Pets:** Large, dogs only. Service with restrictions, supervision.

Sleep Inn Airport SH
(505) 244-3325. **$70-$80, 7 day notice.** 2300 International Ave SE. I-25, exit 222 northbound; exit 222A southbound, 1 mi e to Yale Blvd, then just n. Int corridors. **Pets:** Medium, other species. $3 daily fee/pet. Service with restrictions, supervision.

Stardust Inn M
(505) 243-2891. **$36-$79.** 801 Central Ave NE. I-25, 224A northbound; exit 224B southbound, just e. Ext corridors. **Pets:** Medium, dogs only. $10 one-time fee/pet. Designated rooms, service with restrictions, supervision.

Suburban Extended Stay Hotels by Choice Hotels M
(505) 883-8888. **$49-$69.** 2401 Wellsley Dr NE. I-40, exit 160, just n to Menaul Blvd, just w, then just s. Ext corridors. **Pets:** Other species. $25 deposit/room. Designated rooms, service with restrictions, supervision.

Super 8 Motel East SH
(505) 271-4807. **$45-$85, 4 day notice.** 450 Paisano NE. I-40, exit 166 (Juan Tabo Blvd), just n to Copper, then just s. Int corridors. **Pets:** $8 daily fee/pet. Designated rooms, service with restrictions, supervision.

Super 8 Motel of Albuquerque SH
(505) 888-4884. **$55-$95.** 2500 University Blvd NE. I-25, exit 225 northbound, 1.9 mi n on frontage road to Menaul Blvd, then just e; exit 227 (Comanche Rd) southbound, 0.9 mi s to Menaul Blvd, then just e. Int corridors. **Pets:** $8 daily fee/pet. Designated rooms, service with restrictions, supervision.

Super 8 Motel West (Albuquerque) SH
(505) 836-5560. **$55-$95.** 6030 Iliff Rd NW. I-40, exit 155, 0.5 mi s. Int corridors. **Pets:** $8 daily fee/pet. Service with restrictions, supervision.

TownePlace Suites by Marriott SH
(505) 232-5800. **$80-$149.** 2400 Centre Ave SE. I-25, exit 222 northbound; exit 222A southbound, 1 mi e to Yale Blvd, at northeast jct of Gibson and Yale blvds, then just e. Int corridors. **Pets:** Other species. $100 one-time fee/room. Service with restrictions, supervision.

ALGODONES

Hacienda Vargas Bed and Breakfast Inn BB
(505) 867-9115. **$89-$149, 10 day notice.** 1431 SR 313 (El Camino Real). I-25, exit 248, 0.5 mi w. Int corridors. **Pets:** Accepted.

ARROYO SECO

Adobe and Stars B & B BB
(505) 776-2776. **$95-$215, 32 day notice.** 584 State Hwy 150. 1.1 mi ne on SR 150 at Valdez Rd. Ext/int corridors. **Pets:** Medium, other species. $15 daily fee/pet. Designated rooms, service with restrictions, crate.

ARTESIA

Artesia Inn M
(505) 746-9801. **$45-$55.** 1820 S 1st St. 1.5 mi s on US 285. Ext corridors. **Pets:** Accepted.

BELEN

Best Western-Belen SH
(505) 861-3181. **$64-$84.** 2111 Camino del Llano Blvd. I-25, exit 191, just w. Ext/int corridors. **Pets:** Other species. $20 deposit/room, $5 daily fee/pet. Service with restrictions, supervision.

BERNALILLO

Days Inn-Bernalillo SH
(505) 771-7000. **$50-$100.** 107 N Camino del Pueblo. I-25, exit 242, just w. Int corridors. **Pets:** Small. $30 deposit/pet. Service with restrictions, supervision.

Hyatt Regency Tamaya Resort and Spa LH
(505) 867-1234. **$139-$399.** 1300 Tuyuna Tr. I-25, exit 242, 1 mi w on SR 44 to Tamaya Rd, then 1 mi n, follow signs. Int corridors. **Pets:** Medium, dogs only. $50 one-time fee/room. Service with restrictions, supervision.

La Hacienda Grande BB
(505) 867-1887. **$89-$149, 10 day notice.** 21 Barros Rd. I-25, exit 242, 0.3 mi w to Camino del Pueblo, then 0.5 mi n. Ext/int corridors. **Pets:** Other species. Designated rooms, no service, crate.

BLOOMFIELD

Super 8 Motel M
(505) 632-8886. **$50.** 525 W Broadway Blvd. Jct of US 64 and SR 44. Int corridors. **Pets:** Accepted.

CARLSBAD

Best Western Stevens Inn SH
(505) 887-2851. **$80-$95.** 1829 S Canal St. 1 mi s on US 62, 180 and 285. Ext corridors. **Pets:** $10 daily fee/room. Service with restrictions, supervision.

Carlsbad Inn M ❄
(505) 887-1171. **$39-$59.** 2019 S Canal St. 1.5 mi s on US 62, 180 and 285. Ext corridors. **Pets:** Small, other species. $10 daily fee/pet. Service with restrictions, supervision.
SAVE ⓢ ✕ 🔒 📧 ➔

Comfort Inn SH
(505) 887-1994. **$71-$81.** 2429 W Pierce St. N on US 285. Int corridors. **Pets:** Accepted.
ASK ⓢ ✕ ♿ 📧 🔒 📧 ➔

Days Inn of Carlsbad SH
(505) 887-7800. **$89.** 3910 National Parks Hwy. 3.5 mi sw on US 62 and 180. Ext corridors. **Pets:** Small, dogs only. $10 daily fee/pet. Designated rooms, service with restrictions, supervision.
SAVE ⓢ ✕ ♿ 📧 ➔

Stagecoach Inn M
(505) 887-1148. **$55.** 1819 S Canal St. 1 mi s on US 62, 180 and 285. Ext corridors. **Pets:** Medium. $10 daily fee/pet. Designated rooms, service with restrictions, supervision.
SAVE ⓢ ✕ 🔒 🍽 ➔

CHAMA

Vista del Rio Lodge M
(505) 756-2138. **$65-$85.** 2595 US Hwy 84/64. 0.5 mi s of SR 17. Ext corridors. **Pets:** Small, dogs only. Service with restrictions, supervision.
SAVE ⓢ ✕ 🔒 📧 ✕ 🐾

CHIMAYO

Casa Escondida Bed & Breakfast BB ❄
(505) 351-4805. **$86-$155, 14 day notice.** 64 CR 0100. SR 68, 7.1 mi e on SR 76, 0.5 mi nw on CR 100, follow signs. Ext/int corridors. **Pets:** Other species. $15 daily fee/pet. Designated rooms, service with restrictions, supervision.
ASK ✕ 🔒 📺 ➤

CIMARRON

Cimarron Inn & RV Park M ❄
(505) 376-2268. **$49-$60.** 212 10th St. On US 64. Ext corridors. **Pets:** Other species. Crate.
SAVE ⓢ ✕ 🔒 📧 🐾

CLAYTON

Best Western Kokopelli Lodge SH
(505) 374-2589. **$79-$169, 10 day notice.** 702 S 1st St. US 87, 0.5 mi se of jct US 56 and 64. Ext corridors. **Pets:** Accepted.
SAVE ⓢ ✕ 📧 🔒 📧 ➔

Days Inn & Suites SH
(505) 374-0133. **$69-$159.** 1120 S 1st St. US 87, 1 mi s of jct US 56 and 64. Int corridors. **Pets:** $5 daily fee/pet. Service with restrictions, supervision.
SAVE ⓢ ✕ 📧 🔒 📧 ➔

Super 8 Motel M
(505) 374-8127. **$63-$97.** 1425 S 1st St. US 87, 1 mi se of jct US 56 and 64. Int corridors. **Pets:** Accepted.
ASK ⓢ ✕ ♿

CLOUDCROFT

The Lodge Resort SH
(505) 682-2566. **$120-$350, 14 day notice.** 1 Corona Pl. US 82, 0.3 mi s. Int corridors. **Pets:** Medium. $25 one-time fee/room. Designated rooms, service with restrictions, supervision.
SAVE ⓢ ✕ ♿ 📧 🔒 📧 🍽 ➔ ✕

CLOVIS

Econo Lodge M
(505) 763-3439. **$59-$129.** 1400 E Mabry Dr. 0.5 mi e on US 60, 70 and 84. Ext corridors. **Pets:** Accepted.
ASK ✕ 📧 🔒 📧 ➔

Holiday Inn Clovis SH
(505) 762-4491. **$80.** 2700 E Mabry Dr. 1.5 mi e on US 60, 70 and 84. Ext corridors. **Pets:** Small, other species. Service with restrictions, supervision.
ASK ⓢ ✕ ♿ 📺 📧 🔒 📧 🍽 ➔ ✕

Howard Johnson Expressway Inn SH
(505) 769-1953. **$52-$66.** 2920 Mabry Dr. US 60, 70 and 84, just e. Int corridors. **Pets:** Small, other species. $10 daily fee/room. Service with restrictions.
ASK ⓢ ✕ 🔒 📧 ➔

La Quinta Inn & Suites Clovis SH
(505) 763-8777. **$100-$150.** 4521 N Prince St. Jct US 60/84 and Prince St, 3 mi n. Int corridors. **Pets:** Other species. Service with restrictions, supervision.
SAVE ⓢ ✕ 📺 📧 🔒 📧 ➔

Rodeway Inn SH
(505) 762-4591. **$62-$92.** 1616 Mabry Dr. 1 mi e on US 60, 70 and 84. Ext corridors. **Pets:** Accepted.
SAVE ⓢ ✕ 🔒 📧 ➔

DEMING

Best Western Mimbres Valley Inn SH
(505) 546-4544. **$49-$85.** 1500 W Pine. I-10, exit 81, just e. Ext corridors. **Pets:** Accepted.
ASK ⓢ ✕ 🔒 📧 ➔

Days Inn M
(505) 546-8813. **$49-$59.** 1601 E Pine St. I-10, exit 85 westbound, 2 mi w on business loop; exit 81 eastbound, 1 mi e on business loop. Ext corridors. **Pets:** Accepted.
SAVE ⓢ ✕ 🔒 📧 🍽 ➔

Grand Motor Inn SH 🐾
(505) 546-2632. **$47-$52.** 1721 E Pine St. I-10, exit 85 westbound, 2 mi w on business loop; exit 82 eastbound, 1 mi e on business loop. Ext corridors. **Pets:** Small, other species. $5 deposit/pet. Designated rooms, service with restrictions, supervision.
SAVE ⓢ ✕ 🔒 🍽 ➔

Holiday Inn SH
(505) 546-2661. **$50-$100.** 4600 E Pine St. I-10, exit 85, just w. Ext corridors. **Pets:** Accepted.
SAVE ⓢ ✕ ♿ 📺 📧 🔒 📧 🍽 ➔

La Quinta Inn & Suites SH
(505) 546-0600. **$79-$99.** 4300 E Pine St. I-10, exit 85, just w. Int corridors. **Pets:** Small. Service with restrictions, supervision.
ASK ⓢ ✕ ♿ 📧 🔒 📧 ➔

EDGEWOOD

Alta Mae's Heritage Inn BB
(505) 281-5000. **$95, 14 day notice.** 1950-C Old Route 66. I-40, exit 187, just s to stop sign, then just e. Ext corridors. **Pets:** Accepted.
ASK ✕ ✕ ➤

ELEPHANT BUTTE

Elephant Butte Inn SH ❄
(505) 744-5431. **$70-$100, 3 day notice.** 401 Hwy 195. I-25, exit 83, 4 mi e. Ext corridors. **Pets:** Small. $20 one-time fee/pet. Designated rooms, service with restrictions, supervision.
SAVE ⓢ ✕ ♿ 📧 🔒 📧 🍽 ➔

Marina Suites Motel M
(505) 744-5269. **$75-$95.** 200 Country Club Dr. I-25, exit 83, 4.7 mi e.
Ext corridors. **Pets:** Accepted.
ASK S☐ ☐ ☐ ☑

ESPANOLA

Comfort Inn SH
(505) 753-2419. **$55-$150.** 604-B S Riverside Dr. US 84 and 285, just
s of jct SR 68. Int corridors. **Pets:** Supervision.
SAVE S☐ ☒ ☐ ☐ ☜

Espanola Days Inn SH
(505) 747-1242. **$60-$100.** 807 S Riverside Dr. US 84 and 285, 0.7 mi
s of jct SR 68. Ext corridors. **Pets:** $6 daily fee/pet. Service with restric-
tions, supervision.
ASK S☐ ☒ ☐

Super 8 Motel SH
(505) 753-5374. **$43-$103.** 811 S Riverside Dr. US 84 and 285, 0.5 mi
s of jct SR 68. Int corridors. **Pets:** Accepted.
SAVE S☐ ☒ ☐

FARMINGTON

Best Western Inn & Suites SH
(505) 327-5221. **$89-$109, 14 day notice.** 700 Scott Ave. 1 mi e on SR
516 (Main St), just s. Int corridors. **Pets:** Accepted.
SAVE ☒ ☒ ☐ ☐ ☐ ☜ ☒

Brentwood Inn SH
(505) 325-2288. **$59-$99.** 600 E Broadway. 1 mi e; at Broadway and
Scott Ave. Int corridors. **Pets:** Medium. $10 one-time fee/room. Desig-
nated rooms, no service.
SAVE S☐ ☒ ☒ ☐ ☐ ☐ ☜ ☒

Comfort Inn M
(505) 325-2626. **$70-$110.** 555 Scott Ave. 1 mi e on SR 516 (Main St),
just s. Int corridors. **Pets:** Accepted.
SAVE S☐ ☒ ☐ ☐ ☜

Days Inn M
(505) 325-3700. **$60-$80.** 1901 E Broadway. 1.7 mi e on US 64
(Bloomfield Blvd). Int corridors. **Pets:** Accepted.
ASK S☐ ☒ ☒M ☒ ☒ ☐

Holiday Inn Express M
(505) 325-2545. **$77.** 2110 Bloomfield Blvd. 1.6 mi e on US 64 (Bloom-
field Blvd), just past jct Broadway, on frontage road. Int corridors.
Pets: Accepted.
SAVE S☐ ☒ ☒M ☒ ☒ ☐ ☐ ☜

La Quinta Inn Farmington M
(505) 327-4706. **$80-$121.** 675 Scott Ave. 1 mi e on SR 516 (Main St),
just s. Ext/int corridors. **Pets:** Medium. Service with restrictions.
ASK ☒ ☒M ☒ ☐ ☐ ☜

Super 8 Motel M
(505) 325-1813. **$50-$75.** 1601 E Broadway. Just n of jct SR 64
(Bloomfield Blvd). Int corridors. **Pets:** Medium, other species. $5 daily
fee/pet. Service with restrictions, supervision.
ASK S☐ ☒ ☒ ☐

GALLUP

Americas Best Value Inn & Suites SH
(505) 722-0757. **$49-$72, 3 day notice.** 2003 Hwy 66 W. I-40, exit 20,
1 mi w. Ext/int corridors. **Pets:** Accepted.
SAVE S☐ ☒ ☒M ☐ ☐ ☐ ☐ ☜

Best Western Inn & Suites SH
(505) 722-2221. **$68-$75.** 3009 US 66 W. I-40, exit 16, 1 mi e. Int
corridors. **Pets:** Accepted.
SAVE S☐ ☒ ☐ ☐ ☐ ☜ ☒

Best Western Royal Holiday Motel M
(505) 722-4900. **$59-$149.** 1903 W Hwy 66. I-40, exit 20, 0.5 mi s to
US 66, then 0.8 mi w. Int corridors. **Pets:** Medium. $7 one-time fee/pet.
Service with restrictions, supervision.
SAVE ☒ ☐ ☐ ☜

Comfort Inn M
(505) 722-0982. **$59-$99.** 3208 US 66 W. I-40, exit 16, 0.3 mi e. Int
corridors. **Pets:** Small. $10 daily fee/room. Service with restrictions, super-
vision.
SAVE S☐ ☒ ☐ ☐ ☜

Days Inn-West SH
(505) 863-6889. **$50-$60.** 3201 W Hwy 66. I-40, exit 16, 0.3 mi e. Ext
corridors. **Pets:** Accepted.
SAVE S☐ ☒ ☐ ☐ ☜

Econo Lodge SH
(505) 722-3800. **$40-$69.** 3101 US 66 W. I-40, exit 16, 0.8 mi e. Int
corridors. **Pets:** Medium. $10 daily fee/pet. Service with restrictions, super-
vision.
ASK S☐ ☒

Economy Inn M
(505) 863-9301. **$33-$44.** 1709 US 66 W. I-40, exit 20, s to US 66,
then 0.5 mi w. Ext corridors. **Pets:** Very small. $3 daily fee/pet. Desig-
nated rooms, service with restrictions, supervision.
SAVE ☒ ☐

Gallup Travelodge SH
(505) 722-2100. **$45-$89.** 3275 US 66 W. I-40, exit 16, just e. Int
corridors. **Pets:** Medium. $10 daily fee/pet. Service with restrictions.
ASK S☐ ☒ ☒M ☒ ☐ ☐ ☜

Hampton Inn-West SH
(505) 722-7224. **Call for rates (no credit cards).** 111 Twin Buttes Rd.
I-40, exit 16, just e. Int corridors. **Pets:** Accepted.
☒ ☒M ☐ ☜

La Quinta Inn & Suites SH ❧
(505) 722-2233. **$99-$134.** 3880 Hwy 66 E. I-40, exit 26, just e. Int
corridors. **Pets:** Medium, other species. Service with restrictions, supervision.
ASK S☐ ☒ ☒M ☒ ☐ ☐ ☜ ☒

Ramada Limited SH
(505) 726-2700. **$64-$99.** 1440 W Maloney Ave. I-40, exit 20, 1 mi w.
Int corridors. **Pets:** Small, dogs only. $10 one-time fee/pet. Designated
rooms, service with restrictions, supervision.
ASK S☐ ☒ ☒M ☐ ☐ ☜

Red Roof Inn M
(505) 722-7765. **$36-$60.** 3304 W Hwy 66. I-40, exit 16, just se. Ext
corridors. **Pets:** Medium, other species. Service with restrictions, supervision.
SAVE S☐ ☒ ☐ ☐ ☜

Sleep Inn SH
(505) 863-3535. **$65-$85.** 3820 E US 66. I-40, exit 26, just e. Int
corridors. **Pets:** Accepted.
SAVE S☐ ☒ ☒M ☒ ☐ ☜

Super 8 Motel M
(505) 722-5300. **$49-$70.** 1715 W US 66. I-40, exit 20, s to US 66,
then 0.5 mi w. Int corridors. **Pets:** Large. $10 daily fee/pet. Designated
rooms, no service, supervision.
SAVE S☐ ☒ ☐ ☐ ☜

GRANTS

Best Western Inn & Suites SH
(505) 287-7901. **$69-$89.** 1501 E Santa Fe Ave. I-40, exit 85, just w. Int corridors. **Pets:** Medium. $10 one-time fee/room. Designated rooms, service with restrictions, supervision.

Comfort Inn SH
(505) 287-8700. **$59-$79, 7 day notice.** 1551 E Santa Fe Ave. I-40, exit 85, 0.3 mi n. Int corridors. **Pets:** Accepted.

Days Inn SH
(505) 287-8883. **$55-$75, 7 day notice.** 1504 E Santa Fe Ave. I-40, exit 85, 0.3 mi n. Ext corridors. **Pets:** Small, other species. $10 daily fee/pet. Designated rooms, service with restrictions, supervision.

Grants Travelodge SH
(505) 287-7800. **$59-$79, 7 day notice.** 1608 E Santa Fe Ave. I-40, exit 85, 0.3 mi n. Ext corridors. **Pets:** Accepted.

Holiday Inn Express SH
(505) 285-4676. **$80-$100, 7 day notice.** 1496 E Sante Fe Ave. I-40, exit 85, 0.3 mi n. Int corridors. **Pets:** Small, other species. $10 daily fee/pet. Service with restrictions, supervision.

Sands Motel M
(505) 287-2996. **$36-$38.** 112 McArthur St. I-40, exit 85, 1.5 mi w on Business Loop 40. Ext corridors. **Pets:** $5 daily fee/pet. Service with restrictions, crate.

Super 8 Grants SH
(505) 287-8811. **$45-$65.** 1604 E Santa Fe Ave. I-40, exit 85, just n. Int corridors. **Pets:** Other species. $10 daily fee/pet. Designated rooms, service with restrictions, supervision.

HOBBS

Best Western Executive Inn SH
(505) 397-7171. **$80-$100.** 309 N Marland Blvd. US 62 and 180 and Snyder St. Ext corridors. **Pets:** Accepted.

Days Inn M
(505) 397-6541. **$79-$119.** 211 N Marland Blvd. 2 mi e on US 62 and 180. Ext corridors. **Pets:** $10 one-time fee/pet. Service with restrictions, supervision.

Econo Lodge SH
(505) 397-3591. **$56-$69.** 619 N Marland Blvd. 2.5 mi e on US 62 and 180. Ext corridors. **Pets:** Medium, dogs only. $10 one-time fee/pet. Designated rooms, service with restrictions, supervision.

Hobbs Family Inn SH
(505) 397-3251. **$65-$95.** 501 N Marland Blvd. 2.5 mi e on US 62 and 180. Ext/int corridors. **Pets:** Small. $25 deposit/room. No service, crate.

Lea Wood Inn M
(505) 393-4101. **$55-$60.** 200 N Marland Blvd. On US 62 and 180, 2 mi e. Ext corridors. **Pets:** Small, dogs only. $25 deposit/pet. Service with restrictions, crate.

LAS CRUCES

Best Western Mesilla Valley Inn SH
(505) 524-8603. **$72-$92.** 901 Avenida de Mesilla. I-10, exit 140, just n. Ext/int corridors. **Pets:** Medium, other species. Designated rooms, service with restrictions, crate.

Best Western Mission Inn SH
(505) 524-8591. **$65-$100.** 1765 S Main St. I-10, exit 142, 1 mi n. Ext corridors. **Pets:** Large, other species. $10 daily fee/pet. Service with restrictions, crate.

Comfort Inn & Suites Las Cruces SH
(505) 527-1050. **$75-$135.** 1300 Avenida de Mesilla. I-10, exit 140, just s. Int corridors. **Pets:** Small, dogs only. $15 daily fee/pet. Service with restrictions, supervision.

Comfort Suites by Choice Hotels SH
(505) 522-1300. **$75-$95.** 2101 S Triviz. I-25, exit 1. Int corridors. **Pets:** Accepted.

DreamCatcher Inn Bed & Breakfast de Las Cruces BB
(505) 522-3035. **$100-$135, 5 day notice.** 10201 Starfly Rd. US 70 E to Nasa/Baylor Canyon Rd, 0.5 mi s, then 0.5 mi w. Ext corridors. **Pets:** Other species. $25 one-time fee/pet. Service with restrictions, supervision.

Hampton Inn SH
(505) 526-8311. **$70-$77.** 755 Avenida de Mesilla. I-10, exit 140. Ext corridors. **Pets:** Accepted.

Holiday Inn Express SH
(505) 527-9947. **$59-$189.** 2200 S Valley Dr. I-10, exit 142, 2 blks w. Ext corridors. **Pets:** Accepted.

Hotel Encanto de Las Cruces LH
(505) 522-4300. **$109-$169.** 705 S Telshore Blvd. I-25, exit 3 (Lohman Ave), just e. Int corridors. **Pets:** Accepted.

La Quinta Inn & Suites Las Cruces SH
(505) 523-0100. **$85-$105.** 1500 Hickory Dr. I-10, exit 140, just se of jct I-25 and Avenida de Mesilla. Int corridors. **Pets:** Medium. Service with restrictions.

La Quinta Inn Las Cruces SH
(505) 524-0331. **$91-$111.** 790 Avenida de Mesilla. I-10, exit 140. Int corridors. **Pets:** Medium. Service with restrictions.

Lundeen's Inn of the Arts BB
(505) 526-3326. **$77-$82.** 618 S Alameda Blvd. Center. Int corridors. **Pets:** Accepted.

Ramada Palms de Las Cruces SH
(505) 526-4411. **$70-$78, 3 day notice.** 201 E University Ave. I-10, exit 142, just n. Int corridors. **Pets:** Medium, other species. $25 one-time fee/pet. Designated rooms, service with restrictions, supervision.

Royal Host Motel M
(505) 524-8536. **$46-$54.** 2146 W Picacho St. I-10, exit 139, 1 mi n, then 0.5 mi e on I-10 business route (Picacho St). Ext corridors. **Pets:** Medium. $10 one-time fee/pet. No service, supervision.

♦♦♦ **Sleep Inn by Choice Hotels** [SH]
(505) 522-1700. **$65-$85.** 2121 S Triviz. I-25, exit 1. Int corridors. **Pets:** Accepted.
[A$K] [SD] ⊠ ♿M 👂 ✋ ▣ ☕ 🏊

♦♦ **Super 8 Motel** [M]
(505) 523-8695. **$50-$65.** 245 La Posada Ln. I-10, exit 142, 2.8 mi s on US 80, 85 and 180. Int corridors. **Pets:** Medium, other species. $15 daily fee/pet. Service with restrictions, supervision.
[A$K] [SD] ⊠ ▣

LAS VEGAS

[AAA] ♦♦♦ **Comfort Inn** [SH]
(505) 425-1100. **$65-$100.** 2500 N Grand Ave. I-25, exit 347, just sw, US 85 and I-25 business route. Int corridors. **Pets:** Other species. Designated rooms, service with restrictions, crate.
[SAVE] [SD] ⊠ ✋ ▣ ☕ 🏊

[AAA] ♦♦ **El Camino Motel** [M]
(505) 425-5994. **$50-$65.** 1152 N Grand Ave. I-25, exit 345, 0.3 mi w, US 85 and I-25 business route. Ext corridors. **Pets:** Small, dogs only. $6 daily fee/pet. Designated rooms, supervision.
[SAVE] [SD] ⊠ 🍴

[AAA] ♦♦ **Inn on the Santa Fe Trail** [M]
(505) 425-6791. **$69-$89.** 1133 N Grand Ave. I-25, exit 345, 0.5 mi n; I-25 business route and US 84, 0.3 mi w. Ext corridors. **Pets:** Dogs only. $5 daily fee/room. Service with restrictions, supervision.
[SAVE] [SD] ⊠ ▣ ☕ 🍴 🏊

[AAA] ♦♦♦ **Plaza Hotel** [SH]
(505) 425-3591. **$69-$139.** 230 Plaza St. I-25, exit 343 W, just w, follow signs to Old Town Plaza. Int corridors. **Pets:** Other species. $15 daily fee/pet. Service with restrictions, supervision.
[SAVE] [SD] ⊠ ▣ ☕ 🍴

LORDSBURG

[AAA] ♦♦ **Best Western-Western Skies Inn** [SH]
(505) 542-8807. **$99.** 1303 S Main St. I-10, exit 22, just s. Ext corridors. **Pets:** $25 daily fee/pet. Designated rooms, service with restrictions, supervision.
[SAVE] [SD] ⊠ ▣ ☕ 🍴 🏊

♦♦ **Holiday Inn Express** [SH]
(505) 542-3666. **$85-$99.** 1408 S Main St. I-10, exit 22, just s. Ext corridors. **Pets:** Accepted.
[A$K] [SD] ⊠ ♿M ✋ ▣ ☕ 🏊

[AAA] ♦ **Super 8 Motel** [SH]
(505) 542-8882. **$55-$80.** 110 E Maple. I-10, exit 22, just s. Int corridors. **Pets:** Other species. $5 daily fee/pet. Service with restrictions.
[SAVE] [SD] ⊠

LOS ALAMOS

[AAA] ♦♦ **Best Western Hilltop House Hotel** [SH]
(505) 662-2441. **$59-$119.** 400 Trinity Dr. Center. Int corridors. **Pets:** Large, dogs only. $25 one-time fee/room. Designated rooms, service with restrictions, crate.
[SAVE] ⊠ ✋ ▣ ☕ 🏊

♦♦ **Quality Inn & Suites** [SH]
(505) 662-7211. **$79-$109.** 2175 Trinity Dr. Center. Int corridors. **Pets:** Small. $25 one-time fee/pet. Service with restrictions, supervision.
[A$K] [SD] ⊠ ▣ ☕

LOS LUNAS

♦♦ **Western Skies Inn & Suites** [SH]
(505) 865-0001. **$59-$74.** 2258 Sun Ranch Village Loop. I-25, exit 203, just n. Int corridors. **Pets:** Other species. $10 daily fee/pet. Designated rooms, service with restrictions, supervision.
[A$K] [SD] ⊠ ♿M ✋ ▣ 🏊

LOVINGTON

[AAA] ♦♦ **Lovington Inn** [SH]
(505) 396-5346. **$54-$61.** 1600 W Ave D. Jct US 82 and SR 18, 1 mi w. Ext corridors. **Pets:** Medium. $10 deposit/room. Service with restrictions, supervision.
[SAVE] [SD] ⊠ ✋ ▣ ☕ 🍴

MESILLA

♦♦ **Meson de Mesilla** [CI]
(505) 525-9212. **$65-$175.** 1803 Avenida de Mesilla. I-10, exit 140, 0.4 mi s. Ext/int corridors. **Pets:** Accepted.
[A$K] ⊠ ▣ 🍴 🏊

MORIARTY

[AAA] ♦♦ **Comfort Inn** [SH]
(505) 832-6666. **$60-$130.** 119 Route 66 E. I-40, exit 196, just s, then just e. Int corridors. **Pets:** Accepted.
[SAVE] [SD] ⊠ ♿M ✋ ▣ ☕ 🏊

[AAA] ♦ **Days Inn** [SH]
(505) 832-4451. **$49-$159.** 1809 Route 66 W. I-40, exit 194. Int corridors. **Pets:** Accepted.
[SAVE] [SD] ⊠ ▣

[AAA] ♦♦ **Econo Lodge** [SH]
(505) 832-4457. **$55-$69.** 1316 Route 66 W. I-40, exit 194, 0.5 mi se on US 66 and I-40 business loop. Int corridors. **Pets:** $10 daily fee/pet. No service, supervision.
[SAVE] [SD] ⊠ ▣ ☕

[AAA] ♦♦♦ **Holiday Inn Express** [SH]
(505) 832-5000. **$94.** 1507 Route 66. I-40, exit 194, 0.4 mi e. Int corridors. **Pets:** Other species. $10 one-time fee/pet. Designated rooms, service with restrictions, supervision.
[SAVE] [SD] ⊠ ♿M ▣ ☕ 🏊

[AAA] ♦♦ **Super 8 Motel** [SH]
(505) 832-6730. **$60-$70.** 1611 W Old Route 66. I-40, exit 194, 0.5 mi e on Central Ave. Int corridors. **Pets:** Other species. $20 deposit/room. Designated rooms, service with restrictions, supervision.
[SAVE] [SD] ⊠ ✋ ▣

PINOS ALTOS

♦♦ **Bear Creek Motel & Cabins** [CA] 🐾
(505) 388-4501. **$99-$159, 10 day notice.** 88 Main St. 1 mi n on SR 15. Ext corridors. **Pets:** $10 daily fee/pet.
[A$K] [SD] ▣ ☕ [AC]

POJOAQUE PUEBLO

[AAA] ♦♦ **Cities of Gold Hotel** [SH]
(505) 455-0515. **$69-$129, 3 day notice.** 10A Cities of Gold Rd. On US 84/265, just n. Int corridors. **Pets:** Other species. $20 one-time fee/room. Designated rooms, service with restrictions, crate.
[SAVE] ⊠ ♿M ✋ ▣ ☕ 🍴

RANCHOS DE TAOS

[AAA] ♦ **Budget Host Inn** [M]
(505) 758-2524. **$48-$64, 3 day notice.** 1798 Paseo Del Pueblo Sur (SR 68). On SR 68; center. Ext corridors. **Pets:** $8 one-time fee/pet. Designated rooms, service with restrictions, crate.
[SAVE] ⊠ ▣ ☕

RATON

[AAA] ♦♦ **Best Western Sands** [M]
(505) 445-2737. **$55-$99.** 300 Clayton Rd. I-25, exit 451, just w. Ext/int corridors. **Pets:** Accepted.
[SAVE] [SD] ⊠ 👂 ✋ ▣ ☕ 🍴 🏊

△△△ ▽▽▽ **Budget Host Raton** Ⓜ
(505) 445-3655. **$45-$62.** 136 Canyon Dr. I-25, exit 454, 0.8 mi s on I-25 business loop. Ext corridors. **Pets:** Medium. $2 daily fee/pet. Service with restrictions, supervision.
ⓈⒶⓋⒺ Ⓢ🖇 ✕ ⓖ.ᴹ 🖥

△△△ ▽▽ **Raton Pass Inn** Ⓜ
(505) 445-3641. **$42-$52.** 308 Canyon Dr. I-25, exit 454, 0.8 mi s. Ext corridors. **Pets:** Medium, dogs only. $2 daily fee/pet. Service with restrictions, supervision.
ⓈⒶⓋⒺ Ⓢ🖇 ✕ 🖥

RIO RANCHO

△△△ ▽▽▽ **Best Western Rio Rancho Inn & Conference Center** 🅂🄷
(505) 892-1700. **$55-$110.** 1465 Rio Rancho Blvd. I-25, exit 233 (Alameda Blvd), 6.5 mi w; I-40, exit 155, 10 mi n on Coors Rd/Coors Bypass to SR 528, then 1 mi n. Ext corridors. **Pets:** Accepted.
ⓈⒶⓋⒺ Ⓢ🖇 ✕ 🖉 🖥 🖳 ➣

△△△ ▽▽▽ **Days Inn- Rio Rancho** 🅂🄷
(505) 892-8800. **$49-$110.** 4200 Crestview Dr. I-25, exit 233 (Alameda Blvd), 8 mi w on SR 528; I-40, exit 155, 8 mi n on Coors Rd (SR 448). Ext corridors. **Pets:** Small. $15 one-time fee/pet. Service with restrictions, supervision.
ⓈⒶⓋⒺ Ⓢ🖇 ✕ 🖥 ➣

▽▽ **Extended StayAmerica** 🅂🄷
(505) 792-1338. **$59-$74.** 2608 The American Rd NW. Jct SR 528, just n. Int corridors. **Pets:** Accepted.
🄰🅂🄺 Ⓢ🖇 ✕ ⓖ.ᴹ 🖉 🖥 🖳

▽▽▽ **Extended Stay Deluxe Albuquerque-Rio Rancho Blvd** 🅂🄷
(505) 892-7900. **$79-$89.** 2221 Rio Rancho Blvd. I-25, exit 233 (Alameda Blvd), 6 mi w (becomes SR 528/Rio Rancho Blvd). Int corridors. **Pets:** Accepted.
🄰🅂🄺 Ⓢ🖇 ✕ 🖉 🖉 🖥 🖳 ➣

▽▽ **Rio Rancho Super 8 Motel** 🅂🄷
(505) 896-8888. **$50-$95.** 4100 Barbara Loop SE. I-25, exit 233 (Alameda Blvd), 0.5 mi w, 3.8 mi nw on SR 528, then just e. Int corridors. **Pets:** Other species. $8 daily fee/pet. Service with restrictions, supervision.
🄰🅂🄺 Ⓢ🖇 ✕ ⓖ.ᴹ

ROSWELL

△△△ ▽▽▽ **Best Western El Rancho Palacio** 🅂🄷
(505) 622-2721. **$60-$85.** 2205 N Main St. 1.8 mi n on US 70 and 285. Ext corridors. **Pets:** Service with restrictions, supervision.
ⓈⒶⓋⒺ Ⓢ🖇 ✕ 🖥 🖳 ➣

△△△ ▽▽▽▽ **Best Western Sally Port Inn & Suites** 🅂🄷
(505) 622-6430. **$95-$125.** 2000 N Main St. 1.5 mi n on US 70 and 285. Int corridors. **Pets:** Accepted.
ⓈⒶⓋⒺ Ⓢ🖇 ✕ 🖥 🖳 🍴 ➣ 🖾

△△△ ▽▽▽ **Budget Inn-North** Ⓜ ❀
(505) 623-6050. **$35-$50.** 2101 N Main St. 1.8 mi n on US 70 and 285. Ext corridors. **Pets:** Dogs only. $5 daily fee/pet. Service with restrictions, supervision.
ⓈⒶⓋⒺ ✕ 🖥 ➣

▽▽ **Budget Inn West** 🅂🄷
(505) 623-3811. **$35-$55.** 2200 W 2nd St. 2 mi w on US 70 and 380. Ext corridors. **Pets:** Small, dogs only. $2 daily fee/pet. Service with restrictions, supervision.
🄰🅂🄺 Ⓢ🖇 ✕ 🖥 ➣

△△△ ▽▽▽ **Comfort Inn** 🅂🄷
(505) 623-4567. **$89-$139, 7 day notice.** 3595 N Main St. On US 70 and 285, 3 mi n. Int corridors. **Pets:** Very small. Designated rooms, service with restrictions, supervision.
ⓈⒶⓋⒺ Ⓢ🖇 ✕ ⓖ.ᴹ 🖉 🖥 🖳 ➣

△△△ ▽▽▽ **Days Inn** 🅂🄷
(505) 623-4021. **$60-$90.** 1310 N Main St. 0.8 mi n on US 70 and 285. Ext corridors. **Pets:** Service with restrictions, supervision.
ⓈⒶⓋⒺ Ⓢ🖇 ✕ 🖉 🖥 🖳 ➣

△△△ ▽▽▽ **Frontier Motel** Ⓜ
(505) 622-1400. **$32-$40.** 3010 N Main St. 2.5 mi n on US 70 and 285. Ext corridors. **Pets:** Accepted.
ⓈⒶⓋⒺ Ⓢ🖇 ✕ 🖥 ➣

△△△ ▽▽▽▽ **Holiday Inn Express** 🅂🄷
(505) 627-9900. **$77-$85.** 2300 N Main St. US 70. Int corridors. **Pets:** Medium. Service with restrictions, supervision.
ⓈⒶⓋⒺ Ⓢ🖇 ✕ ⓖ.ᴹ 🖉 🖥 🖳 ➣ 🖾

△△△ ▽▽▽▽ **La Quinta Inn and Suites** 🅂🄷
(505) 622-8000. **$89-$109, 3 day notice.** 200 E 19th St. Jct N Main and 19th St, 2 blks e. Int corridors. **Pets:** Accepted.
ⓈⒶⓋⒺ Ⓢ🖇 ✕ ⓖ.ᴹ 🖉 🖥 🖳 ➣

△△△ ▽▽▽ **Leisure Inn** 🅂🄷
(505) 622-2575. **$44-$50.** 2700 W 2nd St. 2.5 mi w on US 70 and 380. Ext corridors. **Pets:** Small, dogs only. $5 daily fee/pet. Designated rooms, service with restrictions, supervision.
ⓈⒶⓋⒺ Ⓢ🖇 ✕ 🖥 🖳 ➣ 🖾

▽▽▽ **Ramada Limited** 🅂🄷
(505) 623-9440. **$68.** 2803 W 2nd St. 2.5 mi w on US 70 and 380. Ext/int corridors. **Pets:** Accepted.
🄰🅂🄺 Ⓢ🖇 ✕ 🖥 ➣

▽▽▽ **Western Inn** Ⓜ
(505) 623-9425. **$62-$67.** 2331 N Main St. Jct US 70/285/380, 2.2 mi n. Ext corridors. **Pets:** Accepted.
🄰🅂🄺 Ⓢ🖇 ✕ 🖥 🖳 ➣

RUIDOSO

△△△ ▽▽▽ **Dan Dee Cabins** 🄲🄰
(505) 257-2165. **$84-$179, 14 day notice.** 310 Main Rd. 0.8 mi w on Upper Canyon Rd. Ext corridors. **Pets:** Other species. $10 one-time fee/pet. No service, crate.
ⓈⒶⓋⒺ Ⓢ🖇 🖥 🖳 🖾

▽▽▽▽ **The Lodge at Sierra Blanca** 🅂🄷
(505) 258-5500. **$201-$221.** 107 Sierra Blanca Dr. 2.5 mi n on SR 48. Int corridors. **Pets:** Designated rooms, service with restrictions, supervision.
✕ 🖉 🖉 🖥 🖳 ➣ 🖾

△△△ ▽▽▽ **Quality Inn** 🅂🄷
(505) 378-4051. **$59-$189.** 307 Hwy 70 W. Jct US 70 and SR 48. Int corridors. **Pets:** Small, dogs only. $10 one-time fee/pet. Designated rooms, no service, supervision.
ⓈⒶⓋⒺ Ⓢ🖇 ✕ 🖥 🖳 ➣

▽▽▽ **Travelodge** 🅂🄷
(505) 378-4471. **$55-$160.** 159 W Hwy 70. Jct of US 70 and SR 48. Ext corridors. **Pets:** Accepted.
🄰🅂🄺 Ⓢ🖇 ✕ 🖥 🖳 ➣

△△△ ▽▽▽▽ **The Village Lodge** 🄲🄾 ❀
(505) 258-5442. **$109-$159, 7 day notice.** 1000 Mechem Dr. 2 mi n on SR 48. Ext corridors. **Pets:** Medium, other species. $10 one-time fee/room. Crate.
ⓈⒶⓋⒺ Ⓢ🖇 ✕ 🖥 🖳

(A)(A)(A) ▼▼ Whispering Pine Cabins [CA]
(505) 257-4311. **$89-$265, 14 day notice.** 422 Main Rd. 0.9 mi w of jct SR 48 and Suddenth Dr. Ext corridors. **Pets:** Accepted.
[SAVE] [X] [■] [■]

RUIDOSO DOWNS

▼ ▼ Best Western Pine Springs Inn [SH]
(505) 378-8100. **$59-$159, 3 day notice.** 1420 W Hwy 70. Just n; center. Ext corridors. **Pets:** Other species. Service with restrictions, crate.
[ASK] [S] [X] [■] [■] [≈]

SANTA FE

▼▼▼ Alexander's Inn [BB] ❀
(505) 986-1431. **$85-$185, 14 day notice.** 529 E Palace Ave. Just e of jct Paseo De Peralta; 6 blks e of historic plaza. Ext/int corridors. **Pets:** Large, other species. $20 one-time fee/pet. Service with restrictions.
[ASK] [S] [X] [■] [■] [X]

(A)(A)(A) ▼▼▼ Best Western Inn of Santa Fe [SH]
(505) 438-3822. **$45-$145.** 3650 Cerrillos Rd. I-25, exit 278, 2.8 mi n. Int corridors. **Pets:** Accepted.
[SAVE] [S] [X] [≈] [■] [■] [≈]

(A)(A)(A) ▼▼▼▼ Bishop's Lodge Ranch Resort & Spa [LH]
(505) 983-6377. **$169-$419, 3 day notice.** 1297 N Bishop's Lodge Rd. 3.5 mi n of jct Paseo De Peralta. Ext/int corridors. **Pets:** Dogs only. $20 daily fee/pet. Designated rooms, service with restrictions, supervision.
[SAVE] [S] [X] [≈] [■] [■] [≈] [X]

(A)(A)(A) ▼▼▼ The Bobcat Inn [BB]
(505) 988-9239. **$95-$150, 14 day notice.** 442A Old Las Vegas Hwy. I-25, exit 284, just n on Old Pecos Trail, then 4.3 mi ne. Ext/int corridors. **Pets:** Accepted.
[SAVE] [S] [X] [M] [≈] [■]

(A)(A)(A) ▼▼▼ Camel Rock Suites [M]
(505) 989-3600. **$79-$109.** 3007 S St. Frances Dr. 0.8 mi n on S St. Francis Dr, just e on Zia via access drive. Ext corridors. **Pets:** Medium, other species. $10 daily fee/pet. Service with restrictions, supervision.
[SAVE] [S] [X] [M] [≈] [≈] [■] [■]

▼▼▼ Casapueblo Inn [BB]
(505) 988-4455. **$129-$239, 3 day notice.** 138 Park Ave. Jct Guadalupe St. Ext corridors. **Pets:** Large, other species. $50 one-time fee/room. Service with restrictions, crate.
[ASK] [S] [X] [≈] [■]

(A)(A)(A) ▼▼▼ Comfort Inn Santa Fe [SH]
(505) 474-7330. **$59-$199.** 4312 Cerrillos Rd. I-25, exit 278, 1.6 mi n. Int corridors. **Pets:** Other species. $5 daily fee/pet. Service with restrictions, supervision.
[SAVE] [S] [X] [≈] [≈] [■] [■] [≈]

(A)(A)(A) ▼▼▼ Econo Lodge [SH]
(505) 471-4000. **$46-$180.** 3470 Cerrillos Rd. I-25, exit 278, 3 mi n. Int corridors. **Pets:** Accepted.
[SAVE] [S] [X] [M] [≈] [≈] [■] [■] [≈]

(A)(A)(A) ▼▼▼ Eldorado Hotel & Spa [LH] ❀
(505) 988-4455. **$129-$319, 3 day notice.** 309 W San Francisco. Just w of The Plaza at Sandoval St. Int corridors. **Pets:** $50 one-time fee/pet. Service with restrictions, supervision.
[SAVE] [S] [X] [M] [≈] [■] [≈] [≈] [X]

(A)(A)(A) ▼▼▼ El Paradero Bed & Breakfast [BB]
(505) 988-1177. **$85-$175, 14 day notice.** 220 W Manhattan Ave. 0.3 mi s on Cerrillos Rd, 1/2 blk e. Ext/int corridors. **Pets:** Dogs only. $15 daily fee/room. Service with restrictions, crate.
[SAVE] [X] [≈] [■] [■]

(A)(A)(A) ▼▼▼▼ The Hacienda at Hotel Santa Fe [SH] ❀
(505) 982-1200. **$219-$600, 3 day notice.** 1501 Paseo de Peralta. At Cerrillos Rd, 0.6 mi s of The Plaza. Int corridors. **Pets:** Dogs only. $20 daily fee/pet. Service with restrictions, supervision.
[SAVE] [S] [X] [■] [■] [≈] [≈] [X]

(A)(A)(A) ▼▼▼◆ Hacienda Nicholas [BB] ❀
(505) 986-1431. **$110-$220, 14 day notice.** 320 E Marcy St. Just e of jct Paseo de Paralta; 4 blks e of historic plaza. Ext/int corridors. **Pets:** Large, other species. $20 one-time fee/pet. Service with restrictions.
[SAVE] [X]

(A)(A)(A) ▼▼▼◆ Hampton Inn Santa Fe [SH]
(505) 474-3900. **$69-$199.** 3625 Cerrillos Rd. I-25, exit 278, 2.5 mi n. Int corridors. **Pets:** Accepted.
[SAVE] [S] [X] [M] [≈] [≈] [■] [■] [≈] [X]

▼▼▼◆ Hilton of Santa Fe [SH]
(505) 988-2811. **$129-$251, 3 day notice.** 100 Sandoval St. Just sw of The Plaza; between San Francisco and W Alameda sts. Ext/int corridors. **Pets:** Accepted.
[ASK] [S] [X] [≈] [■] [■] [≈] [≈]

(A)(A)(A) ▼▼▼◆ Holiday Inn [SH] ❀
(505) 473-4646. **$79-$159.** 4048 Cerrillos Rd. I-25, exit 278, 2.3 mi n just n of Rodeo Dr. Int corridors. **Pets:** Medium, other species. $25 one-time fee/room. Service with restrictions, supervision.
[SAVE] [S] [X] [M] [≈] [≈] [■] [■] [≈] [X]

(A)(A)(A) ▼▼▼◆ Hotel Plaza Real [SH] ❀
(505) 988-4900. **$119-$289.** 125 Washington Ave. Just ne of The Plaza; center. Ext/int corridors. **Pets:** Dogs only. $50 one-time fee/room. Designated rooms, service with restrictions, supervision.
[ASK] [S] [X] [≈] [■] [■] [≈]

(A)(A)(A) ▼▼▼◆ Hotel Santa Fe [SH] ❀
(505) 982-1200. **$129-$379.** 1501 Paseo de Peralta. At Cerrillos Rd, 0.6 mi s of The Plaza. Int corridors. **Pets:** Dogs only. $20 daily fee/pet. Service with restrictions, supervision.
[SAVE] [S] [X] [≈] [■] [≈] [≈] [X]

(A)(A)(A) ▼▼▼▼ Inn of the Anasazi [SH]
(505) 988-3030. **$209-$1250, 3 day notice.** 113 Washington Ave. Just ne of The Plaza. Int corridors. **Pets:** Accepted.
[SAVE] [X] [≈] [■] [≈]

(A)(A)(A) ▼▼▼▼ Inn On The Alameda [SH] ❀
(505) 984-2121. **$120-$295, 3 day notice.** 303 E Alameda. 4 blks e of The Plaza; at Paseo de Peralta. Ext/int corridors. **Pets:** Small, other species. $20 daily fee/room. Designated rooms, supervision.
[SAVE] [X] [≈] [≈] [■] [■] [X]

(A)(A)(A) ▼▼▼▼ La Quinta Inn Santa Fe [SH]
(505) 471-1142. **$77-$145.** 4298 Cerrillos Rd. I-25, exit 278, 1.8 mi n. Ext/int corridors. **Pets:** Medium. Service with restrictions.
[SAVE] [X] [≈] [≈] [■] [■] [≈]

(A)(A)(A) ▼▼▼ Las Palomas [BB] ❀
(505) 982-5560. **$119-$379.** 460 W San Francisco St. Just w of jct Guadalupe St. Ext corridors. **Pets:** Dogs only. $20 daily fee/pet. Service with restrictions, supervision.
[SAVE] [S] [X] [≈] [■] [■] [X]

▼ Motel 6–150 [M]
(505) 473-1380. **$45-$65.** 3007 Cerrillos Rd. I-25, exit 278, 3.8 mi n. Ext corridors. **Pets:** Medium, other species. Service with restrictions, supervision.
[S] [X] [≈] [■] [≈]

▼▼▼▼ The Old Santa Fe Inn [M] ❀
(505) 995-0800. **$79-$309, 3 day notice.** 320 Galisteo St. Just sw of Historic Santa Fee Plaza; center. Ext/int corridors. **Pets:** Other species. $25 daily fee/pet. Designated rooms, crate.
[ASK] [S] [X] [≈] [≈] [■] [■]

▼▼▼ Park Inn SH ❀
(505) 471-3000. **$49-$114.** 2907 Cerrillos Rd. I-25, exit 278, 7 mi n. Ext corridors. **Pets:** Other species. $50 deposit/room, $10 daily fee/pet. Service with restrictions.
(ASK) (S) (X) (🛏) (📺) (⌇)

⚑ ▼▼ Quality Inn SH
(505) 471-1211. **$59-$199.** 3011 Cerrillos Rd. I-25, exit 278B, 3.8 mi n. Int corridors. **Pets:** Other species. $10 daily fee/pet. No service, supervision.
(SAVE) (S) (X) (🛏) (📺) (🍴) (⌇)

▼▼▼▼ Residence Inn by Marriott SH
(505) 988-7300. **$129-$269.** 1698 Galisteo St. I-25, exit 282, 1.7 mi n on St Francis Dr to St Michaels Dr, just e, then just n. Ext corridors. **Pets:** Accepted.
(ASK) (S) (X) (🗝) (🛏) (📺) (⌇) (X)

⚑ ▼▼ Sage Inn M
(505) 982-5952. **$115-$160.** 725 Cerrillos Rd. 0.4 mi ne of St. Francis Dr (US 84). Ext corridors. **Pets:** Accepted.
(SAVE) (S) (X) (🗝) (🛏) (📺) (⌇)

⚑ ▼▼ Santa Fe Motel & Inn M
(505) 982-1039. **$79-$179, 3 day notice.** 510 Cerrillos Rd. 4 blks sw of The Plaza. Ext corridors. **Pets:** Accepted.
(SAVE) (S) (X) (🛏) (📺)

⚑ ▼▼ Santa Fe Plaza Travelodge SH ❀
(505) 982-3551. **$59-$199.** 646 Cerrillos Rd. 0.8 mi sw of The Plaza. Ext/int corridors. **Pets:** Small, dogs only. $10 daily fee/pet. No service, supervision.
(SAVE) (S) (X) (🗝) (🛏) (📺) (⌇)

▼▼ Sleep Inn SH
(505) 474-9500. **$69-$189, 7 day notice.** 8376 Cerrillos Rd. I-25, exit 278, 0.3 mi n. Int corridors. **Pets:** Accepted.
(ASK) (S) (X) (♿) (🗝) (🖨) (🛏) (📺) (⌇)

SANTA ROSA

⚑ ▼▼ Best Western Adobe Inn SH
(505) 472-3446. **$68-$80, 5 day notice.** 1501 Historic Route 66. I-40, exit 275. Ext corridors. **Pets:** Medium. Service with restrictions, supervision.
(SAVE) (S) (X) (🛏) (📺) (⌇)

⚑ ▼▼ Best Western Santa Rosa Inn M
(505) 472-5877. **$71-$98.** 3022 Historic Route 66. I-40, exit 277, 0.5 mi w. Ext corridors. **Pets:** Medium. $10 daily fee/pet. Designated rooms, service with restrictions, supervision.
(SAVE) (S) (X) (🛏) (📺) (⌇)

⚑ ▼▼ Comfort Inn SH
(505) 472-5570. **$65-$89.** 3343 E Historic Route 66. I-40, exit 277, 0.3 mi w. Ext corridors. **Pets:** Accepted.
(SAVE) (S) (X) (🛏) (📺) (⌇)

⚑ ▼▼ Days Inn of Santa Rosa SH
(505) 472-5985. **$65-$125.** 1830 Historic Route 66. I-40, exit 275. Ext corridors. **Pets:** Small. $5 daily fee/pet. Designated rooms, service with restrictions, supervision.
(SAVE) (X) (🛏) (📺)

⚑ ▼▼▼ Holiday Inn Express SH
(505) 472-5411. **$65-$99.** 3202 Historic Route 66. I-40, exit 277, 0.4 mi w. Int corridors. **Pets:** Accepted.
(SAVE) (S) (X) (♿) (🗝) (📺) (⌇)

⚑ ▼▼▼ La Quinta Inn-Santa Rosa SH
(505) 472-4800. **$69-$105.** 1701 Historic Route 66. I-40, exit 275, just e. Int corridors. **Pets:** Accepted.
(SAVE) (S) (X) (🗝) (🛏) (📺) (⌇)

▼▼ Motel 6-273 M
(505) 472-3045. **$42-$55.** 3400 Historic Route 66. I-40, exit 277, 0.3 mi w. Ext corridors. **Pets:** Medium, other species. Service with restrictions, supervision.
(S) (X) (🗝) (🛏) (📺) (⌇)

▼▼ Super 8 Motel-Santa Rosa M
(505) 472-5388. **$55-$65.** 1201 Historic Route 66. I-40, exit 275, just w. Int corridors. **Pets:** Accepted.
(ASK) (S) (X) (♿) (🗝) (🛏)

⚑ ▼▼ Travelodge SH
(505) 472-3494. **$45-$80.** 1819 Historic Route 66. I-40, exit 275, just n. Ext corridors. **Pets:** Small. $5 daily fee/pet. Designated rooms, service with restrictions, crate.
(SAVE) (X) (🛏) (📺) (⌇)

SILVER CITY

▼▼▼ Comfort Inn SH
(505) 534-1883. **$75-$250.** 1060 E Hwy 180. 1.5 mi e on US 180 and SR 90. Int corridors. **Pets:** Other species. Service with restrictions, supervision.
(ASK) (S) (X) (🛏) (📺) (⌇)

⚑ ▼▼ Econo Lodge Silver City SH
(505) 534-1111. **$53-$85.** 1120 Hwy 180 E. 1.5 mi ne on US 180 and SR 90. Int corridors. **Pets:** Large, other species. $25 deposit/pet, $7 daily fee/room. Designated rooms, service with restrictions, supervision.
(SAVE) (S) (X) (♿) (🗝) (🛏) (📺) (⌇)

⚑ ▼▼▼ Holiday Inn Express SH ❀
(505) 538-2525. **$95-$104.** 1103 Superior St. 3 mi ne on US 180 and SR 90. Int corridors. **Pets:** Other species. Designated rooms, service with restrictions, supervision.
(SAVE) (X) (📺)

SOCORRO

⚑ ▼▼▼ Best Western Socorro Hotel & Suites SH
(505) 838-0556. **$99-$136.** 1100 California Ave NE. Center. Ext/int corridors. **Pets:** Medium. $10 daily fee/pet. Designated rooms, service with restrictions, supervision.
(SAVE) (S) (X) (♿) (🗝) (♿) (🛏) (📺) (⌇)

⚑ ▼▼ Econo Lodge SH ❀
(505) 835-1500. **$39-$65.** 713 California Ave. I-25, exit 150, 1 mi s. Ext corridors. **Pets:** Medium. $5 daily fee/pet. Supervision.
(SAVE) (S) (X) (🛏) (📺) (⌇) (X)

▼▼ Motel 6 #392 SH
(505) 835-4300. **$39-$51.** 807 S US 85. I-25, exit 147. Ext corridors. **Pets:** Medium, other species. Service with restrictions, supervision.
(S) (X) (♿) (🗝) (♿) (🛏) (⌇)

TAOS

⚑ ▼▼▼ Adobe Sun God Lodge M
(505) 758-3162. **$59-$125.** 919 Paseo del Pueblo Sur. SR 68, 1.8 mi sw of jct US 64 and Taos Plaza. Ext corridors. **Pets:** Accepted.
(SAVE) (X) (🛏) (📺)

⚑ ▼▼▼ American Artists Gallery House Bed & Breakfast BB
(505) 758-4446. **$95-$205, 14 day notice.** 132 Frontier Ln. 1 mi s of jct US 64 and Taos Plaza, 0.3 mi e. Ext/int corridors. **Pets:** Dogs only. $25 daily fee/pet. Designated rooms, service with restrictions, supervision.
(SAVE) (S) (X) (🛏) (📺) (X) (♫)

⚑ ▼▼▼ Brooks Street Inn Bed and Breakfast BB
(505) 758-1489. **$99-$169, 14 day notice.** 119 Brooks St. 0.3 mi n on US 64 from jct SR 68 and Taos Plaza, just e. Int corridors. **Pets:** Accepted.
(SAVE) (S) (X) (🛏) (📺) (♫) (🎿)

▼▼▼ Casa Europa Inn & Gallery BB
(505) 758-9798. $115-$175, 14 day notice. 840 Upper Ranchitos Rd. 1.7 mi s from jct US 64. Ext/int corridors. Pets: Accepted.
(ASK) (S6) (✕) (🛏) (📠) (🐾)

▼▼▼ Inn on La Loma Plaza BB
(505) 758-1717. $140-$425, 15 day notice. 315 Ranchitos Rd. 0.3 mi sw on Ranchitos Rd, just w of Taos Plaza. Ext/int corridors. Pets: Accepted.
(SAVE) (S6) (✕) (🛏) (📠) (🐾)

▼▼▼ Inn On The Rio BB
(505) 758-7199. $85-$129, 15 day notice. 910 Kit Carson Rd. US 64, 1.5 mi e of jct SR 68 and Taos Plaza. Ext corridors. Pets: Dogs only. $20 daily fee/pet. Designated rooms, service with restrictions, supervision.
(SAVE) (S6) (✕) (☕) (🐾) (🐾)

▼▼▼ Orinda Bed & Breakfast BB 🐾
(505) 758-8581. $99-$160, 14 day notice. 461 Valverde St. Just w from jct Don Fernando and Camino de la Placita, then just s; look for Orinda sign. Ext/int corridors. Pets: Medium, dogs only. $7 daily fee/pet. Designated rooms.
(SAVE) (✕) (🛏) (📠)

▼▼ Quality Inn SH
(505) 758-2200. $59-$110, 3 day notice. 1043 Paseo del Pueblo Sur. SR 68, 2 mi sw of jct US 64 and Taos Plaza. Ext/int corridors. Pets: Other species. $7 daily fee/pet. Service with restrictions, supervision.
(ASK) (S6) (✕) (📶) (🛏) (📠) (🍴) (🐾)

▼▼ Sagebrush Inn SH
(505) 758-2254. $59-$165, 3 day notice. 1508 Paseo del Pueblo Sur. SR 68, 3 mi sw of jct US 64 and Taos Plaza. Ext corridors. Pets: Other species. $7 daily fee/pet. Designated rooms, service with restrictions, supervision.
(ASK) (S6) (✕) (📶) (🛏) (📠) (🍴) (🐾)

▼▼▼ San Geronimo Lodge BB
(505) 751-3776. $99-$175, 10 day notice. 1101 Witt Rd. 1.3 mi e of jct SR 68 and Taos Plaza on US 64 (Kit Carson Rd), 0.6 mi s. Ext/int corridors. Pets: $10 one-time fee/room. Designated rooms, service with restrictions, crate.
(SAVE) (S6) (✕) (🖊) (🐾) (🐾)

THOREAU

▼▼ Zuni Mountain Lodge BB 🐾
(505) 862-7616. $95 (no credit cards), 7 day notice. 40 W Perch Dr. I-40, exit 53, 13 mi s on SR 612, then w. Ext/int corridors. Pets: Medium, other species. No service, supervision.
(ASK) (✕) (🐾) (📺) (🐾)

TRUTH OR CONSEQUENCES

▼▼▼ Best Western Hot Springs Motor Inn M
(505) 894-6665. $59-$69. 2270 N Date St. I-25, exit 79. Ext corridors. Pets: Other species. Service with restrictions, supervision.
(SAVE) (S6) (✕) (🛏) (📠) (🐾)

▼▼▼ Comfort Inn & Suites SH
(505) 894-1660. $57-$100. 2250 N Date St. I-25, exit 79, just e. Int corridors. Pets: Other species. Supervision.
(ASK) (S6) (🔌) (📶) (🖊) (🛏) (📠) (🐾)

▼▼▼ Super 8 Motel M 🐾
(505) 894-7888. $46-$48. 2151 N Date St. I-25, exit 79, just s. Int corridors. Pets: Service with restrictions, supervision.
(SAVE) (S6) (✕)

TUCUMCARI

▲▲▲ ◆ Americana Motel M
(505) 461-0431. $34-$40. 406 E Tucumcari Blvd. I-40, exit 332, 1.5 mi n on SR 18, then 0.5 mi e on US 66. Ext corridors. Pets: Small. $5 one-time fee/pet. Designated rooms, service with restrictions, supervision.
(SAVE) (S6) (✕)

▲▲▲ ◆▼ Americas Best Value Inn M
(505) 461-0360. $35-$49. 1023 E Route 66 Blvd. I-40, exit 333, n to Tucumcari Blvd, then 0.6 mi w. Ext corridors. Pets: Accepted.
(SAVE) (S6) (✕) (🛏) (📠) (🐾)

▲▲▲ ◆▼ Best Western Discovery Inn SH
(505) 461-4884. $65-$99. 200 E Estrella. I-40, exit 332. Ext corridors. Pets: Accepted.
(SAVE) (S6) (✕) (🛏) (📠) (🍴) (🐾)

▲▲▲ ◆ Budget Inn M
(505) 461-4139. $32-$50. 824 W Tucumcari Blvd. I-40, exit 332, 1 mi n to Tucumari Blvd, then 1 mi w. Ext corridors. Pets: Medium. $5 one-time fee/pet. No service, supervision.
(SAVE) (S6) (✕)

▼▼▼ Comfort Inn SH
(505) 461-4094. $60-$95. 2800 E Tucumcari Blvd. I-40, exit 335, 0.5 mi w. Ext corridors. Pets: Small. $7 daily fee/pet. No service, supervision.
(ASK) (S6) (✕) (🛏) (📠) (🐾)

▲▲▲ ▼▼▼ Days Inn SH
(505) 461-3158. $55-$70. 2623 S First St. I-40, exit 332, just n. Ext/int corridors. Pets: $6 daily fee/pet. Service with restrictions, supervision.
(SAVE) (S6) (✕) (🛏) (📠)

▲▲▲ ▼▼▼ Econo Lodge SH
(505) 461-4194. $49-$69. 3400 Route 66 Blvd. I-40, exit 335, just n, then just w. Int corridors. Pets: Other species. $5 one-time fee/pet. Designated rooms, service with restrictions, supervision.
(SAVE) (S6) (✕) (🛏)

▲▲▲ ▼▼▼ Holiday Inn SH 🐾
(505) 461-3780. $79-$99. 3716 E Tucumcari Blvd. I-40, exit 335, 0.3 mi w on US 66. Ext corridors. Pets: Other species. $6 one-time fee/room. No service, supervision.
(SAVE) (S6) (✕) (🔌M) (📶) (🛏) (📠) (🍴) (🐾) (✕)

▲▲▲ ▼▼▼ Microtel Inn-Tucumcari SH
(505) 461-0600. $69-$89. 2420 S 1st St. I-40, exit 332, just n. Int corridors. Pets: Medium, other species. $6 daily fee/pet. Service with restrictions, supervision.
(SAVE) (S6) (✕) (🖊) (🛏) (📠) (🐾)

▲▲▲ ▼▼▼ Super 8 Motel M
(505) 461-4444. $50-$75. 4001 E Tucumcari Blvd. I-40, exit 335, just w. Int corridors. Pets: Accepted.
(SAVE) (S6) (✕) (🛏) (🐾)

▼▼▼ Tucumcari Inn SH
(505) 461-7800. $38-$42. 1700 E Route 66 Blvd. I-40, exit 333, 0.5 mi n to Tucumari Blvd, then just w. Ext corridors. Pets: Medium, other species. $5 one-time fee/pet. Designated rooms, service with restrictions, supervision.
(ASK) (S6) (✕) (🛏) (🐾)

VAUGHN

▲▲▲ ▼▼▼ Oak Tree Inn SH
(505) 584-8733. $75-$95. Jct State Hwy 54/60 & 285. 1.5 mi e on US 54, 60 and 285. Ext/int corridors. Pets: Accepted.
(SAVE) (S6) (✕) (🔌M) (📶) (🖊) (🛏) (📠) (🍴)

NEW YORK

CITY INDEX

ALBANY

Albany Clarion Hotel SH
(518) 438-8431. $99-$219. 3 Watervliet Ave Ext. I-90, exit 5 (Everett Rd), just s, then e. Int corridors. Pets: Accepted.

Albany Mansion Hill Inn & Restaurant BB
(518) 465-2038. $175, 5 day notice. 115 Philip St at Park Ave. I-787, exit 3B (Madison Ave/US 20 W) to Philip St, 0.4 mi s. Ext/int corridors. Pets: Other species.

CrestHill Suites SH
(518) 454-0007. $98-$129. 1415 Washington Ave. I-90, exit 2 westbound, just s on Fuller Rd, then just e; exit eastbound, just e. Int corridors. Pets: $75 one-time fee/pet. Service with restrictions.

Extended StayAmerica SH
(518) 446-0680. $65-$85. 1395 Washington Ave. I-90, exit 2 westbound, just s on Fuller Rd, then 0.5 mi e; exit eastbound, just e. Int corridors. Pets: Accepted.

TownePlace Suites by Marriott SH
(518) 435-1900. $165-$185. 1379 Washington Ave. I-90, exit 2 westbound, just s on Fuller Rd, then 0.6 mi e; exit eastbound, just e. Int corridors. Pets: Accepted.

ALLEGANY

Microtel Inn & Suites-Olean/Allegany SH
(716) 373-5333. $55-$69. 3234 NYS Rt 417. I-86, exit 24, 2.1 mi e on SR 417 (State St). Int corridors. Pets: Other species. $10 daily fee/room.

ANGELICA

Angelica Inn B&B BB
(585) 466-3063. $64-$119, 14 day notice. 64 W Main St. I-86, exit 31, 0.5 mi w. Ext/int corridors. Pets: Large, other species. $10 daily fee/pet. Designated rooms, service with restrictions.

APALACHIN

Quality Inn SH
(607) 625-4441. $80-$190. 7666 SR 434. SR 17, exit 66, just e. Int corridors. Pets: Small, other species. $10 daily fee/pet. Service with restrictions, supervision.

AUBURN

Holiday Inn-Auburn/Finger Lakes SH
(315) 253-4531. $79-$179. 75 North St. SR 34, just n of US 20/SR 5. Int corridors. Pets: Accepted.

Inn at the Finger Lakes SH
(315) 253-5000. $100-$160. 12 Seminary Ave. Jct SR 34/38, just e on US 20/SR 5; center. Int corridors. Pets: $15 one-time fee/pet. Designated rooms, service with restrictions, supervision.

AVERILL PARK

La Perla at the Gregory House Country Inn & Restaurant CI
(518) 674-3774. $110-$150, 8 day notice. 3016 SR 43. Center. Int corridors. Pets: Small, dogs only. Service with restrictions, supervision.

BALDWINSVILLE

▼▼ Microtel Inn & Suites SH
(315) 635-9556. **$60-$120.** 131 Downer St. SR 690, exit SR 31 W, 0.4 mi e. Int corridors. **Pets:** Other species. $5 daily fee/pet. Service with restrictions, crate.
[ASK] [S0] [✕] [&M] [✍] [🛏] [💻]

BATAVIA

△△△ ▼ Budget Inn M
(585) 343-7921. **$45-$110.** 301 Oak St. I-90, exit 48, just n. Int corridors. **Pets:** Medium. $5 daily fee/pet. Service with restrictions, supervision.
[SAVE] [S0] [✕] [🛏]

△△△ ▼▼▼ Comfort Inn SH
(585) 344-9999. **$59-$149.** 4371 Federal Dr. I-90, exit 48, just n on SR 98. Int corridors. **Pets:** Large. $10 one-time fee/pet. Service with restrictions, supervision.
[SAVE] [S0] [✕] [&M] [✍] [🛏] [💻] [🏊]

△△△ ▼▼▼ Days Inn SH
(585) 343-6000. **$49-$129.** 200 Oak St. I-90, exit 48, just s. Ext/int corridors. **Pets:** Other species. $10 daily fee/pet. Service with restrictions, supervision.
[SAVE] [S0] [✕] [🛏] [💻] [🍴] [🏊]

△△△ ▼▼▼▼ Holiday Inn-Darien Lake SH
(585) 344-2100. **$54-$129.** 8250 Park Rd. I-90, exit 48, just w. Int corridors. **Pets:** $20 one-time fee/room. Service with restrictions, supervision.
[SAVE] [✕] [🛏] [💻] [🍴] [🏊] [✕]

△△△ ▼▼▼▼ Quality Inn & Suites SH
(585) 344-7000. **$69-$189.** 8200 Park Rd. I-90, exit 48, just w. Int corridors. **Pets:** Small, dogs only. $10 one-time fee/room. Service with restrictions, supervision.
[SAVE] [S0] [✕] [&M] [✍] [🛏] [💻] [🏊]

△△△ ▼▼▼ Ramada Limited SH
(585) 343-1000. **$49-$119.** 8204 Park Rd. I-90, exit 48, just w. Int corridors. **Pets:** Accepted.
[SAVE] [S0] [✕] [💻]

BATH

▼▼ Bath Super 8 SH
(607) 776-2187. **$63-$98.** 333 W Morris St. I-86, exit 38, just n. Int corridors. **Pets:** Service with restrictions, supervision.
[ASK] [S0] [✕] [🛏]

▼▼ Days Inn SH
(607) 776-7644. **$60-$115.** 330 W Morris St. I-86, exit 38, just n. Int corridors. **Pets:** Other species. Service with restrictions, supervision.
[ASK] [S0] [✕] [🛏] [💻] [🍴] [🏊]

BINGHAMTON

△△△ ▼▼▼ Comfort Inn of Binghamton SH
(607) 724-3297. **$85-$200.** 1000 Front St. I-81, exit 5, 1 mi n on US 11 (Front St). Int corridors. **Pets:** Accepted.
[SAVE] [S0] [✕] [&M] [🛏] [💻] [🏊]

▼▼ Grand Royale Hotel-A Clarion Collection Hotel LH
(607) 722-0000. **$73-$250.** 80 State St. Just n of jct Hawley St; downtown. Int corridors. **Pets:** Accepted.
[ASK] [S0] [✕] [🛏] [💻]

▼▼ Motel 6-1222 SH
(607) 771-0400. **$45-$59.** 1012 Front St. I-81, exit 6 southbound, 2 mi s on US 11 (Front St); exit 5 northbound, 1 mi n on US 11 (Front St). Int corridors. **Pets:** Medium, other species. Service with restrictions, supervision.
[S0] [✕] [&M] [✍]

BOHEMIA

▼▼▼▼ La Quinta Inn & Suites-Islip SH
(631) 881-7700. **$159-$239.** 10 Aero Rd. I-495, exit 57, 5.1 mi se on SR 454, just s on Johnson Ave, then just e. Int corridors. **Pets:** Medium. Service with restrictions.
[ASK] [✕] [&M] [🍴] [✍] [🛏] [💻]

BOONVILLE

△△△ ▼ Headwaters Motor Lodge M
(315) 942-4493. **$63-$89.** 13524 Rt 12. Jct SR 12 and 120, 0.7 mi n. Int corridors. **Pets:** Medium. Service with restrictions, supervision.
[SAVE] [S0] [✕] [🛏]

BROCKPORT

▼▼▼▼ Holiday Inn Express SH
(585) 395-1000. **$93-$143.** 4908 Lake Rd S. Just s of jct SR 31, on SR 195. Int corridors. **Pets:** Other species. $15 one-time fee/room. No service, supervision.
[ASK] [S0] [✕] [&M] [🛏] [💻]

BUFFALO METROPOLITAN AREA

AMHERST

△△△ ▼▼▼▼ Comfort Inn University SH
(716) 688-0811. **$89-$139.** 1 Flint Rd. I-290, exit 5B, just n on SR 263 (Millersport Hwy), then just w. Int corridors. **Pets:** Other species. $10 daily fee/pet. Designated rooms, service with restrictions, supervision.
[SAVE] [S0] [✕] [🛏] [💻] [🏊]

▼▼▼▼ Homewood Suites Buffalo/Amherst SH 🐾
(716) 833-2277. **$149-$199.** 1138 Millersport Hwy. I-290, exit 5A, just w. Int corridors. **Pets:** Medium. $75 one-time fee/room. Service with restrictions, supervision.
[ASK] [S0] [✕] [&M] [🛏] [💻] [🏊]

△△△ ▼▼▼ Lord Amherst Hotel M
(716) 839-2200. **$69-$115.** 5000 Main St. I-290, exit 7A, just w on SR 5. Ext/int corridors. **Pets:** Service with restrictions, supervision.
[SAVE] [S0] [✕] [&M] [🛏] [💻] [🏊]

▼▼ Motel 6 Buffalo-Amherst #1298 M
(716) 834-2231. **$43-$65.** 4400 Maple Rd. I-290, exit 5B, just n to Maple Rd, then 0.7 mi w. Int corridors. **Pets:** Medium, other species. Service with restrictions, supervision.
[S0] [✕]

▼▼ Red Roof Inn #7104 M
(716) 689-7474. **$57-$104.** 42 Flint Rd. I-290, exit 5B, just n on SR 263 (Millersport Hwy). Ext corridors. **Pets:** Medium, other species. Service with restrictions, supervision.
[✕] [&M] [🛏]

BLASDELL

△△△ ▼▼▼ Clarion Hotel SH
(716) 648-5700. **$69-$199.** 3950 McKinley Pkwy. I-90, exit 56, 0.4 mi e on SR 179, then 0.8 mi s. Int corridors. **Pets:** Accepted.
[SAVE] [S0] [✕] [✍] [🛏] [💻]

(AAA) ▼▼▼ Econo Lodge South M
(716) 825-7530. **$46-$99.** 4344 Milestrip Rd. I-90, exit 56, just e on SR 179. Ext corridors. **Pets:** Medium. $10 daily fee/room. Designated rooms, service with restrictions, supervision.
[SAVE] [S☐] [X] [☑] [☎] [▢]

BOWMANSVILLE

▼▼ Red Roof Inn-Buffalo Airport #7137 M
(716) 633-1100. **$48-$87.** 146 Maple Dr. Just e of SR 78; just n of entrance to I-90 (New York State Thruway), exit 49. Ext corridors. **Pets:** Medium, other species. Service with restrictions, supervision.
[X] [☑] [☎]

BUFFALO

(AAA) ▼▼▼ Best Western Inn-On The Avenue SH
(716) 886-8333. **$119-$159.** 510 Delaware Ave. Between Virginia and Allen sts; downtown. Int corridors. **Pets:** Medium, dogs only. $100 deposit/room. Designated rooms, service with restrictions.
[SAVE] [S☐] [X] [☒] [☎] [▢]

▼▼▼ Holiday Inn-Downtown SH
(716) 886-2121. **$123-$152.** 620 Delaware Ave. Between Allen and North sts; downtown. Int corridors. **Pets:** $30 one-time fee/pet. Service with restrictions, supervision.
[X] [☎] [▢] [¶] [≈]

CHEEKTOWAGA

(AAA) ▼▼▼ Comfort Suites-Buffalo Airport SH
(716) 633-6000. **$99-$159.** 901 Dick Rd. SR 33, exit Dick Rd, just sw. Int corridors. **Pets:** Medium, other species. $10 daily fee/room. Service with restrictions, crate.
[SAVE] [S☐] [X] [☒M] [☑] [☎] [▢] [≈]

▼▼▼ Holiday Inn Express Hotel & Suites-Buffalo Airport SH
(716) 631-8700. **$110-$160.** 131 Buell Ave. I-90, exit 51 (SR 33), just e on Genesee St (SR 33) then just s. Int corridors. **Pets:** Small, other species. $30 one-time fee/room. Service with restrictions, supervision.
[ASK] [S☐] [X] [☒M] [☑] [☒] [☎] [▢] [≈] [X]

▼▼▼ Homewood Suites by Hilton SH
(716) 685-0700. **$209.** 760 Dick Rd. SR 33, exit Dick Rd, 0.3 mi sw. Int corridors. **Pets:** $100 one-time fee/room. Service with restrictions, supervision.
[X] [☒] [☎] [▢] [≈]

(AAA) ▼▼▼ Millennium Hotel LH
(716) 681-2400. **$99-$159.** 2040 Walden Ave. I-90, exit 52, 0.3 mi e. Ext/int corridors. **Pets:** Accepted.
[SAVE] [S☐] [X] [☑] [☎] [▢] [¶] [≈] [X]

(AAA) ▼▼▼ Oak Tree Inn SH
(716) 681-2600. **$60-$99.** 3475 Union Rd. I-90, exit 52, 0.3 mi e on Walden Ave, just n on SR 277 (Union Rd). Int corridors. **Pets:** Accepted.
[SAVE] [S☐] [X] [☒M] [☑] [☒] [☎] [▢]

▼▼▼ Residence Inn by Marriott SH
(716) 892-5410. **$155-$175.** 107 Anderson Rd. I-90, exit 52 westbound, stay to left off exit ramp. Int corridors. **Pets:** Accepted.
[ASK] [S☐] [X] [☒M] [☑] [☒] [☎] [▢] [≈] [X]

CLARENCE

(AAA) ▼▼▼▼ Asa Ransom House CI
(716) 759-2315. **$105-$175, 7 day notice.** 10529 Main St. Jct SR 78 (Transit Rd), 5.3 mi e on SR 5 (Main St). Int corridors. **Pets:** Medium, dogs only. $100 deposit/room. Designated rooms, service with restrictions.
[SAVE] [S☐] [X] [☒M] [☎] [¶]

GRAND ISLAND

(AAA) ▼▼▼▼ Holiday Inn Grand Island Resort LH
(716) 773-1111. **$99-$189.** 100 Whitehaven Rd. I-190, exit 19, 4 mi e. Int corridors. **Pets:** Dogs only. Designated rooms, supervision.
[SAVE] [S☐] [X] [☑] [☒] [☎] [▢] [¶] [≈] [X]

HAMBURG

(AAA) ▼▼▼ Comfort Inn & Suites SH
(716) 648-2922. **$59-$179.** 3615 Commerce Pl. I-90, exit 57, just w. Int corridors. **Pets:** $10 daily fee/room. Service with restrictions, crate.
[SAVE] [S☐] [X] [☒M] [☒] [☎] [▢] [≈]

(AAA) ▼▼▼ Holiday Inn Hamburg SH
(716) 649-0500. **$69-$189.** 5440 Camp Rd. I-90, exit 57, 0.3 mi se on SR 75. Int corridors. **Pets:** Accepted.
[SAVE] [S☐] [X] [☒] [☎] [▢] [¶] [≈]

▼▼▼ Red Roof Inn #7055 M
(716) 648-7222. **$50-$99.** 5370 Camp Rd. I-90, exit 57, just se on SR 75. Ext corridors. **Pets:** Medium, other species. Service with restrictions, supervision.
[X] [☑] [☎]

(AAA) ▼▼▼ Tallyho-tel M
(716) 648-2000. **$50-$125.** 5245 Camp Rd. I-90, exit 57, just nw on SR 75. Ext corridors. **Pets:** Accepted.
[SAVE] [X] [☎] [≈]

KENMORE

▼▼▼ Super 8-Buffalo/Niagara Falls SH
(716) 876-4020. **$53-$84.** 1288 Sheridan Dr. I-190, exit 15, 1.5 mi e on SR 324 (Sheridan Dr). Int corridors. **Pets:** Medium. Service with restrictions, supervision.
[S☐] [X] [☎]

SPRINGVILLE

▼▼▼ Microtel Inn & Suites SH
(716) 592-3141. **$54-$94.** 270 S Cascade Dr. On SR 219 S. Int corridors. **Pets:** Other species. $10 daily fee/room. Service with restrictions, crate.
[ASK] [S☐] [X] [☑] [☒] [☎] [▢]

TONAWANDA

(AAA) ▼▼▼ Econo Lodge M
(716) 694-6696. **$49-$179.** 2000 Niagara Falls Blvd. I-290, exit 3 (Niagara Falls Blvd), 0.5 mi n on US 62. Ext corridors. **Pets:** Accepted.
[SAVE] [S☐] [X] [☎] [▢]

▼▼▼ Microtel-Tonawanda SH
(716) 693-8100. **$52-$90.** 1 Hospitality Centre Way. I-290, exit 1B westbound; exit 1 eastbound, 0.5 mi e on Crestmount Ave, then just n on SR 384 (Delaware St). Int corridors. **Pets:** Medium. $10 daily fee/pet. Service with restrictions, supervision.
[ASK] [X] [☒M] [☎]

WILLIAMSVILLE

▼▼▼ Residence Inn by Marriott Buffalo/Amherst SH
(716) 632-6622. **$79-$219.** 100 Maple Rd. I-290, exit 5B, just n (on Millersport Hwy) to Maple Rd exit, then just e. Ext corridors. **Pets:** Large, other species. $75 one-time fee/room. Service with restrictions, crate.
[ASK] [S☐] [X] [☒M] [☑] [☎] [▢] [≈] [X]

CALCIUM

▼▼ **Microtel Inn Watertown** SH
(315) 629-5000. **$58-$64.** 8000 Virginia Smith Dr. 4 mi e on SR 342; jct US 11. Int corridors. **Pets:** Other species. $100 deposit/pet, $3 daily fee/pet. Service with restrictions, supervision.
ASK S✪ ✕ ⌁ ⬛

CANANDAIGUA

◆◆◆ ▼▼ **Econo Lodge Canandaigua** SH ❀
(585) 394-9000. **$59-$127.** 170 Eastern Blvd. Jct SR 332, 5 and US 20, 0.5 mi e. Int corridors. **Pets:** Medium. $10 daily fee/pet. Designated rooms, service with restrictions, supervision.
SAVE S✪ ✕ ⬛ ⬛

◆◆◆ ▼▼▼ **The Inn On The Lake** SH
(585) 394-7800. **$104-$349, 30 day notice.** 770 S Main St. I-90, exit 44 (Canandaigua/SR 332), just s across US 20 and SR 5. Int corridors. **Pets:** Medium. $25 daily fee/pet. Designated rooms, service with restrictions, crate.
SAVE S✪ ✕ ⌂M ⌁ ⛄ ⬛ ⬛ ⑪ ⊃ ✕

CANASTOTA

▼▼ **Days Inn** SH
(315) 697-3309. **$59-$169, 7 day notice.** 377 N Peterboro St. I-90, exit 34 on SR 13. Int corridors. **Pets:** Other species. $15 daily fee/room. Designated rooms, service with restrictions, supervision.
ASK S✪ ✕ ⬛ ⬛

CATSKILL

◆◆◆ ▼▼ **Catskill Quality Inn & Conference Center** SH
(518) 943-5800. **$59-$269.** 704 Rt 23B. I-87 (New York State Thruway), exit 21, just w. Ext/int corridors. **Pets:** Large. $20 daily fee/pet. Service with restrictions, supervision.
SAVE S✪ ✕ ⬛ ⬛ ⑪ ⊃

CHESTER

◆◆◆ ▼▼▼ **Holiday Inn Express Hotel & Suites** SH ❀
(845) 469-3000. **$109-$250.** 2 Bryle Pl. SR 17, exit 126, just n on SR 94, then just w on SR 17M (Brookside Ave). Int corridors. **Pets:** $30 one-time fee/room. Designated rooms.
SAVE S✪ ✕ ⌂M ⌁ ⛄ ⬛ ⬛ ⊃ ✕

CICERO

◆◆◆ ▼ **Budget Inn** M
(315) 458-3510. **$48-$115.** 901 S Bay Rd. I-481, exit 10, just n. Ext corridors. **Pets:** Small, dogs only. $10 daily fee/pet. Service with restrictions, supervision.
SAVE S✪ ✕ ⬛

CLAY

▼▼▼ **Fairfield Inn by Marriott-Syracuse** SH
(315) 622-2576. **$105-$125.** 3979 SR 31. Jct SR 481, exit 12, just w. Int corridors. **Pets:** Accepted.
ASK S✪ ✕ ⌂M ⛄ ⬛ ⬛ ⊃

CLAYTON

◆◆◆ ▼▼ **Fair Wind Lodge** M
(315) 686-5251. **$50-$85, 7 day notice.** 38201 NYS Rt 12E. 2.3 mi sw. Ext corridors. **Pets:** Service with restrictions, supervision.
SAVE ✕ ⬛ ⊃ ⌁

CLINTON

▼▼▼ **Amidst the Hedges** BB ❀
(315) 853-3031. **$120-$150, 10 day notice.** 180 Sanford Ave. College St, 0.3 mi n on Elm St. Int corridors. **Pets:** Dogs only. Service with restrictions, supervision.
✕ ⬛ ⬛ ⊃

COBLESKILL

◆◆◆ ▼▼▼ **Best Western Inn of Cobleskill** SH
(518) 234-4321. **$79-$199.** 121 Burgin Dr. I-88, exit 21 eastbound on SR 7, 0.8 mi e of jct SR 10; exit 22 westbound, 2.9 mi w on SR 27. Int corridors. **Pets:** Accepted.
SAVE S✪ ✕ ⌂M ⌁ ⬛ ⬛ ⑪ ⊃

▼▼ **Super 8** SH
(518) 234-4888. **$69-$125.** 955 E Main St. I-88, exit 22 westbound, 2.4 mi w on SR 7; exit 21 eastbound, 3.1 mi e on SR 7. Int corridors. **Pets:** Medium, other species. $11 one-time fee/pet. Service with restrictions, supervision.
ASK S✪ ✕ ⌂M ⌁ ⛄

COLONIE

▼ **America's Best Value Inn** M
(518) 456-8982. **$49-$99, 3 day notice.** 1600 Central Ave. I-87, exit 2 (SR 5), 0.8 mi w. Ext corridors. **Pets:** Accepted.
ASK S✪ ✕

◆◆◆ ▼▼▼ **Cocca's Inn & Suites, Wolf Rd** M
(518) 459-2240. **$89-$149.** 2 Wolf Rd. I-87, exit 2E, just e. Ext/int corridors. **Pets:** Accepted.
SAVE S✪ ✕ ⬛ ⬛

▼▼▼ **Holiday Inn Turf on Wolf Road** SH
(518) 458-7250. **$149-$189, 3 day notice.** 205 Wolf Rd. I-87, exit 4, 0.3 mi se. Int corridors. **Pets:** Accepted.
ASK S✪ ✕ ⌂M ⌁ ⛄ ⬛ ⬛ ⑪ ⊃ ✕

▼▼ **Red Roof Inn #7112** M
(518) 459-1971. **$69-$112.** 188 Wolf Rd. I-87, exit 4, just se to Wolf Rd, then just sw. Ext corridors. **Pets:** Medium, other species. Service with restrictions, supervision.
✕ ⌂M ⬛

CORNING

▼▼▼ **Radisson Hotel Corning** SH
(607) 962-5000. **$99-$159.** 125 Denison Pkwy E. On I-86/SR 17; center. Int corridors. **Pets:** Accepted.
ASK S✪ ✕ ⬛ ⬛ ⑪ ⊃

▼▼▼ **Staybridge Suites by Holiday Inn** SH
(607) 936-7800. **$150-$185.** 201 Townley Ave. I-86/SR 17, exit 46, just s. Int corridors. **Pets:** Other species. $75 one-time fee/room. Service with restrictions, supervision.
ASK S✪ ✕ ⌂M ⛄ ⬛ ⬛ ⊃ ✕

CORTLAND

▼▼ **Comfort Inn** SH
(607) 753-7721. **$79-$199.** 2 1/2 Locust Ave. I-81, exit 11, just e. Int corridors. **Pets:** Medium. $10 one-time fee/room. Service with restrictions, supervision.
ASK S✪ ✕ ⬛ ⬛ ⑪

◆◆◆ ▼ **Econo Lodge** M
(607) 756-2856. **$59-$179.** 10 Church St. I-81, exit 11, 0.8 mi s on SR 13/41 and US 11. Ext corridors. **Pets:** Accepted.
SAVE S✪ ✕ ⬛ ⬛

◬ ▽▽▽ Holiday Inn Cortland 🆂🅷
(607) 756-4431. **$69-$189.** 2 River St. I-81, exit 11, just s on SR 13. Int corridors. **Pets:** Other species. $25 one-time fee/room. Service with restrictions, supervision.
🆂🅰🆅🅴 🆂🅾 ✖ 🎣 🍴 ➿

◬ ▽▽▽ Quality Inn Cortland 🆂🅷
(607) 756-5622. **$79-$199.** 188 Clinton St. I-81, exit 11, just n. Int corridors. **Pets:** Other species. $20 one-time fee/room. Designated rooms, service with restrictions, supervision.
🆂🅰🆅🅴 🆂🅾 ✖ 🎣

CUBA

◬ ▽▽▽ Cuba Econo Lodge Ⓜ
(585) 968-1992. **$59-$109.** 1 North Branch Rd. I-86, exit 28, n to N Branch Rd, then e. Int corridors. **Pets:** Medium. $10 daily fee/pet. Designated rooms, service with restrictions, supervision.
🆂🅰🆅🅴 🆂🅾 ✖ 🎣

DELHI

◬ ▽ Buena Vista Motel Ⓜ
(607) 746-2135. **$99-$110.** 18718 State Hwy 28. Jct SR 10, 0.8 mi e. Ext corridors. **Pets:** Small, dogs only. $15 daily fee/pet. Designated rooms, service with restrictions, supervision.
🆂🅰🆅🅴 ✖ 🎣

DE WITT

◬ ▽▽▽ Econo Lodge Ⓜ
(315) 446-3300. **$70-$140.** 3400 Erie Blvd E. I-481, exit 3, 1.2 mi w on SR 5; I-690, exit 17 S (Bridge St), just e on Erie Blvd (SR 5). Ext corridors. **Pets:** Medium. $10 daily fee/pet. Service with restrictions, supervision.
🆂🅰🆅🅴 🆂🅾 ✖ 🎣

DUNKIRK

◬ ▽▽▽▽ Best Western Dunkirk/Fredonia 🆂🅷
(716) 366-7100. **$69-$149.** 3912 Vineyard Dr. I-90, exit 59, just w. Int corridors. **Pets:** Large, other species. $10 daily fee/pet. Designated rooms, service with restrictions, supervision.
🆂🅰🆅🅴 🆂🅾 ✖ 🎣 🍴 ➿

◬ ▽▽▽▽ Clarion Hotel Marina & Conference Center 🆂🅷
(716) 366-8350. **$89-$209.** 30 Lake Shore Dr E. Jct SR 60, 0.3 mi w on SR 5. Int corridors. **Pets:** $10 daily fee/pet. Designated rooms, service with restrictions, supervision.
🆂🅰🆅🅴 🆂🅾 ✖ 🎣 🍴 ➿

◬ ▽▽▽▽ Comfort Inn 🆂🅷
(716) 672-4450. **$69-$149.** 3925 Vineyard Dr. I-90, exit 59, just w of jct SR 60. Int corridors. **Pets:** Large, other species. $10 daily fee/pet. Designated rooms, service with restrictions, supervision.
🆂🅰🆅🅴 🆂🅾 ✖ 🎣

EAST GREENBUSH

▽▽▽▽ Residence Inn by Marriott 🆂🅷
(518) 720-3600. **$169-$259.** 3 Tech Valley Dr. I-90, exit 9, just e. Int corridors. **Pets:** Large, other species. $75 one-time fee/room. Service with restrictions, crate.
🅰🆂🅺 🆂🅾 ✖ 🎣 🍴 ➿

EAST SYRACUSE

▽▽▽▽ Candlewood Suites Syracuse 🆂🅷
(315) 432-1684. **$109-$199.** 6550 Baptist Way. I-90, exit 35 (Carrier Cir) to SR 298 E to Old Collamer Rd, just n. Int corridors. **Pets:** Accepted.
🅰🆂🅺 🆂🅾 ✖ 🎣 🍴

◬ ▽▽▽▽ Comfort Inn-Carrier Circle 🆂🅷
(315) 437-0222. **$59-$134.** 6491 Thompson Rd S. I-90, exit 35 (Carrier Cir). Ext/int corridors. **Pets:** Accepted.
🆂🅰🆅🅴 🆂🅾 ✖ 🎣

▽▽▽▽ CrestHill Suites 🆂🅷
(315) 432-5595. **$119-$219, 7 day notice.** 6410 New Venture Gear Dr. I-90, exit 35 (Carrier Cir) to SR 298 E, just s. Int corridors. **Pets:** Other species. $50 one-time fee/room. Service with restrictions, supervision.
🅰🆂🅺 🆂🅾 ✖ 🎣

▽▽▽ Extended StayAmerica Hotels-Syracuse-Dewitt 🆂🅷
(315) 463-1958. **$45-$90.** 6630 Old Collamer Rd. I-90, exit 35 (Carrier Cir) to SR 298 E, just n. Int corridors. **Pets:** Accepted.
🅰🆂🅺 🆂🅾 ✖ 🎣

◬ ▽▽▽▽ Holiday Inn East-Carrier Circle 🆂🅷
(315) 437-2761. **$90-$169.** 6555 Old Collamer Rd. I-90, exit 35 (Carrier Cir) to SR 298 E, just n. Ext/int corridors. **Pets:** $25 one-time fee/room. Designated rooms, service with restrictions, supervision.
🆂🅰🆅🅴 🆂🅾 ✖ 🎣 🍴 ➿

▽▽▽ Red Roof Inn #7157 Ⓜ
(315) 437-3309. **$52-$84.** 6614 N Thompson Rd. I-90, exit 35 (Carrier Cir), just n. Ext corridors. **Pets:** Medium, other species. Service with restrictions, supervision.
✖ 🎣

▽▽▽▽ Residence Inn by Marriott 🆂🅷 ❀
(315) 432-4488. **$169-$229.** 6420 Yorktown Cir. I-90, exit 35 (Carrier Cir) to SR 298, just e to Old Collamer Rd, then 0.5 mi n. Ext corridors. **Pets:** Other species. $75 one-time fee/room. Service with restrictions.
🅰🆂🅺 🆂🅾 ✖ 🎣 🍴 ➿

ELLICOTTVILLE

◬ ▽▽▽ The Jefferson Inn of Ellicottville 🅱🅱
(716) 699-5869. **$79-$219, 30 day notice.** 3 Jefferson St. Western jct US 219 and SR 242, just n; eastern jct US 219 and 242, 0.8 mi w. Ext/int corridors. **Pets:** Accepted.
🆂🅰🆅🅴 ✖ 🎣

◬ ▽▽▽▽ Sugar Pine Lodge 🅱🅱 ❀
(716) 699-4855. **$95-$258, 30 day notice.** 6158 Jefferson St, Rt 219 S. Jct US 219 and SR 242, 0.5 mi s on US 219. Ext/int corridors. **Pets:** Large. $20 one-time fee/room. Designated rooms.
🆂🅰🆅🅴 ✖ 🎣 ➿

ELMIRA

◬ ▽▽▽ Coachman Motor Lodge Ⓜ
(607) 733-5526. **$75-$120.** 908 Pennsylvania Ave. SR 17, exit 56 (Church St), 0.5 mi w on SR 352, 0.5 mi s on Madison Ave, then 1.4 mi s. Ext corridors. **Pets:** Medium. Service with restrictions, supervision.
🆂🅰🆅🅴 🆂🅾 🎣

FALCONER

▽▽▽ Red Roof Inn Jamestown/Falconer #7273 🆂🅷
(716) 665-3670. **$59-$83.** 1980 E Main St. I-86, exit 13, just w. Int corridors. **Pets:** Medium, other species. Service with restrictions, supervision.
✖

FARMINGTON

◬ ▽▽▽ Budget Inn Ⓜ
(585) 924-5020. **$54-$89, 3 day notice.** 6001 Rt 96. I-90, exit 44, 1 mi s on SR 332, then just e. Ext corridors. **Pets:** Small, dogs only. $10 one-time fee/pet. Service with restrictions, supervision.
🆂🅰🆅🅴 🆂🅾 ✖ 🎣

FAYETTEVILLE

▽▽▽▽ Craftsman Inn 🆂🅷
(315) 637-8000. **$165.** 7300 E Genesee St (SR 5). Across from Fayetteville Towne Center. Int corridors. **Pets:** Large, dogs only. Designated rooms, no service, supervision.
🅰🆂🅺 ✖ 🎣 🍴

FISHKILL

♦♦ Extended StayAmerica-Fishkill-Poughkeepsie SH
(845) 896-0592. **$109-$129.** 55 W Merritt Blvd. I-84, exit 13, just n. Int corridors. **Pets:** Accepted.
ASK SÔ ⅃M 🖧 🔒 🖵

**♦♦♦ Homestead Studio Suites
Hotel-Fishkill-Poughkeepsie** SH
(845) 897-2800. **$114-$144.** 25 Merritt Blvd. I-84, exit 13, just n. Int corridors. **Pets:** Accepted.
ASK SÔ ✕ 🖉 🖧 🔒 🖵

♦♦♦ Residence Inn by Marriott SH
(845) 896-5210. **$169-$209.** 14 Schuyler Blvd. I-84, exit 13, just n. Ext corridors. **Pets:** Accepted.
ASK SÔ ✕ ⅃M 🖉 🖧 🔒 🖵 ⇆ ✕

♦♦♦ Sierra Suites Poughkeepsie-Fishkill SH
(845) 897-5757. **$139-$189.** 100 Westage Business Center Dr. I-84, exit 13, just n to Merritt Blvd, then left at first light. Int corridors. **Pets:** Accepted.
ASK SÔ ✕ ⅃M 🖉 🖧 🔒 🖵 ⇆

FREDONIA

AAA ♦♦ Days Inn Dunkirk-Fredonia SH
(716) 673-1351. **$75-$115.** 10455 Bennett Rd. I-90, exit 59, just s on SR 60. Int corridors. **Pets:** Medium. $10 one-time fee/pet. Designated rooms, service with restrictions, supervision.
SAVE SÔ ✕ 🔒 🖵 🍽 ⇆

AAA ♦♦♦ The White Inn CI
(716) 672-2103. **$89-$199.** 52 E Main St. I-90, exit 59, 0.5 mi s on SR 60, then 1.3 mi sw on US 20 (Main St); center. Int corridors. **Pets:** Other species. $20 one-time fee/room.
SAVE SÔ ✕ 🔒 🍽

FULTON

♦♦♦ Riverside Inn SH
(315) 593-2444. **$59-$145.** 930 S 1st St. On SR 481. Int corridors. **Pets:** Other species. $100 deposit/room. Service with restrictions, supervision.
ASK SÔ ✕ 🔒 🖵 🍽 ⇆

GARDEN CITY

♦♦♦ Wingate Inn SH
(516) 705-9000. **$169-$199.** 821 Stewart Ave. Meadowbrook Pkwy, exit 3, 0.5 mi w. Int corridors. **Pets:** Small, dogs only. $50 one-time fee/room. Designated rooms, service with restrictions, crate.
ASK SÔ ✕ ⅃M 🖧 🔒 🖵

GATES

♦♦♦ Holiday Inn-Rochester Airport SH
(585) 328-6000. **$109-$149.** 911 Brooks Ave. I-390, exit 18A (SR 204), just e. Int corridors. **Pets:** Accepted.
ASK SÔ ✕ 🖉 🔒 🖵 🍽 ⇆ ✕

GENESEO

♦♦ Quality Inn Geneseo SH
(585) 243-0500. **$95-$165.** 4242 Lakeville Rd. I-390, exit 8, 3.4 mi w on SR 20A. Int corridors. **Pets:** Medium. $15 daily fee/room. Designated rooms, service with restrictions, crate.
ASK SÔ ✕ 🖉 🖵

GENEVA

♦♦♦ Hampton Inn Geneva SH
(315) 781-2035. **$114-$192.** 43 Lake St. Jct Exchange St. Int corridors. **Pets:** Accepted.
ASK SÔ ✕ ⅃M 🖉 🖧 🔒 🖵 ⇆

AAA ♦♦♦ Ramada Inn Geneva Lakefront SH 🐾
(315) 789-0400. **$92-$325.** 41 Lakefront Dr. I-90, exit 42, 8 mi s on SR 14. Int corridors. **Pets:** $10 daily fee/pet. Service with restrictions, supervision.
SAVE SÔ ✕ 🖧 🔒 🖵 🍽 ⇆

GREAT NECK

♦♦♦ The Andrew Hotel SH 🐾
(516) 482-2900. **$279-$299.** 75 N Station Plaza. Jct SR 25A, 0.8 mi n on Middle Neck Rd, just e. Int corridors. **Pets:** Medium. $150 one-time fee/pet. Service with restrictions, supervision.
ASK SÔ ✕ 🔒

♦♦♦ Inn at Great Neck SH
(516) 773-2000. **$269.** 30 Cutter Mill Rd. Jct SR 25A, 0.8 mi n on Middle Neck Rd, just w. Int corridors. **Pets:** Small, dogs only. $200 deposit/pet. Designated rooms, service with restrictions, supervision.
ASK SÔ ✕ 🖧 🔒 🖵 🍽

GREECE

♦♦ Extended Stay America-Rochester-Greece SH
(585) 663-5558. **$60-$90.** 600 Center Place Dr. I-390, exit 24A, just e on SR 104 (Ridge Rd), then just n on Buckman Rd. Int corridors. **Pets:** Accepted.
ASK SÔ ✕ ⅃M 🖉 🖧 🔒 🖵

♦♦♦ Hampton Inn-Rochester North SH
(585) 663-6070. **$125-$155.** 500 Center Place Dr. I-390, exit 24A, just e on SR 104 (Ridge Rd), then just n on Buckman Rd. Int corridors. **Pets:** Accepted.
ASK SÔ ✕ ⅃M 🖧 🔒 🖵

♦♦♦ Residence Inn by Marriott-West SH 🐾
(585) 865-2090. **$109-$249.** 500 Paddy Creek Cir. I-390, exit 24A, just e on SR 104 (Ridge Rd), just s on Hoover Dr, then just w. Int corridors. **Pets:** Other species. $100 one-time fee/room. Service with restrictions, crate.
ASK SÔ ✕ 🖧 🔒 🖵 ⇆ ✕

GUILDERLAND

AAA ♦♦♦ Best Western Sovereign Hotel Albany SH
(518) 489-2981. **$99-$159.** 1228 Western Ave. I-87/90, exit 24, follow signs to US 20 (Western Ave), then 1 mi e. Int corridors. **Pets:** Accepted.
SAVE SÔ ✕ 🖉 🖧 🔒 🖵 🍽 ⇆ ✕

HANCOCK

♦♦ Smith's Colonial Motel M
(607) 637-2989. **$75-$130.** 23085 State Hwy 97. SR 17, exit 87, 2.7 mi s. Ext corridors. **Pets:** Accepted.

HAUPPAUGE

AAA ♦♦♦ Residence Inn by Marriott SH
(631) 724-4188. **$129-$229.** 850 Veterans Memorial Hwy. I-495, exit 57, 1.2 mi nw. Int corridors. **Pets:** Accepted.
SAVE SÔ ✕ ⅃M 🖉 🖧 🔒 🖵 ⇆ ✕

AAA ♦♦♦ Sheraton Long Island Hotel LH 🐾
(631) 231-1100. **$109-$229.** 110 Vanderbilt Motor Pkwy. I-495, exit 53 (Wicks Rd), just n, then 0.3 mi e. Int corridors. **Pets:** Medium, dogs only. Designated rooms, service with restrictions, supervision.
SAVE SÔ ✕ ⅃M 🖉 🖧 🔒 🖵 🍽 ⇆ ✕

HENRIETTA

♦♦♦ Comfort Suites by Choice Hotels of Rochester SH
(585) 334-6620. **$135-$155.** 2085 Hylan Dr. I-390, exit 13, just e. Int corridors. **Pets:** Accepted.
ASK SÔ ✕ ⅃M 🖧 🔒 🖵 ⇆

▼▼ Extended StayAmerica-Rochester-Henrietta SH
(585) 427-7580. **$55-$95.** 700 Commons Way. I-390, exit 14B southbound; exit 14 northbound, just e on SR 252 (Jefferson Rd), then just s. Int corridors. **Pets:** Accepted.
(ASK) (S) (M) (✓) (🛏) (💻) (💻)

▼▼▼ Homewood Suites by Hilton-Rochester SH
(585) 334-9150. **$175-$195.** 2095 Hylan Dr. I-390, exit 13, just e. Int corridors. **Pets:** Accepted.
(ASK) (S) (✕) (M) (✓) (🛏) (💻) (🏊)

▼▼ Microtel-Rochester SH
(585) 334-3400. **$45-$99.** 905 Lehigh Station Rd. I-390, exit 12 northbound; exit 12A southbound, just w on SR 253. Int corridors. **Pets:** Small. $75 deposit/room, $10 daily fee/pet. Designated rooms, service with restrictions, supervision.
(ASK) (S) (✕) (✓) (🛏)

▼▼▼ Radisson Rochester Airport SH
(585) 475-1910. **$109-$159, 3 day notice.** 175 Jefferson Rd. I-390, exit 14A southbound; exit 14 northbound, 3 mi w on SR 252 (Jefferson Rd). Int corridors. **Pets:** Small. $35 deposit/room. Designated rooms, service with restrictions, supervision.
(ASK) (S) (✕) (M) (✓) (🛏) (💻) (💻) (🍴) (🏊)

▼▼ Red Roof Inn-Henrietta #7042 M
(585) 359-1100. **$53-$88.** 4820 W Henrietta Rd. I-390, exit 12 northbound; exit 12A southbound, 0.5 mi w on SR 253, then just s on SR 15 (Henrietta Rd). Ext corridors. **Pets:** Medium, other species. Service with restrictions, supervision.
(✕) (🛏)

▼▼▼ Residence Inn by Marriott SH
(585) 272-8850. **$169-$299.** 1300 Jefferson Rd. I-390, exit 14A southbound, 0.5 mi e on SR 252 (Jefferson Rd); exit 14 northbound, just n on SR 15A, then 0.5 mi e on SR 252 (Jefferson Rd). Ext/int corridors. **Pets:** Other species. $100 one-time fee/room. Crate.
(ASK) (S) (✕) (✓) (🛏) (💻) (🏊) (✕)

▼▼▼ R I T Inn & Conference Center SH
(585) 359-1800. **$89-$115.** 5257 W Henrietta Rd. I-390, exit 12 northbound; exit 12A southbound, 0.5 mi w on SR 253, then 0.7 mi s. Int corridors. **Pets:** Accepted.
(ASK) (S) (✕) (✓) (🛏) (💻) (🏊) (✕)

HERKIMER

▲▲▲ ▼▼▼ Herkimer Motel M
(315) 866-0490. **$68-$88.** 100 Marginal Rd. I-90, exit 30, just n on SR 28. Ext/int corridors. **Pets:** Service with restrictions, supervision.
(SAVE) (S) (✕) (✓) (🛏) (💻) (🏊)

HIGHLAND

▼▼ Super 8 Motel M
(845) 691-6888. **$65-$141.** 3423 Rt 9W. Just s of jct SR 299 and US 9W. Int corridors. **Pets:** Accepted.
(ASK) (✕) (M) (✓) (🛏)

HORNELL

▲▲▲ ▼▼▼ Econo Lodge M
(607) 324-0800. **$60-$65.** 7462 Seneca Rd. Jct I-86 and SR 36, exit 34, just s to SR 21, just e to Seneca Rd, then just s. Ext/int corridors. **Pets:** Other species. $7 daily fee/pet. No service.
(SAVE) (S) (✕) (🛏) (💻) (🍴)

HUNTER

▼▼▼ Hunter Inn SH
(518) 263-3777. **$89-$245, 14 day notice.** Rt 23A. Jct SR 296, 1.9 mi e. Int corridors. **Pets:** Accepted.
(ASK) (✕) (🛏) (✕)

HUNTINGTON STATION

▲▲▲ ▼▼▼ Whitman Motor Lodge M
(631) 271-2800. **$90-$110.** 295 E Jericho Tpke. On SR 25 (Jericho Tpke), 0.6 mi e of SR 110. Ext/int corridors. **Pets:** Small, other species. $200 deposit/room, $20 daily fee/pet. Service with restrictions, crate.
(SAVE) (✕) (🛏) (💻)

INLET

▲▲▲ ▼▼ Marina Motel M
(315) 357-3883. **$69-$149, 14 day notice.** 6 S Shore Rd. Center. Ext corridors. **Pets:** Other species. $10 daily fee/pet. Service with restrictions, crate.
(SAVE) (✕) (🛏)

IRONDEQUOIT

▼▼▼ Holiday Inn Express SH
(585) 342-0430. **$115-$135.** 2200 Goodman St N. SR 104, exit Goodman St, just n. Int corridors. **Pets:** Accepted.
(ASK) (S) (✕) (✓) (🛏) (💻) (🏊)

ITHACA

▲▲▲ ▼▼▼▼ Best Western University Inn M
(607) 272-6100. **$139-$209, 14 day notice.** 1020 Ellis Hollow Rd. From SR 79, 1 mi ne on Pine Tree Rd, just n; in East Hill Plaza. Int corridors. **Pets:** Accepted.
(SAVE) (S) (✕) (✓) (🛏) (💻) (🏊)

▲▲▲ ▼▼▼ Comfort Inn SH 🐾
(607) 272-0100. **$99-$250.** 356 Elmira Rd. Jct SR 96, 89 and 79, 1.5 mi sw on SR 13. Int corridors. **Pets:** $30 one-time fee/room. Service with restrictions, supervision.
(SAVE) (S) (✕) (M) (🛏) (💻)

▲▲▲ ▼▼▼ Hampton Inn SH
(607) 277-5500. **$119-$250.** 337 Elmira Rd. On SR 13. Int corridors. **Pets:** Medium, dogs only. $75 deposit/room. Designated rooms, service with restrictions, supervision.
(SAVE) (S) (✕) (M) (✓) (🛏) (💻) (🏊)

▼▼▼ Holiday Inn Ithaca Downtown SH 🐾
(607) 272-1000. **$152-$171.** 222 S Cayuga St. Just n of SR 96B. Int corridors. **Pets:** Medium. $15 one-time fee/room. Designated rooms, service with restrictions, supervision.
(✕) (✓) (🛏) (💻) (🍴) (🏊)

▼▼▼ La Tourelle Resort and Spa CI
(607) 273-2734. **$125-$375, 3 day notice.** 1150 Danby Rd. 2.7 mi s on SR 96B. Int corridors. **Pets:** Dogs only. $25 daily fee/pet. Designated rooms, service with restrictions, supervision.
(ASK) (S) (✕) (🛏) (💻) (🍴) (✕)

▲▲▲ ▼▼▼ Meadow Court Inn M
(607) 273-3885. **$55-$295.** 529 S Meadow St. 1.5 mi s on SR 13 and 96. Ext/int corridors. **Pets:** $10 daily fee/pet. Designated rooms, service with restrictions, crate.
(SAVE) (✕) (M) (✓) (🛏) (💻) (🍴)

JAMESTOWN

▲▲▲ ▼▼▼ Comfort Inn SH
(716) 664-5920. **$70-$150.** 2800 N Main St. I-86, exit 12, just s on SR 60. Int corridors. **Pets:** Other species. $12 one-time fee/pet. Service with restrictions, supervision.
(SAVE) (S) (✕) (🛏) (💻)

▲▲▲ ▼▼▼ Holiday Inn LH
(716) 664-3400. **$79-$119.** 150 W 4th St. I-86, exit 12, 2 mi s on SR 60 (Washington St); center. Int corridors. **Pets:** Small. $50 deposit/room, $25 daily fee/room. Designated rooms, service with restrictions, crate.
(SAVE) (S) (✕) (✓) (M) (🛏) (💻) (🍴) (🏊)

JOHNSON CITY

Best Western of Johnson City SH
(607) 729-9194. **$65-$165.** 569 Harry L Dr. SR 17, exit 70N, 0.3 mi n.
Int corridors. **Pets:** Accepted.

SAVE S X

La Quinta Inn SH
(607) 770-9333. **$65-$199.** 581 Harry L Dr. SR 17, exit 70, 0.3 mi n. Int
corridors. **Pets:** Other species. Service with restrictions, supervision.

ASK S X

Red Roof Inn-Binghamton #7203 M
(607) 729-8940. **$55-$96.** 590 Fairview St. SR 17, exit 70, 0.3 mi n,
then just n on Reynolds Rd. Ext corridors. **Pets:** Medium, other species.
Service with restrictions, supervision.

X

JOHNSTOWN

Holiday Inn SH
(518) 762-4686. **$93-$160.** 308 N Comrie Ave. Jct SR 30A and 29 E,
1.3 mi n. Ext/int corridors. **Pets:** Accepted.

ASK S X

KINGSTON

Holiday Inn SH
(845) 338-0400. **$139-$189, 3 day notice.** 503 Washington Ave. I-87,
exit 19, just e of traffic circle. Int corridors. **Pets:** Accepted.

SAVE S X

LAKE GEORGE

Balmoral Motel/Lake George Inn M
(518) 668-2673. **$49-$125, 10 day notice.** 444 Canada St. I-87, exit
22, 0.3 mi s on US 9. Ext corridors. **Pets:** $15 daily fee/pet. Designated
rooms, service with restrictions, supervision.

ASK S X

Green Haven M
(518) 668-2489. **$54-$109, 10 day notice.** 3136 Lake Shore Dr. I-87,
exit 22, 0.8 mi n on SR 9N. Ext corridors. **Pets:** Large, dogs only. $10
one-time fee/pet. Service with restrictions, supervision.

X

Lake Haven Motel M
(518) 668-2260. **$49-$129, 10 day notice.** 442 Canada St. I-87, exit
22, 0.4 mi s on US 9. Ext corridors. **Pets:** Large, dogs only. $10 daily
fee/pet. Designated rooms, service with restrictions, crate.

ASK S X

Travelodge of Lake George M
(518) 668-5421. **$84-$168.** 2011 SR 9. I-87, exit 21, just s. Ext corridors. **Pets:** Medium. $20 daily fee/pet. Service with restrictions, supervi-
sion.

SAVE S X

LAKE LUZERNE

Luzerne Court M
(518) 696-2734. **$75-$180, 14 day notice.** 508 Lake Ave. I-87, exit 21,
8.7 mi s on SR 9N. Ext corridors. **Pets:** Dogs only. $25 one-time fee/
room. Service with restrictions, supervision.

SAVE X

LAKE PLACID

Art Devlin's Olympic Motor Inn, Inc. M
(518) 523-3700. **$64-$168, 14 day notice.** 2764 Main St. 0.5 mi e on
SR 86. Ext corridors. **Pets:** Dogs only. $4 daily fee/pet. Designated rooms,
supervision.

SAVE X

Comfort Inn on Lake Placid SH
(518) 523-9555. **$100-$200.** 2125 Saranac Ave. 0.5 mi w on SR 86.
Ext/int corridors. **Pets:** Other species. Service with restrictions, supervision.

SAVE S X

**Crowne Plaza Resort & Golf Club Lake
Placid** SH
(518) 523-2556. **$99-$299, 30 day notice.** 1 Olympic Dr. Downtown.
Ext/int corridors. **Pets:** Other species. $10 daily fee/pet. Service with
restrictions, supervision.

SAVE X

Golden Arrow Lakeside Resort SH
(518) 523-3353. **$89-$300, 30 day notice.** 2559 Main St. On SR 86;
center. Int corridors. **Pets:** Other species. $100 deposit/pet, $50 one-time
fee/pet. Designated rooms, service with restrictions, supervision.

SAVE S X

Hilton Lake Placid Resort SH
(518) 523-4411. **$89-$289, 7 day notice.** 1 Mirror Lake Dr. 0.3 mi w on
SR 86. Int corridors. **Pets:** Accepted.

X

Swiss Acres Inn SH
(518) 523-3040. **$58-$148, 7 day notice.** 1970 Saranac Ave. 1 mi w on
SR 86. Ext/int corridors. **Pets:** Accepted.

SAVE S X

LANSING

Econo Lodge SH
(607) 257-1400. **$55-$135.** 2303 N Triphammer Rd. SR 13, exit Triphammer Rd. Int corridors. **Pets:** Other species. $15 daily fee/pet. Desig-
nated rooms, service with restrictions, crate.

SAVE S X

**Ramada Inn Executive Training & Conference
Ctr** SH
(607) 257-3100. **$99-$299.** 2310 N Triphammer Rd. Jct SR 13 and 34,
3.5 mi n on SR 13, exit Triphammer Rd, just w. Int corridors.
Pets: Accepted.

SAVE S X

LATHAM

The Century House, a Clarion Hotel SH
(518) 785-0931. **$130-$230.** 997 New Loudon Rd. I-87, exit 7 (SR 7),
just e, then 0.5 mi n on US 9 (New Loudon Rd). Int corridors.
Pets: $15 daily fee/pet. Service with restrictions, supervision.

SAVE S X

**Comfort Inn Albany Airport & Conference
Center** SH
(518) 783-1900. **$89-$149.** 20 Airport Park Blvd. I-87, exit 4, 2.2 mi nw
on Albany Shaker Rd. Int corridors. **Pets:** $10 daily fee/room. Service
with restrictions, supervision.

SAVE S X

Hampton Inn-Latham SH
(518) 785-0000. **$114-$164.** 981 New Loudon Rd. I-87, exit 7 (SR 7),
just e, then just n on US 9 (New Loudon Rd). Int corridors.
Pets: Accepted.

ASK S X

Holiday Inn Express-Airport SH
(518) 783-6161. **$99-$130.** 946 New Loudon Rd. I-87, exit 7 (SR 7),
just e, then just n on US 9 (New Loudon Rd). Ext corridors.
Pets: Other species. $20 one-time fee/room. Service with restrictions.

SAVE X

▼▼▼ **La Quinta Inn & Suites–Albany Airport** SH
(518) 640-2200. **$99-$149.** 833 New Loudon Rd. I-87, exit 7, just s on US 9 to Latham Circle, then n on US 9. Int corridors. **Pets:** Accepted.
(ASK) (S) (X) (▯) (▯) (▰)

AAA ▼▼▼ **Microtel Inn, Albany Airport** SH
(518) 782-9161. **$45-$169.** 7 Rensselaer Ave. I-87, exit 6, just w. Int corridors. **Pets:** Small. $10 daily fee/pet. Service with restrictions, supervision.
(SAVE) (S) (X) (&M) (▯) (▯) (▯) (▯)

AAA ▼▼▼ **Quality Inn & Suites** SH
(518) 785-5891. **$99-$140.** 611 Troy-Schenectady Rd. I-87, exit 6, just w on SR 7. Ext/int corridors. **Pets:** Medium. $30 one-time fee/room. Designated rooms, service with restrictions, supervision.
(SAVE) (S) (X) (▯) (▯) (▯) (▰)

▼▼▼ **Residence Inn by Marriott Albany Airport** SH
(518) 783-0600. **$149-$269.** 1 Residence Inn Dr. I-87, exit 6, 2 mi w on SR 7. Ext corridors. **Pets:** Other species. $75 one-time fee/room. Service with restrictions.
(X) (▯) (▯) (▯) (▰) (X)

LITTLE FALLS

AAA ▼▼▼ **Best Western Little Falls Motor Inn** SH
(315) 823-4954. **$70-$120.** 20 Albany St. On SR 5 and 167. Int corridors. **Pets:** Other species. $10 deposit/pet. Designated rooms, service with restrictions, crate.
(SAVE) (S) (X) (▯) (▯)

LIVERPOOL

AAA ▼▼▼▼ **Best Western Inn & Suites** SH
(315) 701-4400. **$89-$189.** 136 Transistor Pkwy. I-90, exit 37 (Electronics Pkwy), just n; I-81, exit 25 (7th North St), 1.3 mi w, just n on Electronics Pkwy, then just w. Int corridors. **Pets:** Small, dogs only. $15 daily fee/pet. Service with restrictions, supervision.
(SAVE) (S) (X) (▯) (▯) (▯) (▰)

▼▼▼ **Holiday Inn Syracuse Airport** LH
(315) 457-1122. **$99-$229.** 441 Electronics Pkwy. I-90, exit 37 (Electronics Pkwy); I-81, exit 25 (7th North St), 1.3 mi nw. Int corridors. **Pets:** Medium, other species. $50 deposit/room. Designated rooms, service with restrictions, supervision.
(ASK) (S) (X) (&M) (▯) (▯) (▯) (▯) (▯) (▰) (X)

▼▼▼ **Homewood Suites** SH
(315) 451-3800. **$149-$199.** 275 Elwood Davis Rd. I-81, exit 25 (7th North St), 1 mi w; I-90, exit 36. Int corridors. **Pets:** Medium. $100 one-time fee/pet. Service with restrictions, crate.
(ASK) (S) (X) (&M) (▯) (▯) (▯) (▯) (▰) (X)

AAA ▼▼▼ **Knights Inn** M 🐾
(315) 453-6330. **$49-$199.** 430 Electronics Pkwy. I-90, exit 37 (Electronics Pkwy), just s; I-81, exit 25 (7th North St), 1.3 mi nw, then just s. Ext corridors. **Pets:** Medium. $12 daily fee/pet. Service with restrictions, supervision.
(SAVE) (S) (X) (▯)

LONG LAKE

AAA ▼▼▼ **Journey's End Cottages** CA
(518) 624-5381. **$500-$1000 (weekly), 60 day notice.** 941 Deerland Rd (Rt 30). On SR 30/28 N, 1 mi s. Ext corridors. **Pets:** Medium. $25 one-time fee/room. Service with restrictions, supervision.
(SAVE) (▯) (▯) (X) (X) (Z)

▼▼ **Long View Lodge** CI
(518) 624-2862. **$60-$130, 7 day notice.** 681 Deerland Rd. On SR 30/28 N, 2.2 mi s. Ext/int corridors. **Pets:** Accepted.
(X) (▯) (▯) (X) (X)

MALONE

AAA ▼▼▼ **Four Seasons Motel** M
(518) 483-3490. **$55-$89, 3 day notice.** 206 W Main St. 1 mi w on US 11. Ext corridors. **Pets:** Large. $10 one-time fee/pet. Service with restrictions, supervision.
(SAVE) (S) (X) (▯) (▯) (▰)

AAA ▼▼▼ **Sunset Inn** M
(518) 483-3367. **$50-$80.** 3899 US 11. 1.5 mi e. Ext corridors. **Pets:** Accepted.
(SAVE) (X) (▯) (▯) (▰)

MALTA

▼▼▼▼ **Fairfield Inn & Suites by Marriott** SH
(518) 899-6900. **$89-$339.** 101 Saratoga Village Blvd. I-87, exit 12, just e. Int corridors. **Pets:** Accepted.
(ASK) (S) (X) (&M) (▯) (▯) (▯) (▰)

MASSENA

AAA ▼▼▼ **Econo Lodge-Meadow View Motel** SH 🐾
(315) 764-0246. **$72-$99.** 15054 SR 37. On SR 37, 2.7 mi sw. Ext/int corridors. **Pets:** Small. $5 daily fee/pet. Designated rooms, service with restrictions, supervision.
(SAVE) (S) (X) (▯) (▯) (▯)

MCGRAW

AAA ▼▼▼ **Cortland Days Inn** SH
(607) 753-7594. **$59-$175.** 3775 US Rt 11. I-81, exit 10 (McGraw/Cortland), just n. Int corridors. **Pets:** Accepted.
(SAVE) (X) (▯) (▯)

MEDFORD

AAA ▼▼▼ **The Comfort Inn** SH
(631) 654-3000. **$79-$189.** 2695 Rt 112. I-495, exit 64 (SR 112), just s. Ext/int corridors. **Pets:** Small. $30 daily fee/room. Designated rooms, service with restrictions, supervision.
(SAVE) (S) (X) (&M) (▯) (▯) (▰) (X)

MIDDLETOWN

▼▼▼ **Super 8 Motel** SH
(845) 692-5828. **$70-$110.** 563 Rt 211 E. I-84, exit 4, 0.5 mi w on SR 17 to exit 120, then 0.3 mi e. Int corridors. **Pets:** $25 deposit/room. Service with restrictions, supervision.
(ASK) (S) (X) (▯)

MONTOUR FALLS

AAA ▼▼ **Relax Inn** M
(607) 535-7183. **$39-$135, 4 day notice.** 100 Clawson Blvd. Jct SR 14 and 224. Ext corridors. **Pets:** Small. $10 daily fee/pet. Designated rooms, service with restrictions, supervision.
(SAVE) (S) (X) (▯)

NEWBURGH

▼▼ **Super 8** M
(845) 564-5700. **$55-$120.** 1287 Rt 300. I-87, exit 17, just w; I-84, exit 6, 2 mi e. Int corridors. **Pets:** Accepted.
(ASK) (S) (X) (&M)

NEW HAMPTON

ⒶⒶⒶ ▼▼ Days Inn Ⓜ
(845) 374-2411. **$74-$139.** 4939 Rt 17M. I-84, exit 3, 0.8 mi e on US 6 and SR 17M. Ext/int corridors. **Pets:** $50 deposit/room, $10 daily fee/pet. Designated rooms, service with restrictions, supervision.
SAVE Ⓢ ☒ 🖥 💻 ⇥

NEW HARTFORD

▼▼▼ Holiday Inn Utica Ⓢⓗ
(315) 797-2131. **$119-$219.** 1777 Burrstone Rd. I-90 (New York State Thruway), exit 31, 4.5 mi w on SR 5 W and 12 S, exit Burrstone Rd, then 1 mi nw. Int corridors. **Pets:** Large. $25 one-time fee/room. Designated rooms, service with restrictions, supervision.
ASK Ⓢ ☒ ⓂⓂ ✎ ⓔ 🖥 💻 🍴 ⇥ ☒

NEW YORK METROPOLITAN AREA

ARMONK

ⒶⒶⒶ ▼▼▼ Wellesley Inn Ⓢⓗ
(914) 273-9090. **$149-$300.** 94 Business Park Dr. I-684, exit 3S northbound; exit 3 southbound, 0.3 mi s on SR 22 to Business Park Dr. Int corridors. **Pets:** Accepted.
SAVE Ⓢ ☒ ⓂⓂ ✎ ⓔ 🖥 💻 🍴 ⇥

ELMSFORD

▼▼ Extended StayAmerica-White Plains-Elmsford Ⓢⓗ
(914) 347-8073. **$144-$164.** 118 Tarrytown Rd. I-87, exit 8, just w. Int corridors. **Pets:** Accepted.
ASK Ⓢ ☒ ⓂⓂ ✎ ⓔ 🖥 💻

ⒶⒶⒶ ▼▼▼ Hampton Inn White Plains/Tarrytown Ⓢⓗ ✦
(914) 592-5680. **$209.** 200 Tarrytown Rd. I-287, exit 1; I-87, exit 8, just w. Int corridors. **Pets:** Medium, other species. $25 one-time fee/room. Service with restrictions, crate.
SAVE Ⓢ ☒ ⓂⓂ ✎ ⓔ 🖥 💻 ⇥

FLUSHING

ⒶⒶⒶ ▼▼▼ Sheraton La Guardia East Hotel Ⓛⓗ ✦
(718) 460-6666. **$189-$429.** 135-20 39th Ave. In Flushing; Grand Central Pkwy to Northern Blvd, 1 mi e to Main St, 0.3 mi s to 39th Ave, then just w. Int corridors. **Pets:** Medium. Service with restrictions, supervision.
SAVE ☒ ✎ ⓔ 🖥 💻 🍴

JAMAICA

▼▼ Ramada Plaza Hotel at JFK Ⓛⓗ
(718) 995-9000. **$115-$225.** Bldg 144/JFK International Airport. In Jamaica; Van Wyck Expwy at Belt Pkwy; southwest corner. Int corridors. **Pets:** Accepted.
ASK Ⓢ ☒ ✎ ⓔ 🖥 💻 🍴

MOUNT KISCO

ⒶⒶⒶ ▼▼▼ Holiday Inn Ⓢⓗ
(914) 241-2600. **$130-$250.** 1 Holiday Inn Dr. Saw Mill River Pkwy, exit 37, just e. Int corridors. **Pets:** Accepted.
SAVE ☒ ⓂⓂ ✎ ⓔ 🖥 💻 🍴 ⇥

NANUET

▼▼▼ Candlewood Suites Ⓢⓗ
(845) 371-4445. **$80-$126.** 20 Overlook Blvd. I-287/87 (New York State Thruway), exit 14 (SR 59 W) to New Clarkstown Rd. Int corridors. **Pets:** Accepted.
ASK Ⓢ ☒ ⓔ 🖥 💻

ⒶⒶⒶ ▼▼ Days Inn Nanuet Ⓢⓗ
(845) 623-4567. **$79-$109.** 367 W Rt 59. I-287/87 (New York State Thruway), exit 14 (SR 59) northbound, just e; exit southbound, just w. Ext/int corridors. **Pets:** Other species. $8 daily fee/pet. No service, supervision.
SAVE Ⓢ ☒ 🖥 💻 ⇥

NEW YORK

▼▼▼ 70 Park Avenue Hotel Ⓢⓗ ✦
(212) 973-2400. **$249-$750.** 70 Park Ave. At 38th St. Int corridors. **Pets:** Other species. Service with restrictions.
ASK Ⓢ ☒ ⓂⓂ ✎ ⓔ

ⒶⒶⒶ ▼▼▼ Affinia 50 Ⓢⓗ ✦
(212) 751-5710. **$189-$529.** 155 E 50th St. Between 3rd and Lexington aves. Int corridors. **Pets:** Other species. Service with restrictions.
SAVE ☒ ✎ ⓔ 🖥 💻

ⒶⒶⒶ ▼▼▼ Affinia Dumont Ⓢⓗ ✦
(212) 481-7600. **$189-$499.** 150 E 34th St. Between Lexington and 3rd aves. Int corridors. **Pets:** Other species. Service with restrictions.
SAVE ☒ ✎ ⓔ 🖥 💻 🍴

ⒶⒶⒶ ▼▼▼ Affinia Gardens Ⓢⓗ ✦
(212) 355-1230. **$259-$449.** 215 E 64th St. Between 2nd and 3rd aves. Int corridors. **Pets:** Other species. Service with restrictions.
SAVE ☒ ✎ ⓔ 🖥 💻

ⒶⒶⒶ ▼▼▼ Affinia Manhattan Ⓛⓗ ✦
(212) 563-1800. **$159-$469.** 371 7th Ave. At 31st St. Int corridors. **Pets:** Other species. Service with restrictions.
SAVE ☒ ✎ ⓔ 🖥 💻 🍴

ⒶⒶⒶ ▼▼▼ Algonquin Hotel Ⓛⓗ
(212) 840-6800. **$229-$469.** 59 W 44th St. Between 5th and 6th (Ave of the Americas) aves. Int corridors. **Pets:** Accepted.
SAVE Ⓢ ☒ ✎ ⓔ 🖥 🍴

▼▼▼ Beekman Tower Hotel Ⓢⓗ ✦
(212) 355-7300. **$139-$449.** 3 Mitchell Pl. 49th St and 1st Ave. Int corridors. **Pets:** Other species. Service with restrictions.
ASK ☒ ✎ ⓔ 🖥 💻 🍴

ⒶⒶⒶ ▼▼▼ The Benjamin Hotel Ⓢⓗ ✦
(212) 715-2500. **$239-$669.** 125 E 50th St. Between Lexington and 3rd aves. Int corridors. **Pets:** Other species. Service with restrictions.
SAVE ☒ ✎ 🖥 💻 🍴 ☒

ⒶⒶⒶ ▼▼▼ The Bryant Park Hotel Ⓢⓗ
(212) 869-0100. **$395-$800.** 40 W 40th St. Between 5th and 6th (Ave of the Americas) aves. Int corridors. **Pets:** Accepted.
SAVE Ⓢ ☒ ⓂⓂ ✎ ⓔ 🍴

ⒶⒶⒶ ▼▼▼ The Carlyle Ⓢⓗ
(212) 744-1600. **$540-$1360.** 35 E 76th St. At Madison Ave. Int corridors. **Pets:** Accepted.
SAVE ☒ ✎ ⓔ 🖥 🍴 ☒

▼▼▼ Dream Ⓢⓗ
(212) 247-2000. **$315-$830.** 210 W 55th St. Between Broadway and 7th Ave. Int corridors. **Pets:** Accepted.
ASK Ⓢ ☒ ✎ ⓔ 🖥 🍴 ☒

▼▼▼ Eastgate Tower Hotel Ⓢⓗ ✦
(212) 687-8000. **$239-$529.** 222 E 39th St. Between 2nd and 3rd aves. Int corridors. **Pets:** Other species. Service with restrictions, crate.
ASK ☒ ⓂⓂ ✎ ⓔ 🖥 💻 🍴

▼▼▼▼ Embassy Suites Hotel New York LH
(212) 945-0100. **$209-$559.** 102 N End Ave. Between Murray and Vesey sts. Int corridors. **Pets:** Accepted.
⊠ ⓢ 🛢 🖵

▼▼▼▼▼ Four Seasons Hotel New York LH
(212) 758-5700. **$825-$1095.** 57 E 57th St. Between Park and Madison aves. Int corridors. **Pets:** Accepted.
⊠ ⓜ ⓢ 🛢 🖵 ⓨ ⊠

⚠ ▼▼▼▼ Hampton Inn-Madison Square Garden Area SH
(212) 947-9700. **$169-$519.** 116 W 31st St. Between 6th (Ave of the Americas) and 7th aves. Int corridors. **Pets:** Accepted.
ⓢ ⓢ ⊠ 🛢 🖵

⚠ ▼▼▼▼ Hampton Inn-Manhattan/Chelsea SH
(212) 414-1000. **$209-$460.** 108 W 24th St. Between 6th (Ave of the Americas) and 7th aves. Int corridors. **Pets:** Accepted.
ⓢ ⓢ ⊠ ⓐ ⓢ 🛢 🖵

▼▼▼▼ Hampton Inn-Manhattan/Seaport/Financial District SH
(212) 571-4400. **$148-$444.** 320 Pearl St. Between deck slip and Dover St. Int corridors. **Pets:** Medium. $20 one-time fee/pet. Supervision.
ⓐⓢⓚ ⓢ ⊠ ⓐ ⓢ 🛢 🖵

▼▼▼▼ Hilton New York LH
(212) 586-7000. **$199-$729.** 1335 Ave of the Americas. Between 53rd and 54th sts. Int corridors. **Pets:** Accepted.
⊠ ⓐ ⓢ 🛢 🖵 ⓨ

⚠ ▼▼▼▼ Hilton Times Square LH
(212) 642-2500. **$279-$999.** 234 W 42nd St. Between 7th and 8th aves. Int corridors. **Pets:** Accepted.
ⓢ ⊠ ⓜ ⓐ ⓢ 🛢 🖵 ⓨ

▼▼▼▼ Holiday Inn Express Fifth Ave SH 🐾
(212) 302-9088. **$199-$399.** 15 W 45th St. At 5th Ave. **Pets:** Medium. Service with restrictions, crate.
ⓐⓢⓚ ⓢ ⊠ ⓐ ⓢ 🛢 🖵

▼▼▼▼ Hotel Gansevoort SH
(212) 660-6700. **$495-$555.** 18 9th Ave. At 13th St. Int corridors. **Pets:** Accepted.
⊠ ⓜ ⓐ ⓢ 🛢 ⓨ ⊠

▼▼▼▼ Hotel Plaza Athenee SH 🐾
(212) 734-9100. **$590-$890.** 37 E 64th St. Between Madison and Park aves. Int corridors. **Pets:** Small. $60 one-time fee/pet. Designated rooms, service with restrictions.
⊠ ⓢ 🛢 ⓨ ⊠

▼▼▼▼ Hotel Wales SH 🐾
(212) 876-6000. **$249-$450.** 1295 Madison Ave. Between 92nd and 93rd sts E. Int corridors. **Pets:** $75 one-time fee/room.
ⓢ ⊠ ⓐ 🛢 ⓨ ⊠

⚠ ▼▼▼▼ Jolly Hotel Madison Towers LH
(212) 802-0600. **$275-$604.** 22 E 38th St. Between Park and Madison aves. Int corridors. **Pets:** Small. Service with restrictions, supervision.
ⓢ ⊠ ⓢ 🖵 ⓨ

⚠ ▼▼▼▼ Jumeirah-Essex House LH
(212) 247-0300. **$259-$869.** 160 Central Park S. Between 6th (Ave of the Americas) and 7th aves. Int corridors. **Pets:** Accepted.
ⓢ ⊠ ⓜ ⓐ ⓢ 🛢 ⊠

▼▼▼▼ Le Parker Meridien New York LH 🐾
(212) 245-5000. **$690-$1110.** 118 W 57th St. Between 6th (Ave of the Americas) and 7th aves; vehicle entrance on 56th St. Int corridors. **Pets:** Other species. Service with restrictions.
ⓐⓢⓚ ⊠ ⓐ ⓢ 🛢 ⓨ ⊠ ⊠

▼▼▼▼ The Lowell Hotel SH 🐾
(212) 838-1400. **$635-$7500.** 28 E 63rd St. Between Park and Madison aves. Int corridors. **Pets:** Large.
ⓐⓢⓚ ⊠ ⓐ 🛢 🖵 ⊠

⚠ ▼▼▼▼ Mandarin Oriental, New York LH
(212) 805-8800. **$745-$1125.** 80 Columbus Circle at 60th St. At 60th St. Int corridors. **Pets:** Accepted.
ⓢ ⊠ ⓐ ⓢ ⓨ ⊠

▼▼▼▼ The Mark, New York SH
(212) 744-4300. **$570-$960.** 25 E 77th St. Madison Ave at E 77th St. Int corridors. **Pets:** Accepted.
⊠ ⓐ ⓨ ⊠

⚠ ▼▼▼ Millennium Broadway LH
(212) 768-4400. **$399-$2500.** 145 W 44th St. Between 6th (Ave of the Americas) and 7th aves; in Times Square. Int corridors. **Pets:** Small. Service with restrictions, supervision.
ⓢ ⓢ ⊠ ⓜ ⓐ ⓢ 🛢 🖵 ⓨ ⊠

⚠ ▼▼▼▼ The Muse Hotel SH
(212) 485-2400. **$249-$999.** 130 W 46th St. Between 6th (Ave of the Americas) and 7th aves. Int corridors. **Pets:** Accepted.
ⓢ ⓢ ⊠ ⓢ 🛢 🖵 ⓨ

▼▼▼▼ New York Marriott Marquis LH
(212) 398-1900. **$259-$619.** 1535 Broadway. Between 45th and 46th sts; motor entrance on 46th St. Int corridors. **Pets:** Small, dogs only. $250 one-time fee/room. Service with restrictions, crate.
ⓐⓢⓚ ⊠ ⓐ ⓢ 🛢 🖵 ⓨ

⚠ ▼▼▼▼ The New York Palace LH
(212) 888-7000. **$570-$975.** 455 Madison Ave. Between 50th and 51st sts. Int corridors. **Pets:** Very small, dogs only. Service with restrictions, supervision.
ⓢ ⊠ ⓜ ⓐ ⓢ 🛢 🖵 ⓨ ⊠

⚠ ▼▼▼▼ Novotel New York LH
(212) 315-0100. **$199-$529.** 226 W 52nd St. At Broadway. Int corridors. **Pets:** Accepted.
ⓢ ⓢ ⊠ ⓐ 🛢 ⓨ

▼▼▼▼ Omni Berkshire Place LH
(212) 753-5800. **$389-$589.** 21 E 52nd St. Between Madison and 5th aves. Int corridors. **Pets:** Accepted.
ⓐⓢⓚ ⓢ ⊠ ⓜ ⓐ ⓢ 🛢 ⓨ

▼▼▼▼ On The Ave Hotel SH
(212) 362-1100. **$225-$379.** 2178 Broadway. At 77th St. Int corridors. **Pets:** Accepted.
ⓐⓢⓚ ⓢ ⊠ 🛢 🖵

⚠ ▼▼▼▼ The Peninsula New York LH
(212) 956-2888. **$615-$895.** 700 5th Ave. At 55th St. Int corridors. **Pets:** Accepted.
ⓢ ⊠ ⓐ ⓢ 🛢 ⓨ ⊠ ⊠

▼▼▼▼ The Pierre New York-A Taj Hotel LH
(212) 838-8000. **$640-$1400.** 2 E 61st St. At 5th Ave. Int corridors. **Pets:** Accepted.
⊠ ⓜ ⓐ ⓢ 🛢 ⓨ ⊠

⚠ ▼▼▼▼ Radisson Martinique on Broadway SH
(212) 736-3800. **$274-$734.** 49 W 32nd St. Corner of Broadway. Int corridors. **Pets:** Small, dogs only. $25 daily fee/pet. Service with restrictions, supervision.
ⓢ ⓢ ⊠ ⓜ ⓐ 🛢 🖵 ⓨ

⚠ ▼▼▼▼ The Regency Hotel LH
(212) 759-4100. **$489-$4500.** 540 Park Ave. At 61st St. Int corridors. **Pets:** Accepted.
ⓢ ⓢ ⊠ ⓜ ⓐ ⓢ 🛢 ⓨ

(AAA) ▼▼▼ ▼▼▼ **Renaissance New York Hotel Times Square** 🏨 ❀
(212) 765-7676. **$359-$779.** 2 Times Square, 7th Ave at W 48th St. Broadway and 7th Ave; auto access from 7th Ave, s of W 48th St. Int corridors. **Pets:** Medium. $65 one-time fee/room. Service with restrictions, supervision.
(SAVE) ✕ 🐾 💻 ⑪

(AAA) ▼▼▼▼▼▼ **The Ritz-Carlton New York, Battery Park** 🏨 ❀
(212) 344-0800. **$600-$1025.** Two West St. Jct Battery Park. Int corridors. **Pets:** Medium. $125 one-time fee/pet.
(SAVE) ✕ 🔊 🐾 🛏 🛎 ⑪

(AAA) ▼▼▼▼▼▼ **The Ritz-Carlton New York, Central Park** 🏨 ❀
(212) 308-9100. **$675-$1475.** 50 Central Park S. Between 5th and 6th (Ave of the Americas) aves. Int corridors. **Pets:** Medium. $125 one-time fee/room. Service with restrictions, crate.
(SAVE) ✕ 🔊 🐾 🛏 🛎

▼▼▼ **Shelburne Murray Hill Hotel** 🏨 🐾
(212) 689-5200. **$179-$599.** 303 Lexington Ave. Between 37th and 38th sts. Int corridors. **Pets:** Other species. Service with restrictions.
(ASK) ✕ 🐾 🛏 🛎 💻 ⑪

▼▼▼ **Sheraton Manhattan Hotel** 🏨
(212) 581-3300. **$179-$299.** 790 7th Ave. Between 51st and 52nd sts. Int corridors. **Pets:** Accepted.
(ASK) 🔊 ✕ 🔊 🐾 🛏 🛎 💻 ⑪ 🏊 ✕

▼▼▼ **Sheraton New York Hotel & Towers** 🏨
(212) 581-1000. **$179-$299.** 811 7th Ave. At 52nd St. Int corridors. **Pets:** Accepted.
(ASK) 🔊 ✕ 🔊 🐾 🛏 🛎 💻 ⑪ ✕

(AAA) ▼▼▼▼▼▼ **Sofitel New York** 🏨
(212) 354-8844. **$399-$809.** 45 W 44th St. Between 5th and 6th (Ave of the Americas) aves. Int corridors. **Pets:** Accepted.
(SAVE) ✕ 🐾 🔊 🛏 ⑪ ✕

▼▼▼ **The SoHo Grand Hotel** 🏨
(212) 965-3000. **$639-$749.** 310 W Broadway. In SoHo; jct Grand St. Int corridors. **Pets:** Accepted.
✕ 🔊 ⑪

(AAA) ▼▼▼▼ **Surrey Hotel** 🏨 ❀
(212) 288-3700. **$299-$489.** 20 E 76th St. E 76th St and Madison Ave. Int corridors. **Pets:** Other species. Service with restrictions.
(SAVE) ✕ 🐾 🛏 🛎 ⑪

▼▼▼ **Tribeca Grand Hotel** 🏨
(212) 519-6600. **$309-$2300.** 2 Ave of the Americas. At 6th Ave (Ave of the Americas) and White St. Int corridors. **Pets:** Accepted.
✕ 🔊 ⑪

(AAA) ▼▼▼▼▼▼ **Trump International Hotel & Tower** 🏨
(212) 299-1000. **$705-$795.** 1 Central Park W. Jct Central Park S; at Columbus Circle. Int corridors. **Pets:** Accepted.
(SAVE) ✕ 🐾 🛏 🛎 ⑪ 🏊 ✕

▼▼▼ **The Wall Street District Hotel** 🏨
(212) 232-7700. **$249-$579.** 15 Gold St. Corner of Gold and Platt sts. Int corridors. **Pets:** Accepted.
(ASK) 🔊 ✕ 🔊 🐾 🔊 🛏 💻 ⑪

(AAA) ▼▼▼ ▼▼▼ **The Westin New York at Times Square** 🏨
(212) 201-2700. **$249-$899.** 270 W 43rd St. Corner of 8th Ave. Int corridors. **Pets:** Accepted.
(SAVE) 🔊 ✕ 🐾 🔊 🐾 🛏 🛎 ⑪ ✕

▼▼▼▼▼▼ **W New York** 🏨 ❀
(212) 755-1200. **$429-$519.** 541 Lexington Ave. At 49th St. Int corridors. **Pets:** Medium. $25 daily fee/pet, $100 one-time fee/room. Service with restrictions, supervision.
(ASK) 🔊 ✕ 🔊 🐾 🔊 🐾 🛏 ⑪

▼▼▼▼▼▼ **W New York Times Square** 🏨
(212) 930-7400. **$429-$519.** 1567 Broadway at 47th St. Corner of 47th St. Int corridors. **Pets:** Accepted.
(ASK) ✕ 🔊 🐾 🔊 🐾 🛏 🛎 ⑪

▼▼▼▼ **W New York-Union Square** 🏨
(212) 253-9119. **$549-$649.** 201 Park Ave S. At 17th St. Int corridors. **Pets:** Accepted.
✕ 🐾 🔊 🛏 ⑪ ✕

RYE BROOK

(AAA) ▼▼▼▼ **Hilton Rye Town** 🏨
(914) 939-6300. **$129-$369.** 699 Westchester Ave. I-287 (Cross Westchester Expwy), exit 10 eastbound, 0.6 mi ne on SR 120A; exit westbound, 0.3 mi n on Webb Ave, then 0.4 mi ne on SR 120A. Int corridors. **Pets:** Small, dogs only. $50 one-time fee/room. Designated rooms, service with restrictions, supervision.
(SAVE) ✕ 🐾 🔊 🐾 🛏 🛎 ⑪ 🏊 ✕

STATEN ISLAND

(AAA) ▼▼▼▼ **Hilton Garden Inn Staten Island** 🏨
(718) 477-2400. **$159-$299.** 1100 South Ave. I-278, exit 6 (South Ave) westbound, just s; exit 5 eastbound to SR 440 S, exit South Ave, just s to South Ave, 1 mi n to Lois Ln, then just w. Int corridors. **Pets:** Accepted.
(SAVE) ✕ 🐾 🛏 🛎 ⑪ 🏊 ✕

(AAA) ▼▼▼ **The Staten Island Hotel** 🏨
(718) 698-5000. **$159-$179.** 1415 Richmond Ave. I-278, exit Richmond Ave, 0.5 mi se. Int corridors. **Pets:** Service with restrictions.
(SAVE) 🔊 ✕ 🛏 🛎 ⑪

SUFFERN

(AAA) ▼▼▼▼ **Holiday Inn-Suffern** 🏨
(845) 357-4800. **$109-$129.** 3 Executive Blvd. I-87 (New York State Thruway), exit 14B, just n. Int corridors. **Pets:** Accepted.
(SAVE) 🔊 ✕ 🐾 🛏 🛎 ⑪ 🏊 ✕

TARRYTOWN

▼▼▼▼ **Westchester Marriott Hotel** 🏨
(914) 631-2200. **$119-$299.** 670 White Plains Rd. I-87 (New York State Thruway), exit 9 northbound, 0.8 mi e on SR 119; exit southbound, just n on US 9, then 1 mi e on SR 119. Int corridors. **Pets:** Accepted.
(ASK) ✕ 🐾 🔊 🛏 🛎 ⑪ 🏊 ✕

WHITE PLAINS

▼▼▼▼ **Hyatt Summerfield Suites** 🏨
(914) 251-9700. **$139-$539.** 101 Corporate Park Dr. I-287 (Cross Westchester Expwy), exit 9A eastbound, 0.6 mi e on Westchester Ave, then 0.3 mi n; exit 9N-S westbound, 0.9 mi w on Westchester Ave. Int corridors. **Pets:** Accepted.
(ASK) ✕ 🐾 🛏 🛎 💻 🏊 ✕

END METROPOLITAN AREA

NIAGARA FALLS METROPOLITAN AREA

LOCKPORT

◢◣◥◤ ▼▼▼ Comfort Inn SH
(716) 434-4411. **$59-$119.** 551 S Transit Rd. 1 mi s on SR 78. Int corridors. **Pets:** $10 daily fee/pet. Designated rooms, service with restrictions, supervision.

SAVE S⊘ ✕ ♿M 🛢 🖵

▼▼▼ Holiday Inn Lockport SH ❀
(716) 434-6151. **$70-$150.** 515 S Transit Rd. 1 mi s on SR 78. Int corridors. **Pets:** Other species. $10 daily fee/room. Service with restrictions, supervision.

ASK S⊘ ✕ ♿M ✍ 🖉 🛢 🖵 🍴 ➼

NEWFANE

▼ Lake Ontario Motel M
(716) 778-5004. **$55-$75.** 3330 Lockport-Olcott Rd. 2.5 mi n of jct SR 104 on SR 78. Int corridors. **Pets:** Other species. $5 daily fee/room. Service with restrictions, supervision.

ASK S⊘ ✕ 🛢

NIAGARA FALLS

◢◣◥◤ ▼▼▼ Best Western Summit Inn SH
(716) 297-5050. **$59-$159.** 9500 Niagara Falls Blvd. I-190, exit 22, 2.1 mi e on US 62 S. Int corridors. **Pets:** $8 daily fee/pet. Designated rooms, service with restrictions, supervision.

SAVE S⊘ ✕ 🛢 🖵 ➼

◢◣◥◤ ▼▼▼ Howard Johnson Inn at the Falls SH ❀
(716) 285-5261. **$49-$255.** 454 Main St. I-190, exit 21 (Robert Moses Pkwy), exit City Traffic, just n to Rainbow Blvd, just w. Int corridors. **Pets:** Other species. $10 daily fee/pet. Service with restrictions, supervision.

SAVE S⊘ ✕ ♿M 🛢 🖵 ➼

◢◣◥◤ ▼▼▼ Inn on the River SH
(716) 283-7612. **$89-$199.** 7001 Buffalo Ave. I-190, exit 21, just e. Int corridors. **Pets:** Other species. $15 daily fee/pet. Designated rooms, service with restrictions, supervision.

SAVE S⊘ ✕ 🛢 🖵 ➼

▼▼▼ Quality Hotel and Suites "At the Falls" SH
(716) 282-1212. **$59-$299.** 240 Rainbow Blvd. I-190, exit 21 (Robert Moses Pkwy), eastbound use City Traffic exit, just w; downtown. Int corridors. **Pets:** Other species. $10 daily fee/pet. Service with restrictions, supervision.

ASK ✕ ✍ 🛢 🖵 🍴 ➼

◢◣◥◤ ▼ Swiss Cottage Inn M
(716) 283-8142. **$42-$189.** 6831 Niagara Falls Blvd. I-190, exit 22, 0.5 mi e. Ext corridors. **Pets:** Medium. $10 daily fee/pet. Designated rooms, service with restrictions, supervision.

SAVE S⊘ ✕ 🛢 ➼

END METROPOLITAN AREA

NORTH SYRACUSE

▼▼▼ Candlewood Suites Syracuse Airport SH
(315) 454-8999. **$109-$169.** 5414 South Bay Rd. I-90, exit 36; I-81, exit 26 (Mattydale Rd), follow South Bay Rd signs, just n. Int corridors. **Pets:** Medium, other species. $75 one-time fee/room. Service with restrictions, crate.

ASK S⊘ ✕ ✍ 🖉 🛢 🖵

◢◣◥◤ ▼▼▼ Comfort Inn & Suites/Syracuse Airport SH
(315) 457-4000. **$79-$169.** 6701 Buckley Rd. I-81, exit 25 (7th North St), 0.8 mi w; I-90, exit 36. Int corridors. **Pets:** Large, other species. $10 daily fee/room. Service with restrictions, crate.

SAVE S⊘ ✕ ✍ 🛢 🖵 ➼ 🗶

◢◣◥◤ ▼▼▼ Quality Inn North M
(315) 451-1212. **$72-$119, 7 day notice.** 1308 Buckley Rd. I-81, exit 25 (7th North St), 0.3 mi w, then just n. Ext/int corridors. **Pets:** Accepted.

SAVE S⊘ ✕ 🛢 🖵 🍴 ➼

NORWICH

▼▼ Super 8 Motel of Norwich SH
(607) 336-8880. **$58-$96, 30 day notice.** 6067 State Hwy 12. On SR 12, 0.9 mi n. Int corridors. **Pets:** Medium. $10 one-time fee/room. Service with restrictions, supervision.

ASK S⊘ ✕ 🛢 🖵

OGDENSBURG

◢◣◥◤ ▼▼▼▼ Quality Inn Gran-View M
(315) 393-4550. **$91-$159.** 6765 State Hwy 37. On SR 37, 3 mi sw. Ext/int corridors. **Pets:** Large, other species. $10 one-time fee/room. Designated rooms, service with restrictions, crate.

SAVE S⊘ ✕ 🛢 🖵 🍴 ➼ 🗶

◢◣◥◤ ▼▼▼ The Stonefence Resort & Motel M
(315) 393-1545. **$69-$179.** 7191 SR 37. Jct SR 68, 0.5 mi w. Ext/int corridors. **Pets:** Large. $20 one-time fee/pet. Designated rooms, service with restrictions, supervision.

SAVE S⊘ ✕ 🛢 🖵 🍴 ➼ 🗶

OLD FORGE

▼▼ Best Western Sunset Inn M
(315) 369-6836. **$69-$209, 7 day notice.** 2752 SR 28. 0.3 mi s. Ext/int corridors. **Pets:** Dogs only. Designated rooms, service with restrictions, supervision.

ASK S⊘ ✕ 🛢 🖵 ➼ 🗶

ONEONTA

◢◣◥◤ ▼▼▼▼ Holiday Inn Oneonta/Cooperstown Area SH
(607) 433-2250. **$79-$209.** 5206 State Hwy 23. I-88, exit 15 (SR 23 and 28), 1.5 mi e. Int corridors. **Pets:** Accepted.

SAVE S⊘ ✕ ✍ 🖉 🛢 🖵 🍴 ➼ 🗶

▼▼ Super 8 Motel SH
(607) 432-9505. **$68-$150.** 4973 SR 23. I-88, exit 15 (SR 23 and 28), 0.3 mi e. Int corridors. **Pets:** Designated rooms, service with restrictions, supervision.

ASK S⊘ ✕ ♿M 🛢

OWEGO

◢◣◥◤ ▼ Sunrise Motel M
(607) 687-5667. **$50-$65.** 3778 Waverly Rd. SR 17, exit 64 (SR 96 N) across river w to SR 17C, 2 mi w. Ext corridors. **Pets:** Small. $7 daily fee/pet. Service with restrictions, supervision.

SAVE S⊘ ✕

PAINTED POST

ⓐ ▼▼▼ Best Western Lodge on the Green Ⓜ
(607) 962-2456. **$50-$200.** 3171 Canada Rd. SR 17, exit 44, just s on US 15 to SR 417 and Gang Mills exit, then just n. Ext corridors. **Pets:** Other species. Service with restrictions, crate.
🆂🅰🆅🅴 ⬛ ✖ 🅱 🖥 🏊

▼▼ Econo Lodge SH
(607) 962-4444. **$69-$129.** 200 Robert Dann Dr. Jct US 15 and SR 17, exit 44, s to Gang Mills exit. Int corridors. **Pets:** $10 daily fee/pet. Service with restrictions, crate.
🅰🆂🅺 ⬛ ✖ 🅼 ⬛ 🅱 🖥

ⓐ ▼ Erwin Motel Ⓜ
(607) 962-7411. **$42-$79, 4 day notice.** 806 Addison Rd. US 15, exit Erwin Addison, 0.5 mi e. Ext corridors. **Pets:** Accepted.
🆂🅰🆅🅴 ✖ 🅱 🏊

▼▼ Super 8 Motel SH
(607) 937-5383. **$50-$135, 30 day notice.** 255 S Hamilton St. Jct US 15 and SR 17, exit 44, s to Gang Mills exit. Int corridors. **Pets:** Accepted.
🅰🆂🅺 ⬛ ✖ 🅼 ⬛ 🅱

PEMBROKE

▼▼ Darien Lakes Econo Lodge SH ❀
(585) 599-4681. **$45-$139.** 8493 SR 77. I-90, exit 48A, just s. Int corridors. **Pets:** Other species. Designated rooms, service with restrictions, supervision.
🅰🆂🅺 ⬛ ✖ 🅱 🖥

PENN YAN

ⓐ ▼▼▼ Best Western Vineyard Inn & Suites SH
(315) 536-8473. **$109-$190.** 142 Lake St. I-90, exit 43, SR 14 S to SR 54 N; corner of SR 54 and 14A. Int corridors. **Pets:** Small. $10 daily fee/room. Designated rooms, service with restrictions, supervision.
🆂🅰🆅🅴 ⬛ ✖ 🅱 🖥 🏊

PINE VALLEY

ⓐ ▼▼▼ Best Western Marshall Manor Ⓜ
(607) 739-3891. **$65-$107, 7 day notice.** 3527 Watkins Rd. SR 17, exit 52, 5 mi n on SR 14. Ext corridors. **Pets:** Other species. $6 daily fee/pet. Designated rooms, service with restrictions, crate.
🆂🅰🆅🅴 ⬛ ✖ 🅱 🖥 🏊

PLAINVIEW

▼▼◆ Four Points by Sheraton-Plainview Long Island SH
(516) 694-6500. **$135-$199.** 333 S Service Rd. I-495, exit 48. Int corridors. **Pets:** Very small, dogs only. $100 deposit/pet, $25 daily fee/pet. Service with restrictions, crate.
🅰🆂🅺 ⬛ ✖ 🅼 🅰 🅱 🖥 🍴 🏊

▼▼▼ Homewood Suites Long Island Melville SH
(516) 293-4663. **$229-$359.** 1585 Round Swamp Rd. I-495, exit 48, just s. Int corridors. **Pets:** Medium, other species. $150 one-time fee/room.
🅰🆂🅺 ⬛ ✖ 🅼 🅰 🅱 🖥 🏊 🚫

▼▼▼ Residence Inn by Marriott SH ❀
(516) 433-6200. **$199-$229.** 9 Gerhard Rd. I-495, exit 44, 1.6 mi s on SR 135, exit 10, then just e on Old Country Rd. Int corridors. **Pets:** Large, other species. $100 one-time fee/room. Crate.
✖ 🅼 🅰 🅱 🖥 🍴 🏊 🚫

PLATTSBURGH

ⓐ ▼▼◆ Americas Best Value Inn Ⓜ
(518) 563-0222. **$49-$129.** 19 Booth Dr. I-87, exit 37, just w. Ext corridors. **Pets:** Accepted.
🆂🅰🆅🅴 ⬛ ✖ 🅱 🖥

ⓐ ▼▼ Best Western The Inn at Smithfield SH ❀
(518) 561-7750. **$69-$179.** 446 Rt 3. I-87, exit 37, just w. Int corridors. **Pets:** Other species. $10 one-time fee/room. Service with restrictions, supervision.
🆂🅰🆅🅴 ⬛ ✖ 🅱 🖥 🍴 🏊 🚫

ⓐ ▼▼▼ La Quinta SH
(518) 562-4000. **$77-$144.** 16 Plaza Blvd. I-87, exit 37, just w. Int corridors. **Pets:** Medium. Service with restrictions.
🆂🅰🆅🅴 ✖ 🅼 🅰 🅸 🅱 🖥 🏊

ⓐ ▼▼▼ Microtel Inn and Suites SH
(518) 324-3800. **$54-$134.** 554 SR 3. I-87, exit 37, just w. Int corridors. **Pets:** Medium. $10 daily fee/pet. Service with restrictions, supervision.
🆂🅰🆅🅴 ⬛ ✖ 🅼 🅰 🅱 🖥

▼▼ Super 8 Motel Ⓜ
(518) 562-8888. **$53-$89.** 7129 Rt 9 N. I-87, exit 39, just e, then just n. Int corridors. **Pets:** Dogs only. $10 daily fee/pet. Designated rooms, service with restrictions, supervision.
🅰🆂🅺 ⬛ ✖ 🅼 🅱 🖥 🏊

PORT JERVIS

ⓐ ▼▼ Comfort Inn SH ❀
(845) 856-6611. **$69-$149.** 2247 Greenville Tpke. I-84, exit 1, just se. Int corridors. **Pets:** Medium, other species. $20 one-time fee/room. Designated rooms, service with restrictions, supervision.
🆂🅰🆅🅴 ⬛ ✖ 🅱 🖥 🏊

POUGHKEEPSIE

ⓐ ▼▼▼ Best Western Inn & Conference Center SH
(845) 462-4600. **$90-$150.** 2170 South Rd (Rt 9). I-84, exit 13N, 4.7 mi s of Mid Hudson Bridge. Int corridors. **Pets:** Other species. $50 deposit/room. Service with restrictions, supervision.
🆂🅰🆅🅴 ⬛ ✖ 🅱 🖥 🍴 🏊

◆▼ Econo Lodge SH
(845) 452-6600. **$70-$135.** 2625 US 9. I-84, exit 13N, 1.6 mi s of Mid-Hudson Bridge. Ext corridors. **Pets:** Other species. $100 deposit/pet, $25 daily fee/pet. Service with restrictions, supervision.
🅰🆂🅺 ⬛ ✖ 🅼 🅱

PULASKI

ⓐ ▼ Red Carpet Inn & Scottish Inns & Suites Ⓜ
(315) 298-4717. **$74-$139.** 3723 SR 13. I-81, exit 36, just e. Ext/int corridors. **Pets:** Accepted.
🆂🅰🆅🅴 ⬛ ✖ 🅱 🍴 🏊

RHINEBECK

▼▼▼ Beekman Arms & Delamater Inn and Conference Center Ⓒ🅸
(845) 876-7077. **$110-$300, 14 day notice.** 6387 Mill St (Rt 9). Jct US 9 and SR 308; center of village. Ext/int corridors. **Pets:** Accepted.
✖ 🅰 🅱 🖥 🍴

RIVERHEAD

▼▼▼ Best Western East End SH
(631) 369-2200. **$169-$300, 3 day notice.** 1830 SR 25. I-495, exit 72 (SR 25 E). Int corridors. **Pets:** Medium, dogs only. $50 one-time fee/room. Designated rooms, service with restrictions, crate.
🅰🆂🅺 ⬛ ✖ 🅰 🅱 🖥 🍴 🏊

▼▼▼ Holiday Inn Express East End SH
(631) 548-1000. **$179-$399, 5 day notice.** 1707 Old Country Rd (SR 58). I-495, exit 73, 0.5 mi n. Int corridors. **Pets:** Medium, dogs only. $50 one-time fee/room. Designated rooms, service with restrictions, crate.
🅰🆂🅺 ⬛ ✖ 🅼 🅰 🅱 🖥

ROCHESTER

Clarion Riverside Hotel 🅛🅗
(585) 546-6400. **$99-$169.** 120 E Main St. Downtown. Int corridors.
Pets: Accepted.
[ASK] [S🅓] [✕] [♿M] [▨] [♿] [🛏] [💻] [🍴] [🏊] [✕]

Strathallan Hotel 🅢🅗
(585) 461-5010. **$80.** 550 East Ave. I-490, exit 17, 0.8 mi n on Goodman St, then just w. Int corridors. **Pets:** Accepted.
[ASK] [S🅓] [✕] [🛏] [💻] [🍴]

ROCK HILL

The Lodge at Rock Hill 🅢🅗
(845) 796-3100. **$99-$239.** 283 Rock Hill Dr. SR 17, exit 109, just e. Int corridors. **Pets:** Other species. $25 daily fee/pet. Designated rooms, no service, supervision.
[SAVE] [S🅓] [✕] [▨] [♿] [🛏] [💻] [🏊]

ROCKVILLE CENTRE

Best Western Mill River Manor 🅢🅗
(516) 678-1300. **$109-$159.** 173 Sunrise Hwy. On SR 27; between N Village and N Centre aves. Ext corridors. **Pets:** Accepted.
[SAVE] [S🅓] [✕] [♿M] [▨] [♿] [🛏] [💻] [🍴] [🏊]

ROME

Econo Lodge 🅜
(315) 337-9400. **$70-$110.** 145 E Whitesboro St. Just s of jct SR 26 and 46. Ext corridors. **Pets:** Small. $25 one-time fee/pet. Service with restrictions, supervision.
[ASK] [S🅓] [✕] [🛏] [💻]

Inn at the Beeches 🅜
(315) 336-1776. **$79-$118.** 7900 Turin Rd. Jct SR 46, 2 mi n on SR 26 (Turin Rd). Ext corridors. **Pets:** Accepted.
[SAVE] [S🅓] [✕] [🛏] [🍴] [🏊]

Quality Inn of Rome 🅢🅗
(315) 336-4300. **$73-$159.** 200 S James St. On SR 49; downtown. Ext/int corridors. **Pets:** Medium. $25 daily fee/room. Designated rooms, service with restrictions.
[SAVE] [S🅓] [✕] [🛏] [💻] [🍴] [🏊]

ROSCOE

Roscoe Motel 🅜
(607) 498-5220. **$70, 7 day notice.** 2054 Old Rt 17. SR 17, exit 94, 0.5 mi n on SR 206, then just w. Ext corridors. **Pets:** Accepted.
[SAVE] [🛏] [💻]

ROTTERDAM

Super 8 Schenectady 🅢🅗
(518) 355-2190. **$65-$99.** 3083 Carman Rd. I-890, exit 9 (Curry Rd), 0.4 mi w; I-90, exit 25. Int corridors. **Pets:** Other species. $10 daily fee/pet. Service with restrictions, supervision.
[ASK] [S🅓] [✕]

SACKETS HARBOR

Ontario Place Hotel 🅢🅗
(315) 646-8000. **$84-$150.** 103 General Smith Dr. Center. Int corridors. **Pets:** $10 one-time fee/room. Designated rooms, service with restrictions, crate.
[✕] [🛏] [💻]

SALAMANCA

Holiday Inn Express Hotel & Suites 🅢🅗
(716) 945-7600. **$119-$179.** 779 Broad St. I-86, exit 20, just n. Int corridors. **Pets:** Large, other species. $25 deposit/pet, $25 daily fee/pet. Designated rooms, service with restrictions, supervision.
[ASK] [S🅓] [✕] [♿M] [▨] [♿] [🛏] [💻] [🏊]

SARANAC LAKE

Adirondack Motel 🅜
(518) 891-2116. **$65-$180.** 248 Lake Flower Ave. 0.7 mi e on SR 86. Ext corridors. **Pets:** Dogs only. $10 daily fee/pet. Service with restrictions, crate.
[SAVE] [✕] [🛏] [💻] [✕]

Best Western Mountain Lake Inn 🅢🅗
(518) 891-1970. **$76-$195.** 487 Lake Flower Ave. 0.8 mi e on SR 86. Int corridors. **Pets:** Other species. $20 one-time fee/room. Designated rooms, supervision.
[SAVE] [S🅓] [✕] [♿M] [💻] [🍴] [🏊]

The Hotel Saranac of Paul Smith's College 🅢🅗
(518) 891-2200. **$70-$150, 3 day notice.** 100 Main St. Center. Int corridors. **Pets:** Other species. $15 daily fee/pet. Designated rooms, service with restrictions, crate.
[SAVE] [S🅓] [✕] [▨] [🛏] [💻] [🍴]

Lake Flower Inn 🅜
(518) 891-2310. **$48-$128, 14 day notice.** 234 Lake Flower Ave. 0.6 mi e on SR 86. Ext corridors. **Pets:** Dogs only. Designated rooms, supervision.
[✕] [🛏] [🏊] [✕]

Lake Side Motel 🅜
(518) 891-4333. **$69-$119, 7 day notice.** 256 Lake Flower Ave. 0.6 mi e on SR 86. Ext corridors. **Pets:** Dogs only. $10 daily fee/room. Designated rooms, supervision.
[✕] [🛏] [🏊] [✕]

SARATOGA SPRINGS

Holiday Inn 🅢🅗 🐾
(518) 584-4550. **$89-$319.** 232 Broadway. On US 9, jct SR 50. Int corridors. **Pets:** Other species. Designated rooms, service with restrictions, supervision.
[SAVE] [S🅓] [✕] [▨] [🛏] [💻] [🍴] [🏊]

Residence Inn by Marriott-Saratoga Springs 🅛🅗 🐾
(518) 584-9600. **$139-$399.** 295 Excelsior Ave. I-87, exit 15, just n, just s, then just e. Int corridors. **Pets:** Large. $75 one-time fee/room. Service with restrictions, supervision.
[ASK] [S🅓] [✕] [♿M] [♿] [🛏] [💻] [🏊] [✕]

The Saratoga Hotel & Conference Center 🅢🅗
(518) 584-4000. **$139-$599, 14 day notice.** 534 Broadway. I-87, exit 15, on SR 50. Int corridors. **Pets:** Accepted.
[SAVE] [✕] [♿] [🛏] [💻] [🍴] [🏊]

Union Gables Bed & Breakfast 🅑🅑
(518) 584-1558. **$140-$410, 30 day notice.** 55 Union Ave. I-87, exit 14, 1.5 mi w. Int corridors. **Pets:** $25 one-time fee/room.
[SAVE] [✕] [🛏]

SAUGERTIES

Comfort Inn 🅢🅗 🐾
(845) 246-1565. **$89-$159.** 2790 SR 32. I-87, exit 20, just n. Int corridors. **Pets:** Other species. $25 one-time fee/room. Designated rooms, service with restrictions, supervision.
[SAVE] [S🅓] [✕] [🛏] [💻]

SCHENECTADY

Days Inn 🅢🅗
(518) 370-3297. **$69-$99, 14 day notice.** 167 Nott Terrace. Jct State St (SR 5) and Nott Terrace, 2 blks e; downtown. Int corridors. **Pets:** Very small. $10 daily fee/pet. Designated rooms, no service, supervision.
[ASK] [S🅓] [✕] [▨] [🛏] [💻]

SCHOHARIE

▼▼▼▼ Holiday Inn Express Hotel & Suites Schoharie SH
(518) 295-6088. **$89-$169.** 160 Holiday Way. I-88, exit 23, just e to
Park Pl, then just s. Int corridors. **Pets:** Dogs only. $17 daily fee/pet.
Designated rooms, service with restrictions, supervision.

ASK SAVE X 🐾 🐾 🛏 💻

SCHROON LAKE

▲▲▲ ▼ Blue Ridge Motel M 🐾
(518) 532-7521. **$88-$98, 14 day notice.** 2455 US Rt 9. I-87, exit 28, 4
mi n. Ext/int corridors. **Pets:** Other species. $8 daily fee/pet. Designated
rooms, service with restrictions, crate.

SAVE SAVE X 🛏 💻 🏊 ✗

SCHUYLERVILLE

▼▼ Burgoyne Motor Inn M
(518) 695-3282. **$49-$145, 3 day notice.** 220 Broad St. US 4 and SR
32, just n of jct SR 29. Ext/int corridors. **Pets:** Accepted.

ASK X 🐾 🛏 💻

SKANEATELES

▲▲▲ ▼▼▼▼ Skaneateles Suites M 🐾
(315) 685-7568. **$125-$195.** 4114 W Genesee St. On US 20, 2 mi w.
Ext corridors. **Pets:** Large, dogs only. $35 one-time fee/pet. Service with
restrictions, supervision.

SAVE SAVE X 🛏 💻

SOLVAY

▼▼ ◆ Holiday Inn/Farrell Road SH
(315) 457-8700. **$99-$139.** 100 Farrell Rd. I-690, exit 4 (John Glenn
Blvd). Int corridors. **Pets:** Accepted.

ASK SAVE X 🐾 🐾 🛏 💻 🍴 🏊

SOUTHAMPTON

▲▲▲ ▼▼▼▼ Southampton Inn SH 🐾
(631) 283-6500. **$119-$489, 30 day notice.** 91 Hill St. 0.3 mi n from
corner of Main St and Jobs Ln. Ext corridors. **Pets:** Other species. $39
daily fee/pet. Designated rooms, service with restrictions, supervision.

SAVE SAVE X 🐾 🛏 🍴 🏊 ✗

STEPHENTOWN

▼▼ ◆ The Mill House Inn BB
(518) 733-5606. **$125-$135, 14 day notice.** 86 Rt 43. Jct SR 22, 1.1 mi
e. Ext/int corridors. **Pets:** Accepted.

X 🛏 🏊

SYLVAN BEACH

▼ Cinderella's Suites M
(315) 762-4280. **$59-$179, 16 day notice.** 1208 N Main St. On SR 13;
center. Ext corridors. **Pets:** Accepted.

ASK SAVE X 🛏 💻 🍴

SYRACUSE

▲▲▲ ▼▼▼▼ Renaissance Syracuse Hotel LH
(315) 479-7000. **$155-$339.** 701 E Genesee St. Jct Almond St; downtown. Int corridors. **Pets:** Accepted.

SAVE SAVE X 🐾 🐾 🐾 🛏 💻 🍴

▲▲▲ ▼▼▼▼ Sheraton Syracuse University Hotel &
Conference Center LH 🐾
(315) 475-3000. **$129-$409.** 801 University Ave. I-81, exit 18. Int corridors. **Pets:** Medium, dogs only. Designated rooms, service with restrictions,
supervision.

SAVE SAVE X 🛏 💻 🍴 🏊 ✗

TICONDEROGA

▲▲▲ ▼ Circle Court Motel M
(518) 585-7660. **$60-$84.** 6 Montcalm St. SR 9N; at Liberty Monument
traffic circle. Ext corridors. **Pets:** $10 daily fee/pet. Service with restric-
tions, supervision.

SAVE SAVE X 🛏 💻

TROY

▲▲▲ ▼▼▼ Best Western-Rensselaer Inn SH
(518) 274-3210. **$89-$99.** 1800 6th Ave. I-787, exit 9, 0.5 mi e, exit
downtown, then 0.5 mi s. Int corridors. **Pets:** Very small. $100 deposit/
room. Designated rooms, service with restrictions, crate.

SAVE SAVE X 🛏 💻 🍴 🏊

TUPPER LAKE

▲▲▲ ▼ Red Top Inn M
(518) 359-9209. **$55-$85, 3 day notice.** 1562 SR 30. 3 mi s. Ext/int
corridors. **Pets:** Accepted.

SAVE SAVE X 🛏 💻

UTICA

▼▼ ◆ Best Western Gateway Adirondack Inn SH
(315) 732-4121. **$79-$169.** 175 N Genesee St. I-90 (New York State
Thruway), exit 31, 0.5 mi s. Int corridors. **Pets:** Medium. $25 daily
fee/room. Service with restrictions, supervision.

ASK SAVE X 🐾 🛏 💻

▼▼ ◆ Red Roof Inn #7180 M
(315) 724-7128. **$60-$105.** 20 Weaver St. I-90 (New York State Thruway), exit 31. Ext corridors. **Pets:** Medium, other species. Service with
restrictions, supervision.

X 🛏

▲▲▲ ▼ Scottish Inns M
(315) 735-6698. **$40-$95, 3 day notice.** 238 N Genesee St. I-90 (New
York State Thruway), exit 31, just s. Int corridors. **Pets:** Medium, dogs
only. Designated rooms, service with restrictions, supervision.

SAVE SAVE X 🛏

VALATIE

▲▲▲ ▼▼▼ Blue Spruce Inn & Suites M 🐾
(518) 758-9711. **$80-$100, 7 day notice.** 3093 Rt 9. I-90 (New York
State Thruway), exit 12, 4 mi s on US 9 via New York State Thruway
Extension, exit B1. Ext corridors. **Pets:** Other species. Supervision.

SAVE SAVE X 🛏 💻 🍴 🏊

VESTAL

▼▼▼▼ Holiday Inn at the University SH
(607) 729-6371. **$79-$189.** 4105 Vestal Pkwy E. SR 17, exit 70, 2.5 mi
s on US 201 to SR 434 W, then right on Bunn Hill Rd. Int corridors.
Pets: Accepted.

ASK SAVE X 🐾 🛏 💻 🍴 🏊

VICTOR

▲▲▲ ▼▼▼▼ Hampton Inn and Suites-Rochester/Victor SH
(585) 924-4400. **$139-$179.** 7637 SR 96. I-90 (New York State Thruway), exit 45, just n. Int corridors. **Pets:** Accepted.

SAVE SAVE X 🛏 💻 🏊

▲▲▲ ▼ Royal Inn M
(585) 924-2121. **$59-$99.** 7463 SR 96. I-90 (New York State Thruway),
exit 45; I-490 (SR 96) exit 29, 0.8 mi s. Ext corridors. **Pets:** Accepted.

SAVE SAVE X 🛏

WARRENSBURG

Super 8 Warrensburg/Lake George
(518) 623-2811. **$80-$155.** 3619 SR 9. I-87, exit 23, just w. Int corridors. **Pets:** Other species. $10 daily fee/pet. Designated rooms, service with restrictions, supervision.
(ASK) (X)

WATERLOO

Holiday Inn Waterloo-Seneca Falls SH
(315) 539-5011. **$79-$179.** 2468 SR 414. I-90 (New York State Thruway), exit 41, 4 mi s; just n of jct SR 414/5 and US 20. Int corridors. **Pets:** Accepted.
(SAVE) (X) (info) (parking) (restaurant) (pool) (X)

Microtel Inn & Suites SH
(315) 539-8438. **$46-$94.** 1966 Rt 5 & 20. I-90 (New York State Thruway), exit 41, 4 mi s on SR 414, then just e. Int corridors. **Pets:** $15 daily fee/room. Supervision.
(SAVE) (X) (accessible) (free breakfast) (info) (parking)

WATERTOWN

Best Western Carriage House Inn & Conference Center SH
(315) 782-8000. **$70-$210.** 300 Washington St. Center. Int corridors. **Pets:** $15 daily fee/pet. Designated rooms, service with restrictions, supervision.
(SAVE) (free breakfast) (X) (info) (parking) (restaurant) (pool)

Davidson's Motel M
(315) 782-3861. **$55-$80.** 26177 NYS Rt 3. From Town Square, 3.5 mi e. Ext corridors. **Pets:** Medium, other species. $5 daily fee/pet. Service with restrictions, supervision.
(SAVE) (X) (info) (pool)

Ramada SH
(315) 788-0700. **$84-$94.** 6300 Arsenal St. I-81, exit 45, just w. Int corridors. **Pets:** Accepted.
(SAVE) (free breakfast) (X) (info) (parking) (restaurant) (pool) (X)

WATKINS GLEN

Anchor Inn and Marina M ❖
(607) 535-4159. **$69-$159, 10 day notice.** 3425 Salt Point Rd. Just n on SR 14, 0.8 mi n. Ext corridors. **Pets:** Medium. $25 deposit/pet. Service with restrictions, supervision.
(SAVE) (free breakfast) (X) (accessible) (info) (X)

Chieftain Motel M
(607) 535-4759. **$69-$159, 10 day notice.** 3815 SR 14. Jct SR 14A; 3 mi n of town. Ext corridors. **Pets:** Accepted.
(SAVE) (free breakfast) (X) (accessible) (info) (parking) (pool)

WELLSVILLE

Long Vue Inn & Suites M
(585) 593-2450. **$54-$64.** 5081 Rt 417 W. Jct SR 19, 3 mi w. Ext corridors. **Pets:** $7 daily fee/pet. Supervision.
(SAVE) (free breakfast) (X) (info) (parking)

Microtel Inn & Suites SH
(585) 593-3449. **$54-$104.** 30 W Dyke St. Just n off SR 19 and 417. Int corridors. **Pets:** Accepted.
(ASK) (free breakfast) (X) (accessible) (accessible) (info) (parking)

WEST COXSACKIE

Best Western New Baltimore Inn SH
(518) 731-8100. **$89-$139.** 12600 Rt 9W. I-87 (New York State Thruway), exit 21B, 0.5 mi s. Int corridors. **Pets:** Accepted.
(ASK) (free breakfast) (X) (accessible) (info) (parking) (pool) (X)

WESTMORELAND

Carriage Motor Inn M
(315) 853-3561. **$45-$70, 5 day notice.** 5370 SR 233. I-90 (New York State Thruway), exit 32, just n. Ext corridors. **Pets:** Small. $20 deposit/room, $10 daily fee/pet. Service with restrictions, supervision.
(SAVE) (free breakfast) (X) (info)

WILMINGTON

Grand View Motel M
(518) 946-2209. **$59-$99.** 5941 NYS Rt 86. On SR 86, 1 mi e. Ext corridors. **Pets:** Accepted.
(SAVE) (free breakfast) (X) (info) (pool) (X)

Green Mountain Lodge M
(518) 946-8232. **Call for rates.** 5675 SR 86. Jct SR 86 and Whiteface Mt Hwy (SR 431). Ext corridors. **Pets:** Other species. Supervision.
(X) (info) (parking) (X)

Hungry Trout Resort M ❖
(518) 946-2217. **$69-$169, 14 day notice.** 5239 Rt 86. On SR 86, 2 mi w. Ext corridors. **Pets:** Dogs only. $10 daily fee/pet. Designated rooms, service with restrictions.
(SAVE) (free breakfast) (X) (info) (parking) (restaurant) (pool) (X)

Ledge Rock at Whiteface Mountain M
(518) 946-2379. **$79-$149, 10 day notice.** 5078 NYS Rt 86. On SR 86, 3 mi w. Ext corridors. **Pets:** $25 daily fee/pet. Crate.
(SAVE) (free breakfast) (X) (info) (parking) (pool) (X)

Mountain Brook Lodge M
(518) 946-2262. **$65-$99, 7 day notice.** 5712 Rt 86. Center. Ext corridors. **Pets:** Accepted.
(X) (info) (parking) (pool)

North Pole Inn M
(518) 946-7733. **$59-$139, 7 day notice.** 5636 NYS Rt 86. On SR 86, just w of jct CR 431. Ext corridors. **Pets:** Dogs only. $10 daily fee/pet. Service with restrictions, supervision.
(SAVE) (free breakfast) (X) (info) (parking) (pool) (X)

Willkommen Hof Bed & Breakfast BB ❖
(518) 946-7669. **$70-$149, 21 day notice.** 5367 Rt 86. On SR 86, 1.5 mi of jct CR 431. Int corridors. **Pets:** Large, other species. $50 deposit/pet. Designated rooms, service with restrictions, crate.
(ASK) (free breakfast) (X) (info) (parking) (X) (Z)

WOODBURY

Best Western Woodbury Inn M
(516) 921-6900. **$109-$169.** 7940 Jericho Tpke (SR 25). Jct SR 25 and 135, 0.9 mi e. Ext/int corridors. **Pets:** Accepted.
(SAVE) (free breakfast) (X) (info) (parking) (restaurant) (pool)

Executive Inn at Woodbury M ❖
(516) 921-8500. **$115-$149.** 8030 Jericho Tpke (SR 25). Jct SR 25 and 135, 1 mi e. Ext corridors. **Pets:** $50 one-time fee/room. Service with restrictions, supervision.
(SAVE) (free breakfast) (X) (accessible) (info) (parking) (pool)

NORTH CAROLINA

ABERDEEN

▲▲▲ ▼◆▼ Best Western Pinehurst Motor Inn M
(910) 944-2367. $70-$95. 1500 Sandhills Blvd. Jct US 15/501 N, just s on US 1. Ext corridors. Pets: Accepted.

▼ Motel 6-1234 M
(910) 944-5633. $45-$59. 1408 Sandhills Blvd. Jct US 15/501 N, just s on US 1. Ext corridors. Pets: Medium, other species. Service with restrictions, supervision.

ALBEMARLE

▼◆▼ Best Western Executive Inn SH
(704) 983-6990. $65-$85. 735 SR 24/27 Bypass. Jct US 52 S, 1.4 mi e. Ext corridors. Pets: Accepted.

ANDREWS

▼◆▼ Hawkesdene House Mountain Retreat BB
(828) 321-6027. $149-$189, 3 day notice. 381 Phillips Creek Rd. US 19 business route, 3.2 mi s on Cherry St, then 0.5 mi s. Ext/int corridors. Pets: Accepted.

ARCHDALE

▲▲▲ ▼◆▼ Comfort Inn Archdale SH
(336) 434-4797. $78-$189. 10123 N Main St. I-85, exit 111, just n on US 311, then just sw on Balfour Dr. Int corridors. Pets: Designated rooms, supervision.

ARDEN

▼◆▼ Quality Inn & Suites Biltmore South SH
(828) 684-6688. $59-$169. 1 Skyline Inn Dr. I-26, exit 37. Int corridors. Pets: Accepted.

ASHEBORO

▼◆▼ Comfort Inn SH
(336) 626-3680. $110-$135. 242 Lakecrest Rd. US 64, just w on SR 42. Ext corridors. Pets: Accepted.

ASHEVILLE

▼◆▼ 1889 WhiteGate Inn & Cottage BB
(828) 253-2553. $185-$360, 14 day notice. 173 E Chestnut St. I-240, exit 5B (Charlotte St), just n, then just w; in historic district. Ext/int corridors. Pets: Medium, dogs only. $50 one-time fee/room. Designated rooms, service with restrictions, supervision.

▲▲▲ ▼◆▼◆▼ 1891 Cedar Crest Inn BB
(828) 252-1389. $150-$300, 14 day notice. 674 Biltmore Ave. I-40, exit 50, 1.1 mi n. Ext/int corridors. Pets: Accepted.

▼◆▼ 1900 Inn on Montford BB ❀
(828) 254-9569. $125-$630, 14 day notice. 296 Montford Ave. I-240, exit 4C (Montford Ave/Haywood St), 0.7 mi n; in historic district. Ext/int corridors. Pets: Other species. Designated rooms.

▲▲▲ ▼◆▼◆▼ Abbington Green Bed & Breakfast Inn BB
(828) 251-2454. $125-$385, 14 day notice. 46 Cumberland Cir. I-240, exit 4C (Montford Ave/Haywood St), n to W Chestnut St, just e to Cumberland Ave, then 0.3 mi n; in historic district. Ext/int corridors. Pets: Medium, dogs only. $9 daily fee/pet. Designated rooms, service with restrictions, crate.

▼◆▼ Best Western Asheville Biltmore SH
(828) 253-1851. $64-$194. 22 Woodfin St. I-240, exit 5A (Merrimon Ave). Int corridors. Pets: Medium, other species. $50 one-time fee/pet. Designated rooms, service with restrictions, supervision.

▲▲▲ ▼◆▼◆▼ Best Western of Asheville Biltmore East M
(828) 298-5562. $39-$159. 501 Tunnel Rd. I-240, exit 7, 0.5 mi e on US 70 (Tunnel Rd). Ext corridors. Pets: Medium, dogs only. $10 daily fee/pet. Service with restrictions, supervision.

▼◆▼ Biltmore Village Inn BB
(828) 274-8707. $210-$325, 14 day notice. 119 Dodge St. I-40, exit 50/50B (US 25 N), 0.5 mi n, just e on Lula St, just n on Reed St, just e on Warren Ave, then just s. Ext/int corridors. Pets: Accepted.

▲▲▲ ▼◆▼ Black Walnut B&B Inn BB ❀
(828) 254-3878. $135-$275, 15 day notice. 288 Montford Ave. I-240, exit 4C (Montford Ave/Haywood St), 0.5 mi n; in the historic district. Ext/int corridors. Pets: Other species. Designated rooms.

▼▼ **Carolina Bed & Breakfast** BB
(828) 254-3608. **$120-$215.** 177 Cumberland Ave. I-240, exit 4C (Mont-ford Ave/Haywood St), 0.5 mi n on Montford Ave, just e on Chestnut St, then just n. Ext/int corridors. **Pets:** Accepted.
ASK ✕ ☐ ☐ ☐

▼▼▼ **Comfort Suites-Biltmore Square Mall** SH ❖
(828) 665-4000. **$50-$159.** 890 Brevard Rd. I-26, exit 33, 0.3 mi w. Int corridors. **Pets:** Medium, other species. $20 daily fee/room. Designated rooms, service with restrictions, crate.
SAVE ☐ ✕ ☐ ☐ ☐ ☐ ☐

▼▼▼ **Crowne Plaza Resort** SH
(828) 254-3211. **$79-$199.** 1 Holiday Inn Dr. I-240, exit 3B (Holiday Inn Dr), just w. Int corridors. **Pets:** Accepted.
ASK ✕ ☐ ☐ ☐ ☐ ☐ ☐ ✕

▼▼▼ **Days Inn-Asheville Mall** M
(828) 252-4000. **$40-$205.** 201 Tunnel Rd. I-240, exit 6, 0.5 mi e, on south side of road. Ext corridors. **Pets:** Medium, other species. $15 daily fee/pet. Designated rooms, service with restrictions.
SAVE ☐ ✕ ☐ ☐ ☐ ☐

▼▼▼ **Days Inn-Biltmore East** SH
(828) 298-4000. **$39-$159.** 1435 Tunnel Rd. I-40, exit 55, just n. Int corridors. **Pets:** Medium, dogs only. $10 daily fee/pet. Service with restrictions, supervision.
SAVE ☐ ✕ ☐ ☐ ☐ ☐

▼▼ **Extended StayAmerica** SH
(828) 253-3483. **Call for rates.** 6 Kenilworth Knoll. I-240, exit 6, 0.7 mi e on US 70 (Tunnel Rd), then just n. Int corridors. **Pets:** Accepted.
✕ ☐ ☐ ☐

▼▼▼ **Holiday Inn-Biltmore East at the Blue Ridge Parkway** SH ❖
(828) 298-5611. **$100-$160.** 1450 Tunnel Rd. I-40, exit 55, just n. Int corridors. **Pets:** Other species. $20 daily fee/room. Designated rooms, service with restrictions, crate.
ASK ☐ ✕ ☐ ☐ ☐ ☐ ☐ ☐

▼▼ **The Log Cabin Motor Court** CA
(828) 645-6546. **$55-$250, 14 day notice.** 330 Weaverville Hwy. US 19/23, exit 21 (New Stock Rd), 1 mi s on Weaverville Hwy. Ext corridors. **Pets:** Accepted.
SAVE ✕ ☐ ☐ ☐ ☐

▼ **Motel 6–1134** M
(828) 299-3040. **$43-$61.** 1415 Tunnel Rd. I-40, exit 55. Ext corridors. **Pets:** Medium, other species. Service with restrictions, supervision.
☐ ✕ ☐ ☐

▼▼▼ **Quality Inn & Suites** SH
(828) 298-5519. **$50-$159.** 1430 Tunnel Rd. I-40, exit 55, just n. Ext corridors. **Pets:** Medium, other species. $20 daily fee/pet. Designated rooms, service with restrictions, supervision.
SAVE ☐ ✕ ☐ ☐ ☐ ☐ ☐

▼▼▼ **Ramada Inn Asheville** SH ❖
(828) 298-9141. **$59-$139.** 800 Fairview Rd. I-240, exit 8; jct I-40 and US 74. Ext/int corridors. **Pets:** Other species. $25 one-time fee/room. Designated rooms, service with restrictions.
ASK ☐ ✕ ☐ ☐ ☐ ☐ ✕

▼▼ **Red Roof Inn-West** M
(828) 667-9803. **$43-$80.** 16 Crowell Rd. I-40, exit 44, just n on US 19 and 23, just w on Old Haywood Rd, then just s. Ext corridors. **Pets:** Medium, other species. Service with restrictions, supervision.
✕ ☐ ☐ ☐

▼▼ **Sleep Inn Biltmore** SH
(828) 277-1800. **$69-$159.** 117 Hendersonville Rd. I-40, exit 50 eastbound; exit 50B westbound, just n on US 25. Int corridors. **Pets:** Accepted.
☐ ✕ ☐ ☐ ☐

▼▼ **Super 8 Biltmore East** M
(828) 298-7952. **$37-$99.** 1329 Tunnel Rd. I-40, exit 55, 0.3 mi w. Ext corridors. **Pets:** Other species. $20 one-time fee/pet. Designated rooms, service with restrictions, supervision.
SAVE ☐ ✕ ☐ ☐ ☐ ☐ ☐

▼▼ **Super 8 Motel at Biltmore Square** SH
(828) 670-8800. **$49-$149.** 9 Wedgefield Dr. I-26, exit 33, just nw. Int corridors. **Pets:** Medium, other species. $15 one-time fee/pet. Service with restrictions, supervision.
ASK ☐ ✕ ☐ ☐ ☐ ☐

▼▼ **Super 8 Motel Central** M
(828) 667-8706. **$49-$149.** 8 Crowell Rd. I-40, exit 44, just n on US 19 and 23. Int corridors. **Pets:** Medium. $15 one-time fee/room. Service with restrictions, supervision.
ASK ☐ ✕ ☐ ☐ ☐

BANNER ELK

▼▼▼▼ **Banner Elk Inn B&B and Cottages** BB
(828) 898-6223. **$90-$175, 30 day notice.** 407 Main St E. Jct SR 184 and 194, 0.3 mi n on SR 194. Int corridors. **Pets:** Dogs only. Designated rooms, service with restrictions, supervision.
✕ ☐ ☐

▼▼▼ **Best Western Mountain Lodge at Banner Elk** SH ❖
(828) 898-4571. **$79-$209, 3 day notice.** 1615 Tynecastle Hwy. 1 mi se on SR 184. Ext corridors. **Pets:** Other species. $25 deposit/pet. Designated rooms, service with restrictions.
ASK ☐ ✕ ☐ ☐ ☐ ☐ ☐ ☐ ☐

BLOWING ROCK

▼▼ **Hillwinds Inn** M
(828) 295-7660. **$89-$189, 3 day notice.** 315 Sunset Dr. Just e of Main St. Ext/int corridors. **Pets:** Accepted.
ASK ☐ ✕ ☐ ☐

▼▼▼ **The Village Inn** M
(828) 295-3380. **$79-$189, 3 day notice.** 7876 Valley Blvd. On US 321 Bypass, just e of city park. Ext corridors. **Pets:** Accepted.
ASK ☐ ✕ ☐ ☐ ☐

BOILING SPRINGS

▼▼▼ **AmericInn Lodge & Suites** SH
(704) 434-9996. **$89-$139.** 428 E College Ave. On SR 150; east of town center. Int corridors. **Pets:** Small. $30 one-time fee/room. Designated rooms, service with restrictions.
ASK ☐ ✕ ☐ ☐ ☐ ☐ ☐

BREVARD

▼▼▼ **Holiday Inn Express** SH
(828) 862-8900. **$69-$125.** 1570 Asheville Hwy. 3 mi e on US 64. Int corridors. **Pets:** Accepted.
ASK ☐ ✕ ☐ ☐ ☐ ☐ ☐

BURLINGTON

▼▼▼ **Econo Lodge** SH
(336) 227-1270. **$50-$70, 3 day notice.** 2133 W Hanford Rd. I-40/85, exit 145, just s on SR 49, then just w. Int corridors. **Pets:** Small. $10 daily fee/pet. Service with restrictions, supervision.
SAVE ☐ ✕ ☐ ☐

▼▼▼ **La Quinta Inn** SH
(336) 229-5203. **$65-$155, 3 day notice.** 2444 Maple Ave. I-40/85, exit 145, just n. Int corridors. **Pets:** Accepted.
✕ ☐ ☐ ☐ ☐ ☐

▼ Motel 6–1257 **M**
(336) 226-1325. **$41-$53.** 2155 Hanford Rd. I-40/85, exit 145, just s on SR 49, then just w. Ext corridors. **Pets:** Medium, other species. Service with restrictions, supervision.

CANDLER

◆◆◆ ▼▼▼▼ Owl's Nest Inn and Engadine Cabins **BB** ❀
(828) 665-8325. **$145-$250.** 2630 Smoky Park Hwy. I-40, exit 37, 0.5 mi w on SR 19/23. Ext/int corridors. **Pets:** Other species. $50 one-time fee/room. Designated rooms, service with restrictions, crate.

CARY

◆◆◆ ▼▼▼▼ Best Western Cary Inn & Suites **SH**
(919) 481-1200. **$81-$90.** 1722 Walnut St. I-40, exit 293A, 0.3 mi sw on US 1/64, exit Walnut St, then just w. Ext/int corridors. **Pets:** Small, other species. $125 one-time fee/pet. Service with restrictions, crate.

▼▼▼▼ Candlewood Suites **SH** ❀
(919) 468-4222. **$53-$140.** 1020 Buck Jones Rd. I-40, exit 293A, just sw on US 1/64, exit Walnut St, just w, then 0.5 mi n; in Buck Jones Village. Int corridors. **Pets:** Large, other species. $12 daily fee/room. Service with restrictions, crate.

▼▼▼ Comfort Suites Hotel **SH**
(919) 852-4318. **$69-$109.** 350 Ashville Ave. US 1, exit 98A, 0.8 mi e on Tryon Rd, then just n. Int corridors. **Pets:** Medium. $75 one-time fee/pet. Designated rooms, service with restrictions, supervision.

▼▼▼ Extended StayAmerica Raleigh-Cary-Regency Parkway **SH**
(919) 468-5828. **$79-$99.** 1500 Regency Pkwy. US 1, exit 98A, 0.5 mi e on Tryon Rd, then just s. Int corridors. **Pets:** Accepted.

◆◆◆ ▼▼▼▼ Hampton Inn **SH** ❀
(919) 859-5559. **$79-$119.** 201 Ashville Ave. US 1, exit 98A, 0.8 mi e on Tryon Rd, then just n. Int corridors. **Pets:** $75 one-time fee/room. Designated rooms, service with restrictions, crate.

◆◆◆ ▼▼▼▼ Homewood Suites **SH** ❀
(919) 467-4444. **$135.** 100 MacAlyson Ct. US 1, exit 98B, just w on US 64, then just s on Edinburgh Dr; in MacGregor Park. Int corridors. **Pets:** Medium. $100 one-time fee/pet. Designated rooms, service with restrictions, crate.

▼▼▼ La Quinta Inn & Suites Raleigh (Cary) **SH**
(919) 851-2850. **$99-$119.** 191 Crescent Commons Dr. US 1, exit 98A, 0.5 mi e on Tryon Rd, then just n. Int corridors. **Pets:** Medium. Service with restrictions.

▼▼▼ Residence Inn **SH**
(919) 467-4080. **$59-$189.** 2900 Regency Pkwy. US 1, exit 98A, 0.5 mi e on Tryon Rd, then just s. Int corridors. **Pets:** Medium. $75 one-time fee/room. Service with restrictions.

▼▼ StudioPLUS-Harrison Ave **SH**
(919) 677-9910. **Call for rates.** 600 Weston Pkwy. I-40, exit 287, 0.5 mi s on Harrison Ave, then just w. Int corridors. **Pets:** Accepted.

▼▼▼ TownePlace Suites **SH**
(919) 678-0005. **$99.** 120 Sage Commons Way. I-40, exit 287, 0.5 mi s on Harrison Ave, 2.3 w on Weston Pkwy, then just n. Int corridors. **Pets:** Accepted.

CASHIERS

◆◆◆ ▼▼▼▼ High Hampton Inn & Country Club **SH**
(828) 743-2411. **$216-$399, 14 day notice.** 1525 Hwy 107 S. Jct US 64, 1.5 mi s. Ext/int corridors. **Pets:** Medium, dogs only. $50 one-time fee/room. Designated rooms, service with restrictions, supervision.

▼▼▼ Laurelwood Mountain Inn **M** ❀
(828) 743-9939. **$69-$98, 3 day notice.** 58 Hwy 107. Jct US 64, just n. Ext corridors. **Pets:** Medium, other species. $25 one-time fee/room. Designated rooms, service with restrictions, supervision.

CHAPEL HILL

◆◆◆ ▼▼▼ ▼▼ Carolina Inn **LH**
(919) 933-2001. **$124-$254.** 211 Pittsboro St. Jct Franklin St, just s on Columbia St (SR 86). Int corridors. **Pets:** Accepted.

◆◆◆ ▼▼▼▼ Courtyard by Marriott-Chapel Hill **SH** ❀
(919) 883-0700. **$169-$249.** 100 Marriott Way. I-40, exit 273 & 273A, 1.8 mi w on SR 54, just s on Friday Center Dr, then just e. Int corridors. **Pets:** Medium, dogs only. $100 one-time fee/pet. Designated rooms, service with restrictions, supervision.

▼▼▼ Holiday Inn **SH** ❀
(919) 929-2171. **$89-$169.** 1301 N Fordham Blvd. I-40, exit 270, 2 mi s on US 15/501. Ext corridors. **Pets:** $35 one-time fee/room. Service with restrictions, crate.

◆◆◆ ▼▼▼ ▼▼ The Siena Hotel **SH** ❀
(919) 929-4000. **$119-$250.** 1505 E Franklin St. I-40, exit 270, 2 mi s on US 15/501, then 0.5 mi w. Int corridors. **Pets:** Large, dogs only. $75 one-time fee/room. Service with restrictions, supervision.

CHARLOTTE METROPOLITAN AREA

CHARLOTTE

Ballantyne Resort, The Luxury Collection LH
(704) 248-4000. **$199-$1299.** 10000 Ballantyne Commons Pkwy. I-485, exit 61 or 61B, just s on US 521. Int corridors. **Pets:** Accepted.

Best Western-Charlotte Uptown SH
(704) 372-7550. **$159.** 201 S McDowell St. I-277, exit 2A, just w on 4th St, then just s. Int corridors. **Pets:** Accepted.

Best Western Independence SH
(704) 845-2810. **$75-$85.** 2501 Sardis Rd N. I-485, exit 51A, 3.3 mi w on US 74, then just s. Int corridors. **Pets:** Accepted.

Candlewood Suites-Coliseum SH
(704) 529-7500. **$72.** 5840 Westpark Dr. I-77, exit 5 (Tyvola Rd), just e, then 0.5 mi s. Int corridors. **Pets:** Medium, other species. $75 one-time fee/pet. Service with restrictions.

Charlotte Marriott Southpark SH
(704) 364-8220. **$179-$239.** 2200 Rexford Rd. I-77, exit 5 (Tyvola Rd), 3.6 mi e on Tyvola/Fairview Rds, just n on Sharon Rd, just w on Morrison Blvd, just n on Roxborough Rd, then just w. Int corridors. **Pets:** Medium. $75 one-time fee/pet. Designated rooms, service with restrictions, supervision.

Comfort Inn-Executive Park SH
(704) 525-2626. **$55-$126.** 5822 Westpark Dr. I-77, exit 5 (Tyvola Rd), just e, then 0.5 mi s. Int corridors. **Pets:** Medium. $50 one-time fee/pet. Designated rooms, service with restrictions, supervision.

Comfort Suites-University SH
(704) 547-0049. **$80-$130.** 7735 University City Blvd. I-85, exit 45A, 1 mi e on SR 24, then 0.5 mi s on SR 49. Int corridors. **Pets:** Accepted.

Country Inn & Suites-Charlotte University SH
(704) 549-8770. **$74-$134.** 131 E McCullough Dr. I-85, exit 45A, 0.5 mi e on SR 24, 0.4 mi s on US 29 (N Tryon St), then just e. Int corridors. **Pets:** Accepted.

DoubleTree Guest Suites-South Park SH
(704) 364-2400. **$89-$289.** 6300 Morrison Blvd. I-77, exit 5 (Tyvola Rd), 3.3 mi e on Tyvola/Fairview rds, just n on Barclay Downs, then just e. Int corridors. **Pets:** Medium. $75 deposit/room, $15 daily fee/room. Service with restrictions, crate.

Drury Inn & Suites-Charlotte North SH
(704) 593-0700. **$75-$120.** 415 W WT Harris Blvd. I-85, exit 45A, just e on SR 24. Int corridors. **Pets:** Large, other species. Service with restrictions, supervision.

Extended StayAmerica-Charlotte-Pineville SH
(704) 341-0929. **$80-$100.** 10930 Park Rd. I-485, exit 64A, just n on SR 51, then just e; behind Terraces at Park Place Shopping Center. Int corridors. **Pets:** Accepted.

Extended StayAmerica-Charlotte-Tyvola Rd SH
(704) 676-0569. **Call for rates.** 6035 National Ford Rd. I-77, exit 5 (Tyvola Rd), just w. Int corridors. **Pets:** Accepted.

Extended StayAmerica-Charlotte-University Place SH
(704) 510-1636. **Call for rates.** 8211 University Executive Park Dr. I-85, exit 45A, 0.5 mi e on SR 24, then 0.5 mi s on US 29 (N Tryon St). Int corridors. **Pets:** Accepted.

Extended Stay Deluxe-Charlotte/Pineville SH
(704) 542-9521. **$81.** 8405 Pineville-Matthews Rd. I-485, exit 64A, 0.7 mi n on SR 51. Int corridors. **Pets:** Accepted.

Hampton Inn Airport SH
(704) 392-1600. **$89-$149.** 3127 Sloan Dr. I-85, exit 33, just w, then just s. Int corridors. **Pets:** Medium. Service with restrictions.

Hampton Inn University Place SH
(704) 548-0905. **$89-$139.** 8419 N Tryon St. I-85, exit 45A, 0.5 mi e on SR 24, then just s on US 29 (N Tryon St). Int corridors. **Pets:** Medium, other species. $75 one-time fee/room. Service with restrictions, supervision.

Holiday Inn Airport SH
(704) 394-4301. **$86-$96.** 2707 Little Rock Rd. I-85, exit 32, just e. Int corridors. **Pets:** $25 one-time fee/pet. Designated rooms, service with restrictions, supervision.

Holiday Inn at University Executive Park SH
(704) 547-0999. **$80-$104.** 8520 University Executive Park Dr. I-85, exit 45A, just e on SR 24, then just s. Int corridors. **Pets:** Accepted.

Holiday Inn Center City SH
(704) 335-5400. **$159, 3 day notice.** 230 N College St. I-77, exit 10 or 10B, 1 mi e on Trade St, then just n; jct 6th St. Int corridors. **Pets:** Accepted.

Homestead Studio Suites Hotel-Charlotte/Coliseum SH
(704) 676-0083. **$79-$89.** 710 Yorkmont Rd. I-77, exit 6B northbound, just w, just s on S Tryon St, then just w; exit southbound, just s on S Tryon St, then just w. Ext corridors. **Pets:** Accepted.

Homewood Suites by Hilton Airport/Coliseum SH
(704) 357-0500. **$109-$179.** 2770 Yorkmont Rd. I-77, exit 6B, 2 mi nw on Billy Graham Pkwy, exit Coliseum/Tyvola Rd, just se on Tyvola Rd, then just w. Int corridors. **Pets:** Accepted.

La Quinta Inn & Suites Charlotte (Coliseum) SH
(704) 523-5599. **$98-$118.** 4900 S Tryon St. I-77, exit 6B northbound, just w, then just s; exit southbound, just s. Int corridors. **Pets:** Medium. Service with restrictions.

MainStay Suites SH
(704) 521-3232. **$70-$150.** 7926 Forest Pine Dr. I-77, exit 3 southbound; exit 2 northbound, just e, then just s. Int corridors. **Pets:** Accepted.

Omni Charlotte Hotel LH
(704) 377-0400. **$199-$389.** 132 E Trade St. I-77, exit 10 or 10B, 0.8 mi e; jct Tryon St. Int corridors. **Pets:** Small, dogs only. $50 one-time fee/pet. Designated rooms, service with restrictions, supervision.

▼▼▼▼ **Quality Inn & Suites** SH
(704) 393-5306. **$66-$95.** 3100 Queen City Dr. I-85, exit 33, just w, then just n. Ext/int corridors. **Pets:** Small, other species. $25 one-time fee/pet. Service with restrictions, supervision.
ASK ✕ ᴹ 🐾 🛏 💻 🏊

▼▼ **Quality Inn-Executive Park** SH
(704) 525-0747. **$59-$109.** 440 Griffith Rd. I-77, exit 5 (Tyvola Rd), just e, just s on Westpark Dr, then just e. Int corridors. **Pets:** Other species. $35 one-time fee/room. Service with restrictions, supervision.
ASK Sᴅ ✕ 🐾 💻 🏊

▲▲▲ ▼▼▼ **Ramada Charlotte NE** SH
(704) 596-2999. **$49-$54.** 5415 Equipment Dr. I-85, exit 41, just w, then 0.4 mi n. Ext/int corridors. **Pets:** Accepted.
SAVE Sᴅ ✕ ᴹ 🐾 🐕 🛏 💻 🏊

▲▲▲ ▼▼▼ **Ramada Conference Center "Airport South"** SH
(704) 525-8350. **$69-$149.** 212 Woodlawn Rd. I-77, exit 6A, just e. Int corridors. **Pets:** Accepted.
SAVE Sᴅ ✕ 🐾 🐕 🛏 💻 🍴 🏊

▼▼ **Red Roof Inn-Airport** M
(704) 392-2316. **$45-$77.** 3300 Queen City Dr. I-85, exit 33, just w, then just s. Ext corridors. **Pets:** Medium, other species. Service with restrictions, supervision.
✕ ᴹ 🐾 🛏

▼▼▼▼ **Residence Inn by Marriott** SH
(704) 547-1122. **$74-$119.** 8503 N Tryon St. I-85, exit 45A, 0.5 mi e on SR 24, then just s on US 29 (N Tryon St). Ext corridors. **Pets:** Accepted.
ASK Sᴅ ✕ ᴹ 🐾 🐕 🛏 💻 🏊 ✕

▼▼▼▼ **Residence Inn by Marriott-Charlotte South at I-77/Tyvola Rd** SH
(704) 527-8110. **$108-$134.** 5816 Westpark Dr. I-77, exit 5 (Tyvola Rd), just e, then 0.4 mi s. Ext/int corridors. **Pets:** Medium, other species. $75 one-time fee/pet. Designated rooms, supervision.
ASK Sᴅ ✕ ᴹ 🐾 🛏 💻 🏊 ✕

▼▼▼▼ **Residence Inn by Marriott-Charlotte Uptown** SH ❄
(704) 340-4000. **$89-$489.** 404 S Mint St. I-77, exit 10 or 10B, 0.6 mi e, then just s. Int corridors. **Pets:** Large, other species. $75 one-time fee/room. Service with restrictions.
ASK ✕ ᴹ 🐕 🛏 💻 🍴

▼▼▼▼ **Residence Inn by Marriott-Piper Glen** SH
(704) 319-3900. **$89-$159.** 5115 Piper Station Dr. I-485, exit 59, just s on Rea Rd, then just e. Int corridors. **Pets:** Accepted.
ASK Sᴅ ✕ ᴹ 🐕 🛏 💻 🏊 ✕

▼▼▼▼ **StudioPLUS-Charlotte-Tyvola Rd** SH
(704) 527-1960. **$69-$79.** 5830 Westpark Dr. I-77, exit 5 (Tyvola Rd), just e, then 0.4 mi s. Int corridors. **Pets:** Accepted.
✕ 🛏 💻 🏊

▲▲▲ ▼▼▼▼ **Sheraton Charlotte Airport Hotel** LH
(704) 392-1200. **$89-$179.** 3315 Scott Futrell Dr. I-85, exit 33, just e, then just s. Int corridors. **Pets:** Accepted.
SAVE Sᴅ ✕ 🐾 🐕 🛏 💻 🍴 🏊

▲▲▲ ▼▼▼ **Sleep Inn** SH
(704) 549-4544. **$59-$89.** 8525 N Tryon St. I-85, exit 45A, 0.5 mi e on SR 24, just s on US 29 (N Tryon St). Int corridors. **Pets:** Other species. $25 one-time fee/pet. No service, supervision.
SAVE Sᴅ ✕ ᴹ 🐾 🐕 🛏 💻 🏊

▼▼▼▼ **Staybridge Suites-Arrowood** SH
(704) 527-6767. **Call for rates.** 7924 Forest Pine Dr. I-77, exit 3 southbound; exit 2 northbound, just e, then just s. Int corridors. **Pets:** Accepted.
✕ ᴹ 🐕 🛏 💻 🏊

▼▼▼▼ **Staybridge Suites Charlotte-Ballantyne** SH
(704) 248-5000. **$109-$199.** 15735 John J Delaney Dr. I-485, exit 61 or 61B, just s. Int corridors. **Pets:** $200 one-time fee/room. Service with restrictions, supervision.
ASK Sᴅ ✕ ᴹ 🐾 🐕 🛏 💻 🏊 ✕

▼▼▼ **Studio 6 Airport-#6006** SH
(704) 394-4993. **$49-$59.** 3420 Queen City Dr. I-85, exit 33, just w, then just s. Int corridors. **Pets:** Accepted.
Sᴅ ✕ ᴹ 🐕 🛏 💻

▼▼▼▼ **Summerfield Suites-Charlotte** SH
(704) 525-2600. **$79-$189.** 4920 S Tryon St. I-77, exit 6B northbound, just w, then just s; exit southbound, just s. Int corridors. **Pets:** Accepted.
ASK Sᴅ ✕ ᴹ 🐾 🐕 🛏 💻 🏊 ✕

▼▼▼▼ **TownePlace Suites by Marriott** SH
(704) 548-0388. **$79-$179.** 8710 Research Dr. I-85, exit 45B, just w on SR 24, then just n. Int corridors. **Pets:** Accepted.
ASK Sᴅ ✕ ᴹ 🐾 🐕 🛏 💻 🏊

▼▼▼▼ **TownePlace Suites by Marriott-Arrowood** SH
(704) 227-2000. **$84-$129.** 7805 Forest Point Blvd. I-77, exit 3 southbound; exit 2 northbound, just e. Int corridors. **Pets:** Medium, other species. $75 one-time fee/pet. Service with restrictions, crate.
ASK Sᴅ ✕ ᴹ 🐾 🐕 🛏 💻 🏊

▼▼▼ ▼▼▼ **The Westin Charlotte** LH ❄
(704) 375-2600. **$109-$295.** 601 S College St. I-277, exit College St, just n; jct E Stonewall St. Int corridors. **Pets:** Service with restrictions, supervision.
ASK Sᴅ ✕ ᴹ 🐾 🐕 🛏 💻 🍴 🏊 ✕

CONCORD

▲▲▲ ▼▼▼ **Americas Best Value Inn** M
(704) 788-8550. **$52-$145.** 2451 Kannapolis Hwy. I-85, exit 58, just s on US 29, then just w. Ext corridors. **Pets:** Small, dogs only. $25 one-time fee/room. Designated rooms, service with restrictions, supervision.
SAVE Sᴅ ✕ 🐾 🛏 💻

CORNELIUS

▼▼ **Days Inn-Lake Norman** SH
(704) 892-9120. **$57-$71.** 19901 Holiday Ln. I-77, exit 28, just e, then just n. Ext corridors. **Pets:** $25 one-time fee/room. Designated rooms, service with restrictions.
ASK Sᴅ ✕ ᴹ 🐾 🛏 💻 🍴 🏊

▼▼ **Econo Lodge Lake Norman** M
(704) 892-3500. **$45-$189.** 20740 Torrence Chapel Rd. I-77, exit 28, just w, then just n. Ext corridors. **Pets:** Accepted.
ASK Sᴅ ✕ 🛏 💻 🏊

HUNTERSVILLE

▼▼▼ **Candlewood Suites** SH ❄
(704) 895-3434. **$65-$180, 3 day notice.** 16530 Northcross Dr. I-77, exit 25, just w on SR 73, then just s. Int corridors. **Pets:** Medium, other species. $75 one-time fee/pet. Service with restrictions, supervision.
ASK Sᴅ ✕ 🛏 💻

▼▼▼ **Quality Inn** SH
(704) 892-6597. **$49-$149, 3 day notice.** 16825 Caldwell Creek Dr. I-77, exit 25, just e on SR 73, just n on US 21, then just w. Ext/int corridors. **Pets:** Medium. $25 one-time fee/pet. Designated rooms, no service, crate.
ASK Sᴅ ✕ 🐕 🛏 💻

♦♦♦ **Residence Inn by Marriott-Lake Norman** [SH]
(704) 584-0000. **Call for rates.** 16830 Kenton Dr. I-77, exit 25, 1 mi w on SR 73, then just n. Int corridors. **Pets:** Accepted.
[A$K] ☒ [♿M] 🦻 ♿ ▣ 🖥 🏊 🏋

♦♦ **Sleep Inn** [SH]
(704) 766-2500. **$89-$99.** 16508 Northcross Dr. I-77, exit 25, just w on SR 73, then just s. Int corridors. **Pets:** Accepted.
[A$K] [S/D] ☒ ▣ 🖥

MATTHEWS

[AAA] ♦♦♦ **Country Inn & Suites-Matthews** [SH]
(704) 846-8000. **$89-$119.** 2001 Mount Harmony Church Rd. I-485, exit 51B, 0.5 mi e on US 74, just n on Independence Commerce Dr, then just w. Int corridors. **Pets:** Accepted.
[SAVE] [S/D] ☒ [♿M] ♿ ▣ 🖥 🏊

PINEVILLE

♦♦♦ **Best Western Crown Suites** [SH]
(704) 540-8500. **$89-$159.** 9705 Leitner Dr. I-485, exit 64B, just s on SR 51, then w. Int corridors. **Pets:** Accepted.
[A$K] [S/D] ☒ [♿M] ♿ ▣ 🖥 🏊

End Metropolitan Area

CHEROKEE

[AAA] ♦♦ **Baymont Inn-Cherokee/Smoky Mountains** [SH]
(828) 497-2102. **$59-$149.** 1455 Acquoni Rd. 2.5 mi n, just w off US 441 N. Int corridors. **Pets:** Accepted.
[SAVE] [S/D] ☒ [♿M] 🦻 ♿ ▣ 🖥 🏊

[AAA] ♦♦ **Best Western Great Smokies Inn** [M]
(828) 497-2020. **$49-$169.** 1636 Acquoni Rd. US 441 N, 2.5 mi n; downtown. Ext corridors. **Pets:** Accepted.
[SAVE] [S/D] ☒ 🦻 ▣ 🖥 🍴 🏊

[AAA] ♦♦ **Microtel Inn & Suites** [SH]
(828) 497-7800. **$39-$119.** 674 Casino Tr. Jct US 441 and Business Rt US 441 S. Int corridors. **Pets:** $25 daily fee/pet. Designated rooms, service with restrictions, supervision.
[SAVE] [S/D] ☒ [♿M] ♿ ▣ 🖥 🏊

[AAA] ♦ **Pioneer Motel** [M]
(828) 497-2435. **$38-$80, 3 day notice.** 122 Tsalagi Rd. 0.8 mi w on US 19 S. Ext corridors. **Pets:** Small, dogs only. $20 one-time fee/pet. Designated rooms, no service.
[SAVE] [S/D] ☒ ▣ 🖥 🏊 🏋

CLAREMONT

[AAA] ♦♦ **Super 8 Motel** [M] 🐾
(828) 459-7777. **$61-$85.** 3054 N Oxford St. I-40, exit 135, just s. Ext/int corridors. **Pets:** Medium, dogs only. $15 daily fee/pet. Service with restrictions, supervision.
[SAVE] [S/D] ☒ ♿ ▣ 🖥 🏊

CLAYTON

♦♦ **Sleep Inn** [SH]
(919) 772-7771. **$50-$70.** 105 Commerce Pkwy. I-40, exit 312, just w on SR 42, then just s. Int corridors. **Pets:** Accepted.
[A$K] [S/D] ☒ [♿M] 🦻 ♿ ▣ 🖥 🏊

CLEMMONS

♦♦ **The Village Inn Golf & Conference Center** [SH]
(336) 766-9121. **$62-$75.** 6205 Ramada Dr. I-40, exit 184, just s, then just e. Int corridors. **Pets:** Medium, dogs only. $20 one-time fee/pet. Designated rooms, service with restrictions, supervision.
[A$K] [S/D] ☒ 🦻 ♿ ▣ 🖥 🍴 🏊

COLUMBUS

[AAA] ♦♦ **Days Inn** [M]
(828) 894-3303. **$45-$95.** 626 W Mills St. I-26, exit 67, just w on SR 108. Ext corridors. **Pets:** Medium. $20 one-time fee/pet. Service with restrictions, supervision.
[SAVE] [S/D] ☒ ▣ 🖥 🏊

CONOVER

♦♦ **Days Inn** [SH]
(828) 465-2378. **$52, 5 day notice.** 1710 Fairgrove Church Rd SE. I-40, exit 128, just s. Ext corridors. **Pets:** Other species. $10 one-time fee/pet. Service with restrictions, crate.
☒ [♿M] 🦻 ▣ 🖥 🏊

DORTCHES

♦♦ **Econo Lodge** [M]
(252) 937-6300. **$45-$60.** 5350 Dortches Blvd. I-95, exit 141, just w, then just n on service road. Ext corridors. **Pets:** Accepted.
[A$K] [S/D] ☒ 🦻 ▣ 🖥 🏊

DUNN

♦♦ **Jameson Inn** [M]
(910) 891-5758. **$54-$104.** 901 Jackson Rd. I-95, exit 73, just w, then just s. Ext corridors. **Pets:** Small. $10 daily fee/pet. Service with restrictions, crate.
[A$K] ☒ [♿M] 🦻 ▣ 🖥 🏊

DURHAM

[AAA] ♦♦ **Best Western Skyland Inn** [M] 🐾
(919) 383-2508. **$69-$99.** 5400 US 70 W. I-85, exit 170, 0.3 mi e on US 70, then just n. Ext corridors. **Pets:** Other species. $15 daily fee/pet. Service with restrictions, supervision.
[SAVE] [S/D] ☒ ▣ 🖥 🏊

♦♦♦ **Candlewood Suites** [SH]
(919) 484-9922. **$107.** 1818 E NC Hwy 54. I-40, exit 278, just s, then just w. Int corridors. **Pets:** Medium. $75 one-time fee/room. Designated rooms, service with restrictions, crate.
[A$K] ☒ [♿M] 🦻 ♿ ▣ 🖥 🏋

[AAA] ♦♦♦ **Comfort Inn University** [SH] 🐾
(919) 490-4949. **$90-$100.** 3508 Mt Moriah Rd. I-40, exit 270, just n on US 15/501, then just e. Int corridors. **Pets:** $35 one-time fee/room. Designated rooms, service with restrictions, supervision.
[SAVE] [S/D] ☒ 🦻 ♿ ▣ 🖥 🏊

♦♦ **Crown Park Hotel** [SH]
(919) 956-9444. **$89-$99.** 600 Willard St. SR 147 (Durham Frwy), exit 12C, just n on Duke St, then just e on Yancey St. Int corridors. **Pets:** Accepted.
[A$K] ☒ ▣ 🖥 🏊

♦♦ **Extended Stay Deluxe-Durham-RTP-Miami Blvd** [SH]
(919) 941-2878. **$104-$109.** 4610 S Miami Blvd. I-40, exit 281, just n. Int corridors. **Pets:** Accepted.
[A$K] [S/D] ☒ ▣ 🖥 🏊

▼▼▼ **Extended Stay Deluxe-RTP-Miami Blvd-South** SH
(919) 998-0400. **$104-$130.** 4919 S Miami Blvd. I-40, exit 281, just s. Int corridors. **Pets:** Accepted.
A$K S⛶ ⊠ ⛶M ⛶ ⛶ 🛏 🖳 ⚓

▲▲▲ ▼▼▼ **Hampton Inn** SH 🐾
(919) 471-6100. **$99-$109.** 1816 Hillandale Rd. I-85, exit 174A, just w. Int corridors. **Pets:** Medium. $25 one-time fee/pet. Designated rooms, service with restrictions, crate.
SAVE S⛶ ⊠ ⛶ 🛏 🖳 ⚓

▼▼▼▼ **Holiday Inn Express Hotel & Suites** SH
(919) 474-9800. **$80-$145, 3 day notice.** 4912 S Miami Blvd. I-40, exit 281, just s. Int corridors. **Pets:** Medium, other species. $10 daily fee/room. Designated rooms, service with restrictions.
A$K S⛶ ⊠ ⛶M ⛶ 🛏 🖳

▼▼ **Homestead Studio Suites**
Hotel-Durham/University SH
(919) 402-1700. **$74-$113.** 1920 Ivy Creek Blvd. I-40, exit 270, 2 mi n on US 15/501, exit 105B, then just e on Martin Luther King Jr Pkwy; in University Place. Ext corridors. **Pets:** Accepted.
A$K S⛶ ⊠ ⛶ 🛏 🖳

▲▲▲ ▼▼▼▼ **Homewood Suites Durham/Chapel**
Hill SH 🐾
(919) 401-0610. **$119-$159, 3 day notice.** 3600 Mt Moriah Rd. I-40, exit 270, just n on US 15/501, then just e. Int corridors. **Pets:** Medium. $75 one-time fee/room. Service with restrictions, supervision.
SAVE S⛶ ⊠ ⛶M ⛶ ⛶ 🛏 🖳 ⚓

▼▼▼▼ **La Quinta Inn & Suites Raleigh (Durham-Chapel**
Hill) SH
(919) 401-9660. **$112-$132.** 4414 Durham Chapel Hill Blvd. I-40, exit 270, 1.7 mi n on US 15/501. Int corridors. **Pets:** Medium. Service with restrictions.
A$K ⊠ ⛶M ⛶ ⛶ 🛏 🖳 ⚓

▼▼▼▼ **La Quinta Inn & Suites Raleigh (Research Triangle**
Park) SH
(919) 484-1422. **$99-$119.** 1910 W Park Dr. I-40, exit 278, just n on SR 55, then just e. Int corridors. **Pets:** Medium. Service with restrictions.
A$K ⊠ ⛶M ⛶ 🛏 🖳 ⚓

▲▲▲ ▼▼▼ **Quality Inn & Suites** SH 🐾
(919) 382-3388. **$59-$79.** 3710 Hillsborough Rd. I-85, exit 173, just e on Cole Mill Rd, then just w on US 70 business route. Ext/int corridors. **Pets:** Medium. $25 daily fee/room. Designated rooms, service with restrictions, crate.
SAVE S⛶ ⊠ ⛶ 🛏 🖳 ⚓

▼▼▼ **Residence Inn by Marriott** SH
(919) 361-1266. **$85-$149, 3 day notice.** 201 Residence Inn Blvd. I-40, exit 278, just s, then just w. Ext/int corridors. **Pets:** Accepted.
A$K S⛶ ⊠ ⛶M ⛶ 🛏 🖳 ⚓ ⊠

▼▼ ◆◆ **Sleep Inn-RTP** SH
(919) 993-3393. **$64-$139.** 5208 New Page Rd. I-40, exit 282, just s. Int corridors. **Pets:** Designated rooms, service with restrictions, supervision.
A$K S⛶ ⊠ ⛶M ⛶ 🖳

▼▼▼ **StudioPLUS-Research Triangle Park** SH
(919) 361-1853. **Call for rates.** 2504 NC Hwy 54. I-40, exit 278, just s on SR 55, then just e. Int corridors. **Pets:** Accepted.
⊠ 🛏 ⚓

▼▼▼ **Wyndham Hotel-Research Triangle Park** SH
(919) 941-6066. **$89-$139.** 4620 S Miami Blvd. I-40, exit 281, just n. Int corridors. **Pets:** Accepted.
A$K ⊠ ⛶ 🛏 🖳 ⏷⏷ ⚓

EDEN

▼▼ **Jameson Inn** SH
(336) 627-0472. **$54-$104.** 716 Linden Dr. Jct SR 700/770, 1.4 mi s on SR 87/14, then just e. Ext corridors. **Pets:** Accepted.
A$K ⊠ ⛶M 🛏 🖳 ⚓

ELIZABETH CITY

▼ **Days Inn** M
(252) 335-4316. **Call for rates.** 308 S Hughes Blvd. Jct US 158, 0.6 mi s on US 17. Ext corridors. **Pets:** Accepted.
⊠ 🛏

FAYETTEVILLE

▲▲▲ ▼▼◆ **Comfort Inn Cross Creek** SH 🐾
(910) 867-1777. **$89-$129.** 1922 Skibo Rd. All American Frwy, exit US 401 Bypass, 0.8 mi s. Int corridors. **Pets:** Medium. $25 one-time fee/pet. Service with restrictions, crate.
SAVE S⛶ ⊠ ⛶ 🛏 🖳 ⚓

▲▲▲ ▼▼▼ **Comfort Inn-Fayetteville** M
(910) 323-8333. **$74-$99.** 1957 Cedar Creek Rd. I-95, exit 49, just w. Ext corridors. **Pets:** Other species. $10 one-time fee/room. Designated rooms, service with restrictions, supervision.
SAVE S⛶ ⊠ ⛶ 🛏 🖳 ⚓

▲▲▲ ▼▼▼ **Econo Lodge I-95** M
(910) 433-2100. **$49-$99, 15 day notice.** 1952 Cedar Creek Rd. I-95, exit 49, just w. Ext corridors. **Pets:** Accepted.
SAVE S⛶ ⊠ ⛶ 🛏 ⚓

▼▼ **Extended StayAmerica** M
(910) 485-2747. **$94-$109.** 408 Owen Dr. Jct All American Frwy. Ext corridors. **Pets:** Accepted.
A$K S⛶ ⊠ ⛶ 🖳

▼▼ **Extended Stay Deluxe Fayetteville-Cross Creek**
Mall SH
(910) 868-5662. **$113-$123.** 4105 Sycamore Dairy Rd. All American Frwy, exit Morganton Rd, just e, then just n. Int corridors. **Pets:** Accepted.
A$K S⛶ ⊠ ⛶ 🛏 🖳 ⚓

▼▼▼ **Holiday Inn Bordeaux** SH
(910) 323-0111. **$89-$129.** 1707 Owen Dr. Jct I-95 business route/US 301 S, 2.3 mi w. Ext/int corridors. **Pets:** Accepted.
A$K S⛶ ⊠ ⛶ 🛏 🖳 ⏷⏷ ⚓

▲▲▲ ▼▼▼ **Holiday Inn I-95** SH
(910) 323-1600. **$84-$119.** 1944 Cedar Creek Rd. I-95, exit 49, just w. Ext/int corridors. **Pets:** $20 one-time fee/room. Designated rooms, service with restrictions, crate.
SAVE S⛶ ⊠ ⛶ ⛶ 🛏 🖳 ⏷⏷ ⚓

▼ **Motel 6 #1075** M
(910) 485-8122. **$43-$55.** 2076 Cedar Creek Rd. I-95, exit 49, just e. Ext corridors. **Pets:** Medium, other species. Service with restrictions, supervision.
S⛶ ⊠ ⛶ ⚓

▲▲▲ ▼▼▼ **Quality Inn-East** SH
(910) 323-9850. **$60-$100.** 2111 Cedar Creek Rd. I-95, exit 49, just e. Int corridors. **Pets:** Accepted.
SAVE S⛶ ⊠ 🖳 ⚓

▲▲▲ ▼▼▼ **Ramada** SH
(910) 484-8101. **$70-$100.** 511 Eastern Blvd. Jct SR 24, 0.8 mi s on US 301. Int corridors. **Pets:** Accepted.
SAVE S⛶ ⊠ 🛏 🖳 ⚓

(AAA) ▼▼▼▼ Red Roof Inn 🆂🅷
(910) 321-1460. **$54-$60.** 1569 Jim Johnson Rd. I-95, exit 49, just w on SR 53, then just n. Int corridors. **Pets:** Medium, other species. Service with restrictions, supervision.
🆂🅰🆅🄴 Ⓢ❌ 🗝 🔥 🛏 💻 🏊

FLETCHER

(AAA) ▼▼▼▼ Holiday Inn Asheville-Airport 🆂🅷
(828) 684-1213. **$80-$146, 7 day notice.** 550 Airport Rd. I-26, exit 40, just e. Int corridors. **Pets:** Accepted.
🆂🅰🆅🄴 Ⓢ❌ 🗝 🔥 🛏 💻 🍽 🏊

FOREST CITY

▼▼ Jameson Inn Ⓜ
(828) 287-8788. **$54-$104.** 164 Jameson Dr. US 74 Bypass, exit 181, 1.8 mi nw on US 74A. Ext corridors. **Pets:** Small. $10 daily fee/pet. Service with restrictions, crate.
🄰🆂🅺 ❌ 🗝 🔥 🛏 💻 🏊

FRANKLIN

▼ Country Inn Town Motel Ⓜ
(828) 524-4451. **$30-$84, 3 day notice.** 668 E Main St. 0n US 441 S Business Route. Ext corridors. **Pets:** Accepted.
🄰🆂🅺 Ⓢ❌ 🛏 🏊

▼ Days Inn-Franklin Ⓜ
(828) 524-6491. **$49-$120.** 1320 E Main St. Jct US 23 and 441 Bypass, just nw on US 441 business route. Ext corridors. **Pets:** Accepted.
🄰🆂🅺 Ⓢ❌ 🛏 💻 🏊

▼ Franklin Motel Inn & Suites Ⓜ
(828) 524-4431. **$40-$70.** 17 W Palmer St. Jct US 441 Bypass, 1 mi n on US 441 business route; downtown. Ext corridors. **Pets:** Other species. $10 one-time fee/room.
🄰🆂🅺 Ⓢ❌ 🔥 🛏

▼▼ Microtel Inn & Suites 🆂🅷
(828) 349-9000. **$39-$99.** 81 Allman Dr. Jct US 441 Bypass, 0.4 mi s on US 441 and 23. Int corridors. **Pets:** Accepted.
🄰🆂🅺 Ⓢ❌ 🗝 🔥 🛏 💻

▼ Sapphire Inn Ⓜ
(828) 524-4406. **$40-$70, 5 day notice.** 761 E Main St. 0.5 mi w of US 441 and 64 on SR 28. Ext corridors. **Pets:** Accepted.
🄰🆂🅺 Ⓢ❌ 🛏 🏊

GARNER

▼▼ Holiday Inn Express 🆂🅷
(919) 662-4890. **$85-$100.** 1595 Mechanical Blvd. I-40, exit 298A, 1.9 mi e on US 70, then just n. Int corridors. **Pets:** Accepted.
🄰🆂🅺 Ⓢ❌ 🔥 🛏

GASTONIA

▼▼ Ramada Limited Ⓜ
(704) 864-8744. **$44-$89.** 1400 E Franklin Blvd. I-85, exit 20, 0.5 mi s on SR 279, then just w on US 29/74. Ext corridors. **Pets:** Small. $100 deposit/room, $10 daily fee/room. Service with restrictions, supervision.
🄰🆂🅺 Ⓢ❌ 🗝 🛏 💻

GOLDSBORO

(AAA) ▼▼▼ Best Western Goldsboro Inn Ⓜ
(919) 735-7911. **$69-$120.** 801 US 70 E Bypass. US 70 E Bypass, exit Wayne Memorial Dr eastbound, just n, just w on Eleventh St, then 0.4 mi sw on service road; exit westbound, straight on Eleventh St, then 0.4 mi sw on service road. Ext corridors. **Pets:** Medium, dogs only. $10 daily fee/pet. Service with restrictions, supervision.
🆂🅰🆅🄴 Ⓢ❌ 🔥 🛏 💻 🍽 🏊

(AAA) ▼▼▼ Holiday Inn Express 🆂🅷
(919) 751-1999. **$89-$143.** 909 N Spence Ave. US 70 E Bypass, exit Spence Ave, just s. Int corridors. **Pets:** Accepted.
🆂🅰🆅🄴 Ⓢ❌ 🗝 🔥 🛏 💻 🏊

▼▼ Jameson Inn 🆂🅷
(919) 778-9759. **$54-$104.** 1408 Harding Dr. US 70 E Bypass, exit Spence Ave, just n, then just e on North Park Dr. Int corridors. **Pets:** Accepted.
🄰🆂🅺 ❌ 🗝 🔥 🛏 💻 🏊

GREENSBORO

▼▼▼ Best Western Deep River 🆂🅷
(336) 454-0333. **$79-$199.** 7800 National Service Rd. I-40, exit 210 (SR 68), just s, just w on Thorndike Rd, then just n. Int corridors. **Pets:** Accepted.
🄰🆂🅺 Ⓢ❌ 🔥 🛏 💻 🏊

▼▼▼ Best Western Wendover Plaza 🆂🅷
(336) 297-1055. **$89-$169.** 1103 Lanada Rd. I-40, exit 214 or 214A, just sw on Wendover Ave, then just e on Stanley Rd. Int corridors. **Pets:** Small. $25 daily fee/room. Designated rooms, service with restrictions, crate.
❌ 🗝 🔥 🛏 💻 🏊

▼▼▼ Candlewood Suites 🆂🅷
(336) 454-0078. **Call for rates.** 7623 Thorndike Rd. I-40, exit 210 (SR 68), just s, then just w. Int corridors. **Pets:** Accepted.
❌ 🔥 🛏

(AAA) ▼▼ Comfort Inn 🆂🅷
(336) 294-6220. **$56-$100.** 2001 Veasley St. I-40, exit 217, just s on High Point Rd, then just w. Int corridors. **Pets:** Small. $10 daily fee/pet. Designated rooms, service with restrictions, supervision.
🆂🅰🆅🄴 Ⓢ❌ 🗝 🛏 💻

▼▼ Crestwood Suites 🆂🅷
(336) 886-1250. **Call for rates.** 501 Americhase Dr. I-40, exit 210 (SR 68), 0.5 mi s. Int corridors. **Pets:** Accepted.
❌ 🛏 💻

▼▼ Drury Inn & Suites-Greensboro 🆂🅷
(336) 856-9696. **$80-$125.** 3220 High Point Rd. I-40, exit 217, just s. Int corridors. **Pets:** Large, other species. Service with restrictions, supervision.
🄰🆂🅺 ❌ 🗝 🔥 🛏 💻 🏊

▼▼ Extended StayAmerica-Greensboro-Wendover Ave Ⓜ
(336) 299-0200. **Call for rates.** 4317 Big Tree Way. I-40, exit 214 or 214B, just ne on Wendover Ave, then just w. Ext corridors. **Pets:** Accepted.
❌ 🔥 🛏 💻

▼▼ Extended Stay Deluxe 🆂🅷
(336) 454-0080. **Call for rates.** 7617 Thorndike Rd. I-40, exit 210 (SR 68), just s, then just w. Int corridors. **Pets:** Accepted.
❌ 🔥 🛏 💻 🏊

▼▼▼ La Quinta Inn & Suites Greensboro 🆂🅷
(336) 316-0100. **$123-$143.** 1201 Lanada Rd. I-40, exit 214 or 214A, just sw on Wendover Ave, then just e on Stanley Rd. Int corridors. **Pets:** Medium. Service with restrictions.
🄰🆂🅺 ❌ 🗝 🔥 🛏 💻 🏊

▼▼ Ramada Inn-Conference Center 🆂🅷
(336) 294-5178. **$84-$89.** 2003 Athena Ct. I-40, exit 217, just s on High Point Rd, then just w on Veasley St, then just n on Isler Ct. Ext/int corridors. **Pets:** Accepted.
🄰🆂🅺 Ⓢ❌ 🗝 🔥 🛏 💻 🏊

Red Roof Inn Airport M
(336) 271-2636. **$45-$66.** 615 Regional Rd S. I-40, exit 210 (SR 68), just s, then just e. Ext corridors. **Pets:** Medium, other species. Service with restrictions, supervision.

Residence Inn by Marriott SH
(336) 294-8600. **$59-$194.** 2000 Veasley St. I-40, exit 217, just s on High Point Rd, then 0.4 mi w. Ext corridors. **Pets:** Accepted.

GREENVILLE

Jameson Inn M
(252) 752-7382. **$54-$104.** 920 Crosswinds St. Jct US 264 business route, just s on US 13/SR 11, then just w. Ext corridors. **Pets:** Small. $10 daily fee/pet. Service with restrictions, crate.

HAYESVILLE

Chatuge Mountain Inn M
(828) 389-9340. **$49-$79.** 4238 Hwy 64 E. Jct SR 69, 4.2 mi e. Ext corridors. **Pets:** Accepted.

Deerfield Inn M
(828) 389-8272. **$50-$85.** 40 Chatuge Ln. 3 mi e on US 64. Ext corridors. **Pets:** Other species. $10 daily fee/pet. Supervision.

HENDERSON

Jameson Inn SH
(252) 430-0247. **$54-$104.** 400 N Cooper Dr. I-85, exit 212, just w on Ruin Creek Rd, then just n. Int corridors. **Pets:** Small. $10 daily fee/pet. Service with restrictions, crate.

Lamplight Inn B&B BB
(252) 438-6311. **$90-$120, 7 day notice.** 1680 Flemingtown Rd. I-85, exit 220, 1.5 mi nw. Int corridors. **Pets:** Small, dogs only. Service with restrictions, crate.

HENDERSONVILLE

Best Western Hendersonville Inn M
(828) 692-0521. **$59-$139.** 105 Sugarloaf Rd. I-26, exit 49A, just e. Ext corridors. **Pets:** Small. $10 daily fee/pet. Service with restrictions.

Comfort Inn SH
(828) 693-8800. **$49-$129.** 206 Mitchell Dr. I-26, exit 49B, just w. Ext corridors. **Pets:** Accepted.

HICKORY

Jameson Inn M
(828) 304-0410. **$54-$104.** 1120 13th Ave Dr SE. I-40, exit 125, just s, then 0.4 mi w. Ext corridors. **Pets:** Small. $10 daily fee/pet. Service with restrictions, crate.

Red Roof Inn Hickory M
(828) 323-1500. **$49-$57.** 1184 Lenoir Rhyne Blvd. I-40, exit 125, just n. Ext corridors. **Pets:** Medium, other species. Service with restrictions, supervision.

HIGHLANDS

Mountain High Lodge M
(828) 526-2790. **$49-$189, 7 day notice.** 200 Main St. Just w on US 64; downtown. Ext corridors. **Pets:** Other species. $20 one-time fee/pet. Designated rooms, service with restrictions, supervision.

HIGH POINT

Radisson Hotel High Point SH
(336) 889-8888. **$149-$169.** 135 S Main St. On US 311 business route; center. Int corridors. **Pets:** Accepted.

HILLSBOROUGH

Holiday Inn Express SH
(919) 644-7997. **$80-$200.** 202 Cardinal Dr. I-85, exit 164, just e, then just s. Int corridors. **Pets:** Small. $25 daily fee/pet. Designated rooms, service with restrictions, supervision.

Microtel Inn & Suites SH
(919) 245-3102. **$60-$70.** 120 Old Dogwood St. I-85, exit 164, just w, then s. Int corridors. **Pets:** Accepted.

JACKSONVILLE

Americas Best Value Inn SH
(910) 455-6888. **$70-$90.** 2149 N Marine Blvd. 2.8 mi n on US 17. Int corridors. **Pets:** Dogs only. $10 one-time fee/room. Designated rooms, service with restrictions, supervision.

Extended StayAmerica SH
(910) 347-7684. **Call for rates.** 20 McDaniel Dr. 2.8 mi n on US 17, then just w. Int corridors. **Pets:** Accepted.

Hampton Inn SH
(910) 347-6500. **$99-$119.** 474 Western Blvd. 2.5 mi n on US 17, just e. Ext corridors. **Pets:** Medium. $25 one-time fee/room. Service with restrictions, crate.

JONESVILLE

Comfort Inn SH
(336) 835-9400. **$82-$99.** 1633 Winston Rd. I-77, exit 82, just w. Ext corridors. **Pets:** Medium, other species. $10 daily fee/pet. Designated rooms, service with restrictions, supervision.

Holiday Inn Express SH
(336) 835-6000. **$69-$89.** 1713 NC 67 Hwy. I-77, exit 82, just e. Int corridors. **Pets:** Medium. $10 daily fee/pet. Designated rooms, service with restrictions, supervision.

KINGS MOUNTAIN

Comfort Inn M
(704) 739-7070. **$55-$75.** 722-A York Rd. I-85, exit 8, just n on SR 161. Ext corridors. **Pets:** Accepted.

LAURINBURG

Jameson Inn M
(910) 277-0080. **$54-$104.** 14 Jameson Inn Ct. Jct US 74 Bypass, just n on US 15/401 Bypass, just e. Ext corridors. **Pets:** Small. $10 daily fee/pet. Service with restrictions, crate.

LENOIR

▼▼ Jameson Inn Ⓜ
(828) 758-1200. **$54-$104.** 350 Wilkesboro Blvd. Jct US 321, 0.4 mi ne on SR 18. Ext corridors. **Pets:** Small. $10 daily fee/pet. Service with restrictions, crate.

(A$K) (✕) (&M) (🛏) (💻) (🏊)

LEXINGTON

▼▼▼ Comfort Suites of Lexington ⓈⒽ
(336) 357-2333. **$90-$150.** 1620 Cotton Grove Rd. I-85, exit 91, just s on SR 8, then just ne. Ext/int corridors. **Pets:** Accepted.

(A$K) (S🛁) (✕) (&M) (🛏) (💻) (🏊)

▼▼ Quality Inn Ⓜ ❀
(336) 249-0111. **$68-$125.** 418 Piedmont Dr. I-85, exit 96, 3.9 mi w on US 64. Ext corridors. **Pets:** Medium, other species. $25 one-time fee/room. Service with restrictions, crate.

(A$K) (S🛁) (✕) (🛏) (💻) (🏊)

LINCOLNTON

▼▼ Days Inn Ⓜ
(704) 735-8271. **$54-$59.** 614 Clark Dr. US 321, exit 24, 1 mi w on SR 150, then just s on US 321 business route. Ext corridors. **Pets:** Accepted.

(A$K) (S🛁) (✕) (🛏) (💻) (🏊)

LITTLE SWITZERLAND

▲▲▲ ▼▼▼ Switzerland Inn Ⓒ Ⓘ
(828) 765-2153. **$110-$180, 7 day notice.** Jct SR 226A and Blue Ridge Pkwy, MM 334. Ext/int corridors. **Pets:** Designated rooms, service with restrictions, crate.

(SAVE) (S🛁) (✕) (🛏) (💻) (🍽) (🏊) (✕)

LUMBERTON

▲▲▲ ▼▼▼ Best Western Inn Ⓜ
(910) 618-9799. **$79-$129.** 201 Jackson Ct. I-95, exit 22, just e, then just s. Ext corridors. **Pets:** Other species. $10 daily fee/pet. Service with restrictions, crate.

(SAVE) (S🛁) (✕) (🛏) (🛏) (💻) (🏊)

▼▼ Quality Inn and Suites ⓈⒽ
(910) 738-8261. **$60-$100.** 3608 Kahn Dr. I-95, exit 20, just e, then just n. Ext/int corridors. **Pets:** Accepted.

(A$K) (S🛁) (✕) (🛏) (💻) (🍽) (🏊)

MAGGIE VALLEY

▼ Applecover Inn Motel Ⓜ
(828) 926-9100. **$35-$85, 3 day notice.** 4077 Soco Rd. US 19, 4.5 mi w of US 276. Ext corridors. **Pets:** Accepted.

(✕) (🛏) (💻)

MARION

▲▲▲ ▼▼▼ Hampton Inn ⓈⒽ
(828) 652-5100. **$73-$81.** 3560 US 221 S. I-40, exit 85, just n. Int corridors. **Pets:** Accepted.

(SAVE) (S🛁) (✕) (&M) (🛏) (🛏) (💻) (🏊)

MOCKSVILLE

▲▲▲ ▼▼▼ Comfort Inn & Suites ⓈⒽ
(336) 751-5966. **$66-$95.** 629 Madison Rd. I-40, exit 170, just s on US 601, then just w. Int corridors. **Pets:** Small. $20 one-time fee/pet. No service.

(SAVE) (S🛁) (✕) (&M) (🛏) (🛏) (💻) (🏊)

▼▼ Quality Inn ⓈⒽ
(336) 751-7310. **$65-$125.** 1500 Yadkinville Rd. I-40, exit 170, just s on US 601. Ext corridors. **Pets:** Other species. $25 one-time fee/pet. Service with restrictions, supervision.

(A$K) (S🛁) (✕) (🛏) (🛏) (💻) (🏊)

MOORESVILLE

▼▼▼▼ Holiday Inn Express Hotel & Suites ⓈⒽ
(704) 662-6900. **$99-$179.** 130 Norman Station Blvd. I-77, exit 36, just e on SR 150, then just s. Int corridors. **Pets:** Accepted.

(S🛁) (✕) (&M) (🛏) (🛏) (💻) (🏊)

MOREHEAD CITY

▼▼▼ Holiday Inn Express Hotel & Suites ⓈⒽ ❀
(252) 247-5001. **$75-$185.** 5063 Executive Dr. Jct US 70 and SR 24. Int corridors. **Pets:** Medium, dogs only. $25 one-time fee/room. Designated rooms, service with restrictions, supervision.

(A$K) (S🛁) (✕) (🛏) (🛏) (💻) (🏊)

MORGANTON

▲▲▲ ▼▼▼ Comfort Inn & Suites ⓈⒽ
(828) 430-4000. **$59-$159.** 1273 Burkemont Ave. I-40, exit 103, just s. Int corridors. **Pets:** Medium, other species. $25 one-time fee/pet. Designated rooms, service with restrictions, supervision.

(SAVE) (S🛁) (✕) (&M) (🛏) (🛏) (💻) (🏊)

▼▼▼ Holiday Inn ⓈⒽ
(828) 437-0171. **$69-$84.** 2400 S Sterling St. I-40, exit 105 (SR 18), just s. Ext corridors. **Pets:** Other species. $25 one-time fee/room. Service with restrictions.

(A$K) (S🛁) (✕) (&M) (🛏) (🛏) (💻) (🍽) (🏊)

▼▼ Sleep Inn ⓈⒽ
(828) 433-9000. **$56.** 2400A S Sterling St. I-40, exit 105 (SR 18), just s. Int corridors. **Pets:** Accepted.

(A$K) (S🛁) (✕) (🛏) (🛏) (💻)

MORRISVILLE

▼▼ Extended StayAmerica-RDU Airport Ⓜ
(919) 380-1499. **Call for rates.** 2700 Slater Rd. I-40, exit 284 or 284A, 0.4 mi s on Airport Blvd, then just w. Ext corridors. **Pets:** Accepted.

(✕) (🛏) (💻)

▼▼▼▼ La Quinta Inn & Suites Raleigh-Airport ⓈⒽ
(919) 481-3600. **$95-$125.** 1001 Aerial Center Pkwy. I-40, exit 284 and 284A, just s, then just e. Int corridors. **Pets:** Medium. Service with restrictions.

(A$K) (✕) (&M) (🛏) (🛏) (💻) (🏊)

▼▼▼ La Quinta Inn & Suites (Raleigh-Durham Int'l Airport) ⓈⒽ
(919) 461-1771. **$109-$149.** 1001 Hospitality Ct. I-40, exit 284 or 284A, just s, just e on Aerial Center Pkwy, then just ne; in Aerial Center Park. Int corridors. **Pets:** Medium. Service with restrictions.

(A$K) (✕) (&M) (🛏) (🛏) (🛏) (💻) (🏊)

▼▼▼ Staybridge Suites Raleigh Durham Airport ⓈⒽ
(919) 468-0180. **$95-$175, 3 day notice.** 1012 Airport Blvd. I-40, exit 284 or 284A, just s; enter between Hampton Inn and Holiday Inn Express. Int corridors. **Pets:** $150 one-time fee/room. Designated rooms, service with restrictions, crate.

(A$K) (S🛁) (✕) (&M) (🛏) (🛏) (🛏) (💻) (✕)

MOUNT AIRY

▼▼ Quality Inn Ⓜ
(336) 789-2000. **$59-$115.** 2136 Rockford St. Jct US 52, 0.6 mi s on US 601. Ext corridors. **Pets:** Medium, other species. $25 one-time fee/room. Designated rooms, service with restrictions, supervision.

(A$K) (S🛁) (✕) (🛏) (🛏) (💻) (🏊)

MURPHY

(AAA) ▼▼▼ Best Western of Murphy M ❋
(828) 837-3060. **$63-$120.** 1522 Andrews Rd. US 74, 19 and SR 129, exit Andrews Rd. Ext corridors. **Pets:** Medium, other species. $15 daily fee/pet. Designated rooms, service with restrictions.
(SAVE) (✕) (🛏) (💻) (🌊)

(AAA) ▼▼▼ Days Inn M
(828) 837-8030. **$59-$99.** 754 Hwy 64 W. US 64 W/19 S/74 W and 129 S. Ext corridors. **Pets:** Accepted.
(SAVE) (🔊) (✕) (🛏) (💻) (🌊)

OUTER BANKS AREA

KILL DEVIL HILLS

▼▼▼▼ Clarion Oceanfront Hotel-Nags Head Beach SH
(252) 441-6333. **$59-$259.** 1601 S Virginia Dare Tr. SR 12, at MM 9.5. Int corridors. **Pets:** Accepted.
(ASK) (🔊) (✕) (🐾) (🛏) (💻) (🍴) (🌊) (✕)

▼▼ Quality Inn-John Yancey M
(252) 441-7141. **$59-$229.** 2009 S Virginia Dare Tr. SR 12, at MM 10.3. Ext/int corridors. **Pets:** Accepted.
(ASK) (🔊) (✕) (🐾) (🛏) (💻) (🌊)

(AAA) ▼▼▼ Ramada Plaza Outer Banks Resort & Conference Center SH
(252) 441-2151. **$81-$295.** 1701 S Virginia Dare Tr. SR 12, at MM 9.5. Int corridors. **Pets:** Accepted.
(SAVE) (🔊) (✕) (🛏) (💻) (🍴) (🌊) (✕)

(AAA) ▼▼▼ Travelodge-Nags Head Beach SH
(252) 441-0411. **$39-$349, 3 day notice.** 804 N Virginia Dare Tr. SR 12, at MM 8.1. Ext/int corridors. **Pets:** Accepted.
(SAVE) (🔊) (✕) (🛏) (💻) (🌊)

NAGS HEAD

(AAA) ▼▼▼▼ Comfort Inn Oceanfront South SH
(252) 441-6315. **$54-$224, 3 day notice.** 8031 Old Oregon Inlet Rd. SR 12, at MM 17. Int corridors. **Pets:** Medium. $10 daily fee/room. Designated rooms, service with restrictions, supervision.
(SAVE) (🔊) (✕) (🐾) (🛏) (💻) (🌊) (✕)

OCRACOKE

(AAA) ▼▼▼ The Anchorage Inn SH
(252) 928-1101. **$89-$249, 3 day notice.** 205 Irvin Garrish Hwy (SR 12). From Cedar Island Ferry, just n. Ext corridors. **Pets:** Other species. $20 daily fee/room. Designated rooms, service with restrictions, crate.
(SAVE) (✕) (🛏) (💻) (🌊) (✕)

END AREA

PINEHURST

(AAA) ▼▼▼ Homewood Suites by Hilton SH
(910) 255-0300. **$109-$179.** 250 Central Park Ave. Jct SR 5 and 211; in Olmsted Village. Int corridors. **Pets:** Large, other species. $50 one-time fee/room. Designated rooms, service with restrictions, crate.
(SAVE) (✕) (🔊) (🐾) (🛏) (💻) (🌊)

▼▼▼ Springhill Suites by Marriott SH
(910) 695-0234. **$109-$159.** 10024 US 15/501. Jct US 1, 2.3 mi n. Int corridors. **Pets:** Accepted.
(ASK) (🔊) (✕) (🔊) (🐾) (🛏) (💻) (🌊) (✕)

RALEIGH

(AAA) ▼▼▼ Best Western Raleigh North SH
(919) 872-5000. **$49-$79.** 2715 Capital Blvd. I-440, exit 11 or 11B, just n on US 1. Int corridors. **Pets:** Small. $25 daily fee/pet. Designated rooms, service with restrictions, supervision.
(SAVE) (🔊) (✕) (🐾) (🛏) (💻) (🌊)

▼▼▼ Candlewood Suites-Crabtree SH
(919) 789-4840. **$39-$89.** 4433 Lead Mine Rd. I-440, exit 7 or 7B, just w, then just n. Int corridors. **Pets:** Accepted.
(ASK) (🔊) (✕) (🔊) (🛏) (💻)

(AAA) ▼▼▼ Comfort Suites SH
(919) 876-2211. **$120-$169.** 4400 Capital Blvd. I-440, exit 11 and 11B, 2.5 mi n on US 1. Int corridors. **Pets:** Medium, other species. $25 daily fee/pet. Designated rooms, service with restrictions, crate.
(SAVE) (🔊) (✕) (🐾) (🛏) (💻) (🌊)

(AAA) ▼▼▼ Days Inn M
(919) 878-9310. **$48-$61.** 3201 Wake Forest Rd. I-440, exit 10 (Wake Forest Rd), just n, then just w. Ext corridors. **Pets:** $10 daily fee/room. Service with restrictions, crate.
(SAVE) (✕) (🐾) (🛏) (💻) (🌊)

(AAA) ▼▼▼ Econo Lodge of Raleigh/North M
(919) 856-9800. **$50-$70.** 2641 Appliance Ct. I-440, exit 11 or 11B, just n, then 0.3 mi e. Ext/int corridors. **Pets:** Accepted.
(SAVE) (🔊) (✕) (🔊) (🐾) (🛏) (🌊)

▼▼▼ Extended StayAmerica-North Raleigh SH
(919) 829-7271. **$64-$84.** 911 Wake Towne Dr. I-440, exit 10 (Wake Forest Rd), just s, then w. Int corridors. **Pets:** Accepted.
(ASK) (🔊) (✕) (🛏) (💻)

▼▼▼ Fairfield Inn & Suites–Crabtree SH
(919) 881-9800. **Call for rates.** 2201 Summit Park Ln. I-440, exit 7 or 7B, just w on US 70, just s on Blue Ridge Rd, then just e. Int corridors. **Pets:** Accepted.
(ASK) (✕) (🔊) (🐾) (🛏) (💻) (🌊)

(AAA) ▼▼▼▼ Hampton Inn Crabtree SH ❋
(919) 782-1112. **$129-$159.** 6209 Glenwood Ave. I-440, exit 7 or 7B, 2.5 mi w on US 70. Int corridors. **Pets:** $50 one-time fee/room. Service with restrictions, crate.
(SAVE) (✕) (🔊) (🐾) (🛏) (💻) (🌊) (✕)

▼▼▼ Holiday Inn at Crabtree Valley Mall LH
(919) 782-8600. **$89-$119.** 4100 Glenwood Ave. I-440, exit 7, just w on US 70. Int corridors. **Pets:** Accepted.
(ASK) (🔊) (✕) (🔊) (🐾) (🛏) (💻) (🍴) (🌊)

(AAA) ▼▼▼▼ Holiday Inn Raleigh-North LH ❋
(919) 872-3500. **$99-$119.** 2805 Highwoods Blvd. I-440, exit 11 or 11B, just n on US 1, then just w. Int corridors. **Pets:** Medium. $35 one-time fee/room. Service with restrictions, supervision.
(SAVE) (🔊) (✕) (🔊) (🐾) (🛏) (💻) (🍴) (🌊)

▼▼ Homestead Studio Suites Hotel-Raleigh/Crabtree Valley SH
(919) 510-8551. **$69-$90.** 4810 Bluestone Dr. I-440, exit 7 or 7B, 1.6 mi w on US 70, then just s. Ext corridors. **Pets:** Accepted.
(ASK) (🔊) (✕) (🐾) (🛏) (💻)

▼▼▼ **Homestead Studio Suites**
Hotel-Raleigh/Northeast SH
(919) 807-9970. **$74-$89.** 2601 Appliance Ct. I-440, exit 11 or 11B, just n on US 1, then just e. Int corridors. **Pets:** Accepted.

A$K S⬤ ✕ 🐾 🗄 📠 💻 🌊

▼▼▼ **Homestead Studio Suites Hotel-Raleigh/North**
Raleigh SH
(919) 981-7353. **$64-$84.** 3531 Wake Forest Rd. I-440, exit 10 (Wake Forest Rd), 0.5 mi n. Ext corridors. **Pets:** Accepted.

A$K S⬤ ✕ 🐾 🗄 🗄 🗄 💻

▲▲▲ ▼▼▼ **Homewood Suites by Hilton** SH ☙
(919) 785-1131. **$159.** 5400 Homewood Banks Dr. I-440, exit 7 or 7B, just w on US 70, just s on Blue Ridge Rd, just w on Crabtree Valley, then just s. Int corridors. **Pets:** Medium. $75 one-time fee/room. Designated rooms, service with restrictions, crate.

SAVE S⬤ ✕ 🐾 🗄 🗄 🗄 💻 🌊

▼▼▼ **La Quinta Inn & Suites Raleigh (Crabtree)** SH
(919) 785-0071. **$99-$119.** 2211 Summit Park Ln. I-440, exit 7 or 7B, just w on US 70, just s on Blue Ridge Rd, then just e. Int corridors. **Pets:** Medium. Service with restrictions.

A$K ✕ 🗄 🐾 🗄 🗄 💻 🌊

▼▼▼ **Red Roof Inn-South** SH
(919) 833-6005. **$55-$68.** 1813 S Saunders St. I-40, exit 298B, just n. Int corridors. **Pets:** Medium, other species. Service with restrictions, supervision.

✕ 🗄 🐾 🗄 🗄

▼▼▼ **Residence Inn by Marriott Crabtree** SH
(919) 279-3000. **$89-$229.** 2200 Summit Park Ln. I-440, exit 7 or 7B, just w on US 70, just s on Blue Ridge Rd, then just e. Int corridors. **Pets:** Accepted.

A$K ✕ 🗄 🐾 🗄 🗄 💻 🌊 ✕

▼▼▼ **Residence Inn by Marriott-North Raleigh** SH
(919) 878-6100. **$69-$169.** 1000 Navaho Dr. I-440, exit 10 (Wake Forest Rd), just n, then w. Ext corridors. **Pets:** Accepted.

A$K ✕ 🗄 🐾 🗄 💻 🌊 ✕

▲▲▲ ▼▼▼ **Sheraton Raleigh Center** LH
(919) 834-9900. **$117-$214.** 421 S Salisbury St. Downtown; just s. Int corridors. **Pets:** Accepted.

SAVE S⬤ ✕ 🗄 🗄 💻 🍴 🌊

▼▼◆ **StudioPLUS-North Raleigh** SH
(919) 546-0879. **$69-$99.** 921 Wake Towne Dr. I-440, exit 10 (Wake Forest), just s, then w. Int corridors. **Pets:** Accepted.

A$K S⬤ ✕ 🗄 🗄 🗄 💻

REIDSVILLE

▲▲▲ ▼▼▼ **Americas Best Value Inn & Suites** M
(336) 342-0341. **$45-$149.** 2100 Barnes St. US 29, exit 150 (Barnes St), just e. Ext corridors. **Pets:** Accepted.

SAVE S⬤ ✕ 🗄 💻 🍴 🌊

▲▲▲ ▼▼▼ **Comfort Inn** M
(336) 634-1275. **$66-$219.** 2203 Barnes St. US 29, exit 150 (Barnes St), just e. Ext corridors. **Pets:** Accepted.

SAVE S⬤ ✕ 🐾 🗄 💻 🌊

RESEARCH TRIANGLE PARK

▼▼▼▼ **Radisson Hotel in Research Triangle Park** SH
(919) 549-8631. **$89-$249.** 150 Park Dr. I-40, exit 280, just s, then just w. Int corridors. **Pets:** Accepted.

A$K S⬤ ✕ 🐾 🗄 💻 🍴 🌊 ✕

ROANOKE RAPIDS

▼▼ **Jameson Inn** M
(252) 533-0022. **$54-$104.** 101 S Old Farm Rd. I-95, exit 173, 0.5 mi w on US 158, then just s. Ext corridors. **Pets:** Small. $10 daily fee/pet. Service with restrictions, crate.

A$K ✕ 🐾 🗄 🗄 💻 🌊

ROBBINSVILLE

▼▼ **Microtel Inn & Suites** SH
(828) 479-6772. **$49-$69.** 111 Rodney Orr Bypass (US 129). Center of downtown. Int corridors. **Pets:** Accepted.

A$K S⬤ ✕ 🗄 🐾 🗄 🗄 💻

ROCKY MOUNT

▲▲▲ ▼▼▼ **Best Western Inn I-95 Gold Rock** M
(252) 985-1450. **$58-$88.** 7095 NC 4. I-95, exit 145, just e. Ext corridors. **Pets:** Accepted.

SAVE S⬤ ✕ 🗄 💻 🌊

▲▲▲ ▼▼◆ **Comfort Inn** SH
(252) 937-7765. **$65-$79.** 200 Gateway Blvd. I-95, exit 138, 1 mi e on US 64, exit Winstead Ave, then just s. Int corridors. **Pets:** Other species. $25 one-time fee/room. Designated rooms, service with restrictions.

SAVE S⬤ ✕ 🐾 🗄 🗄 💻 🌊

▼▼ **Red Roof Inn** SH
(252) 984-0907. **$45-$62.** 1370 N Weslyan Blvd. Jct US 64 Bypass, 1.5 mi n on US 301. Int corridors. **Pets:** Medium, other species. Service with restrictions, supervision.

✕ 🐾 🗄 🗄 🌊

▲▲▲ ▼▼▼ **Residence Inn by Marriott** SH ☙
(252) 451-5600. **$145-$169.** 230 Gateway Blvd. I-95, exit 138, 1 mi e on US 64, exit Winstead Ave, just s, then just e. Int corridors. **Pets:** Other species. $75 one-time fee/room. Service with restrictions, crate.

SAVE ✕ 🗄 🐾 🗄 🗄 💻 🌊 ✕

▼ **Super 8 Motel** M
(252) 442-8075. **Call for rates (no credit cards).** 7522 Hwy 48. I-95, exit 145, just e, then just s. Ext corridors. **Pets:** Accepted.

✕ 🗄 🌊

ROXBORO

▼▼▼ **Hampton Inn** SH
(336) 599-8800. **$99-$115, 3 day notice.** 920 Durham Rd. Jct US 158, n on US 501. Int corridors. **Pets:** Small, dogs only. Designated rooms, service with restrictions, supervision.

A$K S⬤ ✕ 🐾 🗄 🗄 💻 🌊

▼▼ **Innkeeper Roxboro** M
(336) 599-3800. **$65-$85, 3 day notice.** 906 Durham Rd. Jct US 158, just n on US 501. Ext/int corridors. **Pets:** Medium, other species. $10 daily fee/room. Designated rooms, service with restrictions.

A$K S⬤ ✕ 🗄

SALISBURY

▼▼▼ **Hampton Inn** SH
(704) 637-8000. **$102-$209.** 1001 Klumac Rd. I-85, exit 75, just w, then just s. Int corridors. **Pets:** Other species. Designated rooms, service with restrictions, supervision.

A$K S⬤ ✕ 🐾 🗄 🗄 💻 🌊

▼▼▼ **Holiday Inn** SH
(704) 637-3100. **$76-$155.** 530 Jake Alexander Blvd S. I-85, exit 75, 0.5 mi w. Ext/int corridors. **Pets:** Medium. $15 one-time fee/pet. Service with restrictions, supervision.

A$K S⬤ ✕ 🐾 🗄 🗄 💻 🍴 🌊 ✕

SALUDA

▼▼▼ The Oaks Bed & Breakfast BB
(828) 749-9613. **$119-$179, 7 day notice.** 339 Greenville St. I-26, exit 59, 1.1 mi sw, 0.3 mi w on US 176, then cross railway tracks. Ext/int corridors. **Pets:** Accepted.
A$K S❄ ✕ 🛏 💻 🏊

SANFORD

▼▼▼ Hampton Inn SH
(919) 775-2000. **$90-$100, 3 day notice.** 1904 S Horner Blvd. Jct US 1, 3.2 mi s on US 421 and SR 87. Int corridors. **Pets:** Medium. $10 daily fee/pet. Service with restrictions, crate.
A$K S❄ ✕ 🛏M 🐾 🐾 🛏 💻 🏊

▼▼ Jameson Inn M
(919) 708-7400. **$54-$104.** 2614 S Horner Blvd. Jct US 1, 4.1 mi s on US 421 and SR 87. Ext corridors. **Pets:** Accepted.
A$K ✕ 🛏M 🛏 💻 🏊

SHELBY

▼▼▼ Hampton Inn SH
(704) 482-5666. **$69-$91.** 2012 E Marion St. Jct US 74 Bypass E and US 74 business route. Int corridors. **Pets:** Accepted.
A$K S❄ ✕ 🏊

▼▼▼ Super 8 M
(704) 484-2101. **$45-$53.** 1716 E Dixon Blvd. Jct SR 180, 0.4 mi w on US 74 Bypass. Ext corridors. **Pets:** Small, other species. $10 daily fee/pet. Service with restrictions, crate.
SAVE S❄ ✕ 🛏 💻

SMITHFIELD

▼▼ Jameson Inn M
(919) 989-5901. **$54-$104.** 125 S Equity Dr. I-95, exit 95, just w, just n on Industrial Park Blvd, then just w. Ext corridors. **Pets:** Small. $10 daily fee/pet. Service with restrictions, crate.
A$K ✕ 🛏M 🐾 🛏 💻 🏊

▼▼▼ Log Cabin Motel M
(919) 934-1534. **$45-$47.** 2491 US 70 E (Business Route). I-95, exit 95, 0.5 mi e. Ext corridors. **Pets:** Designated rooms, no service.
SAVE ✕ 🛏 🍴 🏊

▼▼▼ Super 8 Motel SH
(919) 989-8988. **$60-$105.** 735 Industrial Park Dr. I-95, exit 95, just w, then just n. Int corridors. **Pets:** Small, other species. $6 one-time fee/room. Designated rooms, service with restrictions, supervision.
SAVE S❄ ✕ 🛏M 🐾 🐾 🛏 🏊

SOUTHERN PINES

▼▼▼ Hampton Inn SH
(910) 692-9266. **$89-$104.** 1675 US 1 S. Jct Morgantown Rd, just s. Ext corridors. **Pets:** Small, dogs only. $10 daily fee/pet. Service with restrictions, supervision.
SAVE 🐾 ✕ 🛏 💻 🏊

▼▼ Microtel Inn SH
(910) 693-3737. **$55-$69, 7 day notice.** 205 Windstar Pl. 1 mi s on US 1, just e. Int corridors. **Pets:** Accepted.
A$K S❄ ✕ 🐾

▼▼▼ Residence Inn by Marriott SH 🐾
(910) 693-3400. **$99-$119.** 105 Brucewood Rd. Jct US 1, 1.2 mi n on US 15/501, then just e. Int corridors. **Pets:** Designated rooms.
A$K S❄ ✕ 🐾 🛏 💻 🏊 ✕

SPRING LAKE

▲▲▲ ▼▼▼ Holiday Inn Express Hotel & Suites SH
(910) 436-1900. **$90-$145.** 103 Brook Ln. Jct SR 210, 0.9 mi nw on SR 24/87. Int corridors. **Pets:** Other species. $65 one-time fee/room. Service with restrictions, crate.
SAVE S❄ ✕ 🐾 🐾 🛏 💻 🏊 ✕

▼▼ Super 8 Motel SH
(910) 436-8588. **$55-$85.** 256 S Main St. Jct SR 210, just se on SR 24/87, just s. Int corridors. **Pets:** Small. $15 daily fee/pet. Designated rooms, service with restrictions, supervision.
A$K S❄ ✕ 🐾 🛏

SPRUCE PINE

▲▲▲ ▼▼▼ Richmond Inn BB
(828) 765-6993. **$75-$125, 10 day notice.** 51 Pine Ave. Exit off US 19 E and 226 to Oak Ave, just n on Walnut Ave, follow signs; center. Int corridors. **Pets:** Accepted.
SAVE ✕ 🛏 💻 🏊

STATESVILLE

▲▲▲ ▼▼ Best Western Statesville Inn SH
(704) 881-0111. **$69-$165.** 1121 Morland Dr. I-77, exit 49A, just e on US 70 E. Ext corridors. **Pets:** Small. $15 daily fee/room. Designated rooms, service with restrictions, supervision.
SAVE S❄ ✕ 🐾 🛏 💻 🏊

▼▼▼ Econo Lodge Inn & Suites M
(704) 872-4101. **$59-$79.** 740 Sullivan Rd. I-40, exit 151, just s. Ext corridors. **Pets:** Medium, other species. $25 one-time fee/pet. No service, crate.
A$K S❄ ✕ 🛏M 🐾 🛏 💻 🏊

▼▼▼ Quality Inn SH 🐾
(704) 878-2721. **$70-$80.** 715 Sullivan Rd. I-40, exit 151, just s. Int corridors. **Pets:** Medium. $10 one-time fee/room. Service with restrictions, supervision.
A$K S❄ ✕ 🐾 🛏 💻 🏊

▲▲▲ ▼▼▼ Super 8 Motel M
(704) 878-9888. **$48-$100.** 1125 Greenland Dr. I-77, exit 49A, just e. Ext/int corridors. **Pets:** Small, dogs only. $5 daily fee/pet. Designated rooms, service with restrictions, supervision.
SAVE S❄ ✕ 🐾

SUNSET BEACH

▲▲▲ ▼▼▼▼ Sea Trail Golf Resort & Conference Center CO
(910) 287-1100. **$70-$535, 3 day notice.** 211 Clubhouse Rd. US 17, 2.2 mi e on SR 904, then 1.5 mi s on SR 179. Ext corridors. **Pets:** $70 one-time fee/room. Designated rooms, service with restrictions, supervision.
SAVE S❄ ✕ 🛏 💻 🍴 🏊 ✕

THOMASVILLE

▲▲▲ ▼▼▼ Days Inn SH
(336) 472-6600. **$55-$60.** 895 Lake Rd. I-85, exit 102, just w, then just s. Int corridors. **Pets:** Accepted.
SAVE S❄ ✕ 🛏 🍴 🏊

TRYON

▲▲▲ ▼▼▼ 1906 Pine Crest Inn & Restaurant CI
(828) 859-9135. **$99-$229, 7 day notice.** 85 Pine Crest Ln. I-26, exit 67, 4 mi e on SR 108, just s on New Market Rd, then just e. Ext/int corridors. **Pets:** Accepted.
SAVE S❄ ✕ 🛏 💻 🍴

WASHINGTON

Holiday Inn Express SH
(252) 946-5500. **$64-$80.** 1031 Carolina Ave. Jct US 264, 0.5 mi n on US 17. Int corridors. **Pets:** Accepted.

WAYNESVILLE

The Lodge of Waynesville M
(828) 452-0353. **$49-$125.** 909 Russ Ave. US 23/74, exit 102, just se. Ext corridors. **Pets:** Accepted.

WELDON

Days Inn M
(252) 536-4867. **$60-$90.** 1611 Julian R Allsbrook Hwy. I-95, exit 173, just e on US 158. Ext corridors. **Pets:** $10 daily fee/pet. Service with restrictions, supervision.

WEST JEFFERSON

Nation's Inn M
(336) 246-2080. **$64-$70.** 107 Beaver Creek School Rd. Jct US 221, just n on SR 194, just w. Ext corridors. **Pets:** Accepted.

WILKESBORO

Addison Inn M
(336) 838-1000. **$69-$135.** 1842 Winkler St (Hwy 421 N). 2 mi n on US 421, 0.5 mi w of US 421 business route. Ext corridors. **Pets:** Accepted.

WILLIAMSTON

Hampton Inn SH
(252) 809-1100. **$79-$84.** 1099 Hampton Ct. US 64, exit 514, just s on US 17, then just w. Int corridors. **Pets:** Accepted.

Holiday Inn SH 🐾
(252) 792-3184. **$65-$139.** 101 East Blvd. US 64, exit 514, 1.5 mi n on US 17 business route. Ext/int corridors. **Pets:** Large. Service with restrictions, crate.

WILMINGTON

Baymont Inn M
(910) 392-6767. **$65-$109.** 306 S College Rd. Jct US 17 business route, just s on SR 132. Ext/int corridors. **Pets:** Medium. $15 daily fee/pet. Designated rooms, service with restrictions, supervision.

Comfort Inn Wilmington SH
(910) 791-4841. **$65-$135.** 151 S College Rd. Jct US 17 business route, just s on SR 132. Int corridors. **Pets:** Accepted.

Courtyard by Marriott SH 🐾
(910) 395-8224. **$99-$199.** 151 Van Campen Blvd. Jct US 17 business route, 0.3 mi s on SR 132, just se on Imperial Dr, then just w. Int corridors. **Pets:** Other species. $50 one-time fee/pet. Designated rooms, service with restrictions, supervision.

Days Inn M 🐾
(910) 799-6300. **$55-$89.** 5040 Market St. Jct SR 132, 0.6 mi s on US 17. Ext corridors. **Pets:** Large. $15 daily fee/room. Designated rooms, service with restrictions, crate.

Extended StayAmerica-Wilmington-New Centre Drive SH
(910) 793-4508. **$64-$114.** 4929 New Centre Dr. Jct SR 132, 0.4 mi s on US 17, just e. Int corridors. **Pets:** Accepted.

Hilton Wilmington Riverside LH
(910) 763-5900. **$109-$329.** 301 N Water St. On Cape Fear River waterfront. Int corridors. **Pets:** Accepted.

Innkeeper SH
(910) 799-4292. **$79-$129, 3 day notice.** 5345 W Market St. Jct SR 132, just s on US 17. Int corridors. **Pets:** $10 daily fee/room, $20 one-time fee/pet. Service with restrictions, supervision.

Jameson Inn SH
(910) 452-5660. **$54-$104.** 5102 Dunlea Ct. Jct SR 132, 0.5 mi s on US 17 business route, just w on New Centre Dr. Int corridors. **Pets:** Small. $10 daily fee/pet. Service with restrictions, crate.

MainStay Suites SH
(910) 392-1741. **$89-$280.** 5229 Market St. Jct SR 132, just s on US 17. Int corridors. **Pets:** Small. $100 one-time fee/room, service with restrictions, crate.

Quality Inn M
(910) 791-8850. **$60-$150.** 4926 Market St. Jct SR 132, 0.9 mi s on US 17 business route. Ext corridors. **Pets:** Small. $5 daily fee/pet, $25 one-time fee/pet. Designated rooms, service with restrictions, supervision.

Residence Inn-Landfall SH
(910) 256-0098. **$99-$189.** 1200 Culbreth Dr. Jct US 17 business route, 2.4 mi e on US 74, 0.4 mi n on Military Cutoff Rd, then just e. Int corridors. **Pets:** Medium, other species. $75 one-time fee/room. Designated rooms, service with restrictions, crate.

Super 8 Motel SH
(910) 343-9778. **$60-$180, 3 day notice.** 3604 Market St. Jct SR 132, 1.8 mi s on US 17 business route. Int corridors. **Pets:** Accepted.

WILSON

Best Western-Wilson M
(252) 237-8700. **$49-$120.** 817-A Ward Blvd. US 264, exit 42, 2.6 mi n on Downing St, then just w. Ext corridors. **Pets:** Accepted.

Jameson Inn M
(252) 234-7172. **$65-$75.** 5016 Hayes Pl. I-95, exit 121, just w, then just n. Ext corridors. **Pets:** Small. $10 daily fee/pet. Service with restrictions, crate.

WINSTON-SALEM

Augustus T Zevely Inn BB
(336) 748-9299. **$90-$140, 14 day notice.** 803 S Main St. In Old Salem Historic District. Ext/int corridors. **Pets:** Accepted.

Best Western Salem Inn & Suites SH
(336) 725-8561. **$75-$110.** 127 S Cherry St. I-40 business route, exit 5C (Cherry St) eastbound, just e on High St, then just s; exit westbound, just w on 1st St, just s on Marshall St, just e on High St, then just s. Ext corridors. **Pets:** Accepted.

▼ Crossland Economy Studios M

(336) 759-7780. **Call for rates.** 7910 N Point Blvd. US 52, exit 115B, 2 mi s on University Pkwy, then just e. Ext corridors. **Pets:** Accepted.

⊠ ⚐ 🖥

▼▼ Extended StayAmerica Winston-Salem-Hanes Mall Blvd M

(336) 768-0075. **$69-$94.** 1995 Hampton Inn Ct. I-40, exit 189 (Stratford Rd), just s, just e on Hanes Mall Blvd, then just n. Ext corridors. **Pets:** Accepted.

ASK SÒ ⊠ ⚐ 🖥 💻

▲▲▲ ▼▼▼▼ The Hawthorne Inn & Conference Center SH

(336) 777-3000. **$59-$120.** 420 High St. I-40 business route, exit 5C (Cherry St) eastbound, just e; exit westbound, just w on 1st St, then just s on Marshall St. Int corridors. **Pets:** Medium, other species. $15 daily fee/room. Designated rooms, service with restrictions, supervision.

SAVE SÒ ⊠ ⛬ Ⓜ 🖥 ⚐ 🖥 💻 🍴 ⇌

▼▼▼ Holiday Inn Hanes Mall SH 🐾

(336) 765-6670. **$68.** 2008 S Hawthorne Rd. I-40 business route, exit 2A, 0.5 mi s on Silas Creek Pkwy, then just e. Ext corridors. **Pets:** Small. $25 one-time fee/pet. Service with restrictions, supervision.

ASK ⊠ ⛬ Ⓜ 🖥 ⚐ 💻 🍴 ⇌

▼▼▼ La Quinta Inns & Suites Winston-Salem SH

(336) 765-8777. **$109-$129.** 2020 Griffith Rd. I-40, exit 189 (Stratford Rd), just s, just e on Hanes Mall Blvd, then just s. Int corridors. **Pets:** Medium. Service with restrictions.

ASK ⊠ ⛬ Ⓜ 🖥 ⚐ 🖥 💻 ⇌

▲▲▲ ▼▼▼ Quality Inn-Coliseum SH

(336) 767-8240. **$65-$90.** 531 Akron Dr. US 52, exit 112, just e. Int corridors. **Pets:** Small, other species. $15 daily fee/pet. Service with restrictions, supervision.

SAVE SÒ ⊠ 🖥 🖥 💻 🍴 ⇌

▼▼▼▼ Quality Inn University SH

(336) 767-9009. **$66-$76, 30 day notice.** 5719 University Pkwy. US 52, exit 115B, 0.4 mi w. Ext corridors. **Pets:** Accepted.

ASK SÒ ⊠ 🖥 💻 ⇌

▼▼▼▼ Residence Inn by Marriott SH

(336) 759-0777. **$104-$159.** 7835 N Point Blvd. US 52 N, exit 115B, 2 mi s on University Pkwy, then just e. Ext corridors. **Pets:** Small. $75 one-time fee/pet. Designated rooms, service with restrictions, supervision.

ASK SÒ ⊠ 🖥 🖥 💻 ⇌ ⊠

▼▼ Super 8 University-Madison Park SH

(336) 714-8888. **$67.** 200 Mercantile Dr. US 52, exit 115B, just w on University Pkwy, then just n. Int corridors. **Pets:** Large, other species. $25 one-time fee/pet. Designated rooms, service with restrictions, supervision.

ASK SÒ ⊠ 🖥 ⚐ 🖥 💻 ⇌

YANCEYVILLE

▼▼ Days Inn M

(336) 694-9494. **$55-$160.** 1858 NC Hwy 86 N. Jct SR 62, 1.6 mi nw on US 158/SR 86. Ext corridors. **Pets:** Medium. $10 daily fee/pet. Service with restrictions, supervision.

ASK SÒ ⊠ ⚐ 🖥 ⇌

BEULAH

▼▼ AmericInn Lodge & Suites SH
(701) 873-2220. **$80-$130.** 2100 2nd Ave NW. Jct SR 49/200, 1.2 mi s. Int corridors. **Pets:** $25 one-time fee/room. Service with restrictions, supervision.

BISMARCK

▼▼▼ Best Western Doublewood Inn SH
(701) 258-7000. **$89-$99.** 1400 E Interchange Ave. I-94, exit 159 (US 83), just s. Int corridors. **Pets:** Accepted.

▼▼▼ Best Western Ramkota Hotel SH
(701) 258-7700. **$104-$129.** 800 S 3rd St. Just s of jct I-94 business loop (Bismarck Expy) and S 3rd St. Int corridors. **Pets:** Accepted.

▼▼ Comfort Inn SH
(701) 223-1911. **$69-$95.** 1030 Interstate Ave. I-94, exit 159 (US 83), 0.3 mi nw. Int corridors. **Pets:** Small. Service with restrictions, supervision.

▼▼ Days Inn-Bismarck SH
(701) 223-9151. **$58-$88, 7 day notice.** 1300 E Capitol Ave. I-94, exit 159 (US 83), just s. Int corridors. **Pets:** $5 daily fee/pet. Designated rooms, service with restrictions, supervision.

▼▼ Expressway Inn SH
(701) 222-2900. **$58-$78.** 200 Bismarck Expwy. Jct I-94 business loop (Bismarck Expwy) and S 3rd St. Int corridors. **Pets:** Medium, other species. $10 one-time fee/room. Designated rooms, service with restrictions, supervision.

▼▼ Kelly Inn SH
(701) 223-8001. **$72-$109.** 1800 N 12 St. I-94, exit 159 (US 83), 0.3 mi s. Int corridors. **Pets:** Designated rooms, service with restrictions, supervision.

▼▼▼ Radisson Hotel Bismarck LH
(701) 255-6000. **$84-$119.** 605 E Broadway Ave. Jct 6th St; center. Int corridors. **Pets:** Accepted.

▼▼▼ Ramada Limited Suites SH
(701) 221-3030. **$60-$95.** 3808 E Divide Ave. I-94, exit 161 (Bismarck Expwy), just s. Int corridors. **Pets:** Other species. $10 daily fee/room.

▼▼ Select Inn SH
(701) 223-8060. **$50-$73.** 1505 Interchange Ave. I-94, exit 159 (US 83), just se. Int corridors. **Pets:** Accepted.

BOWMAN

▲▲▲ ▼▼ North Winds Lodge M
(701) 523-5641. **$43-$60.** 503 Hwy 85 S. On US 85, just s of US 12. Ext corridors. **Pets:** Accepted.

CARRINGTON

▼▼ Chieftain Conference Center SH
(701) 652-3131. **$60-$85.** 60 4th Ave S. Jct US 52 and 281, 0.5 mi e on US 52; just s of jct SR 200. Ext/int corridors. **Pets:** Small. $5 daily fee/pet. Designated rooms, service with restrictions, crate.

▼▼ Super 8 Motel SH
(701) 652-3982. **$46-$66.** 101 4th Ave S. Jct US 52 and 281, 0.5 mi e on US 52; just s of jct SR 200. Int corridors. **Pets:** Medium. $5 daily fee/pet. Designated rooms, service with restrictions, supervision.

CASSELTON

▲▲▲ ▼▼▼ Governors' Inn SH
(701) 347-4524. **$89-$99.** 2050 Governors Dr. I-94, exit 331 (SR 18), just n. Int corridors. **Pets:** Other species. $9 daily fee/pet. Designated rooms, service with restrictions, crate.

DEVILS LAKE

▲▲▲ ▼▼▼ Comfort Inn SH
(701) 662-6760. **$75-$85.** 215 Hwy 2 E. Jct US 2 and SR 20. Int corridors. **Pets:** $5 daily fee/room. Designated rooms, service with restrictions.

▲▲▲ ▼ Trails West Motel M
(701) 662-5011. **$49.** 111 1st St W. 0.8 mi sw on US 2. Int corridors. **Pets:** $5 daily fee/pet. Service with restrictions, supervision.

DICKINSON

▼▼ AmericInn Motel & Suites of Dickinson SH
(701) 225-1400. **$89-$135.** 229 15th St W. I-94, exit 61 (SR 22), just n, then e. Int corridors. **Pets:** Accepted.

▼▼ Comfort Inn SH
(701) 264-7300. **$65-$135.** 493 Elks Dr. I-94, exit 61 (SR 22), just n, then w. Int corridors. **Pets:** Other species. $10 one-time fee/room. Designated rooms, service with restrictions, supervision.

▲▲▲ ▼▼▼ Hartfiel Inn BB 🐾
(701) 225-6710. **$79-$89.** 509 3rd Ave W. I-94, exit 61 (SR 22), 0.8 mi s. Int corridors. **Pets:** Medium, dogs only. Designated rooms, service with restrictions, supervision.

Quality Inn & Suites-Dickinson SH
(701) 225-9510. **$61-$135.** 71 Museum Dr. I-94, exit 61 (SR 22), just s, then e. Int corridors. **Pets:** Designated rooms, service with restrictions, supervision.

SAVE S6 X B B D 2 X

EDGELEY

Prairie Rose Inn SH
(701) 493-2075. **$54-$67.** 111 Frontage Rd. Jct US 281 and SR 13. Ext/int corridors. **Pets:** Dogs only. $25 deposit/room. Designated rooms, crate.

A$K S6 X B

FARGO

Airport/Dome Days Inn & Suites SH
(701) 232-0000. **$75-$99.** 1507 19th Ave N. I-29, exit 67, 1.8 mi e. Int corridors. **Pets:** Accepted.

SAVE S6 X D B B D 2

AmericInn Lodge & Suites SH
(701) 234-9946. **$72-$144.** 1423 35th St SW. I-29, exit 64 (13th Ave S), just se. Int corridors. **Pets:** Other species. $10 daily fee/room. Designated rooms, service with restrictions, supervision.

SAVE S6 X D B B D 2 X

Best Western Fargo Doublewood Inn SH
(701) 235-3333. **$89-$120.** 3333 13th Ave S. I-29, exit 64 (13th Ave S), 0.3 mi e. Int corridors. **Pets:** Medium, dogs only. $25 deposit/room. Service with restrictions, supervision.

SAVE S6 X 6M D B B D 1 2 X

Best Western Kelly Inn SH ❀
(701) 282-2143. **$94-$108.** 3800 Main Ave. I-29, exit 65 (Main Ave), just w. Ext/int corridors. **Pets:** Medium. Service with restrictions, supervision.

SAVE S6 X D B B D 1 2 X

Candlewood Suites SH ❀
(701) 235-8200. **$89-$99.** 1831 NDSU Research Park Dr. I-29, exit 67, 1.6 mi e. Int corridors. **Pets:** Other species. $75 one-time fee/room. Service with restrictions.

A$K S6 X 6M B B D

Comfort Inn by Choice Hotels East SH
(701) 280-9666. **$80-$100.** 1407 35th St S. I-29, exit 64 (13th Ave S), just se. Int corridors. **Pets:** Accepted.

A$K S6 X D B B D 2

Comfort Inn by Choice Hotels West SH
(701) 282-9596. **$80-$100.** 3825 9th Ave SW. I-29, exit 64 (13th Ave S), just nw. Int corridors. **Pets:** Accepted.

A$K S6 X B B D 2

Comfort Suites by Choice Hotels SH
(701) 237-5911. **$90-$110.** 1415 35th St SW. I-29, exit 64 (13th Ave S), just se. Int corridors. **Pets:** Accepted.

A$K S6 X 6M D B B D 2

Country Inn & Suites By Carlson SH
(701) 234-0565. **$89-$149.** 3316 13th Ave S. I-29, exit 64 (13th Ave S), 0.3 mi e. Int corridors. **Pets:** Accepted.

A$K S6 X B B D 2 X

Econo Lodge by Choice Hotels SH
(701) 232-3412. **$55-$75.** 1401 35th St S. I-29, exit 64 (13th Ave S), just se. Int corridors. **Pets:** Accepted.

A$K S6 X D B B D

Expressway Inn SH
(701) 235-3141. **$80-$82.** 1340 21st Ave S. I-94, exit 351, just sw. Ext/int corridors. **Pets:** Medium. $15 daily fee/room. Designated rooms, service with restrictions, crate.

A$K S6 X 6M D B B D 1 2 X

Grand Inn of Fargo SH
(701) 232-1321. **$42-$54.** 3402 14th Ave S. I-29, exit 64 (13th Ave S), just se. Int corridors. **Pets:** Dogs only. Designated rooms, service with restrictions, supervision.

SAVE S6 X B

Holiday Inn LH
(701) 282-2700. **$99-$149.** 3803 13th Ave S. I-29, exit 64 (13 Ave S), just nw. Int corridors. **Pets:** Other species. $10 one-time fee/room. Service with restrictions, supervision.

SAVE S6 X 6M D B B D 1 2 X

Holiday Inn Express Fargo SH
(701) 282-2000. **$90-$95.** 1040 40th St S. I-29, exit 64 (13th Ave S), just nw. Int corridors. **Pets:** Accepted.

S6 X 6M D B B D 2 X

Homewood Suites By Hilton SH
(701) 235-3150. **$109-$204.** 2021 16th St N. I-29, exit 67 (19th Ave), 1.7 mi e, then just n. Int corridors. **Pets:** Accepted.

A$K S6 X 6M D B B D

Kelly Inn 13th Avenue SH
(701) 277-8821. **$77-$120.** 4207 13th Ave SW. I-29, exit 64 (13th Ave S), 0.5 mi w. Ext/int corridors. **Pets:** Medium. Service with restrictions, supervision.

A$K S6 X 6M D B B D 2

MainStay Suites SH
(701) 277-4627. **$89-$109.** 1901 44th St SW. I-94, exit 348 (45th St), just n, then just e. Int corridors. **Pets:** Accepted.

A$K S6 X 6M D B B D 2 X

Select Inn SH ❀
(701) 282-6300. **$52-$65.** 1025 38th St SW. I-29, exit 64 (13th Ave S), just w, then n. Int corridors. **Pets:** Large. $25 deposit/room, $5 daily fee/room. Service with restrictions, supervision.

SAVE S6 X D B D

Sleep Inn SH
(701) 281-8240. **$60-$80.** 1921 44 St SW. I-94, exit 348 (45th St), just n, then just e. Int corridors. **Pets:** Accepted.

A$K S6 X D B D 2 X

Staybridge Suites SH
(701) 281-4900. **$94-$184, 7 day notice.** 4300 20th Ave S. I-94, exit 348 (45th St), just n, then e. Int corridors. **Pets:** Small. $200 deposit/room, $50 one-time fee/room. Designated rooms, service with restrictions.

A$K S6 X 6M D B D 2 X

Super 8 Motel SH
(701) 232-9202. **$39-$135, 3 day notice.** 3518 Interstate Blvd. I-29, exit 64 (13th Ave S), just n on east frontage road. Int corridors. **Pets:** Other species. $4 daily fee/pet. Designated rooms, service with restrictions, supervision.

A$K S6 X B D 2

GRAFTON

AmericInn Motel & Suites SH
(701) 352-2788. **$52-$160.** 1015 12th St W. SR 17, 1.2 mi w. Int corridors. **Pets:** Accepted.

A$K S6 X 6M D B B D 2 X

GRAND FORKS

Americas Best Value Inn of Grand Forks M
(701) 775-0555. **$47-$75.** 1000 N 42nd St. I-29, exit 141 (Gateway Dr), jct US 2, then just se. Int corridors. **Pets:** Other species. $10 daily fee/pet. Designated rooms, service with restrictions, supervision.

SAVE S6 X B

▼▼▼ AmericInn Motel & Suites SH
(701) 780-9925. **$62-$175.** 1820 S Columbia Rd. I-29, exit 138 (32nd Ave), 0.7 mi e, then 0.8 mi n. Int corridors. **Pets:** Accepted.
ASK SÓ ✕ &M ⌂ ⌨ ⚪ ▣ ▭ ⌨ ⊠

▼▼ Best Western Town House SH
(701) 746-5411. **$55-$94.** 710 1st Ave N. I-29, exit 140 (DeMers Ave), 3 mi e; downtown. Int corridors. **Pets:** Accepted.
ASK SÓ ✕ ⌂ ⌨ ⚪ ▣ ⫙ ▭ ⊠

▲▲▲ ▼▼▼ Days Inn SH
(701) 775-0060. **$55-$95.** 3101 34th St S. I-29, exit 138 (32nd Ave), 0.5 mi e. Int corridors. **Pets:** $5 daily fee/pet. Designated rooms, service with restrictions, supervision.
SAVE SÓ ✕ ▣ ⚪ ▭

▲▲▲ ▼ Econo Lodge M
(701) 746-6666. **$40-$100.** 900 N 43rd St. I-29, exit 141 (Gateway Blvd), just e, then 0.3 mi s. Ext/int corridors. **Pets:** Medium. $5 daily fee/pet. Supervision.
SAVE SÓ ✕ ▣ ⚪

▼ ▼ Travelodge SH
(701) 772-8151. **$57-$77.** 2100 S Washington St. I-29, exit 140 (DemErs Ave), 2.5 mi e, then 1.5 mi s. Int corridors. **Pets:** Medium, dogs only. $5 daily fee/room. Designated rooms, service with restrictions, supervision.
ASK SÓ ✕ ⚪ ▣ ⚪ ▭ ⊠

JAMESTOWN

▼▼ Comfort Inn by Choice Hotels SH
(701) 252-7125. **$95-$115.** 811 20 St SW. I-94, exit 258 (US 281), just n, then just w. Int corridors. **Pets:** Accepted.
ASK SÓ ✕ ▣ ⚪ ▭

▲▲▲ ▼▼▼ Quality Inn & Suites SH
(701) 252-3611. **$61-$135.** 507 25th St SW. I-94, exit 258 (US 281), just s. Int corridors. **Pets:** Medium. $10 one-time fee/room. Designated rooms, service with restrictions, supervision.
SAVE SÓ ✕ ⌂ ⚪ ▣ ⚪ ⊠

KENMARE

▼▼ Quilt Inn SH
(701) 385-4100. **$55.** 1232 Central Ave N. Just n on US 52. Int corridors. **Pets:** Accepted.
ASK SÓ ✕ ▣ ▭

MANDAN

▲▲▲ ▼▼▼ Best Western Seven Seas Hotel &
Waterpark SH
(701) 663-7401. **$89-$99.** 2611 Old Red Tr. I-94, exit 152 (Sunset Dr), just nw. Int corridors. **Pets:** Accepted.
SAVE SÓ ✕ &M ⌂ ⚪ ▣ ⚪ ▭ ⫙ ▭ ⊠

MEDORA

▲▲▲ ▼▼▼ AmericInn Motel & Suites SH
(701) 623-4800. **$69-$220.** 75 E River Rd S. I-94, exit 24, just se of downtown. Int corridors. **Pets:** Accepted.
SAVE SÓ ✕ &M ⚪ ▣ ⚪ ▭ ⊠

MINOT

▼▼ Best Western Kelly Inn SH
(701) 852-4300. **$79-$169.** 1510 26th Ave SW. US 2 and 52 Bypass, at 16th St SW. Ext/int corridors. **Pets:** Other species. Service with restrictions.
ASK SÓ ✕ ▣ ⚪ ▭ ⊠

▲▲▲ ▼▼▼ Comfort Inn SH
(701) 852-2201. **$70-$150.** 1515 22nd Ave SW. US 2 and 52 Bypass, at 16th St SW. Int corridors. **Pets:** Large, other species. Designated rooms, service with restrictions, supervision.
SAVE SÓ ✕ ⌂ ▣ ⚪ ▭ ⊠

▼ Days Inn SH
(701) 852-3646. **$57-$105, 5 day notice.** 2100 4th St SW. Jct US 2 and 52 Bypass, just n. Int corridors. **Pets:** $5 daily fee/pet. Service with restrictions, supervision.
ASK SÓ ✕ ⌂ ⚪ ▣ ⚪ ▭

▼ ▼ Fairfield Inn by Marriott SH
(701) 838-2424. **$85-$105.** 900 24th Ave SW. 0.5 mi e of jct US 2, 52 Bypass and 16th St SW. Int corridors. **Pets:** Accepted.
ASK SÓ ✕ &M ⌂ ▣ ⚪ ▭

▼▼▼ Holiday Inn Riverside Minot LH
(701) 852-2504. **$64-$114.** 2200 Burdick Expwy E. 1.3 mi e on US 2 business route (Burdick Expwy E). Int corridors. **Pets:** Accepted.
ASK SÓ ✕ ⌂ ⚪ ▣ ⚪ ▭ ⫙ ▭ ⊠

▼▼▼▼ Sleep Inn & Suites LH
(701) 837-3100. **$90-$170.** 2400 10th St SW. US 2 and 52 Bypass at 16th St SW; southeast corner of Dakota Square Mall. Int corridors. **Pets:** Accepted.
ASK SÓ ✕ &M ⌂ ⚪ ▣ ⚪ ▭ ⊠

VALLEY CITY

▲▲▲ ▼▼▼▼ AmericInn Lodge & Suites SH 🐾
(701) 845-5551. **$69-$159.** 280 Winter Show Rd SE. I-94, exit 292, just ne. Int corridors. **Pets:** Other species. $10 one-time fee/room. Designated rooms, service with restrictions, supervision.
SAVE SÓ ✕ &M ⌂ ⚪ ▣ ⚪ ▭ ⊠

▼ Super 8 Motel-Valley City M
(701) 845-1140. **$58-$73.** 860 11th St SW. I-94, exit 292, just nw. Int corridors. **Pets:** $5 daily fee/pet. Designated rooms, service with restrictions, supervision.
ASK SÓ ✕ ▣

WAHPETON

▼▼ AmericInn Lodge & Suites SH
(701) 642-8365. **$71-$101, 7 day notice.** 2029 Two-Ten Dr. 1 mi n on SR 210 Bypass. Int corridors. **Pets:** Accepted.
ASK SÓ ✕ ⌂ ⚪ ▣ ⚪ ▭

▼▼ Rodeway Inn SH
(701) 642-1115. **$65-$85.** 209 13th St S. SR 13, 0.3 mi e of jct SR 210 Bypass. Int corridors. **Pets:** Accepted.
ASK SÓ ✕ ▣ ⚪ ▭

▼▼ Wahpeton Super 8 SH
(701) 642-8731. **$43-$68, 14 day notice.** 995 21st Ave N. 1.5 mi n on SR 210 Bypass. Int corridors. **Pets:** Other species. $5 daily fee/pet. Service with restrictions.
ASK SÓ ✕ ▣ ▭

WATFORD CITY

▲▲▲ ▼ McKenzie Inn M
(701) 444-3980. **$44-$49.** 132 SW 3rd St. US 85, just w. Ext corridors. **Pets:** Medium. Service with restrictions, supervision.
SAVE ✕ ▣

▲▲▲ ▼ Roosevelt Inn & Suites SH
(701) 842-3686. **$55-$140.** 600 2nd Ave SW. US 85, 0.3 mi w. Int corridors. **Pets:** Large. $5 daily fee/pet. Service with restrictions, supervision.
SAVE ✕ ▣ ⚪ ▭

WEST FARGO

◆◆ West Fargo Days Inn SH
(701) 281-0000. **$56-$81.** 525 E Main Ave. I-29, exit 65 (Main Ave), 2.3 mi w. Int corridors. **Pets:** Small. $15 one-time fee/pet. Designated rooms, service with restrictions, supervision.
(ASK) (S□) (X) (�) (🛏) (📺) (⤴)

WILLISTON

AAA ◆◆ El Rancho Motor Hotel SH
(701) 572-6321. **$55-$69.** 1623 2nd Ave W. 1 mi n on US 2 and 85 N Bypass. Ext/int corridors. **Pets:** Accepted.
(SAVE) (S□) (X) (🛏) (📺) (🍴)

AAA ◆◆ Marquis Plaza & Suites SH
(701) 774-3250. **$76-$118.** 1525 9th Ave NW. US 2 and 85, 4 mi e of jct US 85. Int corridors. **Pets:** Small. $10 one-time fee/room. Service with restrictions, supervision.
(SAVE) (S□) (X) (🛏) (📺) (⤴)

OHIO

AKRON

▼▼▼ Red Roof Inn-Akron South #0207 [M]
(330) 644-7748. **$58-$76.** 2939 S Arlington Rd. I-77, exit 120, just n. **Pets:** Medium, other species. Service with restrictions, supervision.
⊠ 🖶

ALLIANCE

▼▼▼ Holiday Inn Express Hotel & Suites [SH]
(330) 821-6700. **$89-$159.** 2341 W State St. 2 mi w on US 62. Int corridors. **Pets:** Small. $10 one-time fee/pet. Designated rooms, service with restrictions, supervision.
[ASK] ⊠ 🖵 🖶 🖵 ⇌

⊕ ▼▼ Super 8 Motel [M]
(330) 821-5688. **$53-$89.** 2330 W State St. 2 mi w on US 62. Ext corridors. **Pets:** Other species. $5 daily fee/pet. Service with restrictions.
[SAVE] [S] ⊠ [c] 🖶 ⇌

AMHERST

▼▼▼ Days Inn [M]
(440) 985-1428. **$50-$80.** 934 N Leavitt Rd. SR 58, 0.3 mi n of SR 2. Ext/int corridors. **Pets:** Accepted.
[ASK] [S] ⊠ 🖶 🖵 ⇌

ASHLAND

⊕ ▼▼ Days Inn [M]
(419) 289-0101. **$45-$80.** 1423 CR 1575. I-71, exit 186, just w. Ext corridors. **Pets:** Other species. Service with restrictions, crate.
[SAVE] [S] ⊠ 🖶 🖵 ⇌

▼▼ The Surrey Inn [SH]
(419) 289-7700. **$59-$109.** 1065 Claremont Ave. 1 mi s. Int corridors. **Pets:** Medium, dogs only. $15 one-time fee/pet. Service with restrictions, crate.
[ASK] ⊠ 🖶 🖵

ASHTABULA

⊕ ▼ Cedars Motel [M] 🐾
(440) 992-5406. **$70-$150.** 2015 W Prospect Rd. Jct SR 11, 3 mi w on US 20. Ext corridors. **Pets:** Other species. $5 daily fee/pet. Service with restrictions, supervision.
[SAVE] ⊠ 🖶

⊕ ▼ Ho Hum Motel [M] 🐾
(440) 969-1136. **$55-$80.** 3801 N Ridge Rd W. I-90, exit 223, 3 mi n on SR 45, then 1 mi e on SR 20. Ext corridors. **Pets:** $5 daily fee/pet. Service with restrictions, supervision.
[SAVE] ⊠ 🖶

ATHENS

⊕ ▼ Budget Host-Coach Inn [M]
(740) 594-2294. **$41-$110, 3 day notice.** 100 Albany Rd (Hwy 50 W). US 50, exit westbound, just past Richland Ave exit; exit eastbound, e on Township Rd 60. Ext corridors. **Pets:** Small, dogs only. $10 daily fee/pet. Designated rooms, service with restrictions, supervision.
[SAVE] ⊠ 🖶 🖵

⊕ ▼▼▼ The Ohio University Inn & Conference Center [SH]
(740) 593-6661. **$109-$149.** 331 Richland Ave. 1 mi w on US 33 and 50. Int corridors. **Pets:** Accepted.
[SAVE] ⊠ [c] 🖶 🖵 [!] ⇌

⊕ ▼▼▼ Super 8 Motel [SH]
(740) 594-4900. **$50-$130, 30 day notice.** 2091 E State St. US 33, exit State St, 2.7 mi e. Int corridors. **Pets:** $10 daily fee/pet. Designated rooms, service with restrictions, crate.
[SAVE] [S] ⊠ 🖶

AUSTINBURG

▼▼ Comfort Inn-Ashtabula [SH]
(440) 275-2711. **$45-$179.** 1860 Austinburg Rd. I-90, exit 223, just n. Int corridors. **Pets:** Accepted.
[ASK] [S] ⊠ [/] 🖶 🖵 [!] ⇌

AUSTINTOWN

Austintown Super 8 Motel M
(330) 793-7788. **$42-$100.** 5280 76 Dr. I-80, exit 223, just s on SR 46. Int corridors. **Pets:** Accepted.

Best Western Meander Inn SH
(330) 544-2378. **$69-$150.** 870 N Canfield-Niles Rd. I-80, exit 223, 0.3 mi s on SR 46. Int corridors. **Pets:** Other species. $10 daily fee/pet. Service with restrictions, supervision.

BEAVERCREEK

Residence Inn by Marriott SH
(937) 358-3914. **$140-$180.** 2779 Fairfield Commons. I-675, exit 17, just e, just s on New Germany-Trebein, then just e. Int corridors. **Pets:** Accepted.

BELLEFONTAINE

Comfort Inn Bellefontaine SH
(937) 599-5555. **$69-$139.** 260 Northview Dr. Jct US 33 and SR 68, just ne. Int corridors. **Pets:** Large, other species. $10 daily fee/pet. Designated rooms, service with restrictions, supervision.

BLUFFTON

Comfort Inn SH
(419) 358-6000. **$76-$119.** 117 Commerce Ln. I-75, exit 142, just w on SR 103. Int corridors. **Pets:** Medium, other species. $15 one-time fee/pet. Service with restrictions, supervision.

BOARDMAN

Americas Best Value Inn & Suites SH
(330) 549-0157. **$59-$79, 7 day notice.** 9988 Market St. 0.5 mi n on SR 7. Int corridors. **Pets:** Accepted.

Days Inn M
(330) 758-2371. **$36-$85, 3 day notice.** 8392 Market St. I-76, exit 232, 1.8 mi n on SR 7. Ext corridors. **Pets:** Accepted.

Microtel Inn Youngstown SH
(330) 758-1816. **$42-$80.** 7393 South Ave. Jct I-680 and US 224, 0.3 mi w. Int corridors. **Pets:** Large. $25 one-time fee/pet. Service with restrictions, supervision.

BOWLING GREEN

Days Inn of Bowling Green M
(419) 352-5211. **$49-$69.** 1550 E Wooster St. I-75, exit 181, just w. Ext corridors. **Pets:** Other species. $10 one-time fee/room. Designated rooms, service with restrictions, supervision.

BRUNSWICK

Sleep Inn SH
(330) 273-1112. **$57-$79.** 1435 S Carpenter Rd. I-71, exit 226, just w. Ext corridors. **Pets:** Medium, dogs only. $10 daily fee/pet. Service with restrictions, supervision.

BRYAN

Colonial Manor Motel M
(419) 636-3123. **$69-$115.** 924 E High St. US 127, 0.8 mi e on SR 2/34. Ext corridors. **Pets:** Medium. Designated rooms, service with restrictions, crate.

CAMBRIDGE

Best Western Cambridge SH
(740) 439-3581. **$40-$90.** 1945 Southgate Pkwy. I-70, exit 178, 0.3 mi n on SR 209. Ext corridors. **Pets:** Accepted.

Budget Inn M
(740) 432-2304. **$40-$55.** 6405 Glenn Hwy. I-70, exit 176, just e on US 40. Ext/int corridors. **Pets:** Small. $10 daily fee/pet. Designated rooms, service with restrictions, supervision.

Comfort Inn SH
(740) 435-3200. **$64-$134.** 2327 Southgate Pkwy. I-70, exit 178, just n on SR 209. Int corridors. **Pets:** Medium, other species. $10 one-time fee/pet. Designated rooms, service with restrictions, supervision.

Days Inn-Cambridge SH
(740) 432-5691. **$49-$79, 3 day notice.** 2328 Southgate Pkwy. I-70, exit 178, just n on SR 209. Int corridors. **Pets:** Service with restrictions, crate.

Deer Creek Express M
(740) 432-6391. **$69-$79.** 2321 Southgate Pkwy. I-70, exit 178, just ne on SR 209. Ext corridors. **Pets:** Other species. $5 daily fee/room. Service with restrictions, crate.

Holiday Inn Cambridge/Salt Fork Area SH
(740) 432-7313. **$59-$99.** 2248 Southgate Pkwy. I-70, exit 178, just n on SR 209. Int corridors. **Pets:** Small. Service with restrictions, supervision.

Super 8 Motel-Cambridge SH
(740) 435-8080. **$42-$89.** 8779 Georgetown Rd. I-70, exit 178, just n. Ext corridors. **Pets:** Small. $10 daily fee/room. Service with restrictions, supervision.

CANTON

Red Roof Inn #7019 M
(330) 499-1970. **$48-$76.** 5353 Inn Circle Ct NW. I-77, exit 109, just w on Everhard Rd. Ext corridors. **Pets:** Medium, other species. Service with restrictions, supervision.

Residence Inn by Marriott SH
(330) 493-0004. **$160-$190.** 5280 Broadmoor Cir NW. I-77, exit 109, 0.5 mi e on Everhard Rd. Int corridors. **Pets:** Accepted.

CARROLLTON

Carrollton Days Inn SH
(330) 627-9314. **$91.** 1111 Canton Rd. On SR 43, 0.5 mi n of SR 39. Int corridors. **Pets:** $20 one-time fee/pet. Service with restrictions, supervision.

CEDARVILLE

▼▼▼ **Hearthstone Inn & Suites** 🆂🅷
(937) 766-3000. **$99-$139.** 10 S Main St. I-70, exit 54, 11 mi s. Int corridors. **Pets:** Accepted.
🄰🅂🄺 🆂 ✕ 🛑 💻

CELINA

🅐🅐🅐 ▼▼ **Americas Best Value Inn-Celina** 🆂🅷
(419) 586-4656. **$60-$99.** 1421 SR 703 E. Jct SR 29. Ext corridors. **Pets:** Accepted.
🆂🅰🆅🅴 🆂 ✕ 🛑 💻

CHILLICOTHE

▼▼▼ **Best Western Adena Inn** 🆂🅷
(740) 775-7000. **$69-$169.** 1250 N Bridge St. US 35, exit Bridge St, 0.8 mi n. Int corridors. **Pets:** $15 daily fee/pet. Service with restrictions, supervision.
🄰🅂🄺 🆂 ✕ 🛢 🛑 💻 ⚓

▼▼▼ **Christopher Inn & Suites** 🆂🅷
(740) 774-6835. **$68-$80.** 30 N Plaza Blvd. US 35, exit Bridge St. Int corridors. **Pets:** Medium, other species. Service with restrictions, supervision.
🄰🅂🄺 🆂 ✕ 🛢 🛑 💻 ⚓

CINCINNATI METROPOLITAN AREA

BATAVIA

▼▼▼▼ **Hampton Inn-Cincinnati Eastgate** 🆂🅷
(513) 752-8584. **$64-$109.** 858 Eastgate North Dr. I-275, exit 63B (SR 32), just e, just n on Gleneste Withamsville Rd, then just w; behind Longhorn Steak House. Int corridors. **Pets:** Accepted.
🄰🅂🄺 🆂 ✕ 🛑 💻 ⚓

🅐🅐🅐 ▼▼▼ **Holiday Inn-Cincinnati Eastgate** 🅻🅷
(513) 752-4400. **$80-$120.** 4501 Eastgate Blvd. I-275, exit 63B (SR 32), 0.5 mi e to Eastgate Mall exit, then 0.5 mi n. Int corridors. **Pets:** Other species. Service with restrictions.
🆂🅰🆅🅴 🆂 ✕ 🎬 🛑 💻 🍴 ⚓ ⊠

BLUE ASH

◆◆ **Extended StayAmerica-Cincinnati-Blue Ash-South** 🆂🅷
(513) 793-6750. **$60-$95.** 4260 Hunt Rd. I-71, exit 14, 1 mi w on Ronald Reagan Hwy, exit Hunt Rd, then just e. Int corridors. **Pets:** Accepted.
✕ 🛑 💻 ⚓

▼▼ **Red Roof Inn Northeast (Blue Ash)** 🅼
(513) 793-8811. **$57-$83.** 5900 Pfeiffer Rd. I-71, exit 15, just w. Ext corridors. **Pets:** Medium, other species. Service with restrictions, supervision.
✕ 🛢 🎬 🛑

▼▼▼ **Residence Inn by Marriott-Blue Ash** 🆂🅷 ❀
(513) 530-5060. **$109-$149.** 11401 Reed-Hartman Hwy. I-275, exit 47, 0.8 mi s. Ext/int corridors. **Pets:** Other species. $75 one-time fee/room. Service with restrictions.
🄰🅂🄺 🆂 ✕ 🛢 🎬 🗒 🛑 💻 ⚓ ⊠

▼▼▼ **TownePlace Suites by Marriott Blue Ash** 🆂🅷 ❀
(513) 469-8222. **$99-$129.** 4650 Cornell Rd. I-275, exit 47, 0.9 mi s on Reed-Hartman Hwy, then just w. Int corridors. **Pets:** Large, other species. $75 one-time fee/room. Service with restrictions.
🄰🅂🄺 🆂 ✕ 🗒 🛑 💻 ⚓

CHERRY GROVE

🅐🅐🅐 ▼▼ **Best Western Clermont** 🅼 ❀
(513) 528-7702. **$69-$139.** 4004 Williams Dr. I-275, exit 65, just w, then just s. Ext corridors. **Pets:** Medium, other species. $25 one-time fee/room. Service with restrictions, supervision.
🆂🅰🆅🅴 🆂 ✕ 🎬 🗒 🛑 💻 ⚓

CINCINNATI

🅐🅐🅐 ▼▼▼▼ **Millennium Hotel Cincinnati** 🅻🅷
(513) 352-2100. **$69-$309.** 150 W 5th St. Between Elm and Race sts. Int corridors. **Pets:** Accepted.
🆂🅰🆅🅴 🆂 ✕ 🗒 🛑 💻 🍴 ⚓

🅐🅐🅐 ▼▼ ▼▼ **The Westin Cincinnati** 🅻🅷
(513) 621-7700. **$119-$339.** 21 E 5th St. Between Vine and Walnut sts. Int corridors. **Pets:** Accepted.
🆂🅰🆅🅴 ✕ 🛢 🎬 🗒 💻 🍴 ⚓

FAIRFIELD

▼▼▼ **Holiday Inn Express** 🆂🅷
(513) 860-2900. **$99-$109.** 6755 Fairfield Business Park Dr. I-275, exit 41 (SR 4), 1.5 mi n. Int corridors. **Pets:** Small. Designated rooms, service with restrictions, supervision.
🄰🅂🄺 ✕ 🛢 🎬 🗒 🛑 💻 ⚓ ⊠

HARRISON

▼▼ **Comfort Inn** 🆂🅷
(513) 367-9666. **$45-$110.** 391 Comfort Dr. I-74, exit 1, just n on New Haven Rd, then just e. Int corridors. **Pets:** Small, dogs only. $20 one-time fee/room. Service with restrictions, supervision.
🄰🅂🄺 🆂 ✕ 🛢 🗒 🛑 💻 ⚓

MASON

🅐🅐🅐 ▼▼ **La Quinta Inn & Suites** 🆂🅷
(513) 459-1111. **$95-$155.** 9918 Escort Dr. I-71, exit 19, just w, then just s. Int corridors. **Pets:** Medium. Service with restrictions.
🆂🅰🆅🅴 ✕ 🎬 🗒 🛑 💻 ⚓

🅐🅐🅐 ▼▼ ◆ **Microtel Inn & Suites Kings Island** 🆂🅷
(513) 754-1500. **$55-$169.** 5324 Beach Blvd. I-71, exit 25, just nw. Int corridors. **Pets:** Small. $20 daily fee/pet. Designated rooms, service with restrictions, supervision.
🆂🅰🆅🅴 🆂 ✕ 🛢 🗒 🛑 💻

MIDDLETOWN

🅐🅐🅐 ▼▼▼ **Best Western Regency Inn** 🆂🅷
(513) 424-3551. **$65-$145.** 6475 Culbertson Rd. I-75, exit 32. Int corridors. **Pets:** Dogs only. $5 daily fee/pet, $25 one-time fee/pet. Designated rooms, service with restrictions.
🆂🅰🆅🅴 🆂 ✕ 🗒 🛑 💻 ⚓

▼▼ **Fairfield Inn by Marriott** 🆂🅷
(513) 424-5444. **$83-$103.** 6750 Roosevelt Pkwy. I-75, exit 32, 0.5 mi w on SR 122. Int corridors. **Pets:** Accepted.
🄰🅂🄺 🆂 ✕ 🛢 🎬 🛑 💻 ⚓

▼ **Super 8 Motel Middletown** 🆂🅷
(513) 422-4888. **$49-$69.** 3553 Commerce Dr. I-75, exit 32, just e, then just n. Int corridors. **Pets:** Dogs only. $10 daily fee/room. Designated rooms, service with restrictions, supervision.
🄰🅂🄺 🆂 ✕ 🛑

MOUNT ORAB

Best Western Mount Orab Inn SH
(937) 444-6666. **$69-$89.** 100 Leininger St. Jct US 68 and SR 32, just n on US 68. Int corridors. **Pets:** Small. $10 one-time fee/pet. Designated rooms, service with restrictions, supervision.

SHARONVILLE

Arcadia Residential Suites SH
(513) 354-1000. **$99-$199, 7 day notice.** 11180 Dowlin Dr. I-75, exit 15, just e on Sharon Rd, then just n. Int corridors. **Pets:** Medium. $50 one-time fee/room. Service with restrictions.

Drury Inn & Suites-Cincinnati North SH
(513) 771-5601. **$100-$180.** 2255 Sharon Rd. I-75, exit 15, just e. Int corridors. **Pets:** Large, other species. Service with restrictions, supervision.

Homewood Suites by Hilton-Cincinnati North SH
(513) 772-8888. **$125-$179.** 2670 E Kemper Rd. I-275, exit 44, jct Mosteller Rd. Int corridors. **Pets:** Large, other species. $15 daily fee/pet. Service with restrictions.

La Quinta Inn & Suites SH
(513) 771-0300. **$125-$139.** 11029 Dowlin Dr. I-75, exit 15, just e. Int corridors. **Pets:** Medium. Service with restrictions.

Residence Inn by Marriott SH ❖
(513) 771-2525. **$149-$229.** 11689 Chester Rd. I-75, exit 15, just w on Sharon Rd, then 1 mi n. Ext corridors. **Pets:** Other species. $150 one-time fee/room. Service with restrictions.

Sheraton Cincinnati North Hotel LH
(513) 771-2080. **$89-$215.** 11320 Chester Rd. I-75, exit 15, just w on Sharon Rd, then 0.5 mi n. Int corridors. **Pets:** Accepted.

SPRINGDALE

La Quinta Inn & Suites SH
(513) 671-2300. **$85-$105.** 12150 Springfield Pike. I-275, exit 41, just n on SR 4. Int corridors. **Pets:** Medium. Service with restrictions.

WEST CHESTER

Staybridge Suites Cincinnati North SH
(513) 874-1900. **$109-$229.** 8955 Lakota Dr W. I-75, exit 19, just w on Union Center Blvd, then just n. Int corridors. **Pets:** Medium, other species. Service with restrictions, crate.

WILMINGTON

AmeriHost Inn & Suites SH
(937) 383-3950. **$79-$109.** 201 Carrie Dr. Jct US 22 and 68, 1.5 mi e on US 22. Int corridors. **Pets:** Accepted.

Holiday Inn Express SH
(937) 382-5858. **$99-$139.** 155 Holiday Dr. 1.6 mi e on US 22. Int corridors. **Pets:** Accepted.

Holiday Inn Wilmington & Roberts Convention Centre LH
(937) 283-3200. **$109-$159.** 123 Gano Rd. I-71, exit 50, just w. Int corridors. **Pets:** Large, other species. $250 deposit/room. Service with restrictions, crate.

CLEVELAND METROPOLITAN AREA

BEACHWOOD

Extended StayAmerica-Cleveland-Beachwood SH
(216) 595-9551. **Call for rates.** 3820 Orange Pl. I-271, exit Chagrin Blvd, just e. Int corridors. **Pets:** Accepted.

Hilton Cleveland East/Beachwood LH
(216) 464-5950. **$99-$219.** 3663 Park East Dr. I-271, exit Chagrin Blvd, just w. Int corridors. **Pets:** Accepted.

Holiday Inn-Beachwood SH
(216) 831-3300. **$129-$149.** 3750 Orange Pl. I-271, exit Chagrin Blvd, just e. Int corridors. **Pets:** Small. $50 deposit/pet. Designated rooms, service with restrictions, supervision.

Homestead Studio Suites Hotel-Cleveland/Beachwood SH
(216) 896-5555. **$55-$120.** 3625 Orange Pl. I-271, exit Chagrin Blvd, just e. Int corridors. **Pets:** Accepted.

Residence Inn by Marriott Cleveland-Beachwood SH
(216) 831-3030. **$109-$159.** 3628 Park East Dr. Jct US 422 and I-271, exit Chagrin Blvd, just w. Int corridors. **Pets:** Other species. $75 one-time fee/room. Service with restrictions, crate.

BROOKLYN

Extended StayAmerica SH
(216) 267-7799. **Call for rates.** 10300 Cascade Crossing. I-480, exit 13, just s. Int corridors. **Pets:** Accepted.

BROOK PARK

Howard Johnson Cleveland Airport M
(216) 676-5200. **$50-$60.** 16644 Snow Rd. I-71, exit 237, just e. Ext/int corridors. **Pets:** Other species. $10 daily fee/room.

CLEVELAND

[AAA] ◆◆◆ **Cleveland Airport Marriott** [LH]
(216) 252-5333. **$109-$194.** 4277 W 150th St. I-71, exit 240, just s. Int corridors. **Pets:** Medium. $50 one-time fee/room. Designated rooms, service with restrictions, crate.
[SAVE] [SD] ⊠ 👂 ♿ ▣ ☕ 🍴 🏊

[AAA] ◆◆◆ **Crowne Plaza Cleveland City Centre Hotel** [LH]
(216) 771-7600. **$99-$189.** 777 St. Clair Ave. E 6th St and St. Clair Ave. Int corridors. **Pets:** Accepted.
[SAVE] [SD] ⊠ 👂 ♿ ▣ ☕ 🍴

[AAA] ◆◆◆ **La Quinta Inn & Suites Cleveland Airport** [SH]
(216) 251-8500. **$85-$109.** 4222 W 150th St. I-71, exit 240, just n. Int corridors. **Pets:** Medium. Service with restrictions.
[SAVE] ⊠ 👂 ▣ ☕

[AAA] ◆◆◆◆ **The Ritz-Carlton, Cleveland** [LH]
(216) 623-1300. **$199-$299.** 1515 W 3rd St. In Tower City Center (3rd St side). Int corridors. **Pets:** Accepted.
[SAVE] ⊠ 👂 ♿ ▣ 🍴 🏊 🏋

◆◆◆ **Sheraton Cleveland Airport Hotel** [SH] 🐾
(216) 267-1500. **$89-$269.** 5300 Riverside Dr. I-71, exit 237, follow signs; just s of I-480 on SR 237. Int corridors. **Pets:** Small, other species. $100 deposit/room. Service with restrictions, supervision.
[A$K] [SD] ⊠ [&M] 👂 ♿ ▣ ☕ 🍴 🏊 🏋

INDEPENDENCE

[AAA] ◆◆ **La Quinta Inn** [SH]
(216) 447-1133. **$85-$109.** 6161 Quarry Ln. I-77, exit Rockside Rd, just e. Int corridors. **Pets:** Medium. Service with restrictions.
[SAVE] ⊠ 👂 ▣ ☕

◆◆ **Red Roof Inn #7028** [M]
(216) 447-0030. **$62-$82.** 6020 Quarry Ln. I-77, exit Rockside Rd, just e. Ext corridors. **Pets:** Medium, other species. Service with restrictions, supervision.
⊠ 👂 ♿ ▣

◆◆◆ **Residence Inn by Marriott** [SH]
(216) 520-1450. **$159-$189.** 5101 W Creek Rd. I-77, exit Rockside Rd, just w to W Creek Rd, then just n. Ext corridors. **Pets:** Accepted.
[A$K] [SD] ⊠ 👂 ♿ ▣ ☕ 🏊 🏋

◆◆◆ **Sheraton Independence Hotel** [SH]
(216) 524-0700. **$89-$179.** 5300 Rockside Rd. I-77, exit Rockside Rd, just w. Int corridors. **Pets:** Accepted.
[A$K] [SD] ⊠ [&M] 👂 ☕ 🍴 🏊 🏋

LAKEWOOD

◆ **Days Inn** [SH]
(216) 226-4800. **$59-$89.** 12019 Lake Ave. I-90, exit 166, 1 mi n on W 117th St, then just w. **Pets:** Accepted.
[A$K] [SD] ⊠

◆ **Travelodge** [SH]
(216) 221-9000. **$59-$79.** 11837 Edgewater Dr. I-90, exit 166, 1 mi n on W 117th St, then just w. Int corridors. **Pets:** Accepted.
[A$K] [SD] ⊠ ▣ ☕

MACEDONIA

◆ **Knights Inn-Cleveland/Macedonia** [M]
(330) 467-1981. **$39-$75.** 240 E Highland Rd. I-271, exit 18, just s; I-80/90 (Ohio Tpke), exit 180, 3 mi n. Ext corridors. **Pets:** Medium, other species. $5 daily fee/pet. Designated rooms, service with restrictions, supervision.
[A$K] [SD] ⊠ ▣ ☕ 🏊

[AAA] ◆◆◆ **La Quinta Inn & Suites Cleveland-Macedonia** [SH]
(330) 468-5400. **$89-$105.** 268 E Highland Rd. I-271, exit 18, just s; I-80/90 (Ohio Tpke), exit 180, just n. Int corridors. **Pets:** Medium. Service with restrictions.
[SAVE] ⊠ [&M] 👂 ♿ ▣ ☕ 🏊

MAYFIELD HEIGHTS

[AAA] ◆◆ **Baymont Inn & Suites-Cleveland (Mayfield Heights)** [SH]
(440) 442-8400. **$79-$149.** 1421 Golden Gate Blvd. I-271, exit 34, 0.3 mi w off US 322. Int corridors. **Pets:** Other species. $10 daily fee/pet. Service with restrictions, crate.
[SAVE] [SD] ⊠ 👂 ▣ ☕

MEDINA

◆◆ **Motel 6 4112** [SH]
(330) 723-3322. **$45-$66.** 3122 Eastpointe Dr. I-71, exit 218, just w. Int corridors. **Pets:** Medium, other species. Service with restrictions, supervision.
[SD] ⊠ 🏊

MIDDLEBURG HEIGHTS

[AAA] ◆◆◆ **Comfort Inn-Cleveland Airport** [SH] 🐾
(440) 234-3131. **$89-$119, 3 day notice.** 17550 Rosbough Dr. I-71, exit 235, 0.3 mi w to Engle Rd, then 0.3 mi n. Int corridors. **Pets:** Large, other species. $35 one-time fee/room. Service with restrictions, supervision.
[SAVE] [SD] ⊠ [&M] ▣ ☕ 🏊

[AAA] ◆◆◆ **Ramada Airport South** [M]
(440) 243-2277. **$65-$105.** 7233 Engle Rd. I-71, exit 235, just w. Ext corridors. **Pets:** $10 one-time fee/room. Designated rooms, service with restrictions, supervision.
[SAVE] [SD] ⊠ ♿ ▣ ☕ 🏊

◆◆ **Red Roof Inn-Middleburg Heights #7060** [SH]
(440) 243-2441. **$58-$75.** 17555 Bagley Rd. I-71, exit 235, just w. Ext/int corridors. **Pets:** Medium, other species. Service with restrictions, supervision.
⊠ ♿ ▣

◆◆◆ **Residence Inn by Marriott** [SH]
(440) 234-6688. **$89-$179.** 17525 Rosbough Dr. I-71, exit 235, just w on Bagley Rd, then just n on Engle Rd. Ext/int corridors. **Pets:** Other species. $100 one-time fee/room. Designated rooms, service with restrictions, crate.
[A$K] ⊠ ♿ ▣ ☕ 🏋

◆◆ **StudioPLUS-Cleveland-Middleburg Heights** [SH]
(440) 243-7024. **Call for rates.** 17552 Rosbough Dr. I-71, exit 235, 0.3 mi w to Engle Rd, then 0.3 mi n. Int corridors. **Pets:** Accepted.
⊠ ♿ ▣ ☕

NORTH OLMSTED

◆◆ **Candlewood Suites** [SH]
(440) 716-0584. **$99.** 24741 Country Club Blvd. I-480, exit 6B, just n on SR 252. Int corridors. **Pets:** Accepted.
[A$K] [SD] ⊠ ♿ ▣ ☕

◆◆ **Homestead Studio Suites Hotel-Cleveland/Airport/North Olmsted** [SH]
(440) 777-8585. **$40-$105.** 24851 Country Club Blvd. I-480, exit 6B, just n on SR 252. Ext corridors. **Pets:** Accepted.
[A$K] [SD] ⊠ [&M] 👂 ♿ ▣ ☕

[AAA] ◆◆◆ **Radisson Hotel Cleveland Airport** [SH]
(440) 734-5060. **$89-$189.** 25070 Country Club Blvd. I-480, exit 6B, just n on SR 252. Int corridors. **Pets:** Accepted.
[SAVE] [SD] ⊠ [&M] 👂 ▣ ☕ 🍴 🏊 🏋

▼▼ StudioPLUS SH
(440) 716-2412. $65-$90. 25801 Country Club Blvd. I-480, exit 6B, just n on SR 252. Int corridors. Pets: Accepted.
⊠ 🖾 🖬 📟 🏊

NORTH RIDGEVILLE

🔴 ▼ Motel 6 Cleveland/North Ridgeville M
(440) 327-6311. $45-$58. 32751 Lorain Rd. I-80, exit 152, 0.6 mi ne on SR 10. Ext corridors. Pets: Medium, other species. Service with restrictions, supervision.
SAVE 🖾 ⊠ 🖾

▼ Super 8 Motel SH
(440) 327-0500. $44-$89. 32801 Lorain Rd. I-80, exit 152, 0.5 mi ne on SR 10. Int corridors. Pets: Accepted.
ASK 🖾 ⊠

RICHFIELD

▼▼▼ Quality Inn & Suites SH
(330) 659-6151. $69-$129. 4742 Brecksville Rd. I-80, exit 173, just s. Int corridors. Pets: Small. Designated rooms, service with restrictions, supervision.
ASK 🖾 ⊠ 🖾 🖬 📟 🍴 🏊 🖾

SOLON

▼▼▼▼ Hampton Inn SH
(440) 542-0400. $99-$129. 6035 Enterprise Pkwy. US 422, exit Harper Rd, 0.6 mi s, then 0.4 mi e. Int corridors. Pets: Other species. Supervision.
ASK 🖾 ⊠ 🖾 🖾 🖾 🖬 📟 🏊

STRONGSVILLE

▼ Motel 6-Strongsville #1497 M
(440) 238-0170. $45-$58. 15385 Royalton Rd. I-71, exit 231A, just e; I-76 (Ohio Tpke), exit 161, 1 mi s. Ext corridors. Pets: Medium, other species. Service with restrictions, supervision.
🖾 ⊠ 🖾

TWINSBURG

▼▼▼ Comfort Suites-Twinsburg SH
(330) 963-5909. $69-$129. 2715 Creekside Dr. I-480, exit 37 (SR 91), just n. Int corridors. Pets: Accepted.
ASK 🖾 ⊠ 🖾 🖾 🖬 📟 🏊

▼▼ Twinsburg Super 8 Motel SH
(330) 425-2889. $50-$99. 8848 Twins Hills Dr. I-480, exit 36, just w on SR 82. Int corridors. Pets: Small. $6 daily fee/pet. No service, supervision.
ASK 🖾 ⊠ 🖬

WESTLAKE

▼▼ Extended Stay Deluxe SH
(440) 899-4160. $65. 30360 Clemens Rd. I-90, exit 156, just n. Int corridors. Pets: Accepted.
ASK 🖾 ⊠ 🖾 🖬 📟

▼▼ Red Roof Inn-Westlake #7094 M
(440) 892-7920. $58-$84. 29595 Clemens Rd. I-90, exit 156, just n. Ext corridors. Pets: Medium, other species. Service with restrictions, supervision.
⊠ 🖾 🖬

WILLOUGHBY

▼▼ Red Roof Inn-East #7053 M
(440) 946-9872. $58-$90. 4166 SR 306. I-90, exit 193, just s. Ext corridors. Pets: Medium, other species. Service with restrictions, supervision.
⊠ 🖾 🖾 🖬

END METROPOLITAN AREA

CLYDE

▼▼ Red Roof Inn SH
(419) 547-6660. $59-$118. 1363 W McPherson Hwy. 1 mi w on SR 20. Int corridors. Pets: Small, dogs only. $50 deposit/pet. Designated rooms, service with restrictions, supervision.
ASK 🖾 ⊠ 🖾 🖾 🖬 🏊

COLUMBUS METROPOLITAN AREA

CIRCLEVILLE

▼▼ Comfort Inn Circleville SH
(740) 477-6116. $64-$74. 24517 US 23 S. Jct US 22 and 23, 2 mi s. Int corridors. Pets: Accepted.
⊠ 🖾 🖾 🖬 📟 🏊

▼▼▼ Holiday Inn Express Hotel & Suites SH
(740) 420-7711. Call for rates. 23911 US 23 S. Jct US 22, 1.2 mi s. Int corridors. Pets: Small. $50 one-time fee/pet. Crate.
⊠ 🖾 🖾 🖾 🖬 📟 🏊

COLUMBUS

▼▼ Baymont Inn & Suites Columbus Airport M
(614) 237-3403. $75-$130. 4240 International Gateway. At Port Columbus International Airport. Ext corridors. Pets: Accepted.
ASK 🖾 ⊠ 🖾 📟 🏊

🔴 ▼▼ Baymont Inn and Suites Columbus/OSU M
(614) 267-4646. $89-$129. 3246 Olentangy River Rd. SR 315, exit N Broadway, 0.3 mi s. Ext corridors. Pets: Other species. Service with restrictions.
SAVE 🖾 ⊠ 🖾 🖬 📟 🏊

🔴 ▼▼▼ Baymont Inn & Suites-Polaris SH ❀
(614) 791-9700. $89-$119. 8400 Lyra Dr. I-71, exit 121, just w. Int corridors. Pets: Medium. $25 one-time fee/room. Designated rooms, service with restrictions.
SAVE 🖾 ⊠ 🖾 🖬 📟 🏊

🔴 ▼▼▼ Best Western Columbus North SH
(614) 888-8230. $90-$100. 888 E Dublin-Granville Rd. I-71, exit 117, 0.5 mi w on SR 161. Int corridors. Pets: Medium, other species. $25 deposit/room. No service, supervision.
SAVE 🖾 ⊠ 🖾 🖬 📟 🍴 🏊 🖾

Days Inn Fairgrounds M
(614) 299-4300. **$50-$100.** 1700 Clara St. I-71, exit 111, just w. Ext corridors. **Pets:** Medium. $10 daily fee/pet. Service with restrictions, crate.
SAVE S⭐ ✕ ⬛ 🖵 ⬤

DoubleTree Guest Suites LH
(614) 228-4600. **$109-$189.** 50 S Front St. Corner of Front and State sts, just n. Int corridors. **Pets:** Large, dogs only. $50 one-time fee/room. Service with restrictions, crate.
ASK ✕ 🐾 ⬛ 🖵 🍴

Drury Inn & Suites-Columbus Convention Center SH
(614) 221-7008. **$107-$167.** 88 E Nationwide Blvd. 0.3 mi n on US 23. Int corridors. **Pets:** Large, other species. Service with restrictions, supervision.
ASK ✕ 🄼 🐾 🖫 ⬛ 🖵 ⬤

Extended StayAmerica-Columbus-Easton SH
(614) 428-6022. **$85-$90.** 4200 Stelzer Rd. I-270, exit 32, just w on Morse Rd, then just n. Int corridors. **Pets:** Accepted.
ASK S⭐ ✕ 🖫 ⬛ 🖵

Extended StayAmerica-Columbus-North SH
(614) 431-0033. **$55-$60.** 6255 Zumstein Dr. I-71, exit 117, just nw. **Pets:** Accepted.
ASK S⭐ ✕ 🖫

Extended StayAmerica-Columbus-Worthington SH
(614) 785-1006. **$70-$75.** 7465 High Cross Blvd. I-270, exit 23, just n on US 23, just e on Dimension Dr, then just s. Int corridors. **Pets:** Accepted.
ASK S⭐ ✕ 🖫 ⬛ 🖵

Extended Stay Deluxe Columbus/Polaris SH
(614) 431-5522. **$95-$100.** 8555 Lyra Dr. I-71, exit 121, just w on Polaris Pkwy. Int corridors. **Pets:** Accepted.
ASK S⭐ ✕ 🄼 🖫 ⬛ 🖵 ⬤

Holiday Inn City Center SH
(614) 221-3281. **$99.** 175 E Town St. 4th and E Town sts. Int corridors. **Pets:** Accepted.
SAVE S⭐ ✕ 🄼 🐾 🖫 ⬛ 🖵 🍴 ⬤

Holiday Inn-Columbus/Worthington Area LH
(614) 885-3334. **$109-$159.** 175 Hutchinson Ave. I-270, exit 23, just n of jct US 23 N, just e on Dimension Dr, then just s on High Cross Blvd. Int corridors. **Pets:** Accepted.
SAVE ✕ 🄼 🐾 🖫 ⬛ 🖵 🍴 ⬤ ✕

Holiday Inn on the Lane SH
(614) 294-4848. **$113-$250.** 328 W Lane Ave. 0.5 mi e of SR 315, exit Lane Ave. Int corridors. **Pets:** Designated rooms, service with restrictions, crate.
SAVE S⭐ ✕ 🄼 🐾 🖫 ⬛ 🖵 🍴 ⬤ ✕

Knights Inn-Columbus East M
(614) 864-0600. **$50-$90.** 4320 Groves Rd. I-70, exit 107, just sw. Ext corridors. **Pets:** Other species. $35 deposit/pet. Supervision.
SAVE S⭐ ✕ ⬛

Microtel Inn & Suites (West) SH
(614) 851-1745. **$69-$99.** 5655 Feder Rd. I-70, exit 91A, just sw. Int corridors. **Pets:** Small, other species. $5 daily fee/pet. Service with restrictions, supervision.
SAVE S⭐ ✕ ⬛ 🖵

Motel 6 #1486 M
(614) 431-2525. **$41-$55.** 7474 N High St. I-270, exit 23, 0.4 mi n on US 23, just e on Dimension Dr, then just s. Ext corridors. **Pets:** Medium, other species. Service with restrictions, supervision.
S⭐ ✕

Motel 6 OSU #1491 M
(614) 846-8520. **$43-$57.** 750 Morse Rd. I-71, exit 116, just w. Ext corridors. **Pets:** Medium, other species. Service with restrictions, supervision.
S⭐ ✕ 🄼 🖫

Ramada Columbus SH
(614) 890-8111. **$85, 7 day notice.** 6767 Schrock Hill Ct. I-270, exit 27, n off Cleveland Ave; enter off Schrock Rd. Int corridors. **Pets:** Small, other species. $10 daily fee/room. Service with restrictions, supervision.
ASK S⭐ ✕ 🐾 ⬛ 🖵 ⬤

Red Roof Inn-Columbus Convention Center SH
(614) 224-6539. **$92-$125.** 111 E Nationwide Blvd. Nationwide Blvd at 3rd St. Int corridors. **Pets:** Medium, other species. Service with restrictions, supervision.
✕ 🄼 🐾 🖫 ⬛

Red Roof Inn-OSU #7121 SH
(614) 267-9941. **$65-$70.** 441 Ackerman Rd. SR 315, exit Ackerman Rd, 0.3 mi e. Ext corridors. **Pets:** Medium, other species. Service with restrictions, supervision.
✕ 🖫

Red Roof Inn-West #7009 M
(614) 878-9245. **$56-$82.** 5001 Renner Rd. I-70, exit 91 eastbound; exit 91B westbound, just nw. Ext corridors. **Pets:** Medium, other species. Service with restrictions, supervision.
✕ 🄼 🖫 ⬛

Red Roof Inn-Worthington #7310 SH
(614) 846-3001. **$55-$71.** 7480 N High St. I-270, exit 23, 0.3 mi n on US 23, just w on Dimension Dr, then just s on Vantage Dr. Ext/int corridors. **Pets:** Medium, other species. Service with restrictions, supervision.
✕ 🖫 ⬛

Sheraton Suites Columbus LH 🐾
(614) 436-0004. **$99-$269.** 201 Hutchinson Ave. I-270, exit 23, 0.3 mi n on US 23, just e on Dimension Dr, then just SE on Vantage Dr. Int corridors. **Pets:** Dogs only. Designated rooms, service with restrictions.
ASK S⭐ ✕ 🄼 🐾 🖫 ⬛ 🖵 🍴 ⬤ ✕

Travelodge SH
(614) 846-9070. **$39-$99.** 6121 Zumstein Dr. I-71, exit 117, jct SR 161, just w. Int corridors. **Pets:** Other species. $10 daily fee/pet. Designated rooms, service with restrictions, supervision.
SAVE S⭐ ✕ 🐾 ⬛ 🖵

The University Plaza Hotel & Conference Center SH
(614) 267-7461. **$105-$149.** 3110 Olentangy River Rd. 0.5 mi s of N Broadway, exit off SR 315. Int corridors. **Pets:** Small. $20 one-time fee/pet. Service with restrictions, supervision.
SAVE S⭐ ✕ ⬛ 🖵 🍴 ⬤

The Westin Columbus LH
(614) 228-3800. **$125-$255.** 310 S High St. Corner of Main and High sts. Int corridors. **Pets:** Accepted.
SAVE S⭐ ✕ 🐾 🖫 ⬛ 🖵 🍴 ✕

DELAWARE

Travelodge M
(740) 369-4421. **$58-$150.** 1001 US Rt 23 N. 0.5 mi n of downtown. Ext/int corridors. **Pets:** Small. $10 daily fee/pet. Service with restrictions, supervision.
SAVE S⭐ ✕ ⬛ 🖵

DUBLIN

♦♦♦ ▼▼▼▼ Columbus Marriott Northwest [LH]
(614) 791-1000. **$144-$229, 3 day notice.** 5605 Paul Blazer Memorial Pkwy. I-270, exit 15 (Tuttle Crossing Blvd), 0.3 mi e. Int corridors. **Pets:** Accepted.
[SAVE] [X] [&M] [🐾] [&] [🛏] [💻] [🍴] [🏊]

▼▼▼ Drury Inn & Suites-Columbus Northwest [SH]
(614) 798-8802. **$85-$130.** 6170 Parkcenter Cir. I-270, exit 15 (Tuttle Crossing Blvd), just e. Int corridors. **Pets:** Large, other species. Service with restrictions, supervision.
[ASK] [X] [&] [🛏] [💻] [🏊]

▼▼▼ Dublin Homewood Suites by Hilton [SH]
(614) 791-8675. **$145-$165.** 5300 Parkcenter Ave. I-270, exit 15 (Tuttle Crossing Blvd), just e, just n on Blazer Pkwy, then just e. Int corridors. **Pets:** Accepted.
[ASK] [S&] [X] [&M] [🐾] [&] [🛏] [💻] [🏊] [X]

▼▼▼ Extended StayAmerica Columbus-Sawmill [SH]
(614) 764-0159. **$65-$70.** 6601 Reflections Dr. I-270, exit 20, 0.7 mi s on Sawmill Rd, just e on SR 161, just s on Martin, then just w. Int corridors. **Pets:** Accepted.
[ASK] [S&] [X] [🛏] [💻] [🏊]

▼▼▼ Extended Stay Deluxe (Columbus/Tuttle) [SH]
(614) 760-0245. **$85-$90.** 5530 Tuttle Crossing Blvd. I-270, exit 15 (Tuttle Crossing Blvd), 0.3 mi w. Int corridors. **Pets:** Accepted.
[ASK] [S&] [X] [&M] [&] [🛏] [💻]

♦♦♦ ▼▼▼ La Quinta Inn & Suites [SH]
(614) 792-8300. **$89-$109.** 6145 Parkcenter Cir. I-270, exit 15 (Tuttle Crossing Blvd), just e. Int corridors. **Pets:** Medium. Service with restrictions.
[SAVE] [X] [&M] [&] [🛏] [💻]

▼▼ Quality Inn & Suites [SH]
(614) 764-0770. **$100.** 3950 Tuller Rd. I-270, exit 20, Just s on Sawmill Rd, then just w on Dublin Center Dr. Int corridors. **Pets:** Medium. $25 one-time fee/pet. Service with restrictions.
[ASK] [S&] [X] [🛏] [💻] [X]

▼▼ Red Roof Inn-Dublin #7127 [M]
(614) 764-3993. **$55-$73.** 5125 Post Rd. I-270, exit 17A, just ne. Ext corridors. **Pets:** Medium, other species. Service with restrictions, supervision.
[X] [&M] [&] [🛏]

♦♦♦ ▼▼▼▼ Residence Inn by Marriott Dublin [SH]
(614) 791-0403. **$79-$199.** 435 Metro Pl S. I-270, exit 17A, 0.5 mi e to Frantz Rd, then 0.5 mi s. Ext/int corridors. **Pets:** $75 one-time fee/room. Service with restrictions, crate.
[SAVE] [S&] [X] [&M] [🐾] [&] [🛏] [💻] [🏊] [X]

▼▼▼ Staybridge Suites [SH]
(614) 734-9882. **$114-$190.** 6095 Emerald Pkwy. I-270, exit 15 (Tuttle Crossing Blvd), just w. Int corridors. **Pets:** Accepted.
[ASK] [X] [&] [🛏] [💻] [🏊] [X]

♦♦♦ ▼▼▼▼ Woodfin Suites Hotel [SH]
(614) 766-7762. **$160.** 4130 Tuller Rd. I-270, exit 20, 0.3 mi s on Sawmill Rd via Dublin Center Dr. Ext corridors. **Pets:** Accepted.
[SAVE] [S&] [X] [🐾] [🛏] [💻] [🏊]

GAHANNA

▼▼ Candlewood Suites Columbus Airport [SH]
(614) 863-4033. **$100-$160.** 590 Taylor Rd. I-270, exit 37, just e, 0.6 mi s on Morrison Rd, then just e. Int corridors. **Pets:** Accepted.
[ASK] [S&] [X] [&] [🛏] [💻]

GROVE CITY

♦♦♦ ▼▼▼ Best Western Executive Inn [M]
(614) 875-7770. **$76-$93.** 4026 Jackpot Rd. I-71, exit 100, just e. Ext corridors. **Pets:** Medium, dogs only. $10 daily fee/pet. Designated rooms, service with restrictions, supervision.
[SAVE] [S&] [X] [🛏] [💻] [🏊]

♦♦♦ ▼▼▼▼ La Quinta Inn South [SH]
(614) 539-6200. **$72-$109.** 3962 Jackpot Rd. I-71, exit 100, just ne. Int corridors. **Pets:** Accepted.
[SAVE] [S&] [X] [&] [🛏] [💻] [🏊] [X]

▼▼ Motel 6-South Columbus #1492 [M]
(614) 875-8543. **$41-$55.** 1900 Stringtown Rd. I-71, exit 100, just w. Ext corridors. **Pets:** Medium, other species. Service with restrictions, supervision.
[S&] [X] [&]

▼▼ Red Roof Inn Columbus/Grove City [M]
(614) 871-9617. **$59-$175.** 4055 Jackpot Rd. I-71, exit 100, 1.3 mi s of jct I-270. Ext corridors. **Pets:** Medium. $100 deposit/pet. Designated rooms, service with restrictions, supervision.
[ASK] [S&] [X] [&] [🛏] [💻]

HEATH

♦♦♦ ▼▼▼ Quality Inn [SH]
(740) 522-1165. **$55-$99.** 733 Hebron Rd. I-70, exit 129B, 7 mi n on SR 79. Ext corridors. **Pets:** Medium. $5 daily fee/pet. Service with restrictions, crate.
[SAVE] [S&] [X] [🛏] [💻] [🍴] [🏊]

HEBRON

▼▼ Red Roof Inn [SH]
(740) 467-7663. **$63-$95.** 10668 Lancaster Rd SW. I-70, exit 126, just s. Int corridors. **Pets:** Medium, other species. Service with restrictions, supervision.
[ASK] [S&] [X] [&M] [&]

HILLIARD

▼▼▼▼ Comfort Suites by Choice Hotels-Columbus [SH]
(614) 529-8118. **$90-$110.** 3831 Park Mill Run Dr. I-270, exit 13A northbound; exit 13 southbound. Int corridors. **Pets:** Accepted.
[ASK] [S&] [X] [&M] [🐾] [&] [🛏] [💻] [🏊]

▼▼▼ Homewood Suites by Hilton-Columbus [SH]
(614) 529-4100. **$135-$155.** 3841 Park Mill Run Dr. I-270, exit 13 southbound; exit 13A northbound. Int corridors. **Pets:** Accepted.
[ASK] [S&] [X] [&M] [🐾] [&] [🛏] [💻] [🏊] [X]

LANCASTER

♦♦♦ ▼▼▼ Lancaster Inn [SH]
(740) 653-3040. **$60-$75.** 1858 N Memorial Dr. 2 mi nw on US 33. Ext/int corridors. **Pets:** Accepted.
[SAVE] [S&] [X] [🛏] [💻] [🍴] [🏊]

MARYSVILLE

♦♦♦ ▼▼▼ AmeriHost Inn-Marysville [SH]
(937) 644-0400. **$99.** 16420 Allenby Dr. Jct US 33 and 36. Int corridors. **Pets:** Accepted.
[SAVE] [S&] [X] [🐾] [&] [🛏] [💻] [🏊] [X]

▼▼ Super 8 Motel-Marysville [SH]
(937) 644-8821. **$55-$100.** 16510 Square Dr. Just e of US 36, exit off US 33. Ext corridors. **Pets:** Very small, other species. $10 daily fee/pet. Designated rooms, service with restrictions, crate.
[ASK] [S&] [X] [🛏] [💻]

NEWARK

AAA ▼▼▼▼ Cherry Valley Lodge 🆂🅷 🐾
(740) 788-1200. **$119-$159.** 2299 Cherry Valley Rd. 3.5 mi w on SR 16, then 0.3 mi s. Int corridors. **Pets:** Dogs only. $150 deposit/room. Designated rooms, service with restrictions, crate.
🆂🅰🆅🅴 🆂🔟 ✕ 🖂🅼 🎥 🖪 💷 🍴 🏊 🏊

REYNOLDSBURG

AAA ▼▼▼ Days Inn & Suites Columbus East 🆂🅷
(614) 864-1280. **$60.** 2100 Brice Rd. I-70, exit 110 westbound; exit 110B eastbound, just n. Int corridors. **Pets:** Accepted.
🆂🅰🆅🅴 🆂🔟 ✕ 🎥 🖪 💷 🍴 🏊

▼▼▼ Extended StayAmerica-Columbus-East 🆂🅷
(614) 759-1451. **$58-$63.** 2200 Lake Club Dr. I-70, exit 110 westbound; exit 110B eastbound, 0.5 mi n on Brice Rd, just w on Channingway, then just s. Int corridors. **Pets:** Accepted.
🅰🆂🅺 🆂🔟 ✕ 🖪 💷 🏊

AAA ▼▼▼▼ La Quinta Inn Columbus East 🆂🅷
(614) 866-6456. **$85-$105.** 2447 Brice Rd. I-70, exit 110 westbound; exit 110B eastbound, 0.3 mi n. Int corridors. **Pets:** Medium. Service with restrictions.
🆂🅰🆅🅴 ✕ 🖪 💷 🏊

▼▼ Red Roof Inn-East #7033 🅼
(614) 864-3683. **$52-$81.** 2449 Brice Rd. I-70, exit 110 westbound; exit 110B eastbound. Ext corridors. **Pets:** Medium, other species. Service with restrictions, supervision.
✕ 🎥 🖪

SUNBURY

AAA ▼▼▼ Days Inn of Sunbury 🆂🅷
(740) 362-6159. **$65-$125.** 7323 SR 37 E. I-71, exit 131, just nw. Int corridors. **Pets:** $10 daily fee/pet. Service with restrictions, supervision.
🆂🅰🆅🅴 🆂🔟 ✕ 🎥 🖪 🏊

▼▼▼ Hampton Inn-Columbus/Delaware 🆂🅷
(740) 363-4700. **$89-$119.** 7329 SR 36 & 37. I-71, exit 131, just nw. Int corridors. **Pets:** Accepted.
🅰🆂🅺 🆂🔟 ✕ 🖂🅼 🎥 🎥 🖪 💷 🏊

WESTERVILLE

AAA ▼▼▼ Baymont Inn & Suites North East 🅼
(614) 890-1244. **$79-$109.** 909 S State St. I-270, exit 29, 0.3 mi n on SR 3. Ext corridors. **Pets:** Accepted.
🆂🅰🆅🅴 🆂🔟 ✕ 🎥 🖪 💷 🏊

WORTHINGTON

AAA ▼▼▼▼ Radisson Hotel Columbus-Worthington 🆂🅷
(614) 436-0700. **$109-$129.** 7007 N High St. I-270, exit 23, just s on US 23. Int corridors. **Pets:** Accepted.
🆂🅰🆅🅴 🆂🔟 ✕ 🖂🅼 🎥 🎥 🖪 💷 🍴 🏊

END METROPOLITAN AREA

CONNEAUT

AAA ▼▼▼ Days Inn of Conneaut 🆂🅷
(440) 593-6000. **$65-$89.** 600 Days Blvd. I-90, exit 241, 0.3 mi n. Int corridors. **Pets:** $10 daily fee/pet. Service with restrictions, supervision.
🆂🅰🆅🅴 ✕ 💷 🏊

COPLEY

▼▼ Extended StayAmerica-Akron-Copley 🆂🅷
(330) 668-9818. **$65-$70.** 185 Montrose Ave W. I-77, exit 137B, just w on SR 18. Int corridors. **Pets:** Accepted.
🅰🆂🅺 🆂🔟 ✕ 🖪 💷

CUYAHOGA FALLS

AAA ▼▼▼ Sheraton Suites Akron-Cuyahoga Falls 🆂🅷 🐾
(330) 929-3000. **$209-$219.** 1989 Front St. SR 8, exit Broad Blvd, just w. Int corridors. **Pets:** Other species. Designated rooms, service with restrictions, supervision.
🆂🅰🆅🅴 🆂🔟 ✕ 🖂🅼 🎥 🖪 💷 🍴 🏊 🏊

DAYTON

▼▼ Comfort Inn by Choice Hotels-North 🆂🅷
(937) 890-9995. **$80-$100.** 7125 Miller Ln. I-75, exit 59 (Wyse/Benchwood rds), just w on Benchwood Rd, then 0.6 mi n. Int corridors. **Pets:** Accepted.
🅰🆂🅺 🆂🔟 ✕ 🖂🅼 🎥 🎥 🖪 💷 🏊

▼▼▼ Dayton Marriott Hotel 🅻🅷
(937) 223-1000. **$104-$169.** 1414 S Patterson Blvd. I-75, exit 51 (Edwin C Moses Blvd), 1 mi e. Int corridors. **Pets:** Other species. $50 one-time fee/room. Designated rooms, service with restrictions, supervision.
🅰🆂🅺 🆂🔟 ✕ 🎥 🎥 🖪 💷 🍴 🏊 🏊

▼▼▼ Drury Inn & Suites-Dayton North 🅻🅷
(937) 454-5200. **$87-$187.** 6616 Miller Ln. I-75, exit 59 (Wyse/Benchwood rds), just w on Benchwood Rd, then just n. Int corridors. **Pets:** Large, other species. Service with restrictions, supervision.
🅰🆂🅺 ✕ 🖂🅼 🎥 🎥 🖪 💷 🏊

▼▼ Econo Lodge Dayton-South 🆂🅷
(937) 435-1550. **$56-$70.** 1944 Miamisburg-Centerville Rd. I-675, exit 2, just w of jct SR 725. Ext corridors. **Pets:** Accepted.
🅰🆂🅺 🆂🔟 ✕ 🎥 🖪 💷 🏊

▼▼ Extended StayAmerica-Dayton North 🆂🅷
(937) 898-9221. **$47-$100.** 6688 Miller Ln. I-75, exit 59 (Wyse/Benchwood rds), just w on Benchwood Rd, then just n. Int corridors. **Pets:** Accepted.
🅰🆂🅺 🆂🔟 ✕ 🎥 🎥 🖪 💷

▼▼ Extended StayAmerica Dayton South 🆂🅷
(937) 439-2022. **Call for rates.** 7851 Lois Cir. I-75, exit 44, just e on SR 725; opposite mall. Int corridors. **Pets:** Accepted.
✕ 🎥 🖪 💷

AAA ▼▼▼ Howard Johnson Express Inn 🆂🅷
(937) 454-0550. **$39-$79.** 7575 Poe Ave. I-75, exit 59 (Wyse/Benchwood rds), just e on Wyse Rd, just sw on Poe Ave/Wyse Rd connector, then 0.8 mi n. Int corridors. **Pets:** Other species. $10 daily fee/pet. Designated rooms, service with restrictions, supervision.
🆂🅰🆅🅴 🆂🔟 ✕ 🎥 🖪 💷 🏊

▼▼ Red Roof Inn-North #7023 🆂🅷
(937) 898-1054. **$51-$65.** 7370 Miller Ln. I-75, exit 59 (Wyse/Benchwood rds), just w on Benchwood Rd, then 0.8 mi n. Ext corridors. **Pets:** Medium, other species. Service with restrictions, supervision.
✕ 🎥 🎥 🖪

▼▼▼▼ **Residence Inn by Marriott-Dayton North** SH
(937) 898-7764. **$119-$159.** 7070 Poe Ave. I-75, exit 59 (Wyse/Benchwood rds), just e on Wyse Rd, just sw on Poe Ave/Wyse Rd connector, then 0.6 mi n. Ext corridors. **Pets:** Large, other species. $100 one-time fee/room. Service with restrictions, crate.

(ASK) (S&) (X) (🖊) (&) (🔔) (🖳) (≈) (X)

DOVER

▼ **Hospitality Inn** M ❀
(330) 364-7724. **$40-$80.** 889 Commercial Pkwy. I-77, exit 83, just e. Ext corridors. **Pets:** Other species. $10 daily fee/pet. Service with restrictions, supervision.

(ASK) (S&) (X) (🖊) (🔔) (≈)

EATON

▲▲▲ ▼▼▼ **Econo Lodge** M
(937) 456-5959. **$40-$80, 3 day notice.** 6161 US Rt 127 N. I-70, exit 10 (US 127), just s. Ext corridors. **Pets:** Accepted.

(SAVE) (S&) (X) (🔔) (🖳)

ELYRIA

▼▼ **Comfort Inn** SH
(440) 324-7676. **$65-$125.** 739 Leona St. I-80, exit 145, just n on SR 57, exit Midway Blvd. Int corridors. **Pets:** Other species. $10 daily fee/pet. Service with restrictions, supervision.

(ASK) (S&) (X) (🔔) (🖳)

▼▼ **Red Roof Inn & Suites** SH
(440) 324-4444. **$59-$109.** 621 Midway Blvd. I-80, exit 145, just n on SR 57, exit Midway Blvd. Int corridors. **Pets:** Medium, other species. Service with restrictions, supervision.

(ASK) (S&) (X) (&M) (🖊) (🔔) (🖳) (≈)

▼▼▼ **Super 8 Motel** SH
(440) 323-7488. **$49-$89.** 910 Lorain Blvd. I-80, exit 145, 0.5 mi s on SR 57. Int corridors. **Pets:** Accepted.

(ASK) (S&) (X) (&) (🖳) (≈)

ENGLEWOOD

▼▼▼ **Holiday Inn-Dayton Northwest Airport** SH
(937) 832-1234. **$75-$169.** 10 Rockridge Rd. I-70, exit 29, just n. Int corridors. **Pets:** Accepted.

(ASK) (S&) (X) (&) (🖳) (🍴) (≈)

▼▼ **Red Roof Inn-Dayton (Englewood)** M
(937) 836-8339. **$44-$84.** 9325 N Main St. I-70, exit 29, just s. Ext corridors. **Pets:** Medium, other species. Service with restrictions, supervision.

(ASK) (S&) (X) (&) (🔔) (≈)

▼▼ **Super 8 Motel-Englewood** M
(937) 832-3350. **$40-$60.** 15 Rockridge Rd. I-70, exit 29, just n. Ext corridors. **Pets:** Medium. $10 daily fee/pet. Service with restrictions, supervision.

(ASK) (S&) (X) (🔔)

FAIRBORN

▲▲▲ ▼▼▼▼ **Hawthorn Inn & Suites** SH
(937) 754-9109. **$89-$109.** 730 E Xenia Dr. I-675, exit 22, just w. Int corridors. **Pets:** Medium. $75 one-time fee/room. Service with restrictions, supervision.

(SAVE) (S&) (X) (🖊) (&) (🔔) (🖳)

▲▲▲ ▼▼▼▼ **Holiday Inn Dayton/Fairborn/I-675** SH
(937) 426-7800. **$109-$129.** 2800 Presidential Dr. I-675, exit 17 (N Fairfield Rd), just w. Int corridors. **Pets:** Medium. $75 one-time fee/room. Service with restrictions, crate.

(SAVE) (S&) (X) (🔔) (🖳) (🍴) (≈)

▲▲▲ ▼▼▼▼ **Homewood Suites by Hilton-Fairborn/Dayton** SH ❀
(937) 429-0600. **$129-$149.** 2750 Presidential Dr. I-675, exit 17 (N Fairfield Rd), just w. Ext/int corridors. **Pets:** Other species. $100 daily fee/pet. Service with restrictions.

(SAVE) (X) (🖊) (🔔) (🖳) (≈)

▼▼▼ **Ramada Limited & Suites-Wright Patterson** SH
(937) 490-2000. **$95-$114, 3 day notice.** 2540 University Blvd. I-675, exit 15 (Colonel Glen Hwy), 1.5 mi e, then just s. Int corridors. **Pets:** Medium, other species. $10 daily fee/pet. Crate.

(ASK) (S&) (X) (&) (🔔) (🖳) (≈)

▼▼▼ **Red Roof Inn-Fairborn #7205** SH
(937) 426-6116. **$59-$73.** 2580 Colonel Glenn Hwy. I-675, exit 17 (N Fairfield Rd), just w. Ext corridors. **Pets:** Medium, other species. Service with restrictions, supervision.

(X) (🖊) (&) (🔔)

FAIRLAWN

▲▲▲ ▼ **Akron Super 8 Motel** SH
(330) 666-8887. **$39-$79.** 79 Rothrock Rd. I-77, exit 137A, just e. Int corridors. **Pets:** Other species. $10 daily fee/pet. Service with restrictions.

(SAVE) (S&) (X) (🖊) (🔔) (🖳)

▼ **Motel 6 Akron North #2000** M
(330) 666-0566. **$41-$55.** 99 Rothrock Rd. I-77, exit 137A, just e. Ext corridors. **Pets:** Medium, other species. Service with restrictions, supervision.

(S&) (X) (🖊) (&)

▲▲▲ ▼▼▼▼ **The Residence Inn by Marriott** SH
(330) 666-4811. **$129-$229.** 120 W Montrose Ave. I-77, exit 137B, just w. Ext corridors. **Pets:** Accepted.

(SAVE) (S&) (X) (🔔) (🖳) (≈) (X)

▼▼ **StudioPLUS-Akron-Copley** SH
(330) 666-3177. **$95-$100.** 170 Montrose Ave W. I-77, exit 137B, just w on SR 18. Int corridors. **Pets:** Accepted.

(ASK) (S&) (X) (🔔) (🖳) (≈)

FINDLAY

▲▲▲ ▼▼▼ **Econo Lodge** M
(419) 422-0154. **$35-$75.** 316 Emma St. I-75, exit 157, just w. Ext corridors. **Pets:** $10 daily fee/pet. Service with restrictions, crate.

(SAVE) (S&) (X) (🔔) (🖳)

▼▼▼▼ **Hawthorn Suites-Findlay** SH
(419) 425-9696. **$69-$159.** 2355 Tiffin Ave. 3 mi e on US 224. Int corridors. **Pets:** Accepted.

(ASK) (S&) (X) (🖊) (&) (🔔) (🖳) (≈) (X)

▼▼ **Quality Inn** M
(419) 423-4303. **$64-$94.** 1020 Interstate Ct. I-75, exit 159, just w. Ext corridors. **Pets:** Accepted.

(ASK) (S&) (X) (🖊) (🔔) (🖳) (≈)

▼▼ **Red Roof Inn** M
(419) 424-0466. **$60-$70.** 1951 Broad Ave. I-75, exit 159, 0.5 mi e. Ext corridors. **Pets:** Medium, other species. Service with restrictions, supervision.

(ASK) (S&) (X) (🖊) (🔔) (≈)

▼▼ **Super 8 Motel-Findlay** SH
(419) 422-8863. **$47-$55.** 1600 Fox St. I-75, exit 159, just e. Int corridors. **Pets:** Accepted.

(ASK) (S&) (X) (🖊) (🔔)

FOSTORIA

AAA ◈◈ Country Club Inn and Suites M
(419) 435-6511. **$62-$70.** 737 Independence Rd. SR 12, 1 mi w of SR 23. Ext corridors. **Pets:** Medium. Service with restrictions, supervision.

[SAVE] [S🐾] [✕] [🍴]

FREDERICKTOWN

◈◈◈ Heartland Country Resort CA 🐾
(419) 768-9300. **$100-$195, 7 day notice.** 3020 Township Rd 190. I-71, exit 151, 2 mi e on SR 95, 2 mi s on SR 314, then 1 mi e on SR 179. Ext corridors. **Pets:** Other species. $15 daily fee/room.

[ASK] [S🐾] [✕] [🍴] [🛏] [💻] [✕]

FREMONT

AAA ◈◈◈ Comfort Inn & Suites SH
(419) 355-9300. **$87-$270.** 840 Sean Dr. I-80/90, exit 91, 2 mi s on SR 53. Int corridors. **Pets:** Medium, other species. $15 one-time fee/pet. Service with restrictions, supervision.

[SAVE] [S🐾] [✕] [🛏] [🍴] [💻] [🌊]

◈◈ Days Inn SH
(419) 334-9551. **$68-$118.** 3701 SR 53 N. I-80/90, exit 91, just n. Int corridors. **Pets:** Small, dogs only. $50 deposit/pet. Designated rooms, service with restrictions, supervision.

[ASK] [S🐾] [✕] [🍴] [🌊]

◈◈◈ Holiday Inn-Fremont SH
(419) 334-2682. **$89-$139.** 3422 Port Clinton Rd. I-80/90, exit 91, just s. Int corridors. **Pets:** Accepted.

[ASK] [S🐾] [✕] [🛏M] [🛏] [💻] [🍴] [🌊] [✕]

GENEVA-ON-THE-LAKE

**AAA ◈◈◈ The Lodge & Conference Center at
Geneva-on-the-Lake SH 🐾**
(440) 466-7100. **$89-$189, 3 day notice.** 4888 N Broadway. I-90, exit 218, 8 mi n. Ext corridors. **Pets:** Other species. $25 one-time fee/pet. Service with restrictions.

[SAVE] [✕] [🛏M] [🗋] [🛏] [🍴] [💻] [🌊] [✕]

GREEN

AAA ◈◈ Super 8 Motel SH
(330) 899-9888. **$65-$109.** 1605 Corporate Woods Pkwy. I-77, exit 118, just w. **Pets:** Medium. $10 daily fee/pet. Designated rooms, service with restrictions, supervision.

[SAVE] [S🐾] [✕] [🛏] [💻] [🌊]

GREENVILLE

AAA ◈◈ Greenville Inn SH
(937) 548-3613. **$65-$75.** 851 E Martin. Jct US 36 and 127, 0.3 mi w on SR 571. Int corridors. **Pets:** Other species. $10 daily fee/pet. Service with restrictions, supervision.

[SAVE] [S🐾] [✕] [🗋] [🛏] [💻] [🍴]

HOLLAND

AAA ◈◈ Econo Lodge M
(419) 866-6565. **$40-$65.** 1201 E Mall Dr. I-475, exit 8, just w on SR 2. Ext corridors. **Pets:** Dogs only. $10 one-time fee/pet. No service, supervision.

[SAVE] [S🐾] [✕] [🗋] [🛏] [💻] [🌊]

◈◈◈ Extended StayAmerica SH
(419) 861-1133. **$55-$65.** 6155 Trust Dr. I-475, exit 8, just e to Holland-Sylvania Rd, then just n. Int corridors. **Pets:** Accepted.

[ASK] [S🐾] [✕] [🗋] [🛏] [💻]

AAA ◈◈ Quality Inn Toledo Airport M
(419) 867-1144. **$59-$149.** 1401 E Mall Dr. I-475, exit 8, just w on SR 2. Ext/int corridors. **Pets:** Other species. $10 daily fee/pet. Service with restrictions, supervision.

[SAVE] [S🐾] [✕] [🗋] [🛏] [💻] [🌊]

◈◈ Red Roof Inn Toledo/Holland #7058 M
(419) 866-5512. **$47-$70.** 1214 Corporate Dr. I-475, exit 8, just e on Holland-Sylvania Rd, then just n to Trust Dr. Ext corridors. **Pets:** Medium, other species. Service with restrictions, supervision.

[✕] [🗋] [🛏]

◈◈ Residence Inn by Marriott SH
(419) 867-9555. **$129-$189.** 6101 Trust Dr. I-475, exit 8, just e to Holland-Sylvania Rd, then just n. Ext corridors. **Pets:** Accepted.

[ASK] [✕] [🗋] [🛏] [💻] [🌊] [✕]

HUBBARD

◈◈◈ Best Western Penn Ohio Inn & Suites SH
(330) 534-5100. **$69-$149.** 6828 Commerce Dr. I-80, exit 234, just n. Int corridors. **Pets:** Small. $20 daily fee/pet. Designated rooms, service with restrictions, supervision.

[ASK] [S🐾] [✕] [🗋] [🛏] [💻] [🌊]

HUBER HEIGHTS

◈◈◈ Holiday Inn Express Hotel & Suites SH
(937) 235-2000. **$94-$149.** 5612 Merily Way. I-70, exit 36, just se on SR 202. Int corridors. **Pets:** $25 one-time fee/room. Designated rooms, service with restrictions, crate.

[ASK] [S🐾] [✕] [🗋] [🗋] [🛏] [💻] [🌊]

◈ Travelodge Dayton/Huber Heights M
(937) 236-9361. **$50-$60.** 7911 Brandt Pike. I-70, exit 38, just s at SR 201. Ext/int corridors. **Pets:** Accepted.

[ASK] [S🐾] [✕] [🛏] [💻] [🌊]

HURON

AAA ◈ Plantation Motel M
(419) 433-4790. **$45-$98, 3 day notice.** 2815 E Cleveland Rd. 3 mi e of town, on US 6. Ext corridors. **Pets:** Accepted.

[SAVE] [✕] [🛏] [💻] [🌊]

JACKSON

AAA ◈◈◈ Comfort Inn-Jackson SH
(740) 286-7581. **$70-$112.** 605 E Main St. Jct SR 32, 0.5 mi n on SR 93. Int corridors. **Pets:** $20 one-time fee/pet. Designated rooms, supervision.

[SAVE] [S🐾] [✕] [🛏] [💻]

AAA ◈◈ Red Roof Inn M
(740) 288-1200. **$67-$84.** 1000 Acy Ave. US 35, exit McCarty Ln, just nw. Int corridors. **Pets:** Medium. $25 deposit/room. Service with restrictions, supervision.

[SAVE] [S🐾] [✕] [🗋] [🛏]

JEFFERSONVILLE

AAA ◈◈ AmeriHost Inn-Jeffersonville SH
(740) 426-6400. **$60-$90.** 10160 Carr Rd NW. I-71, exit 69 (SR 41), just w. Int corridors. **Pets:** Accepted.

[SAVE] [S🐾] [✕] [🗋] [🛏] [💻] [🌊]

AAA ◈◈◈ AmeriHost Inn Washington Court House SH
(740) 948-2104. **$65-$109.** 11431 Allen Rd NW. I-71, exit 65. Int corridors. **Pets:** Accepted.

[SAVE] [S🐾] [✕] [🛏M] [🛏] [💻] [🌊]

KENT

▼▼▼ Days Inn-Akron Kent M
(330) 677-9400. **$59-$85, 7 day notice.** 4422 Edson Rd. I-76, exit 33. Ext corridors. **Pets:** Accepted.
(ASK) (S🐾) (✕) (🖉) (🛢) (🖥) (🖭) (≈)

▼▼▼ Quality Inn & Suites SH
(330) 678-0101. **$65-$99.** 4363 SR 43. I-76, exit 33. Ext corridors. **Pets:** Accepted.
(ASK) (S🐾) (✕) (🖉) (🛢) (🖥) (≈)

▼▼▼ Super 8 Motel SH
(330) 678-8817. **$59-$79, 7 day notice.** 4380 Edson Rd. I-76, exit 33. Int corridors. **Pets:** Accepted.
(ASK) (S🐾) (✕) (🖉) (🛢)

LIMA

▼▼▼ Holiday Inn Lima SH
(419) 222-0004. **$99-$119.** 1920 Roschman Ave. I-75, exit 125A, just se. Int corridors. **Pets:** Other species. Service with restrictions, supervision.
(ASK) (S🐾) (✕) (🖉) (🛢) (🖥) (🖭) (🍴) (≈) (✕)

LOGAN

▲▲▲ ▼▼▼ AmeriHost Inn-Logan SH
(740) 385-1700. **$65-$189.** 12819 SR 664. Jct US 33, just n. Int corridors. **Pets:** Small, other species. $10 daily fee/room. Designated rooms, service with restrictions, supervision.
(SAVE) (S🐾) (✕) (🖥M) (🖉) (🛢) (🖥) (🖭) (≈)

▲▲▲ ▼▼▼▼ Holiday Inn Express Hocking Hills SH
(740) 385-7700. **$108-$148.** 12916 Grey St. SR 664, just w to Lake Logan Rd, then just n. Int corridors. **Pets:** Small. Designated rooms, service with restrictions, supervision.
(SAVE) (S🐾) (✕) (🖥M) (🖉) (🛢) (🖥) (≈)

▼▼▼▼ The Inn At Cedar Falls CI
(740) 385-7489. **$99-$129, 30 day notice.** 21190 SR 374. 9.5 mi s on SR 664, 1 mi e. Int corridors. **Pets:** Large, dogs only. $30 daily fee/pet. Designated rooms, no service, supervision.
(ASK) (S🐾) (✕) (🛢) (🖭) (🍴) (✕) (🕅) (🖉)

LOUDONVILLE

▼▼▼ Little Brown Inn M
(419) 994-5525. **$54-$79.** 940 S Market St. 1 mi s on SR 3. Int corridors. **Pets:** Small. $10 daily fee/pet. Designated rooms, service with restrictions, supervision.
(ASK) (S🐾) (✕) (🛢)

MANSFIELD

▼▼▼ AmeriHost Inn Mansfield SH
(419) 756-6670. **$59-$129.** 180 E Hanley Rd. I-71, exit 169, jct SR 13. Int corridors. **Pets:** $25 one-time fee/room. Service with restrictions, crate.
(ASK) (S🐾) (✕) (🖉) (🖑) (🛢) (🖥) (≈)

▼▼▼ Comfort Inn North SH
(419) 529-1000. **$64-$135.** 500 N Trimble Rd. Int corridors. **Pets:** Accepted.
(ASK) (S🐾) (✕) (🖉) (🛢) (🖥) (≈) (✕)

▲▲▲ ▼▼ Econo Lodge SH
(419) 589-3333. **$44-$65.** 1017 Koogle Rd. I-71, exit 176, just e. Int corridors. **Pets:** $5 daily fee/pet. Service with restrictions, supervision.
(SAVE) (S🐾) (✕) (🛢)

▼▼▼ Knights Inn M
(419) 529-2100. **$37-$100.** 555 N Trimble Rd. Jct US 30. Ext corridors. **Pets:** Large, other species. $50 deposit/room. Service with restrictions, supervision.
(ASK) (S🐾) (✕) (🖉) (🛢) (🖭)

▲▲▲ ▼▼▼▼ La Quinta Inn & Suites Mansfield SH
(419) 774-0005. **$89-$125.** 120 Stander Ave. I-71, exit 169. Int corridors. **Pets:** Other species. Service with restrictions, supervision.
(SAVE) (✕) (🖥M) (🖉) (🖑) (🛢) (🖭) (≈)

▲▲▲ ▼▼▼ Super 8 Motel SH
(419) 756-8875. **$53-$90.** 2425 Interstate Cir. I-71, exit 169. Int corridors. **Pets:** Accepted.
(SAVE) (S🐾) (✕) (🖉) (🛢) (🖭)

▲▲▲ ▼ Travelodge M
(419) 756-7600. **$48-$90.** 90 W Hanley Rd. I-71, exit 169. Ext corridors. **Pets:** Medium. $10 daily fee/room. No service, supervision.
(SAVE) (S🐾) (✕) (🖉) (🛢) (🖭) (≈)

MARIETTA

▲▲▲ ▼▼▼ Americas Best Value Inn M
(740) 373-7373. **$65-$70.** 506 Pike St. I-77, exit 1, just w. Ext corridors. **Pets:** $5 one-time fee/room. Service with restrictions, crate.
(SAVE) (S🐾) (✕) (🖉) (🛢) (🖭) (≈)

▲▲▲ ▼▼▼ Best Western Marietta M
(740) 374-7211. **$55-$88.** 279 Muskingum Dr. I-77, exit 6, 3.5 mi sw on SR 821, then 1 mi s on SR 60. Ext corridors. **Pets:** Small. Service with restrictions, supervision.
(ASK) (S🐾) (✕) (🛢) (🖭) (✕)

▲▲▲ ▼▼▼ Econo Lodge M
(740) 374-8481. **$45-$95.** 702 Pike St. I-77, exit 1, just e. Ext corridors. **Pets:** $7 daily fee/pet. Service with restrictions, supervision.
(SAVE) (S🐾) (✕) (🛢) (🖭) (≈)

▼▼▼▼ The Lafayette Hotel LH
(740) 373-5522. **$65-$125, 3 day notice.** 101 Front St. Center. Int corridors. **Pets:** Accepted.
(ASK) (S🐾) (✕) (🛢) (🖭) (🍴)

▼▼▼ Super 8 Motel-Marietta SH
(740) 374-8888. **$50-$55.** 46 Acme St. I-77, exit 1, just w. Int corridors. **Pets:** Accepted.
(ASK) (✕) (🖉) (🛢)

MARION

▼▼▼ Comfort Inn by Choice Hotels SH
(740) 389-5552. **$70-$90.** 256 James Way. Jct US 23 and SR 95, just w. Int corridors. **Pets:** Accepted.
(ASK) (S🐾) (✕) (🖉) (🖑) (🛢) (🖭) (≈)

MAUMEE

▲▲▲ ▼▼▼▼ Comfort Inn West Toledo/Maumee SH
(419) 893-2800. **$69-$99.** 1426 S Reynolds Rd. I-80/90, exit 59, just s. Int corridors. **Pets:** Small. $10 daily fee/pet. Service with restrictions, supervision.
(SAVE) (S🐾) (✕) (🛢) (🖭) (≈)

▲▲▲ ▼▼▼ Days Inn-Toledo/Maumee M
(419) 897-6900. **$49-$69.** 1704 Tollgate Dr. I-80/90, exit 59, just s. Ext corridors. **Pets:** Accepted.
(SAVE) (S🐾) (✕) (🖉) (🖑) (🛢) (🖭) (≈)

▲▲▲ ▼▼▼ Econo Lodge-Toledo/Maumee M
(419) 893-9960. **$44-$69.** 150 Dussel Dr. I-80/90, exit 59, just s. Ext corridors. **Pets:** Large. $20 deposit/pet. Service with restrictions, supervision.
(SAVE) (S🐾) (✕) (🖉) (🛢) (≈)

▼▼▼▼ Homewood Suites by Hilton-Toledo SH
(419) 897-0980. **$155-$175.** 1410 Arrowhead Rd. I-475, exit 6, just e. Int corridors. **Pets:** Accepted.
(ASK) (S🐾) (✕) (🖥M) (🖉) (🖑) (🛢) (🖭) (≈) (✕)

▼▼ Red Roof Inn-Maumee #7046 M
(419) 893-0292. **$54-$74.** 1570 S Reynolds Rd. I-80/90, exit 59, just s. Ext/int corridors. **Pets:** Medium, other species. Service with restrictions, supervision.
⊠ 🔊 🛢 🖥

▼▼ StudioPLUS-Toledo-Maumee SH
(419) 891-1211. **$70-$75.** 542 W Dussel Dr. I-475, exit 8, just e. Int corridors. **Pets:** Accepted.
ASK 🔊 ⊠ 🔊 🛢 🖥 ⟲ ⟲

⟠ ▼▼ Super 8 Motel-Maumee/Toledo SH
(419) 897-3800. **$45-$69, 5 day notice.** 1390 Arrowhead Rd. I-475, exit 6, just e. Int corridors. **Pets:** Accepted.
SAVE 🔊 ⊠ 🔊 🛢 🖥

MENTOR

⟠ ▼▼▼ Best Western Lawnfield Inn & Suites SH ✿
(440) 205-7378. **$79-$149.** 8434 Mentor Ave. I-90, exit 195, 1.5 mi n to SR 20 (Mentor Ave) then just e. Int corridors. **Pets:** $20 one-time fee/pet. Service with restrictions, crate.
SAVE 🔊 ⊠ 🛢 🖥 ⟲

▼▼▼ Residence Inn by Marriott SH
(440) 392-0800. **$89-$149.** 5660 Emerald Ct. Jct SR 2 and Heisley Rd, just s. Int corridors. **Pets:** Other species. $75 one-time fee/room. Service with restrictions.
ASK 🔊 ⊠ 🛢 🖥 ⟲ ⟲

▼▼ Studio 6 #6019 M
(440) 946-0749. **$51-$64.** 7677 Reynolds Rd. Just s of SR 2 on SR 306. Ext corridors. **Pets:** Accepted.
🔊 ⊠ 🛢 🖥 🖥

MIAMISBURG

▼▼▼ Holiday Inn-Dayton Mall SH
(937) 434-8030. **$95-$139.** 31 Prestige Plaza Dr. I-75, exit 44, just e on SR 725, then just s. Int corridors. **Pets:** Small. $25 one-time fee/room. Service with restrictions, crate.
ASK ⊠ 🔊 🛢 🖥 ⟲ ⟲

▼▼▼ Homewood Suites by Hilton-Dayton South SH
(937) 432-0000. **$134-$154.** 3100 Contemporary Ln. I-75, exit 44, just e on SR 725, then just se on Prestige Plaza Dr. then just s. Int corridors. **Pets:** Accepted.
ASK 🔊 ⊠ 🔊 🛢 🖥 ⟲

▼▼ Red Roof Inn-South #7006 SH
(937) 866-0705. **$53-$67.** 222 Byers Rd. I-75, exit 44, just w on SR 725. Ext corridors. **Pets:** Medium, other species. Service with restrictions, supervision.
⊠ 🔊 🛢 🖥

▼▼▼ Residence Inn by Marriott-Dayton South SH
(937) 434-7881. **$195.** 155 Prestige Pl. I-75, exit 44, just e on SR 725, just se on Prestige Plaza Dr, then just s. Ext corridors. **Pets:** Other species. $100 one-time fee/room. Service with restrictions.
ASK 🔊 ⊠ 🛢 🖥 ⟲ ⟲

▼▼ Super 8 Miamisburg/South Dayton SH
(937) 866-5500. **$39-$79.** 155 Monarch Ln. I-75, exit 44, 0.5 mi w on SR 725. Int corridors. **Pets:** Accepted.
ASK ⊠ 🔊 🛢 🖥

MILAN

▼▼ Motel 6-4016 SH
(419) 499-8001. **$35-$144, 3 day notice.** 11406 US 250 N. I-80/90, exit 118, 1.5 mi n. Int corridors. **Pets:** Medium, other species. Service with restrictions, supervision.
ASK 🔊 ⊠ 🛢 ⟲

▼▼ Red Roof Inn SH
(419) 499-4347. **$49-$149.** 11303 Rt 250/Milan Rd. I-80/90, exit 118, 0.5 mi n. Int corridors. **Pets:** Small, dogs only. $50 deposit/pet. Designated rooms, service with restrictions, supervision.
ASK 🔊 ⊠ 🔊 🛢 ⟲

▼▼ Super 8 Motel SH
(419) 499-4671. **$49-$138.** 11313 Milan Rd. I-80/90, exit 118, 0.5 mi n on SR 250. Int corridors. **Pets:** Medium. $50 deposit/room. Service with restrictions, supervision.
ASK 🔊 ⊠ 🛢 🖥 ⟲

MONTPELIER

▼▼ Ramada Inn & Suites SH
(419) 485-5555. **$81-$129.** 13508 SR 15. I-80/90, exit 13, just s. Int corridors. **Pets:** Other species. Service with restrictions, crate.
ASK 🔊 ⊠ 🔊 🛢 🖥 🖥 ⟲ ⟲

MORAINE

▼▼▼▼ Holiday Inn Hotel & Suites Dayton South SH
(937) 294-1471. **$79-$129.** 2455 Dryden Rd. I-75, exit 50A (Dryden Rd), just nw. Int corridors. **Pets:** Accepted.
ASK 🔊 ⊠ 🔊 🛢 🖥 🖥 ⟲ ⟲

MOUNT GILEAD

▼ Knights Inn M
(419) 946-6010. **$42-$56, 7 day notice.** 5898 SR 95. I-71, exit 151, 0.3 mi w. Ext corridors. **Pets:** Accepted.
ASK 🔊 ⊠ 🛢

MOUNT VERNON

▼▼ Comfort Inn SH
(740) 392-6886. **$70-$125, 14 day notice.** 150 Howard St. Jct SR 13; south of downtown. Int corridors. **Pets:** Other species. $10 daily fee/pet. Service with restrictions, supervision.
ASK 🔊 ⊠ 🔊 🛢 🖥 ⟲

▼▼▼ Holiday Inn Express SH 🐾
(740) 392-1900. **$95-$105.** 11555 Upper Gilchrist Rd. 3 mi e on US 36. Int corridors. **Pets:** Designated rooms, service with restrictions, crate.
ASK 🔊 ⊠ 🛢 🔊 🛢 🖥 ⟲

NAPOLEON

⟠ ▼▼▼ Best Western Napoleon Inn & Suites SH
(419) 599-0850. **$69-$119.** 1290 Independence Dr. From US 6/24, just se. Int corridors. **Pets:** Medium, other species. $12 daily fee/pet. Service with restrictions, supervision.
SAVE 🔊 ⊠ 🔊 🔊 🛢 🖥 ⟲ ⟲

NEWCOMERSTOWN

▼▼▼ Hampton Inn SH
(740) 498-9800. **$80-$115.** 200 Morris Crossing. I-77, exit 65, 0.8 mi w. Int corridors. **Pets:** Small, dogs only. Service with restrictions, supervision.
ASK 🔊 ⊠ 🛢 🖥 ⟲

NEW PHILADELPHIA

▼▼▼ Hampton Inn SH
(330) 339-7000. **$77-$99.** 1299 W High St. I-77, exit 81, just e. **Pets:** Accepted.
ASK 🔊 ⊠ 🔊 🔊 🛢 🖥 ⟲ ⟲

▼ Motel 6-254 M
(330) 339-6446. **$37-$51.** 181 Bluebell Dr SW. I-77, exit 81, 0.4 mi e. Ext corridors. **Pets:** Medium, other species. Service with restrictions, supervision.
🔊 ⊠ 🔊 ⟲

NEWTON FALLS

ⒶⒶⒶ ▼▼ ▼▼ Econo Lodge Ⓜ
(330) 872-0988. **$45-$99.** 4248 SR 5. I-80, exit 209, just w. Ext corridors. **Pets:** $10 daily fee/pet. Service with restrictions.
SAVE 🅢 ⊠ 🅱

NORTH CANTON

▼▼ ▼▼ Knights Inn Canton Ⓜ
(330) 492-5030. **$43-$130.** 3950 Convenience Cir NW. I-77, exit 109 southbound, 0.3 mi e on Everhard, then 0.3 mi s on Whipple; exit 109A northbound, 0.3 mi s on Whipple. Ext corridors. **Pets:** Accepted.
ASK 🅢 ⊠ 🅱 💻 ⇌

NORTHWOOD

ⒶⒶⒶ ▼▼ ▼▼ Comfort Inn South SH
(419) 666-2600. **$65-$108, 3 day notice.** 2426 Oregon Rd. I-75, exit 198, just e; jct Wales and Oregon rds. Int corridors. **Pets:** $10 daily fee/room. Service with restrictions, supervision.
SAVE 🅢 ⊠ 🅱 💻 🍽 ⇌

NORWALK

▼▼ ▼▼ Econo Lodge Ⓜ
(419) 668-5656. **$49-$138.** 342 Milan Ave. 3 mi n on US 250; 6 mi s of I-80/90 (Ohio Tpke). Ext corridors. **Pets:** Small, dogs only. $50 deposit/pet. Designated rooms, service with restrictions, supervision.
ASK 🅢 ⊠ 🅱 💻 ⇌

OBERLIN

▼▼ ▼ Oberlin Inn Ⓒ
(440) 775-1111. **$109-$189.** 7 N Main St. On SR 58; jct College and Main sts; center. Int corridors. **Pets:** Accepted.
ASK 🅢 ⊠ 🅱 💻 🍽

OREGON

ⒶⒶⒶ ▼▼ ▼▼ Comfort Inn East SH ❁
(419) 691-8911. **$74-$129.** 2930 Navarre Ave. I-280, exit 7, just n on access road, then 0.5 mi e on SR 2 (Navarre Ave). Int corridors. **Pets:** $15 one-time fee/room. Designated rooms, service with restrictions, supervision.
SAVE 🅢 ⊠ 🗇 🅱 💻 ⇌

ⒶⒶⒶ ▼▼ ▼ Sleep Inn & Suites SH
(419) 697-7800. **$79-$139.** 1761 Meijer Cir. I-280, exit 6, just w. Int corridors. **Pets:** Accepted.
SAVE 🅢 ⊠ 🗇 🅱 💻 ⇌

PERRYSBURG

ⒶⒶⒶ ▼▼ ▼▼ Howard Johnson Inn Toledo South Ⓜ
(419) 837-5245. **$44-$99.** 3555 Hanley Rd. I-80/90, exit 71, to I-280, exit 1B. Ext/int corridors. **Pets:** Other species. $10 daily fee/pet. Service with restrictions, supervision.
SAVE 🅢 ⊠ 🗇 🅱 💻 ⇌

ⒶⒶⒶ ▼▼▼▼ La Quinta Inn & Suites
Toledo-Perrysburg SH
(419) 872-0000. **$79-$105.** 1154 Professional Dr. I-75, exit 193, just w. Int corridors. **Pets:** Medium. Service with restrictions.
SAVE ⊠ 🗇 🗇 🅱 💻

▼▼ ▼▼ Super 8 Motel-Toledo/Perrysburg/Millbury Ⓜ
(419) 837-6409. **$44-$89.** 3491 Latcha Rd. I-80/90, exit 71 to I-280, exit 1B, just n. Ext corridors. **Pets:** Other species. $10 daily fee/pet. Service with restrictions, supervision.
ASK 🅢 ⊠ 🗇 🅱

PIQUA

ⒶⒶⒶ ▼▼▼ ▼ Comfort Inn-Piqua SH
(937) 778-8100. **$65-$125.** 987 E Ash St. I-75, exit 82, just w. Int corridors. **Pets:** Accepted.
SAVE 🅢 ⊠ 🗇 🗇 🅱 💻 ⇌

▼▼▼▼ La Quinta Inn Piqua SH
(937) 615-0140. **$67, 14 day notice.** 950 E Ash St. I-75, exit 82, just w. Int corridors. **Pets:** Accepted.
ASK 🅢 ⊠ 🗇 🅱 💻 ⇌

POLAND

▼▼ ▼▼ Red Roof Inn #7253 SH
(330) 758-1999. **$52-$81.** 1051 Tiffany S. I-680, exit 11, just w. Int corridors. **Pets:** Medium, other species. Service with restrictions, supervision.
⊠ 🗇 🗇 🅱 💻

▼▼▼▼ Residence Inn by Marriott-Youngstown SH
(330) 726-1747. **$160-$240.** 7396 Tiffany S. I-680, exit 11, just w. Int corridors. **Pets:** Accepted.
ASK 🅢 ⊠ 🗇 🗇 🅱 💻 ⇌ ⊠

PORT CLINTON

▼▼ ▼▼ Best Western Port Clinton SH
(419) 734-2274. **$49-$149.** 1734 E Perry St. 1.7 mi e on SR 163, w of jct SR 2. Int corridors. **Pets:** Accepted.
ASK 🅢 ⊠ 💻 ⇌

ⒶⒶⒶ ▼▼▼ ▼ Commodore Perry Inn & Suites SH ❁
(419) 732-2645. **$44-$219, 3 day notice.** 255 W Lakeshore Dr. Just n of bridge. Int corridors. **Pets:** Other species. $15 one-time fee/pet.
SAVE 🅢 ⊠ 🗇 🅱 💻 🍽 ⇌

▼ ▼ Super 8 SH
(419) 734-4446. **$49-$149.** 1704 E Perry St. 1.7 mi e on SR 163, w of jct SR 2. Int corridors. **Pets:** Small, dogs only. $50 deposit/pet. Designated rooms, service with restrictions, supervision.
ASK 🅢 ⊠ 💻

PORTSMOUTH

▼▼ ▼▼ Portsmouth Super 8 Motel SH
(740) 353-8880. **$48-$68.** 4266 US Rt 23 N. 5 mi n. Int corridors. **Pets:** Accepted.
ASK 🅢 ⊠ 🗇 🗇 🅱 💻 ⇌

RIO GRANDE

▼ College Hill Motel Ⓜ
(740) 245-5326. **$59-$79.** 10987 State Rt 588. US 35, exit Rio Grande. Ext corridors. **Pets:** Accepted.
ASK 🅢 ⊠ 🅱

ST. CLAIRSVILLE

ⒶⒶⒶ ▼▼ ▼ Americas Best Value Inn St.
Clairsville/Wheeling Ⓜ
(740) 695-5038. **$49-$74.** 51260 National Rd. I-70, exit 218, 0.5 mi ne on US 40. Ext corridors. **Pets:** Other species. $10 one-time fee/room. No service, supervision.
SAVE 🅢 ⊠ 🗇 🅱 💻 ⇌

▼▼ ▼▼ Red Roof Inn #7101 Ⓜ
(740) 695-4057. **$46-$77.** 68301 Red Roof Ln. I-70, exit 218, just n. Ext corridors. **Pets:** Medium, other species. Service with restrictions, supervision.
⊠ 🗇 🅱

ST. MARYS

ⓐ ▽▽▽ Americas Best Value Inn St Marys 🆂🅷
(419) 394-2341. **$58-$99.** 1321 Celina Rd. SR 66/29, 0.8 mi w on SR 703. Ext corridors. **Pets:** Accepted.
[SAVE] 🆂🔊 ✕ 🚪 🖥 🏊 ✕

ⓐ ▽▽▽ AmeriHost Inn-St. Marys 🆂🅷
(419) 394-2710. **$79-$99, 3 day notice.** 1410 Commerce Dr. Jct US 33 and SR 29, just s. Int corridors. **Pets:** Accepted.
[SAVE] 🆂🔊 ✕ 🖉 🖥 🚪 🖥 🏊

SANDUSKY

ⓐ ▽▽▽ Best Budget Inn Ⓜ
(419) 626-3610. **$44-$129.** 2027 Cleveland Rd. US 6, just e of Cedar Point Cswy. Ext/int corridors. **Pets:** Medium, dogs only. $50 deposit/pet. Designated rooms, service with restrictions, supervision.
[SAVE] 🆂🔊 ✕ 🏊

ⓐ ▽▽▽ Clarion Inn Sandusky 🆂🅷
(419) 625-6280. **$60-$260.** 1119 Sandusky Mall Blvd. On US 250, 1.5 mi n of SR 2. Int corridors. **Pets:** Medium, dogs only. $25 daily fee/pet. Designated rooms, no service, supervision.
[SAVE] 🆂🔊 ✕ 🖉 🖥 🚪 🖥 🍴 🏊 ✕

▽▽▽ Knights Inn Sandusky Ⓜ
(419) 621-9000. **$49-$129.** 2405 Cleveland Rd. US 6, 2 mi e of Cedar Point Cswy. Ext/int corridors. **Pets:** Medium. $25 deposit/pet. Designated rooms, service with restrictions, supervision.
[ASK] 🆂🔊 ✕ 🚪 🖥 🏊

SEVILLE

▽▽▽▽ Hawthorn Suites Ltd 🆂🅷 🐾
(330) 769-5025. **$85-$119.** 5025 Park Ave W. SR 224, exit 2, just n. Int corridors. **Pets:** Other species. $75 one-time fee/room. Service with restrictions, supervision.
[ASK] 🆂🔊 ✕ 🖉 🚪 🖥 🏊

▽▽▽ Super 8 Motel-Seville 🆂🅷
(330) 769-8880. **$69-$74.** 6116 Speedway Dr. Jct SR 224 and Lake Rd. Int corridors. **Pets:** Accepted.
[ASK] 🆂🔊 ✕ 🖉Ⓜ 🖉 🚪

SIDNEY

ⓐ ▽▽▽ Comfort Inn 🆂🅷
(937) 492-3001. **$80-$125.** 1959 W Michigan Ave. I-75, exit 92, just sw of SR 47. Int corridors. **Pets:** $75 deposit/pet. Service with restrictions, supervision.
[SAVE] 🆂🔊 ✕ 🚪 🖥 🏊

▽▽▽ Econo Lodge 🆂🅷
(937) 492-9164. **$55-$85.** 2009 W Michigan St. I-75, exit 92, just w on SR 47. Ext/int corridors. **Pets:** Accepted.
[ASK] 🆂🔊 ✕ 🚪 🖥

▽▽▽ Holiday Inn 🆂🅷
(937) 492-1131. **$71.** 400 Folkerth Ave. I-75, exit 92, just w. Int corridors. **Pets:** Accepted.
[ASK] 🆂🔊 ✕ 🖉 🖉 🚪 🖥 🍴 🏊

SPRINGFIELD

▽▽▽▽ Holiday Inn South Springfield Ohio 🆂🅷
(937) 323-8631. **$100-$105.** 383 E Leffel Ln. I-70, exit 54, just n, then e. Int corridors. **Pets:** Service with restrictions, supervision.
[ASK] 🆂🔊 ✕ 🖉 🚪 🖥 🍴 🏊 ✕

ⓐ ▽▽▽ Ramada Limited 🆂🅷
(937) 328-0123. **$59-$110.** 319 E Leffel Ln. I-70, exit 54, just n, then e. Int corridors. **Pets:** Medium. $10 daily fee/pet. Designated rooms, service with restrictions, supervision.
[SAVE] 🆂🔊 ✕ 🖉 🚪 🖥 🏊

ⓐ ▽▽▽ Red Roof Inn 🆂🅷
(937) 325-5356. **$64-$109.** 155 W Leffel Ln. I-70, exit 54, just n, then w. Int corridors. **Pets:** Other species. Service with restrictions, supervision.
[SAVE] 🆂🔊 ✕ 🖉 🚪 🖥 🏊

STEUBENVILLE

ⓐ ▽▽▽▽ Holiday Inn-Steubenville 🆂🅷
(740) 282-0901. **$99-$109.** 1401 University Blvd. Jct US 22 and SR 7, 1 mi sw. Ext/int corridors. **Pets:** Medium, other species. $25 daily fee/room. Service with restrictions, crate.
[SAVE] ✕ 🖉 🖉 🚪 🖥 🍴 🏊

STRASBURG

ⓐ ▽▽▽▽ Ramada Limited Dover/Strasburg 🆂🅷
(330) 878-1400. **$65-$110.** 509 S Wooster Ave. I-77, exit 87, 0.4 mi n on US 250 and SR 21. Int corridors. **Pets:** Medium. $15 daily fee/room. Service with restrictions, supervision.
[SAVE] 🆂🔊 ✕ 🖉Ⓜ 🖉 🖉 🚪 🖥 🏊

STREETSBORO

ⓐ ▽▽▽ Microtel Inn & Suites of Streetsboro 🆂🅷 🐾
(330) 422-1234. **$59-$139.** 9371 SR 14. I-80, exit 187, 1.2 mi s. Int corridors. **Pets:** $35 one-time fee/room. Designated rooms, service with restrictions, supervision.
[SAVE] 🆂🔊 ✕ 🚪 🖥 🏊

SWANTON

ⓐ ▽▽▽ Days Inn 🆂🅷
(419) 865-2002. **$59-$69.** 10753 Airport Hwy. I-80/90, exit 3A, just s, then e. Int corridors. **Pets:** Dogs only. $10 daily fee/pet. Service with restrictions, supervision.
[SAVE] 🆂🔊 ✕ 🖉 🖥

TIFFIN

▽▽▽▽ Holiday Inn Express 🆂🅷
(419) 443-5100. **$80-$100.** 78 Shaffer Park Dr. Just w of mall. Int corridors. **Pets:** Other species. $20 one-time fee/room. Service with restrictions, crate.
🆂🔊 ✕ 🚪 🖥 🏊

▽▽▽ Quality Inn 🆂🅷
(419) 447-6313. **$71-$125.** 1927 S SR 53. Jct US 224 and SR 53, 2 mi sw. Ext/int corridors. **Pets:** Dogs only. $15 daily fee/pet. Designated rooms, service with restrictions, crate.
[ASK] ✕ 🖉 🖉 🚪 🖥 🍴 🏊

TOLEDO

ⓐ ▽▽▽ Comfort Inn-North 🆂🅷
(419) 476-0170. **$69-$169.** 445 E Alexis Rd. I-75, exit 210, 2 mi w on SR 184; just e of jct US 24 and SR 184. Int corridors. **Pets:** Other species. $10 one-time fee/room. Designated rooms, service with restrictions, supervision.
[SAVE] 🆂🔊 ✕ 🖉 🚪 🖥

▽▽▽ Radisson Hotel Toledo 🆂🅷
(419) 241-3000. **$139-$159.** 101 N Summit St. Between Jefferson and Monroe sts; downtown. Int corridors. **Pets:** Medium. Designated rooms, service with restrictions, crate.
[ASK] 🆂🔊 ✕ 🖥 🍴

▽▽▽ Red Roof Inn Toledo University #7196 Ⓜ
(419) 536-0118. **$54-$68.** 3530 Executive Pkwy. I-475, exit 17, 0.5 mi s on Secor Rd, then just e. Ext corridors. **Pets:** Medium, other species. Service with restrictions, supervision.
✕ 🖉 🖉 🚪

TROY

▼▼▼▼ Fairfield Inn & Suites by Marriott SH
(937) 332-1446. **$89-$159.** 83 Troy Town Dr. I-75, exit 74, just w. Int corridors. **Pets:** Accepted.
A$K S&# X &M [] [] [] [] ≈

▼▼▼ Holiday Inn Express Hotel & Suites SH
(937) 332-1700. **$75-$95.** 60 Troy Town Dr. I-75, exit 74, just w. Int corridors. **Pets:** Medium, other species. $25 one-time fee/pet. Service with restrictions, crate.
A$K S&# X [] [] [] [] ≈

▼▼▼ Residence Inn By Marriott SH
(937) 440-9303. **$99-$169.** 87 Troy Town Dr. I-75, exit 74, just w. Int corridors. **Pets:** Accepted.
A$K S&# X [] [] [] [] ≈ X

UHRICHSVILLE

AAA ▼▼▼ Best Western Country Inn M
(740) 922-0774. **$50-$75.** 111 McCauley Dr. US 250, exit McCauley Dr. Ext corridors. **Pets:** Medium, other species. $5 one-time fee/room. Service with restrictions, crate.
SAVE S&# X [] [] []

URBANA

AAA ▼▼▼ Econo Lodge Urbana M
(937) 652-2188. **$49-$125.** 2551 S US Hwy 68. 1.3 mi s. Ext corridors. **Pets:** Small. $15 daily fee/pet. Designated rooms, service with restrictions, supervision.
SAVE S&# X [] ≈

VANDALIA

AAA ▼▼▼ Super 8 Motel-Vandalia M
(937) 898-7636. **$39-$89.** 550 E National Rd. I-75, exit 63, just w. Ext corridors. **Pets:** Medium. $7 daily fee/pet. Designated rooms, service with restrictions, supervision.
SAVE S&# X [] [] ≈

AAA ▼▼▼ Travelodge Dayton Airport M
(937) 898-8321. **$39-$69.** 75 Corporate Center Dr. I-70, exit 32, 2.5 mi n, then just e. Ext corridors. **Pets:** Accepted.
SAVE S&# [] [] ≈

VERMILION

▼▼▼▼ Holiday Inn Express SH
(440) 967-8770. **$85-$159.** 2417 SR 60. Jct SR 2 and 60. Int corridors. **Pets:** Medium, other species. $15 one-time fee/room. Service with restrictions, supervision.
A$K S&# X [] [] [] [] ≈

AAA ▼ Motel Plaza M
(440) 967-3191. **$65-$89.** 4645 Liberty Ave. On US 6, 2 mi e of SR 60. Ext corridors. **Pets:** Accepted.
SAVE S&# X [] []

WADSWORTH

AAA ▼ Legacy Inn M
(330) 336-6671. **$42-$51, 3 day notice.** 810 High St. I-76, exit 9, just s. Ext corridors. **Pets:** Medium. $5 one-time fee/room. Service with restrictions, supervision.
SAVE S&# X [] ≈

WAPAKONETA

▼▼▼▼ Hamilton Inn SH
(419) 738-8181. **$69-$130.** 1510 Saturn Dr. I-75, exit 111, just w. Int corridors. **Pets:** Accepted.
A$K S&# X [] [] [] ≈

▼▼ Travelodge SH
(419) 739-9600. **$44-$60.** 413 Apollo Dr. I-75, exit 111, just w. Ext corridors. **Pets:** Accepted.
A$K S&# X [] []

WARREN

AAA ▼▼▼ Americas Best Value Inn M
(330) 392-2515. **$55-$131, 3 day notice.** 777 Mahoning Ave. 0.3 mi n of Courthouse Square. Ext corridors. **Pets:** Other species. Service with restrictions, supervision.
SAVE S&# X [] [] [] ≈

AAA ▼▼▼ Comfort Inn SH
(330) 393-1200. **$65-$105.** 136 N Park Ave. Downtown; east side of Courthouse Square. Int corridors. **Pets:** Medium. $10 daily fee/pet. Service with restrictions, supervision.
SAVE S&# X [] [] [] []]

WAUSEON

AAA ▼▼▼ Best Western Del Mar M
(419) 335-1565. **$79-$119.** 8319 SR 108. I-80/90, exit 34, just s. Ext corridors. **Pets:** Accepted.
SAVE X [] [] [] [] ≈

WINCHESTER

▼▼ Budget Host Inn M
(937) 695-0381. **$55-$65.** 18760 SR 136. Jct US 32. Ext corridors. **Pets:** Accepted.
A$K S&# X []

WOOSTER

AAA ▼▼▼ Econo Lodge M
(330) 264-8883. **$69-$79.** 2137 E Lincoln Way. US 30, 3 mi e. Ext corridors. **Pets:** Large. $10 daily fee/pet. Service with restrictions, supervision.
SAVE S&# X [] [] [] ≈

▼▼▼▼ The Wooster Inn CI
(330) 263-2660. **$80-$225.** 801 E Wayne Ave. 0.5 mi e on Liberty St, 1 mi n on Beall Ave. Int corridors. **Pets:** Accepted.
X [] []]

XENIA

▼▼▼▼ Holiday Inn-Xenia SH
(937) 372-9921. **$99-$139, 7 day notice.** 300 Xenia Towne Square. On W Main St, 0.5 mi w. Int corridors. **Pets:** Small. $15 daily fee/pet. Service with restrictions, supervision.
A$K S&# X [] [] []] ≈

▼▼ Regency Inn SH
(937) 372-9954. **$55.** 600 Little Main St. 1 mi w. Ext corridors. **Pets:** Medium, other species. $10 daily fee/pet. Service with restrictions, supervision.
A$K S&# X [] []

ZANESVILLE

AAA ▼▼▼ AmeriHost Inn-Zanesville SH
(740) 454-9332. **$79-$109.** 230 Scenic Crest Dr. I-70, exit 155, just s. Int corridors. **Pets:** Accepted.
SAVE S&# X [] [] [] [] ≈ X

▼▼ Best Western–B.R. Guest SH 🐾
(740) 453-6300. **$74-$114.** 4929 E Pike. I-70, exit 160, just s. Int corridors. **Pets:** Large, other species. $10 daily fee/pet. Service with restrictions, crate.
A$K S&# X &M [] [] [] ≈

Comfort Inn SH

(740) 454-4144. **$69-$184.** 500 Monroe St. I-70, exit 155 westbound; exit 7th St eastbound, e on Elberon to light, just n on Underwood. Int corridors. **Pets:** Medium, other species. $10 one-time fee/room. Designated rooms, service with restrictions, supervision.

Econo Lodge-Zanesville SH

(740) 452-4511. **$70-$90.** 135 N 7th St. I-70, exit 155, on SR 60 via signs; downtown. Ext corridors. **Pets:** Other species. $10 daily fee/pet. Service with restrictions, supervision.

Holiday Inn Conference Center SH

(740) 453-0771. **$80-$100.** 4645 E Pike. I-70, exit 160, on US 22 and 40. Int corridors. **Pets:** Accepted.

Super 8 Motel-Zanesville SH

(740) 455-3124. **$45-$65.** 2440 National Rd. I-70, exit 152, just n. Int corridors. **Pets:** Large, other species. $10 daily fee/pet. Designated rooms, service with restrictions, supervision.

Travelodge SH

(740) 453-0611. **$50-$70.** 58 N 6th St. I-70, exit 155, on US 22 and SR 60 at Market St. Ext/int corridors. **Pets:** Accepted.

OKLAHOMA

ALTUS

Best Western Altus SH
(580) 482-9300. **$76-$80.** 2804 N Main St. 2 mi n on US 283. Ext corridors. **Pets:** Accepted.

ARDMORE

Best Western Inn SH
(580) 223-7525. **$85.** 6 Holiday Dr. I-35, exit 31A, just ne. Int corridors. **Pets:** Small, dogs only. $25 deposit/pet. Designated rooms, service with restrictions, supervision.

Holiday Inn SH
(580) 223-7130. **$75-$99.** 2705 W Broadway. I-35, exit 31A, just e. Ext corridors. **Pets:** Accepted.

La Quinta Inn Ardmore SH
(580) 223-7976. **$70-$75.** 2432 Veterans Blvd. I-35, exit 33, just e. Ext corridors. **Pets:** Accepted.

Microtel Inn & Suites SH
(580) 224-2600. **$65-$75.** 1904 Cooper Dr. I-35, exit 32, just w. Int corridors. **Pets:** Accepted.

BARTLESVILLE

Microtel Inn & Suites of Bartlesville SH
(918) 333-2100. **$49-$89, 7 day notice.** 2696 SE Washington Blvd. 1.4 mi s of jct US 60 E. Int corridors. **Pets:** Small, dogs only. $25 one-time fee/pet. Service with restrictions, supervision.

BIG CABIN

Super 8 Motel-Big Cabin M
(918) 783-5888. **$49-$58.** 30954 S Hwy 69. I-44, exit 283, just ne. Ext/int corridors. **Pets:** Other species. $20 deposit/room. Designated rooms, service with restrictions.

BLACKWELL

Best Western Blackwell Inn SH
(580) 363-1300. **$67-$79.** 4545 W White Ave. I-35, exit 222, just ne. Int corridors. **Pets:** Accepted.

Comfort Inn SH
(580) 363-7000. **$64-$79.** 1201 N 44th St. I-35, exit 222, just ne. Int corridors. **Pets:** Small, dogs only. $10 daily fee/pet. Designated rooms, service with restrictions, supervision.

CHICKASHA

Holiday Inn Express Hotel & Suites SH
(405) 224-8883. **$86, 14 day notice.** 2610 S 4th St. I-44, exit 80, just se. Int corridors. **Pets:** Large. $25 one-time fee/room. Service with restrictions, supervision.

DAVIS

Davis Microtel Inn & Suites-Treasure Valley Casino SH
(580) 369-3223. **$85-$105.** Rt 1, Box 7C. I-35, exit 55, just e. Int corridors. **Pets:** Small. $10 daily fee/pet. Service with restrictions, supervision.

DUNCAN

Chisholm Suite Hotel SH
(580) 255-0551. **$80-$188.** 1204 N Hwy 81. Center. Int corridors. **Pets:** Accepted.

DURANT

Holiday Inn Express Hotel & Suites SH
(580) 924-8881. **$95-$140.** 2112 W Main St. Just e of jct US 75/69 and 70. Int corridors. **Pets:** Small. $25 one-time fee/room. Service with restrictions, supervision.

ELK CITY

Holiday Inn SH
(580) 225-6637. **$119-$229.** 101 Meadow Ridge Dr. I-40, exit 38, just sw. Ext/int corridors. **Pets:** Medium. $50 deposit/room. Designated rooms, no service, supervision.

ENID

AmeriHost Inn & Suites Enid SH
(580) 234-6800. **$67-$130.** 3614 W Owen K Garriott Rd. Just off US 412, 2 mi w of US 81. Int corridors. **Pets:** Accepted.

Holiday Inn Express Hotel & Suites SH
(580) 237-7722. **Call for rates.** 4702 W Garriott Rd. 2.3 mi w of jct US 81. Int corridors. **Pets:** Accepted.

ERICK

Comfort Inn SH
(580) 526-8124. **$85-$129, 5 day notice.** 1001 N Sheb Wooley. I-40, exit 7, just nw. Ext corridors. **Pets:** Medium. $8 daily fee/pet. Designated rooms, service with restrictions, supervision.

FREDERICK

AAA ▼ Scottish Inns Ⓜ
(580) 335-2129. **$45-$60.** 1015 S Main St. 1 mi s. Ext corridors.
Pets: Accepted.
〔SAVE〕 Ⓢ Ⓧ 🕮 🖵 ≈

GUYMON

AAA ▼▼ Guymon Super 8 🆂🅷
(580) 338-0507. **$51-$75.** 1201 Hwy 54 E. Jct US 54 and 64. Int
corridors. **Pets:** Other species. $6 daily fee/pet. Service with restrictions,
supervision.
〔SAVE〕 Ⓧ 🕮 🖵

AAA ▼ Lodge U.S.A. Ⓜ
(580) 338-5431. **$52.** 923 Hwy 54 E. Just s of jct US 64. Ext corridors.
Pets: Small. $5 one-time fee/pet. Designated rooms, service with restric-
tions, supervision.
〔SAVE〕 Ⓢ Ⓧ 🕮

▼▼ Western Townsman Inn 🆂🅷
(580) 338-6556. **$55-$99, 7 day notice.** 212 NE Hwy 54. 0.7 mi s of jct
US 64. Ext corridors. **Pets:** Medium. Service with restrictions.
〔ASK〕 Ⓢ Ⓧ 🎱 🕮 🖵 ≈

HENRYETTA

AAA ▼ Green Country Inn Ⓜ
(918) 652-9988. **$42-$48.** 2004 Old Hwy 75 W. I-40, exit 237, just ne.
Ext corridors. **Pets:** Small. $5 daily fee/pet. Designated rooms, service with
restrictions, supervision.
〔SAVE〕 Ⓢ Ⓧ 🕮 ≈

HINTON

▼ Microtel Inn & Suites 🆂🅷
(405) 542-6011. **$60-$75.** 4800 N Broadway. I-40, exit 101, just sw. Int
corridors. **Pets:** Accepted.
〔ASK〕 Ⓢ Ⓧ 🎱 🕮 🖵 ≈

IDABEL

AAA ▼▼▼ Comfort Suites 🆂🅷
(580) 286-9393. **$75-$150.** 400 SE Lincoln Blvd. Just s of jct US 70
and 259. Int corridors. **Pets:** Medium, other species. $15 one-time fee/pet.
Service with restrictions, supervision.
〔SAVE〕 Ⓢ Ⓧ 🎱 🕮 🖵 ≈

LAWTON

AAA ▼ Baymont Inn & Suites 🆂🅷
(580) 353-5581. **$84-$94.** 1203 NW 40th St. I-44, exit 39A, 3.7 mi w. Int
corridors. **Pets:** Accepted.
〔ASK〕 Ⓢ Ⓧ 🎱 🕮 🖵 ≈

AAA ▼▼▼ Best Western Hotel & Convention Center 🆂🅷
(580) 353-0200. **$94.** 1125 E Gore Blvd. I-44, exit 37, just e. Ext/int
corridors. **Pets:** Medium. $40 one-time fee/pet. Designated rooms, service
with restrictions, crate.
〔SAVE〕 Ⓢ Ⓧ 🕮 🖵 🍽 ≈ Ⓧ

MCALESTER

▼▼ Best Western Inn of McAlester 🆂🅷
(918) 426-0115. **$70-$80.** 1215 George Nigh Expwy. 3 mi s on US 69.
Ext corridors. **Pets:** Accepted.
Ⓧ 🎱 🕮 🖵 ≈

▼▼ Happy Days Hotel 🆂🅷
(918) 429-0910. **$70-$80.** 1400 S George Nigh Expwy. 3.3 mi s on US
69. Int corridors. **Pets:** Other species. $20 one-time fee/room. Service with
restrictions, supervision.
〔ASK〕 Ⓢ Ⓧ 🎱 🕮 🖵 ≈

▼▼ Super 8 Motel Ⓜ
(918) 426-5400. **$64-$160.** 2400 S Main St. Just n of jct US 69. Ext
corridors. **Pets:** Accepted.
Ⓧ 🕮

MIAMI

▼▼ Microtel Inn & Suites 🆂🅷
(918) 540-3333. **Call for rates.** 2015 E Steve Owens Blvd. I-44, exit
313, just w. Int corridors. **Pets:** $25 one-time fee/pet. Service with restric-
tions, crate.
Ⓧ 🎱 🕮 🖵 ≈

OKLAHOMA CITY METROPOLITAN AREA

DEL CITY

**AAA ▼▼ La Quinta Inn Oklahoma City East (Del
City)** 🆂🅷
(405) 672-0067. **$75-$111.** 5501 Tinker Diagonal Rd. I-40, exit 156A
(Sooner Rd), just nw. Ext/int corridors. **Pets:** Medium. Service with
restrictions.
〔SAVE〕 Ⓧ 🎱 🕮 🖵 ≈

EL RENO

AAA ▼▼ Best Western Hensley's 🆂🅷
(405) 262-6490. **$65-$95.** 2701 S Country Club Rd. I-40, exit 123, just
s. Ext corridors. **Pets:** Dogs only. $25 deposit/room, $5 daily fee/pet.
Service with restrictions, supervision.
〔SAVE〕 Ⓢ Ⓧ 🎱 🕮 🖵 ≈

GUTHRIE

AAA ▼▼▼ Best Western Territorial Inn 🆂🅷
(405) 282-8831. **$66-$79.** 2323 Territorial Tr. I-35, exit 157, just sw. Int
corridors. **Pets:** Small, other species. Service with restrictions, supervision.
〔SAVE〕 Ⓢ Ⓧ 🎱 🕮 🖵 ≈

MIDWEST CITY

▼ Studio 6 #6003 Ⓜ
(405) 737-8851. **$51-$61.** 5801 Tinker Diagonal Rd. I-40, exit 156A
(Sooner Rd), just ne. Ext corridors. **Pets:** Accepted.
Ⓢ Ⓧ 🕮 ≈

MOORE

AAA ▼▼ Best Western Green Tree Inn & Suites 🆂🅷
(405) 912-8882. **$75, 14 day notice.** 1811 N Moore Ave. I-35, exit 118,
just n on westbound frontage road. Int corridors. **Pets:** Very small. $10
one-time fee/pet. Service with restrictions, supervision.
〔SAVE〕 Ⓢ Ⓧ 🎱 🕮 🖵 ≈

▼▼ Microtel Inn & Suites 🆂🅷
(405) 799-8181. **$50-$60.** 2400 S Service Rd. I-35, exit 116, just s on
east service road. Int corridors. **Pets:** Accepted.
〔ASK〕 Ⓢ Ⓧ 🎱 🕮 🖵 ≈

NORMAN

▼▼▼ Days Inn SH
(405) 360-4380. **$45-$58.** 609 N Interstate Dr. I-35, exit 110, 0.5 mi s on east service road. Ext corridors. **Pets:** Other species. $10 daily fee/room. Service with restrictions.
ASK ⬛ ✕ 🔲 🛏 🖥 🏊

**▲▲▲ ▼▼▼ La Quinta Inn & Suites Oklahoma City
(Norman)** SH
(405) 579-4000. **$98-$132.** 930 Ed Noble Dr. I-35, exit 108B (Lindsey), just nw. Int corridors. **Pets:** Medium. Service with restrictions.
SAVE ✕ 🔲 🛏 🖥 🏊

▲▲▲ ▼▼ Quality Inn M
(405) 364-5554. **$95-$105.** 100 SW 26th Dr. I-35, exit 109 (Main St), just se. Ext corridors. **Pets:** Small. $5 daily fee/pet. Service with restrictions, supervision.
SAVE ⬛ ✕ 🖥

▲▲▲ ▼▼▼▼ The Residence Inn by Marriott SH
(405) 366-0900. **$189.** 2681 Jefferson St. I-35, exit 108A, just se. Ext corridors. **Pets:** Other species. $100 one-time fee/room. No service.
SAVE ✕ 🔲 🏊 🛏 🖥 🏊 ✕

OKLAHOMA CITY

▼▼ Baymont Inn SH
(405) 631-8661. **$75-$111.** 8315 I-35 S. I-35, exit 121A (82nd St), just sw. Ext corridors. **Pets:** Medium. Service with restrictions.
ASK ✕ 🔲 🛏 🖥 🏊

▼▼▼ Best Western Memorial Inn & Suites SH
(405) 286-5199. **$80-$95.** 1301 W Memorial Rd. John Kilpatrick Tpke, exit Western Ave, just nw. Int corridors. **Pets:** Medium. $10 daily fee/pet. Service with restrictions, supervision.
ASK ⬛ ✕ 🔲 🛏 🖥 🏊

**▲▲▲ ▼▼▼ Best Western Saddleback Inn & Conference
Center** LH
(405) 947-7000. **$89-$129.** 4300 SW 3rd St. I-40, exit 145 (Meridian Ave), just ne. Ext/int corridors. **Pets:** Accepted.
SAVE ⬛ ✕ 🔲 🛏 🖥 🍽 🏊 ✕

▼▼▼ Candlewood Suites Hotel SH
(405) 680-8770. **$85-$159.** 4400 River Park Dr. I-40, exit 145 (Meridian Ave), 1.1 mi s. Int corridors. **Pets:** Accepted.
ASK ⬛ ✕ 🔲 🛏 🖥

▼▼▼ Clarion Meridian Hotel and Convention Center SH
(405) 942-8511. **$69-$79.** 737 S Meridian Ave. I-40, exit 145 (Meridian Ave), just s. Ext/int corridors. **Pets:** Small, dogs only. Designated rooms, service with restrictions, crate.
ASK ⬛ ✕ 🔲 🔲 🛏 🖥 🏊

▲▲▲ ▼▼▼ Comfort Inn SH 🐾
(405) 943-4400. **$74.** 4240 W I-40 Service Rd. I-40, exit 145 (Meridian Ave), just e on south frontage road. Ext/int corridors. **Pets:** Other species. $20 one-time fee/room. Service with restrictions, supervision.
SAVE ⬛ ✕ 🔲 🛏 🖥 🏊

▲▲▲ ▼▼▼ Comfort Inn at Founders Tower SH
(405) 810-1100. **$74-$149.** 5704 Mosteller Dr. 0.5 mi e of jct SR 74 and 3. Int corridors. **Pets:** Accepted.
SAVE ⬛ ✕ 🔲 🛏 🖥

▲▲▲ ▼▼▼ Comfort Inn North SH
(405) 478-7282. **$69-$125.** 4625 NE 120th. I-35, exit 137 (122nd St), just sw. Int corridors. **Pets:** Large. $10 daily fee/pet. Service with restrictions, supervision.
SAVE ⬛ ✕ 🔲 🛏 🖥 🏊

**▲▲▲ ▼▼▼ Courtyard by
Marriott-Downtown/Bricktown** SH
(405) 232-2290. **$109-$159, 30 day notice.** 2 W Reno Ave. Gaylord and Reno aves; downtown. Int corridors. **Pets:** Medium. $250 one-time fee/room. Service with restrictions, crate.
SAVE ⬛ ✕ 🔲 🔲 🛏 🖥 🍽 🏊

▼▼▼ Courtyard by Marriott-NW SH
(405) 848-0808. **$89-$239.** 1515 Northwest Expwy. I-44, exit 125C westbound; exit 125B eastbound, just e. Int corridors. **Pets:** Small. $100 one-time fee/room. Designated rooms, service with restrictions, supervision.
ASK ✕ 🔲 🔲 🛏 🖥 🍽 🏊 ✕

▲▲▲ ▼▼▼ Crowne Plaza Hotel LH
(405) 848-4811. **$79-$139, 7 day notice.** 2945 Northwest Expwy. 0.5 mi e of jct SR 74 and 3. Ext/int corridors. **Pets:** Accepted.
SAVE ⬛ ✕ 🔲 🔲 🛏 🖥 🍽 🏊

▲▲▲ ▼▼▼ Days Inn West SH
(405) 942-8294. **$42-$95, 30 day notice.** 504 S Meridian Ave. I-40, exit 145 (Meridian Ave), just ne. Ext corridors. **Pets:** $10 daily fee/pet. Service with restrictions, crate.
SAVE ⬛ ✕ 🛏 🖥 🏊

▼▼▼ Embassy Suites LH
(405) 682-6000. **$109-$199.** 1815 S Meridian Ave. I-40, exit 145 (Meridian Ave), 1 mi s. Int corridors. **Pets:** Medium. $50 one-time fee/room. Service with restrictions, crate.
✕ 🔲 🛏 🖥 🍽 🏊 ✕

▼▼▼ Four Points by Sheraton Oklahoma City SH
(405) 681-3500. **$120-$150.** 6300 Terminal Dr. I-40, exit 145 (Meridian Ave), 4 mi s. Int corridors. **Pets:** $30 one-time fee/room. Service with restrictions, supervision.
ASK ⬛ ✕ 🔲 🛏 🖥 🍽 🏊

**▼▼▼ La Quinta Inn & Suites Oklahoma City (Northwest
Expressway)** SH
(405) 773-5575. **$99-$149.** 4829 Northwest Expwy. 1.9 mi w of jct SR 3 and 74. Int corridors. **Pets:** Medium. Service with restrictions.
ASK ✕ 🔲 🔲 🛏 🖥 🏊

▼▼▼ La Quinta Inn and Suites-Quail Springs SH
(405) 755-7000. **$129.** 3003 W Memorial Rd. John Kilpatrick Tpke, exit May Ave, just nw. Int corridors. **Pets:** Medium. $50 one-time fee/room. Designated rooms, service with restrictions, crate.
ASK ⬛ ✕ 🔲 🔲 🛏 🖥 🏊 ✕

▲▲▲ ▼▼▼ La Quinta Inn Oklahoma City (Airport) SH
(405) 942-0040. **$81-$114.** 800 S Meridian Ave. I-40, exit 145 (Meridian Ave), just se. Ext/int corridors. **Pets:** Medium. Service with restrictions.
SAVE ✕ 🔲 🛏 🖥 🍽 🏊

▼▼ Motel 6 Airport-116 M
(405) 946-6662. **$43-$55.** 820 S Meridian Ave. I-40, exit 145 (Meridian Ave), just s. Ext corridors. **Pets:** Medium, other species. Service with restrictions, supervision.
⬛ ✕ 🔲 🔲 🏊

▼▼ Motel 6 West-1128 SH
(405) 947-6550. **$44-$55.** 4200 I-40 Service Rd. I-40, exit 145 (Meridian Ave), just e on south frontage road. Ext/int corridors. **Pets:** Medium, other species. Service with restrictions, supervision.
⬛ ✕ 🛏 🏊

▲▲▲ ▼▼▼ Quality Inn SH
(405) 632-6666. **$75-$95.** 7800 CA Henderson Blvd. I-240, exit 2A, just s. Ext corridors. **Pets:** Medium, dogs only. $10 one-time fee/pet. Designated rooms, service with restrictions, supervision.
SAVE ⬛ ✕ 🔲 🔲 🛏 🖥 🏊

(AAA) ▼▼▼ Quality Inn At Frontier City 🆂🅷
(405) 478-0400. **$45-$70.** 12001 N I-35 Service Rd. I-35, exit 137, just sw. Ext corridors. **Pets:** Small. $10 one-time fee/pet. Service with restrictions, crate.
[SAVE] [S🄍] [✕] [🅻] [🖵] [🔁]

(AAA) ▼▼ Ramada Limited 🆂🅷
(405) 948-8000. **$59-$139.** 2727 W I-44 Service Rd. I-44, exit 124, just n. Int corridors. **Pets:** Accepted.
[SAVE] [S🄍] [✕] [🅻] [🛗] [🖵] [🔁]

(AAA) ▼▼ ▼▼ Renaissance Oklahoma City Hotel 🅻🅷
(405) 228-8000. **$169-$309.** 10 N Broadway Ave. Sheridan and Broadway aves; downtown. Int corridors. **Pets:** Accepted.
[SAVE] [S🄍] [✕] [🅲🄼] [🄻] [🅻] [🛗] [🖵] [🍴] [🔁] [✕]

▼▼▼▼ Residence Inn by Marriott-Oklahoma City West 🆂🅷
(405) 942-4500. **$159-$189.** 4361 W Reno Ave. I-40, exit 145 (Meridian Ave), 0.3 mi n, then just e. Ext corridors. **Pets:** Accepted.
[ASK] [✕] [🄻] [🛗] [🖵] [🔁] [✕]

▼▼▼▼ Residence Inn by Marriott South-Crossroads Mall 🆂🅷
(405) 634-9696. **$145-$175.** 1111 E I-240 Service Rd. I-240, exit 4C eastbound, 0.4 mi nw; exit 5 westbound, 0.8 mi nw. Int corridors. **Pets:** Accepted.
[ASK] [S🄍] [✕] [🅻] [🛗] [🖵] [🔁] [✕]

(AAA) ▼▼▼▼ Sheraton Oklahoma City 🅻🅷 🐾
(405) 235-2780. **$229-$269.** One N Broadway Ave. Sheridan and Broadway aves; downtown. Int corridors. **Pets:** Medium. Service with restrictions.
[SAVE] [✕] [🄻] [🅻] [🛗] [🖵] [🍴] [🔁]

(AAA) ▼▼▼▼ Waterford Marriott Hotel 🅻🅷
(405) 848-4782. **$139-$259.** 6300 Waterford Blvd. I-44, exit 125A, 1.4 mi n. Int corridors. **Pets:** Small. Service with restrictions, supervision.
[SAVE] [S🄍] [✕] [🄻] [🅻] [🛗] [🖵] [🍴] [🔁] [✕]

PURCELL

(AAA) ▼▼ Econo Lodge Ⓜ
(405) 527-5603. **$85-$90, 5 day notice.** 2122 Hwy 74 S. I-35, exit 91, just e. Ext corridors. **Pets:** Medium. $5 daily fee/pet. Service with restrictions, supervision.
[SAVE] [S🄍] [✕] [🄻] [🛗]

SHAWNEE

▼▼ Motel 6-1236 Ⓜ
(405) 275-5310. **$52-$65.** 4981 N Harrison. I-40, exit 186, just ne. Int corridors. **Pets:** Medium, other species. Service with restrictions, supervision.
[S🄍] [✕] [🄻] [🅻] [🔁]

YUKON

(AAA) ▼▼▼▼ Best Western Inn & Suites Yukon 🆂🅷
(405) 265-2995. **$84-$89.** 11440 W I-40 Service Rd. I-40, exit 138, just sw. Ext/int corridors. **Pets:** Other species. $25 deposit/room, $5 daily fee/room. Service with restrictions, supervision.
[SAVE] [S🄍] [✕] [🄻] [🅻] [🛗] [🖵] [🔁] [✕]

END METROPOLITAN AREA

OKMULGEE

(AAA) ▼▼▼▼ Best Western Okmulgee 🆂🅷
(918) 756-9200. **$99-$119.** 3499 N Wood Dr. Just n of jct US 75 and SR 56. Int corridors. **Pets:** Small. $50 deposit/pet. Service with restrictions, supervision.
[SAVE] [S🄍] [✕] [🄻] [🅻] [🛗] [🖵] [🍴] [🔁]

PAULS VALLEY

▼▼▼▼ Comfort Inn & Suites 🆂🅷
(405) 207-9730. **$80-$109.** 103 S Humphrey Blvd. I-35, exit 72, just e. Int corridors. **Pets:** Accepted.
[ASK] [S🄍] [✕] [🛗] [🖵] [🔁]

PONCA CITY

▼▼▼ Comfort Inn & Suites 🆂🅷
(580) 765-2322. **$89-$159.** 3101 N 14th St. I-35, exit 214, 3 mi n on US 77. Int corridors. **Pets:** Small. $25 daily fee/pet. Service with restrictions, supervision.
[ASK] [S🄍] [✕] [🅲🄼] [🄻] [🛗] [🖵] [🔁]

PRYOR

▼▼▼ Comfort Inn & Suites 🆂🅷
(918) 476-6660. **$74-$139.** 307 Mid America Dr. 5 mi s on US 69. Int corridors. **Pets:** Medium, dogs only. $10 daily fee/pet. Designated rooms, service with restrictions, supervision.
[ASK] [S🄍] [✕] [🄻] [🛗] [🖵] [🔁]

(AAA) ▼▼▼ Microtel Inn & Suites 🆂🅷
(918) 476-4661. **$60-$70.** 315 Mid America Dr. 5.1 mi s on US 69. Int corridors. **Pets:** Accepted.
[SAVE] [S🄍] [✕] [🄻] [🅻] [🛗] [🖵]

ROLAND

▼▼▼ Days Inn of Roland 🆂🅷
(918) 427-1000. **$55-$70, 14 day notice.** 207 Cherokee Blvd. I-40, exit 325, just ne. Int corridors. **Pets:** Accepted.
[ASK] [S🄍] [✕] [🄻] [🅻] [🛗] [🔁]

SALLISAW

(AAA) ▼▼▼ Best Western Blue Ribbon Inn 🆂🅷
(918) 775-6294. **$79-$89.** 706 S Kerr Blvd (US 59). I-40, exit 308 (US 59), just n. Ext/int corridors. **Pets:** Accepted.
[SAVE] [S🄍] [✕] [🛗] [🖵] [🔁]

▼▼ Microtel Inn & Suites 🆂🅷
(918) 774-0400. **$59-$69.** 710 S Kerr Blvd. I-40, exit 308 (US 59), just n. Int corridors. **Pets:** Other species. $10 one-time fee/pet. Service with restrictions, supervision.
[ASK] [S🄍] [✕] [🄻] [🛗] [🖵] [🔁]

SAVANNA

(AAA) ▼▼▼ Candlelight Inn & Suites 🆂🅷 🐾
(918) 548-3676. **$55-$85.** Hwy 69. 1.5 mi sw of jct US 69 and Indian Creek Tpke. Int corridors. **Pets:** Medium. Service with restrictions, supervision.
[SAVE] [S🄍] [✕] [🛗] [🖵]

SAYRE

▼▼ AmericInn Lodge & Suites of Sayre 🆂🅷 🐾
(580) 928-2700. **$71-$145.** 2405 S El Camino Rd. I-40, exit 20, just n. Int corridors. **Pets:** Other species. $25 deposit/room, $15 one-time fee/room. Designated rooms.
[ASK] [✕] [🅲🄼] [🄻] [🛗] [🖵] [🔁]

STILLWATER

▼▼ ▼▼ Best Western Stillwater 🅂🅷
(405) 377-7010. **$79-$99.** 600 E McElroy. 1 mi n on US 177 (Perkins Rd). Int corridors. **Pets:** Medium, other species. $20 daily fee/room. No service, supervision.
(ASK) 🅂🅾 ✕ 🗗 🖥 🍴 ➴ ✕

▼▼ ▼▼ Holiday Inn 🅂🅷
(405) 372-0800. **$71.** 2515 W 6th Ave. 1.8 mi w on SR 51. Ext/int corridors. **Pets:** Other species. Designated rooms, crate.
(ASK) 🅂🅾 ✕ 🗗 🖥 🍴 ➴ ✕

THACKERVILLE

▼▼ ▼▼ Winstar Microtel Inn and Suites 🅂🅷
(580) 276-4487. **$185.** Rt 1, Box 682. I-35, exit 1, 1.2 mi n on E Service Rd. Int corridors. **Pets:** Small, other species. $10 daily fee/pet. Service with restrictions, crate.
(ASK) ✕ 🗗 🖥 ➴

Tulsa Metropolitan Area

BROKEN ARROW

⟁⟁⟁ ▼▼▼▼ Clarion Hotel 🅂🅷
(918) 258-7085. **$69-$79.** 2600 N Aspen Ave. Just s of jct SR 51. Int corridors. **Pets:** Medium. $25 one-time fee/room. Designated rooms, service with restrictions, supervision.
(SAVE) 🅂🅾 ✕ 🖉 🗗 🖥 🍴 ➴

CATOOSA

▼▼ Cherokee Casino Inn Ⓜ
(918) 266-7000. **$49-$79.** 19250 Timbercrest Cir. I-44, exit 240A, just nw. Ext corridors. **Pets:** Small. $40 deposit/pet. Designated rooms, service with restrictions, crate.
(ASK) 🅂🅾 ✕ ➴

CLAREMORE

⟁⟁⟁ ▼▼ Claremore Motor Inn Ⓜ
(918) 342-4545. **$39-$49.** 1709 N Lynn Riggs Blvd. 1.2 mi n on SR 66. Ext/int corridors. **Pets:** Small. $7 one-time fee/pet. Service with restrictions, supervision.
(SAVE) 🅂🅾 ✕ 🗗

▼▼ ▼▼ Days Inn Claremore 🅂🅷
(918) 343-3297. **$59-$85.** 1720 S Lynn Riggs Blvd. 1.6 mi s on SR 66. Int corridors. **Pets:** Accepted.
(ASK) 🅂🅾 ✕ 🖉 🗗 🖥 ➴

▼▼ ▼▼ Microtel Inn & Suites 🅂🅷
(918) 343-2868. **$50-$155.** 10600 E Mallard Lake Rd. 2.6 mi s on SR 66. Int corridors. **Pets:** Small. $20 daily fee/pet. Designated rooms, service with restrictions, supervision.
(ASK) 🅂🅾 ✕ 🖉 🗗 🖥 ➴

⟁⟁⟁ ▼▼ ▼▼ Super 8 Motel 🅂🅷
(918) 341-2323. **$64-$74.** 1100 E Will Rogers Blvd. I-44, exit 255, just w. Ext/int corridors. **Pets:** Medium. $5 daily fee/pet. Service with restrictions, supervision.
(SAVE) 🅂🅾 ✕ 🗗

GLENPOOL

⟁⟁⟁ ▼▼ ▼▼ Best Western Glenpool/Tulsa 🅂🅷
(918) 322-5201. **$89-$109.** 14831 S Casper St. I-44, exit 224, 9.5 mi s on US 75. Ext corridors. **Pets:** $50 deposit/pet. Designated rooms, no service, supervision.
(SAVE) 🅂🅾 ✕ 🗗 🖥 ➴

SAND SPRINGS

⟁⟁⟁ ▼▼ ▼▼ Best Western Sand Springs Inn & Suites 🅂🅷
(918) 245-4999. **$71-$82.** 211 S Lake Dr. US 64 and 412, exit 81st W Ave, just sw. Ext/int corridors. **Pets:** Accepted.
(SAVE) 🅂🅾 ✕ 🗗 🖥 ➴

TULSA

▼▼ ▼▼ ▼▼ Ambassador Hotel 🅂🅷 ❀
(918) 587-8200. **$157-$193.** 1324 S Main St. Jct 14th and Main sts. Int corridors. **Pets:** Other species. Service with restrictions.
(ASK) 🅂🅾 ✕ 🖉 🗗 🖥 🍴

▼▼ ▼▼ Baymont Inn & Suites Tulsa 🅂🅷
(918) 488-8777. **$65-$100.** 4530 E Skelly Dr. I-44, exit 229 (Yale Ave/SR 66), just s, then w. Int corridors. **Pets:** Medium. Service with restrictions.
(ASK) ✕ 🖉 🗗 🖥 ➴

▼▼ ▼▼ ▼▼ Candlewood Suites 🅂🅷
(918) 294-9000. **$89-$109.** 10008 E 73rd St S. Just sw of jct 71st and 101st E Ave. Int corridors. **Pets:** Medium, other species. $75 one-time fee/pet. Service with restrictions, crate.
(ASK) 🅂🅾 ✕ 🅗Ⓜ 🗗 🖥

▼▼ ▼▼ Crowne Plaza Tulsa 🅻🅷
(918) 582-9000. **$99-$169.** 100 E 2nd St. Jct 2nd St and Boston; downtown. Int corridors. **Pets:** Accepted.
(ASK) 🅂🅾 ✕ 🖉 🗗 🖥 ➴

▼▼ ▼▼ ▼▼ DoubleTree Hotel At Warren Place 🅻🅷 ❀
(918) 495-1000. **$109-$185.** 6110 S Yale Ave. I-44, exit 229 (Yale Ave/SR 66), 1.3 mi s. Int corridors. **Pets:** Supervision.
✕ 🅗Ⓜ 🖉 🗗 🖥 🍴 ➴ ✕

▼▼ ▼▼ ▼▼ DoubleTree Hotel Downtown Tulsa 🅻🅷
(918) 587-8000. **$159-$410.** 616 W 7th St. Jct 7th St and Houston. Int corridors. **Pets:** Medium. $50 one-time fee/pet. Service with restrictions, supervision.
✕ 🖉 🗗 🖥 🍴 ➴ ✕

▼▼ ▼▼ ▼▼ Embassy Suites Hotel 🅻🅷
(918) 622-4000. **$99-$299.** 3332 S 79th E Ave. I-44, exit 231 eastbound; exit 232 (Memorial Dr) westbound, just sw. Int corridors. **Pets:** Medium. $25 deposit/room, $25 one-time fee/room. Service with restrictions, supervision.
✕ 🖉 🗗 🖥 🍴 ➴ ✕

▼▼ ▼▼ Guest House Suites Plus 🅂🅷
(918) 664-7241. **$80-$140.** 8181 E 41st St. 1.7 mi w of jct US 169. Ext corridors. **Pets:** Medium. Designated rooms, service with restrictions.
(ASK) ✕ 🖉 🗗 🖥 ➴

▼▼ ▼▼ Hampton Inn 🅂🅷
(918) 663-1000. **$79-$99, 3 day notice.** 3209 S 79th Ave E. I-44, exit 231 eastbound; exit 232 (Memorial Dr) westbound, just sw. Int corridors. **Pets:** Small. $25 one-time fee/pet. Service with restrictions, crate.
(ASK) 🅂🅾 ✕ 🖉 🅖 🗗 🖥 ➴

▼▼ ▼▼ Hilton Tulsa Southern Hills 🅻🅷
(918) 492-5000. **$89-$159.** 7902 S Lewis. I-44, exit 227, 3 mi s. Int corridors. **Pets:** Small. $75 one-time fee/room. Designated rooms, service with restrictions, supervision.
(ASK) 🅂🅾 ✕ 🖉 🅖 🗗 🖥 🍴 ➴

▼▼▼▼ Holiday Inn-International Airport SH
(918) 437-7660. **$84.** 1010 N Garnett Rd. I-244, exit 14 (Garnett Rd), just n. Int corridors. **Pets:** Accepted.
🅐🅢🅚 ✖ 🔊 🔊 📵 🖥 💻 🍴 🚬 ✖

▼▼▼▼ Holiday Inn Select SH
(918) 622-7000. **$79-$99.** 5000 E Skelly Dr. I-44, exit 229 (Yale Ave/SR 66); on south frontage road. Ext/int corridors. **Pets:** Medium. $25 one-time fee/room. Service with restrictions, crate.
🅐🅢🅚 🅢 ✖ 🔊 📵 🖥 💻 🍴 🚬

⧫⧫⧫ ▼▼▼▼ La Quinta Inn & Suites Tulsa Central SH
(918) 665-2630. **$89-$109.** 6030 E Skelly Dr. I-44, exit 230, just s. Int corridors. **Pets:** Small. Designated rooms, service with restrictions, supervision.
🆂🅰🆅🅴 🅢 ✖ 🔊 📵 🖥 🚬

▼▼▼ La Quinta Inn Tulsa (Airport) SH
(918) 836-3931. **$58-$105.** 35 N Sheridan Rd. I-244, exit 11 (Sheridan Rd). Ext corridors. **Pets:** Accepted.
🅐🅢🅚 🅢 ✖ 🔊 📵 🖥 🚬

⧫⧫⧫ ▼▼ La Quinta Inn Tulsa (East) SH
(918) 665-0220. **$71-$111.** 10829 E 41st St. US 169, exit E 41st St. Ext corridors. **Pets:** Medium. Service with restrictions.
🆂🅰🆅🅴 ✖ 🔊 📵 🖥 🚬

▼▼ La Quinta Inn Tulsa (South) SH
(918) 254-1626. **$68-$105.** 12525 E 52nd St S. Broken Arrow Expwy (SR 51), exit 129th and 51st sts, just s. Ext corridors. **Pets:** Medium. Service with restrictions.
🅐🅢🅚 ✖ 🔊 📵 🖥 🚬

▼▼ Microtel Inn & Suites SH
(918) 858-3775. **$55-$125.** 4531 E 21st St. Just w of 21st St and Yale Ave. Int corridors. **Pets:** Other species. $25 one-time fee/room. Service with restrictions, supervision.
🅐🅢🅚 🅢 ✖ 🔊 📵 🖥

⧫⧫⧫ ▼▼▼ Post Oak Lodge SH 🐾
(918) 425-2112. **$84-$109.** 5323 W 31st N. 0.7 mi w of jct Apache/41st St. Int corridors. **Pets:** Other species. $50 deposit/room. Designated rooms, service with restrictions, crate.
🆂🅰🆅🅴 🅢 ✖ 🍴 🚬 ✖

▼▼▼ Radisson Tulsa LH
(918) 627-5000. **$99.** 10918 E 41st St. Just e of US 169. Int corridors. **Pets:** Accepted.
🅐🅢🅚 🅢 ✖ 🔊 📵 🖥 💻 🍴 🚬 ✖

▼▼▼ Radisson Tulsa Airport SH
(918) 835-9911. **$119.** 2201 N 77th East Ave. SR 11, exit airport terminal. Int corridors. **Pets:** Accepted.
🅐🅢🅚 🅢 ✖ 📵 💻 🍴 🚬

▼▼ Red Roof Inn M
(918) 622-6776. **$39-$300.** 4717 S Yale Ave. I-44, exit 229 (Yale Ave), just s. Ext corridors. **Pets:** Medium, other species. Service with restrictions, supervision.
🅐🅢🅚 🅢 ✖ 📵 🚬

⧫⧫⧫ ▼▼▼▼ Renaissance Tulsa Hotel & Convention Center LH
(918) 307-2600. **$129-$229.** 6808 S 107th E Ave. Just ne of jct US 169 and 71st St. Int corridors. **Pets:** Accepted.
🆂🅰🆅🅴 🅢 ✖ 🔊 🔊 📵 🖥 💻 🍴 🚬 ✖

▼▼▼ Residence Inn by Marriott SH
(918) 250-4850. **$125-$165.** 11025 E 73rd St. US 169, exit 71st St, just e. Int corridors. **Pets:** Accepted.
🅐🅢🅚 🅢 ✖ 📵 🖥 🚬 ✖

▼▼ Sleep Inn & Suites Tulsa Central SH
(918) 663-2777. **$64-$89.** 8021 E 33rd St S. I-44, exit 231 eastbound; exit 232 (Memorial Dr) westbound, just sw. Int corridors. **Pets:** Small, dogs only. $25 daily fee/pet. Service with restrictions, supervision.
🅐🅢🅚 🅢 ✖ 🔊 🔊 📵 🖥 🚬 ✖

▼▼▼ Staybridge Suites SH
(918) 461-2100. **$109-$199.** 11111 E 73rd St. Just se of jct US 169 and 71st St. Int corridors. **Pets:** Small. $75 one-time fee/pet. Designated rooms, service with restrictions, crate.
🅐🅢🅚 ✖ 🔊 🔊 📵 🖥 💻 🚬 ✖

▼▼ StudioPLUS Tulsa Central SH
(918) 660-2890. **$59-$74.** 7901 E 31st Ct. I-44, exit 231 eastbound; exit 232 (Memorial Dr) westbound, just sw. Int corridors. **Pets:** Accepted.
🅐🅢🅚 🅢 ✖ 📵 🖥 🚬

END METROPOLITAN AREA

WOODWARD

⧫⧫⧫ ▼▼▼ Northwest Inn SH 🐾
(580) 256-7600. **$79-$89.** Hwy 270 S & 1st St. 1.4 mi s of jct US 183, 270, SR 3 and 34. Ext/int corridors. **Pets:** Medium. $10 one-time fee/room. Service with restrictions, supervision.
🆂🅰🆅🅴 ✖ 📵 🖥 🍴 🚬

ALBANY

▼▼▼ Comfort Suites SH
(541) 928-2053. **$65-$114.** 100 Opal Ct NE. I-5, exit 234A southbound; exit 234 northbound, just e. Int corridors. **Pets:** Accepted.

A$K S🐾 ✕ 🛗 🛎 🖥 🏊 ✕

▲▲▲ ▼▼▼ Econo Lodge M
(541) 926-0170. **$55-$84.** 1212 SE Price Rd. I-5, exit 233, just e, then just n. Ext corridors. **Pets:** Small. $10 one-time fee/pet. Service with restrictions, supervision.

SAVE S🐾 ✕ 🛎 🏊

▲▲▲ ▼▼▼ Holiday Inn Express Hotel & Suites SH ❀
(541) 928-8820. **$69-$119.** 105 Opal Ct NE. I-5, exit 234A southbound; exit 234 northbound, 0.4 mi e. Int corridors. **Pets:** Other species. $30 one-time fee/room. Service with restrictions, crate.

SAVE S🐾 ✕ 🛗 📶 🛗 🛎 🖥 🏊 ✕

▲▲▲ ▼▼▼ La Quinta Inn & Suites Albany SH
(541) 928-0921. **$75-$135.** 251 Airport Rd SE. I-5, exit 234B southbound; exit 234 northbound, just w. Int corridors. **Pets:** Other species. Service with restrictions, supervision.

SAVE S🐾 ✕ 📶 🛗 🛎 🖥 🏊 ✕

▲▲▲ ▼▼▼ Motel 6 #4124 M
(541) 926-4233. **$56-$92.** 2735 E Pacific Blvd. I-5, exit 234B southbound; exit 234 northbound, 0.5 mi w. Ext corridors. **Pets:** Medium, other species. Service with restrictions, supervision.

SAVE S🐾 ✕ 🛗 🛎

▲▲▲ ▼▼▼ Phoenix Inn Suites-Albany SH
(541) 926-5696. **$74-$109.** 3410 Spicer Rd SE. I-5, exit 233, just e. Int corridors. **Pets:** Accepted.

SAVE S🐾 ✕ 📶 🛗 🛎 🖥 🏊

▲▲▲ ▼▼▼ Quality Inn & Suites SH
(541) 928-5050. **$63-$83, 14 day notice.** 1100 Price Rd SE. I-5, exit 233, just e, then just n. Int corridors. **Pets:** Accepted.

SAVE S🐾 ✕ 🛗 📶 🛗 🛎 🖥 🏊

ASHLAND

▼▼▼ Ashland Springs Hotel SH
(541) 488-1700. **$89-$229.** 212 E Main St. Corner of 1st St; center. Int corridors. **Pets:** Medium, other species. $30 one-time fee/room. Designated rooms, service with restrictions, supervision.

A$K ✕ 🛗 🛎 🍽

▲▲▲ ▼▼▼ Best Western Bard's Inn SH
(541) 482-0049. **$80-$184.** 132 N Main St. Just n on SR 99 (N Main St) from Downtown Plaza. Ext/int corridors. **Pets:** Other species. $15 daily fee/pet. Designated rooms, service with restrictions, supervision.

SAVE S🐾 ✕ 🛗 🛗 🛎 🖥 🏊

▲▲▲ ▼▼▼ Best Western Windsor Inn M
(541) 488-2330. **$79-$169, 7 day notice.** 2520 Ashland St. I-5, exit 14, just e on SR 66. Ext corridors. **Pets:** Other species. $15 daily fee/pet. Service with restrictions, supervision.

SAVE S🐾 ✕ 🛗 🛗 🛎 🖥 🏊

▲▲▲ ▼▼◆ Cedarwood Inn M
(541) 488-2000. **$69-$119, 3 day notice.** 1801 Siskiyou Blvd. I-5, exit 11 northbound, 2.8 mi w; exit 14 southbound, just w on SR 66, 0.6 mi s on Tolman Creek Rd, then 0.6 mi w. Ext corridors. **Pets:** Small. $10 daily fee/pet. Service with restrictions, supervision.

SAVE ✕ 🛗 🛎 🏊

▲▲▲ ▼▼◆ Flagship Inn of Ashland M
(541) 482-2641. **$69-$119, 3 day notice.** 1193 Siskiyou Blvd. I-5, exit 14, 1.3 mi w on SR 66, just n on SR 99 (Siskiyou Blvd). Ext corridors. **Pets:** Medium. $10 daily fee/pet. Service with restrictions.

SAVE ✕ 📶 🛗 🖥 🏊

▲▲▲ ▼▼▼▼ La Quinta Inn & Suites Ashland SH
(541) 482-6932. **$99-$169.** 434 Valley View Rd. I-5, exit 19, just w. Int corridors. **Pets:** Other species. Service with restrictions, supervision.

SAVE ✕ 🛗 📶 🛗 🖥 🏊

▲▲▲ ▼▼▼▼ Plaza Inn & Suites At Ashland Creek SH
(541) 488-8900. **$109-$289.** 98 Central Ave. I-5, exit 19, 0.5 mi w, 1.9 mi s on SR 99 (N Main St), just e on Water St, then just n. Int corridors. **Pets:** Medium. $25 daily fee/room. Designated rooms, service with restrictions, supervision.

SAVE S🐾 ✕ 🛗 🖥

▲▲▲ ▼▼▼ Super 8 Motel-Ashland SH ❀
(541) 482-8887. **$80-$120.** 2350 Ashland St. I-5, exit 14, just w. Int corridors. **Pets:** Medium, dogs only. $10 daily fee/pet. Service with restrictions, supervision.

SAVE S🐾 ✕ 🛗 🏊

▲▲▲ ▼▼▼ Timbers Motel of Ashland M ❀
(541) 482-4242. **$46-$110, 3 day notice.** 1450 Ashland St. I-5, exit 14, 0.8 mi w. Ext corridors. **Pets:** Other species. Designated rooms.

SAVE S🐾 ✕ 🛗 🖥 🏊

AAA ▼▼▼▼ **Windmill Inn & Suites of Ashland** 🆂🅷 ❁
(541) 482-8310. **$79-$169.** 2525 Ashland St. I-5, exit 14, just e. Int corridors. **Pets:** Other species. Designated rooms, service with restrictions, supervision.
[SAVE] [S₂] [✕] [&M] [🖉] [🖢] [🖬] [🖵] [⇌] [✕]

ASTORIA

▼▼▼▼ **Astoria Holiday Inn Express Hotel &**
Suites 🆂🅷 ❁
(503) 325-6222. **$95-$279.** 204 W Marine Dr. On US 30; west side of town. Int corridors. **Pets:** $15 daily fee/pet. Designated rooms, service with restrictions, supervision.
[ASK] [S₂] [✕] [&M] [🖉] [🖢] [🖬] [🖵] [⇌] [✕]

AAA ▼◆▼ **Best Western Lincoln Inn** 🆂🅷 ❁
(503) 325-2205. **$79-$299.** 555 Hamburg Ave. On US 101/30; at east end of Young's Bay Bridge. Int corridors. **Pets:** Small, dogs only. $15 daily fee/pet. Designated rooms, service with restrictions, supervision.
[SAVE] [S₂] [✕] [🖢] [🖬] [🖵] [⇌] [✕]

▼▼ **Clementine's Bed & Breakfast** 🅱🅱
(503) 325-2005. **$85-$160, 7 day notice.** 847 Exchange St. At 8th and Exchange sts; in historic downtown. Int corridors. **Pets:** Dogs only. $15 one-time fee/room. Designated rooms, service with restrictions, supervision.
[✕] [🖬] [🖵] [🅐] [🇿]

AAA ▼▼ **Crest Motel** 🅼
(503) 325-3141. **$56-$138.** 5366 Leif Erickson Dr. 4 mi e of Astoria Bridge on US 30. Ext corridors. **Pets:** Other species. Supervision.
[SAVE] [✕] [🖬] [🖵] [🅐]

AAA ▼▼▼ **Red Lion Inn Astoria** 🅼
(503) 325-7373. **$85-$146.** 400 Industry St. Just w of Astoria Bridge on US 30, just n on Basin St (Caution: do not turn onto Astoria-Megler Bridge). Ext corridors. **Pets:** Accepted.
[SAVE] [S₂] [✕] [🖉] [🖬] [🖵] [🅐]

BAKER CITY

AAA ▼▼▼▼ **Best Western Sunridge Inn** 🆂🅷 ❁
(541) 523-6444. **$70-$88.** 1 Sunridge Ln. I-84, exit 304, just w. Int corridors. **Pets:** Large, other species. $50 deposit/room, $15 daily fee/room. Designated rooms, service with restrictions, supervision.
[SAVE] [S₂] [✕] [&M] [🖉] [🖬] [🖵] [🍴] [⇌]

▼▼▼ **Geiser Grand Hotel** 🆂🅷 ❁
(541) 523-1889. **$89-$109.** 1996 Main St. I-84, exit 304, 0.9 mi w on Campbell St, then 0.3 mi s; downtown. Int corridors. **Pets:** Other species. $75 deposit/room, $15 daily fee/pet. Service with restrictions, crate.
[ASK] [S₂] [✕] [🖢] [🍴]

BANDON

AAA ▼▼▼ **Bandon Inn** 🅼 ❁
(541) 347-4417. **$74-$139.** 355 Hwy 101. Center. Ext corridors. **Pets:** Medium. $15 daily fee/pet. Designated rooms, service with restrictions, supervision.
[SAVE] [S₂] [✕] [🖉] [🖬] [🖵] [🅐]

AAA ▼◆▼ **Best Western Inn at Face Rock** 🆂🅷
(541) 347-9441. **$157-$289.** 3225 Beach Loop Dr. 1 mi s on US 101, 0.8 mi w on Seabird Rd, then just s. Ext corridors. **Pets:** Accepted.
[SAVE] [✕] [🖉] [🖢] [🖬] [🖵] [🍴] [⇌] [✕] [🅐]

AAA ▼◆▼ **Driftwood Motel** 🅼
(541) 347-9022. **$65-$100.** 460 Hwy 101. On US 101; center. Ext corridors. **Pets:** Accepted.
[SAVE] [✕] [🖬] [🖵] [🅐]

BEND

▼▼ **Bend Riverside Motel Suites** 🅼
(541) 389-2363. **$58-$149.** 1565 NW Wall St. US 97, exit 137 (Revere Ave), just s. Ext corridors. **Pets:** Accepted.
[ASK] [S₂] [✕] [🖢] [🖬] [🖵] [⇌]

▼▼ **Bend Super 8 Motel** 🆂🅷
(541) 388-6888. **$60-$95.** 1275 S Business Hwy 97. US 97, exit 139 (Reed Market Rd), just e to SE 3rd St (Business Rt US 97), then just s. Int corridors. **Pets:** Other species. $10 one-time fee/room. Service with restrictions, supervision.
[ASK] [S₂] [✕] [🖬] [⇌]

AAA ▼◆▼ **Best Western Inn & Suites of Bend** 🆂🅷
(541) 382-1515. **$79-$139.** 721 NE 3rd St. Just s of jct US 20 on Business Rt US 97; at jct of Greely Ave. Ext corridors. **Pets:** Accepted.
[SAVE] [S₂] [✕] [🖉] [🖬] [🖵] [⇌]

▼▼▼▼ **Cricketwood Country Bed & Breakfast** 🅱🅱 ❁
(541) 330-0747. **$95-$135, 7 day notice.** 63520 Cricketwood Rd. 3.8 mi se on Deschutes Market Rd, 0.5 mi e on Hamehook Rd, 0.5 mi on Repine Rd, then just n. Ext/int corridors. **Pets:** Dogs only. $10 daily fee/room. Designated rooms, no service.
[✕] [🖬] [🖵]

▼▼ **Days Inn** 🆂🅷
(541) 383-3776. **$62-$94.** 849 NE 3rd St. US 97, just s of jct US 20. Ext corridors. **Pets:** Accepted.
[ASK] [S₂] [✕] [&M] [🖉] [🖢] [🖬] [🖵] [⇌]

▼▼▼▼ **Fairfield Inn & Suites by Marriott** 🆂🅷
(541) 318-1747. **$79-$149.** 1626 NW Wall St. US 97, exit 137 (Revere Ave), just s; downtown. Int corridors. **Pets:** Other species. $75 one-time fee/room. Service with restrictions, supervision.
[ASK] [S₂] [✕] [&M] [🖉] [🖢] [🖬] [🖵] [⇌] [✕]

AAA ▼▼▼▼ **Hampton Inn** 🆂🅷
(541) 388-4114. **$79-$129.** 15 NE Butler Market Rd. US 97, exit 136 (Butler Market Rd), just n. Ext corridors. **Pets:** Medium. $10 daily fee/pet. Designated rooms, service with restrictions, supervision.
[SAVE] [S₂] [✕] [🖢] [🖬] [🖵] [⇌]

AAA ▼▼◆ **Holiday Inn Express Hotel & Suites** 🆂🅷
(541) 317-8500. **$89-$159.** 20615 Grandview Dr. On US 97; north end of town. Int corridors. **Pets:** $20 one-time fee/room. Designated rooms, service with restrictions, crate.
[SAVE] [S₂] [✕] [&M] [🖉] [🖢] [🖬] [🖵] [⇌] [✕]

AAA ▼▼▼▼ **La Quinta Inn Bend** 🆂🅷
(541) 388-2227. **$69-$129.** 61200 S Business Hwy 97. Jct US 20 E, 3 mi s. Int corridors. **Pets:** Medium, other species. Designated rooms, service with restrictions, supervision.
[SAVE] [✕] [&M] [🖉] [🖢] [🖬] [🖵] [⇌]

AAA ▼▼▼ **Plaza Motel** 🅼 ❁
(541) 382-1621. **$50-$79.** 1430 NW Wall St. US 97, exit 137 (Revere Ave), just s; downtown. Ext corridors. **Pets:** Dogs only. $10 daily fee/pet. Designated rooms, service with restrictions, supervision.
[SAVE] [S₂] [✕] [🖬] [🖵]

AAA ▼▼▼ **Quality Inn** 🆂🅷
(541) 318-0848. **$69-$109.** 20600 Grandview Dr. On US 97; north end of town. Int corridors. **Pets:** Small. $10 daily fee/pet. Designated rooms, service with restrictions, supervision.
[SAVE] [S₂] [✕] [&M] [🖉] [🖢] [🖬] [🖵] [⇌]

AAA ▼▼▼ **Red Lion Inn/North** 🆂🅷
(541) 382-7011. **$74-$169.** 1415 NE 3rd St. US 97, just n of jct US 20. Ext corridors. **Pets:** Service with restrictions, supervision.
[SAVE] [S₂] [✕] [&M] [🖉] [🖢] [🖬] [🖵] [⇌]

The Riverhouse Resort Hotel 🏨 ☙
(541) 389-3111. **$88-$165.** 3075 N Business 97. US 97, exit 136 (Butler Market Rd) northbound, just n; exit 135B southbound. Ext/int corridors. **Pets:** Other species. Service with restrictions, supervision.

Shilo Inn Suites Hotel Bend 🆂🅷 ☙
(541) 389-9600. **$89-$250.** 3105 OB Riley Rd. 1.5 mi n on US 97 from jct US 20 E. Ext corridors. **Pets:** Other species. $25 one-time fee/room. Designated rooms, supervision.

Sleep Inn of Bend 🆂🅷
(541) 330-0050. **$69-$109.** 600 NE Bellevue. On US 20 E, 2 mi e of US 97. Int corridors. **Pets:** Small. $10 one-time fee/pet. Service with restrictions, supervision.

BOARDMAN

Econo Lodge 🅼
(541) 481-2375. **$59-$89.** 105 SW Front St. I-84, exit 164, just s. Ext corridors. **Pets:** Other species. Designated rooms, service with restrictions, supervision.

BROOKINGS

Best Western Beachfront Inn 🆂🅷
(541) 469-7779. **$119-$295.** 16008 Boat Basin Rd. Jct US 101, 0.6 mi w on Benham Ln. Ext corridors. **Pets:** Large. $10 daily fee/pet. Designated rooms, service with restrictions, supervision.

Westward Inn 🅼
(541) 469-7471. **$49-$89.** 1026 Chetco Ave. On US 101; north end of town. Ext corridors. **Pets:** Medium, dogs only. $8 daily fee/pet. Designated rooms, service with restrictions, supervision.

BURNS

Americas Best Inn 🅼
(541) 573-1700. **$47-$75.** 999 Oregon Ave. 1 mi w on US 395/20 from jct SR 78. Ext/int corridors. **Pets:** Accepted.

Days Inn Burns 🅼
(541) 573-2047. **$43-$68.** 577 W Monroe St. Just w on US 395/20 from jct SR 78. Ext corridors. **Pets:** Other species. $5 daily fee/pet. Designated rooms, service with restrictions, supervision.

Silver Spur Motel 🅼
(541) 573-2077. **$46-$53.** 789 N Broadway. US 395/20, at edge of town center. Ext corridors. **Pets:** Large, other species. $5 daily fee/pet. Designated rooms, service with restrictions, supervision.

CANNON BEACH

Cannon Beach Ecola Creek Lodge 🅼
(503) 436-2776. **$54-$225, 3 day notice.** 208 5th St. 0.3 mi w of US 101 via north exit to Ecola State Park. Ext corridors. **Pets:** Large, dogs only. $20 daily fee/pet. Designated rooms, service with restrictions, supervision.

Haystack Resort 🅼 ☙
(503) 436-1577. **$59-$269, 3 day notice.** 3339 S Hemlock St. US 101, exit Tolovana Park, just w. Ext corridors. **Pets:** Medium, dogs only. $10 daily fee/pet. Designated rooms, service with restrictions, supervision.

Inn at Cannon Beach 🅼 ☙
(503) 436-9085. **$89-$239, 7 day notice.** 3215 S Hemlock St. US 101, exit Tolovana Park, just w, then just n. Ext corridors. **Pets:** Other species. $10 daily fee/pet. Designated rooms, service with restrictions, supervision.

Ocean Lodge 🆂🅷 ☙
(503) 436-2241. **$179-$319, 7 day notice.** 2864 S Pacific. US 101, exit Tolovana Park, 1 mi s, then just w on Chisana. Ext/int corridors. **Pets:** Other species. $15 daily fee/pet. Designated rooms, supervision.

Surfsand Resort at Cannon Beach 🅼 ☙
(503) 436-2274. **$109-$339, 3 day notice.** Ocean Front & Gower. US 101, exit Cannon Beach (2nd exit); downtown. Ext corridors. **Pets:** Other species. $12 daily fee/pet. Service with restrictions, supervision.

Tolovana Inn 🅲🅾 ☙
(503) 436-2211. **$65-$379, 3 day notice.** 3400 S Hemlock St. 2 mi s off US 101 Beach Loop. Ext corridors. **Pets:** $12 daily fee/pet. Designated rooms, service with restrictions, supervision.

CANYONVILLE

Best Western Canyonville Inn & Suites 🆂🅷
(541) 839-4200. **$69-$160.** 200 Creekside Dr. I-5, exit 99, just w. Int corridors. **Pets:** Small. $15 daily fee/pet. Designated rooms, service with restrictions, supervision.

CASCADE LOCKS

Best Western Columbia River Inn 🆂🅷
(541) 374-8777. **$79-$169.** 735 WaNaPa St. I-84, exit 44. Int corridors. **Pets:** Medium, other species. $10 daily fee/pet. Designated rooms, service with restrictions, supervision.

CHEMULT

Dawson House Lodge 🅱🅱 ☙
(541) 365-2232. **$50-$120.** 109455 Hwy 97. US 97; center. Ext/int corridors. **Pets:** Medium. $5 daily fee/pet. Service with restrictions, supervision.

COOS BAY

Best Western Holiday Motel 🆂🅷
(541) 269-5111. **$84-$119.** 411 N Bayshore Dr. Just n of downtown on US 101. Ext/int corridors. **Pets:** Small, dogs only. $10 daily fee/pet. Service with restrictions, supervision.

Red Lion Hotel Coos Bay 🆂🅷
(541) 267-4141. **$87-$102.** 1313 N Bayshore Dr. 0.5 mi n of downtown on US 101. Ext corridors. **Pets:** Other species. $10 daily fee/room. Service with restrictions, supervision.

CORVALLIS

Best Western Grand Manor Inn 🆂🅷 ☙
(541) 758-8571. **$86-$111.** 925 NW Garfield. 1.5 mi n on 9th St; downtown. Int corridors. **Pets:** Dogs only. $100 deposit/room, $10 daily fee/pet. Designated rooms, service with restrictions, supervision.

Days Inn 🆂🅷
(541) 754-7474. **$54-$79.** 1113 NW 9th St. 1.3 mi n. Int corridors. **Pets:** Accepted.

ⒶⒶⒶ ♦♦♦♦ Holiday Inn Express On The River 🅂🄷
(541) 752-0800. **$109-$149.** 781 NE 2nd St. I-5, exit 228, 9.8 mi w on SR 34, then 0.4 mi nw. Int corridors. **Pets:** Other species. $25 daily fee/room. Designated rooms, service with restrictions, supervision.
[SAVE] [✕] [🔊] [⬥] [🚪] [💻] [🏊] [✕]

ⒶⒶⒶ ♦♦♦ Motel 6 #4243 🅂🄷
(541) 758-9125. **$56-$75.** 935 NW Garfield Ave. 1.5 mi n on 9th St. Int corridors. **Pets:** Medium, other species. Service with restrictions, supervision.
[SAVE] [S🔊] [✕] [&M] [🔊] [⬥] [🚪] [💻]

♦♦ Super 8 Motel 🅂🄷 🐾
(541) 758-8088. **$66-$85, 10 day notice.** 407 NW 2nd St. US 20, just n of jct SR 34; downtown. **Pets:** Medium, other species. $25 deposit/room. Designated rooms, service with restrictions, supervision.
[ASK] [S🔊] [✕] [&M] [🔊] [⬥] [🚪] [🏊]

COTTAGE GROVE

ⒶⒶⒶ ♦♦♦ Comfort Inn 🅂🄷
(541) 942-9747. **$69-$109.** 845 Gateway Blvd. I-5, exit 174, just w. Ext/int corridors. **Pets:** Other species. $10 daily fee/pet. Designated rooms, service with restrictions, supervision.
[SAVE] [S🔊] [✕] [🔊] [🚪] [💻] [🏊]

ⒶⒶⒶ ♦♦♦♦ Holiday Inn Express 🅂🄷
(541) 942-1000. **$79-$109.** 1601 Gateway Blvd. I-5, exit 174, just w. Int corridors. **Pets:** Medium, dogs only. $10 daily fee/pet. Service with restrictions, supervision.
[SAVE] [S🔊] [✕] [🔊] [⬥] [🚪] [💻] [🏊]

♦♦♦ Village Green Resort Ⓜ
(541) 942-2491. **$69-$149.** 725 Row River Rd. I-5, exit 174, just e. Ext corridors. **Pets:** Accepted.
[ASK] [S🔊] [✕] [🚪] [💻] [🏊]

CRESWELL

ⒶⒶⒶ ♦♦♦ Best Western Creswell Inn Ⓜ
(541) 895-3341. **$59-$149.** 345 E Oregon Ave. I-5, exit 182, just w. Ext corridors. **Pets:** Accepted.
[SAVE] [S🔊] [✕] [🚪] [💻] [🏊]

DALLAS

ⒶⒶⒶ ♦♦♦ Best Western Dallas Inn & Suites 🅂🄷
(503) 623-6000. **$80-$100.** 250 Orchard Dr. SR 223, just n. Int corridors. **Pets:** Accepted.
[SAVE] [S🔊] [✕] [&M] [🔊] [⬥] [🚪] [💻]

THE DALLES

ⒶⒶⒶ ♦♦♦ Best Western River City Inn 🅂🄷
(541) 296-9107. **$64-$104.** 112 W 2nd St. I-84, exit 84 eastbound, just se; exit 85 westbound, 0.8 mi nw; at Liberty and W 2nd St; downtown. Ext/int corridors. **Pets:** Small, other species. $10 daily fee/pet. Designated rooms, supervision.
[SAVE] [S🔊] [✕] [🔊] [🚪] [💻] [🏊]

ⒶⒶⒶ ♦♦♦ Comfort Inn Columbia Gorge 🅂🄷
(541) 298-2800. **$70-$145.** 351 Lone Pine Dr. I-84, exit 87, just n. Int corridors. **Pets:** Medium, other species. $10 daily fee/pet. Supervision.
[SAVE] [S🔊] [✕] [🚪] [💻] [🏊] [✕]

ⒶⒶⒶ ♦♦♦ Cousins Country Inn Ⓜ 🐾
(541) 298-5161. **$60-$129.** 2114 W 6th. I-84, exit 83 eastbound, just n; exit 84 westbound, just nw on W 2nd St, just sw on Webber St, then just n. Ext corridors. **Pets:** Other species. $10 daily fee/pet. Service with restrictions, supervision.
[SAVE] [S🔊] [✕] [&M] [🔊] [⬥] [🚪] [💻] [🍴] [🏊]

ⒶⒶⒶ ♦♦ Motel 6 #4268 🅂🄷
(541) 296-1191. **$49-$99.** 2500 W 6th St. I-84, exit 83 eastbound, just n; exit 84 westbound, just nw on w 2nd St, just sw on Webber St, then just n. Int corridors. **Pets:** Medium, other species. Service with restrictions, supervision.
[SAVE] [S🔊] [✕] [🚪] [🏊]

♦♦ Super 8 Motel 🅂🄷
(541) 296-6888. **$56-$89.** 609 Cherry Heights Rd. I-84, exit 84, just se. Int corridors. **Pets:** Accepted.
[ASK] [✕] [&M] [🔊] [⬥] [🚪] [🏊]

DEPOE BAY

ⒶⒶⒶ ♦♦♦ Crown Pacific Inn Ⓜ
(541) 765-7773. **$70-$95.** 50 NE Bechill St. Center. Ext/int corridors. **Pets:** Large. $10 daily fee/pet. Designated rooms, service with restrictions, supervision.
[SAVE] [S🔊] [✕] [🚪] [💻] [🄺]

ENTERPRISE

♦♦ Ponderosa Motel Ⓜ
(541) 426-3186. **$65-$69.** 102 E Greenwood St. Center. Ext corridors. **Pets:** Large, dogs only. $10 daily fee/pet. Service with restrictions, supervision.
[ASK] [S🔊] [✕] [&M] [🚪] [💻]

♦♦ The Wilderness Inn Ⓜ
(541) 426-4535. **$49-$72.** 301 W North St. Corner of NW 2nd. Ext corridors. **Pets:** Large, dogs only. $10 daily fee/pet. Service with restrictions, supervision.
[ASK] [S🔊] [✕] [🚪] [💻]

EUGENE

ⒶⒶⒶ ♦♦♦ Americas Best Value Inn Ⓜ
(541) 343-0730. **$44-$74.** 1140 W 6th Ave. I-5, exit 194B, 3 mi w on I-105, then just w on SR 99 N (6th Ave). Ext corridors. **Pets:** $8 daily fee/pet. Designated rooms, service with restrictions, supervision.
[SAVE] [✕] [🚪]

ⒶⒶⒶ ♦♦♦♦ Best Western Greentree Inn 🅂🄷 🐾
(541) 485-2727. **$87-$99.** 1759 Franklin Blvd. I-5, exit 194B southbound to I-105, follow signs to University of Oregon; exit 192 northbound, 1.2 mi w. Ext/int corridors. **Pets:** $50 deposit/pet. Service with restrictions, supervision.
[SAVE] [S🔊] [✕] [🚪] [💻] [🏊]

ⒶⒶⒶ ♦♦♦♦ Best Western New Oregon Motel 🅂🄷 🐾
(541) 683-3669. **$87-$99.** 1655 Franklin Blvd. I-5, exit 192 northbound, 1.3 mi w; exit 194B southbound to I-105, follow University of Oregon signs. Ext/int corridors. **Pets:** $50 deposit/pet. Service with restrictions, supervision.
[SAVE] [S🔊] [✕] [🔊] [🚪] [💻] [🏊] [✕]

ⒶⒶⒶ ♦♦♦ Days Inn 🅂🄷
(541) 342-6383. **$75-$120.** 1859 Franklin Blvd. I-5, exit 194B southbound to I-105, follow signs to University of Oregon; exit 192 northbound, 1 mi w. Ext/int corridors. **Pets:** Large, other species. Designated rooms, service with restrictions, supervision.
[SAVE] [S🔊] [✕] [🚪] [💻]

♦♦♦ Eugene/Springfield Residence Inn by Marriott 🅂🄷 🐾
(541) 342-7171. **$149-$159.** 25 Club Rd. I-5, exit 194B, 1.3 mi w on I-105, exit 2 (Coburg Rd), just s, just w on Martin Luther King Jr Blvd (Centennial Blvd), then just se. Int corridors. **Pets:** Other species. $75 one-time fee/room. Designated rooms, service with restrictions.
[ASK] [S🔊] [✕] [&M] [🔊] [⬥] [🚪] [💻] [🏊] [✕]

Express Inn & Suites Ⓜ
(541) 868-1520. **$55-$85, 3 day notice.** 990 W 6th Ave. I-5, exit 194B, 3 mi w on I-105, then just w on SR 99 N (6th Ave). Ext corridors. **Pets:** Small, dogs only. $5 daily fee/pet. Service with restrictions, supervision.

Hilton Eugene Ⓛ🄷
(541) 342-2000. **$129-$184.** 66 E 6th Ave. At 6th Ave and Oak St; center. Int corridors. **Pets:** Accepted.

La Quinta Inn & Suites Waterfront 🅂🄷
(541) 344-8335. **$99-$205.** 155 Day Island Rd. I-5, exit 194B, 1.3 mi w on I-105, exit 2 (Coburg Rd), go straight through jct Coburg Rd to Southwood Ln, just w, then 0.5 mi se on Country Club Rd; follow signs for Autzen Stadium. Int corridors. **Pets:** Other species. $50 deposit/room. Service with restrictions, supervision.

Motel 6-36 Ⓜ
(541) 687-2395. **$49-$63.** 3690 Glenwood Dr. I-5, exit 191, just sw. Ext corridors. **Pets:** Medium, other species. Service with restrictions, supervision.

Red Lion Hotel Eugene Ⓜ
(541) 342-5201. **$149-$159.** 205 Coburg Rd. I-5, exit 194B southbound, 1.3 mi w on I-105, exit 2 (Coburg Rd), then just n. Ext corridors. **Pets:** Accepted.

University Inn & Suites Ⓜ
(541) 342-4804. **$54-$129.** 1857 Franklin Blvd. I-5, exit 194B southbound, to I-105, follow signs to University of Oregon; exit 192 northbound, 1 mi w. Ext corridors. **Pets:** Small, dogs only. $50 deposit/room, $10 one-time fee/pet. Designated rooms, service with restrictions, supervision.

Valley River Inn 🅂🄷 ❀
(541) 743-1000. **$98-$190.** 1000 Valley River Way. I-5, exit 194B southbound, 2.5 mi w on I-105, exit 1, follow Valley River Center signs. Int corridors. **Pets:** Medium. Designated rooms, service with restrictions, supervision.

FLORENCE

Best Western Pier Point Inn 🅂🄷
(541) 997-7191. **$94-$219.** 85625 Hwy 101. Jct SR 126, 1 mi s. Ext corridors. **Pets:** Medium. $10 daily fee/pet. Supervision.

Le Chateau Motel Ⓜ
(541) 997-3481. **$54-$119.** 1084 Hwy 101 N. SR 126, just n. Ext corridors. **Pets:** Accepted.

Oceanbreeze Motel Ⓜ ❀
(541) 997-2642. **$49-$129.** 85165 Hwy 101 S. SR 126, 2 mi s; south end of Siuslaw Bridge. Ext corridors. **Pets:** Dogs only. $10 daily fee/pet. Designated rooms, supervision.

Old Town Inn Ⓜ
(541) 997-7131. **$64-$97.** 170 Hwy 101. SR 126, 0.5 mi s. Ext corridors. **Pets:** Large, dogs only. $7 one-time fee/pet. Designated rooms, service with restrictions, supervision.

Park Motel Ⓜ ❀
(541) 997-2634. **$59-$135.** 85034 Hwy 101 S. Jct SR 126 and US 101, 2.2 mi s. Ext corridors. **Pets:** Other species. $10 daily fee/pet. Service with restrictions, supervision.

FOREST GROVE

Best Western University Inn & Suites 🅂🄷
(503) 992-8888. **$79-$179.** 3933 Pacific Ave. East end of town on SR 8. Int corridors. **Pets:** Medium, dogs only. $10 daily fee/pet. Designated rooms, service with restrictions, supervision.

GARIBALDI

Comfort Inn by Choice Hotels 🅂🄷
(503) 322-3338. **$59-$119.** 502 Garibaldi Ave. On US 101 at jct 5th St; center. Int corridors. **Pets:** Accepted.

GEARHART

Gearhart By The Sea 🄲🄾
(503) 738-8331. **$126-$325, 3 day notice.** 1157 N Marion. 1 mi w off US 101, City Center exit, 1 mi w. Ext corridors. **Pets:** Supervision.

GLENEDEN BEACH

Salishan Spa & Golf Resort Ⓛ🄷 ❀
(541) 764-2371. **$139-$279, 3 day notice.** 7760 Hwy 101 N. Just e of US 101; center. Ext corridors. **Pets:** $25 one-time fee/room. Designated rooms, service with restrictions, supervision.

GLIDE

Illahee Inn Ⓜ
(541) 496-3338. **$70-$80.** 170 Bar L Ranch Rd. I-5, exit 124, 0.8 mi e, just n to SR 138, then e. Ext corridors. **Pets:** Medium. $10 one-time fee/room. Service with restrictions.

Steelhead Run B & B and Fine Art Gallery 🄱🄱 ❀
(541) 496-0563. **$69-$138, 7 day notice.** 23049 N Umpqua (Hwy 138). I-5, exit 124, 0.8 mi e, just n to SR 138, then 20.7 mi e; just e of MM 20. Ext/int corridors. **Pets:** Other species. $20 daily fee/room. Designated rooms, crate.

GOLD BEACH

Gold Beach Inn Ⓜ
(541) 247-7091. **$58-$189.** 29346 Ellensburg Ave. On US 101; center. Ext corridors. **Pets:** Accepted.

Inn of the Beachcomber Ⓜ
(541) 247-6691. **$99-$225.** 29266 Ellensburg Ave. On US 101; south end of town. Ext/int corridors. **Pets:** Accepted.

Jot's Resort Ⓜ ❀
(541) 247-6676. **$60-$195, 3 day notice.** 94360 Wedderburn Loop. Just w of US 101, north end of bridge. Ext corridors. **Pets:** Other species. $15 daily fee/pet. Designated rooms, service with restrictions, supervision.

▼▼▼▼ **Motel 6–4047** Ⓜ
(541) 247-4533. **$81-$91.** 94433 Jerry's Flat Rd. Just e of jct US 101. Ext corridors. **Pets:** Medium, other species. Service with restrictions, supervision.
[🐾] [✕] [📱] [Ӽ]

Ⓐ ▼▼▼ **Sand 'n Sea Motel** Ⓜ
(541) 247-6658. **$59-$139.** 29362 Ellensburg Ave. On US 101; center. Ext/int corridors. **Pets:** Accepted.
[SAVE] [🐾] [✕] [📱] [📺] [Ӽ]

GOVERNMENT CAMP

Ⓐ ▼▼▼▼ **Mt. Hood Inn** SH
(503) 272-3205. **$99-$189.** 87450 E Government Camp. 0.5 mi w of center. Int corridors. **Pets:** Dogs only. $10 daily fee/pet. Service with restrictions, supervision.
[SAVE] [✕] [🔊] [📱] [📺] [Ӽ]

GRANTS PASS

Ⓐ ▼▼▼ **Best Western Grants Pass Inn** Ⓜ
(541) 476-1117. **$85-$142.** 111 NE Agness Ave. I-5, exit 55, just w. Ext corridors. **Pets:** Other species. $10 deposit/room. Service with restrictions.
[SAVE] [🐾] [✕] [📱] [📱] [📺] [≈]

Ⓐ ▼▼▼ **Best Western Inn at the Rogue** SH
(541) 582-2200. **$65-$100.** 8959 Rogue River Hwy. I-5, exit 48, just w. Int corridors. **Pets:** Other species. $20 daily fee/pet. Designated rooms, service with restrictions, supervision.
[SAVE] [🐾] [✕] [📱] [📺] [≈]

Ⓐ ▼▼ **Buona Sera Inn** Ⓜ
(541) 476-4260. **$60-$115.** 1001 NE 6th St. I-5, exit 58, 1.2 mi s on SR 99. Ext corridors. **Pets:** Accepted.
[SAVE] [🐾] [✕] [📱] [📺]

Ⓐ ▼▼▼ **Comfort Inn** SH 🐾
(541) 479-8301. **$65-$130.** 1889 NE 6th St. I-5, exit 58, just s on SR 99. Int corridors. **Pets:** Other species. $10 one-time fee/pet. Service with restrictions, supervision.
[SAVE] [🐾] [✕] [📱] [📺] [≈]

Ⓐ ▼▼▼▼ **Holiday Inn Express** SH
(541) 471-6144. **$82-$119.** 105 NE Agness Ave. I-5, exit 55, just w. Int corridors. **Pets:** Medium. $10 daily fee/pet. Designated rooms, service with restrictions, supervision.
[SAVE] [✕] [📱] [📱] [📺]

Ⓐ ▼▼ **Knights Inn Motel** Ⓜ
(541) 479-5595. **$55-$69.** 104 SE 7th St. I-5, exit 58 southbound, 1.7 mi s on SR 99 to G St, 1 blk e, then just n; exit 55 northbound, 1.8 mi w on US 199 (Grants Pass Pkwy/Redwood Hwy), then just s. Ext corridors. **Pets:** Small, dogs only. $10 daily fee/pet. Service with restrictions, supervision.
[SAVE] [🐾] [✕] [📱]

Ⓐ ▼▼▼▼ **La Quinta Inn & Suites Grants Pass** SH 🐾
(541) 472-1808. **$80-$140.** 243 NE Morgan Ln. I-5, exit 58, 0.4 mi s on SR 99, just e on Hillcrest Dr to SR 99 northbound, then just n. Int corridors. **Pets:** Medium. Service with restrictions, supervision.
[SAVE] [🐾] [✕] [📱] [📱] [📱] [📺] [≈]

Ⓐ ▼▼▼ **Motel 6–253** Ⓜ
(541) 474-1331. **$45-$61.** 1800 NE 7th St. I-5, exit 58, 0.3 mi s on SR 99. Ext corridors. **Pets:** Medium, other species. Service with restrictions, supervision.
[🐾] [✕] [📱] [📱] [📱] [≈]

Ⓐ ▼▼▼ **Redwood Motel** Ⓜ 🐾
(541) 476-0878. **$58-$135.** 815 NE 6th St. I-5, exit 58, 1.2 mi s on SR 99. Ext corridors. **Pets:** Small, dogs only. $10 daily fee/pet. Designated rooms, service with restrictions, supervision.
[SAVE] [🐾] [✕] [📱] [📱] [📱] [📱] [📺] [≈]

Ⓐ ▼▼▼ **Riverside Inn Resort** SH
(541) 476-6873. **$99-$149.** 971 SE 6th St. I-5, exit 58, 2.5 mi s on SR 99. Ext corridors. **Pets:** Large, dogs only. $10 daily fee/pet. Designated rooms, service with restrictions, crate.
[SAVE] [🐾] [✕] [📱] [📱] [📱] [📱] [≈] [✕]

Ⓐ ▼▼ **Rodeway Inn** Ⓜ
(541) 479-2952. **$64-$79.** 1253 NE 6th St. I-5, exit 58, 0.8 mi s on SR 99. Ext corridors. **Pets:** Very small, dogs only. $30 deposit/pet, $10 daily fee/pet, $10 one-time fee/pet. Service with restrictions, supervision.
[SAVE] [🐾] [✕] [📱] [📱] [📺]

Ⓐ ▼▼ **Shilo Inn** SH 🐾
(541) 479-8391. **$52-$113.** 1880 NW 6th St. I-5, exit 58, 0.4 mi s on SR 99. Int corridors. **Pets:** Other species. $25 one-time fee/room. Designated rooms, supervision.
[SAVE] [🐾] [✕] [📱] [📱] [📱] [📺] [≈]

Ⓐ ▼▼▼ **Sunset Inn** Ⓜ
(541) 479-3305. **$55-$95.** 1400 NW 6th St. I-5, exit 58, 0.6 mi s on SR 99. Ext corridors. **Pets:** Small. $10 deposit/pet. Designated rooms, service with restrictions, supervision.
[SAVE] [🐾] [✕] [📱] [📺] [≈]

Ⓐ ▼▼▼ **Super 8 Motel-Grants Pass** Ⓜ 🐾
(541) 474-0888. **$60-$92.** 1949 NE 7th St. I-5, exit 58, 0.4 mi s on SR 99, just e on Hillcrest Dr to SR 99 northbound, then just n. Int corridors. **Pets:** Medium, dogs only. $25 deposit/room. Designated rooms, service with restrictions, supervision.
[SAVE] [🐾] [✕] [📱] [📱] [📺]

Ⓐ ▼▼▼ **Sweet Breeze Inn** Ⓜ
(541) 471-4434. **$58-$110.** 1627 NE 6th St. I-5, exit 58, 0.5 mi s on SR 99. Ext/int corridors. **Pets:** Small, dogs only. $5 daily fee/pet. Designated rooms, supervision.
[SAVE] [🐾] [✕] [📱] [📱]

Ⓐ ▼▼▼ **Travelodge** Ⓜ
(541) 479-6611. **$59-$74.** 1950 NW Vine St. I-5, exit 58, just s on SR 99. Ext corridors. **Pets:** Accepted.
[SAVE] [🐾] [✕] [📱] [📱] [📺]

HALSEY

▼▼ **Pioneer Villa TraveLodge** Ⓜ
(541) 369-2804. **$72-$75.** 33180 SR 228. I-5, exit 216, just e. Ext corridors. **Pets:** $5 daily fee/pet. Supervision.
[ASK] [🐾] [✕] [📱] [📺] [🍴] [≈]

HERMISTON

Ⓐ ▼▼▼ **Oak Tree Inn** SH
(541) 567-2330. **$71.** 1110 SE 4th St. 0.4 mi s on US 395, just w. Int corridors. **Pets:** Small. $10 daily fee/pet. Service with restrictions, supervision.
[SAVE] [🐾] [✕] [📱] [📺]

▼▼▼▼ **Oxford Suites** SH
(541) 564-8000. **$95-$169.** 1050 N 1st St. 0.3 mi n on US 395. Int corridors. **Pets:** Accepted.
[✕] [📱] [🔊] [📱] [📱] [📺] [≈]

HINES

▼▼▼ **Best Western Rory & Ryan Inns** SH
(541) 573-5050. **$69-$100.** 534 Hwy 20 N. On US 20 (Hines/Burns). Int corridors. **Pets:** Dogs only. $10 one-time fee/room. Designated rooms, service with restrictions, supervision.
[ASK] [🐾] [✕] [📱] [📱] [📱] [📺] [≈]

HOOD RIVER

AAA ▼▼▼▼ **Best Western Hood River Inn** 🆂🅷 ❀
(541) 386-2200. **$79-$159.** 1108 E Marina Way. I-84, exit 64, just n, then just e. Int corridors. **Pets:** Large, dogs only. $12 daily fee/room. Designated rooms, supervision.
🆂🅰🆅🅴 🆂🅳 ⊠ 🅖🅜 🈸 🯁 🯄 🍽 ⟿ ⊠

AAA ▼▼▼▼ **Columbia Gorge Hotel** 🅲🅸 ❀
(541) 386-5566. **$159-$399, 14 day notice.** 4000 Westcliff Dr. I-84, exit 62, just w of overpass. Int corridors. **Pets:** Dogs only. $35 one-time fee/pet. Designated rooms, service with restrictions, crate.
🆂🅰🆅🅴 ⊠ 🯁 🍽

AAA ▼▼ **Vagabond Lodge** 🅼 ❀
(541) 386-2992. **$51-$87.** 4070 Westcliff Dr. I-84, exit 62, just n, then just w. Ext corridors. **Pets:** Medium. $5 daily fee/pet. Designated rooms, service with restrictions, supervision.
🆂🅰🆅🅴 ⊠ 🯁 🯄

JACKSONVILLE

AAA ▼▼▼▼ **Jacksonville Inn** 🅲🅸
(541) 899-1900. **$149-$189, 3 day notice.** 175 E California St. On SR 238; at California (SR 238) and 5th sts; center. Ext/int corridors. **Pets:** Accepted.
🆂🅰🆅🅴 🆂🅳 ⊠ 🯁 🯄 🍽

▼▼ **The Stage Lodge** 🅼
(541) 899-3953. **$108-$195, 8 day notice.** 830 N 5th St. On N 5th St (SR 238), 0.3 mi ne. Ext corridors. **Pets:** Medium. $20 daily fee/pet. Service with restrictions, supervision.
🅰🆂🅺 🆂🅳 ⊠ 🅖🅜 ⟳ 🯁 🯄

JOHN DAY

AAA ▼▼▼ **Best Western John Day Inn** 🅼
(541) 575-1700. **$79-$135.** 315 W Main St. Just w on jct US 26 and 395. Ext corridors. **Pets:** Small, dogs only. $10 daily fee/pet. Designated rooms, service with restrictions, supervision.
🆂🅰🆅🅴 🆂🅳 ⟳ 🯁 🯄

AAA ▼▼ **Dreamers Lodge** 🅼
(541) 575-0526. **$46-$66.** 144 N Canyon Blvd. Just n of jct US 26 and 395. Ext corridors. **Pets:** Medium, dogs only. $5 daily fee/pet. Service with restrictions, supervision.
🆂🅰🆅🅴 🆂🅳 ⊠ 🯁 🯄

KEIZER

AAA ▼▼▼▼ **Wittenberg Inn & Conference Center** 🆂🅷
(503) 390-4733. **$89-$99.** 5188 Wittenberg Ln N. I-5, exit 260B southbound; exit 260 northbound, 1.5 mi w on Chemawa Rd and Lockhaven Dr, then just s on River Rd. Int corridors. **Pets:** $10 daily fee/pet. Service with restrictions, supervision.
🆂🅰🆅🅴 🆂🅳 ⊠ 🅖🅜 ⟳ 🯁 🯄 ⟿ ⊠

KLAMATH FALLS

AAA ▼▼▼ **Best Western Klamath Inn** 🅼
(541) 882-1200. **$99-$130.** 4061 S 6th St. Just w on 6th St (SR 140) from jct SR 140 E/39 S and SR 39 N/US 97 business route. Ext corridors. **Pets:** Accepted.
🆂🅰🆅🅴 🆂🅳 ⊠ ⟳ 🯁 🯄 ⟿

AAA ▼▼ **Golden West Motel** 🅼 ❀
(541) 882-1758. **$44-$79.** 6402 S 6th St. S 6th St (SR 140) at eastern edge of town. Ext corridors. **Pets:** $15 one-time fee/room. Service with restrictions, supervision.
🆂🅰🆅🅴 ⊠ 🯁 🯄

AAA ▼▼ **Majestic Inn & Suites** 🅼
(541) 883-7771. **$35-$95.** 5543 S 6th St. 1 mi e on 6th St (SR 140) from jct SR 140 E/39 S and SR 39 N/US 97 business route. Ext corridors. **Pets:** Medium. $5 daily fee/pet. Designated rooms, service with restrictions, supervision.
🆂🅰🆅🅴 🆂🅳 ⊠ 🯁

AAA ▼▼ **Maverick Motel** 🅼
(541) 882-6688. **$39-$99.** 1220 Main St. US 97 N to City Center exit, 0.3 mi e. Ext corridors. **Pets:** Medium. $5 daily fee/pet. Designated rooms, service with restrictions, supervision.
🆂🅰🆅🅴 🆂🅳 ⊠ 🯁

◆ **Motel 6—226** 🆂🅷
(541) 884-2110. **$45-$65.** 5136 S 6th St. 0.5 mi e on 6th St E (SR 140) from jct SR 39/US 97 business route. Ext corridors. **Pets:** Medium, other species. Service with restrictions, supervision.
🆂🅳 ⊠ 🅖🅜 ⟳ ⟳ 🯁 ⟿

AAA ▼▼ **Oregon 8 Motel** 🅼
(541) 883-3431. **$48-$60.** 5225 Hwy 97 N. On US 97; between MM 270 and 271; east side of highway. Ext corridors. **Pets:** $50 deposit/pet, $5 daily fee/pet. Designated rooms, no service, supervision.
🆂🅰🆅🅴 🆂🅳 ⊠ 🯁 🯄

AAA ▼▼ **Quality Inn** 🅼
(541) 882-4666. **$75-$85.** 100 Main St. Just e of US 97, exit City Center. Ext corridors. **Pets:** $50 deposit/pet, $10 daily fee/pet. Designated rooms, service with restrictions, supervision.
🆂🅰🆅🅴 🆂🅳 ⊠ 🅖🅜 ⟳ ⟳ 🯁 🯄 🍽 ⟿

▼▼ **Red Lion Inn Klamath Falls** 🅼
(541) 882-8864. **$101-$129.** 3612 S 6th St. 0.3 mi w on 6th St (SR 140) from jct SR 140 E/39 S and SR 39 N/US 97 business route. Ext corridors. **Pets:** Large, other species. Service with restrictions, crate.
⊠ ⟳ ⟳ 🯁 🯄 ⟿ ⊠

▼▼▼ **The Running Y Ranch** 🆂🅷
(541) 850-5500. **$119-$189, 3 day notice.** 5500 Running Y Rd. On 6th St (SR 140), 7.2 mi n from jct US 66 and SR 140. Int corridors. **Pets:** Accepted.
🅰🆂🅺 🆂🅳 ⊠ 🅖🅜 ⟳ ⟳ 🯁 🯄 🍽 ⟿ ⊠

▼▼▼ **Shilo Inn Klamath Falls** 🆂🅷 ❀
(541) 885-7980. **$119-$155.** 2500 Almond St. North end of US 97. Int corridors. **Pets:** Other species. $25 one-time fee/room. Supervision.
🅰🆂🅺 🆂🅳 ⊠ 🅖🅜 ⟳ ⟳ 🯁 🯄 🍽 ⟿ ⊠

▼▼ **Super 8 Motel** 🆂🅷
(541) 884-8880. **$66-$76.** 3805 Hwy 97. On US 97, 2 mi n. Int corridors. **Pets:** Accepted.
🆂🅳 ⊠ 🅖🅜 🯁

LA GRANDE

▼▼ **Americas Best Value Sandman Inn** 🆂🅷 ❀
(541) 963-3707. **$74-$179.** 2410 E R Ave. I-84, exit 261, just s on Albany, then just e. Int corridors. **Pets:** Other species. $25 one-time fee/room. Designated rooms, supervision.
🅰🆂🅺 🆂🅳 ⊠ ⟳ 🯁 ⟿

AAA ▼▼ **Royal Motor Inn** 🅼
(541) 963-4154. **$44-$50.** 1510 Adams Ave. I-84, exit La Grande on US 30, just n of jct SR 82; downtown. Ext corridors. **Pets:** Dogs only. Designated rooms, supervision.
🆂🅰🆅🅴 ⊠ ⟳ 🯁

LAKEVIEW

AAA ▼▼▼ **Best Western Skyline Motor Lodge** 🅼
(541) 947-2194. **$89, 3 day notice.** 414 N G St. Jct US 395 and SR 140. Ext corridors. **Pets:** Medium, other species. $10 one-time fee/pet. Designated rooms, service with restrictions, supervision.
🆂🅰🆅🅴 🆂🅳 ⊠ ⟳ 🯁 🯄 ⟿

LA PINE

▼▼▼ **Best Western Newberry Station** 🆂🅷
(541) 536-5130. **$79-$129.** 16515 Reed Rd. North end of town, just off SR 97. Int corridors. **Pets:** Small, dogs only. $15 deposit/room, $10 one-time fee/room. Service with restrictions, supervision.

Ⓐ🆂🅺 🆂 ✖ 🔥ᴹ ✍ 🛏 🖥 🏊

LINCOLN CITY

▼▼ **Ashley Inn & Suites** 🆂🅷 🐾
(541) 996-7500. **$69-$149.** 3430 NE Hwy 101. North side on US 101. Int corridors. **Pets:** Dogs only. $20 one-time fee/pet. Designated rooms, service with restrictions, supervision.

Ⓐ🆂🅺 🆂 ✖ ✍ 🛏 🖥 🏊 ✖

🔱 ▼▼ **Coho Inn** Ⓜ
(541) 994-3684. **$61-$250.** 1635 NW Harbor Ave. US 101, exit N 17th St, just w. Ext corridors. **Pets:** Small. $10 daily fee/pet. Designated rooms, service with restrictions, supervision.

🆂 ✖ 🛏 🖥 🏊 ✖ ✍

🔱 ▼▼▼ **Comfort Inn by Choice Hotels-Lincoln City** 🆂🅷
(541) 994-8155. **$79-$269.** 136 NE Hwy 101. On US 101 near D River. Int corridors. **Pets:** Accepted.

🆂 🆂 ✖ 🛏 🖥

🔱 ▼▼ **Econo Lodge** 🆂🅷
(541) 994-5281. **$40-$129.** 1713 NW 21st St. US 101, just w on 21st St. Int corridors. **Pets:** Small, dogs only. $50 deposit/pet, $10 daily fee/pet. Designated rooms, service with restrictions, supervision.

🆂 ✖ 🛏 🖥 ✍

🔱 ▼▼ **Lincoln City Inn** 🆂🅷
(541) 996-4400. **$40-$90.** 1091 SE 1st St. On US 101 at D River. Int corridors. **Pets:** Accepted.

🆂 ✖ 🔥ᴹ ✍ 🛏 🖥

▼▼ **Looking Glass Inn** Ⓜ 🐾
(541) 996-3996. **$69-$129, 3 day notice.** 861 SW 51st St. South side, w of US 101, exit 51 St. Ext corridors. **Pets:** Dogs only. $10 daily fee/pet. Designated rooms, service with restrictions, crate.

Ⓐ🆂🅺 🆂 ✖ 🛏 🖥 ✍

▼▼ **Motel 6-4172** 🆂🅷
(541) 996-2900. **Call for rates.** 3517 NW Hwy 101. North end of town. Int corridors. **Pets:** Medium, other species. Service with restrictions, supervision.

✖ 🔥ᴹ ✍ 🛏

🔱 ▼▼▼ **The O'dysius Hotel** 🆂🅷 🐾
(541) 994-4121. **$179-$345, 3 day notice.** 120 NW Inlet Ct. On US 101 at D River; center. Int corridors. **Pets:** Small, other species. $10 daily fee/pet. Designated rooms, service with restrictions, supervision.

🆂 🆂 ✖ 🏊 🛏 🖥 ✍

🔱 ▼▼▼ **Palace Inn & Suites** 🆂🅷
(541) 996-9466. **$69-$179.** 550 SE Hwy 101. Center. Int corridors. **Pets:** Accepted.

🆂 🆂 ✖ 🛏 🖥 ✖

🔱 ▼▼ **Water's Edge** 🅒🅞
(541) 996-9200. **$99-$199.** 5201 SW Hwy 101. South end of town. Ext corridors. **Pets:** Medium. $75 deposit/room, $10 daily fee/room, $25 one-time fee/room. Designated rooms, supervision.

🆂 🆂 ✖ ✍ 🛏 🖥 ✍

MADRAS

🔱 ▼▼▼ **Best Western Madras Inn** Ⓜ
(541) 475-6141. **$79-$109.** 12 SW 4th St. On US 97/26 southbound; downtown. Ext corridors. **Pets:** Medium, other species. $10 daily fee/pet. Service with restrictions, supervision.

🆂 🆂 ✖ 🔥ᴹ 🏊 ✍ 🛏 🖥 🏊

🔱 ▼ **Budget Inn** Ⓜ
(541) 475-3831. **$59-$79.** 133 NE 5th St. On US 97/26 northbound; downtown. Ext corridors. **Pets:** Medium. $10 daily fee/pet. Supervision.

🆂 🆂 ✖ 🛏

MCMINNVILLE

🔱 ▼▼▼ **Best Western Vineyard Inn** 🆂🅷
(503) 472-4900. **$98-$130, 30 day notice.** 2035 S SR 99 W. Jct SR 99 W and 18. Int corridors. **Pets:** Accepted.

🆂 🆂 ✖ 🔥ᴹ 🛏 🖥 🏊

▼▼▼▼ **Red Lion Inn & Suites** 🆂🅷
(503) 472-1500. **$105-$145, 30 day notice.** 2535 NE Cumulus Ave. Jct SR 99 W, 3.7 mi e on SR 18. Int corridors. **Pets:** Accepted.

Ⓐ🆂🅺 🆂 ✖ 🔥ᴹ 🛏 🖥 🏊 ✖

🔱 ▼▼ **Safari Motor Inn** Ⓜ
(503) 472-5187. **$69-$89.** 381 NE Hwy 99W. North end of SR 99 W. Ext corridors. **Pets:** Medium. $10 daily fee/pet. Service with restrictions, supervision.

🆂 🆂 ✖ 🛏 🖥

MEDFORD

🔱 ▼▼▼▼ **Best Western Horizon Inn** Ⓜ
(541) 779-5085. **$77-$119.** 1154 E Barnett Rd. I-5, exit 27, just e. Ext corridors. **Pets:** $20 one-time fee/pet. Designated rooms, service with restrictions, supervision.

🆂 🆂 ✖ 🏊 ✍ 🛏 🖥 🏊 ✖

🔱 ▼▼ **Cedar Lodge Motor Inn** Ⓜ
(541) 773-7361. **$55-$75.** 518 N Riverside Ave. I-5, exit 27, 0.5 mi w on Barnett Rd, then 1.2 mi n on SR 99. Ext corridors. **Pets:** $5 daily fee/pet. Service with restrictions, supervision.

🆂 🆂 ✖ 🛏 🖥

🔱 ▼▼ **Knights Inn** Ⓜ
(541) 773-3676. **$55-$65.** 500 N Riverside Ave. I-5, exit 27, 0.4 mi w on Barnett Rd, then 1.2 mi n on SR 99. Ext corridors. **Pets:** Accepted.

🆂 🆂 ✖ 🔥ᴹ 🏊 🛏 🖥 🏊

🔱 ▼▼▼ **Medford Inn and Suites** 🆂🅷
(541) 773-8266. **$55-$90.** 1015 S Riverside Ave. I-5, exit 27, 0.4 mi w, then just n. Ext corridors. **Pets:** Accepted.

🆂 🆂 ✖ 🏊 ✍ 🛏 🖥

▼ **Motel 6-Medford North-739** Ⓜ
(541) 779-0550. **$51-$65.** 2400 Biddle Rd. I-5, exit 30 northbound, just s; exit southbound, follow signs for Biddle Rd. Ext corridors. **Pets:** Medium, other species. Service with restrictions, supervision.

🆂 ✖ 🔥ᴹ 🏊 ✍ 🛏 🏊

▼ **Motel 6-Medford South-89** Ⓜ
(541) 773-4290. **$47-$59.** 950 Alba Dr. I-5, exit 27, just e on Barnett Rd, then just n. Ext corridors. **Pets:** Medium, other species. Service with restrictions, supervision.

🆂 ✖ 🔥ᴹ 🏊 ✍ 🛏 🏊

🔱 ▼▼▼ **Red Lion Hotel Medford** Ⓜ
(541) 779-5811. **$119.** 200 N Riverside Ave. I-5, exit 27, 0.4 mi w on Barnett Rd, then 1 mi n. Ext corridors. **Pets:** Accepted.

🆂 🆂 ✖ 🔥ᴹ ✍ 🛏 🖥 🍴 🏊

▼▼ **Shilo Inn Medford** 🆂🅷 🐾
(541) 770-5151. **$72-$103.** 2111 Biddle Rd. I-5, exit 30 northbound, just s; exit southbound, follow signs for Biddle Rd, then just s. Int corridors. **Pets:** Other species. $25 one-time fee/room. Supervision.

Ⓐ🆂🅺 🆂 ✖ 🛏 🖥

▼▼ **Super 8 Inn & Suites** Ⓜ
(541) 664-5888. **Call for rates.** 4999 Biddle Rd. I-5, exit 33, just e. Int corridors. **Pets:** Accepted.

✖ ✍ 🛏 🏊

(AAA) ▼▼ Windmill Inn of Medford SH ❖
(541) 779-0050. **$69-$129.** 1950 Biddle Rd. I-5, exit 30 northbound, just s; exit southbound, follow signs for Biddle Rd, then just s. Int corridors. **Pets:** Other species. Service with restrictions, crate.
⟦SAVE⟧ ⟦S⟧ ⟦✕⟧ ⟦&M⟧ ⟦⟧ ⟦⟧ ⟦⟧ ⟦⟧ ⟦⟧ ⟦✕⟧

MYRTLE POINT

(AAA) ▼ Myrtle Trees Motel M
(541) 572-5811. **$53-$59, 7 day notice.** 1010 8th St (Hwy 42). On SR 42, 0.5 mi e. Ext corridors. **Pets:** Accepted.
⟦SAVE⟧ ⟦✕⟧ ⟦⟧ ⟦⟧

NEWBERG

▼▼ Shilo Inn Suites-Newberg SH ❖
(503) 537-0303. **$63-$113.** 501 Sitka Ave. On SR 99 W. Int corridors. **Pets:** Other species. $25 one-time fee/room. Supervision.
⟦ASK⟧ ⟦S⟧ ⟦✕⟧ ⟦⟧ ⟦⟧ ⟦⟧ ⟦⟧ ⟦✕⟧

◆◆ Travelodge Suites SH
(503) 537-5000. **$63-$95.** 2816 Portland Rd. North end on SR 99 W; behind Finnigan's Restaurant. **Pets:** Medium. $7 daily fee/pet. Designated rooms, service with restrictions, supervision.
⟦ASK⟧ ⟦S⟧ ⟦✕⟧ ⟦⟧ ⟦⟧ ⟦⟧ ⟦✕⟧

NEWPORT

(AAA) ▼▼▼ The Best Western Agate Beach Inn SH ❖
(541) 265-9411. **$84-$135.** 3019 N Coast Hwy. US 20, 1.5 mi n on US 101. Int corridors. **Pets:** Other species. $15 one-time fee/pet. Designated rooms, service with restrictions, supervision.
⟦SAVE⟧ ⟦S⟧ ⟦✕⟧ ⟦⟧ ⟦⟧ ⟦⟧ ⟦⟧ ⟦⟧ ⟦✕⟧ ⟦⟧

(AAA) ▼▼ Econo Lodge M
(541) 265-7723. **$44-$99.** 606 SW Coast Hwy 101. 0.5 mi s of US 20. Ext/int corridors. **Pets:** Accepted.
⟦SAVE⟧ ⟦S⟧ ⟦✕⟧ ⟦⟧ ⟦⟧ ⟦⟧

(AAA) ▼▼▼▼ Hallmark Resort Oceanfront SH ❖
(541) 265-2600. **$89-$189.** 744 SW Elizabeth St. US 20, 0.7 mi s on US 101, just w on SW Bay St. Ext corridors. **Pets:** $15 daily fee/pet. Designated rooms, service with restrictions, crate.
⟦SAVE⟧ ⟦S⟧ ⟦✕⟧ ⟦&M⟧ ⟦⟧ ⟦⟧ ⟦⟧ ⟦⟧ ⟦⟧ ⟦✕⟧ ⟦⟧

(AAA) ▼▼▼▼ The Landing at Newport CO ❖
(541) 574-6777. **$89-$358.** 890 SE Bay Blvd. 0.5 mi e on US 20 from jct US 101, just s on John Moore Rd. Ext corridors. **Pets:** Medium. $75 deposit/room, $10 daily fee/room, $25 one-time fee/room. Designated rooms, service with restrictions, supervision.
⟦SAVE⟧ ⟦S⟧ ⟦✕⟧ ⟦⟧ ⟦⟧ ⟦⟧

(AAA) ▼▼▼▼ La Quinta Inn & Suites Newport SH ❖
(541) 867-7727. **$77-$163.** 45 SE 32nd St. US 101, just s of Yaquina Bay Bridge. Int corridors. **Pets:** Other species. Designated rooms, service with restrictions, supervision.
⟦SAVE⟧ ⟦S⟧ ⟦✕⟧ ⟦&M⟧ ⟦⟧ ⟦⟧ ⟦⟧ ⟦⟧ ⟦⟧ ⟦✕⟧

◆▼ Shilo Inn Oceanfront Resort SH ❖
(541) 265-7701. **$94-$200.** 536 SW Elizabeth St. US 20, 0.5 mi s on US 101, just w on SW Falls St. Ext/int corridors. **Pets:** Other species. $25 one-time fee/room. Designated rooms, supervision.
⟦ASK⟧ ⟦S⟧ ⟦✕⟧ ⟦⟧ ⟦⟧ ⟦⟧ ⟦⟧ ⟦⟧ ⟦⟧

(AAA) ▼◆◆ Waves of Newport Motel and Vacation Rentals M
(541) 265-4661. **$58-$113, 3 day notice.** 820 NW Coast St. US 101, 0.6 mi n from jct US 20, just w on NW 11th St, then just s. Ext corridors. **Pets:** Small, dogs only. $5 daily fee/pet. Service with restrictions, supervision.
⟦SAVE⟧ ⟦✕⟧ ⟦⟧ ⟦⟧ ⟦⟧

(AAA) ▼▼ The Whaler Motel M ❖
(541) 265-9261. **$87-$167.** 155 SW Elizabeth St. Just s on US 101 from jct US 20, just w on SW 2nd St. Ext corridors. **Pets:** Dogs only. $5 daily fee/pet. Designated rooms, service with restrictions, supervision.
⟦SAVE⟧ ⟦S⟧ ⟦✕⟧ ⟦&M⟧ ⟦⟧ ⟦⟧ ⟦⟧ ⟦⟧ ⟦⟧ ⟦⟧

NORTH BEND

(AAA) ▼▼ Comfort Inn M
(541) 756-3191. **$79-$159.** 1503 Virginia Ave. 0.5 mi w of US 101. Ext/int corridors. **Pets:** Small, dogs only. $1500.00 daily fee/pet. Designated rooms, service with restrictions, supervision.
⟦SAVE⟧ ⟦S⟧ ⟦✕⟧ ⟦&M⟧ ⟦⟧ ⟦⟧ ⟦⟧ ⟦⟧

OAKLAND

(AAA) ▼▼▼ Best Western Rice Hill M
(541) 849-3335. **$59-$99.** 621 John Long Rd. I-5, exit 148, just e. Ext corridors. **Pets:** Other species. $10 daily fee/pet. Service with restrictions, crate.
⟦SAVE⟧ ⟦S⟧ ⟦✕⟧ ⟦⟧ ⟦⟧ ⟦⟧ ⟦✕⟧

OAKRIDGE

(AAA) ▼▼▼ Best Western Oakridge Inn M
(541) 782-2212. **$69-$99.** 47433 Hwy 58. West end of SR 58. Ext corridors. **Pets:** Large, dogs only. $10 daily fee/pet. Service with restrictions, supervision.
⟦SAVE⟧ ⟦S⟧ ⟦✕⟧ ⟦⟧ ⟦&⟧ ⟦⟧ ⟦⟧ ⟦⟧

(AAA) ▼▼ Cascade Motel M
(541) 782-2489. **$44-$54.** 47487 SR 58. Center. Ext corridors. **Pets:** Medium. $10 one-time fee/pet. Designated rooms, service with restrictions, supervision.
⟦SAVE⟧ ⟦S⟧ ⟦✕⟧ ⟦⟧ ⟦⟧

ONTARIO

◆▼▼▼ Creek House Bed & Breakfast Inn BB ❖
(541) 823-0717. **$89-$119, 14 day notice.** 717 SW 2nd St. I-84, exit 376A, 0.8 mi w on Idaho Ave, then 0.4 mi s. Int corridors. **Pets:** Dogs only. $100 deposit/room. Service with restrictions, supervision.
⟦ASK⟧ ⟦S⟧ ⟦✕⟧ ⟦⟧ ⟦⟧ ⟦⟧ ⟦⟧

(AAA) ▼▼▼▼ Holiday Inn-Ontario, OR SH
(541) 889-8621. **$74-$119.** 1249 Tapadera Ave. I-84, exit 376B, just ne. Int corridors. **Pets:** Accepted.
⟦SAVE⟧ ⟦S⟧ ⟦✕⟧ ⟦⟧ ⟦&⟧ ⟦⟧ ⟦⟧ ⟦⟧ ⟦⟧

(AAA) ▼▼ Rodeway Inn M ❖
(541) 889-9188. **$54-$63.** 615 E Idaho. I-84, exit 376A, just nw. Ext corridors. **Pets:** Medium. $5 daily fee/pet. Designated rooms, service with restrictions, supervision.
⟦SAVE⟧ ⟦S⟧ ⟦✕⟧ ⟦⟧ ⟦⟧ ⟦⟧

(AAA) ▼▼▼ Sleep Inn SH
(541) 881-0007. **$59-$99.** 1221 SE First Ave. I-84, exit 376B, just se. Int corridors. **Pets:** Medium, dogs only. $10 daily fee/pet. Designated rooms, service with restrictions, supervision.
⟦SAVE⟧ ⟦S⟧ ⟦✕⟧ ⟦&M⟧ ⟦⟧ ⟦&⟧ ⟦⟧ ⟦⟧ ⟦⟧

PACIFIC CITY

(AAA) ▼▼▼▼ Inn at Cape Kiwanda SH ❖
(503) 965-7001. **$119-$299.** 33105 Cape Kiwanda Dr. Just w on Pacific Ave, 1 mi n. Ext corridors. **Pets:** $25 daily fee/pet. Designated rooms, service with restrictions, supervision.
⟦SAVE⟧ ⟦S⟧ ⟦✕⟧ ⟦&M⟧ ⟦⟧ ⟦⟧ ⟦✕⟧ ⟦⟧

(AAA) ▼▼ Pacific City Inn M ❖
(503) 965-6464. **$71-$175, 3 day notice.** 35280 Brooten Rd. Center. Ext corridors. **Pets:** Dogs only. $15 daily fee/pet. Designated rooms, service with restrictions, supervision.
⟦SAVE⟧ ⟦✕⟧ ⟦⟧ ⟦⟧ ⟦⟧ ⟦⟧

PENDLETON

Best Western Pendleton Inn SH
(541) 276-2135. **$80-$135.** 400 SE Nye Ave. I-84, exit 210, just se. Int corridors. **Pets:** Medium. $10 one-time fee/room. Supervision.

[SAVE] [S/D] [X] [&M] [&] [fork] [plate] [pool]

Econo Lodge M
(541) 276-8654. **$53-$59.** 620 SW Tutuilla Rd. I-84, exit 209, just s on US 395. Ext corridors. **Pets:** $7 daily fee/pet. Designated rooms, service with restrictions, supervision.

[SAVE] [S/D] [X] [fork] [plate]

Holiday Inn Express SH
(541) 966-6520. **$81-$200.** 600 SE Nye Ave. I-84, exit 210, just se. Int corridors. **Pets:** Dogs only. $10 daily fee/room. Designated rooms, service with restrictions, supervision.

[SAVE] [S/D] [X] [&] [fork] [plate] [pool]

Motel 6-#349 M
(541) 276-3160. **$41-$61.** 325 SE Nye Ave. I-84, exit 210, just se. Ext corridors. **Pets:** Medium, other species. Service with restrictions, supervision.

[S/D] [X] [fork] [pool]

Oxford Suites SH
(541) 276-6000. **$99.** 2400 SW Court Pl. I-84, exit 209, Just n to SW 20th St, just nw to SW Court Ave, then 0.3 mi sw. Int corridors. **Pets:** Accepted.

[ASK] [S/D] [X] [&M] [fan] [&] [fork] [plate] [pool] [X]

Red Lion Hotel Pendleton SH
(541) 276-6111. **$85-$130.** 304 SE Nye Ave. I-84, exit 210, just s. Ext/int corridors. **Pets:** Accepted.

[SAVE] [X] [fan] [&] [fork] [plate] [tall] [pool] [X]

Travelodge M 🐾
(541) 276-7531. **$59-$79, 5 day notice.** 411 SW Dorion Ave. I-84, exit 209, just w of town center on corner of SW 4th St; downtown. Ext corridors. **Pets:** Dogs only. $10 daily fee/pet. Designated rooms, service with restrictions.

[SAVE] [S/D] [X] [fork] [plate]

PORTLAND METROPOLITAN AREA

BEAVERTON

Comfort Inn & Suites SH
(503) 643-9100. **$75-$130.** 13455 SW Tualatin Valley Hwy. SR 217, exit Canyon Rd (SR 8), 1 mi w. Int corridors. **Pets:** Medium, other species. $15 daily fee/pet. Service with restrictions, supervision.

[ASK] [S/D] [X] [fan] [fork] [plate]

Homestead Studio Suites Hotel Portland-Beaverton M
(503) 690-3600. **$90-$110.** 875 SW 158th Ave. US 26, exit 65 westbound, just s on Cornell Rd, 1.1 mi se on 158th Ave; exit eastbound, just straight on feeder road, then same directions as westbound. Ext corridors. **Pets:** Accepted.

[ASK] [S/D] [X] [&] [fork] [plate]

Homewood Suites By Hilton SH 🐾
(503) 614-0900. **$179.** 15525 NW Gateway Ct. US 26, exit 65, s on 158th Ave, then just e on Waterhouse Ave. Int corridors. **Pets:** Medium. $15 daily fee/pet. Designated rooms, service with restrictions, supervision.

[ASK] [X] [&M] [fan] [&] [fork] [plate] [pool]

Phoenix Inn Suites-Beaverton SH
(503) 614-8100. **$99-$189.** 15402 NW Cornell Rd. US 26, exit 65, just n. Int corridors. **Pets:** Accepted.

[SAVE] [S/D] [X] [&M] [&] [fork] [plate] [pool] [X]

Shilo Inn-Portland/Beaverton SH 🐾
(503) 297-2551. **$109-$129.** 9900 SW Canyon Rd. SR 217, exit Canyon Rd/Beaverton Hillsdale Hwy, take feeder road, 0.3 mi e to SR 8 (Canyon Rd), then 0.6 mi e. Int corridors. **Pets:** Other species. $25 one-time fee/room. Supervision.

[ASK] [S/D] [X] [fan] [&] [fork] [plate] [tall] [pool]

GLADSTONE

Oxford Suites SH
(503) 722-7777. **$95-$135.** 75 82nd Dr. I-205, exit 11, just w. Int corridors. **Pets:** Medium, other species. $25 one-time fee/room. Service with restrictions, supervision.

[ASK] [S/D] [X] [fan] [&] [fork] [plate] [pool] [X]

GRESHAM

Best Western Pony Soldier Inn SH
(503) 665-1591. **$79-$105.** 1060 NE Cleveland Ave. I-84, exit 14 (207th Ave), 0.9 mi s, then just 0.4 mi e on NE Glisan St, 2.8 mi s on NE 223rd Ave, 0.7 mi e on Burnside Rd, then just s. Int corridors. **Pets:** Accepted.

[SAVE] [S/D] [X] [fan] [fork] [plate] [pool] [X]

Days Inn & Suites SH
(503) 465-1515. **$64-$89.** 24124 SE Stark St. I-84, exit 16, 1.5 mi s on NE 238th Dr/242nd, then just n. Int corridors. **Pets:** Accepted.

[SAVE] [S/D] [X] [&] [fork] [plate] [pool]

Extended StayAmerica Gresham SH
(503) 661-0226. **$85-$95.** 17777 NE Sacramento St. I-84, exit 13, just s, then just w. Int corridors. **Pets:** Accepted.

[ASK] [S/D] [X] [fork] [plate]

Holiday Inn Portland/Gresham SH
(503) 907-1777. **$89-$179.** 2752 NE Hogan Dr. I-84, exit 16, 1.7 mi s on 238th/Hogan drs. Int corridors. **Pets:** Small, dogs only. $15 daily fee/pet. Designated rooms, service with restrictions, supervision.

[SAVE] [S/D] [X] [&M] [fan] [&] [fork] [plate] [tall] [pool] [X]

Howard Johnson Gresham SH
(503) 666-9545. **$49-$119.** 1572 NE Burnside Rd. I-84, exit 16, 2.7 mi s on NE 238th Dr, just w on Division, then just se; I-205, exit 19, 5.5 mi e on Division St, then just se. Int corridors. **Pets:** Medium, dogs only. $12 one-time fee/pet. Designated rooms, service with restrictions, supervision.

[SAVE] [S/D] [X] [fan] [&] [fork] [plate] [pool]

Sleep Inn-Portland Gresham SH
(503) 618-8400. **$62-$140.** 2261 NE 181st Ave. I-84, exit 13, just s. Int corridors. **Pets:** Accepted.

[ASK] [S/D] [X] [&M] [&] [fork] [plate] [pool]

Super 8 Motel M
(503) 661-5100. **$54-$69.** 121 NE 181st Ave. I-84, exit 13, 1.4 mi s. Int corridors. **Pets:** Medium, other species. $10 daily fee/pet. Designated rooms, service with restrictions, supervision.

[SAVE] [S/D] [X] [fan] [fork] [plate]

HILLSBORO

🔺 🔻 The Dunes Motel Ⓜ
(503) 648-8991. **$50-$75.** 452 SE 10th Ave (SR 8). US 26, exit 62, 1 mi
s on NW Cornelius Pass Rd, then 4.4 mi w on NE Cornell Rd. Int
corridors. **Pets:** Very small, dogs only. $10 one-time fee/pet. Designated
rooms, no service, supervision.
【SAVE】【S🔴】【✕】【🏠】

🔻🔻 Extended StayAmerica-Portland-Beaverton SH
(503) 439-1515. **$85-$95.** 18665 NW Eider Ct. US 26, exit 64, 0.8 mi s;
behind Wendy's. Int corridors. **Pets:** Accepted.
【ASK】【S🔴】【✕】【📶】【🏠】【💻】

**🔻🔻 Extended Stay Deluxe-Portland-Hillsboro-NW Cornell
Rd SH**
(503) 439-0706. **$105-$115.** 19311 NW Cornell Rd. US 26, exit 64, 0.5
mi s on 185th Ave, then 0.4 mi w. Int corridors. **Pets:** Accepted.
【ASK】【S🔴】【✕】【📶】【♿】【🏠】【💻】【🏊】

**🔺 🔻🔻 Larkspur Landing Home Suite Hotel
Hillsboro/Portland SH**
(503) 681-2121. **$149-$179.** 3133 NE Shute Rd. US 26, exit 61, 1.2 mi
s. Int corridors. **Pets:** Accepted.
【SAVE】【S🔴】【✕】【📶】【♿】【🏠】【💻】

🔺 🔻🔻 Residence Inn by Marriott Portland West SH
(503) 531-3200. **$99-$229.** 18855 NW Tanasbourne Dr. US 26, exit 64,
just s, then just w. Ext/int corridors. **Pets:** Accepted.
【SAVE】【S🔴】【✕】【♿M】【📶】【♿】【🏠】【💻】【🏊】【✕】

**🔺 🔻🔻 TownePlace Suites by Marriott-Portland
Hillsboro SH**
(503) 268-6000. **$69-$189.** 6550 NE Brighton St. US 26, exit 62A
westbound; exit 62 eastbound, just s, 1 mi s on Cornelius Pass Rd,
0.7 mi w on Cornell Rd, just n on 229th Ave, then just w. Ext/int
corridors. **Pets:** Accepted.
【SAVE】【S🔴】【✕】【♿M】【📶】【♿】【🏠】【💻】【🏊】【✕】

KING CITY

🔺 🔻🔻 Best Western Northwind Inn & Suites SH
(503) 431-2100. **$72-$109.** 16105 SW Pacific Hwy. I-5, exit 292, just nw
on SR 217, exit SR 99W, then 2.5 mi s. Int corridors. **Pets:** $10 daily
fee/pet. Service with restrictions, supervision.
【SAVE】【✕】【♿M】【📶】【🏠】【💻】【🏊】

LAKE OSWEGO

🔺 🔻🔻 Crowne Plaza Hotel SH
(503) 624-8400. **$69-$199.** 14811 Kruse Oaks Dr. I-5, exit 292B northbound; exit 292 southbound, just e. Int corridors. **Pets:** $25 one-time
fee/room. Designated rooms, service with restrictions, supervision.
【SAVE】【S🔴】【✕】【♿M】【📶】【♿】【🏠】【💻】【🍽】【🏊】【✕】

🔺 🔻🔻 Phoenix Inn Suites-Lake Oswego SH
(503) 624-7400. **$99-$159.** 14905 SW Bangy Rd. I-5, exit 292 southbound, just e, then just s; exit 292B northbound, just s. Int corridors.
Pets: Accepted.
【SAVE】【✕】【♿M】【📶】【♿】【🏠】【💻】【🏊】【✕】

🔻🔻🔻 Residence Inn by Marriott-Portland South SH ✿
(503) 684-2603. **$149-$209.** 15200 SW Bangy Rd. I-5, exit 292B northbound; exit 292 southbound, just e, then 0.3 mi s. Ext corridors.
Pets: Other species. $10 daily fee/room.
【ASK】【S🔴】【✕】【♿M】【📶】【♿】【🏠】【💻】【🏊】【✕】

MILWAUKIE

🔺 🔻🔻 Econo Lodge Suites Inn Ⓜ
(503) 654-2222. **$59-$79.** 17330 SE McLoughlin Blvd. I-205, exit 9
(Oregon City/Gladstone), 2.3 mi n on SR 99 E (McLoughlin Blvd). Ext
corridors. **Pets:** Small, dogs only. $10 daily fee/pet. Designated rooms,
service with restrictions, supervision.
【SAVE】【S🔴】【✕】【📶】【🏠】【💻】【🏊】

OREGON CITY

🔺 🔻🔻🔻 Rivershore Hotel SH ✿
(503) 655-7141. **$80-$108.** 1900 Clackamette Dr. I-205, exit 9, just n.
Int corridors. **Pets:** Large, other species. $5 daily fee/pet. Service with
restrictions, supervision.
【SAVE】【S🔴】【✕】【♿M】【📶】【♿】【🏠】【💻】【🍽】【🏊】【✕】

PORTLAND

**🔺 🔻🔻🔻 The Benson Hotel, a Coast
Hotel LH ✿**
(503) 228-2000. **$139-$299.** 309 SW Broadway. At SW Broadway and
Oak. Int corridors. **Pets:** Other species. $75 daily fee/room. Designated
rooms, no service, supervision.
【SAVE】【S🔴】【✕】【♿M】【📶】【♿】【💻】【🍽】

🔻🔻🔻 Best Western Inn at the Meadows SH ✿
(503) 286-9600. **$66-$93.** 1215 N Hayden Meadows Dr. I-5, exit 306B,
just e. Int corridors. **Pets:** Other species. $25 one-time fee/room. Service
with restrictions, supervision.
【ASK】【S🔴】【✕】【📶】【🏠】【💻】

🔺 🔻🔻🔻 Best Western Pony Soldier Inn-Airport SH
(503) 256-1504. **$99-$121.** 9901 NE Sandy Blvd. I-205, exit 23A, just e.
Int corridors. **Pets:** Small. Designated rooms, service with restrictions,
supervision.
【SAVE】【S🔴】【✕】【♿M】【🏠】【💻】【🏊】【✕】

🔺 🔻🔻 Briarwood Suites Portland Ⓜ
(503) 788-9394. **$59-$99.** 7740 SE Powell Blvd. I-205, exit 19, 1 mi w.
Ext/int corridors. **Pets:** Accepted.
【SAVE】【S🔴】【✕】【🏠】【💻】

🔻🔻🔻 Country Inn & Suites at Portland Airport SH
(503) 255-2700. **$99-$103.** 7205 NE Alderwood Rd. I-205, exit 24A
(Airport Way) northbound; exit 24 southbound, 1 mi w on Airport Way,
just sw on NE 82nd Ave, then just w. Int corridors. **Pets:** Accepted.
【ASK】【S🔴】【✕】【♿】【🏠】【💻】【🍽】【🏊】

🔺 🔻🔻 Days Inn-Portland North SH
(503) 289-1800. **$79-$139.** 9930 N Whitaker Rd. I-5, exit 306B, just e.
Int corridors. **Pets:** Accepted.
【SAVE】【S🔴】【✕】【📶】【♿】【🏠】

🔻🔻🔻 Four Points by Sheraton Portland Downtown SH
(503) 221-0711. **$110-$150.** 50 SW Morrison St. At Morrison St and
Naito Pkwy (formerly Front Ave). Int corridors. **Pets:** Medium, dogs only.
Service with restrictions, supervision.
【ASK】【S🔴】【✕】【♿M】【📶】【♿】【🏠】【💻】【🍽】

🔺 🔻🔻🔻🔻 The Heathman Hotel SH ✿
(503) 241-4100. **$149-$249.** 1001 SW Broadway. At SW Broadway and
Salmon St. Int corridors. **Pets:** Medium. $40 daily fee/room. Designated
rooms, service with restrictions, supervision.
【SAVE】【S🔴】【✕】【♿M】【📶】【♿】【💻】【🍽】

🔺 🔻🔻🔻 Hilton Portland & Executive Tower LH
(503) 226-1611. **$99-$204.** 921 SW 6th Ave. I-405, exit 1B (6th Ave); at
6th Ave and Taylor St. Int corridors. **Pets:** Large, other species. $25
one-time fee/room. Service with restrictions, supervision.
【SAVE】【✕】【📶】【🏠】【💻】【🍽】【🏊】【✕】

AAA ▼▼▼▼ **Holiday Inn-Portland Airport** LH
(503) 256-5000. **$119-$199.** 8439 NE Columbia Blvd. I-205, exit 23B, 0.5 mi w. Int corridors. **Pets:** Small. $25 one-time fee/room. Designated rooms, service with restrictions, supervision.

SAVE ⬛ ✕ ⬛ ⬛ ⬛ ⬛ ⬛

▼▼▼▼ **Hotel deLuxe** SH
(503) 219-2094. **$139-$199.** 729 SW 15th Ave. I-5 to I-405, exit Salmon St northbound, just n on 14th Ave, w on Morrison St, then s; exit Couch-Burnside southbound; at SW 15th Ave and Yamhill. Int corridors. **Pets:** Medium. $35 one-time fee/pet. Designated rooms, supervision.

ASK ⬛ ✕ ⬛ ⬛ ⬛ ⬛ ⬛

AAA ▼▼▼▼ **Hotel Lucia** SH
(503) 225-1717. **$145-$185.** 400 SW Broadway. At SW Broadway and Stark St. Int corridors. **Pets:** $35 one-time fee/room. Designated rooms, service with restrictions, supervision.

SAVE ⬛ ✕ ⬛ ⬛ ⬛ ⬛ ⬛

AAA ▼▼▼▼ **Hotel Monaco Portland** LH
(503) 222-0001. **$149-$289.** 506 SW Washington St. At SW 5th Ave and SW Washington St. Int corridors. **Pets:** Other species. Designated rooms, service with restrictions, supervision.

SAVE ⬛ ✕ ⬛ ⬛ ⬛ ⬛ ⬛ ⬛

AAA ▼▼▼▼ **Hotel Vintage Plaza** SH
(503) 228-1212. **$139-$279.** 422 SW Broadway. At Broadway and Washington St. Int corridors. **Pets:** Accepted.

SAVE ⬛ ✕ ⬛ ⬛ ⬛

AAA ▼▼▼ **La Quinta Inn & Suites Portland Airport** SH
(503) 382-3820. **$89-$124.** 11207 NE Holman St. I-205, exit 24B northbound; exit 24 southbound, just e on Airport Way. Int corridors. **Pets:** Large, other species. Service with restrictions, crate.

SAVE ⬛ ✕ ⬛ ⬛ ⬛ ⬛ ⬛ ⬛

AAA ▼▼▼ **La Quinta Inn & Suites Portland Northwest** SH
(503) 497-9044. **$86-$112.** 4319 NW Yeon. I-5, exit 302 B southbound, 2.5 mi w on US 30; I-5 to I-405; exit 3 (US 30) northbound, 2.5 mi w. Int corridors. **Pets:** Other species. Designated rooms, service with restrictions, supervision.

SAVE ⬛ ✕ ⬛ ⬛ ⬛ ⬛ ⬛ ⬛

AAA ▼▼▼ **La Quinta Inn Portland Lloyd Center/Convention Center** SH
(503) 233-7933. **$96-$112.** 431 NE Multnomah St. I-5, exit 302A, just e, then just s on Martin Luther King Blvd. Int corridors. **Pets:** Service with restrictions, crate.

SAVE ⬛ ✕ ⬛ ⬛ ⬛ ⬛

AAA ▼▼▼ **The Mark Spencer Hotel** SH
(503) 224-3293. **$89-$149.** 409 SW 11th Ave. At SW Stark St and SW 11th Ave. Int corridors. **Pets:** Other species. $10 daily fee/pet. Designated rooms, service with restrictions, crate.

SAVE ⬛ ✕ ⬛ ⬛

▼▼ **Motel 6 North Portland #4198** SH
(503) 247-3700. **$51-$61.** 1125 N Schmeer Rd. I-5, exit 306B, 0.4 mi s on N Whitaker Rd, then just e. Int corridors. **Pets:** Medium, other species. Service with restrictions, supervision.

⬛ ✕ ⬛ ⬛ ⬛

AAA ▼▼▼ **Oxford Suites** SH
(503) 283-3030. **$109-$179, 7 day notice.** 12226 N Jantzen Dr. I-5, exit 308, just e on Hayden Island Dr. Int corridors. **Pets:** $25 daily fee/pet. Service with restrictions, supervision.

SAVE ✕ ⬛ ⬛ ⬛ ⬛ ⬛ ⬛ ⬛

AAA ▼▼▼▼ **The Paramount Hotel, a Coast Hotel** SH
(503) 223-9900. **$195.** 808 SW Taylor St. At SW 8th Ave and SW Taylor St. Int corridors. **Pets:** Medium. $75 one-time fee/room. Service with restrictions, supervision.

SAVE ⬛ ✕ ⬛ ⬛ ⬛ ⬛ ⬛

AAA ▼▼▼▼ **Park Lane Suites** M
(503) 226-6288. **$109-$179.** 809 SW King Ave. I-405, exit Couch/ Burnside St southbound, 0.5 mi w on Burnside St, then just s; exit Everett St northbound, 0.4 mi w on Glisan St, just s on NW 21st Ave, just w on Burnside St, then just s. Ext corridors. **Pets:** Accepted.

SAVE ⬛ ✕ ⬛ ⬛ ⬛

AAA ▼▼▼ **Quality Inn Portland Airport** SH
(503) 256-4111. **$74-$104.** 8247 NE Sandy Blvd. I-84, exit 5, 1.5 mi n on 82nd Ave; I-205, exit 23A southbound; exit 23B northbound (US 30 business route/Sandy Blvd W), 1 mi w. Ext/int corridors. **Pets:** Medium, other species. $15 daily fee/pet. Service with restrictions, supervision.

SAVE ⬛ ✕ ⬛ ⬛

AAA ▼▼▼▼ **Red Lion Hotel on the River Jantzen Beach-Portland** LH
(503) 283-4466. **$129-$199.** 909 N Hayden Island Dr. I-5, exit 308, just e. Int corridors. **Pets:** Medium. $35 one-time fee/room. Service with restrictions, supervision.

SAVE ⬛ ✕ ⬛ ⬛ ⬛ ⬛ ⬛ ⬛ ⬛

AAA ▼▼▼ **Red Lion Hotel Portland-Convention Center** SH
(503) 235-2100. **$79-$159.** 1021 NE Grand Ave. I-5, exit 302A, just e on Weidler, then just s on Martin Luther King Jr Blvd. Int corridors. **Pets:** Small. $100 deposit/room, $20 daily fee/pet. Designated rooms, service with restrictions, supervision.

SAVE ⬛ ⬛ ⬛ ⬛ ⬛

▼▼▼ **Red Lion Inn & Suites-Portland Airport** SH
(503) 252-6397. **$59-$79.** 5019 NE 102nd Ave. I-205, exit 23A, just e on NE Sandy Blvd. Int corridors. **Pets:** Accepted.

ASK ⬛ ✕ ⬛ ⬛ ⬛ ⬛ ⬛

AAA ▼▼▼▼ **Residence Inn by Marriott-Lloyd Center** SH
(503) 288-1400. **$159-$189.** 1710 NE Multnomah St. I-5, exit 302A, 0.8 mi e on Weidler St, then just s on 15th Ave; I-84, exit 1 (Lloyd Center) westbound, just n on 13th St, then just e. Ext corridors. **Pets:** Accepted.

SAVE ⬛ ✕ ⬛ ⬛ ⬛ ⬛ ⬛ ⬛ ⬛

AAA ▼▼▼ **Residence Inn Portland Downtown at RiverPlace** SH
(503) 552-9500. **$289.** 2115 SW River Pkwy. At SW Moody and SW River Pkwy; on the Willamette River Waterfront. Int corridors. **Pets:** Other species. $10 daily fee/pet. Service with restrictions.

SAVE ⬛ ✕ ⬛ ⬛ ⬛ ⬛ ⬛ ⬛

AAA ▼▼▼▼ **RiverPlace Hotel** SH
(503) 228-3233. **$169-$299.** 1510 SW Harbor Way. At Naito Pkwy (formerly Front Ave) and SW Harbor Way. Int corridors. **Pets:** Other species. $45 one-time fee/room.

SAVE ⬛ ✕ ⬛ ⬛ ⬛ ⬛ ⬛ ⬛ ⬛

AAA ▼▼▼▼ **Sheraton Portland Airport Hotel** LH
(503) 281-2500. **$188-$224.** 8235 NE Airport Way. I-205, exit 24A northbound; exit 24 southbound, 1.5 mi w. Int corridors. **Pets:** $25 one-time fee/room. Service with restrictions, supervision.

SAVE ⬛ ✕ ⬛ ⬛ ⬛ ⬛ ⬛ ⬛

▼▼ **Shilo Inn Rose Garden** SH
(503) 736-6300. **$90-$127.** 1506 NE 2nd Ave. I-5, exit 302A, just e, on NE Weidler, then just s. Int corridors. **Pets:** Other species. $25 one-time fee/room. Supervision.

ASK ⬛ ✕ ⬛ ⬛

▼▼▼▼ Staybridge Suites Portland-Airport 🆂🅷
(503) 262-8888. **$125-$169.** 11936 NE Glenn Widing Dr. I-205, exit 24B northbound; exit 24 southbound, just e, then just ne. Int corridors. **Pets:** Other species. $10 daily fee/pet, $25 one-time fee/pet. Service with restrictions, crate.

🅰🆂🅺 🆂🔁 ✕ 🄳🄼 ⟨⟩ ⟨⟩ 🄷 🄳🄿 🏊 ✕

🅐🅐🅐 ▼▼▼▼ The Westin Portland 🅻🅷 🐾
(503) 294-9000. **$129-$219.** 750 SW Alder St. At Park Ave and SW Alder St. Int corridors. **Pets:** Other species. Service with restrictions.

🆂🅰🆅🅴 🆂🔁 ✕ 🄳🄼 ⟨⟩ ⟨⟩ 🄳🄿 🍽

TIGARD

▼▼▼▼ Embassy Suites Hotel-Portland Washington
   Square 🅻🅷
(503) 644-4000. **$139-$229.** 9000 SW Washington Square Rd. SR 217, exit Progress/Scholls Ferry Rd, just e, then just s on Hall Blvd. Int corridors. **Pets:** Large. $25 daily fee/room. Designated rooms, service with restrictions, supervision.

✕ 🄳🄼 ⟨⟩ ⟨⟩ 🄷 🄳🄿 🍽 🏊 ✕

▼▼ Homestead Studio Suites Hotel Portland-Tigard 🆂🅷
(503) 620-0555. **$90-$110.** 13009 SW 68th Pkwy. I-5, exit 293 (Haines), 0.5 mi s on SW 68th Ave; SR 217 S, exit 72nd Ave, just ne, just e on Hampton St, then just s. Ext corridors. **Pets:** Accepted.

🅰🆂🅺 🆂🔁 ✕ ⟨⟩ ⟨⟩ 🄷 🄳🄿

🅐🅐🅐 ▼▼▼▼ Phoenix Inn Suites-Tigard 🆂🅷
(503) 624-9000. **$99-$159.** 9575 SW Locust. SR 217, exit Greenburg Rd, just e. Int corridors. **Pets:** Accepted.

🆂🅰🆅🅴 🆂🔁 ✕ 🄳🄼 ⟨⟩ ⟨⟩ 🄷 🄳🄿 🏊 ✕

▼▼ Shilo Inn-Tigard/Washington Square 🆂🅷 🐾
(503) 620-4320. **$82-$103.** 10830 SW Greenburg Rd. SR 217, exit Greenburg Rd, just w. Int corridors. **Pets:** Other species. $25 one-time fee/room. Supervision.

🅰🆂🅺 🆂🔁 ✕ ⟨⟩ ⟨⟩ 🄷 🄳🄿 ✕

TROUTDALE

🅐🅐🅐 ▼▼ Comfort Inn & Suites, Columbia Gorge
   West 🆂🅷
(503) 669-6500. **$69-$99.** 477 NW Phoenix Dr. I-84, exit 17. Int corridors. **Pets:** Accepted.

🆂🅰🆅🅴 🆂🔁 ✕ ⟨⟩ 🄷 🄳🄿 🏊

▼▼ Holiday Inn Express-Portland East 🆂🅷
(503) 492-2900. **$79-$109.** 1000 NW Graham Rd. I-84, exit 17, on north frontage road. Int corridors. **Pets:** Other species. $10 daily fee/room. Designated rooms, service with restrictions, crate.

🅰🆂🅺 🆂🔁 ✕ ⟨⟩ ⟨⟩ 🄷 🄳🄿 ✕

▼▼▼ Motel 6-Portland Troutdale-407 🅼
(503) 665-2254. **$41-$59.** 1610 NW Frontage Rd. I-84, exit 17, just s. Ext corridors. **Pets:** Medium, other species. Service with restrictions, supervision.

🆂🔁 ✕ 🄳🄼 ⟨⟩ ⟨⟩ 🄷 🏊

TUALATIN

🅐🅐🅐 ▼▼▼▼ Comfort Inn & Suites 🆂🅷 🐾
(503) 612-9952. **$79-$179.** 7640 SW Warm Springs St. I-5, exit 289, w on Nyberg Rd then s on Martinazzi; just behind Fred Meyer. Int corridors. **Pets:** Small, dogs only. $15 daily fee/pet. Designated rooms, service with restrictions, supervision.

🆂🅰🆅🅴 🆂🔁 ✕ 🄳🄼 ⟨⟩ ⟨⟩ 🄷 🄳🄿 🏊

WILSONVILLE

🅐🅐🅐 ▼▼▼▼ Best Western Willamette Inn 🆂🅷
(503) 682-2288. **$87-$97.** 30800 SW Parkway Ave. I-5, exit 283, just e, then just s. Int corridors. **Pets:** Small, other species. Designated rooms, service with restrictions, supervision.

🆂🔁 ✕ 🄳🄼 🄷 🄳🄿 🏊 ✕

🅐🅐🅐 ▼▼ Comfort Inn 🆂🅷
(503) 682-9000. **$70-$100.** 8855 SW Citizens Dr. I-5, exit 283, just e, then just n on Town Center Loop W. Int corridors. **Pets:** Accepted.

🆂🅰🆅🅴 🆂🔁 ✕ 🄳🄼 ⟨⟩ ⟨⟩ 🄷 🄳🄿

▼▼▼▼ Holiday Inn-Wilsonville 🆂🅷 🐾
(503) 682-2211. **$99-$139.** 25425 SW 95th Ave. I-5, exit 286, just w. Int corridors. **Pets:** $15 one-time fee/room. Service with restrictions, crate.

🅰🆂🅺 🆂🔁 ✕ 🄳🄼 ⟨⟩ ⟨⟩ 🄷 🄳🄿 🍽 🏊

🅐🅐🅐 ▼▼▼▼ La Quinta Inn Wilsonville 🆂🅷
(503) 682-3184. **$69-$139.** 8815 SW Sun Pl. I-5, exit 286, just e, then just n. Int corridors. **Pets:** Other species. Service with restrictions, crate.

🆂🅰🆅🅴 🆂🔁 ✕ 🄳🄼 ⟨⟩ 🄷 🄳🄿 🏊

🅐🅐🅐 ▼▼▼▼ Phoenix Inn Suites-Wilsonville 🆂🅷 🐾
(503) 570-9700. **$69-$129.** 29769 SW Boones Ferry Rd. I-5, exit 283, just w. Int corridors. **Pets:** Medium, other species. $15 daily fee/room. Designated rooms, service with restrictions, supervision.

🆂🅰🆅🅴 🆂🔁 ✕ 🄳🄼 ⟨⟩ ⟨⟩ 🄷 🄳🄿 🏊 ✕

WOOD VILLAGE

🅐🅐🅐 ▼▼ Portland/Troutdale Travelodge 🆂🅷
(503) 666-6623. **$37-$79.** 23705 NE Sandy Blvd. I-84, exit 16, just n. Int corridors. **Pets:** $15 daily fee/pet. Service with restrictions, supervision.

🆂🅰🆅🅴 🆂🔁 ✕ ⟨⟩ 🄷 🄳🄿 🍽

END METROPOLITAN AREA

PORT ORFORD

🅐🅐🅐 ▼▼ Castaway by the Sea 🅼
(541) 332-4502. **$55-$115, 3 day notice.** 545 W 5th St. Jct US 101, just w on Oregon St. Ext corridors. **Pets:** Other species. $10 one-time fee/pet. Designated rooms, service with restrictions, supervision.

🆂🅰🆅🅴 ✕ 🄷 🄳🄿 🄰

▼▼▼▼ WildSpring Guest Habitat 🄲🄰 🐾
(541) 332-0977. **$209-$249, 14 day notice.** 92978 Cemetery Loop Rd. At north end of bridge, e on Cemetery Loop Rd, then 2.5 mi s. Ext corridors. **Pets:** Large, dogs only. $25 daily fee/room. Designated rooms, service with restrictions, crate.

✕ 🄷 ✕ 🄰

PRINEVILLE

▼▼▼▼ Best Western Prineville Inn 🆂🅷 🐾
(541) 447-8080. **$69-$129.** 1475 NE 3rd St. 1.4 mi e on US 26. Int corridors. **Pets:** Other species. $10 one-time fee/room. Service with restrictions, supervision.

🅰🆂🅺 🆂🔁 ✕ 🄳🄼 🄷 🄳🄿 🏊

🅐🅐🅐 ▼▼ Econo Lodge 🅼
(541) 447-6231. **$65-$90.** 123 NE 3rd St. Center; downtown. Int corridors. **Pets:** Accepted.

🆂🅰🆅🅴 🆂🔁 ✕ 🄷 🄳🄿

▼▼▼ Stafford Inn 🆂🅷
(541) 447-7100. **$75-$85.** 1773 NE 3rd St. 1.6 mi w on US 26. Int corridors. **Pets:** Accepted.

🅰🆂🅺 🆂🔁 ✕ ⟨⟩ 🄷 🄳🄿 🏊

PROSPECT

▼▼ Prospect Historic Hotel-Motel & Dinner House 🅼 🐾
(541) 560-3664. **$60-$165.** 391 Mill Creek Dr. Jct SR 62, 0.3 mi s on 1st St (0.7 mi e of MM 43), just w. Ext/int corridors. **Pets:** Other species. $10 one-time fee/room. Designated rooms, service with restrictions, supervision.

⊠ 🛢 ▣ 🍴 ⊠

REDMOND

▼▼▼ Comfort Suites-Redmond Airport 🆂🅷
(541) 504-8900. **$94-$174.** 2243 SW Yew Ave. US 97, just w. Int corridors. **Pets:** Accepted.

🅰🆂🅺 🆂🅳 ⊠ 🖆 🛢 ▣ ⇒

▼▼▼ Eagle Crest Resort 🆂🅷
(541) 923-2453. **$84-$157.** 1522 Cline Falls Rd. 4.5 mi w on SR 126, 1 mi s. Int corridors. **Pets:** Dogs only. $250 one-time fee/room. Designated rooms, service with restrictions, supervision.

🅰🆂🅺 ⊠ 🔊 🗟 🖆 🛢 ▣ 🍴 ⇒ ⊠

▲▲▲ ▼ Motel 6 Redmond-4076 🆂🅷
(541) 923-2100. **$66-$96.** 2247 S Hwy 97. 1 mi s on US 97 from jct SR 126 W. Int corridors. **Pets:** Medium, other species. Service with restrictions, supervision.

🆂🅰🆅🅴 🆂🅳 ⊠ 🔊 🗟 🖆 🛢

▲▲▲ ▼▼ Redmond Inn 🅼
(541) 548-1091. **$55-$80.** 1545 S Hwy 97. 0.5 mi s on US 97 from jct SR 126 W. Ext corridors. **Pets:** Other species. $5 daily fee/pet. Designated rooms, supervision.

🆂🅰🆅🅴 🆂🅳 ⊠ 🛢 ▣ ⇒

▼▼ Redmond Super 8 Motel 🆂🅷
(541) 548-8881. **$61-$105.** 3629 21st Pl SW. US 97, exit Yew Ave. Int corridors. **Pets:** Accepted.

🅰🆂🅺 🆂🅳 ⊠ 🔊 🗟 🖆 ⇒

REEDSPORT

▲▲▲ ▼ Anchor Bay Inn 🅼
(541) 271-2149. **$45-$77.** 1821 Winchester Ave (Hwy 101). On US 101, 0.8 mi s of jct SR 38. Ext corridors. **Pets:** Dogs only. $7 daily fee/pet. Designated rooms, service with restrictions, supervision.

🆂🅰🆅🅴 🆂🅳 ⊠ 🛢 ▣ ⇒ 🕮

▲▲▲ ▼▼▼ Best Western Salbasgeon Inn 🅼
(541) 271-4831. **$76-$138.** 1400 Hwy Ave 101 S. Just s on US 101 from jct SR 38. Ext corridors. **Pets:** Medium, dogs only. $10 daily fee/pet. Designated rooms, service with restrictions, crate.

🆂🅰🆅🅴 🆂🅳 ⊠ 🛢 ▣ ⇒

▲▲▲ ▼ Economy Inn 🅼
(541) 271-3671. **$55-$110.** 1593 Hwy 101. On US 101; center. Ext corridors. **Pets:** Small, dogs only. $5 one-time fee/pet. Designated rooms, service with restrictions, supervision.

🆂🅰🆅🅴 🆂🅳 ⊠ 🛢 ⇒ 🕮

▲▲▲ ▼▼▼ Salbasgeon Inn of the Umpqua 🅼
(541) 271-2025. **$109-$186.** 45209 Hwy 38. US 101, 7.3 mi e. Ext corridors. **Pets:** Accepted.

🆂🅰🆅🅴 🆂🅳 ⊠ 🛢 ▣ ⊠

ROCKAWAY BEACH

▲▲▲ ▼ Sea Treasures Inn 🅼 🐾
(503) 355-8220. **$59-$95.** 301 N Miller St. Jct 3rd Ave N; center. Ext corridors. **Pets:** Other species. $10 one-time fee/pet. Designated rooms, supervision.

🆂🅰🆅🅴 🆂🅳 ⊠ 🛢 ▣ 🕮

▲▲▲ ▼ Silver Sands Motel 🅼
(503) 355-2206. **$78-$158.** 215 S Pacific St. US 101, exit S 2nd Ave, just w. Ext corridors. **Pets:** Dogs only. $50 deposit/room, $10 daily fee/pet. Service with restrictions, supervision.

🆂🅰🆅🅴 🆂🅳 ⊠ 🖆 🛢 ▣ ⇒ ⊠ 🕮

▲▲▲ ▼▼ Tradewinds Motel 🅼 🐾
(503) 355-2112. **$55-$135, 7 day notice.** 523 N Pacific St. Just w of US 101, off N 6th Ave. Ext corridors. **Pets:** Medium, dogs only. $15 daily fee/pet. Designated rooms, service with restrictions, supervision.

🆂🅰🆅🅴 ⊠ 🛢 ▣ 🕮

ROSEBURG

▲▲▲ ▼▼▼ Best Western Garden Villa Inn 🅼
(541) 672-1601. **$69-$99.** 760 NW Garden Valley Blvd. I-5, exit 125, just w. Ext corridors. **Pets:** Accepted.

🆂🅰🆅🅴 🆂🅳 ⊠ 🔊 🖆 🛢 ▣ ⇒

▲▲▲ ▼▼ The Douglas County Inn 🅼
(541) 673-6625. **$55-$79.** 511 SE Stephens St. I-5, exit 124, 0.5 mi e, then just n; downtown. Ext corridors. **Pets:** Medium. Designated rooms, service with restrictions, crate.

🆂🅰🆅🅴 🆂🅳 ⊠ 🖆 🛢 ▣

▲▲▲ ▼▼▼ Holiday Inn Express 🆂🅷 🐾
(541) 673-7517. **$76-$109.** 375 W Harvard Ave. I-5, exit 124, just e. Ext/int corridors. **Pets:** Other species. $10 daily fee/room. Designated rooms, service with restrictions, supervision.

🆂🅰🆅🅴 🆂🅳 ⊠ 🔊 🗟 🖆 🛢 ▣ ⇒

▲▲▲ ▼▼▼ Motel 6 🆂🅷
(541) 464-8000. **$56-$66.** 3100 NW Aviation Dr. I-5, exit 127, just ne. Int corridors. **Pets:** Medium, other species. Service with restrictions, supervision.

🆂🅰🆅🅴 ⊠ 🔊 🖆 🛢

▲▲▲ ▼▼▼ Quality Inn 🅼
(541) 673-5561. **$56-$97.** 427 NW Garden Valley Blvd. I-5, exit 125, just e. Ext corridors. **Pets:** Dogs only. $50 deposit/room, $10 daily fee/pet. Designated rooms, service with restrictions, supervision.

🆂🅰🆅🅴 🆂🅳 ⊠ 🗟 🖆 🛢 ▣ ⇒

▲▲▲ ▼ Roseburg Travelodge 🅼
(541) 672-4836. **$77-$91.** 315 W Harvard Ave. I-5, exit 124, just e. Ext corridors. **Pets:** Accepted.

🆂🅰🆅🅴 ⊠ 🛢 ▣ ⇒

▲▲▲ ▼ Shady Oaks Motel 🅼
(541) 672-2608. **$45-$66, 3 day notice.** 2954 Old Hwy 99 S. I-5, exit 120, 0.5 mi n. Ext corridors. **Pets:** Medium, dogs only. $8 daily fee/pet. Designated rooms, service with restrictions, supervision.

🆂🅰🆅🅴 🆂🅳 ⊠ 🛢

▼▼ ◈ Sleep Inn and Suites 🆂🅷
(541) 464-8338. **$59-$99.** 2855 NW Edenbower Blvd. I-5, exit 127, just n. Int corridors. **Pets:** Medium. $10 one-time fee/room. Service with restrictions, supervision.

🅰🆂🅺 🆂🅳 ⊠ 🔊 🖆 🛢 ▣ ⇒

▼▼ ◈ Super 8 Motel 🆂🅷
(541) 672-8880. **$55-$66.** 3200 NW Aviation Dr. I-5, exit 127, just ne. Int corridors. **Pets:** Accepted.

🅰🆂🅺 🆂🅳 ⊠ 🔊 🗟 🖆 🛢 ⇒

▲▲▲ ▼▼▼ Windmill Inn of Roseburg 🆂🅷 🐾
(541) 673-0901. **$65-$110.** 1450 NW Mulholland Dr. I-5, exit 125, just ne. Int corridors. **Pets:** Designated rooms, service with restrictions, supervision.

🆂🅰🆅🅴 🆂🅳 ⊠ 🔊 🖆 🛢 ▣ ⇒ ⊠

ST. HELENS

ⒶⒶⒶ ▼▼▼ Best Western Oak Meadows Inn 🆂🅷
(503) 397-3000. **$89-$149.** 585 S Columbia River Hwy. South end of town on US 30. Int corridors. **Pets:** Other species. $10 one-time fee/pet. Designated rooms, service with restrictions, supervision.
🆂🅰🆅🅴 🆂🅾 ☒ 🏍 🍽 🔌 🏊

SALEM

ⒶⒶⒶ ▼▼▼ Best Western Black Bear Inn 🅼
(503) 581-1559. **$66-$80.** 1600 Motor Ct NE. I-5, exit 256, just e. Ext corridors. **Pets:** Medium. $10 daily fee/room. Designated rooms, service with restrictions, supervision.
🆂🅰🆅🅴 🆂🅾 ☒ 🅼 🍴 🏍 🍽 🔌 🏊 ☒

ⒶⒶⒶ ▼▼▼ Best Western Pacific Hwy Inn 🅼
(503) 390-3200. **$77-$90.** 4646 Portland Rd NE. I-5, exit 258, just e. Ext corridors. **Pets:** Accepted.
🆂🅰🆅🅴 ☒ 🅼 🍴 🏍 🍽 🔌 🏊

▼ Crossland Studios Salem North 🅼
(503) 363-7557. **Call for rates.** 3535 Fisher Rd NE. I-5, exit 258, just n, 0.4 mi s on Ward Dr, then 0.8 mi s. Ext corridors. **Pets:** Accepted.
☒ 🍽 🔌

ⒶⒶⒶ ▼▼▼ Holiday Inn Express 🆂🅷
(503) 391-7000. **$97-$117.** 890 Hawthorne Ave SE. I-5, exit 253, just w, then just n. Int corridors. **Pets:** Small, dogs only. $15 daily fee/pet. Designated rooms, service with restrictions, supervision.
🆂🅰🆅🅴 🆂🅾 ☒ 🅼 🍴 🏍 🍽 🔌 🏊

▼▼ Howard Johnson Inn 🆂🅷
(503) 375-7710. **$55-$62.** 2250 Mission St SE. I-5, exit 253, 1.4 mi w. Int corridors. **Pets:** Small, dogs only. $10 daily fee/pet. Designated rooms, service with restrictions, supervision.
🅰🆂🅺 🆂🅾 ☒ 🍽 🔌 🏊

▼ Motel 6–1343 🅼
(503) 371-8024. **$45-$61.** 1401 Hawthorne Ave NE. I-5, exit 256, just w, then just s. Ext corridors. **Pets:** Medium, other species. Service with restrictions, supervision.
🆂🅾 ☒ 🍴 🏍 🍽 🏊

ⒶⒶⒶ ▼▼▼▼ Phoenix Inn Suites-North Salem 🆂🅷
(503) 581-7004. **$89-$149.** 1590 Weston Ct NE. I-5, exit 256, just w, then just s. Int corridors. **Pets:** Accepted.
🆂🅰🆅🅴 🆂🅾 ☒ 🅼 🍴 🏍 🍽 🔌 🏊 ☒

ⒶⒶⒶ ▼▼▼▼ Phoenix Inn Suites-South Salem 🆂🅷
(503) 588-9220. **$89-$149.** 4370 Commercial SE. I-5, exit 252, 1.5 mi w on Kuebler Rd, then 0.7 mi n. Int corridors. **Pets:** Accepted.
🆂🅰🆅🅴 🆂🅾 ☒ 🅼 🍴 🏍 🍽 🔌 🏊 ☒

ⒶⒶⒶ ▼▼▼▼ Red Lion Hotel Salem 🆂🅷
(503) 370-7888. **$79-$129.** 3301 Market St NE. I-5, exit 256, just w. Int corridors. **Pets:** Medium. $10 daily fee/pet. Service with restrictions, supervision.
🆂🅰🆅🅴 🆂🅾 ☒ 🍴 🏍 🍽 🔌 🍴 🏊 ☒

▼▼▼ Residence Inn by Marriott 🆂🅷
(503) 585-6500. **$155-$185.** 640 Hawthorne Ave SE. I-5, exit 253, just w, then n. Int corridors. **Pets:** Accepted.
🅰🆂🅺 🆂🅾 ☒ 🅼 🍴 🏍 🍽 🔌 🏊 ☒

▼▼ Salem Super 8 🆂🅷 🐾
(503) 370-8888. **$55-$69.** 1288 Hawthorne Ave NE. I-5, exit 256, just w, then just s. Int corridors. **Pets:** Other species. $10 one-time fee/room. Service with restrictions, supervision.
🅰🆂🅺 🆂🅾 ☒ 🅼 🍴 🍽 🏊

ⒶⒶⒶ ▼▼▼▼ Shilo Inn Suites-Salem 🆂🅷 🐾
(503) 581-4001. **$87-$128.** 3304 Market St NE. I-5, exit 256, just w. Int corridors. **Pets:** Other species. $25 one-time fee/room. Supervision.
🆂🅰🆅🅴 🆂🅾 ☒ 🍽 🔌 🏊 ☒

ⒶⒶⒶ ▼▼▼ Travelodge Salem Capital 🅼
(503) 581-2466. **$46-$62.** 1555 State St. I-5, exit 253, just w on SR 22/99 (Mission St), 0.6 mi n on Airport Rd SE, then 1 mi w. Ext corridors. **Pets:** Small. $10 daily fee/pet. Designated rooms, service with restrictions, supervision.
🆂🅰🆅🅴 ☒ 🏍 🍽 🔌 🏊

SANDY

▼ Best Western Sandy Inn 🆂🅷 🐾
(503) 668-7100. **$85-$125.** 37465 Hwy 26. West side of town. Int corridors. **Pets:** Medium, dogs only. $100 deposit/room, $10 daily fee/pet. Service with restrictions, supervision.
🅰🆂🅺 🆂🅾 ☒ 🅼 🍴 🏍 🍽 🔌 🏊

SEASIDE

ⒶⒶⒶ ▼▼▼ Best Western Ocean View Resort 🆂🅷 🐾
(503) 738-3334. **$49-$439, 3 day notice.** 414 N Prom. US 101, exit 1st Ave, just w, just n on Necanicum Dr, then just w on 4th Ave. Ext/int corridors. **Pets:** Other species. $10 daily fee/pet. Designated rooms, service with restrictions, supervision.
🆂🅰🆅🅴 🆂🅾 ☒ 🏍 🍽 🔌 🍴 🏊

ⒶⒶⒶ ▼▼▼ Comfort Inn Boardwalk 🆂🅷 🐾
(503) 738-3011. **$79-$299.** 545 Broadway. US 101, exit Ave A, just w; downtown. Int corridors. **Pets:** Small, dogs only. $25 daily fee/pet. Designated rooms, service with restrictions, supervision.
🆂🅰🆅🅴 🆂🅾 ☒ 🅼 🍴 🏍 🍽 🔌 🏊

ⒶⒶⒶ ▼▼▼ Ebb-Tide Resort 🆂🅷
(503) 738-8371. **$50-$200.** 300 N Prom. US 101, exit 1st Ave, 0.4 mi w, just n on Columbia St, then just w on 2nd Ave. Ext/int corridors. **Pets:** Other species. $20 daily fee/pet. Service with restrictions, supervision.
🆂🅰🆅🅴 ☒ 🍽 🔌 🏊 ☒ 🎿

ⒶⒶⒶ ▼▼▼ Inn at Seaside 🅼 🐾
(503) 738-9581. **$60-$199, 3 day notice.** 441 2nd Ave. US 101, exit 1st Ave, 0.4 mi w. Ext/int corridors. **Pets:** Other species. $10 daily fee/pet. Service with restrictions, crate.
🆂🅰🆅🅴 🆂🅾 ☒ 🍴 🍽 🔌 🏊

ⒶⒶⒶ ▼▼▼ Seashore Inn...on the Beach 🅼
(503) 738-6368. **$69-$195.** 60 N Prom. US 101, exit 1st Ave, 0.4 mi w. Ext/int corridors. **Pets:** Small. $20 daily fee/room. Service with restrictions, supervision.
🆂🅰🆅🅴 🆂🅾 ☒ 🍽 🔌 🏊 🎿

ⒶⒶⒶ ▼▼▼ Sea Side Oceanfront Inn Bed & Breakfast Hotel 🅱🅱
(503) 738-6403. **$95-$315, 5 day notice.** 581 S Prom. US 101, exit Ave G, 0.6 mi w, then just n. Int corridors. **Pets:** Accepted.
🆂🅰🆅🅴 ☒ 🍽 🔌 🍴

SHADY COVE

ⒶⒶⒶ ▼▼▼▼ The Edgewater Inn on the Rogue River 🅼
(541) 878-3171. **$69-$153.** 7800 Rogue River Dr. Off SR 62. Ext corridors. **Pets:** Accepted.
🆂🅰🆅🅴 🆂🅾 ☒ 🍴 🍽 🔌 🏊 ☒

SISTERS

ⒶⒶⒶ ▼▼▼ Best Western Ponderosa Lodge 🅼
(541) 549-1234. **$95-$220, 30 day notice.** 500 Hwy 20 W. West end of town, just w on US 20 from jct SR 242. Ext corridors. **Pets:** Accepted.
🆂🅰🆅🅴 🆂🅾 ☒ 🍴 🍽 🔌 🏊

ⒶⒶⒶ ▼▼▼ Sisters Inn & RV Park 🅼
(541) 549-7829. **$80-$100.** 540 Hwy 20 W. West end of town, just w on US 20 from jct SR 242. Ext corridors. **Pets:** Small. $15 one-time fee/room. Service with restrictions, supervision.
🆂🅰🆅🅴 🆂🅾 ☒ 🅼 🍴 🏍 🍽 🔌 🏊

SPRINGFIELD

Best Western Grand Manor Inn M
(541) 726-4769. **$86-$129.** 971 Kruse Way. I-5, exit 195A, just e. Int corridors. **Pets:** Dogs only. $100 deposit/room, $10 daily fee/pet. Designated rooms, service with restrictions, supervision.

Comfort Suites Eugene/Springfield SH
(541) 746-5359. **$109-$129.** 969 Kruse Way. I-5, exit 195A, just e. Int corridors. **Pets:** Small, dogs only. $10 daily fee/pet. Designated rooms, service with restrictions, supervision.

Holiday Inn Express SH
(541) 746-8471. **$89-$139.** 3480 Hutton St. I-5, exit 195A, just e. Int corridors. **Pets:** Medium, dogs only. $10 daily fee/pet. Designated rooms, service with restrictions, supervision.

Motel 6 #418 M
(541) 741-1105. **$51-$65.** 3752 International Ct. I-5, exit 195A, just e, then just n on Gateway St. Ext corridors. **Pets:** Medium, other species. Service with restrictions, supervision.

Village Inn M
(541) 747-4546. **$69.** 1875 Mohawk Blvd. I-5, exit 194A, 2.5 mi e, then just n. Ext corridors. **Pets:** Very small. Designated rooms, service with restrictions, supervision.

SUMMER LAKE

Summer Lake Inn CI
(541) 943-3983. **$115-$175, 14 day notice.** 47531 Hwy 31. 10 mi s; between MM 81 and 82. Ext corridors. **Pets:** Accepted.

SUNRIVER

Sunray Vacation Rentals VH
(541) 593-3225. **$100-$800, 60 day notice.** 56890 Venture Ln. 1 mi w on S Century Dr from jct US 97, then just e. Ext corridors. **Pets:** Accepted.

Sunriver Resort LH
(541) 593-1000. **$139-$244, 21 day notice.** 1 Center Dr. 2 mi w of US 97. Ext corridors. **Pets:** Dogs only. $75 deposit/pet. Designated rooms, supervision.

SUTHERLIN

Sutherlin Inn SH
(541) 459-6800. **$54-$90.** 1400 Hospitality Pl. I-5, exit 136, just se. Int corridors. **Pets:** Other species. $10 daily fee/room. Service with restrictions.

Umpqua Regency Inn M
(541) 459-1424. **$65-$85.** 150 Myrtle St. I-5, exit 136, just e. Ext corridors. **Pets:** Other species. $5 daily fee/pet. Service with restrictions, supervision.

SWEET HOME

Sweet Home Inn M
(541) 367-5137. **$69-$74.** 805 Long St. Just e of jct US 20 and SR 228; just s on 10th Ave, just w. Ext corridors. **Pets:** Large, dogs only. $10 daily fee/pet. Service with restrictions, crate.

TILLAMOOK

Mar-Clair Inn M
(503) 842-7571. **$76-$96.** 11 Main Ave. US 101, just n of jct SR 6. Ext/int corridors. **Pets:** Small, dogs only. $10 one-time fee/pet. Service with restrictions, supervision.

Shilo Inn Suites-Tillamook SH
(503) 842-7971. **$81-$143.** 2515 Main Ave. 1 mi n on US 101. Int corridors. **Pets:** Other species. $25 one-time fee/room. Supervision.

UMATILLA

Desert River Inn SH
(541) 922-1000. **$75-$87, 3 day notice.** 705 Willamette Ave. I-82, exit 1 (US 730), 1.6 mi e, then 0.3 mi n. Int corridors. **Pets:** Accepted.

WARRENTON

Shilo Inn Suites-Warrenton/Astoria SH
(503) 861-2181. **$74-$195.** 1609 E Harbor Dr. On US 26/101; near west end of Young's Bay Bridge. Int corridors. **Pets:** Other species. $25 one-time fee/room. Supervision.

WELCHES

The Resort at the Mountain LH
(503) 622-3101. **$99-$199, 3 day notice.** 68010 E Fairway Ave. 0.8 mi s of US 26 on E Welches Rd. Ext corridors. **Pets:** $25 one-time fee/pet. Designated rooms, service with restrictions, crate.

WHEELER

Wheeler on the Bay Lodge and Marina M
(503) 368-5858. **$55-$155, 4 day notice.** 580 Marine Dr. On US 101; center. Ext corridors. **Pets:** Small. $25 deposit/pet, $10 daily fee/pet. Service with restrictions, supervision.

WINSTON

Sweet Breeze Inn II M
(541) 679-2420. **$55-$79, 4 day notice.** 251 NE Main St. I-5, exit 119, 3 mi w. Ext corridors. **Pets:** Small. $9 daily fee/pet. Designated rooms, service with restrictions, supervision.

WOODBURN

Executive Inn Woodburn SH
(503) 982-6515. **$69-$109.** 2887 Newburg Hwy. I-5, exit 271, just e. Int corridors. **Pets:** Accepted.

La Quinta Inn & Suites Woodburn SH
(503) 982-1727. **$65-$89.** 120 Arney Rd NE. I-5, exit 271, just w. Int corridors. **Pets:** Accepted.

YACHATS

The Adobe Resort SH
(541) 547-3141. **$67-$275.** 1555 Hwy 101. 0.5 mi n. Int corridors. **Pets:** $10 daily fee/pet. Designated rooms, service with restrictions, supervision.

The Dublin House M
(541) 547-3703. **$39-$170.** 251 W 7th St. US 101 at 7th St; downtown. Ext corridors. **Pets:** Dogs only. Supervision.

AAA ▽▽▽ Fireside Motel 🅼 ☸
(541) 547-3636. **$65-$150.** 1881 Hwy 101 N. 0.6 mi n; just w of US 101. Ext corridors. **Pets:** Medium. $9 daily fee/pet. Service with restrictions, supervision.
SAVE S/D ⊠ 🗑 💻 ⊠ 🅰🅲

▽▽ Shamrock Lodgettes 🅒🅐
(541) 547-3312. **$59-$139, 3 day notice.** 105 Hwy 101 S. On US 101, just s. Ext corridors. **Pets:** Accepted.
ASK S/D ⊠ 🗑 💻 ⊠ 🅰🅲

CITY INDEX

ABBOTTSTOWN

🔺 ▼▼▼ The Altland House CI
(717) 259-9535. **$165-$325.** Center Square Rt 30. Jct SR 194. Int corridors. **Pets:** Medium, other species. $15 one-time fee/pet. Service with restrictions, supervision.

🅢🅐🆅🅴 ⊠ 🛄 ▣ 🍴

ALLENTOWN

🔺 ▼ Allenwood Motel M
(610) 395-3707. **$55-$135.** 1058 Hausman Rd. I-476, exit 56, 0.5 mi e on US 22, then 0.8 mi s on SR 309; I-78, exit 53 westbound; exit 51 eastbound, 1 mi n on SR 309, w on Tilghman St to light, then 0.8 mi n to dead end. Ext corridors. **Pets:** Medium. $10 daily fee/pet. Designated rooms, service with restrictions, supervision.

🅢🅐🆅🅴 🆂 ⊠ 🛄

🔺 ▼▼▼ Crowne Plaza Hotel LH
(610) 433-2221. **$139-$169.** 904 Hamilton Blvd. 9th St and Hamilton Blvd; downtown. Int corridors. **Pets:** Medium, dogs only. $50 one-time fee/pet. Designated rooms, service with restrictions, crate.

🅰🆂🅺 🆂 ⊠ 📶 🐾 🛄 ▣ 🍴 ≋

▼▼▼▼ Four Points by Sheraton Hotel & Suites Allentown Jetport SH
(610) 266-1000. **$190-$210.** 3400 Airport Rd. On SR 987 N (Airport Rd), 0.5 mi n of jct US 22. Int corridors. **Pets:** Accepted.

⊠ 🔛 📶 🐾 🛄 ▣ 🍴 ≋

🔺 ▼▼▼ Microtel Inn SH
(610) 266-0070. **$38-$139.** 1880 Steelstone Rd. US 22, exit Airport Rd S. Int corridors. **Pets:** $25 one-time fee/pet. Service with restrictions, supervision.

🅢🅐🆅🅴 🆂 ⊠ 🔛 📶 🐾 🛄 ▣

🔺 ▼▼▼ Quality Inn-Allentown SH
(610) 435-7880. **$49-$399.** 1715 Plaza Ln. US 22, exit 15th St, just n. Int corridors. **Pets:** Accepted.

🅢🅐🆅🅴 🆂 ⊠ 📶 🛄 ▣

▼▼▼ Red Roof Inn #7110 M
(610) 264-5404. **$59-$88.** 1846 Catasauqua Rd. US 22, exit Airport Rd S, just s. Ext corridors. **Pets:** Medium, other species. Service with restrictions, supervision.

⊠ 🔛 📶 🐾 🛄

▼▼▼ Staybridge Suites Allentown-Airport SH
(610) 443-5000. **$99-$259.** 1787-A Airport Rd. US 22, exit Airport Rd S, 0.3 mi s. Int corridors. **Pets:** Medium. $50 one-time fee/room.

🅰🆂🅺 🆂 ⊠ 🔛 📶 🐾 🛄 ▣ ≋

🔺 ▼▼▼ Super 8 Motel M
(610) 434-9550. **$45-$195.** 1033 Airport Rd. US 22, exit Airport Rd S, 1.1 mi s. Int corridors. **Pets:** Small. $25 daily fee/pet. Service with restrictions, supervision.

🅢🅐🆅🅴 🆂 ⊠ 🔛 🐾 🛄 ▣

ALTOONA

🔺 ▼▼▼ Econo Lodge M
(814) 944-3555. **$65.** 2906 Pleasant Valley Blvd. I-99/US 220, exit 32 (Frankstown Rd), 0.4 mi w, then 0.5 mi n. Ext corridors. **Pets:** Medium. Service with restrictions, crate.

🅢🅐🆅🅴 🆂 ⊠ 🛄 ▣ 🍴

▼ Motel 6 #1415 M
(814) 946-7601. **$50-$65.** 1500 Sterling St. I-99/US 220, exit 31 (Plank Rd), just w. Ext corridors. **Pets:** Medium, other species. Service with restrictions, supervision.

🆂 ⊠ 🔛 🐾 ≋

🔺 ▼▼▼ Quality Inn of Altoona SH
(814) 944-4581. **$69-$84.** 2915 Pleasant Valley Blvd. I-99/US 220, exit 32 (Frankstown Rd), 0.4 mi w, then 0.5 mi n. Ext corridors. **Pets:** $25 one-time fee/room. Service with restrictions, supervision.

🅢🅐🆅🅴 🆂 ⊠ 🐾 🛄 ▣ 🍴 ≋

▼▼ Super 8 Motel Altoona M
(814) 942-5350. **$58-$73.** 3535 Fairway Dr. I-99/US 220, exit 32 (Frankstown Rd), just w. Int corridors. **Pets:** $10 daily fee/pet. Service with restrictions, supervision.

🅰🆂🅺 🆂 ⊠ 🔛 🛄

BARKEYVILLE

AAA ▼▼▼ **Comfort Inn-Barkeyville** **M**
(814) 786-7901. **$80-$130.** 137 Gibb Rd. I-80, exit 29, just n on SR 8. Ext corridors. **Pets:** Medium. $10 one-time fee/pet. Designated rooms, no service, supervision.
SAVE Sₒ ⊠ 🛏 🖥

▼▼ **Super 8 Motel-Barkeyville** **M**
(814) 786-8375. **$55-$60.** 1010 Dholu Rd. I-80, exit 29, just n on SR 8. Int corridors. **Pets:** Accepted.
ASK Sₒ ⊠ 🖉 🛏

BEDFORD

AAA ▼▼▼ **Best Western Bedford Inn** **SH**
(814) 623-9006. **$73-$96.** 4517 Business Rt 220. I-70/76 (Pennsylvania Tpke), exit 146, 0.3 mi n. Ext/int corridors. **Pets:** $50 deposit/room, $10 daily fee/room. Service with restrictions, supervision.
SAVE Sₒ ⊠ 🖉 🛏 🖥 🍽 ≈ ⊠

AAA ▼ **Budget Host Inn** **M**
(814) 623-8107. **$38-$85.** 4378 Business Rt 220. I-70/76 (Pennsylvania Tpke), exit 146, just n. Ext corridors. **Pets:** Service with restrictions, crate.
SAVE Sₒ ⊠ 🛏 ≈

AAA ▼ **Motel Town House** **M**
(814) 623-5138. **$30-$45, 7 day notice.** 200 S Richard St. I-70/76 (Pennsylvania Tpke), exit 146, 2.5 mi s on US 220 business route. Ext corridors. **Pets:** Accepted.
SAVE Sₒ ⊠ 🛏

AAA ▼▼▼ **Quality Inn Bedford** **SH**
(814) 623-5188. **$63-$85.** 4407 Business Rt 220 N. I-70/76 (Pennsylvania Tpke), exit 146, just n. Ext/int corridors. **Pets:** Medium. $10 daily fee/room. Service with restrictions, supervision.
SAVE Sₒ ⊠ 🛏 🖥 🍽 ≈

AAA ▼ **Super 8 Motel** **M**
(814) 623-5880. **$45-$55.** 4498 Business Rt 220. I-70/76 (Pennslyvania Tpke), exit 146, 0.3 mi n. Int corridors. **Pets:** Accepted.
SAVE Sₒ ⊠ 🛏

AAA ▼▼ **Travelodge** **M**
(814) 623-7800. **$60-$110.** 4271 Business Rt 220. I-70/76 (Pennsylvania Tpke), exit 146, just s. Ext/int corridors. **Pets:** Accepted.
SAVE Sₒ ⊠ 🛏 🖥

BETHEL

AAA ▼▼▼ **Comfort Inn-Bethel/Midway** **SH**
(717) 933-8888. **$79-$139.** 41 Diner Dr. I-78, exit 16, just w. Int corridors. **Pets:** Other species. $10 daily fee/pet. Designated rooms, service with restrictions, crate.
SAVE Sₒ ⊠ 🔶 🖉 🛏 🖥 ≈

BETHLEHEM

AAA ▼▼▼ **Best Western Lehigh Valley Hotel & Conference Center** **SH**
(610) 866-5800. **$79-$149, 3 day notice.** 300 Gateway Dr. US 22, exit Center St and SR 512. Ext/int corridors. **Pets:** Accepted.
SAVE Sₒ ⊠ 🔶 🖉 🖾 🛏 🖥 🍽 ≈

AAA ▼▼▼ **Comfort Inn** **SH** 🐾
(610) 865-6300. **$85-$185.** 3191 Highfield Dr. US 22, exit SR 191, just s. Ext/int corridors. **Pets:** Other species. $10 daily fee/pet. Service with restrictions, supervision.
SAVE Sₒ ⊠ 🖉 🛏 🖥

AAA ▼▼▼ **Comfort Suites** **SH**
(610) 882-9700. **$99-$169.** 120 W 3rd St. SR 378, exit 3rd St, W 3rd and Brodhead sts; center. Int corridors. **Pets:** Other species. $10 daily fee/room. Designated rooms, service with restrictions, supervision.
SAVE Sₒ ⊠ 🖉 🛏 🖥 🍽

AAA ▼▼▼▼ **Historic Hotel Bethlehem** **LH** 🐾
(610) 625-5000. **$159-$179.** 437 Main St. SR 378 S, exit 3 (City Center), just n on 3rd Ave, 0.3 mi e on Union, then 0.3 mi s. Int corridors. **Pets:** Medium. $20 daily fee/room. Service with restrictions.
SAVE Sₒ ⊠ 🔶 🖉 🛏 🖥 🍽

▼▼▼ **Residence Inn by Marriott** **SH**
(610) 317-2662. **$169-$209.** 2180 Motel Dr. US 22, exit Airport Rd S, 0.8 mi se on Catasauqua Rd. Int corridors. **Pets:** Accepted.
ASK Sₒ ⊠ 🖉 🔷 🛏 🖥 ≈ ⊠

BLOOMSBURG

AAA ▼▼▼ **Econo Lodge at Bloomsburg** **SH** 🐾
(570) 387-0490. **$69-$149, 3 day notice.** 189 Columbia Mall Dr. I-80, exit 232, just n on SR 42. Int corridors. **Pets:** Large, other species. $20 daily fee/room. Service with restrictions, crate.
SAVE Sₒ ⊠ 🖉 🛏 🖥

▼▼▼ **The Inn at Turkey Hill** **CI**
(570) 387-1500. **$115-$125.** 991 Central Rd. I-80, exit 236 eastbound; exit 236A westbound, just s. Ext/int corridors. **Pets:** Accepted.
ASK Sₒ ⊠ 🛏 🖥 🍽

BLUE MOUNTAIN

AAA ▼▼ **Kenmar Motel** **M**
(717) 423-5915. **$65-$80.** 17788 Cumberland Hwy. I-76, exit 201, just e on SR 997 N. Ext corridors. **Pets:** Medium, dogs only. $5 daily fee/pet. Designated rooms, service with restrictions, supervision.
SAVE Sₒ ⊠ 🛏

BOYERTOWN

▼ **Mel-Dor Motel** **M**
(610) 367-2626. **$52-$56.** 5 Spring Garden Dr. SR 100, exit New Berlinville; 1 mi n of town. Ext corridors. **Pets:** Accepted.
⊠ 🛏

BRADFORD

AAA ▼▼▼ **Best Western Bradford Inn** **SH**
(814) 362-4501. **$90-$160.** 100 Davis St S. US 219, exit Forman St southbound, just w to Davis St, then 0.3 mi s; exit Elm St northbound, just w. Ext/int corridors. **Pets:** Large. $10 daily fee/pet. Designated rooms, service with restrictions, crate.
SAVE ⊠ 🔶 🛏 🖥 🍽 ≈

▼▼▼ **Glendorn** **CI** 🐾
(814) 362-6511. **$495-$795, 30 day notice.** 1000 Glendorn Dr. SR 219, exit Forman St, just s on Mechanic St, then 4.3 mi w on W Corydon. Ext/int corridors. **Pets:** Large, dogs only. $75 daily fee/pet. Designated rooms, service with restrictions, crate.
ASK ⊠ 🛏 🖥 🍽 ≈ ⊠

BREEZEWOOD

AAA ▼▼▼ **Best Western Plaza Inn** **M**
(814) 735-4352. **$59-$90.** 16407 Lincoln Hwy. I-76 (Pennsylvania Tpke), exit 161, just w on US 30; I-70, exit 147. Ext corridors. **Pets:** Accepted.
SAVE Sₒ ⊠ 🖥 ≈

AAA ▼▼▼ **Breezewood Ramada** **SH** 🐾
(814) 735-4005. **$62-$69, 7 day notice.** 16620 Lincoln Hwy. I-76 (Pennsylvania Tpke), exit 161, just e on US 30; I-70, exit 147, just e on US 30. Int corridors. **Pets:** Medium. $10 daily fee/room. Supervision.
SAVE Sₒ ⊠ 🛏 🖥 🍽 ≈ ⊠

Heritage Inn M
(814) 735-2200. **$59-$79.** 16550 Lincoln Hwy. I-76 (Pennsylvania Tpke), exit 161, just w on US 30; I-70, exit 147, just e on US 30. Int corridors. **Pets:** Accepted.

Wiltshire Motel M
(814) 735-4361. **$41-$49.** 140 S Breezewood Rd. I-76 (Pennsylvania Tpke), exit 161, just w on US 30; I-70, exit 147. Ext corridors. **Pets:** Accepted.

BROOKVILLE

Budget Host Gold Eagle Inn M
(814) 849-7344. **$50-$85.** 250 W Main St. I-80, exit 78, 0.5 mi s on SR 36. Ext corridors. **Pets:** Service with restrictions, crate.

Holiday Inn Express M
(814) 849-8381. **$89, 3 day notice.** 235 Allegheny Blvd. I-80, exit 78, just s on SR 36. Int corridors. **Pets:** $15 one-time fee/pet. Service with restrictions, supervision.

Super 8 Motel M
(814) 849-8840. **$54-$69.** 251 Allegheny Blvd. I-80, exit 78, just n on SR 36. Int corridors. **Pets:** Other species. $10 one-time fee/pet. Supervision.

CAMBRIDGE SPRINGS

The Riverside Inn CI
(814) 398-4645. **$65-$170, 10 day notice.** 1 Fountain Ave. Just ne of center. Int corridors. **Pets:** Other species. $25 one-time fee/room. Service with restrictions, supervision.

CAMP HILL

Radisson Penn Harris Hotel & Convention Center LH
(717) 763-7117. **$119-$181.** 1150 Camp Hill Bypass. Jct US 11, 15 and Erford Rd. Ext/int corridors. **Pets:** Accepted.

CARLISLE

Comfort Suites Hotel SH
(717) 960-1000. **$109-$194.** 10 S Hanover St. I-81, exit 47, 0.8 mi n on SR 34, just s of the square; downtown. Int corridors. **Pets:** Medium. $10 daily fee/pet. Service with restrictions, crate.

Days Inn & Suites-Carlisle SH
(717) 258-4147. **$69-$150.** 101 Alexander Spring Rd. I-81, exit 45, just sw. Int corridors. **Pets:** Accepted.

Econo Lodge M
(717) 249-7775. **$49-$119.** 1460 Harrisburg Pike. I-81, exit 52 southbound; exit 52A northbound; I-76 (Pennsylvania Tpke), exit 226, 0.8 mi n. Ext corridors. **Pets:** Small. $10 daily fee/pet. Designated rooms, service with restrictions, crate.

Hampton Inn Carlisle SH
(717) 240-0200. **$79-$199.** 1164 Harrisburg Pike. I-76 (Pennsylvania Tpke), exit 226, just n; I-81, exit 52 (US 11) southbound; exit 52B northbound, 0.8 mi s. Int corridors. **Pets:** Medium. Service with restrictions, supervision.

Holiday Inn Carlisle SH
(717) 245-2400. **$108-$180.** 1450 Harrisburg Pike. I-81, exit 52 southbound; exit 52A northbound, just se; I-76 (Pennsylvania Tpke), exit 226, 0.8 mi n. Int corridors. **Pets:** Accepted.

Hotel Carlisle & Embers Convention Center LH
(717) 243-1717. **$109-$210.** 1700 Harrisburg Pike. I-81, exit 52 southbound; exit 52A northbound, 0.4 mi n; I-76 (Pennsylvania Tpke), exit 226, 1.2 mi n. Int corridors. **Pets:** Medium, other species. $10 daily fee/pet. Designated rooms, service with restrictions, supervision.

Howard Johnson Inn SH
(717) 243-5411. **$40-$150, 3 day notice.** 1245 Harrisburg Pike. I-81, exit 52 (US 11) southbound; exit 52B northbound, 0.5 mi s; I-76 (Pennsylvania Tpke), exit 226, 0.8 mi n on US 11. Ext/int corridors. **Pets:** Accepted.

Pheasant Field Bed & Breakfast BB
(717) 258-0717. **$105-$185, 3 day notice.** 150 Hickorytown Rd. I-76 (Pennsylvania Tpke), exit 226, 0.4 mi n on US 11, 2.3 mi se on S Middlesex Rd, 0.4 mi e on Ridge Dr, then just s (right turn). Ext/int corridors. **Pets:** Other species. $10 daily fee/room. Designated rooms, service with restrictions, supervision.

Quality Inn Carlisle SH
(717) 243-6000. **$69-$119.** 1255 Harrisburg Pike. I-81, exit 52 southbound; exit 52B northbound; I-76 (Pennsylvania Tpke), exit 226, 0.8 mi n. Int corridors. **Pets:** Small, dogs only. $10 daily fee/pet. Service with restrictions, supervision.

Ramada Ltd SH
(717) 243-8585. **$80-$153.** 1252 Harrisburg Pike. I-81, exit 52 (US 11) southbound; exit 52B northbound; I-76 (Pennsylvania Tpke), exit 226, 1 mi n on US 11. Ext/int corridors. **Pets:** Medium, other species. $10 daily fee/pet. Designated rooms, service with restrictions, supervision.

Rodeway Inn M
(717) 249-2800. **$45-$125.** 1239 Harrisburg Pike. I-81, exit 52 (US 11) southbound; exit 52B northbound, 0.3 mi s; I-76 (Pennsylvania Tpke), exit 226, 0.8 mi s. Ext corridors. **Pets:** Small, other species. $8 daily fee/pet. Service with restrictions, crate.

Sleep Inn Carlisle SH
(717) 249-8863. **$69-$149, 30 day notice.** 5 E Garland Dr. I-81, exit 47 northbound, just ne; exit 47A southbound. Int corridors. **Pets:** Other species. $10 one-time fee/pet. Designated rooms, service with restrictions, supervision.

Super 8 Motel/Carlisle South M
(717) 245-9898. **$51-$105.** 100 Alexander Spring Rd. I-81, exit 45, just se. Int corridors. **Pets:** Accepted.

Super 8 Motel/North Carlisle M
(717) 249-7000. **$32-$149, 3 day notice.** 1800 Harrisburg Pike. I-81, exit 52A northbound; exit 52 (US 11) southbound, 0.5 mi n; I-76 (Pennsylvania Tpke), exit 226, 1.3 mi n. Ext/int corridors. **Pets:** Accepted.

CHAMBERSBURG

Best Western Chambersburg SH
(717) 262-4994. **$69-$199.** 211 Walker Rd. I-81, exit 16, just w on US 30, then just n. Int corridors. **Pets:** Accepted.

Comfort Inn-Chambersburg SH
(717) 263-6655. **$63-$150.** 3301 Black Gap Rd. I-81, exit 20, just e, then just s on SR 997. Int corridors. **Pets:** $10 daily fee/pet. Designated rooms, service with restrictions, supervision.

Days Inn SH
(717) 263-1288. **$60-$109.** 30 Falling Spring Rd. I-81, exit 16, just e on US 30. Int corridors. **Pets:** Medium, other species. $10 daily fee/pet. Designated rooms, service with restrictions, supervision.

Econo Lodge M
(717) 264-8005. **$58-$72.** 1110 Sheller Ave. I-81, exit 14, just w on SR 316. Int corridors. **Pets:** Other species. $10 one-time fee/pet. Service with restrictions, supervision.

CLARION

Holiday Inn SH
(814) 226-8850. **$64-$130.** 45 Holiday Inn Rd. I-80, exit 62, 0.5 mi n on SR 68. Int corridors. **Pets:** Other species. $10 daily fee/room. Service with restrictions, supervision.

Microtel Inn & Suites-Clarion SH
(814) 227-2700. **$59-$99.** 151 Hotel Dr. I-80, exit 62, just n on SR 68, then just e. Int corridors. **Pets:** Accepted.

Quality Inn & Suites Clarion M
(814) 226-8682. **$70-$95.** 24 United Dr. I-80, exit 62, just n on SR 68. Int corridors. **Pets:** $5 one-time fee/pet. Designated rooms, service with restrictions, supervision.

Super 8 Motel-Clarion M
(814) 226-4550. **$55-$68, 7 day notice.** 135 Hotel Rd. I-80, exit 62, just n on SR 68. Ext corridors. **Pets:** Other species. $10 daily fee/room. Designated rooms, service with restrictions, supervision.

CLARKS SUMMIT

Comfort Inn-Clarks Summit/Scranton SH
(570) 586-9100. **$69-$159.** 811 Northern Blvd. I-81, exit 194, on US 6 and 11; I-476 (Pennsylvania Tpke), exit 131. Int corridors. **Pets:** Accepted.

The Inn at Nichols Village SH
(570) 587-1135. **$89-$220.** 1101 Northern Blvd. I-81, exit 194, just w; I-476 (Pennsylvania Tpke), exit 131, 0.7 mi w on US 6 and 11. Int corridors. **Pets:** Accepted.

Ramada Clarks Summit Hotel SH
(570) 586-2730. **$89-$189.** 820 Northern Blvd. I-81, exit 194; I-476 (Pennsylvania Tpke), exit 131, 0.3 mi w on US 6 and 11. Int corridors. **Pets:** Very small. $20 daily fee/pet. Service with restrictions, supervision.

CLEARFIELD

Budget Inn M
(814) 765-2639. **$36-$70.** 6321 Woodland Hwy (US 322 E). I-80, exit 120, 1.5 mi sw on SR 879, then 1.2 mi e. Ext/int corridors. **Pets:** $6 daily fee/pet. Designated rooms, no service, supervision.

Comfort Inn Clearfield SH
(814) 768-6400. **$62-$150.** 1821 Industrial Park Rd. I-80, exit 120, just s. Int corridors. **Pets:** Other species. $15 daily fee/room. Supervision.

Super 8 Motel-Clearfield M
(814) 768-7580. **$48-$81.** 14597 Clearfield/Shawville Hwy (Rt 879). I-80, exit 120, just s. Int corridors. **Pets:** Accepted.

DANVILLE

Quality Inn & Suites Danville M
(570) 275-5100. **$89-$159.** 15 Valley West Rd. I-80, exit 224, just n on SR 54. Int corridors. **Pets:** Accepted.

DICKSON CITY

Residence Inn by Marriott-Scranton SH
(570) 343-5121. **$165-$185.** 947 Viewmont Dr. I-81, exit 190, just e, follow signs to Viewmont Dr. Int corridors. **Pets:** Accepted.

DU BOIS

Clarion Hotel DuBois SH
(814) 371-5100. **$75-$85.** 1896 Rich Hwy. I-80, exit 97, just s. Int corridors. **Pets:** Medium. Designated rooms, service with restrictions, supervision.

DUNMORE

Days Inn SH
(570) 348-6101. **$56-$125.** 1226 O Hwy. I-81, exit 188 (Throop), just n at SR 347. Int corridors. **Pets:** $5 daily fee/pet. Service with restrictions, supervision.

Holiday Inn-Scranton East SH
(570) 343-4771. **$79-$179.** 200 Tigue St. I-84/380, exit 1 (Tigue St), 0.3 mi e of jct I-81. Ext/int corridors. **Pets:** Medium, other species. $10 daily fee/pet. Designated rooms, no service.

Sleep Inn, Inn & Suites SH
(570) 961-1116. **$80-$169.** 102 Monahan Ave. I-81, exit 188 (Throop), just e at SR 347 N (O'Neill Hwy), then just s. Int corridors. **Pets:** Medium, other species. $10 daily fee/pet. Designated rooms, service with restrictions, supervision.

EASTON

Comfort Inn SH
(610) 253-0546. **$89-$169.** 2555 Nazareth Rd. US 22, exit 25th St, just e on N Service Rd. Int corridors. **Pets:** Medium. $20 daily fee/pet. Designated rooms, service with restrictions, supervision.

The Lafayette Inn BB
(610) 253-4500. **$110-$225.** 525 W Monroe St. US 22, exit 4th St (SR 611), just n on 3rd St, 0.3 mi ne on College Ave, then 0.3 mi n on Cattell St to jct Monroe St. Ext/int corridors. **Pets:** $20 daily fee/pet. Designated rooms, service with restrictions, crate.

AAA ▼▼▼ **Quality Inn-Easton Inn** SH
(610) 253-9131. **$80-$150.** 185 S 3rd St. I-78, exit 75, 1 mi n, follow signs; US 22, exit 4th St (SR 611), just e to 3rd St, then 0.5 mi s; downtown. Int corridors. **Pets:** Accepted.
SAVE S X 🖥 💻 ⊞ ⛱

EBENSBURG

▼▼▼ **Comfort Inn** SH
(814) 472-6100. **$87-$97.** 111 Cook Rd. Jct US 219, just e on US 22. Int corridors. **Pets:** Accepted.
ASK S X M 🖥 💻 ⛱

ERIE

AAA ▼▼▼ **Best Western Erie Inn & Suites** SH
(814) 864-1812. **$54-$129, 7 day notice.** 7820 Perry Hwy. I-90, exit 27, just n. Int corridors. **Pets:** Accepted.
SAVE S X 🖥 💻 ⛱

AAA ▼▼▼ **Country Inn & Suites** SH
(814) 864-5810. **$54-$129, 7 day notice.** 8040 Oliver Rd. I-90, exit 24, just s, then 0.5 mi w. Int corridors. **Pets:** $25 one-time fee/room. Service with restrictions, supervision.
SAVE S X 🖥 💻 ⛱

▼▼ **Days Inn** SH
(814) 868-8521. **$59-$169.** 7415 Schultz Rd. I-90, exit 27, just n on SR 97. Int corridors. **Pets:** Other species. $5 daily fee/pet. Service with restrictions, supervision.
ASK S X 🖥 💻 ⛱

▼▼▼ **Homewood Suites by Hilton** SH
(814) 866-8292. **$175-$195.** 2084 Interchange Rd. I-79, exit 180, just e. Int corridors. **Pets:** Accepted.
ASK S X 🖥 💻 ⛱

▼ **Microtel Inn-Erie** M
(814) 864-1010. **$50-$100.** 8100 Peach St. I-90, exit 24, just s. Int corridors. **Pets:** $10 daily fee/room. Service with restrictions, crate.
ASK S X 🖥 💻 🖥

▼▼ **Red Roof Inn #7054** M
(814) 868-5246. **$53-$105.** 7865 Perry Hwy. I-90, exit 27, just n on SR 97. Ext/int corridors. **Pets:** Medium, other species. Service with restrictions, supervision.
X 🖥 🖥

▼▼▼ **Residence Inn by Marriott** SH
(814) 864-2500. **$109-$299.** 8061 Peach St. I-90, exit 24, just s. Int corridors. **Pets:** Other species. $75 one-time fee/room. Service with restrictions, supervision.
ASK S X 🖥 💻 ⛱ X

▼▼ **Super 8 Motel** SH
(814) 864-9200. **$49-$109.** 8040 Perry Hwy. I-90, exit 27, just s. Int corridors. **Pets:** Small. $5 one-time fee/pet. Service with restrictions, supervision.
ASK S X 🖥

FOGELSVILLE

▼▼▼▼ **Comfort Inn Lehigh Valley-West** SH
(610) 391-0344. **$80-$130.** 7625 Imperial Way. I-78, exit 49B (SR 100), just n. Int corridors. **Pets:** Medium, other species. $25 one-time fee/pet. Service with restrictions, crate.
ASK S X 🖥 💻

▼▼▼ **Glasbern** CI ❀
(610) 285-4723. **$140-$325, 7 day notice.** 2141 Packhouse Rd. I-78, exit 49B (SR 100), 0.3 mi n to 1st light, 0.3 mi w on Main St, 0.6 mi n on Church St, then 0.8 mi ne. Ext/int corridors. **Pets:** $25 daily fee/pet. Designated rooms, service with restrictions, supervision.
ASK X 🖥 💻 ⊞ ⛱ X

▼▼▼ **Holiday Inn Conference Center** SH ❀
(610) 391-1000. **$99-$219.** 7736 Adrienne Dr. I-78, exit 49A, 0.3 mi s on SR 100. Int corridors. **Pets:** Dogs only. $49 one-time fee/room. Service with restrictions, crate.
ASK S X M 🖥 💻 ⊞ ⛱ X

▼▼ **Sleep Inn** SH
(610) 395-6603. **$59-$169.** 327 Star Rd. I-78, exit 49A, 0.3 mi s on SR 100, left at 1st traffic light, then immediate left on service road. Int corridors. **Pets:** Medium. $15 daily fee/pet. Designated rooms, no service, supervision.
ASK S X M 🖥 💻

▼▼▼ **Staybridge Suites-Allentown West** SH
(610) 841-5100. **$99-$239.** 327 C Star Rd. I-78, exit 49A, 0.3 mi s on SR 100, e at traffic light, then n on service road. Int corridors. **Pets:** Accepted.
ASK X 🖥 💻 ⛱ X

FRACKVILLE

AAA ▼▼▼ **Econo Lodge** M
(570) 874-3838. **$59-$109.** 501 S Middle St. I-81, exit 124B, 0.4 mi n on SR 61. Ext corridors. **Pets:** Accepted.
SAVE S X 🖥 💻

AAA ▼▼▼ **Granny's Motel & Restaurant** SH ❀
(570) 874-0408. **$58-$69.** 115 W Coal St. I-81, exit 124B, 0.3 mi nw on SR 61, then 0.3 mi n on Altamont Blvd. Ext/int corridors. **Pets:** $5 one-time fee/room. Service with restrictions.
SAVE X 🖥 💻 ⊞

FRANKLIN

▼▼ **Franklin Super 8 Motel** SH
(814) 432-2101. **$65.** 847 Allegheny Ave. 2 mi on SR 8 N. Int corridors. **Pets:** Accepted.
ASK S X 🖥

GALETON

▼ **Pine Log Motel** M
(814) 435-6400. **$50-$65, 7 day notice.** 5156 US Rt 6 W. On US 6, 9 mi w. Ext corridors. **Pets:** Accepted.
X 🖥 X ⓚ

GETTYSBURG

AAA ▼▼▼ **Americas Best Value Inn** M
(717) 334-1188. **$56-$151.** 301 Steinwehr Ave. 1 mi s on US 15 business route, just s of jct SR 134. Ext/int corridors. **Pets:** Small, other species. $10 daily fee/room, $20 one-time fee/room. Service with restrictions, crate.
SAVE S X 🖥 ⛱

▼▼ **Gettysburg Travelodge** M ❀
(717) 334-9281. **$59-$165.** 613 Baltimore St. On SR 97 at US 15 business route. Ext/int corridors. **Pets:** Other species. Designated rooms, service with restrictions.
ASK S X 🖥 💻

▼▼▼ **Holiday Inn-Battlefield** SH
(717) 334-6211. **$72-$280.** 516 Baltimore St. Jct US 15 business route and SR 97. Ext/int corridors. **Pets:** Large, other species. $10 one-time fee/room. Designated rooms, service with restrictions, supervision.
ASK S X 🖥 💻 ⊞ ⛱

▼▼ **Holiday Inn Express of Gettysburg** M
(717) 337-1400. **$76-$170.** 869 York Rd. 1 mi e on US 30. Int corridors. **Pets:** Service with restrictions, supervision.
ASK S X M 🖥 💻 ⛱

GIRARD

▼▼ The Green Roof Inn 🅜 ❀
(814) 774-7072. **$55-$85.** 8790 Rt 18. I-90, exit 9, 1.9 mi s. Ext corridors. **Pets:** Other species. $10 daily fee/pet. Designated rooms, service with restrictions, supervision.

ASK S🌀 ✕ 🖥 💻

GRANTVILLE

▲▲▲ ▼▼ Econo Lodge 🅜
(717) 469-0631. **$50-$95.** 252 Bow Creek Rd. I-81, exit 80. Ext corridors. **Pets:** Medium. $6 daily fee/pet. Designated rooms, service with restrictions, supervision.

SAVE S🌀 ✕ 🍴 🖥 💻

▲▲▲ ▼▼▼ Holiday Inn Harrisburg-Hershey Area, I-81 SH
(717) 469-0661. **$99-$189.** 604 Station Rd. I-81, exit 80. Int corridors. **Pets:** Medium. $75 deposit/room. Service with restrictions, supervision.

SAVE S🌀 ✕ ♿ 🍴 🔥 🖥 💻 🍴 ➰ ✕

GREENCASTLE

▲▲▲ ▼▼ Comfort Inn SH
(717) 597-8164. **$60-$100.** 50 Pine Dr. I-81, exit 3, just s on US 11. Int corridors. **Pets:** Medium, other species. $10 daily fee/pet. Service with restrictions, supervision.

SAVE S🌀 ✕ 🍴 💻 🍴 ✕

GROVE CITY

▼▼ Old Arbor Rose Bed & Breakfast BB
(724) 458-6425. **$75, 4 day notice.** 114 W Main St. Just e. Int corridors. **Pets:** Accepted.

ASK S🌀 ✕ ➰

HAMBURG

▲▲▲ ▼▼▼ Microtel Inn & Suites SH
(610) 562-4234. **$70-$180, 30 day notice.** 50 Industrial Dr. I-78, exit 29B, 0.3 mi n on SR 61, then just e. Int corridors. **Pets:** Other species. $10 daily fee/pet. Service with restrictions, supervision.

SAVE S🌀 ✕ ♿ 🔥 🍴 💻

HANOVER

▲▲▲ ▼▼ Howard Johnson Inn 🅜
(717) 646-1000. **$49-$99.** 1080 Carlisle St. 1.5 mi n on SR 94, just e. Ext corridors. **Pets:** Small, dogs only. $25 daily fee/pet. No service, supervision.

SAVE S🌀 ✕ ♿ 🍴 💻 ➰

HARRISBURG

▲▲▲ ▼▼▼ Best Western Capital Plaza SH
(717) 545-9089. **$76-$85.** 150 Nationwide Dr. I-81, exit 69, just n. Ext/int corridors. **Pets:** Medium. Designated rooms, service with restrictions, supervision.

SAVE S🌀 ✕ ♿ 🍴 💻 ➰

▲▲▲ ▼▼▼▼ Best Western Harrisburg/Hershey Hotel & Suites SH
(717) 652-7180. **$90-$165.** 300 N Mountain Rd. I-81, exit 72 southbound; exit 72B northbound. Int corridors. **Pets:** $10 daily fee/pet. Designated rooms, supervision.

SAVE S🌀 ✕ ♿ 🔥 🍴 🖥 💻 🍴 ➰ ✕

▲▲▲ ▼▼▼▼ Comfort Inn Harrisburg East SH
(717) 561-8100. **$80-$129.** 4021 Union Deposit Rd. I-83, exit 48, just w. Int corridors. **Pets:** Medium, other species. $10 daily fee/room. No service.

SAVE S🌀 ✕ ♿ 🔥 🍴 💻 ➰

▲▲▲ ▼▼▼ Comfort Inn Harrisburg/Hershey SH
(717) 540-8400. **$69-$169.** 7744 Linglestown Rd. I-81, exit 77, 0.5 mi w. Int corridors. **Pets:** Large, other species. $10 daily fee/room. Designated rooms, service with restrictions, crate.

SAVE S🌀 ✕ ♿ 🔥 🍴 🖥 💻 ➰ ✕

▲▲▲ ▼▼▼ Comfort Inn-Riverfront SH
(717) 233-1611. **$89-$149.** 525 S Front St. I-83, exit 43, 0.5 mi n. Ext/int corridors. **Pets:** Medium. $25 daily fee/pet. Designated rooms, service with restrictions, supervision.

SAVE S🌀 ✕ ♿ 🍴 🖥 💻 🍴 ➰

▲▲▲ ▼▼▼▼ Country Inn & Suites By Carlson SH
(717) 651-5100. **$80-$200.** 8000 Jonestown Rd. I-81, exit 77, just s. Int corridors. **Pets:** Accepted.

SAVE S🌀 ✕ ♿ 🔥 🍴 🖥 💻 ➰

▲▲▲ ▼▼▼▼ Crowne Plaza Harrisburg-Hershey LH
(717) 234-5021. **$128-$209.** 23 S 2nd St. Jct Chestnut St; downtown. Int corridors. **Pets:** Small. $50 daily fee/pet. Designated rooms, service with restrictions, crate.

SAVE S🌀 ✕ ♿ 🔥 🍴 🍴 🖥 💻 🍴 ➰

▲▲▲ ▼▼▼▼ Holiday Inn Express Hotel & Suites SH
(717) 657-2200. **$79-$159.** 5680 Allentown Blvd. I-81, exit 72, just s on N Mountain Rd, then just w on US 22. Int corridors. **Pets:** Medium. $10 daily fee/pet. Designated rooms, service with restrictions, supervision.

SAVE S🌀 ✕ ♿ 🍴 🔥 🍴 💻 ➰

▲▲▲ ▼▼▼▼ Holiday Inn Harrisburg East-Airport SH
(717) 939-7841. **$130-$170.** 4751 Lindle Rd. I-283, exit 2, just e. Int corridors. **Pets:** Medium. $75 deposit/pet. Service with restrictions, crate.

SAVE S🌀 ✕ ♿ 🍴 🔥 🍴 🖥 💻 🍴 ➰ ✕

▲▲▲ ▼▼▼ Howard Johnson Inn SH
(717) 540-9100. **$49-$129.** 7930 Linglestown Rd. I-81, exit 77. Int corridors. **Pets:** Very small. $10 daily fee/room. Designated rooms, service with restrictions, supervision.

SAVE S🌀 ✕ 🍴 🍴 💻

▲▲▲ ▼▼▼ La Quinta Inn & Suites Harrisburg-Airport SH
(717) 939-8000. **$72-$149.** 990 Eisenhower Blvd. I-283, exit 2, just se; I-76 (Pennsylvania Tpke), exit 247, 1 mi n. Int corridors. **Pets:** Medium. Service with restrictions.

SAVE ✕ 🍴 🍴 💻

▲▲▲ ▼▼▼ Quality Inn SH
(717) 540-9339. **$70-$150.** 200 N Mountain Rd. I-81, exit 72A northbound; exit 72 southbound. Int corridors. **Pets:** Accepted.

SAVE S🌀 ✕ 🍴 🍴 💻

▼▼▼ Red Roof Inn-North #7037 🅜
(717) 657-1445. **$49-$63.** 400 Corporate Cir. I-81, exit 69, just n on Progress Ave. Ext/int corridors. **Pets:** Medium, other species. Service with restrictions, supervision.

✕ 🍴 🔥

▼▼ Red Roof Inn-South #7027 🅜
(717) 939-1331. **$51-$86.** 950 Eisenhower Blvd. I-283, exit 2, just e. Ext/int corridors. **Pets:** Medium, other species. Service with restrictions, supervision.

✕ 🍴 🔥 🍴

▼▼▼ Residence Inn by Marriott Harrisburg-Hershey SH
(717) 561-1900. **$169-$219.** 4480 Lewis Rd. US 322, exit Penhar Dr, just e. Ext corridors. **Pets:** $100 one-time fee/room. Service with restrictions, crate.

ASK ✕ 🍴 🍴 💻 ➰ ✕

▲▲▲ ▼▼▼▼ Sheraton Harrisburg Hershey LH
(717) 564-5511. **$139-$325.** 4650 Lindle Rd. I-283, exit 2, just e. Int corridors. **Pets:** Accepted.

SAVE S🌀 ✕ 🍴 🔥 🍴 🍴 🖥 💻 🍴 ➰ ✕

AAA ▼ Super 8 Motel-North M
(717) 233-5891. **$65-$129.** 4125 N Front St. I-81, exit 66, 0.8 mi n. Ext corridors. **Pets:** Accepted.
SAVE S× ⊠ 🖶 🌊

HAZLETON

AAA ▼▼ Best Western Genetti Inn & Suites SH
(570) 454-2494. **$80-$125.** 1441 N Church St. I-80, exit 262, 6 mi s on SR 309. Ext/int corridors. **Pets:** Dogs only. $10 daily fee/pet. Service with restrictions, supervision.
SAVE S× ⊠ 🐾 🖶 💻 🌊

AAA ▼▼ Ramada Inn Hazleton SH
(570) 455-2061. **$79-$99.** 1213 N Church. I-80, exit 262, 6 mi s on SR 309; I-81, exit 145, 0.5 mi s on SR 93, 1 mi e on Airport Rd, then 0.7 mi s. Ext corridors. **Pets:** $10 daily fee/pet. Designated rooms, service with restrictions, supervision.
SAVE S× ⊠ 🐾 🖶 💻 �🍴 🌊

HERSHEY

AAA ▼▼▼ Days Inn Hershey SH
(717) 534-2162. **$89-$249.** 350 W Chocolate Ave. On US 422; center. Int corridors. **Pets:** Medium, dogs only. $20 one-time fee/pet. Service with restrictions, supervision.
SAVE S× ⊠ ☾M 🐾 🖶 💻 🌊 ⊠

AAA ▼▼▼ Hampton Inn & Suites SH
(717) 533-8400. **$99-$239.** 749 E Chocolate Ave. 0.9 mi e on US 422. Int corridors. **Pets:** Small. $10 daily fee/pet. Designated rooms, service with restrictions, supervision.
SAVE S× ⊠ ☾M 🐾 🐾 🖶 💻 🌊 ⊠

HUMMELSTOWN

AAA ▼ Hershey Econo Lodge M
(717) 533-2515. **$59-$159.** 115 Lucy Ave. Jct US 322, just e on US 422. Ext corridors. **Pets:** Dogs only. $10 daily fee/pet.
SAVE S× ⊠ 🐾 🖶 💻

AAA ▼▼▼ Holiday Inn Express SH
(717) 583-0500. **$89-$219.** 610 Walton Ave. Just nw of jct US 322, 422 and SR 39 (Hershey Park Dr); just off Hershey Park Dr. Int corridors. **Pets:** Small. $10 daily fee/pet. Service with restrictions, crate.
SAVE S× ⊠ ☾M 🐾 🐾 🖶 💻 🌊 ⊠

HUNTINGDON

▼▼ Huntingdon Motor Inn M
(814) 643-1133. **$53-$75.** Motor Inn Rd. On US 22 at SR 26. Ext corridors. **Pets:** Accepted.
⊠ 🐾 🖶 💻

INDIANA

▼▼▼ Holiday Inn Holidome SH
(724) 463-3561. **$99-$149.** 1395 Wayne Ave. US 422, exit Wayne Ave, 1 mi n. Ext/int corridors. **Pets:** $10 one-time fee/pet. Service with restrictions, supervision.
ASK S× ⊠ 🐾 🖶 💻 �🍴 🌊 ⊠

JONESTOWN

AAA ▼▼ Days Inn Lebanon/Lickdale SH
(717) 865-4064. **$49-$159.** 3 Everest Ln. I-81, exit 90. Int corridors. **Pets:** Medium, other species. $10 one-time fee/pet. Service with restrictions, crate.
SAVE S× ⊠ 🐾 🖶 💻

▼▼ Red Carpet Inn & Suites-Jonestown M
(717) 865-6600. **$68-$120.** 16 Marsenna Ln. I-81, exit 90, just w. Int corridors. **Pets:** Service with restrictions, supervision.
ASK S× ⊠ 🖶 🌊

KITTANNING

▼▼ Comfort Inn SH
(724) 543-5200. **$90-$112.** 13 Hilltop Plaza. SR 28, exit 19A. Int corridors. **Pets:** Small. $15 one-time fee/pet. No service, supervision.
ASK S× ⊠ 🐾 🖶 💻 🌊

AAA ▼▼▼ Quality Inn Royle SH 🐾
(724) 543-1159. **$65-$95.** 405 Butler Rd. SR 28, exit US 422 W (Belmont). Ext/int corridors. **Pets:** Medium. $10 daily fee/pet. Designated rooms, service with restrictions, supervision.
SAVE S× ⊠ 🐾 🖶 💻 �🍴

▼▼ Rodeway Inn Kittanning M 🐾
(724) 543-1100. **$50-$60.** US 422 E. E of jct Business Rt US 422, SR 66 and 28. Ext corridors. **Pets:** Dogs only. $5 daily fee/pet.
ASK S× ⊠ 🖶 💻

LAUREL HIGHLANDS AREA

CHALK HILL

AAA ▼▼ The Lodge at Chalk Hill M
(724) 438-8880. **$57-$110.** Rt 40 E. Just w. Ext corridors. **Pets:** Other species. $10 daily fee/pet. Designated rooms, no service.
SAVE ⊠ 🖶 💻 ⊠

FARMINGTON

▼▼▼ Historic Summit Inn LH
(724) 438-8594. **$109-$299, 3 day notice.** 101 Skyline Dr. On US 40; center. Int corridors. **Pets:** Small, dogs only. $20 daily fee/pet. Service with restrictions, supervision.
ASK S× ⊠ 🖶 💻 �🍴 🌊 ⊠

AAA ▼▼▼▼ Nemacolin Woodlands Resort LH
(724) 329-8555. **$210-$3000, 14 day notice.** 1001 LaFayette Dr. 1 mi e on US 40. Ext/int corridors. **Pets:** Accepted.
SAVE S× ⊠ 🐾 🐾 🖶 💻 �🍴 🌊 ⊠

GREENSBURG

▼▼▼ Four Points by Sheraton SH
(724) 836-6060. **$90.** 100 Sheraton Dr. I-76 (Pennsylvania Tpke), exit 75, 5.6 mi on US 119 N, 3 mi e on US 30, then just n. Int corridors. **Pets:** Small. $10 daily fee/pet. Designated rooms, service with restrictions.
ASK S× ⊠ 🐾 🖶 💻 ⍴ 🌊 ⊠

▼ Knights Inn-Greensburg SH
(724) 836-7100. **$75.** 1215 S Main St. I-76 (Pennsylvania Tpke), exit 75, 4 mi s on US 119; just s of US 30. Ext corridors. **Pets:** $10 daily fee/pet. Designated rooms, service with restrictions, supervision.
ASK S× ⊠ 🖶 💻 🌊

JOHNSTOWN

▼▼▼ Comfort Inn & Suites SH
(814) 266-3678. **$85-$160.** 455 Theatre Dr. US 219, exit Elton (SR 756), just e. Int corridors. **Pets:** $50 deposit/room, $15 daily fee/pet. Designated rooms, service with restrictions, supervision.
ASK S× ⊠ ☾M 🐾 🖶 💻 🌊

▼▼ Econo Lodge Ⓜ
(814) 536-1114. **$49-$149.** 430 Napoleon Pl. Jct SR 271 and 403; downtown. Int corridors. **Pets:** Large, other species. $10 daily fee/room. Service with restrictions, supervision.

ⒶⓈⓀ Ⓢⓕⓑ ⊠ ☒ⓂⓜⒶⓐⓑⒶⓑ

▼▼▼ Holiday Inn Downtown 🆂🅷
(814) 535-7777. **$110.** 250 Market St. Corner of Market and Vine sts; downtown. Int corridors. **Pets:** Large. Designated rooms, service with restrictions, supervision.

ⒶⓈⓀ Ⓢⓕⓑ ⊠ Ⓐⓑ Ⓑ Ⓓ Ⓣ ⇆ ☒

▼▼ Holiday Inn Express Johnstown Ⓜ
(814) 266-8789. **$79-$94.** 1440 Scalp Ave. US 219, exit Windber (SR 56 E), just e. Int corridors. **Pets:** $25 one-time fee/room. Designated rooms, service with restrictions, supervision.

ⒶⓈⓀ Ⓢⓕⓑ ⊠ ☒Ⓜ Ⓜ Ⓐ Ⓑ Ⓓ

▼▼ Sleep Inn 🆂🅷
(814) 262-9292. **$73-$99.** 453 Theatre Dr. US 219, exit Elton (SR 756), just e. Int corridors. **Pets:** $50 deposit/room, $15 daily fee/pet. Designated rooms, service with restrictions, supervision.

ⒶⓈⓀ Ⓢⓕⓑ ⊠ ☒Ⓜ Ⓜ Ⓐ Ⓑ Ⓓ

ⒶⒶⒶ ▼▼▼ Super 8 Motel Johnstown 🆂🅷
(814) 535-5600. **$60-$95, 7 day notice.** 627 Solomon Run Rd. US 219, exit Galleria Dr, just w. Int corridors. **Pets:** Accepted.

🆂🅰🆅🅴 Ⓢⓕⓑ ⊠ Ⓐ Ⓑ

LIGONIER

ⒶⒶⒶ ▼▼▼▼ Lady of the Lake Bed & Breakfast 🅱🅱
(724) 238-6955. **$85-$135, 14 day notice.** 157 Rt 30 E. US 30 E, just w of jct SR 711; beside Idlewild Park. Ext/int corridors. **Pets:** Medium, other species. $10 one-time fee/pet. Designated rooms, service with restrictions, supervision.

🆂🅰🆅🅴 ⊠ Ⓑ Ⓓ ⇆ ☒ Ⓩ

NEW STANTON

ⒶⒶⒶ ▼▼▼ Days Inn New Stanton 🆂🅷
(724) 925-3591. **$55-$99, 7 day notice.** 127 W Byers Ave. I-76, exit 75, 0.5 mi sw; I-70, exit 57B westbound; exit 57 eastbound. Int corridors. **Pets:** Medium. $100 deposit/room, $10 daily fee/pet. Designated rooms, service with restrictions, supervision.

🆂🅰🆅🅴 Ⓢⓕⓑ ⊠ Ⓐ Ⓑ Ⓓ Ⓣ ⇆

ⒶⒶⒶ ▼▼▼ Howard Johnson Inn Ⓜ
(724) 925-3511. **$54-$70.** 112 W Byers Ave. I-76, exit 75, 0.5 mi sw; I-70, exit 57B westbound; exit 57 eastbound. Ext/int corridors. **Pets:** Other species. $7 daily fee/pet. Designated rooms, service with restrictions, supervision.

🆂🅰🆅🅴 Ⓢⓕⓑ ⊠ Ⓑ Ⓓ ⇆

▼▼ Super 8 Motel-New Stanton Ⓜ
(724) 925-8915. **$52-$69.** 103 Bair Blvd. I-76, exit 75, 0.5 mi se; I-70, exit 57B westbound; exit 57 eastbound. Int corridors. **Pets:** Medium. $10 daily fee/pet. Service with restrictions, supervision.

ⒶⓈⓀ Ⓢⓕⓑ ⊠ Ⓑ

SOMERSET

ⒶⒶⒶ ▼▼▼ Best Western Executive Inn 🆂🅷
(814) 445-3996. **$49-$89.** 165 Water Works Rd. I-70/76 (Pennsylvania Tpke), exit 110, just e. Int corridors. **Pets:** Accepted.

🆂🅰🆅🅴 Ⓢⓕⓑ ⊠ Ⓐ Ⓑ Ⓓ ☒

▼▼ Budget Host Inn Ⓜ
(814) 445-7988. **$40-$85, 7 day notice.** 799 N Center Ave. I-70/76 (Pennsylvania Tpke), exit 110, 0.3 mi s. Ext corridors. **Pets:** Small. $10 daily fee/pet. Designated rooms, service with restrictions, supervision.

ⒶⓈⓀ Ⓢⓕⓑ ⊠ Ⓑ

▼▼ Days Inn-Somerset Ⓜ
(814) 445-9200. **$45-$70.** 220 Water Works Rd. I-70/76 (Pennsylvania Tpke), exit 110, just e. Ext corridors. **Pets:** Other species. $9 daily fee/pet. Service with restrictions, supervision.

ⒶⓈⓀ Ⓢⓕⓑ ⊠ Ⓑ

ⒶⒶⒶ ▼ Dollar Inn Ⓜ
(814) 445-2977. **$38-$85.** 1146 N Center Ave. I-70/76 (Pennsylvania Tpke), exit 110, just s, 0.3 mi, then just n on SR 601/N Central Ave; at top of hill. Ext corridors. **Pets:** Medium. $7 daily fee/pet. Designated rooms, service with restrictions, supervision.

🆂🅰🆅🅴 Ⓢⓕⓑ ⊠ Ⓑ

▼▼ Glades Pike Inn 🅱🅱
(814) 443-4978. **$75-$135, 7 day notice.** 2684 Glades Pike. I-70/76 (Pennsylvania Tpke), exit 110, 6 mi w on SR 31; exit 91, 13 mi e on SR 31. Int corridors. **Pets:** Other species. $5 one-time fee/pet. No service, supervision.

⊠

ⒶⒶⒶ ▼▼▼▼ Holiday Inn 🆂🅷
(814) 445-9611. **$84-$109, 3 day notice.** 202 Harmon St. I-70/76 (Pennsylvania Tpke), exit 110, just s. Int corridors. **Pets:** Medium. $50 deposit/room. Designated rooms, service with restrictions, supervision.

🆂🅰🆅🅴 Ⓢⓕⓑ ⊠ Ⓐ Ⓑ Ⓣ ⇆

▼▼▼ The Inn at Georgian Place 🅱🅱
(814) 443-1043. **$105-$195, 7 day notice.** 800 Georgian Place Dr. I-70/76 (Pennsylvania Tpke), exit 110, 0.5 mi e, then 0.5 mi n on SR 601. Int corridors. **Pets:** Medium. Service with restrictions, supervision.

ⒶⓈⓀ Ⓢⓕⓑ ⊠ Ⓣ

▼ Knights Inn Ⓜ 🐾
(814) 445-8933. **$45, 7 day notice.** 147 Gateway Rd. I-70/76 (Pennsylvania Tpke), exit 110, just s. Ext corridors. **Pets:** Medium. $5 daily fee/room. No service, supervision.

ⒶⓈⓀ Ⓢⓕⓑ ⊠ Ⓑ Ⓓ ⇆

ⒶⒶⒶ ▼▼▼ Quality Inn Somerset 🆂🅷
(814) 443-4646. **$69-$149.** 215 Ramada Rd. I-70/76 (Pennsylvania Tpke), exit 110, just s. Int corridors. **Pets:** Other species. Service with restrictions, supervision.

🆂🅰🆅🅴 Ⓢⓕⓑ ⊠ Ⓑ Ⓓ Ⓣ ⇆ ☒

▼ Super 8 Motel Ⓜ
(814) 445-8788. **$49-$141, 15 day notice.** 125 Lewis Dr. I-70/76 (Pennsylvania Tpke), exit 110, just s. Int corridors. **Pets:** $10 daily fee/pet. Service with restrictions, supervision.

ⒶⓈⓀ Ⓢⓕⓑ ⊠ Ⓑ Ⓓ

UNIONTOWN

▼▼▼ Uniontown Holiday Inn 🆂🅷
(724) 437-2816. **$89-$149.** 700 W Main St. 1.8 mi w on US 40. Int corridors. **Pets:** Accepted.

ⒶⓈⓀ Ⓢⓕⓑ ⊠ Ⓐ Ⓐⓑ Ⓑ Ⓓ Ⓣ ⇆ ☒

END AREA

LEBANON

◆◆◆ **Berry Patch Bed and Breakfast** [BB]
(717) 865-7219. **$85-$125, 14 day notice.** 115 Moore Rd. I-81, exit 90, 2.8 mi s on SR 72, 1 mi on New Bunker Hill St, 0.8 mi s on S Lancastor St, just e, then follow signs. Ext/int corridors. **Pets:** Accepted.
[A$K] ☒

[AAA] ◆◆ **Quality Inn-Lebanon Valley** [SH]
(717) 273-6771. **$89-$169.** 625 Quentin Rd. 0.5 mi s on SR 72, from jct US 422. Ext/int corridors. **Pets:** Accepted.
[SAVE] [S/D] ☒ [♿M] 🦻 ♿ ▣ ☕ 🍴 🏊 🏋

LEWISBURG

[AAA] ◆◆ **Days Inn-Lewisburg** [SH]
(570) 523-1171. **$78-$95.** US Rt 15. 0.5 mi n of jct SR 45. Ext corridors. **Pets:** Other species. Service with restrictions.
[SAVE] [S/D] ☒ ▣ ☕ 🏊

LINCOLN FALLS

◆◆ **Morgan Century Farm** [BB]
(570) 924-4909. **$89-$129, 3 day notice.** 30-809 Rt 154. In village. Ext/int corridors. **Pets:** Medium. $10 one-time fee/pet. Designated rooms, service with restrictions, supervision.
[S/D] ☒ ▣ ☕ 📵

LOCK HAVEN

[AAA] ◆◆ **Best Western-Lock Haven** [SH]
(570) 748-3297. **$79-$135.** 101 E Walnut St. US 220, exit SR 120 W, just w. Int corridors. **Pets:** Other species. $10 daily fee/pet. Service with restrictions.
[SAVE] [S/D] ☒ ♿ ▣ ☕

MANSFIELD

[AAA] ◆◆ **Comfort Inn** [SH]
(570) 662-3000. **$59-$119.** 300 Gateway Dr. Jct US 6 and 15. Int corridors. **Pets:** Accepted.
[SAVE] [S/D] ☒ ▣ ☕ 🏋

[AAA] ◆◆ **Mansfield Inn** [M]
(570) 662-2136. **$55-$80, 3 day notice.** 26 S Main St. Jct US 6, just s on Business Rt 15; downtown. Ext corridors. **Pets:** $8 one-time fee/pet. Service with restrictions.
[SAVE] [S/D] ☒ ▣ ☕

[AAA] ◆ **West's Deluxe Motel** [M]
(570) 659-5141. **$60-$90.** 2848 S Main St. SR 15, exit Covington and Canoe Camp, Business Rt 15, 0.8 mi s on 660 W (Main St). Ext corridors. **Pets:** Other species. Service with restrictions, supervision.
[SAVE] [S/D] ☒ ▣ ☕ 🏊

MARIENVILLE

◆ **The Forest Lodge & Campground** [M] 🐾
(814) 927-8790. **$45-$70, 10 day notice.** SR 66. SR 66, 6 mi n of Marienville. Ext/int corridors. **Pets:** Other species. $8 daily fee/pet. Designated rooms, service with restrictions, supervision.
[A$K] [S/D] ☒ ▣ ☕

◆◆ **Microtel Inn & Suites** [SH]
(814) 927-8300. **$84.** 252 Cherry St. 0.6 mi sw of center, on SR 66. Int corridors. **Pets:** Medium. $10 daily fee/pet. Designated rooms, service with restrictions, supervision.
[A$K] [S/D] ☒ ♿ ▣ ☕

MEADVILLE

◆◆ **Motel 6 #4019** [M]
(814) 724-6366. **$59-$79.** 11237 Shaw Ave. I-79, exit 147A, just e on US 322. Int corridors. **Pets:** Medium, other species. Service with restrictions, supervision.
[A$K] [S/D] ☒ ♿

◆◆ **Quality Inn** [M] 🐾
(814) 333-8883. **$60-$129.** 17259 Conneaut Lake Rd. I-79, exit 147B, just w on US 322. Ext/int corridors. **Pets:** Other species. $10 one-time fee/pet. Designated rooms, service with restrictions, supervision.
[A$K] [S/D] ☒ ▣ ☕

MECHANICSBURG

[AAA] ◆◆ **Comfort Inn Capital City** [SH]
(717) 766-3700. **$69-$189, 14 day notice.** 1012 Wesley Dr. I-76 (Pennsylvania Tpke), exit 236 (US 15), 1 mi n to Wesley Dr exit, then just w. Int corridors. **Pets:** $25 daily fee/room. Service with restrictions, supervision.
[SAVE] [S/D] ☒ [♿M] ♿ ▣ ☕ 🏊

[AAA] ◆◆ **Comfort Inn West** [SH]
(717) 790-0924. **$80-$96, 3 day notice.** 6325 Carlisle Pike. Jct Carlisle Pike and US 11, 1 mi w on US 11. Int corridors. **Pets:** Small, other species. $25 deposit/room. Designated rooms, service with restrictions, supervision.
[SAVE] [S/D] ☒ ▣ ☕

◆◆◆ **Hampton Inn-Harrisburg West** [SH] 🐾
(717) 691-1300. **$139-$154, 14 day notice.** 4950 Ritter Rd. I-76 (Pennsylvania Tpke), exit 236 (US 15), 1 mi n to Rossmoyne Rd exit. Int corridors. **Pets:** Other species. Designated rooms, service with restrictions, supervision.
[A$K] [S/D] ☒ [♿M] ▣ ☕ 🏊 🏋

◆◆◆ **Holiday Inn Harrisburg-West** [SH]
(717) 697-0321. **$119-$179.** 5401 Carlisle Pike. Jct Carlisle Pike and US 11, just w. Ext corridors. **Pets:** Accepted.
[A$K] [S/D] ☒ ▣ ☕ 🍴 🏊 🏋

MERCER

◆ **Colonial Inn Motel** [M]
(724) 662-5600. **$38-$49.** 383 N Perry Hwy (US 19). I-80, exit 15, 3.5 mi n; I-79, exit 121, 4.5 mi s on SR 62, then 0.5 mi n on US 19. Ext/int corridors. **Pets:** Other species. $5 one-time fee/pet. Service with restrictions, supervision.
[A$K] [S/D] ☒ ▣ ☕

MIDDLETOWN

◆◆ **Days Inn-Harrisburg Airport** [SH]
(717) 939-4147. **$59-$109.** 800 S Eisenhower Blvd. I-76 (Pennsylvania Tpke), exit 247, just n; I-283, exit 1B (Highspire). Ext corridors. **Pets:** Accepted.
[A$K] [S/D] ☒ 🦻 ▣ ☕ 🏊

MIFFLINVILLE

◆◆ **Super 8 Motel** [M]
(570) 759-6778. **$49-$74, 7 day notice.** 450 3rd St. I-80, exit 242, just n on SR 339. Ext corridors. **Pets:** Dogs only. $10 one-time fee/room. Service with restrictions.
[A$K] [S/D] ☒ ▣

MILESBURG

[AAA] ◆◆◆ **Holiday Inn** [SH]
(814) 355-7521. **$85-$300, 7 day notice.** 971 N Eagle Valley Rd. I-80, exit 158, 0.4 mi n. Int corridors. **Pets:** Accepted.
[SAVE] [S/D] ☒ [♿M] 🦻 ♿ ▣ ☕ 🍴 🏊

MONTGOMERY

[AAA] ◆ **White Deer Motel** [M]
(570) 547-1007. **$60-$98.** 6967 Rt 15 Hwy. Jct SR 54, 1.4 mi s. Ext corridors. **Pets:** Small, dogs only. $3 one-time fee/pet. Service with restrictions, supervision.
[SAVE] [S/D] ☒ ▣ ☕

MORGANTOWN

AAA ▼▼▼▼ Holiday Inn SH
(610) 286-3000. **$109-$149.** 6170 Morgantown Rd. I-76, exit 298, just s on SR 10. Int corridors. **Pets:** $25 one-time fee/pet. Designated rooms, service with restrictions.
[SAVE] [S] [X] [⚷] [🛏] [🖥] [¶] [≈] [X]

NEW CASTLE

▼▼ Comfort Inn-New Castle M
(724) 658-7700. **$59-$130.** 1740 New Butler Rd (US Business 422). Jct SR 65, 1 mi e on US 422, then 1 mi w on US 422 business route. Int corridors. **Pets:** Small, dogs only. $6 daily fee/pet. Service with restrictions, supervision.
[ASK] [S] [X] [🛏] [🖥]

NEW COLUMBIA

AAA ▼▼▼▼ Holiday Inn Express SH
(570) 568-1100. **$83-$189.** 160 Commerce Park Dr. I-80, exit 210A (US 15/New Columbia), just s. Int corridors. **Pets:** Medium, other species. $25 one-time fee/room. Designated rooms, service with restrictions, supervision.
[SAVE] [S] [X] [&M] [⚷] [🛏] [🖥] [≈]

AAA ▼▼▼▼ New Columbia Comfort Inn SH
(570) 568-8000. **$75-$129.** 330 Commerce Park Dr. I-80, exit 210A (US 15/New Columbia), just s. Int corridors. **Pets:** Other species.
[SAVE] [S] [X] [&M] [🛏] [🖥] [¶] [≈]

NEW CUMBERLAND

AAA ▼▼▼ Days Inn Harrisburg South SH
(717) 774-4156. **$70-$126.** 353 Lewisberry Rd. I-83, exit 39A, just ne. Int corridors. **Pets:** Large. $15 daily fee/pet. Service with restrictions, supervision.
[SAVE] [S] [X] [🛏] [🖥] [≈]

AAA ▼▼▼▼ Holiday Inn Hotel & Conference Center-Harrisburg SH
(717) 774-2721. **$119-$149.** 148 Sheraton Dr. I-83, exit 40A, just se. Int corridors. **Pets:** Accepted.
[SAVE] [S] [X] [⚷] [🛏] [🖥] [¶] [≈] [X]

NORTH EAST

AAA ▼ Super 8 Motel M
(814) 725-4567. **$43-$68.** 11021 Side Hill Rd. I-90, exit 41, just n on SR 89. Ext corridors. **Pets:** Dogs only. $5 one-time fee/room. No service, supervision.
[SAVE] [S] [X]

PENNSYLVANIA DUTCH COUNTRY AREA

ADAMSTOWN

▼▼▼▼ The Barnyard Inn B&B and Suites BB
(717) 484-1111. **$85-$135, 10 day notice.** 2145 Old Lancaster Pike. 1 mi ne via Main St/Old Lancaster Pike; SR 272, just w on Willow St to Main St, 1 mi n bearing left at fork, then just n. Int corridors. **Pets:** Other species. $20 one-time fee/room. Designated rooms.
[ASK] [S] [X] [🛏] [🖥] [Ƶ]

AKRON

▼▼▼ Boxwood Inn BB
(717) 859-3466. **$85-$145, 7 day notice.** 1320 Diamond St. SR 272, 0.4 mi se on Main St to Diamond St, then 0.3 mi s. Ext/int corridors. **Pets:** Accepted.
[ASK] [X] [🛏] [🖥]

DENVER

AAA ▼▼▼ Black Horse Lodge and Suites SH
(717) 336-7563. **$59-$189.** 2180 N Reading Rd. I-76 (Pennsylvania Tpke), exit 286, 1 mi w to SR 272, then 0.3 mi n. Ext/int corridors. **Pets:** Other species. Service with restrictions, supervision.
[SAVE] [S] [X] [🛏] [🖥] [¶] [≈]

AAA ▼▼▼ Comfort Inn SH
(717) 336-4649. **$79-$169, 3 day notice.** 2017 N Reading Rd. I-76 (Pennsylvania Tpke), exit 286, 1 mi w to SR 272, then just s. Int corridors. **Pets:** Accepted.
[SAVE] [S] [X] [⚷] [🛏] [🖥]

AAA ▼▼▼▼ Holiday Inn-Lancaster County SH
(717) 336-7541. **$69-$179.** 1 Denver Rd. I-76 (Pennsylvania Tpke), exit 286, 1 mi w to SR 272, then just s. Int corridors. **Pets:** Medium. $10 daily fee/pet. Designated rooms, service with restrictions, supervision.
[SAVE] [S] [X] [&M] [⚷] [⚷] [🛏] [🖥] [¶] [≈]

EPHRATA

AAA ▼▼▼▼ Historic Smithton Inn BB
(717) 733-6094. **$95-$150, 14 day notice.** 900 W Main St. On US 322, just w of jct SR 272, then just s on Academy Dr. Int corridors. **Pets:** Dogs only. Designated rooms, service with restrictions, supervision.
[SAVE] [X] [🛏] [Ƶ]

GORDONVILLE

AAA ▼ Motel 6-Lancaster #4174 M
(717) 687-3880. **$55-$100.** 2959 Lincoln Hwy E. On US 30; center. Int corridors. **Pets:** Medium, other species. Service with restrictions, supervision.
[SAVE] [S] [X] [&M] [🛏]

LANCASTER

AAA ▼▼▼ Americas Best Value Inn M
(717) 397-4911. **$50-$100.** 1320 Harrisburg Pike. US 30 (Lincoln Hwy), exit Harrisburg Pike, 0.6 mi s. Ext corridors. **Pets:** Medium. $10 daily fee/pet. Designated rooms, service with restrictions, supervision.
[SAVE] [S] [X] [🛏]

AAA ▼▼▼▼ Best Western Eden Resort Inn & Suites LH
(717) 569-6444. **$89-$209.** 222 Eden Rd. Jct US 30 (Lincoln Hwy) and SR 272 (Oregon Pike). Ext/int corridors. **Pets:** Small, other species. $15 daily fee/pet. Designated rooms, service with restrictions, supervision.
[SAVE] [S] [X] [&M] [⚷] [⚷] [🛏] [🖥] [¶] [≈] [X]

AAA ▼▼▼▼ Hawthorn Inn & Suites SH ❀
(717) 290-7100. **$79-$149.** 2045 Lincoln Hwy E. Jct US 30 (Lincoln Hwy) E. Int corridors. **Pets:** Medium, dogs only. $25 one-time fee/pet. Designated rooms, service with restrictions, supervision.
[SAVE] [S] [X] [⚷] [⚷] [🛏] [🖥]

◉◉◉ ▼▼▼ Holiday Inn Visitors Center 🆂🅷
(717) 299-2551. **$71-$134.** 521 Greenfield Rd. 3.3 mi e on US 30 (Lincoln Hwy), exit Greenfield Rd, just n. Ext/int corridors. **Pets:** Medium, other species. $30 one-time fee/room. Designated rooms, service with restrictions, supervision.
[SAVE] [S⃝] [✕] [&M] [🕿] [🖫] [🖬] [🖳] [🍴] [🏊] [🗙]

▼▼ Hotel Brunswick 🅻🅷
(717) 397-4800. **$69-$169.** 151 N Queen St. Center. Int corridors. **Pets:** Accepted.
[ASK] [S⃝] [✕] [🕿] [🖫] [🖬] [🖳] [🍴] [🏊]

◉◉◉ ▼▼▼▼ Lancaster Host Resort & Conference Center 🅻🅷
(717) 299-5500. **$89-$159.** 2300 Lincoln Hwy E. On US 30 (Lincoln Hwy), 5 mi e. Int corridors. **Pets:** Medium. $25 one-time fee/room. Designated rooms, service with restrictions, supervision.
[SAVE] [S⃝] [✕] [🕿] [🖬] [🖳] [🍴] [🏊] [🗙]

▼▼ Red Roof Inn of Lancaster 🆂🅷 🐾
(717) 299-9700. **$49-$59.** 2307 Lincoln Hwy E. On US 30 (Lincoln Hwy), 5 mi e. Ext/int corridors. **Pets:** Medium. Service with restrictions, supervision.
[ASK] [S⃝] [✕] [&M] [🕿] [🖫] [🖬] [🏊]

LITITZ

▼▼▼ General Sutter Inn 🅲🅸
(717) 626-2115. **$87.** 14 E Main St. Jct SR 501 and 772; downtown. Int corridors. **Pets:** $10 daily fee/pet. Designated rooms, service with restrictions, supervision.
[✕] [🍴]

MANHEIM

◉◉◉ ▼▼ Rodeway Inn 🅼
(717) 665-2755. **$48-$68.** 2931 Lebanon Rd. I-76 (Pennsylvania Tpke), exit 266, just s on SR 72. Ext corridors. **Pets:** Other species. $5 one-time fee/pet. Service with restrictions, supervision.
[SAVE] [✕] [🏊]

MOUNTVILLE

◉◉◉ ▼▼▼▼ MainStay Suites 🆂🅷
(717) 285-2500. **$99-$219.** 314 Primrose Ln. US 30 (Lincoln Hwy), exit Mountville. Int corridors. **Pets:** Medium, other species. $100 deposit/room, $10 daily fee/pet. Service with restrictions, crate.
[SAVE] [S⃝] [✕] [&M] [🕿] [🖫] [🖬] [🖳] [🏊]

NEW HOLLAND

▼▼▼▼ Comfort Inn 🆂🅷
(717) 355-9900. **$69-$175.** 626 W Main St. 0.5 mi w on SR 23. Int corridors. **Pets:** Medium. $10 daily fee/pet. Service with restrictions, crate.
[ASK] [S⃝] [✕] [🕿] [🖬] [🖳]

STRASBURG

◉◉◉ ▼▼▼ Carriage House Motor Inn 🅼
(717) 687-7651. **$49-$99.** 144 E Main St. 0.3 mi e on SR 896 and 741. Ext corridors. **Pets:** Accepted.
[SAVE] [S⃝] [✕] [🖬]

◉◉◉ ▼▼▼▼ Netherlands Inn & Spa 🆂🅷
(717) 687-7691. **$89-$239, 3 day notice.** One Historic Dr. 0.5 mi n on SR 896; 2.5 mi s of US 30 (Lincoln Hwy). Ext/int corridors. **Pets:** Medium, dogs only. $30 daily fee/room. Designated rooms, service with restrictions, crate.
[SAVE] [S⃝] [✕] [🖬] [🖳] [🍴] [🏊] [🗙]

PHILADELPHIA METROPOLITAN AREA

AUDUBON

◉◉◉ ▼▼▼▼ Homewood Suites by Hilton 🆂🅷 🐾
(610) 539-7300. **$209-$239.** 681 Shannondell Blvd. I-422, exit Trooper Rd, 1.2 mi n. Int corridors. **Pets:** Medium. $250 one-time fee/room. Service with restrictions, crate.
[SAVE] [S⃝] [✕] [&M] [🕿] [🖫] [🖬] [🖳] [🏊] [🗙]

BENSALEM

◉◉◉ ▼▼▼ Holiday Inn-Philadelphia Northeast 🆂🅷
(215) 638-1500. **$129-$159.** 3499 Street Rd. I-276 (Pennsylvania Tpke), exit 351, just s on US 1, then 0.3 mi e on SR 132. Ext/int corridors. **Pets:** $50 deposit/room. Service with restrictions.
[SAVE] [S⃝] [✕] [🕿] [🖬] [🖳] [🍴] [🏊]

◉◉◉ ▼▼▼▼ Sleep Inn & Suites-Bensalem 🆂🅷
(215) 244-2300. **$69-$189.** 3427 Street Rd. I-276 (Pennsylvania Tpke), exit 351, just s on US 1, then 0.3 mi e on SR 132. Int corridors. **Pets:** Small. $15 daily fee/pet. Service with restrictions, supervision.
[SAVE] [S⃝] [✕] [&M] [🕿] [🖬] [🖳]

BERWYN

▼▼▼ Residence Inn by Marriott 🆂🅷
(610) 640-9494. **$209-$269.** 600 W Swedesford Rd. US 202, exit Paoli/SR 252, 1 mi n. Ext corridors. **Pets:** Accepted.
[ASK] [✕] [&M] [🕿] [🖫] [🖬] [🖳] [🏊] [🗙]

CHADDS FORD

◉◉◉ ▼▼▼▼ Brandywine River Hotel 🆂🅷
(610) 388-1200. **$129-$179.** 1609 Baltimore Pike. Jct US 1 and SR 100, 2 mi w of US 202. Int corridors. **Pets:** Accepted.
[SAVE] [S⃝] [✕] [🕿] [🖫] [🖬] [🖳]

CONSHOHOCKEN

◉◉◉ ▼▼▼ Residence Inn by Marriott Philadelphia/Conshohocken 🆂🅷
(610) 828-8800. **$119-$339.** 191 Washington St. I-76 (Schuylkill Expwy), exit 332 (SR 23); I-476, exit 16 (SR 23), 0.3 mi over Fayette Bridge to Elm St, then just se along the river. Int corridors. **Pets:** Accepted.
[SAVE] [✕] [&M] [🕿] [🖫] [🖬] [🖳] [🏊] [🗙]

EAST NORRITON

▼▼▼ Summerfield Suites Hotel Plymouth Meeting East Norriton 🆂🅷
(610) 313-9990. **$119-$399.** 501 E Germantown Pike. I-476, exit 20; I-276 (Pennsylvania Tpke), exit 333, 2.5 mi w. Int corridors. **Pets:** Accepted.
[ASK] [✕] [🕿] [🖫] [🖬] [🖳] [🏊]

ERWINNA

▼▼▼◆ **Golden Pheasant Inn** 🆑 ❀
(610) 294-9595. **$115-$225, 21 day notice.** 763 River Rd. SR 32, 0.5 mi n of jct Dark Hollow Rd. Ext/int corridors. **Pets:** Medium, other species. $20 daily fee/pet. Designated rooms, service with restrictions, supervision.

⊠ 🛄 💻 🍴 ⊠

ESSINGTON

◉◉◉ ▼▼▼◆ **Holiday Inn-Airport** 🖽
(610) 521-2400. **$99-$189.** 45 Industrial Hwy. I-95, exit 9A, 0.3 mi sw on SR 291. Int corridors. **Pets:** Medium. $50 one-time fee/pet. Service with restrictions, supervision.

🆂🅰🆅🅴 🆂🄳 ⊠ ♿ 🔔 🗝 🛄 💻 🍴 🏊

▼◆ **Motel 6** 🅼
(610) 521-6650. **Call for rates.** 43 Industrial Hwy. I-95, exit 9A, 0.3 mi sw on SR 291. Ext corridors. **Pets:** Medium, other species. Service with restrictions, supervision.

⊠ ♿ 🔔 🗝

▼▼◆ **Red Roof Inn-Airport #7119** 🅼
(610) 521-5090. **$81-$109.** 49 Industrial Hwy. I-95, exit 9A, 0.3 mi sw on SR 291. Ext corridors. **Pets:** Medium, other species. Service with restrictions, supervision.

⊠ ♿ 🔔 🗝 🛄

GLEN MILLS

▼▼▼◆ **Sweetwater Farm Bed & Breakfast** 🅱🅱 ❀
(610) 459-4711. **$135-$295, 14 day notice.** 50 Sweetwater Rd. US 1, 2 mi w on Valley Rd, then 0.6 mi s. Int corridors. **Pets:** Other species. $35 daily fee/pet. Designated rooms, service with restrictions.

⊠ 🛄 💻 🏊 ⊠

HORSHAM

◉◉◉ ▼▼▼◆ **Days Inn-Horsham/Willow Grove** 🆂🅷
(215) 674-2500. **$99-$159.** 245 Easton Rd. I-276 (Pennsylvania Tpke), exit 343, 1 mi n. Int corridors. **Pets:** Accepted.

🆂🅰🆅🅴 🆂🄳 🔔 🗝 🛄 💻

▼▼▼◆ **Homestead Studio Suites Hotel-Horsham/Willow Grove** 🆂🅷
(215) 956-9966. **$95-$105.** 537 Dresher Rd. I-276 (Pennsylvania Tpke), exit 343, 1.5 mi n on SR 611 (Easton Rd), just w on Horsham Rd, then 0.5 mi s. Int corridors. **Pets:** Accepted.

🄰🆂🄺 🆂🄳 ⊠ ♿ 🔔 🗝 🛄 💻

▼▼▼◆ **Residence Inn by Marriott-Willow Grove** 🆂🅷
(215) 443-7330. **$199-$239 (no credit cards).** 3 Walnut Grove Dr. I-276 (Pennsylvania Tpke), exit 343, 1 mi n on SR 611 (Easton Rd), then 1.3 mi w on Dresher Rd. Ext corridors. **Pets:** Accepted.

⊠ ♿ 🔔 🗝 🛄 💻 🏊 ⊠

KING OF PRUSSIA

▼▼▼◆ **Homestead Studio Suites Hotel Philadelphia-King of Prussia** 🆂🅷
(610) 962-9000. **$89-$99.** 400 American Ave. I-76 (Pennsylvania Tpke), exit 326 (Valley Forge); Schuylkill Expwy, exit 328A (Mall Blvd), 1.3 mi n on N Gulph Rd, then 1 mi ne on 1st Ave. Int corridors. **Pets:** Accepted.

🄰🆂🄺 🆂🄳 ⊠ ♿ 🔔 🗝 🛄 💻

◉◉◉ ▼▼▼◆ **MainStay Suites** 🆂🅷
(484) 690-3000. **$109-$159, 30 day notice.** 440 American Ave. I-76 (Pennsylvania Tpke), exit 326 (Valley Forge); Schuylkill Expwy, exit 328A (Mall Blvd), 1.3 mi n on N Gulph Rd, 1 mi ne on 1st Ave, then just e. Int corridors. **Pets:** Accepted.

🆂🅰🆅🅴 ⊠ ♿ 🗝 🔔 💻 🏊

▼◆ **Motel 6 Philadelphia-King of Prussia #1280** 🆂🅷
(610) 265-7200. **$39-$61.** 815 W DeKalb Pike. I-76 (Pennsylvania Tpke), exit 326 (Valley Forge), 1.3 mi e to jct US 202 N and S Gulph Rd; Schuylkill Expwy, exit 328A (Mall Blvd), just e. Int corridors. **Pets:** Medium, other species. Service with restrictions, supervision.

🆂🄳 ⊠ 🗝 🏊

▼▼▼◆ **The Sheraton Park Ridge Hotel and Conference Center** 🖽
(610) 337-1800. **$289-$309.** 480 N Gulph Rd. I-76 (Pennsylvania Tpke), exit 327 (Valley Forge), 0.3 mi w. Int corridors. **Pets:** Accepted.

⊠ ♿ 🗝 🔔 🛄 💻 🍴 🏊 ⊠

KULPSVILLE

▼▼▼◆ **Best Western-The Inn at Towamencin** 🆂🅷
(215) 368-3800. **$108-$118.** 1750 Sumneytown Pike. I-476, exit 31, just e. Int corridors. **Pets:** $20 deposit/room. Designated rooms, service with restrictions.

🄰🆂🄺 🆂🄳 ⊠ 🗝 🔔 🛄 🍴 🏊 ⊠

LANGHORNE

◉◉◉ ▼▼▼◆ **Sheraton Bucks County Hotel** 🖽
(215) 547-4100. **$159-$299, 3 day notice.** 400 Oxford Valley Rd. I-95, exit 46A (Oxford Valley Rd), 0.8 mi e, exit off US 1 N. Int corridors. **Pets:** Accepted.

🆂🅰🆅🅴 🆂🄳 ⊠ ♿ 🗝 🔔 🛄 💻 🍴 🏊 ⊠

LIONVILLE

◉◉◉ ▼▼▼◆ **Hampton Inn** 🆂🅷
(610) 363-5555. **$109-$139.** 4 N Pottstown Pike. I-76 (Pennsylvania Tpke), exit 312, 0.5 mi s; jct SR 113 and 100. **Pets:** Accepted.

🆂🅰🆅🅴 🆂🄳 ⊠ ♿ 🗝 🔔 🛄 🏊

◉◉◉ ▼▼▼◆ **The Inn at Chester Springs Hotel Conference Center** 🆂🅷
(610) 363-1100. **$107, 3 day notice.** 815 N Pottstown Pike. I-76 (Pennsylvania Tpke), exit 312, 2 mi s on SR 100. Int corridors. **Pets:** Small, other species. $25 one-time fee/room. Designated rooms, service with restrictions.

🆂🅰🆅🅴 🆂🄳 ⊠ 🗝 🔔 🛄 💻 🍴 🏊

▼▼▼◆ **Residence Inn by Marriott-Exton** 🆂🅷
(610) 594-9705. **$120-$130.** 10 N Pottstown Pike. I-76 (Pennsylvania Tpke), exit 312, 1 mi s on SR 100. Int corridors. **Pets:** Accepted.

🄰🆂🄺 🆂🄳 ⊠ 🗝 🔔 💻 🏊 ⊠

MALVERN

▼▼▼◆ **Homestead Studio Suites Hotel Philadelphia-Malvern** 🆂🅷
(610) 695-9200. **$100-$110.** 8 E Swedesford Rd. Just w of US 202 and SR 29 N. Int corridors. **Pets:** Accepted.

🄰🆂🄺 🆂🄳 ⊠ 🗝 🔔 🛄 💻

◉◉◉ ▼▼▼◆ **Homewood Suites by Hilton** 🆂🅷
(610) 296-3500. **$209-$299.** 12 E Swedesford Rd. US 202, exit SR 29, follow signs. Int corridors. **Pets:** Other species. $25 one-time fee/pet. Service with restrictions, crate.

🆂🅰🆅🅴 🆂🄳 ⊠ ♿ 🗝 🔔 🛄 💻 🏊

◉◉◉ ▼▼▼◆ **Sheraton Great Valley Hotel** 🖽
(610) 524-5500. **$155.** 707 Lancaster Pike. Jct US 202 and 30 E. Int corridors. **Pets:** Accepted.

🆂🅰🆅🅴 🆂🄳 ⊠ ♿ 🗝 🔔 🛄 💻 🍴 🏊

▼▼▼◆ **Staybridge Suites** 🆂🅷
(610) 296-4343. **$199-$209.** 20 Morehall Rd. Jct US 30 and SR 29, just nw. Ext/int corridors. **Pets:** Medium. $10 daily fee/pet, $175 one-time fee/room. Service with restrictions, supervision.

🄰🆂🄺 🆂🄳 ⊠ 🗝 🔔 🛄 💻 🏊 ⊠

MONTGOMERYVILLE

▼▼ Quality Inn Conference Center 🅂🄷
(215) 699-8800. **$105-$120.** 969 Bethlehem Pike. I-276 (Pennsylvania Tpke), exit 339, 8 mi n on SR 309. Ext corridors. **Pets:** Large. $25 daily fee/room. Designated rooms, service with restrictions, supervision.
🄰🅂🄺 🔊 ✕ 🐾 🛏 💻

▼▼▼ Residence Inn by Marriott 🅂🄷
(267) 468-0111. **$115-$205.** 1110 Bethlehem Pike. I-276 (Pennsylvania Tpke), exit 339, 6.5 mi n on SR 309. Int corridors. **Pets:** Accepted.
🄰🅂🄺 🔊 ✕ 🐾 🛏 💻 🏊 🗙

NEW HOPE

🅰🅰🅰 ▼▼▼ 1870 Wedgwood Inn of New Hope 🄱🄱
(215) 862-2570. **$95-$299, 10 day notice.** 111 W Bridge St (SR 179). 0.5 mi w of SR 32; downtown. Ext/int corridors. **Pets:** Accepted.
🆂🄰🅅🄴 ✕ 🛏 💻

▼▼▼ Aaron Burr House Inn & Conference Center 🄱🄱
(215) 862-2520. **$95-$295, 10 day notice.** 80 W Bridge St (SR 179). 0.5 mi w of SR 32; at W Bridge and Chestnut sts. Int corridors. **Pets:** Accepted.
✕ 🛏 🕅

🅰🅰🅰 ▼▼ Best Western New Hope Inn 🅂🄷
(215) 862-5221. **$89-$189.** 6426 Lower York Rd. 2 mi s on US 202, 1 mi w of jct SR 179. Ext corridors. **Pets:** Accepted.
🆂🄰🅅🄴 🔊 ✕ 🐾 🛏 💻 🏋 🏊 🗙

PHILADELPHIA

🅰🅰🅰 ▼▼ Best Western Center City Hotel 🅂🄷
(215) 568-8300. **$129-$159.** 501 N 22nd St. Just n of Benjamin Franklin Pkwy. Int corridors. **Pets:** Medium. $10 daily fee/room. Designated rooms, service with restrictions.
🆂🄰🅅🄴 🔊 ✕ 🐾 🛏 💻 🏋 🏊

🅰🅰🅰 ▼▼▼ Best Western Independence Park Inn 🅂🄷 🐾
(215) 922-4443. **$139-$295.** 235 Chestnut St. Between 2nd and 3rd sts. Int corridors. **Pets:** Small. $50 one-time fee/room. Service with restrictions, crate.
🆂🄰🅅🄴 🔊 ✕ 🛏 💻

🅰🅰🅰 ▼▼▼ The Doubletree Hotel Philadelphia 🄻🄷
(215) 893-1600. **$179-$349.** 237 S Broad St. Jct Broad and Locust sts. Int corridors. **Pets:** Accepted.
🆂🄰🅅🄴 ✕ 🐾 🛏 💻 🏋 🏊 🗙

▼▼ Extended StayAmerica-Philadelphia-Airport 🅂🄷
(215) 492-6766. **$94-$104.** 9000 Tinicum Blvd. I-95, exit 12B, just n on Essington Ave, then just w on Bartram Ave. Int corridors. **Pets:** Accepted.
🄰🅂🄺 🔊 ✕ 🐾 🐾 🛏 💻

▼▼▼ Extended Stay Deluxe Philadelphia Airport 🅂🄷
(215) 365-4360. **$119-$134.** 8880 Bartram Ave. I-95, exit 12B southbound, bear right on exit ramp to light, then just n; exit 10 northbound, follow SR 291 E to light, then 1.1 mi n. Int corridors. **Pets:** Accepted.
🄰🅂🄺 🔊 ✕ 🐾 🐾 🛏 💻 🏊

▼▼▼ Four Points by Sheraton Philadelphia Airport 🅂🄷
(215) 492-0400. **$189.** 4101 Island Ave. Jct I-95 and SR 291, exit 13 northbound; exit 15 southbound. Int corridors. **Pets:** Accepted.
🄰🅂🄺 🔊 ✕ 🐾 🛏 💻 🏋 🏊

🅰🅰🅰 ▼▼▼▼ Four Seasons Hotel Philadelphia 🄻🄷
(215) 963-1500. **$300-$3020.** 1 Logan Square. Corner of 18th St and Benjamin Franklin Pkwy. Int corridors. **Pets:** Accepted.
🆂🄰🅅🄴 ✕ 🐾 🐾 🛏 💻 🏋 🏊 🗙

🅰🅰🅰 ▼▼▼▼ Loews Philadelphia Hotel 🄻🄷 🐾
(215) 627-1200. **$189-$319.** 1200 Market St. Corner of 12th and Market sts. Int corridors. **Pets:** Other species. Designated rooms, service with restrictions, supervision.
🆂🄰🅅🄴 🔊 ✕ 🐾 🐾 🛏 💻 🏋 🏊 🗙

🅰🅰🅰 ▼▼▼▼ Park Hyatt Philadelphia at The Bellevue 🄻🄷
(215) 893-1234. **$188-$332.** Broad & Walnut. Broad St; between Walnut and Locust sts. Int corridors. **Pets:** Accepted.
🆂🄰🅅🄴 ✕ 🐾 🐾 🛏 💻 🏋 🗙

🅰🅰🅰 ▼▼▼ Philadelphia Airport Residence Inn 🅂🄷
(215) 492-1611. **$139-$179.** 4630 Island Ave. I-95, exit 13 northbound; exit 15 southbound, 0.5 mi e; just e of SR 291. Ext/int corridors. **Pets:** Medium. $200 one-time fee/room. Service with restrictions, crate.
🆂🄰🅅🄴 ✕ 🐾 🐾 🛏 💻 🏊 🗙

▼▼▼ Philadelphia Downtown Marriott Hotel 🄻🄷
(215) 625-2900. **$239-$269.** 1201 Market St. Between 12th and 13th sts. Int corridors. **Pets:** Accepted.
🄰🅂🄺 🔊 ✕ 🐾 🐾 🛏 💻 🏋 🏊 🗙

🅰🅰🅰 ▼▼▼ The Radisson Plaza-Warwick Hotel Philadelphia 🄻🄷
(215) 735-6000. **$169-$369, 3 day notice.** 1701 Locust St. Jct 17th and Locust sts. Int corridors. **Pets:** Accepted.
🆂🄰🅅🄴 🔊 ✕ 🐾 🐾 🛏 💻 🏋

▼▼▼ Residence Inn by Marriott Philadelphia City Center 🄻🄷
(215) 557-0005. **$309-$329.** 1 E Penn Square. Jct Market and Juniper sts. Int corridors. **Pets:** Accepted.
🄰🅂🄺 🔊 ✕ 🐾 🐾 🛏 💻 🏊

🅰🅰🅰 ▼▼▼▼ The Rittenhouse Hotel and Condominium Residences 🄻🄷 🐾
(215) 546-9000. **$450-$480.** 210 W Rittenhouse Square. On Rittenhouse Square; just s of Walnut St. Int corridors. **Pets:** Service with restrictions, supervision.
🆂🄰🅅🄴 ✕ 🐾 🐾 🛏 🏊 🗙

▼▼▼▼ The Ritz-Carlton Philadelphia 🄻🄷 🐾
(215) 523-8000. **$209-$699.** Ten Avenue of the Arts. On Broad St; between Market and Chestnut. Int corridors. **Pets:** $75 one-time fee/pet. Service with restrictions, crate.
✕ 🐾 🐾 🛏 🗙

▼▼▼ Sheraton Society Hill 🄻🄷
(215) 238-6000. **$329-$339.** One Dock St. Just s of jct 2nd and Walnut sts. Int corridors. **Pets:** Accepted.
🄰🅂🄺 🔊 ✕ 🐾 🐾 🛏 💻 🏋 🏊 🗙

▼▼▼ Sheraton Suites Philadelphia Airport 🄻🄷 🐾
(215) 365-6600. **$89-$189.** 4101 Island Ave. Jct I-95 and SR 291, exit 13 northbound; exit 15 southbound. Int corridors. **Pets:** Medium. Service with restrictions, supervision.
🄰🅂🄺 🔊 ✕ 🐾 🛏 💻 🏋 🏊 🗙

🅰🅰🅰 ▼▼▼ Sheraton University City 🄻🄷 🐾
(215) 387-8000. **$359-$399.** 36th & Chestnut Sts. I-76 (Pennsylvania Tpke), exit 345, 0.5 mi w. Int corridors. **Pets:** Medium, dogs only. Service with restrictions, supervision.
🆂🄰🅅🄴 🔊 ✕ 🐾 🐾 🛏 💻 🏋 🏊

🅰🅰🅰 ▼▼▼▼ Sofitel Philadelphia 🄻🄷 🐾
(215) 569-8300. **$400-$600.** 120 S 17th St. Jct Sansom and 17th sts. Int corridors. **Pets:** Other species. Service with restrictions.
🆂🄰🅅🄴 🔊 ✕ 🐾 🐾 🐾 🏋

▼▼▼▼ The Westin Philadelphia 🄻🄷
(215) 563-1600. $249-$369. 99 S 17th St at Liberty Pl. Between Market and Chestnut sts. Int corridors. Pets: Accepted.
(SAVE) 🗙 🕖 👷 💻 🍴 🗙

PIPERSVILLE

▼▼ Oak Grove Country Inn 🄼 🐾
(215) 766-8931. $85-$125, 7 day notice. 6755 Easton Rd. SR 611, 1.5 mi s of jct SR 413. Ext corridors. Pets: Other species. $20 one-time fee/pet. Service with restrictions, supervision.
(ASK) 🔊 🗙 🖪 💻

PLYMOUTH MEETING

▼▼▼▼ DoubleTree Guest Suites Plymouth Meeting 🄻🄷
(610) 834-8300. $139-$269. 640 W Germantown Pike. I-476, exit 20; I-276 (Pennsylvania Tpke), exit 333, just w on Plymouth Rd (Norristown), just e on Germantown Pike, then just e on Hickory Rd. Int corridors. Pets: Accepted.
🗙 🕖 🖪 💻 🍴 🗙 🗙

▼▼ Extended StayAmerica-Philadelphia-Plymouth Meeting 🅂🄷
(610) 260-0488. $104-$114. 437 Irwins Ln. I-276 (Pennsylvania Tpke), exit 333, follow signs for Plymouth Rd (Norristown), just w on Plymouth Rd, then just n. Int corridors. Pets: Accepted.
(ASK) 🔊 🗙 🕖 👷 🖪 💻

POTTSTOWN

▼▼▼▼ Comfort Inn 🅂🄷
(610) 326-5000. $109-$139. 99 Robinson St. SR 100, 1 mi n of jct US 422. Int corridors. Pets: Other species. $10 daily fee/pet. Service with restrictions, supervision.
(ASK) 🔊 🗙 🕖 👷 🖪 💻 🗙

▼ Motel 6 🄼
(610) 819-1288. $55-$70. 78 Robinson St. Jct US 422, 1 mi n on SR 100, just w; in Tri-County Business Campus. Int corridors. Pets: Medium, other species. Service with restrictions, supervision.
🔊 🗙 🕖

QUAKERTOWN

▼▼▼ Comfort Inn & Suites 🅂🄷
(215) 538-3000. $89-$169. 1905 John Fries Hwy (SR 663). I-476 (Pennsylvania Tpke), exit 44, just e. Ext corridors. Pets: Other species. Designated rooms, service with restrictions.
(SAVE) 🔊 🗙 🖪 💻

▼▼▼ Hampton Inn-Quakertown 🅂🄷
(215) 536-7779. $119-$139. 1915 John Fries Hwy (SR 663). I-476 (Pennsylvania Tpke), exit 44, just e. Int corridors. Pets: Small. $10 daily fee/pet. Service with restrictions, supervision.
(ASK) 🔊 🗙 🕖 👷 🖪 💻 🗙

TREVOSE

▼▼▼ Radisson Hotel of Philadelphia Northeast 🄻🄷
(215) 638-8300. $139-$169. 2400 Old Lincoln Hwy. I-276 (Pennsylvania Tpke), exit 351, 1 mi s on US 1; jct Roosevelt Blvd and Old Lincoln Hwy. Int corridors. Pets: Accepted.
(ASK) 🔊 🗙 👷 🕖 👷 🖪 💻 🍴 🗙

▼▼ Red Roof Inn #7185 🄼
(215) 244-9422. $68-$93. 3100 Lincoln Hwy. I-276 (Pennsylvania Tpke), exit 351, 0.5 mi s on US 1 at US 132. Ext corridors. Pets: Medium, other species. Service with restrictions, supervision.
🗙 👷 🕖 👷 🖪

UPPER BLACK EDDY

▼▼▼ The Bridgeton House on the Delaware 🄱🄱
(610) 982-5856. $169-$399, 14 day notice. 1525 River Rd. On SR 32; center. Int corridors. Pets: Small, dogs only. $100 deposit/pet. Designated rooms, supervision.
🗙 🖪 💻

WEST CHESTER

🔺🔺🔺 Microtel Inn & Suites 🅂🄷
(610) 738-9111. $64-$99. 500 Willowbrook Ln. Just se of US 202, exit Matlack St. Int corridors. Pets: Other species. $20 daily fee/pet. No service, supervision.
(SAVE) 🔊 🗙 👷 🕖 👷 🖪

END METROPOLITAN AREA

PHILIPSBURG

🔺🔺 Main Liner Motel 🄼
(814) 342-2004. $36-$59. 1896 Philipsburg Bigler (US 322 W) Hwy. 1 mi w of jct SR 53 N. Ext corridors. Pets: $8 daily fee/pet. Designated rooms, service with restrictions, supervision.
(SAVE) 🔊 🗙 🖪

PINE GROVE

▼▼ Comfort Inn 🅂🄷 🐾
(570) 345-8031. $79-$159. SR 443. I-81, exit 100. Int corridors. Pets: Other species. $10 daily fee/pet. Designated rooms, service with restrictions.
(ASK) 🔊 🗙 👷 🕖 🖪 💻 🗙

🔺🔺🔺 Econo Lodge 🅂🄷
(570) 345-4099. $50-$99. 419 Suedberg Rd. I-81, exit 100, just e on SR 443. Ext/int corridors. Pets: $10 daily fee/pet. Designated rooms, service with restrictions, crate.
(SAVE) 🗙 🕖 🖪 💻

PITTSBURGH METROPOLITAN AREA

BEAVER FALLS

▼▼▼▼ **Holiday Inn** SH
(724) 846-3700. **$99-$139, 30 day notice.** 7195 Eastwood Rd. I-76 (Pennsylvania Tpke), exit 13, just n. Int corridors. **Pets:** Other species. $25 one-time fee/room. Service with restrictions, supervision.

ASK SO X & H P TI 2 X

BETHEL PARK

▲▲▲ ▼▼▼▼ **Crowne Plaza Pittsburgh South** SH ❦
(412) 833-5300. **$99-$179.** 164 Ft Couch Rd. 1 mi n on US 19. Int corridors. **Pets:** Medium. $50 daily fee/room. Designated rooms, service with restrictions, supervision.

SAVE SO X @ & H P TI 2

BLAWNOX

▼▼▼▼ **Holiday Inn Hotel & Suites-RIDC Park** SH
(412) 963-0600. **$93-$310.** 180 Gamma Dr. I-76 (Pennsylvania Tpke), exit 48, 3.3 mi s; SR 28, RIDC, exit 10. Int corridors. **Pets:** Accepted.

ASK SO X & H P TI 2

BUTLER

▼▼▼ **Comfort Inn** SH
(724) 287-7177. **$60-$140.** 1 Comfort Ln. 4 mi s on SR 8. Int corridors. **Pets:** $20 daily fee/room. Designated rooms, service with restrictions, supervision.

ASK SO X & H P 2

▼▼▼ **Days Inn Butler** SH
(724) 287-6761. **$52-$129.** 139 Pittsburgh Rd. 2 mi s. Int corridors. **Pets:** Accepted.

ASK SO X H P TI 2 X

▼▼▼ **Locust Brook Lodge** BB
(724) 283-8453. **$80-$125.** 179 Eagle Mill Rd. 5 mi w on US 422 to jct Eagle Mill Rd, then 0.8 mi s; I-79, exit 99, 10 mi e on US 422 to jct Eagle Mill Rd, then 0.8 mi s. Ext/int corridors. **Pets:** Accepted.

ASK SO X &

▼▼ **Super 8 Motel** M
(724) 287-8888. **$60-$65.** 138 Pittsburgh/SR 8. 2 mi s. Int corridors. **Pets:** $10 daily fee/pet. Service with restrictions, supervision.

ASK SO X H

CORAOPOLIS

▼▼ **Americas Best Value Inn-Pittsburgh Airport** M
(412) 604-2378. **$55-$59.** 8858 University Blvd. 0.5 mi n of Business Rt SR 60. Ext corridors. **Pets:** Medium. $10 daily fee/pet. Designated rooms, no service, supervision.

X H

▲▲▲ ▼▼▼▼ **Crowne Plaza Hotel Pittsburgh International** LH
(412) 262-2400. **$99-$259.** 1160 Thorn Run Rd. Business Rt SR 60, exit Thorn Run Rd. Int corridors. **Pets:** Medium. $10 daily fee/room. Designated rooms, service with restrictions, supervision.

SAVE SO X @ & H P TI 2

▼▼▼▼ **Embassy Suites-Pittsburgh International Airport** LH
(412) 269-9070. **$112-$229.** 550 Cherrington Pkwy. Business Rt SR 60, exit Thorn Run Rd. Int corridors. **Pets:** Accepted.

X &M @ & H P TI 2 X

▼▼▼ **Hampton Inn Airport-Pittsburgh** SH
(412) 264-0020. **$89-$129.** 8514 University Blvd. Business Rt SR 60, 0.5 mi n. Int corridors. **Pets:** Accepted.

ASK SO X @ H P

▲▲▲ ▼▼▼▼ **Holiday Inn-Pittsburgh Airport** LH
(412) 262-3600. **$79-$149.** 8256 University Blvd. Business Rt SR 60, 1 mi n. Int corridors. **Pets:** Accepted.

SAVE X &M @ & H P TI 2

▲▲▲ ▼▼▼▼ **La Quinta Inn Pittsburgh (Airport)** SH
(412) 269-0400. **$79-$139.** 8507 University Blvd. 1 mi n of Business Rt SR 60. Int corridors. **Pets:** Medium. Service with restrictions.

SAVE X &M @ H P

CRANBERRY TOWNSHIP

▼▼▼▼ **Holiday Inn Express** SH
(724) 772-1000. **$99.** 20003 Rt 19. I-76 (Pennsylvania Tpke), exit 28, jct US 19 and I-76 (Pennsylvania Tpke); I-79, exit 76 northbound; exit 78 southbound, just s. Int corridors. **Pets:** $10 daily fee/room. Service with restrictions, crate.

X H P

▲▲▲ ▼▼▼▼ **Pittsburgh Marriott North** LH
(724) 772-3700. **$99-$349.** 100 Cranberry Woods Dr. I-79, exit 78 (SR 228) to Cranberry Woods Dr. Int corridors. **Pets:** Small. $75 one-time fee/room. Designated rooms, crate.

SAVE SO X &M @ & H P TI 2

▼▼ **Red Roof Inn-Cranberry Township-Pittsburgh North #7079** M
(724) 776-5670. **$63-$83.** 20009 Rt 19. I-76 (Pennsylvania Tpke), exit 28; I-79, exit 76 northbound; exit 78 southbound. Ext corridors. **Pets:** Medium, other species. Service with restrictions, supervision.

X @ H

▼▼▼▼ **Residence Inn Cranberry** SH
(724) 779-1000. **$129-$169.** 1308 Freedom Rd. I-76 (Pennsylvania Tpke), exit 28, 0.5 mi n on US 19, then 0.3 mi w; I-79, exit 78 southbound, 0.5 mi w. Int corridors. **Pets:** Accepted.

X H P 2 X

DELMONT

▼▼ **Super 8 Motel** M
(724) 468-4888. **$54-$64.** 180 Sheffield Dr. SR 66, just s of US 22. Int corridors. **Pets:** Supervision.

ASK SO X &M H

GIBSONIA

▼▼ **Comfort Inn Gibsonia** M
(724) 444-8700. **$59-$199.** 5137 Rt 8. I-76 (Pennsylvania Tpke), exit 39, just n. Ext corridors. **Pets:** Large, other species. $10 daily fee/pet. Service with restrictions, crate.

ASK SO X & H P

GREEN TREE

▼▼▼▼ **Hampton Inn Hotel Green Tree** SH
(412) 922-0100. **$99-$119.** 555 Trumbull Dr. I-279, exit 4A, northbound; exit 4B southbound, jct US 22 and 30, 1 mi nw via Mansfield Ave. Int corridors. **Pets:** Accepted.

ASK SO X @ H P

▲▲▲ ▼▼▼▼ **Holiday Inn-Pittsburgh Central Green Tree** SH
(412) 922-8100. **$79-$199, 3 day notice.** 401 Holiday Dr. I-279, exit 4A to jct US 22 and 30, 1 mi nw via Mansfield Ave. Int corridors. **Pets:** Medium, other species. $25 one-time fee/pet. Designated rooms, service with restrictions.

SAVE SO X & H P TI 2

(AAA) ▼▼▼ Quality Suites SH
(412) 279-6300. **$89-$289.** 700 Mansfield Ave. I-279, exit 4A to jct US 22 and 30, 1.5 mi nw. Ext corridors. **Pets:** Medium. $15 daily fee/pet. Designated rooms, service with restrictions, supervision.

(SAVE) (S) (X) (🖉) (📦) (📺) (🏊) (🐾)

(AAA) ▼▼▼▼ The Radisson Hotel Pittsburgh/Green Tree LH
(412) 922-8400. **$109-$350.** 101 Radisson Dr. I-279, exit 4A to jct US 22 and 30, 1.1 mi nw via Mansfield Ave. Int corridors. **Pets:** Other species. $100 deposit/pet. Service with restrictions, supervision.

(SAVE) (S) (X) (M) (🖉) (🍴) (📦) (📺) (🍴) (🏊) (🐾)

MARS

▼▼ Comfort Inn Cranberry Township SH
(724) 772-2700. **$59-$129.** 924 Sheraton Dr. I-76 (Pennsylvania Tpke), exit 28; I-79, exit 76 northbound; exit 78 southbound, 0.5 mi s on US 19. Int corridors. **Pets:** Accepted.

(ASK) (S) (X) (🖉) (📦) (📺)

▼ Motel 6 Pittsburgh North Cranberry #42 M
(724) 776-4333. **$45-$63.** 19025 Perry Hwy. I-76 (Pennsylvania Tpke), exit 28, jct US 19; I-79, exit 76 northbound; exit 78 southbound on US 19. Ext corridors. **Pets:** Medium, other species. Service with restrictions, supervision.

(S) (X) (🍴) (📦)

MONACA

▼▼▼ Holiday Inn Express Hotel & Suites-Center Township SH
(724) 728-5121. **$92-$152.** 105 Stone Quarry Rd. SR 60, exit 12, just n. Int corridors. **Pets:** Accepted.

(ASK) (X) (📦) (📺) (🏊)

MONROEVILLE

▼▼ Comfort Inn Pittsburgh East SH
(412) 244-1600. **$69-$139.** 699 Rodi Rd. I-376, exit 11, just n. Int corridors. **Pets:** Accepted.

(ASK) (S) (X) (🍴) (📦) (📺) (🍴) (🏊) (🐾)

▼ Days Inn-Monroeville M
(412) 856-1610. **$48-$199.** 2727 Mosside Blvd. I-76 (Pennsylvania Tpke), exit 57; I-376, exit 14A, 1 mi s on SR 48. Ext corridors. **Pets:** Dogs only. $10 daily fee/pet. Service with restrictions, crate.

(ASK) (S) (X) (📦)

▼▼▼ Hampton Inn Monroeville/Pittsburgh SH
(412) 380-4100. **$114-$144.** 3000 Mosside Blvd. I-76 (Pennsylvania Tpke), exit 57; I-376, exit 14A, 0.3 mi s on SR 48. Int corridors. **Pets:** Accepted.

(ASK) (S) (X) (🖉) (🍴) (📦) (📺) (🏊)

▼▼ Red Roof Inn-Monroeville #7174 M
(412) 856-4738. **$66-$84.** 2729 Mosside Blvd. I-76 (Pennsylvania Tpke), exit 57; I-376, exit 14A, 0.8 mi s on SR 48. Ext corridors. **Pets:** Medium, other species. Service with restrictions, supervision.

(X) (📦)

▼▼ Super 8 Motel Pittsburgh/Monroeville M
(724) 733-8008. **$57-$61.** 1807 Rt 286. I-76 (Pennsylvania Tpke), exit 57; I-376, exit 14A, 2 mi e on US 22 E, then 2 mi e. Int corridors. **Pets:** Large, other species. $10 one-time fee/pet. Service with restrictions, supervision.

(ASK) (S) (X) (📦)

MOON RUN

(AAA) ▼▼▼ Comfort Inn-Pittsburgh Airport SH
(412) 787-2600. **$59-$114.** 7011 Old Steubenville Pike. US 22 and 30, jct SR 60; 4 mi w of jct I-279 and 79. Ext/int corridors. **Pets:** Other species. $10 daily fee/pet. Designated rooms, service with restrictions, supervision.

(SAVE) (S) (X) (🖉) (📦) (📺) (🍴)

(AAA) ▼▼▼ Days Inn Pittsburgh International Airport SH
(412) 859-4000. **$60-$90.** 2500 Marketplace Blvd. SR 60, exit 2 (Montour Run Rd), 0.5 mi e, then 0.5 mi n. Int corridors. **Pets:** Small, dogs only. $25 one-time fee/room. Designated rooms, service with restrictions, supervision.

(SAVE) (S) (X) (🖉) (🍴) (📦) (📺) (🏊)

▼▼▼ Four Points by Sheraton Pittsburgh Airport SH
(724) 695-0002. **$150-$190.** 1 Industry Ln. SR 60, exit 2 (Montour Run Rd). Int corridors. **Pets:** Medium. $50 one-time fee/pet. Service with restrictions, supervision.

(ASK) (S) (X) (🍴) (🍴) (📦) (📺) (🍴) (🏊)

(AAA) ▼▼▼ Holiday Inn Express Pittsburgh Airport SH
(412) 788-8400. **$99-$134.** 5311 Campbells Run Rd. US 22/30 W, exit Crafton (SR 60) S, just w. Int corridors. **Pets:** Accepted.

(SAVE) (X) (🖉) (🍴) (📦) (📺) (🏊)

▼▼ MainStay Suites Pittsburgh Airport SH
(412) 490-7343. **$54-$129.** 1000 Park Lane Dr. SR 60, exit 2 (Montour Run Rd), just w on Cliff Mine Rd, then just s. Int corridors. **Pets:** Accepted.

(ASK) (S) (X) (🍴) (📦) (📺)

▼ Motel 6 Pittsburgh #657 M
(412) 922-9400. **$39-$49.** 211 Beecham Dr. I-79, exit 60A, just s on Steubenville Pike (SR 60), then e. Ext corridors. **Pets:** Medium, other species. Service with restrictions, supervision.

(S) (X) (M) (🍴)

(AAA) ▼▼▼ Pittsburgh Airport Marriott LH
(412) 788-8800. **$109-$349.** 777 Aten Rd. SR 60, exit 2 (Montour Run Rd). Int corridors. **Pets:** $50 one-time fee/room. Service with restrictions, supervision.

(SAVE) (S) (X) (🍴) (🍴) (📦) (📺) (🍴) (🏊) (🐾)

▼▼ Red Roof Inn South Airport #7030 M
(412) 787-7870. **$55-$73.** 6404 Steubenville Pike. I-79, exit 60A, 3.2 mi w on SR 60. Ext/int corridors. **Pets:** Medium, other species. Service with restrictions, supervision.

(X) (🖉) (🍴) (🍴)

▼▼▼ Residence Inn-Pittsburgh Airport SH
(412) 787-3300. **$199-$259.** 1500 Park Lane Dr. SR 60, exit 2 (Montour Run Rd), just w on Cliff Mine Dr to Summit Park Dr, just s to Park Lane Dr, then just e. Int corridors. **Pets:** Accepted.

(ASK) (S) (X) (M) (🖉) (🍴) (🍴) (📦) (📺) (🏊) (🐾)

NEW KENSINGTON

▼▼ Clarion Hotel SH
(724) 335-9171. **$76-$99, 3 day notice.** 300 Tarentum Bridge Rd. SR 366, 1.5 mi s of SR 28, exit 14; at south end of Tarentum Bridge. Int corridors. **Pets:** Other species. Service with restrictions, supervision.

(ASK) (S) (X) (🍴) (🍴) (📦) (📺) (🍴) (🏊)

PITTSBURGH

(AAA) ▼▼▼ Holiday Inn Pittsburgh North Hills SH
(412) 366-5200. **$119-$239.** 4859 McKnight Rd. I-279, exit 11, 7 mi n on US 19. Int corridors. **Pets:** Accepted.

(SAVE) (S) (X) (🖉) (🍴) (🍴) (📦) (📺) (🍴) (🏊)

▼▼▼▼ Omni William Penn Hotel 🄻🄷
(412) 281-7100. **$219-$249.** 530 William Penn Pl. Jct 6th St and William Penn Pl. Int corridors. **Pets:** Small, other species. $50 one-time fee/room. Service with restrictions, crate.
(ASK) (S₆) (✕) (🖉) (🖬) (🖵) (🍴) (✕)

**▼▼▼ Residence Inn by Marriott
Pittsburgh-Oakland** 🅂🄷 🌸
(412) 621-2200. **$179-$289.** 3896 Bigelow Blvd. On SR 380. Int corridors. **Pets:** $75 one-time fee/room. Service with restrictions, crate.
(ASK) (S₆) (✕) (🖉) (🖬) (🖵) (🏊) (✕)

▼▼▼ Sheraton Station Square Hotel 🄻🄷 🌸
(412) 261-2000. **$129-$229.** 300 W Station Square St. I-376, exit Grant St, south end of Smithfield St Bridge; across river. Int corridors. **Pets:** Medium, dogs only. Designated rooms, service with restrictions, supervision.
(ASK) (✕) (🖉) (🖬) (🖵) (🍴) (🏊) (✕)

▼▼▼ The Westin Convention Center Pittsburgh 🄻🄷
(412) 281-3700. **$119-$325.** 1000 Penn Ave. Jct 10th St; at Liberty Center. Int corridors. **Pets:** Accepted.
(ASK) (✕) (🖉) (🖬) (🖵) (🏊) (✕)

▼▼▼ Wyndham Garden Pittsburgh University Place 🄻🄷
(412) 683-2040. **$109-$189.** 3454 Forbes Ave. Jct Forbes Ave and McKee Pl. Int corridors. **Pets:** Medium. $50 deposit/room, $10 daily fee/room. Supervision.
(ASK) (✕) (🖉) (🖬) (🖵) (🍴)

WASHINGTON

🅰🅰🅰 ▼▼▼ Ramada Inn 🅂🄷
(724) 225-9750. **$75-$105.** 1170 W Chestnut St. I-70, exit 15, 0.5 mi e on US 40. Ext/int corridors. **Pets:** Small. $30 one-time fee/room. Designated rooms, service with restrictions, crate.
(SAVE) (S₆) (✕) (🖬) (🖵) (🍴) (🏊)

▼▼ Red Roof Inn #7048 🄼
(724) 228-5750. **$47-$69.** 1399 W Chestnut St. I-70, exit 15, just e on US 40. Ext/int corridors. **Pets:** Medium, other species. Service with restrictions, supervision.
(✕) (🖉) (🖬)

WEST MIFFLIN

▼▼ Comfort Inn-West Mifflin 🅂🄷
(412) 653-6600. **$80-$140.** 1340 Lebanon Church Rd. 0.6 mi e of jct SR 51. Int corridors. **Pets:** $10 daily fee/room. Designated rooms, service with restrictions, supervision.
(S₆) (✕) (🖉) (🖬) (🖵) (🏊)

▼▼ Extended StayAmerica-Pittsburgh-West Mifflin 🅂🄷
(412) 650-9096. **$75-$80.** 1303 Lebanon Churck Rd. 0.5 mi e of jct SR 51. Int corridors. **Pets:** Accepted.
(ASK) (S₆) (✕) (🖬) (🖵)

▼▼▼ Holiday Inn Express Hotel & Suites 🅂🄷
(412) 469-1900. **$105-$139.** 3122 Lebanon Church Rd. 1.5 mi e of jct SR 51. Int corridors. **Pets:** Other species. $10 daily fee/pet. Service with restrictions, supervision.
(ASK) (S₆) (✕) (🖬) (🖵)

END METROPOLITAN AREA

PITTSTON

🅰🅰🅰 ▼▼▼ Knights Inn-Scranton/Pittston 🄼
(570) 654-6020. **$40-$85.** 310 SR 315. I-81, exit 175 northbound, just s on SR 315; exit 175A southbound; I-476 (Northeast Extension Pennsylvania Tpke), exit 115. Ext corridors. **Pets:** Small. Designated rooms, service with restrictions, supervision.
(SAVE) (S₆) (✕) (🖬)

▼▼ Quality Inn 🅂🄷
(570) 655-1234. **$90, 3 day notice.** 400 SR 315. I-81, exit 175 northbound; exit 175B southbound; I-476 (Northeast Extension Pennsylvania Tpke), exit 115. Int corridors. **Pets:** Accepted.
(ASK) (S₆) (✕) (🖬) (🖵) (🍴)

POCONO MOUNTAINS AREA

BLAKESLEE

🅰🅰🅰 ▼▼▼ Best Western Inn-Blakeslee/Pocono 🅂🄷
(570) 646-6000. **$80-$185.** New Ventures Business Park. I-80, exit 284, just n. Int corridors. **Pets:** $50 deposit/room. Service with restrictions, supervision.
(SAVE) (S₆) (✕) (🅼) (🖉) (🖵) (🏊)

EAST STROUDSBURG

🅰🅰🅰 ▼▼▼ Budget Inn & Suites 🅂🄷 🌸
(570) 424-5451. **$59-$89, 3 day notice.** I-80, exit 308. I-80, exit 308, just se on Greentree Rd. Ext/int corridors. **Pets:** $125 deposit/room. Designated rooms, service with restrictions, supervision.
(SAVE) (S₆) (✕) (🖬) (🍴)

▼▼ Super 8 Motel 🄼
(570) 424-7411. **$60-$160.** 340 Greentree Dr. I-80, exit 308, just se. Int corridors. **Pets:** Medium. $10 daily fee/pet. Designated rooms, service with restrictions, supervision.
(ASK) (S₆) (✕) (🅼) (🖬)

LAKE HARMONY

🅰🅰🅰 ▼▼▼ Ramada Inn-Pocono 🅂🄷
(570) 443-8471. **$75-$115.** Rt 940. I-80, exit 277, 0.5 mi e; I-476 (Northeast Extension Pennsylvania Tpke), exit 95 (Pocono). Int corridors. **Pets:** Accepted.
(SAVE) (S₆) (✕) (🖉) (🖉) (🖬) (🖵) (🍴) (🏊) (✕)

MATAMORAS

▼▼▼ Best Western Inn at Hunt's Landing 🅂🄷
(570) 491-2400. **$109-$189.** 120 Rt 6 & 209. I-84, exit 53. Int corridors. **Pets:** Accepted.
(ASK) (S₆) (✕) (🖉) (🖬) (🖵) (🍴) (🏊) (✕)

MILFORD

[AAA] ◆◆ Milford Motel [M]
(570) 296-6411. **$50-$95, 3 day notice.** 591 Rt 6 & 209. On US 6 and 209 N, 0.7 mi e. Ext corridors. **Pets:** Dogs only. $10 one-time fee/room. Designated rooms, no service, supervision.
[SAVE] [SD] ⊠ ▣

[AAA] ◆◆ Red Carpet Inn-Milford [M]
(570) 296-9444. **$65-$125, 7 day notice.** 240 Rt 6. I-84, exit 46, just s. Ext corridors. **Pets:** Medium. $7 daily fee/pet. Designated rooms, no service, supervision.
[SAVE] [SD] ⊠ ▣

[AAA] ◆ Scottish Inns [M]
(570) 491-4414. **$50-$95.** 274 Rt 6 & 209. I-84, exit 53, 1 mi s. Ext corridors. **Pets:** Accepted.
[SAVE] [SD] ⊠ ▣ 🖥

STARLIGHT

◆◆ The Inn at Starlight Lake [CI]
(570) 798-2519. **$90-$195, 14 day notice.** 289 Starlight Lake Rd. Off SR 370, 1 mi n, follow signs. Ext/int corridors. **Pets:** Other species. Designated rooms, service with restrictions.
[A$K] [SD] ⊠ 🍴 🏋 [AC] [TV] ☎

END AREA

PUNXSUTAWNEY

◆◆ Pantall Hotel [SH]
(814) 938-6600. **$64-$125.** 135 E Mahoning St. On US 119/SR 36; downtown. Int corridors. **Pets:** Medium. $25 one-time fee/room. Service with restrictions, supervision.
[A$K] [SD] ⊠ ▣ 🍴

READING

◆◆◆ The Abraham Lincoln- A Wyndham Historic Hotel [LH]
(610) 372-3700. **$109-$159.** 100 N 5th St. 5th and Washington sts; downtown. Int corridors. **Pets:** Accepted.
[A$K] [SD] ⊠ [&M] 🦻 ♿ ▣ 🖥 🍴

[AAA] ◆◆◆ Dutch Colony Inn & Suites [SH]
(610) 779-2345. **$90-$125.** 4635 Perkiomen Ave. US 422, 0.3 mi e of jct US 422 business route. Ext/int corridors. **Pets:** Other species. $12 daily fee/pet. Designated rooms, service with restrictions, supervision.
[SAVE] [SD] ⊠ 🦻 ♿ ▣ 🖥 🍴 🏊 🏋

[AAA] ◆◆ Quality Inn Airport [SH]
(610) 736-0400. **$60-$140.** 2017 Bernville Rd. US 222, exit SR 183, 2 mi s. Int corridors. **Pets:** Small. $25 daily fee/pet. Designated rooms, no service, supervision.
[SAVE] [SD] ⊠ ▣ 🖥

ST. MARYS

◆◆ Comfort Inn [SH]
(814) 834-2030. **$69-$105.** 195 Comfort Ln. 1.8 mi s of center on SR 255, just w. Int corridors. **Pets:** Other species. $15 daily fee/pet. Service with restrictions, supervision.
[A$K] [SD] ⊠ ♿ ▣ 🖥 🏊

SAYRE

[AAA] ◆◆◆ Best Western Grand Victorian [SH]
(570) 888-7711. **$114-$199.** 255 Spring St. SR 17, exit 61, just s. Int corridors. **Pets:** Accepted.
[SAVE] [SD] ⊠ ▣ 🖥 🍴 🏊 🏋

SCRANTON

[AAA] ◆◆◆ Clarion Hotel [LH]
(570) 344-9811. **$79-$139.** 300 Meadow Ave. I-81, exit 184, just w. Int corridors. **Pets:** Other species. $15 daily fee/room. Service with restrictions, supervision.
[SAVE] [SD] ⊠ 🦻 ▣ 🖥 🍴 🏊 🏋

SELINSGROVE

[AAA] ◆◆ Comfort Inn [SH]
(570) 374-8880. **$69-$169.** 613 N Susquehanna Tr. On US 11 and 15, just n of jct US 522. Int corridors. **Pets:** Medium, other species. $25 daily fee/room. Designated rooms, service with restrictions, crate.
[SAVE] [SD] ⊠ ▣ 🖥 🍴 🏊

SHAMOKIN DAM

[AAA] ◆◆ Econo Lodge Inn & Suites [SH]
(570) 743-1111. **$59-$169.** 3249 N Susquehanna Tr. US 11 and 15; just n of jct SR 61. Ext corridors. **Pets:** Small, other species. $10 daily fee/pet. Designated rooms, service with restrictions, crate.
[SAVE] [SD] ⊠ ▣ 🖥 🍴 🏊

[AAA] ◆◆◆ Hampton Inn [SH] 🐾
(570) 743-2223. **$139-$199.** 3 Stettler Ave. US 11 and 15, 1 mi s of jct SR 61. Int corridors. **Pets:** Medium, other species. $25 one-time fee/room. Designated rooms, service with restrictions, supervision.
[SAVE] [SD] ⊠ [&M] 🦻 ♿ ▣ 🖥 🏊

SHICKSHINNY

◆◆ The Blue Heron Bed & Breakfast [BB]
(570) 864-3740. **$60-$90 (no credit cards), 3 day notice.** 1270 Bethel Hill Rd. Jct US 11, 6.2 mi n on SR 239, then 2 mi n on CR 4016 (Harveyville/Bethel Hill Rd). Int corridors. **Pets:** Accepted.
⊠ [TV]

SOUTH WILLIAMSPORT

[AAA] ◆◆ Quality Inn Williamsport [SH]
(570) 323-9801. **$59-$250.** 234 US Hwy 15. 0.8 mi s on US 15. Int corridors. **Pets:** Accepted.
[SAVE] [SD] ⊠ 🦻 ▣ 🖥 🏊

[AAA] ◆◆ Ridgemont Motel [M] 🐾
(570) 321-5300. **$39-$49.** 637 Rt 15 Hwy. 1.2 mi s on US 15. Ext corridors. **Pets:** Medium, dogs only. $5 daily fee/pet. Service with restrictions, supervision.
[SAVE] [SD] ⊠ ▣ 🖥

STATE COLLEGE

◆◆ The Autoport Motel & Restaurant Inc [SH]
(814) 237-7666. **$65-$89.** 1405 S Atherton St. US 322 business route, 1.4 mi e of jct SR 26. Ext/int corridors. **Pets:** Accepted.
[A$K] ⊠ ▣ 🖥 🍴 🏊

[AAA] ◆◆◆ Comfort Suites [SH]
(814) 235-1900. **$69-$250, 7 day notice.** 132 Village Dr. SR 26, 1.1 mi on US 322 W (Atherton St), just ne; center. Int corridors. **Pets:** Other species. $50 deposit/room, $20 daily fee/room. Designated rooms, service with restrictions, supervision.
[SAVE] [SD] ⊠ ♿ ▣ 🖥 🏊

[AAA] ◆◆◆ Days Inn Penn State [LH]
(814) 238-8454. **$109, 30 day notice.** 240 S Pugh St. Just e of SR 26 northbound; 0.4 mi n of jct US 322 business route; downtown. Int corridors. **Pets:** $10 daily fee/room. Designated rooms, service with restrictions, crate.
[SAVE] [SD] ⊠ 🦻 ♿ ▣ 🖥 🍴 🏊

Happy Valley Motor Inn M
(814) 234-1111. **$47-$130.** 1245 S Atherton St. 1.3 mi e on US 322 business route. Ext/int corridors. **Pets:** Medium, other species. $20 one-time fee/pet. Service with restrictions, supervision.

Motel 6 State College#4101 M
(814) 234-1600. **$49-$65.** 1274 N Atherton St. US 322, 1 mi w of jct SR 26. Int corridors. **Pets:** Medium, other species. Service with restrictions, supervision.

Nittany Budget Motel M
(814) 238-0015. **$45-$64.** 2070 Cato Ave. SR 26, 2.6 mi s of jct US 322 business route. Ext corridors. **Pets:** Accepted.

Residence Inn by Marriott SH
(814) 235-6960. **$124-$169.** 1555 University Dr. US 322 business route, 1.5 mi e of jct SR 26. Int corridors. **Pets:** Other species. $75 one-time fee/room. Service with restrictions.

Sleep Inn SH
(814) 235-1020. **$55-$155, 14 day notice.** 111 Village Dr. US 322 business route, 1 mi w of jct SR 26. Int corridors. **Pets:** Medium. $25 one-time fee/pet. Designated rooms, service with restrictions, supervision.

Super 8 State College SH
(814) 237-8005. **$60-$80.** 1663 S Atherton St. US 322 business route, 1.6 mi e of jct SR 26. Int corridors. **Pets:** $25 one-time fee/room. Service with restrictions, supervision.

TOWN HILL

Days Inn Breezewood SH
(814) 735-3860. **$53-$69.** 9648 Old Rt 126. I-70, exit 156, just n. Int corridors. **Pets:** Accepted.

WARREN

Holiday Inn of Warren SH
(814) 726-3000. **$120.** 210 Ludlow St. Jct US 6, just n on Ludlow St (US 62 N). Int corridors. **Pets:** Accepted.

Warren Super 8 Motel SH
(814) 723-8881. **$71-$78.** 204 Struthers St. 1.5 mi w on US 6, exit Ludlow St, w on Allegheny, then s. Ext/int corridors. **Pets:** Accepted.

WAYNESBORO

Best Western of Waynesboro M
(717) 762-9113. **$70-$82.** 239 W Main St. 0.5 mi w on SR 16. Ext corridors. **Pets:** Accepted.

WAYNESBURG

Comfort Inn SH
(724) 627-3700. **$69-$69.** 100 Comfort Ln. I-79, exit 14, just e. Int corridors. **Pets:** Medium, other species. $25 one-time fee/room. Service with restrictions, crate.

Econo Lodge M
(724) 627-5544. **$48-$75.** 126 Miller Ln. I-79, exit 14, just w. Ext corridors. **Pets:** Small. $5 one-time fee/pet. Service with restrictions, supervision.

Super 8 Motel-Waynesburg M
(724) 627-8880. **$50-$55.** 100 Stanley Dr. I-79, exit 14, just w. Int corridors. **Pets:** Other species. Service with restrictions, supervision.

WELLSBORO

Coach Stop Inn M
(570) 724-5361. **$50-$85.** 4755 US Rt 6 W. On US 6, 12 mi w. Ext/int corridors. **Pets:** Accepted.

Penn Wells Lodge M
(570) 724-3463. **$40-$100, 7 day notice.** 4 Main St. Just n on US 6 and SR 287. Ext/int corridors. **Pets:** Small. $20 daily fee/room. Service with restrictions, crate.

WEST HAZLETON

Comfort Inn Hazleton/West Hazleton SH
(570) 455-9300. **$79-$149.** 58 SR 93. I-81, exit 145, 0.3 mi se; I-80, exit 256, 3.8 mi se. Int corridors. **Pets:** Other species. $10 daily fee/room. Service with restrictions, supervision.

WEST MIDDLESEX

Super 8 Motel-West Middlesex/Sharon SH
(724) 528-3888. **$65-$80.** 3369 New Castle Rd. I-80, exit 4B (SR 60), just w to SR 18, then just s. Int corridors. **Pets:** Small. $15 daily fee/pet. Designated rooms, service with restrictions, supervision.

WILKES-BARRE

Best Western Genetti Hotel & Conference Center SH
(570) 823-6152. **$89-$169.** 77 E Market St. Jct Washington St; downtown. Int corridors. **Pets:** Other species. $10 daily fee/room.

Econo Lodge SH
(570) 823-0600. **$65-$185.** 1075 Wilkes-Barre Township Blvd. I-81, exit 165 southbound; exit 165B northbound, on SR 309 business route. Int corridors. **Pets:** Large, other species. $100 deposit/room, $10 daily fee/pet. Designated rooms, service with restrictions, supervision.

Holiday Inn SH
(570) 824-8901. **$94-$199.** 880 Kidder St. I-81, exit 170B to exit 1 (SR 309 S business route). Ext corridors. **Pets:** Accepted.

Host Inn Residential Suites SH
(570) 270-4678. **$129-$239.** 860 Kidder St. I-81, exit 170B to exit 1 (SR 309 S business route) off expressway, then 0.5 mi w. Int corridors. **Pets:** Other species. $15 one-time fee/pet. Service with restrictions, crate.

Red Roof Inn #7139 M
(570) 829-6422. **$53-$68.** 1035 Hwy 315. I-81, exit 170B, jct SR 115, 0.7 mi w, exit 1 (SR 309 S business route) to SR 315, then just n. Ext corridors. **Pets:** Medium, other species. Service with restrictions, supervision.

The Woodlands Inn & Resort LH
(570) 824-9831. **$109-$259.** 1073 Hwy 315. I-81, exit 170B to exit 1 (SR 309 S business route), then 0.3 mi n. Int corridors. **Pets:** Accepted.

WILLIAMSPORT

(AAA) ▼▼▼ Best Western Williamsport Inn SH ☘
(570) 326-1981. **$59-$169.** 1840 E Third St. I-180, exit 25 (Faxon St), just e; 1 mi w of W 3rd St. Ext corridors. **Pets:** Other species. $15 one-time fee/pet. Service with restrictions, crate.
[SAVE] [S🐾] [✕] [🛏] [💻] [🍽] [🏊] [✕🐾]

▼▼▼ Candlewood Suites SH ☘
(570) 601-9100. **$65-$199.** 1836 E Third St. I-180, exit 25 (Faxon St), 0.5 mi e. Int corridors. **Pets:** Large, other species. $150 one-time fee/pet. Crate.
[ASK] [S🐾] [✕] [🌙] [🛗] [🛏] [💻]

▼▼ Econo Lodge M
(570) 326-1501. **$59-$75.** 2019 E 3rd St. I-180, exit 25 (Faxon St) eastbound, 0.8 mi e, just n on Westminster St; exit 23 (3rd St) westbound, 0.3 mi w. Ext corridors. **Pets:** Dogs only. $10 daily fee/room. Service with restrictions.
[ASK] [S🐾] [✕] [🛏] [💻] [🍽]

(AAA) ▼▼▼ Genetti Hotel & Suites SH ☘
(570) 326-6600. **$71-$101, 7 day notice.** 200 W Fourth St. Jct William St; downtown. Int corridors. **Pets:** Other species. $10 daily fee/pet. Service with restrictions, crate.
[SAVE] [S🐾] [✕] [🛗] [🛏] [💻] [🍽] [🏊]

▼▼▼ Holiday Inn Downtown Williamsport SH ☘
(570) 327-8231. **$99-$119.** 100 Pine St. Jct US 220 and SR 15 S; downtown. Int corridors. **Pets:** Small. $15 one-time fee/room. Designated rooms, service with restrictions, supervision.
[ASK] [✕] [🛏] [💻] [🍽] [🏊]

WIND GAP

(AAA) ▼▼▼ Red Carpet Inn M
(610) 863-7782. **$65-$130.** 1395 Jacobsburg Rd. SR 33, exit Wind Gap/Bath SR 512 S, just s on Jacobsburg Rd, follow signs. Ext/int corridors. **Pets:** Accepted.
[SAVE] [S🐾] [✕] [🛏]

WYOMISSING

▼▼ Econo Lodge SH
(610) 378-5105. **$63-$105, 3 day notice.** 635 Spring St. Just off US 422, exit Papermill Rd. Int corridors. **Pets:** Small. $10 daily fee/pet. Service with restrictions, crate.
[ASK] [S🐾] [✕] [🌙] [🛏] [💻]

▼▼▼ Homewood Suites-Reading/Wyomissing SH
(610) 736-3100. **$174-$325.** 2801 Papermill Rd. US 422, exit Papermill Rd, 1.8 mi nw; US 222, exit Spring Ridge Rd. Int corridors. **Pets:** Small. $250 one-time fee/pet. Service with restrictions, supervision.
[ASK] [✕] [🛗] [🌙] [🛗] [🛏] [💻] [🏊]

▼▼▼ The Inn at Reading SH
(610) 372-7811. **$99-$159.** 1040 Park Rd. US 222, exit N Wyomissing Blvd, just n, then 0.3 mi e. Int corridors. **Pets:** Small. $10 daily fee/pet. Designated rooms, service with restrictions, supervision.
[SAVE] [S🐾] [✕] [🌙] [🛏] [💻] [🍽] [🏊] [✕🐾]

▼▼▼ Sheraton Reading Hotel SH ☘
(610) 376-3811. **$109-$199.** 1741 W Papermill Rd. US 422, exit Papermill Rd. Int corridors. **Pets:** Medium. $52 one-time fee/pet. Service with restrictions, supervision.
[ASK] [S🐾] [✕] [🌙] [🛗] [🛏] [💻] [🍽] [🏊] [✕🐾]

WYSOX

▼▼▼ Comfort Inn SH ☘
(570) 265-5691. **$99-$125.** US 6. Center. Int corridors. **Pets:** Large, other species. $15 one-time fee/pet. Service with restrictions, supervision.
[ASK] [S🐾] [✕] [🛗M] [🌙] [🛗] [🛏] [💻] [🏊]

YORK

▼▼▼ Holiday Inn Holidome & Conference Center SH ☘
(717) 846-9500. **$124.** 2000 Loucks Rd. I-83, exit 21B northbound, 2.5 mi w on US 30, then just w; exit 22 southbound, 0.5 mi s on SR 181, 2.2 mi w on US 30, then just n. Int corridors. **Pets:** Medium. $10 one-time fee/pet. Service with restrictions, supervision.
[ASK] [S🐾] [✕] [🌙] [🛗] [🛏] [💻] [🍽] [🏊] [✕🐾]

(AAA) ▼▼▼ Holiday Inn York I-83 & Rt 30 SH
(717) 845-5671. **$96-$125.** 334 Arsenal Rd. I-83, exit 21A northbound; exit 21 southbound, just e on US 30. Ext corridors. **Pets:** Accepted.
[SAVE] [S🐾] [✕] [🌙] [🛗] [🛏] [💻] [🍽] [🏊]

▼▼ Red Roof Inn #315 M
(717) 843-8181. **$61-$91.** 125 Arsenal Rd. I-83, exit 21B northbound, 0.3 mi w on US 30; exit 21 southbound, 0.5 mi s on SR 181 to US 30. Int corridors. **Pets:** Medium, other species. Service with restrictions, supervision.
[✕] [🛗] [🛏]

▼▼ Super 8 Motel M
(717) 852-8686. **$56-$100.** 40 Arsenal Rd. I-83, exit 21B northbound, 0.3 mi w on US 30; exit 21 southbound, 0.5 mi s on SR 181 to US 30. Int corridors. **Pets:** Accepted.
[ASK] [S🐾] [✕] [🛏]

RHODE ISLAND

CITY INDEX

EAST PROVIDENCE

▼▼ Extended StayAmerica Providence-East Providence SH
(401) 272-1661. **$99-$124.** 1000 Warren Ave. I-95, exit 7 eastbound, just e; exit 1 westbound, just nw on Fall River Ave, then just sw via County St. Int corridors. **Pets:** Accepted.

(A$K) (S�½) (✕) (♿) (⌖) (🐾) 🅱 💻

MIDDLETOWN

▼ The Bay Willows Inn Ⓜ ✿
(401) 847-8400. **$39-$189, 7 day notice.** 1225 Aquidneck Ave. Jct SR 138 and 138A. Ext corridors. **Pets:** Large, other species. $10 daily fee/room. Service with restrictions.

(A$K) (S�½) (✕) 🅱

▼▼ Howard Johnson Inn-Newport SH ✿
(401) 849-2000. **$49-$249.** 351 W Main Rd. On SR 114, 0.3 mi s of jct SR 138. Int corridors. **Pets:** Other species. $10 daily fee/pet. Designated rooms, service with restrictions, supervision.

(SAVE) (S�½) (✕) (♿) (⌖) (🐾) 🅱 💻 🍴 ⌘ (✕)

▼ SeaView Inn Ⓜ
(401) 324-6200. **$59-$199, 7 day notice.** 240 Aquidneck Ave (SR 138A). Jct SR 214. Ext corridors. **Pets:** Dogs only. $10 daily fee/pet. Designated rooms, service with restrictions, supervision.

(A$K) (S�½) (✕) 🅱 💻

NEWPORT

▼▼▼ Beech Tree Inn BB
(401) 847-9794. **$99-$295, 14 day notice.** 34 Rhode Island Ave. Just e of SR 114; 0.8 mi s of jct SR 138. Int corridors. **Pets:** Medium, other species. $25 daily fee/pet. No service, crate.

(SAVE) (✕) 🅱

▼▼ The Burbank Rose BB
(401) 849-9457. **$68-$225, 7 day notice.** 111 Memorial Blvd W. Just e on SR 138A. Int corridors. **Pets:** Small. $75 deposit/room. Designated rooms, no service, crate.

(SAVE) (✕) 🅱 💻 (🐾)

▼▼▼ The Hotel Viking LH
(401) 847-3300. **$189-$459, 3 day notice.** One Bellevue Ave. Corner of Kay St, Church and Bellevue Ave. Int corridors. **Pets:** Medium. $35 one-time fee/room. Service with restrictions, supervision.

(SAVE) (✕) 🅱 💻 🍴 ⌘ (✕)

▼▼▼▼ Hyatt Regency Newport Hotel & Spa LH
(401) 851-1234. **$159-$469, 3 day notice.** 1 Goat Island. 0.8 mi w of America's Cup Ave, follow signs to Goat Island. Int corridors. **Pets:** Accepted.

(SAVE) (✕) (🐾) (⌖) 🅱 💻 🍴 ⌘ (✕)

NORTH KINGSTOWN

▼▼ Hamilton Village Inn Ⓜ
(401) 295-0700. **$79-$129, 7 day notice.** 642 Boston Neck Rd. SR 1A, 1.3 mi s of jct SR 102. Ext corridors. **Pets:** Other species. Designated rooms, service with restrictions, supervision.

(✕) 🅱 💻 🍴

PORTSMOUTH

▼▼ Founder's Brook Motel & Suites Ⓜ
(401) 683-1244. **$59-$159, 3 day notice.** 314 Boyd Ln. Jct SR 24, exit Mt. Hope Blvd, on SR 138. Ext corridors. **Pets:** Small, dogs only. $10 daily fee/pet. Designated rooms, service with restrictions, supervision.

(SAVE) (S�½) (✕) 🅱

PROVIDENCE

▼▼▼ Marriott Providence Hotel LH
(401) 272-2400. **$219-$399.** One Orms St. I-95, exit 23 to state offices. Int corridors. **Pets:** Accepted.

(SAVE) (✕) (♿) (🐾) (⌖) 🅱 💻 🍴 ⌘

▼▼▼ Providence Biltmore Hotel LH
(401) 421-0700. **$149-$289.** 11 Dorrance St. I-95, exit 22A; downtown. Int corridors. **Pets:** Accepted.

(SAVE) (S�½) (✕) (♿) (🐾) (⌖) 🅱 💻 🍴

▼▼▼▼ The Westin Providence LH
(401) 598-8000. **$179-$494.** One W Exchange St. I-95, exit 22A; downtown. Int corridors. **Pets:** Accepted.

(SAVE) (✕) (♿) (🐾) (⌖) 💻 🍴 ⌘ (✕)

WAKEFIELD

▼▼▼ The Kings' Rose Inn BB
(401) 783-5222. **$140-$185, 7 day notice.** 1747 Mooresfield Rd (SR 138). I-95, exit 3A, 11 mi e on SR 138; 3.3 mi w of US 1. Int corridors. **Pets:** Service with restrictions, supervision.

(✕)

WARWICK

▼▼▼ Crowne Plaza Hotel at the Crossings LH
(401) 732-6000. **$119-$189.** 801 Greenwich Ave. I-95, exit 12A southbound; exit 12 northbound, 0.3 mi se on SR 5. Int corridors. **Pets:** Accepted.

(✕) (♿) (🐾) 🅱 💻 🍴 ⌘ (✕)

▼▼ Extended StayAmerica Providence-Airport-Warwick SH
(401) 732-2547. **$89-$119.** 245 W Natick Rd. I-295, exit 2 northbound, just sw; exit 3A southbound, 1.1 mi e on SR 37, 2 mi s on SR 2, then just sw. Int corridors. **Pets:** Accepted.

(A$K) (S�½) (✕) (♿) (🐾) (⌖) 🅱 💻

▼▼▼ Hampton Inn & Suites Providence-Warwick Airport SH ✿
(401) 739-8888. **$105-$189.** 2100 Post Rd. I-95, exit 13, e to US 1, then just n. Int corridors. **Pets:** Other species. Service with restrictions, crate.

(SAVE) (✕) (♿) (🐾) (⌖) 🅱 💻 ⌘

▼▼▼ Holiday Inn Express Hotel & Suites SH
(401) 736-5000. **$145-$159.** 901 Jefferson Blvd. I-95, exit 13, 0.4 mi on Airport Connector Rd, then exit Jefferson Blvd. Int corridors. **Pets:** Accepted.

(SAVE) (S☽) (✕) (♿) (🐾) (⌖) 🅱 💻 ⌘

▼▼ Homestead Studio Suites Hotel-Providence/Airport/Warwick SH
(401) 732-6667. **$94-$125.** 268 Metro Center Blvd. I-95, exit 12A, 0.4 mi e on SR 113, 0.4 mi n on SR 5, then 0.4 mi e. Int corridors. **Pets:** Accepted.

(A$K) (S☽) (✕) (♿) (🐾) (⌖) 🅱 💻 (✕)

▼▼▼▼ **Residence Inn by Marriott** 🆂🅷
(401) 737-7100. **$89-$229.** 500 Kilvert St. I-95, exit 13 to Jefferson Blvd, 0.4 mi n, then 0.6 mi w. Ext corridors. **Pets:** Accepted.
(ASK) 🆂 🗙 🐾 🛡 💻 🏊 🗙

▼▼▼▼ **Sheraton Providence Airport Hotel** 🅻🅷
(401) 738-4000. **$285.** 1850 Post Rd. I-95, exit 13, 0.6 mi n on US 1. Int corridors. **Pets:** Accepted.
(ASK) 🗙 🦽 🐾 🖮 🛡 💻 🍽 🏊 🗙

WEST WARWICK

▼▼ **Extended StayAmerica Providence-Airport-West Warwick** 🆂🅷
(401) 885-3161. **$99-$134.** 1235 Division St. I-95, exit 8A northbound, just s on SR 2, then just w; exit 9 southbound, 0.5 mi s on SR 4, exit 8, just w. Int corridors. **Pets:** Accepted.
(ASK) 🆂 🗙 🦽 🐾 🖮 🛡 💻

WYOMING

🔺🔺🔺 ▼▼▼▼ **Stagecoach House Inn** 🅱🅱 🐾
(401) 539-9600. **$110-$199.** 1136 Main St (SR 138). I-95, exit 3B northbound, 0.7 mi nw; exit southbound, 0.4 mi nw. Ext/int corridors. **Pets:** Dogs only. $20 daily fee/room. Designated rooms, service with restrictions, supervision.
(SAVE) 🗙 🛡 💻

SOUTH CAROLINA

AIKEN

▲▲▲ ▼▼ ▼▼ Econo Lodge Ⓜ
(803) 649-3968. **$55-$89.** 3560 Richland Ave W. Jct US 1/78 and SR 19, 2.6 mi w on US 1/78. Ext corridors. **Pets:** Other species. $10 one-time fee/pet. Service with restrictions, supervision.

[SAVE] [S🐾] [✕] [🔒] [💻] [🏊]

▲▲▲ ▼▼ ▼▼ Executive Inn Ⓜ
(803) 648-6821. **$49.** 1850 Richland Ave W. Jct US 1/78 and SR 19, 1.6 mi w on US 1/78. Ext corridors. **Pets:** $10 daily fee/pet. No service, crate.

[SAVE] [S🐾] [✕] [🔧] [🔒] [💻] [🏊]

▼▼ ▼▼ Quality Inn Ⓜ
(803) 502-0900. **$80.** 110 E Frontage Rd. I-20, exit 22 (US 1), just s. Ext corridors. **Pets:** Accepted.

[ASK] [S🐾] [✕] [🔧] [🔒] [💻] [🏊]

▲▲▲ ▼▼ ▼▼ Quality Inn & Suites ⓈⒽ
(803) 641-1100. **$60-$80.** 3608 Richland Ave W. Jct US 1/78 and SR 19, 2.9 mi w on US 1/78. Ext corridors. **Pets:** Other species. $10 daily fee/pet. Service with restrictions, crate.

[SAVE] [S🐾] [✕] [🗓] [🔒] [💻] [🏊]

▼▼ ▼▼ ▼▼ Town & Country Inn 🅑🅑 🐾
(803) 642-0270. **$80-$125.** 2340 Sizemore Cir. Jct US 78 and SR 302/19 (Whiskey Rd), 2.3 mi s on SR 19, then just w. Int corridors. **Pets:** Small, other species. $25 daily fee/pet. Service with restrictions, crate.

[ASK] [S🐾] [✕] [🏊] [🗓]

ANDERSON

▼▼ ▼▼ ▼▼ Country Inn & Suites ⓈⒽ
(864) 622-2200. **$79-$89.** 116 Interstate Blvd. I-85, exit 19B, just n, then just se. Int corridors. **Pets:** Small. $10 daily fee/pet, $25 one-time fee/pet. Designated rooms, service with restrictions, supervision.

[ASK] [S🐾] [✕] [🗬] [🗓] [🔧] [🔒] [💻] [🏊]

▼▼ ▼▼ Days Inn Ⓜ
(864) 375-0375. **$69-$119.** 1007 Smith Mill Rd. I-85, exit 19A, just se. Ext corridors. **Pets:** Accepted.

[ASK] [S🐾] [✕] [🗬] [🗓] [🔒] [💻] [🏊]

▲▲▲ ▼▼ ▼▼ ▼▼ Holiday Inn Express ⓈⒽ
(864) 231-0231. **$75-$199.** 410 Alliance Pkwy. I-85, exit 27, just s on SR 81. Int corridors. **Pets:** Small. $30 one-time fee/pet. Service with restrictions, supervision.

[SAVE] [S🐾] [✕] [🗬] [🗓] [🔧] [🔒] [💻] [🏊]

▼▼ ▼▼ La Quinta Inn Anderson ⓈⒽ
(864) 225-3721. **$88-$108.** 3430 Clemson Blvd. I-85, exit 19A, 2.9 mi se on US 76/SR 28; exit 21 southbound, 2.6 mi s on US 178. Ext corridors. **Pets:** Medium. Service with restrictions.

[ASK] [✕] [🗓] [🔧] [🔒] [💻] [🏊]

BEAUFORT

▼▼ ▼▼ Ramada Limited of Beaufort ⓈⒽ
(843) 524-2144. **$59-$199.** 2001 Boundary St. Jct SR 170, 0.6 mi s on US 21. Ext corridors. **Pets:** Small. $25 one-time fee/pet. Service with restrictions.

[ASK] [S🐾] [✕] [🗓] [🔒] [💻] [🏊]

BENNETTSVILLE

▲▲▲ ▼▼ ▼▼ Holiday Inn Express Ⓜ
(843) 479-1700. **$69-$99.** 213 US Hwy 15 & 401 Bypass E. 0.6 mi s of center, just ne on US 15/401/SR 9. Ext corridors. **Pets:** Accepted.

[SAVE] [S🐾] [✕] [🗓] [🔧] [🔒] [💻] [🏊]

BLUFFTON

▼▼ ▼▼ ▼▼ Comfort Suites of Bluffton ⓈⒽ
(843) 815-1700. **$90-$120.** 23 Towne Dr. I-95, exit 8 (US 278), 12.6 mi e on US 278; in Belfair Towne Village. Int corridors. **Pets:** Medium, other species. Designated rooms, service with restrictions.

[ASK] [S🐾] [✕] [🗬] [🗓] [🔧] [🔒] [💻] [🏊]

▼▼ ▼▼ ▼▼ Holiday Inn Express Hotel & Suites ⓈⒽ
(843) 757-2002. **$69-$149.** 35 Bluffton Rd. Jct William Hilton Pkwy (US 278/Bluffton Rd US 46), just se. Int corridors. **Pets:** Medium. $40 one-time fee/room. Service with restrictions, crate.

[ASK] [S🐾] [✕] [🗬] [🔧] [🔒] [💻] [🏊]

CAMDEN

▲▲▲ ▼▼ ▼▼ Colony Inn Ⓜ
(803) 432-5508. **$65-$75.** 2020 W DeKalb St. Jct US 521/1/601, 1.6 mi w on US 1/601. Ext/int corridors. **Pets:** Medium. Designated rooms, service with restrictions, supervision.

[SAVE] [S🐾] [✕] [🔒] [💻] [🍽] [🏊]

CAYCE

▲▲▲ ▼▼ ▼▼ Riverside Inn Ⓜ
(803) 939-4688. **$57-$65.** 111 Knox Abbott Dr. US 21, just w of Congaree River Bridge. Ext corridors. **Pets:** $20 one-time fee/room. Service with restrictions, crate.

[SAVE] [S🐾] [✕] [🔧] [🔒] [💻] [🏊] [✕]

CHARLESTON METROPOLITAN AREA

CHARLESTON

Best Western Sweetgrass Inn SH
(843) 571-6100. **$59-$139.** 1540 Savannah Hwy. US 17 S, 3.6 mi w of Ashley River Bridge; jct I-526 W (end) and US 17 N, 1.7 mi e. Ext corridors. **Pets:** Medium. $25 one-time fee/room. Service with restrictions, supervision.

Howard Johnson Riverfront SH ❖
(843) 722-4000. **$74-$149.** 250 Spring St. I-26, exit 221A (US 17 S), 1.2 mi sw; just e of Ashley River. Int corridors. **Pets:** Other species. $20 daily fee/room. Designated rooms, service with restrictions.

The Inn at Middleton Place CI ❖
(843) 556-0500. **$159-$500, 3 day notice.** 4290 Ashley River Rd. I-526, exit 11 (Ashley River Rd/SR 61), then 10.3 mi on SR 61 N. Ext corridors. **Pets:** Medium. $50 one-time fee/room. Designated rooms, service with restrictions, crate.

La Quinta Inn Riverview SH
(843) 556-5200. **$79-$149.** 11 Ashley Point Dr. US 17 S, just over Ashley River Bridge to Albermarle Rd, 0.4 mi s to Ashley Pointe Dr. Ext/int corridors. **Pets:** Medium. Service with restrictions.

Residence Inn by Marriott SH
(843) 571-7979. **$99-$239.** 90 Ripley Point Dr. US 17 S, just over Ashley River Bridge to Albermarle Rd, just s. Int corridors. **Pets:** Accepted.

Sleep Inn SH
(843) 556-6959. **$49-$169.** 1524 Savannah Hwy. US 17 S, 3.6 mi w of Ashley River Bridge; jct I-526 W (end) and US 17 N, 1.7 mi e. Int corridors. **Pets:** Medium. $25 one-time fee/room. Service with restrictions, supervision.

Town & Country Inn & Conference Center SH
(843) 571-1000. **$79-$129.** 2008 Savannah Hwy. US 17 S, 3.5 mi nw of Ashley River Bridge; jct I-526 W (end) and US 17 N, just se. Ext corridors. **Pets:** Service with restrictions.

Vendue Inn CI
(843) 577-7970. **$249-$409, 3 day notice.** 19 Vendue Range. Off E Bay St, 1 blk from Waterfront Park; in historic district. Int corridors. **Pets:** $50 one-time fee/pet. Service with restrictions, supervision.

GOOSE CREEK

Quality Inn M
(843) 572-9500. **$39-$99.** 103 Red Bank Rd. Jct US 52/176. Ext corridors. **Pets:** $25 one-time fee/room. Designated rooms, service with restrictions.

KIAWAH ISLAND

Courtside Villas-Kiawah Island Golf Resort-Villas CO
(843) 768-2121. **$117-$2700, 14 day notice.** 1 Sanctuary Beach Dr. 2 mi ne of main gate. Ext corridors. **Pets:** Accepted.

Fairway Oaks-Kiawah Island Golf Resort-Villas CO
(843) 768-2121. **$117-$2700, 14 day notice.** 1 Sanctuary Beach Dr. 2 mi ne of main gate. Ext corridors. **Pets:** Accepted.

Kiawah Island Golf Resort-Villas-Seascape Villas-Island Golf Rental CO
(843) 768-2121. **$117-$2700, 14 day notice.** 1 Sanctuary Beach Dr. 2 mi ne of main gate. Ext corridors. **Pets:** Accepted.

Mariners Watch Villas-Kiawah Island Golf Resort-Villas CO
(843) 768-2121. **$117-$2700, 14 day notice.** 1 Sanctuary Beach Dr. 2 mi ne of main gate. Ext corridors. **Pets:** Accepted.

Parkside Villas-Kiawah Island Golf Resort-Villas CO
(843) 768-2121. **$117-$2700, 14 day notice.** 1 Sanctuary Beach Dr. 2 mi ne of main gate. Ext corridors. **Pets:** Accepted.

Shipwatch Villas-Kiawah Island Golf Resort-Villas CO
(843) 768-2121. **$117-$2700, 14 day notice.** 1 Sanctuary Beach Dr. 2 mi ne of main gate. Ext corridors. **Pets:** Accepted.

Tennis Club Villas-Kiawah Island Golf Resort-Villas CO
(843) 768-2121. **$117-$2700, 14 day notice.** 1 Sanctuary Beach Dr. 2 mi ne of main gate. Ext corridors. **Pets:** Accepted.

Turtle Cove Villas-Kiawah Island Golf Resort-Villas CO
(843) 768-2121. **$117-$2700, 14 day notice.** 1 Sanctuary Beach Dr. 2 mi ne of main gate. Ext corridors. **Pets:** Accepted.

Turtle Point Villas-Kiawah Island Golf Resort-Villas CO
(843) 768-2121. **$117-$2700, 14 day notice.** 1 Sanctuary Beach Dr. 2 mi ne of main gate. Ext corridors. **Pets:** Accepted.

Windswept Villas-Kiawah Island Golf Resort-Villas CO
(843) 768-2121. **$125-$545, 30 day notice.** 1 Sanctuary Beach Dr. 2 mi ne of main gate. Ext corridors. **Pets:** Accepted.

MOUNT PLEASANT

Days Inn Patriots Point M
(843) 881-1800. **$65-$179, 3 day notice.** 261 Johnnie Dodds Blvd. Just e of base of Cooper River Bridge. Ext corridors. **Pets:** Small, dogs only. $10 daily fee/pet. Designated rooms, service with restrictions, supervision.

Extended StayAmerica-Charleston-Mount Pleasant M
(843) 848-4453. **$91-$96.** 304 Wingo Way. Just e of Cooper River Bridge on US 17, then just n. Int corridors. **Pets:** Accepted.

▲▲▲ ▼▼▼ **Hilton Charleston Harbor Resort & Marina** **SH**
(843) 856-0028. **$99-$319.** 20 Patriots Point Rd. Base of Cooper River Bridge, 0.6 mi se on Coleman Blvd (SR 703), then 0.8 mi sw; past museum. Int corridors. **Pets:** Accepted.
(SAVE) ⊠ 🖐 🛢 📺 🍴 🏊 ⊠

▼▼▼ **Homewood Suites by Hilton** **SH**
(843) 881-6950. **$103-$199.** 1998 Riviera Dr. I-526, exit 32 (Georgetown/US 17 N), 1.4 mi ne on US 17, 1 mi se on Isle of Palms connector (SR 517), then just sw. Int corridors. **Pets:** Medium, dogs only. $75 one-time fee/room. Service with restrictions, supervision.
(ASK) ⊠ 🖐M 🖐 🛢 📺 🏊

▼▼ ▼▼ **Lands Inn East** **SH**
(843) 884-5853. **$49-$149.** 310 Hwy 17 (Johnnie Dodds Blvd). US 17, 0.7 mi n of Cooper River Bridge. Ext corridors. **Pets:** Small, dogs only. $15 one-time fee/pet. Service with restrictions, supervision.
(ASK) 🖐 ⊠ 🛢 📺 🏊

▼▼ ▼▼ **Red Roof Inn** **M**
(843) 884-1411. **$61-$100.** 301 Johnnie Dodds Blvd. Just e of base of Cooper River Bridge, on US 17 (Johnnie Dodds Blvd), then just s on McGrath-Darby Blvd. Ext corridors. **Pets:** Medium, other species. Service with restrictions.
⊠ 🖐 🖐 🛢 🏊

▲▲▲ ▼▼▼▼ **Residence Inn by Marriott** **SH** ✿
(843) 881-1599. **$99-$229.** 1116 Isle of Palms Connector. I-526, exit 32 (Georgetown/US 17 N), 1.4 mi ne on US 17 to Isle of Palms connector (SR 517), then just se. Int corridors. **Pets:** Large, other species. $75 one-time fee/room. Designated rooms, service with restrictions, crate.
(SAVE) 🖐 ⊠ 🖐M 🛢 🏊

▼▼ ▼▼ **Sleep Inn Mt Pleasant** **SH**
(843) 856-5000. **$89-$179.** 299 Wingo Way. Just e of base of Cooper River Bridge, then just n at McGrath-Darby Blvd. Int corridors. **Pets:** Medium. $15 daily fee/pet. Designated rooms, service with restrictions, supervision.
(ASK) 🖐 ⊠ 🖐M 🖐 🖐 🛢 📺 🏊

NORTH CHARLESTON

▼▼ ▼▼ **Comfort Inn Coliseum** **M**
(843) 554-6485. **$69-$89.** 5055 N Arco Ln. I-26, exit 213 westbound; exit 213A eastbound, just s, then n. Ext corridors. **Pets:** Accepted.
(ASK) 🖐 ⊠ 🖐 🛢 📺 🏊

▼▼▼▼ **Comfort Suites Charleston/N Charleston, SC** **SH**
(843) 572-8408. **$89-$149.** 2520 N Forest Dr. I-26, exit 209 (Ashley Phosphate Rd), just w of Northside Dr. Int corridors. **Pets:** Accepted.
(ASK) 🖐 ⊠ 🛢 📺 🏊

▲▲▲ ▼▼ **Country Hearth Inn & Suites** **M**
(843) 572-2228. **$55-$85.** 2311 Ashley Phosphate Rd. I-26, exit 209 (Ashley Phosphate Rd), just e. Ext corridors. **Pets:** Accepted.
(SAVE) 🖐 ⊠ 🛢 📺 🏊

▼▼ ▼▼ **Extended StayAmerica-Charleston-Airport-North Charleston** **M**
(843) 747-3787. **$80-$85.** 5059 N Arco Ln. I-26, exit 213, just s on Montague Ave, then nw. Ext corridors. **Pets:** Accepted.
(ASK) 🖐 ⊠ 🛢 📺

▼▼ ▼▼ **Homestead Studio Suites Hotel-Charleston/Airport** **SH**
(843) 740-3440. **$90-$100.** 5045 N Arco Ln. I-26, exit 213 westbound; exit 213A eastbound, just s, then n. Int corridors. **Pets:** Accepted.
(ASK) 🖐 ⊠ 🖐M 🖐 🖐 🛢 📺 🏊

▼▼▼▼ **La Quinta Inn Charleston** **SH**
(843) 797-8181. **$84-$104.** 2499 La Quinta Ln. I-26, exit 209 (Ashley Phosphate Rd), just w. Ext corridors. **Pets:** Medium. Service with restrictions.
(ASK) ⊠ 🖐 🛢 📺 🏊

▼▼▼ **Motel 6 #642** **M**
(843) 572-6590. **$45-$58.** 2551 Ashley Phosphate Rd. I-26, exit 209 (Ashley Phosphate Rd), just w. Ext corridors. **Pets:** Medium, other species. Service with restrictions, supervision.
🖐 ⊠ 🖐 🏊

▲▲▲ ▼▼▼▼ **Quality Suites Convention Center** **SH** ✿
(843) 747-7300. **$99-$159, 30 day notice.** 5225 N Arco Ln. I-26, exit 213 westbound; exit 213A eastbound, just s, then n. Int corridors. **Pets:** Medium, dogs only. $25 one-time fee/pet. Designated rooms, service with restrictions, crate.
(SAVE) 🖐 ⊠ 🖐 🛢 📺 🏊

▼▼▼ **Red Roof Inn** **M**
(843) 572-9100. **$55-$85.** 7480 Northwoods Blvd. I-26, exit 209 (Ashley Phosphate Rd), just e, then just n. Ext corridors. **Pets:** Medium, other species. Service with restrictions, supervision.
⊠ 🖐 🖐 🛢

▼▼▼▼ **Residence Inn by Marriott** **SH**
(843) 572-5757. **$150.** 7645 Northwoods Blvd. I-26, exit 209 (Ashley Phosphate Rd), just e, then n. Ext corridors. **Pets:** Other species. $75 one-time fee/room. Service with restrictions, supervision.
(ASK) 🖐 ⊠ 🖐 🛢 📺 🏊 ⊠

▲▲▲ ▼▼▼▼ **Residence Inn Charleston Airport** **SH** ✿
(843) 266-3434. **$99-$199.** 5035 International Blvd. I-26, exit 213A eastbound, 0.4 mi s, then just w; exit westbound, 0.4 mi s, then just w; I-526, exit International Blvd, 0.8 mi e. Int corridors. **Pets:** Other species. $75 one-time fee/room. Service with restrictions.
(SAVE) 🖐 ⊠ 🖐M 🖐 🖐 🛢 📺 🏊 ⊠

▲▲▲ ▼▼▼▼ **Sheraton Hotel North Charleston Convention Center** **LH**
(843) 747-1900. **$99-$119.** 4770 Goer Dr. I-26, exit 213 westbound; exit 213B eastbound, just n. Int corridors. **Pets:** Accepted.
(SAVE) 🖐 ⊠ 🖐 🛢 📺 🍴 🏊

▼▼▼ **Sleep Inn Charleston North** **SH**
(843) 572-8400. **$74-$124.** 7435 Northside Dr. I-26, exit 209 (Ashley Phosphate Rd), just w. Int corridors. **Pets:** Other species. $10 daily fee/pet. Designated rooms, service with restrictions, crate.
(ASK) 🖐 ⊠ 🛢 📺

▼▼▼ **StudioPlus** **SH**
(843) 553-0036. **$81-$111.** 7641 Northwoods Blvd. I-26, exit 209 (Ashley Phosphate Rd), just e, then just n. Int corridors. **Pets:** Accepted.
(ASK) 🖐 ⊠ 🖐 🖐 🛢 📺 🏊

SUMMERVILLE

▼▼▼▼ **Country Inn & Suites** **SH**
(843) 285-9000. **$85-$129.** 220 Holiday Dr. I-26, exit 199A, just w on US 17 alternate route to Holiday Dr, then just n. Int corridors. **Pets:** Medium. $10 daily fee/pet. Service with restrictions, crate.
(ASK) 🖐 ⊠ 🛢 📺 🏊

▲▲▲ ▼▼▼▼ **Holiday Inn Express-Charleston/Summerville** **SH** ✿
(843) 875-3300. **$95.** 120 Holiday Dr. I-26, exit 199A, just w. Int corridors. **Pets:** Other species. Service with restrictions, supervision.
(SAVE) 🖐 ⊠ 🖐M 🖐 🖐 🛢 📺 🏊

▼▼▼ **Summerville Econo Lodge** **M**
(843) 875-3022. **$70-$80.** 110 Holiday Cir. I-26, exit 199A, just w on US 17A, then just n. Ext corridors. **Pets:** Small. $10 daily fee/room. Service with restrictions, supervision.
(ASK) 🖐 ⊠ 🛢 📺

▲▲▲ ▼▼▼▼▼ **Woodlands Resort & Inn** **CI** ✿
(843) 875-2600. **$295-$890, 7 day notice.** 125 Parsons Rd. I-26, exit 199A, 2 mi s on US 17 alternate route, 1.5 mi w on W Richardson Ave (SR 165), then just s. Int corridors. **Pets:** $25 daily fee/room.
(SAVE) 🖐 ⊠ 🖐 🍴 🏊 ⊠

NEARBY NORTH CAROLINA
CHARLOTTE METROPOLITAN AREA

FORT MILL

▼▼▼ **Comfort Inn Carowinds** SH
(704) 339-0574. **$59-$109.** 3725 Avenue of the Carolinas. I-77, exit 90, just nw. Int corridors. **Pets:** Large, other species. $25 one-time fee/room. Service with restrictions.

ASK SÓ ⊠ 🕹 🖪 🖵 ⇌

🔺🔺🔺 ▼▼▼ **The Plaza Hotel at Carowinds** LH
(803) 548-2400. **$69-$199.** 225 Carowinds Blvd. I-77, exit 90, just nw. Int corridors. **Pets:** Accepted.

SAVE SÓ ⊠ 🖪 🖵 ❚❘ ⇌ ⊠

ROCK HILL

🔺🔺🔺 ▼▼ **Best Western Inn** SH
(803) 329-1330. **$65-$110.** 1106 N Anderson Rd. I-77, exit 82B (US 21), 0.4 mi sw to US 21 Bypass, then just s. Int corridors. **Pets:** Small. $10 daily fee/pet. Service with restrictions, supervision.

SAVE SÓ ⊠ 🖪 🖵 ⇌

▼▼▼ **The Book & the Spindle** BB ❀
(803) 328-1913. **$95-$425, 14 day notice.** 626 Oakland Ave. I-77, exit 82B (US 21), 3.1 mi s; before Aiken. Int corridors. **Pets:** Small, other species. $15 deposit/room. Crate.

⊠ 🖪 🖵

▼▼▼▼ **Holiday Inn** SH
(803) 329-1122. **$69-$89.** 2640 N Cherry Rd. I-77, exit 82B (US 21), just ne. Int corridors. **Pets:** Accepted.

ASK SÓ ⊠ 🛢M 🕹 🖑 🖪 🖵 ❚❘ ⇌

▼▼ **Howard Johnson Inn** M
(803) 329-7900. **Call for rates.** 911 Riverview Rd. I-77, exit 82B (US 21), just sw, then just s. Ext corridors. **Pets:** Small. $10 one-time fee/pet. Service with restrictions, supervision.

ASK SÓ ⊠ 🖪 🖵

▼▼ **Super 8 Motel** SH
(803) 980-0400. **Call for rates.** 888 Riverview Rd. I-77, exit 82B (US 21), just sw, then just s. Int corridors. **Pets:** $10 daily fee/pet. Service with restrictions, crate.

ASK SÓ ⊠ 🛢M ♿ 🖑 🖪

END METROPOLITAN AREA

CHERAW

🔺🔺🔺 ▼ **Days Inn** M
(843) 537-5554. **$45-$70.** 820 Market St. Jct US 52/1/SR 9. Ext corridors. **Pets:** Other species. $5 daily fee/pet. Crate.

ASK SÓ ⊠ 🖪 🖵 ⇌

▼▼ **Jameson Inn** M
(843) 537-5625. **$54-$104.** 885 Chesterfield Hwy. Jct US 1/52/SR 9, 1.6 mi w on SR 9. Ext corridors. **Pets:** Small. $10 daily fee/pet. Service with restrictions, crate.

ASK ⊠ 🖑 🖪 🖵 ⇌

CLEMSON

🔺🔺🔺 ▼▼▼ **Comfort Inn-Clemson** SH
(864) 653-3600. **$80-$175.** 1305 Tiger Blvd. Jct SR 133 and US 76/123, 0.5 mi e. Int corridors. **Pets:** Small. $10 daily fee/pet. Service with restrictions, supervision.

SAVE SÓ ⊠ 🕹 🖪 🖵 ⇌

🔺🔺🔺 ▼▼▼ **Ramada Inn of Clemson** SH
(864) 654-7501. **$65-$204.** 1310 Tiger Blvd. Jct SR 133 and US 76/123, 0.5 mi e. Int corridors. **Pets:** Accepted.

SAVE SÓ ⊠ 🖑 🖪 🖵 ❚❘ ⇌ ⊠

CLINTON

🔺🔺🔺 ▼▼▼ **Comfort Inn** M
(864) 833-5558. **$69-$89.** 105 Trade St. I-26, exit 52, just n; behind truck stop. Ext corridors. **Pets:** Small. $10 daily fee/room. Service with restrictions, crate.

SAVE SÓ ⊠ 🕹 🖪 🖵 ⇌

🔺🔺🔺 ▼ **Days Inn** M
(864) 833-6600. **$69-$89.** 12374 Hwy 56 N. I-26, exit 52, just s. Ext corridors. **Pets:** Dogs only. $10 daily fee/room. Service with restrictions, supervision.

SAVE SÓ ⊠ 🖪 🖵 ⇌

COLUMBIA

▼▼▼ **Chestnut Cottage Bed & Breakfast** BB
(803) 256-1718. **$95-$225, 14 day notice.** 1718 Hampton St. SR 12 (Taylor St), just s; between Henderson and Barnwell sts; downtown. Int corridors. **Pets:** Accepted.

ASK SÓ ⊠ 🖪 🖵

🔺🔺🔺 ▼▼▼ **Comfort Inn Northeast** SH
(803) 788-5544. **$59-$89.** 7700 Two Notch Rd. I-20, exit 74 (Two Notch Rd), just n; I-77, exit 17 (Two Notch Rd), 0.5 mi s. Int corridors. **Pets:** Accepted.

SAVE SÓ ⊠ 🕹 🖪 🖵 ⇌

▼▼▼ **Extended StayAmerica-Columbia-Ft. Jackson** M
(803) 782-2025. **$80-$85.** 5430 Forest Dr. I-77, exit 12, just ne, then just s along service rd; behind mall. Ext corridors. **Pets:** Accepted.

ASK SÓ ⊠ 🕹 🖪 🖵

▼▼ **Extended StayAmerica-Columbia-West** SH
(803) 251-7878. **$65-$70.** 450 Gracern Rd. Just n to Stoneridge Dr, just w to Gracern Rd, then s. Ext corridors. **Pets:** Accepted.

ASK SÓ ⊠ 🕹 🖪 🖵

▼▼ **La Quinta Inn & Suites Columbia NE/Ft. Jackson Area** SH
(803) 736-6400. **$79-$99.** 1538 Horseshoe Dr. I-20, exit 74 (Two Notch Rd), just n; I-77, exit 17 (Two Notch Rd), 0.5 mi s. Int corridors. **Pets:** Medium. Service with restrictions.

ASK ⊠ 🕹 🖪 🖵 ⇌

▼▼ **Microtel Inn & Suites Harbison Area** SH
(803) 772-1914. **$59.** 411 Piney Grove Rd. I-26, exit 104 (Piney Grove Rd), just sw. Int corridors. **Pets:** Accepted.

ASK SÓ ⊠ 🛢M 🕹 🖑 🖪 🖵

▼▼ Motel 6 #1291 SH
(803) 736-3900. **$45-$58.** 7541 Nates Rd. I-20, exit 74 (Two Notch Rd), just n, then just e; I-77, exit 17 (Two Notch Rd), 0.5 mi s, then e. Int corridors. **Pets:** Medium, other species. Service with restrictions, supervision.
🆂 ✕ 🚪ᴹ 👤 🏊

◆◆◆ ▼▼▼▼ Radisson Hotel Columbia & Conference Center LH
(803) 731-0300. **$125-$145.** 2100 Bush River Rd. I-20, exit 63 (Bush River Rd), just e; I-26, exit 108 (Bush River Rd), 0.7 mi w. Int corridors. **Pets:** Small, dogs only. Designated rooms, service with restrictions.
SAVE 🆂 ✕ 🚗 👤 👤 📺 🍴 🏊

◆◆◆ ▼▼▼ Ramada Columbia Northeast SH
(803) 736-3000. **$99-$129.** 7510 Two Notch Rd. I-20, exit 74 (Two Notch Rd), just n; I-77, exit 17 (Two Notch Rd), 0.5 mi s. Int corridors. **Pets:** Accepted.
SAVE 🆂 ✕ 👤 📺 🍴 🏊 ✕

▼▼ Red Roof Inn-West M
(803) 798-9220. **$43-$60.** 10 Berryhill Rd. I-26, exit 106A westbound; exit 106 eastbound, just w. Ext corridors. **Pets:** Medium, other species. Service with restrictions, supervision.
✕ 🚗 👤 👤

▼▼▼▼ Residence Inn by Marriott SH
(803) 779-7000. **$99-$189.** 150 Stoneridge Dr. I-126, exit Greystone Blvd, just n, then just e. Ext corridors. **Pets:** Accepted.
ASK 🆂 ✕ 🚗 👤 📺 🏊 ✕

▼▼▼▼ Residence Inn by Marriott SH
(803) 788-8850. **$129-$189.** 2320 Legrand Rd. I-77, exit 19 southbound, just ne on Farrow Rd to Rabon Rd, then just se; exit 18 northbound. Int corridors. **Pets:** $75 one-time fee/pet. Service with restrictions, supervision.
ASK 🆂 ✕ 👤 📺 🏊 ✕

▼▼▼▼ StudioPlus Greystone Columbia SH
(803) 771-0303. **$60-$65.** 180 Stoneridge Dr. I-126, exit Greystone Blvd, just n, then just e. Int corridors. **Pets:** Accepted.
ASK 🆂 ✕ 🚗 👤 📺 🏊

◆◆◆ ▼ Super 8 M
(803) 735-0008. **$49-$105.** 5719 Fairfield Rd. I-20, exit 70, just s. Ext corridors. **Pets:** Accepted.
SAVE 🆂 ✕ 👤

▼▼▼ Super 8 M
(803) 772-7275. **$55-$100.** 773 St Andrews Rd. I-26, exit 106A westbound; exit 106 eastbound, just w. Ext corridors. **Pets:** Accepted.
ASK 🆂 ✕ 👤 📺 🏊

▼▼▼▼ TownePlace Suites by Marriott SH 🐾
(803) 781-9391. **$79-$109.** 350 Columbiana Dr. I-26, exit 103 (Harbison Blvd), just sw to Columbiana Dr, then 0.7 mi nw. Int corridors. **Pets:** Medium, other species. $100 one-time fee/pet. Service with restrictions, crate.
ASK 🆂 ✕ 🚪ᴹ 🚗 👤 👤 📺 🏊

DUNCAN

▼▼▼ Jameson Inn M
(864) 433-8405. **$54-$104.** 1546 E Main St. I-85, exit 63, 0.4 mi se on SR 290. Ext corridors. **Pets:** Small. $10 daily fee/pet. Service with restrictions, crate.
ASK ✕ 👤 📺 🏊

▼▼▼ Quality Inn SH
(864) 433-1333. **$58-$85.** 1391 E Main St. I-85, exit 63, just nw. Ext corridors. **Pets:** Accepted.
ASK 🆂 ✕ 👤 📺 🏊

EASLEY

◆◆◆ ▼▼ Comfort Inn M
(864) 859-7520. **$70-$75.** 5539 Calhoun Memorial Hwy. Jct US 123 and SR 93, just e on US 123. Ext corridors. **Pets:** Accepted.
SAVE 🆂 ✕ 👤 📺 🏊

▼▼▼ Jameson Inn M
(864) 306-9000. **$54-$104.** 211 Dayton School Rd. Jct US 123 and SR 93, 0.6 mi e on US 123; jct US 123 and SR 153, 1.4 mi w. Ext corridors. **Pets:** Small. $10 daily fee/pet. Service with restrictions, crate.
ASK ✕ 🚪 👤 📺 🏊

FLORENCE

◆◆◆ ▼▼▼ Comfort Inn M
(843) 665-4558. **$59-$189.** 1916 W Lucas St. I-95, exit 164, just se. Ext/int corridors. **Pets:** Accepted.
SAVE 🆂 ✕ 👤 📺 🏊

◆◆◆ ▼▼ Country Hearth Inn & Suites M
(843) 662-9421. **$45-$61.** 831 S Irby St. 1.3 mi s on US 301 and 52. Ext corridors. **Pets:** Accepted.
SAVE 🆂 ✕ 👤 📺 🍴 🏊

◆◆◆ ▼▼ Econo Lodge M
(843) 665-8558. **$60-$65.** 1811 W Lucas St. I-95, exit 164, just se. Ext corridors. **Pets:** Other species. $10 daily fee/pet. Service with restrictions, supervision.
SAVE 🆂 ✕ 👤 📺 🏊

◆◆◆ ▼▼▼▼ Holiday Inn Hotel & Suites SH
(843) 665-4555. **$75-$225.** 1819 W Lucas St. I-95, exit 164, just se. Ext corridors. **Pets:** Medium, other species. $25 one-time fee/pet. Designated rooms, service with restrictions, supervision.
SAVE 🆂 ✕ 🚪ᴹ 🚗 👤 👤 📺 🍴 🏊

◆◆◆ ▼▼▼▼ Howard Johnson Express Inn & Suites M 🐾
(843) 664-9494. **$54-$75, 30 day notice.** 3821 Bancroft Rd. I-95, exit 157, just ne on US 76. Ext corridors. **Pets:** Medium, other species. $10 one-time fee/room. Designated rooms, service with restrictions, supervision.
SAVE 🆂 ✕ 🚪 👤 📺 🏊

▼▼ Motel 6 #1250 M
(843) 667-6100. **$38-$52.** 1834 W Lucas St. I-95, exit 164, just sw. Ext corridors. **Pets:** Medium, other species. Service with restrictions, supervision.
🆂 ✕ 🚪 🏊

◆◆◆ ▼▼▼ Ramada Inn SH
(843) 669-4241. **$45-$69.** 2038 W Lucas St. I-95, exit 164, just nw. Ext/int corridors. **Pets:** Medium, other species. $10 daily fee/pet. Designated rooms, service with restrictions, supervision.
SAVE 🆂 ✕ 👤 📺 🏊 ✕

▼▼ Red Roof Inn M
(843) 678-9000. **$50-$73.** 2690 David McLeod Blvd. I-95, exit 160A, just e on service road. Ext corridors. **Pets:** Medium, other species. Service with restrictions, supervision.
✕ 🚪ᴹ 🚗 🚪

◆◆◆ ▼▼▼ Super 8 Motel M
(843) 661-7267. **$52-$149.** 1832 1/2 W Lucas St. I-95, exit 164, just se. Ext corridors. **Pets:** Very small. $10 daily fee/pet. Designated rooms, service with restrictions, supervision.
SAVE 🆂 ✕ 👤 🏊

ⓐⓐⓐ ▼▼▼ Thunderbird Inn Ⓜ
(843) 669-1611. **$45-$55.** 2004 W Lucas St. I-95, exit 164, just nw. Ext corridors. **Pets:** Accepted.
[SAVE] [S☼] [✕] [🖥] [🍴] [🏊]

GAFFNEY

▼▼ Jameson Inn Ⓜ
(864) 489-0240. **$54-$104.** 101 Stuard St. I-85, exit 92, 0.5 mi se on SR 11/W Floyd Baker Blvd. Ext corridors. **Pets:** Small. $10 daily fee/pet. Service with restrictions, crate.
[ASK] [✕] [♿] [🖥] [💷] [🏊]

THE GRAND STRAND AREA

GEORGETOWN

▼▼▼ Jameson Inn Georgetown Ⓜ
(843) 546-6090. **$54-$104.** 120 Church St. Jct US 17/17 alternate route/701, 1.2 mi se on US 17; just w of ICW Bridge. Ext corridors. **Pets:** Small. $10 daily fee/pet. Service with restrictions, crate.
[ASK] [✕] [♿] [🖥] [💷] [🏊]

▼▼▼ Winyah Bay Inn Bed & Breakfast ⒷⒷ
(843) 546-0464. **$95-$115, 3 day notice.** 3030 South Island Rd. 0.5 mi s of Sylvan L Rosen Bridge on US 17, 2 mi e. Int corridors. **Pets:** Accepted.
[ASK] [✕] [🖥] [💷] [🔋]

LITTLE RIVER

▼▼▼ Holiday Inn Hotel & Suites-North Myrtle Beach ⓢⒽ
(843) 281-9400. **$50-$300.** 722 Hwy 17. Jct SR 9/US 17, 1 mi e; at Coquina Harbor. Int corridors. **Pets:** Accepted.
[ASK] [S☼] [✕] [🖥] [💷] [🍴] [🏊]

MYRTLE BEACH

▼▼▼ La Quinta Inn & Suites Myrtle Beach ⓢⒽ
(843) 916-8801. **$85-$205.** 1561 21st Ave. Jct US 17 Bypass, just se. Int corridors. **Pets:** Medium. Service with restrictions.
[ASK] [✕] [♿] [♿] [🖥] [💷]

▼▼▼ La Quinta Inn Myrtle Beach ⓢⒽ
(843) 449-5231. **$54-$169.** 4709 N Kings Hwy. Jct 48th Ave N and US 17 business route. Int corridors. **Pets:** Medium. Service with restrictions.
[ASK] [S☼] [✕] [🖥] [💷] [🏊]

ⓐⓐⓐ ▼▼▼ Sea Mist Oceanfront Resort ⓁⒽ
(843) 448-1551. **$32-$199, 14 day notice.** 1200 S Ocean Blvd. Jct 12th Ave S. Ext/int corridors. **Pets:** Accepted.
[SAVE] [✕] [♿] [♿] [🖥] [🍴] [🏊] [✕]

▼▼▼▼ Staybridge Suites-Fantasy Harbour ⓢⒽ ❀
(843) 903-4000. **$69-$169.** 3163 Outlet Blvd. Jct US 17 Bypass, 0.7 mi n on US 501, exit River Oaks Rd/George Bishop Pkwy, just w on River Oaks Rd, then 0.4 mi s. Int corridors. **Pets:** Medium. $20 daily fee/room. Designated rooms, service with restrictions, supervision.
[ASK] [S☼] [✕] [♿] [♿] [🖥] [💷] [🏊] [✕]

ⓐⓐⓐ ▼▼▼ Summer Wind Inn & Suites Ⓜ
(843) 946-6960. **$31-$159, 14 day notice.** 1903 S Ocean Blvd. Jct 19th Ave S. Ext corridors. **Pets:** Small, dogs only. $10 daily fee/pet. Service with restrictions.
[SAVE] [S☼] [✕] [🏊]

ⓐⓐⓐ ▼▼ Super 8 Motel-Myrtle Beach ⓢⒽ
(843) 293-6100. **$50-$200, 3 day notice.** 3450 Hwy 17 Bypass. Jct US 501/US 17 Bypass, 3.2 mi sw. Int corridors. **Pets:** Accepted.
[SAVE] [S☼] [✕] [🖥] [🏊]

PAWLEYS ISLAND

▼▼▼ Best Western Hammock Inn Ⓜ
(843) 237-4261. **$64-$144.** 7903 Ocean Hwy. 2.6 mi sw on US 17. Ext corridors. **Pets:** Accepted.
[ASK] [S☼] [✕] [♿] [🖥] [💷] [🍴] [🏊]

END AREA

GREENVILLE

▼▼▼ Crowne Plaza Hotel and Resort Greenville ⓁⒽ
(864) 297-6300. **$109-$159, 3 day notice.** 851 Congaree Rd. I-385, exit 37, just s, then just nw. Int corridors. **Pets:** Medium, other species. $50 one-time fee/room. Service with restrictions, crate.
[ASK] [S☼] [✕] [♿] [♿] [♿] [🖥] [💷] [🍴] [🏊] [✕]

▼▼ Days Inn ⓢⒽ
(864) 288-6900. **$56-$77, 7 day notice.** 2756 Laurens Rd. I-85, exit 48B, just nw; entry between auto dealership. Int corridors. **Pets:** Small, dogs only. $10 daily fee/pet. Service with restrictions, supervision.
[ASK] [S☼] [✕] [🖥] [💷] [🏊]

▼▼▼ Hawthorn Suites ⓢⒽ
(864) 297-0099. **$79.** 48 McPrice Ct. I-385, exit 39 (Haywood Rd), just n, just e on Orchard Park Rd, then just s. Ext corridors. **Pets:** Accepted.
[ASK] [S☼] [✕] [♿] [🖥] [💷] [🏊] [✕]

▼▼▼ Holiday Inn Express Hotel & Suites ⓢⒽ
(864) 213-9331. **$109.** 2681 Dry Pocket Rd. I-85, exit 54 (Pelham Rd), just w, to The Parkway, just n to Parkway E, then just se. Int corridors. **Pets:** Accepted.
[ASK] [S☼] [✕] [♿] [♿] [🖥] [💷] [🏊] [✕]

▼▼▼ Holiday Inn I-85/Augusta Rd ⓢⒽ
(864) 277-8921. **$87-$93.** 4295 Augusta Rd. I-85, exit 46A, just s. Int corridors. **Pets:** Other species. $30 one-time fee/room. Service with restrictions, crate.
[ASK] [✕] [♿] [♿] [♿] [🖥] [💷] [🍴] [🏊]

▼▼▼ La Quinta Inn Greenville (Woodruff Rd.) ⓢⒽ
(864) 297-3500. **$84-$104.** 31 Old Country Rd. I-85, exit 51A, just n on SR 146; I-385, exit 35, just n. Ext/int corridors. **Pets:** Medium. Service with restrictions.
[ASK] [✕] [♿] [🖥] [💷] [🏊]

▼▼▼ La Quinta Inns & Suites Greenville (Haywood) ⓢⒽ
(864) 233-8018. **$99-$116.** 65 W Orchard Park Dr. I-385, exit 39 (Haywood Rd), just n, then w. Int corridors. **Pets:** Medium. Service with restrictions.
[ASK] [✕] [♿] [♿] [🖥] [💷] [🏊] [✕]

▼▼▼ MainStay Suites-Greenville ⓢⒽ
(864) 987-5566. **$88-$109.** 2671 Dry Pocket Rd. I-85, exit 54 (Pelham Rd), just w to The Parkway, just n to Parkway E, then just se. Int corridors. **Pets:** Medium, other species. $10 daily fee/pet. Service with restrictions, supervision.
[ASK] [S☼] [✕] [♿] [♿] [🖥] [💷] [🏊]

▼▼ **Microtel Inn & Suites** 🆂🅷
(864) 297-3811. **$47-$67.** 1024 Woodruff Rd. I-85, exit 51A, 0.5 mi n on SR 146. Int corridors. **Pets:** Other species. $35 one-time fee/room. Service with restrictions, supervision.
🄰🅂🄺 🆂🅳 ⊗ 👣 🖥 💻

▲▲▲ ▼▼▼▼ **The Phoenix Greenville's Inn** 🆂🅷
(864) 233-4651. **$79, 3 day notice.** 246 N Pleasanturg Dr. I-385, exit 40B, 0.6 mi s on SR 291. Ext corridors. **Pets:** Accepted.
🆂🄰🆅🄴 🆂🅳 ⊗ 🕖 🖥 💻 🍽 ⇌

▲▲▲ ▼▼ **Quality Inn Executive Center** 🅼 ✿
(864) 271-0060. **$64-$93.** 540 N Pleasanturg Dr. I-385, exit 40B, just s. Ext corridors. **Pets:** Other species. $15 one-time fee/room. Service with restrictions, crate.
🆂🄰🆅🄴 🆂🅳 ⊗ 🕖 🖥 💻 ⇌

▼ **Red Roof Inn** 🅼
(864) 297-4458. **$47-$60.** 2801 Laurens Rd. I-85, exit 48A, just se frontage road, then just e to end. Ext corridors. **Pets:** Medium, other species. Service with restrictions, supervision.
⊗ 🕖 🖥

▲▲▲ ▼▼▼ **Sleep Inn Palmetto Expo Center** 🆂🅷 ✿
(864) 240-2006. **$55-$119.** 231 N Pleasanturg Dr (SR 291). I-385, exit 40B, 0.6 mi s on SR 291. Int corridors. **Pets:** Large. $20 one-time fee/room. Service with restrictions, supervision.
🆂🄰🆅🄴 🆂🅳 ⊗ 👣 🕖 🖥 💻

▼▼ **StudioPLUS-Greenville-Haywwod Mall** 🆂🅷
(864) 288-4300. **Call for rates.** 530 Woods Lake Rd. I-385, exit 39, just s, then just w. Int corridors. **Pets:** Accepted.
⊗ 🖥 💻 ⇌

GREENWOOD

▼ **Days Inn** 🆂🅷
(864) 223-1818. **$50.** 230 Birchtree Dr. Jct US 25/US 25 Bypass (SR 72 NE), just ne on US 25 Bypass (SR 72 NE), then just s. Int corridors. **Pets:** Accepted.
🄰🅂🄺 🆂🅳 ⊗ 🖥 💻

▼▼▼ **Inn on the Square** 🆂🅷
(864) 330-1010. **$75-$109.** 104 E Court St. Jct Montague St, just s of center; downtown. Int corridors. **Pets:** Accepted.
🄰🅂🄺 🆂🅳 ⊗ 🖥 💻 🍽 ⇌

GREER

▼▼ **Super 8** 🆂🅷
(864) 848-1626. **$50-$55.** 1515 Hwy 101 S. I-85, exit 60, just nw. Int corridors. **Pets:** Accepted.
🄰🅂🄺 🆂🅳 ⊗ 👣 🖥 💻 ⇌

HARDEEVILLE

▲▲▲ ▼▼ **Quality Inn & Suites** 🅼
(843) 784-7060. **$59-$210.** 19000 Whyte Hardee Blvd. I-95, exit 5 (US 17), just n. Ext corridors. **Pets:** Medium. $10 daily fee/pet. Designated rooms, service with restrictions, supervision.
🆂🄰🆅🄴 🆂🅳 ⊗ 👣 🖥 💻 ⇌

▲▲▲ ▼▼ **Sleep Inn Hardeeville** 🆂🅷 ✿
(843) 784-7181. **$69-$109.** 16553 Wyatt Hardee Blvd. I-95, exit 5 (US 17), just se. Int corridors. **Pets:** Small. $20 daily fee/pet. Service with restrictions, supervision.
🆂🄰🆅🄴 🆂🅳 ⊗ 👣 🖥 💻 ⇌

HILTON HEAD ISLAND

▲▲▲ ▼▼▼▼ **Beachwalk Hotel & Condominiums** 🆂🅷
(843) 842-8888. **$59-$149.** 40 Waterside Dr. Sea Pines Cir, 0.7 mi se on Pope Rd, just e. Ext corridors. **Pets:** Accepted.
🆂🄰🆅🄴 🆂🅳 ⊗ 🕖 👣 🖥 💻 ⇌

▲▲▲ ▼▼▼ **Comfort Inn** 🆂🅷
(843) 842-6662. **$49-$179.** 2 Tanglewood Dr. Sea Pines Cir, 1.1 mi se on Pope Ave, just sw; at Coligny Plaza. Int corridors. **Pets:** Medium. $25 daily fee/pet. Service with restrictions, supervision.
🆂🄰🆅🄴 🆂🅳 ⊗ 🕖 🖥 💻 🍽 ⇌ ⊗

▼ **Motel 6–#1129** 🅼
(843) 785-2700. **$45-$65.** 830 William Hilton Pkwy. J Wilton Graves Bridge, 9 mi e on US 278 business route. Ext corridors. **Pets:** Medium, other species. Service with restrictions, supervision.
🆂🅳 🕖 👣 🖥 💻 ⇌

▼▼▼ **Quality Inn & Suites of Hilton Head Island** 🆂🅷
(843) 681-3655. **$50-$150.** 200 Museum St. 3.3 mi e of J Wilton Graves Bridge on US 278 business route. Ext corridors. **Pets:** Small, dogs only. $10 daily fee/room, $25 one-time fee/room. Service with restrictions, crate.
🄰🅂🄺 🆂🅳 ⊗ 🕖 🖥 💻 ⇌

▼▼ **Red Roof Inn-Hilton Head** 🅼
(843) 686-6808. **$51-$91.** 5 Regency Pkwy. Over bridge, 9 mi e on US 278 business route; between Shipyard Plantation and Palmetto Dunes. Ext corridors. **Pets:** Medium, other species. Service with restrictions, supervision.
⊗ 🕖 🖥 ⇌

IRMO

▼▼▼▼ **Extended Stay Deluxe (Columbia-Harbison)** 🆂🅷
(803) 781-8590. **$85-$95.** 1170 Kinley Rd. I-26, exit 102B, just e, then n. Int corridors. **Pets:** Accepted.
🄰🅂🄺 🆂🅳 ⊗ 👣 🕖 👣 🖥 💻 ⇌

LANCASTER

▼▼ **Jameson Inn** 🅼
(803) 283-1188. **$54-$104.** 114 Commerce Blvd. Jct SR 9 Bypass and US 521, 1.3 mi w on SR 9 Bypass. Ext corridors. **Pets:** Small. $10 daily fee/pet. Service with restrictions, crate.
🄰🅂🄺 ⊗ 👣 🕖 👣 🖥 💻 ⇌

LANDRUM

▼▼▼ **The Red Horse Inn** 🅲🄰 ✿
(864) 895-4968. **$145-$270.** 310 N Campbell Rd. Jct SR 14/414, 1.5 mi w on SR 414 to Campbell Rd, then 0.7 mi n. Ext corridors. **Pets:** Medium. $25 one-time fee/pet. Designated rooms, service with restrictions, supervision.
🄰🅂🄺 🆂🅳 ⊗ 🖥 💻 ⊗

LUGOFF

▼▼ **Camden Inn** 🆂🅷
(803) 438-9441. **$69-$71.** 850 Hwy 1 S. I-20, exit 92 (US 601), 2.9 mi n. Ext corridors. **Pets:** Accepted.
🄰🅂🄺 🆂🅳 ⊗ 🕖 🖥 💻 🍽 ⇌

▼▼ **Ramada Limited** 🅼
(803) 438-1807. **$69-$139.** 542 Hwy 601 S. I-20, exit 92 (US 601), just n. Ext corridors. **Pets:** Accepted.
🄰🅂🄺 🆂🅳 ⊗ 🖥 💻 ⇌

MANNING

▲▲▲ ▼▼▼ **Best Western Palmetto Inn** 🅼
(803) 473-4021. **$54-$99.** 2825 Paxville Hwy. I-95, exit 119 (SR 261), just se. Ext corridors. **Pets:** Other species. $5 daily fee/pet. Service with restrictions, crate.
🆂🄰🆅🄴 🆂🅳 ⊗ 🖥 💻 ⇌

▼▼ **Comfort Inn** 🅼
(803) 473-7550. **$56-$89.** 3031 Paxville Hwy. I-95, exit 119 (SR 261), just se. Ext corridors. **Pets:** Accepted.
🄰🅂🄺 🆂🅳 ⊗ 🕖 🖥 💻 ⇌

▼ **Econo Lodge** Ⓜ
(803) 473-2596. **$40-$70.** 6137 Alex Harvin Hwy. I-95, exit 115, just sw. Ext corridors. **Pets:** Small, other species. $10 one-time fee/pet. Service with restrictions, supervision.
(A$K) (S⭐) (✕) (🛏) (💻) (🏊)

▲▲▲ ▼▼▼ **Ramada Inn** Ⓜ
(803) 473-5135. **$60-$65, 15 day notice.** 2816 Paxville Hwy. I-95, exit 119 (SR 261), just se. Ext corridors. **Pets:** Accepted.
(SAVE) (S⭐) (✕) (🐾) (🛏) (💻) (🏊)

NEWBERRY

▲▲▲ ▼▼▼ **Best Western Newberry Inn** Ⓜ
(803) 276-5850. **$65-$70.** 11701 S Carolina Hwy 34. I-26, exit 74 (SR 34), just ne. Ext corridors. **Pets:** Small, dogs only. $5 daily fee/pet. Service with restrictions, supervision.
(SAVE) (S⭐) (✕) (🛏) (💻) (🏊)

ORANGEBURG

▲▲▲ ▼▼▼ **Comfort Inn & Suites** Ⓜ ❀
(803) 531-9200. **$75-$105.** 3671 St Matthews Rd. I-26, exit 145A (US 601), just sw. Ext corridors. **Pets:** Other species. $10 one-time fee/room. Designated rooms, service with restrictions.
(SAVE) (S⭐) (✕) (🐾) (🦽) (🛏) (💻) (🏊)

▼▼ **Jameson Inn Orangeburg** Ⓜ
(803) 534-1611. **$54-$104.** 2350 Chestnut St NE. I-26, exit 145A (US 601), 3.9 mi sw to jct US 601 and 21/178 Bypass, then 2 mi nw. Ext corridors. **Pets:** Small. $10 daily fee/pet. Service with restrictions, crate.
(A$K) (✕) (🦽) (🛏) (💻) (🏊)

▲▲▲ ▼▼▼ **Traveler's Inn** Ⓜ
(803) 531-2590. **$50-$125.** 3691 St Matthews Rd. I-26, exit 145A (US 601), just sw. Ext corridors. **Pets:** Large. $15 daily fee/pet. Service with restrictions, supervision.
(A$K) (✕) (🛏) (💻) (🏊)

PICKENS

▼▼▼ **The Schell Haus, A Resort Bed & Breakfast** (BB)
(864) 878-0078. **$90-$165, 7 day notice.** 117 Hiawatha Tr. Jct US 178/SR 11, 4.6 mi ne on SR 11, then just se; on southeast side of Table Rock State Park. Int corridors. **Pets:** Accepted.
(A$K) (S⭐) (✕) (💻) (🏊) (🅿)

POINT SOUTH

▼▼▼▼ **Holiday Inn Express Point South/Yemassee** (SH)
(843) 726-9400. **$59-$99.** 138 Frampton Dr. I-95, exit 33 (US 17), just ne. Int corridors. **Pets:** Small. $20 daily fee/room. Service with restrictions, supervision.
(A$K) (S⭐) (✕) (🦽M) (🦽) (🛏) (💻) (🏊)

RIDGELAND

▲▲▲ ▼▼▼▼ **Comfort Inn** (SH)
(843) 726-2121. **$72-$92.** Hwy 336 & I-95. I-95, exit 21 (US 336), just nw. Ext/int corridors. **Pets:** Dogs only. $10 one-time fee/room. Service with restrictions.
(SAVE) (S⭐) (✕) (🐾) (🛏) (💻) (🏊)

ST. GEORGE

▼▼▼ **Comfort Inn** Ⓜ ❀
(843) 563-4180. **$48-$60.** 139 Motel Dr. I-95, exit 77 (US 78), just e. Ext corridors. **Pets:** Other species. $10 one-time fee/pet. Service with restrictions, supervision.
(A$K) (S⭐) (✕) (🛏) (💻) (🏊)

▲▲▲ ▼ **Econo Lodge** Ⓜ
(843) 563-4195. **$55-$75.** 5971 W Jim Bilton Blvd. I-95, exit 77 (US 78), just e. Ext corridors. **Pets:** Small. $5 daily fee/pet. Designated rooms, service with restrictions, supervision.
(SAVE) (S⭐) (✕) (🛏) (💻) (🏊)

SANTEE

▲▲▲ ▼▼▼ **Baymont Inn & Suites** Ⓜ
(803) 854-3221. **$65-$85, 3 day notice.** 249 Britain St. I-95, exit 98 (SR 6), just nw, then just s. Ext corridors. **Pets:** Accepted.
(SAVE) (S⭐) (✕) (🐾) (🦽) (🛏) (💻) (🏊)

▲▲▲ ▼▼▼ **Holiday Inn Santee** (SH)
(803) 854-9800. **$75-$250.** 139 Bradford Blvd. I-95, exit 98 (SR 6), just nw, then just sw. Int corridors. **Pets:** Small, other species. $20 daily fee/pet. Designated rooms, service with restrictions, supervision.
(SAVE) (S⭐) (✕) (🦽) (🛏) (💻) (🍴) (🏊)

▲▲▲ ▼▼▼ **Howard Johnson Express Inn** Ⓜ
(803) 854-3870. **$49-$99.** 9112 Old Hwy 6. I-95, exit 98 (SR 6), 0.4 mi se. Ext corridors. **Pets:** Dogs only. $10 daily fee/room. Service with restrictions, crate.
(SAVE) (S⭐) (✕) (🐾) (🛏) (💻) (🏊)

▲▲▲ ▼▼▼ **Super 8 Motel** Ⓜ
(803) 854-3456. **$55.** 9125 Old Hwy 6. I-95, exit 98 (SR 6), 0.4 mi se. Ext corridors. **Pets:** Medium. $10 daily fee/pet. Designated rooms, service with restrictions.
(SAVE) (S⭐) (✕) (🛏) (💻) (🏊)

SENECA

▼▼ **Jameson Inn** Ⓜ
(864) 888-8300. **$54-$104.** 226 Hi-Tech Rd. Jct SR 28 and US 76/123, 0.9 mi w on US 76/123, just se. Ext corridors. **Pets:** Small. $10 daily fee/pet. Service with restrictions, crate.
(A$K) (✕) (🦽M) (🐾) (🛏) (💻) (🏊)

SIMPSONVILLE

▼▼ **Days Inn** Ⓜ
(864) 963-7701. **$64.** 45 Ray E Talley Ct. I-385, exit 27, just s, then just e. Ext corridors. **Pets:** Accepted.
(A$K) (S⭐) (✕) (🛏) (💻) (🏊)

▼▼▼ **Holiday Inn Express-Simpsonville** (SH)
(864) 962-8500. **$59-$69.** 3821 Grandview Dr. I-385, exit 27, just s. Int corridors. **Pets:** Accepted.
(A$K) (S⭐) (✕) (🐾) (🦽) (🛏) (💻) (🏊)

▼ **Motel 6** (SH)
(864) 962-8484. **$42-$100.** 3706 Grandview Dr. I-385, exit 27, just s, then just w. Int corridors. **Pets:** Medium, other species. Service with restrictions, supervision.
(A$K) (S⭐) (✕) (🦽M) (🐾) (🦽) (🛏)

SPARTANBURG

▼▼ **Extended StayAmerica-Spartanburg-Asheville Hwy** Ⓜ
(864) 573-5949. **Call for rates.** 130 Mobile Dr. I-85 business loop, exit 4 northbound, just se, then just ne on service road; exit 4B southbound, just se, then just ne on service road. Ext corridors. **Pets:** Accepted.
(✕) (🐾) (🦽) (🛏) (💻)

▼▼▼ **Holiday Inn Express Hotel & Suites** (SH)
(864) 699-7777. **$93-$123.** 895 Spartan Blvd. I-26, exit 21B (US 29), just e to Blackstock Rd, then 0.7 mi n; adjacent to Westgate Mall. Int corridors. **Pets:** Accepted.
(A$K) (S⭐) (✕) (🦽M) (🐾) (🦽) (🛏) (💻) (🏊)

▼▼ **Quality Inn Expo Center** Ⓜ
(864) 576-2992. **$50-$66.** 2070 New Cut Rd. I-26, exit 17, just w. Ext corridors. **Pets:** Accepted.
(A$K) (S⭐) (✕) (🐾) (🛏) (💻) (🏊)

SUMMERTON

Days Inn of Summerton M
(803) 485-2865. **$34-$75.** 18 Bluff Blvd. I-95, exit 108, just n. Ext corridors. **Pets:** Medium, other species. $5 daily fee/pet. Service with restrictions, supervision.

SUMTER

Ramada Inn SH
(803) 775-2323. **$67-$72.** 226 N Washington St. US 76 business route/521, just n. Ext corridors. **Pets:** Accepted.

Travelers Inn & Suites M
(803) 469-9210. **$56-$80.** 1210 Camden Rd. Jct US 521/US 76. Ext corridors. **Pets:** Medium, other species. $7 daily fee/pet. Designated rooms, service with restrictions, supervision.

TRAVELERS REST

Sleep Inn SH
(864) 834-7040. **$60-$100.** 110 Hawkins Rd. US 25, exit Hawkins Rd. Int corridors. **Pets:** Other species. $15 daily fee/room. Service with restrictions, supervision.

WALTERBORO

Best Western of Walterboro SH ❀
(843) 538-3600. **$59-$89, 3 day notice.** 1428 Sniders Hwy. I-95, exit 53 (SR 63), just e. Ext corridors. **Pets:** Small. $20 daily fee/pet. Designated rooms, service with restrictions, supervision.

Econo Lodge M
(843) 538-3830. **$49-$89.** 1145 Sniders Hwy. I-95, exit 53 (SR 63), just e. Ext corridors. **Pets:** Large, other species. $10 daily fee/pet. Designated rooms, service with restrictions, supervision.

Ramada Inn of Walterboro SH
(843) 538-5403. **$49-$80.** 1245 Sniders Hwy. I-95, exit 53 (SR 63), just e. Ext corridors. **Pets:** Medium. $10 daily fee/pet. Designated rooms, service with restrictions, supervision.

Rice Planters Inn M
(843) 538-8964. **$44.** 97 Ladson Ln. I-95, exit 53 (SR 63), just e. Ext corridors. **Pets:** Other species. $5 daily fee/pet. Service with restrictions, supervision.

Royal Inn M
(843) 538-2503. **$40-$60.** 1142 Sniders Hwy. I-95, exit 53 (SR 63), just e. Ext corridors. **Pets:** Accepted.

Super 8 Motel M
(843) 538-5383. **$51-$61.** 1972 Bells Hwy. I-95, exit 57 (SR 64), just nw. Ext corridors. **Pets:** Accepted.

WINNSBORO

Days Inn M
(803) 635-1447. **$52-$67, 7 day notice.** 1894 US Hwy 321 Bypass. I-77, exit 34 (SR 34), 6.5 mi w, jct US 321/SR 34/213. Ext corridors. **Pets:** Small. $10 daily fee/pet. Designated rooms, service with restrictions, supervision.

Fairfield Motel M
(803) 635-3458. **$60-$80.** 56 US 321 Bypass S. Jct SR 213/US 321 Bypass S, 1.8 mi n. Ext corridors. **Pets:** Small, dogs only. $5 daily fee/pet. Service with restrictions, supervision.

SOUTH DAKOTA

ABERDEEN

▼▼/▼▼ Aberdeen East Super 8 Motel SH ☙
(605) 229-5005. **$70-$75.** 2405 6th Ave SE. 1.8 mi e on US 12. Int corridors. **Pets:** $6 daily fee/pet. Service with restrictions, supervision.
ASK SÓ ✕ &M ⚿ 🛈 🖵 ⇌ ✕

▼▼/▼▼ Aberdeen North Super 8 Motel SH ☙
(605) 226-2288. **$50-$75.** 770 NW Hwy 281. On US 281, 1.5 mi nw. Int corridors. **Pets:** $6 daily fee/pet. Service with restrictions, supervision.
ASK SÓ ✕

▼▼/▼▼ Aberdeen West Super 8 Motel SH ☙
(605) 225-1711. **$61-$180.** 714 S Hwy 281. Jct US 12 and 281. Int corridors. **Pets:** $6 daily fee/pet. Service with restrictions, supervision.
ASK SÓ ✕ 🛈

▼▼/▼▼ AmericInn Lodge & Suites of Aberdeen SH
(605) 225-4565. **$79-$229.** 310 Centennial St. 2.2 mi e on US 12, just n. Int corridors. **Pets:** Accepted.
ASK SÓ ✕ &M ⚿ 🛈 🖵 ⇌ ✕

▲▲▲ ▼▼/▼▼ Best Western Ramkota Hotel SH
(605) 229-4040. **$84-$119.** 1400 8th Ave NW. 1.5 mi nw on US 281. Ext/int corridors. **Pets:** Accepted.
SAVE SÓ ✕ &M ⚿ 🛈 🖵 ♒ ⇌ ✕

▲▲▲ ▼▼/▼▼ Comfort Inn SH ☙
(605) 226-0097. **$79-$129.** 2923 6th Ave SE. 2 mi e on US 12. Int corridors. **Pets:** Medium. $10 daily fee/pet. Service with restrictions, crate.
SAVE SÓ ✕ ⚿ 🛈 🖵 ⇌ ✕

▼▼/▼▼/▼▼ Holiday Inn Express Hotel & Suites SH
(605) 725-4000. **$78-$149.** 3310 7th Ave SE. 2.1 mi e on US 12. Int corridors. **Pets:** Dogs only. $15 daily fee/room. Service with restrictions, supervision.
ASK ✕ &M ⚿ ⚿ 🛈 🖵 ⇌ ✕

ARLINGTON

▼▼/▼▼ Arlington Inn SH
(605) 983-4609. **$56.** 402 S Hwy 81. 1 mi s on US 81. Int corridors. **Pets:** Accepted.
ASK SÓ ✕ ⚿ ⚿ 🛈

BERESFORD

▼▼/▼▼ Super 8 Motel SH
(605) 763-2001. **$58-$63.** 1410 W Cedar. I-29, exit 47 (SR 46), just e. Int corridors. **Pets:** Other species. $10 one-time fee/room. Supervision.
ASK SÓ ✕ ⚿ 🛈 🖵 ⇌ ✕

BLACK HILLS AREA

BELLE FOURCHE

▼▼ Ace Motel M
(605) 892-2612. **$38-$58.** 109 6th Ave. 0.5 mi n via US 85, just e; just s of US 212 Bypass. Ext corridors. **Pets:** Medium. $4 daily fee/pet. Designated rooms, service with restrictions, supervision.
✕ 🛈

CUSTER

▲▲▲ ▼▼/▼▼ Bavarian Inn Motel SH
(605) 673-2802. **$49-$119, 3 day notice.** 907 N 5th St. 1 mi n on US 16 and 385. Ext/int corridors. **Pets:** Accepted.
SAVE SÓ ✕ 🛈 🖵 ♒ ⇌ ✕

▲▲▲ ▼▼/▼▼ Rock Crest Lodge and Cabins CA ☙
(605) 673-4323. **$44-$89, 3 day notice.** 15 W Mt. Rushmore Rd. US 16, 0.5 mi w. Ext/int corridors. **Pets:** Medium, dogs only. $25 deposit/pet, $5 daily fee/pet. Designated rooms, service with restrictions, crate.
SAVE SÓ ✕ 🛈 🖵 ⇌ ✕

▲▲▲ ▼▼/▼▼ Rocket Motel M
(605) 673-4401. **$40-$85.** 211 Mt. Rushmore Rd. On US 16; center. Ext corridors. **Pets:** Accepted.
SAVE SÓ ✕

▲▲▲ ▼▼/▼▼/▼▼ Super 8 Custer SH
(605) 673-2200. **$55-$109.** 415 W Mt. Rushmore Rd. US 16, 0.8 mi w. Int corridors. **Pets:** Other species. $10 daily fee/pet. Service with restrictions, supervision.
SAVE SÓ ✕ 🛈 ⇌

DEADWOOD

▲▲▲ ▼▼ Black Hills Inn & Suites M
(605) 578-7791. **$33-$99, 3 day notice.** 206 Mountain Shadow Ln. 0.3 mi s of jct US 385 and 85. Int corridors. **Pets:** $100 deposit/room, $10 daily fee/pet. Designated rooms, service with restrictions, supervision.
SAVE ✕ ⇌

▲▲▲ ▼▼/▼▼ First Gold Hotel & Gaming SH
(605) 578-9777. **$65-$299, 7 day notice.** 270 Main St. 0.7 mi n on US 85. Int corridors. **Pets:** Medium. $15 one-time fee/room. Designated rooms, service with restrictions, supervision.
SAVE SÓ ✕ ⚿ 🖵 🍴

HILL CITY

▲▲▲ ▼▼/▼▼/▼▼ Best Western Golden Spike Inn & Suites SH ☙
(605) 574-2577. **$64-$145.** 106 Main St. Just n on US 16 and 385. Ext/int corridors. **Pets:** $10 one-time fee/pet. Designated rooms, service with restrictions, supervision.
SAVE SÓ ✕ ⚿ 🛈 🖵 🍴 ⇌ ✕

▲▲▲ ▼▼▼ Lantern Inn M
(605) 574-2582. **$64-$130.** 580 E Main St. On north side of town, on US 16 and 385. Ext corridors. **Pets:** Very small. $5 daily fee/pet. Designated rooms, supervision.
[SAVE] [S🐾] [✕] [🛏] [➣]

▲▲▲ ▼▼▼▼ The Lodge at Palmer Gulch SH ☀
(605) 574-2525. **$60-$242, 10 day notice.** 12620 SR 244. On SR 244, 5 mi w of Mt. Rushmore. Int corridors. **Pets:** Large. $10 daily fee/pet. Designated rooms, service with restrictions, supervision.
[SAVE] [S🐾] [✕] [🛏] [🛏] [➣] [🍴] [≋] [✕]

HOT SPRINGS

▲▲▲ ▼▼▼ Americas Best Value Inn By The
River M ☀
(605) 745-4292. **$40-$90.** 602 W River. On US 385; downtown. Ext corridors. **Pets:** Medium, other species. $20 deposit/pet, $15 daily fee/pet. Designated rooms, service with restrictions, supervision.
[SAVE] [S🐾] [✕] [🛏] [➣]

▲▲▲ ▼▼▼▼ Best Western Sundowner Inn SH ☀
(605) 745-7378. **$59-$209.** 737 S 6th St. 0.5 mi se off US 18 and 385. Int corridors. **Pets:** Medium. Designated rooms, supervision.
[SAVE] [S🐾] [✕] [🛏] [🛏] [➣] [✕]

▲▲▲ ▼▼▼ Budget Host Hills Inn M
(605) 745-3130. **$59-$144.** 640 S 6th St. 0.5 mi se off US 18 and 385. Ext corridors. **Pets:** Medium. Designated rooms, service with restrictions, supervision.
[SAVE] [S🐾] [✕] [🛏] [➣]

▲▲▲ ▼▼▼ Hot Springs Super 8 Motel SH
(605) 745-3888. **$53-$116.** 800 Mammoth St. US 18 Bypass. Int corridors. **Pets:** Medium, other species. $20 deposit/room, $10 one-time fee/room. Service with restrictions, supervision.
[SAVE] [S🐾] [✕] [🗝] [🛏]

KEYSTONE

▲▲▲ ▼▼▼ Holy Smoke Resort CA ☀
(605) 666-4616. **$50-$140, 3 day notice.** 24105 Hwy 16A. On US 16A, 1 mi n. Ext corridors. **Pets:** Medium, dogs only. $8 daily fee/pet. Designated rooms, service with restrictions, supervision.
[SAVE] [✕] [🛏] [🛏] [🍴] [☒]

▼▼▼ Keystone/Mt Rushmore Super 8 SH
(605) 666-6666. **$49-$179.** 250 Winter St. On US 16A; downtown. Ext/int corridors. **Pets:** Accepted.
[A$K] [S🐾] [✕] [🛏]

▼▼▼ Mt. Rushmore's Washington Inn SH
(605) 666-5070. **Call for rates.** 231 Winter St. On US 16A; downtown. Ext/int corridors. **Pets:** Designated rooms, supervision.
[✕] [🛏] [🛏] [🛏] [➣]

▼▼▼ Mt. Rushmore's White House Resort SH
(605) 666-4917. **$40-$200, 3 day notice.** 115 Swanzey St. Jct US 16A and SR 40. Ext/int corridors. **Pets:** Accepted.
[A$K] [S🐾] [✕] [🛏] [🛏] [🛏] [🍴] [➣]

▲▲▲ ▼▼▼ Powder House Lodge CA
(605) 666-4646. **$50-$200, 3 day notice.** 24125 Hwy 16A. On US 16A, 1.5 mi n. Ext corridors. **Pets:** Other species. $15 one-time fee/room. Service with restrictions, crate.
[SAVE] [🛏] [🛏] [🍴] [➣]

LEAD

▲▲▲ ▼▼▼▼ Spearfish Canyon Lodge SH ☀
(605) 584-3435. **$99-$169, 5 day notice.** 10619 Roughlock Falls Rd. I-90, exit 14 (Spearfish Canyon), 13 mi s. Int corridors. **Pets:** Service with restrictions, supervision.
[SAVE] [S🐾] [✕] [🛏] [🛏] [🍴] [✕]

RAPID CITY

▲▲▲ ▼▼▼ Alex Johnson Hotel SH
(605) 342-1210. **$89-$179.** 523 6th St. I-90, exit 57, s on I-190, then left at Omaha; downtown. Int corridors. **Pets:** Accepted.
[SAVE] [S🐾] [✕] [🗝] [🛏] [🛏] [🍴]

▲▲▲ ▼▼▼ Americas Best Value Inn SH
(605) 343-5434. **$55-$199, 21 day notice.** 620 Howard St. I-90, exit 58, just nw of Haines Ave. Int corridors. **Pets:** Accepted.
[SAVE] [S🐾] [✕] [🛏] [🛏] [➣]

▼▼▼▼ Best Western Ramkota Hotel SH
(605) 343-8550. **$97-$149.** 2111 N LaCrosse St. I-90, exit 59 (LaCrosse St), just n. Ext/int corridors. **Pets:** Accepted.
[A$K] [S🐾] [✕] [🛏M] [🗝] [🛏] [🛏] [🛏] [🍴] [➣] [✕]

▲▲▲ ▼▼▼ Budget Host Inn M
(605) 343-5126. **$45-$85.** 2101 Mt. Rushmore Rd. 1 mi s on US 16. Ext corridors. **Pets:** Small. $20 one-time fee/room. Designated rooms, service with restrictions, supervision.
[SAVE] [S🐾] [✕] [🛏] [➣]

▲▲▲ ▼▼▼ Fair Value Inn M
(605) 342-8118. **$40-$75.** 1607 LaCrosse St. I-90, exit 59 (LaCrosse St), 0.3 mi s. Ext corridors. **Pets:** Accepted.
[SAVE] [S🐾] [✕] [🛏] [🛏]

▲▲▲ ▼▼▼ Foothills Inn SH
(605) 348-5640. **$59-$139.** 1625 N LaCrosse St. I-90, exit 59 (LaCrosse St), just s. Int corridors. **Pets:** Accepted.
[SAVE] [S🐾] [✕] [🛏] [🛏] [➣]

▲▲▲ ▼▼▼ Gold Star Motel M
(605) 341-7051. **$38-$78.** 801 E North. I-90, exit 60, 1.5 mi sw on I-90 business loop, 1.2 mi s, then just e, from exit 59 (LaCrosse St). Ext corridors. **Pets:** Medium, other species. $5 daily fee/pet. Service with restrictions, supervision.
[SAVE] [S🐾] [✕] [🛏] [🛏]

▲▲▲ ▼▼▼ Happy Holiday Resort Motel M
(605) 342-8101. **$44-$196, 3 day notice.** 8990 S Hwy 16. On US 16, 7 mi s. Ext corridors. **Pets:** Accepted.
[SAVE] [S🐾] [✕] [🛏] [🛏] [🛏] [➣] [✕]

▼▼▼▼ Holiday Inn Express Hotel & Suites, I-90 SH
(605) 355-9090. **$89-$280.** 645 E Disk Dr. I-90, exit 59 (LaCrosse St), just ne. Int corridors. **Pets:** $10 daily fee/room. Designated rooms, service with restrictions, supervision.
[A$K] [S🐾] [✕] [🛏M] [🗝] [🛏] [🛏] [🛏] [➣]

▲▲▲ ▼▼▼▼ Holiday Inn-Rushmore Plaza LH
(605) 348-4000. **$94-$154.** 505 N 5th St. I-90, exit 58, 1.3 mi s on Haines. Int corridors. **Pets:** $15 daily fee/room. Service with restrictions, crate.
[SAVE] [S🐾] [✕] [🛏M] [🗝] [🛏] [🛏] [🛏] [🍴] [➣] [✕]

▼▼▼▼ La Quinta Inn & Suites SH ☀
(605) 718-7000. **$99-$199.** 1416 N Elk Vale Rd. I-90, exit 61 (Elk Vale Rd), just s. Int corridors. **Pets:** Large, other species. Service with restrictions, supervision.
[A$K] [S🐾] [✕] [🛏M] [🗝] [🗝] [🛏] [🛏] [🍴] [➣] [✕]

▲▲▲ ▼▼▼ Lazy U Motel M
(605) 343-4242. **$42-$72.** 2215 Mt. Rushmore Rd. 1 mi s on US 16. Ext corridors. **Pets:** Accepted.
[SAVE] [S🐾] [✕] [🛏]

▲▲▲ ▼▼▼ Microtel Inn & Suites SH
(605) 348-2523. **$57-$230.** 1740 Rapp St. I-90, exit 59 (LaCrosse St), just se. Int corridors. **Pets:** Small, dogs only. $10 daily fee/pet. Designated rooms, service with restrictions, supervision.
[SAVE] [S🐾] [✕] [🛏M] [🗝] [🛏] [🛏] [➣]

◈ Motel 6–352 **M**
(605) 343-3687. **$40-$73.** 620 E Latrobe St. I-90, exit 59 (LaCrosse St),
just se. Ext corridors. **Pets:** Medium, other species. Service with restrictions, supervision.
[SAVE] [S/0] [X] [&] [📶] [≈]

◈◈ Quality Inn **SH**
(605) 342-3322. **$39-$149, 30 day notice.** 1902 LaCrosse St. I-90, exit
59 (LaCrosse St), just s. Ext/int corridors. **Pets:** Other species. $10 daily
fee/room. Service with restrictions, supervision.
[SAVE] [S/0] [X] [&M] [&] [📶] [💻] [🍴] [≈] [✕]

◈◈ Super 8 Motel-I-90 **SH**
(605) 348-8070. **$47-$195.** 2124 LaCrosse St. I-90, exit 59 (LaCrosse
St), just n. Int corridors. **Pets:** Accepted.
[ASK] [S/0] [X] [&M] [🎱] [&] [📶]

◈◈ Super 8 Motel-South **SH**
(605) 342-4911. **$75-$105.** 2520 Tower Rd. 1.4 mi s on US 16, then
just e. Int corridors. **Pets:** Accepted.
[SAVE] [S/0] [X] [📶]

◈◈ Thrifty Motor Inn **M**
(605) 342-0551. **$42-$165.** 1303 LaCrosse St. I-90, exit 59 (LaCrosse
St), 0.5 mi s. Ext corridors. **Pets:** Accepted.
[SAVE] [S/0] [X] [📶]

ROCKERVILLE

◈ Rockerville Trading Post & Motel **M**
(605) 341-4880. **$60-$80, 3 day notice.** 13525 Main St. Center. Ext
corridors. **Pets:** Accepted.
[ASK] [S/0] [X] [📶] [≈]

SPEARFISH

◈◈◈ Best Western Black Hills Lodge **SH**
(605) 642-7795. **$55-$119, 30 day notice.** 540 E Jackson. I-90, exit 12,
just s. Ext/int corridors. **Pets:** Medium, dogs only. $5 daily fee/pet. Desig-
nated rooms, service with restrictions, supervision.
[SAVE] [S/0] [X] [🎱] [💻] [≈]

◈◈ Days Inn **SH** 🐾
(605) 642-7101. **$55-$350.** 240 Ryan Rd. I-90, exit 10, 1.2 mi s. Ext/int
corridors. **Pets:** Other species. $10 daily fee/room. Designated rooms,
service with restrictions, supervision.
[ASK] [S/0] [X] [📶] [💻]

◈◈◈ Holiday Inn Hotel & Convention
Center **SH** 🐾
(605) 642-4683. **$69-$129.** 305 N 27th St. I-90, exit 14 (Spearfish
Canyon), just n. Ext/int corridors. **Pets:** Other species. $100 deposit/
room, $25 one-time fee/pet. Designated rooms, service with restrictions,
supervision.
[SAVE] [S/0] [X] [&M] [🎱] [&] [📶] [💻] [🍴] [≈] [✕]

◈◈ Howard Johnson Express Inn **SH**
(605) 642-8105. **$45-$99.** 323 S 27th St. I-90, exit 14 (Spearfish Canyon), just s. Int corridors. **Pets:** Other species. $10 daily fee/pet. Desig-
nated rooms, service with restrictions, supervision.
[SAVE] [S/0] [X] [📶] [💻] [🍴] [≈]

◈◈ Spearfish Super 8 Motel **SH** 🐾
(605) 642-4721. **$55-$195.** 440 Heritage Dr. I-90, exit 14 (Spearfish
Canyon), just s, then e, then s. Int corridors. **Pets:** Other species. $10
one-time fee/room. Service with restrictions, supervision.
[ASK] [S/0] [X] [📶] [💻] [≈]

◈◈ Travelodge of Spearfish **M**
(605) 642-4676. **$49-$99.** 346 W Kansas St. Downtown off of Main St;
follow signs. Ext corridors. **Pets:** Other species. $10 daily fee/pet. Desig-
nated rooms, service with restrictions, supervision.
[ASK] [S/0] [X] [📶] [💻] [≈]

STURGIS

◈◈◈ Best Western of Sturgis **SH**
(605) 347-3604. **$49-$119.** 2431 S Junction Ave. I-90, exit 32. Ext/int
corridors. **Pets:** Other species. Designated rooms, service with restrictions,
supervision.
[SAVE] [S/0] [X] [📶] [💻] [🍴] [≈]

END AREA

BRANDON

◈◈◈ Comfort Inn **SH**
(605) 582-5777. **$69-$159.** 1105 N Splitrock Blvd. I-90, exit 406, just s.
Int corridors. **Pets:** Small. $15 one-time fee/room. Designated rooms, serv-
ice with restrictions, supervision.
[SAVE] [S/0] [X] [&M] [&] [📶] [💻] [≈]

BROOKINGS

◈◈ Brookings Super 8 Motel **SH**
(605) 692-6920. **$55-$85.** 3034 Lefevre Dr. I-29, exit 132, just e. Int
corridors. **Pets:** Other species. $5 daily fee/pet. Service with restrictions,
supervision.
[ASK] [S/0] [X] [📶] [≈]

◈◈◈ Fairfield Inn & Suites **SH**
(605) 692-3500. **$64-$145.** 3000 Lefevre Dr. I-29, exit 132, just e. Int
corridors. **Pets:** Other species. $50 one-time fee/pet. Service with restric-
tions, supervision.
[SAVE] [S/0] [X] [&M] [🎱] [&] [📶] [💻] [≈] [✕]

◈◈◈ Holiday Inn Express Hotel & Suites **SH**
(605) 692-9060. **$95-$130.** 3020 Lefevre Dr. I-29, exit 132, just se. Int
corridors. **Pets:** $10 daily fee/pet. Service with restrictions, supervision.
[ASK] [S/0] [X] [&M] [🎱] [&] [📶] [💻] [≈] [✕]

BUFFALO

◈ Tipperary Lodge **M**
(605) 375-3721. **$50.** 604 1st St W. 0.5 mi n on US 85, turn at sign. Int
corridors. **Pets:** Other species. Designated rooms, service with restrictions,
supervision.
[ASK] [S/0] [X] [📶]

CANISTOTA

◈◈◈ Best Western U-Bar Motel **M**
(605) 296-3466. **$60-$90.** 130 Ash St. I-90, exit 368, 6 mi s, follow
signs. Ext corridors. **Pets:** Very small, dogs only. Designated rooms,
service with restrictions, supervision.
[SAVE] [S/0] [X] [📶] [💻]

CHAMBERLAIN

◈◈◈ AmericInn Lodge & Suites of Chamberlain **SH**
(605) 734-0985. **$60-$160.** 1981 E King St. I-90, exit 265, just e. Int
corridors. **Pets:** Other species. $10 daily fee/room. Designated rooms,
service with restrictions, crate.
[SAVE] [X] [&M] [🎱] [&] [📶] [💻] [≈] [✕]

◈◈ Bel Aire Motel **M**
(605) 734-5595. **$40-$66.** 312 E King St. On US 16 and I-90 business
loop; downtown. Ext/int corridors. **Pets:** Dogs only. $5 daily fee/pet.
Supervision.
[SAVE] [S/0] [X] [📶]

AAA ▼▼▼ Best Western Lee's Motor Inn **SH**
(605) 734-5575. **$50-$90.** 220 W King St. On US 17 and I-90 business loop; downtown. Ext/int corridors. **Pets:** Very small, other species. $10 one-time fee/room. No service, supervision.
[SAVE] [S&D] [X] [▣] [⊶] [X]

AAA ▼▼▼ Cedar Shore Resort **LH**
(605) 734-6376. **$70-$150.** 1500 Shoreline Dr. I-90, exit 260, 2.5 mi e on Business Rt I-90, then 1 mi ne on Mickelson county road, follow signs. Int corridors. **Pets:** $10 daily fee/pet. Service with restrictions, crate.
[SAVE] [S&D] [X] [&M] [⟲] [⊡] [🛡] [▣] [¶] [⊶] [X]

▼▼▼ Holiday Inn Express **SH**
(605) 734-5593. **$89-$210.** 100 W Hwy 16. I-90, exit 260, just n. Int corridors. **Pets:** Other species. $10 daily fee/room. Designated rooms, supervision.
[ASK] [S&D] [X] [&M] [⊡] [▣]

AAA ▼ Lake Shore Motel **M**
(605) 234-5566. **$48-$85, 3 day notice.** 115 N River St. Just n of US 16 bridge (the northernmost bridge); just w of downtown. Ext corridors. **Pets:** Accepted.
[SAVE] [X] [🛡]

AAA ▼▼▼ Oasis Inn **SH**
(605) 734-6061. **$51-$119.** 1100 E Hwy 16. I-90, exit 260, 0.4 mi e on US 16 and I-90 business loop. Ext/int corridors. **Pets:** Service with restrictions, supervision.
[SAVE] [S&D] [X] [&M] [⟲] [⊡] [🛡] [▣] [⊶]

DELL RAPIDS

AAA ▼▼ Bilmar Inn & Suites **SH**
(605) 428-4288. **$55-$75.** 510 N Hwy 77. I-29, exit 98 (SR 115), 3 mi e, then just n. Int corridors. **Pets:** $6 daily fee/pet. Designated rooms, service with restrictions, supervision.
[SAVE] [X] [⊡] [🛡] [▣]

DE SMET

▼▼ De Smet Super Deluxe Inn & Suites **SH**
(605) 854-9388. **$62-$85.** 288 Hwy 14 E. US 14, just e. Int corridors. **Pets:** Accepted.
[ASK] [S&D] [X] [⊡] [🛡] [▣] [⊶]

FAITH

AAA ▼▼▼ Prairie Vista Inn **SH**
(605) 967-2343. **$69-$95, 10 day notice.** Hwy 212 & E 1st. On US 212; at east city edge. Int corridors. **Pets:** Medium. $10 one-time fee/pet. Designated rooms, service with restrictions, supervision.
[SAVE] [S&D] [X] [⊡] [▣]

FAULKTON

▼▼ Super 8 Motel **SH**
(605) 598-4567. **$50-$55.** 700 Main St. On US 212; center. Int corridors. **Pets:** Accepted.
[ASK] [S&D] [X] [🛡]

FLANDREAU

AAA ▼▼▼ Royal River Casino & Hotel **SH**
(605) 997-3746. **$55-$99.** 607 S Veterans St. I-29, exit 114, 7 mi e, follow signs. Int corridors. **Pets:** Medium. $50 deposit/pet. Designated rooms, service with restrictions, supervision.
[SAVE] [S&D] [X] [&M] [⊡] [🛡] [▣] [¶] [⊶] [X]

FORT PIERRE

▼▼ Fort Pierre Motel **M**
(605) 223-3111. **$48, 3 day notice.** 211 S 1st Ave. On US 83, 1.2 mi s of jct US 14. Ext corridors. **Pets:** Other species. Service with restrictions, supervision.
[X] [🛡]

HURON

▼▼ Best Western of Huron **SH**
(605) 352-2000. **$85-$100.** 2000 Dakota Ave. 1.3 mi s on SR 37. Ext/int corridors. **Pets:** Dogs only. $10 daily fee/pet. Service with restrictions, supervision.
[ASK] [S&D] [X] [&M] [⟲] [⊡] [🛡] [▣] [X]

▼▼ Comfort Inn Huron **SH**
(605) 352-6655. **$75-$150.** 100 21st St SW. 1.3 mi s on SR 37. Ext/int corridors. **Pets:** Large. $25 one-time fee/room. Service with restrictions, supervision.
[ASK] [S&D] [X] [&M] [⟲] [⊡] [🛡] [▣] [X]

AAA ▼▼▼ Crossroads Hotel & Huron Event Center **LH** 🐾
(605) 352-3204. **$65-$105.** 100 4th St. Just w of Dakota Ave; downtown. Int corridors. **Pets:** $15 daily fee/pet. Service with restrictions, supervision.
[SAVE] [S&D] [X] [&M] [🛡] [▣] [¶] [⊶]

INTERIOR

AAA ▼ Badlands Budget Host Inn **M**
(605) 433-5335. **$41-$63.** 900 SD Hwy 377. Jct SR 44 and 377, 2 mi s of Badlands National Park. Ext corridors. **Pets:** Accepted.
[SAVE] [S&D] [▣] [⊶] [🗲]

KADOKA

AAA ▼▼▼ Best Western H & H El Centro Motel **M** 🐾
(605) 837-2287. **$65-$105.** 105 E Hwy 16. 1.5 mi w on I-90 business route from exit 152, 1.3 mi e from exit 150. Ext corridors. **Pets:** Medium, other species. Designated rooms, service with restrictions, crate.
[SAVE] [S&D] [X] [▣] [¶] [⊶] [X]

AAA ▼ Budget Host Sundowner Motor Inn **M**
(605) 837-2296. **$35-$155.** 510 SR 73. I-90, exit 150, just s. Ext corridors. **Pets:** Accepted.
[SAVE] [S&D] [X] [🛡] [⊶]

AAA ▼ West Motel **M**
(605) 837-2427. **$34-$80, 3 day notice.** 306 Hwy 16 W. I-90, exit 150, 1 mi e on I-90 business route. Ext corridors. **Pets:** $10 one-time fee/room. Service with restrictions, supervision.
[SAVE] [S&D] [X] [🛡]

KIMBALL

▼▼ Super 8 Motel **M**
(605) 778-6088. **$70-$85.** 200 W Kiote. I-90, exit 284, just n. Int corridors. **Pets:** Other species. $10 daily fee/pet. Service with restrictions.
[ASK] [S&D] [X] [&M] [⟲] [▣]

MADISON

▼▼▼ AmericInn Lodge & Suites **SH**
(605) 256-3076. **$73-$110.** 504 10th St SE. SR 34, 0.5 mi se; south side of town. Int corridors. **Pets:** Other species. $25 one-time fee/room. Designated rooms, service with restrictions, supervision.
[ASK] [S&D] [X] [&M] [⊡] [🛡] [▣] [⊶]

MITCHELL

▼▼ AmericInn Lodge & Suites **SH**
(605) 996-9700. **$59-$159.** 1421 S Burr St. I-90, exit 332, just n. Int corridors. **Pets:** $20 daily fee/pet. Designated rooms, no service, supervision.
[ASK] [X] [&M] [⊡] [🛡] [▣] [⊶]

AAA ▼ Anthony Motel **M**
(605) 996-7518. **$40-$95.** 1518 W Havens St. I-90, exit 330, 0.6 mi n on I-90 business loop. Ext corridors. **Pets:** Service with restrictions, supervision.
[SAVE] [S&D] [X] [🛡] [⊶]

(AAA) ▼▼ Days Inn Mitchell SH
(605) 996-6208. **$54-$94.** 1506 S Burr St. I-90, exit 332, just n. Int corridors. **Pets:** $20 deposit/room, $10 daily fee/pet. Designated rooms, service with restrictions, supervision.
[SAVE] [S] [X] [🖥] [💻] [〰] [X]

(AAA) ▼▼▼ Hampton Inn SH ❧
(605) 995-1575. **$75-$123, 30 day notice.** 1920 Highland Way. I-90, exit 332, just se. Int corridors. **Pets:** Dogs only. $20 daily fee/room. Service with restrictions, supervision.
[SAVE] [X] [♿] [🅿] [📷] [🖥] [💻] [〰] [X]

(AAA) ▼▼▼▼ Holiday Inn SH ❧
(605) 996-6501. **$79-$159.** 1525 W Havens St. I-90, exit 330, 0.5 mi n. Ext/int corridors. **Pets:** $10 one-time fee/pet. Supervision.
[SAVE] [S] [X] [♿] [🅿] [🖥] [💻] [🍴] [〰] [X]

(AAA) ◆◆ Kelly Inn & Suites SH
(605) 995-0500. **$69-$125.** 1010 Cabela Dr. I-90, exit 332, just sw. Ext/int corridors. **Pets:** Other species. Service with restrictions, supervision.
[SAVE] [X] [♿] [🖥] [💻] [〰] [X]

(AAA) ◆◆ Thunderbird Lodge M
(605) 996-6645. **$45-$99.** 1601 S Burr St. I-90, exit 332, just n. Ext/int corridors. **Pets:** Accepted.
[SAVE] [S] [X] [♿M] [🖥] [💻]

MOBRIDGE

(AAA) ▼▼ Wrangler Inn SH
(605) 845-3641. **$59-$149.** 820 W Grand Crossing. 0.5 mi w on US 12. Ext/int corridors. **Pets:** Medium, dogs only. Designated rooms, service with restrictions, supervision.
[SAVE] [S] [X] [🖥] [💻] [🍴] [〰] [X]

MURDO

(AAA) ◆◆ Best Western Graham's M
(605) 669-2441. **$59-$110.** 301 W 5th. On I-90 business loop, 0.5 mi w of jct US 83; I-90, exits 191 and 192. Ext corridors. **Pets:** Accepted.
[SAVE] [S] [X] [💻] [〰]

(AAA) ◆◆ Days Inn Range Country SH
(605) 669-2425. **$59-$145.** 302 W 5th. I-90 business loop, 0.5 mi w of jct US 83, exits 192 and 191. Ext/int corridors. **Pets:** Accepted.
[SAVE] [S] [X] [🖥] [💻]

NORTH SIOUX CITY

(AAA) ▼▼ Comfort Inn SH
(605) 232-3366. **$50-$99.** 1311 River Dr. I-29, exit 2, just w. Int corridors. **Pets:** Large, other species. $10 daily fee/pet. Service with restrictions, supervision.
[SAVE] [S] [X] [🖥] [💻] [〰] [X]

◆◆◆ Hampton Inn SH
(605) 232-9739. **$69-$199.** 101 S Sodrac Dr. I-29, exit 2, just w. Int corridors. **Pets:** Medium, other species. $20 one-time fee/room. Designated rooms, service with restrictions, supervision.
[ASK] [S] [X] [♿M] [🅿] [🖥] [💻] [〰] [X]

▼ Super 8 Motel SH
(605) 232-4716. **$39-$120.** 1300 River Dr. I-29, exit 2, just w. Int corridors. **Pets:** Other species. $5 daily fee/room. Service with restrictions, supervision.
[ASK] [S] [X] [🖥] [💻]

PICKSTOWN

▼▼ Fort Randall Inn M
(605) 487-7801. **$45-$62.** 116 US Hwy 18. On US 18/281; just e of the dam. Ext corridors. **Pets:** Other species. $10 daily fee/room. Service with restrictions.
[S] [X] [🖥]

PIERRE

(AAA) ▼▼▼ Best Western Ramkota Hotel SH
(605) 224-6877. **$96-$132.** 920 W Sioux Ave. 1 mi w on US 14/83. Ext/int corridors. **Pets:** Accepted.
[SAVE] [S] [X] [♿M] [📷] [♿] [🖥] [💻] [🍴] [〰]

(AAA) ▼▼▼ Comfort Inn of Pierre SH
(605) 224-0377. **$69-$119.** 410 W Sioux Ave. 0.3 mi w on US 14/83 and SR 34. Int corridors. **Pets:** Other species. $10 one-time fee/room. Designated rooms, supervision.
[SAVE] [X] [♿M] [♿] [🖥] [💻]

(AAA) ▼▼▼ Governor's Inn SH
(605) 224-4200. **$60-$125.** 700 W Sioux Ave. 0.8 mi w on US 14/83 and SR 34. Ext/int corridors. **Pets:** $10 deposit/room. No service, supervision.
[SAVE] [S] [X] [📷] [♿] [🖥] [💻] [〰]

▼▼ Kelly Inn SH
(605) 224-4140. **$67.** 713 W Sioux Ave. 0.8 mi w on US 14/83. Int corridors. **Pets:** Other species. Service with restrictions, crate.
[ASK] [S] [X] [♿] [🖥] [💻]

PLANKINTON

▼▼ Super 8 Motel SH
(605) 942-7722. **$49-$80.** 801 S Main St. I-90, exit 308, just n. Int corridors. **Pets:** Other species. $8 daily fee/pet. Designated rooms, service with restrictions, supervision.
[ASK] [S] [X]

SIOUX FALLS

▼▼▼ Baymont Inn SH
(605) 362-0835. **$69-$139.** 3200 Meadow Ave. I-29, exit 77 (41st St), just w, then just n. Int corridors. **Pets:** Small. $15 one-time fee/room. Service with restrictions, supervision.
[ASK] [S] [X] [♿M] [📷] [♿] [🖥] [💻] [〰]

(AAA) ▼▼▼ Best Western Empire Towers SH ❧
(605) 361-3118. **$62-$89.** 4100 W Shirley Pl. I-29, exit 77 (41st St), just ne. Int corridors. **Pets:** Other species. $10 daily fee/room. Designated rooms, service with restrictions, supervision.
[SAVE] [S] [X] [📷] [♿] [🖥] [💻] [〰]

(AAA) ▼▼▼▼ Best Western Ramkota Hotel & Conference Center LH
(605) 336-0650. **$99-$149.** 3200 W Maple. I-29, exit 81 (Airport/Russell St), just e. Ext/int corridors. **Pets:** Accepted.
[SAVE] [S] [X] [♿M] [📷] [♿] [🖥] [💻] [🍴] [〰] [X]

▼▼▼▼ Clubhouse Hotel & Suites SH
(605) 361-8700. **$129-$199.** 2320 S Louise Ave. I-29, exit 78 (26th St), just e. Ext/int corridors. **Pets:** Accepted.
[ASK] [S] [X] [♿M] [♿] [🖥] [💻] [X]

▼▼▼ Comfort Inn by Choice Hotels South SH
(605) 361-2822. **$75-$95.** 3216 S Carolyn Ave. I-29, exit 77 (41st St), just e, then n. Int corridors. **Pets:** Accepted.
[ASK] [S] [X] [📷] [🖥] [💻] [〰]

(AAA) ▼▼ ◆ Comfort Inn North SH
(605) 331-4490. **$59-$119, 7 day notice.** 5100 N Cliff Ave. I-90, exit 399 (Cliff Ave), 0.3 mi s. Int corridors. **Pets:** Other species. $10 one-time fee/room. Service with restrictions, crate.
[SAVE] [S] [X] [♿M] [🖥] [💻] [〰]

▼▼▼ Comfort Suites by Choice Hotels SH
(605) 362-9711. **$85-$105.** 3208 S Carolyn Ave. I-29, exit 77 (41st St), just e, then n. Int corridors. **Pets:** Accepted.
[ASK] [S] [X] [📷] [🖥] [💻] [〰]

Country Inn & Suites By Carlson 🆂🅷
(605) 373-0153. **$74-$159, 30 day notice.** 200 E 8th St. Just e of Phillips Ave; downtown. Int corridors. **Pets:** $10 daily fee/room. Designated rooms, service with restrictions, supervision.

Days Inn Airport 🆂🅷 ☸
(605) 331-5959. **$76-$139.** 5001 N Cliff Ave. I-90, exit 399 (Cliff Ave), just s. Int corridors. **Pets:** Other species. $10 daily fee/room. Service with restrictions, supervision.

Days Inn-Empire 🆂🅷
(605) 361-9240. **$55-$129.** 3401 Gateway Blvd. I-29, exit 77 (41st St), just w. Int corridors. **Pets:** Dogs only. $10 daily fee/pet. Service with restrictions, supervision.

Homewood Suites By Hilton 🆂🅷 ☸
(605) 338-8585. **$119-$219.** 3620 W Avera Dr. I-229, exit 1C (Louise Ave), just s. Int corridors. **Pets:** Other species. $5 daily fee/room, $15 one-time fee/room. Service with restrictions.

Kelly Inn 🆂🅷
(605) 338-6242. **$61-$174.** 3101 W Russell St. I-29, exit 81 (Airport/Russell St), 0.3 mi e. Ext/int corridors. **Pets:** Accepted.

Microtel Inn & Suites 🆂🅷
(605) 361-7484. **$70-$95.** 2901 S Carolyn Ave. I-29, exit 77 (41st St), just e, then n. Int corridors. **Pets:** Accepted.

Quality Inn & Suites 🆂🅷
(605) 336-1900. **$69-$119.** 5410 N Granite Ln. I-29, exit 83, just e, then 0.3 mi n. Int corridors. **Pets:** Medium. $10 daily fee/pet. Designated rooms, service with restrictions, crate.

Red Roof Inn 🆂🅷 ☸
(605) 361-1864. **$52-$100.** 3500 S Gateway Blvd. I-29, exit 77 (41st St), just w. Int corridors. **Pets:** Service with restrictions, supervision.

Residence Inn by Marriott 🆂🅷
(605) 361-2202. **$135-$155.** 4509 W Empire Pl. I-29, exit 77 (41st St), 0.5 mi se. Int corridors. **Pets:** Accepted.

Sheraton Sioux Falls Hotel 🅻🅷 ☸
(605) 331-0100. **$109-$129.** 1211 N West Ave. I-29, exit 81 (Airport/Russell St), 1.3 mi e. Int corridors. **Pets:** Medium, dogs only. Service with restrictions, supervision.

Sleep Inn Airport 🆂🅷
(605) 339-3992. **$50-$99.** 1500 N Kiwanis Ave. I-29, exit 81 (Airport/Russell St), 0.7 mi e. Int corridors. **Pets:** Small. $10 daily fee/room. Designated rooms, service with restrictions, supervision.

Staybridge Suites 🆂🅷 ☸
(605) 361-2298. **$109-$249.** 2505 S Carolyn Ave. I-29, exit 78, just se. Int corridors. **Pets:** Medium. $25 daily fee/pet. Designated rooms, service with restrictions, supervision.

Super 8/I-90/Airport East 🆂🅷
(605) 339-9212. **$55-$100.** 4808 N Cliff Ave. I-90, exit 399 (Cliff Ave), 0.3 mi s. Int corridors. **Pets:** $10 daily fee/pet. Designated rooms, service with restrictions, supervision.

Super 8 Motel-East 🆂🅷
(605) 338-8881. **$50-$130.** 2616 E 10th St. I-229, exit 6, just e. Int corridors. **Pets:** Large, other species. $10 daily fee/pet. Service with restrictions, supervision.

TownePlace Suites by Marriott 🆂🅷
(605) 361-2626. **$69-$149.** 4545 W Homefield Dr. I-29, exit 78 (26th St), just w. Int corridors. **Pets:** Medium, other species. $75 one-time fee/room. Service with restrictions, supervision.

SISSETON

Sisseton Super 8 🆂🅷
(605) 742-0808. **$65-$85.** 2104 SD Hwy 10. I-29, exit 232 (SR 10), 1.5 mi w; then just w of jct SR 127. Int corridors. **Pets:** Large, other species. Supervision.

VERMILLION

Comfort Inn 🆂🅷
(605) 624-8333. **$69-$89.** 701 W Cherry St. I-29, exit 26 (SR 50), 7.5 mi w on Business Rt SR 50. Int corridors. **Pets:** $5 daily fee/pet. Service with restrictions, supervision.

Holiday Inn Express Hotel & Suites-Vermillion 🆂🅷
(605) 624-7600. **$69-$121.** 1200 N Dakota St. I-29, exit 26, 7 mi w. Int corridors. **Pets:** Accepted.

WALL

Best Western Plains Motel 🅼
(605) 279-2145. **$60-$170.** 712 Glenn St. I-90, exit 110, just n. Ext corridors. **Pets:** Other species. $10 one-time fee/room. Service with restrictions, supervision.

Days Inn 🆂🅷
(605) 279-2000. **$65-$160.** 212 10th Ave. I-90, exit 110, just n, then just w. Int corridors. **Pets:** Designated rooms, supervision.

Econo Lodge 🅼
(605) 279-2121. **$59-$125.** 804 Glenn St. I-90, exit 110, just n. Ext corridors. **Pets:** Accepted.

Sunshine Inn 🅼
(605) 279-2178. **$49-$77.** 608 Main St. Downtown. Ext corridors. **Pets:** Other species. $5 one-time fee/room.

WATERTOWN

Best Western Ramkota Hotel 🆂🅷
(605) 886-8011. **$104-$195.** 1901 9th Ave SW. I-29, exit 177 (US 212), 4 mi w. Int corridors. **Pets:** Accepted.

Comfort Inn 🆂🅷
(605) 886-3010. **$76-$90.** 800 35th St Cir. I-29, exit 177 (US 212), just w. Ext/int corridors. **Pets:** Small. $15 one-time fee/room. Designated rooms, service with restrictions, supervision.

Country Inn & Suites By Carlson 🆂🅷
(605) 886-8900. **$85.** 3400 8th Ave SE. I-29, exit 177 (US 212), just w. Int corridors. **Pets:** Other species. $20 one-time fee/room. Designated rooms, service with restrictions, supervision.

(AAA) ▼▼ Days Inn SH
(605) 886-3500. **$56-$139, 14 day notice.** 2900 9th Ave SE. I-29, exit 177 (US 212), 0.5 mi w. Ext/int corridors. **Pets:** $10 one-time fee/room. Service with restrictions, crate.
SAVE $ ⊠ ⚕M ▱ 🖉 🔲 🖵 🌊

▼▼▼ Holiday Inn Express Hotel & Suites SH
(605) 882-3636. **$75-$129.** 3900 9th Ave SE. I-29, exit 177 (US 212), just e. Int corridors. **Pets:** $10 daily fee/room. Service with restrictions, supervision.
ASK $ ⊠ ⚕ 🔲 🖵 🌊 ⊠

▼ Super 8 Motel-Watertown SH
(605) 882-1900. **$56.** 503 14th Ave SE. On US 81, 0.3 mi s of jct US 212. Int corridors. **Pets:** Accepted.
ASK $ ⊠ 🔲 🖵 🌊

(AAA) ▼▼ Travelers Inn Motel SH
(605) 882-2243. **$52-$58.** 920 14th St SE. I-29, exit 177 (US 212), 1.5 mi w, then just s. Int corridors. **Pets:** Medium, other species. $6 daily fee/pet. Designated rooms, service with restrictions, supervision.
SAVE $ ⊠ 🖉 🔲 🖵

(AAA) ▼ Travel Host Motel M
(605) 886-6120. **$50-$65.** 1714 9th Ave SW. I-29, exit 177 (US 212), 4 mi w. Int corridors. **Pets:** Dogs only. $5 one-time fee/pet. Designated rooms, no service, supervision.
SAVE ⊠ 🔲

WINNER

▼▼▼ Holiday Inn Express Hotel & Suites SH
(605) 842-2255. **$60-$130.** 1360 E Hwy 44. Just ne of jct US 18 and 183. Int corridors. **Pets:** Very small, other species. $25 daily fee/pet. Service with restrictions, supervision.
ASK $ ⊠ ⚕M 🖉 🔲 🖵 🌊

YANKTON

▼▼ Best Western Kelly Inn-Yankton SH
(605) 665-2906. **$89-$119.** 1607 Hwy 50 E. On US 50, 1.8 mi e. Ext/int corridors. **Pets:** Other species. Designated rooms, service with restrictions, supervision.
ASK $ ⊠ ⚕M ▱ 🖉 🔲 🖵 ▯ 🌊 ⊠

▼▼ Days Inn SH
(605) 665-8717. **$70.** 2410 Broadway. US 81, 1.7 mi n. Int corridors. **Pets:** Accepted.
$ ⊠ 🔲 🖵

(AAA) ▼ Lewis & Clark Resort M
(605) 665-2680. **$60-$129, 30 day notice.** 43496 Shore Dr. 4 mi w on SR 52; in Lewis and Clark State Park, turn into park, just w of Marina. Ext corridors. **Pets:** Medium, dogs only. $5 daily fee/pet. Service with restrictions, supervision.
SAVE ⊠ 🖉 🔲 🖵 🌊 ⊠ 🌀

ALCOA

ΔΔΔ ▼▼ Family Inns of America M
(865) 970-2006. **$49-$59.** 2450 Airport Hwy. US 129, just e. Ext corridors. **Pets:** Very small, other species. $20 deposit/room. Designated rooms, service with restrictions, supervision.
(SAVE) (S⬦) (✕) (🛏) (≈)

▼▼▼ Jameson Inn Alcoa SH
(865) 984-6800. **$54-$104.** 206 Corporate Pl. US 129, just s. Int corridors. **Pets:** Small. $10 daily fee/pet. Service with restrictions, crate.
(ASK) (✕) (🛏) (💻) (≈)

ATHENS

▼▼▼ Days Inn-Athens M
(423) 745-5800. **$57-$65, 7 day notice.** 2541 Decatur Pike. I-75, exit 49. Ext corridors. **Pets:** Medium, other species. $5 daily fee/pet. Service with restrictions, crate.
(ASK) (S⬦) (✕) (🛏) (🛏) (💻)

▼▼ Ramada Inn SH
(423) 745-1212. **$75-$95.** 115 CR 247. I-75, exit 52, just w. Ext corridors. **Pets:** Medium. $10 one-time fee/pet. Service with restrictions, supervision.
(ASK) (S⬦) (✕) (🛏) (💻) (🍴) (≈)

BRENTWOOD

▼▼ Baymont Inn & Suites SH
(615) 376-4666. **$79-$99.** 111 Penn Warren Dr. I-65, exit 74B, 1.5 mi w, then just s on West Park. Int corridors. **Pets:** Medium, other species. $10 daily fee/pet. Service with restrictions, supervision.
(ASK) (S⬦) (✕) (🛏) (🎿) (🛏) (🛏) (💻) (≈)

▼▼ Candlewood Suites SH
(615) 309-0600. **$79-$92, 30 day notice.** 5129 Virginia Way. I-65, exit 74B, 0.5 mi w, 0.5 mi s on Franklin Rd, 1.2 mi w on Maryland Way, just s on Ward Cir, then just s. Int corridors. **Pets:** Medium. $75 one-time fee/room. Designated rooms, service with restrictions, supervision.
(ASK) (✕) (🎿) (🛏) (💻)

▼▼ MainStay Suites-Brentwood SH
(615) 371-8477. **$70-$150.** 107 Brentwood Blvd. I-65, exit 74B, 1 mi w. Int corridors. **Pets:** Medium, other species. $10 daily fee/pet. Designated rooms, service with restrictions, crate.
(ASK) (✕) (S⬦) (🛏) (🎿) (🎿) (🛏) (💻) (≈)

ΔΔΔ ▼▼▼▼ Residence Inn Brentwood SH
(615) 371-0100. **$89-$165.** 206 Ward Cir. I-65, exit 74B, 0.3 mi s on Franklin Pike Cir (US 31 S), 0.5 mi w on Maryland Way. Ext/int corridors. **Pets:** Small. $100 one-time fee/room. Service with restrictions.
(SAVE) (S⬦) (✕) (🎿) (🛏) (💻) (≈) (✕)

BROWNSVILLE

▼▼ Comfort Inn SH
(731) 772-4082. **$42-$82.** 2600 Anderson Ave. I-40, exit 56. Ext corridors. **Pets:** Accepted.
(ASK) (S⬦) (✕) (🛏) (💻) (≈)

▼▼ Days Inn SH
(731) 772-3297. **$60-$80.** 2530 Anderson Ave. I-40, exit 56. Ext corridors. **Pets:** Accepted.
(ASK) (✕) (🛏) (💻)

BULLS GAP

ΔΔΔ ▼▼▼ Best Western Executive Inn SH
(423) 235-9111. **$54-$190, 7 day notice.** 50 Speedway Ln. I-81, exit 23. Int corridors. **Pets:** Other species. $15 daily fee/pet. Designated rooms, service with restrictions, supervision.
(SAVE) (S⬦) (✕) (🎿) (🛏) (💻) (≈)

▼▼▼ Super 8 Motel M
(423) 235-4112. **$60-$70.** 90 Speedway Ln. I-81, exit 23. Ext corridors. **Pets:** $10 daily fee/pet. Service with restrictions, supervision.
(✕) (🎿) (🛏)

BUTLER

▼▼▼ Iron Mountain Inn B&B and Creekside Chalet BB
(423) 768-2446. **$165-$350, 14 day notice.** 138 Moreland Dr. 1.6 mi w on Pine Orchard Rd from SR 67 at Stout Store, follow signs; 13 mi w on SR 67 from US 421 in Mountain City, follow sign at Stout Store area. Ext/int corridors. **Pets:** Accepted.
(ASK) (S⬦) (✕) (🛏) (💻)

CARYVILLE

ΔΔΔ ▼▼ Budget Host Inn M
(423) 562-9595. **$25-$45, 4 day notice.** 115 Woods Ave. I-75, exit 134, just w. Ext corridors. **Pets:** Very small. $10 one-time fee/pet. Service with restrictions, supervision.
(SAVE) (✕)

CENTERVILLE

▼▼ Days Inn SH
(931) 729-5600. **$50-$60.** 634 David St. On SR 100, 3 mi w of jct SR 48. Int corridors. **Pets:** Accepted.
(ASK) (S⬦) (✕) (🎿) (🛏) (💻) (🍴) (≈)

CHATTANOOGA

◆◆ America's Best Inn-Hamilton Mall Area M
(423) 894-5454. **$48-$90.** 7717 Lee Hwy. I-75, exit 7B northbound; exit 7 southbound. Ext corridors. **Pets:** Accepted.
⊠ 🐾 📶 💻 🏊

◆◆◆ Baymont Inn & Suites-Chattanooga SH
(423) 821-1090. **$60-$110.** 3540 Cummings Hwy. I-24, exit 174, 0.4 mi s. Int corridors. **Pets:** Accepted.
ASK 🆂 ⊠ 🐾 📶 💻 🏊

◆◆◆ Best Western Heritage Inn SH
(423) 899-3311. **$59-$109.** 7641 Lee Hwy. I-75, exit 7B northbound; exit 7 southbound. Ext corridors. **Pets:** Small, dogs only. $10 daily fee/pet. Service with restrictions, crate.
SAVE 🆂 ⊠ 📶 💻 🏊

◆◆◆ Best Western Royal Inn SH
(423) 821-6840. **$55-$90.** 3644 Cummings Hwy. I-24, exit 174, 0.4 mi s. Ext corridors. **Pets:** Small. $10 daily fee/pet. Service with restrictions, supervision.
SAVE 🆂 ⊠ 📶 💻 🏊

◆◆◆ Comfort Inn SH
(423) 499-1993. **$55-$134.** 7620 Hamilton Park Dr. I-75, exit 7B northbound; exit southbound, just w to Lee Hwy, just s, then just e. Int corridors. **Pets:** Accepted.
SAVE 🆂 📶 💻 🏊

◆◆ Comfort Inn & Suites SH
(423) 899-5151. **$59-$99.** 2341 Shallowford Village Dr. I-75, exit 5 (Shallowford Rd), just w, then just n. Int corridors. **Pets:** Accepted.
ASK 🆂 ⊠ 📶 💻 🏊

◆◆◆ Days Inn-Lookout Mountain Tiftonia West SH
(423) 821-6044. **$55-$85.** 3801 Cummings Hwy. I-24, exit 174, just n. Ext corridors. **Pets:** Accepted.
SAVE 🆂 ⊠ 🐾 📶 💻 🏊

◆◆ Extended StayAmerica-Chattanooga-Airport SH
(423) 892-1315. **$55-$65.** 6240 Airpark Dr. SR 153, exit 1 (Lee Hwy), 0.3 mi s to Vance Rd, then just w. Ext corridors. **Pets:** Accepted.
ASK 🆂 ⊠ ♿M 🐾 📶 💻

◆◆◆ Holiday Inn Chattanooga Choo-Choo LH
(423) 266-5000. **$129-$149.** 1400 Market St. I-24, exit 178 (Broad St) eastbound, then E Main St; exit 178 (Market St) westbound, 0.5 mi n. Ext/int corridors. **Pets:** Small, other species. $25 one-time fee/room. Service with restrictions, supervision.
SAVE 🆂 ⊠ 🐾 📶 💻 🍴 🏊 ⊠

◆◆ La Quinta Inn Chattanooga SH
(423) 855-0011. **$81-$101.** 7015 Shallowford Rd. I-75, exit 5 (Shallowford Rd), just w. Ext corridors. **Pets:** Medium. Service with restrictions.
ASK ⊠ 🐾 📶 💻 🏊

◆◆◆ MainStay Suites-Chattanooga SH
(423) 485-9424. **$59-$119.** 7030 Amin Dr. I-75, exit 5 (Shallowford Rd), just w, then s. Int corridors. **Pets:** Medium, dogs only. $50 one-time fee/room. Designated rooms, no service, crate.
ASK 🆂 ⊠ 📶 💻

◆◆ Microtel Inn-Chattanooga SH
(423) 510-0761. **$32-$60.** 7014 McCutcheon Rd. I-75, exit 5 (Shallowford Rd), just w, 0.3 mi n on Shallowford Village Dr, then just w. Int corridors. **Pets:** Large, other species. $10 daily fee/pet. Service with restrictions, supervision.
ASK ⊠ 📶 🏠

◆◆ Motel 6 Downtown SH
(423) 265-7300. **$41-$100.** 2440 Williams St. I-24, exit 178 (Market St). Int corridors. **Pets:** Medium, other species. Service with restrictions, supervision.
🆂 ⊠ 🐾 📶 🏠

◆◆ ◆◆◆ Quality Inn SH
(423) 821-1499. **$65-$110, 30 day notice.** 3109 Parker Ln. I-24, exit 175, just s. Ext corridors. **Pets:** Other species. $10 daily fee/pet. Service with restrictions, supervision.
SAVE 🆂 ⊠ 📶 💻 🏊

◆◆ ◆◆◆ Quality Suites SH 🐾
(423) 892-1500. **$74-$109.** 7324 Shallowford Rd. I-75, exit 5 (Shallowford Rd), just e. Ext corridors. **Pets:** Small. $10 daily fee/pet. Designated rooms, service with restrictions, supervision.
SAVE 🆂 ⊠ 🐾 📶 💻 🏊

◆◆ Ramada Limited-Lookout Mountain West SH
(423) 821-7162. **$49-$99.** 30 Birmingham Hwy. I-24, exit 174, just s. Ext/int corridors. **Pets:** Medium, other species. $10 daily fee/pet. Service with restrictions.
ASK 🆂 ⊠ 📶 💻 🏊

◆◆ Red Roof Inn-Chattanooga M
(423) 899-0143. **$49-$55.** 7014 Shallowford Rd. I-75, exit 5 (Shallowford Rd), just w. Ext corridors. **Pets:** Medium, other species. Service with restrictions, supervision.
⊠ 🐾 📶

◆◆◆ Residence Inn by Marriott SH
(423) 266-0600. **$114-$229.** 215 Chestnut St. US 27, exit 1C (4th St), just n. Int corridors. **Pets:** Other species. $75 one-time fee/room. Service with restrictions, supervision.
ASK 🆂 ⊠ ♿M 🐾 🐾 📶 💻 🏊

◆◆◆ The Sheraton Read House Hotel LH 🐾
(423) 266-4121. **$99-$249.** 827 Broad St. US 27, exit 1A, just e. Int corridors. **Pets:** Medium. $50 one-time fee/pet. Service with restrictions, crate.
ASK 🆂 ⊠ 📶 💻 🍴 🏊

◆◆◆ Staybridge Suites SH
(423) 267-0900. **$109-$309.** 1300 Carter St. US 27 N, exit 1A (Martin Luther King Blvd), just e to Carter St, then 0.3 mi s. Int corridors. **Pets:** Other species. $25 one-time fee/room. Service with restrictions.
ASK 🆂 ⊠ ♿M 🐾 🐾 📶 💻 🏊

◆◆ Super 8 Motel/Lookout Mountain SH
(423) 821-8880. **$50-$130, 20 day notice.** 20 Birmingham Hwy. I-24, exit 174. Int corridors. **Pets:** Accepted.
ASK 🆂 ⊠ 📶 🏊

CLARKSVILLE

◆◆ Days Inn North SH
(931) 552-1155. **$55-$70.** 130 Westfield Ct. I-24, exit 4, just s. Ext corridors. **Pets:** Accepted.
ASK 🆂 ⊠ ♿M 📶 🏊

◆◆ Days Inn of Clarksville SH
(931) 358-3194. **$68-$105.** 1100 Hwy 76 Connector Rd. I-24, exit 11. Ext corridors. **Pets:** Small. $8 daily fee/pet. Designated rooms, service with restrictions, supervision.
ASK 🆂 ⊠ 📶 🏊

◆◆ ◆◆◆ Econo Lodge Inn & Suites SH
(931) 647-2002. **$60-$69.** 3065 Wilma Rudolph Blvd. I-24, exit 4, 0.3 mi w. Ext corridors. **Pets:** Small. $10 daily fee/pet. Designated rooms, service with restrictions, supervision.
SAVE 🆂 ⊠ 📶 💻 🏊

◆◆ ◆◆◆ Holiday Inn-I-24 SH
(931) 648-4848. **$89-$99.** 3095 Wilma Rudolph Blvd. I-24, exit 4, just s. Ext corridors. **Pets:** Other species. $10 daily fee/room. Designated rooms, service with restrictions, crate.
ASK 🆂 ⊠ 🐾 📶 💻 🍴 🏊 ⊠

▼▼ Red Roof Inn 🆂🅷
(931) 905-1555. **$55-$75.** 197 Holiday Dr. I-24, exit 4, just se. Ext corridors. **Pets:** Medium, other species. Service with restrictions, supervision.
🄰🅂🄺 🅂🅓 ⊠ 🯁 🖵 ➴

CLEVELAND

🄰🄰🄰 ▼▼ Comfort Inn 🆂🅷
(423) 478-5265. **$50-$90.** 153 James Asbury Dr. I-75, exit 27, just w. Ext/int corridors. **Pets:** Medium. $7 daily fee/pet. Service with restrictions, crate.
🅂🄰🅅🄴 🅂🅓 ⊠ 🯁 🖵 ➴

🄰🄰🄰 ▼▼ Douglas Inn & Suites 🆂🅷 🐾
(423) 559-5579. **$55-$80, 5 day notice.** 2600 Westside Dr NW. I-75, exit 25, just e. Ext/int corridors. **Pets:** Small. $10 daily fee/pet. Service with restrictions, supervision.
🅂🄰🅅🄴 🅂🅓 ⊠ 🯁 🖵

🄰🄰🄰 ▼▼ Econo Lodge of Cleveland Ⓜ
(423) 472-3281. **$45-$80.** 2655 Westside Dr NW. I-75, exit 25, just e. Ext corridors. **Pets:** Small. $10 daily fee/pet. Service with restrictions, supervision.
🅂🄰🅅🄴 🅂🅓 ⊠ 🯁 🖵 ➴

▼▼▼ Holiday Inn Mountain View 🆂🅷
(423) 472-1500. **$72-$153.** 2400 Executive Park Dr. I-75, exit 25, just w. Ext/int corridors. **Pets:** Small, other species. $25 one-time fee/room. No service, crate.
⊠ 🖉 🯁 🖵 🍽 ➴

🄰🄰🄰 ▼▼ Howard Johnson Chalet 🆂🅷
(423) 476-8511. **$65-$125.** 2595 Georgetown Rd. I-75, exit 25, just e. Ext corridors. **Pets:** Accepted.
🅂🄰🅅🄴 🅂🅓 ⊠ 🖘 🯁 🖵 🍽 ➴

▼▼ Jameson Inn 🆂🅷
(423) 614-5583. **$54-$104.** 360 Paul Huff Pkwy. I-75, exit 27, 1 mi e. Ext corridors. **Pets:** Small. $10 daily fee/pet. Service with restrictions, crate.
🄰🅂🄺 ⊠ 🖉 🖘 🯁 🖵 ➴

▼▼ Ramada Limited 🆂🅷
(423) 472-5566. **$69-$89, 7 day notice.** 156 James Asbury Dr. I-75, exit 27, just w. Ext corridors. **Pets:** Accepted.
🄰🅂🄺 🅂🅓 ⊠ 🖘 🯁 🖵 ➴

🄰🄰🄰 ◈ Super 8 Motel 🆂🅷
(423) 476-5555. **$60-$70, 14 day notice.** 163 Bernham Dr. I-75, exit 27, just w. Ext/int corridors. **Pets:** Accepted.
🅂🄰🅅🄴 🅂🅓 ⊠ 🖘 🯁 🖵 ➴

CLINTON

▼◈ Clinton Norris Inn Ⓜ
(865) 457-0565. **$58-$95, 5 day notice.** 2317 N Charles G Seivers Blvd. I-75, exit 122, just w. Int corridors. **Pets:** Accepted.
🄰🅂🄺 🅂🅓 ⊠ 🖁🅼 🖉 🯁 🖵 ➴

▼▼ Holiday Inn Express Hotel & Suites 🆂🅷
(865) 457-2233. **$80-$129, 7 day notice.** 141 Buffalo Rd. I-75, exit 122, just w. Ext corridors. **Pets:** Accepted.
🄰🅂🄺 🅂🅓 ⊠ 🖁🅼 🖘 🯁 🖵 ➴

▼▼ Super 8 Motel Ⓜ
(865) 457-2311. **$39-$89.** 720 Park Pl. I-75, exit 122, just w. Ext corridors. **Pets:** Medium. $7 daily fee/pet. Designated rooms, service with restrictions, supervision.
🄰🅂🄺 🅂🅓 ⊠ 🖁🅼 🯁 🖵 ➴

COLUMBIA

🄰🄰🄰 ▼▼▼ Americas Best Value Inn 🆂🅷
(931) 381-1410. **$53-$63.** 1548 Bear Creek Pike. I-65, exit 46, just w. Ext corridors. **Pets:** $5 daily fee/pet. Service with restrictions, supervision.
🅂🄰🅅🄴 🅂🅓 ⊠ 🯁

🄰🄰🄰 ▼▼▼ Holiday Inn Express 🆂🅷
(931) 380-1227. **$80-$110.** 1554 Bear Creek Pike. I-65, exit 46, just w. Ext corridors. **Pets:** Other species. $10 one-time fee/room. Service with restrictions, supervision.
🅂🄰🅅🄴 🅂🅓 ⊠ 🖁🅼 🯁 🖵 ➴

▼▼▼ Jameson Inn 🆂🅷
(931) 388-3326. **$54-$104.** 715 James M Campbell Blvd. 0.9 mi w jct SR 50 and US 31. Int corridors. **Pets:** Small. $10 daily fee/pet. Service with restrictions, crate.
🄰🅂🄺 ⊠ 🯁 🖵 ➴

COOKEVILLE

🄰🄰🄰 ▼▼▼ Alpine Lodge & Suites 🆂🅷
(931) 526-3333. **$40-$58.** 2021 E Spring St. I-40, exit 290, just s. Int corridors. **Pets:** Medium, other species. $5 daily fee/pet. Designated rooms, service with restrictions, supervision.
🅂🄰🅅🄴 🅂🅓 ⊠ 🖉 🯁 🖵 ➴

▼▼▼▼ Baymont Inn & Suites Cookeville 🆂🅷
(931) 525-6668. **$69-$79.** 1151 S Jefferson Ave. I-40, exit 287, just s. Int corridors. **Pets:** Accepted.
🄰🅂🄺 🅂🅓 ⊠ 🖁🅼 🖘 🯁 🖵 ➴

🄰🄰🄰 ▼▼▼ Best Western Thunderbird Motel 🆂🅷
(931) 526-7115. **$50-$55, 7 day notice.** 900 S Jefferson Ave. I-40, exit 287, just n. Ext corridors. **Pets:** $10 daily fee/pet. Service with restrictions, crate.
🅂🄰🅅🄴 🅂🅓 ⊠ 🖁🅼 🖘 🯁 🖵 ➴

🄰🄰🄰 ▼▼▼ Country Hearth Inn & Suites 🆂🅷 🐾
(931) 528-1040. **$35-$80.** 1100 S Jefferson Ave. I-40, exit 287. Ext corridors. **Pets:** Other species. $10 daily fee/pet. Designated rooms, service with restrictions, crate.
🄰🅂🄺 🅂🅓 ⊠ 🯁 🖵 ➴

🄰🄰🄰 ▼▼ Days Inn 🆂🅷
(931) 528-1511. **$50-$125.** 1296 S Walnut Ave. I-40, exit 287. Ext corridors. **Pets:** Small, dogs only. $10 one-time fee/pet. Designated rooms, service with restrictions, supervision.
🅂🄰🅅🄴 🅂🅓 ⊠ 🯁 🖵 ➴

🄰🄰🄰 ▼▼▼▼ Hampton Inn 🆂🅷
(931) 520-1117. **$72-$92.** 1025 Interstate Dr. I-40, exit 287, 0.5 mi n. Ext corridors. **Pets:** Accepted.
🅂🄰🅅🄴 🅂🅓 ⊠ 🖁🅼 🖉 🖘 🯁 🖵 ➴

▼▼ Holiday Inn 🆂🅷
(931) 526-7125. **$49-$99, 14 day notice.** 970 S Jefferson Ave. I-40, exit 287, just n. Ext/int corridors. **Pets:** Accepted.
🄰🅂🄺 ⊠ 🖁🅼 🯁 🖵 🍽 ➴

CORNERSVILLE

🄰🄰🄰 ▼▼▼ Vista Express Ⓜ
(931) 293-2111. **$59-$69.** 3731 Pulaski Hwy. I-65, exit 22 at US 31A. Ext corridors. **Pets:** Accepted.
🅂🄰🅅🄴 🅂🅓 ⊠ 🯁 ➴

CROSSVILLE

▼▼ La Quinta Inn-Crossville 🆂🅷
(931) 456-9338. **$79-$179, 7 day notice.** 4038 Hwy 127 N. I-40, exit 317, just n. Int corridors. **Pets:** Accepted.
🄰🅂🄺 ⊠ 🖁🅼 🖉 🖘 🯁 🖵 ➴

DANDRIDGE

Holiday Inn Express SH
(865) 397-1910. **$69-$120.** 119 Sharon Dr. I-40, exit 417, just s. Int corridors. **Pets:** Medium, other species. $25 one-time fee/pet. Designated rooms, no service, supervision.

Super 8 Motel SH
(865) 397-1200. **$40-$55.** 125 Sharon Dr. I-40, exit 417, just s. Int corridors. **Pets:** $10 daily fee/pet. Supervision.

DECHERD

Jameson Inn SH
(931) 962-0130. **$54-$104.** 1838 Decherd Blvd. Jct Main St and SR 41A, just s. Ext corridors. **Pets:** Small. $10 daily fee/pet. Service with restrictions, crate.

DICKSON

Best Western Executive Inn SH
(615) 446-0541. **$45-$80.** 2338 Hwy 46. I-40, exit 172, just n. Ext corridors. **Pets:** Medium, dogs only. $5 daily fee/pet. Designated rooms, service with restrictions, supervision.

Comfort Inn SH
(615) 441-5252. **$55-$70.** 1025 E Christi Rd. I-40, exit 172. Int corridors. **Pets:** Small, dogs only. $10 daily fee/pet. Designated rooms, service with restrictions, supervision.

Days Inn SH
(615) 740-7475. **$59-$79.** 2415 Hwy 46 S. I-40, exit 172, just s. Ext corridors. **Pets:** $20 deposit/room. Service with restrictions, supervision.

Holiday Inn SH
(615) 446-9081. **$70.** 2420 Hwy 46 S. I-40, exit 172, just s. Ext corridors. **Pets:** Other species. $8 one-time fee/room. Supervision.

Super 8 Motel SH
(615) 446-1923. **$49-$54.** 150 Suzanne Dr. I-40, exit 172, just n on SR 46, then just e. Int corridors. **Pets:** Other species. $7 daily fee/pet. Service with restrictions, supervision.

DYERSBURG

Best Western Dyersburg SH
(731) 285-8601. **$66-$85.** 770 Hwy 51 Bypass. I-155, exit 13, 0.5 mi s; jct of US 51 Bypass and SR 78. Ext corridors. **Pets:** Accepted.

Comfort Inn SH
(731) 285-6951. **$61-$150.** 815 Reelfoot Dr. I-155, exit 13, just s. Ext corridors. **Pets:** Accepted.

Executive Inn & Suites SH
(731) 287-0044. **$40, 4 day notice.** 2331 Lake Rd. I-155, exit 13, 0.5 mi s. Ext corridors. **Pets:** Accepted.

Hampton Inn SH
(731) 285-4778. **$69-$84.** 2750 Mall Loop Rd. I-155, exit 13, just s. Int corridors. **Pets:** Other species. Service with restrictions, supervision.

EAST RIDGE

Americas Best Value Inn SH
(423) 894-6110. **$39-$59.** 639 Camp Jordan Pkwy. I-75, exit 1A (Ringgold Rd), 0.3 mi e. Ext/int corridors. **Pets:** Accepted.

Howard Johnson Plaza Hotel SH
(423) 892-8100. **$79.** 6700 Ringgold Rd. I-75, exit 1A (Ringgold Rd), just e. Int corridors. **Pets:** Accepted.

Ramada Limited SH
(423) 894-1860. **$45-$80.** 6650 Ringgold Rd. I-75, exit 1 (Ringgold Rd). Int corridors. **Pets:** Accepted.

Super 8 Motel M
(423) 894-6720. **Call for rates (no credit cards).** 6521 Ringgold Rd. I-75, exit 1B (Ringgold Rd), just w. Ext corridors. **Pets:** Very small. $10 one-time fee/pet. Service with restrictions, supervision.

ERWIN

Holiday Inn Express SH
(423) 743-4100. **$75-$120.** 2002 Temple Hill Rd. I-26, exit 15, just e. Int corridors. **Pets:** Accepted.

ETOWAH

Sleep Inn SH
(423) 263-4343. **$59-$119.** 600 N Tennessee Ave (US 411). I-75, exit exit 49 (SR 30), Jct US 411 and SR 30, just s. Int corridors. **Pets:** $25 one-time fee/pet. Service with restrictions, supervision.

FAIRVIEW

Deerfield Inn & Suites SH
(615) 799-4700. **$55-$69.** 1407 Hwy 96 N. I-40, exit 182. Ext corridors. **Pets:** Small. $10 daily fee/pet. Designated rooms, service with restrictions, supervision.

FAYETTEVILLE

Best Western-Fayetteville Inn SH
(931) 433-0100. **$70-$80.** 3021 Thornton Taylor Pkwy. 0.7 mi e of US 431, on US 64 and 231 Bypass. Ext corridors. **Pets:** Accepted.

FRANKLIN

Best Western Franklin Inn SH
(615) 790-0570. **$35-$80.** 1308 Murfreesboro Rd. I-65, exit 65, just w. Ext corridors. **Pets:** Accepted.

Comfort Inn SH
(615) 791-6675. **$68-$140.** 4206 Franklin Commons Ct. I-65, exit 65, just e. Ext corridors. **Pets:** Very small, dogs only. $10 daily fee/pet. Designated rooms, service with restrictions, supervision.

Days Inn SH
(615) 790-1140. **$59-$99, 15 day notice.** 4217 S Carothers Rd. I-65, exit 65, just e. Ext corridors. **Pets:** Accepted.

▼▼ Homestead Studio Suites Hotel-Nashville/Franklin-Cool Springs SH
(615) 771-7600. **$67-$77.** 680 Bakers Bridge Ave. I-65, exit 69 (Galleria Blvd), 0.3 mi e on Moore's Ln to Carothers Pkwy, 0.5 mi s, then 0.3 mi w. Ext corridors. **Pets:** Accepted.
ASK S❄ ✕ �
ⓘ

▼▼▼ La Quinta Inn & Suites Nashville-Franklin M
(615) 791-7700. **$75-$119.** 4207 Franklin Commons Ct. I-65, exit 65, just e. Int corridors. **Pets:** Medium. Service with restrictions.
ASK ✕ 🖊 🛒 ⓘ ➳

Ⓐ ▼▼▼ Ramada Limited & Suites SH
(615) 791-4004. **$59-$99.** 6210 Hospitality Dr. I-65, exit 65, 0.5 mi e on US 96. Int corridors. **Pets:** Small, dogs only. $15 daily fee/pet. Designated rooms, service with restrictions, supervision.
SAVE S❄ ✕ 🛒M 🖊 ⓘ ➳

GALLATIN

▼▼ Jameson Inn SH
(615) 451-4494. **$54-$104.** 1001 Village Green Crossing. 2 mi s on US 31. Ext corridors. **Pets:** Small. $10 daily fee/pet. Service with restrictions, crate.
ASK ✕ 🛒M 🌀 🖊 ⓘ ➳

GATLINBURG

ⒶⒶ ▼▼▼ Cobbly Nob Rentals Inc CA
(865) 436-5298. **$85-$700, 30 day notice.** 3722 E Parkway. On US 321, 10.3 mi n of jct US 441. Ext corridors. **Pets:** Medium. $15 one-time fee/pet. Designated rooms, service with restrictions, supervision.
SAVE ✕ ⓘ

ⒶⒶ ▼▼▼ Greenbrier Valley Resorts at Cobbly Nob CA ❀
(865) 436-2015. **$90-$400, 30 day notice.** 3629 E Parkway. On US 321, 10.1 mi n of jct US 441. Ext corridors. **Pets:** Other species. $100 deposit/pet, $10 daily fee/pet. Designated rooms, service with restrictions.
SAVE S❄ ✕ ⓘ ➳

ⒶⒶ ▼▼ Holiday Inn SunSpree Resort M ❀
(865) 436-9201. **$59-$119.** 520 Historic Nature Tr. 0.4 mi e of US 441 at traffic light 8. Ext/int corridors. **Pets:** Other species. $15 one-time fee/pet. Service with restrictions.
SAVE S❄ ✕ 🛒M 🌀 🖊 ⓘ 🍽 ➳ ✕

ⒶⒶ ▼▼▼ Microtel Gatlinburg SH
(865) 436-0107. **$45-$125, 4 day notice.** 211 Historic Nature Tr. Just e of US 441 at traffic light 8. Int corridors. **Pets:** Small. $10 daily fee/pet. Designated rooms, service with restrictions, supervision.
SAVE S❄ ✕ 🛒M 🖊 ⓘ

▼▼▼ The Park Vista Hotel & Convention Center LH
(865) 436-9211. **$69-$129, 3 day notice.** 705 Cherokee Orchard Rd. 0.6 mi e of jct US 441 at traffic light 8. Int corridors. **Pets:** Accepted.
ASK S❄ ✕ 🛒M 🌀 🖊 ⓘ 🍽 ➳ ✕

▼ Terrace on the Water M
(865) 436-4965. **$60-$94, 3 day notice.** 396 Parkway. On US 441; between traffic lights 2 and 3. Ext corridors. **Pets:** Small, dogs only. $5 daily fee/room. Designated rooms, service with restrictions, crate.
ASK S❄ ⓘ ➳

Ⓐ ▼▼▼ Westgate Smoky Mountain Resort CA
(865) 430-4800. **$79-$199, 7 day notice.** 915 Garden Rd. On US 441/321; across from Gatlinburg Welcome Center. Ext corridors. **Pets:** Accepted.
SAVE ✕ 🖊 ⓘ ➳ ✕

GREENEVILLE

Ⓐ ▼▼▼ Comfort Inn of Greeneville SH ❀
(423) 639-4185. **$69-$200.** 1790 E Andrew Johnson Hwy. US 11 E, 2.9 mi ne. Ext/int corridors. **Pets:** $10 daily fee/room. Designated rooms, service with restrictions, supervision.
SAVE S❄ ✕ ⓘ ➳

Ⓐ ▼▼ Days Inn M
(423) 639-2156. **$49-$190, 7 day notice.** 935 E Andrew Johnson Hwy. US 11 E, 2 mi ne. Ext corridors. **Pets:** Large. $10 daily fee/room. Designated rooms, service with restrictions, crate.
SAVE S❄ ✕ 🖊 ⓘ

▼▼▼ Jameson Inn SH
(423) 638-7511. **$54-$104.** 3160 E Andrew Johnson Hwy. US 11 E Bypass, 3.6 mi ne. Int corridors. **Pets:** Small. $10 daily fee/pet. Service with restrictions, crate.
ASK ✕ 🖊 ⓘ ➳

HARRIMAN

Ⓐ ▼▼ Best Western Sundancer Motor Lodge M
(865) 882-6200. **$51-$80.** 120 Childs Rd. I-40, exit 347, just n. Ext corridors. **Pets:** Small. $10 daily fee/pet. Service with restrictions, supervision.
SAVE S❄ ✕ ⓘ

▼▼ Caney Creek Inn SH
(865) 882-5340. **$63-$93.** 1845 S Roane St. I-40, exit 347, just s on US 27/SR 61. Ext corridors. **Pets:** $30 deposit/room. No service, supervision.
ASK S❄ ✕ 🛒M ⓘ ➳

Ⓐ ▼▼ Super 8 Motel M
(865) 882-6600. **$55-$75.** 1867 S Roane St. I-40, exit 347, just s on US 27/SR 61. Ext corridors. **Pets:** Small, dogs only. $10 daily fee/pet. Designated rooms, service with restrictions, supervision.
SAVE S❄ ✕ ⓘ ➳

HIXSON

▼▼▼ Home Away Extended Stay Studios SH
(423) 643-4663. **$69-$99.** 1949 North Point Blvd. Jct SR 153 and Hixson Pike, just w. Ext corridors. **Pets:** Accepted.
ASK S❄ ✕ ⓘ ➳

HURRICANE MILLS

Ⓐ ▼▼ Best Western of Hurricane Mills M ❀
(931) 296-4251. **$90-$110.** 15542 Hwy 13 S. I-40, exit 143. Ext corridors. **Pets:** Small. $10 one-time fee/pet. Service with restrictions, supervision.
SAVE S❄ ✕ 🌀 ⓘ ➳

JACKSON

Ⓐ ▼▼ Best Western Inn & Suites SH
(731) 664-3030. **$55-$95, 7 day notice.** 1936 Hwy 45 Bypass. I-40, exit 80A, just s. Ext corridors. **Pets:** Very small. $15 daily fee/pet. Designated rooms, service with restrictions, supervision.
SAVE S❄ ✕ 🖊 ⓘ ➳

▼▼ Days Inn SH ❀
(731) 668-3444. **$58-$70.** 1919 US 45 Bypass. I-40, exit 80A, just s. Ext corridors. **Pets:** Small. $5 one-time fee/room. Designated rooms, service with restrictions, supervision.
ASK S❄ ✕ ⓘ ➳

▼▼ Days Inn-West SH
(731) 668-4840. **$55.** 2239 Hollywood Dr. I-40, exit 79. Ext corridors. **Pets:** Accepted.
ASK S❄ ✕ ⓘ ➳

▼▼▼▼ **DoubleTree Hotel Jackson** LH
(731) 664-6900. **$129.** 1770 Hwy 45 Bypass. I-40, exit 80A, 0.5 mi s. Int corridors. **Pets:** Accepted.
(ASK) ⊠ 🌮 🔲 🛢 📺 🍽 ⊷

▼◆▼▼ **Jameson Inn** SH
(731) 660-8651. **$54-$104.** 1292 Vann Dr. I-40, exit 80B, 0.6 mi w. Int corridors. **Pets:** Small. $10 daily fee/pet. Service with restrictions, crate.
(ASK) ⊠ 🛢 🔲 ⊷

▼◆▼▼ **La Quinta Inn of Jackson** SH
(731) 664-1800. **$67-$101.** 2370 N Highland Ave. I-40, exit 82A. Int corridors. **Pets:** Medium. Service with restrictions.
(ASK) ⊠ 🛢 🔲 ⊷

◆◆◆ ▼◆▼▼ **Supertel Inn-Jackson** SH
(731) 664-4312. **$84-$114.** 1890 Hwy 45 Bypass. I-40, exit 80A, just s. Ext corridors. **Pets:** Medium, other species. $10 daily fee/pet. Designated rooms, service with restrictions, supervision.
(SAVE) (S🄳) ⊠ (&M) 🔲 🛢 🔲 ⊷

JELLICO

▼◆ **Americas Best Value Inn** M
(423) 784-7241. **Call for rates.** 133 Holiday Ln. I-75, exit 160, just w. Ext corridors. **Pets:** Accepted.
(ASK) ⊠ 🛢 🔲 ⊷

JOHNSON CITY

▼▼ **Comfort Inn of Johnson City** SH
(423) 928-9600. **$56-$290.** 1900 S Roan St. I-26, exit 31, just w on US 321. Ext corridors. **Pets:** Accepted.
(ASK) (S🄳) ⊠ 🛢 🔲 ⊷

▼▼▼ **DoubleTree Hotel** SH
(423) 929-2000. **$79-$399, 7 day notice.** 211 Mockingbird Ln. I-26, exit 35 eastbound; exit 35B westbound, 0.6 mi e on N Roan St. Int corridors. **Pets:** Accepted.
(ASK) (S🄳) ⊠ 🔲 🛢 🔲 📺 ⊷

◆◆◆ ▼◆▼▼ **Holiday Inn-Johnson City** SH
(423) 282-4611. **$90.** 101 W Springbrook Dr. I-26, exit 35A westbound; exit 35 eastbound, just e on N Roan St, then just n. Int corridors. **Pets:** Dogs only. $25 one-time fee/pet. Designated rooms, service with restrictions, crate.
(SAVE) (S🄳) ⊠ 🔲 🛢 🔲 📺 🍽 ⊷

▼▼ **Jameson Inn** SH
(423) 282-0488. **$54-$104.** 119 Pinnacle Dr. I-26, exit 38, just w on CR 354, then just s. Ext corridors. **Pets:** Small. $10 daily fee/pet. Service with restrictions, crate.
(ASK) ⊠ 🔲 🛢 🔲 ⊷

▼▼ **Red Roof Inn-Johnson City** SH
(423) 282-3040. **$52-$66.** 210 Broyles Dr. I-26, exit 35B westbound; exit 35 eastbound, just w on N Roan St. Ext corridors. **Pets:** Medium, other species. Service with restrictions, supervision.
⊠ 🔲 🔲 🛢

▼▼ **Sleep Inn & Suites** SH
(423) 915-0081. **$62-$79.** 2020 Franklin Terrace Ct. I-26, exit 36, just w, then just n, follow signs; entrance on Oakland Ave at light. Int corridors. **Pets:** Other species. Service with restrictions, supervision.
(ASK) (S🄳) ⊠ (&M) 🔲 🔲 🛢 🔲

JONESBOROUGH

▼▼▼ **AmericInn Lodge & Suites** SH
(423) 753-3100. **$79-$159.** 376 E Jackson Blvd. I-26, exit 38 (Boones Creek Rd), Jct US 32 and SR 81. Int corridors. **Pets:** Accepted.
(ASK) (S🄳) ⊠ 🔲 🔲 🛢 🔲 ⊷

KIMBALL

◆◆◆ ▼◆ **Country Hearth Inn & Suites** M
(423) 837-7185. **$45-$85.** 395 Main St. I-24, exit 152, 0.5 mi n. Ext corridors. **Pets:** Dogs only. $5 one-time fee/pet. Designated rooms, supervision.
(ASK) (S🄳) ⊠ 🛢 ⊷

KINGSPORT

▼▼▼▼ **Jameson Inn** SH
(423) 230-0534. **$54-$104.** 3004 Bay Meadow Pl. I-181, exit 51 westbound; exit 51B eastbound, just n on SR 93. Int corridors. **Pets:** Small. $10 daily fee/pet. Service with restrictions, crate.
(ASK) ⊠ 🔲 🛢 🔲 ⊷

▼▼▼▼ **La Quinta Inn Kingsport** SH
(423) 323-0500. **$95-$115.** 10150 Airport Pkwy. I-81, exit 63, just e. Int corridors. **Pets:** Medium. Service with restrictions.
(ASK) ⊠ (&M) 🌮 🔲 🛢 🔲 ⊷

▼◆▼ **Sleep Inn** SH
(423) 279-1811. **$59-$75.** 200 Hospitality Pl. I-81, exit 63, just s. Int corridors. **Pets:** Other species. Service with restrictions, supervision.
(ASK) (S🄳) ⊠ 🔲 🛢 🔲

KINGSTON

◆◆◆ ▼◆▼ **Comfort Inn of Kingston** M
(865) 376-4965. **$60-$90, 14 day notice.** 905 N Kentucky St. I-40, exit 352, 0.3 mi s. Ext corridors. **Pets:** Medium. $10 daily fee/pet. Designated rooms, service with restrictions, supervision.
(SAVE) ⊠ 🛢 🔲

◆◆◆ ▼◆▼ **Days Inn** M
(865) 376-2069. **$70-$100.** 495 Gallaher Rd. I-40, exit 356, just n. Ext corridors. **Pets:** Medium. $10 daily fee/pet. Service with restrictions, supervision.
(SAVE) (S🄳) ⊠ 🌮 🛢 ⊷

KINGSTON SPRINGS

◆◆◆ ▼◆▼ **Best Western Harpeth Inn** SH
(615) 952-3961. **$55-$85.** 116 Luy Ben Hills Rd. I-40, exit 188, just n. Ext corridors. **Pets:** Accepted.
(SAVE) (S🄳) ⊠ 🌮 🔲 🛢 🔲 ⊷

KNOXVILLE

▼◆▼ **Best Western West** M
(865) 675-7666. **$65-$99.** 500 Lovell Rd. I-40, exit 374 (Lovell Rd). Ext corridors. **Pets:** $10 daily fee/room. Service with restrictions.
(ASK) (S🄳) ⊠ (&M) 🌮 🔲 🛢 🔲 ⊷

▼▼ **Budget Inn** SH
(865) 688-1010. **$60-$95.** 5334 Central Ave Pike. I-75, exit 108 (Merchant Dr), just e. Ext corridors. **Pets:** Accepted.
(ASK) (S🄳) ⊠ 🌮 🔲 ⊷

▼▼ **Candlewood Suites-Knoxville** SH
(865) 777-0400. **$89-$119.** 10206 Parkside Dr. I-40/75, exit 374 (Lovell Rd), 0.5 mi s, then 1 mi e. Int corridors. **Pets:** Small. $150 one-time fee/room. Designated rooms, service with restrictions, crate.
(ASK) (S🄳) ⊠ (&M) 🔲 🛢 🔲

◆◆◆ ▼◆▼▼ **The Clarion Inn** SH
(865) 687-8989. **$80-$100.** 5634 Merchants Center Blvd. I-75, exit 108 (Merchants Dr), just w, then just n. Int corridors. **Pets:** Accepted.
(SAVE) (S🄳) ⊠ (&M) 🌮 🔲 🛢 🔲 ⊷

▼▼ **ClubHouse Inn & Suites Knoxville** SH
(865) 531-1900. **$79-$149.** 208 Market Place Ln. I-40/75, exit 378 (Cedar Bluff Rd), just s to N Peters Rd, then just w. Int corridors. **Pets:** Accepted.
(ASK) (S🄳) ⊠ (&M) 🌮 🔲 🛢 🔲 📺 ⊷

▼▼▼ Crowne Plaza Knoxville SH ❀
(865) 522-2600. **$129-$159.** 401 W Summit Hill Dr. Corner of Walnut St; downtown. Int corridors. **Pets:** Other species. $25 one-time fee/room. Service with restrictions.

🗛🅂🗶🛳🎵🐾📶📠📺🍴🏊

▼▼▼ Days Inn East M
(865) 637-3511. **$50-$129.** 5423 Asheville Hwy. I-40, exit 394 (Asheville Hwy). Ext corridors. **Pets:** Other species. $30 one-time fee/room. Designated rooms, service with restrictions, supervision.

🗛🅂🗶🎵🐾🏊🗶

▲▲ ▼▼▼ Econo Lodge-North SH
(865) 687-5680. **$55-$95.** 5505 Merchants Center Blvd. I-75, exit 108 (Merchant Dr), just w, then just n. Ext corridors. **Pets:** Accepted.

🗛🅂🗶🐾

▲▲ ▼ Econo Lodge West M
(865) 693-1011. **$45-$99.** 9240 Park West Blvd. I-40/75, exit 378 (Cedar Bluff Rd), just n to Park West Blvd, then just w. Ext corridors. **Pets:** Medium. $10 daily fee/pet. Designated rooms, service with restrictions, supervision.

🗛🅂🗶🐾📶📺🏊

▼▼ Extended StayAmerica Knoxville-Cedar Bluff M
(865) 769-0822. **$51-$65.** 214 Langley Pl. I-40, exit 378 (Cedar Bluff), just s, then 1 mi w on N Peters Rd. Ext corridors. **Pets:** Accepted.

🗛🅂🗶🐾🏊📶📺

▼▼ Extended StayAmerica Knoxville-West Hills SH
(865) 694-4178. **$65-$75.** 1700 Winston Rd. I-40, exit 380 (West Hills), just w on Kingston Pike, then just s. Int corridors. **Pets:** Accepted.

🗛🅂🗶📶📺🏊

▼▼▼ Hampton Inn North SH
(865) 689-1011. **$74-$144.** 117 Cedar Ln. I-75, exit 108 (Merchant Dr), just e. Ext corridors. **Pets:** Small, other species. Designated rooms, no service, supervision.

🗛🅂🗶🐾📶📺🏊

▲▲ ▼▼▼ Holiday Inn-Central/Papermill Road LH
(865) 584-3911. **$109-$122.** 1315 Kirby Rd. I-40/75, exit 383 (Papermill Rd), 0.5 mi e. Int corridors. **Pets:** Accepted.

🗛🅂🗶🐾🎵🐾📶📺🍴🏊

▲▲ ▼▼▼ Holiday Inn Select-Cedar Bluff LH
(865) 693-1011. **$129.** 304 Cedar Bluff Rd. I-40/75, exit 378 (Cedar Bluff Rd) eastbound; exit 378B westbound, just n to Executive Park Dr. Int corridors. **Pets:** Large, other species. $50 one-time fee/room. Designated rooms, service with restrictions, supervision.

🗛🗶🎵🐾📶📺🍴🏊🗶

▼▼▼ Homewood Suites by Hilton SH
(865) 777-0375. **$119-$279, 3 day notice.** 10935 Turkey Dr. I-40, exit 374 (Lovell Rd), just s to Parkside Dr, then 0.5 mi n on Snow Goose. Int corridors. **Pets:** Accepted.

🗛🗶📶📺🏊🗶

▼▼ La Quinta Inn Knoxville (West) SH ❀
(865) 690-9777. **$91-$111.** 258 Peters Rd N. I-40, exit 378 (Cedar Bluff Rd), just s, then just e. Ext corridors. **Pets:** Medium. Service with restrictions, crate.

🗛🗶🐾🎵📶📺🏊

▼ Motel 6-1252 M
(865) 675-7200. **$41-$53.** 402 Lovell Rd. I-40/75, exit 374 (Lovell Rd), just s. Ext corridors. **Pets:** Medium, other species. Service with restrictions, supervision.

🅂🗶🐾🎵🐾🏊

▼▼▼ Motel 6-Knoxville East M
(865) 633-6646. **Call for rates.** 1550 Cracker Barrel Ln. I-40, exit 398 (Strawberry Plains), just s. Int corridors. **Pets:** Medium, other species. Service with restrictions, supervision.

🗶🐾🐾🏊

▲▲ ▼▼▼ Quality Inn North SH
(865) 689-6600. **$49-$89.** 6712 Central Ave Pike. I-75, exit 110 (Callahan Dr), just e. Ext/int corridors. **Pets:** Accepted.

🖫🗶📶📺🏊

▼▼ Red Roof Inn-West M
(865) 691-1664. **$55-$70.** 209 Advantage Pl. I-40/75, exit 378 (Cedar Bluff Rd), just s to N Peters Rd, then w. Ext corridors. **Pets:** Medium, other species. Service with restrictions, supervision.

🗶🐾🎵🐾📶

▼▼▼ Super 8 East M
(865) 524-0855. **$39-$99, 3 day notice.** 7585 Crosswood Blvd. I-40, exit 398 (Strawberry Plains), just n, then w. Ext corridors. **Pets:** Small. $25 daily fee/pet. Service with restrictions, supervision.

🗛🅂🗶🐾📶📺

▼▼▼ Super 8 Motel-Knoxville SH
(865) 584-8511. **$49-$99.** 6200 Papermill Rd. I-40/75, exit 383 (Papermill Rd), 0.3 mi e. Ext corridors. **Pets:** $6 one-time fee/pet. Service with restrictions, supervision.

🗛🅂🗶🐾🎵📶📺🏊

LAKE CITY

▼▼▼ Days Inn M
(865) 426-2816. **$77-$87.** 221 Colonial Ln. I-75, exit 129, just w. Ext corridors. **Pets:** Medium. $10 daily fee/pet. Service with restrictions, supervision.

🗛🅂🗶🐾📶📺🏊

LAWRENCEBURG

▼▼▼ Best Western Villa Inn SH
(931) 762-4448. **$73-$104.** 2126 N Locust Ave. On US 43, 2.2 mi n of jct US 64. Ext corridors. **Pets:** Medium. $10 daily fee/pet. Designated rooms, service with restrictions, supervision.

🗶📶📺🏊

LEBANON

▲▲ ▼▼▼ Americas Best Value Inn & Suites M
(615) 449-5781. **$45-$100.** 822 S Cumberland St. I-40, exit 238, just n. Ext corridors. **Pets:** Very small. $12 daily fee/pet. Designated rooms, service with restrictions, supervision.

🖫🅂🗶📶📺🏊

▼▼▼ Comfort Inn M
(615) 444-1001. **$49-$89.** 829 S Cumberland St. I-40, exit 238, just n. Ext corridors. **Pets:** Other species. $5 one-time fee/pet. Designated rooms, service with restrictions, supervision.

🗛🅂🗶📶📺🏊

▼▼▼ Days Inn M
(615) 444-5635. **$55-$60.** 914 Murfreesboro Rd. I-40, exit 238, just n. Ext corridors. **Pets:** $5 one-time fee/room. Service with restrictions, supervision.

🗛🅂🗶📶🏊

▼▼▼ Executive Inn M
(615) 444-0505. **$59-$129.** 631 S Cumberland St. I-40, exit 238, 0.5 mi n. Ext/int corridors. **Pets:** Accepted.

🗛🅂🗶🐾📶📺🏊

▼▼▼ Hampton Inn M
(615) 444-7400. **$69-$77.** 704 S Cumberland St. I-40, exit 238, just n. Ext corridors. **Pets:** Designated rooms, service with restrictions, supervision.

🗛🅂🗶🐾🎵📶📺🏊

▼▼▼ Super 8 Motel M
(615) 444-5637. **$55-$60.** 914 Murfreesboro Rd. I-40, exit 238, just s. Ext corridors. **Pets:** $5 one-time fee/room. Service with restrictions, supervision.

🗛🅂🗶📶🏊

LENOIR CITY

AAA ◆◆◆ **Days Inn** SH
(865) 986-2011. **$60-$95.** 1110 Hwy 321 N. I-75, exit 81, just e. Ext corridors. **Pets:** Small. $10 daily fee/pet. Service with restrictions, supervision.

[SAVE] [SÓ] [✕] [🖥] [≈]

AAA ◆◆◆ **Econo Lodge** SH
(865) 986-0295. **$49-$91.** 1211 Hwy 321 N. I-75, exit 81, just w. Ext corridors. **Pets:** Medium. $6 daily fee/pet. Service with restrictions, supervision.

[SAVE] [SÓ] [✕] [🖉] [🖥] [≈]

LEWISBURG

◆◆ **A Richland Inn Hotel** SH
(931) 359-1800. **$80-$90.** 723 E Commerce St. Jct US 431 and 31A, just w; just e of town. Ext corridors. **Pets:** Accepted.

[ASK] [SÓ] [✕] [🖉] [🖥] [🖥]

LEXINGTON

◆ **Econo Lodge** SH
(731) 968-0171. **$55-$60.** 732 W Church St. Jct of US 412 and SR 104, just w. Ext corridors. **Pets:** Accepted.

[ASK] [SÓ] [✕] [🖥] [≈]

LOUDON

AAA ◆◆◆ **Americas Best Value Inn** M
(865) 458-5855. **$50-$60.** 15100 Hwy 72. I-75, exit 72, just w. Ext corridors. **Pets:** Medium. $7 daily fee/pet. Service with restrictions, supervision.

[SAVE] [SÓ] [✕] [🖥] [≈]

MANCHESTER

◆◆ **Ambassador Inn** SH ❀
(931) 728-2200. **$49-$68.** 925 Interstate Dr. I-24, exit 110, just n. Ext/int corridors. **Pets:** Small. Designated rooms, service with restrictions, supervision.

[ASK] [SÓ] [✕] [🖥] [🖥] [≈]

◆◆◆ **Country Inn & Suites By Carlson** SH
(931) 728-7551. **$85.** 126 Expressway Dr. I-24, exit 114, just w. Int corridors. **Pets:** Accepted.

[ASK] [SÓ] [✕] [🖉M] [🖉] [🖥] [🖥] [≈]

AAA ◆◆◆ **Days Inn & Suites** M
(931) 728-9530. **$65.** 2259 Hillsboro Blvd. I-24, exit 114, just w. Ext corridors. **Pets:** Medium, dogs only. $10 daily fee/pet. Service with restrictions, supervision.

[SAVE] [SÓ] [✕] [🖉M] [🖉] [🖥] [🖥] [≈]

◆◆ **Economy Inn** M
(931) 728-6023. **$45-$75.** 890 Interstate Dr. I-24, exit 110, just n. Ext corridors. **Pets:** Accepted.

[ASK] [SÓ] [✕] [🖥] [≈]

AAA ◆◆◆ **Ramada Limited** SH
(931) 728-0800. **$59-$109.** 2314 Hillsboro Blvd. I-24, exit 114, just n. Ext corridors. **Pets:** Medium. $10 one-time fee/pet. Designated rooms, service with restrictions, supervision.

[SAVE] [SÓ] [✕] [🖥] [🖥] [≈]

◆◆◆ **Super 8 Motel** M
(931) 728-9720. **Call for rates.** 2430 Hillsboro Blvd. I-24, exit 114, just n. Ext corridors. **Pets:** Accepted.

[ASK] [✕] [🖥] [≈]

MARTIN

AAA ◆◆◆ **Days Inn** SH
(731) 587-9577. **$63-$199.** 800 University St. Jct US 431 and 43 Bypass. Ext corridors. **Pets:** Medium. $10 daily fee/pet. Designated rooms, no service, supervision.

[SAVE] [SÓ] [✕] [🖥] [🖥] [≈]

MCMINNVILLE

AAA ◆◆◆ **Best Western Tree City Inn** SH
(931) 473-2159. **$75-$99.** 809 Sparta Hwy. Jct US 70 S Bypass and Red Rd, 1 mi s, follow signs. Ext corridors. **Pets:** Dogs only. $10 one-time fee/pet. Service with restrictions, supervision.

[SAVE] [SÓ] [✕] [🖥] [🖥] [≈]

◆◆ **McMinnville Inn** M
(931) 473-7338. **$49-$79.** 2545 Sparta Hwy. I-24, exit 111, n on SR 55 to US 70 S Bypass. Ext corridors. **Pets:** Accepted.

[ASK] [SÓ] [✕] [🖥] [🖥] [≈]

MEMPHIS METROPOLITAN AREA

COLLIERVILLE

◆◆◆◆ **Hampton Inn Collierville** SH
(901) 854-9400. **$89-$249.** 1280 W Poplar Ave. 0.9 mi w of jct CR 175 on US 72. Int corridors. **Pets:** Accepted.

[ASK] [SÓ] [✕] [🖉M] [🖉] [🖉] [🖥] [🖥] [≈]

◆◆ **Plantation Hotel** SH
(901) 853-1235. **$52-$105.** 1230 W Poplar Ave. 2.5 mi w on SR 57 and US 72. Ext corridors. **Pets:** Accepted.

[ASK] [SÓ] [✕] [🖉] [🖥] [🖥] [≈]

CORDOVA

AAA ◆◆◆◆ **Comfort Suites** SH
(901) 213-3600. **$99-$139.** 2427 N Germantown Pkwy. I-40, exit 16, just s. Int corridors. **Pets:** Accepted.

[SAVE] [SÓ] [✕] [🖉M] [🖉] [🖉] [🖥] [🖥] [≈]

AAA ◆◆◆◆ **Quality Suites-Wolfchase** SH
(901) 386-4600. **$89.** 8166 Varnavas Dr. I-40, exit 16, 0.3 mi s on Germantown Pkwy, then e. Int corridors. **Pets:** Designated rooms, service with restrictions, supervision.

[SAVE] [SÓ] [✕] [🖉] [🖥] [🖥] [≈]

◆◆ **StudioPLUS-Cordova** SH
(901) 754-4030. **Call for rates.** 8110 Cordova Centre Dr. I-40, exit 16, 0.8 mi s. Int corridors. **Pets:** Accepted.

[🖉M] [🖉] [🖥] [🖥] [≈]

COVINGTON

◆◆ **Best Western Inn** SH
(901) 476-8561. **$55-$65.** 873 Hwy 51 N. 0.8 mi n of jct US 59 W. Ext corridors. **Pets:** Accepted.

[✕] [🖉] [🖥] [🖥] [≈]

◆◆ **Comfort Inn** SH
(901) 475-0380. **$75-$100.** 901 Hwy 51 N. 1 mi n of jct US 59. Ext corridors. **Pets:** Accepted.

[ASK] [SÓ] [✕] [🖥] [🖥] [≈]

GERMANTOWN

◆◆ **Comfort Inn & Suites-Germantown** SH
(901) 757-7800. **$79, 5 day notice.** 7787 Wolf River Blvd. I-40, exit 16, 5 mi s on Germantown Pkwy. Int corridors. **Pets:** Accepted.

[ASK] [SÓ] [✕] [🖉M] [🖉] [🖥] [🖥] [≈]

AAA ▼▼▼▼ Homewood Suites by Hilton-Germantown SH
(901) 751-2500. **$109-$139.** 7855 Wolf River Blvd. I-40, exit 16, 5.8 mi s on CR 177; at Germantown Pkwy and Wolf River Blvd. Int corridors. **Pets:** Medium, dogs only. $50 one-time fee/room. Service with restrictions, crate.

SAVE ✕ ⟨⟩ ❚ ▯ ⌣

▼▼▼▼ Residence Inn SH
(901) 751-2500. **$99-$159.** 9314 Poplar Pike. I-240, exit 15 (Poplar Ave), 7 mi e. Int corridors. **Pets:** Accepted.

ASK ✕ ⟨M⟩ ⟨⟩ ⟨⟩ ❚ ▯ ⌣ ✕

LAKELAND

AAA ▼▼▼ Super 8 Motel SH
(901) 372-4575. **$72-$89.** 9779 Huff Puff Rd. I-40, exit 20. Ext corridors. **Pets:** Small, dogs only. $10 daily fee/pet. Designated rooms, no service, supervision.

SAVE ⟨⟩ ✕ ❚ ⌣

MEMPHIS

▼▼▼▼ Baymont Inn & Suites Memphis East SH
(901) 377-2233. **$68-$110.** 6020 Shelby Oaks Dr. I-40, exit 12, just n. Int corridors. **Pets:** Medium. Service with restrictions.

ASK ✕ ⟨⟩ ❚ ▯ ⌣

AAA ▼▼▼▼ Comfort Suites Thousand Oaks East Memphis SH
(901) 365-2575. **$65-$80.** 2575 Thousand Oaks Cove. I-240, exit 18. Int corridors. **Pets:** Medium. $25 one-time fee/pet. Designated rooms, service with restrictions, crate.

SAVE ⟨⟩ ✕ ⟨M⟩ ⟨⟩ ⟨⟩ ❚ ▯ ⌣

▼▼▼▼ Drury Inn & Suites-Memphis Northeast SH
(901) 373-8200. **$80-$115.** 1556 Sycamore View. I-40, exit 12, just n. Int corridors. **Pets:** Large, other species. Service with restrictions, supervision.

ASK ✕ ⟨⟩ ⟨⟩ ❚ ▯ ⌣ ✕

▼▼▼ Econo Lodge Inn & Suites M
(901) 396-1000. **Call for rates.** 2745 Airways Blvd. I-240, exit 23B (Airways Blvds), just s. Ext corridors. **Pets:** Accepted.

ASK ⟨⟩ ✕ ❚ ▯ ⌣

▼▼▼▼ Embassy Suites SH
(901) 684-1777. **$99-$219.** 1022 S Shady Grove Rd. I-240, exit 15 (Poplar Ave E), 0.5 mi e, then n. Int corridors. **Pets:** Accepted.

✕ ⟨M⟩ ⟨⟩ ⟨⟩ ❚ ▯ ⟨⟩ ⌣ ✕

▼▼▼ Extended StayAmerica-Sycamore View SH
(901) 386-0026. **Call for rates.** 5885 Shelby Oaks Dr. I-40, exit 12, 0.3 mi n, then just w. Ext corridors. **Pets:** Accepted.

✕ ⟨⟩ ⟨⟩ ❚ ▯

▼▼▼ Extended Stay Deluxe Memphis-Wolfchase Galleria SH
(901) 380-1525. **$85-$90.** 2520 Horizon Lake Dr. I-40, exit 16B, just n, then just w. Int corridors. **Pets:** Accepted.

ASK ⟨⟩ ✕ ⟨⟩ ⟨⟩ ❚ ▯ ⌣

▼▼▼ Holiday Inn Select Memphis Airport LH
(901) 332-1130. **$109-$139.** 2240 Democrat Rd. I-240, exit 23B (Airways Blvd S), just s to Democrat Rd, then just w. Int corridors. **Pets:** Small. $35 one-time fee/pet. Designated rooms, service with restrictions, supervision.

ASK ⟨⟩ ✕ ⟨M⟩ ⟨⟩ ⟨⟩ ❚ ▯ ⟨⟩ ⌣ ✕

▼▼▼ Holiday Inn-University of Memphis SH
(901) 678-8200. **$129.** 3700 Central Ave. I-240, exit 20, 2 mi n on Getwell Rd, just e on Park, 1 mi n on Goodlett, then 0.7 mi w; follow signs to University. Int corridors. **Pets:** Small. $75 one-time fee/room. Service with restrictions, supervision.

ASK ✕ ⟨M⟩ ⟨⟩ ⟨⟩ ❚ ▯

▼▼▼ Homestead Studio Suites Hotel-Memphis/Airport SH
(901) 344-0010. **$57-$81.** 2541 Corporate Ave E. I-240, exit 23B (Airways Blvd S), just s to Democrat Rd, just w to Nonconnah Blvd, then 0.4 mi n to Corporate Ave, follow signs. Int corridors. **Pets:** Accepted.

ASK ⟨⟩ ✕ ⟨M⟩ ⟨⟩ ⟨⟩ ❚ ▯

▼▼▼ Homestead Studio Suites Hotel-Memphis/Poplar Ave SH
(901) 767-5522. **$62-$85.** 6500 Poplar Ave. I-240, exit 15 (Poplar Ave), 1 mi e. Int corridors. **Pets:** Accepted.

ASK ⟨⟩ ✕ ⟨M⟩ ⟨⟩ ⟨⟩ ❚ ▯

▼▼▼ Homewood Suites SH
(901) 763-0500. **$159-$189.** 5811 Poplar Ave. I-240, exit 15 (Poplar Ave). Ext/int corridors. **Pets:** Small, dogs only. $100 one-time fee/room. Service with restrictions.

ASK ✕ ❚ ▯ ⌣

▼▼▼ Homewood Suites by Hilton SH
(901) 758-5018. **$119-$199.** 3583 Hacks Cross Rd. I-240, exit 16, 4 mi e on SR 385, then 1 mi n. Int corridors. **Pets:** Accepted.

ASK ⟨⟩ ✕ ⟨M⟩ ⟨⟩ ❚ ▯ ⌣

▼▼▼ La Quinta Inn & Suites Memphis (Primacy Parkway) SH
(901) 374-0330. **$99-$129.** 1236 Primacy Pkwy. I-240, exit 15 (Poplar Ave), 0.3 mi e, s on Ridgeway, just w, then just s. Int corridors. **Pets:** Medium. Service with restrictions.

ASK ✕ ⟨M⟩ ⟨⟩ ⟨⟩ ❚ ▯ ⌣

AAA ▼▼▼▼ La Quinta Inn & Suites Sycamore View-Memphis SH
(901) 381-0044. **$105-$140.** 6069 Macon Cove. I-40, exit 12, just s. Int corridors. **Pets:** Small. Designated rooms, service with restrictions, supervision.

SAVE ⟨⟩ ✕ ⟨M⟩ ⟨⟩ ⟨⟩ ❚ ▯ ⌣

AAA ▼▼▼ Marriott Residence Inn SH
(901) 685-9595. **$99-$189.** 6141 Old Poplar Pike. I-240, exit 15 (Poplar Ave), 0.5 mi e. Ext/int corridors. **Pets:** Accepted.

SAVE ⟨⟩ ✕ ⟨M⟩ ⟨⟩ ⟨⟩ ❚ ▯ ⌣

AAA ▼▼▼ Quality Inn SH
(901) 382-2323. **$70-$150.** 6068 Macon Cove Rd. I-40, exit 12, just s. Ext/int corridors. **Pets:** Medium, other species. $10 daily fee/pet. Service with restrictions, supervision.

SAVE ⟨⟩ ✕ ⟨M⟩ ❚ ▯ ⌣

AAA ▼▼▼ Quality Inn Airport/Graceland SH
(901) 345-3344. **$69-$139.** 1581 E Brooks Rd. I-55, exit 5A (Brooks Rd), 0.3 mi e. Ext corridors. **Pets:** Other species. $10 daily fee/room. Service with restrictions, supervision.

SAVE ⟨⟩ ✕ ❚ ▯ ⌣

▼▼▼ Radisson Inn Memphis Airport LH
(901) 332-2370. **$109-$139.** 2411 Winchester Rd. I-240, exit 23B (Airways Blvd S), 2.3 mi se, follow signs to Memphis International Airport. Ext/int corridors. **Pets:** Accepted.

ASK ⟨⟩ ✕ ⟨⟩ ❚ ▯ ⟨⟩ ⌣

▼▼▼ Red Roof Inn-East SH
(901) 388-6111. **$48-$64.** 6055 Shelby Oaks Dr. I-40, exit 12, just n. Ext corridors. **Pets:** Medium, other species. Service with restrictions, supervision.

✕ ❚ ▯

▼▼▼▼ Residence Inn by Marriott Memphis Downtown SH
(901) 578-3700. **$229.** 110 Monroe Ave. I-40, exit 1; I-55, exit Riverside Dr, 0.6 mi s, then just e. Int corridors. **Pets:** Medium, other species. $100 one-time fee/room. Service with restrictions, crate.

ASK ⟨⟩ ✕ ⟨M⟩ ⟨⟩ ⟨⟩ ▯ ✕

▼▼▼▼ **Staybridge Suites** 🆂🅷
(901) 682-1722. **$89-$139, 30 day notice.** 1070 Ridge Lake Blvd. I-240, exit 15 (Poplar Ave), just e, then n under overpass. Int corridors. **Pets:** Accepted.

Ⓐ🆂🅺 ⊗ ⛹️ ⟲ 🌊 🍴 ▦ ▤ ⇌ ⊗

MILLINGTON

▼▼ ◆◆ **Admiralty of Plantation Oaks** 🆂🅷
(901) 872-8000. **$99.** 6656 Hwy 51 N. On US 51, 2 mi s. Ext/int corridors. **Pets:** Accepted.

Ⓐ🆂🅺 🆂🅱 ⊗ 🖥️ ▦ ⇌

END METROPOLITAN AREA

MONTEAGLE

▼▼▼▼ **Best Western Smoke House Lodge** 🆂🅷
(931) 924-2091. **$70-$90.** 850 W Main St. I-24, exit 134, just s. Ext corridors. **Pets:** Medium, other species. $15 one-time fee/pet. Designated rooms, service with restrictions, crate.

Ⓐ🆂🅺 🆂🅱 ⊗ ⟲ 🌊 ▦ 🖥️ 🍴 ⇌ ⊗

▼▼▼▼ **Edgeworth Inn** 🅱🅱 🌸
(931) 924-4000. **$125-$225, 14 day notice.** Monteagle Assembly, Cottage 23. I-24, exit 134, 0.4 mi e on US 41A, 2nd left through assembly gates, follow signs. Ext/int corridors. **Pets:** Medium, other species. $25 deposit/pet. Designated rooms, no service.

Ⓐ🆂🅺 🆂🅱 ⊗ ▦ 🖥️ ▨

MORRISTOWN

⒜⒜⒜ ▼▼▼ **Days Inn** 🅼
(423) 587-2200. **$45-$65.** 2512 E Andrew Johnson Hwy. I-81, exit 8, 6 mi n on US 25 E to exit 2B (Greenville-Morristown), then just w. Ext corridors. **Pets:** Small, dogs only. $10 one-time fee/pet. Designated rooms, service with restrictions, supervision.

🆂🅰🆅🅴 🆂🅱 ⊗ 🌊 ▦ 🖥️ ⇌

⒜⒜⒜ ▼▼▼▼ **Holiday Inn Morristown Conference Center** 🆂🅷
(423) 587-2400. **$87-$210.** 5435 S Davy Crockett Pkwy. I-81, exit 8, just n. Int corridors. **Pets:** Medium, other species. $25 one-time fee/room. Designated rooms, service with restrictions, supervision.

🆂🅰🆅🅴 ⊗ ▦ 🖥️ 🍴 ⇌

▼▼▼ **Super 8 Motel** 🅼
(423) 318-8888. **$45-$60.** 5400 S Davy Crockett Pkwy. I-81, exit 8, just n. Int corridors. **Pets:** Small. $9 one-time fee/pet. Service with restrictions, supervision.

Ⓐ🆂🅺 🆂🅱 ⊗ ⛹️ 🌊 ▦ 🖥️

MOUNT JULIET

⒜⒜⒜ ▼▼▼ **Quality Inn & Suites** 🆂🅷
(615) 773-3600. **$55-$99.** 1000 Hershel Dr. I-40, exit 226. Int corridors. **Pets:** Small, other species. $25 one-time fee/room. No service, supervision.

🆂🅰🆅🅴 🆂🅱 ⊗ ▦ 🖥️ ⇌

MURFREESBORO

▼▼ ▼▼ **Best Western Chaffin Inn** 🅼
(615) 895-3818. **$58-$89, 8 day notice.** 168 Chaffin Pl. I-24, exit 78B. Ext corridors. **Pets:** Small. $12 daily fee/pet. Designated rooms, service with restrictions, supervision.

Ⓐ🆂🅺 🆂🅱 ⊗ ⛹️ ▦ 🖥️ ⇌

▼▼▼▼ **DoubleTree Hotel Murfreesboro** 🆂🅷
(615) 895-5555. **$79-$159.** 1850 Old Fort Pkwy. I-24, exit 78B. Int corridors. **Pets:** Small. $50 one-time fee/room. Designated rooms, service with restrictions, supervision.

🆂🅱 ⊗ ⟲ ⛹️ ▦ 🖥️ 🍴 ⇌

▼▼▼ **Hampton Inn** 🅼
(615) 896-1172. **$69-$159.** 2230 Armory Dr. I-24, exit 78B, just n. Ext corridors. **Pets:** Accepted.

Ⓐ🆂🅺 🆂🅱 ⊗ 🌊 ⟲ ▦ 🖥️ ⇌

⒜⒜⒜ ▼▼▼ **Howard Johnson Express Inn** 🆂🅷
(615) 896-5522. **$55-$99.** 2424 S Church St. I-24, exit 81A eastbound; exit 81 westbound. Int corridors. **Pets:** Small. $10 daily fee/pet. Service with restrictions, supervision.

🆂🅰🆅🅴 🆂🅱 ⊗ ▦ 🖥️ 🍴 ⇌

⒜⒜⒜ ▼▼▼▼ **Quality Inn Murfreesboro** 🆂🅷
(615) 890-1006. **$75-$130.** 2135 S Church St. I-24, exit 81 westbound; exit 81B eastbound. Int corridors. **Pets:** $10 one-time fee/room. Service with restrictions, supervision.

🆂🅰🆅🅴 🆂🅱 ⊗ ▦ 🖥️ ⇌

⒜⒜⒜ ▼▼▼ **Ramada Limited** 🆂🅷 🐾
(615) 896-5080. **$60-$100.** 1855 S Church St. I-24, exit 81. Int corridors. **Pets:** Other species. $10 daily fee/pet. Service with restrictions, supervision.

🆂🅰🆅🅴 🆂🅱 ⊗ ▦ 🖥️ ⇌

⒜⒜⒜ ▼▼▼ **Vista Inn and Suites** 🆂🅷
(615) 848-9030. **$50-$99.** 118 Westgate Blvd. I-24, exit 81A eastbound; exit 81 westbound. Int corridors. **Pets:** Small. $10 daily fee/pet. Service with restrictions, supervision.

🆂🅰🆅🅴 🆂🅱 ⊗ ▦ 🖥️ ⇌

NASHVILLE METROPOLITAN AREA

ANTIOCH

⒜⒜⒜ ▼▼▼▼ **Holiday Inn-The Crossings** 🆂🅷 🌸
(615) 731-2361. **$89-$105.** 201 Crossings Pl. I-24, exit 60, 0.5 mi e. Int corridors. **Pets:** Other species. Service with restrictions, crate.

🆂🅰🆅🅴 🆂🅱 ⊗ 🌊 ⟲ ⛹️ ▦ 🖥️ 🍴 ⇌

GOODLETTSVILLE

⒜⒜⒜ ▼▼▼ **Best Western Fairwinds Inn** 🆂🅷
(615) 851-1067. **$54-$83.** 100 Northcreek Blvd. I-65, exit 97 (Long Hollow Pike), 0.5 mi e. Ext corridors. **Pets:** Small. $10 daily fee/pet. Service with restrictions, supervision.

🆂🅰🆅🅴 🆂🅱 ⊗ ▦ 🖥️ ⇌

▼▼▼ **Days Inn Business Place** 🆂🅷
(615) 851-6600. **Call for rates (no credit cards).** 909 Conference Dr. I-65, exit 97, 0.5 mi e to Conference Dr, then 0.6 mi s. Ext corridors. **Pets:** Accepted.

⊗ 🌊 ▦ 🖥️ ⇌

⒜⒜⒜ ▼▼▼▼ **Holiday Inn Express Hotel & Suites** 🆂🅷
(615) 851-1891. **$99-$189.** 120 Cartwright St. I-65, exit 97 (Long Hollow Pike), just w. Int corridors. **Pets:** Small. $25 one-time fee/pet. Designated rooms, service with restrictions, supervision.

🆂🅰🆅🅴 🆂🅱 ⊗ 🌊 ⟲ ⛹️ ▦ 🖥️ ⇌

▼▼ ▼▼ **Red Roof Inn-Nashville North** 🆂🅷
(615) 859-2537. **$45-$60.** 110 Northgate Dr. I-65, exit 97 (Long Hollow Pike), 0.5 mi e. Ext corridors. **Pets:** Medium, other species. Service with restrictions, supervision.

⊗ 🌊 ⟲

HERMITAGE

 Motel 6 🆂🅷
(615) 889-5060. **$55-$70.** 5768 Old Hickory Blvd. I-40, exit 221 westbound; exit 221B eastbound, just n. Ext corridors. **Pets:** Medium, other species. Service with restrictions, supervision.
A$K 🆂 🗙 🐾 🛏 💻 🏊

NASHVILLE

◈◈ Baymont Inn & Suites Nashville-West 🆂🅷
(615) 353-0700. **$75-$90.** 5612 Lenox Ave. I-40, exit 204. Int corridors. **Pets:** Accepted.
A$K 🆂 🗙 🛏 💻 🏊

◈ Best Western Airport Inn 🆂🅷
(615) 889-9199. **$49-$95.** 701 Stewarts Ferry Pike. I-40, exit 219 (Stewarts Ferry Pike). Ext corridors. **Pets:** Accepted.
SAVE 🆂 🗙 🛏 💻 🏊

◈ Best Western Music Row 🆂🅷
(615) 242-1631. **$60-$170.** 1407 Division St. I-40, exit 209B, just w around circle, then just e. Int corridors. **Pets:** Very small. $10 daily fee/pet. Service with restrictions.
SAVE 🆂 🗙 🛏 💻 🏊

◈ ClubHouse Inn & Suites 🆂🅷
(615) 883-0500. **$69-$129.** 2435 Atrium Way. Briley Pkwy to exit 7 (Elm Hill Pike), just e. Int corridors. **Pets:** Accepted.
SAVE 🆂 🗙 🛏 💻 🏊

◈ Comfort Inn Music City 🆂🅷
(615) 226-3300. **$59-$99.** 2407 Brick Church Pike. I-65, exit 87. Int corridors. **Pets:** Accepted.
SAVE 🆂 🗙 🛏 💻 🏊

◈ Comfort Inn Opryland 🆂🅷
(615) 889-0086. **$74-$103.** 2516 Music Valley Dr. I-40, exit 215 (Briley Pkwy), 4 mi n; I-65, exit 90, exit McGavock Pike off Briley Pkwy. Int corridors. **Pets:** Accepted.
SAVE 🆂 🗙 💻 🏊

◈◈ Crossland Studios Nashville 🆂🅷
(615) 366-0559. **Call for rates.** 1210 Murfreesboro Rd. I-40, exit 215 (Briley Pkwy), 2 mi s to exit 4, then 0.8 mi n. Ext corridors. **Pets:** Accepted.
🗙 🐾 💻

◈◈ Drury Inn & Suites-Nashville Airport 🆂🅷
(615) 902-0400. **$70-$140.** 555 Donelson Pike. I-40, exit 216 (Donelson Pike). Int corridors. **Pets:** Large, other species. Service with restrictions, supervision.
A$K 🗙 🛏 💻 🏊

◈ Days Inn 🆂🅷
(615) 889-0090. **$55-$95.** 2460 Music Valley Dr. I-40, exit 215B (Briley Pkwy), 4 mi n to exit 11 (McGavock Pike). Int corridors. **Pets:** Accepted.
SAVE 🆂 🗙 🛏 🏊

◈ Fiddlers Inn 🆂🅷
(615) 885-1440. **$49-$99.** 2410 Music Valley Dr. I-40, exit 215B (Briley Pkwy), 4 mi n to exit 12 (McGavock Pike), then just w. Ext corridors. **Pets:** Small. $5 daily fee/room. Service with restrictions, supervision.
SAVE 🆂 🗙 🛏 💻 🏊

◈◈ GuestHouse International Inn & Suites 🆂🅷
(615) 885-4030. **$99-$129.** 2420 Music Valley Dr. Briley Pkwy, exit 12, 0.3 mi w, then 0.3 mi n. Int corridors. **Pets:** Accepted.
A$K 🆂 🗙 🛏 💻 🏊

◈ The Hermitage Hotel 🅻🅷
(615) 244-3121. **$299-$379.** 231 6th Ave N. Corner of Union St; center. Int corridors. **Pets:** Accepted.
SAVE 🗙 🐾 🛏 🍴 🏊

◈ Holiday Inn Select Vanderbilt 🆂🅷
(615) 327-4707. **$149.** 2613 West End Ave. I-40, exit 209B eastbound; exit 209A westbound, w on Broadway. Int corridors. **Pets:** Accepted.
SAVE 🆂 🗙 🐾 🛏 💻 🍴 🏊

◈ Homestead Studio Suites
Hotel-Nashville/Airport 🆂🅷
(615) 316-9020. **$45-$74.** 727 McGavock Pike. I-40, exit 215B (Briley Pkwy), 1 mi n to exit 7 (Elm Hill Pike), then just e. Ext corridors. **Pets:** Accepted.
A$K 🆂 🗙 🐾 🛏 💻

◈ Homewood Suites by Hilton 🆂🅷
(615) 884-8111. **$80-$125.** 2640 Elm Hill Pike. I-40, exit 216C (Donelson Pike). Int corridors. **Pets:** Medium. $25 daily fee/pet. Service with restrictions, crate.
SAVE 🗙 🐾 🛏 💻 🏊

◈ Hotel Preston 🅻🅷 🐾
(615) 361-5900. **$79-$159, 3 day notice.** 733 Briley Pkwy. I-40, exit 215 (Briley Pkwy). Int corridors. **Pets:** Small, other species. $50 deposit/room. Designated rooms, service with restrictions, supervision.
SAVE 🆂 🗙 🛏 💻 🍴 🏊

◈ La Quinta Inn & Suites Nashville-Airport 🆂🅷
(615) 885-3100. **$80-$125.** 531 Donelson Pike. I-40, exit 216C (Donelson Pike), 0.3 mi n. Int corridors. **Pets:** Medium. Service with restrictions.
A$K 🗙 🛏 💻 🏊

◈ La Quinta Inn Nashville (Airport) Ⓜ
(615) 885-3000. **$79-$112.** 2345 Atrium Way. I-40, exit 215B (Briley Pkwy), 1 mi n to exit 7 (Elm Hill Pike), e to Atrium Way, then 0.3 mi n. Int corridors. **Pets:** Medium. Service with restrictions.
A$K 🗙 🐾 💻 🏊

◈ Loews Vanderbilt Hotel Nashville 🅻🅷 🐾
(615) 320-1700. **$239-$289.** 2100 West End Ave. I-40, exit 209 (Broadway), 1.3 mi w. Int corridors. **Pets:** Other species.
SAVE 🗙 🐾 🛏 💻 🍴 🗙

◈ Microtel Inn & Suites 🆂🅷
(615) 662-0004. **$74-$79.** 100 Coley Davis Ct. I-40, exit 196. Int corridors. **Pets:** Medium. $10 daily fee/pet. Service with restrictions, supervision.
SAVE 🆂 🗙 🛏 💻 🏊

◈ Motel 6–156 🆂🅷
(615) 333-9933. **$38-$51.** 95 Wallace Rd. I-24, exit 56 (Harding Pl). Ext corridors. **Pets:** Medium, other species. Service with restrictions, supervision.
🆂 🗙 🏊

◈ Pear Tree Inn by Drury-Nashville South 🆂🅷
(615) 834-4242. **$55-$95.** 343 Harding Pl. I-24, exit 56 (Harding Pl). Ext corridors. **Pets:** Large, other species. Service with restrictions, supervision.
A$K 🗙 🐾 💻 🏊

◈ Radisson Hotel Nashville Airport 🆂🅷 🐾
(615) 889-9090. **$129-$169.** 1112 Airport Center Dr. I-40, exit 216C (Donelson Pike N). Int corridors. **Pets:** Small. $50 one-time fee/room. Service with restrictions, supervision.
SAVE 🆂 🗙 🐾 🛏 💻 🍴 🏊

◈ Red Roof Inn Airport Ⓜ
(615) 872-0735. **$52-$70.** 510 Claridge Dr. I-40, exit 216C (Donelson Pike), 0.3 mi n. Ext corridors. **Pets:** Medium, other species. Service with restrictions, supervision.
🗙 🐾 🛏

◈ Red Roof Inn South 🆂🅷
(615) 832-0093. **$50-$70.** 4271 Sidco Dr. I-65, exit 78. Ext corridors. **Pets:** Medium, other species. Service with restrictions, supervision.
🗙 🐾 🐾

(AAA) ▼▼▼ Residence Inn SH
(615) 889-8600. **$75-$179.** 2300 Elm Hill Pike. I-40, exit 215B (Briley Pkwy), 1.5 mi n. Ext corridors. **Pets:** Other species. $100 one-time fee/room. Service with restrictions.

(AAA) ▼▼▼ Sheraton Music City Hotel LH
(615) 885-2200. **$219.** 777 McGavock Pike. I-40, exit 215B (Briley Pkwy), 1 mi n to exit 7 (Elm Hill Pike), 0.5 mi e, then s. Int corridors. **Pets:** Large, other species. Designated rooms, service with restrictions, supervision.

▼▼▼ Sheraton Nashville Downtown Hotel LH ❖
(615) 259-2000. **$169-$239, 3 day notice.** 623 Union St. I-40, exit 209, just s of State Capitol. Int corridors. **Pets:** Dogs only. Service with restrictions, supervision.

▼▼ StudioPLUS SH
(615) 871-9669. **Call for rates.** 2511 Elm Hill Pike. I-40, exit 215B, 1.6 mi n. Int corridors. **Pets:** Accepted.

(AAA) ▼▼▼ Super 8 Motel SH
(615) 889-8887. **$53-$58.** 720 Royal Pkwy. I-40, exit 216C (Donelson Pike N), 0.5 mi n, then just e. Int corridors. **Pets:** Large, other species. $10 daily fee/room. Service with restrictions, crate.

(AAA) ▼▼▼ Super 8 Motel-West SH
(615) 356-6005. **$65-$100.** 6924 Charlotte Pike. I-40, exit 201. Ext corridors. **Pets:** Medium, dogs only. $10 daily fee/pet. Service with restrictions, supervision.

END METROPOLITAN AREA

NEWPORT

(AAA) ▼▼▼ Best Western Newport Inn M
(423) 623-8713. **$49-$169, 14 day notice.** 1015 Cosby Hwy. I-40, exit 435, just w. Ext corridors. **Pets:** Accepted.

(AAA) ▼▼▼ Comfort Inn SH
(423) 623-5355. **$54-$169.** 1149 Smokey Mountain Ln. I-40, exit 432B. Int corridors. **Pets:** Accepted.

▼▼ Holiday Inn SH
(423) 623-8622. **$65-$129.** 1010 Cosby Hwy. I-40, exit 435. Ext/int corridors. **Pets:** Accepted.

(AAA) ▼▼▼ Motel 6-4090 M
(423) 623-1850. **$45-$70.** 255 Heritage Blvd. I-40, exit 435. Int corridors. **Pets:** Medium, other species. Service with restrictions, supervision.

(AAA) ▼ Relax Inn M
(423) 625-1521. **$55-$60.** 1148 W Hwy 25-70. I-40, exit 432B. Ext corridors. **Pets:** $5 daily fee/room. Designated rooms, service with restrictions, crate.

OAK RIDGE

▼▼▼ Comfort Inn SH
(865) 481-8200. **$89-$109.** 433 S Rutgers Ave. 0.9 mi se of SR 95 on SR 62. Int corridors. **Pets:** Small, other species. $10 daily fee/pet. Service with restrictions, crate.

▼▼▼ DoubleTree Oak Ridge SH
(865) 481-2468. **$89-$159.** 215 S Illinois Ave. 0.3 mi se of SR 95 on SR 62. Int corridors. **Pets:** $25 one-time fee/room. No service, supervision.

▼▼▼ Jameson Inn SH
(865) 483-6809. **$54-$104.** 216 S Rutgers Ave. Jct SR 95 and 62, 0.9 mi se on SR 62 to Rutgers Ave, then 0.7 mi n. Int corridors. **Pets:** Small. $10 daily fee/pet. Service with restrictions, crate.

ONEIDA

▼ The Galloway Inn M
(423) 569-8835. **$43.** 299 Galloway Dr. Jct SR 63, 3.3 mi n on US 27, just e. Ext corridors. **Pets:** Accepted.

OOLTEWAH

▼ Super 8 Motel M
(423) 238-5951. **$40-$50.** 5111 Hunter Rd. I-75, exit 11, just w. Ext corridors. **Pets:** Accepted.

PICKWICK DAM

▼▼▼ Pickwick Landing State Resort Park Inn LH
(731) 689-3135. **$65-$78.** 220 Playground Loop. Intersection of US 57 and SR 128. Ext/int corridors. **Pets:** $10 daily fee/pet. Designated rooms, service with restrictions, supervision.

PIGEON FORGE

(AAA) ▼▼▼ Americas Best Value Inn at Dollywood Lane SH
(865) 429-0150. **$30-$195.** 202 Emert St. Just w of jct US 441; between traffic lights 7 and 8. Int corridors. **Pets:** Medium, other species. $15 daily fee/pet. Designated rooms, service with restrictions, crate.

▼▼▼ Blackberry Ridge-Accommodations by Sunset Cottage CA
(865) 429-8478. **Call for rates.** 3630 S River Rd. Just e of jct US 441 at traffic light 8, just n. Ext corridors. **Pets:** Other species. $100 deposit/pet. Designated rooms, no service, supervision.

▼▼ Briarstone Inn M
(865) 453-4225. **$27-$179.** 3626 Parkway. On US 441; between traffic lights 7 and 8. Ext corridors. **Pets:** Accepted.

▼▼▼ Cedar Falls Resort-Accommodations by Sunset Cottage CA
(865) 429-8478. **$53-$750, 30 day notice.** 3630 S River Rd. Just e of jct US 441 at traffic light 8, just n. Ext corridors. **Pets:** Other species. $100 deposit/pet. Designated rooms, no service, supervision.

▼▼▼▼ **Holiday Inn Resort** SH
(865) 428-2700. **$60-$140, 3 day notice.** 3230 Parkway. On US 441; between traffic lights 2 and 3. Int corridors. **Pets:** Accepted.
ASK S◘ ✕ ⊘ 🛏 📖 ❘❘ 🏊

▲▲▲ ▼▼▼▼ **La Quinta Inn** SH
(865) 429-3010. **$39-$189.** 219 Emert St. Just w of jct US 441; between traffic lights 7 and 8. Int corridors. **Pets:** Small, other species. $50 deposit/room. Designated rooms, service with restrictions, crate.
SAVE S◘ ✕ ᴥM 🐾 🛏 📖

▼▼ **Microtel Suites at Music Road** SH
(865) 453-1116. **$35-$114.** 2045 Parkway. On US 441, just s of traffic light 0. Int corridors. **Pets:** Other species. $35 one-time fee/room. Designated rooms, service with restrictions.
ASK S◘ ✕ ᴥM 🛏 📖 🏊

▲▲▲ ▼▼▼ **Motel 6 #4021** SH
(865) 908-1244. **$40-$90.** 336 Henderson Chapel Rd. From jct US 441, just w at traffic light 1. Int corridors. **Pets:** Medium, other species. Service with restrictions, supervision.
SAVE S◘ ✕ ᴥM 🐾 🏊

▲▲▲ ▼▼▼▼ **National Parks Resort Lodge** SH
(865) 453-4106. **$25-$130.** 2385 Parkway. On US 441 at traffic light 1. Int corridors. **Pets:** $20 deposit/room, $20 one-time fee/pet. Designated rooms, service with restrictions, supervision.
SAVE ✕ 🛏 📖 🏊

▲▲▲ ▼▼ **Rodeway Inn Mountain Sky** M
(865) 453-3530. **$29-$139.** 4236 Parkway. On US 441, at traffic light 10. Ext corridors. **Pets:** Accepted.
ASK S◘ ✕ 🛏 📖 🏊

▲▲▲ ▼▼▼▼ **Sherwood Forest-Eden Crest Vacation Rentals, Inc** CA 🐾
(865) 774-0059. **$105-$365.** 652 Wears Valley Rd. US 321 to light 3, just w. Ext corridors. **Pets:** Small, dogs only. $135 one-time fee/pet. Service with restrictions, crate.
SAVE S◘ ✕ 🛏 📖 🏊

▲▲▲ ▼▼▼ **Smoky Shadows Motel & Conference Center** SH
(865) 453-7155. **$39-$99, 3 day notice.** 4215 Parkway. On US 441, just n of traffic light 10. Ext/int corridors. **Pets:** Small, dogs only. $10 daily fee/pet. Service with restrictions, supervision.
SAVE S◘ ✕ 🛏 📖 🏊

▲▲▲ ▼▼▼▼ **Starr Crest Resort Cabin Rentals** VH
(865) 429-0156. **$209-$1099, 30 day notice.** 1431 Upper Middle Creek Rd. I-40, US 441, e at traffic light 8, 1.5 mi on Dollywood Ln. Ext corridors. **Pets:** Accepted.
SAVE S◘ ✕ 🛏 📖 🏊

▼▼▼▼ **Valley Heights-Accommodations by Sunset Cottage** CA
(865) 429-8478. **Call for rates.** 3630 S River Rd. Just e of jct US 441 at traffic light 8, just n. Ext corridors. **Pets:** Other species. $100 deposit/pet. Designated rooms, no service, supervision.
✕ 🛏 📖

POWELL

▼▼ **Comfort Inn** M
(865) 938-5500. **$55-$110.** 323 E Emory Rd. I-75, exit 112. Ext corridors. **Pets:** Small, other species. $10 daily fee/pet. Service with restrictions, supervision.
ASK S◘ ✕ 🛏 📖 🏊

PULASKI

▲▲▲ ▼▼▼ **Super 8 Motel** SH
(931) 363-4501. **$42-$72.** I-65 & Hwy 64, Exit 14 East. I-65, exit 14, just e. Ext corridors. **Pets:** Medium, other species. $5 daily fee/pet. Service with restrictions, crate.
SAVE S◘ ✕ 🛏 ❘❘ 🏊

RICEVILLE

▼▼ **Rice Inn** M
(423) 462-2224. **$27-$35.** 3692 Hwy 11. I-75, exit 42, 1.5 mi e, then just n. Ext corridors. **Pets:** Accepted.
ASK S◘ ✕ 🛏

ROGERSVILLE

▼▼▼ **Holiday Inn Express** SH
(423) 272-1842. **$73-$83.** 7139 Hwy 11 W. Jct SR 66 and US 11, 0.5 mi sw. Int corridors. **Pets:** Accepted.
ASK S◘ ✕ 🐾 🛏 📖 🏊

SELMER

▼▼ **Super 8 Motel-Selmer** SH
(731) 645-8880. **$65.** 644 Mulberry Ave. Jct SR 64 and 45, just s on SR 45. Ext corridors. **Pets:** $25 deposit/room. Service with restrictions, supervision.
ASK S◘ ✕ 🐾 🛏 🏊

SEVIERVILLE

▲▲▲ ▼▼▼ **Best Western Dumplin Valley Inn** M
(865) 933-3467. **$39-$119.** 3426 Winfield Dunn Pkwy. I-40, exit 407, 0.4 mi s on SR 66. Ext corridors. **Pets:** Other species. $10 daily fee/room. Service with restrictions, supervision.
SAVE S◘ ✕ ⊘ 🛏 📖 🏊

▲▲▲ ▼▼▼ **Comfort Inn Interstate** M
(865) 933-1719. **$49-$140.** 155 Dumplin Valley Rd. I-40, exit 407, just s on SR 66, then just w. Ext corridors. **Pets:** Medium, other species. $10 daily fee/pet. Designated rooms, service with restrictions, supervision.
SAVE S◘ ✕ ᴥM 🛏 📖 🏊

▲▲▲ ▼▼▼▼ **Comfort Inn Mountain River Suites** M
(865) 428-5519. **$59-$189.** 860 Winfield Dunn Pkwy. I-40, exit 407, 7 mi s on SR 66; 1.3 mi n of jct US 411. Ext corridors. **Pets:** $10 daily fee/pet. Designated rooms, service with restrictions, supervision.
SAVE S◘ ✕ ⊘ 🛏 📖 🏊

▼▼▼ **Holiday Inn Express Hotel & Suites** SH 🐾
(865) 933-9448. **$50-$140, 3 day notice.** 2863 Winfield Dunn Pkwy. I-40, exit 407, 2.3 mi s on SR 66. Int corridors. **Pets:** Small, other species. $15 one-time fee/pet. Designated rooms, crate.
ASK S◘ ✕ ᴥM ⊘ 🐾 🛏 📖 🏊

SMYRNA

▼▼ **Days Inn & Suites** M 🐾
(615) 355-6161. **$60-$65.** 1300 Plaza Dr. I-24, exit 66A, 2.5 mi ne. Ext corridors. **Pets:** $10 daily fee/pet. Service with restrictions, supervision.
ASK S◘ ✕ 🛏 📖 🏊

SWEETWATER

▲▲▲ ▼▼▼ **Comfort Inn** SH
(423) 337-6646. **$45-$75.** 731 S Main St. On US 11, jct SR 68. Ext/int corridors. **Pets:** Medium. $5 daily fee/pet. Service with restrictions, supervision.
SAVE S◘ ✕ 🛏 📖 🏊

▲▲▲ ▼▼▼ **Comfort Inn West** SH
(423) 337-3353. **$50-$109.** 249 Hwy 68. I-75, exit 60, just e. Ext/int corridors. **Pets:** Medium. $5 daily fee/pet. Service with restrictions.
SAVE S◘ ✕ 🛏 📖 🏊

ⓐⓐⓐ ◈ Knights Inn M ❀
(423) 337-9357. **$45-$80.** 207 Hwy 68. I-75, exit 60. Ext corridors.
Pets: Small. $5 one-time fee/pet. Service with restrictions, supervision.
[SAVE] [S🔊] [✕] [🖥]

ⓐⓐⓐ ◈◈◈ Quality Inn & Suites SH
(423) 337-4900. **$70-$160.** 1116 Hwy 68. I-75, exit 60. Int corridors.
Pets: Large, other species. $15 one-time fee/pet. Supervision.
[SAVE] [S🔊] [✕] [🖥] [💻] [🏊]

TOWNSEND

ⓐⓐⓐ ◈◈ Comfort Inn M
(865) 448-9000. **$35-$189, 3 day notice.** 7824 E Lamar Alexander
Pkwy. On US 321, 0.7 mi s of jct SR 73. Ext corridors. **Pets:** Small,
dogs only. $20 daily fee/pet. Designated rooms, service with restrictions,
crate.
[SAVE] [S🔊] [✕] [🖥] [💻] [🏊]

**ⓐⓐⓐ ◈◈◈◈ Laurel Valley & Smoky Mountain Cabin
Rentals VH**
(865) 448-2040. **$109-$345, 30 day notice.** 125 Townsend Park Rd.
1.7 mi s on US 321 from jct SR 73, then just e. Ext corridors.
Pets: Medium, dogs only. $50 one-time fee/room. Designated rooms,
supervision.
[SAVE] [S🔊] [✕] [🖥] [💻] [🏊]

ⓐⓐⓐ ◈◈◈ Valley View Lodge M
(865) 448-2237. **$39-$99, 3 day notice.** 7726 E Lamar Alexander
Pkwy. On US 321, 1.1 mi s of jct SR 73. Ext corridors. **Pets:** Medium.
$10 one-time fee/room. Designated rooms, service with restrictions, crate.
[ASK] [S🔊] [✕] [🎣] [🖥] [💻] [🏊]

TULLAHOMA

◈◈ Jameson Inn SH
(931) 455-7891. **$54-$104.** 2113 N Jackson St. 3 mi n on SR 41A (N
Jackson St). Ext corridors. **Pets:** Small. $10 daily fee/pet. Service with
restrictions, crate.
[ASK] [✕] [🎣] [🖥] [💻] [🏊]

VONORE

◈◈◈◈ Grand Vista Hotel & Suites SH
(423) 884-6200. **$90.** 117 Grand Vista Dr. I-75, exit 172, 14 mi e. Int
corridors. **Pets:** Accepted.
[ASK] [S🔊] [✕] [🔊M] [🎣] [🐾] [🖥] [💻] [🏊]

WHITE HOUSE

◈◈ Holiday Inn Express SH
(615) 672-7200. **$60-$80.** 354 Hester Ln. I-65, exit 108, just e. Ext
corridors. **Pets:** Medium. $5 one-time fee/pet. Designated rooms, service
with restrictions, supervision.
[ASK] [S🔊] [✕] [🔊M] [🐾] [🖥] [💻] [🏊]

WHITEVILLE

◈◈ Super 8 SH
(731) 254-8884. **$50-$60.** 2040 Hwy 64. US 64 and SR 179. Ext
corridors. **Pets:** Medium. $5 daily fee/pet. Service with restrictions, super-
vision.
[ASK] [S🔊] [✕] [🔊M] [🐾] [🖥]

WILDERSVILLE

ⓐⓐⓐ ◈◈◈ Best Western Crossroads Inn SH
(731) 968-2532. **$54-$64.** 21045 Hwy 22 N. I-40, exit 108, just s. Ext
corridors. **Pets:** Accepted.
[SAVE] [S🔊] [✕] [🖥] [💻] [🏊]

CITY INDEX

ABILENE

Best Western Abilene Inn & Suites SH
(325) 672-5501. **$79-$109, 3 day notice.** 350 I-20 W. I-20, exit 286C, just n. Int corridors. **Pets:** Small. Designated rooms, service with restrictions, supervision.

Best Western Mall South SH
(325) 695-1262. **$74.** 3950 Ridgemont Dr. US 83/84, exit Ridgemont Dr, just s. Ext corridors. **Pets:** Medium. $20 daily fee/pet. Designated rooms, service with restrictions, crate.

Budget Host Colonial Inn M
(325) 677-2683. **$49-$59.** 3210 Pine St. Jct I-20 and US 83 business route, exit 286A. Ext/int corridors. **Pets:** Medium. $10 daily fee/pet. Designated rooms, service with restrictions, supervision.

Civic Plaza Hotel SH
(325) 676-0222. **$49-$99.** 505 Pine St. Downtown. Ext corridors. **Pets:** Accepted.

Comfort Suites SH
(325) 795-8500. **$90-$125.** 3165 S Danville Dr. I-20, exit 279, s on US 83/84/277 to Southwest Dr, then just e. Int corridors. **Pets:** Accepted.

Days Inn M
(325) 672-6433. **$62.** 1702 E Hwy 20. I-20, exit 288. Ext corridors. **Pets:** $15 one-time fee/room. Service with restrictions, crate.

Econo Lodge M
(325) 673-5424. **$55-$60.** 1633 W Stamford. S Frontage Rd off I-20 and US 80, exit 285 eastbound; exit 286A westbound. Ext corridors. **Pets:** Small, dogs only. $10 one-time fee/pet. Service with restrictions, supervision.

Holiday Inn Express Mall South SH
(325) 695-0500. **$89-$129.** 3112 S Clark. US 83/277 and Southwest Dr, just e to Catclaw, just n. Int corridors. **Pets:** Small. $30 one-time fee/room. Designated rooms, service with restrictions, supervision.

La Quinta Inn Abilene SH
(325) 676-1676. **$91-$126.** 3501 W Lake Rd. I-20, exit 286C. Ext corridors. **Pets:** Medium. Service with restrictions.

Motel 6 Abilene #79 M
(325) 672-8462. **$41-$53.** 4951 W Stamford St. I-20, exit 282, on eastbound frontage road. Ext corridors. **Pets:** Medium, other species. Service with restrictions, supervision.

Regency Inn & Suites SH
(325) 695-7700. **$62-$79.** 3450 S Clark St. 5 mi sw on US 83/84, exit Southwest Dr. Int corridors. **Pets:** Small. $25 one-time fee/pet. Designated rooms, service with restrictions, crate.

Super 8 Motel M
(325) 673-5251. **$55-$85, 5 day notice.** 1525 E I-20. I-20, exit 288. Ext corridors. **Pets:** Large. $8 daily fee/pet. Service with restrictions, supervision.

ALICE

Days Inn SH
(361) 664-6616. **$60-$75.** 555 N Johnson St. On US 281 business route, n of Johnson St. Int corridors. **Pets:** Accepted.

ALPINE

Oak Tree Inn SH
(432) 837-5711. **$79.** 2407 E Holland (Hwy 90/67). US 90, 2 mi e. Int corridors. **Pets:** Accepted.

Ramada Limited SH
(432) 837-1100. **$90-$140.** 2800 W Hwy 90. On US 90, 2 mi n. Int corridors. **Pets:** Accepted.

ALVIN

Americas Best Value Inn & Suites M
(281) 331-0335. **Call for rates.** 1588 S Hwy 35 Bypass. SR 35 Bypass, 0.5 mi sw of SR 6. Ext corridors. **Pets:** Medium. $10 daily fee/pet. Service with restrictions, supervision.

AMARILLO

Ambassador Hotel LH
(806) 358-6161. **$109-$169.** 3100 I-40 W. I-40, exit 68, just w on north frontage road. Int corridors. **Pets:** Accepted.

Baymont Inn & Suites SH
(806) 356-6800. **$59-$159.** 3411 I-40 W. I-40, exit 67, 0.3 mi e on south frontage road. Int corridors. **Pets:** Accepted.

Best Western Amarillo Inn SH
(806) 358-7861. **$79-$99, 3 day notice.** 1610 Coulter Dr. I-40, exit 65 (Coulter Dr), 0.6 mi n. Ext/int corridors. **Pets:** Accepted.

Best Western Santa Fe SH
(806) 372-1885. **$70-$126.** 4600 I-40 E. I-40, exit 73 (Eastern St) eastbound; exit 73 (Bolton St) westbound, U-turn on south frontage road. Int corridors. **Pets:** Accepted.

Big Texan Motel M
(806) 372-5000. **$46-$75.** 7701 I-40 E. I-40, exit 75 (Lakeside Dr), 0.3 mi w on north frontage road. Ext corridors. **Pets:** Other species. $30 deposit/pet, $10 daily fee/pet. Designated rooms, service with restrictions, supervision.

Days Inn SH
(806) 359-9393. **$59-$129.** 2102 S Coulter Dr. I-40, exit 65 (Coulter Dr), just n. Ext corridors. **Pets:** Accepted.

Days Inn SH
(806) 379-6255. **$49-$109.** 1701 I-40 E. I-40, exit 71 (Ross-Osage), just w on north frontage road. Int corridors. **Pets:** Other species. $10 one-time fee/pet. Designated rooms, service with restrictions, supervision.

Days Inn South SH
(806) 468-7100. **$55-$79, 7 day notice.** 8601 Canyon Dr. I-27, exit 116, just n on east service road. Int corridors. **Pets:** Accepted.

Extended StayAmerica Amarillo West SH
(806) 351-0117. **$64-$74.** 2100 Cinema Dr. I-40, exit 64, just n. Int corridors. **Pets:** Accepted.

Hampton Inn SH
(806) 372-1425. **$79-$119.** 1700 I-40 E. I-40, exit 71 (Ross-Osage), just e on south frontage road. Int corridors. **Pets:** Medium, other species. Service with restrictions, supervision.

Holiday Inn-I-40 SH
(806) 372-8741. **$134.** 1911 I-40 at Ross-Osage. I-40, exit 71 (Ross-Osage), on north frontage road. Int corridors. **Pets:** $25 one-time fee/ room. Designated rooms, service with restrictions, crate.

La Quinta Inn Amarillo (East/Airport Area) SH
(806) 373-7486. **$76-$123.** 1708 I-40 E. I-40, exit 71 (Ross-Osage), just e on south frontage road. Ext corridors. **Pets:** Medium. Service with restrictions.

La Quinta Inn Amarillo (West/Medical Center) SH
(806) 352-6311. **$78-$118.** 2108 S Coulter Dr. I-40, exit 65 (Coulter Dr), just n. Ext corridors. **Pets:** Medium. Service with restrictions.

Microtel Inn & Suites SH
(806) 372-8373. **$68-$88.** 1501 S Ross St. I-40, exit 71 (Ross-Osage), just n. Int corridors. **Pets:** Medium. $25 one-time fee/pet. Service with restrictions, supervision.

Motel 6 Amarillo East #409 M
(806) 374-6444. **$42-$54.** 3930 I-40 E. I-40, exit 72B, on eastbound frontage road. Ext corridors. **Pets:** Medium, other species. Service with restrictions, supervision.

Motel 6 Amarillo West #1146 M
(806) 359-7651. **$41-$54.** 6030 I-40. I-40, exit 66 (Bell St), just w, on north frontage road. Ext corridors. **Pets:** Medium, other species. Service with restrictions, supervision.

Quality Inn & Suites West SH
(806) 358-7943. **$69-$119.** 6800 I-40 W. I-40, exit 66 (Bell St), 0.5 mi w on north frontage road. Ext corridors. **Pets:** $20 one-time fee/pet. Service with restrictions, crate.

Quality Inn-East SH
(806) 376-9993. **$59-$99.** 1515 I-40 E. I-40, exit 71 (Ross-Osage), just w on north frontage road. Ext corridors. **Pets:** Accepted.

Ramada Limited SH
(806) 374-2020. **$49-$79.** 1620 I-40. I-40, exit 71 (Ross-Osage), just e on south frontage road. Ext corridors. **Pets:** Medium. $10 one-time fee/room. Designated rooms, service with restrictions, supervision.

Residence Inn by Marriott SH
(806) 354-2978. **$135-$175.** 6700 I-40 W. I-40, exit 66 (Bell St), 0.5 mi w on north frontage road. Int corridors. **Pets:** Accepted.

Sleep Inn Amarillo SH
(806) 372-6200. **$75-$95, 12 day notice.** 2401 I-40. I-40, exit 72A (Nelson), 0.3 mi w on north frontage road. Int corridors. **Pets:** Very small, cats only. $10 daily fee/pet. Designated rooms, service with restrictions, supervision.
SAVE S✆ ✕ ✗M 🔊 ☕ 🛏 💻 🏊

Travelodge West SH
(806) 353-3541. **$49-$69.** 2035 Paramount Blvd. I-40, exit 68A (Paramount Blvd), just s. Ext corridors. **Pets:** Small, other species. $10 one-time fee/room. Service with restrictions.
SAVE S✆ ✕ 🔊 🛏 💻 🏊

ANTHONY

Best Western SH
(915) 886-3333. **$79-$89.** 9401 S Desert Blvd. I-10, exit 0. Ext corridors. **Pets:** Accepted.
ASK S✆ ✕ ✗M 🔊 ☕ 🛏 💻 🏊 ✕

ARLINGTON

Arlington TownePlace Suites by Marriott SH
(817) 861-8728. **$99-$109.** 1709 E Lamar Ave. 2 mi w of SR 360. Int corridors. **Pets:** Accepted.
ASK ✕ ✗M 🔊 ☕ 🛏 💻 🏊

Baymont Inn & Suites-Arlington SH
(817) 633-2434. **$69, 14 day notice.** 2401 Diplomacy Dr. I-30, exit 30 (SR 360), 0.5 mi s; off SR 360, exit Six Flags Dr northbound; exit Ave H/Lamar Blvd southbound, on southbound service road. Int corridors. **Pets:** Accepted.
SAVE S✆ ✕ ✗M 🔊 ☕ 🛏 💻 🏊

Days Inn Ballpark at Arlington/Six Flags SH
(817) 261-8444. **$37-$99.** 910 N Collins St. I-30, exit 28 (Collins St/FM 157), 1 mi s. Int corridors. **Pets:** Accepted.
SAVE S✆ ✕ 🏊

Hawthorn Suites SH
(817) 640-1188. **$79-$229.** 2401 Brookhollow Plaza Dr. I-30, exit 30 (SR 360), just n to Lamar Blvd, just w to Brookhollow Plaza Dr, then just n. Ext corridors. **Pets:** Accepted.
ASK S✆ ✕ 🔊 🛏 💻 🏊 ✕

Holiday Inn-Arlington SH
(817) 640-7712. **$89-$99.** 1507 N Watson Rd. I-30, exit 30 (SR 360), 1 mi n, exit Ave K/Brown Blvd. Int corridors. **Pets:** Accepted.
SAVE S✆ ✕ ✗M 🔊 🛏 💻 🍴 🏊

Homewood Suites by Hilton SH
(817) 633-1594. **$154-$174.** 2401 E Rd to Six Flags St. I-30, exit 30 (SR 360), 0.5 mi sw. Int corridors. **Pets:** Accepted.
ASK S✆ ✕ ✗M 🔊 ☕ 🛏 💻 🏊

Howard Johnson Express Inn SH
(817) 461-1122. **$45-$99.** 2001 E Copeland Rd. I-30, exit 30 (SR 360) westbound, just s to Six Flags Dr, just w to Copeland Rd, then 0.9 mi w; exit 29 (Ball Pkwy) eastbound. Int corridors. **Pets:** Medium. $10 daily fee/pet. No service.
ASK S✆ ✕ 🛏 💻 🏊

La Quinta Inn & Suites Dallas/Arlington North SH
(817) 640-4142. **$134-$169.** 825 N Watson Rd. I-30, exit 30 (SR 360), exit Six Flags Dr northbound; exit Ave H/Lamar Blvd southbound. Int corridors. **Pets:** Medium. Service with restrictions.
SAVE ✕ 🔊 ☕ 🛏 💻 🏊

Marriott SpringHill Suites-Arlington SH
(817) 860-2737. **$89-$119.** 1975 E Lamar Blvd. I-30, exit 29 (Ballpark Way), 0.4 mi n to Lamar Blvd, then just w. Int corridors. **Pets:** Accepted.
ASK S✆ ✕ ✗M 🔊 ☕ 🛏 💻 🏊

Microtel Inn SH
(817) 557-8400. **$55-$70.** 1740 Oak Village Blvd. I-20, exit 449 (Cooper St) westbound; exit 449A (Cooper St) eastbound, just s. Int corridors. **Pets:** Small, dogs only. $10 daily fee/pet. Designated rooms, service with restrictions, supervision.
ASK S✆ ✕ 🛏 🏊

Sleep Inn Main Gate-Six Flags SH
(817) 649-1010. **$71-$141.** 750 Six Flags Dr. I-30, exit 30 (SR 360), 0.5 mi s. Int corridors. **Pets:** Small, other species. $10 daily fee/pet. Service with restrictions.
SAVE S✆ ✕ 🔊 🛏 💻 🏊

Studio 6-South Arlington #6036 SH
(817) 465-8500. **$53-$63.** 1980 W Pleasant Ridge Rd. I-20, exit 449 (Cooper St), 0.3 mi n, then just w. Ext corridors. **Pets:** Accepted.
S✆ ✕ ☕ 🛏 💻

AURORA

MD Resort Bed & Breakfast BB
(817) 489-5150. **$89-$299, 14 day notice.** 601 Old Base Rd. 2 mi w of jct US 287 to Old Base Rd, 0.5 mi s. Ext/int corridors. **Pets:** Accepted.
SAVE S✆ ✕ 🛏 💻 🏊 ✕ ☎

AUSTIN

Austin Marriott at the Capitol LH
(512) 478-1111. **$125-$199.** 701 E 11th St. I-35, exit 234B, 0.3 mi e. Int corridors. **Pets:** Accepted.
ASK S✆ ✕ 🔊 ☕ 🛏 💻 🍴 🏊 ✕

Baymont Inn Highland Mall SH
(512) 452-9401. **$84-$107.** 7100 I-35 N. I-35, exit 239, on west frontage road. Ext corridors. **Pets:** Medium. Service with restrictions.
SAVE ✕ 🔊 🛏 💻 🏊

Best Western Atrium North SH
(512) 339-7311. **$84-$104.** 7928 Gessner Dr. I-35, exit 240A, 0.4 mi w on Anderson Ln. Int corridors. **Pets:** Small, dogs only. $25 one-time fee/room. Service with restrictions, crate.
SAVE S✆ ✕ 🛏 💻 🏊

Best Western Seville Plaza Inn SH 🐾
(512) 447-5511. **$59-$79.** 4323 I-35 S. I-35, exit 230A (Stassney Rd) southbound; exit 230 (Ben White Blvd) northbound. Int corridors. **Pets:** Small. $20 one-time fee/pet. Service with restrictions, supervision.
ASK S✆ ✕ 🔊 🛏 💻 🍴 🏊

Candlewood Suites Austin Northwest SH
(512) 338-1611. **$79-$119.** 9701 Stonelake Blvd. Jct SR 360 (Capital of Texas Hwy) and Stonelake Blvd, just s. Int corridors. **Pets:** Accepted.
ASK S✆ ✕ ✗M 🔊 ☕ 🛏 💻

Candlewood Suites-South SH
(512) 444-8882. **$79-$120.** 4320 S I-35. I-35, exit 230 northbound; exit 230B southbound, on southbound frontage road. Int corridors. **Pets:** Medium. Service with restrictions, supervision.
ASK S✆ ✕ ✗M 🔊 ☕ 🛏 💻

Clarion Inn & Suites Conference Center SH
(512) 444-0561. **$99-$169.** 2200 S I-35. I-35, exit 232A (Oltorf Blvd), on west side access road. Ext/int corridors. **Pets:** Other species. $50 one-time fee/room. Designated rooms, service with restrictions, supervision.
SAVE S✆ ✕ ☕ 🛏 💻 🍴 🏊

Comfort Suites Airport SH
(512) 386-6000. **$89-$139.** 7501 E Ben White Blvd. I-35, exit 230B (Ben White Blvd/SR 71), 3.6 mi e. Int corridors. **Pets:** Small, other species. $35 one-time fee/pet. Service with restrictions, crate.
ASK S✆ ✕ ✗M 🔊 ☕ 🛏 💻 🏊

▼▼ **Crossland Studios Austin West** SH
(512) 331-4747. **Call for rates.** 12621 Hymeadow Rd. US 183 N, exit Lake Creek, just n, then just e. Ext corridors. **Pets:** Accepted.
⊠ ✕ ⬛ 🖵

▼▼▼ **Crowne Plaza** SH
(512) 323-5466. **$69-$109.** 6121 I-35 N. I-35, exit 238A, on east frontage road. Int corridors. **Pets:** Accepted.
A$K S🔊 ⊠ ⟲ 🛡 🖵 ❙❙ ⇌ ✕

AAA ▼▼ **Days Inn University-Downtown** M
(512) 478-1631. **$64-$120.** 3105 N I-35. I-35, exit 236A at 32nd St from lower level. Ext corridors. **Pets:** Medium. $10 one-time fee/room. Service with restrictions.
SAVE S🔊 ⊠ 🛡 🖵 ⇌

▼▼▼▼ **DoubleTree Hotel Austin** LH
(512) 454-3737. **$109-$209.** 6505 I-35. I-35, exit 238A, on east frontage road. Int corridors. **Pets:** Accepted.
⊠ ⬛M ⟲ 🛰 🛡 🖵 ❙❙ ⇌

AAA ▼▼▼▼ **The Driskill** LH 🐾
(512) 474-5911. **$189-$2500.** 604 Brazos St. Jct 6th St. Int corridors. **Pets:** Medium, other species. $50 daily fee/pet. Service with restrictions, crate.
SAVE ⊠ ⟲ 🛰 ❙❙

▼▼▼▼ **Drury Inn & Suites-Austin North** SH
(512) 467-9500. **$85-$130.** 6711 I-35. I-35, exit 238A, on east frontage road. Int corridors. **Pets:** Large, other species. Service with restrictions, supervision.
A$K ⊠ 🛰 🛡 🖵 ⇌

▼▼ **Econo Lodge** SH
(512) 835-7070. **$79-$129.** 9102 Burnet Rd. US 183 and Burnet Rd; on northeast corner. Ext corridors. **Pets:** Small. $25 one-time fee/pet. Designated rooms, no service, supervision.
A$K S🔊 ⊠ 🛡 🖵 ⇌

▼▼ **Econo Lodge** SH
(512) 458-4759. **$59-$109.** 6201 Hwy 290 E. I-35, exit 238, 0.3 mi e of jct I-35 and US 290 E. Ext corridors. **Pets:** Accepted.
A$K S🔊 ⊠ 🛡 🖵 ⇌

▼▼▼ **Embassy Suites Hotel-Downtown** LH
(512) 469-9000. **$199-$289.** 300 S Congress Ave. Just s of Congress Ave Bridge. Int corridors. **Pets:** Small, other species. $25 one-time fee/room. Designated rooms, service with restrictions, crate.
⊠ ⟲ 🛰 🛡 🖵 ❙❙ ⇌

AAA ▼▼ **Exel Inn Of Austin** SH
(512) 462-9201. **$46-$89.** 2711 I-35 S. I-35, exit 231 (Woodward Ave) southbound; exit 232A (Oltorf St) northbound, on northbound frontage road; just n of jct I-35 and US 290/SR 71. Int corridors. **Pets:** Small, other species. Designated rooms, service with restrictions, supervision.
SAVE S🔊 ⊠ ⟲ 🛡 🖵 ⇌

▼▼ **Extended StayAmerica-Austin Arboretum** SH
(512) 231-1520. **Call for rates.** 10100 Capital of Texas Hwy. Jct Loop 1 (Mo-Pac Expwy) and Capital of Texas Hwy (SR 360), just w. Int corridors. **Pets:** Accepted.
⊠ ⬛M 🛰 🛡 🖵

▼▼ **Extended StayAmerica-Austin Downtown** SH
(512) 457-9994. **Call for rates.** 600 Guadalupe St. Jct 6th St and Guadalupe; on northwest corner. Int corridors. **Pets:** Accepted.
⊠ ⬛M 🛰 🛡 🖵

▼▼▼ **Extended StayAmerica Austin North Central** SH
(512) 339-6005. **$75-$95.** 8221 N I-35. I-35, exit 241, on east frontage road. Int corridors. **Pets:** Accepted.
A$K S🔊 ⊠ ⟲ 🛰 🛡 🖵

▼▼ ▼▼ **Extended StayAmerica-Austin Northwest Lakeline Mall** SH
(512) 258-3365. **Call for rates.** 13858 US Hwy 183 N. Jct US 183 and SR 620, on southwest corner. Int corridors. **Pets:** Accepted.
⊠ ⬛M 🛰 🛡 🖵

▼▼▼ **Extended StayAmerica (Austin/Northwest/Research Park)** SH
(512) 219-6500. **$85-$95.** 12424 Research Blvd. US 183, exit Oak Knoll, on eastbound frontage road. Int corridors. **Pets:** Accepted.
A$K S🔊 ⊠ ⬛M ⟲ 🛰 🖵 ⇌

▼▼▼ **Extended StayAmerica-Austin Southwest** SH
(512) 892-4272. **Call for rates.** 5100 US Hwy 290 W. US 290 W, exit Brodie Ln, 1 mi w. Int corridors. **Pets:** Accepted.
⊠ ⬛M 🛰 🛡 🖵

▼▼▼ **Extended Stay Deluxe Austin-Arboretum-North** SH
(512) 833-0898. **$85-$95.** 2700 Gracy Farms Ln. 2 mi n of US 183 on Loop 1 (Mo-Pac Expwy), exit Burnet Rd (FM 1325). Int corridors. **Pets:** Accepted.
A$K S🔊 ⊠ 🛰 🛡 🖵 ⇌

▼▼▼ **Fairfield Inn & Suites Austin NW** SH
(512) 527-0734. **$94-$114.** 11201 N Mo-Pac Blvd. US 183 N, 1.5 mi n on Loop 1 (Mo-Pac Expwy) to Braker Ln exit, on east frontage road. Int corridors. **Pets:** Accepted.
A$K S🔊 ⊠ ⬛M ⟲ 🛰 🛡 🖵 ⇌ ✕

▼▼▼ **Four Seasons Hotel** LH 🐾
(512) 478-4500. **$380-$2000.** 98 San Jacinto Blvd. Bordering Town Lake. Int corridors. **Pets:** Very small, other species. Designated rooms, service with restrictions, supervision.
⊠ ⟲ 🛰 🛡 🖵 ❙❙ ⇌ ✕

▼▼▼ **Hampton Inn Northwest** SH
(512) 349-9898. **$69-$109.** 3908 W Braker Ln. 1 mi n of US 183 on Loop 1 (Mo-Pac Expwy) to Braker Ln exit. Int corridors. **Pets:** Accepted.
A$K S🔊 ⊠ ⬛M ⟲ 🛰 🖵

▼▼▼ **Hawthorn Suites Austin Central** SH
(512) 459-3335. **$69-$179.** 935 La Posada Dr. I-35, exit 238A, just off east frontage road. Ext corridors. **Pets:** Medium. $150 one-time fee/room. Service with restrictions, crate.
A$K S🔊 ⊠ ⟲ 🛡 🖵 ⇌ ✕

AAA ▼▼▼▼ **Hawthorn Suites Ltd-Austin-Bergstrom International Airport** SH
(512) 247-6166. **$79-$175.** 7800 E Riverside Dr. I-35, exit 230B (Ben White Blvd/SR 71), 3.2 mi e. Int corridors. **Pets:** Accepted.
SAVE S🔊 ⊠ ⬛M ⟲ 🛰 🛡 🖵 ⇌ ✕

▼▼▼ **Holiday Inn Express** SH
(512) 386-7600. **$99-$109.** 6 Ben White Blvd. I-35, exit 230B (Ben White Blvd), 3.2 mi e. Int corridors. **Pets:** Accepted.
A$K S🔊 ⊠ ⟲ 🛰 🛡 🖵 ⇌

▼▼▼ **Holiday Inn Express Hotel & Suites** SH
(512) 251-9110. **$105.** 14620 N I-35. I-35, exit 247, on west frontage road. Int corridors. **Pets:** Accepted.
A$K S🔊 ⊠ ⬛M ⟲ 🛰 🛡 🖵 ⇌

▼▼▼ **Holiday Inn Northwest/Arboretum** SH
(512) 343-0888. **$89-$129.** 8901 Business Park Dr. Jct US 183 and Loop 1 (Mo-Pac Expwy), on southwest corner. Int corridors. **Pets:** Accepted.
A$K S🔊 ⊠ ⟲ 🛰 🛡 🖵 ❙❙ ⇌

▼▼ **Homestead Studio Suites Hotel-Austin/Arboretum-South** SH
(512) 837-6677. **$65-$75.** 9100 Waterford Centre Blvd. US 183, exit Burnet Rd, on westbound frontage road. Ext corridors. **Pets:** Accepted.
A$K S🔊 ⊠ 🛰 🛡 🖵

▼▼▼ **Homestead Studio Suites Hotel-Austin/Downtown/ Town Lake** SH
(512) 476-1818. **$95-$115.** 507 S 1st St. I-35, exit 234B southbound; exit 234A northbound, 1.8 mi w on Cesar Chavez/E 1st St, then 0.5 mi s. Int corridors. **Pets:** Accepted.

▼▼▼▼ **Homewood Suites by Hilton Arboretum NW** SH
(512) 349-9966. **$159-$179.** 10925 Stonelake Blvd. US 183 N to Loop 1 (Mo-Pac Expwy), 1.5 mi n to Braker Ln; on northwest corner. Int corridors. **Pets:** Accepted.

▼▼▼▼ **Howard Johnson Plaza Hotel** SH
(512) 836-8520. **$122-$130.** 7800 I-35 N. I-35, exit 240A, on west frontage road at US 183. Int corridors. **Pets:** Accepted.

🔺🔺🔺 ▼▼▼ **Hyatt Regency Austin** LH
(512) 477-1234. **$135-$265.** 208 Barton Springs Rd. At south end of Congress Bridge; on south bank of Town Lake. Int corridors. **Pets:** Accepted.

▼▼▼▼ **Hyatt Summerfield Suites Northwest** SH
(512) 452-9391. **$89-$199.** 7685 Northcross Dr. Loop 1 (Mo-Pac Expwy), exit Anderson Rd, just e to Northcross Dr, then just s. Ext corridors. **Pets:** $50 one-time fee/room. Designated rooms, service with restrictions, crate.

🔺🔺🔺 ▼▼▼▼ **La Quinta Inn & Suites** SH
(512) 246-2800. **$106-$126.** 150 Parker Dr. I-35, exit 250, on west frontage road. Int corridors. **Pets:** Medium. Service with restrictions.

🔺🔺🔺 ▼▼▼▼ **La Quinta Inn & Suites Austin (Airport)** SH
(512) 386-6800. **$101-$121.** 7625 E Ben White Blvd. I-35, exit 230B (Ben White Blvd/SR 71), 3.8 mi e. Int corridors. **Pets:** Medium. Service with restrictions.

🔺🔺🔺 ▼▼▼▼ **La Quinta Inn & Suites Austin (Mopac North)** SH
(512) 832-2121. **$100-$120.** 11901 N Mo-Pac Expwy. US 183, 2 mi n on Loop 1 (Mo-Pac Expwy) to Duval exit. Int corridors. **Pets:** Medium. Service with restrictions.

▼▼▼▼ **La Quinta Inn & Suites Austin (Southwest at Mopac)** SH
(512) 899-3000. **$143-$163.** 4424 S Loop 1 (Mo-Pac Expwy). Jct Loop 1 (Mo-Pac Expwy), US 290 and SR 71 E, on southbound frontage road. Int corridors. **Pets:** Medium. Service with restrictions.

▼▼▼ **La Quinta Inn Austin (Capitol)** SH
(512) 476-1166. **$120-$140.** 300 E 11 St. Just e of state capitol building. Ext/int corridors. **Pets:** Medium. Service with restrictions.

🔺🔺🔺 ▼▼▼▼ **La Quinta Inn Austin (Highland Mall)** SH
(512) 459-4381. **$91-$115.** 5812 I-35 N. I-35, exit 238A, on west frontage road. Ext corridors. **Pets:** Medium. Service with restrictions.

🔺🔺🔺 ▼▼▼▼ **La Quinta Inn Austin (I-35 South/Ben White)** SH
(512) 443-1774. **$84-$104.** 4200 I-35. I-35, exit 231 (St. Edwards/ Woodward Ave) southbound; exit 230 northbound, just s of jct I-35, US 290 and SR 71, on frontage road. Ext corridors. **Pets:** Medium. Service with restrictions.

▼▼▼▼ **La Quinta Inn Austin (Oltorf)** SH
(512) 447-6661. **$95-$121.** 1603 E Oltorf Blvd. I-35, exit 232A (Oltorf Blvd), just s. Ext/int corridors. **Pets:** Medium. Service with restrictions.

🔺🔺🔺 ▼▼▼▼ **The Mansion at Judge's Hill** SH ❀
(512) 495-1800. **$99-$389, 3 day notice.** 1900 Rio Grande. Jct Rio Grande and Martin Luther King Jr Blvd. Int corridors. **Pets:** Designated rooms.

▼▼▼ ▼▼▼ **Omni Austin Hotel & Suites** LH ❀
(512) 476-3700. **$189-$449.** 700 San Jacinto Blvd. 8th St and San Jacinto Blvd. Int corridors. **Pets:** Small. $50 one-time fee/room. Service with restrictions, crate.

🔺🔺🔺 ▼▼▼ ▼▼▼ **Omni Austin Hotel Southpark** LH
(512) 448-2222. **$109-$219.** 4140 Governor's Row. I-35, exit 230B southbound; exit 230 northbound, on east frontage road. Int corridors. **Pets:** Medium. $50 one-time fee/pet. Supervision.

▼▼▼ **Ramada Limited Austin North** SH
(512) 836-0079. **$55-$151.** 9121 N I-35. I-35, exit 241 northbound; exit 240A southbound, on east frontage road. Int corridors. **Pets:** Accepted.

▼▼ **Red Roof Inn Austin North** M
(512) 835-2200. **$50-$65.** 8210 I-35 N. I-35, exit 241 northbound; exit 240A southbound, on west frontage road. Ext corridors. **Pets:** Medium, other species. Service with restrictions, supervision.

▼▼ **Red Roof Inn-Austin South** SH
(512) 448-0091. **$55-$71.** 4701 I-35 S. I-35, exit 230B (Ben White Blvd/SR 71) southbound; exit 229 (Stassney Rd) northbound, on northbound frontage road. Int corridors. **Pets:** Medium, other species. Service with restrictions, supervision.

🔺🔺🔺 ▼▼▼ ▼▼▼ **Renaissance Austin Hotel** LH ❀
(512) 343-2626. **$219-$289.** 9721 Arboretum Blvd. Jct US 183 and Capital of Texas Hwy (SR 360); southwest corner. Int corridors. **Pets:** $50 deposit/pet. Service with restrictions, supervision.

▼▼▼ **Residence Inn by Marriott Austin Airport/South** SH
(512) 912-1100. **$109-$189.** 4537 S I-35. I-35, exit 229 (Stassney Rd) southbound; exit 230 (Ben White Blvd/SR 71) northbound, on northbound frontage road. Int corridors. **Pets:** Medium, other species. $100 one-time fee/room. Service with restrictions.

▼▼▼ **Residence Inn by Marriott-Austin North/Parmer Lane** SH
(512) 977-0544. **$143-$180.** 12401 N Lamar Blvd. I-35, exit 245, just w. Int corridors. **Pets:** Accepted.

▼▼▼ **Staybridge Suites Hotel** SH
(512) 349-0888. **$109-$199.** 10201 Stonelake Blvd. Jct US 183 and Capital of Texas Hwy (SR 360); northwest corner. Int corridors. **Pets:** Accepted.

▼▼ **Studio 6-Austin Midtown #6033** M
(512) 458-5453. **$53-$71.** 6603 I-35 N. I-35, exit 238A, on east frontage road. Ext corridors. **Pets:** Accepted.

▼▼ ▼▼ Studio 6-Northwest #6032 **M**
(512) 258-3556. **$53-$71.** 11901 Pavillon Blvd. US 183, exit Oak Knoli westbound; exit Duval/Balcones Woods eastbound, on eastbound frontage road. Ext corridors. **Pets:** Accepted.
🅂🄳 ⊠ 🄳 🄷 💻

AAA ▼▼▼ Super 8 Austin North **SH**
(512) 339-1300. **$60-$70.** 8128 N I-35. I-35, exit 241, on west frontage road. Int corridors. **Pets:** Accepted.
SAVE 🅂🄳 ⊠ 🄳 🄷 💻 ≈

AAA ▼▼▼ Super 8 Central **M**
(512) 472-8331. **$55-$160.** 1201 N I-35. I-35, exit 234, at 12th St. Ext corridors. **Pets:** Small. $60 one-time fee/pet. Service with restrictions, supervision.
SAVE 🅂🄳 ⊠ 🄳 🄷 ≈

▼▼ ▼▼ The Woodward Hotel & Conference Center **SH**
(512) 448-2444. **$79-$159, 3 day notice.** 3401 I-35 S. I-35, exit 231 (Woodward St) southbound; exit 230 (Ben White Blvd/SR 71) northbound; on northbound frontage road. Ext/int corridors. **Pets:** Accepted.
ASK 🅂🄳 ⊠ 🄳 🄷 💻 🍴 ≈ ⊠

BANDERA

AAA ▼▼▼ Bandera Lodge Motel **SH**
(830) 796-3093. **$75-$110, 7 day notice.** 700 Hwy 16 S. 1 mi s on SR 16; 7 mi s of jct SR 173. Ext corridors. **Pets:** Very small. $10 daily fee/pet. Service with restrictions, supervision.
SAVE 🅂🄳 ⊠ 🄳 ≈

BASTROP

▼▼ ▼▼ Days Inn Bastrop **SH**
(512) 321-1157. **$55-$75.** 4102 Hwy 71 E. On SR 71, 2 mi e of river at Loop 150 E. Ext corridors. **Pets:** Dogs only. Designated rooms, supervision.
ASK 🅂🄳 ⊠ 🄳 🄷 💻

BEAUMONT

AAA ▼▼▼ Best Western Jefferson Inn **SH**
(409) 842-0037. **$69-$79.** 1610 I-10 S. I-10, exit 851 (College St), westbound service road; 0.5 mi s of jct US 90. Ext corridors. **Pets:** Service with restrictions, supervision.
SAVE 🅂🄳 ⊠ 🄳 🄷 💻 ≈

AAA ▼▼▼▼ Holiday Inn Beaumont Midtown **SH**
(409) 892-2222. **$99-$129.** 2095 N 11th St. I-10, exit 853B (11th St), just n. Int corridors. **Pets:** Accepted.
SAVE ⊠ 🄲🄼 🄳 🄳 🄷 💻 🍴 ≈

AAA ▼▼▼▼ Holiday Inn Beaumont Plaza **LH**
(409) 842-5995. **$139-$149.** 3950 I-10 S. I-10, exit 848 (Walden Rd), just n. Int corridors. **Pets:** $25 daily fee/room. Service with restrictions, supervision.
SAVE 🅂🄳 ⊠ 🄳 🄲 🄷 💻 🍴 ≈

▼▼▼ ▼▼ Howard Johnson Express Inn & Suites **SH**
(409) 832-0666. **$79-$119, 3 day notice.** 2615 I-10 E. I-10, exit 853B (11th St). Ext corridors. **Pets:** Accepted.
ASK 🅂🄳 ⊠ 🄲🄼 🄳 💻 ≈

▼▼▼▼ La Quinta Inn & Suites **SH**
(409) 842-0002. **$109-$139.** 5820 Walden Rd. I-10, exit 848, just n. Int corridors. **Pets:** Small. $50 deposit/room. Service with restrictions, supervision.
ASK 🅂🄳 ⊠ 🄲🄼 🄳 💻 ≈

AAA ▼▼▼ La Quinta Inn Beaumont (Midtown) **SH**
(409) 838-9991. **$95-$115.** 220 I-10 N. I-10, exit 852B (Calder Ave) eastbound; exit 852A (Laurel Ave) westbound, on eastbound service road. Ext corridors. **Pets:** Medium. Service with restrictions.
SAVE ⊠ 🄳 🄲 🄳 💻 ≈

BEDFORD

AAA ▼▼▼▼ Baymont Inn DFW West **SH**
(817) 267-5200. **$99.** 1450 W Airport Frwy. SR 121/183, 0.3 mi e of jct Bedford Rd/Forest Ridge Dr exit. Ext corridors. **Pets:** Accepted.
SAVE 🅂🄳 ⊠ 🄳 🄳 🄷 💻 ≈

BEEVILLE

▼▼ ▼▼ Best Western Texan Inn **SH**
(361) 358-9999. **$65-$95.** 2001 Hwy 59. US 181 at US 59, just e. Ext/int corridors. **Pets:** Accepted.
ASK 🅂🄳 ⊠ 🄷 💻 ≈

▼▼ ▼▼ Motel 6 **SH**
(361) 358-4000. **$45-$55.** 400 S US 181 Bypass. 0.3 mi s of jct US 59 and 181. Ext corridors. **Pets:** Medium, other species. Service with restrictions, supervision.
ASK 🅂🄳 ⊠ 🄷 ≈

BELTON

AAA ▼▼▼ Budget Host Inn **SH** 🐾
(254) 939-0744. **$60-$70.** 1520 S I-35. I-35, exit 292 southbound; exit 293A northbound. Ext corridors. **Pets:** Medium. $20 one-time fee/room. Service with restrictions, crate.
SAVE 🅂🄳 ⊠ 🄷 💻 ≈

▼▼ ▼▼ Ramada Limited **SH**
(254) 939-3745. **$65-$69.** 1102 E 2nd Ave. I-35, exit 294A southbound; exit 294B northbound. Ext corridors. **Pets:** Accepted.
ASK 🅂🄳 ⊠ 🄷 💻 ≈

BENBROOK

AAA ▼▼▼▼ Best Western Winscott Inn & Suites **SH**
(817) 249-0076. **$85-$150.** 590 Winscott Rd. I-20, exit 429B. Int corridors. **Pets:** Small. $10 daily fee/pet. Service with restrictions, supervision.
SAVE 🅂🄳 ⊠ 🄲 🄷 💻 ≈

▼▼ Motel 6-4051 **SH**
(817) 249-8885. **$55-$75.** 8601 Benbrook Blvd (Hwy 377 S). I-20, exit 429A, 0.7 mi s. Int corridors. **Pets:** Medium, other species. Service with restrictions, supervision.
ASK 🅂🄳 ⊠ 🄲🄼 🄲 🄷 ≈

BIG SPRING

AAA ▼▼▼ Best Western Plaza Inn **SH**
(432) 264-7086. **$59-$79.** 300 Tulane Ave. I-20, exit 179, just s. Ext corridors. **Pets:** Medium. $20 one-time fee/pet. Service with restrictions, supervision.
SAVE 🅂🄳 ⊠ 🄲🄼 🄲 🄷 💻 ≈

AAA ▼▼▼ Comfort Inn **M**
(432) 267-4553. **$55-$99.** 2900 E I-20. I-20, exit 179. Ext corridors. **Pets:** Small, other species. $10 one-time fee/pet. Service with restrictions, supervision.
SAVE ⊠ 🄷 💻 ≈

AAA ▼▼▼ Super 8 Motel **M**
(432) 267-1601. **$60-$66, 3 day notice.** 700 W I-20. I-20, exit 177, just n. Ext corridors. **Pets:** Accepted.
SAVE 🅂🄳 ⊠ 🄳 🄷 💻 ≈

BOERNE

AAA ▼▼▼ Best Western Texas Country Inn **SH**
(830) 249-9791. **$76-$96.** 35150 I-10 W. I-10, exit 540 (SR 46), westbound access road. Ext corridors. **Pets:** Accepted.
SAVE 🅂🄳 ⊠ 🄷 💻 ≈

BONHAM

[AAA] ◆ **5 Star Inn** [M]
(903) 583-3121. **$46-$52.** 1515 Old Ector Rd. Jct SR 56 W and 121 S. Ext corridors. **Pets:** $25 deposit/room. Designated rooms, service with restrictions, supervision.
[SAVE] [SD] ✕ ■ 🖥 🏊

BORGER

[AAA] ◆◆◆ **Best Western Borger Inn** [SH]
(806) 274-7050. **$67-$99.** 206 S Cedar. Jct SR 136 and 207, just n. Int corridors. **Pets:** Other species. $10 one-time fee/pet. Service with restrictions, supervision.
[SAVE] [SD] ✕ ♿ ■ 🖥 🏊

BOWIE

[AAA] ◆◆ **Days Inn** [SH]
(940) 872-5426. **$60-$75.** 2436 S US 287. Jct SR 59. Ext corridors. **Pets:** Accepted.
[SAVE] [SD] ✕ ■ 🏊

[AAA] ◆ **Park's Inn** [M]
(940) 872-1111. **$45-$50.** 708 W Wise St. 0.5 mi n of jct SR 59; downtown. Ext corridors. **Pets:** Small. $5 daily fee/pet. No service, supervision.
[SAVE] [SD] ✕ ■ 🏊

BRADY

[AAA] ◆◆ **Best Western Brady Inn** [SH]
(325) 597-3997. **$60-$69.** 2200 S Bridge St. 1.1 mi s on US 87/377. Ext corridors. **Pets:** Very small, other species. $10 one-time fee/pet. Service with restrictions, supervision.
[SAVE] [SD] ✕ ■ 🖥 🏊

[AAA] ◆◆ **Days Inn** [M]
(325) 597-0789. **$49-$59.** 2108 S Bridge St. 1 mi s on US 87/377 at US 190. Ext corridors. **Pets:** Very small, other species. $5 one-time fee/pet. Service with restrictions, supervision.
[SAVE] [SD] ✕ ■ 🖥 🏊

BRENHAM

[AAA] ◆◆◆ **Best Western Inn of Brenham** [SH]
(979) 251-7791. **$69-$129.** 1503 Hwy 290 E. Eastbound, 0.7 mi w of jct US 290 E and SR 577; westbound, 1.3 mi e of jct SR 36 and US 290. Ext corridors. **Pets:** Accepted.
[SAVE] [SD] ✕ ■ 🖥 🍴 🏊

◆◆◆ **Comfort Suites** [SH]
(979) 421-8100. **$69-$149.** 2350 S Day St. US 290, exit SR 36 S, just n on Business Rt SR 36. Int corridors. **Pets:** Accepted.
[A$K] [SD] ✕ ■ 🖥 🏊

BROWNFIELD

◆◆ **Best Western Caprock Inn** [SH]
(806) 637-9471. **$69.** 321 Lubbock Rd. Jct US 385 and 82, 2 blks n. Ext corridors. **Pets:** Accepted.
[A$K] [SD] ✕ ♿ ■ 🖥 🏊

BROWNSVILLE

◆◆◆ **Hawthorn Suites** [SH]
(956) 574-6900. **$89-$129.** 3759 North Expwy. US 77, exit McAllen Rd; on southbound access road. Int corridors. **Pets:** Accepted.
[A$K] [SD] ✕ ■ 🖥 🏊 🏋

[AAA] ◆◆◆ **La Quinta Inn & Suites** [SH]
(956) 350-2118. **$80-$150.** 5051 N Expwy US 77. US 77, exit Alton Gloor Rd southbound; exit Cameron Rd northbound U-turn; on southbound access road. Int corridors. **Pets:** Accepted.
[SAVE] [SD] ✕ ♿ ■ 🖥 🏊

[AAA] ◆◆ **Red Roof Inn** [SH]
(956) 504-2300. **$47-$80.** 2377 North Expwy. US 83, exit FM 802, just s. Ext corridors. **Pets:** Medium, other species. Service with restrictions, supervision.
[SAVE] ✕ ♿ ■ 🖥 🏊

◆◆◆ **Residence Inn by Marriott** [SH]
(956) 350-8100. **$125-$149.** 3975 North Expwy. US 77 and 83, exit McAllen Rd. Int corridors. **Pets:** $100 one-time fee/room. Service with restrictions, supervision.
[A$K] [SD] ✕ ♿M ♿ ■ 🖥 🏊 🏋

◆◆◆ **Staybridge Suites** [SH]
(956) 504-9500. **$99-$159.** 2900 Pablo Kisel Blvd. US 77/83 exit FM 802, 0.8 mi n on access road to Pablo Kisel Blvd, 0.5 mi e. Int corridors. **Pets:** Other species. $75 daily fee/pet. Service with restrictions, supervision.
[A$K] [SD] ✕ ♿ ■ 🖥 🏊 🏋

◆◆ **Super 8 Motel** [SH]
(956) 350-8855. **Call for rates.** 8280 North Expwy. US 77/83, exit SR 511, just e. Int corridors. **Pets:** Accepted.
✕ ♿ ■ 🖥 🏊

BURLESON

[AAA] ◆◆◆ **Comfort Suites** [SH]
(817) 426-6666. **$95.** 321 S Burleson Blvd. I-35W, exit 34 southbound, 2 mi s to exit 36, U-turn; exit 36 northbound, on northbound access road. Int corridors. **Pets:** Medium. $25 daily fee/pet. Service with restrictions, supervision.
[SAVE] [SD] ✕ ♿M ♿ ■ 🖥 🏊

[AAA] ◆◆ **Days Inn** [SH]
(817) 447-1111. **$70.** 329 S Burleson Blvd. I-35W, exit 34 southbound, 2 mi s to crossover, U-turn; exit 36 northbound, on northbound access road. Ext corridors. **Pets:** Small, other species. $10 daily fee/pet. Service with restrictions, supervision.
[SAVE] [SD] ✕ ■ 🏊

CANTON

[AAA] ◆◆ **Best Western Canton Inn** [SH]
(903) 567-6591. **$59-$189.** 2251 N Trade Days Blvd. Jct I-20 and SR 19, exit 527. Ext corridors. **Pets:** Very small. $5 daily fee/pet. Service with restrictions, crate.
[SAVE] [SD] ✕ ■ 🖥 🏊

◆◆ **Comfort Inn & Suites** [SH]
(903) 567-0909. **Call for rates.** 2406 N Trade Days Blvd. I-20, exit 527. Ext corridors. **Pets:** Accepted.
[A$K] ✕ ♿M ♿ ■ 🖥 🏊

◆◆ **Super 8 Motel** [SH]
(903) 567-6567. **$55-$170, 3 day notice.** 17350 I-20. I-20, exit 527. Ext corridors. **Pets:** $5 daily fee/pet. Service with restrictions, supervision.
[A$K] [SD] ✕ ■ 🖥 🏊

CANYON

◆◆◆ **Best Western Palo Duro Canyon** [SH]
(806) 655-1818. **$64-$99.** 2801 4th Ave. I-27, exit 106, 1 mi w. Int corridors. **Pets:** Accepted.
[A$K] [SD] ✕ ♿M ♿ ■ 🖥 🏊

[AAA] ◆◆◆ **Holiday Inn Express Hotel & Suites** [SH]
(806) 655-4445. **$71-$100.** 2901 4th Ave. I-27, exit 106, 2 mi w. Int corridors. **Pets:** Other species. $10 one-time fee/room. Service with restrictions, supervision.
[SAVE] [SD] ✕ ♿M ♿ ■ 🖥 🏊

CEDAR PARK

(AAA) ▼▼ Comfort Inn SH
(512) 259-1810. **$75-$105.** 300 E Whitestone Blvd. I-35, exit 256, 8 mi w on FM 1431. Int corridors. **Pets:** Other species. $10 daily fee/pet. Service with restrictions, supervision.
(SAVE) (S₀) (✕) (&M) (✍) (🌙) (❂) (💻) (⇌)

CHILDRESS

(AAA) ▼▼▼ Best Western Childress M
(940) 937-6353. **$99-$109.** 1801 Ave F NW (Hwy 287). On US 287, just s of jct US 62/83. Ext corridors. **Pets:** Large, other species. $10 daily fee/pet. Designated rooms.
(SAVE) (S₀) (✕) (❂) (💻) (⇌)

(AAA) ▼▼▼ Comfort Inn SH
(940) 937-6363. **$85-$155.** 1804 Ave F NW (Hwy 287). On US 287, just s of jct US 62/83. Ext corridors. **Pets:** Accepted.
(SAVE) (S₀) (✕) (&M) (✍) (❂) (💻) (⇌)

(AAA) ▼▼▼ Days Inn SH
(940) 937-0622. **$67-$77.** 2220 Ave F (Hwy 287). 1.8 mi w on US 287 from jct US 62/83. Int corridors. **Pets:** Accepted.
(SAVE) (S₀) (✕) (&) (❂) (⇌)

(AAA) ▼▼▼ Econo Lodge SH
(940) 937-3695. **$48-$65.** 1612 Ave F NW, Hwy 287. On US 287, just s of jct US 62/83. Ext corridors. **Pets:** Accepted.
(SAVE) (S₀) (✕) (💻)

(AAA) ▼▼▼ Super 8 Motel Childress M
(940) 937-8825. **$60-$80.** 411 Ave F NE (Hwy 287 S). Jct US 83/287, 1.5 mi e. Ext corridors. **Pets:** $13 daily fee/pet. Designated rooms, service with restrictions, supervision.
(SAVE) (S₀) (✕) (&) (❂) (💻) (⇌)

CISCO

▼▼ Americas Best Value Inn of Cisco M
(254) 442-3735. **$59-$79.** 1898 Hwy 206 W. I-20, exit 330. Ext corridors. **Pets:** Accepted.
(ASK) (S₀) (✕) (❂) (💻) (⇌)

CLARENDON

(AAA) ▼▼▼▼ Best Western Red River Inn SH
(806) 874-0160. **$99-$109.** 902 W 2nd St. Jct US 287 and SR 70. Int corridors. **Pets:** Accepted.
(SAVE) (✕) (&M) (&) (❂) (💻) (⇌)

(AAA) ▼▼▼ Western Skies Motel M
(806) 874-3501. **$45-$99.** 800 W 2nd St. 0.5 mi nw on US 287 and SR 70. Ext corridors. **Pets:** Small. $5 daily fee/pet. Designated rooms, service with restrictions, supervision.
(SAVE) (S₀) (✕) (❂) (⇌)

CLAUDE

(AAA) ▼▼ L A Motel M
(806) 226-4981. **$35-$45, 5 day notice.** Hwy 287/200 E 1st St. 0.3 mi s. Ext corridors. **Pets:** Small. No service, supervision.
(SAVE) (S₀) (✕) (❂) (🍴)

CLEBURNE

▼▼ Budget Host Inn-Sagamar Inn M
(817) 556-3631. **$75-$85.** 2107 N Main St. US 67, exit SR 174 (Main St), just e. Ext corridors. **Pets:** Small, dogs only. $15 daily fee/pet. Service with restrictions, supervision.
(ASK) (S₀) (✕) (❂) (💻) (⇌)

(AAA) ▼▼▼▼ Comfort Inn SH
(817) 641-4702. **$89-$150.** 2117 N Main St. On SR 174, just s of jct US 67. Int corridors. **Pets:** Other species. $10 daily fee/pet. Designated rooms, service with restrictions, supervision.
(SAVE) (S₀) (✕) (&M) (✍) (&) (❂) (💻) (⇌)

CLUTE

(AAA) ▼▼▼▼ Best Western Clute Inn & Suites SH
(979) 388-0055. **$70-$120.** 900 Hwy 332. Just w of jct SR 288. Int corridors. **Pets:** Small, other species. $20 daily fee/pet. Service with restrictions, supervision.
(SAVE) (S₀) (✕) (&) (❂) (💻) (⇌)

(AAA) ▼▼▼ La Quinta Inn Clute/Lake Jackson M
(979) 265-7461. **$84-$104.** 1126 Hwy 332 W. On SR 288/332, just w of jct Business Rt SR 288. Ext corridors. **Pets:** Medium. Service with restrictions.
(SAVE) (✕) (✍) (❂) (💻) (⇌)

(AAA) ▼▼▼▼ Mainstay Suites Clute/Lake Jackson SH
(979) 388-9300. **$109-$159.** 1003 W Hwy 332. Just w of jct SR 288. Int corridors. **Pets:** Small. $100 deposit/room. Service with restrictions, supervision.
(SAVE) (S₀) (✕) (❂) (💻) (⇌)

COLLEGE STATION

▼▼ Clarion Hotel College Station SH
(979) 693-1736. **$59-$199.** 1503 Texas Ave S. 1.3 mi s of jct SR 60. Int corridors. **Pets:** Small. $25 one-time fee/room. Service with restrictions.
(ASK) (S₀) (✕) (✍) (❂) (💻) (🍴) (⇌)

▼▼▼ Hilton College Station and Conference Center LH
(979) 693-7500. **$99-$259.** 801 University Dr E. SR 6, exit University Dr, 1.1 mi w. Int corridors. **Pets:** Accepted.
(✕) (&) (❂) (💻) (🍴) (⇌)

(AAA) ▼▼▼ Howard Johnson SH
(979) 693-6810. **$55-$145.** 3702 Hwy 6. SR 6 S, exit Rock Prairie Rd. Ext corridors. **Pets:** Medium. $10 daily fee/pet. Service with restrictions, supervision.
(SAVE) (S₀) (✕) (❂) (💻) (⇌)

(AAA) ▼▼▼ La Quinta Inn College Station SH
(979) 696-7777. **$91-$137.** 607 Texas Ave. Just s on jct SR 60 and 6 business route to Live Oak St, then just e. Ext corridors. **Pets:** Medium. Service with restrictions.
(SAVE) (✕) (❂) (💻) (⇌)

(AAA) ▼▼▼ Manor House Inn SH
(979) 764-9540. **$52, 4 day notice.** 2504 Texas Ave S. 2.4 mi s of jct SR 60. Ext corridors. **Pets:** Accepted.
(SAVE) (S₀) (✕) (❂) (💻) (⇌)

(AAA) ▼▼▼ Ramada Inn SH
(979) 693-9891. **$69-$125, 3 day notice.** 1502 Texas Ave S. 1.3 mi s of jct SR 60. Int corridors. **Pets:** Medium, other species. $15 one-time fee/pet. Service with restrictions, crate.
(SAVE) (S₀) (✕) (❂) (💻) (🍴) (⇌)

▼▼▼ Super 8 Motel-College Station M
(979) 846-8800. **$70-$125.** 301 Texas Ave. Just n of jct SR 60. Int corridors. **Pets:** Accepted.
(ASK) (S₀) (✕) (✍) (&) (❂)

▼▼▼▼ TownePlace Suites By Marriott SH
(979) 260-8500. **$89-$131.** 1300 E University Dr. SR 6, exit University Dr, 1 mi w. Ext corridors. **Pets:** Accepted.
(✕) (✍) (&) (❂) (💻) (⇌)

COLUMBUS

AAA ▼▼▼▼ Holiday Inn Express Hotel & Suites SH
(979) 733-9300. **$89-$150.** 4321 I-10. I-10, exit 696 (SR 71), just w on westbound service road. Int corridors. **Pets:** Accepted.
SAVE S♦ ✕ 🐾 ⊟ ▣ ➿

CONWAY

AAA ▼▼▼ Budget Host S & S Motel M
(806) 537-5111. **$45-$55.** I-40 & SR 207. I-40, exit 96 (SR 207), 0.3 mi w on southbound access road. Ext corridors. **Pets:** Medium. Service with restrictions, supervision.
SAVE S♦ ✕ 🍴

CORPUS CHRISTI

AAA ▼▼▼ Best Western Garden Inn SH
(361) 241-6675. **$84-$129, 7 day notice.** 11217 I-37. I-37, exit 11B (Violet Rd), exit 11B (Violet Rd); on southbound access road. Ext corridors. **Pets:** Medium. $25 daily fee/pet. Service with restrictions, supervision.
SAVE S♦ ✕ ⊟ ▣ ➿ ✕

AAA ▼▼▼ Best Western Marina Grand Hotel SH
(361) 883-5111. **$79-$195.** 300 N Shoreline Blvd. Center of downtown. Int corridors. **Pets:** Small. $25 one-time fee/room. Service with restrictions, supervision.
SAVE S♦ ✕ ⊟ ▣ ➿

▼▼▼ Best Western on the Island SH
(361) 949-2300. **$79-$139.** 14050 S Padre Island Dr. On Park Rd 22. Ext corridors. **Pets:** Medium, other species. $50 deposit/room. Designated rooms, supervision.
ASK S♦ ✕ 🐾 ⊟ ▣ ➿

▼▼▼ Christy Estate Suites CO
(361) 854-1091. **$109-$169.** 3942 Holly Rd. SR 358, exit Weber Rd, 0.5 mi s. Ext/int corridors. **Pets:** Accepted.
ASK S♦ ✕ 🐾 ⊟ ▣ ➿

▼▼ Days Inn-Airport SH
(361) 888-8599. **$40-$130.** 901 Navigation Blvd. I-37, exit 3A (Navigation Blvd), just w. Ext corridors. **Pets:** Accepted.
ASK S♦ ✕ 🐾 ⊟ ▣ 🍴 ➿

▼▼▼ Days Inn Corpus Christi South SH
(361) 854-0005. **$59-$139.** 2838 S Padre Island Dr. On SR 358 westbound access road, 0.4 mi w, exit Kostoryz Rd. Ext corridors. **Pets:** Small. $25 daily fee/pet. Designated rooms, service with restrictions, supervision.
ASK S♦ ✕ ⊟ ▣ ➿

▼▼▼ Drury Inn-Corpus Christi SH
(361) 289-8200. **$70-$123.** 2021 N Padre Island Dr. I-37, exit SR 358, just se at Leopard St. Int corridors. **Pets:** Large, other species. Service with restrictions, supervision.
ASK ✕ 🐾 ⊟ ▣ ➿

AAA ▼▼▼ Holiday Inn-Airport and Conference Center LH
(361) 289-5100. **$81-$117.** 5549 Leopard St. Jct SR 358 and Leopard St, 5.5 mi w. Int corridors. **Pets:** Small, other species. $25 one-time fee/pet. Designated rooms, service with restrictions, supervision.
SAVE S♦ ✕ 🐾 ⊟ ▣ 🍴 ➿

▼▼▼ Holiday Inn-Emerald Beach LH
(361) 883-5731. **$125-$159.** 1102 S Shoreline Blvd. 1.5 mi s on bay from downtown marina. Ext/int corridors. **Pets:** Accepted.
ASK S♦ ✕ 🐾M 🐾 ⊟ ▣ 🍴 ➿ ✕

▼▼▼ Homewood Suites by Hilton SH
(361) 854-1331. **$144-$164.** 5201 Crosstown Expwy (SR 286). I-37, exit SR 358 E (Greenwood), 0.6 mi e. Int corridors. **Pets:** Accepted.
ASK S♦ ✕ 🐾 ⊟ ▣ ✕

▼▼▼ La Quinta Inn Corpus Christi (North) SH
(361) 888-5721. **$86-$136.** 5155 I-37 N. I-37, exit 3A (Navigation Blvd), on southbound access road. Ext corridors. **Pets:** Medium. Service with restrictions.
ASK ✕ 🐾 ⊟ ▣ ➿

AAA ▼▼▼ La Quinta Inn Corpus Christi (South) SH
(361) 991-5730. **$101-$154.** 6225 S Padre Island Dr. SR 358, exit Airline Rd. Ext corridors. **Pets:** Medium. Service with restrictions.
SAVE ✕ 🐾 ⊟ ▣ ➿

▼▼ Motel 6 #231 M
(361) 289-9397. **$41-$55.** 845 Lantana St. I-37, exit 4B (Lantana St), on southbound access road. Ext corridors. **Pets:** Medium, other species. Service with restrictions, supervision.
S♦ ✕ 🐾 ➿

▼ Motel 6 SPI Drive–413 SH
(361) 991-8858. **$40-$61.** 8202 S Padre Island Dr. S Padre Island Dr at Paul Jones St. Ext corridors. **Pets:** Medium, other species. Service with restrictions, supervision.
S♦ ✕ 🐾 ➿

AAA ▼▼▼ Omni Corpus Christi Hotel-Bayfront Tower LH
(361) 887-1600. **$194.** 900 N Shoreline Blvd. In town across from bay; downtown; in the marina district. Int corridors. **Pets:** Small. $50 one-time fee/pet. Service with restrictions, crate.
SAVE S♦ ✕ 🐾M ⊟ ▣ 🍴 ➿ ✕

▼▼▼ Omni Corpus Christi Hotel-Marina Tower LH
(361) 887-1600. **$189.** 707 N Shoreline Blvd. Just n across from bay. Int corridors. **Pets:** Accepted.
ASK S♦ ✕ 🐾 ⊟ ▣ 🍴 ➿ ✕

AAA ▼▼▼ Quality Inn Sandy Shores SH
(361) 883-7456. **$79-$209, 3 day notice.** 3202 Surfside Blvd. 1 mi n on US 181; at north end of Harbor Bridge, exit Bridge St. Ext/int corridors. **Pets:** Accepted.
SAVE S♦ ✕ ⊟ ▣ ➿

AAA ▼▼▼ Red Roof Inn SH
(361) 992-9222. **$47-$86.** 6805 S Padre Island Dr. SR 358, exit Nile Dr. Ext corridors. **Pets:** Medium, other species. Service with restrictions, supervision.
SAVE ✕ ⊟ ▣ ➿

AAA ▼▼▼ Red Roof Inn Corpus Christi Airport M
(361) 289-6925. **$37-$100.** 6301 I-37. I-37, exit 5 (Corn Products Rd), southbound access road. Ext corridors. **Pets:** Medium, other species. Service with restrictions, supervision.
SAVE S♦ ✕ 🐾 ⊟ ➿

AAA ▼▼▼ Rodeway Inn SH
(361) 883-6161. **$69-$139.** 5224 I-37 (Navigation Blvd). I-37, exit 3A (Navigation Blvd), on northbound access road. Ext corridors. **Pets:** Accepted.
SAVE S♦ ✕ ⊟ ▣ ➿

AAA ▼▼▼ Surfside Condominium Apartments CO
(361) 949-8128. **$140-$170.** 15005 Windward Dr. Park Rd 22 on N Padre Island Dr, jct Whitecap Blvd, 0.6 mi n to Winward Dr, 0.8 mi w. Ext corridors. **Pets:** Medium. $15 daily fee/pet. Designated rooms, service with restrictions, supervision.
SAVE ✕ ⊟ ▣ ➿

DALHART

AAA ▼▼▼ Best Western Nursanickel Motel SH
(806) 244-5637. **$59-$75.** 102 Scott Ave (Hwy 87 S). Just s of jct US 54 and 87. Ext corridors. **Pets:** Accepted.
SAVE S♦ ✕ ⊟ ▣ ➿

AAA ▼▼ Budget Inn M
(806) 244-4557. **$40-$69.** 415 Liberal St (Hwy 54). On US 54, just e of US 87 and 385. Ext corridors. **Pets:** Medium. $20 deposit/pet. Service with restrictions, supervision.
SAVE S✗ ⊠ 🖥

AAA ▼▼ Comfort Inn M
(806) 249-8585. **$75-$120.** 1110 Hwy 54 E. 0.5 mi e of jct US 54 and 87. Ext corridors. **Pets:** Medium. Designated rooms, service with restrictions, supervision.
SAVE S✗ ⊠ 🖥 💻 ⇆

AAA ▼▼▼ Days Inn SH
(806) 244-5246. **$70-$180.** 701 Liberal St (Hwy 54). On US 54, 0.5 mi e. Int corridors. **Pets:** Very small. $25 daily fee/pet. No service, supervision.
SAVE S✗ ⊠ ♿ 🖥 💻 ⇆

▼▼▼▼ Holiday Inn Express SH
(806) 249-1145. **$89-$149, 7 day notice.** 801 Liberal St (Hwy 54). 1 mi e of jct US 54 and 87. Int corridors. **Pets:** Very small. $25 one-time fee/pet. No service, supervision.
ASK ⊠ 🔧 🖥 💻 ⇆

AAA ▼▼ Sands Motel M
(806) 244-4568. **$40-$80.** 301 Liberal St (Hwy 54). On US 54, just e of US 87 and 385. Ext corridors. **Pets:** Medium. Designated rooms, service with restrictions, supervision.
SAVE S✗ ⊠ 🖥

AAA ▼▼▼ Super 8 Motel M
(806) 249-8526. **$60-$70.** 403 Tanglewood Rd. Jct US 87/54, 0.5 mi e. Int corridors. **Pets:** Medium. $25 deposit/pet. Designated rooms, service with restrictions, supervision.
SAVE S✗ ⊠ 🖥

DALLAS METROPOLITAN AREA

ADDISON

AAA ▼▼▼▼ Comfort Inn Hotel by the Galleria SH
(972) 701-0881. **$65-$99.** 14975 Landmark Blvd. Jct Belt Line Rd and Landmark Blvd, just s. Int corridors. **Pets:** Accepted.
SAVE S✗ ⊠ 🔧 🔧 🖥 💻 ⇆

▼▼▼▼ Courtyard by Marriott-Addison/Midway SH
(972) 490-7390. **$139-$189.** 4165 Proton Dr. 0.8 mi s of jct Belt Line and Midway rds, just w. Int corridors. **Pets:** Accepted.
ASK S✗ ⊠ 🔧 🔧 🖥 💻 🍽 ⇆

▼▼▼▼ Homewood Suites by Hilton SH
(972) 788-1342. **$89-$159.** 4451 Belt Line Rd. Just e of jct Belt Line and Midway rds. Ext/int corridors. **Pets:** Accepted.
ASK S✗ ⊠ 🔧 🔧 🔧 🖥 💻 ⇆ ✗

▼▼▼▼ La Quinta Inn & Suites Dallas (Addison-Galleria Area) SH
(972) 404-0004. **$84-$121.** 14925 Landmark Blvd. Jct Belt Line Rd and Landmark Blvd, just s. Int corridors. **Pets:** Medium. Service with restrictions.
ASK ⊠ 🔧 🔧 🔧 🖥 💻 ⇆

▼▼▼▼ Residence Inn by Marriott SH
(972) 866-9933. **Call for rates.** 14975 Quorum Dr. Just s of jct Beltline Rd and Quorum Dr. Int corridors. **Pets:** Medium. $75 one-time fee/room. Service with restrictions.
⊠ 🔧 🖥 💻 ⇆ ✗

▼▼▼▼ Summerfield Suites by Wyndham-Addison/North Dallas SH
(972) 661-3113. **$95-$124.** 4900 Edwin Lewis Dr. Just n of jct Belt Line Rd and Quorum Dr to Edwin Lewis Dr, then just w. Ext/int corridors. **Pets:** Accepted.
ASK ⊠ 🔧 🔧 🖥 💻 ⇆ ✗

ALLEN

AAA ▼▼▼ AmeriHost Inn-Allen SH 🐾
(972) 396-9494. **$90-$199.** 407 Central Expwy. US 75, exit 33 (Bethany Dr). Int corridors. **Pets:** Other species. $30 one-time fee/room. Service with restrictions.
SAVE ⊠ 🔧 🖥 💻 ⇆ ✗

BALCH SPRINGS

AAA ▼▼▼ Americas Best Value Inn & Suites M
(972) 286-1010. **$50-$210.** 12875 Seagonville Rd. I-20, exit 481, just n. Int corridors. **Pets:** Accepted.
SAVE S✗ ⊠ 🖥 💻 ⇆

THE COLONY

AAA ▼▼▼▼ Comfort Suites SH
(972) 668-5555. **$79-$170.** 4796 Memorial Dr. Just n of jct SR 121. Int corridors. **Pets:** Small. $25 one-time fee/room. Service with restrictions, supervision.
SAVE S✗ ⊠ 🔧 🔧 🔧 🖥 💻 ⇆

COMMERCE

AAA ▼▼▼▼ Holiday Inn Express Hotel & Suites SH
(903) 886-4777. **$85-$125.** 2207 Culver St. 0.9 mi e of jct SR 224, 24 and 50. Int corridors. **Pets:** Accepted.
SAVE S✗ ⊠ 🔧 🔧 🖥 💻 ⇆

DALLAS

▼▼▼▼ Baymont Inn & Suites SH
(214) 350-5577. **$80.** 2370 W Northwest Hwy. I-35E, exit 436 Northwest Hwy (Loop 12), 0.8 mi e. Int corridors. **Pets:** Accepted.
ASK S✗ ⊠ 🔧 🔧 🖥 💻 ⇆

AAA ▼▼▼ Best Western City Place Inn SH
(214) 827-6080. **$79-$99.** 4150 N Central Expwy. US 75, exit 1B (Fitzhugh Ave) southbound; exit 2 (Fitzhugh Ave) northbound. Ext corridors. **Pets:** Small. $25 one-time fee/pet. Designated rooms, no service, supervision.
SAVE S✗ ⊠ 🔧 🖥 💻 ⇆

▼▼▼ Best Western Dallas Telecom Area Suites SH
(972) 669-0478. **$89-$149.** 13636 Goldmark Dr. US 75, exit 22 (Midpark Rd), just w. Ext/int corridors. **Pets:** Accepted.
ASK S✗ ⊠ 🖥 💻 ⇆

▼▼▼▼ Candlewood Dallas Market Center SH
(214) 631-3333. **$94-$189.** 7930 N Stemmons Frwy. I-35, exit 433B (Mockingbird Ln), on northbound frontage road. Int corridors. **Pets:** Accepted.
ASK S✗ ⊠ 🔧 🖥 💻 ⇆

▼▼▼▼ Candlewood Suites-Dallas by the Galleria SH
(972) 233-6888. **$90-$110.** 13939 Noel Rd. Jct Dallas Pkwy and Spring Valley, just e to Noel Rd, then just s. Int corridors. **Pets:** Medium. $75 one-time fee/pet. Service with restrictions, crate.
ASK S✗ ⊠ 🔧 🔧 🖥 💻

▼▼▼▼ Candlewood Suites Dallas North/Richardson SH
(972) 669-9606. **$76-$78.** 12525 Greenville Ave. I-635, exit 18A (Greenville Ave), just n. Int corridors. **Pets:** Accepted.
ASK S✗ ⊠ 🔧 🔧 🖥 💻

▼▼▼▼ Clarion Hotel Park Central SH
(972) 960-6555. **$74, 7 day notice.** 8102 LBJ Frwy. I-635, exit 19C (Coit Rd) eastbound; exit 19B (US 75/Coit Rd) westbound. Int corridors. **Pets:** Accepted.

ⒶⓈⓀ Ⓢⓓ ⊠ 𝄞 ▣ ⊺⊺ ⌁

ⒶⒶⒶ ▼▼▼▼ Comfort Inn & Suites Market Center SH
(214) 461-2677. **$89-$129.** 7138 N Stemmons Frwy. I-35E, exit 433B (Mockingbird Ln) northbound; exit 432B (Commonwealth Dr) southbound, turn under freeway, 0.7 mi on north access road. Int corridors. **Pets:** Accepted.

SAVE ⊠ 𝄞 ⓓ ⊟ ▣

▼▼▼▼ Country Inn & Suites Dallas Park Central SH
(972) 907-9500. **$63-$81.** 13185 N Central Expwy. US 75 N, exit 22 (Midpark Rd). Int corridors. **Pets:** Accepted.

ⒶⓈⓀ Ⓢⓓ ⊠ 𝄞 ⓓ ⊟ ▣ ⌁

▼▼▼▼ Crowne Plaza Hotel Dallas Market Center LH
(214) 630-8500. **$89-$195.** 7050 Stemmons Frwy. I-35E, exit 433B northbound; exit 432B southbound. Int corridors. **Pets:** Medium. $25 one-time fee/room. Service with restrictions, crate.

ⒶⓈⓀ Ⓢⓓ ⊠ ⓓ ⊟ ▣ ⊺⊺ ⌁ ⊠

ⒶⒶⒶ ▼▼▼▼ Crowne Plaza Suites Hotel Dallas Park Central LH
(972) 233-7600. **$169-$209.** 7800 Alpha Rd. I-635, exit 19C (Coit Rd) eastbound; exit 19B (Coit Rd) westbound, 0.3 mi nw of jct US 75. Int corridors. **Pets:** Accepted.

SAVE Ⓢⓓ ⊠ 𝄞 ⓓ ⊟ ▣ ⊺⊺ ⌁

ⒶⒶⒶ ▼▼▼▼ Dallas Marriott Suites Market Center SH
(214) 905-0050. **$139-$299.** 2493 N Stemmons. I-35E, exit 431 (Motor St). Int corridors. **Pets:** Accepted.

SAVE Ⓢⓓ ⊠ ⓜ 𝄞 ⓓ ⊟ ▣ ⊺⊺ ⌁

▼▼▼ Extended StayAmerica SH
(972) 238-1133. **Call for rates.** 12270 Greenville Ave. I-635, exit 18A (Greenville Ave), just s. Int corridors. **Pets:** Accepted.

⊠ ⓓ ⊟ ▣

▼▼▼ Extended StayAmerica Dallas-North-Park Central SH
(972) 671-7722. **$54-$64.** 9019 Vantage Point Rd. I-635, exit 18A (Greenville Ave), just sw. Ext corridors. **Pets:** Accepted.

ⒶⓈⓀ Ⓢⓓ ⊠ ⓜ ⓓ ⊟ ▣

▼▼ ▼▼ The Fairmont Dallas LH
(214) 720-2020. **$99-$309.** 1717 N Akard St. Corner of Ross Ave and N Akard St. Int corridors. **Pets:** Accepted.

ⒶⓈⓀ Ⓢⓓ ⊠ 𝄞 ⓓ ⊟ ▣ ⊺⊺ ⌁

ⒶⒶⒶ ▼▼▼▼ Holiday Inn Select Dallas Central LH
(214) 373-6000. **$86-$95.** 10650 N Central Expwy. US 75, exit 6 (Walnut Hill Ln/Meadow Rd), 0.5 mi n on northbound access road. Int corridors. **Pets:** Accepted.

SAVE Ⓢⓓ ⊠ 𝄞 ⓓ ⊟ ▣ ⊺⊺ ⌁

▼▼ ▼▼ Homestead Studio Suites Hotel-Dallas/North Addison/Tollway SH
(972) 447-1800. **$63-$72.** 17425 North Dallas Pkwy. North Dallas Tollway, exit Trinity Mills, just s of jct Trinity Mills and Dallas Pkwy, on southbound access road. Ext corridors. **Pets:** Accepted.

ⒶⓈⓀ Ⓢⓓ ⊠ ⓓ ⊟ ▣

▼▼▼▼ Homestead Studio Suites Hotel-Dallas/Plano SH
(972) 248-2233. **$79-$89.** 18470 N Dallas Pkwy. North Dallas Tollway, exit Frankford, just ne. Int corridors. **Pets:** Accepted.

ⒶⓈⓀ Ⓢⓓ ⊠ ⓜ 𝄞 ⓓ ⊟ ▣ ⌁

▼▼▼▼ Homewood Suites by Hilton SH
(214) 819-9700. **$99-$239.** 2747 N Stemmons Frwy. I-35E, exit 432A (Inwood Rd), just s. Int corridors. **Pets:** Accepted.

ⒶⓈⓀ Ⓢⓓ ⊠ ⓜ 𝄞 ⓓ ⊟ ▣ ⌁

▼▼▼▼ Homewood Suites by Hilton–I-635 SH
(972) 437-6966. **$144-$164.** 9169 Markville Dr. I-635, exit 18A (Greenville Ave S), just s, then just e. Int corridors. **Pets:** Accepted.

ⒶⓈⓀ Ⓢⓓ ⊠ ⓓ ⊟ ▣ ⌁ ⊠

▼▼▼▼ Hotel Crescent Court LH ❀
(214) 871-3200. **$365-$2500.** 400 Crescent Ct. Corner of Crescent Ct and McKinney Ave; uptown. Int corridors. **Pets:** $100 one-time fee/room.

⊠ ⊺⊺ ⌁ ⊠

ⒶⒶⒶ ▼▼▼▼ Hotel Lawrence SH
(214) 761-9090. **$119-$399.** 302 S Houston St. I-35E, exit 428A (Commerce St), 0.8 mi to Griffin, just s to Jackson St, then just w. Int corridors. **Pets:** Accepted.

SAVE Ⓢⓓ ⊠ ▣ ⊺⊺

ⒶⒶⒶ ▼▼▼ ▼▼▼ Hotel St. Germain CI ❀
(214) 871-2516. **$290-$650, 7 day notice.** 2516 Maple Ave. I-35, exit 430A (Oak Lawn Ave), 0.5 mi e, then 1 mi s. Int corridors. **Pets:** Small, dogs only. $50 daily fee/pet. Designated rooms, service with restrictions, supervision.

SAVE ⊠ ⊺⊺

ⒶⒶⒶ ▼▼▼ ▼▼▼ Hotel ZaZa SH ❀
(214) 468-8399. **$295-$415.** 2332 Leonard St. Jct Maple Ave/Routh St and McKinney Ave, northeast corner. Int corridors. **Pets:** Medium, other species. $50 one-time fee/pet. Service with restrictions.

SAVE Ⓢⓓ ⊠ ⓜ ⓓ ⊟ ⊺⊺ ⌁ ⊠

▼▼▼▼ La Quinta Inn & Suites Dallas (North Central) SH
(214) 361-8200. **$109-$139.** 10001 N Central Expwy. US 75, exit 6 (Walnut Hill Ln/Meadow Rd) northbound, 0.5 mi n to Meadow Rd, then U-turn under highway; exit 7 (Royal/Meadow Rd) southbound, 1 mi s on feeder. Int corridors. **Pets:** Medium. Service with restrictions.

ⒶⓈⓀ ⊠ ⓜ 𝄞 ⊟ ▣ ⌁

▼▼▼▼ La Quinta Inn & Suites Dallas Northwest SH
(214) 904-9955. **$80-$180.** 2380 W Northwest Hwy. I-35, exit 436 Northwest Hwy (Loop 12), 0.8 mi e. Int corridors. **Pets:** Small. $50 deposit/pet. Service with restrictions, supervision.

ⒶⓈⓀ Ⓢⓓ ⊠ 𝄞 ⓓ ⊟ ▣ ⌁

ⒶⒶⒶ ▼▼▼▼ La Quinta Inn Dallas (City Place) SH
(214) 821-4220. **$99-$119.** 4440 N Central Expwy. N off US 75, exit 2 (Henderson-Knox) northbound; exit 1B (Haskell/Blackburn) southbound. Ext corridors. **Pets:** Medium. Service with restrictions.

SAVE ⊠ 𝄞 ⓓ ⊟ ▣ ⌁

▼▼▼▼ La Quinta Inn Dallas (East) SH
(214) 324-3731. **$80-$110.** 8303 E R L Thornton Frwy. I-30, exit 52A (Jim Miller Rd). Ext corridors. **Pets:** Medium. Service with restrictions.

ⒶⓈⓀ ⊠ ⓜ ⓓ ⊟ ▣ ⌁

▼▼ ▼▼ La Quinta Inn Dallas (Richardson) SH
(972) 234-1016. **$65-$75.** 13685 N Central Expwy. US 75 N, exit 22 (Midpark Rd). Ext/int corridors. **Pets:** Accepted.

ⒶⓈⓀ ⊠ 𝄞 ⓓ ⊟ ▣ ⌁

ⒶⒶⒶ ▼▼▼ ▼▼▼ The Mansion On Turtle Creek LH ❀
(214) 559-2100. **$400-$2400.** 2821 Turtle Creek Blvd. 2 mi nw, entrance on Gillespie St, just e of jct Gillespie and Lawn sts. Int corridors. **Pets:** Medium, other species. $100 one-time fee/room. Service with restrictions, crate.

SAVE ⊠ ⓓ ⊟ ▣ ⊺⊺ ⌁ ⊠

ⒶⒶⒶ ▼▼▼▼ The Melrose Hotel SH
(214) 521-5151. **$295-$495.** 3015 Oak Lawn Ave. I-35E, exit 430 (Oak Lawn Ave), 0.8 mi n; entrance off Cedar Springs. Int corridors. **Pets:** Accepted.

SAVE ⊠ ⊟ ▣ ⊺⊺

Motel 6–560 SH
(972) 620-2828. **$41-$53.** 2753 Forest Ln. I-635, exit 26 (Josey Ln) eastbound; exit 25 (Josey Ln) westbound, just s to Forest Ln, then just w. Ext corridors. **Pets:** Medium, other species. Service with restrictions, supervision.

Motel 6 Forest Lane-South #1119 SH
(972) 484-9111. **$42-$52.** 2660 Forest Ln. I-635, exit 26 (Josey Ln) eastbound, 0.5 mi s to Forest Ln, then just w; exit 25 (Josey Ln) westbound, just s to Forest Ln, then just w. Ext corridors. **Pets:** Medium, other species. Service with restrictions, supervision.

Quality Inn & Suites-North Dallas SH
(972) 484-3330. **$89-$150.** 2421 Walnut Hill Ln. I-35E, exit 438 (Walnut Hill Ln). Int corridors. **Pets:** Medium, other species. $25 one-time fee/pet. Service with restrictions, crate.

Radisson Dallas Love Field LH
(214) 630-7000. **$79.** 1241 W Mockingbird Ln. I-35E, exit 433B, just ne of jct I-35E and W Mockingbird Ln. Int corridors. **Pets:** $50 one-time fee/pet. Service with restrictions, supervision.

Radisson Hotel Central/Dallas LH
(214) 750-6060. **$109-$179.** 6060 N Central Expwy. US 75, exit 3 (Mockingbird Ln), on northbound frontage road. Int corridors. **Pets:** Accepted.

Red Roof Inn-Market Center M
(214) 638-5151. **$50-$55.** 1550 Empire Central Dr. I-35E, exit 434A (Empire Central Dr), 0.3 mi e. Ext corridors. **Pets:** Medium, other species. Service with restrictions, supervision.

Renaissance Dallas Hotel LH
(214) 631-2222. **$119-$249.** 2222 Stemmons Frwy. I-35E, exit 430B (Market Center Blvd), 0.3 mi nw on access road. Int corridors. **Pets:** Accepted.

Residence Inn by Marriott at Dallas Central SH
(214) 750-8220. **$149-$179.** 10333 N Central Expwy. US 75, exit 6 (Walnut Hill Ln/Meadow Rd) northbound, 0.5 mi n to Meadow Rd, U-turn under highway; exit 7 (Royal/Meadow Rd) southbound, 1 mi s on access road. Ext corridors. **Pets:** Accepted.

Residence Inn by Marriott-Dallas Market Center SH
(214) 631-2472. **$129-$159.** 6950 N Stemmons Frwy. I-35E, exit 432B (Commonwealth Ln), 0.6 mi n on northbound frontage road. Ext/int corridors. **Pets:** Accepted.

Residence Inn by Marriott-Dallas Park Central SH
(972) 503-1333. **$139-$169.** 7642 LBJ. I-635, exit 20 (Hillcrest), just e, on eastbound access road. Int corridors. **Pets:** Accepted.

Sheraton Suites Market Center-Dallas LH ❖
(214) 747-3000. **$125, 3 day notice.** 2101 Stemmons Frwy. Nw off I-35E and US 77, exit 430B (Market Center Blvd). Int corridors. **Pets:** $50 deposit/room. Service with restrictions, crate.

SpringHill Suites by Marriott-Stemmons SH
(214) 350-2300. **$139-$159.** 2363 Stemmons Tr. Nw off I-35E and US 77; 0.3 mi se of jct Northwest Hwy (Loop 12) and SR 348, exit 436. Int corridors. **Pets:** Accepted.

Staybridge Suites Dallas By The Galleria SH
(972) 391-0000. **$135.** 7880 Alpha Rd. I-635, exit 19B (Coit Rd), 0.3 mi n, then just w. Int corridors. **Pets:** Other species. $125 one-time fee/room. Service with restrictions, crate.

StudioPLUS SH
(214) 630-0154. **Call for rates.** 2979 N Stemmons Frwy. I-35E, exit 432B, on eastbound access road. Int corridors. **Pets:** Accepted.

Super 7 M
(214) 388-8741. **$43-$55.** 8108 E R L Thornton Frwy. I-30, exit 52A (Jim Miller Rd). Ext corridors. **Pets:** Accepted.

Super 8 Motel SH
(972) 572-1030. **$75.** 8541 S Hampton Rd. I-20, exit 465, 0.3 mi e to S Hampton Rd, then just s. Ext corridors. **Pets:** Accepted.

The Westin City Center, Dallas LH
(214) 979-9000. **$119-$169.** 650 N Pearl St. Between San Jacinto and Bryan St, 0.3 mi w of US 75 Central Expwy. Int corridors. **Pets:** Accepted.

The Westin Galleria, Dallas LH
(972) 934-9494. **$359-$439.** 13340 Dallas Pkwy. Just n of jct I-635 and N Dallas Pkwy. Int corridors. **Pets:** Accepted.

Wyndham Dallas Market Center Hotel SH
(214) 741-7481. **$102-$160.** 2015 Market Center Blvd. I-35E, exit 430B (Market Center Blvd), just w. Int corridors. **Pets:** Accepted.

DENTON

Exel Inn of Denton SH
(940) 383-1471. **$45-$89.** 4211 I-35E N. Jct US 380 and I-35, exit 469, just n. Int corridors. **Pets:** Small, other species. Designated rooms, service with restrictions, supervision.

La Quinta Inn Denton SH
(940) 387-5840. **$88-$111.** 700 Fort Worth Dr. I-35E, exit 465B (Fort Worth Dr), just n. Ext corridors. **Pets:** Medium. Service with restrictions.

Motel 6 Denton #97 M
(940) 566-4798. **$45-$55.** 4125 I-35 N. I-35, exit 469. Ext corridors. **Pets:** Medium, other species. Service with restrictions, supervision.

Quality Inn & Suites Denton SH
(940) 387-3511. **$59-$129.** 1500 Dallas Dr. 2 mi se of jct I-35E and US 77 business route, exit 464 westbound; exit 465A (Teasley Ln) eastbound, 0.4 mi n to Dallas Dr, then 0.5 mi e. Ext corridors. **Pets:** Other species. $20 one-time fee/pet. Service with restrictions.

Radisson Hotel Denton SH
(940) 565-8499. **$79-$109.** 2211 I-35E. Off I-35E and US 77, exit 466B (N Texas Blvd), 2.5 mi sw. Int corridors. **Pets:** Other species. $50 deposit/room. Service with restrictions, crate.

Super 8 Motel-Denton SH
(940) 380-8888. **$55-$170.** 620 S I-35 E. I-35, exit 465A (Teasley Ln). Int corridors. **Pets:** Accepted.

DESOTO

▼▼▼ **Holiday Inn** SH
(972) 224-9100. **$89-$129.** 1515 N Beckley Dr. I-35E, exit 416 (Wintergreen Rd), just s. Ext/int corridors. **Pets:** Accepted.
[ASK] [SD] [X] [B] [P] [TT] [≈] [X]

▼ **Red Roof Inn Dallas/DeSoto** SH
(972) 224-7100. **$49-$59.** 1401 N Beckley Ave. I-35E, exit 416, just s. Ext/int corridors. **Pets:** Medium, other species. Service with restrictions, supervision.
[X] [∅] [∅] [B]

DUNCANVILLE

▼ **Motel 6-#1130** SH
(972) 296-0345. **$45-$58.** 202 Jellison Blvd. I-20, exit 462A (Duncanville Rd) eastbound; exit 462B (Main St) westbound, just s to Camp Wisdom, just w to Duncanville Rd, just n to Jellison Blvd, then just w. Ext/int corridors. **Pets:** Medium, other species. Service with restrictions, supervision.
[SD] [X] [∅] [B] [≈]

FARMERS BRANCH

▼▼ **Comfort Inn of North Dallas** SH
(972) 406-3030. **$65-$98.** 14040 Stemmons Frwy. I-35E, exit 442 (Valwood Pkwy). Int corridors. **Pets:** Small, other species. $15 daily fee/pet. Service with restrictions, supervision.
[ASK] [SD] [X] [B] [P] [≈]

⚹⚹⚹ ▼▼▼ **Holiday Inn Select North Dallas** SH
(972) 243-3363. **$79-$189.** 2645 LBJ Frwy. I-635, exit 26 (Josey Ln) eastbound, just n; exit 25 westbound, 0.4 mi w. Int corridors. **Pets:** Accepted.
[SAVE] [SD] [X] [∅] [∅] [B] [P] [TT] [≈] [X]

▼▼▼ **La Quinta Inn Dallas (NW-Farmers Branch)** SH
(972) 620-7333. **$77-$97.** 13235 Stemmons Frwy. I-35E, exit 441 (Valley View Ln), on southbound frontage road. Ext corridors. **Pets:** Medium. Service with restrictions.
[ASK] [X] [∅] [∅] [B] [P] [≈]

⚹⚹⚹ ▼▼▼▼ **Omni Dallas Hotel Park West** LH
(972) 869-4300. **$99-$289.** 1590 LBJ Frwy. Nw off I-635, 1.5 mi w of jct I-35E, exit 29 (Luna Rd). Int corridors. **Pets:** Accepted.
[SAVE] [SD] [X] [∅] [∅] [B] [P] [TT] [≈] [X]

FRISCO

⚹⚹⚹ ▼▼▼▼ **Embassy Suites Dallas-Frisco Hotel & Conference Center** LH ✿
(972) 712-7200. **$149-$349.** 7600 John Q Hammons Dr. SR 121, exit Parkwood, just n. Int corridors. **Pets:** Small, dogs only. $25 daily fee/pet. Service with restrictions, crate.
[SAVE] [X] [∅M] [∅] [B] [P] [TT] [≈] [X]

⚹⚹⚹ ▼▼▼▼ **The Westin Stonebriar Resort** LH
(972) 668-8000. **$359-$1750.** 1549 Legacy Dr. 0.3 mi n of jct SR 121. Int corridors. **Pets:** Accepted.
[SAVE] [SD] [X] [∅M] [∅] [B] [P] [TT] [≈] [X]

GARLAND

⚹⚹⚹ ▼▼▼ **Best Western Lakeview Inn** SH
(972) 303-1601. **$65-$79.** 1635 E I-30 at Chaha Rd. I-30, exit 62 (Chaha Rd). Ext corridors. **Pets:** Accepted.
[SAVE] [SD] [X] [∅] [B] [P] [≈]

▼▼▼ **Holiday Inn Select LBJ NE (Garland)** SH
(214) 341-5400. **$109.** 11350 LBJ Frwy. I-635, exit 13 (Jupiter/Kingsley rds), just sw. Int corridors. **Pets:** Accepted.
[ASK] [SD] [X] [B] [P] [TT] [≈]

⚹⚹⚹ ▼▼▼ **La Quinta Inn Dallas (Garland)** SH
(972) 271-7581. **$80-$100.** 12721 I-635. I-635, exit 11B, just nw. Ext/int corridors. **Pets:** Medium. Service with restrictions.
[SAVE] [X] [∅] [B] [P] [≈]

⚹⚹⚹ ▼▼▼ **Microtel Inn & Suites** SH
(972) 270-7200. **$50-$95.** 1901 Pendleton Dr. I-635, exit 11B, just n to Pendleton Dr, then just e. Int corridors. **Pets:** Small. $10 daily fee/pet. Designated rooms, service with restrictions, supervision.
[SAVE] [SD] [X] [∅] [B] [P]

▼ **Motel 6-0620** SH
(972) 226-7140. **$43-$55.** 436 W I-30. I-30, exit 59 (Belt Line Rd). Ext corridors. **Pets:** Medium, other species. Service with restrictions, supervision.
[SD] [X] [∅] [≈]

GRAND PRAIRIE

▼▼▼ **La Quinta Inn Dallas (Grand Prairie)** SH
(972) 641-3021. **$74-$97.** 1410 NW 19th St. I-30, exit 32, just e. Ext corridors. **Pets:** Medium. Service with restrictions.
[ASK] [X] [∅M] [∅] [∅] [B] [P] [≈]

▼ **Motel 6-446** SH
(972) 642-9424. **$38-$51.** 406 E Palace Pkwy. I-30, exit 34 (Belt Line Rd), just n to Safari Pkwy, then 0.6 mi w. Ext corridors. **Pets:** Medium, other species. Service with restrictions, supervision.
[SD] [X] [∅] [B] [P] [≈]

GREENVILLE

▼▼▼ **Holiday Inn Express Hotel & Suites** SH
(903) 454-8680. **$85.** 2901 Mustang Crossing. I-30, exit 93A. Int corridors. **Pets:** Small. $100 deposit/room. Service with restrictions, supervision.
[ASK] [SD] [X] [∅M] [∅] [B] [P] [≈]

▼▼▼ **La Quinta Inn & Suites** SH
(903) 454-3700. **$109-$129, 7 day notice.** 3001 Mustang Crossing. I-30, exit 93-A. Int corridors. **Pets:** Small, other species. $50 deposit/pet. Service with restrictions, supervision.
[ASK] [SD] [∅M] [∅] [B] [P] [≈]

▼▼ **Quality Inn** SH
(903) 454-7000. **$60-$80, 7 day notice.** 1215 E I-30. I-30, exit 94B, just e of jct I-30 and US 69. Int corridors. **Pets:** Small. $20 deposit/room, $5 daily fee/room. Service with restrictions, supervision.
[ASK] [SD] [X] [B] [P] [≈]

IRVING

▼▼▼ **Candlewood Dallas/Las Colinas** SH
(972) 714-9990. **$99-$150.** 5300 Greenpark Dr. SR 114, exit Walnut Hill Ln, just s. Int corridors. **Pets:** Medium, other species. $75 one-time fee/pet. Service with restrictions, crate.
[ASK] [SD] [X] [∅M] [∅] [∅] [B] [P]

⚹⚹⚹ ▼▼▼ **Clarion Hotel DFW Airport South** LH
(972) 399-1010. **$60, 7 day notice.** 4440 W Airport Frwy. SR 183, exit Valley View Ln, on eastbound access road. Int corridors. **Pets:** Accepted.
[SAVE] [SD] [X] [∅] [∅] [B] [P] [TT] [≈] [X]

▼▼ **Days Inn DFW North** SH
(972) 621-8277. **$54.** 4325 W Hwy 114. SR 114, exit Belt Line Rd, on westbound service road. Ext corridors. **Pets:** Accepted.
[ASK] [SD] [X] [B] [P] [TT] [≈]

⚹⚹⚹ ▼▼▼ **DFW North Super 8 Motel** SH
(214) 441-9000. **$44-$98.** 4770 W John Carpenter Frwy (SR 114). SR 114, exit Freeport Pkwy. Int corridors. **Pets:** Accepted.
[SAVE] [SD] [X] [∅M] [∅] [B] [P]

▼▼▼▼ **Drury Inn & Suites-DFW Airport** SH
(972) 986-1200. **$80-$125.** 4210 W Airport Frwy. SR 183, exit Esters Rd, on southbound access road. Int corridors. **Pets:** Large, other species. Service with restrictions, supervision.

▼▼ **Extended Stay Deluxe (Dallas-Las Colinas-Green Park Dr.)** SH
(972) 751-0808. **$63-$73.** 5401 Green Park Dr. SR 114, exit Walnut Hill Ln, just s. Int corridors. **Pets:** Accepted.

▲▲▲ ▼▼▼▼▼ **Four Seasons Resort and Club** LH ❀
(972) 717-0700. **$380-$525.** 4150 N MacArthur Blvd. SR 114, exit MacArthur Blvd, 1.5 mi s. Int corridors. **Pets:** Very small. Service with restrictions, supervision.

▼▼▼▼ **Hampton Inn-DFW Airport South** SH
(972) 986-3606. **$82-$141.** 4340 W Airport Frwy. SR 183, exit Valley View Ln, on southbound access road. Int corridors. **Pets:** Accepted.

▼▼ **Homestead Studio Suites Hotel-Dallas/DFW Airport North** SH
(972) 929-3333. **$54-$64.** 7825 Heathrow Dr. SR 114, exit Esters Blvd, s to Plaza Dr, then just w. Int corridors. **Pets:** Accepted.

▼▼ **Homestead Studio Suites Hotel-Dallas/Las Colinas/ Carnaby St.** SH
(972) 756-0458. **$49-$54.** 5315 Carnaby St. SR 114, exit MacArthur Blvd, 0.5 mi s, then just e on Meadow Creek. Ext corridors. **Pets:** Accepted.

▼▼▼ **Homewood Suites by Hilton Las Colinas** SH
(972) 556-0665. **$159.** 4300 Wingren Dr. Ne off SR 114, exit O'Connor Rd/Wingren Dr eastbound, just n to Las Colinas Blvd, 0.4 mi e to Rochelle Rd, then just s; exit Rochelle Rd westbound. Ext/int corridors. **Pets:** Accepted.

▼▼▼ **La Quinta Inn & Suites Dallas (DFW-Airport North)** SH
(972) 915-4022. **$90-$132.** 4850 W John Carpenter Frwy. SR 114, exit Freeport Pkwy, on eastbound service road. Int corridors. **Pets:** Medium. Service with restrictions.

▼▼▼ **La Quinta Inn & Suites Dallas DFW Airport South (Irving)** SH
(972) 252-6546. **$116-$167.** 4105 W Airport Frwy. 3 mi nw off SR 183, exit Esters Rd; on northbound access road. Int corridors. **Pets:** Medium. Service with restrictions.

▼ **Motel 6 #1274 DFW North** M
(972) 915-3993. **$45-$55.** 7800 Heathrow Dr. SR 114, exit Freeport Pkwy, just se. Int corridors. **Pets:** Medium, other species. Service with restrictions, supervision.

▼▼▼▼ **Omni Mandalay Hotel at Las Colinas** LH ❀
(972) 556-0800. **$109-$249.** 221 E Las Colinas Blvd. Nw off SR 114, exit O'Connor Rd. Int corridors. **Pets:** Small. $50 one-time fee/room. Service with restrictions.

▲▲▲ ▼▼▼ **Quality Inn & Suites DFW Airport North** SH
(972) 929-4008. **$39-$159.** 4100 W John Carpenter Frwy. SR 114, exit Esters Blvd, s to Reese St, then e. Ext corridors. **Pets:** Medium. $10 daily fee/pet. Designated rooms, service with restrictions, supervision.

▼▼▼▼ **Red Roof Inn/DFW Airport North** M
(972) 929-0020. **$56-$74.** 8150 Esters Blvd. SR 114, exit Esters Blvd, just n. Ext corridors. **Pets:** Medium, other species. Service with restrictions, supervision.

▼▼▼▼ **Residence Inn by Marriott at Las Colinas** SH
(972) 580-7773. **$189-$219.** 950 W Walnut Hill Ln. SR 114, exit MacArthur Blvd, 0.5 mi s, then just e. Ext corridors. **Pets:** Accepted.

▼▼▼▼ **Residence Inn by Marriott-DFW/Irving** SH
(972) 871-1331. **$99-$189.** 8600 Esters Blvd. SR 114, exit Esters Blvd, 0.9 mi n. Int corridors. **Pets:** Accepted.

▼▼▼▼ **Sheraton Grand Hotel** LH
(972) 929-8400. **$249-$279.** 4440 W John Carpenter Frwy. SR 114, exit Esters Blvd, just s. Int corridors. **Pets:** Accepted.

▼▼▼▼ **Staybridge Suites Dallas-Las Colinas** SH
(972) 465-9400. **$179.** 1201 Executive Cir. SR 114, exit MacArthur Blvd, just s to W Walnut Hill Ln, then just w. Int corridors. **Pets:** Accepted.

▼▼▼▼ **Summerfield Suites by Wyndham-Las Colinas** SH
(972) 831-0909. **$89-$159.** 5901 N MacArthur Blvd. SR 114, exit MacArthur Blvd, jct MacArthur Blvd and SR 114, northwest corner. Ext/int corridors. **Pets:** Accepted.

▼▼▼▼ **The Westin Dallas Fort Worth Airport** LH
(972) 929-4500. **$89-$289.** 4545 W John Carpenter Frwy. Nw off SR 114, exit Esters Blvd. Int corridors. **Pets:** Accepted.

▼▼▼▼ **Wyndham-Las Colinas** SH
(972) 650-1600. **$69-$179.** 110 W John Carpenter Frwy. Sw off SR 114, exit O'Connor Rd. Int corridors. **Pets:** Accepted.

LEWISVILLE

▼▼ **Comfort Suites by Choice Hotels** SH
(972) 315-6464. **$95-$115.** 755A Vista Ridge Mall Dr. I-35E, exit 448A (Round Grove Rd) southbound, 0.5 mi s of jct I-35 and Round Grove Rd on southbound service road to Vista Ridge Mall Dr, then just w; exit 447B northbound, just w on SR 121 Bypass. Int corridors. **Pets:** Accepted.

▼▼▼ **Country Inn & Suites by Carlson** SH
(972) 315-6565. **$75-$95.** 755B Vista Ridge Mall Dr. I-35E, exit 448A (Round Grove Rd) southbound, 0.5 mi s on service road to Vista Ridge Rd; exit 447B northbound, just w on SR 121 Bypass. Int corridors. **Pets:** Accepted.

▼▼ **Extended Stay Hotel** SH
(972) 315-7455. **Call for rates.** 1900 Lake Pointe Dr. I-35E, exit 449 (Corporate Dr), just e. Int corridors. **Pets:** Accepted.

▼▼▼ **Holiday Inn Express Hotel & Suites, Dallas-Lewisville** SH
(972) 459-8000. **$109-$149, 14 day notice.** 780 E Vista Ridge Mall Dr. I-35E, exit 448A, just w, then just n. Int corridors. **Pets:** Medium. $50 deposit/room. Designated rooms, service with restrictions, supervision.

▼▼▼ La Quinta Inn Dallas (Lewisville) 🆂🅷
(972) 221-7525. **$77-$107.** 1657 S Stemmons Frwy. I-35E, exit 449 (Corporate Dr), just w. Ext corridors. **Pets:** Medium. Service with restrictions.
🆂🅰🆅🅴 ⊠ 🅻🅼 📶 🛢 📟 🏊

▼▼▼ Motel 6–1288 🆂🅷
(972) 436-5008. **$41-$53.** 1705 Lakepointe Dr. I-35E, exit 449, just n on access road. Int corridors. **Pets:** Medium, other species. Service with restrictions, supervision.
🆂🅰 ⊠ 📶 🛢 🏊

▼▼▼▼ Residence Inn by Marriott Dallas 🆂🅷
(972) 315-3777. **$205-$225.** 755C Vista Ridge Mall Dr. I-35E, exit 448A (Round Grove Rd), 0.5 mi s on service road; jct I-35 and Round Grove Rd to Vista Ridge Rd, just w. Int corridors. **Pets:** Accepted.
🅰🆂🅺 🆂🅰 ⊠ 🅻🅼 📶 🛢 📟 🏊 ⊠

MCKINNEY

▼▼ Days Inn McKinney 🆂🅷
(972) 548-8888. **Call for rates.** 2104 N Central Expwy. US 75, 0.5 mi n of jct US 380, exit 41. Ext corridors. **Pets:** Medium. $9 daily fee/pet. Service with restrictions.
🅰🆂🅺 ⊠ 🛢 🏊

▼▼ Super 8 Motel-McKinney 🆂🅷
(972) 548-8880. **$50-$100.** 910 N Central Expwy. US 75, exit 40A (Virginia St/Louisiana St), 0.5 mi n on northbound service road. Int corridors. **Pets:** Accepted.
🅰🆂🅺 ⊠ 🛢 🏊

MESQUITE

▼▼▼▼ Comfort Inn 🆂🅷
(972) 285-6300. **$69-$109.** 923 Windbell Cir. I-635, exit 5, just e. Int corridors. **Pets:** Accepted.
🅰🆂🅺 🆂🅰 ⊠ 🅻🅼 📶 🛢 📟 🏊

▼▼ Crossland Economy Studios 🆂🅷
(972) 270-3653. **Call for rates.** 2544 US Hwy 67. I-30, exit 56A, on eastbound access road. Ext corridors. **Pets:** Accepted.
⊠ 🛢 📟

▼▼▼▼ La Quinta Inn and Suites 🆂🅷
(972) 216-7460. **$79-$139.** 118 E Hwy 80. US 80 E, exit Belt Line Rd. Int corridors. **Pets:** Accepted.
🅰🆂🅺 🆂🅰 ⊠ 🅻🅼 🛢 📟 🏊

▼▼▼ Super 8 Motel 🆂🅷
(972) 289-5481. **$47-$70.** 121 Grand Junction Blvd. I-635, exit 4 (Military Pkwy). Ext corridors. **Pets:** Accepted.
🆂🅰🆅🅴 🆂🅰 ⊠ 🛢 📟 🏊

MIDLOTHIAN

▼▼▼ Best Western Midlothian Inn 🆂🅷
(972) 775-1891. **$64-$79, 3 day notice.** 220 N Hwy 67. On US 67, just n of jct US 287. Ext corridors. **Pets:** Medium. $10 daily fee/pet. Service with restrictions, supervision.
🆂🅰🆅🅴 🆂🅰 ⊠ 🛢 📟 🏊

PLANO

▼▼▼▼ Best Western Park Suites Hotel 🆂🅷
(972) 578-2243. **$71-$99.** 640 Park Blvd E. US 75, exit 29A northbound, just e; exit 29 southbound, 0.5 mi s on access road, just e on 15th St, then 0.5 mi n on access road. Int corridors. **Pets:** Dogs only. $25 one-time fee/room. Service with restrictions, supervision.
🅰🆂🅺 🆂🅰 ⊠ 🅻🅼 🛢 📟 🏊

▼▼▼▼ Candlewood Suites-Plano 🆂🅷
(972) 618-5446. **$60-$95.** 4701 Legacy Dr. Jct SR 289 (Preston Rd) and Legacy Dr, just e. Int corridors. **Pets:** Medium. $150 one-time fee/pet. Service with restrictions, supervision.
🅰🆂🅺 🆂🅰 ⊠ 🛢 📟

▼▼ Extended Stay Deluxe 🆂🅷
(972) 398-0135. **$75-$85.** 4636 W Plano Pkwy. Jct SR 289 (Preston Rd) and W Plano Pkwy, 0.4 mi e. Int corridors. **Pets:** Accepted.
🅰🆂🅺 🆂🅰 ⊠ 🛢 📟

▼▼▼ Extended Stay Deluxe (Dallas/Plano) 🆂🅷
(972) 378-9978. **$77-$87.** 2900 Dallas Pkwy. Dallas Pkwy, exit Park Blvd northbound; exit Parker Rd southbound, on northbound service road. Int corridors. **Pets:** Accepted.
🅰🆂🅺 🆂🅰 ⊠ 🅻🅼 📶 🛢 📟 🏊

▼▼▼ Holiday Inn Express Hotel & Suites Plano East 🆂🅷
(972) 881-1881. **$114-$124.** 700 Central Pkwy E. Just e of US 75; 0.3 mi ne of jct FM 544, exit 29A northbound; exit 29 southbound, 0.5 mi s on access road, just e on 15th St, then 0.5 mi n on access road. Int corridors. **Pets:** Small. $25 one-time fee/room. Designated rooms, service with restrictions, supervision.
🅰🆂🅺 🆂🅰 ⊠ 📶 🛢 📟 🏊 ⊠

▼▼ Homestead Studio Suites Hotel-Dallas/Plano Parkway 🆂🅷
(972) 596-9966. **$72-$82.** 4709 W Plano Pkwy. Just n of jct Plano Pkwy and SR 289 (Preston Rd), then just e. Int corridors. **Pets:** Accepted.
🅰🆂🅺 🆂🅰 ⊠ 📶 🛢 📟 🏊

▼▼▼▼ Homewood Suites by Hilton 🆂🅷
(972) 758-8800. **$89-$209.** 4705 Old Shepherd Pl. Jct Plano Pkwy and SR 289 (Preston Rd), 0.4 mi n, then just e. Int corridors. **Pets:** Accepted.
🅰🆂🅺 🆂🅰 ⊠ 🅻🅼 📶 🛢 📟 🏊 ⊠

▼▼▼ La Quinta Inn & Suites Dallas (West Plano) 🆂🅷
(972) 599-0700. **$84-$150.** 4800 W Plano Pkwy. Just n of jct SR 289 (Preston Rd), then just e. Int corridors. **Pets:** Medium. Service with restrictions.
🅰🆂🅺 ⊠ 🅻🅼 📶 🛢 📟 🏊

▼▼▼ La Quinta Inn Dallas (Plano) 🆂🅷
(972) 423-1300. **$74-$102.** 1820 N Central Expwy. US 75, exit 29A (Park Blvd), northbound, just ne; exit 29 southbound, 0.5 mi s on access road, just e on 15th St, then just n on northbound access road. Ext corridors. **Pets:** Medium. Service with restrictions.
🆂🅰🆅🅴 ⊠ 🅻🅼 📶 🛢 📟 🏊

▼▼ Motel 6 🆂🅷
(972) 867-1111. **$60.** 4801 W Plano Pkwy. Just n of jct SR 289 (Preston Rd) and N Plano Pkwy, just e. Int corridors. **Pets:** Medium, other species. Service with restrictions, supervision.
🆂🅰 ⊠ 🅻🅼 📶 🛢 📟 🏊

▼▼ Motel 6–1121 🆂🅷
(972) 578-1626. **$45-$58.** 2550 N Central Expwy. US 75, exit 29A (Park Blvd) northbound; exit 29 southbound, 1 mi n of jct Park Rd (SR 544), on east side of US 75. Ext/int corridors. **Pets:** Medium, other species. Service with restrictions, supervision.
🆂🅰 ⊠ 📶 🛢 🏊

▼▼ Red Roof Inn Dallas-Plano 🆂🅷
(972) 881-8191. **$52-$65.** 301 Ruisseau Dr. SR 75, exit 30 (Parker Rd), 0.5 mi w to Premier, then just n. Ext/int corridors. **Pets:** Medium, other species. Service with restrictions, supervision.
⊠ 🅻🅼 📶 🏊

▼▼▼ Southfork Hotel 🆂🅷
(972) 578-8555. **$79-$99.** 1600 N Central Expwy. US 75, exit 29A northbound; exit 29 southbound, on northbound access road. Int corridors. **Pets:** Designated rooms, supervision.
🆂🅰🆅🅴 🆂🅰 ⊠ 🛢 🍴 🏊

▼▼ Super 8 Motel-Plano 🆂🅷
(972) 423-8300. **$50.** 1704 N Central Expwy. US 75, exit 29A (Park Blvd) northbound, just e; exit 29 southbound, 0.5 mi s on access road, just e on 15th St, then just n on access road. Int corridors. **Pets:** Accepted.
🅰🆂🅺 ⊠ 🅻🅼 📶 🛢

▼▼ ▼▼ TownePlace Suites by Marriott SH
(972) 943-8200. $57-$107. 5005 Whitestone Ln. North Dallas Tollway, exit Spring Creek Pkwy, 1.9 mi e, just n on SR 289 (Preston Rd), to Whitestone Ln, then just w. Int corridors. Pets: Accepted.
(ASK) [S🐾] (X) (&M) (&) (🖥) (💻) (🏊)

RICHARDSON

▲▲▲ ▼▼ ▼▼ Econo Lodge Inn & Suites SH
(972) 470-9440. $45-$99. 2458 N Central Expwy. US 75, exit 27 northbound; exit 26 southbound, 0.8 mi n on access road. Int corridors. Pets: Accepted.
(SAVE) [S🐾] (X) (🖥) (💻)

▼▼▼▼ Homestead Studio Suites
Hotel-Dallas/Richardson SH
(972) 479-0500. $67-$77. 901 E Campbell Rd. US 75, exit 26 (Campbell Rd), just e. Int corridors. Pets: Accepted.
(ASK) [S🐾] (X) (&M) (🐾) (&) (🖥) (💻) (🏊)

▲▲▲ ▼▼▼▼ The Radisson Hotel Dallas North At
Richardson LH 🐾
(972) 644-4000. $80-$199. 1981 N Central Expwy. US 75, exit 26 (Campbell Rd), 1.8 mi n; jct SR 5. Int corridors. Pets: Medium. $25 one-time fee/room. Service with restrictions, crate.
(SAVE) [S🐾] (X) (&M) (🐾) (&) (🖥) (💻) (🍽) (🏊)

▲▲▲ ▼▼ ▼▼ ▼▼ Renaissance Dallas-Richardson Hotel LH
(972) 367-2000. $199-$209. 900 E Lookout Dr. US 75, exit 27A (Gallatin Pkwy/Renner Rd) northbound; exit 26 (Gallatin Pkwy/Campbell Rd) southbound, just e. Int corridors. Pets: Small. $50 one-time fee/room. Designated rooms, service with restrictions, supervision.
(SAVE) [S🐾] (X) (🐾) (&) (🖥) (💻) (🍽) (🏊) (X)

▼▼▼▼ Residence Inn by Marriott Richardson SH
(972) 669-5888. $69-$130. 1040 Waterwood Dr. US 75, exit 26 (Campbell Rd), just e to Greenville Ave, 0.4 mi n to Glenville Rd, then just w. Int corridors. Pets: Accepted.
(X) (🐾) (&) (🖥) (💻) (🏊) (X)

▲▲▲ ▼▼▼▼ The Richardson Hotel LH
(972) 231-9600. $89-$299. 701 E Campbell Rd. US 75, exit 26 (Campbell Rd) southbound; exit northbound, on access road. Int corridors. Pets: Accepted.
(SAVE) [S🐾] (X) (&M) (🐾) (&) (🖥) (💻) (🍽) (🏊) (X)

ROANOKE

▲▲▲ ▼▼▼▼ Speedway Sleep Inn & Suites SH
(817) 491-3120. $70-$90. 13471 Raceway Dr. I-35, exit 70 (SR 114), just e, then just s. Int corridors. Pets: Medium. $50 deposit/room. Service with restrictions, supervision.
(SAVE) [S🐾] (X) (&M) (&) (🖥) (💻) (🏊)

ROCKWALL

▲▲▲ ▼▼▼▼ La Quinta Inn & Suites SH 🐾
(972) 771-1685. $89-$139. 689 E I-30. I-30, exit 67 westbound; exit 67B eastbound. Int corridors. Pets: Medium, other species. Service with restrictions, crate.
(SAVE) [S🐾] (X) (&M) (&) (🖥) (💻) (🏊)

ROWLETT

▲▲▲ ▼▼▼▼ Comfort Suites Lake Ray Hubbard SH
(972) 463-9595. $72. 8701 E I-30. I-30, exit 64 (Dalrock Rd). Int corridors. Pets: Accepted.
(SAVE) [S🐾] (X) (&M) (&) (🖥) (💻) (🏊)

TERRELL

▲▲▲ ▼▼ Americas Best Value Inn M
(972) 563-2676. $50-$65. 309 I-20. Jct I-20 and SR 34, exit 501. Ext corridors. Pets: Small, other species. $5 one-time fee/pet. Supervision.
(SAVE) [S🐾] (X) (🖥) (💻) (🏊)

▲▲▲ ▼▼▼ Best Western Country Inn SH
(972) 563-1521. $52-$69, 15 day notice. 1604 Hwy 34 S. I-20, exit 501 (SR 34), just n. Ext corridors. Pets: Accepted.
(SAVE) [S🐾] (X) (🖥) (💻) (🏊)

END METROPOLITAN AREA

DECATUR

▲▲▲ ▼▼ ▼▼ Best Western Decatur Inn M
(940) 627-5982. $70-$90. 1801 S Hwy 287. 0.6 mi s of jct Business Rt SR 380. Ext corridors. Pets: Accepted.
(SAVE) [S🐾] (X) (🖥) (💻) (🏊)

▲▲▲ ▼▼ ▼▼ Comfort Inn SH
(940) 627-6919. $69-$120. 1709 S US 287. 0.6 mi s of jct Business Rt SR 380. Ext corridors. Pets: Very small. $10 daily fee/pet. Service with restrictions, supervision.
(SAVE) [S🐾] (X) (🖥) (💻) (🏊)

▲▲▲ ▼▼▼▼ Holiday Inn Express Hotel & Suites SH
(940) 627-0776. $89-$179. 1051 N Hwy 287. US 380, exit US 287 N, just n. Int corridors. Pets: Medium. $25 daily fee/room. Service with restrictions, supervision.
(SAVE) [S🐾] (X) (&) (🖥) (💻) (🏊)

▲▲▲ ▼▼ ▼▼ Super 8 Motel SH
(940) 627-0250. $60-$80. 1600 US S 81/287. 0.4 mi s of jct Business Rt US 380. Int corridors. Pets: Accepted.
(SAVE) [S🐾] (X) (&) (🖥) (🏊)

DEL RIO

▲▲▲ ▼▼▼ Comfort Inn & Suites SH
(830) 775-2933. $74-$159. 3616 Veterans Blvd. 3.2 mi nw on US 90. Ext/int corridors. Pets: Supervision.
(SAVE) [S🐾] (X) (&) (🖥) (💻) (🏊)

▲▲▲ ▼▼ ▼▼ Days Inn and Suites SH
(830) 775-0585. $53-$71. 3808 Veterans Blvd. 3.5 mi nw on US 90. Ext corridors. Pets: Medium, other species. $5 daily fee/pet. Service with restrictions, supervision.
(SAVE) [S🐾] (X) (🖥) (💻) (🏊)

▼▼▼▼ La Quinta Inn Del Rio SH
(830) 775-7591. $70-$100. 2005 Veterans Blvd. 1.8 mi nw on US 90, 277 and 377. Ext/int corridors. Pets: Medium. Service with restrictions.
(ASK) (X) (&) (🖥) (💻) (🏊)

▼▼ Motel 6 Del Rio #323 SH
(830) 774-2115. $39-$51. 2115 Veterans Blvd. Jct US 90/277 and Garner Dr. Ext corridors. Pets: Medium, other species. Service with restrictions, supervision.
[S🐾] (X) (🏊)

&&& ▼▼▼ Ramada Inn SH ❖
(830) 775-1511. **$94-$124.** 2101 Veterans Blvd. 1.8 mi nw on US 90, 277 and 377. Ext/int corridors. **Pets:** Small, other species. $15 daily fee/room. Designated rooms, service with restrictions, supervision.
SAVE Sᴅ ✕ 🗎 💻 ¶¶ 🛋 ✕

DONNA

&&& ▼▼▼ Victoria Palms Inn & Suites SH
(956) 464-4656. **$105.** 602 N Victoria Rd. US 83, exit Victoria Rd. Ext corridors. **Pets:** Very small. $100 deposit/room, $5 daily fee/pet, $50 one-time fee/pet. Service with restrictions, supervision.
SAVE Sᴅ ✕ 🗎 💻 ¶¶ 🛋 ✕

DUMAS

&&& ▼▼▼ Best Western Windsor Inn SH
(806) 935-9644. **$69-$89, 7 day notice.** 1701 S Dumas Ave. US 287, 2 mi s of US 87 and SR 152. Ext corridors. **Pets:** Dogs only. $20 deposit/pet, $10 daily fee/pet, $10 one-time fee/pet. Supervision.
SAVE Sᴅ ✕ 🗎 💻 🛋 ✕

▼▼ 💎 Dumas Inn M
(806) 935-6441. **$58-$83, 5 day notice.** 1712 S Dumas Ave. US 287, 1.5 mi s from jct US 87 and SR 152. Ext/int corridors. **Pets:** Accepted.
ASK Sᴅ ✕ 🗎 💻 🛋

&&& ▼▼💎 Econo Lodge SH
(806) 935-9098. **$45-$75.** 1719 S Dumas Ave. US 287, 2 mi s of US 87 and SR 152. Int corridors. **Pets:** Medium. $7 daily fee/pet.
SAVE Sᴅ ✕ 🗎

▼▼▼▼ Holiday Inn Express SH
(806) 935-4000. **$69-$99.** 1525 S Dumas Ave. US 87, 1.1 mi s of US 87 and SR 152. Int corridors. **Pets:** Small, other species. $15 daily fee/room. Service with restrictions, supervision.
ASK Sᴅ ✕ 🗎 💻 🛋

▼▼ Super 8 Motel M
(806) 935-6222. **$79-$89.** 119 W 17th St. US 287, 2 mi s of jct US 87 and SR 152. Ext corridors. **Pets:** Accepted.
ASK ✕ 🗎 💻

EAGLE PASS

&&& ▼▼▼▼ Holiday Inn Express Hotel & Suites SH
(830) 757-3050. **$84-$89, 10 day notice.** 2007 Veterans Blvd. 1.5 mi n on Loop 431 (US 277). Int corridors. **Pets:** Accepted.
SAVE ✕ 🖥ᴍ 🐾 🗎 💻 🛋

▼▼▼▼ La Quinta Inn Eagle Pass SH
(830) 773-7000. **$77-$97.** 2525 E Main St. US 57 and 277 at Loop 431. Ext corridors. **Pets:** Medium. Service with restrictions.
ASK ✕ 🐾 🗎 💻 🛋

▼▼ Super 8 Motel SH ❖
(830) 773-9531. **$62-$68.** 2150 N US Hwy 277. On US 277, 4 mi n. Ext corridors. **Pets:** Small. Service with restrictions, crate.
ASK Sᴅ ✕ 🐾 🐾 🗎 🛋

EASTLAND

▼ Super 8 Motel & RV Park M
(254) 629-3336. **$69-$79.** 3900 I-20 E. I-20, exit 343, on north service road. Ext corridors. **Pets:** $5 daily fee/pet. Designated rooms, no service, supervision.
ASK Sᴅ ✕ 🗎 💻 🛋

EDINBURG

&&& ▼▼💎 Comfort Inn Edinburg M
(956) 318-1117. **$70-$81.** 4001 Closner Blvd. US 281, exit Trenton Rd, just w, then just n. Int corridors. **Pets:** Medium. $15 daily fee/pet, $75 one-time fee/pet. Designated rooms, service with restrictions, supervision.
SAVE Sᴅ ✕ 🐾 🗎 💻 🛋

&&& ▼▼ 💎 La Copa Inn & Suites SH
(956) 381-8888. **$45-$59.** 1210 E Canton Rd. US 281, exit Canton Rd, just off southbound access road. Ext corridors. **Pets:** Large, other species. $10 daily fee/pet. Service with restrictions, supervision.
SAVE Sᴅ ✕ 🛋

&&& ▼▼💎 Super 8 Motel SH
(956) 381-1688. **$49-$69.** 202 N Hwy 281. US 281, exit University Dr. Ext/int corridors. **Pets:** Large, other species. $10 daily fee/pet. Service with restrictions, supervision.
SAVE Sᴅ ✕ 🐾 🗎 🛋

EL PASO

&&& ▼▼ 💎 Best Western Sunland Park Inn M
(915) 587-4900. **$64-$99.** 1045 Sunland Park Dr. I-10, exit 13, just s. Ext corridors. **Pets:** Small. $20 daily fee/pet. Designated rooms, service with restrictions, supervision.
SAVE Sᴅ ✕ 🗎 💻 🛋

&&& ▼▼💎 Chase Suites by Woodfin SH
(915) 772-4400. **$149-$199.** 6791 Montana Ave. I-10, exit 25 (Airway Blvd), 1 mi n, then just e. Ext corridors. **Pets:** Accepted.
SAVE Sᴅ ✕ 🐾 🗎 💻 🛋 ✕

▼▼ 💎 Comfort Inn Airport East SH
(915) 594-9111. **$84-$94.** 900 Yarbrough Dr. I-10, exit 28B. Ext corridors. **Pets:** Accepted.
ASK Sᴅ ✕ 🗎 💻 🛋

&&& ▼▼💎 Days Inn M
(915) 845-3500. **$65-$90.** 5035 S Desert Blvd. I-10, exit 11 (Mesa St) eastbound; exit 9 (Redd) northbound, 1.5 mi e on eastbound service road. Ext corridors. **Pets:** Accepted.
SAVE Sᴅ ✕ 🗎 🛋

▼▼ 💎 Econo Lodge M
(915) 778-3311. **$65-$75.** 6363 Montana Ave. I-10, exit 24 (Geronimo Dr) westbound; exit 24B eastbound, 0.5 mi n on Geronimo Dr, 0.5 mi e. Ext corridors. **Pets:** Accepted.
ASK Sᴅ ✕ 🗎 💻 🛋

▼▼ 💎 Extended StayAmerica-El Paso-Airport SH
(915) 772-5754. **$64-$74.** 6580 Montana Ave. I-10, exit 24 (Geronimo Dr), westbound, exit 24B eastbound, 0.5 mi n on Geronimo Dr, then 0.5 mi e. Ext corridors. **Pets:** Accepted.
ASK Sᴅ ✕ 🗎 💻

▼▼💎 Hawthorn Inn & Suites SH
(915) 778-6789. **$99-$109.** 6789 Boeing. 7 mi e on US 62 and 180 to Airway Blvd, then just n. Int corridors. **Pets:** Other species. $75 one-time fee/room. Service with restrictions, supervision.
✕ 🖥ᴍ 🐾 🗎 💻 🛋

▼▼▼ Hilton El Paso Airport LH
(915) 778-4241. **$125-$235.** 2027 Airway Blvd. I-10, exit 25 (Airway Blvd), 1.3 mi n. Int corridors. **Pets:** Medium. $200 deposit/room. Service with restrictions, supervision.
Sᴅ ✕ 🐾 🐾 🗎 💻 ¶¶ 🛋 ✕

&&& ▼▼▼ Holiday Inn-Airport SH 🐾
(915) 778-6411. **$89-$169.** 6655 Gateway Blvd W. I-10, exit 25 (Airway Blvd). Ext/int corridors. **Pets:** Medium, other species. $8 daily fee/pet, $49 one-time fee/pet. Service with restrictions, supervision.
SAVE ✕ 🐾 🗎 💻 ¶¶ 🛋

&&& ▼▼▼ Holiday Inn El Paso Sunland Park SH
(915) 833-2900. **$92-$259.** 900 Sunland Park Dr. I-10, exit 13. Ext corridors. **Pets:** Medium, other species. $25 one-time fee/room. Service with restrictions, crate.
SAVE Sᴅ ✕ 🐾 🗎 💻 ¶¶ 🛋

▼▼▼ Howard Johnson Inn SH
(915) 591-9471. **$64-$78.** 8887 Gateway Blvd W. I-10, exit 26 (Hawkins Blvd). Int corridors. **Pets:** Accepted.
[ASK] [S☼] [✕] [🔒] [💻] [🍴] [➾]

▼▼ La Quinta Inn Airport East SH
(915) 593-8400. **$95-$115.** 9125 Gateway Blvd W. I-10, exit 28B westbound; exit 27 eastbound. Ext corridors. **Pets:** Medium. Service with restrictions.
[ASK] [✕] [🐾] [♿] [🔒] [💻] [➾]

▼▼ La Quinta Inn & Suites El Paso East SH
(915) 591-3300. **$91-$126.** 7944 Gateway Blvd E. I-10, exit 28B. Int corridors. **Pets:** Medium. Service with restrictions.
[ASK] [✕] [♿M] [🐾] [♿] [🔒] [💻] [➾]

ⒶⒶⒶ ▼▼ La Quinta Inn & Suites El Paso West SH
(915) 585-2999. **$79-$109.** 7620 N Mesa St. I-10, exit 11 (Mesa St). Int corridors. **Pets:** Medium. Service with restrictions.
[SAVE] [✕] [🐾] [🔒] [💻] [➾]

▼▼ La Quinta Inn El Paso (Airport) M
(915) 778-9321. **$95-$115.** 6140 Gateway Blvd E. I-10, exit 24B (Geronimo Dr) eastbound; exit 24 westbound. Ext corridors. **Pets:** Medium. Service with restrictions.
[ASK] [✕] [🐾] [♿] [🔒] [💻] [➾]

▼▼ La Quinta Inn El Paso (Lomaland) SH
(915) 591-2244. **$84-$104.** 11033 Gateway Blvd W. I-10, exit 29 eastbound; exit 30 westbound, 1 mi w. Ext corridors. **Pets:** Medium. Service with restrictions.
[ASK] [✕] [♿M] [🐾] [♿] [🔒] [💻] [➾]

ⒶⒶⒶ ▼▼ La Quinta Inn El Paso (West) M
(915) 833-2522. **$85-$105.** 7550 Remcon Cir. I-10, exit 11 (Mesa St). Ext corridors. **Pets:** Medium. Service with restrictions.
[SAVE] [✕] [🐾] [♿] [🔒] [💻] [➾]

▼▼ Microtel Inn & Suites West M
(915) 584-2026. **$55-$73.** 6185 Desert Blvd S. I-10, exit 8 (Artcraft Rd/Paseo del Norte), on eastbound frontage road. Int corridors. **Pets:** $100 deposit/room. Designated rooms, service with restrictions, crate.
[ASK] [S☼] [✕] [♿M] [🔒] [💻] [➾]

▼▼ Microtel Inn & Suites SH
(915) 772-3650. **$72-$98.** 2001 Airway Blvd. I-10, exit 25 (Airway Blvd), 1.3 mi n. Int corridors. **Pets:** Small, other species. $100 deposit/pet. Service with restrictions, supervision.
[ASK] [✕] [♿M] [🐾] [♿] [🔒] [💻] [➾]

▼▼ Microtel Inn & Suites El Paso East SH
(915) 858-1600. **$51-$71.** 12211 Gateway W at Don Haskins Rd. I-10, exit 34 (Joe Battle), on westbound frontage road. Int corridors. **Pets:** $100 deposit/room. Designated rooms, service with restrictions, supervision.
[ASK] [✕] [♿M] [♿] [🔒] [💻] [➾]

▼▼◆▼ Quality Inn & Suites SH
(915) 772-3300. **$70-$80.** 6099 Montana Ave. I-10, exit 24 (Geronimo Dr) westbound; exit 24B (Geronimo Dr) eastbound, 0.5 mi n. Ext corridors. **Pets:** Accepted.
[ASK] [S☼] [✕] [♿] [🔒] [💻] [🍴] [➾]

▼▼ Red Roof Inn West SH
(915) 587-9977. **$51-$65.** 7530 Remcon Cir. I-10, exit 11 (Mesa St). Ext/int corridors. **Pets:** Medium, other species. Service with restrictions, supervision.
[✕] [♿M] [🐾] [♿] [🔒] [➾]

▼▼◆▼ Residence Inn by Marriott El Paso SH
(915) 771-0504. **$205-$225.** 6355 Gateway Blvd W. I-10, exit 24B (Geronimo Dr) eastbound, n to Edgemere, then just e; exit 25 (Airway Blvd) westbound on westbound frontage road. Int corridors. **Pets:** Accepted.
[ASK] [S☼] [✕] [♿] [🔒] [💻] [➾] [✕]

▼▼ Sleep Inn by Choice Hotels SH
(915) 585-7577. **$70-$90.** 953 Sunland Park Dr. I-10, exit 13. Int corridors. **Pets:** Accepted.
[ASK] [S☼] [✕] [♿] [🔒] [💻] [➾]

▼▼ Studio 6 El Paso #6001 SH
(915) 594-8533. **$54-$66.** 11049 Gateway Blvd W. I-10, exit 29 eastbound; exit 30 westbound. Ext corridors. **Pets:** Accepted.
[S☼] [✕] [♿] [🔒] [💻] [➾]

EULESS

ⒶⒶⒶ ▼▼ La Quinta DFW Airport West-Euless SH
(817) 540-0233. **$51-$130, 3 day notice.** 1001 W Airport Frwy. SR 183, exit Industrial Blvd (FM 157). Ext corridors. **Pets:** Accepted.
[SAVE] [S☼] [✕] [🐾] [🔒] [💻] [➾]

▼▼ Microtel Inn and Suites SH
(817) 545-1111. **$59-$89.** 901 W Airport. SR 183, exit Industrial Blvd (FM 157), just e. Int corridors. **Pets:** Small, dogs only. $25 one-time fee/room. Service with restrictions, supervision.
[ASK] [S☼] [✕] [♿M] [♿] [🔒] [💻] [➾]

▼ Motel 6-Euless #1345 SH
(817) 545-0141. **$39-$51.** 110 Airport. SR 183, exit Euless/Main St, on westbound access road. Ext corridors. **Pets:** Medium, other species. Service with restrictions, supervision.
[S☼] [✕] [♿] [➾]

FALFURRIAS

ⒶⒶⒶ ▼▼▼ Best Western Garden Inn M
(361) 325-4848. **$89-$149.** 2299 Hwy 281 S. 1.5 mi s of SR 285. Ext corridors. **Pets:** Very small, dogs only. $50 deposit/pet. Designated rooms, service with restrictions, supervision.
[SAVE] [S☼] [✕] [🔒] [💻] [➾]

▼▼ Days Inn M
(361) 325-2515. **$64-$74.** 2116 Hwy 281 S. 1.8 mi s of SR 285. Ext corridors. **Pets:** Very small, dogs only. $50 deposit/pet. Designated rooms, service with restrictions, supervision.
[ASK] [S☼] [✕] [♿M] [🔒] [💻]

FORT DAVIS

▼▼ Historical Prude Guest Ranch RA
(432) 426-3202. **$51-$130, 3 day notice.** 6 mi n Hwy 118. 4.5 mi n of jct SR 118 and 17. Ext corridors. **Pets:** Medium. $10 one-time fee/pet. Designated rooms, service with restrictions, crate.
[ASK] [S☼] [✕] [🔒] [🍴] [➾] [✕] [🅿] [🐾]

FORT STOCKTON

ⒶⒶⒶ ▼▼ Best Western Swiss Clock Inn SH
(432) 336-8521. **$69-$79, 10 day notice.** 3201 W Dickinson Blvd. I-10, exit 256, 0.5 mi e. Ext corridors. **Pets:** Medium. $20 daily fee/pet. Designated rooms, service with restrictions, supervision.
[SAVE] [✕] [♿] [🔒] [💻] [🍴] [➾]

ⒶⒶⒶ ▼▼ Comfort Inn of Fort Stockton SH
(432) 336-8531. **$69-$99.** 3200 W Dickinson Blvd. I-10, exit 256, just s. Int corridors. **Pets:** Medium. $10 daily fee/room. Service with restrictions, crate.
[SAVE] [S☼] [✕] [♿] [🔒] [💻] [➾]

ⒶⒶⒶ ▼▼ Days Inn SH
(432) 336-7500. **$59-$89, 4 day notice.** 1408 N US Hwy 285. I-10, exit 257, just s. Ext corridors. **Pets:** Very small. $6 one-time fee/pet. Designated rooms, service with restrictions, supervision.
[SAVE] [S☼] [✕] [🐾] [🔒] [➾]

▼▼ Econo Lodge M
(432) 336-9711. **$45-$48.** 800 E Dickinson Blvd. I-10, exit 261, 1.3 mi w on I-20 business route. Ext corridors. **Pets:** Accepted.
[ASK] [S☼] [✕] [🔒] [➾]

◭ ▼▼▼ Holiday Inn Express 🅂🅗
(432) 336-5955. **$65-$100.** 1308 N US Hwy 285. I-10, exit 257, just s. Ext corridors. **Pets:** Medium, other species. $20 daily fee/room. Designated rooms, service with restrictions.
🆂🅰🆅🅴 🆂 ⊠ 🕹 🖥 🖵 ⤳

◭ ▼▼▼ La Quinta Inn Fort Stockton 🅂🅗
(432) 336-9781. **$74-$97.** 1537 N Hwy 285. I-10, exit 257. Ext corridors. **Pets:** Medium. Service with restrictions.
🆂🅰🆅🅴 ⊠ 🕹 🖥 🖵 ⤳

FORT WORTH

▼▼▼ The Ashton Hotel 🅂🅗
(817) 332-0100. **$280-$800.** 610 Main St. Jct of 6th and Main sts; center. Int corridors. **Pets:** Medium, dogs only. $150 deposit/pet. Service with restrictions, supervision.
⊠ 🕹 🍴

▼▼ Best Western InnSuites Hotel & Suites-Fort Worth/DFW 🅂🅗 🐾
(817) 534-4801. **$79-$139.** 2000 Beach St. I-30, exit 16C (Beach St), just s. Ext/int corridors. **Pets:** Medium, other species. $25 one-time fee/pet. Designated rooms, service with restrictions, crate.
🅰🆂🅺 🆂 ⊠ 🕹 🖥 🖵 ⤳ ⊠

▼▼▼ Candlewood Suites 🅂🅗
(817) 838-8229. **$99-$169.** 5201 Endicott Ave. I-820, exit 17B, just s. Int corridors. **Pets:** Accepted.
🅰🆂🅺 🆂 ⊠ 🕹 🖥 🖵

▼▼ Crossland Economy Suites 🅂🅗
(817) 838-3500. **Call for rates.** 3804 Tanacross Dr. I-820, exit 17B, just s. Ext corridors. **Pets:** Accepted.
⊠ 🕹 🖥 🖵

▼▼ Extended StayAmerica 🅂🅗
(817) 263-9006. **$60-$75.** 5831 Overton Ridge Blvd. I-20, exit 431, 0.5 mi s to Overturn Ridge Blvd, then just e. Int corridors. **Pets:** Accepted.
🅰🆂🅺 🆂 ⊠ 🕹 🖥 🖵

▼▼ Fairfield Inn by Marriott-University Drive 🅂🅗
(817) 335-2000. **$115-$135.** 1505 S University Dr. I-30, exit 12 (University Dr), just s. Int corridors. **Pets:** Accepted.
🅰🆂🅺 🆂 ⊠ 🕹 🖥 🖵 ⤳

◭ ▼▼ Green Oaks Hotel 🅂🅗
(817) 738-7311. **$79-$129.** 6901 West Frwy. I-30, exit 8A westbound; exit 7B eastbound. Ext/int corridors. **Pets:** Other species. $25 deposit/room. Supervision.
🆂🅰🆅🅴 ⊠ 🕹 🖥 🖵 🍴 ⤳ ⊠

▼▼▼ Hampton Inn & Suites-FW Alliance Airport 🅂🅗
(817) 439-0400. **$69-$129.** 13600 North Frwy. I-35W, exit 66 (Westport Pkwy). Int corridors. **Pets:** Accepted.
🅰🆂🅺 🆂 ⊠ 🕹 🖥 🖵

▼▼ Holiday Inn Express Hotel & Suites-Fort Worth West 🅂🅗
(817) 560-4200. **$99-$129.** 2730 Cherry Ln. I-30, exit 7A. Int corridors. **Pets:** Small. $15 daily fee/pet. Designated rooms, no service, supervision.
⊠ 🖥 🖵 ⤳

▼▼ Homestead Studio Suites Hotel-Fort Worth/Medical Center 🅂🅗
(817) 338-4808. **$58-$67.** 1601 River Run. I-30, exit 12 (University Dr), just s. Ext corridors. **Pets:** Accepted.
🅰🆂🅺 🆂 ⊠ 🕹 🖥 🖵

▼▼▼ La Quinta Inn & Suites Fort Worth (North) 🅂🅗
(817) 222-2888. **$101-$131.** 4700 North Frwy. I-35W, exit 56A, just n. Int corridors. **Pets:** Medium. Service with restrictions.
🅰🆂🅺 ⊠ 🕹 🖥 🖵 ⤳

▼▼▼ La Quinta Inn & Suites Fort Worth (Southwest) 🅂🅗
(817) 370-2700. **$112-$143.** 4900 Bryant Irvin Rd. I-20, exit 431. Int corridors. **Pets:** Medium. Service with restrictions.
🅰🆂🅺 ⊠ 🕹 🖥 🖵 ⤳

◭ ▼▼▼ La Quinta Inn Fort Worth (West/Medical Center) 🅂🅗
(817) 246-5511. **$80-$111.** 7888 I-30 W. I-30, exit 7A. Ext/int corridors. **Pets:** Medium. Service with restrictions.
🆂🅰🆅🅴 ⊠ 🕹 🖥 🖵 ⤳

▼▼ Microtel Inn & Suites 🅂🅗
(817) 222-3740. **$59-$89.** 3740 Tanacross Dr. I-820, exit 17B (Beach St), just s. Int corridors. **Pets:** Accepted.
🅰🆂🅺 🆂 ⊠ 🕹 🖥

▼ Motel 6-#117 🅂🅗
(817) 244-9740. **$37-$47.** 8701 I-30 W. I-30, exit 6, just s on Las Vegas. Ext corridors. **Pets:** Medium, other species. Service with restrictions, supervision.
🆂 ⊠ 🕹 🖥 ⤳

▼ Motel 6 East-1341 🅂🅗
(817) 834-7361. **$41-$51.** 1236 Oakland Blvd. I-30, exit 18. Ext corridors. **Pets:** Medium, other species. Service with restrictions, supervision.
🆂 ⊠ ⤳

◭ ▼▼▼ Radisson Hotel Fort Worth North 🅂🅗
(817) 625-9911. **$99-$269.** 2540 Meacham Blvd. I-35W, exit 56A. Int corridors. **Pets:** Accepted.
🆂🅰🆅🅴 🆂 ⊠ 🕹 🖥 🖵 🍴 ⤳

◭ ▼▼▼ ▼▼ The Renaissance Worthington Hotel 🅻🅗
(817) 870-1000. **$159-$259.** 200 Main St. Northwest corner of 2nd and Main sts. Int corridors. **Pets:** Accepted.
🆂🅰🆅🅴 🆂 ⊠ 🕹 🕹 🖥 🖵 🍴 ⤳ ⊠

▼▼▼ Residence Inn-Alliance Airport 🅂🅗
(817) 750-7000. **$75-$149, 7 day notice.** 13400 North Frwy. I-35W, exit 66. Int corridors. **Pets:** $75 one-time fee/room. Service with restrictions, crate.
🅰🆂🅺 🆂 ⊠ 🕹 🖥 🖵 ⤳ ⊠

▼▼▼ Residence Inn by Marriott Fort Worth Cultural District 🅂🅗
(817) 885-8250. **$159-$179.** 2500 Museum Way. I-30, exit 12A, just e of jct University and 7th St, to Stayton St, just s. Int corridors. **Pets:** Small. $100 one-time fee/room. Service with restrictions, supervision.
🅰🆂🅺 🆂 ⊠ 🕹 🖥 🖵 ⤳ ⊠

▼▼▼ Residence Inn By Marriott Fort Worth-River Plaza 🅂🅗
(817) 870-1011. **$179-$219.** 1701 S University Dr. I-30, exit 12 (University Dr), 0.4 mi s. Ext corridors. **Pets:** Accepted.
🅰🆂🅺 🆂 ⊠ 🕹 🕹 🖥 🖵 ⤳ ⊠

▼▼▼ TownePlace Suites by Marriott-Fort Worth 🅂🅗
(817) 732-2224. **$109-$129.** 4200 International Plaza Dr. I-820, exit 433. Int corridors. **Pets:** Large. $100 daily fee/pet. Service with restrictions.
🅰🆂🅺 ⊠ 🖥 🖵 ⤳

FREDERICKSBURG

▼▼▼ Best Western Fredericksburg 🅂🅗
(830) 992-2929. **$89-$149.** 314 E Highway St. Jct US 87 and 290, 6 blks s. Int corridors. **Pets:** Medium. $15 one-time fee/pet. Designated rooms, no service, supervision.
🅰🆂🅺 🆂 ⊠ 🕹 🖥 🖵 ⤳

◭ ▼▼▼ Budget Host Deluxe Inn 🅼
(830) 997-3344. **$40-$85.** 901 E Main St. US 290, 0.5 mi e. Ext corridors. **Pets:** Accepted.
🆂🅰🆅🅴 ⊠ 🖥 🖵

▼▼▼▼ Comfort Inn & Suites SH
(830) 990-2552. **$89-$175.** 723 S Washington St. W on Main St, then s. Int corridors. **Pets:** Accepted.
[ASK] [S✦] [✕] [✦] [✦] [▦] [✦]

◆◆◆ ▼▼ Dietzel Motel M ✿
(830) 997-3330. **$49-$85.** 1141 W US 290. 1 mi w on US 290 at US 87. Ext corridors. **Pets:** Medium. $10 daily fee/pet. Designated rooms, service with restrictions, supervision.
[SAVE] [✕] [✦]

▼▼ Fredericksburg Econo Lodge M ✿
(830) 997-3437. **$70-$100.** 810 S Adams St. Jct US 290 and SR 165, 1 mi s. Ext corridors. **Pets:** $10 one-time fee/pet. No service, supervision.
[ASK] [S✦] [✕] [▦] [✦]

◆◆◆ ▼▼▼ Fredericksburg Inn & Suites SH
(830) 997-0202. **$89-$139.** 201 S Washington. US 290 and 87, 3 blks s. Ext corridors. **Pets:** Medium, dogs only. $35 one-time fee/room. Designated rooms, service with restrictions, crate.
[SAVE] [✕] [✦] [▦] [✦]

▼ Frontier Inn & RV Park M
(830) 997-4389. **$46-$110.** 1704 US Hwy 290 W. US 290, 1 mi w. Ext corridors. **Pets:** Accepted.
[ASK] [S✦] [✕] [✦] [▦]

▼▼▼ Holiday Inn Express SH
(830) 990-4200. **$79-$139.** 1220 N Hwy 87. 1 mi w on US 290 at US 87. Int corridors. **Pets:** Small, dogs only. $25 one-time fee/pet. Service with restrictions, supervision.
[ASK] [S✦] [✕] [✦M] [✦] [✦] [▦] [✦]

▼▼▼▼ La Quinta Inn & Suites SH
(830) 990-2899. **$99-$139.** 1465 E Main St. 1 mi e of downtown. Int corridors. **Pets:** Small, dogs only. Designated rooms, service with restrictions, supervision.
[ASK] [S✦] [✕] [✦M] [✦] [✦] [▦] [✦]

◆◆◆ ▼▼▼▼ Quality Inn SH
(830) 997-9811. **$68-$116, 7 day notice.** 908 S Adams St. 0.8 mi sw on SR 16; 0.8 mi sw of jct US 87 and 290. Ext corridors. **Pets:** Accepted.
[SAVE] [S✦] [✕] [✦] [✦] [▦] [✦]

◆◆◆ ▼▼▼ Sunday House Inn & Suites SH
(830) 997-4484. **$89-$110.** 501 E Main St. 0.4 mi e on US 290. Ext corridors. **Pets:** Small. $10 daily fee/pet. Designated rooms, service with restrictions, supervision.
[SAVE] [S✦] [✕] [✦] [✦] [▦] [✦]

◆◆◆ ▼ Sunset Inn M
(830) 997-9581. **$45-$64.** 900 S Adams St. 0.8 mi sw of jct US 290 and SR 16. Ext corridors. **Pets:** Dogs only. No service, supervision.
[SAVE] [✕] [✦] [▦] [¶]

◆◆◆ ▼▼▼ Super 8 Fredericksburg M
(830) 997-6568. **$45-$90.** 514 E Main St. US 290, just e of jct US 87. Ext corridors. **Pets:** Medium. $10 one-time fee/pet. Service with restrictions, supervision.
[SAVE] [S✦] [✕] [✦] [▦] [✦]

FRITCH

▼▼▼ Lone Star Inn and Suites SH
(806) 857-3191. **$40-$50.** 205 E Broadway. SR 136; in town. Ext corridors. **Pets:** Accepted.
[ASK] [S✦] [✕] [✦] [▦]

FULTON

◆◆◆ ▼▼▼ Best Western Inn by the Bay M
(361) 729-8351. **$84-$94.** 3902 N Hwy 35. SR 35, 0.5 mi n of jct Business Rt SR 35 and FM 3063. Ext corridors. **Pets:** Other species. $10 daily fee/pet. Service with restrictions, supervision.
[SAVE] [S✦] [✕] [✦] [✦] [▦] [✦]

GAINESVILLE

◆◆◆ ▼▼▼ Best Western Southwinds M ✿
(940) 665-7737. **$70-$100.** 2103 N I-35. I-35, exit 499 northbound, 1.4 mi n on access road to S Frontage Rd; exit 498B southbound. Ext corridors. **Pets:** Dogs only. $10 daily fee/pet. No service, supervision.
[SAVE] [S✦] [✕] [✦] [▦] [✦]

◆◆◆ ▼ Budget Host Inn M
(940) 665-2856. **$44.** 1900 N I-35. I-35, exit 499 northbound; exit 498B southbound. Ext corridors. **Pets:** Other species. Service with restrictions.
[SAVE] [✕] [✦]

◆◆◆ ▼▼▼ Ramada Limited SH
(940) 665-8800. **$79-$99.** 600 Medal of Honor Blvd. I-35, exit 496B (California St). Ext corridors. **Pets:** Small, other species. $10 daily fee/room. Service with restrictions, crate.
[SAVE] [S✦] [✕] [✦] [▦] [✦]

◆◆◆ ▼▼▼ Super 8 SH
(940) 665-5599. **$55-$70.** 1936 I-35 N. I-35, exit 499 northbound, exit 498A southbound. Int corridors. **Pets:** Accepted.
[SAVE] [S✦] [✕] [✦] [✦]

GEORGETOWN

◆◆◆ ▼▼▼▼ La Quinta Inn Georgetown SH
(512) 869-2541. **$84-$108.** 333 I-35 N. I-35, exit 264 northbound; exit 262 southbound; on west frontage road. Ext corridors. **Pets:** Medium. Service with restrictions.
[SAVE] [✕] [✦] [✦] [▦] [✦]

GEORGE WEST

◆◆◆ ▼▼ Best Western George West Executive Inn SH ✿
(361) 449-3300. **$77-$83.** 208 N Nueces St. Just n of US 59 on SR 281. Ext corridors. **Pets:** Medium. Service with restrictions, supervision.
[SAVE] [S✦] [✕] [✦] [✦] [▦] [✦]

GIDDINGS

◆◆◆ ▼▼ Executive Inn M
(979) 542-5791. **$54-$64.** 3556 E Austin St. 2 mi e on US 290. Ext corridors. **Pets:** Accepted.
[SAVE] [S✦] [✕] [✦] [▦] [✦]

GLEN ROSE

◆◆◆ ▼▼▼ Best Western Dinosaur Valley Inn & Suites SH
(254) 897-4818. **$105-$375.** 1311 NE Big Ben Tr. On US 67. Int corridors. **Pets:** Medium. $40 one-time fee/room. Service with restrictions, crate.
[SAVE] [S✦] [✕] [✦M] [✦] [✦] [▦] [✦] [✕]

GRANBURY

◆◆◆ ▼▼▼ Comfort Inn SH
(817) 573-2611. **$65-$129.** 1201 Plaza Dr N. 2 mi e on US 377 Bypass. Ext corridors. **Pets:** Small. $10 daily fee/pet. Service with restrictions, supervision.
[SAVE] [S✦] [✕] [✦] [✦] [▦] [✦]

Plantation Inn on the Lake SH
(817) 573-8846. **$70-$90.** 1451 E Pearl St. 0.3 mi w of Business Rt US 377 at US 377 Bypass. Ext/int corridors. **Pets:** Small. $10 daily fee/pet. Service with restrictions, supervision.

GRAPEVINE

Baymont Inn-Dallas-Ft Worth/Airport North SH
(817) 329-9300. **$89-$175.** 301 Capitol St. SR 114, exit Main St. Int corridors. **Pets:** Accepted.

Embassy Suites Outdoor World LH
(972) 724-2600. **$129-$365.** 2401 Bass Pro Dr. US 121, exit Bass Pro Dr. Int corridors. **Pets:** Accepted.

Homewood Suites by Hilton SH
(972) 691-2427. **$164-$184.** 2214 Grapevine Mills Cir W. SR 121 N, exit Bass Pro Dr. Int corridors. **Pets:** Accepted.

Super 8 Motel-Grapevine SH
(817) 329-7222. **$85-$130, 7 day notice.** 250 E Hwy 114. SR 114, exit Main St. Int corridors. **Pets:** Other species. $10 daily fee/pet. Designated rooms, service with restrictions, crate.

GROOM

Chalet Inn M
(806) 248-7524. **$50-$60.** I-40 FM 2300. I-40, exit 113, just s. Ext corridors. **Pets:** Medium. $5 daily fee/pet. Designated rooms, service with restrictions, supervision.

HARLINGEN

Country Inn & Suites By Carlson SH
(956) 428-0043. **$64-$125, 3 day notice.** 3825 S Expwy 83. US 83 and 77, exit Ed Carrey. Int corridors. **Pets:** Other species. $25 one-time fee/pet. Designated rooms, service with restrictions, crate.

Econo Lodge SH
(956) 425-1040. **$40-$80.** 1821 W Tyler. 0.8 mi e of US 77, exit downtown. Ext corridors. **Pets:** Small, dogs only. $10 one-time fee/pet. Service with restrictions, supervision.

Howard Johnson Inn SH
(956) 425-7070. **$57.** 6779 W Expwy 83. Jct US 77, 2.3 mi w on US 83, exit Stuart Place Rd. Ext corridors. **Pets:** Small. $25 one-time fee/room. Service with restrictions, supervision.

La Quinta Inn Harlingen SH
(956) 428-6888. **$89-$109.** 1002 S Expwy 83. US 83 and 77, exit M St. Ext corridors. **Pets:** Medium. Service with restrictions.

Ramada Limited SH
(956) 425-1333. **$67-$77.** 4401 S Expwy 83. US 83 and 77, exit Ed Carey Dr. Ext corridors. **Pets:** Dogs only. Designated rooms, service with restrictions.

Super 8 Motel SH
(956) 412-8873. **$60-$70.** 1115 S Expwy 83. US 83 and 77, exit M St, just n. Int corridors. **Pets:** Accepted.

HEARNE

Oak Tree Inn SH
(979) 279-5599. **$71-$75.** 1051 N Market St. 0.6 mi n of jct US 79 and SR 6. Ext/int corridors. **Pets:** Accepted.

HENDERSON

Best Western Inn of Henderson SH
(903) 657-9561. **$79-$119.** 1500 Hwy 259 S. 2 mi s on US 259, 0.7 mi s of jct US 79 and 259 S. Ext/int corridors. **Pets:** Accepted.

HEREFORD

Best Western Red Carpet Inn SH
(806) 364-0540. **$61-$80.** 830 W 1st St. Just w of jct US 385 and 60. Ext corridors. **Pets:** Medium. Service with restrictions, crate.

Holiday Inn Express SH
(806) 364-3322. **$89.** 1400 W 1st St. Jct US 385/60, just w. Int corridors. **Pets:** Small. $20 daily fee/pet. Service with restrictions, supervision.

HILLSBORO

Best Western Hillsboro Inn SH
(254) 582-8465. **$79-$89.** 307 I-35. I-35, exit 368A northbound; exit 368B southbound, just w. Ext corridors. **Pets:** Accepted.

Days Inn Hillsboro SH
(254) 582-3493. **$65-$69.** 307 SE I-35. I-35, exit 368 A/B. Ext corridors. **Pets:** $5 daily fee/pet. Service with restrictions, supervision.

Motel 6–4136 SH
(254) 580-9000. **$49-$53.** 1506 Hillview Dr. I-35, exit 368 southbound; exit 368A northbound. Int corridors. **Pets:** Medium, other species. Service with restrictions, supervision.

Super 8 SH
(254) 580-0404. **$80-$86, 3 day notice.** 1512 Hillview Dr. I-35, exit 368A northbound; 368 southbound, just e. Int corridors. **Pets:** Small. $10 daily fee/pet. No service, supervision.

HONDO

Hondo Executive Inn M
(830) 426-2535. **$45-$100.** 102 E 19th St. On US 90 W. Ext corridors. **Pets:** Medium. $10 one-time fee/pet. Service with restrictions, supervision.

Regency Inn M
(830) 426-3031. **$45-$85.** 401 Hwy 90 E. Jct SR 173. Ext corridors. **Pets:** Small, dogs only. $10 one-time fee/pet. Designated rooms, service with restrictions, supervision.

HOUSTON METROPOLITAN AREA

BAYTOWN

▼▼▼ Comfort Suites Baytown SH
(281) 421-9764. **$99-$199.** 7209 Garth Rd. I-10, exit 792 (Garth Rd), just n. Int corridors. **Pets:** Accepted.
(ASK) (S₀) (X) (&M) (🐾) 🖥 💻 🏊

▲▲▲ ▼▼▼ Holiday Inn Express SH
(281) 421-7200. **$79-$86.** 5222 I-10 E. I-10, exit 792 (Garth Rd). Int corridors. **Pets:** Accepted.
(SAVE) (S₀) (X) (&M) (🐾) (🐾) 🖥 💻 🏊

▲▲▲ ▼▼▼ La Quinta Inn Houston (Baytown) M
(281) 421-7300. **$91-$111.** 5215 I-10 E. I-10, exit 792 (Garth Rd). Ext corridors. **Pets:** Accepted.
(SAVE) (X) (🐾) 🖥 💻 🏊

▲▲▲ ▼▼▼ La Quinta Inn Houston/Baytown SH
(281) 421-5566. **$74-$94.** 4911 I-10 E. I-10, exit 792 (Garth Rd). Int corridors. **Pets:** Medium. Service with restrictions.
(SAVE) (X) (🐾) (🐾) 🖥 💻 🏊

▼▼ Motel 6-1136 M
(281) 576-5777. **$45-$59.** 8911 Hwy 146. I-10, exit 797 (SR 146). Ext corridors. **Pets:** Medium, other species. Service with restrictions, supervision.
(S₀) (X) (🐾) 🖥 🏊

CHANNELVIEW

▼▼ ▼▼ Travelodge Suites SH
(281) 862-0222. **Call for rates.** 15831 2nd St. I-10, exit 783 (Sheldon Rd) eastbound, just n, then just e on 2nd St; exit westbound, 0.8 mi on Frontage Rd. Ext corridors. **Pets:** Accepted.
(ASK) (X) 🖥 💻 🏊

CONROE

▲▲▲ ▼▼▼▼ Baymont Inn-Conroe SH
(936) 539-5100. **$79-$89, 30 day notice.** 1506 I-45 S. I-45, exit 85 (Gladstell St) northbound; exit 84 (Frazier St) southbound. Int corridors. **Pets:** Accepted.
(SAVE) (S₀) (X) (🐾) (🐾) 🖥 💻 🏊

▼▼▼▼ La Quinta Inn & Suites SH
(936) 228-0790. **$90-$100.** 4006 Sprayberry Ln. I-45, exit 91 (League Line Rd), just e. Int corridors. **Pets:** Small. Service with restrictions, supervision.
(ASK) (S₀) (X) (&M) (🐾) 🖥 💻 🏊

▼▼ Motel 6 Conroe #385 M
(936) 760-4003. **$41-$53.** 820 I-45 S. I-45, exit 85 (Gladstell Rd). Ext corridors. **Pets:** Medium, other species. Service with restrictions, supervision.
(S₀) (X) 🏊

DEER PARK

▼▼ ▼▼ Best Western Deer Park Inn & Suites SH
(281) 476-1900. **$79-$99.** 1401 Center St. SR 225 (La Porte Rd), exit Center St, 0.9 mi s. Ext corridors. **Pets:** Other species. $10 daily fee/pet. Service with restrictions, supervision.
(ASK) (S₀) (X) (🐾) 🖥 💻 🏊

HOUSTON

▲▲▲ ▼▼▼ Americas Best Value Inn SH
(281) 866-8686. **$59.** 609 FM 1960 W. I-45, exit 66 (FM 1960) southbound; exit 66A northbound, just w. Int corridors. **Pets:** Accepted.
(SAVE) (S₀) (X) (🐾) 🖥 🏊

▲▲▲ ▼▼▼ Baymont Inn SH
(713) 941-0900. **$88-$108.** 9902 Gulf Frwy. I-45 S, exit 36 (Airport Blvd/College Rd), just s on southbound frontage road. Ext corridors. **Pets:** Medium. Service with restrictions.
(SAVE) (X) (&M) (🐾) 💻 🏊

▼▼ ▼▼ Baymont Inn & Suites (Brookhollow) M
(713) 688-2581. **$70-$80.** 11002 Northwest Frwy. Nw on US 290, exit Magnum Rd-Watonga Blvd. Ext corridors. **Pets:** Accepted.
(ASK) (X) (🐾) 🖥 💻 🏊

▼▼▼▼ Best Western Houston Hotel & Suites Near the Galleria SH
(713) 688-2800. **$79-$159.** 7625 Katy Frwy. I-10, exit 762 westbound; exit 161B eastbound on eastbound frontage road. Int corridors. **Pets:** Small. $20 one-time fee/room. Service with restrictions, supervision.
(ASK) (S₀) (X) (&M) 🖥 💻 🏊

▼▼▼▼ Candlewood Suites Houston by the Galleria SH
(713) 839-9411. **$59-$104.** 4900 Loop Central Dr. I-610, exit 7 (Fournace Pl), on northbound frontage road. Int corridors. **Pets:** Accepted.
(ASK) (S₀) (X) 🖥 💻

▼▼▼▼ Candlewood Suites-Houston-Clear Lake SH
(281) 461-3060. **$126-$130.** 2737 Bay Area Blvd. I-45, exit 26, 3.7 mi e. Int corridors. **Pets:** Accepted.
(X) (🐾) 🖥 💻

▼▼▼▼ Candlewood Suites-Town & Country SH
(713) 464-2677. **$87-$101.** 10503 Town & Country Way. I-10, exit 755 eastbound, 1.1 mi on frontage road to Town & Country Blvd, then 0.4 mi s; exit 756A westbound, U-turn under I-10, just e to Town & Country Blvd, then 0.4 mi s. Int corridors. **Pets:** Accepted.
(ASK) (S₀) (X) (&M) (🐾) 🖥 💻

▼▼▼▼ Candlewood Suites-Westchase SH
(713) 780-7881. **$65-$125.** 4033 W Sam Houston Pkwy S. Sam Houston Pkwy (Beltway 8), exit Westpark, southeast corner of Westpark and Sam Houston Pkwy (Beltway 8) on northbound frontage road. Int corridors. **Pets:** Accepted.
(ASK) (S₀) (X) (&M) (🐾) 🖥 💻

▼▼▼ Comfort Inn & Suites SH
(713) 623-4720. **$72-$119, 3 day notice.** 4020 Southwest Frwy. US 59, exit Weslayan St northbound; exit Edloe/Weslayan St southbound, on southbound frontage road. Ext corridors. **Pets:** Accepted.
(ASK) (S₀) (X) (🐾) 🖥 💻

▲▲▲ ▼▼▼ Comfort Suites SH
(281) 440-4448. **$74-$179.** 150 Overland Tr. I-45, exit 66 (FM 1960), on southbound frontage road. Int corridors. **Pets:** Small. $25 one-time fee/pet. Service with restrictions, supervision.
(SAVE) (S₀) (X) (&M) (🐾) (🐾) 🖥 💻 🏊

▲▲▲ ▼▼▼ Comfort Suites Galleria SH
(713) 787-0004. **$110-$130.** 6221 Richmond Ave. US 59, exit Hillcroft St, 1 mi n to Richmond Ave, then 0.6 mi e. Int corridors. **Pets:** Accepted.
(SAVE) (X) (🐾) 🖥 💻 🏊

▼▼▼ Comfort Suites Intercontinental Plaza SH
(281) 442-0600. **$69-$199.** 15555 John F Kennedy Blvd. Sam Houston Pkwy (Beltway 8), exit John F Kennedy Blvd, just n. Int corridors. **Pets:** Accepted.
(ASK) (S₀) (X) (&M) (🐾) (🐾) 🖥 💻 🏊

AAA ▼▼▼ **Courtyard by Marriott Houston Brookhollow** SH ✿

(713) 688-7711. **$139-$149.** 2504 N Loop W. I-610, exit 13C (TC Jester), just nw. Int corridors. **Pets:** Medium, other species. $50 one-time fee/pet. Service with restrictions, crate.

SAVE S◖ ⊠ 🎛 ⟨ 🖥 🖵 ⊞ ⤳

AAA ▼▼▼ **Crowne Plaza Northwest Hotel** LH

(713) 462-9977. **$179-$209.** 12801 Northwest Frwy. Nw on US 290, exit Hollister Rd, 0.7 mi e on south service road. Ext/int corridors. **Pets:** Accepted.

SAVE S◖ ⊠ 🎛 ⟨ 🖥 🖵 ⊞ ⤳ ⊠

▼▼▼ **DoubleTree Guest Suites** LH

(713) 961-9000. **$299.** 5353 Westheimer Rd. I-610, exit 8C (Westheimer Rd) northbound; exit 9A (San Felipe Rd/Westheimer Rd) southbound, 0.8 mi w. Int corridors. **Pets:** Accepted.

S◖ ⊠ 🎛 🖥 🖵 ⊞ ⤳ ⊠

▼▼▼ **DoubleTree Houston Downtown** LH

(713) 759-0202. **$109-$309.** 400 Dallas St. At Dallas and Bagby sts. Int corridors. **Pets:** Small. $100 deposit/room. Service with restrictions, supervision.

⊠ 🎛 ⟨ 🖥 🖵 ⊞

▼▼▼ **Drury Inn & Suites-Houston Hobby** SH

(713) 941-4300. **$85-$130.** 7902 Mosley Rd. I-45, exit 36 (Airport Blvd/College Rd) northbound, just w on Airport Blvd, then just n; exit southbound, follow frontage road to Mosley Rd. Int corridors. **Pets:** Large, other species. Service with restrictions, supervision.

ASK ⊠ ⟨M 🎛 ⟨ 🖥 ⤳

▼▼▼ **Drury Inn & Suites-Houston Near the Galleria** SH

(713) 963-0700. **$80-$130.** 1615 W Loop S. I-610, exit 9 (San Felipe Rd) northbound; exit 9A (San Felipe Rd/Westheimer Rd) southbound, on east service road. Int corridors. **Pets:** Large, other species. Service with restrictions, supervision.

ASK ⊠ ⟨M 🎛 ⟨ 🖥 🖵 ⤳

▼▼▼ **Drury Inn & Suites-Houston West** SH

(281) 558-7007. **$80-$125.** 1000 N Hwy 6. I-10, exit 751 (Addicks/SR 6), just n on SR 6. Int corridors. **Pets:** Large, other species. Service with restrictions, supervision.

ASK ⊠ ⟨ 🖥 🖵 ⤴

AAA ▼▼ **Executive Inn & Suites Houston/Hobby Airport** M

(713) 645-7666. **$49-$66.** 6711 Telephone Rd. I-610, exit 33, 2.1 mi s; 0.5 mi s of jct Telephone and Bellfort rds. Ext corridors. **Pets:** Small. $8 daily fee/room. Designated rooms, service with restrictions, supervision.

SAVE S◖ ⊠ 🖥

AAA ▼▼▼▼ **Four Seasons Hotel Houston** LH

(713) 650-1300. **$335-$370.** 1300 Lamar St. Lamar and Austin sts. Int corridors. **Pets:** Accepted.

SAVE ⊠ 🎛 ⟨ 🖥 🖵 ⊞ ⊠

▼▼ **Hampton Inn I-10 East** SH

(713) 673-4200. **$99.** 828 Mercury Dr. I-10, exit 776A (Mercury Dr), just n. Int corridors. **Pets:** Accepted.

S◖ ⊠ 🎛 🖥 🖵 ⤳

▼▼▼▼ **Hilton Americas-Houston** LH

(713) 739-8000. **$99-$379.** 1600 Lamar St. At George R Brown Convention Center; between Crawford and Avenida De Las Americas. Int corridors. **Pets:** Medium, other species. $25 one-time fee/room. Service with restrictions.

ASK ⊠ ⟨M 🖥 🖵 ⊞ ⤳ ⊠

AAA ▼▼▼▼ **Hilton Houston Post Oak** LH

(713) 961-9300. **$129-$289.** 2001 Post Oak Blvd. I-610, exit 8C (Westheimer Rd) northbound, just w; exit 9A (San Felipe Rd/Westheimer Rd) southbound; between San Felipe and Westheimer rds. Int corridors. **Pets:** Accepted.

SAVE S◖ ⊠ 🎛 🖵 ⊞ ⤳ ⊠

AAA ▼▼▼ **Holiday Inn Astrodome at Reliant Park** SH

(713) 790-1900. **$70-$400.** 8111 Kirby Dr. I-610, exit 1C (Kirby Dr), 0.3 mi n. Int corridors. **Pets:** No service, supervision.

SAVE S◖ ⊠ 🎛 ⟨ 🖥 🖵 ⊞ ⤳

AAA ▼▼▼ **Holiday Inn Express Hotel & Suites-Intercontinental** SH

(281) 372-1000. **$99, 15 day notice.** 1330 N Sam Houston Pkwy. Off Sam Houston Pkwy (Beltway 8), exit Aldine Westfield eastbound, 0.8 mi e on service road; exit Hardy Toll Rd westbound, U-turn, then 1 mi e on service road. Int corridors. **Pets:** Medium. $75 one-time fee/pet. Service with restrictions, supervision.

SAVE S◖ ⊠ ⟨ 🖥 🖵 ⤳

AAA ▼▼▼ **Holiday Inn Select-Greenway Plaza** SH

(713) 523-8448. **$159-$229.** 2712 Southwest Frwy. US 59, exit Kirby Dr. Int corridors. **Pets:** Accepted.

SAVE S◖ ⊠ ⟨ 🖥 🖵 ⊞ ⤳

▼▼▼ **Homestead Studio Suites Hotel-Houston/Galleria Area** SH

(713) 960-9660. **$80-$89.** 2300 W Loop S. Loop 610, exit 9A (San Felipe Rd/Westheimer Rd) southbound; exit 9 (San Felipe Rd) northbound, on southbound frontage road. Int corridors. **Pets:** Accepted.

ASK S◖ ⊠ ⟨ 🖥 🖵

▼▼ **Homestead Studio Suites Hotel-Houston/Willowbrook** SH

(281) 397-9922. **$56-$64.** 13223 Champions Center Dr. Jct SR 249 and FM 1960 W, 0.9 mi e to Champion Center Dr, just n to Champion Center Plaza, then just w. Ext corridors. **Pets:** Accepted.

ASK S◖ ⊠ ⟨M 🎛 ⟨ 🖥 🖵

▼▼▼ **Homewood Suites by Hilton Intercontinental** SH

(281) 219-9100. **$139-$259.** 1340 N Sam Houston Pkwy E. Sam Houston Pkwy (Beltway 8), exit Aldine Westfield eastbound, 0.8 mi e on frontage road; exit Hardy Toll Rd westbound, U-turn, then 1 mi e on frontage road. Int corridors. **Pets:** Medium. $50 one-time fee/room. Service with restrictions, supervision.

ASK ⊠ ⟨M ⟨ 🖥 🖵 ⤳ ⊠

▼▼▼ **Homewood Suites by Hilton-Westchase** SH

(713) 334-2424. **$154-$174.** 2424 Rogerdale Rd. Sam Houston Pkwy (Beltway 8), exit Westheimer Rd, just w to Rogerdale Rd, then just n. Int corridors. **Pets:** Accepted.

ASK S◖ ⊠ ⟨M 🎛 ⟨ 🖥 🖵 ⤳ ⊠

▼▼▼ **Homewood Suites by Hilton-Willowbrook** SH

(281) 955-5200. **$164-$184.** 7655 W FM 1960. Just e of jct SR 249 and FM 1960. Int corridors. **Pets:** Accepted.

ASK S◖ ⊠ ⟨M ⟨ 🖥 🖵 ⤳

▼▼▼ **Hotel Sofitel Houston** LH

(281) 445-9000. **$79-$139.** 425 N Sam Houston Pkwy E. Sam Houston Pkwy (Beltway 8), exit Imperial Valley Dr westbound; exit Hardy Toll Rd eastbound, on westbound frontage road. Int corridors. **Pets:** Large. $50 deposit/room. Service with restrictions, supervision.

ASK S◖ ⊠ 🖥 ⊞ ⤳ ⊠

AAA ▼▼▼ **Houston Marriott Medical Center Hotel** LH ✿

(713) 796-0080. **$98-$279.** 6580 Fannin St. I-610, exit 2 (Main St), 2.5 mi ne to Holcombe St, 0.3 mi e, then just n. Int corridors. **Pets:** Medium, other species. $50 one-time fee/room. Service with restrictions, crate.

SAVE S◖ ⊠ ⟨M 🎛 ⟨ 🖥 🖵 ⊞ ⤳ ⊠

AAA ▼▼▼ **La Quinta Inn** SH

(713) 680-8282. **$95-$115.** 11130 Northwest Frwy. US 290 W, exit W 34th St, on southeast corner. Int corridors. **Pets:** Medium. Service with restrictions.

SAVE ⊠ ⟨ 🖥 🖵 ⤳

▼▼▼▼ La Quinta Inn & Suites Houston (Bush Intercontinental Airport) SH
(281) 219-2000. $100-$147. 15510 John F Kennedy Blvd. Sam Houston Pkwy (Beltway 8), exit John F Kennedy Blvd/Vickery, just n. Int corridors. Pets: Medium. Service with restrictions.
A$K ⊠ ⊾M ⧉ 🖶 💻 ⇌

AAA ▼▼▼▼ La Quinta Inn & Suites Houston (Galleria Area) SH
(713) 355-3440. $105-$185. 1625 W Loop S. I-610, exit 9 (San Felipe Rd) northbound; exit 9A (San Felipe Rd/Westheimer Rd) southbound, on northbound service road. Int corridors. Pets: Medium. Service with restrictions.
SAVE ⊠ ⊾M ⧉ ⬚ 🖶 💻 ⇌

▼▼▼▼ La Quinta Inn & Suites Houston North Beltway SH
(832) 554-5000. $65-$75. 10137 North Frwy. I-45, exit 59 (West Rd), on southbound frontage road. Int corridors. Pets: Accepted.
A$K S🔊 ⊠ ⬚ 🖶 💻 ⇌

▼▼▼▼ La Quinta Inn & Suites Houston (Park 10) SH
(281) 646-9200. $95-$136. 15225 Katy Frwy. I-10, exit 748 (Barker Cypress Rd) eastbound, 2.6 mi on eastbound service road; exit 751 (SR 6) westbound, just s to Grisby Rd, then 0.5 mi w. Int corridors. Pets: Medium. Service with restrictions.
A$K ⊠ ⧉ ⬚ 🖶 💻 ⇌

AAA ▼▼▼ La Quinta Inn & Suites Houston Southwest SH
(713) 784-3838. $84-$104. 6790 Southwest Frwy. US 59 (Southwest Frwy), exit Hillcroft St/W Park eastbound; exit Hillcroft St westbound. Int corridors. Pets: Medium. Service with restrictions.
SAVE ⊠ ⬚ 🖶 💻 ⇌

AAA ▼▼▼ La Quinta Inn Houston (Cyfair) SH
(281) 469-4018. $95-$115. 13290 FM 1960 W. Just w of jct US 290 and FM 1960. Ext corridors. Pets: Medium. Service with restrictions.
SAVE ⊠ ⧉ ⬚ 🖶 💻 ⇌

▼▼▼ La Quinta Inn Houston (East) SH
(713) 453-5425. $84-$104. 11999 East Frwy. I-10, exit 778A (Federal Rd) eastbound; exit 776B (Holland Ave) westbound, just n. Ext corridors. Pets: Medium. Service with restrictions.
A$K ⊠ ⧉ ⬚ 🖶 💻 ⇌

AAA ▼▼▼ La Quinta Inn Houston (Greenway Plaza) SH
(713) 623-4750. $90-$120. 4015 Southwest Frwy. Sw off US 59 (Southwest Frwy), exit Weslayan. Ext/int corridors. Pets: Accepted.
SAVE ⊠ ⧉ ⬚ 🖶 💻 ⇌

AAA ▼▼▼ La Quinta Inn Houston (I-45 North) SH
(281) 444-7500. $84-$104. 17111 North Frwy. I-45, exit 66, on southbound service road, 0.4 mi s of jct FM 1960 and I-45. Ext corridors. Pets: Medium. Service with restrictions.
SAVE ⊠ 🖶 💻 ⇌

AAA ▼▼ La Quinta Inn Houston (Medical Center/Reliant Center) SH
(713) 668-8082. $90-$120. 9911 Buffalo Speedway. I-610, exit 2 (Buffalo Speedway/S Main St), just s. Ext corridors. Pets: Accepted.
SAVE ⊠ ⧉ 🖶 💻 ⇌

AAA ▼▼▼ La Quinta Inn Houston (Wilcrest) SH
(713) 932-0808. $84-$114. 11113 Katy Frwy. I-10, exit 754 (Kirkwood Dr) westbound; exit 755 (Wilcrest Rd) eastbound, on eastbound service road. Ext corridors. Pets: Medium. Service with restrictions.
SAVE ⊠ ⧉ ⬚ 🖶 💻 ⇌

AAA ▼▼▼▼ Marriott Houston Hobby Airport LH 🐾
(713) 943-7979. $199-$299. 9100 Gulf Frwy. I-45, exit 36 (Airport Blvd/College Rd) southbound; exit 38 (Monroe) northbound, on southbound frontage road. Int corridors. Pets: Small, dogs only. $50 one-time fee/room. Service with restrictions, crate.
SAVE ⊠ ⧉ ⬚ 🖶 💻 ⎰⎱ ⇌

▼▼▼ Motel 6–1401 M
(713) 334-9188. $52-$62. 2900 W Sam Houston Pkwy S. Sam Houston Pkwy (Beltway 8), exit Westheimer Rd. Int corridors. Pets: Medium, other species. Service with restrictions, supervision.
S🔊 ⊠ ⊾M ⬚ ⇌

AAA ▼▼▼▼ Omni Houston Hotel LH
(713) 871-8181. $329-$399. Four Riverway. I-610, exit 10 (Woodway Dr), 0.3 mi w. Int corridors. Pets: Small, dogs only. $50 one-time fee/room. Service with restrictions, supervision.
SAVE S🔊 ⊠ ⧉ 🖶 💻 ⎰⎱ ⇌ ⊠

AAA ▼▼▼▼ Omni Houston Westside LH 🐾
(281) 558-8338. $119-$289. 13210 Katy Frwy. I-10, exit 753A (Eldridge St), just n. Int corridors. Pets: Small, dogs only. $50 one-time fee/room. Designated rooms, service with restrictions, supervision.
SAVE S🔊 ⊠ ⧉ 🖶 💻 ⇌ ⊠

▼▼▼ Quality Inn by Choice Hotels SH
(713) 675-2711. $69-$109, 3 day notice. 10155 East Frwy. I-10, exit 776A (Mercury Dr), just nw. Ext corridors. Pets: Small. $25 one-time fee/room. Service with restrictions, crate.
A$K S🔊 ⊠ ⧉ ⬚ 🖶 💻 ⇌

▼▼▼ Ramada Plaza Houston Hobby Airport SH
(713) 946-8900. $69-$159. 8611 Airport Blvd. I-45, exit 36 (Airport Blvd), 1.3 mi w. Int corridors. Pets: Accepted.
A$K S🔊 ⊠ 🖶 💻 ⎰⎱ ⇌

▼▼ Red Roof Inn Hobby Airport SH
(713) 943-3300. $55-$65. 9005 Airport Blvd. I-45, exit 36 (Airport Blvd/College Rd), just w. Int corridors. Pets: Medium, other species. Service with restrictions, supervision.
⊠ ⧉ ⬚ 🖶 ⇌

AAA ▼▼▼▼ Renaissance Houston Hotel Greenway Plaza LH
(713) 629-1200. $99-$269. 6 Greenway Plaza E. US 59 (Southwest Frwy), exit Buffalo Speedway. Int corridors. Pets: Accepted.
SAVE ⊠ ⧉ ⬚ 🖶 💻 ⎰⎱ ⇌ ⊠

▼▼▼▼ Residence Inn by Marriott SH 🐾
(832) 366-1000. $259-$329. 904 Dallas St. At Main St. Int corridors. Pets: Small, other species. $100 one-time fee/room. Crate.
S🔊 ⊠ ⊾M ⬚ 🖶 💻 ⇌

▼▼▼ Residence Inn by Marriott Houston by the Galleria SH
(713) 840-9757. $179-$199. 2500 McCue. I-610, exit 8C (Westheimer Rd) northbound; exit 9A (San Felipe Rd/Westheimer Rd) southbound, just w to McCue, then just n. Ext/int corridors. Pets: Accepted.
A$K S🔊 ⊠ ⬚ 🖶 💻 ⇌ ⊠

▼▼▼▼ Residence Inn by Marriott Houston Westchase SH
(713) 974-5454. $179-$209. 9965 Westheimer Rd. Sam Houston Pkwy (Beltway 8), exit Westheimer Rd, 0.7 mi e to Elmside Dr, then just s. Int corridors. Pets: Accepted.
A$K ⊠ ⬚ 🖶 💻 ⇌ ⊠

▼▼▼ Residence Inn by Marriott-Medical Center/Reliant Park SH 🐾
(713) 660-7993. $159-$309. 7710 Main St. I-610, exit 2 (S Main St/Buffalo Speedway), 1.5 mi n. Ext corridors. Pets: Medium. $75 one-time fee/pet. Service with restrictions, supervision.
A$K S🔊 ⊠ ⬚ 🖶 💻 ⇌ ⊠

AAA ▼▼▼ Residence Inn by Marriott-West University SH
(713) 661-4660. $89-$134. 2939 Westpark Dr. US 59, exit Kirby Dr, just s, then just w. Int corridors. Pets: Other species. $75 one-time fee/pet. Service with restrictions.
SAVE S🔊 ⊠ ⊾M ⧉ 🖶 💻 ⇌ ⊠

▼▼▼ **Residence Inn by Marriott Willowbrook** 🆂🅷
(832) 237-2002. **$215-$235.** 7311 W Greens Rd. SR 249, exit Greens Rd, just e. Int corridors. **Pets:** Accepted.

Ⓐ🆂🅺 🆂👁 ⊗ 🐾 🖐 🛏 🖵 ⊠ ⊠

▼▼▼ **Residence Inn-Houston Clear Lake** 🆂🅷
(281) 486-2424. **$89-$162.** 525 Bay Area Blvd. I-45 S, exit 26 (Bay Area Blvd), 1.2 mi e. Ext/int corridors. **Pets:** Medium, other species. $100 one-time fee/room. Service with restrictions.

Ⓐ🆂🅺 🆂👁 ⊗ 🐾 🖐 🛏 🖵 ⊠ ⊠

🆋🅰🅰 ▼▼▼▼ **The St. Regis Hotel, Houston** 🆂🅷 🐾
(713) 840-7600. **$500-$5000.** 1919 Briar Oaks Ln. I-610, exit 9A (San Felipe Rd/Westheimer Rd), 0.3 mi e. Int corridors. **Pets:** Medium. Service with restrictions, crate.

🆂🅰🆅🅴 ⊗ 🐾 🛏 🖵 🍴 ⊠ ⊠

▼▼▼▼ **Sheraton Houston Brookhollow** 🅻🅷 🐾
(713) 688-0100. **$59-$129.** 3000 N Loop W. I-610, exit 13C (TC Jester Blvd). Int corridors. **Pets:** Other species.

Ⓐ🆂🅺 🆂👁 ⊗ 🛏 🖵 🍴 ⊠ ⊠

🆋🅰🅰 ▼▼▼▼ **Sheraton North Houston Hotel** 🅻🅷 🐾
(281) 442-5100. **$100-$225, 30 day notice.** 15700 John F Kennedy Blvd. Sam Houston Pkwy (Beltway 8), exit John F Kennedy Blvd, just n. Int corridors. **Pets:** Medium, other species. Service with restrictions, supervision.

🆂🅰🆅🅴 ⊗ 🐾 🐾 🛏 🖵 🍴 ⊠

▼▼▼▼ **Sheraton Suites Houston Near The Galleria** 🆂🅷 🐾
(713) 586-2444. **$129-$319.** 2400 W Loop S. I-610, exit 9 (San Felipe Rd) northbound; exit 9A (San Felipe Rd/Westheimer Rd) southbound. Int corridors. **Pets:** Medium, dogs only. Service with restrictions, crate.

Ⓐ🆂🅺 🆂👁 ⊗ 🐾 🛏 🖵 🍴 ⊠

▼▼▼▼ **Staybridge Suites Houston-Near The Galleria** 🆂🅷
(713) 355-8888. **$169.** 5190 Hidalgo St. I-610, exit 9A (San Felipe Rd/Westheimer Rd) southbound; exit 8C (Westheimer Rd) northbound, 0.4 mi w to Sage Rd, then just s. Int corridors. **Pets:** Accepted.

⊗ 🐾 🛏 🖵 ⊠

▼▼▼ **Studio 6 #6043** 🆂🅷
(281) 579-6959. **$53-$68.** 1255 Hwy 6 N. I-10, exit 751 (Addicks Rd/SR 6), just n. Ext corridors. **Pets:** Accepted.

🆂👁 ⊗ 🐾 🛏 🖵

▼▼▼ **Studio 6-Houston Hobby South #6039** 🅼
(281) 929-5400. **$63-$76.** 12700 Featherwood. I-45, exit 33 (Fuqua St) southbound, stay in right lane and cross over I-45, just e to Featherwood, then just s. Ext corridors. **Pets:** Accepted.

🆂👁 ⊗ 🐾 🛏 🖵

▼▼ **Studio 6-Spring #6037** 🆂🅷
(281) 580-2221. **$49-$63.** 220 Bammel-Westfield Rd. I-45, exit 66, southbound frontage road, then just w. Ext corridors. **Pets:** Accepted.

🆂👁 ⊗ 🐾 🐾 🛏

🆋🅰🅰 ▼▼▼ **Super 8 Motel-Houston-Webster-NASA** 🅼
(281) 333-5385. **$75-$85.** 18103 Kingsrow Ln. I-45, exit 25 (NASA Rd One), 1.5 mi e. Ext corridors. **Pets:** Accepted.

🆂🅰🆅🅴 🆂👁 ⊗ 🛏 🖵 ⊠

▼▼ **TownePlace Suites by Marriott-Central** 🆂🅷
(713) 690-4035. **$105-$155.** 12820 Northwest Frwy (US 290). US 290, exit Bingle/43rd St eastbound; exit Bingle/Pinemont/43rd St westbound, on westbound feeder. Int corridors. **Pets:** Accepted.

Ⓐ🆂🅺 🆂👁 ⊗ 🐾 🛏 🖵 ⊠ ⊠

▼▼ **TownePlace Suites by Marriott-West** 🆂🅷
(281) 646-0058. **$105-$155.** 15155 Katy Frwy. I-10, exit 751, just s on SR 6 to Grisby Rd, then w. Int corridors. **Pets:** Accepted.

Ⓐ🆂🅺 🆂👁 ⊗ 🐾 🛏 🖵 ⊠

🆋🅰🅰 ▼▼▼▼ **The Westin Galleria, Houston** 🅻🅷 🐾
(713) 960-8100. **$359.** 5060 W Alabama St. I-610, exit 8C (Westheimer Rd) northbound; exit 9A (San Felipe Rd/Westheimer Rd) southbound, 0.5 mi w on Westheimer Rd to Sage, just s, then just e. Int corridors. **Pets:** Small, dogs only. Designated rooms, service with restrictions.

🆂🅰🆅🅴 ⊗ 🐾 🛏 🖵 🍴 ⊠

🆋🅰🅰 ▼▼▼▼ **The Westin Oaks, Houston** 🅻🅷 🐾
(713) 960-8100. **$359.** 5011 Westheimer Rd. I-610, exit 8C (Westheimer Rd) northbound; exit 9A (San Felipe Rd/Westheimer Rd) southbound, just w. Int corridors. **Pets:** Small, dogs only. Designated rooms, service with restrictions, supervision.

🆂🅰🆅🅴 ⊗ 🐾 🛏 🖵 🍴 ⊠

HUMBLE

▼▼▼ **Fairfield Inn by Marriott** 🆂🅷
(281) 540-3311. **$90-$110.** 20525 Hwy 59. US 59, exit Townsen Rd, on southbound access road. Int corridors. **Pets:** Accepted.

Ⓐ🆂🅺 🆂👁 ⊗ 🐾 🐾 🛏 🖵 ⊠

LA PORTE

▼▼▼ **La Quinta Inn Houston (La Porte)** 🆂🅷
(281) 470-0760. **$88-$108.** 1105 Hwy 146 S. Jct SR 146, exit Fairmont Pkwy. Ext corridors. **Pets:** Medium. Service with restrictions.

Ⓐ🆂🅺 ⊗ 🐾 🛏 🖵 ⊠

NASSAU BAY

▼▼ **Microtel Inn & Suites** 🆂🅷
(281) 335-0800. **$45-$80, 3 day notice.** 1620 NASA Rd One. I-45, exit 25 (NASA Rd One), 3 mi e. Int corridors. **Pets:** Accepted.

Ⓐ🆂🅺 🆂👁 ⊗ 🐾 🛏 🖵

SEABROOK

🆋🅰🅰 ▼▼▼▼ **La Quinta Inn & Suites #618** 🆂🅷
(281) 326-7300. **$105-$170.** 3636 NASA Rd One. I-45, exit 25 (NASA Rd One), 6 mi e; SR 146, 2 mi w. Int corridors. **Pets:** Medium. Service with restrictions, supervision.

🆂🅰🆅🅴 🆂👁 ⊗ 🐾 🛏 🖵 ⊠

STAFFORD

🆋🅰🅰 ▼▼▼ **La Quinta Inn Houston (Stafford/Sugarland)** 🆂🅷
(281) 240-2300. **$80-$120.** 12727 Southwest Frwy. US 59 eastbound service road, exit Corporate Dr southbound; exit Airport Blvd/Kirkwood Rd northbound. Int corridors. **Pets:** Medium. Service with restrictions.

🆂🅰🆅🅴 ⊗ 🐾 🛏 🖵 ⊠

▼▼▼ **Residence Inn by Marriott Houston/Sugar Land** 🆂🅷
(281) 277-0770. **$109-$149.** 12703 Southwest Frwy. US 59, exit Corporate Dr southbound; exit Airport Blvd/Kirkwood Rd northbound. Int corridors. **Pets:** Accepted.

Ⓐ🆂🅺 🆂👁 ⊗ 🐾 🛏 🖵 ⊠ ⊠

SUGAR LAND

▼▼▼ **Drury Inn & Suites-Houston/Sugar Land** 🆂🅷
(281) 277-9700. **$85-$125.** 13770 Southwest Frwy. Sw on US 59, exit Dairy Ashford/Sugar Creek southbound; exit Dairy Ashford/Sugar Creek northbound, left under US 59. Int corridors. **Pets:** Large, other species. Service with restrictions, supervision.

Ⓐ🆂🅺 ⊗ 🐾 🐾 🛏 🖵

TOMBALL

🆋🅰🅰 ▼▼▼▼ **Holiday Inn Express** 🆂🅷
(281) 351-4114. **$76-$105.** 1437 Keefer St. SR 249 and FM 2920; northeast corner. Ext corridors. **Pets:** Accepted.

🆂🅰🆅🅴 🆂👁 ⊗ 🛏 🖵

WEBSTER

▼▼▼▼ Extended Stay Houston NASA-Bay Area Blvd SH
(281) 338-7711. **$55-$68.** 720 W Bay Area Blvd. I-45, exit 26 (Bay Area Blvd), just e. Int corridors. **Pets:** Accepted.
(ASK) 🛇 ✕ 🖉 🌀 🖥 💻 ⤳

▼▼▼ La Quinta Inn & Suites Webster SH
(281) 554-5290. **$109, 7 day notice.** 520 W Bay Area Blvd. I-45, exit 26 (Bay Area Blvd), just e. Int corridors. **Pets:** Small. $100 deposit/room. Designated rooms, no service, supervision.
(ASK) 🛇 ✕ 🌀 🖥 💻 ⤳

WINNIE

▼▼ Holiday Inn Express SH
(409) 296-2866. **$79-$129.** 14932 FM 1663. I-10, exit 829, just n. Ext corridors. **Pets:** Small, dogs only. $10 daily fee/pet. No service, supervision.
(ASK) 🛇 ✕ 🖉 🌀 🖥 💻 ⤳

AAA ▼▼ Quality Inn SH
(409) 296-9292. **$60-$100.** 46318 I-10 E. I-10, exit 829, on eastbound frontage road. Ext corridors. **Pets:** $25 deposit/room, $10 daily fee/pet. Service with restrictions, supervision.
(SAVE) 🛇 ✕ 🖥 💻 ⤳

AAA ▼▼ Winnie Inn & Suites SH
(409) 296-2947. **$55-$100, 3 day notice.** 205 Spur 5, Hwy 124. I-10, exit 829, just s. Ext corridors. **Pets:** Accepted.
(SAVE) 🛇 ✕ 🖥 💻 ⤳

THE WOODLANDS

▼▼▼▼ Drury Inn & Suites-Houston/The Woodlands SH
(281) 362-7222. **$80-$120.** 28099 I-45 N. I-45, exit 76 southbound; exit 77 northbound, on west service road. Int corridors. **Pets:** Large, other species. Service with restrictions, supervision.
(ASK) ✕ 🖁 🖉 🌀 🖥 💻 ⤳

AAA ▼▼▼▼ Holiday Inn Express Hotel & Suites SH
(281) 681-8088. **$99, 3 day notice.** 24888 I-45 N. I-45, exit 73 (Rayford/Sawdust Rd), on northbound access road. Int corridors. **Pets:** Medium. $25 one-time fee/room. Service with restrictions, crate.
(SAVE) 🛇 ✕ 🌀 🖥 💻 ⤳ 🛇

AAA ▼▼▼▼ La Quinta Inn Houston, The Woodlands North SH
(281) 367-7222. **$84-$104.** 28673 I-45 N. I-45, exit 78 southbound; exit 79 (SR 242) northbound, on southbound frontage road. Ext/int corridors. **Pets:** Medium. Service with restrictions.
(SAVE) ✕ 🖉 🖥 💻 ⤳

▼▼▼▼ Residence Inn by Marriott SH
(281) 292-3252. **$165-$185.** 1040 Lake Front Cir. I-45, exit 78 southbound; exit 79 (SR 242) northbound, 0.8 mi s of jct I-45 and Research Forest Dr, just w. Int corridors. **Pets:** Accepted.
(ASK) 🛇 ✕ 🌀 🖥 💻 ⤳ 🛇

END METROPOLITAN AREA

HUNTSVILLE

AAA ▼▼▼▼ La Quinta Inn Huntsville SH
(936) 295-6454. **$80-$109.** 124 I-45 N. I-45, exit 116. Ext corridors. **Pets:** Medium. Service with restrictions.
(SAVE) ✕ 🖉 🖥 💻 ⤳

JACKSONVILLE

AAA ▼▼▼▼ Best Western Executive Inn SH
(903) 586-0007. **$86-$90.** 1659 S Jackson St. 1.7 mi s of jct US 69 and 79, on US 69. Int corridors. **Pets:** Accepted.
(SAVE) 🛇 ✕ 🖁 🌀 🖥 💻 ⤳

▼▼▼▼ Holiday Inn Express SH
(903) 589-8500. **$89-$120.** 1848 S Jackson St. On US 69, 2 mi s of jct US 69 and 79. Int corridors. **Pets:** Small. $15 daily fee/pet. Service with restrictions, supervision.
(ASK) 🛇 ✕ 🖁 🖥 💻 ⤳

JASPER

▼ Ramada Inn Jasper SH
(409) 384-9021. **$51.** 239 E Gibson (US 190). US 190 and SR 63, just w of jct US 96. Ext corridors. **Pets:** Medium. $25 one-time fee/pet. Designated rooms, service with restrictions, supervision.
(ASK) 🛇 ✕ 🖥 💻 🍴 ⤳

JUNCTION

▼▼ Days Inn SH 🐾
(325) 446-3730. **$62-$69.** 111 S Martinez St. I-10, exit 457, 0.3 mi s. Ext corridors. **Pets:** Other species. $4 one-time fee/pet. Designated rooms, supervision.
(ASK) 🛇 ✕ 🖥 💻 ⤳

▼ The Hills Motel M
(325) 446-2567. **$40.** 1520 Main St. I-10, exit 456, 1.3 mi s on US 377. Ext corridors. **Pets:** Service with restrictions, supervision.
✕ 🖥 ⤳

▼▼ Rodeway Inn SH
(325) 446-4588. **$55.** 2343 N Main St. I-10, exit 456, just s on US 377. Ext corridors. **Pets:** Accepted.
(ASK) 🛇 ✕ 🖥 💻 ⤳

AAA ▼ Sun Valley Motel M
(325) 446-2505. **$45-$50.** 1611 Main St. I-10, exit 456 eastbound, 1 mi s on US 377; exit 460 westbound, 3 mi w on Loop 481 to jct US 377, then just n. Ext corridors. **Pets:** Other species. $5 daily fee/pet. Service with restrictions, crate.
(SAVE) 🛇 ✕ 🖥 ⤳

KERRVILLE

AAA ▼▼▼▼ Best Western Sunday House Inn SH
(830) 896-1313. **$64-$81.** 2124 Sidney Baker St. I-10, exit 508 (SR 16), just s. Ext corridors. **Pets:** Small. $10 daily fee/pet. Designated rooms, service with restrictions, supervision.
(SAVE) ✕ 💻 🍴 ⤳

AAA ▼▼▼ Budget Inn M
(830) 896-8200. **$50-$80.** 1804 Sidney Baker St. I-10, exit 508 (SR 16), 0.5 mi s on SR 16. Ext corridors. **Pets:** Accepted.
(SAVE) ✕ 🖥 ⤳

AAA ▼▼▼▼ Comfort Inn SH
(830) 792-7700. **$69-$149.** 2001 Sidney Baker St. I-10, exit 508 (SR 16), 0.4 mi s. Int corridors. **Pets:** Small. $10 one-time fee/room. Service with restrictions, supervision.
(SAVE) 🛇 ✕ 🖥 💻 ⤳

▼▼▼▼ Days Inn of Kerrville M
(830) 896-1000. **$79-$169.** 2000 Sidney Baker St. I-10, exit 508 (SR 16), 0.5 mi s. Ext/int corridors. **Pets:** Small, dogs only. $10 daily fee/pet. Service with restrictions, supervision.
✕ 🌀 🖥 💻 ⤳

△△△ ▽▽▽ Econo Lodge of Kerrville SH
(830) 896-1711. **$45-$149.** 2105 Sidney Baker St. I-10, exit 508 (SR 16), just s. Int corridors. **Pets:** Small. $15 daily fee/pet. Designated rooms, service with restrictions, supervision.
[SAVE] [S📶] [✕] [🛏] [💻] [⇌]

△△△ ▽▽▽▽ Y. O. Ranch Resort Hotel & Conference Center LH
(830) 257-4440. **$89-$109.** 2033 Sidney Baker St. I-10, exit 508 (SR 16), 0.3 mi s. Ext/int corridors. **Pets:** Accepted.
[SAVE] [S📶] [✕] [🔊] [🛏] [💻] [🍴] [⇌] [⊗]

KILGORE

△△△ ▽▽▽ Best Western Inn of Kilgore SH
(903) 986-1195. **$72.** 1411 N Hwy 259. I-20, exit 589, 3.9 mi s. Ext corridors. **Pets:** Accepted.
[SAVE] [S📶] [✕] [🛏] [💻] [⇌]

KILLEEN

△△△ ▽▽▽ Holiday Inn Express SH
(254) 554-2727. **$79-$89.** 1602 E Central Texas Expwy. US 190, exit Trimmier Rd. Ext corridors. **Pets:** Other species. Service with restrictions, supervision.
[SAVE] [✕] [🛏] [💻]

▽▽▽▽ La Quinta Inn Killeen SH
(254) 526-8331. **$101-$121.** 1112 S Fort Hood St. US 190, exit Fort Hood St, on westbound access road. Ext corridors. **Pets:** Medium. Service with restrictions.
[ASK] [✕] [🔊] [🛏] [💻] [⇌]

KINGSVILLE

△△△ ▽▽▽ Quality Inn SH
(361) 592-5251. **$69-$89.** 221 S Hwy 77 Bypass. On US 77, just s of jct SR 141. Ext corridors. **Pets:** Small, dogs only. $50 deposit/pet. Designated rooms, service with restrictions, supervision.
[SAVE] [S📶] [✕] [🛏] [💻] [⇌]

△△△ ▽▽▽◆ Rodeway Inn SH
(361) 595-5753. **$74-$84.** 3430 Hwy 77. 4.5 mi s on US 77. Ext corridors. **Pets:** Medium, other species. $20 one-time fee/room. Service with restrictions, crate.
[SAVE] [S📶] [✕] [🛏] [💻] [🍴] [⇌]

△△△ ▽▽◆ Super 8 Motel M
(361) 592-6471. **$60-$80.** 105 S 77 Bypass. 0.8 mi e on US 77. Ext corridors. **Pets:** Small. $20 one-time fee/pet. No service, supervision.
[SAVE] [S📶] [✕] [🛏] [💻] [⇌]

LAJITAS

▽▽▽ ▽▽◆ Lajitas The Ultimate Hideout SH
(432) 424-5000. **$169-$850.** 1 Main St. Center. Ext/int corridors. **Pets:** Accepted.
[ASK] [✕] [🛏] [💻] [🍴] [⇌] [⊗]

LAKE JACKSON

▽▽▽▽ Cherotel Brazosport Hotel & Conference Center SH
(979) 297-1161. **$90-$159.** 925 Hwy 332. On SR 228/332, just w of jct Business Rt SR 288. Int corridors. **Pets:** Accepted.
[ASK] [S📶] [✕] [🛏] [💻] [🍴] [⇌]

LAMESA

▽▽▽ Shiloh Inn M
(806) 872-6721. **$58-$64, 3 day notice.** 1707 Lubbock Hwy. Jct US 87 and 180, 1 mi n. Ext corridors. **Pets:** $10 daily fee/pet. Service with restrictions, supervision.
[ASK] [S📶] [✕] [🛏] [💻] [🍴] [⇌]

LAREDO

△△△ ▽▽▽ Days Inn & Suites SH
(956) 724-8221. **$59-$149.** 7060 N San Bernardo Ave. I-35, exit 4 (San Bernardo Ave), just s on southbound access road. Ext/int corridors. **Pets:** Small. $10 daily fee/pet. Designated rooms, service with restrictions, supervision.
[SAVE] [S📶] [✕] [🛏] [💻] [⇌]

△△△ ▽▽▽▽ La Quinta Inn Laredo (I-35) SH
(956) 722-0511. **$106-$129.** 3610 Santa Ursula Ave. I-35, exit 2 (US 59). Ext corridors. **Pets:** Medium. Service with restrictions.
[SAVE] [✕] [🛏] [💻] [⇌]

▽▽ ▽▽ Motel 6 South-142 M
(956) 725-8187. **$55-$73.** 5310 San Bernardo Ave. I-35, exit 3B (Mann Rd). Ext corridors. **Pets:** Medium, other species. Service with restrictions, supervision.
[S📶] [✕] [♿M] [🐾] [⇌]

▽▽▽ ▽▽ Red Roof Inn Laredo M
(956) 712-0733. **$65-$80.** 1006 W Calton Rd. I-35, exit 3A, 0.3 mi w. Ext/int corridors. **Pets:** Medium, other species. Service with restrictions, supervision.
[✕] [🐾] [🛏] [⇌]

LITTLEFIELD

△△△ ▽▽ Crescent Park Motel & Suites M
(806) 385-4464. **$43-$70.** 2000 Hall Ave. Jct US 84, just n on SR 385. Ext corridors. **Pets:** Accepted.
[SAVE] [✕] [🛏] [💻]

LLANO

△△△ ▽▽▽ Best Western Llano SH
(325) 247-4101. **$69-$89, 3 day notice.** 901 W Young St. 1 mi w on SR 71 and 29. Ext corridors. **Pets:** Accepted.
[SAVE] [S📶] [✕] [🛏] [💻] [⇌]

▽▽▽ Hill Country Suites SH
(325) 247-1141. **$70-$90.** 609 Bessemer Ave. Jct SR 29 and 16/71, 2 blks s. Ext corridors. **Pets:** Accepted.
[ASK] [S📶] [✕] [♿M] [🔊] [🐾] [🛏] [💻] [⇌]

LOCKHART

▽▽▽ ▽▽ Plum Creek Inn M
(512) 398-4911. **$69-$99.** 2001 Hwy 183 S. US 183 S, 1 mi s. Ext corridors. **Pets:** Accepted.
[ASK] [S📶] [✕] [🛏] [💻] [🍴] [⇌]

LONGVIEW

△△△ ▽▽▽ La Quinta Inn Longview SH
(903) 757-3663. **$79-$99.** 502 S Access Rd. I-20, exit 595. Ext corridors. **Pets:** Medium. Service with restrictions.
[SAVE] [✕] [🛏] [💻] [⇌]

▽▽ Motel 6-158 M
(903) 758-5256. **$43-$55.** 110 S Access Rd. I-20, exit 595A. Ext corridors. **Pets:** Medium, other species. Service with restrictions, supervision.
[S📶] [✕] [🐾] [⇌]

LUBBOCK

△△△ ▽▽▽ Best Western Lubbock Windsor Inn SH 🐾
(806) 762-8400. **$79-$119.** 5410 I-27. 3.5 mi s on I-27, exit 1B southbound; U-turn at exit 1A (50th St) northbound. Int corridors. **Pets:** Other species. $25 one-time fee/room. Service with restrictions, supervision.
[SAVE] [S📶] [✕] [🐾] [🛏] [💻] [⇌]

△△△ ▽▽▽▽ Clarion Hotel Lubbock SH
(806) 747-0171. **$60-$159, 3 day notice.** 505 Ave Q. I-27, exit 4, 0.9 mi w to US 84 (Ave Q), then just s. Int corridors. **Pets:** Other species. Service with restrictions.
[SAVE] [S🐾] [✕] [🖉] [🖥] [🛏] [💻] [🍴] [🏊]

▽▽▽▽ Comfort Inn & Suites SH
(806) 763-6500. **$70-$100.** 5828 I-27 S. I-27, exit 1B, just s. Int corridors. **Pets:** Accepted.
[ASK] [S🐾] [✕] [🖉] [🛏] [💻] [🏊]

△△△ ◆ Econo Lodge SH
(806) 747-3525. **$49-$99, 5 day notice.** 5401 Ave Q. I-27, exit 1A (US 84/Ave Q), 0.5 mi w. Ext/int corridors. **Pets:** Accepted.
[SAVE] [S🐾] [✕] [🛏] [🍴] [🏊]

▽▽▽▽ Extended StayAmerica-Lubbock Southwest SH
(806) 785-9881. **$64-$79.** 4802 S Loop 289. S Loop 289, exit Slide Rd; on south access road. Int corridors. **Pets:** Accepted.
[ASK] [✕] [🛏] [💻]

△△△ ▽▽▽▽ Holiday Inn Park Plaza SH
(806) 797-3241. **$69-$169.** 3201 S Loop 289. 5 mi s on Loop 289, exit Indiana Ave, on south frontage road. Ext/int corridors. **Pets:** Accepted.
[SAVE] [S🐾] [✕] [🖉] [🛏] [💻] [🍴] [🏊] [✕]

▽▽▽▽ La Quinta Inn Lubbock SH
(806) 763-9441. **$90-$120.** 601 Ave Q. 0.8 mi nw on US 84 (Ave Q). Ext corridors. **Pets:** Medium. Service with restrictions.
[ASK] [✕] [🖉] [🖉] [🛏] [💻] [🏊]

▽▽▽▽ La Quinta Inn Lubbock (West/Medical Center) SH
(806) 792-0065. **$93-$123.** 4115 Brownfield Hwy. 3.3 mi sw; 2.5 mi ne of Loop 289 on US 62 and 82. Int corridors. **Pets:** Medium. Service with restrictions.
[ASK] [✕] [🖉] [🖉] [🛏] [💻] [🏊]

◆ Lubbock Super 8 Motel M
(806) 762-8726. **$45-$95, 3 day notice.** 501 Ave Q. 1 mi nw on US 84. Ext corridors. **Pets:** $8 daily fee/pet. No service.
[ASK] [S🐾] [✕] [🛏]

◆▽▽▽▽ Residence Inn by Marriott SH
(806) 745-1963. **$109-$299.** 2551 S Loop 289. Loop 289, exit University, 3 mi s, on south frontage road. Ext corridors. **Pets:** Accepted.
[ASK] [✕] [🖉] [🖉] [🛏] [🏊] [✕]

▽▽▽▽ TownePlace Suites by Marriott SH
(806) 799-6226. **$95-$145.** 5310 W Loop 289. W Loop 289, exit US 62/82 (Brownfield Rd), 0.5 mi s on west frontage road. Int corridors. **Pets:** Accepted.
[ASK] [S🐾] [✕] [🖉M] [🖉] [🖉] [🛏] [💻] [🏊]

LUFKIN

▽▽▽ Best Western Crown Colony Inn & Suites SH
(936) 634-3481. **$84-$104.** 3211 S 1st St. 2 mi s of Jct US 59 and Loop 287. Int corridors. **Pets:** Small. $25 one-time fee/pet. Service with restrictions, crate.
[ASK] [S🐾] [✕] [🖉] [🛏] [💻] [🏊]

▽▽ La Quinta Inn Lufkin SH
(936) 634-3351. **$91-$111.** 2119 S 1st St. US 59, exit Carriageway northbound, 0.3 mi s of jct S Loop 287 and US 59 business route. Ext corridors. **Pets:** Medium. Service with restrictions.
[ASK] [✕] [🖉] [🛏] [💻] [🏊]

MADISONVILLE

△△△ ▽▽ Western Lodge M
(936) 348-7654. **$45-$55.** 2007 E Main St. I-45, exit 142, 0.3 mi w. Ext corridors. **Pets:** Very small. $10 daily fee/pet. Service with restrictions, supervision.
[SAVE] [S🐾] [✕] [🛏] [🏊]

MANSFIELD

▽▽▽ Comfort Inn SH
(817) 453-8848. **$85.** 175 N Hwy 287. US 287 S, exit E Broad St. Int corridors. **Pets:** Small, other species. $15 daily fee/pet. Designated rooms, service with restrictions, supervision.
[ASK] [S🐾] [✕] [🖉M] [🖉] [🛏] [💻] [🏊]

MARBLE FALLS

△△△ ▽▽▽▽ Best Western Marble Falls Inn SH
(830) 693-5122. **$49-$129.** 1403 Hwy 281 N. 0.4 mi n of jct SR 281 and FM 1431. Ext/int corridors. **Pets:** Medium. $10 daily fee/pet. Designated rooms, service with restrictions, crate.
[SAVE] [S🐾] [✕] [🖉] [🛏] [💻] [🏊]

MARSHALL

△△△ ▽▽▽ Best Western Executive Inn SH
(903) 935-0707. **$69-$89.** 5201 E End Blvd S. I-20, exit 617, 0.4 mi n on US 59. Ext corridors. **Pets:** Small. $15 daily fee/pet. No service, supervision.
[SAVE] [S🐾] [✕] [🛏] [💻] [🏊]

▽▽▽▽ Holiday Inn Express Marshall SH
(903) 935-7923. **$89-$129.** 4911 E End Blvd S. I-20, exit 617, 0.5 mi n on US 59. Ext corridors. **Pets:** Accepted.
[ASK] [S🐾] [✕] [🖉] [🛏] [💻] [🏊]

△△△ ▽▽▽▽ La Quinta Inn & East Texas Conference Center SH
(903) 927-0009. **$76-$95.** 5301 E End Blvd S. I-20, exit 617, just n on US 59. Int corridors. **Pets:** Accepted.
[SAVE] [S🐾] [✕] [🖉] [🛏] [💻] [🏊]

▽ Motel 6 Marshall #422 M
(903) 935-4393. **$40-$50.** 300 I-20 E. I-20, exit 617, just e on access road. Ext corridors. **Pets:** Medium, other species. Service with restrictions, supervision.
[S🐾] [✕] [🏊]

MCALLEN

▽▽▽▽ Drury Inn-McAllen SH
(956) 687-5100. **$80-$120.** 612 W Expwy 83. US 83, exit 2nd St, on northwest frontage road. Int corridors. **Pets:** Large, other species. Service with restrictions, supervision.
[ASK] [✕] [🛏] [💻] [🏊]

▽▽▽▽ Drury Suites-McAllen SH
(956) 682-3222. **$88-$130.** 228 W Expwy 83. At US 83 and 6th St. Int corridors. **Pets:** Large, other species. Service with restrictions, supervision.
[ASK] [✕] [🖉] [🛏] [💻] [🏊]

▽▽▽▽ Hampton Inn-McAllen SH
(956) 682-4900. **$82-$131.** 300 W Expwy 83. US 83, exit 2nd St, on northwest frontage road. Int corridors. **Pets:** Small. Service with restrictions, crate.
[ASK] [✕] [🛏] [💻] [🏊]

△△△ ▽▽▽▽ La Quinta Inn McAllen SH
(956) 687-1101. **$80.** 1100 S 10th St. 1.5 mi s on SR 336 (S 10th St); just n of jct US 83. Ext corridors. **Pets:** Accepted.
[SAVE] [✕] [🖉M] [🖉] [🖉] [🛏] [💻] [🏊]

▽ Motel 6 McAllen #212 M
(956) 687-3700. **$45-$58.** 700 W Expwy 83. US 83, exit 2nd St, on northwest frontage road. Ext corridors. **Pets:** Medium, other species. Service with restrictions, supervision.
[S🐾] [✕] [🏊]

▽▽ Posada Ana Inn SH
(956) 631-6700. **$63-$101.** 620 W Expwy 83. US 83, exit 2nd St, on northwest frontage road. Int corridors. **Pets:** Small, other species. Service with restrictions, supervision.
[ASK] [✕] [💻]

▼▼▼▼ **Residence Inn by Marriott** 🆂🅷
(956) 994-8626. **$104.** 220 W Expwy 83. US 83, exit 2nd St, just w,
then just n on 2nd St. Int corridors. **Pets:** Accepted.
🅰🆂🅺 🆂 ⊠ 🔋 📶 💻 🏊 ⊠

▼▼▼ **Super 8 Motel** 🆂🅷
(956) 682-1190. **$80-$89.** 1420 E Jackson Ave. US 83, exit Jackson
Ave/Sam Houston St, just s. Int corridors. **Pets:** Accepted.
🅰🆂🅺 🆂 ⊠ 🔋 🏊

MEMPHIS

🅐🅐🅐 ▼▼▼ **Travelodge** Ⓜ
(806) 259-3583. **$50-$65.** 1600 Boykin Dr. On US 287, 1.3 mi n of jct
SR 256. Ext corridors. **Pets:** Medium. $5 daily fee/pet. Service with
restrictions, supervision.
🆂🅰🆅🅴 🆂 ⊠ 🔋 💻 🍴 🏊

MIDLAND

🅐🅐🅐 ▼▼ **Best Western Atrium Inn** 🆂🅷
(432) 694-7774. **$67.** 3904 W Wall St. I-20, exit 134, 1 mi n on Midkiff
Rd, 0.3 mi w on I-20 business route. Ext/int corridors. **Pets:** Small,
other species. $10 one-time fee/pet. Designated rooms, service with restric-
tions.
🆂🅰🆅🅴 🆂 ⊠ 🐾 🔋 💻 🏊 ⊠

🅐🅐🅐 ▼▼▼ **Clarion Hotel & Conference Center** 🆂🅷
(432) 697-3181. **$90.** 4300 W Wall St. I-20, exit 134 (Midkiff Rd), 1 mi
n to I-20 business loop, then 0.7 mi w. Ext/int corridors. **Pets:** Accepted.
🆂🅰🆅🅴 🆂 ⊠ 🐾 🔋 💻 🍴 🏊 ⊠

▼▼▼▼ **Hilton Midland Plaza** 🅻🅷
(432) 683-6131. **$79-$209, 3 day notice.** 117 W Wall St. Jct Wall and
Loraine sts; downtown. Int corridors. **Pets:** Other species. $25 one-time
fee/room. Designated rooms, service with restrictions, supervision.
⊠ 🅜 🐾 🐾 🔋 💻 🍴 🏊 ⊠

🅐🅐🅐 ▼▼▼▼ **La Quinta Inn Midland** 🆂🅷
(432) 697-9900. **$84-$108.** 4130 W Wall St. I-20, exit 131, 0.9 mi n on
SR 250 Loop to exit 1A; 1.2 mi e on I-20 business route. Ext corridors.
Pets: Medium. Service with restrictions.
🆂🅰🆅🅴 ⊠ 🐾 🔋 💻 🏊

▼▼▼ **Ramada Limited** 🆂🅷
(432) 699-4144. **$69-$99.** 3100 W Wall St. 2 mi w on I-20 business
loop. Int corridors. **Pets:** Accepted.
🅰🆂🅺 🆂 ⊠ 🔋 💻 🏊

MINERAL WELLS

🅐🅐🅐 ▼▼▼▼ **Best Western Clubhouse Inn & Suites** 🆂🅷
(940) 325-2270. **$85-$159.** 4410 Hwy 180 E. Jct US 180 and SR 1195;
in East Mineral Wells. Int corridors. **Pets:** Other species. $10 one-time
fee/pet. Service with restrictions, supervision.
🆂🅰🆅🅴 🆂 ⊠ 🅜 🐾 🔋 💻 🏊

MISSION

▼▼▼▼ **Hawthorn Suites** 🆂🅷
(956) 519-9696. **$105-$112.** 3700 Plantation Grove Blvd. US 83, exit
Sharyland Rd, 2.1 mi s to Plantation Grove Blvd. Ext corridors. **Pets:** Small. Service with restrictions, crate.
🅰🆂🅺 🆂 ⊠ 💻 🏊

MONAHANS

▼▼ **Americas Best Value Colonial Inn** Ⓜ
(432) 943-4345. **$63.** 702 W I-20. I-20, exit 80, just s. Ext/int corridors.
Pets: Accepted.
🅰🆂🅺 ⊠ 🐾 🔋 💻 🏊

MOUNT PLEASANT

🅐🅐🅐 ▼▼▼ **Comfort Inn** 🆂🅷
(903) 577-7553. **$65-$95.** 2515 W Ferguson Rd. I-30, exit 160. Ext
corridors. **Pets:** Supervision.
🆂🅰🆅🅴 🆂 ⊠ 🐾 🔋 💻 🏊

▼▼▼▼ **Holiday Inn Express Hotel & Suites** 🆂🅷
(903) 577-3800. **$89-$134.** 2306 Greenhill Rd. I-30, exit 162, just n. Int
corridors. **Pets:** Accepted.
🅰🆂🅺 🆂 ⊠ 🅜 🐾 🔋 💻 🏊

MOUNT VERNON

🅐🅐🅐 ▼▼▼ **Super 8 Motel of Mount Vernon** 🆂🅷
(903) 588-2882. **$49-$69.** 401 W I-30. I-30, exit 146 (SR 37). Ext
corridors. **Pets:** $5 daily fee/pet. Service with restrictions, supervision.
🆂🅰🆅🅴 🆂 ⊠ 🐾 🏊

NACOGDOCHES

▼▼▼ **Best Western Northpark Inn** 🆂🅷
(936) 560-1906. **$68-$89.** 4809 NW Stallings Dr. Jct US 59 N and Loop
224, exit Westward Dr. Ext corridors. **Pets:** Small. $10 one-time fee/pet.
No service, crate.
🅰🆂🅺 🆂 ⊠ 🔋 💻 🏊

▼▼▼ **La Quinta Inn Nacogdoches** 🆂🅷
(936) 560-5453. **$80-$100.** 3215 South St. US 59, jct Loop 224 and US
59 business route, s of town. Ext corridors. **Pets:** Medium. Service with
restrictions.
🅰🆂🅺 ⊠ 🐾 🔋 💻 🏊

NEW BOSTON

🅐🅐🅐 ▼▼▼ **Best Western Inn of New Boston** 🆂🅷
(903) 628-6999. **$49-$99.** 1024 N Center. I-30, exit 201, on westbound
access road. Ext corridors. **Pets:** Accepted.
🆂🅰🆅🅴 🆂 ⊠ 🐾 🔋 💻 🏊

NORTH RICHLAND HILLS

▼▼ **Studio 6 #6034** 🆂🅷
(817) 788-6000. **$47-$57.** 7450 NE Loop 820. I-820, exit 21 (Holiday
Ln), 0.4 mi e on south access road. Ext corridors. **Pets:** Accepted.
🆂 ⊠ 🐾 🐾 🔋 💻

ODEM

🅐🅐🅐 ▼▼▼ **Days Inn-Odem** Ⓜ
(361) 368-2166. **$54-$150, 3 day notice.** 1505 Voss Ave (US 77). US
77, 1 mi s of jct 631. Ext corridors. **Pets:** Accepted.
🆂🅰🆅🅴 🆂 ⊠ 🔋 💻 🏊

ODESSA

🅐🅐🅐 ▼▼▼ **Best Western Garden Oasis** 🆂🅷
(432) 337-3006. **$78-$88 (no credit cards).** 110 W I-20. Jct I-20 and
US 385, exit 116. Ext/int corridors. **Pets:** Other species. Service with
restrictions, supervision.
🆂🅰🆅🅴 🆂 ⊠ 🐾 🔋 💻 🍴 🏊 ⊠

🅐🅐🅐 ▼▼▼ **Days Inn** 🆂🅷
(432) 335-8000. **$50-$54, 3 day notice.** 3075 E Business Loop 20.
I-20, exit 121, 0.7 mi n on Loop 338, then 0.5 mi w. Int corridors.
Pets: Small. $25 one-time fee/pet. Service with restrictions, supervision.
🆂🅰🆅🅴 🆂 ⊠ 🔋 🏊

▼▼▼ **La Quinta Inn Odessa** 🆂🅷
(432) 333-2820. **$84-$108.** 5001 E Business Loop I-20. I-20, exit 121,
0.8 mi n on Loop 338, then just w. Ext corridors. **Pets:** Medium. Service
with restrictions.
🅰🆂🅺 ⊠ 🐾 🔋 💻 🏊

▼▼ **MCM Grande Hotel** SH
(432) 362-2311. **$80-$90.** 6201 E Business I-20. I-20, exit 121, 0.8 mi n on Loop 338, then 1 mi e. Ext/int corridors. **Pets:** Other species. $50 deposit/room. Service with restrictions, supervision.
[ASK] [X] [🐾] [⟊] [🛏] [💻] [🍴] [🏊] [⊗]

▼ **Motel 6 Odessa #439** M
(432) 333-4025. **$42-$55.** 200 E I-20 Service Rd. I-20, exit 116, on eastbound frontage road. Ext corridors. **Pets:** Medium, other species. Service with restrictions, supervision.
[S🐾] [X] [🏊]

▼ **Quality Inn & Suites** SH
(432) 333-3931. **$69-$199.** 3001 E Business I-20. I-20, exit 121, 0.7 mi n on Loop 338, then 0.5 mi w. Ext/int corridors. **Pets:** Accepted.
[ASK] [S🐾] [X] [🛏] [💻] [🏊] [⊗]

OZONA

▲▲▲ ▼▼ **Americas Best Value Inn** M
(325) 392-2631. **$55-$65.** 820 11th St. I-10, exit 365 westbound to SR 163, 1 mi n; exit 363 eastbound to Loop 466, 2 mi e. Ext corridors. **Pets:** $10 one-time fee/pet. Designated rooms, service with restrictions, supervision.
[SAVE] [S🐾] [X] [🛏]

▲▲▲ ▼▼ **Travelodge** M
(325) 392-2656. **$60-$65.** 8 11th St. I-10, exit 368 westbound, 2 mi w; exit 365 eastbound to Loop 466, 1 mi e. Ext corridors. **Pets:** Other species. $5 daily fee/pet. Service with restrictions, supervision.
[SAVE] [S🐾] [X] [🛏] [💻] [🏊]

PALESTINE

▲▲▲ ▼▼ **Best Western Palestine Inn** SH ✿
(903) 723-4655. **$79-$99.** 1601 W Palestine Ave. Jct US 287/SR 19, 0.7 mi sw on US 79. Ext corridors. **Pets:** Medium. $10 daily fee/pet. Designated rooms, service with restrictions, supervision.
[SAVE] [S🐾] [X] [⟊] [🛏] [💻] [🍴] [🏊]

PARIS

▲▲▲ ▼▼ **Best Western Inn of Paris** SH
(903) 785-5566. **$54-$68.** 3755 NE Loop 286. Jct US 82 and E Loop 286, just n. Ext corridors. **Pets:** Medium. $10 daily fee/pet. Service with restrictions, supervision.
[SAVE] [S🐾] [X] [🐾] [⟊] [🛏] [💻] [🏊]

▲▲▲ ▼▼ **Days Inn** SH
(903) 784-8164. **$60-$75.** 2650 N Main. NE Loop 286, exit US 271, just n. Ext corridors. **Pets:** Accepted.
[SAVE] [S🐾] [X] [🛏] [💻] [🏊]

▲▲▲ ▼▼▼ **Holiday Inn** SH ✿
(903) 785-5545. **$78-$124.** 3560 NE Loop 286. E Loop 286, 0.3 mi n of jct US 82. Ext corridors. **Pets:** Small. $20 one-time fee/room. Designated rooms, service with restrictions, supervision.
[SAVE] [S🐾] [X] [⟊] [🐾] [🛏] [💻] [🍴] [🏊]

PECOS

▲▲▲ ▼▼ **Laura Lodge Motel and Suites** M
(432) 445-4924. **$42-$69.** 1000 E Business 20. I-20, exit 42 (US 285), 1 mi nw to Business Rt I-20, then 0.5 mi e. Ext corridors. **Pets:** Small. $10 daily fee/pet. Designated rooms, service with restrictions, supervision.
[SAVE] [S🐾] [X] [🛏] [💻] [🏊]

▲▲▲ ▼▼ **Oak Tree Inn** SH
(432) 447-0180. **$70-$82.** 22 N Frontage Rd. I-20, exit 42, just w on north access road. Int corridors. **Pets:** Small, other species. $10 one-time fee/pet. No service.
[SAVE] [S🐾] [X] [⟊] [🐾] [🛏] [💻]

PHARR

▼▼▼ **Palace Inn & Suites** SH
(956) 702-3330. **$65-$70.** 1130 E Expwy 83. Jct US 83, exit I Rd. Ext corridors. **Pets:** Accepted.
[ASK] [S🐾] [X] [🐾] [🛏] [💻] [🏊]

PLAINVIEW

▼▼ **Best Western Conestoga** SH
(806) 293-9454. **$50-$80.** 600 N I-27. I-27, exit 49, just s of US 70, on eastbound access road. Ext corridors. **Pets:** $10 daily fee/pet. Service with restrictions, supervision.
[ASK] [S🐾] [X] [⟊] [🛏] [💻] [🏊]

▼▼▼ **Holiday Inn Express Hotel & Suites** SH
(806) 296-9900. **$89-$129.** 4213 W 13th St. I-27, exit 49 northbound, just w to Mesa, then just n; exit 50 southbound, just s to 13th St, then just w. Int corridors. **Pets:** Very small. $20 daily fee/pet. No service, supervision.
[ASK] [S🐾] [X] [🐾M] [🐾] [🛏] [💻] [🏊]

PORT ARANSAS

▼▼▼ **Beachgate CondoSuites & Motel** CO
(361) 749-5900. **$59-$195, 7 day notice.** 2000 On the Beach. Beach access; between markers 8 and 9; street access on Anchor Rd off 11th St. Ext/int corridors. **Pets:** Accepted.
[ASK] [X] [🛏] [💻] [🏊]

▼▼ **Executive Keys** CO
(361) 749-6272. **$79-$249, 30 day notice.** 820 Access Rd 1A. 2.5 mi s on SR 361. Ext corridors. **Pets:** Medium, dogs only. $5 daily fee/pet. Designated rooms, service with restrictions, supervision.
[💻] [🏊]

▲▲▲ ▼▼▼▼ **Plantation Suites & Conference Center** M
(361) 749-3866. **$69-$249.** 1909 Hwy 361. On SR 361, 0.4 mi s. Ext corridors. **Pets:** Other species. $100 deposit/room, $25 one-time fee/room. Service with restrictions, crate.
[SAVE] [S🐾] [X] [🛏] [💻] [🏊]

POST

▼▼ **Best Western Post Inn** SH
(806) 495-9933. **$81-$86.** 1011 N Broadway. 1 mi n on US 84. Int corridors. **Pets:** Small, dogs only. $15 daily fee/pet. Designated rooms, service with restrictions, supervision.
[ASK] [S🐾] [X] [🐾] [🛏] [💻] [🏊]

QUANAH

▼▼▼ **Best Western Quanah Inn & Suites** SH
(940) 663-5407. **$89-$139.** 1100 W 11th St (Hwy 287). On north end of town. Int corridors. **Pets:** Accepted.
[ASK] [S🐾] [X] [🐾M] [🐾] [🛏] [💻] [🏊]

RAYMONDVILLE

▲▲▲ ▼▼ **Americas Best Value Inn & Suites** SH ✿
(956) 689-5900. **$49-$59.** 450 S Hwy 77/I-69. US 77/I-69, exit 186 (Raymondville), on frontage road. Ext corridors. **Pets:** Other species. Service with restrictions, supervision.
[SAVE] [S🐾] [X] [🛏] [💻] [🏊]

▲▲▲ ▼▼▼ **Best Western** SH
(956) 689-4141. **$49-$94.** 118 N Hwy 77. US 77, jct FM 186 on southbound access road. Ext corridors. **Pets:** Small. $15 one-time fee/room. Service with restrictions, supervision.
[SAVE] [S🐾] [X] [🛏] [💻] [🏊]

ROBSTOWN

▲▲▲ ▼▼ **Executive Inn** SH
(361) 387-9416. **$60-$90.** 620 Hwy 77 S. On US 77, 1 mi s. Ext corridors. **Pets:** Accepted.
[SAVE] [X] [🛏] [🏊]

ROCKPORT

▼▼ Days Inn M
(361) 729-6379. **$59-$150.** 1212 Laurel St @ Bus 35 Hwy. Jct Laurel St and Business Rt SR 35; center. Ext corridors. **Pets:** Medium, dogs only. $15 daily fee/pet. Service with restrictions, supervision.

[ASK] [SĎ] [✕] [🔒] [🏊]

▲▲▲ ▼▼ Hunt's Castle SH
(361) 729-5002. **$65-$174.** 725 S Water St. Business Rt SR 35, jct Market St, 1.6 mi e to Water St, just s. Ext corridors. **Pets:** Supervision.

[SAVE] [SĎ] [✕] [⚙] [🔒] [🏊]

▲▲▲ ▼▼▼ Laguna Reef Hotel CO
(361) 729-1742. **$90-$325.** 1021 Water St. 0.5 mi s, just e of Business Rt SR 35; entrance on S Austin St. Ext corridors. **Pets:** Small, dogs only. $50 deposit/pet, $7 daily fee/pet. Service with restrictions, supervision.

[SAVE] [SĎ] [✕] [🔒] [🖥] [🏊] [✕]

▲▲▲ ▼▼▼ Sportsman Manor Motel M
(361) 729-5331. **$69-$169.** 1075 N Fulton Beach Rd. SR 35; across from airport. Ext corridors. **Pets:** Small, dogs only. $10 daily fee/pet. Designated rooms, service with restrictions, supervision.

[SAVE] [SĎ] [✕] [🏊]

▲▲▲ ▼▼ The Village Inn M
(361) 729-6370. **$44-$100, 5 day notice.** 503 N Austin St. Just w of jct SR 35 and Business Rt SR 35. Ext corridors. **Pets:** Accepted.

[SAVE] [SĎ] [✕] [🔒] [🖥] [🏊]

ROUND ROCK

▲▲▲ ▼▼ Best Western Executive Inn SH
(512) 255-3222. **$59-$99.** 1851 N I-35. I-35, exit 253 northbound; exit 253A U-turn southbound. Ext corridors. **Pets:** Very small. Service with restrictions.

[SAVE] [SĎ] [✕] [⚙M] [🔒] [🖥] [🏊]

▼▼▼ Candlewood Suites SH
(512) 828-0899. **$69-$109.** 521 S I-35. I-35, exit 252A, just n on northbound frontage road. Int corridors. **Pets:** Other species. $150 one-time fee/room. Service with restrictions.

[ASK] [SĎ] [✕] [⚙] [🏊]

▼▼ Days Inn and Suites SH 🐾
(512) 246-0055. **$70-$99.** 1802 S I-35. I-35, exit 251, just s. Ext/int corridors. **Pets:** Medium, other species. $15 daily fee/pet. Service with restrictions, supervision.

[ASK] [SĎ] [✕] [⚙] [🔒] [🖥] [🏊]

▲▲▲ ▼▼▼ La Quinta Inn Austin (Round Rock) SH
(512) 255-6666. **$84-$111.** 2004 I-35 N. I-35, exit 254, on west frontage road. Int corridors. **Pets:** Medium. Service with restrictions.

[SAVE] [✕] [🖊] [🔒] [🖥] [🏊]

▼▼ Red Roof Inn SH
(512) 310-1111. **$53-$75.** 1990 I-35 N. I-35, exit 254, on west frontage road. Int corridors. **Pets:** Medium, other species. Service with restrictions, supervision.

[✕] [⚙] [🔒] [🏊]

▼▼▼ Residence Inn by Marriott Austin Round Rock SH 🐾
(512) 733-2400. **$89-$199.** 2505 S I-35. I-35, exit 250 southbound; exit 251 northbound, on east frontage road. Int corridors. **Pets:** Other species. $100 one-time fee/room.

[ASK] [SĎ] [✕] [⚙M] [🖊] [🔒] [🖥] [🏊] [✕]

▼▼▼ Staybridge Suites Austin-Round Rock SH
(512) 733-0942. **$89-$129.** 520 I-35 S. I-35, exit 252B northbound; exit 252AB southbound, on west frontage road. Int corridors. **Pets:** Accepted.

[ASK] [SĎ] [✕] [⚙M] [🖊] [🖊] [🔒] [🖥] [🏊]

▲▲▲ ▼▼▼ Wingate Inn and Williamson Conference Center SH
(512) 341-7000. **$99-$129.** 1209 N I-35. I-35, exit 253, just e. Int corridors. **Pets:** Accepted.

[SAVE] [SĎ] [✕] [⚙M] [🖊] [🔒] [🔒] [🖥] [🏊]

SAN ANGELO

▲▲▲ ▼▼ Americas Best Value Inn M
(325) 653-1323. **$51-$85.** 1601 S Bryant Blvd. US 87 and 277 at Ave L. Ext/int corridors. **Pets:** Small, dogs only. $25 deposit/pet, $4 daily fee/pet. Service with restrictions, supervision.

[SAVE] [SĎ] [✕] [🔒] [🖥] [🏊]

▲▲▲ ▼▼ Benchmark Comfort Inn SH
(325) 944-2578. **$70-$110.** 2502 Loop 306. Loop 306, exit Knickerbocker Rd. Ext corridors. **Pets:** Accepted.

[SAVE] [SĎ] [✕] [🔒] [🖥] [🏊]

▲▲▲ ▼▼ Best Western San Angelo SH
(325) 223-1273. **$70.** 3017 W Loop 306. Loop 306, exit College Hills Blvd, just s. Ext corridors. **Pets:** Small. $10 daily fee/pet. Service with restrictions, crate.

[SAVE] [SĎ] [✕] [🔒] [🔒] [🖥] [🏊]

▲▲▲ ▼▼ Days Inn San Angelo SH
(325) 658-6594. **$58-$80.** 4613 S Jackson St. Jct US 87 and Jackson St. Ext corridors. **Pets:** Small. Service with restrictions, supervision.

[SAVE] [SĎ] [✕] [🔒] [🖥] [🍴] [🏊]

▼▼▼ Hawthorn Inn & Suites SH
(325) 653-1500. **$85-$125.** 1355 Knickerbocker Rd. US 87 S, 1 mi w. Int corridors. **Pets:** Accepted.

[ASK] [SĎ] [✕] [🖊] [🔒] [🖥] [🏊]

▲▲▲ ▼▼▼ Howard Johnson San Angelo SH
(325) 653-2995. **$56-$61.** 415 W Beauregard. Just w on US 67 business route at US 87 southbound. Ext/int corridors. **Pets:** Accepted.

[SAVE] [SĎ] [✕] [🔒] [🖥] [🍴] [🏊]

▼▼▼▼ La Quinta Inn San Angelo (Conference Center) SH
(325) 949-0515. **$80-$108.** 2307 Loop 306. Loop 306, exit Knickerbocker Rd, just s. Ext corridors. **Pets:** Medium. Service with restrictions.

[ASK] [✕] [🖊] [🔒] [🖥] [🏊]

▼▼▼ Motel 6 San Angelo #229 M
(325) 658-8061. **$43-$53.** 311 N Bryant Blvd. Just n on US 87. Ext corridors. **Pets:** Medium, other species. Service with restrictions, supervision.

[SĎ] [✕] [🖊] [🔒] [🖥] [🏊]

▼▼ Quality Inn & Suites SH
(325) 655-8000. **$89.** 333 Rio Concho Dr. US 87 to Concho Ave, 1 mi e. Ext/int corridors. **Pets:** Accepted.

[ASK] [SĎ] [✕] [🖊] [🔒] [🖥] [🏊] [✕]

▲▲▲ ▼▼▼ San Angelo Inn & Conference Center SH
(325) 658-2828. **$59-$119.** 441 Rio Concho Dr. US 87 to Concho Ave, 0.5 mi e; downtown. Int corridors. **Pets:** Medium, other species. $50 one-time fee/room. Service with restrictions, supervision.

[SAVE] [✕] [🖊] [🔒] [🖥] [🍴] [🏊]

SAN ANTONIO METROPOLITAN AREA

ELMENDORF

Comfort Inn & Suites Braunig Lake SH
(210) 633-1833. **$79-$99.** 13800 I-37 S. I-37, exit 130 (Donop, South-ton Rd), on northbound access lane. Ext corridors. **Pets:** Small. $5 daily fee/room. Service with restrictions, supervision.

FLORESVILLE

Best Western Floresville Inn SH
(830) 393-0443. **$70-$89.** 1720 S 10th St. US 181, just s of downtown. Ext corridors. **Pets:** Small. $10 daily fee/room. Service with restrictions.

LIVE OAK

La Quinta Inn San Antonio (I-35 North at Toepperwein) SH
(210) 657-5500. **$84-$121.** 12822 I-35 N. I-35, exit 170B (Toepper-wein), exit 170B (Toepperwein); on northbound access road. Ext/int corridors. **Pets:** Medium. Service with restrictions.

NEW BRAUNFELS

Best Western Inn & Suites SH
(830) 625-7337. **$49-$149.** 1493 I-35 N. I-35, exit 190, on southbound access lane. Ext/int corridors. **Pets:** Small. $20 one-time fee/pet. Service with restrictions, supervision.

Executive Inn & Suites SH
(830) 625-3932. **$39-$199.** 808 Hwy 46 S. I-35, exit 189, 0.4 mi e. Ext corridors. **Pets:** Small. $10 daily fee/pet. Designated rooms, service with restrictions, supervision.

Holiday Inn SH
(830) 625-8017. **$59-$199.** 1051 I-35 E. I-35, exit 189, on southbound access road. Ext corridors. **Pets:** Accepted.

Quality Inn & Suites SH
(830) 643-9300. **$65-$400.** 1533 IH-35 N. I-35, exit 190, exit 190; on southbound access road. Int corridors. **Pets:** Medium, other species. $50 deposit/pet, $25 daily fee/pet. Service with restrictions, supervision.

Rodeway Inn SH
(830) 629-6991. **$44-$219.** 1209 I-35 N. I-35, exit 189, on southbound access road. Ext corridors. **Pets:** Large, other species. $20 daily fee/pet. Service with restrictions, supervision.

Super 8 Motel-New Braunfels M
(830) 629-1155. **$49-$199.** 510 Hwy 46 S. I-35, exit 189 (SR 46), just e. Ext corridors. **Pets:** Small. $20 daily fee/pet. Service with restrictions, supervision.

SAN ANTONIO

Alamo Travelodge SH
(210) 222-1000. **$44-$109.** 405 Broadway. US 281, exit Broadway, just s. Ext corridors. **Pets:** Accepted.

AmeriChoice Inn & Suites SH
(210) 224-3030. **$55-$120.** 3817 I-35 N. I-35, exit 161 (Binz-Engleman Rd), follow signs to I-35 S access road northbound; exit Binz-Engleman Rd, continue southbound. Int corridors. **Pets:** Accepted.

Arbor House Suites Bed & Breakfast BB
(210) 472-2005. **$90-$175, 7 day notice.** 109 Arciniega St. Just n of Durango St; near La Villita Historic District. Ext/int corridors. **Pets:** Medium. $25 one-time fee/room. Service with restrictions, supervision.

Best Western-Garden Inn SH
(210) 599-0999. **$89-$169.** 11939 N I-35. I-35, exit 170, on southbound access road, 0.5 mi s to Judson Rd exit. Ext corridors. **Pets:** Very small. $25 daily fee/pet. Service with restrictions.

Best Western Posada Ana Inn-SA Airport SH
(210) 691-9550. **$93-$146.** 9411 Wurzbach Rd. I-10 NW, exit 561 (Wurzbach Rd), on eastbound access road. Int corridors. **Pets:** Small, other species. Service with restrictions, supervision.

Best Western Posada Ana Inn-SA Medical Ctr SH
(210) 342-1400. **$85-$139.** 8600 Jones Maltsberger Rd. I-410, exit 21A (Jones Maltsberger Rd), 0.5 mi s. Int corridors. **Pets:** Accepted.

Best Western San Antonio Airport SH
(210) 366-1800. **$75-$125.** 8818 Jones Maltsberger Rd. I-410, exit 21B (Jones Maltsberger Rd), on westbound access road. Int corridors. **Pets:** Medium. Service with restrictions, supervision.

Brackenridge House B & B BB
(210) 271-3442. **$111-$225, 14 day notice.** 230 Madison. Just s of S St. Marys St at Durango St. Ext/int corridors. **Pets:** Large, other species. Designated rooms, service with restrictions.

Candlewood Suites Hotel SH
(210) 615-0550. **$109-$159.** 9350 I-10 W. I-10 W, exit 561 (Wurzbach Rd), eastbound access road; between Wurzbach Rd and Callaghan. Int corridors. **Pets:** Medium. $75 one-time fee/room. Service with restrictions, crate.

Comfort Inn-East SH
(210) 333-9430. **$55-$175.** 4403 I-10 E. I-10, exit 580 (WW White Rd), on westbound access road. Ext corridors. **Pets:** Accepted.

Crowne Plaza San Antonio Riverwalk LH
(210) 354-2800. **$139-$219.** 111 Pecan St E. Corner of Pecan and Soledad sts. Int corridors. **Pets:** Accepted.

Days Inn Coliseum / AT & T Center SH
(210) 225-4040. **$54-$139.** 3443 I-35 N. I-35, exit 160 (Splashtown), on southbound access road. Ext corridors. **Pets:** $25 one-time fee/pet. Designated rooms, service with restrictions, crate.

Days Inn Downtown Riverwalk SH
(210) 271-3334. **$54-$139.** 1500 I-35 S. I-10/35, exit 154 (Laredo St). Ext/int corridors. **Pets:** $25 one-time fee/pet. Designated rooms, service with restrictions, crate.

▼▼▼▼ **Drury Inn & Suites-San Antonio Airport** SH
(210) 308-8100. **$90-$145.** 95 NE Loop 410. I-410, exit 21A (Jones Maltsberger Rd), 1.8 mi w of airport. Int corridors. **Pets:** Large, other species. Service with restrictions, supervision.

ASK ⊠ ⌖M ⌖ ▤ �... ⇌

▼▼▼▼ **Drury Inn & Suites-San Antonio North** SH
(210) 404-1600. **$90-$155.** 801 N Loop 1604 E. On FM 1604, 0.4 mi w on US 281. Int corridors. **Pets:** Large, other species. Service with restrictions, supervision.

ASK ⊠ ⌖ ▤ ▤ ⇌

▼▼▼▼ **Drury Inn & Suites-San Antonio Northwest** SH
(210) 561-2510. **$85-$165.** 9806 I-10 W. I-10, exit Wurzbach Rd, on southeast corner. Int corridors. **Pets:** Large, other species. Service with restrictions, supervision.

ASK ⊠ ⌖ ▤ ▤ ⇌

♦♦♦ ▼▼▼▼ **Drury Inn & Suites-San Antonio**
Riverwalk SH
(210) 212-5200. **$110-$190.** 201 N St. Mary's St. Just s of College St. Int corridors. **Pets:** Large, other species. Service with restrictions, supervision.

SAVE ⊠ ⌖ ▤ ▤ ⇌

▼▼▼ **Drury Inn-San Antonio Northeast** SH
(210) 654-1144. **$75-$130.** 8300 I-35 N. I-35, exit 165 (Walzem Rd), northbound access road. Ext/int corridors. **Pets:** Large, other species. Service with restrictions, supervision.

ASK ⊠ ⌖M ▤ ▤ ⇌

▼▼ **Econo Lodge Airport** M
(210) 247-4774. **$60-$90.** 2635 NE Loop 410. I-410, exit 25B (Perrin-Beitel Rd), on westbound access road. Ext/int corridors. **Pets:** Accepted.

ASK S⌖ ⊠ ⇌

♦♦♦ ▼▼▼ **Econo Lodge Inn & Suites Fiesta Park** M
(210) 690-5500. **$79-$110.** 13575 IH 10 W. I-10, exit 557, westbound access road. Ext corridors. **Pets:** Accepted.

SAVE S⌖ ⊠ ⌖ ▤ ⇌

♦♦♦ ▼▼ **Econo Lodge Lackland** SH
(210) 645-1430. **$69-$109.** 6301 Old Hwy 90 W. US 90, exit Old US 90, 0.4 mi ne. Ext corridors. **Pets:** Accepted.

SAVE ⊠ ▤ ▤ ⇌

♦♦♦ ▼▼▼▼ **El Tropicano Riverwalk Hotel by Clarion** LH
(210) 223-9461. **$119-$209, 3 day notice.** 110 Lexington Ave. 0.3 mi s of jct Lexington Ave and I-35. Int corridors. **Pets:** Accepted.

SAVE S⌖ ⊠ ▤ ▤ ▤ ⇌

♦♦♦ ▼▼▼▼ **Emily Morgan Hotel** LH ❀
(210) 225-8486. **$129-$239.** 705 E Houston St. On Houston St, just n of Bonham St. Int corridors. **Pets:** Other species. Service with restrictions, crate.

SAVE S⌖ ⊠ ⌖M ⌖ ▤ ▤ ⇌ ⊠

♦♦♦ ▼▼▼▼ **The Fairmount** SH
(210) 224-8800. **$229-$500.** 401 S Alamo St. Opposite convention center and Hemisfair Plaza. Ext/int corridors. **Pets:** Accepted.

SAVE S⌖ ⊠ ⌖ ▤ ⇌ ⊠

♦♦♦ ▼▼▼▼ **Hampton Inn Six Flags Area** SH
(210) 561-9058. **$79-$109.** 11010 I-10. I-10, exit 560 westbound; exit 559 (Huebner Rd) eastbound. Int corridors. **Pets:** Accepted.

SAVE S⌖ ⊠ ⌖ ▤ ▤ ⇌

♦♦♦ ▼▼▼ **Holiday Inn-Downtown-Market Square** SH
(210) 225-3211. **$79-$159.** 318 W Durango St. I-35, exit Durango St, 2 blks e. Int corridors. **Pets:** Accepted.

SAVE S⌖ ⊠ ⌖M ⌖ ▤ ▤ ⇌ ⊠

▼▼▼▼ **Holiday Inn Express-San Antonio Airport** SH
(210) 308-6700. **$92-$152.** 91 NE Loop 410. I-410, exit 21A (Jones Maltsberger Rd) eastbound; exit 20B westbound, on westbound access road; between San Pedro Ave and Jones Maltsberger Rd. Int corridors. **Pets:** Service with restrictions, supervision.

ASK ⊠ ⌖M ▤ ▤ ▤ ⇌

♦♦♦ ▼▼▼▼ **Holiday Inn Riverwalk** SH
(210) 224-2500. **$159-$239, 3 day notice.** 217 N St. Mary's St. Houston St, just s. Int corridors. **Pets:** Accepted.

SAVE S⌖ ⊠ ▤ ▤ ⇌

♦♦♦ ▼▼▼▼ **Holiday Inn Select** SH
(210) 349-9900. **$109-$209.** 77 NE Loop 410. I-410, exit 20B (McCullough St), on westbound access road. Int corridors. **Pets:** Medium. $100 deposit/room, $25 one-time fee/room. Supervision.

SAVE S⌖ ⊠ ⌖M ⌖ ⌖ ▤ ▤ ▤ ⇌

▼▼ **Homegate Studios & Suites** SH
(210) 691-1103. **$49-$99.** 10950 Laureate Dr. 0.5 mi n of Huebner Rd, just off Fredericksburg Rd. Ext corridors. **Pets:** Accepted.

ASK S⌖ ⊠ ▤ ▤ ⇌

▼▼ **HomeGate Studios & Suites** SH
(210) 342-4800. **$54-$89.** 11221 San Pedro Ave. I-410, exit US 281 (San Pedro Ave), 2.3 mi n on US 281, exit Nakoma, on west frontage road. Ext corridors. **Pets:** Accepted.

ASK S⌖ ⊠ ▤ ⇌ ⊠

▼▼ **Homestead Studio Suites Hotel-San**
Antonio-Airport M
(210) 491-9009. **$75-$85.** 1015 Central Pkwy S. I-410, exit US 281 (San Pedro Ave), 4 mi n on US 281, exit Bitters Rd, on northbound access road. Ext corridors. **Pets:** Accepted.

ASK S⌖ ⊠ ▤ ▤

▼▼▼▼ **Hotel Contessa** LH
(210) 229-9222. **$185-$335.** 306 W Market. Market St at St. Mary's St. **Pets:** Accepted.

ASK ⊠ ⌖ ▤ ▤ ⇌ ⊠

▼▼▼ **Hotel Marquis Airport** SH
(210) 653-9110. **$60-$90.** 2635 NE Loop 410. I-410, exit 25B (Perrin-Beitel Rd), on westbound access road. Ext/int corridors. **Pets:** Accepted.

ASK S⌖ ⊠ ▤ ▤ ⇌

♦♦♦ ▼▼▼ **Howard Johnson Lackland Inn & Suites** SH
(210) 675-9690. **$70-$76.** 6815 Hwy 90 W. I-410, exit US 90 to Military Dr, 0.5 mi e on westbound access road. Ext corridors. **Pets:** Small. $25 one-time fee/pet. No service, crate.

SAVE S⌖ ⊠ ▤ ▤ ⇌

▼▼▼ **Inn on the River** BB
(210) 225-6333. **$79-$119, 14 day notice.** 129 Woodward Pl. Just n of W Durango St. Ext/int corridors. **Pets:** Accepted.

ASK ⊠ ▤ ▤

♦♦♦ ▼▼▼ **Knights Inn Windsor Park** M
(210) 646-6336. **$70-$99.** 6370 I-35 N. I-410/35, exit 164A (Rittiman Rd), on northbound access road. Ext corridors. **Pets:** Small. $15 one-time fee/pet. Designated rooms, service with restrictions, supervision.

SAVE S⌖ ⊠ ⌖ ▤ ⇌

♦♦♦ ▼▼▼▼ **La Quinta Inn** SH
(210) 661-4545. **$55-$150.** 6075 IH 10 E. I-10, exit 583 (Foster Rd), on westbound access road. Int corridors. **Pets:** Accepted.

SAVE S⌖ ⊠ ▤ ▤ ⇌

♦♦♦ ▼▼▼ **La Quinta Inn & Suites San Antonio**
(Convention Center) SH
(210) 222-9181. **$179-$259.** 303 Blum St. 0.5 mi ne. Ext/int corridors. **Pets:** Medium. Service with restrictions.

SAVE ⊠ ▤ ▤ ⇌

▼▼▼ La Quinta Inn Alamo South **SH**
(210) 337-7171. **$90-$150.** 3180 Goliad Rd. I-37, exit 135 (Brooks City Base/SE Military Dr), just w of interstate. Int corridors. **Pets:** Very small. Service with restrictions, supervision.

🆎 📶 ⊠ 🔌 💻 🏊

AAA ▼▼▼ La Quinta Inn & Suites San Antonio Airport **SH**
(210) 342-3738. **$120-$157.** 850 Halm. I-410, exit US 281 S, southwest corner. Int corridors. **Pets:** Medium. Service with restrictions.

🆂🅰🆅🅴 ⊠ 🔌 💻 🏊

AAA ▼▼▼ La Quinta Inn & Suites San Antonio-Downtown **SH**
(210) 212-5400. **$123-$185.** 100 W Durango Blvd. I-35, exit 155B (Durango Blvd), 3 blks e of jct E Flores St. Int corridors. **Pets:** Medium. Service with restrictions.

🆂🅰🆅🅴 ⊠ ⚙ 📶 🔌 💻 🏊

▼▼▼ La Quinta Inn San Antonio (I-35 North @ Windsor Park Mall) **SH**
(210) 653-6619. **$86-$128.** 6410 I-35 N. I-35, exit 163B northbound, on I-35 northbound access road; between Rittiman and Eisenhauer rds; exit 164A (Rittiman Rd) southbound. Ext corridors. **Pets:** Medium. Service with restrictions.

🆎 ⊠ 🔌 💻 🏊

▼▼▼ La Quinta Inn San Antonio (Lackland) **SH**
(210) 674-3200. **$95-$126.** 6511 Military Dr W. Sw of jct US 90 and Military Dr W. Ext corridors. **Pets:** Medium. Service with restrictions.

🆎 ⊠ 🔌 💻 🏊

AAA ▼▼▼ La Quinta Inn San Antonio (Market Square) **SH**
(210) 271-0001. **$96-$138.** 900 Dolorosa. I-10/35, exit Durango St, just n on Santa Rosa St, then just w on Nueva St. Ext corridors. **Pets:** Medium. Service with restrictions.

🆂🅰🆅🅴 ⊠ ⚙ 🔌 💻 🏊

AAA ▼▼▼ La Quinta Inn San Antonio (SeaWorld/Ingram Park) **SH**
(210) 680-8883. **$91-$143.** 7134 NW Loop 410. I-410, exit 10 (Culebra Rd), on eastbound access road. Ext corridors. **Pets:** Medium. Service with restrictions.

🆂🅰🆅🅴 ⊠ 🔌 💻 🏊

▼▼▼ La Quinta Inn San Antonio (South Park) **SH**
(210) 922-2111. **$84-$147.** 7202 S Pan American Expwy. I-35, exit 150A (Military Dr) northbound; exit 150B southbound, southeast of jct I-35 and Military Dr SW. Ext corridors. **Pets:** Medium. Service with restrictions.

🆎 ⊠ ⚙ 🔌 💻 🏊

▼▼▼ La Quinta Inn San Antonio (Vance Jackson) **SH**
(210) 734-7931. **$80-$136.** 5922 I-10 W. I-10, exit 565B eastbound; exit 565C (Vance Jackson Rd) westbound, on eastbound access road. Ext corridors. **Pets:** Medium. Service with restrictions.

🆎 ⊠ ⚙ 🔌 💻 🏊

▼▼▼ La Quinta Inn San Antonio (Wurzbach) **SH**
(210) 593-0338. **$88-$126.** 9542 I-10 W. I-10, exit Wurzbach Rd, just e on eastbound access road. Ext corridors. **Pets:** Medium. Service with restrictions.

🆎 ⊠ 🔌 💻 🏊

▼▼▼ Marriott Plaza San Antonio **LH**
(210) 229-1000. **$199-$309.** 555 S Alamo St. Opposite convention center and Hemisfair Plaza. Int corridors. **Pets:** Accepted.

🆎 ⊠ ⚙ 📶 💻 🍴 🏊 ⊠

▼▼▼ Marriott Riverwalk **LH**
(210) 224-4555. **$200-$385.** 711 E Riverwalk. Opposite convention center and Hemisfair Plaza. Int corridors. **Pets:** $25 one-time fee/room. Service with restrictions, supervision.

🆎 ⊠ 📶 ⚙ 🔌 💻 🍴 🏊 ⊠

▼▼ Motel 6-1122 **M**
(210) 225-1111. **$45-$78.** 211 N Pecos St. I-10/35, exit 155 B (Pecos St), on I-10 E/35 S access road. Ext corridors. **Pets:** Medium, other species. Service with restrictions, supervision.

📶 ⊠ ⚙ 🔌 🏊

▼ Motel 6-134 **M**
(210) 650-4419. **$41-$53.** 9503 I-35 N. I-35, exit 167A (Randolf Blvd) southbound; exit 167 (Starlight Terr) northbound. Ext corridors. **Pets:** Medium, other species. Service with restrictions, supervision.

📶 ⊠ 🏊

▼ Motel 6-651 **M**
(210) 673-9020. **$41-$67.** 2185 SW Loop 410. I-410, exit 7 (Marbach Rd), 0.7 mi w; on westbound access road. Ext corridors. **Pets:** Medium, other species. Service with restrictions, supervision.

📶 ⊠ 📶 ⚙ 🔌 🏊

▼ Motel 6 East #183 **SH**
(210) 333-1850. **$41-$63.** 138 N WW White Rd. I-10, exit 580 (WW White Rd), just off westbound access road. Ext corridors. **Pets:** Medium, other species. Service with restrictions, supervision.

📶 ⊠ 🏊

▼▼ Motel 6 Fort Sam Houston #1350 **M**
(210) 661-8791. **$43-$58.** 5522 N PanAm Expwy. I-35/410, exit 164 (Rittiman Rd), just s on northbound access road; just off Goldfield St. Ext corridors. **Pets:** Medium, other species. Service with restrictions, supervision.

📶 ⊠ ⚙ 🏊

▼ Motel 6 San Antonio #1188 **M**
(210) 653-8088. **$41-$55.** 4621 E Rittiman Rd. I-35, exit 164 (Rittiman Rd), exit 164 (Rittiman Rd); on north side of Rittiman Rd. Ext corridors. **Pets:** Medium, other species. Service with restrictions, supervision.

📶 ⊠ 🏊

▼▼ Oak Hills Medical Center Inn & Suites **SH**
(210) 614-9900. **$69-$119.** 7401 Wurzbach Rd. 1.5 mi s of jct I-10 and Wurzbach Rd, just ne of Babcock Rd. Ext/int corridors. **Pets:** Accepted.

🆎 ⊠ 🔌 💻 🍴 🏊

AAA ▼▼ ▼▼ Omni La Mansion del Rio **LH** 🐾
(210) 518-1000. **$219-$379, 3 day notice.** 112 College St. Just s on the Riverwalk. Ext/int corridors. **Pets:** Small. $50 one-time fee/pet. Service with restrictions, supervision.

🆂🅰🆅🅴 📶 ⊠ ⚙ 🔌 💻 🍴 🏊

AAA ▼▼ ▼▼ Omni San Antonio Hotel **LH**
(210) 691-8888. **$149-$249.** 9821 Colonnade Blvd. I-10, exit Wurzbach Rd, 12 mi nw on westbound access road. Int corridors. **Pets:** Accepted.

🆂🅰🆅🅴 📶 ⊠ 💻 🍴 🏊 ⊠

▼▼▼ Pear Tree Inn San Antonio Airport **SH**
(210) 366-9300. **$70-$125.** 143 NE Loop 410. Loop 410 W, exit 21 (Jones Maltsberger Rd), on westbound access road; between Airport Blvd and Jones Maltsberger Rd. Int corridors. **Pets:** Large, other species. Service with restrictions, supervision.

🆎 ⊠ 🔌 💻 🏊

AAA ▼▼▼ Quality Inn & Suites North Airport **SH**
(210) 545-5400. **$89-$129.** 1505 Bexar Crossing. US 281, exit 1604 (Anderson Loop), on southbound access road. Int corridors. **Pets:** Small. $25 one-time fee/pet. Designated rooms, service with restrictions, supervision.

🆂🅰🆅🅴 📶 ⊠ 🔌 💻 🏊

AAA ▼▼▼ Quality Inn Northwest SH
(210) 736-1900. **$69-$149.** 6023 NW I-10 W. I-10, exit 565B eastbound; exit 565C (Vance Jackson Rd) westbound, just n. Ext corridors. **Pets:** Accepted.
SAVE S6 X 8 ⌷ 🏊

AAA ▼▼▼ Red Roof Inn Lackland SH
(210) 675-4120. **$49-$80.** 6861 Hwy 90 W. Northeast jct of US 90 and Military Dr W; access via Renwick St, off Military Dr, just n of jct US 90. Ext corridors. **Pets:** Medium, other species. Service with restrictions, supervision.
SAVE X 8 ⌷ 🏊

▼▼ Red Roof Inn-San Antonio Airport SH
(210) 340-4055. **$51-$74.** 333 Wolfe Rd. On southbound access road, just s of US 281 at Isom Rd. Ext/int corridors. **Pets:** Medium, other species. Service with restrictions, supervision.
X ⌷M 🌙 8

▼▼▼ Red Roof Inn San Antonio (Downtown) M
(210) 229-9973. **$63-$100.** 1011 E Houston St. I-37, exit 141 northbound; exit 141B southbound. Int corridors. **Pets:** Medium, other species. Service with restrictions, supervision.
X 8 🏊

▼▼ Red Roof Inn San Antonio (NW-SeaWorld) SH
(210) 509-3434. **$50-$58.** 6880 NW Loop 410. I-410, exit 11 (Alamo Downs Pkwy), on eastbound access road. Ext/int corridors. **Pets:** Medium, other species. Service with restrictions, supervision.
X ⌷M 🌙 8 🏊

▼▼▼ Residence Inn Alamo Plaza SH
(210) 212-5555. **$139-$219.** 425 Bonham St. I-37/281, exit Commerce St, just w to Bowie St, then 4 blks n. Int corridors. **Pets:** Other species. $100 one-time fee/pet. Service with restrictions.
ASK S6 X 🌙 8 ⌷ 🏊

**▼▼▼ Residence Inn by Marriott San Antonio Downtown/
Market Square** SH
(210) 231-6000. **$169-$299.** 628 S Santa Rosa. I-10/35, exit Durango St, 0.5 mi e. Int corridors. **Pets:** Accepted.
ASK S6 X 🌙 8 ⌷ 🏊 🐾

▼▼▼ Residence Inn NW/Six Flags SH
(210) 561-9660. **$119-$159.** 4041 Bluemel Rd. I-10, exit Wurzbach Rd, 0.3 mi w on eastbound access road. Ext corridors. **Pets:** Accepted.
ASK S6 X ⌷ 🏊 🐾

▼▼▼ Residence Inn San Antonio-Airport SH
(210) 805-8118. **$119-$209.** 1014 NE Loop 410. Loop 410, exit Broadway St, 0.4 mi e on access road. Ext corridors. **Pets:** Accepted.
X 🌙 ⌷ 🏊 🐾

▼▼ Rittiman Inn & Suites SH
(210) 657-0808. **$59-$99.** 6364 I-35 N. I-35, exit 163B (Rittiman Rd) northbound, on northbound access road; exit 164A (Rittiman Rd) southbound. Ext corridors. **Pets:** Accepted.
ASK S6 8

AAA ▼▼▼ Rodeway Inn Downtown SH
(210) 223-2951. **$75-$105.** 900 N Main Ave. I-35, exit San Pedro/Main aves; northeast corner. Ext corridors. **Pets:** Small. $20 daily fee/pet. Service with restrictions, supervision.
SAVE S6 X 8 ⌷ 🏊

▼▼ Royal Hawaiian Continental Inn SH
(210) 655-3510. **Call for rates.** 9735 I-35 N. I-35, exit 167 (Starlight Terr) northbound; exit 167A (Randolph Blvd) southbound; just n of Loop 410 NE; on southbound access road. Ext corridors. **Pets:** Accepted.
ASK X ⌷M 🌙 8 ⌷ 🏊

▼▼▼ San Antonio Marriott Rivercenter LH
(210) 223-1000. **$200-$385.** 101 Bowie St. Corner of Bowie and Commerce sts. Int corridors. **Pets:** Accepted.
ASK X 8 ⌷ 🍴 🐾

AAA ▼▼▼ ▼▼ Sheraton Gunter SH 🐾
(210) 227-3241. **$169-$289.** 205 E Houston St. Center. Int corridors. **Pets:** Medium, dogs only. Designated rooms, supervision.
SAVE S6 X 🌙 8 ⌷ 🏊

▼▼▼ Staybridge Suites San Antonio-Airport SH
(210) 341-3220. **$122-$182.** 66 NE Loop 410. I-410, exit 20B (McCullough St), on eastbound access road; next to Texas Land & Cattle Restaurant. Int corridors. **Pets:** Very small. $100 one-time fee/pet. Service with restrictions.
ASK X ⌷M 8 ⌷ 🏊

▼▼▼ Staybridge Suites San Antonio NW-Colonnade SH
(210) 558-9009. **$109-$159.** 4320 Spectrum One. I-10 W, exit 560 (Wurzbach Rd), follow westbound access road through light, then just n. Int corridors. **Pets:** Other species. $75 one-time fee/room. Service with restrictions, crate.
ASK X 🌙 8 ⌷ 🏊

▼▼ Studio 6 #6046 M
(210) 691-0121. **$49-$71.** 11802 I-10 W. I-10, exit 558 (De Zavala Rd), 0.6 mi e on eastbound access road. Ext corridors. **Pets:** Accepted.
S6 X 🌙 ⌷

AAA ▼▼ Super 8 Downtown Riverwalk M
(210) 222-8833. **$54-$139.** 1 N St. Mary's St. I-35, exit 157B (Brooklyn/McCullough St), 4 blks n on Quincey. Ext corridors. **Pets:** $25 one-time fee/pet. Designated rooms, service with restrictions, crate.
SAVE S6 X ⌷M 🌙 8 ⌷ 🏊

AAA ▼▼▼ Super 8 Motel on Roland SH
(210) 798-5500. **$65-$140.** 302 Roland Ave. I-10, exit 577 (Roland Ave) eastbound. Ext corridors. **Pets:** $10 daily fee/pet. Service with restrictions, supervision.
SAVE S6 X 8 🏊

▼▼ Super 8 Motel SBC/Coliseum Area M
(210) 227-8888. **$58-$88, 3 day notice.** 3617 N PanAm Expwy. I-35, exit 160 (Splashtown), on southbound access road. Ext corridors. **Pets:** $100 deposit/pet, $8 daily fee/pet. Designated rooms, no service, supervision.
ASK S6 X ⌷M 8 🏊

▼▼ Super 8 Motel-Six Flags Fiesta SH
(210) 696-6916. **Call for rates.** 5319 Casa Bella. I-10, exit 557 westbound; exit 558 eastbound, on westbound access road. Int corridors. **Pets:** Accepted.
ASK X 🌙 8 🏊

AAA ▼▼▼ ▼▼ The Westin Riverwalk LH 🐾
(210) 224-6500. **$399-$499, 3 day notice.** 420 W Market St. 2 blks w of Navarro St. Int corridors. **Pets:** Medium, dogs only. Service with restrictions, supervision.
SAVE S6 X ⌷M 🌙 🌙 ⌷ 🍴 🏊 🐾

SEGUIN

▼▼▼ Holiday Inn Seguin SH
(830) 372-0860. **$106-$112.** 2950 N 123 Bypass. I-10, exit 610 (SR 123). Ext corridors. **Pets:** Small. $25 one-time fee/room. Service with restrictions, supervision.
ASK S6 X 8 ⌷ 🍴 🏊

Super 8 Motel of Seguin SH
(830) 379-6888. **$55-$139.** 1525 N Hwy 46. I-10, exit 607 (SR 46), on eastbound access road. Int corridors. **Pets:** Medium. $15 daily fee/pet. Service with restrictions, supervision.
ASK S🐾 ✕ 🎾 🛄 📖

UNIVERSAL CITY

Clarion Suites Hotel SH
(210) 655-9491. **$89-$149.** 13101 E Loop, 1604 N. Loop 1604 at Pat Booker Rd; 0.8 mi e of I-35. Ext corridors. **Pets:** Medium. $25 one-time fee/room. Designated rooms, service with restrictions, crate.
SAVE S🐾 ✕ 🎾 🛄 📖 🐾

END METROPOLITAN AREA

SANDERSON

Desert Air Motel M
(432) 345-2572. **$36-$41.** 806 W Oak. 0.5 mi w on US 90, just e of jct US 285. Ext corridors. **Pets:** Medium, other species. Service with restrictions.
SAVE S🐾 🛄

SAN JUAN

Days Inn San Juan SH
(956) 782-1510. **$80-$85.** 112 W Expwy 83. US 281 S and 83 S, exit Raul Longoria; US 83 N, exit Raul Longoria. Ext corridors. **Pets:** Accepted.
S🐾 ✕ 🛄 📖 🐾

SAN MARCOS

Best Western San Marcos SH
(512) 754-7557. **$89-$139.** 917 I-35 N. I-35, exit 204B, on west side access road. Int corridors. **Pets:** Accepted.
ASK S🐾 ✕ 🛄 📖 🐾

Days Inn SH
(512) 353-5050. **$45-$125.** 1005 I-35 N. I-35, exit 205 northbound; exit 204B southbound, on southbound frontage road, jct SR 80. Ext corridors. **Pets:** Large, dogs only. $10 daily fee/pet. Designated rooms, service with restrictions, supervision.
SAVE S🐾 ✕ 🛄 🐾

La Quinta Inn San Marcos SH
(512) 392-8800. **$84-$136.** 1619 I-35 N. I-35, exit 206 southbound, 0.5 mi s, on west frontage road; exit northbound, 1 mi n to turnaround to west frontage road, then 1.5 mi s. Ext/int corridors. **Pets:** Medium. Service with restrictions.
SAVE ✕ 🐾M 🎾 🛄 📖 🐾

Ramada Limited SH
(512) 395-8000. **$39-$159.** 1701 I-35 N. I-35, exit 206 southbound, 0.4 mi s on west frontage road, then 1.4 mi s. Ext corridors. **Pets:** Very small, dogs only. $20 daily fee/pet. Designated rooms, no service, supervision.
SAVE S🐾 ✕ 🛄 📖 🐾

SEALY

Best Western Inn of Sealy SH
(979) 885-3707. **$79.** 2107 Hwy 36. I-10, exit 720. Ext corridors. **Pets:** Accepted.
ASK S🐾 ✕ 🎾 📖 🐾

SEGOVIA

Econo Lodge M
(325) 446-2475. **$59-$69.** 311 S Segovia Access Rd. I-10, exit 465; on south access road. Ext corridors. **Pets:** Accepted.
SAVE S🐾 ✕ 📖 🐾

SEMINOLE

Raymond Motor Inn M
(432) 758-3653. **$48-$50.** 301 W Ave A. 0.3 mi w on US 62 and 180. Ext corridors. **Pets:** Other species. $10 daily fee/pet. Service with restrictions, supervision.
SAVE S🐾 ✕ 🛄 📖

Seminole Inn M
(432) 758-9881. **$62-$67.** 2200 Hobbs Hwy. 1.5 mi w on US 62 and 180. Ext corridors. **Pets:** Small. $10 daily fee/pet. Service with restrictions, supervision.
SAVE S🐾 ✕ 🛄 📖 🐾

SHAMROCK

Econo Lodge M
(806) 256-2111. **$54-$60.** 1006 E 12th St. I-40, exit 164 westbound; exit 161 or 163 eastbound, just e of US 83. Ext corridors. **Pets:** Accepted.
SAVE S🐾 ✕ 🛄 📖 🐾

Irish Inn SH
(806) 256-2106. **$69-$78, 7 day notice.** 301 I-40 E. I-40, exit 163, 0.3 mi e on north service road. Ext/int corridors. **Pets:** Other species. $9 one-time fee/room. Service with restrictions.
SAVE ✕ 🎾 🛄 📖 🍴 🐾

Western Motel M
(806) 256-3244. **$49-$69.** 104 E 12th St. Business Rt I-40 and US 83. Ext corridors. **Pets:** Medium. $5 daily fee/pet. Service with restrictions, supervision.
SAVE S🐾 ✕ 🍴

SHERMAN

Comfort Suites of Sherman SH
(903) 893-0499. **$90, 14 day notice.** 2900 US Hwy 75 N. US 75, exit 63; 0.3 mi s of jct US 82. Int corridors. **Pets:** Accepted.
ASK S🐾 ✕ 🎾 🛄 📖 🐾

La Quinta Inn & Suites Sherman/Denison SH
(903) 870-1122. **$101-$142.** 2912 US 75 N. US 75, exit 63; just sw of jct US 82. Int corridors. **Pets:** Medium. Service with restrictions.
SAVE ✕ 🎾 🛄 📖 🐾

Quality Inn SH
(903) 868-0555. **$60-$70.** 3605 Hwy 75 S. US 75, exit 56. Int corridors. **Pets:** Small, other species. $20 daily fee/pet. Service with restrictions, crate.
SAVE S🐾 ✕ 🛄 📖 🍴 🐾

SMITHVILLE

Pine Point Inn SH
(512) 237-2040. **$55-$78.** 1503 Dorothy Nichols Ln. Jct SR 71 and Dorothy Nichols Ln. Ext corridors. **Pets:** Accepted.
ASK S🐾 ✕ 🛄

SNYDER

Best Western Snyder Inn M
(325) 574-2200. **$70.** 810 E Coliseum Dr. 1.5 mi w of US 84/80. Ext corridors. **Pets:** Accepted.
ASK S🐾 ✕ 🛄 🐾

Purple Sage Motel M
(325) 573-5491. **$58-$74.** 1501 E Coliseum Dr. 1 mi w on US 180 from jct US 84. Ext corridors. **Pets:** Accepted.
[SAVE] [S6] [X] [🖨] [💻] [≈]

SONORA

Americas Best Value Inn-Twin Oaks Motel M
(325) 387-2551. **$45-$55, 7 day notice.** 1009 N Crockett Ave. I-10, exit 400 westbound; exit 399 eastbound, 0.5 mi e, then 0.3 mi s on US 277. Ext corridors. **Pets:** Accepted.
[SAVE] [S6] [X] [🖨]

Best Western Sonora Inn SH
(325) 387-9111. **$80-$115.** 270 Hwy 277 N. I-10, exit 400. Ext corridors. **Pets:** Other species. $10 daily fee/pet. Designated rooms, service with restrictions.
[SAVE] [S6] [X] [🔧] [🖨] [💻] [≈]

Comfort Inn of Sonora SH
(325) 387-5800. **$80.** 311 N Hwy 277. I-10, exit 400. Ext corridors. **Pets:** $10 daily fee/pet. Service with restrictions.
[SAVE] [S6] [X] [🅼] [🔧] [🖨] [💻] [≈]

Days Inn M
(325) 387-3516. **$64-$69.** 1312 N Service Rd. I-10, exit 400, just n. Ext corridors. **Pets:** $5 daily fee/pet. Service with restrictions.
[SAVE] [S6] [X] [🖨] [💻] [🍴] [≈]

SOUTH PADRE ISLAND

Americas Best Value Inn SH
(956) 761-8500. **$39-$299.** 3813 Padre Blvd. 2.6 mi n of Queen Isabella Cswy. Int corridors. **Pets:** Accepted.
[SAVE] [S6] [X] [🖨] [≈]

Best Western Fiesta Isles Hotel SH
(956) 761-4913. **$59-$369.** 5701 Padre Blvd. 3 mi n of Queen Isabella Cswy. Ext corridors. **Pets:** Accepted.
[SAVE] [S6] [X] [🖨] [≈]

Comfort Suites SH
(956) 772-9020. **$59-$169, 3 day notice.** 912 Padre Blvd. Opposite Queen Isabella Cswy. Int corridors. **Pets:** Accepted.
[ASK] [S6] [X] [🖨] [💻] [≈]

Howard Johnson Inn SH
(956) 761-5658. **$49-$199, 3 day notice.** 1709 Padre Blvd. SR 100, 0.9 mi n at corner of W Palm St. Int corridors. **Pets:** $25 one-time fee/pet. Supervision.
[ASK] [S6] [X] [🅼] [🔧] [🖨] [💻] [≈]

La Copa Beach Resort SH
(956) 761-6000. **$45-$250, 3 day notice.** 350 Padre Blvd. Just s of Queen Isabella Cswy. Int corridors. **Pets:** Small. $10 daily fee/pet. Service with restrictions, supervision.
[SAVE] [S6] [X] [🖨] [≈]

La Quinta Inn and Suites South Padre Island SH
(956) 772-7000. **$59-$399.** 7000 Padre Blvd. I-77, exit SR 100, over Queen Isabella Cswy, then 3 mi n. Int corridors. **Pets:** Accepted.
[ASK] [S6] [X] [🅼] [🔧] [🖨] [💻] [≈] [X]

Motel 6 South Padre Island #1237 M
(956) 761-7911. **$35-$85.** 4013 Padre Blvd. 2 mi n of Queen Isabella Cswy. Ext corridors. **Pets:** Medium, other species. Service with restrictions, supervision.
[S6] [X] [🔧] [≈]

Ramada Limited SH
(956) 761-4097. **$50-$300.** 4109 Padre Blvd. 2 mi n of Queen Isabella Cswy. Ext corridors. **Pets:** Medium. $10 one-time fee/pet. Service with restrictions, supervision.
[SAVE] [X] [🖨] [💻] [≈]

Super 8 Motel SH
(956) 761-6300. **$69-$269.** 4205 Padre Blvd. 2.7 mi n of Queen Isabella Cswy. Ext corridors. **Pets:** Small, dogs only. $10 daily fee/pet. Designated rooms, service with restrictions, supervision.
[ASK] [S6] [X] [🅼] [🔧] [🖨] [≈]

The Tiki Condominium Hotel CO
(956) 761-2694. **$79-$325, 3 day notice.** 6608 Padre Blvd. 3.8 mi n of Queen Isabella Cswy. Ext corridors. **Pets:** Accepted.
[S6] [X] [🖨] [💻] [≈] [X]

Travelodge SH
(956) 761-4744. **$35-$300, 3 day notice.** 6200 Padre Blvd. 3 mi n of Queen Isabella Cswy. Ext corridors. **Pets:** Small. $10 daily fee/pet. Designated rooms, service with restrictions, supervision.
[ASK] [S6] [X] [🔧] [🖨] [💻] [≈]

STEPHENVILLE

Best Western Cross Timbers SH 🐾
(254) 968-2114. **$59-$89.** 1625 W South Loop (US 377). 1.8 mi sw on US 377 Bypass and 67. Ext corridors. **Pets:** Other species. $9 daily fee/room. Service with restrictions, crate.
[SAVE] [X] [🖨] [💻] [≈]

Holiday Inn Stephenville SH
(254) 968-5256. **$80-$130.** 2865 W Washington St. 1.5 mi s on US 377/167. Ext corridors. **Pets:** Medium. $100 deposit/room. Service with restrictions, supervision.
[ASK] [X] [📶] [🖨] [💻] [🍴] [≈]

SULPHUR SPRINGS

Best Western Trail Dust Inn SH
(903) 885-7515. **$69-$89.** 1521 Shannon Rd. Jct I-30 and Loop 301, exit 127. Ext/int corridors. **Pets:** Accepted.
[SAVE] [S6] [X] [🔧] [🖨] [💻] [≈]

Comfort Suites SH
(903) 438-0918. **$70-$74.** 1521 E Industrial Dr. I-30, exit 127, just n. Int corridors. **Pets:** Accepted.
[SAVE] [X] [🅼] [🔧] [🖨] [💻] [≈]

Days Inn Sulphur Springs SH
(903) 885-0562. **$69-$79, 7 day notice.** 1495 E Industrial Dr E. I-30, exit 127. Ext/int corridors. **Pets:** Accepted.
[SAVE] [S6] [X] [🖨] [💻] [🍴] [≈]

SWEETWATER

Comfort Inn SH
(325) 235-5234. **$79-$125.** 216 SE Georgia Ave. I-20, exit 244. Ext corridors. **Pets:** Accepted.
[SAVE] [S6] [X] [📶] [🔧] [🖨] [💻] [≈]

Holiday Inn SH
(325) 236-6887. **$69-$169.** 500 NW Georgia St. I-20, exit 244, just w of jct SR 70 on north access road. Ext/int corridors. **Pets:** Accepted.
[SAVE] [S6] [X] [🖨] [💻] [🍴] [≈]

Ranch House Motel & Restaurant SH
(325) 236-6341. **$50-$69.** 301 SW Georgia Ave. I-20, exit 244, just w of jct SR 70 on south access road. Ext/int corridors. **Pets:** Medium. Designated rooms, service with restrictions, crate.
[SAVE] [S6] [X] [🖨] [💻] [🍴] [≈]

TEMPLE

Americas Best Value Inn M
(254) 773-7221. **Call for rates (no credit cards).** 4001 S General Bruce Dr. I-35, exit 297 southbound; exit 299 northbound, on northbound access road. Ext corridors. **Pets:** Accepted.
[X] [🖨] [💻]

AAA ▼▼▼ **La Quinta Inn Temple** SH
(254) 771-2980. **$82-$109.** 1604 W Barton Ave. SR 53, just e; jct I-35 and US 81, exit 301. Ext/int corridors. **Pets:** Medium. Service with restrictions.
SAVE ✕ 📶 💻 ➔

▼ **Motel 6–257** SH
(254) 778-0272. **$37-$48.** 1100 N General Bruce Dr. I-35, exit 302 (Nugent Ave), just s on access road, follow signs. Ext corridors. **Pets:** Medium, other species. Service with restrictions, supervision.
S6 ✕ ➔

TERLINGUA

AAA ▼▼▼ **Big Bend Motor Inn** M
(432) 371-2218. **$90-$95, 7 day notice.** 300 N Jim Wright Frwy. SR 118, 2 mi from entrance of Big Bend National Park. Ext corridors. **Pets:** Small. $5 daily fee/pet. Designated rooms, service with restrictions, supervision.
SAVE ✕ 📶 💻

TEXARKANA

AAA ▼▼▼ **Baymont Inn** SH
(903) 794-1900. **$80-$100.** 5201 State Line Ave. I-30, exit 223A, sw of jct US 59 and 71. Ext corridors. **Pets:** Medium. Service with restrictions.
SAVE ✕ 📶 💻 ➔

AAA ▼▼▼ **Budget Host Northgate Inn** SH
(903) 793-6565. **$58-$69.** 400 W 53rd St. I-30, exit 223B, on northwest frontage road. Int corridors. **Pets:** Supervision.
SAVE S6 ✕ 📶 💻 ➔

AAA ▼▼▼ **Clarion Hotel** SH
(903) 792-3222. **$75-$140.** 5301 N State Line Ave. I-30, exit 223B. Int corridors. **Pets:** Accepted.
SAVE S6 ✕ &M 📶 💻 ❌ ➔

AAA ▼▼▼ **Comfort Inn** SH
(903) 792-6688. **$69, 14 day notice.** 5105 State Line Ave. I-30, exit 223A, just sw. Ext corridors. **Pets:** Small, other species. $25 one-time fee/room. Service with restrictions, supervision.
SAVE S6 ✕ 📶 💻 ➔

AAA ▼▼▼▼ **Holiday Inn Express** SH
(903) 792-3366. **$76-$106.** 5401 N State Line Ave. I-30, exit 223B, 0.3 mi n on US 71. Int corridors. **Pets:** $25 one-time fee/room. Service with restrictions, supervision.
SAVE S6 ✕ 📶 💻 ➔

▼ **Motel 6–201** SH
(903) 793-1413. **$44-$64.** 1924 Hampton Rd. I-30, exit 222 (Summerhill Rd). Ext corridors. **Pets:** Medium, other species. Service with restrictions, supervision.
S6 ✕ &M ➔

TEXAS CITY

▼▼ **La Quinta Inn Texas City** SH
(409) 948-3101. **$80-$120.** 1121 Hwy 146 N. Jct SR 146 S and FM 1764, 5 mi se of I-45, exit 16 southbound; exit 15 northbound. Ext corridors. **Pets:** Accepted.
ASK ✕ 🚭 📶 💻 ➔

THREE RIVERS

▼▼▼ **Econo Lodge** M
(361) 786-3563. **$54-$154.** 1401 N Harborth Ave. I-37, exit 72 (US 281), 3.8 mi s. Ext corridors. **Pets:** Very small. $10 daily fee/pet. Service with restrictions, supervision.
ASK S6 ✕ 📶 💻

TULIA

▼▼▼ **Select Inn of Tulia** M
(806) 995-3248. **$54-$64.** Rt 1, Box 60. I-27, exit 74. Ext corridors. **Pets:** Very small. $6 daily fee/pet. Designated rooms, service with restrictions, supervision.
ASK S6 ✕ &M 📶 💻

TYLER

AAA ▼▼▼ **Americas Best Value Inn & Suites** SH
(903) 595-2681. **$58-$99.** 2828 W NW Loop 323. Jct US 69 N and Loop 323. Ext corridors. **Pets:** Accepted.
SAVE S6 ✕ 📶 💻 ➔

▼▼▼ **Candlewood Suites** SH
(903) 509-4131. **$85-$112.** 315 E Rieck Rd. 1.1 mi s of jct Loop 323 and US 69 (S Broadway) to Rieck Rd, just e. Int corridors. **Pets:** Accepted.
ASK S6 ✕ &M 🚭 📶 💻

▼▼▼ **Holiday Inn Select** SH
(903) 561-5800. **$119-$129.** 5701 S Broadway. 1.1 mi s of jct Loop 323 and US 69 (S Broadway). Int corridors. **Pets:** Accepted.
ASK S6 ✕ 🚭 🚭 📶 💻 🍴 ❌ ❌

▼▼▼ **La Quinta Inn Tyler** SH
(903) 561-2223. **$92-$119.** 1601 W SW Loop 323. 1 mi w of S US 69. Ext corridors. **Pets:** Medium. Service with restrictions.
ASK ✕ 🚭 📶 💻 ➔

▼▼▼ **Quality Hotel Conference Center** SH
(903) 597-1301. **$49-$89.** 2843 W NW Loop 323. Just w of jct US 69. Int corridors. **Pets:** Accepted.
ASK S6 ✕ &M 📶 💻 🍴 ➔

AAA ▼▼▼ **Ramada Tyler Conference Center** SH
(903) 593-3600. **$100-$150.** 3310 Troup Hwy. 0.3 mi n of jct E Loop 323 and SR 110. Ext corridors. **Pets:** Accepted.
SAVE S6 ✕ 🚭 📶 💻 🍴 ➔

▼▼▼ **Residence Inn by Marriott** SH 🐾
(903) 595-5188. **$85-$135.** 3303 Troup Hwy. 0.3 mi n of jct E Loop 323 and SR 110. Ext corridors. **Pets:** Large, other species. $100 one-time fee/room. Designated rooms, service with restrictions, supervision.
ASK ✕ 🚭 📶 💻 ➔ ❌

UVALDE

▼▼▼ **Holiday Inn** SH
(830) 278-4511. **$88-$140.** 920 E Main St. 0.5 mi e on US 90. Ext corridors. **Pets:** Large. Service with restrictions, supervision.
ASK S6 ✕ 📶 💻 🍴 ➔

VAN HORN

AAA ▼▼▼ **Best Western American Inn** M
(432) 283-2030. **$65-$99.** 1309 W Broadway. I-10, exit 138, 1 mi e. Ext corridors. **Pets:** Medium, other species. $10 daily fee/pet. Designated rooms, service with restrictions, supervision.
SAVE S6 ✕ 📶 💻 ➔

AAA ▼▼▼ **Best Western Inn of Van Horn** M
(432) 283-2410. **$55-$95.** 1705 W Broadway St. I-10, exit 138, 0.3 mi e, then 1 mi w on US 80. Ext corridors. **Pets:** Accepted.
SAVE S6 ✕ 📶 💻 ➔

AAA ▼ **Budget Inn** M
(432) 283-2019. **$30-$50.** 1303 W Broadway. I-10, exit 138, 0.7 mi e. Ext corridors. **Pets:** Accepted.
SAVE S6 ✕ 📶

(AAA) ▼▼▼ Days Inn M
(432) 283-1007. **$64-$90, 10 day notice.** 600 E Broadway St. I-10, exit 140B, just w. Ext corridors. **Pets:** Other species. $10 daily fee/pet. Service with restrictions, supervision.
⟦SAVE⟧ ⟦S⟧ ⟦✕⟧ ⟦▤⟧ ⟦▱⟧ ⟦≈⟧

(AAA) ▼▼▼ Econo Lodge SH
(432) 283-2211. **$60-$90, 7 day notice.** 1601 W Broadway St. I-10, exit 138, 0.5 mi e on Business Rt I-10. Ext corridors. **Pets:** Accepted.
⟦SAVE⟧ ⟦S⟧ ⟦✕⟧ ⟦▤⟧ ⟦▱⟧ ⟦≈⟧

(AAA) ▼▼ Economy Inn M
(432) 283-2754. **$35-$55.** 1500 W Broadway St. I-10, exit 138, 0.5 mi e on US 80. Ext corridors. **Pets:** Medium, other species. $5 one-time fee/room. No service, supervision.
⟦SAVE⟧ ⟦S⟧ ⟦✕⟧ ⟦▤⟧

(AAA) ▼▼▼▼ Holiday Inn Express SH
(432) 283-7444. **$69-$109.** 1905 SW Frontage Rd. I-10, exit 138 (Golf Course Dr). Ext corridors. **Pets:** Accepted.
⟦SAVE⟧ ⟦S⟧ ⟦✕⟧ ⟦⅋⟧ ⟦▱⟧ ⟦▤⟧ ⟦▱⟧ ⟦≈⟧

▼ Motel 6–4024 M
(432) 283-2992. **$46.** 1805 W Broadway St. I-10, exit 138. Ext corridors. **Pets:** Medium, other species. Service with restrictions, supervision.
⟦ASK⟧ ⟦✕⟧ ⟦≈⟧

(AAA) ▼▼▼ Ramada Limited SH ❀
(432) 283-2780. **$91.** 200 Golf Course Dr. I-10, exit 138 (Golf Course Dr). Ext/int corridors. **Pets:** Other species. $10 daily fee/pet. Supervision.
⟦SAVE⟧ ⟦S⟧ ⟦✕⟧ ⟦▤⟧ ⟦▱⟧ ⟦≈⟧

(AAA) ▼▼▼ Van Horn Super 8 M
(432) 283-2282. **$64-$90, 10 day notice.** 1807 E Service Rd. I-10, exit 138 (Golf Course Dr). Ext corridors. **Pets:** Other species. $10 daily fee/pet. Service with restrictions, supervision.
⟦SAVE⟧ ⟦S⟧ ⟦✕⟧ ⟦♿⟧ ⟦▤⟧ ⟦▱⟧

VEGA

(AAA) ▼▼▼ Best Western Country Inn M ❀
(806) 267-2131. **$65-$79.** 1800 W Vega Blvd. 0.5 mi w on US 40 business loop. Ext corridors. **Pets:** Medium. $10 daily fee/pet. Designated rooms, service with restrictions, supervision.
⟦SAVE⟧ ⟦S⟧ ⟦✕⟧ ⟦▤⟧ ⟦▱⟧ ⟦≈⟧

VERNON

▼▼ Best Western Village Inn M
(940) 552-5417. **$82.** 1615 Expwy. US 287, exit Main St, just w. Ext/int corridors. **Pets:** Very small. $25 deposit/pet. Service with restrictions, crate.
⟦ASK⟧ ⟦S⟧ ⟦✕⟧ ⟦▤⟧ ⟦▱⟧ ⟦▯⟧ ⟦≈⟧

VICTORIA

▼▼▼ Holiday Inn Holidome SH
(361) 575-0251. **$89.** 2705 E Houston Hwy (Business Rt 59). On Business Rt US 59, 2.5 mi ne. Ext/int corridors. **Pets:** Accepted.
⟦ASK⟧ ⟦S⟧ ⟦✕⟧ ⟦▤⟧ ⟦▱⟧ ⟦▯⟧ ⟦≈⟧ ⟦✕⟧

▼▼ La Quinta Inn Victoria SH
(361) 572-3585. **$88-$118.** 7603 N Navarro St (US 77 N). 4 mi n; at Loop 463. Ext corridors. **Pets:** Medium. Service with restrictions.
⟦ASK⟧ ⟦✕⟧ ⟦⅋⟧ ⟦▱⟧ ⟦▤⟧ ⟦≈⟧

▼▼ Motel 6 Victoria #225 M
(361) 573-1273. **$41-$52.** 3716 Houston Hwy. On Business Rt US 59. Ext corridors. **Pets:** Medium, other species. Service with restrictions, supervision.
⟦S⟧ ⟦✕⟧ ⟦≈⟧

▼▼ Quality Inn-Victoria SH
(361) 578-2030. **$62-$81.** 3112 E Houston Hwy (Business Rt 59). On Business Rt US 59, 2 mi ne. Ext corridors. **Pets:** Accepted.
⟦ASK⟧ ⟦S⟧ ⟦✕⟧ ⟦▤⟧ ⟦▱⟧ ⟦≈⟧

VIDOR

▼▼▼ La Quinta Inn & Suites SH
(409) 783-2600. **$81-$90.** 165 E Courtland St. I-10, exit 861A, just s. Int corridors. **Pets:** Accepted.
⟦ASK⟧ ⟦S⟧ ⟦✕⟧ ⟦▤⟧ ⟦▱⟧ ⟦≈⟧

WACO

(AAA) ▼▼▼ Best Western Old Main Lodge SH
(254) 753-0316. **$95-$105.** I-35 & 4th St. I-35 and US 81, exit 335A (4th-5th sts). Ext corridors. **Pets:** Small. Service with restrictions, supervision.
⟦SAVE⟧ ⟦S⟧ ⟦✕⟧ ⟦▤⟧ ⟦▱⟧ ⟦≈⟧

(AAA) ▼▼▼ Days Inn SH ❀
(254) 799-8585. **$69-$140.** 1504 I-35. I-35, exit 338B (Behrens Cir), just n. Ext corridors. **Pets:** Medium, dogs only. $10 daily fee/pet. Service with restrictions, supervision.
⟦SAVE⟧ ⟦S⟧ ⟦✕⟧ ⟦▤⟧ ⟦▱⟧ ⟦≈⟧

(AAA) ▼▼▼▼ Hotel Waco SH ❀
(254) 753-0261. **$85-$210.** 1001 Martin Luther King Blvd. I-35, exit 335C (Lake Brazos Dr), just n. Int corridors. **Pets:** Medium. $25 one-time fee/pet. Designated rooms, service with restrictions.
⟦SAVE⟧ ⟦S⟧ ⟦✕⟧ ⟦⅋⟧ ⟦▤⟧ ⟦▱⟧ ⟦▯⟧ ⟦≈⟧

(AAA) ▼▼▼▼ La Quinta Inn Waco (University) SH
(254) 752-9741. **$95-$115.** 1110 S 9th St. I-35, exit 334 (17th St) southbound; exit 334A (18th St) northbound. Ext corridors. **Pets:** Medium. Service with restrictions.
⟦SAVE⟧ ⟦✕⟧ ⟦⅋⟧ ⟦▤⟧ ⟦▱⟧ ⟦≈⟧

▼▼▼ Residence Inn by Marriott SH
(254) 714-1386. **$125-$305.** 501 S University Parks Dr. I-35, exit 335B, 0.3 mi w. Int corridors. **Pets:** Accepted.
⟦ASK⟧ ⟦S⟧ ⟦✕⟧ ⟦⅋⟧ ⟦♿⟧ ⟦▤⟧ ⟦▱⟧ ⟦≈⟧ ⟦✕⟧

▼ Super 8 Motel-Waco SH
(254) 754-1023. **$60-$100.** 1320 S Jack Kultgen Frwy. I-35, exit 334, just e. Int corridors. **Pets:** Accepted.
⟦ASK⟧ ⟦S⟧ ⟦✕⟧ ⟦▤⟧

WAXAHACHIE

(AAA) ▼▼▼ Best Western Gingerbread Inn SH
(972) 937-4202. **$49-$99.** 200 N I-35E. I-35E and US 287 business route, 1.8 mi s of jct US 287, exit 401B. Ext corridors. **Pets:** Accepted.
⟦SAVE⟧ ⟦S⟧ ⟦✕⟧ ⟦▤⟧ ⟦▱⟧ ⟦≈⟧

▼▼ Super 8 Motel SH
(972) 938-9088. **$65-$99.** 400 I-35E. I-35E, exit 401B. Int corridors. **Pets:** Accepted.
⟦ASK⟧ ⟦S⟧ ⟦✕⟧ ⟦▤⟧ ⟦≈⟧

WEATHERFORD

(AAA) ▼▼▼ Best Western Santa Fe Inn SH
(817) 594-7401. **$85-$90, 5 day notice.** 1927 Santa Fe Dr. I-20, exit 409 (Clear Lake Rd/FM 2552), 0.3 mi nw. Ext corridors. **Pets:** Other species. $10 daily fee/pet. Service with restrictions, supervision.
⟦SAVE⟧ ⟦S⟧ ⟦✕⟧ ⟦▤⟧ ⟦▱⟧ ⟦≈⟧

▼▼▼ Hampton Inn SH
(817) 599-4800. **$105-$175.** 2524 S Main St. I-20, exit 408. Int corridors. **Pets:** Small. $10 daily fee/pet. Service with restrictions, supervision.
⟦ASK⟧ ⟦S⟧ ⟦✕⟧ ⟦⅋⟧ ⟦♿⟧ ⟦▤⟧ ⟦▱⟧ ⟦≈⟧

▼▼▼ Holiday Inn Express Hotel & Suites SH
(817) 599-3700. **$100-$170.** 2500 S Main St. I-20, exit 408. Ext/int corridors. **Pets:** Small. $10 daily fee/pet. Service with restrictions, supervision.
⟦ASK⟧ ⟦S⟧ ⟦✕⟧ ⟦♿⟧ ⟦⅋⟧ ⟦♿⟧ ⟦▤⟧ ⟦▱⟧ ⟦≈⟧

AAA ▼▼▼▼ **La Quinta Inn & Suites** SH
(817) 594-4481. **$75, 3 day notice.** 1915 Wall St. I-20, exit 408, just se. Int corridors. **Pets:** Medium. $15 daily fee/room. Service with restrictions, supervision.
SAVE S⁄₀ ✕ ✉M 🐾 🔲 💻 ⊇

WEIMAR

AAA ▼▼ **Czech Inn** M
(979) 725-9788. **$50-$70.** 102 Townsend Ln. I-10, exit 682, just w on north access road. Int corridors. **Pets:** Accepted.
SAVE ✕ 🐾 🔲 💻 ⊇

WELLINGTON

▼ **Cherokee Inn & Restaurant** M
(806) 447-2508. **$37-$53.** 1105 Houston St. US 83, just n of jct FM 338. Ext corridors. **Pets:** Accepted.
ASK S⁄₀ ✕ 🍴

WESLACO

AAA ▼▼▼▼ **Best Western Palm Aire Hotel & Suites** SH
(956) 969-2411. **$56-$111.** 415 S International Blvd. US 83, exit International Blvd. Ext corridors. **Pets:** Small. Service with restrictions, supervision.
SAVE S⁄₀ ✕ 🐾 🔲 💻 🍴 ⊇ ⊠

▼▼▼ **Super 8 Motel** SH
(956) 969-9920. **$39-$49.** 1702 E Expwy 83. US 83, exit Airport Dr. Ext corridors. **Pets:** Accepted.
ASK S⁄₀ ✕ 🔲 ⊇

WICHITA FALLS

AAA ▼▼ **Best Western Wichita Falls Inn** SH
(940) 766-6881. **$59-$79.** 1032 Central Frwy. I-44, exit 2, just w. Ext corridors. **Pets:** Medium. $10 daily fee/pet. Service with restrictions, supervision.
SAVE S⁄₀ ✕ 🔲 💻 ⊇

▼▼▼ **Comfort Inn & Suites** SH
(940) 767-5653. **$65-$149.** 1740 Maurine St. US 287, exit Maurine St, just e. Ext/int corridors. **Pets:** Accepted.
ASK S⁄₀ ✕ ✉M 🐾 🔲 💻 ⊇

▼▼▼▼ **Hawthorn Suites Limited** SH
(940) 692-7900. **$99-$165.** 1917 Elmwood Ave N. US 281 S, exit Southwest Pkwy (CR 369), 2.3 mi w to Kemp Blvd, 2 blks n to Elmwood Ave, then just e. Int corridors. **Pets:** Large. $50 one-time fee/room. Designated rooms, service with restrictions, crate.
ASK S⁄₀ ✕ ✉M 🐾 🔲 💻 ⊇

▼▼▼▼ **Holiday Inn** LH
(940) 761-6000. **$99-$149.** 100 Central Frwy. I-287, exit 1C, on west side access road. Int corridors. **Pets:** Accepted.
ASK S⁄₀ ✕ 🔲 💻 🍴 ⊇

AAA ▼▼▼▼ **La Quinta Inn Wichita Falls** SH
(940) 322-6971. **$84-$104.** 1128 Central Frwy N. I-44, exit 2, just w. Ext corridors. **Pets:** Medium. Service with restrictions.
SAVE ✕ 🐾 🔲 💻 ⊇

▼ **Motel 6 #130** M
(940) 322-8817. **$44-$55.** 1812 Maurine St. I-44, exit 2, just e. Ext corridors. **Pets:** Medium, other species. Service with restrictions, supervision.
S⁄₀ ✕ 🐾 🐾 ⊇

AAA ▼▼▼ **Ramada Limited** M
(940) 855-0085. **$54-$69.** 3209 Northwest. US 287, exit Beverly (CR 11), just w. Ext corridors. **Pets:** $10 daily fee/pet. Service with restrictions, supervision.
SAVE S⁄₀ ✕ 🐾 🔲 💻 ⊇

AAA ▼▼▼ **Towne Crest Inn** M
(940) 322-1182. **$41.** 1601 8th St. US 287, exit Broad St/Business, w on 9th St, 1 blk n on Brook to 8th St, then just e. Ext corridors. **Pets:** Accepted.
SAVE ✕ 🔲 💻

WOODWAY

▼▼ **Extended StayAmerica** SH
(254) 399-8836. **Call for rates.** 5903 Woodway Dr. I-35, exit 330 (SR 6), 5 mi sw; Loop 340, exit 330 to jct SR 84. Int corridors. **Pets:** Accepted.
✕ 🐾 🐾 🔲 💻

ZAPATA

AAA ▼▼ **Best Western Inn by the Lake** SH
(956) 765-8403. **$80-$95.** Hwy 83 S. On US 83, 0.5 mi se. Ext corridors. **Pets:** Accepted.
SAVE ✕ 🔲 💻 ⊇

UTAH

BEAVER

Best Western Butch Cassidy Inn M
(435) 438-2438. **$62-$100.** 161 S Main St. I-15, exit 109 or 112, just e. Ext corridors. **Pets:** Other species. $5 daily fee/pet. Service with restrictions, supervision.

Best Western Paradise Inn M
(435) 438-2455. **$73-$81.** 1451 N 300 W. I-15, exit 112, just e; north end of town. Ext corridors. **Pets:** Small, other species. $9 one-time fee/pet. Designated rooms, service with restrictions, supervision.

Country Inn M
(435) 438-2484. **$46-$60.** 1450 N 300 W. I-15, exit 112, 2 blks e. Ext corridors. **Pets:** Large, other species. $5 daily fee/pet. Service with restrictions, supervision.

DeLano Motel M ❀
(435) 438-2418. **$35-$49, 3 day notice.** 480 N Main St. I-15, exit 112, just e; north end of town. Ext corridors. **Pets:** Medium, dogs only. $5 daily fee/pet. Service with restrictions, supervision.

Quality Inn M
(435) 438-5426. **$63-$75.** 781 W 1800 S. I-15, exit 109, just w. Int corridors. **Pets:** Small, other species. Designated rooms, service with restrictions, supervision.

BICKNELL

Aquarius Motel and Restaurant SH
(435) 425-3835. **$46-$63.** 240 W Main St. SR 24, 9 mi w of Capitol Reef National Park; downtown. Ext/int corridors. **Pets:** Other species. $5 daily fee/room. Service with restrictions, crate.

BLANDING

Four Corners Inn M
(435) 678-3257. **$52-$67.** 131 E Center St. On US 191. Ext corridors. **Pets:** Other species. Crate.

Gateway Inn M
(435) 678-2278. **$61-$89.** 88 E Center St. East side on US 191. Ext corridors. **Pets:** Accepted.

BLUFF

Kokopelli Inn M
(435) 672-2322. **$45-$55.** 160 E Main St. On US 191. Int corridors. **Pets:** Medium. $10 daily fee/pet. Service with restrictions, supervision.

Recapture Lodge M
(435) 672-2281. **$50-$60.** 220 E Main St. On US 191. Ext corridors. **Pets:** Other species. Service with restrictions, supervision.

BOULDER

Boulder Mountain Lodge SH ❀
(435) 335-7460. **$72-$175, 14 day notice.** 20 N Hwy 12. Jct SR 12 and Burr Trail. Ext/int corridors. **Pets:** Other species. $10 daily fee/pet. Designated rooms, service with restrictions, supervision.

BRIGHAM CITY

Crystal Inn M
(435) 723-0440. **$129-$149.** 480 Westland Dr. I-15 and 84, exit 362 (Logan and Brigham City), 1 mi e. Int corridors. **Pets:** Accepted.

Howard Johnson Inn M
(435) 723-8511. **$54-$69.** 1167 S Main St. I-15 and 84, exit 362 (Logan and Brigham City), 2 mi e on US 89 and 91. Ext corridors. **Pets:** Accepted.

BRYCE

Best Western Ruby's Inn LH
(435) 834-5341. **$65-$150.** UT Hwy 63. On SR 63, 1 mi s of SR 12, 1 mi n of Bryce Canyon National Park entrance. Ext/int corridors. **Pets:** Service with restrictions, supervision.

Bryce Canyon Resort SH
(435) 834-5351. **$49-$179.** 139 W SR 12. Jct of SR 12 and 63. Ext corridors. **Pets:** Accepted.

Bryce View Lodge SH
(435) 834-5180. **$60-$99.** SR 63. On SR 63, 1 mi s of SR 12; 1 mi n of Bryce Canyon National Park entrance. Ext corridors. **Pets:** Service with restrictions, supervision.

CEDAR CITY

AAA ▼▼▼ Carlton Hotel Inn & Suites M
(435) 586-2082. **$60-$96.** 250 N 1100 W. I-15, exit 59, just e. Ext corridors. **Pets:** Other species. Designated rooms, no service, crate.
[SAVE] [S🐾] [✕] [🐕] [🛏] [💻] [≈]

AAA ▼▼▼ Cedar Rest Motel M
(435) 586-9471. **$38-$75.** 479 S Main St. I-15, exit 59, just e. Ext corridors. **Pets:** Small, dogs only. $10 daily fee/pet. Designated rooms, service with restrictions, supervision.
[SAVE] [S🐾] [✕] [🛏]

AAA ▼▼▼▼ Crystal Inn Cedar City SH
(435) 586-8888. **$119-$149.** 1575 W 200 N. I-15, exit 59, just w. Ext/int corridors. **Pets:** Other species. $25 one-time fee/room. Designated rooms, no service, crate.
[SAVE] [S🐾] [✕] [🐕] [👟] [🛏] [💻] [🍴] [≈] [✕]

AAA ▼▼▼ Days Inn M
(435) 867-8877. **$54-$94.** 1204 S Main St. I-15, exit 57, 0.4 mi ne. Ext corridors. **Pets:** Medium. $10 daily fee/pet. Designated rooms, service with restrictions, supervision.
[SAVE] [S🐾] [✕] [👟] [🛏] [≈]

▼▼▼▼ Holiday Inn Express Hotel & Suites M
(435) 865-7799. **$81-$109.** 1555 S Old Hwy 91. I-15, exit 57, just e, then s. Int corridors. **Pets:** Accepted.
[ASK] [S🐾] [✕] [🦽M] [👟] [🛏] [💻] [≈]

▼▼▼ Motel 6 of Cedar City–4041 M
(435) 586-9200. **$46-$62.** 1620 W 200 N. I-15, exit 59, just w. Int corridors. **Pets:** Medium, other species. Service with restrictions, supervision.
[S🐾] [✕] [👟]

▼▼▼ Ramada Limited M
(435) 586-9916. **$59-$129.** 281 S Main St. I-15, exit 57, just e. Ext corridors. **Pets:** Small, dogs only. $7 daily fee/pet. Designated rooms, service with restrictions, supervision.
[ASK] [S🐾] [✕] [🛏] [💻] [≈]

AAA ▼▼▼ Super 7 Motel M
(435) 586-6566. **$35-$95.** 190 S Main St. I-15, exit 57, just e. Ext corridors. **Pets:** Small, dogs only. $10 daily fee/pet. Designated rooms, service with restrictions, supervision.
[SAVE] [S🐾] [✕] [🛏]

▼▼▼ Super 8 Motel M
(435) 586-8880. **$45-$90.** 145 N 1550 W. I-15, exit 59, just w. Int corridors. **Pets:** Accepted.
[ASK] [S🐾] [✕] [🦽M] [👟] [🛏]

AAA ▼▼ Valu-Inn M
(435) 586-9114. **$38-$60.** 344 S Main St. I-15, exit 57, just e. Ext corridors. **Pets:** Accepted.
[SAVE] [S🐾] [✕] [🛏]

CLEARFIELD

▼▼▼ Days Inn M
(801) 825-8000. **$49-$89.** 572 N Main St. I-15, exit 335, just w. Int corridors. **Pets:** Other species. $5 one-time fee/pet.
[ASK] [S🐾] [✕] [🐕] [👟] [🛏]

COALVILLE

▼▼▼▼ Best Western Holiday Hills M
(435) 336-4444. **$80-$105, 3 day notice.** 210 S 200 W. I-80, exit 162, just w. Int corridors. **Pets:** Other species. $15 daily fee/pet. Designated rooms, supervision.
[ASK] [S🐾] [✕] [👟] [🛏] [💻] [≈] [✕]

DELTA

AAA ▼▼▼ Best Western Motor Inn M
(435) 864-3882. **$58-$75.** 527 E Topaz Blvd. US 6, at US 50. Ext corridors. **Pets:** Other species. $25 one-time fee/room. Designated rooms, service with restrictions, supervision.
[SAVE] [S🐾] [✕] [🐕] [🛏] [💻] [≈]

DUCK CREEK VILLAGE

AAA ▼▼▼ Pinewoods Resort M
(435) 682-2512. **$55-$475, 30 day notice.** 121 Duck Creek Ridge Rd. Just s of SR 14 via Cedar Mountain Rd, 31 mi e of Cedar City; in Cedar Mountain Village; 10 mi w of jct US 89. Ext/int corridors. **Pets:** Medium. $25 deposit/room. Designated rooms, service with restrictions, supervision.
[SAVE] [S🐾] [✕] [🛏] [💻] [🍴] [✕] [📞]

ESCALANTE

▼▼▼ Rainbow Country Bed & Breakfast BB
(435) 826-4567. **$65-$85, 3 day notice.** 585 E 300 S. Just off SR 12; east end of town. Int corridors. **Pets:** Service with restrictions, supervision.
[ASK] [S🐾] [✕] [🐾] [📞]

FILLMORE

AAA ▼▼▼▼ Best Western Paradise Resort M
(435) 743-6895. **$59-$79.** 905 N Main St. I-15, exit 167, just e. Ext corridors. **Pets:** Accepted.
[SAVE] [S🐾] [✕] [🛏] [💻] [🍴] [≈]

▼▼▼ Inn at Apple Creek M
(435) 743-4334. **$69-$93.** 940 S Hwy 99. I-15, exit 163, just e. Int corridors. **Pets:** Medium. $6 daily fee/pet. Designated rooms, service with restrictions, supervision.
[ASK] [S🐾] [✕] [👟] [🛏] [💻] [≈]

GARDEN CITY

▼▼▼ Canyon Cove Inn M
(435) 946-3565. **$69-$150, 99 day notice.** 315 W Logan (Hwy 89). On US 89, just w of jct US 89 and SR 30. Int corridors. **Pets:** Accepted.
[ASK] [S🐾] [✕] [👟] [🛏] [≈]

GLENDALE

▼▼▼ Historic Smith Hotel Bed & Breakfast BB
(435) 648-2156. **$39-$84.** 295 N Main St. US 89; north end of town. Int corridors. **Pets:** Accepted.
[ASK] [S🐾] [✕] [🐾] [📞]

GREEN RIVER

▼▼▼▼ Holiday Inn Express M
(435) 564-4439. **$69-$119.** 1845 E Main. I-70, exit 160, 2.6 mi ne. Int corridors. **Pets:** Large. $10 daily fee/pet. Designated rooms, service with restrictions, supervision.
[ASK] [S🐾] [✕] [👟] [🛏] [💻] [≈]

▼▼ Motel 6 #289 M
(435) 564-3436. **$41-$55.** 946 E Main St. I-70, exit 160, 2.7 mi ne. Ext corridors. **Pets:** Medium, other species. Service with restrictions, supervision.
[S🐾] [✕] [👟] [🛏] [≈]

▼▼ Ramada Limited M
(435) 564-8441. **$45-$74.** 1117 E Main St. I-70, exit 164, 1 mi nw. Ext/int corridors. **Pets:** Other species. $5 daily fee/pet. No service, supervision.
[ASK] [S🐾] [✕] [👟] [🛏] [💻] [≈]

AAA ▼▼▼ Super 8 Motel M
(435) 564-8888. **$49-$80.** 1248 E Main St. I-70, exit 160, 3.1 mi ne. Int corridors. **Pets:** Accepted.
[SAVE] [S🐾] [✕] [🐕] [👟] [🛏] [≈]

HATCH

Riverside Resort & RV Park M
(435) 735-4223. **$40-$75, 3 day notice.** 594 US Hwy 89. On US 89, 1 mi n. Ext corridors. **Pets:** Accepted.
[SAVE] [S❒] [X] [❒] [❒] [❒] [❒]

HEBER CITY

Swiss Alps Inn M
(435) 654-0722. **$65-$79.** 167 S Main St. On US 40; center. Ext corridors. **Pets:** Accepted.
[SAVE] [S❒] [X] [❒] [❒] [❒] [X]

HUNTSVILLE

Jackson Fork Inn BB
(801) 745-0051. **$75-$130, 3 day notice.** 7345 E 900 S. On SR 39. Int corridors. **Pets:** Accepted.
[ASK] [X] [❒] [❒]

HURRICANE

Days Inn-Hurricane/Zion Park M
(435) 635-0500. **$44-$99.** 40 N 2600 W. West end of town. Int corridors. **Pets:** Accepted.
[ASK] [S❒] [X] [❒] [❒] [❒]

Motel 6-4050 M
(435) 635-4010. **$44-$119.** 650 W State. Just w on SR 9. Ext corridors. **Pets:** Medium, other species. Service with restrictions, supervision.
[SAVE] [S❒] [X] [❒] [❒]

Super 8 M
(435) 635-0808. **$99.** 65 S 700 W. Just s of SR 9. Ext corridors. **Pets:** Accepted.
[ASK] [S❒] [X] [❒] [❒] [❒] [❒]

KANAB

Aikens Lodge M
(435) 644-2625. **$35-$71.** 79 W Center St. On US 89. Ext corridors. **Pets:** Small, dogs only. $10 daily fee/pet. Designated rooms, supervision.
[SAVE] [S❒] [X] [❒] [❒] [❒]

Best Western Red Hills M
(435) 644-2675. **$46-$120.** 125 W Center St. Center. Ext/int corridors. **Pets:** Other species. $10 one-time fee/room. Designated rooms, service with restrictions.
[SAVE] [S❒] [X] [❒] [❒] [❒] [❒]

Bob-Bon Inn M
(435) 644-5094. **$33-$60, 3 day notice.** 236 Hwy 89 N. On US 89. Ext corridors. **Pets:** $10 daily fee/pet. Designated rooms, service with restrictions, supervision.
[SAVE] [X] [❒] [❒]

Clarion Collection-Victorian Charm Inn M
(435) 644-8660. **$79-$159.** 190 N Hwy 89. North end of town. Int corridors. **Pets:** Accepted.
[ASK] [S❒] [X] [❒]

Four Seasons Motel & Restaurant M
(435) 644-2635. **$49-$149.** 36 N 300 W. N of downtown, on US 89. Ext corridors. **Pets:** Accepted.
[ASK] [S❒] [X] [❒]

Holiday Inn Express M
(435) 644-8888. **$69-$119.** 815 E Hwy 89. On US 89, just e. Int corridors. **Pets:** Accepted.
[ASK] [S❒] [X] [❒M] [❒] [❒] [❒] [❒] [❒]

Kanab Mission Inn M
(435) 644-5373. **$35-$59.** 386 E 300 S. E on US 89. Int corridors. **Pets:** Other species. $10 deposit/pet. Service with restrictions, supervision.
[SAVE] [S❒] [X]

Parry Lodge M
(435) 644-2601. **$62-$92.** 89 E Center St. On US 89; corner of 100 E; center. Ext/int corridors. **Pets:** $10 daily fee/pet. Designated rooms.
[SAVE] [S❒] [X] [❒] [❒]

Quail Park Lodge M
(435) 644-8700. **$39-$59.** 125 Hwy 89 N. On US 89. Ext corridors. **Pets:** Medium, other species. Service with restrictions, supervision.
[SAVE] [S❒] [X] [❒] [❒]

Shilo Inn SH 🐾
(435) 644-2562. **$70-$121.** 296 W 100 N. N of downtown on US 89. Int corridors. **Pets:** Other species. $25 one-time fee/room. Supervision.
[ASK] [S❒] [X] [❒] [❒] [❒]

LAKE POWELL

Defiance House Lodge-Bullfrog Marina SH
(435) 684-3000. **$72-$136, 3 day notice.** Bullfrog Marina. 70 mi s of Hanksville; 44 mi s off SR 95 on SR 276. Int corridors. **Pets:** Accepted.
[SAVE] [S❒] [X] [❒] [❒] [❒] [X]

LAYTON

Comfort Inn M
(801) 544-5577. **$50-$85.** 877 N 400 W. I-15, exit 331, then e. Int corridors. **Pets:** Other species. $100 one-time fee/room. Service with restrictions, supervision.
[SAVE] [X] [❒] [❒] [❒] [❒]

Hampton Inn M
(801) 775-8800. **$99-$119.** 1700 Woodland Park Dr. I-15, exit 332, 0.3 mi se. Int corridors. **Pets:** Accepted.
[ASK] [S❒] [X] [❒] [❒] [❒] [❒] [❒]

Holiday Inn Express M
(801) 773-3773. **$99-$159.** 1695 Woodland Park Dr. I-15, exit 332, 0.3 mi se. Int corridors. **Pets:** Accepted.
[ASK] [S❒] [X] [❒] [❒] [❒] [❒] [❒]

La Quinta Inn Salt Lake City (Layton) M
(801) 776-6700. **$71-$110.** 1965 N 1200 W. I-15, exit 332, 1 blk e; corner of Antelope Dr and Angel Rd. Int corridors. **Pets:** Medium. Service with restrictions.
[SAVE] [X] [❒] [❒] [❒] [❒] [X]

TownePlace Suites M
(801) 779-2422. **$69-$159.** 1743 Woodland Park Dr. I-15, exit 332, 0.3 mi se. Int corridors. **Pets:** Accepted.
[ASK] [S❒] [X] [❒] [❒] [❒] [❒]

LEHI

Best Western Timpanogos Inn M 🐾
(801) 768-1400. **$75-$135.** 195 S 850 E. I-15, exit 279; southwest side. Int corridors. **Pets:** Other species. $10 one-time fee/room. Designated rooms, service with restrictions, crate.
[SAVE] [S❒] [X] [❒] [❒] [❒] [❒] [❒]

Motel 6-1405 M
(801) 768-2668. **$45-$58.** 210 S 1200 E. I-15, exit 279, just e. Int corridors. **Pets:** Medium, other species. Service with restrictions, supervision.
[S❒] [X] [❒] [❒] [❒] [❒]

Super 8 M
(801) 766-8800. **$68-$95.** 125 S 850 E. I-15, exit 279; southwest side. Int corridors. **Pets:** Other species. $10 one-time fee/pet. Service with restrictions.
[ASK] [S❒] [X] [❒] [❒] [❒] [❒] [❒]

LOGAN

Best Western Baugh Motel M
(435) 752-5220. **$69-$139, 3 day notice.** 153 S Main St. On US 89 and 91. Ext corridors. **Pets:** Accepted.

Best Western Weston Inn M
(435) 752-5700. **$69-$119.** 250 N Main St. On US 89 and 91; downtown. Ext corridors. **Pets:** Small, dogs only. $10 daily fee/room. Designated rooms, service with restrictions, supervision.

Logan Super 8 SH
(435) 753-8883. **$50-$85.** 865 S Hwy 89 and 91. South end of town. Int corridors. **Pets:** Other species. $10 daily fee/pet. Designated rooms, service with restrictions, supervision.

Ramada Limited SH
(435) 787-2060. **$63-$68.** 2002 S Hwy 89 and 91. South end of town. Int corridors. **Pets:** Accepted.

MANTI

Manti Country Village M
(435) 835-9300. **$59-$89.** 145 N Main St. On US 89. Ext corridors. **Pets:** Medium. $75 deposit/room. Designated rooms, service with restrictions, supervision.

MARYSVALE

Big Rock Candy Mountain Resort M
(435) 326-2000. **$59-$199, 7 day notice.** 4479 N Hwy 89. On US 89, 6 mi n. Ext corridors. **Pets:** Accepted.

MEXICAN HAT

San Juan Inn & Trading Post M
(435) 683-2220. **$48-$74.** Hwy 163 & San Juan River. On US 163. Ext corridors. **Pets:** Dogs only. $5 one-time fee/pet. Designated rooms, service with restrictions, supervision.

MOAB

Apache Motel M
(435) 259-5727. **$35-$99.** 166 S 400 E. Jct US 191 and 100 S, just e, then just s. Ext corridors. **Pets:** Large, other species. Service with restrictions, supervision.

Big Horn Lodge SH
(435) 259-6171. **$34-$90.** 550 S Main St. South end of town. Ext corridors. **Pets:** Other species. $5 daily fee/pet. Designated rooms, service with restrictions, supervision.

Cedar Breaks Condos CO
(435) 259-5125. **$75-$162, 7 day notice.** 400 East & Center St. Jct Main and Center sts, just e, then just s. Ext corridors. **Pets:** Accepted.

Days Inn M
(435) 259-4468. **$34-$88.** 426 N Main St. On US 191; town center. Int corridors. **Pets:** $5 daily fee/pet. Designated rooms, service with restrictions, crate.

The Gonzo Inn M ❖
(435) 259-2515. **$87-$145.** 100 W 200 S. Downtown. Ext/int corridors. **Pets:** Other species. $25 daily fee/room. Service with restrictions.

Kokopelli Lodge M
(435) 259-7615. **$35-$79.** 72 S 100 E. From Main St, just e on 100 S, then just n; downtown. Ext corridors. **Pets:** Accepted.

La Quinta Inns Moab M ❖
(435) 259-8700. **$58-$129.** 815 S Main St. South end of town. Int corridors. **Pets:** Medium, other species. Designated rooms, service with restrictions, supervision.

Moab Valley Inn M
(435) 259-4419. **$75-$120.** 711 S Main St. 1 mi s on US 191. Int corridors. **Pets:** Medium. $10 daily fee/room. Designated rooms, service with restrictions, supervision.

Motel 6 Moab #4119 M
(435) 259-6686. **$39-$120.** 1089 N Main St. North end of town; west side of street. Int corridors. **Pets:** Small. $20 one-time fee/pet. Designated rooms, service with restrictions, supervision.

Nichol's Lane Accommodations CO
(435) 259-5125. **$85-$125, 7 day notice.** 543 Nichol Ln. Just e from jct Center and Main sts, just s, then just e. Ext corridors. **Pets:** Accepted.

Ramada of Downtown Moab M ❖
(435) 259-7141. **$45-$151.** 182 S Main St. At 200 S; downtown. Ext/int corridors. **Pets:** Small. $20 one-time fee/pet. Designated rooms, service with restrictions, supervision.

Red Cliffs Adventure Lodge RA
(435) 259-2002. **$90-$280, 30 day notice.** Milepost 14 Hwy 128. 2 mi n to jct US 191 and SR 128, 14.5 mi e. Ext corridors. **Pets:** Medium. $20 daily fee/pet. Designated rooms, service with restrictions, supervision.

Red Stone Inn M ❖
(435) 259-3500. **$35-$84.** 535 S Main St. Downtown. Ext/int corridors. **Pets:** $5 daily fee/pet. Designated rooms, service with restrictions, supervision.

River Canyon Lodge, An Extended Stay Inn & Suites M ❖
(435) 259-8838. **$49-$149.** 71 W 200 N. Jct 200 N and Main St, just w; downtown. Int corridors. **Pets:** Small. $20 one-time fee/pet. Designated rooms, service with restrictions, supervision.

Riverside Inn SH
(435) 259-8848. **$32-$90.** 988 N Main St. 1 mi n on US 191. Int corridors. **Pets:** Accepted.

Silver Sage Inn M
(435) 259-4420. **$35-$75.** 840 S Main St. South end of town on US 191. Int corridors. **Pets:** Other species. $5 one-time fee/pet. Service with restrictions.

Sleep Inn M
(435) 259-4655. **$49-$200.** 1051 S Main St. South end of town. Int corridors. **Pets:** Large, other species. $50 deposit/room. Designated rooms, service with restrictions, supervision.

Super 8 Motel, Moab M
(435) 259-8868. **$49-$139.** 889 N Main St. US 191, 1 mi n. Int corridors. **Pets:** Small. $20 one-time fee/pet. Designated rooms, service with restrictions, supervision.

The Virginian Motel M 🐾
(435) 259-5951. **$79-$89.** 70 E 200 S. Just e of US 191. Ext corridors. **Pets:** Other species. $10 daily fee/pet. Service with restrictions, supervision.

MONTICELLO

Best Western Wayside Inn M
(435) 587-2261. **$60-$90.** 197 E Central, Hwy 491 St. On US 491, just e of US 191. Ext corridors. **Pets:** $10 daily fee/pet. Designated rooms, service with restrictions, supervision.

The Monticello Inn M
(435) 587-2274. **$50-$65.** 164 E US 491. On US 491, e of US 191. Ext corridors. **Pets:** Small. $50 deposit/room. Designated rooms, service with restrictions, supervision.

Rodeway Inn M
(435) 587-2489. **$39-$76.** 649 N Main St. On US 194 N; end of town. Int corridors. **Pets:** Medium. $50 deposit/pet, $10 daily fee/pet. Service with restrictions, supervision.

MONUMENT VALLEY

Goulding's Trading Post & Lodge SH
(435) 727-3231. **$78-$180, 3 day notice.** 1000 Main St. Just n of Arizona border; 2 mi w of US 163. Ext corridors. **Pets:** Accepted.

MOUNT CARMEL JUNCTION

Golden Hills Motel M
(435) 648-2268. **$41-$60.** 4473 S State St. US 89, jct SR 9. Ext/int corridors. **Pets:** Accepted.

NEPHI

Best Western Paradise Inn M
(435) 623-0624. **$64-$92.** 1025 S Main St. I-15, exit 222, 0.5 mi n. Ext corridors. **Pets:** Accepted.

Safari Motel M
(435) 623-1071. **$47-$53.** 413 S Main St. I-15, exit 228, 3.2 mi w. Ext corridors. **Pets:** Accepted.

OGDEN

Best Rest Inn M
(801) 393-8644. **$110-$130.** 1206 W 2100 S. I-15, exit 343, just e. Ext corridors. **Pets:** Dogs only. $20 one-time fee/room. Designated rooms, service with restrictions, supervision.

Best Western High Country Inn M
(801) 394-9474. **$59-$99.** 1335 W 12th St. I-15, exit 344 (12th St), then e. Ext corridors. **Pets:** Accepted.

Comfort Suites of Ogden M
(801) 621-2545. **$76-$150.** 2250 S 1200 W. I-15, exit 343E, just w. Int corridors. **Pets:** Accepted.

Holiday Inn Express Hotel & Suites M 🐾
(801) 392-5000. **$79-$99.** 2245 S 1200 W. I-15, exit 343, just e. Int corridors. **Pets:** Large, other species. $50 deposit/room. Service with restrictions.

Motel 6 Ogden #0111 M
(801) 627-4560. **$42-$55.** 1455 Washington Blvd. Downtown. Int corridors. **Pets:** Medium, other species. Service with restrictions, supervision.

Red Roof Inn #7279 M
(801) 627-2880. **$48-$70.** 1500 W Riverdale Rd. I-15, exit 343 southbound, just w; exit 342 northbound, just e. Ext/int corridors. **Pets:** Medium, other species. Service with restrictions, supervision.

Sleep Inn M
(801) 731-6500. **$60.** 1155 S 1700 W. I-15, exit 344, just w. Int corridors. **Pets:** Medium. $10 daily fee/pet. Service with restrictions, supervision.

Super 8 Motel M
(801) 731-7100. **$50-$59.** 1508 W 2100 S. I-15, exit 343, just w. Int corridors. **Pets:** Accepted.

OREM

Comfort Inn & Suites M
(801) 431-0405. **$59-$99.** 427 W University Pkwy. I-15, exit 269, 0.5 mi e. Int corridors. **Pets:** Accepted.

La Quinta Inn & Suites Orem (University Parkway) M
(801) 226-0440. **$85-$145.** 521 W University Pkwy. I-15, exit 269, 0.5 mi e. Int corridors. **Pets:** Medium. Service with restrictions.

La Quinta Inn Orem (North/Provo) M
(801) 235-9555. **$59-$109.** 1100 W 780 N. I-15, exit 272, east side. Int corridors. **Pets:** Accepted.

PANGUITCH

Bryce Way Motel M
(435) 676-2400. **$30-$50.** 429 N Main St. On US 89. Ext corridors. **Pets:** Medium. $4 one-time fee/room. No service, supervision.

Color Country Motel M
(435) 676-2386. **$36-$62.** 526 N Main St. On US 89. Ext corridors. **Pets:** Medium, other species. $10 one-time fee/pet. Designated rooms, no service, supervision.

Harold's Place Cabins CA 🐾
(435) 676-2350. **$50-$80.** 3066 Hwy 12. 1 mi e off US 89 at SR 12; 17 mi w of Bryce Canyon. Ext corridors. **Pets:** Medium, dogs only. $20 deposit/room. Designated rooms, service with restrictions, supervision.

Harold's Place Inn M 🐾
(435) 676-8886. **$50-$79.** 3068 Hwy 12. 0.5 mi e off US 89 at SR 12. Int corridors. **Pets:** Medium, dogs only. $20 deposit/room. Designated rooms, service with restrictions, supervision.

▼▼▼ Horizon Motel M
(435) 676-2651. **$35-$99.** 730 N Main St. On US 89. Ext corridors. **Pets:** Medium. $10 one-time fee/pet. Designated rooms, supervision.
ASK ⊠ 🗎 🖵

⚑⚑⚑ ▼▼▼ Marianna Inn Motel M
(435) 676-8844. **$30-$75.** 699 N Main St. On US 89. Ext corridors. **Pets:** Dogs only. $5 daily fee/pet. Designated rooms, service with restrictions, supervision.
SAVE 🔊 ⊠ 🗎 🖵

PARK CITY

⚑⚑⚑ ▼▼▼ Best Western Landmark Inn SH
(435) 649-7300. **$69-$219, 30 day notice.** 6560 N Landmark Dr. I-80, exit 145, at Kimball Junction. Int corridors. **Pets:** Accepted.
SAVE 🔊 ⊠ 🔥M 🗐 🗎 🖵 🏊 ⊠

▼▼▼▼ Holiday Inn Express Hotel & Suites SH
(435) 658-1600. **$119-$299, 14 day notice.** 1501 W Ute Blvd. I-80, exit 145 (Kimball Juncton). Int corridors. **Pets:** Other species. $10 daily fee/pet. Service with restrictions, supervision.
ASK 🔊 ⊠ 🗐 🔥 🗎 🖵 🏊 ⊠

▼▼▼▼ Park City Peak Hotel SH
(435) 649-5000. **$59-$269, 30 day notice.** 2121 Park Ave. I-80, exit 145 (Kimball Junction), 5.1 mi s; north end of town. Int corridors. **Pets:** Accepted.
ASK ⊠ 🗐 🗎 🖵 🍴 🏊 ⊠

▼▼▼▼ The Sundial Lodge SH
(435) 615-8070. **$99-$1004, 10 day notice.** 4000 The Canyon Resort Dr. I-80, exit 145 (Kimball Junction), 3 mi sw via SR 224, 0.6 mi w on Canyons Resort Dr, then just w. Int corridors. **Pets:** Accepted.
ASK 🔊 ⊠ 🔥 🗎 🖵 🍴 🏊 ⊠

PAROWAN

⚑⚑⚑ ▼▼▼ Days Inn M
(435) 477-3326. **$52-$95.** 625 W 200 S. I-15, exit 75, 1.5 mi e. Ext corridors. **Pets:** Accepted.
SAVE 🔊 ⊠ 🗎 🏊 ⊠

PAYSON

▼▼▼▼ Comfort Inn M
(801) 465-4861. **$80-$99.** 830 N Main St. I-15, exit 250, just e. Int corridors. **Pets:** $20 deposit/room. Service with restrictions, supervision.
ASK 🔊 ⊠ 🗐 🗎 🖵 🏊 ⊠

PRICE

⚑⚑⚑ ▼ Budget Host Inn M ☙
(435) 637-2424. **$59-$85.** 145 N Carbonville Rd. US 6, exit 240, just e, then just n on Main St. Ext corridors. **Pets:** Other species. $10 daily fee/pet. Service with restrictions.
SAVE 🔊 ⊠ 🗎 🖵 🏊

⚑⚑⚑ ▼ National 9-Price River Inn M
(435) 637-7000. **$44-$62.** 641 W Price River Dr. US 6, exit 240, just e. Ext/int corridors. **Pets:** Accepted.
SAVE 🔊 ⊠ 🗎 🖵

PROVO

⚑⚑⚑ ▼▼▼ Days Inn M
(801) 375-8600. **$69-$85.** 1675 N 200 W. I-15, exit 269, 3.5 mi e on University Pkwy. Ext corridors. **Pets:** Accepted.
SAVE 🔊 ⊠ 🗐 🔥 🗎 🖵 🏊

▼▼ Econo Lodge Provo Airport M
(801) 373-0099. **$59-$89.** 1625 W Center St. I-15, exit 265A southbound; exit 265B northbound, 0.3 mi w. Ext corridors. **Pets:** Medium. $10 daily fee/pet. Designated rooms, no service, supervision.
ASK 🔊 ⊠ 🗎 🖵

▼▼▼ Hampton Inn M
(801) 377-6396. **$89-$149.** 1511 S 40 E. I-15, exit 266, just e. Int corridors. **Pets:** Other species. $20 one-time fee/room. Designated rooms, service with restrictions, supervision.
ASK 🔊 ⊠ 🗐 🔥 🗎 🖵 🏊

⚑⚑⚑ ▼▼▼ Provo Travelers Inn M
(801) 373-8248. **$45-$120.** 70 E 300 S University Ave. I-15, exit 265 southbound; exit 265A northbound. Ext corridors. **Pets:** Accepted.
SAVE 🔊 ⊠ 🗎 🏊

▼▼▼ Residence Inn by Marriott M
(801) 374-1000. **$149-$199.** 252 W 2230 N. I-15, exit 269, 3.1 mi e via University Pkwy. Int corridors. **Pets:** Accepted.
ASK 🔊 ⊠ 🔥M 🗐 🔥 🗎 🖵 🏊 ⊠

⚑⚑⚑ ▼▼▼ Sleep Inn M
(801) 377-6597. **$69-$129.** 1505 S 40 E. I-15, exit 263, just e. Int corridors. **Pets:** Medium. $10 daily fee/pet. Service with restrictions, supervision.
SAVE 🔊 ⊠ 🗐 🔥 🗎 🖵 🏊 ⊠

⚑⚑⚑ ▼▼◆ Super 8 Provo BYU/Orem UVSC M ☙
(801) 374-6020. **$49-$109.** 1555 N Canyon Rd. I-15, exit 269, 3.5 mi e. Ext/int corridors. **Pets:** Supervision.
SAVE ⊠ 🔥 🗎 🖵 🏊

RICHFIELD

⚑⚑⚑ ▼▼◆ AppleTree Inn M ☙
(435) 896-5481. **$36-$79, 30 day notice.** 145 S Main St. I-70, exit 37 or 40; center of downtown. Ext corridors. **Pets:** $6 one-time fee/room. Supervision.
SAVE 🔊 ⊠ 🗐 🗎 🖵 🏊

▼▼ Best Western Richfield Inn M
(435) 893-0100. **$40-$75.** 1275 N Main St. I-70, exit 40, just s. Int corridors. **Pets:** Other species. $15 one-time fee/room. Designated rooms, service with restrictions, supervision.
ASK 🔊 ⊠ 🔥 🗎 🖵 🏊

⚑⚑⚑ ▼▼◆ Budget Host Nights Inn M
(435) 896-8228. **$33-$46.** 69 S Main St. I-70, exit 37 or 40; center of downtown. Ext corridors. **Pets:** Large, other species. $5 one-time fee/room. Designated rooms, service with restrictions.
SAVE 🔊 ⊠ 🗎 🏊

⚑⚑⚑ ▼▼▼▼ Days Inn SH
(435) 896-6476. **$80-$130.** 333 N Main St. I-70, exit 40, 1 mi s on US 89. Int corridors. **Pets:** Medium, other species. $50 deposit/room, $10 one-time fee/room. Designated rooms, service with restrictions, supervision.
SAVE 🔊 ⊠ 🗎 🖵 🍴 🏊 ⊠

⚑⚑⚑ ▼▼ New West Motel M ☙
(435) 896-4076. **$30-$42.** 447 S Main St. I-70, exit 37 or 40; downtown. Ext corridors. **Pets:** Large, other species. $5 daily fee/room. Service with restrictions, supervision.
SAVE 🔊 ⊠ 🗎

⚑⚑⚑ ▼▼▼▼ Richfield Travelodge M
(435) 896-9271. **$65-$95.** 647 S Main St. I-70, exit 37; south end of town. Int corridors. **Pets:** Other species. $10 one-time fee/room. Designated rooms, service with restrictions, supervision.
SAVE 🔊 ⊠ 🗎 🖵 🍴 🏊

⚑⚑⚑ ▼▼▼ Romanico Inn M ☙
(435) 896-8471. **$33-$44.** 1170 S Cove View Rd. I-70, exit 37, 2 mi n. Ext corridors. **Pets:** Large, other species. $5 one-time fee/room. Designated rooms, service with restrictions, supervision.
SAVE 🔊 ⊠ 🗎

♦♦ **Super 8 Motel** [M]
(435) 896-9204. **$48-$94.** 1377 N Main St. I-70, exit 40, just s. Ext/int corridors. **Pets:** Accepted.
[A$K] [SD] ⊠ 🦻 ☎ 📺

ROOSEVELT

[AAA] ♦♦ **Frontier Motel** [M]
(435) 722-2201. **$55-$68.** 75 S 200 E. On US 40. Ext corridors. **Pets:** Small, dogs only. Designated rooms, service with restrictions, supervision.
[SAVE] [SD] ⊠ ☎ 🍴 🏊

ST. GEORGE

♦♦ **Americas Best Inn & Suites** [M]
(435) 652-3030. **$49-$120.** 245 N Red Cliffs Dr. I-15, exit 8, just e. Ext corridors. **Pets:** Accepted.
[A$K] [SD] ⊠ 🦻 ♿ ☎ 📺 🏊

♦ **Americas Best Value Inn** [M]
(435) 673-4666. **$29-$99.** 60 W St. George Blvd. 1 blk w of Main St; downtown. Ext corridors. **Pets:** Medium, dogs only. $5 one-time fee/pet. Service with restrictions, supervision.
[A$K] [SD] ⊠ ☎ 🏊

♦♦ **The Bluffs Inn & Suites** [M]
(435) 628-6699. **$50-$100.** 1140 S Bluff St. I-15, exit 6 (Bluff St), just w. Ext corridors. **Pets:** Accepted.
[A$K] [SD] ⊠ ♿ ☎ 📺 🏊

[AAA] ♦♦♦ **Budget Inn & Suites** [SH]
(435) 673-6661. **$56-$154.** 1221 S Main St. I-15, exit 6 (Bluff St), just w. Ext corridors. **Pets:** Accepted.
[SAVE] [SD] ⊠ ♿ ☎ 📺 🏊 🏋

♦♦ **Coronada Inn & Suites** [SH]
(435) 628-4436. **$39-$99, 3 day notice.** 559 E St. George Blvd. Downtown. Ext corridors. **Pets:** Accepted.
[A$K] ⊠ ☎ 🏊

[AAA] ♦♦♦ **Crystal Inn St. George** [SH]
(435) 688-7477. **$129-$179.** 1450 S Hilton Dr. I-15, exit 6 (Bluff St), just w. Int corridors. **Pets:** Small, dogs only. $25 one-time fee/pet. Designated rooms, service with restrictions, supervision.
[SAVE] [SD] ⊠ ☎ 📺 🍴 🏊 🏋

[AAA] ♦♦ **Econo Lodge** [M]
(435) 673-4861. **$42-$149.** 460 E St. George Blvd. I-15, exit 8, cross streets 500 E and St. George Blvd; downtown. Ext corridors. **Pets:** Small. $10 daily fee/pet. Designated rooms, service with restrictions, supervision.
[SAVE] [SD] ⊠ 🦻 ♿ ☎ 📺 🏊

[AAA] ♦♦♦ **Fairfield Inn by Marriott** [M]
(435) 673-6066. **$69-$89.** 1660 S Convention Center Dr. I-15, exit 6 (Bluff St), just e. Int corridors. **Pets:** Other species. $75 one-time fee/room. Service with restrictions, supervision.
[SAVE] ⊠ 🦻 ♿ ☎ 📺 🏊

[AAA] ♦♦♦♦ **The Green Valley Spa & Resort** [SH]
(435) 628-8060. **$249-$275, 14 day notice.** 1871 W Canyon View Dr. Bluff and S Main sts, 4 mi sw via Hilton Dr to Dixie Dr, then to Canyon View Dr. Ext corridors. **Pets:** Accepted.
[SAVE] ⊠ ♿[M] ♿ ☎ 📺 🏊 🏋

[AAA] ♦♦♦ **GuestHouse International Inn & Suites** [M]
(435) 673-6161. **$55-$129.** 260 E St George Blvd. I-15, exit 8, 1.5 mi w. Ext corridors. **Pets:** Accepted.
[SAVE] [SD] ⊠ ☎ 📺 🏊

[AAA] ♦♦♦ **Holiday Inn** [SH]
(435) 628-4235. **$89-$134.** 850 S Bluff St. I-15, exit 6 (Bluff St), just w. Ext/int corridors. **Pets:** Small, other species. $25 one-time fee/pet. Designated rooms, service with restrictions, supervision.
[SAVE] ⊠ 🦻 ♿ ☎ 📺 🍴 🏊 🏋

[AAA] ♦♦♦ **Howard Johnson Express Inn & Suites** [M]
(435) 628-8000. **$65-$139.** 1040 S Main St. I-15, exit 6 (Bluff St), just w, then just e. Ext corridors. **Pets:** Accepted.
[SAVE] [SD] ⊠ ♿ ☎ 📺 🏊

[AAA] ♦♦♦ **Red Cliffs Inn & Suites** [M]
(435) 673-3537. **$70-$149.** 912 Red Cliffs Dr. I-15, exit 10, just e. Ext/int corridors. **Pets:** Accepted.
[SAVE] [SD] ⊠ ♿ ☎ 📺 🍴 🏊

♦♦♦ **Seven Wives Inn** [BB] 🐾
(435) 628-3737. **$90-$185, 7 day notice.** 217 N 100 W. I-15, exit 8, 2.1 mi w, then n. Ext/int corridors. **Pets:** $15 one-time fee/pet. Designated rooms, service with restrictions, supervision.
[A$K] ⊠ ♿ ☎ 🏊

♦♦ **Shuttle Lodge Inn** [M]
(435) 688-8383. **$59-$79.** 915 S Bluff St. I-15, exit 6 (Bluff St), just w. Int corridors. **Pets:** $10 daily fee/pet. Designated rooms, service with restrictions, supervision.
[A$K] [SD] ⊠ ☎ 🏊

SALINA

♦ **Ranch Motel** [M]
(435) 529-7789. **$38-$52.** 80 N State St. I-70, exit 56, on US 89; near town center. Ext/int corridors. **Pets:** Medium. $6 daily fee/pet. No service, supervision.
[A$K] [SD] ⊠ ☎

♦♦ **Rodeway Inn** [M]
(435) 529-1300. **$46-$70.** 1400 S State. I-70, exit 56, just n. Int corridors. **Pets:** Accepted.
[A$K] [SD] ⊠ ♿ ☎ 🏊

[AAA] ♦♦ **Scenic Hills Super 8** [M]
(435) 529-7483. **$50-$70.** 75 E 1500 S. I-70, exit 56, just n. Ext corridors. **Pets:** Accepted.
[SAVE] [SD] ⊠ ☎ 🏊

SALT LAKE CITY METROPOLITAN AREA

COTTONWOOD HEIGHTS

Candlewood Suites Hotel SH
(801) 567-0111. **$77.** 6990 S Park Centre Dr. I-15, exit 297, 2.5 mi via 7200 S and Fort Union Blvd. Int corridors. **Pets:** Accepted.

Residence Inn by Marriott at The Cottonwoods SH ❀
(801) 453-0430. **$169-$315.** 6425 S 3000 E. I-215 S, exit 6200 S, 0.3 mi se. Int corridors. **Pets:** Large, other species. $100 one-time fee/room. Service with restrictions, crate.

DRAPER

Holiday Inn Express M
(801) 571-2511. **$69-$129.** 12033 S Factory Outlet Dr. I-15, exit 291, just n; on east side of interstate. Int corridors. **Pets:** Accepted.

Ramada Limited M
(801) 571-1122. **$89-$99.** 12605 S Minuteman Dr. I-15, exit 291, 0.3 mi s on frontage road. Int corridors. **Pets:** Accepted.

MIDVALE

Best Western Executive Inn M ❀
(801) 566-4141. **$70.** 280 W 7200 S. I-15, exit 297, just e. Int corridors. **Pets:** Other species. $15 daily fee/pet. Service with restrictions, supervision.

La Quinta Inn Salt Lake City (Midvale) M
(801) 566-3291. **$74-$114.** 7231 S Catalpa St. I-15, exit 297, just e. Int corridors. **Pets:** Medium. Service with restrictions.

Motel 6 #476 M
(801) 561-0058. **$49-$61.** 7263 S Catalpa Rd. I-15, exit 297, just e, then just s. Ext corridors. **Pets:** Medium, other species. Service with restrictions, supervision.

National 9 Discovery Inn M
(801) 561-2256. **$55-$85.** 380 W 7200 S. I-15, exit 297, just e. Ext/int corridors. **Pets:** Accepted.

Super 8 M
(801) 255-5559. **$64-$84.** 7048 S 900 E. I-15, exit 297, 1.5 mi e on 7200 S to 900 E, then just n. Int corridors. **Pets:** Large, other species. $50 deposit/room. Service with restrictions, supervision.

MURRAY

Holiday Inn Express M
(801) 268-2533. **$59-$119.** 4465 S Century Dr. I-15, exit 301, just w. Int corridors. **Pets:** Other species. $25 one-time fee/pet. Designated rooms, service with restrictions, crate.

Pavilion Inn M
(801) 506-8000. **$60-$130.** 5335 S 440 W. I-15, exit 300, 0.3 mi w. Int corridors. **Pets:** Accepted.

Studio 6 #6038 M
(801) 685-2102. **$51-$65.** 975 E 6600 S. I-215, exit 9, on 900 E, then 0.5 mi e. Ext corridors. **Pets:** Accepted.

NORTH SALT LAKE

Best Western Cottontree Inn M
(801) 292-7666. **$74-$149.** 1030 N 400 E. I-15, exit 315, just e. Int corridors. **Pets:** Large. Service with restrictions, crate.

SALT LAKE CITY

Airport Comfort Inn SH
(801) 746-5200. **$79-$159.** 200 N Admiral Byrd Rd. I-80, exit 113, 0.8 mi n via 5600 W, Amelia Earhart Dr, then s. Int corridors. **Pets:** $20 one-time fee/room. Designated rooms, no service, supervision.

Alpine Executive Suites CO
(801) 533-8184. **$99-$189, 10 day notice.** 164 S 900 E. Cross streets 200 S and 900 E. Ext/int corridors. **Pets:** Accepted.

Baymont Inn & Suites M
(801) 355-0088. **$59-$79.** 2080 W N Temple. W from Temple Square, then 3 mi. Int corridors. **Pets:** Accepted.

Best Western Airport Inn SH
(801) 539-5005. **$80.** 315 N Admiral Byrd Rd. I-80, exit 113, 0.8 mi via 5600 W and Amelia Earhart Dr, then s. Int corridors. **Pets:** Other species. $20 daily fee/pet. Designated rooms, service with restrictions.

Best Western Garden Inn SH
(801) 521-2930. **$79-$109.** 154 W 600 S. Between cross streets 100-200 W. Ext/int corridors. **Pets:** Other species. $20 daily fee/room. Designated rooms, service with restrictions, supervision.

Candlewood Suite Hotel SH
(801) 359-7500. **$90.** 2170 W N Temple. 3 mi w of Temple Square. Int corridors. **Pets:** Accepted.

Chase Suite Hotel by Woodfin M
(801) 532-5511. **$99-$129.** 765 E 400 S. Cross streets 700 E and 400 S. Ext corridors. **Pets:** Accepted.

City Creek Inn M
(801) 533-9100. **$48-$89.** 230 W N Temple St. Cross street 200 W. Ext corridors. **Pets:** Accepted.

Days Inn-Salt Lake City Airport M
(801) 539-8538. **$68-$158.** 1900 W N Temple. W of Temple 59, 2.5 mi. Int corridors. **Pets:** Large. $10 daily fee/pet. Designated rooms, service with restrictions, supervision.

Econo Lodge Downtown M
(801) 363-0062. **$67-$117.** 715 W N Temple. West from Temple Square, 1 mi. Ext corridors. **Pets:** Medium. $20 one-time fee/room. Service with restrictions, supervision.

Hilton Salt Lake City Airport LH
(801) 539-1515. **$99-$209.** 5151 Wiley Post Way. I-80, exit 114 westbound, 0.4 mi nw via Wright Brothers Dr and Wiley Post; exit 113 eastbound, 1.3 mi n via 5600 W, Amelia Earhart Dr, then just s on Charles Lindbergh Dr. Int corridors. **Pets:** Large, other species. $25 deposit/pet, $25 one-time fee/pet. Designated rooms, service with restrictions, crate.

Hilton Salt Lake City Center LH
(801) 328-2000. **$109-$239.** 255 S W Temple. Just n of E 400 S; center. Int corridors. **Pets:** Small. $50 deposit/pet. Service with restrictions, supervision.

Holiday Inn-Downtown SH
(801) 359-8600. **$89-$169.** 999 S Main St. Cross streets 900 S and Main St. Int corridors. **Pets:** Accepted.

Homestead Studio Suites Hotel-Salt Lake City/Sugar House M
(801) 474-0771. **$67-$84.** 1220 E 2100 S. Cross streets 1300 E and 2100 S Sugarhouse. Ext corridors. **Pets:** Accepted.

Hotel Monaco LH
(801) 595-0000. **$109-$269.** 15 W 200 South. Cross streets 200 S and Main St. Int corridors. **Pets:** Other species. Crate.

Howard Johnson Express Inn M
(801) 521-3450. **$49-$89.** 121 N 300 W. At N Temple and 300 W. Ext/int corridors. **Pets:** Accepted.

Metropolitan Inn M
(801) 531-7100. **$69-$119.** 524 SW Temple. Cross streets 500 S and W Temple. Ext corridors. **Pets:** Medium, other species. $25 one-time fee/room. Designated rooms, service with restrictions.

Peery Hotel SH
(801) 521-4300. **$129-$149.** 110 W Broadway. At W Temple. Int corridors. **Pets:** $50 one-time fee/room. Designated rooms, service with restrictions, supervision.

Radisson Hotel Salt Lake City Downtown LH
(801) 531-7500. **$79-$130, 30 day notice.** 215 W South Temple. Opposite Delta Center. Int corridors. **Pets:** Very small, other species. $25 one-time fee/room. Service with restrictions.

Red Lion Hotel Salt Lake Downtown LH
(801) 521-7373. **$189-$199.** 161 W 600 S. At W Temple and 600 S. Int corridors. **Pets:** Medium, other species. $15 daily fee/pet. Service with restrictions, supervision.

Residence Inn by Marriott-City Center SH
(801) 355-3300. **$99-$349.** 285 W Broadway (300 S). Cross streets 300 W and Broadway (300 S). Int corridors. **Pets:** Other species. $100 one-time fee/room. Designated rooms, service with restrictions, supervision.

Residence Inn by Marriott Salt Lake City Airport SH
(801) 532-4101. **$89-$179.** 4883 W Douglas Corrigon Way. I-80, exit 114 westbound, via Wright Brothers Dr; exit 113 eastbound, via Amelia Earhart and Wright Brothers drs, then 2.6 mi se. Int corridors. **Pets:** $100 one-time fee/room. Service with restrictions, supervision.

Salt Lake Plaza Hotel at Temple Square LH
(801) 521-0130. **$79-$165.** 122 W S Temple Dr. W of Temple Square. Int corridors. **Pets:** Accepted.

Sheraton City Centre LH
(801) 401-2000. **$189-$229.** 150 W 500 S. At 200 W and 500 S. Int corridors. **Pets:** Accepted.

Shilo Inn Hotel LH
(801) 521-9500. **$84-$165.** 206 S W Temple. Cross streets 200 S and W Temple. Int corridors. **Pets:** Other species. $25 one-time fee/room. Supervision.

The Skyline Inn M
(801) 582-5350. **$59-$79.** 2475 E 1700 S. E off Foothill Dr. Ext corridors. **Pets:** Accepted.

Super 8 Airport M
(801) 533-8878. **$80-$120, 14 day notice.** 223 N Jimmy Doolittle Rd. I-80, exit 113, 0.7 mi ne via 5600 W, Amelia Earhart Dr and Admiral Byrd Rd, then e. Int corridors. **Pets:** $10 one-time fee/pet. Designated rooms, service with restrictions, supervision.

SANDY

Best Western CottonTree Inn M
(801) 523-8484. **$79-$129.** 10695 S Auto Mall Dr. I-15, exit 293 eastbound, 0.3 mi e. Int corridors. **Pets:** Small, other species. $10 one-time fee/pet. Designated rooms, no service, supervision.

Comfort Inn M
(801) 255-4919. **$56-$130.** 8955 S 255 West. I-15, exit 295, just ne, follow signs. Int corridors. **Pets:** Accepted.

Comfort Suites Sandy M
(801) 495-1317. **$74-$150.** 10680 S Auto Mall Dr. I-15, exit 293 eastbound, 0.3 mi e. Int corridors. **Pets:** Medium. $10 daily fee/room. Service with restrictions, supervision.

Residence Inn by Marriott M
(801) 561-5005. **$159-$309.** 270 W 10000 S. From State St, 0.3 mi w. Int corridors. **Pets:** Medium, other species. $100 one-time fee/room. Designated rooms, service with restrictions, crate.

Sleep Inn M
(801) 572-2020. **$55-$99.** 10676 S 300 W. I-15, exit 293 westbound, just w. Int corridors. **Pets:** Other species. $5 daily fee/pet. Service with restrictions.

Super 8 Motel South Jordan/Sandy M
(801) 553-8888. **$60-$80, 16 day notice.** 10722 S 300 W. I-15, exit 293 westbound, just w. Int corridors. **Pets:** Accepted.

SOUTH SALT LAKE

Days Inn-Central M
(801) 486-8780. **$59-$129.** 315 W 3300 S. I-15, exit 303, just e. Ext corridors. **Pets:** Accepted.

Ramada Limited Salt Lake City M
(801) 486-2400. **$74-$99.** 2455 S State St. Cross street Morris Ave. Int corridors. **Pets:** Accepted.

TAYLORSVILLE

Homestead Studio Suites Hotel-Salt Lake City/Mid Valley M
(801) 269-9292. **$54-$69.** 5683 S Redwood Rd. I-215, exit 13, 0.5 mi n. Ext corridors. **Pets:** Accepted.

WEST VALLEY CITY

🔺 ▽🔷▽ Baymont Inn & Suites Salt Lake City-West Valley City SH
(801) 886-1300. **$82-$120.** 2229 W City Center Ct. I-215, exit 18, just e. Int corridors. **Pets:** Medium. Service with restrictions.

(SAVE) (X) (🐾) (🖍) (🛏) (💻) (🏊)

🔺 ▽🔷▽ Country Inn & Suites By Carlson M
(801) 908-0311. **$59-$125.** 3422 S Decker Lake Dr. I-215, exit 18, 0.3 mi e. Int corridors. **Pets:** Medium. $20 deposit/room. Designated rooms, service with restrictions, crate.

(SAVE) (S⬤) (X) (🐾) (🖍) (🛏) (💻) (🏊)

▽🔷▽ La Quinta Inn West Valley City (Salt Lake-West) SH
(801) 954-9292. **$54-$94.** 3540 S 2200 W. I-215, exit 18; east side. Int corridors. **Pets:** Small, other species. Service with restrictions, supervision.

(ASK) (S⬤) (X) (🐾) (🖍) (🛏) (💻) (🏊)

▽🔷▽ Sleep Inn M ❀
(801) 975-1888. **$65-$100.** 3440 S 2200 W. I-215, exit 18, just e. Int corridors. **Pets:** Medium, other species. Service with restrictions, supervision.

(ASK) (S⬤) (X) (🐾) (🖍) (🛏) (💻) (🏊)

WOODS CROSS

🔺 ▽🔷▽ Hampton Inn M
(801) 296-1211. **$99-$189.** 2393 S 800 W. I-15, exit 315, just w of freeway. Int corridors. **Pets:** Medium, other species. $100 deposit/room. Service with restrictions, supervision.

(SAVE) (S⬤) (X) (🐾) (🖍) (🛏) (💻) (🏊)

▽🔷▽ Motel 6 #1205 M
(801) 298-0289. **$41-$55.** 2433 S 800 W. I-15, exit 315 westbound, just w. Ext corridors. **Pets:** Accepted.

(S⬤) (X) (🖍) (🛏) (🏊)

END METROPOLITAN AREA

SCIPIO

▽▽ Super 8 M
(435) 758-9188. **$59-$99.** 230 W 400 N. I-15, exit 188, just ne. Int corridors. **Pets:** Accepted.

(ASK) (S⬤) (X) (🖍) (🛏) (💻) (🏊)

SPANISH FORK

🔺 ▽🔷▽ Western Inn M
(801) 798-9400. **$50-$70.** 632 Kirby Ln. I-15, exit 258 southbound, 0.5 mi e; exit 257 northbound, 1 mi ne. Int corridors. **Pets:** Dogs only. $12 one-time fee/room. Service with restrictions, supervision.

(SAVE) (S⬤) (X) (🛏)

SPRINGDALE

🔺 ▽🔷▽ Best Western Zion Park Inn M
(435) 772-3200. **$70-$119.** 1215 Zion Park Blvd. 2 mi s of park entrance. Int corridors. **Pets:** Medium. $25 one-time fee/room. Designated rooms, service with restrictions, supervision.

(SAVE) (S⬤) (X) (🐾) (🖍) (🛏) (💻) (🍴) (🏊) (X)

▽🔷▽ Canyon Ranch Motel M ❀
(435) 772-3357. **$49-$99.** 668 Zion Park Blvd. SR 9, just s of south gate to Zion National Park. Ext corridors. **Pets:** Medium, dogs only. $10 one-time fee/pet. Service with restrictions, supervision.

(X) (🛏) (🏊)

SPRINGVILLE

🔺 ▽🔷▽ Best Western Mountain View Inn M
(801) 489-3641. **$64-$99.** 1455 N 1750 W. I-15, exit 261, just e; just s of Provo. Int corridors. **Pets:** Accepted.

(SAVE) (S⬤) (X) (🐾) (🖍) (🛏) (💻) (🏊)

TORREY

🔺 ▽🔷▽ Best Western Capitol Reef Resort SH
(435) 425-3761. **$59-$99.** 2600 E Hwy 24. On SR 24, 2 mi e of jct SR 12 and 24, 1 mi w of Capitol Reef National Park. Ext corridors. **Pets:** Medium. Designated rooms, service with restrictions, supervision.

(SAVE) (S⬤) (X) (🖍) (🛏) (💻) (🍴) (🏊) (X)

▽▽ Cactus Hill Ranch Motel M
(435) 425-3578. **$48, 3 day notice.** 830 S 1000 E. 5 mi s of SR 24 at Teasdale; 5 mi w of SR 12, exit Teasdale; 13 mi w of Capitol Reef National Park, 2 mi se of town center. Ext corridors. **Pets:** Accepted.

(X) (🛏) (💻)

▽🔷▽ Comfort Inn at Capitol Reef/Torrey SH
(435) 425-3866. **$49-$109.** 2424 E Hwy 24. On SR 24, 1.5 mi e of jct SR 12 and 24, 1.5 mi w of Capitol Rd. Ext corridors. **Pets:** Accepted.

(ASK) (S⬤) (X) (🖍) (🛏)

▽▽ Rim Rock Inn M
(435) 425-3398. **$49-$79.** 2523 E Hwy 24. 2.5 mi e of jct SR 12 and 24; east end of town. Ext corridors. **Pets:** Accepted.

(ASK) (S⬤) (X) (🖍) (🛏) (🍴)

▽▽ Torrey/Capitol Reef-Econo Lodge M
(435) 425-3688. **$42-$85.** 600 E Hwy 24. On SR 24, 0.3 mi w of SR 12; 3.3 mi w of Capitol Reef National Park. Int corridors. **Pets:** Accepted.

(ASK) (S⬤) (X) (🖍) (🛏) (🏊)

🔺 ▽🔷▽ Torrey Days Inn M
(435) 425-3111. **$80-$130.** 675 E Hwy 24. Jct SR 12 and 24. Int corridors. **Pets:** Medium, other species. $50 deposit/room, $10 one-time fee/room. Designated rooms, service with restrictions, supervision.

(SAVE) (S⬤) (X) (🛏) (💻) (🏊)

🔺 ▽🔷▽ Wonderland Inn SH
(435) 425-3775. **$54-$74.** 875 E Hwy 24. Jct SR 12 and 24; 3 mi w of Capitol Reef National Park. Ext corridors. **Pets:** Accepted.

(SAVE) (X) (🛏) (🍴) (🏊)

TREMONTON

🔺 ▽ Sandman Motel M
(435) 257-7149. **$47-$50.** 585 W Main St. I-15/84 N, exit 376, 2.1 mi ne to 4-way stop, then 1.5 mi w; I-15 S, exit 381, 0.6 mi e to 4-way stop, s to Main St, then 0.5 mi e; I-84, exit 40, 1.5 mi e. Ext corridors. **Pets:** Other species. Designated rooms, supervision.

(SAVE) (X)

TROPIC

🔺 ▽ ▽ Americas Best Value Inn & Suites-Bryce Valley Inn SH
(435) 679-8811. **$50-$80.** 199 N Main St. SR 12, 10 mi e of Bryce Canyon Park. Ext/int corridors. **Pets:** Medium. $20 daily fee/pet. Designated rooms, service with restrictions.

(SAVE) (S⬤) (X) (🛏) (💻) (🍴)

▽ Bryce Pioneer Village M
(435) 679-8546. **$55-$85.** 80 S Main St. South end of town. Ext corridors. **Pets:** Accepted.

(ASK) (S⬤) (X)

VERNAL

◆◆ Econo Lodge M
(435) 789-2000. **$55-$100.** 311 E Main St. On US 40. Ext corridors.
Pets: Other species. $10 daily fee/pet. Service with restrictions, crate.
⊠ ⛍ 🛏 💻

◆◆ Rodeway Inn M
(435) 789-8172. **$75-$95.** 590 W Main St. US 40. Ext corridors.
Pets: Accepted.
ASK ⊠ 🛏 💻

◆ Sage Motel & Restaurant M
(435) 789-1442. **$55-$75.** 54 W Main St. Center. Ext corridors.
Pets: Other species. $5 one-time fee/pet. Designated rooms, service with
restrictions, supervision.
⊠ 🛏 🍽

WELLINGTON

AAA ◆◆ National 9 Inn M
(435) 637-7980. **$44-$62.** 50 S 700. On US 6. Ext/int corridors.
Pets: Accepted.
SAVE S⛘ ⊠ 🛏 🍽 🌊

WENDOVER

◆◆◆ Econo Lodge M
(435) 665-2226. **$59-$150.** 245 E Wendover Blvd. I-80, exit 2. Ext/int
corridors. **Pets:** Other species. $5 daily fee/room. Service with restrictions,
supervision.
ASK S⛘ ⊠ 🛏 🌊

◆ Western Ridge Motel M
(435) 665-2211. **$29-$49, 7 day notice.** 895 E Wendover Blvd. I-80,
exit 2. Ext corridors. **Pets:** Small. $10 daily fee/pet. Designated rooms,
service with restrictions, supervision.
ASK S⛘ ⊠ 🛏 🌊

VERMONT

ALBURG

▼▼ Ransom Bay Inn BB
(802) 796-3399. **$95-$105.** 4 Center Bay Rd. 0.5 mi s on US 2, from jct SR 78. Int corridors. **Pets:** Accepted.
⊠ W Z

BARRE

AAA ▼▼ The Hollow Inn & Motel M ❖
(802) 479-9313. **$70-$149.** 278 S Main St. Jct US 302, 1 mi s on SR 14; I-89, exit 6, 4.3 mi e on SR 63, then 0.7 mi n on SR 14. Ext/int corridors. **Pets:** Small. $10 daily fee/pet, $10 one-time fee/pet. Service with restrictions, supervision.
SAVE Sc ⊠ 🖥 💻 🌊 🗶

BENNINGTON

AAA ▼▼ Americas Best Value Inn M
(802) 442-2322. **$59-$129, 3 day notice.** 357 US 7 S. Jct SR 9 and US 7, 1.2 mi s. Ext corridors. **Pets:** Dogs only. $10 daily fee/pet. Service with restrictions, supervision.
SAVE Sc ⊠ 🖥 🌊

AAA ▼▼ Bennington Motor Inn M
(802) 442-5479. **$59-$130, 3 day notice.** 143 W Main St. Jct US 7, 0.4 mi w on SR 9. Ext corridors. **Pets:** Accepted.
SAVE Sc ⊠ 🖥 💻

AAA ▼▼ Fife 'N Drum Motel M ❖
. **$49-$129, 3 day notice.** 693 US Rt 7 S. Jct SR 9 and US 7, 1.6 mi s. Ext corridors. **Pets:** Large, other species. $9 daily fee/pet. Designated rooms, service with restrictions, supervision.
SAVE Sc ⊠ 🖥 💻 🌊 🗶

AAA ▼ Harwood Hill Motel M
(802) 442-6278. **$53-$85, 3 day notice.** 864 Harwood Hill Rd (Historic Rt 7A). Jct SR 9, 1.2 mi n on US 7, then 1.7 mi n. Ext corridors. **Pets:** Medium, dogs only. $8 daily fee/pet. Service with restrictions, crate.
SAVE Sc ⊠ 🖥 💻

▼ Knotty Pine Motel M
(802) 442-5487. **$56-$91.** 130 Northside Dr (SR 7A). Jct SR 9, 1.2 mi n on US 7, then just n on Historic SR 7A. Ext corridors. **Pets:** Other species. Service with restrictions, supervision.
⊠ 🖥 💻 🌊

BOLTON VALLEY

AAA ▼▼▼ Black Bear Inn CI ❖
(802) 434-2126. **$114-$340, 21 day notice.** 4010 Bolton Access Rd. I-89, exit 10 northbound, 6.2 mi w on US 2, then 4 mi n; exit 11 southbound, 8.4 mi e on US 2, then 4 mi n. Ext/int corridors. **Pets:** $20 daily fee/room. Designated rooms, service with restrictions.
SAVE ⊠ 🖥 💻 🍴 🌊

BRANDON

AAA ▼▼▼ Brandon Motor Lodge M
(802) 247-9594. **$65-$125.** 2095 Franklin St. 2 mi s on US 7. Ext corridors. **Pets:** Medium, dogs only. $5 daily fee/pet. Designated rooms, service with restrictions, supervision.
SAVE ⊠ 🖥 🌊 🗶

▼▼▼ The Lilac Inn CI ❖
(802) 247-5463. **$120-$295, 30 day notice.** 53 Park St. Just e on SR 73. Int corridors. **Pets:** Dogs only. $30 one-time fee/room. Service with restrictions, supervision.
ASK ⊠ 🍴 Z

AAA ▼▼▼ Maple Grove Dining Room & Cottages CA
(802) 247-6644. **$79-$139, 7 day notice.** 1246 Franklin St. Jct SR 73 and US 7, 1.2 mi s on US 7. Ext corridors. **Pets:** Accepted.
SAVE ⊠ 🖥 💻 🍴 🌊 🗶 Z

BRATTLEBORO

▼▼ Colonial Motel & Spa SH ❖
(802) 257-7733. **$79-$180.** 889 Putney Rd. I-91, exit 3, just e on SR 9, then 0.5 mi s on US 5. Ext corridors. **Pets:** Dogs only. $10 daily fee/room. Service with restrictions, supervision.
ASK Sc ⊠ 🖥 💻 🍴 🌊 🗶

AAA ▼▼ Econo Lodge M
(802) 254-2360. **$39-$139.** 515 Canal St. I-91, exit 1, 0.3 mi n on US 5. Ext/int corridors. **Pets:** Small, dogs only. $10 daily fee/pet. Designated rooms, service with restrictions, supervision.
SAVE Sc ⊠ 🖥 💻 🌊

AAA ▼▼▼ Super 8 Motel M
(802) 254-8889. **$50-$160.** 1043 Putney Rd. I-91, exit 3, just e on SR 9, then just s on US 5. Int corridors. **Pets:** Other species. $20 one-time fee/room. Service with restrictions, supervision.
SAVE Sc ⊠ 🖥 🖥

CAVENDISH

AAA ▼▼▼ Clarion Hotel at Cavendish Pointe SH
(802) 226-7688. **$69-$299, 14 day notice.** 2940 SR 103. On SR 103, just n of jct SR 131. Int corridors. **Pets:** Large, other species. $20 daily fee/pet. Designated rooms, service with restrictions, supervision.
SAVE Sc ⊠ 🖥 💻 🍴 🌊

COLCHESTER

▼▼ Days Inn SH
(802) 655-0900. **$54-$179.** 124 College Pkwy. I-89, exit 15 northbound, just e on SR 15; exit 16 southbound, 1.1 mi s on US 7, then 1 mi e on SR 15. Int corridors. **Pets:** Dogs only. $10 daily fee/pet. Designated rooms, service with restrictions, crate.
ASK Sc ⊠ 🖥 🖥 🌊

▼▼▼▼ Hampton Inn & Conference Center SH
(802) 655-6177. **$119-$209.** 42 Lower Mountain View Dr. I-89, exit 16, just n on US 7. Int corridors. **Pets:** Accepted.
ASK Sc ⊠ 🖥 📶 🖥 🖥 💻 🌊

▼▼ Motel 6 #1407 SH
(802) 654-6860. **$45-$67.** 74 S Park Dr. I-89, exit 16, just s on US 7. Int corridors. **Pets:** Medium, other species. Service with restrictions, supervision.
Sc ⊠ 🖥 🌊

EAST ST. JOHNSBURY

▼▼ ▼▼ Echo Ledge Farm Inn BB
(802) 748-4750. Call for rates. 87 US Rt 2. I-93, exit 1, 0.5 mi n, then 2.2 mi e. Pets: Accepted.
⊠ ☎

ESSEX JUNCTION

▼▼▼▼ Handy Suites SH
(802) 872-5200. $74-$199. 27 Susie Wilson Rd. I-89, exit 15 northbound, 2 mi e, then just n. Int corridors. Pets: Dogs only. $50 deposit/pet. Designated rooms.
ASK S⊠ ⊠ &M 🖥 💻 🏊

▲▲▲ ▼▼▼▼ The Inn at Essex SH ❀
(802) 878-1100. $149-$329, 7 day notice. 70 Essex Way. SR 289, exit 10, 0.3 mi s. Int corridors. Pets: Other species. $150 deposit/room, $25 daily fee/pet. Service with restrictions, crate.
SAVE S⊠ ⊠ &M & 🖥 💻 ❚❚ 🏊 ⊠

FAIRLEE

▲▲▲ ▼▼ ▼ Silver Maple Lodge & Cottages BB
(802) 333-4326. $69-$89, 14 day notice. 520 US 5 S. I-91, exit 15, 0.5 mi s. Ext/int corridors. Pets: Other species. Designated rooms.
SAVE S⊠ ⊠ 🖥 💻 ☎

FLETCHER

▼▼▼▼ The Inn at Buck Hollow Farm BB ❀
(802) 849-2400. $78-$105, 14 day notice. 2150 Buck Hollow Rd. 6.4 mi n of jct SR 104 via Buck Hollow Rd. Int corridors. Pets: $15 one-time fee/pet. Supervision.
ASK ⊠ 🏊 ⊠ ☎

JAMAICA

▲▲▲ ▼▼▼▼ Three Mountain Inn CI
(802) 874-4140. $145-$390, 14 day notice. 3732 Main St. On SR 30; center. Ext/int corridors. Pets: Accepted.
SAVE ⊠ ❚❚ 🏊 ⊠

JEFFERSONVILLE

▼ Deer Run Motor Inn M
(802) 644-8866. $85, 15 day notice. 80 Deer Run Loop. 0.7 mi e on SR 15. Ext/int corridors. Pets: Small, dogs only. $10 daily fee/pet. Service with restrictions, supervision.
⊠ 🖥 💻 🏊

KILLINGTON

▲▲▲ ▼▼ ▼ Butternut on the Mountain SH
(802) 422-2000. $62-$207, 30 day notice. 63 Weathervane Rd. Jct SR 100/US 4, 1.1 mi s on Killington Rd, then just e. Ext/int corridors. Pets: Accepted.
SAVE S⊠ ⊠ 🖥 💻 🏊

▲▲▲ ▼▼▼▼ The Cascades Lodge SH
(802) 422-3731. $84-$219, 21 day notice. 58 Old Mill Rd. 3.6 mi s on Killington Rd, from jct SR 100/US 4, then just e. Int corridors. Pets: $50 daily fee/pet. Designated rooms, service with restrictions, supervision.
SAVE ⊠ ♫ 🖥 💻 ❚❚ 🏊 ⊠

▲▲▲ ▼▼ Val Roc Motel M
(802) 422-3881. $65-$150, 14 day notice. 8006 US 4. 5.9 mi e on US 4, from jct SR 100 N. Ext/int corridors. Pets: Other species. $5 daily fee/pet. Service with restrictions.
SAVE S⊠ ⊠ 🖥 💻 🏊 ⊠

LUDLOW

▲▲▲ ▼▼▼ All Seasons Motel SH
(802) 228-8100. $80-$140, 7 day notice. 112 Main St. On SR 103; center. Ext/int corridors. Pets: Small. $25 daily fee/pet. Service with restrictions, supervision.
SAVE S⊠ ⊠ 🖥 💻 🏊

▲▲▲ ▼▼▼▼ The Andrie Rose Inn BB ❀
(802) 228-4846. $110-$350, 20 day notice. 13 Pleasant St. Corner of Depot St; center. Int corridors. Pets: $25 daily fee/pet. Designated rooms, service with restrictions, crate.
SAVE ⊠ 🖥 💻 ❚❚ ☎

▲▲▲ ▼▼▼▼ Best Western Ludlow Colonial Motel SH
(802) 228-8188. $100-$200, 14 day notice. 93 Main St. On SR 103; center. Ext/int corridors. Pets: Accepted.
SAVE S⊠ ⊠ 🖥 💻 🏊

▲▲▲ ▼▼▼▼ Timber Inn Motel M
(802) 228-8666. $69-$169, 14 day notice. 112 Rt 103 S. On SR 103 S, 1 mi e. Ext corridors. Pets: Medium, dogs only. $15 daily fee/pet. Designated rooms, service with restrictions, crate.
SAVE S⊠ ⊠ 🖥 💻 🏊 ⊠

MANCHESTER VILLAGE

▼▼▼▼ The Village Country Inn CI
(802) 362-1792. $129-$345, 7 day notice. 3835 Main St. On Historic SR 7A, 1 mi s of jct SR 11/30. Ext/int corridors. Pets: Small, dogs only. $40 one-time fee/pet. Designated rooms, service with restrictions, supervision.
ASK S⊠ ⊠ 🖥 💻 🏊

MENDON

▼▼▼ Cortina Inn and Resort SH ❀
(802) 773-3333. $129-$289. 103 US Rt 4. Jct SR 100 N, 3 mi w. Int corridors. Pets: Other species. $10 daily fee/pet. Designated rooms, service with restrictions, supervision.
ASK S⊠ ⊠ & 🖥 💻 ❚❚ 🏊 ⊠

▲▲▲ ▼▼▼▼ Econo Lodge-Killington Area SH
(802) 773-6644. $65-$145, 14 day notice. 51 US 4. Jct US 7, 5.3 mi e. Int corridors. Pets: Accepted.
SAVE S⊠ ⊠ 🖥 💻 🏊

▼▼▼ Mendon Mountainview Lodge SH
(802) 773-4311. $55-$249, 7 day notice. 78 US 4. On US 4, 6 mi e of jct US 7. Int corridors. Pets: Medium, dogs only. $12 daily fee/room. Designated rooms, service with restrictions.
ASK S⊠ ⊠ 🖥 💻 🏊 ⊠

MIDDLEBURY

▲▲▲ ▼▼▼▼ The Middlebury Inn SH
(802) 388-4961. $108-$395, 3 day notice. 14 Court Square. On US 7; center. Ext/int corridors. Pets: Accepted.
SAVE ⊠ ♫ & 🖥 💻 ❚❚

▲▲▲ ▼▼▼▼ Swift House Inn CI ❀
(802) 388-9925. $120-$285, 14 day notice. 25 Stewart Ln. 0.3 mi n on US 7 from jct SR 125 W. Ext/int corridors. Pets: Medium, dogs only. $50 daily fee/room. Designated rooms, service with restrictions, supervision.
SAVE S⊠ ⊠ 💻 ❚❚ ⊠

NORTH HERO

▲▲▲ ▼▼▼ Shore Acres Inn SH
(802) 372-8722. $99-$199, 14 day notice. 237 Shore Acres Dr. 0.5 mi s on US 2. Ext/int corridors. Pets: Dogs only. $15 daily fee/pet. Supervision.
SAVE ⊠ 🖥 ❚❚ ⊠ ☎

PUTNEY

▼▼ **The Putney Inn** 🆂🅷
(802) 387-5517. **$88-$178.** 57 Putney Landing Rd. I-91, exit 4, just e.
Ext corridors. **Pets:** $10 daily fee/pet. Service with restrictions, supervision.
⊠ 💻 🍴

RUTLAND

🅐🅐🅐 ▼▼▼ **Comfort Inn at Trolley Square** 🆂🅷
(802) 775-2200. **$100-$230.** 19 Allen St. On US 7, 1 mi s from jct US 4
w; 1.5 mi n from US 4 e. Int corridors. **Pets:** Accepted.
[SAVE] 💲🔟 ⊠ 🔥M 🖊 🖥 🖥 💻 ⬗

🅐🅐🅐 ▼▼▼ **Holiday Inn Rutland/Killington** 🅻🅷
(802) 775-1911. **$145-$270.** 476 US Rt 7 S. 2.4 mi s on US 7, from US
4 W; 0.4 mi n, US 7 from US 4 E. Int corridors. **Pets:** Other species.
$20 daily fee/pet. Supervision.
[SAVE] 💲🔟 ⊠ 🔥M 🖊 🖥 💻 🍴 ⬗ ⊠

🅐🅐🅐 ▼▼ **Ramada Limited of Rutland** 🆂🅷
(802) 773-3361. **$69-$99.** 253 S Main St, US 7. 1.3 mi s on US 7, from
US 4 W; 1.5 mi n on US 7, from US 4 E. Int corridors. **Pets:** Accepted.
[SAVE] 💲🔟 ⊠ 🖥 💻 ⬗

🅐🅐🅐 ▼▼ **Red Roof Inn Rutland-Killington** 🆂🅷
(802) 775-4303. **$69-$139.** 401 US Hwy 7 S. On US 7/4. Int corridors.
Pets: Other species. Service with restrictions, supervision.
[SAVE] 💲🔟 ⊠ 🖊 🖥 💻 ⬗ ⊠

🅐🅐🅐 ▼ **Rodeway Inn** 🅼
(802) 775-2575. **$54-$179, 5 day notice.** 138 N Main St. 0.5 mi n of jct
US 4 E. Ext corridors. **Pets:** Small, dogs only. $10 daily fee/pet. Desig-
nated rooms, service with restrictions, supervision.
[SAVE] 💲🔟 ⊠ 🖥 💻

🅐🅐🅐 ▼ **Rodeway Inn** 🅼
(802) 773-9176. **$42-$159, 5 day notice.** 115 Woodstock Ave. Jct US
7, 0.5 mi e on US 4. Ext/int corridors. **Pets:** Small, dogs only. $10 daily
fee/pet. Designated rooms, service with restrictions, supervision.
[SAVE] 💲🔟 ⊠ 🖥 ⬗

ST. ALBANS

▼▼▼ **Comfort Inn & Suites** 🆂🅷
(802) 524-3300. **$89-$215.** 813 Fairfax Rd. I-89, exit 19, just w, then
just s on SR 104. Int corridors. **Pets:** Medium. Designated rooms, service
with restrictions, crate.
[ASK] 💲🔟 ⊠ 🔥M 🖊 🖥 💻 ⬗

🅐🅐🅐 ▼▼ **Econo Lodge** 🅼
(802) 524-5956. **$59-$109.** 287 S Main St. I-89, exit 19, 1 mi w to US
7, then 0.5 mi s. Ext/int corridors. **Pets:** Accepted.
[SAVE] 💲🔟 ⊠ 🖥 💻

ST. JOHNSBURY

🅐🅐🅐 ▼▼▼ **Fairbanks Inn** 🅼 ❄️
(802) 748-5666. **$89-$149.** 401 Western Ave. I-91, exit 21, 1 mi e on
US 2. Ext corridors. **Pets:** Dogs only. $5 daily fee/pet. Service with restric-
tions.
[SAVE] 💲🔟 ⊠ 🖥 💻 ⬗

SHAFTSBURY

▼ **Governor's Rock Motel** 🅼
(802) 442-4734. **$59-$95, 7 day notice.** 4325 Rt 7A. 3.3 mi n on
Historic SR 7A, from jct SR 67. Ext corridors. **Pets:** $5 daily fee/pet.
Supervision.
⊠ 🖥

▼▼ **Hillbrook Motel** 🅼
(802) 447-7201. **Call for rates.** 2629 Rt 7A. SR 7, exit 2, 2 mi n on SR
7A. Ext corridors. **Pets:** Medium, dogs only. $5 daily fee/pet. Service with
restrictions, supervision.
⊠ 🖥 💻 ⬗

▼▼ **Serenity Motel** 🅲🅰
(802) 442-6490. **$60-$80.** 4379 Rt 7A. 3.3 mi n on Historic SR 7A, from
jct SR 67. Ext corridors. **Pets:** Other species. Designated rooms, service
with restrictions, supervision.
⊠ 🖥 💻

SOUTH BURLINGTON

▼▼ **Best Western Windjammer Inn & Conference**
Center 🆂🅷 ❄️
(802) 863-1125. **$89-$169.** 1076 Williston Rd. I-89, exit 14E, 0.3 mi e
on US 2. Int corridors. **Pets:** $5 daily fee/pet. Designated rooms, service
with restrictions, supervision.
[ASK] 💲🔟 ⊠ 🔥M 🖊 🖊 🖥 💻 🍴 ⬗ ⊠

▼▼▼ **Comfort Inn & Suites** 🆂🅷 🐾
(802) 865-3400. **$69-$189.** 1285 Williston Rd. I-89, exit 14E, 0.5 mi e
on US 2. Int corridors. **Pets:** Other species. $10 daily fee/pet. Service with
restrictions.
[ASK] 💲🔟 ⊠ 🔥M 🖊 🖥 💻 ⬗

🅐🅐🅐 ▼▼▼ **DoubleTree Hotel Burlington** 🆂🅷
(802) 658-0250. **$109-$239.** 1117 Williston Rd. I-89, exit 14E, just e on
US 2. Int corridors. **Pets:** Other species. Designated rooms, service with
restrictions, supervision.
[SAVE] 💲🔟 ⊠ 🔥M 🖊 🖊 🖥 💻 🍴 ⬗

🅐🅐🅐 ▼▼▼ **Hawthorn Suites Hotel** 🆂🅷 🐾
(802) 860-1212. **$129-$199, 3 day notice.** 401 Dorset St. I-89, exit
14E, just e on US 2, then 0.8 mi s. Int corridors. **Pets:** Other species.
$10 daily fee/pet. Designated rooms, service with restrictions, crate.
[SAVE] ⊠ 🔥M 🖊 🖥 💻 ⬗

🅐🅐🅐 ▼▼▼ **Holiday Inn Burlington** 🅻🅷
(802) 863-6363. **$79-$205.** 1068 Williston Rd. I-89, exit 14E, just e on
US 2. Int corridors. **Pets:** Accepted.
[SAVE] 💲🔟 ⊠ 🔥M 🖊 🖥 💻 🍴 ⬗

🅐🅐🅐 ▼▼▼ **MainStay Suites** 🆂🅷
(802) 846-1986. **$99-$189.** 1702 Shelburne Rd. I-89, exit 13 to US 7,
then 1.5 mi s. Int corridors. **Pets:** Cats only. $25 one-time fee/room.
[SAVE] 💲🔟 ⊠ 🖥 💻

🅐🅐🅐 ▼▼▼ **Sheraton Burlington Hotel & Conference**
Center 🅻🅷
(802) 865-6600. **$109-$269.** 870 Williston Rd. I-89, exit 14W, just w on
US 2. Int corridors. **Pets:** Accepted.
[SAVE] 💲🔟 ⊠ 🖊 🖥 💻 🍴 ⬗

🅐🅐🅐 ▼▼▼ **Smart Suites** 🆂🅷
(802) 860-9900. **$99-$189.** 1700 Shelburne Rd. I-89, exit 13 to US 7,
then 1.5 mi s. Int corridors. **Pets:** Small. $50 one-time fee/room. Desig-
nated rooms, service with restrictions.
[SAVE] 💲🔟 ⊠ 🖥 💻

SOUTH WOODSTOCK

🅐🅐🅐 ▼▼▼ **Kedron Valley Inn** 🅲🅸
(802) 457-1473. **$111-$329, 14 day notice.** Rt 106. Jct US 4, 5 mi s.
Ext/int corridors. **Pets:** Accepted.
[SAVE] ⊠ 🖥 💻 🍴 ⊠ ⬗

SPRINGFIELD

▼▼▼ **The Hartness House** 🅲🅸
(802) 885-2115. **$99-$119, 7 day notice.** 30 Orchard St. 0.4 mi n on
Summer St, bear left at old cemetery. Int corridors. **Pets:** Accepted.
[ASK] ⊠ 🖥 🍴 ⬗ ⊠

▼▼▼ **Holiday Inn Express** 🆂🅷
(802) 885-4516. **$95-$164.** 818 Charlestown Rd. I-91, exit 7. Int corridors. **Pets:** Accepted.
[ASK] 💲🔟 ⊠ 🔥M 🖊 🖥 💻 ⬗

STOWE

1066 Ye Olde England Inne `CI` ❀
(802) 253-7558. **$99, 15 day notice.** 433 Mountain Rd. 0.4 mi w on SR 108, from jct SR 100. Ext/int corridors. **Pets:** Large, other species. $10 daily fee/pet. Designated rooms, service with restrictions, crate.
`SAVE` `⊗` `⌕` `❸` `⌷` `⊺⌷` `⇝` `⊗`

Commodores Inn `LH`
(802) 253-7131. **$98-$198.** 823 S Main St. Jct SR 108, 0.8 mi s on SR 100. Int corridors. **Pets:** Other species. $10 one-time fee/room.
`SAVE` `S⌀` `⊗` `⌕` `❸` `⌷⌷` `⇝` `⊗`

Edson Hill Manor `CI`
(802) 253-7371. **$99-$219, 15 day notice.** 1500 Edson Hill Rd. Jct SR 100, 3.5 mi w on SR 108, then 1.3 mi n. Ext/int corridors. **Pets:** Designated rooms, service with restrictions, supervision.
`⊗` `⌷⌷` `⇝` `⊗`

Hob Knob Inn & Restaurant `M` ❀
(802) 253-8549. **$99-$180, 14 day notice.** 2364 Mountain Rd. Jct SR 100, 2.5 mi w on SR 108. Ext/int corridors. **Pets:** $20 daily fee/pet. Service with restrictions, crate.
`⊗` `❸` `⌷` `⌷⌷` `⇝`

Honeywood Country Lodge `M`
(802) 253-4124. **$79-$179, 15 day notice.** 4527 Mountain Rd. Jct SR 100, 4.5 mi w on SR 108. Ext corridors. **Pets:** Accepted.
`SAVE` `S⌀` `⊗` `❸` `⌷` `⇝` `⊗`

Innsbruck Inn at Stowe `M`
(802) 253-8582. **$79-$184, 15 day notice.** 4361 Mountain Rd. 4.5 mi w on SR 108, from jct SR 100. Ext/int corridors. **Pets:** Medium. $10 daily fee/pet. Designated rooms, service with restrictions, supervision.
`SAVE` `S⌀` `⊗` `❸` `⌷` `⇝` `⊗`

The Mountain Road Resort at Stowe `M`
(802) 253-4566. **$120-$310, 15 day notice.** 1007 Mountain Rd. 1 mi w on SR 108, from jct SR 100. Ext corridors. **Pets:** Accepted.
`SAVE` `S⌀` `⊗` `❸` `⌷` `⇝` `⊗`

Ten Acres Lodge `CI`
(802) 253-7638. **$99-$399, 21 day notice.** 14 Barrows Rd. Jct SR 100, 2.1 mi w on SR 108, then 0.5 mi s on Luce Hill Rd. Ext/int corridors. **Pets:** Accepted.
`SAVE` `S⌀` `⊗` `⇝` `⊗`

Topnotch Resort and Spa `LH`
(802) 253-8585. **$325-$1600, 14 day notice.** 4000 Mountain Rd. 4.2 mi w on SR 108, from jct SR 100. Ext/int corridors. **Pets:** Accepted.
`SAVE` `S⌀` `⊗` `❸` `⌷` `⌷⌷` `⇝` `⊗`

SUNDERLAND

Arcady at the Sunderland `M`
(802) 362-1176. **$70-$140.** 6249 Rt 7A. On Historic SR 7A, 6.3 mi s of jct SR 11. Ext corridors. **Pets:** $15 daily fee/pet. Designated rooms, service with restrictions, supervision.
`S⌀` `⊗` `❸` `⌷` `⇝` `⊗`

WARREN

PowderHound Inn & Condominiums `CO`
(802) 496-5100. **$89-$159, 14 day notice.** 203 Powderhound Rd. On SR 100, 0.3 mi s of jct Sugarbush Access Rd. Ext corridors. **Pets:** Dogs only. $10 daily fee/pet. Service with restrictions.
`SAVE` `⊗` `❸` `⌷` `⇝` `⋇`

WEST BRATTLEBORO

Molly Stark Motel `M`
(802) 254-2440. **$45-$85.** 829 Marlboro Rd. I-91, exit 2, 3.3 mi w on SR 9. Ext corridors. **Pets:** Large, dogs only. $8 daily fee/pet. Supervision.
`⊗` `❸` `⌷`

WEST DOVER

The Gray Ghost Inn `SH`
(802) 464-2474. **$85-$156, 14 day notice.** 290 Rt 100 N. 7.8 mi n on SR 100, from jct SR 9. Int corridors. **Pets:** Designated rooms, service with restrictions, supervision.
`⊗` `⌷⌷` `⇝` `⋇` `⊠`

Red Oak Inn `CI` ❀
(802) 464-8817. **$85-$149, 7 day notice.** 45 Rt 100. 5 mi n. Int corridors. **Pets:** Dogs only. $30 one-time fee/room. Service with restrictions, crate.
`ASK` `S⌀` `⊗` `❸` `⌷` `⇝` `⊗`

WESTMORE

WilloughVale Inn on Lake Willoughby `CI`
(802) 525-4123. **$89-$189, 14 day notice.** 793 VT Rt 5A. Just s on SR 5A, from jct SR 16. Ext/int corridors. **Pets:** Accepted.
`SAVE` `⊗` `❸` `⌷` `⌷⌷` `⊗`

WHITE RIVER JUNCTION

Comfort Inn `SH`
(802) 295-3051. **$99-$219, 7 day notice.** 56 Ralph Lehman Dr. I-91, exit 11, just e. Int corridors. **Pets:** Service with restrictions, supervision.
`ASK` `S⌀` `⊗` `⌕M` `❸` `⌷`

Econo Lodge `SH`
(802) 295-3015. **$69-$159.** 91 Ballardvale Dr. I-91, exit 11, just s on US 5. Int corridors. **Pets:** Accepted.
`SAVE` `S⌀` `⊗` `❸` `⌷` `⇝` `⊗`

WILLISTON

Residence Inn by Marriott `SH`
(802) 878-2001. **$129-$399.** 35 Hurricane Ln. I-89, exit 12, just s on SR 2A, then just e. Ext corridors. **Pets:** Accepted.
`ASK` `S⌀` `⊗` `❸` `⌷` `⇝` `⊗`

TownePlace Suites by Marriott `SH`
(802) 872-5900. **$129-$189.** 66 Zephyr Rd. I-89, exit 12, 1.1 mi n on SR 2A. Int corridors. **Pets:** Accepted.
`ASK` `S⌀` `⊗` `⌕M` `⌕` `❸` `⌷` `⇝`

WILMINGTON

Nordic Hills Lodge `SH` ❀
(802) 464-5130. **$82-$160.** 34 Look Rd. 2.5 mi n on SR 100, from jct SR 9, then 0.6 mi w on Colbrook Rd. Int corridors. **Pets:** Other species. $25 one-time fee/pet. Service with restrictions, supervision.
`SAVE` `S⌀` `⊗` `⌷⌷` `⇝` `⊗`

WOODSTOCK

Braeside Motel `M`
(802) 457-1366. **$78-$148, 15 day notice.** 432 US 4 E (Woodstock Rd). 1 mi e. Ext corridors. **Pets:** Accepted.
`SAVE` `⊗` `❸` `⇝`

VIRGINIA

CITY INDEX

ABINGDON

🔺🔺 🔷🔷🔷 Holiday Inn Express 🆂🅷
(276) 676-2829. **$72-$89.** 940 E Main St. I-81, exit 19 (US 11). Int corridors. **Pets:** Large. $10 one-time fee/room. Designated rooms, service with restrictions.
🆂🅰🆅🅴 ⊠ 🆖🅼 📷 🐾 🍴 💷 🏊

🔷🔷🔷 Quality Inn & Suites of Abingdon 🆂🅷
(276) 676-9090. **$80-$99.** 930 E Main St. I-81, exit 19 (US 11), just w. Int corridors. **Pets:** Accepted.
🅰🆂🅺 🆂🅰 ⊠ 🐾 🍴 💷 🏊

🔷 Super 8 Motel of Abingdon Ⓜ
(276) 676-3329. **$55-$190.** 298 Towne Centre Dr. I-81, exit 17, just ne. Int corridors. **Pets:** Accepted.
🅰🆂🅺 🆂🅰 ⊠ 🍴 💷

ALTAVISTA

🔷🔷 Comfort Suites Hotel 🆂🅷
(434) 369-4000. **$79-$146.** 1558 Main St. US 29 business route, at jct US 29. Int corridors. **Pets:** Accepted.
🅰🆂🅺 🆂🅰 ⊠ 🍴 💷 🍴 🏊

BEDFORD

🔺🔺 🔷🔷🔷 Days Inn 🆂🅷
(540) 586-8286. **$45-$73.** 921 Blue Ridge Ave. Jct US 221, 1.5 mi w on US 460. Ext corridors. **Pets:** Other species. $7 daily fee/pet. Service with restrictions.
🆂🅰🆅🅴 🆂🅰 ⊠ 🍴 💷 🏊

BIG STONE GAP

🔺🔺 🔷 Country Inn Motel Ⓜ
(276) 523-0374. **$52.** 627 Gilley Ave. US 23, 1 mi w on US 23 business route and 58A. Ext corridors. **Pets:** Small. $3 daily fee/pet. Service with restrictions, supervision.
🆂🅰🆅🅴 🆂🅰 ⊠ 🍴

BLACKSBURG

🔺🔺 🔷🔷🔷 Comfort Inn 🆂🅷
(540) 951-1500. **$72-$175.** 3705 S Main St. 3.5 mi s on US 460, jct US 460 Bypass. Int corridors. **Pets:** Accepted.
🆂🅰🆅🅴 🆂🅰 ⊠ 🍴 💷 🏊

BRISTOL

🔺🔺 🔷 Econo Lodge Ⓜ
(276) 466-2112. **$69-$375.** 912 Commonwealth Ave. I-81, exit 3, 1.5 mi e. Ext corridors. **Pets:** Small, dogs only. $10 daily fee/pet. Designated rooms, service with restrictions, supervision.
🆂🅰🆅🅴 🆂🅰 ⊠ 📷 🍴 💷

🔺🔺 🔷🔷🔷 Holiday Inn Hotel & Suites 🅻🅷
(276) 466-4100. **$84.** 3005 Linden Dr. I-81, exit 7, just w. Int corridors. **Pets:** Large, other species. $10 daily fee/room. Designated rooms, service with restrictions, supervision.
🆂🅰🆅🅴 🆂🅰 ⊠ 🆖🅼 🗝 🍴 💷 🍴 🏊

🔷 Howard Johnson Inn Ⓜ
(276) 669-7171. **$50-$69.** 2221 Euclid Ave. I-81, exit 1, just e. Ext corridors. **Pets:** Accepted.
🅰🆂🅺 🆂🅰 ⊠ 🍴 💷 🏊

🔷 Knights Inn Ⓜ
(276) 591-5090. **$54-$72.** 2221 Euclid Ave. I-81, exit 1, just e. Ext corridors. **Pets:** Dogs only. $10 daily fee/pet. Service with restrictions, supervision.
🅰🆂🅺 🆂🅰 ⊠ 🍴 💷

🔺🔺 🔷🔷🔷 La Quinta Inn Bristol 🆂🅷
(276) 669-9353. **$84-$111.** 1014 Old Airport Rd. I-81, exit 7, just e. Ext corridors. **Pets:** Medium. Service with restrictions.
🆂🅰🆅🅴 ⊠ 🆖🅼 🗝 🍴 💷 🏊

🔷 Motel 6 #4125 🆂🅷
(276) 466-6060. **$59-$85.** 21561 Clear Creek Rd. I-81, exit 7, 0.3 mi w. Int corridors. **Pets:** Medium, other species. Service with restrictions, supervision.
🆂🅰 ⊠ 🆖🅼 🗝 🍴

🔺🔺 🔷 Super 8 Motel 🆂🅷
(276) 466-8800. **$45-$289, 7 day notice.** 2139 Lee Hwy. I-81, exit 5, just s. Int corridors. **Pets:** Other species. $10 daily fee/room. Designated rooms, service with restrictions, supervision.
🆂🅰🆅🅴 🆂🅰 ⊠ 🍴

BURKEVILLE

🔺🔺 🔷🔷🔷 Comfort Inn Burkeville 🆂🅷
(434) 767-3750. **$80-$135.** 419 N Agnew St. On US 460, just e of jct US 360. Int corridors. **Pets:** Accepted.
🆂🅰🆅🅴 🆂🅰 ⊠ 🗝 🍴 💷 🍴 🏊

CAPE CHARLES

Sunset Beach Resort SH
(757) 331-1776. **$69-$114.** 32246 Lankford Hwy. US 13, just n of the Chesapeake Bay Bridge Tunnel. Ext corridors. **Pets:** Other species. $10 daily fee/pet. Service with restrictions, supervision.

CHARLOTTESVILLE

Comfort Inn SH 🐾
(434) 293-6188. **$75-$129.** 1807 Emmet St. Jct US 250 Bypass, just n on US 29. Int corridors. **Pets:** $10 daily fee/pet. Designated rooms, service with restrictions, supervision.

Days Inn University Area SH 🐾
(434) 293-9111. **$69-$159.** 1600 Emmet St. I-64, exit 118B (US 29), just n of jct US 250 Bypass. Ext corridors. **Pets:** $10 daily fee/pet. Designated rooms, service with restrictions, crate.

DoubleTree Hotel Charlottesville SH
(434) 973-2121. **$84-$299.** 990 Hilton Heights Rd. I-64, exit 118B (US 29), 4 mi n of jct US 250 Bypass. Int corridors. **Pets:** Accepted.

Econo Lodge-University M
(434) 296-2104. **$69-$190.** 400 Emmet St. Jct US 250 Bypass, 1 mi s on US 29 business route. Ext corridors. **Pets:** Small, dogs only. $10 daily fee/pet. Designated rooms, service with restrictions.

Holiday Inn-Monticello/Charlottesville LH
(434) 977-5100. **$90-$190, 14 day notice.** 1200 5th St SW. I-64, exit 120, just n on SR 631. Int corridors. **Pets:** Other species. $15 daily fee/pet. Service with restrictions, supervision.

Omni Charlottesville Hotel LH
(434) 971-5500. **$124-$209.** 235 W Main St. I-64, exit 120, 2.3 mi n on SR 631; downtown. Int corridors. **Pets:** Small, dogs only. $50 one-time fee/room. Service with restrictions, crate.

Quality Inn-University Area SH 🐾
(434) 971-3746. **$69-$159.** 1600 Emmet St. US 29 (Emmet St), just n of jct US 250 Bypass, then just e on Holiday Dr. Ext corridors. **Pets:** $10 daily fee/pet. Designated rooms, service with restrictions, crate.

Red Roof Inn of Charlottesville SH
(434) 295-4333. **$70-$100.** 1309 W Main St. US 29 (Emmet St), 1 mi e on US 250 (University Ave). Int corridors. **Pets:** Medium, other species. Service with restrictions, supervision.

Residence Inn by Marriott SH 🐾
(434) 923-0300. **$149-$189.** 1111 Millmont St. I-64, exit 118B (US 29), 2.5 mi n on US 29/250 E, just s on Barracks Rd, then just se. Int corridors. **Pets:** Large, other species. $75 one-time fee/room. Service with restrictions, supervision.

Sleep Inn & Suites Monticello SH
(434) 244-9969. **$79-$181.** 1185 5th St. I-64, exit 120, just n. Int corridors. **Pets:** Other species. $10 daily fee/pet. Service with restrictions.

Super 8 Motel/Charlottesville SH
(434) 973-0888. **$49-$149.** 390 Greenbrier Dr. US 29 (Emmet St), 1 mi n of US 250 Bypass. Int corridors. **Pets:** Accepted.

CHRISTIANSBURG

Econo Lodge M
(540) 382-6161. **$48-$179.** 2430 Roanoke St. I-81, exit 118, just w on US 11/460. Ext corridors. **Pets:** Accepted.

Quality Inn SH
(540) 382-2055. **$72-$160.** 50 Hampton Blvd. I-81, exit 118C, just e. Ext corridors. **Pets:** Other species. $10 daily fee/room.

Super 8 Motel-Christiansburg West SH
(540) 382-5813. **$57-$62, 14 day notice.** 55 Laurel St NE. I-81, exit 118, 1 mi w on US 11/460, then 3.5 mi nw on US 460 Bypass; jct SR 114. Int corridors. **Pets:** Accepted.

CLARKSVILLE

Best Western On The Lake SH
(434) 374-5023. **$74-$109, 3 day notice.** 103 Second St. Just n of US 58 business route. Int corridors. **Pets:** Other species. $100 deposit/room, $10 daily fee/pet, $20 one-time fee/pet. Designated rooms, service with restrictions.

COLLINSVILLE

Knights Inn M
(276) 647-3716. **$60-$78.** 2357 Virginia Ave. Jct US 58, 3 mi n on US 220 business route. Ext corridors. **Pets:** Dogs only. Designated rooms, no service, supervision.

Quality Inn-Dutch Inn Hotel and Convention Center SH
(276) 647-3721. **$80-$300.** 2360 Virginia Ave. Jct US 58, 3 mi n on US 220 business route. Ext corridors. **Pets:** $10 daily fee/pet. Designated rooms, service with restrictions.

COVINGTON

Americas Best Value Inn M
(540) 962-7600. **Call for rates.** 908 Valley Ridge Rd. I-64, exit 16, just ne. Ext corridors. **Pets:** Other species. $12 one-time fee/room. Service with restrictions.

Best Western Mountain View SH
(540) 962-4951. **$98-$115.** 820 E Madison St. I-64, exit 16, just n. Ext corridors. **Pets:** Medium, other species. $12 one-time fee/room. Service with restrictions, supervision.

Compare Inn & Suites SH
(540) 962-2141. **$98-$144.** 203 Interstate Dr. I-64, exit 16, just sw. Int corridors. **Pets:** Large, other species. $12 one-time fee/room. Service with restrictions, supervision.

CULPEPER

Comfort Inn-Culpeper SH
(540) 825-4900. **$90-$100.** 890 Willis Ln. 2 mi s on US 29 business route; jct US 29, then just e. Ext corridors. **Pets:** Other species. $15 daily fee/pet. Service with restrictions, supervision.

DALEVILLE

Howard Johnson Express Inn SH
(540) 992-1234. **$53-$98, 5 day notice.** 437 Roanoke Rd. I-81, exit 150B, just nw on US 220. Ext corridors. **Pets:** Medium. $15 one-time fee/room. Service with restrictions, supervision.

DANVILLE

▼▼▼▼ Comfort Inn & Suites 🆂🅷
(434) 793-2000. **$84-$129.** 100 Tower Dr. US 58, just w of jct US 29 business route. Int corridors. **Pets:** $10 daily fee/room. Crate.

🄰🅂🄺 🆂🖸 🗙 🖬 💻 🍴 🏊

▼▼▼ Innkeeper Danville North 🅼
(434) 836-1700. **$55-$75, 3 day notice.** 1030 Piney Forest Rd. US 29 N business route, 0.5 mi n of US 58. Ext corridors. **Pets:** $10 daily fee/room. Designated rooms, service with restrictions, supervision.

🄰🅂🄺 🆂🖸 🗙 🖬 🏊

ⒶⒶⒶ ▼▼▼▼ Stratford Inn 🆂🅷
(434) 793-2500. **$64-$135, 5 day notice.** 2500 Riverside Dr. US 58, just e of jct US 29 business route. Ext corridors. **Pets:** Large. $10 daily fee/pet. Service with restrictions, supervision.

🆂🄰🆅🄴 🆂🖸 🗙 🖽 🖬 💻 🍴 🏊

▼▼▼ Super 8 Motel 🅼
(434) 799-5845. **$65-$150, 7 day notice.** 2385 Riverside Dr. On US 58, just e of jct US 29 business route. Int corridors. **Pets:** Medium. $10 daily fee/pet. Service with restrictions, supervision.

🄰🅂🄺 🆂🖸 🗙 🖬

DISTRICT OF COLUMBIA METROPOLITAN AREA

ALEXANDRIA

▼▼▼ Extended StayAmerica-Washington, DC-Alexandria 🆂🅷
(703) 941-9440. **$135-$155.** 205 N Breckinridge Pl. I-395, exit 3B, 0.3 mi w on SR 236, 0.4 mi ne on Beauregard St, just e on Gloucester Rd, then just s. Int corridors. **Pets:** Accepted.

🄰🅂🄺 🆂🖸 🗙 🖽 🖬 💻

▼▼▼ Hawthorn Suites LTD-Alexandria 🆂🅷
(703) 370-1000. **$109-$169.** 420 N Van Dorn St. I-395, exit 3A, 0.3 mi e on SR 236 to S Van Dorn St, then 0.5 mi n. Int corridors. **Pets:** Accepted.

🄰🅂🄺 🆂🖸 🗙 🗩 🖬 💻 🏊

ⒶⒶⒶ ▼▼▼▼ Holiday Inn Hotel & Suites-Historic District Alexandria 🆂🅷
(703) 548-6300. **$109-$299.** 625 1st St. George Washington Memorial Pkwy, just e of jct 1st and Washington sts. Int corridors. **Pets:** Very small, other species. $25 one-time fee/room. Designated rooms, service with restrictions.

🆂🄰🆅🄴 🆂🖸 🗙 🗩 🖬 💻 🍴 🏊 🗙

▼▼▼ Homestead Studio Suites Hotel-Alexandria 🆂🅷
(703) 329-3399. **$150-$160.** 200 Bluestone Rd. I-95/495, exit 174 (Eisenhower Ave Connector), just n to Eisenhower Ave, then 1.2 mi e. Int corridors. **Pets:** Accepted.

🄰🅂🄺 🆂🖸 🗙 🖽 🗩 🖬 💻

ⒶⒶⒶ ▼▼▼▼ Hotel Monaco Alexandria 🅻🅷
(703) 549-6080. **$149-$469.** 480 King St. On SR 7; between S Pitt and S Royal sts; just sw of City Hall. Int corridors. **Pets:** Accepted.

🆂🄰🆅🄴 🆂🖸 🗙 🗩 🖬 💻 🍴 🏊 🗙

▼▼▼ Red Roof Inn-Alexandria 🅼
(703) 960-5200. **$74-$103.** 5975 Richmond Hwy. I-95/495, exit 177A, 0.5 mi s on US 1. Ext corridors. **Pets:** Medium, other species. Service with restrictions, supervision.

🗙 🖽 🗩 🖬 🖬

ⒶⒶⒶ ▼▼▼▼ Residence Inn by Marriott Alexandria-Old Town 🆂🅷
(703) 548-5474. **$149-$399.** 1456 Duke St. I-95/495, exit 176, 0.5 mi n on SR 241, then 0.7 mi e on SR 236. Int corridors. **Pets:** Accepted.

🆂🄰🆅🄴 🆂🖸 🗙 🖽 🗩 🖬 💻 🏊

ⒶⒶⒶ ▼▼▼▼ Sheraton Suites Old Town Alexandria 🆂🅷 ❀
(703) 836-4700. **$119-$379.** 801 N St Asaph St. Just e of Washington St. Int corridors. **Pets:** Medium, dogs only. Service with restrictions, supervision.

🆂🄰🆅🄴 🗙 🗩 🖬 🖬 💻 🍴

ⒶⒶⒶ ▼▼▼▼ Washington Suites-Alexandria 🆂🅷
(703) 370-9600. **$215-$275.** 100 S Reynolds St. I-395, exit 3A, 0.8 mi e on SR 236 E (Duke St), then just s; near a shopping center. Int corridors. **Pets:** Accepted.

🆂🄰🆅🄴 🆂🖸 🗙 🖽 🗩 🖬 💻 🍴 🏊

ARLINGTON

▼▼▼▼ Residence Inn by Marriott Arlington At Rosslyn 🆂🅷 🐾
(703) 812-8400. **$139-$299.** 1651 N Oak St. I-66, exit 73, 0.3 mi s on Fort Myer Dr, 0.3 mi w on Wilson Blvd to N Pierce St, then 2 blks e on Clarendon Blvd. Int corridors. **Pets:** Large. $100 one-time fee/room. No service.

🗙 🗩 🖬 🖬 💻

ⒶⒶⒶ ▼▼▼▼ Residence Inn by Marriott-Pentagon City 🆂🅷
(703) 413-6630. **$189-$369.** 550 Army Navy Dr. I-395, exit 8C, just 1 mi s of 14th St Bridge. Int corridors. **Pets:** $250 daily fee/room, $8 one-time fee/pet. Designated rooms, service with restrictions.

🆂🄰🆅🄴 🆂🖸 🗙 🖽 🗩 🖬 🖬 💻 🏊

▼▼▼▼ The Ritz-Carlton, Pentagon City 🅻🅷 ❀
(703) 415-5000. **$299-$599.** 1250 S Hayes St. 1 mi s of 14th St Bridge. Int corridors. **Pets:** $125 one-time fee/room. Designated rooms, service with restrictions, supervision.

🄰🅂🄺 🗙 🖽 🗩 🖬 🖬 💻 🍴 🏊 🗙

▼▼▼ Sheraton Crystal City Hotel 🅻🅷
(703) 486-1111. **$119-$389.** 1800 Jefferson Davis Hwy. I-395, exit 8C, 1.4 mi s of 14th St Bridge on US 1; hotel entrance, corner of Eads St. Int corridors. **Pets:** Accepted.

🄰🅂🄺 🆂🖸 🗙 🗩 🖬 🖬 💻 🍴 🏊

▼▼▼ Sheraton National Hotel 🅻🅷
(703) 521-1900. **$129-$309.** 900 S Orme St. I-395, exit 8A, at SR 27 and 244; 1.3 mi s of 14th St Bridge. Int corridors. **Pets:** Accepted.

🗙 🖬 💻 🍴 🏊

▼▼▼ The Westin Arlington Gateway 🅻🅷
(703) 717-6200. **Call for rates.** 801 N Glebe Rd. I-66, exit 71, just e on Fairfax Dr to Vermont Ave; just n of jct SR 120 and Wilson Blvd. Int corridors. **Pets:** Accepted.

🗙 🖽 🗩 🖬 🖬 💻 🍴 🏊

ASHBURN

▼▼▼▼ Homewood Suites by Hilton-Dulles North 🆂🅷
(703) 723-7500. **$109-$229.** 44620 Waxpool Rd. 1.7 mi w of jct SR 28 and Waxpool Rd (SR 625); SR 7, 3.4 mi s on Loudoun County Pkwy (CR 607), 0.3 mi w. Int corridors. **Pets:** Accepted.

🗙 🖽 🗩 🖬 💻 🏊

CENTREVILLE

▼▼▼ Extended StayAmerica-Centreville 🆂🅷
(703) 988-9955. **$114-$134.** 5920 Fort Dr. I-66, exit 53, 0.9 mi s on SR 28; off SR 28, 0.3 mi s of jct US 29. Int corridors. **Pets:** Accepted.

🄰🅂🄺 🆂🖸 🗙 🗩 🖬 💻

CHANTILLY

▼▼ Extended StayAmerica-Chantilly 🆂🅷
(703) 263-7173. **$114-$134.** 14420 Chantilly Crossing Ln. On US 50, 0.4 mi w of jct SR 28; at Chantilly Crossing Shopping Complex. Int corridors. **Pets:** Accepted.
(A$K) 🆂💰 ⊠ 🔥M 🖉 🖘 🖬 🖵

▼▼▼ Extended Stay Deluxe Chantilly 🆂🅷
(703) 263-7200. **$150-$160.** 4506 Brookfield Corporate Dr. I-66, exit 53, 3 mi n on SR 28; 1 mi s of jct SR 28 and US 50. Int corridors. **Pets:** Accepted.
(A$K) 🆂💰 ⊠ 🔥M 🖉 🖘 🖬 🖵 ⌣

▼▼▼ Holiday Inn Select Chantilly-Dulles Expo Center 🅻🅷
(703) 815-6060. **$107-$197.** 4335 Chantilly Shopping Center. I-66, exit 53, 3 mi n on SR 28; 1 mi s of jct US 50 and SR 28. Int corridors. **Pets:** Accepted.
(A$K) 🆂💰 ⊠ 🔥M 🖉 🖘 🖬 🖵 🍴 ⌣

▼▼▼ Residence Inn by Marriott Chantilly Dulles South 🆂🅷
(703) 263-7900. **$89-$269.** 14440 Chantilly Crossing Ln. I-66, exit 57B, on US 50, just w of jct SR 28. Int corridors. **Pets:** Accepted.
(A$K) ⊠ 🖉 🖘 🖬 🖵 ⌣ 🏋

▼▼▼ Staybridge Suites Hotel Chantilly/Dulles International Airport 🆂🅷
(703) 435-8090. **$89-$326.** 3860 Centerview Dr. Jct SR 28, just e on US 50. Int corridors. **Pets:** Small. $150 one-time fee/pet. Designated rooms, crate.
(A$K) 🆂💰 ⊠ 🔥M 🖉 🖘 🖬 🖵 ⌣

▼▼▼▼ TownePlace Suites by Marriott-Chantilly 🆂🅷
(703) 709-0453. **$125-$152.** 14036 Thunderbolt Pl. Jct SR 28, just e on US 50. Int corridors. **Pets:** Accepted.
(A$K) 🆂💰 ⊠ 🖘 🖬 🖵 ⌣

FAIRFAX

▼▼ Candlewood Suites Fairfax-Washington, D.C. 🆂🅷
(703) 359-4490. **$99-$169.** 11400 Random Hills Rd. I-66, exit 57A, 0.5 mi e on US 50, just s on Waples Mill Rd, then 0.4 mi w. Int corridors. **Pets:** Accepted.
(A$K) 🆂💰 ⊠ 🔥M 🖘 🖬 🖵

🅐🅐🅐 ▼▼▼ Comfort Inn University Center 🆂🅷
(703) 591-5900. **$69-$179.** 11180 Fairfax Blvd. I-66, exit 57A, 0.8 mi se on US 50, then 0.5 mi nw of jct US 29. Int corridors. **Pets:** Medium. Service with restrictions, crate.
(SAVE) 🆂💰 ⊠ 🖬 🖵 🍴 ⌣ 🏋

▼▼ Extended StayAmerica Fair Oaks 🆂🅷
(703) 267-6770. **$134-$154.** 12055 Lee Jackson Memorial Hwy. I-66, exit 57B, 0.5 mi w on US 50; at Fair Oaks Mall. Int corridors. **Pets:** Accepted.
(A$K) 🆂💰 ⊠ 🖬 🖵

▼▼▼ Extended Stay Deluxe Fairfax 🆂🅷
(703) 359-5000. **$160-$170.** 3997 Fair Ridge Dr. I-66, exit 57B, 1.2 mi w on US 50. Int corridors. **Pets:** Accepted.
(A$K) 🆂💰 ⊠ 🔥M 🖉 🖘 🖬 🖵 ⌣

▼▼ Homestead Studio Suites Hotel-Fair Oaks 🆂🅷
(703) 273-3444. **$140-$150.** 12104 Monument Dr. I-66, exit 57B, 0.8 mi w on US 50, 0.3 mi s on SR 620 (West Ox Rd), then just se. Ext corridors. **Pets:** Accepted.
(A$K) 🆂💰 ⊠ 🔥M 🖉 🖘 🖬 🖵

▼ Homestead Studio Suites Hotel-Falls Church/Merrifield 🅼
(703) 204-0088. **$140-$150.** 8281 Willow Oaks Corporate Dr. I-495, exit 50A, just w on US 50 to Gallows Rd, then just s. Ext corridors. **Pets:** Accepted.
(A$K) 🆂💰 ⊠ 🔥M 🖉 🖬 🖵

▼▼▼▼ Residence Inn by Marriott-Fair Lakes 🆂🅷 🐾
(703) 266-4900. **$79-$279.** 12815 Fair Lakes Pkwy. I-66, exit 55 (Fairfax County Pkwy N), just w. Int corridors. **Pets:** Medium, other species. $150 one-time fee/room. Service with restrictions, supervision.
(A$K) ⊠ 🔥M 🖉 🖘 🖬 🖵 ⌣ 🏋

FALLS CHURCH

▼▼▼ DoubleTree Hotel and Executive Meeting Center at Tysons Corner 🅻🅷
(703) 893-1340. **$129-$349.** 7801 Leesburg Pike. I-495, exit 47B, just e on SR 7. Int corridors. **Pets:** Accepted.
⊠ 🖉 🖘 🖬 🖵 🍴 ⌣

▼▼▼ Homewood Suites by Hilton-Falls Church 🆂🅷
(703) 560-6644. **$229-$259.** 8130 Porter Rd. I-495, exit 50A, just w to SR 650; 0.4 mi n of SR 650. Int corridors. **Pets:** Medium, dogs only. $100 one-time fee/room. Service with restrictions, crate.
(A$K) ⊠ 🔥M 🖉 🖘 🖬 🖵 ⌣

▼▼▼ Residence Inn by Marriott Fairfax-Merrifield 🆂🅷
(703) 573-5200. **$89-$299.** 8125 Gatehouse Rd. I-495, exit 50A, just w to SR 640 N. Int corridors. **Pets:** Other species. $150 one-time fee/room.
⊠ 🔥M 🖉 🖘 🖬 🖵 ⌣ 🏋

▼▼▼ TownePlace Suites by Marriott-Falls Church 🆂🅷
(703) 237-6172. **$109-$199.** 205 Hillwood Ave. I-495, exit 50B, 2.5 mi e on US 50, 0.6 mi n on Annandale Rd, then e; just s of US 29. Int corridors. **Pets:** Accepted.
(A$K) 🆂💰 ⊠ 🔥M 🖘 🖬 🖵 ⌣

HERNDON

▼▼ Candlewood Suites Washington-Dulles Herndon 🆂🅷
(703) 793-7100. **$59-$229.** 13845 Sunrise Valley Dr. SR 28, 0.4 mi e on Frying Pan Rd, 0.7 mi nw. Int corridors. **Pets:** Accepted.
(A$K) 🆂💰 ⊠ 🔥M 🖘 🖬 🖵

▼▼ Extended StayAmerica-Herndon 🆂🅷
(703) 481-5363. **Call for rates.** 1021 Elden St.. Int corridors. **Pets:** Accepted.
⊠ 🔥M 🖘 🖬 🖵

▼▼▼ Hawthorn Suites Herndon 🆂🅷
(703) 437-5000. **$99-$185.** 467 Herndon Pkwy. SR 267 (Dulles Toll Rd), exit 11 CR 7100 (Fairfax County Pkwy), just n to Spring St exit, just s to Herndon Pkwy (CR 606), just w on CR 606. Int corridors. **Pets:** Medium. $25 daily fee/pet. Service with restrictions, crate.
(A$K) 🆂💰 ⊠ 🖉 🖘 🖬 🖵 ⌣ 🏋

🅐🅐🅐 ▼▼▼ Hilton Washington Dulles Airport 🅻🅷
(703) 478-2900. **$87-$317.** 13869 Park Center Rd. SR 267 (Dulles Toll Rd), exit 9, 3 mi s on SR 28; at McLearen Blvd. Int corridors. **Pets:** Accepted.
(SAVE) ⊠ 🔥M 🖉 🖘 🖬 🖵 🍴 ⌣ 🏋

▼▼▼ Homewood Suites by Hilton Washington-Dulles Airport 🆂🅷
(703) 793-1700. **$99-$350, 15 day notice.** 13460 Sunrise Valley Dr. SR 267 (Dulles Toll Rd), exit 10, 0.5 mi s on SR 657, then just w. Int corridors. **Pets:** Accepted.
(A$K) 🆂💰 ⊠ 🔥M 🖉 🖘 🖬 🖵 ⌣

🅐🅐🅐 ▼▼▼ Residence Inn by Marriott-Herndon/Reston 🆂🅷
(703) 435-0044. **$249-$259.** 315 Elden St. 0.4 mi w on CR 606 from jct CR 7100 (Fairfax County Pkwy). Int corridors. **Pets:** Accepted.
(SAVE) 🆂💰 ⊠ 🖉 🖬 🖵 ⌣ 🏋

▼▼▼ Staybridge Suites Herndon Dulles 🆂🅷 🐾
(703) 713-6800. **$79-$279.** 13700 Coppermine Rd. SR 267 (Dulles Toll Rd), exit 10, 0.7 mi s on Centreville Rd (SR 657), then 0.4 mi w. Ext corridors. **Pets:** Small. $250 one-time fee/room. Service with restrictions, crate.
(A$K) 🆂💰 ⊠ 🖉 🖬 🖵 ⌣ 🏋

LEESBURG

AAA ▼▼ **Best Western Leesburg Hotel & Conference Center** SH
(703) 777-9400. **$89-$139.** 726 E Market St. 0.5 mi e on SR 7 business route. Int corridors. **Pets:** Accepted.
SAVE Sö ✕ 🖥 📖 ⊃

▼▼▼ **Holiday Inn Leesburg** SH
(703) 771-9200. **$99-$139.** 1500 E Market St. 2 mi e on SR 7. Int corridors. **Pets:** Other species. $25 one-time fee/room. Service with restrictions, crate.
ASK Sö ✕ ⬥M ⟲ ⟨ 🖥 📖 ⊣⊢ ⊃

LORTON

▼▼▼ **Comfort Inn Gunston Corner** SH
(703) 643-3100. **$89-$129.** 8180 Silverbrook Rd. I-95, exit 163, just w. Int corridors. **Pets:** Medium. $12 daily fee/room. Service with restrictions, supervision.
ASK Sö ✕ ⟲ ⟨ 🖥 📖 ⊃ ✕

MANASSAS

AAA ▼▼▼ **Best Western Battlefield Inn** SH
(703) 361-8000. **$99-$125.** 10820 Balls Ford Rd. I-66, exit 47A westbound; exit 47 eastbound, just s on SR 234 business route. Ext corridors. **Pets:** Accepted.
SAVE Sö ✕ ⟨ 🖥 📖 ⊣⊢ ⊃

▼▼ **Red Roof Inn-Manassas** M
(703) 335-9333. **$75-$90.** 10610 Automotive Dr. I-66, exit 47 eastbound; exit 47A westbound, just s on SR 234 business route, then just e on Balls Ford Rd. Ext corridors. **Pets:** Medium, other species. Service with restrictions, supervision.
✕ ⟲ ⟨

MCLEAN

AAA ▼▼ **Best Western Tysons Westpark Hotel** LH
(703) 734-2800. **$79-$229.** 8401 Westpark Dr. I-495, exit 47A, 1.3 mi w on SR 7. Int corridors. **Pets:** Large. Service with restrictions, crate.
SAVE Sö ✕ ⬥M ⟲ ⟨ 🖥 📖 ⊣⊢ ⊃ ✕

AAA ▼▼▼▼ **Holiday Inn Tysons Corner** LH
(703) 893-2100. **$79-$289.** 1960 Chain Bridge Rd. I-495, exit 46A, 0.5 mi s on SR 123, just nw on International Dr, then just sw on Greensboro Dr. Int corridors. **Pets:** Small. $40 one-time fee/room. Designated rooms, service with restrictions, supervision.
SAVE Sö ✕ ⬥M ⟲ ⟨ 🖥 📖 ⊣⊢ ⊃ ✕

AAA ▼▼▼▼ **Staybridge Suites-McLean/Tysons Corner** SH
(703) 448-5400. **$119-$309.** 6845 Old Dominion Dr. I-495, exit 46B, 2 mi n on SR 123, then 0.3 mi e on SR 309. Int corridors. **Pets:** Accepted.
SAVE Sö ✕ ⬥M ⟲ ⟨ 🖥 📖 ⊃

RESTON

▼▼ **Homestead Studio Suites Hotel-Reston** M
(703) 707-9700. **$150-$160.** 12190 Sunset Hills Rd. SR 267 (Dulles Toll Rd), exit 12 (Reston Pkwy), just n, then just w. Ext corridors. **Pets:** Accepted.
ASK Sö ✕ ⟨ 🖥 📖

AAA ▼▼▼ **Sheraton Reston Hotel** SH
(703) 620-9000. **$79-$249.** 11810 Sunrise Valley Dr. SR 267 (Dulles Toll Rd), exit 12 (Reston Pkwy), just s. Int corridors. **Pets:** Accepted.
SAVE Sö ✕ ⟨ 🖥 📖 ⊣⊢ ⊃

SPRINGFIELD

▼▼▼ **Comfort Inn Washington DC/Springfield** SH
(703) 922-9000. **$119-$149.** 6560 Loisdale Ct. I-95, exit 169A, just e on SR 644 E; jct I-395 and 495, 0.8 mi s. Int corridors. **Pets:** Accepted.
ASK Sö ✕ ⟲ ⟨ 🖥 📖

▼▼ **Extended StayAmerica-Washington, DC-Springfield** SH
(703) 822-0992. **Call for rates.** 6800 Metropolitan Center Dr. I-95, exit 169A, just e on SR 644, 0.6 mi s on Loisdale Rd, then just e. Int corridors. **Pets:** Accepted.
✕ ⬥M ⟨ 🖥 📖 ⊃

▼▼▼▼ **Hampton Inn Washington DC/Springfield** SH
(703) 924-9444. **$129-$149.** 6550 Loisdale Ct. I-95, exit 169A, just e on SR 644 E; jct I-395 and 495, 0.8 mi s. Int corridors. **Pets:** Medium, other species. Service with restrictions, crate.
ASK Sö ✕ ⬥M ⟲ ⟨ 🖥 📖 ⊃

▼▼ **Red Roof Inn Springfield** SH
(703) 644-5311. **$90-$113.** 6868 Springfield Blvd. I-95, exit 169B, just sw of SR 644; jct I-395 and 495, 0.8 mi s. Int corridors. **Pets:** Medium, other species. Service with restrictions, supervision.
✕ ⬥M ⟨ 🖥

▼▼▼ **TownePlace Suites by Marriott Springfield** SH
(703) 569-8060. **$195-$235.** 6245 Brandon Ave. I-95, exit 169B, just nw of SR 644; jct I-395 and 495, 0.8 mi s. Int corridors. **Pets:** Accepted.
ASK Sö ✕ ⬥M ⟲ ⟨ 🖥 📖 ⊃

STERLING

▼▼ **Candlewood Suites Washington Dulles/Sterling** SH
(703) 674-2288. **$79-$209.** 45520 E Severn Way. 1.6 mi s on SR 28 from jct SR 7, 0.3 mi e. Int corridors. **Pets:** Accepted.
ASK Sö ✕ ⬥M ⟨ 🖥 📖

▼▼ **Extended StayAmerica-Sterling** SH
(703) 444-7240. **$154-$174.** 46001 Waterview Plaza. 1.3 mi e on SR 7 from jct SR 28. Int corridors. **Pets:** Accepted.
ASK Sö ✕ ⬥M ⟨ 🖥 📖

▼▼ **Hampton Inn-Dulles/Cascades** SH
(703) 450-9595. **$89-$209.** 46331 McClellan Way. 1.7 mi e on SR 7, from jct SR 28, 0.5 mi n on CR 1794 (Cascades Pkwy) to Palisade Pkwy, just e, then 0.4 mi s on Whitfield Pl. Int corridors. **Pets:** Medium, other species. Service with restrictions, supervision.
ASK Sö ✕ ⟲ ⟨ 🖥 📖 ⊃ ✕

▼▼▼ **Hampton Inn Washington-Dulles Airport** SH
(703) 471-8300. **$79-$189.** 45440 Holiday Dr. 1.4 mi n on SR 28 from jct SR 267 (Dulles Toll Rd), then just ne. Ext corridors. **Pets:** $25 one-time fee/room. Service with restrictions, supervision.
ASK Sö ✕ ⬥M ⟨ 🖥

AAA ▼▼▼▼ **Holiday Inn Washington Dulles International Airport** SH
(703) 471-7411. **$109-$295.** 1000 Sully Rd. 1.4 mi n on SR 28 from jct SR 267 (Dulles Toll Rd), then just ne. Ext/int corridors. **Pets:** Other species. $50 one-time fee/pet. Service with restrictions.
SAVE Sö ✕ ⟲ ⟨ 🖥 📖 ⊣⊢ ⊃ ✕

▼▼▼ **Residence Inn by Marriott Dulles Airport @ Dulles 28 Center** SH
(703) 421-2000. **$239-$289.** 45250 Monterey Pl. SR 28, exit CR 625 (Waxpool Rd), just w, just n on Pacific Blvd, then just e on Commercial Dr. Int corridors. **Pets:** Accepted.
ASK Sö ✕ ⬥M ⟨ 🖥 📖 ⊃ ✕

▼▼ **Suburban Extended Stay Hotel**
Washington-Dulles/Sterling 🆂🅷
(703) 674-2299. **Call for rates (no credit cards).** 45510 Severn Way. 1.6 mi s on SR 28 from jct SR 7, 0.3 mi e. Int corridors. **Pets:** Accepted.
✕ 🎛 🍴 ▣

▼▼▼ **TownePlace Suites by Marriott at Dulles Airport** 🆂🅷
(703) 707-2017. **$99-$209.** 22744 Holiday Park Dr. 1.4 mi n on SR 28 from jct SR 267 (Dulles Toll Rd), then just ne. Int corridors. **Pets:** $100 one-time fee/pet. Service with restrictions.
🅰🆂🅺 🆂🐾 ✕ 🎛 🍴 🍴 ▣ 🏊

◆◆◆ ▼▼▼▼ **TownePlace Suites by Marriott Sterling** 🆂🅷 🐾
(703) 421-1090. **$69-$249.** 21123 Whitfield Pl. 1.7 mi e on SR 7 from jct SR 28, 0.5 mi n on SR 1794 (Cascades Pkwy) to Palisades Pkwy, just e, then just s. Int corridors. **Pets:** Other species. $100 one-time fee/room. Service with restrictions, crate.
🆂🅰🆅🅴 🆂🐾 ✕ 🍴 🍴 ▣ 🏊

VIENNA

◆◆◆ ▼▼ **Comfort Inn Tysons Corner** 🅼
(703) 448-8020. **$81-$189.** 1587 Spring Hill Rd. I-495, exit 47A, 1.8 mi w on SR 7, then just s; just e of jct SR 267 (Dulles Toll Rd). Ext corridors. **Pets:** Accepted.
🆂🅰🆅🅴 🆂🐾 ✕ 🎛 🍴 ▣ 🏊

▼▼ **Homestead Studio Suites Hotel-Tysons Corner** 🆂🅷
(703) 356-6300. **$180-$190.** 8201 Old Courthouse Rd. I-495, exit 47A, 0.6 mi w on SR 7, then just s on Gallows Rd. Int corridors. **Pets:** Accepted.
🅰🆂🅺 🆂🐾 ✕ 🐾🅼 🍴 🎛 🍴 ▣

▼▼▼ **Residence Inn by Marriott-Tysons Corner** 🆂🅷
(703) 893-0120. **$89-$399.** 8616 Westwood Center Dr. I-495, exit 47A, 1.9 mi w on SR 7, then just s. Ext corridors. **Pets:** Accepted.
🅰🆂🅺 ✕ 🎛 ▣ 🏊 🍴

▼▼▼ **Residence Inn by Marriott Tysons Corner Mall** 🆂🅷
(703) 917-0800. **$119-$269.** 8400 Old Courthouse Rd. I-495, exit 46A, 1.1 mi s on SR 123; 0.3 mi s of jct SR 7 and 123. Int corridors. **Pets:** Accepted.
🅰🆂🅺 🆂🐾 ✕ 🐾🅼 🍴 🍴 🎛 🍴 ▣ 🏊

▼▼▼ **Sheraton Premiere At Tysons Corner** 🅻🅷 🐾
(703) 448-1234. **$219-$229.** 8661 Leesburg Pike. SR 7, just e of jct SR 267 (Dulles Toll Rd). Int corridors. **Pets:** Small. Service with restrictions, supervision.
🅰🆂🅺 ✕ 🍴 🍴 🎛 🍴 🍴 🏊 🍴

WOODBRIDGE

◆◆◆ ▼▼▼ **Quality Inn at Potomac Mills** 🆂🅷
(703) 494-0300. **$69-$129.** 1109 Horner Rd. I-95, exit 161 southbound, 1.5 mi s on US 1, just n on SR 123, then just s; exit 160A northbound, 0.5 mi s on SR 123, then just s. Int corridors. **Pets:** Small, dogs only. $20 daily fee/pet. Designated rooms, service with restrictions, supervision.
🆂🅰🆅🅴 🆂🐾 ✕ 🍴 🎛 🍴 ▣ 🏊

▼▼▼ **Residence Inn by Marriott Potomac Mills** 🆂🅷
(703) 490-4020. **$225-$255.** 14301 Crossing Pl. I-95, exit 158B (Prince William Pkwy), 0.5 mi sw. Int corridors. **Pets:** Accepted.
🅰🆂🅺 🆂🐾 ✕ 🐾🅼 🍴 🍴 🎛 🍴 ▣ 🏊 🍴

END METROPOLITAN AREA

DUBLIN

▼▼ **Comfort Inn-Dublin** 🆂🅷
(540) 674-1100. **$72-$81.** 4424 Cleburne Blvd. I-81, exit 98, just e. Int corridors. **Pets:** Dogs only. $10 daily fee/room. Designated rooms, service with restrictions, supervision.
🅰🆂🅺 🆂🐾 ✕ 🍴 🎛 ▣ 🏊

EMPORIA

◆◆◆ ▼▼▼▼ **Best Western Emporia** 🆂🅷
(434) 634-3200. **$60-$85.** 1100 W Atlantic St. I-95, exit 11B, just w on US 58. Ext corridors. **Pets:** Other species. $10 daily fee/pet. Service with restrictions, supervision.
🆂🅰🆅🅴 🆂🐾 ✕ 🍴 🎛 🍴 ▣ 🏊

◆◆◆ ▼▼ **Comfort Inn** 🆂🅷
(434) 348-3282. **$54-$70, 7 day notice.** 1411 Skippers Rd. I-95, exit 8, just e on US 301. Ext corridors. **Pets:** Accepted.
🆂🅰🆅🅴 🆂🐾 ✕ 🎛 ▣ 🏊

◆◆◆ ▼▼▼ **Days Inn-Emporia** 🆂🅷
(434) 634-9481. **$65-$85.** 921 W Atlantic St. I-95, exit 11B, just w on US 58. Ext corridors. **Pets:** Other species. $8 one-time fee/pet. Service with restrictions.
🆂🅰🆅🅴 🆂🐾 ✕ 🎛 🏊

▼▼▼ **Hampton Inn** 🆂🅷
(434) 634-9200. **$99-$119.** 898 Wiggins Rd. I-95, exit 11B (US 58), just w. Int corridors. **Pets:** Accepted.
🅰🆂🅺 🆂🐾 ✕ 🐾🅼 🍴 🎛 🍴 ▣ 🏊

◆◆◆ ▼▼▼▼ **Quality Inn** 🆂🅷
(434) 348-8888. **$65-$90.** 1207 W Atlantic St. I-95, exit 11B, just w on US 58. Ext corridors. **Pets:** $7 daily fee/pet. Service with restrictions, supervision.
🆂🅰🆅🅴 ✕ 🍴 🎛 ▣ 🏊

FARMVILLE

▼ **Super 8 Motel** 🅼
(434) 392-8196. **$52-$65, 5 day notice.** 2012 S Main St. On US 15, just n of jct US 460. Int corridors. **Pets:** Medium. $5 one-time fee/pet. Service with restrictions, supervision.
🅰🆂🅺 🆂🐾 ✕ 🍴

FREDERICKSBURG

◆◆◆ ▼▼▼ **Best Western Central Plaza** 🅼 🐾
(540) 786-7404. **$59-$79.** 3000 Plank Rd. I-95, exit 130B on SR 3. Ext corridors. **Pets:** Small, other species. $9 daily fee/pet. No service, supervision.
🆂🅰🆅🅴 🆂🐾 ✕ 🐾🅼 🍴 🎛 ▣

◆◆◆ ▼▼▼ **Best Western Fredericksburg** 🆂🅷 🐾
(540) 371-5050. **$66-$99, 15 day notice.** 2205 William St. I-95, exit 130A, 0.3 mi e on SR 3. Ext corridors. **Pets:** $9 daily fee/pet. Service with restrictions, supervision.
🆂🅰🆅🅴 🆂🐾 ✕ 🐾🅼 🍴 🎛 ▣ 🏊

◆◆◆ ▼▼▼ **Dunning Mills Inn All Suites Hotel** 🅲🅾
(540) 373-1256. **$59-$89.** 2305-C Jefferson Davis Hwy. I-95, exit 126, 3 mi n on US 1. Ext corridors. **Pets:** Accepted.
🆂🅰🆅🅴 🆂🐾 ✕ 🍴 🏊

(AAA) ▼▼▼ Holiday Inn-Fredericksburg North [SH]
(540) 371-5550. **$70-$110.** 564 Warrenton Rd. I-95, exit 133, just nw on US 17. Ext corridors. **Pets:** Accepted.
[SAVE] [S6] [✕] [🖥] [💻] [🍴] [🏊] [✕]

▼▼▼ Holiday Inn Select Fredericksburg [LH]
(540) 786-8321. **$109-$169.** 2801 Plank Rd. I-95, exit 130B, on SR 3. Int corridors. **Pets:** Medium. $50 one-time fee/room. Service with restrictions, supervision.
[ASK] [S6] [✕] [&M] [🗄] [✓] [🖥] [💻] [🍴] [🏊]

(AAA) ▼ Howard Johnson Hotel [SH]
(540) 898-1800. **$59-$99.** 5327 Jefferson Davis Hwy. I-95, exit 126. Int corridors. **Pets:** Accepted.
[SAVE] [S6] [✕] [✓] [🖥] [💻] [🏊]

(AAA) ▼▼ Quality Inn [SH]
(540) 371-0330. **$79-$119.** 2310 William St. I-95, exit 130A on SR 3 E. Ext corridors. **Pets:** Accepted.
[SAVE] [S6] [✕] [🖥] [💻] [🏊]

(AAA) ▼▼▼ Quality Inn Fredericksburg [SH]
(540) 373-0000. **$59-$79.** 543 Warrenton Rd. I-95, exit 133, just n on US 17. Ext corridors. **Pets:** Other species. $8 daily fee/pet. Designated rooms, service with restrictions, supervision.
[SAVE] [S6] [✕] [💻] [🍴] [🏊]

(AAA) ▼▼ Ramada Inn South [SH]
(540) 898-1102. **$65-$78.** 5324 Jefferson Davis Hwy. I-95, exit 126, just n on US 1. Ext/int corridors. **Pets:** Very small. $5 daily fee/room. Designated rooms, service with restrictions, crate.
[SAVE] [S6] [✕] [🖥] [💻] [🍴] [🏊] [✕]

(AAA) ▼▼▼ TownePlace Suites by Marriott [SH]
(540) 891-0775. **$89-$159.** 4700 Market St. I-95, exit 126 southbound; exit 126A northbound, just n on US 1, then just e. Int corridors. **Pets:** Medium, other species. $10 daily fee/pet. Designated rooms, no service, supervision.
[SAVE] [✕] [🗄] [✓] [🖥] [💻] [🏊]

FRONT ROYAL

(AAA) ▼ Bluemont Inn [M]
(540) 635-9447. **$49-$99.** 1525 N Shenandoah Ave. I-66, exit 6, 1.8 mi s on US 340/522. Ext corridors. **Pets:** Large. $5 one-time fee/room. Service with restrictions, supervision.
[SAVE] [S6] [✕] [🖥] [💻]

(AAA) ▼ Budget Inn [M]
(540) 635-2196. **$45-$75.** 1122 N Royal Ave. I-66, exit 6, 2.2 mi s on US 340/522 and SR 55. Ext corridors. **Pets:** Small, dogs only. $5 daily fee/pet. Service with restrictions, supervision.
[SAVE] [S6] [✕]

(AAA) ▼▼ Quality Inn-Skyline Drive [SH]
(540) 635-3161. **$63-$100.** 10 Commerce Ave. I-66, exit 6, 3.2 mi s on US 522. Ext corridors. **Pets:** Medium. $15 daily fee/pet. Designated rooms, service with restrictions, supervision.
[SAVE] [S6] [✕] [🖥] [💻] [🏊]

(AAA) ▼ Relax Inn [M]
(540) 635-4101. **$50-$75.** 1801 Shenandoah Ave. I-66, exit 6, 1.5 mi s on US 340/522. Ext corridors. **Pets:** Accepted.
[SAVE] [S6] [✕] [🖥] [💻] [🏊]

(AAA) ▼ Twi-Lite Motel [M]
(540) 635-4148. **$45-$89, 3 day notice.** 53 W 14th St. I-66, exit 6, 2.3 mi s on US 340/522. Ext corridors. **Pets:** Very small. $10 daily fee/pet. No service, supervision.
[SAVE] [S6] [✕] [🖥] [🏊]

GLADE SPRING

(AAA) ▼ Swiss Inn Motel & Suites [M]
(276) 429-5191. **$45-$80.** 33361 Lee Hwy. I-81, exit 29, just e. Ext corridors. **Pets:** Small, dogs only. $7 one-time fee/pet. Service with restrictions, supervision.
[SAVE] [S6] [✕] [✓] [🖥]

GREENVILLE

(AAA) ▼ Budget Host-Historic Hessian House [SH]
(540) 337-1231. **$50-$75, 3 day notice.** 3554 Lee Jackson Hwy. I-81, exit 213, 0.3 mi e. Ext corridors. **Pets:** Small. $10 daily fee/pet. Designated rooms, service with restrictions.
[SAVE] [S6] [✕] [🖥] [💻]

GRUNDY

▼▼▼ Comfort Inn [SH]
(276) 935-5050. **$79-$129, 7 day notice.** US 460 Main St. On US 460, 0.5 mi e. Int corridors. **Pets:** $25 one-time fee/pet. Designated rooms, service with restrictions, supervision.
[ASK] [S6] [✕] [&M] [🗄] [✓] [🖥] [💻]

HAMPTON ROADS AREA

CHESAPEAKE

◆◆ Extended StayAmerica-Chesapeake-Greenbriar-Crossways Blvd [M]
(757) 424-8600. **$80-$100.** 1540 Crossways Blvd. I-64, exit 289B (Greenbrier Pkwy). Ext corridors. **Pets:** Accepted.
[ASK] [S6] [✕] [✓] [🖥] [💻]

▼▼▼ Residence Inn by Marriott, Chesapeake-Greenbrier [SH]
(757) 502-7300. **$139-$259.** 1500 Crossways Blvd. I-64, exit 289B (Greenbrier Pkwy), just s to Jarman Rd (at Crossways Center) to Crossways Blvd, then 0.6 mi n. Int corridors. **Pets:** Accepted.
[ASK] [S6] [✕] [🗄] [✓] [🖥] [💻] [🏊] [✕]

▼ Super 8 Motel [M] 🐾
(757) 686-8888. **$59-$81.** 3216 Churchland Blvd. I-664, exit 9B, 1 mi s on SR 17. Int corridors. **Pets:** Other species. $10 daily fee/room. Designated rooms, service with restrictions, supervision.
[ASK] [S6] [✕] [&M] [🖥]

▼▼ TownePlace Suites By Marriott [SH]
(757) 523-5004. **$109-$169.** 2000 Old Greenbrier Rd. I-64, exit 289A (Greenbrier Pkwy), just n on Greenbrier Pkwy. Int corridors. **Pets:** Accepted.
[ASK] [S6] [✕] [&M] [🗄] [✓] [🖥] [💻] [🏊]

GLOUCESTER

▼▼▼ Comfort Inn Gloucester [SH]
(804) 695-1900. **$79-$164.** 6639 Forest Hill Ave. US 17, just s. Int corridors. **Pets:** Small, dogs only. $10 daily fee/pet. Designated rooms, service with restrictions, crate.
[ASK] [S6] [✕] [🖥] [💻] [🏊]

HAMPTON

▼▼▼ Candlewood Suites [SH]
(757) 766-8976. **$59-$189.** 401 Butler Farm Rd. I-64, exit 261B (Hampton Roads Center Pkwy) eastbound; exit 262B (Magruder Blvd) westbound, then n. Int corridors. **Pets:** Accepted.
[ASK] [S6] [✕] [&M] [✓] [🖥] [💻]

Clarion Hotel-Hampton Roads Convention Center SH

(757) 838-5011. **$104-$169.** 1809 W Mercury Blvd. I-64, exit 263B (Mercury Blvd), jct SR 58. Int corridors. **Pets:** Medium, dogs only. $25 one-time fee/pet. Service with restrictions, supervision.

Extended StayAmerica-Hampton Coliseum M

(757) 896-3600. **Call for rates.** 1915 Commerce Dr. I-64, exit 263 (Mercury Blvd), just n, then just e. Int corridors. **Pets:** Accepted.

Holiday Inn Hampton Hotel & Conference Center LH

(757) 838-0200. **$79-$169.** 1815 W Mercury Blvd. I-64, exit 263B (Mercury Blvd) westbound; exit 263 eastbound. Ext/int corridors. **Pets:** Accepted.

La Quinta Inn Norfolk (Hampton) SH

(757) 827-8680. **$80-$134.** 2138 W Mercury Blvd. I-64, exit 263 (Mercury Blvd), just s. Ext corridors. **Pets:** Accepted.

Ramada Hampton Coliseum & Convention Center SH

(757) 827-7400. **$59-$149, 15 day notice.** 1905 Coliseum Dr. I-64, 263 (Mercury Blvd) eastbound, just n, then just e towards Hampton Coliseum; exit 263B westbound. Ext/int corridors. **Pets:** Small. $10 daily fee/pet. Designated rooms, service with restrictions, supervision.

Super 8 Motel M

(757) 723-2888. **$59-$91.** 1330 Thomas St. I-64, 265B westbound; exit 265C eastbound. Int corridors. **Pets:** Small. $10 daily fee/pet. Designated rooms, no service, supervision.

NEWPORT NEWS

Comfort Inn SH

(757) 249-0200. **$79-$144.** 12330 Jefferson Ave. I-64, exit 255A, just s on Clarie Ln (mall parking lot). Int corridors. **Pets:** Other species. $50 daily fee/pet. Designated rooms, service with restrictions, crate.

Days Inn SH

(757) 874-0201. **$65-$85.** 14747 Warwick Blvd. I-64, exit 250A (SR 105/Ft Eustis Blvd S), 2.5 mi to US 60 E (Warwick Blvd). Ext corridors. **Pets:** Accepted.

Days Inn-Oyster Point & Meeting Center SH

(757) 873-6700. **$89-$119, 3 day notice.** 11829 Fishing Point Dr. I-64, exit 255A, 2.5 mi s to Thimble Shoals Dr E, then 1 blk. Int corridors. **Pets:** Other species. $15 daily fee/pet. Service with restrictions.

Extended StayAmerica Newport News-Oyster Point SH

(757) 873-2266. **$75-$85.** 11708 Jefferson Ave. I-64, exit 258A (Jefferson Ave), 1 mi s. Ext corridors. **Pets:** Accepted.

Omni Newport News Hotel LH

(757) 873-6664. **$120.** 1000 Omni Blvd. I-64, exit 258A (US 17), just s to Oyster Point Rd. Int corridors. **Pets:** Accepted.

StudioPLUS–Newport News SH

(757) 882-8847. **$79-$144.** 12359 Hornsby Ln. I-64, exit 255A, just s on Jefferson Ave. Int corridors. **Pets:** Accepted.

Travelodge M

(757) 874-4100. **$49-$89, 3 day notice.** 13700 Warwick Blvd. I-64, exit 255B, 1 mi w to Bland Blvd, 1 mi s to Warwick Blvd, then just n. Ext corridors. **Pets:** $10 daily fee/pet. Service with restrictions, crate.

NORFOLK

B & B @ Historic Page House Inn BB

(757) 625-5033. **$140-$160, 7 day notice.** 323 Fairfax Ave. I-264, exit 9, 1.4 mi n on Waterside Dr to Olney Rd, just w to Mowbray Arch, then just s; in Ghent historic district. Int corridors. **Pets:** Small, other species. $25 daily fee/pet. Service with restrictions, crate.

Quality Suites Lake Wright SH

(757) 461-6251. **$109-$169.** 6280 Northampton Blvd. I-64, exit 282, just w on US 13. Int corridors. **Pets:** Other species. $35 one-time fee/room. Service with restrictions, supervision.

Radisson Hotel Norfolk SH

(757) 627-5555. **$121-$139.** 700 Monticello Ave. Jct Brambleton Ave and St. Pauls Blvd; downtown. Int corridors. **Pets:** Small. $50 deposit/room. Designated rooms, service with restrictions, supervision.

Residence Inn by Marriott Norfolk Airport SH

(757) 333-3000. **$144-$269.** 1590 N Military Hwy. I-64, exit 281B (Military Hwy). Int corridors. **Pets:** Accepted.

Sheraton Norfolk Waterside Hotel LH

(757) 622-6664. **$69-$309.** 777 Waterside Dr. I-264, exit Waterside Dr; downtown. Int corridors. **Pets:** Accepted.

Sleep Inn Lake Wright SH

(757) 461-1133. **$79-$149.** 6280 Northampton Blvd. I-64, exit 282, just w on US 13. Int corridors. **Pets:** Other species. $25 one-time fee/room. Service with restrictions, supervision.

PORTSMOUTH

Holiday Inn-Olde Towne Portsmouth SH

(757) 393-2573. **$89-$149.** 8 Crawford Pkwy. Just nw from High St. Int corridors. **Pets:** Large, other species. $10 daily fee/room. Service with restrictions, crate.

SUFFOLK

Holiday Inn-Suffolk SH

(757) 934-2311. **$79-$109.** 2864 Pruden Blvd. US 460 at jct US 58 Bypass. Ext corridors. **Pets:** Medium. $50 deposit/pet, $15 one-time fee/pet. Service with restrictions, crate.

VIRGINIA BEACH

Best Western Beach Quarters Inn M

(757) 437-1200. **$29-$269, 3 day notice.** 300 Atlantic Ave. I-264, 1.2 mi s of terminus at Rudee Inlet. Ext corridors. **Pets:** Small, dogs only. $20 daily fee/pet. Designated rooms, service with restrictions, supervision.

Candlewood Suites SH

(757) 213-1500. **Call for rates.** 4437 Bonney Rd. I-264, exit 17B (Independence Blvd/Pembroke Area), just n to Bonney Rd, then just e. Int corridors. **Pets:** Medium, other species. $75 one-time fee/pet. Service with restrictions, crate.

Days Inn Oceanfront SH
(757) 428-7233. **$59-$275, 3 day notice.** 3107 Atlantic Ave. I-264, 0.8 mi n of terminus; just n of jct Laskin Rd (SR 58) at 32nd St. Int corridors. **Pets:** Small, other species. $25 daily fee/pet. Service with restrictions, crate.

DoubleTree Hotel Virginia Beach SH
(757) 422-8900. **$79-$239, 3 day notice.** 1900 Pavilion Dr. I-264, exit 22 (Birdneck Rd). Int corridors. **Pets:** Accepted.

Extended StayAmerica-Virginia-Independence Blvd M
(757) 473-9200. **$74-$79.** 4548 Bonney Rd. I-264, exit 17B (Independence Blvd/Pembroke Area), just n to Bonney Rd, then just e. Ext corridors. **Pets:** Accepted.

Fairfield Inn by Marriott SH
(757) 499-1935. **$109-$139.** 4760 Euclid Rd. I-264, exit 17B (Independence Blvd), just n to Euclid Rd, then just w. Ext/int corridors. **Pets:** Accepted.

Holiday Inn-Executive Center LH ✿
(757) 499-4400. **$114-$199.** 5655 Greenwich Rd. I-64, exit 284B (Newtown Rd); jct I-64 and 264. Int corridors. **Pets:** Medium. Designated rooms, service with restrictions, crate.

Holiday Inn Surfside Hotel & Suites SH
(757) 491-6900. **$89-$244, 3 day notice.** 2607 Atlantic Ave. I-264, n of terminus; at Atlantic Ave and 26th St. Int corridors. **Pets:** Accepted.

La Quinta Inn Norfolk (Virginia Beach) SH
(757) 497-6620. **$84-$185.** 192 Newtown Rd. I-64, exit 284B to I-264 (Virginia Beach-Norfolk Expwy), exit Newtown Rd S. Int corridors. **Pets:** Medium. Service with restrictions.

Ramada Plaza Resort Oceanfront LH
(757) 428-7025. **$80-$245, 3 day notice.** Atlantic Ave & 57th St. I-264, 2.2 mi n of terminus. Int corridors. **Pets:** Accepted.

Red Roof Inn VA Beach (Norfolk Airport) M ✿
(757) 460-6700. **$50-$170, 3 day notice.** 5745 Northampton Blvd. I-64, exit 282, 1 mi n on US 13 (Northampton Blvd). Ext corridors. **Pets:** Small. $25 deposit/room. Designated rooms, service with restrictions, supervision.

Residence Inn Virginia Beach Oceanfront SH
(757) 425-1141. **$154-$319.** 3217 Atlantic Ave. I-264, 1.5 mi n of terminus; Atlantic Ave and 33rd St. Int corridors. **Pets:** Other species. $75 one-time fee/room.

Sheraton Oceanfront Hotel SH ✿
(757) 425-9000. **$99-$259, 3 day notice.** 3501 Atlantic Ave. I-264, 1 mi n of terminus; jct 36th St. Int corridors. **Pets:** Medium, dogs only. Designated rooms, service with restrictions, supervision.

TownePlace Suites By Marriott SH
(757) 490-9367. **$114-$219.** 5757 Cleveland St. I-64, exit 284B to I-264 (Virginia Beach-Norfolk Expwy), exit Newtown Rd N. Int corridors. **Pets:** Medium. $100 one-time fee/room. Service with restrictions, crate.

END AREA

HARRISONBURG

Comfort Inn SH
(540) 433-6066. **$79-$185.** 1440 E Market St. I-81, exit 247A, just e. Int corridors. **Pets:** Other species. $10 daily fee/pet. Service with restrictions, supervision.

Days Inn Harrisonburg SH
(540) 433-9353. **$69-$195.** 1131 Forest Hill Rd. I-81, exit 245, just e. Int corridors. **Pets:** Small, dogs only. $20 daily fee/pet. Designated rooms, service with restrictions.

Harrisonburg Econo Lodge M
(540) 433-2576. **$60-$200.** 1703 E Market St. I-81, exit 247A, 0.5 mi e on US 33. Ext/int corridors. **Pets:** Accepted.

Motel 6 Harrisonburg #1211 M
(540) 433-6939. **$48-$61.** 10 Linda Ln. I-81, exit 247A, just e on US 33. Ext corridors. **Pets:** Medium, other species. Service with restrictions, supervision.

Ramada Inn SH
(540) 434-9981. **$60-$75.** 1 Pleasant Valley Rd. I-81, exit 243, just w, then just n on US 11. Ext corridors. **Pets:** Accepted.

Super 8 Motel M
(540) 433-8888. **$49-$199, 3 day notice.** 3330 S Main St. I-81, exit 243, just e, then just s on US 11. Int corridors. **Pets:** $10 daily fee/pet. Service with restrictions, supervision.

The Village Inn SH ✿
(540) 434-7355. **$69-$79.** 4979 S Valley Pike. I-81, exit 240 southbound, 0.6 mi w on SR 257, then 1.5 mi n on US 11; exit 243 northbound, just w to US 11, then 1.7 mi s. Ext corridors. **Pets:** Other species. $10 daily fee/pet. Service with restrictions.

HILLSVILLE

Best Western Four Seasons South SH
(276) 728-4136. **$55-$90.** 57 Airport Rd. I-77, exit 14, just w on US 58 and 221. Ext corridors. **Pets:** $10 one-time fee/room. Designated rooms, service with restrictions.

◬ ▼▼▼ **Quality Inn** 🆂🅷
(276) 728-2120. **$75-$200, 7 day notice.** 85 Airport Rd. I-77, exit 14, just w on US 58 and 221. Ext corridors. **Pets:** Medium, other species. $10 daily fee/pet. Designated rooms, service with restrictions, supervision.
🆂🅰🆅🅴 🆂🅾 ⊠ 🅶🅼 ⅊ 🗄 ⌨ ⇶

▼ **Red Carpet Inn** Ⓜ
(276) 728-9118. **$61-$130.** 2666 Old Galax Pike. I-77, exit 14, just n. Int corridors. **Pets:** Accepted.
🅰🆂🅺 🆂🅾 ⊠ 🗄 ⌨

HOPEWELL

◬ ▼▼ **Candlewood Suites** 🆂🅷
(804) 541-0200. **$89-$109.** 5113 Plaza Dr. I-295, exit 9B (SR 36), just w; adjacent to Oak Lawn Plaza. Int corridors. **Pets:** Accepted.
🆂🅰🆅🅴 🆂🅾 ⊠ ⅊ 🗄 ⌨

◬ ▼▼▼ **Econo Lodge** 🆂🅷
(804) 541-4849. **$69.** 4096 Oaklawn Blvd. I-295, exit 9A, just e. Int corridors. **Pets:** Small. $20 one-time fee/room. Service with restrictions, supervision.
🆂🅰🆅🅴 🆂🅾 ⊠ 🅶🅼 ⅊ 🗄 ⌨

HOT SPRINGS

▼▼ **Roseloe Motel** Ⓜ
(540) 839-5373. **$60-$80.** 10849 Sam Snead Hwy. 3 mi n. Ext corridors. **Pets:** Accepted.
🅰🆂🅺 🆂🅾 ⊠ 🗄 ⌨

HUDDLESTON

▼▼▼ **Mariners Landing** 🆅🅷
(540) 297-4900. **$119-$275.** 1217 Graves Harbor Tr. On SR 626; on Smith Mountain Lake. Ext/int corridors. **Pets:** Medium, dogs only. $15 daily fee/pet. Service with restrictions, supervision.
⊠ 🅶🅼 ⅊ 🗄 ⌨ 🍽 ⇶ ⊠

IRVINGTON

◬ ▼▼▼▼ **The Tides Inn** 🆂🅷 ❀
(804) 438-5000. **$160-$499, 7 day notice.** 480 King Carter Dr. 0.3 mi w of CR 200. Ext/int corridors. **Pets:** Medium, other species. $30 daily fee/pet. Designated rooms, service with restrictions.
🆂🅰🆅🅴 🆂🅾 ⊠ 🅶🅼 🕸 ⅊ 🗄 ⌨ 🍽 ⇶ ⊠

KESWICK

◬ ▼▼▼▼ **Keswick Hall at Monticello** 🆂🅷 ❀
(434) 979-3440. **$295-$925, 7 day notice.** 701 Club Dr. I-64, exit 129, just n. Int corridors. **Pets:** Medium. $75 one-time fee/room. Service with restrictions.
🆂🅰🆅🅴 ⊠ 🅶🅼 ⅊ 🗄 🍽 ⇶ ⊠

LAWRENCEVILLE

▼▼▼ **Brunswick Mineral Springs B & B Circa 1785** 🅱🅱 ❀
(434) 848-4010. **$85-$145, 5 day notice.** 14910 Western Mill Rd. 5 mi e on US 58, 1 mi s on SR 712, then just e. Int corridors. **Pets:** Large, dogs only. $25 one-time fee/pet. No service, supervision.
🅰🆂🅺 🆂🅾 ⊠ 🗄 ⌨

LEXINGTON

◬ ▼▼▼▼ **Best Western Inn at Hunt Ridge** 🆂🅷 ❀
(540) 464-1500. **$59-$175, 7 day notice.** 25 Willow Spring Rd. I-64, exit 55, just n on US 11 to SR 39; I-81, exit 191, 0.6 mi w. Int corridors. **Pets:** $25 one-time fee/pet. Service with restrictions, supervision.
🆂🅰🆅🅴 🆂🅾 ⊠ 🅶🅼 🕸 ⅊ 🗄 ⌨ 🍽 ⇶

◬ ▼▼▼ **Best Western Lexington Inn** 🆂🅷 ❀
(540) 458-3020. **$59-$155, 7 day notice.** 850 N Lee Hwy. I-64, exit 55, just s on US 11; I-81, exit 191, 1.6 mi w. Ext corridors. **Pets:** $25 one-time fee/room. Service with restrictions, supervision.
🆂🅰🆅🅴 🆂🅾 ⊠ 🕸 🗄 ⌨

◬ ▼▼▼▼ **Comfort Inn-Virginia Horse Center** 🆂🅷 ❀
(540) 463-7311. **$59-$155, 7 day notice.** 62 Comfort Way. I-64, exit 55, just s on US 11; I-81, exit 191, 0.6 mi w. Int corridors. **Pets:** $25 one-time fee/pet. Service with restrictions, supervision.
🆂🅰🆅🅴 🆂🅾 ⊠ 🗄 ⌨ ⇶

◬ ▼▼▼ **Days Inn Keydet General** 🆂🅷
(540) 463-2143. **$60-$135.** 325 W Midland Tr. I-81, exit 188B, 4.5 mi on US 60 W; I-64, exit 50, 5 mi e on US 60. Ext/int corridors. **Pets:** Other species. $10 daily fee/pet. Designated rooms, service with restrictions.
🆂🅰🆅🅴 🆂🅾 ⊠ 🗄 ⌨

▼▼▼ **Econo Lodge** Ⓜ
(540) 463-7371. **$50-$135.** 65 Econo Ln. I-81, exit 191, just s on US 11. Ext corridors. **Pets:** Accepted.
🅰🆂🅺 🆂🅾 ⊠ 🗄 ⌨

◬ ▼▼▼ **Holiday Inn Express** 🆂🅷 ❀
(540) 463-7351. **$74-$180, 7 day notice.** 880 N Lee Hwy. I-64, exit 55, just s on US 11; I-81, exit 191, 1 mi w. Int corridors. **Pets:** $25 one-time fee/pet. Service with restrictions, supervision.
🆂🅰🆅🅴 🆂🅾 ⊠ ⅊ 🗄 ⌨

◬ ▼▼▼ **Howard Johnson Inn** 🆂🅷
(540) 463-9181. **$49-$130.** 2836 N Lee Hwy. I-81, exit 195, just s on US 11. Int corridors. **Pets:** $10 daily fee/pet. Designated rooms, service with restrictions, supervision.
🆂🅰🆅🅴 🆂🅾 ⊠ 🕸 🗄 ⌨ ⇶

▼▼ **Ramada Inn Lexington** 🆂🅷
(540) 463-6400. **$51-$119.** 2814 N Lee Hwy. I-81, exit 195, just sw on US 11. Int corridors. **Pets:** Accepted.
🅰🆂🅺 🆂🅾 ⊠ 🕸 ⅊ 🗄 ⌨ ⇶

▼▼ **Super 8 Motel** Ⓜ
(540) 463-7858. **$52-$90.** 1139 N Lee Hwy. I-64, exit 55, just n. Int corridors. **Pets:** Accepted.
🅰🆂🅺 🆂🅾 ⊠ 🗄

LURAY

◬ ▼▼▼ **Best Western Intown of Luray** 🆂🅷 ❀
(540) 743-6511. **$65-$115.** 410 W Main St. 0.3 mi w on US 211 business route. Ext corridors. **Pets:** Dogs only. $20 daily fee/pet. Service with restrictions, supervision.
🆂🅰🆅🅴 🆂🅾 ⊠ 🗄 ⌨ 🍽 ⇶

▼▼▼ **Days Inn-Luray** 🆂🅷
(540) 743-4521. **$49-$109.** 138 Whispering Hill Rd. US 211 Bypass, 1.7 mi e of jct US 340. Ext corridors. **Pets:** Medium. $10 daily fee/pet. Designated rooms, service with restrictions, supervision.
🅰🆂🅺 🆂🅾 ⊠ 🗄 ⇶ ⊠

LYNCHBURG

▼▼ **Days Inn** 🆂🅷
(434) 847-8655. **$69-$89.** 3320 Candlers Mountain Rd. US 29, exit US 501, just e. Int corridors. **Pets:** Accepted.
🅰🆂🅺 🆂🅾 ⊠ 🗄 ⌨ 🍽 ⇶

◬ ▼▼ **Econo Lodge** Ⓜ
(434) 847-1045. **$75-$100, 3 day notice.** 2400 Stadium Rd. US 29, exit 4 southbound; exit 6 northbound, just w on James St, then just n. Ext corridors. **Pets:** Very small. $15 one-time fee/pet. Designated rooms, service with restrictions.
🆂🅰🆅🅴 🆂🅾 ⊠ 🗄 ⌨

▼▼▼ Extended StayAmerica–University Blvd M
(434) 239-8863. **Call for rates.** 1910 University Blvd. US 460, exit Candlers Mountain Rd/University Blvd. Int corridors. **Pets:** Accepted.
[X] [&M] [⟨⟩] [📶] [▣]

▼▼▼ Holiday Inn Select SH
(434) 528-2500. **$99-$159.** 601 Main St. US 29 Expwy, exit 1 (Main St), just w; downtown. Int corridors. **Pets:** Accepted.
[ASK] [S📶] [X] [⟨⟩] [📶] [▣] [¶¶] [⇌]

▲▲▲ ▼▼▼ Quality Inn SH
(434) 847-9041. **$79-$175.** 3125 Albert Lankford Dr. US 29, exit 7, just s. Int corridors. **Pets:** Medium. $25 one-time fee/pet. Designated rooms, service with restrictions, supervision.
[SAVE] [S📶] [X] [📶] [▣] [⇌]

MARION

▲▲▲ ▼▼▼ Best Western-Marion SH ❀
(276) 783-3193. **$69-$99, 10 day notice.** 1424 N Main St. I-81, exit 47, 0.3 mi s on US 11. Ext corridors. **Pets:** Other species. $7 daily fee/pet. Designated rooms, service with restrictions, supervision.
[SAVE] [S📶] [X] [⟨⟩] [⟨⟩] [📶] [▣] [¶¶] [⇌]

▲▲▲ ▼ Econo Lodge SH
(276) 783-6031. **$59-$89, 10 day notice.** 1424 N Main St. I-81, exit 47, 0.3 mi s on US 11. Ext corridors. **Pets:** Small, other species. $8 daily fee/pet. Service with restrictions, supervision.
[SAVE] [S📶] [X] [⟨⟩] [📶]

MARTINSVILLE

▼ Best Lodge M
(276) 647-3941. **$45-$58.** 1985 Virginia Ave. Jct US 58, 2.5 mi n on US 220 business route. Ext corridors. **Pets:** Medium. $10 daily fee/pet. Designated rooms, service with restrictions, supervision.
[ASK] [S📶] [X] [📶] [▣]

▲▲▲ ▼▼▼ Best Western Martinsville Inn SH
(276) 632-5611. **$85.** US 220 Business Rt S. Jct US 58, 2.3 mi n. Ext corridors. **Pets:** Large, other species. $10 daily fee/room. Service with restrictions, crate.
[SAVE] [S📶] [X] [📶] [▣] [¶¶] [⇌]

▼ Super 8 Motel M
(276) 666-8888. **$55-$65, 30 day notice.** 1044 N Memorial Blvd. Jct US 58, 1.5 mi n on US 220 business route. Int corridors. **Pets:** Accepted.
[ASK] [S📶] [X] [📶]

MAX MEADOWS

▲▲▲ ▼▼▼ Super 8 Motel SH
(276) 637-4141. **$60-$80.** 194 Ft Chiswell Rd. I-77/81, exit 80, just e. Ext corridors. **Pets:** Accepted.
[SAVE] [S📶] [X] [⟨⟩] [📶] [▣]

MIDDLETOWN

▲▲▲ ▼▼▼ Super 8 Motel SH
(540) 868-1800. **$55-$199.** 2120 Reliance Rd. I-81, exit 302. Int corridors. **Pets:** Accepted.
[SAVE] [S📶] [X] [📶] [▣] [⇌]

MINT SPRING

▼▼ Days Inn-Staunton M
(540) 337-3031. **$49-$129.** 372 White Hill Rd. I-81, exit 217, just e on SR 654. Ext corridors. **Pets:** Medium, other species. $10 daily fee/pet. Designated rooms, service with restrictions, supervision.
[ASK] [S📶] [X] [⟨⟩] [⟨⟩] [📶] [▣] [⇌]

MOUNT JACKSON

▲▲▲ ▼▼▼ Best Western-Shenandoah Valley SH
(540) 477-2911. **$70-$130, 4 day notice.** 250 Conickville Rd. I-81, exit 273, just e. Ext corridors. **Pets:** Medium, other species. $10 daily fee/pet. Designated rooms, service with restrictions.
[SAVE] [S📶] [X] [📶] [▣] [¶¶] [⇌]

▼▼▼ The Widow Kip's BB ❀
(540) 477-2400. **$90-$95, 5 day notice.** 355 Orchard Dr. I-81, exit 273, 1.5 mi s on US 11, just w on SR 263, then just sw on SR 698. Int corridors. **Pets:** Other species. $15 daily fee/pet. Designated rooms, no service, crate.
[ASK] [S📶] [X] [📶] [▣] [⇌]

NEW CHURCH

▼▼▼ The Garden & The Sea Inn BB ❀
(757) 824-0672. **$85-$205, 10 day notice.** 4188 Nelson Rd. US 13, 0.3 mi n, just w on CR 710 (Nelson Rd). Int corridors. **Pets:** Other species.
[X] [📶] [⇌] [🄩]

NEW MARKET

▲▲▲ ▼ Budget Inn M
(540) 740-3105. **$29-$69, 3 day notice.** 2192 Old Valley Pike. I-81, exit 264, 1 mi n on US 11. Ext corridors. **Pets:** Small. $10 deposit/room, $5 daily fee/pet. Designated rooms, no service, supervision.
[SAVE] [S📶] [X]

▲▲▲ ▼▼▼ Days Inn SH
(540) 740-4100. **$49-$125.** 9360 George Collins Pkwy. I-81, exit 264, just w on US 211. Ext corridors. **Pets:** $10 daily fee/pet. Service with restrictions, supervision.
[SAVE] [S📶] [X] [▣] [⇌]

NORTON

▼▼▼ Days Inn SH
(276) 679-5340. **$40-$159.** 375 Wharton Ln. Jct US 58 and 23. Int corridors. **Pets:** Other species. $10 one-time fee/room. No service, supervision.
[ASK] [S📶] [X] [⟨⟩] [⟨⟩] [📶] [▣]

ONANCOCK

▲▲▲ ▼▼▼ Spinning Wheel Bed & Breakfast BB ❀
(757) 787-7311. **$75-$110, 3 day notice.** 31 North St. Just n of jct Market (SR 179) and North sts. Int corridors. **Pets:** Medium, other species. $10 daily fee/pet. Crate.
[SAVE] [X] [🄦] [🄩]

PALMYRA

▼▼▼ Inn 1831 and Restaurant BB
(434) 589-1300. **$89-$195, 10 day notice.** Rt 2, Box 1390. On SR 640, 1.8 mi w of jct US 15. Ext/int corridors. **Pets:** Medium. $20 daily fee/pet.
[ASK] [X] [▣] [¶¶] [⇌] [X] [🄩]

PETERSBURG

▲▲▲ ▼▼▼ Best Western-Steven Kent SH
(804) 733-0600. **$65-$90.** 12205 S Crater Rd. I-95, exit 45, jct US 301. Ext/int corridors. **Pets:** Other species. $10 daily fee/pet. Service with restrictions, supervision.
[SAVE] [S📶] [X] [⟨⟩] [📶] [▣] [¶¶] [⇌]

▲▲▲ ▼▼▼ Days Inn SH
(804) 733-4400. **$60-$110.** 12208 S Crater Rd. I-95, exit 45, jct US 301. Ext corridors. **Pets:** $10 daily fee/pet. Service with restrictions, supervision.
[SAVE] [S📶] [X] [📶] [▣] [⇌]

▲▲▲ ▼▼▼ Econo Lodge-South SH
(804) 862-2717. **$49-$129.** 16905 Parkdale Rd. I-95, exit 41, just e. Ext corridors. **Pets:** Accepted.
[SAVE] [S📶] [X] [📶] [▣] [¶¶] [⇌]

♦♦ **Quality Inn** [SH]
(804) 732-2900. **$55-$120.** 11974 S Crater Rd. I-95, exit 45, just n. Ext corridors. **Pets:** Medium. $10 daily fee/room. Designated rooms, service with restrictions.
[ASK] [S/D] ⊠ ▣ 📺 🏊

POUNDING MILL

♦♦♦ **Claypool Hill Holiday Inn Express Hotel & Suites** [SH]
(276) 596-9880. **$80-$140, 14 day notice.** 180 Clay Dr. 0.5 mi e of US 460 and 19. Int corridors. **Pets:** Accepted.
[ASK] [S/D] ⊠ ♿ ▣ 📺 🏊

RADFORD

[AAA] ♦♦♦ **Best Western Radford Inn** [SH] 🐾
(540) 639-3000. **$75-$119.** 1501 Tyler Ave. I-81, exit 109, 2.7 mi nw on SR 177. Int corridors. **Pets:** Small. $10 one-time fee/room. Designated rooms, service with restrictions, crate.
[SAVE] [S/D] ⊠ ▣ 📺 🍴 🏊 🏋

♦ **Super 8 Motel-Radford** [M]
(540) 731-9355. **$50-$56.** 1600 Tyler Ave. I-81, exit 109, just w. Int corridors. **Pets:** Other species. $15 one-time fee/pet. Service with restrictions, crate.
[ASK] [S/D] ⊠ ▣

RAPHINE

♦♦ **Days Inn-Shenandoah Valley** [M]
(540) 377-2604. **$59-$84.** 584 Oakland Cir. I-81, exit 205, just sw. Int corridors. **Pets:** Accepted.
[ASK] [S/D] ⊠ ▣ 🏊

Richmond Metropolitan Area

ASHLAND

[AAA] ♦♦ **Days Inn Ashland** [M]
(804) 798-4262. **$50-$160.** 806 England St. I-95, exit 92B, just w on SR 54. Ext corridors. **Pets:** Accepted.
[SAVE] [S/D] ⊠ ▣ 🏊

[AAA] ♦ **Econo Lodge** [M]
(804) 798-9221. **$39-$109.** 103 N Carter Rd. I-95, exit 92, just w. Ext corridors. **Pets:** Accepted.
[SAVE] [S/D] ⊠ ▣ 📺 🏊

♦♦♦ **The Henry Clay Inn** [CI]
(804) 798-3100. **$90-$165.** 114 N Railroad Ave. I-95, exit 92, 1.5 mi w on SR 54, then n. Ext/int corridors. **Pets:** Accepted.
[ASK] [S/D] ⊠ ▣ 📺

♦♦ **Motel 6** [SH]
(804) 752-7777. **$65-$160.** 101 Cottage Green Dr. I-95, exit 92B, 0.5 mi w on SR 54. Ext corridors. **Pets:** Medium, other species. Service with restrictions, supervision.
[ASK] [S/D] ⊠ 🏊

DOSWELL

[AAA] ♦♦ **Best Western-Kings Quarters** [SH]
(804) 876-3321. **$59-$189, 3 day notice.** 16102 Theme Park Way. I-95, exit 98, just e on SR 30; entrance to theme park. Ext corridors. **Pets:** Accepted.
[SAVE] [S/D] ⊠ ♿ ▣ 📺 🍴 🏊 🏋

GLEN ALLEN

♦♦ **Candlewood Suites Richmond-West** [SH]
(804) 364-2000. **$109.** 4120 Brookriver Dr. I-64, exit 178, just w on W Broad St. Int corridors. **Pets:** Accepted.
[ASK] [S/D] ⊠ ♿M 🦻 ♿ ▣ 📺

♦♦ **Homestead Studio Suites Hotel-Richmond-Innsbrook** [M]
(804) 747-8898. **$84.** 10961 W Broad St. I-64, exit 178B, just e on W Broad St, then just s on Cox Rd. Ext corridors. **Pets:** Accepted.
[ASK] [S/D] ⊠ ▣ 📺

♦♦♦ **Homewood Suites by Hilton Richmond West End-Innsbrook** [SH]
(804) 217-8000. **$159-$169.** 4100 Innslake Dr. I-64, exit 178B, just e on W Broad St to Cox Rd, then just n. Int corridors. **Pets:** Accepted.
[ASK] [S/D] ⊠ ♿M 🦻 ♿ ▣ 📺 🏊

♦♦♦ **Residence Inn by Marriott** [SH]
(804) 762-9852. **$144-$169.** 3940 Westerre Pkwy. I-64, exit 180, n on Gaskins Rd to W Broad St. Int corridors. **Pets:** Accepted.
[ASK] [S/D] ⊠ ♿M ♿ ▣ 📺 🏊 🏋

RICHMOND

♦♦ **Candlewood Suites** [SH]
(804) 271-0016. **$99-$139.** 4301 Commerce Rd. I-95, exit 69, just n. Int corridors. **Pets:** Accepted.
[ASK] [S/D] ⊠ ♿M ♿ ▣ 📺

♦♦ **Days Inn-Richmond West** [SH]
(804) 282-3300. **$59-$159.** 2100 Dickens Rd. I-64, exit 183B westbound; exit 183 eastbound, 0.3 mi e on W Broad St, then just n. Int corridors. **Pets:** Accepted.
[ASK] [S/D] ⊠ 🦻 ▣ 📺 🏊

♦♦ **Extended StayAmerica-I-64-West Broad** [M]
(804) 285-2065. **$74-$84.** 6811 Paragon Pl. I-64, exit 183C (W Broad St), just w to Glenside Dr, just n. Ext corridors. **Pets:** Accepted.
[ASK] [S/D] ⊠ ▣ 📺 🏊

[AAA] ♦♦♦ **Holiday Inn Central** [SH]
(804) 359-9441. **$99-$109.** 3207 N Boulevard. I-64/95, exit 78, just n. Ext/int corridors. **Pets:** Small. $15 one-time fee/room. Designated rooms, service with restrictions, supervision.
[SAVE] [S/D] ⊠ ♿M ♿ ▣ 📺 🍴 🏊

♦♦♦ **Homestead Studio Suites Hotel-Richmond/Midlothian** [SH]
(804) 272-1800. **$84.** 241 Arboretum Pl. Jct Powhite Pkwy (US 76) and Midlothian Tpke (US 60), just w. Int corridors. **Pets:** Accepted.
[ASK] [S/D] ⊠ ♿M 🦻 ♿ ▣ 📺

[AAA] ♦♦♦♦ **The Jefferson Hotel** [LH] 🐾
(804) 788-8000. **$305-$355.** 101 W Franklin St. Franklin and Adams sts; center. Int corridors. **Pets:** Other species. $40 daily fee/pet. Service with restrictions.
[SAVE] [S/D] ⊠ 🦻 ♿ ▣ 🍴 🏊

♦♦♦ **Omni Richmond Hotel** [LH]
(804) 344-7000. **$249-$259.** 100 S 12th St. I-95, exit 74A; I-195, exit Canal St. Int corridors. **Pets:** Accepted.
[ASK] [S/D] ⊠ 🦻 ▣ 📺 🍴 🏊

◬ ▼▼▼ Quality Inn West End SH
(804) 346-0000. **$79-$99.** 8008 W Broad St. I-64, exit 183C westbound; exit 183 eastbound, 1.5 mi w. Int corridors. **Pets:** Medium. $10 daily fee/pet, $35 one-time fee/pet. Service with restrictions, supervision.
SAVE ▮▮ ✕ ▮ ▮ ▮ ▮ ⇔

▼▼▼ Radisson Hotel Historic Richmond SH
(804) 644-9871. **$90-$110.** 301 W Franklin St. Franklin St at Madison. Int corridors. **Pets:** Accepted.
✕ ▮ ▮ ▮ ▮ ⇔

▼▼▼ Sheraton Park South Hotel SH
(804) 323-1144. **$225-$275.** 9901 Midlothian Tpke. US 60, 1 mi w of Powhite Pkwy (US 76). Int corridors. **Pets:** Accepted.
✕ ▮ ▮ ▮ ▮ ▮ ⇔ ✕

◬ ▼▼▼▼ Sheraton Richmond West LH ✿
(804) 285-2000. **$90-$285.** 6624 W Broad St. I-64, exit 183 eastbound; exit 183B westbound. Int corridors. **Pets:** Medium. Service with restrictions, crate.
SAVE ✕ ▮ ▮ ▮ ▮ ▮ ▮ ⇔ ✕

◬ ▼▼▼ Wyndham Richmond Airport SH
(804) 226-4300. **$119-$179.** 4700 S Laburnum Ave. I-64, exit 195, 0.5 mi s. Int corridors. **Pets:** Medium. $50 one-time fee/room. Service with restrictions, crate.
SAVE ▮▮ ✕ ▮ ▮ ▮ ▮ ⇔ ✕

SANDSTON

◬ ▼▼▼ Clarion SH
(804) 222-6450. **$119-$249.** 5203 Williamsburg Rd. I-64, exit 195, 1.5 mi s to Williamsburg Rd, then just e. Ext/int corridors. **Pets:** Accepted.
SAVE ▮▮ ✕ ▮ ▮ ▮ ▮ ⇔

END METROPOLITAN AREA

ROANOKE

◬ ▼▼▼▼ Best Western Inn at Valley View SH
(540) 362-2400. **$69-$139, 7 day notice.** 5050 Valley View Blvd. I-581, exit 3E, just e, then just s via shopping center exit. Int corridors. **Pets:** $25 one-time fee/pet. Service with restrictions, supervision.
SAVE ▮▮ ✕ ▮ ▮ ▮ ⇔

◬ ▼▼▼▼ Comfort Inn Airport SH
(540) 527-2020. **$74-$144, 7 day notice.** 5070 Valley View Blvd. I-81, exit 143 to I-581, exit 3, e to Hershberger Rd. Int corridors. **Pets:** Medium, dogs only. $25 one-time fee/pet. Service with restrictions, supervision.
SAVE ✕ ▮ ▮ ▮ ⇔

◬ ▼▼▼ Courtyard By Marriott Roanoke Airport SH ✿
(540) 563-5002. **$129-$169.** 3301 Ordway Dr. I-581, exit 3W, just w to Ordway Dr. Int corridors. **Pets:** Medium. $75 one-time fee/pet. Designated rooms, service with restrictions, supervision.
SAVE ▮▮ ✕ ▮ ▮ ▮ ▮ ▮ ⇔

◬ ▼▼▼ Days Inn SH
(540) 366-0341. **$65-$105.** 8118 Plantation Rd. I-81, exit 146, just e on SR 115. Ext/int corridors. **Pets:** Medium, other species. $15 one-time fee/room. Service with restrictions, supervision.
SAVE ▮▮ ✕ ▮ ▮ ▮ ⇔

▼ Extended StayAmerica Roanoke-Airport M
(540) 366-3216. **$74-$84.** 2705 W Frontage Rd NW. I-581, exit 3W, just w to Ordway Dr, then 0.4 mi n via service frontage road. Ext corridors. **Pets:** Accepted.
A$K ▮▮ ✕ ▮ ▮ ▮

◬ ▼▼▼▼ Holiday Inn Hotel Tanglewood SH
(540) 774-4400. **$79-$135, 14 day notice.** 4468 Starkey Rd. I-581, exit Franklin Rd/Salem, 0.8 mi n on SR 419. Int corridors. **Pets:** Medium. $35 one-time fee/room. Service with restrictions, supervision.
SAVE ▮▮ ✕ ▮ ▮ ▮ ▮ ▮ ⇔

▼▼▼▼ Holiday Inn Roanoke SH
(540) 362-4500. **$80-$119.** 3315 Ordway Dr. I-581, exit 3W, just w to Ordway Dr, then 0.6 mi n via service road. Int corridors. **Pets:** Medium. $10 daily fee/room, $25 one-time fee/room. Service with restrictions, crate.
A$K ▮▮ ✕ ▮ ▮ ▮ ▮ ▮ ⇔ ✕

◬ ▼▼▼▼ MainStay Suites Roanoke Airport SH
(540) 527-3030. **$79-$175, 7 day notice.** 5080 Valley View Blvd. I-581, exit 3E, just n. Int corridors. **Pets:** Medium, dogs only. $25 one-time fee/pet. Designated rooms, service with restrictions, supervision.
SAVE ▮▮ ✕ ▮ ▮

◬ ▼▼▼▼ Quality Inn Airport SH ✿
(540) 366-8861. **$59-$129, 7 day notice.** 6626 Thirlane Rd. I-581, exit 2 southbound, just s on SR 117 (Peters Creek Rd), then just w. Ext corridors. **Pets:** Other species. $25 one-time fee/room. Service with restrictions, crate.
SAVE ▮▮ ✕ ▮ ▮ ▮ ▮ ⇔ ✕

◬ ▼▼▼ Ramada Inn Conference Center SH
(540) 343-0121. **$49-$109.** 1927 Franklin Rd. Off US 220; exit US 220 business route northbound; exit Wonju St southbound. Ext corridors. **Pets:** $15 daily fee/room. No service, crate.
SAVE ▮▮ ✕ ▮ ▮ ⇔

◬ ▼▼ Sleep Inn Tanglewood SH
(540) 772-1500. **$49-$124, 7 day notice.** 4045 Electric Rd. I-581/US 220, exit Franklin Rd/Salem, 0.7 mi n on SR 419. Int corridors. **Pets:** $25 one-time fee/pet. Service with restrictions, supervision.
SAVE ▮▮ ✕ ▮ ▮

▼▼ Super 8 Motel SH
(540) 563-8888. **$59-$67, 7 day notice.** 6616 Thirlane Rd. I-581, exit 25, s on SR 117 (Peters Creek Rd), then just w. Int corridors. **Pets:** Accepted.
A$K ▮▮ ✕ ▮

ROCKY MOUNT

◬ ▼▼ Franklin Motel M
(540) 483-9962. **$45-$80, 7 day notice.** 20281 Virgil H Goode Hwy. 6.5 mi n on US 220. Ext corridors. **Pets:** Small, dogs only. $10 daily fee/pet. Designated rooms, service with restrictions, supervision.
SAVE ▮▮ ✕ ▮

▼▼▼ Rocky Mount Holiday Inn Express Hotel & Suites SH
(540) 489-5001. **$85.** 395 Old Franklin Tpke. US 220 S and SR 40, 0.3 mi e. Int corridors. **Pets:** Dogs only. $25 daily fee/pet. Service with restrictions, crate.
A$K ▮▮ ✕ ▮ ▮ ▮ ⇔

RUTHER GLEN

Super 8 Motel-Ruther Glen SH
(804) 448-2608. **Call for rates.** 24011 Ruther Glen Rd. I-95, exit 104 (SR 207), just e on Rogers Clark Blvd. Ext corridors. **Pets:** Large, other species. $15 daily fee/room. Service with restrictions, supervision.
⊠ 🛋 💻 🏊

SALEM

Blue Jay Budget Host Inn M 🐾
(540) 380-2080. **$45-$80, 3 day notice.** 5399 W Main St. I-81, exit 132, just e, then 0.3 mi n on US 11/460. Ext corridors. **Pets:** $10 daily fee/pet. Designated rooms, service with restrictions, supervision.
SAVE 🛏 ⊠ 🛋

Comfort Suites Inn at Ridgewood Farm SH
(540) 375-4800. **$80-$130.** 2898 Keagy Rd. I-81, exit 141, 4.7 mi s on SR 419, then just w. Int corridors. **Pets:** Accepted.
SAVE 🛏 ⊠ 🛋 💻 🏊

Econo Lodge-Roanoke/Salem M
(540) 389-0280. **$37-$64.** 301 Wildwood Rd. I-81, exit 137, just e on SR 112. Ext corridors. **Pets:** Accepted.
SAVE 🛏 ⊠ 🛋 💻

Holiday Inn Express SH
(540) 986-1000. **$60-$120.** 1535 E Main St. I-81, exit 141, 2 mi s on SR 419, then just w on US 460. Ext/int corridors. **Pets:** Other species. $25 daily fee/pet. Service with restrictions.
SAVE ⊠ 🛋 💻

Quality Inn Roanoke/Salem SH
(540) 562-1912. **$58-$90.** 179 Sheraton Dr. I-81, exit 141, 0.4 mi e on SR 419. Int corridors. **Pets:** Medium, other species. $15 one-time fee/room. Service with restrictions, crate.
SAVE 🛏 ⊠ 🛋 💻 🏊

SOUTH BOSTON

Holiday Inn-Express SH
(434) 575-4000. **$89-$129.** 1074 Bill Tuck Hwy. Just e on US 58, from jct US 501. Int corridors. **Pets:** Accepted.
ASK 🛏 ⊠ 🛋ᴹ 🛋 💻 🏊

Quality Inn Howard House SH
(434) 572-4311. **$66-$81.** 2001 Seymour Dr. Jct US 58, 501 and 360, 1 mi e on US 360. Ext corridors. **Pets:** Accepted.
SAVE 🛏 ⊠ 💻 🍴 🏊

SOUTH HILL

Comfort Inn SH
(434) 447-2600. **$50-$80.** 918 E Atlantic St. I-85, exit 12B, just w. Ext corridors. **Pets:** Other species. $7 daily fee/room. No service.
SAVE 🛏 ⊠

Super 8 Motel SH
(434) 447-2313. **$56-$141, 7 day notice.** 250 Thompson St. I-85, exit 12A, just n. Int corridors. **Pets:** Accepted.
ASK ⊠ 🛋ᴹ 🛋

STAFFORD

Days Inn Aquia-Quantico SH
(540) 659-0022. **$73-$89.** 2868 Jefferson Davis Hwy. I-95, exit 143A, jct US 1 and SR 610. Ext corridors. **Pets:** Medium. $6 daily fee/pet. Designated rooms, service with restrictions, crate.
SAVE 🛏 ⊠ 💻 🍴 🏊

Holiday Inn Express SH
(540) 657-5566. **$90-$109.** 28 Greenspring Dr. I-95, exit 143B, just w on Garrisonville Rd. Int corridors. **Pets:** Small. $25 daily fee/pet. Service with restrictions, supervision.
ASK 🛏 ⊠ 🖨 💻

STAUNTON

Best Western Staunton Inn SH
(540) 885-1112. **$69-$129, 7 day notice.** 92 Rowe Rd. I-81, exit 222, just e on US 250. Int corridors. **Pets:** Dogs only. $25 one-time fee/pet. Service with restrictions, supervision.
SAVE 🛏 ⊠ 🖨 💻 🏊

Comfort Inn SH
(540) 886-5000. **$72-$135.** 1302 Richmond Ave. I-81, exit 222, just w on US 250. Int corridors. **Pets:** Accepted.
SAVE 🛏 ⊠ 🖨 💻 🏊

Days Inn-Business Place SH
(540) 248-0888. **$45-$119, 30 day notice.** 273-D Bells Ln. I-81, exit 225, just w. Ext corridors. **Pets:** Accepted.
SAVE 🛏 ⊠ 🛋 💻 🏊

Econo Lodge Staunton SH
(540) 885-5158. **$45-$129.** 1031 Richmond Ave. I-81, exit 222, 0.7 mi w on US 250. Ext/int corridors. **Pets:** Medium. $10 daily fee/pet. Service with restrictions, supervision.
SAVE 🛏 ⊠ 💻

GuestHouse International Inn SH
(540) 885-3117. **$52-$110.** 42 Sangers Ln. I-81, exit 222, just e on US 250. Ext corridors. **Pets:** Dogs only. $10 daily fee/room. Designated rooms, service with restrictions, supervision.
ASK 🛏 ⊠ 🖨 🛋 💻 🏊 ⊠

Holiday Inn Golf & Conference Center SH
(540) 248-6020. **$95-$200.** 152 Fairway Ln. I-81, exit 225, 0.3 mi w on SR 275 (Woodrow Wilson Pkwy). Int corridors. **Pets:** Other species. $15 one-time fee/pet. Designated rooms, service with restrictions, supervision.
SAVE 🛏 ⊠ 🖨 💻 🍴 🏊

Howard Johnson Express Inn SH
(540) 886-5330. **$60-$90, 3 day notice.** 268 N Central Ave. I-81, exit 222, 2.2 mi w on SR 250 into downtown; between Pine and Baldwin sts. Ext corridors. **Pets:** Accepted.
⊠ 🛋 🖨 💻 🏊

Quality Inn-Conference Center SH
(540) 248-5111. **$56-$109.** 96 Baker Ln. I-81, exit 225, just e on SR 275 (Woodrow Wilson Pkwy). Ext corridors. **Pets:** Large. $10 daily fee/pet. Designated rooms, service with restrictions, supervision.
SAVE 🛏 ⊠ 🖨 💻 🍴 🏊

Sleep Inn SH
(540) 887-6500. **$65-$129, 7 day notice.** 222 Jefferson Hwy. I-81, exit 222, just e on US 250. Int corridors. **Pets:** Medium, dogs only. $25 one-time fee/pet. Service with restrictions, supervision.
SAVE 🛏 ⊠ 🛋 🖨 💻

STEPHENS CITY

Comfort Inn-Stephens City SH
(540) 869-6500. **$78-$150.** 167 Town Run Ln. I-81, exit 307, just se. Int corridors. **Pets:** Other species. $15 daily fee/pet. Service with restrictions, supervision.
SAVE 🛏 ⊠ 🖨 💻 🏊

STONY CREEK

Hampton Inn-Stony Creek SH
(434) 246-5500. **$89-$149.** 10476 Blue Star Hwy. I-95, exit 33, 0.3 mi s on SR 301. Int corridors. **Pets:** Medium, other species. $10 daily fee/pet. Designated rooms, service with restrictions, crate.
SAVE 🛏 ⊠ 🛋ᴹ 🖨 💻 🏊

Sleep Inn & Suites SH
(434) 246-5100. **$65-$149.** 11019 Blue Star Hwy. I-95, exit 33, 0.3 mi s on SR 301. Int corridors. **Pets:** Medium, other species. $10 daily fee/pet. Service with restrictions, supervision.
SAVE 🛏 ⊠ 🖨 💻 🏊

STRASBURG

(AAA) ▼▼▼▼ Hotel Strasburg [CI]
(540) 465-9191. **$83-$1220.** 213 S Holliday St. I-81, exit 298, 2.2 mi s on US 11, then just s. Int corridors. **Pets:** Small, dogs only. $10 daily fee/pet. Service with restrictions, supervision.

[SAVE] [S🐾] [X] [🍽]

▼▼▼ Ramada Inn [SH]
(540) 465-2444. **$55-$95.** 21 Signal Knob Dr. I-81, exit 298, just e. Int corridors. **Pets:** Small. $10 daily fee/pet. Service with restrictions, supervision.

[ASK] [S🐾] [X] [🛏] [🔧] [🖥] [🍽] [➳]

TAPPAHANNOCK

▼▼ Super 8 Motel [M]
(804) 443-3888. **$60-$70.** 1800 Tappahannock Blvd. US 17 and 360. Int corridors. **Pets:** $10 daily fee/pet. Service with restrictions, supervision.

[ASK] [S🐾] [X] [🔧]

THORNBURG

▼▼ Quality Inn [SH]
(540) 582-1097. **$55-$129.** 6409 Dan Bell Ln. I-95, exit 118 (SR 606), just w. Ext corridors. **Pets:** Accepted.

[ASK] [S🐾] [X] [🛏] [🔧] [🖥] [➳]

TROUTVILLE

(AAA) ▼▼▼▼ Comfort Inn Troutville [SH]
(540) 992-5600. **$45-$99, 7 day notice.** 2545 Lee Hwy S. I-81, exit 150A, just s on US 11. Int corridors. **Pets:** $25 one-time fee/pet. Service with restrictions, supervision.

[SAVE] [S🐾] [X] [🔧] [🖥] [➳]

VERONA

(AAA) ▼▼▼▼ Ramada Limited [SH]
(540) 248-8981. **$39-$119, 3 day notice.** 70 Lodge Ln. I-81, exit 227, just w, then just n. Ext corridors. **Pets:** Small. $10 daily fee/pet. No service, supervision.

[SAVE] [S🐾] [X] [🛏] [🔧] [🖥] [➳]

WARRENTON

(AAA) ▼▼▼ Comfort Inn [M] 🐾
(540) 349-8900. **$119-$249.** 7379 Comfort Inn Dr. 1.5 mi n on US 15/29, on service road. Ext/int corridors. **Pets:** $10 daily fee/pet. Designated rooms, service with restrictions, supervision.

[SAVE] [S🐾] [X] [🔧] [🖥] [➳]

WARSAW

▼▼▼▼ Best Western Warsaw [SH]
(804) 333-1700. **$78-$99.** 4522 Richmond Rd. US 360, just w of town. Int corridors. **Pets:** Small. $10 daily fee/pet. Service with restrictions, supervision.

[ASK] [S🐾] [X] [🛏] [🔧] [🖥] [➳]

WAYNESBORO

(AAA) ▼▼▼ Days Inn Waynesboro [SH]
(540) 943-1101. **$54-$119.** 2060 Rosser Ave. I-64, exit 94, 0.5 mi n on US 340. Ext corridors. **Pets:** Other species. $10 daily fee/room. Service with restrictions, supervision.

[SAVE] [S🐾] [X] [🔧] [🖥] [➳]

(AAA) ▼▼▼ Quality Inn Waynesboro [SH]
(540) 942-1171. **$68-$105.** 640 W Broad St. I-64, exit 96, 3 mi w on SR 624; jct US 250 and 340. Ext/int corridors. **Pets:** Medium. $10 one-time fee/pet. Service with restrictions, crate.

[SAVE] [S🐾] [X] [🛁] [🔧] [🖥] [➳]

(AAA) ▼▼ Super 8 Motel [SH]
(540) 943-3888. **$54-$125.** 2045 Rosser Ave. I-64, exit 94, n on US 340 to Lew Dewitt Blvd, then just w to Apple Tree Ln. Int corridors. **Pets:** $5 daily fee/pet. Service with restrictions, supervision.

[SAVE] [S🐾] [X] [🛁] [🔧] [🖥]

WILLIAMSBURG, JAMESTOWN & YORKTOWN AREA

WILLIAMSBURG

(AAA) ▼▼▼ Best Western Colonial Capitol Inn [SH]
(757) 253-1222. **$59-$109, 3 day notice.** 111 Penniman Rd. Just n of jct US 60/Richmond Rd and SR 5. Int corridors. **Pets:** Accepted.

[SAVE] [S🐾] [X] [🛐M] [🔧] [🖥] [➳]

(AAA) ▼▼▼▼ Best Western Williamsburg Westpark Hotel [SH]
(757) 229-1134. **$59-$129.** 1600 Richmond Rd. Jct US 60/Richmond Rd and SR 612 (Ironbound Rd). Ext/int corridors. **Pets:** Accepted.

[SAVE] [S🐾] [X] [🛐M] [🔧] [🖥] [➳]

(AAA) ▼▼▼ Days Inn Colonial Downtown [SH]
(757) 229-5060. **$35-$109.** 902 Richmond Rd. Just w of Colonial Williamsburg on US 60. Ext corridors. **Pets:** Large, other species. $10 daily fee/pet. Service with restrictions, crate.

[SAVE] [S🐾] [X] [🔧] [➳]

(AAA) ▼▼▼▼ Four Points by Sheraton Hotel & Suites Williamsburg Historic District [SH]
(757) 229-4100. **$60-$140, 3 day notice.** 351 York St. US 60 E, 0.3 mi se of jct SR 5 and 31. Ext/int corridors. **Pets:** Accepted.

[SAVE] [S🐾] [X] [🛐M] [🔧] [🛐] [🔧] [🖥] [🍽] [➳] [X]

(AAA) ▼▼▼▼ Holiday Inn Patriot [SH]
(757) 565-2600. **$79-$149.** 3032 Richmond Rd. I-64, exit 234 (SR 199 E) to US 60, 2.5 mi e. Int corridors. **Pets:** Small. $15 one-time fee/room. Designated rooms, service with restrictions, supervision.

[SAVE] [S🐾] [X] [🛐] [🔧] [🖥] [🍽] [➳] [X]

(AAA) ▼▼▼▼ La Quinta Inn Williamsburg (Historic Area) [SH] 🐾
(757) 253-1663. **$55-$155.** 119 Bypass Rd. US 60 Bypass Rd, 0.3 mi e of Richmond Rd. Ext corridors. **Pets:** Other species. $30 one-time fee/room. Service with restrictions.

[SAVE] [S🐾] [X] [🛐M] [🔧] [🔧] [🖥] [➳]

(AAA) ▼▼▼ Patrick Henry Inn [SH]
(757) 229-9540. **$59-$129, 3 day notice.** 249 York St. E on US 60/Richmond Rd at jct SR 5 and 31; 1 blk from Colonial Williamsburg. Int corridors. **Pets:** Accepted.

[SAVE] [S🐾] [X] [🛐M] [🔧] [🖥] [🍽] [➳]

(AAA) ▼▼▼ Quarterpath Inn [M]
(757) 220-0960. **$39-$99, 3 day notice.** 620 York St. I-64, exit 242 (SR 199 W), 0.6 mi w to US 60 E, then just w. Ext corridors. **Pets:** Accepted.

[SAVE] [S🐾] [X] [🔧] [➳]

♦♦ Ramada Inn 1776 SH
(757) 220-1776. **$39-$129.** 725 Bypass Rd. US 60 (Bypass Rd), 0.5 mi w of jct SR 132. Int corridors. **Pets:** Medium. $10 daily fee/room. Designated rooms, no service, supervision.

⊠ 👓 🛏 🖵 🍽 ⊃

♦♦♦ Red Roof Inn-Williamsburg M
(757) 259-1948. **$40-$110.** 824 Capitol Landing Rd. I-64, exit 238, 0.9 mi se on SR 143, then just w on SR 5. Ext corridors. **Pets:** Medium, other species. Service with restrictions, supervision.

SAVE 👓 ⊠ 🛏 ⊃

♦♦♦♦ Residence Inn by Marriott Williamsburg SH
(757) 941-2000. **$109-$329.** 1648 Richmond Rd. US 60, just w of jct Bypass Rd. Int corridors. **Pets:** Accepted.

ASK 👓 ⊠ 👓 🛏 🖵 ⊃ ⊠

♦♦♦ Super 8 Motel-Historic M
(757) 229-0500. **$40-$85.** 304 2nd St. I-642, exit 242 (SR 199 W), 0.6 mi w on SR 199 to SR 143, 1.6 mi w to SR 162, then just w. Ext corridors. **Pets:** Medium, other species. $10 daily fee/pet. Service with restrictions, supervision.

SAVE 👓 ⊠ 🛏 ⊃

YORKTOWN

♦♦ Candlewood Suites-Yorktown SH
(757) 952-1120. **$79-$189.** 329 Commonwealth Dr. I-64, exit 256B, just n, then just e. Int corridors. **Pets:** Accepted.

ASK 👓 ⊠ 👓 🛏 🖵 ⊃

♦♦ Days Inn SH
(757) 283-1111. **Call for rates.** 4531 George Washington Memorial Hwy. I-64, exit 256B, 0.8 mi ne on Victory Blvd (SR 171), 2 mi n on US 17. Int corridors. **Pets:** Accepted.

⊠ 🛏 ⊃

♦♦♦ TownePlace Suites by Marriott SH 🐾
(757) 874-8884. **$129-$139.** 200 Cybernetics Way. I-64, exit 256B, e to Kiln Creek Pkwy. Int corridors. **Pets:** Other species. $75 one-time fee/room. Service with restrictions, crate.

SAVE 👓 ⊠ 👓 🛏 🖵 ⊃

END AREA

WINCHESTER

♦♦♦♦ Best Western Lee-Jackson Motor Inn SH
(540) 662-4154. **$62-$74.** 711 Millwood Ave. I-81, exit 313B, just nw on US 50/522/17. Ext corridors. **Pets:** Small. $5 daily fee/pet. Service with restrictions, supervision.

SAVE 👓 ⊠ 🛏 🖵 🍽 ⊃

♦♦♦ Days Inn SH
(540) 667-1200. **$55-$85.** 2951 Valley Ave. I-81, exit 310, just w, then 1.8 mi n on US 11. Ext corridors. **Pets:** Accepted.

SAVE 👓 ⊠ 🛏 ⊃

♦♦♦ Holiday Inn Winchester SH
(540) 667-3300. **$79-$99.** 1017 Millwood Pike. I-81, exit 313 northbound; exit 313A southbound, just se on US 50/17, at US 522. Ext/int corridors. **Pets:** Accepted.

SAVE 👓 ⊠ 🖉 🛏 🖵 🍽 ⊃

♦♦ Mohawk Motel M
(540) 667-1410. **$56-$58.** 2754 Northwestern Pike. I-81, exit 317, 3 mi s on SR 37, then 1.7 mi w on US 50. Ext corridors. **Pets:** Accepted.

ASK 👓 ⊠

♦♦♦ Red Roof Inn SH
(540) 667-5000. **$65-$75.** 991 Millwood Pike. I-81, exit 313 northbound; exit 313A southbound, just se on US 50/17. Ext corridors. **Pets:** Medium, other species. Service with restrictions, supervision.

SAVE 👓 ⊠ 🛏

♦♦♦ Super 8 Motel SH
(540) 665-4450. **$56-$76.** 1077 Millwood Pike. I-81, exit 313 northbound; exit 313A southbound, 0.3 mi se on US 50/17. Int corridors. **Pets:** Other species. $7 one-time fee/pet. Service with restrictions, supervision.

SAVE 👓 ⊠ 🛏

♦♦ Tourist City Motel M
(540) 662-9011. **$38-$54, 7 day notice.** 214 Millwood Ave. I-81, exit 313 northbound; exit 313B southbound, 1 mi nw on US 50/522. Ext corridors. **Pets:** Medium, other species. $5 daily fee/pet. Designated rooms, service with restrictions, supervision.

SAVE ⊠ 🛏

♦♦♦ Travelodge of Winchester SH
(540) 665-0685. **$75-$149.** 160 Front Royal Pike. I-81, exit 313 northbound; exit 313A southbound, just s on US 522. Int corridors. **Pets:** Medium, other species. $5 daily fee/pet. Designated rooms, service with restrictions, crate.

SAVE 👓 ⊠ 🖉 🛏 🖵 ⊃

WOODSTOCK

♦♦ Budget Host Inn M
(540) 459-4086. **$41-$50.** 1290 S Main St. I-81, exit 283, 0.8 mi se on SR 42, then 0.6 mi s on US 11. Ext corridors. **Pets:** Medium. $5 daily fee/pet. Service with restrictions, supervision.

SAVE 👓 ⊠ ⊃

♦♦♦ Comfort Inn Shenandoah SH
(540) 459-7600. **$79-$139.** 1011 Motel Dr. I-81, exit 283, just e. Int corridors. **Pets:** Accepted.

SAVE 👓 ⊠ 👓 🛏 🖵 ⊃

WYTHEVILLE

♦♦♦ Best Western Wytheville Inn SH
(276) 228-7300. **$60-$160, 7 day notice.** 355 Nye Rd. I-77, exit 41, just e. Int corridors. **Pets:** $10 daily fee/pet. Designated rooms, service with restrictions, supervision.

SAVE 👓 ⊠ 🛏 🖵 ⊃

♦♦ Budget Host Inn/Interstate Inn M
(276) 228-8618. **$45-$75.** 705 Chapman Rd. I-77/81, exit 73, just w. Ext corridors. **Pets:** Small. $10 daily fee/pet. No service, supervision.

ASK 👓 ⊠ 🛏

♦♦♦ Comfort Inn SH
(276) 637-4281. **$90-$100, 10 day notice.** 2594 E Lee Hwy. I-77/81, exit 80, just w. Int corridors. **Pets:** Accepted.

SAVE 👓 ⊠ 👓 🖉 👓 🛏 🖵 ⊃

♦♦ Days Inn SH
(276) 228-5500. **$65-$80.** 150 Malin Dr. I-81, exit 73, just w. Ext corridors. **Pets:** Small. $5 daily fee/pet. Service with restrictions, supervision.

ASK 👓 ⊠ 🖉 🖵

AAA ◆◆ Econo Lodge M
(276) 228-5517. **$69-$160.** 1160 E Main St. I-81, exit 73, 0.8 mi w. Ext corridors. **Pets:** Small, dogs only. $10 daily fee/pet. Designated rooms, service with restrictions, supervision.

[SAVE] [S⊘] [✕] [⊘] [⊟] [▭]

◆◆ Holiday Inn SH
(276) 228-5483. **$75-$105.** 1800 E Main St. I-77/81, exit 73, just w. Ext/int corridors. **Pets:** Accepted.

[ASK] [S⊘] [✕] [⊘] [⊠] [⊟] [▭] [❚❙] [⊇]

AAA ◆◆ Ramada SH
(276) 228-6000. **$59-$79, 3 day notice.** 955 Peppers Ferry Rd. I-77, exit 41, just e. Ext corridors. **Pets:** Accepted.

[SAVE] [S⊘] [✕] [⊟] [▭] [❚❙] [⊇]

AAA ◆◆ Red Carpet Inn M
(276) 228-5525. **$45-$150, 30 day notice.** 280 Lithia Rd. I-77/81, exit 73, just w. Ext corridors. **Pets:** Small. $10 daily fee/pet. Service with restrictions, supervision.

[SAVE] [S⊘] [✕] [⊟]

◆ Super 8 Motel SH
(276) 228-6620. **$35-$95.** 130 Nye Cir. I-77, exit 41, just e. Ext corridors. **Pets:** Accepted.

[ASK] [S⊘] [✕] [▭]

ABERDEEN

GuestHouse International Inn & Suites SH
(360) 537-7460. **$65-$279.** 701 E Heron St. Just e on US 12, cross street to Kansas St; downtown. Int corridors. **Pets:** Accepted.

Olympic Inn Motel M
(360) 533-4200. **$70-$95.** 616 W Heron St. 0.5 mi w; downtown. Ext corridors. **Pets:** Other species. $10 one-time fee/pet. Service with restrictions, supervision.

AIRWAY HEIGHTS

Microtel Inn & Suites SH
(509) 242-1200. **$59-$64.** 1215 S Garfield Rd. I-90, exit 277 to SR 2, 4 mi w. Int corridors. **Pets:** Accepted.

ANACORTES

Anaco Inn SH
(360) 293-8833. **$59-$104, 3 day notice.** 905 20th St. Just s of downtown. Ext/int corridors. **Pets:** Accepted.

Anacortes Inn M
(360) 293-3153. **$60-$82, 5 day notice.** 3006 Commercial Ave. Just s of downtown. Ext corridors. **Pets:** Medium, dogs only. $10 one-time fee/room. Designated rooms, no service, supervision.

Cap Sante Inn M
(360) 293-0602. **$64-$83.** 906 9th St. On 9th St, just e. Ext corridors. **Pets:** Dogs only. $10 daily fee/pet. Designated rooms, service with restrictions, supervision.

Fidalgo Country Inn SH
(360) 293-3494. **$94-$119.** 7645 SR 20. Jct Fidalgo Bay Rd. Ext/int corridors. **Pets:** Other species. $20 daily fee/pet. Designated rooms, service with restrictions.

Islands Inn M
(360) 293-4644. **$69-$110.** 3401 Commercial Ave. Just s of downtown. Ext corridors. **Pets:** Dogs only. $5 daily fee/room. Service with restrictions, supervision.

Majestic Inn and Spa SH
(360) 299-1400. **Call for rates.** 419 Commercial Ave. Downtown. Int corridors. **Pets:** Small, dogs only. $50 one-time fee/pet. Designated rooms, service with restrictions, supervision.

Ship Harbor Inn M
(360) 293-5177. **$69-$179, 3 day notice.** 5316 Ferry Terminal Rd. 0.3 mi s of ferry landing. Ext corridors. **Pets:** Other species. $10 daily fee/pet. Service with restrictions, supervision.

ASHFORD

Mountain Meadows Inn Bed & Breakfast BB
(360) 569-2788. **$99-$165, 14 day notice.** 28912 SR 706 E. West end of town. Ext/int corridors. **Pets:** Large, other species. $10 daily fee/pet. Designated rooms, supervision.

BELLINGHAM

Best Western Heritage Inn SH
(360) 647-1912. **$79-$109.** 151 E McLeod Rd. I-5, exit 256A, just e. Int corridors. **Pets:** $20 daily fee/pet. Designated rooms, service with restrictions, supervision.

Best Western Lakeway Inn & Conference Center SH
(360) 671-1011. **$89-$189.** 714 Lakeway Dr. I-5, exit 253 (Lakeway Dr), just se. Int corridors. **Pets:** Small. $20 daily fee/room. Designated rooms, service with restrictions, supervision.

The Chrysalis Inn & Spa SH
(360) 756-1005. **$179-$309.** 804 10th St. I-5, exit 250, 1.3 mi nw on Old Fairhaven Pkwy, 0.6 mi n via 12th and 11th sts, just w on Taylor Ave, then just n. Int corridors. **Pets:** Small, dogs only. $50 one-time fee/room. Designated rooms, service with restrictions, supervision.

AAA ▼▼▼▼ **Fairhaven Village Inn** SH ❀
(360) 733-1311. **$129-$182.** 1200 10th St. I-5, exit 250, 1.5 mi w. Int corridors. **Pets:** Small. $20 daily fee/pet. Designated rooms, service with restrictions, supervision.
[SAVE] [X] [&M] [⊘] [&] [🛏] [💻]

AAA ▼▼▼▼ **Holiday Inn Express-Bellingham** SH
(360) 671-4800. **$92-$128.** 4160 Meridian St. I-5, exit 256B, 0.7 mi e. Int corridors. **Pets:** Small, other species. $15 one-time fee/room. Service with restrictions, supervision.
[SAVE] [S6] [X] [&M] [⊘] [&] [🛏] [💻] [≈]

AAA ▼▼▼▼ **Hotel Bellwether** SH
(360) 392-3100. **$149-$815, 3 day notice.** One Bellwether Way. I-5, exit 253 (Lakeway Dr), 0.9 mi nw via Lakeway Dr and E Holly St, just w on Bay St, 0.6 mi n via W Chestnut St and Roeder Ave, then just w. Int corridors. **Pets:** $65 one-time fee/room. Crate.
[SAVE] [S6] [X] [💻] [¶] [✕]

▼▼ **Motel 6-44** M
(360) 671-4494. **$51-$71.** 3701 Byron Ave. I-5, exit 252, just nw. Ext corridors. **Pets:** Medium, other species. Service with restrictions, supervision.
[S6] [X] [&M] [🛏] [≈]

AAA ▼▼▼▼ **Quality Inn Baron Suites** SH
(360) 647-8000. **$95-$205.** 100 E Kellogg Rd. I-5, exit 256A, 1 mi ne via Meridian St. Ext/int corridors. **Pets:** Accepted.
[SAVE] [S6] [X] [⊘] [🛏] [💻] [≈]

AAA ▼▼▼▼ **Travel House Inn** SH
(360) 671-4600. **$49-$93.** 3750 Meridian St. I-5, exit 256A, just w. Ext corridors. **Pets:** $6 daily fee/room. Designated rooms, service with restrictions, supervision.
[SAVE] [S6] [X] [🛏] [≈]

▼▼ **Val-U Inn** SH
(360) 671-9600. **$63-$90.** 805 Lakeway Dr. I-5, exit 253 (Lakeway Dr), just ne. Int corridors. **Pets:** Medium, dogs only. $10 daily fee/room. Designated rooms, service with restrictions, supervision.
[ASK] [S6] [X] [🛏] [💻]

BLAINE

▼▼ **Anchor Inn Motel** M
(360) 332-5539. **$54-$60, 3 day notice.** 250 Cedar St. I-5, exit 276, 0.6 mi sw via Peace Portal Dr. Ext corridors. **Pets:** Small, dogs only. $10 daily fee/room. Service with restrictions, supervision.
[ASK] [S6] [X] [🛏]

AAA ▼▼▼▼ **Semiahmoo Resort** SH
(360) 318-2000. **$109-$279, 3 day notice.** 9565 Semiahmoo Pkwy. I-5, exit 270, 9.5 mi nw on Semiahmoo Spit. Int corridors. **Pets:** Medium, dogs only. $50 one-time fee/room. Designated rooms, service with restrictions, supervision.
[SAVE] [S6] [X] [⊘] [🛏] [💻] [¶] [≈] [✕]

BUCKLEY

AAA ▼▼▼ **Mt View Inn** SH
(360) 829-1100. **$70-$80.** 29405 SR 410 E. On SR 410 at SR 165. Int corridors. **Pets:** Small. $20 one-time fee/pet. Designated rooms, service with restrictions, supervision.
[SAVE] [S6] [X] [🛏] [≈]

BURLINGTON

AAA ▼▼▼ **Cocusa Motel** SH ❀
(360) 757-6044. **$53-$82.** 370 W Rio Vista. I-5, exit 230, just e. Ext corridors. **Pets:** $20 one-time fee/room. Designated rooms, service with restrictions, supervision.
[SAVE] [X] [&] [🛏] [💻] [≈]

CASHMERE

AAA ▼▼▼ **Village Inn Motel** M
(509) 782-3522. **$54-$74, 7 day notice.** 229 Cottage Ave. On Business Rt US 2 and 97; downtown. Ext corridors. **Pets:** Small, dogs only. $10 daily fee/pet. Designated rooms, no service, supervision.
[SAVE] [S6] [X] [🛏]

CASTLE ROCK

AAA ▼▼▼ **Timberland Inn & Suites** M
(360) 274-6002. **$70-$125.** 1271 Mount St. Helens Way. I-5, exit 49, just ne. Ext corridors. **Pets:** Small, dogs only. $15 daily fee/pet. Designated rooms, service with restrictions, supervision.
[SAVE] [S6] [X] [🛏] [💻]

CENTRALIA

▼ **Motel 6-394** M
(360) 330-2057. **$45-$58.** 1310 Belmont Ave. I-5, exit 82, just w on Harrison Ave, then just n. Ext corridors. **Pets:** Medium, other species. Service with restrictions, supervision.
[S6] [X] [&] [🛏] [≈]

CHEHALIS

AAA ▼▼▼▼ **Best Western Park Place Inn & Suites** SH ❀
(360) 748-4040. **$86-$99.** 201 SW Interstate Ave. I-5, exit 76, just se. Int corridors. **Pets:** Small, dogs only. $10 daily fee/pet. Designated rooms, service with restrictions, supervision.
[SAVE] [S6] [X] [&M] [&] [🛏] [💻] [≈]

CHELAN

AAA ▼▼▼▼ **Best Western Lakeside Lodge** SH
(509) 682-4396. **$79-$329, 7 day notice.** 2312 W Woodin Ave. West end of town. Ext corridors. **Pets:** Accepted.
[SAVE] [S6] [X] [⊘] [&] [🛏] [💻] [≈] [✕]

CHEWELAH

AAA ▼▼▼ **Nordlig Motel** M
(509) 935-6704. **$56-$61.** W 101 Grant St. North edge of town on US 395. Ext corridors. **Pets:** $3 one-time fee/room. Service with restrictions, supervision.
[SAVE] [S6] [X] [🛏]

CLARKSTON

▼▼ **Best Western Rivertree Inn** SH 🐾
(509) 758-9551. **$99-$149.** 1257 Bridge St. 0.9 mi w of Snake River Bridge on US 12. Ext corridors. **Pets:** Other species. Designated rooms, supervision.
[ASK] [S6] [X] [&M] [⊘] [&] [🛏] [💻] [≈] [✕]

▼ **Motel 6** M
(509) 758-1631. **Call for rates.** 222 Bridge St. Just w of Snake River Interstate Bridge. Ext corridors. **Pets:** Medium, other species. Service with restrictions, supervision.
[X] [🛏] [≈]

CLE ELUM

AAA ▼ **Cle Elum Travelers Inn** M
(509) 674-5535. **$56-$70.** 1001 E 1st St. I-90, exit 85, 1 mi w on SR 903. Ext/int corridors. **Pets:** Very small. $5 daily fee/pet. Service with restrictions, supervision.
[SAVE] [S6] [X] [&] [🛏]

COLFAX

▼▼▼▼ **Best Western Wheatland Inn** SH
(509) 397-0397. **$59-$99.** 701 N Main. Downtown. Int corridors. **Pets:** Accepted.
[ASK] [S6] [X] [&M] [⊘] [&] [🛏] [💻] [≈]

COLVILLE

▼▼▼ Colville Comfort Inn 🆂🅷
(509) 684-2010. **$68-$200.** 166 NE Canning Dr. 1.5 mi n on US 395.
Int corridors. **Pets:** Accepted.
(ASK) (S🌅) (✕) (🅼) (🖉) (📛) (📛) (💻) (🏊)

CONCRETE

**♦♦ ▼▼▼ Ovenell's Heritage Inn B&B and Log
Cabins** 🅱🅱
(360) 853-8494. **$90-$150, 3 day notice.** 46276 Concrete Sauk Valley
Rd. 0.5 mi w of downtown on SR 20, 3 mi se. Ext/int corridors.
Pets: Dogs only. $25 daily fee/pet. Designated rooms, service with restric-
tions, supervision.
(SAVE) (S🌅) (✕) (📛) (💻) (⊠)

COUGAR

▼▼ Lone Fir Resort Ⓜ ❀
(360) 238-5210. **$45-$85, 7 day notice.** 16806 Lewis River Rd. Center.
Ext corridors. **Pets:** Other species. $10 one-time fee/room. Service with
restrictions, supervision.
(ASK) (S🌅) (✕) (📛) (💻) (🍴) (🏊) (⊠) (🖉)

COULEE DAM

♦♦ ▼▼▼ Coulee House Inn & Suites Ⓜ
(509) 633-1101. **$69-$149.** 110 Roosevelt Way. Just e of river bridge.
Ext corridors. **Pets:** Other species. $15 daily fee/pet. Designated rooms,
service with restrictions, supervision.
(SAVE) (S🌅) (✕) (📛) (💻) (🏊)

DAYTON

▼▼▼ The Weinhard Hotel 🆂🅷
(509) 382-4032. **$85-$165, 7 day notice.** 235 E Main St. Downtown.
Int corridors. **Pets:** Dogs only. $20 one-time fee/pet. Supervision.
(ASK) (✕)

EAST WENATCHEE

▼▼▼ Cedars Inn, East Wenatchee 🆂🅷
(509) 886-8000. **$65-$100, 7 day notice.** 80 Ninth St NE. Just e of SR
28. Int corridors. **Pets:** Very small, dogs only. $10 daily fee/pet. Service
with restrictions, supervision.
(ASK) (S🌅) (✕) (📛) (💻) (🏊)

EATONVILLE

♦♦ ▼▼ Mill Village Motel Ⓜ
(360) 832-3200. **$70-$90.** 210 Center St E. Just e of jct SR 161; center.
Ext corridors. **Pets:** Medium, other species. $10 one-time fee/room. Serv-
ice with restrictions, supervision.
(SAVE) (S🌅) (✕) (🖉) (📛) (💻)

ELLENSBURG

♦♦ ▼▼▼ Best Western Lincoln Inn & Suites 🆂🅷 ❀
(509) 925-4244. **$89-$189.** 211 W Umptanum Rd. I-90, exit 109, just n,
then just w. Int corridors. **Pets:** Small, dogs only. $25 daily fee/pet.
Designated rooms, service with restrictions, supervision.
(SAVE) (S🌅) (✕) (🅼) (🖉) (🖉) (📛) (💻) (🏊)

▼▼▼ Ellensburg Comfort Inn 🆂🅷
(509) 925-7037. **$81-$134.** 1722 Canyon Rd. I-90, exit 109. Int corridors. **Pets:** Accepted.
(ASK) (S🌅) (✕) (🖉) (🖉) (📛) (💻) (🏊)

♦♦ ▼▼ Ellensburg Inn 🆂🅷
(509) 925-9801. **$75-$122.** 1700 Canyon Rd. I-90, exit 109, just n. Int
corridors. **Pets:** Designated rooms, supervision.
(SAVE) (✕) (📛) (💻) (🍴) (🏊)

I-90 Inn Motel Ⓜ
(509) 925-9844. **$58-$78.** 1390 Dollar Way N. I-90, exit 106, just n. Ext
corridors. **Pets:** Accepted.
(SAVE) (S🌅) (✕) (📛)

▼▼ Nites Inn Ⓜ
(509) 962-9600. **$56-$60.** 1200 S Ruby. I-90, exit 109, 0.5 mi n. Ext
corridors. **Pets:** $9 one-time fee/pet. Service with restrictions, supervision.
(ASK) (S🌅) (✕) (📛) (💻)

ELMA

▼▼ Microtel Inn & Suites-Elma 🆂🅷
(360) 482-6868. **$59-$99.** 800 E Main St. Just ne of jct US 12 and SR
8. Int corridors. **Pets:** Accepted.
(ASK) (S🌅) (✕) (📛) (💻)

ENUMCLAW

♦♦ ▼▼▼ Park Center Hotel 🆂🅷
(360) 825-4490. **$75-$85.** 1000 Griffin Ave. Downtown. Ext corridors.
Pets: $10 daily fee/pet. Service with restrictions, supervision.
(SAVE) (S🌅) (✕) (📛) (💻) (🍴)

FERNDALE

▼▼▼ Ferndale Super 8 🆂🅷
(360) 384-8881. **$53-$81.** 5788 Barrett Ave. I-5, exit 262, just ne. Int
corridors. **Pets:** Medium, other species. $10 one-time fee/room. Desig-
nated rooms, service with restrictions, supervision.
(ASK) (✕) (🅼) (🖉) (📛) (🏊)

▼▼▼ Silver Reef Hotel Casino & Spa 🆂🅷
(360) 383-0777. **$119-$159.** 4876 Haxton Way. I-5, exit 260, 3.6 mi w.
Int corridors. **Pets:** Small, other species. $15 daily fee/room. Designated
rooms.
(ASK) (S🌅) (✕) (🖉) (📛) (💻) (🍴) (🏊) (⊠)

FORKS

♦♦ ▼▼▼ Forks Motel Ⓜ
(360) 374-6243. **$55-$99, 5 day notice.** 351 US 101 (Forks Ave S).
Just s. Ext corridors. **Pets:** Medium. $1500.00 one-time fee/pet. Service
with restrictions.
(SAVE) (✕) (📛) (💻) (🏊)

▼▼▼ Manitou Lodge 🅱🅱 ❀
(360) 374-6295. **$99-$169, 14 day notice.** 813 Kilmer Rd. 7.7 mi sw on
SR 110 (LaPush Rd), 0.7 mi w on Mora Rd, then 0.8 mi n. Ext/int
corridors. **Pets:** Other species. $10 daily fee/room. Designated rooms,
crate.
(✕) (📛) (💻) (🐾) (🐾) (🖉)

▼▼ Miller Tree Inn Bed & Breakfast 🅱🅱
(360) 374-6806. **$85-$185, 7 day notice.** 654 E Division St. 0.3 mi e of
US 101 (S Forks Ave). Ext/int corridors. **Pets:** Other species. $10 daily
fee/room. Designated rooms, service with restrictions.
(✕) (📛) (💻) (🐾) (🖉)

♦♦ ▼▼▼ Olympic Suites Inn Ⓜ
(360) 374-5400. **$59-$109.** 800 Olympic Dr. North end of town, just ne
off US 101 (S Forks Ave). Ext corridors. **Pets:** Accepted.
(SAVE) (✕) (📛) (💻) (🐾)

▼▼ Pacific Inn Motel Ⓜ
(360) 374-9400. **$53-$74.** 352 US 101 (S Forks Ave). Just s. Ext
corridors. **Pets:** Accepted.
(ASK) (S🌅) (✕) (📛) (💻)

GOLDENDALE

♦♦ ▼▼▼ Quality Inn & Suites Ⓜ
(509) 773-5881. **$75-$110.** 808 E Simcoe Dr. US 97, exit Simcoe Dr,
just sw. Ext corridors. **Pets:** Accepted.
(SAVE) (S🌅) (✕) (📛) (💻) (🍴) (🏊)

ILWACO

AAA **WV** **Heidi's Inn** **M**
(360) 642-2387. **$49-$95, 7 day notice.** 126 Spruce St. Downtown. Ext corridors. **Pets:** Small, dogs only. $6 one-time fee/pet. Service with restrictions, supervision.
[SAVE] [X] [=] [▭] [X]

KALALOCH

AAA **WVV** **Kalaloch Lodge** **CA**
(360) 962-2271. **$79-$279, 3 day notice.** 157151 US 101. At MM 157. Ext/int corridors. **Pets:** Medium. $12 daily fee/pet. Designated rooms, service with restrictions.
[SAVE] [X] [=] [▭] [⊓⊔] [X] [⊠]

KALAMA

AAA **WV** **Kalama River Inn** **M**
(360) 673-2855. **$49-$64.** 602 NE Frontage Rd. I-5, exit 30 northbound, 0.4 mi n; exit southbound, 0.4 mi s. Ext corridors. **Pets:** Other species. $5 daily fee/room. Service with restrictions, supervision.
[SAVE] [X] [=]

KELSO

AAA **WVV** **Best Western Aladdin** **SH**
(360) 425-9660. **$79-$119.** 310 Long Ave. I-5, exit 39, 1.1 mi w via Allen St and W Main St, then just n on 5th Ave NW. Int corridors. **Pets:** Small, dogs only. $5 daily fee/pet. Designated rooms, service with restrictions, crate.
[SAVE] [S6] [X] [=] [▭] [⇆]

WVVV **GuestHouse Inn & Suites** **SH**
(360) 414-5953. **$85-$185.** 501 Three Rivers Dr. I-5, exit 39, 0.3 mi w on Allen St, then 0.3 mi s. Int corridors. **Pets:** Accepted.
[ASK] [S6] [X] [⊘] [⬥] [=] [▭] [⇆]

W **Motel 6–43** **M**
(360) 425-3229. **$45-$61.** 106 Minor Rd. I-5, exit 39, 0.3 mi ne. Ext corridors. **Pets:** Medium, other species. Service with restrictions, supervision.
[S6] [X] [⬥] [=] [⇆]

AAA **WVV** **Red Lion Hotel & Conference Center Kelso/Longview** **SH**
(360) 636-4400. **$98-$130.** 510 Kelso Dr. I-5, exit 39, 0.3 mi se. Int corridors. **Pets:** Small, dogs only. $20 daily fee/pet. Service with restrictions, crate.
[SAVE] [S6] [X] [⊘] [⬥] [=] [▭] [⊓⊔] [⇆]

WV **Super 8 Motel** **SH** ☘
(360) 423-8880. **$72-$100.** 250 Kelso Dr. I-5, exit 39, just se. Int corridors. **Pets:** Medium. $25 deposit/room, $10 daily fee/room. Service with restrictions, crate.
[ASK] [S6] [X] [⬥M] [=] [⇆]

KENNEWICK

AAA **WVVV** **Best Western Kennewick Inn** **SH**
(509) 586-1332. **$82-$144.** 4001 W 27th Ave. I-82, exit 113 (US 395), 0.8 mi n. Int corridors. **Pets:** Large, other species. $10 one-time/room. Service with restrictions, supervision.
[SAVE] [S6] [X] [⬥M] [⊘] [⬥] [=] [▭] [⇆] [X]

WVV **Clover Island Inn** **SH** ☘
(509) 586-0541. **$79-$99.** 435 Clover Island Dr. US 395, exit Port of Kennewick, 1 mi e on Columbia Dr, then just n. Int corridors. **Pets:** Other species. Service with restrictions, supervision.
[ASK] [S6] [X] [=] [▭] [⇆] [X]

WVV **Comfort Inn** **M**
(509) 783-8396. **$75-$130.** 7801 W Quinault Ave. 0.5 mi s on Columbia Center Blvd from SR 240. Int corridors. **Pets:** $10 daily fee/pet. Designated rooms, service with restrictions, supervision.
[ASK] [S6] [X] [⬥M] [⊘] [⬥] [=] [▭] [⇆]

AAA **WVV** **Days Inn Kennewick** **SH** ☘
(509) 735-9511. **$59-$79.** 2811 W 2nd Ave. Jct US 395 and Clearwater Ave, just s, just w. Ext/int corridors. **Pets:** Small, dogs only. $10 one-time fee/room. Designated rooms, service with restrictions, supervision.
[SAVE] [S6] [X] [=] [▭] [⇆]

AAA **WVV** **Econo Lodge** **M** ☘
(509) 783-6191. **$59-$89.** 300 N Ely St, #A. On US 395, jct Clearwater Ave. Ext corridors. **Pets:** Small, dogs only. $7 daily fee/pet. Service with restrictions, supervision.
[SAVE] [S6] [X] [=] [⇆]

WVV **Fairfield Inn by Marriott** **SH**
(509) 783-2164. **$69-$79.** 7809 W Quinault Ave. 0.5 mi s on Columbia Center Blvd from SR 240. Int corridors. **Pets:** Accepted.
[ASK] [S6] [X] [⬥M] [⊘] [⬥] [=] [▭] [⇆]

AAA **WVV** **Guesthouse International Suites** **SH** ☘
(509) 735-2242. **$62-$69.** 5616 W Clearwater Ave. US 395, 1.9 mi w. Int corridors. **Pets:** Other species. $10 one-time fee/pet. Designated rooms, service with restrictions, crate.
[SAVE] [S6] [X] [⊘] [⬥] [=] [▭]

WVV **Kennewick Super 8** **SH**
(509) 736-6888. **$69-$79, 14 day notice.** 626 N Columbia Center Blvd. 1.1 mi s of SR 240. Int corridors. **Pets:** Large. $10 one-time fee/room. Service with restrictions, supervision.
[ASK] [S6] [X] [⬥M] [⊘] [⬥] [=] [⇆]

AAA **WVVV** **La Quinta Inn & Suites Kennewick** **SH**
(509) 736-3326. **$69-$119.** 4220 W 27th Pl. I-82, exit 113 (US 395), 0.8 mi n. Int corridors. **Pets:** Medium. Service with restrictions, supervision.
[SAVE] [S6] [X] [⬥M] [⊘] [⬥] [=] [▭] [⇆] [X]

AAA **WVVV** **Red Lion Hotel Columbia Center-Kennewick** **SH**
(509) 783-0611. **$89-$119.** 1101 N Columbia Center Blvd. SR 240, 0.5 mi s. Int corridors. **Pets:** Supervision.
[SAVE] [S6] [X] [⬥M] [⊘] [⬥] [=] [▭] [⊓⊔] [⇆]

LACEY

AAA **WV** **La Quinta Inn** **SH**
(360) 412-1200. **$82-$129.** 4704 Park Center Ave NE. I-5, exit 109, just sw. Int corridors. **Pets:** Medium, other species. Service with restrictions, supervision.
[SAVE] [S6] [X] [⬥] [=] [▭] [⇆]

WVV **Quality Inn & Suites** **SH** ☘
(360) 493-1991. **$65-$85.** 120 College St SE. I-5, exit 109, just sw. Int corridors. **Pets:** Small, other species. $15 daily fee/pet. Service with restrictions, crate.
[ASK] [S6] [X] [⊘] [⬥] [=] [▭]

LA CONNER

AAA **WVVV** **La Conner Country Inn** **SH**
(360) 466-3101. **$99-$159.** 107 S 2nd St. 2nd and Morris sts; downtown. Ext/int corridors. **Pets:** Other species. $25 one-time fee/room. Designated rooms, service with restrictions, supervision.
[SAVE] [S6] [X] [=] [▭] [⊓⊔] [X]

LANGLEY

WVVV **Island Tyme Bed & Breakfast** **BB** ☘
(360) 221-5078. **$119-$195, 10 day notice.** 4940 S Bayview Rd. SR 525 at MM 15, just e on Marshview, 2.1 mi n. Int corridors. **Pets:** Dogs only. $20 daily fee/pet. Designated rooms, service with restrictions, supervision.
[X] [X]

AAA ◆◆ Villa Isola Bed & Breakfast Inn BB
(360) 221-5052. **$129-$169, 14 day notice.** 5489 Coles Rd. 5 mi w on SR 525 from Clinton ferry landing, 0.6 mi n. Ext/int corridors. **Pets:** Accepted.
[SAVE] [S♦] [✕] [🛏] [💻] [🏊]

LEAVENWORTH

AAA ◆◆◆ Bavarian Ritz Hotel SH
(509) 548-5455. **$89-$249, 3 day notice.** 633 Front St. Center. Ext/int corridors. **Pets:** Dogs only. $10 daily fee/pet. Service with restrictions, supervision.
[SAVE] [S♦] [✕] [🛏] [💻]

AAA ◆◆◆ Der Ritterhof Motor Inn SH ❀
(509) 548-5845. **$83-$104, 3 day notice.** 190 US 2. 0.3 mi w. Ext corridors. **Pets:** Dogs only. $10 daily fee/pet. Service with restrictions, supervision.
[SAVE] [S♦] [✕] [🐾] [🛏] [💻] [🏊]

◆ The Evergreen Inn M
(509) 548-5515. **$79-$139, 14 day notice.** 1117 Front St. US 2, just s. Ext corridors. **Pets:** Accepted.
[✕] [🛏] [💻]

◆◆ Howard Johnson Inn M
(509) 548-4326. **$79-$169.** 405 W US 2. West end of town. Ext corridors. **Pets:** Accepted.
[ASK] [S♦] [✕] [🛏] [💻] [🏊]

AAA ◆◆◆ Obertal Inn M
(509) 548-5204. **$69-$149.** 922 Commercial St. Off US 2; center. Ext corridors. **Pets:** Other species. $15 daily fee/pet. Designated rooms, service with restrictions.
[SAVE] [S♦] [✕] [🛏] [💻]

◆◆◆◆ Quality Inn & Suites SH ❀
(509) 548-7992. **$99-$289.** 185 US 2. 0.3 mi w. Ext corridors. **Pets:** Medium, other species. $15 daily fee/pet. Designated rooms, service with restrictions, crate.
[ASK] [S♦] [✕] [♿M] [🐾] [🛏] [💻] [🏊]

◆◆ River's Edge Lodge M
(509) 548-7612. **$99-$199, 7 day notice.** 8401 US 2. 3.5 mi e. Ext corridors. **Pets:** Other species. $15 daily fee/pet. Designated rooms, service with restrictions, supervision.
[ASK] [S♦] [✕] [🛏] [🏊]

LIBERTY LAKE

AAA ◆◆◆◆ Best Western Peppertree Liberty Lake Inn SH ❀
(509) 755-1111. **$89-$110.** 1816 N Pepper Ln. I-90, exit 296. Int corridors. **Pets:** Very small, dogs only. $10 daily fee/pet. Service with restrictions, supervision.
[SAVE] [✕] [♿M] [🛏] [💻] [🏊]

◆◆◆◆ Comfort Inn Liberty Lake SH
(509) 340-3333. **$56-$87.** 2327 N Madson Rd. I-90, exit 296, 1 mi e on Appleway, then just n. Int corridors. **Pets:** Accepted.
[ASK] [S♦] [✕] [♿M] [🐾] [🛏] [💻] [🏊] [✕]

LONG BEACH

AAA ◆◆◆ Anchorage Cottages CA
(360) 642-2351. **$70-$128, 7 day notice.** 2209 Boulevard N. Just w of SR 103. Ext corridors. **Pets:** Medium. $10 daily fee/pet. Designated rooms, supervision.
[SAVE] [✕] [🛏] [💻] [AC] [🏊]

AAA ◆◆ The Breakers CO ❀
(360) 642-4414. **$68-$278, 7 day notice.** 26th & SR 103. North end of downtown. Ext corridors. **Pets:** Dogs only. $10 daily fee/room. Designated rooms, service with restrictions, supervision.
[SAVE] [S♦] [✕] [🛏] [💻] [🏊] [✕] [AC]

AAA ◆◆◆ Edgewater Inn SH
(360) 642-2311. **$74-$124, 3 day notice.** 409 Sid Snyder Dr. Just w of SR 103. Ext/int corridors. **Pets:** $10 daily fee/pet. Designated rooms, service with restrictions, supervision.
[SAVE] [✕] [♿] [🛏] [💻] [🍽] [AC]

AAA ◆◆ Our Place at the Beach SH
(360) 642-3793. **$48-$92.** 1309 South Blvd. Just w of SR 103 at south end of town. Ext corridors. **Pets:** Other species. $6 daily fee/pet. Supervision.
[SAVE] [S♦] [✕] [🛏] [💻] [✕] [AC]

AAA ◆◆◆ Rodeway Inn SH
(360) 642-3714. **$55-$135, 7 day notice.** 115 3rd St SW. Downtown. Ext corridors. **Pets:** Accepted.
[SAVE] [S♦] [✕] [🛏] [💻] [🏊] [AC]

AAA ◆◆◆ Super 8 Motel SH ❀
(360) 642-8988. **$69-$159.** 500 Ocean Beach Blvd. On SR 103; downtown. Int corridors. **Pets:** Dogs only. Supervision.
[SAVE] [✕] [♿M] [🐾] [🛏] [💻] [AC]

LONGVIEW

AAA ◆◆ Hudson Manor Inn & Suites M
(360) 425-1100. **$54-$80.** 1616 Hudson St. Downtown. Ext corridors. **Pets:** Accepted.
[SAVE] [✕] [🛏] [💻]

AAA ◆◆ Longview Travelodge M
(360) 423-6460. **$49-$65.** 838 15th Ave. Downtown; opposite Medical Center. Ext corridors. **Pets:** Dogs only. $15 daily fee/room. Service with restrictions, supervision.
[SAVE] [S♦] [✕] [🛏] [💻]

AAA ◆◆ The Townhouse Motel M
(360) 423-7200. **$46-$60, 3 day notice.** 744 Washington Way. Downtown. Ext corridors. **Pets:** Large, other species. $5 daily fee/pet. Service with restrictions, supervision.
[SAVE] [S♦] [✕] [🛏] [💻] [🏊]

MOCLIPS

AAA ◆◆◆ Ocean Crest Resort SH
(360) 276-4465. **$45-$198, 8 day notice.** 4651 SR 109 N. South edge of town. Ext corridors. **Pets:** Accepted.
[SAVE] [S♦] [✕] [♿] [🛏] [💻] [🍽] [🏊] [✕] [AC]

MONTESANO

AAA ◆◆ Monte Square Motel M
(360) 249-4424. **$49-$89.** 100 Brumfield Ave W. US 12, exit SR 107 (Montesano/Raymond), just nw. Ext corridors. **Pets:** Dogs only. $10 one-time fee/pet. Designated rooms, service with restrictions, supervision.
[SAVE] [S♦] [✕] [♿M] [🛏] [💻]

MORTON

AAA ◆◆◆ The Seasons Motel M
(360) 496-6835. **$70-$90.** 200 Westlake Ave. On US 12, at jct SR 7. Ext corridors. **Pets:** Small. $10 one-time fee/room. Service with restrictions, supervision.
[SAVE] [S♦] [✕] [🛏] [💻]

MOSES LAKE

◆◆◆ AmeriStay Inn & Suites SH
(509) 764-7500. **$89-$109.** 1157 N Stratford Rd. I-90, exit 179, 1 mi n to SR 17, 2.8 mi nw to Stratford exit, just n, then just e. Int corridors. **Pets:** Accepted.
[ASK] [S♦] [✕] [♿M] [🐾] [♿] [🛏] [💻] [🏊]

AAA ▼▼▼ **Best Western Lake Inn** SH
(509) 765-9211. **$69-$140.** 3000 Marina Dr. I-90, exit 176, just nw. Int corridors. **Pets:** $20 one-time fee/room. Designated rooms, service with restrictions, supervision.
SAVE SD ✕ GM ⊘ 🖥 🖳 ¶ ➤ ✕

▼▼▼ **Holiday Inn Express** SH
(509) 766-2000. **$85-$130.** 1745 E Kittleson. I-90, exit 179, just n. Int corridors. **Pets:** Accepted.
ASK SD ✕ GM 🔧 🖥 🖳 ➤

▼ ◆ **Inn at Moses Lake** SH
(509) 766-7000. **$75-$100.** 1741 E Kittleson. I-90, exit 179, just n. Int corridors. **Pets:** Supervision.
ASK SD ✕ 🖥

▼▼ **Moses Lake Super 8** SH
(509) 765-8886. **$65-$85, 10 day notice.** 449 Melva Ln. I-90, exit 176, just n. Int corridors. **Pets:** Other species. $10 one-time fee/room. Supervision.
ASK SD ✕ 🖥 ➤

▼▼ **Shilo Inn Suites-Moses Lake** SH ✿
(509) 765-9317. **$75-$117.** 1819 E Kittleson. I-90, exit 179, just n. Int corridors. **Pets:** Other species. $25 one-time fee/room. Supervision.
ASK SD ✕ GM ⊘ 🖥 🖳 ➤ ✕

MOUNT VERNON

AAA ▼▼◆ **Best Western College Way Inn** SH
(360) 424-4287. **$75-$97.** 300 W College Way. I-5, exit 227, just w. Ext corridors. **Pets:** Large. $15 daily fee/pet. Designated rooms, service with restrictions, supervision.
SAVE SD ✕ ⊘ 🖥 🖳 ➤

AAA ▼▼▼ **Best Western CottonTree Inn & Convention Center** SH
(360) 428-5678. **$74-$129.** 2300 Market St. I-5, exit 227, 0.3 mi e on College Way, then 0.5 mi n on Riverside Dr. Int corridors. **Pets:** Accepted.
SAVE SD ✕ GM ⊘ 🖥 🖳 ➤

AAA ▼▼◆ **Quality Inn-Mount Vernon** SH
(360) 428-7020. **$70-$90, 7 day notice.** 1910 Freeway Dr. I-5, exit 227, just w on College Way, then just n. Ext corridors. **Pets:** $10 daily fee/room. Designated rooms, service with restrictions, crate.
SAVE SD ✕ 🖥 🖳 ➤

AAA ▼ **Tulip Inn** M ✿
(360) 428-5969. **$55-$79.** 2200 Freeway Dr. I-5, exit 227, just w on College Way, then just n. Ext corridors. **Pets:** Medium, other species. $10 daily fee/pet. Designated rooms, service with restrictions, supervision.
SAVE SD ✕ 🖥 🖳

OAK HARBOR

AAA ▼▼◆ **Acorn Motor Inn** SH
(360) 675-6646. **$46-$109.** 31530 SR 20. On SR 20 at 300th Ave W (SE Barrington Dr). Int corridors. **Pets:** Other species. $10 daily fee/room. Designated rooms, service with restrictions, supervision.
SAVE SD ✕ 🖥

AAA ▼▼◆ **Coachman Inn** SH
(360) 675-0727. **$80-$215.** 32959 SR 20. Jct Goldie Rd and Midway Blvd. Ext corridors. **Pets:** Accepted.
SAVE SD ✕ 🖥 🖳 ➤ ✕

OCEAN PARK

AAA ▼ **Ocean Park Resort** M
(360) 665-4585. **$65-$89, 10 day notice.** 25904 R St. Just e of SR 103; downtown. Ext corridors. **Pets:** Small, other species. $7 daily fee/pet. Designated rooms, service with restrictions, supervision.
SAVE ✕ 🖥 🖳 ➤ ✕ ⫝ ✎

OCEAN SHORES

AAA ▼▼▼ **The Canterbury Inn** CO
(360) 289-3317. **$82-$278.** 643 Ocean Shores Blvd NW. 0.3 mi s of Chance A La Mer Blvd. Int corridors. **Pets:** Large, dogs only. $150 deposit/room, $15 daily fee/pet. Designated rooms, service with restrictions, supervision.
SAVE SD ✕ 🖥 🖳 ➤ ⫝

AAA ▼▼◆ **The Grey Gull Resort** CO ✿
(360) 289-3381. **$120-$335, 3 day notice.** 651 Ocean Shores Blvd NW. Just s of Chance A La Mer Blvd. Ext corridors. **Pets:** Small, dogs only. $10 daily fee/pet. Designated rooms, service with restrictions, supervision.
SAVE SD ✕ 🖥 🖳 ➤ ⫝

AAA ▼▼▼ **The Nautilus** CO
(360) 289-2722. **$80-$160.** 835 Ocean Shores Blvd NW. 0.3 mi s of Chance Ala Mer Blvd. Ext corridors. **Pets:** Accepted.
SAVE SD ✕ 🖥 🖳 ⫝

AAA ▼▼▼ **The Polynesian Condominium Resort** CO ✿
(360) 289-3361. **$99-$229, 3 day notice.** 615 Ocean Shores Blvd NW. 0.3 mi s of Chance A La Mer Blvd. Ext/int corridors. **Pets:** Other species. $15 daily fee/pet. Designated rooms, service with restrictions, supervision.
SAVE SD ✕ ⊘ 🖥 🖳 ¶ ➤ ✕ ⫝

OKANOGAN

◆ ◆ **Okanogan Inn & Suites** SH
(509) 422-6431. **$54-$65.** 1 Apple Way. SR 97, exit SR 20, just w. Int corridors. **Pets:** Accepted.
ASK SD ✕ ¶ ➤

AAA ▼▼▼ **Ponderosa Motor Lodge** M
(509) 422-0400. **$48-$53.** 1034 S 2nd Ave. 0.3 mi n on SR 215 from jct SR 20. Ext corridors. **Pets:** Medium. $5 one-time fee/pet. Service with restrictions, supervision.
SAVE SD ✕ 🖥 🖳 ➤

OLYMPIA

▼▼◆ **Governor Hotel** SH
(360) 352-7700. **$140.** 621 S Capitol Way. I-5, exit 105 (City Center) northbound; exit 105A southbound, 0.4 mi w on 14th Ave, then 0.6 mi n; downtown. Int corridors. **Pets:** Large, other species. $50 one-time fee/room. Service with restrictions, supervision.
ASK SD ✕ ⊘ 🖥 🖳 ¶ ➤ ✕

▼▼◆ **Quality Inn–Olympia** SH
(360) 943-4710. **$65-$89.** 1211 S Quince St SE. I-5, exit 105B, just n, follow Port of Olympia signs, just n on Plum St, then e on Union Ave. Int corridors. **Pets:** Accepted.
ASK SD ✕ 🖥 🖳 ➤

▼▼▼ **Red Lion Hotel Olympia** SH
(360) 943-4000. **$120-$179.** 2300 Evergreen Park Dr SW. I-5, exit 104, 0.7 mi w on US 101, just n on Cooper Point Rd N, 0.7 mi e on S Evergreen Pk Dr SW, then just n on Lakeridge Way SW. Int corridors. **Pets:** Small. $20 daily fee/pet. Service with restrictions, supervision.
ASK SD ✕ GM ⊘ 🔧 🖥 🖳 ¶ ➤

OLYMPIC NATIONAL PARK

AAA ▼▼▼ **Lake Crescent Lodge** SH
(360) 928-3211. **$68-$211, 7 day notice.** 416 Lake Crescent Rd. 22 mi w of Port Angeles on US 101. Ext/int corridors. **Pets:** Other species. $12 daily fee/pet. Designated rooms, service with restrictions, supervision.
SAVE ✕ 🖥 🖳 ¶ ✕ ⫝ ⫝ ✎

▼▼ **Log Cabin Resort** 🄲🄰
(360) 928-3325. **$53-$143, 7 day notice.** 3183 E Beach Rd. 3.3 mi nw of US 101 (MM 232). Ext corridors. **Pets:** Other species. $14 daily fee/pet. Designated rooms, service with restrictions, supervision.
☒ 🖥 💻 🍴 ☒ 🄺 📶 ☑

OMAK

🆎🆎 ▼▼▼ **Omak Inn** 🆂🅷
(509) 826-3822. **$68-$78.** 912 Koala Dr. On US 97, just n of Riverside Dr. Int corridors. **Pets:** Small, dogs only. $25 one-time fee/pet. Service with restrictions, supervision.
SAVE 🅂🄳 ☒ 🄺 🖥 💻 ☑

▼▼ **Rodeway Inn & Suites** Ⓜ
(509) 826-0400. **$44-$69.** 122 N Main St. Downtown. Ext corridors. **Pets:** Medium, dogs only. $10 daily fee/pet. Designated rooms, service with restrictions, supervision.
A$K 🅂🄳 ☒ 🄺 🖥 💻 ☑

OTHELLO

🆎🆎 ▼▼▼▼ **Best Western Lincoln Inn Othello** 🆂🅷 🐾
(509) 488-5671. **$69-$139.** 1020 E Cedar St. Just off Main St at 10th and Cedar sts. Int corridors. **Pets:** Small, dogs only. $10 daily fee/pet. Designated rooms, service with restrictions, supervision.
SAVE 🅂🄳 ☒ 🖥 💻 ☑

PACIFIC BEACH

▼▼ **Sandpiper Beach Resort** 🄲🄾
(360) 276-4580. **$65-$115.** 4159 SR 109. 1.8 mi s. Ext corridors. **Pets:** Accepted.
A$K ☒ 🖥 💻 🄺 📶 ☑

PACKWOOD

▼▼ **Inn of Packwood** Ⓜ
(360) 494-5500. **$55-$150.** 13032 US 12. Center. Ext corridors. **Pets:** Accepted.
A$K 🅂🄳 ☒ 🖥 💻 ☑

PASCO

🆎🆎 ▼▼▼▼ **Best Western Pasco Inn & Suites** 🆂🅷
(509) 543-7722. **$109-$171.** 2811 N 20th Ave. I-182, exit 12B, just n. Int corridors. **Pets:** Small, other species. $10 one-time fee/room. Service with restrictions, crate.
SAVE 🅂🄳 ☒ 🄼 🖥 🄺 🖥 💻 ☑

🆎🆎 ▼▼ **Budget Inn** Ⓜ
(509) 546-2010. **$44-$55.** 1520 N Oregon St. I-182, exit 14A (SR 395 S). Ext corridors. **Pets:** Accepted.
SAVE 🅂🄳 ☒ 🖥 💻 ☑

🆎🆎 ▼▼▼ **Red Lion Hotel Pasco** 🅻🅷
(509) 547-0701. **$110-$140.** 2525 N 20th Ave. I-182, exit 12B, just n. Int corridors. **Pets:** Accepted.
SAVE ☒ 🄼 🄺 🖥 🖥 💻 🍴 ☑

🆎🆎 ▼▼▼ **Sleep Inn** 🆂🅷 🐾
(509) 545-9554. **$75-$125.** 9930 Bedford St. I-182, exit 7, just ne. Int corridors. **Pets:** $10 daily fee/room. Designated rooms, service with restrictions, supervision.
SAVE ☒ 🄼 🄺 🖥 🖥 💻 ☑

PORT ANGELES

🆎🆎 ▼▼▼ **Portside Inn** 🆂🅷 🐾
(360) 452-4015. **$49-$139, 3 day notice.** 1510 E Front St. Front St at Alder, on east side. Ext corridors. **Pets:** Medium. $10 daily fee/pet. Designated rooms, service with restrictions, supervision.
SAVE 🅂🄳 ☒ 🖥 💻 ☑

🆎🆎 ▼▼▼ **Quality Inn-Uptown** Ⓜ 🐾
(360) 457-9434. **$79-$209.** 101 E 2nd St. At Laurel St, just w of US 101; on bluff. Ext corridors. **Pets:** Small, dogs only. $10 daily fee/room. Designated rooms, service with restrictions, supervision.
SAVE 🅂🄳 ☒ 🖥 💻 🄺

🆎🆎 ▼▼▼▼ **Red Lion Hotel Port Angeles** 🆂🅷
(360) 452-9215. **$109-$229.** 221 N Lincoln St. On US 101 westbound; at ferry landing. Ext/int corridors. **Pets:** Other species. Service with restrictions, supervision.
SAVE 🅂🄳 ☒ 🄼 🄺 🖥 🖥 💻 🍴 ☑

🆎🆎 ▼▼ **Riviera Inn** Ⓜ
(360) 417-3955. **$49-$119, 3 day notice.** 535 E Front St. On US 101 W; downtown. Ext corridors. **Pets:** Small. $15 one-time fee/pet. Designated rooms, service with restrictions, supervision.
SAVE 🅂🄳 ☒ 🖥 🄺

▼▼ **Super 8 Motel** Ⓜ
(360) 452-8401. **$71-$116.** 2104 E 1st St. 1.8 mi e of downtown, just s of US 101. Int corridors. **Pets:** Accepted.
A$K 🅂🄳 ☒ 🄼

NEARBY OREGON
PORTLAND METROPOLITAN AREA

VANCOUVER

🆎🆎 ▼▼ **Comfort Inn** 🆂🅷
(360) 574-6000. **$70-$100.** 13207 NE 20th Ave. I-5, exit 7, just e; I-205, exit 36, just w. Int corridors. **Pets:** Accepted.
SAVE 🅂🄳 ☒ 🄼 🖥 🖥 💻 ☑

▼▼ **Extended StayAmerica-Portland-Vancouver** 🆂🅷
(360) 604-8530. **$75-$85.** 300 NE 115th Ave. I-205, exit 28 (Mill Plain Blvd E), just ne. Int corridors. **Pets:** Accepted.
A$K 🅂🄳 ☒ 🖥 💻

🆎🆎 ▼▼▼ **Hilton Vancouver Washington and Vancouver Convention Center** 🅻🅷
(360) 993-4500. **$119-$219.** 301 W 6th St. I-5, exit 1C (Mill Plain Blvd) southbound, 0.3 mi w, then 0.3 mi s on W Columbia St; exit 1B northbound, 0.5 mi, follow signs to City Center/6th St. Int corridors. **Pets:** Accepted.
SAVE 🅂🄳 ☒ 🄼 🄼 🄺 🖥 💻 🍴 ☑

▼▼▼ **Homewood Suites by Hilton** 🆂🅷
(360) 750-1100. **$89-$149.** 701 SE Columbia Shores Blvd. SR 14, exit 1, just s. Ext/int corridors. **Pets:** Medium, other species. $10 daily fee/pet, $25 one-time fee/room. Designated rooms, service with restrictions, supervision.
A$K 🅂🄳 ☒ 🄺 🖥 💻 ☑ 🄼

🆎🆎 ▼▼▼ **Phoenix Inn Suites-Vancouver** 🆂🅷
(360) 891-9777. **$99-$169.** 12712 SE 2nd Cir. I-205, exit 28 (Mill Plain Blvd E), 0.8 mi e, then just n on SE 126th Ave. Int corridors. **Pets:** Accepted.
SAVE 🅂🄳 ☒ 🄼 🄺 🖥 🖥 💻 ☑ 🄼

▼▼ **Quality Inn & Conference Center** 🆂🅷
(360) 253-8900. **$72-$130.** 221 NE Chkalov Dr. I-205, exit 28 (Mill Plain Blvd E), just ne. Int corridors. **Pets:** Medium, dogs only. $15 daily fee/pet. Service with restrictions, supervision.
A$K 🅂🄳 ☒ 🖥 💻 ☑

Quality Inn & Suites SH
(360) 696-0516. **$69-$95.** 7001 NE Hwy 99. I-5, exit 4, 0.8 mi se. Int corridors. **Pets:** Other species. $10 daily fee/room. Service with restrictions, supervision.
SAVE S X 🏊 🖥 📎 ≈

Red Lion Hotel Vancouver @ the Quay SH
(360) 694-8341. **$79-$150.** 100 Columbia St. 0.5 mi s on dock at foot of Columbia St. Int corridors. **Pets:** Accepted.
ASK S X &M 🏊 🖥 📎 🍽 ≈ X

Red Lion Inn at Salmon Creek SH
(360) 566-1100. **$89-$135.** 1500 NE 134th St. I-5, exit 7, just w; I-205, exit 36, 0.5 mi w. Int corridors. **Pets:** Small, other species. $20 daily fee/room. Service with restrictions, crate.
ASK S X &M 🏊 🖥 📎 ≈

Residence Inn Vancouver SH ☂
(360) 253-4800. **$99-$179.** 8005 NE Parkway Dr. I-205, exit 30 (SR 500 W), 0.5 mi w to Thurston Way, just n to NE Parkway Dr, then just w. Ext corridors. **Pets:** Other species. $75 one-time fee/room.
ASK S X &M 🏊 🖥 📎 ≈ X

Shilo Inn-Hazel Dell/Vancouver SH ☂
(360) 573-0501. **$70-$113.** 13206 Hwy 99. I-5, exit 7, just e; I-205, exit 36, just w. Int corridors. **Pets:** Other species. $25 one-time fee/room. Supervision.
ASK S X 🖥 📎 ≈ X

Staybridge Suites Vancouver-Portland SH
(360) 891-8282. **$79-$169.** 7301 NE 41st St. I-205, exit 30 (SR 500 W), 1.5 mi w to NE Andresen Rd, just n to NE 40th St, just e to NE 72nd St, just n to NE 41st St, then just e. Int corridors. **Pets:** Accepted.
ASK S X &M 🏊 🖥 🖥 📎 ≈ X

END METROPOLITAN AREA

PORT TOWNSEND

Bishop Victorian Hotel SH
(360) 385-6122. **$105-$205, 3 day notice.** 714 Washington St. Corner of Washington and Quincy sts. Int corridors. **Pets:** Accepted.
SAVE X 🖥 📎 🎾

Harborside Inn SH
(360) 385-7909. **$70-$150.** 330 Benedict St. Just e of SR 20. Ext corridors. **Pets:** Accepted.
ASK X 🏊 🖥 📎 ≈ 🎾

Palace Hotel SH ☂
(360) 385-0773. **$59-$289.** 1004 Water St. Downtown. Int corridors. **Pets:** Other species. $10 one-time fee/pet. Service with restrictions, supervision.
SAVE S X 🖥 📎 🎾

The Swan Hotel M
(360) 385-1718. **$85-$495, 3 day notice.** 216 Monroe St. Downtown. Ext corridors. **Pets:** Accepted.
SAVE X 🖥 📎 🎾

PROSSER

Best Western Inn at Horse Heaven SH
(509) 786-7977. **$89-$119.** 225 Merlot Dr. I-82, exit 80, just s. Int corridors. **Pets:** Accepted.
ASK S X &M 🏊 🖥 📎 ≈

PULLMAN

Hawthorn Inn & Suites SH ☂
(509) 332-0928. **$79-$89.** 928 NW Olsen St. 1.6 mi e on SR 270 from US 195. Int corridors. **Pets:** Large. $15 one-time fee/room. Designated rooms, supervision.
SAVE S X &M 🏊 🏊 🖥 📎 ≈ X

Holiday Inn Express Hotel & Suites SH ☂
(509) 334-4437. **$94.** SE 1190 Bishop Blvd. Jct US 195 business route, 0.5 mi s, 1 mi e on SR 270. Int corridors. **Pets:** Other species. Designated rooms, supervision.
ASK S X &M 🏊 🏊 🖥 📎 ≈

Quality Inn Paradise Creek SH
(509) 332-0500. **$90-$110.** 1400 SE Bishop Blvd. Jct US 195 business route, just s, 1 mi e on SR 270. Int corridors. **Pets:** Other species. $35 one-time fee/room. Designated rooms, service with restrictions, crate.
X 🏊 🖥 📎 ≈ X

QUINAULT

Lake Quinault Lodge SH ☂
(360) 288-2900. **$90-$195, 3 day notice.** 345 S Shore Rd. 2 mi off US 101. Ext/int corridors. **Pets:** $12 daily fee/pet. Designated rooms, service with restrictions, supervision.
SAVE X 🖥 🍽 ≈ X 🎾 ✏

QUINCY

Traditional Inns M
(509) 787-3525. **$66-$159.** 500 F St SW. West end of town on SR 28. Ext corridors. **Pets:** Very small, dogs only. $10 daily fee/room. Designated rooms, service with restrictions, supervision.
ASK S X 🖥 📎

REPUBLIC

Prospector Inn SH ☂
(509) 775-3361. **$55-$125.** 979 S Clark Ave. Downtown. Int corridors. **Pets:** $12 daily fee/pet. Service with restrictions, supervision.
SAVE S X 🖥 📎 X

RICHLAND

Clarion Hotel & Conference Center SH
(509) 946-4121. **$69-$129.** 1515 George Washington Way. I-182, exit 5B, 2.5 mi n. Int corridors. **Pets:** Accepted.
SAVE S X &M 🏊 🏊 🖥 📎 🍽 ≈ X

Days Inn M
(509) 943-4611. **$54-$76.** 615 Jadwin Ave. I-182, exit 5B, 0.9 mi n; just w of SR 240 business route; downtown. Ext corridors. **Pets:** Medium. $10 daily fee/room.
SAVE S X 🖥 📎 ≈

Holiday Inn Express Hotel & Suites SH
(509) 737-8000. **$99-$129.** 1970 Center Pkwy. Just s on Columbia Center Blvd from SR 240, just w. Int corridors. **Pets:** Accepted.
ASK S X &M 🏊 🏊 🖥 📎 ≈

▼▼▼ **Red Lion Hotel Richland Hanford House** 🆂🅷
(509) 946-7611. **$79-$139.** 802 George Washington Way. I-182, exit
5B, 1.3 mi n on SR 240 business route. Ext/int corridors.
Pets: Accepted.
🅰🆂🅺 🆂🅳 ⨉ 🆗🅼 🎣 🅾 🅱 🖥 🍽 ⇗ ⌧

▼▼▼ **Shilo Inn Hotel Richland Conference**
    Center 🆂🅷 🐾
(509) 946-4661. **$83-$143.** 50 Comstock St. I-182, exit 5B, 0.5 mi n.
Ext corridors. **Pets:** Other species. $25 one-time fee/room. Supervision.
🅰🆂🅺 🆂🅳 ⨉ 🎣 🅾 🅱 🖥 🍽 ⇗ ⌧

RIMROCK

▼ **Game Ridge Motel** 🅼
(509) 672-2212. **$115, 7 day notice.** 27350 US Hwy 12. Downtown.
Ext corridors. **Pets:** Accepted.
🅰🆂🅺 🆂🅳 ⨉ 🅱 🖥 ⌧ 🅺 🅲

RITZVILLE

🄰🄰🄰 ▼▼▼ **Americas Best Value Inn- Colwell** 🅼
(509) 659-1620. **$47-$64.** 501 W 1st Ave. I-90, exit 220, 0.9 mi n;
downtown. Ext corridors. **Pets:** Accepted.
🆂🄰🅅🄴 🆂🅳 ⨉ 🅱 🖥 ⇗ ⌧

▼▼▼ **Best Western Bronco Inn** 🆂🅷
(509) 659-5000. **$69-$129.** 105 W Galbreath Way. I-90, exit 221, go
over overpass, take second left. Int corridors. **Pets:** Accepted.
🆂🄰🅅🄴 🆂🅳 ⨉ 🅲 🅱 🖥 ⇗

▼▼ **La Quinta Inn Ritzville** 🆂🅷
(509) 659-1007. **$49-$109.** 1513 Smitty's Blvd. I-90, exit 221, just n. Int
corridors. **Pets:** Accepted.
🅰🆂🅺 🆂🅳 ⨉ 🆗🅼 🎣 🅱 🖥 ⇗ ⌧

▼ **Top Hat Motel** 🅼 🐾
(509) 659-1100. **$42-$56.** 210 E 1st Ave. I-90, exit 221, 1 mi ne via
Division St. Ext corridors. **Pets:** Dogs only. Service with restrictions,
supervision.
🅰🆂🅺 🆂🅳 🅱

ROCHESTER

🄰🄰🄰 ▼▼▼ **Eagles Landing Hotel** 🆂🅷
(360) 273-8640. **$105.** 12840 188th Ave SW. 3 mi w on US 12, 0.8 mi
s on Anderson Rd, then just e. Int corridors. **Pets:** Medium. $25 daily
fee/room. Designated rooms, service with restrictions, supervision.
🆂🄰🅅🄴 🆂🅳 ⨉ 🅱 🖥 ⇗

SAN JUAN ISLANDS AREA

DEER HARBOR

▼▼ **Deer Harbor Inn** 🅲🅸
(360) 376-4110. **$139-$375, 14 day notice.** 33 Inn Ln. 7 mi sw of ferry
landing; 3.5 mi sw of Westsound. Ext/int corridors. **Pets:** Accepted.
⨉ 🅱 🖥 🍽 🅺 🅲

EASTSOUND

▼▼ **Outlook Inn on Orcas Island** 🆂🅷
(360) 376-2200. **$54-$265, 7 day notice.** 171 Main St. In Eastsound;
downtown. Ext/int corridors. **Pets:** Accepted.
🅰🆂🅺 🆂🅳 ⨉ 🖥 🅺

FRIDAY HARBOR

🄰🄰🄰 ▼▼▼ **A Friday Harbor Inn & Spa** 🆂🅷
(360) 378-4000. **$129-$345.** 410 Spring St. In Friday Habor; 0.5 mi w of
ferry dock. Ext corridors. **Pets:** Other species. $15 one-time fee/room.
Designated rooms, service with restrictions, supervision.
🆂🄰🅅🄴 ⨉ 🅲 🅱 🖥 ⇗ ⌧

🄰🄰🄰 ▼▼▼ **Lakedale Resort** 🆂🅷 🐾
(360) 378-2350. **$179-$239, 7 day notice.** 4313 Roche Harbor Rd. 4
mi n of Friday Harbor via Tucker Ave. Ext/int corridors. **Pets:** Dogs only.
$25 one-time fee/room. Designated rooms, no service, supervision.
🆂🄰🅅🄴 ⨉ 🅱 🖥 ⌧ 🅺

LOPEZ ISLAND

🄰🄰🄰 ▼ **Lopez Islander Resort** 🆂🅷
(360) 468-2233. **$90-$190, 30 day notice.** 2864 Fisherman Bay Rd.
From ferry landing, 4.8 mi s via Ferry Rd and Fisherman Bay Rd. Ext
corridors. **Pets:** Accepted.
🆂🄰🅅🄴 🆂🅳 ⨉ 🅲 🅱 🖥 🍽 ⇗ ⌧ 🅺

SEATTLE METROPOLITAN AREA

AUBURN

🄰🄰🄰 ▼▼▼ **Best Western Peppertree Auburn Inn** 🆂🅷
(253) 887-7600. **$79-$169.** 401 8th St SW. SR 18, exit C St, just s,
then just w. Int corridors. **Pets:** Very small, dogs only. $10 daily fee/pet.
Designated rooms, service with restrictions, supervision.
🆂🄰🅅🄴 🆂🅳 ⨉ 🅱 🖥 ⇗

🄰🄰🄰 ▼▼▼ **Travelodge Suites** 🆂🅷 🐾
(253) 833-7171. **$60-$70.** Nine 16th St NW. SR 167, exit 15th St NW,
0.8 mi e, then just n on A St NE. Int corridors. **Pets:** Medium. $10 daily
fee/pet. Service with restrictions, crate.
🆂🄰🅅🄴 🆂🅳 ⨉ 🆗🅼 🎣 🅲 🅱 🖥

▼▼ **Val-U Inn** 🆂🅷
(253) 735-9600. **$70-$85.** Nine 14th St NW. SR 167, exit 15th St NW,
0.8 mi e, just s on A St NE, then just w. Int corridors. **Pets:** Accepted.
🅰🆂🅺 🆂🅳 ⨉ 🅲 🅱 🖥

BAINBRIDGE ISLAND

🄰🄰🄰 ▼▼ **Island Country Inn** 🆂🅷
(206) 842-6861. **$99-$199.** 920 Hildebrand Ln NE. 0.8 mi n of ferry
dock on SR 305, just w on High School Rd, then just s. Ext corridors.
Pets: Dogs only. $25 daily fee/pet. Designated rooms, service with restric-
tions, supervision.
🆂🄰🅅🄴 🆂🅳 ⨉ 🎣 🅲 🅱 🖥 ⇗

BELLEVUE

🄰🄰🄰 ▼▼▼▼ **Bellevue Club Hotel** 🆂🅷 🐾
(425) 454-4424. **$255-$1450.** 11200 SE 6th St. I-405, exit 12, 0.4 mi
nw. Int corridors. **Pets:** Small, dogs only. $75 one-time fee/room. Service
with restrictions, supervision.
🆂🄰🅅🄴 🆂🅳 ⨉ 🆗🅼 🎣 🅲 🅱 🍽 ⇗ ⌧

Days Inn Bellevue SH
(425) 643-6644. **$86-$120.** 3241 156th Ave SE. I-90, exit 11 westbound; exit 11A (156th Ave SE) eastbound, just ne. Ext corridors. **Pets:** Medium. $25 one-time fee/pet. Service with restrictions, supervision.

Extended StayAmerica-Seattle-Bellevue SH
(425) 453-8186. **$105-$120.** 11400 Main St. I-405, exit 13A, just se. Int corridors. **Pets:** Accepted.

Homestead Studio Suites Hotel-Seattle-Bellevue M
(425) 865-8680. **$109-$140.** 3700 132nd Ave SE. I-90, exit 11A westbound; exit 10B eastbound, 0.5 mi se. Ext corridors. **Pets:** Accepted.

Homestead Studio Suites Seattle-Redmond M
(425) 885-6675. **$130-$160.** 15805 NE 28th St. I-405, exit 14 (SR 520), 3.3 mi e to 148th Ave NE (south exit), just e on 24th St, just ne on Bel-Red Rd, just n on 156th Ave, then just e. Ext corridors. **Pets:** Accepted.

La Residence Suite Hotel SH
(425) 455-1475. **$95-$160.** 475 100th Ave NE. I-405, exit 13B, 0.9 mi w on NE 8th St, then just s. Int corridors. **Pets:** Accepted.

Larkspur Landing Home Suite Hotel Bellevue/Seattle SH
(425) 373-1212. **$99-$199.** 15805 SE 37th Pl. I-90, exit 11 westbound; exit 11A (150th Ave SE) eastbound, 0.9 mi se on south frontage road. Int corridors. **Pets:** Accepted.

Red Lion Bellevue Inn SH
(425) 455-5240. **$99-$189.** 11211 Main St. I-405, exit 12, 0.4 mi n on 114th St. Int corridors. **Pets:** Small, other species. $25 one-time fee/room. Service with restrictions, crate.

Residence Inn by Marriott, Bellevue-Redmond SH ❖
(425) 882-1222. **$129-$309.** 14455 NE 29th Pl. I-405, exit 14 (SR 520), 2.3 mi e to 148th Ave NE (north exit), then just nw. Ext corridors. **Pets:** Other species. $75 one-time fee/room. Service with restrictions.

Sheraton Bellevue-Seattle East Hotel LH ❖
(425) 455-3330. **$89-$259.** 100 112th Ave NE. I-405, exit 12 northbound; exit 13 southbound, just s. Int corridors. **Pets:** Medium, other species. Service with restrictions, crate.

The Westin Bellevue LH ❖
(425) 638-1000. **$389-$509.** 600 Bellevue Way NE. I-405, exit 13B, 1.5 mi w on NE 8th St. Int corridors. **Pets:** Medium, dogs only. Service with restrictions, supervision.

BOTHELL

Extended StayAmerica-Seattle-Bothell SH
(425) 402-4252. **$100-$110.** 923 228th St SE. I-405, exit 26, just sw. Int corridors. **Pets:** Accepted.

Extended Stay Deluxe Seattle-Bothell SH
(425) 482-2900. **$105-$120.** 22122 17th Ave SE. I-405, exit 26, just n on Bothell Everett Hwy, just e on Canyon Park Blvd SE, then just s. Int corridors. **Pets:** Accepted.

Residence Inn by Marriott Seattle NE SH
(425) 485-3030. **$159-$209.** 11920 NE 195th St. I-405, exit 24, 0.4 mi ne. Ext corridors. **Pets:** Accepted.

BREMERTON

Flagship Inn SH
(360) 479-6566. **$69-$99.** 4320 Kitsap Way. 3.5 mi w of ferry terminal; SR 3, exit Kitsap Way, 0.5 mi e. Int corridors. **Pets:** Small, dogs only. $6 daily fee/pet. Supervision.

Illahee Manor Bed & Breakfast BB 🐾
(360) 698-7555. **$115-$215, 10 day notice.** 6680 Illahee Rd NE. SR 3, exit East Bremerton, 4.9 mi se on Wheaton Way (SR 303), 1.2 mi e on McWilliams Rd, just n on East Blvd, 0.3 mi e on 3rd St, then just n. Ext/int corridors. **Pets:** Large. $25 one-time fee/pet. Designated rooms, no service.

Midway Inn SH
(360) 479-2909. **$84-$94.** 2909 Wheaton Way. SR 303, 2 mi n. Int corridors. **Pets:** Small. $150 deposit/room, $15 daily fee/pet. Designated rooms, service with restrictions, crate.

Super 8 Motel SH
(360) 377-8881. **$71-$87.** 5068 Kitsap Way. 4.2 mi w of ferry terminal; SR 3, exit Kitsap Way, just ne. Int corridors. **Pets:** Other species. $15 deposit/room, $10 one-time fee/room. Service with restrictions, supervision.

EDMONDS

Edmonds Harbor Inn SH
(425) 771-5021. **$109-$139.** 130 W Dayton St. Just s at Port of Edmonds. Ext/int corridors. **Pets:** Accepted.

K & E Motor Inn M
(425) 778-2181. **$45-$75.** 23921 Hwy 99. I-5, exit 177, 1 mi w on SR 104, exit SR 99 (Everett-Lynnwood), then just n. Ext corridors. **Pets:** Small. $20 daily fee/pet. Service with restrictions, supervision.

Travelodge Seattle/Edmonds SH
(425) 771-8008. **$69-$99.** 23825 Hwy 99. I-5, exit 177, 1 mi w on SR 104, exit at SR 99 (Everett-Lynnwood), then just n. Ext corridors. **Pets:** Medium. $25 one-time fee/pet. Service with restrictions, supervision.

EVERETT

Days Inn SH
(425) 355-1570. **$63-$99.** 1602 SE Everett Mall Way. I-5, exit 189 northbound, 0.5 mi w on SR 527, then 0.5 mi s; exit southbound, 0.7 mi s. Ext corridors. **Pets:** Accepted.

Extended StayAmerica-Seattle-Everett SH
(425) 355-1923. **$100-$110.** 8410 Broadway. I-5, exit 189, follow signs towards Broadway, just nw. Int corridors. **Pets:** Accepted.

Inn at Port Gardner SH
(425) 252-6779. **$99-$189.** 1700 W Marine View Dr. I-5, exit 193 northbound, 1.2 mi w on Pacific Ave, then 1.2 mi n; exit 194 southbound, 1.2 mi w on Everett Ave, then 1 mi n; in Everett Marina Village. Int corridors. **Pets:** Small, dogs only. $25 one-time fee/room. Service with restrictions, supervision.

FEDERAL WAY

▼▼▼ **Econo Lodge** SH
(253) 838-7700. **$65-$85.** 1505 S 328th St. I-5, exit 143, 0.5 mi w on S 320th St, 0.5 mi s on Pacific, then just w. Int corridors. **Pets:** Small, dogs only. $15 one-time fee/pet. Designated rooms, service with restrictions, supervision.
ASK ⊗ ⊟ 🖵

▼▼▼ **Extended StayAmerica-Seattle-Federal Way** SH
(253) 946-0553. **$90-$100.** 1400 S 320th St. I-5, exit 143, 0.6 mi w. Int corridors. **Pets:** Accepted.
ASK S🔊 ⊗ 🐾 ⊟ 🖵

▼▼▼ **Federal Way Super 8** SH
(253) 838-8808. **$79-$81.** 1688 S 348th St. I-5, exit 142B, just w. Int corridors. **Pets:** Accepted.
ASK S🔊 ⊗ ⊟

🔺🔺🔺 ▼▼▼▼ **La Quinta Inn & Suites** SH
(253) 529-4000. **$99-$179.** 32124 25th Ave S. I-5, exit 143, just sw. Int corridors. **Pets:** Accepted.
SAVE S🔊 ⊗ ⊟ 🖵 ▥ 🏊

🔺🔺🔺 ▼▼▼▼ **Quality Inn & Suites** SH
(253) 835-4141. **$80-$95.** 1400 S 348th St. I-5, exit 142B, 0.5 mi w. Int corridors. **Pets:** Accepted.
SAVE S🔊 ⊗ 🔊M 🐾 ♿ ⊟ 🖵 🏊

FIFE

▼▼ **Econo Lodge Inn & Suites** SH
(253) 922-9520. **$60-$90.** 3100 Pacific Hwy E. I-5, exit 136B northbound; exit 136 southbound, just nw. Ext corridors. **Pets:** Accepted.
ASK S🔊 ⊗ ⊟ 🖵 🏊

🔺🔺🔺 ▼▼▼▼ **Emerald Queen Hotel & Casino in Fife** SH
(253) 922-2000. **$69-$129.** 5700 Pacific Hwy E. I-5, exit 137, just ne. Int corridors. **Pets:** Accepted.
SAVE S🔊 ⊗ 🔊M 🐾 ♿ ⊟ 🖵 ▥

▼▼ **Extended StayAmerica-Tacoma-Fife** SH
(253) 926-6316. **$90-$100.** 2820 Pacific Hwy E. I-5, 136B northbound; exit 136 southbound, just nw. Int corridors. **Pets:** Accepted.
ASK S🔊 ⊗ ⊟ 🖵

🔺🔺🔺 ▼▼▼▼ **GuestHouse International Inn & Suites** SH
(253) 922-2500. **$60-$90.** 5805 Pacific Hwy E. I-5, exit 137, just ne. Ext corridors. **Pets:** Accepted.
SAVE S🔊 ⊗ ⊟ 🖵

🔺🔺🔺 ▼▼▼ **Howard Johnson** M
(253) 926-1000. **$59-$89.** 3501 Pacific Hwy E. I-5, exit 136B northbound; exit 136 southbound, just ne. Ext corridors. **Pets:** Small, dogs only. $15 daily fee/pet. Designated rooms, no service, supervision.
SAVE S🔊 ⊗ ⊟ 🖵

🔺🔺🔺 ▼▼▼ **Quality Inn** M
(253) 926-2301. **$76-$86.** 5601 Pacific Hwy E. I-5, exit 137, just ne. Ext corridors. **Pets:** Accepted.
SAVE S🔊 ⊗ ⊟ 🖵

GIG HARBOR

🔺🔺🔺 ▼▼▼▼ **Best Western Wesley Inn** SH 🐾
(253) 858-9690. **$149-$270.** 6575 Kimball Dr. SR 16, exit City Center, just e on Pioneer Way, then 0.3 mi s. Int corridors. **Pets:** Other species. $10 daily fee/pet. Designated rooms, service with restrictions, crate.
SAVE S🔊 ⊗ 🔊M ♿ ⊟ 🖵 🏊

🔺🔺🔺 ▼▼▼▼ **The Inn at Gig Harbor** SH 🐾
(253) 858-1111. **$139-$205.** 3211 56th St NW. SR 16, exit Olympic Dr, just w, then 0.4 mi n. Int corridors. **Pets:** Medium, other species. $25 one-time fee/room. Service with restrictions, crate.
SAVE S🔊 ⊗ 🔊M ♿ ⊟ 🖵 ▥ 🏊

ISSAQUAH

▼▼ **Motel 6-295** M
(425) 392-8405. **$65-$81.** 1885 15th Pl NW. I-90, exit 15, 0.3 mi n on 17th Ave NW, then just w on NW Sammamish Rd. Ext corridors. **Pets:** Medium, other species. Service with restrictions, supervision.
S🔊 ⊗ ♿ ⊟ 🏊

KENT

🔺🔺🔺 ▼▼▼▼ **Best Western Plaza By The Green** SH 🐾
(253) 854-8767. **$89-$99.** 24415 Russell Rd. I-5, exit 149 southbound; exit 149A northbound, 2 mi ne via Kent Des Moines Rd (SR 516) and Meeker St. Int corridors. **Pets:** Medium. $25 one-time fee/room. Designated rooms, service with restrictions, crate.
SAVE S🔊 ⊗ 🐾 ⊟ 🖵 ⊗

🔺🔺🔺 ▼▼▼▼ **Comfort Inn Kent** SH
(253) 872-2211. **$69-$145.** 22311 84th Ave S. SR 167, exit 84th Ave S, just n. Int corridors. **Pets:** Small. $10 daily fee/pet. Designated rooms, service with restrictions, supervision.
SAVE S🔊 ⊗ ⊟ 🖵 🏊

▼▼▼ **Extended StayAmerica-Seattle-Kent** SH
(253) 872-6514. **$80-$100.** 22520 83rd Ave S. SR 167, exit 84th Ave S, just nw. Int corridors. **Pets:** Accepted.
⊗ ♿ ⊟ 🖵

▼▼▼ **Hawthorn Suites** SH
(253) 395-3800. **$119-$159.** 6329 S 212th St. I-5, exit 152, 2.6 mi se via Orilla Rd and 212th St. Ext corridors. **Pets:** $150 one-time fee/pet. Service with restrictions, supervision.
ASK S🔊 ⊗ 🐾 ⊟ 🖵 🏊 ⊗

🔺🔺🔺 ▼▼▼▼ **TownePlace Suites by Marriott-Seattle Southcenter** SH 🐾
(253) 796-6000. **$89-$129.** 18123 72nd Ave S. I-405, exit 1 (SR 181), 1.6 mi s on W Valley Hwy, just e on S 180th, then just s. Ext corridors. **Pets:** Large, other species. $10 daily fee/pet. Service with restrictions.
SAVE S🔊 ⊗ 🔊M 🐾 ♿ ⊟ 🖵 🏊 ⊗

KIRKLAND

🔺🔺🔺 ▼▼▼ **Baymont Inn & Suites** SH
(425) 822-2300. **$86-$96.** 12223 NE 116th St. I-405, exit 20A northbound; exit 20 southbound, just e; in Totem Lake area. Ext corridors. **Pets:** Accepted.
SAVE S🔊 ⊗ ♿ ⊟ 🖵 🏊

▼▼▼▼ **La Quinta Inn Seattle (Bellevue/Kirkland)** SH
(425) 828-6585. **$101-$150.** 10530 NE Northup Way. I-405, exit 14 (SR 520) via 108th Ave exit, n on 108th Ave, then just w. Int corridors. **Pets:** Medium. Service with restrictions.
ASK ⊗ 🐾 ♿ ⊟ 🖵 🏊

▼▼▼ **Motel 6-687** M
(425) 821-5618. **$65-$79.** 12010 120th Pl NE. I-405, exit 20B northbound; exit 20 southbound, just se. Ext corridors. **Pets:** Medium, other species. Service with restrictions, supervision.
S🔊 ⊗ 🐾 ♿ 🏊

🔺🔺🔺 ▼▼▼ ▼▼▼▼ **The Woodmark Hotel on Lake Washington** LH
(425) 822-3700. **$250-$1800.** 1200 Carillon Point. On Lake Washington Blvd, 1 mi n of SR 520. Int corridors. **Pets:** Accepted.
SAVE S🔊 ⊗ 🐾 🖵 ▥ ⊗

LAKEWOOD

🔺🔺🔺 ▼▼▼ **Western Inn** SH
(253) 588-5241. **$69-$74.** 9920 S Tacoma Way. I-5, exit 127 (S Tacoma Way), just w on SR 512, then just n. Ext corridors. **Pets:** Accepted.
SAVE S🔊 ⊗ ⊟ 🖵

LYNNWOOD

Best Western Alderwood SH
(425) 775-7600. **$79-$94.** 19332 36th Ave W. I-5, exit 181B northbound, just n on Poplar Way, just w on 196th St SW, then just n; exit 181 (SR 524 W) southbound, just nw. Int corridors. **Pets:** Accepted.
SAVE S♦ ✕ 🐾 📶 🛁 💳 ≈

Embassy Suites Hotel Seattle North/Lynnwood SH
(425) 775-2500. **$124-$204.** 20610 44th Ave W. I-5, exit 181A northbound, just se; exit 181 (SR 524 W) southbound, 0.5 w on 196th St SW, then 0.6 mi s. Int corridors. **Pets:** Accepted.
✕ 📶 🐾 📶 🛁 💳 🍽 ≈ ✕

Extended StayAmerica-Seattle-Lynnwood SH
(425) 670-2520. **$85-$95.** 3021 196th St SW. I-5, exit 181E southbound; exit 181B northbound, just ne. Int corridors. **Pets:** Accepted.
ASK S♦ ✕ 🛁 💳 ≈

La Quinta Inn Lynnwood SH
(425) 775-7447. **$69-$119.** 4300 Alderwood Mall Blvd. I-5, exit 181A northbound, just w; exit 181 (SR 524 W) southbound, 0.5 mi w on 196th St SW, just s on 44th Ave SW, then just e. Int corridors. **Pets:** Small. Service with restrictions, supervision.
SAVE S♦ ✕ 🛁 💳 ≈

Residence Inn by Marriott-Seattle North/Lynnwood SH
(425) 771-1100. **$99-$279.** 18200 Alderwood Mall Pkwy. I-5, exit 183 southbound, just w on 164th St SW, then 1.5 mi se on 28th St W; exit 182 northbound on SR 525, exit 1, then just s; just n of Alderwood Mall Shopping Center. Ext corridors. **Pets:** Accepted.
ASK S♦ ✕ 🐾 🛁 💳 ≈ ✕

MARYSVILLE

Village Inn & Suites SH
(360) 659-0005. **$69-$149.** 235 Beach Ave. I-5, exit 199, just se. Int corridors. **Pets:** Very small, dogs only. $15 one-time fee/pet. Designated rooms, crate.
SAVE S♦ ✕ 🛁 💳

MONROE

Best Western Sky Valley Inn SH
(360) 794-3111. **$80-$175.** 19233 US 2. West end of town. Int corridors. **Pets:** Other species. $15 daily fee/pet. Service with restrictions, supervision.
SAVE S♦ ✕ 🐾 🛁 💳 ≈

GuestHouse International Inn & Suites SH
(360) 863-1900. **$99-$109, 8 day notice.** 19103 US 2. West end of town. Int corridors. **Pets:** $20 daily fee/room. Service with restrictions, supervision.
ASK S♦ ✕ 🐾 🛁 💳 ≈

MOUNTLAKE TERRACE

Studio 6 #6042 M
(425) 771-3139. **$57-$73.** 6017 244th St SW. I-5, exit 177, just ne. Ext corridors. **Pets:** Accepted.
S♦ ✕ ♿ 🐾 🐾 🛁 💳

MUKILTEO

Extended StayAmerica-Seattle-Mukilteo SH
(425) 493-1561. **$100-$110.** 3917 Harbour Pointe Blvd SW. Jct SR 526 and SR 525 (Mukilteo Speedway), 0.5 mi s, then just w. Int corridors. **Pets:** Accepted.
ASK S♦ ✕ 🛁 💳

TownePlace Suites by Marriott-Mukilteo SH
(425) 551-5900. **$119-$159.** 8521 Mukilteo Speedway. Just se of jct 84th St SW and SR 525 (Mukilteo Speedway). Ext corridors. **Pets:** Small. $75 one-time fee/pet. Designated rooms, service with restrictions, crate.
SAVE S♦ ✕ ♿ 🐾 🐾 🛁 💳 ≈ ✕

POULSBO

Holiday Inn Express SH 🐾
(360) 697-4400. **$89-$149.** 19801 NE 7th. On SR 305. Int corridors. **Pets:** Small. $20 daily fee/pet. Service with restrictions.
ASK S♦ ✕ ♿ 🐾 🛁 💳

PUYALLUP

Best Western Park Plaza SH
(253) 848-1500. **$119-$179.** 620 S Hill Park Dr. SR 512 southbound, exit S Hill/Eatonville, just w; northbound, exit 9th St SW, just w. Int corridors. **Pets:** Accepted.
SAVE S♦ ✕ ♿ 🐾 🛁 💳 ≈

Holiday Inn Express Hotel & Suites Puyallup SH 🐾
(253) 848-4900. **$139-$179.** 812 S Hill Park Dr. SR 512 southbound, exit S Hill/Eatonville, just w; northbound, exit 9th St SW, just w. Int corridors. **Pets:** Small, dogs only. $25 one-time fee/room. Service with restrictions, supervision.
ASK S♦ ✕ 🐾 🛁 💳 ≈

RENTON

Econo Lodge M
(425) 228-2858. **$55-$75.** 4710 Lake Washington Blvd NE. I-405, exit 7, just ne. Ext corridors. **Pets:** Small. $10 daily fee/pet. Service with restrictions, crate.
SAVE S♦ ✕ 🛁 💳 ≈

Holiday Inn-Renton SH
(425) 226-7700. **$79-$194.** One S Grady Way. I-405, exit 2 (SR 167/Rainier Ave), jct SR 167 N. Int corridors. **Pets:** Accepted.
SAVE ✕ 🐾 🛁 💳 🍽 ≈

Larkspur Landing Home Suite Hotel Renton SH
(425) 235-1212. **$89-$179.** 1701 E Valley Rd. SR 167, exit E Valley Rd, 1 mi nw. Int corridors. **Pets:** Accepted.
SAVE S♦ ✕ 🐾 🐾 🛁 💳

SEATAC

Clarion Hotel SH
(206) 242-0200. **$99-$120.** 3000 S 176th St. Just e of SR 99. Int corridors. **Pets:** Small. $25 daily fee/room. Service with restrictions, supervision.
SAVE S♦ ✕ ♿ 🛁 💳 🍽 ≈

Coast Gateway Hotel SH
(206) 248-8200. **$99-$149.** 18415 International Blvd. On SR 99. Int corridors. **Pets:** Accepted.
SAVE S♦ ✕ ♿ 🐾 🛁 💳

Doubletree Hotel Seattle Airport LH
(206) 246-8600. **$89-$189.** 18740 International Blvd. On SR 99. Int corridors. **Pets:** Small, other species. Service with restrictions, crate.
✕ 🐾 🐾 🛁 💳 🍽 ≈

Hilton Seattle Airport & Conference Center LH
(206) 244-4800. **$89-$209.** 17620 International Blvd. On SR 99. Int corridors. **Pets:** Accepted.
✕ 🐾 🐾 🛁 💳 🍽 ≈ ✕

Holiday Inn Express Hotel & Suites-Seattle Sea-Tac Airport SH
(206) 824-3200. **$99-$144.** 19621 International Blvd. On SR 99. Int corridors. **Pets:** Other species. $75 one-time fee/room. Service with restrictions, supervision.
ASK S♦ ✕ 🛁 💳

AAA ▼▼▼▼ Holiday Inn Seattle SeaTac International Airport LH
(206) 248-1000. **$89-$209.** 17338 International Blvd. On SR 99. Int corridors. **Pets:** Medium. $20 daily fee/room. Designated rooms, service with restrictions, supervision.

[SAVE] [S] [X] [&M] [2] [B] [=] [Y1] [=]

AAA ▼▼▼▼ La Quinta Inn Seattle (Sea-Tac International) SH
(206) 241-5211. **$100-$149.** 2824 S 188th St. On SR 99. Int corridors. **Pets:** Medium. Service with restrictions.

[SAVE] [X] [2] [B] [=] [=]

▼ Motel 6–1332 M
(206) 246-4101. **$53-$65.** 16500 International Blvd. On SR 99. Ext corridors. **Pets:** Medium, other species. Service with restrictions, supervision.

[S] [X] [&]

▼ Motel 6–736 M
(206) 824-9902. **$53-$65.** 20651 Military Rd. I-5, exit 151, just se. Ext corridors. **Pets:** Medium, other species. Service with restrictions, supervision.

[S] [X] [2] [&] [B] [=]

▼ Motel 6–90 SH
(206) 241-1648. **$51-$63.** 18900 47th Ave S. I-5, exit 152, just sw. Int corridors. **Pets:** Medium, other species. Service with restrictions, supervision.

[S] [X] [2] [&] [B] [=]

▼▼▼ Red Lion Hotel Seattle Airport SH
(206) 246-5535. **$99-$219.** 18220 International Blvd. On SR 99. Int corridors. **Pets:** Accepted.

[ASK] [S] [X] [2] [B] [=] [Y1] [=] [X]

▼ Rodeway Inn Sea Tac SH
(206) 246-9300. **$43-$89.** 2930 S 176th St. Just e of SR 99. Int corridors. **Pets:** Small. $10 one-time fee/pet. Service with restrictions, crate.

[ASK] [S] [X] [B]

▼▼ Super 8 Motel Sea-Tac SH
(206) 433-8188. **$70-$98.** 3100 S 192nd St. Just e of SR 99. Int corridors. **Pets:** Accepted.

[ASK] [S] [X]

SEATTLE

AAA ▼▼▼▼ Alexis Hotel LH
(206) 624-4844. **$175-$349.** 1007 1st Ave. Corner of Madison St and 1st Ave. Int corridors. **Pets:** Accepted.

[SAVE] [S] [X] [2] [&] [=] [Y1] [X]

AAA ▼▼ Aurora Seafair Inn M
(206) 524-3600. **$65-$85.** 9100 Aurora Ave N. I-5, exit 172, 1.5 mi w on N 85th St, then just n. Ext corridors. **Pets:** Small. $10 daily fee/pet. Designated rooms, service with restrictions, supervision.

[SAVE] [S] [X] [B]

AAA ▼▼▼ Best Western Evergreen Inn & Suites SH
(206) 361-3700. **$89-$129.** 13700 Aurora Ave N. I-5, exit 175, 1.1 mi w on NE 145th St, then 0.3 mi s. Int corridors. **Pets:** Medium. $15 one-time fee/pet. Designated rooms, service with restrictions, supervision.

[SAVE] [X] [B] [=] [X]

AAA ▼▼▼ Best Western Executive Inn/Seattle SH
(206) 448-9444. **$119-$199.** 200 Taylor Ave N. I-5, exit 166, 1 mi w; near Seattle Center; just w of SR 99. Int corridors. **Pets:** Medium. $35 one-time fee/room. Service with restrictions.

[SAVE] [S] [X] [&M] [2] [&] [B] [=] [Y1]

AAA ▼▼ Best Western Loyal Inn SH
(206) 682-0200. **$109-$179.** 2301 8th Ave. Corner of 8th Ave and Denny Way. Int corridors. **Pets:** Medium. $35 one-time fee/room. Service with restrictions, crate.

[SAVE] [S] [X] [B] [=] [X]

▼▼▼ Crowne Plaza Seattle LH
(206) 464-1980. **$220-$350.** 1113 6th Ave. Corner of 6th Ave and Seneca St. Int corridors. **Pets:** Other species. $50 one-time fee/room. Service with restrictions, supervision.

[ASK] [X] [2] [B] [=] [Y1]

▼▼ Days Inn Town Center SH
(206) 448-3434. **$59-$99.** 2205 7th Ave. Between Bell and Blanchard sts. Int corridors. **Pets:** Service with restrictions, crate.

[X] [2] [Y1]

AAA ▼▼ The Edgewater LH ❀
(206) 728-7000. **$179-$599.** 2411 Alaskan Way, Pier 67. On waterfront at Pier 67; at base of Wall St. Int corridors. **Pets:** Other species. Designated rooms, service with restrictions, supervision.

[SAVE] [S] [X] [2] [=] [Y1] [X]

▼▼ Executive Hotel Pacific SH
(206) 623-3900. **$129-$169.** 400 Spring St. Between 4th and 5th aves. Int corridors. **Pets:** Small, dogs only. Designated rooms, service with restrictions.

[ASK] [X] [2] [=]

▼▼ Extended StayAmerica-Seattle-Northgate SH
(206) 365-8100. **$85-$95.** 13300 Stone Ave N. I-5, exit 175, 1.0 mi w on n 145th St, 0.5 mi s on Aurora Ave, just e on 135th St. Int corridors. **Pets:** Accepted.

[ASK] [S] [X] [B] [=]

AAA ▼▼▼▼ The Fairmont Olympic Hotel LH ❀
(206) 621-1700. **$299-$429.** 411 University St. Corner of 4th Ave and University St. Int corridors. **Pets:** Small. Service with restrictions, supervision.

[SAVE] [X] [2] [&] [B] [=] [Y1] [=] [X]

▼▼▼ Homewood Suites by Hilton-Seattle Downtown SH ❀
(206) 281-9393. **$179-$349.** 206 Western Ave W. I-5, exit 167 (Mercer St), 0.3 mi w, 0.5 mi s on Fairview Ave, 1.2 mi w on Denny Way, then just n. Int corridors. **Pets:** Medium, other species. $200 one-time fee/room. Designated rooms, service with restrictions, crate.

[ASK] [S] [X] [B] [=]

AAA ▼▼▼ Hotel Max SH ❀
(206) 728-6299. **$199-$269.** 620 Stewart St. Corner of 7th Ave and Stewart St. Int corridors. **Pets:** Medium, other species. $45 one-time fee/room. Service with restrictions, supervision.

[SAVE] [X] [&M] [&] [B] [=] [Y1]

AAA ▼▼▼▼ Hotel Monaco LH
(206) 621-1770. **$159-$349.** 1101 4th Ave. Corner of 4th Ave and Spring St. Int corridors. **Pets:** Accepted.

[SAVE] [S] [X] [2] [B] [=] [Y1] [X]

AAA ▼▼▼▼ Hotel Nexus Seattle SH ❀
(206) 365-0700. **$109-$139.** 2140 N Northgate Way. I-5, exit 173, just nw. Ext corridors. **Pets:** $25 one-time fee/room. Designated rooms, service with restrictions, crate.

[SAVE] [S] [X] [2] [B] [=] [=]

AAA ▼▼▼▼ Hotel Vintage Park LH ❀
(206) 624-8000. **$139-$595.** 1100 5th Ave. Corner of Spring St and 5th Ave. Int corridors. **Pets:** Other species. Supervision.

[SAVE] [S] [X] [2] [Y1] [X]

La Quinta Inn & Suites Seattle Downtown SH
(206) 624-6820. **$79-$189.** 2224 8th Ave. Corner of 8th Ave and Blanchard St. Int corridors. **Pets:** Service with restrictions, supervision.

Red Lion Hotel on Fifth Avenue-Seattle LH ❀
(206) 971-8000. **$290-$390.** 1415 5th Ave. Between Pike and Union sts. Int corridors. **Pets:** Medium, dogs only. $50 one-time fee/room. Service with restrictions.

Residence Inn Marriott Seattle Downtown/Lake Union SH ❀
(206) 624-6000. **$129-$239.** 800 Fairview Ave N. I-5, exit 167 (Mercer St), south end of Lake Union. Int corridors. **Pets:** Other species. $10 daily fee/pet. Service with restrictions, crate.

The Roosevelt, A Coast Hotel SH ❀
(206) 621-1200. **$105-$300.** 1531 7th Ave. Corner of 7th Ave and Pine St. Int corridors. **Pets:** Medium, other species. $50 one-time fee/room. Service with restrictions, supervision.

Sheraton Seattle Hotel LH
(206) 621-9000. **$149-$279.** 1400 6th Ave. Corner of 6th Ave and Pike St. Int corridors. **Pets:** Accepted.

The Sixth Avenue Inn SH
(206) 441-8300. **$72-$109.** 2000 6th Ave. Downtown. Int corridors. **Pets:** Accepted.

Sorrento Hotel SH ❀
(206) 622-6400. **$320-$340.** 900 Madison St. I-5, exit Madison St, just e; at 9th Ave and Madison St. Int corridors. **Pets:** Other species. $50 one-time fee/room. Service with restrictions, supervision.

University Inn SH
(206) 632-5055. **$109-$145.** 4140 Roosevelt Way NE. I-5, exit 169, 0.5 mi e, then just s. Int corridors. **Pets:** Medium, dogs only. $20 daily fee/room. Designated rooms, service with restrictions, supervision.

The Westin Seattle LH ❀
(206) 728-1000. **$129-$229.** 1900 5th Ave. Corner of 5th Ave and Stewart St. Int corridors. **Pets:** Medium. Service with restrictions, supervision.

W Seattle LH
(206) 264-6000. **$259-$479.** 1112 4th Ave. Corner of 4th Ave and Seneca St. Int corridors. **Pets:** Accepted.

SILVERDALE

Cimarron Motor Inn SH
(360) 692-7777. **$79-$119.** 9734 NW Silverdale Way. SR 3, exit Newberry Hill Road, just e, then 1.2 mi n. Int corridors. **Pets:** Small. $50 one-time fee/pet. Designated rooms, service with restrictions, supervision.

Silverdale Beach Hotel SH
(360) 698-1000. **$134-$405.** 3073 NW Bucklin Hill Rd. SR 3, exit Newberry Hill Rd, just e, 1 mi n on Silverdale Way, then just e. Int corridors. **Pets:** Accepted.

SNOHOMISH

Inn At Snohomish M
(360) 568-2208. **$69-$105.** 323 2nd St. East end of town. Ext corridors. **Pets:** Large, other species. Service with restrictions, supervision.

TACOMA

Crossland Studios-Tacoma-Hosmer M
(253) 538-9448. **Call for rates.** 8801 S Hosmer St. I-5, exit 128 northbound, just se; exit 129 southbound, just e on 72nd St, then 1.0 mi s. Ext corridors. **Pets:** Accepted.

Extended StayAmerica-Tacoma-South SH
(253) 475-6565. **$100-$110.** 2120 S 48th St. I-5, exit 130, 0.4 mi nw. Int corridors. **Pets:** Accepted.

La Quinta Inn & Suites Tacoma (Conference Center) SH
(253) 383-0146. **$104-$144.** 1425 E 27th St. I-5, exit 135 southbound; exit 134 northbound, just n. Int corridors. **Pets:** Medium. Service with restrictions.

Sheraton Tacoma Hotel LH
(253) 572-3200. **$128-$224.** 1320 Broadway Plaza. I-5, exit 133 (City Center) to I-705 N, exit A St, left on 11th St, then left; downtown. Int corridors. **Pets:** Accepted.

Shilo Inn-Tacoma SH ❀
(253) 475-4020. **$89-$140.** 7414 S Hosmer St. I-5, exit 129, just se. Int corridors. **Pets:** Other species. $25 one-time fee/room. Supervision.

TUKWILA

Comfort Suites Tukwila SH ❀
(425) 227-7200. **$103-$159.** 7200 Fun Center Way. I-405, exit 1 (SR 181), just n on Interurban Ave, then just e. Int corridors. **Pets:** Medium. $15 daily fee/pet. Service with restrictions, supervision.

Extended StayAmerica-Seattle-Tukwila SH
(206) 244-2537. **$80-$90.** 15451 53rd Ave S. I-5, exit 153 (northbound), Just n on Southcenter Pkwy, just n on 61st St, just w on Southcenter Blvd, then just sw; exit 154B (Southcenter Mall) southbound, just sw. Ext corridors. **Pets:** Accepted.

Homestead Studio Suites Hotel-Seattle-Southcenter M
(425) 235-7160. **$95-$120.** 15635 W Valley Hwy. I-405, exit 1 (SR 181), just s. Ext corridors. **Pets:** Accepted.

Homewood Suites by Hilton SH
(206) 433-8000. **$159-$189.** 6955 Fort Dent Way. I-405, exit 1 (SR 181), just ne. Ext/int corridors. **Pets:** Medium. $20 daily fee/room. Designated rooms, service with restrictions, supervision.

Ramada Limited Sea-Tac Airport SH
(206) 244-8800. **$79-$109.** 13900 Tukwila International Blvd. I-5, exit 158 southbound, 2 mi s; exit 154A (SR 518 W) northbound, 1 mi n on SR 99. Int corridors. **Pets:** Other species. $25 daily fee/pet. Designated rooms, service with restrictions, supervision.

◤◤ **Red Lion Hotel Seattle South** 🆂🅷
(206) 762-0300. **$89-$139.** 11244 Tukwila International Blvd. I-5, exit 158, 0.4 mi w on Boeing Access Rd, then 0.4 mi s. Int corridors.
Pets: Accepted.

◤◤◤ **Residence Inn by Marriott-Seattle South** 🆂🅷
(425) 226-5500. **$99-$209.** 16201 W Valley Hwy. I-405, exit 1 (SR 181), just s. Ext corridors. **Pets:** Accepted.

VASHON

◤ **The Swallow's Nest Guest Cottages** 🅲🅰 🐾
(206) 463-2646. **$105-$250.** 6030 SW 248th St. From north end Ferry Landing, 7.8 mi s on Vashon Hwy; from south end (Tahlequah) Ferry Landing, 5.8 mi n on Vashon Hwy, 1.4 mi e on Quartermaster Dr, 1.5 mi s on Dockton Rd, 0.4 mi s on 75th Ave, then 1 mi e. Ext corridors. **Pets:** Other species. $15 daily fee/pet. Designated rooms, service with restrictions, supervision.

END METROPOLITAN AREA

SEDRO-WOOLLEY

🅰🅰🅰 ◤◤ **Three Rivers Inn** 🆂🅷
(360) 855-2626. **$69-$79.** 210 Ball St. On SR 20, just w of jct SR 9 N. Ext corridors. **Pets:** Accepted.

SEQUIM

🅰🅰🅰 ◤◤ **Econo Lodge** 🆂🅷
(360) 683-7113. **$67-$134.** 801 E Washington St. US 101, exit Sequim Ave, 0.4 mi n, then 0.6 mi e; east end of downtown. Int corridors. **Pets:** Medium. $10 daily fee/pet. Designated rooms, service with restrictions, supervision.

◤◤◤◤ **Quality Inn & Suites–Sequim** 🆂🅷 🐾
(360) 683-2800. **$110-$180.** 134 River Rd. US 101, exit River Rd, just nw. Int corridors. **Pets:** Dogs only. $10 daily fee/pet. Designated rooms, service with restrictions, supervision.

🅰🅰🅰 ◤◤ **Sequim West Inn** 🅼
(360) 683-4144. **$69-$115, 3 day notice.** 740 W Washington St. US 101, exit River Rd, 0.9 mi ne via River Rd and W Washington St. Ext corridors. **Pets:** Small. $10 daily fee/pet. Supervision.

SHELTON

◤◤ **Super 8 Motel of Shelton** 🆂🅷
(360) 426-1654. **$59-$74, 3 day notice.** 2943 Northview Cir. US 101, exit Wallace-Kneeland Blvd, just se. Int corridors. **Pets:** $15 daily fee/pet. Supervision.

SKYKOMISH

🅰🅰🅰 ◤◤ **SkyRiver Inn** 🅼
(360) 677-2261. **$73-$130, 14 day notice.** 333 River Dr E. 16 mi w of Stevens Pass on US 2; south end of Skykomish River Bridge. Ext/int corridors. **Pets:** Other species. $10 daily fee/room. Supervision.

SNOQUALMIE PASS

◤◤ **Summit Lodge at Snoqualmie Pass** 🆂🅷
(425) 434-6300. **$69-$249, 3 day notice.** 603 SR 906. I-90, exit 52 eastbound, 0.3 mi e; exit 53 westbound, 0.3 mi w. Int corridors. **Pets:** Accepted.

SOAP LAKE

◤◤◤ **Notaras Lodge** 🅼
(509) 246-0462. **$65-$120.** 236 E Main Ave. Just w of SR 17. Ext corridors. **Pets:** Accepted.

SOUTH BEND

🅰🅰🅰 ◤◤◤ **The Russell House** 🅱🅱
(360) 875-6487. **$99-$200, 5 day notice.** 902 E Water St. 0.5 mi s on Harrison. Int corridors. **Pets:** Accepted.

SPOKANE

🅰🅰🅰 ◤◤ **Apple Tree Inn** 🅼
(509) 466-3020. **$45-$69.** 9508 N Division St. Jct US 2 and 395, just n. Ext/int corridors. **Pets:** Small, dogs only. $10 daily fee/pet. Designated rooms, service with restrictions, supervision.

🅰🅰🅰 ◤◤◤ **Best Western Peppertree Airport Inn** 🆂🅷
(509) 624-4655. **$79-$189.** 3711 S Geiger Blvd. I-90, exit 276, just n. Int corridors. **Pets:** Accepted.

◤◤ **Comfort Inn North** 🆂🅷
(509) 467-7111. **$49-$129.** 7111 N Division St. I-90, exit 281 (Division St), 4.6 mi n. Int corridors. **Pets:** Accepted.

🅰🅰🅰 ◤◤◤◤ **The Davenport Hotel and Tower** 🅻🅷
(509) 455-8888. **$199.** 10 S Post St. Downtown. Int corridors. **Pets:** Accepted.

◤◤◤ **Doubletree Hotel Spokane City Center** 🅻🅷 🐾
(509) 455-9600. **$99-$179, 3 day notice.** 322 N Spokane Falls Ct. I-90, exit 281 (Division St), just n; downtown. Int corridors. **Pets:** Medium, other species. $25 one-time fee/room. Supervision.

◤◤ **Econo Lodge** 🆂🅷
(509) 747-2011. **$45-$69.** 120 W 3rd Ave. I-90, exit 281 (Division St), just n, then just w on 2nd Ave. Ext corridors. **Pets:** Medium. $10 daily fee/pet. Service with restrictions, supervision.

◤◤◤ **Holiday Inn Express-Downtown** 🆂🅷
(509) 328-8505. **$99-$115.** 801 N Division St. I-90, exit 281 (Division St), 0.8 mi n. Ext/int corridors. **Pets:** Accepted.

◤◤ **Howard Johnson Inn** 🅼 🐾
(509) 326-5500. **$59-$139, 14 day notice.** 3033 N Division St. I-90, exit 281 (Division St), 2.3 mi n on US 2 and 395. Ext/int corridors. **Pets:** Other species. Service with restrictions.

◤◤ **Howard Johnson Inn** 🆂🅷
(509) 838-6630. **$79-$149.** 211 S Division St. I-90, exit 281 (Division St), just n. Int corridors. **Pets:** Small. $10 daily fee/pet. Service with restrictions, supervision.

AAA ▼▼▼ Madison Inn SH ❀
(509) 474-4200. **$65-$75.** 15 W Rockwood Blvd. I-90, exit 281 (Division St) eastbound, just e to Cowley, 0.4 mi s, then just w; exit westbound, just n to 2nd Ave, just w to Browne St, 0.5 mi s to 9th Ave, then just e. Int corridors. **Pets:** Other species. $10 daily fee/pet. Designated rooms, supervision.
[SAVE] [S🔊] [✕] [🕭M] [🐾] [🛏] [💻]

▼▼▼ Oxford Suites-Downtown Spokane SH
(509) 353-9000. **$119-$179.** 115 W North River Dr. I-90, exit 281 (Division St), 1 mi n, then just n. Int corridors. **Pets:** Accepted.
[A$K] [S🔊] [◈] [🕭] [🐾] [🛏] [💻] [≈] [✕]

AAA ▼▼ Ramada Limited M
(509) 838-8504. **$44-$69.** 123 S Post St. I-90, exit 280B (Lincoln St), just n to 1st Ave W, just e to Post St, then just s. Ext corridors. **Pets:** Medium, other species. $25 one-time fee/room. Service with restrictions, supervision.
[SAVE] [S🔊] [✕] [🕭] [🛏] [💻]

▼▼ Ramada Limited Suites SH
(509) 468-4201. **$69-$89.** 9601 N Newport Hwy. US 2 and 395, just n on US 2 (Newport Hwy). Int corridors. **Pets:** Accepted.
[A$K] [S🔊] [✕] [🕭M] [🕭] [🐾] [🛏] [💻] [≈]

▼▼▼▼ Ramada Spokane Airport & Indoor Waterpark SH
(509) 838-5211. **$99.** 8909 Airport Dr. I-90, exit 277B eastbound; exit 277 westbound, 3.4 mi n. Int corridors. **Pets:** $10 one-time fee/room. Service with restrictions, crate.
[A$K] [S🔊] [✕] [🕭] [🛏] [💻] [🍴] [≈] [✕]

AAA ▼▼▼▼ Red Lion Hotel at the Park-Spokane LH ❀
(509) 326-8000. **$99-$125, 30 day notice.** 303 W North River Dr. I-90, exit 281 (Division St), 1.5 mi n on US 195, then just w. Int corridors. **Pets:** $10 deposit/room. Service with restrictions.
[SAVE] [S🔊] [✕] [🕭] [🐾] [🛏] [💻] [🍴] [≈] [✕]

▼▼ Red Lion River Inn-Spokane SH ❀
(509) 326-5577. **$104-$113.** N 700 Division St. I-90, exit 281 (Division St), 0.8 mi n; downtown. Int corridors. **Pets:** Large, other species. $50 deposit/room. Service with restrictions, supervision.
[A$K] [S🔊] [✕] [🛏] [💻] [🍴] [≈] [✕]

AAA ▼ Shangri-La Motel M ❀
(509) 747-2066. **$55-$75.** 2922 W Government Way. I-90, exit 277A eastbound; exit 277 westbound, Garden Springs Rd to Sunset Blvd, 1 mi e to Government Way, then just n to Hartson. Ext corridors. **Pets:** Other species. $20 one-time fee/room. Supervision.
[SAVE] [S🔊] [✕] [💻] [≈]

▼▼ Shilo Inn Hotel SH ❀
(509) 535-9000. **$70-$110.** 923 E 3rd Ave. I-90, exit 281 (Division St), just n to E 3rd Ave, then 0.7 mi e. Int corridors. **Pets:** Other species. $25 one-time fee/room. Supervision.
[A$K] [S🔊] [✕] [🕭M] [🐾] [🕭] [🛏] [💻] [🍴] [≈] [✕]

AAA ▼▼▼ Spokane House Travelodge SH
(509) 838-1471. **$68.** W 4301 Sunset Blvd. I-90, exit 277A eastbound, 1 mi n on Garden Springs Rd; exit 277 westbound, just n on Rustle St. Int corridors. **Pets:** Accepted.
[SAVE] [✕] [🛏] [💻] [🍴] [≈] [✕]

AAA ▼▼▼ Super 8 Airport West SH
(509) 838-8800. **$45-$90.** 11102 W Westbow Blvd. I-90, exit 272 (Medical Lake), just s. Int corridors. **Pets:** Other species. $15 one-time fee/room. Supervision.
[SAVE] [✕] [🕭M] [🛏] [💻] [≈]

▼▼ Travelodge SH ❀
(509) 623-9727. **$59-$170.** W 33 Spokane Falls Blvd. I-90, exit 281 (Division St), 0.5 mi n, then just w. Int corridors. **Pets:** Other species. $10 daily fee/room. Crate.
[A$K] [S🔊] [✕] [🕭M] [🐾] [🛏] [💻]

▼▼▼▼ WestCoast Ridpath Hotel LH
(509) 838-2711. **$72-$87.** 515 W Sprague Ave. Downtown. Int corridors. **Pets:** Accepted.
[A$K] [S🔊] [✕] [🕭] [🐾] [🛏] [💻]

SPOKANE VALLEY

AAA ▼▼▼▼ Best Western Pheasant Hill SH ❀
(509) 926-7432. **$79-$129.** 12415 E Mission. I-90, exit 289, just se. Int corridors. **Pets:** $10 one-time fee/room. Service with restrictions, supervision.
[SAVE] [S🔊] [✕] [🕭M] [🐾] [🛏] [💻] [≈]

AAA ▼▼▼ Broadway Inn & Suites SH
(509) 535-7185. **$99-$129, 14 day notice.** 6309 E Broadway. I-90, exit 286, just w. Ext/int corridors. **Pets:** Service with restrictions, supervision.
[SAVE] [S🔊] [✕] [🕭] [🐾] [🛏] [💻] [≈]

▼▼ Comfort Inn Valley SH
(509) 924-3838. **$65-$95.** 905 N Sullivan Rd. I-90, exit 291B, just s. Int corridors. **Pets:** Accepted.
[A$K] [S🔊] [✕] [🛏] [💻] [≈]

▼ Crossland Studios-Spokane Valley SH
(509) 928-5948. **Call for rates.** 12803 E Sprague. I-90, exit 289, 1.1 mi s, just w. Ext corridors. **Pets:** Accepted.
[✕] [🐾] [🛏] [💻]

▼▼▼ Holiday Inn Express-Valley SH
(509) 927-7100. **$95-$189.** 9220 E Mission. I-90, exit 287, just s. Ext/int corridors. **Pets:** Other species. Designated rooms, supervision.
[A$K] [✕] [🕭M] [🕭] [🐾] [🛏] [💻] [≈]

AAA ▼▼▼▼ La Quinta Inn & Suites Spokane SH
(509) 893-0955. **$79-$149.** 3808 N Sullivan Rd. I-90, exit 291B, 1.3 mi n. Int corridors. **Pets:** Accepted.
[SAVE] [✕] [🕭M] [🕭] [🐾] [🛏] [💻] [≈]

AAA ▼▼▼▼ Mirabeau Park Hotel and Convention Center SH
(509) 924-9000. **$94.** 1100 N Sullivan Rd. I-90, exit 291B, just s. Int corridors. **Pets:** Other species. $25 one-time fee/room. Designated rooms, service with restrictions, crate.
[SAVE] [S🔊] [✕] [🕭] [🐾] [🛏] [💻] [🍴] [≈] [✕]

AAA ▼▼▼▼ Oxford Suites Spokane Valley SH ❀
(509) 847-1000. **$99-$199.** 15015 E Indiana Ave. I-90, exit 291A eastbound; exit 291B westbound, just nw. Int corridors. **Pets:** Small, dogs only. $20 one-time fee/pet. Service with restrictions, supervision.
[SAVE] [S🔊] [✕] [🕭] [🐾] [🛏] [💻] [≈] [✕]

▼▼▼ Quality Inn Valley Suites SH
(509) 928-5218. **$89-$109.** 8923 E Mission. I-90, exit 287. Int corridors. **Pets:** Accepted.
[A$K] [S🔊] [✕] [🕭M] [🕭] [🐾] [🛏] [💻] [≈] [✕]

▼▼▼ Residence Inn by Marriott SH ❀
(509) 892-9300. **$109-$129.** 15915 E Indiana. I-90, exit 291 westbound, just e; exit 291B eastbound, just n, then just e. Int corridors. **Pets:** Small. $75 one-time fee/room. Designated rooms, crate.
[A$K] [◈] [🕭M] [🕭] [🐾] [🛏] [💻] [≈] [✕]

AAA ▼▼ Super 8 Motel SH
(509) 928-4888. **$58-$103.** N 2020 Argonne Rd. I-90, exit 287, just n. Int corridors. **Pets:** Large, other species. $25 deposit/room. Designated rooms, service with restrictions, supervision.
[A$K] [S🔊] [✕] [🛏] [💻] [≈] [✕]

STEVENSON

▲▲▲ ▼▼▼▼ Skamania Lodge 🏠 ☥
(509) 427-7700. **$119-$379, 5 day notice.** 1131 SW Skamania Lodge Way. 1 mi w on SR 14, just n on Rock Creek Dr, then just w. Int corridors. **Pets:** Other species. $50 one-time fee/room. Designated rooms, service with restrictions, crate.
[SAVE] [S🐾] [✕] [🖍] [🖱] [🛏] [💻] [🍴] [🏊] [✕]

SULTAN

▲▲▲ ▼ Dutch Cup Motel Ⓜ
(360) 793-2215. **$62-$79.** 819 Main St. Jct US 2 and Main St. Ext corridors. **Pets:** Medium, other species. Service with restrictions, supervision.
[SAVE] [S🐾] [✕] [🛏]

SUNNYSIDE

▼▼▼▼ Best Western Grapevine Inn 🆂🅷
(509) 839-6070. **$79-$129.** 1849 Quail Ln. I-82, exit 69, just n, then just w. Int corridors. **Pets:** Medium, dogs only. $25 one-time fee/room. Service with restrictions, supervision.
[ASK] [S🐾] [✕] [🖍] [🛏] [💻] [🏊]

▲▲▲ ▼ Country Inn & Suites Ⓜ
(509) 837-7878. **$50-$65.** 408 Yakima Valley Hwy. Downtown. Ext corridors. **Pets:** Medium, other species. $10 daily fee/pet. Service with restrictions, supervision.
[SAVE] [S🐾] [✕] [🛏] [💻] [🏊]

▲▲▲ ▼▼▼ Rodeway Inn 🆂🅷
(509) 837-5781. **$74-$89.** 3209 Picard Pl. I-82, exit 69, just n. Int corridors. **Pets:** Accepted.
[SAVE] [S🐾] [✕] [🛏] [💻] [🏊]

TOPPENISH

▲▲▲ ▼▼▼▼ Best Western Toppenish 🆂🅷 ☥
(509) 865-7444. **$69-$139.** 515 S Elm St. I-82, exit 50, 3.1 mi e. Int corridors. **Pets:** Small, dogs only. $20 daily fee/pet. Designated rooms, service with restrictions, supervision.
[SAVE] [S🐾] [✕] [🖍] [🛏] [💻] [🏊]

TUMWATER

▲▲▲ ▼▼▼ Best Western Tumwater Inn 🆂🅷
(360) 956-1235. **$81-$96.** 5188 Capitol Blvd. I-5, exit 102, just e. Int corridors. **Pets:** Small. $10 daily fee/pet. Service with restrictions, supervision.
[SAVE] [S🐾] [✕] [🖍] [🛏] [💻] [✕]

▼▼▼ Comfort Inn and Conference Center 🆂🅷
(360) 352-0691. **$79-$99.** 1620 74th Ave SW. I-5, exit 101, just se. Int corridors. **Pets:** Accepted.
[ASK] [S🐾] [✕] [🛏] [💻] [🏊]

▼▼▼ Extended StayAmerica-Olympia-Tumwater 🆂🅷
(360) 754-6063. **$90-$100.** 1675 Mottman Rd SW. I-5, exit 104, 0.4 mi nw on US 101 just s on Crosby Blvd then just se. Int corridors. **Pets:** Accepted.
[ASK] [S🐾] [✕] [🖊] [🖍] [🛏] [💻]

▼▼▼ GuestHouse Inn & Suites 🆂🅷 ☥
(360) 943-5040. **$85-$165.** 1600 74th Ave SW. I-5, exit 101, just se. Int corridors. **Pets:** Other species. $50 deposit/room, $10 daily fee/pet. Designated rooms, service with restrictions, crate.
[ASK] [S🐾] [✕] [🖍] [🖊] [🛏] [💻] [🏊]

▼ Motel 6-77 Ⓜ
(360) 754-7320. **$45-$61.** 400 W Lee St. I-5, exit 102, just e on Trosper Rd, just s on Capitol Blvd, then just w. Ext corridors. **Pets:** Medium, other species. Service with restrictions, supervision.
[S🐾] [✕] [🖍] [🛏] [🏊]

TWISP

▼▼ Idle-A-While Motel Ⓜ ☥
(509) 997-3222. **$53-$96.** 505 N SR 20. Just n of town. Ext corridors. **Pets:** Dogs only. $10 daily fee/pet. Service with restrictions, supervision.
[ASK] [S🐾] [✕] [🛏] [💻] [✕]

UNION

▼▼▼▼ Alderbrook Resort & Spa 🆂🅷
(360) 898-2200. **$130-$400, 7 day notice.** 10 E Alderbrook Dr. On SR 106, just e of town. Ext/int corridors. **Pets:** Designated rooms, service with restrictions, supervision.
[ASK] [✕] [🛏] [💻] [🍴] [🏊] [✕]

UNION GAP

▼▼ Best Western Ahtanum Inn 🆂🅷
(509) 248-9700. **$109-$139.** 2408 Rudkin Rd. I-82, exit 36, just n. Int corridors. **Pets:** Accepted.
[ASK] [S🐾] [✕] [🖍] [🛏] [💻] [🏊] [✕]

▲▲▲ ▼▼▼ Quality Inn-Yakima Valley Ⓜ ☥
(509) 248-6924. **$69-$139.** 12 E Valley Mall Blvd. I-82, exit 36, just s. Ext corridors. **Pets:** Small, dogs only. $10 daily fee/pet. Designated rooms, service with restrictions, supervision.
[SAVE] [S🐾] [✕] [🖍] [🖊] [🖍] [🛏] [💻] [🏊]

▼▼ Super 8 Motel Yakima 🆂🅷
(509) 248-8880. **$70-$90.** 2605 Rudkin Rd. I-82, exit 36, just s. Int corridors. **Pets:** Other species. $15 one-time fee/room. Service with restrictions, supervision.
[ASK] [S🐾] [✕] [🖊] [🏊]

WALLA WALLA

▲▲▲ ▼▼▼▼ Best Western Walla Walla Suites Inn 🆂🅷 ☥
(509) 525-4700. **$79-$119.** 7 E Oak St. US 12, exit 2nd Ave, just s. Int corridors. **Pets:** Dogs only. $10 daily fee/pet. Service with restrictions, supervision.
[SAVE] [S🐾] [✕] [🖍] [🖊] [🖍] [🛏] [💻] [🏊]

▲▲▲ ▼ Budget Inn Ⓜ
(509) 529-4410. **$49-$105.** 305 N 2nd Ave. US 12, exit 2nd Ave, 0.3 mi s. Ext corridors. **Pets:** Small. $10 daily fee/pet. Service with restrictions, supervision.
[SAVE] [S🐾] [✕] [🛏] [🏊]

▲▲▲ ▼▼▼▼ Holiday Inn Express 🆂🅷
(509) 525-6200. **$115-$125.** 1433 W Pine St. US 12, exit Pendleton/Prescott. Int corridors. **Pets:** Accepted.
[SAVE] [S🐾] [✕] [🛏] [💻] [🏊] [✕]

▲▲▲ ▼▼▼▼ La Quinta Inn Walla Walla 🆂🅷
(509) 525-2522. **$79-$119.** 520 N 2nd Ave. US 12, exit 2nd Ave, just s. Int corridors. **Pets:** Accepted.
[SAVE] [S🐾] [✕] [🖊] [🛏] [💻] [🏊] [✕]

▲▲▲ ▼▼▼▼ Marcus Whitman Hotel & Conference Center 🏠 ☥
(509) 525-2200. **$109-$264.** Six W Rose. Downtown. Int corridors. **Pets:** Small, dogs only. $20 one-time fee/room. Designated rooms, service with restrictions, supervision.
[SAVE] [S🐾] [✕] [🛏] [💻] [🍴]

▼▼ Walla Walla Inn 🆂🅷 ☥
(509) 529-4360. **$89-$119, 30 day notice.** 325 E Main St. US 12, exit 2nd Ave, 0.5 mi s, then just e. Ext/int corridors. **Pets:** Large. $10 daily fee/pet. Designated rooms, service with restrictions, supervision.
[ASK] [✕] [🛏] [💻] [🏊] [✕]

Walla Walla Super 8 SH
(509) 525-8800. **$73-$95.** 2315 Eastgate St N. US 12, exit Wilbur Ave, just s. Int corridors. **Pets:** Medium, other species. $15 deposit/room, $10 one-time fee/room. Service with restrictions, supervision.

Walla Walla Travelodge M
(509) 529-4940. **$55-$95.** 421 E Main St. US 12, exit 2nd Ave, 0.5 mi s, then just e. Ext/int corridors. **Pets:** Small. $7 daily fee/pet. Service with restrictions, supervision.

WENATCHEE

Avenue Motel M
(509) 663-7161. **$45-$65.** 720 N Wenatchee Ave. On US 2 business loop; just nw of downtown. Ext/int corridors. **Pets:** Dogs only. $5 daily fee/pet. Service with restrictions, supervision.

Coast Wenatchee Center Hotel LH
(509) 662-1234. **$89-$149.** 201 N Wenatchee Ave. Downtown. Int corridors. **Pets:** $10 one-time fee/room. Service with restrictions, supervision.

Comfort Inn SH
(509) 662-1700. **$85-$119.** 815 N Wenatchee Ave. Downtown. Int corridors. **Pets:** Small. $10 daily fee/room. Designated rooms, service with restrictions, supervision.

Econo Lodge M
(509) 663-7121. **$59-$79.** 232 N Wenatchee Ave. Downtown. Ext corridors. **Pets:** Small, dogs only. $10 daily fee/pet. Service with restrictions, supervision.

Holiday Inn Express SH
(509) 663-6355. **$79-$229.** 1921 N Wenatchee Ave. Northwest side of town. Int corridors. **Pets:** Accepted.

La Quinta Inn & Suites Wenatchee SH
(509) 664-6565. **$79-$119.** 1905 N Wenatchee Ave. West end of town. Int corridors. **Pets:** Accepted.

Red Lion Hotel Wenatchee LH
(509) 663-0711. **$82-$144.** 1225 N Wenatchee Ave. Just nw of downtown. Int corridors. **Pets:** Accepted.

Super 8 SH
(509) 662-3443. **$69-$125.** 1401 N Miller St. 1.5 mi n on US 2. Int corridors. **Pets:** Dogs only. $10 daily fee/pet. Designated rooms, service with restrictions, supervision.

Travelodge-Wenatchee M
(509) 662-8165. **$82-$99.** 1004 N Wenatchee Ave. Downtown. Ext corridors. **Pets:** Accepted.

WINTHROP

Americas Best Value Cascade Inn M
(509) 996-3100. **$70-$150.** 1006 SR 20. 1 mi e. Ext corridors. **Pets:** Accepted.

River Run Inn M
(509) 996-2173. **$65-$145, 10 day notice.** 27 Rader Rd. 0.5 mi w on SR 20. Ext corridors. **Pets:** $10 daily fee/pet. Service with restrictions, supervision.

Winthrop Inn M
(509) 996-2217. **$60-$110, 3 day notice.** 960 SR 20. 0.9 mi e. Int corridors. **Pets:** Medium, dogs only. $10 daily fee/pet. Service with restrictions, supervision.

WOODLAND

Cedars Inn Woodland SH
(360) 225-6548. **$79-$95.** 1500 Atlantic Ave. I-5, exit 21, just ne. Ext corridors. **Pets:** Medium, other species. $10 one-time fee/pet. Service with restrictions, supervision.

Lewis River Inn M
(360) 225-6257. **$62-$99.** 1100 Lewis River Rd. I-5, exit 21, just e. Ext corridors. **Pets:** Other species. $7 daily fee/pet. Designated rooms, service with restrictions, supervision.

YAKIMA

Best Western Peppertree Yakima Inn SH
(509) 453-8898. **$85-$120.** 1614 N 1st St. I-82, exit 31, just s. Int corridors. **Pets:** Very small, dogs only. $10 daily fee/pet. Designated rooms, service with restrictions, supervision.

Cedars Suites Yakima Downtown M
(509) 452-8101. **$59-$99.** 1010 E A St. I-82, exit 33B eastbound; exit 33 westbound, just w to 9th St, just n to A St, then just e. Ext corridors. **Pets:** Small, other species. $10 deposit/pet. Designated rooms, service with restrictions, supervision.

Clarion Hotel & Conference Center SH
(509) 248-7850. **$89.** 1507 N 1st St. I-82, exit 31, 0.5 mi s. Int corridors. **Pets:** Large. $10 daily fee/pet. Service with restrictions, supervision.

Comfort Suites SH
(509) 249-1900. **$89-$189.** 3702 Fruitvale Blvd. US 12, exit 40th Ave, just s. Int corridors. **Pets:** Small, dogs only. $15 daily fee/pet. Designated rooms, service with restrictions, supervision.

Fairfield Inn & Suites by Marriott SH
(509) 452-3100. **$96-$160.** 137 N Fair Ave. I-82, exit 33A eastbound, just s; exit 33 westbound, just w to 9th St, just n to B St, then just e. Int corridors. **Pets:** Other species. $15 daily fee/pet. Designated rooms, service with restrictions, supervision.

Holiday Inn Express Yakima SH
(509) 249-1000. **$95-$139.** 1001 E A St. I-82, exit 33B eastbound; exit 33 westbound, just w to 9th St, just n to A St, then just e. Int corridors. **Pets:** Small. $10 daily fee/pet. Designated rooms, service with restrictions, supervision.

Howard Johnson Plaza Yakima Gateway SH
(509) 452-6511. **$83-$98.** 9 N 9th St. I-82, exit 33 westbound; exit 33B eastbound, just s. Int corridors. **Pets:** Other species. $10 daily fee/pet. Service with restrictions, crate.

Oxford Inn SH
(509) 457-4444. **$89.** 1603 E Yakima Ave. I-82, exit 33 westbound, just e; exit 33B eastbound. Int corridors. **Pets:** Accepted.

Oxford Suites SH
(509) 457-9000. **$95-$179.** 1701 E Yakima Ave. I-82, exit 33 westbound; exit 33B eastbound. Int corridors. **Pets:** Accepted.

◆◆ Ramada Limited Ⓜ
(509) 453-0391. **$49-$99.** 818 N 1st St. I-82, exit 31, 1.2 mi s. Ext corridors. **Pets:** $10 daily fee/pet. Supervision.

(ASK) 🛇 ✕ 🐾 🐕 🛄 💻 🌊

◆◆◆ Red Lion Hotel Yakima Center 🆂🅷 🐾
(509) 248-5900. **$88-$108.** 607 E Yakima Ave. I-82, exit 33 westbound; exit 33B eastbound, 0.8 mi w. Ext/int corridors. **Pets:** Small, other species. $5 daily fee/pet. Service with restrictions, crate.

(ASK) ✕ 🐾 🐕 🛄 💻 🍴 🌊

◆◆ Sun Country Inn Ⓜ
(509) 248-5650. **$58-$70, 3 day notice.** 1700 N 1st St. I-82, exit 31, just s. Ext corridors. **Pets:** $7 daily fee/pet. Supervision.

(ASK) 🛇 ✕ 🛄 💻 🌊

ZILLAH

◆◆◆ Comfort Inn 🆂🅷
(509) 829-3399. **$89-$160.** 911 Vintage Valley Pkwy. I-82, exit 52, just n. Int corridors. **Pets:** Other species. $10 daily fee/pet.

(ASK) 🛇 ✕ 🐾ᴹ 🐾 🐕 🛄 💻 🌊

WEST VIRGINIA

BARBOURSVILLE

▼▼▼ Comfort Inn by Choice Hotels SH
(304) 733-2122. $80-$100. 249 Mall Rd. I-64, exit 20, 0.4 mi n. Int corridors. Pets: Accepted.

BECKLEY

◈◈◈ ▼▼▼ Best Western Four Seasons Inn SH
(304) 252-0671. $62-$109. 1939 Harper Rd. I-64/77, exit 44, just e on SR 3. Ext/int corridors. Pets: Other species. $6 daily fee/pet. Service with restrictions, supervision.

▼▼ Comfort Inn SH 🐾
(304) 255-2161. $69-$100. 1909 Harper Rd. I-64/77, exit 44, 0.3 mi e on SR 3. Ext/int corridors. Pets: Other species. Service with restrictions.

◈◈◈ ▼▼▼ Country Inn & Suites By Carlson SH
(304) 252-5100. $60-$200. 2120 Harper Rd. I-64/77, exit 44, just w on SR 3. Int corridors. Pets: Medium, other species. $30 one-time fee/pet. Designated rooms, service with restrictions, supervision.

◈◈◈ ▼▼▼ Howard Johnson Express Inn SH
(304) 255-5900. $70-$110. 1907 Harper Rd. I-64/77, exit 44, 0.4 mi e on SR 3. Int corridors. Pets: Small, dogs only. $15 one-time fee/pet. Designated rooms, service with restrictions, supervision.

◈◈◈ ▼▼ Microtel Inn SH
(304) 256-2000. $50-$99. 2130 Harper Rd. I-64/77, exit 44. Int corridors. Pets: Medium, other species. $25 one-time fee/room. Service with restrictions, supervision.

◈◈◈ ▼▼▼▼ Park Inn & Suites SH
(304) 255-9091. $79. 134 Harper Park Dr. I-64/77, exit 44, just w on SR 3. Int corridors. Pets: Small, dogs only. $10 daily fee/pet. Service with restrictions, supervision.

◈◈◈ ▼▼ Super 8 Motel SH
(304) 253-0802. $55-$99. 2014 Harper Rd. I-64/77, exit 44, just e. Int corridors. Pets: Small. $10 daily fee/pet. Designated rooms, service with restrictions, supervision.

BLUEFIELD

◈◈◈ ▼▼▼ Econo Lodge M
(304) 327-8171. $49-$179. 3400 Cumberland Rd. I-77, exit 1, 3.8 mi nw via US 52/460, then 0.4 mi n on US 52. Ext corridors. Pets: Small, dogs only. $10 daily fee/pet. Designated rooms, service with restrictions, supervision.

◈◈◈ ▼▼▼▼ Holiday Inn Bluefield-On The Hill SH
(304) 325-6170. $81-$99. 3350 Big Laurel Hwy. I-77, exit 1, 3.8 mi nw via US 52/460. Int corridors. Pets: Accepted.

BRIDGEPORT

◈◈◈ ▼▼▼▼ Holiday Inn Clarksburg-Bridgeport SH
(304) 842-5411. $89. 100 Lodgeville Rd. I-79, exit 119, just e on US 50. Int corridors. Pets: Other species. $5 daily fee/room. Service with restrictions, supervision.

▼▼ Sleep Inn SH
(304) 842-1919. $75-$89. 115 Tolley Dr. I-79, exit 119, just e on US 50. Int corridors. Pets: Other species. Service with restrictions, supervision.

CHARLESTON

▼▼▼ Charleston Comfort Suites SH 🐾
(304) 925-1171. $94-$110. 107 Alex Ln. I-77, exit 95, just s on SR 61. Int corridors. Pets: Other species. Designated rooms, supervision.

▼▼▼ Country Inn & Suites By Carlson SH 🐾
(304) 925-4300. $94-$110. 105 Alex Ln. I-77, exit 95, just s on SR 61. Int corridors. Pets: Medium, other species. $10 one-time fee/pet. Crate.

▼▼▼ Days Inn Charleston East M
(304) 925-1010. $63-$74. 6400 MacCorkle Ave. I-77, exit 95, just s on SR 61. Int corridors. Pets: Accepted.

▼▼▼ Holiday Inn Express Civic Center SH
(304) 345-0600. $89-$99. 100 Civic Center Dr. I-64, exit 58B eastbound; exit 58C westbound, just s; downtown. Int corridors. Pets: Accepted.

◈◈◈ ▼▼ Knights Inn-Charleston East M
(304) 925-0451. $50-$57. 6401 MacCorkle Ave SE. I-77, exit 95, just s on SR 61. Ext corridors. Pets: Accepted.

▼▼ Red Roof Inn-Kanawha City M
(304) 925-6953. $55-$74. 6305 SE MacCorkle Ave. I-77, exit 95, just s on SR 61. Ext corridors. Pets: Medium, other species. Service with restrictions, supervision.

CROSS LANES

◈◈◈ ▼▼▼ Comfort Inn West Charleston SH 🐾
(304) 776-8070. $77-$95. 102 Racer Dr. I-64, exit 47, just s. Int corridors. Pets: Large. $25 daily fee/room. Designated rooms, service with restrictions, supervision.

DAVIS

◈◈◈ ▼▼▼▼ Deerfield Village Resort & Conference Center CO
(304) 866-4698. $175-$198. Cortland Ln. 7 mi s on SR 32. Ext corridors. Pets: Medium. $50 one-time fee/pet. No service, supervision.

DUNBAR

◆ **Dunbar Super 8 Motel** [SH]
(304) 768-6888. **$52-$60, 14 day notice.** 911 Dunbar Ave. I-64, exit 53, just w. Int corridors. **Pets:** $10 daily fee/pet. Service with restrictions, supervision.
[ASK] [SD] [X] ▣

EDRAY

[AAA] ◆◆ **Marlinton Motor Inn** [M] 🐾
(304) 799-4711. **$75-$95, 3 day notice.** US 219 N. Center. Ext corridors. **Pets:** Small. $10 one-time fee/pet. Designated rooms, service with restrictions, crate.
[SAVE] [SD] [X] ▣ ☕ 🍴 🏊

ELKINS

[AAA] ◆ **Americas Best Value Inn** [M]
(304) 636-7711. **$46-$110, 3 day notice.** Rt 219/250. 0.9 mi s of SR 219. Ext/int corridors. **Pets:** Accepted.
[SAVE] [SD] [X] ▣ ☕

[AAA] ◆◆◆ **Cheat River Lodge & Inn** [CA]
(304) 636-2301. **$78-$93.** Rt 1, Box 115, Faulkner Rd. 4.8 mi e on US 33, then 1.5 mi ne. Ext corridors. **Pets:** Dogs only. $10 daily fee/pet. Service with restrictions, supervision.
[SAVE] [X] ▣ ☕ 🍴 ⊗

◆◆ **Econo Lodge** [M]
(304) 636-5311. **$73-$78.** US 33 E. 1 mi e. Ext/int corridors. **Pets:** Accepted.
[ASK] [SD] [X] ▣ 🏊

◆◆ **Elkins Days Inn** [SH]
(304) 637-4667. **$75.** 1200 Harrison Ave. 1 mi w on US 33/250/SR 92; downtown; in an office building. Int corridors. **Pets:** Other species. $5 daily fee/pet. Service with restrictions, supervision.
[ASK] [SD] [X] ♿M ▣ ☕ 🍴

◆◆ **Elkins Super 8 Motel** [SH]
(304) 636-6500. **$66-$76, 14 day notice.** 350 Beverly Pike. 0.8 mi s on SR 219. Int corridors. **Pets:** Accepted.
[ASK] [SD] [X] ▣

FAIRMONT

[AAA] ◆◆◆ **Holiday Inn Fairmont** [SH]
(304) 366-5500. **$59-$125.** 930 E Grafton Rd. I-79, exit 137, just e. Int corridors. **Pets:** Small, other species. $10 one-time fee/pet. Designated rooms, supervision.
[SAVE] [SD] [X] ♿M 🦻 ♿ ▣ ☕ 🍴 🏊

◆◆ **Red Roof Inn** [M]
(304) 366-6800. **$45-$60.** 50 Middletown Rd. I-79, exit 132, 0.3 mi s on US 250, just w, then just s. Ext corridors. **Pets:** Medium, other species. Service with restrictions, supervision.
[X] 🦻

◆◆ **Super 8 Motel** [SH]
(304) 363-1488. **$57-$84.** 2208 Pleasant Valley Rd. I-79, exit 133, just e. Int corridors. **Pets:** Medium. Service with restrictions, crate.
[ASK] [SD] [X] ▣

FALLING WATERS

◆◆◆ **Holiday Inn Express Martinsburg North** [SH]
(304) 274-6100. **$55-$69.** 1220 TJ Jackson Dr. I-81, exit 20, just w. Int corridors. **Pets:** Accepted.
[ASK] [SD] [X] ♿ ▣ ☕ 🏊

FROST

◆◆◆ **The Inn at Mountain Quest** [CI] 🐾
(304) 799-7267. **$110-$160, 7 day notice.** Rt 92 Frost. On SR 92, 0.4 mi n. Ext corridors. **Pets:** Large, other species. $10 one-time fee/pet. Designated rooms, service with restrictions.
[ASK] [SD] [X] 🍴 ⊗

HARPERS FERRY

◆◆◆ **Quality Inn & Conference Center** [SH]
(304) 535-6302. **$80-$140.** 4328 William L Wilson Frwy. Just w on US 340. Int corridors. **Pets:** Accepted.
[ASK] [SD] [X] ♿ ▣ ☕ 🍴 🏊

HUNTINGTON

◆◆ **Red Roof Inn** [SH]
(304) 733-3737. **$45-$65.** 5190 US Rt 60 E. I-64, exit 15, just s. Ext corridors. **Pets:** Medium, other species. Service with restrictions, supervision.
[X] ▣

HURRICANE

◆◆ **Red Roof Inn** [M]
(304) 757-6392. **$45-$55.** 500 Putnam Village Dr. I-64, exit 39, just n on SR 34, then just e. Ext corridors. **Pets:** Medium, other species. Service with restrictions, supervision.
[X] ♿ ▣

KEYSER

[AAA] ◆◆ **Keyser Inn** [SH]
(304) 788-0913. **$53-$60.** Rt 220 S. On US 220, 2.3 mi s. Int corridors. **Pets:** Medium. $25 one-time fee/room. Service with restrictions, supervision.
[SAVE] [SD] [X] ▣ ☕

LEWISBURG

[AAA] ◆◆ **Brier Inn** [SH]
(304) 645-7722. **$64-$125.** 540 N Jefferson St. I-64, exit 169, just s on US 219. Ext corridors. **Pets:** Other species. $10 daily fee/pet. Designated rooms, crate.
[SAVE] [SD] [X] ♿ ▣ ☕ 🍴 🏊

[AAA] ◆ **Rodeway Inn** [M]
(304) 645-7070. **$30-$100.** 107 W Fair St. I-64, exit 169, 3.1 mi s on US 219, then just e. Ext corridors. **Pets:** Medium. $10 daily fee/pet. Service with restrictions, supervision.
[SAVE] [SD] [X] ▣ ☕

◆◆ **Super 8 Motel** [SH]
(304) 647-3188. **$61-$66, 10 day notice.** 550 N Jefferson St. I-64, exit 169, just s on US 219. Int corridors. **Pets:** $10 daily fee/pet. Service with restrictions, supervision.
[ASK] [SD] [X] 🦻 ▣

LOGAN

◆ **Super 8 Motel-Logan** [M]
(304) 752-8787. **Call for rates.** 316 Riverview Ave. 1.8 mi e on SR 73. Int corridors. **Pets:** Accepted.
[X] ▣

MARTINSBURG

◆◆ **Days Inn Martinsburg** [SH]
(304) 263-1800. **$55-$65.** 209 Viking Way. I-81, exit 13, just e on W King St (CR 15). Ext/int corridors. **Pets:** Medium, dogs only. $6 daily fee/pet. No service, supervision.
[ASK] [SD] [X] ▣

◆◆ ▼▼ Econo Lodge M
(304) 274-2181. **$60-$63.** 5595 Hammonds Mill Rd. I-81, exit 20, just e. Ext/int corridors. **Pets:** Other species. Service with restrictions, supervision.
[SAVE] [S$] [✕] [▣]

◆◆ ▼ Knights Inn-Martinsburg M
(304) 267-2211. **$50-$85.** 1997 Edwin Miller Blvd. I-81, exit 16E, 0.4 mi e on SR 9. Ext corridors. **Pets:** Medium, other species. $10 daily fee/pet. Designated rooms, service with restrictions, crate.
[SAVE] [S$] [✕] [▤]

◆◆ ▼ Relax Inn M
(304) 263-0831. **$35-$59, 3 day notice.** 1022 Winchester Ave (US 11 N). I-81, exit 12, 0.3 mi e on SR 45, then just n. Ext corridors. **Pets:** Accepted.
[SAVE] [S$] [✕] [▤] [≈]

◆◆ ▼▼ Rodeway Inn SH
(304) 263-8811. **$55-$89.** 94 McMillan Ct. I-81, exit 16E, just e. Ext/int corridors. **Pets:** Medium. $10 one-time fee/pet. Service with restrictions, supervision.
[SAVE] [S$] [✕] [⚙] [▤] [▣] [≈]

▼ Super 8 Motel-Martinsburg SH
(304) 263-0801. **$60-$65.** 2048 Edwin Miller Blvd. I-81, exit 16E, just e on SR 9. Int corridors. **Pets:** Medium. $10 daily fee/pet. Designated rooms, no service, supervision.
[ASK] [S$] [✕] [▤]

MINERAL WELLS

▼▼ Microtel Inn SH
(304) 489-3892. **$45-$55.** 104 Nicolette Rd. I-77, exit 170, just w. Int corridors. **Pets:** Accepted.
[ASK] [S$] [✕] [⚙] [▤]

MORGANTOWN

◆◆ ▼▼▼ Comfort Inn-Morgantown SH
(304) 296-9364. **$69-$125.** 225 Comfort Inn Dr. I-68, exit 1, 0.3 mi n on US 119. Int corridors. **Pets:** Other species. $25 deposit/room. Designated rooms, service with restrictions, supervision.
[SAVE] [S$] [✕] [⚙] [▤] [▣] [¶] [≈]

◆◆ ▼ Friends Inn M
(304) 599-4850. **$54-$59.** 452 Country Club Rd. I-79, exit 155, s on US 19 to SR 705, then e on University Ave. Ext corridors. **Pets:** Very small. $5 daily fee/pet. Designated rooms, service with restrictions, supervision.
[SAVE] [S$] [✕] [⚙]

◆◆ ▼▼▼ Ramada Conference Center SH
(304) 296-3431. **$70-$90.** 20 Scott Ave. I-68, exit 1, 0.3 mi n. Int corridors. **Pets:** Other species. Service with restrictions, supervision.
[SAVE] [S$] [✕] [⚙] [▤] [▣] [¶] [≈] [✗]

NITRO

▼ Econo Lodge M
(304) 755-8341. **$56-$70, 7 day notice.** 4115 1st Ave. I-64, exit 45, 0.8 mi e on SR 25. Ext corridors. **Pets:** Dogs only. $10 daily fee/pet. Designated rooms, no service, supervision.
[ASK] [S$] [✕] [▤] [▣]

PARKERSBURG

▼▼▼ The Blennerhassett SH 🐾
(304) 422-3131. **$119-$250.** 320 Market St. Between Fourth and Fifth sts; downtown. Int corridors. **Pets:** Dogs only. $50 one-time fee/pet. Designated rooms.
[ASK] [S$] [✕] [⚙] [♿] [▣] [¶]

◆◆ ▼ Holiday Inn Parkersburg SH
(304) 485-6200. **$80-$116.** 225 Holiday Hills Dr. I-77, exit 176, just e. Int corridors. **Pets:** Accepted.
[ASK] [S$] [✕] [▤] [▣] [¶] [≈] [✗]

◆◆ ▼ Red Carpet Inn M 🐾
(304) 485-1851. **$50-$55.** 6333 Emerson Ave. I-77, exit 179, 0.4 mi sw on SR 68. Ext corridors. **Pets:** Dogs only. $5 daily fee/pet. Service with restrictions, supervision.
[SAVE] [S$] [✕] [▤] [▣]

▼▼ Red Roof Inn M 🐾
(304) 485-1741. **$54-$71.** 3714 E 7th St. I-77, exit 176, just w on US 50. Ext corridors. **Pets:** Other species. Service with restrictions, supervision.
[ASK] [S$] [✕] [▤] [▣]

PHILIPPI

▼▼ Philippi Lodging M
(304) 457-5888. **$52-$83.** Rt 4, Box 155. 2.5 mi s on US 250. Int corridors. **Pets:** Accepted.
[ASK] [S$] [✕] [⚙] [⚙] [▤]

PRINCETON

◆◆ ▼▼▼ Days Inn SH
(304) 425-8100. **$68-$78.** 347 Meadowfield Ln. I-77, exit 9, 0.3 mi w on US 460, just s on Ambrose Ln, then just e. Ext corridors. **Pets:** Accepted.
[SAVE] [S$] [✕] [⚙] [▤] [▣] [≈]

◆◆ ▼▼▼ Holiday Inn Express Princeton SH 🐾
(304) 425-8156. **$90-$135.** 805 Oakvale Rd. I-77, exit 9, just w. Int corridors. **Pets:** Medium. $20 daily fee/pet. Designated rooms, service with restrictions, supervision.
[SAVE] [S$] [✕] [⚙] [▤] [▣] [≈]

▼▼ Sleep Inn SH
(304) 431-2800. **$75-$225.** 1015 Oakvale Rd. I-77, exit 9, just w on US 460, then just n via service road. Int corridors. **Pets:** Medium, other species. Service with restrictions.
[ASK] [S$] [✕] [⚙] [⚙] [▤] [▣] [≈]

RIPLEY

◆◆ ▼▼▼▼ Best Western McCoys Inn & Conference Center SH
(304) 372-9122. **$90.** 701 W Main St. I-77, exit 138, just e. Ext/int corridors. **Pets:** Accepted.
[SAVE] [S$] [✕] [⚙] [⚙] [▤] [▣] [¶] [≈]

▼ Ripley Super 8 Motel M
(304) 372-8880. **$60-$70.** 102 Duke Dr. I-77, exit 138, just e on SR 33. Int corridors. **Pets:** Medium, other species. Service with restrictions, supervision.
[ASK] [S$] [✕] [⚙] [▤] [▣]

ST. ALBANS

◆◆ ▼ Americas Best Value Inn SH
(304) 766-6231. **$46-$56.** 6210 MacCorkle Ave SW. I-64, exit 54, 3.2 mi w on US 60. Ext corridors. **Pets:** Accepted.
[SAVE] [S$] [✕] [▤] [▣] [¶] [≈]

SNOWSHOE

◆◆ ▼▼▼ Inn at Snowshoe SH
(304) 572-6520. **$89-$200, 21 day notice.** SR 66. 0.5 mi e on SR 66, from US 219 jct, follow signs. Int corridors. **Pets:** Large. $50 one-time fee/room. Designated rooms, no service.
[SAVE] [S$] [✕] [⚙] [▤] [▣] [¶] [≈] [✗]

SOUTH CHARLESTON

▼▼▼▼ **Ramada Plaza Hotel Charleston** 🆂🅷
(304) 744-4641. **$72-$119.** 400 2nd Ave. I-64, exit 56, just nw. Int corridors. **Pets:** Small, other species. $25 daily fee/pet. Designated rooms, service with restrictions, supervision.
🅰🆂🅺 🆂🅾 ✖ 🖊 🖥 📺 🍴 🏊

STAR CITY

ⓐ ▼▼▼ **Econo Lodge-Coliseum** 🆂🅷
(304) 599-8181. **$59-$67.** 3506 Monongahela Blvd. I-79, exit 155, 1.4 mi s on US 119/SR 7. Ext corridors. **Pets:** Accepted.
🆂🅰🆅🅴 🆂🅾 ✖ 🖊 📺

ⓐ ▼▼▼▼ **Quality Inn & Suites Morgantown** 🆂🅷
(304) 599-1680. **$72-$153.** 1400 Saratoga Ave. I-79, exit 155, 1.7 mi s on US 119/SR 7. Ext corridors. **Pets:** Accepted.
🆂🅰🆅🅴 🆂🅾 ✖ 🖖 🖊 🖥 📺 🏊

SUMMERSVILLE

ⓐ ▼▼ **Best Western Summersville Lake Motor Lodge** 🆂🅷
(304) 872-6900. **$62-$70, 15 day notice.** 1203 S Broad St. US 19 and Broad St; 0.6 mi s of jct SR 39. Ext corridors. **Pets:** Small. $7 daily fee/pet. Designated rooms, service with restrictions, supervision.
🆂🅰🆅🅴 🆂🅾 ✖ 🖊 📺

ⓐ ▼▼▼ **Comfort Inn** 🆂🅷
(304) 872-6500. **$80-$180.** 903 Industrial Dr N. US 19, 1.9 mi n of jct SR 39. Int corridors. **Pets:** Small, other species. $10 daily fee/pet. Designated rooms, service with restrictions, supervision.
🆂🅰🆅🅴 🆂🅾 ✖ 🖊 🖊 🖥 📺 🏊 ✖

ⓐ ▼▼▼ **Sleep Inn of Summersville** 🆂🅷
(304) 872-4500. **$60-$155.** 701 Professional Park Dr. US 19, 1.7 mi n of jct SR 39. Int corridors. **Pets:** Small, other species. $10 daily fee/pet. Designated rooms, service with restrictions, supervision.
🆂🅰🆅🅴 🆂🅾 ✖ 🖊 🖊 🖥 📺 🏊

▼▼ **Super 8 Motel-Summersville** 🆂🅷
(304) 872-4888. **$62-$64.** 306 Merchants Walk. US 19, just n. Int corridors. **Pets:** $10 daily fee/room. Service with restrictions, supervision.
🅰🆂🅺 🆂🅾 ✖ 🖊

TRIADELPHIA

ⓐ ▼▼▼ **Comfort Inn-Wheeling** 🆂🅷
(304) 547-0610. **$69-$129.** RR 1, Box 292. I-70, exit 11, just n. Int corridors. **Pets:** Medium. $10 daily fee/room. Service with restrictions, supervision.
🆂🅰🆅🅴 🆂🅾 ✖ 🖊 📺 🏊

ⓐ ▼▼▼ **Holiday Inn Express Wheeling East** 🆂🅷
(304) 547-1380. **$69-$175.** I-70, exit 11. Int corridors. **Pets:** Small. $10 daily fee/pet, $10 one-time fee/pet. Designated rooms, service with restrictions, supervision.
🆂🅰🆅🅴 🆂🅾 ✖ 🖊 🖊 🖊 🖥 📺 🏊

WEIRTON

▼▼▼ **Holiday Inn** 🆂🅷
(304) 723-5522. **$96-$109.** 350 Three Springs Dr. 4.5 mi e on US 22, exit Three Springs Dr. Int corridors. **Pets:** $50 one-time fee/room. Designated rooms, service with restrictions, supervision.
🅰🆂🅺 🆂🅾 ✖ 🖊 🖊 🖊 🖥 📺 🍴 🏊 ✖

WESTON

ⓐ ▼▼▼ **Comfort Inn** 🆂🅷
(304) 269-7000. **$65-$120.** 2906 US Hwy 33 E. I-79, exit 99, just e. Ext corridors. **Pets:** Medium. $10 daily fee/room. Designated rooms, service with restrictions, supervision.
🆂🅰🆅🅴 🆂🅾 ✖ 🖊 🖊 🖊 🖥 📺 🏊

▼▼ **Weston Super 8 Motel** 🆂🅷
(304) 269-1086. **$65-$71, 10 day notice.** 100 Market Place Mall, Suite 12. I-79, exit 99, just e. Int corridors. **Pets:** Accepted.
🅰🆂🅺 🆂🅾 ✖ 🖊 🖊

CITY INDEX

ABBOTSFORD

Sleep Inn SH
(715) 223-3337. **$68.** 300 E Elderberry Rd. SR 29, exit 132 (SR 13), just se. Int corridors. **Pets:** Accepted.

ALGOMA

Scenic Shore Inn M
(920) 487-3214. **$47-$64, 3 day notice.** 2221 Lake St. Jct SR 54, 0.8 mi s on SR 42. Ext corridors. **Pets:** Small, dogs only. Service with restrictions, supervision.

ANTIGO

Northwoods Birch Inn SH
(715) 623-0506. **$77.** 525 Memory Ln. 0.4 mi n of jct SR 64 E and US 45, then just w. Int corridors. **Pets:** Accepted.

Super 8 Motel-Antigo SH
(715) 623-4188. **$59-$112.** 535 Century Ave. On US 45 at SR 64 E. Int corridors. **Pets:** Dogs only. $15 daily fee/pet. Designated rooms, service with restrictions, supervision.

APPLETON

Best Western Midway Hotel SH
(920) 731-4141. **$80-$171.** 3033 W College Ave. US 41, exit 137 (SR 125), 0.5 mi e. Int corridors. **Pets:** Medium. $10 daily fee/pet. Designated rooms, service with restrictions, supervision.

Candlewood Suites SH
(920) 739-8000. **$79-$129.** 4525 W College Ave. Just w of US 41. Int corridors. **Pets:** $75 one-time fee/pet. Service with restrictions, crate.

Comfort Suites Appleton Airport SH
(920) 730-3800. **$99-$199.** 3809 W Wisconsin Ave. US 41, exit 138 (Wisconsin Ave), just e. Int corridors. **Pets:** Other species. Service with restrictions, crate.

Country Inn & Suites By Carlson SH
(920) 830-3240. **$75-$200.** 355 Fox River Dr. US 41, exit 137 (SR 125), just nw. Int corridors. **Pets:** Medium. $20 one-time fee/room. Service with restrictions, crate.

Exel Inn of Appleton M
(920) 733-5551. **$50-$80.** 210 Westhill Blvd. US 41, exit 137 (SR 125), just e. Int corridors. **Pets:** Small, other species. Designated rooms, service with restrictions, supervision.

Extended StayAmerica-Appleton-Fox Cities SH
(920) 830-9596. **$73-$82.** 4141 Boardwalk Ct. US 41, exit 137 (SR 125), w on College Ave, then s on Nicolet Rd. Int corridors. **Pets:** Accepted.

Fairfield Inn by Marriott SH
(920) 954-0202. **$85-$105.** 132 Mall Dr. US 41, exit 137 (SR 125), just nw. Int corridors. **Pets:** Accepted.

La Quinta Inn & Suites College Ave SH
(920) 734-7777. **$119-$149.** 3730 W College Ave. US 41, exit 137 (SR 125), just e. Int corridors. **Pets:** Medium. Service with restrictions.

La Quinta Inn Appleton Fox River Mall Area M
(920) 734-6070. **$79-$99.** 3920 W College Ave. US 41, exit 137 (SR 125), just e. Ext/int corridors. **Pets:** Medium. Service with restrictions.

Microtel Inn & Suites SH
(920) 997-3121. **$50-$99.** 321 Metro Dr. US 41, exit 137 (SR 125), just nw. Int corridors. **Pets:** $10 daily fee/pet. Service with restrictions, supervision.

Residence Inn by Marriott SH
(920) 954-0570. **$145-$165.** 310 Metro Dr. US 41, exit 137 (SR 125), just nw on Mall Dr. Int corridors. **Pets:** Accepted.

ARKDALE

▼▼▼▼ Northern Bay Golf Resort & Marina [CO]
(608) 339-2090. **$109-$300.** 1844 20th Ave. 2.9 mi nw on SR 21, 4.0 mi s on CR Z, then 1.5 nw via Dakota Ave and 20th Ave. Int corridors. **Pets:** Accepted.

[ASK] [S🐾] [✕] [🔧] [💻] [🍴] [🏊] [🗙] [☎]

ASHLAND

⚫⚫⚫ ▼▼▼ AmericInn of Ashland [SH]
(715) 682-9950. **$99-$249.** 3009 Lake Shore Dr E. On US 2, 2.1 mi e of jct SR 13 S. Int corridors. **Pets:** Accepted.

[SAVE] [S🐾] [✕] [&] [🔧] [💻] [🏊] [🗙]

⚫⚫⚫ ▼ Ashland Motel [M]
(715) 682-5503. **$35-$99.** 2300 W Lake Shore Dr. 1.8 mi w on US 2. Ext corridors. **Pets:** Small. $5 daily fee/pet. Designated rooms, service with restrictions, supervision.

[SAVE] [S🐾] [✕] [🔧] [💻]

BALDWIN

▼▼ AmericInn of Baldwin [SH]
(715) 684-5888. **$69-$129.** 500 Baldwin Plaza Dr. I-94, exit 19 (US 63), just ne. Int corridors. **Pets:** Small, dogs only. $25 one-time fee/pet. Designated rooms, no service, supervision.

[ASK] [✕] [&] [🔧] [💻] [🏊] [🗙]

▼▼ Super 8 Motel [SH]
(715) 684-2700. **$65-$109.** 2110 10th Ave. I-94, exit 19 (US 63), just se. Int corridors. **Pets:** Medium. $15 one-time fee/pet. Service with restrictions, supervision.

[ASK] [S🐾] [✕] [&] [🔧] [🏊]

BARABOO

⚫⚫⚫ ▼▼▼▼ Best Western Baraboo Inn [SH]
(608) 356-1100. **$69-$159.** 725 W Pine St. On US 12, 0.3 mi n of SR 33. Int corridors. **Pets:** Accepted.

[SAVE] [S🐾] [✕] [🌀] [&] [🔧] [💻] [🍴] [🏊]

▼▼▼▼ Park Plaza Baraboo [SH]
(608) 356-6422. **$65-$126.** 626 W Pine St. On US 12, 0.3 mi n of SR 33. Int corridors. **Pets:** Medium. No service, supervision.

[ASK] [S🐾] [✕] [&M] [🔧] [💻] [🍴] [🏊] [🗙]

BAYFIELD

▼▼▼ Old Rittenhouse Inn [CI]
(715) 779-5111. **$110-$350, 10 day notice.** 301 Rittenhouse Ave. Just w on SR 13. Int corridors. **Pets:** Accepted.

[✕] [🔧] [🍴] [☎]

BEAVER DAM

⚫⚫⚫ ▼▼▼▼ AmericInn Lodge & Suites [SH]
(920) 356-9000. **$85-$105.** 325 Seippel Blvd. US 151, exit 134 (CR B/Industrial Dr). Int corridors. **Pets:** Other species. $10 daily fee/pet. Designated rooms, service with restrictions, supervision.

[SAVE] [✕] [&] [🔧] [💻] [🏊]

▼ Super 8 Motel [SH]
(920) 887-8880. **$60-$77.** 711 Park Ave. US 151, exit 132 (SR 33), just w. Int corridors. **Pets:** $10 one-time fee/pet. Designated rooms, service with restrictions, supervision.

[ASK] [S🐾] [✕] [🌀]

BELMONT

▼▼ AmeriHost Inn [SH]
(608) 762-6900. **$58-$72.** 103 W Moundview Ave. US 151, exit 26, just w. Int corridors. **Pets:** Other species. $25 one-time fee/room.

[ASK] [S🐾] [✕] [🔧] [💻] [🏊] [🗙]

BELOIT

⚫⚫⚫ ▼▼▼ Americas Best Value Inn [SH] ❀
(608) 365-8680. **$59-$79.** 3002 Milwaukee Rd. I-90, exit 185A, just sw at I-43 and SR 81. Int corridors. **Pets:** Dogs only. $10 one-time fee/room. Designated rooms, service with restrictions, supervision.

[SAVE] [S🐾] [✕] [&M] [🔧] [💻]

⚫⚫⚫ ▼▼▼ Beloit Inn [SH] ❀
(608) 362-5500. **$89-$189.** 500 Pleasant St. Downtown. Int corridors. **Pets:** $100 deposit/room.

[SAVE] [S🐾] [✕] [&] [🔧] [💻] [🍴]

⚫⚫⚫ ▼▼▼ Comfort Inn of Beloit [SH]
(608) 362-2666. **$69-$109.** 2786 Milwaukee Rd. I-90, exit 185A, just w at I-43 and SR 81. Int corridors. **Pets:** Large. $10 daily fee/pet. Service with restrictions, supervision.

[SAVE] [S🐾] [✕] [🌀] [🔧] [💻] [🏊]

⚫⚫⚫ ▼▼▼ Econo Lodge [M]
(608) 364-4000. **$53.** 2956 Milwaukee Rd. I-90, exit 185A, 0.3 mi w. Ext/int corridors. **Pets:** Medium. $6 daily fee/pet. Service with restrictions.

[SAVE] [S🐾] [✕] [💻] [🍴]

BERLIN

⚫⚫⚫ ▼▼▼ Best Western Countryside [M]
(920) 361-4411. **$74-$94.** 227 Ripon Rd. On SR 49, at CR F. Int corridors. **Pets:** Very small, dogs only. $10 one-time fee/pet. Designated rooms, supervision.

[SAVE] [S🐾] [✕] [🔧] [💻]

BIRCHWOOD

▼▼ Cobblestone Bed & Breakfast [BB] ❀
(715) 354-3494. **$79-$125, 10 day notice.** 319 S Main St. 0.8 mi e of jct SR 48 and Main St; center. Int corridors. **Pets:** Other species. Supervision.

[ASK] [S🐾] [✕]

BLACK RIVER FALLS

⚫⚫⚫ ▼▼▼ Best Western-Arrowhead Lodge & Suites [SH]
(715) 284-9471. **$65-$109, 3 day notice.** 600 Oasis Rd. I-94, exit 116, jct SR 54. Int corridors. **Pets:** Accepted.

[SAVE] [S🐾] [✕] [🌀] [&] [🔧] [💻] [🍴] [🏊] [🗙]

▼▼ Days Inn [SH]
(715) 284-4333. **$77-$99.** 919 Hwy 54 E. I-94, exit 116, just w. Int corridors. **Pets:** Small. $15 daily fee/room. Designated rooms, service with restrictions, supervision.

[ASK] [S🐾] [✕] [&] [🔧] [💻] [🏊] [🗙]

BURLINGTON

▼▼ AmericInn Lodge & Suites [SH]
(262) 534-2125. **$71-$164.** 2059 S Browns Lake Rd. 3 mi n on SR 36 and 83, jct CR W. Int corridors. **Pets:** Medium. $25 one-time fee/pet. Designated rooms, service with restrictions, supervision.

[ASK] [S🐾] [✕] [🌀] [&] [🔧] [💻] [🏊]

CADOTT

▼▼ Countryside Motel [M]
(715) 289-4000. **$49-$89.** 545 Lavorata Rd. SR 29, exit 91 (SR 27), just s. Int corridors. **Pets:** Small, dogs only. Designated rooms, service with restrictions, supervision.

[✕]

CHILTON

⚫⚫⚫ ▼▼▼ Best Western Stanton Inn [SH]
(920) 849-3600. **$75-$160, 3 day notice.** 1101 E Chestnut St. Jct US 151 and SR 32/57. Int corridors. **Pets:** Small, dogs only. $50 deposit/room. Designated rooms, service with restrictions, supervision.

[SAVE] [✕] [🔧] [💻] [🏊]

CHIPPEWA FALLS

▼▼ AmericInn of Chippewa Falls SH
(715) 723-5711. **$79-$106.** 11 W South Ave. 2 mi s on SR 124, access via CR J. Int corridors. **Pets:** Accepted.

ASK ⊠ 🐾 ⌂ 🛢 🖵 ➰ ⊠

⚈ ▼▼ Avalon Hotel & Conference Center SH
(715) 723-2281. **$69-$129.** 1009 W Park Ave. Jct SR 124 and CR J. Ext/int corridors. **Pets:** Accepted.

SAVE ⊠ 🛢 🖵 🍴 ➰ ⊠

COLUMBUS

▼▼ Super 8 Motel-Columbus SH
(920) 623-8800. **$66-$115.** 219 Industrial Dr. US 151, exit 118 (SR 16/60), just ne. Int corridors. **Pets:** $10 one-time fee/room. Designated rooms, service with restrictions, supervision.

ASK 🗝 ⊠ 🐾 🛢 🖵 ➰

DE FOREST

▼▼▼ Holiday Inn Express SH
(608) 846-8686. **$84-$109, 14 day notice.** 7184 Morrisonville Rd. I-90/94, exit 126 (CR V), just e. Int corridors. **Pets:** Medium. $20 one-time fee/room. Service with restrictions, supervision.

ASK ⊠ 🗝 🐾 🐾 🛢 🖵 ➰

DE PERE

⚈ ▼▼▼ Kress Inn-A Clarion Collection SH
(920) 403-5100. **$104-$189.** 300 Grant St. US 41, exit 163 (Main St), 1 mi e, then just s on 3rd St. Int corridors. **Pets:** Accepted.

SAVE 🗝 ⊠ 🗝 🐾 🛢 🖵

DODGEVILLE

⚈ ▼▼▼ Best Western Quiet House & Suites SH
(608) 935-7739. **$89-$159.** 1130 N Johns St. On US 18, just e of jct SR 23. **Pets:** Other species. $15 daily fee/pet. Designated rooms, supervision.

SAVE 🗝 ⊠ 🐾 🐾 🛢 ➰

⚈ ▼▼ Pine Ridge Motel M
(608) 935-3386. **$30-$69.** 405 CR YZ. On CR YZ, 0.5 mi e of jct SR 23. Ext corridors. **Pets:** Very small, dogs only. $20 deposit/pet, $10 daily fee/pet. Designated rooms, service with restrictions, supervision.

SAVE 🗝 ⊠ 🛢 🖵

⚈ ▼▼▼ Super 8 Motel of Dodgeville SH
(608) 935-3888. **$54-$85.** 1308 Johns St. Just n of US 18. Int corridors. **Pets:** $50 deposit/room, $10 one-time fee/room. Supervision.

SAVE ⊠ 🐾 🛢 🖵

EGG HARBOR

⚈ ▼▼▼ The Shallows M
(920) 868-3458. **$70-$160, 30 day notice.** 7353 Horseshoe Bay Rd, Hwy G. On CR G, 2.5 mi s. Ext corridors. **Pets:** Small, dogs only. $20 daily fee/pet. Service with restrictions, supervision.

SAVE ⊠ 🛢 🖵 ➰ ⊠

FISH CREEK

▼▼ Julie's Park Cafe & Motel M
(920) 868-2999. **$45-$116, 10 day notice.** 4020 Hwy 42. On SR 42, 0.3 mi n. Ext corridors. **Pets:** Other species. $15 daily fee/pet. Service with restrictions, supervision.

ASK 🗝 ⊠ 🛢 🍴

GILLS ROCK

▼▼ Harbor House Inn BB 🐾
(920) 854-5196. **$79-$199, 21 day notice.** 12666 SR 42. On SR 42; center. Ext/int corridors. **Pets:** Other species. $10 one-time fee/pet. Designated rooms, supervision.

⊠ 🛢 ⊠ 🖾

⬦ Maple Grove Motel M
(920) 854-2587. **$60-$90.** 809 SR 42. On SR 42, 0.3 mi e; 1.5 mi w of car ferry. Ext corridors. **Pets:** Accepted.

⊠ 🛢 🖵 🖾

STURGEON BAY

⚈ ▼▼▼ Best Western Maritime Inn SH
(920) 743-7231. **$58-$114.** 1001 N 14th Ave. 1 mi n on Business Rt SR 42/57. Int corridors. **Pets:** Accepted.

SAVE 🗝 ⊠ 🛢 🖵 ➰

⚈ ▼▼ Super 8 Motel SH
(920) 743-9211. **$56-$106.** 409 Green Bay Rd. 1 mi s on Business Rt SR 42/57. Int corridors. **Pets:** Dogs only. $20 deposit/pet, $5 daily fee/pet. Designated rooms.

SAVE 🗝 ⊠ 🐾 🛢 ➰

EAGLE RIVER

⚈ ▼▼▼ Best Western Derby Inn SH
(715) 479-1600. **$70-$170.** 1800 Hwy 45 N. On US 45, 1 mi n. Int corridors. **Pets:** Medium. $50 deposit/room. Designated rooms, service with restrictions, supervision.

SAVE 🗝 ⊠ 🐾 🛢 🖵 ➰ ⊠

▼▼ Days Inn SH
(715) 479-5151. **$84-$105.** 844 Railroad St N. 0.5 mi n on US 45. Int corridors. **Pets:** Small. $15 daily fee/room. Designated rooms, service with restrictions, supervision.

ASK 🗝 ⊠ 🐾 🛢 🖵 ➰ ⊠

EAST TROY

▼▼▼ Country Inn & Suites by Carlson SH 🐾
(262) 642-2100. **$95-$169.** 2921 O Ln. I-43, exit 36, at jct SR 120. Int corridors. **Pets:** Dogs only. $25 one-time fee/room. Designated rooms, service with restrictions, supervision.

ASK 🗝 ⊠ 🗝 🛢 🖵 ➰

EAU CLAIRE

⚈ ▼▼▼ AmericInn Motel & Suites SH
(715) 874-4900. **$59-$169.** 6200 Texaco Dr. I-94, exit 59, jct US 12. Int corridors. **Pets:** Dogs only. $10 one-time fee/pet. Service with restrictions, supervision.

SAVE 🗝 ⊠ 🐾 🛢 🖵 ➰

▼▼▼ Best Western Trail Lodge Hotel & Suites 🄢🄷
(715) 838-9989. **$69-$129.** 3340 Mondovi Rd. I-94, exit 65, just n. Int corridors. **Pets:** $20 daily fee/room. Designated rooms, service with restrictions, supervision.

🄰🅂🄺 🅂🖧 ✕ 🄶🄼 📧 🈁 📺 🏊 ❌

▼ Comfort Inn 🄢🄷 ❀
(715) 833-9798. **$64-$129.** 3117 Craig Rd. I-94, exit 65, 1.3 mi n on SR 37; just s of jct US 12. Int corridors. **Pets:** Dogs only. $10 daily fee/room. Designated rooms, service with restrictions, supervision.

🄰🅂🄺 🅂🖧 ✕ 🄐 🈁 📺 🏊

▼ Days Inn-West 🄢🄷 ❀
(715) 874-5550. **$52-$75.** 6319 Truax Ln. I-94, exit 59, jct US 12. Int corridors. **Pets:** Other species. $10 one-time fee/pet. Designated rooms, service with restrictions, supervision.

🄰🅂🄺 🅂🖧 ✕ 📧 🈁 📺 🏊

▼▼ Econo Lodge 🄢🄷
(715) 833-8818. **$55-$125.** 4608 Royal Dr. I-94, exit 68, just n on SR 93, just w on Golf Rd, then just s. Int corridors. **Pets:** Medium, dogs only. $50 deposit/room. Designated rooms, no service, supervision.

🄰🅂🄺 🅂🖧 ✕ 🈁 📺

🄐🄐🄐 ▼▼ Exel Inn of Eau Claire 🄢🄷
(715) 834-3193. **$49-$79.** 2305 Craig Rd. I-94, exit 65, 1.3 mi n on SR 37; just w of jct US 12. Int corridors. **Pets:** Small, other species. Designated rooms, no service, supervision.

🅂🄰🅅🄴 🅂🖧 ✕ 🈁 📺

▼▼▼ Grandstay Residential Suites 🄢🄷
(715) 834-1700. **$85-$150.** 5310 Prill Rd. I-94, exit 70, 0.8 mi n on US 53. Int corridors. **Pets:** Small. $50 one-time fee/pet. Designated rooms, service with restrictions, crate.

🄰🅂🄺 🅂🖧 ✕ 🄶🄼 📧 🈁 📺 🏊 ❌

▼▼▼ Holiday Inn Campus Area 🄢🄷
(715) 835-2211. **$92-$139.** 2703 Craig Rd. I-94, exit 65, 1.3 mi n on SR 37; just w of jct US 12. Int corridors. **Pets:** Medium. $15 one-time fee/pet. Designated rooms, no service, supervision.

🄰🅂🄺 ✕ 🄶🄼 📧 🈁 📺 🍴 🏊 ❌

▼▼▼ The Plaza Hotel & Suites 🄻🄷 ❀
(715) 834-3181. **$89-$199, 10 day notice.** 1202 W Clairemont Ave. I-94, exit 65, 1.3 mi n on SR 37; just w of jct US 12. Int corridors. **Pets:** $15 one-time fee/room. Designated rooms, service with restrictions, crate.

🄰🅂🄺 🅂🖧 ✕ 🄐 📧 🈁 📺 🍴 🏊 ❌

▼▼ Ramada Convention Center 🄻🄷
(715) 835-6121. **$60-$100.** 205 S Barstow St. Jct S Barstow and Gibson sts; downtown. Int corridors. **Pets:** Accepted.

🄰🅂🄺 🅂🖧 ✕ 🈁 📺 🍴 🏊

EDGERTON

▼▼ Comfort Inn 🄢🄷
(608) 884-2118. **$66-$150.** 11102 N Goede Rd. I-90, exit 163, just e. Int corridors. **Pets:** Other species. $10 one-time fee/room. Service with restrictions, supervision.

🄰🅂🄺 🅂🖧 ✕ 📧 🈁 📺 🏊

ELKHORN

▼▼ AmericInn Lodge & Suites 🄢🄷
(262) 723-7799. **$71-$151.** 210 E Commerce Ct. I-43, exit 25, just s. Int corridors. **Pets:** Medium. $25 one-time fee/pet. Designated rooms, service with restrictions, supervision.

🄰🅂🄺 🅂🖧 ✕ 🄶🄼 🄐 📧 🈁 📺 🏊

FITCHBURG

🄐🄐🄐 ▼▼▼ Quality Inn & Suites 🄢🄷
(608) 274-7200. **$99-$139.** 2969 Cahill Main. US 12/18, exit 260 (Fish Hatchery/CR D), 1.5 mi s at CR PD (McKee Rd). Int corridors. **Pets:** Other species. $13 daily fee/room. Service with restrictions, crate.

🅂🄰🅅🄴 🅂🖧 ✕ 📧 🈁 📺 🏊 ❌

FOND DU LAC

▼▼ Comfort Inn Fond du Lac 🄢🄷
(920) 921-4000. **$65-$165.** 77 Holiday Ln. Sw of jct US 41 and 151. Int corridors. **Pets:** Accepted.

🄰🅂🄺 🅂🖧 ✕ 🈁 📺 🏊 ❌

▼▼ Econo Lodge of Fond du Lac 🄢🄷
(920) 923-2020. **$58-$80.** 649 W Johnson St. On SR 23, 0.3 mi e jct of US 41. Int corridors. **Pets:** Dogs only. Service with restrictions, supervision.

🄰🅂🄺 🅂🖧 ✕ 🈁 🏊

▼▼▼ Holiday Inn 🄢🄷
(920) 923-1440. **$116-$229.** 625 W Rolling Meadows Dr. On US 151, just sw of jct US 41. Int corridors. **Pets:** $200 deposit/room. Designated rooms, service with restrictions, supervision.

🄰🅂🄺 🅂🖧 ✕ 🄶🄼 📧 🈁 📺 🍴 🏊 ❌

▼▼ Microtel Inn & Suites 🄢🄷
(920) 929-4000. **$54-$104.** 920 S Military Rd. Jct US 41 and 151. Int corridors. **Pets:** $20 one-time fee/room. Service with restrictions, supervision.

🄰🅂🄺 🅂🖧 ✕ 📧 🈁 📺 ❌

🄐🄐🄐 ▼▼▼ Ramada Plaza Hotel 🄻🄷
(920) 923-3000. **$79-$279.** 1 N Main St. Downtown. Int corridors. **Pets:** Small, dogs only. $20 daily fee/room. Service with restrictions, crate.

🅂🄰🅅🄴 🅂🖧 ✕ 🈁 📺 🍴 🏊 ❌

▼▼ Super 8 Motel-FOND DU LAC 🄢🄷
(920) 922-1088. **$55-$83, 3 day notice.** 391 N Pioneer Rd. US 41, exit SR 23, just n on east frontage road (CR VV). Int corridors. **Pets:** Medium, dogs only. $15 daily fee/room. Designated rooms, service with restrictions, supervision.

🄰🅂🄺 🅂🖧 ✕ 📧 🈁 📺

GRANTSBURG

🄐🄐 ▼ Wood River Motel 🄼
(715) 463-2541. **$56-$100.** 703 W SR 70. 1 mi w on SR 70. Ext corridors. **Pets:** Medium. $10 daily fee/pet. Designated rooms, service with restrictions, supervision.

🅂🄰🅅🄴 🅂🖧 ✕ 🄶🄼 📧

GREEN BAY

🄐🄐🄐 ▼▼ AmericInn 🄢🄷
(920) 434-9790. **$75-$165, 30 day notice.** 2032 Velp Ave. US 41, exit 170, 0.3 mi w. Int corridors. **Pets:** Medium. $10 daily fee/pet. Designated rooms, service with restrictions, supervision.

🅂🄰🅅🄴 🅂🖧 ✕ 🄶🄼 📧 🈁 📺 🏊

🄐🄐🄐 ▼▼▼ Baymont Inn-Green Bay 🄢🄷
(920) 494-7887. **$80-$169.** 2840 S Oneida St. US 41, exit 164 (Oneida St), just e. Int corridors. **Pets:** Accepted.

🅂🄰🅅🄴 🅂🖧 ✕ 📧 🈁

🄐🄐🄐 ▼ Bay Motel 🄼
(920) 494-3441. **$45-$73.** 1301 S Military Ave. US 41, exit 167 (Lombardi Ave), 0.4 mi e to Marlee, then 0.6 mi n. Ext corridors. **Pets:** Accepted.

🅂🄰🅅🄴 🅂🖧 ✕ 🈁 📺 🍴

▼▼▼ Candlewood Suites SH
(920) 430-7040. **$79-$119.** 1125 E Mason St. US 41, exit 168 (Mason St), 4 mi e. Int corridors. **Pets:** $75 one-time fee/pet. Service with restrictions, crate.

(ASK) (S6) (✕) (🛏) (🖥) (💻)

▼▼ Comfort Inn by Choice Hotels SH
(920) 498-2060. **$75-$95.** 2841 Ramada Way. US 41, exit 164 (Oneida St), just e to Ramada Way, then just n. Int corridors. **Pets:** Accepted.

(ASK) (S6) (✕) (🕙) (🛏) (💻)

▼▼▼ Country Inn & Suites By Carlson SH
(920) 336-6600. **$105-$159.** 2945 Allied St. US 41, exit 164 (Oneida St), just nw. Int corridors. **Pets:** Small. $15 daily fee/room. Designated rooms, service with restrictions, supervision.

(ASK) (S6) (✕) (🛏) (🖥) (💻) (🏊) (✕)

▲▲▲ ▼▼▼ Days Inn-Lambeau Field SH
(920) 498-8088. **$59-$119.** 1978 Holmgren Way. US 41, exit 167 (Lombardi Ave), 1.4 mi e, then just s. Int corridors. **Pets:** Accepted.

(SAVE) (S6) (✕) (🕙) (🛏) (💻)

▲▲▲ ▼ Exel Inn of Green Bay SH
(920) 499-3599. **$50-$80.** 2870 Ramada Way. US 41, exit 164 (Oneida St), just e. Int corridors. **Pets:** Small, other species. Designated rooms, service with restrictions, supervision.

(SAVE) (S6) (✕) (🛏) (💻)

▼ Holiday Inn City Centre LH
(920) 437-5900. **$89-$129.** 200 Main St. Downtown. Int corridors. **Pets:** Accepted.

(ASK) (S6) (✕) (🛏) (🖥) (💻) (🍴) (🏊) (✕)

▲▲▲ ▼▼▼ Quality Inn & Suites SH
(920) 437-8771. **$79-$109.** 321 S Washington St. On east side of Fox River, just s of Walnut St (SR 29); downtown. Int corridors. **Pets:** Accepted.

(SAVE) (S6) (✕) (🕙) (🛏) (🖥) (💻) (🏊) (✕)

▼▼ Residence Inn by Marriott SH
(920) 435-2222. **$125-$161.** 335 W St Joseph St. SR 172, exit Riverside Dr, 1.1 mi n on SR 57, then just e. Ext corridors. **Pets:** Accepted.

(ASK) (S6) (✕) (🛏) (💻) (🏊) (✕)

▲▲▲ ▼▼ Super 8 Motel SH
(920) 494-2042. **$69-$81.** 2868 S Oneida St. US 41, exit 164 (Oneida St), just e. Int corridors. **Pets:** $15 one-time fee/room. Supervision.

(SAVE) (S6) (✕) (🕙) (🛏) (💻) (✕)

HAYWARD

▼▼ AmericInn of Hayward SH
(715) 634-2700. **$80-$159.** 15601 US Hwy 63. On US 63, just n of jct SR 77. Int corridors. **Pets:** Medium. $10 daily fee/room. Designated rooms, service with restrictions, supervision.

(ASK) (S6) (✕) (🛏) (🖥) (💻) (🏊)

▲▲▲ ▼ Best Northern Pine Inn SH 🐾
(715) 634-4959. **$50-$100.** 9966 N Hwy 27. On SR 27 S, 1.7 mi s of jct US 63. Ext/int corridors. **Pets:** Medium. $5 daily fee/pet. Service with restrictions, supervision.

(SAVE) (S6) (✕) (🛏) (💻) (✕)

▲▲▲ ▼ Comfort Suites SH 🐾
(715) 634-0700. **$79-$179.** 15586 CR B. On CR B, 0.5 mi s of jct SR 27. Int corridors. **Pets:** Other species. $13 daily fee/room. Designated rooms, service with restrictions, supervision.

(SAVE) (S6) (✕) (🛏) (🖥) (💻) (🏊) (✕)

▼▼ Ramada-Hayward SH
(715) 634-4100. **$84-$130.** 10290 Hwy 27 S. On SR 27 S, 0.7 mi s of jct US 63. Int corridors. **Pets:** Small, other species. $10 one-time fee/room. Designated rooms, no service, supervision.

(ASK) (S6) (✕) (🛏) (💻) (🍴) (🏊)

▼▼▼▼ Ross' Teal Lake Lodge and Teal Wing Golf Club CA 🐾
(715) 462-3631. **$170-$250, 21 day notice.** 12425 N Ross Rd. On SR 77, 20 mi ne of jct US 63. Ext corridors. **Pets:** Other species. $10 daily fee/pet. Service with restrictions.

(✕) (🛏) (🖥) (🍴) (🏊) (✕) (🕙)

▼▼ Super 8 Motel SH
(715) 634-2646. **$56-$84.** 10444 N SR 27. On SR 27, 0.3 mi s of jct US 63. Ext/int corridors. **Pets:** Service with restrictions, supervision.

(ASK) (S6) (✕) (🖥)

HILLSBORO

▼▼ Sleep Inn Hillsboro SH
(608) 489-3000. **$65-$250.** 1235 Water Ave (Hwy 33). Hwy 33 and 80/82, just w. Int corridors. **Pets:** Dogs only. $10 one-time fee/room. Designated rooms, service with restrictions, supervision.

(ASK) (S6) (✕) (🛏) (💻) (🏊) (✕)

HUDSON

▼▼ Comfort Inn SH
(715) 386-6355. **$49-$99.** 811 Dominion Dr. I-94, exit 2 (CR F), 1 mi w on south frontage road (Crestview Dr). Int corridors. **Pets:** $50 deposit/room, $5 daily fee/pet. Designated rooms, service with restrictions, supervision.

(ASK) (S6) (✕) (🛏) (💻) (🏊)

▲▲▲ ▼▼ Super 8 Motel of Hudson SH
(715) 386-8800. **$70-$85.** 808 Dominion Dr. I-94, exit 2 (CR F), 1 mi w on south frontage road (Crestview Dr). Int corridors. **Pets:** Medium. $5 daily fee/pet, $15 one-time fee/pet. Designated rooms, service with restrictions, supervision.

(SAVE) (S6) (✕) (🕙) (🛏) (💻) (🏊)

HURLEY

▼▼◇ Days Inn of Hurley SH
(715) 561-3500. **$75-$105.** 13355 N US Hwy 51. Jct US 2 and 51, 0.4 mi s on US 51. Int corridors. **Pets:** $15 one-time fee/room. Designated rooms, service with restrictions, supervision.

(ASK) (S6) (✕) (🛏) (💻) (🏊) (✕)

JANESVILLE

▲▲▲ ▼▼▼ Best Western Janesville SH
(608) 756-4511. **$75-$179.** 3900 Milton Ave. I-90, exit 171A (SR 26), just e. Int corridors. **Pets:** Medium. $10 daily fee/pet. Designated rooms, service with restrictions, supervision.

(SAVE) (S6) (✕) (🛏) (💻) (🍴) (🏊) (✕)

▼▼ Microtel Inn SH
(608) 752-3121. **$56-$80.** 3121 Wellington Pl. I-90, exit 171C (US 14), just se. Int corridors. **Pets:** Accepted.

(ASK) (S6) (✕) (♿M) (🕙) (🛏) (🛏)

▲▲▲ ▼ Select Inn SH
(608) 754-0251. **$37-$42.** 3520 Milton Ave. I-90, exit 171A (SR 26), just sw. Int corridors. **Pets:** Accepted.

(SAVE) (S6) (✕) (🛏) (🛏) (💻)

JEFFERSON

▼▼▼ Rodeway Inn M
(920) 674-4404. **$60-$100, 30 day notice.** 1456 S Ryan Ave. On SR 26, 1.2 mi s of jct US 18. Int corridors. **Pets:** Accepted.

(ASK) (S6) (✕) (♿M) (🕙) (🛏) (🛏) (💻) (🏊)

JOHNSON CREEK

▲▲▲ ▼▼▼ Days Inn-Johnson Creek SH
(920) 699-8000. **$74-$90.** W4545 Linmar Ln. I-94, exit 267 (SR 26), just ne. Int corridors. **Pets:** Dogs only. $75 deposit/room, $10 one-time fee/room. Service with restrictions, supervision.

(SAVE) (S6) (✕) (🛏) (🛏) (💻) (🏊) (✕)

KENOSHA

◆◆ **Best Western Harborside Inn & Convention Center** 🆂🅷
(262) 658-3281. **$109-$169.** 5125 6th Ave. Just ne of jct SR 32 and 158; downtown. Int corridors. **Pets:** Small, other species. $25 one-time fee/pet. Designated rooms, service with restrictions, supervision.

[A$K] 🆂🔟 ✕ ⊘ 🖥 🔲 ⤳

◆◆◆ **Country Inn & Suites By Carlson** 🆂🅷
(262) 857-3680. **$94-$150.** 7011 122nd Ave. I-94, exit 344 (SR 50), just nw. Int corridors. **Pets:** Small. $15 daily fee/room. Designated rooms, service with restrictions, supervision.

[A$K] 🆂🔟 ✕ 🅼 ⊘ 🚹 🖥 🔲 ⤳ ✕

LA CROSSE

◆◆◆ **Best Western-Midway Hotel Riverfront Resort** 🆂🅷 🐾
(608) 781-7000. **$79-$139.** 1835 Rose St. I-90, exit 3, 1 mi s on US 53. Int corridors. **Pets:** Dogs only. $50 deposit/pet, $15 daily fee/pet. Designated rooms, service with restrictions, supervision.

[SAVE] 🆂🔟 ✕ ⊘ 🖥 🔲 🍴 ⤳ ✕

◆◆◆ **Days Inn Hotel & Conference Center** 🆂🅷
(608) 783-1000. **$54-$110.** 101 Sky Harbour Dr. I-90, exit 2, just sw; on French Island. Int corridors. **Pets:** Accepted.

[SAVE] 🆂🔟 ✕ 🖥 🔲 🍴 ⤳

◆◆◆ **Econo Lodge** 🆂🅷
(608) 781-0200. **$45-$100.** 1906 Rose St. I-90, exit 3, 0.9 mi s on US 53. Int corridors. **Pets:** Small. $50 deposit/room. Designated rooms, service with restrictions, supervision.

[SAVE] ✕ 🚹 🔲

◆◆◆ **Exel Inn of La Crosse** 🆂🅷
(608) 781-0400. **$49-$79.** 2150 Rose St. I-90, exit 3, 0.8 mi s on US 53. Int corridors. **Pets:** Small, other species. Designated rooms, service with restrictions, supervision.

[SAVE] 🆂🔟 ✕ 🚹 🔲

◆◆◆◆ **Grandstay Residential Suites of La Crosse** 🆂🅷
(608) 796-1615. **$85-$169.** 525 Front St N. I-90, exit 3; downtown. Int corridors. **Pets:** Small. $20 daily fee/pet. Service with restrictions, crate.

[A$K] ✕ 🖊 🚹 🔲 ⤳ ✕

◆◆◆ **Holiday Inn Hotel & Suites** 🆂🅷
(608) 784-4444. **$109-$119.** 200 Pearl St. Downtown. Int corridors. **Pets:** Accepted.

[SAVE] 🆂🔟 ✕ ⊘ 🖊 🚹 🖥 🔲 🍴 ⤳

◆◆◆◆ **The Radisson Hotel La Crosse** 🅻🅷 🐾
(608) 784-6680. **$169-$199.** 200 Harborview Plaza. Just w of US 53; downtown. Int corridors. **Pets:** Other species. Designated rooms, service with restrictions, crate.

[SAVE] 🆂🔟 ✕ ⊘ 🚹 🖥 🔲 🍴 ⤳ ✕

LADYSMITH

◆◆ **AmericInn Motel & Suites** 🆂🅷
(715) 532-6650. **$66-$116.** 800 W College Ave. On SR 27, 0.5 mi s of US 8. Int corridors. **Pets:** $10 daily fee/pet. Designated rooms, service with restrictions, crate.

[A$K] ✕ 🖊 🚹 🔲 ⤳

LAND O'LAKES

◆◆ **Sunrise Lodge** 🅲🅰
(715) 547-3684. **$85-$198, 21 day notice.** 5894 W Shore Dr. 2 mi s on US 45, 2.8 mi e on CR E, then 1 mi n. Ext corridors. **Pets:** Other species. Service with restrictions, crate.

[A$K] 🆂🔟 🚹 🔲 🍴 ✕ 🅩

LODI

◆◆◆ ◆◆◆◆ **Best Western Countryside Inn** 🆂🅷
(608) 592-1450. **$65-$119.** W 9250 Prospect Dr. I-90/94, exit 119, just w. Int corridors. **Pets:** Accepted.

[SAVE] 🆂🔟 ✕ 🅼 ⊘ 🖊 🚹 🔲 ⤳ ✕

◆◆◆ **Lodi Valley Suites** 🆂🅷
(608) 592-7331. **$40-$70.** 1440 N Hwy 113. On SR 113; 1.5 mi n of jct SR 60. Int corridors. **Pets:** Accepted.

✕ 🚹 ⤳

LUCK

◆◆◆ **Luck Country Inn** 🆂🅷
(715) 472-2000. **$79-$89.** 10 Robertson Rd. Jct SR 35 and 48. Int corridors. **Pets:** Small. $5 daily fee/pet. Designated rooms, service with restrictions, supervision.

[SAVE] 🆂🔟 ✕ 🚹 🔲 🍴 ⤳

MADISON

◆◆◆ ◆◆◆◆ **Best Western East Towne Suites** 🆂🅷
(608) 244-2020. **$69-$169.** 4801 Annamark Dr. I-90/94, exit 135A, just sw on US 151. Int corridors. **Pets:** Large, other species. $15 one-time fee/pet. Designated rooms, service with restrictions, supervision.

[SAVE] 🆂🔟 ✕ ⊘ 🚹 🔲 ⤳

◆◆◆ **Best Western West Towne Suites** 🆂🅷 🐾
(608) 833-4200. **$64-$149.** 650 Grand Canyon Dr. US 12 and 14, exit 255 (Gammon Rd), just e on Odana Rd, then just sw. Int corridors. **Pets:** Medium. $25 deposit/pet. Designated rooms, service with restrictions, supervision.

[SAVE] 🆂🔟 ✕ 🚹 🔲

◆◆◆ **Clarion Suites Madison-Central** 🆂🅷 🐾
(608) 284-1234. **$89-$179.** 2110 Rimrock Rd. US 12 and 18, exit 262 (Rimrock Rd), just nw. Int corridors. **Pets:** $25 daily fee/pet. Service with restrictions, crate.

[SAVE] 🆂🔟 ✕ 🖊 🚹 🔲 ⤳

◆◆◆◆ **Comfort Inn & Suites-Madison** 🆂🅷
(608) 836-3033. **$99-$259.** 1253 John Q Hammons Dr. US 12 and 14, exit 252 (Greenway Blvd), just sw. Int corridors. **Pets:** Other species. Designated rooms, service with restrictions.

[A$K] 🆂🔟 ✕ 🖊 🚹 🔲 ⤳ ✕

◆◆◆ **Crowne Plaza Hotel and Resort** 🅻🅷 🐾
(608) 244-4703. **$129-$209.** 4402 E Washington Ave. I-90/94, exit 135A (US 151), 0.4 mi w. Int corridors. **Pets:** Medium, other species. $20 daily fee/room. Designated rooms, service with restrictions, supervision.

[SAVE] 🆂🔟 ✕ ⊘ 🚹 🔲 🍴 ⤳ ✕

◆◆◆ ◆◆◆◆ **Days Inn-Madison** 🆂🅷
(608) 223-1800. **$72-$159.** 4402 E Broadway Service Rd. US 12 and 18, exit 264 (US 51), just ne. Int corridors. **Pets:** $10 daily fee/pet. Service with restrictions, supervision.

[SAVE] 🆂🔟 ✕ 🖊 🚹 🔲 ⤳

◆◆◆ **Econo Lodge of Madison** 🆂🅷
(608) 241-4171. **$55-$99.** 4726 E Washington Ave. I-90/94, exit 135A (US 151), just w. Int corridors. **Pets:** Other species. $10 daily fee/room. Designated rooms, service with restrictions, supervision.

[SAVE] 🆂🔟 ✕ 🖊 🚹 🔲

◆◆◆ **Exel Inn of Madison** 🆂🅷
(608) 241-3861. **$49-$79.** 4202 E Towne Blvd. I-90/94, exit 135A (US 151), 0.5 mi w. Int corridors. **Pets:** Small, other species. Designated rooms, service with restrictions, supervision.

[SAVE] 🆂🔟 ✕ 🚹 🔲

GrandStay Residential Suites SH
(608) 241-2500. **$89-$129.** 5317 High Crossing Blvd. I-90/94, exit 135C (US 151), 0.5 mi e. Int corridors. **Pets:** Other species. $75 deposit/room. Designated rooms, service with restrictions, crate.

Holiday Inn Express-Madison SH
(608) 255-7400. **$89-$124.** 722 John Nolen Dr. US 12 and 18, exit 263 (John Nolen Dr), just ne. Int corridors. **Pets:** Small. Designated rooms, service with restrictions, supervision.

Howard Johnson Plaza SH
(608) 244-2481. **$89-$139.** 3841 E Washington Ave. I-90/94, exit 135A (US 151), 1 mi w. Int corridors. **Pets:** Accepted.

La Quinta Inn & Suites SH
(608) 245-0123. **$109-$159.** 5217 E Terrace Dr. US 151, exit 98B (American Pkwy), just sw. Int corridors. **Pets:** Medium. Service with restrictions.

Microtel Inn & Suites SH
(608) 242-9000. **$52-$72.** 2139 E Springs Dr. I-90/94, exit 135A, just s, then 0.5 mi e. Int corridors. **Pets:** Accepted.

Red Roof Inn-Madison #7052 M
(608) 241-1787. **$55-$85.** 4830 Hayes Rd. I-90/94, exit 135A, just sw on US 151. Ext corridors. **Pets:** Medium, other species. Service with restrictions, supervision.

Residence Inn by Marriott SH
(608) 244-5047. **$155-$175.** 4862 Hayes Rd. I-90/94, exit 135A (US 151), just sw to Hayes Rd, then just ne. Int corridors. **Pets:** Accepted.

Select Inn SH
(608) 249-1815. **$61-$99.** 4845 Hayes Rd. I-90/94, exit 135A, just sw on US 151. Int corridors. **Pets:** Other species. $25 deposit/room, $10 daily fee/room. Service with restrictions, supervision.

Staybridge Suites SH
(608) 241-2300. **$119-$169.** 3301 City View Dr. I-90/94, exit 135C (US 151), just e on High Crossing Blvd. Int corridors. **Pets:** Accepted.

Super 8 Motel-Madison SH
(608) 258-8882. **$59-$99.** 1602 W Beltline Hwy. US 12 and 18, exit 260B (CR D), just w on North Frontage Road. Int corridors. **Pets:** Medium. $10 daily fee/room. Designated rooms, service with restrictions, supervision.

MANITOWOC

Best Western Lakefront Hotel SH
(920) 682-7000. **Call for rates.** 101 Maritime Dr. I-43, exit 152, 4.2 mi e on SR 42 N, then 1 mi s. Int corridors. **Pets:** Other species. $25 one-time fee/room.

Comfort Inn by Choice Hotels SH
(920) 683-0220. **$95-$115.** 2200 S 44th St. I-43, exit 149, just e. Int corridors. **Pets:** Accepted.

Holiday Inn SH
(920) 682-6000. **$89-$149.** 4601 Calumet Ave. I-43, exit 149, just e. Int corridors. **Pets:** $150 deposit/room. Service with restrictions.

MARSHFIELD

Comfort Inn SH
(715) 387-8691. **$62-$69.** 114 E Upham St. On SR 97; 0.8 mi n of jct SR 13. Int corridors. **Pets:** Accepted.

Holiday Inn & Conference Center SH
(715) 486-1500. **$94.** 750 S Central Ave. Jct SR 13 and 97, 0.5 mi s on Business Rt 13. Int corridors. **Pets:** Accepted.

Park Motel M
(715) 387-1741. **$39-$45.** 1806 S Roddis Ave. Jct SR 13 and 97, 1.0 mi s on Business Rt 13. Ext corridors. **Pets:** Accepted.

MAUSTON

Best Western Park Oasis Inn SH
(608) 847-6255. **$80-$155.** W5641 Hwy 82 E. I-90/94, exit 69, just se. Int corridors. **Pets:** Dogs only. Supervision.

Country Inn By Carlson SH
(608) 847-5959. **$89-$97.** 1001 SR 82. I-90/94, exit 69, just ne. Int corridors. **Pets:** $10 daily fee/pet. Designated rooms, service with restrictions, supervision.

Super 8 Motel M
(608) 847-2300. **$72-$97.** 1001A Hwy 82 E. I-90/94, exit 69, just ne. Int corridors. **Pets:** Other species. $10 daily fee/pet. Service with restrictions, supervision.

MEDFORD

Malibu Inn Motel M
(715) 748-3995. **$71-$99.** 854 N 8th St. On SR 13, 0.6 mi n of jct SR 64. Int corridors. **Pets:** Small, dogs only. $100 deposit/room, $20 daily fee/pet. Designated rooms, service with restrictions, supervision.

MENOMONIE

AmericInn Lodge & Suites SH
(715) 235-4800. **$70-$140.** 1915 N Broadway. I-94, exit 41 (SR 25), just sw. Int corridors. **Pets:** Dogs only. $10 one-time fee/room. Service with restrictions, supervision.

Comfort Inn SH
(715) 233-1500. **$69-$119.** 1721 Plaza Dr NE. I-94, exit 45 (CR B), just sw. Int corridors. **Pets:** Accepted.

Menomonie Motel 6 #4109 SH
(715) 235-6901. **$36-$65.** 2100 Stout St. I-94, exit 41 (SR 25), just se. Int corridors. **Pets:** Medium, other species. Service with restrictions, supervision.

Super 8 Motel-Menomonie SH
(715) 235-8889. **$60-$100.** 1622 N Broadway. I-94, exit 41 (SR 25), just s. Int corridors. **Pets:** $10 daily fee/pet. Designated rooms, service with restrictions, supervision.

MERRILL

AmericInn Lodge & Suites of Merrill SH
(715) 536-7979. **$89-$149.** 3300 E Main St. US 51, exit 208, 0.5 mi w on SR 64. Int corridors. **Pets:** $10 daily fee/pet. Designated rooms, service with restrictions, supervision.

(AAA) ▼▼▼ **Super 8 Motel** SH
(715) 536-6880. **$90-$100.** 3209 E Main St. US 51, exit 208, 0.5 mi w on SR 64. Int corridors. **Pets:** Accepted.
[SAVE] [S6] [X] [&M] [🐾] [🔥] [💻] [🌊] [X]

MIDDLETON

(AAA) ▼▼▼▼ **Country Inn & Suites** SH
(608) 831-6970. **$99-$114.** 2212 Deming Way. I-12/14, exit 252 (Greenway Blvd), just w. Int corridors. **Pets:** Medium, dogs only. $25 daily fee/pet. Designated rooms, no service, supervision.
[SAVE] [S6] [X] [🐾] [🔥] [💻] [🌊]

(AAA) ▼▼▼▼ **Marriott Madison West** LH
(608) 831-2000. **$129-$395.** 1313 John Q Hammons Dr. US 12/14, exit 252 (Greenway Blvd), just w. Int corridors. **Pets:** Accepted.
[SAVE] [S6] [X] [🐾] [🔥] [💻] [🍴] [🌊]

MILWAUKEE METROPOLITAN AREA

BROOKFIELD

(AAA) ▼▼▼▼ **Best Western Midway Hotel** SH
(262) 786-9540. **$110-$160.** 1005 S Moorland Rd. I-94, exit 301A (Moorland Rd), just s. Int corridors. **Pets:** Accepted.
[SAVE] [S6] [X] [🐾] [🔥] [💻] [🍴] [🌊] [X]

(AAA) ▼▼▼▼ **Country Inn & Suites Milwaukee West** LH
(262) 782-1400. **$109-$169.** 1250 S Moorland Rd. I-94, exit 301A (Moorland Rd), just se. Int corridors. **Pets:** Medium. $75 one-time fee/room. Service with restrictions, crate.
[SAVE] [S6] [X] [🐾] [🔥] [💻] [🌊] [X]

▼▼ **Homestead Studio Suites**
Hotel-Milwaukee/Brookfield SH
(262) 782-9300. **$95-$104.** 325 N Brookfield Rd. I-94, exit 297, 1.1 mi e on US 18, then just e. Int corridors. **Pets:** Accepted.
[ASK] [S6] [X] [🐾] [🔥] [💻]

(AAA) ▼▼▼▼ **La Quinta Inn & Suites**
Milwaukee-Brookfield SH
(262) 782-9100. **$95-$129.** 20391 W Bluemound Rd. I-94, exit 297, just e on US 18. Int corridors. **Pets:** Medium. Service with restrictions.
[SAVE] [X] [🐾] [🔥] [💻]

▼▼▼ **Sheraton Milwaukee Brookfield** LH
(262) 786-1100. **$209-$249.** 375 S Moorland Rd. I-94, exit 301B (Moorland Rd), just n. Int corridors. **Pets:** Accepted.
[ASK] [S6] [X] [&M] [🐾] [🔥] [💻] [🍴] [🌊] [X]

▼▼ **TownePlace Suites by Marriott** SH
(262) 784-8450. **$99-$189.** 600 N Calhoun Rd. I-94, exit 297 eastbound, 2.1 mi e on US 18; exit 301B (Moorland Rd) westbound, 1.5 mi n, then 0.4 mi w on US 18. Int corridors. **Pets:** Other species. $100 one-time fee/room. Service with restrictions, crate.
[ASK] [X] [🐾] [🔥] [💻] [🌊]

DELAFIELD

▼▼▼ **La Quinta Inn & Suites Milwaukee-Delafield** SH
(262) 646-8500. **$109-$129.** 2801 Hillside Dr. I-94, exit 287, just s on SR 83, then just e. Int corridors. **Pets:** Medium. Service with restrictions.
[ASK] [X] [&M] [🐾] [🔥] [💻]

GERMANTOWN

(AAA) ▼▼▼ **AmericInn Lodge & Suites of Germantown** SH
(262) 502-9750. **$79-$109.** W190 N10862 Commerce Cir. US 41 and 45, exit Lannon/Mequon rds, just e on SR 167 to Maple Rd. Int corridors. **Pets:** Accepted.
[SAVE] [S6] [X] [🐾] [🔥] [💻] [🌊]

▼▼▼ **Residence Inn by Marriott-Madison**
West/Middleton SH 🐾
(608) 662-1100. **$139-$199.** 8400 Market St. US 12/14 (Beltline), exit 252 (Greenway Blvd), just w, then just n; in Greenway Station. Int corridors. **Pets:** Other species. $75 one-time fee/room. Service with restrictions.
[ASK] [S6] [X] [&M] [🐾] [🔥] [💻] [🌊] [X]

(AAA) ▼▼▼▼ **Staybridge Suites by Holiday Inn** SH
(608) 664-5888. **$129-$189.** 7790 Elmwood Ave. US 12/14, exit 251 (University Ave), just nw. Int corridors. **Pets:** Other species. $150 one-time fee/room. Service with restrictions, supervision.
[SAVE] [X] [&M] [🐾] [🔥] [💻] [🌊]

(AAA) ▼▼▼ **Holiday Inn Express Milwaukee**
NW-Germantown SH
(262) 255-1100. **$119-$129.** W 177 N9675 Riversbend Ln. US 41 and 45, exit CR Q (County Line Rd), then just w. Int corridors. **Pets:** Accepted.
[SAVE] [S6] [X] [&M] [🐾] [🔥] [💻] [🌊] [X]

(AAA) ▼▼▼ **Super 8 Motel-Germantown/Milwaukee** SH 🐾
(262) 255-0880. **$69-$109.** N96 W17490 County Line Rd. US 41 and 45, exit CR Q (County Line Rd), then just w. Int corridors. **Pets:** $5 daily fee/pet. Service with restrictions, supervision.
[SAVE] [S6] [X] [🐾] [🔥] [💻] [🌊]

GLENDALE

(AAA) ▼▼▼ **Exel Inn of Milwaukee Northeast** SH
(414) 961-7272. **$67-$97.** 5485 N Port Washington Rd. I-43, exit 78A (Silver Spring Dr), just se. Int corridors. **Pets:** Small, other species. Designated rooms, service with restrictions, supervision.
[SAVE] [S6] [X] [🔥] [💻]

(AAA) ▼▼▼▼ **La Quinta Inn & Suites-Bayshore Town**
Center SH
(414) 962-6767. **$125-$169.** 5423 N Port Washington Rd. I-43, exit 78A (Silver Spring Dr), just se. Int corridors. **Pets:** Other species. Service with restrictions, crate.
[SAVE] [X] [&M] [🐾] [🔥] [💻] [🌊] [X]

▼▼▼ **Residence Inn by Marriott** SH
(414) 352-0070. **$119-$229.** 7275 N Port Washington Rd. I-43, exit 80 (Good Hope Rd), just e. Ext corridors. **Pets:** Accepted.
[ASK] [S6] [X] [🐾] [🔥] [💻] [🌊] [X]

HARTFORD

(AAA) ▼▼▼ **Super 8 Motel-Hartford** SH
(262) 673-7431. **$65-$85, 3 day notice.** 1539 E Sumner St. On SR 60, 1.1 mi e of center. Int corridors. **Pets:** Small. $10 daily fee/pet. Designated rooms, service with restrictions, supervision.
[SAVE] [S6] [X] [🔥]

JACKSON

(AAA) ▼▼▼ **Comfort Inn & Suites of Jackson** SH
(262) 677-1133. **$100-$150.** W227 N16890 Tillie Lake Ct. Nw of jct US 45 and SR 60. Int corridors. **Pets:** Medium. $30 one-time fee/pet. Designated rooms, service with restrictions, supervision.
[SAVE] [S6] [X] [🐾] [🔥] [💻] [🌊] [X]

MEQUON

Best Western Quiet House & Suites SH
(262) 241-3677. **$96-$284.** 10330 N Port Washington Rd. I-43, exit 85 (Mequon Rd), just w on SR 167, then 1 mi s. Int corridors. **Pets:** Other species. $15 daily fee/pet. Designated rooms, service with restrictions, supervision.

The Chalet Motel of Mequon M ❖
(262) 241-4510. **$69-$159.** 10401 N Port Washington Rd. I-43, exit 85 (Mequon Rd), just w on SR 167, then 1 mi s. Ext corridors. **Pets:** Other species. $10 daily fee/room. Designated rooms, service with restrictions, crate.

MILWAUKEE

Best Western Inn Towne Hotel SH ❖
(414) 224-8400. **$79-$139, 30 day notice.** 710 N Old World 3rd St. Corner of Wisconsin Ave and N Old World 3rd St. Int corridors. **Pets:** Small, other species. Designated rooms, service with restrictions, supervision.

Holiday Inn Hotel and Suites SH
(414) 482-4444. **$109-$139.** 545 W Layton Ave. I-94, exit 317, 1.3 mi e. Int corridors. **Pets:** Accepted.

Hotel Metro-Milwaukee SH ❖
(414) 272-1937. **$189-$309.** 411 E Mason St. Corner of Mason and Milwaukee sts. Int corridors. **Pets:** Small, other species. $25 daily fee/room. Designated rooms, service with restrictions, supervision.

NEW BERLIN

La Quinta Inn & Suites SH
(262) 717-0900. **$95-$125.** 15300 W Rock Ridge Rd. I-43, exit 57 (Moorland Rd), just se. Int corridors. **Pets:** Medium. Service with restrictions.

OAK CREEK

Comfort Suites Milwaukee Airport SH
(414) 570-1111. **$89-$200.** 6362 S 13th St. I-94, exit 319 (College Ave), just e on CR 22, then just s. Int corridors. **Pets:** Accepted.

Exel Inn of Milwaukee South SH
(414) 764-1776. **$51-$90.** 1201 W College Ave. I-94, exit 319 (College Ave), just e. Int corridors. **Pets:** Small, other species. Designated rooms, service with restrictions, supervision.

La Quinta Inn & Suites Milwaukee-Airport SH
(414) 762-2266. **$79-$105.** 7141 S 13th St. I-94, exit 320 (Rawson Ave), just se. Int corridors. **Pets:** Medium. Service with restrictions.

MainStay Suites Oak Creek SH
(414) 571-8800. **$60-$180.** 1001 W College Ave. I-94, exit 319 (College Ave), just e. Int corridors. **Pets:** Accepted.

Red Roof Inn-Milwaukee #7031 M
(414) 764-3500. **$52-$80.** 6360 S 13th St. I-94, exit 319 (College Ave), just e. Ext corridors. **Pets:** Medium, other species. Service with restrictions, supervision.

OCONOMOWOC

Olympia Resort, Spa & Conference Center LH
(262) 369-4999. **$89-$149.** 1350 Royale Mile Rd. I-94, exit 282 (SR 67), 1 mi n. Int corridors. **Pets:** Large, other species. $15 daily fee/pet. Service with restrictions, crate.

PORT WASHINGTON

Holiday Inn Harborview SH ❖
(262) 284-9461. **$69-$199.** 135 E Grand Ave. On SR 33, waterfront of Lake Michigan; downtown. Int corridors. **Pets:** Medium, dogs only. $25 one-time fee/room. Designated rooms, service with restrictions, crate.

WAUKESHA

Best Western Waukesha Grand SH
(262) 524-9300. **$72-$82.** 2840 N Grandview Blvd. I-94, exit 293, just s on CR T. Int corridors. **Pets:** Accepted.

Extended StayAmerica-Milwaukee-Waukesha SH
(262) 798-0217. **$95-$113.** 2520 Plaza Ct. I-94, exit 297, just e on SR 18, then just s. Int corridors. **Pets:** Accepted.

Select Inn SH
(262) 786-6015. **$45-$130.** 2510 Plaza Ct. I-94, exit 297, just w on CR JJ (Bluemound Rd). Int corridors. **Pets:** Medium. $25 deposit/room, $10 daily fee/room. Designated rooms, service with restrictions, supervision.

WAUWATOSA

Exel Inn of Milwaukee West SH
(414) 257-0140. **$62-$92.** 115 N Mayfair Rd. I-94, exit 304B, just n on SR 100. Int corridors. **Pets:** Small, other species. Designated rooms, service with restrictions, supervision.

END METROPOLITAN AREA

MINERAL POINT

Comfort Inn SH
(608) 987-4747. **$49-$95.** 1345 Business Park Rd. On US 151; 0.6 mi n of jct SR 23 and 39. Int corridors. **Pets:** Other species. $25 deposit/room. Service with restrictions, crate.

MINOCQUA

AmericInn of Minocqua SH
(715) 356-3730. **$74-$189.** 700 Hwy 51. On US 51; downtown. Int corridors. **Pets:** Accepted.

▼▼ **Comfort Inn-Minocqua** SH
(715) 358-2588. **$61-$115.** 8729 US 51 N. On US 51 at SR 70 W. Int corridors. **Pets:** Other species. $10 daily fee/pet. Designated rooms, crate.
ASK S✿ ✕ 🛏 💻 ⇌

AAA ▼ **Super 8 Motel** M
(715) 356-9541. **$69-$99.** 8730 Hwy 51 N. On US 51 at SR 70 W. Ext/int corridors. **Pets:** Accepted.
SAVE S✿ ✕

MONONA

▼▼ **AmericInn of Madison South/Monona** SH ✿
(608) 222-8601. **$84-$199.** 101 W Broadway. US 12/18, exit 265 (Monona Dr), just nw. Int corridors. **Pets:** Other species. $5 daily fee/room. Service with restrictions.
ASK S✿ ✕ 🐾 🛏 💻 ⇌ ✕

MONROE

AAA ▼▼ **Gasthaus Motel** M
(608) 328-8395. **$58.** 685 30th St. 1.5 mi s on SR 69. Ext corridors. **Pets:** Other species. $10 daily fee/room. Service with restrictions, supervision.
SAVE ✕ 🐾 🛏 💻

NEENAH

▼▼▼ **Holiday Inn Neenah Riverwalk** SH
(920) 725-8441. **$99.** 123 E Wisconsin Ave. US 41, exit 132 (Main St), 2 mi e; downtown. Int corridors. **Pets:** Accepted.
ASK ✕ 🐾 🐾 🛏 💻 🍴 ⇌

NEILLSVILLE

▼▼ **Super 8 Motel-Neillsville** SH
(715) 743-8080. **$69-$89.** 1000 E Division St. US 10, jct Boon and Division St. Int corridors. **Pets:** Large, other species. $10 daily fee/pet. Designated rooms, service with restrictions, supervision.
ASK S✿ ✕ 🐾 🛏 ⇌

NEW GLARUS

▼▼▼ **Chalet Landhaus Inn** SH
(608) 527-5234. **$94-$170.** 801 Hwy 69. On Hwy 69. Int corridors. **Pets:** Dogs only. $35 daily fee/pet. Service with restrictions, supervision.
ASK ✕ 🛏 💻 🍴 ⇌ ✕

NEW LISBON

AAA ▼ **Travelers Inn of New Lisbon** SH
(608) 562-5141. **$55-$150.** 1700 E Bridge St. I-90/94, exit 61 (SR 80), just ne. Int corridors. **Pets:** Other species. Designated rooms, service with restrictions, supervision.
SAVE S✿ ✕ 🐾 🛏 💻 ⇌

NEW LONDON

AAA ▼ **Americas Best Value Inn New London** SH
(920) 982-5820. **$49-$130.** 1409 N Shawano St. US 45, exit US 54, just n. Int corridors. **Pets:** Dogs only. $8 daily fee/pet. Service with restrictions, supervision.
SAVE S✿ ✕ 🛏 💻 ⇌

▼▼ **AmericInn Lodge & Suites of New London** SH
(920) 982-5700. **$69-$179.** 1404 N Shawano St. US 45, exit US 54, just n. Int corridors. **Pets:** Small, dogs only. $10 one-time fee/pet. Designated rooms, service with restrictions, supervision.
ASK S✿ ✕ 🐾 🐾 🛏 💻 ⇌

NEW RICHMOND

▼▼ **AmericInn Motel & Suites** SH
(715) 246-3993. **$69-$99.** 1020 S Knowles Ave. Just s on SR 65. Int corridors. **Pets:** $15 one-time fee/room. Service with restrictions, supervision.
ASK S✿ ✕ 🐾 🛏 💻 ⇌ ✕

▼▼ **Super 8 Motel** SH
(715) 246-7829. **$82-$90, 5 day notice.** 1561 Dorset Ln. Just s on SR 65. Int corridors. **Pets:** Large. $20 one-time fee/room. Service with restrictions, supervision.
ASK S✿ ✕ 🐾 🛏

ONALASKA

▼▼ **Baymont Inn & Suites LaCrosse-Onalaska** SH
(608) 783-7191. **$70-$189.** 3300 Kinney Coulee Rd N. I-90, exit 5, just ne. Int corridors. **Pets:** Accepted.
ASK S✿ ✕ 🐾 🐾 🐾 🛏 💻 ⇌

▼▼ **Comfort Inn by Choice Hotels** SH
(608) 781-7500. **$85-$105.** 1223 Crossing Meadows Dr. I-90, exit 4, just e on SR 157, then w on CR SS. Int corridors. **Pets:** Accepted.
ASK S✿ ✕ 🐾 🛏 💻 ⇌

▼▼▼ **Holiday Inn Express** SH
(608) 783-6555. **$96-$106.** 9409 Hwy 16. I-90, exit 5, 1 mi e. Int corridors. **Pets:** Service with restrictions, supervision.
ASK S✿ ✕ 🐾 🛏 💻 ⇌ ✕

▼▼ **Microtel Inn** SH
(608) 783-0833. **$43-$58.** 3240 N Kinney Coulee Rd. I-90, exit 5, just ne. Int corridors. **Pets:** $5 daily fee/room. Service with restrictions, supervision.
ASK S✿ ✕ 🐾 🛏

OSCEOLA

AAA ▼▼ **River Valley Inn** SH
(715) 294-4060. **$69-$129.** 1030 Cascade St. Just n on SR 35. Int corridors. **Pets:** Small. $10 daily fee/pet. Service with restrictions, supervision.
SAVE S✿ ✕ 🛏 💻 ⇌

OSHKOSH

▼▼ **AmericInn of Oshkosh** SH
(920) 232-0300. **$70-$200.** 1495 W South Park Ave. US 41, exit 116 (SR 44), 0.5 mi e. Int corridors. **Pets:** Dogs only. $15 daily fee/room. Service with restrictions, supervision.
ASK S✿ ✕ 🐾 🛏 💻 ⇌

▼▼ **Fairfield Inn by Marriott** SH
(920) 233-8504. **$75-$95.** 1800 S Koeller Rd. US 41, exit 117 (9th Ave), 0.8 mi s on east frontage road. Int corridors. **Pets:** Accepted.
ASK S✿ ✕ 🐾 🛏 💻 ⇌

▼▼▼ **Hawthorn Inn & Suites** SH
(920) 303-1133. **$25-$499.** 3105 S Washburn St. US 41, exit 116 (SR 44), just w, then just s. Int corridors. **Pets:** Medium, dogs only. $15 daily fee/pet. Designated rooms, service with restrictions, supervision.
ASK S✿ ✕ 🐾 🐾 🛏 💻 🍴 ⇌

AAA ▼▼▼ **Holiday Inn Express Hotel & Suites** SH ✿
(920) 303-1300. **$99-$200.** 2251 Westowne Ave. US 41, exit 119, 0.4 mi w of jct SR 21. Int corridors. **Pets:** Medium, dogs only. Designated rooms, service with restrictions, supervision.
SAVE S✿ ✕ 🐾 🐾 🐾 🛏 💻 ⇌ ✕

▼▼ **La Quinta Inn Oshkosh** SH
(920) 233-4190. **$75-$105.** 1950 Omro Rd. US 41, exit 119, jct SR 21. Int corridors. **Pets:** Medium. Service with restrictions.
ASK ✕ 🐾 🛏 💻

PLATTEVILLE

AAA ▼▼▼ **Governor Dodge Hotel & Conference Center** SH ✿
(608) 348-2301. **$72-$85.** 300 Business Hwy 151. Jct US 151 and SR 80, just w. Int corridors. **Pets:** Other species. $10 daily fee/room. Service with restrictions, crate.
SAVE S✿ ✕ 🛏 💻 🍴 ⇌

▼▼▼ Mound View Inn 🆂🅷
(608) 348-9518. **$50-$75.** 1755 E Business Hwy 151. On US 151, exit 21, just w. Int corridors. **Pets:** Medium, other species. $20 deposit/room. No service, supervision.
⊠ 🐾 🔋 ⊠

AAA ▼▼▼ Super 8 Motel 🆂🅷
(608) 348-8800. **$52-$90.** 100 Hwy 80/81 S. Jct US 151 and SR 80. Int corridors. **Pets:** Other species. $10 daily fee/pet. Service with restrictions.
SAVE S🐾 ⊠ 🔋

PLEASANT PRAIRIE

▼▼▼▼ Holiday Inn Express Hotel & Suites 🆂🅷
(262) 942-6000. **$89-$170.** 7887 94th Ave. I-94, exit 344 (SR 50), 1.5 mi e, then 0.3 mi s. Int corridors. **Pets:** Small. $50 one-time fee/room. No service, supervision.
A$K S🐾 ⊠ 🔋M 🐾 🔋 🔋 🔋 ≈ ⊠

AAA ▼▼▼ La Quinta Inn-Pleasant Prairie 🆂🅷
(262) 857-7911. **$79-$99.** 7540 118th Ave. I-94, exit 344 (SR 50), just e. Int corridors. **Pets:** Medium. Service with restrictions.
SAVE ⊠ 🐾 🔋 ≈

PLOVER

AAA ▼▼▼ Hampton Inn-Plover 🆂🅷
(715) 295-9900. **$79-$99, 10 day notice.** 3090 Village Park Dr. I-39, exit 153 (CR B), just sw. Int corridors. **Pets:** Small. $50 one-time fee/room. Designated rooms, service with restrictions, supervision.
SAVE S🐾 ⊠ 🔋M 🐾 🔋 🔋 ≈

PORTAGE

▼▼ Super 8 Motel-Portage 🆂🅷
(608) 742-8330. **$55-$85.** 3000 New Pinery. I-39, exit 92, just s. Int corridors. **Pets:** Other species. $10 daily fee/pet. Service with restrictions, supervision.
A$K S🐾 ⊠ 🐾 🔋 🔋

PRAIRIE DU CHIEN

AAA ▼▼▼ Best Western Quiet House & Suites 🆂🅷
(608) 326-4777. **$70-$170.** US 18 and SR 35. On US 18, 1.9 mi e of jct SR 27 N. Ext/int corridors. **Pets:** Small. $15 daily fee/pet. Designated rooms, service with restrictions, supervision.
SAVE ⊠ 🔋 🔋 ≈

AAA ▼▼▼ Bridgeport Inn 🆂🅷
(608) 326-6082. **$67-$129.** Hwy 18, 35 & 60 S. On US 18, 2.2 mi e of jct SR 27 N. Int corridors. **Pets:** Accepted.
SAVE S🐾 ⊠ 🔋 ≈

AAA ▼▼ Brisbois Motor Inn 🅼
(608) 326-8404. **$54-$109.** 533 N Marquette Rd. On SR 35 N, 0.5 mi n of jct US 18/SR 35 S and 27 N. Ext/int corridors. **Pets:** Other species. $10 daily fee/room. Designated rooms, no service.
SAVE S🐾 ⊠ 🔋 🔋 ≈

AAA ▼▼▼▼ Country Inn & Suites By Carlson 🆂🅷
(608) 326-5700. **$79-$165.** 1801 Cabela Dr. On SR 35; 2 mi n of jct US 18/SR 35 S and 27 N. Int corridors. **Pets:** Large, other species. $20 daily fee/pet. Service with restrictions, supervision.
SAVE S🐾 ⊠ 🔋 🔋 🔋 🔋 ≈ ⊠

AAA ▼▼▼ Super 8 Motel-Prairie Du Chien 🆂🅷
(608) 326-8777. **$60-$90.** 1930 S Marquette Rd. On US 18, 1.9 mi e of jct SR 27 N. Ext/int corridors. **Pets:** Small. $15 daily fee/pet. Designated rooms, service with restrictions, supervision.
SAVE ⊠ 🔋

RACINE

AAA ▼▼▼ Microtel Inn & Suites 🆂🅷
(262) 554-8855. **$65-$85.** 5419 Durand Ave. On SR 11, 0.5 mi e of jct SR 31. Int corridors. **Pets:** Small. $25 daily fee/pet. Designated rooms, service with restrictions, supervision.
SAVE ⊠ 🔋M 🐾 🔋 🔋 🔋

▼▼▼ Racine Marriott Hotel 🅻🅷
(262) 886-6100. **$189.** 7111 Washington Ave. I-94, exit 333, 4 mi e on SR 20. Int corridors. **Pets:** Accepted.
A$K S🐾 ⊠ 🐾 🔋 🔋 🔋 🍴 ≈ ⊠

AAA ▼▼▼ Super 8-Racine 🆂🅷
(262) 884-0486. **$55-$160.** 1150 Oakes Rd. I-94, exit 333, 4 mi e on SR 20. Int corridors. **Pets:** Accepted.
SAVE S🐾 ⊠ 🔋 🔋

REEDSBURG

AAA ▼ Copper Springs Motel 🅼
(608) 524-4312. **$44-$68, 5 day notice.** E7278 Hwy 23 & 33. 2 mi e on SR 23 and 33. Ext corridors. **Pets:** Accepted.
SAVE S🐾 🔋 🔋

RHINELANDER

AAA ▼▼▼ Best Western Claridge Motor Inn 🆂🅷
(715) 362-7100. **$89-$170.** 70 N Stevens St. Between Davenport and Rives St; downtown. Int corridors. **Pets:** Other species. $10 daily fee/pet. Designated rooms, service with restrictions, supervision.
SAVE S🐾 ⊠ 🔋 🔋 🍴 ≈ ⊠

AAA ▼▼▼ Comfort Inn 🆂🅷
(715) 369-1100. **$69-$160.** 1490 Lincoln St. On Business Rt US 8, 2.6 mi e of jct SR 47. Int corridors. **Pets:** $10 daily fee/room. Designated rooms, supervision.
SAVE S🐾 ⊠ 🔋 🔋 ≈ ⊠

▼ Holiday Acres Resort 🆂🅷
(715) 369-1500. **$69-$309.** 4060 S Shore Dr. 4.5 mi e on Business Rt US 8, 2.3 mi n on W Lake George Rd. Ext/int corridors. **Pets:** Accepted.
S🐾 ⊠ 🔋 🔋 🍴 ≈ ⊠

▼▼ Holiday Inn Express 🆂🅷
(715) 369-3600. **$74-$174.** 668 W Kemp St. On Business Rt US 8, just e of jct SR 47. Int corridors. **Pets:** Accepted.
A$K S🐾 ⊠ 🔋M 🐾 🔋 🔋 ≈ ⊠

RICE LAKE

AAA ▼▼▼ Microtel Inn & Suites 🆂🅷
(715) 736-2010. **$55-$85.** 2771 Decker Dr. US 53, exit 140 (CR O), just ne. Int corridors. **Pets:** Medium. $10 one-time fee/room. Designated rooms, service with restrictions, supervision.
SAVE ⊠ 🐾 🔋 🔋

RICHLAND CENTER

▼▼ Super 8 Motel-Richland Center 🆂🅷
(608) 647-8988. **$63-$99.** 100 Foundry Dr. 0.9 mi e on US 14. Int corridors. **Pets:** Accepted.
A$K S🐾 ⊠ 🔋 🔋 ≈

RIPON

▼▼ AmericInn of Ripon 🆂🅷
(920) 748-7578. **$78-$138.** 1219 W Fond du Lac St. 1.8 mi w on SR 23. Int corridors. **Pets:** Large, other species. $10 one-time fee/room. Service with restrictions, supervision.
⊠ 🐾 🔋 🔋 ≈ ⊠

▼▼▼ **Comfort Suites at Royal Ridges** ᴴ
(920) 748-5500. **$69-$199.** 2 Westgate Dr. 2 mi w on SR 23. Int corridors. **Pets:** $15 daily fee/room. Designated rooms, service with restrictions, crate.
(ASK) 🆂 ✕ 🕭 🐾 🔋 🖵 ≈

RIVER FALLS

△△△ ▼▼▼ **Super 8 Motel** ᴴ
(715) 425-8388. **$59-$92.** 1207 St. Croix St. On SR 65, 0.5 mi w jct SR 35. Int corridors. **Pets:** Other species. $15 one-time fee/room. Supervision.
(SAVE) 🆂 ✕ 🔋 🖵 ≈

ROTHSCHILD

△△△ ▼▼▼ **Comfort Inn** ᴴ ❀
(715) 355-4449. **$54-$125.** 1510 County Hwy XX. I-39, exit 185 (Business Rt US 51), just se. Int corridors. **Pets:** Medium, dogs only. $15 daily fee/room. Designated rooms, service with restrictions, supervision.
(SAVE) 🆂 ✕ 🐾 🔋 🖵 ≈

SHAWANO

▼▼ **Comfort Inn & Suites** ᴴ
(715) 524-9090. **$78-$139.** W7393 River Bend Rd. SR 29, exit 225, just n on SR 22. Int corridors. **Pets:** Accepted.
(ASK) 🆂 ✕ 🕭 🐾 🔋 🖵 ≈ ✕

▼ **Super 8 Motel-Shawano** ᴴ
(715) 526-6688. **$46-$90.** 211 Waukechon St. 1.2 mi e on SR 29 business route; SR 29, exit 227, 1.8 mi n. then 1.1 mi w. Int corridors. **Pets:** Other species. $25 deposit/room. Service with restrictions, supervision.
(ASK) 🆂 ✕ 🐾 🔋 🖵

SHEBOYGAN

△△△ ▼ **Americas Best Value Inn-Sheboygan** ᴴ ❀
(920) 458-8080. **$61-$81.** 3402 Wilgus Rd. I-43, exit 126, just ne. Int corridors. **Pets:** Dogs only. $10 one-time fee/room. Designated rooms, service with restrictions, supervision.
(SAVE) 🆂 ✕ 🔋 🖵

▼▼ **AmericInn of Sheboygan** ᴴ
(920) 208-8130. **$90-$179.** 3664 S Taylor Dr. I-43, exit 123, just e. Int corridors. **Pets:** Accepted.
(ASK) 🆂 ✕ 🐾 🔋 🖵 ≈

△△△ ▼▼ **Comfort Inn-Sheboygan** ᴴ ❀
(920) 457-7724. **$70-$190.** 4332 N 40th St. I-43, exit 128, 0.3 mi e on Business Rt SR 42. Int corridors. **Pets:** Large, other species. $10 daily fee/pet. Designated rooms, service with restrictions, supervision.
(SAVE) 🆂 ✕ 🐾 🔋 🖵 ≈

▼▼ **La Quinta Inn Sheboygan** ᴴ
(920) 457-2321. **$79-$99.** 2932 Kohler Memorial Dr. I-43, exit 126, 1 mi e on SR 23. Int corridors. **Pets:** Medium. Service with restrictions.
(ASK) ✕ 🐾 🔋 🖵

SHELL LAKE

▼▼ **AmericInn of Shell Lake** ᴴ
(715) 468-4494. **$69-$165.** 315 Hwy 63 S. On SR 63, just s. Int corridors. **Pets:** Accepted.
(ASK) 🆂 ✕ 🐾 🔋 🖵 ≈ ✕

SIREN

△△△ ▼▼▼ **The Lodge at Crooked Lake** ᴴ
(715) 349-2500. **$89-$149.** 24271 SR 35 N. On SR 35, 0.5 mi n of jct SR 70. Int corridors. **Pets:** Accepted.
(SAVE) 🆂 ✕ 🐾 🔋 🖵 🍴 ≈ ✕

△△△ ▼ **Pine Wood Motel** Ⓜ
(715) 349-5225. **$45-$60.** 23862 Hwy 35 S. On SR 35, 0.3 mi s of jct SR 70 W and CR B E. Ext corridors. **Pets:** Small, dogs only. No service, supervision.
(SAVE) ✕ 🔋

SPARTA

△△△ ▼ **Best Nights Inn** Ⓜ
(608) 269-3066. **$39-$99.** 303 W Wisconsin St. I-90, exit 25 (SR 27), 0.5 mi n; exit 28 (SR 16), 1 mi w. Ext corridors. **Pets:** Small, dogs only. $7 daily fee/pet. Designated rooms, service with restrictions, supervision.
(SAVE) 🆂 ✕ 🔋 🖵 ≈

▼▼▼ **Best Western Sparta Trail Lodge** ᴴ
(608) 269-2664. **$74-$129.** 4445 Theatre Rd. I-90, exit 28 (US 16), just w. Int corridors. **Pets:** Medium. $20 one-time fee/room. Service with restrictions, supervision.
(ASK) 🆂 ✕ 🐾 🔋 🖵 🍴 ≈ ✕

△△△ ▼ **Country Inn By Carlson** ᴴ
(608) 269-3110. **$79-$145.** 737 Avon Rd. I-90, exit 25 (SR 27), just n. Int corridors. **Pets:** Other species. $10 one-time fee/pet. Service with restrictions, supervision.
(SAVE) 🆂 ✕ 🐾 🔋 🖵 ≈

▼▼ **Super 8 Sparta** ᴴ
(608) 269-8489. **$70-$175.** 716 Avon Rd. I-90, exit 25 (SR 27), just n. Int corridors. **Pets:** Other species. $10 daily fee/pet. Service with restrictions, crate.
(ASK) 🆂 ✕ 🔋 🖵 ≈

SPOONER

▼▼▼ **Best Western American Heritage Inn** ᴴ
(715) 635-9770. **$84-$139.** 101 E Maple St. On SR 70 just e of US 63, 1 mi w of US 53. Int corridors. **Pets:** Small. $15 daily fee/room. Designated rooms, service with restrictions, supervision.
(ASK) 🆂 ✕ 🖵 ≈ ✕

△△△ ▼▼▼ **Country House Motel & RV Park** Ⓜ ❀
(715) 635-8721. **$59-$99.** 717 South River. On US 63, 0.5 mi s of jct SR 70. Ext/int corridors. **Pets:** Large. $6 daily fee/pet, $6 one-time fee/pet. Service with restrictions, supervision.
(SAVE) ✕ 🐾 🍷 🔋 🖵 ≈

STEVENS POINT

△△△ ▼ **Americas Best Value Inn** ᴴ ❀
(715) 341-8888. **$58-$78.** 247 N Division St. I-39, exit 161 (US 51 business route), 0.6 mi s. Int corridors. **Pets:** Dogs only. $10 one-time fee/room. Designated rooms, service with restrictions, supervision.
(SAVE) 🆂 ✕ 🔋 🖵

▼▼▼ **Country Inn & Suites By Carlson** ᴴ
(715) 345-7000. **$71-$139.** 301 Division St N. I-39, exit 161 (US 51 business route), 0.6 mi s. Int corridors. **Pets:** $25 one-time fee/room. Designated rooms, supervision.
(ASK) 🆂 ✕ 🔋 🖵 ≈

▼▼ **Fairfield Inn by Marriott** ᴴ
(715) 342-9300. **$75-$95.** 5317 Hwy 10 E. I-39, exit 158A (US 10), just se. Int corridors. **Pets:** Accepted.
(ASK) 🆂 ✕ 🐾 🔋 🖵 ≈

▼▼▼ **Holiday Inn Express** ᴴ
(715) 344-0000. **$74-$99.** 1100 Amber Ave. I-39, exit 158 (US 10), 1 mi e on US 10, then just n. Int corridors. **Pets:** Other species. $25 one-time fee/room. Service with restrictions, supervision.
(ASK) 🆂 ✕ 🐾 🔋 🖵 ≈

△△△ ▼▼▼ **La Quinta Inn & Suites Stevens Point** ᴴ
(715) 344-1900. **$79-$99.** 4917 Main St. I-39, exit 158B (US 10), just sw. Int corridors. **Pets:** Medium. Service with restrictions.
(SAVE) ✕ 🐾 🔋 🖵 ≈

▼ Point Motel **M**
(715) 344-8312. **$38-$80.** 209 Division St. I-39, exit 161 (US 51 business route), 0.7 mi s. Ext corridors. **Pets:** Accepted.
[ASK] [S🐾] [✕] [🖥] [💻]

STURTEVANT

🔺🔺 ▼▼ Grandview Inn **SH**
(262) 886-0385. **$72-$110.** 910 S Sylvania Ave. I-94, exit 333 (SR 20), just s on west frontage road. Int corridors. **Pets:** $5 daily fee/pet. Service with restrictions, supervision.
[SAVE] [S🐾] [✕] [🖥] [💻] [≈]

🔺🔺 ▼▼▼ Holiday Inn Express-Racine **SH**
(262) 884-0200. **$99-$130.** 13339 Hospitality Ct. I-94, exit 333 (SR 20), just se. Int corridors. **Pets:** Accepted.
[SAVE] [S🐾] [✕] [&M] [🅿] [✕] [🖥] [💻] [≈]

SUN PRAIRIE

🔺🔺 ▼▼ AmeriHost Inn & Suites-Sun Prairie **SH**
(608) 834-9889. **$59-$119.** 105 Business Park Dr. US 151, exit 103 (CR N), just n. Int corridors. **Pets:** Medium, dogs only. $10 daily fee/pet. Designated rooms, service with restrictions, supervision.
[SAVE] [S🐾] [✕] [&M] [✕] [🖥] [💻] [≈]

🔺🔺 ▼ McGovern's Motel & Suites **M**
(608) 837-7321. **$55-$85.** 820 W Main St. On US 151, exit 101, 1.2 mi ne. Ext/int corridors. **Pets:** Medium, dogs only. $10 daily fee/pet. Designated rooms, service with restrictions, supervision.
[SAVE] [S🐾] [✕] [🖥] [💻] [🍴]

SUPERIOR

🔺🔺 ▼▼ Barkers Island Inn **SH**
(715) 392-7152. **$85-$186.** 300 Marina Dr. Just ne of US 2/53; on Barkers Island. Int corridors. **Pets:** $50 deposit/room, $10 daily fee/room. Service with restrictions, supervision.
[SAVE] [S🐾] [✕] [🖥] [💻] [🍴] [≈] [✕]

▼▼▼ Best Western Bay Walk Inn **SH**
(715) 392-7600. **$59-$129.** 1405 Susquehanna Ave. Just e of US 2 on Belknap St. Int corridors. **Pets:** Accepted.
[ASK] [S🐾] [✕] [🖥] [💻] [≈] [✕]

🔺🔺 ▼▼ Best Western Bridgeview Motor Inn **SH**
(715) 392-8174. **$59-$149.** 415 Hammond Ave. 0.8 mi n at south end of Blatnik Bridge. Int corridors. **Pets:** Accepted.
[SAVE] [S🐾] [✕] [🖥] [💻] [≈] [✕]

▼ Stockade Motel **M**
(715) 398-3585. **$45-$75.** 1616 E 2nd St. On US 2/53, 2.8 mi se. Ext corridors. **Pets:** Accepted.
[✕] [🖥] [💻]

🔺🔺 ▼▼ Superior Inn **SH**
(715) 394-7706. **$45-$130.** 525 Hammond Ave. 0.8 mi n at south end of Blatnik Bridge. Int corridors. **Pets:** Other species. Designated rooms, service with restrictions, supervision.
[SAVE] [S🐾] [✕] [🖥] [💻] [≈]

THORP

🔺🔺 ▼▼ AmericInn Lodge & Suites **SH**
(715) 669-5959. **$96-$146.** 203 1/2 W Hill St. US 29, exit 108 (SR 73), just nw. Int corridors. **Pets:** Accepted.
[SAVE] [✕] [✕] [🖥] [💻] [≈] [✕]

TOMAH

▼▼ AmericInn Lodge and Suites **SH**
(608) 372-4100. **$75-$100.** 750 Vandervort St. I-94, exit 143 (SR 21), just e. Int corridors. **Pets:** $50 deposit/room. Designated rooms, service with restrictions, supervision.
[ASK] [S🐾] [✕] [🅿] [✕] [🖥] [💻] [≈]

▼▼ Comfort Inn by Choice Hotels **SH**
(608) 372-6600. **$90-$110.** 305 Wittig Rd. I-94, exit 143 (SR 21), just w. Int corridors. **Pets:** Accepted.
[ASK] [S🐾] [✕] [🅿] [🖥] [💻] [≈]

▼▼◆▼ Cranberry Country Lodge Convention Center and Water Park **SH**
(608) 374-2801. **$79-$185.** 319 Wittig Rd. I-94, exit 143 (SR 21), just w. Int corridors. **Pets:** Accepted.
[ASK] [S🐾] [✕] [🖥] [💻] [≈] [✕]

🔺🔺 ▼▼ Econo Lodge **SH**
(608) 372-9100. **$65-$145.** 2005 N Superior Ave. I-94, exit 143 (SR 21), just w. Ext/int corridors. **Pets:** Accepted.
[SAVE] [S🐾] [✕] [🅿] [🖥] [💻] [≈]

▼▼ Holiday Inn **SH**
(608) 372-3211. **$85-$95.** 1017 E McCoy Blvd. I-94, exit 143 (SR 21), just e. Int corridors. **Pets:** Service with restrictions, supervision.
[ASK] [S🐾] [✕] [✕] [🖥] [💻] [🍴] [≈] [✕]

🔺🔺 ▼▼ Lark Inn **M**
(608) 372-5981. **$59-$91.** 229 N Superior Ave. I-94, exit 143 (SR 21), 1.5 mi s on US 12; I-90, exit 41, 2 mi n on US 12. Ext/int corridors. **Pets:** $7 daily fee/pet. Service with restrictions, supervision.
[SAVE] [S🐾] [✕] [🖥] [💻]

▼▼ Microtel Inn & Suites **SH**
(608) 374-2050. **$54-$89.** 115 W Andres St. I-94, exit 143 (SR 21), just nw. Int corridors. **Pets:** Medium. $10 daily fee/room. Service with restrictions, supervision.
[ASK] [S🐾] [✕] [✕] [🖥] [💻]

▼▼ Super 8 Motel-Tomah **SH**
(608) 372-3901. **$50-$120.** 1008 E McCoy Blvd. I-94, exit 143 (SR 21), just e. Int corridors. **Pets:** Accepted.
[ASK] [S🐾] [✕] [✕] [🖥] [💻]

TOMAHAWK

▼▼ Comfort Inn **SH**
(715) 453-8900. **$70-$130.** 1738 E Comfort Dr. US 51, exit 229, just nw. Int corridors. **Pets:** Other species. $25 one-time fee/room.
[ASK] [S🐾] [✕] [&M] [✕] [🖥] [💻] [≈] [✕]

▼▼ Super 8 Motel-Tomahawk **SH**
(715) 453-5210. **$45-$126.** 108 W Mohawk Dr. On US 51 business route, 0.6 mi n of downtown. Int corridors. **Pets:** $5 daily fee/room. Designated rooms, service with restrictions, crate.
[ASK] [S🐾] [✕] [🖥] [≈]

WATERFORD

🔺🔺 ▼▼◆▼ Baymont Inns & Suites-Waterford **SH**
(262) 534-4100. **$76-$151.** 750 Fox Ln. On SR 36, 1 mi s of jct SR 164. Int corridors. **Pets:** Accepted.
[SAVE] [S🐾] [✕] [✕] [🖥] [💻] [≈]

WATERTOWN

▼▼▼ Holiday Inn Express **SH**
(920) 262-1910. **$72-$106.** 101 Aviation Way. On SR 26, 1.5 mi s of jct SR 19. Int corridors. **Pets:** Large, dogs only. $20 daily fee/pet. Designated rooms, service with restrictions, supervision.
[ASK] [S🐾] [✕] [✕] [🖥] [💻] [✕]

▼▼ Super 8 Motel **SH**
(920) 261-1188. **$73-$90.** 1730 S Church St. On SR 26, 1.5 mi s of jct SR 19. Int corridors. **Pets:** Dogs only. $75 deposit/room, $10 one-time fee/room. Service with restrictions, supervision.
[ASK] [S🐾] [✕] [🖥] [💻] [≈]

WAUPACA

◇◇◇ ▼▼▼▼ Best Western Grand Seasons Hotel SH ❀
(715) 258-9212. **$159-$189.** 110 Grand Seasons Dr. Jct US 10 and SR 54 W. Int corridors. **Pets:** Medium. $50 deposit/room. Designated rooms, supervision.
[SAVE] [S6] [✕] [⌖] [☷] [🖬] [🖵] [≈] [✕]

WAUPUN

▼ Inn Town Motel M
(920) 324-4211. **$49-$86.** 27 S State St. US 151, exit 146 (SR 49), 1 mi w on Main St, then just s. Ext corridors. **Pets:** Dogs only. $6 daily fee/pet. Service with restrictions, supervision.
[ASK] [S6] [✕] [🖬] [🖵]

WAUSAU

▼▼ Best Western Midway Hotel SH
(715) 842-1616. **$85-$160, 3 day notice.** 2901 Hummingbird Rd. I-39, exit 190 (CR NN), just sw. Int corridors. **Pets:** Accepted.
[ASK] [S6] [✕] [🖬] [🖵] [🍽] [≈] [✕]

◇◇◇ ▼▼▼ Days Inn-Wausau SH
(715) 355-5501. **$61-$79.** 4700 Rib Mountain Dr. I-39, exit 188, just ne. Int corridors. **Pets:** Dogs only. $10 daily fee/pet. Designated rooms, service with restrictions, supervision.
[SAVE] [S6] [✕] [🖬] [🖵] [≈]

◇◇◇ ▼▼▼ Exel Inn of Wausau M
(715) 842-0641. **$48-$78.** 116 S 17th Ave. I-39, exit 192, just ne. Int corridors. **Pets:** Small, other species. Designated rooms, service with restrictions, supervision.
[SAVE] [S6] [✕] [🖬] [🖵]

◇◇◇ ▼▼▼▼ Jefferson Street Inn SH ❀
(715) 845-6500. **$99-$149, 3 day notice.** 201 Jefferson St. Just w of jct 6th St; center. Int corridors. **Pets:** $20 daily fee/pet. Service with restrictions, supervision.
[SAVE] [✕] [🖵] [🍽] [≈]

◇◇◇ ▼▼▼ La Quinta Inn-Wausau SH
(715) 842-0421. **$75-$89.** 1910 Stewart Ave. I-39, exit 192, just se. Int corridors. **Pets:** Medium. Service with restrictions.
[SAVE] [✕] [⌖] [🖬] [🖵] [≈]

▼▼▼ Plaza Hotel & Suites SH
(715) 845-4341. **$68-$81.** 201 N 17th Ave. I-39, exit 192, just ne. Int corridors. **Pets:** Accepted.
[ASK] [✕] [⌖] [🖬] [🖵] [🍽] [≈] [✕]

▼▼▼ Rib Mountain Inn SH
(715) 848-2802. **$69-$229, 3 day notice.** 2900 Rib Mountain Way. I-39, exit 190 (CR NN), 1 mi w on N Mountain Rd (CR NN), then just s. Ext/int corridors. **Pets:** Accepted.
[ASK] [S6] [🖬] [🖵] [✕]

▼▼▼▼ Stewart Inn Bed and Breakfast BB ❀
(715) 849-5858. **$150-$240, 10 day notice.** 521 Grant St. Just n on N 6th St (SR 52), then just w. Int corridors. **Pets:** Other species. Designated rooms, crate.
[✕]

◇◇◇ ▼▼▼ Super 8 Motel SH
(715) 848-2888. **$59-$80.** 2006 Stewart Ave W. I-39, exit 192, just se. Int corridors. **Pets:** Medium. $10 daily fee/pet. Designated rooms, service with restrictions, supervision.
[SAVE] [S6] [✕] [⌖] [☷] [🖬] [🖵] [≈]

WAUTOMA

▼▼ AmericInn SH
(920) 787-5050. **$120-$128.** W7696 SR 21/73. On SR 21 and 73, 1.2 mi e. Int corridors. **Pets:** Dogs only. $10 one-time fee/room. Service with restrictions, supervision.
[ASK] [S6] [✕] [&M] [⌖] [🖬] [🖵] [≈]

▼▼ Super 8 Motel-Wautoma SH
(920) 787-4811. **$64-$85.** W7607 SR 21 and 73. On SR 21 and 73, 1.5 mi e. Int corridors. **Pets:** Other species. $10 one-time fee/pet. Service with restrictions, supervision.
[ASK] [S6] [✕] [🖬] [🖵] [≈]

WEST SALEM

▼▼ AmericInn SH
(608) 786-3340. **$81-$160.** 125 Buol Rd. I-90, exit 12, just sw on CR C. Int corridors. **Pets:** Accepted.
[ASK] [S6] [✕] [⌖] [🖬] [🖵] [≈] [✕]

WHITEWATER

◇◇◇ ▼▼◇ AmeriHost Inn & Suites SH
(262) 472-9400. **$69-$139.** 1355 W Main St. On US business 12, 0.5 mi w of jct SR 59 W. Int corridors. **Pets:** Accepted.
[SAVE] [S6] [✕] [&M] [⌖] [⌖] [🖬] [🖵] [≈] [✕]

▼▼ Super 8 Motel SH
(262) 473-8818. **$39-$199.** 917 E Milwaukee St. On US business 12, east end of town. Int corridors. **Pets:** Accepted.
[ASK] [S6] [✕] [&M] [🖬] [🖵]

WINDSOR

◇◇◇ ▼▼▼ Days Inn SH
(608) 846-7473. **$56-$110, 7 day notice.** 6311 Rostad Cir. I-90/94, exit 131 (SR 19). Int corridors. **Pets:** Dogs only. Designated rooms, supervision.
[SAVE] [S6] [✕] [&M] [⌖] [🖬] [🖵] [≈] [✕]

▼▼ Super 8 Motel-Windsor/North Madison SH
(608) 846-3971. **$53-$79.** 4506 Lake Cir. I-90/94, exit 131 (SR 19). Int corridors. **Pets:** Accepted.
[ASK] [S6] [✕] [🖬] [🖵]

WISCONSIN DELLS

◇◇◇ ▼▼ Americas Best Value Day's End Motel M ❀
(608) 254-8171. **$34-$124, 3 day notice.** N 604 Hwy 12-16. I-90/94, exit 85 (US 12), 0.8 mi nw. Ext corridors. **Pets:** $7 daily fee/pet. Designated rooms, service with restrictions, crate.
[SAVE] [S6] [✕] [🖬] [🖵] [≈] [✕]

◇◇◇ ▼▼▼ Baker's Sunset Bay Resort SH ❀
(608) 254-8406. **$65-$147, 14 day notice.** 921 Canyon Rd. I-90/94, exit 92 (US 12), 0.5 mi w, right on E Adams St, right on Canyon Rd, then 0.8 mi on left. Ext/int corridors. **Pets:** $10 daily fee/pet. Service with restrictions.
[SAVE] [S6] [✕] [🖬] [🖵] [≈] [✕]

◇◇◇ ▼▼ Black Hawk Motel M ❀
(608) 254-7770. **$36-$145, 3 day notice.** 720 Race St. I-90/94, exit 87 (SR 13), 2 mi e on SR 13, 16 and 23. Ext corridors. **Pets:** Small, other species. $5 daily fee/pet. Designated rooms, service with restrictions, crate.
[SAVE] [S6] [✕] [🖬] [🖵] [≈] [✕]

▼ Bridge View Motel M
(608) 254-6114. **$49-$99, 3 day notice.** 1020 River Rd. Just n of SR 13; center. Ext corridors. **Pets:** Medium. $10 daily fee/pet. Designated rooms, service with restrictions, crate.
[ASK] [S6] [✕] [🖬] [≈]

◇◇◇ ▼▼▼ Days Inn of Wisconsin Dells SH
(608) 254-6444. **$45-$159, 3 day notice.** 944 Hwy 12 N. I-90/94, exit 87 (SR 13), 1 mi n at jct US 12 and SR 16. Int corridors. **Pets:** Medium. $50 deposit/pet, $10 daily fee/pet. Designated rooms, service with restrictions, supervision.
[SAVE] [S6] [✕] [🖬] [≈]

(AAA) ▼▼ Howard Johnson Hotel and Antiqua Bay Waterpark SH
(608) 254-8306. **$49-$189.** 655 Frontage Rd. I-90/94, exit 87 (SR 13), just e. Int corridors. **Pets:** Accepted.

(SAVE) (SI) (X) (⊘) (🖥) (💻) (¶) (🏊) (X̄)

(AAA) ▼▼ Motel 6 SH
(608) 355-0700. **$59-$123.** E 10892 Fern Dell Rd. I-90/94, exit 92 (US 12), 0.3 mi s. Int corridors. **Pets:** Medium, other species. Service with restrictions, supervision.

(SAVE) (SI) (X) (&M) (🖥) (💻) (🏊)

(AAA) ▼▼ Super 8 Motel-Wisconsin Dells SH
(608) 254-6464. **$56-$165.** 800 CR H. I-90/94, exit 87 (SR 13), just e. Int corridors. **Pets:** Medium, dogs only. $10 one-time fee/room. Designated rooms, service with restrictions, supervision.

(SAVE) (X) (⊘) (💻) (🏊) (X̄)

WISCONSIN RAPIDS

(AAA) ▼▼▼ Hotel Mead LH
(715) 423-1500. **$115-$225.** 451 E Grand Ave. Just e of downtown. Int corridors. **Pets:** Dogs only. $15 daily fee/room. Designated rooms, supervision.

(SAVE) (SI) (X) (⊘) (&M) (🖥) (💻) (¶) (🏊) (X̄)

▼▼ Quality Inn SH
(715) 423-5506. **$75-$85.** 3120 8th St S. 1.5 mi s on SR 13. Int corridors. **Pets:** Medium, dogs only. $5 daily fee/pet. Service with restrictions, supervision.

(ASK) (SI) (X) (🖥) (💻) (🏊)

▼▼▼ Sleep Inn & Suites SH
(715) 424-6800. **$74-$159.** 4221 8th St S. I-39, exit 136 (SR 73), 16.6 mi w; 3.5 mi n on SR 13. Int corridors. **Pets:** Medium, dogs only. $15 daily fee/pet. Supervision.

(ASK) (SI) (X) (⊘) (&M) (🖥) (💻) (🏊)

(AAA) ▼▼ Super 8 Motel SH 🐾
(715) 423-8080. **$58-$78.** 3410 8th St S. 1.9 mi s on SR 13 of jct SR 54 W. Int corridors. **Pets:** Dogs only. $10 one-time fee/room. Designated rooms, service with restrictions, supervision.

(SAVE) (SI) (X) (⊘) (🖥) (💻)

WITTENBERG

▼▼▼ Comfort Inn & Wilderness Conference Center SH 🐾
(715) 253-3755. **$60-$104.** W17267 Red Oak Ln. US 29, exit 198, just se. Int corridors. **Pets:** Large, dogs only. $20 one-time fee/room. Designated rooms, service with restrictions, supervision.

(ASK) (SI) (X) (&M) (🖥) (🖥) (💻) (🏊) (X̄)

WYOMING

AFTON

🆔 🛇 Lazy B Motel M
(307) 885-3187. **$65-$75.** 219 Washington St (US Hwy 89). On US 89; center. Ext corridors. **Pets:** Dogs only. Designated rooms, service with restrictions, supervision.
(SAVE) (S⬤) ⊠ 🛏 💻 ➰

ALPINE

🆔 🛇 Alpen Haus Resort Hotel M
(307) 654-7545. **$70-$80.** 50 W Hwy 26. Jct US 26 and 89. Int corridors. **Pets:** Small. $10 daily fee/room. Supervision.
(SAVE) (S⬤) ⊠ 🛏 🍴

🛇🛇 Best Western Flying Saddle Lodge 🆂🅷
(307) 654-4422. **$79-$189.** 118878 Jct US 26 & 89. 0.5 mi e of jct US 26 and 89. Ext corridors. **Pets:** Accepted.
(ASK) (S⬤) ⊠ 🛏 💻 🍴 ➰ ⊠

BUFFALO

🆔 🛇 Big Horn Motel M
(307) 684-7822. **$44-$90, 3 day notice.** 209 N Main St, US Hwy 16. On US 16; downtown. Ext corridors. **Pets:** Dogs only. $100 deposit/room. Designated rooms, service with restrictions, supervision.
(SAVE) (S⬤) ⊠ 🛏

🛇🛇 Comfort Inn 🆂🅷
(307) 684-9564. **$52-$150.** 65 Hwy 16 E. I-25, exit 299 (US 16), just e; I-90, exit 58, 1.3 mi w. Ext/int corridors. **Pets:** Medium, other species. $5 daily fee/pet. Designated rooms, service with restrictions, supervision.
(ASK) (S⬤) ⊠ 🛏

🆔 🛇 Rodeway Inn M
(307) 684-2219. **$49-$99.** 333 E Hart St. I-25, exit 299 (US 16), just w. Ext corridors. **Pets:** Medium. $10 daily fee/pet. Designated rooms, service with restrictions, supervision.
(SAVE) (S⬤) ⊠ 🛏 💻

🆔 🛇 Super 8 Motel of Buffalo 🆂🅷
(307) 684-2531. **$57-$124.** 655 E Hart St. I-25, exit 299 (US 16), just w; I-90, exit 58, 1.3 mi w. Int corridors. **Pets:** Other species. $5 one-time fee/pet. Designated rooms, service with restrictions, supervision.
(SAVE) ⊠ 🛏

🆔 🛇 WYO Motel M
(307) 684-5505. **$45-$118.** 610 E Hart St. I-25, exit 299 (US 16), just w; I-90, exit 58, 1.3 mi w. Ext corridors. **Pets:** Accepted.
(SAVE) ⊠ 🛏 💻 ➰

🆔 🛇 Z-Bar Motel CA
(307) 684-5535. **$40-$69.** 626 Fort St. Jct US 16/87/Business Loop I-25, 0.5 mi w on US 16. Ext corridors. **Pets:** Accepted.
(SAVE) (S⬤) ⊠ 🛏 💻

CASPER

🆔 🛇🛇🛇 Best Western Ramkota 🅻🅷
(307) 266-6000. **$77-$106.** 800 N Poplar St. I-25, exit 188B, just e. Int corridors. **Pets:** Accepted.
(SAVE) (S⬤) ⊠ 🔟 🎱 🅒 🛏 💻 🍴 ➰ ⊠

🛇 🛇 Days Inn Casper 🆂🅷
(307) 234-1159. **$79-$99.** 301 E 'E' St. I-25, exit 188A, just s. Int corridors. **Pets:** Service with restrictions, supervision.
(ASK) (S⬤) ⊠ 🛏 💻 ➰

🆔 🛇🛇🛇 Holiday Inn on the River 🆂🅷
(307) 235-2531. **$99-$114.** 300 W 'F' St. I-25, exit 188A, just e. Int corridors. **Pets:** Accepted.
(SAVE) (S⬤) ⊠ 🔟 🎱 🅒 🛏 💻 🍴 ➰ ⊠

🆔 🛇🛇🛇 Parkway Plaza Hotel & Convention Centre 🆂🅷
(307) 235-1777. **$85-$325.** 123 W 'E' St. I-25, exit 188A, just w. Ext/int corridors. **Pets:** Accepted.
(SAVE) ⊠ 🅒 🛏 💻 🍴 ➰ ⊠

🆔 🛇🛇 Quality Inn & Suites 🆂🅷 🐾
(307) 266-2400. **$95-$199.** 821 N Poplar St. I-25, exit 188B, just e. Int corridors. **Pets:** Other species. $10 daily fee/room. Designated rooms, service with restrictions, supervision.
(SAVE) (S⬤) ⊠ 🅒 🛏 💻

🆔 🛇🛇 The Royal Inn M
(307) 234-3501. **$45-$50.** 440 E St. I-25, exit 188A, just s to 'A' St, then just e. Ext corridors. **Pets:** Accepted.
(SAVE) (S⬤) ⊠ 🛏 ➰

🛇 🛇 Skyler Inn 🆂🅷
(307) 232-5100. **$72-$99.** 111 S Wilson St. I-25, exit 186, 0.5 mi s to Yellowstone Hwy, then 1 mi w, jct 1st St. Int corridors. **Pets:** Small, dogs only. $25 one-time fee/pet. Service with restrictions, crate.
(SAVE) (S⬤) ⊠ 🛏 💻

🛇 🛇 Super 8 Motel 🆂🅷
(307) 266-3480. **$79-$99.** 3838 CY Ave. I-25, exit 188B, 1.7 mi w on S Poplar St (SR 220), then 1.8 mi n. Int corridors. **Pets:** Accepted.
(ASK) (S⬤) ⊠ 🛏 💻

CHEYENNE

🆔 🛇🛇🛇 Best Western Hitching Post Inn Resort & Conference Center 🆂🅷
(307) 638-3301. **$100-$134.** 1700 W Lincolnway. I-25, exit 9, 0.8 mi e. Ext/int corridors. **Pets:** Accepted.
(SAVE) (S⬤) ⊠ 🔟 🎱 🅒 🛏 💻 🍴 ➰ ⊠

🛇 🛇 Cheyenne Super 8 Motel M
(307) 635-8741. **$55-$95, 7 day notice.** 1900 W Lincolnway. I-25, exit 9, 0.7 mi e. Int corridors. **Pets:** Accepted.
(ASK) (S⬤) ⊠ 🔟 🅒 🛏

🆔 🛇🛇 Days Inn Cheyenne 🆂🅷
(307) 778-8877. **$58-$165.** 2360 W Lincolnway. I-25, exit 9, just e. Int corridors. **Pets:** Other species. $10 one-time fee/room. Service with restrictions, supervision.
(SAVE) ⊠ 🎱 🅒 🛏 💻 ⊠

🆔 🛇 Fleetwood Motel M 🐾
(307) 638-8908. **$47-$59.** 3800 E Lincolnway. I-80, exit 364, 1.2 mi n on N College Dr, then just w on I-80/US 30 business loop. Ext corridors. **Pets:** $5 daily fee/pet. Service with restrictions, supervision.
(SAVE) (S⬤) ⊠ 🛏 ➰

Historic Plains Hotel SH
(307) 638-3311. **$79-$119.** 1600 Central Ave. I-80, exit 362, 1 mi n on I-180/I-25 business loop/US 85/87 business route, then just w on I-80 business loop/US 30; downtown. Int corridors. **Pets:** Medium. $35 one-time fee/pet. Service with restrictions, crate.
[SAVE] [S] [X] [⚷] [❚] [▭] [¶]

La Quinta Inn Cheyenne SH
(307) 632-7117. **$92-$142.** 2410 W Lincolnway. I-25, exit 9, just e. Int corridors. **Pets:** Medium. Service with restrictions.
[SAVE] [X] [M] [⚷] [❚] [▭] [≈]

Nagle Warren Mansion B & B BB
(307) 637-3333. **$134-$169, 3 day notice.** 222 E 17th St. I-80, exit 362, 1.2 mi n on I-25 business loop/US 85/87 business route, then just e; jct House St; downtown. Int corridors. **Pets:** Medium, other species. $10 daily fee/pet. Designated rooms, service with restrictions.
[SAVE] [X] [M] [X]

Oak Tree Inn SH
(307) 778-6620. **$80-$200.** 1625 Stillwater. 1.2 mi e of jct Dell Range Blvd and Yellowstone Rd, 0.4 mi s. Ext/int corridors. **Pets:** Accepted.
[SAVE] [X] [❚] [¶]

Porch Swing Bed & Breakfast BB ❀
(307) 778-7182. **$75-$85.** 502 E 24th St. I-80, exit 362, 1.8 mi n on I-25 business loop/US 85/87 business route, then just e; downtown. Int corridors. **Pets:** Other species. Service with restrictions, supervision.
[X] [K]

Windy Hills Guest House BB
(307) 632-6423. **$118-$200, 15 day notice.** 393 Happy Jack Rd. I-25, exit 10B, 22 mi w on SR 210 (Happy Jack Rd), then 1 mi s on private gravel road. Ext corridors. **Pets:** Other species. $50 deposit/pet. Designated rooms, service with restrictions, crate.
[ASK] [S] [X] [❚] [▭] [X] [K]

CHUGWATER

Buffalo Lodge Inn SH
(307) 422-3248. **$46-$76, 10 day notice.** 100 Buffalo Dr. I-25, exit 54, just ne. Int corridors. **Pets:** Medium. $9 daily fee/pet. Designated rooms, service with restrictions, supervision.
[ASK] [S] [X] [¶] [≈]

CODY

Beartooth Inn of Cody SH
(307) 527-5505. **$59-$159.** 2513 Greybull Hwy. 1.5 mi e on US 14/16/20. Ext/int corridors. **Pets:** Medium, dogs only. Designated rooms, service with restrictions, supervision.
[SAVE] [S] [X] [❚] [▭] [X]

Best Western Sunset Motor Inn SH
(307) 587-4265. **$59-$155.** 1601 8th St. 0.8 mi w on US 14/16/20. Ext corridors. **Pets:** Small. $25 one-time fee/pet. Designated rooms, service with restrictions, supervision.
[SAVE] [S] [X] [⚷] [❚] [▭] [¶] [≈] [X]

Big Bear Motel M ❀
(307) 587-3117. **$44-$94.** 139 W Yellowstone Ave. 2 mi w on US 14/16/20, from city center. Ext corridors. **Pets:** Other species. $10 daily fee/pet. Designated rooms, supervision.
[SAVE] [X] [❚] [▭] [≈] [Z]

Cody Motor Lodge M ❀
(307) 527-6291. **$60-$120.** 1455 Sheridan Ave. Just w on US 14/16/20 and SR 120. Int corridors. **Pets:** Other species. Designated rooms, service with restrictions, supervision.
[SAVE] [S] [X]

Green Gables Inn M
(307) 587-6886. **$54-$130.** 1636 Central Ave. Just e on US 14/16/20 and SR 120. Ext corridors. **Pets:** Small, dogs only. Designated rooms, service with restrictions, supervision.
[SAVE] [S] [X] [▭]

Sunrise Motor Inn M
(307) 587-5566. **$49-$150.** 1407 8th St. 0.8 mi w on US 14/16/20. Ext corridors. **Pets:** Medium, dogs only. $15 one-time fee/room. Designated rooms, service with restrictions, supervision.
[SAVE] [S] [X] [⚷] [▭] [≈]

DOUGLAS

Best Western Douglas Inn & Conference Center SH ❀
(307) 358-9790. **$79-$99.** 1450 Riverbend Dr. I-25, exit 140, 0.8 mi e. Int corridors. **Pets:** $15 one-time fee/room. Designated rooms, service with restrictions, supervision.
[SAVE] [S] [X] [M] [⚷] [❚] [▭] [¶] [≈] [X]

DUBOIS

Bald Mountain Inn M
(307) 455-2844. **$50-$90, 3 day notice.** 1349 W Ramshorn St. 1.6 mi w on US 26 and 287. Ext corridors. **Pets:** Dogs only. Supervision.
[ASK] [X] [❚] [▭] [X] [K]

Branding Iron Inn CA
(307) 455-2893. **$40-$90.** 401 W Ramshorn St. 0.3 mi w on US 26 and 287. Ext corridors. **Pets:** Other species. $5 one-time fee/room. Service with restrictions, supervision.
[SAVE] [S] [X] [❚] [▭] [K]

Riverside Inn & Campground M
(307) 455-2337. **$46-$55.** 5810 US Hwy 26. 3 mi e on US 26 and 287. Ext corridors. **Pets:** Medium, dogs only. $5 daily fee/pet. Designated rooms, supervision.
[S] [X] [❚] [▭] [X] [K] [W] [Z]

Stagecoach Motor Inn SH ❀
(307) 455-2303. **$48-$84.** 103 Ramshorn St. On US 26 and 287; center. Ext corridors. **Pets:** Medium, dogs only. $10 daily fee/pet. Designated rooms, service with restrictions, supervision.
[SAVE] [X] [⚷] [❚] [▭] [≈] [X] [K]

EVANSTON

Comfort Inn SH
(307) 789-7799. **$79-$109.** 1931 Harrison Dr. I-80, exit 3 (Harrison Dr), just n. Int corridors. **Pets:** Accepted.
[ASK] [S] [X] [⚷] [❚] [▭] [≈]

Days Inn SH
(307) 789-0783. **$69-$99.** 1983 Harrison Dr. I-80, exit 3 (Harrison Dr), just n. Int corridors. **Pets:** Medium. $10 daily fee/pet. Designated rooms, service with restrictions, supervision.
[SAVE] [S] [X] [❚] [▭] [≈]

Holiday Inn Express Hotel & Suites SH
(307) 789-7999. **$79-$110.** 1965 Harrison Dr. I-80, exit 3 (Harrison Dr), just n. Int corridors. **Pets:** Accepted.
[SAVE] [X] [⚷] [❚] [▭] [≈]

Prairie Inn M
(307) 789-2920. **$50-$65.** 264 Bear River Dr. I-80, exit 6, 0.3 mi n. Ext/int corridors. **Pets:** Small. $5 one-time fee/pet. Designated rooms, service with restrictions, supervision.
[SAVE] [X] [❚]

EVANSVILLE

◆◆ ◆◆ Comfort Inn by Choice Hotels-Casper 🆂🅷
(307) 235-3038. **$100-$120.** 480 Lathrop Rd. I-25, exit 185, just e. Int corridors. **Pets:** Accepted.
A$K 🆂🅳 ✕ ℥M ◎ ℰ 🛏 🖵 ≈

◆◆◆◆ Sleep Inn & Suites 🆂🅷
(307) 235-3100. **Call for rates.** 6733 Bonanza. I-25, exit 182, n on Hat Six Rd, then w. Int corridors. **Pets:** Large, other species. Designated rooms, service with restrictions, supervision.
✕ 🛏 🖵 ≈

◆◆◆◆ Super 8 East Casper 🆂🅷
(307) 237-8100. **$89-$109.** 269 Miracle Dr. I-25, exit 185, just e. Int corridors. **Pets:** Accepted.
A$K 🆂🅳 ✕ ℰ 🛏 🖵 ≈

GILLETTE

◆◆◆ ◆◆◆◆ Best Western Tower West Lodge 🆂🅷
(307) 686-2210. **$69-$239.** 109 N US Hwy 14-16. I-90, exit 124, just n. Int corridors. **Pets:** Medium. $25 one-time fee/pet. Service with restrictions, supervision.
SAVE 🆂🅳 ✕ ℰ 🛏 🖵 ⑪ ≈ ✕

◆◆◆ ◆◆ Budget Inn Express 🅼
(307) 686-1989. **$59-$130.** 2011 Rodgers Dr. I-90, exit 124, just n. Int corridors. **Pets:** Medium. $8 daily fee/pet. Designated rooms, service with restrictions, supervision.
SAVE 🆂🅳 ✕ 🛏 ≈

◆◆◆◆ Comfort Inn & Suites of Gillette 🆂🅷
(307) 685-2223. **$89-$209.** 1607 W 2nd Ave. I-90, exit 124, just ne. Int corridors. **Pets:** Accepted.
A$K 🆂🅳 ✕ ℥M ℰ 🛏 🖵 ≈

◆◆◆◆ Holiday Inn Express Hotel & Suites 🆂🅷
(307) 686-9576. **$99-$400.** 1908 Cliff Davis Dr. I-90, exit 126. Int corridors. **Pets:** Accepted.
A$K 🆂🅳 ✕ ℥M ◎ ℰ 🛏 🖵 ≈ ✕

GRAND TETON NATIONAL PARK

◆◆◆ ◆◆◆◆ Flagg Ranch Resort 🅻🅷
(307) 543-2861. **$165-$180, 7 day notice.** Hwy 89. US 89 and 191; 2 mi s of Yellowstone National Park south entrance; 5 mi n of Grand Teton National Park north entrance. Ext corridors. **Pets:** $10 daily fee/pet. Supervision.
SAVE ✕ ℥M ◎ ℰ 🖵 ⑪ ✕ ♘ 📺

◆◆◆◆ Jackson Lake Lodge 🅻🅷
(307) 543-2811. **$189-$650, 7 day notice.** PO Box 250. 5 mi nw of Moran at jct US 89 and 287. Ext/int corridors. **Pets:** $15 daily fee/room. Designated rooms.
✕ ℥M ◎ ℰ 🛏 🖵 ⑪ ≈ ✕ ♘ 📺

◆◆◆ ◆◆ Signal Mountain Lodge 🆂🅷
(307) 543-2831. **$115-$289, 7 day notice.** Inner Park Rd. Teton Park Rd, 2 mi s of US 89, 191 and 287. Ext corridors. **Pets:** $10 daily fee/room. Designated rooms, service with restrictions, supervision.
SAVE ✕ 🛏 🖵 ⑪ ✕ ♘ 📺

◆◆◆ ◆◆ Togwotee Mountain Lodge 🅲🅰 🐾
(307) 543-2847. **$89-$189, 7 day notice.** 27655 Hwys US 26 & 287. 16.5 mi e of Moran at jct US 26 and 287. Ext/int corridors. **Pets:** Other species. Designated rooms.
SAVE ✕ 🛏 🖵 ⑪ ✕

GREEN RIVER

◆◆◆ ◆◆ ◆◆ Oak Tree Inn 🆂🅷
(307) 875-3500. **$68-$75.** 1170 W Flaming Gorge Way. I-80, exit 89, just s. Ext/int corridors. **Pets:** $5 daily fee/pet. Service with restrictions, supervision.
SAVE 🆂🅳 ✕ ℥M ◎ ℰ 🛏 🖵 ⑪

GREYBULL

◆◆◆ ◆◆ Yellowstone Motel 🅼
(307) 765-4456. **$75-$101.** 247 Greybull Ave. 0.4 mi e on US 14. Ext corridors. **Pets:** Accepted.
SAVE 🆂🅳 ✕ 🛏 ≈

GUERNSEY

◆◆◆ ◆◆ The Bunkhouse Motel 🅼
(307) 836-2356. **$55-$65, 7 day notice.** 350 W Whalen. On US 26; center. Ext corridors. **Pets:** $10 daily fee/pet. Service with restrictions, supervision.
SAVE 🆂🅳 ✕ 🛏 🖵

JACKSON

◆◆◆ ◆◆◆◆ 49'er Inn and Suites (Quality Inn and Suites) 🆂🅷
(307) 733-7550. **$72-$215, 14 day notice.** 330 W Pearl St. Just w and just s of town square. Ext/int corridors. **Pets:** Service with restrictions, supervision.
SAVE ✕ ◎ ℰ 🛏 🖵 ✕

◆◆◆ ◆◆ Antler Inn 🆂🅷
(307) 733-2535. **$72-$135, 5 day notice.** 43 W Pearl St. Just s of town square. Ext/int corridors. **Pets:** Dogs only. Service with restrictions, supervision.
SAVE ✕ 🛏 🖵 ✕

◆◆◆ ◆◆ Cowboy Village Resort 🅲🅰 🐾
(307) 733-3121. **$80-$188.** 120 S Flat Creek Dr. 0.3 mi w on Broadway to Flat Creek Dr, just s; downtown. Ext corridors. **Pets:** Dogs only. Service with restrictions, supervision.
SAVE ✕ 🛏 🖵

◆◆◆ ◆◆ Elk Country Inn 🅼 🐾
(307) 733-2364. **$60-$160, 14 day notice.** 480 W Pearl St. Just w, then just s of town square. Ext/int corridors. **Pets:** Other species. Designated rooms, service with restrictions, supervision.
SAVE ✕ 🛏 🖵

◆◆◆ ◆◆◆◆ Homewood Suites by Hilton 🆂🅷
(800) 916-2221. **$329-$409, 3 day notice.** 260 N Millward. Just nw of town square, n on Millward St or w on Mercil Ave, from US 26/89/191 (Broadway). Int corridors. **Pets:** Other species. $100 one-time fee/room. Service with restrictions.
A$K ✕ ℥M ◎ ℰ 🛏 🖵 ≈ ✕

◆◆◆ ◆◆◆ Jackson Hole Lodge 🆂🅷
(307) 733-2992. **$79-$124, 15 day notice.** 420 W Broadway. 0.3 mi w on US 26/89/191. Ext corridors. **Pets:** Medium, other species. $50 deposit/pet. Designated rooms, service with restrictions, supervision.
SAVE 🆂🅳 ✕ ◎ 🛏 🖵 ≈ ✕

◆◆◆ ◆◆ Painted Buffalo Inn 🆂🅷
(307) 733-4340. **$70-$169.** 400 W Broadway. Just w of town square. Ext corridors. **Pets:** Other species. $20 one-time fee/room. Service with restrictions, supervision.
SAVE ✕ ℥M 🛏 ≈

◆◆◆ ◆◆◆◆ Snow King Resort 🅻🅷
(307) 733-5200. **$150-$690.** 400 E Snow King Ave. Just se of town square. Ext/int corridors. **Pets:** $50 one-time fee/room. Designated rooms, service with restrictions, supervision.
SAVE 🆂🅳 ✕ ℰ 🛏 🖵 ⑪ ≈ ✕

◆◆◆ ◆◆ Virginian Lodge 🆂🅷
(307) 733-2792. **$55-$195.** 750 W Broadway. Just w. Ext/int corridors. **Pets:** $10 daily fee/room. Designated rooms, service with restrictions, supervision.
SAVE 🆂🅳 ✕ 🛏 🖵 ⑪ ≈

LANDER

🔺 💎 Holiday Lodge 🅜
(307) 332-2511. **$65-$75.** 210 McFarlane Dr. Just e of jct US 287 and SR 789. Ext corridors. **Pets:** Medium. $10 daily fee/pet. Designated rooms, service with restrictions, crate.
[SAVE] [✕] [📶]

🔺 💎💎 Rodeway Inn 🆂🅷
(307) 332-3940. **$55-$125.** 150 E Main St. Just n of jct US 287 and SR 789. Ext corridors. **Pets:** Medium. $10 one-time fee/pet. Designated rooms, service with restrictions, supervision.
[SAVE] [📶] [✕] [🌙] [📶] [💻] [🍴] [✕]

LARAMIE

💎💎 Days Inn 🆂🅷
(307) 745-5678. **$75-$115.** 1368 McCue St. I-80, exit 310, just e. Int corridors. **Pets:** Small. $15 one-time fee/pet. Designated rooms, service with restrictions, supervision.
[ASK] [📶] [✕] [🌙] [🌙] [🅒] [📶] [💻] [🌊]

🔺 💎 Gas Lite Inn Motel 🅜
(307) 742-6616. **$50-$70.** 960 N 3rd St. I-80, exit 313, 1.6 mi n on US 287; downtown. Ext corridors. **Pets:** Other species. $5 daily fee/pet. Service with restrictions, supervision.
[SAVE] [📶] [✕] [📶] [🌊]

🔺 💎 Sunset Inn 🅜
(307) 742-3741. **$48-$75.** 1104 S 3rd St. I-80, exit 313, just n on US 287. Ext corridors. **Pets:** Medium, dogs only. $100 deposit/room. Designated rooms, service with restrictions, supervision.
[SAVE] [📶] [✕] [📶] [🌊]

🔺 💎 Travelodge Downtown 🅜
(307) 742-6671. **$55-$100.** 165 N 3rd St. I-80, exit 313, 1 mi n on US 287; downtown. Ext corridors. **Pets:** Medium. $50 deposit/pet. Designated rooms, service with restrictions, supervision.
[SAVE] [📶] [✕] [📶] [💻]

LUSK

🔺 💎 Town House Motel, LLC 🅜 🐾
(307) 334-2376. **$50-$70.** 525 S Main St. Just n of jct US 20/85. Ext corridors. **Pets:** Other species. $5 one-time fee/pet. Designated rooms, service with restrictions.
[SAVE] [📶] [✕] [📶] [💻]

NEWCASTLE

🔺 💎 Auto Inn Motel 🅜
(307) 746-2734. **$59-$150.** 2503 W Main St. West end of town on US 16. Ext corridors. **Pets:** $6 daily fee/pet. Designated rooms, service with restrictions, supervision.
[SAVE] [📶] [✕] [📶]

🔺 💎 Sage Motel 🅜
(307) 746-2724. **$50-$70, 3 day notice.** 1227 S Summit Ave. 0.3 mi s of jct US 16 on US 85, just w. Ext corridors. **Pets:** Accepted.
[SAVE] [📶] [✕] [📶] [💻]

PAINTER

💎 Hunter Peak Ranch 🆁🅰
(307) 587-3711. **$130-$175, 90 day notice.** 4027 Crandall Rd. SR 296, 5 mi s of US 212; 40 mi n of SR 120. Ext corridors. **Pets:** Other species. $15 daily fee/room. No service, supervision.
[✕] [📶] [💻] [🍴] [✕] [🅺] [🆆] [✉]

PINEDALE

💎💎 AmeriHost Inn & Suites 🆂🅷
(307) 367-8300. **$89-$159.** 1624 W Pine St. 1 mi n on US 191. Int corridors. **Pets:** $50 deposit/pet. Service with restrictions, supervision.
[ASK] [✕] [📶] [🌙] [🅒] [📶] [🌊]

🔺 💎💎 Best Western Pinedale Inn 🆂🅷
(307) 367-6869. **$80-$160.** 850 W Pine St. 0.5 mi n on US 191. Int corridors. **Pets:** Dogs only. Designated rooms, service with restrictions, supervision.
[SAVE] [📶] [✕] [📶] [💻] [🌊]

💎💎 The Lodge at Pinedale 🆂🅷
(307) 367-8800. **$72-$109.** 1054 W Pine St. 0.7 mi n on US 191. Int corridors. **Pets:** Accepted.
[ASK] [✕] [📶] [💻] [🌊]

🔺 💎 Sun Dance Motel 🅜
(307) 367-4336. **$50-$170.** 148 E Pine St. US 191; city center. Ext corridors. **Pets:** Accepted.
[SAVE] [📶] [✕] [📶] [💻]

POWELL

🔺 💎💎 Kings Inn 🅜
(307) 754-5117. **$69-$125.** 777 E 2nd St. 0.3 mi e on US 14A. Ext corridors. **Pets:** Accepted.
[SAVE] [📶] [✕] [📶] [💻] [🌊]

RAWLINS

🔺 💎💎 Best Western CottonTree Inn 🆂🅷
(307) 324-2737. **$134-$139, 14 day notice.** 2221 W Spruce St. I-80, exit 211, just n. Ext/int corridors. **Pets:** Medium, other species. $10 daily fee/room. Designated rooms, service with restrictions, supervision.
[SAVE] [📶] [✕] [🌙] [📶] [💻] [🍴] [🌊] [✕]

🔺 💎💎 Days Inn Rawlins 🆂🅷 🐾
(307) 324-6615. **$80-$99.** 2222 E Cedar. I-80, exit 215, just n. Int corridors. **Pets:** Other species. $5 daily fee/pet. Designated rooms, service with restrictions, supervision.
[SAVE] [📶] [✕] [🌙] [📶] [💻] [🍴] [🌊]

🔺 💎💎 Oak Tree Inn 🆂🅷
(307) 324-4700. **$79-$99.** 2505 Daley St. I-80, exit 215, 0.5 mi n, then just w on US 287. Int corridors. **Pets:** $10 daily fee/pet. Service with restrictions.
[SAVE] [📶] [✕] [🌙] [🌙] [📶] [💻] [🍴]

🔺 💎💎 Quality Inn of Rawlins 🆂🅷
(307) 324-2783. **$75-$120.** 1801 E Cedar. I-80, exit 215, just w of jct US 287. Int corridors. **Pets:** Accepted.
[SAVE] [📶] [✕] [📶] [💻] [🍴] [🌊]

RIVERTON

💎💎 Comfort Inn & Suites 🆂🅷 🐾
(307) 856-8900. **$75-$139.** 2020 N Federal Blvd. 1.5 mi ne on US 26/SR 789. Int corridors. **Pets:** Large. $10 daily fee/pet. Designated rooms, service with restrictions, supervision.
[ASK] [📶] [✕] [📶] [💻] [🌊]

💎💎 Days Inn 🆂🅷
(307) 856-9677. **$55-$80.** 909 W Main St. 0.5 mi nw on US 26. Ext corridors. **Pets:** Small. $10 daily fee/pet. Designated rooms, service with restrictions, supervision.
[ASK] [📶] [✕] [🅒] [📶]

🔺 💎💎💎 Holiday Inn Convention Center 🆂🅷
(307) 856-8100. **$69-$129.** 900 E Sunset Dr. 0.8 mi ne on US 26/SR 789. Int corridors. **Pets:** Accepted.
[SAVE] [📶] [✕] [🌙] [📶] [💻] [🍴] [🌊]

💎 Paintbrush Motel 🅜
(307) 856-9238. **$49-$64.** 1550 N Federal Blvd. 1.3 mi ne on US 26/SR 789. Ext corridors. **Pets:** Medium, dogs only. $10 one-time fee/pet. Designated rooms, service with restrictions, supervision.
[✕] [📶] [💻]

▼ Super 8 Motel SH
(307) 857-2400. **$55-$90.** 1040 N Federal Blvd. 1 mi ne on US 26/SR 789. Int corridors. **Pets:** $6 daily fee/pet. Service with restrictions, supervision.
ASK S6 ⊠ 🖥

ROCK SPRINGS

▼▼ Econo Lodge SH
(307) 382-4217. **$79-$99.** 1635 Elk St. I-80, exit 104 (Elk St), just n. Ext corridors. **Pets:** Accepted.
ASK S6 ⊠ 🖥 🖵 🏊

▼▼▼ Hampton Inn SH 🐾
(307) 382-9222. **$139-$159.** 1901 Dewar Dr. I-80, exit 102 (Dewar Dr), 1 mi s. Int corridors. **Pets:** Other species. Service with restrictions, supervision.
ASK S6 ⊠ ♿ 🖥 🖵 🏊

▼▼▼ Holiday Inn SH
(307) 382-9200. **$109-$159.** 1675 Sunset Dr. I-80, exit 102 (Dewar Dr), 0.3 mi sw. Ext/int corridors. **Pets:** Medium, other species. $10 daily fee/room. Designated rooms, service with restrictions.
ASK S6 ⊠ 🖉 ♿ 🖥 🖵 🍴 🏊 ✕

▼▼ La Quinta Inn SH
(307) 362-1770. **$109-$139.** 2717 Dewar Dr. I-80, exit 102 (Dewar Dr), just n. Int corridors. **Pets:** Accepted.
ASK S6 ⊠ 🖉 🖥 🖵 🏊

▼ Motel 6–#395 M
(307) 362-1850. **$45-$71.** 2615 Commercial Way. I-80, exit 102 (Dewar Dr), n to Foothills Blvd, then just e. Ext corridors. **Pets:** Medium, other species. Service with restrictions, supervision.
S6 ⊠ ♿ 🖥 🏊

▲▲▲ ▼▼▼ Quality Inn SH
(307) 382-9490. **$110, 30 day notice.** 1670 Sunset Dr. I-80, exit 102 (Dewar Dr), 0.3 mi s, then just w. Ext corridors. **Pets:** Accepted.
SAVE S6 ⊠ ♿ 🖥 🖵 🏊 ✕

SARATOGA

▼▼ Hacienda Motel M
(307) 326-5751. **$69-$82, 7 day notice.** 1500 S First St. 0.5 mi s on SR 130. Int corridors. **Pets:** $5 daily fee/pet. Designated rooms, service with restrictions, supervision.
ASK S6 ⊠ 🖥

SHERIDAN

▲▲▲ ▼▼▼ Americas Best Value Inn M
(307) 672-9757. **$51-$92.** 580 E 5th St. I-90, exit 23, 0.4 mi w. Ext corridors. **Pets:** Accepted.
SAVE S6 ⊠ 🖥

▲▲▲ ▼ Budget Host Inn M
(307) 674-7496. **$55-$125, 3 day notice.** 2007 N Main St. I-90, exit 20, 0.7 mi s; on I-90 business loop. Ext corridors. **Pets:** Accepted.
SAVE ⊠ 🖥 🖵

▲▲▲ ▼▼▼▼ Holiday Inn Atrium & Convention Center SH 🐾
(307) 672-8931. **$119-$139.** 1809 Sugarland Dr. I-90, exit 25, 0.3 mi nw. Int corridors. **Pets:** Large, other species. $50 deposit/room. Service with restrictions, supervision.
SAVE S6 ⊠ 🖉 ♿ 🖥 🖵 🍴 🏊 ✕

▲▲▲ ▼▼▼▼ Mill Inn M
(307) 672-6401. **$65-$120.** 2161 Coffeen Ave. I-90, exit 25, 0.3 mi w. Ext/int corridors. **Pets:** Accepted.
SAVE S6 ⊠ 🖥 🖵

SUNDANCE

▲▲▲ ▼▼ Best Western Inn at Sundance SH 🐾
(307) 283-2800. **$60-$121.** 2719 E Cleveland Ave. I-90, exit 189, just n, then just w on I-90 business loop. Int corridors. **Pets:** Large, other species. $10 daily fee/pet. Service with restrictions, supervision.
SAVE S6 ⊠ 🖥 🖵 🏊

▲▲▲ ▼ Budget Host Arrowhead Motel M
(307) 283-3307. **$39-$69.** 214 Cleveland Ave. I-90 business loop and US 14. Ext corridors. **Pets:** Dogs only. Designated rooms, service with restrictions, supervision.
SAVE ⊠

▲▲▲ ▼▼▼ Rodeway Sundance Mountain Inn M 🐾
(307) 283-3737. **$59-$209.** 26 SR 585. I-90, exit 187, 0.4 mi n. Ext corridors. **Pets:** Medium, other species. $10 daily fee/pet. Service with restrictions, supervision.
SAVE S6 ⊠ 🖥 🖵

TETON VILLAGE

▼▼▼▼ Four Seasons Resort Jackson Hole LH 🐾
(307) 732-5000. **$185-$4250, 30 day notice.** 7680 Granite Loop Rd. Located at the base of Jackson Hole Mountain Resort. Int corridors. **Pets:** Very small, dogs only. Service with restrictions, supervision.
⊠ ♿M 🖉 ♿ 🖥 🖵 🍴 🏊 ✕

THERMOPOLIS

▼▼ Holiday Inn of the Waters SH 🐾
(307) 864-3131. **$87-$139.** 115 E Park St. In Hot Springs State Park. Ext/int corridors. **Pets:** Other species. $10 daily fee/pet. Service with restrictions, supervision.
ASK ⊠ 🖉 ♿ 🖵 🍴 🏊 ✕

▼▼ Hot Springs Super 8 SH
(307) 864-5515. **$54-$124.** Lane 5, Hwy 20 S. On US 20, just se. Int corridors. **Pets:** Accepted.
ASK S6 ⊠ ♿M 🖉 ♿ 🖥 🖵 🏊

TORRINGTON

▼▼ Holiday Inn Express Hotel & Suites SH
(307) 532-7600. **$85-$150.** 1700 E Valley Rd. US 85, e on US 26. Int corridors. **Pets:** Accepted.
ASK S6 ⊠ ♿M 🖉 ♿ 🖥 🖵 🏊 ✕

UCROSS

▲▲▲ ▼▼▼ The Ranch at Ucross RA
(307) 737-2281. **$239, 3 day notice.** 2673 US Hwy 14 E. Jct US 14/16, 0.5 mi w on US 14. Ext/int corridors. **Pets:** Accepted.
SAVE ⊠ 🍴 🏊 ✕ 🎾

WAPITI

▲▲▲ ▼ Green Creek Inn M
(307) 587-5004. **$40-$77.** 2908 Yellowstone Hwy. 2.8 mi w on US 14/16/20. Ext corridors. **Pets:** Accepted.
SAVE S6 ⊠ 🏊

▼ Yellowstone Valley Inn SH
(307) 587-3961. **$49-$169.** 3324 Yellowstone Park Hwy. 3.3 mi w on US 14/16/20. Ext corridors. **Pets:** $15 daily fee/pet. Designated rooms, service with restrictions, supervision.
ASK S6 ⊠ 🖥 🖵 🍴 🏊 ✕ 🏊

WHEATLAND

▲▲▲ ▼▼▼ Best Western Torchlite Motor Inn SH
(307) 322-4070. **$65-$99.** 1809 N 16th St. I-25, exit 78, just e; 1.5 mi n on US 87/I-25 business loop (16th St). Ext corridors. **Pets:** Other species. $5 daily fee/pet. Service with restrictions, supervision.
SAVE ⊠ 🖥 🖵 🏊

WORLAND

▼▼ Days Inn Ⓜ
(307) 347-4251. **$70-$130.** 500 N 10th St. 0.5 mi n on US 20. Ext corridors. **Pets:** Accepted.

ⒶⓈⓀ ⊠ 📧 💻

YELLOWSTONE NATIONAL PARK

ⒶⒶⒶ ▼▼▼ Elephant Head Lodge ☒
(307) 587-3980. **$126-$150, 30 day notice.** 1170 Yellowstone Hwy. 11.7 mi e of Yellowstone National Park East Gate on US 14/16/20. Ext corridors. **Pets:** Other species. $10 one-time fee/pet. Supervision.

ⓈⒶⓋⒺ ⓈⓄ ⊠ 📧 💻 🍴 ⊠ ⓀⒸ Ⓦ Ⓩ

▼ Shoshone Lodge ☒
(307) 587-4044. **$80-$294, 15 day notice.** 349 Yellowstone Hwy. 3.5 mi e of Yellowstone National Park East Gate on US 14/16/20. Ext corridors. **Pets:** $20 deposit/room. Service with restrictions, supervision.

ⒶⓈⓀ ⓈⓄ ⊠ 📧 💻 🍴 ⊠ ⓀⒸ Ⓦ Ⓩ

Canada

ALBERTA

ATHABASCA

◇◇◇ Best Western Athabasca Inn SH
(780) 675-2294. **$99-$119.** 5211 41st Ave. 0.6 mi (1 km) s on Hwy 2. Int corridors. **Pets:** Accepted.
[ASK] [S⊘] [✕] [⊟] [▣] [¶]

BANFF

◇ Banff Rocky Mountain Resort CO
(403) 762-5531. **$165-$445, 3 day notice.** 1029 Banff Ave. Banff Ave and Tunnel Mountain Rd; just s of Trans-Canada Hwy 1. Ext corridors. **Pets:** $15 daily fee/pet. Designated rooms, service with restrictions, supervision.
[ASK] [S⊘] [✕] [⊟] [▣] [¶] [⇋] [✕] [❄]

CAA ◇◇◇ Best Western Siding 29 Lodge SH
(403) 762-5575. **$99-$215.** 453 Marten St. 1 km ne, just off Banff Ave. Int corridors. **Pets:** Accepted.
[SAVE] [S⊘] [✕] [⊟] [▣] [⇋]

CAA ◇◇◇ Castle Mountain Chalets CA
(403) 762-3868. **$145-$335, 14 day notice.** 20 mi (32 km) w on Trans-Canada Hwy 1, jct Castle, 0.6 mi (1 km) ne on Hwy 1A (Bow Valley Pkwy). Ext corridors. **Pets:** Accepted.
[SAVE] [✕] [⊗] [⊟] [▣] [✕] [❄] [☎]

CAA ◇◇◇ ◇◇◇ The Fairmont Banff Springs LH
(403) 762-2211. **$233-$593, 3 day notice.** 405 Spray Ave. Just s on Banff Ave over the bridge, 0.3 mi (0.5 km) e. Int corridors. **Pets:** Accepted.
[SAVE] [S⊘] [✕] [⊗] [⊟] [▣] [¶] [⇋] [✕]

CAA ◇◇◇ Johnston Canyon Resort CA
(403) 762-2971. **$125-$298.** Hwy 1A. 15 mi (24 km) nw on Hwy 1A (Bow Valley Pkwy). Ext corridors. **Pets:** Other species. $10 daily fee/pet. Supervision.
[SAVE] [✕] [⊟] [▣] [¶] [✕] [❄] [☎]

CAA ◇◇◇ Red Carpet Inn SH
(403) 762-4184. **$85-$164.** 425 Banff Ave. 1 km ne. Ext/int corridors. **Pets:** $10 daily fee/room. Designated rooms, service with restrictions, supervision.
[SAVE] [S⊘] [✕] [⊟] [▣]

BROOKS

◇◇◇ Best Western Brooks Inn SH
(403) 363-0080. **$109-$149.** 115 Fifteenth Ave W. Just s off Trans-Canada Hwy 1. Ext/int corridors. **Pets:** Medium. $10 daily fee/pet. Designated rooms, service with restrictions, supervision.
[ASK] [S⊘] [✕] [⊗] [⊟] [▣] [▣] [⇋] [✕]

◇◇ Heritage Inn SH ❀
(403) 362-6666. **$119.** 1217 2nd St W. Trans-Canada Hwy 1, exit Hwy 873, 0.5 mi (0.8 km) s. Int corridors. **Pets:** Large, other species. $10 daily fee/pet. Service with restrictions, supervision.
[ASK] [S⊘] [✕] [⊟] [▣] [¶] [✕]

◇◇◇ Holiday Inn Express Hotel & Suites Brooks SH
(403) 362-7440. **$125-$141.** 1307 2nd St W. Trans-Canada Hwy 1, exit Hwy 873, 0.5 mi (0.8 km) s. Int corridors. **Pets:** Small, dogs only. $25 one-time fee/pet. Designated rooms, service with restrictions, supervision.
[ASK] [S⊘] [✕] [◢] [⊟] [▣] [⇋]

◇◇ Travelodge Brooks SH ❀
(403) 362-8000. **$93.** 1240 Cassils Rd E. Trans-Canada Hwy 1, just sw on SR 542, exit E Brooks. Ext/int corridors. **Pets:** $7 daily fee/room. Designated rooms, service with restrictions.
[ASK] [S⊘] [✕] [⊙M] [⊟] [▣]

CALGARY METROPOLITAN AREA

AIRDRIE

CAA ◇◇◇ ◇ Ramada Inn & Suites SH
(403) 945-1288. **$119-$159.** 191 E Lake Crescent. Hwy 2, exit E Airdrie. Int corridors. **Pets:** Medium, other species. $13 daily fee/pet. Service with restrictions, supervision.
[SAVE] [✕] [⊙M] [⊗] [⊟] [▣] [¶] [⇋]

◇◇ Super 8 Motel-Airdrie SH
(403) 948-4188. **$79-$120.** 815 E Lake Blvd. Hwy 2, exit E Airdrie, 0.8 km e on Hwy 587 E. Int corridors. **Pets:** Accepted.
[ASK] [S⊘] [⊟] [▣]

CALGARY

◇◇ 5 Calgary Downtown Suites LH ❀
(403) 263-0520. **$300-$350.** 618 5th Ave SW. Corner of 5th Ave SW and 5th St SW. Int corridors. **Pets:** Other species. $10 daily fee/pet. Service with restrictions, crate.
[ASK] [S⊘] [✕] [⊟] [▣] [¶] [⇋] [✕]

◇◇◇ Blackfoot Inn SH ❀
(403) 252-2253. **$115-$229.** 5940 Blackfoot Tr SE. At 58th Ave SE; access to property from 58th Ave only. Int corridors. **Pets:** Other species. Designated rooms, service with restrictions, crate.
[ASK] [✕] [⊗] [▣] [¶] [⇋] [✕]

CAA ◇◇◇ ◇ Calgary Marriott Hotel LH
(403) 266-7331. **$139-$429.** 110 9th Ave SE. Jct 9th Ave and Centre St; adjacent to Telus Convention Centre. Int corridors. **Pets:** Other species.
[SAVE] [✕] [◢] [⊗] [⊟] [▣] [¶] [⇋] [✕]

CAA ◇◇◇ ◇ Calgary Westways Guest House BB ❀
(403) 229-1758. **$79-$150, 4 day notice.** 216 25th Ave SW. 1.7 km s on Hwy 2A (MacLeod Trail S), 0.5 km w. Int corridors. **Pets:** Other species. $8 daily fee/pet.
[SAVE] [S⊘] [✕]

Ⓐ ▼▼▼ **Carriage House Inn** 🆂🅷 ❀
(403) 253-1101. **$109-$159, 3 day notice.** 9030 MacLeod Tr S. On Hwy 2A (MacLeod Trail); corner of 90th Ave SW. Int corridors. **Pets:** Other species. $10 daily fee/pet. Designated rooms, service with restrictions, supervision.
🆂🅰🆅🅴 🆂🖧 ▤ 🔒 🖵 🍽 🏊 ⊠

▼▼▼ **Coast Plaza Hotel & Conference Centre** 🅻🅷 ❀
(403) 248-8888. **$119-$199.** 1316 33rd St NE. Just s of jct 16th Ave (Trans-Canada Hwy 1) and 36th St NE, just w on 12th Ave NE. Int corridors. **Pets:** Large, other species. $20 one-time fee/room. Designated rooms, service with restrictions, supervision.
🅰🆂🅺 ⊠ 🖧🅼 🔒 🖵 🍽 🏊 ⊠

▼▼▼ **Delta Bow Valley** 🅻🅷
(403) 266-1980. **$109-$259.** 209 4th Ave SE. 1st St SE and 4th Ave SE. Int corridors. **Pets:** Accepted.
🅰🆂🅺 🆂🖧 ⊠ 🔒 🖵 🍽 🏊 ⊠

▼▼▼ **Delta Calgary Airport** 🅻🅷
(403) 291-2600. **$143-$260.** 2001 Airport Rd NE. At Calgary International Airport. Int corridors. **Pets:** Accepted.
🅰🆂🅺 🆂🖧 ⊠ 🔒 🖵 🍽 🏊

Ⓐ ▼▼▼ **Delta Calgary South** 🆂🅷 ❀
(403) 278-5050. **$129-$209, 5 day notice.** 135 Southland Dr SE. On Hwy 2A (MacLeod Trail); corner of Southland Dr. Int corridors. **Pets:** Small. $35 one-time fee/room. Service with restrictions, supervision.
🆂🅰🆅🅴 🆂🖧 ⊠ 🔒 🖵 🍽 🏊 ⊠

Ⓐ ▼▼ **Econo Lodge South** 🅼
(403) 252-4401. **$79-$129.** 7505 MacLeod Tr S. Corner of MacLeod Trail and 75th Ave. Ext/int corridors. **Pets:** Small. $10 daily fee/pet. Designated rooms, service with restrictions, supervision.
🆂🅰🆅🅴 🆂🖧 ⊠ 🔒 🖵 🏊

▼▼▼ **Executive Royal Inn North Calgary** 🆂🅷
(403) 291-2003. **$119.** 2828 23rd St NE. 27th Ave NE and Barlow Trail. Int corridors. **Pets:** Accepted.
🅰🆂🅺 ⊠ 🖧🅼 🔒 🖵 🍽 ⊠

▼▼ ▼▼ **The Fairmont Palliser** 🅻🅷 ❀
(403) 262-1234. **$149-$459, 7 day notice.** 133 9th Ave SW. 9th Ave SW and 1st St SW. Int corridors. **Pets:** Large. $25 daily fee/pet. Service with restrictions, crate.
🅰🆂🅺 🆂🖧 ⊠ 🖵 🍽 🏊 ⊠

Ⓐ ▼▼▼▼ **Greenwood Inn Hotels** 🆂🅷
(403) 250-8855. **$119-$249.** 3515 26th St NE. From Barlow Trail N, just e on 32nd Ave NE, then just n. Int corridors. **Pets:** Other species. $10 daily fee/room. Designated rooms, service with restrictions, crate.
🆂🅰🆅🅴 🆂🖧 ⊠ 🖧 🔒 🖵 🍽 🏊 ⊠

Ⓐ ▼▼▼ **Holiday Inn Calgary-Airport** 🆂🅷
(800) 465-4329. **$119-$139.** 1250 McKinnon Dr NE. 0.6 mi (1 km) e of jct Hwy 2 (Deerfoot Trail) and 16th Ave NE (Trans-Canada Hwy 1). Int corridors. **Pets:** Medium. $10 daily fee/pet. Designated rooms, service with restrictions, supervision.
🆂🅰🆅🅴 🆂🖧 ⊠ 🔒 🖵 🍽 🏊

Ⓐ ▼▼▼ **Holiday Inn Express Calgary-University** 🆂🅷
(403) 289-6600. **$130-$250.** 2227 Banff Tr NW. 16th Ave NW (Trans-Canada Hwy 1) and Banff Trail NW. Int corridors. **Pets:** Other species. Designated rooms, service with restrictions, supervision.
🆂🅰🆅🅴 🆂🖧 ⊠ 🖧🅼 🖧 🔒 🖵

Ⓐ ▼▼▼ **Holiday Inn Express Hotel & Suites Calgary Downtown** 🆂🅷
(403) 269-8262. **$159-$289.** 1020 8th Ave SW. 8th Ave at 10th St SW. Int corridors. **Pets:** Accepted.
🆂🅰🆅🅴 🆂🖧 ⊠ 🔒 🖵

▼▼▼▼ **Holiday Inn Express Hotel & Suites Calgary-South** 🆂🅷
(403) 225-3000. **$127-$199.** 12025 Lake Fraser Dr SE (MacLeod Trail S). Hwy 2 (Deerfoot Trail), exit Anderson Rd W, then just s on MacLeod Trail. Int corridors. **Pets:** Small. $10 one-time fee/pet. Designated rooms, service with restrictions, supervision.
🅰🆂🅺 🆂🖧 ⊠ 🔒 🖵 🖵 ⊠

Ⓐ ▼▼▼ **Hotel Arts** 🆂🅷
(403) 266-4611. **$119-$349.** 119 12th Ave SW. At 1st St SW; centre. Int corridors. **Pets:** Accepted.
🆂🅰🆅🅴 ⊠ 🖧🅼 🖧 🔒 🖵 🍽 🏊

▼▼▼ **International Hotel of Calgary** 🅻🅷
(403) 265-9600. **$259-$349.** 220 4th Ave SW. Corner of 4th Ave and 2nd St SW. Int corridors. **Pets:** Accepted.
🅰🆂🅺 🆂🖧 ⊠ 🖵 🍽 🏊 ⊠

▼▼▼ **Marriott Residence Inn-Calgary Airport** 🆂🅷
(403) 735-3336. **$129-$299.** 2622 39th Ave NE. Corner of Barlow Trail and 39th Ave NE. Int corridors. **Pets:** Small. $100 one-time fee/pet. Service with restrictions, crate.
🅰🆂🅺 ⊠ 🖧🅼 🖧 🔒 🖵 🏊 ⊠

▼▼▼ **Radisson Hotel Calgary Airport** 🆂🅷
(403) 291-4666. **$139-$269.** 2120 16th Ave NE. Just e of jct 16th Ave NE (Trans-Canada Hwy 1) and Hwy 2 (Deerfoot Trail). Int corridors. **Pets:** Accepted.
🅰🆂🅺 🆂🖧 ⊠ 🖧🅼 🔒 🖵 🍽 🏊

▼▼▼ **Sandman Hotel Downtown Calgary** 🅻🅷
(403) 237-8626. **$129-$190.** 888 7th Ave SW. Corner of 7th Ave SW and 8th St SW. Int corridors. **Pets:** Accepted.
🅰🆂🅺 🆂🖧 ⊠ 🔒 🖵 🍽 🏊

▼▼▼ **Sandman Hotel Suites & Spa Calgary Airport** 🆂🅷
(403) 219-2475. **$119-$179.** 25 Hopewell Way NE. Just n of jct Barlow Trail and McKnight Blvd. Int corridors. **Pets:** Accepted.
🅰🆂🅺 🆂🖧 ⊠ 🖵 🍽 🏊 ⊠

▼▼▼ **Sheraton Cavalier Hotel** 🅻🅷 ❀
(403) 291-0107. **$229-$299.** 2620 32nd Ave NE. Barlow Trail at 32nd Ave NE. Int corridors. **Pets:** Supervision.
🅰🆂🅺 ⊠ 🖵 🍽 🏊 ⊠

Ⓐ ▼▼▼▼ **Sheraton Suites Calgary Eau Claire** 🅻🅷 ❀
(403) 266-7200. **$169-$579.** 255 Barclay Parade SW. At 3rd St SW and 2nd Ave SW. Int corridors. **Pets:** Large, dogs only. Designated rooms, service with restrictions, supervision.
🆂🅰🆅🅴 🆂🖧 ⊠ 🖧 🔒 🖵 🍽 🏊 ⊠

Ⓐ ▼▼▼ **Super 8 Motel Calgary Airport** 🆂🅷
(403) 291-9888. **$115-$200.** 3030 Barlow Tr NE. Corner of 32nd Ave and Barlow Trail NE. Int corridors. **Pets:** Small, dogs only. $25 daily fee/pet. Service with restrictions, supervision.
🆂🅰🆅🅴 🆂🖧 ⊠ 🔒

▼▼▼ **Travelodge Hotel Calgary Airport** 🆂🅷
(403) 291-1260. **$99-$159.** 2750 Sunridge Blvd NE. Just se of jct 32nd Ave NE and Barlow Trail NE. Int corridors. **Pets:** Other species. $100 deposit/room. Service with restrictions, crate.
🅰🆂🅺 🆂🖧 ⊠ 🔒 🖵 🍽 🏊

Ⓐ ▼▼▼▼ **The Westin Calgary** 🅻🅷 ❀
(403) 266-1611. **$129-$319.** 320 4th Ave SW. Corner of 4th Ave SW and 3rd St. Int corridors. **Pets:** Medium. Service with restrictions, crate.
🆂🅰🆅🅴 🆂🖧 ⊠ 🖧🅼 🖧 🖵 🍽 🏊 ⊠

(AA) ▽▽▽▽ **Wingate Inn** SH ❀
(403) 514-0099. **$149-$299.** 400 Midpark Way. Hwy 2A (MacLeod Trail), 0.3 mi (0.5 km) e on Sun Valley, just n on Midpark Way, then just s. Int corridors. **Pets:** Other species. $25 daily fee/pet. Service with restrictions.

SAVE [S0] ⊠ [¿] 🛏 💻 🏊 ⊠

COCHRANE

(AA) ▽▽ ▽▽ **Best Western Harvest Country Inn** SH
(403) 932-1410. **$99-$139.** 11 West Side Dr. Hwy 1A, 0.6 mi (1 km) sw on Hwy 22. Ext/int corridors. **Pets:** Accepted.

A$K [S0] ⊠ 🛏 💻

(AA) ▽▽ ▽▽ **Bow River Inn** M
(403) 932-7900. **$69-$139.** 3 West Side Dr. Hwy 1A, 0.6 mi (1 km) sw on Hwy 22. Ext corridors. **Pets:** Accepted.

SAVE [S0] ⊠ 🛏 💻

▽▽ ▽▽ **Super 8 Motel-Cochrane** SH
(403) 932-6355. **$140-$180, 14 day notice.** 10 Westside Dr. Hwy 1A, 0.6 mi (1 km) sw on Hwy 22. Int corridors. **Pets:** Accepted.

A$K [S0] ⊠ 🛏 💻 🏊 ⊠

▽▽ ▽▽ **Travelodge Cochrane** SH
(403) 932-5588. **$89-$189.** 5 West Side Dr. Hwy 1A, 0.6 mi (1 km) sw on Hwy 22. Int corridors. **Pets:** Medium, other species. $10 daily fee/pet. Designated rooms, service with restrictions, supervision.

A$K [S0] ⊠ 🛏 💻 🏊

OKOTOKS

(AA) ▽▽▽▽ **Lakeview Inns & Suites-Okotoks** SH ❀
(403) 938-7400. **$124.** 22 Southridge Dr. Hwy 2, exit 2A, 2.5 mi (4 km) s to Southridge Dr. Int corridors. **Pets:** Other species. $10 daily fee/pet. Designated rooms, service with restrictions, supervision.

SAVE [S0] ⊠ 🛏 💻

STRATHMORE

(AA) ▽▽ ▽▽ **Best Western Strathmore Inn** SH
(403) 934-5777. **$83-$158.** 550 Hwy 1. Trans-Canada Hwy 1, jct SR 817; centre. Int corridors. **Pets:** $10 one-time fee/room. Designated rooms, service with restrictions, supervision.

SAVE [S0] ⊠ 🛏 💻 🏊

▽▽ ▽▽ **Travelodge Strathmore** SH
(403) 901-0000. **$129-$139.** 350 Ridge Rd. Just n of Trans-Canada Hwy 1 at Ridge Rd. Int corridors. **Pets:** $10 daily fee/room. Designated rooms, service with restrictions, supervision.

A$K [S0] ⊠ 🛏 💻 🏊 ⊠

END METROPOLITAN AREA

CAMROSE

▽▽ ▽▽ **Norsemen Inn** SH
(780) 672-9171. **$89-$109.** 6505 48th Ave. Hwy 13 (48th Ave) at 65th St; west end of town. Int corridors. **Pets:** Accepted.

A$K [S0] ⊠ 🛏 💻 🍴

CANMORE

(AA) ▽▽ ▽▽ **Banff Boundary Lodge** CO
(403) 678-9555. **$79-$269, 3 day notice.** 1000 Harvie Heights Rd. Just e of Banff National Park east gate, parallel to Trans-Canada Hwy 1, exit Harvie Heights Rd. Ext corridors. **Pets:** Accepted.

SAVE [S0] ⊠ 🛏 💻 🐾

(AA) ▽▽ ▽▽ **Canadian Rockies Chalets** CO
(403) 678-3799. **$79-$223.** 1206 Bow Valley Tr. 3.6 mi (5.8 km) e of Banff National Park east gate on Hwy 1A (Bow Valley Trail); Trans-Canada Hwy 1, exit Canmore. Ext corridors. **Pets:** Dogs only. $15 daily fee/pet. Service with restrictions, supervision.

SAVE [S0] ⊠ 🛏 💻 🐾

(AA) ▽▽▽▽ **Canmore Inn & Suites** SH
(403) 609-4656. **$89-$240.** 1402 Bow Valley Tr. 3.5 mi (5.6 km) e of Banff National Park east gate on Hwy 1A (Bow Valley Trail); Trans-Canada Hwy 1, exit Canmore. Int corridors. **Pets:** Accepted.

SAVE [S0] ⊠ 🛏 💻 🏊 ⊠

▽▽ ▽▽ **The Lodges at Canmore** SH
(403) 678-9350. **$164-$294, 5 day notice.** 107 Montane Rd. Trans-Canada Hwy 1, exit 1A (Bow Valley Trail), 0.6 mi (1.6 km) w to Montane Rd. Int corridors. **Pets:** Accepted.

A$K ⊠ 🛏 💻 🏊

▽▽ ▽▽ **Mystic Springs Chalets & Hot Pools** CO ❀
(403) 609-0333. **$185-$335, 5 day notice.** 140 Kananaskis Way. Trans-Canada Hwy 1, exit 1A (Bow Valley Trail), 0.6 mi (1 km)w, then n at Montane Dr. Ext corridors. **Pets:** Medium. $20 daily fee/room. Designated rooms, service with restrictions, crate.

A$K [S0] ⊠ 🛏 💻 🏊 ⊠

(AA) ▽▽▽▽ **Radisson Hotel & Conference Centre** SH ❀
(403) 678-3625. **$99-$349.** 511 Bow Valley Tr. Trans-Canada Hwy 1, exit Canmore; 6 km e of Banff National Park east gate on Hwy 1A (Bow Valley Trail). Ext/int corridors. **Pets:** $15 daily fee/pet. Service with restrictions, supervision.

SAVE [S0] ⊠ 🛏 💻 🍴 🏊 ⊠

(AA) ▽▽▽▽ **Residence Inn by Marriott Canmore** SH
(403) 678-3400. **$149-$279, 7 day notice.** 91 Three Sisters Dr. Trans-Canada Hwy 1, exit Three Sisters Pkwy, then 2.5 mi (4 km) n. Int corridors. **Pets:** Accepted.

SAVE [S0] ⊠ [&M] [?] [¿] 🛏 💻 🏊 ⊠

(AA) ▽▽▽▽ **Rocky Mountain Ski Lodge** M
(403) 678-5445. **$69-$205.** 1711 Bow Valley Tr. Trans-Canada Hwy 1, exit Canmore; 3 mi (4.8 km) e of Banff National Park east gate on Hwy 1A (Bow Valley Trail). Ext corridors. **Pets:** $5 daily fee/pet. Designated rooms, service with restrictions, supervision.

SAVE [S0] ⊠ 🛏 💻 ⊠

(AA) ▽▽ ▽▽ **Rundle Mountain Lodge** M ❀
(403) 678-5322. **$69-$129, 7 day notice.** 1723 Bow Valley Tr. Trans-Canada Hwy 1, exit Canmore; 3 mi (4.8 km) e of Banff National Park east gate on Hwy 1A (Bow Valley Trail). Ext corridors. **Pets:** Other species. $10 daily fee/pet. Service with restrictions, supervision.

SAVE [S0] ⊠ 🛏 💻 🏊

(AA) ▽▽ ▽▽ **Rundle Ridge Chalets** CA
(403) 678-5387. **$84-$215.** 1100 Harvie Heights Rd. Trans-Canada Hwy 1, exit Harvie Heights Rd; (1 km) e of Banff National Park east gate. Ext corridors. **Pets:** Accepted.

SAVE ⊠ 🛏 ⊠ 🐾 🐾

(AA) ▽▽ ▽▽ **Windtower Lodge & Suites** CO
(403) 609-6600. **$129-$399, 3 day notice.** 160 Kananaskis Way. Trans-Canada Hwy 1, exit 1A (Bow Valley Trail), 0.6 mi (1 km) w, then n at Montane Dr. Int corridors. **Pets:** Accepted.

SAVE [S0] ⊠ 🛏 💻 🍴 🐾

CLAIRMONT

◆◆◆ **Ramada Inn & Suites** [SH] 🐾
(780) 814-7448. **$169-$229, 3 day notice.** 7201 99 St. Jct Hwy 43 and 2, just n. Int corridors. **Pets:** Other species. $25 one-time fee/room. Service with restrictions, crate.
⊠ ▣ 📺

CLARESHOLM

◆◆ **Bluebird Motel** [M]
(403) 625-3395. **$69-$86.** 5505 1st St W. 0.3 mi (0.5 km) n on Hwy 2. Ext corridors. **Pets:** Other species. Designated rooms, service with restrictions, supervision.
⊠ ▣ 📺

DRAYTON VALLEY

◆◆ **Lakeview Inns & Suites** [SH]
(780) 542-3200. **$129-$159.** 4302 50th St. Hwy 22, exit Drayton Valley, just n. Int corridors. **Pets:** Accepted.
⊠ ▣ 📺 🍴 ⛌

DRUMHELLER

[CAA] ◆◆◆ **Inn at Heartwood Manor** [CI]
(403) 823-6495. **$89-$299, 3 day notice.** 320 N Railway Ave E. Just e of Hwy 9; downtown. Int corridors. **Pets:** Accepted.
[SAVE] ⊠ ▣ 📺

◆◆◆ **Ramada Inn & Suites** [SH]
(403) 823-2028. **$149-$179, 30 day notice.** 680 2nd St SE. Off Hwy 9. Ext/int corridors. **Pets:** Accepted.
[A$K] [SD] ⊠ [&M] ♿ ▣ 📺 🏊 ⛌

◆◆ **Super 8 Motel** [SH]
(403) 823-8887. **$129-$169.** 600-680 2nd St SE. Off Hwy 9. Ext/int corridors. **Pets:** Other species. $10 daily fee/pet. Designated rooms, service with restrictions, supervision.
[A$K] [SD] ⊠ ▣ 📺 🏊 ⛌

EDMONTON METROPOLITAN AREA

EDMONTON

◆◆ **Alberta Place Suite Hotel** [CO]
(780) 423-1565. **$89-$150.** 10049 103rd St. Just s of Jasper Ave. Int corridors. **Pets:** Accepted.
[A$K] [SD] ⊠ ▣ 📺 🍴 🏊

[CAA] ◆◆ **Best Western Cedar Park Inn** [SH] 🐾
(780) 434-7411. **$109, 21 day notice.** 5116 Gateway Blvd. Hwy 2 (Gateway Blvd) at 51st Ave. Int corridors. **Pets:** Other species. Designated rooms, service with restrictions, supervision.
[SAVE] ⊠ ▣ 📺 🍴 🏊

[CAA] ◆◆ **Chateau Louis Hotel & Conference Centre** [SH]
(780) 452-7770. **$109-$199.** 11727 Kingsway. On Kingsway and 117th St. Int corridors. **Pets:** Medium, other species. $5 daily fee/pet. Designated rooms, service with restrictions, crate.
[SAVE] [SD] ⊠ [&M] 👂 ♿ ▣ 📺 🍴

[CAA] ◆◆ **Comfort Inn West** [SH] 🐾
(780) 484-4415. **$105-$129, 14 day notice.** 17610 100th Ave. At 176th St. Int corridors. **Pets:** Medium. $10 daily fee/pet. Service with restrictions, supervision.
[SAVE] [SD] ⊠ ▣ 📺 🍴

[CAA] ◆◆ **Continental Inn** [SH]
(780) 484-7751. **$95-$121, 7 day notice.** 16625 Stony Plain Rd. On Hwy 16A (Stony Plain Rd) at 166th St. Int corridors. **Pets:** Accepted.
[SAVE] [SD] ⊠ ▣ 📺 🍴

◆◆◆ **Delta Edmonton Centre Suite Hotel** [LH]
(780) 429-3900. **$180.** 10222 102nd St. At 102nd St at 103rd Ave. Int corridors. **Pets:** Accepted.
[A$K] [SD] ⊠ 👂 ♿ 📺 🍴 ⛌

◆◆◆ **Delta Edmonton South Hotel and Conference Centre** [LH]
(780) 434-6415. **$114-$231.** 4404 Gateway Blvd. Jct Calgary Trail (Hwy 2) and Whitemud Dr. Int corridors. **Pets:** Accepted.
[A$K] [SD] ⊠ ▣ 📺 🍴 🏊

◆◆ **Executive Royal Inn West Edmonton** [SH]
(780) 484-6000. **$131-$142.** 10010 178th St. Corner of 178th St and 100th Ave. Int corridors. **Pets:** Accepted.
[A$K] [SD] ⊠ ▣ 📺 🍴 ⛌

[CAA] ◆◆◆◆ **The Fairmont Hotel Macdonald** [LH]
(780) 424-5181. **$143-$413.** 10065 100th St. Just s of Jasper Ave. Int corridors. **Pets:** Other species. $25 daily fee/room. Service with restrictions, supervision.
[SAVE] [SD] ⊠ [&M] 📺 🍴 🏊 ⛌

[CAA] ◆◆◆ **Four Points by Sheraton Edmonton South** [LH]
(780) 465-7931. **$115-$195.** 7230 Argyll Rd. Hwy 2 (Gateway Blvd), 2.3 mi (3.7 km) e at 63rd Ave (which becomes Argyll Rd); at 75th St. Int corridors. **Pets:** Small. $10 daily fee/pet. Designated rooms, service with restrictions, supervision.
[SAVE] [SD] ⊠ ▣ 📺 🍴 🏊

[CAA] ◆◆◆ **Greenwood Hotel & Suites** [SH]
(780) 431-1100. **$104-$199.** 4485 Gateway Blvd. Hwy 2 (Gateway Blvd), just n of Whitemud Dr. Int corridors. **Pets:** Accepted.
[SAVE] ⊠ [&M] 👂 ♿ ▣ 📺 🍴 🏊 ⛌

[CAA] ◆◆◆ **Holiday Inn Convention Centre (S.E. Edmonton)** [SH]
(780) 468-5400. **$129-$139.** 4520 76th Ave. Hwy 14, just s via 50th St exit, then just e. Int corridors. **Pets:** Accepted.
[SAVE] ⊠ 👂 ▣ 📺 🍴 🏊 ⛌

◆◆◆ **Holiday Inn Edmonton-The Palace** [SH]
(780) 438-1222. **$139, 12 day notice.** 4235 Gateway Blvd. Just s of Whitemud Dr. Int corridors. **Pets:** Accepted.
[A$K] [SD] ⊠ ▣ 📺 🍴

[CAA] ◆◆◆ **Holiday Inn Express Edmonton-Downtown** [SH]
(780) 423-2450. **$119.** 10010 104th St. Corner of 100th Ave; centre. Int corridors. **Pets:** Medium. $25 one-time fee/pet. Service with restrictions, supervision.
[SAVE] [SD] ⊠ ▣ 📺 🏊 ⛌

[CAA] ◆◆◆ **Mayfield Inn & Suites at West Edmonton** [LH]
(780) 484-0821. **$130-$185.** 16615 109th Ave. 1 mi (1.6 km) n of jct Hwy 2 (Gateway Blvd) and 16A on Mayfield Rd. Int corridors. **Pets:** Accepted.
[SAVE] [SD] ⊠ ▣ 📺 🍴 🏊 ⛌

◆◆◆ **Metterra Hotel on Whyte** [SH]
(780) 465-8150. **$350-$400.** 10454 82nd Ave (Whyte Ave). Just e of 105th St. Int corridors. **Pets:** Medium, other species. $25 one-time fee/room. Designated rooms, service with restrictions, crate.
[A$K] [SD] ⊠ 📺

(CAA) ♦♦♦ **Rosslyn Inn & Suites** **SH** 🐾
(780) 476-6241. **$80-$93.** 13620 97 St. Hwy 16 (Yellowhead Hwy), exit 97th St, 1 mi (1.6 km) n. Int corridors. **Pets:** Medium. $10 daily fee/pet. Designated rooms, service with restrictions, crate.
SAVE 🚭 ⊗ 🛏 💻 🍴

♦♦ **Signature Suite Hotel Edmonton House** **CO**
(780) 420-4000. **$119-$240.** 10205 100th Ave. Just se of jct 102nd St and 100th Ave. Int corridors. **Pets:** Accepted.
A$K 🚭 ⊗ 🛏 💻 🍴 ⊷ ⊗

(CAA) ♦♦ **Super 8 Hotel** **SH**
(780) 433-8688. **$119-$179.** 3610 Gateway Blvd. Jct 36th Ave. Int corridors. **Pets:** Accepted.
SAVE 🚭 ⊗ 🛏 💻 ⊷

♦♦♦ **The Sutton Place Hotel, Edmonton** **LH**
(780) 428-7111. **$192-$344.** 10235 101st St. 102nd Ave at 101st St. Int corridors. **Pets:** Small. $20 one-time fee/room. Service with restrictions, supervision.
A$K ⊗ 🛏 💻 🍴 ⊷ ⊗

(CAA) ♦♦♦ **Travelodge Beverly Crest** **SH** 🐾
(780) 474-0456. **$89-$149, 30 day notice.** 3414 118th Ave. 5 mi (8 km) e of Capilano Dr, 0.6 mi (1 km) s from W Hwy 16 (Yellowhead Trail) on Victoria Trail exit. Int corridors. **Pets:** Very small, dogs only. $30 daily fee/pet. Designated rooms, supervision.
SAVE ⊗ 💻 🍴

♦♦ **Travelodge Edmonton South** **SH** 🐾
(780) 436-9770. **$94-$129.** 10320 45th Ave S. Jct Calgary Trail (Hwy 2) and 45th Ave, just n of Whitemud Dr. Int corridors. **Pets:** Designated rooms, service with restrictions, supervision.
A$K 🚭 ⊗ 🛏 💻 ⊷

♦♦ **Travelodge Edmonton West** **SH**
(780) 483-6031. **$109-$144.** 18320 Stony Plain Rd. Hwy 16A (Stony Plain Rd) at 184th St. Int corridors. **Pets:** Medium. $50 deposit/pet. Designated rooms, service with restrictions, supervision.
A$K 🚭 ⊗ 🛏 💻 🍴 ⊷ ⊗

♦♦♦ **Varscona Hotel on Whyte** **SH**
(780) 434-6111. **$290-$340.** 8208 106th St. Corner of 82nd Ave (Whyte Ave) and 106th St. Int corridors. **Pets:** Medium, other species. $25 one-time fee/room. Designated rooms, crate.
A$K 🚭 ⊗ 💻 🍴

(CAA) ♦♦♦♦ **The Westin Edmonton** **LH**
(780) 426-3636. **$329.** 10135 100th St. 101st Ave at 100th St. Int corridors. **Pets:** Accepted.
SAVE ⊗ 🦮 💻 🍴 ⊷ ⊗

(CAA) ♦♦♦♦ **Wingate Inn Edmonton West** **SH**
(780) 443-1000. **$135-$309.** 18220 100th Ave. 100th Ave at 182nd St. Int corridors. **Pets:** $25 one-time fee/pet. Designated rooms, service with restrictions.
SAVE 🚭 ⊗ 🦮 🛏 💻 ⊷ ⊗

LEDUC

♦♦♦♦ **Executive Royal Inn Hotel & Conference Centre** **SH**
(780) 986-1840. **$105-$115.** 8450 Sparrow Dr. Hwy 2, 0.6 mi (1 km) e. Int corridors. **Pets:** Medium. $10 one-time fee/room. Designated rooms, service with restrictions, supervision.
A$K 🚭 ⊗ 🦮 🛏 💻 🍴

NISKU

(CAA) ♦♦♦♦ **Holiday Inn Express Edmonton Int'l Airport** **SH**
(780) 955-1000. **$113-$180.** 1102 4th St. Hwy 2, exit Edmonton International Airport/Nisku Business Park (10th Ave), 0.5 mi (0.8 km) e. Int corridors. **Pets:** Medium, other species. $25 daily fee/pet. Designated rooms, service with restrictions, supervision.
SAVE 🚭 ⊗ 🦮 🦮 🦮 🛏 💻 ⊷ ⊗

(CAA) ♦♦♦ **Nisku Inn & Conference Centre-Edmonton Airport** **SH**
(780) 955-7744. **$149.** 1101 4th St. Hwy 2, exit Edmonton International Airport/Nisku Business Park (10th Ave), 0.3 mi (0.5 km) e. Int corridors. **Pets:** Other species. $20 daily fee/pet.
SAVE 🚭 ⊗ 🦮 🛏 💻 🍴 ⊷

SHERWOOD PARK

(CAA) ♦♦♦ **Franklin's Inn** **SH**
(780) 467-1234. **$85-$95, 7 day notice.** 2016 Sherwood Dr. At Granada Blvd. Int corridors. **Pets:** Accepted.
SAVE 🚭 ⊗ 🛏 💻 🍴

(CAA) ♦♦♦ **Ramada Limited-Edmonton East/Sherwood Park** **SH**
(780) 467-6727. **$144-$184.** 30 Broadway Blvd. Hwy 16, exit Broadmoor Blvd, 1.2 mi (2 km) s. Int corridors. **Pets:** Medium. $200 deposit/pet, $15 daily fee/pet. Designated rooms, service with restrictions, supervision.
SAVE 🚭 ⊗ 🦮 🛏 💻

(CAA) ♦♦♦ **Roadking Inns** **SH**
(780) 464-1000. **$99-$149.** 26 Strathmoor Dr. Just sw of Hwy 16, exit Broadmoor Blvd. Int corridors. **Pets:** Accepted.
SAVE 🚭 ⊗ 🛏 💻 🍴

SPRUCE GROVE

♦♦♦ **Royal Inn Express Hotel** **SH** 🐾
(780) 962-6050. **$93-$219.** 20 Westgrove Dr. I-16A, Hwy 16A, just n. Int corridors. **Pets:** Small, dogs only. $10 daily fee/pet. Designated rooms, supervision.
A$K 🚭 ⊗ 🛏 💻

STONY PLAIN

♦♦ **Ramada Inn & Suites** **SH**
(780) 963-0222. **$92-$164.** 3301 43rd Ave. Hwy 16A, exit Dunmore Rd, just s. Ext/int corridors. **Pets:** Accepted.
A$K 🚭 ⊗ 🛏 💻 🍴 ⊷

♦ **Stony Convention Inn** **SH**
(780) 963-3444. **$77-$97.** 4620 48th St. Hwy 16A, exit Stony Plain Rd, 0.5 mi (0.8 km) s on SR 779. Int corridors. **Pets:** Accepted.
A$K 🚭 ⊗ 🛏 💻 🍴

END METROPOLITAN AREA

EDSON

▼▼▼▼ Best Western High Road Inn SH
(780) 712-2378. **$130.** 300 52nd St. On 2nd Ave; centre. Int corridors.
Pets: $10 daily fee/pet. Designated rooms, supervision.
⊠ 🖥 🖩 🍽 🛏 ⊠

(CAA) ▼▼▼ Guest House Inn & Suites M
(780) 723-4486. **$90-$105.** 4411 4th Ave. 0.6 mi (1 km) e on Hwy 16.
Ext/int corridors. **Pets:** Accepted.
🆂🅰🆅🅴 🆂🄳 ⊠ 🖥 🖩 🍽 ⊠

▼▼ Lakeview Inns & Suites SH
(780) 723-2500. **$90-$110.** 4300 2nd Ave. 0.6 mi (1.1 km) e on Hwy 16.
Int corridors. **Pets:** Accepted.
🄰🆂🄺 ⊠ 🖥 🖩

FORT MACLEOD

(CAA) ▼▼ Sunset Motel M
(403) 553-4448. **$50-$70.** 104 Hwy 3 W. 0.6 mi (1 km) w on Hwy 2 and
3. Ext corridors. **Pets:** Accepted.
🆂🅰🆅🅴 🆂🄳 ⊠ 🖥 🖩

GRANDE PRAIRIE

▼▼▼▼ Best Western Grande Prairie Hotel & Suites SH
(780) 402-2378. **$169-$270.** 10745 117th Ave. Corner of Hwy 43 and
117th Ave. Int corridors. **Pets:** Accepted.
🄰🆂🄺 ⊠ 🖈 🖥 🖩 🍽 🛏

(CAA) ▼▼▼▼ Pomeroy Inn & Suites SH
(780) 831-2999. **$169-$179.** 11710 102nd St. 102nd St at 117th Ave.
Int corridors. **Pets:** Accepted.
🆂🅰🆅🅴 🆂🄳 ⊠ 🖥 🖩 🛏 ⊠

**(CAA) ▼▼ Quality Hotel & Conference Centre Grande
Prairie** LH
(780) 539-6000. **$108-$169.** 11201 100th Ave. 1.8 mi (2.9 km) w on
Hwy 2. Int corridors. **Pets:** Accepted.
🆂🅰🆅🅴 🆂🄳 ⊠ 🖥 🖩 🍽

▼▼ Service Plus Inns and Suites SH
(780) 538-3900. **$129-$169.** 10810 107th A Ave. 1.4 mi (2.2 km) w on
Hwy 2, just n. Int corridors. **Pets:** Accepted.
🆂🄳 ⊠ 🖈 🖥 🖩 🛏 ⊠

▼▼ Stanford Inn SH 🐾
(780) 539-5678. **$109-$114.** 11401 100th Ave. 1.8 mi (2.8 km) w on
Hwy 2. Ext/int corridors. **Pets:** Other species. $10 daily fee/pet. Service
with restrictions, supervision.
🄰🆂🄺 🆂🄳 ⊠ 🖥 🖩 🍽 ⊠

(CAA) ▼▼▼ Super 8 Motel SH 🐾
(780) 532-8288. **$129.** 10050 116 Ave. 102nd St at 117th Ave. Int
corridors. **Pets:** Small, dogs only. $25 daily fee/room. Designated rooms,
service with restrictions, supervision.
🆂🅰🆅🅴 ⊠ 🖥 🖩 🛏 ⊠

HIGH RIVER

▼▼ Heritage Inn SH 🐾
(403) 652-3834. **$112-$120.** 1104 11th Ave SE. Trans-Canada Hwy 2,
exit 23, 0.5 mi (0.8 km) w of Hwy 2. Int corridors. **Pets:** Medium. $10
daily fee/pet. Service with restrictions, supervision.
🄰🆂🄺 🆂🄳 ⊠ 🖥 🖩 🍽 🛏

▼▼▼ Super 8 Motel SH
(403) 652-4448. **$120-$190.** 1601 13th Ave SE. Trans-Canada Hwy 2,
exit High River, just w. Int corridors. **Pets:** Medium. $10 daily fee/pet.
Service with restrictions, supervision.
🄰🆂🄺 ⊠ 🄶🄼 🖈 🖥 🖩 🛏 ⊠

HINTON

▼▼▼▼ Best Western White Wolf Inn SH
(780) 865-7777. **$145-$200.** 828 Carmichael Ln. At west end of town;
just off Hwy 16. Ext corridors. **Pets:** $10 daily fee/pet. Designated rooms,
service with restrictions, supervision.
⊠ 🖥 🖩

(CAA) ▼▼▼ Days Inn SH
(780) 817-1960. **$139-$199.** 358 Smith St. 1.4 mi (2.3 km) e on Hwy
16. Int corridors. **Pets:** Accepted.
🆂🅰🆅🅴 🆂🄳 ⊠ 🖥 🖩

▼▼▼▼ Lakeview Inns & Suites SH
(780) 865-2575. **$140-$150.** 500 Smith St. 1.1 mi (1.7 km) e on Hwy
16. Ext/int corridors. **Pets:** Accepted.
⊠ 🖥 🖩

JASPER

(CAA) ▼▼▼ Amethyst Lodge SH
(780) 852-3394. **$95-$275.** 200 Connaught Dr. 0.3 mi (0.5 km) e. Ext/int
corridors. **Pets:** Accepted.
🆂🅰🆅🅴 🆂🄳 ⊠ 🖩 🍽

▼▼▼▼ The Fairmont Jasper Park Lodge LH �
(780) 852-3301. **$149-$599, 3 day notice.** Lodge Rd. 3 mi (4.8 km) ne
via Hwy 16; 2 mi (3.2 km) se off highway via Maligne Rd, follow signs.
Ext corridors. **Pets:** Other species. $50 daily fee/room. Designated rooms,
service with restrictions, crate.
🄰🆂🄺 🆂🄳 ⊠ 🖈 🖥 🖩 🍽 🛏 ⊠ 🄺

(CAA) ▼▼▼▼ Jasper Inn Alpine Resort SH
(780) 852-4461. **$95-$413, 3 day notice.** 98 Geikie St. Corner of
Geikie and Bonhomme sts. Ext/int corridors. **Pets:** Accepted.
🆂🅰🆅🅴 🆂🄳 ⊠ 🖥 🖩 🍽 🛏 ⊠ 🄺

(CAA) ▼▼▼▼ Lobstick Lodge SH
(780) 852-4431. **$99-$245.** 94 Geikie St. Corner of Geikie and Juniper
sts. Int corridors. **Pets:** Other species. $10 daily fee/room. Designated
rooms, service with restrictions, crate.
🆂🅰🆅🅴 🆂🄳 ⊠ 🖥 🖩 🍽 ⊠ 🄺

(CAA) ▼▼▼ Maligne Lodge M
(780) 852-3143. **$89-$484.** 900 Connaught. 0.6 mi (1 km) sw. Ext/int
corridors. **Pets:** $25 deposit/room. Designated rooms.
🆂🅰🆅🅴 🆂🄳 ⊠ 🖥 🖩 🍽 🛏

(CAA) ▼▼▼ Marmot Lodge M
(780) 852-4471. **$99-$245.** 86 Connaught Dr. 1 mi (1.6 km) ne. Ext
corridors. **Pets:** Other species. $10 daily fee/room. Designated rooms,
service with restrictions, crate.
🆂🅰🆅🅴 🆂🄳 ⊠ 🖥 🖩 🍽 🛏

▼▼▼ Patricia Lake Bungalows CA
(780) 852-3560. **$65-$285, 7 day notice.** Pyramid Lake Rd. 3 mi (4.8
km) nw via Pyramid Lake Rd. Ext corridors. **Pets:** Medium, dogs only.
$10 daily fee/pet. Designated rooms, service with restrictions, supervision.
⊠ 🖥 🖩 ⊠ 🄩

(CAA) ▼▼▼ Pyramid Lake Resort SH
(780) 852-4900. **$125-$400, 3 day notice.** Pyramid Lake Rd. Jct Connaught Dr and Cedar St, 3.75 mi (6 km) nw via Pyramid Lake Rd. Ext
corridors. **Pets:** Accepted.
🆂🅰🆅🅴 🆂🄳 ⊠ 🖥 🖩 🍽 ⊠ 🄺

**(CAA) ▼▼▼▼ The Sawridge Inn and Conference
Centre** SH 🐾
(780) 852-5111. **$119-$299, 3 day notice.** 82 Connaught Dr. 1.1 mi
(1.7 km) e. Int corridors. **Pets:** Small, dogs only. $20 one-time fee/room.
Designated rooms, supervision.
🆂🅰🆅🅴 🆂🄳 ⊠ 🄶🄼 🖥 🖩 🛏 ⊠

(CAA) ▼▼▼ Sunwapta Falls Resort M
(780) 852-4852. **$79-$368.** Hwy 93. 34.75 mi (55 km) s on Icefields Pkwy (Hwy 93). Ext corridors. **Pets:** Accepted.
[SAVE] [✕] [🛏] [💻] [¶] [⊠] [♨] [🐾]

(CAA) ▼▼▼ Tonquin Inn M
(780) 852-4987. **$76-$406.** 100 Juniper St. Corner of Juniper and Geikie sts. Ext/int corridors. **Pets:** $25 daily fee/pet. Designated rooms.
[SAVE] [✕] [🛏] [💻] [¶] [♨]

KANANASKIS

▼▼▼▼ Delta Lodge at Kananaskis LH
(403) 591-7711. **$109-$289, 3 day notice.** Kanasaskis Village. Trans-Canada Hwy 1, 14.7 mi (23.5) s on Hwy 40 (Kananaskis Trail), then 1.8 mi (3 km) on Kananaskis Village access road, follow signs. Int corridors. **Pets:** Accepted.
[ASK] [S] [✕] [🐕] [🛏] [💻] [¶] [♨] [⊠]

LAKE LOUISE

(CAA) ▼▼▼ The Fairmont Chateau Lake Louise LH 🐾
(403) 522-3511. **$199-$659, 3 day notice.** 111 Lake Louise Dr. 1.8 mi (3 km) up the hill from the village. Int corridors. **Pets:** Small, other species. $25 daily fee/pet. Designated rooms, supervision.
[SAVE] [✕] [💻] [¶] [♨] [⊠]

▼▼▼ Lake Louise Inn SH
(403) 522-3791. **$99-$325, 7 day notice.** 210 Village Rd. Just w of 4-way stop. Ext/int corridors. **Pets:** Accepted.
[ASK] [S] [✕] [🛏] [💻] [¶] [♨] [⊠]

LETHBRIDGE

(CAA) ▼▼▼ Canadas Best Value Inn M
(403) 328-6636. **$70-$100.** 1030 Mayor Magrath Dr S. 2.5 mi (4 km) se on Hwy 4 and 5, exit Mayor Magrath Dr S. Ext/int corridors. **Pets:** $10 one-time fee/pet. Designated rooms, service with restrictions, supervision.
[SAVE] [S] [✕] [🛏] [💻] [♨]

(CAA) ▼▼▼ Comfort Inn SH
(403) 320-8874. **$79-$110.** 3226 Fairway Plaza Rd S. Southeast end of city; Mayor Magrath Dr, exit n at Scenic Dr. Int corridors. **Pets:** Other species. $10 daily fee/pet. Service with restrictions, supervision.
[ASK] [S] [✕] [🛏] [💻] [♨]

(CAA) ▼▼ Days Inn Lethbridge SH
(403) 327-6000. **$79-$104.** 100 3rd Ave S. Corner of 3rd Ave and Scenic Dr; centre. Ext/int corridors. **Pets:** Accepted.
[SAVE] [S] [✕] [🛏] [💻] [♨]

(CAA) ▼▼▼ Econo Lodge & Suites Lethbridge M
(403) 328-5591. **$70-$100.** 1124 Mayor Magrath Dr S. 2.5 mi (4 km) se on Hwy 4 and 5, exit Mayor Magrath Dr S. Ext corridors. **Pets:** $10 one-time fee/room. Designated rooms, service with restrictions, supervision.
[SAVE] [✕] [🛏] [💻]

▼▼▼▼ Holiday Inn Express Hotel & Suites Lethbridge SH
(403) 394-9292. **$145-$295.** 120 Stafford Dr S. Hwy 3, exit Stafford Dr, just s; downtown. Int corridors. **Pets:** Accepted.
[ASK] [S] [✕] [🛏] [💻] [♨] [⊠]

(CAA) ▼▼▼▼ Lethbridge Lodge Hotel and Conference Centre LH
(403) 328-1123. **$120-$200.** 320 Scenic Dr. Scenic Dr at 4th Ave S; centre. Int corridors. **Pets:** Accepted.
[SAVE] [S] [✕] [🛏] [💻] [¶] [♨]

(CAA) ▼ Pepper Tree Inn M
(403) 328-4436. **$55-$67.** 1142 Mayor Magrath Dr S. 2.5 mi (4 km) se on Hwy 4 and 5, exit Mayor Magrath Dr S. Ext corridors. **Pets:** Other species. $8 daily fee/room. Designated rooms, service with restrictions, supervision.
[SAVE] [S] [✕] [🛏] [♨]

▼▼▼ Ramada Hotel & Suites LH
(403) 380-5050. **$129-$149.** 2375 Mayor Magrath Dr S. (4.5 km) se on Hwy 4 and 5, exit Mayor Magrath Dr S. Int corridors. **Pets:** Dogs only. $10 daily fee/room. Designated rooms, service with restrictions.
[ASK] [S] [✕] [🛏] [💻] [¶] [♨] [⊠]

▼▼▼ Sandman Hotel Lethbridge SH
(403) 328-1111. **Call for rates.** 421 Mayor Magrath Dr. Hwy 3, exit Mayor Magrath Dr, just s. Int corridors. **Pets:** Accepted.
[✕] [🛏] [💻] [¶] [♨]

LLOYDMINSTER

▼▼▼ Best Western Wayside Inn & Suites SH
(780) 875-4404. **$137-$157, 7 day notice.** 5411 44th St. 0.5 mi (0.8 km) w on Hwy 16 from jct Hwy 17. Int corridors. **Pets:** Small. $25 daily fee/pet. Designated rooms, service with restrictions, supervision.
[ASK] [S] [✕] [🛏] [💻] [¶] [♨]

MEDICINE HAT

▼▼▼ Best Western Inn SH
(403) 527-3700. **$99-$289.** 722 Redcliff Dr. On Trans-Canada Hwy 1, 0.3 mi (0.4 km) w of jct Hwy 3, access 7th St SW. Ext/int corridors. **Pets:** Medium. Designated rooms, service with restrictions, supervision.
[ASK] [S] [✕] [🛏M] [🛏] [💻] [♨] [⊠]

▼▼▼ Medicine Hat Lodge Hotel Casino Convention Centre Health Spa & Indoor LH
(403) 529-2222. **$111-$132.** 1051 Ross Glen Dr SE. East end approach to city on Trans-Canada Hwy 1, at Dunmore Rd. Int corridors. **Pets:** Other species. $10 daily fee/room. Designated rooms, service with restrictions, crate.
[ASK] [S] [✕] [🛏] [🛏] [💻] [¶] [♨] [⊠]

▼ Motel 6-Medicine Hat SH
(403) 527-1749. **$66-$70.** 20 Strochon Ct SE. Trans-Canada Hwy 1, exit Dunmore Rd, just sw. Int corridors. **Pets:** Medium, other species. Service with restrictions, supervision.
[S] [✕] [🛏M] [🐕] [🛏]

▼▼ Super 8 Motel SH
(403) 528-8888. **$78-$147.** 1280 Trans-Canada Way SE. Trans-Canada Hwy 1 at 13 Ave SE; just n off Trans-Canada Hwy 1. Ext/int corridors. **Pets:** $5 daily fee/room. Designated rooms, service with restrictions, supervision.
[ASK] [S] [✕] [🛏] [💻] [♨]

PINCHER CREEK

▼▼ Heritage Inn SH 🐾
(403) 627-5000. **$93-$100.** 919 Waterton Ave (Hwy 6). SR 3, 2.9 mi (4.7 km) s. Int corridors. **Pets:** Medium, other species. $10 daily fee/pet. Designated rooms, service with restrictions, supervision.
[ASK] [S] [✕] [🛏] [💻] [¶]

RED DEER

(CAA) ▼▼▼▼ Best Western Red Deer Inn & Suites SH
(403) 346-3555. **$115-$130.** 6839 66th St. Hwy 2, exit 67th St, just e. Int corridors. **Pets:** Other species. $10 daily fee/pet. Designated rooms, service with restrictions, supervision.
[SAVE] [S] [✕] [🛏M] [🐕] [🛏] [💻] [♨]

(CAA) ▼▼▼▼ Capri Hotel Trade & Convention Centre LH
(403) 346-2091. **$160-$185.** 3310 50th Ave. 1.3 mi (2 km) n on Hwy 2A (Gaetz Ave). Int corridors. **Pets:** Accepted.
[SAVE] [S] [✕] [🛏] [💻] [¶] [⊠]

(CAA) ▼▼▼ Comfort Inn & Suites SH 🐾
(403) 348-0025. **$99-$139.** 6846 66th St. Hwy 2, exit 67th St, just e. Int corridors. **Pets:** Medium. $20 one-time fee/room. Service with restrictions, supervision.
[SAVE] [✕] [🛏M] [🛏] [💻] [♨] [⊠]

◎ ▽▽▽ Holiday Inn 67 Street ⬛
(403) 342-6567. **$99-$109.** 6500 67th St. Hwy 2, exit 67th St, 0.5 mi (0.8 km) e. Int corridors. **Pets:** Very small, other species. $50 deposit/room. Designated rooms, service with restrictions, supervision.
SAVE ⊠ ⬛ ⬛ ⬛ ⬛ ⊠

◎ ▽▽▽ Holiday Inn Express Red Deer ⬛
(403) 343-2112. **$109-$129.** 2803 50th Ave. 1.1 mi (1.8 km) e on Hwy 2A (Gaetz Ave). Int corridors. **Pets:** Accepted.
SAVE ⬛ ⊠ ⬛ ⬛ ⬛ ⬛ ⊠

▽▽▽ Sandman Hotel Red Deer ⬛
(403) 343-7400. **$115-$320.** 2818 Gaetz Ave. 1 mi (1.6 km) n on Hwy 2A (Gaetz Ave). Int corridors. **Pets:** Accepted.
ASK ⬛ ⊠ ⬛ ⬛ ⬛ ⬛ ⬛

▽▽ Stanford Inn ⬛
(403) 347-5551. **$99-$169.** 4707 Ross St. Just e of Hwy 2A (Gaetz Ave); centre. Int corridors. **Pets:** $10 daily fee/pet. Supervision.
ASK ⬛ ⊠ ⬛ ⬛ ⬛

ROCKY MOUNTAIN HOUSE

◎ ▽ Chinook Inn M
(403) 845-2833. **$80-$90.** 5321 59th Ave. 0.8 mi (1.3 km) w on Hwy 11, then s. Int corridors. **Pets:** Accepted.
SAVE ⬛ ⊠ ⬛ ⬛

◎ ▽▽▽ Holiday Inn Express Rocky Mountain House ⬛
(403) 845-2871. **$89-$99.** 4715 45th St. Just nw of jct 47th Ave and 45th St. Int corridors. **Pets:** $15 daily fee/pet. Service with restrictions, supervision.
SAVE ⬛ ⊠ ⬛ ⬛

▽▽▽ Super 8 Motel ⬛
(403) 846-0088. **$119-$169.** 4406 41st Ave. Just off Hwy 11 at east end of town. Int corridors. **Pets:** Small. $10 daily fee/room. Designated rooms, service with restrictions, supervision.
ASK ⬛ ⊠ ⬛ ⬛ ⬛ ⊠

TABER

▽▽ Heritage Inn ⬛ ✿
(403) 223-4424. **$92-$94.** 4830 46th Ave. 0.6 mi (1 km) e of jct Hwy 3 and 36 S, on Hwy 3. Int corridors. **Pets:** Medium. $10 daily fee/pet. Service with restrictions, supervision.
ASK ⬛ ⊠ ⬛ ⬛ ⬛ ⊠

WATERTON PARK

◎ ▽▽ Bayshore Inn M
(403) 859-2211. **$104-$154, 3 day notice.** 111 Waterton Ave. Centre. Ext corridors. **Pets:** Accepted.
SAVE ⬛ ⊠ ⬛ ⬛ ⬛ ⬛

▽▽▽ Waterton Lakes Lodge ⬛
(403) 859-2150. **$114-$219, 3 day notice.** 101 Clematis Ave. Centre. Ext/int corridors. **Pets:** Accepted.
⊠ ⬛ ⬛ ⬛ ⬛ ⬛ ⬛ ⊠

WESTEROSE

▽▽ Village Creek Country Inn M
(780) 586-0006. **Call for rates.** 9 Village Dr. Hwy 13, just n on Norris Beach Rd; 17.5 mi (28 km) w of Hwy 2. Ext/int corridors. **Pets:** Accepted.
⊠ ⬛ ⬛ ⊠

WETASKIWIN

▽▽ Best Western Wayside Inn ⬛
(780) 352-6681. **$89-$119.** 4103 56 St. Just n of Hwy 13 W, on Hwy 2A. Int corridors. **Pets:** Accepted.
ASK ⬛ ⊠ ⬛ ⬛

▽▽ Super 8 Motel ⬛
(780) 361-3808. **$89-$119.** 3820 56th St. On Hwy 2A, just s of jct Hwy 13 W. Ext/int corridors. **Pets:** Very small. $50 deposit/room. Designated rooms, service with restrictions, supervision.
ASK ⬛ ⊠ ⬛ ⬛

WHITECOURT

◎ ▽▽▽ Quality Inn ⬛
(780) 778-5477. **$125-$175.** 5420 49th Ave. On Hwy 43, just e of Hwy 32. Int corridors. **Pets:** Other species. Designated rooms, service with restrictions, supervision.
SAVE ⬛ ⊠ ⬛ ⬛ ⬛ ⊠

◎ ▽▽▽ Super 8 Motel ⬛
(780) 778-8908. **$119-$129.** 4121 Kepler St. On Hwy 43, just e of Hwy 32. Int corridors. **Pets:** Medium, other species. $25 daily fee/pet. Designated rooms, service with restrictions, supervision.
SAVE ⊠ ⬛ ⬛

BRITISH COLUMBIA

CITY INDEX

100 MILE HOUSE

◆◆ 100 Mile House Super 8 [M]
(250) 395-8888. **$85-$100.** 989 Alder Ave. 0.6 mi (1 km) s on Hwy 97. Ext corridors. **Pets:** Accepted.
⊠ ▣ 📺

◆◆ Ramada Limited [M]
(250) 395-2777. **$90-$209.** 917 Alder Ave. 0.6 mi (1 km) s on Hwy 97. Int corridors. **Pets:** Other species. Service with restrictions, crate.
[S/D] ⊠ ▣ 📺

◆◆ Red Coach Inn [SH]
(250) 395-2266. **$76-$93.** 170 Cariboo Hwy N. On Hwy 97, on north end of town. Ext/int corridors. **Pets:** Other species. $6 daily fee/room. Supervision.
[A$K] [S/D] ⊠ ♿[M] ▣ 📺 🍴 🏊

108 MILE HOUSE

[CAA] ◆◆ 108 Resort & Conference Centre [SH]
(250) 791-5211. **$90-$160.** 4816 Telqua Dr. From Hwy 97, 1 mi (1.6 km) nw on access road, follow signs. Ext corridors. **Pets:** Medium. $10 daily fee/pet. Designated rooms, service with restrictions, crate.
[SAVE] [S/D] ⊠ ♿[M] ▣ 📺 🍴 🏊 ✂

ABBOTSFORD

[CAA] ◆◆ Best Western Bakerview Inn [M] 🐾
(604) 859-1341. **$95-$129.** 1821 Sumas Way. Trans-Canada Hwy 1, exit 92 (Town Centre), just n on Hwy 11. Ext corridors. **Pets:** Other species. $100 deposit/room. Designated rooms, service with restrictions, crate.
[SAVE] [S/D] ⊠ ▣ 📺 🍴 🏊

◆◆◆ Coast Abbotsford Hotel & Suites [SH]
(604) 853-1880. **$90-$160.** 2020 Sumas Way. Trans-Canada Hwy 1, exit 92 (Town Centre), just n on Hwy 11. Int corridors. **Pets:** Accepted.
[A$K] [S/D] ⊠ ▣ 📺 🍴 🏊

◆◆ Ramada Plaza & Conference Centre-Abbotsford [SH] 🐾
(604) 870-1050. **$99-$134.** 36035 N Parallel Rd. Trans-Canada Hwy 1, exit 95 (Whatcom Rd). Int corridors. **Pets:** Medium, other species. $10 daily fee/pet. Designated rooms, service with restrictions, supervision.
[A$K] [S/D] ⊠ ♿[M] ♿ ▣ 📺 🍴 🏊 ✂

[CAA] ◆◆ Super 8 Motel Abbotsford [SH]
(604) 853-1141. **$89-$129.** 1881 Sumas Way. Trans-Canada Hwy 1, exit 92 (Town Centre), just n on Hwy 11. Ext/int corridors. **Pets:** Accepted.
[SAVE] [S/D] ⊠ ♿[M] ♿ ▣ 📺 🏊 ✂

BLUE RIVER

[CAA] ◆◆ Glacier Mountain Lodge [M]
(250) 673-2393. **$72-$124.** 869 Shell Rd. On Hwy 5 (Yellowhead Hwy) at Shell Rd, follow signs. Int corridors. **Pets:** Other species. $10 daily fee/room. Designated rooms, service with restrictions, supervision.
[SAVE] [S/D] ⊠ ▣

BOWEN ISLAND

◆◆ Wildwood Lane Cottages [CA]
(604) 947-2253. **$115-$175, 14 day notice.** 1291 Adams Rd. From ferry terminal, 3.5 mi (5.6 km) w on Grafton Rd, then 0.6 mi (1 km) n. Ext corridors. **Pets:** Accepted.
⊠ ▣ 📺 [AC]

CACHE CREEK

[CAA] ◆◆ Bonaparte Motel [M]
(250) 457-9693. **$50-$120.** 1395 Hwy 97 N. Just n of jct Trans-Canada Hwy 1. Ext corridors. **Pets:** Accepted.
[SAVE] [S/D] ⊠ ▣ 🏊

CAMPBELL RIVER

[CAA] ◆◆◆ Anchor Inn & Suites [SH]
(250) 286-1131. **$119-$299.** 261 Island Hwy. On Island Hwy 19A, 1.3 mi (2 km) s. Int corridors. **Pets:** Small. $8 daily fee/pet. Designated rooms, service with restrictions, supervision.
[SAVE] [S/D] ⊠ ▣ 📺 🍴 🏊 [AC]

[CAA] ◆◆◆ Best Western Austrian Chalet [M]
(250) 923-4231. **$111-$169.** 462 S Island Hwy. 2 mi (3.2 km) s on Island Hwy 19A. Ext/int corridors. **Pets:** Very small, other species. $6 one-time fee/pet. Designated rooms, service with restrictions, supervision.
[SAVE] [S/D] ⊠ ♿[M] ▣ 📺 🏊 ✂ [AC]

[CAA] ◆ Campbell River Lodge Fishing & Adventure Resort [M]
(250) 287-7446. **$64-$109, 3 day notice.** 1760 N Island Hwy. On Island Hwy 19A, 1.3 mi (2 km) nw of downtown; just e from Hwy 19 and 28. Ext/int corridors. **Pets:** $8 one-time fee/pet. Designated rooms, service with restrictions, supervision.
[SAVE] [S/D] ⊠ ▣ 🍴 [AC]

◆ Campbell River Super 8 [M]
(250) 286-6622. **$75-$99.** 340 S Island Hwy. 1.9 mi (3 km) s on Island Hwy 19A. Int corridors. **Pets:** Medium. $50 deposit/pet, $6 daily fee/pet. Designated rooms, service with restrictions, supervision.
[A$K] [S/D] ⊠ ♿[M] ▣ 🏊

◆◆ **Town Centre Inn** Ⓜ
(250) 287-8866. **$64-$84.** 1500 Dogwood St. Follow Island Hwy 19A through town, watch for signs, just e on Dogwood St; corner of 16th Ave. Ext corridors. **Pets:** Small. $5 daily fee/room. Designated rooms, service with restrictions, supervision.
⊠ 🍴 💻 🎿

CASTLEGAR

Ⓐ ◆◆◆ **Quality Inn Castlegar** Ⓜ
(250) 365-2177. **$90.** 1935 Columbia Ave. Jct Hwy 3A and 3B, just s. Ext/int corridors. **Pets:** $5 daily fee/pet. Designated rooms, service with restrictions, supervision.
[SAVE] [S🐾] ⊠ 🍴 💻 🍴

◆◆ **Super 8 Motel-Castlegar** SH
(250) 365-2700. **$89-$179.** 651 18th St. Hwy 3, exit city centre. Int corridors. **Pets:** Accepted.
[ASK] [S🐾] ⊠ 🍴 💻

CHASE

◆◆ **Chase Country Inn Motel** Ⓜ
(250) 679-3333. **$59-$99, 3 day notice.** 576 Coburn St. Trans-Canada Hwy 1 and Coburn St. Ext corridors. **Pets:** Medium. $10 daily fee/pet. Service with restrictions, supervision.
[ASK] [S🐾] ⊠ 🍴 💻 🍴

◆◆ **Quaaout Resort & Conference Centre** SH
(250) 679-3090. **$84-$199.** Trans-Canada Hwy 1, exit Squilax Bridge, 1.5 mi (2.5 km) w on Little Shuswap Rd. Int corridors. **Pets:** Other species. $10 daily fee/pet. Designated rooms, service with restrictions.
⊠ 🦽 🍴 💻 🍴 🏊 🎿

CHEMAINUS

◆◆◆ **Best Western Chemainus Festival Inn** SH ✿
(250) 246-4181. **$119-$229.** 9573 Chemainus Rd. Trans-Canada Hwy 1, exit Henry Rd, 0.9 mi (1.4 km) e. Int corridors. **Pets:** $25 deposit/room. Designated rooms, service with restrictions, supervision.
[S🐾] ⊠ 🦽 🍴 💻 🏊

CHILLIWACK

Ⓐ ◆◆◆ **Best Western Rainbow Country Inn** SH
(604) 795-3828. **$79-$133.** 43971 Industrial Way. Trans-Canada Hwy 1, exit 116 (Lickman Rd). Int corridors. **Pets:** Accepted.
[SAVE] [S🐾] ⊠ 🍴 💻 🍴 🏊

Ⓐ ◆◆ **Chilliwack Travelodge** SH
(604) 792-4240. **$69-$99.** 45466 Yale Rd W. Trans-Canada Hwy 1, exit 119, just n. Int corridors. **Pets:** Medium. $10 daily fee/pet. Designated rooms, service with restrictions, supervision.
[SAVE] [S🐾] ⊠ 🍴 💻 🍴 🏊

◆◆ **Comfort Inn** Ⓜ
(604) 858-0636. **$95-$135.** 45405 Luckakuck Way. Trans-Canada Hwy 1, exit 119, s on Vedder Rd, then 0.6 mi (1 km) w. Int corridors. **Pets:** Medium, other species. $5 daily fee/room. Designated rooms, service with restrictions, crate.
[ASK] [S🐾] ⊠ 🦽 💻

CHRISTINA LAKE

◆◆ **New Horizon Motel** Ⓜ
(250) 447-9312. **$95-$165.** 2037 Hwy 3. Just e. Ext corridors. **Pets:** Accepted.
⊠ 🦽 🍴 💻

CLEARWATER

Ⓐ ◆◆◆ **Clearwater Valley Resort** CA
(250) 674-3909. **$55-$115.** 373 Clearwater Valley Rd. Jct Hwy 5 (Yellowhead Hwy) and Clearwater Valley Rd. Ext corridors. **Pets:** Accepted.
[SAVE] ⊠ 🍴 💻 🍴 🏊 🎿

Ⓐ ◆◆ **Jasper Way Inn Motel on beautiful Dutch Lake** Ⓜ
(250) 674-3345. **$56-$95.** 57 E Old N Thompson Hwy. 0.6 mi (1 km) w on Old N Thompson Hwy, just off Hwy 5 (Yellowhead Hwy). Ext corridors. **Pets:** Accepted.
[SAVE] [S🐾] ⊠ 🍴 💻 🎿

COMOX

Ⓐ ◆◆◆ **Port Augusta Inn & Suites** SH
(250) 339-2277. **$69-$89, 4 day notice.** 2082 Comox Ave. From Hwy 19A (Cliffe Ave), follow signs to Comox Ave, then 2.5 mi (4 km) e. Ext/int corridors. **Pets:** Medium. $10 daily fee/pet. Designated rooms, service with restrictions, crate.
[SAVE] [S🐾] ⊠ 🦽 🍴 💻 🍴 🏊

COURTENAY

Ⓐ ◆◆◆ **Best Western The Westerly Hotel** SH
(250) 338-7741. **$144-$289.** 1590 Cliffe Ave. Corner of Cliffe Ave and Island Hwy 19A N. Int corridors. **Pets:** Large. $10 daily fee/pet. Service with restrictions, supervision.
[SAVE] [S🐾] ⊠ 🦽 💻 🍴 🏊 🎿

Ⓐ ◆◆◆◆ **Kingfisher Oceanside Resort & Spa** SH
(250) 338-1323. **$135-$165.** 4330 S Island Hwy. 3.8 mi (6 km) s on Island Hwy 19A S, watch for signs. Ext corridors. **Pets:** Accepted.
[SAVE] ⊠ 🦽 🎿 🍴 💻 🍴 🏊 🎿 🎿

Ⓐ ◆◆ **Travelodge Courtenay** Ⓜ
(250) 334-4491. **$89-$124.** 2605 Cliffe Ave. 0.8 mi (1.2 km) s on Island Hwy 19A S. Ext corridors. **Pets:** $5 deposit/pet. Designated rooms, service with restrictions, supervision.
[SAVE] [S🐾] ⊠ 🍴 💻 🏊

CRANBROOK

◆◆ **Heritage Inn** SH
(250) 489-4301. **$120.** 803 Cranbrook St N. Hwy 3 and 95; centre. Int corridors. **Pets:** $10 daily fee/room.
[ASK] [S🐾] ⊠ 🍴 💻 🍴 🏊

Ⓐ ◆◆◆ **Model A Inn** Ⓜ ✿
(250) 489-4600. **$65-$170.** 1908 Cranbrook St N. 0.6 mi (1 km) w of jct Hwy 93 and 95. Ext corridors. **Pets:** Dogs only.
[SAVE] [S🐾] ⊠ 🍴 💻

Ⓐ ◆◆◆◆ **St. Eugene Golf Resort & Casino** LH
(250) 420-2000. **$99-$139.** 7731 Mission Rd. Hwy 3, exit Kimberley/Airport (Hwy 95A) to Mission Rd, 4.5 km n. Int corridors. **Pets:** Accepted.
[SAVE] [S🐾] ⊠ 🍴 💻 🍴 🏊 🎿

Ⓐ ◆◆◆ **Super 8 Motel** SH
(250) 489-8028. **$99-$110.** 2370 Cranbrook St N. Just w of jct Hwy 93 and 95. Int corridors. **Pets:** Accepted.
[SAVE] [S🐾] ⊠ 🦽 🍴

CRESTON

◆◆◆ **Downtowner Motor Inn** SH
(250) 428-2238. **$45-$60.** 1218 Canyon St. Corner of 12th Ave N. Int corridors. **Pets:** $4 daily fee/pet.
⊠ 🍴

Ⓐ ◆◆◆ **Skimmerhorn Inn** Ⓜ ✿
(250) 428-4009. **$75-$96.** 2711 Hwy 3. 0.5 mi (0.8 km) e on Hwy 3. Ext corridors. **Pets:** Small, dogs only. $5 daily fee/pet. Service with restrictions, crate.
[SAVE] ⊠ 🍴 💻 🏊

Ⓐ ◆◆ **Sunset Motel** Ⓜ
(250) 428-2229. **$69-$89.** 2705 Canyon St, Hwy 3 E. On Hwy 3, 0.6 mi (1 km) e. Ext corridors. **Pets:** Accepted.
[SAVE] [S🐾] ⊠ 🍴 💻 🏊

DAWSON CREEK

(CAA) ▼▼▼ Dawson Creek Super 8 [SH]
(250) 782-8899. **$110-$160.** 1440 Alaska Ave. Just s of jct Hwy 97 S (Hart Hwy) and 97 N (Alaska Hwy). Int corridors. **Pets:** Other species. $10 daily fee/pet. Designated rooms, service with restrictions, supervision.
[SAVE] [S🔊] [✕] [🛏] [💻] [🍴]

DUNCAN

(CAA) ▼▼▼ Best Western Cowichan Valley Inn [SH]
(250) 748-2722. **$108-$158.** 6474 Trans-Canada Hwy 1. (3 km) n. Int corridors. **Pets:** Service with restrictions, supervision.
[SAVE] [S🔊] [✕] [🛏] [💻] [🍴] [≈]

▼ Falcon Nest Motel [M]
(250) 748-8188. **$58-$79.** 5867 Trans-Canada Hwy 1. 0.9 mi (1.5 km) n. Ext corridors. **Pets:** Small, dogs only. $7 daily fee/pet. Designated rooms, service with restrictions, supervision.
[ASK] [✕] [🛏] [💻] [≈]

▼▼▼▼ Travelodge Silver Bridge Inn Duncan [SH]
(250) 748-4311. **$99-$139.** 140 Trans-Canada Hwy 1. Just n of Silver Bridge. Ext corridors. **Pets:** Other species. $15 daily fee/pet. Designated rooms.
[ASK] [S🔊] [✕] [🛏] [💻] [🍴]

ENDERBY

(CAA) ▼▼ Howard Johnson Inn Fortunes Landing [M]
(250) 838-6825. **$79-$109.** 1510 George St. 0.6 mi (1 km) n on Hwy 974. Ext corridors. **Pets:** Other species. $5 daily fee/pet. Designated rooms, service with restrictions, supervision.
[SAVE] [S🔊] [✕] [🛏] [💻] [🍴] [≈]

FERNIE

(CAA) ▼▼▼▼ Best Western Fernie Mountain Lodge [SH]
(250) 423-5500. **$119-$329.** 1622 7th Ave. Jct Hwy 3 and 7th Ave; east end of town. Int corridors. **Pets:** Accepted.
[SAVE] [S🔊] [✕] [🛏] [💻] [🍴] [≈]

(CAA) ▼▼▼▼ Park Place Lodge [SH]
(250) 423-6871. **$109-$239.** 742 Hwy 3. At 7th St. Int corridors. **Pets:** Accepted.
[SAVE] [S🔊] [✕] [🛏] [💻] [🍴] [≈] [✕]

▼▼▼▼ Stanford Inn [CO] ❤
(250) 423-5000. **$89-$650.** 100 Riverside Way. From centre, 1.2 mi (2 km) on Hwy 3. Ext/int corridors. **Pets:** Medium. $10 daily fee/room, $25 one-time fee/room. Service with restrictions, supervision.
[ASK] [S🔊] [✕] [🛏] [💻] [🍴] [≈] [✕]

▼▼ Super 8 Motel-Fernie [SH]
(250) 423-6788. **$72-$96.** 2021 Hwy 3. On Hwy 3; west end of town. Int corridors. **Pets:** Accepted.
[ASK] [S🔊] [✕] [🛏]

FORT ST. JOHN

(CAA) ▼▼▼ Best Western Coachman Inn [SH]
(250) 787-0651. **$105-$111.** 8540 Alaska Rd. 1.2 mi (2 km) s on Hwy 97. Int corridors. **Pets:** Other species. $15 daily fee/pet. Service with restrictions, crate.
[SAVE] [S🔊] [✕] [🛏] [💻] [🍴] [✕]

▼▼▼▼ Pomeroy Inn & Suites [SH]
(250) 262-3030. **$169-$189.** 9304 Alaska Rd. Just s on Hwy 97 (Alaska Hwy). Int corridors. **Pets:** Accepted.
[ASK] [S🔊] [✕] [🛏] [💻]

▼▼▼▼ Quality Inn Northern Grand [LH] ❤
(250) 787-0521. **$119-$199.** 9830 100th Ave. Centre. Int corridors. **Pets:** $25 daily fee/pet. Designated rooms, crate.
[ASK] [S🔊] [✕] [🛏] [💻] [🍴] [≈] [✕]

▼▼▼ Super 8 Motel-Fort St. John [SH] ❤
(250) 785-7588. **$35-$45.** 9500 Alaska Hwy. Just s on Hwy 97 (Alaska Hwy). Int corridors. **Pets:** Medium. $25 one-time fee/pet. Designated rooms, service with restrictions, supervision.
[ASK] [S🔊] [✕] [🛏M] [♿] [🛏] [💻] [🍴] [≈] [✕]

FORT STEELE

(CAA) ▼▼▼ Bull River Guest Ranch [RA]
(250) 429-3760. **$125-$165.** Hwy 95, 21.9 mi se of town on Ft Steele-Wardner Rd, 12 mi ne on gravel road, follow signs; Hwy 3 W, 41 km e of Cranbrook, use Ft Steele Rd. Ext corridors. **Pets:** Dogs only. No service, supervision.
[SAVE] [✕] [🛏] [💻] [✕] [🎾] [🅿] [☎]

GIBSONS

▼▼▼ Bonniebrook Lodge Bed & Breakfast [CI] ❤
(604) 886-2887. **$149-$249, 7 day notice.** 1532 Ocean Beach Esplanade. Hwy 101, 3.8 mi (6 km) s on Veterans Rd to Fichett St, just sw to King St, 0.6 mi (1 km) sw to Chaster, then 5 mi (8 km) sw to Gowers Pt Rd, follow signs. Ext/int corridors. **Pets:** Dogs only. Designated rooms, supervision.
[ASK] [S🔊] [✕] [🛏] [💻] [🎾] [☎]

(CAA) ▼▼▼ Cedars Inn Hotel & Convention Centre [M]
(604) 886-3008. **$94-$156.** 895 Gibsons Way. Hwy 101 and Shaw Rd; 3.8 mi (6 km) n from ferry terminal. Ext/int corridors. **Pets:** Accepted.
[SAVE] [S🔊] [✕] [🛏] [💻] [🍴] [≈] [✕]

GOLD BRIDGE

▼▼▼ Morrow Chalets [CA]
(250) 238-2462. **$225-$325, 30 day notice.** 5 mi (8 km) n from the Tyaughton Lake turnoff, follow signs. Ext corridors. **Pets:** Other species. No service, supervision.
[ASK] [S🔊] [✕] [🛏] [💻] [🎾]

▼▼▼ Tyax Mountain Lake Resort [SH]
(250) 238-2221. **$134-$328, 30 day notice.** Tyaughton Lake Rd. 5 mi (8 km) n from the Tyaughton Lake turnoff, follow signs. Int corridors. **Pets:** Accepted.
[ASK] [✕] [🛏] [🍴] [✕] [🎾]

GOLDEN

(CAA) ▼▼▼▼ Best Western Mountain View Inn [SH]
(250) 344-2333. **$109-$189.** 1040 9 Ave N. just w of jct Hwy 95 and Trans-Canada Hwy 1; on S Service Rd. Int corridors. **Pets:** Accepted.
[SAVE] [S🔊] [✕] [🛏] [💻] [≈]

▼ Golden Gate Motel [M]
(250) 344-2252. **$45-$70.** 1408 Golden View Rd. On Trans-Canada Hwy 1, 1 mi (1.6 km) e of jct Hwy 95. Ext corridors. **Pets:** Medium. $5 one-time fee/pet. Designated rooms, service with restrictions, supervision.
[ASK] [S🔊] [✕] [🛏]

▼▼ Golden Rim Motor Inn [M]
(250) 344-2216. **$69-$110, 3 day notice.** 1416 Golden View Rd. On Trans-Canada Hwy 1, 1 mi (1.6 km) e of jct Hwy 95. Ext corridors. **Pets:** Medium, dogs only. $10 daily fee/pet. Service with restrictions, supervision.
[ASK] [S🔊] [✕] [🛏] [💻] [🍴] [≈] [✕]

(CAA) ▼▼▼▼ Hillside Lodge & Chalets [CA]
(250) 344-7281. **$128-$145, 5 day notice.** 1740 Seward Frontage Rd. 9.4 mi (15 km) w on Hwy 1, follow signs n off highway. Ext corridors. **Pets:** Accepted.
[SAVE] [✕] [🛏] [💻] [✕] [🎾] [☎]

GRAND FORKS

▼▼ Ramada Limited M
(250) 442-2127. **$74-$99.** 2729 Central Ave. West end of town on Hwy 3. Ext corridors. **Pets:** Accepted.
[S♣] [✕] [🛏] [💻] [🍴] [⌂]

Ⓐ ▼▼ Western Traveller Motel M
(250) 442-5566. **$59-$129.** 1591 Central Ave. West end of town on Hwy 3. Ext corridors. **Pets:** Small, dogs only. $7 daily fee/pet. Designated rooms, no service, supervision.
[SAVE] [S♣] [✕] [🛏] [💻]

GULF ISLANDS NATIONAL PARK RESERVE AREA

PENDER ISLAND

Ⓐ ▼▼▼▼ Poets Cove Resort & Spa SH
(250) 629-2100. **$219-$307.** 9801 Spalding Rd, South Pender Island. From Otter Bay ferry terminal, follow signs to South Pender Island, then 10 mi (16 km) s; Otter Bay Rd to Bidwell Harbour Rd to Canal Rd. Ext/int corridors. **Pets:** Accepted.
[SAVE] [S♣] [✕] [♿M] [🛏] [💻] [🍴] [⌂] [✕]

QUADRA ISLAND

▼▼ Taku Resort M
(250) 285-3031. **$95-$290, 14 day notice.** 616 Taku Rd. From Campbell River ferry terminal, 4.1 mi (6.6 km) n on West Rd, then just e on Heriot Bay Rd, follow signs to Heriot Bay. Ext corridors. **Pets:** $10 daily fee/pet. Designated rooms, service with restrictions, supervision.
[✕] [🛏] [💻] [✕] [♿] [☎]

SALT SPRING ISLAND

▼▼ Harbour House SH
(250) 537-5571. **$59-$295.** 121 Upper Ganges Rd. 0.6 mi (1 km) n on Lower Ganges Rd, then just e, towards Long Harbour ferry terminal. Ext/int corridors. **Pets:** Accepted.
[ASK] [S♣] [✕] [♿M] [♿] [💻] [🍴] [♿]

▼▼ Old Farmhouse Bed & Breakfast BB
(250) 537-4113. **$170-$195, 14 day notice.** 1077 North End Rd. From Ganges township, 2.5 mi (4 km) n on Lower Ganges North End Rd. Int corridors. **Pets:** Accepted.
[S♣] [✕] [♿] [☎] [☎]

▼ Seabreeze Inne M
(250) 537-4145. **$85-$165, 3 day notice.** 101 Bittancourt Rd. From Ganges township, 0.6 mi (1 km) s on Fulford-Ganges Rd. Ext corridors. **Pets:** Accepted.
[ASK] [✕] [🛏] [💻] [✕] [♿]

SATURNA

▼▼ Saturna Lodge CI
(250) 539-2254. **$120-$195, 14 day notice.** 130 Payne Rd. From BC ferry terminal, just s on Narvaez Bay Rd, then just e, follow signs. Int corridors. **Pets:** Accepted.
[✕] [🍴] [♿] [☎] [☎]

END AREA

HARRISON HOT SPRINGS

Ⓐ ▼▼▼ Harrison Beach Hotel SH ❀
(604) 796-1111. **$99-$259, 3 day notice.** 160 Esplanade Ave. Just w; on the lakefront. Int corridors. **Pets:** Medium. $40 one-time fee/room. Designated rooms, service with restrictions.
[SAVE] [S♣] [✕] [♿M] [♿] [🛏] [💻] [🍴] [⌂]

Ⓐ ▼▼▼ Harrison Hot Springs Resort & Spa LH ❀
(604) 796-2244. **$129-$359, 3 day notice.** 100 Esplanade Ave. Just w; on lakefront. Int corridors. **Pets:** Large, other species. Designated rooms, service with restrictions, supervision.
[SAVE] [✕] [🛏] [💻] [🍴] [⌂] [✕]

HOPE

Ⓐ ▼▼▼ Alpine Motel M
(604) 869-9931. **$70-$100.** 505 Old Hope-Princeton Way. Trans-Canada Hwy 1, exit 173 westbound; exit 170 eastbound, just n from lights. Ext corridors. **Pets:** Accepted.
[SAVE] [S♣] [✕] [🛏] [💻]

Ⓐ ▼ Best Continental Motel M
(604) 869-9726. **$54-$99.** 860 Fraser Ave. Trans-Canada Hwy 1, exit 170 to downtown; at Fort St. Ext corridors. **Pets:** Accepted.
[SAVE] [S♣] [✕] [🛏] [💻]

Ⓐ ▼▼ Quality Inn M
(604) 869-9951. **$73-$110.** 350 Old Hope-Princeton Way. Trans-Canada Hwy 1, exit 173 westbound; exit 170 eastbound, just n from lights. Int corridors. **Pets:** Other species. Service with restrictions, supervision.
[SAVE] [S♣] [✕] [♿M] [🛏] [💻] [⌂]

INVERMERE

Ⓐ ▼▼▼ Best Western Invermere Inn SH
(250) 342-9246. **$99-$169.** 1310 7th Ave. 1.8 mi (3 km) w of Hwy 93 and 95 at Invermere exit; centre. Int corridors. **Pets:** Accepted.
[SAVE] [S♣] [✕] [🛏] [💻] [🍴]

▼▼ Invermere Super 8 SH
(250) 342-8888. **$85-$100.** 8888 Arrow Rd. On Hwy 95. Int corridors. **Pets:** Other species. $10 daily fee/pet. Designated rooms, supervision.
[S♣] [✕] [🛏] [💻] [🍴]

KAMLOOPS

Ⓐ ▼▼▼ Accent Inns M ❀
(250) 374-8877. **$89-$149.** 1325 Columbia St W. Trans-Canada Hwy 1, exit 369 (Columbia St) eastbound, at Notre Dame Dr; exit 370 (Summit Dr) westbound, at Notre Dame Dr. Ext corridors. **Pets:** Service with restrictions, supervision.
[SAVE] [S♣] [✕] [♿M] [🛏] [💻] [⌂] [✕]

Ⓐ ▼▼▼ Econo Lodge Inn & Suites M
(250) 372-8533. **$59-$89.** 1773 Trans-Canada Hwy E. 1.5 mi (2.4 km) e on Trans-Canada Hwy 1, south side of service access road. Ext corridors. **Pets:** $100 deposit/room, $10 daily fee/pet. Designated rooms, service with restrictions, supervision.
[SAVE] [S♣] [✕] [🛏] [💻] [⌂]

Ⓐ ▼ Grandview Motel M
(250) 372-1312. **$55-$99.** 463 Grandview Terr. Trans-Canada Hwy 1, exit 369 (Columbia St) eastbound, 1.3 mi (2 km) n; exit 370 (Summit Dr) westbound to Columbia St via City Centre. Ext corridors. **Pets:** Medium. $115 daily fee/pet. Designated rooms, service with restrictions, supervision.
[SAVE] [S♣] [✕] [🛏] [💻] [⌂]

[CAA] ◆◆◆ **Hampton Inn** [SH] 🐾
(250) 571-7897. **$99-$250.** 1245 Rogers Way. Trans-Canada Hwy 1, exit 368 (Hillside Ave), just s via Hillside Way. Int corridors. **Pets:** Dogs only. $20 daily fee/room. Designated rooms, service with restrictions, supervision.
[SAVE] [SD] 🚭 [&M] ♿ ▣ ☕ 🏊 🏋

◆ **Hospitality Inn** [M]
(250) 374-4164. **$55-$89.** 500 W Columbia St. Trans-Canada Hwy 1, exit 369 (Columbia St) eastbound, 1.3 mi (2 km) n; exit 370 (Summit Dr) westbound to Columbia St via City Centre. Ext corridors. **Pets:** Medium. $15 daily fee/pet. Service with restrictions, supervision.
[A$K] [SD] 🚭 ▣ ☕ 🏊

[CAA] ◆◆ **Kamloops Super 8 Motel** [M]
(250) 374-8688. **$64-$97.** 1521 Hugh Allan Dr. Trans-Canada Hwy 1, exit 367 (Pacific Way). Int corridors. **Pets:** $10 daily fee/pet. Designated rooms, service with restrictions, supervision.
[SAVE] [SD] 🚭 [&M]

◆◆ **Place Inn** [SH] 🐾
(250) 374-5911. **$99-$129.** 1285 Trans-Canada Hwy W. Trans-Canada Hwy 1, exit 368 (Hillside Ave), just s. Int corridors. **Pets:** Large. $20 daily fee/pet. Designated rooms, service with restrictions, supervision.
[A$K] [SD] 🚭 ▣ ☕ 🍴 🏊

[CAA] ◆◆ **Ramada Inn-Kamloops** [SH]
(250) 374-0358. **$89-$129.** 555 W Columbia St. Trans-Canada Hwy 1, exit 369 (Columbia St) eastbound, 1.3 mi (2 km) n; exit 370 (Summit Dr) westbound to Columbia St via City Centre. Int corridors. **Pets:** Medium. $10 daily fee/pet. Designated rooms, service with restrictions, supervision.
[SAVE] [SD] 🚭 ▣ ☕ 🍴 🏊

◆ **Ranchland Motel** [M]
(250) 828-8787. **$59-$71.** 2357 Trans-Canada Hwy E. 2.8 mi (4.5 km) e on Trans-Canada Hwy 1, exit River Rd, then just w along service access road. Ext corridors. **Pets:** Small. $10 daily fee/pet. Designated rooms, service with restrictions, supervision.
[A$K] [SD] 🚭 ▣ ☕

[CAA] ◆◆ **Scott's Inn & Restaurant** [M] 🐾
(250) 372-8221. **$69-$99.** 551 11th Ave. Trans-Canada Hwy 1, exit 369 (Columbia St) eastbound, 3.1 mi (5 km) n; exit City Centre westbound, 1 mi (1.6) km s on Columbia St. Ext corridors. **Pets:** Other species. $10 daily fee/pet. Designated rooms, service with restrictions, supervision.
[SAVE] [SD] 🚭 ▣ ☕ 🍴 🏊

KELOWNA

[CAA] ◆◆ **Accent Inns** [SH] 🐾
(250) 862-8888. **$99-$159.** 1140 Harvey Ave. Corner of Hwy 97 N (Harvey Ave) and Gordon Dr. Ext corridors. **Pets:** $15 daily fee/room. Designated rooms, service with restrictions, supervision.
[SAVE] [SD] 🚭 ▣ ☕ 🍴 🏊 🏋

[CAA] ◆◆◆ **Best Western Inn-Kelowna** [SH] 🐾
(250) 860-1212. **$129-$279.** 2402 Hwy 97 N. 0.6 mi (1 km) s of jct Hwy 33 and 97 N (Harvey Ave); corner of Leckie Rd. Ext/int corridors. **Pets:** Small, dogs only. $25 daily fee/room. Designated rooms, service with restrictions, crate.
[SAVE] [SD] 🚭 [&M] ♿ ▣ ☕ 🍴 🏊 🏋

[CAA] ◆◆ **Comfort Inn Kelowna-Westside** [SH]
(250) 769-2355. **$106-$244.** 1655 Westgate Rd. Jct Hwy 97 (Harvey Ave) and Bartley Rd, s to Ross Rd. Int corridors. **Pets:** Medium. $10 daily fee/pet. Service with restrictions, supervision.
[SAVE] [SD] 🚭 ▣ ☕ 🍴 🏊

[CAA] ◆◆ **Days Inn** [M]
(250) 868-3297. **$99-$179.** 2649 Hwy 97 N. Jct Hwy 97 (Harvey Ave) and 33, just n. Ext/int corridors. **Pets:** Large. $10 daily fee/room. Designated rooms, service with restrictions, crate.
[SAVE] [SD] 🚭 ▣ ☕ 🏊

◆◆◆ **The Grand Okanagan Lakefront Resort & Conference Centre** [LH]
(250) 763-4500. **$149-$549.** 1310 Water St. Hwy 97 (Harvey Ave), 0.6 mi (1 km) w along Water St. Int corridors. **Pets:** Accepted.
[A$K] [SD] 🚭 [&M] ▣ ☕ 🍴 🏊 🏋

◆◆ **Ramada Lodge Hotel** [SH]
(250) 860-9711. **$99-$139.** 2170 Harvey Ave. Hwy 97 N (Harvey Ave) at Dilworth Dr. Ext/int corridors. **Pets:** Other species. $10 daily fee/room. Designated rooms, supervision.
[A$K] [SD] 🚭 ☕ 🍴 🏊

[CAA] ◆◆ **The Royal Anne Hotel** [SH]
(250) 763-2277. **$89-$189.** 348 Bernard Ave. Corner of Pandosy and Bernard Ave; downtown. Int corridors. **Pets:** Small. $10 one-time fee/pet. Service with restrictions, crate.
[SAVE] [SD] 🚭 ☕

◆ **Town & Country Motel** [M]
(250) 860-7121. **$80-$119.** 2629 Hwy 97 N. From jct Hwy 33, just n on Hwy 97 N (Harvey Ave). Ext corridors. **Pets:** Accepted.
[A$K] [SD] 🚭 ♿ ▣ ☕ 🏊

◆◆ **Vineyard Inn** [M]
(250) 860-5703. **$79-$169.** 2486 Hwy 97 N. Southwest corner of jct Hwy 97 (Harvey Ave) and 33. Ext corridors. **Pets:** Accepted.
[A$K] [SD] 🚭 ▣ ☕ 🏊 🏋

KIMBERLEY

[CAA] ◆◆◆ **Trickle Creek Residence Inn by Marriott** [SH] 🐾
(250) 427-5175. **$104-$275.** 500 Stemwinder Dr. From Gerry Sorensen Way, follow signs. Int corridors. **Pets:** $75 one-time fee/room. Designated rooms, service with restrictions, crate.
[SAVE] [SD] 🚭 👂 ♿ ▣ ☕ 🍴 🏊 🏋

LOGAN LAKE

◆ **Logan Lake Lodge** [M] 🐾
(250) 523-9466. **$65-$69, 7 day notice.** 111 Chartrand Ave. At Meadow Creek Rd and Chartrand Cresent; centre. Int corridors. **Pets:** $15 one-time fee/room. Designated rooms, supervision.
[A$K] [SD] 🚭 ▣ ☕ 🍴 [K]

LUND

◆ **The Historic Lund Hotel** [SH]
(604) 414-0474. **$80-$195, 3 day notice.** 1436 Hwy 101. End of Hwy 101; on the Sunshine Coast (Hwy 101). Ext/int corridors. **Pets:** Accepted.
[A$K] [SD] 🚭 ☕ 🍴

MADEIRA PARK

◆◆◆ **Sunshine Coast Resort & Marina** [CO] 🐾
(604) 883-9177. **$80-$285, 21 day notice.** 12695 Sunshine Coast (Hwy 101). Just n of Madeira Park Rd, follow signs. Ext/int corridors. **Pets:** Other species. $20 daily fee/pet. Designated rooms, supervision.
🚭 [&M] ♿ ▣ ☕ 🏋 [K]

MANNING PARK

◆◆ **Manning Park Resort** [SH]
(250) 840-8822. **$134-$159.** Hwy 3. Crowsnest Hwy 3; midway between Hope and Princeton. Ext/int corridors. **Pets:** Accepted.
[A$K] [SD] 🚭 ▣ ☕ 🍴 🏊 🏋 [K]

MCBRIDE

[CAA] ◆◆ **North Country Lodge** [M]
(250) 569-0001. **$79-$109.** 868 Frontage Rd N. Just w of village main exit, on Hwy 16 north service road. Ext corridors. **Pets:** Accepted.
[SAVE] [SD] 🚭 ▣ ☕ 🍴

MERRITT

Ⓐ ▼▼▼ Best Western Nicola Inn 🆂🅷
(250) 378-4253. **$79-$119.** 4025 Walters St. Hwy 5, exit 290, 0.6 mi (1 km) w. Ext corridors. **Pets:** Other species. $10 daily fee/pet. Designated rooms, service with restrictions, supervision.
🆂🅰🆅🅴 🆂🅾 ⊠ 🛏 📠 🍽 ≈

Ⓐ ▼▼▼ Ramada Limited 🅜
(250) 378-3567. **$75-$95.** 3571 Voght St. Hwy 5, exit 290, just w. Ext corridors. **Pets:** Accepted.
🆂🅰🆅🅴 🆂🅾 ⊠ 🛏 📠 ≈ ⊠

Ⓐ ▼▼▼ Super 8 Motel 🅜
(250) 378-9422. **$80-$120.** 3561 Voght St. Hwy 5, exit 290, just w. Ext corridors. **Pets:** Small. $10 daily fee/pet. Designated rooms, service with restrictions, crate.
🆂🅰🆅🅴 🆂🅾 ⊠ 🛏 📠 🍽 ≈

NAKUSP

Ⓐ ▼▼▼ The Selkirk Inn 🆂🅷
(250) 265-3666. **$47-$80.** 210 W 6th Ave. Just n. Int corridors. **Pets:** Small. $20 deposit/room, $5 daily fee/pet. Designated rooms, service with restrictions, supervision.
🆂🅰🆅🅴 ⊠ 🛏 📠

NANAIMO

Ⓐ ▼▼▼ Best Western Dorchester Hotel 🆂🅷 🐾
(250) 754-6835. **$95-$135.** 70 Church St. Trans-Canada Hwy 1 to Comox Rd; follow signs downtown. Int corridors. **Pets:** $15 daily fee/pet. Designated rooms, service with restrictions, supervision.
🆂🅰🆅🅴 🆂🅾 ⊠ 🛏 📠 🍽

Ⓐ ▼▼▼ Best Western Northgate Inn 🆂🅷 🐾
(250) 390-2222. **$85-$129.** 6450 Metral Dr. Hwy 19A (Island Hwy), just w on Aulds Rd, then just s. Int corridors. **Pets:** Other species. $20 daily fee/room. Designated rooms, service with restrictions, crate.
🆂🅰🆅🅴 🆂🅾 ⊠ 🛏 📠 🍽 ⊠

▼▼ Days Inn Nanaimo Harbourview 🆂🅷
(250) 754-8171. **$96-$140, 3 day notice.** 809 Island Hwy S. On Island Hwy 1, 1.3 mi (2 km) s. Int corridors. **Pets:** Medium. $10 daily fee/pet. Designated rooms, service with restrictions, supervision.
🅰🆂🅺 🆂🅾 ⊠ 🛏 📠 🍽 ≈

Ⓐ ▼▼▼ Inn on Long Lake 🆂🅷
(250) 758-1144. **$119-$179.** 4700 Island Hwy N. 3.1 mi (5 km) n on Hwy 19A (Island Hwy) from Departure Bay ferry terminal. Ext corridors. **Pets:** Accepted.
🆂🅰🆅🅴 🆂🅾 ⊠ 🅼 🛏 📠 ≈ ⊠

NANOOSE BAY

▼▼▼ Fairwinds Schooner Cove Hotel & Marina 🆂🅷
(250) 468-7691. **$69-$179.** 3521 Dolphin Dr. Island Hwy 1, (8.5 km) se, follow signs via Powderpoint Rd (which becomes Fairwinds Dr). Int corridors. **Pets:** Accepted.
🅰🆂🅺 🆂🅾 ⊠ 🅼 📠 🍽 ≈ ⊠ 🔧

NARAMATA

▼▼▼ The Village Motel 🅜
(250) 496-5535. **$65-$147, 14 day notice.** 244 Robinson Dr. 8.8 mi (14 km) n on Naramata Rd from Penticton. Ext corridors. **Pets:** Small, dogs only. $20 daily fee/pet. Service with restrictions, supervision.
🆂🅾 ⊠ 🛏 📠 🔧 🇿

NELSON

Ⓐ ▼▼▼ Best Western Baker Street Inn & Convention Centre 🆂🅷 🐾
(250) 352-3525. **$109-$139.** 153 Baker St. Jct Hwy 6 and 3A. Int corridors. **Pets:** Large. $10 one-time fee/pet. Designated rooms.
🆂🅰🆅🅴 🆂🅾 ⊠ 🅼 🛏 📠 🍽

NEW DENVER

▼▼ Sweet Dreams Guesthouse 🅲🅸
(250) 358-2415. **$80-$95, 7 day notice.** 702 Eldorado St. Just w of Hwy 6 on Slocan Ave. Int corridors. **Pets:** Accepted.
🅰🆂🅺 🆂🅾 ⊠ 🍽 🔧 🇼 🇿

OSOYOOS

▼▼▼ Spirit Ridge Vineyard Resort & Spa 🅲🅾
(250) 495-5445. **$179-$359, 5 day notice.** 1200 Rancher Creek Rd. Hwy 97 S, e on Hwy 3 (Main St), cross bridge, left on 45th St. Ext corridors. **Pets:** Accepted.
🅰🆂🅺 ⊠ 🛏 📠 ≈ ⊠

PARKSVILLE

Ⓐ ▼▼▼ Quality Resort Bayside 🆂🅷 🐾
(250) 248-8333. **$109-$259.** 240 Dogwood St. Island Hwy 19, exit 51 (Parksville/Coombs), 1.3 mi (2 km) e, then 0.6 mi (1 km) n on Hwy 19A. Int corridors. **Pets:** Dogs only. $15 daily fee/pet. Service with restrictions, supervision.
🆂🅰🆅🅴 🆂🅾 ⊠ 🅼 📠 🍽 ≈ ⊠

▼▼ Skylite Motel 🅜 🐾
(250) 248-4271. **$62-$129.** 459 E Island Hwy. Island Hwy 19, exit 46 (Parksville), 2.2 mi (3.5 km) n on Hwy 19A. Ext corridors. **Pets:** Other species. Service with restrictions, supervision.
🅰🆂🅺 🆂🅾 ⊠ 🛏

Ⓐ ▼▼▼▼ Tigh-Na-Mara Seaside Spa Resort & Conference Center 🅻🅷
(250) 248-2072. **$119-$329, 3 day notice.** 1155 Resort Dr. Island Hwy 19, exit 46 (Parksville), 1.3 mi (2 km) n on Hwy 19A. Ext corridors. **Pets:** $25 one-time fee/room. Designated rooms, service with restrictions, crate.
🆂🅰🆅🅴 🆂🅾 ⊠ 🛏 📠 🍽 ≈ ⊠ 🔧

▼▼ Travelodge Parksville 🆂🅷
(250) 248-2232. **$109-$209.** 424 W Island Hwy. Island Hwy 19, exit 51 (Parksville/Coombs), 1.3 mi (2 km) e, then just n on Hwy 19A. Int corridors. **Pets:** Other species. $10 daily fee/pet. Service with restrictions, supervision.
🅰🆂🅺 🆂🅾 ⊠ 🅼 📠 ≈

Ⓐ ▼▼▼ V.I.P. Motel 🅜
(250) 248-3244. **$74-$129, 7 day notice.** 414 W Island Hwy. Island Hwy 19, exit 51 (Parksville/Coombs), 1.3 mi (2 km) e, then just n on Hwy 19A. Ext corridors. **Pets:** Medium. $10 daily fee/room. Service with restrictions, supervision.
🆂🅰🆅🅴 🆂🅾 ⊠ 🛏 📠 🔧

PARSON

▼▼ Alexa Chalets-Timber Inn & Restaurant 🆂🅷
(250) 348-2228. **$75-$95, 30 day notice.** 3483 Hwy 95. Just off Hwy 95; 21.3 mi (34 km) s of Golden. Ext/int corridors. **Pets:** Accepted.
🅰🆂🅺 ⊠ 🛏 📠 🍽 ⊠ 🔧 🇼 🇿

PEMBERTON

Ⓐ ▼▼▼▼ Pemberton Valley Lodge 🆂🅷 🐾
(604) 894-2000. **$89-$269.** 1490 Portage Rd. Just e on Hwy 99 from Pioneer Junction. Int corridors. **Pets:** Dogs only. $20 one-time fee/pet. Designated rooms, service with restrictions, supervision.
🆂🅰🆅🅴 ⊠ 🅼 🛏 📠 ≈

PENTICTON

▼▼▼▼ Best Western Inn at Penticton 🆂🅷
(250) 493-0311. **$99-$169, 3 day notice.** 3180 Skaha Lake Rd. 2.5 mi (4 km) s. Ext corridors. **Pets:** Accepted.
🅰🆂🅺 🆂🅾 ⊠ 🛏 📠 🍽 ≈

(CAA) ▼▼▼ **Golden Sands Resort Motel** [CO]
(250) 492-4210. **$69-$295, 21 day notice.** 1028 Lakeshore Dr W. Riverside Dr and Lakeshore Dr W. Ext corridors. **Pets:** Medium, dogs only. $10 daily fee/pet. Designated rooms, service with restrictions, supervision.
[SAVE] [S🐾] [✕] [📶] [📺] [🏊]

(CAA) ▼▼▼▼ **Penticton Lakeside Resort, Convention Centre & Casino** [LH] 🐾
(250) 493-8221. **$155-$275, 7 day notice.** 21 Lakeshore Dr W. Main St at Lakeshore Dr W. Int corridors. **Pets:** $10 daily fee/room. Designated rooms, service with restrictions, supervision.
[SAVE] [S🐾] [✕] [📶] [📺] [🍴] [🏊] [✕]

(CAA) ▼▼▼ **Penticton Slumber Lodge** [M]
(250) 492-4008. **$68-$248, 7 day notice.** 274 Lakeshore Dr W. Corner of Lakeshore Dr and Winnipeg St; Hwy 97, n on Riverside, 1 mi (1.5 km) e. Ext corridors. **Pets:** Medium, dogs only. $10 daily fee/pet. Service with restrictions, supervision.
[SAVE] [✕] [⎙M] [📶] [📺] [🏊]

(CAA) ▼▼▼ **Ramada Inn & Suites** [SH]
(250) 492-8926. **$89-$239.** 1050 Eckhardt Ave W. 0.8 mi (1.2 km) w on Hwy 97. Ext corridors. **Pets:** Accepted.
[SAVE] [S🐾] [✕] [⎙M] [🖥] [📶] [📺] [🍴] [✕]

(CAA) ▼▼ **Spanish Villa Resort** [M]
(250) 492-2922. **$68-$248, 7 day notice.** 890 Lakeshore Dr W. Corner of Power St and Lakeshore Dr W. Ext corridors. **Pets:** Medium, dogs only. $10 daily fee/pet. Service with restrictions, supervision.
[SAVE] [✕] [📶] [📺] [🏊]

▼▼ **Super 8 Motel Penticton** [M] 🐾
(250) 492-3829. **$79-$149.** 1706 Main St. Jct Main St and Industrial. Ext/int corridors. **Pets:** Dogs only. $10 daily fee/pet. Designated rooms, service with restrictions, supervision.
[ASK] [S🐾] [✕] [📶] [📺] [🏊]

PORT ALBERNI

(CAA) ▼▼▼▼ **Best Western Barclay Hotel** [SH]
(250) 724-7171. **$109-$199.** 4277 Stamp Ave. Johnston Rd (Hwy 4), just s on Gertrude St. Int corridors. **Pets:** Accepted.
[SAVE] [S🐾] [✕] [📶] [📺] [🍴] [📺] [✕]

▼▼▼ **Hospitality Inn** [SH] 🐾
(250) 723-8111. **$90-$165.** 3835 Redford St. 2 mi (3.2 km) sw of jct Hwy 4 via City Centre/Port Alberni South Rt. Int corridors. **Pets:** Other species. $10 daily fee/pet. Designated rooms, service with restrictions, supervision.
[ASK] [S🐾] [✕] [📺] [🍴]

(CAA) ▼▼ **Riverside Motel** [M]
(250) 724-9916. **$59-$86.** 5065 Roger St. Johnston Rd (Hwy 4), just s on Gertrude St, then just w. Ext corridors. **Pets:** Accepted.
[SAVE] [S🐾] [✕] [📶] [📺] [AC]

PORT HARDY

▼▼ **Airport Inn** [SH]
(250) 949-9434. **$85-$115.** 4030 Byng Rd. Hwy 19, 3.1 mi (5 km) ne, follow signs. Int corridors. **Pets:** Other species. $5 daily fee/room. Service with restrictions, supervision.
[ASK] [✕] [📶] [📺] [🍴] [AC]

▼▼ **Glen Lyon Inn** [SH]
(250) 949-7115. **$75-$145, 3 day notice.** 6435 Hardy Bay Rd. Hwy 19, 0.9 mi (1.5 km) n, follow signs. Ext corridors. **Pets:** Medium. $10 daily fee/room. Designated rooms, service with restrictions, supervision.
[ASK] [S🐾] [✕] [📶] [📺] [🍴] [AC]

POWELL RIVER

▼▼▼ **Powell River Town Centre Hotel** [SH]
(604) 485-3000. **$145-$200.** 4660 Joyce Ave. 0.5 mi (0.8 km) e on Duncan St (BC ferry terminal), then 0.6 mi (1 km) n. Int corridors. **Pets:** $10 daily fee/pet. Designated rooms, service with restrictions.
[ASK] [S🐾] [✕] [⎙M] [📺] [🍴]

PRINCE GEORGE

(CAA) ▼▼▼ **Best Western City Centre** [M] 🐾
(250) 563-1267. **$92-$115.** 910 Victoria St. Just n of Victoria St (Hwy 16) and Patricia Blvd; downtown. Ext corridors. **Pets:** Medium. $25 daily fee/room. Designated rooms, service with restrictions, supervision.
[SAVE] [S🐾] [✕] [📶] [📺] [🍴] [🏊]

(CAA) ▼▼▼ **P.G. Hi-Way Motel** [M]
(250) 564-6869. **$70-$80.** 1737 20th Ave. Jct Hwy 97, 0.7 mi (1.2 km) e on Trans-Canada Hwy 16 (Yellowhead Hwy). Ext corridors. **Pets:** Accepted.
[SAVE] [S🐾] [✕] [📶] [📺]

PRINCE RUPERT

(CAA) ▼▼ **Aleeda Motel** [M]
(250) 627-1367. **$55-$90.** 900 3rd Ave W. Corner of 3rd Ave W and 8th St. Int corridors. **Pets:** Other species. $5 daily fee/pet. Designated rooms, service with restrictions, supervision.
[SAVE] [S🐾] [✕] [📶] [📺] [AC]

▼▼ **The Coast Prince Rupert Hotel** [SH]
(250) 624-6711. **$107-$182.** 118 6th St. Between 1st and 2nd aves W. Int corridors. **Pets:** Accepted.
[ASK] [✕] [⎙M] [📺] [🍴]

(CAA) ▼▼ **Totem Lodge Motel** [M]
(250) 624-6761. **$72-$95.** 1335 Park Ave. 1 mi (1.6 km) w on Hwy 16 (2nd Ave W) from downtown. Int corridors. **Pets:** Accepted.
[SAVE] [S🐾] [✕] [📶] [📺] [AC]

PRINCETON

(CAA) ▼▼▼ **Best Western Princeton Inn** [M]
(250) 295-3537. **$80-$119.** 169 Hwy 3. On Hwy 3. Ext corridors. **Pets:** Medium, other species. $10 daily fee/pet. Designated rooms, service with restrictions, supervision.
[SAVE] [S🐾] [✕] [📶] [📺] [🏊]

(CAA) ▼▼ **Villager Inn** [M]
(250) 295-6996. **$89-$99.** 244 4th St. Just off Hwy 3. Ext corridors. **Pets:** Accepted.
[SAVE] [S🐾] [✕] [📶] [📺] [🏊]

QUALICUM BEACH

▼▼ **Old Dutch Inn (By The Sea)** [SH]
(250) 752-6914. **$69-$109.** 2690 Island Hwy W. Hwy 19, exit 60 (Qualicum Beach/Port Alberni), 2.5 mi (4 km) on Memorial Ave at jct Hwy 19A. Int corridors. **Pets:** Accepted.
[ASK] [S🐾] [✕] [📶] [📺] [🍴] [🏊] [AC]

▼▼ **Qualicum Heritage Inn** [SH]
(250) 752-9262. **$79-$115, 3 day notice.** 427 College Rd. Hwy 19, exit 60 (Qualicum Beach/Port Alberni), 2.5 mi (4 km) e on Memorial Ave, then 0.6 mi (1 km) s on Island Hwy 19A. Int corridors. **Pets:** Accepted.
[✕] [📺] [🍴] [AC]

QUESNEL

(CAA) ▼▼▼ **Talisman Inn** [M]
(250) 992-7247. **$65-$81.** 753 Front St. Hwy 97, 0.6 mi (1 km) n of Carson Ave. Int corridors. **Pets:** $10 daily fee/pet. Designated rooms, service with restrictions, supervision.
[SAVE] [S🐾] [✕] [📶] [📺]

RADIUM HOT SPRINGS

◆◆ ◆◆ **Chalet Europe** Ⓜ
(250) 347-9305. **$79-$179, 7 day notice.** 5063 Madsen Rd. 0.6 mi (1 km) off Hwy 93; up the hill. Ext corridors. **Pets:** Accepted.
(A$K) (S🐾) ✕ 🖪 🖵 (⊠)

◆◆ **Lido Motel** Ⓜ
(250) 347-9533. **$45-$75, 3 day notice.** 4876 McKay St. Jct Hwy 93 and 95, just w along Main St, then just s. Ext corridors. **Pets:** Medium, other species. $10 daily fee/pet. Supervision.
✕ 🖪 🖵 (Ⓩ)

REVELSTOKE

Ⓐ ◆◆ ◆◆ **Best Western Wayside Inn** ⬛
(250) 837-6161. **$89-$169.** 1901 LaForme Blvd. North side of Trans-Canada Hwy 1, at intersection nearest east end of Columbia River Bridge. Ext/int corridors. **Pets:** Large, other species. Designated rooms, service with restrictions, supervision.
(SAVE) (S🐾) ✕ (&M) 🖪 🖵 (¶¶) ⊗

Ⓐ ◆◆◆◆ **The Coast Hillcrest Resort Hotel** ⬛ 🐾
(250) 837-3322. **$125-$235.** 2100 Oak Dr. 2.7 mi (4.3 km) e on Trans-Canada Hwy 1, 0.6 mi (0.9 km) sw. Int corridors. **Pets:** $15 daily fee/pet. Designated rooms, service with restrictions, crate.
(SAVE) (S🐾) ✕ 🖪 🖵 (¶¶) (⊠)

Ⓐ ◆◆ ◆◆ **Monashee Lodge** Ⓜ
(250) 837-6778. **$74-$84.** 1601 3rd St W. South side of Trans-Canada Hwy 1, just e of Columbia River Bridge at Victoria Rd, then just se on Wright Ave. Ext corridors. **Pets:** Medium, dogs only. $10 one-time fee/pet. Designated rooms, service with restrictions, supervision.
(SAVE) ✕ 🖪 🖵

Ⓐ ◆◆ **Swiss Chalet Motel** Ⓜ
(250) 837-4650. **$59-$99.** 1101 Victoria Rd. 0.6 mi (1 km) s from Trans-Canada Hwy 1. Ext corridors. **Pets:** Small, dogs only. $10 daily fee/pet. Service with restrictions, supervision.
(SAVE) ✕ 🖪 🖵

ROSSLAND

◆◆ **Thriftlodge Rossland** Ⓜ
(250) 362-7364. **$74-$99, 14 day notice.** 1199 Nancy Green Hwy. 0.6 mi (1 km) w on Hwy 3B, jct Hwy 22. Ext corridors. **Pets:** Other species. $7 daily fee/room. Designated rooms, service with restrictions, supervision.
(A$K) ✕ 🖪 🖵

SALMON ARM

◆◆ ◆◆ **Best Western Salmon Arm Inn** Ⓜ
(250) 832-9793. **$79-$149.** 61 10th St SW. From centre, 0.7 mi (1.1 km) w on Trans-Canada Hwy 1. Ext corridors. **Pets:** Accepted.
(A$K) (S🐾) ✕ 🖪

◆◆◆◆ **Holiday Inn Express Hotel & Suites Salmon Arm** ⬛
(250) 832-7711. **$109-$199.** 1090 22nd St NE. 0.5 mi on Trans-Canada Hwy 1. Int corridors. **Pets:** Medium. $10 daily fee/pet. Designated rooms, service with restrictions, supervision.
(A$K) (S🐾) ✕ (&M) (🐾) 🖪 🖵 (🏊) ⊗

◆◆ **Super 8 Motel** ⬛
(250) 832-8812. **$70-$135, 10 day notice.** 2901 10th Ave NE. 0.6 mi (1 km) e on Trans-Canada Hwy 1. Int corridors. **Pets:** Accepted.
(A$K) (S🐾) ✕ (&M) 🖪

SECHELT

◆◆ ◆◆ **Driftwood Inn** Ⓜ
(604) 885-5811. **$99-$189.** 5454 Trail Ave. Follow Sunshine Coast Hwy 101, just w of City Centre. Ext/int corridors. **Pets:** Medium, dogs only. $20 daily fee/pet. Service with restrictions, supervision.
(A$K) (S🐾) ✕ 🖪 🖵 (¶¶) (Ⓚ)

SICAMOUS

◆◆ ◆◆ **Sicamous Super 8 Motel** ⬛
(250) 836-4988. **$70-$130.** 1120 Riverside Ave. Trans-Canada Hwy 1, s on Hwy 97A, just w on Main St to traffic circle, then just s. Ext corridors. **Pets:** Accepted.
(A$K) (S🐾) ✕ (&M) 🖪

SILVERTON

◆◆ ◆◆ **William Hunter Cabins** Ⓒ🄰 🐾
(250) 358-2844. **$85-$118, 10 day notice.** 303 Lake Ave. Centre. Ext corridors. **Pets:** Other species. Supervision.
(A$K) (S🐾) ✕ 🖪 🖵 ⊗ (Ⓚ)

SMITHERS

Ⓐ ◆◆ ◆◆ **Aspen Motor Inn** Ⓜ
(250) 847-4551. **$91-$100.** 4628 Yellowhead Hwy. 0.9 mi (1.5 km) w on Hwy 16 (Yellowhead Hwy). Ext corridors. **Pets:** Accepted.
(SAVE) (S🐾) ✕ 🖪 🖵 (¶¶) (🏊)

SQUAMISH

Ⓐ ◆◆ ◆◆ **Mountain Retreat Hotel & Suites** ⬛
(604) 815-0883. **$94-$154.** 38922 Progress Way. 0.9 mi (1.5 km) n on Hwy 99 at Industrial Way. Int corridors. **Pets:** Medium. $20 one-time fee/room. Designated rooms, supervision.
(SAVE) (S🐾) ✕ (&M) 🖪 🖵 (🏊) ⊗

Ⓐ ◆◆ ◆◆ **Sea To Sky Hotel** ⬛
(604) 898-4874. **$99-$109.** 40330 Tantalus Way. 2.9 mi (4.5 km) n on Hwy 99 at Garibaldi Way. Int corridors. **Pets:** Small. $15 daily fee/room. Designated rooms, service with restrictions, supervision.
(SAVE) (S🐾) ✕ (&M) 🖪 🖵 (¶¶) ⊗

SUMMERLAND

Ⓐ ◆◆ ◆◆ **Summerland Motel** Ⓜ
(250) 494-4444. **$65-$124, 10 day notice.** 2107 Tait St. 3.1 mi (5 km) s on Hwy 97. Ext corridors. **Pets:** $10 daily fee/pet. Service with restrictions, supervision.
(SAVE) (S🐾) ✕ 🖪 🖵 (🏊)

SUN PEAKS

Ⓐ ◆◆ ◆◆ ◆◆ **Delta Sun Peaks Resort** ⬛
(250) 578-6000. **$115-$319, 7 day notice.** 3240 Village Way. Hwy 5, 19.4 mi (31 km) ne on Todd Mountain Rd, follow signs to village. Int corridors. **Pets:** Accepted.
(SAVE) (S🐾) ✕ (&M) 🖪 🖵 (¶¶) (🏊) ⊗

TERRACE

Ⓐ ◆◆ ◆◆ ◆◆ **Best Western Terrace Inn** ⬛
(250) 635-0083. **$119-$124.** 4553 Greig Ave. Hwy 16, just e on Greig Ave, follow City Centre signs. Int corridors. **Pets:** $10 one-time fee/room. Service with restrictions, supervision.
(SAVE) (S🐾) ✕ 🖪 🖵 (¶¶)

TOFINO

Ⓐ ◆◆ ◆◆ ◆◆ **Best Western Tin Wis Resort Lodge** ⬛ 🐾
(250) 725-4445. **$119-$210.** 1119 Pacific Rim Hwy. (3.5 km) s on Hwy 4. Ext corridors. **Pets:** Dogs only. Designated rooms, service with restrictions, supervision.
(SAVE) (S🐾) ✕ (&M) 🖪 🖵 (¶¶) (Ⓚ)

◆◆◆◆ **Long Beach Lodge Resort** ⬛ 🐾
(250) 725-2442. **$279-$529, 7 day notice.** 1441 Pacific Rim Hwy. 4.7 mi (7.5 km) s on Hwy 4. Ext/int corridors. **Pets:** $50 one-time fee/room. Designated rooms, service with restrictions, supervision.
(A$K) ✕ 🖪 🖵 (¶¶) (Ⓚ)

(AA) ▼▼▼ Pacific Sands Beach Resort SH ❀
(250) 725-3322. **$235-$535, 7 day notice.** 1421 Pacific Rim Hwy. 4.7 mi (7.5 km) s on Hwy 4. Ext corridors. **Pets:** Medium, dogs only. $25 daily fee/pet. Designated rooms, service with restrictions, supervision.
[SAVE] [X] [&M] [⛵] [🐾] [💻] [🐕]

(AA) ▼▼▼ ▼▼▼ Wickaninnish Inn SH
(250) 725-3100. **$220-$540, 14 day notice.** Osprey Ln at Chesterman Beach. 2.7 mi (4.3 km) e on Hwy 4. Int corridors. **Pets:** Accepted.
[SAVE] [X] [&M] [⛵] [🐾] [🐕] [🐕]

VALEMOUNT

(AA) ▼▼▼ Canoe Mountain Lodge SH
(250) 566-9171. **$78-$124.** 1465 5th Ave. Just e of Hwy 5 (Yellowhead Hwy). Int corridors. **Pets:** Accepted.
[SAVE] [S🐾] [X] [🐾] [💻]

(AA) ▼▼▼ Chalet Continental Motel SH
(250) 566-9787. **$79-$135.** 1450 5th Ave. Off Hwy 5 (Yellowhead Hwy), just e. Int corridors. **Pets:** Accepted.
[SAVE] [S🐾] [X] [🐾] [💻] [🐕] [🐕]

(AA) ▼▼▼ Holiday Inn Hotel & Suites Valemount SH
(250) 566-0086. **$89-$175.** 1950 Hwy 5 S. 0.9 mi (1.5 km) s on Hwy 5 (Yellowhead Hwy). Int corridors. **Pets:** Other species. $35 one-time fee/room. Designated rooms, service with restrictions, supervision.
[SAVE] [S🐾] [X] [&M] [⛵] [🐾] [💻] [🍴] [🏊] [🐕]

VANCOUVER METROPOLITAN AREA

ALDERGROVE

(AA) ▼▼▼ Best Western Country Meadows SH
(604) 856-9880. **$89-$109.** 3070 264th St. Trans-Canada Hwy 1, exit 73 (264th St/Aldergove), 3.1 mi (5 km) s on 264th St (Hwy 13). Int corridors. **Pets:** Medium. $15 daily fee/pet. Designated rooms, service with restrictions, supervision.
[SAVE] [S🐾] [X] [&M] [🐾] [💻] [🍴] [🏊]

BURNABY

(AA) ▼▼▼ Accent Inns M ❀
(604) 473-5000. **$109-$149.** 3777 Henning Dr. Trans-Canada Hwy 1, exit 28 (Grandview Hwy), just n on Boundary Rd. Ext corridors. **Pets:** Small. $15 daily fee/room. Designated rooms, service with restrictions, supervision.
[SAVE] [S🐾] [X] [&M] [⛵] [🐾] [💻] [🍴] [🐕]

(AA) ▼▼▼ ▼▼▼ Best Western Kings Inn and Conference Centre SH
(604) 438-1383. **$119-$199.** 5411 Kingsway. Trans-Canada Hwy 1, exit 29 (Willingdon Ave), 1.9 mi (3 km) s to Kingsway, then 1.2 mi (2 km) e. Ext corridors. **Pets:** Small. $15 daily fee/pet. Service with restrictions, supervision.
[SAVE] [S🐾] [X] [🐾] [💻] [🍴] [🐕]

(AA) ▼▼▼ ▼▼▼ Hilton Vancouver Metrotown LH
(604) 438-1200. **$155-$215.** 6083 McKay Ave. Trans-Canada Hwy 1, exit 29 (Willingdon Ave), 1.8 mi (3 km) s to Kingsway, then just e. Int corridors. **Pets:** Accepted.
[SAVE] [X] [&M] [⛵] [🐾] [💻] [🍴] [🐕]

▼▼ Lake City Motor Inn M
(604) 294-5331. **$89-$109.** 5415 Lougheed Hwy. Trans-Canada Hwy 1, exit 29 (Willington Ave), just n, 0.6 mi (1 km) e on Lougheed Hwy, just n on Springer Ave, then just e on Broadway. Ext corridors. **Pets:** Accepted.
[X] [🐾] [🐕]

COQUITLAM

(AA) ▼▼▼ Best Western Chelsea Inn SH
(604) 525-7777. **$89-$129.** 725 Brunette Ave. Trans-Canada Hwy 1, exit 40B (Brunette Ave N). Int corridors. **Pets:** Small. $20 daily fee/pet. Designated rooms, service with restrictions, supervision.
[SAVE] [S🐾] [X] [&M] [🐾] [💻] [🐕]

▼▼ Ramada Inn Coquitlam SH
(604) 931-4433. **$89-$159.** 631 Lougheed Hwy. Trans-Canada Hwy 1, exit 37 (Gaglardi Way) eastbound, 2.2 mi (3.5 km) e on Lougheed Hwy (Hwy 7); exit 44 (Coquitlam) westbound, then 1.9 mi (3 km) w on Lougheed Hwy (Hwy 7). Ext/int corridors. **Pets:** Other species. $30 one-time fee/room. Designated rooms, service with restrictions, supervision.
[ASK] [S🐾] [X] [&M] [🐾] [💻] [🍴] [🐕]

DELTA

▼▼▼ The Coast Tsawwassen Inn SH ❀
(604) 943-8221. **$92-$149.** 1665 56th St. Hwy 99, exit 28 (Tsawwassen Ferries), 5 mi (8 km) w on Hwy 17; 3.1 mi (5 km) from the BC ferry terminal. Int corridors. **Pets:** Other species. $10 daily fee/pet. Service with restrictions, supervision.
[ASK] [S🐾] [X] [&M] [🐾] [💻] [🍴] [🐕] [🐕]

▼▼▼ River Run Cottages BB ❀
(604) 946-7778. **$129-$210, 21 day notice.** 4551 River Rd W. Hwy 17, 1.6 mi (2.5 km) n on Ladner Trunk Rd (which becomes 47A St, then becomes River Rd W). Ext corridors. **Pets:** Medium, dogs only. $20 daily fee/pet. Designated rooms, supervision.
[ASK] [S🐾] [X] [🐾] [💻] [🐕] [🐕] [🐕]

LANGLEY

(AA) ▼▼ Best Value Westward Inn M ❀
(604) 534-9238. **$65-$85.** 19650 Fraser Hwy. Trans-Canada Hwy 1, exit 58 (200th St/Langley City), 3.1 mi (5 km) s on 200th St, 0.6 mi (1 km) w on Hwy 10, then just w. Ext corridors. **Pets:** $6 daily fee/room. Service with restrictions, supervision.
[SAVE] [S🐾] [X] [🐾] [💻]

(AA) ▼▼▼ Best Western Langley Inn SH
(604) 530-9311. **$99-$129.** 5978 Glover Rd. Trans-Canada Hwy 1, exit 66 (232nd St), 6 km s, follow signs. Int corridors. **Pets:** Small, dogs only. $15 daily fee/pet. Designated rooms, service with restrictions, supervision.
[SAVE] [S🐾] [X] [🐾] [💻] [🍴] [🐕]

(AA) ▼▼▼ Coast Hotel & Convention Centre SH ❀
(604) 530-1500. **$124-$179.** 20393 Fraser Hwy. Trans-Canada Hwy 1, exit 58 (200th St/Langley City), 3.9 mi (6.3 km) s on 200th St, then just w. Int corridors. **Pets:** Small, dogs only. $15 daily fee/pet. Supervision.
[SAVE] [S🐾] [X] [&M] [💻] [🍴]

(AA) ▼▼▼ Holiday Inn Express Hotel & Suites Langley SH
(604) 882-2000. **$109-$129.** 8750 204th St. Trans-Canada Hwy 1, exit 58 (200th St/Langley City), just e on 88th Ave. Int corridors. **Pets:** Accepted.
[SAVE] [S🐾] [X] [&M] [⛵] [🐾] [💻] [🐕] [🐕]

▼▼ Sandman Hotel Langley SH
(604) 888-7263. **$129-$189.** 8855 202nd St. Trans-Canada Hwy 1, exit 58 (200th St), just e on 88th Ave. Int corridors. **Pets:** Accepted.
[ASK] [S🐾] [X] [🐾] [💻] [🍴]

◆◆ **Super 8 Langley/Aldergrove** M ❖
(604) 856-8288. **$109-$139.** 26574 Gloucester Way. Trans-Canada Hwy 1, exit 73 (264th St/Aldergrove), just e on 56th Ave. Int corridors. **Pets:** Other species. Service with restrictions, supervision.

ASK Sᴅ ✕ ᴍ ⬛ ⬤ 🍴 ➳ ⊠

ⒸⒶ ◆◆ **Travelodge-Langley City** M
(604) 533-4431. **$89-$129.** 21653 Fraser Hwy. Trans-Canada Hwy 1, exit 66 (232nd St), 3.8 mi (6 km) s, 0.6 mi (1 km) se on Langley Bypass, then (1.5 km) e to 216th St. Ext corridors. **Pets:** $10 daily fee/pet. Designated rooms, service with restrictions, supervision.

SAVE Sᴅ ✕ ⬛ ⬤

MAPLE RIDGE

ⒸⒶ ◆◆◆ **Best Western Maple Ridge** SH
(604) 463-5111. **$99-$149.** 21735 Lougheed Hwy. 1.2 mi (2 km) w on Lougheed Hwy (Hwy 7). Ext corridors. **Pets:** Accepted.

SAVE Sᴅ ✕ ⬛ ⬤ 🍴

ⒸⒶ ◆◆◆ **Travelodge Maple Ridge** M
(604) 467-1511. **$85-$99.** 21650 Lougheed Hwy. 1.2 mi (2 km) w on Lougheed Hwy (Hwy 7). Int corridors. **Pets:** Accepted.

SAVE Sᴅ ✕ ⬛ ⬤ ⊠

MISSION

ⒸⒶ ◆◆◆ **Best Western Mission City Lodge** SH
(604) 820-5500. **$80-$120.** 32281 Lougheed Hwy. Just w of Hwy 11; corner of Lougheed Hwy (Hwy 7) and Hurd St. Int corridors. **Pets:** Medium. $10 daily fee/pet. Designated rooms, service with restrictions, supervision.

SAVE Sᴅ ✕ ᴍ ⬛ ⬤ 🍴 ➳ ⊠

NORTH VANCOUVER

ⒸⒶ ◆◆◆◆ **Holiday Inn Hotel & Suites North Vancouver** LH ❖
(604) 985-3111. **$112-$179.** 700 Old Lillooet Rd. Trans-Canada Hwy 1, exit 22 (Mt Seymour Pkwy), follow signs. Int corridors. **Pets:** Medium, dogs only. $200 deposit/room, $25 daily fee/pet. Designated rooms, service with restrictions, supervision.

SAVE Sᴅ ✕ ᴍ ⬛ ⬤ 🍴 ➳ ⊠

◆ **Lionsgate Travelodge** M
(604) 985-5311. **$55-$200.** 2060 Marine Dr. Trans-Canada Hwy 1, exit 14 (Capilano Rd), 0.9 mi (1.5 km) s, then just w; from north end of Lions Gate Bridge, just e. Ext corridors. **Pets:** Accepted.

ASK Sᴅ ✕ ⬛ ⬤ ➳

ⒸⒶ ◆◆◆ **North Vancouver Hotel** M
(604) 987-4461. **$89-$149.** 1800 Capilano Rd. Trans-Canada Hwy 1, exit 14 (Capilano Rd), 0.9 mi (1.5 km) s; from north end of Lions Gate Bridge, 0.6 mi (1 km) e on Marine Dr, then just n. Ext corridors. **Pets:** Medium, other species. $20 daily fee/pet. Designated rooms, service with restrictions, crate.

SAVE Sᴅ ✕ ᴍ ⬛ ⬤ ➳

RICHMOND

ⒸⒶ ◆◆◆ **Accent Inns** SH ❖
(604) 273-3311. **$89-$149.** 10551 St. Edwards Dr. Hwy 99, exit 39 (Bridgeport/Airport) northbound to St. Edwards Dr; exit 39A (Richmond/Airport) southbound to St. Edwards Dr. Ext corridors. **Pets:** Medium. $15 daily fee/room. Designated rooms, service with restrictions, supervision.

SAVE Sᴅ ✕ ᴍ ᴋ ⬛ 🍴

ⒸⒶ ◆◆◆ **Best Western Abercorn Inn** SH ❖
(604) 270-7576. **$109-$239.** 9260 Bridgeport Rd. Hwy 99, exit 39 (Bridgeport/Airport) northbound; exit 39A (Richmond/Airport) southbound. Int corridors. **Pets:** Medium. $15 daily fee/pet. Service with restrictions, supervision.

SAVE Sᴅ ✕ ᴍ ⬛ ⬤ 🍴

ⒸⒶ ◆◆◆◆ **Best Western Richmond Hotel & Convention Center** LH ❖
(604) 273-7878. **$119-$189.** 7551 Westminster Hwy. Corner of Minoru Blvd and Westminster Hwy. Int corridors. **Pets:** Other species. $15 daily fee/room. Service with restrictions, supervision.

SAVE Sᴅ ✕ ᴍ ⬛ ⬤ 🍴 ➳ ⊠

ⒸⒶ ◆◆◆ **Comfort Inn Vancouver Airport** SH
(604) 278-5161. **$69-$149.** 3031 #3 Rd. Hwy 99, exit 39 (Bridgeport Rd/Airport) northbound; exit 39A (Richmond/Airport) southbound. Int corridors. **Pets:** Accepted.

SAVE ✕ ⬤ 🍴 ➳

ⒸⒶ ◆◆◆◆ **Delta Vancouver Airport** LH
(604) 278-1241. **$129-$209.** 3500 Cessna Dr. Corner of Russ Baker Way and Cessna Dr; near Moray Bridge. Int corridors. **Pets:** Accepted.

SAVE Sᴅ ✕ ᴍ ᴋ ⬛ ⬤ ➳

ⒸⒶ ◆◆◆◆ **The Fairmont Vancouver Airport** LH 🐾
(604) 207-5200. **$249-$319.** 3111 Grant McConachie Way. In Vancouver International Airport. Int corridors. **Pets:** Small, other species. $25 daily fee/pet. Designated rooms, service with restrictions, supervision.

SAVE Sᴅ ✕ ᴍ ⬛ ⬤ 🍴 ➳ ⊠

◆◆◆ **Holiday Inn Express Vancouver-Airport** SH
(604) 273-8080. **$99-$159.** 9351 Bridgeport Rd. Hwy 99, exit 39 (Bridgeport Rd/Airport) northbound; exit 39A (Richmond/Airport) southbound. Int corridors. **Pets:** $10 daily fee/room. Designated rooms, service with restrictions, supervision.

ASK Sᴅ ✕ ᴍ ⬛ ⬤

◆◆◆ **Holiday Inn International Vancouver Airport** SH
(604) 821-1818. **$109-$169.** 10720 Cambie Rd. Hwy 99, exit 39 (Bridgeport Rd/Airport) northbound to St. Edwards Dr, just 0.6 mi (1 km) n; southbound exit 39B (No. 4 Rd), just e. Int corridors. **Pets:** Small. $15 daily fee/pet. Designated rooms, service with restrictions, crate.

ASK Sᴅ ✕ ᴍ ⬛ ⬤ 🍴

ⒸⒶ ◆◆◆ **La Quinta Inn Vancouver Airport** SH
(604) 276-2711. **$89-$129.** 8640 Alexandra Rd. No. 3 Rd, just e on Alderbridge Way, then just n on Kwantlen St. Int corridors. **Pets:** Accepted.

SAVE Sᴅ ✕ ⬛ ⬤ ➳

ⒸⒶ ◆◆◆ **Sandman Hotel Vancouver Airport** SH
(604) 303-8888. **$149-$169.** 3233 St. Edwards Dr. Hwy 99, exit 39 (Bridgeport Rd/Airport) northbound to St. Edwards Dr; exit 39A (Richmond/Airport) southbound. Int corridors. **Pets:** Accepted.

SAVE ✕ ᴍ ⬛ ⬤ 🍴 ➳

ⒸⒶ ◆◆◆◆ **Vancouver Airport Marriott** SH
(604) 276-2112. **$115-$205.** 7571 Westminster Hwy. Corner of Minoru Blvd and Westminster Hwy. Int corridors. **Pets:** $60 one-time fee/room. Service with restrictions, supervision.

SAVE Sᴅ ✕ ᴍ ⬛ ⬤ 🍴 ➳

SURREY

ⒸⒶ ◆◆◆ **Days Inn Surrey** SH
(604) 588-9511. **$99-$129.** 9850 King George Hwy. Jct Fraser Hwy (Hwy 1A) and Hwy 99A (King George Hwy). Int corridors. **Pets:** Large, other species. $20 daily fee/pet. Service with restrictions, crate.

SAVE Sᴅ ✕ ᴍ ᴋ ⬛ ⬤ 🍴 ➳

◆◆ **Ramada Hotel & Suites Surrey/Guildford** SH
(604) 930-4700. **$109-$139.** 10410 158th St. Trans-Canada Hwy 1, exit 50 (160th St), just w on 104th Ave. Int corridors. **Pets:** Medium, other species. $10 daily fee/pet. Service with restrictions, crate.

ASK ✕ ᴍ ᴋ ⬛ ⬤ 🍴 ➳

▼▼◆ **Ramada Limited Surrey-Langley** SH ❖
(604) 576-8388. **$99-$129.** 19225 Hwy 10. Trans-Canada Hwy 1, exit 58, 3.1 mi (5 km) s on 200th St, then 1.2 mi (2 km) w on Rt 10; corner of 192nd St and Rt 10. Int corridors. **Pets:** $10 daily fee/pet. Designated rooms, service with restrictions.
ASK S❂ ✕ ᵫM ☒ ▤ ➠ ¶¶ ➷

CAA ▼▼◆▼ **Sheraton Vancouver Guildford Hotel** LH ❖
(604) 582-9288. **$109-$179.** 15269 104th Ave. Trans-Canada Hwy 1, exit 48 eastbound, 0.6 mi (1 km) s on 152nd St, then just e; exit 50 westbound, 104th Ave, then just w. Int corridors. **Pets:** Small. Designated rooms, service with restrictions, crate.
SAVE S❂ ✕ ▤ ¶¶ ➷

VANCOUVER

▼◆ **2400 Motel** M
(604) 434-2464. **$60-$199.** 2400 Kingsway. 4.5 mi (7.2 km) se on Hwy 1A and 99A (Kingsway and 33rd Ave). Ext corridors. **Pets:** Other species. $8 daily fee/pet. Designated rooms, service with restrictions, crate.
✕ ▤ ⚠

CAA ▼▼◆▼ **Best Western Chateau Granville** SH
(604) 669-7070. **$119-$239.** 1100 Granville St. Between Davie and Helmcken sts. Int corridors. **Pets:** Accepted.
SAVE S❂ ✕ ᵫM ▤ ▤ ¶¶

CAA ▼▼◆▼ **Best Western Sands** SH ❖
(604) 682-1831. **$129-$239.** 1755 Davie St. Between Bidwell and Denman sts. Int corridors. **Pets:** $10 daily fee/pet. Designated rooms, supervision.
SAVE S❂ ✕ ▤ ▤ ¶¶

CAA ▼▼◆▼ **Delta Vancouver Suites** SH
(604) 689-8188. **$159-$299.** 550 W Hastings St. Between Seymour and Richards sts; entrance in alley way. Int corridors. **Pets:** Accepted.
SAVE ✕ ᵫM ▤ ¶¶ ➷ ⊠

CAA ▼▼◆ ▼▼◆ **The Fairmont Hotel Vancouver** LH ❖
(604) 684-3131. **$199-$409.** 900 W Georgia St. Corner of Burrard at W Georgia St; enter from Hornby St. Int corridors. **Pets:** Other species. $25 daily fee/pet. Service with restrictions, supervision.
SAVE S❂ ✕ ᵫM ▤ ¶¶ ➷ ⊠

CAA ▼▼◆ ▼▼◆ **The Fairmont Waterfront** LH ❖
(604) 691-1991. **$249-$449.** 900 Canada Place Way. Howe St at Cordova St. Int corridors. **Pets:** $25 one-time fee/room. Service with restrictions, supervision.
SAVE S❂ ✕ ᵫM ▤ ¶¶ ➷ ⊠

CAA ▼▼◆ ▼▼◆ **Four Seasons Hotel Vancouver** LH ❖
(604) 689-9333. **$270-$3500.** 791 W Georgia St. Between Howe and W Georgia sts. Int corridors. **Pets:** Small. Service with restrictions, supervision.
SAVE ✕ ᵫM ⚗ ¶¶ ➷ ⊠

CAA ▼▼◆▼ **The Georgian Court Hotel** SH
(604) 682-5555. **$263-$375.** 773 Beatty St. Between Georgia and Robson sts. Int corridors. **Pets:** $25 one-time fee/pet. Designated rooms, service with restrictions, supervision.
SAVE ✕ ᵫM ▤ ¶¶ ⊠

CAA ▼▼◆ **Granville Island Hotel** SH
(604) 683-7373. **$160-$250.** 1253 Johnston St. Granville Island; below the bridge, follow signs. Int corridors. **Pets:** $25 daily fee/pet. Designated rooms, service with restrictions, supervision.
SAVE ✕ ᵫM ▤ ¶¶ ⊠

CAA ▼▼◆▼ **Holiday Inn Express Vancouver** SH ❖
(604) 254-1000. **$89-$219.** 2889 E Hastings St. Between Renfrew and Kaslo sts. Int corridors. **Pets:** $15 daily fee/room. Service with restrictions, supervision.
SAVE S❂ ✕ ᵫM ▤ ▤

CAA ▼▼◆▼ **Holiday Inn Hotel & Suites Vancouver-Downtown** LH ❖
(604) 684-2151. **$109-$359.** 1110 Howe St. Between Helmcken and Davie sts. Int corridors. **Pets:** Medium, other species. Service with restrictions, supervision.
SAVE S❂ ✕ ᵫM ▤ ▤ ¶¶ ➷

▼▼◆▼ **Holiday Inn Vancouver-Centre (Broadway)** SH
(604) 879-0511. **$125-$209.** 711 W Broadway. Between Heather and Willow sts. Int corridors. **Pets:** Accepted.
ASK S❂ ✕ ᵫM ▤ ▤ ¶¶ ➷

CAA ▼▼◆ ▼▼◆ **Hotel Le Soleil** SH ❖
(604) 632-3000. **$325-$490.** 567 Hornby St. Between Dunsmuir and Pender sts. Int corridors. **Pets:** $75 one-time fee/room. Service with restrictions, supervision.
SAVE S❂ ✕ ᵫM ▤ ¶¶

CAA ▼▼◆ ▼▼◆ **Howard Johnson Hotel** SH ❖
(604) 688-8701. **$89-$189.** 1176 Granville St. Between Davie and Helmcken sts. Int corridors. **Pets:** Medium. $25 daily fee/pet. Designated rooms, service with restrictions, supervision.
SAVE S❂ ✕ ▤ ▤ ¶¶

CAA ▼▼◆ ▼▼◆ **Pacific Palisades Hotel** LH ❖
(604) 688-0461. **$150-$390.** 1277 Robson St. Between Jervis and Bute sts. Int corridors. **Pets:** Medium. Service with restrictions.
SAVE S❂ ✕ ᵫM ⚗ ▤ ▤ ¶¶ ➷ ⊠

CAA ▼▼◆ ▼▼◆ **Pan Pacific Vancouver** LH
(604) 662-8111. **$169-$510.** 300-999 Canada Place. Motor entrance off Burrard St. Int corridors. **Pets:** Accepted.
SAVE S❂ ✕ ᵫM ▤ ▤ ¶¶ ➷ ⊠

▼▼◆ ▼▼◆ **Quality Hotel Downtown-The Inn at False Creek** SH
(604) 682-0229. **$79-$219.** 1335 Howe St. Between Drake and Pacific sts. Int corridors. **Pets:** Accepted.
✕ ᵫM ⚗ ▤ ▤ ¶¶ ➷

CAA ▼▼◆ ▼▼◆ **Ramada Inn & Suites Downtown Vancouver** SH
(604) 685-1111. **$75-$199.** 1221 Granville St. Between Davie and Drake sts. Int corridors. **Pets:** Other species. $20 daily fee/room. Service with restrictions, crate.
SAVE S❂ ✕ ▤ ▤ ¶¶

CAA ▼▼◆ ▼▼◆ **Ramada Limited Downtown Vancouver** SH
(604) 488-1088. **$124-$219.** 435 W Pender St. Between Homer and Richards sts. Int corridors. **Pets:** Accepted.
SAVE S❂ ✕ ᵫM ⚗ ▤

CAA ▼▼◆▼ **Renaissance Vancouver Hotel Harbourside** LH
(604) 689-9211. **$159-$229.** 1133 W Hastings St. Between Bute and Thurlow sts. Int corridors. **Pets:** Accepted.
SAVE S❂ ✕ ᵫM ▤ ¶¶ ➷ ⊠

CAA ▼▼◆▼ **Residence Inn by Marriott Vancouver** SH
(604) 688-1234. **$139-$309.** 1234 Hornby St. Between Drake and Davie sts. Int corridors. **Pets:** $75 one-time fee/pet.
SAVE S❂ ✕ ᵫM ▤ ▤ ¶¶ ➷

▼▼◆ ▼▼◆ **Sandman Hotel Downtown Vancouver** SH
(604) 681-2211. **$109-$209.** 180 W Georgia St. Between Cambie and Beatty sts. Int corridors. **Pets:** Accepted.
ASK S❂ ✕ ▤ ¶¶ ➷

CAA ▼▼◆ ▼▼◆ **Sheraton Vancouver Wall Centre Hotel** LH
(604) 331-1000. **$179-$569.** 1088 Burrard St. Between Helmcken and Nelson sts. Int corridors. **Pets:** Accepted.
SAVE ✕ ᵫM ⚗ ▤ ▤ ¶¶ ➷ ⊠

(AA) ▼▼▼▼ **The Sutton Place Hotel** 🏨 ❀
(604) 682-5511. **$189-$429, 3 day notice.** 845 Burrard St. Between Smithe and Robson sts. Int corridors. **Pets:** Medium, other species. $150 one-time fee/room. Designated rooms, service with restrictions, supervision.
[SAVE] [S⌀] [✕] [&M] [⌀] [🖵] [🍴] [⇌] [✕]

▼▼ **Sylvia Hotel** 🅂🄷
(604) 681-9321. **$85-$300.** 1154 Gilford St. Beach Ave and Gilford St; across from English Bay. Int corridors. **Pets:** Other species. Service with restrictions, supervision.
[✕] [🖥] [🍴] [🅰]

(AA) ▼▼▼▼ **Vancouver Marriott Pinnacle Downtown** 🏨 ❀
(604) 684-1128. **$129-$329.** 1128 W Hastings St. Between Thurlow and Bute sts. Int corridors. **Pets:** Other species. $30 one-time fee/pet. Supervision.
[SAVE] [✕] [&M] [🖵] [🍴] [⇌] [✕]

(AA) ▼▼▼▼ **The Westin Bayshore Resort & Marina** 🏨 ❀
(604) 682-3377. **$460.** 1601 Bayshore Dr. W Georgia and Cardero sts. Int corridors. **Pets:** Medium, dogs only. Service with restrictions, supervision.
[SAVE] [✕] [&M] [⌀] [🖵] [🍴] [⇌] [✕]

(AA) ▼▼▼▼ **The Westin Grand, Vancouver** 🏨
(604) 602-1999. **$169-$459.** 433 Robson St. Between Homer and Richards sts. Int corridors. **Pets:** Accepted.
[SAVE] [S⌀] [✕] [&M] [🖵] [🍴] [⇌] [✕]

WHITE ROCK

(AA) ▼▼▼▼ **Ocean Promenade Hotel** 🅂🄷
(604) 542-0102. **$139-$489.** 15611 Marine Dr. Hwy 99, exit 2B southbound; exit 2 (White Rock/8th Ave) northbound, 1.3 mi (2 km) w. Ext/int corridors. **Pets:** Medium. $50 one-time fee/pet. Designated rooms, service with restrictions, supervision.
[SAVE] [S⌀] [✕] [&M] [🖥] [🖵]

END METROPOLITAN AREA

VERNON

(AA) ▼▼ **Best Western Vernon Lodge & Conference Centre** 🅂🄷 ❀
(250) 545-3385. **$105-$129.** 3914 32nd St. 1 mi (1.5 km) n on Hwy 97 (32nd St). Int corridors. **Pets:** $15 daily fee/room. Designated rooms, service with restrictions, supervision.
[SAVE] [S⌀] [✕] [&M] [🖥] [🖵] [🍴] [⇌]

(AA) ▼▼▼ **Holiday Inn Express Hotel & Suites Vernon** 🅂🄷
(250) 550-7777. **$109-$154.** 4716 34th St. Hwy 97 (32nd St) northbound at 48th Ave. Int corridors. **Pets:** Medium, dogs only. $20 daily fee/pet. Designated rooms, service with restrictions, supervision.
[SAVE] [S⌀] [✕] [🖥] [🖵] [⇌]

▼▼ **Vernon Travelodge** 🅂🄷
(250) 545-2161. **$69-$109.** 3000 28th Ave. Hwy 97 (32nd St), just e on 28th Ave; near Polson Park. Ext corridors. **Pets:** Accepted.
[A$K] [S⌀] [✕] [🖥] [🖵] [⇌]

VICTORIA METROPOLITAN AREA

ESQUIMALT

(AA) ▼▼▼▼ **Comfort Inn & Suites** 🄼
(250) 388-7861. **$79-$295.** 101 Island Hwy. Douglas St, 3.1 mi (5 km) w on Gorge Rd, then just s on Admirals Rd. Ext/int corridors. **Pets:** Dogs only. $15 daily fee/pet. Service with restrictions, supervision.
[SAVE] [S⌀] [✕] [🖥] [🖵] [⇌]

MALAHAT

(AA) ▼▼▼▼ **The Aerie Resort** 🄲🄸
(250) 743-7115. **$195-$995.** 600 Ebadora Ln. 20 mi (32 km) n of Victoria off Trans-Canada Hwy 1, use Spectacle Lake turn off, follow signs. Int corridors. **Pets:** Small, dogs only. $25 one-time fee/pet. Designated rooms, service with restrictions.
[SAVE] [S⌀] [✕] [🖵] [🍴] [⇌] [✕]

▼▼ **Malahat Bungalows Motel** 🄼
(250) 478-3011. **$62-$150, 3 day notice.** Trans-Canada Hwy 1, 16.3 mi (26 km) n of Victoria, watch for signs. Ext corridors. **Pets:** Medium, other species. $10 daily fee/pet. Service with restrictions, supervision.
[✕] [🖥] [🅰] [🗷]

SAANICH

▼▼▼ **Howard Johnson Hotel & Suites** 🅂🄷
(250) 704-4656. **$99-$199.** 4670 Elk Lake Dr. Blanshard St (Hwy 17), just w on Royal Oak Dr, then just n. Ext/int corridors. **Pets:** Accepted.
[A$K] [S⌀] [✕] [&M] [&] [🖥] [🖵] [🍴] [⇌]

▼▼ **Sea View Inn: A Clarion Collection Hotel** 🅂🄷 ❀
(250) 658-2171. **$79-$299, 3 day notice.** 4550 Cordova Bay Rd. (10 km) n on (Blanshard St) Hwy 17, exit Royal Oak Dr, (2 km) e to Cordova Bay Rd, then follow to Mount Douglas Park. Ext/int corridors. **Pets:** Other species. $20 daily fee/pet. Designated rooms, service with restrictions.
[A$K] [S⌀] [✕] [🖥] [🖵] [🅰]

SAANICHTON

(AA) ▼▼▼ **Quality Inn Waddling Dog** 🅂🄷
(250) 652-1146. **$84-$154.** 2476 Mt Newton Crossroad. Corner of Hwy 17 and Mt Newton Crossroad. Int corridors. **Pets:** Medium. $10 daily fee/pet. Designated rooms, service with restrictions.
[SAVE] [S⌀] [✕] [🖵] [🍴]

ⓐ ▼▼ Victoria Airport Super 8 SH ❀
(250) 652-6888. **$95-$125.** 2477 Mt Newton Crossroad. Just e of Hwy 17. Int corridors. **Pets:** Medium. $10 one-time fee/room. Service with restrictions, supervision.
SAVE S�６ ✕ 🌡M 🔲

SIDNEY

▼▼▼ Best Western Emerald Isle Motor Inn SH
(250) 656-4441. **$99-$169.** 2306 Beacon Ave. Hwy 17, exit Sidney, just e. Int corridors. **Pets:** Accepted.
ASK S�６ ✕ 🌡M 🔲 🍴

▼▼▼ The Cedarwood Inn & Suites SH
(250) 656-5551. **$69-$245.** 9522 Lochside Dr. Hwy 17, just e on McTavish Rd, then (1.4 km) n. Ext corridors. **Pets:** Accepted.
ASK S�６ ✕ 🔸 🔲 🅺

▼▼▼ Miraloma on the Cove SH
(250) 656-6622. **$109-$375.** 2326 Harbour Rd. Beacon Ave, 1.3 mi (2 km) n on Resthaven Dr, then 0.6 mi (1 km) e. Int corridors. **Pets:** Accepted.
ASK S�６ ✕ 🌡M 🔸 🔸 🔲 ✕ 🅺

ⓐ ▼▼ Victoria Airport Travelodge Sidney SH
(250) 656-1176. **$99-$225.** 2280 Beacon Ave. Just e of Hwy 17, exit Sidney. Int corridors. **Pets:** Large, other species. $10 daily fee/room. Designated rooms, service with restrictions, supervision.
SAVE S�６ ✕ 🌡M 🔸 🔲 🠒

SOOKE

▼▼ Ocean Wilderness Inn & Spa BB
(250) 646-2116. **$99-$180, 7 day notice.** 9171 W Coast Rd. (14 km) w on Hwy 14. Ext/int corridors. **Pets:** $15 daily fee/room. Service with restrictions, supervision.
ASK S�６ ✕ 🔸 🅺 🌊 🟰

ⓐ ▼▼▼ Sooke Harbour House CI ❀
(250) 642-3421. **$275-$575, 14 day notice.** 1528 Whiffen Spit Rd. (2 km) w on Hwy 14. Ext/int corridors. **Pets:** Other species. $40 daily fee/pet. Service with restrictions.
SAVE ✕ 🌡M 🔸 🔸 🔲 🍴 🅺 🌊

VICTORIA

ⓐ ▼▼▼ Abigail's Hotel BB ❀
(250) 388-5363. **$199-$450, 7 day notice.** 906 McClure St. Blanshard St (Hwy 17), just e on Fairfield Rd, then just n on Vancouver St. Int corridors. **Pets:** Small, dogs only. $25 one-time fee/room. Designated rooms, service with restrictions, supervision.
SAVE S�６ ✕ 🔸 🔲

ⓐ ▼▼▼ Accent Inns SH ❀
(250) 475-7500. **$89-$159.** 3233 Maple St. 1.9 mi (3 km) n on Blanshard St (Hwy 17); corner of Blanchard St and Cloverdale Ave. Ext corridors. **Pets:** Medium. $15 daily fee/pet. Designated rooms, service with restrictions, supervision.
SAVE S�６ ✕ 🌡M 🔸 🔲 🍴

ⓐ ▼▼▼ Admiral Inn M ❀
(250) 388-6267. **$89-$209.** 257 Belleville St. Corner of Belleville and Quebec sts. Ext corridors. **Pets:** Other species. $10 deposit/room. Designated rooms, crate.
SAVE S�６ ✕ 🔸 🔲

ⓐ ▼▼▼ Best Western Carlton Plaza Hotel SH ❀
(250) 388-5513. **$89-$249.** 642 Johnson St. Between Douglas and Broad sts. Int corridors. **Pets:** $10 daily fee/pet. Service with restrictions, supervision.
SAVE S�６ ✕ 🌡M 🔸 🔲 🍴

ⓐ ▼▼▼ Blue Ridge Inns M ❀
(250) 388-4345. **$69-$119.** 3110 Douglas St. Between Finlayson St and Speed Ave. Ext corridors. **Pets:** $10 daily fee/room. Service with restrictions, supervision.
SAVE S�６ ✕ 🔸 🔲 🍴 🠒 🅺

ⓐ ▼▼▼ Chateau Victoria Hotel and Suites LH ❀
(250) 382-4221. **$89-$299.** 740 Burdett Ave. Between Douglas and Blanshard sts. Int corridors. **Pets:** Dogs only. $15 deposit/pet. Designated rooms, service with restrictions, crate.
SAVE ✕ 🔸 🔲 🍴 🠒

ⓐ ▼▼ Crystal Court Motel M
(250) 384-0551. **$69-$135.** 701 Belleville St. Between Douglas and Blanshard sts. Ext corridors. **Pets:** Other species. Service with restrictions.
SAVE S�６ ✕ 🔸 🔲 🅺

ⓐ ▼▼▼ Days Inn on the Harbour SH ❀
(250) 386-3451. **$83-$203.** 427 Belleville St. Between Oswego and Menzies sts; entrance on Quebec St. Int corridors. **Pets:** $10 daily fee/room. Designated rooms, service with restrictions.
SAVE S�６ ✕ 🔸 🔲 🍴 🠒 🅺

ⓐ ▼▼▼ Delta Victoria Ocean Pointe Resort & Spa LH
(250) 360-2999. **$119-$419.** 45 Songhees Rd. Just w of Johnson St Bridge, Esquimalt at Tyee Rd. Int corridors. **Pets:** Accepted.
SAVE S�６ ✕ 🌡M 🔸 🔲 🍴 🠒 ✕

ⓐ ▼▼▼ Executive House Hotel SH ❀
(250) 388-5111. **$85-$195.** 777 Douglas St. Between Blanshard and Douglas sts; downtown. Int corridors. **Pets:** Designated rooms, supervision.
SAVE S�６ ✕ 🔸 🔲 🍴 ✕ 🅺

ⓐ ▼▼▼▼ The Fairmont Empress LH ❀
(250) 384-8111. **$169-$559.** 721 Government St. Between Belleville and Humboldt sts. Int corridors. **Pets:** Small, dogs only. $25 daily fee/room. Designated rooms, service with restrictions, supervision.
SAVE S�６ ✕ 🌡M 🔸 🔸 🔲 🍴 🠒 ✕ 🅺

ⓐ ▼▼▼▼ Harbour Towers Hotel & Suites LH
(250) 385-2405. **$94-$414.** 345 Quebec St. Between Oswego and Pendray sts. Int corridors. **Pets:** Accepted.
SAVE S�６ ✕ 🌡M 🔸 🔸 🔲 🍴 🠒 ✕ 🅺

ⓐ ▼▼▼▼ Hotel Grand Pacific LH ❀
(250) 386-0450. **$149-$319.** 463 Belleville St. Between Oswego and Menzies sts. Int corridors. **Pets:** Small. $50 one-time fee/room. Designated rooms, service with restrictions, supervision.
SAVE S�６ ✕ 🌡M 🔸 🔸 🔲 🠒 ✕

ⓐ ▼▼▼ Howard Johnson Hotel-City Centre SH
(250) 382-2151. **$59-$189.** 310 Gorge Rd E. From Douglas St, 0.9 mi (1.4 km) w; between Jutland St and Washington Ave. Int corridors. **Pets:** Accepted.
SAVE S�６ ✕ 🔸 🔲 🍴 🠒

ⓐ ▼▼▼ Huntingdon Hotel & Suites SH
(250) 381-3456. **$69-$189.** 330 Quebec St. Between Oswego and Pendray sts. Int corridors. **Pets:** Accepted.
SAVE S�６ ✕ 🔲 🍴

ⓐ ▼▼▼▼ The Magnolia Hotel & Spa SH ❀
(250) 381-0999. **$169-$329.** 623 Courtney St. Corner of Courtney and Gordon sts. Int corridors. **Pets:** $80 one-time fee/room. Service with restrictions, supervision.
SAVE S�６ ✕ 🌡M 🔲 🍴 ✕

Ⓐ ▽▽▽▽ Marriott Victoria Inner Harbour 🄻🄷
(250) 480-3800. **$129-$299.** 728 Humboldt St. Between Blanshard and Douglas sts. Int corridors. **Pets:** Small. $50 one-time fee/room. Supervision.

Ⓐ ▽▽▽▽ Prior House B&B Inn 🄱🄱 🐾
(250) 592-8847. **$119-$275, 14 day notice.** 620 St. Charles St. Blanshard St (Hwy 17), (2 km) e on Fort St, then just s. Int corridors. **Pets:** Medium, dogs only. $25 one-time fee/room. Designated rooms, service with restrictions, supervision.

Ⓐ ▽▽▽ Robin Hood Motel 🄼
(250) 388-4302. **$61-$99.** 136 Gorge Rd E. Douglas St, (2.4 km) w. Ext corridors. **Pets:** Dogs only. $5 daily fee/pet. Designated rooms, service with restrictions, supervision.

Ⓐ ▽▽▽▽ Travelodge Victoria 🅂🄷
(250) 388-6611. **$65-$175.** 229 Gorge Rd E. From Douglas St, (2 km) w on Gorge Rd E; at Washington Ave. Ext corridors. **Pets:** Medium. $10 daily fee/pet. Designated rooms, service with restrictions.

Ⓐ ▽▽▽▽ The Westin Bear Mountain Victoria Golf Resort & Spa 🅂🄷 🐾
(250) 391-7160. **$389.** 1376 Lynburne Pl. Trans-Canada Hwy 1, exit 14 (Highlands), 1.1 mi (1.7 km) n on Millstream Rd, then 1.9 mi (3 km) ne on Bear Mountain Pkwy, follow signs. Int corridors. **Pets:** Medium. $60 one-time fee/room. Designated rooms, service with restrictions, supervision.

END METROPOLITAN AREA

WESTBANK

Ⓐ ▽▽▽▽ Holiday Inn Westbank (Kelowna) 🅂🄷
(250) 768-8879. **$77-$131.** 2569 Dobbin Rd. Hwy 97 (Dobbin Rd) and Herbert Rd. Int corridors. **Pets:** Accepted.

WHISTLER

Ⓐ ▽▽▽▽ Best Western Listel Whistler Hotel 🅂🄷
(604) 932-1133. **$99-$449, 14 day notice.** 4121 Village Green. Hwy 99, just e on Village Gate Blvd, then follow Whistler Way. Int corridors. **Pets:** Accepted.

▽▽▽▽ Crystal Lodge 🅂🄷 🐾
(604) 932-2221. **$138-$1225, 30 day notice.** 4154 Village Green. Hwy 99, just e on Village Gate Blvd, then follow Whistler Way. Int corridors. **Pets:** Medium, dogs only. $20 daily fee/pet. Designated rooms, service with restrictions, supervision.

Ⓐ ▽▽▽▽ Delta Whistler Village Suites 🄻🄷
(604) 905-3987. **$99-$419, 45 day notice.** 4308 Main St. Hwy 99, just e on Village Gate Blvd, just n on Northlands Blvd, then just e. Int corridors. **Pets:** Accepted.

Ⓐ ▽▽ Edgewater Lodge 🄼 🐾
(604) 932-0688. **$104-$320, 14 day notice.** 8020 Alpine Way. 2.5 mi (4 km) n of Whistler Village via Hwy 99, then e. Ext corridors. **Pets:** Dogs only. $20 one-time fee/room. Supervision.

Ⓐ ▽▽▽▽ The Fairmont Chateau Whistler 🄻🄷
(604) 938-8000. **$159-$949, 30 day notice.** 4599 Chateau Blvd. Hwy 99, 0.6 mi (1 km) e on Lorimer Rd (Upper Village), just w on Blackcomb Way. Int corridors. **Pets:** Accepted.

Ⓐ ▽▽▽▽ Four Seasons Resort Whistler 🄻🄷
(604) 935-3400. **$245-$1475.** 4591 Blackcomb Way. Hwy 99, 0.6 mi (1 km) e on Lorimer Rd (Upper Village). Int corridors. **Pets:** Accepted.

▽▽▽▽ Hilton Whistler Resort & Spa 🄻🄷
(604) 932-1982. **$119-$599.** 4050 Whistler Way. Hwy 99, just e on Village Gate Blvd, then follow Whistler Way. Int corridors. **Pets:** Accepted.

Ⓐ ▽▽▽▽ Pan Pacific Whistler Village Centre 🅂🄷 🐾
(604) 966-5500. **$139-$2699, 30 day notice.** 4299 Blackcomb Way. Hwy 99, just e on Village Gate Blvd. Int corridors. **Pets:** $25 daily fee/room.

▽▽▽▽ Residence Inn by Marriott 🄲🄾
(604) 905-3400. **$149-$899, 30 day notice.** 4899 Painted Cliff Rd. Hwy 99, 0.6 mi (1 km) e on Lorimer Rd (Upper Village), just se on Blackcomb Way, then just w, follow road all the way to the end. Int corridors. **Pets:** Accepted.

Ⓐ ▽▽▽ Summit Lodge & Spa 🅂🄷
(604) 932-2778. **$129-$725, 30 day notice.** 4359 Main St. Hwy 99, just n on Village Gate Blvd, just w on Northlands Blvd. Int corridors. **Pets:** Accepted.

▽▽ ◆ Tantalus Resort Lodge 🄲🄾
(604) 932-4146. **$159-$729, 14 day notice.** 4200 Whistler Way. Hwy 99, just e on Village Gate Blvd, then follow Whistler Way to the end. Int corridors. **Pets:** Accepted.

Ⓐ ▽▽▽▽ The Westin Resort & Spa 🄻🄷 🐾
(604) 905-5000. **$149-$899, 60 day notice.** 4090 Whistler Way. Hwy 99, just e on Village Gate Blvd, then s. Int corridors. **Pets:** Medium, dogs only. Service with restrictions, supervision.

WILLIAMS LAKE

▽▽ Drummond Lodge Motel 🄼
(250) 392-5334. **$75-$102.** 1405 Cariboo Hwy. 0.6 mi (1 km) s on Hwy 97. Ext corridors. **Pets:** Accepted.

Ⓐ ▽▽ ▽ Williams Lake Super 8 Motel 🄼
(250) 398-8884. **$82-$107.** 1712 Broadway Ave S. 1.2 mi (2 km) s on Hwy 97. Int corridors. **Pets:** Accepted.

MANITOBA

BEAUSEJOUR

▼▼ **Superior Inn** SH
(204) 268-9050. **$85-$123.** 1055 Park Ave. Jct Hwy 44, 12 and 302. Int corridors. **Pets:** Accepted.
ASK S☼ ✕ 🖥 📺 ≈

BOISSEVAIN

CAA ▼◆◆ **Canadian Wilderness Inn** SH
(204) 534-7155. **$70-$80.** 306 Mountain Ave. Centre. Int corridors. **Pets:** Accepted.
SAVE S☼ ✕ 🖥 📺

BRANDON

CAA ▼◆▼▼ **Canad Inns-Brandon** SH
(204) 727-1422. **$109-$159.** 1125 18th St. On Hwy 10 (18th St) at jct Brandon Ave. Int corridors. **Pets:** Medium. $25 one-time fee/room. Designated rooms, service with restrictions, supervision.
SAVE S☼ ✕ 🖥 🖥 📺 ❢ ≈

▼▼ **Comfort Inn** SH
(204) 727-6232. **$87-$135.** 925 Middleton Ave. Northside Trans-Canada Hwy 1 service road; between Hwy 10 N and 10 S; just e of McDonald's Restaurant. Int corridors. **Pets:** Other species. $5 one-time fee/room. Designated rooms, supervision.
ASK S☼ ✕ 🖥 🖥 📺

CAA ▼◆▼ **Days Inn** SH ❀
(204) 727-3600. **$94-$104.** 2130 Currie Blvd. Jct Trans-Canada Hwy 1, 5 mi (8 km) s on Hwy 10 S (18th St). Int corridors. **Pets:** Other species. $10 daily fee/pet. Designated rooms, service with restrictions, crate.
SAVE S☼ ✕ 🖥 📺 ≈

CAA ▼ **Rodeway Inn Motel** SH ❀
(204) 728-7230. **$62-$67.** 300 18th St N. On Hwy 10 S, 2 mi (3.2 km) s of Trans-Canada Hwy 1. Ext/int corridors. **Pets:** Medium. $50 deposit/room. Designated rooms, service with restrictions, supervision.
SAVE ✕ 🖥 📺

▼▼ **Royal Oak Inn & Suites** SH
(204) 728-5775. **$126-$199.** 3130 Victoria Ave. 3 mi (5 km) s of Trans-Canada Hwy 1; 0.9 mi (1.4 km) w of jct Hwy 10 (18th St) and 1A (Victoria Ave). Int corridors. **Pets:** Accepted.
ASK S☼ ✕ 🖥 📺 ❢ ≈ ✕

▼▼ **Super 8 Motel Brandon** SH ❀
(204) 729-8024. **$86-$116.** 1570 Highland Ave. On Trans-Canada Hwy 1, south service road, just e of Hwy 10 (18th St). Int corridors. **Pets:** Medium. $20 one-time fee/room. Designated rooms, service with restrictions, supervision.
S☼ ✕ 🖥 🖥 📺 ≈

▼▼▼ **Victoria Inn** SH
(204) 725-1532. **$120-$187.** 3550 Victoria Ave. 3 mi (5 km) s of Trans-Canada Hwy 1; 1.1 mi (1.8 km) w of jct Hwy 10 (18th St) and 1A (Victoria Ave). Int corridors. **Pets:** Accepted.
ASK S☼ ✕ 🖥 📺 ❢ ≈ ✕

CHURCHILL

▼▼ **Polar Inn & Suites** M
(204) 675-8878. **$135.** 153 Kelsey Blvd. Centre. Int corridors. **Pets:** Accepted.
ASK ✕ 🖥 📺 🐾

▼▼ **The Tundra Inn** SH
(204) 675-8831. **$95-$195, 90 day notice.** 34 Franklin St. Centre. Int corridors. **Pets:** Accepted.
S☼ ✕ 🖥 📺 🐾

HECLA

▼▼ **Solmundson Gesta Hus** BB
(204) 279-2088. **$75-$90.** On Hwy 8; in Hecla Village. Int corridors. **Pets:** Accepted.
ASK S☼ ✕ 🗇

NEEPAWA

▼▼ **Bay Hill Inns & Suites** M
(204) 476-8888. **$74-$82.** 160 Main St W. Hwy 16, just w of jct Rt 5. Int corridors. **Pets:** Accepted.
✕ 🖥 📺 ❢ ≈

THE PAS

▼▼ **Super 8** SH
(204) 623-1888. **$85.** 1717 Gordon Ave. At southern approach to town. Int corridors. **Pets:** Accepted.
ASK S☼ ✕ 🖥 📺 ≈

CAA ▼ **Wescana Inn** SH
(204) 623-5446. **$72-$94.** 439 Fischer Ave. On Hwy 10; centre. Ext/int corridors. **Pets:** Accepted.
SAVE S☼ ✕ 🖥 📺 ❢

PORTAGE LA PRAIRIE

▼◆ **Super 8** M ❀
(204) 857-8883. **$86-$92.** 2668 Hwy 1A W. 0.9 mi (1.5 km) w on Trans-Canada Hwy 1A. Int corridors. **Pets:** Other species. Designated rooms, service with restrictions, crate.
ASK S☼ ✕ 🖥 📺 ≈

▼ **Westgate Inn Motel** M
(204) 239-5200. **$55-$71.** 1010 Saskatchewan Ave E. 0.6 mi (1 km) e on Trans-Canada Hwy 1A. Ext corridors. **Pets:** Accepted.
ASK ✕ 🖥 📺

RUSSELL

▼▼ **The Russell Inn Hotel & Conference Centre** SH ❀
(204) 773-2186. **$96-$108, 14 day notice.** Hwy 16 Russell. 0.8 mi (1.2 km) se on Hwy 16 and 83. Ext/int corridors. **Pets:** Small, other species. Service with restrictions, supervision.
ASK S☼ ✕ 🖥 📺 ❢ ≈ ✕

THOMPSON

▼◆▼ **Country Inn & Suites By Carlson** SH
(204) 778-8879. **$110-$120.** 70 Thompson Dr N. Just w of Hwy 6. Int corridors. **Pets:** Accepted.
ASK S☼ ✕ 🖥 📺

WINKLER

▼▼ **Heartland Resort & Conference Centre** SH
(204) 325-4381. **$85-$135.** 851 Main St N. Main St and Hwy 14; centre. Int corridors. **Pets:** Accepted.
ASK S☼ ✕ 🖥 🖥 📺 ❢ ✕

WINNIPEG METROPOLITAN AREA

WINNIPEG

Canad Inns Polo Park SH
(204) 775-8791. **$109-$159.** 1405 St. Matthews Ave. Just e of St James St. Int corridors. **Pets:** Medium. $25 one-time fee/room. Designated rooms, service with restrictions, supervision.

Clarion Hotel & Suites SH
(204) 774-5110. **$139-$269.** 1445 Portage Ave. Jct Empress St. Int corridors. **Pets:** $15 one-time fee/room. Designated rooms, service with restrictions, crate.

Comfort Inn Airport SH
(204) 783-5627. **$107-$121.** 1770 Sargent Ave. At Sargent Ave and King Edward St. Int corridors. **Pets:** Medium. $5 daily fee/room. Designated rooms, service with restrictions, crate.

Comfort Inn South SH
(204) 269-7390. **$95-$140.** 3109 Pembina Hwy. Just n of jct Perimeter Hwy 100 and 75. Int corridors. **Pets:** Medium. $10 daily fee/room. Designated rooms, service with restrictions, supervision.

Country Inn & Suites By Carlson SH
(204) 783-6900. **$110-$120.** 730 King Edward St. Just s of jct Wellington Ave. Int corridors. **Pets:** Accepted.

Days Inn SH
(204) 586-8525. **$119.** 550 McPhillips St. Just n of Logan Ave. Int corridors. **Pets:** Accepted.

Delta Winnipeg LH
(204) 942-0551. **$95-$161.** 350 St. Mary Ave. At Hargrave St. Int corridors. **Pets:** Accepted.

The Fairmont Winnipeg LH ❀
(204) 957-1350. **$99-$1599.** 2 Lombard Pl. Just e of corner Portage Ave and Main St. Int corridors. **Pets:** Large, other species. $25 one-time fee/room. Service with restrictions.

Greenwood Inn & Suites SH
(204) 775-9889. **$99-$199.** 1715 Wellington Ave. Wellington Ave at Century St. Int corridors. **Pets:** Other species. $10 daily fee/pet. Designated rooms, service with restrictions, supervision.

Hilton Suites Winnipeg Airport SH
(204) 783-1700. **$119-$169.** 1800 Wellington Ave. At Berry St. Int corridors. **Pets:** Accepted.

Holiday Inn Winnipeg-South SH
(204) 452-4747. **$120-$140.** 1330 Pembina Hwy. At McGillivray Blvd. Int corridors. **Pets:** Other species. Designated rooms, service with restrictions, supervision.

The Marlborough Hotel SH
(204) 942-6411. **$79-$119, 7 day notice.** 331 Smith St. Just n off Metro Rt 85 (Portage Ave). Int corridors. **Pets:** Accepted.

Place Louis Riel All-Suite Hotel SH ❀
(204) 947-6961. **$100-$200.** 190 Smith St. At St. Mary Ave. Int corridors. **Pets:** Other species. $10 daily fee/room. Designated rooms, service with restrictions.

Radisson Hotel Winnipeg Downtown LH
(204) 956-0410. **$97-$136.** 288 Portage Ave. At Smith St. Int corridors. **Pets:** Accepted.

Super 8 SH
(204) 269-8888. **$102-$134.** 1714 Pembina Hwy. 0.6 mi (1 km) n of jct Bishop Grandin Blvd. Int corridors. **Pets:** Accepted.

Travelodge SH ❀
(204) 255-6000. **$84-$97.** 20 Alpine Ave. Just e of jct Fermor Ave and St. Anne's Rd. Int corridors. **Pets:** Large, other species. $6 daily fee/room. Designated rooms, service with restrictions, supervision.

Victoria Inn Hotel & Convention Centre SH
(204) 786-4801. **$93.** 1808 Wellington Ave. At Berry St. Int corridors. **Pets:** Accepted.

Viscount Gort Hotel SH
(204) 775-0451. **$83-$129.** 1670 Portage Ave. Portage Ave at Rt 90. Int corridors. **Pets:** Accepted.

York The Hotel SH
(204) 942-5300. **$109-$299.** 161 Donald St. At York Ave. Int corridors. **Pets:** Accepted.

END METROPOLITAN AREA

NEW BRUNSWICK

CITY INDEX

BATHURST

▼▼ Atlantic Host Hotel SH
(506) 548-3335. **$94-$120.** 1450 Vanier Blvd. Rt 11, exit 310 (Vanier Blvd). Int corridors. **Pets:** Small. Designated rooms, no service, supervision.

▼▼ Comfort Inn SH
(506) 547-8000. **$81-$100.** 1170 St Peter's Ave. 2.1 mi (3.4 km) n on Rt 134 (St Peter's Ave). Int corridors. **Pets:** Accepted.

▼▼ Danny's Inn & Conference Centre SH
(506) 546-6621. **$72-$100.** Rt 134. Rt 11, exit 310 (Vanier Blvd) northbound to Rt 134 (St Peter's Ave), 2.5 mi (4 km) n; exit 318 southbound to Rt 134 (St Peter's Ave), 2.3 mi (3.8 km) s. Ext/int corridors. **Pets:** Medium. $100 deposit/room. Designated rooms, service with restrictions, supervision.

▼▼ Lakeview Inns & Suites SH
(506) 548-4949. **$94-$106.** 777 St Peter's Ave. 1.8 mi (3 km) n on Rt 134 (St Peter's Ave). Int corridors. **Pets:** Accepted.

BOUCTOUCHE

▼▼ Auberge Bouctouche Inn & Suites SH 🐾
(506) 743-5003. **$79-$119.** 50 Industrielle St. Rt 11, exit 32A/B. Int corridors. **Pets:** Medium. $10 daily fee/pet. Designated rooms, service with restrictions, supervision.

CAMPBELLTON

▼▼ Comfort Inn SH
(506) 753-4121. **$110-$130.** 111 chemin Val D'Amour. Hwy 11, exit 415, 0.6 mi (1 km) e on Sugarloaf St W. Ext/int corridors. **Pets:** Accepted.

▼▼ Howard Johnson SH
(506) 753-4133. **$98-$117.** 157 Water St. Hwy 134; in City Centre Complex. Int corridors. **Pets:** Accepted.

CARAQUET

▼▼▼ Super 8 Motel SH
(506) 727-0888. **$89-$154.** 9 Carrefour Ave. Just e of jct Rt 11 and St Pierre Blvd E. Int corridors. **Pets:** Medium. $10 one-time fee/pet. Service with restrictions, supervision.

CHANCE HARBOUR

▼▼▼ The Mariner's Inn CI
(506) 659-2619. **$119-$139, 3 day notice.** 32 Mawhinney Cove Rd. Hwy 1, exit 96, 5.6 mi (9 km) s on Rt 790; 18.7 mi (30 km) w of Saint John. Int corridors. **Pets:** Medium, dogs only. $10 daily fee/pet. Designated rooms, service with restrictions, supervision.

COCAGNE

▼▼ Cocagne Motel M
(506) 576-6657. **$50-$90.** 1718 Rt 535. Rt 11, exit 15, 0.6 mi (1 km) n on Rt 535. Ext corridors. **Pets:** Accepted.

DALHOUSIE

▼▼▼ Best Western Manoir Adelaide SH
(506) 684-5681. **$119.** 385 Adelaide St. Centre. Int corridors. **Pets:** Very small, dogs only. $75 deposit/pet. Designated rooms, service with restrictions, supervision.

EDMUNDSTON

▼▼▼ Chateau Edmundston Hotel & Suites SH
(506) 739-7321. **$95-$140.** 100 rue Rice. Trans-Canada Hwy 2, exit 18 (Hebert Blvd), 1 mi (1.6 km) sw, then just w on Church Rd. Int corridors. **Pets:** Accepted.

▼▼ Comfort Inn SH
(506) 739-8361. **$92-$165.** 5 Bateman Ave. Trans-Canada Hwy 2, exit 18 (Hebert Blvd). Int corridors. **Pets:** Other species. Service with restrictions, crate.

▼▼ Quality Inn SH
(506) 735-5525. **$81-$144.** 919 Canada Rd. Trans-Canada Hwy 2, exit 13B eastbound; exit 13BA westbound. Ext/int corridors. **Pets:** Medium. $10 daily fee/room. Designated rooms, service with restrictions, supervision.

FREDERICTON

▼▼ Auberge Wandlyn Inn SH
(506) 462-4444. **$90-$110.** 958 Prospect St. Rt 8, exit 3 (Hanwell Rd) eastbound; exit 5 (Smythe St) westbound. Ext/int corridors. **Pets:** Accepted.

▼▼ City Motel SH
(506) 450-9900. **$95-$115.** 1216 Regent St. Trans-Canada Hwy 2, exit 285A and B eastbound; exit 285B westbound, 2 mi (3.3 km) n on Rt 101 (Regent St). Int corridors. **Pets:** Accepted.

▼▼▼ Comfort Inn SH
(506) 453-0800. **$99-$134.** 797 Prospect St. Rt 8, exit 3 (Hanwell Rd) eastbound; exit 5 (Smythe St) westbound. Int corridors. **Pets:** Accepted.

▼▼▼ Crowne Plaza Fredericton Lord Beaverbrook LH
(506) 455-3371. **$149-$179.** 659 Queen St. Corner of Regent St. Int corridors. **Pets:** $15 one-time fee/room. Designated rooms, service with restrictions.

▼▼▼ Delta Fredericton LH
(506) 457-7000. **$160-$235.** 225 Woodstock Rd. 1 mi (1.6 km) n on Rt 102; downtown. Int corridors. **Pets:** Accepted.

▼▼ **Holiday Inn Fredericton** 🄢🄷 ❀
(506) 363-5111. **$109-$169.** 35 Mactaquac Rd (Hwy 102). Trans-Canada Hwy 2, exit 258 eastbound, 7 mi (11 km) e; exit 294 westbound, 19 mi (30 km) w. Ext/int corridors. **Pets:** Other species. Designated rooms, service with restrictions, supervision.
🄰🄢🄺 🆂🅹 ⊠ 🄶🄼 🄷 🄻 🆈🄸 ⇌ ⊠

▼▼ **Lakeview Inns & Suites-Fredericton** 🄢🄷
(506) 459-0035. **$109-$124.** 665 Prospect St. Rt 8, exit 3 (Hanwell Rd) eastbound; exit 5 (Smythe St) westbound. Int corridors. **Pets:** Medium. $5 daily fee/pet. Designated rooms, service with restrictions, supervision.
🄰🄢🄺 🆂🅹 ⊠ 🄷 🄻

🄲🄰 ▼▼▼ **Ramada Hotel Fredericton** 🄢🄷 ❀
(506) 460-5500. **$119-$169.** 480 Riverside Dr. On Rt 105 at the north end of Princess Margaret Bridge. Int corridors. **Pets:** $10 one-time fee/room. Designated rooms, service with restrictions, crate.
🆂🄰🆅🄴 🆂🅹 ⊠ 🄷 🄻 🆈🄸 ⇌ ⊠

GRAND FALLS

▼▼ **Auberge Pres-du-Lac Inn** 🄢🄷
(506) 473-1300. **$90-$125.** 10039 Rt 144. Trans-Canada Hwy 2, exit 75, just w. Ext/int corridors. **Pets:** Small. Designated rooms, service with restrictions, supervision.
🄰🄢🄺 🆂🅹 ⊠ 🄶🄼 🄷 🄻 🆈🄸 ⇌ ⊠

▼▼▼ **Best Western Grand-Sault Hotel & Suites** 🄢🄷
(506) 473-6200. **$121-$199.** 187 Ouellette St. Trans-Canada Hwy 2, exit 79. Int corridors. **Pets:** Accepted.
🄰🄢🄺 🆂🅹 ⊠ 🄶🄼 ♿ 🄷 🄻 🄻

MIRAMICHI

▼▼ **Comfort Inn** 🄢🄷 ❀
(506) 622-1215. **$87-$135.** 201 Edward St. 0.6 mi (1 km) w on Rt 8. Int corridors. **Pets:** Medium. Service with restrictions, supervision.
🄰🄢🄺 🆂🅹 ⊠ 🄷 🄻

▼▼ **Lakeview Inns & Suites** 🄢🄷
(506) 627-1999. **$90-$109, 7 day notice.** 333 King George Hwy. 1.1 mi (1.8 km) w on Rt 8. Int corridors. **Pets:** Other species. $50 deposit/room. Designated rooms, service with restrictions, supervision.
🄰🄢🄺 🆂🅹 ⊠ 🄷 🄻

▼▼▼ **Rodd Miramichi River-A Rodd Signature Hotel** 🄢🄷
(506) 773-3111. **$109-$204.** 1809 Water St. Hwy 11, exit 120, 0.4 mi (0.6 km) e. Int corridors. **Pets:** Accepted.
🄰🄢🄺 🆂🅹 ⊠ 🄶🄼 ♿ 🄷 🄻 🆈🄸 ⇌

MONCTON

🄲🄰 ▼▼ **Beacon Light Motel** 🄼
(506) 384-1734. **$75-$120.** 1062 Mountain Rd. Trans-Canada Hwy 2, exit 454 (Mapleton Rd), 1.7 mi (2.8 km) to Rt 126 (Mountain Rd), then just s. Ext/int corridors. **Pets:** Accepted.
🆂🄰🆅🄴 ⊠ 🄷 🄻 🆈🄸 ⇌

▼▼▼ **Best Western Moncton** 🄢🄷
(506) 388-0888. **$115-$230.** 300 Lewisville Rd. Trans-Canada Hwy 2, exit 459A eastbound, s on Rt 115 to Lewisville Rd, then left; exit 467A westbound, 5 mi (8 km) w on Hwy 15, exit 10. Int corridors. **Pets:** Very small. Designated rooms, service with restrictions, supervision.
🄰🄢🄺 🆂🅹 ⊠ 🄶🄼 ♿ 🄷 🄻 🄻

🄲🄰 ▼▼ **Coastal Inn Champlain** 🄢🄷
(506) 857-9686. **$99-$129.** 502 Kennedy St. At Paul St; opposite Champlain Place Shopping Centre. Ext/int corridors. **Pets:** Other species. Designated rooms, service with restrictions, supervision.
🆂🄰🆅🄴 🆂🅹 ⊠ 🄷 🄻 🆈🄸 ⇌

▼▼ **Colonial Inns** 🄢🄷
(506) 382-3395. **$97.** 42 Highfield St. 1 blk n of Main St; centre. Ext/int corridors. **Pets:** Accepted.
🄰🄢🄺 🆂🅹 ⊠ 🄷 🆈🄸 ⇌ ⊠

🄲🄰 ▼▼ **Comfort Inn** 🄢🄷
(506) 859-6868. **$85-$295.** 20 Maplewood Dr. Trans-Canada Hwy 2, exit 459A onto Hwy 115 S, left on Rt 134 E (Lewisville Rd). Int corridors. **Pets:** Other species. Service with restrictions, supervision.
🆂🄰🆅🄴 🆂🅹 ⊠ 🄷 🄻

▼▼ **Comfort Inn** 🄢🄷
(506) 384-3175. **$105-$295.** 2495 Mountain Rd. Trans-Canada Hwy 2, exit 450. Int corridors. **Pets:** Accepted.
🄰🄢🄺 🆂🅹 ⊠ 🄷 🄻

▼▼ **Country Inn & Suites By Carlson** 🄢🄷 ❀
(506) 852-7000. **$90-$132.** 2475 Mountain Rd. Trans-Canada Hwy 2, exit 450. Int corridors. **Pets:** $50 deposit/room, $5 daily fee/pet. Designated rooms, service with restrictions, supervision.
🄰🄢🄺 🆂🅹 ⊠ 🄷 🄻

🄲🄰 ▼▼▼ **Crowne Plaza Moncton Downtown** 🄻🄷
(506) 854-6340. **$149-$179.** 1005 Main St. Highfield and Main sts; downtown. Int corridors. **Pets:** $10 one-time fee/pet. Designated rooms, service with restrictions, supervision.
🆂🄰🆅🄴 🆂🅹 ⊠ 🄷 🄻 🆈🄸 ⇌ ⊠

▼▼▼▼ **Delta Beausejour** 🄻🄷
(506) 854-4344. **$129-$199.** 750 Main St. Main and Bacon sts; centre of downtown. Int corridors. **Pets:** Accepted.
🄰🄢🄺 ⊠ 🄻 🆈🄸 ⇌

🄲🄰 ▼▼▼▼ **Holiday Inn Express Hotel & Suites Moncton** 🄢🄷 ❀
(506) 384-1050. **$119-$199.** 2515 Mountain Rd. Trans-Canada Hwy 2, exit 450. Ext/int corridors. **Pets:** Medium. $100 deposit/room. Designated rooms, service with restrictions, supervision.
🆂🄰🆅🄴 🆂🅹 ⊠ 🄶🄼 🄐 🄻 🆈🄸 ⇌ ⊠

▼▼▼ **Rodd Park House Inn** 🄢🄷
(506) 382-1664. **$83-$182.** 434 Main St. On Rt 106 (Main St) at King St. Ext/int corridors. **Pets:** Accepted.
🄰🄢🄺 🆂🅹 ⊠ 🄻 🆈🄸 ⇌

▼▼▼ **Super 8 Motel Moncton/Dieppe** 🄢🄷 ❀
(506) 858-8880. **Call for rates.** 370 Dieppe Blvd. Hwy 15, exit 16, 0.6 mi (1 km) s. Int corridors. **Pets:** Other species. Service with restrictions, supervision.
⊠ 🄶🄼 🄰 🄷 🄻 ⇌

OROMOCTO

▼▼▼ **Days Inn Oromocto** 🄢🄷
(506) 357-5657. **$114-$122.** 60 Brayson Blvd. Trans-Canada Hwy 2, exit 301 eastbound; exit 303 westbound, just s to Pioneer Ave, then 1 mi (1.6 km) w. Int corridors. **Pets:** Accepted.
🄰🄢🄺 🆂🅹 ⊠ 🄶🄼 🄰 🄷 🄻 🆈🄸 ⇌

ROTHESAY

▼▼▼ **Shadow Lawn Inn** 🄲🄸
(506) 847-7539. **$119-$195, 3 day notice.** 3180 Rothesay Rd. Hwy 1, exit 137B eastbound; exit 137A westbound, follow signs for Rothesay Rd and Rt 100, 1 mi (1.6 km) left on Old Hampton Rd (Rt 100), then left on Rt 100. Int corridors. **Pets:** $15 daily fee/room. Service with restrictions, supervision.
🄰🄢🄺 🆂🅹 ⊠ 🄷 🄻 🆈🄸

SACKVILLE

▼▼ **Coastal Inn Sackville** 🄢🄷
(506) 536-0000. **$89-$115.** 15 Wright St. Trans-Canada Hwy 2, exit 504. Int corridors. **Pets:** Accepted.
⊠ 🄷

🄲🄰 ▼▼▼ **Marshlands Inn** 🄲🄸
(506) 536-0170. **$84-$190.** 55 Bridge St. On Hwy 106; centre. Int corridors. **Pets:** Accepted.
🆂🄰🆅🄴 ⊠ 🆈🄸

ST. ANDREWS

CAA ▼▼▼ **The Fairmont Algonquin** 🅛🅗 ☘
(506) 529-8823. **$129-$299, 3 day notice.** 184 Adolphus St. Off Hwy
127. Int corridors. **Pets:** Other species. $25 daily fee/pet. Service with
restrictions, supervision.
[SAVE] [✕] [🛏] [💻] [🍴] [≈] [✕]

▼▼▼ **St. Andrews Cottages** 🅒🅐
(506) 529-8555. **$95-$139, 14 day notice.** 3907 Rt 127. On Rt 127, 1.5
mi (2.5 km) n. Ext corridors. **Pets:** Accepted.
[✕] [🛏] [≈] [🅐🅒]

CAA ▼▼▼▼ **The Windsor House of St. Andrews** 🅒🅘
(506) 529-3330. **$125-$300, 14 day notice.** 132 Water St. Centre. Int
corridors. **Pets:** Other species. Service with restrictions.
[SAVE] [S🔒] [✕] [🍴]

ST. BASILE

▼▼▼▼ **Days Inn Edmundston** 🅢🅗
(506) 263-0000. **$80-$162.** 10 rue Mathieu. Trans-Canada Hwy 2, exit
26. Int corridors. **Pets:** Other species. Service with restrictions.
[ASK] [S🔒] [✕] [🛏] [💻]

SAINT JOHN

▼ **Colonial Inns** 🅢🅗
(506) 652-3000. **$102-$110.** 175 City Rd. Adjacent to Hwy 1, exit 123.
Ext/int corridors. **Pets:** Accepted.
[ASK] [S🔒] [✕] [🛏] [🍴] [≈]

▼▼ **Comfort Inn** 🅢🅗
(506) 674-1873. **$120-$145.** 1155 Fairville Blvd. Hwy 1, exit 117 westbound; exit 119 eastbound, turn left. Int corridors. **Pets:** Accepted.
[ASK] [S🔒] [✕] [💻]

▼▼ **Country Inn & Suites** 🅢🅗 ☘
(506) 635-0400. **$99-$138.** 1011 Fairville Blvd. Hwy 1, exit 119B eastbound, left on Catherwood Dr, left at lights; exit 119A westbound. Int
corridors. **Pets:** Other species. $15 one-time fee/room. Service with restric-
tions, crate.
[ASK] [S🔒] [✕] [🛏] [💻]

▼▼▼▼ **Delta Brunswick** 🅛🅗 ☘
(506) 648-1981. **$109-$169.** 39 King St. Centre of downtown; in Brunswick Square Mall. Int corridors. **Pets:** Medium. $35 one-time fee/room.
Designated rooms, service with restrictions, supervision.
[ASK] [S🔒] [✕] [🅛🅜] [🅛🅜] [💻] [🍴] [≈] [✕]

CAA ▼▼▼ **Fort Howe Hotel & Convention Centre** 🅢🅗
(506) 657-7320. **$99-$175.** 10 Portland St. Hwy 1, exit 121 eastbound
off Harbour Bridge; exit 123 westbound. Int corridors. **Pets:** Other
species. Service with restrictions, supervision.
[SAVE] [S🔒] [✕] [🛏] [💻] [🍴] [≈]

▼▼▼▼ **Hilton Saint John** 🅛🅗
(506) 693-8484. **$119-$219.** One Market Square. Hwy 1, exit 122 at
Market Square. Int corridors. **Pets:** Accepted.
[✕] [💻] [🍴] [≈] [✕]

CAA ▼▼▼▼ **Holiday Inn Express Hotel & Suites** 🅢🅗
(506) 642-2622. **$99-$179.** 400 Main St/Chesley Dr. 0.6 mi (1 km) w on
Hwy 1; north end Chesley Dr, exit 121; off Harbour Bridge. Int corridors. **Pets:** Accepted.
[SAVE] [S🔒] [✕] [🛏] [💻] [≈]

CAA ▼▼▼▼ **Inn on the Cove and Spa** 🅒🅘 ☘
(506) 672-7799. **$109-$225, 7 day notice.** 1371 Sand Cove Rd. Hwy
1, exit 119, right to Sand Cove Rd, then 3.2 mi (2 km) w. Int corridors.
Pets: Medium, dogs only. $35 one-time fee/room. Designated rooms, serv-
ice with restrictions, supervision.
[SAVE] [S🔒] [✕] [🅛🅜] [💻] [🍴] [🆉]

ST. STEPHEN

CAA ▼▼ **St. Stephen Inn** 🅢🅗
(506) 466-1814. **$59-$89.** 99 King St. On Hwy 1; centre. Ext/int corridors. **Pets:** Accepted.
[SAVE] [S🔒] [✕] [🍴]

SHEDIAC

▼▼ **Gaudet Chalets & Motel** 🅜
(506) 533-8877. **$65-$119, 30 day notice.** 14 Belleview Heights. On Rt
133, 1.4 mi (2.4 km) w of Rt 15, exit 37. Ext corridors. **Pets:** Accepted.
[✕] [🛏] [≈]

ST-LEONARD

CAA ▼▼▼ **Daigle's Motel** 🅢🅗
(506) 423-6351. **$78-$99.** 68 rue DuPont. Hwy 17, 0.6 mi (1 km) s of
Trans-Canada Hwy 2, exit 58. Ext corridors. **Pets:** Small. $7 one-time
fee/pet. Designated rooms, service with restrictions, supervision.
[SAVE] [S🔒] [✕] [🍴] [≈]

SUSSEX

CAA ▼ **All Seasons Inn** 🅜
(506) 433-2220. **$65-$125.** 1015 Main St. Hwy 1, exit 192 eastbound;
exit 198 westbound, left towards Sussex Corner; centre. Ext corridors.
Pets: Accepted.
[SAVE] [S🔒] [✕] [💻] [🍴]

▼▼ **Fairway Inn** 🅢🅗
(506) 433-3470. **$92-$155.** 216 Roachville Rd. Hwy 1, exit 193. Ext/int
corridors. **Pets:** Small. $10 daily fee/pet. Designated rooms, service with
restrictions, supervision.
[ASK] [S🔒] [✕] [💻] [🍴] [≈]

▼ **Pine Cone Motel** 🅜
(506) 433-3958. **$65-$75.** 12808 Rt 114. Hwy 1, exit 198, 1.2 mi (2 km)
e on Hwy 114 towards Penobsquis. Ext corridors. **Pets:** Small. Designated rooms, no service, supervision.
[ASK] [✕] [🆉]

WOODSTOCK

CAA ▼▼▼ **Econo Lodge** 🅢🅗 ☘
(506) 328-8876. **$85-$130.** 168 Rt 555. Trans-Canada Hwy 2, exit 188
(Houlton Rd). Ext/int corridors. **Pets:** Medium. $10 daily fee/pet. Desig-
nated rooms, service with restrictions, crate.
[SAVE] [S🔒] [✕] [💻] [🍴] [≈]

CAA ▼▼▼ **Howard Johnson Inn** 🅢🅗
(506) 328-3315. **$80-$110.** 159 Rt 555, exit 188 TCH. Trans-Canada
Hwy 2, exit 188 (Houlton Rd). Ext/int corridors. **Pets:** Medium. $10 daily
fee/pet. Designated rooms, service with restrictions, supervision.
[ASK] [S🔒] [✕] [💻] [🍴] [≈] [✕]

▼ **Stiles Motel Hill View** 🅢🅗
(506) 328-6671. **$85-$105, 3 day notice.** 827 Main St. Trans-Canada
Hwy 2, exit 185 eastbound, 1.6 mi (2.5 km) e; exit 188 (Houlton Rd)
westbound, 3.4 mi (5.5 km) via Rt 555 and 103 (Main St). Ext corridors. **Pets:** Accepted.
[ASK] [S🔒] [✕] [🍴]

YOUNGS COVE ROAD

CAA ▼ **McCready's Motel** 🅜
(506) 362-2916. **$56-$65.** 10995 Rt 10. Trans-Canada Hwy 2, exit 365,
just w. Ext corridors. **Pets:** Accepted.
[SAVE] [🍴] [🅐🅒] [🆉]

NEWFOUNDLAND AND LABRADOR

CITY INDEX

CHANNEL-PORT-AUX-BASQUES

▼▼▼ St. Christopher's Hotel 🆂🅷
(709) 695-7034. **$80-$113.** 146 Caribou Rd. Trans-Canada Hwy 1, exit Port Aux Basques (downtown), follow signs 1.2 mi (2 km). Int corridors. **Pets:** Medium, other species. Designated rooms, service with restrictions, supervision.
(A$K) 🆂🅱 ⊠ 🛢 💻 (ᵀᴵ)

CLARENVILLE

▼▼ Restland Motel 🆂🅷
(709) 466-7636. **$95-$105.** 262 Memorial Dr. Centre. Ext/int corridors. **Pets:** Accepted.
(A$K) 🆂🅱 ⊠ 🛢 (ᵀᴵ) (A̶C̶)

▼▼▼ St. Jude Hotel 🆂🅷
(709) 466-1717. **$92-$110.** 247 Trans-Canada Hwy. On Trans-Canada Hwy 1; centre. Int corridors. **Pets:** $10 one-time fee/room. Designated rooms, service with restrictions, supervision.
⊠ 🛢 💻 (ᵀᴵ)

CORNER BROOK

▼▼ Comfort Inn 🆂🅷
(709) 639-1980. **$110-$130.** 41 Maple Valley Rd. Trans-Canada Hwy 1, exit 5 eastbound; exit 6 westbound, via Confederation Ave. Int corridors. **Pets:** Other species. Supervision.
(A$K) 🆂🅱 ⊠ 💻 (ᵀᴵ)

▼▼ Glynmill Inn 🆂🅷
(709) 634-5181. **$111.** 1B Cobb Ln. Centre. Int corridors. **Pets:** Service with restrictions.
⊠ 🛢 💻 (ᵀᴵ)

▼▼▼ Greenwood Inn & Suites-Corner Brook 🅻🅷
(709) 634-5381. **$109-$119.** 48 West St. Centre. Int corridors. **Pets:** Accepted.
⊠ 🛢 💻 (ᵀᴵ) 🏊

▼▼ Mamateek Inn 🆂🅷
(709) 639-8901. **$99-$109, 30 day notice.** Maple Valley Rd. Trans-Canada Hwy 1, exit 5 eastbound; exit 6 westbound via Confederation Ave. Int corridors. **Pets:** Accepted.
(A$K) 🆂🅱 ⊠ (ᵀᴵ)

COW HEAD

▼▼▼ Shallow Bay Motel & Cabins 🆂🅷
(709) 243-2471. **$85-$105.** Rt 430, The Viking Trail. Hwy 430, 2.5 mi (4 km) w towards the ocean, follow signs. Ext/int corridors. **Pets:** Accepted.
⊠ 🛢 💻 (ᵀᴵ) 🏊 (A̶C̶)

GANDER

▼▼▼ Albatross Hotel 🆂🅷
(709) 256-3956. **$91-$92.** TransCanada Hwy. On Trans-Canada Hwy 1. Ext/int corridors. **Pets:** Other species.
(A$K) ⊠ 💻 (ᵀᴵ)

▼▼▼ Comfort Inn 🆂🅷
(709) 256-3535. **$100-$129.** 112 Trans-Canada Hwy 1. Centre. Ext/int corridors. **Pets:** Accepted.
(A$K) 🆂🅱 ⊠ 🛢 💻 (ᵀᴵ)

(CAA) ▼▼▼ Hotel Gander 🆂🅷
(709) 256-3931. **$79-$99, 30 day notice.** 100 Trans-Canada Hwy 1. Centre. Int corridors. **Pets:** Accepted.
(SAVE) 🆂🅱 ⊠ 🛢 💻 (ᵀᴵ) 🏊

▼▼▼ Sinbad's Hotel & Suites 🆂🅷
(709) 651-2678. **$90.** Bennett Dr. Centre; opposite Gander Mall. Ext corridors. **Pets:** Medium, other species. Designated rooms, service with restrictions, crate.
(A$K) 🆂🅱 ⊠ 🛢 💻 (ᵀᴵ)

GRAND FALLS-WINDSOR

▼▼▼ Mount Peyton Hotel 🆂🅷
(709) 489-2251. **$109-$112.** 214 Lincoln Rd. 0.6 mi (1 km) ne on Trans-Canada Hwy 1. Ext/int corridors. **Pets:** Accepted.
(A$K) 🆂🅱 ⊠ 🛢 💻 (ᵀᴵ)

LABRADOR CITY

▼▼▼ Carol Inn 🆂🅷
(709) 944-7736. **$65-$85.** 215 Drake Ave. Centre. Int corridors. **Pets:** Accepted.
(A$K) 🆂🅱 ⊠ 🛢 💻 (ᵀᴵ)

L'ANSE AU CLAIR

▼▼ Northern Light Inn 🆂🅷
(709) 931-2332. **$90-$110, 21 day notice.** Rt 510. On Rt 510; centre. Int corridors. **Pets:** Accepted.
(A$K) 🆂🅱 ⊠ 🛢 (ᵀᴵ)

ST. JOHN'S

(CAA) ▼▼▼ Best Western Travellers Inn 🆂🅷
(709) 722-5540. **$89-$159.** 199 Kenmount Rd. Just w of Pippy Place Rd. Ext/int corridors. **Pets:** Medium, other species. $100 deposit/room. Designated rooms, service with restrictions, supervision.
(SAVE) 🆂🅱 ⊠ 🛢 💻 (ᵀᴵ) 🏊

▼▼▼ Capital Hotel 🆂🅷
(709) 738-4480. **$118.** 208 Kenmount Rd. Just w of Pippy Place Rd. Int corridors. **Pets:** Designated rooms, service with restrictions, crate.
(A$K) 🆂🅱 ⊠ 🛢 💻 (ᵀᴵ)

(CAA) ▼▼▼ Comfort Inn Airport 🆂🅷
(709) 753-3500. **$99-$149.** 106 Airport Rd. Trans-Canada Hwy 1, exit 47A, 0.6 mi (1 km) n on Rt 40 (Portugal Cove Rd). Int corridors. **Pets:** $30 one-time fee/room. Supervision.
(SAVE) 🆂🅱 ⊠ 🛢 💻 (ᵀᴵ)

▼▼▼ Delta St. John's Hotel and Conference Centre 🅻🅷
(709) 739-6404. **$135-$155, 30 day notice.** 120 New Gower St. At Barter's Hill Rd; centre. Int corridors. **Pets:** Accepted.
(A$K) 🆂🅱 ⊠ (&̶M̶) (▽̶) 💻 (ᵀᴵ) 🏊 (⊠̶)

▼▼▼ The Fairmont Newfoundland 🅻🅷
(709) 726-4980. **$161-$332.** Cavendish Square. Centre. Int corridors. **Pets:** Medium, other species. $25 daily fee/room. Service with restrictions, supervision.
(A$K) ⊠ 💻 (ᵀᴵ) 🏊 (⊠̶)

▼▼▼ **Holiday Inn St. John's-Govt Centre** 🏨 ❀
(709) 722-0506. **$120-$135.** 180 Portugal Cove Rd. Trans-Canada Hwy 1, exit 47A, 0.9 mi (1.4 km) s. Ext/int corridors. **Pets:** Large, other species. $25 deposit/room. Designated rooms, service with restrictions, supervision.
⊠ 🅼 ⬚ 🖥 💻 🍴 ⋍

Ⓐ ▼▼▼ **Ramada St. John's** 🆂🅷
(709) 722-9330. **$109-$179.** 102 Kenmount Rd. Corner of Pippy Place Rd. Int corridors. **Pets:** Accepted.
🆂🅰🆅🅴 🆂 ⊠ 🖥 💻 🍴

▼▼▼ **Super 8 Motel** 🆂🅷
(709) 739-8888. **$109-$139.** 175 Higgins Line Rd. Trans-Canada Hwy 1, exit 47A, just s on Rt 40 (Portugal Cove Rd). Int corridors. **Pets:** Accepted.
🅰🆂🅺 🆂 ⊠ 🅼 ⬚ 🖥 💻 ⋍

STEPHENVILLE

▼ ◆ **Holiday Inn Stephenville** 🆂🅷
(709) 643-6666. **$140.** 44 Queen St. Centre. Int corridors. **Pets:** Accepted.
🅰🆂🅺 🆂 ⊠ 💻 🍴

NORTHWEST TERRITORIES

YELLOWKNIFE

▽▽▽ **Fraser Tower Suite Hotel** 🆂🅷
(867) 873-8700. **$145-$175.** 5303 52nd St. Corner of 52nd St and 53rd Ave. Int corridors. **Pets:** $10 daily fee/room. Service with restrictions, supervision.
Ⓐ$🅺 ⊠ 🛢 💻 🅰🅲

▽▽ **Yellowknife Super 8 Motel** Ⓜ 🐾
(867) 669-8888. **$139-$179.** 308 Old Airport Rd. 1.2 mi (2 km) s on Franklin, 0.6 mi (1 km) w; in WalMart Plaza. Int corridors. **Pets:** Other species. $25 one-time fee/room. Designated rooms, service with restrictions, supervision.
Ⓐ$🅺 🆂🛢 ⊠ 🛢 💻

NOVA SCOTIA

CITY INDEX

AMHERST

🏵🏵 Auberge Wandlyn Inn SH
(902) 667-3331. **$115-$149.** W Victoria St. Trans-Canada Hwy 104, exit 3, 0.6 mi (1 km) w. Ext/int corridors. **Pets:** Accepted.
(A$K) ⊠ 🖥 🖥 ⊺ 🏊

🏵🏵 Comfort Inn SH
(902) 667-0404. **$106-$167, 14 day notice.** 143 Albion St S. Trans-Canada Hwy 104, exit 4, 1 mi (1.5 km) n on Rt 2. Int corridors. **Pets:** Other species. Service with restrictions, supervision.
(A$K) 🔖 ⊠ 🖥 🖥

🏵🏵 Super 8 Motel SH
(902) 660-8888. **$115-$139.** 40 Lord Amherst Dr. Trans-Canada Hwy 104, exit 4. Int corridors. **Pets:** Medium. $10 daily fee/room. Service with restrictions, supervision.
(A$K) 🔖 ⊠ 🖥 🖥 🏊

ANNAPOLIS ROYAL

🏵🏵 Annapolis Royal Inn M
(902) 532-2323. **$89-$148, 30 day notice.** Route 6. 0.6 mi (1 km) w on Hwy 1. Ext corridors. **Pets:** Accepted.
(A$K) 🔖 ⊠ 🖥

🏵🏵 Champlain Motel M
(902) 532-5473. **$105-$125, 30 day notice.** RR 2. 2.5 mi (4.2 km) w on Hwy 1. Ext corridors. **Pets:** Accepted.
(A$K) 🔖 ⊠ 🖥 🖥 🏊

🏵🏵🏵 Hillsdale House Inn BB 🐾
(902) 532-2345. **$79-$139.** 519 St George St. Just e of Rt 1; centre. Int corridors. **Pets:** $20 one-time fee/room. Service with restrictions, supervision.
(A$K) ⊠

🏵🏵🏵 The King George Inn BB
(902) 532-5286. **$89-$159.** 548 Upper St George St. Centre. Int corridors. **Pets:** Accepted.
(A$K) 🔖 ⊠ 🗺

ANTIGONISH

🏵🏵 Maritime Inn Antigonish SH
(902) 863-4001. **$105-$145.** 158 Main St. Centre. Ext/int corridors. **Pets:** Designated rooms, service with restrictions, supervision.
(SAVE) ⊠ 🖥 ⊺

AULD'S COVE

🏵🏵 The Cove Motel & Restaurant/Gift Shop M
(902) 747-2700. **$118.** 227 Auld. 0.6 mi (1 km) n off Trans-Canada Hwy 104; 1.9 mi (3 km) w of Canso Cswy. Ext corridors. **Pets:** Medium. Designated rooms, service with restrictions, supervision.
(SAVE) ⊠ 🖥 🖥 ⊺ 🗺

BADDECK

🏵🏵 The Ceilidh Country Lodge M
(902) 295-3500. **$89-$129, 3 day notice.** 357 Shore Rd. Trans-Canada Hwy 105, exit 8, 1 mi (1.6 km) e on Rt 205 (Shore Rd). Ext/int corridors. **Pets:** Accepted.
⊠ 🖥 🖥

🏵🏵 Hunter's Mountain Chalets CA
(902) 295-3392. **$78-$138, 4 day notice.** 562 Cabot Tr. Trans-Canada Hwy 105, exit 7, 1.6 mi (2.6 km) n. Ext corridors. **Pets:** Small, dogs only. $10 daily fee/pet. No service, supervision.
(SAVE) ⊠ 🖥 (K) 🗺

🏵🏵 Inverary Resort SH
(902) 295-3500. **$109-$189, 3 day notice.** 368 Shore Rd. Trans-Canada Hwy 105, exit 8, 1 mi (1.6 km) e on Rt 205 (Shore Rd). Ext/int corridors. **Pets:** Accepted.
(SAVE) ⊠ 🐾 🖥 🖥 ⊺ 🗺 🗺

🏵🏵🏵 McIntyre's Housekeeping Cottages CA
(902) 295-1133. **$68-$250, 4 day notice.** 8908 Hwy 105. Trans-Canada Hwy 105, 3 mi (5 km) w. Ext corridors. **Pets:** Large. $8 daily fee/pet. Service with restrictions, supervision.
(A$K) 🔖 ⊠ 🖥 🗺

🏵🏵 Silver Dart Lodge & MacNeil House SH
(902) 295-2340. **$97-$249, 3 day notice.** 257 Hwy 205. Trans-Canada Hwy 105, exit 8, 0.6 mi (1 km) e on Rt 205 (Shore Rd). Ext/int corridors. **Pets:** Accepted.
(SAVE) ⊠ 🖥 🖥 ⊺ 🗺 🗺

BAYFIELD

🏵🏵 Sea'Scape Cottages CA
(902) 386-2825. **$85-$115, 21 day notice.** Bayfield Antigonish Civil 6. Trans-Canada Hwy 104, exit 36, 3.1 mi (5.1 km) n on Sunrise Trail, then 1 mi (1.6 km) w. Ext corridors. **Pets:** Accepted.
(SAVE) ⊠ 🖥 🖥 🗺 (K) 🗺

BLACK POINT

🏵 Grand View Motel and Cottages M
(902) 857-9776. **$75-$93, 30 day notice.** 8414 Hwy 3. Hwy 103, exit 5 westbound, 1.2 mi (2 km) s to Rt 3, then 9 mi (15 km) w; exit 6 eastbound to Rt 3, then 5.4 mi (9 km) e. Ext corridors. **Pets:** Accepted.
🔖 ⊠ 🖥 (K) 🗺

BRIDGETOWN

🏵🏵 Bridgetown Motor Inn SH
(902) 665-4403. **$72-$82.** 396 Granville St. Hwy 101, exit 20, 0.6 mi (1 km) w on Rt 1. Ext corridors. **Pets:** Accepted.
(A$K) ⊠ 🗺

BRIDGEWATER

🏵🏵 Auberge Wandlyn Inn SH 🐾
(902) 543-7131. **$93-$130.** 50 North St. Hwy 103, exit 12, 1.1 mi (1.7 km) s on Rt 10. Int corridors. **Pets:** Other species. Designated rooms, service with restrictions, crate.
(A$K) 🔖 ⊠ 🖥 🖥 ⊺ 🗺

▼▼ Bridgewater Bogan Villa Inn SH
(902) 543-8171. **$75-$119.** 35 High St. Hwy 103, exit 13, just e. Int corridors. **Pets:** Accepted.
(ASK) (S♦) (✕) (⊡) (¶) (≈)

▼▼ Comfort Inn SH
(902) 543-1498. **$90-$155.** 49 North St. Hwy 103, exit 12, 1.1 mi (1.7 km) s on Rt 10. Int corridors. **Pets:** Accepted.
(ASK) (S♦) (✕) (♿M) (⊟) (⊡)

CHESTER

▼ Windjammer Motel M
(902) 275-3567. **$65-$85.** 4070 Rt 3. 0.6 mi (1 km) w. Ext corridors. **Pets:** Other species. Service with restrictions, supervision.
(ASK) (S♦) (✕) (⊟) (¶)

CHETICAMP

▼▼ Cabot Trail Sea & Golf Chalets CA
(902) 224-1777. **$129-$169, 7 day notice.** 71 Fraser Doucet Ln. Centre. Ext corridors. **Pets:** Medium. $15 daily fee/pet. Service with restrictions, supervision.
(ASK) (✕) (⊟) (⊡) (✕) (Ⓩ)

CAA ▼▼ Laurie's Motor Inn SH
(902) 224-2400. **$80-$149.** 15456 Laurie Rd. Centre. Ext/int corridors. **Pets:** Service with restrictions.
(SAVE) (S♦) (✕) (⊟) (¶)

CAA ▼ Parkview Motel, Dining Room & Lounge M
(902) 224-3232. **$79-$109.** 16546 Cabot Tr. 4.5 mi (7.2 km) n at West Gate Cape Breton Highlands National Park. Ext corridors. **Pets:** Accepted.
(SAVE) (✕) (⊟) (⊡) (¶) (Ⓩ)

CHURCH POINT

▼▼ Manoir Samson M
(902) 769-2526. **$85-$125.** 1768 Rt 1. On Hwy 1; centre. Ext corridors. **Pets:** Accepted.
(ASK) (S♦) (✕) (⊟) (Æ)

DARTMOUTH

CAA ▼▼ Comfort Inn SH ❖
(902) 463-9900. **$129-$165.** 456 Windmill Rd. Hwy 111, exit Shannon Park. Int corridors. **Pets:** Service with restrictions, crate.
(SAVE) (S♦) (✕) (⊟) (⊡)

▼▼ Country Inn & Suites By Carlson SH
(902) 465-4000. **$105-$170.** 101 Yorkshire Ave Ext. Hwy 111, exit Princess Margaret Blvd. Int corridors. **Pets:** Accepted.
(ASK) (S♦) (✕) (⊟) (⊡)

CAA ▼▼▼ Holiday Inn Halifax-Harbourview LH
(902) 463-1100. **$129-$179.** 99 Wyse Rd. Adjacent to Angus L MacDonald Bridge. Int corridors. **Pets:** Small. $25 one-time fee/room. Designated rooms, service with restrictions, supervision.
(SAVE) (S♦) (✕) (⊟) (⊡) (¶) (≈)

CAA ▼▼ Park Place Hotel & Conference Centre Ramada Plaza LH ❖
(902) 468-8888. **$115-$152.** 240 Brownlow Ave. From Murray Mackay Bridge, 0.7 mi (1.2 km) n on Hwy 111, exit 3 (Burnside Dr). Int corridors. **Pets:** Small. $50 deposit/pet. Designated rooms, service with restrictions, supervision.
(SAVE) (S♦) (✕) (♿M) (⊟) (⊡) (¶) (≈) (✕)

CAA ▼▼ Quality Inn Halifax/Dartmouth SH
(902) 469-5850. **$80-$180.** 313 Prince Albert Rd. Hwy 111, exit 6A, 1 blk s. Int corridors. **Pets:** Medium. Designated rooms, service with restrictions, supervision.
(SAVE) (S♦) (✕) (⊟) (⊡) (¶)

DIGBY

CAA ▼▼ Admiral Digby Inn SH
(902) 245-2531. **$75-$129.** 441 Shore Rd. Hwy 101, exit 26, 1.5 mi (2.5 km) n, follow St John Ferry signs, 3 mi (5 km) w on Victoria Rd, just e of ferry terminal. Ext corridors. **Pets:** Accepted.
(SAVE) (S♦) (✕) (⊟) (⊡) (¶) (≈)

HALIFAX

▼ Chebucto Inn SH
(902) 453-4330. **$75-$145.** 6151 Lady Hammond Rd. Jct Hwy 111 and Rt 2 (Bedford Hwy), 0.4 mi (0.7 km) e. Ext corridors. **Pets:** Accepted.
(ASK) (✕) (¶)

CAA ▼▼▼ Citadel Halifax Hotel LH
(902) 422-1391. **$124-$269.** 1960 Brunswick St. Between Cogswell and Duke sts. Int corridors. **Pets:** Accepted.
(SAVE) (S♦) (✕) (⊟) (⊡) (¶) (≈) (✕)

CAA ▼▼▼ Delta Barrington LH
(902) 429-7410. **$98-$208.** 1875 Barrington St. Between Cogswell and Duke sts. Int corridors. **Pets:** Accepted.
(SAVE) (S♦) (✕) (⊟) (¶) (≈) (✕)

CAA ▼▼▼ Delta Halifax LH
(902) 425-6700. **$98-$208.** 1990 Barrington St. Corner of Cogswell and Barrington sts. Int corridors. **Pets:** Accepted.
(SAVE) (S♦) (✕) (⊡) (¶) (≈) (✕)

CAA ▼▼ Econo Lodge & Suites SH ❖
(902) 443-0303. **$69-$189.** 560 Bedford Hwy. On Rt 2 (Bedford Hwy), 6 mi (9.6 km) w. Int corridors. **Pets:** $10 one-time fee/room. Designated rooms, service with restrictions, supervision.
(SAVE) (S♦) (✕) (♿M) (⊟) (⊡) (¶) (≈)

CAA ▼▼ Esquire Motel M
(902) 835-3367. **$65-$90.** 771 Bedford Hwy. Hwy 102, exit 4A, 3.3 mi (5.3 km) e on Rt 2 (Bedford Hwy). Ext corridors. **Pets:** $10 one-time fee/room. Service with restrictions, supervision.
(ASK) (S♦) (✕) (⊟) (⊡) (≈) (Æ)

CAA ▼▼▼ Holiday Inn Express Halifax/Bedford SH ❖
(902) 445-1100. **$109-$129, 14 day notice.** 133 Kearney Lake Rd. Hwy 102, exit 2. Int corridors. **Pets:** Medium. $25 one-time fee/room. Designated rooms, service with restrictions, supervision.
(SAVE) (S♦) (✕) (♿M) (⊡▪) (⊟) (⊡) (≈)

CAA ▼▼▼ Holiday Inn Select Halifax-Centre LH ❖
(902) 423-1161. **$139-$189.** 1980 Robie St. Jct Quinpool St. Int corridors. **Pets:** Medium. Designated rooms, service with restrictions, supervision.
(SAVE) (S♦) (✕) (⊟) (⊡) (¶) (≈) (✕)

CAA ▼▼▼ Lakeview Inns & Suites SH ❖
(902) 450-3020. **$159-$399.** 98 Chain Lake Dr. Hwy 102, exit 2A eastbound; Hwy 103, exit 2. Int corridors. **Pets:** Medium. $150 deposit/room, $10 daily fee/pet. Service with restrictions, supervision.
(ASK) (S♦) (✕) (♿M) (⊟) (⊡) (≈)

CAA ▼▼▼ The Lord Nelson Hotel & Suites LH ❖
(902) 423-6331. **$109-$229.** 1515 S Park St. Corner of Park St and Spring Garden Rd; centre. Int corridors. **Pets:** Large, other species. Service with restrictions, supervision.
(SAVE) (✕) (♿M) (Ⓩ) (⊡▪) (⊟) (⊡) (¶)

CAA ▼▼▼▼ The Prince George Hotel LH ❖
(902) 425-1986. **$149-$209.** 1725 Market St. Between Prince and Carmichael sts. Int corridors. **Pets:** Other species. Service with restrictions, supervision.
(SAVE) (✕) (♿M) (⊡) (¶) (≈) (✕)

▼▼▼▼ **Quality Inn & Suites Halifax** 🆂🅷 🐾
(902) 444-6700. **$108-$163.** 980 Parkland Dr. Hwy 102, exit 2. Int corridors. **Pets:** Medium. Service with restrictions, supervision.
(ASK) (S🔟) (✕) (⛫M) (🛢) (🛢) (🖳) (🏊) (✕)

▼▼▼▼ **Residence Inn by Marriott** 🆂🅷
(902) 422-0493. **$149-$199.** 1599 Grafton St. Corner of Sackville St. Int corridors. **Pets:** Accepted.
(ASK) (S🔟) (✕) (⛫M) (🖭) (🛢) (🖳)

▼▼ **Travelers Motel** 🅼
(902) 835-3394. **$55-$82.** 773 Bedford Hwy. Hwy 102, exit 4A, 3.3 mi (5.3 km) e on Rt 2 (Bedford Hwy). Ext corridors. **Pets:** Accepted.
(S🔟) (✕) (🛢) (🅰)

🆀🅰 ▼▼▼ **The Westin Nova Scotian** 🅻🅷 🐾
(902) 421-1000. **$129-$295.** 1181 Hollis St. Between Barrington and Lower Water sts. Int corridors. **Pets:** Service with restrictions.
(SAVE) (S🔟) (✕) (⛫M) (🖳) (🍴) (🏊) (✕)

INGONISH BEACH

▼▼▼▼ **Keltic Lodge** 🅻🅷
(902) 285-2880. **$161-$344, 3 day notice.** Middle Head Peninsula. Inside the Cape Breton Highlands National Park; off Cabot Trail main highway. Ext/int corridors. **Pets:** Other species. Designated rooms, service with restrictions.
(ASK) (S🔟) (✕) (🛢) (🖳) (🍴) (🏊) (✕)

KEMPTVILLE

🆀🅰 ▼▼▼▼ **Trout Point Lodge** 🅲🅸
(902) 482-8360. **$165-$265, 21 day notice.** 189 Trout Point Rd. 6.6 mi (11 km) e on Rt 203, 2.1 mi (3.5 km) n on gravel entry road. Ext corridors. **Pets:** Accepted.
(SAVE) (S🔟) (✕) (🍴) (✕) (🅰) (🆆) (☎)

KENTVILLE

▼▼ ▼ **Auberge Wandlyn Inn** 🆂🅷
(902) 678-8311. **$110-$125.** 7270 Hwy 1. Hwy 101, exit 14. Ext/int corridors. **Pets:** Accepted.
(ASK) (✕) (🛢) (🖳) (🍴) (🏊)

🆀🅰 ▼ **Sun Valley Motel** 🅼
(902) 678-7368. **$66-$90.** 905 Park St. Hwy 101, exit 14, 0.5 mi (0.8 km) e on Rt 1. Ext corridors. **Pets:** Accepted.
(SAVE) (S🔟) (✕) (🛢) (🖳) (🅰) (☎)

LISCOMB

▼▼▼▼ **Liscombe Lodge** 🆂🅷
(902) 779-2307. **$140-$175, 3 day notice.** RR 1, 2884 Hwy 7. On Hwy 7. Ext/int corridors. **Pets:** Accepted.
(ASK) (✕) (⛫M) (🅲) (🛢) (🖳) (🍴) (🏊) (✕)

LUNENBURG

🆀🅰 ▼▼▼ **Boscawen Inn** 🅱🅱
(902) 634-3325. **$90-$205, 3 day notice.** 150 Cumberland St. Centre. Int corridors. **Pets:** Medium, dogs only. $20 one-time fee/room. Designated rooms, service with restrictions, supervision.
(SAVE) (✕) (🅰)

▼▼ **The Homeport Motel** 🅼
(902) 634-8234. **$75-$103.** 167 Victoria Rd. 0.6 mi (1 km) w on Rt 3. Ext corridors. **Pets:** Accepted.
(ASK) (S🔟) (✕) (🛢) (🖳)

🆀🅰 ▼▼▼▼ **Lunenburg Arms Hotel & Spa** 🆂🅷 🐾
(902) 640-4040. **$99-$255, 7 day notice.** 94 Pelham St. Corner of Pelham and Duke sts; centre. Int corridors. **Pets:** Other species. Service with restrictions, supervision.
(SAVE) (✕) (⛫M) (🅲) (🖳) (🍴)

MAHONE BAY

▼▼▼▼ **Bayview Pines Country Inn** 🅱🅱
(902) 624-9970. **$85-$150, 5 day notice.** 678 Oakland Rd. Hwy 103, exit 10, 1.2 mi (2 km) w on Rt 3 to Kedy's Landing, 3.6 mi (6 km) e of Mahone Bay. Ext/int corridors. **Pets:** Accepted.
(✕) (🛢) (🖳) (🅰) (☎)

MAVILLETTE

▼ **Cape View Motel & Cottages** 🅼
(902) 645-2258. **$70-$80.** 124 John Doucette Rd. Rt 1, 19.2 mi (32 km) ne of Yarmouth; centre. Ext corridors. **Pets:** Accepted.
(S🔟) (✕) (🛢) (🅰) (☎)

MIDDLETON

▼▼ ▼ **Mid-Valley Motel** 🆂🅷
(902) 825-3433. **$80-$105.** 121 Main St. Hwy 101, exit 18, 0.6 mi (1 km) w on Rt 1. Ext corridors. **Pets:** Accepted.
(✕) (🛢) (🍴) (🏊)

MUSQUODOBOIT HARBOUR

▼▼▼ **The Elephant's Nest Bed & Breakfast** 🅱🅱
(902) 827-3891. **$85-$130, 3 day notice.** 127 Pleasant Dr. From jct Hwy 107 and 7, 2.5 mi (4 km) w, follow signs. **Pets:** Small, dogs only. Designated rooms, service with restrictions, supervision.
(ASK) (✕) (✕) (🅰)

NEW GLASGOW

▼▼▼ **Comfort Inn** 🆂🅷 🐾
(902) 755-6450. **$89-$165.** 740 Westville Rd. On Hwy 289, just e of jct Trans-Canada Hwy 104, exit 23. Int corridors. **Pets:** Other species. Service with restrictions, supervision.
(ASK) (S🔟) (✕) (🛢) (🖳)

▼▼ ▼ **Country Inn & Suites By Carlson** 🆂🅷
(902) 928-1333. **$99-$160.** 700 Westville Rd. On Hwy 289, just e of jct Trans-Canada Hwy 104, exit 23. Int corridors. **Pets:** Accepted.
(ASK) (S🔟) (✕) (🛢) (🖳)

NEW HARBOUR

▼▼▼ **Lonely Rock Seaside Bungalows** 🅲🅰
(902) 387-2668. **$90-$230, 14 day notice.** 150 New Harbour Rd. Rt 316, 0.4 mi (0.7 km) s. Ext corridors. **Pets:** Dogs only. No service, supervision.
(✕) (🛢) (✕) (🅰) (☎)

NORTH SYDNEY

🆀🅰 ▼▼▼ **Clansman Motel** 🆂🅷 🐾
(902) 794-7226. **$79-$125.** 9 Baird St. Hwy 125, exit 2, just e on King St. Ext/int corridors. **Pets:** Designated rooms, service with restrictions, supervision.
(SAVE) (S🔟) (✕) (🛢) (🖳) (🍴) (🏊)

PARRSBORO

▼▼ **The Sunshine Inn** 🅼 🐾
(902) 254-3135. **$76-$150.** 2 mi (3.2 km) n. Ext corridors. **Pets:** $10 one-time fee/pet. No service, supervision.
(ASK) (S🔟) (✕) (🛢) (✕) (☎)

PICTOU

▼▼ **Willow House Inn** 🅱🅱
(902) 485-5740. **$55-$80.** 11 Willow St. Corner of Willow and Church sts; centre. Int corridors. **Pets:** Accepted.
(✕) (☎)

PORT DUFFERIN

▼ **Marquis of Dufferin Seaside Inn** Ⓜ ❀
(902) 654-2696. **$60-$94.** 25658 Hwy 7, RR 1. On Hwy 7. Ext corridors. **Pets:** Other species. Service with restrictions.
❎ 🅷 ⊠ 🅺 🆉

PORT HASTINGS

Ⓐ ▼ **Cape Breton Causeway Inn** 🆂🅷
(902) 625-0460. **$94-$135.** 21 Old Victoria Rd. E of Canso Cswy on Trans-Canada Hwy 105 rotary; entrance through north side of church. Ext/int corridors. **Pets:** Accepted.
🆂🅰🆅🅴 🆂ₒ ❎ 🅷 💻 🅷

▼▼ **Econo Lodge MacPuffin** Ⓜ
(902) 625-0621. **$84-$119.** 373 Hwy 4. 1 mi (1.6 km) n on Hwy 4; 1 mi (1.6 km) s of Canso Cswy. Ext corridors. **Pets:** Other species. Service with restrictions, crate.
🅰🆂🅺 🆂ₒ ❎ 💻 ➰

PORT HAWKESBURY

Ⓐ ▼▼ **Maritime Inn Port Hawkesbury** 🆂🅷
(902) 625-0320. **$98-$149.** 717 Reeves St. 4.2 mi (6.4 km) e of Canso Cswy on Hwy 4. Ext/int corridors. **Pets:** Accepted.
🆂🅰🆅🅴 ❎ 🅷 💻 🅷 ➰

SCOTSBURN

▼▼▼ **Stonehame Lodge & Chalets** 🅲🅰 ❀
(902) 485-3468. **$65-$205.** RR 3. Rt 256, 7.5 mi (12 km) w of Pictou via Rt 376, last 1.2 mi (2 km) on gravel entry road. Ext corridors. **Pets:** Large, other species. Service with restrictions, crate.
🅰🆂🅺 🆂ₒ ❎ 🅷 💻 ➰ 🆇

SHELBURNE

Ⓐ ▼▼▼ **Mackenzie's Motel, Cottages, and Suites** Ⓜ
(902) 875-2842. **$75-$135.** 260 Water St. Hwy 103, exit 26, 1 mi (1.6 km) e on Rt 3. Ext corridors. **Pets:** Very small, dogs only. Designated rooms, supervision.
🆂🅰🆅🅴 ❎ 🅷 💻 ➰

SMITHS COVE

▼▼ **Harbourview Inn** 🅱🅱
(902) 245-5686. **$69-$149, 7 day notice.** 25 Harbourview Rd. Hwy 101, exit 25 eastbound; exit 24 westbound. Ext/int corridors. **Pets:** Accepted.
❎ 🅷 💻 ➰ 🆇 🆉

▼▼ **Hedley House Inn By The Sea** Ⓜ
(902) 245-2500. **$69-$189.** RR 1. Hwy 101, exit 25 eastbound; exit 24 westbound. Ext corridors. **Pets:** Accepted.
🆂ₒ ❎ 🅷 💻 🅷 🅺 🆉

Ⓐ ▼▼▼ **Mountain Gap Inn** 🆂🅷
(902) 245-5841. **$79-$145, 3 day notice.** 217 Hwy 1, Smiths Cove. Hwy 101, exit 25 eastbound; exit 24 westbound. Ext corridors. **Pets:** Accepted.
🆂🅰🆅🅴 🆂ₒ ❎ 🅷 💻 🅷 ➰ 🆇

SYDNEY

Ⓐ ▼▼▼▼ **Cambridge Suites Hotel** 🅻🅷
(902) 562-6500. **$124-$195.** 380 Esplanade. Hwy 4, 3.1 mi (5 km) e of jct Hwy 125, exit 6E; downtown. Int corridors. **Pets:** Accepted.
🆂🅰🆅🅴 🆂ₒ ❎ 🅷 💻 🅷

▼▼▼▼ **Comfort Inn** 🆂🅷 ❀
(902) 562-0200. **$105-$189.** 368 Kings Rd. Hwy 4, 2.1 mi (3.5 km) e of jct Hwy 125, exit 6E. Int corridors. **Pets:** Other species. Service with restrictions, supervision.
🅰🆂🅺 🆂ₒ ❎ 🅷 💻

Ⓐ ▼▼▼▼ **Days Inn Sydney** 🆂🅷
(902) 539-6750. **$89-$119.** 480 Kings Rd. Hwy 4, 1.7 mi (2.8 km) e of jct Hwy 125, exit 6E. Int corridors. **Pets:** Designated rooms, service with restrictions, supervision.
🆂🅰🆅🅴 🆂ₒ ❎ 🅷 💻 ➰ 🆇

Ⓐ ▼▼▼▼ **Delta Sydney** 🅻🅷
(902) 562-7500. **$144-$194.** 300 Esplanade. Centre at Prince St. Int corridors. **Pets:** $15 one-time fee/room. Supervision.
🆂🅰🆅🅴 🆂ₒ ❎ 🅷 💻 🅷 ➰ 🆇

▼▼▼ **Quality Inn Sydney** 🆂🅷
(902) 539-8101. **$101-$142.** 560 Kings Rd. Hwy 4, 2 mi (3.3 km) e of jct Hwy 125. Int corridors. **Pets:** Accepted.
🅰🆂🅺 🆂ₒ ❎ 🅶 💻 🅷 ➰

SYDNEY MINES

▼▼▼▼ **Gowrie House Country Inn** 🅲🅸
(902) 544-1050. **$99-$265, 3 day notice.** 840 Shore Rd. Hwy 105, exit 21E, 1.9 mi (3 km) n on Rt 305. Ext/int corridors. **Pets:** Accepted.
❎ 🅷 💻 🅷

TRURO

▼▼▼ **Comfort Inn** 🆂🅷
(902) 893-0330. **$133-$169.** 12 Meadow Dr. Hwy 102, exit 14. Int corridors. **Pets:** Accepted.
🅰🆂🅺 🆂ₒ ❎ 🅷 💻

▼▼▼ **Howard Johnson Hotel and Convention Centre** 🆂🅷
(902) 895-1651. **$80-$96.** 437 Prince St. Centre. Ext/int corridors. **Pets:** Accepted.
🅰🆂🅺 🆂ₒ ❎ 🅷 💻 🅷 ➰

Ⓐ ▼▼ **The Palliser Motel** Ⓜ
(902) 893-8951. **$75.** 103/104 Tidal Bore Rd. Hwy 102, exit 14. Ext corridors. **Pets:** Accepted.
🆂🅰🆅🅴 🆂ₒ ❎ 🅷 🆉

▼▼▼▼ **Super 8 Motel** 🆂🅷
(902) 895-8884. **$139-$189.** 85 Treaty Tr. Hwy 102, exit 13A. Int corridors. **Pets:** Other species. $10 daily fee/room. Service with restrictions, supervision.
🅰🆂🅺 🆂ₒ ❎ 🅶 🅶 🅷 💻 ➰

WHITE POINT

▼▼ **White Point Beach Resort** 🆂🅷
(902) 354-2711. **$100-$180, 3 day notice.** 75 White Point Rd 2. Hwy 103, exit 20A, 5.6 mi (9 km) w on Rt 3. Ext/int corridors. **Pets:** Other species. Designated rooms.
🅰🆂🅺 ❎ 🅷 💻 🅷 ➰ 🆇

WHYCOCOMAGH

▼▼▼▼ **Keltic Quay Bayfront Lodge & Cottages** 🅲🅰
(902) 756-1122. **$149-$299, 3 day notice.** 90 Main St. Just se off Trans-Canada Hwy 105; centre. Ext corridors. **Pets:** No service, supervision.
❎ 🅷 💻 🅺

YARMOUTH

Ⓐ ▼▼▼ **Best Western Mermaid** Ⓜ
(902) 742-7821. **$79-$180.** 545 Main St. Corner of Main St and Starrs Rd. Ext corridors. **Pets:** Accepted.
🆂🅰🆅🅴 🆂ₒ ❎ 🅷 💻 ➰ 🅺

Ⓐ ▼▼▼ **Capri Motel** Ⓜ
(902) 742-7168. **$59-$160.** 8-12 Herbert St. Corner of Herbert and Main sts. Ext corridors. **Pets:** Accepted.
🆂🅰🆅🅴 🆂ₒ ❎ 🅷 💻

▼▼ Comfort Inn 🆂🅷
(902) 742-1119. **$95-$195.** 96 Starrs Rd. Jct Hwy 101 E and Hwy 3. Int corridors. **Pets:** Accepted.
🄰🅂🄺 🆂🅾 ⊠ 🛏 🖵

ⓐ ▼ Lakelawn Motel Ⓜ
(902) 742-3588. **$74-$99.** 641 Main St. 0.6 mi (1 km) n on Hwy 1. Ext/int corridors. **Pets:** Small, dogs only. Designated rooms, service with restrictions, supervision.
🆂🄰🅅🄴 ⊠ 🄺 🕿

▼▼ Rodd Colony Harbour Inn 🆂🅷
(902) 742-9194. **$95-$149.** 6 Forest St. At ferry terminal. Int corridors. **Pets:** Other species.
🄰🅂🄺 🆂🅾 ⊠ 🛏 🖵 🍽 🄺

▼▼▼ Rodd Grand Yarmouth-A Rodd Signature Hotel 🅻🅷
(902) 742-2446. **$129-$225.** 417 Main St. Near centre of downtown. Int corridors. **Pets:** Accepted.
🄰🅂🄺 🆂🅾 ⊠ 🛏 🖵 🍽 ⊇ ⊠

▼ Voyageur Motel Ⓜ
(902) 742-7157. **$79-$104, 3 day notice.** RR #1. 3 mi (4.8 km) ne on Hwy 1. Ext corridors. **Pets:** Accepted.
🄰🅂🄺 ⊠ 🛏 🄺

CITY INDEX

AJAX

▼▼ Super 8 Motel-Ajax 🆂🅷
(905) 428-6884. **$94-$129.** 210 Westney Rd S. Jct Bayly St from Hwy 401, exit Westney Rd, 1 km s. Int corridors. **Pets:** Accepted.

🅧 🔳 🔳 🔳

ALGONQUIN PROVINCIAL PARK

▼▼▼ Killarney Lodge 🅒🅐
(705) 633-5551. **$298-$598, 3 day notice.** Hwy 60-Lake of Two Rivers-Algonquin. On Hwy 60; 21 mi (33 km) into park from west gate; 14 mi (23 km) from east gate. Ext corridors. **Pets:** Large. $25 daily fee/pet. Designated rooms, supervision.

🔳 🅧 🔳 🔳 🔳

ARNPRIOR

▼ Country Squire Motel 🅼 🐾
(613) 623-6556. **$69-$110, 3 day notice.** 111 Staye Court Dr. Hwy 17, exit White Lake Rd N. Ext corridors. **Pets:** Medium, dogs only. $15 one-time fee/pet. Service with restrictions, supervision.

🔳 🅧 🔳 🅧

AURORA

ⒶⒶ ▼▼▼ Howard Johnson Hotel Aurora 🆂🅷
(905) 727-1312. **$80-$108.** 15520 Yonge St. 0.5 km n of Wellington St. Int corridors. **Pets:** Accepted.

🆂🅰🆅🅴 🔳 🅧 🔳 🔳 🔳

BANCROFT

ⒶⒶ ▼▼▼ Best Western Sword Motor Inn 🅼
(613) 332-2474. **$113-$153.** 146 Hastings St. On Hwy 62 N; centre. Ext/int corridors. **Pets:** Small. $10 daily fee/pet. Service with restrictions, supervision.

🆂🅰🆅🅴 🔳 🅧 🔳 🔳 🔳 🔳 🅧

BARRIE

ⒶⒶ ▼▼▼ Comfort Inn 🆂🅷
(705) 722-3600. **$100-$140.** 75 Hart Dr. Hwy 400, exit 96A E (Dunlop St). Int corridors. **Pets:** Medium, other species. Designated rooms, service with restrictions, supervision.

🆂🅰🆅🅴 🔳 🅧 🔳 🔳

ⒶⒶ ▼▼▼ Comfort Inn & Suites 🆂🅷
(705) 721-1122. **$89-$129.** 210 Essa Rd. Hwy 400, exit 94 (Essa Rd), just e. Int corridors. **Pets:** Medium. Designated rooms, service with restrictions, supervision.

🆂🅰🆅🅴 🔳 🅧 🔳 🔳

▼▼ Days Inn Barrie 🆂🅷
(705) 733-8989. **$99-$150.** 60 Bryne Dr. Hwy 400, exit 94 (Essa Rd), just s, then just e. Int corridors. **Pets:** Other species. $10 daily fee/room. Designated rooms, service with restrictions, supervision.

🅰🅂🅺 🔳 🅧 🔳 🔳 🔳

ⒸⒶⒶ ▼▼▼▼ Holiday Inn Barrie-Hotel & Conference Centre 🆂🅷
(705) 728-6191. **$109-$179.** 20 Fairview Rd. Hwy 400, exit 94 (Essa Rd), just e. Int corridors. **Pets:** Accepted.

🆂🅰🆅🅴 🔳 🅧 🔳 🔳 🔳 🔳 🔳 🔳 🅧

ⒸⒶⒶ ▼▼▼ Holiday Inn Express Hotel & Suites Barrie 🆂🅷
(705) 725-1002. **$131-$185.** 506 Bryne Dr. Hwy 400, exit 90 (Molson Park Dr), just sw. Int corridors. **Pets:** Medium. $15 daily fee/room. Supervision.

🆂🅰🆅🅴 🔳 🅧 🔳 🔳 🔳

ⒸⒶⒶ ▼▼▼ Travelodge Barrie 🆂🅷
(705) 734-9500. **$109-$139.** 55 Hart Dr. Hwy 400, exit 96A E (Dunlop St). Int corridors. **Pets:** Other species. Service with restrictions, crate.

🆂🅰🆅🅴 🔳 🅧 🔳 🔳 🔳 🔳

BARRY'S BAY

▼ Mountain View Motel 🅼
(613) 756-2757. **$70-$175, 7 day notice.** 18508 Hwy 60 E. On Hwy 60, 2.5 mi (4 km) e. Ext corridors. **Pets:** Accepted.

🅧 🔳 🔳 🅧

BAYFIELD

ⒸⒶⒶ ▼▼▼ ▼▼▼ The Little Inn of Bayfield 🅒🅸 🐾
(519) 565-2611. **$192-$275, 3 day notice.** 26 Main St. Hwy 21, exit Main St, jct Catherine St. Int corridors. **Pets:** Medium, dogs only. $50 one-time fee/pet. Designated rooms, service with restrictions, supervision.

🆂🅰🆅🅴 🔳 🅧 🔳 🔳

ⒸⒶⒶ ▼ The Martha Ritz House 🅒🅸
(519) 565-2325. **$125, 4 day notice.** 27 Main St. Hwy 21, exit Main St, jct Catherine St. Int corridors. **Pets:** Service with restrictions, supervision.

🆂🅰🆅🅴 🔳 🔳 🔳 🔳

BELLEVILLE

ⒸⒶⒶ ▼▼▼ Best Western Belleville 🆂🅷 🐾
(613) 969-1112. **$99-$120.** 387 N Front St. Hwy 401, exit 543A, 0.5 km s on Hwy 62 (N Front St). Int corridors. **Pets:** Designated rooms.

🆂🅰🆅🅴 🔳 🅧 🔳 🔳 🔳

▼▼ **Comfort Inn** SH
(613) 966-7703. **$109-$123.** 200 N Park St. Hwy 401, exit 543A, 1 km
s on Hwy 62 (N Front St). Int corridors. **Pets:** Accepted.
⊠ 🖥 🖵

▼▼▼▼ **Ramada Inn on the Bay** SH
(613) 968-3411. **$159-$194, 3 day notice.** 11 Bay Bridge Rd. Hwy 2,
0.5 km s. Int corridors. **Pets:** Accepted.
(ASK) 🖏 ⊠ 🖥 🖵 🍴 ⇌ 🐾

BLIND RIVER

▼ **Lakeview Inn** M
(705) 356-0800. **$82-$88, 3 day notice.** 143 Causley St. On Hwy 17,
just e of Hwy 557. Ext corridors. **Pets:** Small. Service with restrictions,
supervision.
(ASK) 🖏 ⊠ 🖥 🍴

▼ **Old Mill Motel** M
(705) 356-2274. **$79-$100.** Hwy 17 & Woodward St. Centre. Ext corridors. **Pets:** Accepted.
(ASK) 🖏 ⊠ 🖥

BRACEBRIDGE

⊕ ▼▼▼ **Travelodge Bracebridge** M
(705) 645-2235. **$99-$189.** 320 Taylor Rd. Hwy 11, exit 189 (Hwy
42/Taylor Rd), 0.6 mi (1 km) w. Ext corridors. **Pets:** Medium. $10 daily
fee/pet. Service with restrictions, supervision.
(SAVE) 🖏 ⊠ 🖥 🖵 ⇌ 🐾

BRAMPTON

▼▼ **Comfort Inn** SH
(905) 452-0600. **$111-$119.** 5 Rutherford Rd S. Hwy 401, exit Hwy 410
N, 6.9 mi (11 km) to Hwy 7 E (Queen St), then 0.6 mi (1 km) w. Int
corridors. **Pets:** Medium. Designated rooms, service with restrictions,
supervision.
(ASK) 🖏 ⊠ 🖥 🖵

▼▼ **Motel 6 #1902** SH
(905) 451-3313. **$66-$106.** 160 Steelwell Rd. Hwy 410, exit Steeles
Ave E, s on Tomken, then just w. Int corridors. **Pets:** Medium, other
species. Service with restrictions, supervision.
🖏 ⊠ 🖥

BRANTFORD

▼▼ **Comfort Inn** SH
(519) 753-3100. **$119-$159.** 58 King George Rd. Just s of jct Hwy 403
and 24. Int corridors. **Pets:** Accepted.
(ASK) 🖏 ⊠ 🖥 🖵 🍴

▼▼ **Days Inn** SH
(519) 759-2700. **$125-$150.** 460 Fairview Dr. Hwy 403, exit Wayne
Gretzky Pkwy, 5 mi (0.8 km) n. Int corridors. **Pets:** Other species. $15
one-time fee/room. Designated rooms, service with restrictions.
(ASK) 🖏 ⊠ 🖥 🖵 🍴

▼▼▼ **Holiday Inn Brantford** SH
(519) 758-9999. **$96-$114.** 664 Colborne St. Hwy 403, exit Wayne
Gretzky Pkwy, 1.3 mi (2 km) s to Colborne St, then just w. Int corridors. **Pets:** Accepted.
(ASK) 🖏 ⊠ 🖥 🖵 🍴 ⇌

BRIGHTON

▼ **Presquile Beach Motel** M
(613) 475-1010. **$64-$104.** 243 Main St W. Hwy 401, exit 509, 2.5 mi
(4 km) s on Hwy 30, then 2 km w on Hwy 2. Ext corridors. **Pets:** Service with restrictions, supervision.
⊠ 🖥 📶

BROCKVILLE

⊕ ▼▼▼ **Comfort Inn** SH 🐾
(613) 345-0042. **$119-$144.** 7777 Kent Blvd. Hwy 401, exit 696, just
nw. Int corridors. **Pets:** Other species. $5 daily fee/pet. Service with restric-
tions, supervision.
(SAVE) 🖏 ⊠ 🖥 🖵

⊕ ▼▼ **Travelodge** SH
(613) 345-3900. **$75-$130, 30 day notice.** 7789 Kent Blvd. Hwy 401,
exit 696, just nw. Int corridors. **Pets:** Service with restrictions, crate.
(SAVE) 🖏 ⊠ 🖥 🖵

BURLINGTON

⊕ ▼▼▼▼ **Burlington on the Lake Travelodge**
Hotel SH 🐾
(905) 681-0762. **$137-$164.** 2020 Lakeshore Rd. Jct Brant. Int corridors. **Pets:** Dogs only. $10 daily fee/pet. Designated rooms, service with
restrictions, supervision.
(SAVE) 🖏 ⊠ 🖥 🖵 🍴 ⇌ 🐾

⊕ ▼▼ **Comfort Inn** SH 🐾
(905) 639-1700. **$110-$155.** 3290 S Service Rd. QEW, exit Walker's
Line Rd westbound, just s to Harvester Rd, then just w; exit Guelph
Line Rd eastbound, just s to Harvester Rd, then just e. Int corridors.
Pets: Other species. Service with restrictions, supervision.
(SAVE) 🖏 ⊠ 🖥

▼▼▼ **Motel 6 Canada #1900** SH
(905) 331-1955. **$66-$106.** 4345 N Service Rd. QEW, exit Walker's
Line Rd N to N Service Rd. Int corridors. **Pets:** Medium, other species.
Service with restrictions, supervision.
🖏 ⊠ 📶 🖥

▼▼▼▼ **Travelodge Burlington** SH
(905) 639-9290. **$99-$139.** 950 Walker Rd. QEW, exit Walker's Line
Rd, just s. Int corridors. **Pets:** Accepted.
(ASK) 🖏 ⊠ 🖥 🖵 ⇌

CAMBRIDGE

⊕ ▼▼▼ **Comfort Inn** SH 🐾
(519) 658-1100. **$113-$133.** 220 Holiday Inn Dr. Hwy 401, exit 282, just
n to Groh Ave. Int corridors. **Pets:** Other species. Service with restrictions,
supervision.
(SAVE) 🖏 ⊠ 🖥 🖵 🐾

⊕ ▼▼▼ ▼▼▼ **Langdon Hall Country House Hotel &**
Spa CI 🐾
(519) 740-2100. **$229-$629, 7 day notice.** 1 Langdon Dr. Hwy 401, exit
275, then 0.8 mi (1.3 km) se on Fountain St, then 0.6 mi (1 km) S on
Blair Rd, then follow signs. Ext/int corridors. **Pets:** Designated rooms,
service with restrictions.
(SAVE) ⊠ 🖥 🖵 🍴 ⇌ 🐾

⊕ ▼▼▼ **Super 8 Motel-Cambridge** SH
(519) 622-1070. **$89-$109, 30 day notice.** 650 Hespeler Rd. Hwy 401,
exit 282, 0.6 mi (1 km) s. Int corridors. **Pets:** Accepted.
(SAVE) 🖏 ⊠ 🖥 🖵 🍴 ⇌

⊕ ▼▼▼ **Travelodge Cambridge** SH
(519) 622-1180. **$69-$119.** 605 Hespeler Rd. Hwy 401, exit 282, 0.6 mi
(1 km) s. Int corridors. **Pets:** $10 daily fee/pet. Crate.
(SAVE) 🖏 ⊠ 🖥 🖵 🍴

CHAPLEAU

▼▼ **Riverside Motel** M
(705) 864-0440. **$74-$99.** 116 Cherry St. Corner of Grey and Cherry
sts. Ext corridors. **Pets:** Other species. Service with restrictions, supervision.
(ASK) 🖏 ⊠ 🖥 🖵 🐾

CHATHAM

▼▼ Comfort Inn 🆂🅷
(519) 352-5500. **$115-$129.** 1100 Richmond St. Hwy 401, exit 81 (Bloomfield Rd), 3.1 mi (5 km) n. Int corridors. **Pets:** Accepted.

CHATSWORTH

▼▼ Key Motel 🅼
(519) 794-2350. **$70-$80.** 317051 Hwy 6/10. On Hwy 6 and 10. Ext/int corridors. **Pets:** Accepted.

COBOURG

Ⓐ ▼▼▼▼ Best Western Cobourg Inn and Convention
Centre 🆂🅷
(905) 372-2105. **$131-$262, 3 day notice.** 930 Burnham St. Hwy 401, exit 472 (Burnham St S). Int corridors. **Pets:** Other species. Service with restrictions, supervision.

▼▼ Comfort Inn 🆂🅷
(905) 372-7007. **$138-$155.** 121 Densmore Rd. Hwy 401, exit 474, just se. Int corridors. **Pets:** Accepted.

CORNWALL

Ⓐ ▼▼▼▼ Best Western Parkway Inn & Conference
Centre 🆂🅷
(613) 932-0451. **$129-$159.** 1515 Vincent Massey Dr. Hwy 401, exit 789 (Brookdale Ave), 1.8 mi (2.8 km) s, then just w. Int corridors. **Pets:** $10 daily fee/pet. Designated rooms, service with restrictions, supervision.

Ⓐ ▼▼▼ Comfort Inn-Cornwall 🆂🅷
(613) 937-0111. **$80-$225.** 1625 Vincent Massey Dr. Hwy 401, exit 789 (Brookdale Ave), 2.8 km s, then 0.7 km w. Int corridors. **Pets:** Other species. $20 one-time fee/room. Designated rooms, service with restrictions, crate.

Ⓐ ▼▼ Econo Lodge 🆂🅷
(613) 936-1996. **$59-$89.** 1142 Brookdale Ave. Hwy 401, exit 789 (Brookdale Ave), 1.9 mi (3 km) s. Ext/int corridors. **Pets:** Accepted.

DRYDEN

Ⓐ ▼▼▼ Best Western Motor Inn 🆂🅷
(807) 223-3201. **$99-$125.** 349 Government St. On Hwy 17. Ext/int corridors. **Pets:** Designated rooms, service with restrictions, crate.

▼▼ Comfort Inn 🅼
(807) 223-3893. **$109-$143.** 522 Government St. On Hwy 17. Int corridors. **Pets:** Other species. Service with restrictions, supervision.

FONTHILL

▼ Hipwell's Motel 🅼
(905) 892-3588. **$60-$75.** 299 Reg Rd 20 W. 1 mi (1.6 km) w; centre. Ext corridors. **Pets:** $5 daily fee/pet. Service with restrictions, supervision.

FORT FRANCES

▼▼ Super 8 🆂🅷
(807) 274-4945. **$99-$102.** 810 Kings Hwy. On Hwy 11. Int corridors. **Pets:** $10 one-time fee/room. Service with restrictions, crate.

FRENCH RIVER

Ⓐ ▼ French River Trading Post Motel 🅼
(705) 857-2115. **$70-$80.** 20112 Hwy 69. On Trans-Canada Hwy 69, 0.6 mi (1 km) n of French River Bridge. Ext corridors. **Pets:** Small. $10 daily fee/room. Designated rooms, service with restrictions, supervision.

GANANOQUE

Ⓐ ▼▼▼▼ Best Western Country Squire Resort 🆂🅷
(613) 382-3511. **$69-$249.** 715 King St E. Hwy 401, exit 647 eastbound; exit 648 westbound, 0.6 mi (1 km) w on Hwy 2 (King St). Ext/int corridors. **Pets:** $10 one-time fee/pet. Designated rooms, service with restrictions, supervision.

Ⓐ ▼▼ Clarion Inn & Conference Centre 1000
Islands 🆂🅷
(613) 382-7272. **$79-$249.** 50 Main St. Corner of King St (Hwy 2); centre. Int corridors. **Pets:** Accepted.

Ⓐ ▼▼ Comfort Inn 1000 Islands 🅼
(613) 382-4728. **$59-$239.** 785 King St E. Hwy 401, exit 647 eastbound; exit 648 westbound, 0.3 mi (0.5 km) w on Hwy 2 (King St). Ext/int corridors. **Pets:** Accepted.

▼▼▼ Trinity House Inn 🅒🅸
(613) 382-8383. **$90-$250, 7 day notice.** 90 Stone St S. Corner of Pine St; centre. Int corridors. **Pets:** Designated rooms, service with restrictions.

GRIMSBY

Ⓐ ▼▼▼▼ Super 8 Motel-Grimsby 🆂🅷
(905) 309-8800. **$84-$129, 3 day notice.** 11 Windward Dr. QEW, exit 74 (Casablanca N). Int corridors. **Pets:** Medium, other species. $10 daily fee/pet. Service with restrictions, crate.

GUELPH

▼▼ Comfort Inn Guelph 🆂🅷
(519) 763-1900. **$124-$144.** 480 Silvercreek Pkwy. Jct Hwy 6 and 7. Int corridors. **Pets:** Service with restrictions, supervision.

Ⓐ ▼▼▼▼ Holiday Inn Guelph 🅻🅷 ❀
(519) 836-0231. **$139-$199.** 601 Scottsdale Dr. Jct Hwy 6 N and Stone Rd E; 5 mi (8 km) n of jct Hwy 401. Int corridors. **Pets:** No service, supervision.

Ⓐ ▼▼▼ Ramada Hotel & Conference Centre 🆂🅷
(519) 836-1240. **$112-$124.** 716 Gordon St. Jct Gordon St and Stone Rd; 5 mi (8 km) n of Hwy 401 via Brock Rd. Int corridors. **Pets:** Other species. Designated rooms, no service, supervision.

HALIBURTON

▼ Lakeview Motel 🅼
(705) 457-1027. **$90-$180, 5 day notice.** 4951 CR 21. Jct Hwy 118, 1.6 mi (2.5 km) w on CR 21. Ext corridors. **Pets:** Medium. $8 daily fee/pet. Designated rooms, service with restrictions, crate.

HAMILTON

Ⓐ ▼▼▼ Knights Inn at Clappison Corners 🅼
(905) 689-6615. **$89-$119.** 15 Hwy 5 W. Jct Hwy 5 and 6. Ext/int corridors. **Pets:** Accepted.

ⒸⒶ ▼▼▼▼ **Sheraton Hamilton** 🔲 ❀
(905) 529-5515. **$109-$169.** 116 King St W. On Hwy 6 and 8 west-bound; downtown. Int corridors. **Pets:** Medium. Service with restrictions, supervision.
🆂🅰🆅🅴 🆂🔳 ✖ 🔳 🔳 🔳 🔳 🔳

▼▼▼ **Staybridge Suites** 🆂🅷 ❀
(905) 577-9000. **$189-$279.** 118 Market St. Hwy 403, exit King St, then e across from Jackson Square, jct Caroline. Int corridors. **Pets:** $95 one-time fee/pet. Service with restrictions.
🅰🆂🅺 🆂🔳 ✖ 🔳 🔳 🔳 🔳

HANOVER

ⒸⒶ ▼▼▼▼ **The Victorian Manor Bed & Breakfast** 🅱🅱
(519) 364-1117. **$80-$100.** 500 9th Ave. Just n of 10th St. Int corridors. **Pets:** Accepted.
🆂🅰🆅🅴 🆂🔳 ✖ 🆉

HAWKESBURY

▼▼ **Best Western L'Heritage** 🆂🅷
(613) 632-5941. **$107-$140.** 1575 Tupper St. Jct Hwy 34, 1.9 mi (3 km) e on Hwy 17. Int corridors. **Pets:** Accepted.
🅰🆂🅺 🆂🔳 ✖ 🔳 🔳 🔳

HUNTSVILLE

▼▼ **Comfort Inn** 🆂🅷 ❀
(705) 789-1701. **$110-$162.** 86 King William St. Jct Hwy 60. Int corridors. **Pets:** Other species. Designated rooms, service with restrictions, supervision.
🅰🆂🅺 🆂🔳 ✖ 🔳 🔳

▼▼▼ **Delta Grandview Resort** 🔲
(705) 789-4417. **$99-$279, 14 day notice.** 939 Hwy 60. Jct Hwy 11, 3.8 mi (6 km) e. Ext corridors. **Pets:** Accepted.
🅰🆂🅺 🆂🔳 ✖ 🔳 🔳 🔳 🔳 🔳

ⒸⒶ ▼▼ **King William Inn** 🔲
(705) 789-9661. **$69-$129.** 23 King William St. Hwy 60, 0.6 mi (1 km) s. Ext corridors. **Pets:** Dogs only. Designated rooms, service with restrictions, supervision.
🆂🅰🆅🅴 🆂🔳 ✖ 🔳 🔳

▼ **Tulip Inn** 🔲 ❀
(705) 789-4001. **$70-$140, 3 day notice.** 211 Arrowhead Park Rd. Hwy 11, exit 226 (Muskoka Rd 3), follow signs for Arrowhead Park. Ext corridors. **Pets:** Supervision.
🅰🆂🅺 ✖ 🔳 🔳

INGERSOLL

▼▼▼ **Travelodge Ingersoll** 🆂🅷
(519) 425-1100. **$91-$120.** 20 Samnah Crescent. Hwy 401, exit 216 (Culloden Rd). Int corridors. **Pets:** Accepted.
🅰🆂🅺 🆂🔳 ✖ 🔳 🔳 🔳

KAPUSKASING

▼▼ **Comfort Inn** 🆂🅷
(705) 335-8583. **$105.** 172 Government Rd E. Hwy 11, corner of Brunelle Rd. Int corridors. **Pets:** $10 one-time fee/room. Designated rooms, service with restrictions.
🅰🆂🅺 🆂🔳 ✖ 🔳 🔳

KENORA

▼▼ **Best Western Lakeside Inn & Conference Centre** 🆂🅷
(807) 468-5521. **$110-$254, 14 day notice.** 470 First Ave S. Centre. Int corridors. **Pets:** Accepted.
🅰🆂🅺 🆂🔳 ✖ 🔳 🔳 🔳 🔳

▼▼ **Comfort Inn** 🔲
(807) 468-8845. **$94-$114.** 1230 Hwy 17 E. 0.9 mi (1.5 km) e. Int corridors. **Pets:** Accepted.
🅰🆂🅺 🆂🔳 ✖ 🔳 🔳

▼▼ **Days Inn** 🆂🅷
(807) 468-2003. **$95-$121.** 920 Hwy 17 E. On Hwy 17, 0.6 mi (1 km) e. Ext/int corridors. **Pets:** Other species. Designated rooms, service with restrictions.
🅰🆂🅺 🆂🔳 ✖ 🔳 🔳 🔳 🔳 🔳

ⒸⒶ ▼▼ **Kenora Travelodge** 🆂🅷
(807) 468-3155. **$90-$150.** 800 Hwy 17 E. 0.6 mi (1 km) e. Int corridors. **Pets:** Designated rooms, service with restrictions, crate.
🆂🅰🆅🅴 🆂🔳 ✖ 🔳 🔳 🔳 🔳 🔳

KILLALOE

▼▼▼ **Annie's Inn** 🅱🅱
(613) 757-0950. **$65-$85 (no credit cards), 7 day notice.** 67 Roche St. Hwy 60, exit Maple St, 1 blk to Roche St, then w; driveway entrance is at the end of the street. Int corridors. **Pets:** Accepted.
🅰🆂🅺 🆂🔳 ✖ 🔳 🆉

KINGSTON

▼▼ **Comfort Inn** 🆂🅷
(613) 549-5550. **$79-$130.** 1454 Princess St. Hwy 401, exit 613 (Sydenham Rd), 4 km se. Int corridors. **Pets:** Other species. Supervision.
🅰🆂🅺 🆂🔳 ✖ 🔳 🔳

ⒸⒶ ▼▼ **Comfort Inn** 🆂🅷
(613) 546-9500. **$90-$180.** 55 Warne Crescent. Hwy 401, exit 617 (Division St), 0.3 km s to Dalton Ave. Int corridors. **Pets:** Accepted.
🆂🅰🆅🅴 🆂🔳 ✖ 🔳 🔳

ⒸⒶ ▼▼▼ **Confederation Place Hotel** 🆂🅷 ❀
(613) 549-6300. **$139-$239.** 237 Ontario St. Centre of downtown. Int corridors. **Pets:** Medium, other species. $15 daily fee/room. Designated rooms, crate.
🆂🅰🆅🅴 🆂🔳 ✖ 🔳 🔳 🔳 🔳

ⒸⒶ ▼▼▼ **The Executive Inn & Suites** 🔲
(613) 549-1620. **$89-$149, 3 day notice.** 794 Hwy 2 E. Hwy 401, exit 623, 8 km s, then 2 km e. Ext corridors. **Pets:** Small, dogs only. $10 daily fee/pet. Designated rooms, service with restrictions, supervision.
🆂🅰🆅🅴 🆂🔳 ✖ 🔳 🔳 🔳

ⒸⒶ ▼▼▼ **Holiday Inn Kingston-Waterfront** 🆂🅷
(613) 549-8400. **$139-$259.** 2 Princess St. Corner of Ontario St; centre of downtown. Int corridors. **Pets:** Designated rooms, service with restrictions, supervision.
🆂🅰🆅🅴 🆂🔳 ✖ 🔳 🔳 🔳 🔳 🔳 🔳

▼▼ **Super 8 Motel** 🆂🅷
(613) 542-7395. **$59-$149.** 720 Princess St. Centre. Int corridors. **Pets:** Accepted.
🅰🆂🅺 🆂🔳 ✖ 🔳

KIRKLAND LAKE

▼▼ **Comfort Inn** 🆂🅷
(705) 567-4909. **$111-$132.** 455 Government Rd W. Rt 66, just w of centre. Int corridors. **Pets:** Accepted.
✖ 🔳 🔳

KITCHENER

▼▼▼ **Delta Kitchener-Waterloo** 🔲
(519) 744-4141. **$90-$169.** 105 King St E. Corner of King and Benton sts; downtown. Int corridors. **Pets:** Accepted.
🅰🆂🅺 🆂🔳 ✖ 🔳 🔳 🔳 🔳 🔳

(CAA) ▼▼▼▼ Holiday Inn Kitchener-Waterloo Hotel & Conference Centre 【LH】
(519) 893-1211. **$92-$174.** 30 Fairway Rd S. Hwy 401, exit 278, 3.5 mi (5.6 km) w on Hwy 8, exit Weber St, then just e on King St. Int corridors. **Pets:** Accepted.
[SAVE] [S🐾] [✕] [🛏] [💻] [▤] [🍴] [⚓] [✕🐕]

▼▼ Mornington Crescent B&B 【BB】
(519) 743-4557. **$75-$150.** 11 Sunbridge Crescent. Hwy 86 N, exit University E, 0.6 mi (1 km) to Bridge St just s, 0.3 mi (0.5 km) to Bridal Trail, then 0.5 mi (0.9 km) e. Int corridors. **Pets:** Other species. Supervision.
[✕] [🛏] [💻] [⚓] [🐾]

(CAA) ▼▼▼▼ Radisson Hotel Kitchener 【SH】
(519) 894-9500. **$129-$179.** 2960 King St E. Hwy 401, exit 278, 3.8 mi (6 km) w on Hwy 8, exit Weber St. Int corridors. **Pets:** Medium, other species. Service with restrictions.
[SAVE] [S🐾] [✕] [🛏] [💻] [🍴] [⚓]

▼▼▼▼ Walper Terrace Hotel 【SH】 🐾
(519) 745-4321. **$99-$129.** 1 King St W. Corner of King and Queen sts; downtown. Int corridors. **Pets:** $39 one-time fee/room. Service with restrictions, supervision.
[ASK] [S🐾] [✕] [🛏] [💻] [🍴]

LEAMINGTON

(CAA) ▼▼▼ Comfort Inn 【SH】 🐾
(519) 326-9071. **$75-$160.** 279 Erie St S. Just s of jct Talbot and Erie sts; on direct route to Point Pelee National Park. Int corridors. **Pets:** $10 daily fee/room. Designated rooms, service with restrictions, supervision.
[SAVE] [S🐾] [✕] [🛏] [💻]

(CAA) ▼▼▼▼ Ramada Leamington 【SH】
(519) 325-0260. **$95-$200, 3 day notice.** 201 Erie St N. 0.6 mi (1 km) n of Talbot St. Int corridors. **Pets:** Small, dogs only. $15 daily fee/pet. Designated rooms, service with restrictions, supervision.
[SAVE] [✕] [⚙] [🛏] [💻] [⚓] [✕🐕]

(CAA) ▼ Sun Parlor Motel 【M】
(519) 326-6131. **$55-$85, 7 day notice.** 135 Talbot St W. On Hwy 3, 0.6 mi (1 km) w of Erie St. Ext corridors. **Pets:** Accepted.
[SAVE] [S🐾] [✕] [🛏]

LISTOWEL

(CAA) ▼▼▼ Country Inn Motel 【M】
(519) 291-1580. **$89-$175.** RR 1 Hwy 23 N-8500 Rd 164. On Hwy 23 N, 2.2 mi (3.5 km) n of Main St. Ext/int corridors. **Pets:** Accepted.
[SAVE] [S🐾] [✕] [🛏] [💻] [✕🐕]

LONDON

▼▼▼▼ Airport Inn & Suites 【SH】
(519) 457-1200. **$95-$102, 3 day notice.** 2230 Dundas St E. Hwy 401, exit Airport Rd, 4.8 mi (7.7 km) n; corner of Airport Rd and Dundas St E. Int corridors. **Pets:** Medium. $15 daily fee/pet. Service with restrictions, supervision.
[S🐾] [✕] [🛏] [💻]

(CAA) ▼▼▼▼ Best Western Lamplighter Inn & Conference Centre 【SH】
(519) 681-7151. **$179-$184.** 591 Wellington Rd S. 2.3 mi (3.7 km) n off Hwy 401, exit 186 (Wellington Rd). Int corridors. **Pets:** Small, other species. $10 daily fee/pet. Designated rooms, service with restrictions, supervision.
[SAVE] [S🐾] [✕] [🛏] [💻] [🍴] [⚓] [✕🐕]

▼▼▼ Comfort Inn 【SH】
(519) 685-9300. **$85-$160.** 1156 Wellington Rd. Hwy 401, exit 186B (Wellington Rd), just n. Int corridors. **Pets:** Designated rooms, service with restrictions, supervision.
[ASK] [S🐾] [✕] [🛏] [💻]

(CAA) ▼▼▼ Days Inn London 【SH】
(519) 681-1240. **$89-$155.** 1100 Wellington Rd S. Hwy 401, exit 186B (Wellington Rd), 0.9 mi (1.5 km) n. Int corridors. **Pets:** Accepted.
[SAVE] [S🐾] [✕] [🛏] [💻] [🍴] [⚓]

(CAA) ▼▼▼▼ Delta London Armouries 【LH】
(519) 679-6111. **$139-$199.** 325 Dundas St. On Hwy 2. Int corridors. **Pets:** Other species. $35 one-time fee/room. Service with restrictions.
[SAVE] [S🐾] [✕] [🛏] [💻] [🍴] [⚓] [✕🐕]

(CAA) ▼▼▼▼ Holiday Inn Hotel & Suites-London 【SH】
(519) 680-0077. **$129-$159.** 864 Exeter Rd. Hwy 401, exit 186 (Wellington Rd) westbound; exit 186B eastbound. Int corridors. **Pets:** Medium. Service with restrictions, supervision.
[SAVE] [S🐾] [✕] [⚙] [🛏] [💻] [🍴] [⚓]

(CAA) ▼▼▼▼ Quality Suites 【SH】
(519) 680-1024. **$109-$169.** 1120 Dearness Dr. Hwy 401, exit 186B (Wellington Rd), 1 mi (1.6 km) n. Int corridors. **Pets:** Service with restrictions, supervision.
[SAVE] [S🐾] [✕] [🛏] [💻]

▼▼▼▼ Residence Inn by Marriott London Downtown 【SH】 🐾
(519) 433-7222. **$149-$219.** 383 Colborne St. Jct King St. Int corridors. **Pets:** Large. $75 one-time fee/room. Service with restrictions, crate.
[ASK] [S🐾] [✕] [⚙] [🛏] [💻] [✕🐕]

(CAA) ▼▼▼▼ StationPark All Suite Hotel 【LH】 🐾
(519) 642-4444. **$179.** 242 Pall Mall St. Hwy 401, exit 186B (Wellington Rd), 5.6 mi (9 km) n to Pall Mall St. Int corridors. **Pets:** Large. Designated rooms, service with restrictions.
[SAVE] [S🐾] [✕] [💻] [🍴] [✕🐕]

MARATHON

(CAA) ▼ Peninsula Inn 【M】
(807) 229-0651. **$85-$95.** On Hwy 17, 1.5 mi (2.4 km) w of jct Hwy 626. Ext corridors. **Pets:** Medium. $10 daily fee/pet. Designated rooms, service with restrictions, supervision.
[SAVE] [✕] [🛏] [🍴]

▼▼ Travelodge Marathon 【SH】
(807) 229-1213. **$97.** Hwy 17. On Hwy 17, jct Peninsula Rd. Int corridors. **Pets:** Other species. Designated rooms, service with restrictions.
[ASK] [S🐾] [✕] [🛏] [💻] [🍴]

MASSEY

(CAA) ▼ Mohawk Motel Canada 【M】
(705) 865-2722. **$69-$175.** 335 Sable St. Centre. Ext/int corridors. **Pets:** Medium. $8 one-time fee/pet. Designated rooms, service with restrictions, supervision.
[SAVE] [✕] [🛏] [💻]

MCKELLAR

(CAA) ▼▼▼▼ The Inn at Manitou 【SH】
(705) 389-2171. **$590-$990, 30 day notice.** 81 The Inn Rd. Hwy 124, exit McKellar Centre Rd, 5 mi (8 km) s, follow signs. Ext corridors. **Pets:** Designated rooms, service with restrictions.
[SAVE] [✕] [🛏] [🍴] [⚓] [✕🐕]

MIDLAND

▼▼ Comfort Inn 【SH】
(705) 526-2090. **$104-$170.** 980 King St. Jct King St and Hwy 12. Int corridors. **Pets:** Service with restrictions, supervision.
[ASK] [S🐾] [✕] [🛏] [💻]

MINDEMOYA

▼ Mindemoya Motel Ⓜ
(705) 377-4779. **$82-$109, 3 day notice.** 6375 Hwy 542. In Mindemoya; 0.6 mi (1 km) w of jct Hwy 551 and 542. Ext corridors. **Pets:** Small, dogs only. $10 daily fee/pet. Designated rooms, service with restrictions, supervision.

Ⓧ 🛅 🖵

MISSISSAUGA

Ⓐ ▼▼▼ Best Western Admiral Hotel & Suites @ Conference Centre-Mississauga Airport 🆂🅷
(905) 795-1011. **$99-$249.** 40 Admiral Blvd. Hwy 401, exit Hwy 10 (Hurontario St), 0.9 mi (1.5 km) n; just s of Derry Rd. Int corridors. **Pets:** Small. $25 daily fee/pet. Designated rooms, service with restrictions, crate.

🆂🅰🆅🅴 🔊 Ⓧ 🛅 🖵 🏊 Ⓧ

Ⓐ ▼▼▼ Comfort Inn Airport West 🆂🅷
(905) 624-6900. **$99-$124.** 1500 Matheson Blvd. Hwy 401, exit Dixie Rd, then s. Int corridors. **Pets:** Accepted.

🆂🅰🆅🅴 🔊 Ⓧ 🛅 🖵 🍽

Ⓐ ▼▼▼▼ Delta Meadowvale Resort and Conference Centre 🅻🅷
(905) 821-1981. **$89-$189.** 6750 Mississauga Rd. Hwy 401 W, exit 336 (Mississauga Rd), just s. Int corridors. **Pets:** Accepted.

🆂🅰🆅🅴 🔊 Ⓧ 🅼 🖵 🍽 🏊 Ⓧ

Ⓐ ▼▼▼▼ Delta Toronto Airport West 🅻🅷
(905) 624-1144. **$89-$199.** 5444 Dixie Rd. 1 km s of jct Hwy 401 and Dixie Rd. Int corridors. **Pets:** Accepted.

🆂🅰🆅🅴 🔊 Ⓧ 🛅 🖵 🍽 🏊 Ⓧ

Ⓐ ▼▼▼ Econo Lodge Inn & Suites Toronto Airport 🆂🅷
(905) 677-7331. **$79-$159.** 6355 Airport Rd. 1.3 mi (2km) s of Derry Rd. Ext/int corridors. **Pets:** Other species. $150 deposit/room. Service with restrictions, supervision.

🆂🅰🆅🅴 🔊 Ⓧ 🛅 🖵 🍽

▼▼▼ Four Points by Sheraton Mississauga Meadowvale 🅻🅷
(905) 858-2424. **$100-$190.** 2501 Argentia Rd. Sw of Hwy 401 and Mississauga Rd; corner of Derry and Argentia rds. Int corridors. **Pets:** Accepted.

🅰🆂🅺 🔊 Ⓧ 🅼 🖉 🛅 🖵 🍽 🏊 Ⓧ

▼▼▼ Four Points by Sheraton Toronto Airport 🅻🅷
(905) 678-1400. **$99-$279.** 6257 Airport Rd. 7 mi (11.2 km) n of jct QEW and Hwy 427 N, exit Hwy 401 via airport expressway. Int corridors. **Pets:** Accepted.

🅰🆂🅺 🔊 Ⓧ 🅼 🖉 🛅 🖵 🍽 🏊

Ⓐ ▼▼▼ Holiday Inn Toronto-Mississauga 🅻🅷
(905) 855-2000. **$109-$149.** 2125 N Sheridan Way. QEW, exit Erin Mills Pkwy. Int corridors. **Pets:** $25 one-time fee/room. Service with restrictions, supervision.

🆂🅰🆅🅴 Ⓧ 🅼 🖉 🛅 🖵 🍽 🏊

Ⓐ ▼▼▼▼ Holiday Inn Toronto-West 🆂🅷
(905) 890-5700. **$119-$179.** 100 Britannia Rd E. Hwy 401, exit Hwy 10 S (Hurontario St). Int corridors. **Pets:** Accepted.

🆂🅰🆅🅴 🔊 Ⓧ 🛅 🖵 🍽 🏊

Ⓐ ▼▼▼ Homewood Suites by Hilton Toronto-Mississauga 🆂🅷
(905) 564-5529. **$139-$299.** 6430 Edwards Blvd. Hwy 401, exit Hwy 10 (Hurontario St), 0.3 mi (0.5 km) n to Annagem Blvd, then just e. Int corridors. **Pets:** Accepted.

🆂🅰🆅🅴 🔊 Ⓧ 🖉 🛅 🖵 🏊 Ⓧ

▼▼ Motel 6 #1910 🆂🅷
(905) 814-1664. **$72-$106.** 2935 Argentia Rd. Hwy 401, exit 333 (Winston Churchill Blvd), just s. Int corridors. **Pets:** Medium, other species. Service with restrictions, supervision.

🔊 Ⓧ 🅼 🖉 🛅

Ⓐ ▼▼▼ Novotel Hotel Mississauga 🅻🅷 🐾
(905) 896-1000. **$119-$199.** 3670 Hurontario St. On Hwy 10 at Burnhamthorpe Rd; Hwy 401, exit Hwy 10 S (Hurontario St), 3.1 mi (5 km). Int corridors. **Pets:** Other species. Service with restrictions, supervision.

🆂🅰🆅🅴 🔊 Ⓧ 🛅 🖵 🍽 🏊 Ⓧ

Ⓐ ▼▼▼ Quality Inn & Suites Airport 🆂🅷
(905) 624-9500. **$81-$154.** 5599 Ambler Dr. Hwy 401, exit 346 (S Dixie Rd), w on Aerowood Dr, then just n. Int corridors. **Pets:** Medium. $10 daily fee/room. Service with restrictions, supervision.

🆂🅰🆅🅴 🔊 Ⓧ 🛅 🖵 🍽 🏊

▼▼▼ Residence Inn by Marriott 🆂🅷
(905) 567-2577. **$109-$229.** 7005 Century Ave. Hwy 401, exit Erin Mills Pkwy/Mississauga Rd, s to Argentia Rd. Int corridors. **Pets:** $100 one-time fee/room. Service with restrictions, crate.

🅰🆂🅺 🔊 Ⓧ 🅼 🖉 🛅 🖵 🏊 Ⓧ

Ⓐ ▼▼▼ Residence Inn by Marriott Mississauga Airport Corporate Centre West 🆂🅷
(905) 602-7777. **$119-$229.** 5070 Creekbank Rd. Hwy 401 W, exit Dixie Rd S 0.9 mi (1.5 km) to Eglinton Ave, then 0.6 mi (1 km). Int corridors. **Pets:** Accepted.

🆂🅰🆅🅴 🔊 Ⓧ 🖉 🛅 🖵 🏊 Ⓧ

Ⓐ ▼▼▼ Sandalwood Suites Hotel Toronto Airport 🆂🅷
(905) 238-9600. **$89-$199.** 5050 Orbitor Dr. Jct Eglinton Ave and Renforth Dr, 1.4 mi (2.3 km) w on Eglinton Ave. Int corridors. **Pets:** Medium. $8 daily fee/pet. Designated rooms, service with restrictions, crate.

🆂🅰🆅🅴 🔊 Ⓧ 🛅 🖵

Ⓐ ▼▼▼▼ Sheraton Gateway Hotel In Toronto International Airport 🅻🅷 🐾
(905) 672-7000. **$109-$279.** Toronto Intnatl Airport, Terminal 3. In Lester B. Pearson International Airport. Int corridors. **Pets:** Medium. Service with restrictions.

🆂🅰🆅🅴 🔊 Ⓧ 🅼 🖵 🍽 🏊 Ⓧ

▼▼ Studio 6 Mississauga #1908 Ⓜ
(905) 502-8897. **$70-$90.** 60 Brittannia Rd E. Hwy 401, exit Hwy 10 (Hurontario St). Int corridors. **Pets:** Accepted.

🔊 Ⓧ 🖉 🛅 🖵

▼▼▼ Toronto Airport Hilton 🅻🅷
(905) 677-9900. **$109-$279.** 5875 Airport Rd. Hwy 401, exit Dixon Rd, 2.2 mi (3.5 km) w. Int corridors. **Pets:** Accepted.

🅰🆂🅺 🔊 Ⓧ 🅼 🖉 🛅 🍽 🏊

MONETVILLE

▼▼ Memquisit Lodge 🅒🅐
(705) 898-2355. **$87-$95, 90 day notice.** 506 Memquisit Rd. 13 mi (20.8 km) ne on west arm of Lake Nipissing, on Hwy 64 and Memquisit Lodge Rd; 23 mi (36.8 km) sw off Hwy 17, on Hwy 64. Ext corridors. **Pets:** Accepted.

🛅 🖵 🍽 Ⓧ Ⓐ Ⓩ

MORRISBURG

The McIntosh Country Inn & Conference Centre SH
(613) 543-3788. **$69-$109.** 12495 Hwy 2 E. Hwy 401, exit 750, 1.2 mi (2 km) s on Rt 31, then 0.6 mi (1 km) e. Int corridors. **Pets:** Medium. $25 daily fee/pet. Designated rooms, service with restrictions, crate.

NEWMARKET

Comfort Inn SH
(905) 895-3355. **$119-$155.** 1230 Journey Cir. Hwy 404, exit 51 (Davis Dr), just w on Davis Dr, then just n on Harry Walker Pkwy. Int corridors. **Pets:** Other species. Service with restrictions, supervision.

NIAGARA FALLS METROPOLITAN AREA

FORT ERIE

Comfort Inn SH
(905) 871-8500. **$119-$124.** 1 Hospitality Dr. QEW, exit 2 (Berti St) westbound; exit 1B (Concession Rd S) eastbound. Int corridors. **Pets:** Other species. $10 daily fee/pet. Crate.

LINCOLN

Best Western Beacon Harbourside Inn & Conference Centre SH
(905) 562-4155. **$59-$229.** 2793 Beacon Blvd. QEW, exit 57. Int corridors. **Pets:** Small. $10 one-time fee/pet. Designated rooms, service with restrictions, supervision.

NIAGARA FALLS

Best Western Fallsview SH
(905) 356-0551. **$79-$299, 3 day notice.** 6289 Fallsview Blvd. Jct Niagara River Pkwy, just n on Murray St. Ext/int corridors. **Pets:** $10 daily fee/pet. Service with restrictions, crate.

Camelot Inn M
(905) 354-3754. **$50-$225.** 5640 Stanley Ave. Just n of Hwy 20; just s of Hwy 420. Ext corridors. **Pets:** Accepted.

Econo Lodge near the Falls M
(905) 358-6243. **$45-$120.** 6000 Stanley Ave. 0.8 mi (1.3 km) w on Hwy 20, just s. Ext/int corridors. **Pets:** Accepted.

Fallsview Casino Resort LH
(905) 358-3255. **$209-$449, 3 day notice.** 6380 Fallsview Blvd. Jct Murray St. Int corridors. **Pets:** Small. $50 daily fee/room. Service with restrictions, crate.

Niagara Parkway Court Motel M
(905) 295-3331. **$49-$149.** 3708 Main St (Niagara River Pkwy S). 1.6 mi (2.5 km) s of the falls. Ext corridors. **Pets:** Medium. $10 one-time fee/pet. Designated rooms, service with restrictions, supervision.

Peninsula Inn & Resort SH
(905) 354-8812. **$69-$189.** 7373 Niagara Square Dr. QEW, exit McLeod Rd, just w. Int corridors. **Pets:** Small. $10 daily fee/pet. Designated rooms, service with restrictions, supervision.

Sheraton Fallsview Hotel & Conference Centre LH
(905) 374-1077. **$89-$399.** 6755 Fallsview Blvd. Near Konica Minolta Tower. Int corridors. **Pets:** Medium, dogs only. $25 daily fee/room. Designated rooms, service with restrictions, supervision.

Sheraton on the Falls LH
(905) 374-4445. **$99-$999.** 5875 Falls Ave. Entrance to Rainbow Bridge on Hwy 20. Int corridors. **Pets:** Medium, dogs only. Service with restrictions, supervision.

Stanley Motor Inn M
(905) 358-9238. **$60-$140.** 6220 Stanley Ave. 2 blks from the falls; w of Skylon Tower. Ext/int corridors. **Pets:** Small, dogs only. $10 one-time fee/pet. No service, crate.

Thriftlodge Clifton Hill M
(905) 357-4330. **$49-$299.** 4945 Clifton Hill. Just s on jct Victoria Ave. Ext corridors. **Pets:** Medium. Service with restrictions, supervision.

NIAGARA-ON-THE-LAKE

Gate House Hotel CI
(905) 468-3263. **$145-$245, 7 day notice.** 142 Queen St. Jct Gate. Int corridors. **Pets:** Accepted.

Harbour House Hotel SH
(905) 468-4683. **$205-$380, 10 day notice.** 85 Melville St. Jct Ricardo St. Int corridors. **Pets:** Dogs only. $25 one-time fee/pet. Designated rooms, no service, supervision.

The Oban Inn and Spa SH
(905) 468-2165. **$150-$325.** 160 Front St. Jct Gate. Ext/int corridors. **Pets:** Small. $50 daily fee/pet. Designated rooms.

Old Bank House BB
(905) 468-7136. **$159-$235, 28 day notice.** 10 Front St. Corner of King and Front sts; centre. Int corridors. **Pets:** Accepted.

Pillar and Post Inn, Spa and Conference Centre CI
(905) 468-2123. **$135-$335.** 48 John St. Just n on Hwy 55 (Mississauga St), just e; 13 mi from QEW. Ext/int corridors. **Pets:** Small. $35 one-time fee/room. Designated rooms.

Prince of Wales Hotel & Spa SH
(905) 468-3246. **$155-$355.** 6 Picton St. Jct Picton and King sts; 9 mi (14.4 km) e of jct QEW and Hwy 55, via Hwy 55. Ext/int corridors. **Pets:** Small. $35 one-time fee/room. Designated rooms.

Queen's Landing Hotel SH
(905) 468-2195. **$135-$335.** 155 Byron St. Just n on King St, just e. Int corridors. **Pets:** Small, dogs only. $100 daily fee/room. Service with restrictions.

▼▼▼▼ **Shaw Club Hotel** SH
(905) 468-5711. **$91-$455, 10 day notice.** 92 Picton St. Jct Wellington St. Int corridors. **Pets:** Accepted.
ASK S👁 ✕ 🍴 💻 🍴

ST. CATHARINES

CAA ▼▼▼ **Comfort Inn** SH
(905) 687-8890. **$99-$159.** 2 Dunlop Dr. QEW, exit 46 (Lake St); between Lake and Geneva sts. Int corridors. **Pets:** Designated rooms, service with restrictions, supervision.
SAVE S👁 ✕ 🔶M 🍴 💻 🍴

CAA ▼▼▼▼ **Holiday Inn St. Catharines/Niagara** SH
(905) 934-8000. **$99-$599.** 2 N Service Rd. QEW, exit 46 (Lake St), just e. Int corridors. **Pets:** Accepted.
SAVE S👁 ✕ 🍴 💻 🍴 ➷ ✕

CAA ▼▼▼ **Howard Johnson Hotel & Conference Centre** SH
(905) 934-5400. **$89-$289.** 89 Meadowvale Dr. QEW, exit 46 (Lake St). Int corridors. **Pets:** $10 one-time fee/room. Designated rooms, service with restrictions, supervision.
SAVE S👁 ✕ 🍴 💻 🍴 ➷ ✕

CAA ▼▼▼▼ **Quality Hotel Parkway Convention Centre** LH
(905) 688-2324. **$109-$319.** 327 Ontario St. QEW, exit 47 (Ontario St), 0.5 mi (0.8 km) s. Int corridors. **Pets:** $16 one-time fee/room. Designated rooms, service with restrictions, supervision.
SAVE S👁 ✕ 🍴 💻 🍴 ✕

CAA ▼▼▼ **The Travelodge St. Catharines** M
(905) 688-1646. **$89-$149.** 420 Ontario St. QEW, exit 47 (Ontario St). Ext corridors. **Pets:** Medium. $10 daily fee/pet. Service with restrictions, supervision.
SAVE S👁 ✕ 🍴 💻 🍴 ➷

THOROLD

▼▼▼ **Four Points by Sheraton St. Catharines** LH
(905) 984-8484. **$99-$199.** 3530 Schmon Pkwy. Hwy 406, exit St. David's Rd W. Int corridors. **Pets:** $10 daily fee/room. Designated rooms, service with restrictions, crate.
ASK S👁 ✕ 🔶 🍴 💻 🍴 ➷ ✕

WELLAND

▼▼▼ **Comfort Inn-Niagara Falls/Welland** SH
(905) 732-4811. **$50-$80.** 870 Niagara St. 1.5 mi (2.5 km) n. Int corridors. **Pets:** Accepted.
ASK S👁 ✕ 🍴 💻

CAA ▼▼▼ **Days Inn-Welland** SH
(905) 735-6666. **$60-$150.** 1030 Niagara St N. Hwy 20, 1 mi (1.5 km) se on Hwy 58. Int corridors. **Pets:** Accepted.
SAVE S👁 ✕ 🔶 🍴 💻 🍴 ➷ ✕

END METROPOLITAN AREA

NORTH BAY

CAA ▼▼▼ **Best Western North Bay** SH ✿
(705) 474-5800. **$89-$199.** 700 Lakeshore Dr. Hwy 11, exit Lakeshore Dr, 2.5 mi (4 km) n on Hwy 11B. Int corridors. **Pets:** Other species. Service with restrictions, crate.
SAVE S👁 ✕ 🍴 💻 🍴 ➷ ✕

CAA ▼▼▼▼ **Clarion Resort Pinewood Park** SH ✿
(705) 472-0810. **$180-$280.** 201 Pinewood Park Dr. Hwy 11, exit Lakeshore Dr, immediately turn s on Pinewood Park Dr, then 0.4 mi (0.7 km). Int corridors. **Pets:** Other species. Service with restrictions, crate.
SAVE S👁 ✕ 🍴 💻 🍴 ➷ ✕

▼▼ **Comfort Inn** SH
(705) 494-9444. **$99-$139.** 676 Lakeshore Dr. Hwy 11B, exit Lakeshore Dr; 2.5 mi (4 km) n of jct Hwy 11. Int corridors. **Pets:** Other species. Service with restrictions, crate.
ASK S👁 ✕ 🍴 💻

▼▼ **Comfort Inn-Airport** SH
(705) 476-5400. **$99-$150.** 1200 O St. 1.8 mi (3 km) e on Hwy 11 and 17 Bypass; at O'Brien St exit. Int corridors. **Pets:** Service with restrictions, supervision.
ASK S👁 ✕ 🍴 💻

▼▼ **Super 8** SH
(705) 495-4551. **$76-$99.** 570 Lakeshore Dr. Hwy 11, exit Lakeshore Dr, 2.8 mi (4.5 km) n on Hwy 11B. Int corridors. **Pets:** Service with restrictions, supervision.
ASK ✕ 🔶 🍴 💻

CAA ▼▼▼ **Travelodge** SH
(705) 472-7171. **$82.** 718 Lakeshore Dr. Hwy 11B, exit Lakeshore Dr; 2.2 mi (3.5 km) n of jct Hwy 11. Int corridors. **Pets:** Accepted.
SAVE S👁 ✕ 🔶 🍴 💻

▼▼ **Travelodge-Airport** SH ✿
(705) 495-1133. **$109-$169.** 1525 Seymour St. Jct Hwy 11, 17 and Seymour St. Int corridors. **Pets:** Other species. $25 deposit/room. Service with restrictions, supervision.
ASK S👁 ✕ 🍴 💻 ➷

OAKVILLE

▼▼▼ **Holiday Inn Oakville-Centre** SH
(905) 842-5000. **$189-$209.** 590 Argus Rd. QEW, exit 118 (Trafalgar Rd), just s. Int corridors. **Pets:** Accepted.
ASK S👁 ✕ 🔶M 🔶 🍴 💻 🍴 ➷ ✕

▼▼▼ **Homewood Suites by Hilton Toronto-Oakville** SH
(905) 829-9998. **$157-$274.** 2095 Winston Park Dr. QEW, exit 124 (Winston Churchill Blvd), just n to Upper Middle Rd E. Int corridors. **Pets:** Medium. $75 one-time fee/room. Designated rooms, service with restrictions, supervision.
ASK S👁 ✕ 🔶M 🔶 🍴 💻 ➷

CAA ▼▼▼ **Park Plaza Hotel and Conference Centre Toronto/Oakville** SH
(905) 845-7561. **$149-$249.** 360 Oakville Place Dr. QEW, exit 118 (Trafalgar Rd) just n. Int corridors. **Pets:** Small. $25 one-time fee/pet. Designated rooms, service with restrictions, crate.
SAVE S👁 ✕ 🍴 💻 🍴 ➷ ✕

CAA ▼▼▼ **Quality Hotel & Suites-Oakville** SH
(905) 847-6667. **$119-$199.** 754 Bronte Rd. QEW, exit 111 (Bronte Rd/Hwy 25), 0.3 mi (0.4 km) s. Int corridors. **Pets:** Other species. $50 one-time fee/pet. Service with restrictions, crate.
SAVE ✕ 🍴 💻 🍴 ➷ ✕

ORILLIA

▼▼ **Comfort Inn** SH
(705) 327-7744. **$120-$147, 14 day notice.** 75 Progress Dr. Hwy 11 N, exit Hwy 12, s on Memorial Ave; corner of Progress Dr and Memorial Ave. Int corridors. **Pets:** Accepted.
ASK S👁 ✕ 🍴 💻

 Econo Lodge SH
(705) 326-3554. **$79-$109.** 265 Memorial Ave. 0.3 mi (0.5 km) n of Hwy 12. Int corridors. **Pets:** $50 deposit/room. Designated rooms, service with restrictions.
⟦SAVE⟧ ⟦S🐾⟧ ⟦✕⟧ ⟦🖥⟧ ⟦🖥⟧

OSHAWA

▼▼ Comfort Inn SH
(905) 434-5000. **$99-$195.** 605 Bloor St W. Hwy 401, exit 416 (Park Rd), s to Bloor St, then 0.8 km w. Int corridors. **Pets:** Accepted.
⟦ASK⟧ ⟦S🐾⟧ ⟦✕⟧ ⟦🖥⟧ ⟦🖥⟧

▼▼▼ Holiday Inn Oshawa SH
(905) 576-5101. **$129-$179.** 1011 Bloor St E. Hwy 401, exit 419 (Harmony Rd). Int corridors. **Pets:** Accepted.
⟦SAVE⟧ ⟦S🐾⟧ ⟦✕⟧ ⟦🖥⟧ ⟦🖥⟧ ⟦🍴⟧ ⟦🏊⟧ ⟦✕⟧

▼▼▼ Oshawa Travelodge SH
(905) 436-9500. **$99-$129.** 940 Champlain Ave. Hwy 401, exit 412 (Thickson Rd N). Int corridors. **Pets:** Accepted.
⟦ASK⟧ ⟦S🐾⟧ ⟦✕⟧ ⟦🖥⟧ ⟦🖥⟧ ⟦🏊⟧

OTTAWA METROPOLITAN AREA

OTTAWA

Adam's Airport Inn SH
(613) 738-3838. **$94-$145.** 2721 Bank St. Jct Hunt Club Rd and Bank St, 0.6 mi (1 km) s. Int corridors. **Pets:** Accepted.
⟦SAVE⟧ ⟦✕⟧ ⟦🖥⟧ ⟦🖥⟧

Best Western Barons Hotel & Conference Centre SH
(613) 828-2741. **$129-$179.** 3700 Richmond Rd. Hwy 417, exit 130, 1.3 mi (2 km) s. Int corridors. **Pets:** Other species. $10 daily fee/pet. Service with restrictions, supervision.
⟦SAVE⟧ ⟦S🐾⟧ ⟦✕⟧ ⟦🐾⟧ ⟦🖥⟧ ⟦🖥⟧ ⟦🍴⟧ ⟦🏊⟧ ⟦✕⟧

▼▼▼ Bostonian Executive Suites SH
(613) 594-5757. **$159-$189.** 341 MacLaren St. Between Bank and O'Connor sts. Int corridors. **Pets:** Accepted.
⟦ASK⟧ ⟦S🐾⟧ ⟦✕⟧ ⟦🖥⟧ ⟦🖥⟧

Brookstreet LH
(613) 271-1800. **$139-$279.** 525 Legget Dr. Hwy 417, exit 138 (March Rd), 2.3 (3.7 km) n, just e on Solandt Dr to Legget Dr, then just n. Int corridors. **Pets:** Small. $250 deposit/pet, $25 daily fee/pet. Designated rooms, service with restrictions, supervision.
⟦SAVE⟧ ⟦S🐾⟧ ⟦✕⟧ ⟦🖥⟧ ⟦🍴⟧ ⟦🏊⟧ ⟦✕⟧

Cartier Place Suite Hotel SH
(613) 236-5000. **$129-$209.** 180 Cooper St. Between Elgin and Cartier sts. Int corridors. **Pets:** Accepted.
⟦SAVE⟧ ⟦S🐾⟧ ⟦✕⟧ ⟦🖥⟧ ⟦🖥⟧ ⟦🍴⟧ ⟦🏊⟧ ⟦✕⟧

Comfort Inn SH
(613) 744-2900. **$90-$170.** 1252 Michael St. Hwy 417, exit 115 (St. Laurent Blvd), just ne. Int corridors. **Pets:** Large, other species. Service with restrictions, crate.
⟦SAVE⟧ ⟦S🐾⟧ ⟦✕⟧ ⟦🖥⟧ ⟦🖥⟧

Comfort Inn Ottawa West SH
(613) 592-2200. **$109-$150.** 222 Hearst Way. Hwy 417, exit 138 (Eagleson Rd), 0.4 mi (0.6 km) s, then just w on Katimavik Rd. Int corridors. **Pets:** Other species. Designated rooms, no service, crate.
⟦SAVE⟧ ⟦S🐾⟧ ⟦✕⟧ ⟦🖥⟧ ⟦🖥⟧

Days Inn-Downtown (Ottawa) SH
(613) 789-5555. **$109-$139.** 319 Rideau St. Between Nelson St and King Edward Ave. Ext/int corridors. **Pets:** Medium, other species. Designated rooms, service with restrictions, supervision.
⟦SAVE⟧ ⟦S🐾⟧ ⟦✕⟧ ⟦🖥⟧ ⟦🖥⟧ ⟦🍴⟧

▼▼ The Days Inn Ottawa West SH
(613) 726-1717. **$130.** 350 Moodie Dr. Hwy 417, exit 134, 0.9 mi (1.5 km) s. Int corridors. **Pets:** Medium. $20 daily fee/room. Designated rooms, service with restrictions, supervision.
⟦ASK⟧ ⟦S🐾⟧ ⟦✕⟧ ⟦🖥⟧ ⟦🖥⟧ ⟦🍴⟧

Delta Ottawa Hotel and Suites LH
(613) 238-6000. **$129-$229.** 361 Queen St. Corner of Lyon St. Int corridors. **Pets:** Accepted.
⟦SAVE⟧ ⟦✕⟧ ⟦🖥⟧ ⟦🖥⟧ ⟦🍴⟧ ⟦🏊⟧ ⟦✕⟧

Extended Stay Deluxe Ottawa Downtown SH
(613) 236-7500. **$115-$145.** 141 Cooper St. Between Elgin and Cartier sts. Int corridors. **Pets:** Accepted.
⟦SAVE⟧ ⟦S🐾⟧ ⟦✕⟧ ⟦🖥⟧ ⟦🖥⟧ ⟦🍴⟧ ⟦✕⟧

Fairmont Chateau Laurier LH
(613) 241-1414. **$169-$399.** 1 Rideau St. Just e of Parliament buildings. Int corridors. **Pets:** Accepted.
⟦SAVE⟧ ⟦S🐾⟧ ⟦✕⟧ ⟦🐾M⟧ ⟦🖥⟧ ⟦🖥⟧ ⟦🍴⟧ ⟦🏊⟧ ⟦✕⟧

Holiday Inn Hotel & Suites SH 🐾
(613) 238-1331. **$159-$171.** 111 Cooper St. Corner of Cartier St. Int corridors. **Pets:** Other species. Designated rooms.
⟦SAVE⟧ ⟦S🐾⟧ ⟦✕⟧ ⟦🐾⟧ ⟦🖥⟧ ⟦🖥⟧ ⟦🍴⟧

Les Suites Hotel Ottawa SH 🐾
(613) 232-2000. **$139-$199.** 130 Besserer St. Between Nicholas and Waller sts. Int corridors. **Pets:** Other species. $25 one-time fee/room. Designated rooms, service with restrictions.
⟦SAVE⟧ ⟦S🐾⟧ ⟦✕⟧ ⟦🐾M⟧ ⟦🖥⟧ ⟦🖥⟧ ⟦🍴⟧ ⟦🏊⟧ ⟦✕⟧

▼▼▼ Lord Elgin Hotel LH
(613) 235-3333. **$135-$175.** 100 Elgin St. Between Laurier Ave and Slater St. Int corridors. **Pets:** Designated rooms, service with restrictions, supervision.
⟦ASK⟧ ⟦S🐾⟧ ⟦✕⟧ ⟦🐾⟧ ⟦🖥⟧ ⟦🖥⟧ ⟦🍴⟧ ⟦🏊⟧ ⟦✕⟧

Monterey Inn Resort & Conference Centre SH
(613) 288-3500. **$99-$149.** 2259 Prince of Wales Dr. 0.5 mi (0.8 km) s of Hunt Club Rd. Ext corridors. **Pets:** Accepted.
⟦SAVE⟧ ⟦S🐾⟧ ⟦✕⟧ ⟦🖥⟧ ⟦🖥⟧ ⟦🍴⟧ ⟦🏊⟧ ⟦✕⟧

Novotel Ottawa Hotel SH 🐾
(613) 230-3033. **$139-$219.** 33 Nicholas St. Corner of Daly Ave. Int corridors. **Pets:** Large, other species.
⟦SAVE⟧ ⟦S🐾⟧ ⟦✕⟧ ⟦🖥⟧ ⟦🖥⟧ ⟦🍴⟧ ⟦🏊⟧ ⟦✕⟧

Ottawa Marriott LH
(613) 238-1122. **$119-$259.** 100 Kent St. Corner of Queen St. Int corridors. **Pets:** Accepted.
⟦SAVE⟧ ⟦S🐾⟧ ⟦✕⟧ ⟦🖥⟧ ⟦🖥⟧ ⟦🍴⟧ ⟦🏊⟧ ⟦✕⟧

Quality Hotel Ottawa, Downtown SH
(613) 789-7511. **$129-$155.** 290 Rideau St. Corner of King Edward Ave. Int corridors. **Pets:** Accepted.
⟦SAVE⟧ ⟦S🐾⟧ ⟦✕⟧ ⟦🖥⟧ ⟦🖥⟧ ⟦🍴⟧

Radisson Hotel Ottawa Parliament Hill SH
(613) 236-1133. **$199.** 402 Queen St. Corner of Bay and Queen sts. Int corridors. **Pets:** Medium. Designated rooms, service with restrictions.
⟦SAVE⟧ ⟦S🐾⟧ ⟦✕⟧ ⟦🖥⟧ ⟦🖥⟧ ⟦🍴⟧

♦♦♦ Residence Inn by Marriott SH
(613) 231-2020. **$159-$289.** 161 Laurier Ave W. Corner of Elgin St. Int corridors. **Pets:** $85 one-time fee/room. Service with restrictions, crate.
(ASK) (S/D) (X) (H) (D) (≈) (X)

(CAA) ♦♦♦ Rideau Heights Motor Inn M
(613) 226-4152. **$99-$119.** 72 Rideau Heights Dr. Hwy 16 (Prince of Wales Dr), 0.3 mi (0.5 km) n of Hunt Club Rd. Ext corridors. **Pets:** Small, other species. $10 daily fee/pet. Designated rooms, service with restrictions, supervision.
(SAVE) (S/D) (X) (H) (D)

(CAA) ♦♦♦♦ Sheraton Ottawa Hotel LH
(613) 238-1500. **$115-$245.** 150 Albert St. Corner of O'Connor St. Int corridors. **Pets:** Small. Designated rooms, service with restrictions, supervision.
(SAVE) (S/D) (X) (H) (D) (†↑) (≈)

(CAA) ♦♦♦♦ Southway Inn of Ottawa SH ❀
(613) 737-0811. **$138-$148, 3 day notice.** 2431 Bank St. On Hwy 31, corner of Hunt Club Rd. Int corridors. **Pets:** Medium. $30 daily fee/pet. Designated rooms, service with restrictions, supervision.
(SAVE) (S/D) (X) (H) (D) (†↑) (≈) (X)

(CAA) ♦♦ Travelodge Ottawa East SH
(613) 745-1133. **$99-$149.** 1486 Innes Rd. Hwy 417, exit 112 (Innes Rd), just e. Int corridors. **Pets:** Accepted.
(SAVE) (S/D) (X) (H) (D) (†↑) (≈)

(CAA) ♦♦♦ Travelodge Ottawa Hotel & Conference Centre SH
(613) 722-7600. **$109-$189.** 1376 Carling Ave. Just e of jct Kirkwood Ave. Int corridors. **Pets:** Accepted.
(SAVE) (S/D) (X) (H) (D) (†↑) (X)

(CAA) ♦♦ Value Inn M
(613) 745-1531. **$85-$99.** 2098 Montreal Rd. Hwy 417, exit 113, 1.6 mi (2.5 km) e on Hwy 174 to Montreal Rd W exit. Ext corridors. **Pets:** Large. $10 daily fee/pet. Service with restrictions, crate.
(SAVE) (S/D) (X) (H) (D)

(CAA) ♦♦ Webb's Motel M
(613) 728-1881. **$95-$100.** 1705 Carling Ave. Hwy 417, exit 126, 0.3 mi (0.5 km) n on Maitland Ave, then 0.3 mi (0.5 km) e. Ext/int corridors. **Pets:** Accepted.
(SAVE) (X) (H)

♦♦♦♦ The Westin Ottawa LH
(613) 560-7000. **$169-$369.** 11 Colonel By Dr. Corner of Rideau St. Int corridors. **Pets:** Accepted.
(X) (⤢) (♿) (H) (D) (†↑) (≈) (X)

END METROPOLITAN AREA

OWEN SOUND

♦♦♦ Comfort Inn SH
(519) 371-5500. **$99-$169.** 955 9th Ave E. Jct Hwy 6, 10, 21 and 26. Int corridors. **Pets:** Accepted.
(ASK) (S/D) (X) (H) (D)

(CAA) ♦♦♦♦ Days Inn Hotel and Convention Centre SH ❀
(519) 376-1551. **$89-$189.** 950 6th St E. Jct Hwy 6 and 10. Int corridors. **Pets:** Other species. $20 daily fee/room. Designated rooms, service with restrictions.
(SAVE) (S/D) (X) (H) (D) (†↑) (≈) (X)

♦♦ Owen Sound Inn SH
(519) 371-3011. **$45-$159.** 485 9th Ave E. Jct Hwy 6, 10, 26 and 21; follow Hwy 6 and 10, 0.6 mi (1 km) s. Int corridors. **Pets:** Accepted.
(ASK) (S/D) (X) (H) (D)

♦♦ Travelodge SH
(519) 371-9297. **$114-$155.** 880 10th St E. Jct Hwy 6, 10, 21 and 26. Int corridors. **Pets:** Accepted.
(ASK) (S/D) (X) (H) (D)

PARRY SOUND

♦♦ Comfort Inn SH
(705) 746-6221. **$106-$150.** 120 Bowes St. Hwy 69, exit 224 (Bowes St), just w. Int corridors. **Pets:** Designated rooms.
(ASK) (S/D) (X) (H) (D)

(CAA) ♦♦♦ Microtel Inn & Suites SH
(705) 746-2700. **$99-$134.** 292 Louisa St. Hwy 69, exit 224 (Bowes St) northbound, just w; southbound, just e. Int corridors. **Pets:** Small, other species. $10 daily fee/pet. Designated rooms, supervision.
(SAVE) (S/D) (X) (♿) (H) (D)

♦♦ Resort Tapatoo SH
(705) 378-2208. **$88-$193, 8 day notice.** Otter Lake Rd. Hwy 69, exit 217, 3.9 mi (6.2 km) sw. Ext/int corridors. **Pets:** $20 daily fee/pet. Designated rooms, service with restrictions.
(ASK) (S/D) (X) (H) (D) (†↑) (≈) (X)

PEMBROKE

♦ Colonial Fireside Inn M
(613) 732-3623. **$69-$89.** 1350 Pembroke St W. Jct Hwy 17, 3.1 mi (5 km) n on Forest Lea Rd, just e. Ext corridors. **Pets:** $5 daily fee/pet. Service with restrictions, supervision.
(ASK) (S/D) (X) (H) (D) (≈)

♦♦ Comfort Inn SH ❀
(613) 735-1057. **$100-$179.** 959 Pembroke St E. 1 mi (1.6 km) e on Old Hwy 17. Int corridors. **Pets:** Service with restrictions, supervision.
(ASK) (S/D) (X) (H) (D)

PETAWAWA

(CAA) ♦♦♦ Thriftlodge Petawawa SH
(613) 687-4686. **$109-$169.** 3520 Petawawa Blvd. Hwy 17, exit Paquette Rd, 1.5 mi (2.4 km) e, then just s. Int corridors. **Pets:** Accepted.
(SAVE) (S/D) (X) (H) (D)

PETERBOROUGH

♦♦ King Bethune House, Guest House & Spa BB ❀
(705) 743-4101. **$149, 14 day notice.** 270 King St. From Charlotte and George St (clock tower), 1 blk s on George St to King St, then just w. Int corridors. **Pets:** Other species. Supervision.
(X) (H) (D)

(CAA) ♦♦♦ Quality Inn SH ❀
(705) 748-6801. **$94-$124.** 1074 Lansdowne St W. 1.9 mi (3 km) from jct Hwy 115 and Bypass. Int corridors. **Pets:** Medium. Service with restrictions.
(SAVE) (S/D) (X) (H) (D)

PICKERING

▼▼ ▼▼ Comfort Inn SH
(905) 831-6200. **$95-$165.** 533 Kingston Rd. Hwy 401, exit 394 N (White's Rd) to Hwy 2, 0.5 km w. Int corridors. **Pets:** Medium. Designated rooms, service with restrictions, supervision.
ASK 🛏 ✕ 🍴 💻

PLANTAGENET

▼▼▼ Motel de Champlain M
(613) 673-5220. **$70-$110.** 5999 Hwy 17. Jct CR 9. Ext/int corridors. **Pets:** Other species. $20 daily fee/pet. Service with restrictions, crate.
ASK 🛏 ✕ 🍴 🍴

PORT CARLING

CAA ▼▼▼▼ Delta Sherwood Inn SH
(705) 765-3131. **$169-$1094, 14 day notice.** 1090 Sherwood Rd. Hwy 169, n of jct Hwy 118; on Lake Joseph. Ext/int corridors. **Pets:** Accepted.
SAVE 🛏 ✕ 🍴 💻 🍴 ✕

PORT HOPE

CAA ▼▼▼ Comfort Inn SH
(905) 885-7000. **$119-$210.** Hwy 401 & 28. Hwy 401, exit 464, just n. Int corridors. **Pets:** Service with restrictions, supervision.
SAVE 🛏 ✕ 🍴 💻

PROVIDENCE BAY

CAA ▼▼ Huron Sands Motel M
(705) 377-4616. **$79-$119, 3 day notice.** 5216 Hwy 551. In Providence Bay; on Hwy 551, 17 mi (27.2 km) w of South Baymouth via 10th Side Rd, follow signs; centre. Ext corridors. **Pets:** Other species. $10 one-time fee/pet. Service with restrictions, supervision.
SAVE ✕ 🍴 🍴 ✕

RENFREW

CAA ▼▼ ▼ Best Western-Renfrew Inn and Conference Centre SH
(613) 432-8109. **$122-$175.** 760 Gibbons Rd. Hwy 17, exit O'Brien Rd. Int corridors. **Pets:** Other species. $15 daily fee/room. Service with restrictions, supervision.
SAVE 🛏 ✕ 🍴 💻 🍴 ✕ ✕

▼▼ The Rocky Mountain House M
(613) 432-5801. **$84-$119.** 409 Stewart St N. Jct Bruce St. Ext corridors. **Pets:** Accepted.
ASK 🛏 ✕ 🍴 💻 🍴

ROSSPORT

▼▼ The Willows Inn Bed & Breakfast BB
(807) 824-3389. **$85-$130, 10 day notice.** 1 Main St. Centre. Int corridors. **Pets:** $30 deposit/room. Designated rooms, supervision.
✕ 🏫

ST. THOMAS

CAA ▼▼ ▼▼ Comfort Inn SH
(519) 633-4082. **$119-$159.** 100 Centennial Ave. 4.1 mi (6.5 km) e on Hwy 3. Int corridors. **Pets:** Medium. $20 one-time fee/pet. Service with restrictions.
SAVE 🛏 ✕ 🍴 💻

SARNIA

▼▼▼▼ Holiday Inn Sarnia-Point Edward SH
(519) 336-4130. **$115-$200.** 1498 Venetian Blvd. E of Bluewater Bridge. Int corridors. **Pets:** Accepted.
ASK 🛏 ✕ 🍴 🍴 💻 🍴 ✕ ✕

▼▼ Super 8 Motel-Sarnia SH
(519) 337-3767. **$80-$90.** 420 Christina St N. Between Exmouth and London rds. Ext/int corridors. **Pets:** Accepted.
ASK 🛏 ✕ 🍴 🍴 💻

SAULT STE. MARIE

▼▼ Adams Motel M
(705) 254-4345. **$59-$99.** 647 Great Northern Rd. 2.8 mi (4.4 km) n on Hwy 17B. Ext corridors. **Pets:** Accepted.
ASK 🛏 ✕ 🍴 💻

CAA ▼▼▼▼ Algoma's Water Tower Inn SH
(705) 949-8111. **$119-$189.** 360 Great Northern Rd. Jct Hwy 17 and Second Line. Int corridors. **Pets:** Other species. Designated rooms, supervision.
SAVE 🛏 ✕ 🍴 🍴 💻 🍴 ✕ ✕

▼▼ Ambassador Motel M
(705) 759-6199. **$64-$99.** 1275 Great Northern Rd. 4 mi (6.4 km) n on Hwy 17. Ext corridors. **Pets:** $10 daily fee/pet. Designated rooms, service with restrictions, crate.
✕ 🍴 💻 ✕ ✕

CAA ▼▼ Bel-Air Motel M
(705) 945-7950. **$55-$95.** 398 Pim St. 1.3 mi (2 km) n on Hwy 17B. Ext corridors. **Pets:** Medium. $5 daily fee/pet. Designated rooms, service with restrictions.
SAVE 🛏 ✕ 🍴 💻

CAA ▼▼ Catalina Motel M
(705) 945-9260. **$92-$114.** 259 Great Northern Rd. 2 mi (3.2 km) n on Hwy 17B. Ext corridors. **Pets:** $11 daily fee/room. No service.
SAVE 🛏 ✕ 🍴 💻

CAA ▼▼▼ City Centre Travelodge SH
(705) 759-1400. **$109-$130, 45 day notice.** 332 Bay St. Opposite Station Mall. Int corridors. **Pets:** Medium. Designated rooms, service with restrictions, supervision.
SAVE 🛏 ✕ 🍴 💻 🍴

CAA ▼▼▼ Comfort Inn SH
(705) 759-8000. **$98-$155.** 333 Great Northern Rd. 2.3 mi (3.6 km) n on Hwy 17B. Ext/int corridors. **Pets:** Medium. $5 daily fee/pet. Service with restrictions, supervision.
SAVE 🛏 ✕ 🍴 💻

▼▼ ▼▼ Glenview Cottages CA 🐾
(705) 759-3436. **$99-$150, 5 day notice.** 2611 Great Northern Rd. 6 mi (9.6 km) n on Hwy 17. Ext corridors. **Pets:** $5 daily fee/room. Designated rooms, crate.
ASK ✕ 🍴 💻 ✕ ✕

CAA ▼▼▼▼ Holiday Inn Sault Ste. Marie-Waterfront SH
(705) 949-0611. **$119-$179.** 208 St. Marys River Dr. On the waterfront. Int corridors. **Pets:** Other species. Designated rooms, service with restrictions, crate.
SAVE 🛏 ✕ 🍴 💻 🍴 ✕ ✕

▼▼ Holiday Motel M
(705) 759-8608. **$50-$79.** 435 Trunk Rd. Jct Hwy 17 and 17B, just e. Ext corridors. **Pets:** Service with restrictions, supervision.
✕ 🍴 💻

CAA ▼▼ Northlander Motel M
(705) 254-6452. **$55-$85.** 243 Great Northern Rd. 1.9 mi (3 km) n on Hwy 17B. Ext corridors. **Pets:** Large, other species. Service with restrictions, supervision.
SAVE 🛏 ✕ 🍴 💻

▼▼ Satelite Motel M
(705) 759-2897. **$55-$95.** 248 Great Northern Rd. 1.9 mi (3 km) n on Hwy 17B. Ext corridors. **Pets:** Medium, other species. $4 daily fee/room. Service with restrictions.
✕ 🍴 💻

▽▽ **Sleep Inn** SH
(705) 253-7533. **$85-$150.** 727 Bay St. Between East and Church sts; downtown. Int corridors. **Pets:** Accepted.

🄰🅂🄺 💲👁 ✕ 🔒 🖥 ✕

🄰🄰 ▽▽ **Super 8** SH
(705) 254-6441. **$75-$130.** 184 Great Northern Rd. 1.3 mi (2 km) n on Hwy 17B. Int corridors. **Pets:** Accepted.

🆂🅰🆅🅴 💲👁 ✕ 🔒 🖥

▽ **Villa Inn Motel** M
(705) 942-2424. **$55-$79.** 724 Great Northern Rd. 2.9 mi (4.6 km) n on Hwy 17B. Ext corridors. **Pets:** Other species. Designated rooms, service with restrictions.

✕ 🔒 🖥

SIMCOE

▽▽ **Comfort Inn** SH
(519) 426-2611. **$94-$169.** 85 Queensway E. 0.3 mi (0.5 km) e on Hwy 3. Int corridors. **Pets:** Medium, other species. Designated rooms, service with restrictions, supervision.

🄰🅂🄺 💲👁 ✕ 🔒 🖥

▽▽ **Travelodge Simcoe** SH
(519) 426-4751. **$119.** 385 Queensway W (Hwy 3). 1 km w. Ext/int corridors. **Pets:** Small. $10 daily fee/pet. Service with restrictions, supervision.

🄰🅂🄺 💲👁 ✕ 🖑 🔒 🖥 🍴 🏊 ✕

SMITHS FALLS

▽▽ **Best Western Colonel By Inn** SH
(613) 284-0001. **$87-$107.** 88 Lombard St. 1.2 km s on Hwy 15. Ext/int corridors. **Pets:** $10 daily fee/pet. Designated rooms, service with restrictions, supervision.

🄰🅂🄺 💲👁 ✕ 🔒 🖥 🍴 🏊

SOUTH BAYMOUTH

🄰🄰 ▽ **Huron Motor Lodge** SH
(705) 859-3131. **$89-$135.** 24 Water St N. In South Baymouth; centre; opposite ferry terminal dock. Ext corridors. **Pets:** Medium, other species. $10 daily fee/pet. Designated rooms, service with restrictions, supervision.

🆂🅰🆅🅴 💲👁 ✕ 🔒 🖥 🏊 🍳 🖫

STRATFORD

▽▽◆ **Arden Park Hotel** SH
(519) 275-2936. **$94-$225.** 552 Ontario St. Jct Romeo St. Int corridors. **Pets:** Accepted.

✕ 🖑 🔒 🖥 🍴 🏊

SUDBURY

🄰🄰 ▽▽ **Best Western Downtown Sudbury Centre-Ville** SH
(705) 673-7801. **$100-$116, 14 day notice.** 151 Larch St. Centre. Int corridors. **Pets:** Medium, other species. $15 daily fee/pet. Service with restrictions, supervision.

🆂🅰🆅🅴 💲👁 ✕ 🖥 🍴

▽▽ **Comfort Inn** SH
(705) 522-1101. **$128-$164.** 2171 Regent St S. 3 mi (5 km) s on Hwy 46. Int corridors. **Pets:** Other species. Designated rooms, service with restrictions, supervision.

🄰🅂🄺 💲👁 ✕ 🔒 🖥

▽▽ **Comfort Inn** SH 🐾
(705) 560-4502. **$90-$185.** 440 Second Ave N. Kingsway Hwy at Second Ave. Int corridors. **Pets:** Medium. $15 daily fee/pet. Designated rooms, service with restrictions, supervision.

🄰🅂🄺 💲👁 ✕ 🖑 🔒 🖥

▽▽ **Days Inn Sudbury** SH 🐾
(705) 674-7517. **$120-$150.** 117 Elm St. Centre of downtown. Int corridors. **Pets:** Medium, other species. $10 one-time fee/room. Designated rooms, service with restrictions.

🄰🅂🄺 💲👁 ✕ 🔒 🖥 🍴 🏊

🄰🄰 ▽▽▽ **Holiday Inn Hotel Sudbury** SH
(705) 522-3000. **$115-$205.** 1696 Regent St S. Hwy 69 (Regent St), just n of Paris St. Ext/int corridors. **Pets:** Accepted.

🆂🅰🆅🅴 💲👁 ✕ 🖑 🔒 🖥 🍴 🏊 ✕

🄰🄰 ▽▽ **Quality Inn & Conference Centre** SH
(705) 675-1273. **$103-$135.** S. Jct Kingsway Hwy and Paris St, 0.3 mi (0.5 km) s, just e. Int corridors. **Pets:** Other species. Designated rooms, service with restrictions, crate.

🆂🅰🆅🅴 💲👁 ✕ 🔒 🖥 🍴 🏊

▽▽▽ **Radisson Hotel, Sudbury** SH
(705) 675-1123. **$109-$175.** 85 St. Anne Rd. Jct St. Anne Rd and Notre Dame Ave; downtown. Int corridors. **Pets:** $30 one-time fee/room. Designated rooms, service with restrictions, supervision.

🄰🅂🄺 💲👁 ✕ 🔒 🖥 🍴 🏊

▽▽ **Travelodge Hotel Sudbury** SH
(705) 522-1100. **$109-$169.** 1401 Paris St. 0.9 mi (1.5 km) n of jct Hwy 69 (Regent St). Int corridors. **Pets:** Accepted.

🄰🅂🄺 💲👁 ✕ 🔒 🖥 🏊

THESSALON

🄰🄰 ▽ **Carolyn Beach Motor Inn** M
(705) 842-3330. **$82-$120.** 1 Lakeside Dr. Just w on Hwy 17; jct Hwy 17B. Ext corridors. **Pets:** Large. $10 daily fee/pet. Service with restrictions, supervision.

🆂🅰🆅🅴 ✕ 🔒 🖥 🍴 ✕

THUNDER BAY

🄰🄰 ▽▽ **Best Western Crossroads Motor Inn** SH
(807) 577-4241. **$95-$165.** 655 W Arthur St. Jct Hwy 61, 17 and 11, just e. Int corridors. **Pets:** Medium, other species. $15 one-time fee/room. Designated rooms, service with restrictions, supervision.

🆂🅰🆅🅴 💲👁 ✕ 🔒

🄰🄰 ▽▽ **Best Western Nor'Wester Resort Hotel** SH
(807) 473-9123. **$135-$165.** 2080 Hwy 61. 5.8 mi (9.2 km) sw of jct Hwy 11, 17 and 61, exit Loch Lomond Rd. Int corridors. **Pets:** Medium. $20 one-time fee/pet. Designated rooms, service with restrictions, supervision.

🆂🅰🆅🅴 💲👁 ✕ 🔒 🖥 🍴 🏊 ✕

▽▽ **Comfort Inn** M 🐾
(807) 475-3155. **$89-$159.** 660 W Arthur St. Jct Hwy 11, 17 and 61, just e. Int corridors. **Pets:** Other species. Service with restrictions, supervision.

🄰🅂🄺 💲👁 ✕ 🔒 🖥

🄰🄰 ▽▽ **Super 8 Motel** SH
(807) 344-2612. **$80-$140.** 439 Memorial Ave. Jct Hwy 11, 17 and Harbour Expwy. 1.9 mi (3 km) e on Harbour Expwy, 1.3 mi (2 km) n. Int corridors. **Pets:** Accepted.

🆂🅰🆅🅴 💲👁 ✕ 🔒

▽▽ **Victoria Inn** SH
(807) 577-8481. **$106-$110.** 555 W Arthur St. 0.5 mi (0.8 km) e of jct Hwy 11B, 17B and 61 (western access to town). Int corridors. **Pets:** Accepted.

🄰🅂🄺 ✕ 🔒 🖥 🍴 🏊 ✕

TILLSONBURG

🄰🄰 ▽▽ **Super 8 Motel-Tillsonburg** SH
(519) 842-7366. **$110-$130.** 92 Simcoe St. Hwy 19, just e. Int corridors. **Pets:** $10 daily fee/pet. Service with restrictions, crate.

🆂🅰🆅🅴 💲👁 ✕ 🔒 🍴

TIMMINS

◆◆ Comfort Inn SH
(705) 264-9474. **$105, 30 day notice.** 939 Algonquin Blvd E. Hwy 101, 0.3 mi (0.5 km) e of Hwy 655. Int corridors. **Pets:** Accepted.
ASK SD ✕ ⯀ ▣

◆◆ Travelodge SH
(705) 360-1122. **$75-$85.** 1136 Riverside Dr. Hwy 101, 2.8 mi, 4.4 km w on Hwy 655. Int corridors. **Pets:** Accepted.
ASK SD ✕ ⯀ ▣

TOBERMORY

◆ Coach House Inn M
(519) 596-2361. **$59-$102.** 7189 Hwy 6. Hwy 6, 1.2 mi (2 km) s of ferry docks. Ext corridors. **Pets:** Accepted.
✕ ⯀ ⯑ ✕ ⯑

TORONTO METROPOLITAN AREA

MARKHAM

(CAA) ◆◆ Comfort Inn SH
(905) 477-6077. **$119-$199.** 8330 Woodbine Ave. Hwy 401, exit 375, 5.6 mi (9 km) n; Hwy 404, exit Hwy 7, just e, then s. Int corridors. **Pets:** Accepted.
SAVE SD ✕ ⯀ ▣ ⯑ ✕

(CAA) ◆◆◆ Howard Johnson Hotel Toronto-Markham SH
(905) 479-5000. **$109-$159.** 555 Cochrane Dr. Hwy 404 N, exit Hwy 7 E to E Valhalla Dr. Int corridors. **Pets:** Accepted.
SAVE SD ✕ ⯀ ▣ ⯑ ⯑ ✕

(CAA) ◆◆◆ Radisson Hotel Toronto-Markham LH ❀
(905) 477-2010. **$109-$149.** 50 E Valhalla Dr. Hwy 404, exit Hwy 7, then e. Int corridors. **Pets:** Medium, other species. $25 one-time fee/room. Service with restrictions, crate.
SAVE SD ✕ ⯀ ▣ ⯑ ⯑ ✕

◆◆◆ Residence Inn by Marriott SH
(905) 707-7933. **$129-$219.** 55 Minthorn Blvd. Directly s of jct Hwy 7 and Leslie St. Int corridors. **Pets:** Accepted.
ASK SD ✕ ⯑ ⯀ ▣ ⯑ ✕

◆◆◆ Staybridge Suites Toronto-Markham SH ❀
(905) 771-9333. **$110-$170.** 355 S Park Rd. Jct Hwy 404 and 7, w on Hwy 7, then e. Int corridors. **Pets:** Other species. $75 one-time fee/room. Service with restrictions, supervision.
ASK SD ✕ ⯑ ⯀ ▣ ⯑

RICHMOND HILL

(CAA) ◆◆◆◆ Sheraton Parkway Toronto North Hotel, Suites & Conference Centre LH ❀
(905) 881-2121. **$129-$149.** 600 Hwy 7 E. Jct Hwy 401 and Don Valley Pkwy (Hwy 404), exit 375 via Don Valley Pkwy (Hwy 404), 5 mi (8 km) n to jct Hwy 7, then 0.6 mi (1 km) w. Int corridors. **Pets:** Medium, dogs only. Designated rooms, service with restrictions, supervision.
SAVE SD ✕ ⯀ ▣ ⯑ ⯑ ✕

TORONTO

◆◆ Carlingview Airport Inn SH
(416) 675-3303. **$95.** 221 Carlingview Dr. QEW, exit Hwy 427 N to Dixon Rd E, 0.6 mi (1 km) to Carlingview Dr, then just s. Ext/int corridors. **Pets:** Accepted.
ASK SD ✕ ⯀ ▣ ⯑

◆◆◆ Cawthra Square Inn BB
(416) 966-0013. **$139-$319, 14 day notice.** 10 Cawthra Square. Directly w of Jarvis St. Int corridors. **Pets:** Accepted.
ASK SD ✕

◆◆ Comfort Inn SH ❀
(416) 736-4700. **$95-$165.** 66 Norfinch Dr. Hwy 400, exit Finch Ave E, just n. Int corridors. **Pets:** Other species. Service with restrictions, crate.
ASK SD ✕ ⯀ ▣

(CAA) ◆◆◆ Cosmopolitan Toronto SH
(416) 350-2000. **$179-$440.** 8 Colborne St. Between King and Wellington sts. Int corridors. **Pets:** Small. $25 daily fee/room, $75 one-time fee/room. Designated rooms, service with restrictions, supervision.
SAVE ✕ ⯀ ▣ ⯑

(CAA) ◆◆◆ Crowne Plaza Toronto Don Valley LH ❀
(416) 449-4111. **$129-$249.** 1250 Eglinton Ave E. Don Valley Pkwy, exit 375 (Wynford Dr); jct Don Valley Pkwy and Eglinton Ave E. Int corridors. **Pets:** Medium. $20 daily fee/room. Designated rooms, service with restrictions, supervision.
SAVE SD ✕ ⯑ ⯑ ⯀ ▣ ⯑ ⯑ ✕

(CAA) ◆◆◆ Days Hotel & Conference Centre-Toronto Downtown LH
(416) 977-6655. **$95-$179.** 30 Carlton St. Adjacent to Maple Leaf Gardens. Int corridors. **Pets:** Accepted.
SAVE SD ✕ ⯀ ▣ ⯑ ⯑ ✕

(CAA) ◆◆◆ Days Inn Toronto West Lakeshore SH
(416) 532-9900. **$65-$139.** 14 Roncesvalles Ave. Jct King and Queen sts W and The Queensway. Int corridors. **Pets:** Medium. $10 daily fee/room. Service with restrictions, supervision.
SAVE SD ✕ ▣ ⯑

(CAA) ◆◆◆ Delta Chelsea Hotel LH
(416) 595-1975. **$116-$269.** 33 Gerrard St W. Just w of Yonge St; just s of College St. Int corridors. **Pets:** Accepted.
SAVE SD ✕ ⯀ ▣ ⯑ ⯑ ✕

◆◆◆ Delta Toronto East LH
(416) 299-1500. **$139-$199.** 2035 Kennedy Rd. Just ne of jct Hwy 401 and Kennedy Rd, exit 379. Int corridors. **Pets:** Accepted.
✕ ⯀ ▣ ⯑ ⯑ ✕

(CAA) ◆◆◆ DoubleTree International Plaza Hotel Toronto Airport LH
(416) 244-1711. **$109-$229.** 655 Dixon Rd. Jct Hwy 27 N, just w of jct Hwy 401. Int corridors. **Pets:** Small. Service with restrictions, supervision.
SAVE SD ✕ SM ⯀ ▣ ⯑ ⯑ ✕

(CAA) ◆◆◆◆ The Fairmont Royal York LH ❀
(416) 368-2511. **$189-$339.** 100 Front St W. QEW/Gardiner Expwy, exit n on York or Bay sts; entrance on Wellington St. Int corridors. **Pets:** Medium, other species. $25 daily fee/room. Service with restrictions, crate.
SAVE SD ✕ SM ⯀ ▣ ⯑ ⯑ ✕

(CAA) ◆◆◆ Four Seasons Hotel LH ❀
(416) 964-0411. **$365-$600.** 21 Avenue Rd. Corner of Avenue Rd and Cumberland Ave. Int corridors. **Pets:** Other species. Service with restrictions, supervision.
SAVE ✕ ⯀ ▣ ⯑ ⯑ ✕

◆◆◆ Gloucester Square Inns of Toronto BB
(416) 966-0013. **$139-$319, 14 day notice.** 512-514 Jarvis St. Jct Gloucester. Int corridors. **Pets:** Accepted.
ASK SD ✕

Hilton Toronto 🏨
(416) 869-3456. **$149-$349, 3 day notice.** 145 Richmond St W. Jct University Ave. Int corridors. **Pets:** Accepted.

Holiday Inn Express Toronto Downtown 🏨
(416) 367-5555. **$109-$179.** 111 Lombard St. West side of Jarvis St; between Adelaide and Richmond sts; 0.6 mi (1 km) n off Gardiner Expwy at Jarvis St exit. Int corridors. **Pets:** Accepted.

Holiday Inn Express Toronto-North York 🏨
(416) 665-3500. **$109-$159.** 30 Norfinch Dr. Hwy 400, exit Finch Ave E. Int corridors. **Pets:** Accepted.

Holiday Inn Toronto Midtown 🏨
(416) 968-0010. **$109-$229.** 280 Bloor St W. Just w of St. George. Int corridors. **Pets:** Accepted.

Holiday Inn Toronto On King (Downtown) 🏨
(416) 599-4000. **$189-$309.** 370 King St W. Between Spadina Ave and Peter St. Int corridors. **Pets:** Medium, dogs only. $35 one-time fee/pet. Designated rooms, service with restrictions, supervision.

Hotel Le Germain 🏨
(416) 345-9500. **$225-$395.** 30 Mercer St. Between John St and Blue Jays Way. Int corridors. **Pets:** Medium. $35 daily fee/pet. Service with restrictions, supervision.

InterContinental Toronto Yorkville 🏨
(416) 960-5200. **$259-$3000.** 220 Bloor St W. Just w of Avenue Rd. Int corridors. **Pets:** $25 daily fee/room, $50 one-time fee/room. Supervision.

Le Royal Meridien King Edward Hotel 🏨
(416) 863-9700. **$169-$249.** 37 King St E. Just e of Yonge St. Int corridors. **Pets:** Service with restrictions, supervision.

Metropolitan Hotel 🏨
(416) 977-5000. **$129-$279.** 108 Chestnut St. Just s of Dundas St. Int corridors. **Pets:** Accepted.

Montecassino Hotel & Suites 🏨
(416) 630-8100. **$99-$399.** 3710 Chesswood Dr. At Sheppard Ave. Int corridors. **Pets:** Small. $200 deposit/room. Designated rooms, service with restrictions, supervision.

Novotel Toronto Centre 🏨
(416) 367-8900. **$149-$349, 3 day notice.** 45 The Esplanade. Just ne of Gardiner Expwy via Yonge St. Int corridors. **Pets:** Other species. Service with restrictions, supervision.

Novotel Toronto North York 🏨
(416) 733-2929. **$102-$252.** 3 Park Home Ave. Hwy 401, exit Yonge St, 0.6 mi (1 km) n, then just w. Int corridors. **Pets:** Accepted.

Pantages Suites Hotel and Spa 🏨
(416) 362-1777. **$179-$440.** 200 Victoria St. Jct Shuter. Int corridors. **Pets:** Small. $25 daily fee/room, $75 one-time fee/room. Designated rooms, service with restrictions, supervision.

Park Plaza Hotel Toronto Airport 🏨
(416) 675-1234. **$89-$249.** 33 Carlson Ct. Just w of jct Hwy 27 and Dixon Rd W. Int corridors. **Pets:** Accepted.

Quality Hotel & Suites Toronto Airport East 🏨
(416) 240-9090. **$79-$239.** 2180 Islington Ave. Hwy 401, exit 356. Int corridors. **Pets:** $15 daily fee/room. Designated rooms, service with restrictions, supervision.

Quality Suites Toronto Airport 🏨
(416) 674-8442. **$99-$159.** 262 Carlingview Dr. 0.6 mi (1 km) w of jct Hwy 27 N and Dixon Rd. Int corridors. **Pets:** Accepted.

Radisson Hotel Toronto East 🏨
(416) 493-7000. **$159-$179.** 55 Hallcrown Pl. Hwy 401, exit Victoria Park N to Consumers Rd, then w. Int corridors. **Pets:** Accepted.

Radisson Suite Hotel Toronto Airport 🏨
(416) 242-7400. **$129-$189.** 640 Dixon Rd. Just e of jct Hwy 27; just w of jct Hwy 401. Int corridors. **Pets:** Accepted.

Ramada Hotel Toronto Airport 🏨
(416) 621-2121. **$129-$209.** 2 Holiday Dr. Hwy 427, exit Holiday Dr southbound; exit Burnhamthorpe Rd northbound. Int corridors. **Pets:** Medium. $10 daily fee/room. Service with restrictions, supervision.

Renaissance Toronto Airport Hotel 🏨
(416) 675-6100. **$125-$289.** 801 Dixon Rd. Jct Hwy 27 N and Dixon Rd. Int corridors. **Pets:** Accepted.

Renaissance Toronto Hotel Downtown 🏨
(416) 341-7100. **$179-$299.** 1 Blue Jays Way. Jct Front St. Int corridors. **Pets:** Small. $50 one-time fee/room. Service with restrictions, supervision.

Residence Inn by Marriott Toronto Airport 🏨
(416) 798-2900. **$129-$315.** 17 Reading Ct. Just w of jct Hwy 27 and Dixon Rd. Int corridors. **Pets:** Other species. $125 one-time fee/room. Designated rooms, service with restrictions, supervision.

The Sheraton Centre Toronto Hotel 🏨
(416) 361-1000. **$330-$399.** 123 Queen St W. Opposite Toronto Civic Centre and City Hall. Int corridors. **Pets:** Medium, dogs only. Service with restrictions, supervision.

SoHo Metropolitan Hotel 🏨
(416) 599-8800. **$200-$785.** 318 Wellington St W. Jct Blue Jays Way. Int corridors. **Pets:** Medium, dogs only. Service with restrictions, crate.

The Sutton Place Hotel 🏨
(416) 924-9221. **$160-$515.** 955 Bay St. Jct Wellesley St. Int corridors. **Pets:** Small, other species. $150 deposit/room. Service with restrictions, supervision.

Toronto Airport Marriott Hotel 🏨
(416) 674-9400. **$109-$259.** 901 Dixon Rd. Corner of Dixon Rd and Carlingview Dr. Int corridors. **Pets:** Other species. $30 one-time fee/room. Service with restrictions, supervision.

 ▼▼▼▼ **Travelodge Hotel Toronto Airport (Dixon Road)** SH
(416) 674-2222. **$99-$189.** 925 Dixon Rd. Corner of Carlingview Dr and Dixon Rd. Int corridors. **Pets:** $25 one-time fee/room. Designated rooms, service with restrictions, supervision.

▼▼▼ **Travelodge Toronto East** SH
(416) 299-9500. **$95-$119.** 20 Milner Business Ct. Jct Hwy 401 and Markham Rd, just n on Markham Rd. Int corridors. **Pets:** Accepted.

▼▼▼▼ **The Westin Harbour Castle** LH ❀
(416) 869-1600. **$149-$389.** One Harbour Sq. At the foot of Bay St; on shore of Lake Ontario. Int corridors. **Pets:** Medium, dogs only. Service with restrictions, supervision.

▼▼▼▼ **The Westin Prince Toronto** LH
(416) 444-2511. **$135-$175.** 900 York Mills Rd. Just s of Hwy 401 via Leslie St exit to York Mills Rd E. Int corridors. **Pets:** Accepted.

▼▼▼ **Windsor Arms Hotel** SH ❀
(416) 971-9666. **$295.** 18 St. Thomas St. Jct Bloor St. Int corridors. **Pets:** Medium. Service with restrictions.

END METROPOLITAN AREA

TRENTON

▼▼▼ **Comfort Inn** SH
(613) 965-6660. **$109-$139.** 68 Monogram Pl. Hwy 401, exit 526 (Glen Miller Rd), just s. Int corridors. **Pets:** Accepted.

▼▼▼▼ **Holiday Inn Trenton** SH
(613) 394-4855. **$104-$185.** 99 Glen Miller Rd. Hwy 401, exit 526 (Glen Miller Rd), just s. Int corridors. **Pets:** Accepted.

TWEED

▼ **Park Place Motel** M
(613) 478-3134. **$80-$90, 4 day notice.** 43 Victoria St. Hwy 37, 0.3 mi (0.5 km) s of centre. Ext corridors. **Pets:** $10 daily fee/pet. Designated rooms, service with restrictions, supervision.

WATERLOO

▼▼ **Comfort Inn** SH
(519) 747-9400. **$99-$169.** 190 Weber St N. East side off Weber St; just s of Hwy 86. Int corridors. **Pets:** Other species. Service with restrictions, supervision.

▼▼▼▼ **Les Diplomates B&B (Executive Guest House)** BB
(519) 725-3184. **$126-$156.** 100 Blythwood Rd. Hwy 85 N, exit King St, s to Columbia, w to Hazel St, then e. Ext/int corridors. **Pets:** $10 one-time fee/pet. Service with restrictions, supervision.

▼▼▼▼ **The Waterloo Inn & Conference Centre** SH
(519) 884-0220. **$145.** 475 King St N. 1.9 mi (3 km) n on King St, jct Hwy 85. Int corridors. **Pets:** Large, other species. $15 daily fee/pet. Designated rooms, service with restrictions, crate.

WAWA

▼ **Best Northern** M
(705) 856-7302. **$68-$89.** 150 Hwy 17 S. Hwy 17, 3.3 mi (5.3 km) s of jct Hwy 101. Ext corridors. **Pets:** Accepted.

▼ **The Mystic Isle Motel** M
(705) 856-1737. **$70-$85.** 153 Hwy 17 S. On Hwy 17, 3.3 mi (5.2 km) s of jct Hwy 101. Ext corridors. **Pets:** Accepted.

▼ **Parkway Motel** M
(705) 856-7020. **$75-$80.** 232 Hwy 17 S. Hwy 17, 2.5 mi (4 km) s of jct Hwy 101. Ext corridors. **Pets:** Other species. $10 daily fee/room. Designated rooms, service with restrictions, supervision.

▼ **Sportsman's Motel** M
(705) 856-2272. **$85.** 171 Mission Rd. Hwy 101, 1.5 mi (2.4 km) e of jct Hwy 17. Ext corridors. **Pets:** Small. $10 daily fee/room. Designated rooms, service with restrictions, supervision.

▼ **Wawa Northern Lights Motel & Chalets** M ❀
(705) 856-1900. **$79-$109.** 1014 Hwy 17. On Hwy 17, 5 mi (8 km) n of jct Hwy 101. Ext corridors. **Pets:** Other species. Service with restrictions, supervision.

WHITBY

▼▼ **Motel 6 #1907** SH
(905) 665-8883. **$72-$106.** 165 Consumers Dr. Hwy 401, exit 410 (Brock St/Hwy 12), just ne. Int corridors. **Pets:** Medium, other species. Service with restrictions, supervision.

▼▼▼▼ **Quality Suites** SH
(905) 432-8800. **$132-$225.** 1700 Champlain Ave. Hwy 401, exit 412 (Thickson Rd), 0.3 mi (0.5 km) n to Champlain Ave, then 0.6 mi (1 km) e. Int corridors. **Pets:** Accepted.

▼▼▼ **Residence Inn by Marriott** SH
(905) 444-9756. **$159-$229.** 160 Consumers Dr. Hwy 401, exit 410 (Brock St/Hwy 12). Int corridors. **Pets:** $75 one-time fee/room. Service with restrictions.

WINDSOR

▼▼▼ **Comfort Inn** SH
(519) 966-7800. **$99-$139.** 2955 Dougall Ave. 3.3 mi (5.3 km) s on Hwy 3B, off Hwy 401 via Detroit-Windsor Tunnel exit. Int corridors. **Pets:** Accepted.

▼▼▼ **Comfort Inn** SH
(519) 972-1331. **$102-$192, 7 day notice.** 2765 Huron Church Rd. West side of Huron Church Rd; 0.5 mi (0.8 km) s of EC Row Expwy. Int corridors. **Pets:** Medium. $10 daily fee/room. Service with restrictions, supervision.

▼▼▼▼ **Hampton Inn and Suites** SH
(519) 972-0770. **$149-$154.** 1840 Huron Church Rd. 0.9 mi (1.5 km) n of EC Row Expwy. Int corridors. **Pets:** Other species. Service with restrictions, supervision.

ASK S/D ✕ 🛏 💻 ⇌

CAA ▼▼▼▼ **Hilton Windsor** LH
(519) 973-5555. **$129-$199.** 277 Riverside Dr W. 1 km w of Detroit-Windsor Tunnel; 0.6 mi (1 km) e of Ambassador Bridge; downtown. Int corridors. **Pets:** Accepted.

SAVE S/D ✕ 💻 🍽 ⇌ ✕

CAA ▼▼▼▼ **Holiday Inn Select Windsor (Ambassador Bridge)** LH ❖
(519) 966-1200. **$134.** 1855 Huron Church Rd. Jct Huron Church and Malden rds; 0.9 mi (1.5 km) n of EC Row Expwy. Int corridors. **Pets:** Medium. Service with restrictions, crate.

SAVE S/D ✕ 🛏 💻 🍽 ⇌ ✕

CAA ▼▼ **Ivy Rose Motor Inn Ltd.** M ❖
(519) 966-1700. **$69-$150.** 2885 Howard Ave. 3 mi (4.8 km) s of downtown; just n of Devonshire Shopping Mall. Ext corridors. **Pets:** Large. $25 deposit/room. Designated rooms, service with restrictions, crate.

SAVE S/D ✕ 🛏 🍽 ⇌

CAA ▼▼▼▼ **Quality Suites Windsor** SH ❖
(519) 977-9707. **$119-$199.** 250 Dougall Ave. Jct McDougall Ave and Chatham St; downtown. Int corridors. **Pets:** $50 one-time fee/room. Designated rooms, service with restrictions, supervision.

SAVE S/D ✕ &M 🛏 💻 🍽

▼▼▼▼ **Radisson Riverfront Hotel** LH ❖
(519) 977-9777. **$119-$189.** 333 Riverside Dr W. 0.6 mi (1 km) w of Detroit-Windsor Tunnel; 0.6 mi (1 km) e of Ambassador Bridge. Int corridors. **Pets:** Medium, other species. $50 one-time fee/room. Service with restrictions, supervision.

ASK S/D ✕ 🛏 💻 🍽 ⇌ ✕

CAA ▼▼▼▼ **Travelodge Windsor Ambassador Bridge** SH
(519) 972-1100. **$85-$190.** 2330 Huron Church Rd. North of EC Row Expwy. Int corridors. **Pets:** Small. Service with restrictions, supervision.

SAVE ✕ 🛏 💻 ⇌

WOODSTOCK

CAA ▼▼▼▼ **Quality Hotel and Suites** SH
(519) 537-5586. **$99-$240.** 580 Bruin Blvd. Hwy 401, exit 232, just n; w of Hwy 59. Int corridors. **Pets:** Service with restrictions, crate.

SAVE S/D ✕ 🛏 💻 🍽 ⇌ ✕

CAA ▼▼▼ **Super 8 Motel** SH
(519) 421-4588. **$89-$105.** 560 Norwich Ave. Jct Hwy 401 and 59, exit 232, just n. Int corridors. **Pets:** Accepted.

SAVE S/D ✕ 🛏

PRINCE EDWARD ISLAND

CAVENDISH

▼▼▼ **Bay Vista Motor Inn** Ⓜ
(902) 963-2225. **$53-$99.** 9517 Cavendish Rd. Jct Rt 13, 2.8 mi (4.8 km) w on Rt 6. Ext corridors. **Pets:** Medium. Designated rooms, service with restrictions, supervision.
⊠ 🛏 🏊 ☎

▼▼▼ **Cavendish Bosom Buddies Cottages** Ⓒⓐ ❀
(902) 963-3449. **$80-$280, 14 day notice.** RR 1. Jct Rt 6 and 13, 0.4 mi (0.7 km) e on Rt 6. Ext corridors. **Pets:** Supervision.
ASK 🛏 ⊠ 🛏 🖥 🎦 ☎

ⒶⒶ ▼▼▼ **Cavendish Maples Cottages** Ⓒⓐ
(902) 963-2818. **$70-$280, 30 day notice.** 79 Avonlea Blvd. Jct Rt 6 and 13, 1.5 mi (2.5 km) w on Rt 6. Ext corridors. **Pets:** Accepted.
SAVE ⊠ 🛏 🖥 🏊 ⊠ ☎

CHARLOTTETOWN

ⒶⒶ ▼▼▼ **Best Western Charlottetown** SH
(902) 892-2461. **$199-$239.** 238 Grafton St. Centre. Int corridors. **Pets:** Other species.
SAVE 🛏 ⊠ 🖐 👂 👤 🛏 🖥 🍴 🏊 ⊠

▼▼▼ **Comfort Inn** SH ❀
(902) 566-4424. **$129-$195.** 112 Trans-Canada Hwy 1. Trans-Canada Hwy 1, 2.8 mi (4.5 km) w. Int corridors. **Pets:** Supervision.
ASK 🛏 ⊠ 🛏

▼▼▼ **Delta Prince Edward** LH
(902) 566-2222. **$139-$389.** 18 Queen St. At Water and Queen sts. Int corridors. **Pets:** Accepted.
ASK 🛏 ⊠ 🖥 🍴 🏊 ⊠

▼▼▼ **Econo Lodge** Ⓜ
(902) 368-1110. **$79-$199.** 20 Lower Malpeque Rd. Jct Trans-Canada Hwy 1 and Lower Malpeque Rd, 2.8 mi (4.5 km) w. Ext/int corridors. **Pets:** Accepted.
ASK 🛏 ⊠ 🛏 🖥 🏊

ⒶⒶ ▼▼▼ **Holiday Inn Express Hotel & Suites Charlottetown** SH ❀
(902) 892-1201. **$99-$269.** 200 Trans-Canada Hwy. On Trans-Canada Hwy 1, 3 mi (5 km) w. Int corridors. **Pets:** Other species.
SAVE 🛏 ⊠ 🖐 👤 🛏 🖥 🏊

▼▼▼ **Quality Inn on the Hill** SH
(902) 894-8572. **$124-$281.** 150 Euston St. Just e of University Ave. Int corridors. **Pets:** Accepted.
ASK 🛏 ⊠ 🛏 🖥 🍴

▼▼▼ **Rodd Charlottetown-A Rodd Signature Hotel** SH
(902) 894-7371. **$109-$250.** 75 Kent St. Corner of Kent and Pownal sts. Int corridors. **Pets:** Accepted.
ASK 🛏 ⊠ 🛏 🖥 🍴 🏊 ⊠

▼▼▼ **Rodd Confederation Inn & Suites** Ⓜ ❀
(902) 892-2481. **$75-$158.** Trans-Canada Hwy 1. On Trans-Canada Hwy 1, 2.5 mi (4 km) w. Ext/int corridors. **Pets:** $10 daily fee/room. Designated rooms, service with restrictions, supervision.
ASK 🛏 ⊠ 🛏 🖥 🍴 🏊

▼▼▼ **Rodd Royalty Inn** SH
(902) 894-8566. **$96-$185.** Intersection Hwy 1 & 2. 2.5 mi (4 km) w on Trans-Canada Hwy 1. Ext/int corridors. **Pets:** $10 daily fee/room. Designated rooms.
ASK 🛏 ⊠ 🛏 🖥 🍴 🏊

CORNWALL

▼ **Sunny King Motel** Ⓜ
(902) 566-2209. **$49-$116, 3 day notice.** Trans Canada Hwy. On Hwy 1; centre. Ext corridors. **Pets:** Accepted.
ASK 🛏 ⊠ 🛏 🖥 🏊 🎦

MAYFIELD

▼▼▼ **Cavendish Gateway Resort by Clarion Collection** Ⓜ
(902) 963-2213. **$89-$179.** Rt 13. On Rt 13, 3.6 mi (6 km) w of Cavendish; centre. Ext/int corridors. **Pets:** Accepted.
ASK 🛏 ⊠ 🛏 🖥 🏊

NORTH RUSTICO

ⒶⒶ ▼ **St. Lawrence Motel** Ⓜ
(902) 963-2053. **$49-$159, 14 day notice.** 351 Gulf Shore Rd. On RR 2. Ext corridors. **Pets:** Accepted.
SAVE ⊠ 🛏 🖥 🎦 ☎

RICHMOND

ⒶⒶ ▼▼▼ **Caernarvon Cottages, B&B and Gardens** Ⓒⓐ
(902) 854-3418. **$100, 30 day notice.** 4697 Hwy 12, RR 1. Jct Hwy 2 and Rt 131, 6 mi (10 km) e. Ext/int corridors. **Pets:** Accepted.
SAVE 🛏 🖥 🎦

ROSENEATH

▼▼▼▼ **Rodd Brudenell River-A Rodd Signature Resort** LH
(902) 652-2332. **$131-$246, 3 day notice.** Rt #3. Jct Rt 4 and 3, 3.3 mi (5.5 km) e. Ext/int corridors. **Pets:** Accepted.
ASK 🛏 ⊠ 🛏 🖥 🍴 🏊 ⊠

ST. PETERS

▼▼▼ **Greenwich Gate Lodge** Ⓜ
(902) 961-3496. **$79-$119, 7 day notice.** Rt 2. Jct Rt 2 and 16; centre. Ext corridors. **Pets:** Accepted.
ASK 🛏 ⊠ 🛏 🖥

ⒶⒶ ▼▼▼ **The Inn at St. Peters** Ⓒ
(902) 961-2135. **$340-$390, 7 day notice.** 1668 Greenwich Rd. Jct Rt 16 and 313, 0.6 mi (1 km) w on Rt 313. Ext corridors. **Pets:** Service with restrictions.
SAVE ⊠ 🖐 🛏 🖥 🍴

SUMMERSIDE

▼▼ **Econo Lodge** SH
(902) 436-9100. **$90-$130.** 80 All Weather Hwy. Jct Hwy 1A and 2, 3.1 mi (5 km) w on Hwy 2. Int corridors. **Pets:** Medium, dogs only. Designated rooms, service with restrictions, crate.
ASK 🛏 ⊠ 🛏 🖥 🍴 🏊

ⒶⒶ ▼▼ **Quality Inn Garden of the Gulf** Ⓜ
(902) 436-2295. **$86-$194.** 618 Water St. 1 mi (1.6 km) e on Hwy 11. Ext/int corridors. **Pets:** Designated rooms, service with restrictions, supervision.
SAVE 🛏 ⊠ 🛏 🖥 🏊

ⒶⒶ ▼▼▼ **Slemon Park Hotel & Conference Centre** SH
(902) 432-1780. **$100-$105.** 12 Redwood Ave. On Rt 2, 3 mi (5 km) w at Summerside Airport. Int corridors. **Pets:** Medium. $100 deposit/pet. Designated rooms, service with restrictions, supervision.
SAVE 🛏 ⊠ 🖐 👤 🛏 🖥 🍴

WOODSTOCK

▼▼▼ **Rodd Mill River Resort** SH
(902) 859-3555. **$91-$211, 3 day notice.** Rt 180. On Rt 136, just e of jct Rt 2. Int corridors. **Pets:** Accepted.
ASK 🛏 ⊠ 🛏 🖥 🍴 🏊 ⊠

ALMA

♦♦ **Comfort Inn** SH
(418) 668-9221. **$90-$145.** 870 ave du Pont S. On Hwy 169; centre of town. Int corridors. **Pets:** Accepted.
[ASK] [SÒ] [X] [📆] [🖥]

♦ **Hotel Motel Les Cascades** M
(418) 662-6547. **$62-$92.** 140 ave du Pont N. On Hwy 169, just n of bridge; centre. Ext/int corridors. **Pets:** Accepted.
[ASK] [SÒ] [X] [📆] [🖥] [🍴]

BAIE-COMEAU

♦♦ **Comfort Inn** SH
(418) 589-8252. **$113-$128.** 745 boul Lafleche. On Rt 138. Int corridors. **Pets:** Designated rooms, service with restrictions, supervision.
[ASK] [SÒ] [X] [📆] [🖥]

BAIE-ST-PAUL

(A) ♦♦ **Hotel Baie-Saint-Paul** SH
(418) 435-3683. **$69-$114.** 911 boul Mgr-de-Laval. On Rt 138, 0.3 mi (0.5 km) e of Rt 362. Int corridors. **Pets:** Other species. $5 deposit/pet. Designated rooms, service with restrictions, supervision.
[SAVE] [X] [📆] [🖥] [🍴] [✕]

BERTHIERVILLE

♦♦ **Days Inn Berthierville** SH
(450) 836-1621. **$92-$165.** 760 rue Gadoury. Hwy 40, exit 144. Ext/int corridors. **Pets:** Small, other species. Designated rooms, service with restrictions, supervision.
[ASK] [SÒ] [X] [📆] [🖥]

BROMONT

♦♦♦ **Hotel Le Menhir** SH
(450) 534-3790. **$89-$169.** 125 boul Bromont. Hwy 10, exit 78, 1.6 mi (2.7 km) s. Ext/int corridors. **Pets:** Accepted.
[ASK] [SÒ] [X] [📆] [🖥] [🍴] [✕]

CARLETON-ST-OMER

♦♦ **Hostellerie Baie Bleue** M
(418) 364-3355. **$75-$185.** 482 boul Perron. On Hwy 132. Ext corridors. **Pets:** Small. $10 daily fee/room. Service with restrictions, supervision.
[ASK] [SÒ] [X] [📆] [🖥] [🍴] [✕] [✕] [⚿]

CHICOUTIMI

♦♦♦ **Centre de Congres et Hotel La Saguenenne** SH 🐾
(418) 545-8326. **$114-$172.** 250 des Sagueneens. Just w of jct Rt 175 (boul Talbot); in Saguenay sector. Int corridors. **Pets:** Small. Designated rooms, service with restrictions, crate.
[ASK] [SÒ] [X] [ÒM] [✕] [📆] [🖥] [🍴] [✕] [✕]

♦♦ **Comfort Inn** SH
(418) 693-8686. **$87-$130.** 1595 boul Talbot. Jct Rt 170, 1.8 mi (2.8 km) n. Int corridors. **Pets:** Small. Designated rooms, no service, supervision.
[ASK] [SÒ] [X] [📆] [🖥]

COWANSVILLE

♦♦ **Days Inn-Cowansville** SH
(450) 263-7331. **$70-$120.** 111 place Jean-Jacques Bertrand. Hwy 10, exit 68, 9.9 mi (15.9 km) s on Rt 139. Int corridors. **Pets:** $15 one-time fee/room. Service with restrictions, supervision.
[ASK] [SÒ] [X] [📆] [🖥] [🍴]

DRUMMONDVILLE

(A) ♦♦♦ **Best Western Hotel Universel** SH
(819) 478-4971. **$109-$409.** 915 rue Hains. Hwy 20, exit 177, just s on boul St-Joseph, then just e. Int corridors. **Pets:** Accepted.
[SAVE] [SÒ] [X] [📆] [🖥] [🍴] [✕]

♦♦ **Comfort Inn** SH
(819) 477-4000. **$95-$121.** 1055 rue Hains. Hwy 20, exit 177, 0.3 mi (0.5 km) s on boul St-Joseph, then just w. Int corridors. **Pets:** Large, other species. Designated rooms, service with restrictions, supervision.
[ASK] [SÒ] [X] [📆] [🖥]

♦♦♦ **Quality Suites** SH
(819) 472-2700. **$100-$240.** 2125 rue Canadien. Hwy 20, exit 175, just s. Int corridors. **Pets:** Designated rooms, service with restrictions, supervision.
[ASK] [SÒ] [X] [📆] [🖥] [✕]

GATINEAU

(A) ♦♦♦ **Clarion Hotel & Conference Center** SH
(819) 568-5252. **$109-$133.** 111 rue Bellehumeur. Hwy 50, exit 139, 1 mi (1.6 km) se on boul Maloney ouest (Hwy 148), then just sw. Int corridors. **Pets:** Accepted.
[SAVE] [SÒ] [X] [📆] [🖥] [🍴] [✕] [✕]

(A) ♦♦ **Comfort Inn Gatineau** SH
(819) 243-6010. **$110-$160.** 630 boul La Gappe. Hwy 50, exit 140, 1.3 mi (2 km) e. Int corridors. **Pets:** Other species. Designated rooms, service with restrictions, supervision.
[SAVE] [SÒ] [X]

(A) ♦♦♦ **Four Points by Sheraton & Conference Centre Gatineau-Ottawa** LH
(819) 778-6111. **$99-$195.** 35 rue Laurier. Corner of rue Victoria, across from Canadian Museum of Civilization; in Hull sector. Int corridors. **Pets:** Accepted.
[SAVE] [SÒ] [X] [📆] [🖥] [🍴] [✕]

(CAA) ▼▼▼▼ **Holiday Inn Plaza La Chaudiere**
Gatineau-Ottawa LH
(819) 778-3880. **$105-$159.** 2 rue Montcalm. 0.5 mi (0.8 km) w of Portage Bridge at Rt 148 and rue Montcalm; in Hull sector. Int corridors. **Pets:** Large. $35 daily fee/room. Service with restrictions, supervision.
SAVE [S♦] [✕] [🛏] [📺] [🍴] [🏊] [✕]

GRENVILLE-SUR-LA-ROUGE

(CAA) ▼▼▼ ▼▼▼ **Hotel du Lac Carling** LH
(450) 533-9211. **$170-$220, 30 day notice.** 2255 Rt 327 nord. 3.1 mi (5 km) n. Int corridors. **Pets:** Accepted.
SAVE [S♦] [✕] [🛏] [📺] [🍴] [🏊] [✕]

LAC-BROME (KNOWLTON)

▼▼▼▼ **Auberge Knowlton** CI
(450) 242-6886. **$120-$135.** 286 chemin Knowlton. Corner of Hwy 104 and Rt 243; centre. Int corridors. **Pets:** Medium, dogs only. Designated rooms, no service, supervision.
[✕] [🍴]

LA MALBAIE

(CAA) ▼▼▼▼ ▼▼▼▼ **Fairmont Le Manoir Richelieu** LH
(418) 665-3703. **$143-$233.** 181 rue Richelieu. On Rt 362, 2.6 mi (4.1 km) w of jct Rt 138. Int corridors. **Pets:** Small. $25 daily fee/pet. Service with restrictions, supervision.
SAVE [S♦] [✕] [🛏] [📺] [🍴] [🏊] [✕]

▼▼▼ ▼▼▼ **La Pinsonniere** CI
(418) 665-4431. **$300-$500, 15 day notice.** 124 rue St-Raphael. Just off Rt 138, follow signs; in Cap-a-L'Aigle sector. Int corridors. **Pets:** Dogs only. Supervision.
[✕] [🍴] [🏊] [✕]

LA POCATIERE

▼▼ ▼▼ **Motel Le Pocatois** M
(418) 856-1688. **$63-$90.** 235 Rt 132. Hwy 20, exit 439, 0.5 mi (0.8 km) s. Ext/int corridors. **Pets:** Accepted.
[✕] [🛏] [📺]

LENNOXVILLE

(CAA) ▼▼ ▼▼ **La Paysanne Motel & Hotel** M
(819) 569-5585. **$70-$106, 7 day notice.** 42 rue Queen. On Rt 143. Ext/int corridors. **Pets:** Accepted.
SAVE [S♦] [✕] [🛏] [🍴] [🏊]

L'ISLET

▼▼▼ ▼▼▼ **Auberge La Paysanne** CO
(418) 247-7276. **$70-$120.** 497 des Pionniers est. On Rt 132, 2.6 mi (4.2 km) e, jct Rt 285; centre. Ext corridors. **Pets:** Accepted.
[S♦] [✕] [🛏] [📺] [🏊]

LOUISEVILLE

▼▼▼ **Gite du Carrefour et Maison historique J.I.L.**
Hamelin BB
(819) 228-4932. **$80-$90 (no credit cards).** 11 ave St-Laurent ouest. On Rt 138; Hwy 40, exit 174 westbound; exit 166 eastbound; centre. Int corridors. **Pets:** No service.
[ASK] [✕] [🏊] [📺] [✕]

MARIA

▼▼▼ ▼▼▼ **Hotel Honguedo** SH
(418) 759-3488. **$84-$147.** 548 boul Perron. On Rt 132, in town centre. Ext/int corridors. **Pets:** Accepted.
[ASK] [S♦] [✕] [🛏] [📺] [🍴] [🏊]

MATANE

(CAA) ▼▼ **Motel La Marina** M
(418) 562-3234. **$55-$92.** 1032 ave du Phare ouest. On Rt 132. Ext corridors. **Pets:** Accepted.
SAVE [✕] [🛏] [📺] [🏊] [✕]

MONTEBELLO

(CAA) ▼▼▼ ▼▼▼ **Fairmont Le Chateau Montebello** LH 🐾
(819) 423-6341. **$189-$289, 3 day notice.** 392 rue Notre-Dame. On Rt 148. Int corridors. **Pets:** $35 daily fee/pet. Crate.
SAVE [✕] [🛏] [📺] [🍴] [🏊] [✕]

MONTMAGNY

▼▼▼ ▼▼▼ **Manoir des Erables** CI
(418) 248-0100. **$99-$160, 10 day notice.** 220 boul Tache est (Rt 132). Hwy 20, exit 376, 1.4 mi (2.2 km) e on Rt 228, 0.9 mi (1.5 km) e. Ext/int corridors. **Pets:** Medium. $15 daily fee/room. Designated rooms, service with restrictions.
[✕] [📺] [🍴] [🏊] [✕]

MONTREAL METROPOLITAN AREA

BROSSARD

(CAA) ▼▼▼▼ **Best Western Hotel National** SH
(450) 466-6756. **$110-$139.** 7746 boul Taschereau. Rt 134, 0.8 mi (1.3 km) w of Hwy 10, exit boul Taschereau ouest. Int corridors. **Pets:** Accepted.
SAVE [S♦] [✕] [🛏] [📺] [🏊]

▼▼ ▼▼ **Comfort Inn** SH
(450) 678-9350. **$107-$120.** 7863 boul Taschereau. Rt 134, 0.9 mi (1.5 km) w of Hwy 10, exit boul Taschereau ouest. Int corridors. **Pets:** $10 daily fee/pet. Designated rooms, service with restrictions, supervision.
[ASK] [S♦] [✕] [🛏]

DORVAL

▼▼ ▼▼ **Comfort Inn Dorval** SH
(514) 636-3391. **$130-$154.** 340 ave Michel-Jasmin. Hwy 520, exit 2 eastbound; exit 1 westbound, 0.2 mi (0.3 km) along service road to ave Marshall, follow to ave Michel-Jasmin. Int corridors. **Pets:** Accepted.
[ASK] [S♦] [✕] [🛏] [📺]

(CAA) ▼▼▼▼ **Hampton Inn & Suites** SH
(514) 633-8243. **$150-$190.** 1900 route Transcanadienne (Hwy 40). Hwy 40, exit 55, 0.5 mi (0.8 km) e of boul Sources on south side service road. Int corridors. **Pets:** Designated rooms, service with restrictions, supervision.
SAVE [S♦] [✕] [♦M] [🛏] [📺] [🏊]

(CAA) ▼▼▼▼ **Hilton Montreal Aeroport** LH
(514) 631-2411. **$119-$329.** 12505 boul Cote-de-Liesse. Just n of Hwy 520 on northside service road at airport entrance. Int corridors. **Pets:** Other species. $25 daily fee/room. Designated rooms, service with restrictions, supervision.
SAVE [✕] [♦M] [🛏] [📺] [🍴] [🏊] [✕]

(CAA) ▼▼▼ **Travelodge Montreal-Trudeau Airport** SH
(514) 631-4537. **$109-$225.** 1010 chemin Herron. Hwy 20, exit 54 westbound, just s on boul Fenelon to ave Dumont, follow to chemin Herron; exit 56 eastbound, 1.1 mi (1.7 km) along service road. Int corridors. **Pets:** Other species. $100 deposit/room. Designated rooms, service with restrictions, crate.
SAVE [✕] [🛏] [📺] [✕]

LAVAL

▼▼▼ Comfort Inn SH
(450) 686-0600. **$116-$132.** 2055 Autoroute des Laurentides. Hwy 15, exit 8 (boul St-Martin), e on boul St-Martin, 0.4 mi (0.7 km) n on boul Le Corbusier, then w on boul Tessier. Int corridors. **Pets:** Designated rooms, service with restrictions, supervision.

ASK S⚫ ✕ 🛏 🖥 🍴

▼▼ Econo Lodge SH
(450) 681-6411. **$89-$144.** 1981 boul Cure-Labelle. Hwy 15, exit 8 (boul St-Martin) northbound; exit 10 southbound, 1.3 mi (2 km) w on boul St-Martin ouest, then 0.3 mi (0.5 km) n. Ext/int corridors. **Pets:** Designated rooms, service with restrictions, supervision.

ASK S⚫ ✕ 🛏 🖥 ⊠

ⒸⒶ ▼▼▼ Hampton Inn & Suites-Laval SH
(450) 687-0010. **$114-$154.** 1961 boul Cure-Labelle. Hwy 15, exit 8 (boul St-Martin) northbound; exit 10 southbound, 1.4 mi (2.3 km) w on boul St-Martin ouest, then just n. Int corridors. **Pets:** Service with restrictions, supervision.

SAVE S⚫ ✕ 🛏 🖥 ⊠

ⒸⒶ ▼▼▼ Quality Suites Laval SH
(450) 686-6777. **$139-$162.** 2035 Autoroute des Laurentides. Hwy 15, exit 8 (boul St-Martin), 0.4 mi (0.7 km) n on boul Le Corbusier, w on boul Tessier. Int corridors. **Pets:** Designated rooms, service with restrictions, supervision.

SAVE S⚫ ✕ 🛏 🖥

▼▼▼ Sheraton Laval Hotel LH 🐾
(450) 687-2440. **$109-$259.** 2440 Autoroute des Laurentides. Hwy 15, exit 10. Int corridors. **Pets:** Service with restrictions, supervision.

ASK ✕ 🛏 🖥 🍴 ⊠ ⊠

LONGUEUIL

▼▼ Days Inn Longueuil SH
(450) 677-8911. **$86-$105, 3 day notice.** 2800 boul Marie-Victorin. Hwy 20/Rt 132, exit 15 eastbound, follow signs for boul Marie-Victorin est; exit 90 westbound from Pont-Tunnel Louis-Hippolyte-Lafontaine. Int corridors. **Pets:** Accepted.

ASK S⚫ ✕ 🖥 🍴

MONTREAL

ⒸⒶ ▼▼ All Suite VIP Loft SH
(514) 448-4848. **$89-$139, 5 day notice.** 329 rue Ontario est. Just w of rue St-Denis. Int corridors. **Pets:** Small, dogs only. $200 deposit/pet, $15 one-time fee/pet. Service with restrictions, supervision.

SAVE S⚫ ✕ 🖥

ⒸⒶ ▼▼▼ Chateau Versailles Hotel SH 🐾
(514) 933-3611. **$194-$254.** 1659 rue Sherbrooke ouest. Corner rue St-Mathieu. Int corridors. **Pets:** Other species. $20 daily fee/room. Designated rooms, service with restrictions, crate.

SAVE S⚫ ✕ 🖥

ⒸⒶ ▼▼▼ Days Hotel LH
(514) 938-4611. **$95-$400.** 1005 rue Guy. Just s of boul Rene-Levesque. Int corridors. **Pets:** Small. $15 daily fee/pet. Service with restrictions, supervision.

SAVE S⚫ ✕ 🛏 🖥 🍴 ⊠ ⊠

ⒸⒶ ▼▼▼ Delta Montreal LH
(514) 286-1986. **$139-$289.** 475 ave President-Kennedy. Corner of rue City Councillors. Int corridors. **Pets:** Accepted.

SAVE S⚫ ✕ 🛏 🖥 🍴 ⊠ ⊠

ⒸⒶ ▼▼▼ DoubleTree Plaza Hotel Downtown LH
(514) 842-8581. **$139-$269.** 505 rue Sherbrooke est. Between rue Berri and St-Hubert. Int corridors. **Pets:** Accepted.

SAVE S⚫ ✕ 🖥 🍴 ⊠ ⊠

ⒸⒶ ▼▼▼ ▼▼ Fairmont The Queen Elizabeth LH
(514) 861-3511. **$189-$499.** 900 boul Rene-Levesque ouest. Between rue University and Mansfield. Int corridors. **Pets:** Small. $25 daily fee/pet. Designated rooms, service with restrictions, crate.

SAVE S⚫ ✕ 🛏M 🛏 🖥 🍴 ⊠ ⊠

ⒸⒶ ▼▼▼ ▼▼ Four Points by Sheraton Montreal Airport LH
(514) 344-1999. **$119-$169.** 6600 Cote-de-Liesse. Hwy 520, exit 5 eastbound on south side service road; follow signs for rue Hickmore and Hwy 520 E; in St-Laurent sector. Int corridors. **Pets:** Accepted.

SAVE S⚫ ✕ 🛏 🛏 🖥 🍴 ⊠ ⊠

ⒸⒶ ▼▼▼ ▼▼ Four Points by Sheraton Montreal Centre-Ville LH
(514) 842-3961. **$139-$235.** 475 rue Sherbrooke ouest. Between rue Durocher and Aylmer. Int corridors. **Pets:** Service with restrictions, supervision.

SAVE S⚫ ✕ 🛏 🖥 🍴

ⒸⒶ ▼▼▼ ▼▼ Hilton Montreal Bonaventure LH 🐾
(514) 878-2332. **$149-$269.** 900 rue de La Gauchetiere W. Corner of Mansfield and de la Gauchetiere. Int corridors. **Pets:** Small. Service with restrictions, supervision.

SAVE S⚫ ✕ 🛏 🖥 🍴 ⊠

ⒸⒶ ▼▼▼ ▼▼ Holiday Inn Express Hotel & Suites SH
(514) 448-7100. **$109-$350.** 155 boul Rene-Levesque est. Corner de Bullion. Int corridors. **Pets:** Other species. Service with restrictions.

SAVE ✕ 🛏 🖥

ⒸⒶ ▼▼▼ ▼▼ Holiday Inn Montreal-Airport SH
(514) 739-3391. **$104-$169.** 6500 Cote-de-Liesse. Hwy 520, exit 5 eastbound on south side service road; exit westbound to rue Ness, follow signs for rue Hickmore and Hwy 520 E; in St-Laurent sector. Ext/int corridors. **Pets:** Accepted.

SAVE ✕ 🛏M 🛏 🖥 🍴 ⊠ ⊠

ⒸⒶ ▼▼▼ ▼▼ Holiday Inn Montreal-Midtown LH
(514) 842-6111. **$119-$179.** 420 rue Sherbrooke ouest. Between rue Bleury and City Councillors. Int corridors. **Pets:** Medium. $35 one-time fee/room. Service with restrictions, supervision.

SAVE ✕ 🛏 🖥 🍴 ⊠ ⊠

▼▼▼ ▼▼ Hotel Gault SH
(514) 904-1616. **$349-$749.** 449 rue Ste-Helene. Just s of rue Notre-Dame. Int corridors. **Pets:** Medium. $20 daily fee/pet. Service with restrictions, crate.

✕ 🛏 🖥 🍴

ⒸⒶ ▼▼▼ Hotel Godin SH
(514) 843-6000. **$159-$339.** 10 rue Sherbrooke ouest. Corner of boul St-Laurent. Int corridors. **Pets:** Medium. $50 one-time fee/pet.

SAVE ✕ 🛏 🖥 🍴

ⒸⒶ ▼▼▼ ▼▼ Hotel InterContinental Montreal LH
(514) 987-9900. **$179-$575.** 360 rue St-Antoine ouest. Corner of rue St-Pierre. Int corridors. **Pets:** Small, dogs only. $35 daily fee/room. Service with restrictions, crate.

SAVE ✕ 🛏 🖥 🍴 ⊠ ⊠

ⒸⒶ ▼▼▼ Hotel La Tour Centre-Ville CO
(514) 866-8861. **$102-$145.** 400 boul Rene-Levesque ouest. Corner of rue de Bleury. Int corridors. **Pets:** Very small. $50 deposit/room. Designated rooms, service with restrictions, supervision.

SAVE ✕ 🛏 🖥 🍴 ⊠

▼▼▼ Hotel Le Germain SH 🐾
(514) 849-2050. **$230-$330.** 2050 rue Mansfield. Just n of ave President-Kennedy. Int corridors. **Pets:** Medium. $30 daily fee/room. Service with restrictions, supervision.

ASK ✕ 🛏 🖥 🍴

▼▼ ▼▼▼ **Hotel Le St-James** 🆂🅷
(514) 841-3111. **$400-$475.** 355 rue St-Jacques ouest. Corner of rue St-Pierre. Int corridors. **Pets:** Accepted.
🅰🆂🅺 🆂 ✕ 🍽

▼▼ **Hotel Le Saint-Malo** 🆂🅷
(514) 931-7366. **Call for rates.** 1455 rue du Fort. Just s of boul de Maisonneuve. Int corridors. **Pets:** Accepted.
✕

🅒🅐🅐 ▼▼▼ **Hotel Omni Mont-Royal** 🅻🅷
(514) 284-1110. **$159-$329, 7 day notice.** 1050 rue Sherbrooke ouest. Corner of rue Peel. Int corridors. **Pets:** Small, other species. $50 one-time fee/room. Service with restrictions, supervision.
🆂🅰🆅🅴 🆂 ✕ 🏍 🛈 🍽 ≈ ✕

🅒🅐🅐 ▼▼▼ **Hotel Travelodge Montreal Centre** 🆂🅷
(514) 874-9090. **$99-$149.** 50 boul Rene-Levesque ouest. Between rue Clark and St-Urbain. Int corridors. **Pets:** Other species. $10 daily fee/pet. Service with restrictions, crate.
🆂🅰🆅🅴 🆂 ✕ 🛈 🖵 🍽

🅒🅐🅐 ▼▼▼ **L'Appartement Hotel** 🅒🅞
(514) 284-3634. **$127-$160.** 455 rue Sherbrooke ouest. Corner of rue Durocher. Int corridors. **Pets:** Accepted.
🆂🅰🆅🅴 🆂 ✕ 🛈 🖵 ≈

▼▼▼ **La Presidence Hotel and Suites** 🅒🅞
(514) 842-9988. **$129-$189.** 505 rue Sherbrooke est. Between rue Berri and St-Hubert. Int corridors. **Pets:** Accepted.
🅰🆂🅺 🆂 ✕ 🛈 🖵 🍽 ≈ ✕

🅒🅐🅐 ▼▼▼ ▼▼▼ **Le Centre Sheraton** 🅻🅷
(514) 878-2000. **$169-$599.** 1201 boul Rene-Levesque ouest. Between rue Drummond and Stanley. Int corridors. **Pets:** Medium. Service with restrictions, supervision.
🆂🅰🆅🅴 ✕ 🖨 🛈 🖵 🍽 ≈ ✕

🅒🅐🅐 ▼▼▼ ▼▼▼ **Le Meridien Versailles-Montreal** 🆂🅷 🐾
(514) 933-8111. **$129-$219.** 1808 rue Sherbrooke ouest. Corner of rue St-Mathieu. Int corridors. **Pets:** Other species. $20 daily fee/room. Designated rooms, service with restrictions, crate.
🆂🅰🆅🅴 ✕ 🛈 🖵 🍽

🅒🅐🅐 ▼▼▼ ▼▼▼ **Le Saint-Sulpice Hotel Montreal** 🆂🅷 🐾
(514) 288-1000. **$175-$495.** 414 rue St-Sulpice. Just n of rue St-Paul. Int corridors. **Pets:** Medium. $40 one-time fee/room.
🆂🅰🆅🅴 ✕ 🛈 🖵 🍽 ✕

🅒🅐🅐 ▼▼▼ ▼▼▼ **Le Square Phillips Hotel & Suites** 🆂🅷
(514) 393-1193. **$139-$232.** 1193 Place Phillips. Between rue Ste-Catherine and boul Rene-Levesque. Int corridors. **Pets:** Designated rooms, service with restrictions, supervision.
🆂🅰🆅🅴 🆂 ✕ 🛈 🖵 🍽 ≈

🅒🅐🅐 ▼▼▼ ▼▼▼ **Loews Hotel Vogue** 🅻🅷 🐾
(514) 285-5555. **$152-$428.** 1425 rue de la Montagne. Between Ste-Catherine and boul de Maisonneuve. Int corridors. **Pets:** Large, other species.
🆂🅰🆅🅴 🆂 ✕ 🛈 🖵 🍽

🅒🅐🅐 ▼▼▼ **Marriott Residence Inn-Montreal**
Centre-ville/Downtown 🆂🅷
(514) 982-6064. **$155-$475.** 2045 rue Peel. Between rue Sherbrooke and boul de Maisonneuve. Int corridors. **Pets:** Medium, other species. $100 one-time fee/room.
🆂🅰🆅🅴 🆂 ✕ 🛈 🖵 ≈

🅒🅐🅐 ▼▼▼ **Novotel Montreal Centre** 🅻🅷 🐾
(514) 861-6000. **$119-$289.** 1180 rue de la Montagne. Between rue Ste-Catherine and boul Rene-Levesque. Int corridors. **Pets:** Other species. Service with restrictions, supervision.
🆂🅰🆅🅴 🆂 ✕ 🖵 🍽

🅒🅐🅐 ▼▼▼ **Quality Hotel Dorval** 🆂🅷
(514) 731-7821. **$127.** 7700 Cote-de-Liesse. Hwy 520, exit 4 eastbound on south side service road; exit 4 (Montee-de-Liesse) westbound; in St-Laurent sector. Int corridors. **Pets:** Accepted.
🆂🅰🆅🅴 🆂 ✕ 🛈 🖵 🍽 ≈ ✕

🅒🅐🅐 ▼▼▼ **Quality Hotel Downtown Montreal** 🆂🅷
(514) 849-1413. **$99-$340.** 3440 ave du Parc. Between rue Sherbrooke and Milton. Int corridors. **Pets:** Other species. $50 deposit/room, $25 one-time fee/pet. Service with restrictions, supervision.
🆂🅰🆅🅴 🆂 ✕ 🛈 🖵

🅒🅐🅐 ▼▼▼ **Residence Inn by Marriott Montreal**
Westmount 🆂🅷
(514) 935-9224. **$109-$189.** 2170 ave Lincoln. Just e of rue Atwater. Int corridors. **Pets:** Accepted.
🆂🅰🆅🅴 🆂 ✕ 🅶🅼 🛈 🖵 ≈

▼▼▼ ▼▼▼ **Residence Inn Montreal Airport** 🆂🅷
(514) 336-9333. **Call for rates.** 6500 Place Robert-Joncas. Hwy 40, exit 65 (Cavendish boul), then 0.3 mi (0.5 km) w on northside service road, then just n on rue Beaulac. Int corridors. **Pets:** Accepted.
✕ 🅶🅼 🏍 🖨 🛈 🖵 🍽 ≈ ✕

▼▼▼ ▼▼▼ **The Ritz-Carlton, Montreal** 🅻🅷
(514) 842-4212. **$135-$625.** 1228 rue Sherbrooke ouest. Corner de la Montagne. Int corridors. **Pets:** Accepted.
✕ 🖵 🍽 ✕

🅒🅐🅐 ▼▼▼ ▼▼▼ **Sofitel Montreal** 🆂🅷
(514) 285-9000. **$195-$530.** 1155 rue Sherbrooke ouest. Corner of rue Stanley. Int corridors. **Pets:** Other species.
🆂🅰🆅🅴 🆂 ✕ 🛈 🍽 ✕

▼▼▼ ▼▼▼ **W Montreal** 🅻🅷 🐾
(514) 395-3100. **$179-$289.** 901 Square-Victoria. Corner of rue St-Antoine. Int corridors. **Pets:** Medium. $25 daily fee/room, $100 one-time fee/room. Supervision.
🅰🆂🅺 🆂 ✕ 🅶🅼 🛈 🖵 🍽

🅒🅐🅐 ▼▼▼ **XIXe siecle Hotel Montreal** 🆂🅷
(514) 985-0019. **$159-$495.** 262 rue St-Jacques ouest. Between rue St-Jean and rue St-Pierre. Int corridors. **Pets:** Small. $50 daily fee/pet. Service with restrictions, crate.
🆂🅰🆅🅴 🆂 ✕ 🛈 🍽

POINTE-CLAIRE

🅒🅐🅐 ▼▼▼ **Comfort Inn** 🆂🅷
(514) 697-6210. **$79-$195.** 700 boul St-Jean. Hwy 40, exit 52, just s. Int corridors. **Pets:** Other species. Service with restrictions, supervision.
🆂🅰🆅🅴 🆂 ✕ 🛈 🖵

🅒🅐🅐 ▼▼▼ **Quality Suites Montreal Aeroport,**
Pointe-Claire 🆂🅷 🐾
(514) 426-5060. **$109-$169.** 6300 Rt Transcanadienne. Hwy 40, exit 52 eastbound, south side service road; westbound, follow signs for boul St-Jean sud and Hwy 40 est to access south side service road. Int corridors. **Pets:** Designated rooms, service with restrictions, supervision.
🆂🅰🆅🅴 🆂 ✕ 🅶🅼 🛈 🖵 🍽

ROSEMERE

▼▼▼ **Hotel Le Rivage** 🆂🅷
(450) 437-2171. **$89-$134.** 125 boul Cure-Labelle. Hwy 15, exit 14, 2.4 mi (4 km) e. Int corridors. **Pets:** Accepted.
✕ 🛈 🖵 ≈

ST-LAURENT

(CAA) ▽▽▽ Ramada Montreal Airport Hotel 🄻🄷
(514) 733-8818. **$129-$169, 7 day notice.** 7300 Cote-de-Liesse. Hwy 520, exit 4 eastbound on south side service road; exit Montee-de-Liesse westbound. Int corridors. **Pets:** Service with restrictions, supervision.
🆂🄰🆅🅴 🆂🅾 ☒ 🖥 🖵 🍴 🏊

VAUDREUIL-DORION

(CAA) ▽▽▽ Chateau Vaudreuil Suites Hotel 🄻🄷 🐾
(450) 455-0955. **$200-$550.** 21700 Trans-Canada Hwy 40. Hwy 40, exit 36 westbound; exit 35 eastbound. Int corridors. **Pets:** Other species. Crate.
🆂🄰🆅🅴 ☒ 🖥 🖵 🍴 🏊 ☒

END METROPOLITAN AREA

MONT-TREMBLANT CENTRE DE VILLEGIATURE

(CAA) ▽▽▽▽ Hotel Quintessence 🅂🄷
(819) 425-3400. **$289-$1839.** 3004 chemin de la Chapelle. Hwy 117 N, exit 119 (Montee Ryan), 6 mi (10 km) e to Mont-Tremblant Resort centre. Int corridors. **Pets:** Accepted.
🆂🄰🆅🅴 ☒ 🖵 🍴 🏊 ☒

(CAA) ▽▽▽▽ Le Grand Lodge Mont-Tremblant 🅂🄷
(819) 425-2734. **$120-$640, 8 day notice.** 2396 rue Labelle. On Rt 327, 0.3 mi (0.4 km) s of Montee Ryan. Int corridors. **Pets:** Accepted.
🆂🄰🆅🅴 🆂🅾 ☒ 🖥 🖵 🍴 🏊 ☒

NEW RICHMOND

▽▽▽ Hotel Le Francis 🅂🄷
(418) 392-4485. **$99-$149.** 210 chemin Pardiac. Just s of Rt 132. Ext/int corridors. **Pets:** Small, dogs only. $10 one-time fee/pet. Service with restrictions, supervision.
🄰🆂🄺 ☒ 🖥 🖵 🍴 🏊 ☒

PASPEBIAC

▽▽▽ Auberge du Parc Inn 🅂🄷
(418) 752-3355. **$79-$165.** 68 boul Gerard D Levesque ouest. On Rt 132; centre. Ext corridors. **Pets:** Accepted.
☒ 🍴 🏊 ☒ 🄰🄲

PERCE

▽ Au Pic de l'Aurore 🄲🄰
(418) 782-2151. **$59-$135.** 1 Rt 132. 1.2 mi (2 km) e from village. Ext corridors. **Pets:** Medium. $50 deposit/pet, $25 one-time fee/pet. Designated rooms, service with restrictions, supervision.
☒ 🖥 🖵 🄲

▽▽▽ Hotel La Normandie 🅂🄷
(418) 782-2112. **$79-$239.** 221 Rt 132 ouest. Centre. Int corridors. **Pets:** Medium. $50 one-time fee/room. Designated rooms, service with restrictions, crate.
☒ 🖥 🖵 🍴 🄲

▽▽▽ Hotel/Motel Le Mirage 🄼
(418) 782-5151. **$75-$168.** 288 Rt 132 ouest. On Rt 132. Ext corridors. **Pets:** Small, dogs only.
☒ 🖥 🍴 🏊

▽▽▽ Hotel Motel Manoir de Perce 🅂🄷
(418) 782-2022. **$66-$158.** 212 Rt 132. Centre. Ext/int corridors. **Pets:** Accepted.
🆂🅾 ☒ 🖥 🍴

PLESSISVILLE

▽▽ Motel A la Claire Fontaine 🄼
(819) 362-6388. **$45-$75.** 2165 rue St-Calixte. Rt 165, 0.6 mi (1 km) e on Rt 116, follow signs. Ext corridors. **Pets:** Very small. Designated rooms, no service, supervision.
🄰🆂🄺 🆂🅾 ☒ 🖥 🍴

PORTNEUF

▽▽ Hotel Le Portneuvois 🅂🄷
(418) 286-6400. **$100-$110.** 101 rue Simeon-Delisle. Hwy 40, exit 261, then 0.3 mi (0.5 km) s on rue Provencher. Int corridors. **Pets:** Accepted.
🄰🆂🄺 🆂🅾 ☒ 🖥 🖵

QUEBEC METROPOLITAN AREA

BEAUPRE

(CAA) ▽▽▽ Auberge La Camarine 🄲🄸
(418) 827-5703. **$100-$200.** 10947 boul Ste-Anne. On Hwy 138, 0.9 mi (1.5 km) w of jct Hwy 360. Int corridors. **Pets:** Accepted.
🆂🄰🆅🅴 ☒ 🖥

(CAA) ▽▽▽▽ Chateau Mont Sainte Anne 🄻🄷
(418) 827-5211. **$139-$269, 7 day notice.** 500 boul du Beau-Pre. Hwy 360, 2.3 mi (3.7 km) ne from jct Hwy 138. Int corridors. **Pets:** $20 daily fee/pet. Designated rooms, service with restrictions, crate.
🆂🄰🆅🅴 🆂🅾 ☒ 🖥 🖵 🍴 🏊 ☒

(CAA) ▽▽▽▽ Hotel Val des Neiges 🄻🄷 🐾
(418) 827-5711. **$89.** 201 rue Val-des-Neiges. Just off Hwy 360. Int corridors. **Pets:** Small. $20 daily fee/room. Designated rooms, service with restrictions, supervision.
🆂🄰🆅🅴 🆂🅾 ☒ 🖥 🖵 🍴 🏊 ☒

L'ANCIENNE-LORETTE

▽▽ Comfort Inn 🅂🄷
(418) 872-5900. **$115-$145.** 1255 boul Duplessis. Jct boul Duplessis and Wilfrid-Hamel (Hwy 138). Int corridors. **Pets:** Service with restrictions, supervision.
🄰🆂🄺 🆂🅾 ☒ 🖥 🖵

LEVIS

▽▽ Comfort Inn 🅂🄷
(418) 835-5605. **$95-$170.** 10 du Vallon est. Hwy 20, exit 325S eastbound; exit 325 westbound. Int corridors. **Pets:** Accepted.
🄰🆂🄺 🆂🅾 ☒ 🖥 🖵

QUEBEC

▽▽ Appartements La Pergola 🄲🄾
(418) 681-1428. **$65-$120, 15 day notice.** 405 boul Rene-Levesque ouest. Between aves Moncton and des Erables. Int corridors. **Pets:** Accepted.
🄰🆂🄺 🆂🅾 🖥 🖵

Auberge Saint-Antoine SH
(418) 692-2211. **$249-$309.** 8 rue St-Antoine. Corner of rue Dalhousie. Int corridors. **Pets:** Accepted.
[SAVE] [X] [🅗] [💷] [🍴]

Comfort Inn SH
(418) 666-1226. **$95-$195.** 240 boul Ste-Anne. Hwy 440, exit Francois-de-Laval. Int corridors. **Pets:** Other species.
[ASK] [S🅓] [X] [🅗] [💷]

Comfort Inn de l'Aeroport-Hamel SH
(418) 872-5038. **$93-$145.** 7320 boul Wilfrid-Hamel. Hwy 138, 0.9 mi (1.5 km) w of boul Duplessis. Int corridors. **Pets:** Other species. Service with restrictions, supervision.
[ASK] [S🅓] [X] [🅗] [💷]

Delta Quebec LH 🐾
(418) 647-1717. **$100-$315.** 690 boul Rene-Levesque est. Just w of boul Honore-Mercier. Int corridors. **Pets:** Medium. $35 one-time fee/room. Designated rooms, service with restrictions.
[SAVE] [S🅓] [X] [🅗] [💷] [🍴] [≈] [X]

Fairmont Le Chateau Frontenac LH 🐾
(418) 692-3861. **$199-$549.** 1 rue des Carrieres. In Old Quebec. Int corridors. **Pets:** Medium. $25 daily fee/pet. Supervision.
[SAVE] [S🅓] [X] [🐾] [💷] [🍴] [≈] [X]

Gite du Vieux-Bourg BB
(418) 661-0116. **$75-$105, 15 day notice.** 492 ave Royale. Hwy 440, exit Francois-de-Laval, just n, then 0.3 mi (0.5 km) e; in Beauport sector. Int corridors. **Pets:** Supervision.
[ASK] [X] [🅗] [💷] [≈]

Hilton Quebec LH
(418) 647-2411. **$119-$329.** 1100 boul Rene-Levesque est. Corner of ave Honore-Mercier. Int corridors. **Pets:** Accepted.
[SAVE] [X] [🅗] [💷] [🍴] [≈] [X]

Hotel Clarion Quebec LH
(418) 653-4901. **$95-$350.** 3125 boul Hochelaga. Hwy 73, exit 136 (Hochelaga ouest); in Ste-Foy sector. Int corridors. **Pets:** Accepted.
[ASK] [S🅓] [X] [🅗] [💷] [🍴] [≈] [X]

Hotel Gouverneur Quebec-Sainte-Foy LH
(418) 651-3030. **$99-$250.** 3030 boul Laurier. Corner of rue Lavigerie; in Ste-Foy sector. Ext/int corridors. **Pets:** Accepted.
[ASK] [X] [🅗] [💷] [🍴] [≈]

Hotel Quality Suites Quebec SH
(418) 622-4244. **$115-$190.** 1600 rue Bouvier. Hwy 40, exit 312N (Pierre-Bertrand nord), 1.3 mi (2 km) w of jct Rt 358. Int corridors. **Pets:** Other species. Supervision.
[SAVE] [S🅓] [X] [🅗] [💷]

Hotel Universel SH
(418) 653-5250. **$98-$148.** 2300 chemin Ste-Foy. Hwy 73, exit 137, 1.4 mi (2.3 km) e on chemin des Quatre-Bourgeois; in Ste-Foy sector. Ext/int corridors. **Pets:** Designated rooms, service with restrictions, supervision.
[SAVE] [S🅓] [X] [🅗] [💷] [🍴] [≈]

L'Hotel du Vieux Quebec SH 🐾
(418) 692-1850. **$94-$284.** 1190 rue St-Jean. Corner of rue de l'Hotel-Dieu. Int corridors. **Pets:** $10 daily fee/room. Designated rooms, service with restrictions, supervision.
[SAVE] [X] [🅗] [🍴]

Loews Le Concorde LH 🐾
(418) 647-2222. **$109-$309.** 1225 Cours du General-de-Montcalm. Corner of Grande Allee est. Int corridors. **Pets:** $25 deposit/room. Designated rooms, service with restrictions, supervision.
[SAVE] [S🅓] [X] [🅗] [💷] [🍴] [≈] [X]

STE-FOY

Motel Oncle Sam M
(418) 872-1488. **$45-$119.** 7025 boul Wilfrid-Hamel. On Hwy 138 at jct boul Duplessis; in Ste-Foy sector. Ext corridors. **Pets:** Accepted.
[X] [🅗] [💷] [≈]

ST-FERREOL-LES-NEIGES

Chalets Montmorency Condominiums CO
(418) 826-2600. **$89-$129.** 1768 ave Royale. On Hwy 360. Ext corridors. **Pets:** Dogs only. $25 daily fee/pet. No service, crate.
[SAVE] [S🅓] [X] [🅗] [💷] [≈] [X]

Chalets-Village Mont-Sainte-Anne CA
(418) 826-3331. **$550-$4950, 90 day notice.** 1815 boul Les Neiges. On north side of Hwy 360; village center. Ext corridors. **Pets:** Other species. $100 one-time fee/room. Designated rooms, no service, supervision.
[🅗] [💷] [X]

END METROPOLITAN AREA

RIGAUD

Howard Johnson SH
(450) 458-7997. **Call for rates (no credit cards).** 93 Rt 201. Hwy 40, exit 17, then just ne. Int corridors. **Pets:** Accepted.
[X] [🅗] [💷] [🍴]

RIMOUSKI

Comfort Inn SH
(418) 724-2500. **$115-$150.** 455 boul St-Germain ouest. On Rt 132. Int corridors. **Pets:** Service with restrictions, supervision.
[ASK] [S🅓] [X] [🅗] [💷]

Hotel Rimouski LH
(418) 725-5000. **$112-$142, 15 day notice.** 225 boul Rene-Lepage est. On Rt 132, corner of rue Julien-Rehel. Int corridors. **Pets:** Small. Designated rooms, supervision.
[ASK] [X] [🅗] [💷] [🍴] [≈] [X]

RIVIERE-DU-LOUP

Comfort Inn SH
(418) 867-4162. **$100-$170.** 85 boul Cartier. Hwy 20, exit 507, just se; Hwy 85, exit 96 (Fraserville); follow signs. Int corridors. **Pets:** Very small. Designated rooms, service with restrictions, supervision.
[SAVE] [S🅓] [X] [🅗] [💷]

Days Inn Riviere-du-Loup SH
(418) 862-6354. **$99-$185.** 182 rue Fraser. Hwy 20, exit 503, 0.6 mi (1 km) e on Rt 132. Ext corridors. **Pets:** $10 daily fee/pet. Supervision.
[SAVE] [S🅓] [X] [🅗] [💷] [≈]

ROBERVAL

Hotel Chateau Roberval LH
(418) 275-7511. **$119-$139.** 1225 boul Marcotte. On Hwy 169; centre. Int corridors. **Pets:** Accepted.
[SAVE] [S🅓] [X] [🅗] [💷] [🍴] [≈] [X]

ROUYN-NORANDA

◆◆◆ Comfort Inn **SH**
(819) 797-1313. **$90-$110.** 1295 rue Lariviere. On Rt 117, 2.5 mi (4 km) s from town centre. Int corridors. **Pets:** Accepted.
🅰️🆂🆇🅱️📟📺

SHAWINIGAN

(CAA) ◆◆◆ Auberge Escapade Inn **SH**
(819) 539-6911. **$79-$150.** 3383 rue Garnier. Hwy 55, exit 217, then 0.3 mi (0.5 km) n on Rt 351. Ext/int corridors. **Pets:** Small. $10 daily fee/room. Service with restrictions, crate.
🆂🅰️🆅🅴📟📺🍽️

(CAA) ◆◆◆ Auberge Gouverneur & Centre de Congres Shawinigan **SH**
(819) 537-6000. **$150-$175.** 1100 Promenade-du-St-Maurice. Hwy 55 N, exit 211, 2.8 mi (4.4 km) n on Hwy 153, follow signs. Int corridors. **Pets:** Small. Crate.
🆂🅰️🆅🅴📟📺🍽️🏊🆇

◆◆◆ Comfort Inn & Suites **SH**
(819) 536-2000. **$72-$145.** 500 boul du Capitaine. Hwy 55 N, exit 211, 2.8 mi (4.4 km) n on Hwy 153, then 1.3 mi (2 km) s on Rt 157. Int corridors. **Pets:** Accepted.
🅰️🆂🆇🅱️📟📺

SHERBROOKE

(CAA) ◆◆◆ Delta Sherbrooke Hotel and Conference Centre **LH**
(819) 822-1989. **$89-$161.** 2685 rue King ouest. Hwy 410, exit 4E, 0.6 mi (1 km) e on Rt 112. Int corridors. **Pets:** Accepted.
🆂🅰️🆅🆇📟📺🍽️🏊🆇

ST-ANTOINE-DE-TILLY

◆◆◆ Manoir de Tilly **CI**
(418) 886-2407. **$136-$307, 3 day notice.** 3854 chemin de Tilly. Jct Hwy 20, exit 291, 5.3 mi (8.5 km) n on Rt 273; centre. Int corridors. **Pets:** Accepted.
🆂🆇🍽️

STE-ANNE-DE-BEAUPRE

(CAA) ◆◆◆ Manoir Ste-Anne **M**
(418) 827-8383. **$65-$125.** 9776 boul Ste-Anne. On Hwy 138. Ext corridors. **Pets:** Small. Supervision.
🆂🆇🅱️📟

STE-ANNE-DES-MONTS

(CAA) ◆◆◆ Motel Beaurivage **M**
(418) 763-2291. **$55-$160.** 245 1ere ave ouest. Just off Rt 132. Ext/int corridors. **Pets:** Accepted.
🆂🆇🅱️📟🍽️🆇

STE-MARTHE

◆◆◆ Auberge des Gallant **CI**
(450) 459-4241. **$130-$250, 14 day notice.** 1171 chemin St-Henri. 5.3 mi (8.5 km) w on chemin St-Henri from Hwy 201. Int corridors. **Pets:** Accepted.
🆇📟🍽️🏊🆇

ST-FAUSTIN-LAC-CARRE

◆ Motel sur la Colline **M**
(819) 688-2102. **$60-$152, 15 day notice.** 357 Rt 117. On Rt 117, 2.5 mi (4 km) n of exit for city. Ext/int corridors. **Pets:** Accepted.
🅰️🆂🆇🅱️📟🏊

ST-FELICIEN

(CAA) ◆◆◆ Hotel du Jardin **LH**
(418) 679-8422. **$105-$190.** 1400 boul du Jardin. On Hwy 167. Int corridors. **Pets:** Small. Service with restrictions, supervision.
🆂🆇🅱️📟🍽️🏊🆇

ST-GEORGES (BEAUCE)

(CAA) ◆◆◆ Comfort Inn **M**
(418) 227-1227. **$85-$165.** 16525 boul Lacroix. On Rt 173, just n of jct Rt 204 W. Ext/int corridors. **Pets:** Small. $25 daily fee/pet. Designated rooms, service with restrictions, supervision.
🆂🆇🅱️📟🍽️

ST-HONORE-DE-SHENLEY

◆ Motel Jasper **M**
(418) 497-2322. **$64-$74.** 657 Rt 185. On Rt 185. Ext corridors. **Pets:** Small. Service with restrictions, supervision.
🅰️🆂🆇🍽️

ST-HYACINTHE

◆◆◆ Hotel des Seigneurs Saint-Hyacinthe **LH**
(450) 774-3810. **$110-$300.** 1200 rue Johnson. Hwy 20, exit 130S, just e on rue Gauvin from boul Laframboise. Int corridors. **Pets:** Medium. Designated rooms, service with restrictions, crate.
🅰️🆂🆇🅱️📟🍽️🏊🆇

ST-JEAN-PORT-JOLI

◆◆ Auberge du Faubourg **M**
(418) 598-6455. **$89-$105, 10 day notice.** 280 ave de Gaspe ouest (Rt 132). 1.4 mi (2.4 km) w on Rt 132 from jct Rt 204; Hwy 20, exit 414. Ext corridors. **Pets:** $15 daily fee/room. Service with restrictions.
🅰️🆇🅱️📟🍽️🏊🆇

ST-JEAN-SUR-RICHELIEU

(CAA) ◆◆ Comfort Inn **SH**
(450) 359-4466. **$94-$169.** 700 rue Gadbois. Hwy 35, exit 9, e on rue Pierre-Caisse. Int corridors. **Pets:** Other species. Service with restrictions, supervision.
🆂🆇🅱️🏊

ST-LIBOIRE

◆◆ Econo Lodge **SH**
(450) 793-4444. **$76-$120.** 110 Rang Charlotte. Hwy 20, exit 147, just s. Int corridors. **Pets:** Accepted.
🅰️🆂🆇🅱️📟🍽️🏊

THETFORD MINES

◆◆ Comfort Inn **SH** ❀
(418) 338-0171. **$120-$129.** 123 boul Frontenac ouest. On Rt 112. Int corridors. **Pets:** Other species. Service with restrictions, crate.
🅰️🆂🆇📟

TROIS-RIVIERES

◆◆ Comfort Inn **SH**
(819) 371-3566. **$88-$112.** 6255 rue Corbeil. Hwy 55, exit 183 (boul Jean XXIII); 1.3 mi (2 km) n of Laviolette Bridge, then 0.3 mi (0.5 km) e. Int corridors. **Pets:** Accepted.
🆇🅱️📟

(CAA) ◆◆◆ Days Inn **SH**
(819) 377-4444. **$80-$170, 14 day notice.** 3155 boul Saint-Jean. Hwy 55, exit 183 (boul Jean XXIII), 0.3 mi (0.5 km) w, then 0.3 mi (0.4 km) n. Int corridors. **Pets:** Accepted.
🆂🆇🅱️

▼▼▼ **Delta Trois-Rivieres Hotel and Conference Center** LH
(819) 376-1991. **$99-$125.** 1620 rue Notre-Dame centre. Corner of rue St-Roch; centre. Int corridors. **Pets:** Accepted.
A$K S∅ ✕ ▦ ▭ ❘❙ ⚓ ✕

CAA ▼▼▼ **Hotel Du Roy Trois-Rivieres** SH
(819) 379-3232. **$75-$125.** 3600 boul Gene H Kruger. On Rt 138, 1.3 mi (2 km) e of Pont Laviolette and jct Hwy 55. Ext/int corridors. **Pets:** Accepted.
SAVE S∅ ✕ ▦ ▭ ❘❙ ⚓

CAA ▼▼▼ **Super 8 Motel Trois-Rivieres** SH
(819) 377-5881. **$111-$139.** 3185 boul Jean XXIII. Hwy 55, exit 183 (boul Jean XXIII), just nw. Int corridors. **Pets:** $15 daily fee/room. Designated rooms, service with restrictions, crate.
SAVE S∅ ✕ ▦ ▭ ⚓

VAL-D'OR

▼▼ **Comfort Inn** SH
(819) 825-9360. **$89-$101.** 1665 3ieme Ave. In town centre. Int corridors. **Pets:** Accepted.
A$K S∅ ✕ ▦ ▭

▼▼▼ **Hotel Forestel** LH
(819) 825-5660. **$80-$140.** 1001 3ieme ave est. On Rt 117. Int corridors. **Pets:** Medium. Service with restrictions, supervision.
A$K S∅ ✕ ▦ ▭ ❘❙

▼▼ **Hotel-Motel Prelude** SH
(819) 825-0090. **$81-$88.** 1159 3ieme ave. On Rt 117 N; in town centre. Ext/int corridors. **Pets:** Other species. Supervision.
A$K S∅ ✕ ▦ ▭

▼▼▼ **Motel L'Escale Hotel Suite** SH
(819) 824-2711. **$101-$131.** 1100 rue L. In town centre. Ext/int corridors. **Pets:** Accepted.
✕ ▦ ▭ ❘❙

SASKATCHEWAN

CARONPORT

The Pilgrim Inn SH
(306) 756-5002. **$77.** Hwy 1 W. Jct Main Access; on Trans-Canada Hwy 1. Int corridors. **Pets:** Other species. Designated rooms, service with restrictions.

ESTEVAN

Perfect Inns & Suites SH
(306) 634-8585. **$89-$99.** 134 2nd Ave. Just n of jct Hwy 39 E and 2nd Ave. Int corridors. **Pets:** Accepted.

KINDERSLEY

Best Western Westridge Inn SH
(306) 463-4687. **$98-$108, 7 day notice.** 100 12th Ave NW. Jct of Hwy 7 and 21. Ext/int corridors. **Pets:** Small. Designated rooms, service with restrictions, supervision.

MELFORT

Travelodge SH
(306) 752-5592. **$110, 3 day notice.** 101 Spruce Haven Rd. On Hwy 3 and 6; at eastern approach to town. Int corridors. **Pets:** Accepted.

MOOSE JAW

Comfort Inn SH
(306) 692-2100. **$87.** 155 Thatcher Dr W. Just w of jct Main St. Int corridors. **Pets:** Large. $15 one-time fee/pet. Designated rooms, service with restrictions, supervision.

Days Inn SH
(306) 691-5777. **$93-$104.** 1720 Main St N. From jct Trans-Canada Hwy 1, just s. Int corridors. **Pets:** Other species. $13 daily fee/pet. Designated rooms, service with restrictions, supervision.

Heritage Inn SH
(306) 693-7550. **$105-$108.** 1590 Main St N. 0.9 mi (1.5 km) s of jct Trans-Canada Hwy 1 and 2; access from Hwy 2 via Thatcher Dr. Int corridors. **Pets:** Other species. $10 daily fee/pet. Service with restrictions, supervision.

Prairie Oasis Motel M
(306) 693-8888. **$84-$86.** 955 Thatcher Dr E. Just s of jct Trans-Canada Hwy 1 and Thatcher Dr E. Ext corridors. **Pets:** Designated rooms, service with restrictions, crate.

Super 8 Motel-Moose Jaw M
(306) 692-8888. **$72-$104.** 1706 Main St N. 0.9 mi (1.5 km) s of jct Trans-Canada Hwy 1; access from Hwy 2 via Thatcher Dr. Int corridors. **Pets:** Large, other species. $15 one-time fee/room. Designated rooms, no service, supervision.

NORTH BATTLEFORD

Super 8 Motel SH
(306) 446-8888. **$72-$90.** 1006 Hwy 16 Bypass. 0.3 mi (0.5 km) nw of jct Hwy 16. Int corridors. **Pets:** Other species. $25 one-time fee/room. Service with restrictions, supervision.

Tropical Inn SH
(306) 446-4700. **$95-$155.** 1001 Hwy 16 Bypass. Corner of Battleford Rd and Hwy 16 Bypass. Int corridors. **Pets:** Accepted.

PRINCE ALBERT

Comfort Inn SH
(306) 763-4466. **$88-$126.** 3863 2nd Ave W. 1.4 mi (2.3 km) s at jct Hwy 2 and Marquis Rd. Int corridors. **Pets:** Other species. Service with restrictions, supervision.

Super 8 SH
(306) 953-0088. **$84-$94.** 4444 2nd Ave W. Just s of jct Hwy 2 and Marquis Rd. Int corridors. **Pets:** Accepted.

Travelodge Prince Albert SH
(306) 764-6441. **$75-$105.** 3551 2nd Ave W. 1.4 mi (2.2 km) s at jct Hwy 2 and Marquis Rd. Ext/int corridors. **Pets:** Accepted.

REGINA

Comfort Inn SH
(306) 789-5522. **$99-$116, 10 day notice.** 3221 E Eastgate Dr. Trans-Canada Hwy 1, 1.3 mi (2 km) e of Ring Rd; at eastern approach to city. Int corridors. **Pets:** Accepted.

Country Inn & Suites By Carlson SH
(306) 789-9117. **$105-$125, 3 day notice.** 3321 Eastgate Bay. Trans-Canada Hwy 1, 1.3 mi (2 km) e of Ring Rd; at eastern approach to city. Int corridors. **Pets:** Medium, other species. $10 one-time fee/room. Service with restrictions, crate.

Days Inn SH
(306) 522-3297. **$99-$139.** 3875 Eastgate Dr. Trans-Canada Hwy 1, exit Prince of Wales Dr; at eastern approach to city. Int corridors. **Pets:** Accepted.

Delta Regina LH
(306) 525-5255. **$125.** 1919 Saskatchewan Dr. At Rose St; centre. Int corridors. **Pets:** Accepted.

Holiday Inn Hotel & Suites SH
(306) 789-3883. **$109-$113.** 1800 Prince of Wales Dr. From jct Trans-Canada Hwy 1, just n; at eastern approach to city. Int corridors. **Pets:** Accepted.

Ⓐ ▼▼ **Howard Johnson Inn** 🆂🅷
(306) 565-0455. **$79-$149.** 1110 Victoria Ave E. Trans-Canada Hwy 1,
just w of Ring Rd; at eastern approach to city. Int corridors.
Pets: Accepted.

🆂🅰🆅🅴 🆂🅳 ☒ 🔋 💻 🏊

▼▼▼ **Quality Hotel** 🆂🅷
(306) 569-4656. **$126-$139, 3 day notice.** 1717 Victoria Ave. Just e of
Broad St; downtown. Int corridors. **Pets:** Accepted.

☒ 🔋 💻 🍽

Ⓐ ▼▼▼▼ **Radisson Plaza Hotel Saskatchewan** 🅻🅷
(306) 522-7691. **$123-$158.** 2125 Victoria Ave. Victoria Ave at Scarth
St; centre. Int corridors. **Pets:** $35 one-time fee/room. Service with restric-
tions, crate.

🆂🅰🆅🅴 🆂🅳 ☒ 🔍🅼 🔋 💻 🍽 ☒

▼▼▼ **Ramada Hotel & Convention Centre** 🅻🅷
(306) 569-1666. **$89-$126.** 1818 Victoria Ave. Victoria Ave and Broad
St; centre of downtown. Int corridors. **Pets:** Accepted.

🅰🆂🅺 🆂🅳 ☒ 🔋 💻 🍽 🏊 ☒

Ⓐ ▼▼▼ **Regina Inn Hotel & Conference Centre** 🅻🅷
(306) 525-6767. **$109-$194.** 1975 Broad St. Jct Victoria Ave; centre of
downtown. Int corridors. **Pets:** Medium. $50 deposit/room. Supervision.

🆂🅰🆅🅴 🆂🅳 ☒ 🔋 💻 🍽

▼ **Regina Super 8** 🆂🅷
(306) 789-8833. **$80-$120, 3 day notice.** 2730 Victoria Ave E. Trans-
Canada Hwy 1, 1 mi (1.6 km) e of Ring Rd; at eastern approach to
city. Int corridors. **Pets:** Accepted.

🅰🆂🅺 ☒ 🔍🅼 🔋 💻

▼▼▼ **Sandman Hotel Suites and Spa** 🆂🅷
(306) 757-2444. **$114-$150.** 1800 Victoria Ave E. Just e of Ring Rd; at
eastern approach to city. Int corridors. **Pets:** Accepted.

☒ 🔍 🔋 💻 🍽 🏊

SASKATOON

Ⓐ ▼▼ **Best Western Inn & Suites** 🆂🅷
(306) 244-5552. **$90-$100.** 1715 Idylwyld Dr N. 1.6 mi (2.6 km) n on
Hwy 11 (Idylwyld Dr). Ext/int corridors. **Pets:** Accepted.

🆂🅰🆅🅴 🆂🅳 ☒ 🔋 💻 🍽 ☒

Ⓐ ▼▼ **Colonial Square Motel & Suites** 🆂🅷
(306) 343-1676. **$79-$89.** 1301 8th St E. Just w of Cumberland St.
Ext/int corridors. **Pets:** Other species. $5 daily fee/room. Designated
rooms, service with restrictions, supervision.

🆂🅰🆅🅴 🆂🅳 ☒ 🔋 💻

▼▼ **Comfort Inn** 🆂🅷 🐾
(306) 934-1122. **$100-$150.** 2155 Northridge Dr. 1.9 mi (3 km) n; just
ne of jct Hwy 11 (Idylwyld Dr) and Circle Dr. Int corridors. **Pets:** Small.
Designated rooms, no service, supervision.

☒ 🔍🅼 🔋 💻

▼▼ **Country Inn & Suites By Carlson** 🆂🅷 🐾
(306) 934-3900. **$90.** 617 Cynthia St. Just w of jct Hwy 11 (Idylwyld Dr)
and Circle Dr. Int corridors. **Pets:** Medium, other species. $20 one-time
fee/room. Designated rooms, service with restrictions, crate.

🅰🆂🅺 🆂🅳 ☒ 🔍🅼 🔋 💻

▼▼▼▼ **Delta Bessborough** 🅻🅷
(306) 244-5521. **$124-$214.** 601 Spadina Crescent E. At 21st St E;
centre of downtown. Int corridors. **Pets:** Accepted.

🅰🆂🅺 🆂🅳 ☒ 🔋 💻 🍽 🏊 ☒

▼▼▼ **Holiday Inn Express Hotel & Suites Saskatoon** 🆂🅷
(306) 384-8844. **$109-$169.** 315 Idylwyld Dr N. Jct 25th St W. Int
corridors. **Pets:** Accepted.

🅰🆂🅺 ☒ 🔍🅼 🔋 💻 🏊

▼▼▼ **Radisson Hotel Saskatoon** 🆂🅷
(306) 665-3322. **$109-$149, 3 day notice.** 405 20th St E. At 4th Ave S;
centre. Int corridors. **Pets:** Accepted.

🅰🆂🅺 🆂🅳 ☒ 🔍🅼 🔋 💻 🍽 🏊 ☒

▼▼ **Sandman Hotel** 🅻🅷
(306) 477-4844. **$89-$117.** 310 Circle Dr W. Jct Ave C N. Int corridors.
Pets: Accepted.

🅰🆂🅺 🆂🅳 ☒ 🔋 💻 🍽 🏊

Ⓐ ▼▼▼ **Saskatoon Inn Hotel & Conference**
Centre 🅻🅷 🐾
(306) 242-1440. **$114.** 2002 Airport Dr. Jct Circle and Airport drs. Int
corridors. **Pets:** Designated rooms, service with restrictions, supervision.

🆂🅰🆅🅴 🆂🅳 ☒ 🔋 💻 🍽 🏊

Ⓐ ▼▼▼ **Saskatoon Travelodge Hotel** 🆂🅷
(306) 242-8881. **$140-$150.** 106 Circle Dr W. 1.9 mi (3 km) n, then just
w of jct Hwy 11 (Idylwyld Dr). Int corridors. **Pets:** Medium. $10 daily
fee/room. Service with restrictions, supervision.

🆂🅰🆅🅴 ☒ 🔋 💻 🍽 🏊 ☒

▼▼▼ **Sheraton Cavalier** 🆂🅷
(306) 652-6770. **$209.** 612 Spadina Crescent E. At 21st St E; centre of
downtown. Int corridors. **Pets:** Accepted.

🅰🆂🅺 🆂🅳 ☒ 🔋 🍽 🏊 ☒

▼▼ **Super 8** 🆂🅷
(306) 384-8989. **$92.** 706 Circle Dr E. 1.3 mi (2 km) e of jct Hwy 11
(Idylwyld Dr). Ext/int corridors. **Pets:** Other species. $5 one-time fee/
room. Service with restrictions, crate.

🅰🆂🅺 🆂🅳 ☒ 🔋 💻

SHAUNAVON

▼ **Hidden Hilten Motel** 🅼
(306) 297-4166. **$55-$70.** 352 5th St W. 0.3 mi (0.5 km) e from jct Hwy
13 and 37, just n. Ext corridors. **Pets:** Accepted.

🅰🆂🅺 🆂🅳 ☒ 🔋

SWIFT CURRENT

▼▼ **Comfort Inn** 🆂🅷
(306) 778-3994. **$108-$150.** 1510 S Service Rd E. Trans-Canada Hwy
1, just w of 22nd Ave NE. Int corridors. **Pets:** Accepted.

🅰🆂🅺 🆂🅳 ☒ 🔋 💻

Ⓐ ▼ **Rodeway Inn Motel** 🆂🅷
(306) 773-4664. **$57-$59.** 1200 S Service Rd E. Trans-Canada Hwy 1,
just w of 22nd Ave NE. Ext/int corridors. **Pets:** Accepted.

🆂🅰🆅🅴 🆂🅳 ☒ 🔋 🍽

Ⓐ ▼ **Safari Inn Motel** 🅼
(306) 773-4608. **$56-$70.** 810 S Service Rd E. 0.6 mi (1 km) w of jct
Hwy 1 and 4. Ext corridors. **Pets:** $10 daily fee/pet. Designated rooms,
service with restrictions, supervision.

🆂🅰🆅🅴 🆂🅳 ☒ 🔋 💻

▼▼ **Super 8 Motel** 🆂🅷
(306) 778-6088. **$84-$165, 30 day notice.** 405 N Service Rd E. Just e
of Central Ave. Int corridors. **Pets:** Accepted.

🅰🆂🅺 🆂🅳 ☒ 🔋 💻 🏊

Ⓐ ▼ **Westwind Motel** 🅼
(306) 773-1441. **$60-$72.** 155 N Service Rd W. Trans-Canada Hwy 1,
0.3 mi (0.5 km) w of Central Ave. Ext corridors. **Pets:** Small, dogs only.
$5 one-time fee/pet. Designated rooms, service with restrictions, supervi-
sion.

🆂🅰🆅🅴 🆂🅳 ☒ 🔋 🍽 🏊

WEYBURN

(CAA) ▼▼ Perfect Inns & Suites Ⓜ
(306) 842-2691. **$65-$95.** 238 Sims Ave. 0.3 mi (0.5 km) w of jct Hwy 35 and 39. Ext/int corridors. **Pets:** $2 daily fee/room. Service with restrictions, supervision.
[SAVE] [⊠] [🔒] [💻]

YORKTON

▼▼ Best Western Parkland Inn 🆂🅷
(306) 783-9781. **Call for rates.** 110 Broadway St E. On Hwy 9, 10, and 16 (Yellowhead Hwy); downtown. Int corridors. **Pets:** Accepted.
[⊠] [🔒] [💻] [🍽] [🏊] [⊠]

▼▼ Comfort Inn & Suites 🆂🅷
(306) 783-0333. **$72-$175.** 22 Dracup Ave. Just w of jct Hwy 9, 10 and 16 (Yellowhead Hwy). Int corridors. **Pets:** Accepted.
[ASK] [🆂🅳] [⊠] [🔒] [💻] [🏊]

YUKON TERRITORY

DAWSON CITY

▼ Bonanza Gold Motel M
(867) 993-6789. **$69-$189.** 1.5 mi (2.4 km) s on Hwy 2. Ext corridors. **Pets:** Other species. $20 one-time fee/pet. Service with restrictions, supervision.

⊠ 🐾 🛏 💻 🍽 🎖

▼▼ Klondike Kate's Cabins CA
(867) 993-6527. **$95-$140.** 1103 3rd Ave & King St. Downtown. **Pets:** $20 one-time fee/room. Service with restrictions.

⊠ 🛏 💻 🍽 🎖

◆ ▼▼ Westmark Inn Dawson City M
(867) 993-5542. **$149.** 5th St & Harper. At 5th and Harper sts; downtown. Ext/int corridors. **Pets:** Accepted.

SAVE ⊠ 💻 🍽 🎖

HAINES JUNCTION

◆ ▼▼ Alcan Motor Inn M
(867) 634-2371. **$110-$150.** Jct Hwy 1 (Alaska Hwy) and 3 (Haines Hwy). Ext corridors. **Pets:** Accepted.

SAVE 🔥 ⊠ 🛏 💻

WHITEHORSE

◆ ▼▼ High Country Inn SH
(867) 667-4471. **$99-$239.** 4051 4th Ave. 0.4 mi (0.6 km) e of Main St. Int corridors. **Pets:** Designated rooms, supervision.

SAVE ⊠ 🛏 💻 🍽

◆ ▼▼ Westmark Whitehorse Hotel & Conference Centre SH
(867) 393-9700. **$109-$159.** 201 Wood St. At 2nd Ave; centre. Int corridors. **Pets:** Designated rooms, service with restrictions, supervision.

SAVE ⊠ ♿ 🐾 🛏 💻 🍽 🎖

CAMPGROUNDS

United States
Canada

United States

Alabama

CHILDERSBURG — DESOTO CAVERNS PARK CAMPGROUND. (256) 378-7252. **4P $20-$26, XP $3-$5.** 5181 DeSoto Caverns Pkwy, 35044. On SR 76, 5 mi e.

⊠

PELHAM — BIRMINGHAM SOUTH CAMPGROUND. (205) 664-8832. **2P $33-$39, XP $2.** 222 Hwy 33, 35124. I-65, exit 242, 0.5 mi w on CR 52, then 0.3 mi n.

🌊 ⊠

Arizona

AMADO — DE ANZA TRAILS RV RESORT. (520) 398-8628. **Call for rates.** 2869 E Frontage Rd, 85645. I-19, exit 48, just e, then 1.6 mi s. (HC 65 Box 381, TUMACACORI, 85640).

🏔 🌊 ⊠

APACHE JUNCTION — SUPERSTITION SUNRISE LUXURY RV RESORT. (480) 986-4524. **2P $20-$45, XP $5. (no credit cards).** 702 S Meridian Rd, 85220. US 60, exit 193 (Signal Butte Rd), 0.4 mi n to Southern, 1 mi e, then 0.5 mi n.

🏔 🌊 ⊠

BENSON — BUTTERFIELD RV RESORT. (520) 586-4400. **Call for rates.** 251 S Ocotillo Rd, 85602. I-10, exit 304 (Ocotillo Rd), 0.6 mi s.

🏔 🌊 ⊠

BENSON — COCHISE TERRACE RV RESORT. (520) 586-0600. **2P $19-$30, XP $2.** 1030 S Barrel Cactus Ridge, 85602. I-10, exit 302, 1 mi s on SR 90, then just w.

🅢 🏔 🌊 ⊠

BENSON — PATO BLANCO LAKES RV RESORT. (520) 586-8966. **$16.** 635 E Pearl St, 85602. I-10, exit 306, just s, 0.7 mi w on Frontage Rd, then 0.4 mi n on County Rd.

🏔 🌊 ⊠

BENSON — SAN PEDRO RESORT COMMUNITY. (520) 586-9546. **2P $26, XP $2. (no credit cards).** 1110 S Hwy 80, Box 1, 85602. I-10, exit 304 (Ocotillo Ave), 0.5 mi s, 1 mi e on 4th St, then 1.3 mi se.

🏔 🌊 ⊠

CAMP VERDE — DISTANT DRUMS RV RESORT. (928) 554-8000. **2P $30-$40.** 583 W Middle Verde Rd, 86322. I-17, exit 289, just sw.

🏔 🌊 ⊠

CASA GRANDE — FIESTA GRANDE-RV RESORT. (520) 836-7222. **2P $32, XP $2.** 1511 E Florence Blvd, 85222. I-10, exit 194, 2 mi w.

🏔 🌊 ⊠

CASA GRANDE — PALM CREEK GOLF AND RV RESORT. (520) 421-7000. **2P $27-$42, XP $5.** 1110 N Henness Rd, 85222. I-10, exit 194, 1 mi w, then just n.

🏔 🌊 ⊠

ELOY — DESERT VALLEY RV RESORT. (520) 466-4500. **2P $28, XP $3.** 4555 W Tonto Rd, 85231. I-10, exit 203 (Toltec Rd), 0.5 mi n on Toltec Rd, then 0.5 mi w.

🏔 🌊 ⊠

FORT MCDOWELL — EAGLE VIEW RV RESORT AT FT MCDOWELL ⟨AAA⟩ (480) 836-5310. **4P $37-$42, XP $10.** 9605 N Ft McDowell Rd, 85264. Jct Shea Blvd, 2 mi ne on SR 89, 0.5 mi se.

🏔 🌊 ⊠

GOLD CANYON — CANYON VISTAS RV RESORT. (480) 288-8844. **2P $18-$36, XP $5.** 6601 E US Hwy 60, 85218. 1.2 mi w of Kings Ranch Rd; between MM 202 and 201.

🏔 🌊 ⊠

HUACHUCA CITY — TOMBSTONE TERRITORIES RV PARK ⟨AAA⟩ (520) 457-2584. **2P $30-$32, XP $1.** 2111 E Hwy 82, 85616. Jct SR 90, 7.7 mi e on SR 82; between mm 59 and 60.

🏔 🌊 ⊠

LAKE HAVASU CITY — HAVASU RV RESORT. (928) 764-2020. **6P $35, XP $5.** 1905 Victoria Farms Rd, 86404. From London Bridge, 5.3 mi n on SR 95, just e on Chenoweth Dr, then 0.4 mi n. Small pets allowed.

🏔 🌊 ⊠

MESA — GOOD LIFE RV RESORT ⟨AAA⟩ (480) 832-4990. **2P $35, XP $3.** 3403 E Main St, 85213. US 60, exit 184 (Val Vista Dr), 2 mi n, then just w. Small pets allowed.

🏔 🌊 ⊠

MESA — MESA SPIRIT RV RESORT ⟨AAA⟩ (480) 832-1770. **2P $18-$45, XP $4.** 3020 E Main St, 85213. US 60, exit 184 (Val Vista Dr), 2 mi n to Main St, then 0.8 mi w.

🏔 🌊 ⊠

MESA — SUN LIFE VACATION RESORT. (480) 981-9500. **2P $35, XP $3.** 5055 E University Dr, 85205. Just w of Higley Rd.

🏔 🌊 ⊠

MESA — VAL VISTA VILLAGE. (480) 832-2547. **2P $18-$55, XP $3.** 233 N Val Vista Dr, 85213. US 60, exit 184 (Val Vista Dr), 2.2 mi n.

🏔 🌊 ⊠

MESA — VALLE DEL ORO RV RESORT. (480) 984-1146. **2P $35.** 1452 S Ellsworth Rd, 85209. US 60, exit 191, just n. Small pets allowed.

🏔 🌊 ⊠

PICACHO — PICACHO PEAK RV RESORT ⟨AAA⟩ (520) 466-7841. **Call for rates.** 17065 E Peak Ln, 85241. I-10, exit 219, 0.7 mi s on frontage road. (PO Box 300).

🏔 🌊 ⊠

SHOW LOW — VOYAGER AT JUNIPER RIDGE ⟨AAA⟩ (928) 532-3456. **4P $21-$32, XP $2.** 1993 Juniper Ridge Resort, 85901. Jct US 60, 7.3 mi n on SR 77 to White Mountain Lake Rd, then 3 mi e.

🏔 🌊 ⊠

SUN CITY/SUN CITY WEST — PARADISE RV RESORT. (623) 977-0344. **Call for rates.** 10950 W Union Hills Dr, 85373. Loop 101, exit 15 (Union Hills Dr), 3.8 mi w. Small pets allowed.

🏔 🌊 ⊠

SURPRISE — SUNFLOWER RV RESORT. (623) 583-0100. **$40-$240.** 16501 N El Mirage Rd, 85374. Loop 101, exit 14 (Bell Rd), 5.2 mi w, then just s.

🏔 🌊 ⊠

TONOPAH — SADDLE MOUNTAIN RV PARK ⟨AAA⟩ (623) 386-3892. **$23.** 3607 N 411th Ave, 85354. I-10, exit 94, 0.6 mi s.

🏔 🌊 ⊠

TUCSON — BEAUDRY RV RESORT. (520) 239-1700. **$25-$37.** 5151 S Country Club, 85706. I-10, exit 264B (Palo Verde and Irvington), just n to Irvington, 0.5 mi w, then just s.

🏔 🌊 ⊠

TUCSON — VOYAGER RV RESORT ⟨AAA⟩ (520) 574-5000. **4P $27-$47, XP $2.** 8701 S Kolb Rd, 85706. I-10, exit 270, 0.7 mi s.

🏔 🌊 ⊠

YUMA — BONITA MESA RV RESORT. (928) 342-2999. **Call for rates. (no credit cards).** 9400 N Frontage Rd, 85365. I-8, exit 12 (Fortuna Rd), just n, then 1.6 mi w.

🏔 🌊 ⊠

YUMA — COCOPAH RV & GOLF RESORT. (928) 343-9300. **2P $28-$32, XP $2.** 6800 Strand Ave, 85364. I-8, exit Winterhaven/4th Ave eastbound, 0.5 mi s on 4th Ave, 2.4 mi w on 1st St, just s on Ave C, 1.4 mi w on Riverside, then 0.9 mi nw.

YUMA — HIDDEN SHORES RV VILLAGE. (928) 539-6700. **6P $60-$80.** 10300 Imperial Dam Rd, 85365. I-8, exit 12 (Fortuna Rd), 1.9 mi n, 10.4 mi n on US 95, then 6.5 mi w; Yuma Proving Ground Base.

YUMA — LAS QUINTAS OASIS RESORT. (928) 305-9005. **$29, XP $3.** 10442 E Frontage Rd, 85365. I-8, exit 12 (Fortuna Rd), just n, then 0.6 mi w; north side of interstate. Small pets allowed.

YUMA — SUN VISTA RV RESORT ⒶⒶⒶ (928) 726-8920. **2P $41, XP $3.** 7201 E 32nd St (Business 8), 85365. I-8, exit 7 (Araby Rd), just s, then 0.5 mi e. Small pets allowed.

YUMA — WESTWIND RV & GOLF RESORT. (928) 342-2992. **2P $28-$40, XP $3.** 9797 E 32nd St (S Frontage Rd), 85365. I-8, exit 12 (Fortuna Rd) on south side, 1 mi w. Small pets allowed.

California

BAKERSFIELD — BAKERSFIELD PALMS RV RESORT ⒶⒶⒶ (661) 366-6700. **2P $26-$28, XP $2.** 250 Fairfax Rd, 93307. SR 99, exit 24 (SR 58 E), 6 mi e, exit Fairfax Rd, then 0.5 mi n.

BIG BEAR LAKE — BIG BEAR SHORES RV RESORT & YACHT CLUB. (909) 866-4151. **Call for rates.** 40751 North Shore Ln, 92315. SR 18, 5 mi e of the dam on SR 38 (North Shore Dr), 1.2 mi se. (PO Box 1572).

BUELLTON — FLYING FLAGS RV PARK & CAMPGROUND ⒶⒶⒶ (805) 688-3716. **2P $21-$53, XP $3.** 180 Ave of the Flags, 93427. Just w of US 101, exit 140A (SR 246).

CASTAIC — VALENCIA TRAVEL VILLAGE ⒶⒶⒶ (661) 257-3333. **$35-$70, XP $2-$4.** 27946 Henry Mayo Rd, 91384. I-5, exit SR 126, 1.3 mi w.

CATHEDRAL CITY — OUTDOOR RESORTS/PALM SPRINGS. (760) 324-4005. **6P $45-$77.** 69-411 Ramon Rd, 92234. I-10, exit 126 (Date Palm Dr), 2.2 mi s, then 0.5 mi e.

CHULA VISTA — CHULA VISTA RV RESORT. (619) 422-0111. **4P $43-$65, XP $3.** 460 Sandpiper Way, 91910. I-5, exit 7B (J St/Marina Pkwy), 4 mi w, then 0.5 mi n. Small pets allowed.

CHULA VISTA — SAN DIEGO METRO KOA. (619) 427-3601. **2P $40-$95, XP $4.** 111 N 2nd Ave, 91910. I-5, exit 8B (E St), 1 mi e to 2nd Ave, then 1 mi n; I-805, exit E St, 1 mi w, then just n.

COLOMA — COLOMA RESORT. (530) 621-2267. **2P $36-$38, XP $7-$10.** 6921 Mt Murphy Rd, 95613. E off SR 49 on Mt. Murphy Rd; on South Fork of American River. (PO Box 516).

DEL LOMA — DEL LOMA RV PARK & CAMPGROUND. (530) 623-2834. **$24-$85, XP $2-$5.** Rt 1, Box 54, 96010. US 299, southwest Del Loma.

DESERT HOT SPRINGS — SKY VALLEY RESORT. (760) 329-2909. **2P $38-$42, XP $5.** 74-711 Dillon Rd, 92241. I-10, exit Palm Dr, 3.3 mi n, then 8.5 mi e.

EL CENTRO — DESERT TRAILS RV PARK. (760) 352-7275. **2P $27-$34.** 225 Wake Ave, 92243. I-8, exit 115 (4th St/SR 86), just s, then just e. Small pets allowed.

FORTUNA — RIVERWALK RV PARK & CAMPGROUND. (707) 725-3359. **2P $25-$65, XP $5.** 2189 Riverwalk Dr, 95540. W of US 101, exit Kenmar Rd.

GARBERVILLE — BENBOW VALLEY RV RESORT & GOLF COURSE ⒶⒶⒶ (707) 923-2777. **2P $30-$47, XP $4.** 7000 Benbow Dr, 95542. US 101, exit Benbow Dr, 2 mi s.

GROVELAND — YOSEMITE LAKES CAMPGROUND AND RESORT. (209) 962-0121. **Call for rates.** 31191 Hardin Flat Rd, 95321. 18 mi e on SR 120, 5 mi w of Yosemite National Park's SR 120 Gate/Entrance.

HEMET — GOLDEN VILLAGE PALMS RV RESORT ⒶⒶⒶ (951) 925-2518. **2P $37-$55, XP $10.** 3600 W Florida Ave, 92545. SR 79 N (San Jacinto St), 3 mi w. Small pets allowed.

INDIO — INDIAN WELLS RV PARK. (760) 347-0895. **2P $37-$41.** 47-340 Jefferson St, 92201. I-10, exit 139 (Jefferson St/Indio Blvd), 3 mi s.

JULIAN — PINEZANITA TRAILER RANCH & CAMPGROUND. (760) 765-0429. **2P $24, XP $2.** 4446 SR 79, 92036. On SR 79, 3.6 mi s of SR 78. (PO Box 2380).

LODI — FLAG CITY RV RESORT. (209) 339-8300. **6P $38, XP $4.** 6120 W Banner St, 95242. I-5, exit SR 12 E, s on Star St, then just e.

NEWPORT BEACH — NEWPORT DUNES WATERFRONT RV RESORT. (949) 729-3863. **6P $55-$300.** 1131 Back Bay Dr, 92660. SR 73, exit 15 (Jamboree Rd) southbound, 3 mi s, then just n on SR 1; exit 13 (Bison Ave) northbound, just w to MacArthur Blvd, 2.5 mi s to SR 1, then 1.5 mi n.

NILAND — FOUNTAIN OF YOUTH SPA. (760) 354-1340. **2P $26-$38, XP $2.** 10249 Coachella Canal Rd, 92257. 14 mi nw on SR 111, then 2.3 mi ne on Hot Mineral Spa Rd.

ORANGE — ORANGELAND RECREATION VEHICLE PARK ⒶⒶⒶ (714) 633-0414. **8P $55-$70, XP $2.** 1600 W Struck Ave, 92867. SR 57, exit 2 (Katella Ave), 0.5 mi e, then just s.

PASO ROBLES — WINE COUNTRY RV RESORT. (805) 238-4560. **2P $39-$58, XP $3.** 2500 Airport Rd, 93446. US 101, exit 231B (SR 46/Fresno/Bakersfield), 2 mi e, then just n. (PO Box 2552, 93447).

PETALUMA — SAN FRANCISCO NORTH/PETALUMA KOA ⒶⒶⒶ (707) 763-1492. **2P $35-$66, XP $5-$7.** 20 Rainsville Rd, 94952. US 101, exit Penngrove, just w to Stony Point Rd, then 0.5 mi n.

PISMO BEACH — PACIFIC DUNES RANCH RV PARK. (805) 489-7787. **6P $28-$50, XP $5.** 1205 Silver Spur Pl, 93445. In Oceano; SR 1, exit 22nd St, 0.3 mi s, then 0.4 mi w.

PISMO BEACH — PISMO COAST VILLAGE RV RESORT. (805) 773-1811. **6P $34-$47, XP $2.** 165 S Dolliver St, 93449. 0.5 mi s on SR 1.

PLYMOUTH — FAR HORIZONS 49'ER VILLAGE ⒶⒶⒶ (209) 245-6981. **4P $37-$62, XP $5.** 18265 Hwy 49, 95669. On SR 49, 0.3 mi s.

SAN DIEGO — CAMPLAND ON THE BAY. (858) 581-4260. **Call for rates.** 2211 Pacific Beach Dr, 92109. I-5, exit 23A (Grand Ave) northbound, 1 mi w to Olney, then 0.3 mi s; exit 23 (Balboa/Garnet) southbound, s on Mission Bay Dr to Grand Ave, then 1 mi w to Olney.

SAN DIMAS — EAST SHORE RV PARK ▲▲▲ (909) 599-8355. **2P $37-$44, XP $2.** 1440 Camper View Rd, 91773. I-10, exit 44 (Fairplex Dr), 0.6 mi n, 0.6 mi w on Via Verde, then 0.6 mi n; in Frank G Bonelli Regional Park.

SAN JUAN BAUTISTA — BETABEL RV RESORT ▲▲▲ (831) 623-2202. **2P $38, XP $3.** 9664 Betabel Rd, 95045. US 101, exit Betabel Rd, just w. Small pets allowed.

SANTA BARBARA — EL CAPITAN CANYON. (805) 685-3887. **$115-$345.** 11560 Calle Real, 93117. 20 mi nw on north side of US 101 at El Capitan State Beach.

SANTA BARBARA — OCEAN MESA AT EL CAPITAN. (805) 685-3887. **6P $35-$85.** 11560 Calle Real, 93117. 20 mi nw on northside of US 101; at El Capitan State Beach.

SHAVER LAKE — CAMP EDISON ▲▲▲ (559) 841-3134. **2P $22-$45, XP $3.** 42696 Tollhouse Rd, 93664. Just ne; lakeside. (PO Box 600).

TEMECULA — PECHANGA RV RESORT ▲▲▲ (951) 770-2658. **$42.** 45000 Pechanga Pkwy, 92592. I-15, exit 58 (SR 79 S), 1 mi e, then 2 mi s.

TEMECULA — VAIL LAKE RESORT. (951) 303-0173. **6P $35-$75, XP $5-$10.** 38000 Hwy 79 S, 92592. I-15, exit 58 (SR 79 S), 9 mi se.

TRINIDAD — EMERALD FOREST OF TRINIDAD ▲▲▲ (707) 677-3554. **2P $24-$39, XP $3.** 753 Patrick's Point Dr, 95570. US 101, exit Patrick's Point Dr W. (PO Box 870).

WEAVERVILLE — TRINITY LAKE RESORTS AT PINEWOOD COVE RV PARK & CAMPGROUND. (530) 286-2201. **2P $20-$38, XP $4-$5.** 45110 State Hwy 3, 96091. 14 mi ne of town.

WILLITS — WILLITS-UKIAH KOA. (707) 459-6179. **2P $25-$55, XP $3-$4.** 1600 Hwy 20, 95490. 1.5 mi w on SR 20, from jct US 101. (PO Box 946).

WINTERHAVEN — RIVER'S EDGE RV RESORT. (760) 572-5105. **Call for rates.** 2299 Winterhaven Dr, 92283. I-8, exit 170 (Winterhaven Dr), 0.5 mi e. Small pets allowed.

Colorado

BRECKENRIDGE — TIGER RUN RESORT. (970) 453-9690. **$34-$59.** 85 Tiger Run Rd, 80424. I-70, exit 203, 6 mi s on SR 9, then just e on Revette Dr.

FORT COLLINS — FORT COLLINS KOA/ LAKESIDE. (970) 484-9880. **2P $34-$125, XP $3-$8.** 1910 N Taft Hill Rd, 80524. I-25, exit 269B, 6 mi w to Taft Hill, then 2.2 mi n.

GOLDEN — DAKOTA RIDGE RV PARK. (303) 279-1625. **2P $39, XP $4.** 17800 W Colfax Ave, 80401. I-70, exit 262 (W Colfax Ave), 1.8 mi w on US 40.

GRAND LAKE — WINDING RIVER RESORT INC ▲▲▲ (970) 627-3215. **2P $28-$35, XP $4-$5.** 1447 CR 491, 80447. 1.5 mi ne on US 31 to CR 491, then 1.5 mi w. (PO Box 629).

LOVELAND — JOHNSON'S CORNER RV RETREAT. (970) 669-8400. **Call for rates.** 3618 SE Frontage Rd, 80537. I-25, exit 254, 0.3 mi se; adjacent to Great Colorado Marketplace. Small pets allowed.

Florida

ARCADIA — TOBY'S RV RESORT. (863) 494-1744. **2P $27-$42, XP $5.** 3550 NE Hwy 70, 34266. On SR 70, 2.7 mi e.

BRADENTON — ENCORE RV RESORT-SARASOTA NORTH. (941) 745-2600. **6P $27-$65.** 800 Kay Rd NE, 34212. I-75, exit 220 southbound; exit 220B northbound, 0.6 mi w on SR 64, then 0.8 mi n on Cypress Creek Blvd (merges to Kay Rd NE).

BRADENTON — HORSESHOE COVE RV RESORT. (941) 758-5335. **2P $30-$45, XP $3.** 5100 60th St E, 34203. I-75, exit 217 southbound; exit 217B northbound, 1.7 mi w on SR 70, then just n on Caruso Rd.

BUSHNELL — BLUEBERRY HILL RV RESORT. (352) 793-4112. **2P $30-$35.** 6233 CR 609, 33513. I-75, exit 314, just e on SR 48, then just s. Small pets allowed.

CRYSTAL RIVER — ROCK CRUSHER CANYON RV PARK. (352) 795-3870. **Call for rates.** 275 S Rock Crusher Rd, 34429. 1.5 mi s of SR 44.

DAVENPORT — DEER CREEK RV RESORT. (863) 424-2839. **2P $45-$65, XP $10.** 42749 Hwy 27, 33837. I-4, exit 55, 1 mi se.

DAVENPORT — FORT SUMMIT KOA ▲▲▲ (863) 424-1880. **2P $39-$66, XP $4.** 2525 Frontage Rd, 33837. Jct US 27 and I-4, exit 55, on frontage road; behind Best Western.

DEBARY — HIGH BANKS MARINA & CAMP RESORT. (386) 668-4491. **2P $45, XP $5.** 488 W Highbanks Rd, 32713. 2.7 mi w of US 17-92.

DESTIN — DESTIN RV BEACH RESORT. (850) 837-3529. **Call for rates.** 362 Miramar Beach Dr, 32550. 4.1 mi e of SR 293 (Mid-Bay Bridge), just s.

FORT MYERS BEACH — GULF WATERS RV RESORT ▲▲▲ (239) 437-5888. **Call for rates.** 11301 Summerlin Square Rd, 33931. 1.6 mi sw of jct US 41 on Gladiolus Dr (CR 865), 3.8 mi w on Summerlin Rd (CR 869), just s on Pine Ridge Rd, then just w.

FORT MYERS BEACH — INDIAN CREEK PARK RV RESORT & MANUFACTURED HOME COMMUNITY ▲▲▲ (239) 466-6060. **2P $32-$47, XP $4.** 17340 San Carlos Blvd, 33931. 2.4 mi ne of jct Matanzas Pass Bridge.

FORT MYERS — SIESTA BAY RV RESORT ▲▲▲ (239) 466-8988. **$32-$48, XP $4.** 19333 Summerlin Rd, 33908. 1.6 mi sw of jct US 41 on Gladiolus Dr (CR 865), 4.8 mi s on Summerlin Rd (CR 869).

JACKSONVILLE — FLAMINGO LAKE RV RESORT ▲▲▲ (904) 766-0672. **2P $45-$48, XP $3-$4.** 3640 Newcomb Rd, 32218. I-295, exit 32, just nw on SR 115.

JENNINGS — JENNINGS OUTDOOR RESORT CAMPGROUND. (386) 938-3321. **2P $26-$29, XP $2.** 2039 Hamilton Ave, 32053. I-75, exit 467, just w on SR 143.

JENSEN BEACH — NETTLES ISLAND. (772) 229-1300. **$36-$64.** 9803 S Ocean Dr, 34957. On SR A1A, 2.3 mi n of jct SR 732 (Jensen Beach Cswy); on S Hutchinson Island.

KISSIMMEE — OUTDOOR RESORTS AT ORLANDO. (863) 424-1259. **$30-$40.** On US 192, 1 mi e of jct US 27; jct I-4, exit 64B, 6.3 mi w. (9000 W US 192, CLERMONT, 34711). Small pets allowed.

KISSIMMEE — TROPICAL PALMS FUN RESORT. (407) 396-4595. **Call for rates.** 2650 Holiday Tr, 34746. I-4, exit 64A, 1.5 mi e on US 192, then 0.8 mi s.

LA BELLE — WHISPER CREEK RV RESORT. (863) 675-6888. **2P $35. (no credit cards).** 3745 N SR 29 SW, 33935. On SR 29, 1.8 mi n of jct SR 80.

LAKE BUENA VISTA — DISNEY'S FORT WILDERNESS RESORT & CAMPGROUND (407) 824-2727. **2P $41-$96, XP $2.** 4510 N Fort Wilderness Tr, 32830-1000. In Walt Disney World. (PO Box 10000).

LAKELAND — LAKELAND CAREFREE RV RESORT. (863) 687-6146. **Call for rates.** 900 Old Combee Rd, 33805. I-4, exit 33 eastbound, 1 mi ne on SR 33, then just w; exit 38 westbound, 5 mi sw on SR 33, then just nw.

LAKELAND — SANLAN RANCH CAMPGROUND (863) 665-1726. **2P $18-$40, XP $3.** 3929 US 98 S, 33813. I-4, exit 32, 8.7 mi s on US 98; just s of SR 570.

LEESBURG — HOLIDAY TRAVEL RESORT (352) 787-5151. **4P $33, XP $5.** 28229 CR 33, 34748. 3.5 mi s via US 27, 0.5 mi w.

MELBOURNE BEACH — OUTDOOR RESORTS MELBOURNE BEACH LUXURY RV RESORT. (321) 724-2600. **4P $35-$70, XP $3.** 214 Horizon Ln, 32951. 2.5 mi s.

OKEECHOBEE — OKEECHOBEE KOA RESORT & GOLF COURSE. (863) 763-0231. **2P $34-$75, XP $4-$6.** 4276 Hwy US 441 S, 34974. On US 98 and 441, 3 mi s of jct SR 70; 0.3 mi n of Lake Okeechobee and jct SR 78.

OLD TOWN — YELLOW JACKET CAMPGROUND RESORT. (352) 542-8365. **2P $27-$37, XP $6-$10.** 55 SE 503 Ave, 32680. 10.7 mi s on SR 349, then 1.2 mi on dirt road.

PANAMA CITY BEACH — EMERALD COAST RV BEACH RESORT (850) 235-0924. **2P $48-$80, XP $3.** 1957 Allison Ave, 32407. US 98/98A and Allison Ave, 1.5 mi w of Hathaway Bridge.

PORT CHARLOTTE — RIVERSIDE RV RESORT & CAMP-GROUND (863) 993-2111. **4P $30-$47, XP $2-$3.** 9770 SW CR 769, 34269. I-75, exit 170, 4.5 mi ne on CR 769 (Kings Hwy).

RIVER RANCH — RIVER RANCH RV RESORT (863) 692-1116. **Call for rates.** 3400 River Ranch Blvd, 33867. 3.5 mi s of SR 60; 25 mi e of US 27; 23 mi w of Florida Tpke and US 441; just w of the Kissimmee River. (30529 River Ranch Blvd).

ROCKLEDGE — SPACE COAST RV RESORT. (321) 636-2873. **2P $35-$40, XP $3.** 820 Barnes Blvd, 32955. I-95, exit 195 (Fiske Blvd), 0.3 mi se, 2 mi w of US 1 on SR 502. Small pets allowed.

SARASOTA — SUN-N-FUN RV RESORT (941) 371-2505. **Call for rates.** 7125 Fruitville Rd, 34240. I-75, exit 210, 1.2 mi e on SR 780.

SEBASTIAN — ENCORE RV PARK-VERO BEACH. (772) 589-7828. **6P $28-$43, XP $5.** I-95, exit 156, just e on CR 512. (9455 108th Ave, VERO BEACH, 32967-3154).

SEBRING — BUTTONWOOD BAY RV RESORT (863) 655-1122. **2P $25-$36, XP $4.** 10001 US 27 S, 33876. 1.5 mi s of SR 98. Small pets allowed.

SILVER SPRINGS — THE SPRINGS RV RESORT. (352) 236-5250. **Call for rates.** 2950 NE 52nd Ct, 34488. On SR 40, 0.5 mi w of Silver Springs attraction, 0.5 mi n.

ST. PETERSBURG — ST. PETERSBURG-MADEIRA BEACH RESORT KOA. (727) 392-2233. **2P $37-$85, XP $4-$6.** 5400 95th St N, 33708. Jct 38th Ave N, 1.4 mi n on Tyrone/Bay Pines Blvd (Alternate Rt US 19), 0.5 mi e.

TITUSVILLE — THE GREAT OUTDOORS RV & GOLF RESORT. (321) 269-5004. **2P $35-$55, XP $3.** 125 Plantation Dr, 32780. I-95, exit 215, 0.5 mi w on SR 50, 1.8 mi s on paved entrance road. Small pets allowed.

UMATILLA — OLDE MILL STREAM RV RESORT (352) 669-3141. **2P $28-$31, XP $3.** 1000 N Central Ave, 32784. 0.8 mi n on SR 19. Small pets allowed.

Georgia

PINE MOUNTAIN — PINE MOUNTAIN CAMPGROUND. (706) 663-4329. **2P $20-$37, XP $2.** 8804 Hamilton Rd, 31822. I-185, exit 42, 8 mi s on US 27.

Idaho

CASCADE — ARROWHEAD R.V. PARK ON THE RIVER (208) 382-4534. **2P $25-$28, XP $1.** 955 S Hwy 55, 83611. South end of town. (PO Box 337).

COEUR D'ALENE — BLACKWELL ISLAND RV RESORT. (208) 665-1300. **2P $35-$46, XP $2.** 800 S Marina Dr, 83814. I-90, exit 12, 1.5 mi s on US 95.

KAMIAH — LEWIS-CLARK RESORT RV PARK. (208) 935-2556. **$22-$25.** 1.5 mi e on US 12. (Rt 1, Box 17X, 83536).

WHITE BIRD — SWIFTWATER RV PARK & STORE. (208) 839-2700. **2P $20-$25, XP $3.** HC 01, Box 24, 83554. Just n of Milepost 222, exit Hammer Creek Recreational area, 0.8 mi nw. (PO Box 150).

Illinois

LEE CENTER — O'CONNELL'S YOGI BEAR JELLYSTONE PARK (815) 857-3860. **2P $30-$60, XP $10-$15.** 970 Greenwing Rd, 61310. I-39, exit 87 (US 30), 12.8 mi w to CR 1955 E, then 3.3 mi se, follow signs. (PO Box 200, AMBOY).

Indiana

FREMONT — YOGI BEAR'S JELLYSTONE PARK CAMP RESORT ⒶⒶⒶ (260) 833-1114. **2P $29-$57, XP $5-$9.** 140 Ln, 201 Barton Lake, 46737-9652. I-69, exit 157 southbound; exit 154 northbound, 3 mi w on SR 120, then 0.5 mi n on CR 300 W; Toll Rd, exit 144 to SR 120.

GRANGER — SOUTH BEND EAST KOA. (574) 277-1335. **2P $18-$45, XP $3-$4.** 50707 Princess Way, 46530. I-80/90, exit 83, 2.3 mi ne on SR 23.

MONTICELLO — INDIANA BEACH CAMP RESORT. (574) 583-8306. **Call for rates.** 5224 E Indiana Beach Rd, 47960. 0.5 mi w on US 24, 3.3 mi n on W Shafer Dr (6th St).

PIERCETON — YOGI BEAR'S JELLYSTONE PARK CAMP-RESORT. (574) 594-2124. **5P $32-$55, XP $5.** 1916 N 850 E, 46562. US 30, 4.3 mi n on SR 13, 1.3 mi e on CR 200.

SANTA CLAUS — LAKE RUDOLPH CAMPGROUND & RV RESORT. (812) 937-4458. **8P $20-$45.** 78 N Holiday Blvd, 47579. I-64, exit 63, 7.9 mi s on SR 162. (PO Box 98).

Louisiana

CARENCRO — BAYOU WILDERNESS RV RESORT. (337) 896-0598. **4P $29-$32, XP $4.** 201 St Clair Rd, 70520. I-49, exit 2, 2.5 mi e on SR 98, then 1 mi n on Wilderness Trail.

HAMMOND — NEW ORLEANS-HAMMOND KOA KAMP-GROUND. (985) 542-8094. **2P $26-$30, XP $2-$3.** 14154 Club Deluxe Rd, 70403. I-12 to I-55 S, exit 28, 1 blk n, then 0.7 mi w.

KINDER — COUSHATTA CASINO RV RESORT. (337) 738-1200. **$17-$22.** 777 Pow Wow Pkwy, 70648. N of jct US 190 and 165, 4.5 mi on US 165. (PO Box 1240).

ROBERT — YOGI BEAR'S JELLYSTONE PARK CAMP-RESORT. (985) 345-3011. **Call for rates.** 46049 SR 445 N, 70455. I-12, exit 47, 3 mi n. (PO Box 519).

SCOTT — KOA KAMPGROUND OF LAFAYETTE. (337) 235-2739. **4P $34-$45, XP $5.** 537 Apollo Rd, 70583. I-10, exit 97, 0.5 mi s. Small pets allowed.

VIDALIA — RIVER VIEW RV PARK ⒶⒶⒶ (318) 336-1400. **2P $29-$35, XP $3.** 100 River View Pkwy, 71373. Jct US 65/84, 0.8 mi s on SR 131.

Maine

CASCO — POINT SEBAGO RESORT. (207) 655-3821. **4P $25-$79, XP $5.** 261 Point Sebago Rd, 04015. Jct SR 121, 3.7 mi n on US 302, then 1 mi w, follow signs.

DAMARISCOTTA — LAKE PEMAQUID CAMPGROUND ⒶⒶⒶ (207) 563-5202. **4P $24-$42, XP $10.** 100 Twin Cove Ln, 04543. 0.8 mi n on US 1 business route, 2 mi e on Biscay Rd, then 0.3 mi n on Egypt Rd. (PO Box 967).

NORTH WATERFORD — PAPOOSE POND RESORT & CAMP-GROUND. (207) 583-4470. **6P $22-$62, XP $10.** 700 Norway Rd, 04088. 1.9 mi w on SR 118 from jct SR 37; from Norway, 10 mi w on SR 118.

OLD ORCHARD BEACH — POWDER HORN FAMILY CAMP-ING RESORT. (207) 934-4733. **2P $35-$59, XP $4-$8.** 48 Cascade Rd, 04064. 1 mi w on SR 98; jct US 1, 1.8 mi e on SR 98. (PO Box 366).

OLD ORCHARD BEACH — WILD ACRES FAMILY CAMPING RESORT. (207) 934-2535. **2P $34-$65, XP $5-$10.** 179 Saco Ave, 04064. I-95 (Maine Tpke), exit 36, 3 mi e on I-195 and SR 5.

SCARBOROUGH — BAYLEY'S CAMPING RESORT ⒶⒶⒶ (207) 883-6043. **2P $24-$65, XP $5-$8.** 275 Pine Point Rd, 04074. Jct US 1, 2 mi e via SR 9 (Pine Point Rd), watch for sign.

WELLS — WELLS BEACH RESORT CAMPGROUND ⒶⒶⒶ (207) 646-7570. **2P $43-$67, XP $7.** 1000 Post Rd (US 1), 04090-4109. Jct SR 109 and 9, 1.3 mi s on US 1.

Maryland

BERLIN — FRONTIER TOWN CAMPGROUND. (410) 641-0880. **2P $25-$76, XP $5-$10.** 8428 Stephen Decatur Hwy, 21811. Jct SR 50, 4 mi s on SR 611. (PO Box 691, OCEAN CITY, 21843).

COLLEGE PARK — CHERRY HILL PARK ⒶⒶⒶ (301) 937-7116. **2P $53-$62, XP $5.** 9800 Cherry Hill Rd, 20740. I-95, exit 29B, 1 mi w on SR 212 (Powder Mill Rd), then 1 mi s; I-495, exit 25, just s to Cherry Hill Rd, then 1 mi nw.

FLINTSTONE — HIDDEN SPRINGS CAMPGROUND. (814) 767-9676, off season (301) 478-2282. **4P $25-$29, XP $2.** I-68, exit 50 to Rocky Gap State Park, 3.5 mi n on Pleasant Valley Rd. (PO Box 190, 21530).

FREELAND — MORRIS MEADOWS RECREATION FARM ⒶⒶⒶ (410) 329-6636. **2P $23-$52, XP $5-$10.** 1523 Freeland Rd, 21053. I-83, exit 36 (SR 439), w to jct SR 45, 1 mi n, then 3 mi w, follow signs.

WILLIAMSPORT — YOGI BEAR'S JELLYSTONE PARK CAMP RESORT HAGERSTOWN. (301) 223-7117. **6P $22-$72, XP $7.** 16519 Lappans Rd, 21795. I-81, exit 1, 1.2 mi e on SR 68.

Massachusetts

BRIMFIELD — QUINEBAUG COVE CAMPGROUND. (413) 245-9525. **2P $25-$35, XP $3-$6.** 49 E Brimfield-Holland Rd, 01010. I-84, exit 3B, 3.8 mi w on US 20, then 0.3 mi s.

FOXBORO — NORMANDY FARMS CAMPGROUND. (508) 543-7600. **2P $20-$66, XP $5-$10.** 72 West St, 02035. I-495, exit 14A, 1 mi n on US 1, then 1.3 mi e on Thurston and West sts.

OAKHAM — PINE ACRES FAMILY CAMPING RESORT. (508) 882-9509. **2P $22-$55, XP $7-$15.** 203 Bechan Rd, 01068. Jct SR 122, 2 mi sw on SR 148, then just s via Spencer Rd.

SAVOY — SHADY PINES CAMPGROUND. (413) 743-2694. **2P $30-$32, XP $8-$10.** 547 Loop Rd, 01256. On SR 8A and 116, 3.1 mi se.

Michigan

BAY VIEW — PETOSKEY KOA RV & CABIN RESORT. (231) 347-0005. **2P $25-$69, XP $3.** 1800 N US 31, 49770. US 31, 1 mi n of SR 119.

DECATUR — TIMBER TRAILS RV PARK. (269) 423-7311. **$28, XP $10.** 84981 47 1/2 St, 49045. 1.9 mi sw on SR 51, 0.8 mi n.

PORT HURON — PORT HURON KOA KAMPGROUND. (810) 987-4070. **2P $26-$60, XP $3-$4.** 5111 Lapeer Rd, 48074. I-94, exit 262, 8 mi n on Wadhams Rd, then 0.3 mi e; I-69, exit 196, 0.4 mi n on Wadhams Rd, then 0.3 mi e.

Minnesota

CALEDONIA — DUNROMIN' PARK. (507) 724-2514. **$20-$40, XP $2-$4.** 12757 Dunromin Dr, 55921. 2.8 mi s on SR 76 S from jct SR 44, 0.5 mi e.

CASS LAKE — STONY POINT RESORT, TRAILER PARK CAMP-GROUNDS (218) 335-6311. **2P $20-$30, XP $2.** 5510 US 2 NW, 56633. On US 2, 2 mi e of jct SR 371. (PO Box 518).

HINCKLEY — GRAND CASINO HINCKLEY RV RESORT (320) 384-4886. **$13-$23.** 1326 Fire Monument Rd, 55037. I-35, exit 183, 1 mi e on SR 48.

PARK RAPIDS — BREEZE CAMPING & RV RESORT ON EAGLE LAKE. (218) 732-5888. **2P $36-$38, XP $3.** 25824 CR 89, 56470. 9 mi n on US 71 from jct SR 34.

PRIOR LAKE — DAKOTAH MEADOWS RV PARK AND CAMP-GROUND (952) 445-8000. **Call for rates.** 2341 Park Pl, 55372. Just w of CR 83.

RICHMOND — EL RANCHO MANANA CAMPGROUND & RIDING STABLE (320) 597-2740. **Call for rates.** 27302 Ranch Rd, 56368. 4 mi n on CR 9 from jct SR 23 and 24, 2 mi ne on Manana and Ranch rds; 9 mi s of jct I-94, exit 153, via CR 9.

WALKER — SHORES OF LEECH LAKE CAMPGROUND & MARINA. (218) 547-1819. **2P $41, XP $5.** 6166 Morriss Point Rd, 56484. 2.8 mi nw on SR 371 and 200 from jct SR 34, 0.5 mi e, follow signs.

Mississippi

MERIDIAN — MERIDIAN EAST/TOOMSUBA KOA. (601) 632-1684. **2P $22-$34, XP $2-$3.** 3953 KOA Campground Rd, 39364. I-20/59, exit 165, 1.5 mi s, follow signs.

OCEAN SPRINGS — CAMP JOURNEY'S END. (228) 875-2100. **2P $28-$38, XP $5.** 7501 Hwy 57, 39565. I-10, exit 57, 0.5 mi n.

PICAYUNE — SUN ROAMERS RV RESORT (601) 798-5818. **2P $26-$31, XP $3.** 41 Mississippi Pines Blvd, 39466. I-59, exit 4, 0.8 mi e on SR 43 S, then 0.5 mi s on Stafford Rd.

Missouri

BRANSON — THE WILDERNESS AT SILVER DOLLAR CITY LOG CABINS AND RV'S. (417) 338-8189. **2P $30-$35, XP $2.** 5125 SR 265, 65616. 0.5 mi s of jct SR 76.

Montana

MISSOULA — JELLYSTONE RV RESORT. (406) 543-9400. **2P $27-$33, XP $2-$4.** 9900 Jellystone Ave, 59808. I-90, exit 96 (west side entry), 0.9 mi n.

POLSON — POLSON/FLATHEAD LAKE KOA. (406) 883-2151. **2P $28-$55, XP $3-$5.** 200 Irvine Flats Rd, 59860. 1 mi n on US 93, 0.3 mi w.

WEST GLACIER — WEST GLACIER KOA. (406) 387-5341. **2P $30-$47, XP $4-$5.** 355 Halfmoon Flats Rd, 59936. 2.5 mi w on US 2, 1 mi s. (PO Box 215).

Nebraska

NORTH PLATTE — HOLIDAY RV PARK & CAMPGROUND (308) 534-2265. **2P $20-$32, XP $2.** 601 Halligan Dr, 69101. I-80, exit 177, just n on US 83, immediate right turn on frontage road (Halligan Dr), then 0.5 mi e.

Nevada

BOULDER CITY — BOULDER OAKS RV RESORT. (702) 294-4425. **4P $35, XP $5.** 1010 Industrial Rd, 89005. Just w of US 93.

CARSON CITY — COMSTOCK COUNTRY RV RESORT (775) 882-2445. **$28-$54, XP $3.** 5400 S Carson St, 89701. 3.3 mi s and w off US 395, 0.3 mi s of jct US 50 W.

LAS VEGAS — OASIS LAS VEGAS RV RESORT. (702) 260-2020. **4P $35-$59, XP $2.** 2711 W Windmill Ln, 89123. I-15, exit 33 (Blue Diamond Rd), 0.5 mi e to Las Vegas Blvd, then 0.5 mi s. Small pets allowed.

MESQUITE — DESERT SKIES RESORT. (928) 347-6000. **Call for rates.** 350 E Hwy 91, 89024. I-15, exit 122, 1.5 mi ne via Hillside Dr. (PO Box 3780).

MINDEN — SILVER CITY RV RESORT (775) 267-3359. **2P $35, XP $4.** 3165 US 395, 89423. 6 mi s of Carson City; 3 mi s of jct US 50 W.

PAHRUMP — SEIBT DESERT RETREAT LUXURY MOTOR-COACH RESORT (775) 751-1174. **4P $30-$80, XP $10.** 301 W Leslie St, 89060. 10 mi n of SR 160 and 372, jct SR 160.

PAHRUMP — TERRIBLE'S LAKESIDE CASINO & RV RESORT (775) 751-7770. **6P $24-$36, XP $2.** 5870 S Homestead Rd, 89048. SR 160, 3.5 mi s.

RENO — KOA AT THE RENO HILTON. (775) 789-2147. **Call for rates.** 2500 E 2nd St, 89595. US 395, exit Mill St, just e.

SPARKS — RIVERS EDGE RV PARK (775) 358-8533. **2P $32-$41, XP $2.** 1405 S Rock Blvd, 89431. I-80, exit Rock Blvd S; US 395, exit SR 66 (Mill St).

VERDI — GOLD RANCH CASINO & RV RESORT. (775) 345-8880. **Call for rates.** 320 Gold Ranch Rd, 89439. I-80, exit 2. (PO Box 160).

ZEPHYR COVE — ZEPHYR COVE RESORT CAMPGROUND (775) 589-4907. **Call for rates.** 760 Hwy 50, 89448. US 50, 4 mi n of state line. (PO Box 830).

New Hampshire

BARRINGTON — AYERS LAKE FARM CAMPGROUND ⓐⓐⓐ (603) 335-1110, off season (603) 332-5940. **4P $32-$42, XP $3-$7. (no credit cards).** 557 US 202, 03825. Spaulding Tpke, exit 13, 4.5 mi w.

⊠

BARRINGTON — BARRINGTON SHORES CAMPGROUND ⓐⓐⓐ (603) 664-9333. **5P $35-$45, XP $3-$12.** 70 Hall Rd, 03825. Jct SR 125 and US 4, 2.5 mi w on US 4, then 3 mi n.

⊠

CHICHESTER — HILLCREST CAMPGROUND. (603) 798-5124. **2P $28-$33, XP $5-$12.** 78 Dover Rd, 03234. I-93, exit 15, 8 mi e on SR 4; jct SR 28 and 4, 2 mi w on SR 4.

🛥 ⊠

HAMPTON FALLS — WAKEDA CAMPGROUND LLC ⓐⓐⓐ (603) 772-5274. **5P $30-$42, XP $5.** 294 Exeter Rd (SR 88), 03844. SR 88, 3.8 mi w of jct US 1.

⊠

LACONIA — PAUGUS BAY CAMPGROUND. (603) 366-4757. **Call for rates. (no credit cards).** 96 Hilliard Rd, 03246. Jct US 3 and SR 11B, 0.5 mi n on US 3, then w. Small pets allowed.

⊠

MEREDITH — CLEARWATER CAMPGROUND ⓐⓐⓐ (603) 279-7761. **2P $20-$42, XP $1-$10.** 26 Campground Rd (SR 104), 03253. I-93, exit 23, 3 mi e.

⊠

MILTON — MI-TE-JO LAKESIDE FAMILY CAMPGROUND ⓐⓐⓐ (603) 652-9022. **2P $35-$43, XP $5-$8. (no credit cards).** 111 Mi-Te Jo Rd, 03851. SR 16, exit 17 northbound, 0.8 mi e on SR 75, 3.3 mi n on SR 125, then 1 mi e on Townhouse Rd; exit southbound, 3.3 mi on SR 125, 1 mi e on Townhouse Rd. (PO Box 830).

⊠

NEW HAMPTON — TWIN TAMARACK FAMILY CAMPING & RV RESORT ⓐⓐⓐ (603) 279-4387. **2P $32-$40, XP $1-$8.** 41 Twin Tamarack Rd, 03256. I-93, exit 23, 2.5 mi e on SR 104.

🛥 ⊠

SOUTH WEARE — COLD SPRINGS CAMP RESORT. (603) 529-2528. **2P $44-$48, XP $3-$7.** 62 Barnard Hill Rd, 03281. Jct SR 77/149, 1.5 mi se, 0.3 mi n on sign posted road; 10 mi nw of jct SR 114/101. (22 Wildlife Dr, SOUTH WEARE).

🛥 ⊠

TAMWORTH — CHOCORUA CAMPING VILLAGE ⓐⓐⓐ (603) 323-8536. **4P $23-$59, XP $6-$8.** 893 White Mountain Hwy, 03817. SR 16, 2.5 mi n of jct SR 25. (PO Box 484, CHOCORUA).

🛥 ⊠

TWIN MOUNTAIN — TWIN MOUNTAIN KOA KAMPGROUND ⓐⓐⓐ (603) 846-5559. **2P $29-$149, XP $3-$10.** 372 SR 115, 03595. Jct US 302, 2.1 mi n on US 3, then 0.8 mi ne. (PO Box 148).

🛥 ⊠

WOODSTOCK — BROKEN BRANCH KOA. (603) 745-8008. **2P $29-$45, XP $3-$8.** 1002 Eastside Rd (SR 175), 03293. I-93, exit 31, 2 mi s, follow signs. (PO Box 6, WOODSTOCK).

$D 🛥 ⊠

New Jersey

CAPE MAY COURT HOUSE — BIG TIMBER LAKE CAMPING RESORT ⓐⓐⓐ (609) 465-4456. **4P $38-$57, XP $3-$7.** 116 Swainton Goshen Rd, 08210. Garden State Pkwy, exit 13 southbound, 0.5 mi w on paved road, 1 mi s on US 9, then 1 mi w (CR 646). (PO Box 366).

🛥 ⊠

CAPE MAY — BEACHCOMBER CAMPING RESORT. (609) 886-6035. **2P $23-$60, XP $3-$5.** 462 Seashore Rd, 08204. Garden State Pkwy, exit 4A (SR 47 N), w to 3rd traffic light, then 1 mi s; Railroad Ave and Seashore Rd.

🛥 ⊠

CAPE MAY — HOLLY SHORES BEST HOLIDAY TRAV-L-PARK ⓐⓐⓐ (609) 886-1234. **2P $22-$48, XP $3-$5.** 491 US 9, 08204. Garden State Pkwy, exit 4A (SR 47 N) to 2nd traffic light, 1 mi s. Small pets allowed.

🛥 ⊠

CAPE MAY — SEASHORE CAMPSITES INC ⓐⓐⓐ (609) 884-4010. **4P $26-$48, XP $3-$5.** 720 Seashore Rd, 08204. Garden State Pkwy, exit 4A (SR 47 N), 1 mi n to CR 626, then 2.7 mi s.

🛥 ⊠

OCEAN VIEW — OCEAN VIEW RESORT CAMPGROUND ⓐⓐⓐ (609) 624-1675. **4P $39-$66, XP $6-$7.** 2555 Rt 9, 08230. US 9, 0.8 mi nw of Garden State Pkwy, exit 17 southbound; exit northbound, use service area turnaround. (PO Box 607).

🛥 ⊠

New Mexico

ALBUQUERQUE — ALBUQUERQUE KOA-CENTRAL. (505) 296-2729. **Call for rates.** 12400 Skyline Rd NE, 87123. I-40, exit 166, just s, then left.

🛥 ⊠

ALBUQUERQUE — AMERICAN RV PARK ⓐⓐⓐ (505) 831-3545. **4P $23-$32, XP $3.** 13500 Central Ave SW, 87121. I-40, exit 149, just s, then w.

🛥 ⊠

DEMING — A LITTLE VINEYARD RV PARK ⓐⓐⓐ (505) 546-3560. **2P $17-$19, XP $2.** 2901 E Pine St, 88030. I-10, exit 85, 1 mi w.

$D 🛥 ⊠

GALLUP — USA RV PARK ⓐⓐⓐ (505) 863-5021. **2P $26-$30, XP $2.** 2925 W Hwy 66, 87301. I-40, exit 16, 1 mi e.

$D 🛥 ⊠

LAS CRUCES — HACIENDA RV RESORT ⓐⓐⓐ (505) 528-5800. **Call for rates.** 740 Stern Dr, 88005. I-10, exit 140, just e. (PO Box 1479, MESILLA, 88046-1479).

🏍 ⊠

RIO RANCHO — STAGECOACH STOP RV RESORT. (505) 867-1000. **Call for rates.** 3650 SR 528, 87124. I-25, exit 242, w to SR 528, then 0.5 mi s.

🏍 🛥 ⊠

SILVER CITY — SILVER CITY KOA. (505) 388-3351. **4P $17-$42, XP $3-$4.** 11824 E Hwy 180, 88022. 4.9 mi e on US 180 and SR 90.

🛥 ⊠

New York

BATH — HICKORY HILL CAMPING RESORT ⓐⓐⓐ (607) 776-4345. **2P $36-$45, XP $3.** 7531 CR 13, 14810. SR 17, exit 38, 1 mi n on SR 54, then at fork, 2 mi n on Haverling St (CR 13).

🛥 ⊠

DEWITTVILLE — CHAUTAUQUA HEIGHTS CAMPING RESORT CAMPGROUND. (716) 386-3804. **2P $21-$35, XP $4-$8.** 5652 Thumb Rd, 14728. I-86, exit 10 westbound, 5 mi on CR 430 W; I-90, exit 60 to Mayville, 2.4 mi on CR 430 E, just e.

🛥 ⊠

GARDINER — YOGI BEAR'S JELLYSTONE PARK CAMP-RESORTS AT LAZY RIVER. (845) 255-5193. **4P $59, XP $4-$10.** 50 Bevier Rd, 12525. 1.5 mi w on US 44 and SR 55, 0.8 mi se on Albany Post and Bevier rds, follow signs.

🛥 ⊠

GARRATTSVILLE — YOGI BEAR'S JELLYSTONE PARK AT CRYSTAL LAKE. (607) 965-8265. **4P $18-$55, XP $3-$10.** 111 E Turtle Lake Rd, 13342. Jct SR 80, 6.2 mi s on CR 16, 0.7 mi n on CR 51, then 1.1 mi w on CR 17.

$D 🛥 ⊠

GREENFIELD PARK — SKYWAY CAMPING RESORT. (845) 647-5747. **2P $60, XP $10.** 99 Mountaindale Rd, 12435. Jct US 209 and SR 52, 5.2 mi w on SR 52, then 1.1 mi sw.

GREENFIELD PARK — YOGI BEAR'S JELLYSTONE PARK CAMP-RESORT AT BIRCHWOOD ACRES. (845) 434-4743. **4P $32-$62, XP $6-$12.** 85 Martinfeld Rd, 12789. Jct US 209 and SR 52, 8 mi w on SR 52, then 0.5 mi s. (PO Box 482, WOODRIDGE).

LAKE GEORGE — LAKE GEORGE ESCAPE. (518) 623-3207. **2P $25-$58, XP $6.** 175 E Schroon River Rd, 12845. I-87, exit 23, 0.4 mi e on Diamond Point Rd, then 0.8 mi n. (PO Box 431).

OLD FORGE — OLD FORGE CAMPING RESORT. (315) 369-6011. **2P $24-$38, XP $2-$4.** 3347 SR 28, 13420. 1 mi n of town. (PO Box 51).

PLATTEKILL — NEWBURGH/NEW YORK CITY NORTH KOA ⚠ (845) 564-2836. **2P $30-$45, XP $4-$5.** 119 Freetown Hwy, 12568. 1.5 mi n on SR 32, 3 mi s of jct US 44 and SR 55, 0.5 mi e, follow signs.

PULASKI — BRENNAN BEACH RV RESORT ⚠ (315) 298-2242. **2P $33-$42, XP $5.** 80 Brennan Beach, 13142. I-81, exit 36, 4 mi w on SR 13, 1 mi n on SR 3.

QUEENSBURY — LAKE GEORGE RV PARK. (518) 792-3775. **2P $45-$68, XP $7.** 74 SR 149, 12845. I-87 (New York State Thruway), exit 20, 0.5 mi n on US 9, then 0.4 mi e.

QUEENSBURY — LEDGEVIEW VILLAGE RV PARK. (518) 798-6621. **$35-$39, XP $3.** 321 SR 149, 12845. I-87 (New York State Thruway), exit 20, 0.5 mi n on US 9, then 1.5 mi e.

VERONA — THE VILLAGES AT TURNING STONE. (315) 361-7275. **Call for rates.** 5065 SR 365, 13478. I-90, exit 33, 1.3 mi w. (PO Box 126).

WATKINS GLEN — WATKINS GLEN-CORNING KOA KAMP-GROUND. (607) 535-7404. **2P $30-$60, XP $3-$7.** 1710 SR 414, 14891. SR 414, 4.5 mi s of jct SR 14.

North Carolina

BOONE — KOA-BOONE. (828) 264-7250. **2P $28-$36, XP $2-$5.** 123 Harmony Mt Ln, 28607. Jct US 221 and 421, 3 mi n on SR 194, 1 mi w on Ray Brown Rd.

CANDLER — KOA ASHEVILLE WEST. (828) 665-7015. **2P $29-$45, XP $4-$5.** 309 Wiggins Rd, 28715. I-40, exit 37, just s, 0.5 mi w on US 19/23, then 0.3 mi n.

CEDAR MOUNTAIN — BLACK FOREST CAMPING RESORT. (828) 884-2267. **2P $24-$35, XP $3-$5.** 100 Summer Rd, 28718. On US 276, 12.6 mi s of Brevard. (PO Box 709).

CHEROKEE — CHEROKEE GREAT SMOKIES KOA. (828) 497-9711. **2P $27-$199, XP $5.** 4 mi n on Big Cove Rd. (92 KOA Campground Rd, 28719).

North Dakota

BISMARCK — BISMARCK KOA. (701) 222-2662. **Call for rates.** 3720 Centennial Rd, 58503-8001. I-94, exit 161 (Centennial Rd), 1 mi n.

Ohio

AURORA — JELLYSTONE PARK CAMP RESORT ⚠ (330) 562-9100. **4P $30-$55, XP $3-$8.** 3392 SR 82, 44255. 4 mi e.

BROOKVILLE — DAYTON TALL TIMBERS RESORT KOA. (937) 833-3888. **2P $29-$51, XP $4-$10.** 7796 Wellbaum Rd, 45309. 0.5 mi n on SR 49; jct I-70, exit 24, 0.5 mi w on Pleasant Plain Rd, then 0.3 mi s.

GENEVA-ON-THE-LAKE — INDIAN CREEK CAMPING & RESORT. (440) 466-8191. **2P $35-$45, XP $3-$5.** 4710 Lake Rd E, 44041-9459. 2 mi e on SR 531.

SHELBY — SHELBY/MANSFIELD KOA. (419) 347-1392. **2P $26-$75, XP $5-$12.** 6787 Baker 47, 44875-9103. 4 mi nw on SR 39, then 4.5 mi n, follow signs.

Oregon

ASHLAND — HOWARD PRAIRIE LAKE RESORT ⚠ (541) 482-1979. **2P $17-$27, XP $5.** 3249 Hyatt Prairie Rd, 97520. I-5, exit 14, 0.7 mi e on SR 66, 17 mi e on Dead Indian Memorial Rd, then 3.4 mi s.

CANNON BEACH — RV RESORT AT CANNON BEACH ⚠ (503) 436-2231. **Call for rates.** 340 Elk Creek Rd, 97110. US 101, exit Sunset Blvd. (PO Box 1037).

EUGENE — PREMIER RV RESORT OF EUGENE. (541) 686-3152. **2P $37-$42, XP $3.** 33022 Van Duyn Rd, 97408. I-5, exit 199, just e, then 0.4 mi s; n of town at Coburg exit.

LEBANON — MALLARD CREEK GOLF & RV RESORT. (541) 259-0070. **2P $40.** 31958 Bellinger Scale Rd, 97355. I-5, exit 228, 5.6 mi e on SR 34 (follow south and east truck route), 1.3 mi s on Denny School Rd, 2.2 mi e on Airport Dr, 4.6 mi s on US 20, 1.1 mi ne on Waterloo Rd, just e on Berlin Rd, then 0.4 mi n.

NETARTS — NETARTS BAY RV PARK & MARINA. (503) 842-7774. **4P $24-$35, XP $5.** 2260 Bilyeu, 97143. Just w. (PO Box 218, NETARTS). Small pets allowed.

SALEM — PHOENIX RV PARK ⚠ (503) 581-2497. **2P $30, XP $2.** 4130 Silverton Rd NE, 97305. I-5, exit 256, 0.3 mi e on Market, 1.3 mi n on Lancaster, then just e.

SALEM — SALEM PREMIER RV RESORT. (503) 364-7714. **2P $30-$43, XP $3.** 4700 Salem-Dallas Hwy 22, 97304. I-5, exit 260A (Salem Pkwy), follow signs to city center; 3 mi sw to Commercial St NE, then 1.4 mi s to Marion St; 4.7 mi sw from Marion St Bridge via SR 22; 4.3 mi e of jct SR 22 and 99 W.

SISTERS — SISTERS INN & RV PARK ⚠ (541) 549-7275. **Call for rates.** 540 Hwy 20 W, 97759. On US 20, 0.3 mi w. (PO Box 938).

SISTERS — SISTERS/BEND KOA. (541) 549-3021. **Call for rates.** 67667 Hwy 20 W, 97701. On US 20, 3.5 mi e.

WARM SPRINGS — KAHNEETA HIGH DESERT RESORT & CASINO RV PARK. (541) 553-1112. **Call for rates.** 6823 Hwy 8, 97761. 11 mi ne off US 26; on Warm Springs Indian Reservation. (PO Box 1240).

WARRENTON — ASTORIA/WARRENTON/SEASIDE KOA ⚠ (503) 861-2606. **2P $26-$57, XP $4-$7.** 1100 NW Ridge Rd, 97121. 4.6 mi nw of jct US 101, follow signs to Fort Stevens State Park.

WELCHES — MT. HOOD VILLAGE VACATION COTTAGES & RV RESORT. (503) 622-4011. **6P $23-$43.** 65000 E Hwy 26, 97067. On US 26, 2 mi w.

WILSONVILLE — PHEASANT RIDGE RV RESORT ⒶⒶⒶ (503) 682-7829. **2P $30-$34, XP $1.** 8275 SW Elligsen Rd, 97070. I-5, exit 286, just e. Small pets allowed.

Pennsylvania

BAKERSVILLE — PIONEER PARK CAMPGROUND. (814) 445-6348. **2P $21-$32, XP $3.** Just e on SR 31, 0.5 mi s via signs. (273 Trent Rd, 15501).

BEDFORD — FRIENDSHIP VILLAGE CAMPGROUND ⒶⒶⒶ (814) 623-1677. **$20-$32, XP $2.** 348 Friendship Village Rd, 15522. 1.3 mi w on US 30 from jct US 220, 0.5 mi n via signs.

BELLEFONTE — BELLEFONTE/STATE COLLEGE KOA ⒶⒶⒶ (814) 355-7912. **2P $22-$47, XP $3-$5.** 2481 Jacksonville Rd, 16823. I-80, exit 161, 2 mi ne on SR 26.

BOWMANSVILLE — LAKE IN WOOD CAMPGROUND. (717) 445-5525. **2P $30-$52, XP $3-$6.** 576 Yellow Hill Rd, 17555. SR 23, 4.5 mi n on SR 625, 1 mi ne on Oaklyn Dr, then 1.5 mi e, follow signs.

BOWMANSVILLE — OAK CREEK CAMPGROUNDS ⒶⒶⒶ (717) 445-6161. **4P $25-$42, XP $5-$7.** 400 E Maple Grove Rd, 17507. From SR 625, 1.5 mi e. (PO Box 128).

BOWMANSVILLE — SUN VALLEY CAMPGROUND. (717) 445-6262. **4P $28-$150, XP $6.** 451 E Maple Grove Rd, 17507. From SR 625, 1.9 mi e. (PO Box 129).

CLAY — STARLITE CAMPING RESORT. (717) 733-9655. **2P $36, XP $2-$5.** 1500 Furnace Hill Rd, 17578. US 322, 1.1 mi n on Clay Rd, 2.4 mi ne, follow signs.

COOKSBURG — KALYUMET CAMPGROUND ⒶⒶⒶ (814) 744-9622. **Call for rates.** I-80, exit 62, 2 mi e on SR 68 E to light at Clarion Courthouse, go straight for 9.5 mi. (8630 Miola Rd, LUCINDA, 16235). Small pets allowed.

ELVERSON — WARWICK WOODS FAMILY CAMPING RESORT ⒶⒶⒶ (610) 286-9655. **Call for rates.** 401 Trythall Rd, 19520. I-76 (Pennsylvania Tpke), exit 298 eastbound, 1 mi s on SR 10, then 7.5 mi e on SR 23 to sign at Trythall Rd; exit 312 westbound, 8.5 mi n on SR 100, then 5 mi w on SR 23. (PO Box 280, ST. PETERS, 19470).

ERIE — ERIE KOA KAMPGROUNDS. (814) 476-7706. **Call for rates.** I-90, exit 18, 1.3 mi s on SR 832, then 0.8 mi e; I-79, exit 174, 1.5 mi w. (6645 West Rd, MCKEAN, 16426).

FARMINGTON — BENNER'S MEADOW RUN CAMPING & CABINS. (724) 329-4097. **2P $30-$36, XP $3-$7.** 315 Nelson Rd, 15437. 2.5 mi n of US 40, follow signs. Small pets allowed.

GETTYSBURG — DRUMMER BOY CAMPING RESORT ⒶⒶⒶ (717) 334-3277. **2P $32-$47, XP $2-$5.** 1300 Hanover Rd, 17325. 2 mi e on SR 116 at US 15 Bypass, exit Hanover Rd.

GETTYSBURG — GETTYSBURG CAMPGROUND ⒶⒶⒶ (717) 334-3304. **4P $29-$40, XP $3-$5.** 2030 Fairfield Rd, 17325. 3 mi w on SR 116 W.

GETTYSBURG — GETTYSBURG KOA KAMPGROUND ⒶⒶⒶ (717) 642-5713. **2P $22-$40, XP $3-$6.** 20 Knox Rd, 17325. 3 mi w on US 30, 3 mi s on Knoxlyn Rd, follow signs.

GETTYSBURG — GRANITE HILL CAMPING RESORT ⒶⒶⒶ (717) 642-8749. **2P $20-$44, XP $2-$8.** 3340 Fairfield Rd, 17325. 5.8 mi w on SR 116.

GETTYSBURG — ROUND TOP CAMPGROUND. (717) 334-9565. **4P $22-$46, XP $3-$6.** 180 Knight Rd, 17325. 3 mi s on SR 134 at US 15.

HARRISVILLE — KOZY REST KAMPGROUND ⒶⒶⒶ (724) 735-2417. **2P $23-$28, XP $2-$4.** 449 Campground Rd, 16038. Jct SR 8/SR 58, 0.5 mi e on SR 58 to Campground Rd, then 1.9 mi ne.

HERSHEY — HERSHEY HIGHMEADOW CAMPGROUND. (717) 534-8999. **2P $29-$44, XP $4.** 1200 Matlack Rd, 17036. 0.5 mi n on SR 39 W from jct US 322 and 422. (PO Box 866, 17033).

HOLTWOOD — MUDDY RUN RECREATION PARK. (717) 284-5850. **6P $23, XP $3.** 172 Bethesda Church Rd W, 17532. 1.8 mi ne on SR 372.

JONESTOWN — JONESTOWN KOA. (717) 865-2526. **Call for rates.** 145 Old Rt 22, 17038. 2 mi e on US 22 from jct SR 72, 0.5 mi s; I-81, exit 90, 5 mi se; I-78, exit 6, 5 mi w, follow signs. (PO Box 867).

KNOX — WOLFS CAMPING RESORT ⒶⒶⒶ (814) 797-1103. **Call for rates.** 308 Timberwolf Run, 16232. I-80, exit 53.

LANCASTER — OLD MILL STREAM CAMPGROUND. (717) 299-2314. **4P $29-$41, XP $3.** 2249 Lincoln Hwy E, 17602. 5 mi e on US 30.

LENHARTSVILLE — ROBIN HILL CAMPING RESORT. (610) 756-6117. **$29-$39.** 149 Robin Hill Rd, 19534. I-78, exit 40 (Krumsville) or exit 35 (Lenhartsville), follow signs for 3 mi.

LICKDALE — LICKDALE CAMPGROUND. (717) 865-6411. **4P $26-$30, XP $3-$7.** 11 Lickdale Rd, 17038. I-81, exit 90, just e.

LIVERPOOL — FERRY BOAT CAMPSITES ⒶⒶⒶ (717) 444-3200. **4P $20-$38, XP $2-$3.** 32 Ferry Ln, 17045. 2 mi s on US 11/15.

MANHEIM — PINCH POND FAMILY CAMPGROUND & RV PARK ⒶⒶⒶ (717) 665-7640. **$30-$40, XP $7.** 3075 Pinch Rd, 17545. I-76 (Pennsylvania Tpke), exit 266, 1 mi s on SR 72, 0.5 mi w on Cider Press Rd, then 1 mi n.

MANSFIELD — BUCKTAIL CAMPING RESORT. (570) 662-2923, off season (610) 489-3737. **4P $18-$46, XP $7-$10.** 130 Bucktail Rd, 16933. US 15, 2nd Mansfield exit (Rt 6), 0.3 mi e on US 6, 1.5 mi n on Lambs Creek Rd, then 1 mi w.

MARSHALLS CREEK — OTTER LAKE CAMP RESORT. (570) 223-0123. **$34-$54, XP $4-$8.** I-80, exit 309, 3 mi n on US 209, just n on SR 402, then 7 mi w on Marshalls Creek Rd. (PO Box 850, 18335).

MEADVILLE — BROOKDALE FAMILY CAMPGROUND. (814) 789-3251. **4P $25-$39, XP $3-$5.** 25164 State Hwy 27, 16335. On SR 27, 8 mi e.

MERCERSBURG — SAUNDEROSA PARK INC. (717) 328-2216. **Call for rates.** 5909 Little Cove Rd, 17236. 4.8 mi w on SR 16, 2.5 mi s on SR 456.

MERCER — MERCER-GROVE CITY KOA. (724) 748-3160. **2P $30-$55, XP $3-$5.** 1337 Butler Pike, 16137. I-79, exit 113, 3 mi n on SR 258, follow signs.

MERCER — ROCKY SPRINGS CAMPGROUND. (724) 662-4415. **Call for rates. (no credit cards).** 84 Rocky Spring Rd, Rt 318, 16137. I-80, exit 15 westbound, 2 mi n on US 19 to Butler St (SR 318), then 4.5 mi w; exit eastbound, jct I-80 and exit 4A (SR 318), 6.5 mi ne.

MILL RUN — YOGI BEAR'S JELLYSTONE PARK CAMP RESORT. (724) 455-2929. **4P $16-$55, XP $3-$10.** 839 Mill Run Rd, 15464. Just s on SR 381. (PO Box 91).

NEW COLUMBIA — WILLIAMSPORT SOUTH/NITTANY MOUNTAIN KOA KAMPGROUND ⒶⒶⒶ (570) 568-5541. **4P $29-$45, XP $2-$5.** 2751 Millers Bottom Rd, 17856. I-80, exit 210A, 0.5 mi s on US 15, 4.5 mi w on New Columbia Rd, then 0.4 mi nw.

NEW HOLLAND — SPRING GULCH RESORT. (717) 354-3100. **2P $29-$55, XP $2-$6.** 475 Lynch Rd, 17557. Jct SR 23 and 897, 4 mi s on SR 897.

PINE GROVE — PINE GROVE KOA AT TWIN GROVE PARK ⒶⒶⒶ (717) 865-4602. **2P $27-$41, XP $4-$6.** 1445 Suedburg Rd, 17963. I-81, exit 100, 5 mi w on SR 443.

PORTERSVILLE — BEAR RUN CAMPGROUND ⒶⒶⒶ (724) 368-3564. **2P $26-$39, XP $3-$6.** 184 Badger Hill Rd, 16051. I-79, exit 96, 0.8 mi n on SR 488.

PORTLAND — DRIFTSTONE ON THE DELAWARE ⒶⒶⒶ (570) 897-6859. **2P $28-$40, XP $3-$5.** 4 mi s from jct SR 611 and Portland Bridge. (2731 River Rd, MOUNT BETHEL, 18343).

ROBESONIA — ADVENTURE BOUND CAMPING RESORTS AT EAGLES PEAK. (610) 589-4800. **4P $28-$46, XP $2-$10.** 397 Eagles Peak Rd, 19551. 2.4 mi s on SR 419 from jct US 422, 2.3 mi e, follow signs.

SHARTLESVILLE — APPALACHIAN CAMPSITES. (610) 488-6319. **2P $29-$50, XP $3-$8.** 60 Motel Dr, 19554. I-78, exit 23, 0.5 mi w on service road (entrance just past motel). (PO Box 289).

SHARTLESVILLE — MOUNTAIN SPRINGS CAMPING RESORT INC & ARENA ⒶⒶⒶ (610) 488-6859. **4P $28-$36, XP $3-$5.** 3450 Mountain Rd, 19554. I-78, exit 23, 1 mi n. (PO Box 365).

SIGEL — CAMPERS PARADISE CAMPGROUNDS & CABINS. (814) 752-2393. **2P $22, XP $5.** 37 Steele Dr, 15860. On SR 949 N, 3 mi n of SR 36.

STRASBURG — WHITE OAK CAMPGROUND ⒶⒶⒶ (717) 687-6207. **4P $24-$30, XP $3.** 3156 White Oak Rd, 17566. 3.7 mi s of Centre Square on S Decatur St/May Post Office Rd, then 0.3 mi e. (PO Box 90, 17579).

WATERFORD — SPARROW POND FAMILY CAMPGROUND AND RECREATION FACILITY ⒶⒶⒶ (814) 796-6777. **4P $23-$65, XP $3-$5.** 11103 Route 19 N, 16441. I-90, exit 24, 10 mi s on US 19 (Peach St).

South Carolina

HILTON HEAD ISLAND — HILTON HEAD HARBOR RV RESORT & YACHT CLUB. (843) 681-3256. **4P $45-$59, XP $3.** 43A Jenkins Rd, 29926. 0.9 mi se of Intracoastal Waterway Bridge off US 278, 0.4 mi n, follow signs.

HILTON HEAD ISLAND — OUTDOOR RESORTS' MOTORCOACH RESORT ⒶⒶⒶ (843) 785-7699. **4P $47-$53, XP $2.** 133 Arrow Rd, 29928. 5.6 mi e on Cross Island Pkwy (US 278 toll), then just w.

MYRTLE BEACH — LAKEWOOD CAMPING RESORT ⒶⒶⒶ (843) 238-5161. **5P $25-$60, XP $2-$3.** 5901 S Kings Hwy, 29575. Jct SR 544, 0.5 mi ne on US 17 business route.

MYRTLE BEACH — MYRTLE BEACH TRAVEL PARK. (843) 449-3714. **4P $30-$57, XP $4.** 10108 Kings Rd, 29572. Jct US 17 business route/SR 22, 1.3 mi s.

MYRTLE BEACH — OCEAN LAKES FAMILY CAMPGROUND ⒶⒶⒶ (843) 238-5636. **$25-$60.** 6001 S Kings Hwy, 29575. Jct SR 544 and US 17 business route.

MYRTLE BEACH — PIRATELAND FAMILY CAMPING RESORT. (843) 238-5155. **4P $25-$65, XP $3.** 5401 S Kings Hwy, 29575. Jct SR 544, 1.2 mi ne on US 17 business route.

South Dakota

CHAMBERLAIN — CEDAR SHORE CAMPGROUND ⒶⒶⒶ (605) 734-5273, off season (605) 734-6376. **$25-$27.** 1500 Shoreline Dr, 57365. I-90, exit 260, 2.5 mi e on US 16 and I-90 business loop, then 1 mi ne on Mickelson country road, follow signs. (PO Box 308, 57325).

DEADWOOD — WHISTLER GULCH CAMPGROUND & RV PARK. (605) 578-2092. **$23-$36.** 235 Cliff, 57732. 0.7 mi s on US 85.

HILL CITY — RAFTER J BAR RANCH CAMPGROUND ⒶⒶⒶ (605) 574-2527. **2P $22-$41, XP $3.** 12325 Rafter J Rd, 57745. 3.3 mi s on US 16 and 385 at SR 87/244. (PO Box 128).

INTERIOR — BADLANDS WHITE RIVER KOA ⒶⒶⒶ (605) 433-5337. **2P $22-$32, XP $3-$4.** 20720 SD Hwy 44, 57750. 4 mi e of jct SR 377.

MITCHELL — RIVERSIDE KOA. (605) 996-1131. **2P $18-$38, XP $3.** 41244 SD Hwy 38, 57301-7800. I-90, exit 335, 0.5 mi n, then 0.3 mi w.

NORTH SIOUX CITY — SIOUX CITY NORTH KOA. (605) 232-4519. **2P $21-$40, XP $3.** 601 Streeter Dr, 57049. I-29, exit 2 northbound, 1 mi n on west service road; exit 4 southbound, 1 mi w on west service road.

SIOUX FALLS — YOGI BEAR CAMP RESORT. (605) 332-2233. **2P $22-$33, XP $2.** 26014 478th Ave, 57005. I-90, exit 402, just n.

SPEARFISH — ELKHORN RIDGE RV PARK & CAMPGROUND. (605) 722-1800. **6P $12-$44.** 20189 US 85, 57783. I-90, exit 17 (US 85), 0.5 mi s.

Tennessee

EAST RIDGE — BEST HOLIDAY TRAV-L-PARK/CHATTANOOGA. (706) 891-9766. **2P $23-$33, XP $3.** 1709 Mack Smith Rd, 37412. I-75, exit 1 southbound; exit 1B northbound, 0.3 mi w, then 1 mi s.

GATLINBURG — OUTDOOR RESORTS OF GATLINBURG. (865) 436-5861. **4P $35-$45, XP $2-$4.** 11.5 mi e on US 321 N. (4229 Parkway E, 37738).

NASHVILLE — NASHVILLE JELLYSTONE PARK ⚑ (615) 889-4225. **2P $38-$50, XP $4.** 2572 Music Valley Dr, 37214-1096. I-40, exit 215 (Briley Pkwy N), 6 mi to exit 12 (Music Valley Dr), follow signs.

NASHVILLE — TWO RIVERS CAMPGROUND. (615) 883-8559. **2P $29-$38, XP $3.** 2616 Music Valley Dr, 37214. I-40, exit 215B (Briley Pkwy), 5 mi n, 0.3 mi w on McGavock Pike, then 1.5 mi n.

PIGEON FORGE — CLABOUGH'S CAMPGROUND. (865) 428-1951. **4P $23-$30, XP $2.** 405 Wear's Valley Rd, 37863. 0.7 mi w of jct US 441 at traffic light 3.

PIGEON FORGE — RIVEREDGE RV PARK. (865) 453-5813. **2P $25-$34, XP $4.** 4220 Huskey St, 37863. Just off US 441 at traffic light 10.

TOWNSEND — LITTLE RIVER VILLAGE CAMPGROUND ⚑ (865) 448-2241. **2P $15-$50, XP $2-$4.** 8533 State Hwy 73, 37882. On SR 73, 0.4 mi w of entrance to Great Smoky Mountain National Park.

Texas

ABILENE — KOA-ABILENE. (325) 672-3681. **2P $26-$39, XP $3.** 4851 W Stamford St, 79603. I-20, exit 282 (Shirley Rd), 0.5 mi w of US 83-277, follow signs.

AMARILLO — AMARILLO RV RANCH ⚑ (806) 373-4962. **2P $28-$35, XP $2.** 1414 Sunrise Dr, 79104. I-40, exit 74 (Whitaker Rd), 0.3 mi w on north frontage road.

AMARILLO — FORT AMARILLO RV RESORT. (806) 331-1700. **2P $30, XP $2.** 10101 Amarillo Blvd W, 79124. I-40, exit 64 westbound, 0.3 mi n on Soncy to Amarillo Blvd, then 1 mi w; exit 62B eastbound, 0.7 mi e.

AUSTIN — AUSTIN LONE STAR RV RESORT. (512) 444-6322. **$28-$48.** 7009 I-35 S, 78744. I-35, exit 226B/227 (Slaughter/S Congress aves) southbound; exit 228/229 (Wm Cannon Dr) northbound, on northbound Frontage Rd.

BEAUMONT — GULF COAST RV RESORT. (409) 842-2285. **2P $29, XP $3-$5.** 5175 Brooks Rd, 77705. I-10, exit 846 westbound; exit 845 eastbound, follow blue signs.

BOERNE — ALAMO FIESTA RV RESORT ⚑ (830) 249-4700. **2P $25-$40, XP $3.** 33000 IH-10 W, 78006. I-10, exit 543, 1 mi w on westbound access road. Small pets allowed.

DONNA — VICTORIA PALMS RESORT. (956) 464-7801. **2P $25-$45, XP $2.** 602 E Victoria Rd, 78537. Just s of jct US 83. Small pets allowed.

LUBBOCK — LUBBOCK RV PARK ⚑ (806) 747-2366. **2P $24-$28, XP $2.** 4811 N I-27, 79403. I-27, exit 9, 2 mi n of Loop 289. (PO Box 597).

MERCEDES — ENCORE PARADISE SOUTH. (956) 565-2044. **Call for rates.** 8000 Paradise S, 78570. On Mile 2 W Rd, just n of US 83.

MONTGOMERY — HAVENS LANDING RV RESORT ⚑ (936) 582-1200. **2P $31, XP $2.** 19785 Hwy 105 W, 77356. I-45, exit 87, 13 mi w.

SAN ANTONIO — ADMIRALTY RV RESORT ⚑ (210) 647-7878. **Call for rates.** 1485 N Ellison Dr, 78251. Jct Loop 1604 and SR 151, 1.3 mi nw on SR 151 to Military Dr, just w to Ellison Dr, then 0.7 mi n.

SAN ANTONIO — ALAMO KOA KAMPGROUND. (210) 224-9296. **2P $31-$37, XP $3.** 602 Gembler Rd, 78219. I-35, exit Coliseum, 0.5 mi s, then 0.8 mi e; I-10, exit WW White Rd, 0.3 mi n, then 1 mi w.

SAN ANTONIO — TEXAS BLAZING STAR RV, LTD ⚑ (210) 680-7827. **2P $34-$47, XP $4.** 1120 W Loop 1604 N, 78251. Just s of Military Hwy.

SAN BENITO — FUN-N-SUN RV RESORT. (956) 399-5125. **2P $26-$28, XP $2.** 1400 Zillock Rd, 78586. 4 mi nw from US 83 and 77, exit Paso Real Rd, 0.4 mi s.

SOUTH PADRE ISLAND — LONG ISLAND VILLAGE. (956) 943-6449. **Call for rates.** 900 S Garcia St, 78597. On SR 100, turn right before crossing causeway. (PO Box 695, PORT ISABEL, 78578).

WESLACO — PINE TO PALM RESORT PARK. (956) 968-5760. **$22, XP $2. (no credit cards).** 802 International Blvd, 78596. FM 1015, 0.8 mi s of jct US 83, just s of jct Business Rt US 83.

WICHITA FALLS — WICHITA FALLS RV PARK ⚑ (940) 723-1532. **2P $25-$28, XP $2.** 2944 Seymour Hwy (Business 277 S), 76301. I-44, exit 1A, 1.2 mi s.

Utah

BRYCE — RUBY'S INN CAMPGROUND TRAILER PARK ⚑ (435) 834-5301, off season (435) 834-5341. **2P $28-$35, XP $2.** 1280 S Hwy 63, 84764. On SR 63, 1 mi n of Bryce Canyon Park entrance. (PO Box 640022).

CANNONVILLE — CANNONVILLE-BRYCE VALLEY KOA. (435) 679-8988. **2P $24-$36, XP $3.** Hwy 12 at Redrock Rd, 84718. On SR 12, north end of town. (PO Box 50).

FRUIT HEIGHTS — CHERRY HILL CAMPING RESORT ⚑ (801) 451-5379. **2P $20-$32, XP $2.** 1325 S Main St, 84037. I-15 N, exit 326, 1.5 mi n via US 89 and 273, follow signs; I-15 S, exit 331, 2 mi se via 2nd N and Main sts, follow signs.

MOAB — MOAB KOA CAMPGROUND ⚑ (435) 259-6682. **2P $27-$30, XP $4.** 3225 S Hwy 191, 84532. 4 mi s; e off US 191.

MOAB — MOAB VALLEY RV RESORT. (435) 259-4469. **2P $19-$66, XP $5.** 1773 N Hwy 191, 84532. 2 mi n, just s of Colorado River Bridge. Small pets allowed.

RICHFIELD — RICHFIELD KOA. (435) 896-6674. **2P $28-$33, XP $2-$3.** 600 W 600 S, 84701. 6 blks w of US 89 (Main St); I-70, exit 40 southbound, 2.5 mi via Main St; exit 37 northbound, 1.5 mi via 1200 S and 400 W.

ST. GEORGE — MCARTHUR'S TEMPLE VIEW RV RESORT 🄰🄰🄰 (435) 673-6400. **2P $26-$36, XP $3.** 975 S Main St, 84770. I-15, exit 6 (Bluff St), 0.5 mi w, then just n. Small pets allowed.

ST. GEORGE — SETTLERS RV PARK 🄰🄰🄰 (435) 628-1624. **Call for rates.** 1333 E 100 South, 84790. E of I-15, exit 8, right on River Rd. Small pets allowed.

VIRGIN — ZION RIVER RESORT RV PARK & CAMPGROUND 🄰🄰🄰 (435) 635-8594. **4P $45-$50, XP $3.** 730 E Hwy 9, 84779. I-15, exit 16 (SR 16) northbound, 22 mi ne; exit 27 southbound, 12 mie ne. (PO Box 790219).

Virginia

CHARLOTTESVILLE — CHARLOTTESVILLE KOA. (434) 296-9881. **2P $25-$34, XP $2-$5.** 3825 Red Hill Rd, 22903. US 29 (s of I-64), 4.2 mi e on CR 708; SR 20, 1.4 mi w on CR 708.

CHERITON — CHERRYSTONE FAMILY CAMPING RESORT 🄰🄰🄰 (757) 331-3063. **2P $17-$55, XP $5.** 1511 Townfields Dr, 23316. 1.5 mi w on SR 680 from jct US 13. (PO Box 545).

FRONT ROYAL — FRONT ROYAL RV CAMPGROUND 🄰🄰🄰 (540) 635-2741. **2P $28-$47.** 585 KOA Dr, 22630. I-66, exit 6 or 13, entrance is 2 mi s of town on US 340 S. (PO Box 274).

LURAY — LURAY RV RESORT COUNTRY WAYE 🄰🄰🄰 (540) 743-7222. **2P $26-$39, XP $3-$5.** 3402 Kimball Rd, 22835. Jct US 211, 2 mi n on US 340, then 0.3 mi e on SR 658.

LURAY — YOGI BEAR'S JELLYSTONE PARK 🄰🄰🄰 (540) 743-4002. **2P $35-$57, XP $3-$6.** 2250 Hwy 211 E, 22835. On US 211, 3 mi e. (PO Box 191).

MADISON — SHENANDOAH HILLS CAMPGROUND 🄰🄰🄰 (540) 948-4186. **2P $28-$40, XP $2-$5.** 110 Campground Ln, 22727. 2 mi s on US 29.

MINT SPRING — WALNUT HILLS CAMPGROUND. (540) 337-3920. **2P $27-$35, XP $3.** 484 Walnut Hills Rd, 24463. I-81, exit 217, 0.7 mi w to US 11, 1.5 mi s, then 1.2 mi e on SR 655.

NATURAL BRIDGE — NATURAL BRIDGE KOA KAMP-GROUND 🄰🄰🄰 (540) 291-2770. **2P $23-$64, XP $3-$4.** 214 Kildeer Ln, 24578. I-81, exit 180 northbound; exit 180B southbound, just nw on US 11. (PO Box 148).

URBANNA — BETHPAGE CAMP RESORT. (804) 758-4349. **4P $29-$59, XP $4-$6.** 679 Brown's Ln, 23175. 1 mi n of town on CR 602. (PO Box 178).

VIRGINIA BEACH — HOLIDAY TRAV-L-PARK 🄰🄰🄰 (757) 425-0249. **2P $21-$50, XP $5.** 1075 General Booth Blvd, 23451. I-264 terminus to Pacific Ave, 2.5 mi s.

VIRGINIA BEACH — OUTDOOR RESORTS/VIRGINIA BEACH. (757) 721-2020. **4P $40-$70, XP $7.** 3665 S Sandpiper Rd, 23456. I-264 terminus to Pacific Ave, 2 mi s to Rudee Inlet Bridge/General Booth Blvd, 5.6 mi s to Princess Anne Rd, 0.8 mi e to Sandbridge Rd, 5.5 mi e to Sandpiper Rd, then 3.5 mi s.

VIRGINIA BEACH — VIRGINIA BEACH KOA 🄰🄰🄰 (757) 428-1444. **2P $19-$48, XP $6.** 1240 General Booth Blvd, 23451. I-264 terminus to Pacific Ave/General Booth Blvd, 2 mi s.

Washington

BURLINGTON — BURLINGTON KOA. (360) 724-5511. **2P $24-$39, XP $3-$4.** 6397 N Green Rd, 98233. I-5, exit 232, 3.5 mi n on Old US 99.

CLARKSTON — GRANITE LAKE PREMIER RV RESORT. (509) 751-1635. **2P $25-$36, XP $3.** 306 Granite Lake Dr, 99403. Just w of Snake River Bridge on US 12, just n on 5th St.

LYNDEN — LYNDEN KOA. (360) 354-4772. **2P $25-$67, XP $5.** 8717 Line Rd, 98264. 1.7 mi n of downtown on SR 539 (Guide Meridian Rd), 3 mi e on SR 546 (E Badger Rd), then 0.5 mi s.

MOSSYROCK — HARMONY LAKESIDE RV PARK 🄰🄰🄰 (360) 983-3804. **4P $29-$49, XP $4.** 563 SR 122, 98585. I-5, exit 68, 21 mi e on US 12, then 2.3 mi n.

OAK HARBOR — NORTH WHIDBEY RV PARK. (360) 675-9597. **$25, XP $2.** 565 W Cornet Bay Rd, 98277. On SR 20, 1 mi s of Deception Pass Bridge, 8 mi n of Oak Harbor.

PORT ANGELES — PORT ANGELES/SEQUIM KOA. (360) 457-5916. **2P $24-$70, XP $5.** 80 O'Brien Rd & US 101 E, 98362. 7 mi e on US 101; 8 mi w of Sequim on US 101; just e of US 101, MM 255.

SPOKANE — ALDERWOOD RV RESORT. (509) 467-5320. **2P $30-$37, XP $3.** 14007 N Newport Hwy, 99021. I-90, exit 287, 8 mi n to SR 206, then 1.5 mi w.

West Virginia

HARPERS FERRY — HARPERS FERRY/CIVIL WAR BATTLE-FIELDS KOA 🄰🄰🄰 (304) 535-6895. **2P $20-$160, XP $3-$6.** 343 Campground Rd, 25425. 1 mi sw on US 340 from Shenandoah River Bridge, 0.3 mi s, follow signs.

MILTON — FOX FIRE CAMPING RESORT. (304) 743-5622. **4P $26-$35, XP $3.** US 60, 25541. I-64, exit 28, 0.3 mi s, then 2.7 mi w. (Rt 2, Box 655).

Wisconsin

BAGLEY — YOGI BEAR'S JELLYSTONE PARK CAMP RESORT. (608) 996-2201. **Call for rates.** 11354 CR X, 53801. 1.3 mi n.

FORT ATKINSON — JELLYSTONE PARK OF FORT ATKINSON. (920) 568-4100. **Call for rates.** N 551 Wishing Well Dr, 53538. 5 mi s on SR 26 from jct US 12, 0.8 mi w on Koshkonong Lake Rd, then just s. Small pets allowed.

WISCONSIN DELLS — YOGI BEAR'S JELLYSTONE PARK CAMP-RESORT 🄰🄰🄰 (608) 254-2568. **4P $19-$95, XP $5-$10.** S 1915 Ishnala Rd, 53965. I-90/94, exit 89 eastbound; exit 92 westbound, follow signs. (PO Box 510).

Canada

Alberta

CALGARY — PINE CREEK R.V. CAMPGROUND. (403) 256-3002. **2P $27-$34, XP $2.** 1.9 mi (3.1 km) s on Hwy 2A from Hwy 22X overpass. (PO Box 174, DE WINTON, T0L 0X0).

EDMONTON — GLOWING EMBERS TRAVEL CENTRE & RV PARK ⒶⒶ (780) 962-8100. **$30-$40, XP $1.** 26309 Hwy 16A, T7X 5A6. 1.9 mi (3 km) w of city limits; 1.1 mi (1.8 km) sw from Devon exit (Hwy 60 S), follow signs.

HINTON — HINTON/JASPER KOA ⒶⒶ (780) 865-5062, off season (403) 288-8351. **2P $20-$38, XP $3-$5.** Hwy 16, T9B 1X3. On Hwy 16, 2.5 mi (4 km) w. (4720 Vegas Rd NW, CALGARY, T3A 1W3).

OKOTOKS — COUNTRY LANE RV PARK ⒶⒶ (403) 995-2330. **$32.** E on Hwy 7 and 2A; jct Hwy 2, 7 and 2A. (PO Box 1530, T1S 1B4).

British Columbia

BURNABY — BURNABY CARIBOO R.V. PARK ⒶⒶ (604) 420-1722. **2P $33-$49, XP $3-$5.** 8765 Cariboo Pl, V3N 4T2. Trans-Canada Hwy 1, exit 37 (Cariboo Rd), follow signs.

CAMPBELL RIVER — RIPPLE ROCK RV PARK. (250) 287-7108. **2P $20-$39, XP $3.** 15011 Browns Bay Rd, V9H 1N9. Jct Hwy 19A, 28 and 19, 12 mi (19 km) n on Hwy 19, then 2.8 mi (4.5 km) e.

FAIRMONT HOT SPRINGS — FAIRMONT HOT SPRINGS RV PARK. (250) 345-6033. **Call for rates.** 1 mi (1.6 km) n off Hwy 93 and 95; adjacent to Fairmont Hot Springs Resort. (PO Box 10, V0B 1L0).

MALAHAT — VICTORIA WEST KOA. (250) 478-3332. **2P $23-$36, XP $4-$6.** On Trans-Canada Hwy 1 (Malahat Dr), 15.9 mi (25.6) km n of Victoria. (PO Box 103).

NORTH VANCOUVER — CAPILANO RV PARK ⒶⒶ (604) 987-4722. **2P $28-$45, XP $4.** 295 Tomahawk Ave, V7P 1C5. Trans-Canada Hwy 1, exit 14 (Capilano Rd), 1.6 km s to Marine Dr, follow signs.

OLIVER — DESERT GEM RV RESORT ⒶⒶ (250) 498-5544. **2P $20-$32, XP $5.** 34037 Hwy 97, V0H 1T0. 0.6 mi (1 km) s from 342nd Ave. (PO Box 400).

SURREY — PEACE ARCH RV PARK. (604) 594-7009. **$27-$34, XP $2.** 14601 40th Ave, V3S 0L2. Hwy 99, exit 10, follow signs.

WHISTLER — RIVERSIDE RV RESORT AND CAMPGROUND. (604) 905-5533. **2P $45-$50, XP $5.** 8018 Mons Rd, V0N 1B8. Hwy 99, from Upper Village, 0.9 mi (1.5 km) n, exit Blackcomb Way, follow signs. Small pets allowed.

New Brunswick

WOODSTOCK — YOGI BEAR'S JELLYSTONE PARK AT KOZY ACRES. (506) 328-6287. **5P $30-$40, XP $5-$8.** Trans-Canada Hwy 2, exit 191 (Beardsley Rd). (PO Box 9004, E7M 6B5).

Nova Scotia

BADDECK — BADDECK-CABOT TRAIL CAMPGROUND/GOOD SAM PARK ⒶⒶ (902) 295-2288. **4P $23-$31, XP $3-$4.** 9584 Trans-Canada Hwy 105, B0E 1B0. 5 mi (8 km) w. (PO Box 417).

Ontario

AMHERSTBURG — YOGI BEAR JELLYSTONE PARK CAMP RESORTS. (519) 736-3201. **2P $35-$45, XP $2-$10.** 4610 County Rd 18, RR 1, N9V 2Y7. 2.5 mi (4 km) e on Pike Rd (Simco St).

BRADFORD — YOGI BEAR'S JELLYSTONE PARK & CAMP-RESORT ⒶⒶ (905) 775-1377. **2P $35-$55, XP $6-$8.** 3666 Simcoe Rd 88, L3Z 2A4. Hwy 400, exit 64B, jct Hwy 400 and Simcoe Rd 88. (RR 1, 3666 Simcoe Rd 88). Small pets allowed.

FOREST — OUR PONDEROSA RV RESORT & GOLF RESORT. (519) 786-2031. **4P $37.** 9338 W Ipperwash Rd, N0N 1J0. 1.9 mi (3 km) n on W Ipperwash Rd from jct CR 7. (RR 2).

KINCARDINE — FISHERMAN'S COVE TENT & TRAILER PARK LTD.** (519) 395-2757. **$40-$55, XP $4-$6.** 13 Southline Ave, N2Z 2X5. Jct Hwy 21 and 9, 10.6 mi (17.7 km) e to Kinloss, then 1.9 mi (3 km) s; follow signs. (RR 4).

KITCHENER — BINGEMANS. (519) 744-1002. **6P $32-$47, XP $6.** 425 Bingemans Centre Dr, N2B 3X7. 3.5 mi (5.6 km) on Hwy 7; 1 mi (1.6 km) e of jct Hwy 7 and Conestoga Pkwy (Hwy 86).

NIAGARA FALLS — CAMPARK RESORTS ⒶⒶ (905) 358-3873. **2P $38-$48, XP $3-$5.** 9387 Lundy's Ln, L2E 6S4. 3.9 mi (6.3 km) w of falls on Hwy 20.

NIAGARA FALLS — NIAGARA FALLS KOA KAMPGROUND. (905) 356-2267. **Call for rates.** 8625 Lundy's Ln, L2H 1H5. 3.5 mi (5.6 km) w on Hwy 20.

SAUBLE BEACH — CARSON'S CAMP LTD. (519) 422-1143. **2P $25-$40, XP $3-$10. (no credit cards).** 110 Southampton Pkwy, N0H 2G0. 0.6 mi (1 km) s on CR 13. (Rt 1).

SAUBLE BEACH — WOODLAND PARK. (519) 422-1161. **2P $31-$50, XP $3-$15.** 47 Sauble Falls Pkwy, RR 1, N0H 2G0. 0.6 mi (1 km) n on CR 13.

Québec

LEVIS — KOA-QUEBEC CITY. (418) 831-1813. **2P $26-$43, XP $3-$5.** 684 chemin Olivier, G7A 2N6. Hwy 20, exit 311, 0.9 mi (1.5 km) w, north-side service road; in St-Nicolas sector.

ST-MATHIEU-DE-BELOEIL — CAMPING ALOUETTE ⒶⒶ (450) 464-1661. **2P $30-$38, XP $3.** 3449 de l'Industrie, J3G 4S5. Hwy 20, exit 105; follow signs.

STE-SABINE — CAMPING CARAVELLE. (450) 293-7637. **2P $23-$29, XP $3. (no credit cards).** 180 Rang de la Gare, J0J 2B0. Jct Rt 104, 2.9 mi (4.7 km) s on Rt 235, then 0.5 mi (0.8 km) w on Rang de la Gare; 3.6 mi (6 km) s of Farnham.